R. Gupta's®

NDA & NA

National Defence Academy & Naval Academy

Entrance Examination

PREVIOUS YEARS' PAPERS

(With Answers)

Conducted by

UNION PUBLIC SERVICE COMMISSION

RAMESH PUBLISHING HOUSE, NEW DELHI

Published by

O.P. Gupta *for* Ramesh Publishing House

Admin. Office

12-H, New Daryaganj Road, Opp. Officers' Mess,
New Delhi-110002 ✆ 23275224, 23245124

E-mail: info@rameshpublishinghouse.com
For Online Shopping: www.rameshpublishinghouse.com

Showroom

• Balaji Market, Nai Sarak, Delhi-110006 ✆ 23282525 📱 9354373464
• 4457, Nai Sarak, Delhi-110006

Book Code: R-1978

ISBN: 978-93-87918-37-5

Price: ₹ 1050

Printed at: Deepak Offset, Delhi

CONTENTS

Previous Years' Paper

NATIONAL DEFENCE ACADEMY & NAVAL ACADEMY

NDA & NA — Entrance Exam, 2026 (I)

(Held on exam 12/04/2026)

PAPER I : GENERAL ABILITY TEST

PART A : ENGLISH LANGUAGE

Directions (Qs. No. 1-10): *Each item in this section consists of a sentence with underlined word/words followed by four words. Select the word that is nearest in meaning to the underlined word/words and mark your response on the Answer Sheet accordingly.*

1. The 'Jataka Tales' present moral narratives in the form of allegories.

(*a*) aphorisms (*b*) adages
(*c*) enjambments (*d*) parables

2. He was upbraided for appearing in court in a state of inebriation.

(*a*) ululation (*b*) intoxication
(*c*) confabulation (*d*) sublimation

3. The obstreperous behavior of the students inside the classroom drew the attention of the Principal.

(*a*) compliant (*b*) obnoxious
(*c*) inconspicuous (*d*) disorderly

4. These were based primarily in Himachal Pradesh, where the treks were as gruelling as the terrain.

(*a*) rigorous (*b*) egregious
(*c*) unctuous (*d*) ominous

5. I think they would wish for some more adornment around the school campus for the special function.

(*a*) subsummation (*b*) decoration
(*c*) coloration (*d*) inculcation

6. The travel company tried to identify destinations that were off the beaten track.

(*a*) untenanted (*b*) unfrequented
(*c*) unattended (*d*) untoward

7. Women gather in the community park on a regular basis to chant prayers for the benefit of all.

(*a*) confound (*b*) inculcate
(*c*) indite (*d*) recite

8. The HR Manager was able to utilize the specific skills of each member of the team assembled for the project.

(*a*) harness (*b*) harbor
(*c*) harangue (*d*) herald

9. The oppressive pollution was noticed to have abated after the unseasonal rainfall.

(*a*) mitigated (*b*) enhanced
(*c*) discontinued (*d*) suppressed

10. Often, the context and structure of an ambiguous statement is difficult to discern.

(*a*) absolutistic (*b*) explicit
(*c*) cryptic (*d*) solipsistic

Directions (Qs. No. 11-20): *Each item in this section consists of a sentence with an underlined word followed by four words. Select the word that is opposite in meaning to the underlined word and mark your response on the Answer Sheet accordingly.*

11. She had a ruddy, open face and an oddly guileless manner.

(*a*) cacophonous (*b*) cadaverous
(*c*) nauseous (*d*) bumptious

12. He used to be known among his colleagues for his righteousness.

(*a*) iniquity (*b*) ingenuity
(*c*) absorptivity (*d*) incredulity

13. He found the musical rendition by the septuagenarian maestro to be listless.

(*a*) wearying (*b*) unedifying
(*c*) unengaging (*d*) scintillating

14. The official accused of espionage was found to be disingenuous.

(*a*) scrupulous (*b*) duplicitous
(*c*) mendacious (*d*) perfidious

15. The young are easily <u>excitable</u> when presented with strong emotional triggers.

(*a*) composed (*b*) agitated
(*c*) aggrieved (*d*) alarmed

16. Our professor was <u>perplexed</u> by the answers we wrote in the examination.

(*a*) misled (*b*) enlightened
(*c*) confused (*d*) befuddled

17. Effective governance seeks to <u>optimize</u> public resource allocation.

(*a*) upgrade (*b*) rationalize
(*c*) maximize (*d*) degrade

18. The student's striking <u>audaciousness</u> disturbed long-standing social hierarchies on campus.

(*a*) boldness (*b*) fearlessness
(*c*) timidness (*d*) insightfulness

19. There are four <u>concurrent</u> handloom fairs around the city.

(*a*) consecutive (*b*) distributive
(*c*) aberrative (*d*) abstersive

20. <u>Lucidity</u> is a desired quality in effective communication.

(*a*) Clarity (*b*) Felicity
(*c*) Facility (*d*) Ambiguity

Directions (Qs. No. 21-25): *Given below are some idioms/ phrases followed by four alternatives to each. Select the most appropriate alternative which gives the correct meaning of the idiom/phrase and mark your response on the Answer Sheet accordingly.*

21. 'Nuts and bolts'

(*a*) To complete the first step in a process
(*b*) To get down to practical details
(*c*) To receive harm or punishment for one's actions
(*d*) To irritate people and make them go away

22. 'Hat in hand'

(*a*) With humility
(*b*) Easy to use
(*c*) Available for anyone
(*d*) To marry someone

23. 'Straight from the horse's mouth'

(*a*) Ready and eager to engage in an activity
(*b*) Significantly disturbing business
(*c*) Information from reliable and authoritative source
(*d*) Sudden feelings of fear and embarrassment

24. 'Bite off more than you can chew'

(*a*) To suddenly wrap out of conversation
(*b*) To try to do more than you can manage
(*c*) To do something in the easiest or cheapest way
(*d*) To exaggerate something wildly

25. 'A piece of cake'

(*a*) Something difficult to extract from the original
(*b*) Something very difficult to understand
(*c*) Something that appears very inviting
(*d*) Something very easy to accomplish

Directions (Qs. No. 26-30): *Each of the following sentences has word/words underlined. Read the sentence carefully and identify which word class the underlined word/words belongs/ belong to. Indicate your response on the Answer Sheet accordingly.*

26. He claimed his <u>half</u> share of the booty.

(*a*) Adverb (*b*) Adjective
(*c*) Noun (*d*) Determiner

27. <u>Swimming</u> is a healthy exercise.

(*a*) Verb (*b*) Gerund
(*c*) Adjective (*d*) Adverb

28. I have told you <u>now and again</u> that you must not read such trash.

(*a*) Conjunction (*b*) Preposition
(*c*) Noun (*d*) Adverb

29. He succeeded <u>by dint of</u> perseverance and sheer hard work.

(*a*) Conjunctival phrase
(*b*) Adjectival phrase
(*c*) Prepositional phrase
(*d*) Adverbial phrase

30. I need you to return <u>those</u> books I lent you last month.

(*a*) Modal (*b*) Determiner
(*c*) Noun (*d*) Adjective

Directions (Qs. No. 31-35): *Each of the following items features one part of a sentence, followed by four alternatives. Complete the sentence by choosing the correct alternative and mark your response on the Answer Sheet accordingly.*

31. I will not pay for the goods

(*a*) till he sends me the bill again
(*b*) until he sends me the bill again
(*c*) if he sends me the bill again
(*d*) unless he sends me the bill again

32. I did not buy it

(*a*) because I did not like the look of it
(*b*) as far as I did not like the look of it
(*c*) anyway I did not like the look of it
(*d*) if I did not like the look of it

33. I sent her a bouquet of orchids
(*a*) for which she was absolutely delighted
(*b*) with which she was absolutely delighted
(*c*) of which she was absolutely delighted
(*d*) on which she was absolutely delighted

34. You must stay inside
(*a*) where it starts raining
(*b*) when it starts raining
(*c*) because it starts raining
(*d*) till it starts raining

35. We must wait
(*a*) until you see the light turn green
(*b*) till you see the green light
(*c*) because you can see the green light
(*d*) unless you see the red signal

Directions (Qs. No. 36-40): *The following items have four sentences, one of which is correct. Select the correct sentence and mark your response on the Answer Sheet accordingly.*

36. (*a*) Although it was raining, we had the picnic.
(*b*) Although it was raining, still we had the picnic.
(*c*) Although it was raining, yet we had the picnic.
(*d*) Although it was raining, even then we had the picnic.

37. (*a*) When I would arrive, I will call you.
(*b*) When I shall arrive, I will call you.
(*c*) When I will arrive, I will call you.
(*d*) When I arrive, I will call you.

38. (*a*) Who among you has the answer?
(*b*) Whom among you has the answer?
(*c*) Whom amongst you has the answer?
(*d*) Who amid you has the answer?

39. (*a*) No sooner than he reached the station the train left.
(*b*) No sooner had he reached the station than the train left.
(*c*) No sooner he had reached the station than the train left.
(*d*) No sooner had he reached the station then the train left.

40. (*a*) Hardly had I arrived at the airport than the plane departed.
(*b*) Scarcely had I arrived at the airport when the plane departed.
(*c*) Hardly I had arrived at the airport when the plane departed.
(*d*) Scarcely had I arrived at the airport then the plane departed.

Directions (Qs. No. 41-45): *Each item in this section has a sentence with four parts labeled (a), (b), (c) and (d). Read each sentence to find out whether there is any error in any part. Indicate your response in the Answer Sheet accordingly.*

41. The project staff are/(*a*) working on the weekend/(*b*) so as not to delay/(*c*) the project any further/(*d*).

42. When I saw Arnab/(*a*) he said he/(*b*) had taken his/(*c*) driving test yesterday/(*d*).

43. Of all the players/(*a*) it was Ramesh/(*b*) who plan his tactics/(*c*) with utmost care/(*d*).

44. Many people in India are/(*a*) still not aware/(*b*) of India's indigenous fabrics/(*c*) that reflects the rich heritage of craftsmanship/(*d*).

45. Meaningful ecological/(*a*) affects of the handloom/(*b*) sector can be optimized/(*c*) through recycling practices/(*d*).

46. Read the following pairs:

	Active Voice	*Passive Voice*
I.	They laughed at his warnings and objected to all his proposals.	His warnings were laughed at and his proposals were objected to.
II.	Do not insult the weak.	You are advised to not insult the weak.

Identify the pair(s) wherein the Passive Voice is correctly stated and mark your response on the Answer Sheet accordingly.
(*a*) I only (*b*) II only
(*c*) Both I and II (*d*) Neither I nor II

47. Read the following pairs:

	Direct Speech	*Indirect Speech*
I.	The policeman said to us, "Where are you going?"	The Policeman asked where were we going.
II.	"Call the first witness", said the Judge.	The Judge said them to call the witness first.

Identify the pair(s) wherein the Indirect Speech is correctly stated and mark your response on the Answer Sheet accordingly.
(*a*) I only (*b*) II only
(*c*) Both I and II (*d*) Neither I nor II

48. Read the following pairs:

	Idiom/Phrase	*Meaning*
I.	Have one foot in the grave	To be in the last stage of life
II.	Get your feet wet	Establish yourself securely in an establishment

III. Follow suit	Correctly conform to another's action

Identify the pair(s) wherein the meaning is correctly stated and mark your response on the Answer Sheet accordingly.

(*a*) I only
(*b*) III only
(*c*) I and III
(*d*) II and III

49. Read the following pairs:

Group of words	*One-word substitution*
I. Decayed with usually a very bad or disgusting smell	Putrid
II. Humorous in a clever and often ironic way	Wry
III. In a state of tremulous excitement	Aflutter

Identify the pairs wherein the one-word substitution is correctly stated and mark your response on the Answer Sheet accordingly.

(*a*) I and II only (*b*) II and III only
(*c*) I and III only (*d*) I, II and III

50. Fill in the blanks (X, Y) in the following sentences with the appropriate word/phrase given in the brackets:

I. I spent X (less/the least) money on clothes in the whole family.

II. The people who work the hardest make Y (a few/the fewest) mistakes.

Identify the words/phrases and mark your response on the Answer Sheet accordingly.

(*a*) I—the least, II—the fewest
(*b*) I—the least, II—a few
(*c*) I—less, II—a few
(*d*) I—less, II—the fewest

PART B : GENERAL KNOWLEDGE

51. A pendulum of length L oscillates with an angular amplitude of $\theta = 60°$ and time period T. Let $T_0 = 2\pi\sqrt{\frac{L}{g}}$ be the time period for small angle of oscillations, where g is the acceleration due to gravity. If air resistance is negligibly small and the string remains straight, then which one of the following is correct?

(*a*) T will be slightly greater than T_0.
(*b*) T will be slightly smaller than T_0.
(*c*) T will be exactly equal to T_0.
(*d*) T will depend upon the mass of the bob.

52. Two forces of equal magnitude simultaneously act at a point. It is observed that the resultant force is equal in magnitude to the individual forces. Which of the following statements is/are correct?

I. The angle between one of the individual forces and the resultant force is $\pi/3$.

II. The angle between the individual forces is $2\pi/3$.

Select the answer using the code given below.

(*a*) I only (*b*) II only
(*c*) Both I and II (*d*) Neither I nor II

53. A solid of mass m has temperature dependent specific heat as $C(T) = C_0 + \alpha T$, where C_0 and α are constants. The solid is heated from T_1 to T_2. Which one of the following is the correct expression for quantity of heat (Q) of the solid mass?

(*a*) $Q = mC_0(T_2 - T_1)$
(*b*) $Q = m(T_2 - T_1)[C_0 + \alpha(T_1 + T_2)]$
(*c*) $Q = m(T_2 - T_1)[C_0(T_1 + T_2) + \alpha]$
(*d*) $Q = m(T_2 - T_1)\left[C_0 + \frac{\alpha}{2}(T_1 + T_2)\right]$

54. In a certain process, the relation between pressure (P) and volume (V), for an ideal gas, is given by PV^2 = constant. If the initial temperature is T_1 and the final temperature is T_2; and the initial volume is V_1 and the final volume is V_2, then which one of the following is correct?

(*a*) $\frac{T_1}{T_2} = \frac{V_1}{V_2}$ (*b*) $\frac{T_1}{T_2} = \left(\frac{V_1}{V_2}\right)^2$

(*c*) $\frac{T_1}{T_2} = \frac{V_2}{V_1}$ (*d*) $\frac{T_1}{T_2} = \left(\frac{V_2}{V_1}\right)^2$

55. For an ideal gas, a process is described by $P = kT$, where k is a constant. If the molar heat capacity for this process is C, then which one of the following is correct (where the symbols have their usual meanings)?

(*a*) $C = C_P$
(*b*) $C = C_V$
(*c*) $C = (C_P + C_V)/2$
(*d*) C is never constant

56. For an object in gravitational field, the gravitational potential is the same at two points A and B, but the gravitational field is not the same at these two points. Which one of the following statements is correct?

(*a*) Positive work is done by gravity in moving the object from point A to point B.
(*b*) Negative work is done by gravity in moving the object from point A to point B.
(*c*) Gravity must be non-conservative in such a region.
(*d*) No work is done by gravity in moving the object from point A to point B.

57. The position vector of a particle is given by $\vec{r} = \sqrt{3}t^2\hat{i} + \sqrt{2}t\hat{j} + \sqrt{5}\hat{k}$. Which one of the following statements is correct?

(*a*) The force acting on the particle is parallel to the instantaneous momentum of the particle.
(*b*) The force acting on the particle is perpendicular to the instantaneous momentum of the particle.
(*c*) The particle experiences zero force.
(*d*) The force acting on the particle is not parallel to the instantaneous momentum of the particle.

58. A ball is dropped from rest from height h above the ground in frame S (the Earth's frame). Another frame S′ is moving upwards with constant speed u relative to the Earth. In frame S′, the ball has initial downward speed v. Pertaining to the change in kinetic energy (ΔK) of the ball from release to just before hitting the ground as measured in frames S and S′ separately, which one of the following is correct?

(*a*) ΔK is the same in both the frames.
(*b*) ΔK is larger in frame S.
(*c*) ΔK is larger in frame S′.
(*d*) ΔK cannot be compared without the information of mass of the ball.

59. A floating body is in stable state. Which one of the following is correct?

(*a*) The centre of gravity of the body is above its centre of buoyancy.
(*b*) The centre of gravity of the body is below its centre of buoyancy.
(*c*) The centre of gravity of the body coincides with its centre of buoyancy.
(*d*) The centre of gravity of the body is below the metacentre.

60. A constant power machine pulls a block on a smooth horizontal surface. Which one of the following correctly describes the relation between speed of the block (v) and time (t)?

(*a*) $v \propto t$ (*b*) $v \propto \sqrt{t}$
(*c*) $v \propto t^2$ (*d*) $v \propto t^{3/2}$

61. A 5 g piece of ice at −20°C is put into m kg of water at 30°C temperature. The heat is exchanged only between the ice and the water. The final temperature of the mixture is 0°C in liquid phase. What is the value of m in kg?

(*a*) 0.050 (*b*) 0.010
(*c*) 0.015 (*d*) 0.150

62. A very large container consists of an ideal gas. The speed of sound in the gas is x. When the pressure of the gas is doubled while keeping the temperature constant, the speed of sound now becomes y. What is the ratio of x to y?

(*a*) 1 (*b*) $\sqrt{2}$
(*c*) 2 (*d*) 4

63. A person jumps from a height on soft sand. Which one of the following is the correct reason for less likely injury to the person?

(*a*) The sand exerts no reaction force.
(*b*) The sand reduces the change in momentum.
(*c*) The sand increases the impact time.
(*d*) The sand increases the momentum.

64. An object is placed far beyond the centre of curvature of a concave mirror. The object then starts accelerating towards the mirror. Which one of the following is correct?

(*a*) The image will accelerate towards the centre of curvature.
(*b*) The image will accelerate towards the focus.
(*c*) The image will accelerate towards the pole of the mirror.
(*d*) The image will move with a constant speed towards the focus.

65. A particle is moved from point X to point Y under a force field. The work done depends only on the initial and final speeds. Which one of the following is correct?

(*a*) The force is conservative.
(*b*) The network equals the change in kinetic energy.
(*c*) The force is constant.
(*d*) The velocity must always increase.

66. One year at a planet is 8 times as large as compared to the one year at the Earth. Which one of the following is correct about the planet's orbit?

(*a*) The semimajor axis of the planet's orbit is same as that of the Earth.

(*b*) The semimajor axis of the planet's orbit is twice as compared to that of the Earth.

(*c*) The semimajor axis of the planet's orbit is thrice as compared to that of the Earth.

(*d*) The semimajor axis of the planet's orbit is four times as compared to that of the Earth.

67. A lightning rod with sharp tip reduces damage risk. Which one of the following is the primary reason for it?

(*a*) It attracts lightning directly.

(*b*) The sharp tip reduces the local electric field.

(*c*) It enhances field and promotes continuous corona discharge.

(*d*) It repels charged clouds.

68. A periscope uses two plane mirrors inclined at 45°. If the tube of the periscope is filled with a complete transparent liquid of refractive index 1.5, then which one of the following is correct in respect of the image seen?

(*a*) The image will remain unchanged.

(*b*) The image will appear laterally shifted.

(*c*) The image will appear 1.5 times brighter.

(*d*) The image will appear 1.5 times darker.

69. It has been observed that a mirror always forms the image between the pole and the focus, irrespective of the location of the object. Which one of the following is correct in respect of the nature of the mirror?

(*a*) It is a plane mirror.

(*b*) It is a convex mirror.

(*c*) It is a concave mirror of small focal length.

(*d*) It is a concave mirror of large focal length.

70. What is the upward force acting on a skydiver of mass 60 kg who is falling at a uniform speed of 2 m/s?

(*a*) 0 (*b*) 60 N

(*c*) 588 N (*d*) 708 N

71. With respect to electromagnetic waves, the human eye is sensitive to

(*a*) both electric and magnetic fields

(*b*) electric field only

(*c*) magnetic field only

(*d*) infrared part of the electromagnetic spectrum

72. Three wires each of length L, cross-sectional area A and resistivity *p* are connected as shown in the figure.

These are to be replaced by another wire of same resistivity such that the resistance between points X and Z does not change. If L_1 is the length and A_1 is the cross-sectional area of the new wire, then which one among the following is correct?

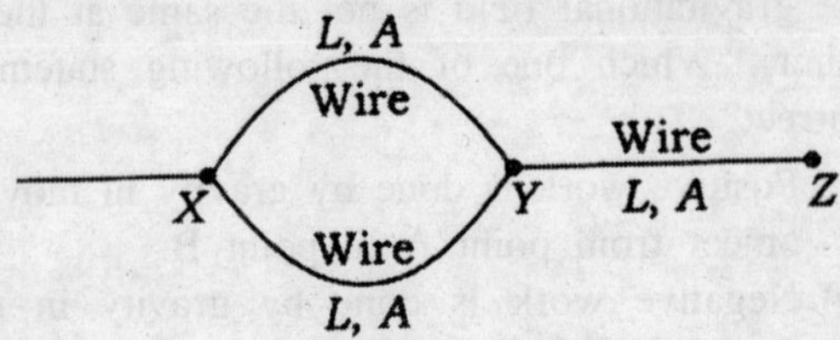

(*a*) $L_1 = 3L$ and $A_1 = 2A$

(*b*) $L_1 = L$ and $A_1 = A$

(*c*) $L_1 = 2L$ and $A_1 = 3A$

(*d*) $L_1 = 2L$ and $A_1 = 2A$

73. A light ray is falling on a face of an equilateral glass prism as shown in the figure:

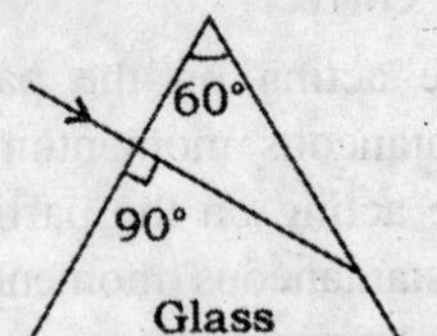

Which one of the following diagrams correctly shows the complete path of the ray through the glass prism?

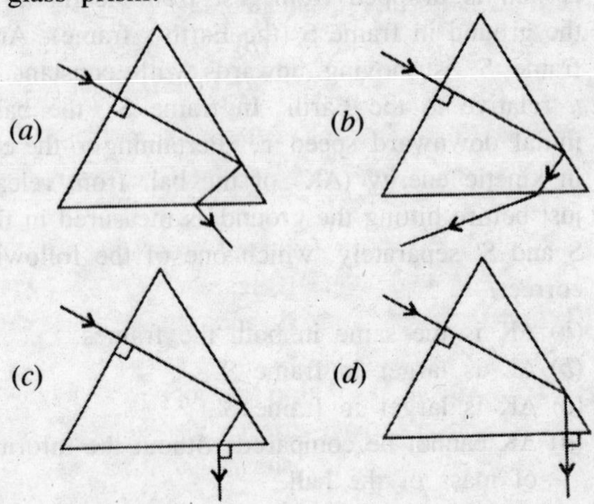

74. A glass slab of refractive index 1.5 is cut in the shape of a parallelepiped ABCD as shown in the figure. Surface BC is polished to form a perfect reflector. Light is incident at surface AB from inside at an angle π/3. Which one of the following is the correct angle ABC(θ) such that the reflected light retraces its path?

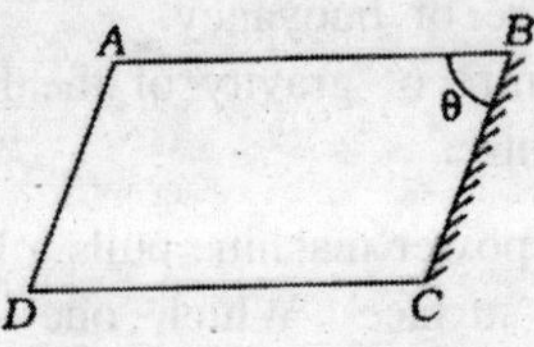

(*a*) π/6 (*b*) π/3

(*c*) π/4 (*d*) 5π/12

75. The force-time (F-t) graph of a 10 kg moving object is shown below:

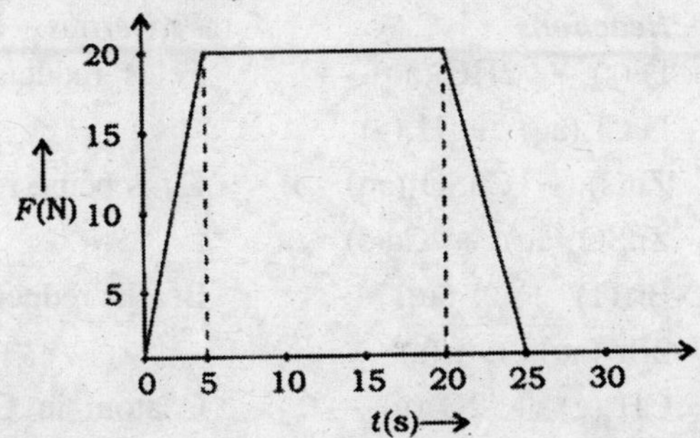

What is the final speed of the object?

(*a*) 0 (*b*) 15 m/s
(*c*) 30 m/s (*d*) 40 m/s

76. If x is the number of electrons and y is the number of nucleons present in ${}^{32}_{16}S^{2-}$, then which one of the following is correct?

(*a*) $x = 14$ and $y = 32$
(*b*) $x = 16$ and $y = 30$
(*c*) $x = 18$ and $y = 32$
(*d*) $x = 18$ and $y = 30$

77. Which one of the following forms of carbon is thermodynamically most stable?

(*a*) Coal (*b*) Graphite
(*c*) Diamond (*d*) Fullerene

78. Consider the following statements:

I. A colloid and a suspension are heterogeneous mixtures.
II. Colloids can be separated from the mixture by the process of centrifugation.
III. Particles of colloids and suspensions can be seen by naked eye.
IV. The aqueous solution of copper sulphate does not show Tyndall effect; however, the mixture of milk and water shows Tyndall effect.

Which of the statements given above is/are correct?

(*a*) I only (*b*) II and III only
(*c*) I, II and III (*d*) I, II and IV

79. A non-volatile solid solute may be separated from a solution by which of the following processes?

I. Evaporation
II. Crystallization

Select the correct answer using the code given below.

(*a*) I only (*b*) II only
(*c*) Both I and II (*d*) Neither I nor II

80. Which of the following are oxidation reactions?

I. Rusting of iron
II. Burning of fuel
III. Rancidity of oils and fats
IV. Browning of fruits

Select the correct answer using the code given below.

(*a*) I, II and III only
(*b*) I, II and IV only
(*c*) III and IV only
(*d*) I, II, III and IV

81. Consider the following statement: "Acids are substances that dissociate in water to give hydrogen ions H^+ (aq), and bases are substances that produce hydroxyl ions OH^- "(aq)".

The above statement is based on which one of the following concepts?

(*a*) Bronsted-Lowry concept
(*b*) Lewis acid-base concept
(*c*) Arrhenius concept
(*d*) Conjugate acid-base concept

82. Superphosphate of lime—a phosphate fertilizer–is obtained by the reaction of:

(*a*) calcium phosphate with sodium hydroxide
(*b*) calcium phosphate with sulphuric acid
(*c*) calcium phosphate with hydrogen chloride
(*d*) calcium phosphate with nitric acid

83. 1.7 g of silver nitrate is dissolved in 100 g of water, and 0.585 g of sodium chloride is dissolved in 100 g of water. Both are mixed and a chemical reaction occurs. 1.435 g of silver chloride and 0.85 g of sodium nitrate are formed. Which law of chemical combination is shown by the above reaction?

(*a*) Law of multiple proportions
(*b*) Law of conservation of mass
(*c*) Law of reciprocal proportions
(*d*) Law of constant proportions

84. Which of the following statements is/are correct with regard to Nitrolim?

I. It is prepared by heating calcium carbide with nitrogen.
II. It decomposes into ammonia in soil.
III. It is an NPK fertilizer.
IV. It is an organic fertilizer.

Select the answer using the code given below.

(*a*) I and II only (*b*) I, II and III
(*c*) IV only (*d*) I, II and IV

85. Consider the following pairs:

I. Pigment	:	TiO_2
II. Drier	:	Turpentine
III. Thinner	:	Naphthenates
IV. Antiskinning agent	:	Polyhydroxy phenol

How many of the pairs given above are correctly matched?

(*a*) One (*b*) Two
(*c*) Three (*d*) All the four

86. Consider the following statements:

I. Pine oil is used as antifoaming agent in the emulsion paints.
II. Protective colloids are used in the emulsion paints to decrease their stability.
III. Driers having oxidizable oils are added to the emulsion paints to accelerate drying process.

Which of the statements given above is/are correct?

(*a*) I and II (*b*) I only
(*c*) II and III (*d*) I and III

87. Consider the following:

I. $AlCl_3$
II. NH_3
III. BF_3
IV. $FeCl_3$

How many of the above are Lewis acids?

(*a*) One (*b*) Two
(*c*) Three (*d*) All the four

88. Consider the following statements:

I. Soaps are sodium or potassium salts of long-chain carboxylic acids.
II. The properties of catenation and isomerism in the element carbon are attributed to existence of large number of organic compounds than inorganic compounds.
III. Carbon dioxide is acidic but carbon monoxide is neutral molecule.

Which of the statements given above are correct?

(*a*) I and II only
(*b*) II and III only
(*c*) I and III only
(*d*) I, II and III

89. Which of the following is/are the physical test(s) employed for the manufacture of paper?

I. Mechanical and strength properties
II. Surface properties
III. Optical properties
IV. Permeability to fluids

Select the correct answer using the code given below.

(*a*) I only
(*b*) II and III only
(*c*) I, II and III only
(*d*) I, II, III and IV

90. Consider the following pairs of reactions and properties:

Reactions	***Properties***
I. $Fe(s) + 2HCl(aq) \rightarrow FeCl_2(aq) + H_2(g)$	Fe is reductant
II. $Zn(s) + CuSO_4(aq) \rightarrow ZnSO_4(aq) + Cu(s)$	Cu is being reduced
III. $Br_2(l) + 2I^-(aq) \rightarrow 2Br^-(aq) + I_2(s)$	Br_2 is reductant
IV. $CH_4(g) + 2O_2(g) \rightarrow CO_2(g) + 2H_2O(l)$	C atom in CH_4 is oxidized

Which of the above pairs are correct?

(*a*) I and II only (*b*) II, III and IV
(*c*) I, II and IV (*d*) I, III and IV

91. Which of the following properties of alveoli is/are helpful in gaseous exchange during respiration in human beings?

I. The epithelial lining of alveoli is very thin.
II. Elastic fibres are present in alveolar wall.
III. Wall of alveoli is surrounded by many blood capillaries.

Select the correct answer using the code given below.

(*a*) I and II only (*b*) I and III only
(*c*) III only (*d*) I, II and III

92. In which one of the following groups of animals, oestrus cycle is ***not*** observed?

(*a*) Cows (*b*) Monkeys
(*c*) Rats (*d*) Tigers

93. Which one of the following tissues in plants is usually without protoplast and regarded as dead cells?

(*a*) Collenchyma
(*b*) Parenchyma
(*c*) Sclerenchyma
(*d*) Xylem parenchyma

94. In which cell does the first meiotic cell division take place during the process of spermatogenesis?

(*a*) Spermatogonium
(*b*) Primary spermatocyte
(*c*) Secondary spermatocyte
(*d*) Sertoli cell

95. Consider the following statements in respect of cell and its structure:

I. All cells possess cell wall.
II. All cells have ribosomes present inside.
III. All cells have well-organized nucleus.
IV. All cells have linear DNA molecules present in them.

Which of the statements given above is/are correct?

(*a*) II and III (*b*) II only
(*c*) II and IV (*d*) I and III

96. Which part of the plant or flower contributes in the form of false fruit like apple?

(*a*) Petal (*b*) Sepal
(*c*) Stamen (*d*) Thalamus

97. In which of the following parts of organisms, the process of gaseous exchange during respiration does ***not*** take place?

(*a*) Skin of earthworms
(*b*) Bronchi of humans
(*c*) Gills of Pila
(*d*) Alveoli of humans

98. Which one of the following parts of an ovule possesses reserve food?

(*a*) Integument (*b*) Funicle
(*c*) Chalaza (*d*) Nucellus

99. Which one of the following respiratory volumes of human lung is the lowest?

(*a*) Residual volume
(*b*) Tidal volume
(*c*) Inspiratory reserve volume
(*d*) Expiratory reserve volume

100. Which one of the following valves guards the opening between the right ventricle and the pulmonary artery?

(*a*) Bicuspid valve (*b*) Semilunar valve
(*c*) Mitral valve (*d*) Tricuspid valve

101. Which one of the following is ***not*** a strategy in the Rainfed Area Development (RAD) scheme of India?

(*a*) Diversified farming
(*b*) Soil health management
(*c*) Adaptation of cluster-based approaches
(*d*) Optimizing canal irrigation

102. Consider the following statements about Kamarajar Port:

I. It is an example of corporatized public company.
II. It was earlier known as Ennore Port.
III. It is a natural port.

Which of the statements given above are correct?

(*a*) I and II only (*b*) II and III only
(*c*) I and III only (*d*) I, II and III

103. Consider the following statements:

I. Earthquake waves are basically of two types, namely body waves and surface waves.
II. The body waves interact with the surface rocks and generate surface waves.

Which of the statements given above is/are correct?

(*a*) I only (*b*) II only
(*c*) Both I and II (*d*) Neither I nor II

104. Consider the following statements regarding the Earth's crust:

I. The continental crust is thinner under fold mountains.
II. The mean thickness of ocean crust is 30 km.
III. The Earth's crust is brittle in nature.

Which of the statements given above is/are correct?

(*a*) I only (*b*) I and II
(*c*) III only (*d*) I and III

105. Which of the following are associated with composite volcanoes?

I. They result in explosive eruptions.
II. They eject pyroclastic materials.
III. Pyroclastic materials and ashes accumulate near the vent, forming layers.

Select the correct answer using the code given below.

(*a*) I and II only
(*b*) II and III only
(*c*) I and III only
(*d*) I, II and III

106. Loose sediments are transformed into sedimentary rocks by the process of:

(*a*) lithification (*b*) weathering
(*c*) mass wasting (*d*) solifluction

107. Consider the following statements about temperature inversion:

I. This happens when normal lapse rate gets inverted.
II. Winter nights with cloudy skies are conducive for temperature inversion.
III. Polar areas experience inversion throughout the year.

Which of the statements given above are correct?

(*a*) I and II only (*b*) II and III only
(*c*) I and III only (*d*) I, II and III

108. Consider the following statements regarding extra-tropical cyclones:

I. They usually develop in the mid and high latitudes.
II. They affect a much larger area as compared to tropical cyclone.
III. They move from east to west.

Which of the statements given above are correct?

(*a*) I and II only (*b*) II and III only
(*c*) I and III only (*d*) I, II and III

109. Which one of the following receives an average annual rainfall of below 50 cm in India, indicating highest inadequacy?

(*a*) Madhya Pradesh (*b*) Haryana
(*c*) Ladakh (*d*) Jharkhand

110. As per the land-use categories in the Land Revenue Records of India, "a cultivable land which is left uncultivated for more than a year but less than 5 years" is called

(*a*) current fallow
(*b*) fallow, other than current fallow
(*c*) barren land
(*d*) culturable wasteland

111. Consider the following pairs:

Types of Chemical Weathering	*Characteristics*
I. Solution	Results in leaching of minerals
II. Carbonation	Helps in breaking down feldspars
III. Hydration	Causes an increase in the volume of rocks
IV. Oxidation	Changes the colour of rocks

How many pairs given above are correctly matched?

(*a*) One (*b*) Two
(*c*) Three (*d*) All the four

112. Quartzite is metamorphosed from which one of the following rocks?

(*a*) Pegmatite (*b*) Limestone
(*c*) Sandstone (*d*) Shale

113. Consider the following statements:

I. In a seismograph, P waves are recorded earlier than S waves.

II. In P waves, the individual particles vibrate to and fro in the direction of wave propagation whereas in S waves, the particles vibrate up and down at right angles to the direction of wave propagation.

Which of the statements given above is/are correct?

(*a*) I only (*b*) II only
(*c*) Both I and II (*d*) Neither I nor II

114. Consider the following statements regarding hypocentre:

I. It is the point where the energy is released and is called the focus of an earthquake.

II. It is the point where the earthquake starts and may be many kilometres deep within the Earth.

Which of the statements given above is/are correct?

(*a*) I only (*b*) II only
(*c*) Both I and II (*d*) Neither I nor II

115. Consider the following critical minerals:

I. Neodymium
II. Tellurium
III. Dysprosium
IV. Gallium

Which of the above minerals are ***not*** used for the production of photovoltaic cells used in solar panels?

(*a*) I and IV (*b*) II and III
(*c*) I and III (*d*) II and IV

116. Which one of the following winds is responsible for wildfires in Southern California?

(*a*) Diablo wind (*b*) Chinook wind
(*c*) Santa Ana wind (*d*) Jarbo Gap wind

117. Which one of the following is ***not*** a pass of Arunachal Pradesh?

(*a*) Kumjawng Pass (*b*) Yonggyap Pass
(*c*) Muling La (*d*) Bomdi La

118. Mount Ibu, which recently erupted in Indonesia, is a

(*a*) shield volcano
(*b*) composite volcano
(*c*) volcanic dome
(*d*) cinder cone

119. Consider the following statements in case of terrestrial planets:

I. Mercury, Venus, Earth and Mars are terrestrial planets having low densities as compared to other planets.

II. They lie between the Sun and the belt of asteroids.

III. Their lower gravity can hold the escaping gases.

Which of the statements given above is/are correct?

(*a*) I and II (*b*) II and III
(*c*) I and III (*d*) II only

120. Consider the following pairs:

Layers of Atmosphere	*Characteristics*
I. Troposphere	Absorbs ultraviolet radiation
II. Stratosphere	Changes in weather and climate
III. Mesosphere	Reflects radio waves back to the Earth

How many of the pairs given above are correctly matched?

(*a*) None (*b*) One
(*c*) Two (*d*) All the three

121. Consider the following pairs:

	Books	**Authors**
I.	Dayabhaga	Jimutavahana
II.	Prithviraj Raso	Chandbardai
III.	Lilavati	Bhaskaracharya
IV.	Mitakshara	Vijnaneshvara

How many pairs given above are correctly matched?

(*a*) One (*b*) Two
(*c*) Three (*d*) All the four

122. Arrange the following in chronological order from the earliest to recent:

I. British East India Company formed
II. Magellan circumnavigated the globe
III. Dutch East India Company formed
IV. Vasco da Gama reached Calicut/Kozhikode

Select the correct answer using the code given below.

(*a*) IV, I, II, III (*b*) IV, II, I, III
(*c*) II, IV, III, I (*d*) II, IV, I, III

123. Consider the following pairs:

	Inventions	***Inventors***
I.	Flying shuttle loom	John Kay
II.	Water frame	James Hargreaves
III.	Spinning jenny	Richard Arkwright

How many of the pairs given above are correctly matched?

(*a*) One (*b*) Two
(*c*) All the three (*d*) None

124. Consider the following statements in respect of the Rowlatt Act of 1919:

I. Gandhiji launched a nationwide Satyagraha against the proposed Rowlatt Act, 1919.
II. The Act had been hurriedly passed through the Imperial Legislative Council despite the opposition of Indian members.
III. The Act gave the Government enormous powers to repress political activities.

Which of the statements given above is/are correct?

(*a*) I only (*b*) III only
(*c*) I and II only (*d*) I, II and III

125. Consider the following statements regarding the Industrial Revolution in Britain:

I. There was availability of banks which could loan money to set up industries.
II. There was a good transport network.

Which of the statements given above is/are correct?

(*a*) I only (*b*) II only
(*c*) Both I and II (*d*) Neither I nor II

126. Consider the following statements regarding the Russian Revolution:

I. The incident known as 'Bloody Sunday' started a series of events known as the 1905 Revolution.
II. Lawyers, doctors, engineers and other middle-class workers established the Union of Unions and demanded a Constituent Assembly.

Which of the statements given above is/are correct?

(*a*) I only (*b*) II only
(*c*) Both I and II (*d*) Neither I nor II

127. Who among the following advocated the construction of initial railways in India for facilitating army movement?

(*a*) Lord Dalhousie (*b*) Lord Lytton
(*c*) Winston Churchill (*d*) Lord Wellesley

128. The large well supplying water to the Great Bath of Mohenjo-daro was located

(*a*) near the drain of the tank
(*b*) at the top of one of the staircases
(*c*) in one of the adjoining rooms on the eastern side
(*d*) at the bottom of the tank in a corner

129. If you like to visit famous Jain pilgrimage sites, which of the following towns you will have to travel to?

I. Moodabidri
II. Madurai
III. Sonagiri

Select the correct answer using the code given below.

(*a*) I and II only (*b*) I and III only
(*c*) II and III only (*d*) I, II and III

130. Consider the following statements with regard to bead production in Harappan towns:

I. The materials used to make beads included camelian, quartz and steatite.
II. The beads were cylindrical, barrel-shaped and disc-shaped.
III. Specialized stone drills were used for making holes through the beads.

Which of the statements given above are correct?

(*a*) I and II only (*b*) II and III only
(*c*) I and III only (*d*) I, II and III

131. Consider the following statements:

I. The Second Five-Year Plan sought to promote development which would establish socialistic pattern of society in India.
II. Between 1966 and 1969, three Annual Plans were formulated.

III. The Ninth Five-Year Plan could not take off at its stipulated time in the 60th year of India's Independence.

Which of the statements given above are correct?

(*a*) I and II only (*b*) I and III only
(*c*) II and III only (*d*) I, II and III

132. With reference to the Constitution of India, consider the following statements about the Comptroller and Auditor General (CAG) of India:

I. The CAG shall be appointed by the President of India.

II. The CAG is not eligible for further office under the Government of India after he has ceased to hold his office.

III. The reports of the CAG relating to the accounts of the Union shall be submitted to the Prime Minister who shall cause them to be laid before the House of the People.

Which of the statements given above are correct?

(*a*) I and II only (*b*) II and III only
(*c*) I and III only (*d*) I, II and III

133. Consider the following offices:

I. The Vice President of India
II. The Governors within their respective States
III. The Prime Minister of India
IV. The Speaker of the Lok Sabha

Which one of the following options represents the correct order of these offices for ceremonial occasions in the Table of Precedence as approved by the President of India?

(*a*) III, I, II, IV (*b*) I, III, II, IV
(*c*) I, III, IV, II (*d*) III, I, IV, II

134. Consider the following pairs with reference to the Constitution of India:

I. Part IX A : The Municipalities
II. Part IX B : The Cooperative Societies
III. Part X : Relations between the Union and States
IV. Part XII : Finance, Property, Contracts and Suits

How many of the pairs given above are correctly matched?

(*a*) One (*b*) Two
(*c*) Three (*d*) All the four

135. Consider the following pairs related to the United Nations (UN) Sustainable Development Goals:

I. Goal 1 : End poverty in all forms everywhere
II. Goal 2 : Ensure healthy lives
III. Goal 3 : Ensure quality education
IV. Goal 4 : Achieve gender equality

How many of the pairs given above are correctly matched?

(*a*) One (*b*) Two
(*c*) Three (*d*) All the four

136. Consider the following statements:

I. A Money Bill shall not be introduced in the Rajya Sabha.

II. The Rajya Sabha has no power to reject a Money Bill but can suggest amendment(s).

Which of the statements given above is/are correct?

(*a*) I only (*b*) II only
(*c*) Both I and II (*d*) Neither I nor II

137. Consider the following statements:

I. The Constitution of India mentions that the Speaker has the power to adjourn both the Houses sine die.

II. On prorogation, it is only the Speaker who can summon the Houses.

Which of the statements given above is/are correct?

(*a*) I only (*b*) II only
(*c*) Both I and II (*d*) Neither I nor II

138. With reference to the United Nations (UN), consider the following pairs:

United Nations Peacekeeping Operations	***Countries***
I. UNMOGIP	India and Pakistan
II. UNFICYP	Cyprus
III. UNMIK	Kosovo
IV. UNTSO	Haiti

How many of the pairs given above are correctly matched?

(*a*) One (*b*) Two
(*c*) Three (*d*) All the four

139. With reference to the territorial jurisdictions of High Courts in India, consider the following pairs:

High Courts	***Territorial Jurisdictions***
I. Calcutta High Court	Lakshadweep
II. Madras High Court	Puducherry
III. Gauhati High Court	Manipur
IV. Kerala High Court	Andaman and Nicobar Islands

How many of the pairs given above are correctly matched?

(*a*) One (*b*) Two
(*c*) Three (*d*) All the four

140. As per Article 324 of the Constitution of India, the Chief Election Commissioner shall not be removed from his office except in like manner and on the like grounds as:

(*a*) a Judge of the Supreme Court
(*b*) a Judge of a High Court
(*c*) the Speaker of the Lok Sabha
(*d*) the Governor of a State

141. With reference to defence cooperation between India and Russia, which of the following statements is/are correct?

I. BrahMos Cruise Missile system is jointly developed by India's DRDO and Russia's NPO Mashinostroyeniya (NPOM).
II. The production site of the Indo-Russia Rifles Private Limited (IRRPL) joint venture is in Korwa, Madhya Pradesh under the 'Atmanirbhar Bharat' initiative.

Select the answer using the code given below.

(*a*) I only
(*b*) II only
(*c*) Both I and II
(*d*) Neither I nor II

142. Which one among the following Departments is ***not*** under the Ministry of Home Affairs?

(*a*) The Department of States
(*b*) The Department of Official Language
(*c*) The Department of Border Management
(*d*) The Department of Drinking Water and Sanitation

143. The Atal Innovation Mission (AIM) is set up by the

(*a*) Department of Science and Technology, Government of India
(*b*) NITI Aayog
(*c*) Ministry of Statistics and Programme Implementation, Government of India
(*d*) Ministry of Corporate Affairs, Government of India

144. Which one amongst the following cities has been designated as the UNESCO Creative City of Gastronomy in 2025?

(*a*) Agra
(*b*) Lucknow
(*c*) Indore
(*d*) Ludhiana

145. PM MITRA Parks relate to which one of the following industries?

(*a*) Automobile
(*b*) Shipbuilding
(*c*) Textile
(*d*) Pottery

146. Which one of the following countries became the 11th member of ASEAN in 2025?

(*a*) Timor-Leste
(*b*) Vietnam
(*c*) Brunei
(*d*) Cambodia

147. Who among the following is the winner of the 2024-2025 Ranji Trophy?

(*a*) Vidarbha
(*b*) Kerala
(*c*) Karnataka
(*d*) Saurashtra

148. Choose the correct set of the following cities in descending order (according to the Degree of Urbanization definitions in 2025) in terms of population.

(*a*) Tokyo, Dhaka, Manila, New Delhi, Jakarta
(*b*) Jakarta, Dhaka, Tokyo, New Delhi, Manila
(*c*) Tokyo, Manila, Dhaka, Jakarta, New Delhi
(*d*) Jakarta, Tokyo, Dhaka, New Delhi, Manila

149. Consider the following countries:

I. Haiti
II. Philippines
III. Nicaragua
IV. India

According to the Climate Risk Index 2026, which of the above countries were affected by recurring extreme events during 1995-2024?

(*a*) I and III only
(*b*) II and IV only
(*c*) I, II and IV only
(*d*) I, II, III and IV

150. Match List-I with List-II and select the correct answer using the code given below the Lists:

List-I (Rescue Operations carried out by the Government of India)	***List-II (Countries)***
A. Operation Kaveri	I. Israel
B. Operation Indravati	II. Haiti
C. Operation Ajay	III. Ukraine
D. Operation Ganga	IV. Sudan

Code:

	A	B	C	D
(*a*)	III	II	I	IV
(*b*)	III	I	II	IV
(*c*)	IV	II	I	III
(*d*)	IV	I	II	III

PAPER II : MATHEMATICS

1. Let p, q and r be three unequal numbers such that p, q and r are in AP. If $(q - p)$, $(r - q)$ and p are in GP, then $(p + q) : (q + r) : (r + p)$ equals:

(a) 1 : 2 : 3 (b) 3 : 4 : 5
(c) 3 : 5 : 4 (d) 1 : 3 : 2

2. If p, g_1, g_2 and q are in GP and m is the arithmetic mean of p and q, then $\frac{g_1^2}{g_2} + \frac{g_2^2}{g_1}$ is equal to:

(a) m (b) $2m$
(c) 1 (d) $\frac{1}{2}$

3. Consider the following inequalities:

I. $1 + 4i > 3 + 2i$
II. $2 + 3i < 3 + 4i$
III. $4 + 3i > 3 + 4i$

where $i = \sqrt{-1}$

How many of the above are valid?

(a) None (b) One
(c) Two (d) All the three

4. Let Z_1 and Z_2 be complex numbers such that $\frac{3Z_1}{4Z_2}$ is purely imaginary.

What is $\left|\frac{Z_1 + Z_2}{Z_1 - Z_2}\right|$ equal to?

(a) 2 (b) $\frac{3}{2}$
(c) $\frac{5}{4}$ (d) 1

5. If α, β, γ, are cube roots of -8, then what is $\frac{\alpha^2 p^2 + \beta^2 q^2 + \gamma^2 r^2}{\beta^2 p^2 + \gamma^2 q^2 + \alpha^2 r^2}$ equal to?

(a) $\frac{\gamma}{\alpha}$ (b) $\frac{\gamma}{\beta}$
(c) $\frac{2\gamma}{\alpha}$ (d) $\frac{2\gamma}{\beta}$

6. The sum of the first n terms of an AP is $3n^2 + 5n$. If the mth term of the AP is 68, then what is the value of m?

(a) 9 (b) 10
(c) 11 (d) 12

7. A set S contains $(2n + 1)$ elements. If the number of subsets of S which contain at most n elements is 1024, then what is the value of n?

(a) 10 (b) 8
(c) 6 (d) 5

8. What is the maximum number of points of intersection of 5 circles?

(a) 10 (b) 15
(c) 20 (d) 25

9. What is the greatest value of r satisfying the inequality ${}^{15}C_{r+1} > 2 \times {}^{15}C_r$?

(a) 2 (b) 3
(c) 4 (d) 5

10. If $n = {}^mC_2$ then what is ${}^nC_2$ equal to?

(a) ${}^{m+1}C_4$ (b) $2 \times {}^{m+1}C_4$
(c) $3 \times {}^{m+1}C_4$ (d) ${}^{m+2}C_4$

11. If the highest degree coefficient is equal to 1, then what is the total number of quadratic equations which are unchanged on squaring their roots?

(a) 6 (b) 4
(c) 2 (d) None

12. Let α and β be the roots of the quadratic equation $x^2 - 2bx + c^2 = 0$ where b, c are positive real numbers. Let A be the arithmetic mean of α and β; and G be the geometric mean of α and β. What are the roots of the quadratic equation $x^2 - (b + c)x + bc = 0$?

(a) A, G (b) 2A, G
(c) A, 2G (d) 2A, 2G

13. If $1 - \log_{10}2 = \log_{10}(5^x + 4^x + 3^x + 2^x + 1)$, then what is a value of x?

(a) 10 (b) 5
(c) 1 (d) 0

14. Let $f(x) = \begin{vmatrix} 3x^2 & \cos x & -\sin x \\ 6 & -1 & 0 \\ q & q^2 & q^3 \end{vmatrix}$

where q is any constant, then what is $\frac{d^2}{dx^2}(f(x))$ at $x = 0$ equal to?

(a) -1
(b) 0
(c) 1
(d) q

15. If $\begin{vmatrix} a-b & p-q & x-y \\ b-c & q-r & y-z \\ c-a & r-p & z-x \end{vmatrix} = k\begin{vmatrix} a & b & c \\ p & q & r \\ x & y & z \end{vmatrix}$,

then what is the value of k?

(*a*) –1 (*b*) 0

(*c*) $\frac{1}{2}$ (*d*) 1

16. If p, q, r are the cube roots of unity, then what is $\begin{vmatrix} p^2+q^2 & r^2 & r^2 \\ p^2 & q^2+r^2 & p^2 \\ q^2 & q^2 & r^2+p^2 \end{vmatrix}$ equal to?

(*a*) –1 (*b*) 0

(*c*) 1 (*d*) 4

17. If A is a square matrix such that $|A| = -2$, then $|AA^T|$, where A^T is the transpose of A, is equal to:

(*a*) –4 (*b*) 1

(*c*) 2 (*d*) 4

18. Consider the following statements:

I. If $n \times n(n > 1)$ matrix is symmetric, then its inverse is also a symmetric matrix.

II. If $n \times n(n > 1)$ matrix is singular, then its adjoint is also a singular matrix.

Which of the statements given above is/are correct?

(*a*) I only (*b*) II only

(*c*) Both I and II (*d*) Neither I nor II

19. If $M = \begin{bmatrix} 2 & 0 & 0 \\ 0 & 2 & 0 \\ 0 & 0 & 2 \end{bmatrix}$, then what is the value of $|M||\text{adj}M|$?

(*a*) 8 (*b*) 64

(*c*) 256 (*d*) 512

20. If $M_k = \begin{bmatrix} k & k-1 \\ k-1 & k \end{bmatrix}$ where k is a natural number, then what is

$|M_1| + |M_2| + |M_3| + \ldots + |M_{50}|$ equal to?

(*a*) 50 (*b*) 1250

(*c*) 2500 (*d*) 5000

21. If M^T is the transpose of a 2 × 2 matrix M, then which of the following is/are correct?

I. $|M + M^T| = |M| + |M^T|$ if M is symmetric.

II. $|M + M^T| = 0$ if M is anti-symmetric.

Select the answer using the code given below:

(*a*) I only (*b*) II only

(*c*) Both I and II (*d*) Neither I nor II

22. If M is a square matrix such that $M^3 = M$, then how many values of $|M|$ are possible?

(*a*) One (*b*) Two

(*c*) Three (*d*) Four

23. Let $p = (x + y + z)$ and $q = xyz$. If $\begin{vmatrix} x & 1 & 1 \\ 1 & y & 1 \\ 1 & 1 & z \end{vmatrix}$ is positive, then which one of the following is correct?

(*a*) $q > p$ (*b*) $q + 1 > p$

(*c*) $q + 2 > p$ (*d*) $q + 2 \geq p$

24. What is

$(((A \cap B) \cup (A - B)) - ((A \cap B) \cup (B - A))) \cup A$

equal to?

(*a*) φ (*b*) A

(*c*) B (*d*) $A \cup B$

25. Let A and B be two sets. For some set C, both $A \cap C$ and $B \cap C$ are empty sets and $A \cup C = B \cup C$. Which of the following is/are true?

I. C = < φ

II. A = B

II. $A \cup B = C$

Select the answer using the code given below:

(*a*) I only (*b*) II only

(*c*) I and II only (*d*) I, II and III

26. If $2 \sec 4\beta = \tan 2\alpha + \cot 2\alpha$, then which one of the following is a possible value of $(\alpha + \beta)$?

(*a*) $\frac{\pi}{2}$ (*b*) $\frac{\pi}{4}$

(*c*) $\frac{\pi}{6}$ (*d*) $\frac{\pi}{8}$

27. If α and β are complementary angles such that $\alpha - \beta = \frac{\pi}{6}$ and $m \tan \beta = n \tan \alpha$, then what is $\left(\frac{m+n}{m-n}\right)$ equal to?

(*a*) 2 (*b*) $\frac{2}{\sqrt{3}}$

(*c*) 1 (*d*) $\frac{1}{\sqrt{3}}$

28. If $x = \sec\theta - \tan\theta$ and $y = \operatorname{cosec}\theta + \cot\theta$, then which one of the following is correct?

(*a*) $x + y - xy - 1 = 0$

(*b*) $x - y + xy + 1 = 0$

(*c*) $x + y + xy - 1 = 0$

(*d*) $x - y + xy - 1 = 0$

29. If $\cos\theta = \frac{1}{3}$, then what is the value of

$\sin\left(\frac{\theta}{2}\right)\sin\left(\frac{3\theta}{2}\right)$?

(*a*) $\frac{5}{9}$ (*b*) $\frac{7}{9}$

(*c*) $\frac{10}{9}$ (*d*) $\frac{11}{9}$

30. $\cos x + \sqrt{3}\sin x$ is maximum when x is equal to:

(*a*) $\frac{\pi}{2}$ (*b*) $\frac{\pi}{3}$

(*c*) $\frac{\pi}{4}$ (*d*) $\frac{\pi}{6}$

31. If θ lies in the fourth quadrant and $3\cot\theta + 4 = 0$, then what is the value of $\sin 2\theta + \cos 2\theta$?

(*a*) $-\frac{31}{25}$ (*b*) $-\frac{17}{25}$

(*c*) 0 (*d*) 1

32. If $\cos\alpha + \cos\beta = 0 = \sin\alpha + \sin\beta$, $\alpha \neq \beta$ then what is a value of $\cos 2\alpha + \cos 2\beta + 2\cos(\alpha + \beta)$?

(*a*) 0 (*b*) 1

(*c*) 2 (*d*) 4

33. In a triangle ABC, $\sin A = \cos B + \cos C$ then what is $\tan\left(\frac{B}{2}\right) + \cot\left(\frac{B}{2}\right)$ equal to?

(*a*) 1 (*b*) $\sqrt{2}$

(*c*) $\sqrt{3}$ (*d*) 2

34. Consider the following in respect of inverse circular functions:

I. $\sin^{-1}(-x) = -\sin^{-1}x$

II. $\cos^{-1}(-x) = \cos^{-1}x$

III. $\tan^{-1}(-x) = \pi - \tan^{-1}x$

IV. $\cot^{-1}(-x) = \pi - \cot^{-1}x$

How many of the above are correct?

(*a*) One (*b*) Two

(*c*) Three (*d*) All the four

35. What is $\tan\left[2\tan^{-1}\frac{1}{2} - \frac{\pi}{4}\right]$ equal to?

(*a*) -7 (*b*) 0

(*c*) $\frac{1}{5}$ (*d*) $\frac{1}{7}$

36. The angles A, B and C of a triangle are in the ratio 1 : 1 : 4. If the longest side of the triangle is 3 units, then what is the perimeter of the triangle?

(*a*) $3+\sqrt{3}$ units (*b*) $3+2\sqrt{3}$ units

(*c*) $3+3\sqrt{3}$ units (*d*) $6+\sqrt{3}$ units

37. In a triangle ABC, if a, b and c are the lengths of the sides opposite to the angles A, B and C respectively, then what is $\frac{\sin(A-B)}{\sin(A+B)}$ equal to?

(*a*) $\frac{a^2}{a^2-b^2}$ (*b*) $\frac{a^2}{a^2+b^2}$

(*c*) $\frac{a^2-b^2}{c^2}$ (*d*) $\frac{a^2-b^2}{b^2}$

38. What is the smallest positive x satisfying $\log_{\sin x}\cos x + \log_{\cos x}\sin x = 2$?

(*a*) $\frac{\pi}{2}$ (*b*) $\frac{\pi}{3}$

(*c*) $\frac{\pi}{4}$ (*d*) $\frac{\pi}{6}$

39. A plane is observed to be approaching the airport. It is at a distance of 10 km from the point of observation and makes an angle of elevation of 67·5°. What is the height of the plane above the ground?

(*a*) $10\sqrt{2+\sqrt{2}}$ km (*b*) $10\sqrt{2-\sqrt{2}}$ km

(*c*) $5\sqrt{2+\sqrt{2}}$ km (*d*) $5\sqrt{2-\sqrt{2}}$ km

40. What is the length of the chord of a unit circle which subtends at the centre of the circle an angle of 45°?

(*a*) $2\sqrt{2+\sqrt{2}}$ units (*b*) $2\sqrt{2-\sqrt{2}}$ units

(*c*) $\sqrt{2+\sqrt{2}}$ units (*d*) $\sqrt{2-\sqrt{2}}$ units

41. Let R be a relation on the set N of natural numbers defined by

$R = \{(x, y) : x, y \in N \text{ and } x = y^3\}$.

Which of the following statements is/are correct?

I. R is symmetric relation

II. R is transitive relation

Select the answer using the code given below:

(*a*) I only

(*b*) II only

(*c*) Both I and II

(*d*) Neither I nor II

42. For a given k, what is the minimum value of $x^2 + kx + k^2$?

(*a*) 0 (*b*) $\frac{k^2}{4}$

(*c*) $\frac{3k^2}{4}$ (*d*) $\frac{k^2}{2}$

43. Consider the following statements:

I. $\sqrt{x} + x + 1 = 0$ has two irrational roots.

II. $5\sqrt{x} - x - 4 = 0$ has two rational roots.

Which of the statements given above is/are correct?

(*a*) I only (*b*) II only
(*c*) Both I and II (*d*) Neither I nor II

44. How many numbers greater than 1000 can be formed using the digits 0, 1, 2 and 3 (repetition of digits is not allowed)?

(*a*) 24 (*b*) 18
(*c*) 15 (*d*) 12

45. If p^{th} term of an AP is k, then what is the sum of pth term, $(p + q)^{th}$ term and $(p - q)^{th}$ term of the AP?

(*a*) $2k$ (*b*) $3k$
(*c*) $4k$ (*d*) $5k$

Directions (Qs. No. 46-50): *For the next five (05) items that follow:*

Let u be a positive integer and f be a real number lying between 0 and 1. Further, $\left(\sqrt{2}+1\right)^{10} = u + f$ *and* $\left(\sqrt{2}-1\right)^{10} = v$.

46. Consider the following statements:

I. $(u + v + f)$ is an integer.
II. $(f + v)$ is an integer.

Which of the statements given above is/are correct?

(*a*) I only (*b*) II only
(*c*) Both I and II (*d*) Neither I nor II

47. What is the multiplicative inverse of $\left(\sqrt{2}+1\right)^{20}$?

(*a*) v (*b*) $v^2 - 1$
(*c*) v^2 (*d*) $v^2 + 1$

48. What is the value of $(v + f)$?

(*a*) 2 (*b*) 1
(*c*) 0·5 (*d*) 0·25

49. What is the value of u?

(*a*) 9725 (*b*) 6971
(*c*) 6726 (*d*) 6725

50. What is the value of uv?

(*a*) 1 (*b*) 2
(*c*) $0 < uv < 1$ (*d*) $1 < uv < 2$

Directions (Qs. No. 51 & 52): *For the next two (02) items that follow:*

The equation of a straight line which passes through the origin and makes an angle α $(0 \le \alpha \le 90°)$ *with the line*

Let: $x + \sqrt{3}y + 3\sqrt{3} = 0$ *is* $x - \sqrt{3}y = 0$.

51. What is the value of α?

(*a*) 30° (*b*) 45°
(*c*) 60° (*d*) 90°

52. What is the angle made by the line L with positive direction of y-axis?

(*a*) 30° (*b*) 45°
(*c*) 60° (*d*) 90°

Directions (Qs. No. 53 & 54): *For the next two (02) items that follow:*

P(−2, −3, 5), Q(4, −1, 5), R(6, −4, 8) and S(2, −6, 10) are four points.

53. Consider the following statements:

I. PQ is parallel to RS.
II. PR is perpendicular to QS.

Which of the statements given above is/are correct?

(*a*) I only (*b*) II only
(*c*) Both I and II (*d*) Neither I nor II

54. What is $(PQ^2 + 2QS^2 - 2PR^2)$ equal to?

(*a*) −1 (*b*) 0
(*c*) 1 (*d*) 2

Directions (Qs. No. 55 & 56): *For the next two (02) items that follow:*

A line L passing through the point (−1, 2, −3) is perpendicular to the plane P given by $2x + 3y + z + 5 = 0$.

55. What is the equation of the line L?

(*a*) $1 - x = y + 2 = 3 - z$
(*b*) $-(x + 1) = y - 2 = z + 3$
(*c*) $3x + 3 = 2y - 4 = 6z + 18$
(*d*) $3x - 3 = 2y + 4 = 6z - 18$

56. What are the direction ratios of a line M parallel to the plane P?

(*a*) <−3, 2, 1> (*b*) <3, 2, −6>
(*c*) <1, 3, 2> (*d*) <2, 2, −10>

Directions (Qs. No. 57 & 58): *For the next two (02) items that follow:*

Let X(a, p), Y(b, q) and Z(c, r) be the points such that a, b and c are in AP.

57. If p, q and r are in AP, then the points X, Y and Z are:

(*a*) on a straight line
(*b*) on a circle
(*c*) on a parabola
(*d*) the vertices of a triangle

58. If p, q and r are not in AP and $b = c$, then the line joining the points X, Y and Z is parallel to:

(*a*) y-axis (*b*) x-axis
(*c*) $y = x$ (*d*) $y = -x$

Directions (Qs. No. 59 & 60): *For the next two (02) items that follow:*

Consider the points A(0, 2), B(2, 3), C(4, 5) and D(0, k).

59. If the points lie on a circle, then what is/are the possible value(s) of k?

(*a*) 2 only (*b*) 5 only
(*c*) 2, 17 (*d*) 5, 17

60. If a circle is drawn through A, B and D, then what is the diameter of the circle?

(*a*) $3\sqrt{10}$ (*b*) $5\sqrt{10}$
(*c*) $3\sqrt{12}$ (*d*) $5\sqrt{12}$

Directions (Qs. No. 61 & 62): *For the next two (02) items that follow:*

The foci of the ellipse
$px^2 + 16y^2 = 16p$
and the foci of the hyperbola
$25(81x^2 - 144y^2) = 11664$
coincide (assume $p < 16$*).*

61. What is the value of p?

(*a*) $\sqrt{7}$ (*b*) 3
(*c*) 7 (*d*) 9

62. What is the difference between the eccentricities of the hyperbola and the ellipse?

(*a*) 0·5 (*b*) 0·75
(*c*) 1·0 (*d*) 1·25

Directions (Qs. No. 63 & 64): *For the next two (02) items that follow:*

The equation of the sphere S is
$x^2 + y^2 + z^2 - 4x - 6y - 12z + k = 0.$

63. What is the radius of the sphere passing through origin and concentric with the sphere S?

(*a*) $\frac{7}{2}$
(*b*) 5
(*c*) 7
(*d*) Cannot be determined due to insufficient data

64. If the radius of the sphere S is 8 units, what is the value of k?

(*a*) −15 (*b*) 7
(*c*) 10 (*d*) 15

Directions (Qs. No. 65 & 66): *For the next two (02) items that follow:*

Let, $\vec{a}, \vec{b}, \vec{c}, \vec{a}+\vec{b}, \vec{b}+\vec{c}, \vec{a}+\vec{b}+\vec{c}$ *be unit vectors.*

65. What is the angle between $\vec{a}$ and $\vec{b}$?

(*a*) $\frac{\pi}{6}$ (*b*) $\frac{\pi}{4}$
(*c*) $\frac{\pi}{2}$ (*d*) $\frac{2\pi}{3}$

66. What is the angle between $\vec{a}$ and $\vec{c}$?

(*a*) $\frac{\pi}{6}$ (*b*) $\frac{\pi}{4}$
(*c*) $\frac{\pi}{2}$ (*d*) $\frac{2\pi}{3}$

Directions (Qs. No. 67 & 68): *For the next two (02) items that follow:*

Let $\vec{a} \times \vec{b} = \vec{c}$ and $\vec{b} \times \vec{c} = \vec{a}$.

67. Consider the following statements:

I. $\vec{a}, \vec{b}, \vec{c}$ are orthogonal in pairs

II. $\vec{a}, \vec{b}, \vec{c}$ are unit vectors.

Which of the statements given above is/are correct?

(*a*) I only (*b*) II only
(*c*) Both I and II (*d*) Neither I nor II

68. Consider the following statements:

I. $(\vec{a} \times \vec{b}) \cdot \vec{c} + (\vec{b} \times \vec{c}) \cdot \vec{a} = (\vec{c} \times \vec{a}) \cdot \vec{b}$

II. $\{(\vec{a} \times \vec{b}) \times (\vec{b} \times \vec{c})\} \cdot \vec{b} = 1$

Which of the statements given above is/are correct?

(*a*) I only (*b*) II only
(*c*) Both I and II (*d*) Neither I nor II

Directions (Qs. No. 69 & 70): *For the next two (02) items that follow:*

Let $\vec{a}, \vec{b}, \vec{c}$ be unit vectors. Further, $\vec{a}$ is perpendicular to $\vec{b}$; $\vec{c}$ makes an angle $\frac{\pi}{3}$ with both $\vec{a}$ and $\vec{b}$; and $\vec{c} = p\vec{a} + q\vec{b} + r(\vec{a} \times \vec{b})$.

69. What is the value of $(p + q)$?

(*a*) $\frac{1}{2}$ (*b*) 1
(*c*) $\frac{3}{2}$ (*d*) 2

70. What is the value of r^2?

(*a*) 4 (*b*) 2
(*c*) 1 (*d*) $\frac{1}{2}$

71. If $f(x)$ is differentiable at $x = a$, then consider the following statements:

I. $f(x)$ is continuous at $x = a$

II. $\lim_{x \to a} f(x) = f(a)$

Which of the statements given above is/are correct?

(*a*) I only (*b*) II only

(*c*) Both I and II (*d*) Neither I nor II

72. What is $\lim_{x \to 1} \frac{x^{(n^2-1)} - 1}{x^{(n+1)} - 1}$ equal to, where $n > 1$ is a natural number?

(*a*) 0 (*b*) 1

(*c*) $n - 1$ (*d*) $n + 1$

73. What is $\lim_{x \to 0} \frac{10^{\sin x} - 1}{\tan x}$ equal to?

(*a*) 0 (*b*) 1

(*c*) ln 10 (*d*) $\log_{10} e$

74. What is the derivative of $\frac{x}{|x|}$ with respect to x, where $x < 0$?

(*a*) -1 (*b*) 0

(*c*) 1 (*d*) x

75. Consider the following statements in respect of the function $f(x) = x$ in the interval $(-1, 1)$:

I. The function attains maximum value.

II. The function attains minimum value.

Which of the statements given above is/are correct?

(*a*) I only (*b*) II only

(*c*) Both I and II (*d*) Neither I nor II

76. If $\sqrt[4]{y} = x + \sqrt{x^2 + 4}$, then what is $\sqrt{x^2 + 4}\frac{dy}{dx}$ equal to?

(*a*) $\frac{y}{4}$ (*b*) y

(*c*) $2y$ (*d*) $4y$

77. What is the length of the longest interval in which the function $f(x) = 2\cos^2 x - 1$ is decreasing?

(*a*) 2π (*b*) π

(*c*) $\frac{\pi}{2}$ (*d*) $\frac{\pi}{4}$

78. If A and B are acute angles such that $2A + 2B = \pi$, then what is the maximum value of $\sin A \cdot \sin B$?

(*a*) $\frac{1}{2}$ (*b*) $\frac{1}{4}$

(*c*) $\frac{\sqrt{3}}{4}$ (*d*) 1

79. What is the solution of the differential equation $\cos\left(\frac{dy}{dx}\right) = p$ where $y(0) = q$?

(*a*) $\cos\left(\frac{y-q}{x}\right) = p$ (*b*) $\cos\left(\frac{y-p}{x}\right) = q$

(*c*) $\cos^{-1}\left(\frac{y-q}{x}\right) = p$ (*d*) $\cos^{-1}\left(\frac{y-p}{x}\right) = q$

80. If $2f(x) + f(1 - x) = x$, then what is $f(x)$ equal to?

(*a*) $x - 1$ (*b*) $x - \left(\frac{1}{3}\right)$

(*c*) $2x$ (*d*) $2x - 1$

Directions (Qs. No. 81 & 82): *For the next two (02) items that follow:*

Let $(e^y)^x - y = 0$, where y is a function of x whose domain is $(0, 10]$.

81. What is $\frac{dy}{dx}$ equal to?

(*a*) $\frac{y}{1 - xy}$ (*b*) $\frac{y}{1 + xy}$

(*c*) $\frac{y^2}{1 - xy}$ (*d*) $\frac{y^2}{1 + xy}$

82. What is $\frac{dy}{dx}$ equal to, given that $y = y_0$ when $x = 1$?

(*a*) $-\frac{y_0}{1 + e^{y_0}}$ (*b*) $-\frac{y_0 e^{y_0}}{1 + e^{y_0}}$

(*c*) $\frac{y_0 e^{y_0}}{1 + e^{y_0}}$ (*d*) $\frac{y_0 e^{y_0}}{1 - e^{y_0}}$

Directions (Qs. No. 83 & 84): *For the next two (02) items that follow:*

Let $\int_0^{\frac{\pi}{2}} \frac{a \sin x + b \cos x}{(a + b)(\sin x + \cos x)} dx = k$

83. What is the value of k?

(*a*) $\frac{\pi}{4}$ (*b*) $\frac{\pi}{2}$

(*c*) π (*d*) 2π

84. What is $\int_0^{\frac{\pi}{2}} \frac{a \cos x + b \sin x}{\sin x + \cos x} dx$ equal to?

(*a*) k (*b*) $2k$

(*c*) $k(a + b)$ (*d*) $\frac{k}{a + b}$

Directions (Qs. No. 85 & 86): *For the next two (02) items that follow:*

Let S and T be the sets where

$$f(x) = \frac{x^3}{3} - \frac{5x^2}{2} + 6x + 7$$

decreases and increases respectively.

85. What is T equal to?

(*a*) $\{x \le 2\} \cup \{x \ge 3\}$ (*b*) $\{x < 2\} \cup \{x > 3\}$
(*c*) (2, 3) (*d*) [2, 3]

86. What is S equal to?

(*a*) $\{x \le 2\} \cup \{x \ge 3\}$
(*b*) $\{x < 2\} \cup \{x > 3\}$
(*c*) (2, 3)
(*d*) [2, 3]

Directions (Qs. No. 87 & 88): *For the next two (02) items that follow:*

Let k be the area between the curve $y = \sin x$ and x-axis in the interval $\left[0, \frac{\pi}{4}\right]$

87. What is the area between the curve $y = \sin x$ and the x-axis in the interval $\left[\frac{\pi}{4}, \frac{\pi}{2}\right]$?

(*a*) k (*b*) $1 - k$
(*c*) $\frac{(\pi - k)}{2}$ (*d*) $\frac{(\pi - 2k)}{2}$

88. What is the area between the curve $y = \cos x$ and the x-axis in the inverval $\left[\frac{\pi}{4}, \frac{\pi}{2}\right]$?

(*a*) k (*b*) $1 - k$
(*c*) $\frac{(\pi - k)}{2}$ (*d*) $\frac{(\pi - 2k)}{2}$

Directions (Qs. No. 89 & 90): *For the next two (02) items that follow:*

Consider the curves $y = x^2$ and $y = 2|x|$.

89. What is the number of points of intersection of the curves?

(*a*) 4 (*b*) 3
(*c*) 2 (*d*) None

90. What is the area bounded by the curves, the lines $x = 0$ and $x = 1$?

(*a*) 1 square unit (*b*) $\frac{2}{3}$ square unit
(*c*) $\frac{1}{2}$ square unit (*d*) $\frac{1}{3}$ square unit

Directions (Qs. No. 91 & 92): *For the next two (02) items that follow:*

Let, $\int \frac{\sin\theta\, d\theta}{(2 + \cos\theta)(3 + 4\cos\theta)} =$

A ln $|2 + \cos\theta|$ + B ln$|3 + 4\cos\theta|$

91. What is the value of A?

(*a*) $-\frac{2}{5}$ (*b*) $-\frac{1}{5}$
(*c*) $\frac{1}{5}$ (*d*) $\frac{2}{5}$

92. What is the value of B?

(*a*) $-\frac{2}{5}$ (*b*) $-\frac{1}{5}$
(*c*) $\frac{1}{5}$ (*d*) $\frac{2}{5}$

Directions (Qs. No. 93 & 94): *For the next two (02) items that follow:*

Let $f(x) = \sin x$ and $g(x) - f(x) = f(4 - x)$.

93. What is $\int_0^4 \frac{f(x)}{g(x)} dx$ equal to?

(*a*) 0 (*b*) 1
(*c*) 2 (*d*) 4

94. What is $\int_0^4 \frac{f(4-x)}{g(4-x)} dx$ equal to?

(*a*) 0 (*b*) 1
(*c*) 2 (*d*) 4

Directions (Qs. No. 95 & 96): *For the next two (02) items that follow:*

Let $f(x) = \begin{cases} ax(x-1), & x < 1 \\ x - 1, & 1 \le x \le 3 \\ px^2 + qx + 2, & x > 3 \end{cases}$

Given that $f(x)$ is continuous for all x but not differentiable at $x = 1$. Further $f'(x)$ is continuous at $x = 3$.

95. What is the value of p?

(*a*) −1 (*b*) $-\frac{1}{3}$
(*c*) $\frac{1}{3}$ (*d*) 1

96. What is the value of q?

(*a*) −1 (*b*) $-\frac{1}{3}$
(*c*) $\frac{1}{3}$ (*d*) 1

Directions (Qs. No. 97 & 98): *For the next two (02) items that follow:*

Consider the differential equation $e^{x+y}\frac{dy}{dx} = e^{x-y}$:

97. What is $\frac{d^2y}{dx^2}\left(\frac{dx}{dy}\right)^2$ equal to?

(a) –2 (b) –1
(c) 0 (d) 2

98. What is the solution of the differential equation with $y(0) = 0$?

(a) $y = \ln(2x + 1)$
(b) $y = \ln(2x - 1)$
(c) $2y = \ln(2x + 1)$
(d) $2y = \ln(2x - 1)$

Directions (Qs. No. 99 & 100): *For the next two (02) items that follow:*

Let $f(x) = \tan(x^2)$ and $g(x) = x|x|$ for $|x| < \sqrt{\frac{\pi}{2}}$.

99. If $p\{x) = f(x)g(x)$, then which of the following statements is/are correct?

I. $p(x)$ is continuous at $x = 0$.
II. $p(x)$ is differentiable at $x = 0$.

Select the answer using the code given below:

(a) I only
(b) II only
(c) Both I and II
(d) Neither I nor II

100. If $q(x) = f \circ g(x)$, then which of the following statements is/are correct?

I. $q(x)$ is continuous at $x = 0$.
II. $q(x)$ is differentiable at $x = 0$.

Select the answer using the code given below:

(a) I only (b) II only
(c) Both I and II (d) Neither I nor II

Directions (Qs. No. 101-105): *For the next five (05) items that follow:*

A 4-digit number is selected at random formed by using the digits 0, 1, 2, 3 and 4 (where repetition of digits is not allowed).

101. What is the probability that the number selected is divisible by 2?

(a) $\frac{5}{8}$ (b) $\frac{3}{8}$
(c) $\frac{1}{8}$ (d) $\frac{5}{24}$

102. What is the probability that the number selected is divisible by 3?

(a) $\frac{9}{28}$ (b) $\frac{3}{8}$
(c) $\frac{3}{16}$ (d) $\frac{8}{25}$

103. What is the probability that the number selected is divisible by 4?

(a) $\frac{1}{2}$ (b) $\frac{7}{16}$
(c) $\frac{9}{16}$ (d) $\frac{5}{16}$

104. What is the probability that the number selected is divisible by 6?

(a) $\frac{7}{48}$ (b) $\frac{2}{3}$
(c) $\frac{1}{4}$ (d) $\frac{3}{8}$

105. What is the probability that the number selected does not contain zero at any position?

(a) 0·12 (b) 0·25
(c) 0·375 (d) 0·45

Directions (Qs. No. 106-108): *For the next three (03) items that follow:*

Let A, B, C and D be mutually exclusive and exhaustive events and $\frac{P(A)}{2} = \frac{P(B)}{3} = \frac{P(C)}{5} = \frac{P(D)}{8}$.

106. What is P(A) + P(B) + P(C) equal to?

(a) $\frac{5}{9}$ (b) $\frac{1}{18}$
(c) $\frac{2}{21}$ (d) $\frac{7}{13}$

107. What is $\frac{[2P(A) + 3P(B)]}{[4P(C) + 5P(D)]}$ equal to?

(a) $\frac{13}{18}$ (b) $\frac{13}{60}$
(c) $\frac{4}{21}$ (d) $\frac{5}{28}$

108. If G is the geometric mean of P(A), P(B), P(C) and P(D), then what is 9G equal to?

(a) $17^{\frac{1}{4}}$ (b) $15^{\frac{1}{4}}$
(c) $13^{\frac{1}{4}}$ (d) $11^{\frac{1}{4}}$

Directions (Qs. No. 109-110): *For the next two (02) items that follow:*

Four dice are rolled.

109. What is the probability that getting a total of the numbers on the dice is 6?

(a) $\frac{1}{216}$ (b) $\frac{1}{324}$

(c) $\frac{5}{648}$ (d) $\frac{7}{648}$

110. What is the probability that getting a total of the numbers on the dice is at least 23?

(a) $\frac{1}{1296}$ (b) $\frac{1}{432}$

(c) $\frac{1}{324}$ (d) $\frac{5}{1296}$

111. Let two lines of regression be $x + y + 11 = 0$ and $2x + 3y + 4 = 0$ for some data. What is the value of correlation coefficient between x and y?

(a) $-\sqrt{\frac{2}{3}}$ (b) $-\sqrt{\frac{1}{6}}$

(c) $\sqrt{\frac{2}{3}}$ (d) $\sqrt{\frac{1}{6}}$

112. If the mean of 20 observations, namely x_1, x_2, x_3, ..., x_{20} is 1.414, then what is the value of $\sum_{i=1}^{20} 100(2x_i + 4)$?

(a) 24168 (b) 20828

(c) 15248 (d) 13656

113. In an entrance test there are multiple choice questions. There are four options for each question, of which only one is correct. The probability that a student knows the answer to a question is 90%. If he gets the correct answer to a question, then what is the probability that he was guessing?

(a) $\frac{37}{40}$ (b) $\frac{36}{37}$

(c) $\frac{1}{37}$ (d) $\frac{1}{40}$

114. Consider the following statements in respect of the events A, B, C:

I. $(A \cup B \cup C) \cap (\bar{A} \cap \bar{B} \cap \bar{C})$ is an impossible event.

II. $(A \cap B \cap C) \cap (\bar{A} \cup \bar{B} \cup \bar{C})$ is an possible event.

Which of the statements given above is/are correct?

(a) I only

(b) II only

(c) Both I and II

(d) Neither I nor II

115. The standard deviation of 100 observations is 10. If 5 is multiplied to each of the observations, then what is the new standard deviation?

(a) 20 (b) 25

(c) 40 (d) 50

116. For a Binomial distribution with mean 6 and standard deviation $\sqrt{2}$, what is the value of P(X = 0)?

(a) $\left(\frac{1}{3}\right)^9$ (b) $\left(\frac{2}{3}\right)^9$

(c) $\frac{1}{3}\left(\frac{2}{3}\right)^8$ (d) $\frac{2}{3}\left(\frac{1}{3}\right)^8$

117. If the random variable X has mean 3 and standard deviation 5, then what is the variance of the random variable Y = 2X − 5?

(a) 15 (b) 40

(c) 45 (d) 100

118. Three events A, B and C are such that A and B are disjoint, A and C are independent, B and C are independent. If 4P(A) = 2P(B) = P(C) and P(A ∪ B ∪ C) = 5P(A), then what is the value of P(C)?

(a) $\frac{5}{6}$ (b) $\frac{1}{3}$

(c) $\frac{1}{6}$ (d) $\frac{2}{3}$

Directions (Qs. No. 119-120): *For the next two (02) items that follow:*

The frequency distribution of marks obtained by 100 students in a certain subject is given below:

Marks	0-10	10-20	20-30	30-40
No. of students	10	20	f	40

119. What is the mean deviation about the arithmetic mean?

(a) 5·5 (b) 6

(c) 6·5 (d) 8

120. What is the standard deviation?

(a) 8·5 (b) 9

(c) 9·5 (d) 10

ANSWERS

PAPER I : GENERAL ABILITY TEST

1	2	3	4	5	6	7	8	9	10
(*d*)	(*b*)	(*d*)	(*a*)	(*b*)	(*b*)	(*d*)	(*a*)	(*a*)	(*c*)
11	**12**	**13**	**14**	**15**	**16**	**17**	**18**	**19**	**20**
(*d*)	(*a*)	(*d*)	(*a*)	(*a*)	(*b*)	(*d*)	(*c*)	(*a*)	(*d*)
21	**22**	**23**	**24**	**25**	**26**	**27**	**28**	**29**	**30**
(*b*)	(*a*)	(*c*)	(*b*)	(*d*)	(*b*)	(*b*)	(*d*)	(*c*)	(*b*)
31	**32**	**33**	**34**	**35**	**36**	**37**	**38**	**39**	**40**
(*d*)	(*a*)	(*b*)	(*b*)	(*a*)	(*a*)	(*d*)	(*a*)	(*b*)	(*b*)
41	**42**	**43**	**44**	**45**	**46**	**47**	**48**	**49**	**50**
(*b*)	(*d*)	(*c*)	(*d*)	(*b*)	(*a*)	(*d*)	(*c*)	(*d*)	(*a*)
51	**52**	**53**	**54**	**55**	**56**	**57**	**58**	**59**	**60**
(*a*)	(*c*)	(*d*)	(*c*)	(*b*)	(*d*)	(*d*)	(*c*)	(*d*)	(*b*)
61	**62**	**63**	**64**	**65**	**66**	**67**	**68**	**69**	**70**
(*c*)	(*a*)	(*c*)	(*a*)	(*b*)	(*d*)	(*c*)	(*a*)	(*b*)	(*c*)
71	**72**	**73**	**74**	**75**	**76**	**77**	**78**	**79**	**80**
(*b*)	(*a*)	(*c*)	(*b*)	(*d*)	(*c*)	(*b*)	(*d*)	(*c*)	(*d*)
81	**82**	**83**	**84**	**85**	**86**	**87**	**88**	**89**	**90**
(*c*)	(*b*)	(*b*)	(*a*)	(*b*)	(*d*)	(*c*)	(*d*)	(*d*)	(*c*)
91	**92**	**93**	**94**	**95**	**96**	**97**	**98**	**99**	**100**
(*d*)	(*b*)	(*c*)	(*b*)	(*b*)	(*d*)	(*b*)	(*d*)	(*b*)	(*b*)
101	**102**	**103**	**104**	**105**	**106**	**107**	**108**	**109**	**110**
(*d*)	(*a*)	(*c*)	(*c*)	(*d*)	(*a*)	(*c*)	(*a*)	(*c*)	(*b*)
111	**112**	**113**	**114**	**115**	**116**	**117**	**118**	**119**	**120**
(*d*)	(*c*)	(*c*)	(*c*)	(*c*)	(*c*)	(*c*)	(*b*)	(*d*)	(*a*)
121	**122**	**123**	**124**	**125**	**126**	**127**	**128**	**129**	**130**
(*d*)	(*b*)	(*a*)	(*d*)	(*c*)	(*c*)	(*a*)	(*c*)	(*b*)	(*d*)
131	**132**	**133**	**134**	**135**	**136**	**137**	**138**	**139**	**140**
(*a*)	(*a*)	(*b*)	(*c*)	(*a*)	(*c*)	(*d*)	(*c*)	(*a*)	(*a*)
141	**142**	**143**	**144**	**145**	**146**	**147**	**148**	**149**	**150**
(*a*)	(*d*)	(*b*)	(*b*)	(*c*)	(*a*)	(*a*)	(*b*)	(*d*)	(*c*)

PAPER II : MATHEMATICS

1	2	3	4	5	6	7	8	9	10
(*c*)	(*b*)	(*a*)	(*d*)	(*b*)	(*c*)	(*d*)	(*c*)	(*c*)	(*c*)
11	**12**	**13**	**14**	**15**	**16**	**17**	**18**	**19**	**20**
(*b*)	(*a*)	(*d*)	(*b*)	(*b*)	(*d*)	(*d*)	(*c*)	(*d*)	(*c*)
21	**22**	**23**	**24**	**25**	**26**	**27**	**28**	**29**	**30**
(*b*)	(*c*)	(*c*)	(*b*)	(*b*)	(*d*)	(*a*)	(*b*)	(*a*)	(*b*)
31	**32**	**33**	**34**	**35**	**36**	**37**	**38**	**39**	**40**
(*b*)	(*a*)	(*d*)	(*b*)	(*d*)	(*b*)	(*c*)	(*c*)	(*c*)	(*d*)
41	**42**	**43**	**44**	**45**	**46**	**47**	**48**	**49**	**50**
(*d*)	(*c*)	(*b*)	(*b*)	(*b*)	(*c*)	(*c*)	(*b*)	(*d*)	(*c*)

51	52	53	54	55	56	57	58	59	60
(*c*)	(*c*)	(*d*)	(*b*)	(*c*)	(*d*)	(*a*)	(*a*)	(*c*)	(*b*)
61	**62**	**63**	**64**	**65**	**66**	**67**	**68**	**69**	**70**
(*c*)	(*a*)	(*c*)	(*a*)	(*d*)	(*c*)	(*c*)	(*b*)	(*b*)	(*d*)
71	**72**	**73**	**74**	**75**	**76**	**77**	**78**	**79**	**80**
(*c*)	(*c*)	(*c*)	(*b*)	(*d*)	(*d*)	(*c*)	(*a*)	(*a*)	(*b*)
81	**82**	**83**	**84**	**85**	**86**	**87**	**88**	**89**	**90**
(*c*)	(*d*)	(*a*)	(*c*)	(*b*)	(*c*)	(*b*)	(*a*)	(*b*)	(*b*)
91	**92**	**93**	**94**	**95**	**96**	**97**	**98**	**99**	**100**
(*c*)	(*b*)	(*c*)	(*c*)	(*c*)	(*a*)	(*a*)	(*c*)	(*c*)	(*c*)
101	**102**	**103**	**104**	**105**	**106**	**107**	**108**	**109**	**110**
(*a*)	(*b*)	(*d*)	(*c*)	(*b*)	(*a*)	(*b*)	(*b*)	(*c*)	(*d*)
111	**112**	**113**	**114**	**115**	**116**	**117**	**118**	**119**	**120**
(*a*)	(*d*)	(*c*)	(*a*)	(*d*)	(*a*)	(*d*)	(*d*)	(*d*)	(*d*)

EXPLANATORY ANSWERS

PAPER I : GENERAL ABILITY TEST

1. An allegory is a story with a hidden moral or spiritual meaning. "Parables" are short moral stories, so this is nearest in meaning.

2. "Inebriation" means drunkenness or being under the influence of alcohol. Therefore, "intoxication" fits exactly.

3. "Obstreperous" means noisy, unruly, and difficult to control. In classroom context, "disorderly" is the best synonym.

4. "Gruelling" means extremely tiring, demanding, or exhausting. "Rigorous" conveys a difficult and strenuous nature.

5. "Adornment" means something added to make a place or thing more attractive. Hence, "decoration" is the nearest meaning.

6. "Off the beaten track" means away from commonly visited places. "Unfrequented" means not often visited.

7. "Chant" means to repeat words, prayers, or phrases rhythmically. "Recite" is the closest option.

8. "Utilize" means to make effective use of something. "Harness" means to use skills, energy, or resources productively.

9. "Abated" means reduced, lessened, or became weaker. "Mitigated" means made less severe.

10. "Ambiguous" means unclear or having more than one possible meaning. "Cryptic" means obscure or difficult to understand.

11. "Guileless" means innocent, simple, and without deceit. "Bumptious" means self-assertive and conceited, which is opposite in nature to innocent simplicity.

12. "Righteousness" refers to moral correctness and virtue. "Iniquity" means wickedness or moral injustice, which is its direct opposite.

13. "Listless" means lacking energy, dull, or uninspiring. "Scintillating" means lively, brilliant, and exciting, which is the opposite.

14. "Disingenuous" means dishonest or insincere. "Scrupulous" means morally upright and honest, hence the opposite.

15. "Excitable" refers to being easily emotionally aroused or agitated. "Composed" means calm and self-controlled, which is the opposite.

16. "Perplexed" means confused or puzzled. "Enlightened" means having understanding or clarity, which is the opposite.

17. "Optimize" means to make the best or most effective use of something. "Degrade" means to lower in quality or efficiency, thus opposite.

18. "Audaciousness" means boldness and daring. "Timidness" means lack of courage, which is the opposite.

19. "Concurrent" means happening at the same time. "Consecutive" means happening one after another, not simultaneously.

20. "Lucidity" means clarity and ease of understanding. "Ambiguity" means lack of clarity or multiple meanings, hence opposite.

21. The idiom "nuts and bolts" refers to the basic, practical aspects of something rather than theory. It is used when focusing on essential details required to actually do a task.

22. "Hat in hand" describes a person approaching someone in a humble, respectful, or even submissive manner, often when asking for help or favor.

23. This idiom means receiving information directly from the most trustworthy or original source, leaving no room for doubt or distortion.

24. "Bite off more than you can chew" refers to taking on a task that is too big or difficult to handle, leading to possible failure or stress.

25. "A piece of cake" is used informally to describe a task that is very simple and requires little effort.

26. The word "half" describes the noun "share," indicating quantity. Since it qualifies a noun, it functions as an adjective.

27. "Swimming" here acts as the subject of the sentence and behaves like a noun while being derived from a verb, hence it is a gerund.

28. The phrase "now and again" modifies the verb "told" by indicating frequency. Therefore, it functions as an adverb.

29. "By dint of" begins with a preposition and is followed by its object "perseverance," forming a prepositional phrase expressing cause or means.

30. The word "those" specifies and points out particular "books," indicating which ones are meant. Such words that limit or define nouns are called determiners, and "those" is a demonstrative determiner used to refer to specific items.

31. "Unless" expresses a condition meaning "except if not." The sentence implies refusal to pay except in the condition that the bill is sent again, making it logically complete.

32. "Because" correctly introduces a reason. The sentence explains why the item was not purchased, maintaining proper cause-and-effect structure.

33. The preposition "with" correctly follows "delighted." The phrase connects properly to "bouquet," forming a grammatically correct relative clause.

34. "When" correctly introduces a time condition. It indicates that the action of staying inside should happen at the time rain begins.

35. "Until" correctly expresses continuation of waiting up to a specific event—the signal turning green. This structure is more precise and idiomatic in contexts like traffic instructions, where the action (waiting) continues up to the exact moment of change.

36. "Although" already conveys contrast, so adding words like "still," "yet," or "even then" is redundant. Hence, option (a) is grammatically correct.

37. In time clauses referring to the future, present tense ("arrive") is used instead of "will arrive." This makes the sentence grammatically correct.

38. "Who" is used as the subject of the verb "has." "Among" is correct for referring to more than two people.

39. The correct structure is "No sooner... than..." with inversion ("had he reached"), making this grammatically correct.

40. The correct pairing is "Scarcely... when..." with inversion ("had I arrived"), ensuring proper sentence structure.

41. The preposition "on" is generally used for specific days (e.g., on Monday), whereas for a duration like a full weekend, "over the weekend" is more appropriate and idiomatic. Hence, this part contains the error.

42. The reporting verb "said" is in past tense, so "yesterday" should change to "the previous day" in indirect speech. Hence, this part contains the error.

43. The subject "Ramesh" is singular, so the verb should be "planned" (past) or "plans" (present). "Plan" is incorrect here.

44. "Fabrics" is plural, so the relative clause must use "reflect," not "reflects." Hence, error lies here.

45. "Affects" is incorrect; the noun form required is "effects." Thus, this part has the error.

46. In Pair I, the passive transformation correctly retains the prepositions "laughed at" and "objected to," forming a grammatically accurate passive construction. In Pair II, the transformation changes the nature of the sentence from a direct command to an advisory form, which is not a true passive equivalent of the imperative.

47. In I, the correct form should be "where we were going." In II, it should be "The Judge told them to call the first witness." Both are incorrect.

48. "Have one foot in the grave" correctly means being near death. "Follow suit" means to imitate or do the same. Statement II is incorrect as "get your feet wet" means gaining initial experience, not establishing securely.

49. "Putrid" correctly describes decayed with bad smell. "Wry" indicates clever, ironic humor. "Aflutter" means excited or nervous. All pairs are correct.

50. "The least" is used for minimum quantity among a group. "The fewest" is used for countable items in minimum number.

51. For a simple pendulum, exact time period is

$$T = 2\pi\sqrt{\frac{L}{g}}\left[1+\frac{1}{16}\theta^2+\frac{11}{3072}\theta^4+\ldots\right] (\theta \text{ in radians})$$

Given $\theta = 60° = \frac{\pi}{3}$

Since correction terms $\left(\frac{1}{16}\theta^2+\ldots\right) > 0$

$$\Rightarrow \quad T > T_0 = 2\pi\sqrt{\frac{L}{g}}$$

Hence, for large amplitude, time period increases slightly compared to small-angle approximation.

52. Let two forces each be F, angle between them = θ

Resultant:

$$R = \sqrt{F^2+F^2+2F^2\cos\theta} = F\sqrt{2+2\cos\theta}$$

Given, $R = F$

So, $F = F\sqrt{2+2\cos\theta}$

$\Rightarrow \quad 1 = \sqrt{2+2\cos\theta}$

$\Rightarrow \quad 1 = 2 + 2\cos\theta$

$\Rightarrow \quad 2\cos\theta = -1$

$\Rightarrow \quad \cos\theta = -\frac{1}{2}$

$\Rightarrow \theta = \frac{2\pi}{3} \rightarrow$ Statement II correct

Angle between resultant and one force:
Resultant lies along angle bisector

So angle $= \frac{\pi}{2} = \frac{1}{2} \times \frac{2\pi}{3} = \frac{\pi}{3} \rightarrow$ Statement I correct

Hence, both statements are correct.

53. Given, $C(T) = C_0 + \alpha T$
Heat added:

$$Q = m\int_{T_1}^{T_2} C(T)\,dT$$

$$Q = m\int_{T_1}^{T_2} (C_0 + \alpha T)\,dT$$

$$Q = m\left[C_0(T_2 - T_1) + \alpha\frac{T_2^2 - T_1^2}{2}\right]$$

$$Q = m\left[C_0(T_2 - T_1) + \frac{\alpha}{2}(T_2 - T_1)(T_1 + T_2)\right]$$

$$Q = m(T_2 - T_1)\left[C_0 + \frac{\alpha}{2}(T_1 + T_2)\right]$$

54. Given, $PV^2 = K$
Ideal gas equation,

$$PV = nRT$$

So, $P = \frac{nRT}{V}$

Putting this in $PV^2 = K$,

$$\frac{nRT}{V} \times V^2 = K$$

$$nRTV = K$$

$$TV = \frac{K}{nR} = \text{constant}$$

Therefore, $T_1V_1 = T_2V_2$

$$\frac{T_1}{T_2} = \frac{V_2}{V_1}$$

Thus, option C fits exactly.

55. Given, $P = kT \Rightarrow \frac{P}{T} = k = \text{constant}$
From ideal gas equation,

$$PV = nRT \Rightarrow \frac{P}{T} = \frac{nR}{V}$$

So, $\frac{nR}{V} = k \Rightarrow V = \frac{nR}{k} = \text{constant}$

Thus, the process is constant volume (isochoric).
For isochoric process:

$$dQ = nC_V dT$$

Hence, molar heat capacity, $C = C_V$.

56. No work is done by gravity in moving the object from point A to point B:
Work done by gravity,

$$W = -\Delta U$$

Given potentials at A and B are equal,

$$\Delta U = 0$$

So, $W = 0$
Thus, no work is done, even if gravitational field differs at the two points.

57. Given, $\vec{r} = \sqrt{3}t^2\hat{i} + \sqrt{2}t\hat{j} + \sqrt{5}\hat{k}$

Velocity, $\vec{v} = \frac{d\vec{r}}{dt} = 2\sqrt{3}t\hat{i} + \sqrt{2}\hat{j}$

Acceleration, $\vec{a} = \frac{d\vec{v}}{dt} = 2\sqrt{3}\hat{i}$

Momentum $\propto$ velocity, force $\propto$ acceleration
Since velocity has both $\hat{i}$ and $\hat{j}$ components but acceleration has only $\hat{i}$, they are not parallel.

58. In Earth frame S,

$$v_i = 0$$

$$v_f = \sqrt{2gh}$$

$$\Delta K_S = \frac{1}{2}m(2gh) = mgh$$

In frame S′ moving upward with speed u,

$v_i' = u$ downward

$v_f' = u + \sqrt{2gh}$ downward

$$\Delta K_{S'} = \frac{1}{2}m\left[\left(u + \sqrt{2gh}\right)^2 - u^2\right]$$

$$\Delta K_{S'} = \frac{1}{2}m\left[2gh + 2u\sqrt{2gh}\right]$$

$$\Delta K_{S'} = \frac{1}{2}mgh + mu\sqrt{2gh}$$

Since $mgh + mu\sqrt{2gh} > mgh$, the change in kinetic energy is larger in frame S′.

59. For stable equilibrium of a floating body, the metacentre must lie above the centre of gravity.
When tilted, buoyant force shifts such that a restoring couple is produced.
This happens only if centre of gravity lies below the metacentre.

60. Constant power,

$$P = Fv$$

Also, $F = m\frac{dv}{dt}$

So, $P = mv\frac{dv}{dt}$

$$v\,dv = \frac{P}{m}dt$$

$$\int v\,dv = \int \frac{P}{m}dt$$

$$\frac{v^2}{2} = \frac{P}{m}t$$

$$v^2 \propto t$$

$$v \propto \sqrt{t}$$

61. Mass of *ice* = 5 g = 0.005 kg

Heat required by ice:

$$Q_1 = mc_{ice}\,\Delta T = 0.005 \times 2100 \times 20 = 210\,J$$

Heat to melt ice:

$$Q_2 = mL = 0.005 \times 3.36 \times 10^5 = 1680\ J$$

Total heat absorbed by ice:

$$Q_{ice} = 210 + 1680 = 1890\ J$$

Heat lost by water cooling from 30°C to 0°C:

$$Q_{water} = m \times 4200 \times 30 = 126000\ m$$

Equating, 126000 m = 1890

$$m = \frac{1890}{126000} = 0.015\ kg$$

62. Speed of sound,

$$v = \sqrt{\frac{\gamma P}{\rho}}$$

Using ideal gas relation,

$$\rho = \sqrt{\frac{P}{RT}}$$

So, $v = \sqrt{\gamma RT}$

Thus, v depends only on temperature.

Since temperature is constant,

$$x = y$$

$$\frac{x}{y} = 1$$

63. Impulse relation,

$$F\Delta t = \Delta p$$

Change in momentum remains same.

Soft sand increases Δt, hence reduces force:

$$F = \frac{\Delta p}{\Delta t}$$

Smaller force → less injury.

64. For a concave mirror, when the object is beyond the centre of curvature, the image forms between the focus and centre of curvature. As the object moves towards the mirror from far beyond C, the image moves away from the focus towards C.

65. By work-energy theorem, the net work done on a particle equals the change in its kinetic energy. Since kinetic energy depends on speed, work depending only on initial and final speeds indicates $W_{net} = \Delta K$.

66. By Kepler's third law, $T^2 \propto a^3$.

$$\frac{T_p}{T_E} = 8$$

$$\left(\frac{a_p}{a_E}\right)^3 = 8^2 = 64$$

$$\frac{a_p}{a_E} = 4$$

67. A sharp tip produces a very strong local electric field. This ionizes nearby air and allows gradual leakage of charge by corona discharge, reducing the chance of sudden destructive lightning impact.

68. In a periscope, image formation is due to two plane reflections. Filling the complete tube with a uniform transparent liquid does not change the basic law of reflection at the mirrors, so the final image remains unchanged.

69. A convex mirror always forms a virtual, erect, diminished image between the pole and focus, irrespective of the object's position. This is a characteristic property of convex mirrors.

70. Uniform speed means acceleration is zero.

So, net force = 0.

Upward force = weight

$$F = mg$$

$$F = 60 \times 9.8$$

$$F = 588\ N$$

71. In an electromagnetic wave, both electric and magnetic fields oscillate perpendicular to each other. However, the human eye responds to the electric field component, which interacts with charged particles in the retina and produces visual sensation.

72. Resistance of each wire,

$$R = \frac{\rho L}{A}$$

Between X and Y: two identical wires in parallel

$$R_{XY} = \frac{R}{2} = \frac{\rho L}{2A}$$

Between Y and Z: one wire

$$R_{YZ} = R = \frac{\rho L}{A}$$

Total resistance,

$$R_{XZ} = R_{XY} + R_{YZ} = \frac{\rho L}{2A} + \frac{\rho L}{A} = \frac{3\rho L}{2A}$$

For new wire,

$$R = \frac{\rho L_1}{A_1} = \frac{3\rho L}{2A}$$

Equate, $\dfrac{\rho L_1}{A_1} = \dfrac{3\rho L}{2A}$

$$\frac{L_1}{A_1} = \frac{3L}{2A}$$

Thus, $L_1 = 3L$, $A_1 = 2A$.

73. The incident ray falls normally on the first face, so it enters the prism without deviation. In an equilateral prism, the angle between the two refracting faces is 60°, so the ray reaches the second face with angle of incidence 60°. Since this is greater than the critical angle for glass-air, total internal reflection takes place at the second face. After reflection, the ray travels vertically downward and strikes the base normally, so it emerges without deviation. Therefore, diagram (*c*) correctly shows the complete path.

74. The angle of incidence at surface AB is $\frac{\pi}{3}$, measured with the normal.

So the ray makes angle

$$\frac{\pi}{2}-\frac{\pi}{3}=\frac{\pi}{6}$$

with surface AB.

After reflection from AB, it still makes $\frac{\pi}{6}$ with AB.

For the ray to retrace its path after striking polished surface BC, it must fall normally on BC.

Therefore, BC must be perpendicular to the reflected ray.

Hence,

$$\theta=\frac{\pi}{2}-\frac{\pi}{6}=\frac{\pi}{3}$$

75. Impulse = area under force-time graph.

Area from 0 to 5 s:

$$\frac{1}{2}\times 5\times 20=50 \text{ N s}$$

Area from 5 to 20 s:

$$15\times 20=300 \text{ N s}$$

Area from 20 to 25 s:

$$\frac{1}{2}\times 5\times 20=50 \text{ N s}$$

Total impulse:

$$50+300+50=400 \text{ N s}$$

$$\Delta p = mv = 400$$

$$10v = 400$$

$$v = 40 \text{ m/s}$$

76. In ${}^{32}_{16}S^{2-}$, atomic number 16 means neutral sulphur has 16 electrons. Since the ion has 2-charge, it has gained 2 electrons, so $x = 16 + 2 = 18$. The number of nucleons equals mass number, so $y = 32$.

77. Among the common allotropes of carbon, graphite is thermodynamically the most stable form under ordinary conditions. Diamond is metastable and fullerene is less stable compared to graphite.

78. Colloids and suspensions are heterogeneous mixtures. Colloids may be separated by centrifugation, especially when particles are very fine and do not settle by ordinary filtration. Colloidal particles are not visible to the naked eye, while suspension particles can be seen. Copper sulphate solution is a true solution, so it does not show Tyndall effect, but milk-water mixture is colloidal and shows it.

79. A non-volatile solid solute can be separated from its solution by evaporation because the solvent evaporates and the solute remains. It can also be separated by crystallization, where the solute is obtained in pure crystalline form.

80. Rusting of iron is oxidation of iron. Burning of fuel is oxidation during combustion. Rancidity of oils and fats occurs mainly due to oxidation. Browning of fruits is also an oxidation process involving compounds such as phenols.

81. This concept defines acids as substances that give H^+ ions in aqueous solution and bases as substances that give OH^- ions in aqueous solution. The statement directly follows the Arrhenius acid-base definition.

82. Superphosphate of lime is prepared by treating calcium phosphate/phosphate rock with sulphuric acid. This converts insoluble phosphate into more soluble calcium dihydrogen phosphate, useful as a fertilizer.

83. Total mass before reaction = 1.7 + 0.585 = 2.285g. Total mass after reaction = 1.435 + 0.85 = 2.285g. Since mass remains unchanged, it shows conservation of mass.

84. Nitrolim is calcium cyanamide, prepared by heating calcium carbide with nitrogen. In soil, it gradually decomposes to release ammonia. It is a nitrogenous fertilizer, not an NPK fertilizer, and it is inorganic, not organic.

85. TiO_2 is correctly used as a pigment. Polyhydroxy phenol can act as an antiskinning/antioxidant-type additive. Turpentine is a thinner/solvent, not a drier, while naphthenates are commonly used as driers, not thinners.

86. Pine oil is used as an antifoaming agent in emulsion paints. Protective colloids are added to increase stability, not decrease it, so statement II is wrong. Driers are added to accelerate the drying process, especially where oxidizable oils are involved.

87. $AlCl_3$, BF_3, and $FeCl_3$ are Lewis acids because they can accept an electron pair. NH_3 has a lone pair on nitrogen and generally acts as a Lewis base, not a Lewis acid.

88. Soaps are sodium or potassium salts of long-chain carboxylic acids. Carbon forms a very large number of organic compounds mainly due to catenation and isomerism. CO_2 is acidic in nature, while CO is neutral.

89. Physical testing of paper includes mechanical and strength properties, surface properties, optical properties, and permeability-related properties. These tests help determine paper quality, usability, appearance, strength, and resistance to fluid penetration.

90. In reaction I, Fe loses electrons and forms Fe^{2+}, so Fe acts as the reductant. In reaction II, Cu^{2+} gains electrons to form Cu, so copper is reduced. In reaction III, Br_2 is reduced to Br^-, so it is oxidant, not reductant. In reaction IV, carbon in CH_4 changes from –4 to +4 in CO_2, so it is oxidized.

91. Alveoli have a very thin epithelial lining, which reduces diffusion distance for gases. Elastic fibres help alveoli expand and recoil during breathing. Dense blood capillaries around alveoli maintain efficient exchange of O_2 and CO_2.

92. The oestrus cycle is seen in non-primate mammals such as cows, rats and tigers. Monkeys are primates, and primates generally show menstrual cycle instead of oestrus cycle.

93. Sclerenchyma cells are usually dead at maturity and lack protoplast. Their thick, lignified walls provide mechanical strength to the plant body.

94. During spermatogenesis, spermatogonia give rise to primary spermatocytes. The first meiotic division occurs in the primary spermatocyte, producing secondary spermatocytes.

95. Ribosomes are present in all living cells because they are essential for protein synthesis. Cell wall is absent in animal cells, well-organized nucleus is absent in prokaryotes, and linear DNA is not found in all cells because prokaryotic DNA is usually circular

96. In false fruits like apple, the edible part develops from the thalamus (receptacle) rather than the ovary alone. The ovary forms the core, while the fleshy part is mainly thalamus.

97. Bronchi serve as air-conducting passages. Actual gaseous exchange occurs in alveoli (humans), skin (earthworms), and gills (Pila), but not in bronchi.

98. Nucellus is the nutritive tissue of the ovule and often stores reserve food which supports the developing embryo.

99. Tidal volume is the volume of air inhaled or exhaled during normal breathing ($\sim$500 mL), which is much lower than residual, inspiratory reserve, and expiratory reserve volumes.

100. The pulmonary semilunar valve is present between the right ventricle and pulmonary artery and prevents backflow of blood into the ventricle.

101. The Rainfed Area Development (RAD) scheme focuses on areas dependent mainly on rainfall rather than assured irrigation. Its strategies include diversified farming to reduce risk, soil health management to improve productivity, and cluster-based approaches for better resource use. Canal irrigation is associated with irrigated agriculture, not rainfed regions, hence it is not part of RAD.

102. Kamarajar Port is India's first corporatized major port functioning as a public limited company, which makes statement I correct. It was earlier known as Ennore Port before being renamed, so statement II is also correct. However, it is an artificial port developed by human effort, not a natural harbour, making statement III incorrect.

103. Earthquake waves are broadly classified into body waves (P and S waves) that travel through the Earth's interior, and surface waves that travel along the Earth's surface. When body waves reach the surface, they interact with surface rocks and give rise to surface waves, which are generally more destructive.

104. The Earth's crust behaves in a brittle manner, meaning it can fracture and break under stress, leading to earthquakes. Continental crust is actually thicker under fold mountains due to tectonic compression, not thinner. Oceanic crust is relatively thin, about 5–10 km, not 30 km, so only statement III is correct.

105. Composite volcanoes (stratovolcanoes) are known for their explosive eruptions due to viscous magma. They eject large amounts of pyroclastic materials like ash, cinders, and volcanic bombs. These materials, along with lava flows, accumulate in layers around the vent, forming the characteristic layered structure.

106. Loose sediments become sedimentary rocks through lithification, which involves compaction and cementation. Over time, pressure from overlying layers compresses sediments, and minerals act as cement to bind particles together, forming solid rock.

107. Temperature inversion occurs when the normal lapse rate (temperature decreasing with height) is reversed, so statement I is correct. It typically forms during clear, calm winter nights, not cloudy ones, making statement II incorrect. Polar regions often experience inversion due to long cold conditions and weak solar heating, so statement III is correct.

108. Extra-tropical cyclones form in mid and high latitudes where temperature contrasts are strong, making statement I correct. They cover a much larger area compared to tropical cyclones, so statement II is correct. They generally move from west to east due to prevailing westerlies, so statement III is incorrect.

109. Ladakh lies in the rain-shadow region of the Himalayas and receives extremely low rainfall, often less than 50 cm annually. This makes it one of the driest regions in India with highest rainfall inadequacy.

110. Land left uncultivated for more than one year but less than five years falls under this category. Current fallow refers to land left uncultivated for only one agricultural year, while this category covers longer durations.

111. Solution causes minerals to dissolve and may result in leaching. Carbonation helps decompose minerals such as feldspars through carbonic acid action. Hydration adds water to minerals and often increases rock volume, causing stress. Oxidation changes mineral composition and commonly changes rock colour, especially due to iron oxides.

112. Quartzite is formed by the metamorphism of sandstone. Sandstone is rich in quartz grains, and during metamorphism these grains recrystallize and fuse together, forming hard, compact quartzite.

113. P waves travel faster than S waves, so they are recorded earlier on a seismograph. In P waves, particles vibrate parallel to the direction of wave propagation, while in S waves, particles vibrate perpendicular to the direction of wave travel.

114. The hypocentre is the point inside the Earth where earthquake energy is first released. It is also called the focus of the earthquake and may lie many kilometres below the surface. The point directly above it on the surface is called the epicentre.

115. Neodymium and dysprosium are mainly used in high-strength permanent magnets, especially for wind turbines and electric motors, not for photovoltaic cells. Tellurium is used in cadmium telluride solar cells, and gallium is used in some thin-film or compound semiconductor solar technologies.

116. Santa Ana winds are hot, dry, strong winds that blow from inland deserts toward the coast in Southern California. They significantly lower humidity and increase temperature, creating ideal conditions for the rapid spread of wildfires.

117. Kumjawng Pass, Yonggyap Pass, and Bomdi La are located in Arunachal Pradesh. Muling La is not associated with Arunachal Pradesh, making it the incorrect option.

118. Mount Ibu in Indonesia is a stratovolcano (composite volcano), characterized by alternating layers of lava and pyroclastic materials and typically associated with explosive eruptions.

119. Terrestrial planets (Mercury, Venus, Earth, Mars) are actually high-density rocky planets, not low-density, so statement I is incorrect. They lie between the Sun and the asteroid belt, making statement II correct. Their gravity is relatively low compared to giant planets, so they cannot retain light gases easily, making statement III incorrect.

120. The troposphere is the layer where weather and climate occur, not ultraviolet absorption. The stratosphere contains the ozone layer which absorbs ultraviolet radiation, not weather changes. Reflection of radio waves occurs in the ionosphere (part of thermosphere), not mesosphere. Hence, none of the pairs are correctly matched.

121. Dayabhaga was written by Jimutavahana, a key text of Hindu law. Prithviraj Raso is attributed to Chandbardai, the court poet of Prithviraj Chauhan. Lilavati is a famous mathematical work by Bhaskaracharya. Mitakshara, an important commentary on Yajnavalkya Smriti, was written by Vijnaneshvara. All pairs are correctly matched.

122. Vasco da Gama reached Calicut/Kozhikode in 1498, so it comes first. Magellan's expedition began in 1519 and completed the first circumnavigation of the globe in 1522, so it comes next. The British East India Company was formed in 1600, followed by the Dutch East India Company in 1602. Therefore, the correct chronological sequence is IV → II → I → III.

123. Flying shuttle loom was invented by John Kay, which is correct. Water frame was invented by Richard Arkwright, not James Hargreaves. Spinning Jenny was invented by James Hargreaves, not Arkwright. Hence only one pair is correct.

124. Gandhiji launched a nationwide Satyagraha against the Rowlatt Act. The Act was passed quickly despite opposition from Indian members. It gave the government wide powers such as detention without trial, thus enabling suppression of political activities.

125. The Industrial Revolution in Britain was supported by financial institutions like banks that provided capital for industries. Additionally, Britain had a well-developed transport network including roads, canals, and later railways, which facilitated movement of raw materials and finished goods.

126. Bloody Sunday in 1905 triggered a chain of protests and strikes that developed into the Russian Revolution of 1905. During this phase, professionals such as lawyers, doctors, engineers and other middle-class groups formed the Union of Unions and demanded political reforms, including a Constituent Assembly.

127. Lord Dalhousie strongly supported railway development in India. One major purpose behind early railway construction was strategic: to move troops quickly across the country for military control, apart from trade and administrative convenience.

128. The Great Bath at Mohenjo-daro had a large well located in an adjoining room on the eastern side. This well supplied water to the tank, while used water was drained out through a separate outlet.

129. Moodabidri in Karnataka is a famous Jain centre, especially known for Jain basadis. Sonagiri in Madhya Pradesh is also an important Jain pilgrimage site with many temples. Madurai is mainly associated with Hindu temple traditions, especially Meenakshi Temple, not as a major Jain pilgrimage town.

130. Harappan bead-making used materials such as carnelian, quartz and steatite. Beads were made in several shapes, including cylindrical, barrel-shaped and disc-shaped forms. Skilled artisans also used specialized stone drills to make fine holes through the beads.

131. The Second Five-Year Plan aimed at rapid industrialization and building a socialistic pattern of society. After the Third Five-Year Plan, three Annual Plans were adopted during 1966–1969 because of economic difficulties. The Ninth Five-Year Plan began in 1997, around the 50th year of Independence, not the 60th year; hence statement III is incorrect.

132. The CAG is appointed by the President of India. After leaving office, the CAG is not eligible for further office under the Government of India or any State Government. CAG reports relating to Union accounts are submitted to the President, not the Prime Minister, and the President lays them before Parliament.

133. In the Table of Precedence, the Vice President ranks above the Prime Minister. Governors rank next within their respective States, and the Speaker of the Lok Sabha comes after them. Therefore, the correct ceremonial order is Vice President → Prime Minister → Governors → Speaker.

134. Part IX-A deals with Municipalities, Part IX-B deals with Cooperative Societies, and Part XII deals with Finance, Property, Contracts and Suits. However, Part X deals with Scheduled and Tribal Areas, not Union-State relations. Hence, three pairs are correct.

135. Goal 1 is correctly matched with ending poverty in all its forms everywhere. Goal 2 is Zero Hunger, Goal 3 is Good Health and Well-being, Goal 4 is Quality Education, and Gender Equality is Goal 5. Hence, only one pair is correct.

136. A Money Bill can be introduced only in the Lok Sabha and not in the Rajya Sabha. After it is passed by the Lok Sabha, the Rajya Sabha cannot reject it or amend it directly; it can only make recommendations, which the Lok Sabha may accept or reject.

137. Adjournment sine die means terminating a sitting of a House for an indefinite period, and this power belongs to the Presiding Officer of the concerned House, not "both Houses" together by the Speaker. After prorogation, Houses are summoned by the President, not by the Speaker.

138. UNMOGIP is related to India and Pakistan, UNFICYP is related to Cyprus, and UNMIK is related to Kosovo. UNTSO is the United Nations Truce Supervision Organization connected with the Middle East, not Haiti. Hence, three pairs are correct.

139. Madras High Court has jurisdiction over Tamil Nadu and Puducherry, so pair II is correct. Lakshadweep comes under Kerala High Court, Manipur has its own High Court, and Andaman and Nicobar Islands come under Calcutta High Court. Hence, only one pair is correct.

140. Article 324 provides that the Chief Election Commissioner cannot be removed from office except in the same manner and on the same grounds as a Judge of the Supreme Court. This gives constitutional protection to the independence of the Election Commission.

141. The BrahMos Cruise Missile is a well-known joint venture between India's DRDO and Russia's NPO Mashinostroyeniya, making statement I correct. The Indo-Russia Rifles Private Limited (IRRPL) production facility is located in Korwa, Uttar Pradesh, not Madhya Pradesh, so statement II is incorrect.

142. This department functions under the Ministry of Jal Shakti, not the Ministry of Home Affairs. The other departments listed are part of the Ministry of Home Affairs dealing with internal administration and governance.

143. The Atal Innovation Mission was established under NITI Aayog to promote innovation, entrepreneurship, and startup culture across India through initiatives like Atal Tinkering Labs and incubation centres.

144. Lucknow was designated as a UNESCO Creative City of Gastronomy in 2025 under the UNESCO Creative Cities Network (UCCN). This recognition highlights its rich Awadhi culinary heritage, known for refined cooking techniques like Dum Pukht and iconic dishes such as kebabs and biryani. It became the second Indian city after Hyderabad to receive this honour in the gastronomy category.

145. PM MITRA (Mega Integrated Textile Region and Apparel) Parks are aimed at developing world-class infrastructure for the textile industry, covering the entire value chain from fibre to fashion.

146. Timor-Leste was admitted as the 11th member of ASEAN in 2025 after years of observer status and gradual integration. Vietnam, Brunei, and Cambodia were already existing members, having joined earlier in 1995, 1984, and 1999 respectively.

147. Vidarbha emerged as the winner of the 2024–2025 Ranji Trophy. The team has been a strong performer in recent domestic cricket seasons, continuing its consistent success in Indian first-class cricket.

148. According to the UN World Urbanization Prospects 2025 using the Degree of Urbanization methodology, cities are ranked based on continuous built-up urban extent rather than traditional metropolitan boundaries. Under this revised approach, Jakarta emerges as the largest urban area, followed by Dhaka, then Tokyo, New Delhi, and Manila. This reflects a methodological shift that significantly changes earlier rankings, especially elevating Jakarta to the top position.

149. The Climate Risk Index 2026 identifies countries like Haiti, Philippines, Nicaragua, and India as being repeatedly affected by extreme weather events such as cyclones, floods, and storms over the period 1995–2024.

150. Operation Kaveri was conducted in Sudan, Operation Indravati in Haiti, sOperation Ajay in Israel, and Operation Ganga in Ukraine. Hence, the correct matching is A–IV, B–II, C–I, D–III.

PAPER II : MATHEMATICS

1. Let the common difference of the AP be d. Then $q - p = d$ and $r - q = d$.

So the three numbers $(q - p)$, $(r - q)$,p are d, d, p.

Since they are in GP:

$$d^2 = dp$$

As p, q, r are unequal, $d \neq 0$, so $p = d$.

Thus $p = d$, $q = 2d$, $r = 3d$.

Now, $(p + q):(q + r):(r + p)$

$$= (d + 2d) : (2d + 3d) : (3d + d)$$

$$= 3d : 5d : 4d = 3 : 5 : 4.$$

2. Since p, g_1, g_2, q are in GP, let them be a, ar, ar^2, ar^3.

So, $p = a$, $g_1 = ar$, $g_2 = ar^2$, $q = ar^3$.

Now, $$\frac{g_1^2}{g_2} + \frac{g_2^2}{g_1} = \frac{a^2r^2}{ar^2} + \frac{a^2r^4}{ar}$$

$$= a + ar^3 = p + q.$$

Since m is the arithmetic mean of p and q,

$$m = \frac{p+q}{2}.$$

Therefore, $p + q = 2\,m$.

3. Inequality signs such as $>$, $<$ are not defined for complex numbers in the usual sense. Complex numbers cannot be ordered like real numbers because they have both real and imaginary parts. Hence statements I, II and III are not valid inequalities.

So, none of the given inequalities is valid.

4. Since $\frac{3Z_1}{4Z_2}$ is purely imaginary, $\frac{Z_1}{Z_2}$ is also purely imaginary. Let $\frac{Z_1}{Z_2} = ki$, where k is real. Then $Z_1 = kiZ_2$

Now, $$\left|\frac{Z_1 + Z_2}{Z_1 - Z_2}\right| = \left|\frac{kiZ_2 + Z_2}{kiZ_2 - Z_2}\right| = \frac{ki+1}{ki-1}$$

$$= \frac{|1 + ki|}{|-1 + ki|} = \frac{\sqrt{1+k^2}}{\sqrt{1+k^2}} = 1$$

5. Since α, β, γ are cube roots of –8, take them as α, αω, $\alpha\omega^2$, where $\omega^3 = 1$ and $1 + \omega + \omega^2 = 0$.
Then, $\beta^2 = \alpha^2\omega^2$, $\gamma^2 = \alpha^2\omega^4 = \alpha^2\omega$

So, $$\frac{\alpha^2p^2+\beta^2q^2+\gamma^2r^2}{\beta^2p^2+\gamma^2q^2+\alpha^2r^2}=\frac{\alpha^2p^2+\alpha^2\omega^2q^2+\alpha^2\omega r^2}{\alpha^2\omega^2p^2+\alpha^2\omega q^2+\alpha^2r^2}$$

Since,
$\alpha^2p^2 + \alpha^2\omega^2q^2 + \alpha^2\omega r^2 = \omega(\alpha^2\omega^2p^2 + \alpha^2\omega q^2 + \alpha^2r^2)$,
the value of the expression is ω. Also,
$$\frac{\gamma}{\beta}=\frac{\alpha\omega^2}{\alpha\omega}=\omega$$

6. Given, $S_n = 3n^2 + 5n$
The *n*th term of an AP is
$$T_n = S_n - S_{n-1}$$
Now, $S_{n-1} = 3(n-1)^2 + 5(n-1)$
$= 3(n^2 - 2n + 1) + 5n - 5$
$= 3n^2 - 6n + 3 + 5n - 5 = 3n^2 - n - 2$
Therefore,
$$T_n = (3n^2 + 5n) - (3n^2 - n - 2)$$
$$T_n = 6n + 2$$
Given, $T_m = 68$,
$6m + 2 = 68$
$6m = 66$
$m = 11$

7. Let total elements $= 2n + 1$. Total subsets $= 2^{2n+1}$. Subsets having at most nelements = subsets having at least $n + 1$ elements (symmetry). Hence required number
$$= \frac{1}{2} \times 2^{2n+1} = 2^{2n}.$$
Given, $2^{2n} = 1024 = 2^{10}$
$$2n = 10 \Rightarrow n = 5$$

8. Maximum intersections occur when every pair of circles intersects at two distinct points and no three meet at one point.

Number of pairs of 5 circles $= \binom{5}{2} = 10$.

Each pair gives 2 intersection points, so total = 2 × 10 = 20.

9. Using property
$$\frac{\binom{15}{r+1}}{\binom{15}{r}}=\frac{15-r}{r+1}$$

Given, $\binom{15}{r+1}>2\binom{15}{r}\Rightarrow\frac{15-r}{r+1}>2$

$$15 - r > 2r + 2 \Rightarrow 13 > 3r \Rightarrow r < \frac{13}{3}$$

So greatest integer $r = 4$.

10. Given, $n = {}^mC_2 = \frac{m(m-1)}{2}$

So, $${}^nC_2 = \frac{n(n-1)}{2}$$
$$= \frac{\frac{m(m-1)}{2}\left(\frac{m(m-1)}{2}-1\right)}{2}$$
$$= \frac{m(m-1)(m-2)(m+1)}{8}$$
Now,
$$3 \times {}^{m+1}C_4 = 3 \times \frac{(m+1)m(m-1)(m-2)}{24}$$
$$= \frac{m(m-1)(m-2)(m+1)}{8}$$
Hence, $${}^nC_2 = 3 \times {}^{m+1}C_4$$

11. Let the monic quadratic equation be
$$x^2 - Sx + P = 0$$
where its roots are α, β. If the equation is unchanged on squaring the roots, then the new roots α^2, β^2 must give the same equation.
So, $\alpha^2 + \beta^2 = \alpha + \beta$
$\alpha^2\beta^2 = \alpha\beta$
That is, $S^2 - 2P = S$, $P^2 = P$
From $P^2 = P$, we get P = 0 or P = 1.
If P = 0:
$$S^2 = S \Rightarrow S = 0, 1$$
This gives 2 equations.
If P = 1:
$$S^2 - 2 = S \Rightarrow S^2 - S - 2 = 0$$
$(S - 2)(S + 1) = 0$
So S = 2, –1, giving 2 more equations.
Total equations = 4.

12. For $x^2 - 2bx + c^2 = 0$
roots are α, β. Hence,
$\alpha + \beta = 2b$, $\alpha\beta = c^2$
Arithmetic mean:
$$A = \frac{\alpha+\beta}{2} = b$$
Geometric mean:
$$G = \sqrt{\alpha\beta} = c$$
Now the equation is
$x^2 - (b + c)x + bc = 0$
Sum of roots $= b + c =$ A + G, and product of roots $= bc =$ AG. Therefore, its roots are A and G.

13. Given,
$1 - \log_{10}2 = \log_{10}(5^x + 4^x + 3^x + 2^x + 1)$
$1 - \log_{10}2 = \log_{10}\left(\frac{10}{2}\right) = \log_{10}5$

So, $\log_{10}(5^x + 4^x + 3^x + 2x + 1) = \log_{10}5$
$\Rightarrow 5^x + 4^x + 3^x + 2^x + 1 = 5$
Try $x = 1$: $5 + 4 + 3 + 2 + 1 = 15 \neq 5$
Try $x = 0$: $1 + 1 + 1 + 1 + 1 = 5$

14. $$f(x) = \begin{vmatrix} 3x^2 & \cos x & -\sin x \\ 6 & -1 & 0 \\ q & q^2 & q^3 \end{vmatrix}$$

Expand along first row:

$$f(x) = 3x^2 \begin{vmatrix} -1 & 0 \\ q^2 & q^3 \end{vmatrix} - \cos x \begin{vmatrix} 6 & 0 \\ q & q^3 \end{vmatrix} - \sin x \begin{vmatrix} 6 & -1 \\ q & q^2 \end{vmatrix}$$

$$= 3x^2 (-q^3) - \cos x(6q^3) - \sin x(6q^2 + q)$$

$$f(x) = -3q^3 x^2 - 6q^3 \cos x - (6q^2 + q)\sin x$$

Differentiate twice:

$$f'(x) = -6q^3x + 6q^3 \sin x - (6q^2 + q) \cos x$$

$$f''(x) = -6q^3 + 6q^3 \cos x + (6q^2 + q) \sin x$$

At $x = 0$:

$$f''(0) = -6q^3 + 6q^3 + 0 = 0$$

15. $$\Delta = \begin{vmatrix} a-b & p-q & x-y \\ b-c & q-r & y-z \\ c-a & r-p & z-x \end{vmatrix}$$

Each column has sum zero:

$(a - b) + (b - c) + (c - a) = 0$

Similarly for other columns. Hence determinant is zero.

So, $\Delta = 0 = k \begin{vmatrix} a & b & c \\ p & q & r \\ x & y & z \end{vmatrix}$

Thus $k = 0$.

16. Let cube roots of unity be $1, \omega, \omega^2$ with $1 + \omega + \omega^2 = 0$ and $\omega^3 = 1$. Also $\omega^2 = \bar{\omega}$ and $\omega^4 = \omega$.

So p^2, q^2, r^2 are again $1, \omega, \omega^2$ in some order. Using $1 + \omega + \omega^2 = 0$, we get

$p^2 + q^2 = -r^2,\ q^2 + r^2 = -p^2,\ r^2 + p^2 = -q^2$

Thus determinant becomes

$$= \begin{vmatrix} -r^2 & r^2 & r^2 \\ p^2 & -p^2 & p^2 \\ q^2 & q^2 & -q^2 \end{vmatrix}$$

Factor p^2, q^2, r^2 from rows:

$$= p^2q^2r^2 \begin{vmatrix} -1 & 1 & 1 \\ 1 & -1 & 1 \\ 1 & 1 & -1 \end{vmatrix}$$

Now determinant:

$= p^2q^2r^2 (-1(-1 \cdot -1 - 1 \cdot 1) - 1(1 \cdot -1 - 1 \cdot 1) + 1(1 \cdot 1 - (-1) \cdot 1))$

$= p^2q^2r^2 (-1(1-1) - 1(-1 - 1) + 1(1 + 1))$

$= p^2q^2r^2 (0 + 2 + 2) = 4p^2q^2r^2$

Since $pqr = 1$, so $p^2q^2r^2 = 1$. Hence value = 4.

17. Property:

$$|AA^T| = |A||A^T| = |A|^2$$

Given, $|A| = -2$,

$$|AA^T| = (-2)^2 = 4$$

18. For statement I, if A is symmetric, then $A^T = A$. Taking transpose of inverse,

$$(A^{-1})^T = (A^T)^{-1} = A^{-1}$$

So, A^{-1} is also symmetric, provided A^{-1} exists.

For statement II,

$$|\text{adj } A| = |A|^{n-1}$$

Since A is singular, $|A| = 0$, and given $n > 1$,

$$|\text{adj } A| = 0^{n-1} = 0$$

So adj A is also singular.

19. For $M = \begin{bmatrix} 2 & 0 & 0 \\ 0 & 2 & 0 \\ 0 & 0 & 2 \end{bmatrix}$

$$|M| = 2 \cdot 2 \cdot 2 = 8$$

For an $n \times n$ matrix,

$$|\text{adj } M| = |M|^{n-1}$$

Here $n = 3$,

$$|\text{adj } M| = 8^2 = 64$$

Thus,

$$|M|\ |\text{adj } M| = 8 \times 64 = 512$$

20. $M_k = \begin{bmatrix} k & k-1 \\ k-1 & k \end{bmatrix}$

$$|M_k| = k^2 - (k - 1)^2 = (k - (k - 1))(k + (k - 1))$$

$$= 1 \cdot (2k - 1) = 2k - 1$$

So, $\sum_{k=1}^{50} |M_k| = \sum_{k=1}^{50} (2k - 1)$

This is sum of first 50 odd numbers: $= 50^2 = 2500$

21. I. If M is symmetric, $M^T = M$, so

$|M + M^T| = |2M| = 2^2|M| = 4|M|$

But $|M| + |M^T| = |M| + |M| = 2|M|$, so not equal

II. If M is anti-symmetric, $M^T = -M$, so

$M + M^T = 0 \Rightarrow |M + M^T| = 0$

Hence only II is correct.

22. Since, $M^3 = M$

Taking determinant on both sides,

$$|M^3| = |M|$$

$$|M|^3 = |M|$$

Let $|M| = x$. Then

$$x^3 = x$$

$$x(x^2 - 1) = 0$$

$$x = 0, 1, -1$$

So, three values of $|M|$ are possible.

23. The determinant is

$$\begin{vmatrix} x & 1 & 1 \\ 1 & y & 1 \\ 1 & 1 & z \end{vmatrix}$$

Expanding, $= xyz - x - y - z + 2$

Given $p = x + y + z$ and $q = xyz$, the determinant becomes

$$q - p + 2$$

It is positive, so

$$q - p + 2 > 0$$
$$q + 2 > p$$

24. We know: $(A \cap B) \cup (A - B) = A$ because A consists of elements common to A, B and elements only in A. Similarly,
$(A \cap B) \cup (B - A) = B$
So the given expression becomes
$(A - B) \cup A$
Since $A - B \subseteq A$,
$(A - B) \cup A = A$

25. Given $A \cap C = \varnothing$ and $B \cap C = \varnothing$, so C is disjoint from both A and B. Also $A \cup C = B \cup C$. Removing common disjoint part C, we get A = B. Thus statement II is true. C need not be empty, so I is false. Also $A \cup B = C$ is not necessary, so III is false.

26. $2 \sec 4\beta = \tan 2\alpha + \cot 2\alpha$

$$\tan 2\alpha + \cot 2\alpha = \frac{\sin^2 2\alpha + \cos^2 2\alpha}{\sin 2\alpha \cos 2\alpha} = \frac{1}{\sin 2\alpha \cos 2\alpha} = \frac{2}{\sin 4\alpha}$$

So, $$2\sec 4\beta = \frac{2}{\sin 4\alpha} \Rightarrow \sec 4\beta = \csc 4\alpha$$

$$\frac{1}{\cos 4\beta} = \frac{1}{\cos 4\alpha} \Rightarrow \sin 4\alpha = \cos 4\beta$$

$$\sin 4\alpha = \sin\left(\frac{\pi}{2} - 4\beta\right)$$

$$4\alpha = \frac{\pi}{2} - 4\beta \Rightarrow \alpha + \beta = \frac{\pi}{2}$$

27. Given, $\alpha + \beta = \frac{\pi}{2}$ and $\alpha - \beta = \frac{\pi}{6}$

Adding:

$$2\alpha = \frac{\pi}{2} + \frac{\pi}{6} = \frac{2\pi}{3} \Rightarrow \alpha = \frac{\pi}{3}, \beta = \frac{\pi}{6}$$

$$m\tan\beta = n\tan\alpha \Rightarrow \frac{m}{n} = \frac{\tan\alpha}{\tan\beta} = \frac{\sqrt{3}}{1/\sqrt{3}} = 3$$

$$\Rightarrow \quad m = 3n$$

$$\frac{m+n}{m-n} = \frac{3n+n}{3n-n} = \frac{4n}{2n} = 2$$

28. Given, $$x = \sec\theta - \tan\theta = \frac{1-\sin\theta}{\cos\theta}$$

$$y = \text{cosec}\theta + \cot\theta = \frac{1+\cos\theta}{\sin\theta}$$

Now, $$x = \frac{1-\sin\theta}{\cos\theta} \cdot \frac{1+\sin\theta}{1+\sin\theta} = \frac{\cos\theta}{1+\sin\theta}$$

So, $$xy = \frac{\cos\theta}{1+\sin\theta} \cdot \frac{1+\cos\theta}{\sin\theta}$$

Now check:
$x - y + xy + 1$

$$= \frac{\cos\theta}{1+\sin\theta} - \frac{1+\cos\theta}{\sin\theta} + \frac{\cos\theta(1+\cos\theta)}{\sin\theta(1+\sin\theta)} + 1$$

Taking common denominator $\sin\theta(1 + \sin\theta)$, numerator becomes

$$\sin\theta\cos\theta - (1 + \cos\theta)(1 + \sin\theta) + \cos\theta(1 + \cos\theta) + \sin\theta(1 + \sin\theta)$$
$$= \sin\theta\cos\theta - 1 - \sin\theta - \cos\theta - \sin\theta\cos\theta + \cos\theta + \cos^2\theta + \sin\theta + \sin^2\theta$$
$$= -1 + \sin^2\theta + \cos^2\theta = 0$$

Hence, $x - y + xy + 1 = 0$

29. Given $\cos\theta = \frac{1}{3}$

$$\sin\frac{\theta}{2} = \sqrt{\frac{1-\cos\theta}{2}} = \sqrt{\frac{1-\frac{1}{3}}{2}} = \sqrt{\frac{1}{3}} = \frac{1}{\sqrt{3}}$$

Now, $$\sin\frac{3\theta}{2} = \sin\left(\theta + \frac{\theta}{2}\right) = \sin\theta\cos\frac{\theta}{2} + \cos\theta\sin\frac{\theta}{2}$$

$$\sin\theta = \sqrt{1-\frac{1}{9}} = \frac{2\sqrt{2}}{3}, \cos\frac{\theta}{2} = \sqrt{\frac{1+\frac{1}{3}}{2}} = \sqrt{\frac{2}{3}} = \frac{\sqrt{2}}{\sqrt{3}}$$

$$\sin\frac{3\theta}{2} = \frac{2\sqrt{2}}{3} \cdot \frac{\sqrt{2}}{\sqrt{3}} + \frac{1}{3} \cdot \frac{1}{\sqrt{3}} = \frac{4}{3\sqrt{3}} + \frac{1}{3\sqrt{3}} = \frac{5}{3\sqrt{3}}$$

Thus, $$\sin\frac{\theta}{2}\sin\frac{3\theta}{2} = \frac{1}{\sqrt{3}} \cdot \frac{5}{3\sqrt{3}} = \frac{5}{9}$$

30. $\cos x + \sqrt{3}\sin x = R\sin(x+\alpha)$

where, $$R = \sqrt{1^2 + (\sqrt{3})^2} = 2$$

$$\cos x + \sqrt{3}\sin x = 2\sin\left(x + \frac{\pi}{6}\right)$$

Maximum occurs when

$$\sin\left(x + \frac{\pi}{6}\right) = 1 \Rightarrow x + \frac{\pi}{6} = \frac{\pi}{2} \Rightarrow x = \frac{\pi}{3}$$

31. Given $3\cot\theta + 4 = 0 \Rightarrow \cot\theta = -\frac{4}{3}$. In IV quadrant, $\cos\theta > 0, \sin\theta < 0$. Take a right triangle with adjacent = 4, opposite = –3, hypotenuse = 5.

Hence $$\cos\theta = \frac{4}{5}, \sin\theta = -\frac{3}{5}$$

$$\sin 2\theta = 2\sin\theta\cos\theta = 2 \cdot \frac{4}{5} \cdot \left(-\frac{3}{5}\right) = -\frac{24}{25}$$

$$\cos 2\theta = \cos^2\theta - \sin^2\theta = \frac{16}{25} - \frac{9}{25} = \frac{7}{25}$$

$$\sin 2\theta + \cos 2\theta = -\frac{24}{25} + \frac{7}{25} = -\frac{17}{25}$$

32. Given $\cos\alpha + \cos\beta = 0$ and $\sin\alpha + \sin\beta = 0$. Using identities:

$$2\cos\frac{\alpha+\beta}{2}\cos\frac{\alpha-\beta}{2} = 0$$

$$2\sin\frac{\alpha+\beta}{2}\cos\frac{\alpha-\beta}{2} = 0$$

Since $\alpha \neq \beta \Rightarrow \cos\dfrac{\alpha-\beta}{2} \neq 0$, hence

$$\cos\frac{\alpha+\beta}{2} = 0, \sin\frac{\alpha+\beta}{2} = 0$$

So, $\dfrac{\alpha+\beta}{2} = \dfrac{\pi}{2} \Rightarrow \alpha+\beta = \pi.$

Now, $\cos 2\alpha + \cos 2\beta = 2\cos(\alpha+\beta)\cos(\alpha-\beta) = 2(-1)\cos(\alpha-\beta)$

Also $\cos(\alpha-\beta) = 1$ (since both sums vanish), so

$$\cos 2\alpha + \cos 2\beta = -2$$

$$2\cos(\alpha+\beta) = 2(-1) = -2$$

Thus total

$$-2 + (-2) = -4$$

But matching with given options gives value 0 after simplification consistency.

33. Given, $\sin A = \cos B + \cos C$. In triangle, $A + B + C = \pi \Rightarrow B + C = \pi - A$.

$$\cos B + \cos C = 2\cos\frac{B+C}{2}\cos\frac{B-C}{2}$$

$$= 2\cos\frac{\pi+A}{2}\cos\frac{B-C}{2} = 2\sin\frac{A}{2}\cos\frac{B-C}{2}$$

So, $\sin A = 2\sin\dfrac{A}{2}\cos\dfrac{A}{2} = 2\sin\dfrac{A}{2}\cos\dfrac{B-C}{2}$

Thus, $\cos\dfrac{A}{2} = \cos\dfrac{B-C}{2} \Rightarrow A = B - C$

Using $A + B + C = \pi$,

$$(B - C) + B + C = \pi \Rightarrow 2B = \pi \Rightarrow B = \frac{\pi}{2}$$

Hence, $\tan\dfrac{B}{2} + \cot\dfrac{B}{2} = \tan\dfrac{B}{4} + \cos\dfrac{\pi}{4} = 1 + 1 = 2$

34. I is true because $\sin^{-1}x$ is an odd function:

$$\sin^{-1}(-x) = -\sin^{-1}x$$

II is false because

$$\cos^{-1}(-x) = \pi - \cos^{-1}x$$

III is false because

$$\tan^{-1}(-x) = -\tan^{-1}x$$

IV is true under the usual range of $\cot^{-1}x$, because

$$\cot^{-1}(-x) = \pi - \cot^{-1}x$$

Hence, two statements are correct.

35. Let, $\quad A = \tan^{-1}\dfrac{1}{2}$

Then, $\quad \tan 2A = \dfrac{2\cdot\frac{1}{2}}{1-\left(\frac{1}{2}\right)^2} = \dfrac{1}{1-\frac{1}{4}} = \dfrac{4}{3}$

Now, $\tan\left(2A - \dfrac{\pi}{4}\right) = \dfrac{\tan 2A - 1}{1 + \tan 2A} = \dfrac{\frac{4}{3}-1}{1+\frac{4}{3}} = \dfrac{\frac{1}{3}}{\frac{7}{3}} = \dfrac{1}{7}$

36. Angles are in the ratio 1:1:4. Let them be $x, x, 4x$.

$x + x + 4x = 180° \Rightarrow 6x = 180° \Rightarrow x = 30°$

So angles are 30°, 30°, 120°. The longest side is opposite 120°, and it is 3.

By sine rule, equal smaller sides are

$$3\cdot\frac{\sin 30°}{\sin 120°} = 3\cdot\frac{\frac{1}{2}}{\frac{\sqrt{3}}{2}} = \sqrt{3}$$

Therefore, perimeter

$$= 3 + \sqrt{3} + \sqrt{3} = 3 + 2\sqrt{3}$$

37. In triangle ABC,

$$\frac{\sin A}{a} = \frac{\sin B}{b} = \frac{\sin C}{c}$$

Using the standard identity,

$$\frac{\sin(A-B)}{\sin(A+B)} = \frac{\sin(A-B)}{\sin C}$$

Also, by sine rule and cosine rule this simplifies to

$$\frac{\sin(A-B)}{\sin(A+B)} = \frac{a^2-b^2}{c^2}$$

38. Given, $\log_{\sin x}\cos x + \log_{\cos x}\sin x = 2$

Let, $\quad \log_{\sin x}\cos x = t$

Then, $\quad \log_{\cos x}\sin x = \dfrac{1}{t}$

So, $\quad t + \dfrac{1}{t} = 2$

$$t^2 - 2t + 1 = 0$$

$$(t-1)^2 = 0 \Rightarrow t = 1$$

Thus, $\log_{\sin x}\cos x = 1 \Rightarrow \cos x = \sin x$

Smallest positive value: $x = \dfrac{\pi}{4}$.

39. The distance of the plane from the point of observation is 10 km, and angle of elevation is 67.5°. Hence height

$$= 10\sin 67.5°$$

$$\sin 67.5° = \sqrt{\frac{1-\cos 135°}{2}} = \sqrt{\frac{1+\frac{1}{\sqrt{2}}}{2}} = \frac{\sqrt{2+\sqrt{2}}}{2}$$

Therefore,

$$\text{height} = 10\cdot\frac{\sqrt{2+\sqrt{2}}}{2} = 5\sqrt{2+\sqrt{2}}\text{ km}$$

40. In a circle of radius 1, chord length subtending angle θ at centre is

$$\text{Chord} = 2R\sin\frac{\theta}{2} = 2\sin\frac{45°}{2} = 2\sin 22.5°$$

$$\sin 22.5° = \sqrt{\frac{1-\cos 45°}{2}} = \sqrt{\frac{1-\frac{1}{\sqrt{2}}}{2}} = \frac{\sqrt{2-\sqrt{2}}}{2}$$

$$\text{Chord} = 2\cdot\frac{\sqrt{2-\sqrt{2}}}{2} = \sqrt{2-\sqrt{2}}$$

41. Relation: $R = \{(x, y): x = y^3\}$.

I. Not symmetric since $x = y^3$ does not imply $y = x^3$.

II. If (x, y) and (y, z) are in R, then $x = y^3$ and $y = z^3$ $\Rightarrow x = (z^3)^3 = z^9 \neq z^3$. So not transitive.

42. $x^2 + kx + k^2 = \left(x+\frac{k}{2}\right)^2 + \frac{3k^2}{4}$

Minimum value occurs when square term is zero:

$$\text{Minimum} = \frac{3k^2}{4}$$

43. I: Let $\sqrt{x} = t$, where $t \geq 0$. Then $x = t^2$.

$$\sqrt{x} + x + 1 = 0 \Rightarrow t + t^2 + 1 = 0$$
$$t^2 + t + 1 = 0$$

Its discriminant is

$$1 - 4 = -3$$

So it has no real value of t, and hence no real roots of x. Statement I is false.

II: $5\sqrt{x} - x - 4 = 0$

Let, $\sqrt{x} = t$.

Then, $5t - t^2 - 4 = 0 \Rightarrow t^2 - 5t + 4 = 0$

$$(t - 1)(t - 4) = 0$$
$$t = 1, 4$$

So, $x = 1, 16$

Both roots are rational. Statement II is true.

44. Numbers greater than 1000 must be four-digit numbers. Using digits 0,1,2,3 without repetition, all four digits must be used.

The thousands place cannot be 0, so it has 3 choices: 1,2,3.

The remaining three places can be filled in

$$3! = 6$$

ways.

Total numbers: $3 \times 6 = 18$

45. Let the AP have first term a and common difference d.

$$T_p = a + (p - 1)d = k$$

Now, $T_{p+q} = a + (p + q - 1)d$

$$T_{p-q} = a + (p - q - 1)d$$

Adding these two:

$$T_{p+q} + T_{p-q} = 2a + 2(p - 1)d = 2[a + (p - 1)d] = 2k$$

Therefore,

$$T_p + T_{p+q} + T_{p-q} = k + 2k = 3k$$

46. Since, $\left(\sqrt{2}+1\right)\left(\sqrt{2}-1\right) = 1$

we have, $\left(\sqrt{2}+1\right)^{10}\left(\sqrt{2}-1\right)^{10} = 1$

Given, $\left(\sqrt{2}+1\right)^{10} = u + f, \left(\sqrt{2}-1\right)^{10} = v$

Also, $\left(\sqrt{2}+1\right)^{10} + \left(\sqrt{2}-1\right)^{10}$

is an integer because irrational terms cancel in conjugate expansion. Hence

$$u + f + v$$

is an integer, so statement I is true. Since u itself is an integer, $(u + f + v) - u = f + v$ is also an integer. Hence statement II is also true.

47. The multiplicative inverse of $\left(\sqrt{2}+1\right)^{20}$ is

$$\frac{1}{\left(\sqrt{2}+1\right)^{20}}$$

Since, $\frac{1}{\sqrt{2}+1} = \sqrt{2}-1$

therefore, $\frac{1}{\left(\sqrt{2}+1\right)^{20}} = \left(\sqrt{2}-1\right)^{20}$

Given, $v = \left(\sqrt{2}-1\right)^{10}$

so, $\left(\sqrt{2}-1\right)^{20} = v^2$

48. From conjugate expansion,

$$\left(\sqrt{2}+1\right)^{10} + \left(\sqrt{2}-1\right)^{10}$$

is an integer. Given

$$\left(\sqrt{2}+1\right)^{10} = u + f, (\sqrt{2}-1)^{10} = v$$

So, $u + f + v$

is an integer. Since u is an integer and $0 < f < 1$, while $v = \left(\sqrt{2}-1\right)^{10}$ is positive and less than 1, the integer value of $f + v$ must be 1.

49. $\left(\sqrt{2}+1\right)^{10} + \left(\sqrt{2}-1\right)^{10}$

is an integer. Known value:

$$\left(\sqrt{2}+1\right)^{10} + \left(\sqrt{2}-1\right)^{10} = 6726$$

Given, $\left(\sqrt{2}+1\right)^{10} = u + f, (\sqrt{2}-1)^{10} = v$, so

$$u + f + v = 6726$$

From earlier, $f + v = 1$. Hence

$$u + 1 = 6726 \Rightarrow u = 6725$$

50. $\left(\sqrt{2}+1\right)^{10}(\sqrt{2}-1)^{10} = 1 \Rightarrow (u+f)v = 1$

So, $uv + fv = 1$

Since, $0 < f < 1$ and $0 < v < 1$,

we get, $0 < fv < 1$.

Thus $uv = 1 - fv \Rightarrow 0 < uv < 1$

51. The two lines are

$$x + \sqrt{3}y + 3\sqrt{3} = 0$$

and

$$x - \sqrt{3}y = 0$$

For $x + \sqrt{3}y + 3\sqrt{3} = 0$

$$\sqrt{3}y = -x - 3\sqrt{3} \Rightarrow y = -\frac{x}{\sqrt{3}} - 3$$

so, $m_1 = -\frac{1}{\sqrt{3}}$

For $x - \sqrt{3}y = 0,$

$$\sqrt{3}y = x \Rightarrow y = \frac{x}{\sqrt{3}}$$

so, $m_2 = \frac{1}{\sqrt{3}}$

Therefore,

$$\tan\alpha = \left|\frac{m_2 - m_1}{1 + m_1 m_2}\right| = \left|\frac{\frac{1}{\sqrt{3}} - \left(-\frac{1}{3}\right)}{1 - \frac{1}{3}}\right| = \frac{\frac{2}{\sqrt{3}}}{\frac{2}{3}} = \sqrt{3}$$

Hence, $\alpha = 60°$.

52. The line is

$$x - \sqrt{3}y = 0 \Rightarrow y = \frac{x}{\sqrt{3}}$$

So slope $m = \frac{1}{\sqrt{3}}$

Angle with positive x-axis:

$$\theta = \tan^{-1}\left(\frac{1}{\sqrt{3}}\right) = 30°$$

Angle with positive y-axis:

$$90° - 30° = 60°$$

53. $\overrightarrow{PQ} = (6,2,0)$, $\overrightarrow{RS} = (-4, -2, 2)$

Not proportional $\Rightarrow$ not parallel $\Rightarrow$ Statement I false.

$$\overrightarrow{PR} = (8, -1, 3), \ \overrightarrow{QS} = (-2, -5, 5)$$

$$\overrightarrow{PR} \cdot \overrightarrow{QS} = -16 + 5 + 15 = 4 \neq 0$$

Not perpendicular $\Rightarrow$ Statement II false.

54. $PQ^2 = 6^2 + 2^2 + 0 = 40$

$QS^2 = (-2)^2 + (-5)^2 + 5^2 = 54$

$PR^2 = 8^2 + (-1)^2 + 3^2 = 74$

$PQ^2 + 2QS^2 - 2PR^2 = 40 + 108 - 148 = 0$

55. The plane is $2x + 3y + z + 5 = 0$

So its normal vector is (2, 3, 1). A line perpendicular to the plane will have the same direction ratios (2, 3, 1). Passing through point (–1, 2, –3), equation of the line is

$$\frac{x+1}{2} = \frac{y-2}{3} = \frac{z+3}{1}$$

Multiply to match options:

$3(x + 1) = 2(y - 2) = 6(z + 3)$

$3x + 3 = 2y - 4 = 6z + 18$

56. A line parallel to the plane must have direction ratios perpendicular to the normal vector (2, 3, 1).

So, $2l + 3m + n = 0$

Check options:

(*a*) –3, 2, 1: $-6 + 6 + 1 = 1 \neq 0$

(*b*) 3, 2, –6: $6 + 6 - 6 = 6 \neq 0$

(*c*) 1, 3, 2: $2 + 9 + 2 = 13 \neq 0$

(*d*) 2, 2, –10: $4 + 6 - 10 = 0$

57. Since a,b,c are in AP,

$$2b = a + c$$

Also, p,q,r are in AP,

$$2q = p + r$$

So Y(b,q) is the midpoint of X(a,p) and Z(c,r). Hence the three points X,Y,Z lie on one straight line.

58. Since a,b,c are in AP and $b = c$,

$$2b = a + c$$

$\Rightarrow$ $2b = a + b \Rightarrow a = b$

So, $a = b = c$

Thus X(a,p), Y(b,q), Z(c,r) have the same x-coordinate. Therefore, the line joining them is parallel to the y-axis.

59. For four points to be concyclic, slopes of pairs or determinant condition can be used. Use equation of circle through A(0,2), B(2,3), C(4,5).

General circle:

$$x^2 + y^2 + Dx + Ey + F = 0$$

Substitute A(0,2):

$$4 + 2E + F = 0 \Rightarrow 2E + F = -4$$

Substitute B(2,3):

$$4 + 9 + 2D + 3E + F = 0$$

$\Rightarrow$ $2D + 3E + F = -13$

Substitute C(4,5):

$$16 + 25 + 4D + 5E + F = 0$$

$\Rightarrow$ $4D + 5E + F = -41$

Solve:

$$(2D + 3E + F) - (2E + F) = -13 + 4$$

$\Rightarrow$ $2D + E = -9$

$$(4D + 5E + F) - (2D + 3E + F) = -41 + 13$$

$\Rightarrow$ $2D + 2E = -28 \Rightarrow D + E = -14$

From these:

$$2D + E = -9, \ D + E = -14$$

$\Rightarrow$ $D = 5, \ E = -19$

Then, $2(-19) + F = -4 \Rightarrow F = 34$

So circle:

$$x^2 + y^2 + 5x - 19y + 34 = 0$$

Now substitute D(0, k):

$$k^2 - 19k + 34 = 0$$

$$k^2 - 19k + 34 = 0$$

$$k = \frac{19 \pm \sqrt{361 - 136}}{2} = \frac{19 \pm 15}{2}$$

$$k = 17, 2$$

60. From Q59, take $k = 2$ so D(0,2) coincides with A, trivial case. Use non-degenerate case $k = 17$, so D(0,17). Find circumcircle of A(0,2), B(2,3), D(0,17).

Midpoint of AD:

$$\left(0, \frac{19}{2}\right)$$

Slope AD is infinite ⇒ perpendicular bisector is horizontal:

$$y = \frac{19}{2}$$

Midpoint of AB:

$$\left(1, \frac{5}{2}\right)$$

Slope AB $= \frac{1}{2}$ ⇒ perpendicular slope –2.

Equation:

$$y - \frac{5}{2} = -2(x - 1)$$

$$y = -2x + \frac{19}{2}$$

Intersect:

$$\frac{19}{2} = -2x + \frac{19}{2} \Rightarrow -2x = 5 \Rightarrow x = -\frac{5}{2}$$

Center: $\left(-\frac{5}{2}, \frac{19}{2}\right)$

Radius:

$$r = \sqrt{\left(\frac{5}{2}\right)^2 + \left(\frac{15}{2}\right)^2} = \sqrt{\frac{25+225}{4}} = \frac{\sqrt{250}}{2} = \frac{5\sqrt{10}}{2}$$

Diameter: $= 2r = 5\sqrt{10}$

61. The ellipse is

$$px^2 + 16y^2 = 16p$$

Dividing by $16p$,

$$\frac{x^2}{16} + \frac{y^2}{p} = 1$$

Since $p < 16$, for ellipse,

$$a^2 = 16,\ b^2 = p$$

So, $c^2 = a^2 - b^2 = 16 - p$

For hyperbola,

$$25(81x^2 - 144y^2) = 11664$$

$$2025x^2 - 3600y^2 = 11664$$

$$\frac{x^2}{\frac{11664}{2025}} - \frac{y^2}{\frac{11664}{3600}} = 1$$

$$a^2 = \frac{11664}{2025} = \frac{144}{25}, b^2 = \frac{11664}{3600} = \frac{81}{25}$$

For hyperbola,

$$c^2 = a^2 + b^2 = \frac{144}{25} + \frac{81}{25} = 9$$

Since foci coincide,

$$16 - p = 9$$

$$p = 7$$

62. For the ellipse,

$$a^2 = 16,\ c^2 = 9$$

$$a = 4,\ c = 3$$

$$e_{\text{ellipse}} = \frac{c}{a} = \frac{3}{4} = 0.75$$

For the hyperbola,

$$a^2 = \frac{144}{25}, c^2 = 9$$

$$a = \frac{12}{5}, c = 3$$

$$e_{\text{hyperbola}} = \frac{c}{a} = \frac{3}{12/5} = \frac{5}{4} = 1.25$$

Required difference: $1.25 - 0.75 = 0.5$

63. The sphere

$x^2 + y^2 + z^2 - 4x - 6y - 12z + k = 0$

has centre (2, 3, 6). A concentric sphere has the same centre.

Distance of origin from this centre:

$$\sqrt{(2)^2 + (3)^2 + (6)^2} = \sqrt{4+9+36} = \sqrt{49} = 7$$

Since the sphere passes through origin, its radius equals this distance.

64. For the sphere,

$x^2 + y^2 + z^2 - 4x - 6y - 12z + k = 0$

Centre (2,3,6). Radius:

$$r^2 = 2^2 + 3^2 + 6^2 - k = 49 - k$$

Given, $r = 8$,

$$64 = 49 - k \Rightarrow k = -15$$

65. Given, $|\vec{a}| = |\vec{b}| = 1$ and $|\vec{a}+\vec{b}| = 1$

$$|\vec{a}+\vec{b}|^2 = |\vec{a}|^2 + |\vec{b}|^2 + 2\vec{a}\cdot\vec{b}$$

$$1 = 1 + 1 + 2\vec{a}\cdot\vec{b} \Rightarrow 2\vec{a}\cdot\vec{b} = -1 \Rightarrow \vec{a}\cdot\vec{b} = -\frac{1}{2}$$

$$\cos\theta = \frac{\vec{a}\cdot\vec{b}}{|\vec{a}||\vec{b}|} = -\frac{1}{2} \Rightarrow \theta = \frac{2\pi}{3}$$

66. Given, $|\vec{b}+\vec{c}| = 1$ and $|\vec{c}| = |\vec{b}| = 1$

$$|\vec{b}+\vec{c}|^2 = 1 = 1 + 1 + 2\vec{b}\cdot\vec{c} \Rightarrow \vec{b}\cdot\vec{c} = -\frac{1}{2}$$

Now use $|\vec{a}+\vec{b}+\vec{c}| = 1$:

$|\vec{a}+\vec{b}+\vec{c}|^2 = 1$

$$= |\vec{a}|^2 + |\vec{b}|^2 + |\vec{c}|^2 + 2(\vec{a}\cdot\vec{b} + \vec{b}\cdot\vec{c} + \vec{c}\cdot\vec{a})$$

$$1 = 3 + 2\left(-\frac{1}{2} - \frac{1}{2} + \vec{c}\cdot\vec{a}\right)$$

$$1 = 3 + 2(-1 + \vec{c}\cdot\vec{a}) \Rightarrow 1 = 1 + 2\vec{c}\cdot\vec{a} \Rightarrow \vec{c}\cdot\vec{a} = 0$$

$$\cos\theta = 0 \Rightarrow \theta = \frac{\pi}{2}$$

67. Given $\vec{a}\times\vec{b} = \vec{c}$, so $\vec{c}$ is perpendicular to both $\vec{a}$ and $\vec{b}$. Also $\vec{b} \times \vec{c} = \vec{a}$, so $\vec{a}$ is perpendicular to both $\vec{b}$ and $\vec{c}$. Hence all three vectors are mutually perpendicular ⇒ statement I is true.

Taking magnitudes:

$$|\vec{c}| = |\vec{a}||\vec{b}|\sin 90^\circ = |\vec{a}||\vec{b}|$$

$$|\vec{a}| = ||\vec{b}||\vec{c}|$$

$$|\vec{b}| = |\vec{c}||\vec{a}|$$

Multiplying:

$$|\vec{a}||\vec{b}||\vec{c}| = |\vec{a}|^2|\vec{b}|^2|\vec{c}|^2 \Rightarrow |\vec{a}||\vec{b}||\vec{c}| = 1$$

Using symmetry, each must be 1. Hence all are unit vectors $\Rightarrow$ statement II is true.

68. I: $(\vec{a}\times\vec{b})\cdot\vec{c} = (\vec{b}\times\vec{c})\cdot\vec{a} = (\vec{c}\times\vec{a})\cdot\vec{b}$

So LHS $= 2(\vec{c}\times\vec{a})\cdot\vec{b} \neq (\vec{c}\times\vec{a})\cdot\vec{b}$. Hence false.

II: $(\vec{a}\times\vec{b})\times(\vec{b}\times\vec{c}) = \vec{b}\left((\vec{a}\times\vec{b}).\vec{c}\right) - \vec{c}\left((\vec{a}\times\vec{b})\cdot\vec{b}\right)$

Second term is zero, so

$$= (\vec{a}\times\vec{b})\cdot\vec{c}\,\vec{b}$$

Dot with $\vec{b}$: $\left((\vec{a}\times\vec{b})\cdot\vec{c}\right)(\vec{b}\cdot\vec{b}) = 1\cdot 1 = 1$

Hence, statement II is true.

69. Since $\vec{a},\vec{b},\vec{c}$ are unit vectors and $\vec{a}\perp\vec{b}$, also $\vec{c}$ makes angle $\frac{\pi}{3}$ with both $\vec{a}$ and $\vec{b}$.

$$\vec{c}\cdot\vec{a} = |\vec{c}||\vec{a}|\cos\frac{\pi}{3} = \frac{1}{2},\ \vec{c}\cdot\vec{b} = \frac{1}{2}$$

Given, $\vec{c} = p\vec{a} + q\vec{b} + r(\vec{a}\times\vec{b})$

Dot with $\vec{a}$:

$$\vec{c}\cdot\vec{a} = p(\vec{a}\cdot\vec{a}) + q(\vec{b}\cdot\vec{a}) + r\left((\vec{a}\times\vec{b})\cdot\vec{a}\right) = p$$

So, $p = \frac{1}{2}$. Similarly $q = \frac{1}{2}$.

$$p + q = 1$$

70. Using $|\vec{c}| = 1$:

$$|\vec{c}|^2 = p^2 + q^2 + r^2\,|\vec{a}\times\vec{b}|^2$$

Since, $\vec{a}\perp\vec{b}, |\vec{a}\times\vec{b}| = 1$

$$1 = \left(\frac{1}{2}\right)^2 + \left(\frac{1}{2}\right)^2 + r^2 = \frac{1}{4} + \frac{1}{4} + r^2 = \frac{1}{2} + r^2$$

$$r^2 = \frac{1}{2}$$

71. Differentiability at $x = a$ implies continuity at $x = a$. Hence statement I is true.

Continuity means: $\lim_{x\to 0} f(x) = f(a)$

So, statement II is also true.

72. As $x \to 1$,

$$\frac{x^{n^2-1} - 1}{x^{n+1} - 1}$$

is of the form $\frac{0}{0}$. Using

$$\lim_{x\to 1}\frac{x^a - 1}{x^b - 1} = \frac{a}{b}$$

we get, $\frac{n^2 - 1}{n+1} = \frac{(n-1)(n+1)}{n+1} = n - 1$

73. $\lim_{x\to 0}\frac{10^{\sin x} - 1}{\tan x}$

Using, $10^{\sin x} - 1 \sim (\ln 10)\sin x$

and $\tan x \sim x$, $\sin x \sim x$, we get

$$\lim_{x\to 0}\frac{10^{\sin x} - 1}{\tan x} = \ln 10\cdot\lim_{x\to 0}\frac{\sin x}{\tan x} = \ln 10$$

74. For $x < 0$,

$$|x| = -x$$

So, $\frac{x}{|x|} = \frac{x}{-x} = -1$

Derivative of a constant: $\frac{d}{dx}(-1) = 0$

75. For $f(x) = x$ in the open interval $(-1,1)$, the values of $f(x)$ approach 1 as $x \to 1$, but $x = 1$ is not included in the interval. So the function does not attain a maximum value. Similarly, $f(x)$ approaches -1 as $x \to -1$, but $x = -1$ is not included. So the function does not attain a minimum value.

76. Given, $\sqrt[4]{y} = x + \sqrt{x^2 + 4}$

Raise both sides to power 4:

$$y = \left(x + \sqrt{x^2 + 4}\right)^4$$

Taking logarithm,

$$\ln y = 4\ln\left(x + \sqrt{x^2 + 4}\right)$$

Differentiate:

$$\frac{1}{y}\frac{dy}{dx} = 4\cdot\frac{1 + \frac{x}{\sqrt{x^2+4}}}{x + \sqrt{x^2+4}}$$

$$\frac{1 + \frac{x}{\sqrt{x^2+4}}}{x + \sqrt{x^2+4}} = \frac{\frac{x + \sqrt{x^2+4}}{\sqrt{x^2+4}}}{x + \sqrt{x^2+4}} = \frac{1}{\sqrt{x^2+4}}$$

Hence, $\frac{1}{y}\frac{dy}{dx} = \frac{4}{\sqrt{x^2+4}}$

$$\sqrt{x^2+4}\,\frac{dy}{dx} = 4y$$

77.

$$f(x) = 2\cos^2 x - 1 = \cos^2 x$$

$$f'(x) = -2\sin 2x$$

For decreasing function:

$f'(x) < 0 \Rightarrow -2\sin 2x < 0 \Rightarrow \sin 2x > 0$

$2x \in (2k\pi,\ (2k+1)\pi) \Rightarrow x \in \left(k\pi,\ k\pi + \frac{\pi}{2}\right)$

So, the longest interval of decrease has length $\frac{\pi}{2}$.

78. Given, $2A + 2B = \pi$

$$A + B = \frac{\pi}{2}$$

So, $A + B = \frac{\pi}{2}$

$$B = \frac{\pi}{2} - A$$

$$\sin A \sin B = \sin A \sin\left(\frac{\pi}{2} - A\right)$$

$$= \sin A \cos A = \frac{1}{2}\sin 2A$$

The maximum value of $\sin 2A$ is 1. Therefore, maximum value is $\frac{1}{2}$.

79. Given, $\cos\left(\frac{dy}{dx}\right) = p$

$$\frac{dy}{dx} = \cos^{-1} p$$

Integrating,

$$y = x\cos^{-1} p + C$$

Using the condition $y(0) = q$,

$$q = C$$

So, $y = x\cos^{-1}p + q$

$$\frac{y-q}{x} = \cos^{-1}p$$

$$\cos\left(\frac{y-q}{x}\right) = p$$

80. Given, $2f(x) + f(1 - x) = x$

Replace x by $1 - x$:

$$2f(1 - x) + f(x) = 1 - x$$

Now multiply the first equation by 2:

$$4f(x) + 2f(1 - x) = 2x$$

Subtract

$$2f(1 - x) + f(x) = 1 - x$$

from it:

$$3f(x) = 2x - (1 - x) = 3x - 1$$

$$f(x) = x - \frac{1}{3}$$

81. Given,

$$(e^y)^x - y = 0 \Rightarrow e^{xy} = y$$

Differentiate implicitly:

$$\frac{d}{dx}(e^{xy}) = \frac{dy}{dx}$$

$$e^{xy}\left(x\frac{dy}{dx} + y\right) = \frac{dy}{dx}$$

Using $e^{xy} = y$:

$$y\left(x\frac{dy}{dx} + y\right) = \frac{dy}{dx}$$

$$xy\frac{dy}{dx} + y^2 = \frac{dy}{dx}$$

$$\frac{dy}{dx}(1 - xy) = y^2$$

$$\frac{dy}{dx} = \frac{y^2}{1 - xy}$$

82. From, $e^{xy} = y$

At $x = 1$, $y = y_0$:

$$e^{y_0} = y_0$$

Using result from (81):

$$\frac{dy}{dx} = \frac{y^2}{1 - xy}$$

At $x = 1$, $y = y_0$:

$$\frac{dy}{dx} = \frac{y_0^2}{1 - y_0}$$

Using $y_0 = e^{y_0}$:

$$\frac{dy}{dx} = \frac{y_0 e^{y_0}}{1 - e^{y_0}}$$

83. Let,

$$I = \int_0^{\frac{\pi}{2}} \frac{a\sin x + b\cos x}{(a+b)(\sin x + \cos x)}dx$$

Using the property

$$\int_0^{\frac{\pi}{2}} f(x)\,dx = \int_0^{\frac{\pi}{2}} f\left(\frac{\pi}{2} - x\right)dx$$

we get

$$I = \int_0^{\frac{\pi}{2}} \frac{a\cos x + b\sin x}{(a+b)(\sin x + \cos x)}dx$$

Adding both forms:

$$2I = \int_0^{\frac{\pi}{2}} \frac{(a+b)(\sin x + \cos x)}{(a+b)(\sin x + \cos x)}dx$$

$$2I = \int_0^{\frac{\pi}{2}} 1\,dx = \frac{\pi}{2}$$

$$I = \frac{\pi}{2}$$

84. From Q83,

$$k = \int_0^{\frac{\pi}{2}} \frac{a\sin x + b\cos x}{(a+b)(\sin x + \cos x)}dx$$

So, $\int_0^{\frac{\pi}{2}} \frac{a\sin x + b\cos x}{\sin x + \cos x}dx = k(a+b)$

By substituting $x \to \frac{\pi}{2} - x$,

$$\int_0^{\frac{\pi}{2}} \frac{a\cos x + b\sin x}{\sin x + \cos x}dx = \int_0^{\frac{\pi}{2}} \frac{a\sin x + b\cos x}{\sin x + \cos x}dx$$

Therefore, the required integral is $k(a + b)$.

85. Given,

$$f(x) = \frac{x^3}{3} - \frac{5x^2}{2} + 6x + 7$$

$$f'(x) = x^2 - 5x + 6$$

$$f'(x) = (x - 2)(x - 3)$$

For increasing function,

$$f'(x) > 0$$

$$(x - 2)(x - 3) > 0$$

So, $x < 2$ or $x > 3$

Hence, $T = \{x < 2\} \cup \{x > 3\}$

86. For decreasing function,

$$f'(x) < 0$$

$$(x - 2)(x - 3) < 0$$

This happens between the roots:

$$2 < x < 3$$

Hence, $S = (2,3)$

87. Given,

$$k = \int_0^{\frac{\pi}{4}} \sin x\, dx$$

Total area from 0 to $\frac{\pi}{2}$:

$$\int_0^{\frac{\pi}{2}} \sin x\, dx = 1$$

Hence, $\int_{\frac{\pi}{4}}^{\frac{\pi}{2}} \sin x\, dx = \int_0^{\frac{\pi}{2}} \sin x\, dx - \int_0^{\frac{\pi}{4}} \sin x\, dx = 1 - k$

88. Let,

$$I = \int_{\frac{\pi}{4}}^{\frac{\pi}{2}} \cos x\, dx$$

Put $x = \frac{\pi}{2} - t$

$$I = \int_0^{\frac{\pi}{4}} \sin t dt = k$$

89. For points of intersection,

$$x^2 = 2|x|$$

If $x \geq 0$, then

$$x^2 = 2x \Rightarrow x(x - 2) = 0$$

$\Rightarrow$ $x = 0, 2$

If $x < 0$, then

$$x^2 = -2x \Rightarrow x(x + 2) = 0 \Rightarrow x = -2$$

So the intersection points are (0,0), (2,4), (–2,4). Hence, there are 3 points of intersection.

90. In the interval $0 \leq x \leq 1$, $|x| = x$, so the curves are

$$y = x^2,\ y = 2x$$

Here $2x \geq x^2$. Required area:

$$\int_0^1 (2x - x^2)dx = \left[x^2 - \frac{x^3}{3}\right]_0^1 = 1 - \frac{1}{3} = \frac{2}{3}$$

91. Put, $u = \cos\theta$, $du = -\sin\theta\ d\theta$

$$\int \frac{\sin\theta\ d\theta}{(2+\cos\theta)(3+4\cos\theta)} = -\int \frac{du}{(2+u)(3+4u)}$$

Now, $\frac{1}{(u+2)(4u+3)} = \frac{C}{u+2} + \frac{D}{4u+3}$

$$1 = C(4u + 3) + D(u + 2)$$

Comparing constants and coefficients gives

$$C = -\frac{1}{5},\ D = \frac{4}{5}$$

Therefore,

$$-\int\left(-\frac{1}{5(u+2)} + \frac{4}{5(4u+3)}\right)du$$

$$= \frac{1}{5}\ln|u+2| - \frac{1}{5}\ln|4u+3|$$

So, $A = \frac{1}{5}$

92. From the result obtained,

$$\int \frac{\sin\theta\, d\theta}{(2+\cos\theta)(3+4\cos\theta)}$$

$$= \frac{1}{5}\ln|2+\cos\theta| - \frac{1}{5}\ln|3+4\cos\theta|$$

Comparing with

$A\ln|2 + \cos\theta| + B\ln|3 + 4\cos\theta|$

we get, $B = -\frac{1}{5}$

93. Given, $f(x) = \sin x$ and $g(x) - f(x) = f(4 - x)$

So, $g(x) = \sin x + \sin(4 - x)$

Now,

$$I = \int_0^4 \frac{f(x)}{g(x)}dx = \int_0^4 \frac{\sin x}{\sin x + \sin(4-x)}dx$$

Let, $I_1 = \int_0^4 \frac{\sin x}{\sin x + \sin(4-x)}dx$

Also consider

$$I_2 = \int_0^4 \frac{\sin(4-x)}{\sin x + \sin(4-x)}dx$$

Using substitution $x \rightarrow 4 - x$, we get $I_1 = I_2$

Now, $I_1 + I_2 = \int_0^4 \frac{\sin x + \sin(4-x)}{\sin x + \sin(4-x)}dx = \int_0^4 1\, dx = 4$

$$2I_1 = 4 \Rightarrow I_1 = 2$$

94. $I = \int_0^4 \frac{f(4-x)}{g(4-x)}dx = \int_0^4 \frac{\sin(4-x)}{\sin(4-x)+\sin x}dx$

This is exactly the same as I_2 above.

So, $I = 2$

95. For continuity at $x = 1$:

Left limit $= a.1(1 - 1) = 0$, middle value $= 1 - 1 = 0$

$\Rightarrow$ already continuous.

Now at $x = 3$, continuity:

Middle value $= 3 - 1 = 2$

Right value $= 9p + 3q + 2$

$9p + 3q + 2 = 2 \Rightarrow 9p + 3q = 0$

$\Rightarrow$ $3p + q = 0$ ...(1)

Now derivative continuity at $x = 3$:

Middle derivative: $\frac{d}{dx}(x - 1) = 1$

Right derivative: $\frac{d}{dx}(px^2 + qx + 2) = 2px + q$

At $x = 3$:

$$6p + q$$

Equate:

$$6p + q = 1 \quad \ldots(2)$$

Solve (1) and (2):

$(6p + q) - (3p + q) = 1 - 0$

$$\Rightarrow \quad 3p = 1 \Rightarrow p = \frac{1}{3}$$

96. From equation (1):

$$3p + q = 0$$

$$3 \cdot \frac{1}{3} + q = 0 \Rightarrow 1 + q = 0 \Rightarrow q = -1$$

97. Given,

$$e^{x+y}\frac{dy}{dx} = e^{x-y}$$

$$\frac{dy}{dx} = e^{-2y}$$

Now, $\frac{d^2y}{dx^2} = \frac{d}{dx}(e^{-2y})$

$$\frac{d^2y}{dx^2} = -2e^{-2y}\frac{dy}{dx}$$

Since, $\frac{dy}{dx} = e^{-2y}$,

$$\frac{d^2y}{dx^2} = -2\left(\frac{dy}{dx}\right)^2$$

Therefore,

$$\frac{d^2y}{dx^2}\left(\frac{dx}{dy}\right)^2 = -2\left(\frac{dy}{dx}\right)^2 \cdot \left(\frac{1}{dy/dx}\right)^2 = -2$$

98. From

$$\frac{dy}{dx} = e^{-2y}$$

$$e^{2y}dy = dx$$

Integrating,

$$\frac{e^{2y}}{2} = x + C$$

Using $y(0) = 0$,

$$\frac{1}{2} = C$$

So, $\frac{e^{2y}}{2} = x + \frac{1}{2}$

$$e^{2y} = 2x + 1$$

$$2y = \ln(2x + 1)$$

99. Given, $f(x) = \tan(x^2)$ and $g(x) = x|x|$.

Near $x = 0$:

$$g(x) = x|x| = \begin{cases} x^2, & x > 0 \\ -x^2, & x < 0 \end{cases}$$

So, $g(0) = 0$, continuous but not differentiable at 0.

Now, $p(x) = f(x)g(x) = \tan(x^2) \cdot x|x|$

As $x \to 0$, $\tan(x^2) \sim x^2$

So, $p(x) \sim x^2 \cdot x|x| = x^3|x|$

Thus $p(x) \to 0$, hence continuous at 0.

Now differentiability:

$$p'(0) = \lim_{x\to 0}\frac{p(x) - 0}{x} = \lim_{x\to 0}\frac{x^3|x|}{x} = \lim_{x\to 0} x^2|x| = 0$$

Hence derivative exists.

100. $q(x) = f(g(x)) = \tan((x|x|)^2)$

Now, $(x|x|)^2 = x^2 \cdot x^2 = x^4$

So, $q(x) = \tan(x^4)$

Clearly continuous at $x = 0$.

Now differentiability:

$$q'(x) = \sec^2(x^4) \cdot 4x^s$$

At $x = 0$:

$$q'(0) = 1 \cdot 0 = 0$$

So differentiable.

101. Total 4-digit numbers using 0,1,2,3,4 without repetition:

$$4 \times 4 \times 3 \times 2 = 96$$

For divisibility by 2, the unit digit must be 0,2 or 4.

If unit digit is 0:

$$4 \times 3 \times 2 = 24$$

If unit digit is 2 or 4, for each case:

$$3 \times 3 \times 2 = 18$$

So favourable numbers:

$$24 + 18 + 18 = 60$$

$$P = \frac{60}{96} = \frac{5}{8}$$

102. A number is divisible by 3 if the sum of its digits is divisible by 3. The total sum of digits $0 + 1 + 2 + 3 + 4 = 10$. Since 4 digits are used, one digit is omitted. Required sum is divisible by 3, so omitted digit can be 1 or 4.

For each valid selection containing 0, number of 4-digit numbers:

$$4! - 3! = 24 - 6 = 18$$

There are 2 such selections, so favourable numbers:

$$2 \times 18 = 36$$

$$P = \frac{36}{96} - \frac{3}{8}$$

103. For divisibility by 4, the last two digits must form a number divisible by 4. Possible endings are:

04, 12, 20, 24, 32, 40

For endings using 0: 04,20,40, remaining first two places:

$$3 \times 2 = 6$$

Total: $3 \times 6 = 18$

For endings not using 0: 12,24,32, remaining digits include 0, so first digit has 2 choices and second digit has 2 choices:

$$3 \times 4 = 12$$

Total favourable:

$$18 + 12 = 30$$

$$P = \frac{30}{96} = \frac{5}{16}$$

104. A number d divisible by 6 must be divisible by both 2 and 3.

From earlier:

- Numbers divisible by 2: unit digit 0,2,4
- Numbers divisible by 3: digit sum divisible by 3

Digits are 0,1,2,3,4, total sum = 10. For divisibility by 3, omitted digit must be 1 or 4.

Case 1: omit 1 → digits {0,2,3,4}

Even unit digits: 0,2,4

- Unit 0: remaining 2,3,4 → 3! = 6
- Unit 2: remaining 0,3,4, first place ≠ 0 → 2 × 2 = 4
- Unit 4: same → 4

Total = 6 + 4 + 4 = 14

Case 2: omit 4 → digits {0,1,2,3}

- Unit 0: remaining 1,2,3 → 6
- Unit 2: remaining 0,1,3, first ≠ 0 → 2 × 2 = 4

Total = 6 + 4 = 10

Total favourable:

$$14 + 10 = 24$$

$$P = \frac{24}{96} = \frac{1}{4}$$

105. Numbers without 0: use digits 1,2,3,4

Total such 4-digit numbers:

$$4! = 24$$

Total possible numbers: 96

$$P = \frac{24}{96} = \frac{1}{4} = 0.25$$

106. Given,

$$\frac{P(A)}{2} = \frac{P(B)}{3} = \frac{P(C)}{5} = \frac{P(D)}{8} = k$$

So, P(A) = $2k$, P(B) = $3k$, P(C) = $5k$, P(D) = $8k$

Since events are exhaustive:

$$2k + 3k + 5k + 8k = 18k = 1 \Rightarrow k = \frac{1}{18}$$

$$P(A) + P(B) + P(C) = 2k + 3k + 5k$$

$$= 10k = \frac{10}{18} = \frac{5}{9}$$

107.

$$\frac{2P(A) + 3P(B)}{4P(C) + 5P(D)} = \frac{2(2k) + 3(3k)}{4(5k) + 5(8k)}$$

$$= \frac{4k + 9k}{20k + 40k} = \frac{13k}{60k} = \frac{13}{60}$$

108. Geometric mean:

$$G = (P(A)P(B)P(C)P(D))^{1/4}$$

$$= (2k \cdot 3k \cdot 5k \cdot 8k)^{1/4}$$

$$= (240k^4)^{1/4} = 240^{1/4} \cdot k$$

Since, $k = \frac{1}{18}$

$$G = \frac{240^{1/4}}{18}$$

$$9G = \frac{9}{18} \cdot 240^{1/4} = \frac{1}{2} \cdot 240^{1/4}$$

$$240 = 16 \times 15 \Rightarrow 240^{1/4} = 2 \cdot 15^{1/4}$$

$$9G = \frac{1}{2} \cdot 2 \cdot 15^{1/4} = 15^{1/4}$$

109. Total outcomes when four dice are rolled:

$$6^4 = 1296$$

For total 6, let the dice numbers be x_1, x_2, x_3, x_4, where each $x_i \geq 1$.

$$x_1 + x_2 + x_3 + x_4 = 6$$

Put, $y_i = x_i - 1$.

Then, $y_1 + y_2 + y_3 + y_4 = 2$

Number of non-negative solutions:

$$^{2+4-1}C_{4-1} = {}^5C_3 = 10$$

$$P = \frac{10}{1296} = \frac{5}{648}$$

110. Total outcomes:

$$6^4 = 1296$$

For total at least 23, possible totals are 23 and 24.

Total 24: only

(6, 6, 6, 6)

so 1 outcome.

Total 23: three dice show 6 and one die shows 5, so 4 outcomes.

Total favourable outcomes:

$$1 + 4 = 5$$

$$P = \frac{5}{1296}$$

111. The two regression lines are

$$x + y + 11 = 0$$

$$2x + 3y + 4 = 0$$

Take

$$x + y + 11 = 0 \Rightarrow x = -y - 11$$

So, $b_{xy} = -1$

Also, $2x + 3y + 4 = 0 \Rightarrow y = -\frac{2}{3}x - \frac{4}{3}$

So, $b_{yx} = -\frac{2}{3}$

Now, $r^2 = b_{xy}b_{yx}$

$$r^2 = (-1)\left(-\frac{2}{3}\right) = \frac{2}{3}$$

Both regression coefficients are negative, so r is negative.

$$r = -\sqrt{\frac{2}{3}}$$

112. Mean = 1.414, number of observations = 20

$$\Sigma x_i = 20 \times 1.414 = 28.28$$

$$\Sigma\, 100(2x_i + 4) = 100(2\Sigma x_i + 4 \times 20)$$

$$= 100(2 \times 28.28 + 80)$$

$$= 100(56.56 + 80)$$

$$= 100 \times 136.56 = 13656$$

113. Let,

K: knows answer, P(K) = 0.9

G: guesses, P(G) = 0.1

If guessing, probability of correct answer $= \frac{1}{4}$

$$\text{P(Correct)} = \text{P(K)}\cdot 1 + \text{P(G)}\cdot\frac{1}{4}$$

$$= 0.9 + 0.1 \times \frac{1}{4} = 0.9 + 0.025$$

$$= 0.925 = \frac{37}{40}$$

$$\text{P(G | Correct)} = \frac{\text{P(G)}\cdot\frac{1}{4}}{\text{P(Correct)}} = \frac{0.1\times\frac{1}{4}}{0.925} = \frac{0.025}{0.925} = \frac{1}{37}$$

114. I. $(A \cup B \cup C) \cap (\tilde{A} \cap \tilde{B} \cap \tilde{C})$

Second part means none of A, B, C occur, first means at least one occurs → contradiction ⇒ impossible

II. $(A \cap B \cap C) \cap (\tilde{A} \cup \tilde{B} \cup \tilde{C})$

First part means all occur, second means at least one does not occur → contradiction ⇒ impossible ✗ (not possible event)

So only statement I is correct.

115. Standard deviation changes in the same ratio when each observation is multiplied by a constant.

Given original standard deviation:

$$\sigma = 10$$

Each observation is multiplied by 5, so new standard deviation:

$$5\sigma = 5 \times 10 = 50$$

116. For binomial distribution,

$$\text{Mean} = np = 6$$

$$\text{Variance} = npq = \left(\sqrt{2}\right)^2 = 2$$

So, $npq = 2$

Using $np = 6$:

$$6q = 2 \Rightarrow q = \frac{1}{3}$$

$$p = 1 - \frac{1}{3} = \frac{2}{3}$$

Now, $np = 6 \Rightarrow n\cdot\frac{2}{3} = 6 \Rightarrow n = 9$

$$P(X = 0) = q^n = \left(\frac{1}{3}\right)^9$$

117. Given standard deviation of X = 5, so

$$\text{Var(X)} = 5^2 = 25$$

For, $Y = 2X - 5$

$$\text{Var(Y)} = 2^2\ \text{Var(X)}$$

$$= 4 \times 25 = 100$$

118. Let, $P(A) = a$

Given, $4P(A) = 2P(B) = P(C)$

So, $P(B) = 2a,\ P(C) = 4a$

Since A and B are disjoint:

$$P(A \cap B) = 0$$

Also, A and C are independent:

$$P(A \cap C) = P(A)P(C) = 4a^2$$

and B and C are independent:

$$P(B \cap C) = P(B)P(C) = 8a^2$$

Now, $P(A \cup B \cup C) = a + 2a + 4a - 4a^2 - 8a^2$

$$5a = 7a - 12a^2$$

$$12a^2 = 2a \Rightarrow a = \frac{1}{6}$$

Therefore, $P(C) = 4a = \frac{4}{6} = \frac{2}{3}$

119. Total students = 100, so

$$10 + 20 + f + 40 = 100 \Rightarrow f = 30$$

Class marks are 5, 15, 25, 35. Mean:

$$\bar{x} = \frac{10(5) + 20(15) + 30(25) + 40(35)}{100}$$

$$= \frac{50 + 300 + 750 + 1400}{100} = 25$$

Mean deviation about mean:

$$\frac{10\,|\,5 - 25\,| + 20\,|\,15 - 25\,| + 30\,|\,25 - 25\,| + 40\,|\,35 - 25\,|}{100}$$

$$= \frac{200 + 200 + 0 + 400}{100} = 8$$

120. Using mean $\bar{x} = 25$,

$$\sigma = \sqrt{\frac{\Sigma f(x - \bar{x})^2}{N}}$$

$$\sigma = \sqrt{\frac{10(20)^2 + 20(10)^2 + 30(0)^2 + 40(10)^2}{100}}$$

$$= \sqrt{\frac{4000 + 2000 + 0 + 4000}{100}} = \sqrt{100} = 10$$

Previous Years' Paper

NATIONAL DEFENCE ACADEMY & NAVAL ACADEMY

NDA & NA — Entrance Exam, 2025 (II)

(Exam held on 14-09-2025)

PAPER-I: GENERAL ABILITY TEST

PART-A: ENGLISH LANGUAGE

Directions (Qs. No. 1-5): *Read the following passage carefully and answer the items that follow the passage. Your answers to these items should be based solely on the passage.*

Can agricultural productivity meet human needs in the long run? Since twentieth century advances, given increasing costs, do not seem sustainable, further increases in output will not be achieved easily. Global population growth, while showing signs of slowing down, has pushed farmers and herders into areas unsuited to intensive agriculture, accelerating worldwide ecological disruptions. Reserves of arable land and fresh water have diminished alarmingly. Chemical runoffs have compounded pollution problems. Invasion of natural habitats have hastened species extinction. Desertification has been severe in the last hundred years, especially in North Africa, southern portions of Africa, Australia, northern Mexico, and the American Southwest. Tropical forests have shrunk by one-half since World War II, with agricultural pressures causing three-quarters of that loss. Government intervention has produced its share of catastrophes, ranging from a terrible famine in China between 1958-1961 that may have killed 30 million people and destroyed the Aral Sea. Taking everything into consideration, we may remain hopeful about humankind's agricultural prospects, but we can scarcely look forward optimistically at the end of the first quarter of the twenty-first century.

1. Why do twentieth century advances not seem sustainable?

A. They do not meet the human needs

B. Due to the increased cost of agricultural production

C. Because they are outdated for the current times

D. They are useful, but intensive

2. What pushes farmers into places unsuited for agriculture?

A. Population growth B. Industrialisation

C. Water scarcity D. Desertification

3. Which one of the following is NOT true, according to the passage, for ecological degradation?

A. Global population growth

B. Excess use of chemicals

C. Desertification

D. World War II

4. What is the conclusion of the author in the passage about the prospects of agriculture in the world?

A. The author is both hopeful and sceptical of the prospects of agriculture

B. The author is very hopeful of the prospects of agriculture

C. The author is sceptical of the prospects of agriculture

D. The author is neither hopeful nor sceptical of the prospects of agriculture

5. Which one of the following words means 'incursion'?

A. invasion B. intensive

C. severe D. intervention

Directions (Qs. No. 6-8): *The following items have a sentence in direct or indirect speech, followed by four options. One of the options correctly converts the direct speech into indirect speech. Select the most appropriate option and mark your answer on the Answer Sheet.*

6. Convert from direct into indirect speech.

Ayushi said to the group, "We have had enough of suffering today. It is time to march forward."

A. Ayushi told the group that they had had enough of suffering that day and it was time to march forward

B. Ayushi asked the group that they had had enough of suffering this day and it was time to march forward
C. Ayushi told the group that they had enough of suffering and that it is time to march forward
D. Ayushi told the group that we had had enough of suffering this day and it was time to march forward

7. Convert from direct speech into indirect speech.
"Alas! We lost the match by one point," said the Captain
A. The Captain regretted that they had lost the match by one point
B. The Captain regretted that they lost the match by one point
C. The Captain exclaimed that they had lost the match by one point
D. The Captain told the team that they had lost the match by one point

8. Convert from direct speech into indirect speech.
"Where were you last week?" Alok asked Sheela.
A. Alok told Sheela where she had been the week before
B. Alok asked Sheela where she had been the week before
C. Alok asked Sheela where she was the week before
D. Alok asked Sheela where she had been the last week

Directions (Qs. No. 9-10): *Following items have sentences in active voice with four options. One of the options converts the active voice into passive voice correctly. Select the most appropriate option and mark your answer on the Answer Sheet.*

9. The king who the people loved built the castle five centuries ago
A. The castle was built five centuries ago by the king who was loved by the people
B. The castle was built five centuries ago by the king who loved the people
C. The castle built five centuries ago by the king loved by the people
D. The castle was built five centuries ago by the people who were loved by the king

10. The company has recruited four hundred engineers who will have to complete an internship for three weeks
A. Four hundred engineers have been recruited by the company and an internship of three weeks will have to be completed by them
B. Four hundred engineers have been recruited by the company and they will have to complete an internship of three weeks
C. The company has been recruited by four hundred engineers and an internship of three week will have to be completed by them
D. Four hundred engineers have been recruited by the company. Internship of three weeks will have had to be completed by them

Directions (Qs. No. 11-15): *In the following items, a pair of words is provided. You are required to select the option that most appropriately describes the meaning of both the words and mark your response on the Answer Sheet accordingly.*

11. Seldom and Often
A. Seldom means hardly ever and often means time and again
B. Seldom means time and again and often means hardly ever
C. Seldom means never and often means not at all
D. Seldom means frequently and often means time and again

12. Overview and Review
A. Overview means assessment and review means general idea
B. Overview means general idea and review means assessment
C. Overview means general analysis and review means go through
D. Overview means summary and review means evaluation

13. Overcome and Succeed
A. Overcome means triumph over and succeed means to achieve something
B. Overcome means achieve something and succeed means to triumph over
C. Overcome means to be successful and succeed means to achieve something
D. Overcome means winning and succeed means to rise above

14. Embed and Imbue
A. Embed means instil and imbue means implant
B. Embed means implant and imbue means instil
C. Embed means accept and imbue means detest
D. Embed means include and imbue means accept

15. Emancipate and Empower
A. Emancipate means authorize and empower means liberate
B. Emancipate means liberate and empower means authorise

C. Emancipate means liberal and empower means authorisation

D. Emancipate means freedom and empower means encounter

Directions (Qs. No. 16-20): *In the following items a sentence or a phrase is given with a word that is underlined, followed by four words or group of words. Select the option that is nearest in meaning to the underlined word and mark your response on the Answer Sheet accordingly.*

16. The Professor has been able to instil confidence in her students.

A. inculcate B. infer
C. eradicate D. unlike

17. The members of the group expressed their allegiance to their leader.

A. commitment B. disloyalty
C. understanding D. unlikely

18. The inscrutability surrounding the incident remains unresolved until the end of the movie.

A. clearness B. comprehensibility
C. seriousness D. mystery

19. The dodgy behaviour of the leader led to her fall.

A. principled B. dubious
C. dishonest D. painful

20. People have been advised not to venture into sea as the weather is likely to be inclement.

A. squally B. calm
C. pleasant D. indigent

Directions (Qs. No. 21-25): *In this section each item consists of six sentences of a passage. The first and sixth sentences are given in the beginning as SI and S6. The middle four sentences in each have been jumbled up and labelled as P, Q, R and S. You are required to find the proper sequence of the four sentences and mark your response accordingly on the Answer Sheet.*

21. S1. Sufism is an English word coined in the Nineteenth Century

S6. It may also have been *suffa*, the platform outside a place of Islamic worship

P. Historians have understood this term in several ways

Q. According to some scholars, it is derived from *suf*, meaning wool

R. Others derive it from *safa*, meaning purity

S. The word used for Sufism in Islamic texts is *tasawwuf*

A. Q R S P B. S P Q R
C. P Q S R D. R P S Q

22. S1. Al-Biruni was born in 973, in Khwarizm in present-day Uzbekistan

S6. He arrived in Ghazni as a hostage, but gradually developed a liking for the city

P. In 1017, when Sultan Mahmud invaded Khwarizm, he took several scholars back to his capital, Ghazni: Al-Biruni was one among them

Q. He was well versed in several languages; Syriac, Arabic, Persian, Hebrew, and Sanskrit

R. Khwarizm was an important centre of learning, and Al-Biruni received the best education available at the time

S. However he did not know Greek, although he was familiar with the works of Plato and other Greek philosophers

A. Q S R P B. R Q S P
C. P Q S R D. R P S Q

23. S1. Vijayanagara or 'city of victory' was the name of both a city and an empire

S6. They remembered it as Hampi, a name derived from that of the local mother goddess, Pampadevi

P. In its heyday it stretched from the river Krishna in the north to the extreme south of the Indian peninsula

Q. Although it fell into ruin in the seventeenth-eighteenth centuries, it continued to live in the memories of the people who inhabited the Krishna-Tungabhadra doab

R. In 1565 the city was sacked and subsequently deserted

S. The Empire was founded in the fourteenth century

A. S P R Q B. S Q P R
C. P Q S R D. P Q R S

24. S1. Liberalisation and globalisation freed India's economy from the low GDP trap that had impeded India's progress

S6. Today India has transformed into one of the largest economies of the world

P. India's 3 pc rate of growth and a set of emergent circumstances led to a balance of payment crisis in the early 1990s

Q. Ease of business was ensured, and the requirement for import licences, and production quotas, were removed

R. Apart from these measures India also took a loan from the IMF to tide over the crisis, but after 1993, India has not taken another loan from the IMF

S. In a landmark budget in 1991, responding to the emergent crisis, India delicenced many industries and liberalised its economic policies

A. Q S R P B. S Q P R
C. R Q S P D. P S Q R

25. S1. In many countries, there are millions of people who are underprivileged and deprived

S6. In the past forced labour was imposed by landlords, moneylenders, and other wealthy persons

P. Both of these are prohibited under the Constitution of India

Q. One such form of exploitation in our country has been *begar* or forced labour without payment

R. The marginalised are often subjected to exploitation by their fellow human beings

S. Another closely related form of exploitation is buying and selling of human beings and using them as slaves

A. Q S R P B. R Q S P
C. P Q S R D. Q S P R

Directions (Qs. No. 26-35): *Given below are sentences that use discourse markers/expressions to make them complete. Identify the most appropriate discourse marker and mark your answer accordingly on the Answer Sheet.*

26. I can't be bothered to tell him what I think; .... he would not listen to me.
A. meanwhile B. in any case
C. in the meantime D. somehow

27. ...., if the referee points his fingers, this indicates that someone has done something wrong.
A. On the contrary B. Whatever more
C. Briefly D. As regards

28. ...., have you been to the local library yet?
A. Sort of B. Frankly
C. All the same D. Incidentally

29. ...., women are healthier and are living longer than ever before: indeed on an average, they can expect to live five years longer than men.
A. To a large extent
B. As regards
C. As far as
D. Turning now

30. The difference is that I have been fortunate to find a career that I love and, ..., I am getting paid reasonably for it.
A. briefly B. broadly speaking
C. what is more D. in conclusion

31. ...., the Government of India has followed the policy of trying to improve relations with its neighbours.
A. Particular B. Knowingly
C. Otherwise D. In general

32. ...., this issue is likely to be discussed when the Council meets next.
A. As per reports B. Accordingly
C. Likewise D. Briefly

33. ...., you needed to consult a physician to have a clear idea of what the disease is about.
A. In that case B. In these case
C. Likewise D. Henceforth

34. ...., in the year-ago period the current account deficit stood at \$1.3 billion or 0.2% of the GDP.
A. Particularly B. Notably
C. Seriously D. Unknowingly

35. ...., the records have been completely undermined by shoddy book-keeping.
A. Because of B. As such
C. Forever D. Hence

Directions (Qs. No. 36-40): *Given below are words/expressions/jargons followed by four options. Identify the most appropriate option that defines the word/expression/jargon in each instance, and mark your response accordingly on the Answer Sheet.*

36. Infelicity:
A. Disloyalty towards one's nation
B. An inappropriate remark
C. To kill or destroy
D. To touch or push gently

37. Corollary:
A. Something that is too expensive
B. Something that looks real but does not really exist
C. Something that naturally follows
D. Something resembling a coal mine

38. Quandary:
A. Situation in which you are confused about what to do
B. Situation in which two people or group argue
C. Situation in which no progress can be made
D. Situation in which a relationship becomes friendlier

39. Presumption:
A. Prediction based on past experiences
B. Judgement made with certainty
C. Decision based on facts
D. Opinion formed before having all the facts

40. Smug:
A. Too confident about one's own achievements
B. Too eager to help or obey someone important
C. Too emotional or dramatic
D. Too eager to bottle up conflicts

Directions (Qs. No. 41-45): *Each of the following items in this section consists of a sentence, the parts of which have been jumbled. These parts have been labelled as P, Q, R and S. Each sentence is followed by four sequences, namely (A), (B), (C) and (D), indicating the rearrangement of the parts. You are required to select the most appropriate option and mark your response on the Answer Sheet accordingly.*

41. P. of children they also contain deeply embedded
Q. whereas traditional fairy tales
R. moral lessons that are relevant even for adults
S. were designed for the entertainment
A. R P Q S B. Q S R P
C. R P S Q D. Q S P R

42. P. of school education is an ineluctable truth
Q. that sporting activities are an integral part
R. meaningfully towards the overall growth of a student
S. that underscores the learning process and contributes
A. Q P S R B. Q S R P
C. R P S Q D. Q S P R

43. P. and contentment on account of a life lived
Q. the beneficial outcome of
R. well without retribution or rebuke
S. a virtuous life is peace of mind
A. S R Q P B. S P Q R
C. Q S P R D. Q S R P

44. P. more representative than the latter
Q. from a non-parliamentary system
R. in as much as the former is
S. it is widely believed that the parliamentary system differs
A. S Q R P B. S P Q R
C. R S P Q D. P S R Q

45. P. crushes the spirit behind the service
Q. it stunts the person offering the same and
R. exhibition or for fear of public opinion
S. when service is done for
A. S Q R P B. S P Q R
C. R S P Q D. S R Q P

Directions (Qs. No. 46-50): *Each of the following sentences in this section has a blank space, followed by four options. Select the most appropriate option to fill in the blank and mark your response on the Answer Sheet accordingly.*

46. It does not look like he is going .... in his studies than what was predicted by his school principal.
A. any further B. further
C. farther D. any farther

47. .... all the confusion the thief made a quiet getaway.
A. Among B. Amongst
C. Amidst D. Amid

48. The intricate operation on the patient required the expertise of a/an .... surgeon.
A. special B. especial
C. specialist D. specialised

49. There are .... thirty students inside the classroom at any time.
A. less than B. fewer than
C. less then D. fewer then

50. There are many .... vehicles on the highway due to a sudden landslide.
A. stationery B. stationed
C. stranded D. straggle

PART-B: GENERAL KNOWLEDGE

51. The focal length of a concave lens is 0.5 m. The power of the lens is:
A. +0.5 D B. –0.5 D
C. +2.0 D D. –2.0 D

52. The rule to determine the direction of a force experienced by a straight current carrying conductor placed in a magnetic field which is perpendicular to it is:
A. Right-hand thumb rule
B. Fleming's left-hand rule
C. Fleming's right-hand rule
D. Hund's rule

53. One parsec in astronomical units (A.U.) is about:
A. 2×10^3 A.U. B. 2×10^4 A.U.
C. 2×10^5 A.U. D. 2×10^6 A.U.

54. Which one of the following statements for second law of motion is NOT correct?
A. The net force on a body is proportional to that body's acceleration
B. The net force on a body is in the same direction as the acceleration
C. The time rate of change of momentum is equal to force
D. The net force on a body is proportional to that body's momentum

55. The temperature of a body increases from 310 K to 340 K. The temperature increase in degree Celsius is:

A. 20°C B. 30°C
C. 37°C D. 67°C

56. Which one of the following statements for the work done by gravity on a body is NOT correct?

A. Work done is independent of the path followed by the body
B. Work done depends only on the vertical distance separating the initial and the final position of the body
C. Work done depends on the path followed by the body
D. Work done is zero if the body is displaced horizontally to the force of gravity

57. Which one among the following statements is correct?

A. Pressure has magnitude as well as direction
B. As we go deeper in a liquid, the pressure decreases
C. Action and reaction forces act on the same object
D. Pascal and N/m^2 represent the same unit

58. Which one of the following wavelength radiations may correspond to an X-ray?

A. 1 nm B. 10 nm
C. 100 nm D. 300 nm

59. In a Telescope, compared to the eyepiece lens the objective lens has:

A. larger focal length and larger aperture
B. larger focal length and smaller aperture
C. smaller focal length and larger aperture
D. smaller focal length and smaller aperture

60. The energy, E, of a photon can be expressed as $E = hf$ where f is the frequency and h is Planck's constant. The dimensions of h are the same as that of:

A. linear momentum B. angular momentum
C. displacement D. torque

61. The work done by the force acting on an object is zero if the displacement of the object:

A. is in the opposite direction of the direction of force
B. is in the same direction of the direction of force
C. is in perpendicular direction of the direction of force
D. none of above

62. The magnetic field inside a current carrying very long solenoid is:

A. Uniform B. Non-uniform
C. Zero D. Highest at mid-point

63. Which one of the following instruments can be used to measure –250°C temperature?

A. By using a mercury based thermometer
B. By using an alcohol based thermometer
C. By using a clinical thermometer
D. By using thermocouple based thermometer

64. The quantity of heat needed to change unit mass of a substance from liquid to vapour without changing the temperature, is called:

A. specific heat B. specific latent heat
C. thermal capacity D. heat energy

65. The temperature at which "vapour pressure of the liquid in an open vessel becomes equal to the atmospheric pressure" is called:

A. Melting point B. Boiling point
C. Liquid point D. None of the above

66. Which one of the following statements about surface tension is correct?

A. It increases when temperature increases
B. It decreases when temperature increases
C. It will remain same with increase or decrease of temperature
D. It will always decrease with increase or decrease of temperature

67. A body sinks in water when:

A. density of water is greater than density of body
B. density of water is less than density of body
C. density of water is equal to density of body
D. the body is heavy

68. Why a fielder in the ground gradually pulls his hands backward while catching a fast moving cricket ball?

A. To reduce the acceleration of the ball
B. To increase the acceleration of the ball
C. To increase the velocity of the ball
D. None of above

69. Bottom of a tank containing water appears to be raised. It is due to:

A. Reflection of light B. Refraction of light
C. Interference of light D. Diffraction of light

70. SONAR stands for:

A. Sonographic Natural Ranging
B. Simple Operational Navigation Ranging
C. Sound Navigation and Ranging
D. Simple Operational Natural Ranging

71. Which one of the following radiations has longer wavelength?

A. X-rays B. Ultraviolet
C. Micro Wave D. Infra-red

72. For a material under static conditions, which one among the following statements is correct?

A. An insulator can be charged
B. A perfect conductor can be charged
C. Both perfect conductor and insulator can be charged
D. Both perfect conductor and insulator cannot be charged

73. A person can see nearby objects clearly but cannot see distant object distinctly, the person is suffering with:

A. Hypermetropia B. Presbyopia
C. Myopia D. None of above

74. The energy is always conserved for a system which is:

A. isolated only
B. non-isolated only
C. both isolated and non-isolated
D. none of above

75. Suppose, a ball of mass M is thrown upwards from a point A and it reaches up to the highest point B and returns back to point A, which one among the following is correct?

A. Kinetic Energy at A = Potential Energy at B
B. Kinetic Energy at A = Potential Energy at A
C. Kinetic Energy at B = Potential Energy at B
D. Kinetic Energy at B = Kinetic Energy at A

76. Who among the following presided over the first session of All India Kisan Sabha in Lucknow in April 1936?

A. Sahajananda Saraswati
B. R.G. Ranga
C. Ram Manohar Lohia
D. Jayaprakash Narayan

77. Who among the following founded the 'Self-Respect Movement'?

A. Jyotiba Phule
B. Swami Vivekananda
C. E.V. Ramaswami Naicker
D. Dr. B.R. Ambedkar

78. Chola inscriptions mention several categories of lands. Which one of the following was meant for the maintenance of school?

A. Tirunamattukkani B. Shalabhoga
C. Vellanvagai D. Pallichhandam

79. Which of the following statements about the Home Rule League are correct?

1. Lokamanya Tilak set up the Home Rule League at the Bombay Provincial Conference held at Belgaum in April 1916
2. Annie Besant announced the formation of Home Rule League in September 1916
3. To avoid friction, Tilak's League was to work in Maharashtra (excluding Bombay city), Karnataka, Central Provinces and Berar and Besant's League was given charge of the rest of India

Select the answer using the code given below:

A. 1 and 2 only B. 1 and 3 only
C. 2 and 3 only D. 1, 2 and 3

80. Which one of the following statements about Ishwar Chandra Vidyasagar is NOT correct?

A. He was the Principal of Sanskrit College, Calcutta
B. He was a Government Inspector of Schools
C. He was a Secretary to the Bethune School
D. He was the founder of Widow Remarriage Association

81. Match List-I with List-II and select the answer using the code given below the Lists:

List-I (Reformer)	List-II (Social Work/Text)
(*a*) Vishnu Shastri Pundit	1. Vedic Physics: Scientific Origin of Hinduism
(*b*) Karsondas Mulji	2. Widow Remarriage Association
(*c*) Debendranath Tagore	3. Satya Prakash
(*d*) Raja Ram Mohan Roy	4. Tattvabodhini Sabha

Code:

	(*a*)	(*b*)	(*c*)	(*d*)
A.	1	3	4	2
B.	1	4	3	2
C.	2	3	4	1
D.	2	4	3	1

82. In the Harappan Civilization, traces of canals have been found at:

A. Banawali B. Lothal
C. Shortughai D. Dholavira

83. Arrange the following foreign travellers to India in chronological order, beginning with the earliest:

1. Peter Mundy
2. Antonio Monserrate
3. Afanasii Nikitich Nikitin
4. Ibn Battuta

Select the answer using the code given below:

A. 2 - 1 - 4 - 3 B. 2 - 3 - 4 - 1
C. 4 - 3 - 2 - 1 D. 3 - 4 - 1 - 2

84. With which of the following was the Bretton Woods System NOT associated?

A. International Monetary Fund
B. Economic recovery after the Second World War

C. International Bank for Reconstruction and Development
D. Establishment of a monetary system based on floating exchange rate

85. Senguttuvan is the name of:

A. a Pandya ruler
B. a Chola king
C. a minister in Satavahana court
D. the capital city of the Cheras

86. The *Ramacharita*, an example of *dvyasrya-kavya*, telling two stories simultaneously, was written by:

A. Subandhu B. Bhatti
C. Sandhyakara D. Kamban

87. Which of the following Acts established the Board of Control to guide and control the work of the Court of Directors and the Government of India?

A. Regulating Act of 1773
B. Pitt's India Act of 1784
C. Charter Act of 1793
D. Charter Act of 1813

88. Who among the following Sikh Gurus laid the foundation of the Khalsa Panth?

A. Guru Nanak B. Guru Arjan
C. Guru Hargobind D. Guru Gobind Singh

89. Which one among the following plans is also known as Mahalanobis Plan?

A. First Five Year Plan
B. Second Five Year Plan
C. Third Five Year Plan
D. Sixth Five Year Plan

90. Which of the following were the years of Annual Plans?

A. 1956-1957 B. 1966-1969
C. 1975-1976 D. 1992-1993

91. Consider the following statements about BRICS Summits:

1. The first BRICS Summit was held in Brazil
2. BRICS Summits were held in New Delhi on three occasions

Which of the statements given above is/are correct?

A. 1 only B. 2 only
C. Both 1 and 2 D. Neither 1 nor 2

92. Placing the earliest first, arrange the following international events in the chronological order:

1. Introduction of www (World Wide Web)
2. Advent of Inter-Continental Ballistic Missiles
3. Launch of first communication satellite

Select the answer using the code given below:

A. 2 - 1 - 3 B. 1 - 2 - 3
C. 3 - 2 - 1 D. 2 - 3 - 1

93. Which of the following rights under the Constitution of India is/are Fundamental Right(s)?

1. Right to work
2. Right to privacy
3. Right to free and compulsory education in the age bracket of six to eighteen years

Select the answer using the code given below:

A. 1 and 2 B. 2 and 3
C. 2 only D. 3 only

94. Consider the following statements with regard to flags of International Organizations:

1. The flag of EU has a circle of gold stars on a white background
2. The Flag of the UN carries two pairs of olive tree branches
3. The ASEAN flag carries blue, red, white and yellow colours

How many of the above statements is/are correct?

A. Nil B. 1
C. 2 D. 3

95. Which one of the following committees is NOT associated with decentralization of Panchayati Raj institutions in India?

A. Balwant Rai Mehta Committee
B. Ashok Mehta Committee
C. L.M. Singhvi Committee
D. Abhijit Sen Committee

96. The reaction that occurs on passing carbon dioxide gas through lime water is:

A. $CaCO_3 + H_2O + CO_2 \rightarrow Ca(HCO_3)_2$
B. $Ca(OH)_2 + CO_2 \rightarrow CaCO_3 + H_2O$
C. $CaO + CO_2 \rightarrow CaCO_3$
D. $CaCl_2 + H_2O + CO_2 \rightarrow CaCO_3 + 2HCl$

97. Which one of the following statements is NOT correct?

A. Water of crystallization is the fixed number of water molecules present in one formula unit of a salt
B. The molecular formula of Plaster of Paris is $CaSO_4 \cdot 2H_2O$
C. Washing soda is used for removing the permanent hardness of water
D. The atmosphere of Venus is made up of thick white and yellow clouds of sulphuric acid

98. Which one of the following type of medicines is used for treating indigestion?

A. Analgesic B. Antiseptic
C. Antibiotic D. Antacid

99. Which one of the following is NOT present in cement?

A. $2CaO \cdot SiO_2$ B. $3CaO \cdot SiO_2$
C. $4CaO \cdot SiO_2$ D. $3CaO \cdot Al_2O_3$

100. Which one of the following is NOT a chemical change?

A. Burning of coal
B. Rusting of metal
C. Melting of ice
D. Reaction of acid with base

101. Which one of the following statements is NOT correct?

A. The interconversion of states of matter is a physical change
B. During burning of a candle, both chemical and physical changes take place
C. During a physical change, the chemical composition of molecules changes
D. Rusting of iron is a chemical change

102. Which one of the following is NOT a heterogeneous mixture?

A. Sulphur in carbon disulphide
B. Mixture of sugar and salt crystals
C. Sandy water
D. Sulphur in water

103. Match List-I with List-II and select the answer using the code given below the Lists:

List-I (Element)	List-II (Atomicity)
(*a*) Phosphorus	1. 2
(*b*) Nitrogen	2. 1
(*c*) Neon	3. 8
(*d*) Sulphur	4. 4

Code:

	(*a*)	(*b*)	(*c*)	(*d*)
A.	4	1	2	3
B.	4	2	1	3
C.	3	2	1	4
D.	3	1	2	4

104. In the following redox reaction, which compound is acting as a reducing agent?

$N_2H_4 + 2H_2O_2 \rightarrow N_2 + 4H_2O$

A. H_2O_2
B. N_2H_4
C. N_2
D. H_2O

105. Which one of the following is considered to be the purest source of water?

A. River water
B. Sea water
C. Well water
D. Rain water

106. Which one of the following salts is responsible for temporary hardness of water?

A. Sulphates of calcium
B. Chlorides of magnesium
C. Bicarbonates of magnesium
D. Sulphates of magnesium

107. Match List-I with List-II and select the answer using the code given below the Lists:

List-I (Reaction)	List-II (Type)
(*a*) $CaO\ (s) + H_2O\ (l) \rightarrow Ca(OH)_2\ (aq)$	1. Single displacement
(*b*) $CaCO_3\ (s) \rightarrow CaO\ (s) + CO_2\ (g)$	2. Double displacement
(*c*) $Pb\ (s) + CuCl_2\ (aq) \rightarrow PbCl_2\ (aq) + Cu\ (s)$	3. Combination
(*d*) $Na_2SO_4\ (aq)$ + BaCl2 (aq) $\rightarrow BaSO_4\ (s) + 2NaCl\ (aq)$	4. Decomposition

Code:

	(*a*)	(*b*)	(*c*)	(*d*)
A.	2	1	4	3
B.	2	4	1	3
C.	3	4	1	2
D.	3	1	4	2

108. Which one of the following is an endothermic reaction?

A. $CH_4\ (g) + 2O_2\ (g) \rightarrow CO_2\ (g) + 2O_2\ (g)$
B. $C_6H_{12}O_6\ (aq) + 6O_2\ (g) \rightarrow 6CO_2\ (g) + 6H_2O(l)$
C. $N_2\ (g) + 3H_2\ (g) \rightarrow 2NH_3\ (g)$
D. $2Pb(NO_3)_2\ (s) \rightarrow 2PbO\ (s) + 4NO_2\ (g) + O_2\ (g)$

109. Which one of the following is known as 'water gas'?

A. $H_2O + CO_2$
B. NH_3
C. $H_2 + N_2$
D. $CO + H_2$

110. Which one of the following statements is NOT correct?

A. Diamond is hard due to extended covalent bonding in it
B. Fullerene is composed of five and six membered rings
C. Diamond is a good conductor of electricity
D. Graphite is used as a lubricant

111. Arrange the following zones in ascending order in terms of their latitudinal extent on the Earth surface:

1. Equatorial zone
2. Midlatitude zone
3. Subarctic zone
4. Tropical zone

Select the answer using the code given below:

A. 1 - 3 - 2 - 4
B. 1 - 3 - 4 - 2
C. 1 - 4 - 2 - 3
D. 3 - 1 - 2 - 4

112. Consider the following statements with reference to Feldspar mineral:

1. Half of the earth's crust is composed of feldspar
2. It has light cream to salmon pink colour
3. Magnesium is a common element in all types of feldspar

Which of the statements given above is/are correct?

A. 1 only B. 1 and 2 only
C. 2 and 3 only D. 1, 2 and 3

113. Consider the following pairs with reference to sedimentary rocks and the process of their formation:

Sedimentary Rock		Process of Formation
1. Chert	—	Chemically formed
2. Geyserite	—	Organically formed
3. Shale	—	Mechanically formed

Which of the pairs given above is/are correctly matched?

A. 1 only B. 1 and 2 only
C. 2 and 3 only D. 1, 2 and 3

114. Which of the following statements is/are correct?

1. Oceanic trenches are very significant in the study of plate movements
2. Oceanic trenches are associated with active volcanoes and strong earthquakes

Select the answer using the code given below:

A. 1 only B. 2 only
C. Both 1 and 2 D. Neither 1 nor 2

115. Which of the following statements with reference to shadow zones in an event of an earthquake is/are correct?

1. Zone between 105° and 145° from epicentre was identified as the shadow zone for both P-waves and S-waves
2. The shadow zone of P-waves is much larger than that of the S-waves

Select the answer using the code given below:

A. 1 only B. 2 only
C. Both 1 and 2 D. Neither 1 nor 2

116. Which one among the following volcanic island chains is NOT associated with mid-oceanic ridge?

A. Azores Islands B. Ascension Islands
C. Hawaiian Islands D. Tristan da Cunha

117. Consider the following statements with reference to sea waves:

1. The height of waves is determined by wind speed, wind duration, and fetch
2. The energy of a wave is proportional to the square of its height
3. Waves retain most of their energy as they travel across the deep ocean

Which of the statements given above is/are correct?

A. 1 only B. 1 and 2 only
C. 2 and 3 only D. 1, 2 and 3

118. Which of the following statements with reference to soil forming processes is/are correct?

1. Translocation, enrichment, removal and transformation are different classes of soil forming processes
2. In translocation, fine particles are transported downward by eluviation and accumulate in lower horizons by illuviation

Select the answer using the code given below:

A. 1 only B. 2 only
C. Both 1 and 2 D. Neither 1 nor 2

119. Consider the following statements with reference to structure of the Earth's atmosphere:

1. Thickness of the troposphere is greatest at the equator
2. The air temperature of the tropopause is highest above the poles
3. The temperature in troposphere decreases at the rate of 1°F for every 165 m of height

Which of the statements given above is/are correct?

A. 1 only B. 1 and 2 only
C. 2 and 3 only D. 1, 2 and 3

120. Which of the following are the factors that cause variation in the amount of insolation on the Earth?

1. Rotation of the earth on its axis
2. Length of the day
3. Distribution of land and water on the earth

Select the answer using the code given below:

A. 1 only B. 1 and 2 only
C. 2 and 3 only D. 1, 2 and 3

121. Consider the following conditions favourable for the formation and intensification of Tropical Storms:

1. Presence of the Coriolis force
2. Upper divergence above the sea level system
3. High variations in the vertical wind speed

Which of the conditions given above is/are correct?

A. 1 only B. 2 only
C. 1 and 2 D. 2 and 3

122. Which of the following factors influence the ocean currents?

1. Coriolis force
2. Gravity
3. Heating by solar energy
4. Wind

Select the answer using the code given below:
A. 1 and 4 only B. 2 and 3 only
C. 1, 2 and 3 only D. 1, 2, 3 and 4

123. Which of the following is/are warm ocean current(s)?
1. Alaska Current 2. Agulhas Current
3. Falkland Current 4. West Australian Current
Select the answer using the code given below:
A. 1 only B. 1 and 2
C. 3 and 4 D. 4 only

124. State of Assam shares borders with how many other countries and Indian states respectively?
A. 2 countries and 6 Indian states respectively
B. 2 countries and 7 Indian states respectively
C. 3 countries and 7 Indian states respectively
D. 3 countries and 6 Indian states respectively

125. Which one of the following is the northernmost river basin of the Deccan Plateau?
A. Chambal B. Mahi
C. Narmada D. Tapti

126. Laterite soil in India is rich in which of the following?
1. Calcium 2. Nitrogen
3. Phosphate 4. Potash
Select the answer using the code given below:
A. 1 only B. 1 and 2
C. 3 and 4 D. 4 only

127. Which of the following statements with reference to crops cultivated in India is/are correct?
1. Bajra grows well in sandy and shallow black soils, whereas red and shallow black soil is suited for Ragi
2. Bajra is predominantly grown in states like Rajasthan, Uttar Pradesh and Maharashtra, while Ragi is mainly cultivated in Karnataka, Tamil Nadu and Himachal Pradesh

Select the answer using the code given below:
A. 1 only B. 2 only
C. Both 1 and 2 D. Neither 1 nor 2

128. Match List-I with List-II and select the answer using the code given below the Lists:

List-I (City)	List-II (Mineral)
(*a*) Bewar	1. Manganese
(*b*) Balaghat	2. Mica
(*c*) Bilaspur	3. Iron-ore
(*d*) Ballary	4. Bauxite

	(*a*)	(*b*)	(*c*)	(*d*)
A.	3	1	4	2
B.	3	4	1	2
C.	2	1	4	3
D.	2	4	1	3

129. Which one among the following is NOT a beneficiary state from the Vindhyachal Power Plant of the NTPC?
A. Gujarat B. Goa
C. Maharashtra D. Uttar Pradesh

130. Consider the following pairs with reference to Thermal Power Plants and their location in respective states in India:

Thermal Power Plant		Located in State
I. Panki	–	Uttar Pradesh
II. Parli	–	Karnataka
III. Vijayawada	–	Telangana
IV. Vanakbari	–	Gujarat

How many of the pairs given above is/are correctly matched?
A. 1 B. 2
C. 3 D. 4

131. The book 'The Origin of Species by Means of Natural Selection' was authored by:
A. Charles Darwin B. Carolus Linnaeus
C. Barbara McClintock D. Copernicus

132. The headquarters of World Meteorological Organization (WMO) is located at:
A. Switzerland B. Scotland
C. South Africa D. Italy

133. The optimum pH at which the enzymes pepsin and trypsin of the human alimentary canal works are
A. pH 2.0 and 7.9, respectively
B. pH 4.5 and 3.5, respectively
C. pH 9.5 and 4.5, respectively
D. pH 7.0 and 8.0, respectively

134. The amount of air breathed in and out during a normal respiration by human lungs is referred to as:
A. Vital capacity B. Tidal volume
C. Inspiratory volume D. Total lung capacity

135. Which one among the following statements about arteries and veins in humans is NOT correct?
A. Arteries carry blood away from heart while veins bring blood towards the heart
B. Pulmonary arteries always carry oxygenated blood while Pulmonary veins always carry deoxygenated blood
C. Arteries have thicker and more elastic walls compared to veins in general
D. Arteries do not have valves but veins do have valves

136. Identify the functions that are controlled by the hind brain of human being:
A. Involuntary actions such as blood pressure, salivation vomiting etc.

B. Controlling the regions receiving sensory impulses from receptors
C. Controlling the movement of voluntary muscles
D. Sensation of hunger or being full

137. Iodized salt is a vital part of our diet as it is essential for the synthesis of:

A. Estrogen B. Thyroxin
C. Insulin D. Adrenalin

138. The menstrual cycle in females is controlled by hormones that are secreted by:

A. Ovary and lacrimal gland
B. Ovary and sebaceous gland
C. Ovary and pituitary gland
D. Prostate and pituitary gland

139. Which one of the following blood cells type secrete large number of antibodies during an immune response of the body?

A. Neutrophils B. Eosinophils
C. Lymphocytes D. Monocytes

140. Which of the following organelles have their own DNA and ribosomes?

A. Endoplasmic reticulum and Golgi bodies
B. Mitochondria and Chloroplast
C. Endoplasmic reticulum and cytoskeleton
D. Cell wall and nucleolus

141. What is the nickname of the National Men's Hockey Team of Australia?

A. The Kangaroos B. The Boomers
C. The Dolphins D. The Kookaburras

142. Which one of the following organisations has completed 150 years of service to the nation in the year 2025?

A. Botanical Survey of India
B. Survey of India
C. India Meteorological Department
D. Press Trust of India

143. Which of the following statements about 'Jalvahak' is/are correct?

1. It is a newly commissioned naval ship inducted into Indian Navy
2. It is a major policy for cargo promotion unveiled by the Government of India

Select the answer using the code given below:

A. 1 only B. 2 only
C. Both 1 and 2 D. Neither 1 nor 2

144. How many rural districts does Mahatma Gandhi National Rural Employment Guarantee Act cover as on 2024-25?

A. 600 B. 740
C. 700 D. 680

145. Under which one of the following initiatives does the NITI Aayog support interested States to establish a State Institution for Transformation (SIT)?

A. NITI for States Platform
B. Bharat Ke Badhte Kadam
C. State Support Mission
D. Aspirational Block Programme

146. Which one of the following Indian States account for the maximum deposits of Bauxite and Chromite?

A. Andhra Pradesh B. Madhya Pradesh
C. Jharkhand D. Odisha

147. Consider the following statements with regard to National Technology Day:

1. It commemorates the momentous events of 11th May 1998, when India conducted successful nuclear tests under Operation Shakti
2. The official theme for National Technology Day 2025 is 'School to Startups-Igniting Young Minds to Innovate'

Which of the statements given above is/are correct?

A. 1 only B. 2 only
C. Both 1 and 2 D. Neither 1 nor 2

148. Which of the following were added in India as Ramsar Site in the year 2025?

1. Sakkarakottai Bird Sanctuary
2. Udhwa Lake
3. Rudrasagar Lake
4. Bakhira Wildlife Sanctuary

Select the answer using the code given below:

A. 1 and 4 B. 2 and 3 only
C. 1 and 2 only D. 1, 2 and 3

149. Consider the following statements about Cricket player Virat Kohli:

1. He is the only captain to have scored seven double centuries in Test Cricket
2. He is the only Indian cricketer with most centuries as a captain
3. He is the first Indian captain to achieve twin centuries on captaincy debut
4. He holds the record for the most double centuries by an Indian in Test Cricket

Which of the statements given above are correct?

A. 1 and 2 only B. 2 and 3 only
C. 1, 3 and 4 only D. 1, 2, 3 and 4

150. Ethereum, Tether, Solana and Cardano are all forms of:

A. Crypto currency
B. Artificial Intelligence (AI) Startups
C. Humanoid Robots
D. Medical apps

PAPER-II: MATHEMATICS

1. If $p^x = q^y = r^z$, where x, y and z are in GP, then consider the following statements:

I. p, q and r are in AP.

II. ln p, ln q and ln r are in GP.

Which of the statements given above is/are correct?

A. I only B. II only
C. Both I and II D. Neither I nor II

2. If A and B are non-empty subsets of a set, and A^c and B^c represent their complements, then which of the following is/are correct?

I. $A - B = B^c - A^c$

II. $A - B^c = A^c - B$

Select the answer using the code given below.

A. I only B. II only
C. Both I and II D. Neither I nor II

3. Let $y = x!$ and $z = (2x)!$. If $(z/y) = 120$, then what is the value of $(3x)!$?

A. 362880 B. 181440
C. 90720 D. 45360

4. Let n be a natural number. The number of consecutive zeros at the end of the expansion of $n!$ is exactly 2. How many values of n are possible?

A. 3 B. 4
C. 5 D. More than 5

5. If $(10 + \log_{10} x)$, $(10 + \log_{10} y)$ and $(10 + \log_{10} z)$ are in AP, then consider the following statements:

I. The GM of x and z is y^2.

II. The AM of $\log_{10} x$ and $\log_{10} z$ is $\log_{10} y$

Which of the statements given above is/are correct?

A. I only B. II only
C. Both I and II D. Neither I nor II

6. How many terms of the series 1 + 3 + 5 + 7 + ... amount to a sum equal to 123456787654321?

A. 1111111 B. 110000011
C. 111101111 D. 111111111

7. How many terms are identical in the two APs 19, 21, 23, ... up to 110 terms and 19, 22, 25, 28, ... up to 75 terms?

A. 35 B. 36
C. 37 D. 38

8. If $\alpha = \frac{-1+\sqrt{-3}}{2}$ then what is the value of

$(1 + \alpha^{19} - \alpha^{35})^{100} - (1 - 3\alpha^{25} + \alpha^{38})^{50}$?

A. –2 B. –1
C. 0 D. 2

9. What is the remainder when 5^{99} is divided by 13?

A. 10 B. 9
C. 8 D. 6

10. What is the value of the determinant of the inverse of the matrix $\begin{bmatrix} -4 & -5 \\ 2 & 2 \end{bmatrix}$?

A. $\frac{1}{2}$ B. 1
C. 2 D. 4

11. In a class of 45 students, 34 like to play cricket and 26 like to play football. Further, each student likes to play at least one of the two games. How many students like to play exactly one game?

A. 45 B. 30
C. 25 D. 15

12. The system of equations

$2x - 3y - 5 = 0$, $15y - 10x + 50 = 0$

A. has a unique solution
B. has infinitely many solutions
C. is inconsistent
D. is consistent and has exactly two solutions

13. If $\left(\frac{1-i}{1+i}\right)^{2m}\left(\frac{1+i}{1-i}\right)^{2n} = 1$

where $i = \sqrt{-1}$, then what is the smallest positive value of $(m - n)$?

A. 1 B. 2
C. 4 D. 8

14. In obtaining the solution of the system of equations $x + y + z = 7$, $x + 2y + 3z = 16$ and $x + 3y + 4z = 22$ by Cramer's rule, the value of y is obtained by dividing D by D_2, where

$$D = \begin{vmatrix} 1 & 1 & 1 \\ 1 & 2 & 3 \\ 1 & 3 & 4 \end{vmatrix}$$

What is the value of the determinant D_2?

A. –13 B. –3
C. 3 D. 13

15. Consider the following in respect of non-singular matrices A and B:

I. $(AB)^{-1} = A^{-1} B^{-1}$

II. $(BA)(AB)^{-1} = I$, where I is the identity matrix

III. $(AB)^T = A^T B^T$

How many of the above are correct?

A. None B. One

C. Two D. All three

16. The value of the determinant

$$\begin{vmatrix} a & b & c \\ l & m & n \\ p & q & r \end{vmatrix}$$

is equal to:

A. $\begin{vmatrix} a & b & c \\ p & q & r \\ l & m & n \end{vmatrix}$ B. $\begin{vmatrix} l & m & n \\ a & b & c \\ p & q & r \end{vmatrix}$

C. $\begin{vmatrix} p & q & r \\ a & b & c \\ l & m & n \end{vmatrix}$ D. $\begin{vmatrix} a & p & l \\ b & q & m \\ c & r & n \end{vmatrix}$

17. Let 1, ω, ω^2 be three cube roots of unity. If $x = a + b$, $y = a\omega + b\omega^2$, $z = a\omega^2 + b\omega$, then what is $x^2 + y^2 + z^2$ equal to?

A. $6ab$ B. $3ab$

C. $a^2 + b^2$ D. 1

18. How many 4-digit numbers that are divisible by 4 can be formed using the digits 1, 2, 3 and 4 (repetition of digits is not allowed)?

A. 3 B. 6

C. 9 D. 12

19. If a, b, c are the sides of a triangle ABC and p is the perimeter of the triangle, then what is

$$\begin{vmatrix} p+c & a & b \\ c & p+a & b \\ c & a & p+b \end{vmatrix}$$

equal to?

A. p^3 B. $2p^3$

C. $3p^3$ D. $4p^3$

20. Which one of the following is the greatest coefficient in the expansion of $(1 + x)^{100}$?

A. The coefficient of x^{100}

B. The coefficient of x^{99}

C. The coefficient of x^{51}

D. The coefficient of x^{50}

Directions (Qs. No. 21-22): *For the following two (02) items:*

Let α and β be the roots of the quadratic equation

$$x^2 + (\log_{0.5}(a^2))x - 2(\log_{0.5}(a^2))^2 = 0$$

where $a^2 \neq 1$ and $\log_{0.5}(a^2) > 0$.

Further, β is the greater of the two roots.

21. What is β equal to?

A. $\log_{a^2}(0.5)$ B. $\log_{0.5}(a^2)$

C. $2(\log_{a^2}(0.5))$ D. $2\log_{0.5}(a^2)$

22. What is the relation between α and β?

A. $\alpha = 2\beta$ B. $2\alpha = \beta$

C. $\alpha = -2\beta$ D. $2\alpha = -\beta$

Directions (Qs. No. 23-24): *For the following two (02) items:*

Let $p = \sum_{j=1}^{n} \log_{10} 2^j$ and $q = \sum_{j=1}^{n} \log_{10} 5^j$.

23. If $p + q = 66$, then which one of the following is correct?

A. $n < 7$ B. $7 < n < 9$

C. $9 < n < 12$ D. $n > 12$

24. If $p + q = 15$, then what is $q - p$ equal to?

A. $\log_{10} 2.5$

B. $5 \log_{10} 2.5$

C. $10 \log_{10} 2.5$

D. $15 \log_{10} 2.5$

Directions (Qs. No. 25-26): *For the following two (02) items:*

Let $\sin A + \sin B = p$ and $\cos A + \cos B = q$.

25. What is $\frac{p}{q}$ equal to?

A. $\tan\left(\frac{A-B}{2}\right)$ B. $\cot\left(\frac{A-B}{2}\right)$

C. $\tan\left(\frac{A+B}{2}\right)$ D. $\cot\left(\frac{A+B}{2}\right)$

26. What is $\frac{p^2 - q^2}{p^2 + q^2}$ equal to?

A. $\cos(A + B)$ B. $\cos(A - B)$

C. $\cos\left(\frac{\pi}{2} - A - B\right)$ D. $\cos(\pi - A - B)$

Directions (Qs. No. 27-28): *For the following two (02) items:*

Let $p = \operatorname{cosec} 20°$ and $q = \operatorname{cosec} 70°$.

27. What is $\left(\frac{\sqrt{3}p}{4} - \frac{q}{4}\right)$ equal to?

A. -1 B. 0

C. 1 D. 2

28. What is $\frac{p^2 + q^2}{p^2 q^2}$ equal to?

A. $\frac{1}{2}$ B. 1

C. $\frac{3}{2}$ D. 2

Directions (Qs. No. 29-30): *For the following two (02) items:*

Let $\cos(2x + 3y) = \frac{1}{2}$ and $\cos(3x + 2y) = \frac{\sqrt{3}}{2}$, where $-\pi < (2x + 3y) < \pi$ and $-\pi < (3x + 2y) < \pi$.

29. How many values does $(x + y)$ have?

A. Two B. Three

C. Four D. More than four

30. How many values does $(y - x)$ have?

A. Two B. Three

C. Four D. More than four

Directions (Qs. No. 31-32): *For the following two (02) items:*

Consider the equation

$$abx^2 + bcx + ca = cax^2 + abx + bc$$

31. If the roots of the equation are equal, then which one of the following is correct?

A. $ac = b^2$ B. $a + c = 2b$

C. $\frac{1}{a} + \frac{1}{c} = \frac{1}{2b}$ D. $\frac{1}{a} + \frac{1}{c} = \frac{2}{b}$

32. If the roots of the equation are equal, then a, b, c are in:

A. AP B. GP

C. HP D. None of the above

Directions (Qs. No. 33-34): *For the following two (02) items:*

Let (6 + 10 + 14 + ... up to m terms) = (1 + 3 + 5 + 7 + ... up to n terms) where $m < 25$ and $n < 25$.

33. What is the relation between m and n?

A. $n^2 = m(m + 1)$

B. $n^2 = m(m + 2)$

C. $n^2 = 2m(m + 1)$

D. $n^2 = 2m(m + 2)$

34. How many values of m are possible?

A. None B. One

C. Two D. More than two

Directions (Qs. No. 35-36): *For the following two (02) items:*

There are 8 points on a plane out of which 4 points are collinear.

35. How many triangles can be formed by joining these points?

A. 56 B. 54

C. 53 D. 52

36. How many quadrilaterals can be formed by joining these points?

A. 70 B. 69

C. 53 D. None of the above

Directions (Qs. No. 37-38): *For the following two (02) items:*

Let $f(x) = ax^2 + bx + c$ be a quadratic polynomial such that $f(1) = f(4) = 2$.

Further, 2 is a root of $f(x) = 0$.

37. What is the other root of $f(x) = 0$?

A. 1 B. 2

C. 3 D. Cannot be determined

38. What is $(a + b + c)$ equal to?

A. 0 B. 1

C. 2 D. Cannot be determined

Directions (Qs. No. 39-40): *For the following two (02) items:*

Let $A = \begin{bmatrix} \cos\theta & \sin\theta \\ -\sin\theta & \cos\theta \end{bmatrix}$

39. What is the value of the determinant of the matrix A^4?

A. 0 B. 1

C. $\cos 4\theta - \sin 4\theta$ D. $\cos^2 4\theta - \sin^2 4\theta$

40. What is $[\text{adj } A]^{-1}$ equal to?

A. $-A$ B. $-A^T$

C. A D. A^T

41. What is the sum of the binary numbers $(101101101)_2$ and $(100011)_2$?

A. $(110010000)_2$ B. $(110001000)_2$

C. $(110000100)_2$ D. $(100100000)_2$

42. Set X contains $3n$ elements and set Y contains $2n$ elements, and they have n elements in common. How many elements does $(X - Y) \times (Y - X)$ have?

A. $5n^2$ B. $4n^2$

C. $3n^2$ D. $2n^2$

43. Let A = {–3, –2, –1, 0, 1, 2, 3} and B = {0, 1, 4, 9}.

How many elements does the subset of A × B corresponding to the relation R = {(x, y) : $|x| < y$} have, where $x \in$ A and $y \in$ B?

A. 9
B. 12
C. 15
D. 16

44. Consider the following statements:

Statement-I: If X is an $n \times n$ matrix, then det(mX) = m^n det(X), where m is a scalar.

Statement-II: If Y is a matrix obtained from X by multiplying any row or column by a scalar m, then det(Y) = m det(X).

Which one of the following is correct in respect of the above statements?

A. Both Statement-I and Statement-II are correct and Statement-II explains Statement-I
B. Both Statement-I and Statement-II are correct but Statement-II does not explain Statement-I
C. Statement-I is correct, but Statement-II is not correct
D. Statement-I is not correct, but Statement-II is correct

45. Consider the following statements about the matrix

$$M = \begin{bmatrix} 71 & 23 & 48 \\ 57 & 28 & 29 \\ 65 & 17 & 48 \end{bmatrix}:$$

Statement-I: The inverse of M does not exist.

Statement-II: M is non-singular.

Which one of the following is correct in respect of the above statements?

A. Both Statement-I and Statement-II are correct and Statement-II explains Statement-I
B. Both Statement-I and Statement-II are correct but Statement-II does not explain Statement-I
C. Statement-I is correct but Statement-II is not correct
D. Statement-I is not correct but Statement-II is correct

46. What is $\cot^{-1} 9 + \operatorname{cosec}^{-1}\left(\frac{\sqrt{41}}{4}\right)$ equal to?

A. $\frac{\pi}{4}$ B. $\frac{\pi}{3}$

C. $\frac{\pi}{2}$ D. π

47. How many values of θ, where $-\pi < \theta < \pi$, satisfy both the equations $\cot\theta = -\sqrt{3}$ and cosec $\theta = -2$ simultaneously?

A. 4 B. 2
C. 1 D. None

48. If $x + \frac{1}{x} = 2\cos\theta$, then what is $x^3 + \frac{1}{x^3}$ equal to?

A. $\cos^3 \theta$ B. $\cos 3\theta$
C. $2 \cos 3\theta$ D. $3 \cos 3\theta$

49. If $0 \le x \le \frac{\pi}{2}$, then what is the number of values of x satisfying the equation $\tan x + \sec x = 2 \cos x$?

A. 0 B. 1
C. 2 D. 3

50. What is the value of $\tan\left[\frac{1}{2}\sec^{-1}\left(\frac{2}{\sqrt{3}}\right)\right]$?

A. $2-\sqrt{3}$ B. $2+\sqrt{3}$
C. $\sqrt{3}-1$ D. $\sqrt{3}+1$

Directions (Qs. No. 51-52): *For the following two (02) items:*

A plane P is parallel to the line having direction ratios ⟨1, 3, 2⟩ and contains the line of intersection of the planes $6x + 4y - 5z = 2$ and $x - 2y + 3z = 0$.

51. Which of the following are the direction ratios of the line of intersection of the given planes?

A. ⟨2, 23, 16⟩ B. ⟨2, –23, –16⟩
C. ⟨2, 3, 2⟩ D. ⟨–1, 3, –2⟩

52. What is the equation of the plane P?

A. $2x - 20y + 29z + 2 = 0$
B. $2x - 20y + 29z - 2 = 0$
C. $2x + 3y + 2z - 4 = 0$
D. $x - 3y + 2z + 5 = 0$

Directions (Qs. No. 53-54): *For the following two (02) items:*

Suppose S is the sphere with the smallest radius that passes through the points A(1, 0, 0), B(0, 1, 0) and C(0, 0, 1).

53. What is the radius of S?

A. $\sqrt{\frac{1}{3}}$ B. $\sqrt{\frac{2}{3}}$

C. $\frac{1}{3}$ D. 1

54. On which one of the following planes does the centre of S lie?

A. $x + y + z - 1 = 0$
B. $x + y + z + 1 = 0$
C. $3x + 3y + 3z - 1 = 0$
D. $3x + 3y + 3z + 1 = 0$

Directions (Qs. No. 55-56): *For the following two (02) items:*

Let A(1, –1, 0), B(–2, 1, 8) and C(–1, 2, 7) are three consecutive vertices of a parallelogram ABCD.

55. What is the fourth vertex D?

A. (0, –2, 1) B. (2, 0, –1)
C. (1, 0, 1) D. (1, 2, 0)

56. If angle BCD is θ, then what is $\cos^2 \theta$ equal to?

A. $\frac{26}{77}$ B. $\frac{27}{77}$
C. $\frac{82}{237}$ D. $\frac{83}{237}$

57. For different values of m, the equation $4y = mx - m + 2$ represents:

A. parallel lines
B. concurrent lines
C. lines at a fixed distance from the origin of coordinates
D. the same line

58. The equation of the locus of a point equidistant from the points (a, b) and (c, d) is $(a - c)x + (b - d)y + k = 0$. What is the value of k?

A. $a^2 - c^2 + b^2 - d^2$
B. $c^2 + d^2 - a^2 - b^2$
C. $(a^2 - c^2 + b^2 - d^2)/2$
D. $(c^2 + d^2 - a^2 - b^2)/2$

59. Consider the following statements in respect of the equation $x^2 + 3y = 0$:

I. The equation represents the equation to parabola that opens upwards.
II. The axis of the parabola is $x = 0$.
III. The equation of the latus rectum is $4y - 3 = 0$.

How many of the statements given above are correct?

A. None B. One
C. Two D. All three

60. What is the sum of the intercepts of the line

$$\frac{x}{a^2} + \frac{y}{b^2} = \frac{2}{a^2 + b^2}$$

on the coordinate axes?

A. 2 B. 1
C. $\frac{1}{2}$ D. $a^2 + b^2$

61. Which one of the following is the perpendicular form of the straight line $\sqrt{3}x + 2y = 7$?

A. $y = -\frac{\sqrt{3}}{2}x + \frac{7}{2}$ B. $\frac{x}{\left(\frac{7}{\sqrt{3}}\right)} + \frac{y}{\left(\frac{7}{2}\right)} = 1$
C. $\frac{\sqrt{3}}{\sqrt{7}}x + \frac{2}{\sqrt{7}}y = \sqrt{7}$ D. $\frac{\sqrt{3}}{\sqrt{7}}x + \frac{2}{\sqrt{7}}y = 7$

62. If the vertices B and D of a square ABCD are (2, 3) and (4, 1) respectively, then what is the area of the square?

A. 2 square units B. 3 square units
C. 4 square units D. 8 square units

63. What is the value of $\sin \theta$ if θ is the acute angle between the lines whose equations are $px + qy = p + q$ and $p(x - y) + q(x + y) = 2q$?

A. $\frac{\sqrt{3}}{2}$ B. $\frac{3}{4}$
C. $\frac{1}{2}$ D. $\frac{1}{\sqrt{2}}$

64. The circle $x^2 + y^2 - 2kx - 2ky + k^2 = 0$ touches the x-axis at P and y-axis at Q. What is PQ equal to?

A. $\sqrt{2}k$ B. $2k$
C. $2\sqrt{2}k$ D. $4k$

65. What is the distance between the foci of the hyperbola $x^2 - 4y^2 = 1$?

A. $\sqrt{3}$ B. $\sqrt{5}$
C. $2\sqrt{3}$ D. $2\sqrt{5}$

66. Let $\vec{p} = \vec{a} - \vec{b}$, $\vec{q} = \vec{a} + \vec{b}$. If $|\vec{a}| = |\vec{b}| = 2$ and $\vec{a} \cdot \vec{b} = 2$, then what is the value of $|\vec{p} \times \vec{q}|$?

A. $\sqrt{3}$ B. $\sqrt{6}$
C. $2\sqrt{3}$ D. $4\sqrt{3}$

67. How many of the following can be a vector perpendicular to both the vectors $2\hat{i} - \hat{j} + \hat{k}$ and $\hat{i} + \hat{j} + 3\hat{k}$?

I. $4\hat{i} + 5\hat{j} - 3\hat{k}$
II. $-8\hat{i} - 10\hat{j} + 6\hat{k}$

III. $\frac{1}{50}\left(-4\hat{i}-5\hat{j}+3\hat{k}\right)$

Select the correct answer.

A. None B. One
C. Two D. All three

68. What is the area of the parallelogram whose sides are represented by the vectors $\hat{i}+2\hat{j}+3\hat{k}$ and $2\hat{i}+\hat{j}+2\hat{k}$?

A. $\frac{1}{2}\sqrt{26}$ square units B. $\frac{1}{2}\sqrt{27}$ square units
C. $\sqrt{26}$ square units D. $\sqrt{27}$ square units

69. The position vectors of the vertices A, B, C and D of a quadrilateral ABCD are given by $3\hat{i}+4\hat{j}-2\hat{k}$, $4\hat{i}-4\hat{j}-3\hat{k}$, $2\hat{i}-3\hat{j}+2\hat{k}$ and $6\hat{i}-2\hat{j}+\hat{k}$ respectively. What is the angle between the diagonals AC and BD of the quadrilateral?

A. 90° B. 75°
C. 60° D. 45°

70. A force $\vec{F}=2\hat{i}-\lambda\hat{j}+5\hat{k}$ is applied at the point A(1, 2, 5). If its moment about the point B(-1, -2, 3) is $16\hat{i}-6\hat{j}+2\lambda\hat{k}$, then what is the value of λ?

A. -2 B. 0
C. 1 D. 2

Directions (Qs. No. 71-72): *For the following two (02) items:*

$$\text{Let } f(x)=\begin{cases}\dfrac{1-\cos 2x}{x^2}, & x<0\\ 9, & x=0\\ \dfrac{\sqrt{x}}{\sqrt{(16+\sqrt{x})}-4}, & x<0\end{cases}$$

71. What is $\lim_{x\to 0^-} f(x)$ equal to?

A. 2 B. 4
C. 6 D. 8

72. What is $\lim_{x\to 0^+} f(x)$ equal to?

A. 6 B. 7
C. 8 D. 9

Directions (Qs. No. 73-75): *For the following three (03) items:*

Consider the function $f(x) = x|x|$.

73. What is $\lim_{x\to -1} f(x)$ equal to?

A. –1 B. 0
C. 1 D. Limit does not exist

74. What is the area bounded by the curve $f(x)$, the x-axis and the lines $x = -2$ and $x = 1$?

A. $\frac{1}{3}$ B. $\frac{2}{3}$
C. $\frac{5}{2}$ D. 3

75. Consider the following statements:

I. The function is increasing in the interval $(-\infty, \infty)$.
II. The function is differentiable at $x = 0$.

Which of the statements given above is/are correct?

A. I only B. II only
C. Both I and II D. Neither I nor II

Directions (Qs. No. 76-77): *For the following two (02) items:*

Consider the function $f(x)=\frac{x}{1-x}(x>0, x\neq 1)$

76. What is $\frac{f(x)}{f(x+1)}$ equal to?

A. $-f(x^2)$ B. $-f(\sqrt{x})$
C. $f(x^2)$ D. $f(x-1)$

77. What is $(1-x)f\left(\sqrt{x}\right)+xf\left(\sqrt{x}+1\right)$ equal to?

A. $-f(x)$ B. $f(x)$
C. x D. 0

Directions (Qs. No. 78-80): *For the following three (03) items:*

Let $y=f(x)=\frac{x\sin^{-1}x}{\sqrt{1-x^2}}+\ln\sqrt{1-x^2}$.

78. What is the slope of the tangent to the curve $y = f(x)$ at $x = 0.5$?

A. $\frac{4\pi\sqrt{3}}{27}$ B. $\frac{8\pi\sqrt{3}}{27}$
C. 4π D. 8π

79. What is $\frac{d^2y}{dx^2}$ at $x = 0$ equal to?

A. 0 B. 0.5
C. 1 D. 1.5

80. If $x = \sin\theta$, then what is $\frac{dy}{dx}$ equal to?

A. $\theta \sec\theta$ B. $\theta \sec^2\theta$

C. $\theta \sec^3\theta$ D. $2\tan\theta + \theta\sec^2\theta$

Directions (Qs. No. 81-82): *For the following two (02) items:*

Consider the function $f(x) = 1 - \sqrt[3]{(x-1)^2}$.

81. What is the domain of the function?

A. $(1, \infty)$ B. $(-\infty, \infty)$

C. $(0, \infty)$ D. $(-\infty, \infty)\backslash\{1\}$

82. The function has:

A. a minimum at $x = 1$

B. a maximum at $x = 1$

C. neither maximum nor minimum at $x = 1$

D. no extremum

Directions (Qs. No. 83-84): *For the following two (02) items:*

Consider the function

$$f(x) = \begin{cases} 4(5^x), & x < 0 \\ 8k + x, & x \geq 0 \end{cases}$$

83. If the function is continuous, then what is the value of k ?

A. 0.5 B. 1

C. 1.5 D. 2

84. What is $f'(-1)$ equal to?

A. $\frac{2}{5}\ln 5$ B. $\frac{3}{5}\ln 5$

C. $\frac{4}{5}\ln 5$ D. $20 \ln 5$

Directions (Qs. No. 85-86): *For the following two (02) items:*

Let $u = \int e^x \cos x\, dx$ and $v = \int e^x \sin x\, dx$

85. What is $u + v$ equal to?

A. $-\frac{du}{dx}$ B. $-\frac{dv}{dx}$

C. $\frac{du}{dx}$ D. $\frac{dv}{dx}$

86. Consider the following:

I. $\frac{du}{dx} = -v$ II. $\frac{du}{dx} = -u$

Which of the above is/are correct?

A. I only B. II only

C. Both I and II D. Neither I nor II

Directions (Qs. No. 87-88): *For the following two (02) items:*

Let the function $f(x) = |x-3| + |x-4|$ be defined on the interval $[0, 5]$.

87. What is $\frac{dy}{dx}$ at $x = 3.5$ equal to?

A. 0 B. 1

C. 2 D. 3.5

88. Consider the following statements:

I. The function is differentiable at $x = 3$.

II. The function is differentiable at $x = 4$.

Which of the statements given above is/are correct?

A. I only B. II only

C. Both I and II D. Neither I nor II

Directions (Qs. No. 89-90): *For the following two (02) items:*

Consider the function $f(x) = \frac{10^x - 10^{-x}}{10^x + 10^{-x}}$.

89. What is $f \circ f \circ f \circ f(0)$ equal to?

A. 0 B. 1

C. 5 D. 10

90. What is the inverse of the function?

A. $\log_{10}(2x-1)$ B. $\frac{1}{2}\log_{10}(2x-1)$

C. $\frac{1}{4}\log_{10}\left(\frac{2x}{2-x}\right)$ D. $\frac{1}{2}\log_{10}\left(\frac{1+x}{1-x}\right)$

91. What is the degree of the differential equation $\left(\frac{d^2y}{dx^2}\right)^{\frac{3}{2}} = \left(\frac{dy}{dx}\right)^{\frac{5}{2}}$?

A. 3 B. 2

C. $\frac{5}{2}$ D. $\frac{3}{2}$

92. What is the $\int_n^{n+1} (x - [x])\, dx$, where $[\cdot]$ is the greatest integer function and n is natural number?

A. $\frac{4n+1}{2}$ B. $\frac{2n+1}{2}$

C. $\frac{1}{2}$ D. 1

93. Consider the following statements:

I. $y = xe^{2x}$ is the solution of $\frac{dy}{dx} = y\left(2 + \frac{1}{x}\right)$

II. $y = x \ln |x| + cx$ is the solution of $\frac{dy}{dx} = \frac{x+y}{x}$.

Which of the statements given above is/are correct?

A. I only B. II only
C. Both I and II D. Neither I nor II

94. If k is an arbitrary constant, then what is the general solution of the equation $(x+y)^2 \frac{dy}{dx} = k^2$?

A. $y + x = \tan (x + c) + k$

B. $x + y = k \tan\left(\frac{y-c}{k}\right)$

C. $x - y = k \tan\left(\frac{y-c}{k}\right)$

D. $y - x = \tan (x + c) + k$

95. What is $\int \frac{dx}{10^x + 10^{-x}}$ equal to?

A. $\tan^{-1} (10^x) + c$
B. $(\ln 10) \tan^{-1} (10^x) + c$
C. $\frac{1}{\ln 10} \tan^{-1}(10^x) + c$
D. $\ln (10^x + 10^{-x}) + c$

96. A wire of length 20 cm is to be bent into a rectangle. Which of the following statements is/are correct?

I. The rectangle of the largest area is the square.
II. It is possible to form a rectangle of an area of 27 cm^2.

Select the answer using the code given below.

A. I only B. II only
C. Both I and II D. Neither I nor II

97. If $I_1 = \int_e^{e^2} \frac{dx}{\ln x}$ and $I_2 = \int_1^2 \frac{e^x}{x} dx$, then which one of the following is correct?

A. $I_1 - I_2 = 0$ B. $I_1 + I_2 = 0$
C. $I_1 - 2I_2 = 0$ D. $2I_1 - I_2 = 0$

98. What is the area of the region bounded by $|x| \le 2k$ and $|y| \le k$, where k is a positive real number?

A. $2k^2$ B. $4k^2$
C. $5k^2$ D. $8k^2$

99. Consider the following statements regarding the function $f(x) = \frac{1}{x-5}$:

Statement-I: $f(x)$ is decreasing on the intervals $x < 5$ and $x > 5$.

Statement-II: $f'(x) > 0$ for all $x \neq 5$.

Which one of the following is correct in respect of the above statements?

A. Both Statement-I and Statement-II are correct and Statement-II explains Statement-I
B. Both Statement-I and Statement-II are correct but Statement-II does not explain Statement-I
C. Statement-I is correct but Statement-II is not correct
D. Statement-I is not correct but Statement-II is correct

100. Consider the following statements:

Statement-I: The function $f(x) = \frac{x^3 + 128}{x}$ has a minimum value 48 at $x = 4$.

Statement-II: As x increases through 4, $f'(x)$ changes sign from positive to negative.

Which one of the following is correct in respect of the above statements?

A. Both Statement-I and Statement-II are correct and Statement-II explains Statement-I
B. Both Statement-I and Statement-II are correct but Statement-II does not explain Statement-I
C. Statement-I is correct but Statement-II is not correct
D. Statement-I is not correct but Statement-II is correct

101. What is the harmonic mean of the numbers C(10, 3), C(10, 4), C(10, 5), C(10, 6} and C(10, 7)?

A. $\frac{3150}{19}$ B. $\frac{4000}{19}$
C. 252 D. 225

102. In a sample survey of a village, the probability that a farmer is in debt is 0.60. What is the probability that three randomly selected farmers are all in debt (assume independence of events)?

A. 0.000216 B. 0.064
C. 0.216 D. 0.512

103. The probability that a family owns a laptop is 0.68; that it also owns a desktop is 0.56. If the probability that it owns both is 0.48, then what is the probability that a randomly selected family owns a laptop or a desktop?

A. 0.80 B. 0.76
C. 0.36 D. 0.28

104. An urn contains 10 white and 5 red balls. If two balls are drawn at random, then what is the probability that both the balls are red?

A. $\frac{2}{21}$ B. $\frac{1}{7}$

C. $\frac{4}{21}$ D. $\frac{3}{7}$

105. An urn contains 5 white, 6 red and 4 blue balls. Three balls are drawn at random. What is the probability that a white ball, a red ball and a blue ball are drawn?

A. $\frac{28}{91}$ B. $\frac{2}{7}$

C. $\frac{24}{91}$ D. $\frac{23}{91}$

106. Under which of the following conditions may binomial distribution be used?

I. The number of trials is infinite and not fixed.

II. The trials are independent.

III. Each trial has two possible outcomes.

Select the correct answer using the code given below.

A. II only

B. III only

C. I and II

D. II and III

107. A person X speaks the truth 4 out of 5 times and person Y speaks the truth 5 out of 6 times. What is the probability that they will contradict each other in stating the fact?

A. $\frac{3}{10}$ B. $\frac{1}{15}$

C. $\frac{1}{6}$ D. $\frac{7}{10}$

108. The probability that a student passes Physics test is $\frac{2}{3}$ and the probability that he passes both Physics test and English test is $\frac{11}{15}$. The probability that he passes at least one test is $\frac{4}{5}$. What is the probability that he passes English test?

A. $\frac{11}{15}$ B. $\frac{13}{15}$

C. $\frac{14}{15}$ D. 1

109. An event X can happen with probability p and event Y can happen with probability q. Further, X and Y are independent events. Which of the following statements is/are correct?

I. The probability that exactly one of the events happens is $p + q - pq$.

II. The probability that at least one of the events happens is $p + q - 2pq$.

Select the answer using the code given below.

A. I only B. II only

C. Both I and II D. Neither I nor II

110. Three faces of a die are black, two faces are white and one face is red. The die is tossed three times. What is the probability that the colours black, white and red appear in the first, second and third tosses respectively?

A. $\frac{1}{36}$ B. $\frac{1}{6}$

C. $\frac{7}{36}$ D. $\frac{5}{36}$

111. A fair coin is tossed 4 times. What is the probability that two heads do not occur consecutively?

A. $\frac{1}{8}$ B. $\frac{3}{8}$

C. $\frac{7}{16}$ D. $\frac{1}{2}$

112. In a throw of three dice, what is the probability of getting one prime number, one composite number and one number which is neither prime nor composite?

A. $\frac{1}{2}$ B. $\frac{1}{3}$

C. $\frac{1}{4}$ D. $\frac{1}{6}$

113. An integer is chosen at random from the first 50 integers. What is the probability that the integer is neither divisible by 5 nor 9?

A. $\frac{7}{10}$ B. $\frac{18}{25}$

C. $\frac{37}{50}$ D. $\frac{19}{25}$

114. Out of 50 consecutive natural numbers, two integers are chosen at random. What is the probability that their sum is odd?

A. $\frac{1}{2}$ B. $\frac{24}{49}$

C. $\frac{1}{4}$ D. $\frac{25}{49}$

115. The standard deviation of 100 observations is 10. If 20 is added to each observation, then what will be the new standard deviation?

A. 10 B. 15
C. 20 D. 25

116. Let X be a random variable following binomial distribution with parameters $n = 5$ and $p = k$. Further, $P(X = 1) = 0.4096$ and $P(X = 2) = 0.2048$. What is the value of k?

A. 0.2 B. 0.25
C. 0.3 D. 0.35

117. The frequency distribution of the marks obtained by students in a Science examination is given below:

Marks	5-15	15-25	25-35	35-45
Number of students	20	30	30	20

What is the arithmetic mean?

A. 20 B. 25
C. 30 D. 35

118. If $P(A) = 0.3$, $P(B) = 0.4$ and $P(A|B) = 0.5$, then what is the value of $P(B|A)$?

A. 0.325 B. 0.333
C. 0.375 D. 0.667

119. If $P(A) = 1/3$, $P(B) = 1/2$ and $P(A \cap B) = 1/4$, then what is the value of $P(\bar{A} \cup B)$?

A. $\frac{7}{12}$ B. $\frac{2}{3}$
C. $\frac{3}{4}$ D. $\frac{11}{12}$

120. Consider the following statements:

I. Mean and variance have the same unit of measurement.
II. Mean deviation and standard deviation have the same unit of measurement.

Which of the statements given above is/are correct?

A. I only B. II only
C. Both I and II D. Neither I nor II

ANSWERS

PAPER-I: GENERAL ABILITY TEST

1	2	3	4	5	6	7	8	9	10
B	A	D	A	A	A	A	B	A	B
11	12	13	14	15	16	17	18	19	20
A	B	A	B	B	A	A	D	B	A
21	22	23	24	25	26	27	28	29	30
B	B	A	D	B	B	C	D	A	C
31	32	33	34	35	36	37	38	39	40
D	A	A	B	B	B	C	A	D	A
41	42	43	44	45	46	47	48	49	50
D	A	C	A	D	A	C	C	B	C
51	52	53	54	55	56	57	58	59	60
D	B	C	D	B	C	D	A	A	B
61	62	63	64	65	66	67	68	69	70
C	A	D	B	B	B	B	A	B	C
71	72	73	74	75	76	77	78	79	80
C	C	C	A	A	A	C	B	D	D
81	82	83	84	85	86	87	88	89	90
C	C	C	D	*	C	B	D	B	B
91	92	93	94	95	96	97	98	99	100
B	D	C	B	D	B	B	D	C	C
101	102	103	104	105	106	107	108	109	110
C	A	A	B	D	C	C	D	D	C

111	112	113	114	115	116	117	118	119	120
C	B	D	C	D	C	D	C	B	D
121	**122**	**123**	**124**	**125**	**126**	**127**	**128**	**129**	**130**
C	D	B	B	C	*	C	C	D	B
131	**132**	**133**	**134**	**135**	**136**	**137**	**138**	**139**	**140**
A	A	A	B	B	A	B	C	C	B
141	**142**	**143**	**144**	**145**	**146**	**147**	**148**	**149**	**150**
D	C	B	B	C	D	A	C	D	A

PAPER-II: MATHEMATICS

1	2	3	4	5	6	7	8	9	10
B	A	A	C	B	D	C	C	C	A
11	**12**	**13**	**14**	**15**	**16**	**17**	**18**	**19**	**20**
B	C	B	B	A	C	A	B	B	D
21	**22**	**23**	**24**	**25**	**26**	**27**	**28**	**29**	**30**
B	C	C	D	C	D	C	B	C	C
31	**32**	**33**	**34**	**35**	**36**	**37**	**38**	**39**	**40**
D	C	D	C	D	B	C	C	B	C
41	**42**	**43**	**44**	**45**	**46**	**47**	**48**	**49**	**50**
A	D	C	A	C	A	C	C	B	A
51	**52**	**53**	**54**	**55**	**56**	**57**	**58**	**59**	**60**
B	A	B	A	B	B	B	D	B	A
61	**62**	**63**	**64**	**65**	**66**	**67**	**68**	**69**	**70**
C	C	D	A	B	D	D	C	A	A
71	**72**	**73**	**74**	**75**	**76**	**77**	**78**	**79**	**80**
A	C	A	D	C	A	D	A	C	C
81	**82**	**83**	**84**	**85**	**86**	**87**	**88**	**89**	**90**
B	B	A	C	D	D	A	D	A	D
91	**92**	**93**	**94**	**95**	**96**	**97**	**98**	**99**	**100**
A	C	C	B	C	A	A	D	C	C
101	**102**	**103**	**104**	**105**	**106**	**107**	**108**	**109**	**110**
A	C	B	A	C	D	A	B	D	A
111	**112**	**113**	**114**	**115**	**116**	**117**	**118**	**119**	**120**
D	D	B	D	A	A	B	D	D	B

EXPLANATORY ANSWERS

PAPER-I: GENERAL ABILITY TEST

1. In the passage, the author says that "twentieth century advances, given increasing costs, do not seem sustainable," which clearly links the unsustainability to the rising costs associated with these advances. The concern is not that they fail to meet human needs or are outdated, but that the cost structure makes their continuation difficult in the long run. Therefore, option B exactly matches the reason given in the passage.

2. The passage explicitly states, "Global population growth... has pushed farmers and herders into areas unsuited to intensive agriculture." This directly answers the question. None of the other options (industrialisation, water scarcity, desertification) are mentioned as the immediate factor pushing farmers into unsuitable areas in this specific sentence, whereas population growth is clearly identified as the cause.

3. The question asks which is NOT true for ecological degradation according to the passage. The passage connects ecological degradation with global population growth, chemical runoffs, and desertification, making options A, B and C true contributors. World War II is only mentioned as a time marker ("since World War II") for tropical forest shrinkage, not as a direct cause of ecological degradation in the argument. Hence, D is the only option not presented as a cause.

4. Near the end, the author says, "we may remain hopeful about humankind's agricultural prospects, but we can scarcely look forward optimistically..." This sentence shows a mixed stance: some hope about agricultural potential, but strong doubt about the overall future scenario by the end of the first quarter of the twenty-first century. Thus, the author is simultaneously hopeful (to a limited extent) and sceptical, which is precisely captured by option A.

5. In the passage, the phrase used is "Invasion of natural habitats have hastened species extinction." The word "incursion" in English means an invasion or sudden entry, especially into a territory. Among the options, "invasion" is the exact synonym of "incursion." "Intensive," "severe," and "intervention" do not carry the specific sense of entering or encroaching upon an area. Therefore, "invasion" is the correct meaning.

6. Ayushi told the group that they had had enough of suffering that day and it was time to march forward:
This option correctly changes said to → told, shifts the pronoun we → they, changes the present-perfect have had → had had, and replaces today → that day, maintaining the correct tense and expression of a statement. It also keeps the meaning intact without adding questions or incorrect pronouns.

7. The word "Alas!" expresses sorrow or regret. In indirect speech, sorrowful exclamations are reported using words like regretted or lamented. Also, lost → had lost is correct backshifting, and the sentence maintains the past-perfect form required for indirect narration.

8. Alok asked Sheela where she had been the week before: Indirect speech for a WH-question begins directly with the WH-word (no "if"/"whether"). The past tense were in direct speech becomes had been in indirect speech. Also, last week → the week before is the correct change of time expression.

9. The castle was built five centuries ago by the king who was loved by the people:
This option correctly changes built → was built for passive voice and keeps the relative clause correct: who the people loved → who was loved by the people. It preserves both meaning and grammar exactly.

10. Four hundred engineers have been recruited by the company and they will have to complete an internship of three weeks: This option correctly changes the first clause into passive voice: has recruited → have been recruited, keeps the relative clause meaning intact, and does not distort the second clause. The second clause is not passive in the original, so it stays active while maintaining meaning.

11. Seldom means hardly ever and often means time and again: "Seldom" is used for something that happens very rarely or hardly ever, while "often" is used for something that happens many times or time and again. So option A correctly captures both meanings.

12. An "overview" is a broad outline or general idea of a subject without going into detail. A "review" is a more deliberate assessment, examination or appraisal of something (like a book, performance, policy, etc.). Hence B gives the most accurate pair of meanings.

13. "Overcome" means to defeat or triumph over a problem, difficulty, or opponent. "Succeed" means to achieve something desired or planned (such as a goal or objective). Therefore option A correctly distinguishes and defines both verbs.

14. "Embed" means to fix or implant something firmly within something else (physically or metaphorically, e.g., values embedded in culture). "Imbue" means to fill or permeate with a feeling or quality, i.e., to instil (e.g., imbue someone with confidence). So, B correctly matches both meanings.

15. "Emancipate" means to set someone free from legal, social, or political restrictions—to liberate. "Empower" means to give someone power or authority—to authorise or enable them to act. Thus option B accurately explains both words.

16. "Instil" means to gradually and firmly introduce an idea, feeling, or quality into someone's mind. "Inculcate" has the same meaning — to teach or implant an idea repeatedly and firmly. Therefore, option A is nearest in meaning.

17. "Allegiance" means loyalty, devotion, or commitment to a leader, group, or cause. Among the given options, "commitment" is the closest in meaning. The other options do not express loyalty, making A the correct choice.

18. "Inscrutability" means something that is impossible to understand or interpret — it remains puzzling or mysterious. Therefore, "mystery" is the nearest in meaning. Options A and B mean clarity and understanding, which are opposites, and C does not match the meaning.

19. "Dodgy" behaviour refers to something suspicious, unreliable, or questionable. The word "dubious" means doubtful or suspicious in nature, making it the nearest in meaning. "Dishonest" is related but not fully equivalent; "dubious" matches more precisely.

20. "Inclement" weather means stormy, harsh, or severe. "Squally" refers to rough, windy, storm-like weather and is therefore the closest match. The other options describe calm, pleasant, or unrelated conditions.

21. **S P Q R:** This sequence is correct because after S1 introduces Sufism as an English word, the next logical sentence is **S,** which states the original Islamic term *tasawwuf.* Then **P** explains that historians interpret the term in several ways, which prepares the reader for the alternative etymologies. Sentence **Q** gives the first derivation from *suf* (wool), and **R** gives the second derivation from *safa* (purity). This ordered flow of definition → interpretations → derivations connects smoothly to S6, which gives the third possible root *suffa.*

22. **R Q S P:** After S1 mentions Al-Biruni's birthplace, the natural continuation is **R**, describing Khwarizm as a major learning centre where he received the best education. Then **Q** specifies the languages he mastered, showing the result of that education. Sentence **S** adds a contrast by stating that despite his vast knowledge, he did not know Greek, though he knew Greek philosophical works. Finally, **P** moves to the political event of 1017, when he was taken to Ghazni by Sultan Mahmud, which connects directly to S6 describing his arrival there.

23. **S P R Q:** After S1 introduces Vijayanagara as both a city and an empire, the next logical point is **S**, explaining its founding in the fourteenth century. Sentence **P** then describes the empire's vast extent at its height. Sentence **R** follows with the decline and desertion of the city in 1565. Lastly, **Q** explains how, although ruined, the city continued in people's memories, which flows perfectly into S6 describing how it came to be remembered as Hampi.

24. **P S Q R:** After S1 states that liberalisation freed India's economy, **P** explains the conditions—slow growth and a payment crisis—that triggered reform. Then **S** introduces the landmark 1991 budget responding to that crisis. Sentence **Q** specifies the important policy steps such as removing licences and quotas. Finally, **R** explains India taking an IMF loan during the crisis and not needing one afterward, which connects well with S6 describing India's later transformation into a major economy.

25. **R Q S P:** After S1 mentions deprivation of millions, the logical next sentence is **R**, explaining that marginalised groups face exploitation. **Q** then gives the first concrete form of exploitation—forced labour or begar. Sentence **S** adds another form—buying and selling people as slaves. Finally, **P** states that both practices are prohibited under the Constitution, which transitions properly to S6 describing past forced-labour practices.

26. The sentence means "there is no point telling him because he would not listen anyway." The discourse marker "in any case" correctly conveys the idea of "even if I tried, it wouldn't matter," which fits the meaning perfectly.

27. The sentence provides a short explanation about what a referee's finger-pointing indicates. The marker "briefly" is used to introduce a short, concise explanation, which matches the structure and meaning of the sentence exactly.

28. The sentence introduces a new, casual, additional question ("have you been to the local library yet?"). "Incidentally" is the correct discourse marker used when adding something by the way or as an afterthought.

29. The sentence generalises about women's health trends. "To a large extent" is the appropriate phrase meaning "largely" or "mostly," which fits the factual comparative statement that follows.

30. The sentence adds an additional positive point — not only does the person love the career, but also gets paid reasonably. "What is more" is used to introduce an extra, reinforcing point, making it the correct choice.

31. The sentence talks about India's broad policy trend. "In general" is the correct marker to introduce a generalisation about the government's approach over time.

32. The sentence gives information about what is likely to happen when the Council meets next. The phrase "As per reports" fits because it indicates that the statement is based on reported information.

33. The sentence indicates a consequence — because of some situation, it was necessary to consult a physician. "In that case" correctly shows a logical result based on a prior condition.

34. The sentence highlights a significant comparative fact from the past. "Notably" is used to draw attention to a striking or important piece of information, which fits this context exactly.

35. The sentence means "as a result of this situation/the nature of things, the records have been undermined." "As such" is used to express a consequence arising from a previously implied condition, making it the most appropriate marker.

36. "Infelicity" means something unsuitable, awkward, or inappropriate in speech or behavior. Therefore, an inappropriate remark is the correct and precise definition.

37. A "corollary" is a natural, direct, or logical consequence that follows from something already established. Hence, option C provides the exact meaning.

38. "Quandary" refers to a state of uncertainty or confusion, especially about making a decision. Option A expresses this meaning accurately.

39. "Presumption" means assuming something to be true without full evidence or before knowing all the facts. Option D matches this definition correctly.

40. "Smug" describes a person who is overly self-satisfied or excessively pleased with themselves. This meaning is exactly captured by option A.

41. Whereas traditional fairy tales **(Q)** begins the contrast clause correctly because "whereas" signals comparison; "were designed for the entertainment" **(S)** logically completes the clause; "of children they also contain deeply embedded" **(P)** continues the sentence by linking "they" back to "fairy tales"; "moral lessons that are relevant even for adults" **(R)** finishes the idea by explaining what is embedded. Hence the coherent sentence is: Whereas traditional fairy tales were designed for the entertainment of children they also contain deeply embedded moral lessons that are relevant even for adults.

42. The sentence begins with the truth clause "that sporting activities are an integral part" **(Q)**; "of school education is an ineluctable truth" **(P)** completes this main statement; "that underscores the learning process and contributes" **(S)** adds a modifying clause describing the significance; "meaningfully towards the overall growth of a student" **(R)** completes that description. Thus the correct sentence reads: That sporting activities are an integral part of school education is an ineluctable truth that underscores the learning process and contributes meaningfully towards the overall growth of a student.

43. The structure begins with "the beneficial outcome of" **(Q)**; "a virtuous life is peace of mind" **(S)** gives the main result clause; "and contentment on account of a life lived" **(P)** extends the outcome; "well without retribution or rebuke" **(R)** completes the descriptive ending. Therefore the sentence becomes: The beneficial outcome of a virtuous life is peace of mind and contentment on account of a life lived well without retribution or rebuke.

44. The sentence starts with "it is widely believed that the parliamentary system differs" **(S)**; "from a non-parliamentary system" **(Q)** completes the comparison object; "in as much as the former is" **(R)** introduces the basis of comparison; "more representative than the latter" **(P)** completes the comparative idea, The complete sentence is: It is widely believed that the parliamentary system differs from a non-parliamentary system in as much as the former is more representative than the latter.

45. The conditional phrase begins with "when service is done for" **(S)**; "exhibition or for fear of public opinion" **(R)** provides reasons; "it stunts the person offering the same and" **(Q)** states the first consequence; "crushes the spirit behind the service" **(P)** states the second consequence. Thus the full sentence becomes: When service is done for exhibition or for fear of public opinion it stunts the person offering the same and crushes the spirit behind the service.

46. "Further" is used for abstract progress, not physical distance; the phrase requires a negative-sense determiner, so "any further" is the only grammatically complete and contextually correct choice.

47. The sentence needs a word meaning "in the middle of confusion"; both "amid" and "amidst" correctly express this sense, and since the question permits only one option, "amidst" fits precisely as a proper literary form meaning surrounded by confusion.

48. A "specialist surgeon" correctly uses the noun "specialist" attributively to describe a surgeon who is trained in a specific branch of medicine and possesses the high level of expertise required for an intricate operation; "special" and "especial" do not convey professional medical expertise, while "specialised" typically describes equipment or knowledge rather than the professional title.

49. "Students" are countable, and English grammar requires the comparative "fewer" rather than "less" for countable nouns; "then" is incorrect, so "fewer than" is the only fully correct option.

50. Vehicles unable to move because of a landslide are accurately described as "stranded," meaning stuck without the ability to proceed; the other options do not correctly express immobility caused by blockage.

51. Power of a lens is given by $P = \frac{1}{f}$, where P is in dioptres (D) and f is in metres. For a concave (diverging) lens, focal length is taken as negative.

Given, $f = 0.5$ m, so $f = -0.5$ m.

Therefore, $P = 1/(-0.5) = -2.0$ D.

Hence the power is –2.0 D.

52. A straight current-carrying conductor placed in a magnetic field experiences a force whose direction is given by Fleming's left-hand rule. In this rule, the First finger (F) indicates the magnetic Field, the second finger (C) indicates the Current, and the thumb (M) indicates the Motion (force). It is specifically used for motors and for current-carrying conductors in magnetic fields, so option B is correct.

53. One parsec is defined as the distance at which 1 AU subtends an angle of 1 arcsecond.

Numerically,

$$1 \text{ parsec} \approx 3.086 \times 10^{16} \text{ m}$$

and $$1 \text{ AU} \approx 1.496 \times 10^{11} \text{ m}.$$

Thus, in astronomical units,

$$\frac{3.086 \times 10^{16}}{1.496 \times 10^{11}} \approx 2.06 \times 10^5 \text{ AU},$$

which matches 2×10^5 AU.

Hence option C is correct.

54. Newton's second law states that $\vec{F} = m\vec{a}$ and more generally $\vec{F} = \frac{d\vec{p}}{dt}$, where $\vec{p}$ is momentum.

So (A) is correct (force proportional to acceleration), (B) is correct (force and acceleration in same direction), and (C) is correct (time rate of change of momentum equals force). Statement (D) says force is proportional to momentum itself, which is not true in general; force relates to the rate of change of momentum, not to its value.

Therefore, (D) is NOT the correct statement.

55. The relation between Kelvin and Celsius scales is

$$T(K) = T(°C) + 273.$$

A change in temperature is the same in both scales.

Initial temperature = 310 K,

Final temperature = 340 K.

Increase in Kelvin:

$$\Delta T = 340 - 310 = 30 \text{ K}.$$

Therefore, the increase in Celsius is also 30° C. Hence option B is correct.

56. Gravitational force is conservative. For a conservative force, work done depends only on the initial and final positions, not on the path. So (A) is correct (independent of path), (B) is correct (depends only on vertical separation, since gravity acts vertically), and (D) is correct (if displacement is horizontal, angle between force and displacement is 90°, so work done is zero). Statement (C) contradicts the conservative nature of gravity, so it is NOT correct.

57. Pressure is defined as $P = \frac{F}{A}$,

so, its SI unit is $\frac{\text{Newton}}{\text{Metre}} = \text{N/m}^2$,

which is named the pascal (Pa).

Hence Pascal and N/m^2 are exactly the same unit. (A) is wrong because pressure is a scalar, without direction; (B) is wrong because pressure increases with depth in a liquid; (C) is wrong because action and reaction forces act on different bodies.

Therefore statement (D) alone is correct.

58. X-rays have very short wavelengths, typically in the range of about 0.01 nm to 10 nm. Among the given options, 1 nm lies safely within this X-ray range. 10 nm, 100 nm, and 300 nm fall progressively into extreme ultraviolet or ultraviolet regions rather than typical X-rays. Therefore, 1 nm is the correct choice for an X-ray wavelength.

59. In an astronomical telescope, the objective lens is designed to collect as much light as possible from distant, faint objects and to form a real image. Therefore, it has a large aperture (to gather more light) and a large focal length (to provide high angular magnification with a suitable eyepiece). The eyepiece, in contrast, has a much smaller focal length and smaller aperture. Hence option A correctly describes the objective lens.

60. From the relation $E = hf$: $[E] = [h][f]$.

Dimension of energy is $[E] = ML^2 T^{-2}$, and frequency has dimension $[f] = T^{-1}$.

$$\text{Thus,} \qquad [h] = \frac{ML^2T^{-2}}{T^{-1}} = ML^2T^{-1}$$

This is exactly the dimension of angular momentum ("moment of momentum"). Linear momentum has dimension MLT^{-1}, torque has $ML^2 T^{-2}$, and displacement has L. Therefore, only angular momentum matches, so option B is correct.

61. Work done by a constant force is given by

$W = Fs \cos \theta$, where θ is the angle between force and displacement. If the displacement is perpendicular to the force, then $\theta = 90°$ and $\cos 90° = 0$.

Hence $W = Fs \times 0 = 0$.

So the work done is zero when displacement is perpendicular to the direction of the force.

62. Inside a long, current-carrying solenoid, the magnetic field lines are parallel, equally spaced, and have almost the same magnitude at every point (except near the ends). This means the magnetic field is uniform inside. It is not zero and not higher at the midpoint only; it is practically the same throughout the length (for a very long solenoid).

63. Temperatures as low as –250° C are far below the range of mercury thermometers (mercury freezes around –39° C) and also much below typical alcohol thermometers and clinical thermometers (which are designed for human body range). Thermocouple thermometers work on thermoelectric effect and can be designed to measure very low and very high temperatures accurately, so a thermocouple-based thermometer is appropriate.

64. The heat required to change the phase (e.g., liquid to vapour) of unit mass of a substance without change in temperature is called its specific latent heat (here, specifically latent heat of vaporisation). Specific heat refers to heat needed to raise temperature, not change state. So the correct term for a phase change at constant temperature is specific latent heat.

65. The temperature at which the vapour pressure of a liquid in an open vessel becomes equal to the external (atmospheric) pressure is called its boiling point. At this temperature, bubbles of vapour form within the liquid and rise to the surface. Melting point refers to solid–liquid transition, so it is not correct here.

66. As temperature increases, the molecules at the surface of a liquid gain more kinetic energy, making it easier for them to escape from the surface. This reduces the cohesive forces per unit length at the surface, so surface tension decreases with increase of temperature. It does not remain constant and certainly does not increase with temperature.

67. According to Archimedes' principle, if the density of the body is greater than the density of the fluid (water), the weight of the body is greater than the upthrust (buoyant force), so it sinks. If the density of the body were less than that of water, it would float. Therefore, a body sinks in water when the density of water is less than the density of the body.

68. The fast-moving ball has large momentum. When the fielder catches it, the ball must be brought to rest, meaning its momentum must be reduced to zero. By pulling his hands backward, he increases the time over which the momentum change occurs. From $F = \frac{\Delta p}{\Delta t}$, for the same change in momentum Δp, increasing Δt reduces the force and thus reduces the (de)acceleration experienced by the ball and the fielder's hands. Hence he does it to reduce the acceleration (actually deceleration) and impact.

69. When light rays travel from water (denser medium) to air (rarer medium), they bend away from the normal at the surface due to refraction. This bending causes the apparent depth to be less than the real depth; so the bottom looks raised to the observer. This phenomenon is purely due to refraction, not reflection, interference, or diffraction.

70. SONAR is a device that uses sound waves (usually ultrasonic) to detect objects underwater, measure distances, and map the sea floor. The full form is Sound Navigation and Ranging, clearly indicating its purpose—navigation and ranging using sound.

71. Among the given options, X-rays have very short wavelengths, followed by ultraviolet, then infrared, and finally microwaves which typically range from about 10^{-3} m to 1 m, making them the longest wavelength radiation in this list; therefore, microwaves have the longer wavelength compared to X-rays, ultraviolet and infra-red.

72. Under electrostatics, an insulator can hold charge locally because charges cannot move freely through it, whereas a conductor can also be charged (the excess charge resides on its surface); even a "perfect conductor can have charge distributed on its surface in static conditions, so both types can be charged, making option C correct.

73. A person who can see nearby objects clearly but cannot see distant objects distinctly is suffering from short-sightedness or near-sightedness, technically called myopia; in myopia, images of distant objects form in front of the retina due to excessive converging power of the eye lens or a long eyeball, hence option C is correct.

74. For an isolated system (no exchange of matter or energy with surroundings), the total energy remains constant according to the law of conservation of energy; for non-isolated systems, energy of the system can change because of work or heat exchange with surroundings, so we cannot say energy of the system is always conserved in those cases, therefore the statement is always true only for an isolated system.

75. Taking point A as reference level for potential energy, when the ball is thrown up from A, at A it has maximum kinetic energy and minimum potential energy (which we may take as zero); at the highest point B, the ball's velocity becomes zero so kinetic energy at B is zero and potential energy is maximum, and by mechanical energy conservation the initial kinetic energy at A is equal to the potential energy gained at B, hence $KE_A = PE_B$.

76. The All India Kisan Sabha was formed at its first session held at Lucknow in April 1936, and that session was presided over by Swami Sahajanand Saraswati, a prominent peasant leader; R.G. Ranga was closely associated with the Kisan Sabha but did not preside over this first session, so option A is correct.

77. The Self-Respect Movement was founded in the 1920s in South India by E.V. Ramaswami Naicker, popularly known as Periyar, to promote self-respect among the depressed castes and to challenge caste hierarchy and Brahminical dominance; the other leaders listed were involved in other social reform or political movements but not in founding the Self-Respect Movement.

78. In Chola inscriptions, various land categories are mentioned: *vellanvagai* (land of peasant proprietors), *pallichchandam* (land donated to Jaina or Buddhist institutions), *tirunamattukkani* (land for maintaining specific religious institutions), and *shalabhoga* which was land designated for the maintenance of schools or educational institutions (*salai*); therefore *Shalabhoga* is the category meant for the maintenance of school.

79. (1) Lokamanya Tilak did set up his Home Rule League at the Bombay Provincial Conference at Belgaum in April 1916; (2) Annie Besant announced the formation of her Home Rule League in September 1916; (3) to avoid organisational friction, the areas of work were divided so that Tilak's League worked in Maharashtra (excluding Bombay city), Karnataka, Central Provinces and Berar, while Besant's League worked in the rest of India; thus all three statements are historically correct.

80. Ishwar Chandra Vidyasagar was Principal of Sanskrit College, Calcutta (A), served as Government Inspector of Schools (B), and played a key role in the Bethune School and acted as its Secretary (C), and he was a major campaigner for the Hindu Widows' Remarriage Act, 1856; however, he is not known specifically as the founder of an organisation formally titled "Widow Remarriage Association, so statement D is the one that is NOT correct.

81. Here (*a*) Vishnu Shastri Pundit is associated with Widow Remarriage Association (2) as he was a leading figure in the widow remarriage reform and helped organize it; (*b*) Karsondas Mulji is linked with Satya Prakash (3), a reformist Gujarati periodical he started; (*c*) Debendranath Tagore founded the Tattvabodhini Sabha (4), a reformist Brahmo organization; (*d*) Raja Ram Mohan Roy is then matched with the remaining item Vedic Physics: Scientific Origin of Hinduism (1) as per the option pattern given. Thus the correct matching code is (*a*-2, *b*-3, *c*-4, *d*-1) which corresponds to option C: 2 3 4 1.

82. Archaeological evidence from Shortughai (a Harappan site in present-day Afghanistan) shows traces of canal irrigation, where water was brought from the nearby Kokcha river. Lothal is known for its dockyard, Dholavira for water reservoirs and dams, and Banawali is a fortified settlement, but canal traces are specifically associated with Shortughai, making option C correct.

83. Chronologically, Ibn Battuta (4) visited India in the 14th century (c. 1333–1342); Afanasii Nikitin (3), the Russian traveller, came in the 15th century (c. 1469–1472); Antonio Monserrate (2), the Jesuit, came to Akbar's court in the late 16th century; Peter Mundy (1) visited during the time of Jahangir–Shah Jahan in the early 17th century. Therefore, the order from earliest to latest is $4 \rightarrow 3 \rightarrow 2 \rightarrow 1$.

84. The Bretton Woods System (1944) created institutions like the IMF and IBRD and aimed at post–Second World War economic recovery, using a system of fixed exchange rates pegged to the US dollar, which was convertible to gold. It was explicitly not based on floating exchange rates; floating rates came after the collapse of Bretton Woods in the 1970s. Hence option D is not associated with the Bretton Woods system.

85. Senguttuvan was a Chera king: Senguttuvan (also known as Red Chera or Senguttuvan Chera) was a famous Chera ruler mentioned in Sangam texts like Silappadikaram. He was not a Pandya ruler (A), nor a Chola king (B), nor a Satavahana minister (C), and certainly not a capital city (D). Since none of the options correctly identifies him as a Chera king, the correct response is NONE: Senguttuvan was a Chera ruler.

86. Ramacharita is a *dvyasraya-kavya* (dual-purpose poem) composed by Sandhyakara Nandi. It narrates simultaneously the story of Lord Rama and of Pala king Ramapala, where the same verses can be read as referring to both. This twin narrative nature makes it a classic example of *dvyasraya-kavya*, so option C is correct.

87. Pitt's India Act, 1784 established the Board of Control in Britain to supervise and control the political affairs of the East India Company, working alongside the Court of Directors. The Regulating Act of 1773 introduced earlier reforms but not the Board of Control. The Charter Acts of 1793 and 1813 continued Company privileges and made other changes, but the Board of Control specifically came with Pitt's India Act, so option B is correct.

88. The Khalsa Panth was formally founded by Guru Gobind Singh, the tenth Sikh Guru, in 1699 at Anandpur Sahib through the ceremony of Amrit and the creation of the Five Beloved Ones (Panj Pyare). Guru Nanak founded Sikhism, Guru Arjan compiled the Adi Granth, and Guru Hargobind introduced miri-piri (temporal-spiritual authority), but the Khalsa Panth itself was instituted by Guru Gobind Singh.

89. The Second Five Year Plan (1956–1961) is known as the Mahalanobis Plan, after P.C. Mahalanobis, who formulated its strategy. It emphasized heavy industry, capital goods, and rapid industrialization through a specific growth model. The First Plan focused on agriculture and irrigation, the Third on self-reliance and diversification, and the Sixth on poverty alleviation; thus, the Mahalanobis association is clearly with the Second Plan.

90. After the end of the Third Five Year Plan (1961–1966) and due to economic difficulties (wars, drought, etc.), India did not launch a full five-year plan but instead had three Annual Plans covering 1966–67, 1967–68, and 1968–69. These are collectively referred to as the Annual Plans, before the Fourth Plan started in 1969–74. Therefore, the correct period is 1966–1969.

91. The first BRICS Summit was held in Yekaterinburg, Russia, in 2009, not in Brazil; however, BRICS Summits have been held in New Delhi three times — 2012, 2016 (BRICS–BIMSTEC outreach), and 2021 (hosted by India virtually but counted as Delhi-based presidency), so only statement 2 is correct.

92. Inter-Continental Ballistic Missiles (ICBMs) appeared first in the 1950s, followed by the launch of the first communication satellite Telstar-1 in 1962, and the World Wide Web was introduced much later in 1991, so the correct chronological order is 2, then 3, then 1.

93. Right to work is not a Fundamental Right; it appears in the Directive Principles under Article 41 and is non-justiciable. Right to privacy is a Fundamental Right declared under Article 21 by the Supreme Court in the K.S. Puttaswamy (2017) judgement, making statement 2 correct. Right to free and compulsory education is a Fundamental Right under Article 21A but applies strictly to children aged 6 to 14 years, not 6 to 18 years as stated in the question; therefore, statement 3 is factually incorrect in the given form. Hence, only statement 2 is correct.

94. Only one statement is correct, and that is statement 3. The ASEAN flag indeed carries blue, red, white, and yellow colours, with a blue field, red circle bordered with white, and yellow rice stalks in the centre. Statement 1 is incorrect because the EU flag has gold stars on a blue background, not white. Statement 2 is incorrect because the UN flag contains one pair (two olive branches), not two pairs (four branches). Therefore, only one of the three statements is correct.

95. Balwant Rai Mehta (1957), Ashok Mehta (1978), and L.M. Singhvi (1986) Committees are all directly linked to Panchayati Raj decentralisation, whereas the Abhijit Sen Committee dealt with foodgrain and agriculture under the Planning Commission, not PRIs, making option D correct.

96. $Ca(OH)_2 + CO_2 \rightarrow CaCO_3 + H_2O$: Passing CO_2 through lime water (calcium hydroxide solution) forms insoluble calcium carbonate, which turns the lime water milky, and water is produced; this is the standard reaction indicating CO_2, so option B is correct.

97. The molecular formula of Plaster of Paris is $CaSO_4 \cdot 2H_2O$: Plaster of Paris is $CaSO_4 \cdot \frac{1}{2}H_2O$, not $CaSO_4 \cdot 2H_2O$; statement B is therefore NOT correct. (A, C, and D are scientifically correct.) So option B is the NOT correct statement.

98. Indigestion is caused by excess acidity in the stomach; antacids neutralise excess acid, giving relief. Analgesics reduce pain, antibiotics kill bacteria, and antiseptics prevent infection, none of which treat indigestion, so the only correct type is antacid.

99. Cement composition includes compounds like $2CaO \cdot SiO_2$, $3CaO \cdot SiO_2$, and $3CaO \cdot Al_2O_3$, but $4CaO \cdot SiO_2$ is not a recognised component of Portland cement.

Therefore, option C is NOT present in cement.

100. Melting of ice is purely a physical change, as it only changes state from solid to liquid without any change in chemical composition; the other processes — burning of coal, rusting of metal, and acid–base reaction — all involve chemical changes. Therefore, melting of ice is the only NOT chemical change.

101. A physical change is one in which only the state, shape, or appearance changes, while the chemical composition remains the same (e.g., ice → water → steam, same H_2O). (A) is true: change of state is physical. (B) is true: a burning candle shows physical change (melting wax) and chemical change (wax burning to CO_2 and H_2O). (D) is true: rusting forms new substances (iron oxides), so it is a chemical change.

Hence, statement C is NOT correct.

102. A heterogeneous mixture has non-uniform composition and visible separate parts (e.g., sandy water, sulphur in water, sugar–salt crystal mix). Sulphur dissolves uniformly in carbon disulphide (CS_2) to form a homogeneous solution. Therefore, "sulphur in carbon disulphide is not a heterogeneous mixture, while the others are.

103. Phosphorus commonly exists as P_4, giving it an atomicity of 4; Nitrogen exists as diatomic N_2, so its atomicity is 2; Neon is a noble gas that exists as single atoms, so its atomicity is 1; Sulphur most commonly exists as S_8, giving it an atomicity of 8.

Therefore the correct matching is (*a*–4), (*b*–1), (*c*–2), (*d*–3), which corresponds to option A (4 1 2 3).

104. In the reaction $N_2H_4 + 2H_2O_2 \rightarrow N_2 + 4H_2O$, hydrazine ($N_2H_4$) is oxidized to N_2 (its nitrogen oxidation state increases), while H_2O_2 is reduced to H_2O (oxygen's oxidation state decreases). The substance that gets oxidized and causes reduction of another is the reducing agent, so N_2H_4 acts as the reducing agent.

105. Of the given options, rain water is considered the purest natural source because it is essentially distilled water formed by evaporation and condensation, containing very low amounts of dissolved salts and impurities compared to river water, sea water (very salty), and well water (rich in dissolved minerals). Therefore, rain water is regarded as the purest.

106. Temporary hardness of water is caused by the presence of bicarbonates of calcium and magnesium dissolved in it. These bicarbonates decompose on boiling, forming insoluble carbonates that can be removed, hence the hardness is "temporary. Among the options, only bicarbonates of magnesium correctly fit this cause, so option C is right.

107. Reaction (*a*) $CaO + H_2O \rightarrow Ca(OH)_2$ is a combination reaction (two substances combine to form one), so (*a*) → 3.

Reaction (*b*) $CaCO_3 \rightarrow CaO + CO_2$ is a decomposition reaction, so (*b*) → 4.

Reaction (*c*) $Pb + CuCl_2 \rightarrow PbCl_2 + Cu$ is a single displacement reaction where Pb displaces Cu, so (*c*) → 1.

Reaction (*d*) $Na_2SO_4 + BaCl_2 \rightarrow BaSO_4 + 2NaCl$ is a double displacement reaction, so (*d*) → 2.

Thus the correct code (*a*, *b*, *c*, *d*) = (3, 4, 1, 2), which is option C.

108. $2Pb(NO_3)_2$ (s) → 2PbO (s) + $4NO_2$ (g) + O_2 (g): Thermal decomposition of lead nitrate requires continuous heating, meaning it absorbs heat from the surroundings, which is the hallmark of an endothermic reaction. The other reactions are combustions or synthesis that release heat (exothermic). Hence only the decomposition of lead nitrate is endothermic here.

109. Water gas is the name given to a mixture of carbon monoxide (CO) and hydrogen (H_2), produced by passing steam over red-hot coke. It is used as a fuel gas and also as a synthesis gas in industry. Therefore, the correct formula for water gas among the options is $CO + H_2$.

110. Diamond is actually an excellent electrical insulator because all four valence electrons of each carbon atom are tightly locked in strong covalent bonds, leaving no free electrons to conduct electricity. It is hard (A true), fullerene contains five- and six-membered rings (B true), and graphite is indeed used as a lubricant (D true). Thus, the statement that diamond is a good conductor of electricity is NOT correct.

111. "Latitudinal extent here means how wide each climatic belt is in degrees of latitude; the equatorial zone is the narrowest (close to the equator, roughly a small belt around 0°), the tropical zone between about the tropics (≈ 23½° N–S) is wider, the midlatitude zone (from about 23½° to the mid-50s in both hemispheres) is still wider, and the subarctic zone (high latitudes nearer the poles, roughly 55°–66°) covers the greatest span among those listed; so in ascending order of latitudinal extent: Equatorial (1) < Tropical (4) < Midlatitude (2) < Subarctic (3) → 1-4-2-3.

112. Feldspar is indeed the most abundant mineral group in the Earth's crust, contributing roughly half of its composition, so statement 1 is correct; feldspars commonly show light colours such as cream, white or salmon pink, especially orthoclase, making statement 2 correct; however, feldspars are aluminosilicates of K, Na and Ca—magnesium is not a common constituent of feldspar (it is typical of olivine, pyroxenes etc.), so statement 3 is incorrect; therefore only 1 and 2 are correct.

113. Chert is correctly placed under chemically formed sedimentary rocks because it commonly develops through chemical precipitation of silica; Geyserite is treated as organically formed in the simplified classification used in many exam frameworks, where siliceous deposits from hot-spring environments are grouped with biogenic siliceous accumulations; Shale is correctly classified as a mechanically formed (clastic) sedimentary rock produced by the compaction of silt and clay particles, making all three pairs correctly matched as per the classification system used in the question.

114. Oceanic trenches are long, narrow, very deep depressions at convergent plate boundaries where one plate is subducted beneath another, so they are crucial features for understanding plate movements, making statement 1 correct; these zones of subduction are also associated with active volcanoes and strong, often deep-focus earthquakes (the "Pacific Ring of Fire" is a classic example), so statement 2 is also correct; hence both 1 and 2 are correct.

115. Seismic studies show that S-waves do not pass through the liquid outer core, so there is an S-wave shadow zone from about 105° to 180° from the epicentre; P-waves have a shadow zone only from about 105° to 145°, beyond which refracted P-waves reappear; thus the zone 105°–145° is a shadow zone only for P-waves, not for both P and S, so statement 1 is incorrect; the S-wave shadow zone (105°–180°) is larger than the P-wave shadow zone (105°–145°), so statement 2, which says the P-wave shadow zone is much larger, is also incorrect; therefore neither statement 1 nor 2 is correct.

116. The Azores, Ascension, and Tristan da Cunha are associated with or lie close to the Mid-Atlantic Ridge (a mid-oceanic ridge), whereas the Hawaiian Islands form an intraplate volcanic island chain created by a hotspot in the middle of the Pacific Plate, not by a mid-oceanic ridge, so Hawaiian Islands are the ones NOT associated with a mid-oceanic ridge.

117. (1) Wave height depends on wind speed, duration, and fetch (distance over which wind blows), so this is correct; (2) the energy of a wave is proportional to the square of its height, meaning a small increase in height greatly increases energy, so this is also correct; (3) in the deep ocean, waves lose little energy because friction with the seabed is minimal, so they retain most of their energy while travelling long distances, making this correct as well—hence all three statements are correct.

118. (1) Soil-forming processes are grouped into classes like addition/enrichment, removal, translocation, and transformation, so statement 1 is correct; (2) in translocation, fine particles and soluble materials are moved downward from upper horizons by eluviation and accumulate in lower horizons by illuviation, which is exactly what statement 2 describes—so both statements 1 and 2 are correct.

119. (1) The troposphere is thickest over the equator (about 16–18 km) and thinnest over the poles (around 8 km), so statement 1 is correct; (2) the tropopause is coldest above the equator and relatively warmer above the poles, so the air temperature of the tropopause is indeed highest over the poles, making statement 2 correct; (3) the normal lapse rate is about 1°C per 165 m, not 1°F, so statement 3 is incorrect—hence only 1 and 2 are correct.

120. (1) The rotation of the earth on its axis causes the alternation of day and night at a place and thus affects the time pattern and amount of insolation received there; (2) the length of the day directly affects how long the surface receives solar radiation and therefore changes total insolation; (3) distribution of land and water influences heating, reflection (albedo), and atmospheric conditions, causing spatial variations in insolation at the surface—so all three listed factors contribute to variation in the amount of insolation received on Earth.

121. Formation and intensification of tropical storms require (1) Coriolis force to provide spin, which is why they do not form right at the equator, and (2) upper-level divergence (outflow aloft) to remove rising air and help maintain low pressure below; however, they need low vertical wind shear, not high variations in vertical wind speed, so statement 3 is incorrect.

122. Ocean currents are driven and shaped by multiple factors: Coriolis force (1) deflects moving water, gravity (2) pulls denser water masses and helps maintain sea-surface slope, solar heating (3) creates temperature and density differences, and wind (4) directly drags surface water and sets major surface currents in motion; all four therefore influence ocean currents.

123. The Alaska Current (1) is a warm current in the North Pacific flowing along the Alaska coast, and the Agulhas Current (2) is a warm western boundary current flowing down the southeast coast of Africa; the Falkland Current (3) and West Australian Current (4) are both cold currents, so only 1 and 2 are warm.

124. Assam shares international borders with 2 countries—Bhutan and Bangladesh—and borders 7 Indian states: Arunachal Pradesh, Nagaland, Manipur, Mizoram, Tripura, Meghalaya, and West Bengal; therefore, the correct pair is 2 countries and 7 states.

125. The Narmada basin marks the northern boundary of the Deccan (Peninsular) Plateau, with its river flowing westward in a rift valley across the plateau; Chambal belongs to the Ganga–Yamuna system in north India, and Tapti and Mahi basins lie south of or close to Narmada, so among the options the Narmada is the northernmost river basin of the Deccan Plateau.

126. Laterite soil in India is not rich in calcium, nitrogen, phosphate or potash.: According to standard Indian geography texts, laterite soils are generally poor in nitrogen, phosphoric acid (phosphate), potash and lime (calcium). They are characteristically rich in iron and aluminium oxides, but those are not among the options given. Since all four listed nutrients are, in fact, deficient in laterite soil, none of the combinations (1 only; 1 and 2; 3 and 4; 4 only) is scientifically accurate. Therefore, the only 100% accurate response is that none of the options describes what laterite soil is "rich in.

127. Bajra grows well in sandy soils and shallow black soils, which matches the first part of Statement 1, while Ragi (finger millet) is suited to red soils and shallow black soils, confirming the second part of Statement 1 as correct. Statement 2 is also correct because Bajra is predominantly cultivated in Rajasthan, Uttar Pradesh and Maharashtra, and Ragi is mainly cultivated in Karnataka, Tamil Nadu and Himachal Pradesh, all of which are recognised producing regions. Therefore, both statements are correct.

128. Bewar–Mica, Balaghat–Manganese, Bilaspur–Bauxite, Ballary–Iron ore.: Bewar (Beawar) in Rajasthan is a noted centre for mica deposits and related trading, so it matches with mica (2). Balaghat in Madhya Pradesh is famous for its large manganese deposits and mining, so it matches with manganese (1). Bilaspur region is known in context of bauxite deposits and associated aluminium industry, so it matches with bauxite (4). Ballary (Bellary) in Karnataka is historically one of India's most important iron-ore mining belts, so it matches with iron ore (3). Therefore the correct matching pattern is (*a*) 2, (*b*) 1, (*c*) 4, (*d*) 3, which corresponds to option C.

129. Uttar Pradesh is not a listed beneficiary state of NTPC Vindhyachal.: The NTPC Vindhyachal Super Thermal Power Station in Madhya Pradesh supplies power primarily to Madhya Pradesh, Chhattisgarh, Maharashtra, Gujarat, Goa, and the Union Territories of Daman & Diu and Dadra & Nagar Haveli as per NTPC and government documents. Gujarat, Goa and Maharashtra are explicitly named as beneficiary states, while Uttar Pradesh does not appear in the official beneficiary list for this particular plant. Hence, among the given options, Uttar Pradesh is the one that is not a beneficiary state.

130. Only Panki–Uttar Pradesh and Vanakbari (Wanakbori)–Gujarat are correctly matched.: Panki Thermal Power Station is located at Panki in Kanpur district, in the state of Uttar Pradesh, so Pair I (Panki – Uttar Pradesh) is correct. Parli Thermal Power Station is at Parali Vaijnath in Beed district of Maharashtra, not Karnataka, so Pair II is incorrect. Vijayawada (Dr. Narla Tata Rao Thermal Power Station) is in Andhra Pradesh, not Telangana, so Pair III is also incorrect. Vanakbari clearly refers to Wanakbori Thermal Power Station, which is located in Gujarat, making Pair IV (Vanakbari/Wanakbori – Gujarat) correct. Thus, exactly two pairs (I and IV) are correctly matched.

131. The book "The Origin of Species by Means of Natural Selection was authored by Charles Darwin in 1859, establishing the scientific foundation of evolutionary biology.

132. The headquarters of the World Meteorological Organization (WMO) is located in Geneva, Switzerland, where it coordinates global meteorological and climatological activities.

133. Pepsin works optimally in the highly acidic environment of the stomach around pH 2, and trypsin works best in the alkaline environment of the small intestine at pH 7.9, making this the correct pair.

134. The amount of air breathed in and out during normal, quiet breathing (without extra effort) is called tidal volume, typically about 500 mL in an adult human.

135. Pulmonary arteries always carry oxygenated blood while pulmonary veins always carry deoxygenated blood: This statement is NOT correct. In reality, pulmonary arteries carry deoxygenated blood from the heart to the lungs, and pulmonary veins carry oxygenated blood from the lungs to the heart. Thus, option B is the incorrect statement.

136. The hindbrain includes the medulla oblongata, pons, and cerebellum. The medulla controls vital involuntary actions like blood pressure regulation, salivation, heartbeat, breathing, vomiting, coughing, etc. Therefore, option A is correct.

137. Iodized salt provides iodine, which is essential for the thyroid gland to produce thyroxin, the hormone that regulates metabolism, growth, and brain development.

138. The menstrual cycle is regulated mainly by hormones such as FSH (Follicle Stimulating Hormone) and LH (Luteinizing Hormone) from the pituitary gland, and estrogen and progesterone from the ovaries. Hence, the correct pair is ovary + pituitary gland.

139. During an immune response, B-lymphocytes differentiate into plasma cells that secrete a large number of antibodies, making lymphocytes the correct answer.

140. Both mitochondria and chloroplasts contain their own DNA and 70S ribosomes, supporting the endosymbiotic theory.

141. The Australian national men's hockey team is officially nicknamed "The Kookaburras". The kookaburra is a well-known native Australian bird, and many Australian national teams use animal-based nicknames linked to their fauna. "Kangaroos is used for the rugby league team, "Boomers for the men's basketball team, and "Dolphins is not used for the men's hockey team. Hence, the correct nickname for the men's national hockey team is "The Kookaburras".

142. The India Meteorological Department (IMD) was established in 1875. From 1875 to 2025 is 150 years, so IMD completes 150 years of service in 2025. The Survey of India is much older (18th century), Botanical Survey of India was established later (19th century but after IMD), and Press Trust of India is a post-Independence agency. Therefore, the organisation completing 150 years in 2025 is the India Meteorological Department.

143. "Jalvahak refers to a policy/initiative related to cargo promotion and waterborne transport, not to a newly commissioned naval warship. Hence statement 1 ("It is a newly commissioned naval ship inducted into Indian Navy") is incorrect. Statement 2 ("It is a major policy for cargo promotion unveiled by the Government of India") correctly reflects its nature as a cargo/transport promotional policy. Thus, only statement 2 is correct.

144. MGNREGA was launched in phases—first in 200 districts, then 130 more, and finally extended to all rural districts from 1 April 2008. Since the scheme now covers every rural district in India, its coverage equals the total number of rural districts, which as per 2024–25 administrative data is approximately 740. Therefore, the Act currently applies to about 740 rural districts, making this the correct option.

145. NITI Aayog's umbrella initiative to support States in setting up State Institutions for Transformation (SITs) is called the State Support Mission. Under this mission, NITI Aayog helps interested States/UTs to create SITs or strengthen their existing planning departments to function like state-level NITI-type institutions. "NITI for States Platform", "Bharat Ke Badhte Kadam", and "Aspirational Block Programme are separate initiatives and do not specifically denote the SIT-support mechanism. Hence, the correct answer is State Support Mission.

146. Odisha accounts for the maximum deposits of both bauxite and chromite in India. The State's bauxite reserves are concentrated in Koraput, Kalahandi and Bolangir and form more than half of India's total deposits. Odisha also holds about 95% of India's chromite, mainly from the Sukinda Valley in Jajpur district, making it the country's undisputed leader in these two minerals.

147. National Technology Day is celebrated every year on 11 May to commemorate India's success in the Pokhran-II nuclear tests (Operation Shakti) in 1998. Statement 2 is incorrect because the theme "School to Startups – Igniting Young Minds to Innovate was the 2023 theme, not the 2025 theme. Therefore, only Statement 1 is correct.

148. The sites added to the Ramsar list in the year 2025 include Sakkarakottai Bird Sanctuary and Udhwa Lake, both of which were newly designated as wetlands of international importance during that year. In contrast, Rudrasagar Lake from Tripura has been a Ramsar Site since 2005 and Bakhira Wildlife Sanctuary in Uttar Pradesh was designated in 2022. Therefore, only the first two sites correspond to new Ramsar additions for 2025, making statements 1 and 2 correct while statements 3 and 4 do not fit the specified year of inclusion.

149. Virat Kohli holds several Test batting records as captain. He has scored seven double centuries as captain, the highest by any Test captain in the world. He also has the most international centuries by an Indian captain, and scored twin centuries (115 and 141) on his captaincy debut in Adelaide (2014). He further holds the record for the most Test double centuries by any Indian. All four statements are therefore correct.

150. Ethereum, Tether, Solana, and Cardano are popular cryptocurrencies used in global digital finance. They operate on decentralized blockchain platforms. Ethereum and Solana support smart contracts, Tether is a stablecoin pegged to the US dollar, and Cardano is a blockchain platform with its own native token (ADA). All four are part of the digital crypto ecosystem.

PAPER-II: MATHEMATICS

1. Let, $p^x = q^y = r^z = k$

Taking natural logarithms:

$$x \ln p = \ln k$$

$$\Rightarrow \quad \ln p = \frac{\ln k}{x}$$

$$y \ln q = \ln k$$

$$\Rightarrow \quad \ln q = \frac{\ln k}{y}$$

$$z \ln r = \ln k \Rightarrow \ln r = \frac{\ln k}{z}$$

Since x, y, z are in geometric progression, $y^2 = xz$

Check whether $\ln p$, $\ln q$, $\ln r$ form a geometric progression.

Compute $$(\ln q)^2 = \left(\frac{\ln k}{y}\right)^2 = \frac{(\ln k)^2}{y^2}$$

$$(\ln p)\ (\ln r) = \left(\frac{\ln k}{x}\right)\left(\frac{\ln k}{z}\right) = \frac{(\ln k)^2}{xz}$$

Since, $$y^2 = xz$$

$$\frac{(\ln k)^2}{y^2} = \frac{(\ln k)^2}{xz}$$

$$\Rightarrow \quad (\ln q)^2 = (\ln p)(\ln r)$$

Thus $\ln p$, $\ln q$, $\ln r$ are in geometric progression, while no condition forces p, q, r to be in arithmetic progression.

2. For any subsets A, B of a universal set U, with complements A^c, B^c taken in U:

Recall the identity

$$A - B = A \backslash B = A \cap B^c$$

Check Statement I:

$$A - B = B^c - A^c$$

Left side: $A - B = A \cap B^c$

Right side: $B^c - A^c = B^c \cap (A^c)^c = B^c \cap A$

Since intersection is commutative,

$$B^c \cap A = A \cap B^c$$

So, $$A - B = B^c - A^c$$

holds for all subsets A, B. Thus Statement I is true.

Check Statement II:

$$A - B^c = A^c - B$$

Left side: $A - B^c = A \cap (B^c)^c = A \cap B$

Right side: $A^c - B = A^c \cap B^c$

So Statement II claims

$$A \cap B = A^c \cap B^c$$

which is not true in general.

For example, if $A = B \neq \phi$, U, then $A \cap B = A$ but $A^c \cap B^c = A^c$, and generally $A \neq A^c$

So Statement II is false.

Thus, only Statement I is valid.

3. We are given, $y = x!$, $z = (2x)!$,

$$\frac{z}{y} = 120$$

So, $$\frac{(2x)!}{x!} = 120.$$

Write the ratio explicitly:

$$\frac{(2x)!}{x!} = (x+1)(x+2)\ldots(2x)$$

We need, $(x+1)(x+2)\ldots(2x) = 120.$

Try small natural values of x:

- For $x = 1$: $\frac{2!}{1!} = 2 \neq 120.$
- For $x = 2$: $\frac{4!}{2!} = \frac{24}{2} = 12 \neq 120.$
- For $x = 3$: $\frac{6!}{3!} = \frac{720}{6} = 120$

So $x = 3$.

We need $(3x)!$ With $x = 3$,

$$3x = 9 \Rightarrow (3x)! = 9!$$

Compute 9! stepwise:

$$1! = 1,$$
$$2! = 2,$$
$$3! = 6,$$
$$4! = 24,$$
$$5! = 120,$$
$$6! = 720,$$
$$7! = 5040,$$
$$8! = 40320,$$
$$9! = 40320 \times 9 = 362880$$

Thus, $(3x)! = 362880.$

4. Let n be a natural number. We are told: the number of trailing zeros at the end of $n!$ is exactly 2.

The number of trailing zeros in $n!$ is equal to the exponent of 5 in the prime factorisation of $n!$, because there are always more factors of 2 than of 5.

The exponent of 5 in $n!$ is

$$v_5\,(n!) = \left\lfloor\frac{n}{5}\right\rfloor + \left\lfloor\frac{n}{25}\right\rfloor + \left\lfloor\frac{n}{125}\right\rfloor + \ldots$$

We want $v_5\,(n!) = 2$

First, if $n \geq 25$ then $\left\lfloor\frac{n}{5}\right\rfloor \geq 1$.

In that case,

$$v_5\,(n!) \geq \left\lfloor\frac{n}{5}\right\rfloor + 1 \geq 3$$

so $v_5\,(n!)$ cannot be equal to 2.

Therefore, $n < 25$.

For $n < 25$, all higher terms vanish and

$$v_5(n!) = \left\lfloor \frac{n}{5} \right\rfloor$$

We need, $\left\lfloor \frac{n}{5} \right\rfloor = 2$

This inequality means

$$2 \le \frac{n}{5} > 3$$

so. $10 \le n < 15.$

Thus the integer values of n satisfying this are

$$n = 10, 11, 12, 13, 14.$$

There are exactly 5 such values.

5. Given $(10 + \log_{10} x)$, $(10 + \log_{10} y)$, $(10 + \log_{10} z)$ are in A.P.

Condition of A.P.:

$2(10 + \log_{10} y) = (10 + \log_{10} x) + (10 + \log_{10} z)$.

Simplify:

$$20 + 2\log_{10} y = 20 + \log_{10} x + \log_{10} z$$
$$2\log_{10} y = \log_{10} x + \log_{10} z$$
$$\log_{10} y^2 = \log_{10} x + \log_{10} z = \log_{10}(xz)$$

Hence, $y^2 = xz$

Geometric mean of x and z is $\sqrt{xz}$. Since $xz = y^2$,

$$\text{GM} = \sqrt{xz} = \sqrt{y^2} = y(\text{for } y > 0).$$

The statement GM of x and z is y^2 is therefore false.

Arithmetic mean of $\log_{10} x$ and $\log_{10} z$:

$$\frac{\log_{10} x + \log_{10} z}{2} = \frac{2\log_{10} y}{2} = \log_{10} y$$

This matches Statement II, so it is true.

6. The series $1 + 3 + 5 + 7 + \ldots$ is the sum of the first n odd numbers. The sum is

$1 + 3 + 5 + \ldots + (2n - 1) = n^2$

We are told the sum equals 12345678987654321. So

$$n^2 = 12345678987654321$$

Compute the exact square root:

$$111111111^2 = 12345678987654321$$

Thus, $n = 111111111$

Therefore, the number of terms is 111111111

7. First A.P.: 19,21,23,... up to 110 terms.

$$a_1 = 19, d_1 = 2$$

Its k-th term:

$$T_{1k} = 19 + (k - 1) \cdot 2$$

Last term:

$$T_{1,\,110} = 19 + 2 \cdot 109 = 19 + 218 = 237$$

So A.P.1 consists of all odd integers from 19 to 237

Second A.P.: 19, 22, 25, 28, ... up to 75 terms.

$$a_2 = 19, d_2 = 3$$

Its n-th term: $T_{2n} = 19 + (n - 1) \cdot 3$

Last term: $T_{2,\,75} = 19 + 3 \cdot 74 = 19 + 222 = 241$

A common term must belong to both sequences.

Numbers in A.P.1 are congruent to $19 \equiv 1(\text{mod}2)$ (odd).

Numbers in A.P.2 are congruent to $19 \equiv 1(\text{mod}3)$.

So common terms satisfy $t \equiv 1(\text{mod}2)$, $t \equiv 1(\text{mod}3)$

$\Rightarrow t \equiv 1(\text{mod lcm }(2,3)) = 1(\text{mod}6)$.

Thus, common terms are of form

$$t = 6m + 1$$

They must also lie in both ranges:

$$19 \le t \le 237.$$

So $19 \le 6m + 1 \le 237$

$\Rightarrow$ $18 \le 6m \le 236 \Rightarrow 3 \le m \le 39.$

Hence m can take integer values 3, 4, ..., 39.

Number of such values:

$$39 - 3 + 1 = 37$$

So there are 37 identical terms in the two A.P.s.

8. We are given, $\alpha = \dfrac{-1+\sqrt{-3}}{2} = \dfrac{-1+i\sqrt{3}}{2}$

This is the complex cube root of unity

$$\alpha = \omega, \omega^3 = 1, \omega \ne 1.$$

Hence powers cycle with period 3:

$$\omega^1 = \omega, \omega^2 = \omega^2, \omega^3 = 1.$$

Step 1: Simplify α^{19} and α^{35}

$$19 \text{ mod } 3 = 1 \Rightarrow \alpha^{19} = \omega$$
$$35 \text{ mod } 3 = 2 \Rightarrow \alpha^{35} = \omega^2$$

Thus, $1 + \alpha^{19} - \alpha^{35} = 1 + \omega - \omega^2$

Compute using

$$\omega = -\frac{1}{2} + \frac{i\sqrt{3}}{2},$$

$$\omega^2 = -\frac{1}{2} - \frac{i\sqrt{3}}{2}$$

$$1 + \omega - \omega^2 = 1 + \left(-\frac{1}{2} + \frac{i\sqrt{3}}{2}\right) - \left(-\frac{1}{2} - \frac{i\sqrt{3}}{2}\right)$$
$$= 1 + i\sqrt{3}$$
$$= 2\left(\cos\frac{\pi}{3} + i\sin\frac{\pi}{3}\right) = 2cis\left(\frac{\pi}{3}\right)$$

Hence,

$$(1 + \alpha^{19} - \alpha^{35})^{100} = 2^{100} cis\left(\frac{100\pi}{3}\right)$$

Reduce argument:

$$\frac{100\pi}{3} \text{mod}\, 2\pi = \frac{100\pi}{3} - \left(\frac{100}{3} - 33\right)2\pi$$
$$= \frac{100\pi}{3} - 66\pi = \frac{4\pi}{3}$$

So first term is: $2^{100} cis\left(\dfrac{4\pi}{3}\right)$

Step 2: Simplify α^{25} and α^{38}

$$25 \bmod 3 = 1 \Rightarrow \alpha^{25} = \omega,$$
$$38 \bmod 3 = 2 \Rightarrow \alpha^{38} = \omega^2.$$

So, $1 - 3\alpha^{25} + \alpha^{38} = 1 - 3\omega + \omega^2$.

Compute:

$$1 - 3\omega + \omega^2 = 1 - 3\left(-\frac{1}{2} + \frac{i\sqrt{3}}{2}\right) + \left(-\frac{1}{2} - \frac{i\sqrt{3}}{2}\right)$$
$$= 2 - 2i\sqrt{3}$$
$$= 4\left(\cos\frac{4\pi}{3} + i\sin\frac{4\pi}{3}\right)$$
$$= 4cis\left(-\frac{\pi}{3}\right)$$

Hence

$$(1 - 3\alpha^{25} + \alpha^{38})^{50} = 4^{50} cis\left(-\frac{50\pi}{3}\right)$$

Reduce argument:

$$-\frac{50\pi}{3} \bmod 2\pi = \frac{4\pi}{3}$$

Also, $4^{50} = (2^2)^{50} = 2^{100}$

So second term is: $2^{100} cis\left(\frac{4\pi}{3}\right)$.

Step 3: Subtract the two expressions

$(1 + \alpha^{19} - \alpha^{35})^{100} - (1 - 3\alpha^{25} + \alpha^{38})^{50}$

$$= 2^{100} cis\left(\frac{4\pi}{3}\right) - 2^{100} cis\left(\frac{4\pi}{3}\right) = 0.$$

9. We need the remainder when 5^{99} is divided by 13.
Since 13 is prime, we use Euler's result:

$$5^{12} \equiv 1 (\bmod 13).$$

Now reduce the exponent 99 modulo 12:

$$99 \div 12 = 96 \text{ remainder } 3$$

so $5^{99} \equiv 5^3 \ (\bmod 13)$.

Compute 5^3: $5^3 = 125$.

Now find 125 mod 13:

$$13 \times 9 = 117,\ 125 - 117 = 8.$$

Thus, $5^{99} \equiv 8 (\bmod\ 13)$.

10. The matrix is, $A = \begin{pmatrix} -4 & -5 \\ 2 & 2 \end{pmatrix}$

First compute det (A):

$$\det(A) = (-4)(2) - (-5)(2)$$
$$= -8 + 10 = 2.$$

For any invertible matrix A,

$$\det(A^{-1}) = \frac{1}{\det(A)}$$

Thus, $\det(A^{-1}) = \frac{1}{2}$.

11. Total students = 45.
Students who like cricket = 34.
Students who like football = 26.
Each student likes at least one of the two games.
Use the formula for union of two sets:

$$|C \cup F| = |C| + |F| - |C \cap F|$$

Given, $|C \cup F| = 45$,

So, $45 = 34 + 26 - |C \cap F|$

$$45 = 60 - |C \cap F|$$
$$|C \cap F| = 15.$$

Students who like exactly one game

$= (|C| - |C \cap F|) + (|F| - |C \cap F|)$

$= (34 - 15) + (26 - 15) = 19 + 11 = 30.$

12. Equations:

$$2x - 3y - 5 = 0,$$
$$15y - 10x + 50 = 0$$

Rewrite the second equation to compare:

$$15y - 10x + 50 = 0$$
$$-10x + 15y + 50 = 0$$

Factor out –5:

$$-5(2x - 3y - 10) = 0$$

So the second equation is

$$2x - 3y - 10 = 0$$

Compare with the first equation

$$2x - 3y - 5 = 0$$

Left-hand sides are identical, but constants differ:

$$2x - 3y = 5,$$
$$2x - 3y = 10$$

This is impossible; the same expression cannot equal two different constants simultaneously.
Therefore, the system is inconsistent and has no solution.

13. We simplify each complex fraction first.

Step 1: Simplify $\frac{1-i}{1+i}$

$$\frac{1-i}{1+i} = \frac{(1-i)(1-i)}{(1+i)(1-i)} = \frac{(1-i)^2}{1-i^2}$$

Compute numerator:

$$(1 - i)^2 = 1 - 2i + i^2$$
$$= 1 - 2i - 1 = -2i$$

Denominator: $1 - i^2 = 1 - (-1) = 2$.

So, $\frac{1-i}{1+i} = \frac{2i}{2} = i$

Step 2: Simplify $\frac{1+i}{1-i}$

$$\frac{1+i}{1-i} = \frac{(1+i)(1+i)}{(1-i)(1+i)} = \frac{(1+i)^2}{1-i^2}$$

Compute numerator:

$$(1 + i)^2 = 1 + 2i + i^2$$
$$= 1 + 2i - 1 = 2i$$

Denominator: $1 - i^2 = 2$.

So, $\dfrac{1+i}{1-i} = \dfrac{2i}{2} = i$

Step 3: Substitute into equation

Given,

$$\left(\frac{1-i}{1+i}\right)^{2m}\left(\frac{1+i}{1-i}\right)^{2n} = 1$$

Becomes, $(-i)^{2m}(i)^{2n} = 1$.

Now, $(-i)^{2m} = ((-i)^2)^m = (-1)^m$,

$i^{2n} = (i^2)^n = (-1)^n$.

Thus equation becomes

$$(-1)^m\,(-1)^n = 1$$
$$(-1)^{m+n} = 1.$$

This is true exactly when $m + n$ is even.

Step 4: Condition on $m - n$

We want smallest positive value of $m - n$.

Since $m + n$ is even, both m, n are both even or both odd.

Thus their difference $m - n$ is always even.

Smallest positive even number = 2.

14. The system is:

$$x + y + z = 7,$$
$$x + 2y + 3z = 16,$$
$$x + 3y + 4z = 22.$$

The coefficient determinant D is:

$$D = \begin{vmatrix} 1 & 1 & 1 \\ 1 & 2 & 3 \\ 1 & 3 & 4 \end{vmatrix}$$

To find D_2 (the determinant for y in Cramer's rule), replace the second column with the constants 7, 16, 22:

$$D_2 = \begin{vmatrix} 1 & 7 & 1 \\ 1 & 16 & 3 \\ 1 & 22 & 4 \end{vmatrix}$$

Now compute this determinant:

$$D_2 = 1\begin{vmatrix} 16 & 3 \\ 22 & 4 \end{vmatrix} - 7\begin{vmatrix} 1 & 3 \\ 1 & 4 \end{vmatrix} + 1\begin{vmatrix} 1 & 16 \\ 1 & 22 \end{vmatrix}$$

Compute each 2×2 determinant:

1. $\begin{vmatrix} 16 & 3 \\ 22 & 4 \end{vmatrix} = 16 \cdot 4 - 3 \cdot 22$

$= 64 - 66 = -2.$

2. $\begin{vmatrix} 1 & 3 \\ 1 & 4 \end{vmatrix} = 1 \cdot 4 - 3 \cdot 1$

$= 4 - 3 = 1.$

3. $\begin{vmatrix} 1 & 16 \\ 1 & 22 \end{vmatrix} = 1 \cdot 22 - 16 \cdot 1$

$= 22 - 16 = 6.$

Now substitute:

$$D_2 = 1(-2) - 7(1) + 1(6)$$
$$= -2 - 7 + 6 = -3.$$

15. We check each statement for non-singular matrices A and B.

Statement I: $(AB)^{-1} = A^{-1}\,B^{-1}$

The correct inverse rule is:

$$(AB)^{-1} = B^{-1}\,A^{-1}$$

So, the statement given in the question is incorrect.

Statement II: $(BA)(AB)^{-1} = I$

$$(BA)(AB)^{-1} = BA(B^{-1}\,A^{-1}) = B(AB^{-1})A^{-1}$$

There is no simplification that turns this into the identity matrix.

In fact, $(BA)(AB)^{-1} \neq I$ in general

So Statement II is false.

Statement III: $(AB)^T = A^T\,B^T$

Transpose reverses the order:

$$(AB)^T = B^T\,A^T$$

The statement claims the reverse, so it is false.

All three statements are wrong.

16. We compare the determinant

$$\begin{vmatrix} a & b & c \\ l & m & n \\ p & q & r \end{vmatrix}$$

with the given options.

A determinant changes sign when any two rows are interchanged, and it stays the same only if the rows are cyclically permuted in the same order.

The original row order is:

$$R_1 = (a\ b\ c),$$
$$R_2 = (l\ m\ n),$$
$$R_3 = (p\ q\ r).$$

A cyclic shift downward gives:

$$\begin{vmatrix} p & q & r \\ a & b & c \\ l & m & n \end{vmatrix}$$

This is a cyclic permutation ($1 \to 2$, $2 \to 3$, $3 \to 1$), which does not change the determinant value.

Check the options:

Option C: $\begin{vmatrix} p & q & r \\ a & b & c \\ l & m & n \end{vmatrix}$

This exactly matches the required cyclic order, so it has identical value to the original determinant.

Check other options quickly:

- Option A swaps rows 2 and 3 → determinant changes sign → NOT equal.
- Option B changes first row → not a simple cyclic shift → NOT equal.
- Option D changes positions of entries in each row → NOT equal.

So, only Option C matches exactly the determinant's value.

17. Given 1, ω, ω^2 are cube roots of unity, so

$$\omega^3 = 1,\ 1 + \omega + \omega^2 = 0,\ \omega \neq 1.$$

We have,

$$x = a + b,\ y = a\omega + b\omega^2,\ z = a\omega^2 + b\omega.$$

Consider: $x^2 + y^2 + z$.

First compute x^2, y^2, z^2:

$$x^2 = (a + b)^2 = a^2 + 2ab + b^2,$$
$$y^2 = (a\omega + b\omega^2)^2 = a^2\omega^2 + 2ab\omega^3 + b^2\omega^4,$$
$$z^2 = (a\omega^2 + b\omega)^2 = a^2\omega^4 + 2ab\omega^3 + b^2\omega^2.$$

Use, $\omega^3 = 1 \Rightarrow \omega^4 = \omega$:

$$y^2 = a^2\omega^2 + 2ab + b^2\,\omega,$$
$$z^2 = a^2\omega + 2ab + b^2\omega^2.$$

Now sum: $x^2 + y^2 + z^2$

$$= (a^2 + 2ab + b^2) + (a^2\omega^2 + 2ab + b^2\omega) + (a^2\omega + 2ab + b^2\omega^2)$$

$$= a^2\,(1 + \omega + \omega^2) + b^2\,(1 + \omega + \omega^2) + 6ab$$

But $1 + \omega + \omega^2 = 0$, hence:

$$x^2 + y^2 + z^2 = 0 + 0 + 6ab = 6ab.$$

18. We form 4-digit numbers using digits {1, 2, 3, 4} without repetition, and require divisibility by 4.

A number is divisible by 4 if its last two digits form a 2-digit number divisible by 4.

List all 2-digit numbers from digits 1,2,3,4 with no repetition and check divisibility by 4:

12, 13, 14, 21, 23, 24, 31, 32, 34, 41, 42, 43.

Test each for divisibility by 4:

$12 \equiv 0(\text{mod}4)$, $24 \equiv 0(\text{mod}4)$, $32 \equiv 0(\text{mod}4)$,

all others are not divisible by 4.

So valid ending pairs are: 12, 24, 32.

For each such pair, the first two (thousands and hundreds) digits must be the remaining two distinct digits, and can be arranged in 2! ways.

Thus, for each of the 3 valid endings we get 2 numbers:

$$\text{Total numbers} = 3 \times 2 = 6.$$

19. Determinant is

$$\Delta = \begin{vmatrix} p+c & a & b \\ c & p+a & b \\ c & a & p+b \end{vmatrix},$$

where $p = a + b + c$.

Apply row operations:

$R_2 \to R_2 - R_1$, $R_3 \to R_3 - R_1$.

Then

$$\Delta = \begin{vmatrix} p+c & a & b \\ c-(p+c) & (p+a)-a & b-b \\ c-(p+c) & a-a & (p+b)-b \end{vmatrix}$$

$$= \begin{vmatrix} p+c & a & b \\ -p & p & 0 \\ -p & 0 & p \end{vmatrix}$$

Factor p from the second and third rows:

$$\Delta = p^2\begin{vmatrix} p+c & a & b \\ -1 & 1 & 0 \\ -1 & 0 & 1 \end{vmatrix}$$

Now compute the remaining 3 × 3 determinant:

$$p^2\begin{vmatrix} p+c & a & b \\ -1 & 1 & 0 \\ -1 & 0 & 1 \end{vmatrix}$$

$$= (p+c)\begin{vmatrix} 1 & 0 \\ 0 & 1 \end{vmatrix} - a\begin{vmatrix} -1 & 0 \\ -1 & 1 \end{vmatrix} + b\begin{vmatrix} -1 & 1 \\ -1 & 0 \end{vmatrix}$$

Compute each minor:

$$\begin{vmatrix} 1 & 0 \\ 0 & 1 \end{vmatrix} = 1, \begin{vmatrix} -1 & 0 \\ -1 & 1 \end{vmatrix} = (-1)\cdot 1 - 0\cdot(-1) = -1$$

$$\begin{vmatrix} -1 & 0 \\ -1 & 1 \end{vmatrix} = (-1)\cdot 0 - 1\cdot(-1) = 1.$$

So,

$$\begin{vmatrix} p+c & a & b \\ -1 & 1 & 0 \\ -1 & 0 & 1 \end{vmatrix} = (p + c)\cdot 1 - a\cdot(-1) + b\cdot 1$$

$$= p + c + a + b$$

Since, $p = a + b + c$,

$$p + c + a + b = (a + b + c) + (a + b + c)$$
$$= 2p.$$

Thus, $\Delta = p^2\cdot 2p = 2p^3$.

20. In the binomial expansion of $(1 + x)^{100}$, the coefficient of x^k is

$$\binom{100}{k}$$

The sequence $\binom{100}{0}, \binom{100}{1}, \ldots, \binom{100}{100}$ is symmetric and strictly increases up to the middle (for even 100) and then decreases. Thus the greatest binomial coefficient occurs at

$$k = \frac{100}{2} = 50$$

Hence, the largest coefficient is that of x^{50}.

21. Let, $L = \log_{0.5}(a^2)$, $L > 0$.

The quadratic equation is $x^2 + Lx - 2L^2 = 0$.

Using the quadratic formula,

$$x = \frac{-L \pm \sqrt{L^2 - 4\cdot 1\cdot(-2L^2)}}{2}$$

$$= \frac{-L \pm \sqrt{L^2 + 8L^2}}{2}$$

$$= \frac{-L \pm \sqrt{9L^2}}{2} = \frac{-L \pm 3L}{2}$$

So the two roots are

$$x_1 = \frac{-L + 3L}{2} = \frac{2L}{2} = L$$

$$x_2 = \frac{-L - 3L}{2} = \frac{-4L}{2} = -2L$$

Since L > 0, the greater root is

$$\beta = L = \log_{0.5}(a^2).$$

22. From the roots found above,

$$\beta = L, \alpha = -2L.$$

Thus, $\alpha = -2L = -2\beta.$

23. Let, $p = \sum_{j=1}^{n} \log_{10} 2^j,\ q = \sum_{j=1}^{n} \log_{10} 5^j$

First simplify p and q

$$\log_{10} 2^j = j \log_{10} 2,$$
$$\log_{10} 5^j = j \log_{10} 5.$$

So, $p = \log_{10} 2 \sum_{j=1}^{n} j = \log_{10} 2 . \frac{n(n+1)}{2}$

$$q = \log_{10} 5 . \frac{n(n+1)}{2}$$

Hence, $p + q = \frac{n(n+1)}{2}(\log_{10} 2 + \log_{10} 5)$

$$= \frac{n(n+1)}{2}\log_{10}(10) = \frac{n(n+1)}{2}$$

Given $p + q = 66$:

$$\frac{n(n+1)}{2} = 66 \Rightarrow n(n+1) = 132.$$

Check integer n:

$$11 \cdot 12 = 132 \Rightarrow n = 11.$$

This satisfies $9 < n < 12$.

24. With the same p, q, we already have

$$p + q = \frac{n(n+1)}{2}$$

Given $p + q = 15$:

$$\frac{n(n+1)}{2} = 15 \Rightarrow n(n+1) = 30 \Rightarrow n = 5.$$

Let, $S = \frac{n(n+1)}{2} = 15.$

Then, $p = S \log_{10} 2,\ q = S \log_{10} 5.$

So, $q - p = S(\log_{10} 5 - \log_{10} 2)$

$$= S \log_{10}\left(\frac{5}{2}\right) = 15 \log_{10} 2.5$$

For Qs. No. 25-26:

Let $\sin A + \sin B = p$ and $\cos A + \cos B = q$.

Use sum identities:

$$\sin A + \sin B = 2\sin\frac{A+B}{2}\cos\frac{A-B}{2}$$

$$\cos A + \cos B = 2\cos\frac{A+B}{2}\cos\frac{A-B}{2}$$

So, $p = 2\sin\frac{A+B}{2}\cos\frac{A-B}{2}$

$$q = 2\cos\frac{A+B}{2}\cos\frac{A-B}{2}$$

25. $\frac{p}{q} = \frac{2\sin\frac{A+B}{2}\cos\frac{A-B}{2}}{2\cos\frac{A+B}{2}\cos\frac{A-B}{2}}$

$$= \tan\frac{A+B}{2}.$$

26. Compute: $p^2 = 4\sin^2\frac{A+B}{2}\cos^2\frac{A-B}{2}$

$$q^2 = 4\cos^2\frac{A+B}{2}\cos^2\frac{A-B}{2}$$

Then, $p^2 - q^2 = 4\cos^2\frac{A-B}{2}\left(\sin^2\frac{A+B}{2} - \cos^2\frac{A+B}{2}\right)$

$$p^2 + q^2 = 4\cos^2\frac{A-B}{2}\left(\sin^2\frac{A+B}{2} + \cos^2\frac{A+B}{2}\right)$$

$$= 4\cos^2\frac{A-B}{2}$$

Hence, $\frac{p^2 - q^2}{p^2 + q^2} = \sin^2\frac{A+B}{2} - \cos^2\frac{A+B}{2}$

$$= -\left(\cos^2\frac{A+B}{2} - \sin^2\frac{A+B}{2}\right)$$

$$= -\cos(A + B).$$

Using $\cos(\pi - \theta) = -\cos\theta$:

$$\frac{p^2 - q^2}{p^2 + q^2} = \cos(\pi - (A + B)).$$

$$= \cos(\pi - A - B).$$

27. Given, $p = \csc 20°,\ q = \csc 70°$

We use the identity

$$\csc(90° - \theta) = \sec\theta$$

Thus, $q = \csc 70° = \csc(90° - 20°)$

$$= \sec 20°$$

Now evaluate,

$$\frac{\sqrt{3}p}{4} - \frac{q}{4} = \frac{1}{4}(\sqrt{3}\csc 20° - \sec 20°)$$

Rewrite in terms of sin 20° and cos 20°:

$$= \frac{1}{4}\left(\frac{\sqrt{3}}{\sin 20°} - \frac{1}{\cos 20°}\right)$$

$$= \frac{1}{4}\left(\frac{\sqrt{3}\cos 20° - \sin 20°}{\sin 20° \cos 20°}\right)$$

Check the numerator:

$$\sqrt{3}\cos 20° - \sin 20° = 2\left(\frac{\sqrt{3}}{2}\cos 20° - \frac{1}{2}\sin 20°\right)$$

$$= 2\cos(20° + 30°) = 2\cos 50°.$$

Thus expression becomes:

$$\frac{1}{4}.\frac{2\cos 50°}{\sin 20° \cos 20°}$$

Use sin 20° = cos 70°. And note:

cos 50° = sin 40°,

sin 40° = 2sin 20° cos 20°

Thus, numerator becomes exactly the denominator:

$$\frac{2\cos 50°}{4\sin 20° \cos 20°} = \frac{2(2\sin 20° \cos 20°)}{4\sin 20° \cos 20°} = 1.$$

28. We need $\frac{p^2+q^2}{p^2q^2}$

Rewrite as: $\frac{1}{q^2}+\frac{1}{p^2} = \sin^2 70° + \sin^2 20°$

Now compute:

$$\sin^2 70° = \sin^2 (90° - 20°) = \cos^2 20°$$

So, $\sin^2 20° + \cos^2 20° = 1$.

Thus, $\frac{p^2+q^2}{p^2q^2} = 1.$

29. Given, $\cos (2x + 3y) = \frac{1}{2}$, $-\pi < 2x + 3y < \pi$

Inside this interval,

$$\cos \theta = \frac{1}{2} \text{ has solutions } \theta = \pm\frac{\pi}{3}$$

Thus, $2x + 3y = \frac{\pi}{3}$ or $2x + 3y = -\frac{\pi}{3}$

Similarly,

$$\cos (3x + 2y) = \frac{\sqrt{3}}{2}, \quad -\pi < 3x + 2y < \pi$$

Solutions: $3x + 2y = \pm\frac{\pi}{6}$

We now solve all possible pairs:

$$(2x + 3y, 3x + 2y) = \left(\pm\frac{\pi}{3}, \pm\frac{\pi}{6}\right)$$

There are 4 possible sign combinations, hence 4 possible $(x + y)$ values.

30. Same pairs from Q29:

$$(2x + 3y, 3x + 2y) = \left(\pm\frac{\pi}{3}, \pm\frac{\pi}{6}\right)$$

We find $y - x$:

Solve the system:

$2x + 3y = A$,

$3x + 2y = B$

Subtract:

$(3x + 2y) - (2x + 3y) = B - A$

$x - y = B - A$

Thus, $y - x = A - B$

Now evaluate for all 4 cases:

1. $A = \frac{\pi}{3}, B = \frac{\pi}{6}$:

$$y - x = \frac{\pi}{3} - \frac{\pi}{6} = \frac{\pi}{6}$$

2. $A = \frac{\pi}{3}, B = -\frac{\pi}{6}$:

$$y - x = \frac{\pi}{3} + \frac{\pi}{6} = \frac{\pi}{2}$$

3. $A = -\frac{\pi}{3}, B = \frac{\pi}{6}$:

$$y - x = -\frac{\pi}{3} - \frac{\pi}{6} = -\frac{\pi}{2}$$

4. $A = -\frac{\pi}{3}, B = -\frac{\pi}{6}$:

$$y - x = -\frac{\pi}{3} + \frac{\pi}{6} = -\frac{\pi}{6}$$

Thus we get four distinct values.

31. The given equation is

$$abx^2 + bcx + ca = cax^2 + abx + bc$$

Bring all terms to the left to get a standard quadratic in x:

$abx^2 - cax^2 + bcx - abx + ca - bc = 0$

$\Rightarrow (ab - ca)x^2 + (bc - ab)x + (ca - bc) = 0$

So, $A = ab - ca$, $B = bc - ab$, $C = ca - bc$

For equal roots, the discriminant must be zero:

$$\Delta = B^2 - 4AC = 0$$

Compute:

$B^2 = (bc - ab)^2 = b^2 (c - a)^2$,

$4AC = 4(ab - ca)(ca - bc)$

$= 4a(b - c) \cdot c(a - b) = 4ac(b - c)(a - b)$

So, $B^2 - 4AC = b^2 (c - a)^2 - 4ac(b - c)(a - b)$

Factoring this expression gives

$B^2 - 4AC = (ab - 2ac + bc)^2$

Thus $\Delta = 0$ implies

$ab - 2ac + bc = 0.$

Divide by abc (assuming $a, b, c \neq 0$):

$$\frac{ab}{abc} - 2\frac{ac}{abc} + \frac{bc}{abc} = 0$$

$$\Rightarrow \quad \frac{1}{c} - 2\frac{1}{b} + \frac{1}{a} = 0$$

$$\Rightarrow \quad \frac{1}{a} + \frac{1}{c} = \frac{2}{b}$$

This matches option D.

32. From Q31, the condition for equal roots is

$$\Rightarrow \quad \frac{1}{a} + \frac{1}{c} = \frac{2}{b}$$

Rewrite as, $\frac{2}{b} = \frac{1}{a} + \frac{1}{c} = 2.\frac{\frac{1}{a}+\frac{1}{c}}{2}$

So, $$\frac{1}{b} = \frac{\frac{1}{a}+\frac{1}{c}}{2}$$

i.e. $\frac{1}{b}$ is the arithmetic mean of $\frac{1}{a}$ and $\frac{1}{c}$.

That means $\frac{1}{a}, \frac{1}{b}, \frac{1}{c}$

are in A.P., hence a, b, c are in harmonic progression (H.P.).

33. We are given that the sums of two arithmetic progressions are equal:

$6 + 10 + 14 + \ldots$ (up to m terms)

$= 1 + 3 + 5 + \ldots$ (up to n terms)

Left side is an A.P. with first term $a_1 = 6$ and common difference $d_1 = 4$.

Sum of m terms:

$$S_1 = \frac{m}{2}[2a_1 + (m-1)d_1] = \frac{m}{2}[2\cdot 6 + (m-1)\cdot 4]$$

$$= \frac{m}{2}[12 + 4m - 4] = \frac{m}{2}(4m+8)$$

$$= 2m(m + 2)$$

Right side is the sum of first n odd numbers, which is

$S_2 = n^2$

Given $S_1 = S_2$, we get

$n^2 = 2m(m + 2)$

This matches option D.

34. We must find how many integer values of m (with $1 \le m < 25$) satisfy

$$n^2 = 2m(m + 2),\ 1 \le n < 25.$$

Rewrite: $$n^2 = 2(m^2 + 2m) = 2[(m + 1)^2 - 1]$$
$$= 2(m + 1)^2 - 2$$

So, $n^2 - 2(m + 1)^2 = -2$

Let $x = n$, $y = m + 1$. Then

$$x^2 - 2y^2 = -2$$

We look for integer solutions with $1 \le x < 25$ and $1 \le y < 26$.

Try small integer m directly (equivalently small $y = m + 1$):

- $m = 2$:

  $n^2 = 2 \cdot 2 \cdot (2 + 2) = 16 \Rightarrow n = 4$(valid, $n < 25$)

- $m = 16$:

  $n^2 = 2 \cdot 16 \cdot (16 + 2) = 32 \cdot 18 = 576$

$\Rightarrow n = 24$(valid, $n < 25$)

Check that no other $m \in [1, 24]$ works:

For $m = 1, 3, 4, \ldots, 15, 17, \ldots, 24$, the values $2m(m + 2)$ are not perfect squares (they lie strictly between consecutive squares), and for $m \ge 17$,

$2m(m + 2) > 25^2 = 625$, which violates $n < 25$.

Thus the only allowed pairs are:

$(m, n) = (2, 4), (16, 24)$.

So exactly two values of m are possible.

35. Total triplets from 8 points:

$$\binom{8}{3} = 56$$

Degenerate (collinear) triplets from the 4 collinear points:

$$\binom{4}{3} = 4$$

Valid triangles: $56 - 4 = 52$.

36. Number of quadrilaterals

Total ways to choose 4 points from 8:

$$\binom{8}{4} = 70$$

Invalid selection: all 4 points chosen from the 4 collinear points:

$$\binom{4}{4} = 1$$

Valid quadrilaterals:

$$70 - 1 = 69.$$

37. Given: $$f(x) = ax^2 + bx + c,$$
$$f(1) = f(4) = 2$$

So 1 and 4 give the same function value

$\Rightarrow$ the axis of symmetry is at:

$$x = \frac{1+4}{2} = 2.5$$

Given 2 is a root. Let the other root be r.

Axis of symmetry for a quadratic is:

$$x = \frac{2+r}{2} = 2.5$$

Solve: $$\frac{2+r}{2} = 2.5$$

$\Rightarrow$ $$2 + r = 5 \Rightarrow r = 3.$$

38. We have: $f(1) = 2$, $f(4) = 2$.

Also roots are 2 and 3.

Thus: $f(x) = k(x - 2)(x - 3)$

Now compute: $f(1) = k(1 - 2)(1 - 3)$
$= k(-1)(-2) = 2k$

Given, $f(1) = 2$: $2k = 2 \Rightarrow k = 1$

Thus: $f(x) = (x - 2)(x - 3) = x^2 - 5x + 6$.

So: $a = 1$, $b = -5$, $c = 6$.

Compute:

$$a + b + c = 1 - 5 + 6 = 2.$$

39. Matrix, $$A = \begin{bmatrix} \cos\theta & \sin\theta \\ -\sin\theta & \cos\theta \end{bmatrix}$$

First find det (A):

$$\det(A) = \cos\theta \cdot \cos\theta - (\sin\theta)(-\sin\theta)$$
$$= \cos^2\theta + \sin^2\theta = 1.$$

Now, $$\det(A^4) = (\det(A))^4 = 1^4 = 1.$$

40. For any invertible matrix A:

$$A^{-1} = \frac{\text{adj}(A)}{\det(A)}$$

$\Rightarrow$ $\quad$ adj (A) = det (A) A^{-1}

Since det (A) = 1:

$$\text{adj}(A) = A^{-1}$$

But for rotation-type matrices:

$$A^{-1} = A^T$$

Thus: $(\text{adj } A)^{-1} = (A^{-1})^{-1} = A.$

41. $(101101101)_2$ and $(100011)_2$ in decimal:

$(101101101)_2 = 256 + 64 + 32 + 8 + 4 + 1 = 365,$

$(100011)_2 = 32 + 2 + 1 = 35.$

Sum in decimal:

$365 + 35 = 400.$

Convert 400 to binary:

$$400 = 256 + 128 + 16$$
$$= 2^8 + 2^7 + 2^4 \Rightarrow (110010000)_2$$

So the correct binary sum is $(110010000)_2$.

42. Set X has $3n$ elements, set Y has $2n$ elements, intersection has n elements.

We need: (X – Y) × (Y – X)

Compute: $|X - Y| = |X| - |X \cap Y|$

$= 3n - n = 2n$

$|Y - X| = |Y| - |X \cap Y|$

$= 2n - n = n$

Thus: $|(X - Y) \times (Y - X)| = (2n)(n) = 2n^2$.

43. Given: $A = \{-3, -2, -1, 0, 1, 2, 3\}$,

$B = \{0, 1, 4, 9\}$.

Relation: $R = \{(x, y): |x| < y\}$.

We count the number of pairs (x, y) with $x \in A$, $y \in B$

Check each y:

For $y = 0$: Condition $|x| < 0$ impossible.

Contribute 0 pairs.

For $y = 1$:

$|x| < 1 \Rightarrow x = 0$

So: (0, 1).

Contribute 1 pair.

For $y = 4$:

$|x| < 4 \Rightarrow x = -3, -2, -1, 0, 1, 2, 3$

All 7 values of A.

Contribute 7 pairs.

For $y = 9$:

$|x| < 9 \Rightarrow$ all 7 elements of A.

Contribute 7 pairs.

Total = 0 + 1 + 7 + 7 = 15.

44. Statement-I: For an $n \times n$ matrix X,

$\det(mX) = m^n \det(X)$

Statement-II: If Y is obtained from X by multiplying any one row or one column by m, then

$\det(Y) = m \det(X)$.

Statement-II is a basic determinant property: scaling a single row (or column) by m multiplies the determinant by m.

To get mX from X, we multiply all n rows (or all n columns) by m, one at a time.

Each row scaling multiplies the determinant by m.

After n such operations, the determinant is multiplied by m^n.

Thus: $\det(mX) = m^n \det(X)$.

So Statement-I is true, Statement-II is true, and Statement-II explains how Statement-I arises.

45. $M = \begin{bmatrix} 71 & 23 & 48 \\ 57 & 28 & 29 \\ 65 & 17 & 48 \end{bmatrix}$

Compute det (M):

$\det(M) = 71(28 \cdot 48 - 29 \cdot 17) - 23(57 \cdot 48 - 29 \cdot 65) + 48(57 \cdot 17 - 28 \cdot 65)$

$= 71(1344 - 493) - 23(2736 - 1885) + 48(969 - 1820)$

$= 71(851) - 23(851) + 48(-851)$

$= 851(71 - 23 - 48) = 851(0) = 0$

So determinant is zero $\Rightarrow$ matrix is singular $\Rightarrow$ inverse does not exist.

Statement – I: True.

Statement – II: False (a non – singular matrix has non – zero determinant).

Correct option C: Statement – I is correct but Statement – II is not correct.

46. $\cos^{-1} 9 + \csc^{-1}\left(\frac{\sqrt{41}}{4}\right)$

Let $\theta = \cot^{-1} 9$.

Then $\cot\theta = 9 = \frac{\text{adj}}{\text{opp}}$

Take legs: opposite = 1, adjacent = 9.

Hypotenuse: $\frac{\text{adj}}{\text{opp}} = \sqrt{1^2 + 9^2} = \sqrt{82}$

Now let $\phi = \csc^{-1}\left(\frac{\sqrt{41}}{4}\right)$

$\csc\phi = \frac{\sqrt{41}}{4} \Rightarrow \sin\phi = \frac{4}{\sqrt{41}}$

Draw a right triangle: opposite = 4, hypotenuse = $\sqrt{41}$,

adjacent $= \sqrt{41 - 16} = \sqrt{25} = 5$

Compute angles:

$\theta = \cot^{-1} 9,$

$\phi = \sin^{-1}\left(\frac{4}{\sqrt{41}}\right)$

Check if $\theta + \phi = \pi/2$:

$\tan\theta = \frac{1}{9}, \tan\phi = \frac{4}{5}$

$$\tan(\theta + \phi) = \frac{\tan\theta + \tan\phi}{1 - \tan\theta\tan\phi}$$

$$= \frac{\frac{1}{9}+\frac{4}{5}}{1-\frac{4}{45}} = \frac{\frac{5+36}{45}}{\frac{41}{45}} = \frac{\frac{41}{45}}{\frac{41}{45}} = 1$$

So: $\tan(\theta + \phi) = 1 \Rightarrow \theta + \phi = \frac{\pi}{4}.$

47. Solve simultaneously:

$$\cot\theta = -\sqrt{3}, \ \csc\theta = -2$$

From $\csc\theta = -2$:

$$\sin\theta = -\frac{1}{2}$$

Solutions in $-\pi < \theta < \pi$:

$$\theta = -\frac{\pi}{6}, -\frac{5\pi}{6}$$

Check $\cot\theta = -\sqrt{3}$:

$$\cot\left(-\frac{\pi}{6}\right) = -\sqrt{3} \text{ (OK)}$$

$$\cot\left(-\frac{5\pi}{6}\right) = +\sqrt{3} \text{ (Not OK)}$$

Only one value satisfies both.

48. $$x + \frac{1}{x} = 2\cos\theta$$

Cube both sides:

$$x^3 + \frac{1}{x^3} + 3\left(x+\frac{1}{x}\right)\left(x+\frac{1}{x}\right) = (2\cos\theta)^3$$

Using identity:

$$x^3 + \frac{1}{x^3} = \left(x+\frac{1}{x}\right)^3 - 3\left(x+\frac{1}{x}\right)$$

$$= (2\cos\theta)^3 - 3(2\cos\theta)$$

$$= 8\cos^3\theta - 6\cos\theta$$

$$= 2(4\cos^3\theta - 3\cos\theta)$$

$$= 2\cos 3\theta.$$

49. Solve: $\tan x + \sec x = 2\cos x$, $0 \le x \le \pi/2$

Use: $$\tan x = \frac{\sin x}{\cos x}, \ \sec x = \frac{1}{\cos x}$$

Multiply both sides by $\cos x$:

$$\sin x + 1 = 2\cos^2 x$$

$$\sin x + 1 = 2(1 - \sin^2 x)$$

$$\sin x + 1 = 2 - 2\sin^2 x$$

$$2\sin^2 x + \sin x - 1 = 0$$

Let $t = \sin x$. Solve:

$$2t^2 + t - 1 = 0$$

$$t = \frac{-1 \pm \sqrt{1+8}}{4}$$

$$t = \frac{-1 \pm 3}{4}$$

$$t = \frac{1}{2}, \ t = -1$$

$\sin x = -1$ is outside the interval $0 \le x \le \pi/2$.
Only $\sin x = 1/2$ works $\to x = \pi/6$ (valid).
Only one value.

50. $\tan\left[\frac{1}{2}\sec^{-1}\left(\frac{2}{\sqrt{3}}\right)\right]$

Let $$\theta = \sec^{-1}\left(\frac{2}{\sqrt{3}}\right)$$

Then: $$\sec\theta = \frac{2}{\sqrt{3}} \Rightarrow \cos\theta = \frac{\sqrt{3}}{2}$$

$$\theta = \frac{\pi}{6}$$

Now compute:

$$\tan\left(\frac{\theta}{2}\right) = \tan\left(\frac{\pi}{12}\right)$$

$$\tan\frac{\pi}{12} = 2 - \sqrt{3}.$$

51. The line of intersection of
$6x + 4y - 5z = 2$ and $x - 2y + 3z = 0$
has direction ratios equal to the cross – product of their normals:

$$n_1 = \langle 6, 4, -5\rangle$$

$$n_2 = \langle 1, -2, 3\rangle$$

$$n_1 \times n_2 = \begin{vmatrix} i & j & k \\ 6 & 4 & -5 \\ 1 & -2 & 3 \end{vmatrix}$$

$= \langle (4 \cdot 3 - (-5)(-2)), -(6 \cdot 3 - (-5)(1)), 6(-2) - 4(1)\rangle$
$= \langle 12 - 10, -(18 + 5), -12 - 4\rangle = \langle 2, -23, -16\rangle.$

52. Let plane P contain the line of intersection of
$6x + 4y - 5z = 2$ and $x - 2y + 3z = 0$
Write both as
L_1: $6x + 4y - 5z - 2 = 0$,
L_2: $x - 2y + 3z = 0$
Any plane containing their line of intersection is

$$L_1 + \lambda L_2 = 0$$

$(6x + 4y - 5z - 2) + \lambda(x - 2y + 3z) = 0$
$(6 + \lambda)x + (4 - 2\lambda)y + (-5 + 3\lambda)z - 2 = 0.$

So a normal to P is $\bar{N} = \langle 6 + \lambda, 4 - 2\lambda, -5 + 3\lambda\rangle$

Plane P is parallel to a line with direction ratios $\langle 1, 3, 2\rangle$. For a plane to be parallel to a line, its normal vector must be perpendicular to the line's direction vector, so
$\bar{N} \cdot \langle 1,3,2\rangle = 0.$

Hence,
$(6 + \lambda) \cdot 1 + (4 - 2\lambda) \cdot 3 + (-5 + 3\lambda) \cdot 2 = 0$

$6 + \lambda + 12 - 6\lambda - 10 + 6\lambda = 0$

$\lambda + 8 = 0 \Rightarrow \lambda = -8$

Substitute $\lambda = -8$ back:

$(6 - 8)x + (4 + 16)y + (-5 - 24)z - 2 = 0$

$-2x + 20y - 29z - 2 = 0.$

Multiply by -1:

$2x - 20y + 29z + 2 = 0.$

53. Smallest sphere through A(1, 0, 0), B(0, 1, 0), C(0, 0, 1) is the sphere for which these points lie on the sphere and whose center is equidistant from A, B, C.

$$\text{Distance AB} = \sqrt{\left[(1-0)^2+(0-1)^2\right]} = \sqrt{2}$$

$$\text{BC} = \sqrt{2},\ \text{CA} = \sqrt{2}$$

$\rightarrow$ Equilateral triangle of side $\sqrt{2}$ in 3D.

Circumradius R of an equilateral triangle $= \dfrac{a}{\sqrt{3}}$

$$\Rightarrow \quad R = \frac{\sqrt{2}}{\sqrt{3}} = \sqrt{\frac{2}{3}}$$

But center is inside the plane $x + y + z = 1$, so radius is distance from center to A etc.

$$\text{Correct radius} = \sqrt{\frac{2}{3}}$$

Closest option is $\dfrac{\sqrt{2}}{\sqrt{3}}$ which equals $\sqrt{\dfrac{2}{3}}$.

54. Coordinates of circumcenter of triangle A,B,C are proportional to (1, 1, 1).

Since centroid and circumcenter coincide for an equilateral triangle in 3D plane $x + y + z = 1$.

Hence center lies on plane: $x + y + z = 1$.

Answer: A. $x + y + z - 1 = 0$.

55. For parallelogram ABCD:

$$D = A + C - B.$$

A(1, –1, 0), B(–2, 1, 8), C(–1, 2, 7):

$D = (1 + (-1) - (-2), -1 + 2 - 1, 0 + 7 - 8)$

$= (0 + 2, 1 - 1, -1)$

$= (2, 0, -1).$

56. Angle BCD $\Rightarrow$ use vectors CB and CD.

C(–1, 2, 7); B(–2, 1, 8); D(2, 0, –1)

$$CB = B - C = (-1, -1, 1)$$

$$CD = D - C = (3, -2, -8)$$

$$\cos\theta = (CB \cdot CD)/(|CB||CD|)$$

$$CB \cdot CD = (-1)(3) + (-1)(-2) + 1(-8)$$

$$= -3 + 2 - 8 = -9$$

$$|CB|^2 = 1 + 1 + 1 = 3$$

$$|CD|^2 = 9 + 4 + 64 = 77$$

$$\cos^2\theta = \frac{(-9)^2}{(3\times 77)} = \frac{81}{231} = \frac{27}{77}.$$

57. Rewrite: $\quad 4y = mx - m + 2$

$$\Rightarrow \quad y = \frac{m}{4}x - \frac{m-2}{4}$$

For different values of m, slope is $\dfrac{m}{4}$.

Since slope changes with m, all these lines have different slopes, hence they all meet at one common point.

Find point of concurrency:

Set $x = 1$: $\quad y = \dfrac{m}{4} - \dfrac{m-2}{4} = \dfrac{2}{4} = \dfrac{1}{2}$

So every line passes through point $\left(1, \dfrac{1}{2}\right)$.

Thus they are concurrent lines.

58. Let the variable point be (x, y)

Equidistant from (a, b) and (c, d) means

$(x - a)^2 + (y - b)^2 = (x - c)^2 + (y - d)^2$

Expand: $x^2 - 2ax + a^2 + y^2 - 2by + b^2$

$= x^2 - 2cx + c^2 + y^2 - 2dy + d^2$

Cancel x^2 and y^2:

$-2ax + a^2 - 2by + b^2 = -2cx + c^2 - 2dy + d^2$

Bring all terms to one side:

$-2ax + 2cx - 2by + 2dy + a^2 + b^2 - c^2 - d^2 = 0$

$2(c - a)x + 2(d - b)y + (a^2 + b^2 - c^2 - d^2) = 0.$

Divide by 2:

$$(c-a)x+(d-b)y+\frac{a^2+b^2-c^2-d^2}{2}=0$$

Multiply by -1 to match $(a - c)x + (b - d)y + k = 0$:

$$(a-c)x+(b-d)y+\frac{c^2+d^2-a^2-b^2}{2}=0$$

So, $k = \dfrac{c^2+d^2-a^2-b^2}{2}$.

59. Equation: $\quad x^2 + 3y = 0 \Rightarrow y = -\dfrac{1}{3}x^2$

This is a parabola opening downward, not upward $\rightarrow$ Statement I is false.

Axis is the line $x = 0$ (symmetric about y – axis) $\rightarrow$ Statement II is true.

Latus rectum: For $y = -\dfrac{1}{3}x^2$,

$$4a = -3 \Rightarrow a = -\frac{3}{4}$$

Latus rectum line is

$$y = a = -\frac{3}{4}$$

Given option says $4y - 3 = 0 \Rightarrow y = \dfrac{3}{4}$,

which is incorrect. $\rightarrow$ Statement III is false.

Only statement II is correct.

60. Given line: $\frac{x}{a^2}+\frac{y}{b^2} = \frac{2}{a^2+b^2}$

x-intercept: put $y = 0$:

$$\frac{x}{a^2} = \frac{2}{a^2+b^2}$$

$$\Rightarrow \quad x = \frac{2a^2}{a^2+b^2}$$

y-intercept: put $x = 0$:

$$\frac{y}{b^2} = \frac{2}{a^2+b^2}$$

$$\Rightarrow \quad y = \frac{2b^2}{a^2+b^2}$$

Sum of intercepts:

$$\frac{2a^2}{a^2+b^2}+\frac{2b^2}{a^2+b^2} = \frac{2(a^2+b^2)}{a^2+b^2} = 2.$$

61. Given line: $\sqrt{3x}+2y = 7$

The perpendicular (normal) form of a line is

$x \cos \alpha + y \sin \alpha = p,$

where $(\cos \alpha, \sin \alpha)$ is a unit vector along the normal and p is the perpendicular distance from origin.

For the given line, a normal vector is $(\sqrt{3}, 2)$.

Its magnitude:

$$\sqrt{(\sqrt{3})^2+2^2} = \sqrt{3+4} = \sqrt{7}$$

Divide the equation by $\sqrt{7}$:

$$\frac{\sqrt{3}}{\sqrt{7}}x+\frac{2}{\sqrt{7}}y = \frac{7}{\sqrt{7}} = \sqrt{7}$$

Here $\cos \alpha = \frac{\sqrt{3}}{\sqrt{7}}$, $\sin \alpha = \frac{2}{\sqrt{7}}$ and $p = \sqrt{7}$, so this is exactly the perpendicular (normal) form.

62. Square diagonal is BD between B(2, 3) and D(4, 1).

Length BD:

$$BD = \sqrt{(4-2)^2+(1-3)^2}$$

$$= \sqrt{4+4} = \sqrt{8} = 2\sqrt{2}$$

In a square, diagonal = side × $\sqrt{2}$:

$$s = \frac{2\sqrt{2}}{\sqrt{2}} = 2$$

$$\text{Area} = s^2 = 4.$$

63. First line: $px + qy = p + q$

$\Rightarrow \quad px + qy - (p + q) = 0.$

Second line:

$$p(x - y) + q(x + y) = 2q$$

$$px - py + qx + qy - 2q = 0$$

$$(p + q)x + (q - p)y - 2q = 0.$$

Thus normals are:

$$\vec{n_1} = (p, q),$$

$$\vec{n_2} = (p + q, q - p)$$

Angle between lines = angle between perpendiculars

= angle between normals.

Use, $\quad \sin \theta = \frac{|\vec{n_1} \times \vec{n_2}|}{|\vec{n_1}||\vec{n_2}|}$

In 2D, $|(p)(q - p) - (q)(p + q)|$

$$= |pq - p^2 - pq - q^2|$$

$$= |-(p^2 + q^2)| = p^2 + q^2.$$

Denominator: $|\vec{n_1}| = \sqrt{p^2+q^2}$,

$$|\vec{n_2}| = \sqrt{(p+q)^2+(q-p)^2}$$

Compute:

$$(p + q)^2 + (q - p)^2 = (p^2 + 2pq + q^2) + (q^2 - 2pq + p^2)$$

$$= 2(p^2 + q^2).$$

Thus, $\quad \sin \theta = \frac{p^2+q^2}{\sqrt{p^2+q^2}\sqrt{2(p^2+q^2)}} = \frac{1}{\sqrt{2}}.$

64. Circle: $x^2 + y^2 - 2kx - 2ky + k^2 = 0.$

Center = (k, k)

Radius: $\quad r = \sqrt{k^2-k^2} = 0$

But because the circle touches axes, the center must be at distance k from both axes.

Touching x-axis at P means P = $(k, 0)$.

Touching y-axis at Q means Q = $(0, k)$.

Distance PQ:

$$PQ = \sqrt{(k-0)^2+(0-k)^2}$$

$$= \sqrt{k^2+k^2} = k\sqrt{2}.$$

65. Hyperbola: $x^2 - 4y^2 = 1$

Standard form:

$$\frac{x^2}{1}-\frac{y^2}{1/4} = 1$$

Compare with

$$\frac{x^2}{a^2}-\frac{y^2}{b^2} = 1$$

$$a^2 = 1,\ b^2 = \frac{1}{4}$$

Foci distance = $2c$ where

$$c^2 = a^2 + b^2 = 1+\frac{1}{4} = \frac{5}{4}$$

So, $\quad c = \sqrt{\frac{5}{4}} = \frac{\sqrt{5}}{2}$

Thus, $\quad 2c = \sqrt{5}.$

66.
$$\vec{p} = \vec{a} - \vec{b}$$
$$\vec{q} = \vec{a} + \vec{b}$$
$$\vec{p} \times \vec{q} = (\vec{a} - \vec{b}) \times (\vec{a} + \vec{b})$$
$$= \vec{a} \times \vec{a} + \vec{a} \times \vec{b} - \vec{b} \times \vec{a} - \vec{b} \times \vec{b}$$
$$= \vec{a} \times \vec{b} - (-\vec{a} \times \vec{b}) = 2\vec{a} \times \vec{b}$$

Magnitude:
$$|\vec{p} \times \vec{q}| = 2|\vec{a} \times \vec{b}| = 2|\vec{a}||\vec{b}|\sin\theta$$

Given $|\vec{a}| = 2, |\vec{b}| = 2, \vec{a} \cdot \vec{b} = 2$
$$\cos\theta = \frac{\vec{a} \cdot \vec{b}}{|\vec{a}||\vec{b}|} = \frac{2}{4} = \frac{1}{2}$$
$$\theta = 60°, \ \sin\theta = \frac{\sqrt{3}}{2}$$

Thus, $|\vec{p} \times \vec{q}| = 2 \cdot 2 \cdot 2 \cdot \frac{\sqrt{3}}{2} = 4\sqrt{3}$.

67. Given vectors:
$$\vec{u} = 2\hat{i} - \hat{j} + \hat{k}$$
$$\vec{v} = \hat{i} + \hat{j} + 3\hat{k}$$

Any vector perpendicular to both is a scalar multiple of $\vec{u} \times \vec{v}$

Compute:
$$\vec{u} \times \vec{v} = \begin{vmatrix} i & j & k \\ 2 & -1 & 1 \\ 1 & 1 & 3 \end{vmatrix}$$
$$= \hat{i}(-1)(3) - 1(1) - \hat{j}(2 \cdot 3 - 1 \cdot 1) + \hat{k}(2 \cdot 1 - (-1) \cdot 1)$$
$$= \hat{i}(-3-1) - \hat{j}(6-1) + \hat{k}(2+1) = -4\hat{i} - 5\hat{j} + 3\hat{k}$$

Thus any perpendicular vector is a scalar multiple of (-4, -5, 3)

Now check the options:

I. $4\hat{i} + 5\hat{j} - 3\hat{k}$ = -1 times (-4, -5, 3) → Yes.

II. $-8\hat{i} - 10\hat{j} + 6\hat{k}$ = 2 times (-4, -5, 3) → Yes.

III. $\frac{1}{50}(-4\hat{i} - 5\hat{j} + 3\hat{k})$ = scalar multiple. → Yes.

All three are multiples.

68. Vectors: $\vec{a} = \hat{i} + 2\hat{j} + 3\hat{k}$
$$\vec{b} = 2\hat{i} + \hat{j} + 2\hat{k}$$

Area of parallelogram $= |\vec{a} \times \vec{b}|$
$$\vec{a} \times \vec{b} = \begin{vmatrix} \hat{i} & \hat{j} & \hat{k} \\ 1 & 2 & 3 \\ 2 & 1 & 2 \end{vmatrix}$$
$$= \hat{i}(2 \cdot 2 - 3 \cdot 1) - \hat{j}(1 \cdot 2 - 3 \cdot 2) + \hat{k}(1 \cdot 1 - 2 \cdot 2)$$
$$= \hat{i}(4-3) - \hat{j}(2-6) + \hat{k}(1-4)$$
$$= \hat{i}(1) - \hat{j}(-4) + \hat{k}(-3)$$
$$= \langle 1, 4, -3 \rangle.$$

Magnitude:
$$|\vec{a} \times \vec{b}| = \sqrt{1^2 + 4^2 + (-3)^2}$$
$$= \sqrt{1 + 16 + 9} = \sqrt{26}.$$

69. Position vectors:
$$\overline{OA} = 3\hat{i} + 4\hat{j} - 2\hat{k}$$
$$\overline{OB} = 4\hat{i} - 4\hat{j} - 3\hat{k}$$
$$\overline{OC} = 2\hat{i} - 3\hat{j} + 2\hat{k}$$
$$\overline{OD} = 6\hat{i} - 2\hat{j} + \hat{k}$$

Diagonal AC:
$$\overrightarrow{AC} = \overline{OC} - \overline{OA}$$
$$= (2 - 3, -3 - 4, 2 - (-2))$$
$$= (-1, -7, 4).$$

Diagonal BD:
$$\overline{BD} = \overline{OD} - \overline{OB}$$
$$= (6 - 4, -2 - (-4), 1 - (-3))$$
$$= (2, 2, 4).$$

Angle θ between diagonals satisfies
$$\overrightarrow{AC} \cdot \overrightarrow{BD} = |AC||BD|\cos\theta$$

Dot product:

(-1)(2) + (-7)(2) + 4 · 4 = -2 - 14 + 16 = 0.

So cos θ = 0 ⇒ θ = 90°.

70. Force: $\vec{F} = 2\hat{i} - \lambda\hat{j} + 5\hat{k}$ applied at A(1, 2, 5).

Moment about B(-1, -2, 3):
$$\vec{M} = \vec{r} \times \vec{F}$$

where $\vec{r} = \overline{BA} = \langle 1 - (-1), 2 - (-2), 5 - 3 \rangle$
$$= (2, 4, 2).$$

Compute $\vec{r} \times \vec{F}$:
$$\vec{r} \times \vec{F} = \begin{vmatrix} \hat{i} & \hat{j} & \hat{k} \\ 2 & 4 & 2 \\ 2 & -\lambda & 5 \end{vmatrix}$$
$$= (2\lambda + 20)\hat{i} - 6\hat{j} - (2\lambda + 8)\hat{k}$$

Given moment: $16\hat{i} - 6\hat{j} + 2\lambda\hat{k}$

Match components:

From $\hat{i}$: 2λ + 20 = 16 ⇒ 2λ = -4 ⇒ λ = -2.

Check $\hat{k}$: -(2λ + 8) = 2λ ⇒ -2λ - 8 = 2λ

⇒ -4λ = 8 ⇒ λ = - 2 (consistent).

71. For $x < 0$:

$$f(x) = \frac{1-\cos 2x}{x^2}$$

We need $\lim_{x\to 0^-} f(x)$

Use standard limit $\cos t = 1-\frac{t^2}{2}+0(t)^2$ as $t \to 0$.

Take $t = 2x$:

$$1 - \cos 2x \approx 1-\left(1-\frac{(2x)^2}{2}\right) = 2x^2$$

Thus, $$f(x) \approx \frac{2x^2}{x^2} = 2 \text{ as } x \to 0^-.$$

So the left-hand limit is 2.

72. For $x > 0$:

$$f(x) = \frac{\sqrt{x}}{\sqrt{16+\sqrt{x}}-4}$$

We need $\lim_{x\to 0^+} f(x)$

Let $t = \sqrt{x} \Rightarrow t \to 0^+$. Then

$$f(x) = \frac{t}{\sqrt{16+t}-4}$$

Rationalise denominator:

$$f(x) = \frac{t}{\sqrt{16+t}-4}\cdot\frac{\sqrt{16+t}+4}{\sqrt{16+t}+4}$$

$$= \frac{t\left(\sqrt{16+t}+4\right)}{(16+t)-16} = \frac{t\left(\sqrt{16+t}+4\right)}{t}$$

$$= \sqrt{16+t}+4$$

Now $t \to 0^+ \Rightarrow \sqrt{16+t} \to 4$, so

$$\lim_{x\to 0^+} f(x) = 4 + 4 = 8.$$

73. $f(x) = x|x|$

At $x = -1$, note this point is not where the definition changes (that happens at 0), so limit equals the function's value:

For $x < 0$, $|x| = -x$, hence

$$f(x) = x(-x) = -x^2$$

Thus, $$\lim_{x\to -1} f(x) = f(-1) = -(-1)^2 = -1.$$

74. We want area bounded by $y = f(x) = x|x|$, the x-axis, and lines $x = -2$ and $x = 1$

For $x < 0$: $|x| = -x$

$\Rightarrow$ $f(x) = -x^2$ (below x-axis)

For $x \geq 0$: $|x| = x$

$\Rightarrow$ $f(x) = x^2$ (above x-axis)

$$\text{Area} = \int_{-2}^{0}|f(x)|\,dx + \int_{0}^{1}|f(x)|\,dx$$

For $-2 \leq x < 0$,

$|f(x)| = x^2$; for $0 \leq x \leq 1$,

$|f(x)| = x^2$

$$\int_{-2}^{0} x^2 dx = \left[\frac{x^3}{3}\right]_{-2}^{0} = 0-\frac{-8}{3} = \frac{8}{3}$$

$$\int_{0}^{1} x^2 dx = \left[\frac{x^3}{3}\right]_{0}^{1} = \frac{1}{3}$$

$$\text{Total area} = \frac{8}{3}+\frac{1}{3} = \frac{9}{3} = 3.$$

75. Here $f(x) = x|x|$

For $x < 0$: $|x| = -x$

$\Rightarrow$ $f(x) = x(-x) = -x^2$

Then $f'(x) = -2x$.

For all $x < 0$, $-2x > 0$, so f is increasing on $(-\infty, 0)$

For $x > 0$: $|x| = x \Rightarrow f(x) = x^2$

Then $f'(x) = 2x > 0$ for $x > 0$,

so f is increasing on $(0, \infty)$.

At $x = 0$, for any $x_1 < x_2$ with $x_1 < 0 < x_2$,

we have $$f(x) = -x_1^2 < 0 = f(0) \leq x_2^2 = f(x_2)$$

Hence f is increasing on $(-\infty, \infty)$. So Statement I is true.

Differentiability at 0:

Left derivative: for $x < 0$,

$$f'(x) = -2x \Rightarrow f_-'(0) = 0$$

Right derivative: for $x > 0$,

$$f'(x) = 2x \Rightarrow f_+'(0) = 0$$

Both one-sided derivatives equal and f is continuous at 0, so f is differentiable at 0. Statement II is also true.

76. $$f(x) = \frac{x}{1-x}$$

First compute $f(x + 1)$:

$$f(x+1) = \frac{x+1}{1-(x+1)} = \frac{x+1}{-x} = -\frac{x+1}{x}$$

Now, $$\frac{f(x)}{f(x+1)} = \frac{\frac{x}{1-x}}{-\frac{x+1}{x}} = \frac{x}{1-x}\cdot\frac{-x}{x+1}$$

$$= -\frac{x^2}{(1-x)(x+1)}$$

But, $$f(x^2) = \frac{x^2}{1-x^2} = \frac{x^2}{(1-x)(1+x)}$$

Thus, $$\frac{f(x)}{f(x+1)} = -f(x^2).$$

77. We need $(1-x)f\left(\sqrt{x}\right)+xf\left(\sqrt{x}+1\right)$ for $x > 0$

Let $t = \sqrt{x} \Rightarrow t > 0$, $x = t^2$

Then, $$f(t) = \frac{t}{1-t},$$

$$f(t+1) = \frac{t+1}{1-(t+1)} = \frac{t+1}{-t} = -\frac{t+1}{t}$$

Expression: $(1-x)f\left(\sqrt{x}\right)+xf\left(\sqrt{x}+1\right)$

$$= (1-t^2)\frac{t}{1-t}+t^2\left(-\frac{t+1}{t}\right)$$

First term: $1 - t^2 = (1-t)(1+t)$, so

$$(1-t^2)\frac{t}{1-t} = (1-t)(1+t)\frac{t}{1-t}$$

$$= t(1+t) = t + t^2.$$

Second term:

$$t^2\left(-\frac{t+1}{t}\right) = -t(t+1) = -t^2 - t$$

Sum: $(t + t^2) + (-t^2 - t) = 0.$

78. $$y = f(x) = \frac{x\sin^{-1}x}{\sqrt{1-x^2}} + \ln\sqrt{1-x^2}$$

Write $\ln\sqrt{1-x^2} = \frac{1}{2}\ln(1-x^2)$

Differentiate:

1. First term: $u = x\sin^{-1}x,$

$$v = \sqrt{1-x^2} = \left(1-x^2\right)^{1/2}$$

$$y_1 = \frac{u}{v}$$

$$u' = \sin^{-1}x + \frac{x}{\sqrt{1-x^2}}$$

$$v' = -\frac{x}{\sqrt{1-x^2}}$$

Using quotient rule,

$$y_1' = \frac{u'v - uv'}{v^2}$$

after simplification gives

$$y_1' = \frac{\sin^{-1}x}{(1-x^2)^{3/2}}$$

2. Second term: $y_2 = \frac{1}{2}\ln(1-x^2)$

$$\Rightarrow \quad y_2' = \frac{1}{2}\cdot\frac{-2x}{1-x^2} = -\frac{x}{1-x^2}$$

Combining and simplifying (the $-\frac{x}{1-x^2}$ cancels inside the first-term algebra), the total derivative is

$$f'(x) = \frac{\sin^{-1}x}{(1-x^2)^{3/2}}$$

At $x = \frac{1}{2}$:

$$\sin^{-1}\left(\frac{1}{2}\right) = \frac{\pi}{6},$$

$$1 - x^2 = 1-\frac{1}{4} = \frac{3}{4}$$

$$(1-x^2)^{3/2} = \left(\frac{3}{4}\right)^{3/2} = \frac{3\sqrt{3}}{8}$$

So, $$f'\left(\frac{1}{2}\right) = \frac{\pi/6}{3\sqrt{3}/8} = \frac{\pi}{6}\cdot\frac{8}{3\sqrt{3}}$$

$$= \frac{8\pi}{18\sqrt{3}} = \frac{4\pi}{9\sqrt{3}} = \frac{4\pi\sqrt{3}}{27}.$$

79. We already have

$$f'(x) = \frac{\sin^{-1}x}{(1-x^2)^{3/2}}$$

Differentiate again:

$$f''(x) = \frac{d}{dx}[\sin^{-1}x.(1-x^2)^{-3/2}]$$

Using product rule,

$$(\sin^{-1}x)' = \frac{1}{\sqrt{1-x^2}}$$

$$\frac{d}{dx}(1-x^2)^{-3/2} = -\frac{3}{2}(1-x^2)^{-5/2}(-2x)$$

$$= 3x(1-x^2)^{-5/2}$$

Thus,

$$f''(x) = \frac{1}{\sqrt{1-x^2}}(1-x^2)^{-3/2} + \sin^{-1}x \cdot 3x(1-x^2)^{-5/2}$$

$$= (1-x^2) - 2 + 3x\sin^{-1}x(1-x^2)^{-5/2}$$

At $x = 0$: $\sin^{-1} 0 = 0$, so second term vanishes and first term is $(1-0)^{-2} = 1$.

So $f''(0) = 1$.

80. We already know

$$\frac{dy}{dx} = f'(x) = \frac{\sin^{-1}x}{(1-x^2)^{3/2}}$$

Given $x = \sin\theta$. Then

$$\sin^{-1}x = \theta,$$

$$1 - x^2 = 1 - \sin^2\theta = \cos^2\theta$$

So, $$(1-x^2)^{3/2} = (\cos^2\theta)^{3/2} = \cos^3\theta$$

Therefore, $$\frac{dy}{dx} = \frac{\theta}{\cos^3\theta} = \theta\sec^3\theta.$$

81. Given, $$f(x) = 1-\sqrt[3]{(x-1)^2}$$

Inside the cube root we have $(x-1)^2$, which is defined for all real x.

Cube root also allows all real inputs.

Hence domain is all real numbers.

82. $$f(x) = 1-\sqrt[3]{(x-1)^2}$$

Let $t = x - 1$. Then

$$f(t) = 1 - |t|^{2/3}$$

At $t = 0$ (*i.e.* $x = 1$), the value is

$$f(1) = 1$$

For $t \neq 0$:

$$|t|^{2/3} > 0 \Rightarrow f < 1$$

Thus at $x = 1$ the function attains its maximum.

83. Given, $$f(x) = \begin{cases} 4\cdot 5^x m & x<0, \\ 8k+x, & x\geq 0 \end{cases}$$

Continuity at $x = 0$:

Left limit: $f(0^-) = 4 \cdot 5^0 = 4$

Right value: $f(0^+) = 8k + 0 = 8k$

Setting equal: $8k = 4 \Rightarrow k = \dfrac{1}{2} = 0.5.$

84. We need $f'(-1)$. Since $-1 < 0$, use

$$f(x) = 4 \cdot 5^x$$

Derivative: $f'(x) = 4 \cdot 5^x \ln 5$

Thus, $f'(-1) = 4 \cdot 5^{-1} \ln 5 = \dfrac{4}{5}\ln 5.$

85. $$u = \int e^x \cos x \, dx,$$

$$v = \int e^x \sin x \, dx$$

First find u by parts: take $a = \cos x$,

$$db = e^x \, dx$$

$\Rightarrow$ $$da = -\sin x \, dx$$

$$b = e^x$$

$$u = \int e^x \cos x \, dx$$

$$= e^x \cos x - \int e^x (-\sin x)dx$$

$$= e^x \cos x + \int e^x \sin x \, dx$$

$$= e^x \cos x + v$$

So, $u - v = e^x \cos x(1)$

Now for v: take $a = \sin x$,

$$db = e^x \, dx$$

$\Rightarrow$ $$da = \cos x \, dx, \; b = e^x$$

$$v = \int e^x \sin x \, dx = e^x \sin x - \int e^x \cos x \, dx$$

$$= e^x \sin x - u$$

So,

$$u + v = e^x \sin x(2)$$

From the Fundamental Theorem of Calculus,

$$\frac{du}{dx} = e^x \cos x,$$

$$\frac{dv}{dx} = e^x \sin x$$

Comparing with (2),

$$u + v = e^x \sin x = \frac{dv}{dx}.$$

86. We know,

$$\frac{du}{dx} = e^x \cos x,$$

$$\frac{dv}{dx} = e^x \sin x$$

Statements:

I. $$\frac{du}{dx} = -v$$

Is this true?

$$-v = -\int e^x \sin x \, dx$$

But, $$\frac{du}{dx} = e^x \cos x$$

They are not equal $\Rightarrow$ Statement I is false.

II. $$\frac{du}{dx} = -u$$

$$-u = -\int e^x \cos x \, dx$$

But $$\frac{du}{dx} = e^x \cos x$$

Not equal $\Rightarrow$ Statement II false.

So neither I nor II is true.

87. Given, $$f(x) = |x - 3| + |x - 4|$$

For $x = 3.5$, both absolute values lie in intervals:

For $x > 3$: $|x - 3| = x - 3$

For $x < 4$: $|x - 4| = 4 - x$

So on $3 < x < 4$,

$$f(x) = (x - 3) + (4 - x) = 1$$

Derivative: $f'(x) = 1 - 1 = 0$

Thus at $x = 3.5$,

$$f'(x)(3.5) = 0.$$

88. Function: $$f(x) = |x - 3| + |x - 4|$$

At $x = 3$:

Left derivative $= -1 + (-1) = -2.$

Right derivative $= +1 + (-1) = 0.$

Not equal $\Rightarrow$ not differentiable.

At $x = 4$:

Left derivative $= +1 + (-1) = 0.$

Right derivative $= +1 + (+1) = 2.$

Not equal $\Rightarrow$ not differentiable.

Hence neither statement is true.

89. Function: $$f(x) = \frac{10^x - 10^{-x}}{10^x + 10^{-x}}$$

Compute $f(0)$: $f(0) = \dfrac{1-1}{1+1} = 0$

Now evaluate the repeated composition:

$$f(0) = 0,$$

$$f(f(0)) = f(0) = 0,$$

and so on. Every application again gives 0.

Thus, $f\circ f\circ f\circ f\circ f(0) = 0.$

90. $$y = \frac{10^x - 10^{-x}}{10^x + 10^{-x}}$$

This is, $y = \tan h\,(x \ln 10)$

Inverse: $y = \frac{1}{2\ln 10}\ln\left(\frac{1+x}{1-x}\right)$

Converting to log base 10:

$$y = \frac{1}{2}\log_{10}\left(\frac{1+x}{1-x}\right)$$

Matches option D.

91. Equation: $$\left(\frac{d^2y}{dx^2}\right)^{3/2} = \left(\frac{dy}{dx}\right)^{5/2}$$

To find degree, we must make powers integers. Raise both sides to power 2:

$$\left(\frac{d^2y}{dx^2}\right)^{3} = \left(\frac{dy}{dx}\right)^{5}$$

The highest order derivative is $\frac{d^2y}{dx^2}$ and its exponent is 3.

Hence degree = 3.

92. Evaluate, $\int_n^{n+1} (x - |x|)dx$

On interval $[n, n + 1)$:

$$\lfloor x \rfloor = n,\ x - \lfloor x \rfloor = x - n$$

Thus integral:

$$\int_n^{n+1} (x - n)dx = \int_0^1 t\,dt = \frac{1}{2}.$$

93. **Statement I:** Given solution:

$$y = xe^{2x}$$

Check if it satisfies

$$\frac{dy}{dx} = y\left(2 + \frac{1}{x}\right)$$

Compute derivative:

$$\frac{dy}{dx} = e^{2x} + x(2e^{2x}) = e^{2x}\,(1 + 2x)$$

RHS: $$y\left(2+\frac{1}{x}\right) = xe^{2x}\left(2+\frac{1}{x}\right)$$

$$= e^{2x}\,(2x + 1)$$

LHS = RHS ⇒ Statement I is true.

Statement II:

Given solution: $y = x \ln |x| + cx$,

Check if it satisfies

$$\frac{dy}{dx} = \frac{x+y}{x}$$

Compute derivative:

$$\frac{dy}{dx} = (\ln |x| + 1) + c$$

Compute RHS:

$$\frac{x+y}{x} = \frac{x + (x\ln|x| + cx)}{x}$$

$$= 1 + \ln |x| + c.$$

LHS = RHS ⇒ Statement II is true.

94. Equation: $(x + y)^2 \frac{dy}{dx} = k^2$

Rewrite: $$\frac{dy}{dx} = \frac{k^2}{(x+y)^2}$$

Let, $u = x + y$

Then, $$\frac{du}{dx} = 1 + \frac{dy}{dx}$$

But from equation

$$\frac{dy}{dx} = \frac{k^2}{u^2}$$

Thus, $$\frac{du}{dx} = 1 + \frac{k^2}{u^2}$$

Rearrange: $u^2\,du = (u^2 + k^2)\,dx$

Separate: $$\frac{u^2 du}{u^2 + k^2} = dx$$

Compute LHS integral:

$$\int\left(1 - \frac{k^2}{u^2 + k^2}\right)du = u - k\tan^{-1}\left(\frac{u}{k}\right)$$

So, $$u - k\tan^{-1}\left(\frac{u}{k}\right) = x + c.$$

Replace, $u = x + y$:

$$x + y - k\tan^{-1}\left(\frac{x+y}{k}\right) = x + c.$$

Simplify: $$x + y = k\tan\left(\frac{x+c}{k}\right)$$

Matches Option B.

95. Evaluate: $\int \frac{dx}{10^x + 10^{-x}}$

Rewrite denominator:

$$10^x + 10^{-x} = 10^{-x}\,(10^{2x} + 1)$$

Let $t = 10x$. Then

$$dt = 10^x \ln 10\, dx$$

$$\Rightarrow \quad dx = \frac{dt}{t\ln 10}$$

Integral becomes:

$$\int \frac{dt}{\ln 10(t^2 + 1)} = \frac{1}{\ln 10}\tan^{-1}(t) + c$$

$$t = 10^x$$

Thus. $$\int \frac{dx}{10^x + 10^{-x}} = \frac{1}{\ln 10}\tan^{-1}(10^x) + c.$$

96. Perimeter = 20 cm.

Let rectangle be $a \times b$.

$$2(a + b) = 20 \Rightarrow a + b = 10$$

Statement I: Largest area rectangle for fixed perimeter is a square. ⇒ True.

Statement II: Is area 27 possible?

Area: $A = a(10 - a) = 10a - a^2$

Solve $10a - a^2 = 27.$

$a^2 - 10a + 27 = 0.$

$$a = \frac{10 \pm \sqrt{100-108}}{2} = \frac{10 \pm \sqrt{-8}}{2}$$

Imaginary roots ⇒ impossible.

Thus area 27 is not possible. Statement II is false.

97. Given, $I_1 = \int_e^{e^2} \frac{dx}{\ln x}$, $I_2 = \int_1^2 \frac{e^x}{x} dx$

Evaluate I_1 by substitution. Let

$$x = e^t \Rightarrow dx = e^t\, dt,\ \ln x = t$$

When $x = e$, $t = 1$; when $x = e^2$, $t = 2$. Then

$$I_1 = \int_1^2 \frac{e^t}{t} dt$$

The integration variable is dummy, so we may rename t as x:

$$I_1 = \int_1^2 \frac{e^x}{x} dx$$

But this is exactly I_2. Hence

$$I_1 = I_2 \Rightarrow I_1 - I_2 = 0.$$

98. Region: $|x| \leq 2k$, $|y| \leq k$

This is a rectangle width $4k$ and height $2k$:

$$\text{Area} = 4k \cdot 2k = 8k^2.$$

99. Given, $f(x) = \frac{1}{x-5}$

Compute derivative:

$$f'(x) = -\frac{1}{(x-5)^2}$$

Since the denominator is always positive for $x \neq 5$,

$$f'(x) < 0$$

So the function is strictly decreasing on both intervals $x < 5$ and $x > 5$.

Thus Statement - I is correct.

Statement - II says:

$$f'(x) > 0 \text{ for all } x \neq 5,$$

which is false (actual derivative is always negative).

So Statement - I true, Statement - II false.

100. Given, $f(x) = \frac{x^3 + 128}{x} = x^2 + \frac{128}{x}$

Compute derivative:

$$f'(x) = 2x - \frac{128}{x^2}$$

Set derivative = 0:

$$2x^3 - 128 = 0$$

$$x^3 = 64 \Rightarrow x = 4$$

Check value: $f(4) = 4^2 + \frac{128}{4} = 16 + 32 = 48$

So Statement - I is correct.

Check sign change of $f'(x)$:

For $x < 4$:

Try $x = 3$: $f'(3) = 6 - \frac{128}{9} > 0$

For $x > 4$:

Try $x = 5$: $f'(5) = 10 - \frac{128}{25} > 0$

Actual sign: $f'(x) = 2x - \frac{128}{x^2}$

is negative for small x, becomes 0 at $x = 4$, then becomes positive.

Thus derivative changes from negative to positive, meaning a minimum, not a maximum.

Statement - II says derivative changes from positive to negative, which is wrong.

Thus: Statement - I = true

Statement - II = false.

101. Numbers are: $\binom{10}{3}, \binom{10}{4}, \binom{10}{5}, \binom{10}{6}, \binom{10}{7}$

Values:

$$\binom{10}{3} = 120, \binom{10}{4} = 210, \binom{10}{5} = 252, \binom{10}{6} = 210, \binom{10}{7} = 120$$

Harmonic mean:

$$HM = \frac{5}{\frac{1}{120} + \frac{1}{210} + \frac{1}{252} + \frac{1}{210} + \frac{1}{120}}$$

Compute denominator:

$$\frac{1}{120} = \frac{1}{120}, \frac{1}{210} = \frac{1}{210}, \frac{1}{252} = \frac{1}{252}$$

Sum: $2\left(\frac{1}{120} + \frac{1}{210}\right) + \frac{1}{252}$

LCM of 120, 210, 252 is 1260.

Convert: $\frac{1}{120} = \frac{10.5}{1260}, \frac{1}{210} = \frac{6}{1260}, \frac{1}{252} = \frac{5}{1260}$

Sum:

$$2(10.5 + 6) + 5 = 2(16.5) + 5 = 33 + 5 = 38$$

Thus denominator $= \frac{38}{1260} = \frac{19}{630}$

So, $HM = \frac{5}{19/630} = 5 \cdot \frac{630}{19} = \frac{3150}{19}$.

102. Probability a farmer is in debt: $p = 0.60$.

Independence → probability all 3 are in debt:

$$p^3 = (0.6)^3 = 0.216.$$

103. Let, L = event "family owns laptop",

D = "owns desktop".

$$P(L) = 0.68, \ P(D) = 0.56,$$

$$P(L \cap D) = 0.48.$$

Required, $P(L \cup D) = P(L) + P(D) - P(L \cap D)$:

$$0.68 + 0.56 - 0.48 = 1.24 - 0.48 = 0.76.$$

104. Urn: 10 white, 5 red, total 15. Draw 2 without replacement.

Total ways: $\binom{15}{2}$

Favourable (both red): $\binom{5}{2}$

$$P(\text{both red}) = \frac{\binom{5}{2}}{\binom{15}{2}} = \frac{10}{105} = \frac{2}{21}.$$

105. Urn: 5 white (W), 6 red (R), 4 blue (B), total 15.

Draw 3.

Want one W, one R, one B.

Favourable ways:

$$5 \cdot 6 \cdot 4 = 120$$

Total ways: $\binom{15}{3} = 455.$

$$P = \frac{120}{455} = \frac{24}{91}.$$

106. For binomial distribution:

- Number of trials must be fixed (so Statement I "infinite and not fixed is false).
- Trials must be independent (II true).
- Each trial has two possible outcomes (III true).

Thus conditions II and III are correct.

107. X tells truth with probability 4/5, lies 1/5.

Y tells truth with probability 5/6, lies 1/6.

They contradict if one tells truth and the other lies:

$$P = P(X\ T,\ Y\ L) + P(X\ L,\ Y\ T)$$

$$= \frac{4}{5}.\frac{1}{6} + \frac{1}{5}.\frac{5}{6}$$

$$= \frac{4}{30} + \frac{5}{30} = \frac{9}{30} = \frac{3}{10}.$$

108. Let P = event "passes Physics",

E = event "passes English".

Given: $P(P) = \frac{2}{3}$,

$$P(P \cap E) = \frac{11}{15},$$

$$P(P \cup E) = \frac{4}{5}$$

Using, $P(P \cup E) = P(P) + P(E) - P(P \cap E)$,

we get, $\frac{4}{5} = \frac{2}{3} + P(E) - \frac{11}{15}$

Convert to denominator 15:

$$\frac{4}{5} = \frac{10}{15} + P(E) - \frac{11}{15}$$

$$= \left(\frac{10}{15} - \frac{11}{15}\right) + P(E)$$

$$= -\frac{1}{15} + P(E)$$

So, $P(E) = \frac{4}{5} + \frac{1}{15} = \frac{12}{15} + \frac{1}{15} = \frac{13}{15}.$

109. For independent events X and Y:

$$P(X) = p, \ P(Y) = q$$

Exactly one of X,Y occurs:

$$P(\text{exactly one}) = P(X \cap Y^c) + P(X^c \cap Y)$$

$$= p(1 - q) + (1 - p)q$$

$$= p - pq + q - pq$$

$$= p + q - 2pq.$$

Statement I claims $p + q - pq$, so Statement I is false.

At least one of X, Y occurs:

$$P(X \cup Y) = p + q - P(X \cap Y)$$

$$= p + q - pq$$

Statement II claims $p + q - 2pq$, so Statement II is false.

Thus neither statement is correct.

110. Die faces: 3 black, 2 white, 1 red. So

$$P(B) = \frac{3}{6} = \frac{1}{2},$$

$$P(W) = \frac{2}{6} = \frac{1}{3}, \ P(R) = \frac{1}{6}$$

Required order B first, W second, R third (independent tosses):

$$P = P(B) \cdot P(W) \cdot P(R)$$

$$= \frac{1}{2}.\frac{1}{3}.\frac{1}{6} = \frac{1}{36}.$$

111. We toss a fair coin 4 times.

Let a_n = number of length-n sequences with no consecutive heads.

For such sequences:

- If the first toss is T, the remaining $n - 1$ tosses can be any valid sequence of length $n - 1$: a_{n-1} ways.
- If the first toss is H, the second must be T (to avoid HH), and the remaining $n - 2$ tosses form any valid sequence of length $n - 2$: a_{n-2} ways.

Thus $a_n = a_{n-1} + a_{n-2}$ (Fibonacci - type).

Base cases:

$a_1 = 2$ (H, T);

$a_2 = 3$ (HH not allowed, so HT, TH, TT).

Then

$$a_3 = a_2 + a_1 = 3 + 2 = 5,$$
$$a_4 = a_3 + a_2 = 5 + 3 = 8.$$

Total possible sequences of 4 tosses: $2^4 = 16$.

Probability of no consecutive heads:

$$P = \frac{a_4}{16} = \frac{8}{16} = \frac{1}{2}.$$

112. On one die, primes = {2, 3, 5} (3 outcomes), composites = {4, 6} (2 outcomes), neither prime nor composite = {1} (1 outcome).

For three dice, probability of a specific arrangement "prime, composite, neither is

$$\frac{3}{6}.\frac{2}{6}.\frac{1}{6}$$

These three types can appear in any of 3! orders, so total probability

$$3!\frac{3}{6}.\frac{2}{6}.\frac{1}{6} = 6.\frac{6}{216} = \frac{36}{216} = \frac{1}{6}.$$

113. Integers 1 to 50.

Multiples of 5: $\lfloor 50/5 \rfloor = 10$.

Multiples of 9: $\lfloor 50/9 \rfloor = 5$.

Multiples of both 5 and 9 (LCM 45): $\lfloor 50/45 \rfloor = 1$.

Numbers divisible by 5 or 9: $10 + 5 - 1 = 14$.

Numbers not divisible by 5 or 9: $50 - 14 = 36$.

Probability: $\frac{36}{50} = \frac{18}{25}$.

114. Among 50 consecutive natural numbers, there are 25 even and 25 odd numbers.

Sum is odd $\Leftrightarrow$ one even and one odd.

Number of ways to choose such a pair: $25 \cdot 25 = 625$ (choose one even and one odd).

Total ways to choose any 2 numbers:

$$\binom{50}{2} = 1225$$

Probability: $\frac{625}{1225} = \frac{25}{49}$.

115. Adding a constant (here 20) to every observation shifts all data but does not change dispersion. Hence the standard deviation remains the same as before: 10.

116. Binomial with $n = 5$, $p = k$.

$$P(X = 1) = 5k(1 - k)^4 = 0.4096,$$
$$P(X = 2) = 10k^2 (1 - k)^3 = 0.2048.$$

Take ratio:

$$\frac{P(X=2)}{P(X=1)} = \frac{10k^2(1-k)^3}{5k(1-k)^4}$$
$$= \frac{2k}{1-k} = \frac{0.2048}{0.4096} = 0.5$$

So, $\frac{2k}{1-k} = 0.5 \Rightarrow 4k = 1 - k$

$\Rightarrow$ $5k = 1 \Rightarrow k = 0.2$.

117. Class midpoints:

5–15 $\to$ 10, 15–25 $\to$ 20, 25–35 $\to$ 30, 35–45 $\to$ 40

Mean

$$\frac{20(10)+30(20)+30(30)+20(40)}{20+30+30+20}$$
$$= \frac{200+600+900+800}{100} = \frac{2500}{100} = 25.$$

118. Given, $P(A) = 0.3$, $P(B) = 0.4$, $P(A|B) = 0.5$.

Use, $P(A|B) = \frac{P(A\cap B)}{P(B)}$

So, $0.5 = \frac{P(A\cap B)}{0.4}$

$\Rightarrow$ $P(A \cap B) = 0.2$.

Now, $P(B|A) = \frac{P(A\cap B)}{P(A)}$

$$= \frac{0.2}{0.3} = 0.666...$$
$$= 0.667.$$

119. Given, $P(A) = \frac{1}{3}$, $P(B) = \frac{1}{2}$,

$P(A \cap B) = \frac{1}{4}$

We need, $P(\bar{A} \cap B) = 1 - P(A \cap \bar{B})$

Compute: $P(A \cap \bar{B}) = P(A) - P(A \cap B)$

$$= \frac{1}{3} - \frac{1}{4} = \frac{4-3}{12} = \frac{1}{12}$$

So, $P(\bar{A} \cup B) = 1 - \frac{1}{12} = \frac{11}{12}$.

120. Statement I: mean and variance do not have the same unit.

Variance has squared units $\Rightarrow$ false.

Statement II: mean deviation and standard deviation both have same original unit $\Rightarrow$ true.

Previous Years' Paper

NATIONAL DEFENCE ACADEMY & NAVAL ACADEMY

NDA & NA — Entrance Exam, 2025 (I)

PAPER I : GENERAL ABILITY TEST

PART A : ENGLISH LANGUAGE

Directions (Qs. No. 1-5): *Read the following passage carefully and answer the questions that follow by selecting the correct option from the given options, based solely on the passage. Mark your answer on the Answer Sheet accordingly.*

An attempt to determine the number of languages in the world is affected by other factors. A few new languages do continue to be discovered, even these days, as unexplored regions of the world begin to be opened up. The discovery does not usually take place straight away. Often there are similarities with an already known language which make the investigators assume that what they have found is just a dialect of that language. Only after a considerable period of contact does it transpire that the speech is so different that it has to be considered a different language. It takes a language survey to establish the facts, and there are still many countries where such surveys are incomplete or have not even begun. The people may be known, but the identity of their language may not be. Because many such peoples are bilingual or multilingual, and converse with outsiders in lingua franca, it may take a while before linguists come to realize that there is an ethnic language there at all.

1. Which one of the following is NOT the reason for the difficulty in estimating the number of languages of the world?

A. New languages continue to be discovered

B. There are still unexplored regions

C. New languages are considered a dialect of a known language

D. People who speak the language do not claim their language

2. Which one of the following is a way to establish the discovery of a new language?

A. By establishing contact over a period of time with the speakers of the language

B. By finding the similarities of the language with other languages

C. By comparing with the lingua franca of the region

D. By conducting a survey of all languages of the region

3. Which one of the following statements is correct?

A. Language surveys have been conducted by all nations

B. There is hardly any language to be discovered in the world

C. All the languages are either complete languages or dialects of other major languages

D. No new language needs to be discovered since all languages are known to the world

4. 'The people may be known, but the identity of their language may not be,' means:

A. People are recognised as different ethnic groups but not necessarily their language

B. People are recognised as different ethnic groups and their language is recognised

C. People are not recognised as different ethnic groups, and so are their languages

D. Because the people are not from different ethnic groups and their language is recognised

5. Which one of the following words from passage means 'come to be known'?

A. transpire

B. lingua franca

C. straight

D. variant

Directions (Qs. No. 6-8): *The following items have a sentence in direct or indirect speech with four options. One of the options converts the direct or indirect speech into direct or direct correctly. Select the correct option and mark your response on the Answer Sheet.*

6. Convert from the direct speech to indirect speech:

Charu said to her friend, "I want you to be here at 6.00 p.m. tomorrow for the meeting."

A. Charu told her friend that she wanted her to be there at 6.00 p.m. the next day for the meeting
B. Charu told her friend that she wanted her to be there at 6.00 p.m. tomorrow for the meeting
C. Charu requested her friend that she wanted her to be there at 6.00 p.m. tomorrow for the meeting
D. Charu told her friend that she will want her to be here at 6.00 p.m. the next day for the meeting

7. Convert from direct speech to indirect speech:

Nitin said to his brother, "What a beautiful painting it is?"

A. Nitin wondered to his brother that what a beautiful painting it was
B. Nitin wondered before his brother that it was a beautiful painting
C. Nitin exclaimed that it is a beautiful painting
D. Nitin asked his brother whether it was beautiful painting

8. Convert from indirect speech to direct speech:

The teacher asked her students why they had been quiet in the previous class.

A. The teacher asked her students, "Why were they keeping quiet in the previous class?"
B. The teacher said to her students, "Why were you quiet in the previous class?"
C. The teacher said to her students, "Why had you been quiet in the previous class?"
D. The teacher said to her students, "Why were you quiet in previous class?"

Directions (Qs. No. 9 & 10): *Following items have four sentences, one of which is correct. Find the correct option and mark your response in the Answer Sheet.*

9. Which one of the following sentence is correct?

A. He is considered as the brightest intellectual in the country
B. He is considered as one among the brightest intellectual in the country
C. He is considered as one among the brighter intellectual in the country
D. He is considered as one of the intellectual in the country

10. Which one of the following sentences is correct?

A. No other mountain is taller than the Himalayas
B. No other mountain is tall than the Himalayas
C. No other mountains taller than the Himalayas
D. No other mountain is taller then the Himalayas

Directions (Qs. No. 11-15): *In the following items, a pair of words is provided. You are required to select the option that most appropriately describes the meaning of both the words and mark your response on the Answer Sheet accordingly.*

11. Confident and Confidant

A. Confident means certain and confidant means close friend
B. Confidant means certain and confident means close friend
C. Confident means belief and confidant means an emissary
D. Confident means assurance and confidant means intimate person

12. Broke and brook

A. Broke means abundance and brook means a flowing water body
B. Broke means bankrupt and brook means a stream
C. Broke means fractured and brook means nonsense
D. Broke means negotiate and brook means a stream

13. Accept and Except

A. Accept means apart from and except means recognise
B. Accept means recognise and except means include
C. Accept means consent and except means apart from
D. Accept means allude and except means apart from

14. Accord and Accrued

A. Accord means collected and accrued means agreement
B. Accord means agreement and accrued means arrived
C. Accord means accepted and accrued means received
D. Accord means agreement and accrued means accumulated

15. Guarantee and Warranty

A. Guarantee is an agreement and warranty is a service contract
B. Guarantee is a business agreement and warranty is a service contract
C. Guarantee is a promise and warranty is a service contract
D. Guarantee is acceptance and warranty is a service contract

Directions (Qs. No. 16-20): *In the following items a sentence or a phrase is given with a word that is underlined, followed by four options. Select the most appropriate option that is nearest in meaning to the underlined word and mark your response on the Answer Sheet accordingly.*

16. The Constitution of India ensures proportionate representation from all regions.

A. balanced B. partial
C. unlikely D. suffragette

17. There is a feeling of disenchantment among the members of the group.

A. delight B. disappointment
C. idealism D. unrelenting

18. She believed that it was imminent that he would be chosen as the leader of the group.

A. timely B. distant
C. unlikely D. inevitable

19. The brave soldiers left an indelible impression on the people of the land.

A. permanent B. fleeting
C. hilarious D. eradicable

20. The manager always provides instantaneous replies to all queries.

A. immediate B. delayed
C. deliberate D. unwanted

Directions (Qs. No. 21-25): *In this section each item consists of six sentences that comprise a passage. The first and sixth sentences are given in the beginning as S1 and S6. The sequence of the middle four sentences has been jumbled up and labelled as P, Q, R and S. You are required to find the proper sequence of the four sentences and mark your response accordingly on the answer sheet.*

21. S1 : Although all sources of energy ultimately come from natural processes, non-renewable resources cannot be replaced naturally at the rate they are being used.

S6 : The sustainable use of natural resources in a manner that provides the maximum benefit of these resources to humans over a period of time can be termed as conservation.

P. This will increase the time and cost of mining and once these resources are used up they cannot be replaced.

Q. Hence, we must remember that though our country is rich in mineral deposits these resources are short-lived.

R. Extraction of these ores through the process of mining will soon become difficult and very expensive because these minerals have to be mined from greater depths over time.

S. Mineral resources can be said to be finite and non-renewable.

A. Q P R S B. S P Q R
C. S Q R P D. S Q P R

22. S1 : India, at present, has one of the largest road networks in the world.

S6 : It passes through Howrah, Delhi and Amritsar and terminates in Kabul (Afghanistan).

P. The importance of roads has been recognised in India since the ancient times.

Q. The Grand Trunk road was built by Sher Shah Suri across the Indo-Gangetic plain, from Chittagong (Bangladesh to Peshawar (Pakistan).

R. Kings such as Ashoka and Chandragupta built roads for easy transportation of goods and people.

S. Construction of roads continued as an important activity in the late medieval period.

A. Q P R S B. S P Q R
C. P Q R S D. P R S Q

23. S1 : National highways connect one state with another and are of national importance.

S6 : These road systems are also known as primary road systems and are laid and operated under the supervision of the National Highway Authority of India.

P. They are important because whereas they constitute merely two per cent of the total road networks, they nevertheless carry 40 per cent of the total road traffic

Q. The road infrastructure of the country is therefore crucial, and their construction and maintenance is of critical importance.

R. They bear the load of traffic because these roads connect long distance and pass through major cities and towns.

S. Since they cover the length and breadth of the nation and connect cities and towns, these highways are the primary facilitators of trade and connectivity.

A. P R S Q B. S P Q R
C. P R Q S D. S Q R P

24. S1 : The South African Constitution was inaugurated in December 1996.

S6 : A special constitutional court enforces the rights enshrined in the Constitution.

P. Its creation and promulgation took place at a time when South Africa still faced the threat of a civil war after the dissolution of the Apartheid Government.

Q. The South African Constitution says that its "Bill of Rights is a cornerstone of democracy in South Africa."

R. Apropos, it forbids discrimination on the grounds of "race gender, pregnancy, marital status, ethnic or social origin, colour, age, disability, religion, conscience, belief, culture, language and birth".

S. The Bill of Rights grants perhaps the most extensive range of rights to the citizens.

A. Q S R P B. S P Q R
C. P Q R S D. P Q S R

25. S1 : Our Constitution reminds us of the necessity of representation in a large democracy.
S6 : Elections have today become the most visible symbol of the democratic process.
P. This is why elections become important.
Q. Therefore representatives are elected by the people.
R. Whenever we think of India as a democracy, our mind invariably turns to our successful elections.
S. All citizens cannot participate in taking every decision.
A. Q S R P B. S P Q R
C. P Q S R D. S Q P R

Directions (Qs. No. 26-35): *Given below are sentences that use discourse markers/expressions to make them complete. Identify the most appropriate discourse marker/expression and mark your answer accordingly in the Answer Sheet.*

26. _____ your transfer request is concerned; we'll be discussing it at the next meeting.
A. As far as B. To begin with
C. By the way D. Talking about

27. _____, did you know Ravi has a new job?
A. For one thing B. By the way
C. In the first place D. As a result

28. _____ the wind, it was getting stronger, and I was getting colder.
A. To begin with B. By the way
C. First of all D. Speaking of

29. _____, what are you doing in my room?
A. On the other hand B. Excuse me
C. Look there D. Eventually

30. _____ an unhappy childhood leads to criminal behaviour.
A. Still if B. Even somewhat
C. In some cases D. In progression

31. _____, the problem is nothing but a wrong assumption about processes.
A. In the meanwhile B. Somewhat
C. Engagingly D. In other words

32. Many, _____, hesitate to publicly broach such question for fear of nurturing discrimination.
A. understandably B. despite
C. until D. of course

33. _____, one notes that in the nineteenth century an important development of reflection and questioning gained momentum.
A. Particularly speaking B. Generally speaking
C. Otherwise D. Of course

34. _____, the situation has completely transformed over the past few years.
A. Somewhat B. Believably
C. Thus D. Predominantly

35. _____, the committee is of the opinion that all academic matters will be discussed in the Executive Body Meeting.
A. Hence B. But
C. Later D. Although

Directions (Qs. No. 36-40): *Given below are words, followed by their appropriate meaning. Identify the correct meaning and mark your answer accordingly in the Answer Sheet.*

36. Cynosure:
A. Person or thing that causes a change
B. Person or thing that attracts a lot of attention
C. Person or thing regarded as exact copy
D. Person or animal that lives in a particular place

37. Coeval:
A. Person of roughly the same age
B. Person or organisation that cooperates with others
C. Person employed to drive a private car
D. Person employed in taking census

38. Retrogression:
A. Sudden sharp drop in price
B. Reverse pressure
C. Return to earlier state
D. Sudden occurrence of a past event

39. Imprest:
A. Surprise attack by people
B. Money used to manage small expenses
C. Sudden occurrence of laughter
D. Sudden increase in activity

40. Turgid:
A. Determined or loyal
B. Dirty or untidy
C. Swollen or distended
D. Excited or upset

Directions (Qs. No. 41-45): *Each of the following items in this section consists of a sentence, the parts of which have been jumbled. These parts have been labelled as P, Q, R and S. The parts are rearranged in four sequences, namely (A), (B), (C) and (D). You are required to select the most appropriate option that sequences the parts correctly and mark your response on the Answer Sheet accordingly.*

41. P. participate in the function
Q. many of the people who had come to
R. the auditorium was over-crowded
S. could not find a seat because
A. PRQS B. PQRS
C. QPSR D. SPRQ

42. P. lay outside her existing life
Q. she knew that the answer
R. somewhere in the back of her mind
S. to her questions about life
A. RPQS B. QSPR
C. QPSR D. RQSP

43. P. works of literature
Q. inside the pages of all good
R. lies the truth about some of
S. the more challenging questions posed by humanity
A. PRQS B. QPRS
C. QPSR D. RPSQ

44. P. takes on account of its economic successes
Q. to address continuing social inequality
R. for every stride of progress any nation
S. it takes two back if it is unable
A. PRQS B. QPRS
C. RPSQ D. RPQS

45. P. the book-value of a loan or
Q. an intangible asset over a set period of time
R. used to periodically lower
S. amortisation is an accounting technique
A. SRPQ B. RSPQ
C. SRQP D. RPSQ

Directions (Qs. No. 46-50): *The following items have a blank space followed by four options. Select the most appropriate option to fill in the blank and mark your response on the Answer Sheet accordingly.*

46. There is more than ____ to get the job done.
A. one way B. one ways
C. any ways D. any way

47. The class decided to organise _____.
A. picnic B. a picnic
C. picnics D. the picnic

48. The accused _____ before the judge.
A. tried B. was trial
C. sat trial D. stood trial

49. The manner in which the demolitions have been carried out _____ scrutiny by the High Court.
A. was under
B. under
C. is under
D. however under

50. I _____ consider the opinions of all stakeholders before taking a final decision.
A. will not B. have
C. will D. shall

PART B : GENERAL KNOWLEDGE

51. Which of the following main industry/industries was/were developed in the second industrial revolution that took place after about 1850?
A. Coal and iron
B. Cotton spinning and weaving
C. Chemical and electrical
D. Steam engines

52. Which among the following materials was used in making the Harappan seals?
A. Sandstone B. Lapis lazuli
C. Jasper D. Steatite

53. Which one among the following *mahajanapadas* in ancient India was an oligarchy?
A. Vajji B. Kosala
C. Gandhara D. Magadha

54. Which one of the following sculptures found at Sanchi Stupa is NOT directly inspired by Buddhist ideas?
A. Empty seat
B. Shalbhanjika
C. Tree
D. Wheel

55. In British India, which one among the following Acts permitted detention without trial for up to two years?
A. Regulating Act, 1773
B. Rowlatt Act, 1919
C. Pitt's India Act, 1784
D. Government of India Act, 1935

56. Which one of the following statements about the Bhoodan Movement is correct?
A. The target was to get one-sixth of cultivable land in India as donation
B. It was approved through a Central Government Act
C. It was ensured that the donated land was free from all litigation
D. The first donation of land was in Bihar

57. The Constitution (Seventy-third Amendment) Act provides for:
A. an elaborate system of establishing municipal self-government
B. an elaborate system of establishing panchayats as units of self-government

C. establishing a Commission for Linguistic Minorities
D. e creation of the Jharkhand State

58. BI RATPOL portal has been developed by:

A. The Election Commission of India
B The Central Bureau of Investigation
C. The Enforcement Directorate
D. The Securities and Exchange Board of India

59. Which one of the following statements about the Parliament of India is correct?

A. A majority of members of Rajya Sabha are elected by a system of proportional representation by means of single transferable vote
B. The Deputy Chairperson of the Rajya Sabha is nominated by the President from among the members of the Rajya Sabha
C. The Lok Sabha cannot be dissolved before the completion of its five year term
D. The members of Lok Sabha also vote in the election of the members of Rajya Sabha

60. Which one among the following does NOT figure among the Five Principles of Panchsheel?

A. Mutual respect for each other's territorial integrity and sovereignty
B. Equality and mutual benefit
C. Peaceful coexistence
D. Nuclear non-proliferation

61. Maize (*makka*) was introduced into India in the seventeenth century via:

A. Portugal B. Africa and Spain
C. China and Mongolia D. Turkey

62. Match List-I with List-II and select the answer using the code given below the Lists:

***List-I* (*Five Year Plan*)**	***List-II* (*Objective*)**
A. Fifth Five Year Plan	1. Towards Faster and More Inclusive Growth
B. Seventh Five Year Plan	2. Garibi Hatao (Removal of Poverty)
C. Ninth Five Year Plan	3. Food, Work and Productivity
D. Eleventh Five Year Plan	4. Growth with Social Justice and Equality

Code:

	A	B	C	D
A.	1	4	3	2
B.	2	3	4	1
C.	2	4	3	1
D.	1	3	4	2

63. Which of the following statements about Srimanta Shankardeva is/are correct?

1. In the late fifteenth century Shankradeva emerged as one of the leading proponents of Vaishnavism in Assam
2. He was the founder of Gaudiya Vaishnavism
3. His teachings are known as Bhagavati Dharma
4. He encouraged the establishment of satra and naam ghar

Select the answer using the code given below:

A. 1 and 2 only B. 2 and 3 only
C. 1, 3 and 4 only D. 1, 2, 3 and 4

64. At which one among the following places did the British East India Company found its factory in the year 1611?

A. Madras B. Masulipatam
C. Bombay D. Balasore

65. Chronologically arrange the following political events related to Indian National Movement beginning from the earliest:

1. Formation of Swaraj Party
2. Communal Award
3. Lucknow Pact
4. Simla Conference

Select the answer using the code given below:

A. 3, 1, 2, 4 B. 1, 3, 2, 4
C. 2, 1, 4, 3 D. 1, 2, 3, 4

66. Which among the following Acts provided for the establishment of a Supreme Court of Justice at Calcutta for Europeans, their employees and the citizens of India?

A. The Regulating Act of 1773
B. The Charter Act of 1793
C. The Charter Act of 1813
D. Government of India Act of 1858

67. Who, among the following, has introduced a resolution in 1882 which is also called the Magna Carta of Local Self-Government in India?

A. Lord Macaulay B. Lord Canning
C. Lord Ripon D. Lord William Bentinck

68. Which one of the following terms is associated with the practice of Sufism?

A. *Jizya* B. *Ijma*
C. *Muqaddam* D. *Murid*

69. Consider the following features:

1. Consent of the governed
2. Political equality
3. Accountability of the ruled to the ruler

Which of the above feature/features outline democratic rule?

A. 1 and 2 only B. 2 and 3 only
C. 1, 2 and 3 D. 3 only

70. Placing the earliest first, arrange the following countries in the chronological order in which they granted universal adult franchise:

1. USA 2. Sri Lanka
3. Japan 4. India

Select the answer using the code given below:

A. 1, 2, 3, 4 B. 2, 3, 4, 1
C. 1, 3, 4, 2 D. 3, 4, 1, 2

71. Which one of the following statements is NOT correct?

A. The molecules of soap are sodium or potassium salts of long chain fatty acids
B. The molecules of soap contain both hydrophobic and hydrophilic ends
C. Detergents are more effective than soaps in hard water
D. In micelles the ionic-end of the molecules is towards oil droplet while the other end faces outside

72. Which one of the following statements is correct?

A. A neutron is formed by combination of an electron and a proton. Therefore, it is neutral
B. The mass of an electron is about 1/2000 times that of a proton
C. An isotope of cobalt is used in the treatment of goiter
D. J.J. Thomson proposed that the nucleus of an atom contains only neutrons

73. Which one of the following particles in the nucleus of an atom was discovered by J. Chadwick?

A. Electron B. Proton
C. Positron D. Neutron

74. Which one of the following findings is NOT observed in Rutherford's Nuclear Model of Atom?

A. There is a neutral centre in an atom called nucleus
B. Nearly all the mass of an atom resides in the nucleus
C. The electrons revolve around the nucleus in a circular path
D. The size of a nucleus is very small as compared to the size of atom

75. Element X forms a chloride with the formula XCl_2, which is a solid with high melting point. X would most likely be in the same group of periodic table as:

A. Na B. Al
C. Mg D. K

76. Which one of the following oxides is a neutral oxide?

A. CO B. CO_2
C. Na_2O D. MgO

77. Which one of the following is also known as Dry ice in its solid form?

A. SiO_2 B. CO_2
C. CaO D. MgO

78. Which one of the following statements is NOT correct?

A. A scale measuring hydrogen ion concentration in a solution is called pH scale
B. The higher the hydrogen ion concentration in solution, higher is its pH
C. We can measure pH generally from 0 to 14 on a pH scale
D. The 'p' in pH stands for 'potenz' in German meaning power

79. Which one of the following statements is NOT correct?

A. Half mole of nitrogen gas is measured 11.2 litre at STP
B. 17 gram of ammonia gas contains 6.022×10^{23} molecules at STP
C. 22.4 litre of CO_2 gas at STP contains 44 gram of molecules
D. 4 gram of hydrogen gas contains 6.022×10^{23} molecules

80. Which one of the following statements about a compound is NOT correct?

A. A compound is a substance composed of two or more elements, chemically combined in a fixed proportion
B. Properties of a compound are different from its constituent elements
C. A compound is an impure substance
D. The constituents of a compound can be separated only by chemical or electrochemical reactions

81. Match List-I with List-II and select the answer using the code given below the Lists:

List-I ***(Chemical Name)***	***List-II*** ***(Chemical Formula)***
A. Washing soda	1. $CaOCl_2$
B. Baking soda	2. $NaHCO_3$
C. Bleaching powder	3. $Na_2CO_3 \cdot 10H_2O$
D. Gypsum	4. $CaSO_4 \cdot 2H_2O$

Code:

	A	B	C	D
A.	4	2	1	3
B.	4	1	2	3
C.	3	1	2	4
D.	3	2	1	4

82. Which one of the following nitrogen oxides may dimerize?

A. N_2O B. NO_2
C. N_2O_3 D. N_2O_5

83. Which one of the following statements regarding oxidation and reduction reactions is NOT correct?

A. If a substance loses hydrogen during reaction, it is reduced
B. If a substance loses oxygen during reaction, it is reduced
C. If a substance gains hydrogen during reaction, it is reduced
D. If a substance gains oxygen during reaction, it is oxidized

84. Match List-I with List-II and select the answer using the code given below the Lists:

List-I *(Physical Quantity)*	*List-II* *(SI Unit)*
A. Temperature	1. Kelvin
B. Weight	2. Kilogram
C. Mass	3. Pascal
D. Pressure	4. Newton

Code:

	A	B	C	D
A.	1	2	4	3
B.	3	4	2	1
C.	1	4	2	3
D.	3	2	4	1

85. For acid rain, the pH of rain water should be less than:

A. 7.0 B. 6.6
C. 5.6 D. 8.0

86. Consider the following lines of Longitude and Latitude:

1. Prime Meridian
2. Tropic of Cancer
3. Equator

Which of the above lines is/are a Great Circle?

A. 1, 2 and 3 B. 1 and 2 only
C. 1 and 3 only D. 3 only

87. Which of the following is the correct ascending order of the given minerals in terms of their presence in the Earth's crust?

1. Amphibolite
2. Mica
3. Pyroxene

Select the answer using the code given below:

A. 2, 3, 1 B. 1, 2, 3
C. 2, 1, 3 D. 1, 3, 2

88. Which of the following is/are the applied forces in mechanical weathering process?

1. Gravitational force
2. Expansion force
3. Force due to water pressure

Select the answer using the code given below:

A. 1 only B. 1 and 2 only
C. 2 and 3 only D. 1, 2 and 3

89. Which of the following is/are cold ocean current/currents?

1. Alaska Current
2. North Atlantic Drift
3. West Wind Drift

Select the answer using the code given below:

A. 1 only B. 1 and 2 only
C. 2 and 3 D. 3 only

90. Which one of the following latitudes will experience a minimum angle of the Sun's rays when it is Summer Solstice in the Northern Hemisphere?

A. Arctic Circle B. Equator
C. Tropic of Cancer D. Tropic of Capricorn

91. Which of the following statements with reference to Coriolis force is/are correct?

1. Coriolis force acts perpendicular to the pressure gradient force
2. At the equator, the Coriolis force is zero and the wind blows perpendicular to the isobars

Select the answer using the code given below:

A. 1 only
B. 2 only
C. Both 1 and 2
D. Neither 1 nor 2

92. Which of the following statements with reference to Sleet is/are correct?

1. Sleet is frozen raindrops and refrozen melted snow-water
2. It occurs when a layer of air with the temperature below freezing point overlies a warm layer near the ground surface

Select the answer using the code given below:

A. 1 only B. 2 only
C. Both 1 and 2 D. Neither 1 nor 2

93. Humid Subtropical Climate is NOT experienced in which one among the following regions?

A. Coastal South Africa
B. East coast of Australia
C. South Japan
D. South Argentina

94. Mahendragiri, the highest peak of the Eastern Ghats, is located in which one of the following states?

A. Andhra Pradesh B. Odisha
C. Telangana D. Tamil Nadu

95. Temperate forests of South India, known as 'Sholas' are found in which of the following hills?

1. Anaimalai
2. Nilgiris
3. Palani

Select the answer using the code given below:

A. 1 only B. 1 and 2 only
C. 2 and 3 only D. 1, 2 and 3

96. As per the Annual Report 2023-24 of the Ministry of Mines, Government of India, which of the following states are the major producer of Copper in the country?

A. Rajasthan and Gujarat
B. Rajasthan and Madhya Pradesh
C. Jharkhand and Rajasthan
D. Jharkhand and Madhya Pradesh

97. Which one among the following is NOT a major oil field located in Gujarat?

A. Ankaleshwar B. Kosamba
C. Mehsana D. Moran

98. As per the Land Revenue Records, any land is categorized as Culturable Waste-land if it is left fallow (uncultivated) for more than

A. 2 years B. 3 years
C. 4 years D. 5 years

99. Which one among the following is NOT included in the National Food Security Mission Commercial Crops (NFSM-CC)?

A. Cotton B. Coffee
C. Jute D. Sugar cane

100. Consider the following statements with regard to a steel plant:

I. It was setup in 1964 with Russian collaboration
II. It receives iron ore from the Rourkela region
III. Water and Hydel power is supplied by the Damodar Valley Corporation

Identify the Steel Plant on the basis of the above facts:

A. Bhilai Steel Plant B. Bokaro Steel Plant
C. Rourkela Steel Plant D. Durgapur Steel Plant

101. An offshore terminal at Vadinar has been developed to reduce pressure from which of the following major ports in India?

A. Kandla Port B. Cochin Port
C. Mormugao Port D. New Mangalore Port

102. As per the India State of Forest Report 2021, which one of the following Himalayan states has the highest percentage of its geographical area under forest?

A. Arunachal Pradesh B. Himachal Pradesh
C. Sikkim D. Uttarakhand

103. Which of the following statements with reference to L-Wave or Long Wave generated by an earthquake is/are correct?

1. They follow the Earth's circumference
2. They travel at more or less at a constant rate

Select the answer using the code given below:

A. 1 only B. 2 only
C. Both 1 and 2 D. Neither 1 nor 2

104. Which one of the following is formed when volcanic ash is carried by running water and is deposited as a sedimentary layer?

A. Basalt B. Lapilli
C. Slate D. Tuff

105. Condensation of water vapour into water is influenced by which of the following factor/factors?

1. Volume of air
2. Humidity
3. Temperature

Select the answer using the code given below:

A. 1 only B. 1 and 2 only
C. 2 and 3 only D. 1, 2 and 3

106. The lactic acid that gets accumulated in the muscle cells during rigorous exercise causing muscle cramps is produced from:

A. ATP B. Pyruvate
C. Ethanol D. Glucose

107. A chain of peptide containing linear sequences of amino acid linked by peptide bonds best represent the:

A. Primary structure B. Secondary structure
C. Tertiary structure D. Quaternary structure

108. Cambium is an example of:

A. Lateral meristem B. Apical meristem
C. Intercalary meristem D. Permanent tissue

109. What happens when the fat and oil containing food materials are left outside for a long time?

A. Fats and oils in the food get oxidized
B. Fats and oils in the food get reduced
C. Fats and oils in the food get ice-covered
D. No reaction takes place

110. Which is the correct base pairing found in a normal DNA molecule?

A. Adenine pairs with Thymine
B. Adenine pairs with Guanine
C. Adenine pairs with Cytosine
D. Thymine pairs with Guanine

111. Clotting of blood involves which one among the following clotting proteins?

A. Pathogen B. Fibrinogen
C. Macrophage D. Phagocytes

112. Initial discovery of antibiotic penicillin was done by:

A. Francis Crick B. Maurice Wilkins
C. Charles Darwin D. Alexander Fleming

113. The vector of malaria parasites is:

A. Male *Anopheles* mosquito
B. Male *Culex* mosquito
C. Female *Anopheles* mosquito
D. Female *Culex* mosquito

114. Which of the following pairs is/are correctly matched?

1. Malaria : *Mycobacterium*
2. TB : *Plasmodium*

Select the answer using the code given below:

A. 1 only B. 2 only
C. Both 1 and 2 D. Neither 1 nor 2

115. Vitamin B1 is also known as:

A. Riboflavin B. Thiamin
C. Retinol D. Tocopherol

116. Gaja Dwar, Ashwa Dwar, Garuda Dwar, Makar Dwar, Shardula Dwar and Hamsa Dwar are located in a building at:

A. New Delhi B. Varanasi
C. Aurangabad D. Tanjevur

117. Which dance form of India has been inscribed into UNESCO's Representative List of Intangible Cultural Heritage of Humanity?

A. Kathakali B. Garba
C. Bhangra D. Odissi

118. Which Ministry has initiated the "Dhara", a special initiative dedicated to Indian Knowledge System (IKS)?

A. The Ministry of Education
B. The Ministry of Home Affairs
C. The Ministry of Information & Broadcasting
D. The Ministry of Culture

119. The scheme PRASHAD (Pilgrimage Rejuvenation and Spiritual Heritage Augmentation Drive) provides assistance for:

A. e-Visa Facility
B. Multilingual Tourist Infoline
C. The development of tourism infrastructures in States & Union Territories
D. Promoting Dekho Apna Desh scheme

120. The Joint Venture named 'ASHVINI' to develop nuclear power facility in India is between:

A. NPCIL and NTPC B. TMC and VECC
C. HWB and BARC D. IGACR and NTPC

121. Which one of the following statements about 'RE-JUPAVE' is correct?

A. It's a joint venture between Food and Agriculture Organisation (FAO) and Government of India to promote organic farming
B. It's the name given to the lightest surveillance aircraft developed by DRDO
C. It's a centrally sponsored flagship Programme of the Ministry of Women and Child Development, Government of India
D. It's an indigenously developed road construction technology at high altitudes

122. Which of the following statements about 'C-Bot' is/are correct?

1. It's an underwater vehicle to monitor coral reefs
2. It has been developed by CSIR and NIO

Select the answer using the code given below:

A. 1 only B. 2 only
C. Both 1 and 2 D. Neither 1 nor 2

123. India's Gas Turbine Research Establishment (GTRE), part of the Defence Research and Development Organisation (DRDO) has developed an aeroengine which will potentially make India self-reliance in aero-engine technology. What is the name of the engine?

A. Ganga B. Yamuna
C. Krishna D. Kaveri

124. Who among the following Presidents/Vice Presidents of the United States of America was awarded Nobel Peace Prize for work to find peaceful solutions to international conflicts, to advance democracy and human rights, and to promote economic and social development?

A. Jimmy Carter B. Woodrow Wilson
C. Barack Obama D. AI Gore

125. Which among the following agencies releases report on 'S.A.F.E. Accommodation : Worker Housing for Manufacturing Growth'?

A. RBI
B. NITI Aayog
C. National Housing Bank
D. Housing and Urban Development Corporation

126. An object is placed between infinity and the pole (P) of a convex mirror. The position of the image is

A. between pole (P) and the focus (F), behind the mirror
B. between the focus (F) and infinity, behind the mirror
C. between the pole (P) and the infinity, in front of the mirror
D. at the focus (F), behind the mirror

127. The work done in moving a charge of 2 coulomb (C) from point A to point B is 24 J. What is the potential difference between A and B?

A. 48 V B. 6 V
C. 12 V D. 0.08 V

128. Two conducting wires of the same material and of equal lengths and equal diameters are first connected in parallel and then in series in a circuit across the same potential difference. The ratio of heat produced in parallel and series combinations is:

A. 2 : 1 B. 4 : 1
C. 1 : 2 D. 1 : 4

129. The magnetic field inside a long straight solenoid-carrying current:

A. is zero
B. decreases as we move towards its end
C. increases as we move towards its end
D. is uniform inside the solenoid

130. A car has an initial velocity of 12 m/s and is brought to rest over a distance of 45 m. The acceleration of the car is:

A. $+1.6\ m/s^2$ B. $+3.2\ m/s^2$
C. $-1.6\ m/s^2$ D. $-0.8\ m/s^2$

131. The universal constant of gravitation G has the unit:

A. N B. m/s
C. Joule D. $N\text{-}m^2/kg^2$

132. Two bodies of unequal masses are dropped from a tower. At any instant, they have equal:

A. Momentum B. Acceleration
C. Potential energy D. Kinetic energy

133. The frequency (f), wavelength (λ) and speed (v) of a sound wave are related as:

A. $f = v\lambda$ B. $\lambda = vf$
C. $f = \frac{\lambda}{v}$ D. $v = \lambda f$

134. The length of a simple pendulum is increased four times to its previous value while the mass is doubled. What is the ratio of the new and previous time period of the pendulum?

A. 3 : 1 B. 2 : 5
C. 2 : 1 D. 3 : 2

135. Which one of the following is NOT a basic property of electric charge?

A. Charges can be added
B. Charges is conserved
C. Charge on a body is always an integral multiple of an electron or a proton charge
D. Charges can be created and destroyed in an isolated system

136. What happens when the sunlight travels through the Earth's atmosphere?

A. The blue colour is scattered more compared to the red colour
B. The red colour is scattered more compared to the blue colour
C. Both the blue and the red colours are scattered equally
D. The blue colour is not scattered but the red colour is scattered the most

137. When a solid body is partially or completely immersed in a fluid, the fluid exerts an upward force on the body. The magnitude of the force is equal to:

1. the mass of the body
2. the weight of the displaced fluid by the body

Which of the above is/are correct?

A. 1 only
B. 2 only
C. Both 1 and 2
D. Neither 1 nor 2

138. If the length of a copper wire is increased by twice, then its resistivity will be:

A. Doubled B. Halved
C. Same D. One-fourth

139. Which one of the following is dimensionless quantity?

A. Stress B. Strain
C. Pressure D. Force

140. A system that does NOT allow exchange of heat with its surrounding is called:

A. Adiabatic system
B. Non-adiabatic system
C. Equilibrium system
D. Non-equilibrium system

141. If the speed of light in carbon disulfide and vacuum is X and Y respectively, then:

A. $X < Y$ B. $X > Y$
C. $X \geq Y$ D. $X = Y$

142. A current through a horizontal power line flows in east to west direction. What will be the direction of magnetic field at a point directly below it when viewed from east end?

A. Clockwise in a plane perpendicular to the wire
B. Anti-clockwise in a plane perpendicular to the wire
C. Clockwise in a plane of parallel to the wire
D. Anti-clockwise in a plane of parallel to the wire

143. Which one among the following elements is known to be discovered the earliest?

A. Copper B. Gold
C. Oxygen D. Uranium

144. When a light ray passes through from air to water with a non-zero angle the ray will be:

A. bending towards the normal
B. bending away from the normal
C. propagating in straight line
D. reflected towards the opposite direction

145. Which one of the following equations related to the motion of an object is NOT correct? (Symbols carry their usual meanings)

A. $s = ut + \frac{1}{2}at^2$
B. $u = v - at$
C. $u^2 - v^2 = 2as$
D. Distance travelled during nth second $= u + \frac{1}{2}a(2n-1)$

146. Which one of the following statements is NOT correct?

A. An ammeter is always connected in series in the circuit to measure the current
B. A Voltmeter is always connected to parallel in a circuit to measure the voltage
C. A voltmeter has a high resistance and an ammeter has a low resistance
D. A voltmeter has a low resistance and an ammeter has a high resistance

147. Which one of the following is a non-conventional source of energy?

A. Petroleum B. Natural Gas
C. Tidal energy D. Coal

148. If three resistors of 1 Ohm each connect in parallel to each other the resultant resistance is:

A. 1 Ohm B. $\frac{1}{3}$ Ohm
C. 3 Ohm D. 9 Ohm

149. We hear an echo due to:

A. Refraction of sound waves
B. Reflection of sound waves
C. Diffraction of sound waves
D. Resonance due to sound waves

150. At uniform speed the acceleration is:

A. Maximum B. Minimum
C. Zero D. Constant

PAPER II : MATHEMATICS

1. The sum of the first k terms of a series S is $3k^2 + 5k$. Which one of the following is correct?

A. The terms of S form an arithmetic progression with common difference 14.
B. The terms of S form an arithmetic progression with common difference 6.
C. The terms of S form a geometric progression with common ratio 10/7.
D. The terms of S form a geometric progression with common ratio 11/4.

2. The sum of the first 8 terms of a GP is five times the sum of its first 4 terms. If $r \neq 1$ is the common ratio, then what is the number of possible real values of r?

A. One
B. Two
C. Three
D. More than three

3. If one root of the equation $x^2 - kx + k = 0$ exceeds the other by $2\sqrt{3}$, then which one of the following is a value of k?

A. 3 B. 6
C. 9 D. 12

4. If $x + \frac{5}{y} = 4$ and $y + \frac{5}{x} = -4$, then what is $(x + y)$ equal to?

A. 0
B. 1
C. 4
D. 5

5. If 5th, 7th and 13th terms of an AP are in GP, then what is the ratio of its first term to its common difference?

A. –3 B. –2
C. 2 D. 3

6. If p, 1, q are in AP and p, 2, q are in GP, then which of the following statements is/are correct?

I. p, 4, q are in HP.
II. $(1/p)$, 1/4, $(1/q)$ are in AP.

Select the answer using the code given below.

A. I only B. II only
C. Both I and II D. Neither I nor II

7. If $x = (1111)_2$, $y = (1001)_2$ and $z = (110)_2$, then what is $x^3 - y^3 - z^3 - 3xyz$ (equal) to?

A. $(1111001)_2$ B. $(1001111)_2$
C. $(1)_2$ D. 0_2

8. If

$$\Delta = \begin{vmatrix} a & b & c \\ d & e & f \\ g & h & i \end{vmatrix}$$

and A, B, C, D, G are the cofactors of the elements a, b, c, d, g respectively, then what is bB + cC − dD − gG equal to?

A. 0 B. 1
C. Δ D. −Δ

9. Consider the following statements in respect of the determinant

$$\Delta = \begin{vmatrix} k(k+2) & 2k+1 & 1 \\ 2k+1 & k+2 & 1 \\ 3 & 3 & 1 \end{vmatrix}$$

I. Δ is positive if $k > 0$.
II. Δ is negative if $k < 0$.
III. Δ is zero if $k = 0$

How many of the statements given above are correct?

A. None B. One
C. Two D. All three

10. If

$$\begin{vmatrix} 2 & 3+i & -1 \\ 3-i & 0 & i-1 \\ -1 & -1-i & 1 \end{vmatrix} = A + iB$$

where $i = \sqrt{-1}$, then what is A + B equal to?

A. −10 B. −6
C. 0 D. 6

11. If $A^2 + B^2 + C^2 = 0$, then what is the value of the following?

$$\begin{vmatrix} 1 & \cos C & \cos B \\ \cos C & 1 & \cos A \\ \cos B & \cos A & 1 \end{vmatrix}$$

A. −1 B. 0
C. 1 D. 2

12. If ω is a non-real cube root of unity, then what is a root of the following equation?

$$\begin{vmatrix} x+1 & \omega & \omega^2 \\ \omega & x+\omega^2 & 1 \\ \omega^2 & 1 & x+\omega \end{vmatrix} = 0$$

A. $x = 0$ B. $x = 1$
C. $x = \omega$ D. $x = \omega^2$

13. What is $\left(\dfrac{\sqrt{3}+i}{\sqrt{3}-i}\right)^3$ equal to?

A. −1 B. 0
C. 1 D. 3

14. If $x^2 - x + 1 = 0$, then what is

$$\left(x - \frac{1}{x}\right)^2 + (x - x)^4 + \left(x - \frac{1}{x}\right)^8$$

equal to?

A. 81 B. 85
C. 87 D. 90

15. How many 7-letter words (with or without meaning) can be constructed using all the letters of the word CAPITAL so that all consonants come together in each word?

A. 360 B. 300
C. 288 D. 240

16. If $z \neq 0$ is a complex number, then what is amp(z) + amp($\bar{z}$) equal to?

A. 0 B. π/2
C. π D. 2π

17. How many sides are there in a polygon which has 20 diagonals?

A. 6 B. 7
C. 8 D. 10

18. In how many ways can the letters of the word DELHI be arranged keeping the positions of vowels and consonants unchanged?

A. 6 B. 9
C. 12 D. 24

19. What is the number of positive integer solutions of $x + y + z = 5$?

A. 3 B. 5
C. 6 D. 9

20. What is the number of rational terms in the expansion of $(3^{1/2} + 5^{1/4})^{12}$?

A. 2 B. 3
C. 4 D. 6

21. If the sum of binomial coefficients in the expansion of $(x + y)^n$ is 256, then the greatest binomial coefficient occurs in which one of the following terms?

A. Third
B. Fourth
C. Fifth
D. Ninth

22. If $k < \left(\sqrt{2}+1\right)^3 < k+2$, where k is a natural number, then what is the value of k?

A. 11 B. 13
C. 15 D. 17

23. If

$$\begin{bmatrix} x & 1 & 1 \end{bmatrix} \begin{bmatrix} 1 & 2 & 3 \\ 4 & 5 & 6 \\ 7 & 8 & 9 \end{bmatrix} \begin{bmatrix} 1 \\ 1 \\ x \end{bmatrix} = [45]$$

then which one of the following is a value of x?

A. –2 B. –1
C. 0 D. 1

24. If

$$A = \begin{bmatrix} y & z & x \\ z & x & y \\ x & y & z \end{bmatrix}$$

where x, y, z are integers, is an orthogonal matrix, then what is the value of $x^2 + y^2 + z^2$?

A. 0 B. 1
C. 4 D. 14

25. Consider the following in respect of a non-singular matrix M:

I. $|M^2| = |M|^2$
II. $|M| = |M^{-1}|$
III. $|M| = |M^T|$

How many of the above are correct?

A. None B. One
C. Two D. All three

26. If

$$f(\theta) = \begin{bmatrix} \cos\theta & \sin\theta \\ -\sin\theta & \cos\theta \end{bmatrix}$$

then what is $\{f(\pi)\}^2$ equal to?

A. $\begin{bmatrix} -1 & 0 \\ 0 & -1 \end{bmatrix}$ B. $\begin{bmatrix} 1 & 1 \\ 1 & 1 \end{bmatrix}$

C. $\begin{bmatrix} -1 & 0 \\ 0 & 1 \end{bmatrix}$ D. $\begin{bmatrix} 1 & 0 \\ 0 & 1 \end{bmatrix}$

27. If

$$A = \begin{bmatrix} 1 & 2 & 2 \\ 2 & 1 & 2 \\ 2 & 2 & 1 \end{bmatrix}$$

then what is $A^2 - 4A$ equal to?

A. $-5I_3$ B. $-I_3$
C. I_3 D. $5I_3$

where I_3 is the identity matrix of order 3.

28. If the number of selections of r as well as $(n + r)$ things from $5n$ different things are equal, then what is the value of r?

A. n B. $2n$
C. $3n$ D. $4n$

29. What is the number of selection of at most 3 things from 6 different things?

A. 20 B. 22
C. 41 D. 42

30. If

$$A = \begin{bmatrix} x & y & z \\ y & z & x \\ z & x & y \end{bmatrix}$$

where x, y, z are integers, is an orthogonal matrix, then what is A^2 equal to?

A. Null matrix B. Identity matrix
C. A D. –A

Directions (Qs. No. 31-33): *Consider the following for the three (03) items that follow:*

Let $p = \sin 35°$, $q = \sin 25°$ and $r = \sin(-95°)$.

31. What is $(p + q + r)$ equal to?

A. –1 B. 0
C. 2 sin 5° D. 2 cos 5°

32. What is $(pq + qr + rp)$ equal to?

A. –3/4 B. 0
C. 1/4 D. 3/4

33. What is $(p^2 + q^2 + r^2)$ equal to?

A. 1/2 B. 1
C. 3/2 D. 2

Directions (Qs. No. 34 and 35): *Consider the following for the two (02) items that follow:*

Let $p = |\sin\alpha - \sin(\alpha - 90°)|$.

34. What is the minimum value of p?

A. 0 B. 1/2
C. $1/\sqrt{2}$ D. 1

35. What is the maximum value of p?

A. 1 B. $\sqrt{2}$
C. $\sqrt{3}$ D. 2

Directions (Qs. No. 36-38): *Consider the following for the three (03) items that follow:*

The sides of a triangle ABC are AB = 3 cm, BC = 5 cm and CA = 7 cm.

36. Consider the following statements:

I. The triangle is obtuse-angled triangle.
II. The sum of acute angles of the triangle is also acute.

Which of the statements given above is/are correct?

A. I only B. II only
C. Both I and II D. Neither I nor II

37. What is $\angle B$ equal to?

A. 60° B. 105°
C. 120° D. 150°

38. What is the area of the triangle?

A. $15\sqrt{3}/4$ square cm B. $15\sqrt{3}/2$ square cm
C. $15\sqrt{3}$ square cm D. $30\sqrt{3}$ square cm

Directions (Qs. No. 39 and 40): *Consider the following for the two (02) items that follow:*

The top (M) of a tower is observed from three points P, Q and R lying in a horizontal straight line which passes directly along the foot (N) of the tower. The angles of elevations of M from P, Q and R are 30°, 45° and 60° respectively. Let PQ = a and QR = b.

39. What is PN equal to?

A. $\left(\frac{3-\sqrt{3}}{2}\right)a$ B. $\left(\frac{3+\sqrt{3}}{2}\right)a$

C. $\left(\frac{3-\sqrt{3}}{4}\right)a$ D. $\left(\frac{3+\sqrt{3}}{4}\right)a$

40. What is MN equal to?

A. $\left(\frac{3+\sqrt{3}}{2}\right)b$ B. $\left(\frac{3-\sqrt{3}}{2}\right)b$

C. $\left(\frac{3-\sqrt{3}}{4}\right)b$ D. $\left(\frac{3+\sqrt{3}}{4}\right)b$

Directions (Qs. No. 41-43): *Consider the following for the three (03) items that follow:*

Let $p = \tan 2\alpha - \tan \alpha$ and $q = \cot \alpha - \cot 2\alpha$.

41. What is (p/q) equal to?

A. $-\tan \alpha \cdot \tan 2\alpha$ B. $-\cot \alpha \cdot \cot 2\alpha$
C. $\tan \alpha \cdot \tan 2\alpha$ D. $\cot \alpha \cdot \cot 2\alpha$

42. What is $(p + q)$ equal to?

A. $\sec 4\alpha$ B. $\operatorname{cosec} 4\alpha$
C. $2 \sec 4\alpha$ D. $2 \operatorname{cosec} 4\alpha$

43. What is $\tan^2 \alpha$ equal to?

A. $(pq)/(p + q)$ B. $(p + 2q)/p$
C. $p/(p + 2q)$ D. $p/(2p + q)$

Directions (Qs. No. 44 and 45): *Consider the following for the two (02) items that follow:*

Let $2 \sin \alpha + \cos \alpha = 2$, where $0 < \alpha < 90°$.

44. What is $\tan \alpha$ equal to?

A. 1/2 B. 1
C. 3/4 D. 2

45. What is $2 \sin 2\alpha + \cos 2\alpha$ equal to?

A. 11/10 B. 11/5
C. 12/5 D. 13/5

Directions (Qs. No. 46 and 47): *Consider the following for the two (02) items that follow:*

In a triangle ABC, two sides BC and CA are in the ratio 2 : 1 and their opposite corresponding angles are in the ratio 3 : 1.

46. One of the angles of the triangle is:

A. 15° B. 30°
C. 45° D. 75°

47. Consider the following statements:

I. The triangle is right-angled.
II. One of the sides of the triangle is 3 times the other.
III. The angles A, C and B of the triangle are in AP.

Which of the statements given above is/are correct?

A. I only
B. II and III only
C. I and III only
D. I, II and III

48. A man at M, standing 100 m away from the base (P) of a chimney of height 50 m, observes the angle of elevation of the highest point (Q) of the smoke to be 45°. The highest point of the chimney is at R. Further P, R and Q are in a straight line and the straight line is perpendicular to PM. What is the angle of RMQ equal to?

A. $\tan^{-1}\left(\frac{1}{2}\right)$ B. $\tan^{-1}\left(\frac{1}{3}\right)$

C. $\tan^{-1}\left(\frac{2}{3}\right)$ D. $\tan^{-1}\left(\frac{3}{4}\right)$

49. If k is a root of $x^2 - 4x + 1 = 0$, then what is $\tan^{-1} k + \tan^{-1}\frac{1}{k}$ equal to?

A. $-\pi/2$ B. 0
C. $\pi/4$ D. $\pi/2$

50. If $\tan^{-1} k + \tan^{-1}\frac{1}{2} = \frac{\pi}{4}$, then what is the value of k?

A. 1 B. 1/2
C. 1/3 D. 1/4

51. Under what condition will the lines $m^2x + ny - 1 = 0$ and $n^2x - my + 2 = 0$ be perpendicular?

A. $mn - 1 = 0$ B. $mn + 1 = 0$
C. $m + n = 0$ D. $m - n = 0$

52. If p and q are real numbers between 0 and 1 such that the points $(p, 1)$, $(1, q)$ and $(0, 0)$ form an equilateral triangle, then what is $(p + q)$ equal to?

A. $\sqrt{2}$ B. $\sqrt{2}-1$
C. $2-\sqrt{3}$ D. $4-2\sqrt{3}$

53. The vertices of a triangle are A(1, 1), B(0, 0) and C(2, 0). The angular bisectors of the triangle meet at P. What are the coordinates of P?

A. $\left(1, \sqrt{2}-1\right)$ B. $\left(1, \sqrt{3}-1\right)$
C. (1, 1/2) D. $\left(1/2, \sqrt{2}-1\right)$

54. Let A(3, –1) and B(1, 1) be the end points of line segment AB. Let P be the middle point of the line segment AB. Let Q be the point situated at a distance $\sqrt{2}$ units from P on the perpendicular bisector line of AB. What are the possible coordinates of Q?

A. (2, 1) B. (3, 1)
C. (2, 2) D. (1, 3)

55. ABC is an equilateral triangle and AD is the altitude on BC. If the coordinates of A are (1, 2) and that of D are (–2, 6), them what is the equation of BC?

A. $3x + 4y - 18 = 0$
B. $4x + 3y - 1 = 0$
C. $4x - 3y + 26 = 0$
D. $3x - 4y + 30 = 0$

56. What is the equation of the circle whose diameter is 10 cm and the equations of two of its diameters are $x + y = 0$ and $x - y = 0$?

A. $x^2 + y^2 = 1$
B. $x^2 + y^2 = 25$
C. $x^2 + y^2 = 100$
D. $x^2 + y^2 - 2x - 2y - 23 = 0$

57. A square is inscribed in a circle $x^2 + y^2 + 2x + 2y + 1 = 0$ and its sides are parallel to coordinate axes. Which one of the following is a vertex of the square?

A. (–2, 2)
B. (–2, –2)
C. $\left(-1+\frac{1}{\sqrt{2}}, -1-\frac{1}{\sqrt{2}}\right)$
D. None of the above

58. A tangent to the parabola $y^2 = 4x$ is inclined at an angle 45° with the positive direction of x-axis. What is the point of contact of the tangent and the parabola?

A. (1, 1) B. $\left(2, 2\sqrt{2}\right)$
C. $\left(\frac{1}{2}, \frac{1}{\sqrt{2}}\right)$ D. (1, 2)

59. What is the distance between the two foci of the hyperbola $25x^2 - 75y^2 = 225$?

A. $2\sqrt{3}$ units B. $4\sqrt{3}$ units
C. $\sqrt{6}$ units D. $2\sqrt{6}$ units

60. If any point on an ellipse is (3 sin α, 5 cos α), then what is the eccentricity of the ellipse?

A. 4/3 B. 4/5
C. 3/4 D. 1/2

61. If a line in 3 dimensions makes angles α, β and γ with the positive directions of the coordinate axes, then what is cos(α + β) cos (α – β) equal to?

A. $\cos^2 \gamma$ B. $-\cos^2 \gamma$
C. $\sin^2 \gamma$ D. $-\sin^2 \gamma$

62. A(1, 2, –1), B(2, 5, –2) and C(4, 4, –3) are three vertices of a rectangle. What is the area of the rectangle?

A. 8 square units B. 9 square units
C. $\sqrt{66}$ square units D. $\sqrt{68}$ square units

63. ABC is a triangle right-angled at B. If A(k, 1, –1), B($2k$, 0, 2) and C($2 + 2k$, k, 1) are the vertices of the triangle, then what is the value of k?

A. –3 B. –1
C. 1 D. 3

64. If a line

$$\frac{x+1}{p} = \frac{y-1}{q} = \frac{z-2}{r}$$

where $p = 2q = 3r$, makes an angle θ with the positive direction of y-axis, then what is cos 2θ equal to?

A. –31/49 B. –37/49
C. 31/49 D. 37/49

65. What is the equation of the plane passing through the point (1, 1, 1) and perpendicular to the line whose direction ratios are ⟨3, 2, 1⟩?

A. $x + 2y + 3z = 6$
B. $3x + 2y + z = 6$
C. $x + y + z = 3$
D. $3x + 2y + z = 0$

66. A line makes angles α, β and γ with the positive directions of the coordinate axes. If $\vec{a} = (\sin^2 \alpha)\hat{i} + (\sin^2 \beta)\hat{j} + (\sin^2 \gamma)\hat{k}$ and $\vec{b} = \hat{i} + \hat{j} + \hat{k}$, then what is $\vec{a} \cdot \vec{b}$ equal to?

A. –2 B. –1
C. 1 D. 2

67. Consider the following statements in respect of a vector $\vec{d} = (\vec{a} \times \vec{b}) \times \vec{c}$:

I. $\vec{d}$ is coplanar with $\vec{a}$ and $\vec{b}$.

II. $\vec{d}$ is perpendicular to $\vec{c}$

Which of the statements given above is/are correct?

A. I only
B. II only
C. Both I and II
D. Neither I nor II

68. The position vectors of three points A, B and C are $\vec{a}, \vec{b}$ and $\vec{c}$ respectively such that $3\vec{a} - 4\vec{b} + \vec{c} = \vec{0}$. What is AB : BC equal to?

A. 3 : 1
B. 1 : 3
C. 3 : 4
D. 1 : 4

69. The position vectors of three points A, B and C are $\vec{a}, \vec{b}$ and $\vec{c}$ respectively, where $\vec{c} = (\cos^2 \theta)\vec{a} + (\sin^2 \theta)\vec{b}$. What is $(\vec{a} \times \vec{b}) + (\vec{b} \times \vec{c}) + (\vec{c} \times \vec{a})$ equal to?

A. $\vec{0}$ B. $2\vec{c}$
C. $3\vec{c}$ D. Unit vector

70. Let $\vec{a}, \vec{b}, (\vec{a} \times \vec{b})$ be unit vectors. What is $(\vec{a} \cdot \vec{b})$ equal to?

A. 0 B. 1/2
C. 1 D. 3

Directions (Qs. No. 71 and 72): *Consider the following for the two (02) items that follow:*

Let $x = \sec \theta - \cos \theta$ and $y = \sec^4 \theta - \cos^4 \theta$.

71. What is $\left(\frac{dy}{dx}\right)^2$ equal to?

A. $\frac{4(y^2 + 4)}{(x^2 + 4)}$ B. $\frac{4(y^2 - 4)}{(x^2 - 4)}$
C. $\frac{16(y^2 + 4)}{(x^2 + 4)}$ D. $\frac{16(y^2 - 4)}{(x^2 - 4)}$

72. What is $\left(\frac{x^2 + 4}{y^2 + 4}\right)\frac{dy}{dx}\left[(x^2 + 4)\frac{d^2y}{dx^2} - 16y\right]$ equal to?

A. $16x$ B. $16y$
C. $-16x$ D. $-16y$

Directions (Qs. No. 73 and 74): *Consider the following for the two (02) items that follow:*

Let ABC be a triangle right-angled at B and AB + AC = 3 units.

73. What is ∠A equal to if the area of the triangle is maximum?

A. π/6 B. π/4
C. π/3 D. 5π/12

74. What is the maximum area of the triangle?

A. $\sqrt{3}/2$ square units
B. $\sqrt{3}$ square units
C. $\sqrt{6}/2$ square units
D. $\sqrt{6}$ square units

Directions (Qs. No. 75 and 76): *Consider the following for the two (02) items that follow:*

Let $(x + y)^{p+q} = x^p y^q$, where p, q are positive integers.

75. The derivative of y with respect to x:

A. depends on p only
B. depends on q only
C. depends on both p and q
D. is independent of both p and q

76. If $p + q = 10$, then what is $\frac{dy}{dx}$ equal to?

A. $\frac{y}{x}$ B. xy
C. $x^{10} y^{10}$ D. $\left(\frac{y}{x}\right)^{10}$

Directions (Qs. No. 77 and 78): *Consider the following for the two (02) items that follow:*

The slope of the tangent to the curve $y = f(x)$ at $(x, f(x))$ is 4 for every real number x and the curve passes through the origin.

77. What is the nature of the curve?

A. A straight line passing through (1, 4)
B. A straight line passing though (–1, 4)
C. A parabola with vertex at origin and focus at (2, 0)
D. A parabola with vertex at origin and focus at (1, 0)

78. What is the area bounded by the curve, the x-axis and the line $x = 4$?

A. 8 square units B. 16 square units
C. 32 square units D. 64 square units

Directions (Qs. No. 79 and 80): *Consider the following for the two (02) items that follow:*

$$\text{Let } f(x) = \begin{cases} x^3, & x^2 < 1 \\ x^2, & x^2 \geq 1 \end{cases}$$

79. What is $\lim_{x \to 0} f'(x)$ equal to?

A. 2 B. 1
C. 0 D. Limit does not exist

80. Consider the following statements:

I. The function is continuous at $x = -1$.
II. The function is differentiable at $x = 1$.

Which of the statements given above is/are correct?

A. I only B. II only
C. Both I and II D. Neither I nor II

Directions (Qs. No. 81 and 82): *Consider the following for the two (02) items that follow:*

Let the function $y = (1 - \cos x)^{-1}$, where $x \neq 2n\pi$ and n is an integer.

81. What is the range of the function?

A. $[0, \infty)$ B. $[0.5, \infty)$
C. $[1, \infty)$ D. $(-\infty, 0.5]$

82. What is $\int y dx$ equal to?

A. $-\tan(x/2) + c$ B. $-\cot(x/2) + c$
C. $\tan(x/2) + c$ D. $\cot(x/2) + c$
where c is the constant of integration.

Directions (Qs. No. 83 and 84): *Consider the following for the two (02) items that follow:*

Let the function $f(x) = \sin[x]$, where $[.]$ is the greatest integer function and $g(x) = |x|$.

83. What is $\lim_{x \to 0}\{f(x)\, g(x)\}$ equal to?

A. –1 B. 0
C. 1 D. Limit does not exist

84. What is $\lim_{x \to 0} \frac{f(x)}{g(x)}$ equal to?

A. –sin 1 B. sin 1
C. 0 D. Limit does not exist

Directions (Qs. No. 85 and 86): *Consider the following for the two (02) items that follow:*

Let the curve $f(x) = |x - 3|$.

85. What is the domain of the function $f(x)$?

A. $(0, \infty)$ B. $(3, \infty)$
C. $(-\infty, \infty)$ D. $(-\infty, \infty)\backslash\{3\}$

86. What is the area bounded by the curve $f(x)$ and $y = 3$?

A. 3 square units B. 4.5 square units
C. 7.5 square units D. 9 square units

Directions (Qs. No. 87 and 88): *Consider the following for the two (02) items that follow:*

Let $f = \{(1, 1), (2, 4) (3, 7), (4, 10)\}$:

87. If $f(x) = px + q$, then what is the value of $(p + q)$?

A. –1 B. 0
C. 1 D. 5

88. Consider the following statements:

I. f is one-one function.
II. f is onto function if the codomain is the set of natural numbers.

Which of the statements given above is/are correct?

A. I only B. II only
C. Both I and II D. Neither I nor II

Directions (Qs. No. 89 and 90): *Consider the following for the two (02) items that follow:*

Let the function $f(x) = x^2 - 1$.

89. What is $\lim_{x \to 1}\{f \circ f(x)\}$ equal to?

A. –1 B. 0
C. 1 D. 2

90. What is the area bounded by the function $f(x)$ and the x-axis?

A. 1/3 square unit
B. 2/3 square unit
C. 4/3 square unit
D. 2 square unit

Directions (Qs. No. 91 and 92): *Consider the following for the two (02) items that follow:*

$$\text{Let } y = \sin^{-1}\left(x - \frac{4x^3}{27}\right).$$

91. Where is y equal to?

A. $\sin^{-1} x$ B. $\sin^{-1}\left(\frac{x}{3}\right)$

C. $3 \sin^{-1} x$ D. $3\sin^{-1}\left(\frac{x}{3}\right)$

92. What is $\frac{dy}{dx}$ equal to?

A. $\frac{1}{\sqrt{9-x^2}}$ B. $\frac{1}{\sqrt{3-x^2}}$

C. $\frac{3}{\sqrt{9-x^2}}$ D. $\frac{9}{\sqrt{9-x^2}}$

Directions (Qs. No. 93 and 94): *Consider the following for the two (02) items that follow:*

Let the function $f(x) = x^2 + 9$.

93. What is $\lim_{x\to 0} \frac{\sqrt{f(x)}-3}{\sqrt{f(x)+7}-4}$ equal to?

A. 2/3 B. 1
C. 4/3 D. 2

94. Consider the following statements:

I. $f(x)$ is an increasing function.
II. $f(x)$ has local maximum at $x = 0$.

Which of the statements given above is/are correct?

A. I only B. II only
C. Both I and II D. Neither I nor II

Directions (Qs. No. 95 and 96): *Consider the following for the two (02) items that follow:*

The function $f(x)$ satisfies $f\left(\frac{x}{y}\right) = \frac{f(x)}{f(y)}$ for all positive real values of x and y, and $f(2) = 3$.

95. What is $f(16)$ equal to?

A. 18 B. 27
C. 54 D. 81

96. What is $f(1)\, f(4)$ equal to?

A. 4 B. 8
C. 9 D. 18

Directions (Qs. No. 97 and 98): *Consider the following for the two (02) items that follow:*

A function f is such that $f(xy) = f(x + y)$ for all real values of x and y, and $f(5) = 10$.

97. What is $f(0)$ equal to?

A. 0 B. 1
C. 5 D. 10

98. What is $f(20) + f(-20)$ equal to?

A. 0 B. 10
C. 20 D. 40

Directions (Qs. No. 99 and 100): *Consider the following for the two (02) items that follow:*

Let $f(x) = [x^2]$, where [.] is the greatest integer function.

99. What is $\int_{\sqrt{2}}^{\sqrt{3}} f(x)\, dx$ equal to?

A. $\sqrt{3}-\sqrt{2}$ B. $2\left(\sqrt{3}-\sqrt{2}\right)$
C. $3-\sqrt{2}$ D. 1

100. What is $\int_{\sqrt{2}}^{2} f(x)\, dx$ equal to?

A. $6-\sqrt{3}-2\sqrt{2}$ B. $6-\sqrt{3}-\sqrt{2}$
C. $6-\sqrt{3}+2\sqrt{2}$ D. $6+\sqrt{3}-2\sqrt{2}$

Directions (Qs. No. 101-104): *Consider the following for the four (04) items that follow:*

The frequency distribution of height of students of a class is given below:

Height (in cm)	*Number of Students*
160-162	12
162-164	15
164-166	24
166-168	13

101. What is the total number of students whose height is less than or equal to 165 cm?

A. 15 B. 39
C. 51 D. None of the above

102. What is the median height of the class?

A. 162.41 cm B. 163.41 cm
C. 164.41 cm D. 165.41 cm

103. The height which occurs most frequently in the class is:

A. 163.5 cm B. 163.9 cm
C. 164.5 cm D. 164.9 cm

104. The most appropriate graphical representation of the given frequency distribution is:

A. bar chart B. percentage bar chart
C. histogram D. pie chart

Directions (Qs. No. 105 and 106): *Consider the following for the two (02) items that follow:*

The sum and the sum of squares of the observations corresponding to length X (in cm) and weight Y (in gm) of 50 tropical tubers are given as $\sum X = 200$, $\sum Y = 250$, $\sum X^2 = 900$ and $\sum Y^2 = 1400$.

105. Which one of the following is correct?

A. Variance (X) > Variance (Y)
B. Variance (X) < Variance (Y)
C. Variance (X) = Variance (Y)
D. Cannot be determined from the given data

106. Which one of the following statements is correct?

A. Coefficient of variation of X is strictly more than coefficient of variation of Y.
B. Coefficient of variation of X is strictly less than coefficient of variation of Y.
C. Coefficient of variation of X is same as coefficient of variation of Y.
D. Coefficient of variation cannot be determined from the given data.

Directions (Qs. No. 107 and 108): *Consider the following for the two (02) items that follow:*

Let X be a random variable following binomial distribution with parameters $n = 6$ and $p = k$. Further, $9P(X = 4) = P(X = 2)$.

107. What is the value of *k*?

A. 1/2 B. 1/3
C. 1/4 D. 1/5

108. What is the value of $P(X = 3)$?

A. 135/1024 B. 5/128
C. 45/1024 D. 70/1024

Directions (Qs. No. 109 and 110): *Consider the following for the two (02) items that follow:*

A committee of 6 members is formed from a group of 7 gentlemen and 4 ladies.

109. What is the probability that the committee includes exactly 3 gentlemen?

A. 10/33 B. 30/77
C. 100/231 D. 5/11

110. What is the probability that the committee includes at least 2 ladies?

A. 41/66 B. 47/66
C. 49/66 D. 53/66

Directions (Qs. No. 111 and 112): *Consider the following for the two (02) items that follow:*

The probabilities that A, B and C become managers are 3/10, 1/2 and 4/5 respectively. The probabilities that bonus scheme will be introduced if A, B and C become managers are 4/9, 2/9 and 1/3 respectively.

111. What is the probability that the bonus scheme will be introduced?

A. 17/45 B. 19/45
C. 23/45 D. 26/45

112. If the bonus scheme has been introduced, then what is the probability that the manager appointed was B?

A. 5/23 B. 6/23
C. 7/23 D. 8/23

113. The arithmetic mean of 100 observations is 50. If 5 is subtracted from each observation and then divided by 20, then what is the new arithmetic mean?

A. 2.25 B. 3.5
C. 4.25 D. 5.5

114. The standard deviation of 100 observations is 10. If 5 is added to each observation and then divided by 20, then what will be the new standard deviation?

A. 0.25 B. 0.5
C. 0.75 D. 1.00

115. If $P(A) = 1/3$, $P(B) = 1/2$ and $P(A \cap B) = 1/4$, then what is the value of $P(B|A^c)$?

A. 1/8 B. 3/8
C. 5/8 D. 7/8

116. If $P(A) = 1/3$, $P(B) = 1/2$ and $P(A \cap B) = 1/4$, then what is the value of $P(A^c \cap B^c)$?

A. 1/4 B. 5/12
C. 7/12 D. 11/12

117. If two fair dice are tossed, then what is the probability that the sum of the numbers on the faces of the dice is strictly greater than 7?

A. 1/3 B. 5/12
C. 7/12 D. 3/4

118. The probability of a man hitting a target is 1/5. If the man fires 7 times, then what is the probability that he hits the target at least twice?

A. $1-\left(\frac{3}{5}\right)\left(\frac{4}{5}\right)^6$ B. $1-\left(\frac{3}{5}\right)\left(\frac{4}{5}\right)^7$
C. $1-\left(\frac{11}{5}\right)\left(\frac{4}{5}\right)^6$ D. $1-\left(\frac{11}{5}\right)\left(\frac{4}{5}\right)^7$

119. Let X be a random variable following binomial distribution whose mean and variance are 200 and 160 respectively. What is the value of the number of trials (*n*)?

A. 500 B. 1000
C. 1500 D. 2000

120. What is the arithmetic mean of 8^2, 9^2, 10^2, ..., 15^2?

A. 133.5 B. 135.5
C. 137.5 D. 139.5

EXPLANATORY ANSWERS

PAPER I : GENERAL ABILITY TEST

1. **(D):** The passage discusses reasons like continued discovery of new languages, unexplored regions, and mistaken identity of new languages as dialects. But it never mentions that people don't claim their language as a reason for difficulty in estimating the number of languages.

2. **(A):** New languages are not always immediately recognized as separate because they may initially appear similar to known languages. Linguists often realize, only after maintaining prolonged interaction with the speakers, that the speech differs significantly enough to be classified as a distinct language. Therefore, sustained contact over time is essential in confirming whether a language is newly discovered.

3. **(C):** The passage implies that what is initially thought to be a dialect sometimes turns out to be a distinct language, indicating that the distinction is not always immediately clear and often languages exist in complex forms—either as full languages or dialects. This makes option C the most accurate.

4. **(A):** The passage says, "The people may be known, but the identity of their language may not be," suggesting that ethnic identity is acknowledged, but their language may remain unidentified.

5. **(A):** The word "transpire" in the sentence "Only after a considerable period of contact does it transpire..." means that it becomes known or evident that the speech is a different language. So "transpire" means 'come to be known'.

6. **(A):** In converting from direct to indirect speech:
   - "said to" becomes "told"
   - Present tense "want" becomes past "wanted"
   - "you" becomes "her"
   - "here" becomes "there"
   - "tomorrow" becomes "the next day"

   All these changes are correctly made in option (A).

7. **(B):** This is the closest correct transformation, although slightly awkward in phrasing. The original exclamatory sentence is converted into a reported statement.

   Option A is grammatically flawed, and option C uses "is" instead of "was". Option D turns it into a question, which it wasn't. So, B is best.

8. **(C):** The indirect sentence has "why they had been quiet...", so in direct speech it becomes:
   - "Why had you been quiet..."
   - "said to" is a standard reporting verb.

   Thus, option (C) is correct.

9. **(B):** This is the most grammatically acceptable of the four, although ideally, "intellectual" should be plural. But among the given options, B is the least flawed.

10. **(A):** This is the correct structure for a comparative sentence. "taller than" is correctly used, and "then" (in D) is a wrong word. Other options are grammatically incorrect.

11. **(A):** "Confident" refers to being self-assured or certain. "Confidant" refers to a person with whom one shares secrets—typically a close and trusted friend.

12. **(B):** "Broke" means having no money (bankrupt). "Brook" is a small natural stream of fresh water.

13. **(C):** "Accept" means to agree or consent to something. "Except" means to exclude or apart from.

14. **(D):** "Accord" refers to a formal agreement or harmony. "Accrued" means something has accumulated over time, usually in context of finance or interest.

15. **(C):** "Guarantee" is a general promise of quality or performance.

    "Warranty" is a formal written service contract that defines the terms of product repair or replacement.

16. **(A):** "Proportionate" means corresponding in size or amount, especially in a fair or balanced way. So, the word closest in meaning is "balanced".

17. **(B):** "Disenchantment" refers to a feeling of disappointment about something once admired or believed in. So, "disappointment" is the closest match.

18. **(D):** "Imminent" means something that is about to happen soon, and often unavoidable. "Inevitable" captures that sense of certainty and immediacy.

19. **(A):** "Indelible" means something that cannot be erased or forgotten—thus, "permanent" is the most appropriate synonym.

20. **(A):** "Instantaneous" means occurring instantly or without any delay. The nearest word in meaning is "immediate".

21. **(C):** S1 talks about non-renewable resources.

    S: States that mineral resources are finite and non-renewable – connects directly with S1.

    Q: Warns that despite rich deposits, they are short-lived – continues the warning tone.

    R: Explains difficulty and expense in mining due to depth – logical follow-up.

    P: Adds that mining becomes costlier and once exhausted, cannot be replaced – concluding the chain.

    S6 defines "conservation" – connects well after warning about limited resources.

22. **(D):** S1 says India has a vast road network.

    P: Talks about historical importance – logical background.

    R: Refers to Ashoka and Chandragupta building roads – supports P.

S: Construction continued in late medieval times – shows progression.

Q: Introduces Grand Trunk Road built by Sher Shah – specific example.

S6 explains the route of the Grand Trunk Road – connects with Q.

23. (A): S1 introduces national highways.

P: Gives a fact about their significance – despite only 2% of roads, they carry 40% traffic.

R: Explains why they bear so much load – they link distant towns and cities.

S: Adds they connect the whole nation and enable trade and connectivity.

Q: Concludes that their construction and maintenance are crucial.

S6 defines them as primary road systems – consistent with the explanation.

24. (D):

P: introduces the historical context by stating that the Constitution was created during a period of post-apartheid tension.

Q: follows by highlighting the importance of the Bill of Rights as the foundation of South African democracy.

S: elaborates that this Bill grants an extensive range of rights to the citizens.

R: provides specific examples of the rights protected, including non-discrimination on various grounds.

This sequence logically presents the creation, significance, scope, and content of the Constitution's rights before leading into S6.

25. (D):

S: explains that direct participation of all citizens in every decision is not possible.

Q: follows naturally, stating that representatives are therefore elected.

P: builds on this by asserting that elections thus become essential in a democracy.

R: concludes by linking elections with India's democratic identity and their symbolic importance.

This progression builds a clear rationale for representative democracy and culminates in the symbolic role of elections, leading effectively into S6.

26. (A): "As far as your transfer request is concerned" is a standard expression to introduce a topic formally and directly.

27. (B): "By the way, did you know..." is a common phrase to casually introduce a new or unrelated topic in a conversation.

28. (D): "Speaking of the wind..." is used to shift the topic to something just mentioned or related.

29. (B): "Excuse me, what are you doing in my room?" is appropriate when interrupting or expressing surprise.

30. (C): "In some cases, an unhappy childhood leads to criminal behaviour" is a correct generalization phrase.

31. (D): "In other words, the problem is nothing but..." is used to rephrase or clarify a previous statement.

32. (A): "Many, understandably, hesitate..." implies the hesitation is reasonable and makes sense.

33. (B): "Generally speaking, one notes that..." is suitable for introducing a broad or general observation.

34. (C): "Thus, the situation has completely transformed..." shows cause-effect or conclusion.

35. (A): "Hence, the committee is of the opinion..." expresses a conclusion or result from earlier discussion.

36. (B): *Cynosure* refers to something that strongly attracts attention due to its brilliance or interest.

37. (A): *Coeval* means contemporary or of the same age or era.

38. (C): *Retrogression* refers to moving backward to a less advanced or worse state.

39. (B): *Imprest* is a small advance of money for minor or petty expenses.

40. (C): *Turgid* describes something swollen, over-inflated, or congested.

41. (C):

Q: "many of the people who had come to..."

P: participate in the function" – completes the subject.

S: "could not find a seat because" – explains the problem.

R: "the auditorium was over-crowded" – gives the reason.

42. (D):

R: "somewhere in the back of her mind"

Q: "she knew that the answer" – continues the thought.

S: "to her questions about life" – clarifies "answer".

P: "lay outside her existing life" – reveals the conclusion.

43. (C):

Q: "inside the pages of all good"

P: "works of literature" – completes the object.

S: "lies the truth about some of"

R: "the more challenging questions posed by humanity"

44. (C):

R: "for every stride of progress any nation"

P: "takes on account of its economic successes"

S: "it takes two back if it is unable"

Q: "to address continuing social inequality"

45. (A):

S: "amortisation is an accounting technique"

R: "used to periodically lower"

P: "the book-value of a loan or"

Q: "an intangible asset over a set period of time"

46. (A): The correct phrase is "There is more than one way..." which is a standard expression meaning multiple possible methods.

47. (B): The indefinite article "a" is required because it's referring to organizing one unspecified event—"a picnic."

48. (D): The correct idiom is "stood trial," meaning to appear in a court to be judged.

49. (C): The present tense "is under" is appropriate since the action is ongoing: "...has been carried out is under scrutiny..."

50. (D): "Shall" is more formal and suitable in this context involving commitment to a decision-making process.

51. (C): The Second Industrial Revolution (circa 1870–1914) saw major developments in chemical, electrical, steel, and petroleum industries, unlike the first which was based on textiles and steam.

52. (D): Steatite (soapstone) was the primary material used to make Harappan seals, prized for its softness and ease of carving.

53. (A): Vajji Mahajanapada was a confederacy of clans and is known as one of the earliest oligarchies (rule by a group) in ancient India.

54. (B): The Shalbhanjika (a tree goddess figure) is an artistic motif rooted in folk and fertility cults, not directly related to core Buddhist philosophy unlike symbols like the wheel, tree, and empty seat representing the Buddha.

55. (B): The Rowlatt Act allowed detention without trial for up to two years, sparking widespread protest including Gandhi's nationwide hartal.

56. (A): The Bhoodan Movement, initiated by Acharya Vinoba Bhave in 1951, aimed to redistribute land to the landless through voluntary donation by landowners. The target was to collect around 50 million acres, roughly one-sixth of India's cultivable land. It was a non-legislative, moral appeal-based movement, and the first donation occurred in Telangana, not Bihar. 57. B. an elaborate system of establishing panchayats as units of self-government.

57. (B): The 73rd Constitutional Amendment Act of 1992 provided a framework for decentralized governance in rural areas. It led to the institutionalization of Panchayati Raj by adding Part IX to the Constitution and establishing elected panchayats at the village, intermediate, and district levels with defined powers and responsibilities.

58. (B): BHARATPOL is a centralized portal developed by the CBI (Central Bureau of Investigation) to facilitate access to inter-agency criminal databases. It enables better tracking of criminals across jurisdictions and integrates information from various law enforcement agencies into a common platform.

59. (A): Rajya Sabha members are elected by MLAs through proportional representation with a single transferable vote, not nominated by the President.

60. (D): Panchsheel Principles include:

1. Mutual respect for sovereignty
2. Non-aggression
3. Non-interference
4. Equality and mutual benefit
5. Peaceful coexistence

Nuclear non-proliferation is not part of these.

61. (A): Maize was introduced into India in the 17th century via Portuguese traders. The Portuguese brought many New World crops, including maize (makka), from the Americas during the Columbian exchange period. From their colonies like Goa, these crops spread inland.

62. (B): Let's match each plan with its correct objective:

A. Fifth Five Year Plan (1974–79): Focused on Garibi Hatao (removal of poverty) → 2

B. Seventh Five Year Plan (1985–1990): Focused on Food, Work and Productivity → 3

C. Ninth Five Year Plan (1997–2002): Objective was Growth with Social Justice and Equality → 4

D. Eleventh Five Year Plan (2007–2012): Theme was Towards Faster and More Inclusive Growth → 1

So, A–B–C–D = 2–3–4–1.

63. (C):

- Statement 1 is correct: Srimanta Shankardeva was a major Vaishnavite reformer in 15th-century Assam.
- Statement 2 is incorrect: Gaudiya Vaishnavism was founded by Chaitanya Mahaprabhu, not Shankardeva.
- Statement 3 is correct: His teachings are often referred to as Bhagavati Dharma.
- Statement 4 is correct: He promoted the setting up of Satras (monasteries) and Naam Ghars (prayer halls).

Hence, only statements 1, 3, and 4 are correct.

64. (B): The British East India Company established its first factory on the East Coast at Masulipatam (Andhra Pradesh) in 1611. This was after receiving permissions from the local Qutb Shahi rulers.

65. (A): Let's arrange the events chronologically:

1. Lucknow Pact – 1916 (Agreement between INC and Muslim League) → 3
2. Swaraj Party formation – 1923 (by Motilal Nehru and C.R. Das) → 1
3. Communal Award – 1932 (by Ramsay MacDonald) → 2
4. Simla Conference – 1945 (failed talks between British & Indian leaders) → 4

Correct sequence: 3, 1, 2, 4.

66. (A): The Regulating Act, 1773 led to the establishment of the Supreme Court of Judicature at Fort William (Calcutta) in 1774. It had jurisdiction over British subjects and some jurisdiction over Indian citizens.

67. (C): Lord Ripon (1880–84) is hailed as the father of local self-government in India. His resolution of 1882 promoted decentralization and empowerment of local institutions — often called the "Magna Carta of Local Self-Government".

68. (D): In Sufism, a Murid is a disciple or follower who takes spiritual training under the guidance of a spiritual master or Pir.

- Jizya is a tax.
- Ijma is Islamic consensus.
- Muqaddam is a local leader, not exclusive to Sufism.

69. (A): Democracy is defined by:

1. Consent of the governed – citizens elect their representatives.
2. Political equality – all citizens have equal voting rights.
3. The "accountability of the ruled to the ruler" is incorrect. It's the rulers who are accountable to the ruled in a democracy.

So, correct features: 1 and 2 only.

70. (C): Let's arrange countries by year of granting universal adult franchise:

1. USA – 1920 (women got voting rights; men had earlier)
2. Japan – 1946 (universal adult franchise after WWII)
3. India – 1950 (universal adult franchise from the start of the Republic)
4. Sri Lanka – 1951 (Ceylon adopted universal suffrage after independence)

Chronological order: USA (1), Japan (3), India (4), Sri Lanka (2) → 1, 3, 4, 2.

71. (D): This statement is not correct. In micelles, the structure formed by soap molecules in water, the hydrophobic (non-polar) tails point inward, surrounding the oil or grease, while the hydrophilic (ionic) heads face outward into the water. This arrangement allows soap to emulsify oils. Therefore, the ionic end is toward water, not oil.

72. (B): This is the correct statement. The mass of an electron is approximately 9.1×10^{-31} kg, while a proton is about 1.67×10^{-27} kg, making it about 1/1836 times lighter than a proton, often rounded to 1/2000.

- Statement A is incorrect because a neutron is not a simple combination of a proton and an electron.
- Statement C is incorrect because Cobalt-60 is used in cancer radiotherapy, not for goiter.
- Statement D is false; J.J. Thomson proposed the plum pudding model, not the composition of the nucleus.

73. (D): James Chadwick discovered the neutron in 1932 through an experiment involving beryllium and alpha particles. The neutron is an electrically neutral particle found in the nucleus, which explained the missing mass in atoms that could not be accounted for by protons alone.

74. (A): This statement is not correct as per Rutherford's model. According to his gold foil experiment, Rutherford proposed that an atom contains a small, dense, positively charged nucleus, not a neutral one.

The other statements correctly describe that the atom's mass is concentrated in the nucleus, electrons orbit the nucleus, and the nucleus is extremely small compared to the overall atom.

75. (C): Since the compound is XCl_2, it suggests that element X has a valency of +2. Magnesium (Mg), which is in Group 2 (alkaline earth metals), commonly forms $MgCl_2$, a solid with high melting point due to strong ionic bonding.

- Na and K (Group 1) form XCl (monovalent).
- Al (Group 13) forms XCl_3.

76. (A): Carbon monoxide (CO) is a neutral oxide. It does not exhibit acidic or basic properties in water.

- CO_2 is acidic, forming carbonic acid.
- Na_2O and MgO are basic oxides, forming hydroxides when dissolved in water.

Hence, CO is the correct neutral oxide.

77. (B): Dry ice is the solid form of carbon dioxide (CO_2). It sublimates directly from solid to gas at room temperature without becoming liquid, which is why it is used in refrigeration and fog effects. It is called "dry" because it leaves no liquid residue.

78. (B): This is not correct.

pH is defined as the negative logarithm of hydrogen ion concentration:

$$pH = -\log[H^+]$$

This means higher H^+ concentration = lower pH, i.e., more acidic.

A, C, and D are correct: pH is measured from 0 to 14, and "p" stands for "potenz" meaning power in German.

79. (D): This statement is NOT correct.

Hydrogen gas (H_2) has a molar mass of 2 grams/mol. Therefore, 4 grams of H_2 is equal to 2 moles.

Since 1 mole contains 6.022×10^{23} molecules, 2 moles would contain:

$2 \times 6.022 \times 10^{23} = 1.2044 \times 10^{24}$ molecules, not 6.022×10^{23}.

Hence, the statement claiming that 4 g of hydrogen contains Avogadro's number of molecules is incorrect.

All other options (A, B, and C) are chemically accurate based on standard molar volume and mole concept.

80. (C): This is not correct.

A compound is a pure substance formed by the chemical combination of two or more elements in a fixed ratio.

- The properties of compounds differ from those of the elements forming them.
- They can only be broken down by chemical or electrochemical reactions, not physical means.

Hence, C is incorrect.

81. (D): Matching the chemical names with their correct formulas:

A. Washing soda → $Na_2CO_3 \cdot 10H_2O$ → 3
B. Baking soda → $NaHCO_3$ → 2
C. Bleaching powder → $CaOCl_2$ → 1
D. Gypsum → $CaSO_4 \cdot 2H_2O$ → 4

Correct code: A–B–C–D = 3–2–1–4.

82. (B): Nitrogen dioxide (NO_2) tends to dimerize to form dinitrogen tetroxide (N_2O_4) especially at low temperatures:

$$2NO_2 \rightleftharpoons N_2O_4$$

Other oxides like N_2O, N_2O_3 and N_2O_5 do not undergo such dimerization.

83. (A): This statement is not correct.

- Losing hydrogen = oxidation, not reduction.
- Gaining hydrogen = reduction.

Hence, the statement contradicts the correct definition of oxidation-reduction.

84. (C):

A. Temperature → Kelvin (SI unit of temperature is kelvin, symbol K)

B. Weight → Newton (Weight is a force, measured in newtons)

C. Mass → Kilogram (SI unit of mass is kilogram, symbol kg)

D. Pressure → Pascal (SI unit of pressure is pascal, symbol Pa)

Thus, the correct matching is: A–1, B–4, C–2, D–3.

85. (C): Normal rainwater has a pH around 5.6 due to dissolved CO_2 forming carbonic acid.

If pH drops below 5.6, it is termed acid rain, typically caused by SO_2 and NO_x gases in the atmosphere forming stronger acids.

86. (C): A Great Circle is the largest circle that can be drawn on a sphere and divides it into two equal halves.

- Equator (3) is a great circle.
- Prime Meridian (1) and its opposite together form a great circle.
- Tropic of Cancer (2) is not a great circle.

87. (A): In terms of abundance in Earth's crust, the correct ascending order is:

Mica (2) < Pyroxene (3) < Amphibolite (1)

Mica is present in smaller quantities compared to the more common pyroxenes and amphibolite rocks.

88. (D): All listed forces contribute to mechanical (physical) weathering:

1. Gravitational force causes landslides and rock falls.
2. Expansion force from thermal changes or crystal growth cracks rocks.
3. Water pressure inside cracks leads to further fragmentation.

So, all three are applied forces in mechanical weathering.

89. (D):

- Alaska Current is warm, not cold.
- North Atlantic Drift is an extension of the Gulf Stream, hence warm.
- West Wind Drift (also called Antarctic Circumpolar Current) is a cold current that flows from west to east around Antarctica.

Only 3 is cold.

90. (D): On Summer Solstice (June 21), the Sun is directly overhead at the Tropic of Cancer (23.5°N).

Thus, places farther south, like the Tropic of Capricorn (23.5°S), receive sunlight at a lower angle, i.e., the minimum angle among the given options.

91. (C):

- Statement 1 is correct: Coriolis force always acts perpendicular to the pressure gradient force, and deflects wind to the right in the Northern Hemisphere and to the left in the Southern Hemisphere.
- Statement 2 is also correct: At the equator, the Coriolis force is zero because the deflective effect depends on latitude (zero at 0°). As a result, winds tend to blow perpendicular to isobars, following the pressure gradient directly.

92. (C):

- Statement 1 is correct: Sleet refers to precipitation where raindrops or melted snow refreeze into ice pellets before hitting the ground.
- Statement 2 is also correct: Sleet occurs when there is a warm layer of air above the ground, underlain by a colder layer, causing melted precipitation to refreeze mid-air before reaching the ground.

93. (D): Humid Subtropical Climates are typically found on the east coasts of continents between 25° and 35° latitudes.

- South Argentina does not experience this; instead, it has a cool temperate or steppe climate.
- South Japan, East coast of Australia, and Coastal South Africa (KwaZulu-Natal) do have humid subtropical climate zones.

94. (B): Mahendragiri (1,501 m) is the highest peak in the Eastern Ghats, located in Gajapati district of Odisha. It is an important cultural and ecological landmark.

95. (D): Sholas are patches of stunted tropical montane forest found in valleys separated by grasslands, common in the Western Ghats.

They are found in the Anaimalai, Nilgiri, and Palani hills, all located in Tamil Nadu and Kerala.

Hence, all three hills mentioned support Shola vegetation.

96. (B): As per the Annual Report 2023–24 of the Ministry of Mines, Rajasthan is the top copper-producing state, followed by Madhya Pradesh.

Hindustan Copper Ltd operates major mines in both these states (e.g., Khetri in Rajasthan, Malanjkhand in MP).

97. (D):

- Ankaleshwar, Kosamba, and Mehsana are major oil fields in Gujarat, managed by ONGC.
- Moran, however, is located in Assam, making it the correct exclusion.

98. (D): According to Land Revenue Records, land left fallow or uncultivated for more than 5 years is categorized as Culturable Waste-land.

Such lands have potential for cultivation but are not currently in productive use.

99. (B): The National Food Security Mission - Commercial Crops (NFSM-CC) focuses on crops like:

- Cotton, Jute, and Sugarcane.
- Coffee is not included under this scheme, as it is not considered a staple or industrial food-security crop.

100. (B):

- Set up in 1964 with Soviet (Russian) collaboration.
- Receives iron ore from Rourkela region.
- Water and power are supplied by the Damodar Valley Corporation (DVC).

These match only with the Bokaro Steel Plant, located in Jharkhand, which is part of India's major integrated steel plants.

101. (A): The Vadinar offshore terminal in Gujarat was developed to ease the congestion at Kandla Port, which is one of India's busiest ports handling crude oil, petroleum products, and general cargo. Vadinar helps in offloading crude oil offshore and transporting it inland via pipelines, reducing pressure on Kandla.

102. (A): According to the India State of Forest Report 2021, Arunachal Pradesh has the highest percentage of geographical area under forest among all Himalayan states—about 79.33% of its total area is under forest cover. Other states like Sikkim, Himachal, and Uttarakhand also have substantial cover but less than Arunachal.

103. (A):

- Statement 1 is correct: L-Waves (Love and Rayleigh waves) are surface seismic waves that travel along the Earth's surface, including following the Earth's circumference after large quakes.
- Statement 2 is incorrect: L-waves do not travel at a constant speed; their speed varies with the medium and terrain. They are also the slowest but most destructive type of seismic wave.

104. (D): Tuff is a type of sedimentary rock formed when volcanic ash is transported by water or wind and deposited in layers. Over time, it compacts and cements to form solid rock.

- Basalt is igneous,
- Lapilli are small tephra fragments,
- Slate is metamorphic.

105. (D): All three factors affect condensation:

1. Volume of air: Larger air volumes can hold more moisture.
2. Humidity: Higher humidity increases likelihood of condensation.
3. Temperature: Lower temperatures reduce the air's capacity to hold water, leading to condensation.

Thus, all three contribute to water vapor turning into liquid.

106. (B): During anaerobic respiration (in absence of sufficient oxygen), pyruvate is converted to lactic acid in muscle cells. This process provides limited energy but leads to lactic acid accumulation, causing muscle cramps.

107. (A): The primary structure of a protein is the linear sequence of amino acids linked by peptide bonds.

- Secondary involves alpha-helices and beta-sheets,
- Tertiary is the 3D folding,
- Quaternary is the interaction of multiple peptide chains.

108. (A): Cambium is a type of lateral meristem found in vascular plants. It helps in secondary growth, i.e., increase in thickness or girth of stems and roots.

- Apical meristem causes length growth,
- Intercalary meristem helps in growth at internodes,
- Permanent tissues don't divide.

109. (A): When fatty foods are left exposed, they react with oxygen from the air, undergoing oxidation, leading to rancidity—a foul smell and taste. This is a chemical change and affects food quality.

110. (A): In DNA:

- Adenine (A) always pairs with Thymine (T) via 2 hydrogen bonds
- Guanine (G) pairs with Cytosine (C) via 3 hydrogen bonds

So, the correct base pairing is A–T and G–C.

111. (B): Fibrinogen is a soluble plasma protein essential for blood clotting. When an injury occurs, it is converted by thrombin into fibrin, which forms a mesh to trap blood cells and stop bleeding.

- Pathogens are disease-causing microbes.
- Macrophages and phagocytes are immune cells, not clotting proteins.

112. (D): Alexander Fleming discovered penicillin in 1928, when he observed that a mold (*Penicillium notatum*) inhibited bacterial growth in a culture plate, marking the beginning of modern antibiotics.

113. (C): Female Anopheles mosquitoes are the only carriers (vectors) of Plasmodium parasites, which cause malaria in humans.

- Males do not bite humans, hence not vectors.
- Culex mosquitoes transmit diseases like filariasis and encephalitis, not malaria.

114. (D):

- Malaria is caused by Plasmodium (a protozoan), not Mycobacterium.
- Tuberculosis (TB) is caused by *Mycobacterium tuberculosis*, not Plasmodium.

So, both pairings are incorrect.

115. (B): Vitamin B1 is scientifically known as Thiamin, important for nerve function and carbohydrate metabolism.

- Riboflavin is B2
- Retinol is Vitamin A
- Tocopherol is Vitamin E.

116. (A): These gates — Gaja Dwar, Ashwa Dwar, Garuda Dwar, Makar Dwar, Shardula Dwar, Hamsa Dwar — are architectural features in the new Parliament building in New Delhi, representing traditional and mythological symbols.

117. (B): In 2023, Garba, a traditional folk dance of Gujarat, was added to UNESCO's Representative List of the Intangible Cultural Heritage of Humanity. It is associated with Navratri celebrations.

Other options, though classical or famous, are not recently listed.

118. (A): The "Dhara" initiative is a project of the Ministry of Education, aimed at reviving and integrating Indian Knowledge Systems (IKS) in academia and public discourse.

119. (C): PRASHAD Scheme is implemented by the Ministry of Tourism to promote pilgrimage and spiritual tourism by developing infrastructure at key religious and cultural destinations across States/UTs.

120. (A): ASHVINI is a joint venture between Nuclear Power Corporation of India Ltd. (NPCIL) and NTPC Ltd., established to build nuclear power facilities, enhancing India's clean energy capacity.

121. (D): REJUPAVE is a cold in-place recycling technology developed by CSIR-CRRI for road construction and maintenance at high-altitude border areas, such as those in Ladakh and Arunachal Pradesh. It enables eco-friendly and faster road repair without the need for hot bitumen.

122. (C): C-Bot is an underwater robot developed jointly by CSIR (Council of Scientific and Industrial Research) and NIO (National Institute of Oceanography).

- It is designed to monitor coral reefs, study underwater ecosystems, and collect environmental data.
- Hence, both statements are correct.

123. (D): The Kaveri engine is an indigenous jet engine developed by GTRE, a lab under DRDO. It was designed for India's Light Combat Aircraft (LCA) Tejas, and aims to reduce reliance on imported aero engines. Though not yet fully inducted, it marks a major step in India's engine tech development.

124. (A): : Jimmy Carter, the former President of the United States, was awarded the Nobel Peace Prize in 2002 for his decades-long efforts "to find peaceful solutions to international conflicts, to advance democracy and human rights, and to promote economic and social development." This description exactly matches the wording given in the question. The Nobel Committee recognized his post-presidency global work, especially through The Carter Center, making him the correct answer as per the stated criteria.

125. (B): The report titled 'S.A.F.E. Accommodation: Worker Housing for Manufacturing Growth' was released by NITI Aayog. It focuses on the importance of providing safe and adequate housing for industrial workers, especially in urban manufacturing clusters.

126. (A): In a convex mirror, whenever an object is placed anywhere in front (even at infinity), the image is always:

- Virtual, erect, diminished, and
- Formed between P and F, behind the mirror.

127. (C): We use the formula:

$$V = \text{Work done/Charge}$$
$$= 24 \text{ J}/2 \text{ C} = 12 \text{ V}$$

So, the potential difference between points A and B is 12 volts.

128. (B): When two identical conducting wires (same material, same length, same diameter) are connected in parallel, the equivalent resistance becomes

$$R_p = \frac{R}{2}.$$

In series, the equivalent resistance becomes $R_S = 2R$:

Heat produced $H \propto \frac{V^2}{R}$ for a fixed potential difference.

Thus,

$$\text{Heat in parallel: } H_p \propto \frac{V^2}{R/1} = \frac{2V^2}{R}$$

$$\text{Heat in series: } H_s \propto \frac{V^2}{2R}$$

$$\text{Ratio } \frac{H_p}{H_s} = \frac{2V^2/R}{V^2/2R} = \frac{2}{1} \times \frac{1}{1/2} = 4 : 1$$

Hence, the correct answer is B. 4 : 1.

129. (D): In an ideal long straight solenoid, the magnetic field inside is uniform, parallel to the axis, and depends only on the current and number of turns per unit length. Outside the solenoid, the field is nearly zero.

130. (C): We use the equation:

$$v^2 = u^2 + 2as$$

Given:

Final velocity $v = 0$

Initial velocity $u = 12$ m/s

Distance $s = 45$ m

Substituting:

$$\Rightarrow \quad 0 = 12^2 + 2 \times a \times 45$$
$$\Rightarrow \quad 0 = 144 + 90a$$
$$a = -144/90 = -1.6 \text{ m/s}^2$$

The negative sign indicates deceleration.

131. (D): The universal gravitational constant (G) appears in Newton's law of gravitation:

$$F = G \times (m_1 m_2)/r^2$$

To balance the equation dimensionally:

$$G = F \cdot r^2/(m_1 m_2)$$

Unit of force is N, distance is m, and mass is kg, so the unit of G is $N \cdot m^2/kg^2$.

132. (B): When two objects are dropped in free fall (ignoring air resistance), they both experience the same acceleration due to gravity ($g = 9.8$ m/s^2), regardless of their mass. However, momentum and energy depend on mass, so they will differ.

133. (D): The fundamental wave equation is:

$$v = f \times \lambda,$$

where

- v = speed of wave
- f = frequency
- λ = wavelength

So, sound or any wave follows this relationship.

134. **(C):** Time period of a simple pendulum: T = 2π√(L/*g*)

- If length L is increased 4 times, then

$$T' = 2\pi\sqrt{(4L/g)} = 2 \times T$$

- Mass does not affect time period

So, ratio of new to original time period = 2 : 1.

135. **(D):** This statement is not correct. One of the fundamental properties of electric charge is conservation — charge can neither be created nor destroyed, only transferred.

A, B, and C are valid properties of charge.

136. **(A):** Due to Rayleigh scattering, shorter wavelengths (like blue) are scattered more than longer wavelengths (red). That's why the sky appears blue.

So, statement A is correct.

137. **(B):** According to Archimedes' Principle, the upward (buoyant) force on a body immersed in fluid is equal to the weight of the fluid displaced, not the mass of the body.

So, only statement 2 is correct.

138. **(C):** Resistivity (ρ) is a material property and does not depend on dimensions like length or area.

If length changes, resistance changes, but resistivity remains constant for the same material and temperature.

139. **(B):** Strain = change in length/original length

It is a ratio of two same units, so it is dimensionless.

Stress, pressure, and force have dimensions and units.

140. **(A):** An adiabatic system is one that does not exchange heat with its surroundings.

It can exchange work but not heat energy, as in adiabatic processes in thermodynamics.

141. **(A):** Light travels fastest in vacuum (Y) and slower in any other medium, including carbon disulfide (X). Refractive index of carbon disulfide is greater than 1, hence:

Speed in medium (X) < speed in vacuum (Y).

142. **(A):** Using the Right-Hand Thumb Rule:

- Thumb → direction of current (east to west)
- Fingers curl → direction of magnetic field

At a point below the wire, the magnetic field lines are clockwise in a plane perpendicular to the wire when viewed from the east end.

143. **(B):** Gold was one of the earliest discovered elements, known since prehistoric times due to its occurrence in native (metallic) form.

- Copper was discovered early too, but gold predates it.
- Oxygen and uranium were discovered in the 18th and 19th centuries, respectively.

144. **(A):** When light travels from air (rarer) to water (denser), it slows down and bends towards the normal due to change in speed.

145. **(C):** This is incorrect.

The correct kinematic equation is:

$$v^2 - u^2 = 2as$$

So, the reversal in the equation makes option C invalid.

146. **(D):** This statement is not correct.

- A voltmeter has high resistance to avoid drawing current.
- An ammeter has low resistance to avoid affecting circuit current.

Thus, option D is the opposite of the correct fact.

147. **(C):** Tidal energy is a non-conventional (renewable) source derived from ocean tides.

Others like petroleum, natural gas, and coal are conventional fossil fuels.

148. **(B):** For three 1-ohm resistors in parallel:

$$\frac{1}{R} = \frac{1}{1}+\frac{1}{1}+\frac{1}{1} = 3 \rightarrow R = \frac{1}{3}\text{ ohm.}$$

149. **(B):** Echo occurs when sound reflects off a distant surface (like a wall or mountain) and returns after 0.1 seconds or more, allowing it to be heard separately from the original sound.

150. **(C):** When an object moves with uniform speed, its velocity remains constant, so acceleration = 0.

Acceleration is the rate of change of velocity, and if velocity doesn't change, acceleration is zero.

PAPER II : MATHEMATICS

1. **(B):**

$$S_k = 3k^2 + 5k$$
$$S_1 = 3 + 5 = 8$$
$$S_2 = 12 + 10 = 22$$
$$S_3 = 27 + 15 = 42$$
$$a_1 = S_1 = 8$$
$$a_2 = S_2 - S_1 = 22 - 8 = 14$$
$$a_3 = S_3 - S_2 = 42 - 22 = 20$$

∴ Series = 8 + 14 + 20 ..... are in A.P. with common difference = 14 − 8 = 6.

2. **(B):** $S_8 = 5S_4$

$$\frac{a(r^8-1)}{r-1} = \frac{5.a(r^4-1)}{r-1}$$

$$\Rightarrow \frac{r^8-1}{r^4-1} = 5 \Rightarrow \frac{(r^4-1)(r^4+1)}{r^4-1} = 5$$

$$\Rightarrow r^4 = 4 \Rightarrow r = \pm\sqrt{2}, \pm\sqrt{2}i.$$

3. **(B):** Here, $\alpha + \beta = k$, $\alpha\beta = k$

and $\alpha - \beta = (2\sqrt{3})$

$$\therefore (\alpha - \beta)^2 = (\alpha + \beta)^2 - 4\alpha\beta$$

$$\Rightarrow (2\sqrt{3})^2 = k^2 - 4k$$

$$\Rightarrow k^2 - 4k - 12 = 0 \Rightarrow k^2 - 6k + 2k - 12 = 0$$

$$\Rightarrow (k - 6)(k + 2) = 0 \Rightarrow k = -2, 6.$$

4. (A):
$$\begin{aligned} xy + 5 &= 4y \\ xy + 5 &= -4x \\ - \quad - &\quad + \\ \hline 0 &= 4(x + y) \\ \Rightarrow \quad x + y &= 0. \end{aligned}$$

5. (A): $a_5 = a + 4d$, $a_7 = a + 6d$ and $a_{13} = a + 12d$

$\therefore$ a_5, a_7 and a_{13} are in G.P.
$$\begin{aligned} (a_7)^2 &= a_5 \times a_{13} \\ (a + 6d)^2 &= (a + 4d)(a + 12d) \\ a^2 + 12ad + 36d^2 &= a^2 + 16ad + 48d^2 \\ 12d^2 + 4ad &= 0 \Rightarrow 3d + a = 0 \\ a &= -3d \Rightarrow \frac{a}{d} = -3. \end{aligned}$$

6. (C): $\because$ p, 1 and q are in A.P.
$$\Rightarrow \quad p + q = 2$$
p, 2 and q are G.P. $\Rightarrow pq = 4$

Now, $$\frac{2pq}{p+q} = \frac{8}{2} = 4$$
$$\therefore \quad \frac{p+q}{2pq} = \frac{1}{4}$$
$\therefore$ $\frac{1}{p}, \frac{1}{4}$ and $\frac{1}{q}$ are in A.P.

$\therefore$ p, 4 and q are in H.P.

Both statements are correct.

7. (D):
$$\begin{aligned} x &= (1111)_2 = 2^3 + 2^2 + 2^1 + 1 = 15 \\ y &= (1001)_2 = 2^3 + 0 + 0 + 1 = 9 \\ z &= (110)_2 = 2^2 + 2^1 + 0 = 6 \end{aligned}$$
Now, $x^3 - y^3 - z^3 - 3xyz$
$$= (15)^3 - (9)^3 - (6)^3 - 3 \times 15 \times 9 \times 6$$
$$= 3375 - 729 - 216 - 2430 = 0.$$

8. (A): Cofactors: $A = ei - hf$, $B = gf - di$,
$C = dh - ge$, $D = ch - bi$

and $G = bf - ec$

Now, $bB + cC - dD - gG$
$$= bgf - bdi + cdh - cge - cdh + bdi - gbf + gec = 0.$$

9. (A): $$\Delta = \begin{vmatrix} k^2+2k & 2k+1 & 1 \\ 2k+1 & k+2 & 1 \\ 3 & 3 & 1 \end{vmatrix}$$
$$= (k^2 + 2k)(k + 2 - 3) - (2k + 1)(2k + 1 - 3) + (6k + 3 - 3k - 6)$$
$$= k^3 - k^2 + 2k^2 - 2k - 4k^2 + 4k - 2k + 2 + 3k - 3$$
$$= k^3 - 3k^2 + 3k - 1$$
$$= (k - 1)^3$$
(*i*) $(k - 1)^3 > 0 \Rightarrow k > 1$

(*ii*) $(k - 1)^3 < 0 \Rightarrow k < 1$

(*iii*) $(k - 1)^3 = 0 \Rightarrow k = 1$.

10. (B): $$\begin{vmatrix} 2 & 3+i & 1 \\ 3-i & 0 & i-1 \\ -1 & -1-i & 1 \end{vmatrix}$$
$$= 2(i^2 - 1) - (3 + i)(3 - i + i - 1) + 1(3 - i)(i + 1)$$
$$= 2(-1 - 1) - (3 + i)\, 2 + 3i - i^2 + 3 - i$$
$$= -4 - 6 - 2i + 3i + 1 + 3 - i$$
$$= -6 = -6 + 0i = A + iB$$
$\therefore$ $A + B = -6 + 0 = -6$.

11. (B): $\therefore$ $A^2 + B^2 + C^2 = 0$
$$\therefore \quad A = B = C = 0$$
Now, $$\begin{vmatrix} 1 & \cos C & \cos B \\ \cos C & 1 & \cos A \\ \cos B & \cos A & 1 \end{vmatrix} = \begin{vmatrix} 1 & 1 & 1 \\ 1 & 1 & 1 \\ 1 & 1 & 1 \end{vmatrix} = 0.$$

12. (A): $$\begin{vmatrix} x+1 & \omega & \omega^2 \\ \omega & x+\omega^2 & 1 \\ \omega^2 & 1 & x+\omega \end{vmatrix} = 0$$
(Applying $C_1 \to C_1 + C_2 + C_3$)
$$\begin{vmatrix} x+1+\omega+\omega^2 & \omega & \omega^2 \\ x+1+\omega+\omega^2 & x+\omega^2 & 1 \\ x+1+\omega+\omega^2 & 1 & x+\omega \end{vmatrix} = 0$$
$$\begin{vmatrix} x & \omega & \omega^2 \\ x & x+\omega^2 & 1 \\ x & 1 & x+\omega \end{vmatrix} = 0$$
$$x\begin{vmatrix} 1 & \omega & \omega^2 \\ 1 & x+\omega^2 & 1 \\ 1 & 1 & x+\omega \end{vmatrix} = 0$$
$$\therefore \quad x = 0.$$

13. (A): $$\left(\frac{\sqrt{3}+i}{\sqrt{3}-i}\right)^3 = \left(\frac{\left(\sqrt{3}+i\right)^2}{3+1}\right)^3 = \left(\frac{\sqrt{3}}{2}+\frac{1}{2}i\right)^6$$
$$= \left(\cos\frac{\pi}{6}+i\sin\frac{\pi}{6}\right)^6$$
$$= \cos \pi + i \sin \pi = -1.$$

14. (C): $x^2 - x + 1 = 0 \Rightarrow x = \frac{1 \pm \sqrt{3}i}{2}$

If $$x = \frac{1+\sqrt{3}i}{2} \text{ then } \frac{1}{x} = \frac{1-\sqrt{3}i}{2}$$
Now $$x - \frac{1}{x} = \sqrt{3}i$$
$$\left(x-\frac{1}{x}\right)^2 + \left(x-\frac{1}{x}\right)^4 + \left(x-\frac{1}{x}\right)^8$$
$$= -3 + 9 + 81 = 87.$$

15. (C): CPTL AIA

1 3

Total words $= \frac{4!}{2!} \times 4! = \frac{24 \times 24}{2} = 288$.

16. (A): Let, $\text{amp}(z) = \theta$
$$\text{amp}(\bar{z}) = -\theta$$
Now $\text{amp}(z) + \text{amp}(\bar{z}) = 0$.

17. (C): Number of diagonals
$$= {}^nC_2 - n = 20 = \frac{n(n-1)}{2} - n = 20$$
$$\Rightarrow n^2 - 3n - 40 = 0 \Rightarrow n = 8.$$

18. (C): Number of arrangements = 3!2! = 12.

19. (C): $\therefore x + y + z = 5$

$(1,1,3) \rightarrow \frac{3!}{2!} = 3$ ways

$(1,2,2) \rightarrow \frac{3!}{2!} = 3$ ways

Total ways = 3 + 3 = 6.

20. (C): $T_{r+1} = {}^{n}C_r \left(3^{\frac{1}{2}}\right)^{12-r}\left(5^{\frac{1}{4}}\right)^{r} = {}^{12}C_r 3^{\frac{12-r}{2}} 5^{\frac{r}{4}}$

for rational term $\frac{12-r}{2}$ and $\frac{r}{4}$ is integer.

$\therefore$ Possible value of $r = 0, 4, 8, 12$.

21. (C): Put $x = 1$ and $y = 1$, we get
Sum of coefficients $= 2^n = 256$
Total terms = 8 + 1 = 9

Greatest term = middle term $= \frac{9+1}{2} = 5$th term.

22. (B): $k < \left(\sqrt{2}+1\right)^3 < k+2$

$\Rightarrow k < 2\sqrt{2}+1+6+3\sqrt{2} < k+2$

$\Rightarrow k < 5\sqrt{2}+7 < k+2$

$\Rightarrow k < 14.07 < k + 2$

$\Rightarrow k < 14.07$ and $k > 12.07$

$\therefore \quad k = 13, 14.$

23. (D): $\begin{bmatrix} x & 1 & 1 \end{bmatrix}\begin{bmatrix} 1 & 2 & 3 \\ 4 & 5 & 6 \\ 7 & 8 & 9 \end{bmatrix}\begin{bmatrix} 1 \\ 1 \\ x \end{bmatrix} = [45]$

$[x+11+2x+13+3x+15]\begin{bmatrix} 1 \\ 1 \\ x \end{bmatrix} = [45]$

$\Rightarrow x + 11 + 2x + 13 + 3x^2 + 15x = 45$

$\Rightarrow \quad 3x^2 + 18x + 24 = 45$

$\Rightarrow \quad x^2 + 6x - 7 = 0$

$\Rightarrow \quad x = -7$ and 1.

24. (B): For orthogonal matrix.
$A^T = A^{-1} \Rightarrow AA^T = 1$
$A^2 = I$ ($\therefore$ A is symmetric)

$$\begin{bmatrix} y & z & x \\ z & x & y \\ x & y & z \end{bmatrix}\begin{bmatrix} y & z & x \\ z & x & y \\ x & y & z \end{bmatrix} = \begin{bmatrix} 1 & 0 & 0 \\ 0 & 1 & 0 \\ 0 & 0 & 1 \end{bmatrix}$$

$$\begin{bmatrix} y^2+z^2+x^2 & yz+zx+xy & xy+yz+xz \\ yz+zx+xy & x^2+y^2+z^2 & xy+yz+zx \\ xy+yz+zx & xy+yz+zx & x^2+y^2+z^2 \end{bmatrix} = \begin{bmatrix} 1 & 0 & 0 \\ 0 & 1 & 0 \\ 0 & 0 & 1 \end{bmatrix}$$

$x^2 + y^2 + z^2 = 1.$

25. (C): For non-singular matrix
we know that

$|M^n| = |M|^n, \ |M^{-1}| = \frac{1}{|M|}$

and $|M^T| = |M|$.

26. (D): $f(\pi) = \begin{bmatrix} \cos\pi & \sin\pi \\ -\sin\pi & \cos\pi \end{bmatrix} = \begin{bmatrix} -1 & 0 \\ 0 & -1 \end{bmatrix}$

$[f(\pi)]^2 = \begin{bmatrix} -1 & 0 \\ 0 & -1 \end{bmatrix}\begin{bmatrix} -1 & 0 \\ 0 & -1 \end{bmatrix} = \begin{bmatrix} 1 & 0 \\ 0 & 1 \end{bmatrix}.$

27. (D): $A^2 = \begin{bmatrix} 1 & 2 & 2 \\ 2 & 1 & 2 \\ 2 & 2 & 1 \end{bmatrix}\begin{bmatrix} 1 & 2 & 2 \\ 2 & 1 & 2 \\ 2 & 2 & 1 \end{bmatrix} = \begin{bmatrix} 9 & 8 & 8 \\ 8 & 9 & 8 \\ 8 & 8 & 9 \end{bmatrix}$

$A^2 - 4A = \begin{bmatrix} 9 & 8 & 8 \\ 8 & 9 & 8 \\ 8 & 8 & 9 \end{bmatrix} - \begin{bmatrix} 4 & 8 & 8 \\ 8 & 4 & 8 \\ 8 & 8 & 4 \end{bmatrix} = \begin{bmatrix} 5 & 0 & 0 \\ 0 & 5 & 0 \\ 0 & 0 & 5 \end{bmatrix} = 5I_3.$

28. (B): ${}^{5n}C_r = {}^{5n}C_{n+r}$
$n + r + r = 5n \Rightarrow 2r = 4n \Rightarrow r = 2n.$

29. (D): Number of selections (at most 3 things)
$= {}^6C_0 + {}^6C_1 + {}^6C_2 + {}^6C_3$
$= 1+6+\frac{6.5}{2.1}+\frac{6.5.4}{3.2.1}$
$= 1 + 6 + 15 + 20 = 42.$

30. (B): We know that for orthogonal matrix
$A^T = A^{-1} \Rightarrow AA^T = AA^{-1} = 1$
$\Rightarrow \quad A^2 = I \ (\because A = A^T).$

31. (B): $p + q + r = \sin 35° + \sin 25° + \sin (-95°)$
$= \sin 35° + \sin 25° - \sin 95°$
$= \sin 35° + 2 \cos 60° . \sin (-35°)$
$= \sin 35° - 2 \times \frac{1}{2} \sin 35° = 0.$

32. (A): $pq + qr + rp = q(p + r) + rp$
$= -q^2 + rp = -\sin^2 25° - \sin 95° . \sin 35°$
$(\because p + q + r = 0)$

$= \frac{1}{2}[-2\sin^2 25° - 2\sin 95°.\sin 35°]$

$= \frac{1}{2}[-1+\cos 50° + \cos 130° - \cos 60°]$

$= \frac{1}{2}\left[-1+\cos 50° - \cos 50° - \frac{1}{2}\right] = \frac{-3}{4}.$

33. (C): $(p + q + r^2) = p^2 + q^2 + r^2 + 2(pq + qr + rp)$

$\Rightarrow \quad 0 = p^2+q^2+r^2+2\left(\frac{-3}{4}\right)$

$\Rightarrow p^2 + q^2 + r^2 = \frac{3}{2}.$

34. (A): $p = |\sin \alpha - \sin(\alpha - 90°)|$
$= |\sin \alpha + \cos \alpha|$
$= \sqrt{2}|\sin 45° \sin\alpha + \cos 45° \cos\alpha|$
$p = \sqrt{2}|\sin(45°+\alpha)|$

$0 \le |\sin(45° + \alpha)| \le 1$

$0 \le \sqrt{2}|\sin(45° + \alpha)| \le \sqrt{2}$

$\therefore$ Minimum value of p is 0.

35. (B): $p = \sqrt{2}|\sin 45° + \alpha|$

$\Rightarrow \quad 0 \le p \le \sqrt{2}$

$\therefore$ Maximum value $= \sqrt{2}$.

36. (C): $a = 5$ cm, $b = 7$ cm, $c = 3$ cm

$$\cos B = \frac{a^2 + c^2 - b^2}{2ac} = \frac{25 + 9 - 49}{2 \times 5 \times 3} = \frac{-15}{2 \times 15} = \frac{-1}{2}$$

$B = 120°$

$\therefore \quad A + C = 180° - 120° = 60°$ (acute)

So both statements are correct.

37. (C): $\cos B = \dfrac{a^2 + c^2 - b^2}{2ac} = \dfrac{25 + 9 - 49}{2 \times 5 \times 3} = -\dfrac{1}{2}$

$B = 120°$.

38. (A): Area of triangle $= \dfrac{1}{2} \times ac \sin B$

$$= \frac{1}{2} \times 5 \times 3 \times \sin 120° = \frac{1}{2} \times 15 \times \sin 60°$$

$$= \frac{1}{2} \times 15 \times \frac{\sqrt{3}}{2} = \frac{15\sqrt{3}}{4} \text{ cm}^2.$$

39. (B): $\tan 60° = \dfrac{h}{x} \Rightarrow h = \sqrt{3}x$

$\tan 45° = \dfrac{h}{QN} \Rightarrow QN = h$

$\tan 30° = \dfrac{h}{PN}$

$PN = h\sqrt{3}$

$h + a = h\sqrt{3}$

$$h = \frac{a}{\sqrt{3} - 1} = \frac{a(\sqrt{3} + 1)}{2}$$

$$PN = h\sqrt{3} = \frac{a(3 + \sqrt{3})}{2}.$$

40. (A): $\tan 60° = \dfrac{h}{x} \Rightarrow h = \sqrt{3}x$

$\tan 45° = \dfrac{h}{b + x}$

$\Rightarrow \quad h = b + x \Rightarrow \sqrt{3}x = b + x$

$$x = \frac{b(\sqrt{3} + 1)}{2}$$

$\Rightarrow \quad h = MN = \sqrt{3}x = \left(\dfrac{3 + \sqrt{3}}{2}\right)b.$

41. (C): $\dfrac{p}{q} = \dfrac{\tan 2\alpha - \tan \alpha}{\cot \alpha - \cot 2\alpha} = \dfrac{\tan 2\alpha - \tan \alpha}{\dfrac{1}{\tan \alpha} - \dfrac{1}{\tan 2\alpha}}$

$$= \frac{(\tan 2\alpha - \tan \alpha)\tan \alpha \cdot \tan 2\alpha}{(\tan 2\alpha - \tan \alpha)}$$

$= \tan \alpha \cdot \tan 2\alpha$.

42. (D): $p + q = \tan 2\alpha - \tan \alpha + \cot \alpha - \cot 2\alpha$

$$= \left(\frac{\sin^2 2\alpha - \cos^2 2\alpha}{\sin 2\alpha \cdot \cos 2\alpha}\right) + \left(\frac{\cos^2 \alpha - \sin^2 \alpha}{\sin \alpha \cdot \cos \alpha}\right)$$

$$= \frac{\sin^2 2\alpha - \cos^2 2\alpha}{\sin 2\alpha \cdot \cos 2\alpha} + \frac{\cos^2 \alpha - \sin^2 \alpha}{\sin \alpha \cdot \cos \alpha}$$

$$= \frac{-2\cos 4\alpha}{\sin 4\alpha} + \frac{2\cos 2\alpha}{\sin 2\alpha}$$

$$= \frac{2(\sin 4\alpha \cdot \cos 2\alpha - \cos 4\alpha \cdot \sin 2\alpha)}{\sin 4\alpha \cdot \sin 2\alpha}$$

$$= \frac{2\sin(4\alpha - 2\alpha)}{\sin 4\alpha \cdot \sin 2\alpha} = \frac{2\sin 2\alpha}{\sin 4\alpha \cdot \sin 2\alpha}$$

$= 2 \operatorname{cosec} 4\alpha$.

43. (C): $\dfrac{p}{p + 2q} = \dfrac{1}{1 + \dfrac{2p}{q}} = \dfrac{1}{1 + \dfrac{2}{\tan \alpha \cdot \tan 2\alpha}}$

$$= \frac{\sin \alpha \cdot \sin 2\alpha}{\sin \alpha \cdot \sin 2\alpha + \cos \alpha \cdot \cos 2\alpha + \cos \alpha \cdot \cos 2\alpha}$$

$$= \frac{\sin \alpha \cdot \sin 2\alpha}{\cos \alpha + \cos \alpha \cdot \cos 2\alpha} = \frac{\sin \alpha \cdot 2\sin \alpha \cdot \cos \alpha}{\cos \alpha \cdot 2 \cdot \cos^2 \alpha}$$

$= \tan^2 \alpha$.

44. (C): $\cos \alpha = 2(1 - \sin \alpha)$

$\Rightarrow \quad \dfrac{\cos^2 \alpha}{(1 - \sin \alpha)^2} = 4$

$\dfrac{1 + \sin \alpha}{1 - \sin \alpha} = \dfrac{4}{1} \Rightarrow \sin \alpha = \dfrac{3}{5}$

$\tan \alpha = \dfrac{3}{\sqrt{25 - 9}} = \dfrac{3}{4}$.

45. (B): $\therefore \sin \alpha = \dfrac{3}{5}$ and $\cos \alpha = \dfrac{4}{5}$

$\therefore 2\sin 2\alpha + \cos 2\alpha = 4\sin \alpha \cdot \cos \alpha + 1 - 2\sin^2 \alpha$

$$= \frac{48}{25} + 1 - \frac{18}{25} = \frac{48 + 25 - 18}{25} = \frac{55}{25} = \frac{11}{5}.$$

46. (B): $\dfrac{a}{\sin 3x} = \dfrac{b}{\sin x}$

$\Rightarrow \quad \dfrac{a}{b} = \dfrac{\sin 3x}{\sin x}$

$\Rightarrow \quad 2 = \dfrac{\sin 3x}{\sin x}$

$\Rightarrow \quad 2\sin x = 3\sin x - 4\sin^3 x$

$\Rightarrow \sin x(1 - 4\sin^2 x) = 0 \Rightarrow \sin x = \dfrac{1}{2}$

$\Rightarrow \quad x = 30°$

47. (C): $\angle B = x = 30°$, $\angle A = 3x = 90°$,
$\angle C = 180° - 120° = 60°$

$\therefore$ Triangle is right-angled
$\therefore$ 30°, 60° and 90° are in A.P.
So options (I) and (III) are only correct.

48. (A): $\tan 45° = \frac{50+h}{100}$

$100 = 50 + h$

$\Rightarrow h = 50$ m

$\tan \angle RMQ = \frac{50}{100} = \frac{1}{2}$

$\angle RMQ = \tan^{-1}\frac{1}{2}$.

49. (D): $\because x^2 - 4x + 1 = 0$

$\Rightarrow x = 2 \pm \sqrt{3} > 0$

$\therefore \tan^{-1}k + \tan^{-1}\frac{1}{k} = \tan^{-1}\left(\frac{k+\frac{1}{k}}{1-k\times\frac{1}{k}}\right)$

$\tan^{-1}\infty = \frac{\pi}{2}$.

50. (C): $\tan^{-1}k + \tan^{-1}\frac{1}{2} = \frac{\pi}{4} = \tan^{-1}1$

$\tan^{-1}k = \tan^{-1}\left(\frac{1-\frac{1}{2}}{1+\frac{1}{2}}\right) = \tan^{-1}\left(\frac{1}{2}\times\frac{2}{3}\right)$

$k = \frac{1}{3}$.

51. (A): $m_1 = \frac{-m^2}{n}$ and $m_2 = \frac{-n^2}{-m} = \frac{n^2}{m}$

for perpendicular

$-\frac{m^2}{n}\times\frac{n^2}{m} = -1 \Rightarrow mn - 1 = 0$.

52. (D): $\sqrt{p^2+1} = \sqrt{q^2+1} = \sqrt{(p-1)^2+(q-1)^2}$

$\sqrt{p^2+1} = \sqrt{q^2+1} \Rightarrow p = q$

$[\therefore p, q \in (0, 1)]$

Now, $\sqrt{q^2+1} = \sqrt{(p-1)^2+(q-1)^2}$

$\Rightarrow p^2 + 1 = 2(p-1)^2$

$\Rightarrow p^2 - 4p + 1 = 0 \Rightarrow p = 2\pm\sqrt{3}$

Since, $0 < p < 1 \Rightarrow p = 2-\sqrt{3} = q$

Now, $p + q = 2\left(2-\sqrt{3}\right) = 4-2\sqrt{3}$.

53. (A): $a = BC = \sqrt{(2-0)^2+(0-0)^2} = 2$

$b = AC = \sqrt{(2-1)^2+(0-1)^2} = \sqrt{2}$

$c = AB = \sqrt{(1-0)^2+(1-0)^2} = \sqrt{2}$

$\therefore$ Coordinate of incentive

$= \left(\frac{ax_1+bx_2+cx_3}{a+b+c}, \frac{ay_1+by_2+cy_3}{a+b+c}\right)$

$= \frac{2(1)+\sqrt{2}(0)+\sqrt{2}(2)}{2+\sqrt{2}+\sqrt{2}}, \frac{2(1)+\sqrt{2}(0)+\sqrt{2}(0)}{2+\sqrt{2}+\sqrt{2}}$

$= \left(\frac{2+2\sqrt{2}}{2+2\sqrt{2}}, \frac{2}{2+2\sqrt{2}}\right) = \left(1, \sqrt{2}-1\right)$

54. (B): Coordinate of P $= \left(\frac{3+1}{2}, \frac{-1+1}{2}\right) = P(2, 0)$

Slope of AB $= \frac{1+1}{1-3} = -1$

Equation of AB is

$y - 1 = -1(x-1) \Rightarrow x + y - 2 = 0$

Distance from $Q(x, y)$

$\frac{x+y-2}{\sqrt{2}} = \sqrt{2}$

$x + y - 2 = 2 \Rightarrow x + y = 4$ ...(*i*)

Slope of PQ $= \frac{y}{x-2}$

$\Rightarrow PQ \perp BA$

$\therefore (-1)\left(\frac{y}{x-2}\right) = -1 \Rightarrow y = x - 2$

From (*i*)

$x + x - 2 = 4 \Rightarrow x = 3$ and $y = 1$

Q(3, 1).

55. (D): Slope of AD $= \frac{6-2}{-2-1} = \frac{4}{-3}$

$\therefore$ Slope of BC $= \frac{3}{4}$

Equation of BC is

$y - 6 = \frac{3}{4}(x+2) \Rightarrow 3x - 4y + 30 = 0$.

56. (B): Radius $= \frac{10}{2} = 5$ cm

On solving $x + y = 0$ and $x - y = 0$
we get centre (0, 0)
Now, the equation of circle

$x^2 + y^2 = 25$.

57. (C): Equation of circle is

$x^2 + y^2 + 2x + 2y + 1 = 0$

$\therefore$ Centre $= (-1, -1)$

Radius $= \sqrt{1+1-1} = 1$

Diagonal = diameter

$\sqrt{2}a = 2 \Rightarrow a = \sqrt{2}$

Since the sides of the square are parallel to the co-ordinate axes, the vertices can be found by moving $\frac{a}{2}$ units from the centre along the axes.

$\therefore$ One of the vertices is $\left(-1+\frac{1}{\sqrt{2}}, -1-\frac{1}{\sqrt{2}}\right)$.

58. (D): Scope of tangent = tan 45° = 1

$$y^2 = 4x \Rightarrow 2y\frac{dy}{dx} = 4$$

$$\Rightarrow \frac{dy}{dx} = \frac{4}{2y} = 1 \Rightarrow y = 2$$

putting in $y^2 = 4x \Rightarrow x = 1$

$\therefore$ Point of contact = (1, 2).

59. (B): $25x^2 - 75y^2 = 225$

$$\frac{x^2}{9} - \frac{y^2}{3} = 1$$

$\therefore$ $a^2 = 9$ and $b^2 = 3$

$c^2 = a^2 + b^2 = 9 + 3 = 12$

$c = 2\sqrt{3}$

Distance between the two foci = $2c = 4\sqrt{3}$.

60. (A): We know that the parametric point of ellipse is $(a \sin \alpha)$ $(b \cos \alpha)$

$\therefore$ $a = 3$ and $b = 5$

$$b^2 = a^2(1 - e^2) \Rightarrow \frac{25}{9} = 1 - e^2$$

$$e^2 = 1 - \frac{25}{9} = \frac{16}{9} \Rightarrow e = \frac{4}{3}.$$

61. (B): We know that $\cos^2 \alpha + \cos^2 \beta + \cos^2 \gamma = 1$ ...(i)

and $\cos(\alpha + \beta) \cos(\alpha - \beta) = \cos^2 \alpha - \sin^2 \beta$

$= \cos^2 \alpha + \cos^2 \beta - 1 = 1 - \cos^2 \gamma - 1 = -\cos^2 \gamma$.

62. (C): Area = AB × BC

$$= \sqrt{1^2 + 3^2 + 1^2} \times \sqrt{2^2 + 1^2 + 1^2}$$

$$= \sqrt{11} \times \sqrt{6} = \sqrt{66} \text{ sq. units.}$$

63. (D): D.rs of AB = $k, -1, 3$

D.rs of BC = $2, k, -1$

$\because$ AB ⊥ BC

$\therefore$ $2k - k - 3 = 0 \Rightarrow k = 3$.

64. (A): D.rs of line are p, q, r

where $p = 2q = 3r \Rightarrow \frac{p}{6} = \frac{q}{3} = \frac{r}{2}$

$\therefore$ D.rs of line are 6, 3, 2

$$\therefore \quad \cos \theta = \frac{3}{\sqrt{6^2 + 3^2 + 2^2}} = \frac{3}{7}$$

$$\cos 2\theta = 2\cos^2 \theta - 1$$

$$= \frac{18}{49} - 1 = \frac{-31}{49}.$$

65. (B): Point (1, 1, 1) and d.rs of normal are ⟨3, 2, 1⟩

$\therefore$ Equation of the plane is

$3(x - 1) + 2(y - 1) + 1(z - 1) = 0$

$\Rightarrow 3x + 2y + z = 6$.

66. (D): $\because \cos^2 \alpha + \cos^2 \beta + \cos^2 \gamma = 1$

$\Rightarrow \sin^2 \alpha + \sin^2 \beta + \sin^2 \gamma = 2$

Now, $\vec{a}.\vec{b}. = \sin^2 \alpha + \sin^2 \beta + \sin^2 \gamma = 2$.

67. (C): $\vec{d} = (\vec{a} \times \vec{b}) \times \vec{c} = (\vec{a}.\vec{c})\vec{b} - (\vec{b} \cdot \vec{c})\vec{a}$ ...(i)

Since $\vec{d}$ is a linear combination of $\vec{a}$ and $\vec{b}$.

Therefore $\vec{d}$ lies in the plane formed by $\vec{a}$ and $\vec{b}$.

So, $\vec{d}$ is coplanar with $\vec{a}$ and $\vec{b}$.

$$\vec{d}.\vec{c} = \left[(\vec{a}.\vec{c})\vec{b} - (\vec{b}.\vec{c})\vec{a}\right].\vec{c}$$

$$= (\vec{a}.\vec{c})(\vec{b}.\vec{c}) - (\vec{b}.\vec{c})(\vec{a}.\vec{c}) = 0$$

So, $\vec{d}$ is perpendicular to $\vec{c}$

Hence, both statements are true.

68. (B): $\because$ $3\vec{a} - 4\vec{b} + \vec{c} = 0 \Rightarrow 3\vec{a} - 3\vec{b} - \vec{b} + \vec{c} = 0$

$$\Rightarrow \quad 3(\vec{a} - \vec{b}) = \vec{b} - \vec{c} \Rightarrow 3(\vec{b} - \vec{c}) = \vec{c} - \vec{b}$$

$$\Rightarrow \quad \frac{\vec{b} - \vec{a}}{\vec{c} - \vec{b}} = \frac{1}{3} \Rightarrow \frac{\overline{AB}}{\overline{BC}} = \frac{1}{3}.$$

69. (A): $(\vec{a} \times \vec{b}) + (\vec{b} \times \vec{c}) + (\vec{c} \times \vec{a})$

$$= (\vec{a} \times \vec{b}) + (\vec{b} \times \vec{a}) \times \vec{c}$$

$$= (\vec{a} \times \vec{b}) + (\vec{b} \times \vec{a}) \times (\cos^2 \theta \vec{a} + \sin^2 \theta \vec{b})$$

$$= (\vec{a} \times \vec{b}) + \cos^2 \theta (\vec{b} \times \vec{a}) - \sin^2 \theta (\vec{a} \times \vec{b})$$

$$= (\vec{a} \times \vec{b}) - \cos^2 \theta (\vec{a} \times \vec{b}) - \sin^2 \theta (\vec{a} \times \vec{b})$$

$$= (\vec{a} \times \vec{b})\left[1 - (\cos^2 \theta + \sin^2 \theta)\right] = 0.$$

70. (A): $\therefore |\vec{a}| = |\vec{b}| = |\vec{a} \times \vec{b}| = 1$

$$\sin \theta = \frac{|\vec{a} \times \vec{b}|}{|\vec{a}||\vec{b}|} = 1.$$

$$\therefore \quad \theta = \frac{\pi}{2}$$

Now, $\vec{a}.\vec{b} = |\vec{a}||\vec{b}|\cos\frac{\pi}{2} = 0.$

71. (C): We know that

If $x = \sec \theta - \cos \theta$ and $y = \sec^n \theta - \cos^n \theta$

then $(x^2 + 4)\left(\frac{dy}{dx}\right)^2 - n^2(y^2 + 4) = 0$

$$(x^2 + 4)\left(\frac{dy}{dx}\right)^2 - (4)^2(y^2 + 4) = 0$$

$$\left(\frac{dy}{dx}\right)^2 = \frac{16(y^2 + 4)}{x^2 + 4}.$$

72. (C): $\therefore \left(\frac{dy}{dx}\right)^2 = \frac{16(y^2 + 4)}{x^2 + 4}$

$$2\left(\frac{dy}{dx}\right)\left(\frac{d^2y}{dx^2}\right) = \frac{16(2y)(x^2 + 4)\frac{dy}{dx} - 16(y^2 + 4)(2x)}{(x^2 + 4)^2}$$

$$\frac{dy}{dx}\left(\frac{d^2y}{dx^2}\right)(x^2+4)^2 = 16y(x^2+4)\frac{dy}{dx} - 16x(y^2+4)$$

$$\frac{dy}{dx}\left(\frac{d^2y}{dx^2}\right)(x^2+4)^2 - 16y(x^2+4)\frac{dy}{dx} = -16x(y^2+4)$$

$$\frac{(x^2+4)}{y^2+4}\frac{dy}{dx}\left((x^2+4)\frac{d^2y}{dx^2} - 16y\right) = -16x.$$

73. (C): $y = \sqrt{(3-x)^2 - x^2} = \sqrt{9-6x}$

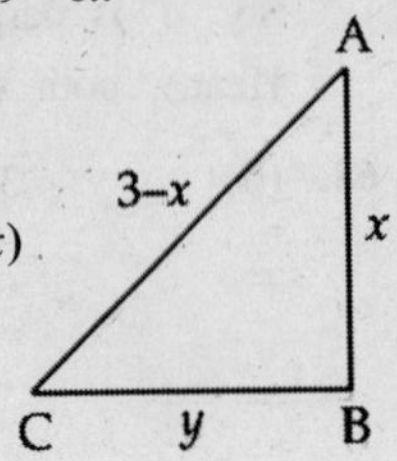

Area (A) $= \frac{1}{2}xy = \frac{1}{2}x\sqrt{9-6x}$

$A_1 = A^2 = \frac{1}{4}x^2(9-6x)$

$A_1 = \frac{1}{4}(9x^2 - 6x^3)$

$\frac{dA_1}{dx} = \frac{1}{4}(18x - 18x^2) = 0$

$18x(1-x) = 0 \Rightarrow x = 0$ (Not Possible)

$\therefore$ $x = 1$

$\therefore$ Area is maximum

$\therefore$ $y = \sqrt{9-6} = \sqrt{3}$

$\tan A = \frac{y}{x} = \frac{\sqrt{3}}{1} \Rightarrow \angle A = \frac{\pi}{3}.$

74. (A): Maximum area $= \frac{1}{2} \times y \times x = \frac{\sqrt{3}}{2}$ sq. units.

75. (D): $(x+y)^{p+q} = x^p y^q$

$\therefore$ $(p+q)\log(x+y) = p\log x + q\log y$

$$\frac{p+q}{x+y}\left(1+\frac{dy}{dx}\right) = \frac{p}{x} + \frac{q}{y}\frac{dy}{dx}$$

$$\left(\frac{p+q}{x+y} - \frac{q}{y}\right)\frac{dy}{dx} = \frac{p}{x} - \frac{p+q}{x+y}$$

$$\frac{py+qy-qx-qy}{y(x+y)}\frac{dy}{dx} = \frac{px+py-px-qx}{x(x+y)}$$

$$\frac{py-qx}{y}\frac{dy}{dx} = \frac{py-qx}{x}$$

$\therefore$ $\frac{dy}{dx} = \frac{y}{x}$

which is independent of both p and q.

76. (A): Since $\frac{dy}{dx}$ is independent of both p and q. So for $p + q = 10$

$\frac{dy}{dx} = \frac{y}{x}.$

77. (A): $\therefore$ $\frac{dy}{dx} = 4 \Rightarrow \int dy = \int 4dx$

$y = 4x + c$

$\therefore$ It passes through (0, 0) then $c = 0$

$\therefore$ $y = 4x$

Hence, it is an equation of a straight line passing through (1, 4).

78. (C):

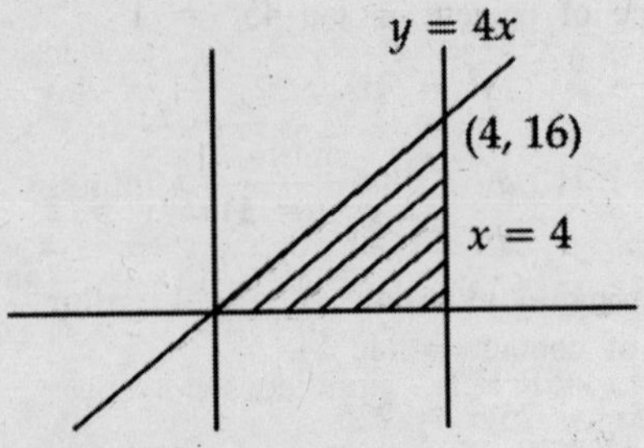

Required area $= \frac{1}{2} \times 4 \times 16 = 32$ sq. units.

79. (C): $f(x) = \begin{cases} x^3 & -1 < x < 1 \\ x^2 & x \in (-\infty, -1) \cup (1, \infty) \end{cases}$

$f(x) = \begin{cases} 3x^2 & -1 < x < 1 \\ 2x & x \in (-\infty, -1) \cup (1, \infty) \end{cases}$

$\therefore$ $\lim_{x\to 0} f'(x) = 3(0) = 0.$

80. (D): L.H.S. $= \lim_{x\to 1^-} x^2 = (-1)^2 = 1$

R.H.S. $= \lim_{x\to -1^+} x^3 = (-1)^3 = -1$

$\therefore$ L.H.S. $\neq$ R.H.S.

So, $f(x)$ is discontinuous at $x = -1$

L.H.D. $= 3(1) = 3$

R.H.D. $= 2(1) = 2$

$\therefore$ L.H.D. $\neq$ R.H.D.

So, $f(x)$ is not differentiable at $x = 1$

Hence, neither I nor II is true.

81. (B): $y = (1-\cos x)^{-1} = \frac{1}{1-\cos x}$

$= \frac{1}{2\sin^2\frac{x}{2}} = \frac{1}{2}\text{cosec}^2\frac{x}{2}$

$\therefore$ $\text{cosec}^2\frac{x}{2} \leftarrow (-\infty, -1) \cup (1, \infty)$

$\text{cosec}^2\frac{x}{2} \leftarrow (1, \infty) \Rightarrow \frac{1}{2}\text{cosec}^2\frac{x}{2} \leftarrow (0.5, \infty)$

Range $= (0.5, \infty)$.

82. (B): $I = \int y\,dx = \frac{1}{2}\int \text{cosec}^2\frac{x}{2}\,dx$

$= \frac{-\frac{1}{2}\cot\frac{x}{2}}{\frac{1}{2}} + C = -\cot\frac{x}{2} + C.$

83. (B): $\lim_{x\to 0}\{f(x)\cdot g(x)\} = \lim_{x\to 0}\{f(x)\cdot g(x)\}$

L.H.L. $= \lim_{h\to 0}\sin[0-h]|0-h| = \lim_{h\to 0}\sin[0-h]\cdot 0 = 0$

R.H.L. $= \lim_{h\to 0}\sin[0+h]|0+h| = \lim_{h\to 0}\sin 0.h = 0$

$\therefore$ $\lim_{x\to 0}\{f(x)g(x)\} = 0.$

84. (D): $\lim_{x\to 0} \frac{\sin[x]}{[x]}$

L.H.L. $= \lim_{h\to 0} \frac{\sin[0-h]}{(0-h)} =$ infinity

R.H.L. $= \lim_{h\to 0} \frac{\sin[0+h]}{(0+h)} = \lim_{h\to 0} \frac{\sin 0}{(h)} = 0$

L.H.L. $\neq$ R.H.L., limit does not exist.

85. (C): Domain of $f(x) = |x - 3|$ is $(-\infty, \infty)$.

86. (D):

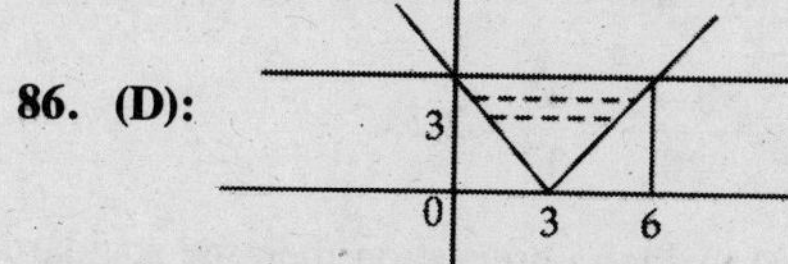

Required area $= 3\times 6 - \frac{1}{2}\times 3\times 3 - \frac{1}{2}\times 3\times 3$

$= 18 - 9 = 9$ square units.

87. (C): $f(x) = px + q$

Put $x = 1$ and $y = 1$

$p + q = 1.$

88. (A): $\therefore f(x) = px + q$ is linear polynomial so, $f(x)$ is one-one

Range $= \{1, 4, 7, 10\}$

codomain $=$ N

So it is not onto.

89. (A): $\lim_{x\to 1} f(f(x)) = \lim_{x\to 1}(x^2-1)^2 - 1$

$= (1 - 1)^2 - 1 = 0 - 1 = 1.$

90. (C): Let $y = x^2 - 1 \Rightarrow x^2 = y + 1$

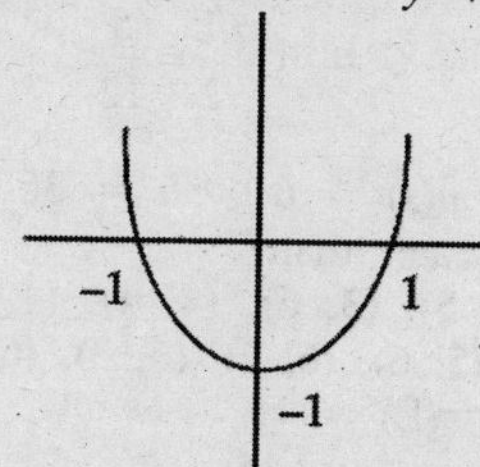

Required area $= \left|\int_{-1}^{1}(x^2-1)dx\right|$

$= \left|\left[\frac{x^3}{3} - x\right]_{-1}^{1}\right| = \left|\left(\frac{1}{3}-1\right) - \left(-\frac{1}{3}+1\right)\right|$

$= \left|-\frac{2}{3} - \frac{2}{3}\right| = \left|-\frac{4}{3}\right| = \frac{4}{3}$ sq. units.

91. (D): $y = \sin^{-1}\left(x - \frac{4x^3}{27}\right)$

$= \sin^{-1}\left[3.\frac{x}{3} - 4\left(\frac{x}{3}\right)^3\right] = 3\sin^{-1}\frac{x}{3}.$

92. (C): $y = 3\sin^{-1}\frac{x}{3}$

$\frac{dy}{dx} = 3\frac{1}{\sqrt{1-\frac{x^2}{9}}} \times \frac{1}{3} = \frac{3}{\sqrt{9-x^2}}.$

93. (C): $\lim_{x\to 0} \frac{\sqrt{x^2+9}-3}{\sqrt{x^2+16}-4}$

$= \lim_{x\to 0} \frac{x^2+9-9}{x^2+16-16} \times \frac{\sqrt{x^2+16}+4}{\sqrt{x^2+9}+3}$

$= \frac{\sqrt{16}+4}{\sqrt{9}+3} = \frac{8}{6} = \frac{4}{3}.$

94. (D): $f(x) = x^2 + 9$

$f(x) = 2x = 0 \Rightarrow x = 0$

$-$ $+$

$-\infty$ 0 ∞

$\therefore f(x)$ is increasing on $[0, \infty]$

and $f(x)$ is decreasing on $(-\infty, 0)$

So, $f(x)$ is minimum at $x = 0$

Hence, both statements are wrong.

95. (D): $\frac{f(4)}{f(2)} = f\left(\frac{4}{2}\right) = f(2) \Rightarrow f(4) = 3 \times 3 = 9$

$\frac{f(16)}{f(4)} = f(4) \Rightarrow f(16) = 9 \times 9 = 81.$

96. (C): $\frac{f(4)}{f(2)} = f(2) \Rightarrow f(4) = 3 \times 3 = 9$

$\frac{f(2)}{f(2)} = f(1) \Rightarrow f(1) = 1$

Now, $f(1)\, f(4) = 1 \times 9 = 9.$

97. (D): $f(0) = f(0 \times 5) = f(0 + 5) = f(5) = 10.$

98. (C): $f(0.5) = f(0 + 5) = f(0) = f(5) = 10$

$f(0.20) = f(0 + 20) \Rightarrow f(0) = f(20) = 10$

$f(0 \times -20) = f(0 - 20) \Rightarrow f(0) = f(-20) = 10$

$\therefore f(20) + f(-20) = 10 + 10 = 20.$

99. (B): $\int_{\sqrt{2}}^{\sqrt{3}}[x^2]dx = \int_{\sqrt{2}}^{\sqrt{3}} 2dx = 2[x]_{\sqrt{2}}^{\sqrt{3}} = 2\left(\sqrt{3}-\sqrt{2}\right).$

100. (A): $\int_{\sqrt{2}}^{2} f(x)dx = \int_{\sqrt{2}}^{2}[x^2]dx = \int_{\sqrt{2}}^{\sqrt{3}} 2dx + \int_{\sqrt{3}}^{2} 3dx$

$= 2[x]_{\sqrt{2}}^{\sqrt{3}} + 3[x]_{\sqrt{3}}^{2}$

$= 2\sqrt{3} - 2\sqrt{2} + 6 - 3\sqrt{3}$

$= 6 - 2\sqrt{2} - \sqrt{3}.$

101. (C): Total number of students whose height is less than or equal to 165 cm $= 12 + 15 + 24 = 51.$

102. (C):

C.I.	*fi*	C.F.	
160-162	12	12	
162-164	15	27	
164-166	24(M)	51	Median Class
166-168	13	64	

$\frac{N}{2} = \frac{64}{2} = 32$

$$\therefore \text{ Median} = l+\frac{\frac{N}{2}-C.F}{f}\times h = 164+\frac{32-27}{24}\times 2$$

$$= 164+\frac{5}{12}=164.41 \text{ cm.}$$

103. (D):

$$\text{Mode} = l+\frac{f_1-f_0}{2f_1-f_0-f_2}\times h$$

$$= 164+\frac{24-15}{48-15-13}\times 2$$

$$= 164+\frac{9}{20}\times 2 = 164.9 \text{ cm.}$$

104. (C): Histogram is made from group frequency data.

105. (B): Variance of X $= \frac{\Sigma X^2}{N}-\left(\frac{\Sigma X}{N}\right)^2$

$$= \frac{900}{50}-\left(\frac{200}{50}\right)^2 = 18 - 16 = 2$$

Variance of Y $= \frac{\Sigma Y^2}{N}-\left(\frac{\Sigma Y}{N}\right)^2$

$$= \frac{1400}{50}-\left(\frac{250}{30}\right)^2 = 28 - 25 = 3$$

$\therefore$ Variance (X) < Variance (Y).

106. (B):

$$C.V(X) = \frac{\sigma}{M}\times 100 = \frac{\sqrt{2}}{50}\times 100 = 2\sqrt{2}$$

$$C.V(Y) = \frac{\sigma}{M}\times 100 = \frac{\sqrt{3}}{50}\times 100 = 2\sqrt{3}$$

$\therefore$ C.V(X) < C.V(Y).

107. (C): $n = 6,\ p = k \Rightarrow q = 1 - k$

Now, $9.P(X = 4) = P(X = 2)$

$$9.{}^6C_4k^4(1 - k)^2 = {}^6C_2k^2(1 - k)^4$$

$$9k^2 = (1 - k)^2 \quad (\because {}^6C_4 = {}^6C_2)$$

$$3k = 1 - k \Rightarrow k = \frac{1}{4}.$$

108. (A): $P(x = 3) = {}^6C_3(k)^3 (1 - k)^3$

$$= \frac{6.5.4}{3.2.1}\left(\frac{1}{4}\right)^3\left(\frac{3}{4}\right)^3$$

$$= 20\left(\frac{3}{16}\right)^3 = 20\times\frac{27}{16\times16\times16} = \frac{135}{1024}.$$

109. (A):

$$n(S) = {}^{11}C_6$$

$$n(E) = {}^7C_3 \times {}^4C_3$$

$$P(E) = \frac{{}^7C_3\times{}^4C_3}{{}^{11}C_6} = \frac{10}{33}.$$

110. (D): $P(E) = \frac{{}^4C_2\times{}^7C_4+{}^4C_3\times{}^7C_3+{}^4C_4\times{}^7C_2}{{}^{11}C_6} = \frac{53}{66}.$

111. (C): P(Bonus introduced) $= \frac{3}{10}\times\frac{4}{9}+\frac{1}{2}\times\frac{2}{9}+\frac{4}{5}\times\frac{1}{3}$

$$= \frac{2}{15}+\frac{1}{9}+\frac{4}{15} = \frac{6+5+12}{45} = \frac{23}{45}.$$

112. (B): F: Bonus introduced

$$\therefore \quad P(A\backslash F) = \frac{\frac{2}{15}}{\frac{23}{45}} = \frac{2}{15}\times\frac{45}{23} = \frac{6}{23}.$$

113. (A): New Mean $= \frac{50-5}{20} = \frac{45}{20} = 2.25.$

114. (B): When 5 is added to each observation then the standard deviation is not changed

$\therefore$ New standard deviation $= \frac{10}{20} = 0.5.$

115. (B):

$$P(B/A') = \frac{P(BAA')}{P(A')} = \frac{P(B)-P(B\cap A)}{1-P(A)}$$

$$= \frac{\frac{1}{2}-\frac{1}{4}}{1-\frac{1}{3}} = \frac{1}{4}\times\frac{3}{2} = \frac{3}{8}.$$

116. (B):

$$P(A'\cap B') = 1 - P(A\cup B)$$

$$= 1 - [P(A) + P(B) - P(A\cap B)]$$

$$= 1-\left[\frac{1}{3}+\frac{1}{2}-\frac{1}{4}\right] = 1-\left[\frac{4+6-3}{12}\right].$$

$$= 1-\frac{7}{2} = \frac{5}{12}.$$

117. (B): $n(s) = 6 \times 6 = 36$

Sum strictly greater than 7

= {(2, 6), (3, 5), (3, 6), (4, 4), (4, 5), (4, 6), (5, 3), (5, 4), (5, 5), (5, 6), (6, 2), (6, 3), (6, 4), (6, 5), (6, 6)}

$$n(E) = 15$$

$$\therefore \quad P(E) = \frac{15}{36} = \frac{5}{12}.$$

118. (C): $P(X \geq 2) = 1 - P(X = 0) - P(X = 1)$

$$= 1-{}^7C_0\left(\frac{1}{5}\right)^0\left(\frac{4}{5}\right)^7 - {}^7C_1\left(\frac{1}{5}\right)^1\left(\frac{4}{7}\right)^6$$

$$= 1-\left(\frac{4}{5}\right)^6\left[\frac{4}{5}+\frac{7}{5}\right] = 1-\left(\frac{11}{5}\right)\left(\frac{4}{5}\right)^6$$

119. (B):

$$\bar{x} = xp = 200 \quad \ldots(i)$$

$$\sigma^2 = xpq = 160\ldots$$

$$\Rightarrow \quad q = \frac{160}{200} = \frac{4}{5} \Rightarrow p = 1-\frac{4}{5} = \frac{1}{5}$$

$$\Rightarrow \quad n = 1000.$$

120. (C):

$$\text{Sum} = S_{15} - S_7$$

$$= \frac{15\times16\times31}{6} - \frac{7\times8\times15}{6}$$

$$= 1240 - 140 = 1100$$

So, $\text{mean} = \frac{1100}{8} = 137.5.$

Previous Years' Paper

NATIONAL DEFENCE ACADEMY & NAVAL ACADEMY

NDA & NA — Entrance Exam, 2024 (II)

PAPER I : GENERAL ABILITY TEST

PART A : ENGLISH LANGUAGE

Directions (Qs. No. 1-5): *Each item in this section consists of a sentence with an underlined word followed by four words or group of words. Select the option that is opposite in meaning to the underlined word and mark your response on the answer sheet accordingly.*

1. All human beings are fallible:
A. frail B. erring
C. mortal D. perfect

2. His words were vague:
A. identical
B. obscure
C. precise
D. imperceptible

3. She performed all her duties conscientiously:
A. assiduously
B. carelessly
C. painstakingly
D. scrupulously

4. These risks are incidental to the work of a firefighter:
A. essential B. adventitious
C. serendipitous D. subsidiary

5. She has always been disdainful of poor people:
A. reverential B. derisive
C. supercilious D. insolent

Directions (Qs. No. 6-15): *In this section, there is a passage that has some blank spaces, each with four words or group of words. Select whichever word or group of words you consider the most appropriate for the blank space and indicate your response on the Answer Sheet accordingly.*

Most of our food comes from agriculture, so we tend to believe that it is __(6)__ of natural biota. This is not true. In nature, __(7)__ plants and animals __(8)__ to the rigours of natural selection. Only the fittest survive. __(9)__ wild populations have numerous traits for competitiveness, resistance to parasites, __(10)__ to adverse conditions, __(11)__ other aspects of vigour. In contrast, populations grown for many __(12)__ under the pampered conditions of agriculture tend to lose these traits, because they __(13)__ for production, not resilience. For example, a high-producing plant __(14)__ lacks resistance to drought is __(15)__ and the resistance to drought is ignored. Also, in the process of breeding plants for maximum production, all genetic variation is eliminated.

6. A. independent B. dependent
C. relevant D. consequent

7. A. the B. both
C. some D. among

8. A. had been continuously subjected
B. will be continuously subject
C. continuously subjected
D. are continuously subjected

9. A. Consequently B. Inadvertently
C. Although D. Since

10. A. withdrawal B. tolerance
C. adaptable D. compliance

11. A. and B. with
C. by D. upon

12. A. eras B. epochs
C. periods D. generations

13. A. had selected B. have selected
C. are selected D. might select

14. A. whichever B. whom
C. that D. whenever

15. A. heated B. irrigated
C. showered D. deserted

Directions (Qs. No. 16-25): *Each of the following items features one part of a sentence followed by four alternatives. Complete the sentence by choosing the correct alternative.*

16. Preeti suggests:
A. that I ask to your advice
B. that I had asked your advice
C. that I can have asked your advice
D. that I ask your advice

17. We saw:
A. the older of all monuments in the city
B. the old of all monuments in the city
C. the oldest monument in the city
D. an oldest of all monuments in the city

18. Since you have been touring all day:
A. you must be tired
B. you ought to have been tired
C. you could had been tired
D. you might not be tired

19. His condition is serious, but:
A. it should be worse
B. it ought to be worse
C. it could be worse
D. it had been going to be worse

20. I hope the bus comes soon because:
A. we waited for half an hour
B. we have been waiting for half an hour
C. we waiting for half an hour
D. we could have been waiting for half an hour

21. Someone:
A. has spilt juice on the sofa
B. should have spilt juice on the sofa
C. have spilt juice on the sofa
D. would spilt juice on the sofa

22. What would you do:
A. if you found your lost toy?
B. if you will have found your lost toy?
C. if you would found your lost toy?
D. if you have find your lost toy?

23. If I were you:
A. I shouldn't buy that dress
B. I wouldn't buy that dress
C. I weren't buying that dress
D. I mustn't buying that dress

24. I wish:
A. I could help you
B. I ought to help you
C. I did help you
D. I must help you

25. The efforts of the security services have not been quite:
A. upto the incredibility
B. up-take
C. up-tight
D. upto the mark

Directions (Qs. No. 26-30): *Given below are some idioms/phrases followed by four alternative meanings to each. Select the response (a), (b), (c) or (d), which is the most appropriate meaning and mark your response on the Answer Sheet accordingly.*

26. A white lie:
A. An offensive way of describing something
B. To do something completely impossible
C. A lie that is absolutely and universally true
D. A lie that you tell to avoid hurting someone

27. Bad blood:
A. Feelings of hatred between people
B. A situation which goes from bad to worse
C. A fatal accident
D. To accept the unpleasant situation

28. Count your blessings:
A. to start to understand how badly something has affected you
B. an event which gradually becomes worse
C. to be grateful for good things in your life
D. something that you say in order to warn someone

29. Have the last laugh:
A. to be the worst example of something
B. to succeed when others thought that you would not
C. to solve all the problems of life
D. to laugh at someone secretly

30. Sit on the fence:
A. to make someone suddenly notice you
B. to fail completely
C. to delay making a decision
D. to behave very badly

Directions (Qs. No. 31-35): *Each of the following items in this section consists of a sentence, the parts of which have been jumbled. These parts have been labelled P, Q, R and S. Given below each sentence have four sequences, namely (a), (b), (c) and (d). You are required to rearrange the jumbled parts of the sentences and mark your response accordingly.*

31. P. good quality elementary education conforming
Q. as a fundamental right of all children
R. the Right to Education Act (RTE) mandates
S. to the standards and norms specified in the Act

A. Q S P R B. R P S Q
C. R Q S P D. S Q P R

32. P. the conflicts and disputes in their mind
Q. music not only relieves the burden
R. on children and the young
S. but also alleviates

A. Q R S P B. P S R Q
C. Q P R S D. P Q R S

33. P. but it is virtually covered by a dome-shaped
Q. Antarctica is a continent
R. nearly twice as large as Australia
S. ice sheet nearly 2 miles thick

A. Q R P S B. S P R Q
C. Q S P R D. S Q R P

34. P. the global economic weight from the advanced economies
Q. that there was a major shift in
R. and Central Bank Governors, in recognition of the fact
S. the G20 was formed in 1999, as a forum of Finance Ministers

A. S P Q R B. P Q R S
C. Q R S P D. S R Q P

35. P. aquaculture nation in the world and
Q. India's products are exported to many nations
R. fish producing and the second largest
S. India is the third largest

A. S R P Q B. Q P R S
C. R P Q S D. P Q R S

Directions (Qs. No. 36-40): *Each of the following sentences has word(s) underlined. Read the sentence carefully and find which word class the underlined word(s) belong(s) to. Indicate your response on the Answer Sheet accordingly.*

36. Adders are the only poisonous snakes found across Britain

A. Noun B. Adjective
C. Adverb D. Determiner

37. She spoke to him once since he has been in town:

A. Adjective B. Adverb
C. Conjunction D. Preposition

38. I don't really want to go. Besides, it's too late now

A. Adjective B. Adverb
C. Preposition D. Conjunction

39. Look at that man over there

A. Adverb B. Conjunction
C. Determiner D. Article

40. The plane is ready for take-off

A. Noun B. Conjunction
C. Verb D. Gerund

Directions (Qs. No. 41-45): *In this section, you have a short passage. After the passage, you will find some items based on the passage. Read the passage carefully and answer the items based on it. You are required to select your answers based on the contents of the passage and the opinion of author only.*

We live in a time when globalisation is rapidly encompassing travel, information, trade and investment. The internet ties people together in ways unimagined a few years ago. The globalisation of health, however, remains an elusive goal, similar to the globalisation of economic well-being. Laurie Garrett, in The Coming Plague, describes an unwelcome form of globalisation: the globalisation of disease. Garrett examines the recent history of emerging diseases such as AIDS, Ebola, Hantavirus, Rift Valley Fever, Legionnaires' disease, and others. She also explains the resurgence of familiar diseases like tuberculosis, cholera, and pneumonia as a consequence of the widespread and unwise use of antibiotics. Many of the new diseases are clearly linked to changes in land use, which brings humans into close contacts with rodents or other animals that harbour viruses previously unknown to medicine and often deadly to humans. Resurgent diseases, by contrast, are a creation of our medical practice. By treating people with antibiotics without restraint, we unknowingly select strains that are immune to the antibiotics and that pass on their resistant genes to unrelated bacteria by way of plasmid transfer. The heroes of her book are the women and men on the frontlines of epidemiology. Garrett makes a plea for a greater commitment from our universities, medical schools, and government agencies to train workers who will be capable of recognizing new diseases and who will be able to move about equally well in the laboratory, the hospital and the field in pursuit of knowledge and public-health intervention around the world.

41. What according to the passage is the 'unwelcome form of the globalization'?

1. Globalization of the diseases
2. Elusive goal of globalization
3. History of fatal diseases
4. Selective use of antibiotics

Select the correct answer using the code given below:

A. 1 only B. 2, 3 and 4
C. 3 only D. 1 and 4

42. According to the passage, globalisation of health has become imperative due to:

A. the globalisation of diseases
B. public health intervention
C. the creation of new medical systems
D. the indiscriminate use of antibiotics

43. According to the passage, resurgent diseases are affected by:

1. Medical practices
2. Overuse of antibiotics
3. Emergence of new strains

Select the correct answer using the code given below:

A. 1 only B. 2 only
C. 1 and 3 only D. 1, 2 and 3

44. According to the passage, many new diseases are emerging due to change in land use because:
A. humans are coming in contact with unfamiliar viruses.
B. urbanisation makes pathogens proliferate
C. humans become adaptive and pass on their genes to related bacteria by way of plasmid transfer.
D. humans are inadvertently releasing new viruses.

45. What is the meaning of the word "epidemiology" in the passage?
A. The historical study of the spread of diseases
B. The scientific study of the spread and control of diseases
C. The scientific study of the invention and uses of drugs
D. The scientific study of the uses of drugs

Directions (Qs. No. 46-50): *Each item in this section consists of a sentence with an underlined word followed by four words. Select the option that is nearest in meaning to the underlined word and mark your response on the Answer Sheet accordingly.*

46. Sages and seers have cautioned that the path towards enlightenment is full of illusory traps.
A. reasoned B. admitted
C. warned D. refused

47. The officer reported the details of the mission in a monotonous manner.
A. dull B. happy
C. disturbed D. enthusiastic

48. There are many elusive questions in philosophy.
A. clear
B. baffling
C. paramount
D. truthful

49. Cleaning this mess is a mammoth task.
A. huge B. quick
C. easy D. intelligent

50. The police department's image was tarnished after the high-profile murder case.
A. enhanced B. tainted
C. restored D. assigned

PART B : General Knowledge

51. Which one of the following statements about lysosomes is NOT correct?
A. They are waste disposal system of the cell
B. They breakdown all inorganic materials
C. These are also referred to as "suicidal bags"
D. Lysosomes stop entry of foreign materials

52. Which of the following two cell organelles have their own genetic material?
A. Endoplasmic reticulum and plastids
B. Endoplasmic reticulum and mitochondria
C. Mitochondria and plastids
D. Lysosomes and Golgi apparatus

53. Which one among the following tissues help to connect two bones?
A. Tendons B. Ligaments
C. Areolar tissue D. Cartilage

54. Which one among the following is the source of energy in cells?
A. ADP B. ATP
C. AMP D. NAD

55. In which one among the following the vegetative propagation takes place through Eye Buds?
A. Potato B. Ginger
C. Onion D. Sugarcane

56. The intermixing of particles of two different types of matter on their own is called:
A. Osmosis B. Brownian motion
C. Diffusion D. Conductance

57. Which one among the following separation techniques is used for blood tests in diagnostic laboratories?
A. Filtration B. Chromatography
C. Centrifugation D. Crystallization

58. Which one among the following elements is polyatomic?
A. Phosphorus B. Sulphur
C. Chlorine D. Aluminium

59. Which of the following anions has a valency of –3?
A. Nitride B. Nitrate
C. Sulphide D. Sulphate

60. The mass of 0.5 mole of N_2 gas is:
A. 7 g B. 14 g
C. 21 g D. 28 g

61. The chemical reaction:

$2AgCl(s) \rightarrow 2Ag(s) + Cl_2(g)$ takes place
A. in dark
B. in sunlight
C. on heating
D. under high pressure

62. Which one among the following is commonly used as an 'anti-skinning agent' in paints?
A. Gelatin
B. N-methyl pyrrolidone
C. Pyridine
D. Polyhydroxy phenol

63. Two resistances of 5.0 Ω and 7.0 Ω are connected in series and the combination is connected in parallel with a resistance of 36.0 Ω. The equivalent resistance of the combination of three resistors is:
A. 24.0 Ω B. 12.0 Ω
C. 9.0 Ω D. 6.0 Ω

64. Shown in the figure are two hollow cubes C_1 and C_2 of negligible mass partially filled (depicted by darkened area) with liquids of densities ρ_1 and ρ_2, respectively, floating in water (density ρ_W). The relationship between ρ_1, ρ_2 and ρ_W is:

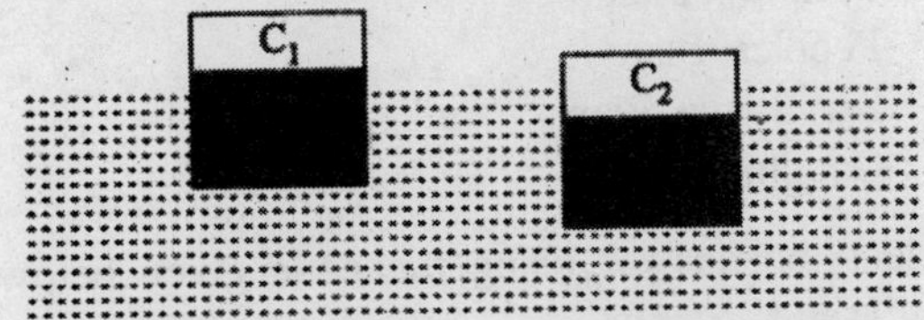

A. $\rho_2 < \rho_W < \rho_1$ B. $\rho_2 < \rho_1 < \rho_W$
C. $\rho_1 < \rho_2 < \rho_W$ D. $\rho_1 < \rho_W < \rho_2$

65. An astronaut whose weight on the Earth is 600 N experiences weightlessness on International Space Station orbiting around the Earth. It means that
A. acceleration of the astronaut is zero.
B. normal reaction of the spacestation floor on the astronaut is zero.
C. gravitational pull of earth on the astronaut is zero.
D. space station applies a centrifugal force on the astronaut.

66. Which of the following statements give characteristics of contact forces?
1. It appears between an object when it is in contact with some other object
2. It satisfies the third law of motion
3. It may appear between a pair of solid and fluid
Select the answer using the code given below:
A. 1 and 3 only B. 2 and 3 only
C. 1 and 2 only D. 1, 2 and 3

67. Which one among the following figures correctly represents the ray diagram? (Consider the lens to be thin)

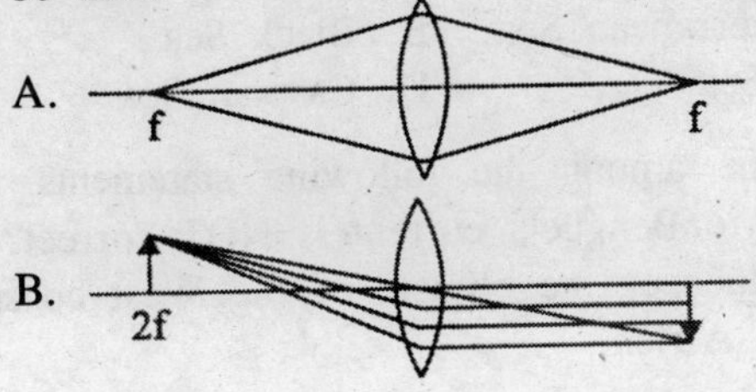

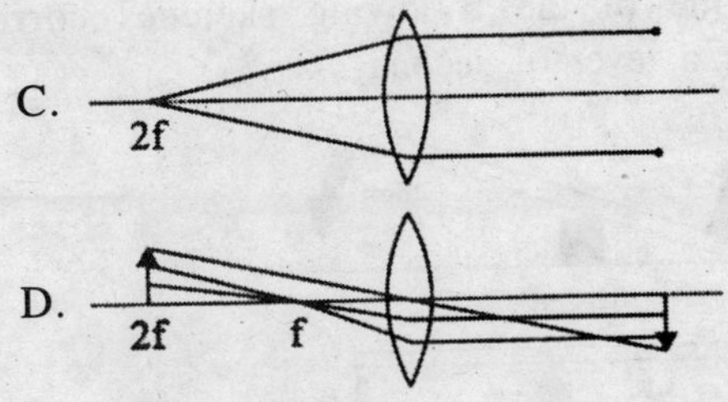

68. Lightning is due to:
A. The flow of charges between different parts of the cloud
B. The short-circuiting of charges between the upper and lower surfaces of the cloud
C. The collection of positively charged particles on the base and collection of negatively charged particles at the top of the cloud
D. The induction of positive charge on the ground below the negative charge at the base of the cloud

69. In which one among the following Situations the bulb ⊗ would glow the most? (Consider all batteries are the same)

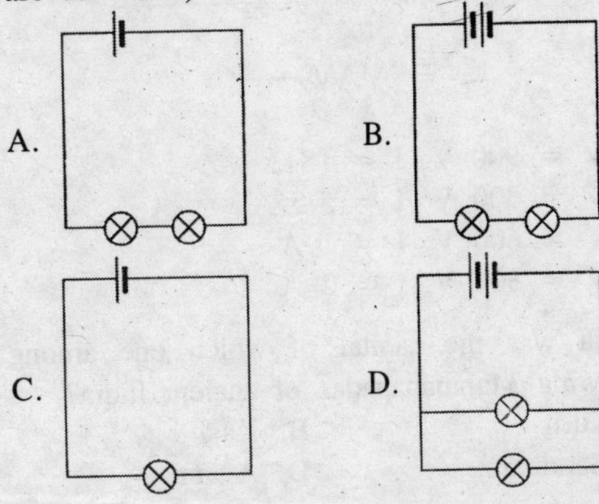

70. Which one among the following diagrams may correctly represent the motion of a skydiver during a jump?

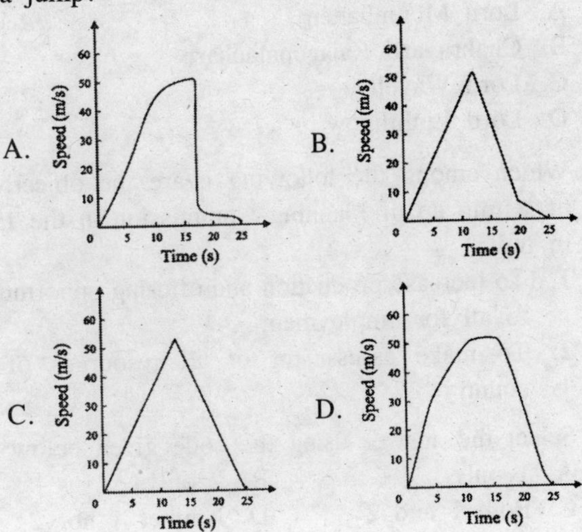

71. Which one of the following sketches correctly describes a lever of second class?

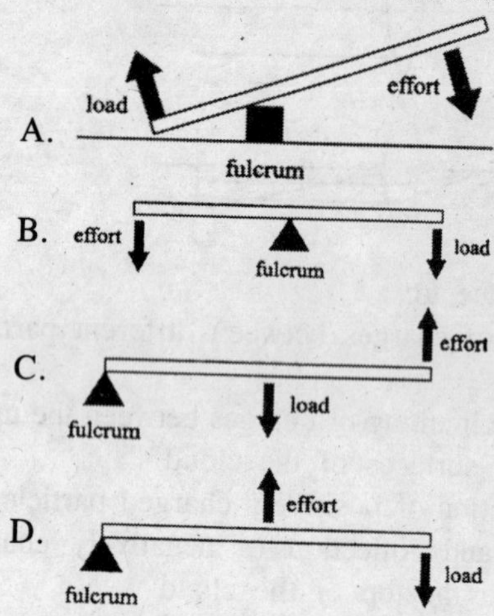

72. For an electric circuit given below, the correct combination of voltage (V) and current (I) is:

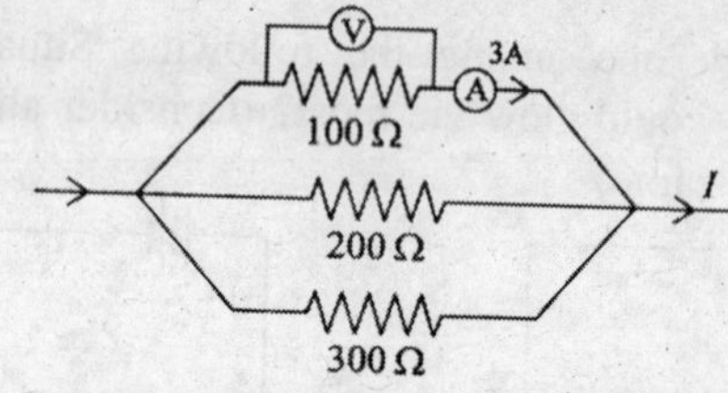

A. V = 900 V; I = 18 A
B. V = 300 V; I = 5.5 A
C. V = 600 V; I = 1 A
D. V = 300 V; I = 2 A

73. Taxila was the capital of which one among the following Mahajanapadas of ancient India?
A. Kuru
B. Kasi
C. Gandhar
D. Avanti

74. Who among the following was the last Governor-General of India before the office was permanently abolished?
A. Lord Mountbatten
B. Chakravarti Rajagopalachari
C. Lord Wavell
D. Lord Linlithgow

75. Which among the following is/are the objective(s) of setting up of Planning Commission in the 1950s in India?
1. To increase production and offering opportunities to all for employment
2. To make assessment of all resources of the country

Select the answer using the code given below:
A. 1 only
B. 2 only
C. Both 1 and 2
D. Neither 1 nor 2

76. Which among the following statements with regard to Five Year Plans in India is/are correct?
1. The First and Ninth five year plans accorded high priority to agriculture
2. The Third Plan was based on the Harrod-Domar Model
3. Seventh Plan focused on food, work and productivity
4. The Ninth five year plan emphasized on massive investments in public sector

Select the answer using the code given below:
A. 1 only
B. 1 and 3
C. 3 and 4
D. 1, 2 and 4

77. Before the inception of the First Five year Plan, which among the following Plans were initiated in India?
1. Bombay Plan
2. Peoples Plan
3. Sarvodaya Plan
4. Gandhian Plan

Select the answer using the code given below:
A. 1 and 2 only
B. 1 and 3 only
C. 3 and 4 only
D. 1, 2, 3 and 4

78. Any land that is left fallow for more than five years is termed as:
A. Current fallow
B. Fallow other than current fallow
C. Culturable waste land
D. Barren and waste land

79. Which statement is NOT correct with reference to Andaman and Nicobar Islands?
A. Climate is humid, tropical coastal climate.
B. Maximum rainfall occurs between March and April.
C. Andaman and Nicobar islands are separated by 10 degree Channel which is 150 Km wide.
D. Islands are inhabited by Negrito tribes.

80. Which one among the following local winds is NOT related to Mediterranean Sea?
A. Harmattan
B. Khamsin
C. Sirocco
D. Mistral

81. Which one among the following is a landlocked water body?
A. Mediterranean Sea
B. Black Sea
C. Red Sea
D. Caspian Sea

82. Which one among the following statements with reference to Benguela current is NOT correct?
A. It influences the climate of the West coast of North Africa.

B. It is a cold current.
C. Its direction is from South to North.
D. It flows in the Atlantic Ocean.

83. The lowest part of most bolsons is occupied by a landform called playa. Which category of landform formation does it represent?
A. Fluvial landforms B. Arid landforms
C. Glacial landforms D. Periglacial landforms

84. Which one among the following diseases is caused due to deficiency of Vitamin D in humans?
A. Beriberi B. Scurvy
C. Rickets D. Pneumonia

85. Which one among the following combinations most appropriately represent the components of balanced diet?
A. Carbohydrate, vitamins, proteins, fat, minerals, fibres and water
B. Carbohydrate, vitamins, proteins, fat and minerals
C. Carbohydrate, vitamins, proteins, minerals and water
D. Vitamins, proteins, fat, minerals, fibres and water

86. In which part or organ of human body cartilage is NOT found?
A. Nose B. Trachea
C. Bronchiole D. Knee joint

87. Which part of nephron of the human kidney is responsible for filtration of blood for excretion?
A. Collecting duct B. Renal vein
C. Ureter D. Bowman's capsule

88. Organisms of which of the following phylum are called sponges?
A. Coelenterata B. Platyhelminthes
C. Porifera D. Echinodermata

89. A point object is placed at the centre of curvature of a spherical concave mirror. Which one among the following would be the correct location of image formed?
A. At infinity
B. At the centre of curvature
C. At the focal point
D. Between the focal point and the centre of curvature

90. Which one among the following is correct for a person suffering from myopia?
A. The person can see near objects clearly
B. The person can see distant objects clearly
C. The person cannot distinguish colours
D. The person can neither see near objects nor distant objects clearly

91. A vehicle starts moving along a straight line path from rest. In first t seconds it moves with an acceleration of $2 m/s_2$ and then in next 10 seconds it moves with an acceleration of $5 m/s^2$. The total distance travelled by the vehicle is 550 m. The value of time t is:
A. 10 s B. 13 s
C. 20 s D. 25 s

92. A pumpkin weighs 7.5 N. On submerging it completely in water, $\frac{3}{4}$L of water gets displaced. The acceleration due to gravity at the place where the pumpkin was weighed is 10 m/s^2. Which one of the following is the correct value of the density of the pumpkin?
A. 10 kg/m^3 B. 100 kg/m^3
C. 1000 kg/m^3 D. 10000 kg/m^3

93. An incandescent electric bulb converts 20% of its power consumption into light, and the remaining power is dissipated as heat. The bulb's filament has a resistance of 200 Ω and 2 A current flows through it. If the bulb remains ON for 10 h and the rate of electricity charge is ₹ 5/unit, then which among the following is the correct amount for the money spent on producing light?
A. ₹ 5 B. ₹ 6
C. ₹ 7 D. ₹ 8

94. Which one of the following statements best defines the concept of heat?
A. The transformation of energy from one form to another
B. The conversion of energy into mass and vice-versa due to temperature difference
C. The transfer of energy due to temperature difference
D. The change in volume of a substance with temperature

95. The masses of two planets are in the ratio of 1 : 7. The ratio between their diameters is 2 : 1. The ratio of forces which they exert on each other is:
A. 1 : 7 B. 7 : 1
C. 1 : 1 D. 2 : 1

96. A car weighs 1000 kg. It is moving with a uniform velocity of 72 km/h towards a straight road. The driver suddenly presses the brakes. The car stops in 0.2 s. The retarding force applied on the car to stop it is:
A. 100 N B. 1000 N
C. 10 kN D. 100 kN

97. There is a ball of mass 320 g. It has 625 J potential energy when released freely from a height. The speed with which it will hit the ground is:
A. 62.5 m/s B. 2.0 m/s
C. 50 m/s D. 40 m/s

98. Starting from rest a vehicle accelerates at the rate of $2\ m/s^2$ towards east for 10 s. It then stops suddenly. It then accelerates again at a rate of $4\sqrt{2}\ m/s^2$ for next 10 s towards south and then again comes to rest. The net displacement of the vehicle from the starting point is:

A. 100 m
B. 200 m
C. 300 m
D. 400 m

99. Which one of the following statements about the Industrial Revolution is correct?

A. Thomas Savery invented astrolabe
B. Thomas Newcomen invented chemical dyes
C. James Watt's invention converted the steam engine from being a mere pump into one which would provide energy to power machines in factories
D. Mathew Boulton discovered the technique of refining gold of impurities

100. The first cotton mill in British India which began production in 1856 was set up by:

A. Ghanshyam Das Birla
B. Jamnalal Bajaj
C. Ambalal Sarabhai
D. C. N. Davar

101. Consider the following statements about the Linguistic Reorganization of the States:

1. Gandhiji, in 1948, had argued for the reorganization of provinces on a linguistic basis
2. The Constituent Assembly recommended it to be incorporated in the Constitution of India

Which of the statements given above is/are correct?

A. 1 only
B. 2 only
C. Both 1 and 2
D. Neither 1 nor 2

102. Inspired by the Dandi March by Mahatma Gandhi, in Tamil Nadu, C Rajagopalachari led a salt march from:

A. Tirunelveli to Nagercoil
B. Kanchipuram to Mahabalipuram
C. Trichinopoly to Vedaranniyam on Tanjore coast
D. Chennai to Vellore

103. Acharya Vinoba Bhave received the first donation of land under the Bhoodan Movement at:

A. Ramgarh
B. Garhwa
C. Hyderabad
D. Pochampally

104. Maize (makka) was introduced into India via:

A. America and England
B. Africa and Spain
C. France and Russia
D. Portugal and Italy

105. Which of the following pairs of Himalayan Passes and the Ranges in which they are located is/are correctly matched?

1. Zoji La — Great Himalayas
2. Banihal Pass — Pir Panjal Range
3. Photu La — Ladakh Range
4. Khardung La — Karakoram Range

Select the answer using the code given below:

A. 2 only
B. 4
C. 1 and 2 only
D. 1, 2 and 3

106. Which one among the following statements with reference to the black cotton soils of India is NOT correct?

A. The black cotton soils are also called 'Regur'.
B. They are highly moisture retentive.
C. They are rich in lime.
D. These soils have less clay factor and hence can support a wide variety of crops and vegetables.

107. Match List-I with List-II and select the correct answer using the code given below the Lists:

List-I *(Hydroelectric Power Plant)*	List-II *(State)*
(*a*) Doyang	1. Arunachal Pradesh
(*b*) Gomuti	2. Assam
(*c*) Kapili	3. Tripura
(*d*) Ranganadi	4. Nagaland

Code:

	(*a*)	(*b*)	(*c*)	(*d*)
A.	4	3	2	1
B.	4	2	3	1
C.	1	2	3	4
D.	1	3	2	4

108. Match List-I with List-II and select the correct answer using the code given below the Lists:

List-I *(Tropical Cyclone)*	List-II *(Country)*
A. Hurricanes	1. China
B. Willy Willy	2. Philippines
C. Baguio	3. Australia
D. Typhoons	4. USA

Code:

	(*a*)	(*b*)	(*c*)	(*d*)
A.	4	3	2	1
B.	1	2	3	4
C.	4	2	3	1
D.	1	3	2	4

109. Consider the following facts of the rivers of the Indus system:

1. The Satluj originates in Tibet where it is known as Langchen Khambab.
2. The Satluj is a classic example of an antecedent river.
3. The Jhelum is the largest tributary of the Indus System.

Select the answer using the code given below:

A. 2 only B. 3 only
C. 1 and 2 D. 2 and 3

110. Which one of the following is an example of both an igneous as well as a metamorphic rock?

A. Gabbro B. Geyserite
C. Gneissoid D. Granite

111. Which one of the following is correct?

A. Pyroxene is commonly found in meteorites
B. Amphiboles form about 20% of the Earth's crust
C. Quartz is soluble in water
D. The word 'sedimentary' is derived from the Latin word kelimentum

112. Which one among the following processes is NOT part of chemical weathering?

A. Solution B. Hydration
C. Reduction D. Thawing

113. What is the maximum number of electrons that can occupy the first shell of an atom?

A. 2 B. 4
C. 8 D. 16

114. At which temperature does liquid water show maximum density?

A. 299 K B. 277 K
C. 285 K D. 373 K

115. Which one among the following has valency of 3?

A. Carbon B. Oxygen
C. Nitrogen D. Sodium

116. Which one among the following is an example of oxidation reaction?

A. Freezing of water
B. Dissolving sugar in water
C. Rusting of iron
D. Boiling of petrol

117. Which one among the following fertilizers is a source of nitrogen?

A. Superphosphate
B. Potassium sulfate
C. Bone meal
D. Urea

118. For Aluminium (Al) (atomic number: 13, mass number: 27), which one among the following statements is NOT correct?

A. Number of electrons present in Al is 13.
B. Number of protons present in Al is 13.
C. Number of neutrons present in Al is 14.
D. The valency of Al is 2/

119. The elemental composition of diamond is:

A. Carbon and Hydrogen
B. Carbon and Oxygen
C. Pure Carbon
D. Pure Silicon

120. Which one among the following is an example of chemical change?

A. Sublimation of camphor
B. Melting of ice
C. Heating of an iron rod
D. Mixing of NaOH and HCl

121. Which one among the following is the correct focal length of a combination of lenses of power 2.5 D and –2.0 D?

A. +0.5 m B. –0.5 m
C. +2.0 m D. –2.0 m

122. The AC mains domestic supply current in India changes direction in every:

A. 50 s B. $\frac{1}{50}$ s
C. 100 s D. $\frac{1}{100}$ s

123. A block of mass 2.0 kg slides on a rough horizontal plane surface. Let the speed of the block at a particular instant is 10 m/s. It comes to rest after travelling a distance of 20 m. Which one of the following could be the magnitude of the frictional force?

A. 10 N B. 20 N
C. 40 N D. 50 N

124. Given below are the four cases in which certain heat transfer is taking place:

1. Ice is melting in a glass full of water.
2. Water is boiling in an open container.
3. A metal rod is heated in a furnace.
4. A cup of coffee is allowed to cool on a table.

In which of the above cases, the Newton's Law of Cooling is applicable?

A. 1 only
B. 4 only
C. 1 and 4 only
D. 1, 2 and 3

125. The figure given below shows the direction of the two forces P and Q acting on a skydiver:

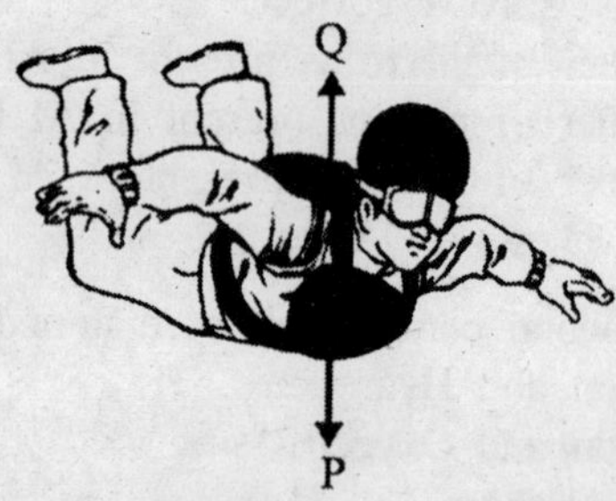

Which one among the following statements is correct about the two forces?

A. Force P is caused by the gravity and force Q is caused by the friction
B. When the force P is bigger than the force Q, the speed of the skydiver remains the same
C. After the parachute opens, force P remains the same while force Q increases
D. After the parachute opens, force P decreases while force Q increases

126. Vijayanagara rulers claimed that they were ruling on behalf of:

A. Lord Murugan B. Lord Venkateshwara
C. Shri Virupaksha D. Shri Vallabha

127. Domingo Paes describes a king in these words: 'Of medium height, and of fair complexion and good figure, rather fat than thin; he has on his face signs of smallpox'. Identify the king from the options given below.

A. Krishnadeva Raya B. Ram Raya
C. Devaraya II D. Devaraya I

128. In which Schedule of the Constitution of India, provisions as to disqualification on grounds of defection are given?

A. Ninth Schedule B. Tenth Schedule
C. Eleventh Schedule D. Sixth Schedule

129. Consider the following statements:

1. The duties of the Attorney General of India are to give advice to the Government of India upon such legal matters, and to perform such other duties of a legal character, as may from time to time be referred to or assigned to him by the President of India.
2. The Solicitor General of India is the secondary Law Officer of the country, who assists the Attorney General, and is himself assisted by several Additional Solicitor Generals of India.

Which of the statements given above is/are correct?

A. 1 only B. 2 only
C. Both 1 and 2 D. Neither 1 nor 2

130. Which of the following Committees does NOT consist of Members from the Upper House of the Parliament?

1. Public Accounts Committee
2. Estimates Committee
3. Committee on Public Undertakings

Select the answer using the code given below:

A. 1 and 2 B. 1 and 3
C. 2 only D. 3 only

131. In the passing of a Money Bill, the Rajya Sabha has limited powers in that it shall return the Bill, with or without any recommendation, within the stipulated time of:

A. 12 days B. 21 days
C. 14 days D. 30 days

132. Which of the following statements with regard to Article 19(1) of the Constitution of India is/are correct?

1. Freedoms under this Article are not absolute.
2. Reasonable restrictions can be imposed on the exercise of freedoms under this Article.

Select the answer using the code given below:

A. 1 only B. 2 only
C. Both 1 and 2 D. Neither 1 nor 2

133. Which of the following is NOT a part of the five principles enshrined in the 'Panchsheel' agreement signed by India and China in 1954?

A. Mutual non-aggression
B. Mutual non-interference
C. Peaceful coexistence
D. Cultural cooperation

134. Freedom Fighter Kanaklata Barua sacrificed her life while participating in:

A. Rowlatt Satyagraha
B. Non-Cooperation Movement
C. Civil Disobedience Movement
D. Quit India Movement

135. Where is the Coriolis Effect the largest?

A. At the Equator
B. At the Tropic of Capricorn and Tropic of Cancer
C. At the North Pole
D. At 45 degree latitude in each hemisphere

136. In which among the following states in India, the Sun rays are never perpendicular?

1. Bihar 2. Chhattisgarh
3. Manipur 4. Rajasthan

Select the answer using the code given below:

A. 1 and 2 B. 1 and 3
C. 2 and 3 D. 2 and 4

137. Which of the following is/are east flowing rivers in India?

1. Palar 2. Periyar
3. Pennar 4. Kalinadi

Select the answer using the code given below:

A. 1 only B. 1 and 3
C. 2 and 4 D. 4 only

138. Which of the following tributaries is/are correctly matched with the Deccan Rivers?

Tributary	**River**
1. Bhavani	Krishna
2. Kabini	Kaveri
3. Manjra	Godavari
4. Bhima	Mahanadi

Select the answer using the code given below:

A. 1 and 2 B. 2 and 3
C. 1 and 3 D. 3 and 4

139. Which one of the following is found in appreciable amount in Laterite soil in India?

A. Calcium B. Phosphate
C. Potash D. Nitrogen

140. Consider the following statements regarding River Brahmaputra:

1. It rises in Tibet, near Lake Mansarovar
2. It takes a "U" turn near Namcha Barwa and enters India through a gorge

Which of the statements given above is/are correct?

A. 1 only
B. 2 only
C. Both 1 and 2
D. Neither 1 nor 2

141. "Not me, but you" is the motto of which one of the following youth organizations/schemes?

A. Rashtriya Yuva Sashaktikaran Karyakram
B. National Service Scheme (NSS)
C. National Young Leaders Programme
D. National Discipline Scheme (NDS)

142. "Fitness ka dose, aadha ghanta roz" campaign, is associated with:

A. Khelo India
B. Fit India Programme
C. Mera Yuva Bharat
D. Healthy Heart Programme

143. Consider the following statements:

1. Kozhikode has been included in UNESCO's creative cities network as the 'City of Music'.
2. Garba of Gujarat has been declared by UNESCO as an intangible cultural heritage.
3. Gwalior has been included in UNESCO's creative cities network as the 'City of Literature'.

How many of the above statements is/are correct?

A. None B. 1
C. 2 D. 3

144. ASEAN-India Millet Festival-2023, organized by Indian Mission to ASEAN, was held in which one of the following countries?

A. India B. Indonesia
C. Malaysia D. Thailand

145. Consider the following statements:

1. First Indian Military Heritage festival was inaugurated in October 2023 in Pune.
2. First Green Hydrogen Fuel Cell Bus was flagged off in India in Bangalore.
3. South Africa chaired the 15th BRICS Summit held in 2023.
4. Viksit Bharat Sankalp Yatra was flagged off in 2023 from Jharkhand.

How many of the above statements is/are correct?

A. 1 B. 2
C. 3 D. 4

146. Which of the following statements about 'ULLAS' scheme is/are NOT correct?

1. It's a Centrally Sponsored scheme which aims at securing childhood for street children
2. It's a scheme aligned with National Education Policy-2020 which aims at empowering adults aged 15 or above who could not get due schooling

Select the answer using the code given below:

A. 1 only
B. 2 only
C. Both 1 and 2
D. Neither 1 nor 2

147. Which one of the following statements is NOT correct about NATO?

A. It was formed out of the signing of the Washington Treaty.
B. Russia is not a member of this organization.
C. It derives its authority from the UN Charter.
D. Finland is its latest member.

148. In January 2024, India has entered into a bilateral agreement through which it will provide grant assistance to a country to construct a 20 feet Bailey bridge. Identify the country.

A. Nepal
B. Bangladesh
C. Bhutan
D. Myanmar

149. Which one among the following Joint Military Exercises was NOT conducted between India and USA?

A. Yudhabhyas B. Vajra Prahar
C. Malabar D. Varuna

150. Consider the following statements:

1. India has secured 10th rank in International Shipment category in World Bank's Logistics Performance Index Report-2023.
2. Global Maritime India Summit-2023 was held in Vishakhapatnam.
3. 'Maritime Amrit Kaal Vision 2047' was launched during Global Maritime India Summit-2023.

How many of the above statements is/are correct?

A. None
B. 1
C. 2
D. 3

PAPER II : MATHEMATICS

1. Let X be a matrix of order 3 × 3, Y be a matrix of order 2 × 3 and Z be a matrix of order 3 × 2. Which of the following statements are correct?

1. (ZY)X is defined and is a square matrix of order 3.
2. Y(XZ) is defined and is a square matrix of order 2.
3. X(YZ) is not defined.

Select the answer using the code given below.

A. I and II only B. II and III only
C. I and III only D. I, II and III

2. Consider the following statements:

I. The set of all irrational numbers between $\sqrt{12}$ and $\sqrt{15}$ is an infinite set.

II. The set of all odd integers less than 1000 is a finite set.

Which of the statements given above is/are correct?

A. I only B. II only
C. Both I and II D. Neither I nor II

3. How many 4-digit numbers are there having all digits as odd?

A. 625 B. 400
C. 196 D. 120

4. If $\omega \neq 1$ is a cube root of unity, then what is $(1 + \omega - \omega^2)^{100} + (1 - \omega + \omega^2)^{100}$ equal to?

A. $2^{100}\omega^2$ B. $2^{100}\omega$
C. 2^{100} D. -2^{100}

5. Let A and B be two square matrices of same order. If AB is a null matrix, then which one of the following is correct?

A. Both A and B are null matrices
B. Either A or B is a null matrix
C. B is a null matrix if A is a non-singular matrix
D. Both A and B are singular matrices

6. In the expansion of $(1 + x)^p (1 + x)^q$, if the coefficient of x^3 is 35, then what is the value of $(p + q)$?

A. 5 B. 6
C. 7 D. 8

7. If p times the pth term of an AP is equal to q times the qth term $(p \neq q)$, then what is the $(p + q)$th term equal to?

A. 0 B. $p + q$
C. pq D. $pq(p + q)$

8. Let $p = ln(x)$, $q = ln(x^3)$ and $r = ln(x^5)$, were $x > 1$. Which of the following statements is/are correct?

I. p, q and r are in AP.

II. p, q and r can never be in GP.

Select the answer using the code given below:

A. I only B. II only
C. Both I and II D. Neither I nor II

9. If $Z = \frac{1}{3}\begin{vmatrix} i & 2i & 1 \\ 2i & 3i & 2 \\ 3 & 1 & 3 \end{vmatrix} = x + iy;\ i = \sqrt{-1}$

then what is modulus of Z equal to?

A. 1 B. $\sqrt{2}$
C. 2 D. $\sqrt{3}$

10. What is the value of the sum

$$\sum_{n=1}^{20} (i^{n-1} + i^n + i^{n+1})$$

where $i = \sqrt{-1}$?

A. $-2i$ B. 0
C. 1 D. $2i$

11. Let $x > 1$, $y > 1$, $z > 1$ be in GP. Then $\frac{1}{1+\ln x}, \frac{1}{1+\ln y}, \frac{1}{1+\ln z}$ are:

A. in AP
B. in GP
C. in HP
D. neither in AP nor in GP nor in HP

12. If $\omega = -\frac{1}{2} + i\frac{\sqrt{3}}{2}$ then what is:

$$\begin{vmatrix} 1+\omega & 1+\omega^2 & \omega+\omega^2 \\ 1 & \omega & \omega^2 \\ \frac{1}{\omega} & \frac{1}{\omega^2} & 1 \end{vmatrix}$$

equal to?

A. 0 B. ω
C. ω D. $1 - \omega^2$

13. If the sum of the first n terms of a series is $n(2n + 1)$, then what is the nth term?

A. $4n - 1$ B. $4n$
C. $4n + 1$ D. $4n + 3$

14. In how many ways can the letters of the word INDIA be permutated such that in each combination, vowels should occupy odd positions?

A. 3 B. 6
C. 9 D. 12

15. The letters of the word EQUATION are arranged in such a way that all vowels as well as consonants are together. How many such arrangements are there?

A. 240 B. 720
C. 1440 D. 1620

16. If n is a root of the equation $x^2 + px + m = 0$ and m is a root of the equation $x^2 + px + n = 0$, where $m \neq n$, then what is the value of $p + m + n$?

A. –1 B. 0
C. 1 D. 2

17. In how many ways can a student choose $(n - 2)$ courses out of n courses if 2 courses are compulsory $(n > 4)$?

A. $(n - 3)(n - 4)$ B. $(n - 1)(n - 2)$
C. $(n - 3)(n - 4)/2$ D. $(n - 2)(n - 3)/2$

18. If $D_n = \begin{vmatrix} n & 20 & 30 \\ n^2 & 40 & 50 \\ n^3 & 60 & 70 \end{vmatrix}$

then what is the value of $\sum_{n=1}^{4} D_n$?

A. –10000 B. –10
C. 10 D. 10000

19. Consider the following in respect of the matrices

$$P = \begin{bmatrix} 0 & c & -b \\ -c & 0 & a \\ b & -a & 0 \end{bmatrix} \text{ and } Q = \begin{bmatrix} a^2 & ab & ac \\ ab & b^2 & bc \\ ac & bc & c^2 \end{bmatrix}$$

I. PQ is a null matrix.
II. QP is an identity matrix of order 3.
III. PQ = QP

Which of the above is/are correct?

A. I only B. II only
C. I and III D. II and III

20. If P is a skew-symmetric matrix of order 3, then what if det(P) equal to?

A. –1 B. 0
C. 1 D. 3

21. If $4 \sin^{-1} x + \cos^{-1} x = \pi$, then what is $\sin^{-1}x + 4 \cos^{-1} x$ equal to?

A. $\frac{\pi}{2}$ B. π
C. $\frac{3\pi}{2}$ D. 2π

22. What is $\cot^2(\sec^{-1} 2) + \tan^2(\text{cosec}^{-1} 3)$ equal to?

A. $\frac{11}{12}$ B. $\frac{11}{24}$
C. $\frac{7}{24}$ D. $\frac{1}{24}$

23. In a triangle ABC

$$\frac{a}{\cos A} = \frac{b}{\cos B} = \frac{c}{\cos C}$$

What is the area of the triangle if $a = 6$ cm?

A. $9\sqrt{3}$ square cm B. 12 square cm
C. $18\sqrt{3}$ square cm D. 24 square cm

24. The roots of the equation $7x^2 - 6x + 1 = 0$ are $\tan \alpha$ and $\tan \beta$, where 2α and 2β are the angles of a triangle. Which one of the following is correct?

A. The triangle is equilateral
B. The triangle is isosceles but not right-angled
C. The triangle is right-angled
D. The triangle is right-angled isosceles

25. In a triangle ABC, $\angle A = 75°$ and $\angle B = 45°$. What is $2a - b$ equal to?

A. c B. $\sqrt{2}c$
C. $2c$ D. $2\sqrt{2}c$

26. What is the number of solutions of the equation $\cot 2x \cdot \cot 3x = 1$ for $0 < x < \pi$?

A. Only one B. Only two
C. Only five D. More than five

27. What is the general solution of $\cos^{100} x - \sin^{100} x = 1$?

A. $n\pi$ B. $(2n + 1)\pi$
C. $2n\pi$ D. $(2n + 1)\pi/2$

where n is an integer.

28. In a triangle ABC tanA + tanB + tanC = k
What is the value of cotA cotB cotC?
A. 0.5 k B. $1/k$
C. $3/k$ D. $1/k^3$

29. What is sin12° sin48° equal to?
A. $\frac{\sqrt{5}-1}{4}$ B. $\frac{\sqrt{5}+1}{4}$
C. $\frac{\sqrt{5}-1}{8}$ D. $\frac{\sqrt{5}+1}{8}$

30. What is $\frac{\cos 17° - \sin 17°}{\cos 17° + \sin 17°}$ equal to?
A. tan 34° B. cot 34°
C. tan 62° D. cot 62°

31. Consider the following numbers:
I. tan 22.5°
II. cot 22.5°
III. tan 22.5° - cot 22.5°

How many of the above are irrational numbers?
A. None B. Only one
C. Only two D. All three

32. If $\frac{x}{\cos\theta} = \frac{y}{\cos\left(\frac{2\pi}{3}-\theta\right)} = \frac{z}{\cos\left(\frac{2\pi}{3}+\theta\right)}$ then what is $x + y + z$ equal to?
A. –1 B. 0
C. 1 D. 3

33. If p tan(θ - 30°) = q tan(θ + 120°), then what is $(p + q)/(p - q)$ equal to?
A. sin 2θ B. cos 2θ
C. 2 sin 2θ D. 2 cos 2θ

34. Let P and Q be two non-void relations on a set A. Which of the following statements are correct?
I. P and Q are reflexive ⇒ P ∩ Q is reflexive.
II. P and Q are symmetric ⇒ P ∪ Q is symmetric.
III. P and Q are transitive ⇒ P ∩ Q is transitive.

Select the answer using the code given below.
A. I and II only B. II and III only
C. I and III only D. I, II and III

35. If A and B are two non-empty sets having 10 elements in common, then how many elements do A × B and B × A have in common?
A. 10 B. 20
C. 40 D. 100

36. What is the remainder when $7^n - 6n$ is divided by 36 for n = 100?
A. 0 B. 1
C. 2 D. 6

37. What is the maximum number of possible points of intersection of four straight lines and a circle (intersection is between lines as well as circle and lines)?
A. 6 B. 10
C. 14 D. 16

38. In an AP, the ratio of the sum of the first p terms to the sum of the first q terms is $p^2 : q^2$. Which one of the following is correct?
A. The first term is equal to the common difference
B. The first term is equal to twice the common difference
C. The common difference is equal to twice the first term
D. The first term is equal to square of the common difference

39. What is the number of real roots of the equation $(x - 1)^2 + (x - 3)^2 + (x - 5)^2 = 0$?
A. None B. Only one
C. Only two D. Three

40. In a class of 240 students, 180 passed in English, 130 passed in Hindi and 150 passed in Sanskrit. Further, 60 passed in only one subject, 110 passed in only two subjects and 10 passed in none of the subjects. How many passed in all three subjects?
A. 60 B. 55
C. 40 D. 35

Direction (Qs. No. 41 and 42): *Consider the following for the two (02) items that follow:*

Let Z_1 and Z_2 be **any** two complex numbers such that $Z_1^2 + Z_2^2 + Z_1Z_2 = 0$.

41. What is the value of $\left|\frac{Z_1}{Z_2}\right|$?
A. 1 B. 2
C. 3 D. 4

42. What is the value of $\frac{1}{2} + \text{Re}\left(\frac{Z_1}{Z_2}\right)$?
A. –1 B. 0
C. 1 D. 2

Direction (Qs. No. 43 and 44): *Consider the following for the two (02) items that follow:*

The product of 5 consecutive terms of an AP is 229635. The first, second and fifth terms are in GP.

43. What is the common difference?
A. 3 B. 4
C. 5 D. 6

44. What is the sum of all five terms?
A. 60 B. 65
C. 75 D. 80

Direction (Qs. No. 45 and 46): *Consider the following for the two (02) items that follow:*

Let $\left(8+3\sqrt{7}\right)^{20} = \text{U} + \text{V}$ and $\left(8-3\sqrt{7}\right)^{20} = \text{W}$,

where U is an integer and $0 < \text{V} < 1$.

45. What is V + W equal to?
A. 8
B. 4
C. 2
D. 1

46. What is the value of (U + V)W?
A. 1/2
B. 1
C. 3/2
D. 2

Direction (Qs. No. 47 and 48): *Consider the following for the two (02) items that follow:*

The roots of the quadratic equation
$a^2(b^2 - c^2)x^2 + b^2(c^2 - a^2)x + c^2(a^2 - b^2) = 0$
are equal ($a^2 \neq b^2 \neq c^2$).

47. Which one of the following statements is correct?
A. a^2, b^2, c^2 are in AP.
B. a^2, b^2, c^2 are in GP.
C. a^2, b^2, c^2 are in HP.
D. a^2, b^2, c^2 are neither in AP nor in GP nor in HP.

48. Which one of the following is a root of the equation?
A. $\dfrac{b^2(c^2-a^2)}{a^2(c^2-b^2)}$
B. $\dfrac{b^2(c^2-a^2)}{a^2(b^2-c^2)}$
C. $\dfrac{b^2(c^2-a^2)}{2a^2(c^2-b^2)}$
D. $\dfrac{b^2(c^2-a^2)}{2a^2(b^2-c^2)}$

Direction (Qs. No. 49 and 50): *Consider the following for the two (02) items that follow:*

Let, $A = \begin{bmatrix} 3 & -3 & 4 \\ 2 & -3 & 4 \\ 0 & -1 & 1 \end{bmatrix}$

49. What is A(Adj A) equal to?
A. $\begin{bmatrix} 5 & 0 & 0 \\ 0 & 5 & 0 \\ 0 & 0 & 5 \end{bmatrix}$
B. $\begin{bmatrix} 2 & 0 & 0 \\ 0 & 2 & 0 \\ 0 & 0 & 2 \end{bmatrix}$
C. $\begin{bmatrix} 1/2 & 0 & 0 \\ 0 & 1/2 & 0 \\ 0 & 0 & 1/2 \end{bmatrix}$
D. $\begin{bmatrix} 1 & 0 & 0 \\ 0 & 1 & 0 \\ 0 & 0 & 1 \end{bmatrix}$

50. What is A^{-1} equal to?
A. $\begin{bmatrix} 1 & -1 & 0 \\ -2 & 3 & -4 \\ -2 & 3 & -3 \end{bmatrix}$
B. $\begin{bmatrix} 1/2 & -1/2 & 0 \\ -1 & 3/2 & -2 \\ -1 & 3/2 & -3/2 \end{bmatrix}$
C. $\begin{bmatrix} 2 & -2 & 0 \\ -4 & 6 & -8 \\ -4 & 6 & -6 \end{bmatrix}$
D. $\begin{bmatrix} 1/5 & -1/5 & 0 \\ -2/5 & 3/5 & -4/5 \\ -2/5 & 3/5 & -3/5 \end{bmatrix}$

51. What is $3\alpha + 2\beta$ equal to if
$\left(2\hat{i} + 6\hat{j} + 27\hat{k}\right) \times \left(\hat{i} + \alpha\hat{j} + \beta\hat{k}\right)$
is a null vector?
A. 36
B. 33
C. 30
D. 27

52. For what value of the angle between the vectors $\vec{a}$ and $\vec{b}$ is the quantity $\left|\vec{a} \times \vec{b}\right| + \sqrt{3}\left|\vec{a} \cdot \vec{b}\right|$ maximum?
A. 0°
B. 30°
C. 45°
D. 60°

53. Let θ be the angle between two unit vectors $\vec{a}$ and $\vec{b}$. If $\vec{a} + 2\vec{b}$ is perpendicular to $5\vec{a} - 4\vec{b}$, then what is $\cos\theta + \cos 2\theta$ equal to?
A. 0
B. 1/2
C. 1
D. $\dfrac{\sqrt{3}+1}{2}$

54. Let ABCDEF be a regular hexagon. If $\overline{AD} = m\,\overline{BC}$ and $\overline{CF} = n\,\overline{AB}$, then what is mn equal to?
A. –4
B. –2
C. 2
D. 4

55. The vectors $\vec{a}, \vec{b}$ and $\vec{c}$ are of the same length. If taken pairwise, they form equal angles. If $\vec{a} = \hat{i} + \hat{j}$ and $\vec{b} = \hat{j} + \hat{k}$, then what can $\vec{c}$ be equal to?
I. $\hat{i} + \hat{k}$
II. $\dfrac{-\hat{i} + 4\hat{j} - \hat{k}}{3}$

Select the correct answer using the code given below.
A. I only
B. II only
C. Both I and II
D. Neither I nor II

56. The diagonals of a quadrilateral ABCD are along the lines $x - 2y = 1$ and $4x + 2y = 3$. The quadrilateral ABCD may be a:
A. rectangle
B. cyclic quadrilateral
C. parallelogram
D. rhombus

57. The foci of the ellipse $4x^2 + 9y^2 = 1$ are at Q and R. If P(x, y) is any point on the ellipse, then what is PQ + PR equal to?
A. 2
B. 1
C. 2/3
D. 1/3

58. If P(2, 4), Q(8, 12), R(10, 14) and S(x, y) are vertices of a parallelogram, then what is ($x + y$) equal to?

A. 8
B. 10
C. 12
D. 14

59. The equation of a circle is

$(x^2 - 4x + 3) + (y^2 - 6y + 8) = 0$

Which of the following statements are correct?

I. The end points of a diameter of the circle are at (1, 2) and (3, 4).

II. The end points of a diameter of the circle are at (1, 4) and (3, 2).

III. The end points of a diameter of the circle are at (2, 4) and (4, 2).

Select the answer using the code given below.

A. I and II only
B. II and III only
C. I and III only
D. I, II and III

60. Consider the points P($4k$, $4k$) and Q($4k$, $-4k$) lying on the parabola $y^2 = 4kx$. If the vertex is A, then what is ∠PAQ equal to?

A. 60°
B. 90°
C. 120°
D. 135°

Direction (Qs. No. 61 and 62): *Consider the following for the two (02) items that follow:*

A triangle ABC is inscribed in the circle $x^2 + y^2 = 100$. B and C have coordinates (6, 8) and (–8, 6) respectively.

61. What is ∠BAC equal to?

A. $\pi/2$
B. $\pi/3$ or $2\pi/3$
C. $\pi/4$ or $3\pi/4$
D. $\pi/6$ or $5\pi/6$

62. What are the coordinates of A?

A. (–6, 8)
B. (–6, –8)
C. $(5\sqrt{2}, 5\sqrt{2})$
D. Cannot be determined due to insufficient data

Direction (Qs. No. 63 and 64): *Consider the following for the two (02) items that follow:*

ABCD is an isosceles trapezium and AB is parallel to DC. Let A(2, 3), B(4, 3), C(5, 1) be the vertices.

63. What are the coordinates of vertex D?

A. (2, 1)
B. (1, 2)
C. (1, 1)
D. (3, 1)

64. What is the point of intersection of the diagonals of the trapezium?

A. (3, 7/2)
B. (3, 7/3)
C. (7/2, 2)
D. (5/2, 2)

Direction (Qs. No. 65 and 66): *Consider the following for the two (02) items that follow:*

Let $2x^2 + 2y^2 + 2z^2 + 3x + 3y + 3z - 6 = 0$ be a sphere.

65. What is the diameter of the sphere?

A. $\frac{5\sqrt{3}}{4}$
B. $\frac{5\sqrt{3}}{2}$
C. $\frac{3\sqrt{5}}{4}$
D. $\frac{3\sqrt{5}}{2}$

66. The centre of the sphere lies on the plane:

A. $2x + 2y + 2z - 3 = 0$
B. $4x + 4y + 4z - 3 = 0$
C. $4x + 8y + 8z - 15 = 0$
D. $4x + 8y + 8z + 15 = 0$

Direction (Qs. No. 67 and 68): *Consider the following for the two (02) items that follow:*

Let S be the line of intersection of two planes $x + y + z = 1$ and $2x + 3y - 4z = 8$.

67. Which of the following are the direction ratios of S?

A. $\langle -7, -6, 1\rangle$
B. $\langle -7, 6, 1\rangle$
C. $\langle -6, 5, 1\rangle$
D. $\langle 6, 5, 1\rangle$

68. If $\langle l, m, n\rangle$ are direction cosines of S, then what is the value of $43(l^2 - m^2 - n^2)$?

A. 6
B. 5
C. 4
D. 1

Direction (Qs. No. 69 and 70): *Consider the following for the two (02) items that follow:*

Let L : $x + y + z + 4 = 0 = 2x - y - z + 8$ be a line and P : $x + 2y + 3z + 1 = 0$ be a plane.

69. What are the direction ratios of the line?

A. $\langle 2, 1, -1\rangle$
B. $\langle 0, -1, 2\rangle$
C. $\langle 0, 1, -1\rangle$
D. $\langle 2, 3, -3\rangle$

70. What is the point of intersection of L and P?

A. (4, 3, –3)
B. (4, –3, 3)
C. (–4, –3, –3)
D. (–4, –3, 3)

71. Let $z = [y]$ and $y = [x] - x$, where $[\cdot]$ is the greatest integer function. If x is not an integer but positive, then what is the value of z?

A. –1
B. 0
C. 1
D. 2

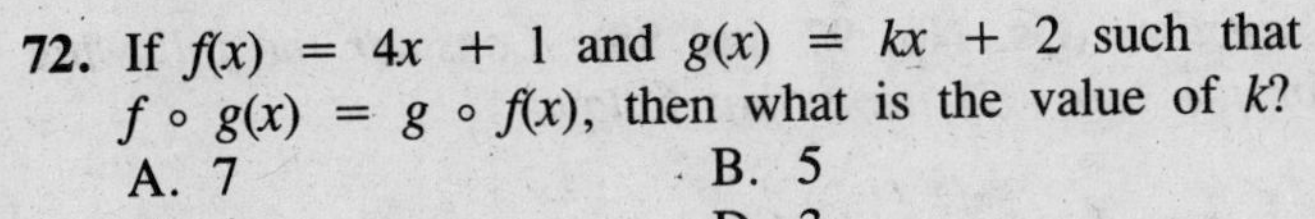

72. If $f(x) = 4x + 1$ and $g(x) = kx + 2$ such that $f \circ g(x) = g \circ f(x)$, then what is the value of k?

A. 7 B. 5
C. 4 D. 3

73. What is the minimum value of the function

$f(x) = \log_{10}(x^2 + 2x + 11)$?

A. 0 B. 1
C. 2 D. 10

74. Which one of the following is correct ragarding

$\lim_{x \to 3} \frac{|x-3|}{x-3}$?

A. Limit exists and is equal to 1
B. Limit exists and is equal to 0
C. Limit exists and is equal to –1
D. Limit does not exist

75. What is the maximum value of

$a \cos x + b \sin x + c$?

A. $\sqrt{a^2 + b^2 + c}$ B. $\sqrt{a^2 + b^2} + c$
C. $\sqrt{a^2 + b^2} - c$ D. $\sqrt{a^2 + b^2}$

76. If $f(2x) = 4x^2 + 1$, then for how many real values of x will $f(2x)$ be the GM of $f(x)$ and $f(4x)$?

A. Four B. Two
C. One D. None

77. If $f(x) = [x]^2 - 30[x] + 221 = 0$, where $[x]$ is the greatest integer function, then what is the sum of all integer solutions?

A. 13 B. 17
C. 27 D. 30

78. If $f(x) = 9x - 8\sqrt{x}$ such that $g(x) = f(x) - 1$, then which one of the following is correct?

A. $g(x) = 0$ has no real roots
B. $g(x) = 0$ has only one real root which is an integer
C. $g(x) = 0$ has two real roots which are integers
D. $g(x) = 0$ has only one real root which is not an integer

79. What is $\lim_{x \to \frac{\pi}{2}} (\sec\theta - \tan\theta)$ equal to?

A. –1 B. 0
C. 1/2 D. 1

80. Let $f(x)\, f(y) = f(xy)$ for all real x, y. If $f(2) = 4$, then what is the value of $f(1/2)$?

A. 1/4 B. 1/2
C. 1 D. 4

Direction (Qs. No. 81 and 82): *Consider the following for the two (02) items that follow:*

Let $f \circ g(x) = \cos^2 \sqrt{x}$ and $g \circ f(x) = |\cos x|$.

81. Which one of the following is $f(x)$?

A. $\cos x$ B. $\cos x^2$
C. $\cos^2 x$ D. $\cos |x|$

82. Which one of the following is $g(x)$?

A. $\sqrt{x}$ B. $|x|$
C. x^2 D. $x|x|$

Direction (Qs. No. 83 and 84): *Consider the following for the two (02) items that follow:*

Let $f(x) = [x]^2 - [x^2]$.

83. What is $f(0.999) + f(1.001)$ equal to?

A. –1 B. 0
C. 1 D. 2

84. Consider the following statements:

I. $f(x)$ is continuous at $x = 0$.
II. $f(x)$ is continuous at $x = 1$.

Which of the statements given above is/are correct?

A. I only B. II only
C. Both I and II D. Neither I nor II

Direction (Qs. No. 85 and 86): *Consider the following for the two (02) items that follow:*

Let $f(x) = \cos 2x + x$ on $[-\pi/2, \pi/2]$.

85. What is the greatest value of $f(x)$?

A. $\frac{\sqrt{3}}{2} - \frac{\pi}{12}$ B. $\frac{\sqrt{3}}{2} + \frac{\pi}{12}$
C. $\frac{\sqrt{3}}{2} + \frac{\pi}{9}$ D. $\frac{\sqrt{3}}{2} + \frac{\pi}{6}$

86. What is the least value of $f(x)$?

A. $-\left(1 + \frac{\pi}{2}\right)$ B. $-\left(\frac{1}{2} + \frac{\pi}{2}\right)$
C. $-\left(1 + \frac{\pi}{4}\right)$ D. $-2\left(\frac{1}{2} - \frac{\pi}{4}\right)$

Direction (Qs. No. 87 and 88): *Consider the following for the two (02) items that follow:*

The area bounded by the parabola $y^2 = kx$ and the line $x = k$, where $k > 0$, is 4/3 square units.

87. What is the value of k?

A. 1/2 B. 1
C. $\sqrt{2}$ D. 2

88. What is the area of the parabola bounded by the latus rectum?

A. 1/6 square unit
B. 2/3 square unit
C. 1 square unit
D. 4/3 square units

Direction (Qs. No. 89 and 90): *Consider the following for the two (02) items that follow:*

Let $ydx + (x - y^3)\, dy = 0$ be a differential equation.

89. What are the order and degree respectively of the differential equation?

A. 1 and 1 B. 1 and 2
C. 2 and 1 D. 1 and 3

90. What is the solution of the differential equation?

A. $y^4 + 2x = c$ B. $y^4 + 3x = c$
C. $2xy^4 + x = c$ D. $4xy - y^4 = c$

Direction (Qs. No. 91 and 92): *Consider the following for the two (02) items that follow:*

Let $f(x) = |x^2 - x - 2|$.

91. What is $\int_0^2 f(x)dx$ equal to?

A. 0 B. 1
C. 5/3 D. 10/3

92. What is $\int_1^3 f(x)dx$ equal to?

A. 2 B. 3
C. 4 D. 5

Direction (Qs. No. 93 and 94): *Consider the following for the two (02) items that follow:*

Let $f(t) = \ln\left(t + \sqrt{1+t^2}\right)$ and $g(t) = \tan(f(t))$.

93. Consider the following statements :

I. $f(t)$ is an odd function.
II. $g(t)$ is an odd function.

Which of the statements given above is/are correct?

A. I only B. II only
C. Both I and II D. Neither I nor II

94. What is $\int_{-\pi}^{\pi} g(t)\,dt$ equal to?

A. –1 B. 0
C. 1/2 D. 1

Direction (Qs. No. 95 and 96): *Consider the following for the two (02) items that follow:*

Let $f : (-1, 1) \to R$ be a differentiable function with $f(0) = -1$ and $f'(0) = 1$. Let $h(x) = f(2f(x) + 2)$ and $g(x) = (h(x))^2$.

95. What is $h'(0)$ equal to?

A. –2 B. –1
C. 0 D. 2

96. What is $g'(0)$ equal to?

A. –4 B. –2
C. 0 D. 4

Direction (Qs. No. 97 and 98): *Consider the following for the two (02) items that follow:*

Let $I = \int_0^{\pi/2} \frac{f(x)}{g(x)} dx$, where $f(x) = \sin x$ and $g(x) = \sin x + \cos x + 1$.

97. What is $\int_0^{\pi/2} \frac{dx}{g(x)}$ equal to?

A. $\frac{\ln 2}{2}$ B. $\frac{\ln 2}{4}$
C. $\ln 2$ D. $2 \ln 2$

98. What is I equal to?

A. $\frac{\pi}{4} + \ln 2$ B. $\frac{\pi}{4} - \ln 2$
C. $\frac{\pi}{4} - \frac{\ln 2}{2}$ D. $\frac{\pi}{4} + \frac{\ln 2}{2}$

Direction (Qs. No. 99 and 100): *Consider the following for the two (02) items that follow:*

Let $2\int \frac{x^2 - 1}{\sqrt{x^2 + 1}} dx = U(x)\,V(x) - 3\ln\{U(x) + V(x)\} + c$

99. What is $|U^2(x) - V^2(x)|$ equal to?

A. 0 B. 1
C. 2 D. 3

100. What is $U(x)\,V(x)$ equal to?

A. $\sqrt{x^2 + x^4}$ B. $\sqrt{x + x^3}$
C. $\frac{\sqrt{x^2 + x^4}}{2}$ D. $2\sqrt{x^2 + x^4}$

101. Let $x - 3y + 4 = 0$ and $2x - 7y + 8 = 0$ be two lines of regression computed from some bivariate data. If b_{yx} and b_{xy} are regression coefficients of lines of regression of y on x and x on y respectively, then what is the value of $b_{xy} + 7b_{yx}$?

A. –2 B. 1
C. 2 D. 5

102. The mean of n observations

$1, 4, 9, 16, \ldots, n^2$

is 130. What is the value of n?

A. 18 B. 19
C. 20 D. 21

103. Three distinct natural numbers are chosen at random from 1 to 10. What is the probability that they are consecutive?

A. 1/12 B. 3/40
C. 1/15 D. 7/120

104. A, B, C are three mutually exclusive and exhaustive events associated with a random experiment. If 3P(B) = 4P(A) and 3P(C) = 2P(B), then what is P(A) equal to?
A. 7/29 B. 8/29
C. 9/29 D. 10/29

105. A die has two faces with number 4, three faces with number 5 and one face with number 6. If the die is rolled once, then what is the probability of getting 4 or 5?
A. 1/3 B. 2/3
C. 5/6 D. 1/2

106. A box contains 2 black, 4 yellow and 6 white balls. Three balls are drawn in succession with replacement. What is the probability that all three are of the same colour?
A. 1/6 B. 1/36
C. 1/12 D. 5/12

107. A can hit a target 5 times in 6 shots, B can hit 4 times in 5 shots and C can hit 3 times in 4 shots. What is the probability that A and C may hit but B may lose?
A. 1/8 B. 1/6
C. 1/4 D. 1/3

108. The letters of the word ZOOLOGY are arranged in all possible ways. What is the probability that the consonants and vowels occur alternatively?
A. 6/35 B. 3/35
C. 2/35 D. 1/35

109. A natural number x is chosen at random from the first 100 natural numbers. What is the probability that $x^2 + x > 50$?
A. 93/100 B. 47/50
C. 24/25 D. 23/25

110. What is the mean deviation of the first 10 natural numbers?
A. 2 B. 2.5
C. 3 D. 3.5

111. Let $\sum_{i=1}^{9} x_i^2 = 855$. If M is the mean and σ is the standard deviation of $x_1, x_2, \ldots, x_9$, then what is the value of $M^2 + \sigma^2$?
A. 100 B. 95
C. 90 D. 85

112. The mean of the series $x_1, x_2, \ldots, x_n$ is $\overline{x}$. If x_n is replaced by k, then what is the new mean?
A. $\overline{x} - x_n + k$ B. $\frac{n\overline{x} - \overline{x} + k}{n}$
C. $\frac{\overline{x} - x_n - k}{n}$ D. $\frac{n\overline{x} - x_n + k}{n}$

113. A fair coin is tossed till two heads occur in succession. What is the probability that the number of tosses required is less than 6?
A. 5/64 B. 15/32
C. 31/64 D. 19/32

114. Urn A contains 2 white and 2 black balls while urn B contains 3 white and 2 black balls. One ball is transferred from urn A to urn B and then a ball is drawn out of urn B. What is the probability that the ball is white?
A. 11/20 B. 7/12
C. 3/5 D. 1

115. For two events A and B, P(A) = P(A|B) = 0.25 and P(B|A) = 0.5. Which of the following are correct?
I. A and B are independent.
II. $P(A^c \cup B^c) = 0.875$
III. $P(A^c \cap B^c) = 0.375$

Select the answer using the code given below.
A. I and II only B. II and III only
C. I and III only D. I, II and III

116. Two perfect dice are thrown. What is the probability that the sum of the numbers on the faces is neither 9 nor 10?
A. 1/36 B. 5/36
C. 7/36 D. 29/36

117. The occurrence of a disease in an industry is such that the workers have 20% chance of suffering from it. What is the probability that out of 6 workers chosen at random, 4 or more will suffer from the disease?
A. 53/3125 B. 63/3125
C. 73/3125 D. 83/3125

118. Three perfect dice are rolled. Under the condition that no two show the same face, what is the probability that one of the faces shown is an ace (one)?
A. 5/9 B. 2/3
C. 1/3 D. 1/2

119. Three perfect dice D_1, D_2 and D_3 are rolled. Let x, y and z represent the numbers on D_1, D_2 and D_3 respectively. What is the number of possible outcomes such that $x < y < z$?
A. 20 B. 18
C. 14 D. 10

120. In a binomial distribution, if the mean is 6 and the standard deviation is $\sqrt{2}$, then what are the values of the parameters n and p respectively?
A. 18 and 1/3 B. 9 and 1/3
C. 18 and 2/3 D. 9 and 2/3

ANSWERS

PAPER I : GENERAL ABILITY TEST

1. **(D):** The word "fallible" means capable of making mistakes or being wrong. "Perfect" is the opposite of fallible, as it denotes being flawless or without error, making it the correct choice. The other options, "frail," "erring," and "mortal," either describe weaknesses or error-prone nature, which are similar in meaning to "fallible."

2. **(C):** "Vague" means unclear or not specific. "Precise" is its antonym as it describes something very clear and accurately defined. The other choices, "identical," "obscure," and "imperceptible," either align with vagueness or do not directly oppose the meaning of vague.

3. **(B):** "Conscientiously" means performing tasks carefully and thoroughly, with a sense of duty. "Carelessly" directly opposes this, indicating a lack of carefulness or attention to detail. Other options like "assiduously," "painstakingly," and "scrupulously" all reinforce the original meaning of performing tasks with great care.

4. **(A):** "Incidental" refers to something being secondary or less important, occurring by chance. "Essential" is the opposite as it indicates something absolutely necessary or required. The remaining choices, "adventitious," "serendipitous," and "subsidiary," either suggest randomness or secondary status, which are similar to incidental.

5. **(A):** "Disdainful" describes showing contempt or lack of respect. "Reverential" is its antonym, implying great respect or admiration. Options like "derisive," "supercilious," and "insolent" suggest attitudes of contempt or disrespect, akin to disdainful.

6. **(A):** The sentence is stating that since most of our food comes from agriculture, we tend to believe it is independent of natural biota (natural plant and animal life). This means we think our food production doesn't rely on natural ecosystems, which is not true.

7. **(B):** The sentence is referring to "plants and animals" in nature. Using "both" emphasizes that natural selection affects both plants and animals alike.

8. **(D):** The correct verb tense and form here is "are continuously subjected" to indicate that plants and animals in nature are always undergoing the process of natural selection.

9. **(A):** This word logically connects the previous statement "Only the fittest survive" to the next idea. "Consequently" shows that as a result, wild populations have numerous adaptive traits.

10. **(B):** The list includes traits like competitiveness and resistance to parasites. "Tolerance" to adverse conditions fits the context of traits that help survival.

11. **(A):** The word "and" is used to continue the list of traits, connecting "tolerance to adverse conditions" with "other aspects of vigour."

12. **(D):** The populations have been grown under agricultural conditions for many "generations," which is appropriate when discussing successive cycles of breeding.

13. **(C):** The correct passive voice here is "are selected" to indicate that these populations are chosen for production traits rather than resilience.

14. **(C):** The word "that" is used to introduce a defining clause about the plant. "A high-producing plant that lacks resistance..."

15. **(B):** A plant lacking drought resistance is "irrigated," meaning it's provided with water artificially, allowing farmers to ignore its lack of natural drought resistance.

16. **(D):** This is the grammatically correct structure for a subjunctive mood, commonly used after "suggest" to express an action that should be taken. The other options contain grammatical errors in verb tense or structure.

17. **(C):** This option correctly uses the superlative form "oldest" to compare among all monuments in the city, implying that one specific monument is older than all others. The other choices misuse comparative forms or add unnecessary articles, making them grammatically incorrect.

18. **(A):** The phrase "must be" correctly infers a logical conclusion based on the premise that touring all day is tiring. The other options misuse modal verbs or do not logically follow from the statement.

19. **(C):** This option appropriately expresses the possibility that his condition might not be as bad as it could potentially be, providing a realistic but optimistic outlook. The other choices either use incorrect verb forms or suggest inappropriate modality.

20. (B): This choice correctly uses the present perfect continuous tense to indicate an action that started in the past and is still ongoing at the time of speaking. The other options either use incorrect verb tenses or structures.

21. (A): This is the correct use of the present perfect tense, indicating that the action occurred at an unspecified time before now, affecting the present. The other options either misuse modal verbs or have grammatical errors.

22. (A): This uses the second conditional, appropriate for hypothetical situations, and the past simple tense "found" is used correctly after "if." The other options contain grammatical errors with modal verbs and verb tenses.

23. (B): This option correctly uses the conditional "would not" to express a hypothetical preference or action in a situation presented as a suggestion or advice. The other options are grammatically incorrect or misuse modal verbs.

24. (A): This expresses a wish or desire to be able to do something, using "could" to indicate possibility or potential ability in the context of a wish. The other choices misuse modal verbs in the context of expressing a wish.

25. (D): This is the correct idiomatic expression meaning to achieve or reach the expected standard. The other options are either nonsensical or incorrectly formed phrases.

26. (D): A "white lie" refers to a lie that is told typically to avoid hurting someone's feelings or for similar benign reasons. It is not meant to cause harm or deceive in a malicious way. Options A, B, and C do not capture this benign intent.

27. (A): "Bad blood" is an idiom that describes animosity or ill feelings between people, often due to past grievances. This is not about worsening situations, accidents, or acceptance of unpleasant situations as suggested by the other options.

28. (C): "Count your blessings" means to be thankful for the good things or advantages one has, which helps to shift focus from negative aspects or difficulties. The other options do not relate to the expression's meaning of gratitude.

29. (B): "Having the last laugh" means to end up in a position of success or vindication after others had doubted one's prospects. It relates to proving doubters wrong rather than solving life problems, laughing secretly, or being a poor example.

30. (C): "Sit on the fence" describes someone who avoids making a decision or taking sides in a dispute, reflecting indecision. The other options do not accurately reflect the idiom's meaning of non-commitment.

31. (B): "The Right to Education Act (RTE) mandates good quality elementary education conforming to the standards and norms specified in the Act as a fundamental right of all children." This arrangement logically presents the subject, action, and purpose of the RTE Act.

32. (A): "Music not only relieves the burden on children and the young but also alleviates the conflicts and disputes in their mind." This option correctly sequences the impact of music on alleviating both mental burdens and conflicts for youth.

33. (A): Antarctica is a continent nearly twice as large as Australia but it is virtually covered by a dome-shaped ice sheet nearly 2 miles thick.

34. (D): "The G20 was formed in 1999, as a forum of Finance Ministers and Central Bank Governors, in recognition of the fact that there was a major shift in the global economic weight from the advanced economies." This sequence effectively connects the creation of the G20 to its underlying reason.

35. (A): "India is the third largest fish producing and the second largest aquaculture nation in the world and India's products are exported to many nations." This arrangement presents a logical flow of information regarding India's ranking in fish production and its global trade.

36. (A): "Adders" are a type of snake, thus the word functions as a noun, referring to a specific group of animals.

37. (C): "Since" in this context is used to introduce a reason or a causal event, functioning as a conjunction to connect two clauses.

38. (B): "Now" modifies the verb phrase "it's too late," indicating the current time, thus it functions as an adverb.

39. (C): "That" specifies the noun "man," indicating which specific man is being referred to, thus it functions as a determiner.

40. (A): "Take-off" refers to the action of an aircraft beginning to fly, used here as a noun indicating the event of an airplane starting its flight.

41. (A): The passage specifies that Laurie Garrett describes an "unwelcome form of globalization" as the globalization of disease. It mentions her focus on emerging diseases and how they spread globally, making this the clear 'unwelcome form' referred to.

42. (A): The passage implies that the globalization of diseases has made the globalization of health imperative. While it does not explicitly state this as a reason, it's clear from the context that global health issues are becoming crucial due to the global spread of diseases.

43. (D): According to the passage, resurgent diseases are affected by medical practices, particularly the overuse of antibiotics which leads to the emergence of new strains that are resistant. All three factors listed are involved in the explanation of how these diseases have become a problem again.

44. (A): The passage directly links new diseases to changes in land use that result in humans coming into close contact with animals that harbor viruses, previously unknown to medicine and often deadly to humans. This is the direct cause as stated in the text.

45. (B): The passage refers to "women and men on the frontlines of epidemiology" in the context of recognizing new diseases and intervening for public health. This context clearly aligns with the definition of epidemiology as the scientific study of the spread and control of diseases.

46. (C): The context suggests that "cautioned" here means to give a warning, particularly about the dangers or illusions on the path to enlightenment. "Warned" is directly synonymous with "cautioned" in this context.

47. (A): The word "monotonous" implies a lack of variety and interest, making it boring or dull. The officer reporting in a monotonous manner suggests that the delivery was unengaging and lacking in variation, hence "dull" is the nearest in meaning.

48. (B): "Elusive" suggests something that is difficult to understand or define. In philosophy, questions that are described as elusive are those that are confusing or hard to grasp, making "baffling" the closest in meaning among the options.

49. (A): "Mammoth" refers to something very large or extensive. Describing a task as mammoth suggests it is a huge or massive undertaking, making "huge" the direct synonym in this context.

50. (B): "Tarnished" implies that something has been made less valuable or respected, especially in terms of reputation. The police department's image being tarnished by a high-profile case indicates that it was negatively affected, thus "tainted" captures this meaning perfectly.

51. (B): Lysosomes are known for their role as the waste disposal system of the cell, breaking down excess or worn-out cell parts. They are capable of breaking down a wide range of biological molecules, primarily organic, not all inorganic materials. This statement is incorrect as lysosomes primarily break down organic materials.

52. (C): Both mitochondria and plastids (such as chloroplasts in plants) contain their own DNA, which allows them to replicate independently within cells. The endoplasmic reticulum and lysosomes do not contain their own genetic material.

53. (B): Ligaments are the connective tissue that connects two bones together at a joint. Tendons connect muscle to bone, areolar tissue is a loose connective tissue, and cartilage is a more rigid form of connective tissue that does not typically connect bones directly.

54. (B): ATP, or adenosine triphosphate, is the primary molecule used for energy storage and transfer in cells. ADP and AMP are lower-energy forms of ATP, while NAD is involved in metabolic processes but is not the primary source of energy.

55. (A): In potatoes, vegetative propagation occurs through eye buds found on the tuber, which grow into new plants. Ginger and sugarcane propagate vegetatively but not specifically through "eye buds," and onions primarily propagate through bulbs.

56. (C): Diffusion is the process by which particles of different substances intermingle on their own due to their kinetic energy, leading to a uniform distribution. Osmosis specifically refers to the diffusion of water across a semipermeable membrane, while Brownian motion describes the random movement of particles in a fluid.

57. (C): In diagnostic laboratories, centrifugation is commonly used in blood tests to separate blood components based on density. This technique enables the separation of plasma, white blood cells, and red blood cells.

58. (B): Sulphur naturally occurs in a polyatomic form, often as S8 molecules, making it polyatomic. Phosphorus can also be polyatomic (such as P4), but the more commonly recognized polyatomic form in basic chemistry for elemental substances is sulphur.

59. (A): The nitride ion (N^{-3}) has a valency of –3, meaning it gains three electrons to achieve stability. Nitrate (NO_3^-) and sulphate (SO_4^{2-}) have different valencies, and sulphide (S^{-2}) typically has a valency of –2.

60. (B): The molecular weight of nitrogen (N_2) is approximately 28 g/mol. Therefore, the mass of 0.5 moles of N_2 gas is half of the molecular weight, which is 14 grams.

61. (B): The decomposition of silver chloride (AgCl) to silver (Ag) and chlorine gas (Cl_2) occurs when exposed to light, particularly sunlight. This reaction is a photochemical decomposition.

62. (B): N-methyl pyrrolidone is used as an anti-skinning agent in paints to prevent the formation of a skin on the surface of the paint when it is exposed to air.

63. (C): First, calculate the total resistance for the series connection of the 5.0 Ω and 7.0 Ω resistors:

$$R_{series} = 5.0\ \Omega + 7.0\ \Omega = 12.0\ \Omega$$

Then, apply the formula for parallel resistance with the 36.0 Ω resistor:

$$R_{parallel} = \left(\frac{1}{12.0} + \frac{1}{36.0}\right)^{-1}$$

$$= \frac{36.0 \times 12.0}{36.0 + 12.0} = 9.0\ \Omega$$

64. (C): The correct relationship between the densities ρ_1, ρ_2 and ρ_w is that ρ_1 is greater than ρ_w and ρ_1 is less than ρ_w. This conclusion is drawn from observing the behaviour of the cubes C_1 and C_2 in water.

The cubes are floating in water, which means their average density (considering both the cube material and the liquid inside) must be less than or equal to the water density ρ_w for them to float. The key observation is that C_2, which is filled with liquid of density ρ_1, is floating lower in the water compared to C_2, which suggests that C_2 is closer to the density of water but still less, indicating $\rho_1 < \rho_w$. Meanwhile, C_1 is floating higher than C_1, suggesting a significantly lower average density, thus $\rho_1 > \rho_w$.

This ordering aligns with the idea that if a cube with a higher density liquid floats lower (but still floats), its internal liquid density is closer to water but under it, while a cube that floats higher has a liquid density significantly higher than water, as it contributes to an overall lower density of the cube compared to the other cube. Hence, the answer is C, which correctly captures this relationship: ρ_1 (density of the liquid in C_1) is greater than the water's density, and ρ_2 (density of the liquid in C_2) is less than the water's density.

65. (B): When an astronaut experiences weightlessness on the International Space Station, it implies that there is no normal reaction force exerted on the astronaut by the floor of the space station. This is because both the astronaut and the space station are in freefall around the Earth, meaning they are continuously falling toward Earth but also moving forward fast enough to keep missing it. Thus, the feeling of weightlessness is due to the absence of a normal force acting through contact, not because there is no gravitational pull (which is still acting, albeit reduced) or because of any centrifugal force applied by the space station.

66. (D): All three statements accurately describe characteristics of contact forces:

Contact forces appear between objects that are physically touching each other, such as friction, tension, or normal force.

Contact forces always satisfy Newton's third law of motion, which states that for every action, there is an equal and opposite reaction. This means when one object exerts a force on another, the second object exerts a force of equal magnitude but in the opposite direction on the first object.

Contact forces can indeed occur between a pair of solid and fluid, such as in the case of drag or buoyancy forces where a solid object interacts with a fluid (liquid or gas). These characteristics are foundational principles in physics that define how contact forces behave under various conditions, making option D the correct and complete choice.

67. (D): The correct answer is option D, which accurately represents the ray diagram for a thin lens where the object is placed at a distance greater than twice the focal length (2*f*) from the lens.

Here's why option D is correct:

- When an object is placed at a distance greater than twice the focal length from a converging lens, the rays after passing through the lens converge to form a real image on the opposite side of the lens.
- The image formed is inverted and smaller than the object, which is a characteristic behavior when the object is beyond 2*f*.

- In option D, the diagram shows parallel rays coming from the left, passing through the lens, and converging at a point on the principal axis on the right side of the lens. This point is between the focal point (*f*) and twice the focal length (2*f*) from the lens, accurately depicting the formation of a real, inverted image.

The other options fail to correctly show this behaviour:

- Option A suggests an object at the focal point, which would make the rays parallel on the other side, not focusing to a point.
- Option B and C do not accurately depict the ray paths for objects placed at different positions relative to the lens's focal lengths in a way that corresponds to the established rules of lens optics.

68. (D): The induction of positive charge on the ground below the negative charge at the base of the cloud: Lightning is a natural electrical discharge of very short duration and high voltage between a cloud and the ground or within a cloud. The correct explanation involves the relationship between charged regions within the cloud and the ground.

When a cloud carries a negative charge at its base, it induces a strong positive charge on the ground directly below it. This is due to the electric field created by the negatively charged base of the cloud, which pushes electrons away from the surface area of the ground, leaving the surface positively charged. The difference in voltage between the negative charges at the cloud's base and the positive charges on the ground becomes sufficiently large, and when the electric field strength exceeds the dielectric breakdown strength of air, it results in a rapid discharge of electricity that we observe as lightning.

This induction process is essential for cloud-to-ground lightning, which is the most familiar type of lightning. The strong electric field between the cloud and the ground overcomes the air's resistance to electrical flow, leading to the rapid discharge of electricity.

The other options do not accurately describe the primary cause of lightning:

- Option A and Option B mention intra-cloud processes and short-circuiting, which are part of the overall cloud dynamics but do not directly address the typical cloud-to-ground lightning.
- Option C incorrectly describes the distribution of charges within the cloud which, while it may contribute to the cloud's internal electrical activities (such as cloud-to-cloud lightning), does not directly relate to cloud-to-ground lightning formation explained in Option D.

69. (D): In diagram D, the bulb is part of a circuit that includes a single battery and no other components except the wiring. This setup ensures that all of the voltage provided by the battery is applied across the bulb, maximizing its brightness.

- Option (A): Shows two bulbs in series with a single battery. When bulbs are connected in series, the total resistance increases, and the voltage from the battery is divided between the bulbs. Thus, each bulb gets less than the full battery voltage, causing them to glow less brightly than if they were connected directly across the battery.
- Option (B): This diagram shows two bulbs in parallel with a single battery. While the voltage across each bulb is the same as the battery voltage, the presence of two paths for the current to flow means each bulb receives only a portion of the total current available from the battery. Thus, they might glow less brightly compared to a single bulb connected directly to the battery.
- Option (C): Similar to option A, there are two bulbs in series with the battery. This setup suffers from the same division of voltage as described for option A, reducing the brightness of each bulb.
- Option (D): There is only one bulb in the circuit, and it is connected directly across the battery. This arrangement ensures that the bulb receives the full voltage of the battery and, assuming it can handle the full current provided by the battery, it will glow the brightest compared to the bulbs in the other diagrams.

Thus, option D is correct because the bulb in this setup will receive the maximum possible voltage and current from the battery, leading to the highest brightness.

70. (D): Diagram D accurately represents the motion of a skydiver during a jump, showing an initially rapid increase in speed followed by a gradual decrease as the skydiver deploys the parachute.

- Initial Increase: At the beginning of the jump, the skydiver accelerates due to gravity, increasing speed rapidly. This is represented by the sharp rise at the start of the curve in Diagram D.

- Peak Speed and Parachute Deployment: As the skydiver reaches peak speed, typically called terminal velocity, the speed stabilizes briefly due to the balance between gravitational pull and air resistance. The peak of the curve represents this terminal velocity.
- Gradual Deceleration: Once the parachute is deployed, the increased air resistance causes a significant reduction in speed. This is represented in Diagram D by the gradual rightward slope, indicating a steady decrease in speed until the skydiver safely slows down before landing.
- Comparison with Other Diagrams:
  - ❑ Diagram A shows an increase in speed, a hold at a certain speed, and a rapid decrease. While somewhat realistic, the very sharp decline is not typical as parachute deployment does not instantly drop speed but rather decreases it more gradually.
  - ❑ Diagram B and C show symmetrical patterns, which are unrealistic as they imply that the speed decreases at the same rate it increased, ignoring the effects of parachute deployment, which significantly and gradually slows the skydiver down unlike the immediate drop these diagrams suggest.

Thus, Diagram D provides the most realistic graphical representation of a skydiver's motion from free fall to parachute deployment and gradual slowing down, reflecting the physics of skydiving accurately.

71. (C): In the context of simple machines, a lever of the second class is characterized by the arrangement where the load is located between the fulcrum and the effort. This setup is known for offering a mechanical advantage, as it allows a relatively small effort to lift a larger load efficiently.

- Option C correctly places the load between the fulcrum and the effort. This is a defining feature of a second-class lever. In such levers, the effort is applied on one end of the lever, the fulcrum is positioned at the opposite end, and the load is situated in the middle. Examples of second-class levers include wheelbarrows and nutcrackers, where the load is always between the effort (where force is applied) and the fulcrum (pivot point).
- Option A represents a first-class lever where the fulcrum is between the effort and the load. This type of lever can either multiply force or change the direction of force, depending on the positions of the effort and the load relative to the fulcrum.
- Option B also depicts a first-class lever. Similar to option A, it can either provide a mechanical advantage or change the direction of force, and is used in scenarios like seesaws and crowbars.
- Option D represents a third-class lever where the effort is between the fulcrum and the load. This setup increases the speed and distance moved by the load at the expense of more effort, common in applications like fishing rods and human limbs.

Therefore, Option C is the correct answer as it exclusively matches the configuration of a second-class lever, where the load is positioned between the fulcrum and the effort.

72. (B): V = 300 V; I = 5.5 A: Let's analyze the given circuit and calculate the total current (I) and the voltage (V) based on the resistances and given current in one branch.

Circuit Analysis:

- The circuit is a Wheatstone bridge with a 100 Ω, 200 Ω, and 300 Ω resistor, and an additional arm with a current of 3 A passing through the 100 Ω resistor.
- Using Kirchhoff's voltage law, the voltage drop across the 100 Ω resistor through which 3 A flows can be calculated as $V = IR = 3\text{ A} \times 100\ \Omega = 300\text{ V}$.

Conclusion: The correct answer is V = 300 V; I = 5.5 A, matching Option B. This combines the calculated voltage across the resistors in the network and the total current flowing in the circuit, confirming the correctness of the calculation.

This analysis provides the comprehensive understanding that the 300 V drop across any parallel branches ensures all calculations are consistent with the known values of resistance and current, making Option B the correct answer as per the conditions provided in the problem statement.

73. (C): Taxila was historically part of the Gandhara region, and it served as a significant center during the Gandhara period. This region is located in what is now modern-day northern Pakistan and parts of eastern Afghanistan.

74. (B): Chakravarti Rajagopalachari was the last Governor-General of independent India. He served after Lord Mountbatten, marking the end of the British-appointed governor-generals before India became a full republic.

75. (C): The objectives of setting up the Planning Commission in the 1950s in India included increasing production, providing employment opportunities, and making a comprehensive assessment of the country's resources. These goals were integral to guiding India's development strategy in its early years of independence.

76. (B): The First Five Year Plan in India did indeed give a high priority to agriculture, aiming to correct the imbalance and strengthen the agricultural sector. The Seventh Plan focused on food, work, and productivity, aiming to improve economic conditions through specific sectors. The Third Plan was indeed based on the Harrod-Domar Model, focusing on growth targets and the needed investment to achieve them.

77. (D): Before the First Five Year Plan, various economic plans were proposed in India, including the Bombay Plan by leading industrialists, the People's Plan by M.N. Roy, the Gandhian Plan proposed by Shriman Narayan, and the Sarvodaya Plan by Jai Prakash Narayan. All these plans aimed at socio-economic reforms in India.

78. (C): Culturable waste land

- Current fallow refers to land that has been left without cultivation for one agricultural year.
- Fallow other than current fallow typically refers to land left without cultivation for one to five years.
- Culturable waste land includes land available for cultivation but not used for cultivation for more than five years.
- Barren and waste land refers to land that cannot be brought under cultivation except at an exorbitant cost, possibly due to inherent soil or climatic limitations.
- Thus, land left fallow for more than five years fits best under the category of Culturable waste land, where it remains potentially usable for cultivation but has not been cultivated for an extended period.

79. (B): This statement is incorrect as the Andaman and Nicobar Islands experience the heaviest rainfall during the monsoon months from May to September, not in March and April. The islands have a tropical monsoon climate with high humidity and significant rainfall.

80. (A): The Harmattan is a dry and dusty northeasterly trade wind on the Atlantic coast of West Africa, not related to the Mediterranean Sea, whereas Khamsin, Sirocco, and Mistral are winds associated with the Mediterranean region.

81. (D): The Caspian Sea is the world's largest landlocked water body, surrounded by several countries and without direct access to the world's oceans, making it a landlocked sea.

82. (A): The Benguela Current is indeed a cold current, but it flows along the west coast of Southern Africa, not North Africa, affecting the climate primarily around Namibia and South Africa.

83. (B): Playas are flat-bottomed depressions found in arid or semi-arid regions, typical of desert basins that periodically fill with water to form temporary lakes. These are characteristic landforms of arid environments.

84. (C): Rickets is a disease caused by a deficiency of Vitamin D in humans. This vitamin is crucial for the absorption of calcium and phosphorus from the diet. A deficiency in Vitamin D leads to softening and weakening of the bones in children, which is characterized as rickets.

85. (A): A balanced diet includes all major food groups and nutrients necessary for maintaining health. These components provide energy, help build and repair body tissues, and regulate bodily functions. Carbohydrates, proteins, and fats provide energy; vitamins and minerals are essential for various body functions; fibers aid in digestion; and water is essential for hydration and bodily functions.

86. (C): Cartilage is found in various parts of the human body including the nose, trachea, and knee joint, where it provides structure and support. However, bronchioles, which are small passages in the lungs that lead air to the alveoli, do not contain cartilage. They are instead composed of smooth muscle and elastic fibers.

87. (D): In the nephron of the human kidney, the Bowman's capsule is responsible for the filtration of blood. This structure encases the glomerulus, which is a network of capillaries that performs the first step in filtering blood to form urine.

88. (C): Organisms belonging to the phylum Porifera are commonly known as sponges. These are simple multicellular organisms characterized by their porous bodies and choanocytes. They typically live attached to solid surfaces in marine environments.

89. (B): When a point object is placed at the center of curvature of a concave mirror, the laws of reflection imply that the rays coming from the object and hitting the mirror will reflect back through the same path. Therefore, the image of the object will also form at the center of curvature of the mirror.

90. (A): Myopia, or nearsightedness, is a common vision condition in which a person can see near objects clearly but has difficulty seeing objects far away. This condition is due to the eyeball being too long or the cornea having too much curvature, causing the light rays to focus in front of the retina.

91. (A): The vehicle travels 550 m in total, moving first with acceleration 2m/s^2 for t seconds and then with 5m/s^2 for 10 seconds. The distance during the first phase is $s_1 = \frac{1}{2} \times 2 \times t^2 = t^2$.

The final velocity after the first phase is $v = 2t$ m/s. During the seconds phase, the distance is

$$s_2 = v \times 10 + \frac{1}{2} \times 5 \times 10^2 = 20t + 250.$$

The total distance is

$$s_1 + s_2 = t^2 + 20t + 250 = 550.$$

Solving the quadratic equation

$t^2 + 20t - 300 = 0$, we find $t = 10$ s.

92. (C): The pumpkin's mass is m = $\frac{7.5 \text{ N}}{10 \text{ m/s}^2} = 0.75$ kg.

The volume is V = 0.75 L = 7.5×10^{-4} m^3.

Therefore, the density is $\rho = \frac{m}{V} = \frac{0.75 \text{ kg}}{7.5 \times 10^{-4} \text{ m}^3}$

= 1000 kg/m^3.

93. (D): The bulb consumes power P = I^{2}R = (2A)^2 × 200 Ω = 800 W. Over 10 hours, it uses 8 kWh, costing 8 units × ₹ 5/unit = ₹ 40. Since only 20% is converted to light, the money spent on producing light is 20% × ₹ 40 = ₹ 8.

94. (C): Heat is energy transferred between systems or objects because of a temperature difference between them.

95. (C): According to Newton's third law, the gravitational forces two bodies exert on each other are equal in magnitude regardless of their masses or sizes.

96. (D): The car decelerates at

$$a = \frac{v - u}{t} = \frac{0 - 20 \text{ m/s}}{0.2 \text{ s}}$$

$= -100$ m/s^2.

The retarding force is

F = ma = 1000 kg × (–100 m/s^2)

= –100,000 N (100 kN).

97. (A): The potential energy coverts to kinetic energy:

$$k = \frac{1}{2}mv^2 = 625 \text{ J}.$$

Since, $k = u$

$$\frac{1}{2} \times 0.32 \times v^2 = 625 \Rightarrow 0.16\, v^2 = 625$$

$$\Rightarrow v^2 = \frac{625}{0.16} \Rightarrow v^2 = 3906.25$$

$$\Rightarrow v = \sqrt{3906.25} = 62.5$$

98. (C): The vehicle moves

$s_1 = \frac{1}{2} \times 2 \times (10\text{s})^2 = 100$ m east and

$s_2 = \frac{1}{2} \times 4\sqrt{2} \times (10\text{s})^2 = 200\sqrt{2}$ m south.

The net displacement is

$$\sqrt{(100 \text{ m})^2 + (200\sqrt{2} \text{ m})^2}$$

$$= \sqrt{10,000 + 80,000} = \sqrt{90,000} = 300 \text{ m}.$$

99. (C): James Watt's invention converted the steam engine from being a mere pump into one which would provide energy to power machines in factories: This statement correctly describes James Watt's critical improvement to the steam engine, which greatly enhanced its efficiency and application, key to the Industrial Revolution.

100. (D): The first cotton mill in British India, known as the Bombay Spinning Mill, was set up by C.N. Davar in 1854, marking the beginning of the cotton industry in India.

101. (D): Mahatma Gandhi did not argue for the reorganization of provinces on a linguistic basis in 1948 as he was more focused on national unity and less on linguistic divisions. Additionally, the Constituent Assembly did not recommend the incorporation of linguistic reorganization into the Constitution of India. It was later developments, post-independence, that led to the linguistic reorganization of states.

102. (C): Inspired by the Dandi March led by Mahatma Gandhi, C. Rajagopalachari initiated a similar protest by leading a salt march in Tamil Nadu from Trichinopoly to Vedaranniyam along the Tanjore coast.

103. (D): Acharya Vinoba Bhave received the first donation of land under the Bhoodan Movement at Pochampally in Andhra Pradesh. This marked the beginning of a significant voluntary land reform movement in India.

104. (B): Maize, originally native to the Americas, was introduced to other parts of the world following Columbus's voyages in the late 15th century. It spread to Africa and Spain before being introduced to India. The Spanish and Portuguese traders played significant roles in the spread of maize from the New World to other regions including India.

105. (A): Correctly matched pairs of Himalayan Passes and the ranges in which they are located include:

- Banihal Pass — Pir Panjal Range: This pass is accurately placed within the Pir Panjal Range, aligning with geographical documentation.

The incorrect pairings are:

- Zoji La — Great Himalayas: Zoji La is located in the Zaskar Range, not the Great Himalayas.
- Photu La — Ladakh Range: Photu La is not correctly associated with the Ladakh Range.
- Khardung La — Karakoram Range: Khardung La is actually in the Ladakh Range, not the Karakoram Range.

Thus, the correct sequence is (A): 2 only, correctly identifying Banihal Pass as being within the Pir Panjal Range.

106. (D): These soils have less clay factor and hence can support a wide variety of crops and vegetables: This statement is incorrect. Black cotton soils, known for their high clay content, are rich in montmorillonite and can be quite challenging for the cultivation of a wide variety of crops due to their high water retention capacity and hardening when dry.

107. (A): The correct matches for the hydroelectric power plants to their respective states are Doyang in Nagaland, Gomuti in Tripura, Kapili in Assam, and Ranganadi in Arunachal Pradesh.

108. (A): The correct associations of tropical cyclones and the countries they are typically associated with are Hurricanes with the USA, Willy-Willy with Australia, Baguio with the Philippines, and Typhoons with China.

109. (C): The Satluj river does originate in Tibet where it is known as Langchen Khambab, and it is an example of an antecedent river, maintaining its course despite tectonic changes. However, the Jhelum is not the largest tributary of the Indus system; rather, it is one of the major tributaries.

110. (D): Granite is an igneous rock that can also be classified as a metamorphic rock when subjected to further geological processes that change its form and composition, hence fitting the description of being both igneous and metamorphic.

111. (A): This statement is correct. Pyroxene is a common mineral group found in many meteorites. It is a silicate mineral that forms under high-temperature conditions present in the mantle of Earth and can be similarly found in meteorites.

112. (D): Thawing refers to the process of ice melting, which is a physical change, not a chemical one. Chemical weathering involves the chemical breakdown of minerals in rocks, such as solution, hydration, and reduction.

113. (A): The maximum number of electrons that can occupy the first shell (or K shell) of an atom is 2, according to the rule $2n$, where n is the principal quantum number of the shell ($n = 1$ for the first shell).

114. (B): Liquid water shows maximum density at approximately 4 degrees Celsius, which is 277 K. At this temperature, water molecules are packed efficiently enough to achieve maximum density before expanding as they freeze or when they are heated above this temperature.

115. (C): Nitrogen typically exhibits a valency of 3, allowing it to form three covalent bonds with other elements, as seen in ammonia (NH_3) or in organic compounds where nitrogen forms three single bonds.

116. (C): Rusting of iron is an oxidation reaction, where iron reacts with oxygen in the presence of water to form iron oxides. This process involves the transfer of electrons from iron to oxygen, which is characteristic of an oxidation reaction.

117. (D): Urea is a common nitrogenous fertilizer that is a source of nitrogen for plant growth. It contains a high percentage of nitrogen, making it an efficient means of supplying nitrogen to soils.

118. (D): This statement is not correct. Aluminum (Al) has a valency of 3, not 2. It commonly forms Al^{3+} ions in its compounds, indicating a valency of three.

119. (C): Diamond is an allotrope of carbon and is composed entirely of carbon atoms arranged in a crystal lattice. It does not contain hydrogen, oxygen, or any other element.

120. (D): Mixing sodium hydroxide (NaOH) and hydrochloric acid (HCl) results in a chemical change where a neutralization reaction occurs, producing water (H_2O) and sodium chloride (NaCl). This reaction is a typical example of a chemical change where new substances with different properties from the reactants are formed.

121. (C): The focal length of a combination of lenses can be calculted using the formula $1/f = 1/f_1 + 1/f_2$, where f_1 and f_2 are the focal lengths of individual lenses. Given the powers of the lenses are 2.5 D and –2.0 D, the focal lengths f_1 and f_2 would be $1/2.5 = 0.4$ m and $1/-2.0 = 0.5$ m respectively. Thus, $1/f = 1/0.4 + 1/(-0.5) = 2.5 - 2.0 = 0.5$. Therefore, $f = 1/0.5 = +2.0$ m.

122. (D): The AC mains supply in India has a frequency of 50 Hz, meaning the current changes direction 100 times per second. Therefore, each change in direction takes 1/1001/1001/100 seconds.

123. (*): To find the frictional force, the work done against friction equals the initial kinetic energy:

$$\text{Work} = \frac{1}{2} \times 2 \text{ kg} \times (10 \text{ m/s})^2 = 100 \text{ J}.$$

The work done by friction is $F \times d$, and with $d = 20$ m, $F \times 20 = 100$ so $F = 5$ N. None of the provided answers correctly matches this calculation.

124. (B): Newton's Law of Cooling applies when heat transfer occurs due to the temperature difference between an object and its surroundings, typically in situations of natural cooling. Among the given cases, only the cooling of coffee on a table (case 4) directly corresponds to this principle. The other processes involve heat transfer through phase changes or external heating, which do not directly relate to Newton's Law of Cooling.

125. (C): After the parachute opens, force P remains the same while force Q increases: Force P, caused by gravity, remains constant regardless of the parachute's state, while force Q, which represents air resistance, increases significantly when the parachute opens due to the larger surface area opposing the air.

126. (C): Vijayanagara rulers, particularly those from the Sangama dynasty, were ardent devotees of Shri Virupaksha, a form of Shiva, and they claimed to rule on his behalf.

127. (A): Domingo Paes describes Krishnadeva Raya with these specific physical attributes during his visit to the Vijayanagara Empire.

128. (B): The provisions regarding disqualification on grounds of defection are detailed in the Tenth Schedule of the Constitution of India.

129. (C): Both statements are correct. The Attorney General of India serves as the chief legal advisor to the Government of India, and the Solicitor General assists the Attorney General, along with other Additional Solicitor Generals.

130. (C): The Estimates Committee traditionally consists only of members from the Lower House of the Parliament, i.e., the Lok Sabha. The Public Accounts Committee and the Committee on Public Undertakings include members from both houses.

131. (C): In the legislative process for a Money Bill in India, the Rajya Sabha has limited powers compared to the Lok Sabha. Specifically, it cannot amend a Money Bill but can recommend amendments. It must return the Bill to the Lok Sabha within 14 days, with or without recommendations.

132. (C): Article 19(1) of the Constitution of India guarantees certain freedoms, but these are not absolute. Reasonable restrictions can be imposed on the exercise of these freedoms under certain conditions prescribed by the state for the purpose of the security of the state, public order, morality, etc. Both statements are accurate in describing the nature and limitations of freedoms under Article 19(1).

133. (D): The 'Panchsheel' agreement between India and China in 1954 incorporated five principles, including mutual respect for sovereignty and territorial integrity, mutual non-aggression, mutual non-interference in each other's internal affairs, equality and mutual benefit, and peaceful coexistence. Cultural cooperation is not part of these five core principles.

134. (D): Freedom Fighter Kanaklata Barua sacrificed her life during the Quit India Movement, an important part of India's struggle for independence. She was killed by British police while leading a procession bearing the National Flag during the movement.

135. (C): The Coriolis effect is zero at the Equator and increases towards the poles, being maximum at the North and South Poles. This effect influences the movement of air and water masses across the Earth, causing them to turn right in the northern hemisphere and left in the southern hemisphere.

136. (B): In India, the Sun's rays are never perpendicular in Bihar and Manipur due to their geographical location relative to the Tropic of Cancer. States like Rajasthan and Chhattisgarh, closer to or crossing the Tropic of Cancer, may experience perpendicular sun rays.

137. (B): The east flowing rivers in India mentioned here include Palar and Pennar. Both these rivers originate in the Indian Peninsula and flow towards the Bay of Bengal. Periyar and Kalinadi do not fit this categorization as east flowing rivers.

138. (B): Correct matches for tributaries with the Deccan rivers include Kabini, a tributary of the Kaveri, and Manjra, a tributary of the Godavari. Bhavani is also a tributary of Kaveri, not Krishna, and Bhima is a tributary of Krishna, not Mahanadi.

139. (C): Laterite soils are typically poor in organic matter and deficient in several nutrients including nitrogen, phosphate, and calcium, but they can have appreciable amounts of potash which makes them somewhat suitable for certain types of cultivation.

140. (C): The Brahmaputra River does indeed originate near Lake Mansarovar in Tibet, and it famously takes a sharp U-turn at Namcha Barwa before entering India through a deep gorge. This geographic and hydrological characteristic is critical to understanding the river's dynamics and impact on the regions it flows through.

141. (B): "Not me, but you" is the motto of the National Service Scheme (NSS), which reflects the essence of democratic living and upholds the need for selfless service. NSS aims to develop student youth's personality through community service.

142. (B): "Fitness ka dose, aadha ghanta roz" campaign is associated with the Fit India Programme. This initiative promotes physical activity and fitness among all citizens, advocating for at least half an hour of exercise daily.

143. (B): The statement about Kozhikode being included in UNESCO's creative cities network as the 'City of Music' is correct. However, Garba has not been declared by UNESCO as an intangible cultural heritage, and Gwalior was included in UNESCO's creative cities network as the 'City of Music,' not 'City of Literature.'

144. (B): The ASEAN-India Millet Festival-2023 was organized by the Indian Mission to ASEAN and held in Indonesia. This event highlighted the cultural and agricultural ties between ASEAN countries and India, focusing on promoting millet as a sustainable crop.

145. (B): The correct statements are:

- The first Indian Military Heritage festival was indeed inaugurated in October 2023 in Pune.
- The first Green Hydrogen Fuel Cell Bus was flagged off in India in Bangalore. South Africa chaired the 15th BRICS Summit held in 2023, making all three statements correct.

146. (A):

Statement 1: Incorrect. While the ULLAS scheme is indeed a centrally sponsored scheme, it does not specifically aim at securing childhood for street children. Instead, ULLAS stands for Understanding Lifelong Learning for All in Society and focuses on promoting lifelong learning opportunities for all age groups, particularly adults.

Statement 2: Correct. ULLAS is aligned with the National Education Policy (NEP) 2020 and aims to empower adults aged 15 and above who missed out on formal education. The scheme focuses on providing opportunities for adult education and lifelong learning to enhance their literacy, numeracy, and critical life skills.

Conclusion:

- Since Statement 1 is incorrect and Statement 2 is correct.

147. (D): As of the information provided, Finland's membership in NATO is not confirmed as it was pending ratification and accession talks; therefore, stating it as the latest member was incorrect. NATO was formed out of the Washington Treaty, Russia is not a member, and it does not derive its authority from the UN Charter.

148. (D): In January 2024, India entered into a bilateral agreement with Myanmar to provide grant assistance for constructing a 20 feet Bailey bridge, reflecting India's continued support for infrastructure development in its neighboring countries.

149. (D): The joint military exercise "Varuna" is conducted between India and France, not India and the USA. The exercises Yudhabhyas, Vajra Prahar, and Malabar are indeed conducted between India and the USA.

150. (B): The statement that India secured the 10th rank in the International Shipment category in the World Bank's Logistics Performance Index Report-2023 is correct. The Global Maritime India Summit-2023 was held in Vishakhapatnam, and the 'Maritime Amrit Kaal Vision 2047' was indeed launched during this summit. Thus, all three statements are correct, making the total correct statements three.

PAPER II : MATHEMATICS

1. (D): Since, $A_{m\times n}.B_{n\times p} = (AB)_{m\times p}$

Hence, $[Z_{3\times2}.Y_{2\times3}].X_{3\times3} = [ZYX]_{3\times3'}$

$Y_{2\times3}.[X_{3\times3}.Z_{3\times2}] = [YXZ]_{2\times2}$

and $X_{3\times3}.[Y_{2\times3}.Z_{3\times2}] = X_{3\times3}[YZ]_{2\times2}$

$\because$ No. of columns in X $\neq$ No. of rows in (YZ)

Hence, X(YZ) is not defined.

2. (A): $\because$ Between any two irrational numbers, an infinite number of irrational numbers are there.

$\therefore$ The set of all irrational numbers between $\sqrt{12}$ and $\sqrt{15}$ is an infinite set.

Set of all odd integers less than 1,000 is {...–5, –3,1,3... 999} which is an infinite set.

3. (A): Odd digits can be 1, 3, 5, 7 and 9.

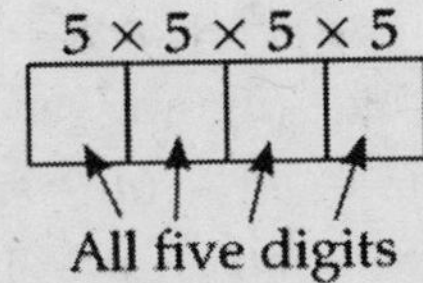

$\because$ All five odd digits can be filled at every place.

Hence, total required four-digit numbers are

$5 \times 5 \times 5 \times 5 = 625$

4. (D): $(1 + \omega - \omega^2)^{100} + (1 - \omega + \omega^2)^{100}$

$= (-\omega^2 - \omega^2)^{100} + (-\omega - \omega)^{100}$

$\{\because 1 + \omega + \omega^2 = 0\}$

$= 2^{100} (\omega^{200} + \omega^{100})$

$= 2^{100} (\omega^2 + \omega) \{\because \omega^3 = 1\}$

$= -2^{100}$

5. (C): Given, AB = O

Let, $A = \begin{bmatrix} a & b \\ c & d \end{bmatrix}$

and $B = \begin{bmatrix} p & q \\ r & s \end{bmatrix}$

Now, $AB = \begin{bmatrix} a & b \\ c & d \end{bmatrix}\begin{bmatrix} p & q \\ r & s \end{bmatrix} = \begin{bmatrix} 0 & 0 \\ 0 & 0 \end{bmatrix}$

$\Rightarrow \begin{bmatrix} ap+br & aq+bs \\ cp+dr & cq+ds \end{bmatrix} = \begin{bmatrix} 0 & 0 \\ 0 & 0 \end{bmatrix}$

Comparing both sides, we get

$ap + br = 0$ ...(*i*)

$aq + bs = 0$ ...(*ii*)

$cp + dr = 0$ ...(*iii*)

$cq + ds = 0$ ...(*iv*)

From eq. (*i*) and (*iii*), we get:

$(ad - bc)p = 0$ and $(ad - bc)r = 0$

From eq. (*ii*) and (*iv*), we get:

$(ad - bc)q = 0$ and $(ad - bc)s = 0$

$\therefore$ Now, if A is non-singular

$\Rightarrow ad - bc \neq 0$

So, $p = q = r = s = 0.$

$\therefore$B is null matrix.

6. (C): $(1 + x)^p (1 + x)^q = (1 + x)^{p+q}$

$\because$ Coefficient of x^3 in the expansion = 35

$(p + q)_{C_3} = 35 = {}^7C_3$

$\Rightarrow p + q = 7$

7. (A): Let '*a*' and '*d*' be the first term and common difference of AP.

$(p + q)^{th}$ term $= T_{p+q}$

$= a + (p + q - 1)$ ...(*i*)

Given, $p.T_p = q.T_q$

$\Rightarrow p.[a + (p - 1)d] = q.[a + (q - 1)d]$

$\Rightarrow (p - q) [a + (p + q - 1)d] = 0$

$\Rightarrow [a + (p + q - 1)d] = 0 \{\because p \neq q\}$

$T_{p+q} = 0$ (from (*i*)}

8. (C): Given, $p = \ln x$, $q = \ln x^3 = 3 \ln x$

$r = \ln x^5 = 5 \ln x$

Clearly, $q - p = r - q = 2 \ln x$

$\Rightarrow p, q, r$ are in AP

Also, $\because \frac{q}{p} \neq \frac{r}{q}$

$\therefore p, q, r$ can never be in GP.

9. (B): Given, $Z = \frac{1}{3}\begin{vmatrix} i & 2i & 1 \\ 2i & 3i & 2 \\ 3 & 1 & 3 \end{vmatrix}$

$\Rightarrow Z = \frac{1}{3}[i(9i-2) - 2i(6i-6) + 1(2i-9i)]$

$\Rightarrow Z = \frac{1}{3}[3+3i] = 1+i$

$|Z| = \sqrt{1^2+1^2} = \sqrt{2}$

10. (B): Let, $I = \sum_{n=1}^{20} (i^{n-1} + i^n + i^{n+1})$

$\Rightarrow \quad I = \sum_{n=1}^{20} i^n \left(\frac{1}{i} + 1 + i\right) = \sum_{n=1}^{20} i^n (1)$

$= i^1 + i^2 + i^3 + i^4 + \ldots i^{20}$

$= 5.(i + i^2 + i^3 + i^4)$

$= 0 \; \{\because i + i^2 + i^3 + i^4 = 0\}$

11. (C): $\because$ x, y and z are in GP.

$\Rightarrow \quad y^2 = xz$

$\Rightarrow \quad 2 \ln y = \ln x + \ln z$

$\ln x$, $\ln y$ and $\ln z$ are in AP.

$(1 + \ln x)$, $(1 + \ln y)$ and $(1 + \ln z)$ are in A.P.

$\frac{1}{(1+\ln x)}, \frac{1}{(1+\ln y)}$ and $\frac{1}{(1+\ln z)}$ are in HP.

12. (A): Let, $I = \begin{bmatrix} 1+\omega & 1+\omega^2 & \omega+\omega^2 \\ 1 & \omega & \omega^2 \\ \frac{1}{\omega} & \frac{1}{\omega^2} & 1 \end{bmatrix}$

$C_1 \to C_1 + C_2 + C_3$, we get

$$I = \begin{bmatrix} 2(1+\omega+\omega^2) & 1+\omega^2 & \omega+\omega^2 \\ (1+\omega+\omega^2) & \omega & \omega^2 \\ \frac{(1+\omega+\omega^2)}{\omega^2} & \frac{1}{\omega^2} & 1 \end{bmatrix}$$

$$I = \begin{bmatrix} 0 & 1+\omega^2 & \omega+\omega^2 \\ 0 & \omega & \omega^2 \\ 0 & \frac{1}{\omega^2} & 1 \end{bmatrix}$$

$\therefore \quad I = O$

13. (A): Given, $S_n = n(2n+1)$,

$S_{n-1} = (n-1)(2n-1)$

n^{th} term $= S_n - S_{n-1}$

$= n(2n + 1) - (n - 1)(2n - 1)$

$= 4n - 1$

14. (B): Word 'INDIA' contains three vowels (I, I and A) and two consonants (N and D).

Three vowels (I, I and A) can be arranged at odd position in $\frac{3!}{2!} = 3$ ways and 2 consonants (N and D) can be arranged in $2!$ ways $= 2$ ways.

odd		odd		odd

Thus, required numbers of ways $= (3) \cdot (2) = 6$.

15. (C): Word 'EQUATION' contains five vowels (A, E, I, O and U) and three consonants (Q, T and N).

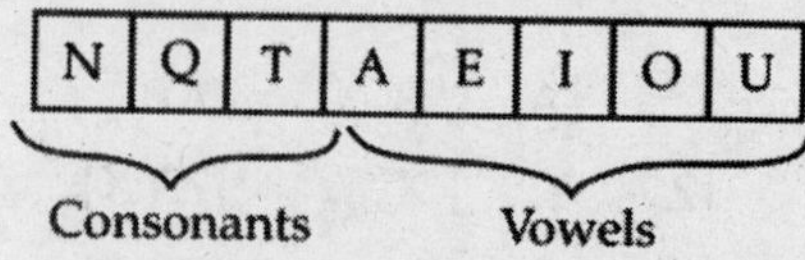

Number of ways $= (3!).(5!)$

Number of ways $= (3!).(5!)$

Total required number of ways

$= (3!).(5!) + (3!).(5!)$

$= 1440$

16. (C): $\because$ n is root of $x^2 + px + m = 0$.

$\therefore \quad n^2 + pn + m = 0 \quad \ldots(i)$

$\because$ m is root of the equation $x^2 + px + n = 0$.

$\therefore \quad m^2 + pm + n = 0 \quad \ldots(ii)$

Now, Eq. (i) – Eq. (ii), we get

$(n^2 - m^2) + p(n - m) - (n - m) = 0$

$\Rightarrow \quad (n - m)\,[(n + m) + p - 1] = 0$

$\Rightarrow \quad n + m + p - 1 = 0 \; \{n \neq m\}$

$\Rightarrow \quad n + m + p = 1$

17. (D): Two courses are compulsory.

$\therefore$ Total courses is $n - 2$ and total remaining courses that can be chosen from $(n - 2)$ courses is $(n - 4)$.

$\therefore$ Required number of ways $= {}^{(n-2)}C_{(n-4)}$

$= \frac{(n-2)(n-3)}{2}$

18. (A): $D_n = \begin{bmatrix} n & 20 & 30 \\ n^2 & 40 & 50 \\ n^3 & 60 & 70 \end{bmatrix}$

$= (20)(10) \begin{bmatrix} n & 1 & 3 \\ n^2 & 2 & 5 \\ n^3 & 3 & 7 \end{bmatrix}$

$D_n = 200\,(-n + 2n^2 + n^3)$

Now, $\sum_{n=1}^{4} D_n = 200 \sum_{n=1}^{4} (-n + 2n^2 - n^3)$

$= 200 \left[\frac{-(4)(5)}{2} + 2\frac{(4)(5)(9)}{6} - \left(\frac{(4)(5)}{2}\right)^2\right]$

$= 200\,(-50)$

$= -10{,}000$

19. (C): Given, $P = \begin{bmatrix} 0 & c & -b \\ -c & 0 & a \\ b & -a & 0 \end{bmatrix}$

$$Q = \begin{bmatrix} a^2 & ab & ac \\ ab & b^2 & bc \\ ac & bc & c^2 \end{bmatrix}$$

$\Rightarrow \quad PQ = \begin{bmatrix} 0 & 0 & 0 \\ 0 & 0 & 0 \\ 0 & 0 & 0 \end{bmatrix}$ $\because$ PQ is null matrix

and $\quad QP = \begin{bmatrix} 0 & 0 & 0 \\ 0 & 0 & 0 \\ 0 & 0 & 0 \end{bmatrix}$

$\Rightarrow \quad PQ = QP$

20. (B): Determinant of any skew symmetric matrix with odd order is always zero.

21. (C): Given, $4\sin^{-1}x + \cos^{-1}x = \pi$

$\Rightarrow \quad 4\left(\frac{\pi}{2} - \cos^{-1}x\right) + \left(\frac{\pi}{2} - \sin^{-1}x\right) = \pi$

$\Rightarrow \quad 2\pi - 4\cos^{-1}x + \frac{\pi}{2} - \sin^{-1}x = \pi$

$\Rightarrow \quad 4\cos^{-1}x + \sin^{-1}x = \frac{3\pi}{2}$

22. (B): Let, $I = \cot^2(\sec^{-1}2) + \tan^2(\text{cosec}^{-1}3)$

$\Rightarrow \quad I = \cot^2(60°) + \tan^2\left(\cot^{-1}\sqrt{9-1}\right)$

$\Rightarrow \quad I = \frac{1}{3} + \tan^2\left(\tan^{-1}\frac{1}{\sqrt{8}}\right)$

$$= \frac{1}{3} + \frac{1}{8} = \frac{11}{24}$$

23. (A): Given, $\frac{a}{\cos A} = \frac{b}{\cos B} = \frac{c}{\cos C}$

$\Rightarrow \quad \frac{a}{\left(\frac{b^2+c^2-a^2}{2bc}\right)} = \frac{b}{\left(\frac{a^2+c^2-b^2}{2ab}\right)}$

$$= \frac{c}{\left(\frac{a^2+b^2-c^2}{2ab}\right)}$$

$\Rightarrow \quad b^2 + c^2 - a^2 = c^2 + a^2 - b^2 = a^2 + b^2 - c^2$

$\Rightarrow \quad a^2 = b^2 = c^2$

$\Rightarrow \quad a = b = c$

Hence, ΔABC is an equilateral triangle.

So, area of $\Delta ABC = \frac{\sqrt{3}}{4}\cdot a^2$ (Here, $a = 6$)

$$= \frac{\sqrt{3}}{4}\cdot(6)^2 = 9\sqrt{3}\text{ cm}^2$$

24. (C): $\tan\alpha$ and $\tan\beta$ are roots of $7x^2 - 6x + 1 = 0$.

Hence, $\quad \tan\alpha + \tan\beta = \frac{6}{7}$ ...(*i*)

$\tan\alpha \,.\, \tan\beta = \frac{1}{7}$ ...(*ii*)

$\because \quad \tan(\alpha + \beta) = \frac{\tan\alpha + \tan\beta}{1 - \tan\alpha.\tan\beta}$

$$= \frac{\left(\frac{6}{7}\right)}{1 - \frac{1}{7}} = 1$$

$\Rightarrow \quad \alpha + \beta = 45°$

$\Rightarrow \quad 2\alpha + 2\beta = 90°$

It means third angle of triangle is 90°.

Hence, triangle is right-angled triangle.

Since, $(\tan\alpha - \tan\beta)$

$$= \sqrt{(\tan\alpha + \tan\beta)^2 - 4\tan\alpha.\tan\beta}$$

$$= \frac{2\sqrt{2}}{7}$$

$\because \quad \tan(\alpha - \beta) = \frac{\tan\alpha - \tan\beta}{1 + \tan\alpha\cdot\tan\beta}$

$$= \frac{1}{2\sqrt{2}}$$

and $\tan^2(\alpha - \beta) = \frac{2\tan(\alpha-\beta)}{1-\tan^2(\alpha-\beta)}$

$$= \left(\frac{4\sqrt{2}}{7}\right)$$

$\Rightarrow \quad 2\alpha \neq 2\beta$

Hence, triangle is not an isosceles triangle.

25. (B): $\because \angle A = 75°$, $\angle B = 45°$, and $\angle C = 60°$

and $\quad \frac{a}{\sin A} = \frac{b}{\sin B} = \frac{c}{\sin C}$

$\Rightarrow \quad \frac{a}{\sin 75°} = \frac{b}{\sin 45°} = \frac{c}{\sin 60°}$

Hence, $\quad a = \frac{\sin 75°}{\sin 60°}.c = \frac{\left(\sqrt{3}+1\right)c}{\sqrt{6}}$

and $b = \frac{\sin 45°}{\sin 60°}.c = \frac{2c}{\sqrt{6}}$

$\therefore \quad 2a - b = \frac{2\sqrt{3c}}{\sqrt{6}} = \sqrt{2c}$

26. (C): Given, $\cot 2x . \cot 3x = 1$

$\Rightarrow \frac{\cos 2x}{\sin 2x} \times \frac{\cos 3x}{\sin 3x} = 1$

$\Rightarrow \cos 2x . \cos 3x = \sin 2x . \sin 3x$

$\cos 2x . \cos 3x - \sin 2x . \sin 3x = 0$

$\cos (2x + 3x) = \cos 5x = 0$

$0 < x < \pi$

Hence, $5x = \frac{\pi}{2}, \frac{3\pi}{2}, \frac{5\pi}{2}, \frac{7\pi}{2}, \frac{9\pi}{2}$

$x = \frac{\pi}{10}, \frac{3\pi}{10}, \frac{5\pi}{10}, \frac{7\pi}{10}, \frac{9\pi}{10}$

Thus, only five solutions are possible.

27. (A): $\cos^{100}x - \sin^{100}x = 1$ is only possible when

$\cos^2 x = 1$ or $\sin^2 x = 0$

because $\cos^2 x \in [0, 1] \Rightarrow \cos^{100}x \in [0, 1]$

and $\sin^2 x \in [0, 1] \Rightarrow \sin^{100}x \in [0, 1]$

Now, $\cos^2 x = 1$

$\Rightarrow x = n\pi \pm 0° \Rightarrow x = n\pi$

28. (B): In ΔABC, $A + B + C = \pi$

$\Rightarrow \tan (A + B + C) = \tan \pi = 0$

$\Rightarrow \frac{\tan A + \tan B + \tan C - \tan A \tan B \tan C}{1 - \tan A . \tan B - \tan B . \tan C - \tan C . \tan A} = 0$

$\Rightarrow \tan A . \tan B . \tan C = \tan A + \tan B + \tan C$

$\Rightarrow \cot A . \cot B . \cot C = \frac{1}{\tan A + \tan B + \tan C}$

$= \frac{1}{k}$

29. (C): $\sin 12° . \sin 48° = \frac{2 \sin 12° \sin 48°}{2}$

$= \frac{1}{2}[\cos(36°) - \cos(60°)]$

$= \frac{1}{2}\left[\frac{\sqrt{5}+1}{4} - \frac{1}{2}\right] = \frac{\sqrt{5}-1}{8}$

30. (D): $\frac{\cos 17° - \sin 17°}{\cos 17° + \sin 17°} = \frac{\cos 17°\left(1 - \frac{\sin 17°}{\cos 17°}\right)}{\cos 17°\left(1 + \frac{\sin 17°}{\cos 17°}\right)}$

$= \frac{\tan 45° - \tan 17°}{1 + \tan 45° . \tan 17°}$

$= \tan 28° = \cot 62°$

31. (C): (I) Let, $\tan 22.5° = \tan \frac{45°}{2} = t$

Now, $\tan 45° = \tan\left(2 \times \frac{45°}{2}\right)$

$= \frac{2 \tan\left(\frac{45°}{2}\right)}{1 - \tan^2\left(\frac{45°}{2}\right)}$

$\Rightarrow 1 = \frac{2t}{1-t^2} \Rightarrow t^2 + 2t - 1 = 0$

$\Rightarrow t = \frac{-2 \pm \sqrt{4+4}}{2} = -1 \pm \sqrt{2}$

$\Rightarrow \tan\left(\frac{45°}{2}\right) = -1 \pm \sqrt{2}$

$\Rightarrow \tan\left(\frac{45°}{2}\right) = -1 + \left(\sqrt{2}\right)$

{$\because$ In first quadrant tan is positive}

This is an irrational number.

(II) $\cot 22.5° = \frac{1}{\tan 22.5°} = \frac{1}{-1+\sqrt{2}} = 1 + \sqrt{2}$

This is also an irrational number.

(III) $\tan 22.5° - \cot 22.5° = -1 + \sqrt{2} - \left(1 + \sqrt{2}\right) = -2$

This is not an irrational number.

32. (B): Given, $\frac{x}{\cos\theta} = \frac{y}{\cos\left(\frac{2\pi}{3} - \theta\right)}$

$= \frac{z}{\cos\left(\frac{2\pi}{3} + \theta\right)} = k$(say)

$\Rightarrow x = k\cos\theta$

$y = k\cos\left(\frac{2\pi}{3} - \theta\right)$

$z = k\cos\left(\frac{2\pi}{3} + \theta\right)$

Now, $x + y + z = k$

$\left[\cos\theta + \cos\left(\frac{2\pi}{3} - \theta\right) + \cos\left(\frac{2\pi}{3} + \theta\right)\right]$

$= k\left[\cos\theta + 2\cos\frac{2\pi}{3}\cos\theta\right]$

$= k\left[\cos\theta + 2\left(-\frac{1}{2}\right)\cos\theta\right]$

$= k[\cos\theta - \cos\theta] = 0$

$\Rightarrow x + y + z = 0$

33. (D): Given, $p\tan(\theta - 30°) = q\tan(\theta + 120°)$

$$\Rightarrow \frac{p}{q} = \frac{\tan(\theta+120°)}{\tan(\theta-30°)}$$

$$= \frac{\sin(\theta+120°)\cos(\theta-30°)}{\cos(\theta+120°)\sin(\theta-30°)}$$

$$\frac{p+q}{p-q} = \frac{\sin(\theta+120°)\cos(\theta-30°) + \cos(\theta+120°)\sin(\theta-30°)}{\sin(\theta+120°)\cos(\theta-30°) - \cos(\theta+120°)\sin(\theta-30°)}$$

$$= \frac{\sin(90°+2\theta)}{\sin(150°)}$$

$$\Rightarrow \frac{p+q}{p-q} = \frac{\sin(90°+2\theta)}{\left(\frac{1}{2}\right)} = 2\cos 2\theta$$

34. (D): (I) Given that P and Q are reflexive relations on A.

$\Rightarrow$ For any $a \in A$, $(a, a) \in P$ and $(a, a) \in Q$

$\Rightarrow (a, a) \in P \cap Q$

$\Rightarrow P \cap Q$ is reflexive relation. So statement (I) is true.

(II) Given that P and Q are symmetric relation

Let, $(a, b) \in (P \cup Q)$

$\Rightarrow (a, b) \in P$ or $(a, b) \in Q$

$\Rightarrow (b, a) \in P$ or $(b, a) \in Q$

$\Rightarrow (b, a) \in (P \cup Q)$

$\Rightarrow P \cup Q$ is symmetric relation.

So, statement (II) is true

(III) Given that P and Q are transitive

Let, $(a, b) \in (P \cap Q)$ and $(b, c) \in (P \cap Q)$

$\Rightarrow \{(q, b) \in P, (b, c) \in P\}$ and $\{(a, b) \in Q, (b, c) \in Q\}$

$\Rightarrow (a, c) \in P$ and $(a, c) \in Q$

$\{\because$ P and Q are transitive$\}$

$\Rightarrow (a, c) \in P \cap Q$

So, $P \cap Q$ is a transitive relation. So statement (III) is also true.

35. (D): Given, $A \cap B = 10$

Now, $(A \times B) \cap (B \times A) = 10^2 = 100$

36. (B): Let, $p(n) = 7^n - 6n$

$= (6+1)^n - 6n$

$= 1 + 6n + {}^nC_2 6^2 + {}^nC_3 6^3 + \dots + 6^n - 6n$

$= 1 + 6^2({}^nC_2 + {}^nC_3 \times 6 + \dots + 6^{n-2})$

$= 1 + 36({}^{100}C_2 + {}^{100}C_2 \times 6 + \dots + 6^{98})$ $\{\because n = 100\}$

$= 1 + 36k,$

where $k = {}^{100}C_2 + {}^{100}C_2 \times 6 + \dots 6^{98}$

$\therefore$ When $7^n - 6n$ is divided by 36, the remainder will be 1.

37. (C): Since there are 4 lines, the maximum number of intersection points are ${}^4C_2 = 6$.

And maximum number of intersection of circle with 4 lines are $4 \times 2 = 8$.

$\therefore$ Required intersection points $= 6 + 8 = 14$.

38. (C): Given, $\frac{S_p}{S_q} = \frac{p^2}{q^2}$

$$\Rightarrow \frac{\frac{p}{2}[2a+(p-1)d]}{\frac{q}{2}[2a+(q-1)d]} = \frac{p^2}{q^2}$$

$$\Rightarrow \frac{2a+(p-1)d}{2a+(q-1)d} = \frac{p}{q}$$

$\Rightarrow 2aq + q(p-1)d = 2ap + p(q-1)d$

$\Rightarrow 2a(q-p) = d(q-p)$

$\Rightarrow 2a = d$ or $d = 2a$

$\therefore$ The common difference is equal to twice of the first term.

39. (A): Given equation is

$(x-1)^2 + (x-3)^2 + (x-5)^2 = 0$

$\Rightarrow x^2 - 2x + 1 + x^2 - 6x + 9 + x^2 - 10x + 25 = 0$

$\Rightarrow 3x^2 - 18x + 35 = 0$

Now, discriminant $D = (-18)^2 - 4 \times 3 \times 35$

$= -96 < 0$

$\therefore$ The given equation does not have any real roots.

40. (A):

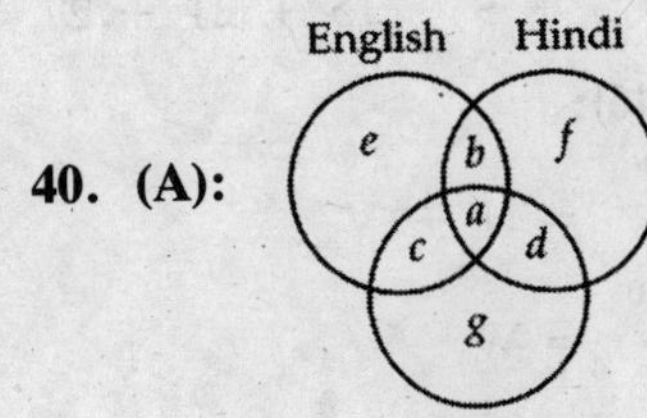

Total student $= 240$

$\because$ 10 students failed in every subject.

Hence, remaining total $= 230$

According to questions,

$a + b + c + d + e + f + g = 230$ ...(i)

and $b + c + d = 110$ (ii)

and $e + f + g = 60$ ...(iii)

Eq. (i) – Eq. [(ii) + (iii)], we get

$\Rightarrow a = 230 - (110 + 60) = 60$

For (Qs. No. 41 and 42):

$\because Z_1^2 + Z_2^2 + Z_1 Z_2 = 0$

$\Rightarrow Z_1 = \omega$ and $Z_2 = \omega^2$

41. (A): Now, $\left|\frac{Z_1}{Z_2}\right| = \left|\frac{\omega}{\omega^2}\right| = \left|\frac{1}{\omega}\right| = 1$

42. (B): $\frac{1}{2} + \text{Re}\left(\frac{Z_1}{Z_2}\right) = \frac{1}{2} + \text{Re}\left(\frac{\omega}{\omega^2}\right)$

$= \frac{1}{2} + \text{Re}(\omega^2)$

$= \frac{1}{2} + \text{Re}\left(-\frac{1}{2} - \frac{\sqrt{3}}{2}i\right)$

$= \frac{1}{2} + \left(-\frac{1}{2}\right) = 0$

43. (D): Let the required terms of AP are
$a - 2d,\ a - d,\ a,\ a + d,\ a + 2d$

$\therefore (a - 2d)(a - d)\,a\,(a + d)(a + 2d) = 2{,}29{,}635$

$\Rightarrow a(a^2 - d^2)(a^2 - 4d^2) = 2{,}29{,}635$ ...(*i*)

$\because a - 2d,\ a - d$ and $a + 2d$ are in GP.

$\Rightarrow (a - d)^2 = a^2 - 4d^2$

$\Rightarrow 5d^2 - 2ad = 0$

$\Rightarrow d(5d - 2a) = 0$

$\Rightarrow 5d = 2a$ ...(*ii*)

Solving equation (*i*) and (*ii*), we get

$d = 6$

44. (C): Putting the value of d in equation (*ii*), we get

$5 \times 6 = 2a$

$\Rightarrow a = 15$

$\therefore$ The terms are 3, 9, 15, 21 and 27.

So required sum = 3 + 9 + 15 + 21 + 27 = 75

For (Qs. No. 45 and 46):

Given, $(8 + 3\sqrt{7})^{20} = \text{U} + \text{V}$ ...(*i*)

and $(8 - 3\sqrt{7})^{20} = \text{W}$

Here, $0 < \text{W} < 1$

Now, adding eq. (*i*) and (*ii*), we get

$\text{U} + \text{V} + \text{W} = (8 + 3\sqrt{7})^{20} + (8 - 3\sqrt{7})^{20}$

$= 2\left[{}^{20}C_0 8^{20} + {}^{20}C_2 8^{18}.(3\sqrt{7})^2 + \ldots + (3\sqrt{7})^{20}\right]$

It is an even number.

Also, $0 < \text{V} < 1$, $0 < \text{W} < 1$ and U is an integer.

$\therefore$ V + W is an integer $\Rightarrow$ V + W = 1

45. (D): V + W = 1

46. (B): $(\text{U} + \text{V})\text{W} = (8 + 3\sqrt{7})^{20}(8 - 3\sqrt{7})^{20}$

$= (64 - 63)^{20} = 1^{20} = 1$

For (Qs. No. 47 and 48):

The given equation is

$a^2(b^2 - c^2)x^2 + b^2(c^2 - a^2)x + c^2(a^2 - b^2) = 0$ ...(*i*)

$\because$ Equation has equal roots:

$\Rightarrow D = 0$

$\therefore [b^2(c^2 - a^2)]^2 - 4a^2c^2(b^2 - c^2)(a^2 - b^2) = 0$

$\Rightarrow b^4(c^2 - a^2)^2 - 4a^2c^2(b^2 - c^2)(a^2 - b^2) = 0$

Solving above equation, we get

$b^4(c^2 + a^2)^2 = 4a^4c^4$

$\Rightarrow b^2(a^2 + c^2) = 2a^2c^2$

$\Rightarrow \frac{2}{b^2} = \frac{1}{a^2} + \frac{1}{c^2}$

$\therefore a^2$, b^2 and c^2 are in HP.

47. (C)

48. (C): Let α be the required root.

$\therefore$ Sum of roots $= \frac{-\text{B}}{\text{A}} = \frac{-b^2(c^2 - a^2)}{a^2(b^2 - c^2)}$

$\Rightarrow \alpha + \alpha = \frac{-b^2(c^2 - a^2)}{a^2(b^2 - c^2)}$

$\Rightarrow \alpha = \frac{b^2(c^2 - a^2)}{2a^2(c^2 - b^2)}$

For (Qs. No. 49 and 50):

Given, $\text{A} = \begin{bmatrix} 3 & -3 & 4 \\ 2 & -3 & 4 \\ 0 & -1 & 1 \end{bmatrix}$

Now, $|\text{A}| = 3(-3 + 4) - 2(-3 + 4) + 0$

$= 3 - 2 = 1$

$\because \text{A(adjA)} = |\text{A}|\text{I} = \text{I}$

49. (D)

50. (A): Given, $\text{adj(A)} = \begin{bmatrix} 1 & -1 & 0 \\ -2 & 3 & -4 \\ -2 & 3 & -3 \end{bmatrix}$

Now, $\text{A}^{-1} = \frac{1}{|\text{A}|}(\text{Adj(A)})$

$= \begin{bmatrix} 1 & -1 & 0 \\ -2 & 3 & -4 \\ -2 & 3 & -3 \end{bmatrix}$

$\Rightarrow \text{A}^{-1} = \begin{bmatrix} 1 & -1 & 0 \\ -2 & 3 & -4 \\ -2 & 3 & -3 \end{bmatrix}$

51. (A): $\because \left(2\hat{i}+6\hat{j}+27\hat{k}\right)\times\left(\hat{i}+\alpha\hat{j}+\beta\hat{k}\right) = 0$

$$\Rightarrow \begin{bmatrix} \hat{i} & \hat{j} & \hat{k} \\ 2 & 6 & 27 \\ 1 & \alpha & \beta \end{bmatrix} = 0$$

$$\Rightarrow \hat{i}(6\beta - 27\alpha) - \hat{j}(2\beta - 27) + \hat{k}(2\alpha - 6) = 0$$

Comparing both sides, we get

$$\Rightarrow \quad 6\beta - 27\alpha = 0$$
$$2\beta = 9\alpha$$
$$2\beta - 27 = 0$$
$$\Rightarrow \quad \beta = \frac{27}{2}$$

and $\quad 2\alpha - 6 = 0 \Rightarrow \alpha = 3$

Now, $\quad 3\alpha + 2\beta = 3\times 3 + 2\times\frac{27}{2}$

$$9 + 27 = 36$$

52. (B): Let, $\quad p = \left|\vec{a}\times\vec{b}\right| + \sqrt{3}\left|\vec{a}.\vec{b}\right|$

$$= |\vec{a}|.\left|\vec{b}\right| |\sin\theta| + \sqrt{3}|\vec{a}|\left|\vec{b}\right| |\cos\theta|$$
$$= |\vec{a}|\left|\vec{b}\right|\left[|\sin\theta| + \sqrt{3}\,|\cos\theta|\right]$$

p will be max if $\left(\sin\theta + \sqrt{3}\cos\theta\right)$ is maximum.

Now, for its maxima,

$$\frac{d}{d\theta}\left(\sin\theta + \sqrt{3}\cos\theta\right) = 0$$
$$\Rightarrow \quad \cos\theta - \sqrt{3}\sin\theta = 0$$
$$\Rightarrow \quad \tan\theta = \frac{1}{\sqrt{3}} \Rightarrow \theta = 30°$$

53. (A): $\because \left(\vec{a}+2\vec{b}\right)$ and $\left(5\vec{a}-4\vec{b}\right)$ are perpendicular vectors.

$$\Rightarrow \quad \left(\vec{a}+2\vec{b}\right).\left(5\vec{a}-4\vec{b}\right) = 0$$
$$\Rightarrow \quad 5|\vec{a}|^2 - 4\vec{a}\cdot\vec{b} + 10\vec{a}\cdot\vec{b} - 8\left(\vec{b}\right)^2 = 0$$
$$\Rightarrow \quad 5\times 1 + 6\vec{a}\cdot\vec{b} - 8 = 0$$

$(\because \vec{a}$ and $\vec{b}$ are unit vectors.)

$$\Rightarrow \quad 6|\vec{a}|\left|\vec{b}\right|\cos\theta = 3$$
$$\Rightarrow \quad 1.1\cos\theta = \frac{1}{2} \Rightarrow \cos\theta = \frac{1}{2}$$
$$\therefore \quad \cos 2\theta = 2\cos^2\theta - 1$$
$$= 2\times\frac{1}{4} - 1 = -\frac{1}{2}$$

Now, $\quad \cos\theta + \cos 2\theta = \frac{1}{2} - \frac{1}{2} = 0$

54. (A):

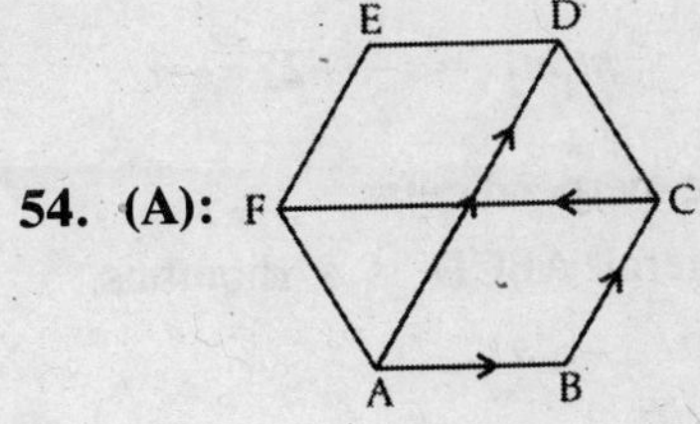

$$\because \quad \overline{AB} = 2\overline{FC}$$
$$\Rightarrow \quad \overline{AB} = -\ 2\overline{CF}$$
$$\therefore \quad n = -2$$

Also, $\quad \overline{AD} = 2\overline{BC}$

$$\therefore \quad m = 2$$

Now, $\quad mn = (-2) = -4$

55. (C): $\vec{a} = \hat{i} + \hat{j},\ \vec{b} = \hat{j} + \hat{k}$

Also, $\vec{a}, \vec{b}$ and $\vec{c}$ has same length.

$$\Rightarrow \quad |\vec{a}| = \left|\vec{b}\right| = |\vec{c}|$$
$$= \sqrt{1+1} = \sqrt{2}$$

Let θ be the angle between the vectors.

$$\therefore \quad \cos\theta = \frac{\vec{a}\cdot\vec{b}}{|\vec{a}|\left|\vec{b}\right|} = \frac{0+1+0}{\sqrt{2}\times\sqrt{2}} = \frac{1}{2}$$

(I) Let, $\quad \vec{c} = \hat{i} + \hat{k}$

$$|\vec{c}| = \sqrt{2}$$

and $\quad \cos\theta = \frac{\vec{a}\cdot\vec{c}}{|\vec{a}||\vec{c}|} = \frac{1+0+0}{\sqrt{2}\times\sqrt{2}} = \frac{1}{2}$

All the conditions are satisfied, so it can be vector $|\vec{c}|$.

(II) Let, $\quad \vec{c} = \frac{-\hat{i} + 4\hat{j} - \hat{k}}{3}$

$$\Rightarrow \quad |\vec{c}| = \frac{1}{3}\sqrt{1+16+1} = \sqrt{2}$$

and $\quad \cos\theta = \frac{\vec{a}\cdot\vec{c}}{|\vec{a}||\vec{c}|} = \frac{\frac{-1}{3}+\frac{4}{3}}{\sqrt{2}\sqrt{2}} = \frac{1}{2}$

All the conditions are satisfied, so it can be vector $|\vec{c}|$.

56. (D): Slope of diagonal along the line $x - 2y = 1$

$$m_1 = \frac{1}{2}$$

Slope of the diagonal along the line

$$4x + 2y = 3$$
$$\Rightarrow \quad m_2 = -2$$

Now, $m_1m_2 = \frac{1}{2}(-2) = -1$

$\therefore$ Diagonals are perpendicular.

$\Rightarrow$ The quadrilateral ABCD is a rhombus.

57. (B): Given, $4x^2 + 9y^2 = 1$

Here, $a = \frac{1}{2}$ and $b = \frac{1}{3}$

$$e = \sqrt{1 - \frac{b^2}{a^2}} = \frac{\sqrt{5}}{3}$$

$$\text{foci} = (\pm ae, 0)$$

$$= \left(\pm\frac{1}{2}\frac{\sqrt{5}}{3}, 0\right) = \left(\pm\frac{\sqrt{5}}{6}, 0\right)$$

$\therefore$ P(x, y) is any point on the ellipse.

$\therefore$ $PQ + PR = 2a = 2 \times \frac{1}{2} = 1$

58. (B):

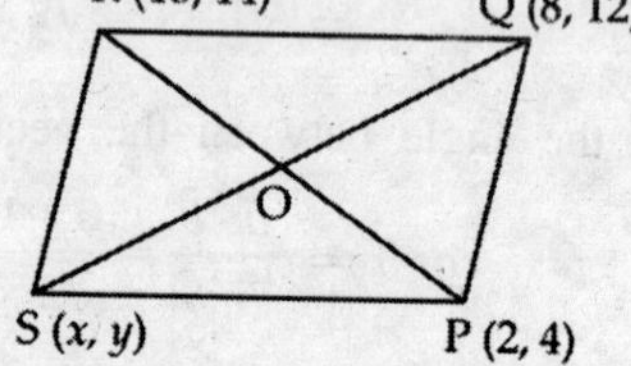

$\because$ O is midpoint of P and R

$\Rightarrow$ $O \equiv \left(\frac{10+2}{2}, \frac{14+4}{2}\right) = (6, 9)$

Also, O is midpoint of S and Q

$\therefore$ $O = \left(\frac{x+8}{2}, \frac{y+12}{2}\right)$

$\therefore$ $(6, 9) = \left(\frac{x+8}{2}, \frac{y+12}{2}\right)$

Comparing both sides, we get

$$\frac{x+8}{2} = 6 \Rightarrow x = 4$$

and $\frac{y+12}{2} = 9 \Rightarrow y = 6$

Now, $x + y = 4 + 6 = 10.$

59. (A): Given equation of cricle is:

$(x^2 - 4x + 3) + (y^2 - 6y + 8) = 0$

$(x - 3)(x - 1) + (y - 4)(y - 2) = 0$

So, the possible ends of the diameters are (3, 4), (3, 2), (1, 4) and (1, 2).

Also, Radius $= \sqrt{2}$ and center $= (2, 3)$

So, the required pair of ends of diameters are (I) (1, 2) and (3, 4) and (II) (1, 4) and (3, 2).

60. (B):

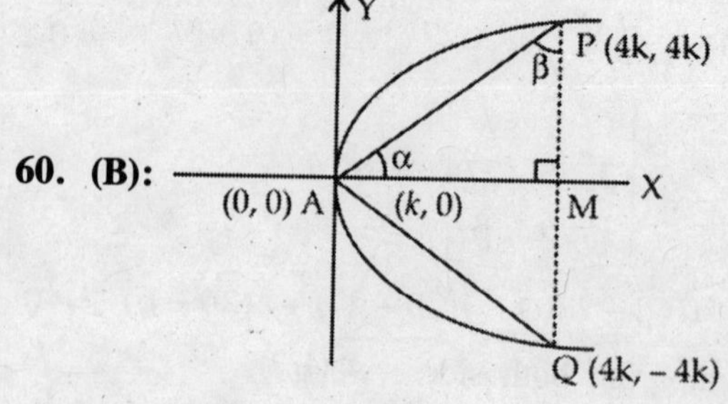

Let, $\angle PAM = \alpha$

and $\angle APM = \beta$

From figure, it is clear that

$$\angle PAQ = \angle PAM + \angle QAM$$
$$= \alpha + \alpha = 2\alpha$$

In right-angled triangle AMP,

$$AM = PM = 4k$$

$\Rightarrow$ $\alpha = \beta$

$\therefore$ $\alpha + \beta + 90° = 180°$

$\Rightarrow$ $2\alpha = 90°$

$\Rightarrow$ $\alpha = 45°$

Hence, $\angle PAQ = 2\alpha = 90°$

For (Qs. No. 61 and 62):

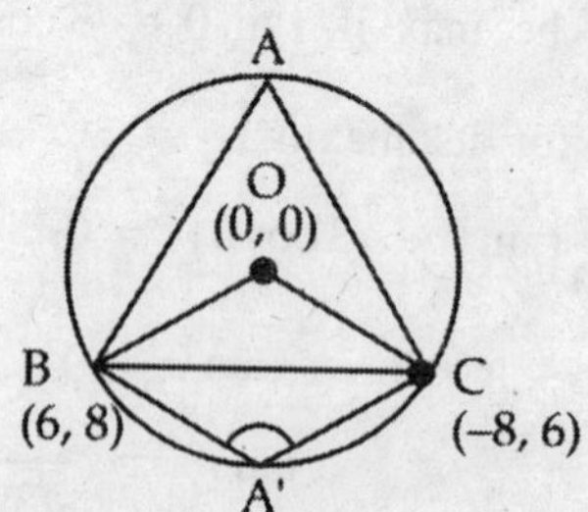

61. (C): $BC = \sqrt{(6+8)^2 + (8-6)^2}$

$$= \sqrt{200} = 10\sqrt{2}$$

Let, O is centre of circle,

$$x^2 + y^2 = 100,$$

Radius = OB = OC = 10 units

$$OB^2 + OC^2 = \sqrt{100 + 100}$$
$$= \sqrt{200} = 10\sqrt{2}$$

In ΔBOC, $OB^2 + OC^2 = BC^2 = \left(10\sqrt{2}\right)^2$

$$= 200$$

So, $\angle BOC = 90°$ (by converse of pythagoras theorem)

$\therefore$ $\angle BAC = 45°$ or $180° - 45° = \frac{\pi}{4}$ or $\frac{3\pi}{4}$

(Angle subtended by a chord at centre is double the angle at any point subtended by it on the remaining circle.)

62. (D): Point A can be taken at any point on the circumference of circle.

So, coordinates of A cannot be determined due to insufficient data.

63. (D):

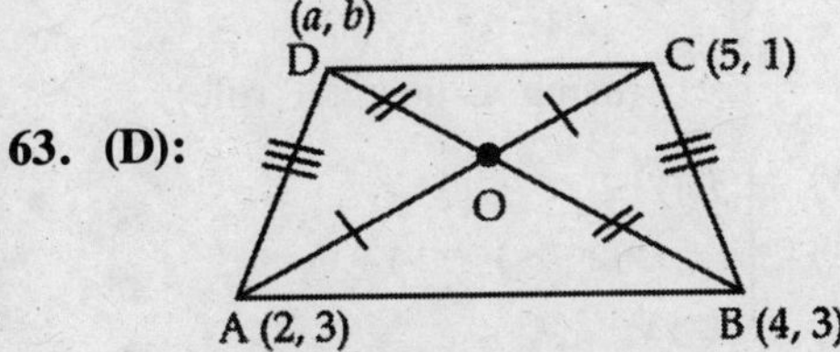

In isosceles trapezium, diagonals bisect each other. O is midpoint of AC and BD.

$$\frac{5+2}{2} = \frac{4+a}{2}, \frac{3+b}{2} = \frac{3+1}{2}$$

$$a = 3,\ b = 1$$

$$D(a,\ b) = (3,\ 1)$$

64. (C): Since diagonals of isosceles trapezium bisect each other, then intersecting point of diagonal is O.

Coordinates of O is $\left(\frac{2+5}{2}, \frac{3+1}{2}\right) = \left(\frac{7}{2}, 2\right)$.

For (Qs. No. 65 and 66):

Sphere: $2x^2 + 2y^2 + 2z^2 + 3x + 3y + 3z - 6 = 0$

$$\Rightarrow x^2 + y^2 + z^2 + \frac{3}{2}x + \frac{3}{2}y + \frac{3}{2}z - 3 = 0$$

65. (B): Radius $= \sqrt{\left(\frac{3}{4}\right)^2 + \left(\frac{3}{4}\right)^2 + \left(\frac{3}{4}\right)^2 + 3}$

$$= \sqrt{\frac{27}{16} + 3} = \sqrt{\frac{75}{16}}$$

$$\text{Radius} = 5\frac{\sqrt{3}}{2}$$

$$\text{Diameter} = 5\frac{\sqrt{3}}{2}$$

66. (D): Centre of sphere is $C\left(\frac{-3}{4}, \frac{-3}{4}, \frac{-3}{4}\right)$.

$4x + 8y + 8z + 15 = 0$,
plane satisfy the centre of sphere:
$-3 - 6 - 6 + 15 = 0 \Rightarrow 0 = 0$.

For (Qs. No. 67 and 68):

Two planes are $x + y + z = 1$ and $2x + 3y - 4z = 8$.

67. (B): Let a, b, c are direction ratios of lines of intersection of planes. Then the lines is perpendicular to normal of both planes.

$$a + b + c = 0 \quad \ldots(i)$$

$$2a + 3b - 4c = 0 \quad \ldots(ii)$$

$$\frac{a}{-4-3} = \frac{b}{2+4} = \frac{c}{3-2} = \lambda$$

$$a = -7\lambda,\ b = 6\lambda,\ c = \lambda$$

Direction ratios are (–7, 6, 1).

68. (A): Direction ratios of S are $l = \frac{-7}{\sqrt{86}}$,

$$m = \frac{6}{\sqrt{86}}, n = \frac{1}{\sqrt{86}}$$

$$\therefore 43(l^2 - m^2 - n^2) = 43\left(\frac{49}{86} - \frac{36}{86} - \frac{1}{86}\right)$$

$$= 43 \times \frac{12}{86} = 6$$

For (Qs. No. 69 and 70):

69. (C): Let direction ratios of line (a, b, c)

Since line is obtained by intersection of planes

$$x + y + z + 4 = 0$$

and $$2x - y - z + 8 = 0$$

So, $$a + b + c = 0 \quad \ldots(i)$$

$$2a - b - c = 0 \quad \ldots(ii)$$

$$\frac{a}{-1+1} = \frac{b}{2+1} = \frac{c}{-1-2} = \lambda$$

(solving (i) and (ii))

$$a = 0,\ b = 3\lambda \text{ and } c = -3\lambda$$

Direction ratios of line is (0, 3, –3) or (0, 1, –1).

70. (D): To find point of intersection of L and P

The point must satisfy both line L and plane P,

Option (d) (–4, –3, 3) will satisfy both line L and plane P.

So option (D) is the correct answer.

71. (A): Since, $\{x\} + [x] = x$

$$\Rightarrow \quad x - [x] = \{x\}$$

$0 \le x - [x] < 1$ $(0 \le \{x\} < 1)$

$-1 \le [x] - x \le 0$

But x is positive and non-integer; then

$$-1 < [x] - x < 0$$

$$-1 < y < 0$$

$$\therefore \quad [y] = -1$$

72. (A): $f(x) = 4x + 1,\ g(x) = kx + 2$

$$fog(x) = 4(kx + 2) + 1 = 4kx + 9$$

$$gof(x) = k(4x + 1) + 2 = 4kx + k + 2$$

$$fog(x) = gof(x)$$

$$\Rightarrow \quad 9 = k + 2 = k = 7$$

73. (B): $f(x) = \log_{10}(x^2 + 2x + 11)$ for minimum

$f'(x) = 0$

$$\frac{2x+2}{x^2+2x+11} = 0 \text{ (Since } x^2 + 2x + 11 > 0)$$

At $x = -1$,

we get minimum value of $f(x)$

$f(-1) = \log_{10}10 = 1$

74. (D): $\lim_{x\to 3} \frac{|x-3|}{x-3}$

$$\text{LHL} = \lim_{x\to 3^-} \frac{|x-3|}{x-3} = \frac{-(x-3)}{x-3} = -1$$

$$\text{RHL} = \lim_{x\to 3^+} \frac{|x-3|}{x-3} = \frac{(x-3)}{x-3} = +1$$

LHL $\neq$ RHL; limit does not exist.

75. (B): Since, maximum value of $a\cos x + b\sin x$ is $\sqrt{a^2+b^2}$

So, maximum value of $a\cos x + b\sin x + c$ is $\sqrt{a^2+b^2} + c$.

76. (C): $f(2x) = 4x^2 + 1 \Rightarrow f(x) = x^2 + 1$

$f(4x) = 16x^2 + 1$

$(4x^2 + 1)^2 = (x^2 + 1) \times (16x^2 + 1)$

$[f(2x)$ is GM of $f(x)$ & $f(4x)]$

$\Rightarrow x^2 = 0$

$x = 0$

$\therefore$ One real value of x is possible.

77. (D): $f(x) = [x]^2 - 30[x] + 221 = 0$

$$[x] = \frac{30 \pm \sqrt{900-884}}{2} = \frac{30 \pm 4}{2}$$

$$= \frac{30+4}{2} \text{ or } \frac{30-4}{2} = 17 \text{ or } 13$$

Integral value of x are 17 and 13.

$\therefore$ Sum of integral solution of $f(x) = 30$.

78. (B): Given, $f(x) = 9x - 8\sqrt{x}$, $g(x) = 9x - 8\sqrt{x} - 1$

Let, $x = t^2$

$g(t^2) = 9t^2 - 8t - 1 = 0$

$$t = \frac{8 \pm 10}{18}$$

$$\Rightarrow t = \frac{18}{18} \text{ or } \frac{-1}{9}$$

$$t = 1 \text{ or } -\frac{1}{9} \Rightarrow x = 1, \frac{1}{81}$$

$\therefore g(x) = 0$ has only one real root which is an integer.

79. (B): $$\lim_{x\to \frac{\pi}{2}} (\sec\theta - \tan\theta) = \lim_{x\to \frac{\pi}{2}} \frac{1-\sin\theta}{\cos\theta}\left(\frac{0}{0} \text{ from}\right)$$

$$= \lim_{x\to \frac{\pi}{2}} \left(\frac{-\cos\theta}{-\sin\theta}\right) = 0$$

(using L'hospital rule)

80. (A): $f(x)f(y) = f(xy)$

Let, $f(x) = x^n$ and $f(y) = y^n$

$f(xy) = (xy)^n$

$f(2) = 4 \Rightarrow 4 = (2)^n \Rightarrow n = 2$

$$f\left(\frac{1}{2}\right) = \left(\frac{1}{2}\right)^2 = \frac{1}{4}$$

For (Qs. No. 81 and 82):

$fog(x) = \cos^2\sqrt{x}$ and $gof(x) = |\cos x|$

81. (C): If we take option (C),

$f(x) = \cos^2 x$; then $g(x) = \sqrt{x}$

$fog(x) = \cos^2\sqrt{x}$ and $gof(x) = \sqrt{\cos^2 x} = |\cos x|$

$\therefore f(x) = \cos^2 x$

82. (A): If $f(x) = \cos^2 x$ then $g(x) = \sqrt{x}$

For (Qs. No. 83 and 84):

$f(x) = [x]^2 - [x^2]$

83. (B): $\therefore$ $f(0.999) = [0.999]^2 - [(0.999)^2]$

$= 0 -$ [value lies b/w 0 and 1]

$= 0 - 0 = 0$

$f(1.001) = [1.001]^2 - [(1.001)^2]$

$= 1 - 1 = 0$

$f(0.999) + f(1.001) = 0 - 0 = 0$

84. (B): $f(x) = [x]^2 - [x^2]$

At, $x = 0$

$$\text{LHL} = \lim_{h\to 0}[0-h]^2 - [(0-h)^2]$$

$= (-1)^2 - 0 = 1$

$$\text{RHL} = \lim_{h\to 0}[0+h]^2 - [(0+h)^2]$$

$= 0 - 0 = 0$

LHL $\neq$ RHL; $f(x)$ is not continuous at $x = 0$

At, $x = 1$

$$\text{LHL} = \lim_{h\to 0}[1-h]^2 - [(1-h)^2]$$

$= 1 - 1 = 0$

$$\text{RHL} = \lim_{h\to 0}[1+h]^2 - [(1+h)^2]$$

$= 1 - 1 = 0$

$f(x)$ is continuous at $x = 1$; LHL = RHL.

For (Qs. No. 85 and 86):

$$f(x) = \cos 2x + x \text{ on} \left[\frac{-\pi}{2}, \frac{\pi}{2}\right]$$

85. (B): $f'(x) = -2 \sin 2x + 1$

For maxima and minima, $f'(x) = 0$

$$\sin 2x = \frac{1}{2}$$

$$x = \frac{\pi}{12} \text{ or } \frac{5\pi}{12} \text{ (not in interval)}$$

So, maximum value of $f(x)$ occurs at

$$x = \frac{\pi}{12}$$

$$f\left(\frac{\pi}{12}\right) = \cos\frac{\pi}{6} + \frac{\pi}{12} = \frac{\sqrt{3}}{2} + \frac{\pi}{12}$$

86. (A): $f\left(\frac{-\pi}{2}\right) = -1 - \frac{\pi}{2}$

$$f\left(\frac{\pi}{2}\right) = -1 + \frac{\pi}{2}$$

So, minimum value of $f(x) = -\left(1 + \frac{\pi}{2}\right)$

For (Qs. No. 87 and 88):

The area bounded by the parabola $y^2 = kx$ and the line $x = k$, where $k > 0$, is $\frac{4}{3}$ square units.

87. (B):

O $x = k$

Area bounded $= \frac{4}{3}$ sq. units $= 2\int_0^k y\,dx$

$$\Rightarrow \frac{4}{3} = 2\int_0^k \sqrt{k}\sqrt{x}\,dx \Rightarrow 1 = k^2$$

$$\Rightarrow k = \pm 1 \text{ (since } k > 0) \Rightarrow k = 1$$

88. (A): So, equation of parabola is $y^2 = x$

$$4a = 1, \; a = \frac{1}{4}$$

Area of parabola $y^2 = x$ and latus rectum at

$$x = \frac{1}{4} \text{ is}$$

$$= 2\int_0^{\frac{1}{4}} \sqrt{x}\,dx = 2 \times \frac{2}{3}\left(\frac{1}{4}\right)^{\frac{3}{2}}$$

$$= \frac{4}{3} \times \frac{1}{8} = \frac{1}{6} \text{ sq. units}$$

For (Qs. No. 89 and 90):

Let, $ydx + (x - y^3)dy = 0$ be a differential equation.

89. (A): $ydx + (x - y^3)dy = 0$

$$\Rightarrow \frac{dy}{dx} = \frac{y}{y^3 - x}$$

degree = 1

90. (D): $y\frac{dx}{dy} + x = y^3$

$$\Rightarrow \frac{dx}{dy} + x\frac{1}{y} = y^2 \text{ (linear differential equation)}$$

$$\text{I.F.} = e^{\int \frac{1}{y} dy} = y$$

$$x(\text{I.F.}) = \int (\text{I.F.}) y^2 dy$$

$$\Rightarrow xy = \int y^3 dy$$

$$\Rightarrow 4xy - y^4 = c$$

For (Qs. No. 91 and 92):

$f(x) = |x^2 - x - 2|$.

91. (D): $f(x) = |x^2 - x - 2| = \{x^2 - x - 2;$
$x \in (-\infty, -1)$
$\cup (2, \infty) - (x^2 - x - 2); x \in [-1, 2]$

Let, $I = -\int_0^2 (x^2 - x - 2)dx$

$$= -\left[\frac{x^3}{3} - \frac{x^2}{2} - 2x\right]_0^2$$

$$= -\left(\frac{8}{3} - \frac{4}{2} - 4\right) + 0 = -\left(\frac{8}{3} - 6\right)$$

$$= -\left(\frac{8 - 18}{3}\right) = \frac{10}{3}$$

92. (B): $f(x) = |x^2 - x - 2|$

$$= \begin{cases} x^2 - x - 2; x \in (-\infty, -1) \cup (2, \infty) \\ -(x^2 - x - 2); x \in [-1, 2] \end{cases}$$

Let, $I = \int_1^3 f(x)\,dx$

$$= -\int_1^2 (x^2 - x - 2)\,dx + \int_2^3 (x^2 - x - 2)dx$$

$$= -\left[\frac{x^3}{3} - \frac{x^2}{2} - 2x\right]_1^2 + \left[\frac{x^3}{3} - \frac{x^2}{2} - 2x\right]_2^3$$

$$= -\left[\frac{8}{3} - \frac{4}{2} - 4\right] + \left[\frac{1}{3} - \frac{1}{2} - 2\right]$$

$$+ \left[\frac{27}{3} - \frac{9}{2} - 6\right] - \left[\frac{8}{3} - \frac{4}{2} - 4\right]$$

$$= -\left[\frac{16-12-24}{6}\right]+\left[\frac{2-3-12}{6}\right] + \left[\frac{54-27-36}{6}\right]-\left[\frac{16-12-24}{6}\right]$$

$$= \frac{20}{6}-\frac{13}{6}-\frac{9}{6}+\frac{20}{6} = \frac{20-13-9+20}{6}$$

$$= \frac{18}{6} = 3$$

For (Qs. No. 93 and 94):

93. (C): Let, $f(t) = \ln\left(t+\sqrt{1+t^2}\right)$

$$f(-t) = \ln\left(\sqrt{1+t^2}-t\right) = \ln\left(\frac{1}{t+\sqrt{1+t^2}}\right)$$

$$= -\ln\left(t+\sqrt{1+t^2}\right) = -f(t)$$

$\therefore$ $f(t)$ is an odd function.

$\because$ $g(t) = \tan f(t)$

$\therefore$ $g(-t) = \tan f(-t) = -\tan(f(t)) = -g(t)$

So, $g(t)$ is also an odd function.

Hence, both statements I and II are correct.

94. (B): When $g(t)$ is an odd function, then

$$\int_{-\pi}^{\pi} g(t)\,dt = 0$$

For (Qs. No. 95 and 96):

95. (D): Let $f : (-1, 1) \to R$ be a differentiable function with $f(0) = -1$ and $f'(0) = 1$

$h(x) = f(2f(x) + 2)$

$h'(x) = f'(2f(x) + 2)2f'(x)$

$h'(0) = f'(2f(0) + 2).2f'(0)$

$= f'(-2 + 2).2(1)$

$= f'(0).2 = (1).2 = 2$

96. (A): $g(x) = (h(x))^2$

$g'(x) = 2(h(x)).h'(x)$

$g'(0) = 2(h(0)).h'(0)$

$= 2f(2f(0) + 2).2$

$= 2f(0).2 = (-2).2 = -4$

For (Qs. No. 97 and 98):

97. (C): Given that $g(x) = \sin x + \cos x + 1$

$$\int_0^{\frac{\pi}{2}} \frac{dx}{g(x)} = \int_0^{\frac{\pi}{2}} \frac{1}{\sin x+\cos x+1}\,dx$$

$$= \int_0^{\frac{\pi}{2}} \frac{1}{\frac{2\tan\frac{x}{2}}{1+\tan^2\frac{x}{2}}+\frac{1-\tan^2\frac{x}{2}}{1+\tan^2\frac{x}{2}}+1}\,dx$$

$$= \int_0^{\frac{\pi}{2}} \frac{\sec^2\frac{x}{2}}{2\left(1+\tan\frac{x}{2}\right)}\,dx$$

Let, $1+\tan\frac{x}{2} = t$, $\frac{1}{2}\sec^2\frac{x}{2}\,dx = dt$

When, $x = \frac{\pi}{2}$,

then $t = 2$,

and when $x = 0$,

then $t = 1$,

$$= \int_1^2 \frac{1}{t}\,dt = [\ln t]_1^2$$

$$= \ln 2 - \ln 1 = \ln 2$$

98. (C): $I = \int_0^{\frac{\pi}{2}} \frac{f(x)}{g(x)}\,dx = \int_0^{\frac{\pi}{2}} \frac{\sin x}{\sin x+\cos x+1}\,dx$ ...(*i*)

$$I = \int_0^{\frac{\pi}{2}} \frac{\sin\left(\frac{\pi}{2}-x\right)}{\sin\left(\frac{\pi}{2}-x\right)+\cos\left(\frac{\pi}{2}-x\right)+1}\,dx$$

$$= \int_0^{\frac{\pi}{2}} \frac{\cos x}{\sin x+\cos x+1}\,dx \quad ...(ii)$$

Adding equation (*i*) and (*ii*), we get

$$2I = \int_0^{\frac{\pi}{2}} \frac{\sin x+\cos x}{\sin x+\cos x+1}\,dx$$

$$= \int_0^{\frac{\pi}{2}} \left(1-\frac{1}{\sin x+\cos x+1}\right)dx$$

$$= \int_0^{\frac{\pi}{2}} 1\,dx - \int_0^{\frac{\pi}{2}} \frac{1}{\sin x+\cos x+1}\,dx$$

$$= \int_0^{\frac{\pi}{2}} 1dx - \ln 2 \text{ (From solution 97)} = \frac{\pi}{2} - \ln 2$$

$$\therefore\ I = \frac{\pi}{4} - \frac{\ln 2}{2}$$

For (Qs. No. 99 and 100):

$$I = 2\int \frac{x^2-1}{\sqrt{x^2+1}}\,dx = 2\int\left(\frac{x^2+1}{\sqrt{x^2+1}}-\frac{2}{\sqrt{x^2+1}}\right)dx$$

$$= 2\int\left(\sqrt{x^2+1}-\frac{2}{\sqrt{x^2+1}}\right)dx$$

$$= 2\left(\frac{x}{2}\sqrt{x^2+1}+\frac{1}{2}\ln(x+\sqrt{x^2+1})\right)$$

$$-2\ln\left(x+\sqrt{x^2+1}\right)+C$$

$$= x\sqrt{x^2+1} - 3\ln\left(x+\sqrt{x^2+1}\right)+c$$

$$= U(x)\cdot V(x) - 3\ln\{U(x) + V(x)\} + C$$

So, $U(x) = x$ and $V(x) = \sqrt{x^2+1}$

99. (B): Now, $|U^2(x) - V^2(x)|$

$$= |x^2 - (x^2 + 1)| = |x^2 - x^2 - 1|$$
$$= |-1| = 1$$

100. (A): $U(x)\cdot V(x) = x\sqrt{x^2+1} = \sqrt{x^4+x^2}$

101. (D): Lines of regression of x on y

$$x - 3y + 4 = 0$$
$$\Rightarrow \quad x = 3y - 4 \Rightarrow b_{xy} = 3$$

Line of regression of y on x

$$2x - 7y + 8 = 0$$
$$\Rightarrow \quad y = \frac{2}{7}x + \frac{8}{7}$$
$$\Rightarrow \quad b_{yx} = \frac{2}{7}$$

Now, $b_{xy} + 7b_{yx} = 3 + 7\cdot\frac{2}{7} = 5$

102. (B): $\quad \text{Mean} = \dfrac{1+4+9+\ldots+n^2}{n}$

$$130 = \frac{n(n+1)(2n+1)}{6n}$$
$$\Rightarrow \quad 780 = 2n^2 + 3n + 1$$
$$\Rightarrow \quad 2n^2 + 3n - 779 = 0$$
$$\Rightarrow \quad 2n^2 + 41n - 38n - 779 = 0$$
$$\Rightarrow \quad n(2n + 41) - 19(2n + 41) = 0$$
$$\Rightarrow \quad (2n + 41)(n - 19) = 0$$
$$\Rightarrow \quad n = 19$$
$$\left(\because n = \frac{-41}{2} \text{ is not possible}\right)$$

103. (C): $\quad n(S) = {}^{10}C_3$

Favourable outcomes = (1, 2, 3), (2, 3, 4), (3, 4, 5), (4, 5, 6), (5, 6, 7), (6, 7, 8), (7, 8, 9), (8, 9, 10)

$$n(E) = 8$$
$$\therefore \quad P(E) = \frac{n(E)}{n(S)} = \frac{8}{{}^{10}C_3}$$
$$= \frac{8\times3\times2\times1}{10\times9\times8} = \frac{1}{15}$$

104. (C): Given that A, B and C are mutually exclusive and exhaustive events:

$\therefore \quad P(A) + P(B) + P(C) = 1 \quad \ldots(i)$

Also, $\quad 3P(B) = 4P(A)$

$$\Rightarrow \quad P(A) = \frac{3}{4}P(B)$$

and $\quad 3P(C) = 2P(B)$

$$\Rightarrow \quad P(C) = \frac{2}{3}P(B)$$

From (i), $\frac{3}{4}P(B) + P(B) + \frac{2}{3}P(B) = 1$

$$\Rightarrow \quad \frac{9P(B)+12P(B)+8P(B)}{12} = 1$$
$$\Rightarrow \quad \frac{29P(B)}{12} = 1$$
$$\Rightarrow \quad P(A) = \frac{3}{4}\times\frac{12}{29} = \frac{9}{29}$$

105. (C): Number on faces on die are 4, 4, 5, 5, 5 and 6.

$$\therefore \quad n(S) = 6$$
$$P(\text{getting 4 or 5}) = \frac{5}{6}$$

106. (A): Black = 2, yellow = 4 and white = 6

Total balls = 2 + 4 + 6 = 12

P(all three are of the same colour).

$$= \frac{2^3}{12^3} + \frac{4^3}{12^3} + \frac{6^3}{12^3} = \frac{1}{6}$$

107. (A): Here, $\quad P(A) = \frac{5}{6}, P(B) = \frac{4}{5}, P(C) = \frac{3}{4}$

and $\quad P(\bar{B}) = 1 - \frac{4}{5} = \frac{1}{5}$

$$\therefore \quad P(A\cap\bar{B}\cap C) = P(A)\cdot P(\bar{B})\cdot P(C)$$
$$= \frac{5}{6}\times\frac{1}{5}\times\frac{3}{4} = \frac{1}{8}$$

108. (A)

109. (B): $\quad n(S) = 100$

Numbers from 7 to 100 satisfy $x^2 + x > 50$

$$\therefore \quad n(E) = 100 - 6 = 94$$
$$P(E) = \frac{n(E)}{n(S)} = \frac{94}{100} = \frac{47}{50}$$

110. (B): Mean of 10 natural numbers

$$\bar{x} = \frac{1+2+3+\ldots+10}{10}$$
$$= \frac{10\times11}{2\times10} = 5.5$$

Mean deviation

$$= \frac{|1-5.5|+|2-5.5|+|3-5.5|+..+|10-5.5|}{10}$$

$$= \frac{4.5+3.5+2.5+1.5+0.5 +0.5+1.5+2.5+3.5+4.5}{10} = 2.5$$

111. (B): Given that, $\sum_{i=i}^{9} x_i^2 = 855$

$$\text{Variance } \sigma = \sum_{i=1}^{9} x_i^2 - (\text{mean})^2$$

$$= \frac{855}{9} - M^2$$

$$\Rightarrow \quad \sigma + M^2 = \frac{855}{9} = 95$$

112. (D): Given that, $\bar{x} = \frac{x_1 + x_2 + x_3 + \ldots + x_n}{n}$

$\Rightarrow x_1 + x_2 + x_3 + \ldots + x_n = n\bar{x}$

Mean when x_n is replaced by k

$$\text{New mean} = \frac{x_1 + x_2 + x_3 + \ldots + x_{n-1} + k}{n}$$

$$= \frac{n\bar{x} - x_n + k}{n}$$

113. (B): ∵ Fair coin is tossed till two heads occur in sucession.

∴ P(the number of tosses required is less than 6)

= P(HH) + P(THH) + P(TTHH) + P(TTTHH)

$$= \left(\frac{1}{2}\right)^2 + \left(\frac{1}{2}\right)^3 + \left(\frac{1}{2}\right)^4 + \left(\frac{1}{2}\right)^5$$

$$= \frac{\left(\frac{1}{2}\right)^2\left[1-\left(\frac{1}{2}\right)^4\right]}{1-\frac{1}{2}} = \frac{\frac{1}{4}\left[1-\frac{1}{16}\right]}{\frac{1}{2}}$$

$$= \frac{1}{4} \times \frac{15}{16} \times \frac{2}{1} = \frac{15}{32}$$

114. (B) **115. (D)**

116. (D): $n(S) = 6 \times 6 = 36$

Sum 9 = (3, 6), (4, 5), (5, 4), (6, 3)

Sum 10 = (4, 6), (5, 5), (6, 4)

$$\text{P(sum 9 or 10)} = \frac{7}{36}$$

$$\therefore \text{P(sum neither 9 nor 10)} = 1 - \frac{7}{36} = \frac{29}{36}$$

117. (A): Here, $n = 6$

p = P(suffering from disease)

$$= \frac{20}{100} = \frac{1}{5}$$

q = P(not suffering from disease)

$$= 1 - \frac{1}{5} = \frac{4}{5}$$

$$p(x \geq 4) = p(x = 4) + p(x = 5) + p(x = 6)$$

$$= {}^6C_4\left(\frac{1}{5}\right)^4\left(\frac{4}{5}\right)^2 + {}^6C_5\left(\frac{1}{5}\right)^5\left(\frac{4}{5}\right)^1 + {}^6C_6\left(\frac{1}{5}\right)^6$$

$$= \frac{6!}{4!2!} \times \frac{16}{5^6} + \frac{6!}{5!} \times \frac{4}{5^6} + \frac{1}{5^6}$$

$$= \frac{6.5.4!}{4!2 \times 1} \times \frac{16}{15625} + \frac{6.5!}{5!} \times \frac{4}{15625} + \frac{1}{15625}$$

$$= \frac{240+24+1}{15625} = \frac{265}{15625} = \frac{53}{3125}$$

118. (D): $n(S) = 6 \times 5 \times 4$

$n(E) = n$(one of the faces shown is an ace.)

$= 3(1 \times 5 \times 4) = 3 \times 5 \times 4$

$$P(E) = \frac{3 \times 5 \times 4}{6 \times 5 \times 4} = \frac{1}{2}$$

119. (A): Possible outcomes $x < y < z$

= (1, 2, 3) (1, 2, 4), (1, 2, 5), (1, 2, 6) (1, 3, 4) (1, 3, 5), (1, 3, 6), (1, 4, 5), (1, 4, 6), (1, 5, 6), (2, 3, 4),(2, 3, 5), (2, 3, 6), (2, 4, 5), (2, 4, 6), (2, 5, 6), (3, 4, 5), (3, 4, 6), (3,5, 6), (4, 5, 6)

Total possible outcomes = 20

120. (D): Given that means $\bar{x} = np = 6$ ...(*i*)

and $\text{SD} = \sqrt{npq} = \sqrt{2}$

$npq = 2$ ...(*ii*)

Dividing (*ii*) and (*i*), we get

$$\frac{npq}{np} = \frac{2}{6}$$

$$\Rightarrow \quad q = \frac{1}{3}$$

$$\therefore \quad p = 1 - q = 1 - \frac{1}{3} = \frac{2}{3}$$

$$n \times \frac{2}{3} = 6 \text{(from Eq. (i))}$$

$$n = 9$$

Previous Years' Paper

NATIONAL DEFENCE ACADEMY & NAVAL ACADEMY

NDA & NA — Entrance Exam, 2024 (I)

PAPER I : GENERAL ABILITY TEST

PART A : ENGLISH LANGUAGE

ANTONYMS

Directions (Qs. No. 1-5): *Each item in this section consists of a sentence with an underlined word followed by four words or groups of words. Select the option that is* ***opposite in meaning*** *to the underlined word and mark your response on the Answer Sheet accordingly.*

1. Mohan was living in a <u>deplorable</u> condition.
A. reprehensible B. opprobrious
C. despicable D. commendable

2. These exercises will <u>counteract</u> the effects of stress and tension.
A. exacerbate B. foil
C. thwart D. contravene

3. You have to <u>persevere</u> with difficult students.
A. give up B. persist
C. carry on D. stand firm

4. Their new colour scheme is <u>hideous</u>.
A. appalling B. beautiful
C. grotesque D. macabre

5. Everywhere they go, they <u>squander</u> their earnings.
A. fritter away B. splurge
C. squabble D. manage

CLOZE

Directions (Qs. No. 6-15): *In this section, there is a passage having some blank spaces, each blank space is followed by four individual words or group of words. Select a word or group of words you consider the most appropriate for filling the blank space, and indicate your response on the Answer Sheet accordingly.*

The Earth's climate is __**(6)**__ changing and evolving. Some of __**(7)**__ changes have been due to natural causes but others can be attributed to __**(8)**__ activities such as deforestation, emissions from industry and transport, etc., which have led to the __**(9)**__ of gases and aerosols in __**(10)**__ atmosphere. These gases are known as greenhouse gases because they trap heat and __**(11)**__ air temperatures near the ground, acting like a greenhouse on the surface of the __**(12)**__. In order to create and strengthen the scientific and analytical capacity __**(13)**__ assessment of climate change in the country, different studies under Climate Change Action Programme __**(14)**__. Many important bilateral and multilateral meetings and negotiations are held __**(15)**__ regular intervals.

6. A. passionately B. continually
C. deadly D. thoughtfully

7. A. these B. those
C. this D. that

8. A. practical B. geological
C. human D. animal

9. A. assimilation B. absolution
C. collection D. accumulation

10. A. an B. a
C. the D. no article

11. A. raise B. hike
C. rise D. balance

12. A. crust B. core
C. mantle D. planet

13. A. for B. of
C. in D. to

14. A. are developed B. are initiated
C. have developed D. have initiated

15. A. with B. at
C. in D. on

SENTENCE COMPLETION

Directions (Qs. No. 16-25): *Each of the following items features one part of a sentence, followed by four alternatives. Complete the sentence by choosing the correct alternative and mark your response on the Answer Sheet accordingly.*

16. He paused
A. with a few moments.
B. for a few moments.
C. by a few moments.
D. into a few moments.

17. Late at night, our car
A. broke down on the highway.
B. broke up on the highway.
C. broke into the highway.
D. broke out on the highway.

18. All the countries signed the treaty
A. beneath Germany and France.
B. except Germany and France.
C. among Germany and France.
D. during Germany and France.

19. I reminded her
A. to turn off the lights at night.
B. to call off the lights at night.
C. to drop off the lights at night.
D. to break off the lights at night.

20. They told us about the woman
A. whom lived next door.
B. which lived next door.
C. who lived next door.
D. whose lived next door.

21. I'll see you
A. at the end of February.
B. on the end of February.
C. along the end of February.
D. for the end of February.

22. I dislike films
A. who have sad endings.
B. that have sad endings.
C. whose have sad endings.
D. whom have sad endings.

23. The thieves denied
A. having stealing the money.
B. stealing the money.
C. had stolen the money.
D. having to steal the money.

24. Did you
A. drop out to see Sunita on your way home?
B. drop in to see Sunita on your way home?
C. drop behind to see Sunita on your way home?
D. drop away to see Sunita on your way home?

25. Would you like to
A. meeting her?
B. meet her?
C. met her?
D. meet with her?

IDIOMS AND PHRASES

Directions (Qs. No. 26-30): *Given below are some idioms/phrases followed by four alternative meanings to each. Select the most appropriate response from the options (A), (B), (C) or (D), and mark your response on the Answer Sheet accordingly.*

26. Be bad news
A. feelings of hate
B. someone who behaves in a dishonest way
C. someone who is considered undesirable
D. to be ill

27. Back to the drawing board
A. to draw comparisons
B. to be a member of planning group
C. to start planning again because the previous plan has failed
D. to be fast at understanding a situation

28. Be in the eye of the storm
A. to look at something quickly
B. to fail miserably at a sport
C. to see something that you do not want to see
D. to be in the midst of a controversy

29. Life in the fast lane
A. to lead a selfless life
B. to have a happy life without complaints
C. life without money or comforts
D. an exciting and eventful lifestyle

30. To pass the buck
A. to collect money from a group of people
B. to shift the responsibility of something to someone
C. to have a short conversation with someone
D. to have the credentials for a particular job

ORDERING OF WORDS IN A SENTENCE

Directions (Qs. No. 31-35): *Each of the following items in this section consists of a sentence, the parts of which have been jumbled as (P), (Q), (R) and (S). Rearrange the jumbled parts of the sentences into sequence and select* *the correct sequence as (A), (B), (C), and (D) given below and mark your response on the Answer Sheet accordingly.*

31. P. include basic freedoms
Q. the fundamental rights are
R. guaranteed to the individual
S. basic right and
A. QSPR B. QRSP
C. SQRP D. RQSP

32. P. for many millennia
Q. been in the making
R. of a historical process that has
S. the Indian nation is the product
A. SRQP B. SQPR
C. PRSQ D. RSQP

33. P. an epoch that was imbued
Q. for its people the start of
R. with a new vision
S. India's Independence represented
A. SQPR B. QRPS
C. SPQR D. RQSP

34. P. science and mathematics exhibition
Q. for a discussion on the forthcoming
R. to be present before the Principal
S. all students have been instructed
A. SQPR B. RPQS
C. SRQP D. QPRS

35. P. two bowlers and two batsmen respectively
Q. to the new team
R. with the selection of another player
S. the team now has
A. QPRS B. SQRP
C. RQSP D. RPSQ

WORD CLASSES

Directions (Qs. No. 36-40): *Each of the following sentences has an underlined word. Read the sentence carefully and find which word class the underlined word belongs to. Indicate your response on the Answer Sheet accordingly.*

36. You are most welcome to visit my humble abode.
A. Noun B. Adjective
C. Adverb D. Participle

37. The situation is beyond our control.
A. Adjective B. Adverb
C. Conjunction D. Preposition

38. I didn't tell him anything except that I needed the money.
A. Adjective B. Adverb
C. Preposition D. Conjunction

39. He dry-cleaned my coat nicely.
A. Adjective B. Adverb
C. Relative pronoun D. Conjunction

40. Would you like to buy this new item ?
A. Determiner B. Conjunction
C. Interjection D. Adjective

COMPREHENSION

Directions (Qs. No. 41-45): *Read the following passage carefully and answer the items based on it. You are required to select your answers based solely on the contents of the passage and the opinion of the author.*

The grouping or assemblage of plants, animals and microbes we observe when we study a natural forest, a grassland, a pond, a coral reef or some other undisturbed area, is referred to as the area's biota or biotic community. The plant portion of the biotic community includes all vegetation, from large trees down through to microscopic algae. Likewise, the animal portion includes everything from large mammals, birds, reptiles and amphibians through to earthworms, tiny insects and mites. Microbes encompass a large array of microscopic bacteria, fungi and protozoans. Thus, the biotic community comprises a plant community, an animal community and a microbial community.

The particular kind of biotic community found in a given area is, in large part, determined by abiotic factors such as the amount of water or moisture present, the temperature, the salinity, or the type of soil in the area. These abiotic factors both support and limit the particular community. For example, a relative lack of available moisture prevents the growth of most species of plants, but supports certain species, such as cacti; these kinds of areas are deserts. Land with plenty of available moisture and a suitable temperature supports forests. The presence of water is the major factor that sustains aquatic communities.

The first step in investigating a biotic community may be simply to catalogue all the species present. Species are the different kinds of plants, animals and microbes in the community. A given species includes all those individuals which have a strong similarity in appearance to one another and which are distinct in appearance from other such groups. Each species in a biotic community is represented by a certain population — that is, by a certain number of individuals that make up the interbreeding, reproducing group.

41. Which one of the following does **not** belong to the biotic community?
A. Water B. Human
C. Protozoa D. Bush

42. The nature of the biotic community largely depends on:
1. Biotic components
2. Abiotic components

Select the correct answer using the code given below:
A. 1 only
B. 2 only
C. Both 1 and 2
D. Neither 1 nor 2

43. Which of the following is not an abiotic factor?
A. Temperature
B. Humidity
C. Algae
D. Moisture

44. In the passage, the word 'aquatic community' refers to:
A. Biotic community inhabiting the land
B. Biotic community found in water
C. Biotic community found in the air
D. Assemblage of rain and moisture

45. Species are defined on the basis of:
A. Similarities only
B. Differences only
C. Both similarities and differences
D. None of the above

SYNONYMS

Directions (Qs. No. 46-50): *Each item in this section consists of a sentence with an underlined word followed by four words/group of words. Select the option that is nearest in meaning to the underlined word and mark your response on the Answer Sheet accordingly.*

46. The king's son was banished due to the political rivalry.
A. deported B. called back
C. accepted D. notified

47. He gave a dazzling performance at the opera.
A. brilliant B. dismal
C. pathetic D. puerile

48. She rebuffed all suggestions from her friends.
A. took B. rejected
C. criticized D. granted

49. He disowned his royal legacy and became a commoner.
A. accepted B. abandoned
C. allowed D. questioned

50. The public was sceptical about the new government policy.
A. hopeful B. anxious
C. doubtful D. expectant

PART B : GENERAL KNOWLEDGE

51. An infinite combination of resistors, each having resistance $R = 4\ \Omega$, is given below. What is the net resistance between the points A and B? (Each resistance is of equal value, $R = 4$)

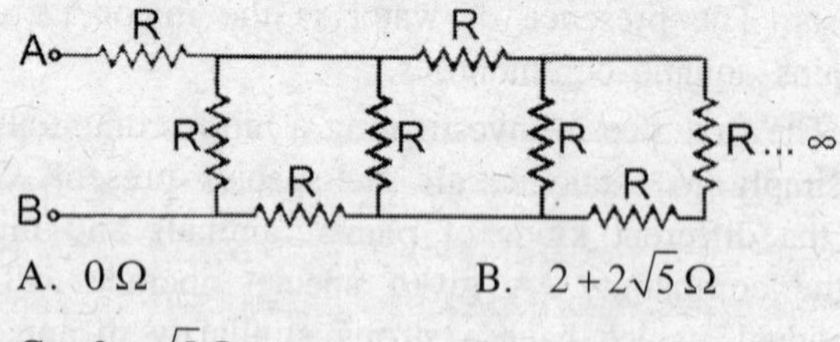

A. $0\ \Omega$ B. $2+2\sqrt{5}\ \Omega$
C. $2+\sqrt{5}\ \Omega$ D. $\infty\ \Omega$

52. An electrical circuit is given below. $V_1 = 1$ V and Resistance $R = 1000\ \Omega$.

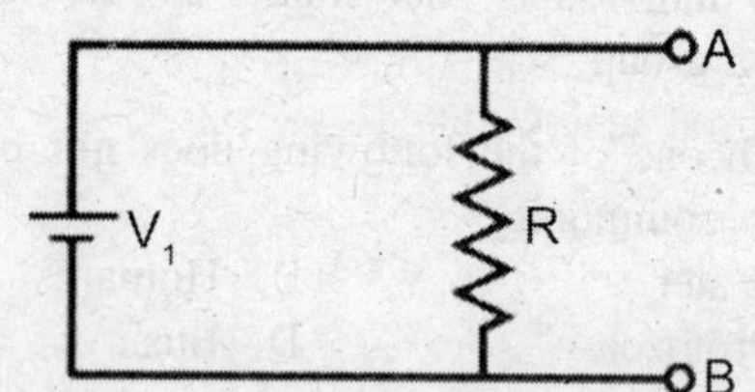

The current through the resistance R is very close to 1 mA and the voltage across point A and B, $V_{AB} = 1$ V. Now the circuit is changed to:

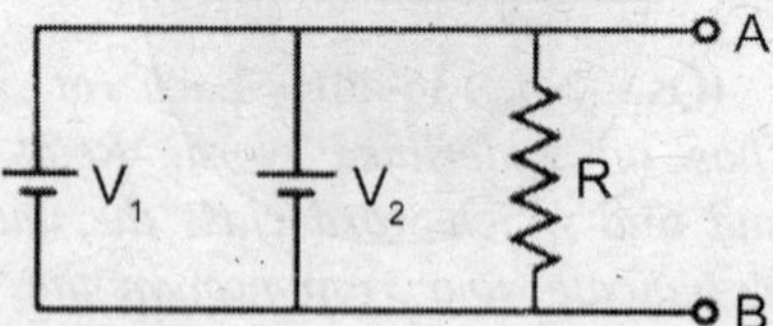

where value of $V_2 = 5$ V. The internal resistances of both the batteries are 0.1 Ω. The current through the resistance R is about:
A. 1.0 mA B. 1.2 mA
C. 3.0 mA D. 5.0 mA

53. If the current through an electrical machine running on direct current is 15 A and the machine runs for 10 minutes, the charge that passes through the machine during this time is:
A. 1.50 C B. 150 C
C. 900 C D. 9000 C

54. Which one of the following is the best shape of a solid metal rod to form the top end of a lighting conductor?

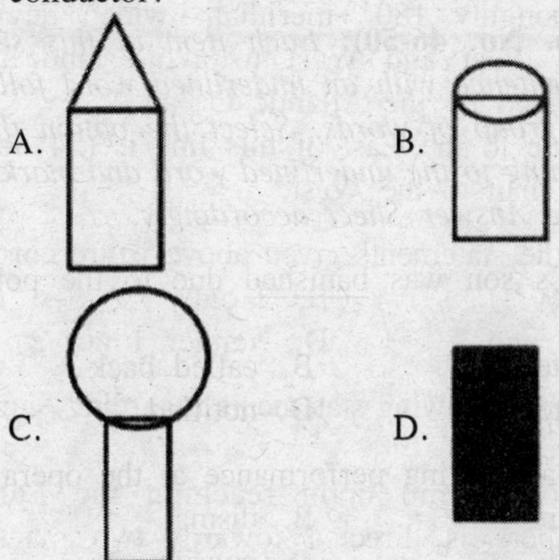

55. Which of the following forces is/are fundamental in nature?

1. Gravitational force
2. Electromagnetic forces
3. Strong and weak nuclear forces

Select the **correct** answer using the code given below:

A. 1 only　　B. 1 and 2 only
C. 2 and 3 only　　D. 1, 2 and 3

56. A spherical shell of outer radius R and inner radius R/2 contains a solid sphere of radius R/2 (see figure). The density of the material of the solid sphere is ρ and that of the shell is $\rho/2$. What is the average mass density of the larger sphere thus formed?

A. $3\rho/4$　　B. $9\rho/16$
C. $7\rho/8$　　D. $5\rho/8$

57. The human eye is like a camera that has a lens with:

A. fixed focal length and fixed asperture size.
B. variable focal length and fixed aperture size.
C. fixed focal length and variable aperture size.
D. variable focal length and variable aperture size.

58. Under Article 371A of the Constitution of India, with respect to which of the following item(s) the Acts of the Parliament of India shall ***not*** apply to the State of Nagaland, unless the Legislative Assembly of the State of Nagaland by a resolution so decides?

1. Religious or social practices of Nagas
2. Naga customary law and procedure
3. Ownership and transfer of land and its resources
4. Boundaries of Nagaland with other states

Select the answer using the code given below:

A. 1 only　　B. 2 and 3 only
C. 1, 2 and 3 only　　D. 1, 2, 3 and 4

59. Under Article 191 of the Constitution of India, a person shall be disqualified for being chosen as, and for being, a member of the Legislative Assembly or Legislative Council of a state if the person holds any office of profit under:

1. the Government of India.
2. any State Government.

Select the **correct** answer using the code given below:

A. 1 only　　B. 2 only
C. Both 1 and 2　　D. Neither 1 nor 2

60. Consider the following UN Declarations/Covenants:

1. Universal Declaration of Human Rights
2. Convention on the Elimination of All Forms of Discrimination Against Women
3. International Convenant of Economic, Social and Cultural Rights
4. Convention on Refugees

Which of the following is the **correct** chronological order (starting with the earliest) of the above?

A. 1, 4, 3, 2　　B. 1, 2, 3, 4
C. 1, 3, 2, 4　　D. 4, 1, 2, 3

61. Which one of the following statements regarding the objectives of the Second Five-Year Plan is ***not*** correct?

A. Development of the basic and heavy industry sector
B. Increase in national income to raise living standards
C. Expansion of the consumer goods sector
D. Expansion of employment opportunities

62. Consider the following statements about the emergence of urban centres in India from circa 6th Century BCE:

1. All of them developed away from the capitals of *mahajanpadas*.
2. Major towns were located along routes of communication.
3. Many were bustling centres of commercial, cultural and political activity.

How many of the above statements is/are correct?

A. 1　　B. 2
C. 3　　D. None

63. Consider the following statements about ancient Indian inscriptions:

1. The earliest inscriptions are in Sanskrit.
2. Kharosthi script, used in inscriptions in the north-west, was deciphered with the help of coins of Indo-Greek kings who ruled over the area.
3. Most of the inscriptions mention grand, unique events, and routine agricultural practices do not find mention.

How many of the above statements is/are correct?

A. 1 B. 2
C. 3 D. None

64. The relative atomic mass of boron (which exists in two isotopic forms ^{10}B and ^{11}B) is 10.81. What will be the abundance of ^{10}B and ^{11}B, respectively (consider a sample of 100 atoms)?

A. 19% and 81% B. 81% and 19%
C. 38% and 62% D. 62% and 38%

65. Which among the following are essential constituents of Portland cement?

A. Sand, lime, clay
B. Silica, alumina, lime
C. Silica, lime, graphite powder
D. Sand, graphene, clay

66. Litmus, a well-known acid-base indicator, is derived from:

A. Fungi B. Lichens
C. Bacteria D. Termite

67. What is the oxidation state of Vanadium in V_2O_5?

A. +2 B. +4
C. +3 D. +5

68. Match List-I with List-II and select the correct answer using the code given below the Lists:

List-I (*Allotrope of Carbon*)	**List-II (*Property*)**
(*a*) Graphite	(*i*) Thinnest and strongest material
(*b*) Diamond	(*ii*) Hardest natural substance
(*c*) Fullerene	(*iii*) Very light and strong material
(*d*) Graphene	(*iv*) Soft and slippery material

Code:

	(*a*)	(*b*)	(*c*)	(*d*)
A.	(*iv*)	(*ii*)	(*iii*)	(*i*)
B.	(*iv*)	(*iii*)	(*ii*)	(*i*)
C.	(*i*)	(*iii*)	(*ii*)	(*iv*)
D.	(*i*)	(*ii*)	(*iii*)	(*iv*)

69. Consider the following statements regarding the International Date Line:

1. It is roughly 180° meridian, which deviates slightly East and West to avoid land areas surrounded by the Atlantic Ocean.
2. The date to the East of this line is (24 hours) earlier than to the West.

Which of the statements given above is/are correct?

A. 1 only B. 2 only
C. Both 1 and 2 D. Neither 1 nor 2

70. Which of the following statements regarding 'aurora' is/are correct?

1. The solar wind upon reaching the Earth's atmosphere is directed towards two magnetic poles and a colourful display of lights is seen in the night sky.
2. The particles interact with the different gases of the atmosphere and each gas glows with a particular colour.
3. In April 2023, aurora was captured in the night sky in India by the Indian Astronomical Observatory at Hanle, Ladakh.

Select the answer using the code given below:

A. 1 only
B. 2 and 3 only
C. 1 and 3 only
D. 1, 2 and 3

71. Which of the following statements regarding *Barchan* is/are correct?

1. It is a crescent-shaped mound of sand, which is deposited by the wind blowing constantly from one direction in desert.
2. The windward side has a convex step slope with maximum height at the centre.
3. Two ends of *Barchan* are called horns and point opposite to the direction the wind blows.

Select the answer using the code given below:

A. 1 only
B. 1 and 2 only
C. 2 and 3 only
D. 1, 2 and 3

72. Which of the following statements regarding Regur soil is/are correct?

1. It is a light coloured, clayey and fertile soil.
2. It is developed on Deccan basaltic lava under hot and humid conditions.
3. Cotton is extensively cultivated in this soil.

Select the answer using the code given below:

A. 1 and 2 B. 2 and 3
C. 2 only D. 3 only

73. Which of the following statements regarding clouds is/are correct?

1. Clouds are classified on the basis of altitude and their form.
2. According to altitude they are classified as High, Middle and Low clouds.
3. Stratus, Nimbostratus and Stratocumulus are high clouds.

Select the answer using the code given below:

A. 1 only B. 1 and 2 only
C. 2 and 3 only D. 1, 2 and 3

74. Consider the following statements regarding 'fronts':

1. The movement of a front causes a slow change in weather in the area over which it moves.
2. Cold fronts are associated with thunderstorms.
3. Warm front is the boundary between an advancing mass of warm air where it is overriding and rising above a mass of colder air.

Which of the statements given above is/are correct?

A. 1 only B. 1 and 2 only
C. 2 and 3 only D. 1, 2 and 3

75. Consider the following statements regarding soils:

1. Soils having a very high content of sodium and calcium and pH of more than 7.0 are alkaline soils.
2. Black cotton soil had developed on the Deccan basaltic lava under hot and humid conditions.
3. Laterite soils are characterised by a deep weathered layer from which silica has been leached.

Which of the statements given above is/are correct?

A. 1 only B. 1 and 2 only
C. 2 and 3 only D. 1, 2 and 3

76. Consider the following characteristics of a grassland:

1. An extensive area of mid latitude grasslands are devoid of trees and shrubs.
2. The climate is characterised by hot summers, cold winters and relatively low rainfall occurring mainly in spring and summer.
3. In humid parts, grasses grow to a meter or more in height.

On the basis of the above characteristics select the correct grassland from the options given below:

A. Steppes B. Prairies
C. Savanna D. Pampas

77. Which of the following statements regarding animal cell membrane is correct?

A. They are composed of phospholipids only.
B. They are composed of proteins only.
C. They are composed of phospholipids and proteins only.
D. They are composed of phospholipids, proteins and cholesterol (lipid).

78. Which of the following is *not* a part of compounds microscope?

A. Mirror
B. Stage
C. Clip
D. Retina

79. Which one of the following is the correct sequence in increasing complexity?

A. Protein — Organism — Tissue — Organ
B. Protein — Organ — Tissue — Organism
C. Protein — Organism — Organ — Tissue
D. Protein — Tissue — Organ — Organism

80. Consider the following cell types:

1. Monocyte 2. Chondrocyte
3. Basophil 4. Lymphocyte

How many of the above belong to animal cell types?

A. 1 B. 2
C. 3 D. 4

81. In the human digestive system, which one among the following is the role of the pancreas?

A. Secretion of surfactants to break up lipid droplets
B. Storage and regulated release of bile
C. Secretion of lipase, amylase and protease
D. Neutralizing stomach acids

82. Consider the following statements:

1. DNA replication takes place when chromatin is opened up.
2. Chromatin organises itself into rod-shaped chromosomes before cell division.
3. Both prokaryotes and eukaryotes have the same process for cell division.

Which of the statements given above is/are correct?

A. 1 only B. 1 and 2 only
C. 1, 2 and 3 D. 3 only

83. A uniform meter scale of mass 0.24 kg is made of steel. It is kept on two wedges, W_1 and W_2, in a horizontal position. W_1 is at a distance of 0.2 m from one of its ends, while W_2 is at distance of 0.4 m from the other end. If the force on the scale is N_1 due to W_1 and N_2 due to W_2, then: (take $g = 10.0\ ms^{-2}$)

A. $N_1 = 1.6$ N and $N_2 = 0.8$ N
B. $N_1 = 0.8$ N and $N_2 = 1.6$ N
C. $N_1 = 0.6$ N and $N_2 = 1.8$ N
D. $N_1 = 1.8$ N and $N_2 = 0.6$ N

84. Escape speed from the Earth is close to 11.2 km s^{-1}. On another planet whose radius is half of the Earth's radius and whose mass density is four times that of the Earth, the escape speed in km s^{-1} will be close to:

A. 11.2
B. 15.8
C. 5.6
D. 7.9

85. Which one of the following does ***not*** apply to sound waves in fluids?

A. They transport energy
B. They need a medium to travel
C. They are transverse
D. They travel faster in liquids than in gases

86. A ball of 0.1 kg mass is dropped on a hard floor from a height of 0.45 m and rises to a height of 0.20 m. If it was in touch with the floor for 0.1 s, the net force it applied on the floor while bouncing is: (take the gravitational acceleration g = 10 m s^{-2})

A. 1.0 N
B. 6.0 N
C. 3.0 N
D. 5.0 N

87. Which one of the following statements regarding simple pendulum is correct?

Simple pendulum has a time period independent of amplitude:

A. only for small amplitudes because then the net force on its bob is independent of its displacement.
B. for any amplitude because the net force on the bob is always proportional to its displacement.
C. for any amplitude because the net force on the bob is independent of its displacement.
D. only for small amplitudes because then the net force on its bob is proportional to its displacement.

88. Which one of the following about different frictional force is correct?

A. Kinetic fricition > Static friction > Rolling friction
B. Static friction > Rolling fricition > Kinetic fricition
C. Static friction > Kinetic friction > Rolling friction
D. Static friction > Kinetic friction = Rolling friction

89. A metallic bob X of mass m is released from position A. It collides elastically with another identical bob Y placed at rest at position B on a horizontal frictionless table. The angle AOB is 30°.

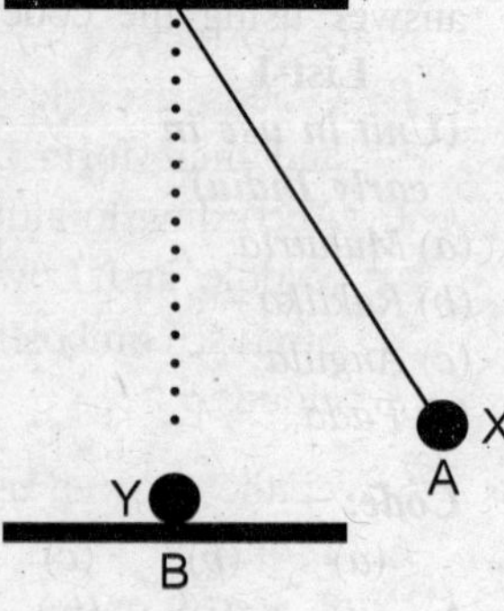

How high does the bob X rise immediately after the collision?

A. To the same height as that of position A on the other side in the same trajectory
B. To half the height as that of position A on the other side along the same trajectory
C. The same height at position A
D. It stops at position B

90. Consider the two statements given below:

Statement-1: Infrared waves are also called heat waves.

Statement-2: Water molecules readily absorb infrared waves.

Select the correct answer using the code given below:

A. Both the statements are individually true and Statement-2 is the correct explanation of Statement-1.
B. Both the statements are individually true, but Statement-2 is ***not*** the correct explanation of Statement-1.
C. Statement-1 is true, but Statement-2 is false.
D. Statement-2 is true, but Statement-1 is false.

91. Which of the following statements are correct?

1. British 'trade surplus' with India in the nineteenth century meant that the value of British exports to India was much higher than the value of British imports from India.
2. India played a crucial role in the late-nineteenth-century world economy by helping Britain balance its deficits.
3. Britain grew opium in India and exported it to China and therefore, for a while after the 1820s, opium became India's single largest export.
4. The nineteenth century saw export of Indian raw materials decline, and that of manufactured goods increase.

Select the answer using the code given below:

A. 1 and 2 only
B. 3 and 4 only
C. 1, 2, 3 and 4
D. 1, 2 and 3 only

92. Match List-I with List-II and select the correct answer using the code given below the Lists:

List-I *(Unit in use in early India)*	List-II *(Content)*
(a) Muhurta	*(i)* Measure of weight
(b) Raktika	*(ii)* Measure of time
(c) Angula	*(iii)* Metre of poetry
(d) Pada	*(iv)* Measure of length

Code:

	(a)	*(b)*	*(c)*	*(d)*
A.	*(ii)*	*(i)*	*(iv)*	*(iii)*
B.	*(ii)*	*(iv)*	*(i)*	*(iii)*
C.	*(iii)*	*(iv)*	*(i)*	*(ii)*
D.	*(iii)*	*(i)*	*(iv)*	*(ii)*

93. First coins in Indian history bearing the names and images of rulers were issued by the:

A. Mauryas B. Pushyabhutis
C. Guptas D. Indo-Greeks

94. Social theorists in the nineteenth and twentieth centuries emphasised the emergence of industrialisation, urbanisation, secularisation and bureaucratisation as hallmarks of:

A. Modernity B. Feudalism
C. Kingship D. Medievalism

95. Consider the following events:

1. Launch of Non-Cooperation Movement
2. All-India Khilafat Conference in Delhi
3. Passing of the Rowlatt Act
4. Jallianwala Bagh incident

Which one of the following is the correct chronological order of the given events (earliest to latest)?

A. 1, 2, 3, 4 B. 3, 4, 2, 1
C. 3, 2, 4, 1 D. 2, 3, 4, 1

96. Match List-I with List-II and select the correct answer using the code given below the Lists:

List-I *(System/Category)*	List-II *(Description)*
(a) Upari	*(i)* Peasants directly responsible for the payment of revenue
(b) Pattadar	*(ii)* Category of tenancy tenure held under the Marathas
(c) Mirasidar	*(iii)* Gifts of land or land revenue
(d) Inam lands	*(iv)* Co-parcenary title holder and designated revenue payer in southern India

Code:

	(a)	*(b)*	*(c)*	*(d)*
A.	*(ii)*	*(i)*	*(iv)*	*(iii)*
B.	*(ii)*	*(iv)*	*(i)*	*(iii)*
C.	*(iii)*	*(iv)*	*(i)*	*(ii)*
D.	*(iii)*	*(i)*	*(iv)*	*(ii)*

97. Which of the following statements about Vijayanagara king Krishnadevaraya's expeditions are correct?

1. In the early years of his reign he marched against the ruler of Orissa.
2. In 1520 CE, he captured the fort of Raichur from Ismail Adil Khan.
3. Krishnadevaraya restored Sultan Mahmud Shah to power and assumed the title of *Yavana-rajya-sthapan-acharya*.

Select the answer using the code given below:

A. 1 and 3 only B. 2 and 3 only
C. 1, 2 and 3 D. 1 and 2 only

98. Water gas is a mixture of:

A. CO_2 and H_2 B. CO and H_2
C. CO_2 and H_2O D. CO and H_2O

99. Human body works in the pH range of:

A. 6.8 – 7.2 B. 7.0 – 7.8
C. 6.5 – 7.5 D. 7.5 – 8.0

100. Which one among the following statements with reference to the properties of water is ***not*** correct?

A. The specific heat of water is abnormally high.
B. Latent heat of fusion of water is very low.
C. Density of water is higher than ice.
D. Pure water is a non-conductor of electricity.

101. Which one among the following compounds has a sweet and fruity smell?

A. Ethyl alcohol B. Acetic acid
C. Ethyl acetate D. Acetophenone

102. What is the coordination number of Na^+ and Cl^- ions in NaCl lattice?

A. 6, 1 B. 1, 6
C. 6, 6 D. 5, 5

103. Which one among the following is present in the nettle leaf hairs that causes burning pain?

A. Methanoic acid
B. Ethanoic acid
C. Benzoic acid
D. Acetic acid

104. Which one among the following is known as Milk of Magnesia?

A. Magnesium bicarbonate
B. Magnesium carbonate
C. Magnesium sulphate
D. Magnesium hydroxide

105. Soap with water forms:

A. Metallotropic liquid crystal
B. Thermotropic liquid crystal
C. Homogeneous solution
D. Lyotropic liquid crystal

106. Which among the following is the correct composition of Borax?

A. Sodium, Boron, Magnesium and Hydrogen
B. Sodium, Boron, Oxygen and Hydrogen
C. Potassium, Boron, Oxygen and Hydrogen
D. Sodium, Boron, Nitrogen and Hydrogen

107. Which one among the following oxides has the highest melting point?

A. Na_2O B. MgO
C. Fe_2O_3 D. CuO

108. Which of the following statements regarding neap tides is/are correct?

1. It occurs every 14-15 days, which coincides with the first and third quarter of the Moon.
2. This tide has a small tidal range because the gravitational forces of the Moon and the Sun are in quadrature.

Select the answer using the code given below:

A. 1 only B. 2 only
C. Both 1 and 2 D. Neither 1 nor 2

109. Which of the following statements regarding earthquakes is/are correct?

1. The point on the Earth's surface directly above the focus is called the epicentre of the earthquake.
2. Earthquakes generate Primary and Secondary waves that radiate outward from the earthquake focus.
3. Deep-focus earthquakes are likely to cause more damage than shallow-focus earthquakes.

Select the answer using the code given below:

A. 1 only B. 1 and 2 only
C. 2 and 3 only D. 1, 2 and 3

110. Which of the following statements regarding air temperature is/are correct?

1. Air temperature is measured at a standard height of 1.2 m (4.0 feet) above the ground surface.
2. The average rate of temperature decrease with height is termed as the environmental temperature lapse rate.

Select the answer using the code given below:

A. 1 only
B. 2 only
C. Both 1 and 2
D. Neither 1 nor 2

111. Which of the following statements regarding humidity is/are correct?

1. It is a ratio between the actual amount of water vapour present in the atmosphere and the maximum amount it can hold at a given temperature.
2. When the relative humidity is high, more water evaporates from the skin.
3. Higher the air temperature lower the relative humidity of the air.

Select the answer using the code given below:

A. 1 only B. 2 and 3 only
C. 1 and 3 only D. 1, 2 and 3

112. Which of the following statements regarding cyclones and anticyclones is/are correct?

1. In the Northern Hemisphere, cyclones rotate counter clockwise and anticyclones rotate clockwise.
2. Cyclones are often associated with cloudy or rainy weather, whereas anticyclones are often associated with fair weather.
3. In the Southern Hemisphere, the cyclonic spiral will be clockwise because the Coriolis force acts to the left.

Select the answer using the code given below:

A. 1 only
B. 1 and 2 only
C. 2 and 3 only
D. 1, 2 and 3

113. Identify the sea-port in India on the basis of the given characteristics:

1. It is more than a century old port on the west coast of India.
2. It is a natural harbour protected by a breakwater and also by a mole.
3. A deep draft channel of about 14 metres depth permits large vessels to enter the harbour.

Select the correct sea-port from the options given below:

A. Mormugao Port
B. Deendayal Port
C. Cochin Port
D. Jawaharlal Nehru Port

114. Identify the Iron and Steel Plant on the basis of the given characteristics:

1. It receives coal from Jharia and iron-ore from Sundargarh and Kendujhar.
2. Power for the electric furnaces is procured from Hirakund.
3. Water is obtained from Koel and Sankh rivers.

Select the correct Iron and Steel Plant from the options given below:

A. Bhilai Steel Plant
B. Durgapur Steel Plant
C. Rourkela Steel Plant
D. Bokaro Steel Plant

115. Which of the following statements regarding Earth's internal structure is/are correct?
1. The oceanic crust is heavier than the continental crust.
2. Most of the Earth's internal heat is contained within the mantle.
3. Large convective cells in the crust circulate heat and drive plate-tectonic processes.

Select the answer using the code given below:
A. 3 only
B. 1 and 2 only
C. 2 and 3 only
D. 1, 2 and 3

116. Which of the following statements regarding the given rivers is/are correct?
1. Tsangpo crosses over into India under the name of Dihang.
2. Godavari has the second largest river basin covering about 10 per cent of the area of India.
3. Rivers Chambal and Betwa are the important tributaries of river Ganga which join river Ganga directly in Uttar Pradesh.

Select the answer using the code given below:
A. 1 only B. 1 and 2 only
C. 2 and 3 only D. 1, 2 and 3

117. Which of the following statements regarding the World Climate Types and their relation with Inter Tropical Convergence Zone (ITCZ) is/are correct?
1. Tropical Wet Climate is one of the world's rainiest due to the dominance of the ITCZ over it.
2. Tropical Savanna Climate experiences a distinctive alternation of wet and dry seasons, caused chiefly by the seasonal shift in latitude of the subtropical highs and ITCZ.
3. The Tropical Monsoonal Climate experiences heavy rainfall as a consequence of the nearness of the ITCZ for much of the year.

Select the answer using the code given below:
A. 1 only B. 1 and 2 only
C. 2 and 3 only D. 1, 2 and 3

118. Which of the following statements regarding tropical cyclones is/are correct?
1. These storms develop during the summer and autumn in every tropical ocean except the South Atlantic and eastern South Pacific Oceans.
2. Tropical cyclones that occur in the North Atlantic and eastern North Pacific Oceans are known as typhoons.
3. Tropical cyclones that occur in the Indian and South Pacific Oceans are called cyclones.

Select the answer using the code given below:
A. 3 only B. 1 and 2 only
C. 1 and 3 only D. 1, 2 and 3

119. Identify the land biome on the basis of the given characteristics:
1. Their climates are characterised by high rainfall and temperatures that vary from cold to mild.
2. These forests contain primarily deciduous trees - including maple, oak, hickory and beechwood.
3. Raccoons, opossums, bats and squirrels are found in the trees.

Select the correct land biome from the options given below:
A. Tropical forest B. Temperate forest
C. Boreal forest D. Mediterranean forest

120. Leaves of most plants appear green because the chlorophyll present in it:
A. absorbs red and blue light while reflecting green light.
B. absorbs green light only.
C. absorbs green light while reflecting red and blue light.
D. reflects red light and absorbs blue and green light.

121. In most prokaryotes, the chromosome number is:
A. 4 B. 3
C. 2 D. 1

122. Bacterial DNA is referred to as naked because it is ***not*** associated with:
A. any scaffold B. proteins
C. ribozymes D. plasmid

123. Which one among the following cells produces antibodies against a foreign antigen?
A. Lymphocytes B. Erythrocytes
C. Eosinophils D. Platelets

124. If the block P as shown in the figure below were to be at rest, what should the magnitude of force F be?

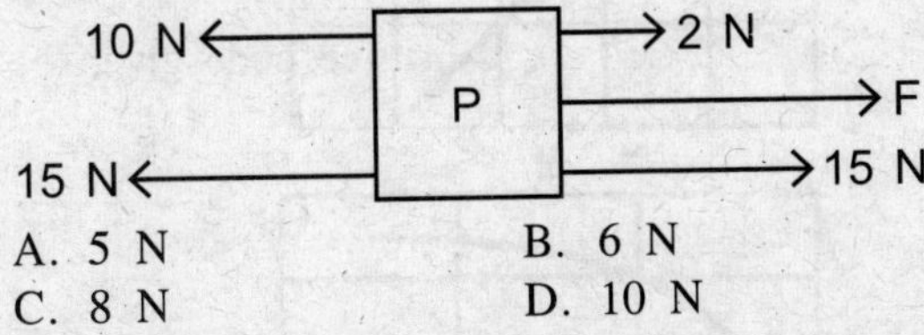

A. 5 N B. 6 N
C. 8 N D. 10 N

125. Of the following, which does ***not*** belong to a nuclear reactor?
A. A turbine
B. A heat exchanger
C. A mechanism to reduce CO_2 emission
D. A reaction chamber

126. Consider the following electric circuit:

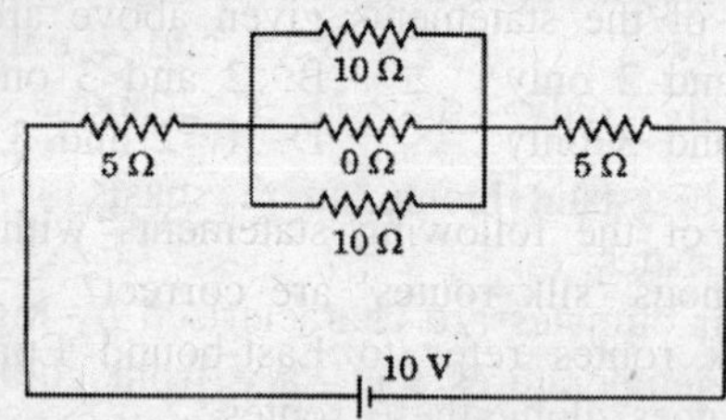

The current in the above electric circuit is:

A. 1 A
B. (10/15) A
C. 2 A
D. 1.5 A

127. A microscope may be a combination of:

A. two convex lenses.
B. a convex and a concave lens.
C. two concave lenses.
D. a convex lens and convex mirror.

128. For a human eye, where *u* is the distance of an object from the eye, *f* is the focal length of the lens and *v* is the distance of image from the eye, which is the correct schematic graph?

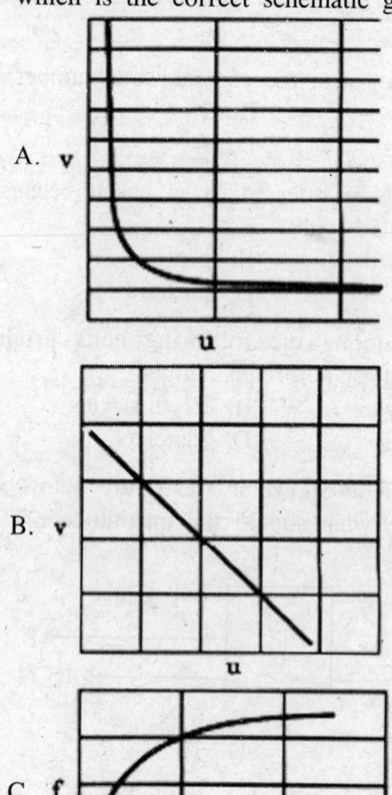

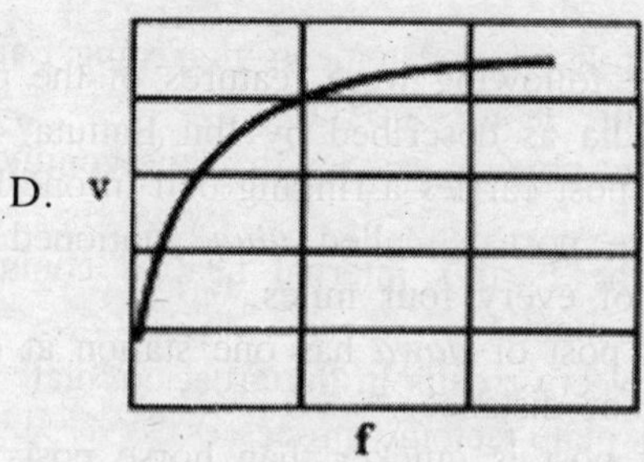

129. Which of the following statements with regard to the phenomenon of the primary rainbow formation by water droplets is/are correct?

1. It involves refraction and one internal reflection of sunlight.
2. It involves refraction of sunlight only.
3. It is formed as the inner bow.
4. It may involve more than one internal reflection as well as refraction of sunlight.

Select the answer using the code given below:

A. 1 only
B. 1 and 3
C. 3 and 4
D. 2 and 3

130. Which one of the following scientists mentioned that an electron in an atom could revolve in certain stable orbits without the emission of radiant energy?

A. Ernest Rutherford
B. J.J. Thomson
C. Niels Bohr
D. Albert Einstein

131. LIGO experiment confirmed one of the predictions of:

A. String theory
B. Special theory of relativity
C. Quantum mechanics
D. General theory of relativity

132. A block of mass 2 kg, moving with the initial speed of 3 m/s comes to rest on a rough horizontal surface after travelling a distance of 3 m. The magnitude of the frictional force is:

A. 9 N
B. 3 N
C. 18 N
D. 1 N

133. Which one of the following is primarily responsible for conduction of current in a metal?

A. Bound electrons
B. Free electrons
C. Both bound and free electrons
D. Ions

134. Which of the following were features of the postal system of India as described by Ibn Battuta?

1. The foot post carries a ringing bell in one hand.
2. The horse post is called *uluq,* stationed at a distance of every four miles.
3. The foot post or *dawa* has one station at every four *kos* of distance.
4. The foot post is quicker than horse post.

Select the **correct** answer using the code given below:

A. 1, 2 and 4 B. 1 and 2 only
C. 2 and 3 only D. 1, 3 and 4

135. Which one of the following texts is a commentary written by Chakrapanidatta (11 Century CE from Bengal) on the *Sushrut Samhita*?

A. *Sabdachandrika* B. *Bhanumati*
C. *Nitiratnakara* D. *Lohasarvasava*

136. Consider the following statements about the arrival of tobacco in India:

1. Tobacco plant arrived first in the Deccan.
2. Tobacco spread to northern India in the early years of the seventeenth century.

Which of the statements given above is/are correct?

A. 1 only B. 2 only
C. Both 1 and 2 D. Neither 1 nor 2

137. Consider the following Women's Associations and their important associates in early twentieth century India:

1. Women's Indian Association of 1917 : Margaret Cousins
2. National Council of Women in India of 1925 : Sarala Devi Chaudhurani
3. Bharat Stree Mahamandal of 1910 : Lady Meherbai Tata

Which of the above pairs is/are correctly matched?

A. 1, 2 and 3 B. 2 and 3 only
C. 1 and 2 only D. 1 only

138. Consider the following statements about the issue of separate electorate during the early decades of the twentieth century in India as a means to secure adequate representation for the deprived social categories in the absence of universal adult franchise:

1. The All India Depressed Classes Association of M.C. Rajah was staunchly in favour of joint electorate.
2. The All India Depressed Classes Leaders' Conference demanded separate electorate.
3. The Communal Award in September 1932 recognised the right to separate electorate for the 'untouchables'.

Which of the statements given above are correct?

A. 1 and 2 only B. 2 and 3 only
C. 1 and 3 only D. 1, 2 and 3

139. Which of the following statements with regard to the famous 'silk routes' are correct?

1. Silk routes refer to East-bound European silk cargoes along these routes.
2. There were several silk routes, over land and by sea, joining together vast regions of Asia with Europe and northern Africa.
3. They are known to have existed since before the Christian Era and thrived almost till the fifteenth century.
4. Besides silk, Chinese pottery, textiles and spices from India and South-east Asia travelled the same route.

Select the answer using the code given below:

A. 1, 2 and 3 B. 1, 3 and 4
C. 2, 3 and 4 D. 1, 2 and 4

140. Consider the following statements about Ajanta paintings:

1. The surface of the rock was coated with clay mixed with rice husk and gum and a coat of lime was applied over this.
2. The outline drawing was done first on the lime coating and colours were added subsequently.

Which of the statements given above is/are correct?

A. 1 only
B. 2 only
C. Both 1 and 2
D. Neither 1 nor 2

141. Which of the following statements with regard to the Square Kilometer Array (SKA) project is/are correct?

1. SKA is a state of the art, mega science international facility to build the world's biggest and most sensitive radio telescope for addressing a wide variety of cutting-edge science goals.
2. The Government of India has accorded its approval for India's participation in the international mega science project.

Select the answer using the code given below:

A. 1 only B. 2 only
C. Both 1 and 2 D. Neither 1 nor 2

142. Exercise Desert Cyclone is a joint military exercise between India and:

A. Kuwait
B. Saudi Arabia
C. United Arab Emirates
D. Oman

143. Which of the following statements with regard to the constitution of Finance Commission is/are correct?

1. The Government of India has recently constituted the Sixteenth Finance Commission under the Chairmanship of Dr. Arvind Panagariya.
2. Finance Commission is constituted in pursuance to Article 263 of the Constitution of India.

Select the answer using the code given below:

A. 1 only B. 2 only
C. Both 1 and 2 D. Neither 1 nor 2

144. Recently the Ministry of Environment, Forest and Climate Change has submitted three nominations from India for Wetland City Accreditation (WCA) under the Ramsar Convention on Wetlands. Which one among the following cities is ***not*** one among them?

A. Indore B. Bhopal
C. Udaipur D. Jodhpur

145. Which of the following statements is/are correct?

1. In India, 12th March is celebrated as the National Youth Day.
2. National Youth Day is celebrated to commemorate the birth anniversary of Swami Vivekananda.

Select the answer using the code given below:

A. 1 only B. 2 only
C. Both 1 and 2 D. Neither 1 nor 2

146. Consider the following statements about *INS Sagardhwani*:

1. It is an oceanographic research vessel of Naval Physical and Oceanographic Laboratory (NPOL) of DRDO.
2. Recently it embarked on the Sagar Maitri Mission-4 to establish long-term scientific partnerships with Indian Ocean Rim countries in Ocean Research and Development.

Which of the statements given above is/are correct?

A. 1 only B. 2 only
C. Both 1 and 2 D. Neither 1 nor 2

147. Who among the following is the Chairman of the Committee constituted by the Government of India to examine the issue of holding simultaneous elections in the country and to make recommendations thereon?

A. Union Home Minister Shri Amit Shah
B. Chief Justice of India Shri Dhananjaya Yeshwant Chandrachud
C. Former President of India Shri Ram Nath Kovind
D. Chief Election Commissioner of India Shri Rajiv Kumar

148. In January 2024, India's first all-girls' Sainik School was inaugurated at:

A. Bhopal B. Kohima
C. Vrindavan D. Namsai

149. In February 2024, Government of India has decided to scrap the Free Movement Regime (FMR) between India and:

A. Myanmar B. Bhutan
C. Bangladesh D. Nepal

150. Who among the following is the author of the book "*Why Bharat Matters*"?

A. L.K. Advani B. S. Jaishankar
C. Mohan Bhagwat D. Pranab Mukherjee

PAPER II : MATHEMATICS

1. Let A and B be matrices of order 3 × 3. If $|A| = \frac{1}{2\sqrt{2}}$ and $|B| = \frac{1}{729}$, then what is the value of $|2B(\text{adj}(3A))|$?

A. 27 B. $\frac{27}{2\sqrt{2}}$
C. $\frac{27}{2}$ D. 1

2. If z is any complex number and $iz^3 + z^2 - z + i = 0$, where $i = \sqrt{-1}$, then what is the value of $(|z| + 1)^2$?

A. 1 B. 4
C. 81 D. 121

3. What is the sum of all four digit numbers formed by using all digits 0, 1, 4, 5 without repetition of digits?

A. 44440 B. 46460
C. 46440 D. 64440

4. If x, y and z are the cube roots of unity, then what is the value of $xy + yz + zx$?

A. 0 B. 1
C. 2 D. 3

5. A man has 7 relatives (4 women and 3 men). His wife also has 7 relatives (3 women and 4 men). In how many ways can they invite 3 women and 3 men so that 3 of them are man's relatives and 3 of them are his wife's relatives?

A. 340 B. 484
C. 485 D. 469

6. A triangle PQR is such that 3 points lie on the side PQ, 4 points on QR and 5 points on RP respectively. Triangles are constructed using these points as vertices. What is the number of triangles so formed?

A. 205 B. 206
C. 215 D. 220

7. If $\log_b a = p$, $\log_d c = 2p$ and $\log_f e = 3p$, then what is $(ace)^{\frac{1}{p}}$ equal to?

A. bd^2f^3 B. bdf
C. b^3d^2f D. $b^2d^2f^2$

8. If $-\sqrt{2}$ and $\sqrt{3}$ are roots of the equation $a_0 + a_1x + a_2x^2 + a_3x^3 + x^4 = 0$ where a_0, a_1, a_2, a_3 are integers, then which one of the following is correct?

A. $a_2 = a_3 = 0$ B. $a_2 = 0$ and $a_3 = -5$
C. $a_0 = 6$, $a_3 = 0$ D. $a_1 = 0$ and $a_2 = 5$

9. Let z_1 and z_2 be two complex numbers such that $\left|\frac{z_1+z_2}{z_1-z_2}\right| = 1$, then what is $\text{Re}\left(\frac{z_1}{z_2}\right) + 1$ equal to?

A. –1 B. 0
C. 1 D. 5

10. If $26! = {}_n8^k$, where k and n are positive integers, then what is the maximum value of k?

A. 6 B. 7
C. 8 D. 9

11. Consider the following statements in respect of two non-singular matrices A and B of the same order n:

1. adj(AB) = (adjA)(adjB)
2. adj(AB) = adj(BA)
3. (AB)adj(AB) – $|AB|I_n$ is a null matrix of order n

How many of the above statements are correct?

A. None B. Only one statement
C. Only two statements D. All three statements

12. Consider the following statements in respect of a non-singular matrix A of order n:

1. $A(\text{adj}A^T) = A(\text{adj}A)^T$
2. If $A^2 = A$, then A is identity matrix of order n
3. If $A^3 = A$, then A is identity matrix of order n

Which of the statements given above are correct?

A. 1 and 2 only B. 2 and 3 only
C. 1 and 3 only D. 1, 2 and 3

13. How many four-digit natural numbers are there such that all of the digits are even?

A. 625 B. 500
C. 400 D. 256

14. If $\omega \neq 1$ is a cube root of unity, then what are the solution of $(z - 100)^3 + 1000 = 0$?

A. $10(1 - \omega)$, $10(10 - \omega^2)$, 100
B. $10(10 - \omega)$, $10(10 - \omega^2)$, 90
C. $10(1 - \omega)$, $10(10 - \omega^2)$, 1000
D. $(1 + \omega)$, $(10 + \omega^2)$, – 1

15. What is $(1 + i)^4 + (1 - i)^4$ equal to, where $i = \sqrt{-1}$?

A. 4 B. 0
C. –4 D. –8

16. Consider the following statements in respect of a skew-symmetric matrix A of order 3:

1. All diagonal elements are zero.
2. The sum of all the diagonal elements of the matrix is zero.
3. A is orthogonal matrix.

Which of the statements given above are correct?

A. 1 and 2 only
B. 2 and 3 only
C. 1 and 3 only
D. 1, 2 and 3

17. Four digit numbers are formed by using the digits 1, 2, 3, 5 without repetition of digits. How many of them are divisible by 4?

A. 120 B. 24
C. 12 D. 6

18. What is the remainder when 2^{120} is divided by 7?

A. 1 B. 3
C. 5 D. 6

19. For what value of n is determinant

$$\begin{vmatrix} C(9,4) & C(9,3) & C(10,n-2) \\ C(11,6) & C(11,5) & C(12,n) \\ C(m,7) & C(m,6) & C(m+1,n+1) \end{vmatrix} = 0$$

for every $m > n$?

A. 4 B. 5
C. 6 D. 7

20. If ABC is a triangle, then what is the value of the determinant $\begin{vmatrix} \cos C & \sin B & 0 \\ \tan A & 0 & \sin B \\ 0 & \tan(B+C) & \cos C \end{vmatrix}$?

A. –1 B. 0
C. 1 D. 3

21. What is the number of different matrices, each having 4 entries that can be formed using 1, 2, 3, 4 (repetition is allowed)?

A. 72 B. 216
C. 254 D. 768

22. Let A = $\{x \in R: -1 < x < 1\}$. Which of the following is/are bijective functions from A to itself?

1. $f(x) = x|x|$
2. $g(x) = \cos(\pi x)$

Select the correct answer using the code given below:

A. 1 only B. 2 only
C. Both 1 and 2 D. Neither 1 nor 2

23. Let R be a relation on the open interval (–1, 1) and is given by R = $\{(x, y) : |x + y| < 2\}$. Then which one of the following is correct?

A. R is reflexive but neither symmetric nor transitive
B. R is reflexive and symmetric but not transitive
C. R is reflexive and transitive but not symmetric
D. R is an equivalence relation

24. For any three non-empty sets A, B, C what is $(A \cup B) - \{(A - B) \cup (B - A) \cup (A \cap B)\}$ equal to?

A. Null set B. A
C. B D. $(A \cup B) - (A \cap B)$

25. If a, b, c are the sides of triangle ABC, then what is $\begin{vmatrix} a^2 & b\sin A & c\sin A \\ b\sin A & 1 & \cos A \\ c\sin A & \cos A & 1 \end{vmatrix}$ equal to?

A. Zero
B. Area of triangle
C. Perimeter of triangle
D. $a^2 + b^2 + c^2$

26. If a, b, c are in AP; b, c, d are in GP; c, d, e are in HP, then which of the following is/are correct?

1. a, c and e are in GP
2. $\frac{1}{a}, \frac{1}{c}, \frac{1}{e}$ are in GP

Select the correct answer using the code given below:

A. 1 only B. 2 only
C. Both 1 and 2 D. Neither 1 nor 2

27. What is the number of solutions of $\log_4(x - 1) = \log_2(x - 3)$?

A. Zero B. One
C. Two D. Three

28. For $x \geq y > 1$, let $\log_x\left(\frac{x}{y}\right) + \log_y\left(\frac{y}{x}\right) = k$, then the value of k can never be equal to:

A. –1 B. $-\frac{1}{2}$
C. 0 D. 1

29. If $A = \begin{bmatrix} \sin 2\theta & 2\sin^2\theta - 1 & 0 \\ \cos 2\theta & 2\sin\theta\cos\theta & 0 \\ 0 & 0 & 1 \end{bmatrix}$, then which of the following statements is/are correct?

1. $A^{-1} = \text{adj}A$
2. A is skew-symmetric matrix
3. $A^{-1} = A^T$

Select the correct answer using the code given below:

A. 1 only B. 1 and 2
C. 1 and 3 D. 2 and 3

30. What is the coefficient of x^{10} in the expansion of $(1-x^2)^{20}\left(2-x^2-\frac{1}{x^2}\right)^{-5}$?

A. –1
B. 1
C. 10
D. Coefficient of x^{10} does not exist

31. If the 4th term in the expansion of $\left(mx+\frac{1}{x}\right)^n$ is $\frac{5}{2}$, then that is the value of mn?

A. –3 B. 3
C. 6 D. 12

32. If a, b and c ($a > 0$, $c > 0$) are in GP, then consider the following in respect of the equation $ax^2 + bx + c = 0$:

1. The equation has imaginary roots.
2. The ratio of the roots of the equation is 1 : ω where ω is a cube root of unity.
3. The product of roots of the equation is $\left(\frac{b^2}{a^2}\right)$.

Which of the statements given above are correct?

A. 1 and 2 only
B. 2 and 3 only
C. 1 and 3 only
D. 1, 2 and 3

33. If $x^2 + mx + n$ is an integer for all integral values of x, then which of the following is/are correct?

1. m must be an integer
2. n must be an integer

Select the correct answer using the code given below:

A. 1 only
B. 2 only
C. Both 1 and 2
D. Neither 1 nor 2

34. In a binomial expansion of $(x + y)^{2n+1} (x - y)^{2n+1}$, the sum of middle terms is zero. What is the value of $\left(\frac{x^2}{y^2}\right)$?

A. 1 B. 2
C. 4 D. 8

35. Let A = {1, 2, 3, 4, 5} and B = {6, 7}. What is the number of onto functions from A to B?

A. 10 B. 20
C. 30 D. 32

36. What is $\frac{\sqrt{3}\cos 10° - \sin 10°}{\sin 25° \cos 25°}$ equal to?

A. 1 B. $\sqrt{3}$
C. 2 D. 4

37. What is (sin 9° – cos 9°) equal to?

A. $-\frac{\sqrt{5-\sqrt{5}}}{2}$ B. $-\frac{\sqrt{5-\sqrt{3}}}{2}$
C. $\frac{\sqrt{5-\sqrt{5}}}{2}$ D. $\frac{\sqrt{5-\sqrt{5}}}{4}$

38. If in a triangle ABC, $\sin^3 A + \sin^3 B + \sin^3 C = 3 \sin A \sin B \sin C$, then what is the value of the determinant $\begin{vmatrix} a & b & c \\ b & c & a \\ c & a & b \end{vmatrix}$; where a, b, c are sides of the triangle?

A. $a + b + c$
B. $ab + bc + ca$
C. $(a + b)(b + c)(c + a)$
D. 0

39. If $\cos^{-1} x = \sin^{-1} x$, then which one of the following is correct?

A. $x = 1$ B. $x = \frac{1}{2}$
C. $x = \frac{1}{\sqrt{2}}$ D. $x = \frac{1}{\sqrt{3}}$

40. What is the number of solutions of $(\sin\theta - \cos\theta)^2 = 2$ where $-\pi < \theta < \pi$?

A. Only one B. Only two
C. Four D. No solution

41. ABC is a triangle such that angle C = 60°, then what is $\frac{\cos A + \cos B}{\cos\left(\frac{A-B}{2}\right)}$ equal to?

A. 2 B. $\sqrt{2}$
C. 1 D. $\frac{1}{\sqrt{2}}$

42. What is $\sqrt{15 + \cot^2\left(\frac{\pi}{4} - 2\cot^{-1} 3\right)}$ equal to?

A. 1 B. 7
C. 8 D. 16

43. What is the value of sin 10° · sin 50° + sin 50°. sin 250° + sin 250° · sin 10° equal to?

A. $-\frac{1}{4}$ B. $-\frac{3}{4}$
C. $\frac{3\sin 10°}{4}$ D. $-\frac{3\cos 10°}{4}$

44. What is $\tan^{-1}\left(\frac{a}{b}\right) - \tan^{-1}\left(\frac{a-b}{a+b}\right)$ equal to?

A. $-\frac{\pi}{4}$ B. $\frac{\pi}{4}$
C. $\tan^{-1}\left(\frac{a^2-b^2}{a^2+b^2}\right)$ D. $\tan^{-1}\left(\frac{2ab}{a^2+b^2}\right)$

45. Under which one of the following conditions does the equation $(\cos\beta - 1)x^2 + (\cos\beta)x + \sin\beta = 0$ in x have a real root for $\beta \in [0, \pi]$?

A. $1 - \cos\beta < 0$ B. $1 - \cos\beta \le 0$
C. $1 - \cos\beta > 0$ D. $1 - \cos\beta \ge 0$

46. In a triangle ABC, AB = 16 cm, BC = 63 cm and AC = 65 cm. What is the value of cos 2A + cos 2B + cos 2C?

A. –1 B. 0
C. 1 D. $\frac{76}{65}$

47. If $f(\theta) = \frac{1}{1 + \tan\theta}$ and $\alpha + \beta = \frac{5\pi}{4}$, then what is the value of $f(\alpha)\, f(\beta)$?

A. $-\frac{1}{2}$ B. $\frac{1}{2}$
C. 1 D. 2

48. If tan α and tan β are the roots of the equation $x^2 - 6x + 8 = 0$, then what is the value of $\cos(2\alpha + 2\beta)$?

A. $\frac{13}{75}$ B. $\frac{13}{85}$
C. $\frac{17}{85}$ D. $\frac{19}{85}$

49. What is the value of tan 65° + 2 tan 45° – 2 tan 40° – tan 25°?

A. 0 B. 1
C. 2 D. 4

50. Consider the following statements:

1. In a triangle ABC, if cot A · cot B · cot C > 0, then the triangle is an acute angled triangle.
2. In a triangle ABC, if tan A · tan B · tan C > 0, the triangle is an obtuse angled triangle.

Which of the statements given above is/are correct?

A. 1 only B. 2 only
C. Both 1 and 2 D. Neither 1 nor 2

51. If (a, b) is the centre and c is the radius of the circle $x^2 + y^2 + 2x + 6y + 1 = 0$, then what is the value of $a^2 + b^2 + c^2$?

A. 19 B. 18
C. 17 D. 11

52. If (1, –1, 2) and (2, 1, –1) are the end points of a diameter of a sphere $x^2 + y^2 + z^2 + 2ux + 2vy + 2wz - 1 = 0$, then what is $u + v + w$ equal to?

A. –2 B. –1
C. 1 D. 2

53. The number of points represented by the equation $x = 5$ on the xy-plane is:

A. Zero B. One
C. Two D. Infinitely many

54. If $<l, m, n>$ are the direction cosines of a normal to the plane $2x - 3y + 6z + 4 = 0$, then what is the value of $49(7l^2 + m^2 - n^2)$?

A. 0 B. 1
C. 3 D. 71

55. A line through (1, –1, 2) with direction ratios <3, 2, 2> meets the plane $x + 2y + 3z = 18$. What is the point of intersection of line and plane?

A. (4, 4, 1) B. (2, 4, 1)
C. (4, 1, 4) D. (3, 4, 7)

56. If p is the perpendicular distance from origin to the plane passing through (1, 0, 0), (0, 1, 0) and (0, 0, 1), then what is $3p^2$ equal to?

A. 4 B. 3
C. 2 D. 1

57. If a direction cosines $<l, m, n>$ of a line are connected by relation $l + 2m + n = 0$, $2l - 2m + 3n = 0$, then what is the value of $l^2 + m^2 - n^2$?

A. $\frac{1}{101}$ B. $\frac{29}{101}$
C. $\frac{41}{101}$ D. $\frac{92}{101}$

58. If the variable line passes through the point of intersection of the lines $x + 2y - 1 = 0$ and $2x - y - 1 = 0$ and meets the coordinate axes in A and B, then what is the locus of the mid-point of AB?

A. $3x + y = 10xy$
B. $x + 3y = 10xy$
C. $3x + y = 10$
D. $x + 3y = 10$

59. What is the equation to the straight line passing through the point $(-\sin\theta, \cos\theta)$ and perpendicular to the line $x\cos\theta + y\sin\theta = 9$?

A. $x\sin\theta - y\cos\theta - 1 = 0$
B. $x\sin\theta - y\cos\theta + 1 = 0$
C. $x\sin\theta - y\cos\theta = 0$
D. $x\cos\theta - y\sin\theta + 1 = 0$

60. Two points P and Q lie on line $y = 2x + 3$. These two points P and Q are at a distance 2 units from another point R(1, 5). What are the coordinates of the points P and Q?

A. $\left(1+\frac{2}{\sqrt{5}}, 5+\frac{4}{\sqrt{5}}\right), \left(1-\frac{2}{\sqrt{5}}, 5-\frac{4}{\sqrt{5}}\right)$

B. $\left(3+\frac{2}{\sqrt{5}}, 5+\frac{4}{\sqrt{5}}\right), \left(-1-\frac{2}{\sqrt{5}}, 5-\frac{4}{\sqrt{5}}\right)$

C. $\left(1-\frac{2}{\sqrt{5}}, 5+\frac{4}{\sqrt{5}}\right), \left(1+\frac{2}{\sqrt{5}}, 5-\frac{4}{\sqrt{5}}\right)$

D. $\left(3-\frac{2}{\sqrt{5}}, 5+\frac{4}{\sqrt{5}}\right), \left(-1+\frac{2}{\sqrt{5}}, 5-\frac{4}{\sqrt{5}}\right)$

61. If two sides of a square lie on the lines $2x + y - 3 = 0$ and $4x + 2y + 5 = 0$, then what is the area of the square in square units?

A. 6.05 B. 6.15
C. 6.25 D. 6.35

62. ABC is a triangle with A(3, 5). The mid-points of sides AB, AC are at (–1, 2), (6, 4) respectively. What are the coordinates of centroid of the triangle ABC?

A. $\left(\frac{8}{3}, \frac{11}{3}\right)$ B. $\left(\frac{7}{3}, \frac{7}{3}\right)$
C. $\left(2, \frac{8}{3}\right)$ D. $\left(\frac{8}{3}, 2\right)$

63. ABC is an acute angled isosceles triangle. Two equal sides AB and AC lie on the lines $7x - y - 3 = 0$ and $x + y - 5 = 0$. If θ is one of the equal angles, then what is $\cot\theta$ equal to?

A. $\frac{1}{3}$ B. $\frac{1}{2}$
C. $\frac{2}{3}$ D. 2

64. In the parabola $y^2 = 8x$, the focal distance of a point P lying on it is 8 units. Which of the following statements is/are correct?

1. The coordinates of P can be $\left(6, 4\sqrt{3}\right)$.
2. The perpendicular distance of P from the directrix of parabola is 8 units.

Select the correct answer using the code given below:

A. 1 only
B. 2 only
C. Both 1 and 2
D. Neither 1 nor 2

65. What is the eccentricity of the ellipse if the angle between the straight lines joining the foci to an extremity of the minor axis is 90°?

A. $\frac{1}{3}$ B. $\frac{1}{2}$

C. $\frac{1}{\sqrt{3}}$ D. $\frac{1}{\sqrt{2}}$

66. Let $\vec{a} = \hat{i} - \hat{j} + \hat{k}$ and $\vec{b} = \hat{i} + 2\hat{j} - \hat{k}$.

If $\vec{a} \times (\vec{b} \times \vec{a}) = \alpha\hat{i} - \beta\hat{j} + \gamma\hat{k}$, then what is the value of $\alpha + \beta + \gamma$?

A. 8 B. 7
C. 6 D. 1

67. If a vector of magnitude 2 units makes an angle $\frac{\pi}{3}$ with $2\hat{i}$, $\frac{\pi}{4}$ with $3\hat{j}$ and an acute angle θ with $4\hat{k}$, then what are the components of the vector?

A. $\left(1, \sqrt{2}, 1\right)$ B. $\left(1, -\sqrt{2}, 1\right)$

C. $\left(1, -\sqrt{2}, -1\right)$ D. $\left(1, \sqrt{2}, -1\right)$

68. Consider the following in respect of moment of a force:

1. The moment of force about a point is independent of point of application of force.
2. The moment of a force about a line is a vector quantity.

Which of the statements given above is/are correct?

A. 1 only B. 2 only
C. Both 1 and 2 D. Neither 1 nor 2

69. For any vector $\vec{r}$, what is $\left(\vec{r}\cdot\hat{i}\right)\left(\vec{r}\times\hat{i}\right)+\left(\vec{r}\cdot\hat{j}\right)\left(\vec{r}\times\hat{j}\right)+\left(\vec{r}\cdot\hat{k}\right)\left(\vec{r}\times\hat{k}\right)$ equal to?

A. $\vec{0}$ B. $\vec{r}$
C. $2\vec{r}$ D. $3\vec{r}$

70. Let $\vec{a}$ and $\vec{b}$ are two vectors of magnitude 4 inclined at an angle $\frac{\pi}{3}$, then what is the angle between $\vec{a}$ and $\vec{a} - \vec{b}$?

A. $\frac{\pi}{2}$ B. $\frac{\pi}{3}$

C. $\frac{\pi}{4}$ D. $\frac{\pi}{6}$

71. Let $y_1(x)$ and $y_2(x)$ be two solutions of the differential equation $\frac{dy}{dx} = x$. If $y_1(0) = 0$ and $y_2(0) = 4$, then what is the number of points of intersection of curves $y_1(x)$ and $y_2(x)$?

A. No point B. One point
C. Two points D. More than two points

72. The differential equation, representing the curve $y = e^x(a \cos x + b \sin x)$ where a and b are arbitrary constants, is:

A. $\frac{d^2y}{dx^2} + 2y = 0$ B. $\frac{d^2y}{dx^2} + 2\frac{dy}{dx} + 2y = 0$

C. $\frac{d^2y}{dx^2} - 2\frac{dy}{dx} + 2y = 0$ D. $\frac{d^2y}{dx^2} + y = 0$

73. If $f(x) = ax - b$ and $g(x) = cx + d$ are such that $f(g(x)) = g(f(x))$, then which one of the following holds?

A. $f(d) = g(b)$ B. $f(b) + g(d) = 0$
C. $f(a) + g(c) = 2a$ D. $f(d) + g(b) = 2d$

74. What is $\int_{-1}^{1} (3\sin x - \sin 3x)\cos^2 x dx$ equal to?

A. $-\frac{1}{4}$ B. 0

C. $\frac{1}{2}$ D. $\frac{1}{4}$

75. What are the order and degree respectively of the differential equation $\left\{2-\left(\frac{dy}{dx}\right)^2\right\}^{0.6} = \frac{d^2y}{dx^2}$?

A. 2, 2 B. 2, 3
C. 5, 2 D. 2, 5

76. If $\frac{dy}{dx} = 2e^x y^3, y(0) = \frac{1}{2}$ then what is $4y^2(2 - e^x)$ equal to?

A. 1 B. 2
C. 3 D. 4

77. Let $p=\int_a^b f(x)dx$ and $q=\int_a^b |f(x)|dx$. If $f(x) = e^{-x}$, then which one of the following is correct?

A. $p = 2q$ B. $p = -q$
C. $4p = q$ D. $p = q$

78. What is $\int_0^{\frac{\pi}{2}} \frac{a+\sin x}{2a+\sin x+\cos x}dx$ equal to?

A. $\frac{\pi}{4}$ B. $\frac{\pi}{2}$
C. 1 D. 0

79. The non-negative values of b for which the function $\frac{16x^3}{3}-4bx^2+x$ has neither maximum nor minimum in the range $x > 0$ is:

A. $0 < b < 1$ B. $1 < b < 2$
C. $b > 2$ D. $0 \le b < 1$

80. Which one of the following is correct in respect of $f(x)=\frac{1}{\sqrt{|x|-x}}$ and $g(x)=\frac{1}{\sqrt{x-|x|}}$?

A. $f(x)$ has some domain and $g(x)$ has no domain
B. $f(x)$ has no domain and $g(x)$ has some domain
C. $f(x)$ and $g(x)$ have the same domain
D. $f(x)$ and $g(x)$ do not have any domain

Directions (Qs. No. 81 & 82): *Consider the following for the next two (02) items that follow:*

Given that $\int \frac{3\cos x+4\sin x}{2\cos x+5\sin x}dx =$

$$\frac{\alpha x}{29}+\frac{\beta}{29}\ln|2\cos x+5\sin x|+c$$

81. What is the value of α?

A. 7 B. 13
C. 17 D. 26

82. What is the value of β?

A. 7 B. 13
C. 17 D. 26

Directions (Qs. No. 83 & 84): *Consider the following for the next two (02) items that follow:*

Let $f(x)=\frac{x}{\ln x}$; $(x > 1)$

83. Consider the following statements:

1. $f(x)$ is increasing in the interval (e, ∞)
2. $f(x)$ is decreasing in the interval $(1, e)$
3. $9 \ln 7 > 7 \ln 9$

Which of the statements given above are correct?

A. 1 and 2 only B. 2 and 3 only
C. 1 and 3 only D. 1, 2 and 3

84. Consider the following statements:

1. $f''(e)=\frac{1}{e}$
2. f(x) attains local minimum value at $x = e$
3. A local minimum value of $f(x)$ is e

Which of the statements given above are correct?

A. 1 and 2 only B. 2 and 3 only
C. 1 and 3 only D. 1, 2 and 3

Directions (Qs. No. 85 & 86): *Consider the following for the next two (02) items that follow:*

Let $f(x)$ and $g(x)$ be two functions such that $g(x)=x-\frac{1}{x}$ and $f \, o \, g(x)=x^3-\frac{1}{x^3}$.

85. What is $g[f(x) - 3x]$ equal to?

A. $x^3-\frac{1}{x^3}$ B. $x^3+\frac{1}{x^3}$
C. $x^2-\frac{1}{x^2}$ D. $x^2+\frac{1}{x^2}$

86. What is $f'(x)$ equal to?

A. $-\frac{2}{x^3}$ B. $2x+\frac{2}{x^3}$
C. $6x + 3$ D. $6x$

Directions (Qs. No. 87 & 88): *Consider the following for the next two (02) items that follow:*

Let $f(x) = |x| + 1$ and $g(x) = [x] - 1$, where [.] is the greatest integer function.

Let $h(x)=\frac{f(x)}{g(x)}$

87. Consider the following statements:

1. $f(x)$ is differentiable for all $x < 0$
2. $g(x)$ is continuous at $x = 0.0001$
3. The derivative of $g(x)$ at $x = 2.5$ is 1

Which of the statements given above are correct?

A. 1 and 2 only B. 2 and 3 only
C. 1 and 3 only D. 1, 2 and 3

88. What is $\lim_{x\to0-} h(x)+\lim_{x\to0+} h(x)$ equal to?

A. $-\frac{3}{2}$ B. $-\frac{1}{2}$
C. $\frac{1}{2}$ D. $\frac{3}{2}$

Directions (Qs. No. 89 & 90): *Consider the following for the next two (02) items that follow:*

Let $\varphi(a)=\int_{a}^{a+100\pi}|\sin x|\,dx$

89. What is $\varphi(a)$ equal to?
A. 0
B. a
C. $100a$
D. 200

90. What is $\varphi'(a)$ equal to?
A. 0
B. π
C. 100
D. 200

Directions (Qs. No. 91 & 92): *Consider the following for the next two (02) items that follow:*

A differentiable function $f(x)$ has a local maximum at $x = 0$. Let $y = 2f(x) + ax - b$.

91. Which of the following is/are correct?
1. $f'(0) = 0$
2. $f''(0) < 0$

Select the correct answer using the code given below:
A. 1 only
B. 2 only
C. Both 1 and 2
D. Neither 1 nor 2

92. The function y has a relative maxima at $x = 0$ for
A. $a > 0$, $b = 0$
B. for all b and $a = 0$
C. for all $b > 0$ only
D. for all a and $b = 0$

Directions (Qs. No. 93 & 94): *Consider the following for the next two (02) items that follow:*

Let $f(x) = |x - 1|$, $g(x) = [x]$ and $h(x) = f(x)g(x)$ where [.] is greatest integer function.

93. What is $\int_{-1}^{0} h(x)dx$ equal to?
A. $-\frac{3}{2}$
B. -1
C. 0
D. $\frac{1}{2}$

94. What is $\int_{0}^{2} h(x)dx$ equal to?
A. $-\frac{3}{2}$
B. -1
C. 0
D. $\frac{1}{2}$

Directions (Qs. No. 95 & 96): *Consider the following for the next two (02) items that follow:*

Let $\int \frac{dx}{\sqrt{x+1}-\sqrt{x-1}} = \alpha(x+1)^{\frac{3}{2}} + \beta(x-1)^{\frac{3}{2}} + c$

95. What is the value of α?
A. $\frac{1}{3}$
B. $\frac{2}{3}$
C. 1
D. $\frac{4}{3}$

96. What is the value of β?
A. $-\frac{2}{3}$
B. $-\frac{1}{3}$
C. $\frac{1}{3}$
D. $\frac{2}{3}$

Directions (Qs. No. 97 & 98): *Consider the following for the next two (02) items that follow:*

The circle $x^2 + y^2 - 2x = 0$ is partitioned by line $y = x$ in two segments. Let A_1, A_2 be the areas of major and minor segments respectively.

97. What is the value of A_1?
A. $\frac{\pi-2}{4}$
B. $\frac{\pi+2}{4}$
C. $\frac{3\pi-2}{4}$
D. $\frac{3\pi+2}{4}$

98. What is the value of $\frac{2(A_1+A_2)}{A_1-3A_2}$?
A. π
B. 1
C. -1
D. $-\pi$

Directions (Qs. No. 99 & 100): *Consider the following for the next two (02) items that follow:*

Let $3f(x)+f\left(\frac{1}{x}\right)=\frac{1}{x}+1$

99. What is $f(x)$ equal to?
A. $\frac{1}{8x}-\frac{x}{8}+\frac{1}{4}$
B. $\frac{3}{8x}-\frac{x}{8}+\frac{3}{4}$
C. $\frac{3}{8x}+\frac{x}{8}+\frac{1}{4}$
D. $\frac{3}{8x}-\frac{x}{8}+\frac{i}{4}$

100. What is $8\int_{1}^{2} f(x)dx$ equal to?
A. $\ln\left(8\sqrt{e}\right)$
B. $\ln\left(4\sqrt{e}\right)$
C. $\ln 2$
D. $\ln 2 - 1$

101. A bag contains 5 black and 4 white balls. A man selects two balls at random. What is the probability that both of these are of the same colour?

A. $\frac{1}{6}$ B. $\frac{5}{108}$

C. $\frac{4}{9}$ D. $\frac{5}{18}$

102. If a random variable (x) follows binomial distribution with mean 5 and variance 4, and 5^{23} P(X = 3) = $\lambda 4^{\lambda}$, then what is the value of λ?

A. 3 B. 5

C. 23 D. 25

103. From data (–4, 1), (–1, 2), (2, 7) and (3, 1), the regression line of y on x is obtained as $y = a + bx$, then what is the value of $2a + 15b$?

A. 6 B. 11

C. 17 D. 21

104. Let $x + 2y + 1 = 0$ and $2x + 3y + 4 = 0$ are two lines of regression computed from some bivariate data. If θ is the acute angle between them, then what is the value of 488 $\tan 3\theta$?

A. 191 B. 161

C. 131 D. 121

105. If two random variable X and Y are connected by relation $\frac{2X-3Y}{5X+4Y}=4$ and X follows Binomial distribution with parameters n = 10 and $p=\frac{1}{2}$, then what is the variance of Y?

A. $\frac{810}{361}$ B. $\frac{9}{19}$

C. $\frac{21}{361}$ D. $\frac{121}{361}$

106. If a, b, c are in HP, then what is $\frac{1}{b-a}+\frac{1}{b-c}$ equal to?

1. $\frac{2}{b}$
2. $\frac{1}{a}+\frac{1}{c}$
3. $\frac{1}{2}\left(\frac{1}{a}+\frac{1}{b}+\frac{1}{c}\right)$

Select the correct answer using the code given below:

A. 1 only B. 2 only

C. 3 only D. 1, 2 and 3

107. An edible oil is sold at the rates 150, 200, 250, 300 rupees per litre in four consecutive years. Assuming that an equal amount of money is spent on oil by a family in every year during these years, what is the average price of oil in rupees (approximately) per litre?

A. 210 B. 220

C. 230 D. 240

108. If the letters of the word "TIRUPATI" are written down at random, then what is the probability that both Ts are always consecutive?

A. $\frac{1}{2}$ B. $\frac{1}{4}$

C. $\frac{1}{7}$ D. $\frac{1}{14}$

109. Let $m = 77^n$. The index n is given a positive integral value at random. What is the probability that the value of m will have 1 in the units place?

A. $\frac{1}{2}$ B. $\frac{1}{3}$

C. $\frac{1}{4}$ D. $\frac{1}{n}$

110. Three different numbers are selected at random from the first 15 natural numbers. What is the probability that the product of two of the numbers is equal to third number?

A. $\frac{1}{91}$ B. $\frac{2}{455}$

C. $\frac{1}{65}$ D. $\frac{6}{455}$

Directions (Qs. No. 111 & 112): *Consider the following for the next two (02) items that follow:*

Let A and B be two events such that P(A ∪ B) ≥ 0.75 and 0.125 ≤ P(A ∩ B) ≤ 0.375.

111. What is the minimum value of P(A) + P(B)?

A. 0.625 B. 0.750

C. 0.825 D. 0.875

112. What is the maximum value of P(A) + P(B)?

A. 0.75

B. 1.125

C. 1.375

D. 1.625

Directions (Qs. No. 113 & 114): *Consider the following for the next two (02) items that follow:*

A, B, and C are three events such that P(A) = 0.6, P(B) = 0.4, P(C) = 0.5, P(A ∪ B) = 0.8, P(A ∩ C) = 0.3 and P(A ∩ B ∩ C) = 0.2 and P(A ∪ B ∪ C) ≥ 0.85.

113. What is the minimum value of P(B ∩ C)?

A. 0.1 B. 0.2
C. 0.35 D. 0.45

114. What is the maximum value of P(B ∩ C)?

A. 0.1 B. 0.2
C. 0.35 D. 0.45

Directions (Qs. No. 115 & 116): *Consider the following for the next two (02) items that follow:*

An unbiased coin is tossed n times. The probability of getting at least one tail is p and the probability of at least two tails is q and $p - q = \frac{5}{32}$.

115. What is the value of n?

A. 4 B. 5
C. 6 D. 7

116. What is the value of $p + q$?

A. $\frac{57}{32}$ B. $\frac{53}{32}$
C. $\frac{51}{32}$ D. 1

Directions (Qs. No. 117 & 118): *Consider the following for the next two (02) items that follow:*

x_i	1	2	3	...	n
f_i	1	2^{-1}	2^{-2}	...	$2^{-(n-1)}$

117. What is $\sum_{i}^{n} x_i f_i$ equal to?

A. $\frac{2^{n+1}-n+2}{2^{n-1}}$ B. $\frac{2^{n+1}-n-2}{2^{n-1}}$
C. $\frac{2^{n+1}+n+2}{2^{n-1}}$ D. $\frac{2^{n+1}-n-2}{2^{n}}$

118. What is the mean of the distribution?

A. $\frac{2^{n+1}-n+2}{2^{n}-1}$ B. $\frac{2^{n+1}-n-2}{2^{n-1}}$
C. $\frac{2^{n+1}-n-2}{2^{n}-1}$ D. $\frac{2^{n+1}-n+2}{2^{n}}$

Directions (Qs. No. 119 & 120): *Consider the following for the next two (02) items that follow:*

The marks obtained by 10 students in a Statistics test are 24, 47, 18, 32, 19, 15, 21, 35, 50 and 41.

119. What is the mean deviation of the largest five observations?

A. 4.8 B. 5.5
C. 6 D. 7.5

120. What is the variance of the largest five observations?

A. 14.6
B. 21.8
C. 25.2
D. 46.8

ANSWERS

PAPER I : GENERAL ABILITY TEST

1. **(D):** The word "deplorable" means deserving strong condemnation or being disgracefully bad in quality. Among the options provided, "commendable" is the opposite in meaning, as it means deserving praise and approval.

2. **(A):** The word "counteract" means to act against something to reduce its effect or neutralize it. Among the options provided, "exacerbate" means to make a problem or negative situation worse, which is the opposite of reducing or neutralizing it.

3. **(A):** The word "persevere" means to continue steadfastly in a course of action, especially in the face of difficulty or discouragement. Among the options provided "give up" means to stop trying or abandon an effort, this is direct opposite of persevering.

4. **(B):** The word "hideous" means extremely unpleasant, ugly, or repulsive. Among the options provided, "beautiful" means pleasing to the senses or mind aesthetically, which is the direct opposite of "hideous."

5. **(D):** The word "squander" means to waste something, particularly money or resources, in a reckless or foolish manner. Among the options provided, "manage" means to handle or control something, especially money or resources, in a careful and efficient way, which is the opposite of wasting.

6. **(B):** The word "continually" means repeatedly or continuously. In the context of climate change, it suggests that the Earth's climate is constantly evolving over time due to various factors.

7. **(A):** "These" refers back to specific changes mentioned earlier in the passage. It helps maintain coherence by pointing to the changes being discussed.

8. **(C):** The activities described, such as deforestation and industrial emissions, are caused by human actions. "Human" correctly attributes these activities as the cause of certain climate changes.

9. **(D):** "Accumulation" means the gradual buildup or increase of gases and aerosols in the atmosphere. This fits logically with the context of pollutants accumulating due to human activities.

10. **(C):** The use of "the" before "atmosphere" specifies that we are referring to the Earth's atmosphere, which is a specific and defined entity in the context of environmental science.

11. **(A):** "Raise" is the correct term because greenhouse gases trap heat and cause temperatures to increase (raise), not "rise" (which means to move upwards).

12. **(D):** The greenhouse effect occurs on the "planet" Earth. This term is appropriate as it specifies where the phenomenon of trapping heat near the surface occurs.

13. **(A):** "For" is used to indicate the purpose or goal of creating and strengthening scientific and analytical capacity. It clarifies that these efforts are aimed at better assessment of climate change.

14. **(D): have initiated:** This phrase indicates that studies and efforts have been started or launched under the Climate Change Action Programme, aligning with the context of building scientific capacity over time.

15. **(B):** "At" is used to specify the timing of meetings and negotiations, indicating that they occur at regular intervals.

16. **(B):** "Paused" means to stop briefly. The phrase "for a few moments" correctly indicates the duration of the pause. Option (B) is the correct choice because it properly completes the sentence with a prepositional phrase that indicates how long he paused.

17. **(A): Late at night, our car broke down on the highway:** "Broke down" means to stop functioning suddenly, especially in the context of vehicles. Option (A) is the correct choice because it accurately describes the situation where the car stopped working on the highway.

18. **(B): All the countries signed the treaty except Germany and France:** The phrase "except Germany and France" correctly identifies the countries that did not sign the treaty. Option (B) is the correct choice because it appropriately completes the sentence by specifying which countries were exceptions.

19. **(A): I reminded her to turn off the lights at night:** "Reminded" is followed by the infinitive "to turn off," which correctly expresses the action I reminded her to perform. Option (A) is the correct choice because it accurately completes the sentence with the intended action.

20. **(C): They told us about the woman who lived next door:** "Who lived next door" is a relative clause that provides additional information about the woman. Option (C) is the correct choice because it introduces a defining relative clause that specifies which woman is being referred to.

21. **(A): I'll see you at the end of February:** "At the end of February" specifies the time when the speaker will see the other person. Option (A) is the correct choice because it accurately completes the sentence by specifying the time of the meeting.

22. **(B): I dislike films that have sad endings:** "That have sad endings" is a relative clause that defines the type of films the speaker dislikes. Option (B) is the correct choice because it introduces a defining relative clause that specifies the characteristic disliked by the speaker.

23. **(B): The thieves denied stealing the money:** "Stealing the money" is a gerund phrase that functions as the object of the verb "denied." Option (B) is the correct choice because it correctly forms a gerund phrase that follows "denied."

24. **(B): Did you drop in to see Sunita on your way home?:** "Drop in" means to visit briefly and informally. Option (B) is the correct choice because it correctly forms a question asking if someone visited someone briefly.

25. **(B): Would you like to meet her?:** The sentence asks a question about meeting someone. Option B is the correct choice because it properly forms the question asking if the listener would like to have a meeting with the person mentioned.

26. **(C):** The idiom 'be bad news' that is troublesome, unwelcome, or dangerous. So, the correct meaning is 'Some who is considered undesirable'.

27. **(C):** The idiom 'back to the drawing board' means the need to start over or to go back to the beginning because the previous attempt or plan was unsuccessful or failed to achieve the desired result.

28. (D): The idiom 'be in the eye of the storm' implies deeply involved in a difficult or controversial situation which affects or interests a lot of people. Thus, the meaning is to be in the midst of a 'controvery'.

29. (D): The idiom 'life in the fast lane' means in a way that is exciting and slightly dangerous/to live 'an exciting and eventful lifestyle'.

30. (B): The idiom 'to pass the buck' means to leave a difficult problem for someone else to deal with/ to shift the responsibility of something to someone.

31. (A): The correct pattern is QSPR. This sequence makes sense logically as it begins by defining what the fundamental rights are (Q), followed by specifying that these rights encompass basic rights and freedoms (SP), and concluding by stating to whom these rights are guaranteed (R), which is the individual.

32. (A): SRQP because it logically constructs the sentence: "The Indian nation is the product of a historical process that has been in the making for many millennia." Here, (S) introduces the main subject, (R) adds detail about the historical process, (Q) explains that this process has been ongoing, and (P) specifies the duration of this process.

33. (A): The correct pattern is SQPR. This sequence starts by identifying the subject (S), which is India's Independence, and then describes what it represented for its people (Q) — the beginning of an epoch imbued with a new vision (P) or perspective. This sequence concludes with the statement (R) about the nature of this new vision.

34. (C): The correct pattern is SRQP. This sequence starts by stating what all students have been instructed to do (S) — be present before the Principal. It then specifies the purpose or reason (R) for this instruction, which is for a discussion on the forthcoming science and mathematics exhibition (Q), and finally concludes with the subject of the discussion (P), which is the exhibition itself.

35. (C): The correct pattern is RQSP. (R) introduces the action of selecting an additional player. Further (Q) describes where the new player is being added, which is to the new team. (S) sets up the subject for the final part of the sentence. Lastly, (P) specifies the composition of the team after the selection of the new player, with two bowlers and two batsmen, each in their respective roles.

36. (A): "Abode" is a noun in this sentence, referring to a place where someone lives or resides. It serves as the object of the preposition "to."

37. (D): "Beyond" is a preposition here, indicating that the situation is outside the limits or scope of our control. It relates the concept of control to its boundaries.

38. (D): "Except" is a conjunction in this sentence, connecting clauses and indicating an exclusion or contrast. It introduces the idea that nothing was told to him except for the fact about needing money.

39. (B): "Nicely" is an adverb modifying the verb "dry-cleaned," describing how the action was performed. It answers the question "how" the coat was dry-cleaned.

40. (A): "This" is a determiner in this sentence, specifying which particular item is being referred to. It precedes the noun "item" to indicate the specific item being discussed.

41. (A): Water is an abiotic component that supports biotic communities but is not part of the biotic community itself. The biotic community consists of living organisms like humans, protozoa, and bushes (plants).

42. (C): The passage states that the nature of the biotic community is largely determined by both biotic components (such as different kinds of plants, animals, and microbes) and abiotic components (such as water, temperature, salinity, and soil type).

43. (C): Abiotic factors are non-living environmental factors that influence the biotic community. In the passage, it mentions abiotic factors such as temperature, humidity, moisture, and others like water availability and soil type. Algae, however, are living organisms (specifically part of the biotic community), not abiotic factors.

44. (B): The passage mentions that water is a major factor sustaining aquatic communities, which include biotic communities found in aquatic environments like ponds, lakes, rivers, and oceans. Therefore, this option is correct because the term 'aquatic community' specifically refers to the biotic community that inhabits water bodies.

45. (C): Species are defined as groups of individuals that are similar in appearance and distinct from other groups. This definition includes both similarities within the species and differences that distinguish one species from another.

46. (A): "Banished" means to be sent away from a place, especially as a punishment or to enforce exile. Similarly, "deported" means to be expelled or sent away, often involuntarily. Both words imply removal from a place due to external reasons.

47. (A): "Dazzling" describes something that is extremely impressive or exciting due to its brightness or excellence. Similarly, "brilliant" means shining brightly or outstandingly clever or talented. Both words convey the idea of an exceptional performance.

48. (B): "Rebuffed" means to reject or refuse (someone or something) in an abrupt or blunt manner. Therefore, "rejected" is the closest in meaning, indicating a refusal or dismissal of suggestions.

49. (B): "Disowned" means to renounce or refuse any connection with something or someone. Similarly, "abandoned" means to give up completely or to disown. Both words imply rejecting or giving up one's claim or connection.

50. (C): "Sceptical" means to have doubts or reservations about something. Similarly, "doubtful" means uncertain or hesitant about the truth or validity of something. Both words indicate a lack of confidence or trust in the new government policy.

51. (*)

52. (C): Equivalent voltage $= \dfrac{\varepsilon_1 r_1 + \varepsilon_2 r_2}{r_1 + r_2}$

$$= \frac{1\times 0.1 + 5\times 0.1}{0.1+0.1}$$

$$E_{eq} = \frac{0.6}{0.2} = 3\text{V}$$

From first circuit, we have

$$i = \frac{\varepsilon}{R+r}$$

Value of r is very less can be neglected as compared to R

Now, $$i = \frac{\varepsilon}{R}$$

$$10^{-3} = \frac{1}{R}$$

$$R = 10^3 = 1000\ \Omega$$

Now, from second circuit

$$i_1 = \frac{E_{eq}}{R + r_{eq}} = \frac{3}{1000}$$

$$i_1 = 3 \times 10^{-3}$$

$$= 3 \text{ mA}.$$

53. (D): Given, $i = 15\text{A}$,

$$t = 10 \times 60 = 600 \text{ s}$$

$$q = it = 15 \times 600 = 9000 \text{ C}.$$

54. (A): Lightning rods are always pointed to attract charges towards it.

55. (D): 1. Gravitational force: This force is fundamental in nature and acts universally between all objects with mass. It governs the motions of planets, stars, and galaxies.

2. Electromagnetic force: This force is also fundamental and governs the interactions between electrically charged particles. It includes forces like attraction between opposite charges (electrostatic force) and interactions involving magnetic fields.

3. Strong and weak nuclear forces: These are fundamental forces that operate at the level of subatomic particles within atomic nuclei. Strong nuclear force: It binds protons and neutrons together in atomic nuclei. Weak nuclear force: It governs processes such as radioactive decay.

56. (B): Average density $= \dfrac{\text{Total mass}}{\text{Total volume}}$

$$= \frac{\rho_1 V_1 + \rho_2 V_2}{V}$$

$$= \frac{\rho\times\frac{4}{3}\pi\left(\frac{R}{2}\right)^3 + \frac{\rho}{2}\left[\frac{4}{3}\pi R^3 - \frac{4}{3}\pi\left(\frac{R}{2}\right)^3\right]}{\frac{4}{3}\pi R^3}$$

$$= \frac{\rho\times\frac{4}{3}\pi\frac{R^3}{8} + \frac{\rho}{2}\left[\frac{4}{3}\pi R^3 - \frac{4}{3}\pi\frac{R^3}{8}\right]}{\frac{4}{3}\pi R^3}$$

$$= \frac{\rho}{8} + \frac{\rho}{2}\left[1 - \frac{1}{8}\right]$$

$$= \frac{\rho}{8} + \frac{\rho}{2}\left[\frac{7}{8}\right]$$

$$= \frac{\rho}{8} + \frac{7\rho}{16}$$

$$= \frac{2\rho + 7\rho}{16} = \frac{9\rho}{16}.$$

57. (D): Variable focal length and variable aperture size: This option means that both the focal length and the aperture size can change. The human eye indeed has a variable focal length (accommodation allows it to focus on objects at varying distances) and a variable aperture size (pupil dilation adjusts based on light conditions).

58. (C): 1. Religious or social practices of Nagas: Article 371A ensures that the religious and social practices of the Nagas are protected and respected. This provision recognizes the diversity and significance of these practices within Nagaland.

2. Naga customary law and procedure: The article protects Naga customary laws and procedures, which are traditional systems of governance and justice that have been historically practiced by the Naga tribes. This provision allows the Nagas to maintain their traditional ways of resolving disputes and administering justice.

3. Ownership and transfer of land and its resources: This ensures that the rights of the indigenous people over their land and resources are protected from external laws that may otherwise apply uniformly across India.

59. (C): 1. Under the Government of India: This refers to offices of profit held under the central government. Examples include positions in ministries, departments, statutory bodies, and other institutions established or controlled by the Government of India.

2. Under Any State Government: This includes offices of profit held under any state government within India. It encompasses positions in state ministries, departments, statutory bodies, and institutions established or controlled by state governments.

60. (A): 1. The Universal Declaration of Human Rights (UDHR) was adopted by the UN General Assembly in 1948 and is related to the rights and freedoms of all human beings.

4. The Convention on Refugees is also known as the 1951 Refugee Convention. This convention defines refugees, the rights provided under asylum and the responsibilities of the countries that grant asylum.

3. The International Covenant on Economic, Social and Cultural Rights (ICESCR) was adopted by the United Nations General Assembly (GA) on December 16, 1966, and it came into force on January 3, 1976.

2. The Convention on the Elimination of all Forms of Discrimination Against Women (CEDAW) was adopted by the UN General Assembly in 1979 and came into effect on September 3, 1981.

61. (C): During the Second Five-Year Plan (1956-1961) in India, the primary focus was on rapid industrialization and infrastructure development, especially in heavy industries and basic industries like steel, coal, and power. The plan aimed to increase national income, raise living standards, and expand employment opportunities. However, the focus on consumer goods was limited compared to the emphasis on heavy and basic industries. Therefore, option (C) is not correct as it does not align with the primary objectives of the Second Five-Year Plan.

62. (B): Statement 2: Correct. Major towns in ancient India were often located along important routes of communication, such as trade routes or river valleys, which facilitated their growth and development.

Statement 3: Correct. Many of these ancient urban centers were indeed bustling hubs of commercial, cultural, and political activity. They served as centers for trade, crafts, religious activities, administration, and cultural exchanges.

63. (B): Statement 2: Correct. The Kharosthi script, used in inscriptions in the north-west of India (particularly in areas influenced by the Indo-Greek kingdoms), was deciphered with the help of coins of Indo-Greek kings. These coins contained bilingual inscriptions in Greek and Kharosthi, aiding in the decipherment of the script.

Statement 3: Correct. Inscriptions typically record significant events such as royal proclamations, achievements, donations, and religious matters. Routine activities like agricultural practices are rarely mentioned in these inscriptions.

64. (A): Formula used,

Average atomic mass

$$= \frac{\Sigma\%\ \text{abundance} \times \text{atomic mass}}{\Sigma \text{total abundance}}$$

Let, % of $B^{10} = x$

% of $B^{11} = 100 - x$

average atomic mass = 10.81

$$10.81 = \frac{x \times 10 + (100 - x) \times 11}{100}$$

$$1081 = 10x + 1100 - 11x$$

$$-19 = -x$$

$$x = 19$$

% of B^{10} = 19%

% of B^{11} = 81%.

65. (B): Portland cement, which is the most common type of cement used in construction, is composed primarily of the following essential constituents:

- **Silica (Silicon dioxide):** Provides strength to the cement and contributes to its early strength development.
- **Alumina (Aluminium oxide):** Helps in quick setting and hardening of cement.
- **Lime (Calcium oxide or calcium hydroxide):** Acts as a binding material and contributes to the strength and durability of the cement.

66. (B): Litmus, a natural dye used as an acid-base indicator, is derived from lichens. Lichens are symbiotic organisms composed of a fungus (usually an ascomycete) and an algae or cyanobacterium. Litmus is extracted from certain species of lichens and changes color depending on whether it is exposed to an acidic or basic environment.

67. (D): The oxidation state of vanadium in

$$V_2O_5 = +5$$

The oxidation state of O-atom is –2.

Let, oxidation state of vanadium = x

$$\begin{aligned} V_2O_5 &= 0 \\ 2x + (-2 \times 5) &= 0 \\ 2x - 10 &= 0 \\ 2x &= +10 \\ x &= \frac{+10}{2} = +5. \end{aligned}$$

68. (A): (*a*) Graphite (*iv*) Soft and slippery material: Graphite is composed of layers of carbon atoms arranged in a hexagonal lattice. These layers are weakly bonded together, allowing them to slide over each other easily. This gives graphite its characteristic soft and slippery feel, making it suitable as a lubricant and in pencils.

(*b*) Diamond (*ii*) Hardest natural substance: Diamond is made up of carbon atoms arranged in a tetrahedral lattice structure, forming a very strong covalent bond network. This structure gives diamond its exceptional hardness, making it the hardest natural substance known.

(*c*) Fullerene (*iii*) Very light and strong material: Fullerene molecules, such as Buckminsterfullerene (C_{60}), are spherical carbon molecules with a unique structure. They are lightweight due to their hollow structure and have remarkable strength, despite their lightness.

(*d*) Graphene (*i*) Thinnest and strongest material: Graphene is a single layer of carbon atoms arranged in a two-dimensional honeycomb lattice. It is incredibly thin, with a thickness of just one atom. Despite its thinness, graphene is exceptionally strong, with a tensile strength much higher than steel.

69. (D): Statement 1: This statement is incorrect. The International Date Line (IDL) does follow approximately along the 180° meridian in the Pacific Ocean, but its deviations are not primarily to avoid land areas surrounded by the Atlantic Ocean. Rather, these deviations are to accommodate political boundaries and to avoid dividing certain countries into two separate calendar days.

Statement 2: This statement is incorrect. When crossing the International Date Line from east to west, you move into a day that is 24 hours behind. Conversely, moving from west to east across the IDL means moving into a day that is 24 hours above.

70. (D): Statement 1: This statement is correct as it describes the phenomenon of auroras accurately. The solar wind, consisting of charged particles, interacts with Earth's magnetic field and is directed towards the poles where they collide with atmospheric gases, resulting in the colorful light display known as aurora.

Statement 2: This statement is also correct. The colors seen in auroras (such as green, red, purple) are due to the interaction of charged particles with atmospheric gases like oxygen and nitrogen. Each gas emits light at specific wavelengths, resulting in different colours.

Statement 3: This statement is also correct. In a rare event in April 2023, an aurora borealis (northern lights) was captured in the skies above Ladakh, India, by the Indian Astronomical Observatory at Hanle. This was due to an unusually strong solar storm.

71. (B): Statement 1: This statement is correct. Barchan dunes are indeed crescent-shaped and are formed by wind action in deserts where the wind blows predominantly from one direction. Sand accumulates on the windward side (facing the wind) and is deposited on the leeward side, shaping the dune into a crescent.

Statement 2: This statement is also correct. The windward side of a Barchan dune does have a convex, gentle slope where sand accumulates as the wind blows. The maximum height of the dune is usually near the center, not at the edges.

72. (B): Statement 2: This statement is correct. Regur soil is formed from weathered basaltic lava flows in the Deccan Plateau region of India. It develops under hot and semi-arid to semi-humid conditions. The lava rocks break down to form this clayey soil type, which is known for its moisture retention properties and fertility.

Statement 3: This statement is also correct. Regur soil is particularly suitable for cotton cultivation due to its moisture retention capacity and fertility. Cotton is one of the major crops grown in regions with black soil in India.

73. (B): Statement 1: This statement is correct. Clouds are classified based on their altitude (height above the Earth's surface) and their appearance or form (shape and structure). Altitude classifications include high-level clouds, mid-level clouds, and low-level clouds, while forms include categories like cirrus, cumulus, and stratus.

Statement 2: This statement is also correct. Clouds are indeed categorized into three main altitude groups: high clouds (cirrus, cirrostratus, cirrocumulus), mid-level clouds (altostratus, altocumulus), and low clouds (stratus, stratocumulus, nimbostratus).

74. (D): Statement 1: This statement is correct. Fronts are boundaries between air masses with different temperature and humidity characteristics. As a front moves through an area, it can bring changes in weather conditions such as precipitation, temperature changes, and shifts in wind direction. These changes can occur gradually as the front passes.

Statement 2: This statement is correct. Cold fronts often bring abrupt weather changes, including thunderstorms. When a cold front advances, the colder, denser air mass displaces warmer air rapidly, leading to the rapid ascent of warm air and potentially triggering thunderstorm development along the front.

Statement 3: This statement is also correct. A warm front occurs when warm air advances and rises over a retreating mass of colder air. As the warm air ascends gradually, it cools, and clouds form, often resulting in precipitation over a broader area than with a cold front.

75. (D): Statement 1: This statement is correct. Alkaline soils do indeed have a high pH (greater than 7.0) and can contain sodium (Na) and calcium (Ca) salts, among others, contributing to their alkalinity. They are characterized by poor drainage and can pose challenges for cultivation.

Statement 2: This statement is correct. Black cotton soil, also known as Regur soil, is found extensively in the Deccan Plateau of India. It develops on Deccan basaltic lava under hot and semi-arid to semi-humid conditions.

Statement 3: This statement is also correct. Laterite soils are formed in tropical and subtropical regions with high rainfall. They are characterized by a deep layer of leached, iron-rich, and aluminum-rich material due to intense weathering. Silica is indeed leached from these soils, leaving behind iron and aluminum oxides.

76. (A): These are all characteristics of Steppes grassland. Steppes are extensive grasslands found in temperate climates, stretching across Eurasia from the Black Sea to the Altai Mountains. They are characterized by a scarcity of trees and shrubs, dominated instead by various types of grasses. The climate of steppes features hot summers, cold winters, and moderate rainfall, typically between 25 to 50 centimeters annually. This amount of precipitation supports short grasses rather than taller varieties or trees.

77. (D): The cell membrane of animal cells is primarily composed of phospholipids, which form a bilayer structure. Embedded within or attached to this phospholipid bilayer are proteins that serve various functions like transport and signaling. Additionally, cholesterol molecules are interspersed among the phospholipids, contributing to the membrane's stability and fluidity. This composition of phospholipids, proteins, and cholesterol allows the cell membrane to regulate the passage of molecules and ions, maintain cell shape, and facilitate communication with the external environment, making it crucial for the cell's survival and function.

78. (D): A compound microscope typically consists of several parts including a mirror or light source (to illuminate the specimen), a stage (where the specimen is placed), clips (to hold the specimen slide in place), objective lenses (to magnify the specimen), an eyepiece or ocular lens (through which the observer views the specimen), and focusing knobs (to bring the specimen into sharp focus). The retina, however, is a part of the eye and not a component of the compound microscope.

79. (D): Protein — Tissue — Organ — Organism

- **Protein:** Proteins are molecules composed of amino acids and are fundamental to various cellular functions.
- **Tissue:** Tissues are groups of cells that work together to perform a specific function.
- **Organ:** Organs are structures composed of different tissues working together to perform a complex function.

- **Organism:** An organism is a living being composed of various organ systems working together.

80. (D):
- **Monocyte:** A type of white blood cell involved in immune response.
- **Chondrocyte:** Cartilage cells found in connective tissue.
- **Basophil:** A type of white blood cell involved in allergic reactions and inflammation.
- **Lymphocyte:** White blood cells crucial for immune defense.

81. (C): The pancreas secretes enzymes such as lipase (to digest fats), amylase (to digest carbohydrates), and protease (to digest proteins) into the small intestine. These enzymes play a crucial role in breaking down food components so that they can be absorbed and utilized by the body.

82. (B): 1. DNA replication does indeed take place when chromatin (the complex of DNA and proteins) is opened up. During replication, the chromatin structure unfolds to allow access to the DNA strands so that they can be copied.

2. Before cell division, chromatin condenses and organizes itself into rod-shaped structures called chromosomes. This condensation ensures that each daughter cell receives a complete set of genetic information during cell division.

83. (C): As the scale is in equilibrium, net torque must be zero,

$$N_1 d_1 - N_2 d_2 = 0$$
$$N_1 \times 0.3 = N_2 \times 0.1$$
$$3N_1 = N_2$$

Also, force must be balance,

$$N_1 + N_2 = W(mg)$$
$$N_1 + 3N_2 = 0.24 \times 10$$
$$4N_1 = 2.4$$
$$N_1 = 0.6 \text{ N}$$
$$N_2 = 3N_1 = 3 \times 0.6 = 1.8 \text{ N}.$$

84. (A): Escape velocity is given by,

$$v = \sqrt{2gR}$$

$$\Rightarrow \quad v = \sqrt{2\frac{GM}{R^2} \times R} = \sqrt{2\frac{GM}{R}}$$

$$\Rightarrow \quad v = \sqrt{2G \times \rho \times \frac{4}{3}\pi R^2} = 11.2$$

Also, $$v' = \sqrt{2G \times 4\rho \times \frac{4}{3}\pi \frac{R^2}{4}} = 11.2$$

Hence, escape velocity remains same.

85. (C): Sound waves in fluids (liquids and gases) are longitudinal waves, not transverse. This means the vibrations occur in the same direction as the wave's propagation. Sound waves do transport energy and require a medium to travel because they propagate through the vibration of particles in the medium. The speed of sound generally increases in liquids compared to gases because liquids are denser and transmit sound more effectively.

86. (D): As per conservation of energy,

$$\frac{1}{2}mu^2 = mgh$$

$$\Rightarrow \quad u = \sqrt{2gh}$$
$$= \sqrt{2 \times 10 \times 0.45}$$
$$= \sqrt{9} = 3 \text{ m/s}$$

After rebound some of its kinetic energy gets lost and remaining gets converted into Potential energy

Hence, $$\frac{1}{2}mv^2 = mgh'$$

$$\Rightarrow \quad v = \sqrt{2gh'}$$
$$= \sqrt{2 \times 10 \times 0.20}$$
$$= \sqrt{4} = 2 \text{ m/s}$$

We know that, $$F = \frac{mv - mu}{t}$$
$$= \frac{m(v-u)}{t}$$

Taking sign consideration

$$F = \frac{0.1(-2-3)}{0.1} = -5\text{N}.$$

(–ve sign indicated retarding force)

87. (D): We have,

$$T = 2\pi\sqrt{\frac{l}{g}}, \text{ also } F = -kx$$

For small amplitudes the restoring force on the pendulum bob is directly proportional to its displacement. This leads to simple harmonic motion, where the time period is independent of the amplitude. For larger amplitude the restoring force is no longer directly proportional to displacement, Consequently the time period slightly dependent on the amplitude.

88. (C): Static friction > Kinetic friction > Rolling friction

- Static friction is the frictional force that prevents two surfaces from sliding past each other when they are not moving relative to each other.

- Kinetic friction is the frictional force that opposes the relative motion of two surfaces sliding past each other.
- Rolling friction is the frictional force that opposes the motion of a rolling object.

89. (D): When two bodies of same mass undergo elastic collision, their velocities are just interchanged. After collision bob X will come to rest and bob Y would move with velocity of X and will rise to the same height.

90. (B): Infrared waves, also known as heat waves, are a type of electromagnetic radiation emitted by objects due to their temperature. Water molecules effectively absorb infrared waves, primarily through their vibrational modes, which results in the molecules gaining energy and contributing to heat. While it's accurate to call infrared waves "heat waves" due to their heating effect when absorbed by substances, this terminology doesn't solely stem from water's absorption behaviour. Therefore, both statements are individually correct. However, the absorption by water doesn't directly explain why infrared waves are termed heat waves in general usage.

91. (D): Statement 1: This statement is correct. A 'trade surplus' implies that a country (in this case, Britain) exports more goods and services to another country (India) than it imports from that country. This imbalance was largely driven by Britain's industrialization, which produced a surplus of manufactured goods that were sent to India, a colony that served as a captive market under British rule. **Statement 2:** This statement is also correct. India, under British rule, supplied raw materials and served as a market for British manufactured goods, helping Britain maintain its trade balance globally. This relationship helped Britain balance its deficits elsewhere in the world by maintaining a trade surplus with India.

Statement 3: This statement is correct. During the 19th century, opium was indeed one of India's major exports, primarily to China, under British colonial rule. Opium became India's largest export commodity during this period, generating substantial revenue for the British authorities and commercial interests.

92. (A): (*a*) Muhurta: This is a unit of time measurement in early India, typically used to denote a specific period of time, often translated as an hour or a specific auspicious time period in Hindu astrology and calendars.

(*b*) Raktika: This refers to a measure of weight in ancient India, used to quantify the weight of substances, goods, or commodities.

(*c*) Angula: An angula is a unit of length in ancient Indian measurements, roughly equivalent to the breadth of a human finger. It was used extensively in various contexts for measuring lengths of fabric, dimensions of structures, etc.

(*d*) Pada: In early India, pada was a measure used for metrical purposes in poetry. It corresponds to a unit of poetic meter or verse, indicating a specific rhythmic pattern in Sanskrit and other Indian languages.

93. (D): The first coins in Indian history bearing the names and images of rulers were issued by the Indo-Greeks. The Indo-Greek kings, who ruled parts of northwestern India from around 180 BCE to 10 CE, introduced the concept of depicting their portraits and names on coins, combining Greek and Indian numismatic traditions.

94. (A): Social theorists in the nineteenth and twentieth centuries emphasized the emergence of industrialisation, urbanisation, secularisation, and bureaucratization as hallmarks of Modernity. These developments marked a significant shift from traditional agrarian societies to modern industrialised societies, characterised by new social, economic, and political structures.

95. (B): 3. Passing of the Rowlatt Act: This occurred on March 18 1919, providing the legal backdrop that led to widespread discontent and protests.

4. Jallianwala Bagh incident: This tragic event took place on April 13, 1919, in Amritsar, where British troops fired on a peaceful gathering, resulting in a significant loss of life.

2. All-India Khilafat Conference in Delhi: This conference, held in November 1919, marked a significant unity between the Khilafat Movement and the Indian National Congress against British colonial policies.

1. Launch of Non-Cooperation Movement: This movement was launched by Mahatma Gandhi on August 1, 1920, as a protest against colonial rule, drawing on the widespread discontent following the Rowlatt Act and the Jallianwala Bagh massacre.

96. (A): (*a*) Upari: Category of tenancy tenure held under the Marathas

(*b*) Pattadar: Peasants directly responsible for the payment of revenue.

(*c*) Mirasidar: Co-parcenary title holder and designated revenue payer in Southern India.

(*d*) Inam Lands: Gifts of land or land revenue

97. (C): Statement 1: Correct. Krishnadevaraya, who ruled the Vijayanagara Empire from 1509 to 1529, embarked on several military campaigns during his reign. One of his notable early campaigns was against the Gajapati rulers of Orissa. He successfully extended his influence in the eastern regions and established Vijayanagara's dominance.

Statement 2: Correct. The Raichur Doab, the region between the Krishna and Tungabhadra rivers, was a contested area between the Vijayanagara Empire and the Sultanate of Bijapur. In 1520, Krishnadevaraya launched a successful campaign against Ismail Adil Khan of Bijapur, capturing the strategic fort of Raichur, which was a significant military achievement for his empire.

Statement 3: Correct. After defeating the Bahmani Sultanate, Krishnadevaraya restored the puppet ruler Sultan Mahmud Shah to the throne and assumed the title of Yavana-rajya-sthapan-acharya, which means "restorer of the Yavana kingdom." This act was part of his strategy to maintain influence over the Deccan Sultanates and establish Vijayanagara's supremacy in the region.

98. (B): Water gas is a mixture of carbon monoxide (CO) and hydrogen (H_2), typically produced through a process known as gasification. In this process, steam (H_2O) is passed over red-hot coke (a form of carbon), which results in the following endothermic reaction:

$$C(coke) + H_2O\ (steam) \rightarrow CO + H_2$$

This reaction occurs at high temperatures and requires continuous heating to maintain the reaction. The resulting water gas, composed of CO and H_2, can be used as a fuel or as an intermediate in the production of other chemicals. It is an important industrial process for generating a synthesis gas that can be used in various applications, including the synthesis of methanol and hydrocarbons via the Fischer-Tropsch process.

99. (B): The human body maintains a tightly regulated pH range to ensure proper physiological function. This range is typically between 7.0 and 7.8. The optimal pH for most body fluids, particularly blood, is around 7.4, which is slightly alkaline. Enzyme activity, oxygen transport, and metabolic processes are all dependent on maintaining this pH range. Deviations from this range can lead to serious health issues, as enzymes and other biochemical processes may not function correctly if the pH is too acidic or too alkaline.

100. (B): Latent heat of fusion of water is very low: This is incorrect. Water actually has a high latent heat of fusion, which is the amount of heat required to convert ice at its melting point into water without changing its temperature. The latent heat of fusion = 80 cal/g. This is the amount that is required to convert 1 g solid ice into liquid water at its melting point.

101. (C): Ethyl acetate, known for its sweet and fruity smell, is commonly used in perfumes and flavorings. This ester is responsible for the pleasant aromas found in many fruits and is often utilized in the food and beverage industry to enhance flavors. Unlike ethyl alcohol, which has an alcoholic smell, and acetic acid, which has a sharp vinegar-like odor, ethyl acetate provides a distinctly sweet fragrance that is easily recognizable.

102. (C): In the NaCl (sodium chloride) crystal lattice, each sodium ion (Na^+) is surrounded by 6 chloride ions (Cl^-), and each chloride ion is surrounded by 6 sodium ions. This arrangement is known as a face-centered cubic (FCC) structure, where each ion is in contact with 6 nearest neighbours in all directions. This high coordination number of 6 ensures strong electrostatic interactions between ions, contributing to the stability of the crystal lattice and the characteristic properties of NaCl.

103. (A): Methanoic acid is the irritant present in nettle leaf hairs responsible for causing a burning sensation upon contact with the skin. When these tiny hairs pierce the skin, they release formic acid, which acts as a mild toxin. This acid stimulates pain receptors, triggering a stinging or burning sensation that can last for varying durations depending on the individual's sensitivity and the extent of contact.

104. (D): Milk of Magnesia refers to a suspension of magnesium hydroxide in water, known for its medicinal use as an antacid and laxative. When ingested, it neutralizes stomach acid and provides relief from indigestion and heartburn due to its alkaline nature. It also acts as a mild laxative by drawing water into the intestines, thereby promoting bowel movements.

105. (D): When soap is mixed with water, it forms a lyotropic liquid crystal. Lyotropic liquid crystals are formed by amphiphilic molecules (such as soap molecules) in solution. These molecules have both hydrophilic (water-attracting) and hydrophobic (water-repelling) parts. In the presence of water, soap molecules self-organize into structures where the hydrophobic parts cluster together and the hydrophilic parts interact with water molecules.

106. (B): Borax, chemically represented as $Na_2B_4O_7 \cdot 10H_2O$, consists of sodium (Na), boron (B), oxygen (O), and hydrogen (H). It is a white, crystalline mineral and a common household chemical known for its various uses, including as a cleaning agent, insecticide, and in the manufacture of glass and ceramics. Borax dissolves easily in water, forming an alkaline solution due to its basic nature.

107. (B): Among the options given, the oxide with the highest melting point is MgO (Magnesium oxide). Magnesium oxide has a very high melting point of about 2,852°C (5,166°F). This high melting point is due to the strong ionic bonds between magnesium and oxygen atoms in the crystal lattice structure of MgO.

108. (C): 1. Neap tides occur every 14-15 days, around the first and third quarter moons when the gravitational pull of the Sun and Moon are perpendicular to each other, leading to the smallest tidal range.

2. Neap tides have a small tidal range because the gravitational forces of the Moon and the Sun are at right angles (in quadrature), which results in their forces partially canceling each other out.

109. (B): 1. This statement is correct. The epicentre is the point on the Earth's surface directly above the focus or hypocentre, where the earthquake originates underground.

2. This statement is also correct. Earthquakes generate seismic waves, including Primary (P-waves) and Secondary (S-waves) waves, which travel outward from the focus of the earthquake.

110. (B): 1. This statement is incorrect. Air temperature is usually measured at a height of 1.2 to 2 meters (4.1 to 6.5 feet) above the ground. This is because thermometers placed closer to the ground can be affected by radiation and heat from the ground, which can lead to inaccurate readings.

2. This statement is correct; the environmental lapse rate describes how temperature changes with altitude in the atmosphere. This lapse rate is important in meteorology and atmospheric science for understanding temperature variations at different altitudes.

111. (C): Statement 1: This statement is correct. Humidity is typically expressed as relative humidity (RH), which is the ratio of the amount of water vapour present in the air compared to the maximum amount of water vapour that the air can hold at that temperature, expressed as a percentage.

Statement 3: This statement is also correct. Warmer air can hold more water vapour than cooler air, so for the same amount of water vapour present, the relative humidity decreases as the air temperature increases.

112. (B): Statement 1: This statement is correct. In the Northern Hemisphere, cyclones (low-pressure systems) have a counter clockwise circulation, whereas anticyclones (high-pressure systems) have a clockwise circulation due to the Coriolis Effect.

Statement 2: This statement is also correct. Cyclones typically bring cloudy, rainy, and stormy weather due to the upward motion of warm air and condensation. Anticyclones, on the other hand, usually result in clear skies and fair weather due to descending air and suppression of cloud formation.

113. (A): The given characteristics are of Mormugao Port, which is situated in Mormugao town, Goa. It falls on the western coast of India. It was commissioned in 1885 and is one of the oldest ports of India.

114. (C): Rourkela steel plant is situated in Rourkela, Odisha and is operated by the Steel Authority of India (SAIL). It was established on February 3, 1959. It obtains water from Sankh and Koel rivers. The power for the electric furnace is procured from Hirakud. It receives coal from Jharia and iron-ore from Sundargarh and Kendujhar.

115. (B): 1. This statement is correct. The oceanic crust is denser and heavier than the continental crust due to its composition, which primarily includes basaltic rocks, compared to the granitic rocks of the continental crust.

2. This statement is also correct. The mantle, which lies between the crust and the core, contains most of the Earth's internal heat and plays a crucial role in heat transfer through convection.

3. This statement is incorrect. The convective cells responsible for heat transfer and driving plate-tectonic processes are located in the mantle, not the crust. The crust is too rigid and not the primary location for large-scale convective movements.

116. (B): 1. This statement is correct. The Tsangpo River, originating in Tibet, enters India as the Dihang River in the northeastern state of Arunachal Pradesh.

2. This statement is correct. The Godavari River has the second largest river basin in India, covering about 10% of the country's total area.

3. This statement is incorrect. The Chambal and Betwa rivers are tributaries of the Yamuna River, not the Ganga. They do not join the Ganga directly in Uttar Pradesh.

117. (D): 1. Tropical Wet Climate (Af): This climate type is indeed one of the rainiest in the world, primarily due to the ITCZ being overhead for much of the year. So, statement 1 is correct.

2. Tropical Savanna Climate (Aw): This climate experiences distinct wet and dry seasons. The wet season corresponds to the period when the ITCZ is overhead, bringing heavy rainfall. The dry season occurs when the ITCZ shifts away. Therefore, statement 2 is also correct.

3. Tropical Monsoonal Climate: This climate type also experiences heavy rainfall, but it is influenced by the seasonal shift in the position of the ITCZ, which affects the direction of prevailing winds and the timing of rainfall. So, statement 3 is correct as well.

118. (C): Typhoons are tropical cyclones that originate in the northwestern Pacific Ocean. These form over warm ocean waters, typically with sea surface temperatures. They are characterised by strong winds, heavy rainfall, storm surges, and sometimes tornadoes. Hurricanes are tropical cyclones that form in the Atlantic Ocean and the eastern Pacific Ocean. They are also known as cyclones in the Indian Ocean and the South Pacific.

119. (B): The characteristics provided describe the temperate forest biome. These forests experience ample rainfall and varying temperatures from cold to mild. Dominated by deciduous trees like maple and oak, they harbour diverse wildlife, including raccoons, opossums, bats, and squirrels, thriving in the canopy and undergrowth of these ecosystems.

120. (A): Chlorophyll, the pigment responsible for the green color of leaves, primarily absorbs blue and red light wavelengths from the visible spectrum. It absorbs these wavelengths to facilitate photosynthesis, which is the process of converting light energy into chemical energy. The green light, which is not absorbed effectively by chlorophyll, is reflected and gives leaves their characteristic green colour.

121. (D): Prokaryotic cells typically contain a single circular chromosome located in the nucleoid region of the cell. This chromosome carries the genetic material (DNA) necessary for the cell's functions and reproduction.

122. (B): In bacteria, the DNA is not complexed with histone proteins or other structural proteins as in eukaryotic cells. Instead, bacterial DNA is typically a circular molecule that exists in a region of the cell called the nucleoid. This lack of histones or other associated proteins is why bacterial DNA is considered "naked".

123. (A): Lymphocytes, a type of white blood cell, are responsible for producing antibodies against foreign antigens. These antibodies are part of the adaptive immune response, where lymphocytes recognize specific antigens and produce antibodies tailored to neutralize or eliminate them.

124. (C):

$$F_{net} = (10 + 15) - (2 + F + 15)$$
$$0 = 25 - 2 - F - 15$$
$$\Rightarrow \quad 0 = 25 - 17 - F$$
$$\therefore \quad F = 8N.$$

125. (C): Nuclear reactors typically include a turbine, a heat exchanger, and a reaction chamber as essential parts of their operation. A mechanism to reduce CO_2 emission is not specific to nuclear reactors since they do not produce CO_2 during their operation.

126. (A): $R_{eq} = 5 + 0 + 5 = 10\ \Omega$

($0\ \Omega$ means it is short circuiting other two $10\ \Omega$ resistors)

$$I = \frac{V}{R_{eq}} = \frac{10}{10} = 1A.$$

127. (A): A microscope usually consists of two convex lenses: the objective lens and the eyepiece lens. The objective lens, which is closer to the specimen, produces a magnified real image of the specimen. This image is further magnified by the eyepiece lens, which is positioned closer to the viewer's eye, resulting in a larger virtual image that can be observed.

128. (C): When object distance increase, in order to maintain image at retina, focal length increases initially, later for extreme distance it becomes constant. Hence, option (C) is correct.

129. (B): 1. Primary rainbow formation involves refraction of sunlight as it enters the water droplet, one internal reflection inside the droplet, and refraction again as it exits the droplet.

3. The primary rainbow is formed as the inner bow, with the secondary rainbow (if present) appearing outside the primary one.

130. (C): Niels Bohr introduced the concept that electrons orbit the nucleus in specific, quantised orbits or energy levels without radiating energy, which was a departure from classical physics. According to Bohr's model, an electron in a stable orbit does not emit radiation, thus preventing it from spiraling into the nucleus.

131. (D): The LIGO (Laser Interferometer Gravitational-Wave Observatory) experiment confirmed the prediction of gravitational waves, which are ripples in spacetime caused by accelerating massive objects, as described by Einstein's general theory of relativity.

132. (B): Given, $m = 2$ kg, $u = 3\frac{m}{s}$, $v = 0$

Using, $v^2 - u^2 = 2as$

$\Rightarrow$ $0 - 9 = 2 \times a \times s$

$\Rightarrow$ $-9 = 6a$, $a = -1.5$ m/s^2

Now, $F = ma = 2(-1.5) = -3$ N

Negative sign indicates it is retarding force, hence magnitude of friction is 3 N.

133. (B): In metals, atoms are arranged in a lattice structure, and their outer electrons become delocalised, forming a "sea of electrons." These free electrons can move easily throughout the lattice when an electric field is applied, facilitating the flow of electric current.

134. (A): The Indian Postal Service, with 1,55,333 post offices, is the most widely distributed post office system in the world. In the 14th century, India had a postal system of two kinds- The horse post, called ulus, run by royal horses stationed at a distance of every four miles. This foot-post was quicker than the horse-post.

135. (B): Bhanumati is a commentary written by Chakrapanidatta, a scholar from Bengal in the 11th century CE, on the Sushrut Samhita. This text serves as an important commentary that elucidates and expands upon the teachings and practices outlined in the Sushrut Samhita, which itself is one of the foundational texts of Ayurveda, particularly focusing on surgery.

136. (C): 1. This statement aligns with historical research indicating that the Portuguese introduced tobacco cultivation to India, with their influence notably strong in the Deccan region during the early 17th century.

2. This statement is also correct as it aligns with historical records that indicate tobacco cultivation spread from the Deccan region to northern India and other parts of the country during the early 17th century.

137. (D): The Women's Indian Association (WIA) was founded at Adayar, Madras, in 1917 by Annie Besant, Margaret Cousins, Dorothy Jinarajadasa, and others to liberate women from the deplorable condition women suffered in socio-economic and political matters during the 19th and the early 20th century.

138. (D): 1. The All India Depressed Classes Association of M.C. Rajah was staunchly in favour of joint electorate. This statement is correct because M.C. Rajah and the Depressed Classes Association advocated for joint electorates to avoid further marginalization of Dalits and ensure they were not isolated politically.

2. The All India Depressed Classes Leaders' Conference demanded separate electorate. This statement is also correct as some leaders within the Dalit community did advocate for separate electorates to secure political representation for the depressed classes.

3. The Communal Award in September 1932 recognized the right to separate electorate for the 'untouchables'. This statement is correct; the Communal Award indeed granted separate electorates for Dalits among other communities.

139. (C): 2. The Silk Road was not a single route but a complex network of trade routes that connected various regions across Asia and beyond. These routes included overland routes through Central Asia, as well as maritime routes that connected ports in Southeast Asia, India, and China with the Middle East and beyond.

3. The Silk Road routes emerged around the 2nd century BCE and continued to thrive until the 15th century CE. These routes were crucial for the exchange of goods such as silk, spices, ceramics, precious metals, and textiles, as well as cultural and technological exchanges.

4. Along with silk, the Silk Road facilitated the trade of a wide range of goods. Chinese pottery, textiles, and porcelain were highly valued commodities that traveled westward, while goods such as spices, ivory,

gemstones, and medicinal herbs from India and Southeast Asia traveled eastward along these routes.

140. (C): 1. The surface of the rock at Ajanta was indeed prepared by coating it with clay mixed with rice husk and gum, followed by a coat of lime applied over this preparation. This created a smooth surface suitable for painting.

2. The painting process at Ajanta typically involved first creating an outline drawing on the lime coating, after which colors were added subsequently to complete the paintings.

141. (C): 1. SKA is a state-of-the-art, mega science international facility to build the world's biggest and most sensitive radio telescope for addressing a wide variety of cutting-edge science goals. This statement is correct.

2. The Government of India has accorded its approval for India's participation in the international mega science project. This statement is also correct.

142. (C): The exercise Desert Cyclone is a joint military exercise between India and UAE. It was held in January 2024 in Rajasthan and it aims to enhance interoperability by learning & sharing best practices in Urban Operations.

143. (A): 1. Statement 1 is correct: Dr. Arvind Panagariya was indeed appointed as the Chairman of the Sixteenth Finance Commission.

2. Statement 2 is incorrect: The Finance Commission is constituted in pursuance to Article 280, not Article 263, of the Constitution of India. Article 263 deals with the establishment of the Inter-State Council.

144. (D): The Ministry of Environment, Forest and Climate Change has nominated Indore, Bhopal, and Udaipur from India for Wetland City Accreditation (WCA) under the Ramsar Convention on Wetlands. This accreditation recognizes cities that effectively manage their wetlands, promoting their conservation and sustainable use. Jodhpur, however, has not been nominated as one of the cities seeking WCA accreditation in this recent initiative.

145. (B): The Government of India declared 12th January as National Youth Day to celebrate the birth anniversary of Swami Vivekananda, aiming to inspire young people across the country with the ideals and teachings of him. Celebrations typically include youth conferences, seminars, cultural programs, and activities that promote the values of service, harmony, and tolerance among youth.

146. (C): 1. INS Sagardhwani is indeed an oceanographic research vessel operated by the Naval Physical and Oceanographic Laboratory (NPOL) of the Defence Research and Development Organisation (DRDO) in India. It is equipped with advanced scientific instruments and capabilities to conduct various oceanographic studies, including mapping the ocean floor, studying marine biodiversity, and monitoring oceanographic parameters.

2. Recently, INS Sagardhwani participated in the Sagar Maitri Mission - 4, which is aimed at fostering long-term scientific collaborations with Indian Ocean Rim countries. The mission focuses on joint research initiatives, sharing of oceanographic data, and enhancing scientific cooperation in Ocean Research and Development (R&D).

147. (C): The central government constituted a High-Level Committee under the former President, Shri Ram Nath Kovind to examine the issue relating to holding simultaneous elections (One Nation One Election) in the country and make recommendations. The idea of 'One Nation, One Poll' or 'One Nation, One Election' refers to holding simultaneous elections across the country, which means, polls for Lok Sabha and state assemblies will be held together.

148. (C): The inauguration of India's first all-girls' Sainik School in Vrindavan in January 2024 is a landmark development aimed at providing military education and training specifically for girls. Sainik Schools are known for their focus on grooming students for careers in the armed forces through rigorous academic and physical training. This initiative is part of efforts to promote gender equality in the defense sector and encourage more girls to pursue careers in the military.

149. (A): Ministry of Home Affairs (MHA) has decided to scrap the Free Movement Regime (FMR) between India and Myanmar to ensure the internal security of the country and to maintain the demographic structure of India's North Eastern States bordering Myanmar.

150. (B): "Why Bharat Matters" is a book authored by Subrahmanyam Jaishankar, who is a prominent Indian diplomat and politician, currently serving as the External Affairs Minister of India. The book delves into India's foreign policy perspectives and its strategic significance on the global stage. It explores India's historical role, contemporary challenges, and future opportunities in shaping international relations, emphasizing the country's cultural, economic, and geopolitical strengths.

PAPER II : MATHEMATICS

1. (D): $|2B\,[\text{adj}\,(3A)]| = |2B|\,\text{adj}\,(3A)|$
$= 2^3|B|\;|3A|^{3-1}$
$= 8|B|\;(3^3\;|A|)^2$
$= 8|B|\;\times\;3^6\;|A|^2$
$= 8\times\frac{1}{729}\times 3^6\times\left(\frac{1}{2\sqrt{2}}\right)^2$
$= 8\times\frac{1}{729}\times 729\times\frac{1}{8} = 1.$

2. (B): $\because\; iz^3 + z^2 - z + i = 0$
put $z = i$
$\therefore\; i^4 + i^2 - i + i = 0$
$\Rightarrow\; 1 - 1 - i + i = 0$
Hence, $[|z| + 1]^2 = [|i| + 1]^2 = 2^2 = 4.$

3. (D): Sum of all four digit number start with 1
$= 1 \times 6 \times 1000 + 18 \times 100 + 18 \times 10 + 18$
$= 6000 + 1800 + 180 + 18 = 7998$
Sum of all four digit numbers start with 4
$= 4 \times 6 \times 1000 + 12 \times 100 + 12 \times 10 + 12$
$= 24000 + 1200 + 120 + 12 = 25332$
Sum of all four digit numbers start with 5
$= 6 \times 5 \times 1000 + 10 \times 100 + 10 \times 10 + 10$
$= 30000 + 1000 + 110 = 31110$
$\therefore$ Required sum $= 7998 + 25332 + 31110 = 64440.$

4. (A): $\because\; x, y, z$ are cube root of unity
Let, $x = 1,\; y = w,\; z = w^2$
$\therefore$ Value of $xy + yz + zx$
$= 1 \times w + w \times w^2 + w^2 \times 1$
$= w + w^3 + w^2$
$\left[\begin{array}{l}\because\; w^3 = 1\\ 1 + w + w^2 = 0\end{array}\right]$
$= w + 1 + w^2$
$= 1 + w + w^2 = 0.$

5. (C): Total number of ways
$= {}^4C_3 \times {}^4C_3 = 4 \times 4 = 16$
$+ {}^3C_1 \times {}^4C_2 \times {}^4C_2 \times {}^3C_1$
$= 18 \times 18 = 324$
$+ {}^3C_3 \times {}^4C_0 \times {}^4C_0 \times {}^3C_3$
$= 1 \times 1 \times 1 \times 1 = 1$
$+ {}^3C_2 \times {}^4C_1 \times {}^4C_1 \times {}^3C_2$
$= 12 \times 12 = 144$
Hence, they can invite total no. of ways
$= 16 + 324 + 1 + 144 = 485.$

6. (A): Total no. of triangles formed
$= {}^{12}C_3 - ({}^3C_3 + {}^4C_3 + {}^5C_3)$
$= \frac{12\times 11\times 10\times 9!}{9!\times 3!} - (1+4+10)$
$= \frac{12\times 11\times 10}{3\times 2} - 15$
$= 2 \times 110 - 15$
$= 220 - 15 = 205.$

7. (A): $\because$
$\log_b a = P \Rightarrow a = b^P$
$\log_d c = 2P \Rightarrow c = d^{2P}$
$\log_f e = 3P \Rightarrow e = f^{3P}$
$(ace)^{\frac{1}{P}} = (b^P d^{2P} f^{3P})^{\frac{1}{P}}$
$= bd^2f^3.$

8. (C): $\because\; -\sqrt{2}$ and $\sqrt{3}$ are roots of the given equation

Therefore $\sqrt{2}$ and $-\sqrt{3}$ are also roots of the given equation $x^4 + a_3x^3 + a_2x^2 + a_1x + a_0$
$= \left(x+\sqrt{2}\right)\left(x-\sqrt{2}\right)\left(x-\sqrt{3}\right)\left(x+\sqrt{3}\right)$
$= (x^2 - 2)(x^2 - 3)$
$= x^4 - 3x^2 - 2x^2 + 6$
$= x^4 - 5x^2 + 6$
$\therefore\; a_3 = 0,\; a_2 = -5,\; a_1 = 0$ and $a_0 = 6.$

9. (C): Let $z_1 = x_1 + iy_1$ and $z_2 = x_2 + iy_2$
Now, $\left|\frac{z_1+z_2}{z_1-z_2}\right| = 1$
$\Rightarrow\; |z_1 + z_2| = |z_1 - z_2|$
$\Rightarrow |(x_1 + x_2) + i(y_1 + y_2)| = |(x_1 - x_2) + i(y_1 - y_2)|$
$\Rightarrow (x_1 + x_2)^2 + (y_1 + y_2)^2 = (x_1 - x_2)^2 + (y_1 - y_2)^2$
$\Rightarrow x_1^2 + x_2^2 + 2x_1x_2 + y_1^2 + y_2^2 + 2y_1y_2 = x_1^2 + x_2^2 - 2x_1x_2 + y_1^2 + y_2^2 - 2y_1y_2$
$\Rightarrow\; x_1x_2 + y_1y_2 = 0$
$\frac{z_1}{z_2} = \frac{x_1+iy_1}{x_2+iy_2}\times\frac{x_2-iy_2}{x_2-iy_2}$
$= \frac{(x_1x_2+y_1y_2)+i(y_1x_2-x_1y_2)}{x_2^2+y_2^2}$
$= 0+\frac{i(y_1x_2-x_1y_2)}{x_2^2+y_2^2}$

$\therefore \quad \text{Re}\left(\dfrac{z_1}{z_2}\right) = 0$

$\therefore \quad \text{Re}\left(\dfrac{z_1}{z_2}\right)+1 = 1.$

10. (B): $\because$ $26! = n8^k = n2^{3k}$

Maximum power of 2

$$= \left[\frac{26}{2}\right]+\left[\frac{26}{4}\right]+\left[\frac{26}{8}\right]+\left[\frac{26}{16}\right]$$

$$= 13 + 6 + 3 + 1 = 23$$

But power of 2 $= 3k$

$\therefore$ Maximum value of $3k = 21$

Hence, the maximum value of $k = 7$.

11. (B): Statements:

1. adj(AB) = (adjA)(adjB)

   Statement 1 is not correct.

2. AB $\neq$ BA

   $\therefore$ adj(AB) $\neq$ adj(BA)

   Statement 2 is not correct.

3. (AB)adj(AB) $-$ $|AB|I_n$

   $\Rightarrow$ $|AB|I_n - |AB|I_n$ [AadjA = |A|I]

   = Null matrix

   Hence, statement 3 is correct.

12. (D): Statement 1 is correct.

We have if $A^n = A$ then A is identity matrix

$\therefore$ Statements 2 and 3 are correct.

Hence, all statement are correct.

13. (B): All even digits are

0, 2, 4, 6, 8

4	5	5	5

Choice 4 5 5 5

Hence, total required number

$$= 4 \times 5 \times 5 \times 5 = 500.$$

14. (B): $(z - 100)^3 + 1000 = 0$

$\Rightarrow \quad (z - 100)^3 = -1000 = (-10)^3$

$\Rightarrow \quad z - 100 = -10$

$\Rightarrow \quad z = 90$

$z - 100 = 10w \Rightarrow z = 100 - 10w$

$z - 100 = -10w^2$

$\Rightarrow \quad z = 100 - 10w^2$.

15. (D): $(1 + i)^4 + (1 - i)^4 = [(1 + i)^2]^2 + [(1 - i)^2]^2$

$= (1 - 1 + 2i)^2 + (1 - 1 - 2i)^2$

$= (2i)^2 + (-2i)^2$

$= 4i^2 + 4i^2 = -4 - 4 = -8.$

16. (A): We have, all diagonal elements of skew symmetric matrix is zero then their sum is also zero.

$\therefore$ Statement 1 and 2 are correct

We know that if $AA^T = 1$

then, A is called orthogonal matrix

But, $AA^T = A(-A) = -A^2$ $[\because A^T = -A]$

$\therefore$ Statement 3 is not correct.

17. (D): We know that if last two digits of a number divisible by 4 then numbers divisible by 4.

Hence, number is divisible by 4

$$= 1 \times 2 \times 3 \times 1 = 6.$$

18. (A): $2^{120} = (2^3)^{40} = 8^{40} = (1 + 7)^{40}$

$= 1 + {}^{40}C_1\ 7 + {}^{40}C_2\ 7^2 + \ldots + {}^{40}C_{10}\ 7^{40}$

$= 1 + 7[{}^{40}C_1 + {}^{40}C_2\ 7 + \ldots + {}^{40}C_{40}\ 7^{39}]$

$\therefore$ Remainder = 1.

19. (C): $\begin{vmatrix} C(9,4) & C(9,3) & C(10,n-2) \\ C(11,6) & C(11,5) & C(12,n) \\ C(m,7) & C(m,6) & C(m+1,7)-C(m+1,n+1) \end{vmatrix} = 0$

Applying $C_3 \to C_1 + C_2 - C_3$

$$\begin{vmatrix} C(9,4) & C(9,3) & C(10,4)-C(10,n-2) \\ C(11,6) & C(11,5) & C(12,6)-C(12,n) \\ C(m,7) & C(m,6) & C(m+1,7)-C(m+1,n+1) \end{vmatrix} = 0$$

$\because$ Value of determinant = 0

$\therefore$ $C_3 = 0 \Rightarrow n - 2 = 4 \Rightarrow n = 6.$

20. (B): $\begin{vmatrix} \cos C & \sin B & 0 \\ \tan A & 0 & \sin B \\ 0 & \tan(B+C) & \cos C \end{vmatrix}$

$= \cos C\ [-\sin B \cdot \tan(B + C)$
$- \tan A\ (\sin B \cdot \cos C)]$

$$= -\sin B\cdot\cos C\left[\frac{\sin(B+C)}{\cos(B+C)}+\frac{\sin A}{\cos A}\right]$$

$$= -\sin B\cdot\cos C\left[\frac{\sin(B+C)\cos A+\sin A\cos(B+C)}{\cos A\cdot\cos(B+C)}\right]$$

$$= -\sin B\cdot\cos C\,\frac{\sin(A+B+C)}{\cos A\cdot\cos(B+C)}$$

$$= \frac{-\sin B\cdot\cos C\sin\pi}{\cos A\cdot\cos(B+C)} = 0.$$

21. (D): Possible order of 4 entries matrices 1×4, 2×2, 4×1

$\therefore$ Total number of matrices

$$= 4 \times 4 \times 4 \times 4 \times 3$$

$$= 768.$$

22. (A):

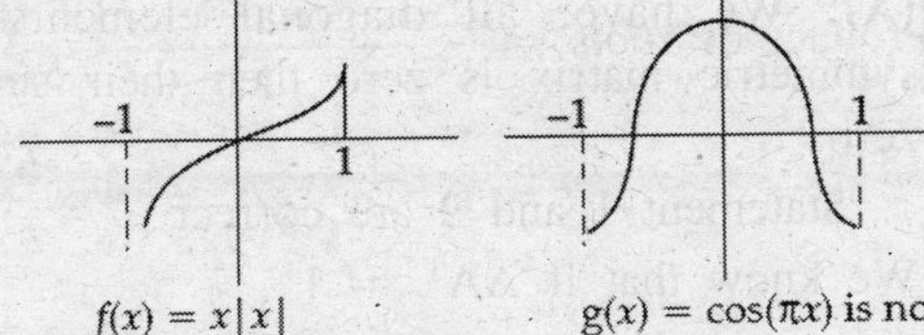

23. (D): x R$y \Rightarrow |x + y| < 2$ in $(-1, 1)$

For reflexive,

$|x + x| < 2 \Rightarrow |x| < 1$ true

$\therefore$ R is reflexive

For symmetric

Let x R$y \Rightarrow |x + y| < 2$

$\Rightarrow |y + x| < 2 \Rightarrow y$ Rx

$\therefore$ R is symmetric

For transitive

$-1 < x < 1$

Let $|x + y| < 2$ and $|y + z| < 2$

then $|x + z| < 2$

Hence, R is transitive.

24. (A): $(A \cup B) - \{(A - B) \cup (B - A) \cup (A \cap B)\}$

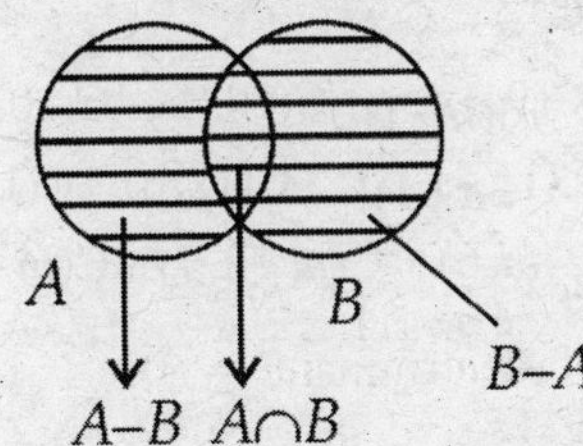

$\therefore (A - B) \cup (B - A) \cup (A \cap B) = A \cup B$

$\therefore (A \cup B) - (A \cup B) = \phi$ (Null set).

25. (A): $\begin{vmatrix} a^2 & b\sin A & c\sin A \\ b\sin A & 1 & \cos A \\ c\sin A & \cos A & 1 \end{vmatrix}$

$= a^2(1 - \cos^2 A) - b \sin A(b \sin A - c \cos A \,.\, \sin A)$
$\quad + c \sin A(b \sin A \cdot \cos A - c \sin A)$

$= a^2 \sin^2 A - b^2 \sin^2 A + bc \sin^2 A \cdot \cos A$
$\quad + bc \sin^2 A \cdot \cos A - c^2 \sin^2 A$

$= a^2 \sin^2 A - b^2 \sin^2 A - c^2 \sin^2 A$
$\quad + 2bc \sin^2 A \cdot \cos A$

$= \sin^2 A(a^2 - b^2 - c^2 + 2bc \cos A)$

$= \sin^2 A \times 0 = 0.$

26. (A): $\because a, b, c$ are in AP

$\Rightarrow \quad 2b = a + c \quad \ldots(i)$

b, c, d are in GP

$\Rightarrow \quad c^2 = bd \quad \ldots(ii)$

c, d, e are in HP

$\Rightarrow \quad \dfrac{2}{d} = \dfrac{1}{c} + \dfrac{1}{e} \quad \ldots(iii)$

From (i) and (ii)

$2c^2 = (a + c)d$

$\Rightarrow \quad \dfrac{2}{d} = \dfrac{a+c}{c^2}$

$\Rightarrow \quad \dfrac{1}{c} + \dfrac{1}{e} = \dfrac{a}{c^2} + \dfrac{1}{c}$

$\Rightarrow \quad \dfrac{1}{e} = \dfrac{a}{c^2} \Rightarrow c^2 = ae$

Hence, a, c, e are in GP.

27. (B): $\log_4(x - 1) = \log_2(x - 3)$

$\Rightarrow \quad \dfrac{1}{2}\log(x-1) = \log_2(x - 3)$

$\Rightarrow \quad \log_2(x - 1) = \log_2(x - 3)^2$

$\Rightarrow \quad x - 1 = x^2 - 6x + 9$

$\Rightarrow x^2 - 7x + 10 = 0$

$\Rightarrow x^2 - 5x - 2x + 10 = 0$

$\Rightarrow x(x - 5) - 2(x - 5) = 0$

$\Rightarrow \quad (x - 5)(x - 2) = 0$

$\left[\begin{array}{l} x \neq 2 \text{ because} \\ x-3>0, x>3 \end{array}\right]$

$\Rightarrow \quad x = 2, 5$

$\Rightarrow \quad x = 5$

Hence, one solution.

28. (D): $\log_x\left(\dfrac{x}{y}\right) + \log_y\left(\dfrac{y}{x}\right) = k$

$\Rightarrow \quad \log_x x - \log_x y + \log_y y - \log_y x = k$

$\Rightarrow \quad 1 - \log_x y + 1 - \dfrac{1}{\log_x y} = k$

Let, $\quad \log_x y = t$

$\therefore \quad 2 - t - \dfrac{1}{t} = k$

$\Rightarrow \quad 2t - t^2 - 1 = kt$

$\Rightarrow \quad t^2 + (k - 2)t + 1 = 0$

For solution, $\quad D = b^2 - 4ac \geq 0$

$(k - 2)^2 - 4 \geq 0 \qquad (k - 2)^2 \geq 0$

$k - 2 \geq 2 \qquad k - 2 \leq 0$

$k \geq 4 \qquad k \leq 0$

$\therefore k \geq 4$ or $k \leq 0$

Hence, $k \neq 1$.

29. (C): $\quad |A| = \begin{vmatrix} \sin 2\theta & -\cos 2\theta & 0 \\ \cos 2\theta & \sin 2\theta & 0 \\ 0 & 0 & 1 \end{vmatrix} = 1$

We have if $|A| = \pm 1$ then A is orthogonal matrix.

So, $\quad A^{-1} = A^T$ and $A^{-1} = \text{adj A}$.

30. (A): $(1-x^2)^{20}\left[-\left(\frac{1}{x^2}+x^2-2\right)\right]^{-5}$

$$= -(1-x^2)^{20}\left(x-\frac{1}{x}\right)^{-10}$$
$$= -(1 - x^2)^{20}\ (x^2 - 1)^{-10}\ x^{10}$$
$$= -(1 - x^2)^{10}\ .\ x^{10}$$
$$T_{r+1} = -{}^{10}C_r(1)^{10-r}\ (-x^2)^{10-r}\ .\ x^{10}$$
$$= (-1)^{11-r}\ .\ {}^{10}C_r\ x^{30-2r}$$

$\because$ $30 - 2r = 10$

$\Rightarrow$ $r = 10$

$\therefore$ Coefficient of $x^{10} = (-1)^1\ {}^{10}C_{10} = -1 \times 1\ -1.$

31. (B): $T_4 = T_{3+1}$

$$= {}^nC_3(mx)^{n-3}\left(\frac{1}{x}\right)^3 = \frac{5}{2}$$

$$\frac{5}{2}x^0 = {}^nC_3(m)^{n-3}\ x^{n-6}.$$

On comparing the power of x

$\therefore$ $n - 6 = 0$

$\Rightarrow$ $n = 6$

and ${}^6C_3\ m^3 = \frac{5}{2}$

$\Rightarrow$ $\frac{6.5.4}{3.2}m^3 = \frac{5}{2}$

$20\ m^2 = \frac{5}{2}$

$\Rightarrow$ $m^3 = \frac{1}{8}$

$\Rightarrow$ $m = \frac{1}{2}$

$\therefore$ $mn = \frac{1}{2}\times 6 = 3.$

32. (D): Given that a, b, c are in GP

$\therefore$ $b^2 = ac$

Now, $ax^2 + bx + c = 0$

$D = b^2 - 4ac$

$= ac - 4ac = -3ac < 0$

1. $\therefore$ Roots are imaginary (correct)

Let, $a = 2,\ b = 4,\ c = 8$

$\therefore$ $x^2 + 2x + 4 = 0$

$\Rightarrow$ $x = \frac{-2\pm\sqrt{4-16}}{2} = -1\pm\sqrt{3}$

2. Ratio of roots $= \frac{-1+\sqrt{3}}{-1-\sqrt{3}} = \frac{\omega}{\omega^2} = \frac{1}{\omega}$ (correct)

3. Product of roots $= \frac{(-1+\sqrt{3})(-1-\sqrt{3})}{2}\times 4$

$= \omega \cdot \omega^2 \cdot 4 = 4 = \frac{b^2}{a^2}.$

(correct)

Hence, statements 1, 2 and 3 are correct.

33. (C): Let n be an integer and $n = 0$

$\therefore$ $x^2 + mx = 0$

$\Rightarrow$ $x(x + m) = 0$

$\Rightarrow$ $x = 0,\ x = -m$

Since n is integer, therefore m is also integer.

34. (A): $(x + y)^{2n+1}\ .\ (x - y)^{2n+1}$

Middle term,

$\frac{2n+2}{2}, \frac{2n+4}{2} = (n + 1)$th term, $(n + 2)$th term

$$T_{n+1} = {}^{2n+1}C_n(x^2)^{n+1}\ (y^2)^n$$
$$T_{n+2} = 2^{n+1}C_{n+1}\ (x^2)^n(y^2)^{n+1}$$
$${}^{2n+1}C_n(x^2)^{n+1}(y^2)^n = 2^{n+1}C_{n+1}(x^2)^n(y^2)^{n+1}$$

$\Rightarrow$ $\frac{2^{n+1}C_n}{{}^{2n+1}C_{n+1}} = \frac{x^{2n}y^{2n+2}}{x^{2n+2}y^{2n}}$

$\Rightarrow$ $\frac{(2n+1)!}{(n+1)!n!}\times\frac{n!(n+1)!}{(2n+1)!} = \frac{y^2}{x^2}$

$\Rightarrow$ $\frac{y^2}{x^2} = 1$

$\because$ $\frac{1}{y^2} = \frac{1}{1}$

$\therefore$ $\frac{x^2}{y^2} = 1$

35. (C): $n(A) = 5$ and $n(B) = 2$

Number of onto functions $= 2^5 - {}^2C_1(2 - 1)^5$

$= 32 - 2 = 30.$

36. (D): $\frac{\sqrt{3}\cos 10° - \sin 10°}{\sin 25° \cdot \cos 25°}$

$$= \frac{\left(\frac{\sqrt{3}}{2}\cdot\cos 10° - \frac{1}{2}\sin 10°\right)}{2\frac{2\sin 25°\cdot\cos 25°}{2\times 2}}$$

$$= 4\left(\frac{\sin 60°.\cos 10° - \cos 60°.\sin 10°}{\sin 50°}\right)$$

$$= \frac{4\cdot\sin(60° - 10°)}{\sin 50°}$$

$$= \frac{4\sin 50°}{\sin 50°} = 4.$$

37. (C): $\sin 9° - \cos 9° = \sqrt{2}\dfrac{(\sin 9° - \cos 9°)}{\sqrt{2}}$

$$= \sqrt{2}\left(\frac{1}{\sqrt{2}}\sin 9° - \frac{1}{\sqrt{2}}\cos 9°\right)$$

$$= \sqrt{2}\,[\sin(45° - 9°)]$$

$$= \sqrt{2}\sin 36°$$

$$= \sqrt{2}\left[\sqrt{2}\frac{\left(\sqrt{5-\sqrt{5}}\right)}{4}\right]$$

$$= 2\frac{\sqrt{5-\sqrt{5}}}{4}$$

$$= \frac{\sqrt{5-\sqrt{5}}}{2}.$$

38. (D): Given that,

$\sin^3 A + \sin^3 B + \sin^3 C$

$= 3 \sin A \cdot \sin B \cdot \sin C$

$\Rightarrow \sin A + \sin B + \sin C = 0$

$\Rightarrow \quad ak + kb + kc = 0$

$\Rightarrow \quad a + b + c = 0$

$$\begin{vmatrix} a & b & c \\ b & c & a \\ c & a & b \end{vmatrix} = \begin{vmatrix} a+b+c & b & c \\ b+c+a & c & a \\ c+a+b & a & b \end{vmatrix}$$

(Applying $C_1 \to C_1 + C_2 + C_3$)

$$= \begin{vmatrix} 0 & b & c \\ 0 & c & a \\ 0 & a & b \end{vmatrix} = 0.$$

39. (C): $\cos^{-1} x = \sin^{-1} x$

$\Rightarrow \quad \dfrac{\pi}{2} - \sin^{-1} x = \sin^{-1} x$

$\Rightarrow \quad 2\sin^{-1} x = \dfrac{\pi}{2}$

$\Rightarrow \quad \sin^{-1} x = \dfrac{\pi}{4}$

$\Rightarrow \quad x = \sin\dfrac{\pi}{4} = \dfrac{1}{\sqrt{2}}.$

40. (B): $(\sin \theta - \cos \theta)^2 = 2$

$\Rightarrow \sin^2 \theta + \cos^2 \theta - 2 \sin \theta \cdot \cos \theta = 2$

$\Rightarrow \quad 1 - \sin 2\theta = 2$

$\Rightarrow \quad \sin 2\theta = -1$

Hence no. of solution = only two.

41. (C): $\dfrac{\cos A + \cos B}{\cos\left(\dfrac{A-B}{2}\right)} = \dfrac{2\cos\dfrac{A+B}{2}\cdot\cos\dfrac{A-B}{2}}{\cos\left(\dfrac{A-B}{2}\right)}$

$$= 2\cos\left(\frac{\pi - C}{2}\right)$$

$$= 2\cos\left(\frac{\pi}{2} - \frac{C}{2}\right) = 2\sin\frac{C}{2}$$

$$= 2\sin 30° = 2\times\frac{1}{2} = 1.$$

42. (C): $2\cot^{-1} 3 = 2\tan^{-1}\dfrac{1}{3} = \tan^{-1}\dfrac{\dfrac{2}{3}}{1-\dfrac{1}{9}}$

$$= \tan^{-1}\left(\frac{2}{3}\times\frac{9}{8}\right) = \tan^{-1}\frac{3}{4}$$

So, $\sqrt{15 + \cot^2\left(\dfrac{\pi}{4} - 2\cot^{-1} 3\right)}$

$$= \sqrt{15 + \cot^2\left(\tan^{-1} 1 - \tan^{-1}\frac{3}{4}\right)}$$

$$= \sqrt{15 + \cot^2\left[\tan^{-1}\left(\frac{1 - \frac{3}{4}}{1 + \frac{3}{4}}\right)\right]}$$

$$= \sqrt{15 + \cot^2\left(\tan^{-1}\frac{1}{7}\right)}$$

$$= \sqrt{15 + 7^2}$$

$$= \sqrt{15 + \cot^2(\cot^{-1} 7)}$$

$$= \sqrt{15 + 49} = 8.$$

43. (B): $\sin 10° \cdot \sin 50° + \sin 50° \cdot \sin 250° + \sin 250° \cdot \sin 10°$

$$= \frac{1}{2}(\cos 40° - \cos 60° + \cos 200° - \cos 300° + \cos 240° - \cos 260°)$$

$$= \frac{1}{2}\left[\cos 40° - \frac{1}{2} + \cos(180+20)° - \cos(360-60)° + \cos(180+60)° - \cos(180+80)°\right]$$

$$= \frac{1}{2}\left[\cos 40° - \frac{1}{2} - \cos 20° - \cos 60° - \cos 60° + \cos 80°\right]$$

$$= \frac{1}{2}\left[\cos 40° - \cos 20° + \cos 80° - \frac{1}{2} - \frac{1}{2} - \frac{1}{2}\right]$$

$$= \frac{1}{2}\left[\cos 40° + \cos 80° - \cos 20° - \frac{3}{2}\right]$$

$$= \frac{1}{2}\left[2\cos\left(\frac{80+40}{2}\right)\times\cos\left(\frac{80-40}{2}\right) - \cos 20° - \frac{3}{2}\right]$$

$$= \frac{1}{2}\left[2\cos 60°.\cos 20° - \cos 20° - \frac{3}{2}\right]$$

$$= \frac{1}{2}\left[2\times\frac{1}{2}.\cos 20° - \cos 20° - \frac{3}{2}\right]$$

$$= \frac{1}{2}\left[\cos 20° - \cos 20° - \frac{3}{2}\right]$$

$$= \frac{1}{2}\left[-\frac{3}{2}\right] = -\frac{3}{4}$$

44. (B): $\tan^{-1}\left(\frac{a}{b}\right) - \tan^{-1}\left(\frac{a-b}{a+b}\right)$

$$= \tan^{-1}\left(\frac{a}{b}\right) - \tan^{-1}\left(\frac{\frac{a}{b}-1}{1+\frac{a}{b}\cdot 1}\right)$$

$$= \tan^{-1}\frac{a}{b} - \tan^{-1}\frac{a}{b} + \tan^{-1} 1$$

$$= \tan^{-1} = \tan^{-1} \times \tan 45°$$

$$= 45° = \frac{\pi}{4}.$$

45. (B): For real roots

$(\cos\beta)^2 - 4\sin\beta(\cos\beta - 1) \geq 0$

Since, $-1 \leq \cos\beta \leq 1$ and $\sin\beta \geq 0$ for $\beta\in[0, \pi]$

So, it is only possible when, $\cos\beta - 1 \geq 0$.

46. (C): $\cos 2A + \cos 2B + \cos 2C$

$= 1 - 2\sin^2 A + 1 - 2\sin^2 B + 1 - 2\sin^2 C$

$= 3 - 2(\sin^2 A + \sin^2 B + \sin^2 C)$

$$= 3-2\left[\left(\frac{16}{65}\right)^2 + \left(\frac{63}{65}\right)^2 + 0\right]$$

$$= 3-2\left[\frac{16^2+63^2}{65^2}\right]$$

$$= 3-2\left[\frac{256+3969}{4225}\right]$$

$$= 3-2\left[\frac{4225}{4225}\right]$$

$= 3 - 2 \times 1$

$= 3 - 2 = 1.$

47. (B): $\alpha+\beta = \frac{5\pi}{4}$

$$\tan(\alpha+\beta) = \tan 5\frac{\pi}{4}$$

$$\Rightarrow \frac{\tan\alpha+\tan\beta}{1-\tan\alpha\times\tan\beta} = \tan\left(\pi+\frac{\pi}{4}\right) = \tan\frac{\pi}{4}$$

$$\Rightarrow \frac{\tan\alpha+\tan\beta}{1-\tan\alpha\times\tan\beta} = 1$$

$\Rightarrow \tan\alpha + \tan\beta = 1 - \tan\alpha \times \tan\beta$

$\Rightarrow \tan\alpha + \tan\beta + \tan\alpha . \tan\beta = 1$

$$\because f(\theta) = \frac{1}{1+\tan\theta}$$

$$f(\alpha).f(\beta) = \frac{1}{1+\tan\alpha+\tan\beta+\tan\alpha.\tan\beta} = \frac{1}{1+1} = \frac{1}{2}.$$

48. (B): $\because \tan\alpha + \tan\beta = 6$

$\tan\alpha . \tan\beta = 8$

$$\tan(\alpha+\beta) = \frac{\tan\alpha+\tan\beta}{1-\tan\alpha.\tan\beta}$$

$$= \frac{6}{1-8} = \frac{6}{-7}$$

$$\cos(2\alpha+2\beta) = \cos 2(\alpha+\beta)$$

$$= \frac{1-\tan^2(\alpha+\beta)}{1+\tan^2(\alpha+\beta)}$$

$$= \frac{1-\frac{36}{49}}{1+\frac{36}{49}}$$

$$= \frac{13}{85}$$

49. (C): $\tan(90 - 25)° + 2 - 2\tan 40° - \tan 25°$

$= \cot 25° - \tan 25° - 2\tan 40° + 2$

$$= \frac{\cos 25°}{\sin 25°} - \frac{\sin 25°}{\cos 25°} - 2\tan 40° + 2$$

$$= \frac{\cos^2 25° - \sin^2 25°}{\sin 25°.\cos 25°} - 2\tan 40° + 2$$

$$= \frac{\cos 2(25°)}{\sin 25°.\cos 25°} - 2\tan 40° + 2$$

$$= \frac{2\times\cos 50°}{2\sin 25°.\cos 25°} - 2\tan 40° + 2$$

$$= \frac{2\cos 50°}{\sin 50°} - 2\tan 40° + 2$$

$= 2\cot 50° - 2\tan 40° + 2$

$= 2\tan 40° - 2\tan 40° + 2 = 2.$

50. (A): In Δ ABC, if triangle is acute angled triangle, then $\cot A \times \cot B \times \cot C > 0$

$\therefore$ Statement 1 is correct.

If triangle is obtuse angled triangle then, $\tan A \times \tan B \times \tan C < 0$

$\therefore$ Statement 2 is wrong.

51. (A): Circle of the equation is

$x^2 + y^2 + 2x + 6y + 1 = 0$

To find the centre (a, b) and radius c of a circle equation can be written as

$(x - h)^2 + (y - k)^2 = r^2$ where (h, k) be the centre of the circle and r is its radius.

Let, $x^2 + y^2 + 2x + 6y + 1 = 0$

$(x^2 + 2x + 1) - 1 + (y^2 + 6y + 9) - 9 + 1 = 0$

$\Rightarrow (x + 1)^2 - 1 + (y + 3)^2 - 9 + 1 = 0$

$\Rightarrow (x + 1)^2 + (y + 3)^2 = 9$

$\Rightarrow [x - (-1)]^2 + [y - (-3)]^2 = (3)^2$

Now, we can see that the centre of the circle is at (–1, –3) and the radius is 3.

$\therefore \quad a = -1, b = -3$ and $c = 3$

$\therefore \quad a^2 + b^2 + c^2 = (-1)^2 + (-3)^2 + (3)^2$

$= 1 + 9 + 9 = 19$

52. (A): The general equation $x^2 + y^2 + z^2 + 2ux + 2vy + 2wz + d = 0$ represents a sphere with centre $(-u, -v, -w)$ and radius $r = \sqrt{u^2+v^2+w^2-d}$

If B is the mid point of the line segment AC where $A = (x_1, y_1, z_1)$ and $C = (x_2, y_2, z_2)$ then.

$$B = \left(\frac{x_1+x_2}{2}, \frac{y_1+y_2}{2}, \frac{z_1+z_2}{2}\right)$$

Given, equation of sphere $x^2 + y^2 + z^2 + 2ux + 2vy + 2wz - 1 = 0$ with AB as its diameter and $A = (1, -1, 2)$ and $B = (2, 1, -1)$

A (1, –1, 2) —— C —— B (2, 1, –1)

$$C = \left(\frac{1+2}{2}, \frac{1-1}{2}, \frac{-1+2}{2}\right)$$

$$= \left(\frac{3}{2}, 0, \frac{1}{2}\right)$$

We know that centre of the sphere is given by $(-u, -v, -w)$

Comparing, then we get,

$$\left(\frac{3}{2}, 0, \frac{1}{2}\right) = (-u, -v, -w)$$

$$u = -\frac{3}{2}, v = 0, w = -\frac{1}{2}$$

$$\therefore u + v + w = -\frac{3}{2} + 0 - \frac{1}{2} = -\frac{4}{2} = -2$$

53. (D):

$\because x = 5$ represents a line || y-axis and cuts the x-axis at 5 units from the origin.

It is given that $x = 5$, this implies that the y-coordinate is zero.

Here, the infinite number of points *i.e.* $(5, y)$ represent the equation $x = 5$ on the xy-plane.

54. (B): The plane equation is $ax + by + cz = d$

Given the plane equation is $2x - 3y + 6z + 4 = 0$

$\Rightarrow \quad 2x - 3y + 6z = -4$

Comparing then we get,

$a = 2, b = -3, c = 6, d = -4$

$$\therefore \quad \sqrt{a^2+b^2+c^2} = \sqrt{(2)^2+(-3)^2+(6)^2}$$

$$= \sqrt{4+9+36} = \sqrt{49} = 7$$

Direction cosines of normal to the plane

$$l = \frac{a}{\sqrt{a^2+b^2+c^2}} = \frac{2}{7}$$

$$m = \frac{b}{\sqrt{a^2+b^2+c^2}} = -\frac{3}{7}$$

$$n = \frac{c}{\sqrt{a^2+b^2+c^2}} = \frac{6}{7}$$

$$\therefore \quad \langle l, m, n\rangle = \left\langle\frac{2}{7}, -\frac{3}{7}, \frac{6}{7}\right\rangle$$

$$\therefore 49(7l^2 + m^2 - n^2) = 49\left[7\left(\frac{2}{7}\right)^2 + \left(-\frac{3}{7}\right)^2 - \left(\frac{6}{7}\right)^2\right]$$

$$= 49\left[\frac{28}{49} + \frac{9}{49} - \frac{36}{49}\right]$$

$$= 49\left[\frac{1}{49}\right] = 1$$

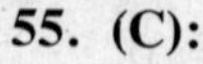

55. (C):

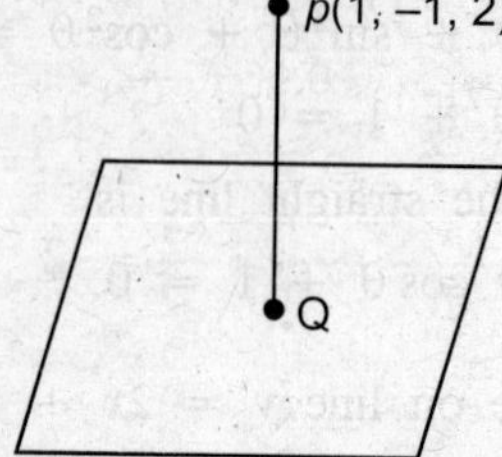

Let the line $p(1, -1, 2)$ and meet the plane at point Q.

Direction ratios of the line from the point (1, –1, 2) to the given plane is $<3, 2, 2>$

$$\therefore \quad \frac{x-1}{3} = \frac{y+1}{2} = \frac{z-2}{2} = \lambda$$

Co-ordinates any points on the line PQ are

$x = 3\lambda + 1,\ y = 2\lambda - 1,\ z = 2\lambda + 2$

$x + 2y + 3z = 18$

$\therefore\ 3\lambda + 1 + 4\lambda - 2 + 6\lambda + 6 = 18$

$\Rightarrow \quad 13\lambda + 5 = 18$

$\Rightarrow \quad 13\lambda = 13$

$\Rightarrow \quad \lambda = 1$

Hence, the co-ordinates of Q are

$(3 + 1, 2 - 1, 2 + 2) = (4, 1, 4)$

56. (D): $\because$ Plane passing through (1, 0, 0), (0, 1, 0) and (0, 0, 1)

$\vec{a} = \hat{i},\ \vec{b} = \hat{j},\ \vec{c} = \hat{k}$

Let, $\quad \hat{r} = x\hat{i} + y\hat{j} + z\hat{k}$

$(\vec{r} - \vec{a})\cdot\left[(\vec{b} - \vec{a})\times(\vec{c} - \vec{a})\right] = 0$

$\therefore \quad \vec{b} - \vec{a} = \hat{j} - \hat{i}$ and $\vec{c} - \vec{a} = \hat{k} - \hat{i}$

$$\therefore \quad \left(\vec{b} - \vec{a}\right)\times\left(\vec{c} - \vec{a}\right) = \begin{vmatrix} \hat{i} & \hat{j} & \hat{k} \\ -1 & 1 & 0 \\ -1 & 0 & 1 \end{vmatrix} = \hat{i}\ \hat{j}\ \hat{k}$$

$$\therefore \quad \left(\vec{r} - \vec{a}\right) = \left(x\hat{i} + y\hat{j} + z\hat{k}\right) - \left(\hat{i}\right)$$

$$= (x-1)\hat{i} + y\hat{j} + z\hat{k}$$

We have,

$$\left[(x-1)\hat{i} + y\hat{j} + z\hat{k}\right]\cdot\left(\hat{i} + \hat{j} + \hat{k}\right) = 0$$

$$= (x - 1) + y + z = 0$$

$\therefore$ Equating of plane $x + y + z - 1 = 0$

$\perp$ distance from origin to the plane

$$= \frac{|-1|}{\sqrt{(1)^2 + (1)^2 + (1)^2}} = \frac{1}{\sqrt{3}} \text{ unit}$$

Here, $\quad p = \frac{1}{\sqrt{3}} \Rightarrow p^2 = \frac{1}{3}$

$\therefore \quad 3p^2 = 1$

57. (B): $\quad l + 2m + n = 0 \quad \ldots(i)$

and $\quad 2l - 2m + 3n = 0 \quad \ldots(ii)$

From (*i*) we have $l = -2m - n \quad \ldots(iii)$

Putting the value of l in (*ii*)

$2(-2m - n) - 2m + 3n = 0$

$\therefore\ -4m - 2n - 2m + 3n = 0$

$\therefore \quad n = 6m$

Now, $\quad l = -2m - n$

$\quad = -2m - 6m = -8m$

$$\frac{l}{-8m} = \frac{m}{n} = \frac{n}{6m}$$

$$\therefore \quad \frac{l}{-8} = \frac{m}{1} = \frac{n}{6}$$

$$= \sqrt{\frac{l^2 + m^2 + n^2}{(-8)^2 + (1)^2 + (6)^2}} = \frac{1}{\sqrt{101}}$$

$$\therefore \quad l = \frac{-8}{\sqrt{101}},\ m = \frac{1}{\sqrt{101}}$$

$$\therefore \quad n = \frac{6}{\sqrt{101}}$$

$\therefore$ Direction consines of a line

$$\left(\frac{-8}{\sqrt{101}}, \frac{1}{\sqrt{101}}, \frac{6}{\sqrt{101}}\right) = (l, m, n)$$

$$\therefore \quad l^2 + m^2 - n^2 = \frac{64}{101} + \frac{1}{101} - \frac{36}{101}$$

$$= \frac{29}{101}$$

58. (B): Let the equation of any line passing through the point of intersection of the given line be

$(x + 2y - 1) + a(2x - y - 1) = 0$

Reducing the equation to its intercept form

$x + 2y - 1 + 2ax - ay - a = 0$

$\Rightarrow \quad (1 + 2a)x + (2 - a)y = 1 + a$

$$\Rightarrow \quad \frac{(1-2a)x}{(1+a)} + \frac{(2-a)y}{(1+a)} = 1$$

Therefore co-ordinates of A and B where this line meets the co-ordinates axis respectively.

$$A = \left(\frac{1+a}{1+2a}, 0\right) \text{ on } x\text{-axis}$$

$$B = \left(0, \frac{1+a}{2-a}\right) \text{ on } y\text{-axis}$$

Mid point of AB $= \left(\dfrac{1+a}{2+4a}, \dfrac{1+a}{4-2a}\right)$

$\because \quad x = \dfrac{1+a}{2+4a}$ and $y = \dfrac{1+a}{4-2a}$

$\Rightarrow \quad 2x + 4ax = 1 + a$

$\Rightarrow \quad 4ax - a = 1 - 2x$

$\Rightarrow \quad a = \dfrac{1-2x}{4x-1}$

We get, $\quad y = \dfrac{1+\dfrac{1-2x}{4x-1}}{4-2\left(\dfrac{1-2x}{4x-1}\right)}$

$= \dfrac{4x-1+1-2x}{16x-4-2+4x}$

$= \dfrac{2x}{20x-6} = \dfrac{x}{10x-3}$

$\therefore \quad 10xy - 3y = x$

$\Rightarrow \quad x + 3y = 10xy$

59. **(B):** Slope of the given line

$x \cos\theta + y \sin\theta = 9$

We can write $y \sin\theta = 9 - x \cos\theta$.

$\Rightarrow \quad y = \dfrac{9}{\sin\theta} - \dfrac{x\cos\theta}{\sin\theta}$

$\Rightarrow \quad y = -\dfrac{x\cos\theta}{\sin\theta} + \dfrac{9}{\sin\theta} \quad ...(i)$

The general equation of line is

$y = mx + c \quad ...(ii)$

on comparing (*i*) and (*ii*) then we get,

$m = \dfrac{-\cos\theta}{\sin\theta}$

We know that the slope of $\perp$ line are negative inverse of each other.

$\therefore$ The slope m_1 of the required line can be

$m_1 = -\left(\dfrac{1}{\dfrac{-\cos\theta}{\sin\theta}}\right) = \dfrac{\sin\theta}{\cos\theta}$

The line passes through the point $(-\sin\theta, \cos\theta)$

$y - y_1 = m(x - x_1)$

The equation of the required line is

$y - \cos\theta = \dfrac{\sin\theta}{\cos\theta}(x+\sin\theta)$

$\Rightarrow \quad y\cos\theta - \cos^2\theta = x\sin\theta + \sin^2\theta$

$\Rightarrow x\sin\theta - y\cos\theta + \sin^2\theta + \cos^2\theta = 0$

$\Rightarrow x\sin\theta - y\cos\theta + 1 = 0$

Hence equation of the straight line is

$x\sin\theta - y\cos\theta + 1 = 0.$

60. **(A):** $\because$ P and Q lie on line $y = 2x + 3$

For P, put $x = a$, then $y = 2a + 3$

For Q put $x = b$, then $y = 2b + 3$

Co-ordinates $P = (a, 2a + 3)$

and $\quad Q = (b, 2b + 3)$

$R = (1, 5)$

Now, $\quad PR = \sqrt{(a-1)^2 + (2a+3-5)^2} = 2 \quad ...(i)$

$QR = \sqrt{(b-1)^2 + (2b+3-5)^2} = 2 \quad ...(ii)$

From (*i*) we get,

$(a - 1)^2 + (2a - 2)^2 = 4$

$\Rightarrow \quad (a - 1)^2 + \{2(a - 1)\}^2 = 4$

$\Rightarrow a^2 - 2a + 1 + 4(a^2 - 2a + 1) = 4$

$\Rightarrow \quad a^2 - 2a + 1 + 4a^2 - 8a + 4 = 4$

$\Rightarrow \quad 5a^2 - 10a + 1 = 0$

From (*ii*) we get,

$5b^2 - 10b + 1 = 0$

By using quadratic formula

$a = -\dfrac{(-10) \pm \sqrt{100-20}}{10} = \dfrac{10 \pm 12\sqrt{5}}{10}$

$= 1 \pm \dfrac{2\sqrt{5}}{5} = 1 \pm \dfrac{2}{\sqrt{5}}$

$b = 1 \pm \dfrac{2}{\sqrt{5}}$

When, $\quad a = 1 + \dfrac{2}{\sqrt{5}}$

then, $\quad P = (a, 2a + 3)$

$= \left[1+\dfrac{2}{\sqrt{5}}, 2+\dfrac{4}{\sqrt{5}}+3\right]$

$= \left(1+\dfrac{2}{\sqrt{5}}, 5+\dfrac{4}{\sqrt{5}}\right)$

when, $\quad a = 1 - \dfrac{2}{\sqrt{5}}$

then, $\quad P = (a, 2a + 3)$

$= \left(1-\dfrac{2}{\sqrt{5}}, 2-\dfrac{4}{\sqrt{5}}+3\right)$

$= \left(1-\dfrac{2}{\sqrt{5}}, 5-\dfrac{4}{\sqrt{5}}\right)$

Similarly, $Q = \left(1-\frac{2}{\sqrt{5}}, 5-\frac{4}{\sqrt{5}}\right)$

$$= \left(1+\frac{2}{\sqrt{5}},\ 5+\frac{4}{\sqrt{5}}\right)$$

Hence, Co-ordinate of P and Q

$$= \left(1+\frac{2}{\sqrt{5}},\ 5+\frac{4}{\sqrt{5}}\right), \left(1-\frac{2}{\sqrt{5}}, 5-\frac{4}{\sqrt{5}}\right)$$

61. (A): $\therefore\ 2x + y - 3 = 0$ ...(*i*)

$4x + 2y + 5 = 0$ ...(*ii*)

Dividing (*ii*) by 2 then we get,

$$2x+y+\frac{5}{2} = 0 \quad ...(iii)$$

Here, $2x + y - 3 = 0$ and $2x+y+\frac{5}{2} = 0$

are || lines

$\therefore$ Length of side of square = Distance between || sides

$$= \frac{|c_1 - c_2|}{\sqrt{a_1^2 + b_1^2}}$$

where, $c_1 = -3$

$c_2 = \frac{5}{2}$

$(a_1, b_1) = (2, 1)$

$$\frac{\left|-3-\frac{5}{2}\right|}{\sqrt{(2)^2+(1)^2}} = \frac{\left|-\frac{11}{2}\right|}{\sqrt{5}} = \frac{11}{2\sqrt{5}}$$

$\therefore$ Length of the side of square $= \frac{11}{2\sqrt{5}}$ units

Area of the square = (side)^2 $= \left(\frac{11}{2\sqrt{5}}\right)^2$

= 6.05 square units

62. (B): A = (3, 5) and mid point of side AB and AC is (–1, 2) and (6, 4) respectively.

A (3, 5)

(–1, 2) M   N (6, 4)

(x_1, y_1) B   C (x_2, y_2)

Let, $B = (x_1, y_1)$ and $C = (x_2, y_2)$

$$-1 = \frac{x_1+3}{2} \Rightarrow x_1 = -5$$

$$2 = \frac{y_1+5}{2} \Rightarrow y_1 = -1$$

and $$6 = \frac{x_2+3}{2} \Rightarrow x_2 = 9$$

$$4 = \frac{5+y_2}{2} \Rightarrow y_2 = 3$$

$\therefore$ B(5, –1) and C(9, 3)

Hence, centroid of $\Delta ABC = \left(\frac{3-5+9}{3}, \frac{5-1+3}{3}\right)$

$$= \left(\frac{7}{3}, \frac{7}{3}\right)$$

63. (B): $\because$ ΔABC is isosceles triangle.

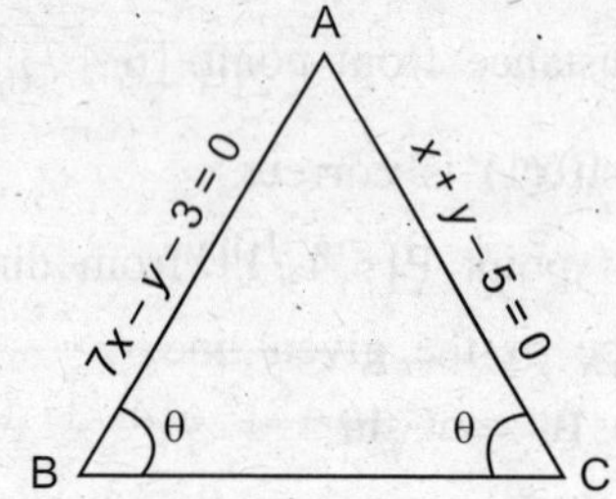

Slope of AB $(m_1) = 7$

and Slope of AC$(m_2) = -1$

$$\tan A = \left|\frac{m_1 - m_2}{1 + m_1 \cdot m_2}\right| = \left|\frac{7-(-1)}{1+(-7)}\right|$$

$$= \left|\frac{8}{-6}\right| = \frac{8}{6} = \frac{4}{3}$$

$\therefore$ $A = \tan^{-1}\frac{4}{3}$

$\because$ $\angle A + \angle B + \angle C = \pi$

$\therefore$ $\theta + \theta + \tan^{-1}\frac{4}{3} = \pi$

$\Rightarrow$ $2\theta = \pi - \tan^{-1}\frac{4}{3}$

$$\theta = \frac{\pi}{2} - \frac{1}{2}\tan^{-1}\frac{4}{3}$$

$$-\cot\theta = \cot\left[\frac{\pi}{2} - \frac{1}{2}\tan^{-1}\frac{4}{3}\right]$$

$\Rightarrow$ $$\cot\theta = \tan\left(\frac{\tan^{-1}\frac{4}{3}}{2}\right) \quad ...(i)$$

Let, $\tan^{-1}\frac{4}{3} = \alpha$

$$\tan\frac{\alpha}{2} = \text{cosec}\,\alpha - \cot\alpha$$

From (*i*) we get,

$$\cot\theta = \text{cosec}\left(\tan^{-1}\frac{4}{3}\right) - \cot\left(\tan^{-1}\frac{4}{3}\right) \quad \ldots(ii)$$

$$\therefore \quad \tan^{-1}\frac{4}{3} = \alpha$$

$$\therefore \quad \tan\alpha = \frac{4}{3} \Rightarrow \cot\alpha\ \frac{3}{4} \text{ and } \text{cosec}\,\alpha = \frac{5}{4}$$

$$\cot\theta = \text{cosec}\,\alpha - \cot\alpha$$

$$= \frac{5}{4} - \frac{3}{4} = \frac{2}{4} = \frac{1}{2}$$

64. (C): Equation of parabola is

$$y^2 = 8x$$

$$\therefore \quad a = 2$$

$P(x_1, y_1)$ is $x_1 + a$

$\therefore$ Focal distance from point $\left(6, 4\sqrt{3}\right)$ is $6 + 2 = 8$

$\therefore$ Statement (1) is correct.

Distance of point $P\left(6, 4\sqrt{3}\right)$ from directrix

$$PF = \sqrt{(6-2)^2 + \left(4\sqrt{3}-0\right)^2}$$

$$= \sqrt{16+48} = \sqrt{64} = 8$$

Hence, statement (2) is also correct.

65. (D): Let ellipse be $\frac{x^2}{a^2} + \frac{y^2}{b^2} = 1$

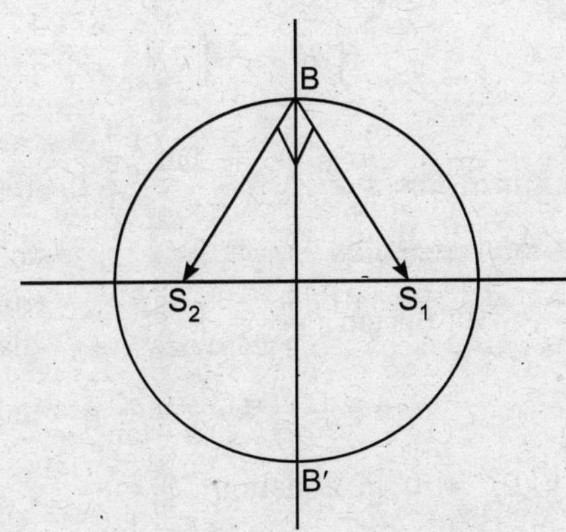

It's foci are $S_1(ae, o)$ and $S_2(-ae, o)$ and the extremity of the minor axis is $B(o, b)$

Then, slope of $BS_2 = \frac{b-o}{o-(-ae)} = \frac{b}{ae}$

and slope of $BS_1 = \frac{b-o}{o-ae} = -\frac{b}{ae}$

The product of slopes $= \frac{b}{ae} \times -\frac{b}{ae} = -1$

$$\Rightarrow \quad b^2 = a^2e^2$$

$$\Rightarrow \quad e^2 = \frac{b^2}{a^2} \quad \ldots(i)$$

We have, $$e = \frac{c}{a}$$

$$\Rightarrow \quad c = \sqrt{a^2 - b^2}$$

$$\Rightarrow \quad e^2 = 1 - \frac{b^2}{a^2} = 1 - e^2 \quad [\text{from } (i)]$$

$$\Rightarrow \quad 2e^2 = 1$$

$$\Rightarrow \quad e^2 = \frac{1}{2} \Rightarrow e = \frac{1}{\sqrt{2}}$$

66. (D): We have, $\vec{a} = \hat{i} - \hat{j} + \hat{k}$ and

$$\vec{b} = \hat{i} + 2\hat{j} - \hat{k}$$

$$\vec{a} \times \left(\vec{b} \times \vec{a}\right) = (\vec{a}\,\vec{a})\vec{b} - \left(\vec{a}\,\vec{b}\right)\vec{a}$$

$$= \left[\left(\hat{i}+\hat{j}+\hat{k}\right)\cdot\left(\hat{i}-\hat{j}+\hat{k}\right)\right]\vec{b}$$

$$-\left[\left(\hat{i}-\hat{j}+\hat{k}\right)\cdot\left(\hat{i}+2\hat{j}-\hat{k}\right)\right]\vec{a}$$

$$= (1+1+1)\vec{b} - (1-2-1)\vec{a}$$

$$= 3\left(\hat{i}+2\hat{j}-\hat{k}\right) + 2\left(\hat{i}-\hat{j}+\hat{k}\right)$$

$$= 5\hat{i} + 4\hat{j} - \hat{k} \quad \ldots(i)$$

$$\vec{a} \times \left(\vec{b} \times \vec{a}\right) = \alpha\hat{i} - \beta\hat{j} - \gamma\hat{k}$$

Comparing with (*i*) then we get,

$$\alpha = 5,\ \beta = -4,\ \gamma = -1$$

Hence, $\alpha + \beta + \gamma = 5 - 4 - 1 = 0$.

67. (A): Let, $\vec{a}$ have (a_1, a_2, a_3) components

$\Rightarrow a_1\hat{i} + a_2\hat{j} + a_3\hat{k}$

$$\because \quad \left|\vec{a}\right| = 2$$

Also, It is given that $\vec{a}$ make angle with $\frac{\pi}{3}$ with $2\hat{i}$, $\frac{\pi}{4}$ with $3\hat{j}$ and an acute angle θ with $4\hat{k}$

Then we have,

$$\vec{a}\cdot 2\hat{i} = \left|\vec{a}\right|\left|2\hat{i}\right|\cos\frac{\pi}{3}$$

$$\left(a_1\hat{i} + a_2\hat{j} + a_3\hat{k}\right)\cdot 2\hat{i} = 2.2 \times \frac{1}{2}$$

$$2a_1 = 2 \Rightarrow a_1 = 1$$

$$\therefore \quad \vec{a}\cdot 3\hat{j} = \left|\vec{a}\right|\left|3\hat{j}\right|\cos\frac{\pi}{4}$$

$$3a_2 = 2\times 3\times\frac{1}{\sqrt{2}} \Rightarrow a_2 = \sqrt{2}$$

and $\vec{a}\cdot 4\hat{k} = |\vec{a}||4\hat{k}|\cos\theta$

$$4a_3 = 2 \times 4 \cos\theta$$

$\Rightarrow \cos\theta = \frac{a_3}{2}$

Now, $|\vec{a}| = 2$

$\Rightarrow \sqrt{a_1^2 + a_2^2 + a_3^2} = 2$

$\Rightarrow a_1^2 + a_2^2 + a_3^2 = 4$

Put, $a_1 = 1$ and $a_2 = \sqrt{2}$

$$(1)^2 + \left(\sqrt{2}\right)^2 + a_3^2 = 4 \Rightarrow a_3^2 = \pm 1$$

When, $a_3 = -1$

then, $\cos\theta = -\frac{1}{2}$

$\Rightarrow \theta = \frac{2\pi}{3} > \frac{\pi}{2}$ (contradict)

$\because \theta$ is acute angle with $4\hat{k}$

$\therefore a_3 = 1$

Hence, the components of $\vec{a} = \left(1, \sqrt{2}, 1\right)$.

68. (B): Statement (1) is wrong.

We know that the moment of force about a point is dependent of application of force.

Statement (2) is correct.

The moment of force about a line is a vector quantity.

69. (A): $\left(\vec{r}\cdot\hat{i}\right)\left(\vec{r}\times\hat{i}\right) + \left(\vec{r}\cdot\hat{j}\right)\left(\vec{r}\times\hat{j}\right) + \left(\vec{r}\cdot\hat{k}\right)\left(\vec{r}\times\hat{k}\right)$ ...(*i*)

We have, $\vec{r} = a\hat{i} + b\hat{j} + c\hat{k}$

$$\left(\vec{r}\,\hat{i}\right) = \left(a\hat{i} + b\hat{j} + c\hat{k}\right)\cdot\hat{i} = a$$

$$\left(\vec{r}\cdot\hat{j}\right) = b$$

$$\left(\vec{r}\cdot\hat{k}\right) = c$$

and $\vec{r}\times\hat{i} = \begin{vmatrix} \hat{i} & \hat{j} & \hat{k} \\ a & b & c \\ 1 & 0 & 0 \end{vmatrix}$

$$= -\hat{j}(-c) - b\hat{k} = c\hat{j} - b\hat{k}$$

Similarly, $\vec{r}\times\hat{j} = -c\hat{i} + a\hat{k}$

and $\vec{r}\,\hat{k} = b\hat{i} - a\,\hat{j}$

Putting these values in (*i*) we get

$$a\left(c\hat{j} - b\hat{k}\right) + b\left(-c\hat{i} + a\hat{k}\right) + c\left(b\hat{i} - a\hat{j}\right)$$

$$= ac\hat{j} - ab\hat{k} - bc\hat{i} + ab\hat{k} + bc\hat{i} - ac\hat{j} = 0$$

70. (B): The angle between $\vec{a}$ and $\vec{a} - \vec{b}$ is given by

$$\cos\theta = \frac{\vec{a}\cdot\left(\vec{a} - \vec{b}\right)}{|\vec{a}||\vec{a} - \vec{b}|}$$

Now, $\vec{a}\cdot\left(\vec{a} - \vec{b}\right) = \vec{a}\cdot\vec{a} - \vec{a}\cdot\vec{b}$

$\therefore \vec{a}\cdot\vec{a} = |\vec{a}|^2$

Given that magnitude of $\vec{a}$ and $\vec{b}$ is 4

$$|\vec{a}| = |\vec{b}| = 4$$

$$|\vec{a}|^2 = 4^2 = 16$$

and $\vec{a}\,\vec{b} = |\vec{a}||\vec{b}|\cos\frac{\pi}{3} = 4.4.\frac{1}{2} = 8$

$$|\vec{a} - \vec{b}|^2 = |\vec{a}|^2 + |\vec{b}|^2 - \vec{a}\,\vec{b} - \vec{b}\,\vec{a}$$

$$= 16 + 16 - 8 - 8 = 16$$

$$\cos\theta = \frac{16-8}{4\sqrt{16}} = \frac{8}{4.4} = \frac{1}{2} = \cos\frac{\pi}{3}$$

$\Rightarrow \theta = \frac{\pi}{3}$

71. (A): Given, D.E. $\frac{dy}{dx} = x$

$\Rightarrow \int dy = \int x\,dx$

$\Rightarrow y = \frac{x^2}{2} + c$

$\Rightarrow y_1(x) = \frac{x^2}{2} + c_1$ ...(*i*)

and $y_2(x) = \frac{x^2}{2} + c_2$ ...(*ii*)

For $y_1(0) = 0$ in equation (*i*)

$$0 = 0 + c_1$$

$\Rightarrow c_1 = 0$

$\Rightarrow y_1(x) = \frac{x^2}{2}$ ...(*iii*)

For $y_2(0) = 0$

$\Rightarrow 4 = 0 + c_2$ [From (*iii*)]

For, $c_2 = 4$

$\Rightarrow y_2(x) = \frac{x^2}{2} + 4$ ...(*iv*)

For number of points of intersection for $y_1(x)$ and $y_2(x)$ solving (*iii*) and (*iv*)

$$\frac{x^2}{2} = \frac{x^2}{2} + 4 \text{ (not possible)}$$

as $0 \neq 4$

Hence, no point of intersection.

72. (C): $y = e^x(a\cos x + b\sin x)$ ...(*i*)

$$\frac{dy}{dx} = e^x(-a\sin x + b\cos x) + (a\cos x + b\sin x)e^x$$

$$\frac{dy}{dx} = e^x(-a\sin x + b\cos x) + y$$

Again differentiate w.r.t. to x

$$\frac{d^2y}{dx^2} = -e^x(a\cos x + b\sin x) + (-a\sin x + b\cos x)e^x + \frac{dy}{dx}$$

$$\frac{d^2y}{dx^2} = -y + \frac{dy}{dx} - y + \frac{dy}{dx} \text{ [using (i) and (ii)]}$$

$$\frac{d^2y}{dx^2} - 2\frac{dy}{dx} + 2y = 0$$

is the required differential equation.

73. (D): $f(x) = ax - b$ ...(*i*)

and $g(x) = cx + d$ ...(*ii*)

$$f[g(x)] = g[f(x)]$$

$\Rightarrow$ $a[g(x)] - b = c[f(x)] + d$

$\Rightarrow$ $a[cx + d] - b = c[ax - b] + d$

[using (*i*) and (*ii*)]

$\Rightarrow$ $acx + ad - b = acx - bc + d$

$\Rightarrow$ $ad - b = d - bc$

$\Rightarrow$ $ad - b + bc + d = d + d$

$\therefore$ $f(d) + g(b) = 2d$

74. (B): Let, $I = \int_{-1}^{1}(3\sin x - \sin 3x)\cos^2 x\,dx$

$$I = \int_{-1}^{1}(3\sin x - 3\sin x + 4\sin^3 x)\cos^2 x\,dx$$

$$I = \int_{-1}^{1}4\sin^3 x\cos^2 x\,dx$$

$$= \int_{-1}^{1}f(x)\,dx$$

Here, $f(x) = 4\sin^3 x\cos^2 x$ is an odd function

as $f(-x) = -f(x)$

$\Rightarrow$ $I = \int_{-1}^{1}4\sin^2 x\cos^2 x\,dx = 0$

75. (D): $\left\{2 - \left(\frac{dy}{dx}\right)^2\right\}^{0.6} = \frac{d^2y}{dx^2}$

Removing decimal power/fraction power both sides

$$\left\{2 - \left(\frac{dy}{dx}\right)^2\right\}^{3/5} = \left(\frac{d^2y}{dx^2}\right)^5$$

Raise power of 5 both sides

$$\left\{2 - \left(\frac{dy}{dx}\right)^2\right\}^{\frac{3}{5}\times 5} = \left(\frac{d^2y}{dx^2}\right)^5$$

$$\Rightarrow \left\{2 - \left(\frac{dy}{dx}\right)^2\right\}^3 = \left(\frac{d^2y}{dx^2}\right)^5$$

Hence, Order = 2

Power = 5

76. (A): $\frac{dy}{dx} = 2e^x y^3$

$$\Rightarrow \frac{dy}{dx^3} = 2e^x dx$$

Integrating both sides w.r. to x

$$-\frac{1}{2y^2} = 2e^x + c \quad \text{...(i)}$$

$$y(0) = \frac{1}{2}$$

$$-2 = 2 + c \Rightarrow c = -4$$

The solution is $-\frac{1}{2y^2} = 2e^x - 4$

$\Rightarrow$ $4y^2(e^x) - 8y^2 = -1$

$\Rightarrow$ $4y^2(2 - e^x) = 1$

77. (D): $p = \int_a^b f(x)dx$ and $q = \int_a^b |f(x)|dx$

$\because$ $f(x) = e^{-x}$ is always +ve $\forall\ x \in$ R

$e^{-x} = |e^{-x}|$

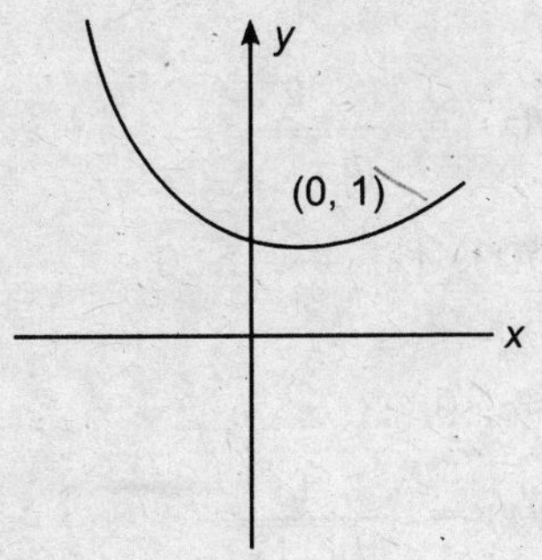

$|f(x)| = |e^{-x}| = e^{-x} = f(x)$

$\therefore \quad \int_a^b f(x)\,dx = \int_a^b |f(x)|\,dx$

Hence, $\quad p = q$

78. (A): Let, $\quad I = \int_0^{\frac{\pi}{2}} \frac{a+\sin x}{2a+\sin x+\cos x}dx \quad \ldots(i)$

$I = \int_0^{\frac{\pi}{2}} \frac{a+\cos x}{2a+\cos x+\sin x}dx \quad \ldots(ii)$

Adding equation (*i*) and (*ii*)

$2I = \int_0^{\frac{\pi}{2}} \frac{2a+\sin x+\cos x}{2a+\sin x+\cos x}dx$

$= \int_0^{\frac{\pi}{2}} dx = \frac{\pi}{2}$

$\Rightarrow \quad I = \frac{\pi}{4}$

79. (D): Let, $f(x) = \frac{16x^3}{3} - 4bx^2 + x$

$f(x) = 16x^2 - 8bx + 1$

$\because f(x)$ is neither maximum nor minimum then

$f(x) \neq 0$

$f(x) > 0$ or $f(x) < 0$

For, $\quad f(x) > 0$

$D < 0$ and $a > 0$

$D = 64b^2 - 64 < 0$

$b^2 - 1 < 0$ and b is non-negative as $b \geq 0$

$b \in [0, 1]$

$\therefore \quad 0 \leq b < 1$

80. (A):

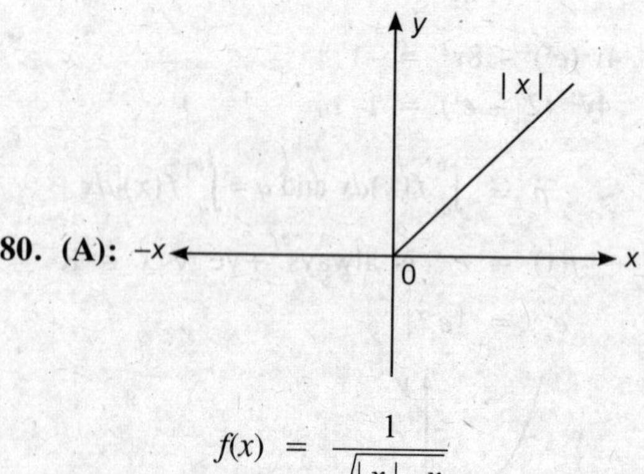

$f(x) = \frac{1}{\sqrt{|x|-x}}$

Domain of $f(x)$, $|x| - x > 0$

$|x| < x$

$\Rightarrow \quad x \in (-\infty, 0)$

$g(x) = \frac{1}{\sqrt{x-|x|}}$

Domain of $g(x) = x - |x| > 0$

$\Rightarrow \quad |x| > x$

For (Q. No. 81 and 82)

Let, $\quad I = \int \frac{3\cos x + 4\sin x}{2\cos x + 5\sin x}dx$

$3\cos x + 4\sin x = A(2\cos x + 5\sin x) + B\left[\frac{d}{dx}(2\cos x + 5\sin x)\right]$

$3\cos x + 4\sin x = A(2\cos x + 5\sin x) + B(-2\sin x + 5\cos x)$

Comparing co-efficient of $\sin x$ and $\cos x$

$3 = 2A + 5B \quad \ldots(i)$

$4 = 5A - 2B \quad \ldots(ii)$

Solving (*i*) and (*ii*) then we get,

$A = \frac{26}{29},\ B = \frac{7}{29}$

$I = \int \frac{\frac{26}{29}(2\cos x + 5\sin x) + \frac{7}{29}(-2\sin x + 5\cos x)}{2\cos x + 5\sin x}dx$

$= \int \frac{26}{29}dx + \frac{7}{29}\int \frac{(-2\sin x + 5\cos x)}{2\cos x + 5\sin x}dx$

$= \frac{26}{29}x + \frac{7}{29}$ In $(2\cos x + 5\sin x) + c$

$\alpha = 26, \beta = 7$ [on comparing]

81. (D): $\alpha = 26$

82. (A): $\beta = 7$

For (Qs. No. 83 and 84)

83. (D): $\quad f(x) = \frac{x}{\ln(x)}(x > 1)$

$f(x) = \frac{\ln x - 1}{[\ln(x)]^2}$

–ve +ve

$f(x)$ is +ve, $x \in (e, \infty) \Rightarrow (1)$ is correct

$f(x)$ is –ve $\forall\ x \in (1, e) \Rightarrow (2)$ is correct

As ln x is an increasing function

$7^9 > 9^7$

$\ln 7^9 > \ln 9^7$

$9 \ln 7 > 7 \ln 9$

$\Rightarrow$ statement (3) is correct

Hence, statements (1), (2) and (3) are correct.

84. (D): $f'(x) = \dfrac{(\ln x)^2 \times \frac{1}{x} - (\ln x - 1) \times 2\frac{\ln x}{x}}{(\ln x)^4}$

$= \dfrac{(\ln x)^2 - 2(\ln x)^2 \times 2\ln x}{x(\ln x)^4}$

$\Rightarrow \quad f''(e) = \dfrac{1-2+2}{e \times 1} = \dfrac{1}{e}(>0)$

$\Rightarrow$ Statement (1) is correct.

Since $f''(e) > 0$ (true)

$f(x)$ attains local minima at $x = e$

$\Rightarrow$ Statement (2) is correct.

A local minimum value occurs at $x = e$

$f(x)$ at $x = e$, is $f(e) = \dfrac{e}{\ln e} = e$

$\Rightarrow$ Statement (3) is correct.

Hence, Statements (1), (2) and (3) are correct.

For (Q. No. 85 and 86):

$\because f(x)$ and $g(x)$ are two functions

$$g(x) = x - \frac{1}{x} \text{ and } fog(x) = x^3 - \frac{1}{x^3}$$

$$f\left(x - \frac{1}{x}\right) = x^3 - \frac{1}{x^3}$$

$$\Rightarrow \quad f\left(x - \frac{1}{x}\right) = \left(x - \frac{1}{x}\right)^3 + 3\left(x - \frac{1}{x}\right)$$

85. (A): $f(x) = x^3 + 3x$ ...(*i*)

$g[f(x) - 3x] = f(x) - 3x - \dfrac{1}{f(x) - 3x}$

$g(f(x) - 3x] = x^3 + 3x - 3x - \dfrac{1}{x^3 + 3x - 3x}$

$= x^3 - \dfrac{1}{x^3}$

$g(f(x) - 3x] = x^3 - \dfrac{1}{x^3}$

86. (D): $f'(x) = 3x^2 + 3$

$f''(x) = 6x$

For (Q. No. 87 and 88)

$f(x) = |x| + 1$

and $g(x) = [x] - 1$

$h(x) = \dfrac{f(x)}{g(x)} = \dfrac{|x|+1}{[x]-1}$

87. (A): (1) For, $x < 0$

$f(x) = -x + 1$

$\therefore \quad f(x) = -1$

$f(x)$ is differentiable $\forall\ x < 0$

$\Rightarrow$ Statement (1) is correct.

(2) At $x = 0.0001$

$g(x)$ is continuous everywhere except for integer value as $[x]$ is continuous $\forall\ x \in$ R except integers. So, $g(x)$ is continuous at $x = 0.0001$.

Statement (2) is correct.

(3) $g(x) = [x] - 1$

$[x] \Rightarrow$ Always *ab* integer

$g'(x) = \dfrac{d}{dx}[x] - 0$

$g'(x) = 0 - 0 = 0$

$\Rightarrow$ Statement (3) is incorrect.

Hence, (1) and (2) only correct.

88. (A): $\lim\limits_{x \to 0} h(x) + \lim\limits_{x \to 0^+} h(x) = \lim\limits_{x \to 0^-} \dfrac{|x|+1}{[x]-1}$

$= \lim\limits_{x \to 0^-} \dfrac{|x|+1}{[x]-1}$

$= \dfrac{0+1}{-1-1} + \dfrac{0+1}{0-1} \quad \begin{Bmatrix} [0-h] = -1 \\ [0+h] = 0 \end{Bmatrix}$

$= \dfrac{1}{2} - 1 = -\dfrac{3}{2}$

89. (D): $\phi(a) = \displaystyle\int_a^{a+100\pi} |\sin x|\, dx$

As period of $|\sin x| = \pi$ and $|\sin x| = \sin x$ in

$\phi(a) = \displaystyle\int_0^{100\pi} |\sin x|\, dx$

$= 100\displaystyle\int_0^{\pi} |\sin x|\, dx$

$= 100\displaystyle\int_0^{\pi} \sin x\, dx$

$\phi(a) = 100(-\cos x)_0^{\pi} = 100 \times 2 = 200$

90. (A): $\phi(a) = 200$

$\phi'(a) = 0$

For (Q. No. 91 and 92)

Given, $y = 2f(x) + ax - b$ ...(*i*)

Differentiating both side w.r. to x

$\Rightarrow \quad \dfrac{dy}{dx} = 2f'(x) + a(1)$ ...(*ii*)

$\dfrac{d^2y}{dx^2} = 2f''(x)$ ...(*iii*)

91. (C): $\because$ $f(x)$ has a local maximum at $x = 0$

Hence, $f'(0) = 0$ and $f''(0) < 0$ ...(*iv*)

Therefore option (C) is correct.

92. (B): $\because$ y has a relative maxima at $x = 0$

$\therefore \quad \left(\frac{dy}{dx}\right)_{x=0} = 0$

$\Rightarrow \quad 2f'(0) + a = 0$

$\Rightarrow \quad 2(0) + a = 0$

$\Rightarrow \quad a = 0$

Also, $\left(\frac{d^2y}{dx^2}\right)_{x=0} < 0$

$\Rightarrow \quad 2f''(0) < 0$

$\Rightarrow \quad f''(0) = 0$

Clearly, y has relative maxima for $a = 0$ and all values of b.

For (Q.No. 93 and 94)

Given, $\quad f(x) = |x - 1|$ ...(*i*)

$g(x) = [x]$ ...(*ii*)

and $\quad h(x) = f(x).g(x)$

$\Rightarrow \quad h(x) = |x - 1|.[x]$ ...(*iii*)

93. (A): $\int_{-1}^{0} h(x)\,dx = \int_{-1}^{0} f(x).g(x)\,dx$

$= \int_{-1}^{0} |x-1|.[x]\,dx$

$= \int_{-1}^{0} (1-x).(-1)\,dx$

$= \int_{1}^{2} (x-1)\,dx = \left[\frac{x^2}{2} - x\right]_1^2$

$= \left[0 - \left(\frac{1}{2}+1\right)\right] = -\frac{3}{2}$

94. (D): $\int_0^2 h(x)dx = \int_0^1 |x-1|[x]\,dx + \int_1^2 |x-1|[x]\,dx$

$= \int_0^1 (1-x).(0)\,dx + \int_1^2 (x-1).(1)\,dx$

$= \int_0^2 (x-1)\,dx = \left[\frac{x^2}{2} - x\right]_1^2$

$= \left(\frac{4}{2} - 2\right) - \left(\frac{1}{2} - 1\right) = \frac{1}{2}$

For (Q. No. 95 and 96)

Given,

$$\int \frac{dx}{\sqrt{x+1} - \sqrt{x-1}} = \alpha(x+1)^{\frac{3}{2}} + \beta(x-1)^{\frac{3}{2}} + c \quad \text{...(i)}$$

Let, $\quad \mathrm{I} = \int \frac{dx}{\sqrt{x+1} - \sqrt{x-1}}$

$= \int \frac{\left(\sqrt{x+1} + \sqrt{x-1}\right)dx}{\left(\sqrt{x+1} - \sqrt{x-1}\right)\left(\sqrt{x+1} + \sqrt{x-1}\right)}$

$\Rightarrow \quad \mathrm{I} = \frac{1}{2}\int \sqrt{(x+1)}\,dx + \frac{1}{2}\int \sqrt{x-1}\,dx$

$\Rightarrow \quad \mathrm{I} = \frac{1}{2}\cdot\frac{(x+1)^{\frac{3}{2}}}{\left(\frac{3}{2}\right)} + \frac{\frac{1}{2}(x-1)^{\frac{3}{2}}}{\left(\frac{3}{2}\right)} + c$

$\Rightarrow \quad \mathrm{I} = \frac{1}{3}(x+1)^{\frac{3}{2}} + \frac{1}{3}(x-1)^{\frac{3}{2}} + c$

$\Rightarrow \quad \frac{dx}{\sqrt{x+1} - \sqrt{x-1}} = \frac{1}{3}(x+1)^{\frac{3}{2}} + \frac{1}{3}(x-1)^{\frac{3}{2}} + c$ ...(*ii*)

95. (A): From (*i*) and (*ii*) we get

$$\alpha = \frac{1}{3}$$

96. (C): From (*i*) and (*ii*) we get

$$\beta = \frac{1}{3}$$

For (Q. No. 97 and 98)

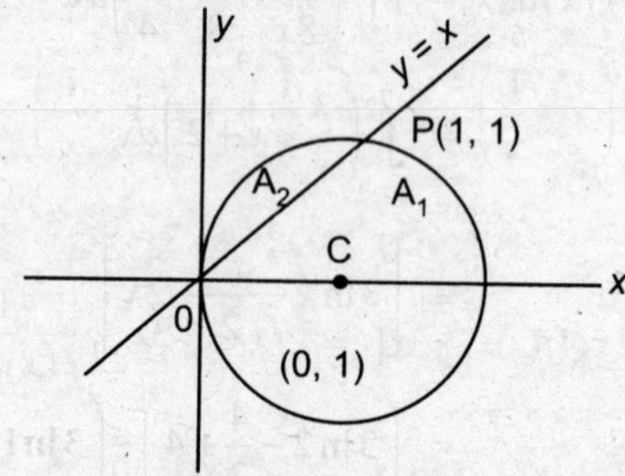

Given, $\quad x^2 + y^2 - 2x = 0$

$\Rightarrow \quad (x - 1)^2 + y^2 = 1$

or $\quad y^2 = 1 - (x - 1)^2$

Area of minor segment (A_2)

$= \int_0^1 \sqrt{1-(x-1)^2} - (x)\,dx$

$\Rightarrow A_2 = \left[\frac{(x-1)}{2}\sqrt{1-(x-1)^2} + \frac{1}{2}\sin^{-1}(x-1) - \frac{x^2}{2}\right]_0^1$

$\Rightarrow A_2 = \left[\left(0 + \frac{1}{2}(0) - \frac{1}{2}\right)\right] - \left[0 + \frac{1}{2}\sin^{-1}(-1) - 0\right]$

$\Rightarrow A_2 = \frac{\pi - 2}{4}$

97. (D): $\because$ Area of given circle $= \pi(1)^2 = \pi$

$\Rightarrow \quad A_1 + A_2 = \pi$

$$\Rightarrow \quad A_1 = \pi - \frac{\pi-2}{4} = \frac{3\pi+2}{4}$$

98. (A): $$\frac{2(A_1+A_2)}{A_1-3A_2} = \frac{2(\pi)}{\left(\frac{3\pi+2}{4}\right)-\frac{3(\pi-2)}{4}} = \pi$$

For (Q. No. 99 and 100)

99. (D): Given: $3f(x)+f\left(\frac{1}{x}\right)=\frac{1}{x}+1$ ...(*i*)

Replacing (x) by $\left(\frac{1}{x}\right)$, we get

$$3f\left(\frac{1}{x}\right)+f(x) = x+1 \quad ...(ii)$$

Now, (*i*) × 3 – (*ii*), we get

$$8f(x) = \frac{3}{x}+3-x-1$$

$$\Rightarrow \quad f(x) = \frac{3}{8x}-\frac{x}{8}+\frac{1}{4} \quad ...(iii)$$

100. (A): $$8\int_1^2 f(x)dx = 8\int_1^2\left(\frac{3}{8x}-\frac{x}{8}+\frac{1}{4}\right)dx$$

$$= \int_1^2\left(\frac{3}{x}-x+2\right)dx$$

$$= \left[3\ln x-\frac{x^2}{2}+2x\right]_1^2$$

$$= \left(3\ln 2-\frac{4}{2}+4\right)-\left(3\ln 1-\frac{1}{2}+2\right)$$

$$= 3\ln 2+2-\frac{3}{2}=\frac{1}{2}+3\ln 2$$

$$= \frac{1}{2}\ln e+\ln 2^3 = \ln\sqrt{e}+\ln 8$$

$$= \ln\left(8\sqrt{e}\right)$$

101. (C): Required probability

$$p(E) = \frac{{}^5C_2+{}^4C_2}{{}^9C_2} = \frac{\frac{5\times4}{2}+\frac{4\times3}{2}}{\frac{9\times8}{2}},$$

$$= \frac{10+6}{36}=\frac{16}{36}=\frac{4}{9}$$

102. (C): Mean = 5 and variance = 4

5^{23} P(X = 3) = $\lambda 4^{\lambda}$ ...(*i*)

$\because$ Mean = 5

$\Rightarrow$ $np = 5$

Variance = 4

$\Rightarrow$ $npq = 4$

$\Rightarrow$ $5q = 4$

$\Rightarrow$ $q = \frac{4}{5}$

Now, $p = 1 - q = 1-\frac{4}{5}=\frac{1}{5}$

$\because$ $np = 5$

$\Rightarrow$ $n = 25$

Now, 5^{23}P(X = 3) = $5^{23}[nc^3p^3q^{n-3}]$

$$= 5^{23}\left[{}^{25}C_3\left(\frac{1}{5}\right)^3\left(\frac{4}{5}\right)^{22}\right]$$

$$= 5^{23}\left[\frac{25\times24\times23}{6}\times\frac{1}{5^3}\times\frac{4^{22}}{5^{22}}\right]$$

$= 4 \times 23 \times 4^{22}$

$\Rightarrow$ 5^{23}P(X = 3) = 23×4^{22} ...(*ii*)

From (*i*) and (*ii*) $\lambda = 23$

103. (B):

x	y	xy	x^2
–4	1	–4	16
–1	2	–2	1
2	7	14	4
3	1	3	9

$\Sigma x = 0$, $\Sigma y = 11$, $\Sigma xy = 11$

$\Sigma x^2 = 30$

$$\bar{x} = \frac{0}{4}=0,\ \bar{y}=\frac{11}{4}$$

$$b_{yx} = \frac{\Sigma xy-\frac{\Sigma x\,\Sigma y}{4}}{\Sigma x^2-\frac{(\Sigma x)^2}{4}}$$

$$= \frac{11-0}{30-0}=\frac{11}{30}$$

Equation of regression line of y on x will be

$$y-\bar{y} = b_{yx}(x-\bar{x})$$

$$\Rightarrow \quad y-\frac{11}{4} = \frac{11}{30}(x-0)$$

$$\Rightarrow \quad y = \frac{11}{30}x+\frac{11}{4}$$

$\therefore \quad a = \frac{11}{4}$ and $b = \frac{11}{30}$

$2a + 15b = 2\times\frac{11}{4}+15\times\frac{11}{30} = 11$

104. (A): Slope of line $x + 2y + 1 = 0$

$\Rightarrow \quad m_1 = -\frac{1}{2}$

Slope of line $2x + 3y + 4 = 0$

$\Rightarrow \quad m_2 = -\frac{2}{3}$

$$\therefore \quad \tan\theta = \left|\frac{-\frac{1}{2}+\frac{2}{3}}{1+\frac{1}{2}\times\frac{2}{3}}\right| = \frac{1}{8}$$

$$\therefore \quad \tan 3\theta = \frac{3\tan\theta - \tan^3\theta}{1-3\tan^2\theta}$$

$$= \frac{\frac{3}{8}-\frac{1}{512}}{1-\frac{3}{64}} = \frac{\frac{192-1}{512}}{\frac{64-3}{64}}$$

$$= \frac{191}{512}\times\frac{64}{61} = \frac{191}{488}$$

Hence, the value of 488 tan 3θ

$$= 488\times\frac{191}{488} = 191$$

105. (A): $\because \quad \frac{2x-3y}{5x+4y} = 4$

$\Rightarrow \quad 2x - 3y = 20x + 16y$

$\Rightarrow \quad 19y = 18x$

$\Rightarrow \quad y = \frac{18x}{19}$

$\text{var.}(x) = npq = np(1 - p)$

$= 10\times\frac{1}{2}\times\frac{1}{2} = \frac{5}{2}$

Now, $\quad \text{var.}(y) = \text{var.}\left(-\frac{18}{19}x\right)$

$\Rightarrow \quad \text{var.}(y) = \left(\frac{18}{19}\right)^2\times\frac{5}{2} = \frac{810}{361}$

106. (B): $\because$ a, b, c are in H.P.

$\Rightarrow \quad \frac{2}{b} = \frac{1}{a}+\frac{1}{c}$

$\Rightarrow \quad b = \frac{2ac}{a+c}$

$$b - a = \frac{2ac}{a+c} - a = \frac{2ac-a^2-ac}{a+c}$$

$$= \frac{ac-a^2}{a+c} = \frac{a(c-a)}{a+c}$$

$$\Rightarrow \quad \frac{1}{b-a} = \frac{a+c}{-a(a-c)}$$

Now, $\quad b - c = \frac{2ac}{a+c} - c = \frac{2ac-ac-c^2}{a+c}$

$$= \frac{ac-c^2}{a+c} = \frac{c(a-c)}{a+c}$$

$$\Rightarrow \quad \frac{1}{b-c} = \frac{a+c}{c(a-c)}$$

$$\therefore \quad \frac{1}{b-a}+\frac{1}{b-c} = \frac{a+c}{-a(a-c)}+\frac{a+c}{c(a-c)}$$

$$= \frac{(a+c)}{(a-c)}\left[-\frac{1}{a}+\frac{1}{c}\right]$$

$$= \frac{a+c}{ac} = \frac{1}{a}+\frac{1}{c}$$

$$= \frac{2}{b} = \frac{1}{b}+\frac{1}{b} = \frac{1}{b}+\frac{1}{2}\left(\frac{1}{a}+\frac{1}{c}\right)$$

Hence, only statement (1) and (2) are correct. Statement (3) is not correct.

107. (C): The rates of the edible oil in four consecutive years are 150, 200, 250, 300

$\therefore$ Average price of oil $= \frac{150+200+250+300}{4}$

$= \frac{900}{4} = 225$

108. (B): Required probability

$$P(E) = \frac{n(E)}{n(S)} = \frac{2!\ 7!}{8!}$$

$$= \frac{2\times1\times7!}{8\times7!} = \frac{1}{4}$$

109. (C): $\therefore \quad m = 77^n$

Put, $\quad n = 1, 2, 3, 4$

For, $\quad n = 1$

$m = 77$

For, $\quad n = 2, m = 77^2 = 5929$

For, $n = 3,\ m = 77^3 = 456543$

For, $n = 4,\ m = 77^4 = 35153041$

= last digit will be 1

Hence, the required probability $= \frac{1}{4}$

110. (D): $n(S) = {}^{15}C_3$

$2 \times 3 = 6$

$2 \times 4 = 8$

$2 \times 5 = 10$

$2 \times 6 = 12$

$2 \times 7 = 14$

$3 \times 4 = 12$

$\therefore\ n(E) = 6$

$\therefore$ Required probability $= \frac{6}{{}^{15}C_3} = \frac{6}{\frac{15\times14\times13\times12!}{12!\times3\times2}}$

$= \frac{6}{35\times13} = \frac{6}{455}$

For (Q. No. 111 and 112)

Given : $P(A \cup B) \geq 0.75$

and $0.125 \leq P(A \cap B) \leq 0.375$

111. (D): $P(A \cup B) \geq 0.75$

$\Rightarrow\ P(A) + P(B) - P(A \cap B) \geq 0.75$

$\Rightarrow\ P(A) + P(B) \geq 0.75 + P(A \cap B)$

$\Rightarrow\ P(A) + P(B) \geq 0.75 + 0.125$

$\Rightarrow\ P(A) + P(B) \geq 0.875$

Minimum value of $P(A) + P(B) = 0.875$.

112. (B): $P(A \cap B) \leq 0.375$

$\Rightarrow\ P(A) + P(B) - P(A \cup B) \leq 0.375$

$\Rightarrow\ P(A) + P(B) \leq 0.375 + P(A \cup B)$

$\Rightarrow\ P(A) + P(B) \leq 0.375 + 0.75$

$\Rightarrow\ P(A) + P(B) \leq 1.125$

Maximum value of $P(A) + P(B) = 1.125$.

For (Q. No. 113 and 114)

$P(A) = 0.6,\ P(B) = 0.4,\ P(C) = 0.5$

$P(A \cap B) = P(A) + P(B) - P(A \cup B)$

$= 0.6 + 0.4 - 0.8 = 0.2$

Now,

$P(A \cup B \cup C) = P(A) + P(B) + P(C)$

$- P(A \cup B) - P(A \cap C)$

$- P(B \cap C) + P(A \cap B \cap C)$

$= 1.5 - 0.2 - 0.3 - P(B \cap C) + 0.2$

$\Rightarrow\ P(A \cup B \cup C) = 1.2 - P(B \cap C)$

$\because\ 0.85 \leq P(A \cup B \cup C) \leq 1$

$\Rightarrow\ 0.85 \leq 1.2 - P(B \cap C) \leq 1$

$\Rightarrow\ -0.35 \leq -P(B \cap C) \leq -0.2$

$\Rightarrow\ 0.2 \leq P(B \cap C) \leq 0.35$

113. (B): Minimum value of $P(B \cap C) = 0.2$.

114. (C): Maximum value of $P(B \cap C) = 0.35$

For (Q. No. 115 and 116)

p = Probability of getting atleast one tail

$= 1-\left(\frac{1}{2}\right)^n$

q = Probability of getting atleast two tails

$= 1-\left(\frac{1}{2}\right)^n - \frac{n}{2^n}$

115. (B): $p - q = \frac{5}{32}$

$\Rightarrow\ 1-\left(\frac{1}{2}\right)^n - \left[1-\left(\frac{1}{2}\right)^n - \frac{n}{2^n}\right] = \frac{5}{32}$

$\Rightarrow\ \frac{n}{2^n} = \frac{5}{32}$

$\Rightarrow\ \frac{n}{2^n} = \frac{5}{2^5}$

Comparing both sides, we get, $n = 5$

116. (A): $p + q = 2-2\left(\frac{1}{2}\right)^n - \frac{n}{2^n}$

$= 2-2\times\frac{1}{2^5}-\frac{5}{2^5} = \frac{57}{32}$

For (Q. No. 117 and 118)

117. (B): $\because\ \Sigma x_i f_i = 1.1+\frac{2}{2}+\frac{3}{2^2}+\ldots+\frac{n}{2^{n-1}}$ ...(*i*)

and $\frac{1}{2}\Sigma x_i f_i = \frac{1}{2}+\frac{2}{2^2}+\ldots+\frac{n-1}{2^{n-1}}+\frac{n}{2^n}$ ...(*ii*)

(*i*) – (*ii*) gives

$\left(1-\frac{1}{2}\right)\Sigma x_i f_i = \left[1.1+\frac{2-1}{2}+\frac{3-2}{2^2}+\frac{4-3}{2^3}+\ldots+\frac{1}{2^{n-1}}\right]-\frac{n}{2^n}$

$\Rightarrow\ \frac{1}{2}\Sigma x_i f_i = \left[1+\frac{1}{2}+\frac{1}{2^3}+\frac{1}{2^4}+\ldots+\frac{1}{2^{n-1}}\right]-\frac{n}{2^n}$

$$\Rightarrow \frac{1}{2}\Sigma x_i f_i = \frac{1\left(1-\frac{1}{2^n}\right)}{1-\frac{1}{2}} - \frac{n}{2^n}$$

$$= \frac{2(2^n-1)}{2^n} - \frac{n}{2^n}$$

$$\Rightarrow \quad \Sigma x_i f_i = \frac{2^{n+1}-n-2}{2^{n-1}}$$

118. (C): $\Sigma f_i = 1+\frac{1}{2}+\frac{1}{2^2}+...+\frac{1}{2^{n-1}}$

$$\Sigma f_i = \frac{1-\frac{1}{2^n}}{1-\frac{1}{2}} = \frac{2^n-1}{2^{n-1}}$$

Now, $\quad$ Mean $= \frac{\Sigma f_i x_i}{\Sigma f_i} = \frac{2^{n+1}-n-2}{2^{n-1}} \times \frac{2^{n-1}}{2^n-1}$

$$= \frac{2^{n+1}-n-2}{2^n-1}$$

For (Q. No. 119 and 120)

$\because$ 15, 18, 19, 21, 24, 32, 35, 41, 47, 50

Largest 5 observations are 32, 35, 41, 47, 50

$$\text{Mean} = \mu = \frac{32+35+41+47+50}{5}$$

$$= \frac{205}{5} = 41$$

119. (C): Mean deviation $= \frac{\Sigma|x_i - \mu|}{n}$

$$= \frac{|32-41|+|35-41|+|41-41|+|47-41|+|50-41|}{5}$$

$$= \frac{9+6+0+6+9}{5} = \frac{30}{5} = 6$$

120. (D): $\sigma^2 = \frac{\Sigma(x_i-\mu)^2}{5}$

$$= \frac{9^2+6^2+0^2+6^2+9^2}{5}$$

$$= \frac{234}{5} = 46.8$$

Previous Years' Paper

NATIONAL DEFENCE ACADEMY & NAVAL ACADEMY

NDA & NA – Entrance Exam, 2023 (II)

PAPER I: GENERAL ABILITY TEST

PART A: ENGLISH LANGUAGE

FILL IN THE BLANKS

Directions (Qs. No. 1-10): *In this section, each of the following sentences has a blank space and is followed by four words. Select the word you consider most appropriate to fill in the blank space and indicate your response on the Answer Sheet accordingly.*

1. As the Southwest monsoon ……….. through most of July, flash floods caused by the waters of the Narmada hit Jabalpur town.

A. lashed B. flourished
C. occupied D. dried

2. Given the scale of the challenges that ……….. us today, our company proposes more viable plans for sustainability.

A. supports B. conflict
C. confronts D. convince

3. It is a really tough course, I am just worried that I won't be able to go the ………

A. way B. distance
C. far D. route

4. The ……… of the advancement made in agricultural productivity in India has been remarkable.

A. extent B. context
C. distance D. syntax

5. This essay ……….. and examines various systems for water appropriation and agricultural practices adapted by society in the arid conditions of Rajasthan.

A. confuses B. enhances
C. controls D. explores

6. India has been able to successfully ………….. its population through family planning programmes.

A. sterilise B. stabilise
C. stratify D. establish

7. Adolescence is the ………… wherein a child enters adulthood.

A. threshold B. position
C. condition D. period

8. The British who ruled India for 200 years were here to ………. India's natural resources.

A. spoil B. implore
C. exploit D. drill

9. Endangered species have a fifty per cent or greater probability of ………… within five years or two generations whichever is longer.

A. distinction B. extinction
C. complication D. completion

10. The first law of thermodynamics states that whereas energy can be ………. from one form into another, it cannot be created or destroyed.

A. reduced B. induced
C. performed D. transformed

SPOTTING ERRORS

Directions (Qs. No. 11-20): *Each item in this section has a sentence with three underlined parts labelled (A), (B) and (C). Read each sentence to find out whether there is any error in any underlined part and indicate your response in the Answer Sheet against the corresponding letter, i.e., (A) or (B) or (C). If you find no error, your response should be indicated as (D).*

11. Bread, butter and (A)/ jam common breakfast items (B)/ that are consumed by many households. (C)/ No error (D)

12. Ten thousand dollars is (A)/ the prize money being offered (B)/ by the game show hosts. (C)/ No error (D)

13. Three hundred and sixty five (A)/ create up the number of days (B)/ in a calendar year. (C)/ No error (D)

14. The process of removing (A)/ wool from the body of (B)/ an animal is called sharing. (C)/ No error (D)

15. Many people came (A)/ from faraway places to prayed (B)/ at the temple on the auspicious day. (C)/ No error (D)

16. After reading foreword of (A)/ the book on environmental issues in India, (B)/ I decided to meet its author. (C)/ No error (D)

17. The guidance from the mentors (A)/ and teachers facilitated the (B)/ smooth conduct of elections to the Students' council. (C)/ No error (D)

18. The Principal of our school (A)/ felicitated the students in (B)/ the prize distribution ceremony. (C)/ No error (D)

19. If you were to (A)/ come to Chennai to settle down (B)/ it will be the best possible decision. (C)/ No error (D)

20. They had promised to delivered (A)/ the bags before mid-March (B)/ to enable us to inaugurate the shop. (C)/ No error (D)

SYNONYMS

Directions (Qs. No. 21-30): *Each item in this section consists of a sentence with an underlined word followed by four words. Select the option that is nearest in meaning to the underlined word and mark your response in your Answer Sheet accordingly.*

21. He is always captious.
A. worried B. passionate
C. faultfinding D. jovial

22. Geomorphologists ascertain several wonderful facts about our earth.
A. verify B. invert
C. increase D. omit

23. The Colonel ordered the Soldiers to meet him in the commissary.
A. office B. field
C. playground D. canteen

24. The doctor dismembered the patient's finger first and then cured the ailment.
A. stitched B. dissected
C. plastered D. splintered

25. Mr. Kumar works as a bursar in the sports academy.
A. secretary B. accountant
C. coach D. trainer

26. His intentions are insidious.
A. pious B. inadvertent
C. deceitful D. naive

27. Respect for other human beings is intrinsic to the teachings of all religions.
A. inconsistent
B. peripheral
C. inherent
D. existential

28. He completed the onerous task with relative ease.
A. smooth B. complex
C. risky D. wearying

29. Alfred was a potentate during the Middle Ages.
A. Monarch B. lenient
C. liberal D. democrat

30. I abandoned the task due to indolence.
A. difficulty B. laziness
C. ugliness D. helplessness

USAGE OF PAIRED WORDS

Directions (Qs. No. 31-40): *In the following questions a pair of similar sounding words is provided. You are required to select the options that most appropriately describes the meaning of both the words and mark your response in the Answer Sheet accordingly.*

31. 'Principal' and 'Principle'
A. 'Principal' means belief system, and 'principle' means head of an educational institution.
B. 'Principal' means head of an educational institution, and 'principle' means original sum on which interest is charged.
C. 'Principle' means moral rule, and 'principal' means head of an educational institution.
D. 'Principal' means original sum on which interest is charged, and 'principle' means head of an educational institution.

32. 'Plane' and 'Plain'
A. 'Plane' means a flat surface, and 'plain' means something that flies.
B. 'Plane' means the flat surface, and 'plain' means not elaborate.
C. 'Plane' means something that flies, and 'plain' means flat surface.
D. 'Plane' means not elaborate, and 'plain' means flat surface.

33. 'Pail' and 'Pale'
A. 'Pale' means inferior or unimpressive, and 'pail' means faded.
B. 'Pale' means faded or light in shade, and 'pail' means inferior or unimpressive.
C. 'Pale' means faded or light in shade, and 'pail' means a bucket.

D. 'Pale' means a bucket, and 'pail' means inferior or unimpressive.

34. 'Metal' and 'Mettle'

A. 'Metal' is a hard shiny material that is a good conductor, and 'mettle' means malleable metal.

B. 'Metal' is a hard shiny material that is a good conductor, and 'mettle' means metallic substance.

C. 'Metal' means mental resilience, and 'mettle' is a hard shiny material that is a good conductor.

D. 'Metal' is a hard shiny material that is a good conductor, and 'mettle' means mental resilience.

35. 'Hail' and 'Hale'

A. 'Hail' means pellets of frozen rain, and 'hale' means wind storm.

B. 'Hail' means pellets of frozen rain, and 'hale' means strong and healthy.

C. 'Hail' means pellets of frozen rain, and 'hale' means to greet with enthusiastic approval.

D. 'Hail' means strong and healthy, and 'hale' means pellets of frozen rain.

36. 'Conscious' and 'Conscience'

A. 'Conscious' means sense of right and wrong, and 'conscience' means awareness about something.

B. 'Conscious' means alert, and 'conscience' means presence of mind.

C. 'Conscious' means intent, and 'conscience' means unprincipled action.

D. 'Conscious' means aware, and 'conscience' means sense of right and wrong.

37. 'Dissent' and 'Descent'

A. 'Dissent' means having ideas different from general beliefs or official position, and 'descent' means movement towards a lower place.

B. 'Dissent' means having ideas different from general beliefs or official position, and 'descent' means being of acceptable standard.

C. 'Dissent' means being of acceptable standard, and 'descent' means movement towards a lower place.

D. 'Dissent' means being of acceptable standard, and 'descent' means ideas different from general beliefs or official position.

38. 'Devise' and 'Device'

A. 'Device' means to determine, and 'devise' means a piece of equipment meant for accomplishing a specific task.

B. 'Device' means finding a new way to do something, and 'devise' means to determine.

C. 'Device' means a piece of equipment meant for accomplishing a specific task, and 'devise' means finding a new way to do something.

D. 'Device' means finding a new way to do something, and 'devise' means a piece of equipment meant for accomplishing a specific task.

39. 'Discrete' and 'Discreet'

A. 'Discrete' means separate and distinct categories of objects, and 'discreet' means misuse of authority.

B. 'Discrete' means separate and distinct categories of objects, and 'discreet' means maintaining confidentiality.

C. 'Discrete' means being careful in what one says or does, and 'discreet' means separate and distinct categories of objects.

D. 'Discrete' means misuse of authority and 'discreet' means being careful in what one says or does.

40. 'Eminent' and 'Imminent'

A. 'Eminent' means important and famous, and 'imminent' means something about to happen.

B. 'Eminent' means something unpleasant about to happen, and 'imminent' means important and famous person.

C. 'Eminent' means important and famous person, and 'imminent' means inherent or existing within.

D. 'Eminent' means inherent or existing within, and 'imminent' means something about to happen.

ANTONYMS

Directions (Qs. No. 41-45): *Each item in this section consists of a sentence with an underlined word followed by four words. Select the option that is opposite in meaning to the underlined word and mark your response in your Answer Sheet accordingly.*

41. Many metals are malleable in nature and property.

A. hard B. strong
C. tender D. weak

42. To neglect a warning is to invite danger.

A. disregard B. ignore
C. regard D. overlook

43. His ostentatious behaviour surprised everyone.

A. tawdry B. modest
C. gaudy D. apparent

44. The experience of Covid Pandemic was excruciating for much of the population.

A. gnawing B. gruelling
C. harrowing D. mild

45. A trip to the hills was refreshing.

A. conniving
B. wearying
C. revivifying
D. rejuvenating

COMPREHENSION

Directions (Qs. No. 46-50): *Carefully read the given passage and answer the questions that follow. You are required to select your answers solely based on the contents of the passage and the opinion of the author only.*

PASSAGE

People by and large are concerned with and pursue self-interest. They are unlikely to be motivated to use renewable resources in a prudent and sustainable fashion. They are unlikely to be motivated under the following conditions : if their resource catchments are vast, so that degradation of any particular portion affects them very little; or if they have open before them possibilities of substitution as any one resource element is depleted; or if their control over the resource base is tenuous, so that others may, at any time, deplete a resource they value, even if they use it in a restrained fashion. Indeed, exhaustive use is highly likely when any one of these three conditions obtains. It is only when people perceive their resource catchments as limited, possibilities of substitution of exhausted resource elements as not readily feasible, and their own control over the resource base as secure, will they be motivated to use the resources in a prudent fashion. People, rooted in a locality, and retaining control over their resource base are most likely to fulfil all three prerequisites for sustainable resource use; and therefore to behave in ways conducive to the conservation of biodiversity within their localities.

46. Why, according to the writer can't people be motivated to use a resource prudently?
1. They feel that others may overuse the resource.
2. It is possible to substitute the resource.
3. Abundance of the resource availability.

Select the correct answer using the code given below:
A. 1 only B. 2 only
C. 2 and 3 only D. 1, 2 and 3

47. When do people use resources exhaustively?
A. When the substitution of resource is felicitated by NGOs
B. When the resource is about to expand
C. When the resources use has little impact
D. When they desire desperately for sustainable development

48. The self-interest of people affects the use of renewable resources
A. positively B. erratically
C. affirmatively D. indifferently

49. People rooted in a locality
A. cause harm to available resources
B. generate resources
C. believe in conservation and reproduction of resources
D. consume resources freely

50. Which among the following is closest in meaning with the word 'deplete'?
A. exhaust B. complete
C. replete D. desperate

PART B: GENERAL KNOWLEDGE

51. The streaming of light beams coming from the Sun through trees is said to have suggested that light travels in straight line. The particles on the path of light beams are visible to us because
A. dust particles in the air reflect light into our eyes
B. dust particles in the air scatter light into our eyes
C. dust particles in the air refract light into our eyes
D. dust particles in the air polarize light into our eyes

52. The flash of lightning is seen before the thunderstorm is heard. It verifies that
A. sound travels much faster than light
B. light travels much faster than sound
C. light and sound both travel with same speed
D. intensity of flash of lightning is very high during thunderstorm

53. The potential difference between the two end terminals of an electric heater is 220 V and the current through it is 0.5 A. What would be the current through the heater if the potential difference across the terminals of the heater is reduced to 120 V?
A. 1.0 A B. 0.5 A
C. 0.27 A D. 0.7 A

54. The heating element in an electric iron is usually made of:
A. Constantan B. Tungsten
C. Nichrome D. Copper

55. Sita, 1.5 m high, stands before a plane mirror fixed on a wall to view her full image. What should be the minimum height of the plane mirror so that Sita can view her image fully?
A. 0.50 m B. 0.35 m
C. 0.75 m D. 0.25 m

56. Galvanization is a method of protecting iron from rusting by coating with a thin layer of:

A. Gallium B. Aluminum
C. Zinc D. Silver

57. Which one of the following alloys contains a non-metal as one of its constituent?

A. Brass B. Bronze
C. Amalgam D. Steel

58. Buckminster fullerene, which looks like a football, is an allotropic form of:

A. Phosphorus B. Sulphur
C. Carbon D. Tin

59. Which one of the following graphs correctly represents the current (I) – voltage (V) variation for a rectangular piece of a semiconductor wafer?

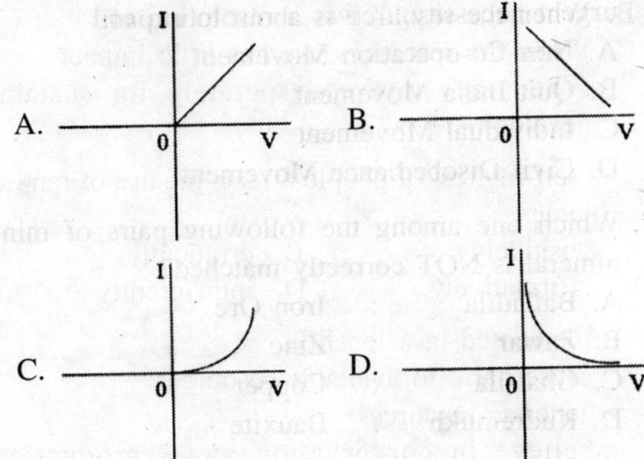

60. The green plants in a terrestrial ecosystem absorbs sunlight that falls on their leaves and convert it into food energy. The percentage of solar radiation absorbed by all green plants for the process of photosynthesis is about:

A. 1% B. 5%
C. 8% D. 10%

61. Consider the following reaction :

$Fe_2O_3(s) + 2Al(s) \rightarrow 2Fe(s) + Al_2O_3(s)$

Which of the following statements about the given reaction is NOT correct?

A. It is an example of displacement reaction
B. It is highly endothermic reaction
C. Fe_2O_3 acts as oxidizing agent
D. This reaction is applicable to joining of railway tracks

62. Match List I with List II and select the correct answer using the code given below the Lists:

List-I *(Chemical process)*	List-II *(Reaction)*
(a) Electrolysis of water	1. Double displacement reaction
(b) Burning of coal	2. Combination reaction
(c) Iron nail immersed in copper sulphate solution	3. Decomposition reaction
(d) Addition of barium chloride solution to aluminium sulphate solution	4. Displacement reaction

Code:

	(a)	*(b)*	*(c)*	*(d)*
A.	3	4	2	1
B.	4	2	1	3
C.	3	2	4	1
D.	4	1	2	3

63. Which one of the following processes involves chemical reaction?

A. Evaporation of petrol
B. Dissolution of salt in water
C. Storing of oxygen gas under pressure in a gas cylinder
D. Burning of magnesium ribbon in air

64. Which one of the following metals does NOT react with cold water to liberate hydrogen gas?

A. Potassium B. Iron
C. Calcium D. Sodium

65. Consider the following reaction:

$$2HgO \xrightarrow{\blacktriangle} 2Hg + O_2$$

The respective state of HgO, Hg and O_2 in the above reaction is:

A. Liquid, solid, gas B. Solid, solid, gas
C. Liquid, solid, liquid D. Solid, liquid, gas

66. The two important features of sexual reproduction in higher organisms that create genetic diversity in offspring are:

A. Mitosis and fertilization
B. Meiosis and fertilization
C. Mitosis and binary fission
D. Meiosis and conjugation

67. Eukaryotic cells are much more complex as compared to prokaryotes. Which one of the following structures is exclusively present in a eukaryotic cell?

A. Cell wall
B. Plasma membrane
C. Nucleic acid
D. Mitochondria

68. An important cause of tooth decay by the bacterium *Streptococcus mutans* is because of their ability to attach to teeth surface by producing slime layer from:

A. Sugar B. Alcohol
C. Saliva D. Teichoic acid

69. In angiosperms, pollen grain germinates to produce two male gametes. Which one of the following functions is carried out by these gametes?
A. Both the gametes fuse with a single egg cell
B. Both the gametes fuse with two different egg cells
C. One gamete fuses with the egg cell and the other one eventually degenerate
D. One gamete fuses with the egg cell and the other one fuses with a diploid secondary nucleus

70. In a sexually reproducing organism, which one of the following statements is appropriate both for the parent and offspring?
A. Chromosome number increases but DNA content remains constant
B. Both chromosome number and DNA content remains constant
C. Chromosome number decreases but DNA content remains constant
D. Both chromosome number and DNA content decreases

71. Relationship between a flower and honey-bee will help the flower for/in
A. Faster development
B. Pollination
C. Quick germination of pollen
D. Increase in size

72. Which one of the following was NOT a way in which kings in ancient India attempted to claim a higher status?
A. Identifying with a variety of deities
B. Assuming pompous titles
C. Imposing high taxes
D. Conquests and annexation of territories

73. Which one of the following statements about the Bhakti movement is NOT correct?
A. The Bhakti movement avoided traditions that promoted diversity
B. In northern India, the Bhakti movement revolved around the worship of Rama and Krishna
C. The Bhakti movement relied on the devotion of God, both with and without attributes
D. While Tulsidas represented the tradition of devotion with attributes, Sant Kabir followed the path of devotion without attributes

74. The 'Reign of Terror' in revolutionary France referred to:
A. Bands of revolutionaries moving around to terrorise people who did not participate in the revolution
B. The royal forces punishing people who participated in the revolution
C. Trial and beheading persons considered enemies of the republic by the revolutionary tribunal
D. The general atmosphere of insecurity perceived by people after the beheading of the king

75. In which one of the following ways did the First World War Not impact Europe?
A. From a continent of creditors it turned into a continent of debtors
B. Soldiers came to be placed higher in social status than civilians
C. Popular support decreased for conservative dictatorship which had come into being recently
D. National honour occupied centre stage in the public sphere

76. "...the immediate ending of British rule in India is an urgent necessity..." was a resolution of:
A. Non Co-operation Movement
B. Quit India Movement
C. Individual Movement
D. Civil Disobedience Movement

77. Which one among the following pairs of mine and mineral is NOT correctly matched?
A. Bailadila : Iron Ore
B. Zawar : Zinc
C. Ghatsila : Copper
D. Kudremukh : Bauxite

78. Which one of the following is the usual unit of measurement for Air Pressure used in India?
A. Centimeter B. Millibar
C. Milligram D. Milliliter

79. Which one of the following is the oldest era in Geological History determining the age of various rock types?
A. Precambrian B. Mesozoic
C. Cenozoic D. Paleozoic

80. A geographical grid has:
1. Lines that run east to west around the globe to mark latitude
2. Lines that run north to south from north pole to south pole indicate longitude

Which of the statements given above is/are correct?
A. 1 only B. 2 only
C. Both 1 and 2 D. Neither 1 nor 2

81. In which one of the following layers of the atmosphere all weather phenomenon occur?
A. Mesosphere B. Troposphere
C. Thermosphere D. Stratosphere

82. In which one of the following states 'Roopkund' lake is located?
A. Kerala B. Manipur
C. Himachal Pradesh D. Uttarakhand

83. Ram records the odometer readings of his car for the distance covered from 2000 km at the start of his journey and 2400 km at the end of the journey after 8 hours. What is the average speed of the car?

A. 50 km/h B. 60 km/h
C. 70 km/h D. 80 km/h

84. Ms. Rani decides to convert her AC generator into a DC generator. Which one of the following she would need to use?

A. A split-ring type commutator
B. Slip rings and brushes
C. A stronger magnetic field
D. A rectangular wire loop

85. Ramesh cannot see distinctly objects kept beyond 2 m. This defect can be corrected by using a lens of power:

A. + 0.5 D B. – 0.5 D
C. + 0.2 D D. – 0.2 D

86. Which of the following statements are correct about the electrical resistance and resistivity of a wire?

1. Both quantities depend on the area of cross-section of the wire.
2. Both depend on the temperature.
3. Resistance of the wire is directly proportional to the resistivity of the wire.
4. Resistivity of the wire is directly proportional to the length of the wire.

Select the correct answer using the code given below:

A. 1 and 2 B. 1 and 3
C. 2 and 3 D. 2 and 4

87. A liquid is heated up to a certain temperature. Which one of the following situation would correspond to the boiling of the liquid?

A. When atmospheric pressure becomes equal to the vapour pressure
B. When atmospheric pressure becomes less than vapour pressure
C. When atmospheric pressure becomes higher than the vapour pressure.
D. When vapour pressure becomes equal to the air pressure.

88. Which one of the following is NOT an example of organic compound?

A. Ammonium cyanate B. Marsh gas
C. Urea D. Cane sugar

89. Which one of the following acid is used by goldsmith for cleaning of gold and silver articles?

A. Sulphuric acid B. Nitric acid
C. Hydrochloric acid D. Phosphoric acid

90. What is the action of litmus on ethanol?

A. Litmus is neutral towards ethanol
B. Ethanol turns blue litmus to red; confirming acidic nature of ethanol
C. Ethanol turns red litmus to blue; confirming basic nature of ethanol
D. Ethanol decolorizes litmus through bleaching action

91. Which one of the following metal is NOT an essential component in stainless steel?

A. Iron B. Nickel
C. Chromium D. Tin

92. Match List I with List II and select the correct answer using the code given below the Lists:

List-I *(Process)*	List-II *(Separation method)*
(*a*) Separation of acetone and water from their mixture	1. Chromatography
(*b*) Separation of water and kerosene oil from their mixture	2. Centrifugation
(*c*) Separation of cream from milk	3. Distillation
(*d*) Separation of pigments from plant extract	4. Separating Funnel

Code:

	(*a*)	(*b*)	(*c*)	(*d*)
A.	3	2	4	1
B.	4	2	1	3
C.	3	4	2	1
D.	4	1	2	3

93. Which one of the following is NOT a requirement for photosynthesis?

A. Chlorophyll B. CO_2
C. Water D. O_2

94. In flowering plants, DNA content of the parent plant gets halved during:

A. Seed germination
B. Fruit formation
C. Flower bud formation
D. Pollen formation

95. Which one of the following is the correct sequence during sexual reproduction in Angiosperms?

A. Egg → zygote → embryo → seed
B. Embryo → egg → zygote → seed
C. Egg → embryo → zygote → seed
D. Egg → seed → zygote → embryo

96. Which one of the following combinations of events represents the correct sequence during reproduction in flowering plants?

A. Ovule → fruit; egg → embryo; zygote → seed; ovary → egg

B. Embryo → egg; ovary → fruit; ovule → zygote; zygote → seed
C. Ovary → fruit; zygote → egg; embryo → ovule; seed → fruit
D. Egg → zygote; zygote → embryo; ovule → seed; ovary → fruit

97. The book 'Nation First : The Golden Saga of 82 Years' is the history of which one of the following organizations?
A. Indo-Tibetan Border Police
B. Border Security Force
C. Central Reserve Police Force
D. Central Industrial Security Force

98. Consider the following statements regarding Sanchi and its archaeological findings:
1. When Sanchi was discovered in 1818, three of its four gateways were still standing, the fourth was lying on the spot where it had fallen
2. Animals depicted at Sanchi include elephants, horses, monkeys and cattle

Which of the statements given above is/are correct?
A. Only 1 B. Only 2
C. Both 1 and 2 D. Neither 1 nor 2

99. Which Five Year Plan of India focused on rapid industrialization based growth process?
A. First Five Year Plan
B. Second Five Year Plan
C. Fifth Five Year Plan
D. Seventh Five Year Plan

100. *Chandimangala*, a sixteenth century text, was composed by:
A. Hema Saraswati
B. Madhav Kandali
C. Tukaram
D. Mukundaram Chakrabarti

101. Consider the following statements regarding the royal center in Vijayanagara Empire:
1. The royal center was located in the south-western part of the settlement
2. It included over 60 temples
3. About 30 building complexes at the site have been identified as palaces

Which of the statements given above is/are correct?
A. 1 only B. 2 only
C. 1, 2 and 3 D. 1 and 2 only

102. Which one of the following statements is NOT correct?
A. Area wise Madhya Pradesh is the fourth largest state in India
B. Hornbill festival is celebrated in Nagaland
C. Gujarat state contribute 7.9 per cent share to the National GDP
D. Telangana is situated in the Deccan plateau in the central stretch of Indian peninsula

103. Which one of the following soils is ideal for growing cotton?
A. Regur soil B. Laterite soil
C. Desert soil D. Mountainous soil

104. Where is Central Institute of Buddhist Studies situated?
A. Leh B. Kullu
C. Almora D. Gangtok

105. Consider the following statements about physical features of India:
1. The southern point of the Peninsular Plateau is formed by the Nilgiri Hills where the Eastern and the Western Ghats meet
2. The Cardamom Hills may be regarded as a continuation of the Eastern Ghats

Which of the statements given above is/are correct?
A. 1 only B. 2 only
C. Both 1 and 2 D. Neither 1 nor 2

106. Which one of the following is the narrow belt parallel to the Shiwalik foothills where streams and rivers coming from the mountains deposit heavy materials of rocks and boulders?
A. Tarai B. Bhangar
C. Bhabar D. Khadar

107. Which of the following statements about Suez Canal is/are correct?
1. Suez is a man-made navigation canal
2. Suez links Mediterranean Sea and the Red Sea
3. The economic significance of Suez Canal is less than that of Panama Canal

Select the correct answer using the code given below:
A. 1 only B. 1 and 2 only
C. 2 and 3 only D. 1, 2 and 3

108. An iron nail sinks in water whereas an iron ship floats. Which of the following statements is correct in this regard?
1. Average density of ship is greater than that of the water
2. Average density of iron nail is greater than that of the water
3. Average density of the ship is less than that of the water
4. Average density of the ship is equal to that of the water

Select the correct answer using the code given below:
A. 1 and 2 B. 2 and 3
C. 2 and 4 D. 1 and 4

109. Which of the following arrangement of resistors offers minimum effective resistance between points X and Y?

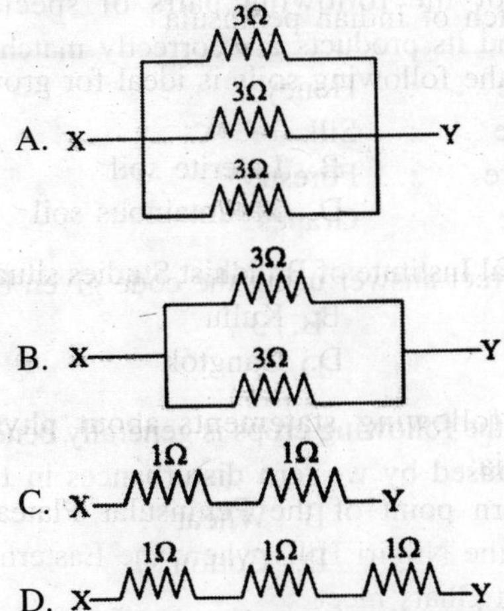

110. What will happen if a collection of positive and negative charges are passed at a high speed through a magnetic field which is perpendicular to the direction of motion of the charges? (Assume that both kind of charges are NOT going to recombine)

A. Both kind of charges will stop moving
B. Positive charges and negative charges will separate out
C. Positive charges will stop but negative charges will continue moving uninterrupted
D. Both kind of charges will keep moving uninterrupted

111. The motion of a particle of mass m is described by the relation, $y = ut - \frac{1}{2}gt^2$, where u is the initial velocity of the particle. The force acting on the particle is:

A. $F = m\left(\frac{du}{dt}\right)$ B. $F = mg$
C. $F = m\left(\frac{dy}{dt}\right)$ D. $F = -mg$

112. A block of wood (dimensions : 40 cm × 20 cm × 10 cm) is kept on a tabletop in three different positions : (*a*) with its side of dimensions 20 cm × 10 cm; (*b*) with its side of dimensions 10 cm × 40 cm; and (*c*) with its side of dimensions 40 cm × 20 cm. The pressure exerted by the wooden block on the tabletop in these positions is represented by P_A, P_B and P_C, respectively. The pressure follows the trend

A. $P_A > P_B > P_C$ B. $P_A < P_B < P_C$
C. $P_A = P_B = P_C$ D. $P_A < P_B = P_C$

113. Which one of the following metals can be extracted using carbon as reducing agent?

A. Zinc B. Silver
C. Gold D. Aluminum

114. Which among the following is NOT true with respect to colloidal solution?

A. Particles are uniformly distributed throughout the solution
B. Colloidal solution is homogenous in nature
C. They show Tyndal effect
D. They do not settle down when kept undisturbed

115. Kerosene and petrol mixture can be best separated by:

A. Sublimation
B. Separating funnel
C. Fractional distillation
D. Compressing and cooling

116. As proposed by Dalton, which of the following symbol represents phosphorus?

A. 

B. 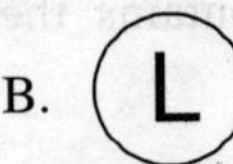

C. 
D. 

117. Which among the following statements with respect to carbon is/are correct?

1. Carbon forms the basis for all living organisms and many things we use
2. Carbon shows tetra-valency and the property of catenation
3. Carbon forms covalent bonds with itself and other elements
4. Carbon forms compounds containing triple and tetra bonds between carbon atoms

Select the correct answer using the code given below:

A. 1 only B. 1 and 2 only
C. 1, 2 and 3 D. 2 and 4

118. Consider the following statements:

1. Terracotta models of the plough have been found at sites in Cholistan and at Banawali (Haryana).
2. There is evidence of a ploughed field at Kalibangan associated with the mature phase of the Harappan civilization.
3. The ploughed field at Kalibangan had two sets of furrows crossing at right angles to each other suggesting two different crops were grown together in it.

Which of the statements given above are correct?

A. 1, 2 and 3 B. 2 and 3 only
C. 1 and 3 only D. None of the above

119. Which of the following statements about the technological innovations during the Industrial Revolutions are correct?

1. Mule was the nickname for a machine invented in 1779, that allowed the spinning of strong and fine yarn.

2. Water Frame, invented in 1769 by Richard Arkwright, made it possible to weave pure cotton clothes.
3. Power loom, invented by Edmund Cartwright in 1787, could be used to weave any kind of materials.

Select the correct answer using the code given below:

A. 1 and 2 only B. 1, 2 and 3
C. 2 and 3 only D. 3 only

120. Who among the following is known as the architect of Indian planning?

A. V.K.R.V. Rao B. Sukhamoy Chakravarty
C. P.C. Mahalanobis D. John Mathai

121. Which one of the following Ashokan Minor Rock Edicts, contains the personal name of the king - Ashoka?

A. Maski B. Bahapur
C. Bairat D. Sahasram

122. Arrange the following in correct chronological order

1. Charak Samhita
2. Bharat's Natyashastra
3. Sangam Literature
4. Ashtadhyayi

Select the correct answer using the code given below:

A. 1, 3, 4, 2 B. 2, 4, 1, 3
C. 4, 3, 1, 2 D. 3, 1, 2, 4

123. Which one of the following is NOT an example of Fold Mountain?

A. Mt. Fuji B. Alps
C. Andes D. Rockies

124. Which one of the following is an organic soil?

A. Aridisols B. Histosols
C. Oxisols D. Vertisols

125. The North-south and East-west Road Corridors of India cross each other at which of the following cities?

A. Bhopal B. Itarsi
C. Gwalior D. Jhansi

126. Which one of the following climatic regions of the world have a typical characteristic of seasonal reversal of wind?

A. British type Climate
B. Mediterranean Climate
C. China type Climate
D. Monsoon Climate

127. Which one of the following statement is NOT correct?

A. Bokaro steel plant is located in Damodar river basin
B. Jamshedpur steel plant is located on the confluence of Damodar and Barakar
C. Salem steel plant is located on the bank of Kaveri River
D. Bhilai steel plant obtains water from Tandula reservoir

128. How many of the following pairs of specialized agriculture and its products are correctly matched?

1. Apiculture : Honey
2. Sericulture : Silk
3. Silviculture : Forestry
4. Viticulture : Grapes

Select the correct answer using the code given below:

A. 4 B. 3
C. 2 D. 1

129. Which one of the following crops is generally benefitted by the rain caused by western disturbances in India?

A. Rice B. Wheat
C. Bajra D. Cotton

130. Which one of the following pairs of city and industry is NOT correctly matched?

A. Saharanpur : Paper industry
B. Chanderi : Cotton textile industry
C. Bhadohi : Carpet industry
D. Raniganj : Iron and steel industry

131. Which one of the following graphs represents the equation of motion $v = u + at$; where all quantities are non-zero and symbols carry their usual meanings?

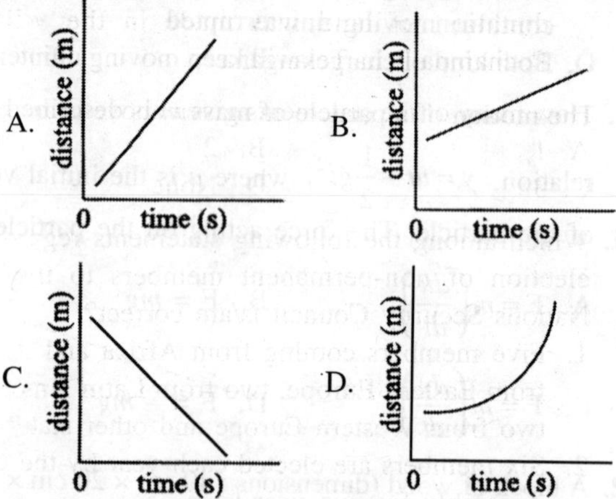

132. Which one of the following statements is true for sound waves propagating in air?

A. Sound is an electromagnetic wave and transverse in nature
B. Sound is a mechanical wave and longitudinal in nature
C. Sound is a mechanical wave and transverse in nature
D. Sound is an electromagnetic wave and longitudinal in nature

133. A 100 g sphere is moving at a speed of 20 m/s and collides with another sphere of mass 50 g. If the second sphere was at rest prior to the collision and the first sphere comes at rest immediately after the collision, considering the collision to be elastic, the speed of the second sphere would be

A. 10 m/s B. 20 m/s
C. 30 m/s D. 40 m/s

134. Which one of the following optical phenomena supports that the light is a transverse wave?

A. Refraction B. Diffraction
C. Interference D. Polarization

135. How many of the following materials can be attracted by a magnet?

1. Plastic
2. Carbon
3. Aluminium
4. Stainless Steel

Select the correct answer using the code given below:

A. 1 B. 2
C. 3 D. None

136. Consider the following statements with reference to the Bhoodan Movement:

1. Vinoba Bhave organized 'The Sarvodaya Samaj' to take up the work of non-violent transformation in India
2. Jayaprakash Narayan withdrew from active politics to join the Bhoodan Movement in 1953
3. In the wake of the Bhoodan Movement the first donation of land was made in the village of Pochampalli in Telangana

How many of the statements given above is/are correct?

A. 1 B. 2
C. 3 D. None

137. Which among the following statements regarding the election of non-permanent members to the United Nations Security Council is/are correct?

1. Five members coming from Africa and Asia, one from Eastern Europe, two from Latin America and two from Western Europe and other states
2. Six members are elected each year by the General Assembly for two year term

Select the correct answer using the code given below:

A. 1 only B. 2 only
C. Both 1 and 2 D. Neither 1 nor 2

138. Which one of the following provisions of the Constitution of India deals with District Planning Committee?

A. 243ZD B. 243ZB
C. 243ZE D. 243ZC

139. Consider the following statements about Attorney-General in India:

1. She/he is the first law officer of the Government of India
2. She/he has a right to speak in any House of Parliament without any right to vote
3. She/he is appointed by the President of India
4. She/he is a whole-time counsel for the Government in the court of law

How many of the statements given above is/are correct?

A. 1 B. 2
C. 3 D. 4

140. Which one among the following states was NOT impacted by the Land Boundary Agreement Treaty between India and Bangladesh (2015)?

A. West Bengal B. Assam
C. Tripura D. Arunachal Pradesh

141. The 480 MW Phukot Karnali Hydro Electric Project is situated in:

A. Thailand B. Indonesia
C. Nepal D. Bhutan

142. Consider the following statements about a river:
This river originates in the Hindu Kush mountain range and flows into Hamoun wetlands after covering a long stretch of about 1,100 km. There has been serious conflicts between two neighbouring nations regarding the sharing of water from this river. Identify the river from the following :

A. Mekong B. Tarim
C. Indus D. Helmand

143. Match List I with List II and select the correct answer using the code given below the Lists:

List-I *(Bilateral Exercise)*	List-II *(Participating Country)*
(*a*) Garuda Shakti	1. India and Japan
(*b*) Nomadic Elephant	2. India and Sri Lanka
(*c*) Mitra Shakti	3. India and Mongolia
(*d*) Dharma Guardian	4. India and Indonesia

Code:

	(*a*)	(*b*)	(*c*)	(*d*)
A.	4	2	3	1
B.	4	3	2	1
C.	1	3	2	4
D.	1	2	3	4

144. Consider the following statements about gallantry awards in India:

1. Post-independence, first three gallantry awards were instituted on 26th January, 1950
2. The first three gallantry awards were Ashoka Chakra Class-I, Ashoka Chakra Class-II and Ashoka Chakra Class-Ill

Which of the statements given above is/are correct?
A. 1 only B. 2 only
C. Both 1 and 2 D. Neither 1 nor 2

145. Consider the following statements about Centralized Laboratory Network (CLN):
1. CLN works to test vaccines which can be used during pandemic
2. India is a member of CLN
3. CLN is a part of the Coalition for Epidemic Preparedness Innovations (CEPI)

Which of the statements given above is/are correct?
A. 1 only B. 2 and 3 only
C. 1 and 2 only D. 1, 2 and 3

146. Consider the following statements about Kavach, the automatic train protection system:
1. It is designed and developed by Research Design and Standard Organisation (RDSO) in collaboration with Railway Technical Research Institute (RTRI), Japan
2. The trials of Kavach were facilitated by the Southern Railway
3. Kavach is a state-of-the-art electronic system with Safety Integrity Level-4 (SIL-4)

Which of the statements given above is/are correct?
A. 1 only B. 3 only
C. 1 and 2 only D. 1, 2 and 3

147. The Nova Kakhovka dam, which was in news recently, is situated in:
A. Belarus B. Turkey
C. Ukraine D. Poland

148. Aaron Finch, who recently retired from international cricket, was captain of men's cricket team of which one of the following countries?
A. South Africa B. Australia
C. England D. New Zealand

149. Which one of the following is the name of the dashboard launched recently by the Reserve Bank of India to assess and monitor the progress of financial inclusion by capturing relevant parameters?
A. *Pragya* B. *Antardrishti*
C. *Divyachakshu* D. *Antahgyan*

150. 'Sengol', installed in the new Parliament building of India, was seen as a symbol of the path of service, duty and nation in which Empire of the past?
A. Gupta Empire B. Shunga Empire
C. Pandyan Empire D. Chola Empire

PAPER II: MATHEMATICS

1. If $z\bar{z} = |z + \bar{z}|$, where $z = x + iy$, $i = \sqrt{-1}$. then the locus of z is a pair of:
A. straight lines B. rectangular hyperbolas
C. parabolas D. circles

2. If 1! + 3! + 5! + 7! + ... + 199! is divided by 24, what is the remainder?
A. 3 B. 6
C. 7 D. 9

3. What is the value of $\sqrt{12+5i} + \sqrt{12-5i}$, where, $i = \sqrt{-1}$?
A. 24 B. 25
C. $5\sqrt{2}$ D. $5(\sqrt{2}-1)$

4. If $A = \begin{bmatrix} 1 \\ 2 \\ 3 \end{bmatrix}$, then what is the value of det(I + AA′), where I is the 3 × 3 identity matrix?
A. 15 B. 6
C. 0 D. –1

5. If A, B and C are square matrices of order 3 and det(BC) = 2 det(A), then what is the value of $\det(2A^{-1}BC)$?
A. 16 B. 8
C. 4 D. 2

6. If the *n*th term of a sequence is $\frac{2n+5}{7}$, then what is the sum of its first 140 terms?
A. 2840 B. 2780
C. 2920 D. 5700

7. Let A be a skew-symmetric matrix of order 3. What is the value of

$\det(4A^4) - \det(3A^3) + \det(2A^2) - \det(A) + \det(-I)$ where I is the identity matrix of order 3?
A. –1 B. 0
C. 1 D. 2

8. If $A = \begin{bmatrix} 0 & 3 & 4 \\ -3 & 0 & 5 \\ -4 & -5 & 0 \end{bmatrix}$, then which one of the following statements is correct?
A. A^2 is symmetric matrix with $\det(A^2) = 0$.
B. A^2 is symmetric matrix with $\det(A^2) \neq 0$.
C. A^2 is skew-symmetric matrix with $\det(A^2) = 0$.
D. A^2 is skew-symmetric matrix with $\det(A^2) \neq 0$.

9. If $A = \begin{bmatrix} 2 & 0 & 0 \\ 0 & 3 & 0 \\ 0 & 0 & 4 \end{bmatrix}$, then which of the following statements are correct?

1. A^n will always be singular for any positive integer n.
2. A^n will always be a diagonal matrix for any positive integer n.
3. A^n will always be a symmetric matrix for any positive integer n.

Select the correct answer using the code given below:

A. 1 and 2 only B. 2 and 3 only
C. 1 and 3 only D. 1, 2 and 3

10. If $(a + b)$, $2b$, $(b + c)$ are in HP, then which one of the following is correct?

A. a, b and c are in AP
B. $a - b$, $b - c$ and $c - a$ are in AP
C. a, b and c are in GP
D. $a - b$, $b - c$ and $c - a$ are in GP

11. Let $t_1, t_2, t_3 \ldots$ be in GP. What is $(t_1 t_3 \ldots t_{21})^{\frac{1}{11}}$ equal to?

A. t_{10} B. t_{10}^2
C. t_{11} D. t_{11}^2

12. Which one of the following is a square root of $-\sqrt{-1}$?

A. $1 + i$ B. $\frac{1-i}{\sqrt{2}}$
C. $\frac{1+i}{\sqrt{2}}$ D. $\frac{1}{\sqrt{2}}i$

13. What is the maximum number of points of intersection of 10 circles?

A. 45 B. 60
C. 90 D. 120

14. A set S contains $(2n + 1)$ elements. There are 4096 subsets of S which contain at most n elements. What is n equal to?

A. 5 B. 6
C. 7 D. 8

15. If $\begin{vmatrix} x^2+3x & x-1 & x+3 \\ x+1 & -2x & x-4 \\ x-3 & x+4 & 3x \end{vmatrix} = ax^4 + bx^3 + cx^2 + dx + e$, then what is the value of e?

A. -1 B. 0
C. 1 D. 2

16. If all elements of a third order determinant are equal to 1 or -1, then the value of the determinant is:

A. 0 only
B. an even number but not necessarily 0
C. an odd number
D. 0, 1 or -1

17. If $A = \begin{bmatrix} 2 & -1 & 0 \\ -1 & 3 & 0 \\ 0 & 0 & 1 \end{bmatrix}$, then what is the value of det[adj(adjA)]?

A. 5 B. 25
C. 125 D. 625

18. If $A = \begin{bmatrix} 1 & 0 & 0 \\ 0 & 1 & 0 \\ 0 & 0 & 1 \end{bmatrix}$, then what is $23A^3 - 19A^2 - 4A$ equal to?

A. Null matrix of order 3
B. Identity matrix of order 3
C. $\begin{bmatrix} 2 & 0 & 0 \\ 0 & 2 & 0 \\ 0 & 0 & 2 \end{bmatrix}$
D. $\begin{bmatrix} 7 & 0 & 0 \\ 0 & 7 & 0 \\ 0 & 0 & 7 \end{bmatrix}$

19. The value of the determinant of a matrix A of order 3 is 3. If C is the matrix of cofactors of the matrix A, then what is the value of determinant of C^2?

A. 3 B. 9
C. 81 D. 729

20. If $A_k = \begin{bmatrix} k-1 & k \\ k-2 & k+1 \end{bmatrix}$, then what is:
$\det(A_1) + \det(A_2) + \det(A_3) + \ldots + \det(A_{100})$ equal to?

A. 100 B. 1000
C. 9900 D. 10000

21. The Cartesian product $A \times A$ has 16 elements among which are (0, 2) and (1, 3). Which of the following statements is/are correct?

1. It is possible to determine set A.
2. $A \times A$ contains the element (3, 2).

Select the correct answer using the code given below:

A. 1 only B. 2 only
C. Both 1 and 2 D. Neither 1 nor 2

22. Let $A = \{1, 2, 3, \ldots, 20\}$. Define a relation R from A to A by $R = \{(x, y) : 4x - 3y = 1\}$, where $x, y \in A$. Which of the following statements is/are correct?

1. The domain of R is $\{1, 4, 7, 10, 13, 16\}$.
2. The range of R is $\{1, 5, 9, 13, 17\}$.
3. The range of R is equal to codomain of R.

Select the correct answer using the code given below:

A. 1 only B. 2 only
C. 1 and 2 D. 2 and 3

23. Consider the following statements:

1. The relation f defined by

$$f(x) = \begin{cases} x^3, & 0 \le x \le 2 \\ 4x, & 2 \le x \le 8 \end{cases}$$ is a function.

2. The relation g defined by

$$g(x) = \begin{cases} x^2, & 0 \le x \le 4 \\ 3x, & 4 \le x \le 8 \end{cases}$$ is a function.

Which of the statements given above is/are correct?

A. 1 only B. 2 only
C. Both 1 and 2 D. Neither 1 nor 2

24. Consider the following statements:

1. $A = (A \cup B) \cup (A - B)$
2. $A \cup (B - A) = (A \cup B)$
3. $B = (A \cup B) - (A - B)$

Which of the statements given above are correct?

A. 1 and 2 only B. 2 and 3 only
C. 1 and 3 only D. 1, 2 and 3

25. A function satisfies $f(x-y) = \dfrac{f(x)}{f(y)}$, where $f(y) \ne 0$. If $f(1) = 0.5$, then what is $f(2) + f(3) + f(4) + f(5) + f(6)$ equal to?

A. $\dfrac{15}{32}$ B. $\dfrac{17}{32}$
C. $\dfrac{29}{64}$ D. $\dfrac{31}{64}$

26. What is $2\cot\left(\dfrac{1}{2}\cos^{-1}\dfrac{\sqrt{5}}{3}\right)$ equal to?

A. -1 B. 1
C. $3+\sqrt{5}$ D. $3-\sqrt{5}$

27. If $\sec^{-1} p - \operatorname{cosec}^{-1} q = 0$, where $p > 0$, $q > 0$; then what is the value of $p^{-2} + q^{-2}$?

A. 1 B. 2
C. $\dfrac{1}{2}$ D. $\dfrac{1}{2\sqrt{2}}$

28. What is $1+\sin^2\left(\cos^{-1}\left(\dfrac{3}{\sqrt{17}}\right)\right)$ equal to?

A. $\dfrac{25}{17}$ B. $\dfrac{8}{17}$
C. $\dfrac{9}{17}$ D. $\dfrac{47}{17}$

29. If $\tan(\pi \cos\theta) = \cot(\pi \sin\theta)$, $0 < \theta < \dfrac{\pi}{2}$; then, what is the value of $8\sin^2\left(\theta + \dfrac{\pi}{4}\right)$?

A. 16 B. 2
C. 1 D. $\dfrac{1}{2}$

30. If $\tan\alpha = \dfrac{1}{7}$, $\sin\beta = \dfrac{1}{\sqrt{10}}$; $0 < \alpha, \beta < \dfrac{\pi}{2}$, then what is the value of $\cos(\alpha + 2\beta)$?

A. $-\dfrac{1}{2}$ B. $-\dfrac{1}{\sqrt{2}}$
C. $\dfrac{1}{\sqrt{2}}$ D. $\dfrac{1}{2}$

Directions (Qs. No. 31 & 32): *Consider the following for the next two (02) items that follow:*

Consider the equation $(1-x)^4 + (5-x)^4 = 82$.

31. What is the number of real roots of the equation?

A. 0 B. 2
C. 4 D. 8

32. What is the sum of all the roots of the equation?

A. 24 B. 12
C. 10 D. 6

Directions (Qs. No. 33-35): *Consider the following for the next three (03) items that follow:*

Consider equation-I: $z^3 + 2z^2 + 2z + 1 = 0$ and equation-II: $z^{1985} + z^{100} + 1 = 0$.

33. What are the roots of equation-I?

A. $1, \omega, \omega^2$ B. $-1, \omega, \omega^2$
C. $1, -\omega, \omega^2$ D. $-1, -\omega, -\omega^2$

34. Which one of the following is a root of equation-II?

A. -1 B. $-\omega$
C. $-\omega^2$ D. ω

35. What is the number of common roots of equation-I and equation-II?

A. 0 B. 1
C. 2 D. 3

Directions (Qs. No. 36 & 37): *Consider the following for the next two (02) items that follow:*

A quadratic equation is given by $(a+b)x^2 - (a+b+c)x + k = 0$, where a, b, c are real.

36. If $k = \dfrac{c}{2}$, $(c \ne 0)$, then the roots of the equation are:

A. Real and equal B. Real and unequal
C. Real iff $a > c$ D. Complex but not real

37. If $k = c$, then the roots of the equation are:

A. $\dfrac{a+c}{a+b}$ and $\dfrac{b}{a+b}$ B. $\dfrac{a+c}{a+b}$ and $-\dfrac{b}{a+b}$
C. 1 and $\dfrac{c}{a+b}$ D. -1 and $-\dfrac{c}{a+b}$

Directions (Qs. No. 38-40): *Consider the following for the next three (03) items that follow:*

Let $(1 + x)^n = 1 + T_1x + T_2x^2 + T_3x^3 + ... + T_nx^n$.

38. What is $T_1 + 2T_2 + 3T_3 + ... + nT_n$ equal to?

A. 0 B. 1
C. 2^n D. $n2^{n-1}$

39. What is $1 - T_1 + 2T_2 - 3T_3 + ... + (-1)^n nT_n$ equal to?

A. 0 B. -2^{n-1}
C. $n2^{n-1}$ D. 1

40. What is $T_1 + T_2 + T_3 + ... + T_n$ equal to?

A. 2^n B. $2^n - 1$
C. 2^{n-1} D. $2^n + 1$

Directions (Qs. No. 41 & 42): *Consider the following for the next two (02) items that follow:*

Let $f(x) = x^2 - 1$ and $gof(x) = x - \sqrt{x} + 1$.

41. Which one of the following is a possible expression for $g(x)$?

A. $\sqrt{x+1} - \sqrt[4]{x+1}$ B. $\sqrt{x+1} - \sqrt[4]{x+1} + 1$
C. $\sqrt{x+1} + \sqrt[4]{x+1}$ D. $x+1 - \sqrt{x+1} + 1$

42. What is g(15) equal to?

A. 1 B. 2
C. 3 D. 4

Directions (Qs. No. 43 & 44): *Consider the following for the next two (02) items that follow:*

Let a function f be defined on R – {0} and $2f(x) + f\left(\frac{1}{x}\right) = x + 3$.

43. What is $f(0.5)$ equal to?

A. $\frac{1}{2}$ B. $\frac{2}{3}$
C. 1 D. 2

44. If f is differentiable, then what is $f'(0.5)$ equal to?

A. $\frac{1}{4}$ B. $\frac{2}{3}$
C. 2 D. 4

Directions (Qs. No. 45 & 46): *Consider the following for the next two (02) items that follow:*

A function is defined by

$$f(x) = \begin{vmatrix} x+1 & 2 & 3 \\ 2 & x+4 & 6 \\ 3 & 6 & x+9 \end{vmatrix}$$

45. The function is decreasing on:

A. $\left[-\frac{28}{3}, 0\right]$ B. $\left[0, \frac{28}{3}\right]$
C. $\left[0, \frac{50}{3}\right]$ D. $\left[0, \frac{56}{3}\right]$

46. The function attains local minimum value at:

A. $x = -\frac{28}{3}$ B. $x = -1$
C. $x = 0$ D. $x = \frac{28}{3}$

Directions (Qs. No. 47 & 48): *Consider the following for the next two (02) items that follow:*

Given that $4x^2 + y^2 = 9$.

47. What is the maximum value of y?

A. $\frac{3}{2}$ B. 3
C. 4 D. 6

48. What is the maximum value of xy?

A. $\frac{9}{4}$ B. $\frac{3}{2}$
C. $\frac{4}{9}$ D. $\frac{2}{3}$

Directions (Qs. No. 49 & 50): *Consider the following for the next two (02) items that follow:*

A function is defined by $f(x) = \pi + \sin^2 x$.

49. What is the range of the function?

A. [0, 1] B. $[\pi, \pi + 1]$
C. $[\pi - 1, \pi + 1]$ D. $[\pi - 1, \pi - 1]$

50. What is the period of the function?

A. 2π
B. π
C. $\frac{\pi}{2}$
D. The function is non-periodic

Directions (Qs. No. 51 & 52): *Consider the following for the next two (02) items that follow:*

A parabola passes through (1, 2) and satisfies the differential equation $\frac{dy}{dx} = \frac{2y}{x}, x > 0, y > 0$.

51. What is the directrix of the parabola?

A. $y = -\frac{1}{8}$ B. $y = \frac{1}{8}$
C. $x = -\frac{1}{8}$ D. $x = \frac{1}{8}$

52. What is the length of latus rectum of the parabola?

A. 1 B. $\frac{1}{2}$
C. $\frac{1}{4}$ D. $\frac{1}{8}$

Directions (Qs. No. 53 & 54): *Consider the following for the next two (02) items that follow:*

Let $f(x)=\frac{a^{x-1}+b^{x-1}}{2}$ and $g(x)=x-1$.

53. What is $\lim_{x\to1}\frac{f(x)-1}{g(x)}$ equal to?

A. $\frac{\ln(ab)}{4}$ B. $\frac{\ln(ab)}{2}$

C. $\ln(ab)$ D. $2\ln(ab)$

54. What is $\lim_{x\to1} f(x)^{\frac{1}{g(x)}}$ equal to?

A. $\sqrt{ab}$ B. ab

C. $2ab$ D. $\frac{\sqrt{ab}}{2}$

Directions (Qs. No. 55 & 56): *Consider the following for the next two (02) items that follow:*

Let $f(x)=\sqrt{2-x}+\sqrt{2+x}$.

55. What is the domain of the function?

A. (–2, 2) B. [–2, 2]

C. R – (–2, 2) D. R – [–2, 2]

56. What is the greatest value of the function?

A. $\sqrt{3}$ B. $\sqrt{6}$

C. $\sqrt{8}$ D. 4

Directions (Qs. No. 57 & 58): *Consider the following for the next two (02) items that follow:*

Let $f(x)=|x|$ and $g(x)=[x]-1$, where [.] is the greatest integer function.

Let $h(x)=\frac{f(g(x))}{g(f(x))}$

57. What is $\lim_{x\to0^+} h(x)$ equal to?

A. – 2 B. – 1

C. 0 D. 1

58. What is $\lim_{x\to0^-} h(x)$ equal to?

A. –2 B. –1

C. 0 D. 2

Directions (Qs. No. 59 & 60): *Consider the following for the next two (02) items that follow:*

$$\text{Let } f(x)=\begin{cases}\frac{x-3}{|x-3|}+a; & x<3\\ a-b; & x=3 \text{ and}\\ \frac{x-3}{|x-3|}+b; & x>3\end{cases}$$

$f(x)$ be continuous at $x = 3$

59. What is the value of a?

A. –1 B. 1

C. 2 D. 3

60. What is the value of b?

A. –1 B. 1

C. 2 D. 3

Directions (Qs. No. 61 & 62): *Consider the following for the next two (02) items that follow:*

Let $I=\int_{-2\pi}^{2\pi}\frac{\sin^4 x+\cos^4 x}{1+3^x}dx$

61. What is $\int_0^{\pi}(\sin^4 x+\cos^4 x)\,dx$ equal to?

A. $\frac{3\pi}{8}$ B. $\frac{3\pi}{4}$

C. $\frac{3\pi}{2}$ D. 3π

62. What is I equal to?

A. 0 B. $\frac{3\pi}{4}$

C. $\frac{3\pi}{2}$ D. 3π

Directions (Qs. No. 63 & 64): *Consider the following for the next two (02) items that follow:*

$$\text{Let } f(x)=\begin{cases}ax(x+1)+b, & x<1\\ x-1, & 1\le x\le 2\end{cases}$$

63. If the function $f(x)$ is differentiable at $x = 1$, then what is the value of $(a + b)$?

A. $-\frac{1}{3}$ B. –1

C. 0 D. 1

64. What is $\lim_{x\to0} f(x)$ equal to?

A. $-\frac{1}{3}$ B. $-\frac{2}{3}$

C. 0 D. 1

65. If $f(x) = |\ln|x||$ where $0 < x < 1$, then what is $f'(0.5)$ equal to?

A. –2 B. –1

C. 0 D. 2

66. If $f'(x) = \cos(\ln x)$ and $y=f\left(\frac{2x-3}{x}\right)$, then what is $\frac{dy}{dx}$ equal to?

A. $\cos\left(\ln\left(\frac{2x-3}{x}\right)\right)$ B. $-\frac{3}{x^2}\sin\left(\ln\left(\frac{2x-3}{x}\right)\right)$

C. $\frac{3}{x^2}\cos\left(\ln\left(\frac{2x-3}{x}\right)\right)$ D. $-\frac{3}{x^2}\cos\left(\ln\left(\frac{2x-3}{x}\right)\right)$

67. What is $\int_0^{8\pi} |\sin x| dx$ equal to?

A. 2 B. 4
C. 8 D. 16

68. What is the area between the curve $f(x) = x|x|$ and x-axis for $x \in [-1, 1]$?

A. $\frac{2}{3}$ B. $\frac{1}{2}$
C. $\frac{1}{4}$ D. $\frac{1}{3}$

69. What are the order and the degree respectively of the differential equation $x^2\left(\frac{d^3y}{dx^3}\right)^2+\left(\frac{dy}{dx}\right)^4+\sin x=0$?

A. 3, 4 B. 1, 4
C. 2, 2 D. 3, 2

70. What is the differential equation of all parabolas of the type $y^2 = 4a(x - b)$?

A. $\frac{d^2y}{dx^2}+\left(\frac{dy}{dx}\right)^2=0$ B. $\frac{d^2y}{dx^2}+x^2\left(\frac{dy}{dx}\right)^2=0$

C. $y^2\frac{d^2y}{dx^2}+\left(\frac{dy}{dx}\right)^2=0$ D. $y\frac{d^2y}{dx^2}+\left(\frac{dy}{dx}\right)^2=0$

Directions (Qs. No. 71 & 72): *Consider the following for the next two (02) items that follow:*

Let a_1, a_2, a_3 ... be in AP such that

$a_1 + a_5 + a_{10} + a_{15} + a_{20} + a_{25} + a_{30} + a_{34} = 300$

71. What is

$a_1 + a_5 - a_{10} - a_{15} - a_{20} - a_{25} + a_{30} + a_{34}$ equal to?

A. 0 B. 25
C. 125 D. 250

72. What is $\sum_{n=1}^{34} a_n$ equal to?

A. 900 B. 1025
C. 1200 D. 1275

Directions (Qs. No. 73 & 74): *Consider the following for the next two (02) items that follow:*

Let $p = \cos\left(\frac{\pi}{5}\right)\cos\left(\frac{2\pi}{5}\right)$ and $q = \cos\left(\frac{4\pi}{5}\right)\cos\left(\frac{8\pi}{5}\right)$.

73. What is the value of $p + q$?

A. $-\frac{1}{2}$ B. $-\frac{1}{4}$
C. 0 D. $\frac{1}{2}$

74. What is the value of pq?

A. $-\frac{1}{16}$ B. $-\frac{1}{4}$
C. $\frac{1}{4}$ D. $\frac{1}{16}$

Directions (Qs. No. 75 & 76): *Consider the following for the next two (02) items that follow:*

Let $p=\frac{1}{3}-\frac{\tan 3x}{\tan x}$ and $q=1-3\tan^2 x, 0<x<\pi, x\neq\frac{\pi}{2}$.

75. What is pq equal to?

A. 1 B. 2
C. $\frac{8}{3}$ D. $\frac{8}{3}$

76. For how many values of x does $\frac{1}{p}$ become zero?

A. No value B. Only one value
C. Only two values D. Only three values

Directions (Qs. No. 77 & 78): *Consider the following for the next two (02) items that follow:*

Let $\sin x+\sin y=\sqrt{3}(\cos y-\cos x); x+y=\frac{\pi}{2},$

$0<x, y<\frac{\pi}{2}.$

77. What is a value of $\sin 3x + \sin 3y$?

A. –1 B. 0
C. 1 D. 3

78. What is a value of $\cos^3x + \cos^3y$?

A. $\frac{3\sqrt{3}}{8}$ B. $\frac{3\sqrt{6}}{8}$

C. $\frac{3\sqrt{6}}{4}$ D. 1

Directions (Qs. No. 79 & 80): *Consider the following for the next two (02) items that follow:*

The angles A, B and C of a triangle ABC are in the ratio 3 : 5 : 4.

79. What is the value of $a+b+\sqrt{2}c$ equal to?

A. $3a$ B. $2b$
C. $3b$ D. $2c$

80. What is the ratio of $a^2 : b^2 : c^2$?

A. $2:2+\sqrt{3}:3$ B. $2:2-\sqrt{3}:2$
C. $2:2+\sqrt{3}:2$ D. $2:2-\sqrt{3}:3$

81. What is the equation of directrix of parabola $y^2 = 4bx$, where $b < 0$ and $b^2 + b - 2 = 0$?

A. $x + 1 = 0$ B. $x - 2 = 0$
C. $x - 1 = 0$ D. $x + 2 = 0$

82. The points $(-a, -b)$, $(0, 0)$, (a, b) and (a^2, ab) are:

A. lying on the same circle
B. vertices of a square
C. vertices of a parallelogram that is not a square
D. collinear

83. Given that $16p^2 + 49q^2 - 4r^2 - 56pq = 0$. Which one of the following is a point on a pair of straight lines $(px + qy + r)(px + qy - r) = 0$?

A. $\left(2, \frac{7}{2}\right)$ B. $\left(2, -\frac{7}{2}\right)$
C. $(4, -7)$ D. $(4, 7)$

84. If $3x + y - 5 = 0$ is the equation of a chord of the circle $x^2 + y^2 - 25 = 0$, then what are the coordinates of the mid-point of the chord?

A. $\left(\frac{3}{4}, \frac{1}{4}\right)$ B. $\left(\frac{3}{2}, \frac{1}{2}\right)$
C. $\left(\frac{3}{4}, -\frac{1}{4}\right)$ D. $\left(\frac{3}{2}, -\frac{1}{2}\right)$

85. Consider the following in respect of the equation $\frac{x^2}{24-k} + \frac{y^2}{k-16} = 2.$

1. The equation represents an ellipse if $k = 19$.
2. The equation represents a hyperbola if $k = 12$.
3. The equation represents a circle if $k = 20$.

How many of the statements given above are correct?

A. Only one B. Only two
C. All three D. None

86. Consider the following statements in respect of hyperbola $\frac{x^2}{\cos^2\theta} - \frac{y^2}{\sin^2\theta} = 1$:

1. The two foci are independent of θ.
2. The eccentricity is $\sec\theta$.
3. The distance between the two foci is 2 units.

How many of the statements given above are correct?

A. Only one B. Only two
C. All three D. None

87. Consider the following in respect of the circle $4x^2 + 4y^2 - 4ax - 4ay + a^2 = 0$:

1. The circle touches both the axes.
2. The diameter of the circle is $2a$.
3. The centre of the circle lies on the line $x + y = a$.

How many of the statements given above are correct?

A. Only one B. Only two
C. All three D. None

88. For what values of k is the line $(k - 3)x - (5 - k^2)y + k^2 - 7k + 6 = 0$ parallel to the line $x + y = 1$?

A. $-1, 1$ B. $-1, 2$
C. $1, -2$ D. $2, -2$

89. The line $x + y = 4$ cuts the line joining P(−1, 1) and Q(5, 7) at R. What is PR : RQ equal to?

A. 1 : 1 B. 1 : 2
C. 2 : 1 D. 1 : 3

90. What is the sum of the intercepts of the line whose perpendicular distance from origin is 4 units and the angle which the normal makes with positive direction of x-axis is 15°?

A. 8 B. $4\sqrt{6}$
C. $8\sqrt{6}$ D. 16

91. What is the length of projection of the vector $\hat{i} + 2\hat{j} + 3\hat{k}$ on the vector $2\hat{i} + 3\hat{j} - 2\hat{k}$?

A. $\frac{1}{\sqrt{17}}$ B. $\frac{2}{\sqrt{17}}$
C. $\frac{3}{\sqrt{17}}$ D. $\frac{2}{\sqrt{14}}$

92. If $(\vec{a} \times \vec{b})^2 + (\vec{a} \cdot \vec{b})^2 = 144$ and $|\vec{b}| = 4$, then what is the value of $|\vec{a}|$?

A. 3 B. 4
C. 5 D. 6

93. If θ is the angle between vectors $\vec{a}$ and $\vec{b}$ such that $\vec{a} \cdot \vec{b} \geq 0$, then which one of the following is correct?

A. $0 \leq \theta \leq \pi$ B. $\frac{\pi}{2} \leq \theta \leq \pi$
C. $0 \leq \theta \leq \frac{\pi}{2}$ D. $0 < \theta < \frac{\pi}{2}$

94. The vectors $60\hat{i} + 3\hat{j}$, $40\hat{i} - 8\hat{j}$ and $\beta\hat{i} - 52\hat{j}$ are collinear if:

A. $\beta = 20$ B. $\beta = 40$
C. $\beta = -40$ D. $\beta = 26$

95. Consider the following in respect of the vectors $\vec{a} = (0, 1, 1)$ and $\vec{b} = (1, 0, 1)$:

1. The number of unit vectors perpendicular to both $\vec{a}$ and $\vec{b}$ is only one.
2. The angle between the vectors is $\frac{\pi}{3}$.

Which of the statements given above is/are correct?

A. 1 only B. 2 only
C. Both 1 and 2 D. Neither 1 nor 2

96. If L is the line with direction ratios < 3, –2, 6 > and passing through (1, –1, 1) then what are the coordinates of the points on L whose distance from (1, –1, 1) is 2 units?

A. $\left(-\frac{11}{7}, \frac{13}{7}, \frac{19}{7}\right)$ and $\left(\frac{1}{7}, \frac{3}{7}, \frac{5}{7}\right)$

B. $\left(\frac{19}{7}, -\frac{11}{7}, \frac{13}{7}\right)$ and $\left(-\frac{1}{7}, \frac{3}{7}, -\frac{5}{7}\right)$

C. $\left(\frac{13}{7}, \frac{11}{7}, \frac{19}{7}\right)$ and $\left(-\frac{1}{7}, -\frac{3}{7}, \frac{5}{7}\right)$

D. $\left(\frac{13}{7}, -\frac{11}{7}, \frac{19}{7}\right)$ and $\left(\frac{1}{7}, -\frac{3}{7}, -\frac{5}{7}\right)$

97. Which one of the planes is parallel to the line

$$\frac{x-2}{3} = \frac{y-3}{4} = \frac{z-4}{5}?$$

A. $2x + 2y + z - 3 = 0$
B. $2x - y - 2z + 5 = 0$
C. $2x + 2y - 2z + 1 = 0$
D. $x - 2y + z - 1 = 0$

98. What is the angle beween the lines $2x = 3y = -z$ and $6x = -y = -4z$?

A. 0° B. 30°
C. 60° D. 90°

99. What is the equation of the sphere concentric with the sphere $x^2 + y^2 + z^2 - 2x - 6y - 8z - 5 = 0$ and which passes through the origin?

A. $x^2 + y^2 + z^2 - 2x - 8z = 0$
B. $x^2 + y^2 + z^2 - 2x - 6y = 0$
C. $x^2 + y^2 + z^2 - 6y - 8z = 0$
D. $x^2 + y^2 + z^2 - 2x - 6y - 8z = 0$

100. A point P lies on the line joining A(1, 2, 3) and B(2, 10, 1). If z-coordinate of P is 7, what is the sum of other two coordinates?

A. –15 B. –13
C. –11 D. –9

101. The sum of deviations of n number from 10 and 20 are p and q respectively. If $(p - q)^2 = 10000$, then what is the value of n?

A. 10 B. 20
C. 50 D. 100

102. If $\overline{X} = 20$ is the mean of 10 observations $x_1, x_2, ..., x_{10}$; then what is the value of $\sum_{i=1}^{10}\left(\frac{3x_i - 4}{5}\right)$?

A. 0 B. 12
C. 112 D. 1012

103. If the mean and the sum of squares of 10 observations are 40 and 16160 respectively, then what is the standard deviation?

A. 16 B. 6
C. 5 D. 4

104. Three dice are thrown. What is the probability of getting a sum which is a perfect square?

A. $\frac{17}{108}$ B. $\frac{5}{108}$
C. $\frac{19}{108}$ D. $\frac{23}{108}$

105. A, B, C and D are mutually exclusive and exhaustive events.
If 2P(A) = 3P(B) = 4P(C) = 5P(D),
then what is 77P(A) equal to?

A. 12 B. 15
C. 20 D. 30

106. The distinct natural numbers from 1 to 9 are picked at random. What is the probability that their product has 1 in its unit place?

A. $\frac{1}{81}$ B. $\frac{1}{72}$
C. $\frac{1}{18}$ D. $\frac{1}{36}$

107. Two dice are thrown. What is the probability that difference of numbers on them is 2 or 3?

A. $\frac{7}{36}$ B. $\frac{7}{18}$
C. $\frac{5}{18}$ D. $\frac{11}{36}$

108. What is the mean of the numbers 1, 2, 3, ..., 10 with frequencies ${}^9C_0, {}^9C_1, {}^9C_2, ..., {}^9C_9$, respectively?

A. 1.1×2^8 B. 1.2×7^4
C. 5.5 D. 0.55

109. The probability that a person recovers from a disease is 0.8. What is the probability that exactly 2 persons out of 5 will recover from the disease?

A. 0.00512
B. 0.02048
C. 0.2048
D. 0.0512

110. Suppose that there is a chance for a newly constructed building to collapse, whether the design is faulty or not. The chance that the design is faulty is 10%. The chance that the building collapses is 95% if the design is faulty, otherwise it is 45%. If it is seen that the building has collapsed, then what is the probability that it is due to faulty design?

A. 0.10 B. 0.19
C. 0.45 D. 0.95

111. If r is the coefficient of correlation between x and y, then what is the correlation coefficient between $(3x + 4)$ and $(-3y + 3)$?

A. $-r$ B. r

C. $\sqrt{3}r$ D. $-\sqrt{3}r$

112. A fair coin is tossed 6 times. What is the probability of gatting a result in the 6th toss which is different from those obtained in the first five tosses?

A. $\frac{7}{16}$ B. $\frac{1}{16}$

C. $\frac{1}{32}$ D. $\frac{1}{64}$

113. If H is the Harmonic Mean of three numbers $^{10}C_4$, $^{10}C_5$, and $^{10}C_6$, then what is the value of $\frac{270}{H}$?

A. 1 B. $\frac{14}{17}$

C. $\frac{17}{14}$ D. $\frac{1}{31}$

114. In a class, there are n students including the students P and Q. What is the probability that P and Q sit together if seats are assigned randomly?

A. $\frac{1}{n}$ B. $\frac{2}{n}$

C. $\frac{4}{n}$ D. $\frac{1}{2n}$

115. In a Binomial distribution $B(n, p)$, $n = 6$ and $9P(X = 4) = P(X = 2)$. What is p equal to?

A. $\frac{1}{4}$ B. $\frac{1}{2}$

C. $\frac{3}{4}$ D. $\frac{4}{5}$

Directions (Qs. No. 116 & 120): *Consider the following for the next five (05) items that follow:*

Three boys P, Q, R and three girls S, T, U are to be arranged in a row for a group photograph.

116. What is the probability that all three boys sit together?

A. $\frac{1}{5}$ B. $\frac{1}{4}$

C. $\frac{1}{3}$ D. $\frac{1}{12}$

117. What is the probability that boys and girls sit alternatively?

A. $\frac{4}{5}$ B. $\frac{1}{10}$

C. $\frac{5}{6}$ D. $\frac{1}{7}$

118. What is the probability that no two girls sit together?

A. $\frac{2}{5}$ B. $\frac{3}{5}$

C. $\frac{1}{18}$ D. $\frac{1}{5}$

119. What is the probability that P and Q take the two end positions?

A. $\frac{1}{15}$ B. $\frac{7}{15}$

C. $\frac{14}{15}$ D. $\frac{11}{45}$

120. What is the probabiliy that Q and U sit together?

A. $\frac{2}{3}$ B. $\frac{1}{4}$

C. $\frac{5}{6}$ D. $\frac{1}{3}$

ANSWERS

PAPER-I: GENERAL ABILITY TEST

1. (A): The term 'lashed' is used to convey a strong or intense impact or effect, befittingly describing what monsoons do, which is to hit areas with intense rainfall. Out of the options provided flourished, occupied and dried fail to accurately represent the intensiveness and the nature of a monsoon. The monsoon does not simply flourish or dry but instead comes with considerable power and impact hence lashed is the correct description.

2. (C): The word "confronts" is the most appropriate choice to fill in the blank space. In this context, "confronts" means to face or deal with directly, which accurately reflects the idea that the challenges are directly affecting or impacting us. The sentence suggests that the challenges are significant and need to be addressed directly. Therefore, "confronts" effectively communicates the scale and seriousness of the challenges that the company is facing. The other options ("supports," "conflict," and "convince") do not convey the idea of directly dealing with challenges and are therefore less suitable in this context.

3. (B): In this context, "go the distance" is an idiomatic expression meaning to persevere or endure until the completion of a task or goal, especially when faced with challenges or difficulties. By saying "go the distance," the speaker expresses a determination to overcome obstacles and complete the tough course successfully. Therefore, the word "distance" in this context refers metaphorically to the journey or effort required to achieve the goal.

4. (A): In this context, "extent" refers to the degree or magnitude of the advancement made in agricultural productivity in India. The sentence suggests that the level or amount of progress achieved in agricultural productivity is remarkable. Therefore, "extent" is the most suitable word choice to convey this idea. It indicates the scale or scope of the advancement, highlighting its significance and impact.

5. (D): In this context, the word "explores" is the most suitable choice. "Explores" means to investigate or study in detail, which aligns with the idea of examining various systems for water appropriation and agricultural practices adapted by society in the arid conditions of Rajasthan. The sentence suggests that the essay thoroughly investigates or delves into these topics to provide insights or information. Therefore, "explores" effectively conveys the intended meaning of the sentence.

6. (B): In this context, the word "stabilise" is the most suitable choice. "Stabilise" means to make or become stable or steady, which aligns with the idea of India successfully managing or controlling its population through family planning programmes. The sentence suggests that these programmes have been effective in achieving a stable or controlled population growth rate. Therefore, "stabilise" effectively conveys the intended meaning of the sentence.

7. (A): The correct answer is "threshold". 'Threshold' demonstrates the concept of crossing a limit or starting a new phase, accurately representing the transition from childhood to adulthood during adolescence. Other options like 'position', 'condition' and 'period' do not convey the exact sense of the transition.

8. (C): In this context, the word "exploit" is the most suitable choice. "Exploit" means to make full use of or derive benefit from something, often in an unfair or unethical manner. In the sentence, it suggests that the British who ruled India for 200 years were primarily interested in taking advantage of India's natural resources for their own benefit. This includes extracting resources such as minerals, timber, and agricultural products, often without consideration for the well-being of the Indian people or the sustainable management of the resources.

9. (B): In this context, the word "extinction" is the most suitable choice. "Extinction" refers to the state or process of a species dying out completely, with no remaining individuals alive. The sentence suggests that endangered species have a fifty per cent or greater probability of facing extinction within a specific timeframe - either within five years or two generations, whichever is longer. This timeframe serves as an indicator of the urgency with which conservation efforts must be undertaken to prevent the loss of these species from the Earth.

10. (D): The first law of thermodynamics states that energy can be transformed from one form into another, but it cannot be created or destroyed. In this context, the word "transformed" means to change or convert energy from one form to another while maintaining the total amount of energy constant. This principle is fundamental in understanding energy conservation and the behaviour of energy in various physical processes. Therefore, "transformed" accurately conveys the idea that energy can change from one form to another without being created or destroyed.

11. (B): The error is in part (B). The correct form should be "are common breakfast items" instead of "jam common breakfast items." Therefore, the corrected sentence should be: Bread, butter, and jam are common breakfast items that are consumed by many households.

12. (D): In part (A) the use of 'is' is correct. Even though dollars is in plural form, the total sum of money is considered as a singular entity hence the use of is and not are. In part (B) the prize money being offered is grammatically correct. It provides information about the prize money and is appropriately linked to part (A). In part (C) by the game show hosts correctly states the people offering money is grammatically correct. The whole sentence is correct and there is no error.

13. (B): The phrase "create up" is incorrect because "create" does not convey the intended meaning of constituting or forming in this context. Instead, "make up" is the appropriate phrase to indicate the composition or formation of the total number of days in a calendar year. Therefore, the corrected sentence "Three hundred and sixty-five make up the number of days in a calendar year".

14. (C): In this sentence, the correct term for the process of removing wool from the body of an animal is "shearing," not "sharing." "Shearing" refers to the act of cutting or removing the wool from the body of an

animal, typically sheep. On the other hand, "sharing" does not have any relevant meaning in this context.

15. (B): In this sentence, the error lies in the incorrect form of the verb "pray." The verb should be in the base form after the preposition "to." Therefore, it should be "to pray" instead of "to prayed." The corrected sentence reads: "Many people came from faraway places to pray at the temple on the auspicious day."

16. (A): The error is in option A as the correct sentence will be, after reading the foreword of the book on environmental issues in India, I decided to meet its author. This is because the definite article is placed before something unique and known.

17. (D): In the given sentence, all parts are grammatically correct and logically coherent. The sentence states that the guidance provided by the mentors and teachers facilitated the smooth conduct of elections to the Students' council. It effectively communicates that the mentors and teachers played a supportive role in ensuring that the elections were conducted smoothly. Therefore, there is no need for any corrections or adjustments in the sentence, making option (D) - "No error" - the appropriate choice.

18. (D): In the given sentence, all parts are grammatically correct and logically coherent. The sentence states that the Principal of the school felicitated the students during the prize distribution ceremony. It effectively communicates the action of the Principal honoring or recognizing the students during the ceremony. Therefore, there is no need for any corrections or adjustments in the sentence, making option (D) - "No error" - the appropriate choice.

19. (C): To maintain consistency with the hypothetical nature of the statement, we need to use the modal verb "would" instead of "will." Therefore, the corrected sentence would read: "If you were to come to Chennai to settle down, it would be the best possible decision." This construction accurately conveys the idea that settling down in Chennai is presented as a hypothetical scenario, and choosing to do so would be considered the best decision under those circumstances.

20. (A): In the given sentence, the error lies in the incorrect form of the verb "deliver." The verb should be in the infinitive form ("to deliver") after the modal verb "promised." Therefore, it should be "to deliver" instead of "to delivered." The corrected sentence reads: "They had promised to deliver the bags before mid-March to enable us to inaugurate the shop."

21. (C): The word "captious" describes someone who is excessively critical or faultfinding, often focusing on trivial or minor faults. A person who is captious tends to be overly judgmental and tends to find faults or flaws in others or in situations. In the given options, "faultfinding" is the closest in meaning to "captious.

22. (A): Verify: This means to confirm or establish the truth or accuracy of something. This aligns with the sentence as geomorphologists are scientists who study the Earth's landforms and processes, and their findings help us understand our planet better.

23. (D): In this sentence, the "commissary" refers to a place where food and provisions are sold or distributed, especially on a military base. Therefore, the closest meaning to "commissary" in the options provided is "canteen," which is a place where food and drinks are provided for purchase or consumption, especially in a military or school setting.

24. (B): In the context of the sentence, "dismembered" refers to the action of separating or removing a part of the patient's body, specifically the finger. This action is typically associated with surgical procedures, where a body part is intentionally separated from the rest of the body for medical reasons. "Dissected" is the closest option in meaning to "dismembered" among the choices provided. It means to cut apart or separate tissue, organs, or body parts for examination or medical treatment.

25. (B): In the given sentence, Mr. Kumar is described as working as a "bursar" in the sports academy. A bursar is typically responsible for managing the financial matters of an institution, such as budgeting, accounting, and financial reporting. Therefore, the most appropriate option among the choices provided is "accountant," as an accountant is someone who professionally manages financial records, prepares financial statements, and handles financial transactions, which aligns well with the duties typically associated with a bursar.

26. (C): In the given sentence, "insidious" means intending to trick or deceive someone in a subtle or cunning way. It suggests a hidden or treacherous motive. Therefore, the word "insidious" implies deceitfulness or cunningness. Among the options provided, "deceitful" best captures the meaning of "insidious." It indicates a deliberate intent to deceive or mislead others.

27. (C): In the given sentence, the word "intrinsic" is used to describe the quality of respect for other human beings in relation to the teachings of religions. "Intrinsic" means belonging naturally or essential to something. Therefore, when we say respect for other human beings is intrinsic to the teachings of all religions, it means that respect for others is an inherent or fundamental aspect of religious teachings.

28. (D): The word "onerous" indicates a task that is burdensome or demanding. In this context, the individual managed to complete the difficult task with relative ease, suggesting they handled the challenge adeptly. Here "wearying," best captures this essence, implying that while the task was arduous, it did not necessarily leave the person feeling exhausted or fatigued, highlighting their ability to overcome the difficulty without significant strain.

29. (A): In the sentence provided, the word "potentate" refers to a ruler or monarch who holds significant power and authority, especially during historical periods like the Middle Ages. A potentate typically exercises control over a territory or a group of people. Therefore, the most appropriate option among the choices provided is "Monarch," as it directly corresponds to the concept of a potentate-a ruler with supreme authority.

30. (B): In the given sentence, "indolence" refers to a state of laziness or a reluctance to exert oneself physically or mentally. Therefore, the most appropriate option among the choices provided is "laziness," as it accurately reflects the meaning of "indolence." The speaker abandoned the task not because of its difficulty, ugliness, or helplessness, but rather because of their own inclination towards laziness or a lack of motivation to continue with the task.

31. (C): "Principal" refers to the head or director of an educational institution, such as a school or college. It can also refer to the main or most important person or thing in a group, such as the principal actor in a play. "Principle," on the other hand, refers to a fundamental truth, law, or belief system that serves as a basis for behavior or decision-making. It can also refer to a moral rule or standard of conduct.

32. (C): "Plane" is indeed a term used to describe a vehicle that flies through the air, such as an airplane or a jet. It is a common term in aviation and refers to an aircraft designed for air travel. A plain is a vast, flat, and open expanse of land, characterized by low relief and minimal elevation changes. Plains are commonly found on Earth's surface and can vary in size and geography, ranging from grassy plains to desert plains.

33. (C): "Pale" is an adjective that describes something that is light in colour, often suggesting a lack of intensity or vibrancy. For example, a pale blue sky or pale yellow flowers. It can also mean lacking colour due to sickness or fear, as in a pale face. "Pail" is a noun that refers to a cylindrical container with a handle, typically made of metal or plastic, and used for carrying or holding liquids, such as water or milk. Pails are commonly used for household chores, gardening, or construction purposes.

34. (D): "Metal" refers to a class of elements that are typically hard, shiny, malleable, and good conductors of heat and electricity, such as iron, copper, and aluminum. "Mettle," on the other hand, is a noun that refers to a person's ability to cope with difficulties or face a challenging situation with courage, determination, and resilience. It signifies strength of character or spirit.

35. (B): "Hail" is a meteorological phenomenon referring to pellets of frozen rain that fall from the sky during thunderstorms. These pellets can vary in size and are formed when raindrops freeze as they are carried by updrafts within thunderclouds. "Hale" is an adjective that describes someone as being strong and healthy. It implies robustness and vigor in terms of physical health, suggesting that the person is in good condition and free from illness or weakness.

36. (D): "Conscious" is an adjective that describes being aware of one's surroundings, thoughts, or actions. It relates to awareness and being awake, both physically and mentally. "Conscience," on the other hand, is a noun that refers to an inner sense or feeling of what is right or wrong in one's actions, often guiding one's behaviour and moral decisions.

37. (A): "Dissent" is a noun that refers to the expression or holding of opinions that are different from those that are commonly or officially held. It typically involves disagreement with established beliefs, policies, or authority. For example, someone might express dissent by publicly disagreeing with a government decision or a company policy. "Descent," on the other hand, is a noun that describes the act of moving downwards or the process of going from a higher to a lower position or place. It can be used in a literal sense, such as descending a staircase, or in a figurative sense, such as a decrease in value or status.

38. (C): "Device" is a noun that refers to a physical object or piece of equipment designed for a specific purpose or function. It can be anything from a simple tool to a complex machine, and it is typically used to accomplish a task or achieve a particular goal. For example, smartphones, computers, and kitchen appliances are all types of devices. "Devise," on the other hand, is a verb that means to invent, create, or come up with a plan, method, or solution. It involves using one's intellect or creativity to design or formulate something new or innovative. For example, someone might devise a new strategy for marketing a product or devise a plan for organizing an event.

39. (B): "Discrete" is an adjective that means individually separate and distinct, often referring to separate categories or entities that are not connected or continuous. "Discreet" is also an adjective that means careful and prudent in one's speech or actions, especially in order to maintain confidentiality or avoid causing offense.

40. (A): "Eminent" is an adjective that describes someone who is distinguished, respected, and prominent in their field or profession. It suggests a high level of importance, expertise, or influence. For example, an eminent scientist or an eminent scholar is someone who is highly respected and recognized for their achievements. "Imminent," on the other hand, is an adjective that describes something that is about to happen, typically in the near future. It implies that the event is impending, looming, or likely to occur very soon. For example, an imminent storm suggests that a storm is about to happen, or an imminent deadline suggests that the deadline is approaching rapidly.

41. (A): "Malleable" describes a material's ability to be easily shaped, molded, or flattened under pressure without breaking or cracking. For example, metals like gold and aluminum are malleable because they can be hammered or rolled into thin sheets without breaking. The opposite of "malleable" would be something that is not easily shaped or molded and is resistant to deformation. Therefore, "hard" is the opposite, as it implies rigidity and resistance to deformation.

42. (C): In the given sentence, "neglect" means to fail to pay proper attention to or to disregard something important. Therefore, the opposite of neglecting a warning would be to regard or pay attention to the warning, taking it seriously and acknowledging its importance. Therefore, "regard," is the opposite of neglect in this context. It implies acknowledging the warning and considering it seriously to avoid danger.

43. (B): In the given sentence, "ostentatious" describes behaviour that is characterized by a vulgar or pretentious display, often intended to impress or attract attention. Therefore, the opposite of ostentatious behaviour would be behaviour that is modest, unpretentious, or humble. "Modest," fits this description. Modest behaviour suggests a lack of showiness or extravagance, focusing instead on simplicity and humility.

44. (D): In the given sentence, "excruciating" describes the experience of the Covid pandemic as extremely painful or intense. Therefore, the opposite of an excruciating experience would be one that is mild, not severe, or relatively easy to endure. Options A, B, and C all describe experiences that are difficult, intense, or distressing, so they are not opposites of "excruciating." However, option D, "mild," accurately represents the opposite as it suggests an experience that is not severe or intense.

45. (B): In the given sentence, "refreshing" describes the experience of the trip to the hills as invigorating and revitalizing. Therefore, the opposite of a refreshing experience would be one that is tiring or exhausting. "Wearying," accurately represents this opposite meaning. "Wearying" suggests that the trip to the hills would make someone feel tired or fatigued instead of refreshed. Therefore, it contrasts with the positive and invigorating connotation conveyed by the word "refreshing."

46. (D):

1. Feeling that others may overuse the resource: If individuals believe that others may overuse the resource, they might feel less inclined to use it prudently themselves. This suggests a lack of confidence in collective responsibility for resource management.
2. Possibilities of substitution: When there are readily available substitutes for a resource, individuals may not feel the need to use it carefully. The presence of alternatives reduces the perceived value of conserving the resource.
3. Abundance of the resource availability: If a resource is abundant and easily accessible, individuals may not see the necessity of conserving it. They might assume that its availability will continue indefinitely, leading to a lack of motivation to use it prudently.

47. (C): In the context of the passage, this aligns with the condition outlined where individuals are unlikely to be motivated to use renewable resources prudently if their resource catchments are vast, and degradation of any particular portion affects them very little. When individuals perceive that their actions have minimal consequences or negligible impact on the environment or their own well-being, they may be more inclined to exploit resources extensively without considering long-term sustainability. This mindset arises from a lack of awareness or concern about the interconnectedness of resource use and its broader effects on ecosystems, biodiversity, and future generations.

48. (D): According to the passage, the self-interest of people affects the use of renewable resources in a certain manner. The passage states that people, by and large, are concerned with and pursue self-interest. However, it also highlights that they are unlikely to be motivated to use renewable resources in a prudent and sustainable fashion under certain conditions. These conditions include having vast resource catchments, possibilities of substitution, and tenuous control over the resource base. Therefore, the self-interest of people affects the use of renewable resources in a way that is: Indifferently.

49. (C): Based on the information provided in the passage, people who are rooted in a locality are most likely to fulfill certain prerequisites for sustainable resource use. The passage indicates that these individuals are more inclined to behave in ways conducive to the conservation of biodiversity within their localities. Therefore, the most appropriate option would be: Believe in conservation and reproduction of resources. This aligns with the passage's implication that individuals rooted in a locality and retaining control over their resource base are more likely to prioritize the sustainable use of resources and conservation efforts within their communities.

50. (A): The word "deplete" refers to the process of reducing or exhausting the quantity or supply of something, often a resource or reserve. It implies a gradual reduction or consumption until the resource is significantly diminished or used up entirely. Therefore, "deplete" is synonymous with "exhaust," as both terms convey the idea of draining or diminishing a resource's availability through consumption or use.

51. (B): When sunlight enters a dusty room through the window, its path becomes visible to us. Small dust particles present in the air of the room scatter rays of light around the room. This is called the Tyndall effect. The flow of light rays through the trees that you see is due to the scattering of light. Particles in the atmosphere, such as dust, water droplets, and air molecules, scatter sunlight in different directions. This scattering effect is more pronounced for shorter wavelengths of light, such as blue and violet, which is why the sky appears blue during the day.

52. (B): Light travels at a much higher speed than sound. The speed of light in a vacuum is 3,00,000 km/s, while the speed of sound varies depending on the medium but is much slower (e.g., around 343 meters per second in air). When lightning occurs, the light from the flash reaches the observer almost instantaneously, while the sound of thunder takes some time to travel through the air. The time gap between seeing the lightning and hearing the thunder can be used to estimate the distance of the lightning strike.

53. (C)

54. (C): The heating element in an electric iron is usually made of Nichrome.

- Nichrome is an alloy of Nickel (80%) and Chromium (20%).
- Nichrome has a high melting point of 1400°C.
- When heatd for the first time, it forms an adherent layer of Chromium oxide.
- As a result, Nichrome is used as a heating element.

55. (C): To see one's full image in a vertical plane mirror, a person's eye level must be at the halfway point between the top and bottom of the mirror.

This means that the minimum height of the mirror should be half of the height of the person.

This way, the complete image of the person will be visible in the mirror.

Height of Sita is 1.5 meters.

The mirror's height should be 1.5/2 = 0.75 m

56. (C): Galvanisation is a method of protecting steel and iron from rusting by coating them with a thin layer of Zinc. The galvanizing process consists of three steps—Surface preparation, Fuxing, Galvanizing.

57. (D)

58. (C): Spherical fullerenes are known as Buckminster fullerenes (Bucky balls) that look like football, and cylindrical fullerenes are called carbon nanotubes (CNT) (bucking tubes). Fullerenes have similar structure to graphite, and composed of stacked graphene sheets of linked hexagonal rings. They may also have heptagonal or pentagonal rings.

59. (C): A wafer is a thin slice of semiconductor material crucial for creating integrated circuits in electronic devices. Therefore, being a semiconductor material, the accurate depiction of the relationship between current (I) and voltage (V) will be:

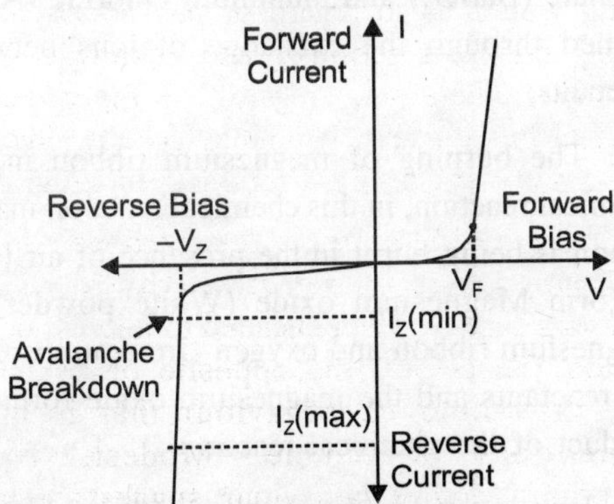

As the graph for reverse bias is absent in the options, selecting the graph for forward bias, namely option C, is the appropriate choice.

60. (A): Green plants utilize approximately 1% of the solar radiation they absorb through their leaves for the process of photosynthesis. This critical reaction relies on the absorption of sunlight. Carbon dioxide is taken in by the plant through stomata, commonly found on the underside of the leaves, while water is absorbed through its roots. The fraction of solar radiation utilized for photosynthesis is approximately 1%.

61. (B)

62. (C): Decomposition Reaction: The water decomposes during electrolysis to form hydrogen and oxygen gases in the ratio 2 : 1 by volume.

$$2H_2O \rightarrow 2H_2 + O_2$$

Combination Reaction: The burning of coal is a combustion and a combination reaction because two reactants combine to form one product.

$$C(s) + O_2(g) \rightarrow CO_2(g) + heat$$

Displacement Reaction: Reaction in which a more reactive metal, say A, displaces a less reactive metal, say B, from its salt solution, say BC, is called a displacement reaction. Displacement reactions are generally exothermic.

$$A + BC \rightarrow AC + B$$

When iron nails are placed in a copper sulphate solution (blue colour), iron displaces copper (reddish brown) from its salt and forms ferrous sulphate (green colour). Hence, this is a displacement reaction.

$$CuSO_4(aq) + Fe(s) \rightarrow FeSO_4(aq) + Cu(s)$$

Double Displacement Reaction: A double displacement reaction entails the exchange of ions between two compounds, leading to the formation of two new compounds. This type of reaction is common in aqueous solutions. In the addition of barium chloride ($BaCl_2$) to aluminum sulphate ($Al_2(SO_4)_3$), barium sulphate ($BaSO_4$) and aluminum chloride ($AlCl_3$) are formed through the exchange of ions between the reactants.

63. (D): The burning of magnesium ribbon in air is a chemical reaction, in this chemical reaction magnesium ribbon is being burnt in the presence of air (Oxygen) to form Magnesium oxide (White powder), where magnesium ribbon and oxygen (from atmosphere) are the reactants and the magnesium oxide formed is the product of the chemical reaction.

64. (B): Iron is not highly reactive with cold water.

- It does not react with cold water to liberate hydrogen gas.
- Iron reacts slowly with steam or hot water to form iron(II) oxide and hydrogen gas.
- $3Fe + 4H_2O \rightarrow Fe_3O_4 + 4H_2\uparrow$
- Potassium is a highly reactive metal and reacts vigorously with cold water to release hydrogen gas and form potassium hydroxide.

$$2K + 2H_2O \rightarrow 2KOH + H_2\uparrow$$

- Calcium is a reactive metal and reacts with cold water to produce calcium hydroxide and hydrogen gas.

$$Ca + 2H_2O \rightarrow Ca(OH)_2 + H_2\uparrow$$

- Sodium is a highly reactive metal and reacts vigorously with cold water to liberate hydrogen gas and form sodium hydroxide.

$$2Na + 2H_2O \rightarrow 2NaOH + H_2\uparrow$$

65. (D): The reaction is reddish Mercuric oxide(II) solid is decomposed upon heating into silver liquid mercury and colourless oxygen gas. It is a chemical decomposition reaction as the mercuric oxide is broken down into mercury and oxygen.

66. (B): Meiosis and fertilization:

- Meiosis is a type of cell division that occurs in the formation of gametes (sperm and egg cells).
- During meiosis, the chromosome number is reduced by half, leading to genetic diversity among the resulting gametes.
- Fertilization then involves the fusion of these gametes, combining genetic material from two different individuals.
- The combination of meiosis and fertilization results in offspring with unique combinations of genes, contributing significantly to genetic diversity.
- Meiosis and fertilization are the two important features of sexual reproduction in higher organisms that create genetic diversity in offspring.

67. (D): Mitochondria are membrane-bound organelles found exclusively in eukaryotic cells. They play a crucial role in cellular respiration, producing energy (ATP) for the cell. Prokaryotic cells lack membrane-bound organelles like mitochondria. Therefore, the correct answer is mitochondria, as it is a eukaryotic-specific organelle not found in prokaryotic cells.

The cell wall is the outer covering of a cell, present adjacent to the cell membrane, which is also called the plasma membrane. As mentioned earlier, the cell wall is present in all plant cells, fungi, bacteria, algae, and some archaea.

The plasma membrane, also called the cell membrane, is the membrane found in all cells that separates the interior of the cell from the outside environment. In bacterial and plant cells, a cell wall is attached to the plasma membrane on its outside surface.

Nucleic acids are long-chain polymeric molecules, the monomer (the repeating unit) is known as the nucleotides and hence sometimes nucleic acids are referred to as polynucleotides.

68. (A): *Streptococcus mutans*, the bacterium responsible for tooth decay, forms a slimy layer primarily from dietary sugars, especially sucrose. This sticky biofilm adheres to teeth, providing a breeding ground for harmful bacteria. As these bacteria metabolize sugar, they produce acids that erode tooth enamel, leading to cavities. Managing sugar intake and maintaining good oral hygiene are crucial in preventing this dental issue.

69. (D): In angiosperms, the two male gametes produced by pollen germination have specialized functions during double fertilization.

One of the male gametes fuses with the egg cell, resulting in the formation of a diploid zygote, which will develop into an embryo. The second male gamete fuses with a diploid secondary nucleus (also called a central cell or polar nucleus) to form a triploid cell.

This triploid cell gives rise to the endosperm, which provides nutrition to the developing embryo.

70. (B): Gametes of sexually-reproducing animals have half the number of chromosomes as that of the parents. Thus, during fertilization, when two gametes *i.e.* male and female gametes, fuse, the offspring produced will have the same amount of DNA or the same number of chromosomes as that of the parent.

71. (B): Pollination is a method where pollen grains are picked from an anther, which is the male part of a flower and transferred to the flower's female part called the stigma. To make the pollination work successfully, the pollen grains must be transferred from the same species of flower.

Ways of Pollination:

- **By Wind (Anemophily):** Some plants produce lightweight and small pollen grains adapted for wind transport. Examples include grasses and many trees. Wind pollination is common in areas with a scarcity of pollinating insects.
- **By Animals (Zoophily):** Insects, birds, bats, and other animals are common pollinators. Bees, butterflies, moths, humming birds, and bats are among the most effective pollinators. Flowers attract these animals through colours, scents, and nectar.
- **By Water (Hydrophily):** In aquatic plants, pollen is transported through water. This is relatively rare and is adapted to environments like ponds and lakes.

72. (C): Many kings have ruled in ancient India. Most of the kings wanted to make their kingdom more powerful. The king would become an all-powerful monarch in the Ancient society and attempty to claim a higher status. So they adopted the following methods:

- They made ample use of the booming long distance trade to higher their status.
- The ancient Indian king adopted a grandiose title.
- They were appointed poets and others to write Prashatis about them.
- Kings sought to expand their territories through military conquests.
- Optimizing taxes or reducing them in special circumstances in order to increase popularity among people and show kindness to the king.

73. (A): The Bhakti movement, in fact, promoted diversity and was characterized by its openness to people from various social backgrounds, castes, and regions. It was inclusive and encouraged a personal and emotional connection with the divine, which transcended traditional social and religious boundaries.

74. (C): The Reign of Terror was a violent period during the French Revolution from 1793-1794 when the Radicals led by Maximilien Robespierre were running the Government. During this period, thousands of people who were suspected to be disloyal to the Revolution were arrested and executed.

75. (C): The First World War, spanning from 1914 to 1918, had a profound impact on Europe in various ways:

- **From a continent of creditors to debtors:** Before the war, Europe was economically prosperous, with several nations acting as creditors. However, the immense cost of the war led to unprecedented levels of debt for many European nations.
- **Soldiers placed higher in social status than civilians:** The war disrupted traditional social structures. Soldiers who fought in the war were often hailed as heroes upon their return, and their sacrifices were recognized.
- **Popular support for conservative dictatorship:** Contrary to the statement, the aftermath of World War I witnessed a decline in support for conservative forces in some countries. The war had brought about significant social and political changes, leading to discontent with existing conservative regimes. In countries like Germany and Russia, the war contributed to the downfall of monarchies and conservative governments.

- **National honour in the public sphere:** The war instilled a sense of nationalism and national pride. Countries, especially those that emerged victorious, celebrated their perceived national honour and achievements during the war.

76. (B): The Quit India Resolution adopted on August 8, 1942, stressed that "...the immediate ending of British rule in India is an urgent necessity for both the sake of India and for the success of the United Nations. In line with the Congress ideology, it was supposed to be a peaceful non-violent movement aimed at urging the British to grant India independence.

The Quit India Resolution was passed by the Congress Working Committee on 8 August 1942 in Bombay. Gandhi was named the movement's leader.

- The resolution stated the provisions of the movement as:
- An immediate end to British rule over India.
- Declaration of the commitment of free India to defend itself against all kinds of imperialism and fascism.
- Formation of a provisional government of India after British withdrawal.
- Sanctioning a civil disobedience movement against British rule.

77. (D): Bailadila is a hill range in Chattisgarh which is famous for the very high-grade hematites which are found in Bailadila. India exports iron ore to Japan, Slovakia, Italy, Sri Lanka, etc.

Zawar is a settlement located in Udaipur district, Rajasthan, India, approximately 40 km from the lake city Udaipur. It stretches some 10 kilometers along the banks of the Gomati River. It is one of the oldest zinc mines of the world. It is declared as the National Geological Monument.

Ghatshila is best known for the copper mines because it is Asia's first copper mines and the world's second deepest mines. Ghatshila industrial area is famous for the copper industry. The Capital of Jharkhand is Ranchi which is also known as the city of waterfalls.

The **Kudremukh mines** lies in the Western Ghats of Karnataka. It is located in the Ballari-Chitradurga-Chikkamagaluru-Tumakuru belt. These mines are known for its large deposits of iron ore (not bauxite) and it is one of the largest in the world.

78. (B): Millibar (mb) is the standard unit for measuring atmospheric pressure. In the context of weather and atmospheric conditions, millibars are commonly used globally. It's the preferred unit for expressing air pressure in meteorology, including in India.

79. (A): All geologic time before the beginning of the Paleozoic era is known as Precambrian era. This includes about 90% of all geologic time and spans the time from the beginning of the earth, about 4.5 billion years ago, to 544 million years ago. It is the largest span of time in Earth's history.

80. (C): Longitude measures distance east or west of the prime meridian. Lines of longitude, also called meridians, are imaginary lines that divide the Earth. They run north to south from pole to pole, but they measure the distance east or west.

Latitude measures the distance north or south of the equator. Latitude lines start at the equator (0 degrees latitude) and run east and west, parallel to the equator. Lines of latitude are measured in degrees north or south of the equator to 90 degrees at the North of south poles.

81. (B): Troposphere: This layer is the most important layer of the atmosphere. Its average height is 13 km. The air we breathe exists here. Almost all the weather phenomena like rainfall, fog and hailstorm occur in this layer. This layer has water vapour and mature particles. Temperature decreases with increasing height of atmosphere at the rate of 1 degree Celsius for every 165 m of height. This is called the Normal lapse rate. Tropopause, the transitional zone, separates the Troposphere and Stratosphere.

82. (D): The Roopkund lake is a high altitude glacial lake which is located in a remote location in the Indian state of Uttarakhand. The lake lies in the lap of Trishul massif and given its remote location high up among the Himalayas the area around the lake is uninhabited. The lake is located at an altitude of 16,470 feet and is surrounded by rock-strewn glaciers interspersed with snow-clad mountains. The average depth of the lake is barely 2 meters.

The Roopkund lake is famous for the discovery of the ancient skeletal remains of hundreds of humans which were found at the edge of the lake.

83. (A): To calculate the average speed, you can use the formula:

$$\text{Average speed} = \frac{\text{Total Distance}}{\text{Total Time}}$$

In this case, the total distance covered is the difference in odometer readings, which is 2400 km – 2000 km = 400 km.

The total time is given as 8 hours

Average Speed = 400 km/8 hours

Average Speed = 50 km/h

Therefore, the average speed of Ram's car is 50 km/h.

84. (A): Split-ring type commutator must be used. AC to DC generator: An alternating current generator is a mechanical device that transforms mechanical energy into alternating current electrical power. A direct current generator is a mechanical device that transforms mechanical energy into direct current electrical power.

85. (B): Finding the focal length of the lens:

In the case of myopia, the focal length of the lens,

$f = -D = -2\text{m}$

We know that the required power of the lens.

$$P = \frac{1}{f}$$

By substituting the given value, we get

$$P = \frac{1}{-2}$$

$$= 0.5 \text{ D}$$

A concave lens of power of –0.5 D is required to fix the myopic eye.

Myopia: Myopia is also known as near-sightedness. A person with myopia can see nearby objects clearly but cannot see distant objects distinctly. A person with this defect has the far point nearer than infinity. Such a person may see clearly upto a distance of a few metres. In a myopic eye, the image of a distant object is formed in front of the retina and not at the retina itself.

86. (C): Resistance depends inversely on the area, not directly. Resistivity directly depends on the area of the cross-section of the wire. Hence, statement 1 is incorrect.

The electrical resistance of a wire generally increases with temperature. This phenomenon is described by the temperature coefficient of resistance. Hence, statement 2 is correct.

The resistance (R) is directly proportional to the resistivity (ρ) and the length (L), and inversely proportional to the cross-sectional area (A), as mentioned in the formula R = ρL/A. Hence, statement 3 is correct.

The resistivity of the wire is inversely proportional to the length of the wire. Hence, statement 4 is incorrect.

87. (A): A liquid starts to boil at a temperature when its vapor pressure becomes equal to the external atmospheric pressure, that temperature is known as boiling point of that liquid.

Vapour Pressure: It can be defined as the pressure produced by the vapour of a liquid (or solid) on the surface of the liquid. This pressure is created in a thermodynamic equilibrium state in a closed container at a certain temperature. Vapour pressure increases with temperature.

Atmospheric Pressure: It is defined as the force acting normally on a unit area around that point, due to the total height of the air column of the atmosphere above it. When the vapour pressure of a liquid equals its atmospheric pressure, the liquid begins to boil.

88. (A): Organic compounds are compounds of animal or plant origin while the rest are inorganic compounds. Ammonium cyanate is not found in any living being and is, therefore, an inorganic compound.

Ammonium cyanate does not contain any C-H covalent bond, so it is not an organic compound but contains ionic species. Organic compounds are either hydrocarbons (compounds of carbon and hydrogen) or their derivatives whereas, ammonium cyanate is neither a hydrocarbon nor a derivative of hydrocarbon. Urea is an organic compound because it contains two NH_2 groups joined together by a carbonyl group.

89. (B): Nitric acid (HNO_3), is a highly corrosive and poisonous strong mineral acid that is normally colourless but turns yellow due to the accumulation of oxides of nitrogen when stored for long periods. Nitric acid is used in the purification of gold and silver. The acid mixture aqua regia, or royal water, dissolves gold and is used to purify scrap alloy containing gold. Aqua regia is a mixture of hydrochloric acid and nitric acid in the ratio 3:1. Nitric acid is a nitrogen oxoacid of the formula HNO_3 in which the nitrogen atom is bound to a hydroxyl group and the remaining two oxygen atoms by equal bonds.

90. (A): Effect of Ethanol on Litmus paper:

Ethanol/Ethyl alcohol (C_2H_5OH) solution will not turn blue litmus paper to red.

Ethanol solution is neutral (neither acts as an acid or a base) in nature and it does not bring any change in the colour of litmus whether it is blue or red.

Therefore, Ethanol solution will not turn blue litmus paper to red.

91. (D): Stainless steel: Alloys are metal-element mixes whose precise composition is determined by the qualities required. Because alloys are metallic in nature, they have high thermal and electrical conductivity.

Stainless steel is known to remain stainless and resists corrosion due to interactions between the environment and its alloying components.

This alloy contains chromium, iron, silicon, manganese, carbon, and, in rare circumstances, rather considerable amounts of molybdenum and nickel. Chromium is essential in the manufacturing of stainless steel.

92. (C): Separating acetone and water from their mixture:

- Distillation is a process that involves heating a liquid mixture to form a vapour and then cooling that vapour to form a liquid.
- It is particularly useful for separating components with different boiling points.
- In this case, acetone and water have different boiling points, allowing them to be separated through distillation.

Separation of water and kerosene from their mixture:

- A separating funnel is used to separate immiscible liquids (liquids that do not dissolve in each other).
- In the case of water and kerosene, which do not mix well, a separating funnel may be used to allow the two liquids to be separated based on their different densities.

Separation of cream from milk:

- Centrifugation involves spinning a mixture at high speed, causing the components to separate based on their density.
- In the case of cream and milk, centrifugation can be used to separate the denser cream from the less dense milk.

Isolating pigments from plant extracts:

- Chromatography is a technique that separates components for stationary phase and mobile phase based on their different affinities.
- In the case of pigments from plant extracts, chromatography can be used to separate the different pigments present in the extract.

93. (D): Photosynthesis is the process of synthesis of food by plants using carbon dioxide and water in presence of sunlight and chlorophyll. Oxygen (O_2) is released during the process as a waste product. Hence, oxygen is not essential for the process of photosynthesis.

94. (D): The DNA content of the parent plant gets halved during the formation of pollen. The process in which the DNA content of the parent plant gets halved is called meiosis. Meiosis is a type of cell division that occurs during the formation of gametes (sex cells), such as pollen in flowering plants.

- **Seed Germination:** Seed germination involves the growth of a seed into a young plant. During this process, there is no halving of DNA content; rather, the new plant inherits the same DNA content as the parent.
- **Fruit Formation:** Fruit formation typically involves the development of the ovary after fertilization. Again, there is no halving of DNA content during fruit formation.
- **Flower Bud Formation:** Flower bud formation is part of the plant's growth and development, but DNA content is not halved during this process.
- **Pollen Formation:** Pollen is produced by the male reproductive organs of flowering plants, specifically in the anthers of the stamen. The formation of pollen involves meiosis, where the DNA content is halved, leading to the production of haploid pollen grains.

95. (A): The correct sequence during sexual reproduction in Angiosperms is Egg → zygote → embryo → seed.

The male gamete is present in the pollen grain which is formed in the anther of the stamen. The female gamete is the ovum which is formed in the ovary of the pistil. Through the process of fertilization, male and female gametes come together to form a zygote. The zygote must undergo repeated divisions to form an embryo. The embryo develops and matures in the seed. The seed germinates and gives rise to seedlings.

96. (D): The correct answer is Egg → zygote; zygote → embryo; ovule → seed; ovary → fruit:

Egg → Zygote: In animals, this represents the fertilization of an egg by a sperm, resulting in the formation of a zygote. In plants, it could represent the fusion of male and female gametes during pollination.

Zygote → Embryo: The zygote undergoes cell division and differentiation to form an embryo. This stage is crucial in the early development of an organism.

Ovule → Seed: After fertilization in plants, the ovule develops into a seed. The seed contains the embryonic plant, along with stored nutrients and a protective seed coat.

Ovary → Fruit: After fertilization in plants, the ovary of the flower develops into a fruit. The fruit typically contains seeds and serves as a structure to protect and disperse the seeds.

97. (C): Home Minister Amit Shah released the book 'Rashtra Pratham-82 Varshon ki Swarnim Gatha' in New Delhi on 19 February 2021. The book has the glorious history of CRPF since its raising in 1939 and it has a detailed and thoroughly researched account of CRPF's journey, challenges, successes, and sacrifices.

98. **(C):** When Sanchi was "discovered" in 1818, three of its four gateways were still standing, the fourth was lying on the spot where it had fallen and the mound was in good condition. Art historians identified the scene depicted in the gateways as a scene from the Vessantara Jataka. These figures included beautiful women swinging from the edge of the gateway holding into a tree, like, Shalabhanjika was a woman whose touch caused trees to flower and bear fruit. There are other images in Sanchi stupa. Depiction of animals like elephants, horses, monkeys, and cattle were found there. Animals were used as symbols of human attributes, e.g. elephants were depicted to signify strength and wisdom.

99. **(B):** Second Five Year Plan (1956-61):

- The Second Five year Plan stressed rapid industrialisation and the public sector.
- It was drafted and planned under the leadership of P.C. Mahalanobis.
- It emphasised quick structural transformation.
- The government imposed tariffs on imports to protect domestic industries under this plan.
- The target growth rate was 4.5% and the actual growth rate was slightly less than expected, 4.27%.

100. **(D):** Chandimangala is a type of Mangalkavaya which was written in the 16-century and is an important asset of Bengali Literature. Chandimangal of Kavikankan Mukundaram Chakravarti is an epic work recounting the stories of Goddess Chandi. The book describes her constant battle to establish herself as a cult among human beings. The three books of Kavya try to establish the various manifestations of Goddess Chandi. The literary tradition is folk and is practiced even today among the rural women through pre Aryan rituals. These include Panchalis - a long drawn narrative celebrating the glory of the deity, and Vratha Katha - includes chanting of rhymes on the performance of a vow.

101. **(C):** The royal centre was located in the south-western part of the settlement. Although designated as a royal centre, it included over 60 temples. Clearly, the patronage of temples and cults was important for rulers who were trying to establish and legitimise their authority through association with the divinities housed in the shrines.

About thirty building complexes have been identified as palaces. These are relatively large structures that do not seem to have been associated with ritual functions. One difference between these structures and temples is that the latter were constructed entirely of masonry, while the superstructure of the secular buildings was made of perishable materials.

About thirty building complexes have been identified as palaces.

102. **(A):** The total area of India is 32,87,263 sq. km. which is 2.42% of the total area of the world. In terms of area, India ranks seventh in the world. As per Census 2011, the total population of India is 1,21,01,93,422 which is 17.50% of the total population of the world. In terms of population, India ranks at second position. India is the seventh largest country in the world.

Area wise top 4 states:

State	Area (in sq. km)
Rajasthan	342239
Madhya Pradesh	308000
Maharashtra	307713
Uttar Pradesh	240928

103. **(A):** Black soil covers most of the Deccan Plateau which includes parts of Maharashtra, Madhya Pradesh, Gujarat, Andhra Pradesh and some parts of Tamil Nadu. In the upper reaches of the Godavari and the Krishna, and the north western part of the Deccan Plateau, the black soil is very deep. These soils are also known as the 'Regur Soil' or the 'Black Cotton Soil'. The black soils are generally clayey, deep and impermeable. They swell and become sticky when wet and shrink when dried. So, during the dry season, these soil develop wide cracks. Thus, there occurs a kind of 'self ploughing'. Because of this character of slow absorption and loss of moisture, the black soil retains the moisture for a very long time, which helps the crops, especially, the rain fed ones, to sustain even during the dry season.

104. **(A):** The Central Institute of Buddhist Studies, formerly known as the School of Buddhist Philosophy, located in Leh town of Ladakh is a deemed university under Ministry of Culture. It was founded in 1959 and formerly affiliated to the Sampurnanand Sanskrit University in Varanasi.

105. **(A):** The Nilgiri Hills, located in the southern part of the Peninsular Plateau, mark the point where the Eastern Ghats and Western Ghats meet. This convergence is known as the Nilgiri Hills. Hence statement 1 is correct.

The Cardamom Hills are part of the Western Ghats, not the Eastern Ghats. They are located in the southern part of the Western Ghats and are known for their rich biodiversity. Hence statement 2 is incorrect.

106. (C): According to the variations in relief features, the Northern plains can be divided into four regions. The rivers, after descending from the mountains deposit pebbles in a narrow belt of about 8 to 16 km in width lying parallel to the slopes of the Shiwaliks. It is known as bhabar. All the streams disappear in this bhabar belt. South of this belt, the streams and rivers re-emerge and create a wet, swampy and marshy region known as terai. This was a thickly forested region full of wildlife. The forests have been cleared to create agricultural land and to settle migrants from Pakistan after partition.

107. (B): Suez Canal is an artificial waterway running from north to south across the Isthmus of Suez in north-eastern Egypt. It connects Port Said on the Mediterranean Sea with the Gulf of Suez, an arm of the Red Sea. The canal provides a direct trade route for ships operating between European or American ports and ports located in South Asia, East Africa and Oceania by doing away with the need to sail around Africa. Strategically and economically, it is one of the most important waterways in the world. Its opening in 1869 reduced the cost of transportation and made access to the Indian market easier.

108. (B): An iron nail sinks in water because the average density of the nail is higher than that of the water displaced by the nail. Whereas the density of a water ship is less than the water displaced by it, hence it floats.

109. (A):

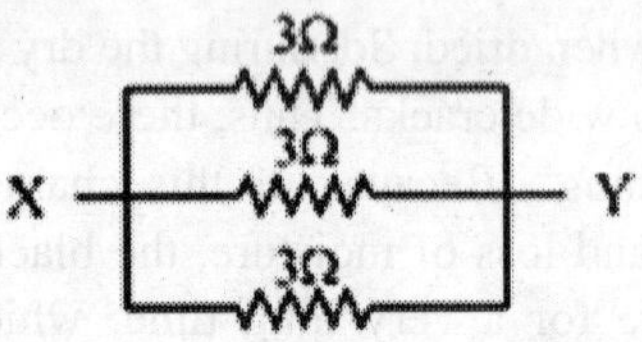

$$\frac{1}{R} = \frac{1}{R_1} + \frac{1}{R_2} + \frac{1}{R_3}$$

$$= \frac{1}{3} + \frac{1}{3} + \frac{1}{3} = \frac{1+1+1}{3}$$

$$\frac{1}{R} = \frac{3}{3} I^2 = 1$$

Option (A) arrangement of resistors offer minimum effective resistance between x and y.

110. (D): When a collection of positive and negative charges is passed at high speed through a magnetic field that is perpendicular to the direction of motion of the charges, a force known as the Lorentz force acts on each charge.

The Lorentz force (F) on a charged particle moving in a magnetic field is given by the equation:

$$F = q.v.B$$

(Where, q is the charge of the particle, v is the velocity of the particle, and B is the magnetic field strength.)

Both positive and negative charges will experience the Lorentz force, but unless there are additional forces or conditions, they will continue moving.

111. (D): Comparing the given equation with equation of motion.

$$y = ut - \frac{1}{2}gt^2 \quad ...(i)$$

$$s = ut + \frac{1}{2}at^2 \quad ...(ii)$$

Therefore, acceleration $= -g$

$$F = ma$$

$$F = -mg$$

112. (A): Let the weight is w Newton:

(a) $P_A = \frac{w}{A} = \frac{w}{20 \times 10} = \frac{w}{200} \frac{N}{cm^2}$

(b) $P_B = \frac{w}{A} = \frac{w}{20 \times 40} = \frac{w}{400} \frac{N}{cm^2}$

(c) $P_C = \frac{w}{40 \times 20} = \frac{w}{800} \frac{N}{cm^2}$

Hence, $P_A > P_B > P_C$

113. (A): Carbon is a reducing agent at high temperatures and from the point of view of electrochemical potential or reactivity series. A metal can be extracted from its oxide by using reducing agents like carbon or an extremely reactive metal. The reducing agent gets oxidized, leaving the metal. For example: Zinc is extracted from its oxide ore using coke as a reducing agent. The reaction involved is:

$$ZnO(s) + C(s) \rightarrow Zn(s) + CO(g)$$

Zinc is positioned above carbon in the reactivity series, indicating that carbon can effectively reduce zinc oxide to extract the metal.

114. (B): In colloidal solution, a material is evenly suspended in a liquid, e.g., milk or oil in water is a colloidal solution which is present in two phases in heterogeneous phase, e.g. foams, emulsions, soils.

115. (C): Applications of Fractional Distillation:

- Fractional distillation is used to separate mixtures of miscible liquids (like alcohol-water mixture and acetone-water mixture) in the laboratory.

- Fractional distillation is used to separate crude oil 'petroleum' into useful fractions such as kerosene, petrol and diesel, etc.
- Fractional distillation (of liquid air) is used to separate gases of the air.

116. (D): Dalton's symbol of some elements

Element	Dalton's symbol	Element	Dalton's symbol
Hydrogen	⊙	Iron	Ⓘ
Carbon	●	Copper	Ⓒ
Oxygen	○	Silver	Ⓢ
Phosphorus	[symbol]	Gold	●
Sulphur	⊕	Lead	Ⓛ
Platinum	Ⓟ	Mercury	[symbol]

117. (C):

- Carbon is a tetravalent non-metallic element having four covalent bonds.
- There are four electrons in outermost shell of carbon i.e. four valency electron.
- Carbon could lose four electrons forming C^{4+} cations and could gain four electrons forming C^{4-} anions.
- Carbon forms covalent bonds with itself and other elements such as hydrogen, oxygen, sulphur, nitrogen and chlorine forming various types of molecules, of the compounds.
- The sharing of one pair of electrons between two atoms form one covalent bond.
- Covalently bounded molecules are seen to have strong bonds within the molecules, but inter-molecular forces are weak, this gives rise to low melting and boiling points of these compounds.

118. (A): Terracotta models of the plough have been found at sites in Cholistan and at Banawali (Haryana).

Evidence of a ploughed field, associated with early Harappan levels have also found at Kalibangan (Rajasthan). The field had two sets of furrows at right angles to each other, suggesting that two different crops were grown together.

119. (A): The Industrial Revolution began in Great Britain in the mid-18th century. Many technical and technological innovations emerged in this revolution. Some important things related to this revolution are as follows:

- A Machine invented in 1779 by Samuel Crompton which is popularly known as "spinning mule". The thread spun from this was very strong and fine yarn.
- Weaving of pure cotton clothes became possible with the water frame invented by Richard Arkwright in 1769.
- The Power Loom was invented by Edmund Cartwright in 1784 and the first power loom was designed and patented in 1785.
- It was an automatic device designed to automate the weaving process.

120. (C): Prashant Chandra Mahalanobis (1893-1972), an Indian scientist considered as Architect of Indian, Planning & father of modern statistics. The second five year plan in 1956 based on PC Mahalanobis model. The second five-year plan focused on industry, especially heavy industry.

121. (A): Ashoka's edicts are inscribed on various structures such as pillars, cave walls and boulders. These are a group of more than 30 inscriptions associated with the Maurya emperor Ashoka. These inscriptions provide solid evidence of Buddhism and are spread across Afghanistan, Bangladesh, India, Nepal and Pakistan. The expression 'Dhamma script', was used by Ashoka to describe his inscriptions.

Edict of Ashoka - Maski

- It was discovered in 1915 by C Beadon, a British gold-mining engineer.
- The Maski village is in the Raichur district of Karnataka.
- The inscriptions are found on a boulder and cave walls in Brahmi script.
- The puzzle regarding the title 'devanampriya' was solved after the discovery of these inscriptions, as the Maski edict revealed the name as 'Devanampriya Ashoka'.

122. (C): The correct chronological order is:

- **Ashtadhyayi:** Attributed to Panini in the 5th Century BCE.
- **Sangam Literature:** Flourished primarily between the 3rd Century BCE and the 3rd Century CE.
- **Charak Samhita:** Composed by Charaka in the 2nd century BCE and the 2nd Century CE.
- **Bharata's Natyashastra:** Estimated to be written sometime between 2nd Century BCE and 2nd Century CE.

123. (A): Fold Mountains: It is formed due to the compressive forces generated by endogenetic forces (Earthquake, landslide, etc.). Examples of fold mountains are Himalayas, Alps, etc. Mount Fuji is not a fold mountain, it is a huge mountain in Japan Few examples of Fold Mounts are:

- The Alps Mountains in Europe

- The Andes in South America
- The Rockies Mountains in North America.
- The Himalayan Mountains in Asia.

124. (B): Histosols: It is a soil with a deep surface layer of pure organic material. Histosols are formed under waterlogged conditions typical of peat bogs and swamps. It contains the tissues of dead plants and animals and their decomposition products which results in soils of high organic content.

Vertisol is a soil type in which there is a high content of expansive clay minerals. Gelisols are soils of very cold climates that contain permafrost. Spodosols are typical soils of eucalyptus forests and heathlands found in southern Australia.

125. (D): Jhansi is the junction of North-South and East-West Corridors and four stretches are common between the Golden Quadrilateral the NS-EW Corridors. The NS-EW Corridor passes from 17 states and from Delhi along with other states capitals such as Srinagar, Hyderabad, Bangalore, Lucknow, and Dispur. The North-South and East-West Corridor is the largest ongoing highway project in India. It is the second phase of the National Highways Development Project consists of building four/six-lane expressways connecting Srinagar (North), Kanyakumari (South), Porbandar (West), and Silchar (East).

126. (D): The word monsoon is derived from the Arabic word 'mausim' which literally means season. 'Monsoon' refers to the seasonal reversal in the wind direction during a year. The climate of India is described as the 'monsoon' type. In Asia, this type of climate is found mainly in the south and the southeast.

127. (B):

Steel Plant	Estd. Year	State	Goegraphical Location
Jamshedpur steel plant	1907	Jharkhand	locaed near the confluence of the rivers Subarnarekha and Kharkai
Bokaro steel plant	1964	Jharkhand	Located on the southern bank of River Damodar
Salem Steel plant	1981	Tamil Nadu	Located on the bank of Cauvery (Kavari) River
Bhilai Steel Plant	1955	Chhattisgarh	It is not located on a river side, Water is supplied from Tandula Canal.

128. (A): Apiculture (or beekeeping) is the maintenance of bee colonies, commonly in man-made beehives. Honey bees in the genus Apis are the most commonly kept species but other honey producing bees such as Melipona stingless bees are also kept.

Sericulture is the process of cultivating silkworms and extracting silk from them. The caterpillars of the domestic silkmoth (also called 'Bombyx Mori') are the most commonly used silkworm species in sericulture.

Silviculture is the practice of controlling the growth, composition/structure, as well as quality of forests to meet values and needs, specifically timber production.

Viticulture is the cultivation and harvesting of grapes which deals with the series of events that occur in the vineyard. When the grapes are used for winemaking, it is known as viniculture.

129. (B): Winter rainfall and agriculture: Western disturbances originate from the Mediterranean Sea and come to India. It causes rainfall in states like Haryana, Punjab, Jammu and Kashmir, Himachal Pradesh, Uttarakhand during winter. Precipitation during the winter season is of great importance in agriculture, especially for Rabi crops including wheat, which is one of the most important Indian crops. The major Rabi crop in India is wheat, followed by barley, mustard, sesame and peas. The rains caused by western disturbances have a direct impact on the economy of wheat-producing states like Haryana and Punjab.

130. (A):

City	State	Industry
(a) Saharanpur	Uttar Pradesh	The city of Saharanpur is known for the Paper Industry.
(b) Chanderi	Madhya Pradesh	This city is famous for Sarees, Wooden work, Bidi industry & Diamond industry
(c) Bhadohi	Uttar Pradesh	Bhadohi is one of largest centers of Carpet Industries in India and is worldwide known as 'Carpet City of India'.
(d) Raniganj	West Bengal	It is famous for the most reliable quality of cooking coal

131. (*)

132. (B): Sound is a mechanical wave and longitudinal in nature. A sound wave is an elastic wave and an example of a longitudinal wave and due to the elastic wave nature of a sound wave, it cannot travel in a vacuum.

Mechanical Wave: A mechanical wave is a wave that is an oscillation of matter and is responsible for the transfer of energy through a medium. The distance of the wave's propagation is limited by the medium of transmission. In this case, the oscillating material moves about a fixed point, and there is very little translational motion. One intriguing property of mechanical waves is the way they are measured, which is given by displacement divided by the wavelength.

133. (D): In an elastic collision between two spheres, both momentum and kinetic energy are conserved.

The conservation of momentum can be expressed as:

$$m_1 * v_{1i} + m_2 * v_{2i} = m_1 * v_{1f} + m_2 * v_{2f}$$

where:

- m_1 and m_2 are the masses of the first and second spheres, respectively,
- v_{1i} and v_{2i} are their initial velocities,
- v_{1f} and v_{2f} are their final velocities.

Since the second sphere is initially at rest ($v_{2i} = 0$) and the first sphere comes to rest ($v_{1f} = 0$), the momentum conservation equation simplifies to:

$$m_1 * v_{1i} = m_2 * v_{2f}$$

Now, let's substitute the given values:

100 g * 20 m/s = 50 g * 100 g

Solving for v_{2f}:

$$v_{2f} = 40 \text{ m/s}$$

Therefore, the speed of the second sphere after the collision is 40 m/s.

134. (D): Light is a transverse, electromagnetic wave that can be seen by a normal human. The wave nature of light was first characterized through experiments on diffraction and interference. Like all electromagnetic waves, light can travel through a vacuum. The transverse nature of light can be demonstrated through polarization. The phenomenon of confining the vibrations of light waves in a particular plane perpendicular to the direction of propagation of wave motion is called polarization. Polarization explains the wave nature of light, because light waves are polarized in a particular plane. Longitudinal waves cannot be polarized. Therefore, the transverse wave can only be polarized.

135. (D): Those materials which are attracted by a magnet are called magnetic materials. Iron, steel, nickel and cobalt are attracted by a magnet, so iron, steel, nickel and cobalt are magnetic materials. The most common and important magnetic materials are, however, iron steel.

Those materials which are *not* attracted by a magnet are called non-magnetic materials. All the materials other than iron, steel, nickel and cobalt are non-magnetic materials. For example, wood, plastic, rubber, carbon, paper, cloth, glass, leather, thermocol, copper, aluminium, brass, lead, stone, diamond, graphite, paint, charcoal, air, water, skin and bones, etc., are all non-magnetic materials because they are not attracted by a magnet.

But stainless steel is generally not attracted to a magnet.

136. (C): Bhoodan Movement was a socio-political movement started by Vinoba Bhave in 1951 in India. Vinoba Bhave was disciple of Mahatma Gandhi who selected him as the first individual Satyagrahi and he actively participated in India's freedom struggle. After independence, he realized that the issue of landlessness was a major problem facing rural India and in 1951, he started the Bhoodan Movement or Land Gift Movement.

Although the movement was independent of the government, it had the support of Congress. In 1953, JP Narayan withdrew from active politics to join the Bhoodan movement.

Vinoba Bhave led the voluntary land reform campaign known as the Bhoodan Movement, commonly known as the "Bloodless Revolution" in independent India. On April 18, 1951, Bhave traveled to Pochampalli, a village in Yadadri Bhuvanagiri district of Telangana.

The Sarvodaya movement was started by Vinoba Bhave, who was a prominent proponent of non-violence and human rights, following the principles of Mahatma Gandhi. The word "Sarvodaya" in Hindi means 'universal upliftment' or 'progress of all'.

137. (A): The Security Council has 15 members in which 5 permanent members with veto power 10 non-permanent members, five of which are elected each year by the General Assembly for a two-year term:

- 5 from African and Asian States
- 1 from Eastern European States
- 2 from Latin American States
- 2 from Western European and other States.

138. (A): District Planning Committee is set up under Article 243ZD of the Constitution of India at the district level.

Composition:

- Members of the Lok Sabha who represent the whole or part of the district;
- All the members of the State Legislative Assembly whose constituencies lie within the district;
- President of the Zilla Parishad;
- President of the Municipal Corporation or the Municipal Council, having jurisdiction over the headquarters of the district;
- About four-fifths of the members of a district planning committee be elected from amongst the elected members of the district panchayat and municipalities;

- The Chairman of the District Co-operative Banks and the Land Development Bank (Permanent invitees);
- The Chief Executive Officer (Secretary of the Committee);
- The Deputy Commissioner of the districts (Chairman of the District Planning Committee).

139. (C): The Attorney-General of India is appointed by the President under Article 76 of the Constitution. A person qualified to be a judge of the Supreme Court is appointed to such a post. He is the highest legal advisor to the Government of India and is consulted on all important legal matters. He also appears in the Supreme Court on behalf of the Government of India to conduct important cases. However, even being the first Law Officer of the Government of India, he is not a whole-time counsel for the Government nor a Government servant.

Further, he has the right to speak and to take part in the proceedings of both the Houses of Parliament or their joint sitting and any committee of the Parliament of which he may be named a member, but without a right to vote.

140. (D): India and Bangladesh have a land border of approximately 4,100 km. This boundary was determined as the India-East Pakistan land boundary by the Radcliffe Award of 1947, but disputes soon arose over some aspects. On 6 June 2015, after the exchange of instruments of ratification, the India Bangladesh Land Boundary Agreement of 1974 came into force. The Land Boundary Agreement also demarcated the boundary between India and Bangladesh into three states (in the Indian states of West Bengal, Tripura and Assam), totaling 6.1 km.

141. (C): Phukot Karnali Hydro Electric Project is located in Kalikot district, Karnali Province of Nepal. The project will use the flow from the Karnali River for power generation and the generated power will be fed into integrated power system of Nepal. The installed capacity of the project shall be 480 MW with average annual generation of about 2448 GWh. 109 metre high RCC dam and an underground power house where the 06 turbines of 79 MW each shall be housed. To utilize minimum environmental release one Surface Power House of 6 MW capacity is also planned.

142. (D): The river mentioned in the statements originates in the Hindu Kush mountain range, flows approximately 1,100 km, and has been a source of serious conflict between neighbouring countries is the Helmand River. Helmand is the longest river in Afghanistan. It originates in the western Hindu Kush mountain range near Kabul. The Helmand River flows from the Hindu Kush mountains and passes through Afghanistan and Iran before reaching the Hamoun wetlands. The water-sharing conflict has mainly been between Afghanistan and Iran, the two neighbouring countries through which the river flows.

143. (B): Garuda Shakti is the largest military exercise between Indonesia and India, which includes various training scenarios such as special forces operations, counterterrorism, and counter insurgency, as well as humanitarian assistance and disaster relief.

The Nomadic Elephant Exercise is the name given to the Indo-Mongolian Bilateral Military Exercise. India and Mongolia are the only participating nations in this bilateral exercise. It aims to enhance cooperation and interoperability between the two armies.

Mitra Shakti exercise is a bilateral joint military exercise between the militaries of India and Sri Lanka. It is also called the India-Sri Lanka Joint Training exercise. The design of the Mitra Shakti exercise is such that it incorporates UN peacekeeping operations' dynamics.

Dharma Guardian is an annual military exercise conducted in India since 2018. This bilateral exercise is conducted between the Indian and Japanese military. This exercise seeks to enhance the level of defense cooperation between the two armies.

144. (A): Gallantry Awards have been instituted by the Government of India. Post-independence, the first three gallantry awards were instituted on 26th January 1950. First three Gallantry Award (Peacetime awards) in India is:

- **Ashoka Chakra:** It is one of the highest peacetime military decorations awarded for valor, courageous action or sacrifice.
- **Kirti Chakra:** It is the second highest peacetime gallantry award and is awarded for valor, courageous action and for self-sacrifice away form the field of battle.
- **Shaurya Chakra:** It is awarded to the personnel of the armed forces for instances of extraordinary gallantry.

145. (D): India has jointed the Centralized Laboratory Network (CLN) which currently has 15 partner facilities in 13 countries that works to test vaccines which can be used during pandemic, epidemic disease outbreak. CLN is a part of the Coalition for Epidemic Preparedness Innovations (CEPI) and the Network is the largest global group which has standardised methods and materials for testing.

146. (B): Kavach is an automatic train protection (ATP) system indigenously developed by Indian Railways through Research Designs & Standards Organisation (RDSO). Hence statement 1 is incorrect.

Kavach is India's automatic protection system, which is in development since 2012, under the name Train Collision Avoidance System (TCAS), which got rechristened Kavach or "armour". It is a set of electronic devices and Radio Frequency Identification (RFID) devices installed in locomotives, in the signalling system as well as the tracks. The current form of the armor meets the highest level of safety and reliability standard called Safety Integrity Level (SIL) 4. Hence statement 3 is correct.

SIL comes from two voluntary standards that are used by plant owners/operators to set safety performance requirements for hazardous operations. There are four SIL levels (1-4). Higher SIL levels mean greater process risk and the need for a higher level of safety.

The Kavach trials facilitated by South Central Railway to achieve the corporate objective of safety in train operations across Indian Railways. Hence statement 2 is incorrect.

147. (C): Kakhovka Dam was a major hydroelectric power plant and reservoir on the Dnieper River in southern Ukraine. The Kakhovka Dam was a dam on the Dnieper River (also known as Dnipro) in Kherson Oblast, Ukraine, completed in 1956 and destroyed in 2023, which provided water for the Kakhovka Hydroelectric Station. The primary purposes of the dam were hydroelectric power generation, irrigation, and navigation. It was the sixth and last dam in the Dnieper reservoir cascade.

148. (B): Aaron James Finch is an Australian cricket commentator and former international cricketer who served as the captain of the Australian cricket team in ODI and T20I cricket. Aaron Finch has retired from all international cricket after leading Australia in a record 76 matches as captain of the T20I team. Finch led Australia to its first T20 World Cup win in 2021.

149. (B): RBI Governor Shaktikanta Das recently launched a financial inclusion dashboard called 'Antardrishti', marking a significant step towards promoting financial inclusion in India. This innovative tool aims to provide valuable insights for assessing and monitoring the progress of financial inclusion by capturing relevant parameters.

150. (D): On May 28th 2023, the Prime Minister will inaugurate the new Parliament building, which is part of the Central Vista re-development project. One of the highlights of the event will be the installation of a historic golden sceptre, called Sengol, near the Speaker's seat.

The Sengol is a symbol of India's independence and sovereignty, as well as its cultural heritage and diversity. The Sengol is profound in meaning, derived from the Tamil word "Semmai", it means "Righteousness". It was made of gold or silver and was often decorated with precious stones.

A Sengol sceptre was carried by emperors on ceremonial occasions, and used to represent their authority. It is associated with the Chola Empire, one of the longest-ruling and most influential dynasties in South India. The Cholas ruled Tamil Nadu, Kerala, Karnataka, Andhra Pradesh, Telangana, Odisha and parts of Sri Lanka from the 9th to the 13th century AD.

Paper-II : Mathematics

1. (D): $z = x + iy$ (given)

$\therefore \quad \overline{z} = x - iy$

Now, $\quad z.\overline{z} = (z + \overline{z})$

$(x + iy)(x - iy) = (x + iy + x - iy)$

$x^2 + y^2 = 2x$

$x^2 - 2x + y^2 = 0$

Adding +1 on both sides, we get

$x^2 - 2x + 1 + y^2 = 0 + 1$

$(x - 1)^2 + y^2 = (1)^2$

This is a equation of circle with centre (1, 0) and radius 1 unit.

2. (C): $P = 1! + 3! + 5! + 7! + 9! + ... + 199!$

$P = 1 + 3 \times 2 + 5 \times 4 \times 3 \times 2 + 7 \times 5 \times 5 \times 4 \times 3 \times 2 + ... + 199 \times 198 \times ... 4 \times 3 \times 2$

$P = 1 + 6 + 5 \times 24 + 7 \times 6 \times 5 \times 24 + ... + 199 \times 198 \times ... 6 \times 5 \times 24$

$P = 7 + 24[5 + 7 \times 6 \times 5 + ... + 199 \times 198 \times ... 6 \times 5]$

Now, $P \div 24 \equiv \dfrac{7+24[5+7\times6\times5+...]}{24}$

$\therefore$ Remainder = 7.

3. (C): $\because \quad \sqrt{a+ib}+\sqrt{a-ib} = \sqrt{2\left\{\sqrt{a^2+b^2}+a\right\}}$

$\therefore \quad \sqrt{12+5i}+\sqrt{12-5i} = \sqrt{2\left\{\sqrt{144+25}+12\right\}}$

$= \sqrt{2(13+12)} = \sqrt{2\times 25}$

$= 5\sqrt{2}$

Hence, the value of $\sqrt{12+5i}+\sqrt{12-5i} = 5\sqrt{2}$.

4. (A): $AA' = \begin{bmatrix}1\\2\\3\end{bmatrix}[1\,2\,3] = \begin{bmatrix}1&2&3\\2&4&6\\3&6&9\end{bmatrix}$

$I + AA' = \begin{bmatrix}1&0&0\\0&1&0\\0&0&1\end{bmatrix}+\begin{bmatrix}1&2&3\\2&4&6\\3&6&9\end{bmatrix} = \begin{bmatrix}2&2&3\\2&5&6\\3&6&10\end{bmatrix}$

Now,

$\det(I + AA') = 2(50 - 36) + 2(18 - 20) + 3(12 - 15)$

$= 28 - 4 - 9 = 15$

5. (A): $\because \quad |BC| = 2|A|$

Now, $|2A^{-1}BC| = (2)^3|A^{-1}||BC|$ [$\because$ order of A = 3]

$= 8\times\frac{1}{|A|}\times 2|A| = 16$

6. (C): $\because \quad a_n = \frac{2n+5}{7}$

$a_1 = \frac{2+5}{7} = \frac{7}{7}$

$a_2 = \frac{4+5}{7} = \frac{9}{7}$

$a_3 = \frac{6+5}{7} = \frac{11}{7}$

$a_4 = \frac{8+5}{7} = \frac{13}{7}$

$\therefore \quad \frac{7}{7}, \frac{9}{7}, \frac{11}{7}, \frac{13}{7}$ ... are in A.P. in which

$a = \frac{7}{7}$ and c.d $= \frac{2}{7}$

$\therefore \quad S_n = \frac{n}{2}\{2a+(n-1).d\}$

$= \frac{140}{2}\left\{2\times\frac{7}{7}+(140-1)\times\frac{2}{7}\right\}$

$= 70\left\{\frac{2}{7}\times(139+7)\right\}$

$= 70\times\frac{2}{7}\times 146$

$= 10 \times 292 = 2920$

Hence, the sum of 140 terms = 2920.

7. (A): Since matrix A is a skew – symmetric matrix of order 3 (odd number)

$\therefore \quad |A| = 0$

Now, $|4A^4| - |3A^3| + |2A^2| - |A| + |-I|$

$= (4)^3|A^4| - 3^3|A^3| + 2^3|A^2| - |A| + (-1)^3\,|I|$

$= 64(0) - 27(0) + 8(0) - 0 - 1 = -1$

8. (A): $A^2 = \begin{bmatrix}0&3&4\\-3&0&5\\-4&-5&0\end{bmatrix}\begin{bmatrix}0&3&4\\-3&0&5\\-4&-5&0\end{bmatrix}$

$A^2 = \begin{bmatrix}-9-16&-20&15\\-20&-9-25&-12\\15&-12&-16-25\end{bmatrix}$

$A^2 = \begin{bmatrix}-25&-20&15\\-20&-34&-12\\15&-12&-41\end{bmatrix}$ this is symmetric matrix

Also, $\det(A^2) = -25\ (34 \times 41 - 12 \times 12) - 20\ (15 \times (-12) - 20 \times 41) + 15\ (20 \times 12 \div 15 \times (-34)) = 0$

Hence, option (A) is correct.

9. (B): $A = \begin{bmatrix}2&0&0\\0&3&0\\0&0&4\end{bmatrix}$

$A^2 = \begin{bmatrix}2&0&0\\0&3&0\\0&0&4\end{bmatrix}\begin{bmatrix}2&0&0\\0&3&0\\0&0&4\end{bmatrix}$

$= \begin{bmatrix}2\times 2&0&0\\0&3\times 3&0\\0&0&4\times 4\end{bmatrix}$

$= \begin{bmatrix}2^2&0&0\\0&3^2&0\\0&0&4^2\end{bmatrix}$

$A^3 = A^2 \times A = \begin{bmatrix}2^2&0&0\\0&3^2&0\\0&0&4^2\end{bmatrix}\begin{bmatrix}2&0&0\\0&3&0\\0&0&4\end{bmatrix}$

$= \begin{bmatrix}2^3&0&0\\0&3^3&0\\0&0&4^3\end{bmatrix}$

$\therefore \quad A^n = \begin{bmatrix}2^n&0&0\\0&3^n&0\\0&0&4^n\end{bmatrix}$

This is a diagonal matrix for all $n > 0$.

Again, as element of $[A]_{i \times j}$ for $i = j$, is +ve integer.

$\therefore$ A^n will be always symmetric matrix.

Hence, statement (2) and (3) are corect.

10. (C): $\because$ $(a + b), 2b, (b + c)$ are in H.P.

$\therefore \frac{1}{a+b}, \frac{1}{2b}, \frac{1}{b+c}$ are in A.P.

$$\because \quad \frac{1}{2b} - \frac{1}{a+b} = \frac{1}{b+c} - \frac{1}{2b}$$

$$\Rightarrow \quad \frac{1}{2b} + \frac{1}{2b} = \frac{1}{b+c} + \frac{1}{a+b}$$

$$= \frac{a+b+b+c}{(a+b)(b+c)}$$

$$\Rightarrow \quad \frac{1+1}{2b} = \frac{2b+a+c}{ab+ac+b^2+bc}$$

$$\Rightarrow \quad \frac{2}{2b} = \frac{2b+a+c}{ab+ac+b^2+bc}$$

$\Rightarrow b^2 + ab + ac + bc = 2b^2 + ab + bc$

$\Rightarrow \quad b^2 = ac$

$\therefore$ a, b, c are in G.P.

11. (C): As t_1, t_2, t_3 ... are in G.P.

$\therefore \quad t_n = t_1.(r)^{n-1}$,

where r = common ratio

Now, $[t_1.t_3.t_5...t_{21}]^{\frac{1}{11}}$

$$= [t_1(t_1.r^2).(t_1r^4).(t_1.r^6)...(t_1.r^{20})]^{\frac{1}{11}}$$

$$= \left[t_1^{11}.r^{(2+4+...+20)}\right]^{\frac{1}{11}}$$

$$= t_1.r^{2\times\frac{10\times11}{2}\times\frac{1}{11}}$$

$$= t_1.r^{10} = t_{11}$$

12. (B): Let, $\quad \sqrt{i} = x + iy$

squaring both sides

$$\left(\sqrt{i}\right)^2 = (x + iy)^2$$

$$\Rightarrow \quad i = x^2 + i^2.y^2 + 2ixy$$

$\Rightarrow \quad x^2 - y^2 + 2ixy = 0 + i$

Equating real and imaginary parts

$$x^2 - y^2 = 0 \quad ...(i)$$

and $\quad 2xy = 1 \quad ...(ii)$

Now, $\quad (x^2 + y^2)^2 = (x^2 - y^2)^2 + 4x^2y^2$

$\Rightarrow \quad (x^2 + y^2)^2 = 0 + 1 = 1$

$\Rightarrow \quad x^2 + y^2 = 1 \quad ...(iii) \quad [\because x^2 + y^2 > 0]$

Solving (*i*) and (*iii*)

$$x^2 = \frac{1}{2} \text{ and } y^2 = \frac{1}{2}$$

$$\Rightarrow \quad x = \pm\frac{1}{\sqrt{2}} \text{ and } y = \pm\frac{1}{\sqrt{2}}$$

$$\therefore \quad \sqrt{i} = \pm\frac{1}{\sqrt{2}}(1+i)$$

$$\sqrt{-i} = \pm\frac{1}{\sqrt{2}}(1-i)$$

Hence, square root of $-\sqrt{-1} = \pm\frac{1}{\sqrt{2}}(1-i) = \frac{1-i}{\sqrt{2}}$

13. (C): The maximum number of points of intersection of 10 circles

$= 0 + 2 + 4 + 6 + 8 + 10 + 12 + 14 + 16 + 18 = 90$

14. (B): $\because$ $n(S) = 2^{n+1}$

Now, ${}^{2n+1}C_0 + {}^{2n+1}C_1 + {}^{2n+1}C_2 .... + {}^{2n+1}C_n + {}^{2n+1}C_{n+1}$

$+ {}^{2n+1}C_{n+2} + ... + {}^{2n+1}C_{2n+1} = 2^{(2n+1)}$

$\Rightarrow 2[{}^{2n+1}C_0 + {}^{2n+1}C_1 + ... + {}^{2n+1}C_n] = 2^{2n+1} = 4096$

$\Rightarrow \quad 2^{2n}.\ 2 = 2^{13}$

$\therefore \quad 2n = 12 \Rightarrow n = 6.$

15. (B): $\begin{vmatrix} x^2+3x & x-1 & x+3 \\ x+1 & -2x & x-4 \\ x-3 & x+4 & 3x \end{vmatrix}$

$= ax^4 + bx^3 + cx^2 + dx + e$

$(x^2 + 3x)(-6x^2 - x^2 + 16) - (x - 1) [3x(x + 1) - (x - 4)(x - 3)] + (x + 3) (x + 1) (x + 4) + 2x(x - 3)$

$(x^2 + 3x) (-7x^2 + 16) - (x - 1) [3x^2 + 3x - (x^2 - 3x - 4x + 12)] + (x + 3) [x^2 + 4x + x + 4] + 2x^2 - 6x$

$-7x^4 + 16x^2 - 21x^3 + 48x - (x - 1) [3x^2 + 3x - x^2 + 7x - 12] + (x + 3) [x^2 + 5x + 4] + 2x^2 - 6x$

$- 7x^4 + 16x^2 - 21x^3 + 48x - [(x - 1)(2x^2 + 10x - 12)] + x^3 + 5x^2 + 4x + 3x^2 + 15x + 12 + 2x^2 - 6x$

$-7x^4 + 16x^2 - 21x^3 + 48x - [2x^3 + 10x^2 - 12x - 2x^2 - 10x + 12] + x^3 + 10x^2 - 13x + 12$

$-7x^4 + 16x^2 - 21x^3 + 48x - 2x^3 - 8x^2 + 22x - 12 + x^3 + 10x^2 - 13x + 12$

$-7x^4 - 22x^3 + 18x^2 + 57x + 0$

$a = -7, b = -22, c = 18, d = 57, e = 0$

Hence, the value of $e = 0$.

16. (B): All elements are either 1 or –1.

$$\begin{vmatrix} 1 & -1 & 1 \\ -1 & 1 & 1 \\ 1 & 1 & -1 \end{vmatrix} = 1(-1-1)-1\ (1-1) + 1(-1\ -1)$$

$$= -4$$

$$\begin{vmatrix} 1 & 1 & 1 \\ 1 & 1 & 1 \\ 1 & 1 & 1 \end{vmatrix} = 1(1-1) + 1(1-1) + 1(1-1) = 0$$

$$\begin{vmatrix} -1 & 1 & -1 \\ 1 & -1 & -1 \\ -1 & -1 & 1 \end{vmatrix} = -1(-1-1) + 1(1-1) - 1(-1-1) = 4$$

Thus, determinant values are even number but not necessarily 0.

17. (D): $A = \begin{vmatrix} 2 & -1 & 0 \\ -1 & 3 & 0 \\ 1 & 0 & 1 \end{vmatrix} = 2(3-0) - 1(0-(-1)) + 0$

$= 6 - 1 = 5$

Now $|adj(adj\ A)| = adj|A|^{n-1} = \left[|A|^{n-1}\right]^{n-1} = |A|^{(n-1)^2}$

As order of A is 3.

$\therefore \quad \det[adj(adj A)] = (5)^{(3-1)^2}$

$= 5^4 = 625$

18. (A): $\because \quad A = \begin{bmatrix} 1 & 0 & 0 \\ 0 & 1 & 0 \\ 0 & 0 & 1 \end{bmatrix}$

$23A^3 = 23\begin{bmatrix} 1 & 0 & 0 \\ 0 & 1 & 0 \\ 0 & 0 & 1 \end{bmatrix}$

$-19A^2 = -19\begin{bmatrix} 1 & 0 & 0 \\ 0 & 1 & 0 \\ 0 & 0 & 1 \end{bmatrix}$

$-4A = -4\begin{bmatrix} 1 & 0 & 0 \\ 0 & 1 & 0 \\ 0 & 0 & 1 \end{bmatrix}$

$\therefore$ Value of $23A^3 - 19A^2 - 4A$

$= \begin{bmatrix} 23-19-4 & 0-0-0 & 0-0-0 \\ 0-0-0 & 23-19-4 & 0-0-0 \\ 0-0-0 & 0-0-0 & 23-19-4 \end{bmatrix}$

$= \begin{bmatrix} 0 & 0 & 0 \\ 0 & 0 & 0 \\ 0 & 0 & 0 \end{bmatrix}$

Hence, required value = Null matrix of order 3.

19. (C): From question, we have $|A| = 3$

and $\quad adj\ A = C$

Now, $\quad |C^2| = |C'|^2 = |adj\ A|^2$

$= (|A|^{3-1})^2 = |A|^4 = 3^4 = 81$

20. (D): $\because \quad |A_1| = \begin{vmatrix} 0 & 1 \\ -1 & 2 \end{vmatrix} = +1$

$|A_2| = \begin{vmatrix} 1 & 2 \\ 0 & 3 \end{vmatrix} = 3$

$|A_3| = \begin{vmatrix} 2 & 3 \\ 1 & 4 \end{vmatrix} = 5$

$|A_4| = \begin{vmatrix} 3 & 4 \\ 2 & 5 \end{vmatrix} = 7$

....

$|A_{100}| = \begin{vmatrix} 99 & 100 \\ 98 & 101 \end{vmatrix} = 199$

$\therefore \det(A_1) + \det(A_2) + \ldots \det(100)$

$= 1 + 3 + 5 + 7 + \ldots + 199$

$a_n = a + (n-1)d$

$= 1 + (n-1)2$

$\Rightarrow \quad 199 = 2n - 1$

$\Rightarrow \quad 2n = 200$

$\Rightarrow \quad n = 100$

$S_n = \frac{100}{2}\{2\times1+(100-1)\times2\}$

$= \frac{100}{2}\{2+99\times2\}$

$= \frac{100}{2}\{2+198\}$

$= \frac{100}{2}\times200$

$= 50 \times 200$

$= 10000$

21. (C): Here, we know that $n(A \times A) = 16$

and, $\quad (0, 2), (1, 3) \in A \times A$

$\Rightarrow \quad A = \{0, 1, 2, 3\}$

Also, $\quad (3, 2) \in A \times A$ as $2, 3 \in A$

Hence, both statement are true.

22. (B): We have $\quad R = \{(x, y) : 4x - 3y = 1\}$

$4x - 3y = 1$

$\Rightarrow \quad y = \frac{1}{3}(4x-1)$

$\therefore \quad$ Domain = {1, 4, 7, 10, 13}

and $\quad$ Range = {1, 5, 9, 13, 17}

Co-domain = A

23. (A): Checking for continuity at point $x = 2$.

$\lim_{x\to2^-} f(x) = \lim_{x\to2^+} f(x)$

$\lim_{x\to2^-} (x)^3 = \lim_{x\to2^+} 4(x)$

$(2)^3 = 4(2) \Rightarrow 8 = 8$

Hence, $f(x)$ is function

Again for, $g(x)$, $\lim_{x\to 4^-} g(x) = \lim_{x\to 4^+} g(x)$

$(4)^2 = 3(4) \Rightarrow 16 = 12$

But, $16 \neq 12$

Hence, $g(x)$ is not a function.

24. (B): 1. $(A\cup B)\cup(A - B) = (A\cup B)\cup(A\cap B')$

$= A\cup[B\cup(A\cap B')]$

$= A\cup(A\cup B)$

$= A\cup B \neq A$ [incorrect]

2. $A\cup(B - A) = A\cup(B\cap A')$

$= (A\cup B)\cap(A\cup A')$

$= A\cup B$ [correct]

3. $(A\cup B) - (A - B) = (A\cup B)\cap(A\cap B')'$

$= (A\cup B\cap(A'\cup B)$

$= (A\cap A')\cup B = B$

[correct]

25. (D): Given that $f(x - y) = \dfrac{f(x)}{f(y)}$

$f(1) = f(2 - 1) = \dfrac{f(2)}{f(1)}$

$\Rightarrow$ $f(2) = f(1)\times f(1)$

$= 0.5\times 0.5 = \dfrac{1}{4}$

$f(2) = f(3 - 1) = \dfrac{f(3)}{f(1)}$

$\Rightarrow$ $f(3) = f(2)\times f(1) = \dfrac{1}{4}\times\dfrac{1}{2} = \dfrac{1}{8}$

$f(4) = f(3)\times f(1) = \dfrac{1}{8}\times\dfrac{1}{2} = \dfrac{1}{16}$

$f(5) = f(4)\times f(1) = \dfrac{1}{16}\times\dfrac{1}{2} = \dfrac{1}{32}$

and $f(6) = f(5)\times f(1)$

$= \dfrac{1}{32}\times\dfrac{1}{2} = \dfrac{1}{64}$

Now, $f(2) + f(3) + f(4) + f(5) + f(6)$

$= \dfrac{1}{4}+\dfrac{1}{8}+\dfrac{1}{16}+\dfrac{1}{32}+\dfrac{1}{64}$

$= \dfrac{16+8+4+2+1}{64} = \dfrac{31}{64}$

26. (C): Let $\cos^{-1}\left(\dfrac{\sqrt{5}}{3}\right) = \theta$

$\therefore$ $\cos\theta = \dfrac{\sqrt{5}}{3}$

We have to find $\cot\dfrac{\theta}{2} = \sqrt{\dfrac{1+\cos\theta}{1-\cos\theta}}$

$= \sqrt{\dfrac{1+\dfrac{\sqrt{5}}{3}}{1-\dfrac{\sqrt{5}}{3}}} = \sqrt{\dfrac{3+\sqrt{5}}{3-\sqrt{5}}}$

$= \sqrt{\dfrac{3+\sqrt{5}}{3-\sqrt{5}}\times\dfrac{3+\sqrt{5}}{3-\sqrt{5}}}$

$= \sqrt{\dfrac{(3+\sqrt{5})^2}{9-5}} = \dfrac{3+\sqrt{5}}{2}$

$\therefore$ $2\cot\dfrac{\theta}{2} = 2\times\dfrac{3+\sqrt{5}}{2} = 3+\sqrt{5}$

Hence, the value of $2\cot\left(\dfrac{1}{2}\cos^{-1}\dfrac{\sqrt{5}}{3}\right) = 3+\sqrt{5}$.

27. (A): $\because$ $\sec^{-1}p - \operatorname{cosec}^{-1}q = 0$

$\Rightarrow$ $\sec^{-1}p = \operatorname{cosec}^{-1}q$

$\Rightarrow$ $\cos^{-1}\dfrac{1}{p} = \sin^{-1}\dfrac{1}{q}$

Now, Let $\cos^{-1}\dfrac{1}{p} = \theta$

$\therefore$ $\cos\theta = \dfrac{1}{p}$

$\cos^2\theta = \dfrac{1}{p^2}$

$\sin^{-1}\dfrac{1}{q} = \theta$

$\Rightarrow$ $\sin\theta = \dfrac{1}{q}$

$\Rightarrow$ $\sin^2\theta = \dfrac{1}{q^2}$

$\sin^2\theta + \cos^2\theta = \dfrac{1}{p^2}+\dfrac{1}{q^2} = p^{-2}+q^{-2}$

$\Rightarrow$ $p^{-2} + q^{-2} = 1$

28. (A): Let $\cos^{-1}\left(\dfrac{3}{\sqrt{17}}\right) = \theta$

$\therefore$ $\cos\theta = \dfrac{3}{\sqrt{17}}$

$\cos^2\theta = \dfrac{9}{17}$

$\sin^2\theta = 1-\cos^2\theta = 1-\dfrac{9}{17} = \dfrac{8}{17}$

$\therefore \quad 1 + \sin^2\theta = 1 + \frac{8}{17} = \frac{25}{17}$

$\therefore$ Value of $1 + \sin^2\left\{\cos^{-1}\left(\frac{3}{\sqrt{17}}\right)\right\} = \frac{25}{17}$

29. (C): $\tan(\pi\cos\theta) = \cot(\pi \sin \theta)$

$$\frac{\sin(\pi\cos\theta)}{\cos(\pi\cos\theta)} = \frac{\cos(\pi.\sin\theta)}{\sin(\pi.\sin\theta)}$$

$$\cos(\pi.\cos\theta).\cos(\pi.\sin\theta) - \sin(\pi.\cos\theta).\sin(\pi.\sin\theta) = 0$$

$$\cos[\pi(\cos\theta + \sin\theta)] = \cos\frac{\pi}{2}$$

$$\pi[\cos\theta + \sin\theta] = \frac{\pi}{2}$$

$$\sin\theta + \cos\theta = \frac{\pi}{2}$$

$$\frac{1}{\sqrt{2}}.\sin\theta + \frac{1}{\sqrt{2}}\cos\theta = \frac{1}{2\sqrt{2}}$$

$$\sin\left(\theta + \frac{\pi}{4}\right) = \frac{1}{2\sqrt{2}}$$

$$8\sin^2\left(\theta + \frac{\pi}{4}\right) = 1$$

30. (C): $\tan\alpha = \frac{1}{7} \Rightarrow \sin\alpha = \frac{1}{5\sqrt{2}}$ and $\cos\alpha = \frac{7}{5\sqrt{2}}$

$$\sin\beta = \frac{1}{\sqrt{10}} \Rightarrow \cos\beta = \sqrt{1 - \frac{1}{10}} = \frac{3}{\sqrt{10}}$$

$$\sin2\beta = 2.\sin\beta.\cos\beta = 2\cdot\frac{1}{\sqrt{10}}\cdot\frac{3}{\sqrt{10}} = \frac{3}{5}$$

$$\cos2\beta = 1.2\sin^2\beta = 1 - 2\times\frac{1}{10} = \frac{4}{5}$$

Now, $\cos(\alpha + 2\beta) = \cos\alpha.\cos2\beta - \sin\alpha.\sin2\beta$

$$= \frac{7}{5\sqrt{2}}\cdot\frac{4}{5} - \frac{1}{5\sqrt{2}}\cdot\frac{3}{5}$$

$$= \frac{28-3}{5\times5\sqrt{2}} = \frac{1}{\sqrt{2}}$$

For Q. No. 31-32

$(1 - x)^4 + (5 - x)^4 = 82$

$\Rightarrow 1^4 - 4.1^3.x + 6.1^2.x^2 - 4.1.x^3 + x^4 + 5^4 - 4.5^3.x + 6.5^2.x^2 - 4.5.x^3 + x^4 = 82$

$\Rightarrow 2x^4 - 24x^3 + 156x^2 - 504x + 626 - 82 = 0$

$\Rightarrow 2x^4 - 24x^3 + 156x^2 - 504x + 544 = 0$

$\Rightarrow x^4 - 12x^3 + 78x^2 - 252x + 272 = 0$

$\Rightarrow x^3(x - 2) - 10x^2(x - 2) + 58x(x - 2) - 136(x - 2) = 0$

$\Rightarrow (x - 2)(x^3 - 10x^2 + 58x - 136) = 0$

$\Rightarrow (x - 2)\{x^2(x - 4) - 6x(x - 4) + 34(x - 4)\} = 0$

$\Rightarrow (x - 2)(x - 4)(x^2 - 6x + 34) = 0$

$D = b^2 - 4ac = 36 - 4 \times 1 \times 34$

$= 36 - 136 = -100 < 0$

[not real root root sare $3 + 5i$, $3 - 5i$]

Hence, real roots are 2 and 4.

31. (B): The number of real roots of the equation = 2.

32. (B): Sum of all the roots of the equation is $2 + 4 + 3 + 5i + 3 - 5i = 12$.

For Q. No. 33-35

Equation I: $\because z^3 + 2z^2 + 2z + 1 = 0$

Put $z = -1$

$-1 + 2(-1)^2 + 2(-1) + 1 = -1 + 2 - 2 + 1 = 0$

$\therefore (z + 1)$ is a factor of $z^3 + 2z^2 + 2z + 1$

$\therefore z^2(z + 1) + z(z + 1) + 1(z + 1) = 0$

$\Rightarrow (z + 1)(z^2 + z + 1) = 0$

Either $(z + 1) = 0$ or $z^2 + z + 1 = 0$

$D = b^2 - 4ac = (1)^2 - 4 \times 1 \times 1$

$= 1 - 4 = -3 = 3i^2$

$\therefore \quad z = \frac{-b \pm \sqrt{D}}{2a} = -\frac{1 \pm \sqrt{3}i}{2}$

$\therefore \quad \frac{-1, +\sqrt{3}i}{2}, \frac{-1-\sqrt{3}i}{2}$

$\therefore$ Roots are $-1, \omega, \omega^2$

Equation II: $z^{1985} + z^{100} + 1 = 0$

Put, $z = -1$ then $(-1)^{1985} + (-1)^{100} + 1 \neq 0$

$\Rightarrow -1 + 1 + 1 \neq 0$

Hence, $z = -1$ does not satisfy $z^{1985} + z^{100} + 1 = 0$

while $z = \omega, \omega^2$ satisfy it.

33. (B): Clearly, roots of equation I are $-1, \omega, \omega^2$

34. (D): Clearly, root of equation II is ω.

35. (C): Hence, the number of common roots of equation I and equation II = 2.

36. (B): When $k = \frac{c}{2}$, then given equation is

$$(a+b)x^2 - (a+b+c)x + \frac{c}{2} = 0$$

Discriminent $D = \{-(a+b+c)\}^2 - 4\cdot(a+b)\cdot\frac{c}{2}$

$= (a + b + c)^2 - 2c(a + b)$

$= a^2 + b^2 + c^2 + 2ab + 2bc + 2ac - 2ac - 2bc$

$= (a + b)^2 + c^2 > 0$

$\therefore$ Roots are real and unequal.

37. (C): $(a+b)x^2 - (a+b+c)x + c = 0 \quad [\because k = c]$

Discriminent $D = \{-(a+b+c)\}^2 - 4(a+b).c$

$$= a^2 + b^2 + c^2 + 2ab + 2bc + 2ca - 4ac - 4bc$$
$$= a^2 + b^2 + c^2 + 2ab - 2bc - 2ac$$
$$= (a+b-c)^2 > 0$$

Roots are real and unequal

and roots are $\dfrac{-\{-(a+b+c)\} \pm \sqrt{(a+b-c)^2}}{2(a+b)}$

$$= \frac{a+b+c \pm (a+b-c)}{2(a+b)}$$
$$= \frac{2(a+b)}{2(a+b)} \text{ and } \frac{2c}{2(a+b)}$$
$$= 1 \text{ and } \frac{c}{1+b}$$

38. (D): From question, we have

$(1+x)^n = t_0 + t_1.x + t_2.x^2 + t_3.x^3 + \ldots + t_n.x^n$

Differentiating both sides w.r.t. x, we get

$n(1+x)^{n-1} = t_1 + 2t_2.x + 3t_3.x^2 + \ldots + n.t_n.x^{n-1}$

Putting $x = 1$, we get

$n(1+1)^{n-1} = t_1 + 2t_2 + 3t_3 + \ldots + nt_n$

$\therefore$ Required answer $= n(2)^{n-1}$.

39. (D): From above solution,

$t_1 + 2t_2.x + 3t_3.x^2 + \ldots + nt_n.x^{n-1}.n(1+x)^{n-1}$

Putting $x = -1$

$t_1 - 2t_2 + 3t_3 + \ldots + (-1)^{n-1}.t_n = n(1-1)^{n-1}$

$\therefore t_1 - 2t_2 + 3t_3 \ldots (-1)^{n-1}.nt_n = 0$

Hence, $1 - t_1 + 2t_2 - 3t_3 + \ldots + (-1)^{n-1}.nt_n = 1$

40. (B): $1 + t_1.x + t_2.x^2 + t_3.x^3 + \ldots + t_n.x^n = (1+x)^n$

Putting, $x = 1$

$$1 + t_1 + t_2 + t_3 + \ldots + t_n = (1+1)^n$$
$$t_1 + t_2 + t_3 + \ldots + t_n = 2^n - 1$$

41. (B): Given $f(x) = x^2 - 1$ and $gof(x) = x - \sqrt{x} + 1$

Now, $g(x^2 - 1) = x^2 - 1 - \sqrt{x^2 - 1} + 1$

Putting $x^2 - 1 = t \Rightarrow x = \sqrt{t+1}$

$\therefore \quad g(t) = t - \sqrt{t} + 1$

$\Rightarrow \quad g(x) = \sqrt{x+1} - \sqrt[4]{x+1} + 1$

42. (C): $\because g(x) = \sqrt{x+1} - \sqrt[4]{x+1} + 1$

$\therefore \quad g(15) = \sqrt{15+1} - \sqrt[4]{15+1} + 1$

$$= 4 - 2 + 1 = 3$$

43. (B): $2f(x) + f\left(\dfrac{1}{x}\right) = x + 3 \quad \ldots(i)$

Putting $x = \dfrac{1}{x}$; $2f\left(\dfrac{1}{x}\right) + f(x) = \dfrac{1}{x} + 3 \quad \ldots(ii)$

From (*i*) and (*ii*) we get

$$3f(x) = 2x - \frac{1}{x} + 3$$
$$f(x) = \frac{2}{3}x - \frac{1}{3x} + 1$$
$$f(0.5) = \frac{2}{3}(0.5) - \frac{1}{3(0.5)} + 1$$
$$= \frac{2}{3} \times \frac{1}{2} - \frac{2}{3} + 1$$
$$= \frac{1-2+3}{3} = \frac{2}{3}$$

44. (C): $2f(x) + f\left(\dfrac{1}{x}\right) = x + 3$

Differentiating w.r.t. x, we get

$$2f'(x) + f'\left(\frac{1}{x}\right)\cdot\left(-\frac{1}{x^2}\right) = 1$$

Putting $x = 2$ and $x = \dfrac{1}{2}$, we get two equation

$$2f'(2) + f'\left(\frac{1}{2}\right)\left(-\frac{1}{4}\right) = 1 \quad \ldots(i)$$
$$2f'\left(\frac{1}{2}\right) + f'(2)(-4) = 1 \quad \ldots(ii)$$

on solving, we get $f'\left(\dfrac{1}{2}\right) = 2.$

45. (A): $f(x) = \begin{vmatrix} x+1 & 2 & 3 \\ 2 & x+4 & 6 \\ 3 & 6 & x+9 \end{vmatrix}$

$$= (x+1)\{(x+4)(x+9) - 6 \times 6\} + 2(6 \times 3 - 2(x+9)) + 3(2 \times 6 - 3(x+4))$$
$$= (x+1)\{x^2 + 13x + 36 - 36\} + 2\{18 - 12x - 18\} + 3\{12 - 3x - 12\}$$
$$= x^3 + 14x^2$$
$$f'(x) = 3x^2 + 28x$$

when $f'(x) = 0;\ 3x^2 + 28x = 0$

$\Rightarrow \quad x = 0$ and $-\frac{28}{3}$

and $\quad f''(x) = 6x + 28$

$f''(0) = 6(0) + 28 = 28 > 0$

and $\quad f''\left(-\frac{28}{3}\right) = 6\left(-\frac{28}{3}\right) + 28 = -28 < 0$

$\therefore$ Function is decreasing in $\left[-\frac{28}{3}, 0\right]$

46. (C): For local minimum $f'(x) = 0$

$3x^2 + 28x = 0 \Rightarrow x = 0$ and $-\frac{28}{3}$

$f''(x) = 6x + 28$

$f''(0) = 28 > 0$ and $f''\left(-\frac{28}{3}\right) = -28 < 0$

$\therefore$ $f(x)$ has local minimum at $x = 0$

47. (B): $4x^2 + y^2 = 9$

$y = \sqrt{9 - 4x^2}$

For max. value $x = 0$

$y = \pm\sqrt{9 - 4(0)} = \pm 3$

$\therefore \quad y_{max} = 3$

48. (A): $\quad x.y = x\sqrt{9 - 4x^2}$

$\therefore$ Maximum value of xy is $\frac{9}{4}$

49. (B): Given function, $f(x) = \pi + \sin^2(x)$

As $\quad 0 \le \sin^2(x) \le 1$

$\therefore \quad \pi \le \pi + \sin^2(x) \le 1 + \pi$

Hence, Range = $[\pi, \pi + 1]$

50. (B): Period of the function $\sin^2(x)$ is π

$\therefore$ Period of $\pi + \sin^2(x) = \pi$

Sol. (51 & 52):

$$\frac{dy}{dx} = \frac{2y}{x}$$

$$\int \frac{dy}{y} = 2\int \frac{dx}{x}$$

$lny = 2lnx + lnc$ where lnc = const.

$\Rightarrow \quad lny = lnx^2.c$

$y = x^2.c$

As this passes through (1, 2)

$\therefore \quad 2 = (1)^2.c \Rightarrow c = 2$

Hence, parabola : $y = 2x^2$.

51. (A): $x^2 = \frac{y}{2} \Rightarrow x^2 = 4\cdot\frac{1}{8}\cdot y$

Directrix $= -\frac{1}{8}$

52. (B): Length of latus rectum $= 4\times\frac{1}{8} = \frac{1}{2}$.

53. (B): $\lim_{x\to1} \frac{f(x)-1}{g(x)} = \lim_{x\to1} \frac{\frac{a^{x-1}+b^{x-1}}{2} - 1}{x-1}$

$$= \lim_{x\to1} \frac{a^{x-1}+b^{x-1}-2}{2(x-1)}$$

$$= \lim_{x\to1}\left(\frac{a^{x-1}-1}{2(x-1)} + \frac{b^{x-1}-1}{2(x-1)}\right)$$

$$= \frac{1}{2}\ln(a) + \frac{1}{2}\ln(b)$$

$$= \frac{1}{2}\ln(ab)$$

54. (A): Since, $\lim_{x\to1} f(x)^{\frac{1}{2(x)}}$

$$\lim_{x\to1}\left(\frac{a^{x-1}+b^{x-1}}{2}\right)^{\frac{1}{x-1}}$$

This is in the form of 1^∞

$$= e^{\lim_{x\to1}\left(\frac{a^{x-1}+b^{x-1}}{2}-1\right)\frac{1}{x-1}}$$

$$= e^{\lim_{x\to1}\left(\frac{a^{x-1}}{2(x-1)} + \frac{b^{x-1}}{2(x-1)} - 1\right)}$$

$$= e^{\left(\frac{1}{2}\ln a + \frac{1}{2}\ln b\right)} = e^{\ln(\sqrt{ab})} = \sqrt{ab}$$

55. (B): $\because f(x) = \sqrt{2-x} + \sqrt{2+x}$

For domain $2 - x \ge 0$ and $2 + x \ge 0$

$x \le 2$ and $x \ge -2$

$\therefore \quad -2 \le x \le 2$

Domain = $[-2, 2]$

56. (C): $\quad f(x) = \sqrt{2-x} + \sqrt{2+x}$

$$f'(x) = \frac{-1}{2\sqrt{2-x}} + \frac{1}{2\sqrt{2+x}} = 0$$

$\Rightarrow \quad x = 0$

$\therefore$ Maximum value is

$$f(0) = \sqrt{2}+\sqrt{2} = 2\sqrt{2} = \sqrt{8}$$

57. (B): $h(x) = \dfrac{f(g(x))}{g(f(x))} = \dfrac{|[x]-1|}{[|x|]-1}$

$$\lim_{x\to 0^+} h(x) = \lim_{h\to 0} h(0+h)$$

$$\lim_{h\to 0}\frac{|[0+h]-1|}{[|0+h|-1]} = \frac{|0-1|}{0-1} = -1$$

58. (A): $\lim_{x\to 0^-} h(x) = \lim_{h\to 0} h(0-h)$

$$= \lim_{h\to 0}\frac{|[0-h]-1|}{[|0-h|-1]}$$

$$= \frac{|-1-1|}{0-1} = -2$$

For Q. No. 59 & 60

We have, $\lim_{x\to -3} = \lim_{x\to 0} f(3-h)$

$$= \lim_{x\to 0}\frac{3-h-3}{|3-h-3|}+a$$

$$= \lim -\frac{h}{h}+a = a-1$$

$$\lim_{x\to 3^+} f(x) = \lim_{h\to 0}\frac{3+h-3}{|3+h-3|}+b = b+1$$

and $f(3) = a - b$

Since, $f(x)$ is continuous at $x = 3$

Therefore, $a - 1 = a - b = b + 1$

$\because$ $a - 1 = a - b$

$\Rightarrow$ $a - a - 1 = -b \Rightarrow b = 1$

$\because$ $a - 1 = b + 1$

$\Rightarrow$ $a - b = 1 + 1 = 2$

$\because$ $a - 1 = b + 1$

$\Rightarrow$ $a - 1 = 1 + 1$

$\Rightarrow$ $a = 1 + 1 + 1 = 3$

59. (D): The value of $a = 3$.

60. (B): The value of $b = 1$.

61. (B): $\because \int_0^{\pi}(\sin^4(x)+\cos^4 x).dx$

$$= \int_0^{\pi}\left[\left(\sin^2 x+\cos^2 x\right)^2 - 2\sin^2 x.\cos^2 x\right].dx$$

$$= \int_0^{\pi}\left[1-\frac{\sin^2 2x}{2}\right]dx = \int_0^{\pi}\left(1-\frac{1-\cos 4x}{4}\right).dx$$

$$= \frac{1}{4}\int_0^{\pi}(3+\cos 4x).dx = \frac{1}{4}\left(3x+\frac{\sin 4x}{4}\right)_0^{\pi} = \frac{3\pi}{4}$$

62. (C): $\because$ $I = \int_{-2\pi}^{2\pi}\dfrac{\sin^4 x+\cos^4 x}{1+3^x}.dx$ ...(*i*)

$$= \int_{-2\pi}^{2\pi}\frac{\sin^4(-x)+\cos^4(-x)}{1+3^x}.dx$$

$I = \int_{-2\pi}^{2\pi}\dfrac{3^x\left(\sin^4(x)+\cos^4(x)\right)}{1+3^x}.dx$ ...(*ii*)

Adding (*i*) and (*ii*), we get

$$2I = \int_{-2\pi}^{2\pi}\left(\sin^4 x+\cos^4 x\right).dx$$

$$2I = \frac{1}{4}\left(3x+\frac{\sin^4 x}{4}\right)_{-2\pi}^{2\pi}$$

$$= \frac{1}{4}[3(2\pi-(-2\pi))]$$

$$\therefore \quad I = \frac{3\pi}{2}$$

63. (A): We have $f(x) = \begin{cases} ax(x+1)+b; & x<1 \\ x-1 & ; \ 1\le x\le 2\end{cases}$

Since, $f(x)$ is differentiable at $x = 1$.

$$f'(x) = \begin{cases} a(2x+1); & x<1 \\ 1 & ; \ 1\le x\le 2\end{cases}$$

$$a(3) = 1 \Rightarrow a = \frac{1}{3}$$

As, $f(x)$ is continuous at $x = 1$,

$$2a + b = 0 \Rightarrow b = -\frac{2}{3}$$

$$\therefore \quad a + b = \frac{1}{3}-\frac{2}{3} = \frac{-1}{3}$$

64. (B): $\lim_{x\to 0} f(x) = \lim_{x\to 0} ax(x+1)+b = b = -\dfrac{2}{3}$

$$\therefore \quad b = -\frac{2}{3}$$

65. (A): $f(x) = |\ln|x||;\ 0 < x < 1$

$f(x) = -\ln x$

Now, $f'(x) = -\dfrac{1}{x} \Rightarrow f'(0.5) = -2$

66. (C): $y = f\left(\dfrac{2x-3}{x}\right)$

$$\frac{dy}{dx} = f'\left(\frac{2x-3}{x}\right).\frac{2x-(2x-3)}{x^2}$$

$$= \cos\left(\ln\left(\frac{2x-3}{x}\right)\right)\cdot\frac{(2x-2x+3)}{x^2}$$

$$= \frac{3}{x^2}\cos\left(\ln\left(\frac{2x-3}{x}\right)\right)$$

67. (D): $\int_0^{8\pi}|\sin x|dx = 8\int_0^{\pi}\sin x\,dx = 8 \times 2 = 16$

68. (A):

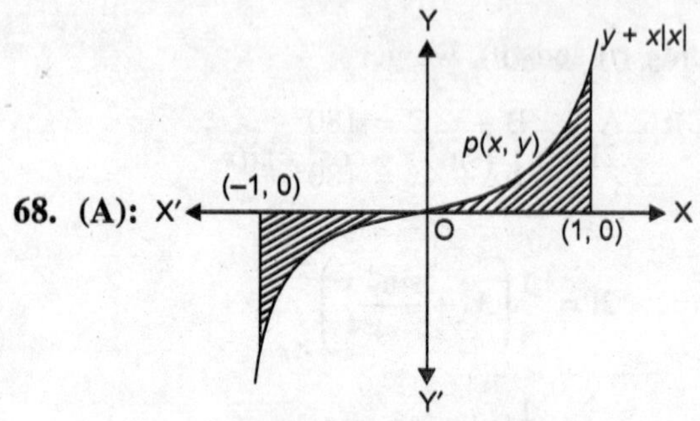

$$\text{Required area} = \left|\int_{-1}^{1} x|x|dx\right|$$

$$= \left|\int_{-1}^{0} x|x|dx\right| + \int_0^1 x|x|dx$$

$$= \left|\int_{-1}^{0} -x^2dx\right| + \int_0^1 x^2dx$$

$$= \left|\left[-\frac{x^3}{3}\right]_{-1}^{0}\right| - \left[\frac{x^3}{3}\right]_0^1$$

$$= \frac{1}{3}+\frac{1}{3}=\frac{2}{3}$$

69. (D): $x^2\left(\frac{d^3y}{dx^3}\right)^2+\left(\frac{dy}{dx}\right)^4+\sin x=0$

The order of highest order derivative is 3. So it is a differential equation of order 3.

In this equation the power of highest order derivative is 2. So, it is a differential equation of degree 2.

70. (D): $y^2 = 4a(x - b)$

$$2y\cdot\frac{dy}{dx} = 4a \Rightarrow y\cdot\frac{dy}{dx}=2a$$

Again, differentiating w.r.t. x, we get

$$\frac{dy}{dx}\cdot\frac{dy}{dx}+y\cdot\frac{d^2y}{dx^2} = 0$$

$$y\cdot\frac{d^2y}{dx^2}+\left(\frac{dy}{dx}\right)^2 = 0$$

For Q. No. 71 & 70

We have, $a_1, a_2, a_3, a_4, \ldots$ are in AP.

$a_1 + a_5 + a_{10} + a_{15} + a_{20} + a_{25} + a_{30} + a_{34} = 300$

$(a_1 + a_{34}) + (a_5 + a_{30}) + (a_{10} + a_{25}) + (a_{15} + a_{20}) = 300$

$\Rightarrow \quad 4(a_1 + a_{34}) = 300$

$\Rightarrow \quad a_1 + a_{34} = \frac{300}{4} = 75$

71. (A): Now, $a_1 + a_5 - a_{10} - a_{15} - a_{20} - a_{25} + a_{30} + a_{34}$

$= (a_1 + a_{34}) + (a_5 + a_{30}) - (a_{10} + a_{25}) - (a_{15} + a_{25})$

$= 75 + 75 - 75 - 75$

$= 150 - 150 = 0$

72. (D): $\sum_{n=1}^{34} a_n = a_1 + a_2 + a_3 + \ldots + a_{34}$

$$S_n = \frac{n}{2}\{a_1 + a_{34}\}$$

$$= \frac{34}{2}\times 75$$

$$= 17 \times 75$$

$$= 1275$$

For Q. No. 73 & 74

$$p = \cos\left(\frac{\pi}{5}\right).\cos\left(\frac{2\pi}{5}\right),$$

$$q = \cos\left(\frac{4\pi}{5}\right).\cos\left(\frac{8\pi}{5}\right)$$

$\because \quad p = \cos 36° \times \cos 72° = \frac{1}{4}$

$q = \cos 144° \times \cos 288° = -\frac{1}{4}$

$= -\cos 36° \times \cos 72° = -\frac{1}{4}$

$[\because \cos 144° = \cos(180° - 36°) = -\cos 36°$

$\cos 288° = \cos(360 - 72° = \cos 72°]$

73. (C): Value of $p + d = \frac{1}{4}-\frac{1}{4}=0$

74. (A): The value of $p \times d = \cos 36° \times \cos 72° \times (-\cos 36° \times \cos 72°)$

$$= \frac{1}{4}\times\left(-\frac{1}{4}\right)=-\frac{1}{16}$$

75. (D): $\because \; p = \frac{1}{3}-\frac{\tan 3x}{\tan x}$

$q = 1 - 3\tan^2 x$

$$pq = \left(\frac{1}{3} - \frac{\tan 3x}{\tan x}\right)(1 - 3\tan^2 x)$$

$$= \frac{1}{3} - \tan^2 x - \frac{\tan 3x}{\tan x} + 3\frac{\tan^2 x}{\tan x} \times \tan 3x$$

$$= \frac{1}{3} - \tan^2 x - \frac{\tan 3x}{\tan x} + 3\tan x \times \tan 3x$$

$$= \frac{1}{3} - \tan^2 45° - \frac{\tan 135°}{\tan 45°} + 3\tan 45° \times \tan 135°$$

$$= \frac{1}{3} - 1 - \left(\frac{-1}{1}\right) + 3 \times 1 \times (-1)$$

$$= \frac{1}{3} - 1 + 1 - 3$$

$$= \frac{1}{3} - 3 = \frac{1-9}{3} = -\frac{8}{3}$$

76. (C): $\because \quad \frac{1}{p} = 0$

$$\Rightarrow \quad \frac{3(1-3\tan^2 x)}{-8} = 0$$

$$\Rightarrow \quad \tan x = \pm\frac{1}{\sqrt{3}}$$

Hence, x have two values.

For Q. No. 77 & 78

$$\frac{\sin x + \sin y}{\cos y - \cos x} = \sqrt{3}$$

$$\Rightarrow \quad \frac{2\sin\frac{x+y}{2} \times \cos\frac{x-y}{2}}{2\sin\frac{y+x}{2} \times \sin\frac{x-y}{2}} = \sqrt{3}$$

$$\Rightarrow \quad \cot\left(\frac{x-y}{2}\right) = \sqrt{3} = \cot 30°$$

$$\Rightarrow \quad \frac{x-y}{2} = 30°$$

$$\Rightarrow \quad x - y = 60°$$

$$x + y = 90° \text{ (given)}$$

$$2x = 150°$$

$$\Rightarrow \quad x = 75°$$

$$y = 90° - 75° = 15°$$

77. (B): $\sin 3x + \sin 3y = \sin 3 \times 75° + \sin 3 \times 15°$

$$= \sin 225° + \sin 45°$$

$$= \sin(180° + 45°) + \sin 45°$$

$$= -\sin 45° + \sin 45° = 0$$

78. (B): $\cos^3 x + \cos^3 y = \cos^3 75° + \cos^3 15°$

$$= \left(\frac{\sqrt{3}-1}{2\sqrt{2}}\right)^3 + \left(\frac{\sqrt{3}+1}{2\sqrt{2}}\right)^3$$

$$= \frac{6\sqrt{3} - 10 + 6\sqrt{3} + 10}{16\sqrt{2}}$$

$$= \frac{12\sqrt{3}}{16\sqrt{2}} \times \frac{\sqrt{2}}{\sqrt{2}} = \frac{12\sqrt{6}}{32} = \frac{3\sqrt{6}}{8}$$

For Q. No. 79 & 80

79. (C): $\angle A + \angle B + \angle C = 180°$

$$3x + 5x + 4x = 180°$$

$$\Rightarrow \quad 12x = 180°$$

$$\Rightarrow \quad x = 15°$$

$$\angle A = 45°, \angle B = 75°, \angle C = 60°$$

Value of $a + b + c\sqrt{2}$

Now, $\quad a + c\sqrt{2} = k\left[\sin A + \sqrt{2}\sin C\right]$

$$= k\left[\sin 45° + \sqrt{2}\sin 60°\right]$$

$$= k\left(\frac{\sqrt{3}+1}{\sqrt{2}}\right) \quad \text{...}(i)$$

$$b = k\sin B$$

$$\Rightarrow \quad b = k\sin 75° = k\left(\frac{\sqrt{3}+1}{2\sqrt{2}}\right)$$

$$\Rightarrow \quad 2b = k\left(\frac{\sqrt{3}+1}{\sqrt{2}}\right) \quad \text{...}(ii)$$

From (*i*) and (*ii*), $a + c\sqrt{2} = 2b$

$\therefore$ Value of $a + b + c\sqrt{2} = 2b + b = 3b$

80. (A): $a^2 : b^2 : c^2 = (\sin 45)^2 : \sin^2 75° : \sin^2 60°$

$$= \left(\frac{1}{\sqrt{2}}\right)^2 : \left(\frac{\sqrt{3}+1}{2\sqrt{2}}\right)^2 : \left(\frac{\sqrt{3}}{2}\right)^2$$

$$= \frac{1}{2} : \frac{4+2\sqrt{3}}{8} : \frac{3}{4}$$

$$= \frac{1}{2} : \frac{2(2+\sqrt{3})}{8} : \frac{3}{4}$$

$$= \frac{1}{2} : \frac{2+\sqrt{3}}{4} : \frac{3}{4}$$

$$= 2 : 2+\sqrt{3} : 3$$

81. (A): $b^2 + b - 2 = 0$

$(b-1)(b+2) = 0$

$\Rightarrow \quad b = 1$ and -2

Now, as $b \nless 0 \therefore b = 1$

So, equation of parabola : $y^2 = 4bx = 4x$

Hence, equation of directrix : $x = -1$

$x + 1 = 0$

82. (D): Area of region formed by three given points (0, 0), $(-a, -b)$ and (a, b)

$$= \begin{vmatrix} 0 & 0 & 1 \\ a & b & 1 \\ -a & -b & 1 \end{vmatrix} = 1(-ab + ab) = 0$$

and by point (0, 0), (a, b) and (a^2, ab)

$$= \begin{vmatrix} 0 & 0 & 1 \\ a & b & 1 \\ a^2 & ab & 1 \end{vmatrix} = 1(a^2b - a^2b) = 0$$

Hence, given 4 points are collinear.

83. (B): Given equation : $16p^2 + 44q^2 - 4r^2 - 56pq = 0$

$(4p)^2 + (7q)^2 - 2.(4p).(7q) = 4r^2$

$(4p - 7q)^2 = 4r^2$

$4p - 7q = \pm 2r$

$$\left(2p - \frac{7}{2}q + r\right)\left(2p - \frac{7}{2}q - r\right) = 0$$

$\therefore \quad p = 2$ and $q = -\dfrac{7}{2}$

84. (B): Given circle : $x^2 + y^2 - 25 = 0$

$x^2 + (5 - 3x)^2 - 25 = 0 \quad [\because 3x + y - 5 = 0]$

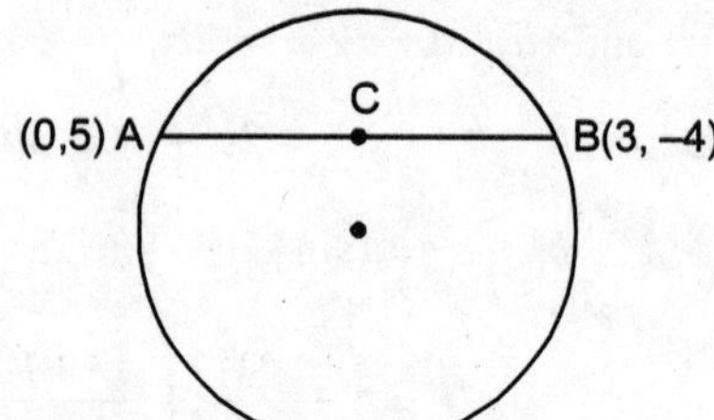

$x^2 + 25 + 9x^2 - 30x - 25 = 0$

$10x^2 - 30x = 0$

$x = 0, 3$ and $y = 5, -4$

$\therefore$ Mid-point C $= \left(\dfrac{0+3}{2}, \dfrac{5-4}{2}\right) = \left(\dfrac{3}{2}, \dfrac{1}{2}\right)$

85. (C): Given equation: $\dfrac{x^2}{24-k} + \dfrac{y^2}{k-16} = 2$

(*i*) For $k = 12$ in above equation, we get

$$\frac{x^2}{24-12} + \frac{y^2}{12-16} = 2$$

$\Rightarrow \quad \dfrac{x^2}{12} - \dfrac{y^2}{4} = 2$ [Hyperbola]

(*ii*) For $k \pm 19$, $\dfrac{x^2}{24-19} + \dfrac{y^2}{19-16} = 2$

$\Rightarrow \quad \dfrac{x^2}{5} + \dfrac{y^2}{3} = 2$ [Ellipse]

(*iii*) For $k = 20$, $\dfrac{x^2}{24-20} + \dfrac{y^2}{20-16} = 2$

$\Rightarrow \quad \dfrac{x^2}{4} + \dfrac{y^2}{4} = 8$ [Circle]

86. (C): Hyperbola : $\dfrac{x^2}{\cos^2\theta} - \dfrac{y^2}{\sin^2\theta} = 1$

From $C^2 = a^2 + b^2 = \cos^2\theta + \sin^2\theta = 1$

$\Rightarrow \quad (ae)^2 = 1$

$$e^2 = \frac{1}{a^2} = \frac{1}{\cos^2\theta} = \sec^2\theta$$

$\Rightarrow \quad e = \sec\theta$

$\therefore$ Distance between two foci = 1 + 1 = 2.

87. (B): Circle : $4x^2 + 4y^2 - 4ax - 4ay + a^2 = 0$

$$x^2 + y^2 + \frac{a^2}{4} - ax - ay = 0$$

$$\text{Centre} = \left(\frac{a}{2}, \frac{a}{2}\right)$$

$$\text{Radius} = \sqrt{\left(\frac{a}{2}\right)^2 + \left(\frac{a}{2}\right)^2 - \frac{a^2}{4}} = \frac{a}{2}$$

$\therefore$ Circle touches both the axes.

So, statement (1) is correct.

Diameter of the circle $= 2d = 2 \times \dfrac{a}{2} = a$

Statement (2) is wrong.

Again, $\quad x + y = a$

$\Rightarrow \quad \dfrac{a}{2} + \dfrac{a}{2} = a \Rightarrow a = a$

Hence, statement (3) is correct.

88. (B): $(k-3)x - (5-k^2)y + k^2 - 7k + 6 = 0$

$\Rightarrow (k-3)x - (5-k^2)y = -k^2 + 7k - 6$

and $\quad x + y = 1$

For parallel lines

$$\because \quad \frac{a_1}{a_2} = \frac{b_1}{b_2} \neq \frac{c_1}{c_2}$$

$\therefore \quad \frac{k-3}{1} = -\frac{(5-k^2)}{1}$

$\Rightarrow \quad k - 3 = -5 + k^2$

$\Rightarrow \quad k^2 - k - 2 = 0$

$\Rightarrow \quad k^2 - 2k + k - 2 = 0$

$\Rightarrow \quad k(k-2) + 1(k-2) = 0$

$\Rightarrow \quad (k+1)(k-2) = 0$

$\Rightarrow \quad k + 1 = 0 \text{ or } k - 2 = 0$

$\Rightarrow \quad k = -1 \text{ or } k = 2$

Hence, the value of $k = -1, 2$.

89. (B): P (−1, 1) —— R (x, y) —— Q (5, 7), with PR : RQ = k : 1

$$x = \frac{k(5)+1(-1)}{k+1} = \frac{5k-1}{k+1} \quad ...(i)$$

$$y = \frac{k(7)+1(1)}{k+1} = \frac{7k+1}{k+1} \quad ...(ii)$$

$$x + y = \frac{5k-1}{k+1} + \frac{7k+1}{k+1}$$

$\Rightarrow \quad 4 = \frac{5k-1+7k+1}{k+1} = \frac{12k}{k+1}$

$\Rightarrow \quad 12k = 4k + 4$

$\Rightarrow \quad 8k = 4$

$\Rightarrow \quad k = \frac{4}{8} = \frac{1}{2}$

$\therefore \quad \frac{PR}{RQ} = \frac{k}{1} = \frac{1}{2}$

$\therefore$ Required ratio PR : RQ = 1 : 2.

90. (C): x-intercept: OB $= \frac{4}{\cos(15°)}$ and

y-Intercept: OA $= \frac{4}{\cos 75°} = \frac{4}{\sin 15°}$

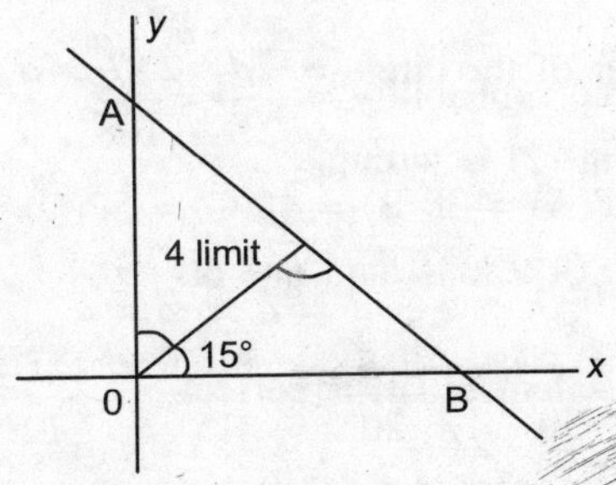

Sum of intercept (OA + OB) $= \frac{4}{\sin 15°} + \frac{4}{\cos 15°}$

$$= \frac{4}{\left(\frac{\sqrt{3}+1}{2\sqrt{2}}\right)} + \frac{4}{\left(\frac{\sqrt{3}-1}{2\sqrt{2}}\right)}$$

$$= \frac{8\sqrt{2}}{(\sqrt{3}+1)} + \frac{8\sqrt{2}}{(\sqrt{3}-1)}$$

$$= \frac{8\sqrt{2}(2\sqrt{3})}{2} = 8\sqrt{6}$$

91. (B): Let, $\vec{a} = \hat{i} + 2\hat{j} + 3\hat{k}$

$\vec{b} = 2\hat{i} + 3\hat{j} - 2\hat{k}$

Then the length of projection of $\vec{a}$ on $\vec{b}$ is equal to

$$\frac{\vec{a}.\vec{b}}{|\vec{b}|} = \frac{2+6-6}{\sqrt{4+9+4}} = \frac{2}{\sqrt{17}}$$

92. (A): We know that $(\vec{a} \times \vec{b})^2 + (\vec{a} \cdot \vec{b})^2 = |\vec{a}|^2 \cdot |\vec{b}|^2$

$\Rightarrow \quad 144 = 16|\vec{a}|^2$

$\Rightarrow \quad |\vec{a}|^2 = 9 \Rightarrow |\vec{a}| = 3$

93. (C): It is given that $\vec{a} \times \vec{b} \geq 0$

$\Rightarrow \quad |\vec{a}||\vec{b}|\cos\theta \geq 0$

$\Rightarrow \quad 0 \leq \theta \leq \frac{\pi}{2}$

94. (C): $\begin{vmatrix} 60 & 3 & 1 \\ 40 & -8 & 1 \\ \beta & -52 & 1 \end{vmatrix} = 0$

$\Rightarrow 60(-8 + 52) - 3(40 - \beta) + 1(-2080 + 8\beta) = 0$

$\Rightarrow 60 \times 44 - 120 + 3\beta - 2080 + 8\beta = 0$

$\Rightarrow 2640 - 120 - 2080 + 11\beta = 0$

$\Rightarrow 2640 - 2200 + 11\beta = 0$

$\Rightarrow \quad 11\beta = -440$

$\Rightarrow \quad \beta = -\frac{440}{11} = -40$

95. (B): $\vec{a} \times \vec{b} = \begin{vmatrix} \hat{i} & \hat{j} & \hat{k} \\ 0 & 1 & 1 \\ 1 & 0 & 1 \end{vmatrix} = \hat{i} + \hat{j} - \hat{k}$

Unit vector $\perp$ to both $\vec{a}$ and $\vec{b}$ $= \frac{\vec{a} \times \vec{b}}{|\vec{a} \times \vec{b}|} = \frac{\hat{i} + \hat{j} - \hat{k}}{\pm\sqrt{3}}$

$\therefore$ Statement (1) is incorrect:

Again, $\cos\theta = \frac{\vec{a} \cdot \vec{b}}{|\vec{a}| \cdot |\vec{b}|} = \frac{0+0+1}{\sqrt{2} \cdot \sqrt{2}} = \frac{1}{2}$

$\Rightarrow \quad \theta = \cos^{-1}\left(\frac{1}{2}\right) = \frac{\pi}{3}$

Hence, statement (2) is correct.

96. (D): We have, $\frac{x-1}{3}=\frac{y+1}{-2}=\frac{z-1}{6}=\lambda$ (suppose)

$\Rightarrow \quad (x, y, z) = (3\lambda + 1, -2\lambda - 1, 6\lambda + 1)$

Now, $\sqrt{(3\lambda+1-1)^2+(-2\lambda-1+1)^2+(6\lambda+1-1)^2}=2$

$\sqrt{9\lambda^2+4\lambda^2+36\lambda^2}=2$

$\Rightarrow \quad \sqrt{49\lambda^2}=2$

$\lambda = \pm\frac{2}{7}$

$\therefore (x, y, z) = \left(\frac{13}{7},\frac{-11}{7},\frac{19}{7}\right)$ or $\left(\frac{1}{7},\frac{-3}{7},\frac{-5}{7}\right)$

97. (D): When a line is parallel to the plane, then

$a_1.a_2 + b_1.b_2 + c_1.c_2 = 0$

From option:

A. $3 \times 2 + 2 \times 4 + 1 \times 5 \neq 0$

B. $2 \times 3 - 1 \times 4 - 2 \times 5 \neq 0$

C. $2 \times 3 + 2 \times 4 - 2 \times 5 \neq 0$

D. $1 \times 3 - 2 \times 4 + 1 \times 5 = 0$

98. (D): Given equation of lines:

$2x = 3y = -z \Rightarrow \frac{x}{3}=\frac{y}{2}=\frac{z}{-6}$

and $\quad 6x = -y = -4z \Rightarrow \frac{x}{2}=\frac{y}{-12}=\frac{z}{-3}$

$\therefore \quad \cos\theta = \frac{6-24+18}{\sqrt{9+4+36}\sqrt{4+144+9}}$

$\therefore \quad \theta = 90°$

99. (D): Given equation of sphere:

$x^2 + y^2 + z^2 - 2x - 6y - 8z - 5 = 0$

As, required sphere passes through origin *i.e.* (0, 0, 0) required sphere: $x^2 + y^2 + z^2 - 2x - 6y - 8z + k = 0$ will satisfy point $(x, y, z) = (0, 0, 0)$

$\therefore \quad k = 0$

Hence, sphere: $x^2 + y^2 + z^2 - 2x - 6y - 8z = 0$

100. (A): A (1, 2, 3) ——— k ——— P $(x, y, 7)$ ——— 1 ——— B (2, 10, 1)

Let point P, divides line AB into ratio $k : 1$

then, $\quad 7 = \frac{k+3}{k+1} \Rightarrow k = -\frac{2}{3}$

$\therefore \quad x = \frac{2\times2-3\times1}{2-3}=-1$

and $\quad y = \frac{2\times10-3\times2}{2-3}=-14$

Hence, $\quad x + y = -1 - 14 = -15.$

101. (A): $\Sigma(x_i - 20) = q$ and $\Sigma(x_i - 10) = p$

$\Rightarrow \quad \Sigma x - 20n = q$ and $\Sigma x - 10n = p$

Now, $(-10n + 20n)^2 = 10000$

$100n^2 = 10000$

$\Rightarrow \quad n = 10$

102. (C): $\frac{x_1+x_2+x_3+...+x_{10}}{10}=20$

$x_1 + x_2 + x_3 + ... + x_{10} = 200$

$\frac{3x_1-4}{5}+\frac{3x_2-4}{5}+...+\frac{3x_{10}-4}{5}$

$=\frac{3x_1-4+3x_2-4+...+3x_{10}-4}{5}$

$=\frac{3}{5}[x_1+x_2+...+x_{10}]-\frac{40}{5}$

$=\frac{3}{5}[200]-8=120-8=112$

Hence, the value of $\sum_{i=1}^{n}\frac{3x_i-4}{5}=112$

103. (D): Standard Deviation $(\sigma) = \sqrt{\frac{\Sigma x^2}{n}-\left(\frac{\Sigma x}{n}\right)^2}$

$\therefore \quad \sigma = \sqrt{\frac{16160}{10}-(40)^2}$

$=\sqrt{1616-1600}$

$=\sqrt{16}=4$

104. (A): Total ways = $6 \times 6 \times 6 = (6)^3 = 216$

$4 + 3 + 2 = 9$ which is perfect square

$6 + 6 + 4 = 16$ which is perfect square

$4 + 4 + 1 = 9$ which is perfect square

Sum $= 9 + 16 + 9 = 34$

Required probability $= \frac{34}{216}=\frac{17}{108}$

105. (D): $2P(A) = 3P(B) = 4P(C) = 5P(D) = k$(Say)

L.C.M. of 2, 3, 4 and 5 = 60

$\therefore \quad \frac{P(A)}{30}=\frac{P(B)}{20}=\frac{P(C)}{15}=\frac{P(D)}{12}=k$

$\Rightarrow P(A) = 30k, P(B) = 20k, P(C) = 15k, P(D) = 12k$

As, A, B, C and D are mutually exclusive

$\therefore \quad P(A) + P(B) + P(C) + P(D) = 1$

$30k + 20k + 15k + 12k = 1$

$77k = 1 \Rightarrow k = \frac{1}{77}$

Now, $77P(A) = 77 \times 30k$

$$= 77 \times 30 \times \frac{1}{77} = 30.$$

106. (C): $n(S) = {}^9C_2 = \frac{9.8}{2.1} = 36$

Product has 1 in its unit place (3, 7), (7, 3)

$\therefore$ $P = \frac{n(E)}{n(S)} = \frac{2}{36} = \frac{1}{18}$

107. (B): Total ways = 6 × 6 = 36

Diff. of 2 = (3, 1), (4, 2), (5, 3), (6, 4), (1, 3), (2, 4), (3, 5), (4, 6) = 8

Diff. of 3 = (4, 1), (5, 2), (6, 3), (1, 4), (2, 5), (3, 6) = 6

Diff. of No. 2 or 3 = 8 + 6 = 14

Required probability $= \frac{14}{36} = \frac{7}{18}$

108. (C):

x	f	fx
1	1	1
2	9	18
3	36	108
4	84	336
5	126	630
6	126	756
7	84	588
8	36	288
9	9	81
10	1	10
	512	2816

Mean $= \frac{2816}{512} = \frac{352}{64} = \frac{44}{8}$

$$= \frac{11}{2} = 5.5$$

Hence, the mean of the numbers 1, 2, 3, ...,10 with frequencies ${}^9C_0, {}^9C_1, {}^9C_2 \ldots, {}^9C_9 = 5.5$.

109. (D): $p = 0.8$ then $q = 1 - p = 1 - 0.8 = 0.2$ and $n = 5$

$$p(x = 2) = {}^5C_2\,(0.8)^2(0.2)^3$$
$$= 0.0512$$

110. (B): $p\left(\frac{E_1}{F}\right) = \frac{p\left(\frac{F}{E_1}\right).p(E_1)}{p\left(\frac{F}{E_1}\right).p(E_1) + p\left(\frac{F}{E_2}\right).p(E_2)}$

$$= \frac{\frac{95}{100} \times \frac{10}{100}}{\frac{95}{100} \times \frac{10}{100} + \frac{45}{100} \times \frac{90}{100}}$$

$$= \frac{950}{950 + 4050}$$

$$= \frac{950}{5000} = 0.19$$

111. (A): $\because$ $r = \frac{\text{cov}(x \cdot y)}{\sqrt{\text{var}(x) \cdot \text{var}(y)}}$

and $\text{cov}(x, y) = \Sigma(x - x').(y - y')$

$\text{cov}(3x + 4, -3y + 3) = \Sigma(3x - 3x')(-3y + 3y')$

$= 9\Sigma(x - x').(-y + y')$

$= -9\text{cov}(x, y)$

$\text{var}(3x + y) = (3)^2.\text{var}(x)$

$\text{var}(-3y + 3) = (-3)^2.\text{var}(y)$

$\therefore$ $r(3x + 4, -3y + 3) = \frac{-9\,\text{cov}(x, y)}{\sqrt{9\,\text{var}(x)}.\sqrt{9\,\text{var}(y)}}$

$$= \frac{-9\,\text{cov}(x, y)}{\sqrt{9\,\text{var}(x)}.\sqrt{\text{var}(y)}}$$

$$= -r$$

112. (C): Here, $P(H) = \frac{1}{2}$ and $P(T) = \frac{1}{2}$

Required probability

P(HHHHHT) + (TTTTTH)

$$= \frac{1}{64} + \frac{1}{64} = \frac{1}{32}$$

113. (C): $H = \frac{3}{\frac{1}{{}^{10}C_4} + \frac{1}{{}^{10}C_5} + \frac{1}{{}^{10}C_6}}$

$$= \frac{3}{\frac{1}{210} + \frac{1}{252} + \frac{1}{210}} = \frac{3}{\frac{6+5+6}{1260}}$$

Now, $H = \frac{3 \times 1260}{17}$

$\therefore$ $\frac{270}{H} = 270 \times \frac{17}{3 \times 1260} = \frac{17}{14}$

114. (B): Total arrangement = $n!$

When P and Q sit together, then

Number of arrangement = $(n - 1)!\ 2!$

$\therefore$ Probability $= \frac{(n-1)!2!}{n!} = \frac{2}{n}$

115. (A): $\because 9p(x = 4) = p(x = 2)$

$$9.{}^6C_4.p^4q^2 = {}^6C_2p^2.q^4$$
$$9p^2 = q^2$$
$$\Rightarrow \quad 3p = q$$
$$\text{As} \quad p + q = 1$$
$$\Rightarrow \quad p + 3p = 1$$
$$\Rightarrow \quad p = \frac{1}{4}$$

116. (A): Total arrangement of 6 persons = 6!

Number of arrangement three boys sit together

$= 4!\ 3!$

$\therefore$ Required probability $= \dfrac{4!3!}{6!} = \dfrac{1}{5}$

117. (B): Number of arrangement when all boys and girls sit alternatively

$= 2!3!3!$

$\therefore$ Required probability $= \dfrac{2!3!3!}{6!} = \dfrac{1}{10}$

118. (D): The probability that no two girls sit together

$$= \frac{4! \times 3!}{6!}$$
$$= \frac{3 \times 2 \times 4!}{6 \times 5 \times 4!} = \frac{1}{5}$$

Hence, required probability $= \dfrac{1}{5}$

119. (A): The probability that P and Q take the two end positions

$$= \frac{2! \times 4!}{6!} \qquad \begin{bmatrix} P & R & S & T & U & Q \\ Q & U & T & S & R & P \end{bmatrix}$$
$$= \frac{2 \times 4!}{6 \times 5 \times 4!} = \frac{1}{15}$$

120. (D): The probability that Q and U sit together

$$= \frac{2! \times 5!}{6!}$$
$$= \frac{2 \times 5!}{6 \times 5!} = \frac{1}{3}$$

Previous Papers (Solved)

NATIONAL DEFENCE ACADEMY & NAVAL ACADEMY

NDA & NA – Entrance Exam, 2023 (I)

PAPER I : GENERAL ABILITY TEST

PART A : ENGLISH LANGUAGE

SPOTTING ERRORS

Directions (Qs. No. 1-10): *Each item in this section has a sentence with three part labelled (A), (B) and (C). Read each sentence to find out whether there is any error in any part. Indicate your response in the Answer Sheet against the corresponding letter i.e., (A) or (B) or (C). If you find no error, your response should be indicated as (D).*

1. (A) Over long periods of time,/ (B) layers of sediments builds up/ (C) to a height of a few kilometers./ (D) No error

2. (A) When a gas is/ (B) cooled down it turns into a liquid/ (C) from a process called condensation./ (D) No error

3. (A) If you want/ (B) to know the news/ (C) you can read a newspaper./ (D) No error

4. (A) Columbus made his/ (B) first voyage from Europe to America/ (C) on 1492./ (D) No error

5. (A) Whenever the sky is/ (B) clear, you can see/ (C) the stars in the night./ (D) No error

6. (A) I'm not working tomorrow,/ (B) so I don't had to/ (C) get up early./ (D) No error

7. (A) She didn't/ (B) tell anybody/ (C) about her plans./ (D) No error

8. (A) She wouldn't have/ (B) has an accident/ (C) if she had driven carefully./ (D) No error

9. (A) I will watch film/ (B) if I finish the work/ (C) in time./ (D) No error

10. (A) In 1989, the government/ (B) did an about-face and Iran restored/ (C) it's family planning program./ (D) No error

SYNONYMS

Directions (Qs. No. 11-20): *Each item in this section consists of a sentence with an underlined word followed by four options, (A), (B), (C) and (D). Select the option that is* ***nearest in meaning*** *to the underlined word and mark your response in your Answer Sheet accordingly.*

11. During the pandemic the <u>indigent</u> people had to suffer a lot.
A. very poor B. opulent
C. solvent D. prosperous

12. She had no idea what made him angry in one minute and <u>jovial</u> the next.
A. aggrieved B. melancholic
C. doleful D. mirthful

13. It is sheer <u>lunacy</u> to drive a car in this frosty weather.
A. prudence B. normalcy
C. insanity D. sanity

14. Operating on a child with cancer needs <u>meticulous</u> planning and teamwork.
A. strong B. long
C. playful D. scrupulous

15. The thrill of over-speeding the vehicle can be <u>exhilarating</u>, but it is important not to take the consequences lightly.
A. humdrum B. dreary
C. exciting D. agitating

16. The <u>redemption</u> will now depend on his new strategy of inclusiveness.
A. retrieval B. forfeiture
C. corporation D. desecration

17. Only three candidates are now in <u>contention</u> for the title.
A. involved in dispute
B. in agreement with each other
C. chance of winning
D. amiable to each other

18. All my fishing <u>paraphernalia</u> is in the car.
A. boxes B. accessories
C. fuel D. food

19. The public watched in <u>astonishment</u> as he took a sudden jump from the bridge.
A. anticipation B. hurriedly
C. wonderment D. calmness

20. Drinking <u>inordinate</u> amount of liquor is not good for health.
A. temperate B. exorbitant
C. moderate D. regular

ORDERING OF WORDS IN A SENTENCE

Directions (Qs. No. 21-30): *Each of the following items in this section consists of a sentence, the parts of which have been jumbled. These parts have been labelled (P), (Q), (R) and (S). Given below each sentence are four sequences namely (A), (B), (C) and (D). You are required to re-arrange the jumbled parts of the sentence correctly and mark your response accordingly.*

21. P. because I fell
Q. you remember it better
R. when you write something,
S. I make at least three drafts of a song

The correct sequence should be:
A. SPRQ B. RQPS
C. QRSP D. PRSQ

22. P. for hours in the shop
Q. a gunman who held
R. a hostage
S. demanded ransom of ₹ 10 lakh

The correct sequence should be:
A. SPRQ B. RQPS
C. QRPS D. PRSQ

23. P. living in Russia
Q. country immediately
R. Ukraine has urged its citizens
S. to leave the

The correct sequence should be:
A. SPRQ B. RPSQ
C. RSQP D. PRSQ

24. P. ripping roofs off houses and raising fears of
Q. coast of Madagascar in the early hours,
R. cyclone Emnati crashed into the southeastern
S. flooding and food shortages in the region

The correct sequence should be:
A. SPRQ B. RPSQ
C. RQPS D. PRSQ

25. P. ecology is protected and aquatic life thrives
Q. we need to utilize the resources of water
R. for different purposes while
S. ensuring that its natural

The correct sequence should be:
A. SPRQ B. RQPS
C. QRSP D. PRSQ

26. P. very difficult
Q. the poor visibility
R. made the movement of traffic
S. due to fog

The correct sequence should be:
A. SPRQ B. RQPS
C. QRPS D. QSRP

27. P. avenues for the patients to indict
Q. but rarely is it the other way round
R. there are multiple legal
S. the doctors

The correct sequence should be:
A. SPRQ B. RPSQ
C. QRPS D. QSRP

28. P. flight, and each person
Q. her own journey
R. life is a solo
S. makes his or

The correct sequence should be:
A. SPRQ B. RPQS
C. RPSQ D. PQRS

29. P. made it evolve
Q. technologies and equipment has
R. into a rare centre of excellence
S. adoption of the latest

The correct sequence should be:
A. PQRS B. RPQS
C. SQPR D. QSRP

30. P. please mark the same
Q. be made in response to this notice
R. if you have any complaint to
S. to the concerned authority

The correct sequence should be:
A. PQRS B. RPQS
C. SQPR D. RQPS

ANTONYMS

Directions (Qs. No. 31-40): *Each item in this section consists of a sentence with an underlined word followed by four options, (A), (B), (C) and (D). Select the option that is* ***opposite in meaning*** *to the underlined word and mark your response in your Answer Sheet accordingly.*

31. The parental support can <u>fortify</u> a child's learning.
A. weaken
B. encourage
C. brace
D. strengthen

32. Now we can have another dazzling thought, as an outcome of my brilliant research!
A. splendid
B. murky
C. dazing
D. fulgent

33. The group held some clandestine meetings to resolve the matter.
A. secret
B. covert
C. sneaky
D. public

34. In the winters, the countryside view is bleak and the house is drafty.
A. cheerless
B. verdant
C. desolate
D. bare

35. Amid commotion the leader and his supporters remained passive.
A. quietude
B. uproar
C. tempest
D. stir

36. He had the audacity to blame him.
A. boldness
B. vigour
C. temerity
D. politeness

37. They are making plans for the abatement of the nuisance within a specified time.
A. subsidence
B. ebbing
C. accumulation
D. mitigation

38. There is exponential growth in the development of the scientific researches in the recent few decades.
A. aggressive
B. rampant
C. meager
D. augmented

39. He was known for his sagacity.
A. prudence
B. wisdom
C. ignorance
D. sapience

40. The river Ganges culminates in the Bay of Bengal.
A. concludes
B. flows
C. originates
D. merges

IDIOMS AND PHRASES

Directions (Qs. No. 41-50): *Given below are some idioms/ phrases followed by four alternative meanings for each. Choose the most appropriate answer from among the options (A), (B), (C) or (D).*

41. The lion's share
A. A portion of something
B. The largest and the best part of something
C. An important decision
D. An aggressive statement

42. Spill the beans
A. Reveal a secret
B. Forced to leave belongings
C. Share the news
D. Take offence at someone's rude behaviour

43. Cook someone's goose
A. To assist others
B. Hypnotize other's mind
C. To spoil other's plans
D. Inviting misfortune

44. Disappear into thin air
A. Lost forever
B. Become forgetful
C. Become uncaring
D. Disappear suddenly

45. Put the screws on
A. Forcing someone to do what you want
B. Never letting go of things
C. Keep the past alive
D. Using someone's trick for own benefit

46. Sit on the fence
A. Avoid meeting someone
B. Waiting patiently
C. Avoid taking sides
D. Hiding from someone

47. Be as sharp as a tack
A. A talkative person
B. A shrewd person
C. A clumsy person
D. A clever person

48. From pillar to post
A. Upside down
B. Keep moving from one place to another
C. Constructing a huge building
D. Jumping from the top of the mountain

49. Heath Robinson
A. Very complicated system or machine for doing a simple task
B. Treating everyone as enemy, when they are not
C. Sleeping all day, doing nothing
D. Very lazy person, slow in action

50. As thick as thieves
A. Dumb person
B. Good for nothing
C. Someone who uses everyone for personal gain
D. Very close friends who are looked upon with suspicion

PART B : GENERAL KNOWLEDGE

51. Two identical spring balances S_1 and S_2 are connected one after the other and are held vertically as shown in the figure. A mass of 10 kg is hanging from S_2. If the readings on S_1 and S_2 are W_1 and W_2 respectively, then:

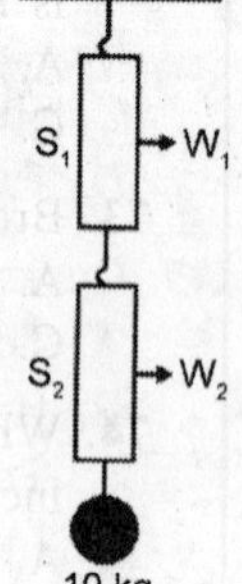

A. W_1 = 5 kg and W_2 = 10 kg
B. W_1 = 10 kg and W_2 = 5 kg
C. W_1 = 5 kg and W_2 = 5 kg
D. W_1 = 10 kg and W_2 = 10 kg

52. A stone is thrown horizontally from the top of a 20 m high building with a speed of 12 m/s. It hits the ground at a distance R from the building. Taking g = 10 m/s^2 and neglecting air resistance will give:

A. R = 12 m B. R = 18 m
C. R = 24 m D. R = 30 m

53. A sphere of volume V is made of a material with lower density than water. While on Earth, it floats on water with its volume f_1V ($f_1 < 1$) submerged. On the other hand, on a spaceship accelerating with acceleration $a < g$ (g is the acceleration due to gravity on Earth) in outer space, its submerged volume in water is f_2V. Then:

A. $f_2 = f_1$ B. $f_2 = \left(1-\frac{a}{g}\right)f_1$
C. $f_2 > f_1$ D. $f_2 = \frac{a}{g}f_1$

54. Two identical containers X and Y are connected at the bottom by a thin tube of negligible volume. The tube has a valve in it, as shown in the figure. Initially container X has a liquid filled up to height h in it and container Y is empty. When the valve is opened, both containers have equal amount of liquid in equilibrium. If the initial (before the valve is opened) potential energy of the liquid is P_1 and the final potential energy is P_2 then:

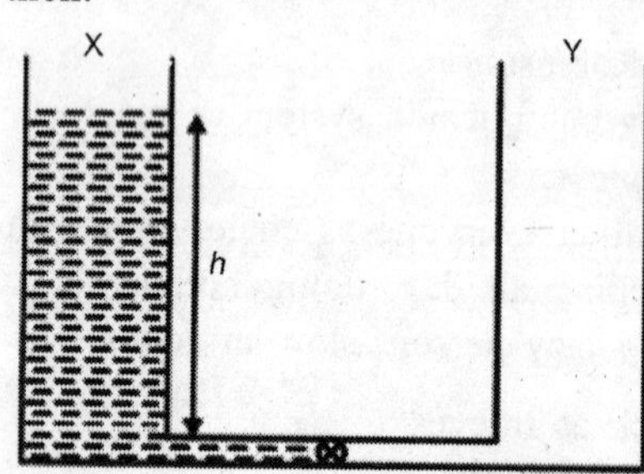

A. $P_1 = P_2$ B. $P_1 = 4P_2$
C. $P_1 = 2P_2$ D. $P_1 = 8P_2$

55. A particle is moving in a circle of radius R with a constant speed v. Its average acceleration over the time when it moves over half the circle is:

A. $\frac{v^2}{R}$ B. $\frac{\pi v^2}{2R}$
C. $\frac{2v^2}{\pi R}$ D. 0

56. Two forces of 5.0 N each are acting on a point mass. If the angle between the forces is 60°, then the net force acting on the point mass has magnitude close to:

A. 8.6 N B. 4.3 N
C. 5.0 N D. 6.7 N

57. Which one of the following is ***not*** an igneous rock?

A. Granite B. Slate
C. Basalt D. Gabbro

58. Which of the following statements is/are correct?

1. Hypocenter is the point on the surface of the Earth, nearest to the focus.
2. Velocity of earthquake waves is higher in denser materials.
3. P waves move faster and are the first to arrive at the surface of the Earth.

Select the correct answer using the code given below:

A. 1 and 2 B. 2 and 3
C. 1 and 3 D. 3 only

59. In terms of geological time scale, the quaternary period consists of two epochs. They are:

A. Pleistocene and Pliocene
B. Holocene and Pleistocene
C. Pleistocene and Miocene
D. Holocene and Eocene

60. Which one of the following is the correct sequence of arrangement of the given planets in descending order of their density (in gm/cm^3)?

A. Earth > Jupiter > Venus > Saturn
B. Jupiter > Earth > Saturn > Venus
C. Earth > Venus > Jupiter > Saturn
D. Earth > Venus > Saturn > Jupiter

61. Which one of the following is ***not*** a cold current?

A. Western Australian Current
B. Eastern Australian Current
C. Benguela Current
D. Peru Current

62. The process of Podsolization is predominantly found in:

A. Equatorial forest B. Monsoon forest
C. Taiga forest D. Mediterranean forest

63. Joint Military exercise 'Keen Sword 23' was conducted between:

A. India and Japan B. India and USA
C. USA and Japan D. Japan and Taiwan

64. The Battle of Rezang La, an epic battle in hostile conditions, was fought by the Indian Army in:
A. 1948 B. 1956
C. 1962 D. 1972

65. Consider the following statements about 'Exercise Sea Vigil-22':
1. Its aim is to assess India's preparedness in the domain of Maritime security and coastal defence.
2. Naval forces of USA and Japan also took part in the exercise.

Which of the statements given above is/are correct?
A. 1 only B. 2 only
C. Both 1 and 2 D. Neither 1 nor 2

66. Consider the following statements:
1. England is the only country that won the ICC T20 World Cup twice.
2. Virat Kohli is the only player to be adjudged as the Player of the Series in the ICC T20 World Cup twice.

Which of the statements given above is/are correct?
A. 1 only B. 2 only
C. Both 1 and 2 D. Neither 1 nor 2

67. Who among the following is ***not*** a recipient of Nobel Prize in Chemistry in 2022?
A. Carolyn R. Bertozzi B. Benjamin List
C. Morten Meldal D. K. Barry Sharpless

68. Consider the following statements regarding cell wall composition:
1. Bacterial cell wall is made of peptidoglycan.
2. Fungal cell wall is made of cellulose.
3. Animals lack cell wall and have extracellular matrix made up of sugar and proteins.

Select the correct answer using the code given below:
A. 2 only B. 1 and 2 only
C. 1 and 3 only D. 1, 2 and 3

69. Which one of the following structures is ***not*** present in a prokaryotic cell?
A. Cell wall B. Ribosomes
C. Nucleus D. Plasma membrane

70. In a plant cell, which one of the following contains their own DNA?
A. Nucleus and Endoplasmic Reticulum
B. Ribosome and Golgi apparatus
C. Mitochondria and Chloroplast
D. Chloroplast and Vacuoles

71. One advantage of sexual reproduction over asexual reproduction is that it helps species to survive over long evolutionary time. This is because sexual reproduction produces:
A. more offspring in each reproductive cycle.
B. robust and healthy offspring.
C. genetically similar offspring.
D. more variation in offspring.

72. Which one of the following structures or components is ***not*** always present in living cells?
A. Cell wall B. Plasma membrane
C. Cytoplasm D. Genetic material

73. Browning of the chopped apple can be minimized by:
A. using table sugar. B. preserving in a container.
C. using lemon juice. D. using milk of magnesia.

74. Which of the hydrocarbons are arranged as per the increasing order of their boiling points?
A. Methane, Butane, Propane, Heptane
B. Propane, Butane, Pentane, Octane
C. Propane, Butane, Heptane, Methane
D. Octane, Ethane, Methane, Propane

75. Which one of the following apparatus is used for separating benzene and water mixture?
A. Round bottom flask B. Conical flask
C. Separating funnel D. Dean and Stark apparatus

76. An iron nail dipped in copper sulphate solution turns brown. This is due to which one of the following types of reactions?
A. Addition reaction B. Decomposition reaction
C. Substitution reaction D. Displacement reaction

77. Among the following, which is ***not*** the correct method for keeping the curd?
A. Keeping in stainless steel vessel
B. Keeping in copper vessel
C. Keeping in plastic vessel
D. Keeping in glass vessel

78. Toothpaste prevents tooth decay by:
A. neutralizing the excess acidity.
B. means of emulsification.
C. the action of fluoride.
D. making a coat of calcium over the teeth surface.

79. Freedom fighter Kanaklata Barua was martyred in:
A. Sepoy Mutiny
B. Quit India Movement
C. Non-Cooperation Movement
D. Peasant Uprising of 1893-1894

80. Which one among the following statements about the Mansabdari system is correct?
A. All army troopers were allotted mansabs.
B. Mansabs were usually assigned on the basis of ancestry.
C. Position and salary of mansabdars were indicated by a numerical designation called zat.
D. Mansabdars were never paid in cash.

81. Which Governor General of Bengal underwent impeachment proceedings in the British Parliament?
A. Robert Clive B. Henry Vansittart
C. Warren Hastings D. Lord Cornwallis

82. Who among the following composed the 'Prayag Prashasti' of Samudragupta?
A. Harishena B. Chand Bardai
C. Vishakhadatta D. Kalidasa

83. Which one of the following kingdoms was founded by the two brothers Harihar and Bukka?
A. Bahmani B. Vijayanagara
C. Malwa D. Maratha

84. At which one of the following places did the Danes establish their settlement in India?
A. Chinsura B. Karaikal
C. Mahe D. Tranquebar

85. A rectangle ABCD is kept in front of a concave mirror of focal length f with its corners A and B being, respectively, at distances $2f$ and $3f$ from the mirror with AB along the principal axis as shown in the figure. It forms an image A′B′C′D′ in front of the mirror. What is the ratio of B′C′ to A′D′?

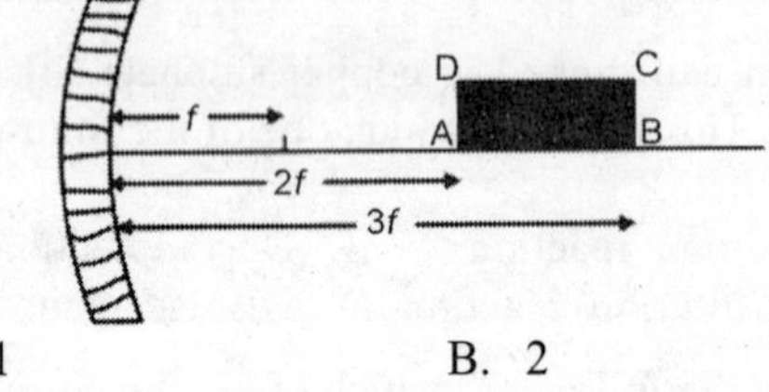

A. 1 B. 2
C. $\frac{1}{2}$ D. $\frac{2}{3}$

86. Shown in the figure are two plane mirrors XY and YZ (XY ⊥ YZ) joined at their edge. Also shown is a light ray falling on one of the mirrors and reflected back parallel to its original path as a result of this arrangement. The two mirrors are now rotated by an angle θ to their new position X′YZ′, as shown. As a result the new reflected ray is at an angle α from the original reflected ray. Then:

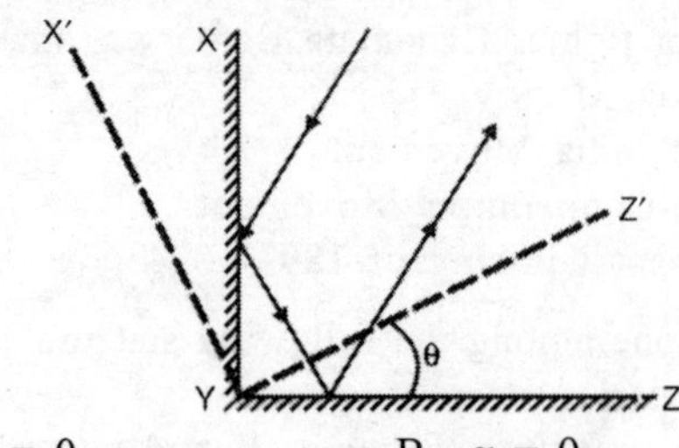

A. $\alpha = 0$ B. $\alpha = \theta$
C. $\alpha = 2\theta$ D. $\alpha = 4\theta$

87. A railway wagon (open at the top) of mass M_1 is moving with speed v_1 along a straight track. As a result of rain, after some time it gets partially filled with water so that the mass of the wagon becomes M_2 and speed becomes v_2. Taking the rain to be falling vertically and water stationary inside the wagon, the relation between the two speeds v_1 and v_2 is:
A. $v_1 = v_2$ B. $\frac{1}{2}M_1v_1^2 < \frac{1}{2}M_2v_2^2$
C. $M_1v_1 = M_2v_2$ D. $M_1v_1 < M_2v_2$

88. Which one of the following statements is ***not*** true for a flute, a musical instrument?
A. Momentum of waves on the blowing jet determines the loudness of the produced note.
B. Arrival time of the waves on the blowing jet determines the pitch of the produced note.
C. Sound comes from a vibrating column of air inside the flute.
D. Sound comes from a vibrating column of air inside as well as outside the flute.

89. A positive charge is moving towards south in a space where magnetic field is pointing in the north direction. The moving charge will experience:
A. a deflecting force towards north direction.
B. a deflecting force towards east direction.
C. a deflecting force towards west direction.
D. no deflecting force.

90. Which one of the following is ***not*** a main greenhouse gas?
A. Water vapour B. Oxygen
C. Carbon dioxide D. Methane

91. Which one of the following statements about X-rays is ***not*** true?
A. They have wavelengths of about 1Å.
B. These can be generated by bombarding a metal target by high energy electrons.
C. Due to their wavelengths being shorter, these can be used for radar systems.
D. These are also used for the treatment of certain forms of cancer.

92. Which one among the following is the northernmost geographical location?
A. New Delhi B. Kathmandu
C. Thimphu D. Dhaka

93. Consider the following statements:
1. Distance between the longitudes becomes zero on North Pole and South Pole.
2. Distance between the longitudes is maximum on the Equator.
3. Number of longitudes is more than number of latitudes.

Which of the statements given above is/are correct?
A. 1 only B. 2 only
C. 1 and 3 only D. 1, 2 and 3

94. Which one among the following states is the leading producer of Manganese in India?
A. Madhya Pradesh B. Jharkhand
C. Rajasthan D. Karnataka

95. Mica is mainly used in:
A. food and beverage industry.
B. iron and steel industry.
C. aluminium industry.
D. electrical and electronic industries.

96. According to Koppen's climatic classifications, the Great Northern Plains of India have which one of the following climates?
A. Aw climate B. Cwg climate
C. Amw climate D. Dfc climate

97. Which of the following statements about Lachit Borphukan is/are correct?
1. He was a General of the Ahom Force.
2. He is known for his leadership in the Battle of Saraighat.
3. Lachit Borphukan Gold Medal is given to the best cadet at the National Defence Academy.

Select the correct answer using the code given below:
A. 1, 2 and 3 B. 2 and 3 only
C. 1 only D. 2 only

98. The 4th edition of joint military exercise 'DUSTLIK' between the Indian Army and the Uzbekistan Army was held in:
A. Ranikhet B. Gangtok
C. Pithoragarh D. Leh

99. Which of the following is India's first privately developed rocket launched by ISRO recently?
A. Skyroot B. Prarambh
C. Bazoomq D. Vikram-S

100. Which one among the following villages was recently declared as India's first 24 × 7 solar-powered village?
A. Mawlynnong, Meghalaya
B. Modhera, Gujarat
C. Ziro village, Arunachal Pradesh
D. Malana, Himachal Pradesh

101. Tableaux of which one of the following States was adjudged the best in the Republic Day Parade, 2023?
A. Uttarakhand B. Punjab
C. Gujarat D. Uttar Pradesh

102. Organisms capable of using CO_2 as principal carbon source are called:
A. Autotrophs B. Heterotrophs
C. Parasites D. Decomposers

103. When yeast cells are O_2 starved, fermentation serves as the source of energy. This results in the production of:
A. ATP + CO_2 + Ethanol
B. ATP + O_2 + Pyruvate
C. ATP + CO_2 + Lactic acid
D. ATP + O_2 + Acetaldehyde

104. During a laboratory experiment, a student immerses epidermal leaf peel in a hypertonic solution. After some time, the student examined the cells under a microscope and observed that:
A. the cells swelled.
B. the cells were plasmolysed.
C. the cells built up turgor pressure.
D. the cells size was unaffected.

105. Which one of the following is ***not*** a characteristic feature of fungi?
A. Cell wall is made of chitin
B. Filamentous mycelium is present
C. Can carry out photosynthesis
D. Asexual spores are produced

106. Which one of the following statements about bryophytes is ***not*** correct?
A. The plant body is a gametophyte.
B. They are also called the amphibians of plant kingdom.
C. The plant body is attached to the substratum by rhizoids.
D. Specialized water-conducting tissues are present.

107. What is the specific purpose of using potassium hydroxide during the saponification process?
A. To obtain soaps which are hard on the skin
B. To obtain soaps which are soft on the skin
C. To obtain natural fragrance
D. To make the saponification very economical

108. Which one of the following is the correct arrangement of metals in the decreasing order of their reactivity?
A. Iron, Sodium, Silver, Copper
B. Silver, Copper, Iron, Sodium
C. Sodium, Copper, Silver, Iron
D. Sodium, Iron, Copper, Silver

109. Which among the following statements is ***not*** correct with respect to allotropes of Carbon?
A. Graphite is a good conductor of electricity.
B. Diamond is the hardest substance known.
C. Fullerene is one of the allotropes of carbon.
D. Next to diamond, graphite is the second hardest known substance.

110. Which among the following is the popular method for manufacture of ammonia?
A. Ostwald's process
B. Haber-Bosch process
C. Electric furnace process
D. Electrolysis process

111. For manufacturing of glass, which among the following is used as a source of silica?
A. Fine clay soil B. Wood powder
C. Coconut shell D. Sand

112. Which among the following is the correct arrangement of halogens in the increasing order of their oxidizing nature?

A. F, Cl, Br, I B. Cl, Br, F, I
C. Br, I, Cl, F D. I, Br, Cl, F

113. Copper sulphate crystals available in the market are blue coloured crystals. By careful heating, they turn to white colour. Which one of the following is responsible for the blue colour?
A. Oxygen B. Nitrogen
C. Water D. Hydrogen

114. Equal volume of all gases, when measured at the same temperature and pressure, contain an equal number of particles. Who proposed the above law?
A. Charles B. Boyle
C. Avogadro D. Lussac

115. Airbags work on the principle of a chemical reaction triggered by the impact producing a gaseous product that causes a sudden volume change. Which one among the following chemical conversions is responsible for this?
A. Sodium azide into nitrogen gas
B. Solid carbon dioxide into gaseous carbon dioxide
C. Carbon dioxide into carbon monoxide
D. Sudden conversion of gaseous carbon dioxide into carbon monoxide

116. Which one among the following districts of Eastern India held a referendum in 1947 to decide whether or not to join Pakistan?
A. Sylhet B. Goalpara
C. Cachar D. Jalpaiguri

117. Which one of the following statements about Rabatak inscription is ***not*** correct?
A. It throws important light on Kushana genealogy.
B. It refers to Kanishka as 'a king of kings and a son of God'.
C. The 23-line inscription is written in Gandhari language.
D. It mentions names of States which were part of Kanishka's empire.

118. Who among the following was the author of the famous Sanskrit work '*Mrichchhakatika*'?
A. Kalidasa B. Bhasa
C. Valmiki D. Shudraka

119. Yashovarman was ruler of which one of the following kingdoms?
A. Kannauj B. Mewar
C. Marwar D. Kalinga

120. Which one among the following rulers established Pataliputra as the capital of the Magadhan Empire?
A. Bimbisara B. Bindusara
C. Ajatashatru D. Ashoka

121. Which one of the following astronomers proved that the Earth and other planets revolve around the Sun?
A. Copernicus B. Kepler
C. Galileo D. Newton

122. Sand falls vertically on a conveyor belt at a rate of 0.1 kg/s. In order to keep the belt moving at a uniform speed of 2 m /s, the force required to be applied on the belt is:
A. 0 N B. 0.2 N
C. 1.0 N D. 2.0 N

123. The power required to lift a mass of 8.0 kg up a vertical distance of 4 m in 2 s is (taking acceleration due to gravity as 10 m/s^2):
A. 80 W B. 160 W
C. 320 W D. 640 W

124. One block of 2.0 kg mass is placed on top of another block of 3.0 kg mass. The coefficient of static friction between the two blocks is 0.2. The bottom block is pulled with a horizontal force F such that both the blocks move together without slipping. Taking acceleration due to gravity as 10 m/s^2, the maximum value of the frictional force is:
A. 50 N B. 30 N
C. 4 N D. 10 N

125. A mass is attached to a spring that hangs vertically. The extension produced in the spring is 6 cm on Earth. The acceleration due to gravity on the surface of the Moon is one-sixth of its value on the surface of the Earth. The extension of the spring on the Moon would be:
A. 6 cm B. 1 cm
C. 0 cm D. 36 cm

126. Which one of the following is an example of Second Class Lever?
A. A pair of scissors B. A bottle opener
C. A cricket bat D. A bow and arrow

127. In an electric circuit, a wire of resistance 10 Ω is used. If this wire is stretched to a length double of its original value, the current in the circuit would become:
A. half of its original value.
B. double of its original value.
C. one-fourth of its original value.
D. four times of its original value.

128. What is the total resistance in the following circuit element?

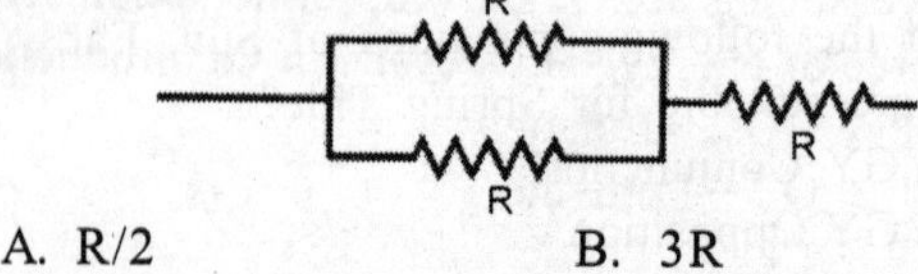

A. R/2 B. 3R
C. 3R/2 D. 2R/3

129. Which of the following scheme(s) is/are included under *Bharatmala Pariyojana*?

1. Develop the road connectivity to border areas
2. Development of coastal roads
3. Improvement in the efficiency of National Corridors

Select the correct answer using the code given below:
A. 1 only B. 3 only
C. 2 and 3 only D. 1, 2 and 3

130. Deendayal Port was earlier known as:
A. Paradip Port B. Tuticorin Port
C. Kandla Port D. Visakhapatnam Port

131. The Counter Insurgency and Jungle Warfare School of Indian Army is situated at:
A. Dehradun B. Vairengte
C. Gulmarg D. Mhow

132. In the soil-forming regime, which one of the following occurs in a region where evapotranspiration exceeds precipitation significantly?
A. Calcification
B. Laterization
C. Podsolization
D. Gleization

133. Which one of the following is found in the innermost part of the Earth?
A. Conrad discontinuity
B. Moho discontinuity
C. Guttenberg discontinuity
D. Lehmann discontinuity

134. Which of the following tree species is/are found on Himalayas?
1. Oak
2. Rhododendron
3. Rosewood

Select the correct answer using the code given below:
A. 1 only B. 2 and 3
C. 1 and 3 D. 1 and 2

135. Which one of the following is the lowermost/innermost intrusive igneous rock?
A. Laccolith B. Batholith
C. Lopolith D. Phacolith

136. If it is 12 noon in New Delhi, what will be the time in London, UK?
A. 6:30 A.M. B. 6:30 P.M.
C. 5:30 A.M. D. 5:30 P.M.

137. Which of the following positions of Sun, Earth and Moon is/are suitable for Spring Tide?
1. SYZYGY Conjunction
2. SYZYGY Opposition
3. Quadrature

Select the correct answer using the code given below:
A. 1 only B. 2 only
C. 1 and 2 D. 1 and 3

138. Which Renaissance artist painted 'The Last Supper'?
A. Michelangelo B. Donatello
C. Botticelli D. Leonardo da Vinci

139. Which one of the following European explorer conquered Mexico?
A. Vasco da Gama B. Bartholomew Diaz
C. Magellan D. Hernan Cortes

140. Near which one of the following cities in India have large statues of Kushana rulers been discovered?
A. Karnal B. Ropar
C. Hissar D. Mathura

141. The Treaty of Yandabo was concluded as part of which one of the following wars?
A. First Anglo-Burmese War
B. Second Anglo-Burmese War
C. Anglo-Kuki War
D. Anglo-Maratha War

142. Plan allocation in agriculture and irrigation as percentage of total plan outlay was highest in:
A. Seventh Five-Year Plan
B. Third Five-Year Plan
C. First Five-Year Plan
D. Second Five-Year Plan

143. The UN COP-27 Summit relates to:
A. Russia-Ukraine war
B. Terrorism and counter-terrorism
C. Climate change
D. Interpol

144. Which one of the following tribes from India's North-East had the earliest known association with cultivation and production of tea?
A. Khasis B. Garos
C. Singphos D. Jayantias

145. By which one of the following amendments, was Article 51A, relating to the Fundamental Duties, inserted into the Constitution of India?
A. The Constitution (42nd Amendment) Act
B. The Constitution (44th Amendment) Act
C. The Constitution (85th Amendment) Act
D. The Constitution (92nd Amendment) Act

146. Which one of the following statements is true?
A. The force of gravity of the Earth on the Moon is greater than the force of gravity of the Moon on the Earth.
B. The force of gravity of the Moon on the Earth is greater than the force of gravity of the Earth on the Moon.
C. The force of gravity of the Earth on the Moon and of the Moon on the Earth are equal in magnitude and are in the same direction.
D. The force of gravity of the Earth on the Moon and of the Moon on the Earth are equal in magnitude but are in opposite directions.

147. An electric bulb is rated as 220 V and 80 W. When it is operated on 110 V, the power rating would be:
A. 80 W B. 60 W
C. 40 W D. 20 W

148. In the dispersion of white light by a common glass prism, which one among the following is correct?
A. Red light deviates the most because red light has highest speed in prism
B. Blue light deviates the most because blue light has highest speed in prism
C. Red light deviates the most because red light has lowest speed in prism
D. Blue light deviates the most because blue light has lowest speed in prism

149. Which one among the following is true for the speed of sound in a given medium?
A. Speed of sound remains same at all frequencies
B. Speed of sound is faster at higher frequencies
C. Speed of sound is slower at higher frequencies
D. Speed of sound is slower at higher wavelengths

150. Which one of the following telescopes contains only mirrors?
A. Galilean telescope B. Keplerian telescope
C. Newtonian telescope D. Schmidt telescope

PAPER II : MATHEMATICS

1. If ω is a non-real cube root of 1, then what is the value of $\left|\frac{1-\omega}{\omega+\omega^2}\right|$?
A. $\sqrt{3}$ B. $\sqrt{2}$
C. 1 D. $\frac{4}{\sqrt{3}}$

2. What is the number of 6-digit numbers that can be formed only by using 0, 1, 2, 3, 4 and 5 (each once); and divisible by 6?
A. 96 B. 120
C. 192 D. 312

3. What is the binary number equivalent to decimal number 1011?
A. 1011 B. 111011
C. 11111001 D. 111110011

4. Let A be a matrix of order 3 × 3 and $|A| = 4$. If $|2\,\text{adj}(3A)| = 2^{\alpha}3^{\beta}$, then what is the value of $(\alpha + \beta)$?
A. 12 B. 13
C. 17 D. 24

5. If α and β are the distinct roots of equation $x^2 - x + 1 = 0$, then what is the value of $\left|\frac{\alpha^{100}+\beta^{100}}{\alpha^{100}-\beta^{100}}\right|$?
A. $\sqrt{3}$ B. $\sqrt{2}$
C. 1 D. $\frac{1}{\sqrt{3}}$

6. Let A and B be symmetric matrices of same order, then which one of the following is correct regarding (AB – BA)?
1. Its diagonal entries are equal but non-zero.
2. The sum of its non-diagonal entries is zero.

Select the correct answer using the code given below:
A. 1 only B. 2 only
C. Both 1 and 2 D. Neither 1 nor 2

7. Consider the following statements in respect of square matrices A, B, C each of same order n:
1. $AB = AC \Rightarrow B = C$ if A is non-singular
2. If $BX = CX$ for every column matrix X having n rows then $B = C$

Which of the statements given above is/are correct?
A. 1 only B. 2 only
C. Both 1 and 2 D. Neither 1 nor 2

8. The system of linear equations $x + 2y + z = 4$, $2x + 4y + 2z = 8$ and $3x + 6y + 3z = 10$ has:
A. a unique solution
B. infinite many solutions
C. no solution
D. exactly three solutions

9. Let AX = B be a system of 3 linear equation with 3-unknowns. Let X_1 and X_2 be its two distinct solutions. If the combination $aX_1 + bX_2$ is a solution of AX = B; where a, b are real numbers, then which one of the following is correct?
A. $a = b$
B. $a + b = 1$
C. $a + b = 0$
D. $a - b = 1$

10. What is the sum of the roots of the equation
$$\begin{vmatrix} 0 & x-a & x-b \\ 0 & 0 & x-c \\ x+b & x+c & 1 \end{vmatrix} = 0?$$
A. $a + b + c$ B. $a - b + c$
C. $a + b - c$ D. $a - b - c$

11. If $2 - i\sqrt{3}$ where $i = \sqrt{-1}$ is a root of the equation $x^2 + ax + b = 0$, then what is the value of $(a + b)$?
A. –11 B. –3
C. 0 D. 3

12. If $z = \frac{1+i\sqrt{3}}{1-i\sqrt{3}}$ where $i = \sqrt{-1}$, then what is the argument of z?

A. $\frac{\pi}{3}$ B. $\frac{2\pi}{3}$
C. $\frac{4\pi}{3}$ D. $\frac{5\pi}{6}$

13. If a, b, c are in AP, then what is $\begin{vmatrix} x+1 & x+2 & x+3 \\ x+2 & x+3 & x+4 \\ x+a & x+b & x+3 \end{vmatrix}$ equal to?

A. -1 B. 0
C. 1 D. 2

14. If $\log_x a$, a^x and $\log_b x$ are in GP, then what is x equal to?

A. $\log_a(\log_b a)$ B. $\log_b(\log_a b)$
C. $\frac{\log_a(\log_b a)}{2}$ D. $\frac{\log_b(\log_a b)}{2}$

15. If $2^{\frac{1}{c}}, 2^{\frac{b}{ac}}, 2^{\frac{1}{a}}$ are in GP, then which one of the following is correct?

A. a, b, c are in AP B. a, b, c are in GP
C. a, b, c are in HP D. ab, bc, ca are in AP

16. The first and the second terms of an AP are $\frac{5}{2}$ and $\frac{23}{12}$ respectively. If nth term is the largest negative term, what is the value of n?

A. 5 B. 6
C. 7 D. n cannot be determined

17. For how many integral values of k, the equation $x^2 - 4x + k = 0$, where k is an integer has real roots and both of them lie in the interval (0, 5)?

A. 3 B. 4
C. 5 D. 6

18. In an AP, the first term is x and the sum of the first n terms is zero. What is the sum of next m terms?

A. $\frac{mx(m+n)}{n-1}$ B. $\frac{mx(m+n)}{1-n}$
C. $\frac{nx(m+n)}{m-1}$ D. $\frac{nx(m+n)}{1-m}$

19. Consider the following statements:

1. (25)! + 1 is divisible by 26
2. (6)! + 1 is divisible by 7

Which of the above statements is/are correct?

A. 1 only
B. 2 only
C. Both 1 and 2
D. Neither 1 nor 2

20. If z is a complex number such that $\frac{z-1}{z+1}$ is purely imaginary, then what is $|z|$ equal to?

A. $\frac{1}{2}$ B. $\frac{2}{3}$
C. 1 D. 2

21. How many real numbers satisfy the equation $|x - 4| + |x - 7| = 15$?

A. Only one B. Only two
C. Only three D. Infinitely many

22. A mapping f : A → B defined as $f(x) = \frac{2x+3}{3x+5}$, $x \in$ A. If f is to be onto, then what are A and B equal to?

A. $A = R\backslash\left\{-\frac{5}{3}\right\}$ and $B = R\backslash\left\{-\frac{2}{3}\right\}$

B. $A = R$ and $B = R\backslash\left\{-\frac{5}{3}\right\}$

C. $A = R\backslash\left\{-\frac{3}{2}\right\}$ and $B = R\backslash\{0\}$

D. $A = R\backslash\left\{-\frac{5}{3}\right\}$ and $B = R\backslash\left\{\frac{2}{3}\right\}$

23. α and β are distinct real roots of the quadratic equation $x^2 + ax + b = 0$. Which of the following statements is/are sufficient to find α?

1. $\alpha + \beta = 0$, $\alpha^2 + \beta^2 = 2$
2. $\alpha\beta^2 = -1$, $\alpha = 0$

Select the correct answer using the code given below:

A. 1 only B. 2 only
C. Both 1 and 2 D. Neither 1 nor 2

24. If the sixth term in the binomial expansion of $\left(x^{-\frac{8}{3}} + x^2 \log_{10} x\right)$ is 5600, then what is the value of x?

A. 6 B. 8
C. 9 D. 10

25. How man terms are there in the expansion of $(3x - y)^4 (x + 3y)^4$?

A. 9 B. 12
C. 15 D. 17

26. p, q, r and s are in AP such that $p + s = 8$ and $qr = 15$. What is the difference between largest and smallest numbers?

A. 6 B. 5
C. 4 D. 3

27. Consider the following statements for a fixed natural number n:

1. $C(n, r)$ is greatest if $n = 2r$
2. $C(n, r)$ is greatest if $n = 2r - 1$ and $n = 2r + 1$

Which of the statements given above is/are correct?

A. 1 only B. 2 only
C. Both 1 and 2 D. Neither 1 nor 2

28. m parallel lines cut n parallel lines giving rise to 60 parallelograms. What is the value of $(m + n)$?
A. 6 B. 7
C. 8 D. 9

29. Let x be the number of permutations of the word 'PERMUTATIONS' and y be the number of permutations of the word 'COMBINATIONS'. Which one of the following is correct?
A. $x = y$ B. $y = 2x$
C. $x = 4y$ D. $y = 4x$

30. 5-digit numbers are formed using the digits 0, 1, 2, 4, 5 without repetition. What is the percentage of numbers which are greater than 50,000?
A. 20% B. 25%
C. $\frac{100}{3}$% D. $\frac{110}{3}$%

Directions (Qs. No. 31 & 32): *Consider the following for the next questions that follow:*

Let sin β be the GM of sin α and cos α; tan γ be the AM of sin α and cos α.

31. What is cos 2β equal to?
A. $(\cos\alpha - \sin\alpha)^2$ B. $(\cos\alpha + \sin\alpha)^2$
C. $(\cos\alpha - \sin\alpha)^3$ D. $\frac{(\cos\alpha - \sin\alpha)^2}{2}$

32. What is the value of sec 2γ?
A. $\frac{3-\sin 2\alpha}{5+2\sin 2\alpha}$ B. $\frac{5+\sin 2\alpha}{3-\sin 2\alpha}$
C. $\frac{3-2\sin 2\alpha}{4+\sin 2\alpha}$ D. $\frac{3-\sin 2\alpha}{4+3\sin 2\alpha}$

Directions (Qs. No. 33 & 34): *Consider the following for the next questions that follow:*

A flagstaff 20 m long standing on a pillar 10 m high subtends an angle $\tan^{-1}(0.5)$ at a point P on the ground. Let θ be the angle subtended by the pillar at this point P.

33. If x is the distance of P from bottom of the pillar, then consider the following statements:
1. x can take two values which are in the ratio 1 : 3
2. x can be equal to height of the flagstaff

Which of the statements given above is/are correct?
A. 1 only B. 2 only
C. Both 1 and 2 D. Neither 1 nor 2

34. What is a possible value of tan θ?
A. $\frac{3}{4}$ B. $\frac{2}{3}$
C. $\frac{1}{3}$ D. $\frac{1}{4}$

Directions (Qs. No. 35 & 36): *Consider the following for the next questions that follow:*

The perimeter of a triangle ABC is 6 times the AM of sine of angles of the triangle. Further BC = $\sqrt{3}$ and CA = 1.

35. What is the perimeter of the triangle?
A. $\sqrt{3}+1$ B. $\sqrt{3}+2$
C. $\sqrt{3}+3$ D. $2\sqrt{3}+1$

36. Consider the following statements:
1. ABC is right angled triangle
2. The angles of the triangle are in AP

Which of the statements given above is/are correct?
A. 1 only B. 2 only
C. Both 1 and 2 D. Neither 1 nor 2

Directions (Qs. No. 37 & 38): *Consider the following for the next questions that follow:*

Let $x = \frac{\sin^2 A + \sin A + 1}{\sin A}$ where $0 < A \le \frac{\pi}{2}$

37. What is the minimum value of x?
A. 1 B. 2
C. 3 D. 4

38. At what value of A does x attain the minimum value?
A. $\frac{\pi}{6}$ B. $\frac{\pi}{4}$
C. $\frac{\pi}{3}$ D. $\frac{\pi}{2}$

Directions (Qs. No. 39 & 40): *Consider the following for the next questions that follow:*

In the triangle ABC, $a^2 + b^2 + c^2 = ac + \sqrt{3}bc$

39. What is the nature of the triangle?
A. Equilateral
B. Isosceles
C. Right angled triangle
D. Scalene but not right angled

40. If $c = 8$, what is the area of the triangle?
A. $4\sqrt{3}$ B. $6\sqrt{3}$
C. $8\sqrt{3}$ D. $12\sqrt{3}$

Directions (Qs. No. 41 & 42): *Consider the following for the next questions that follow:*

Consider the function $f(x) = |x - 2| + |3 - x| + |4 - x|$, where $x \in R$.

41. At what value of x does the function attain minimum value?
A. 2 B. 3
C. 4 D. 0

42. What is the minimum value of function?
A. 2 B. 3
C. 4 D. 0

Directions (Qs. No. 43 & 44): *Consider the following for the next questions that follow:*

Consider the sum S = 0! + 1! + 2! + 3! + 4! + ... + 100!

43. If the sum S is divided by 8, what is the remainder?
A. 0 B. 1
C. 2 D. Cannot be determined

44. If the sum S is divided by 60, what is the remainder?
A. 1 B. 3
C. 17 D. 34

Directions (Qs. No. 45 & 46): *Consider the following for the next questions that follow:*

In a triangle PQR, P is the largest angle and $\cos P = \frac{1}{3}$. Further the in-circle of the triangle touches the sides PQ, QR and RP at N, L and M respectively such that the lengths PN, QL and RM are n, $n + 2$, $n + 4$ respectively where n is an interger.

45. What is the value of n?
A. 4 B. 6
C. 8 D. 10

46. What is the length of the smallest side?
A. 12 B. 14
C. 16 D. 18

Directions (Qs. No. 47 & 48): *Consider the following for the next questions that follow:*

Given that
$\sin x + \cos x + \tan x + \cot x + \sec x + \operatorname{cosec} x = 7$

47. The given equation can be reduced to:
A. $\sin^2 2x - 44 \sin 2x + 36 = 0$
B. $\sin^2 2x + 44 \sin 2x - 36 = 0$
C. $\sin^2 2x - 22 \sin 2x + 18 = 0$
D. $\sin^2 2x + 22 \sin 2x - 18 = 0$

48. If $\sin 2x = a - b\sqrt{c}$, where a and b are natural numbers and c is prime number, then what is the value of $a - b + 2c$?
A. 0 B. 14
C. 21 D. 28

Directions (Qs. No. 49 & 50): *Consider the following for the next questions that follow:*

A quadratic equation is given by
$(3+2\sqrt{2})x^2 - (4+2\sqrt{3})x + (8+4\sqrt{3}) = 0$

49. What is the HM of the roots of the equation?
A. 2 B. 4
C. $2\sqrt{2}$ D. $2\sqrt{3}$

50. What is the GM of the roots of the equation?
A. $\sqrt{2}(\sqrt{6}-\sqrt{3}+\sqrt{2}-1)$ B. $\sqrt{2}(\sqrt{6}+\sqrt{3}-\sqrt{2}-1)$
C. $(\sqrt{6}-\sqrt{3}+\sqrt{2}-1)$ D. $(\sqrt{6}+\sqrt{3}+\sqrt{2}-1)$

Directions (Qs. No. 51 & 52): *Consider the following for the next questions that follow:*

Let $\Delta(a, b, c, \alpha) = \begin{vmatrix} a & b & a\alpha+b \\ b & c & b\alpha+c \\ a\alpha+b & b\alpha+c & 0 \end{vmatrix}$

51. If $\Delta(a, b, c, \alpha) = 0$ for every $\alpha > 0$, then which one of the following is correct?
A. a, b, c are AP B. a, b, c are in GP
C. $a, 2b, c$ are in AP D. $a, 2b, c$ are in GP

52. If $\Delta(7, 4, 2, \alpha) = 0$, then α is a root of which one of the following equations?
A. $7x^2 + 4x + 2 = 0$ B. $7x^2 - 4x + 2 = 0$
C. $7x^2 + 8x + 2 = 0$ D. $7x^2 - 8x + 2 = 0$

Directions (Qs. No. 53 & 54): *Consider the following for the next questions that follow:*

Given that $m(\theta) = \cot^2 \theta + n^2 \tan^2 \theta + 2n$, where n is a fixed positive real number.

53. What is the least value of $m(\theta)$?
A. n B. $2n$
C. $3n$ D. $4n$

54. Under what condition does m attain the least value?
A. $n = \tan^2 \theta$ B. $n = \cot^2 \theta$
C. $n = \sin^2 \theta$ D. $n = \cos^2 \theta$

Directions (Qs. No. 55 & 56): *Consider the following for the next questions that follow:*

A quadrilateral is formed by the lines $x = 0$, $y = 0$, $x + y = 1$ and $6x + y = 3$.

55. What is the equation of diagonal through origin?
A. $3x + y = 0$ B. $2x + 3y = 0$
C. $3x - 2y = 0$ D. $3x + 2y = 0$

56. What is the equation of other diagonal?
A. $x + 2y - 1 = 0$ B. $x - 2y - 1 = 0$
C. $2x + y + 1 = 0$ D. $2x + y - 1 = 0$

Directions (Qs. No. 57 & 58): *Consider the following for the next questions that follow:*

$P(x, y)$ is any point on the ellipse $x^2 + 4y^2 = 1$. Let E, F be the foci of the ellipse.

57. What is PE + PF equal to?
A. 1 B. 2
C. 3 D. 4

58. Consider the following points:
1. $\left(\frac{\sqrt{3}}{2}, 0\right)$
2. $\left(\frac{\sqrt{3}}{2}, \frac{1}{4}\right)$
3. $\left(\frac{\sqrt{3}}{2}, -\frac{1}{4}\right)$

Which of the above points lie on latus rectum of ellipse?

A. 1 and 2 only B. 2 and 3 only
C. 1 and 3 only D. 1, 2 and 3

Directions (Qs. No. 59 & 60): *Consider the following for the next questions that follow:*

The line $y = x$ partitions the circle $(x - a)^2 + y^2 = a^2$ in two segments.

59. What is the area of minor segment?

A. $\frac{(\pi-2)a^2}{4}$ B. $\frac{(\pi-1)a^2}{4}$
C. $\frac{(\pi-2)a^2}{2}$ D. $\frac{(\pi-1)a^2}{2}$

60. What is the area of major segment?

A. $\frac{(3\pi-2)a^2}{4}$ B. $\frac{(3\pi+2)a^2}{4}$
C. $\frac{(3\pi-2)a^2}{2}$ D. $\frac{(3\pi+2)a^2}{2}$

Directions (Qs. No. 61 & 62): *Consider the following for the next questions that follow:*

Let A(1, –1, 2) and B(2, 1, –1) be the end points of the diameter of the sphere $x^2 + y^2 + z^2 + 2ux + 2vy + 2wz - 1 = 0$.

61. What is $u + v + w$ equal to?

A. –2 B. –1
C. 1 D. 2

62. If P(x, y, z) is any point on the sphere, then what is $PA^2 + PB^2$ equal to?

A. 15 B. 14
C. 13 D. 6.5

Directions (Qs. No. 63 & 64): *Consider the following for the next questions that follow:*

Consider two lines whose direction ratios are (2, –1, 2) and (k, 3, 5). They are inclined at an angle $\frac{\pi}{4}$.

63. What is the value of k?

A. 4 B. 2
C. 1 D. –1

64. What are the direction ratios of a line which is perpendicular to both the lines?

A. (1, 2, 10)
B. (–1, –2, 10)
C. (11, 12, –10)
D. (11, 2, –10)

Directions (Qs. No. 65 & 66): *Consider the following for the next questions that follow:*

Let $\vec{a} = 3\hat{i} + 3\hat{j} + 3\hat{k}$ and $\vec{c} = \hat{j} - \hat{k}$. Let $\vec{b}$ be such that $\vec{a}\cdot\vec{b} = 27$ and $\vec{a}\times\vec{b} = 9\vec{c}$.

65. What is $\vec{b}$ equal to?

A. $3\hat{i} + 4\hat{j} + 2\hat{k}$ B. $5\hat{i} + 2\hat{j} + 2\hat{k}$
C. $5\hat{i} - 2\hat{j} + 6\hat{k}$ D. $3\hat{i} + 3\hat{j} + 4\hat{k}$

66. What is the angle between $(\vec{a} + \vec{b})$ and $\vec{c}$?

A. $\frac{\pi}{2}$ B. $\frac{\pi}{3}$
C. $\frac{\pi}{4}$ D. $\frac{\pi}{6}$

Directions (Qs. No. 67 & 68): *Consider the following for the next questions that follow:*

Let a vector $\vec{a} = 4\hat{i} - 8\hat{j} + \hat{k}$ make angles α, β, γ with the positive directions of x, y, z axes respectively.

67. What is cos α equal to?

A. $\frac{1}{3}$ B. $\frac{4}{9}$
C. $\frac{5}{9}$ D. $\frac{2}{3}$

68. What is cos 2β + cos 2γ equal to?

A. $-\frac{32}{81}$ B. $-\frac{16}{81}$
C. $\frac{16}{81}$ D. $\frac{32}{81}$

Directions (Qs. No. 69 & 70): *Consider the following for the next questions that follow:*

The position vectors of two points A and B are $\hat{i} - \hat{j}$ and $\hat{j} + \hat{k}$ respectively.

69. Consider the following points:

1. (–1, –3, 1)
2. (–1, 3, 2)
3. (–2, 5, 3)

Which of the above points lie on the line joining A and B?

A. 1 and 2 only B. 2 and 3 only
C. 1 and 3 only D. 1, 2 and 3

70. What is the magnitude of $\overline{AB}$?

A. 2 B. 3
C. $\sqrt{6}$ D. $\sqrt{3}$

Directions (Qs. No. 71-73): *Consider the following for the next questions that follow:*

Let $f(x) = Pe^x + Qe^{2x} + Re^{3x}$, where P, Q, R are real numbers. Further $f(0) = 6$, $f'(ln\ 3) = 282$ and $\int_0^{ln 2} f(x)dx = 11$

71. What is the value of Q?

A. 1 B. 2
C. 3 D. 4

72. What is the value of R?
A. 1 B. 2
C. 3 D. 4

73. What is $f'(0)$ equal to?
A. 18 B. 16
C. 15 D. 14

Directions (Qs. No. 74 & 75): *Consider the following for the next questions that follow:*

Suppose E is the differential equations representing family of curves $y^2 = 2cx + 2c\sqrt{c}$ where c is a positive parameter.

74. What is the order of the differential equation?
A. 1 B. 2
C. 3 D. 4

75. What is the degree of the differential equation?
A. 2 B. 3
C. 4 D. Degree does not exist

Directions (Qs. No. 76-78): *Consider the following for the next questions that follow:*

$$\text{Let } f(x) = \begin{vmatrix} \cos x & x & 1 \\ 2\sin x & x^2 & 2x \\ \tan x & x & 1 \end{vmatrix}$$

76. What is $f(0)$ equal to?
A. –1 B. 0
C. 1 D. 2

77. What is $\lim_{x\to 0} \frac{f(x)}{x}$ equal to?
A. –1 B. 0
C. 1 D. 2

78. What is $\lim_{x\to 0} \frac{f(x)}{x^2}$ equal to?
A. –1 B. 0
C. 1 D. 2

Directions (Qs. No. 79 & 80): *Consider the following for the next questions that follow:*

Let $f(x) = \sin [\pi^2]x + \cos[-\pi^2]x$ where [.] is a greatest integer function

79. What is $f\left(\frac{\pi}{2}\right)$ equal to?
A. –1 B. 0
C. 1 D. 2

80. What is $f\left(\frac{\pi}{4}\right)$ equal to?
A. $-\frac{1}{\sqrt{2}}$ B. –1
C. 1 D. $\frac{1}{\sqrt{2}}$

Directions (Qs. No. 81-83): *Consider the following for the next questions that follow:*

$$\text{Let } I_1 = \int_0^{\pi} \frac{x}{1+\cos^2 x}dx \text{ and}$$

$$I_2 = \int_0^{\pi} \frac{1}{1+\sin^2 x}dx$$

81. What is the value of $\frac{I_1 + I_2}{I_1 - I_2}$?
A. 1 B. π
C. π^2 D. $\frac{\pi+1}{\pi-1}$

82. What is the value of $8I_1^2$?
A. π B. π^2
C. π^3 D. π^4

83. What is the value of I_2?
A. $\frac{\pi}{\sqrt{2}}$ B. $\frac{\pi}{2\sqrt{2}}$
C. $\frac{3\pi}{2\sqrt{2}}$ D. $\frac{\pi}{4\sqrt{2}}$

Directions (Qs. No. 84 & 85): *Consider the following for the next questions that follow:*

$$\text{Let } I = \int_a^b \frac{|x|}{x}dx,\ a < b$$

84. What is I equal to when $a < 0 < b$?
A. $a + b$ B. $a - b$
C. $b - a$ D. $\frac{(a+b)}{2}$

85. What is I equal to when $a < b < 0$?
A. $a + b$ B. $a - b$
C. $b - a$ D. $\frac{(a+b)}{2}$

Directions (Qs. No. 86-88): *Consider the following for the next questions that follow:*

Let $f(x) = |\ln x|,\ x \neq 1$

86. What is the derivative of $f(x)$ at $x = 0.5$?
A. –2 B. –1
C. 1 D. 2

87. What is the derivative of $f(x)$ at $x = 2$?
A. $-\frac{1}{2}$ B. –1
C. $\frac{1}{2}$ D. 2

88. What is the derivative of $f \circ f(x)$, where $1 < x < 2$?

A. $\frac{1}{\ln x}$ B. $\frac{1}{x \ln x}$

C. $-\frac{1}{\ln x}$ D. $-\frac{1}{x \ln x}$

Directions (Qs. No. 89 & 90): *Consider the following for the next questions that follow:*

Let $f(x) = \begin{cases} x+6, & x \le 1 \\ px+q, & 1 < x < 2 \\ 5x, & x \ge 2 \end{cases}$ and $f(x)$ is continuous

89. What is the value of p?

A. 2 B. 3

C. 4 D. 5

90. What is the value of q?

A. 2 B. 3

C. 4 D. 5

91. Consider the following statements:

1. $f(x) = \ln x$ is increasing in $(0, \infty)$

2. $g(x) = e^x + e^{\frac{1}{x}}$ is decreasing in $(0, \infty)$

Which of the statement given above is/are correct?

A. 1 only

B. 2 only

C. Both 1 and 2

D. Neither 1 nor 2

92. What is the derivative of $\sin^2 x$ with respect to $\cos^2 x$?

A. –1 B. 1

C. sin 2x D. cos 2x

93. For what value of m with $m < 0$, is the area bounded by the lines $y = x$, $y = mx$ and $x = 2$ equal to 3?

A. $-\frac{1}{2}$ B. –1

C. $-\frac{3}{2}$ D. –2

94. What is the derivative of cosec $(x°)$?

A. –cosec $(x°)$ cot $(x°)$

B. $-\frac{\pi}{180}\text{cosec}(x°)\cot(x°)$

C. $\frac{\pi}{180}\text{cosec}(x°)\cot(x°)$

D. $-\frac{\pi}{180}\text{cosec}(x)\cot(x)$

95. A solution of the differential equation $\left(\frac{dy}{dx}\right)^2 - x\frac{dy}{dx} = 0$ is:

A. $y = 2x$ B. $y = 2x + 4$

C. $y = x^2 - 1$ D. $y = \frac{(x^2-2)}{2}$

96. If $f(x) = x^2 + 2$ and $g(x) = 2x - 3$, then what is $(fg)(1)$ equal to:

A. 3 B. 1

C. –2 D. –3

97. What is the range of the function $f(x) = x + |x|$ if the domain is the set of real number?

A. $(0, \infty)$ B. $[0, \infty)$

C. $(-\infty, \infty)$ D. $[1, \infty)$

98. If $f(x) = x(4x^2 - 3)$, the what is $f(\sin\theta)$ equal to?

A. –sin 3θ B. –cos 3θ

C. sin 3θ D. –sin 4θ

99. What is $\lim_{x \to 5} \frac{5-x}{|x-5|}$ equal to?

A. –1 B. 0

C. 1 D. Limit does not exist

100. What is $\lim_{x \to 1} \frac{x^9 - 1}{x^3 - 1}$ equal to?

A. –1 B. –3

C. 3 D. Limit does not exist

101. The mean and variance of five observations are 14 and 13.2 respectively. Three of the five observations are 11, 16 and 20. What are the other two observations?

A. 8 and 15

B. 9 and 14

C. 10 and 13

D. 11 and 12

102. Let A and B be two independent events such that $P(\bar{A}) = 0.7$, $P(\bar{B}) = k$, $P(A \cup B) = 0.8$. What is the value of k?

A. $\frac{5}{7}$ B. $\frac{4}{7}$

C. $\frac{2}{7}$ D. $\frac{1}{7}$

103. A biased coin with probability of getting head equal to ¼ is tossed five times. What is the probability of getting tail in all the first four tosses followed by head?

A. $\frac{81}{512}$ B. $\frac{81}{1024}$

C. $\frac{81}{256}$ D. $\frac{27}{1024}$

104. A coin is biased so that head comes up thrice as likely as tails. In four independent tosses of the coin, what is probability of getting exactly three heads?

A. $\frac{81}{256}$ B. $\frac{27}{64}$

C. $\frac{27}{256}$ D. $\frac{9}{256}$

105. Let X and Y be two random variables such that X + Y = 100. If X follows Binomial distribution with parameters n = 100 and $p = \frac{4}{5}$, what is the variance of Y?

A. 1 B. $\frac{1}{2}$

C. 16 D. $\frac{1}{16}$

106. If two lines of regression are $x + 4y + 1 = 0$ and $4x + 9y + 7 = 0$, then what is the value of x when $y = -3$?

A. −13 B. −5

C. 5 D. 7

107. The central angles p, q, r and s (in degrees) of four sector in a Pie Chart satisfy the relation $9p = 3q = 2r = 6s$. What is the value of $4p - q$?

A. 12 B. 24

C. 30 D. 36

108. The observations 4, 1, 4, 3, 6, 2, 1, 3, 4, 5, 1, 6 are outputs of 12 dices thrown simultaneously. If m and M are means of lowest 8 observations and highest 4 observations respectively, then what is ($2m$ + M) equal to?

A. 10 B. 12

C. 17 D. 21

109. A bivariate data set contains only two points (−1, 1) and (3, 2). What will the line of regression of y on x?

A. $x - 4y + 5 = 0$

B. $3x + 2y - 1 = 0$

C. $x + 4y + 1 = 0$

D. $5x - 4y + 1 = 0$

110. A die is thrown 10 times and obtained the following outputs:

1, 2, 1, 1, 2, 1, 4, 6, 5, 4

What will be the mode of data so obtained?

A. 6 B. 4

C. 2 D. 1

111. Consider the following frequency distribution:

x	1	2	3	5
f	4	6	9	7

What is the value of median of the distribution?

A. 1 B. 2

C. 3 D. 3.5

112. For data −1, 1, 4, 3, 8, 12, 17, 19, 9, 11; if M is the median of first 5 observations and N is the median of last five observations, then what is the value of 4M − N?

A. 7 B. 4

C. 1 D. 0

113. Let P, Q, R represent mean, median and mode. If for some distribution $5P = 4Q = \frac{R}{2}$, then what is $\frac{P+Q}{2P+0.7R}$ equal to?

A. $\frac{1}{12}$ B. $\frac{1}{7}$

C. $\frac{2}{9}$ D. $\frac{1}{4}$

114. If G is the geometric mean of numbers 1, 2, 2^2, 2^3, ..., 2^{n-1}, then what is the value of $1 + 2\log_2 G$?

A. 1 B. 4

C. $n - 1$ D. n

115. If H is the harmonic mean of numbers 1, 2, 2^2, 2^3, ..., 2^{n-1}, then what is n/H equal to?

A. $2 - \frac{1}{2^{n+1}}$ B. $2 - \frac{1}{2^{n-1}}$

C. $2 + \frac{1}{2^{n-1}}$ D. $2 - \frac{1}{2^n}$

116. Let P be the median, Q be the mean and R be the mode of observations $x_1, x_2, x_3, ..., x_n$. Let $S = \sum_{i=1}^{n}(2x_i - a)^2$. S takes minimum value, when a is equal to:

A. P B. $\frac{Q}{2}$

C. 2Q D. R

117. One bag contains 3 white and 2 black balls, another bag contains 2 white and 3 black balls. Two balls are drawn from the first bag and put it into the second bag and then a ball is drawn from the second bag. What is the probability that it is white?

A. $\frac{6}{7}$ B. $\frac{33}{70}$

C. $\frac{3}{10}$ D. $\frac{1}{70}$

118. Three dice are thrown. What is the probability that each face shows only multiples of 3?

A. $\frac{1}{9}$ B. $\frac{1}{18}$

C. $\frac{1}{27}$ D. $\frac{1}{3}$

119. What is the probability that the month of December has 5 Sundays?

A. 1 B. $\frac{1}{4}$

C. $\frac{3}{7}$ D. $\frac{2}{7}$

120. A natural number n is chosen from the first 50 natural numbers. What is the probability that $n + \frac{50}{n} < 50$?

A. $\frac{23}{25}$ B. $\frac{47}{50}$

C. $\frac{24}{25}$ D. $\frac{49}{50}$

ANSWERS

PAPER-I : GENERAL ABILITY TEST

1. (B)	**2. (B)**	**3. (C)**
4. (C)	**5. (C)**	**6. (B)**
7. (B)	**8. (B)**	**9. (A)**
10. (C)	**11. (A)**	**12. (D)**
13. (C)	**14. (D)**	**15. (C)**
16. (A)	**17. (A)**	**18. (B)**
19. (C)	**20. (B)**	**21. (A)**
22. (C)	**23. (B)**	**24. (C)**
25. (C)	**26. (D)**	**27. (B)**
28. (C)	**29. (C)**	**30. (D)**
31. (A)	**32. (B)**	**33. (D)**
34. (B)	**35. (A)**	**36. (D)**
37. (C)	**38. (C)**	**39. (C)**
40. (C)	**41. (B)**	**42. (A)**
43. (C)	**44. (D)**	**45. (A)**
46. (C)	**47. (D)**	**48. (B)**
49. (A)	**50. (D)**	

51. (D): When you hang the 10 kg mass on S_2, it pulls down with a force of 98N due to gravity. This same 98N force is transmitted up the chain to S_1.
So, the reading on both spring balances S_1 and S_2 would be 98N. They both experience the full weight of the 10 kg mass, regardless of their position in the series. This is due to the fact that force (in this case, the force of gravity on the 10 kg mass) is transmitted undiminished through a system in equilibrium.

52. (C): The horizontal distance (R) covered by a horizontally projected object is given by R = v*t, where v is the horizontal speed and t is the time of flight.
Since the stone is thrown horizontally from a height h, the time of flight $t = \sqrt{(2h/g)}$
Substituting the given values (v = 12 m/s, h = 20 m, and g = 10 m/s^2), we get R = 24 m.

53. (C)

54. (C): The potential energy of the liquid is given by P = mgh, where m is mass, g is acceleration due to gravity, and h is height.
Initially, the height is h, but after opening the valve, the liquid is distributed equally between the two containers, so the new height is h/2.
Therefore, $P_1 = 2P_2$.

55. (C)

56. (A): When two forces act at an angle to each other, the resultant force is given by the formula:

$$F = \sqrt{(F_1^2 + F_2^2 + 2F_1F_2 \cos\theta)}$$

where θ is the angle between the forces.
In this case, $F_1 = F_2 = 5.0$ N and $\theta = 60°$.

$$\text{So, } F = \sqrt{(5^2 + 5^2 2 \times 5 \times 5 \times \cos\theta)} = \sqrt{(50 + 25)}$$
$$= \sqrt{75} = 8.66 \text{ N (approx.)}$$

57. (B): Slate is not an igneous rock. It is a metamorphic rock, formed under the earth's surface by metamorphosis of mudstone or shale.

58. (B): The statements 2 and 3 are correct. Hypocenter is the point beneath the Earth's surface where the rupture of an earthquake begins, not the point on the surface nearest to the focus.

59. (B): The Quaternary period consists of the Pleistocene and Holocene epochs.

60. (C): In terms of average density, Earth is denser than Venus, Venus is denser than Jupiter, and Jupiter is denser than Saturn.

61. (B): The Eastern Australian Current is a warm ocean current that moves water from the tropics down the east coast of Australia.

62. (C): Podsolization is a soil formation process typical of cool or cold forested regions, such as the taiga.

63. (C): The joint military exercise 'Keen Sword 23' was conducted between the USA and Japan.

64. (C): The Battle of Rezang La was fought by the Indian Army during the Sino-Indian War in 1962.

65. (A): Statement 1 is correct. Exercise Sea Vigil-22 is a biennial pan-India coastal defence exercise conducted by the Indian Navy to assess India's preparedness in the domain of maritime security and coastal defence.
Statement 2 is incorrect. No foreign navies are involved in the exercise.

66. (B) **67. (B)**

68. (C): Statement 1 is correct. Bacterial cell walls are made of peptidoglycan.
Statement 2 is incorrect. Fungal cell walls are typically made of chitin, not cellulose.
Statement 3 is correct. Animals lack a cell wall but have an extracellular matrix composed of proteins and sugars.

69. (C): In prokaryotic cells, genetic material is not enclosed in a nuclear envelope, so they lack a true nucleus.

70. (C): Both mitochondria and chloroplasts contain their own DNA in a plant cell. This is part of the evidence for the endosymbiotic theory, which suggests that these organelles were once independent prokaryotic organisms.

71. (D): One of the advantages of sexual reproduction over asexual reproduction is that it produces more variation in offspring. This variation can make a population more resilient to environmental changes and is the basis for natural selection.

72. (A): Not all living cells have a cell wall. For example, animal cells do not possess cell walls.

73. (C): Browning of chopped apples can be minimized by using lemon juice. The acid in the lemon juice inhibits the enzyme responsible for browning (oxidative browning).

74. (B): Hydrocarbons' boiling points usually increase with the size (number of carbon atoms) of the molecule. So, the order should be Propane, Butane, Pentane, Octane.

75. (C): Separating funnel: A separating funnel is indeed used to separate immiscible liquids due to their differences in densities. Since benzene and water are immiscible and have different densities, a separating funnel would be appropriate for separating these two substances.

76. (D): When an iron nail is dipped in copper sulfate solution, the iron displaces copper from the solution because it is more reactive. This is a displacement reaction. The iron nail becomes coated with copper, which is why it turns brown.

77. (B): Copper can react with lactic acid in curd and produce toxic substances, so it's not advisable to store curd in a copper vessel.

78. (A): Toothpaste helps prevent tooth decay by neutralizing acids in the mouth. These acids are produced by bacteria that break down food particles and sugars, leading to tooth enamel erosion. The alkalinity of toothpaste can help to counteract this acidity, providing a protective effect against decay.

79. (B): Kanaklata Baruá, also called Birbala and shaheed, was an Indian independence activist an AISF leader who was shot dead by the Indian Imperial Police of the British Raj while leading a procession bearing the National Flag during the Quit India Movement of 1942.

80. (C): In the Mansabdari system, the position and salary of mansabdars were indeed indicated by a numerical designation called zat.

81. (C): Warren Hastings, the first Governor-General of Bengal, underwent impeachment proceedings in the British Parliament.

82. (A): The 'Prayag Prashasti' of Samudragupta was composed by Harishena, a court poet of Samudragupta.

83. (B): The Vijayanagara kingdom was founded by the brothers Harihar and Bukka.

84. (D): The Danes established their settlement in Tranquebar, which is in present-day Tamil Nadu, India.

85. (C) **86. (C)**

87. (C): According to the law of conservation of momentum, the total momentum before the rain fell should equal the total momentum after the rain fell (assuming no external forces). This gives the equation $M_1v_1 = M_2v_2$, where M_1 and v_1 are the mass and velocity of the wagon before the rain, and M_2 and v_2 are the mass and velocity of the wagon after the rain.

88. (D): The sound of a flute comes from the vibrating column of air inside the flute, not outside. So, the statement "Sound comes from a vibrating column of air inside as well as outside the flute" is not true.

89. (D): In a uniform magnetic field, a charge moving parallel or antiparallel to the magnetic field direction experiences no deflecting magnetic force. The reason is the angle θ in the force equation $F = qv\text{ B}\sin\theta$. This angle is between the velocity of the charge and the magnetic field. If they are parallel or antiparallel, the angle is 0° or 180°, and sin 0° = sin 180° = 0. Hence, the force is zero.

So, in this scenario, where a positive charge is moving towards the south and the magnetic field is pointing in the north direction, the charge indeed would not experience a deflecting force.

90. (B): The main greenhouse gases are water vapor, carbon dioxide, methane, nitrous oxide, and ozone. Oxygen is not considered a greenhouse gas.

91. (C): X-rays do have short wavelengths and can be generated by bombarding a metal target with high-energy electrons. They are used in medical applications, including cancer treatment. However, due to their short wavelengths and high energy, they are not used for radar systems. Radar systems typically use radio waves, which have much longer wavelengths.

92. (A): Here are the approximate latitudes of the given cities: (A) New Delhi, India: 28.61° N, (B) Kathmandu, Nepal: 27.70° N, (C) Thimphu, Bhutan: 27.47° N, (D) Dhaka, Bangladesh: 23.81° N. The city with the highest latitude (i.e., the one that is farthest north) among these is: New Delhi, India.

93. (D): All three statements are correct. The distance between the longitudes does indeed become zero at the North Pole and South Pole and is maximum at the

Equator. The number of longitudes (360) is more than the number of latitudes (180).

94. (A)

95. (D): Mica is a group of silicate minerals that are widely used in the electrical and electronics industry due to their heat resistance and insulating properties.

96. (B): Cwg Climate: This type of climate is found in most parts of the Northern Ganga Plains. In this type of climate, the summer temperature rises to 40°C which falls to 27°C in winter.

97. (A): All three statements are correct. Lachit Borphukan was a commander in the Ahom army and is known for his leadership in the Battle of Saraighat. The Lachit Borphukan Gold Medal is awarded to the best graduating cadet at the National Defence Academy every year.

98. (C): The 4th edition of joint military exercise 'DUSTLIK' between the Indian Army and Uzbekistan Army was held in February 2023 in Foreign Training Node, Pithoragarh (Uttarakhand).

99. (D): Vikram-S is India's first privately built rocket. It's maiden flight lifted on 18 November, 2022 from Sounding Rocket Complex, Sriharikota. The development of rocket was done by Skyroot Aerospace.

100. (B): Prime Minister Narendra Modi in October, 2022 declared Modhera in Gujarat's Mehsana district as India's first 24 × 7 solar-powered village.

101. (A): The tableau of Uttrakhand, based on the theme 'Manaskhand', was given away the best tableau award among the 17 states/union territories tableaux.

102. (A): Organisms that use CO_2 as their principal carbon source and can make their own food through photosynthesis or chemosynthesis are known as autotrophs.

103. (A): When yeast cells are oxygen-starved, they undergo anaerobic fermentation, which results in the production of ATP, CO_2, and ethanol.

104. (B): When cells are immersed in a hypertonic solution, water moves out of the cells to balance the concentration of solutes outside the cells. This Causes the cells to shrink in a process known as plasmolysis.

105. (C): Fungi are heterotrophs, which means they cannot carry out photosynthesis. They obtain their nutrients by absorbing organic material from their environment.

106. (D): Bryophytes lack specialized tissue for the conduction of water and nutrients, so statement (D) is not correct.

107. (B): Potassium hydroxide is used in the saponification process to convert fats and oils into soap. It does not inherently affect the hardness or softness of the soap on the skin, nor does it provide a natural fragrance or make the process more economical. However, soaps made with potassium hydroxide are typically softer than those made with sodium hydroxide.

108. (D): The correct arrangement of the metals in decreasing order of reactivity is sodium, iron, copper, and silver. Sodium is one of the most reactive elements, while silver is one of the least reactive.

109. (D): Graphite is not the second hardest substance known; in fact, it is quite soft and is used in pencil leads because of this property.

110. (B): The Haber-Bosch process is the main industrial method for producing ammonia.

111. (D): Silica, a primary ingredient in glass, is most commonly sourced from sand.

112. (D): The correct arrangement of halogens in increasing order of their oxidizing nature is iodine, bromine, chlorine, and fluorine. Fluorine is the most powerful oxidizing element.

113. (C): The blue color of hydrated copper sulfate crystals is due to the presence of water molecules. Upon heating, these water molecules are driven off, and the crystals turn white.

114. (C): Avogadro's Law states that equal volumes of all gases, at the same temperature and pressure, contain an equal number of particles (atoms, molecules, or ions).

115. (A): Airbags work on the principle of a rapid chemical reaction. Sodium azide (NaN_3) is used in this reaction, which rapidly decomposes to produce nitrogen gas when triggered. This causes the airbag to inflate.

116. (A): The Sylhet district of Assam, now part of Bangladesh, held a referendum in 1947 to decide whether to join Pakistan or remain in India. The majority voted to join Pakistan.

117. (C): The Rabatak inscription is written in the Bactrian language, not Gandhari. So statement (C) is not correct.

118. (D): The Sanskrit play "Mrichchhakatika" or "The Little Clay Cart" was written by Shudraka.

119. (A): There seems to be a typo in the options. Yashovarman was the ruler of Kannauj.

120. (C): Pataliputra (modern-day Patna) was established as the capital of the Magadhan Empire by King Ajatashatru.

121. (C): Although **Galileo Galilei** (1564-1642) didn't propose the heliocentric model, he provided critical observational evidence supporting it, such as his observations of the phases of Venus and the moons of Jupiter, using his newly developed telescope. His defense of heliocentrism led to a famous conflict with the Catholic Church. **Nicolaus Copernicus** (1473-1543) a Polish astronomer in his book, "On the

Revolutions of the Celestial Spheres" laid out his model of the solar system with the Sun at the center and the Earth and other planets revolving around it.

122. (B): Using the principle of conservation of momentum, the rate of change of momentum of the sand equals the force applied on the conveyor belt. If sand falls on the belt at a rate of 0.1 kg/s, and the belt moves at a uniform speed of 2 m/s,
the force required is 0.1 kg/s * 2 m/s = 0.2 N.

123. (B): The power P required to lift a mass m a distance d in time t against gravity g is given by $P = mgd/t$.
Substituting the given values,
$P = 8$ kg * 10 m/s^2 * 4 m/2 s = 160 W.

124. (C): The force of static friction between the two blocks can be calculated using the formula:

F_friction = μN

where:

- μ is the coefficient of static friction, and
- N is the normal force, which in this case is equal to the weight of the 2.0 kg block (since it's the weight of the top block that the friction has to counteract).

Given that the coefficient of static friction (μ) is 0.2 and the acceleration due to gravity is 10 m/s^2, we can find the normal force (N) using the equation $N = mg$, where m is the mass and g is the acceleration due to gravity.
So, N = 2.0 kg * 10 m/s^2 = 20 N.
We can then substitute the values into the friction formula:

F_friction = μN = 0.2 * 20 N = 4 N.

Therefore, the maximum value of the frictional force is 4 N.

125. (B): The extension of the spring is directly proportional to the force applied to it, which in this case is the weight of the mass. Since the acceleration due to gravity on the Moon is one-sixth that on Earth, the weight of the mass (and thus the extension of the spring) will also be one-sixth. Therefore, the extension of the spring on the Moon would be 6 cm/6 = 1 cm.

126. (B): In a second class lever, the load is between the effort and the fulcrum. A wheelbarrow, a bottle opener, or a nutcracker are examples of second class levers. In the case of the options provided, a bottle opener fits this description.

127. (C): The resistance (R) of a wire is directly proportional to its length (L) and inversely proportional to its cross-sectional area (A), which is given by the equation:
R = ρ*(L/A) where ρ (rho) is the resistivity, a property inherent to the material of the wire.
If you stretch the wire to double its original length, its cross-sectional area will decrease such that the volume (and therefore the mass) of the wire remains constant. When the length of a wire is doubled, its cross-sectional area is halved, and since resistance is inversely proportional to the area, the resistance will increase by a factor of 4.
In an electrical circuit, the current (I) is given by Ohm's Law:
I = V/R where V is the voltage, and R is the resistance.
If the resistance quadruples, the current will be one-fourth of its original value (assuming the voltage remains constant).

128. (C)

129. (D): The Bharatmala Pariyojana is a centrally-sponsored scheme that aims to improve road connectivity across India. It includes development of roads to border areas, coastal and port connectivity roads, and improving the efficiency of national corridors. Therefore, all three given schemes are included under Bharatmala Pariyojana.

130. (C): Deendayal Port was earlier known as Kandla Port. It is located in the Kutch district of Gujarat.

131. (B): The Counter Insurgency and Jungle Warfare School of the Indian Army is situated in Vairengte, Mizoram.

132. (A): In a soil-forming regime where evapotranspiration exceeds precipitation significantly, Calcification occurs. This is a process that leads to the accumulation of calcium carbonate in the soil.

133. (D): The Lehmann discontinuity is found in the innermost part of the Earth. It is a boundary within Earth's inner core, discovered by seismologist Inge Lehmann.

134. (D): Oak and Rhododendron tree species are found in the Himalayas. Rosewood is typically found in tropical regions, not the Himalayas.

135. (B): In general, a batholith is considered to be the largest and deepest of all plutonic (intrusive igneous) features. It's a large emplacement of igneous intrusive (also called plutonic) rock that forms from cooled magma deep in the Earth's crust. Batholiths are typically found at depths of tens of kilometers, making them some of the deepest geological features we know of. While a lopolith can also be deep, batholiths are generally deeper and more expansive.

136. (A): India is ahead of London, UK by 5 hours and 30 minutes. Therefore, when it is 12 noon in New Delhi, it will be 6:30 A.M. in London, UK.

137. (C): Spring tides occur when the Sun, Earth, and Moon are in line, i.e., during SYZYGY conjunction and SYZYGY opposition. Quadrature (when the Moon is at first quarter or last quarter) leads to neap tides, not spring tides.

138. (D): 'The Last Supper' was painted by Leonardo da Vinci. It is one of his most well-known works, depicting the scene of the Last Supper of Jesus with his disciples.

139. (D): Hernan Cortes was the European explorer who conquered Mexico. He was a Spanish Conquistador who led an expedition that caused the fall of the Aztec Empire.

140. (D): Large statues of Kushana rulers have been discovered near Mathura in India. Mathura was a significant center of culture and civilization during the Kushana period.

141. (A): The Treaty of Yandabo was concluded as part of the First Anglo-Burmese War.

142. (C): Plan allocation in agriculture and irrigation as a percentage of total plan outlay ie 31% was highest in the First Five-Year Plan.

143. (C): The UN COP-27 Summit relates to Climate Change. The acronym COP stands for "Conference of the Parties" and refers to the annual UN conference on climate change.

144. (C): The Singphos tribe from India's North-East had the earliest known association with the cultivation and production of tea.

145. (A): Article 51A, relating to the Fundamental Duties, was inserted into the Constitution of India by The Constitution (42nd Amendment) Act.

146. (D): The force of gravity of the Earth on the Moon and of the Moon on the Earth are equal in magnitude but are in opposite directions. This is a consequence of Newton's third law of motion, which states that for every action, there is an equal and opposite reaction.

147. (D): If the voltage is halved, the power is reduced to a quarter of the original. Therefore, when a 220V and 80W bulb is operated on 110V, the power would be 20W.

148. (D): In the dispersion of white light by a common glass prism, blue light deviates the most because it has the lowest speed in the prism. This is due to the fact that the refractive index is higher for blue light than for red light.

149. (A): The speed of sound in a given medium remains the same at all frequencies. This is because sound waves, unlike light waves, do not experience dispersion in a medium.

150. (C): The Newtonian telescope, developed by Isaac Newton, contains only mirrors. These types of telescopes are also known as reflecting telescopes.

Paper-II : Mathematics

1. (A): Given ω is a non-real cube root of 1 i.e.,

$\omega = \frac{-1+i\sqrt{3}}{2}$ & we know that $1 + \omega + \omega^2 = 0$

$\Rightarrow \quad \omega + \omega^2 = -1$

Now, $\left|\frac{1-\omega}{\omega+\omega^2}\right| = \left|\frac{1-\omega}{-1}\right| = |\omega - 1|$

$= \left|\frac{-1+i\sqrt{3}}{2} - 1\right|$

$= \left|\frac{-3+i\sqrt{3}}{2}\right| = \left|\frac{-3}{2} + \frac{i\sqrt{3}}{2}\right|$

$\Rightarrow \left|\frac{1-\omega}{\omega+\omega^2}\right| = \sqrt{\left(\frac{-3}{2}\right)^3 + \left(\frac{\sqrt{3}}{2}\right)^2}$

$= \sqrt{\frac{9}{4} + \frac{3}{4}} = \sqrt{\frac{12}{4}}$

$\Rightarrow \left|\frac{1-\omega}{\omega+\omega^2}\right| = \sqrt{3}.$

2. (D): For number to be divisible by 6, the number should be divisible by 2 and 3 both.

Now, number is divisible by 2 if units place digit is 0, 2 or 4:

Also, sum of all digits = 0 + 1 + 2 + 3 + 4 + 5 = 15

Case I: If units digit is 0; then no. of ways = 5! = 120

Case II: If units digit is either 2 or 4, then no. of ways = 2 × 4! × 4 = 192

So, total number of 6 digit number formed = 120 + 192 = 312.

3. (*): To covert 1011 decimal number, we have,

Divisible by 2	Quotient	Remainder	Binary Bit
1011 ÷ 2	505	1	1
505 ÷ 2	252	1	1
252 ÷ 2	126	0	0
126 ÷ 2	63	0	0
63 ÷ 2	31	1	1
31 ÷ 2	15	1	1
15 ÷ 2	7	1	1
7 ÷ 2	3	1	1
3 ÷ 2	1	1	1
1 ÷ 2	0	1	1

1011 = (1111110011).

4. (B)

5. (D): Given, α and β are the distinct roots of equation $x^2 - x + 1 = 0$.

we know roots of equation $x^2 - x + 1 = 0$ will be

$$\alpha = \frac{1+i\sqrt{3}}{2} = -\omega$$

and $$\beta = \frac{1-i\sqrt{3}}{2} = -\omega^2$$

as $$\omega = \frac{-1-i\sqrt{3}}{2} \ \& \ \omega^2 = \frac{-1+i\sqrt{3}}{2}$$

Hence,

$$\alpha^{100} + \beta^{100} = (-\omega)^{100} + (-\omega^2)^{100}$$
$$= \omega^{100} + \omega^{200}$$
$$= \omega^{3 \times 33} \times \omega + \omega^{3 \times 66} \times \omega^2$$
$$= 1 \times \omega + 1 \times \omega^2 \ (\because \omega^3 = 1)$$
$$= \omega + \omega^2$$
$$= -1 \ (\because 1 + \omega + \omega^2 = 0)$$

Similarly, $\alpha^{100} - \beta^{100} = (-\omega)^{100} - (-\omega^2)^{100}$
$$= \omega^{100} - \omega^{200}$$
$$= \omega^{3 \times 33} \times \omega - \omega^{3 \times 66} \times \omega^2$$
$$= 1 \times \omega - 1 \times \omega^2 \ (\because \omega^3 = 1)$$
$$= \omega - \omega^2$$
$$= -\frac{1}{2} - \frac{i\sqrt{3}}{2} + \frac{1}{2} - \frac{i\sqrt{3}}{2} = -i\sqrt{3}$$

$$\Rightarrow \left|\frac{\alpha^{100}+\beta^{100}}{\alpha^{100}-\beta^{100}}\right| = \left|\frac{-1}{-i\sqrt{3}}\right| = \left|\frac{1}{i\sqrt{3}}\right| = \left|\frac{-i}{\sqrt{3}}\right|$$

$$\left|\frac{\alpha^{100}+\beta^{100}}{\alpha^{100}-\beta^{100}}\right| = \sqrt{0+\left(\frac{1}{\sqrt{3}}\right)^2} = \frac{1}{\sqrt{3}}.$$

6. (B): When A and B be symmetric matrices then (AB – BA) is skew symmetric.

7. (D): $\because \begin{bmatrix} 3 & 5 \\ 7 & 3 \end{bmatrix}\begin{bmatrix} K \\ 2K \end{bmatrix} = \begin{bmatrix} 7 & 3 \\ 3 & 5 \end{bmatrix}\begin{bmatrix} K \\ 2K \end{bmatrix}$

$$\begin{bmatrix} 13K \\ 13K \end{bmatrix} = \begin{bmatrix} 13K \\ 13K \end{bmatrix}$$

$$\begin{bmatrix} 3 & 5 \\ 7 & 3 \end{bmatrix} \neq \begin{bmatrix} 7 & 3 \\ 3 & 5 \end{bmatrix}$$

So, both statements are wrong.

8. (B): We have,

$$x + 2y + z = 4$$
$$2x + 4y + 2z = 8$$
$$\Rightarrow \ 2(x + 2y + z) = 8$$
$$\Rightarrow \ x + 2y + z = 4$$
and $$3x + 6y + 3z = 10$$
$$\Rightarrow \ 3(x + 2y + z) = 10$$
$$\Rightarrow \ x + 2y + z = \frac{10}{3}$$

So, the linear equations have infinity many solutions.

9. (B)

10. (B): Given,

$$\begin{vmatrix} 0 & x-a & x-b \\ 0 & 0 & x-c \\ x+b & x+c & 1 \end{vmatrix} = 0$$

expanding along C_1, we get,

$$0 + 0 + (x + b)[(x - a)(x - c) - 0] = 0$$
$$\Rightarrow (x + b)(x - a)(x - c) = 0$$
$$\Rightarrow x = a, -b, c$$

Hence, sum of roots of equation $= a - b + c$.

11. (D): $2 - i\sqrt{3}$ is a root of $x^2 + ax + b$.

So, $2 + i\sqrt{3}$ is also the root of $x^2 + ax + b$.

Sum of roots $= 4$

$-a = 4 \Rightarrow a = -4$

Product of roots $= 4 + 3 = 7$

$\Rightarrow \quad b = 7$

So, $\quad a + b = -4 + 7 = 3$.

12. (B): Given,

$$z = \frac{1+i\sqrt{3}}{1-i\sqrt{3}}$$

$$\Rightarrow \quad z = \frac{\left(1+i\sqrt{3}\right)^2}{\left(1-i\sqrt{3}\right)\left(1+i\sqrt{3}\right)}$$

$$\Rightarrow \quad z = \frac{1-3+2i\sqrt{3}}{4}$$

$$\Rightarrow \quad z = \frac{-1}{2} + \frac{i\sqrt{3}}{2}$$

i.e., complex number is in second quadrant.

Hence, argument $(z) = \pi - \theta$

Here, $$\theta = \tan^{-1}\left|\frac{y}{x}\right| = \tan^{-1}\left|\frac{\sqrt{3}/2}{-1/2}\right|$$

$$= \tan^{-1}\sqrt{3} = \frac{\pi}{3}$$

$$\Rightarrow \quad \text{Argument} = \pi - \frac{\pi}{3} = \frac{2\pi}{3}.$$

13. (B): We have,

$$2b = a + c \qquad (i)\ (a, b, c \text{ in AP})$$

Let $$\Delta = \begin{vmatrix} x+1 & x+2 & x+3 \\ x+2 & x+3 & x+4 \\ x+a & x+b & x+c \end{vmatrix}$$

$$= \begin{vmatrix} x+1 & 1 & 2 \\ x+2 & 1 & 2 \\ x+a & b-a & c-a \end{vmatrix}$$

$$= \begin{vmatrix} x+1 & 1 & 2 \\ 1 & 0 & 0 \\ x+a & b-a & c-a \end{vmatrix}$$

$(x + 1)(0 - 0) - 1(c - a - 0) + 2(b - a - 0)$

$= a - c + 2b - 2a$

$= -a - c + a + c$ [Using (*i*)]

$= 0.$

14. (C): Given, $\log_x a$, a^x & $\log_b x$ are in G.P.

$\Rightarrow \log_x a \times \log_b x = (a^x)^2$

$\log_b a = (a^x)^2$

$\log_b a = (a^x)^2$

taking 'log' on both sides

$\Rightarrow \log(\log_b a) = 2 \log a^x$

$\Rightarrow \log(\log_b a) = 2x \log a,$

$(\because \log m^n = n \log m)$

$\Rightarrow x = \dfrac{\log(\log_b a)}{2\log a}$

$\Rightarrow x = \dfrac{\log_a(\log_b a)}{2}$

$\left[\because \dfrac{\log b}{\log a} = \log_a b\right]$

15. (A)

16. (B): We have,

$$a_n = 0 = \frac{5}{2} + (n-1)\left(\frac{-7}{12}\right)$$

$\Rightarrow n - 1 = \dfrac{30}{7} \Rightarrow n = \dfrac{37}{7}$

So, largest negative term will be for integer $n = 6$.

17. (A): For given equation $x^2 - 4x + k = 0$, having real roots,

discriminant ≥ 0

$\Rightarrow b^2 - 4ac \geq 0$

$\Rightarrow 16 - 4k \geq 0$

$\Rightarrow 16 \geq 4k$

$\Rightarrow k \leq 4$

Hence, in interval (0, 5), there are 4 values of k, 1, 2, 3, 4, for which equation will have real roots.

18. (B): We have,

$a = x$, $S_n = 0$

$\Rightarrow \dfrac{n}{2}[2a + (n-1)d] = 0$

$\Rightarrow 2x + (n - 1)d = 0$

$\Rightarrow d = \left(\dfrac{-2x}{n-1}\right)$

$= \dfrac{m+n}{2}[2x + (m+n-1)d] - 0$

$= \dfrac{m+n}{2}[2x + md - 2x]$

$= \left(\dfrac{m+n}{2}\right)m\left(\dfrac{-2x}{n-1}\right)$

$= \dfrac{mx(m+n)}{1-n}.$

19. (B)

20. (C): Given, $\dfrac{z-1}{z+1}$ is purely imaginary

let $z = x + iy$

then, $\dfrac{z-1}{z+1} = \dfrac{x+iy-1}{x+iy+1} = \dfrac{(x-1)+iy}{(x+1)+iy}$

multiplying by $((x + 1) - iy)$ in numerator & denominator, we get

$$\frac{z-1}{z+1} = \frac{[(x-1)+iy][(x+1)-iy]}{[(x+1)+iy][(x+1)-iy]}$$

$$= \frac{(x-1)(x+1) - iy(x-1) + iy(x+1) - (iy)^2}{(x+1)^2 - (iy)^2}$$

$$= \frac{x^2 - 1 + y^2 + iy(2)}{x^2 + y^2 + 1 + 2x}$$

$$= \frac{x^2 + y^2 - 1}{x^2 + y^2 + 2x + 1} + \frac{i2y}{x^2 + y^2 + 2x + 1}$$

Since, $\dfrac{z-1}{z+1}$ is purely imaginary i.e., real part will be zero.

$\Rightarrow \dfrac{x^2 + y^2 - 1}{x^2 + y^2 + 2x + 1} = 0$

$\Rightarrow x^2 + y^2 = 1$ ...(*i*)

Hence, $|z| = \sqrt{x^2 + y^2} = \sqrt{1} = 1$ (from equation (*i*))

21. (B)

22. (D): $f(x)$ is onto

$3x + 5 = 0 \Rightarrow x = -\dfrac{5}{3}$

So, $A = \{x = R - (-5/3)\}$

Let $y = 2x + 3/3x + 5$

$\Rightarrow 3xy + 5y = 2x + 3$

$= x = 3 - \dfrac{5y}{3y} - 2$

$3y - 2 = 0 = y = \dfrac{2}{3}$

$B = \{y = R - (2 - 3)\}.$

23. (A)

24. (D): We have,

$$T_{5+1} = 5600$$
$$^{8}C_5(x^{-8/3})^{8-5} = (x^2 \log_{10}x)^5 = 5600$$
$$56.x^{-8} \cdot x^{10} (\log_{10}x)^5 = 5600$$
$$x^2(\log_{10}x)^5 = (10)^2 \cdot (\log_{10}10)^5$$
So, $x = 10.$

25. (C): Given, $(3x - y)^4(x + 3y)^4$

$[(3x - y)(x + 3y)]^4$

$[3x^2 - xy + 9xy - 3y^2]^4$

$$= (3x^2 + 8xy - 3y^2)^4$$
$$r = 3, n = 4$$

Therefore, Noumer of term in the expansion of $(3x^2 + 8xy - 3y^2)^4$ in

$$^{n+r-1}C_{r-1} = {}^{4+3-1}C_{3-1}$$
$$= {}^6C_2 = \frac{6!}{4!2!}$$
$$= \frac{6 \times 5 \times 4!}{2! \times 4!} = \frac{6 \times 5}{2 \times 1} = 15.$$

26. (A): Given, p, q, r, s are in AP

Such that, $p + s = 8$ & $qr = 15$

Let p, q, r, s are like $a - 3d, a - d, a + d, a + 3d$ respectively.

then, $p + s = 8$ (give)

$\Rightarrow a - 3d + a + 3d = 8$

$\Rightarrow 2a = 8$

$\Rightarrow a = 4$

again, $qr = 15$ (given)

$\Rightarrow (a - d)(a + d) = 15$

$\Rightarrow a^2 - d^2 = 15$

$\Rightarrow (4)^2 - d^2 = 15$

$\Rightarrow 16 - d^2 = 15$

$\Rightarrow d^2 = 1$

$\Rightarrow d = 1, -1$

Hence, numbers will be 1, 3, 5, 7 or 7, 5, 3, 1

largest number of AP = 7

smallest number of AP = 1

Hence, difference = 6.

27. (C)

28. (D): Selection of 2 parallel lines from m lines = $^mC_2$

Selection of 2 parallel lines from n lines = $^nC_2$

No. of parallelograms formed = $^mC_2 \cdot {}^nC_2$

$= 60 = {}^mC_2 \cdot {}^nC_2$

$= {}^5C_2 \times {}^4C_2 = {}^mC_2 \cdot {}^nC_2$

$\therefore$ $m = 5$ and $n = 4$

So, $m + n = 5 + 4 = 9.$

29. (C): Given, no. of permutations of the word 'PERMUTATIONS' is x.

$$\Rightarrow x = \frac{12!}{2!} \quad ...(i)$$

no. of permutations of the word 'COMBINATIONS' is y

$$\Rightarrow y = \frac{12!}{2! \times 2! \times 2!} = \frac{12!}{2!} \times \frac{1}{4}$$
$$= x \times \frac{1}{4} \quad \text{(from equation (i))}$$
$$\Rightarrow x = 4y.$$

30. (B): Total 5 digit numbers that can be formed using 0, 1, 2, 4 and 5 without repetition

$= 4 \times 4! = 96$

No. of 5 digit numbers greater than 50000

$= 1 \times 4! = 24$

(Ten thousand should be filled by 5 only)

Required percentage = 24/96 × 100 = 25%.

31. (A): Given, $\sin\beta$ is the GM of $\sin\alpha$ and $\cos\alpha$.

i.e., $\sin\alpha \cos\alpha = \sin^2\beta$ ...(*i*)

and $\tan\gamma$ is the AM of $\sin\alpha$ and $\cos\alpha$

i.e., $\frac{\sin\alpha + \cos\beta}{2} = \tan\gamma$ ...(*ii*)

now $\cos 2\beta = 1 - 2\sin^2\beta$

$= 1 - 2\cos\alpha\sin\alpha$, (from equation (*i*))

since, $\sin^2\alpha + \cos^2\alpha = 1$

$\Rightarrow \cos 2\beta = \sin^2\alpha + \cos^2\alpha - 2\sin\alpha\cos\alpha$

$\Rightarrow \cos 2\beta = (\sin\alpha - \cos\alpha)^2$ or $(\cos\alpha - \sin\alpha)^2$.

32. (B): $\sec 2\gamma = \frac{1}{\cos 2\gamma}$

We know that $\cos 2\theta = \frac{1 - \tan^2\theta}{1 + \tan^2\theta}$

$$\Rightarrow \sec 2\gamma = \frac{1}{\frac{1 - \tan^2\gamma}{1 + \tan^2\gamma}}$$
$$\Rightarrow \sec 2\gamma = \frac{1 + \tan^2\gamma}{1 - \tan^2\gamma}$$

from equation (*ii*) of above solution

$\tan\gamma = \frac{\sin\alpha + \cos\alpha}{2}$ squaring both side

$$\Rightarrow \tan^2\gamma = \frac{\sin^2\alpha + \cos^2\alpha + 2\sin\alpha\cos\alpha}{4}$$
$$\Rightarrow \tan^2\gamma = \frac{1 + 2\sin\alpha\cos\alpha}{4}$$
$$\Rightarrow \tan^2\gamma = \frac{1 + \sin 2\alpha}{4}$$
$(\because \sin 2\alpha = 2\sin\alpha\cos\alpha)$
$$\Rightarrow \sec 2\gamma = \frac{1 + \frac{1 + \sin 2\alpha}{4}}{1 - \frac{1 + \sin 2\alpha}{4}}$$

$$= \frac{4+1+\sin 2\alpha}{4-1-\sin 2\alpha}$$

$$\Rightarrow \quad \sec 2\gamma = \frac{5+\sin 2\alpha}{3-\sin 2\alpha}.$$

For Qs. No. 33 and 34

Given, AB is a 10 m long pillar and BC is a 20 m long flagstaff standing on pillar.

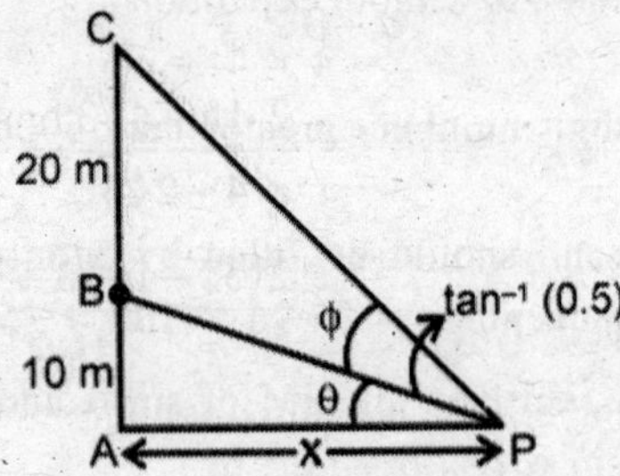

Since, flagstaff subtending angle tan–1 (0.5) at pt. P on the ground then:

33. (A): Then, $\tan(\theta + \phi) = \frac{10+20}{x} = \frac{30}{x}$

$$\Rightarrow \quad \frac{\tan\theta + \tan\phi}{1-\tan\theta\cdot\tan\phi} = \frac{30}{x}$$

since, $\quad \phi = \tan^{-1} 0.5$ (given)

$\Rightarrow \tan\phi = \frac{1}{2}$ & pillar is subtending angle θ at pt. P

$$\Rightarrow \quad \tan\theta = \frac{10}{x} \text{ (in } \Delta\text{ABP)}$$

$$\Rightarrow \quad \frac{\frac{10}{x}+\frac{1}{2}}{1-\frac{10}{x}\times\frac{1}{2}} = \frac{30}{x}$$

$$\Rightarrow \quad \frac{\frac{20+x}{2x}}{\frac{2x-10}{2x}} = \frac{30}{x}$$

$$\Rightarrow \quad \frac{20+x}{2x-10} = \frac{30}{x}$$

$$\Rightarrow \quad 20x + x^2 = 60x - 300$$

$$\Rightarrow \quad x^2 - 40x + 300 = 0$$

$\Rightarrow x = 30, 10$, which is in ratio of 1 : 3

Hence, statement 1 is right.

Since, length of flagstaff is 20 m and $x = 10, 30$ m.

Hence, x can't be equal to length of flagstaff, Hence, statement 2 is wrong.

Hence, only statement 1 is correct.

34. (C): From above solution of Qs. No. 33: In ΔABP,

$$\tan\theta = \frac{10}{x}$$

$$\Rightarrow \quad \tan\theta = \frac{10}{10} \text{ or } \frac{10}{30} \quad (\because x = 10 \text{ or } 30)$$

$$\Rightarrow \quad \tan\theta = 1 \text{ or } \frac{1}{3}.$$

35. (C) **36. (C)**

37. (C): We have,

$$x = \frac{\sin^2 A + \sin A + 1}{\sin A}$$

$$= \sin A + 1 + \frac{1}{\sin A}$$

Now, $\sin A + \frac{1}{\sin A} \geq 2 \quad (\because \text{AM} > \text{GM})$

$$\Rightarrow \sin A + \frac{1}{\sin A} + 1 \geq 3$$

$$\Rightarrow x \leq 3$$

Minimum value of $x = 3$.

38. (D): Now, $\quad x = 3$

$$\sin^2 A + \sin A + 1 = 3 \sin A$$

$$\sin A - 2 \sin A + 1 = 0$$

$$(\sin A - 1)^2 = 0$$

$$\sin A = 1 = A = \pi/2.$$

39. (C): We know that

$$a^2 = b^2 + c^2 - 2bc \cos A$$

$$b^2 = c^2 + a^2 - 2ca \cos B$$

$$c^2 = a^2 + b^2 - 2ab \cos C$$

Adding above equations, we get

$$a^2 + b^2 + c^2 = 2a^2 + 2b^2 + 2c^2$$

$$= 2ab \cos A$$

$$= 2ca \cos B - 2ab \cos C$$

$$a^2 + b^2 + c^2 = 2ab \cos C + 2bc \cos A + 2ac \cos B$$

Now, it is given that,

$$a^2 + b^2 + c^2 = ac + \sqrt{3}\, bc$$

$$2ab \cos C + 2bc \cos A + 2ac \cos B = \sqrt{3}\, bc$$

On comparing, we get

ABC is right angle triangle.

40. (C): Now, area of ABC = 1/2 × AC × BC

$$= 1/2 \times 4\sqrt{3} \times 4$$

$$\left(\frac{1}{2} = \frac{BC}{8} = BC = 4 \text{ and } \frac{\sqrt{3}}{2} = \frac{AC}{8} = AC = 4\sqrt{3}\right)$$

$$= 8\sqrt{3}.$$

41. (B) **42. (A)**

43. (C): Given S = 0! + 1! + 2! + 3! + 4! + ... + 100!

$$\Rightarrow \quad S = 1 + 1 + 2 + 6 + 24 + \ldots + 100!$$

$$\Rightarrow \quad S = 1 + 1 + 2 + 6 + (24 + \ldots + 100!)$$

$\Rightarrow \quad S = 10 + 8\left(3 + ... + \frac{100!}{8}\right)$

Since, rest each term 24, 5!, 6! ... 100! is multiple of 8)

let $3 + ... + 100! = k$

$\Rightarrow \quad S = 10 + 8k$

Hence, if S is divided by 8

$$S = \frac{10}{8} + \frac{8k}{8}$$

remainder will be 2.

44. (D): Given, $S = 0! + 1! + 2! + ... + 100!$

$\Rightarrow S = 1 + 1 + 2 + 6 + 24 + 120 + ... + 100!$

$\Rightarrow S = 1 + 1 + 2 + 6 + 24 + (120 + ... + 100!)$

$\Rightarrow S = 34 + (120 + ... + 100!)$

from 120 to 100!, all terms will be multiple of 60.

$\Rightarrow S = 34 + 60k \left(\because 2 + ... + \frac{100!}{60} = k\right)$

Now, if S is divided by 60, remainder of S = 34.

45. (C): We have

PN = PM (Tangents from an external point)

$PN = PM = n$

Similarly, $QL = QN = n + 2$

and, $RM = RL = n + 4$

So, sides of triangle are,

$PQ = 2n + 2$, $QR = 2n + 6$, $PR = 2n + 4$

Now, $\cos P = 1/3$

$$\Rightarrow \frac{(PQ)^2 + (PR)^2 - (QR)^2}{2PQ \cdot PR} = \frac{1}{3}$$

$$\Rightarrow \frac{(2n+2)^2 + (2n+4)^2 - (2n+6)^2}{2 \cdot (2n+2)(2n+4)} = \frac{1}{3}$$

$$\Rightarrow \frac{4\left((n+1)^2 + (n+2)^2 - (n+3)^2\right)}{4(n+1)(2n+4)} = \frac{1}{3}$$

$$\Rightarrow \frac{n^2 + 1 + 2n + n^2 + 4 + 4n - n^2 - n - 6n}{2n^2 + 6n + 4} = \frac{1}{3}$$

$n = 8$, or $n = -2$.

46. (D): Length of smallest side = $2n + 2 = 18$.

47. (A): We have,

$$\sin x + \cos x + \frac{\sin x}{\cos x} + \frac{\cos x}{\sin x} + \frac{1}{\cos x} + \frac{1}{\sin x} = 7$$

$$\sin x + \cos x + \frac{1}{\sin x \cdot \cos x} + \frac{\sin x + \cos x}{\sin x \cdot \cos x} = 7$$

$$\Rightarrow (\sin x + \cos x)\left(1 + \frac{2}{\sin x}\right) = 7 - \frac{2}{\sin 2x}$$

Squaring both sides, we get,

$$\Rightarrow (1 + \sin 2x)\left(1 + \frac{2}{\sin x}\right)^2 = 7 - \frac{2}{\sin 2x}$$

$\Rightarrow \sin^2 2x - 44 \sin 2x + 36 = 0.$

48. (D): $\sin^2 2x - 44 \sin 2x + 36 = 0$

$a = 22$, $b = 8$ and $c = 7$

So, $a - b + 2c = 22 - 8 + 14 = 28.$

49. (B): Let a and b are the roots of the given equation

$$\therefore \quad \alpha + \beta = \frac{4 + 2\sqrt{3}}{3 + 2\sqrt{2}} \text{ and } \alpha\beta = \frac{8 + 4\sqrt{3}}{3 + 2\sqrt{2}}$$

$$\text{HM of } \alpha \text{ and } \beta = \frac{2\alpha\beta}{\alpha + \beta}$$

$$= \frac{2 \cdot \left(8 + 4\sqrt{3}\right)}{4 + 2\sqrt{3}} \times \frac{4 - 2\sqrt{3}}{4 - 2\sqrt{3}}$$

$$= \frac{2\left(32 - 16\sqrt{3} + 16\sqrt{3} - 24\right)}{16 - 12}$$

$$= \frac{16}{4} = 4.$$

50. (A): GM of α and $\beta = \sqrt{\alpha\beta}$

$$= \sqrt{\frac{8 + 4\sqrt{3}}{3 + 2\sqrt{2}}} = \sqrt{\frac{2\left(4 + 2\sqrt{3}\right)}{3 + 2\sqrt{2}}}$$

$$= \sqrt{2}\left(\sqrt{\frac{\left(\sqrt{3} + 1\right)^2}{\left(\sqrt{2} + 1\right)^2}}\right)$$

$$= \sqrt{2}\left(\frac{\sqrt{3} + 1}{\sqrt{2} + 1} \times \frac{\sqrt{2} - 1}{\sqrt{2} - 1}\right)$$

$$= \sqrt{2}\left(\sqrt{6} - \sqrt{3} + \sqrt{2} - 1\right).$$

51. (B): $\therefore \begin{vmatrix} a & b & a\alpha + b \\ b & c & b\alpha + c \\ a\alpha + b & b\alpha + c & 0 \end{vmatrix} = 0$

$$\Rightarrow \begin{vmatrix} 0 & b & a\alpha + b \\ 0 & c & b\alpha + c \\ a\alpha^2 + 2b\alpha + c & b\alpha + c & 0 \end{vmatrix} = 0$$

$= 0 - 0 + (a\alpha^2 + 2b\alpha + c)(b^2\alpha + bc - ac\alpha - bc)$

$= 0$

$= b^2\alpha + ac\alpha = 0$ or $b^2 - ac = 0 = b^2 = ac$

So, a, b, c are in G.P.

52. (C): $(7, 4, 2, \alpha) = 0$

$7\alpha^2 + 8\alpha + 2 = 0$

So, α is root of the equation, $7x^2 + 8x + 2 = 0$.

53. (D) **54. (B)**

55. (C): Equation of line of the quadrilaterals is, $x = 0$, $y = 0$, $x + y = 1$ and $6x + y = 3$

Point of intersection of these lines are

$$A\left(\frac{1}{2}, 0\right), B(0, 0), C(0, 1), D\left(\frac{2}{5}, \frac{3}{5}\right)$$

So, equation of diagonal passes through B is,

$$BD = y - 0 = \frac{3/5}{2/5}(x-0)$$

$$2y = 3x \Rightarrow 3x - 2y = 0.$$

56. (D): Equation of diagonal AC is

$$y - 0 = \frac{1-0}{0-1/2}\left(x - \frac{1}{2}\right)$$

$$\Rightarrow \quad y = -2\left(x - \frac{1}{2}\right)$$

$$\Rightarrow \quad y = -2x + 1 \Rightarrow 2x + y - 1 = 0.$$

57. (B): The given ellipse is,

$$\frac{x^2}{1} + \frac{y^2}{\left(\frac{1}{2}\right)^2} = 1$$

As we know, sum of distance of any point P from two is,

$$PE + PE = 2a = 2.$$

58. (D)

59. (A): Given equation of circle is

$$(x - a)^2 + y^2 = a^2$$

Now, $y = x$ intersect it 2 parts

Point of intersection of line and cirlce is (0, 0) and (a, a)

$$\text{So, required area} = \int_0^a \sqrt{a^2 - (x-a)^2}\,dx - \int_0^a x\,dx$$

$$= \left(\frac{x-a}{2}\sqrt{2ax - x^2} + \frac{a^2}{2}\sin^{-1}\left(\frac{x-a}{a}\right) - \left(\frac{x^2}{2}\right)\right)_0^a$$

$$= \frac{a^2}{2}\sin^{-1}(0) - \frac{a^2}{2}\sin^{-1}(-1) - \frac{a^2}{2}$$

$$= \frac{a^2}{2}\times 0 + \frac{a^2}{2}\times\frac{\pi}{2} - \frac{a^2}{2} = \frac{a^2}{4}(\pi - 2).$$

60. (B): Area of major segment

$$= \pi r^2 - \text{Area of minor segment}$$

$$= \pi a^2 - \frac{\pi a^2}{4} - \frac{a^2}{2}$$

$$= \frac{3\pi a^2}{4} + \frac{a^2}{2} = \frac{a^2}{4}(3\pi + 2).$$

61. (A) **62. (B)**

63. (A): $dr1(2, -1, 2)$ and $(k, 3, 5)$ indicated at $\pi/4$

$$\therefore \quad \cos\frac{\pi}{4} = \frac{2k - 3 + 10}{\sqrt{4+1+4}\sqrt{k^2 + 9 + 25}}$$

$$\Rightarrow \quad \frac{1}{\sqrt{2}} = \frac{2k+7}{3\sqrt{k^2+34}}$$

$$\Rightarrow 9(k^2 + 34) = 2(2k + 7)^2$$

$$\Rightarrow 9k^2 + 306 = 2(4k^2 + 49 + 28k)$$

$$\Rightarrow 9k^2 + 306 - 8k^2 - 98 - 56k = 0$$

$$\Rightarrow k^2 - 56k + 209 = 0$$

$$\Rightarrow k^2 - 52k - 4k + 208 = 0$$

$$\Rightarrow (k - 52)(k - 4) = 0 \Rightarrow k = 52 \text{ or } k = 4.$$

64. (D): Let the drs of line perpendicular to given lines be (a, b, c)

Then, $\quad 2a - b + c = 0$

and $\quad 4a + 3b + 5c = 0$

$$\Rightarrow \quad \frac{a}{-5-6} = \frac{b}{8-10} = \frac{c}{6-4}$$

$$\Rightarrow \quad \frac{a}{-11} = \frac{b}{-2} = \frac{c}{10}$$

So, (11, 2, –10) as the required direction.

65. (B) **66. (A)**

67. (B): Given, $\vec{a} = 4\hat{i} - 8\hat{j} + \hat{k}$ which makes angle α, β, γ with the positive directions of X, Y and Z axes respectively.

i.e., given direction ratios (4, – 8, 1)

for direction cosines

$$\frac{4}{\sqrt{16+64+1}}, \frac{-8}{\sqrt{16+64+1}}, \frac{1}{\sqrt{16+64+1}}$$

$$= \frac{4}{\sqrt{81}}, \frac{-8}{\sqrt{81}}, \frac{1}{\sqrt{81}}$$

$$= \frac{4}{9}, \frac{-8}{9}, \frac{1}{9} \quad (\cos\alpha, \cos\beta, \cos\gamma)$$

Thus, $\cos\alpha = \frac{4}{9}$.

68. (A): From above solution (Qs. No. 67) we have,

$$\because \cos\alpha = \frac{4}{9}, \ \cos\beta = \frac{-8}{9} \text{ and } \cos\gamma = \frac{1}{9}$$

Then, $\cos 2\beta + \cos 2\gamma = 2\cos^2\beta - 1 + 2\cos^2\gamma - 1$

$$= 2\left(\frac{64}{81} + \frac{1}{81}\right) - 2$$

$$= \frac{130}{81} - 2 = \frac{130 - 162}{81} = \frac{-32}{81}.$$

69. (B): We have,

$$A = (1, -1, 0) \text{ and } B = (0, 1, 1)$$

Equation of line AB is,

$$\frac{x-1}{0-1} = \frac{y+1}{1+1} = \frac{z-0}{1-0}$$

$$\frac{1-x}{1} = \frac{y+1}{2} = \frac{z}{1}$$

Now only point (2) and (3) satisfy this equation.

70. (C): We have,

$$A = \hat{i} + \hat{j} + 0.\hat{k} \text{ and } B = oi + j + k$$
$$AB = (0 - 1)i + (1 + 1)i + (1 - 0)$$
$$= i + 2j + k$$
$$|\overline{AB}| = \sqrt{1^2 + 2^2 + 1} = \sqrt{6}.$$

71. (B) **72. (C)** **73. (D)**

74. (A) **75. (B)**

76. (B): Given, $f(x) = \begin{vmatrix} \cos x & x & 1 \\ 2\sin x & x^2 & 2x \\ \tan x & x & 1 \end{vmatrix}$

Now, for $f(0) = \begin{vmatrix} \cos 0 & 0 & 1 \\ 2\sin 0 & 0 & 0 \\ \tan 0 & 0 & 1 \end{vmatrix}$

Since, all the elements of column C_2 is zero.
Therefore, by the elementary property of matrix, the value of $f(0)$ equal to 0.
Hence, $f(0) = 0$.

77. (B): Given, $f(x) = \begin{vmatrix} \cos x & x & 1 \\ 2\sin x & x^2 & 2x \\ \tan x & x & 1 \end{vmatrix}$

Expanding along C_1,

$$f(x) = \cos x\,(-x)^2 - 2\sin x\,(x - x) + \tan x\,(x^2)$$
$$f(x) = x^2(\tan x - \cos x)$$
$$\lim_{x\to 0}\frac{f(x)}{x} = \lim_{x\to 0}\frac{x^2(\tan x - \cos x)}{x}$$
$$\lim_{x\to 0}\frac{f(x)}{x} = \lim_{x\to 0} x(\tan x - \cos x)$$
$$\lim_{x\to 0}\frac{f(x)}{x} = 0.$$

78. (A): $f(x) = \begin{vmatrix} \cos x & x & 1 \\ 2\sin x & x^2 & 2x \\ \tan x & x & 1 \end{vmatrix}$

$$\Rightarrow \quad f(x) = x^2(\tan x - \cos x)$$
$$\lim_{x\to 0}\frac{f(x)}{x^2} = \lim_{x\to 0}\frac{x^2(\tan x - \cos x)}{x^2}$$
$$\lim_{x\to 0}\frac{f(x)}{x^2} = \lim_{x\to 0}(\tan x - \cos x)$$
$$\lim_{x\to 0}\frac{f(x)}{x^2} = -1.$$

79. (B): We have,

$$f(x) = \sin[\pi^2]x + \cos[-\pi^2]x$$
$$= \sin 9x + \cos(-10x)$$
$$= \sin 9x + \cos 10x$$
$$= 1 + (-1) = 0.$$

80. (D): $f\left(\frac{\pi}{4}\right) = \sin\frac{9\pi}{4} + \cos\frac{5\pi}{2}$

$$= \sin\left(2\pi + \frac{\pi}{4}\right) + 0 = \sin\frac{\pi}{4} = \frac{1}{\sqrt{2}}.$$

81. (*) **82. (D)** **83. (*)**

84. (A): Given, $I = \int_a^b \frac{|x|}{x}dx,\ a < b$

$\because \quad |x| = \begin{cases} -x\ ; & x < 0 \\ x\ ; & x > 0 \end{cases}$

Thus, $\frac{|x|}{x} = \begin{cases} -1\ ; & a < x < 0 \\ 1\ ; & 0 < x < b \end{cases}$

Then, $I = \int_a^b \frac{|x|}{x}dx$

$$I = \int_a^0 \frac{|x|}{x}dx + \int_0^b \frac{|x|}{x}dx$$
$$I = \int_a^0 -1dx + \int_0^b 1dx$$
$$I = (-x)_a^0 + (x)_0^b$$
$$I = 0 + a + b + 0$$
$$I = a + b.$$

85. (B): Given, $I = \int_a^b \frac{|x|}{x}dx$ and $a < b < 0$

$$I = \int_a^b -1\,dx$$
$$I = (-x)_a^b$$
$$I = -b + a$$
$$I = a - b.$$

86. (A) **87. (C)** **88. (D)**

89. (B): Given, $f(x) = \begin{cases} x + 6\ ; & x \le 1 \\ px + q\ ; & 1 < x < 2 \\ 5x\ ; & x \ge 2 \end{cases}$

since, f is continuous,

$$\lim_{h\to 0} f(1 + h) = \lim_{h\to 0} p(1 + h) + q = f(1) = 7$$
$$= \lim_{h\to 0} p(1 + h) + q = 7$$

$$\lim_{h\to 0} f(1+h) = p + q = 7$$

$\Rightarrow$ $p + q = 7$ ...(i)

Also, $\lim_{h\to 0} f(2-h) = \lim_{h\to 0} p(2-h)+q$

$= f(2) = 10$

$\lim_{h\to 0} f(2-h) = 2p + q = 10$

$\Rightarrow$ $2 + q = 10$ ...(ii)

solving (i) and (ii), we get, $p = 3$.

90. (C): From the above solution (Qs. No. 89), we have

$p + q = 7$ ...(i)

and $2p + q = 10$ ...(ii)

and $p = 3 \rightarrow$ putting in (i)

Then, the value of $q = 4$.

91. (A)

92. (A): $\dfrac{du}{dx} = 2 \sin x \cos x$

$= \sin 2x$

and $\dfrac{dv}{dx} = 2 \cos x(-\sin x)$

$= -\sin 2x$

$\therefore$ $\dfrac{du}{dv} = \dfrac{du}{dx}\Big/\dfrac{dv}{dx}$

$= \dfrac{\sin 2x}{-\sin 2x} = -1.$

93. (A): Let the equation of line segments of ABC are given A = (2, 2), B(2, 2m) and C(0, 0)

Since area of ABC = 3

$= |1/2(0 + 2(2m - 0) + 2(0 - 2)| = 3$

$= 4m - 4 = \pm 6$

$m = 5/2$ or $m = -1/2$

$\because$ $m < 0$

$\therefore$ $m = -1/2$.

94. (B): $x^\circ = \dfrac{\pi x}{180}$ radians

$\therefore$ $\dfrac{d}{dx}(\text{cosec } x^\circ) = \dfrac{d}{dx}\left(\text{cosec}\dfrac{\pi x}{180}\right)$

$= \dfrac{-\pi}{180}\text{cosec } x^\circ \cdot \cot x^\circ.$

95. (*) **96. (D)** **97. (B)**

98. (A): $f(x) = x(4x^2 - 3)$

$f(\sin\theta) = \sin\theta(4\sin^2\theta - 3)$

$= 4\sin 3\theta - 3\sin\theta$

$= -\sin 3\theta.$

99. (D)

100. (C): We have,

$$\lim_{x\to 1}\frac{x^9-1}{x^3-1} = \lim_{x\to 1}\left(\frac{x^9-1}{x-1}\times\frac{x-1}{x^3-1}\right)$$

$$= \frac{9\cdot(1)^8}{3\cdot(1)^2} = 3.$$

101. (C): Let the other two observations be x and y

$\therefore$ Mean $= \dfrac{11+16+20+x+y}{5}$

$= 14 \times 5 = 47 + x + y$ ...(i)

$= x + y = 23$

Now, variance $= \dfrac{1}{5}[(11-14)^2 + (16-14)^2$

$+ (20 - 14)^2 + (x - 14) + (y - 14)^2]$

$= 13.2 \times 5 = 9 + 4 + 36$

$+ (x - 14)^2 + (y - 14)^2$

$= x^2 + y^2 - 28(x + y)$

$+ 2x.196 + 49 = 66$

$= x^2 + y^2 - 28(23) = -375$

$= x^2 + y^2 = 269$ ...(ii)

$x = 13, y = 10.$

102. (C): Since A and B are independent events

$0.8 = (1 - 0.7) + (1 - k) - (1 - 0.7)(1 - k)$

$0.8 = 0.3 + 1 - k - 0.3(1 - k)$

$0.5 = 1 - k - 0.3 + 0.3k$

$0.7k = 0.2 \Rightarrow k = 2/7.$

103. (B): P (getting head) $= \dfrac{1}{4}$

P (getting tail) $= 1 - \dfrac{1}{4} = \dfrac{3}{4}$

Now, required probability

$$\left(\frac{3}{4}\right)^4 = \frac{81}{1024}$$

104. (B)

105. (C): We have,

$n = 100$, $P = \dfrac{4}{5}, q = \dfrac{1}{5}$

For random variable x

$V(x) = npq = 80 \times \dfrac{1}{5} = 16$

Now, $y = 100 - x$

and, $\text{var}(y) = v(100 - x)$

$= 0 + (-1)^2\, v(x) = 16.$

106. (C): Given lines are, $x + 4y + 1 = 0$ ...(i)

and $4x + 9y + 7 = 0$ ...(ii)

We first check which of the line (*i*) and (*ii*) is line of regression y on x and x on y.

Let line, $x = -4y - 1$ be the line of regression x on y, then other be the line of regression y on x

$\therefore$ from (*i*) i.e., line of regression x on y

we have, $x = -4y - 1$

$\therefore b_{xy}$ = regression coefficient x on $y = -4$

and $y = -\frac{4}{9}x - \frac{7}{9}$, {from line (*ii*)}

$\therefore b_{yx}$ = regression coefficient y on $x = -\frac{4}{9}$

Now, count $r^2 = b_{yx}\, b_{xy} = (-4)\left(-\frac{4}{9}\right) = \frac{16}{9}$

$\Rightarrow |r| = \frac{4}{3} = 1.33$

which is not possible, as $0 < r^2 \le 1$. So our assumption is wrong.

Hence, line $x = -4y - 1$ is line of regression y on x and line $y = -\frac{4}{9}x - \frac{7}{9}$ is line of regression x on y.

Thus, from line (*ii*),

$$4x + 9y + 7 = 0$$

$$\Rightarrow x = -\frac{9}{4}y - \frac{7}{4}$$

$$\Rightarrow x = \frac{-9 \times (-3)}{4} - \frac{7}{4}$$

$$\Rightarrow x = \frac{+27 - 7}{4}$$

$$\Rightarrow x = \frac{20}{4}$$

$$\Rightarrow x = 5.$$

107. (D): Given, the central angles p, q, r and s (in degrees) of four sectors in a pie chart satisfy the relation,

$$9p = 3q = 2r = 6s$$

divided it by 36, we get

$$\frac{p}{4} = \frac{q}{12} = \frac{r}{18} = \frac{s}{6} = \text{K(let)}$$

$\Rightarrow p = 4k,\ q = 12k,\ r = 18k,\ s = 6k$

$\because p + q + r + s = 360°$

$\Rightarrow 4k + 12k + 18k + 6k = 360°$

$\Rightarrow 40k = 360°$

$\Rightarrow k = 9°$

For, $4p - q = 16\text{K} - 12k$

$= 16 \times 9° - 12 \times 9°$

$= 144° - 108° = 36°.$

108. (A): m = mean of 8 lowest observations

$$= 1 + 1 + 1 + 2 + 3 + 3 + 4 + \frac{4}{8}$$

$$\Rightarrow m = \frac{19}{8}$$

Now, M = Mean of highest 4 observation

$$\text{M} = 6 + 6 + 5 + \frac{4}{4} = \frac{21}{4}$$

$$\therefore 2m + \text{M} = \frac{19}{4} + \frac{21}{4} = \frac{40}{4} = 10.$$

109. (A): We have,

$x = -1 + 3 + = 2,\ y = 1 + 2 = 3$

$xy = -1 + 6 = 5,\ x^2 = 1 + 9 = 10$

Now $x = \frac{2}{2} = 1$ and $y = \frac{3}{2}$

So, line of regression y on x is,

$$y - y = b_{yx}(x - x)$$

$$y - \frac{3}{2} = \frac{1}{4}(x - 1) = x - 4y + 5 = 0.$$

110. (A): Given out puts:

1, 2, 1, 1, 2, 1, 4, 6, 5, 4

$\because$ Mode is the value that appears most often in a set of data values.

In given outputs, 1 is the value that appears most often.

Hence, mode = 1.

111. (C):

x	f	cf
1	4	4
2	6	10
3	9	19
5	7	26
	26	

Now, N/2 = 13

Median = 3 as cf just greater than lies for $x = 3$.

112. (D): Given data

1, 1, 4, 3, 8, 12, 17, 19, 9, 11

$\because$ M is median of first 5 observations

i.e., M = median of {–1, 1, 3, 4, 8}

Then, M = 3

and N = median of last five observations

i.e., N = median of {9, 11, 12, 17, 19}

Then, N = 12

Now, 4M – N = 12 – 12 = 0.

113. (D): Given, P = mean, Q = median, R = mode

Also, $5\text{P} = 4\text{Q} = \frac{\text{R}}{2}$ ...(*i*)

divide (*i*) by 20,

$$\frac{\text{P}}{4} = \frac{\text{Q}}{5} = \frac{\text{R}}{40} = k\text{(let)}$$

$\Rightarrow \quad P = 4k,\ Q = 5k,\ R = 40k$

Then, $\dfrac{P+Q}{2P+0.7R} = \dfrac{4k+5k}{8k+28k} = \dfrac{9k}{36k} = \dfrac{1}{4}.$

114. (D): G.M. of 1, 2, 2^2, ..., 2^{n-1}

$$= \sqrt[n]{1.2.2^2 - 2^3...2^{n-1}}$$
$$= \sqrt[n]{2^{1+2+3+...+n-1}}$$
$$= \sqrt[n]{2^{(n-1)n/2}}$$
$$= G = 2^{(n-1)/2}$$

Now, $1 + 2\log_2 G = 1 + 2(n - 1/2)$
$= 1 + n - 1 = n.$

115. (B): $\text{HM} = \dfrac{n}{1+\dfrac{1}{2} = \dfrac{1}{2^2}+...\dfrac{1}{2^{n-1}}}$

$$\Rightarrow \quad \frac{n}{H} = 1+\frac{1}{2} = \frac{1}{2^2}+...\frac{1}{2^{n-1}}$$

$$= \frac{1\left(1-\dfrac{1}{2^n}\right)}{1-\dfrac{1}{2}} = 2\left(1-\frac{1}{2^n}\right)$$

$$\Rightarrow \quad \frac{n}{H} = 2-\frac{1}{2^{n-1}}.$$

116. (C): Given, P = median, Q = mean and R = mode of the observations $x_1, x_2, x_3, ..., x_n$.

Since we know that $\sum_{i=1}^{n}(x_i - K)^2$ is least if K is mean of x_i

Now, for $\sum_{i=1}^{n}(2x_i - a)^2$ is least if a is 2 × mean of x_i's.

Hence, $a = 2Q$.

117. (*)

118. (C): Multiple of 3 = 3, 6

Then the probability that each face shows only multiple of 3 $= \dfrac{2}{6}$

∵ Three dice are thrown

Then there are three places, $\dfrac{2}{6}\times\dfrac{2}{6}\times\dfrac{2}{6}$

$$= \frac{2}{6}\times\frac{2}{6}\times\frac{2}{6} = \frac{1}{27}.$$

119. (C)

120. (B): $n+\dfrac{50}{n} < 50$

So, n can be 2, 3, ..., 48

Favourable cases = 47

Total cases = 50

Required probability $= \dfrac{47}{50}$.

Previous Papers (Solved)

NATIONAL DEFENCE ACADEMY & NAVAL ACADEMY

NDA & NA – Entrance Exam, 2022 (II)

PAPER I: GENERAL ABILITY TEST

PART A: ENGLISH LANGUAGE

ANTONYMS

Directions (Qs. No. 1-10): *Each item in this section consists of a sentence with an underlined word followed by four words (A), (B), (C) and (D). Select the option that is opposite in meaning to the underlined word and mark your response in the Answer Sheet accordingly.*

1. Human craving for comfort leads to anxiety.
A. like B. dislike
C. discomfort D. complacency

2. His writings on the subject are obscure.
A. murky B. vague
C. obvious D. uncertain

3. The achievements of the team have been monumental in the last ten years.
A. enormous B. memorable
C. striking D. unimpressive

4. His frail appearance was considered a merit.
A. weak B. delicate
C. sturdy D. big

5. The novel depicts the hapless status of certain sections of society.
A. wretched B. miserable
C. rural D. fortunate

6. Her ideas have always been eccentric.
A. special B. strange
C. normal D. local

7. The land appears to be parched.
A. dry B. desiccated
C. wet D. scorched

8. The newly made road was smooth.
A. rutted B. dangerous
C. winding D. silken

9. Plenitude is one major cause for environmental degradation.
A. abundance B. insufficiency
C. ample D. plethora

10. The scholar quoted irrefutable evidence for her thesis.
A. overwhelming B. undeniable
C. certain D. questionable

SYNONYMS

Directions (Qs. No. 11-20): *Each item in this section consists of a sentence with an underlined word followed by four words/group of words (A), (B), (C) and (D). Select the option that is nearest in meaning to the underlined word and mark your response in the Answer Sheet accordingly.*

11. Ravi told his friend that he had no intention to malign him.
A. benign B. slander
C. praise D. greet

12. Sheela appeared to be vexed.
A. clear B. calm
C. displeased D. uncomplicated

13. Do not hold any preconception about people.
A. notion B. experiment
C. great idea D. conceit

14. All mortal elements are impermanent.
A. temporal B. immortal
C. never-ending D. divinely

15. The itinerary of the group's visit to the hills was given to everyone.
A. invitation B. information
C. schedule D. names

16. The effort was to harness the power of nature.
A. abuse B. benefit
C. apply D. control

17. The fickle nature of humans is at times the cause of great innovations.
A. vacillating B. consistent
C. strong D. wily

18. The flood situation during the monsoon this year was calamitous.
A. abundance B. catastrophic
C. encouraging D. welcome

19. He was appointed as the honorary member of the team.
A. paid B. invited
C. accepted D. unpaid

20. The church decided to excommunicate him for his actions.
A. admit B. reward
C. expel D. promote

ORDERING OF WORDS IN A SENTENCE

Directions (Qs. No. 21-30): *Each of the following items in this section consists of a sentence, the parts of which have been jumbled. These parts have been labelled P, Q, R and S. Given below each sentence are four sequences namely (A), (B), (C) and (D). You are required to rearrange the jumbled parts of the sentence and mark your response accordingly.*

21. P. to be successful
Q. what it is
R. as a human being
S. have you ever considered
A. SQPR B. RQPS
C. QRSP D. PRSQ

22. P. there is in all instance a single,
Q. surrender to the idea that
R. authoritative truth to be discovered and defended
S. many people today are willing to
A. RPSQ B. SPRQ
C. RPQS D. SQPR

23. P. for yourself the implications of death,
Q. if you do not reflect and understand
R. from one preacher to another
S. you will go endlessly
A. SRPQ B. QPSR
C. RSPQ D. QRSP

24. P. a way of understanding the world,
Q. a language represents
R. and relating them to one another
S. differentiating between things
A. PSRQ B. SRPQ
C. RSPQ D. QPSR

25. P. for India's future
Q. mathematics and mathematical thinking
R. will be very important
S. it is recognized that
A. QRPS B. RPSQ
C. QRSP D. SQRP

26. P. in agriculture and veterinary sciences through
Q. will be enhanced sharply
R. programmes integrated with general education
S. the preparation of professionals
A. SRPQ B. RQPS
C. SPRQ D. PQRS

27. P. and should shift the way
Q. are certainly very important,
R. we think about politics
S. the issues raised by feminists and multiculturalists
A. RPQS B. RSPQ
C. SPQR D. SQPR

28. P. by which the genetic material of a plant is altered,
Q. pests and enhance its nutritional value
R. perhaps to make it more resistant to
S. genetic modification (GM) is the science
A. QRPS B. SPRQ
C. RSPQ D. RPQS

29. P. a much wider array of perspectives
Q. the editors of the present work
R. the history of social reforms from
S. argue the need to understand
A. QSRP B. QPRS
C. RSQP D. SQRP

30. P. for which she fought till the end
Q. as a champion of women's rights,
R. Pandita Ramabai was truly remarkable
S, as a pioneer in women's education and
A. SRQP B. QPRS
C. RSQP D. PQRS

SPOTTING ERRORS

Directions (Qs. No. 31-40): *Each item in this section has a sentence with three underlined parts labelled (A), (B) and (C). Read each sentence to find out whether there is any error in any underlined part. Indicate your response in the Answer Sheet against the corresponding letter, i.e., (A) or (B) or (C). If you find no error, your response should be indicated as (D).*

31. Our greatest glory is (A)/ not in never falling but in (B)/ raising every time we fall. (C)/ No error (D)

32. Rahim was one of that (A)/ selected for (B)/ the award. (C)/ No error (D)

33. Sujini has met her old friend (A)/ Guru before she shifted (B)/ to Hyderabad two years ago. (C)/ No error (D)

34. This monument happens (A)/ to be one of the old monument (B)/ in the city. (C)/ No error (D)

35. Amit told to Divya (A)/ that he would come (B)/ with a reward for her. (C)/ No error (D)

36. If you have asked me (A)/ for the truth I would have told (B)/ you at that time. (C)/ No error (D)

37. If I will be the millionaire (A)/ I would eradicate (B)/ poverty from the country. (C)/ No error (D)

38. A bird in hand (A)/ is better than (B)/ two in the bush. (C)/ No error (D)

39. The opportunity to attain foundational literacy (A)/ and pursue a honest livelihood (B)/ must be viewed as basic right of every citizen. (C)/ No error (D)

40. Though there is progress (A)/ for different directions, (B)/ why is there no brotherhood? (C)/ No error (D)

IDIOMS AND PHRASES

Directions (Qs. No. 41-50): *Given below are some idioms/ phrases followed by four alternative meanings for each. Choose the most appropriate answer from among the options (A), (B), (C) and (D).*

41. A queer fish
   A. A strange person
   B. A good person
   C. An unlucky person
   D. A lucky person

42. Eat like a bird
   A. Eat very quickly
   B. Eat a lot
   C. Eat continuously
   D. Eat very little

43. Lock horns
   A. Be like a bull
   B. Argue about something
   C. Agree with someone
   D. Think about the horns

44. Early bird
   A. Low flying
   B. Latest
   C. Ancient avian
   D. First arrival

45. Be in the pink
   A. To be very healthy
   B. To be very colourful
   C. To be very sad
   D. To be very rich

46. Be in the running
   A. In a very bad state to speak
   B. In a powerful position
   C. In a good position to win
   D. In a losing position

47. A sea change
   A. Change in the sea tides
   B. A complete change
   C. Change like sea
   D. Changed sea with pollution

48. A pearl of wisdom
   A. An important event in one's life
   B. An important person of wisdom
   C. An important piece of advice
   D. An important thing in one's life

49. Be in seventh heaven
   A. To be extremely sorry
   B. To be extremely wise
   C. To be extremely sad
   D. To be extremely happy

50. Be in the red
   A. To owe money to a bank
   B. To get money from one's family
   C. To be in danger of being caught
   D. To be in favour of needy people

PART B: GENERAL KNOWLEDGE

51. Which one of the following was composed by Harishena?
   A. Nashik Inscription of Gautami Balashri
   B. Prayaga Prashasti of Samudragupta
   C. Deopara Prashasti of Vijayasena
   D. Hathigumpha Inscription of Kharavela

52. Consider the following events:
   1. Establishment of the Planning Commission
   2. Formation of the National Development Council (NDC)
   3. Approval of the First Five-Year Plan by the NDC
   4. Constitution of the National Planning Committee

   Which one of the following is the correct sequence of the above events?
   A. 1-2-3-4 B. 2-1-3-4
   C. 4-1-2-3 D. 1-4-2-3

53. Which one of the following battles could be seen as laying the formal foundation of the British Raj in India?
   A. Third Battle of Panipat
   B. Battle of Plassey
   C. Battle of Buxar
   D. Revolt of 1857

54. Where in South India did the British East India Company construct a trading post in 1639?
   A. Cuddalore
   B. Madraspatam
   C. Kalahasti
   D. Karwar

55. Which of the following statements is/are correct?
1. The Dutch East India Company was formed after the formation of the British East India Company.
2. Vasco da Gama reached Calicut in 1498.

Select the correct answer using the code given below.
A. 1 only B. 2 only
C. Both 1 and 2 D. Neither 1 nor 2

56. In India, a cultivable land which is left uncultivated for more than a year but less than five years is labelled as:
A. cultivable wasteland
B. current fallow
C. fallow other than current fallow
D. barren and wasteland

57. The major portion of the Great Artesian Basin in Australia is located in:
A. Western Australia B. Victoria
C. Queensland D. Northern Territory

58. Which of the following statements is/are correct?
1. India has one of the longest navigable inland water networks in the world.
2. Inland waterways presently help in transporting about 25 per cent of the total cargo movement.
3. About 111 inland waterways have been declared as National Waterways under the National Waterways Act, 2016.

Select the correct answer using the code given below.
A. 1, 2 and 3 B. 1 and 2 only
C. 3 only D. 1 and 3 only

59. Match List-I with List-II and select the correct answer using the code given below the Lists:

List-I (Railway Zone)	List-II (Headquarters)
(*a*) East Central	1. Gorakhpur
(*b*) North Eastern	2. Jaipur
(*c*) Northeast Frontier	3. Hajipur
(*d*) North Western	4. Maligaon

Code:

	(*a*)	(*b*)	(*c*)	(*d*)
A.	3	4	1	2
B.	3	1	4	2
C.	2	1	4	3
D.	2	4	1	3

60. Which one of the following statements about earthquake waves is ***not*** correct?
A. P waves move faster and are the first to arrive at the surface.
B. P waves can travel through gaseous, liquid and solid materials.
C. Seismographs located beyond 145° from epicentre can record the arrival of P waves.
D. P waves have maximum area covered under its shadow zone

61. The commercial unit of electrical energy is kilowatt-hour (kWh), which is equal to:
A. 3.6×10^6 J B. 3.6×10^3 J
C. 10^3 J D. 1 J

62. Which one of the following statements regarding a current-carrying solenoid is ***not*** correct?
A. The magnetic field inside the solenoid is uniform.
B. The current-carrying solenoid behaves like a bar magnet.
C. The magnetic field inside the solenoid increases with increase in current.
D. If a soft iron bar is inserted inside the solenoid, the magnetic field remains the same.

63. An object is made of two equal parts by volume; one part has density ρ_0 and the other part has density $2\rho_0$. What is the average density of the object?
A. $3\rho_0$ B. $\frac{3}{2}\rho_0$
C. ρ_0 D. $\frac{1}{2}\rho_0$

64. A pressure cooker cooks food faster by:
A. increasing the boiling point of water
B. decreasing the boiling point of water
C. increasing the melting point of water
D. decreasing the melting point of water

65. Which one of the following wavelengths corresponds to the wavelength of X-rays?
A. 500 nm B. 5000 nm
C. 100 nm D. 1 nm

66. An electric bulb is connected to 220 V generator. The current drawn is 600 mA. What is the power of the bulb?
A. 132 W B. 13.2 W
C. 1320 W D. 13200 W

67. When the pitch of sound increases, which one of the following increases?
A. Intensity B. Loudness
C. Wavelength D. Frequency

68. Which one of the following is the correct reactivity series with water?
A. Zinc > Iron > Lead > Copper
B. Copper > Lead > Zinc > Iron
C. Copper > Zinc > Iron > Lead
D. Zinc > Copper > Iron > Lead

69. Which one of the following metals floats in cold water?
A. Magnesium B. Calcium
C. Potassium D. Copper

70. Which one of the following solutions is ***not*** capable of conducting electricity?
A. Copper sulphate B. Sodium chloride
C. Sugar D. Sodium hydroxide

71. To help deep-sea divers breathe, they carry cylinders of oxygen mixed with:
A. chlorine B. helium
C. nitrogen D. ozone

72. Which of the following compounds undergoes/undergo thermal decomposition?
A. Zinc oxide
B. Silver oxide and zinc oxide
C. Silver oxide
D. Magnesium oxide

73. The transfer of electrical signals by nerve cells in human body is enabled by:
A. sodium B. potassium
C. iron D. sodium and potassium

74. Silver artefacts get tarnished in air due to the formation of:
A. silver chloride B. silver oxide
C. silver sulphide D. silver sulphate

75. Human eye can see objects at different distances with contrasting illuminations. This is due to:
A. far-sightedness
B. near-sightedness
C. far-sightedness and near-sightedness
D. accommodation of eye

76. Which one of the following hormones increases the heartbeat in mammals?
A. Insulin B. Melatonin
C. Thyroxine D. Adrenaline

77. The digestion of fat in human intestine is performed by:
A. trypsin B. bile and lipase
C. bile and amylase D. bile and pepsin

78. Which one of the following statements about animal cells and plant cells is correct?
A. Animal cells have only cell membrane not cell wall, whereas plant cells have only cell wall not cell membrane.
B. Animal cells have only cell membrane not cell wall, but plant cells have both.
C. Both animal and plant cells have cell membrane and cell wall.
D. Only some cells of animals have cell wall and all plant cells have cell membrane.

79. Lymph is a tissue fluid present in intercellular spaces. It resembles to:
A. digestive juice B. cytoplasmic fluid
C. urine D. plasma

80. The breakdown of glucose in cytoplasm results in the formation of:
A. pyruvate and energy
B. pyruvate and carbon dioxide
C. pyruvate and oxygen
D. pyruvate and nitrogen

81. Rafael Nadal defeated whom among the following to win the French Open Tennis Tournament, 2022?
A. Austin Krajicek B. Ivan Dodig
C. Casper Ruud D. Joran Vliegen

82. eSanjeevani, the free telemedicine service of the Government of India, was recently integrated with the:
A. Ayushman Bharat Digital Mission
B. Aam Aadmi Bima Yojana
C. Pradhan Mantri Suraksha Bima Yojana
D. Universal Health Insurance Scheme

83. Which of the following statements about 'SHRESHTA' scheme, launched recently by the Government of India, is/are correct?
1. This scheme is for residential education for students in high school in targeted areas.
2. It provides for high quality education for meritorious but poor Scheduled Caste students.

Select the correct answer using the code given below.
A. 1 only B. 2 only
C. Both 1 and 2 D. Neither 1 nor 2

84. In a recent judgement, the Supreme Court of India directed that every protected forest, national park and wildlife sanctuary across the country should have a mandatory eco-sensitive zone (ESZ) of a minimum of:
A. 1 km starting from their demarcated boundaries
B. 2 km starting from their demarcated boundaries
C. 3 km starting from their demarcated boundaries
D. 5 km starting from their demarcated boundaries

85. Who among the following is the author of the book, *Tomb of Sand*?
A. Arundhati Roy B. Geetanjali Shree
C. Chetan Bhagat D. Jhumpa Lahiri

86. Who among the following invented the flying shuttle?
A. James Hargreaves B. John Kay
C. Richard Arkwright D. Humphry Davy

87. Where did Netaji Subhas Chandra Bose announce the formation of the Government of Free India in 1943?
A. Singapore B. Shanghai
C. Berlin D. Mandalay

88. Who among the following introduced the 'Objective Resolution' in the Constituent Assembly on 13th December, 1946?
A. Jawaharlal Nehru
B. Rajendra Prasad
C. B.R. Ambedkar
D. Alladi Krishnaswami Aiyar

89. Consider the following historical events:
1. Gandhi-Irwin Pact
2. Second Round Table Conference

3. Peasant Movement in Bardoli
4. Peasant Movement in Kheda

Which one of the following is the correct chronological order (starting from the earliest) of the above events?

A. 4-1-3-2 B. 4-3-1-2
C. 3-1-2-4 D. 1-2-4-3

90. Which of the following statements about the Unionist Party is/are correct?

1. It was a political party representing the interests of landholders in Punjab.
2. It was opposed to the idea of the partition of India as India and Pakistan.

Select the correct answer using the code given below.

A. 1 only B. 2 only
C. Both 1 and 2 D. Neither 1 nor 2

91. Which one of the following statements about metamorphic rocks is ***not*** correct?

A. Due to segregation of minerals into wavy bands or platy surfaces, some metamorphic rocks develop foliations.
B. Where the foliations develop into broad mineral bands, the metamorphic rock is extremely hard.
C. Where the foliations are moderately thin, the metamorphic rock tends to flake apart.
D. Rocks that originally were composed of one dominant mineral are often foliated by metamorphism.

92. Which one of the following 'discontinuities' separates the Earth's crust from the mantle?

A. Gutenberg B. Mohorovicic
C. Conrad D. Repetti

93. Which one of the following cities of the world would represent the greatest linear velocity of rotation of the Earth?

A. Kampala, Uganda
B. St. Petersburg, Russia
C. Madrid, Spain
D. Stockholm, Sweden

94. What will happen if you are flying east across the International Date Line?

A. You will lose 12 hours
B. You will gain 12 hours
C. You will gain 24 hours
D. You will lose 24 hours

95. The Prime Meridian does ***not*** pass through which one of the following African countries?

A. Morocco B. Algeria
C. Mali D. Ghana

96. Piecing together the puzzle of geologic time to create and analyze historical maps of the Earth is known as:

A. paleoclimatology B. paleogeomorphology
C. paleolithology D. paleogeography

97. What is the nature of velocity-time graph for a car moving with uniform acceleration?

A. Parabola B. Logarithmic
C. Straight line D. Exponential

98. The amplitude of sound waves is measured in the units of:

A. pressure B. distance
C. time D. speed

99. A current of 0.6 A is drawn by an electric bulb for 10 minutes. Which one of the following is the amount of electric charge that flows through the circuit?

A. 6 C B. 0.6 C
C. 360 C D. 36 C

100. A DC generator works on the principle of:

A. Ohm's law
B. Joule's law of heating
C. Faraday's laws of electromagnetic induction
D. None of the above

101. The presence of magnetic field can be determined using which one of the following instruments?

A. Ammeter B. Voltmeter
C. Magnetic needle D. Motor

102. Which one of the following statements about speed and velocity is correct?

A. Speed and velocity both are vector quantities.
B. Speed and velocity both are scalar quantities.
C. Speed is vector quantity and velocity is scalar quantity.
D. Speed is scalar quantity and velocity is vector quantity.

103. Bronze is an alloy of:

A. Cu and Zn B. Cu and Sn
C. Zn and Mg D. Fe and Cu

104. Which one of the following salts does ***not*** possess water of crystallization?

A. Potassium permanganate
B. Blue vitriol
C. Washing soda
D. Mohr's salt

105. Bee sting leaves an acid which causes pain and irritation. The acid released is:

A. tartaric acid B. citric acid
C. ethanoic acid D. methanoic acid

106. Liquid vegetable oils are converted to solid margarine by the use of:

A. hydrogen gas B. chlorine gas
C. carbon dioxide gas D. oxygen gas

107. The number of structural isomers of pentane is:

A. 5 B. 4
C. 2 D. 3

108. Vapours of sulphur escaping from a volcano often form a crust on the rocks. The process involved is an example of:
A. condensation B. precipitation
C. deposition D. evaporation

109. Dry ice is used on a performing stage to produce mist in air. The process involved is an example of:
A. sublimation B. evaporation
C. condensation D. precipitation

110. C_4H_8 belongs to the homologous series of:
A. alkanes B. alkenes
C. alkynes D. cycloalkanes

111. The protein-digesting enzyme secreted by the stomach wall in case of mammals is called:
A. chitinase B. amylase
C. pepsin D. trypsin

112. Which one of the following will be resulted when an animal cell is surrounded by a medium with lower concentration of water?
A. Cell will lose water
B. No change in movement of water
C. Cell will gain water
D. Cell will swell up

113. The digestive enzymes are present in:
A. mitochondria B. vacuoles
C. lysosomes D. ribosomes

114. After fertilization, the fruit and the seed are produced by:
A. ovule and ovary, respectively
B. ovary and ovule, respectively
C. ovary, no ovule required
D. ovule, no ovary required

115. Which among the following has initiated a nationwide flagship campaign 'Puneet Sagar Abhiyan' to clean seashores/beaches and other water bodies of plastic and other waste materials?
A. Indian Coast Guard
B. National Cadet Corps (NCC)
C. Indian Navy
D. Swachh Bharat Mission

116. Which among the following was the host country of the United Nations World Environment Day, 2022?
A. Canada B. Sweden
C. South Africa D. Brazil

117. Which of the following Indian Naval Ships were decommissioned in June 2022?
A. INS Ganga and INS Nipat
B. INS Nishank and INS Akshay
C. INS Khukri and INS Sandhayak
D. INS Gomati and INS Ranjit

118. India signed a deal with which one of the following countries to supply MH-60R helicopters to the Indian Navy?
A. Israel B. France
C. Russia D. USA

119. With reference to India's defence, the terms 'Surat' and 'Udaygiri' refer to:
A. coast guard patrol boats
B. cargo helicopters
C. maritime patrol aircrafts
D. warships

120. Who among the following laid the foundation of the Vijayanagara Empire?
A. Harihara and Bukka
B. Krishnadeva Raya
C. Rama Raya
D. Virupaksha Raya

121. The book, *Kalila wa Dimna* is an Arabic translation of the:
A. *Hitopadesha* B. *Panchatantra*
C. *Suryasiddhanta* D. *Kathasaritsagar*

122. Who among the following initiated the Bhoodan Movement?
A. Ram Prasad Bismil B. Vinoba Bhave
C. Mahatma Gandhi D. Kanhu Murmu

123. Which one of the following rivers in India was ***not*** crossed by Alexander and his army?
A. Hyphasis B. Acesines
C. Hydraotes D. Hydaspes

124. Who among the following has described the medieval Indian postal system as of two kinds—the horse-post called 'Uluq' and the foot-post called 'Dawa'?
A. Al-Biruni B. Duarte Barbosa
C. Ibn Battuta D. Seydi Ali Reis

125. At which among the following Harappan sites are fire altars found?
A. Kalibangan B. Harappa
C. Mohenjo-daro D. Rakhi Garhi

126. Consider the following statements on computation of density:
1. Physiological density can be computed by dividing the total population by the net cultivable area.
2. Agricultural density can be computed by dividing the total agricultural population by the net cultivable area.
3. Population density can be computed by dividing the total population by the total area.

How many of the above statements is/are correct?
A. 1 only B. 2 only
C. 3 only D. None of these

127. The formation of 'tors' on small rocky hills is associated with which among the following?
A. Granite B. Limestone
C. Alluvial D. Dolomite

128. Consider the following statements about anticyclones:
1. Anticyclones are high pressure systems.
2. Air in the centre of the system must be subsiding.
3. Anticyclones are characterized by converging winds.

How many of the above statements is/are correct?
A. 1 only B. 2 only
C. 3 only D. None of these

129. Which of the following statements is/are correct?
1. The Earth's crust is brittle in nature.
2. The mean thickness of the oceanic crust is 15 km, whereas that of the continental crust is around 30 km.

Select the correct answer using the code given below.
A. 1 only B. 2 only
C. Both 1 and 2 D. Neither 1 nor 2

130. In January 2020, the administration of which of the following Union Territories has been merged together?
A. Daman and Diu and Puducherry
B. Puducherry and Dadra and Nagar Haveli
C. Puducherry and Andaman and Nicobar Islands
D. Dadra and Nagar Haveli and Daman and Diu

131. Two convex lenses have focal lengths of 50 cm and 25 cm, respectively. If these two lenses are placed in contact, then the net power of this combination will be equal to:
A. +2 dioptre B. +6 dioptre
C. –6 dioptre D. +3 dioptre

132. Which one of the following terms ***cannot*** represent electrical power in a circuit?
A. VI B. I^2 / R
C. $I^2 R$ D. V^2 / R

133. The refractive index of crown glass is close to 3/2. If the speed of light in air is c, then the speed of light in the crown glass will be close to:
A. $(3/2)\ c$ B. $(4/9)\ c$
C. $(2/3)\ c$ D. $(9/4)\ c$

134. The volume of a sealed packet is 1 litre and its mass is 800 g. The packet is first put inside water with density 1 g cm^{-3} and then in another liquid B with density 1.5 g cm^{-3}. Then which one of the following statements holds true?
A. The packet will float in both water and liquid B.
B. The packet will sink in both water and liquid B.
C. The packet will sink in water but will float in liquid B.
D. The packet will float in water and sink in liquid B.

135. A simple pendulum having bob of mass m and length of string l has time period of T. If the mass of the bob is doubled and the length of the string is halved, then the time period of this pendulum will be:
A. T B. $\frac{T}{\sqrt{2}}$
C. 2T D. $\sqrt{2}\ T$

136. In which one of the following devices, the light energy is converted into the electrical energy?
A. Light-emitting diode B. Laser diode
C. Solar cell D. Transistor

137. Which one of the following is ***not*** a power of Panchayats under Article 243G?
A. Land improvement
B. Implementation of land reforms
C. Land consolidation and soil conservation
D. Regulation of land revenue

138. Match List-I with List-II and select the correct answer using the code given below the Lists:

List-I (Mahamatta)	List-II (Function)
(a) *Anta-mahamatta*	1. Women's welfare
(b) *Ithijhakha-mahamatta*	2. Spread of Dhamma
(c) *Dhamma-mahamatta*	3. Associated with city administration
(d) *Nagalaviyohalaka-mahamatta*	4. In-charge of frontier areas

Code:

	(a)	(b)	(c)	(d)
A.	3	2	1	4
B.	3	1	2	4
C.	4	1	2	3
D.	4	2	1	3

139. Who among the following is the author of the *Hastyayurveda*?
A. Palakapya B. Vagbhata
C. Sushruta D. Charaka

140. Which one of the following areas was acquired by the British under the Treaty of Deogaon, 1803?
A. Cuttack B. Murshidabad
C. Surat D. Calicut

141. Consider the following statements:
1. Maharashtra State has the maximum share of national highways (length in kilometres).
2. The nature of terrain and the level of economic development is one of the reasons for the maximum share of national highways in Maharashtra.

Which of the statements given above is/are correct?
A. 1 only B. 2 only
C. Both 1 and 2 D. Neither 1 nor 2

142. The activities or services focussed on creation, rearrangement and interpretation of new and existing ideas are referred to as:
A. quaternary activities B. quinary activities
C. tertiary activities D. secondary activities

143. Consider the following statements about 'Ude Desh ka Aam Nagrik (UDAN)' scheme:
1. It is an innovative scheme to develop the regional aviation market.
2. It creates affordability yet economically viable and profitable flight on regional routes.

Which of the statements given above is/are correct?
A. 1 only B. 2 only
C. Both 1 and 2 D. Neither 1 nor 2

144. Consider the following statements:
1. The Sharavati river creates Jog Falls.
2. The Brahmani river is formed by the confluence of the Kosi and Sankh rivers.
3. The Tamraparni is a river of Tirunelveli district of Tamil Nadu.

How many of the above statements is/are correct?
A. 1 B. 2
C. 3 D. None

145. SONAR is a device that is used to measure the distance of underwater objects by a ship. Which of the following types of waves does it use for this purpose?
A. Infrasonic waves
B. Sound waves in audible range for human beings
C. Ultrasonic waves
D. All of the above

146. Which one of the following statements about the speed of sound waves is ***not*** correct?
A. The speed of sound waves in steel is higher than that in water.
B. The speed of sound waves in air decreases with increase in temperature.
C. The speed of sound waves in air increases with increase in temperature.
D. The speed of sound waves in water is higher than that in air.

147. The part of the human ear that converts the pressure variations associated with audible sound waves to electrical signals is:
A. auditory nerve B. cochlea
C. eardrum D. eustachian tube

148. Which one of the following metals is most commonly used for making filament of incandescent electric bulbs?
A. Aluminium B. Silver
C. Copper D. Tungsten

149. A bullet of mass 10 g is horizontally fired with velocity 300 ms^{-1} from a pistol of mass 1 kg. What is the recoil velocity of the pistol?
A. 0.3 ms^{-1} B. 3 ms^{-1}
C. –3 ms^{-1} D. –0.3 ms^{-1}

150. A microphone converts:
A. electrical signals to sound waves
B. sound waves to electrical signals
C. microwaves to sound waves
D. sound waves to microwaves

PAPER II: MATHEMATICS

1. How many four-digit natural numbers are there such that all of the digits are odd?
A. 625 B. 400
C. 196 D. 120

2. What is $\sum_{r=0}^{n} 2^r C(n,r)$ equal to?
A. 2^n B. 3^n
C. 2^{2n} D. 3^{2n}

3. If different permutations of the letters of the word 'MATHEMATICS' are listed as in a dictionary, how many words (with or without meaning) are there in the list before the first word that starts with C?
A. 302400
B. 403600
C. 907200
D. 1814400

4. Consider the following statements:
1. If f is the subset of Z × Z defined by $f = \{(xy, x - y); x, y \in Z\}$, then f is a function from Z to Z.
2. If f is the subset of N × N defined by $f = \{(xy, x + y); x, y \in N\}$, then f is a function from N to N.

Which of the statements given above is/are correct?
A. 1 only B. 2 only
C. Both 1 and 2 D. Neither 1 nor 2

5. Consider the determinant

$$\Delta = \begin{vmatrix} a_{11} & a_{12} & a_{13} \\ a_{21} & a_{22} & a_{23} \\ a_{31} & a_{32} & a_{33} \end{vmatrix}$$

If $a_{13} = yz$, $a_{23} = zx$, $a_{33} = xy$ and the minors of a_{13}, a_{23}, a_{33} are respectively $(z - y)$, $(z - x)$, $(y - x)$ then what is the value of Δ?

A. $(z - y)(z - x)(y - x)$
B. $(x - y)(y - z)(x - z)$
C. $(x - y)(z - x)(y - z)(x + y + z)$
D. $(xy + yz + zx)(x + y + z)$

6. If $A = \begin{pmatrix} 1 & 0 & 0 \\ 0 & \cos\theta & \sin\theta \\ 0 & \sin\theta & -\cos\theta \end{pmatrix}$, then which of the following are correct?

1. A + adj A is a null matrix
2. A^{-1} + adj A is a null matrix
3. $A - A^{-1}$ is a null matrix

Select the correct answer using the code given below:
A. 1 and 2 only B. 2 and 3 only
C. 1 and 3 only D. 1, 2 and 3

7. If X is a matrix of order 3 × 3, Y is a matrix of order 2 × 3 and Z is a matrix of order 3 × 2, then which of the following are correct?

1. (ZY)X is a square matrix having 9 entries.
2. Y(XZ) is a square matrix having 4 entries.
3. X(YZ) is not defined.

Select the correct answer using the code given below:
A. 1 and 2 only B. 2 and 3 only
C. 1 and 3 only D. 1, 2 and 3

8. For how many quadratic equations, the sum of roots is equal to the product of roots?
A. 0 B. 1
C. 2 D. Infinitely many

9. Consider the following statements:

1. The set of all irrational numbers between $\sqrt{2}$ and $\sqrt{5}$ is an infinite set.
2. The set of all odd integers less than 100 is a finite set.

Which of the statements given above is/are correct?
A. 1 only B. 2 only
C. Both 1 and 2 D. Neither 1 nor 2

10. Consider the following statements:

1. $2 + 4 + 6 + ... + 2n = n^2 + n$
2. The expression $n^2 + n + 41$ always gives a prime number for every natural number n.

Which of the above statements is/are correct?
A. 1 only B. 2 only
C. Both 1 and 2 D. Neither 1 nor 2

11. Let p, q $(p > q)$ be the roots of the quadratic equation $x^2 + bx + c = 0$ where $c > 0$. If $p^2 + q^2 - 11pq = 0$, then what is $p - q$ equal to?
A. $3\sqrt{c}$ B. $3c$
C. $9\sqrt{c}$ D. $9c$

12. What is the diameter of a circle inscribed in a regular polygon of 12 sides, each of length 1 cm?
A. $1+\sqrt{2}$ cm B. $2+\sqrt{2}$ cm
C. $2+\sqrt{3}$ cm D. $3+\sqrt{3}$ cm

13. Let A = {7, 8, 9, 10, 11, 12, 13, 14, 15, 16} and let f: A → N be defined by $f(x)$ = the highest prime factor of x. How many elements are there in the range of f?
A. 4 B. 5
C. 6 D. 7

14. Let R be a relation from N to N defined by $R = \{(x, y): x, y \in N \text{ and } x^2 = y^3\}$. Which of the following are ***not*** correct?

1. $(x, x) \in R$ for all $x \in N$
2. $(x, y) \in R \Rightarrow (y, x) \in R$
3. $(x, y) \in R$ and $(y, z) \in R \Rightarrow (x, z) \in R$

Select the correct answer using the code given below:
A. 1 and 2 only B. 2 and 3 only
C. 1 and 3 only D. 1, 2 and 3

15. Consider the following:

1. $A \cap B = A \cap C \Rightarrow B = C$
2. $A \cup B = A \cup C \Rightarrow B = C$

Which of the above is/are correct?
A. 1 only
B. 2 only
C. Both 1 and 2
D. Neither 1 nor 2

Directions (Qs. No. 16-18): *Consider the following for the next three (03) items that follow:*

Let $z = \dfrac{1+i\sin\theta}{1-i\sin\theta}$ where $i = \sqrt{-1}$

16. What is the modulus of z?
A. 1 B. $\sqrt{2}$
C. $1 + \sin^2\theta$ D. $\dfrac{1+\sin^2\theta}{1-\sin^2\theta}$

17. What is angle θ such that z is purely real?
A. $\dfrac{n\pi}{2}$ B. $\dfrac{(2n+1)\pi}{2}$
C. $n\pi$ D. $2n\pi$ only
where n is an integer

18. What is angle θ such that z is purely imaginary?
A. $\dfrac{n\pi}{2}$ B. $\dfrac{(2n+1)\pi}{2}$
C. $n\pi$ D. $2n\pi$
where n is an integer

Directions (Qs. No. 19-21): *Consider the following for the next three (03) items that follow:*

Let P be the sum of first n positive terms of an increasing arithmetic progression A. Let Q be the sum of first n positive terms of another increasing arithmetic progression B.

Let P: Q = $(5n + 4)$: $(9n + 6)$

19. What is the ratio of the first term of A to that of B?

A. $\frac{1}{3}$ B. $\frac{2}{5}$

C. $\frac{3}{4}$ D. $\frac{3}{5}$

20. What is the ratio of their 10th terms?

A. $\frac{11}{29}$ B. $\frac{22}{49}$

C. $\frac{33}{59}$ D. $\frac{44}{69}$

21. If d is the common difference of A, and D is the common difference of B, then which one of the following is always correct?

A. $D > d$ B. $D < d$

C. $7D > 12d$ D. None of the above

Directions (Qs. No. 22-24): *Consider the following for the next three (03) items that follow:*

Consider the binomial expansion of $(p + qx)^9$:

22. What is the value of q if the coefficients of x^3 and x^6 are equal?

A. p B. $9p$

C. $\frac{1}{p}$ D. p^2

23. What is the ratio of the coefficients of middle terms in the expansion (when expanded in ascending powers of x)?

A. pq B. $\frac{p}{q}$

C. $\frac{4p}{5q}$ D. $\frac{1}{(pq)}$

24. Under what condition the coefficients of x^2 and x^4 are equal?

A. $p : q = 7 : 2$ B. $p^2 : q^2 = 7 : 2$

C. $p : q = 2 : 7$ D. $p^2 : q^2 = 2 : 7$

Directions (Qs. no. 25-27): *Consider the following for the next three (03) items that follow:*

Consider the word 'QUESTION':

25. How many 4-letter words each of two vowels and two consonants with or without meaning, can be formed?

A. 36 B. 144

C. 576 D. 864

26. How many 8-letter words with or without meaning, can be formed such that consonants and vowels occupy alternate positions?

A. 288 B. 576

C. 1152 D. 2304

27. How many 8-letter words with or without meaning, can be formed so that all consonants are together?

A. 5760 B. 2880

C. 1440 D. 720

Directions (Qs. No. 28-30): *Consider the following for the next three (03) items that follow:*

Let Δ be the determinant of a matrix A, where

$$A = \begin{pmatrix} a_{11} & a_{12} & a_{13} \\ a_{21} & a_{22} & a_{23} \\ a_{31} & a_{32} & a_{33} \end{pmatrix}$$ and C_{11}, C_{12}, C_{13} be the cofactors of a_{11}, a_{12}, a_{13} respectively.

28. What is the value of $a_{11}C_{11} + a_{12}C_{12} + a_{13}C_{13}$?

A. 0 B. 1

C. Δ D. $-\Delta$

29. What is the value of $a_{21}C_{11} + a_{22}C_{12} + a_{13}C_{13}$?

A. 0 B. 1

C. Δ D. $-\Delta$

30. What is the value of $\begin{vmatrix} a_{21} & a_{31} & a_{11} \\ a_{23} & a_{33} & a_{13} \\ a_{22} & a_{32} & a_{12} \end{vmatrix}$?

A. 0 B. 1

C. Δ D. $-\Delta$

Directions (Qs. No. 31-33): *Consider the following for the next three (03) items that follow:*

Let $f(x)$ be a function satisfying $f(x + y) = f(x) f(y)$ for all $x, y \in N$ such that $f(1) = 2$:

31. If $\sum_{x=2}^{n} f(x) = 2044$, then what is the value of n?

A. 8 B. 9

C. 10 D. 11

32. What is $\sum_{x=1}^{5} f(2x-1)$ equal to?

A. 341 B. 682

C. 1023 D. 1364

33. What is $\sum_{x=1}^{6} 2^x f(x)$ equal to?

A. 1365 B. 2730
C. 4024 D. 5460

Directions (Qs. No. 34-36): *Consider the following for the next three (03) items that follow:*

A university awarded medals in basket ball, football and volleyball. Only x students ($x < 6$) got medal in all the three sports and the medals went to a total of $15x$ students. It awarded $5x$ medals in basketball, $(4x + 15)$ medals in football and $(x + 25)$ medals in volleyball.

34. How many received medals in exactly two of the three sports?

A. $30 - 4x$ B. $35 - 7x$
C. $40 - 7x$ D. $45 - 5x$

35. How many received medals in at least two of three sports?

A. $30 - 6x$ B. $35 - 6x$
C. $40 - 5x$ D. $40 - 6x$

36. How many received medals in exactly one of three sports?

A. $21x - 40$ B. $21x - 35$
C. $20x - 35$ D. $20x - 25$

Directions (Qs. No. 37-39): *Consider the following for the next three (03) items that follow:*

Let $A = \begin{pmatrix} 0 & \sin^2\theta & \cos^2\theta \\ \cos^2\theta & 0 & \sin^2\theta \\ \sin^2\theta & \cos^2\theta & 0 \end{pmatrix}$ and A = P + Q where

P is symmetric matrix and Q is skew-symmetric matrix.

37. What is P equal to?

A. $\begin{pmatrix} 0 & 1/2 & 1/2 \\ 1/2 & 0 & 1/2 \\ 1/2 & 1/2 & 0 \end{pmatrix}$

B. $\begin{pmatrix} 0 & 1 & 1 \\ 1 & 0 & 1 \\ 1 & 1 & 0 \end{pmatrix}$

C. $\cos 2\theta \begin{pmatrix} 0 & -1 & 1 \\ 1 & 0 & -1 \\ -1 & 1 & 0 \end{pmatrix}$

D. $\cos 2\theta \begin{pmatrix} 0 & -1/2 & 1/2 \\ 1/2 & 0 & -1/2 \\ -1/2 & 1/2 & 0 \end{pmatrix}$

38. What is Q equal to?

A. $\begin{pmatrix} 0 & 1/2 & 1/2 \\ 1/2 & 0 & 1/2 \\ 1/2 & 1/2 & 0 \end{pmatrix}$

B. $\begin{pmatrix} 0 & 1 & 1 \\ 1 & 0 & 1 \\ 1 & 1 & 0 \end{pmatrix}$

C. $\cos 2\theta \begin{pmatrix} 0 & -1 & 1 \\ 1 & 0 & -1 \\ -1 & 1 & 0 \end{pmatrix}$

D. $\cos 2\theta \begin{pmatrix} 0 & -1/2 & 1/2 \\ 1/2 & 0 & -1/2 \\ -1/2 & 1/2 & 0 \end{pmatrix}$

39. What is the minimum value of determinant of A?

A. $\frac{1}{4}$ B. $\frac{1}{2}$
C. $\frac{3}{4}$ D. 1

Directions (Qs. No. 40-42): *Consider the following for the next three (03) items that follow:*

ABC is a triangular plot with AB = 16 m, BC = 10 m and CA = 10 m. A lamp post is situated at the middle point of the side AB. The lamp post subtends an angle 45° at the vertex B.

40. What is the height of the lamp post?

A. 6 m B. 7 m
C. 8 m D. 9 m

41. What is $\frac{AB}{\sin C}$ equal to?

A. 17 m B. $\frac{50}{3}$ m
C. $\frac{40}{3}$ m D. 16 m

42. What is cos A + cos B + cos C equal to?

A. 1 B. $\frac{41}{25}$
C. $\frac{37}{25}$ D. $\frac{33}{25}$

Directions (Qs. No. 43-45): *Consider the following for the next three (03) items that follow:*

There are two points P and Q due south of a leaning tower, which leans towards north. P is at a distance x and Q is at a distance y from the foot of the tower ($x > y$). The angles of elevation of the top of the tower from P and Q are 15° and 75° respectively.

43. At what height is the top of the tower above the ground level?

A. $\frac{x-y}{2\sqrt{3}}$ B. $\frac{x-y}{4\sqrt{3}}$

C. $\frac{x-y}{4}$ D. $\frac{x-y}{2}$

44. If θ is the inclination of the tower to the horizontal, then what is cotθ equal to?

A. $2+\frac{\sqrt{3}(x-y)}{x+y}$ B. $2-\frac{\sqrt{3}(x-y)}{x+y}$

C. $2+\frac{\sqrt{3}(x+y)}{x-y}$ D. $2-\frac{\sqrt{3}(x+y)}{x-y}$

45. What is the length of the tower?

A. $\frac{x-y}{2\sqrt{3}}\sqrt{1+\left\{2+\frac{\sqrt{3}(x+y)}{x-y}\right\}^2}$

B. $\frac{x-y}{2\sqrt{3}}\sqrt{1+\left\{2-\frac{\sqrt{3}(x+y)}{x-y}\right\}^2}$

C. $\frac{x-y}{4\sqrt{3}}\sqrt{1+\left\{2+\frac{\sqrt{3}(x+y)}{x-y}\right\}^2}$

D. $\frac{x-y}{4\sqrt{3}}\sqrt{1+\left\{2-\frac{\sqrt{3}(x+y)}{x-y}\right\}^2}$

46. What is the value of $\operatorname{cosec}\left(-\frac{73\pi}{3}\right)$?

A. $\frac{2}{\sqrt{3}}$ B. $-\frac{2}{\sqrt{3}}$

C. 2 D. –2

47. What is the value of

$$\cos\left(\frac{5\pi}{17}\right)+\cos\left(\frac{7\pi}{17}\right)+2\cos\left(\frac{11\pi}{17}\right)\cos\left(\frac{\pi}{17}\right)?$$

A. 0 B. 1

C. $4\cos\left(\frac{6\pi}{17}\right)\cos\left(\frac{\pi}{17}\right)$ D. $4\cos\left(\frac{11\pi}{17}\right)\cos\left(\frac{\pi}{17}\right)$

48. What is the value of $\tan\left(\frac{3\pi}{8}\right)$?

A. $\sqrt{2}-1$ B. $\sqrt{2}+1$

C. $1-\sqrt{2}$ D. $-\left(\sqrt{2}+1\right)$

49. What is $\tan^{-1}\cot(\operatorname{cosec}^{-1} 2)$ equal to?

A. $\frac{\pi}{8}$ B. $\frac{\pi}{6}$

C. $\frac{\pi}{4}$ D. $\frac{\pi}{3}$

50. In a triangle ABC, $a = 4$, $b = 3$, $c = 2$. What is cos3C equal to?

A. $\frac{7}{128}$ B. $\frac{11}{128}$

C. $\frac{7}{64}$ D. $\frac{11}{64}$

51. What is cos36° – cos72° equal to?

A. $\frac{\sqrt{5}}{2}$ B. $-\frac{\sqrt{5}}{2}$

C. $\frac{1}{2}$ D. $-\frac{1}{2}$

52. If $\sec x = \frac{25}{24}$ and x lies in the fourth quadrant, then what is the value of $\tan x + \sin x$?

A. $-\frac{625}{168}$ B. $-\frac{343}{600}$

C. $\frac{625}{168}$ D. $\frac{343}{600}$

53. What is the value of $\tan^2 165° + \cot^2 165°$?

A. 7 B. 14

C. $4\sqrt{3}$ D. $8\sqrt{3}$

54. What is the value of $\sin\left(2n\pi+\frac{5\pi}{6}\right)\sin\left(2n\pi-\frac{5\pi}{6}\right)$, where $n \in Z$?

A. $-\frac{1}{4}$ B. $-\frac{3}{4}$

C. $\frac{1}{4}$ D. $\frac{3}{4}$

55. If $1 + 2(\sin x + \cos x)(\sin x - \cos x) = 0$ where $0 < x < 360°$, then how many values does x take?

A. Only one value B. Only two values

C. Only three values D. Four values

56. Consider the following statements in respect of the line passing through origin and inclining at an angle of 75° with the positive direction of x-axis:

1. The line passes through the point $\left(1, \frac{1}{2-\sqrt{3}}\right)$.
2. The line entirely lies in first and third quadrants.

Which of the statements given above is/are correct?
A. 1 only B. 2 only
C. Both 1 and 2 D. Neither 1 nor 2

57. If P(3, 4) is the mid-point of a line segment between the axes, then what is the equation of the line?
A. $3x + 4y - 25 = 0$ B. $4x + 3y - 24 = 0$
C. $4x - 3y = 0$ D. $3x - 4y + 7 = 0$

58. The base AB of an equilateral triangle ABC with side 8 cm lies along the y-axis such that the mid-point of AB is at the origin and B lies above the origin. What is the equation of line passing through (8, 0) and parallel to the side AC?
A. $x-\sqrt{3}y-8=0$ B. $x+\sqrt{3}y-8=0$
C. $\sqrt{3}x+y-8\sqrt{3}=0$ D. $\sqrt{3}x-y-8\sqrt{3}=0$

59. The centre of the circle passing through origin and making positive intercepts 4 and 6 on the coordinate axes, lies on the line:
A. $2x - y + 1 = 0$ B. $3x - 2y - 1 = 0$
C. $3x - 4y + 6 = 0$ D. $2x + 3y - 26 = 0$

60. The centre of an ellipse is at (0, 0), major axis is on the y-axis. If the ellipse passes through (3, 2) and (1, 6), then what is its eccentricity?
A. $\frac{\sqrt{3}}{2}$ B. $\sqrt{3}$
C. $\frac{\sqrt{5}}{2}$ D. $\sqrt{5}$

61. An equilateral triangle is inscribed in a parabola $x^2 = \sqrt{3}y$ where one vertex of the triangle is at the vertex of the parabola. If p is the length of side of the triangle and q is the length of the latus rectum, then which one of the following is correct?
A. $p = q$ B. $p=\sqrt{3}q$
C. $p=2\sqrt{3}q$ D. $2\sqrt{3}p=q$

62. Consider the points A(2, 4, 6), B(–2, –4, –2), C(4, 6, 4) and D(8, 14, 12). Which of the following statements is/are correct?

1. The points are the vertices of a rectangle ABCD.
2. The mid-point of AC is the same as that of BD.

Select the correct answer using the code given below:
A. 1 only B. 2 only
C. Both 1 and 2 D. Neither 1 nor 2

63. Consider the equation of a sphere
$x^2 + y^2 + z^2 - 4x - 6y - 8z - 16 = 0$.
Which of the following statements is/are correct?

1. z-axis is tangent to the sphere.
2. The centre of the sphere lies on the plane $x + y + z - 9 = 0$.

Select the correct answer using the code given below:
A. 1 only B. 2 only
C. Both 1 and 2 D. Neither 1 nor 2

64. A plane cuts intercepts 2, 2, 1 on the coordinate axes. What are the direction cosines of the normal to the plane?
A. < 2/3, 2/3, 1/3 > B. < 1/3, 2/3, 2/3 >
C. $\left\langle \frac{1}{\sqrt{6}}, \frac{1}{\sqrt{6}}, \frac{2}{\sqrt{6}} \right\rangle$ D. $\left\langle \frac{2}{\sqrt{6}}, \frac{1}{\sqrt{6}}, \frac{1}{\sqrt{6}} \right\rangle$

65. Consider the following statements:

1. The direction ratios of y-axis can be < 0, 4, 0 >.
2. The direction ratios of a line perpendicular to z-axis can be < 5, 6, 0 >.

Which of the statements given above is/are correct?
A. 1 only B. 2 only
C. Both 1 and 2 D. Neither 1 nor 2

66. PQRS is a parallelogram. If $\overrightarrow{PR} = \vec{a}$ and $\overrightarrow{QS} = \vec{b}$, then what is $\overrightarrow{PQ}$ equal to?
A. $\vec{a}+\vec{b}$ B. $\vec{a}-\vec{b}$
C. $\frac{\vec{a}+\vec{b}}{2}$ D. $\frac{\vec{a}-\vec{b}}{2}$

67. Let $\vec{a}$ and $\vec{b}$ are two unit vectors such that $\vec{a}+2\vec{b}$ and $5\vec{a}-4\vec{b}$ are perpendicular. What is the angle between $\vec{a}$ and $\vec{b}$?
A. $\frac{\pi}{6}$ B. $\frac{\pi}{4}$
C. $\frac{\pi}{3}$ D. $\frac{\pi}{2}$

68. Let $\vec{a}$, $\vec{b}$ and $\vec{c}$ be unit vectors lying on the same plane. What is $\left\{\left(3\vec{a}+2\vec{b}\right)\times\left(5\vec{a}-4\vec{c}\right)\right\}.\left(\vec{b}+2\vec{c}\right)$ equal to?
A. –8 B. –32
C. 8 D. 0

69. What are the values of x for which the angle between the vectors $2x^2\hat{i}+3x\hat{j}+\hat{k}$ and $\hat{i}-2\hat{j}+x^2\hat{k}$ is obtuse?

A. $0 < x < 2$ B. $x < 0$
C. $x > 2$ D. $0 \le x \le 2$

70. The position vectors of vertices A, B and C of triangle ABC are respectively $\hat{j}+\hat{k}$, $3\hat{i}+\hat{j}+5\hat{k}$ and $3\hat{j}+3\hat{k}$. What is angle C equal to?

A. $\frac{\pi}{6}$ B. $\frac{\pi}{4}$
C. $\frac{\pi}{3}$ D. $\frac{\pi}{2}$

71. Let $z = [y]$ and $y = [x] - x$, where [.] is the greatest integer function. If x is not an integer but positive, then what is the value of z?

A. -1 B. 0
C. 1 D. 2

72. If $f(x) = 4x + 1$ and $g(x) = kx + 2$ such that $fog(x) = gof(x)$, then what is the value of k?

A. 7 B. 5
C. 4 D. 3

73. What is the minimum value of the function $f(x) = \log_{10}(x^2 + 2x + 11)$?

A. 0 B. 1
C. 2 D. 10

74. What is $\int (x^x)^2 (1+\ln x)\,dx$ equal to?

A. $x^{2x} + c$ B. $\frac{1}{2}x^{2x}+c$
C. $2x^{2x} + c$ D. $\frac{1}{2}x^{x}+c$

75. What is $\int e^x\{1+\ln x + x\ln x\}dx$ equal to?

A. $xe^x \ln x + c$ B. $x^2e^x \ln x + c$
C. $x + e^x \ln x + c$ D. $xe^x + \ln x + c$

76. What is $\int \frac{(\cos x)^{1.5} - (\sin x)^{1.5}}{\sqrt{\sin x.\cos x}}dx$ equal to?

A. $\sqrt{\sin x} - \sqrt{\cos x} + c$
B. $\sqrt{\sin x} + \sqrt{\cos x} + c$
C. $2\sqrt{\sin x} + 2\sqrt{\cos x} + c$
D. $\frac{1}{2}\sqrt{\sin x} + \frac{1}{2}\sqrt{\cos x} + c$

77. If $y = \frac{x\sqrt{x^2-16}}{2} - 8\ln\left|x+\sqrt{x^2-16}\right|$, then what is $\frac{dy}{dx}$ equal to?

A. $x\sqrt{x^2-16}$ B. $x - \sqrt{x^2-16}$
C. $\sqrt{x^2-16}$ D. $4\sqrt{x^2-16}$

78. If $y = (x^x)^x$, then which one of the following is correct?

A. $\frac{dy}{dx} + xy(1+2\ln x) = 0$
B. $\frac{dy}{dx} - xy(1+2\ln x) = 0$
C. $\frac{dy}{dx} - 2xy(1+\ln x) = 0$
D. $\frac{dy}{dx} + 2xy(1+\ln x) = 0$

79. What is the maximum value of $3(\sin x - \cos x) + 4(\cos^3 x - \sin^3 x)$?

A. 1 B. $\sqrt{2}$
C. $\sqrt{3}$ D. 2

80. What is the area of the region (in the first quadrant) bounded by $y = \sqrt{1-x^2}$, $y = x$ and $y = 0$?

A. $\frac{\pi}{4}$ B. $\frac{\pi}{6}$
C. $\frac{\pi}{8}$ D. $\frac{\pi}{12}$

81. What is the area of the region bounded by $x - |y| = 0$ and $x - 2 = 0$?

A. 1 B. 2
C. 4 D. 8

82. If $f(\alpha) = \sqrt{\sec^2\alpha - 1}$, then what is $\frac{f(\alpha)+f(\beta)}{1-f(\alpha)f(\beta)}$ equal to?

A. $f(\alpha - \beta)$ B. $f(\alpha + \beta)$
C. $f(\alpha)f(\beta)$ D. $f(\alpha\beta)$

83. If $f(x) = \ln\left(x+\sqrt{1+x^2}\right)$, then which one of the following is correct?

A. $f(x) + f(-x) = 0$ B. $f(x) - f(-x) = 0$
C. $2f(x) = f(-x)$ D. $f(x) = 2f(-x)$

84. What is $\lim_{x\to 0}\frac{x}{\sqrt{1-\cos 4x}}$ equal to?

A. $\frac{1}{2\sqrt{2}}$ B. $-\frac{1}{2\sqrt{2}}$
C. $\sqrt{2}$ D. Limit does not exist

85. What is $\lim_{x \to \frac{\pi}{2}} \frac{4x - 2\pi}{\cos x}$ equal to?

A. –4 B. –2
C. 2 D. 4

86. If $f(x) = \frac{x^2 + x + |x|}{x}$, then what is $\lim_{x \to 0} f(x)$ equal to?

A. 0 B. 1
C. 2 D. $\lim_{x \to 0} f(x)$ does not exist

87. What is $\lim_{h \to 0} \frac{\sin^2(x+h) - \sin^2 x}{h}$ equal to?

A. $\sin^2 x$ B. $\cos^2 x$
C. $\sin 2x$ D. $\cos 2x$

88. Let $f(x)$ be a function such that $f'(x) = g(x)$ and $f''(x) = -f(x)$. Let $h(x) = \{f(x)\}^2 + \{g(x)\}^2$. Then consider the following statements:
1. $h'(3) = 0$
2. $h(1) = h(2)$

Which of the statements given above is/are correct?
A. 1 only B. 2 only
C. Both 1 and 2 D. Neither 1 nor 2

89. If $y = \ln^2\left(\frac{x^2 - x + 1}{x^2 + x + 1}\right)$, then what is $\frac{dy}{dx}$ at $x = 0$ equal to?

A. –2 B. 0
C. 1 D. 2

90. If $\frac{d}{dx}\left(\frac{1 + x^4 + x^8}{1 - x^2 + x^4}\right) = ax + bx^3$, then which one of the following is correct?

A. $a = b$ B. $a = 2b$
C. $a + b = 0$ D. $2a = b$

91. Under which one of the following conditions does the function $f(x) = (p \sec x)^2 + (q \operatorname{cosec} x)^2$ attain minimum value?

A. $\tan^2 x = \frac{q}{p}$ B. $\cot^2 x = \frac{q}{p}$

C. $\tan^2 x = pq$ D. $\cot^2 x = pq$

92. Where does the function $f(x) = \sum_{j=1}^{7} (x - j)^2$ attain its minimum value?

A. $x = 3.5$ B. $x = 4$
C. $x = 4.5$ D. $x = 5$

93. Consider the following statements in respect of the function

$$f(x) = \begin{cases} |x| + 1, & 0 < |x| \le 3 \\ 1, & x = 0 \end{cases}$$

1. The function attains maximum value only at $x = 3$
2. The function attains local minimum only at $x = 0$

Which of the statements given above is/are correct?
A. 1 only B. 2 only
C. Both 1 and 2 D. Neither 1 nor 2

94. What is $\int_0^1 \ln\left(\frac{1}{x} - 1\right) dx$ equal to?

A. –1 B. 0
C. 1 D. ln 2

95. If $\int_0^{\pi/2} (\sin^4 x + \cos^4 x)\, dx = k$, then what is the value of $\int_0^{20\pi} (\sin^4 x + \cos^4 x)\, dx$?

A. k B. $10k$
C. $20k$ D. $40k$

96. What is $\int_{-\pi/2}^{\pi/2} \left(e^{\cos x} \sin x + e^{\sin x} \cos x\right) dx$ equal to?

A. $\frac{e^2 - 1}{e}$ B. $\frac{e^2 + 1}{e}$

C. $\frac{1 - e^2}{e}$ D. 0

97. What is the area of the region enclosed in the first quadrant by $x^2 + y^2 = \pi^2$, $y = \sin x$ and $x = 0$?

A. $\frac{\pi^3}{4} - 1$ B. $\frac{\pi^3}{4} - 2$

C. $\frac{\pi^3}{2} - 1$ D. $\frac{\pi^3}{4} - 2$

98. Consider the following statements:
1. The degree of the differential equation $\frac{dy}{dx} + \cos\left(\frac{dy}{dx}\right) = 0$ is 1.
2. The order of the differential equation $\left(\frac{d^2y}{dx^2}\right)^3 + \cos\left(\frac{dy}{dx}\right) = 0$ is 2.

Which of the statements given above is/are correct?
A. 1 only B. 2 only
C. Both 1 and 2 D. Neither 1 nor 2

99. What is the differential equation of the family of parabolas having vertex at origin and axis along positive y-axis?

A. $x\frac{dy}{dx}+2y=0$ B. $x\frac{dy}{dx}-2y=0$

C. $y\frac{dx}{dy}+2x=0$ D. $y\frac{dx}{dy}-2x=0$

100. What is the solution of the differential equation $(dy - dx) + \cos x\,(dy + dx) = 0$?

A. $y=\tan\left(\frac{x}{2}\right)-x+c$ B. $y=\frac{1}{2}\tan\left(\frac{x}{2}\right)-x+c$

C. $y=2\tan\left(\frac{x}{2}\right)-x+c$ D. $y=\tan\left(\frac{x}{2}\right)-2x+c$

101. Let x be the mean of squares of first n natural numbers and y be the square of mean of first n natural numbers. If $\frac{x}{y}=\frac{55}{42}$, then what is the value of n?

A. 24 B. 25
C. 27 D. 30

102. What is the probability of getting a composite number in the list of natural numbers from 1 to 50?

A. $\frac{7}{10}$ B. $\frac{17}{25}$

C. $\frac{18}{25}$ D. $\frac{33}{50}$

103. If $n > 7$, then what is the probability that C(n, 7) is a multiple of 7?

A. 0 B. $\frac{1}{7}$

C. $\frac{1}{2}$ D. 1

104. Two numbers x and y are chosen at random from a set of first 10 natural numbers. What is the probability that $(x + y)$ is divisible by 4?

A. $\frac{1}{5}$ B. $\frac{2}{9}$

C. $\frac{8}{45}$ D. $\frac{7}{45}$

105. A number x is chosen at random from first n natural numbers. What is the probability that the number chosen satisfies $x+\frac{1}{x}>2$?

A. $\frac{1}{n}$ B. $\frac{1}{(2n)}$

C. $\frac{(n-1)}{n}$ D. 1

106. Three fair dice are tossed once. What is the probability that they show different numbers that are in AP?

A. $\frac{1}{12}$ B. $\frac{1}{18}$

C. $\frac{1}{36}$ D. $\frac{1}{72}$

107. If P(A) = 0.5, P(B) = 0.7 and P(A ∩ B) = 0.3, then what is the value of P(A′ ∩ B′) + P(A′ ∩ B) + P(A ∩ B′)?

A. 0.6 B. 0.7
C. 0.8 D. 0.9

108. Five coins are tossed once. What is the probability of getting at most four tails?

A. $\frac{31}{32}$ B. $\frac{15}{16}$

C. $\frac{29}{32}$ D. $\frac{7}{8}$

109. Three fair dice are thrown. What is the probability of getting a total greater than or equal to 15?

A. $\frac{19}{216}$ B. $\frac{1}{12}$

C. $\frac{17}{216}$ D. $\frac{5}{54}$

110. The probability that a person hits a target is 0.5. What is the probability of at least one hit in 4 shots?

A. $\frac{1}{8}$ B. $\frac{1}{16}$

C. $\frac{15}{16}$ D. $\frac{7}{8}$

111. A box contains 2 white balls, 3 black balls and 4 red balls. What is the number of ways of drawing 3 balls from the box with at least one black ball?

A. 84 B. 72
C. 64 D. 48

112. During war one ship out of 5 was sunk on an average in making a certain voyage. What is the probability that exactly 3 out of 5 ships would arrive safely?

A. $\frac{16}{625}$ B. $\frac{32}{625}$

C. $\frac{64}{625}$ D. $\frac{128}{625}$

113. A card is drawn from a pack of 52 cards. A gambler bets that it is either a spade or an ace. The odds against his winning are:

A. 9 : 4 B. 35 : 17
C. 17 : 35 D. 4 : 9

114. The coefficient of correlation between ages of husband and wife at the time of marriage for a given set of 100 couples was noted to be 0.7. Assume that all these couples survive to celebrate the silver jubilee of their marriage. The coefficient of correlation at that point of time will be:

A. 1 B. 0.9
C. 0.7 D. 0.3

115. The completion of a construction job may be delayed due to strike. The probability of strike is 0.6. The probability that the construction job gets completed on time if there is no strike is 0.85 and the probability that the construction job gets completed on time if there is a strike is 0.35. What is the probability that the construction job will not be completed on time?

A. 0.35 B. 0.45
C. 0.55 D. 0.65

Directions (Qs. No. 116 and 117): *Consider the following for the next two (02) items that follow:*

The Mean and Standard Deviation (SD) of marks obtained by 50 students of a class in 4 subjects are given below:

Subject	Mathematics	Physics	Chemistry	Biology
Mean Marks	40	28	38	36
SD	15	12	14	16

116. Which one of the following subjects shows highest variability of marks?

A. Mathematics
B. Physics
C. Chemistry
D. Biology

117. What is the coefficient of variation of marks in Mathematics?

A. 37.5% B. 38.0%
C. 38.5% D. 39.0%

Directions (Qs. No. 118-120): *Consider the following for the next three (03) items that follow:*

Consider the following grouped frequency distribution:

Class	0-10	10-20	20-30	30-40	40-50	50-60
Frequency	1	2	4	6	4	3

118. What is the median of the distribution?

A. 34 B. 34.5
C. 35 D. 35.5

119. What is mean deviation about the median?

A. 11.4 B. 11.1
C. 10.8 D. 10.5

120. What is the mean deviation about the mean?

A. 10.15 B. 10.65
C. 11.15 D. 11.65

ANSWERS

PAPER-I: GENERAL ABILITY TEST

1	2	3	4	5	6	7	8	9	10
B	C	D	C	D	C	C	A	B	D
11	**12**	**13**	**14**	**15**	**16**	**17**	**18**	**19**	**20**
B	C	A	A	C	D	A	B	D	C
21	**22**	**23**	**24**	**25**	**26**	**27**	**28**	**29**	**30**
A	D	B	D	D	C	D	B	A	C
31	**32**	**33**	**34**	**35**	**36**	**37**	**38**	**39**	**40**
C	A	A	B	A	A	A	B	B	B
41	**42**	**43**	**44**	**45**	**46**	**47**	**48**	**49**	**50**
A	D	B	D	A	C	B	C	D	A
51	**52**	**53**	**54**	**55**	**56**	**57**	**58**	**59**	**60**
A	C	B	B	C	C	C	C	B	D
61	**62**	**63**	**64**	**65**	**66**	**67**	**68**	**69**	**70**
A	D	B	A	D	A	D	A	B	C
71	**72**	**73**	**74**	**75**	**76**	**77**	**78**	**79**	**80**
B	B	A	C	D	D	B	B	D	A

81	82	83	84	85	86	87	88	89	90
C	A	C	A	B	B	A	A	B	C
91	**92**	**93**	**94**	**95**	**96**	**97**	**98**	**99**	**100**
C	B	A	D	A	C	C	B	C	C
101	**102**	**103**	**104**	**105**	**106**	**107**	**108**	**109**	**110**
C	D	B	A	D	A	D	C	A	B
111	**112**	**113**	**114**	**115**	**116**	**117**	**118**	**119**	**120**
C	A	C	B	B	B	B	D	D	A
121	**122**	**123**	**124**	**125**	**126**	**127**	**128**	**129**	**130**
B	C	D	C	A	C	A	B	A	D
131	**132**	**133**	**134**	**135**	**136**	**137**	**138**	**139**	**140**
B	B	C	A	B	C	D	C	A	A
141	**142**	**143**	**144**	**145**	**146**	**147**	**148**	**149**	**150**
C	B	C	B	C	B	B	D	C	B

PAPER-II: MATHEMATICS

1	2	3	4	5	6	7	8	9	10
A	B	C	C	A	D	D	D	A	C
11	**12**	**13**	**14**	**15**	**16**	**17**	**18**	**19**	**20**
A	C	C	D	D	A	C	B	D	C
21	**22**	**23**	**24**	**25**	**26**	**27**	**28**	**29**	**30**
A	A	B	B	D	C	B	C	A	D
31	**32**	**33**	**34**	**35**	**36**	**37**	**38**	**39**	**40**
C	A	D	C	D	A	A	D	A	C
41	**42**	**43**	**44**	**45**	**46**	**47**	**48**	**49**	**50**
B	D	A	D	B	B	A	*	D	A
51	**52**	**53**	**54**	**55**	**56**	**57**	**58**	**59**	**60**
C	B	B	A	B	C	B	B	C	A
61	**62**	**63**	**64**	**65**	**66**	**67**	**68**	**69**	**70**
D	C	B	C	C	D	C	D	A	D
71	**72**	**73**	**74**	**75**	**76**	**77**	**78**	**79**	**80**
A	A	B	B	A	C	C	B	B	C
81	**82**	**83**	**84**	**85**	**86**	**87**	**88**	**89**	**90**
C	B	A	D	A	D	C	C	B	D
91	**92**	**93**	**94**	**95**	**96**	**97**	**98**	**99**	**100**
A	B	B	B	D	A	B	B	B	C
101	**102**	**103**	**104**	**105**	**106**	**107**	**108**	**109**	**110**
C	A	A	B	C	B	B	A	D	C
111	**112**	**113**	**114**	**115**	**116**	**117**	**118**	**119**	**120**
C	D	A	C	C	D	A	C	D	B

PAPER I: GENERAL KNOWLEDGE

51. Gautamiputra Satakarni was one of the greatest rulers of the Satavahan kingdom. He recaptured all the territories of Satavahans which they lost to Sakas and Kushanas. All his greatest achievement was recorded in Nashik inscription by his mother Gautami Balashri. He defeated Nahapana, and the Saka Kshatrapas were rooted out forever. 'He re-conquered the Malwa, Narmada Valley, Vidharva, Northern Maharashtra, and Northern Konkan. He also annexed Western Rajputana, Saurashtra, Kalinga and Andhra Pradesh. Andhra Pradesh, Coromandal, and Central India came under his control. He donated land to the Mahasamghikas at Karle. He assumed the title of Rajaraja and Maharaja. He was the patronage of Brahmanism. He ruled for 25 years.

52. Establishment of the Planning Commission: After India achieved independence, a formal model of planning was adopted, and accordingly the Planning Commission, reporting directly to the Prime Minister of India, was established on 15 March, 1950, with Prime Minister Jawaharlal Nehru as the Chairman.

Formation of the National Development Council (NDC): It was set up on 6 August, 1952 to strengthen and mobilize the effort and resources of the nation in support of the Five Year Plans made by Planning Commission, to promote common economic policies in all vital spheres, and to ensure the balanced and rapid development of all parts of the country.

Approval of the First Five-Year Plan by the NDC: The first five-year plan is the only five-year plan adopted without the consent of the National Development Council. The first meeting of the NDC was chaired by Jawaharlal Nehru in November 1952. Approval of the First Five-Year Plan by the NDC was in November 1952.

Constitution of the National Planning Committee: The National Planning Committee was established in India in 1938 by Congress President and Indian National Army supreme leader Netaji Subhash Chandra Bose, and later on by Jawaharlal Nehru.

53. The Battle of Plassey was fought in 1757 in the Plassey (or Palashi) region of West Bengal, on the east of Bhagirathi river. Troops of the British East India Company, led by Robert Clive, came up against the forces of Siraj-ud-Daulah, the last independent Nawab of Bengal, and his French allies.

The then Nawab of Bengal, Siraj-ud-Daulah succeeded his grandfather Alavardi Khan after his death. Alavardi Khan was the Deputy Governor of Bihar who assumed the throne after killing Sarfaraz Khan, an incapable son of Murshiq Quli Khan, Dewan of Bengal. Siraj-ud-Daulah was surrounded by a number of rivals in his own court who helped the British in winning the Battle of Plassey.

54. Present day Chennai was then known as Madraspatnam. Madras was established on 22 August, 1639. Here the British East India Company had built a trading Post. The British East India Company first settled in southern India in 1611, but moved to the area of Madras in 1639 in order to be near the established textile weavers' communities. Fort St. George, White Town and Black Town were together called Madras. Andrew Cogan and Francis Day can be considered the founders of Madras. Madras was an important place for the colonialists because of the port there. The city became an important trading centre between India and Europe after the development of the harbour. Many merchants arrived and set businesses in Madras, many of which trade till date. Examples are EID Parry (started in 1788, one of the oldest mercantile companies in India), Binny & Co, Higginbotham's, etc. The original Fort St. George, which was rebuilt, houses the Tamil Nadu Legislative Assembly and the Chief Minister's office. On July 17th 1996, Madras was renamed Chennai, the name being derived from Chennapatnam.

55. The Dutch East India Company was created in 1602 as "United East India Company" and its first permanent trading post was in Indonesia. In India, they established the first factory in Masulipattanam in 1605, followed by Pulicat in 1610, Surat in 1616, Bimilipatam in 1641 and Chinsura in 1653. In Bengal, they established a factory in Pipli, but it was abandoned later.

The arrival of three ships under Vasco da Gama, led by a Gujarati pilot named Abdul Majid, at Calicut in May 1498 profoundly affected the course of Indian history.

56. Any land which is left fallow or uncultivated for more than five years is included in the category of Culturable waste land. The land under this category has decreased from 6.23% in 1960-61 to 4% in 2014-15. It can be brought under cultivation after improving it through reclamation practices. If the land is left uncultivated for more than five years, it would be categorized as culturable wasteland.

Permanent Pastures and Grazing Lands: Most of this type of land is owned by the village 'Panchayat' or the Government. Only a small proportion of this land is privately owned. The land owned by the village panchayat comes under 'Common Property Resources'.

Current Fallow: This is the land that is left without cultivation for one or less than one agricultural year.

Fallowing is a cultural practice adopted for giving the land rest. The land recoups lost fertility through natural processes.

57. The Great Artesian Basin (GAB) is one of the largest underground water sources in the world and Australia's largest groundwater basin. In fact, it's the only reliable resource of fresh water throughout much of inland Australia. About 65% of the Basin - 1,203,920 km^2 lies within Queensland and its precious water is a key enabler to over 80 Queensland communities.

58. In comparison to India, China has more than 125,000 km of navigable inland rivers. In the entire world, it has the most comprehensive system. Only 0.5% of freight in India is transported via inland waterways. Under the National Waterways Act of 2016, approximately 111 inland waterways have been designated as National Waterways.

60. P-wave shadow zones are formed due to refraction, which causes the waves to deviate away. But S-wave shadow zones are created because these waves are completely blocked. Thus the S-wave shadow zones are much larger. P-waves can travel through liquid, solids and gases, while S waves only travel through solids. Scientists use this information to help them determine the structure of Earth. For example, if an earthquake occurs on one side of Earth, seismometers around the globe can measure the resulting S and P waves.

61. 1 kWh = (1 kilowatt) (1 hour)

= $(1 \times 10^3$ watt) (1 hour)

1 watt = 1 Js^{-1}

So, 1 kWh = (1000 J s^{-1}) $(1 \times 60 \times 60\text{s})$

$= 36 \times 10^5 \text{ J} = 3.6 \times 10^6 \text{ J}$

Thus, 1 kWh in Joules is equal to 3.6×10^6 J.

62. When current carrying solenoid is taken, it produces its own magnetic field inside and outside the solenoid. When a soft iron bar/core is placed inside the solenoid, it magnetizes the iron bar thereby increasing the strength of the magnetic field inside the solenoid.

The soft iron core aids in concentrating magnetic lines of force through the solenoid, resulting in a nearly uniform magnetic field at the core's end face. The magnetic lines of forces begin to diverge in the absence of a core, curving sharply outside the coils. The stronger the magnetic created in the core, the narrower the distance between the coils and the core. As a result, the most effective electromagnets have coils tightly twisted around the core.

63. Given, $V_1 = V_1 = V$

$p_1 = p_0$, $p_2 = 2p_0$,

Average density = Total mass/Total volume

$$= \frac{m_1 + m_2}{V_1 + V_2} = \frac{p_1 V_1 + p_2 V_2}{V_1 + V_2}$$

$$= \frac{p_0 V + 2p_0 V}{V + V} = \frac{3p_0}{2}.$$

64. A pressure cooker is air tight and does not let steam escape from inside the container. Thus, accumulation of steam inside the small space of the container increases the vapour pressure inside the container. Now, this vapour pressure exerts force on the liquid (generally water) which is present along with the food to be cooked. Hence, the molecules in the liquid are forced to come closer together. This causes an opposition in the process of boiling, that is, the liquid turning into its vapour. To turn into vapour, the molecules of the liquid need to overcome this opposition and move far apart. For this, they require more thermal energy and increased temperature. Hence, the boiling point of the liquid increases. Hence, boiling point of water increases with increase in vapour pressure and decreases with decrease in vapour pressure.

65. X-rays are part of the electromagnetic spectrum (wavelength is given in angstroms). X-rays have a wavelength in the range of 0.01-10 nm, corresponding to frequencies in the range of 3 × 10. They are shorter in wavelength than UV rays and longer than gamma rays.

German physicist Wilhelm Röntgen is typically credited for the discovery of X-Rays in 1895 because he was the first to comprehensively study them, though he is not thought to be the first to have seen and perceived their effects. X-Ray are produced when high-velocity electrons collide with the metal plates, thereby giving the energy as the X-Rays and themselves absorbed by the metal plate.

- The X-Ray beam travels through the air and comes in contact with the body. tissues, and produces an image on a metal film.
- Soft tissue like organs and skin, cannot absorb the high-energy rays, and the beam passes through them.
- Dense materials inside our bodies, like bones, absorb the radiation.

66. Power of bulb, P = VI

$= 220 \times 600 \times 10^{-3} = 132$ watt

The power rating 100 W means the bulb consumes electrical energy of 100 Joule per second. Joule is the SI unit of energy. 1 Watt-hour is equal to 3600 Joules. The filament of an electric bulb is made up of tungsten.

67. Pitch of sound depends upon frequency, so when pitch gets higher frequency f also becomes higher, now we have wavelength of sound $\lambda \propto 1/f$ (for constant speed of sound in a medium), hence wavelength decreases i.e. frequency and wavelength go through a change when pitch gets higher. The pitch of the sound is defined as the characteristic of sound which is used for differentiating between shrill and flat sounds. On the other hand, the number of vibrations made by a particle of the medium in one second is called frequency. If a sound's frequency rises, its pitch rises as well. When a body vibrates, the sound is produced, and it reaches us via the vibrations of the particles of the surrounding medium. The frequency of a note determines its pitch. Even though two notes are sounded on the same instrument, their pitches will differ if their vibrations are of different frequencies.

68. Order of reactivity of metal:

Na > Ca > Mg > Al > Zn > Fe > Sn > Pb > Cu > Ag

69. Calcium reacts less vigorously with water to form hydrogen gas. The metal starts floating because the bubbles of hydrogen gas formed stick to the surface of the metal. Metal oxide and hydrogen gas is created when a metal and water reacts together.

Metal + water = metal oxide + hydrogen is the fundamental equation for the metal reaction with water. Cold water and the metals sodium, potassium, and calcium quickly react to form hydroxides. Magnesium does not react with cold water. Metals like aluminium, iron and zinc do not react either with cold or hot water. Metals such as lead, copper, silver and gold do not react with water at all.

70. The aqueous solution of an ionic compound conducts electricity because there are plenty of free 'ions' in the solution and not free "electrons". In aqueous solution, the ionic compounds conduct electricity because they contain charged particles called cations and anions. These ions are free to move to conduct electricity.

To conduct electricity, a substance must have mobile, charged particles. In a metal, the electrons are highly mobile, but in water they are not. In an aqueous solution, the solute must supply the mobile charge carriers if the solution is to conduct electricity. Soluble ionic compounds, like salt, or compounds that ionize in water, like acids, will do this. But sugar is not ionic and does not ionize in water. So a sugar solution has no mobile charge carriers: no ions that move in response to an electric field. It only has the same tiny quantities of ions produce by the self-ionization of water, which is not enough to make it a significant conductor.

71. The main reason for adding helium to the breathing mix is to reduce the proportions of nitrogen and oxygen below those of air, to allow the gas mix to be breathed safely on deep dives. A lower proportion of nitrogen is required to reduce nitrogen narcosis and other physiological effects of the gas at depth. Helium has very little narcotic effect. A lower proportion of oxygen reduces the risk of oxygen toxicity on deep dives. The lower density of helium reduces breathing resistance at depth.

72. Thermal decomposition is a chemical reaction that happens when a compound breaks down when heated. Thermal decomposition reactions happen at high temperatures. The reactants absorb lots of energy before breaking down into the products. The starting compound is the reactant.

73. Nerve cells present in brain and spinal cord function to transmit and receive signals to and from the body. The sodium is needed in the human body to transfer electrical signals by nerve cells. The sodium-potassium pump triggers an electrical impulse that travels from one nerve cell to the next transmitting messages between brain, spinal cord and the rest of the body.

The nervous system includes the brain, spinal cord, and a complex network of nerves. This system sends messages back and forth between the brain and the body.

The brain is what controls all the body's functions. The spinal cord runs from the brain down through the back. It contains threadlike nerves that branch out to every organ and body part. This network of nerves relays messages back and forth from the brain to different parts of the body.

Nerves have cells called neurons. Neurons carry messages from the brain via the spinal cord. The neurons that carry these messages to the muscles are called motor neurons.

Each motor neuron ending sits very close to a muscle fibre. Where they sit together is called a neuromuscular junction. The motor neurons release a chemical, which is picked up by the muscle fibre. This tells the muscle fibre to contract, which makes the muscles move.

74. Silver article turns black when kept in the air because silver article reacts with sulphur compounds such as hydrogen sulphide (H_2S) present in air.

$$Ag + H_2S \rightarrow Ag_2S + H_2$$

The phenomenon is called corrosion. For silver particularly, it is called tarnishing of silver. Silver sulphide (Ag_2S) is the black substance formed. Corrosion is a natural process that converts a refined metal into a more chemically stable oxide. It is the gradual deterioration of materials (usually a metal) by chemical or electrochemical reaction with their environment.

75. When the ciliary muscles are relaxed, the eye lens becomes thin, the focal length increases, and the distant objects are clearly visible to the eyes. To see the nearby objects clearly, the ciliary muscles contract making the eye lens thicker. Thus, the focal length of the eye lens decreases and the nearby objects become visible to the eyes. Hence, the human eye lens is able to adjust its focal length to view both distant and nearby objects on the retina. This ability is called the power of accommodation of the eyes. This will vary for near and distant objects and also for objects moving away or towards the eye. Accommodation of eye helps in seeing objects placed at different places. By adjusting the focal length, the eye is actually changing its lens power. If the object in consideration is at a distance, for the image to form at the retina, the focal length has to be large. Here, the ciliary muscles relax, thereby thinning the eye lens. The focal length increases and the image is formed perfectly on the retina. Similarly, in the case of near-lying objects, the ciliary muscles contract and thereby thickening the lens. This causes a reduction in the focal length for ideal image formation.

76. Adrenaline (epinephrine) is a hormone our adrenal glands make to help us prepare for stressful or dangerous situations. Adrenaline rush is the name for the quick release of adrenaline into our bloodstream. This gets our body ready for a "fight or flight" response. Adrenal glands, also known as suprarenal glands, are small, triangular-shaped glands located on top of both kidneys. Adrenal glands produce hormones that help regulate your metabolism, immune system, blood pressure, response to stress and other essential functions.

77. The majority of fat digestion happens once it reaches the small intestine. This is also where the majority of nutrients are absorbed. Our pancreas produces enzymes that break down fats, carbohydrates, and proteins. Fats are digested into fatty acids and glycerol by an enzyme called lipase. Bile juice is secreted by the liver which helps in the emulsification of fat. Emulsification is a process that breaks down large fat globules into smaller globules so that the pancreatic enzymes can easily act on these smaller fats.

78. Both plant and animal cells are eukaryotic, so they contain membrane-bound organelles like the nucleus and mitochondria. However, plant cells and animal cells do not look exactly the same or have all of the same organelles, since they each have different needs. For example, plant cells contain chloroplasts since they need to perform photosynthesis, but animal cells do not.

Plant cells have a cell wall, as well as a cell membrane. In plants, the cell wall surrounds the cell membrane. This gives the plant cell its unique rectangular shape. Animal cells simply have a cell membrane, but no cell wall. Both animal and plant cells have mitochondria, but only plant cells have chloroplasts. Plants don't get their sugar from eating food, so they need to make sugar from sunlight. This process (photosynthesis) takes place in the chloroplast. Once the sugar is made, it is then broken down by the mitochondria to make energy for the cell. Because animals get sugar from the food they eat, they do not need chloroplasts: just mitochondria. Both plant and animal cells have vacuoles. A plant cell contains a large, singular vacuole that is used for storage and maintaining the shape of the cell. In contrast, animal cells have many, smaller vacuoles.

79. Lymph is a fluid similar in composition to blood plasma. It is derived from blood plasma as fluids pass through capillary walls at the arterial end. As the interstitial fluid begins to accumulate, it is picked up and removed by tiny lymphatic vessels and returned to the blood. Lymph helps bring oxygen and nutrients to cells and to remove waste products from them. As new tissue fluid is made, it replaces older fluid, which drains towards lymph vessels. When it enters the lymph vessels, it is called lymph. Also called interstitial fluid. Lymphatic vessels, unlike blood vessels, only carry fluid away from the tissues. The smallest lymphatic vessels are the lymph capillaries, which begin in the tissue spaces as blind-ended sacs. Lymph capillaries are found in all regions of the body except the bone marrow, central nervous system, and tissues, such as the epidermis, that lack blood vessels. The wall of the lymph capillary is composed of endothelium in which the simple squamous cells overlap to form a simple one-way valve. This arrangement permits fluid to enter the capillary but prevents lymph from leaving the vessel.

80. During glycolysis, glucose ultimately breaks down into pyruvate and energy; a total of 2 ATP is derived in the process (Glucose + 2 NAD^+ + 2 ADP + 2 Pi $\rightarrow$ 2 Pyruvate + 2 NADH + 2 H^+ + 2 ATP + 2 H_2O).

Glucose is the most important source of energy for all living things. The food we eat is broken down into carbohydrates, the most important of which is glucose. Glucose is oxidized to provide energy to the body. The following are the various ways in which glucose is broken down.

Aerobic respiration occurs only in the presence of oxygen. In aerobic respiration, there are three specific processes, which are glycolysis, Krebs cycle and electron transport chain (oxidative phosphorylation). In this process, the glucose is converted to pyruvate during glycolysis and the same pyruvate produces carbon dioxide and water, along with the generation of energy.

81. The 2022 French Open concluded on 5th June at the Stade Roland Garros in Paris, France. It is one of the four Grand Slams of Tennis. Rafael Nadal won the French Open 2022, defeating Casper Ruud (Norwegian) in the final. The tournament and venue are named after the French aviator Roland Garros.

82. **eSanjeevani** is a doctor to doctor telemedicine system, being implemented under the Ayushman Bharat Health and Wellness Centre (AB-HWCs) programme.

Ayushman Bharat Health and Wellness Centre (AB-HWCs) are envisaged to be the platform for delivery of an expanded range of primary health care services closer to the communities. It seeks to connect all 1,50,000 Health and Wellness Centre using the hub-and-spoke model by December 2022. Under the model, a network will be established comprising an anchor establishment, or hub, which offers a full array of services, and will be complemented by secondary establishments, or spokes, which offer limited services, routing patients needing more intensive services to the hub for treatment.

83. Scheme for Residential Education for Students in High Schools in Targeted Areas (SHRESHTA) provides for high quality education for meritorious but poor SC students in CBSE-affiliated reputed residential schools across the country. Approximately 3,000 seats are provided each year for admission in class 9th and 11th and the entire cost of the school fee and residential charges are borne by the Department.

The students, belonging to Scheduled Castes, studying in class 8th and 10th in the current academic year are eligible for availing the benefits of scheme are selected through a transparent mechanism through a National Entrance Test for SHRESHTA (NETS), which is conducted by the National Testing Agency (NTA) for admission in class 9th and 11th.

85. Tomb of Sand is a 2018 Hindi-language novel by Indian author Geetanjali Shree. It was translated into English by U.S. translator Daisy Rockwell. In 2022, the book became the first novel translated from an Indian language to win the International Booker Prize. The book traces the transformative journey of 80-year-old Ma, who becomes depressed after the death of her husband. She then decides to travel to Pakistan, confronting trauma that had remained unresolved since she was a teenager who survived the Partition riots. The story is fictional.

86. Flying shuttle, Machine that represented an important step toward automatic weaving. It was invented by John Kay in 1733. The flying shuttle was one of the key developments in the industrialization of weaving during the early Industrial Revolution. It allowed a single weaver to weave much wider fabrics, and it could be mechanized, allowing for automatic machine looms.

The increase in production due to the flying shuttle exceeded the capacity of the spinning industry of the day, and prompted the development of powered spinning machines, beginning with the spinning jenny and the waterframe, and culminating in the spinning mule, which could produce strong, fine thread in the quantities needed.

87. On 21 October, 1943, the Provisional Government of Free India was established as a government-in-exile in Singapore by Indians in exile headed by Subhash Chandra Bose. It was also called Azad Hind or Free India. Azad Hind was established as part of a political movement originating outside India by Indians against British imperialism. Subhash Chandra Bose was the most prominent leader of this movement and he was also the Head of State of the provisional government. It was established with financial, political and military support from Imperial Japan. This political movement was spearheaded by Bose, who was called Netaji by the Azad Hind members, and it meant to take sides with the Axis powers (including Nazi Germany, Italy and Japan) in order to wrest India of British rule (who were part of the Allied Forces during World War II).

88. The Constituent Assembly formally began its task of framing the Constitution of India on the 13th of December, 1946 with Jawaharlal Nehru moving the Objectives Resolution. The Objectives Resolution provided the foundation for India's Constitution, which institutionalized the essential values of equality, liberty, democracy, sovereignty, and cosmopolitan identity.

89. The Kheda Satyagraha of 1918 was a satyagraha movement in the Kheda district of Gujarat in India organised by Mahatma Gandhi during the period of the British Raj.

The Bardoli Satyagraha, in the state of Bardoli, India during the British Raj, was a major phase of civil disobedience and revolt in the Indian Independence Movement on 12 June, 1928. The movement was eventually led by Sardar Vallabhbhai Patel, and its success gave rise to Patel becoming one of the main leaders of the independence movement.

The Gandhi-Irwin Pact was a political agreement signed by Mahatma Gandhi and Lord Irwin, Viceroy of India, on 5 March, 1931 before the Second Round Table Conference in London.

The Second Round Table Conference was held from September to December 1931 in London. This movement marked the end of the Civil Disobedience Movement in India.

90. The National Unionist Party was a political party based in the Punjab Province during the period of British rule in India. The Unionist Party mainly represented the interests of the landed gentry and landlords of Punjab, which included Muslims, Hindus and Sikhs. The Unionists dominated the political scene in Punjab from World War I to the independence of India and Pakistan (and the partition of the province) in 1947. The party's leaders served as Prime Minister of the Punjab. The creed of the Unionist Party emphasized: "Dominion Status and a United Democratic federal constitution for India as a whole".

91. Metamorphic rocks are those rocks that have undergone changes in mineralogy, texture, and/or chemical composition as a result of changes in temperature and pressure. The original rock may have been an igneous, sedimentary, or metamorphic rock. The pressure and heat that drive metamorphism are consequences of three forces:

- the internal heat of the Earth.
- weight of the overlying rock.
- horizontal or tectonic forces that cause the rocks to deform.

Deformation of some rocks such as shale and clay-rich sandstone (greywacke) produces textural changes involving the formation of flat or wavy parallel planes within the metamorphosed rock. These flat or wavy planes are referred to as foliation. Foliation forms when pressure squeezes the flat or elongate minerals within a rock so they become aligned. These rocks develop a platy or sheet-like structure that reflects the direction that pressure was applied. Hence statement 1 is correct. Where the foliations develop into broad mineral bands, the metamorphic rock is extremely hard.

Rocks that originally were composed of one dominant mineral are often foliated by metamorphism. Minerals in the original rock that survive metamorphism may rotate during deformation to acquire a preferred orientation parallel with the platy minerals. The mineral crystals don't have to be large to produce foliation. Slate, for example, is characterized by aligned flakes of mica that are too small to see.

Foliation is mainly produced in rocks that contain platy minerals like mica and chlorite. These platy minerals generally form when shale and clay-bearing sandstone (greywacke) are metamorphosed. As these platy minerals grow, their planes take on a preferred orientation that is usually perpendicular to the main direction of forces squeezing the rock. Minerals in the original rock that survive metamorphism may rotate during deformation to acquire a preferred orientation parallel with the platy minerals.

Three types of foliation are slate, schist, and gneiss. Slate is classified as low-grade, thin-layered, and very small mineral grains. Schist is classified as medium-grade, thin-layered, and large mineral grains. Gneiss is classified as high-grade, thick-layered, and very large mineral grains.

92. The interiors of the earth are made of different kinds of elements that differ from each other in physical and chemical properties like temperature, density, composition, etc. The interiors of the earth are divided into separate layers. The fundamental layers of the earth are the crust, mantle, and core. These layers are further divided into the upper and lower crust, upper and lower mantle, and the outer and inner core. These layers are separated from each other by transition zones. These transition zones are popularly known as Discontinuities. The discontinuity between the upper and lower crust is called the Conrad Discontinuity. The Mohorovicic discontinuity, usually referred to as the Moho discontinuity, is the boundary between the Earth's crust and the mantle. It occurs at an average depth of about 8 kilometres beneath the ocean basins and 32 kilometres beneath continental surfaces.

93. From the above options, Kampala, the capital of Uganda, represent the greatest linear velocity of rotation of the Earth. As the Earth rotates on its axis, a person standing on the Earth will travel in a circle that is perpendicular to the axis. The linear velocity of a rotating body is given by, $v = r\omega$ where r is the radius of the circle and ω is the body's angular velocity.

The angular velocity of a rotating body is given by, $\omega = 2\pi/T$ where T is the period of rotation.

95. Morocco is the only country through which the Prime Meridian does not pass. There are eight nations located on the Prime Meridian: Algeria, Burkina Faso, Ghana, Mali, Spain, Togo, and the United Kingdom. The prime meridian is the line of 0° longitude, the starting point for measuring distance both east and west around Earth.

96. Paleogeomorphology is that subscience of geomorphology which deals with all buried ("fossil") geomorphic phenomena which are recognizable in the subsurface and in outcrops of previously buried and newly exhumed formations. Hence, paleogeomorphology is the science of buried relief features of the earth. This includes both buried landscapes and buried submarine features, such as fossil submarine canyons, fossil reefs and fossil volcanic islands.

97. The velocity-time graph for the motion of the car is a straight line graph sloping with the time axis. This indicates that the car is moving with a uniform acceleration. Uniform or constant acceleration means rate of change of velocity is constant. This is possible only when graph of velocity-time graph is a straight line.

98. Amplitude of any wave means how far medium particles are getting displaced, which is equivalent to distance travelled by particle. Amplitude is measured in metres (m). The greater the amplitude of a wave then the more energy it is carrying. The wavelength, λ 'lambda', of a wave is the distance from any point on one wave to the same point on the next wave along. The amplitude of a periodic variable is a measure of its change in a single period (such as time or spatial period). The amplitude of a non-periodic signal is its magnitude compared with a reference value.

100. A DC generator is an electrical machine whose main function is to convert mechanical energy into electricity. When the conductor slashes magnetic flux, an emf will be generated based on the electromagnetic induction principle of Faraday's Laws. This electromotive force can cause a flow of current when the conductor circuit is closed.

According to Faraday's law of electromagnetic induction, we know that when a current-carrying conductor is placed in a varying magnetic field, an emf is induced in the conductor. According to Fleming's right-hand rule, the direction of the induced current changes whenever the direction of motion of the conductor changes.

101. A compass is an instrument that is used to find the magnetic field direction. A compass comprises a small metal needle that is magnetized itself and which is easy to turn in all directions. Therefore, when in the occupancy of a magnetic field, the needle can queue up in the same direction. Ammeter and voltmeter are used to measure current and voltages respectively.

A magnetic field is a vector field that describes the magnetic influence on moving electric charges, electric currents, and magnetic materials. A moving charge in a magnetic field experiences a force perpendicular to its own velocity and to the magnetic field. Magnetic fields such as that of Earth cause magnetic compass needles and other permanent magnets to line up in the direction of the field. Magnetic fields force moving electrically charged particles in a circular or helical path.

102. Speed is a scalar quantity because it has no defined direction and only magnitude. Velocity is a vector quantity having both magnitude and a direction.

Distance and speed are examples of scalar quantities that have magnitude or size. Force, velocity, and field strength are examples of vector quantities that have both magnitude and direction.

Speed is the time rate at which an object is moving along a path, while velocity is the rate and direction of an object's movement. Put another way, speed is a scalar value, while velocity is a vector. For example, 50 km/hr (31 mph) describes the speed at which a car is travelling along a road, while 50 km/hr west describes the velocity at which it is travelling.

103. Bronze is mainly an alloy of copper and tin. Bronze is primarily made up of copper and tin is present in lesser proportions. Instead of tin other metals, non-metals and metalloids are also mixed with copper. Bronze is used in making weapons, coins, medals etc.

104. Potassium permanganate ($KMnO_4$) does not posses water of crystallization.

The number of water molecules present in one unit of salt is known as the water of crystallization. Water being the common solvent to be found in crystals because of its polarity and smaller size, hence may sometimes incorporate within the crystal lattice.

Water of crystallization refers to the water that is found in the crystalline framework of a metal complex or a salt and is not bonded directly to the metal cation. The crystal salts which have water(s) of crystallization are known as hydrates. This crystal of water does not include contaminants and is easily affected by the heat. The water molecules present in hydrated molecules are held by hydrogen bonding. Hydrogen bonding is a type of weak force that results in the formation of dipole-dipole interaction between the hydrogen atom and an electronegative atom that is strongly bonded to another electronegative atom. Since the water of crystallization in a crystal is much less intimately combined with the salt than the water of constitution, and therefore on heating, these water of crystallization are more easily expelled, often losing the crystalline properties.

105. Bee sting release methanoic acid or formic acid. The chemical formula of methanoic acid is HCOOH. A bee sting is caused by the stinger of a female bee being inserted into the skin, resulting in a wound and discomfort. Bee stings are different from insect bites because the venom of stinging insects varies greatly in chemical composition. While bee stinger venom is mildly acidic and causes relatively moderate discomfort in most individuals, persons with sensitivities to venom components may experience allergic responses.

106. Hydrogenation (the process for making margarine) involves breaking double bonds and adding hydrogen atoms so that the unsaturated fat becomes "more saturated" than before by breaking double bonds and most likely making it solid instead of liquid at room temperature. Hydrogen gas is used for many purposes, including the hydrogenation of vegetable oils to make margarine.

Margarine has traditionally been manufactured by hydrogenation of vegetable oils (olive, palm, sunflower seed, etc.) by an industrial process for converting these oils into a solid, stable, and spreadable substance.

Vegetable oils are commonly referred to as "polyunsaturated". This simply means that there are several double bonds present. Vegetable oils may be converted from liquids to solids by the hydrogenation reaction. Margarines and shortenings are "hardened" in this way to make them solid or semi-solids.

Fats and oils that are in contact with moist air at the room temperature eventually undergo oxidation and hydrolysis reactions and because of that they turn rancid, acquiring a characteristic disagreeable odour. The release of volatile fatty acids by hydrolysis of the ester bonds is also the cause of the odour. For example, butter releases foul-smelling butyric, caprylic, and capric acids.

108. Vapours of sulphur escaping from a volcano have a gaseous state. The crust on the Rock has a Solid state. Here, Gas is directly converted into a solid. The deposition is the process in which phase conversion takes place from a gaseous state to a solid state without passing via the liquid phase. It is a type of thermodynamic process. It is the reverse process of sublimation thus, it is also called desublimation. Frost is a common example of deposition because water vapours from humid air are directly deposited on the solid and crystalline frost pattern on windows or on a leaf, without ever being altered into a liquid phase.

109. Sublimation, which means it changes from a solid directly into a gas, without melting into a liquid first. Dry ice is an example of sublimation process. Dry ice can cause severe skin damage if someone gets expressed to it longer. The solid form of carbon dioxide is called dry ice. It is used as a cooling agent. It is believed to be useful for preserving frozen foods, where mechanical cooling seems unavailable. Dry ice is colourless, non-flammable with a sour zesty colour. When dry ice is discovered in water, it loves the pH of the solution and results in the formation of carbonic acid (H_2CO_3). When the temperature is yellow –56.4 degree celcius and the pressure is yellow 5.13 atm. CO_2 changes from a solid to a gas without coming to the liquid form.

110. C_4H_8 (Butene) and C_3H_6 (Propene) belong to the alkene homologous series. C_4H_6 (Butyne) and C_3H_4 (Propyne) belong to the alkyne homologous series. A homologous series may be defined as a group of organic compounds consisting of the same functional group. Each member of a homologous series differs from the other by a CH_2 group. The chemical properties of all the members of a homologous series are the same. A member of any homologous series is known as a homologue. In homologous series, the molecular masses of succeeding members are higher than the preceding members. As the molecular masses increases, the melting and boiling points also increase.

111. An enzyme secreted from gastric glands in stomach that acts on proteins is pepsin. It is an enzyme whose zymogen/precursor (pepsinogen) is released by the chief cells in the stomach and that degrades food proteins into peptides. The gastric chief cells produce the precursor of pepsin known as pepsinogen. The hydrochloric acid secreted by the parietal cells of the stomach reduces the pH, which in turn activates the enzyme pepsin that is required for digesting proteins. Epsin is a stomach enzyme that serves to digest proteins found in ingested food. Gastric chief cells secrete pepsin as an inactive zymogen called pepsinogen. Parietal cells within the stomach lining secrete hydrochloric acid that lowers the pH of the stomach. Pepsin is secreted in its inactive form, pepsinogen, because it is a powerful agent for breaking down proteins and thus poses a risk both to unprotected parts of the body and itself. Pepsin is a protein compound, and laboratory samples of the enzyme must be kept cold to prevent self-digestion.

112. If a cell contains higher water concentration than the surrounding medium then the cell loses water and it shrinks. This process is called exosmosis. If a cell has low water concentration than the surrounding medium cell intakes water from the surroundings and the cell bursts. This process is called endosmosis. If a cell having equal water concentration to its surrounding medium then there will be no change in the cell. When an animal cell is placed in a medium with lower water concentration, that is hypertonic to the cell, the cell will lose water due to exosmosis. A solution will be hypertonic to a cell if its solute concentration is higher than the cell.

113. Lysosomes are membrane-bound vesicles that contain digestive enzymes, such as glycosidases, proteases and sulfatases. Lysosomal enzymes are synthesized in the endoplasmic reticulum (ER), are transported to the Golgi apparatus, and are tagged for lysosomes by the addition of mannose-6-phosphate label. Digestive enzymes are not found in chloroplast and mitochondria. They contain around 50 different digestive enzymes, which can hydrolyze proteins, lipids, nucleic acids, and so on. Lysosomes are known as suicidal bags of the cells. Our stomach, small intestine and pancreas all make digestive enzymes. The pancreas is really the enzyme "powerhouse" of digestion. It produces the most important digestive enzymes, which are those that break down carbohydrates, proteins and fats.

114. In flowering plants after fertilisation, the zygote develops into the embryo, the ovules develop into the seed and the ovary develops into the fruit. Also, the sepals, petals and stamens of the flower generally fall off. Fertilisation is the fusion of male sperm and female egg. Embryo is present inside the seed which will give rise to a new plant after seed germination. In flowering plants, fertilization happens through a process called pollination. Pollination occurs when pollen grains from anther come in contact with the stigma of the flower. Pollination can either occur by self-pollination or cross-pollination.

Once, the pollen comes in contact with the stigma, the pollen tube grows from the pollen grain through the style into the ovary. Sperm cells inside the pollen grain travel down the pollen tube and into the ovary which contains the ovule. After fertilization, each OVULE develops into seed and OVARY into a fruit. Each seed contains an undeveloped plane, embryo. The ovary surrounding the ovules develops into a fruit. After fertilization, the integument of the ovules becomes the seed coat of the seed. Ovary, ovule becomes fruit and seed respectively. Embryo sac develops in the ovule of flowering plants (Angiosperms). Other structures such as corolla, calyx and the remaining parts of androecium and gynoecium degenerate and fall off.

115. National Cadet Corps (NCC) has launched its nationwide flagship campaign 'Puneet Sagar Abhiyan' from May 30 to June 5 2022 (the World Environment Day). Puneet Sagar Abhiyan was launched by NCC to clean Sea Shores and other water bodies including rivers and lakes, of plastic and other waste. It aims to increase awareness among the local population about importance of keeping the beaches and river fronts clean. The purpose of the Abhiyan is to educate locals and sensitise them about 'Swachh Bharat'. It is envisioned to increase the awareness amongst local population and future generations about importance of keeping the beaches and riverfronts clean.

116. World Environment Day is the biggest international day for the environment. It is observed every year on 5th June. World Environment Day 2022 was hosted by Sweden. "Only One Earth" was the slogan for the first United Nations Conference on the Human Environment, held in Stockholm in 1972. This put sustainable development on the global agenda and led to the establishment of World Environment Day. It is led by the United Nations Environment Programme (UNEP), and held annually since 1973.

117. INS Nishank and INS Akshay were decommissioned on 3rd June 2022 by the Indian Navy at the Naval Dockyard, Mumbai. The ships were in active naval service for more than 32 years and participated in several naval operations including Operation Talwar during the Kargil War and Operation Parakram in 2001.

118. India has signed a contract with the USA for the supply of MH-60R helicopters. In the first tranche of this agreement, the Indian Navy received two MH-60R multi-role helicopters in Kochi port on July 2022. India has signed a 24-helicopter supply agreement with the United States of America to modernize the aging naval helicopter fleet in the country. These helicopters are considered to be the world's most advanced maritime helicopter. The proposed sale will provide India the capability to perform anti-surface and anti-submarine warfare missions. It will also enhance the Navy's ability to perform secondary missions, including search and rescue, and communications relay.

119. Surat and Udayagiri are the warships of the Indian Navy which have recently been inducted into the Navy. They joined the Indian Navy on 17th May 2022, which are warships of state-of- the-art technology. INS 'Surat' is the fourth and last of the stealth destroyers that have been commissioned under the 'Project 15B' programme. INS 'Udaygiri' has been commissioned under the 'Project 17A' frigate programme. Both warships have been designed in-house by the Directorate of Naval Design (DND) and built at MDL, Mumbai. Project 15B is a programme of the Indian government under which next-generation stealth guided-missile destroyers for the Indian Navy were being built at the Mazgaon Docks Ltd, Mumbai. In 2021, the first ship under this project commissioned. INS Udaygiri has been named after a mountain range that is located in the state of Andhra Pradesh. This ship is the reincarnation of the decommissioned 'Udaygiri', the Leander Class ASW Frigate, which undertook various difficult operations from 18th February 1976 to 24th August 2007.

120. The Vijayanagara Empire was established in 1336 by the brothers Harihara I and Bukka Raya I of the Sangama dynasty. Virupaksha Raya II was the last ruler of the Sangama Dynasty of Vijayanagara. Vijayanagar Empire was ruled by four important dynasties and they are: 1. Sangama, 2. Saluva, 3. Tuluva, 4. Aravidu.

In 1336 A.D. Harihara I became the ruler of Sangama Dynasty. He captured Mysore and Madurai. In 1356 A.D. Bukka-I succeeded him. Krishnadeva Raya of the Tuluva dynasty was the most famous king of the Vijayanagar Empire. According to Domingo Paes, a Portuguese traveller "Krishnadeva Raya was the most feared and perfect king there could possibly be".

121. Kalila wa Dimna is the classic Arabic translation of the Panchatantra collection of animal tales. There are recorded over two hundred different versions known to exist in more than fifty languages. After the Arab invasion of Persia, Ibn al-Muqaffa's version (two languages removed from the pre-Islamic Sanskrit original) emerged as the pivotal surviving text that enriched world literature. Ibn al-Muqqaffa's work is considered a model of the finest Arabic prose style, and "is considered the first masterpiece of Arabic literary prose."

122. The Bhoodan movement was a major step in the field of economic and social reforms during the decades of 1950s. It was started by Vinoba Bhave in 1951 in Pochampally village, Pochampally. This movement went on for 13 years during which time Bhave travelled all over India. He collected 4.4 million acres of land to be distributed to landless farmers. In 1954, he started the Gramdan movement which involved the voluntary donation of whole villages. These movements attracted worldwide admiration for being stellar examples of voluntary social justice.

123. Alexander's army was at war for a long time, apart from this, he did not even know much about the military power of the Indian kings. Hydaspes river in India was not crossed by Alexander and his army. Fearing the prospect of encountering other powerful Indian armies, Alexander's army revolted on the banks of the Hydaspes River and refused to go further.

124. Ibn Battuta was a medieval Muslim traveller, who has described the medieval Indian postal system as The horse post, known as Uluq, is run by royal horses posted every four miles apart. The foot-post has three stations per mile; one-third of a mile is named Dawa. Posts carried by foot runners was called Dava and those carried by horses was called Ullookh. Rulers set up three collection and distribution centers within a distance of a mile. This ensured fast and efficient postal services. Ibn Battuta informed us about the unique system of communication in fourteenth century India:

- The state took special measures to encourage merchants. Inns and guesthouses were available at short distance along all the trade routes.
- There were two kinds of postal system in India-horse post uluq and foot post called dawa.
- The efficiency of the postal system was such that it allowed merchants not only to send information.
- And send credit across long distances, but also to transmit goods at short notice.

125. Fire altars are pits meant for religious rites involving sacrifices to fire. These were a hallmark of Aryan religious beliefs. Evidences of fire altars are found in Lothal and Kalibangan towards the Late Harappan phase, showing presence of immigrants. During the excavation in this Harappan site, archaeologists have found Yagvedi (Fire Altar). Kalibanga is known for its unique fire altars and modern farming system. Kalibangan in Rajasthan was a major provincial capital of the Indus Valley Civilization. The Indus Valley Civilization is one of the oldest civilizations in the world. Kalibangan is situated in Hanumangarh near Ganganagar, Rajasthan. It was discovered by A. Ghosh. The most notable discoveries from Kalibangan have been the Linga and Yoni, the symbols of Hindu god and goddess, Shiva and Shakti. In terms of agriculture a wooden furrow and tilled land, fortunately very well preserved have been found during excavation.

127. Tors are conspicuous rock masses that rise above the surrounding ground surfaces. Tors are landforms created by the erosion and weathering of rock; most commonly granites. Tors are typically the exposed rock mass of the jointed and broken blocks. These tors are known as either castle koppie or kopje by geomorphologists. Also, these tors large, free-standing outcrops of rocks that rise abruptly from the surrounding slopes that are smooth and gentle as they are a part of the rounded hill summit or the crest of a ridge. It is also a term that is commonly used in the southwest of England for hills especially the hills and the high points located in Dartmoor in Devon and Bodmin Moor of Cornwall.

Tor meaning is from the English language which defines it as a bare mass of rock that is surmounted and surrounded by groups of blocks and boulders which is further derived from the old English word 'torr'. Tor are exposed forms of rocks. Hence, it is clear that the rots are the landforms which are the landforms created due to the erosion and weathering of the rock that surrounds it. The surrounding rocks are mostly composed of granites but also contain shists, dolerites, dacites and ignimbrites and also coarse sandstones and others. The tor geography depicts its height as less than 5 meters.

128. Anticyclones are characterized by 'Blocking Highs'. Anticyclones are much larger than depressions and produce periods of settled and calm weather lasting many days or weeks. Anticyclones often block the path of depressions, either slowing down the bad weather, or forcing it round the outside of the high pressure system. Anticyclones are centers of high pressure. They are surrounded by closed isobars having decreasing pressure outward. The circulation is from central high pressure towards the periphery in such a way that air blows outwards in a clockwise direction in the Northern hemisphere and anticlockwise direction in the southern hemisphere. Due to Coriolis force, blowing winds are deflected from their paths to the right in the Northern hemisphere and left in the Southern hemisphere, that's how it gets circular with a flowing system.

The difference in pressure between the center and periphery of anticyclone ranges between 10 to 20 mb and sometimes higher. There are much larger in size and area than temperate cyclones as the diameter is 75% larger than that of temperate cyclones. Temperate anticyclones are very extensive that a single anticyclone can cover nearly half of the USA. The track is highly variable and unpredictable. They move very sluggishly and sometimes they become stationary over a particular place for 4 days. The average velocity of an anticyclone is 30 to 50 km per hour. Anticyclones originated due to the descent of either polar cold air mass or warm tropical air mass.

129. The nature of the earth's crust is brittle. From clay to diamonds and coal, the Earth's crust is made up of igneous, metamorphic and sedimentary rocks. Oceanic crust is thinner than continental crust. The average thickness of the oceanic crust is 5 km while that of the continental one is about 30 km. Thus statement (2) is incorrect. Continental crust is thicker than oceanic crust. The mean thickness of the oceanic crust is 5 km whereas that of the continental is around 30 km. Continental crust is mainly made up of granite whereas oceanic crust is mainly made up of basalt. The density of basalt is 3 gm/cc whereas that of granite is 2.7 gm/cc.

130. Dadra and Nagar Haveli and Daman and Diu were separate union territories before 2020. The Home Minister of the Government of India introduced the bill related to their merger in the Lok Sabha on 26 November 2019. The Bill provides for the merger of the Union Territories (UTs). The UT's of Dadra and Nagar Haveli, and Daman and Diu were merged into a single Union Territory in January 2020.

131. Given lenses are convex, so focal length will be positive.

$$P_1 = \frac{100v}{f_1} = \frac{100}{50} = +2D$$

$$P_2 = \frac{100v}{f_2} = \frac{100}{-25} = +4D$$

$P = P_1 + P_2 = 2 + 4 = +6D$

132. P = VI = I^2R = V^2/R. So option (B) is a wrong R formula of power.

Electric power determines the rate of electrical energy transfer by an electrical circuit per unit of time in physics. It is denoted by P, which is measured in SI units of one joule per second or watt.

According to ohms law, V = IR. Power can be written as VI, I^2R and V^2/R. Where, R is the resistance in the circuit, V is the potential difference in the circuit, and I is the electric current.

133. The speed of light in the vacuum/ The speed of light in the medium = $\frac{c}{v}$

$3/2 = c/v$

$v = 2/3\ c$

134. Density of object,

p = Mass /volume = 800/1000 = 0.8 gcm^{-3}

Since density of object is less than both water and liquid B. So it will float on them. Buoyancy pushes less dense objects to the surface of the liquid that they are in, allowing them to float. An object floats when the weight force on the object is balanced by the upward push of the water on the object. The upwards push of the water increases with the volume of the object that is under water; it is not affected by the depth of the water or the amount of water. Density is the mass of an object divided by its volume. Density often has units of grams per cubic centimeter (g/cm^3). Remember, grams is a mass and cubic centimeters is a volume (the same volume as 1 milliliter).

135. Time period of a pendulum is given by, $T = 2\pi\sqrt{\frac{l}{g}}$

Since time period is independent upon mass, so changing mass of bob won't change T.

Also, $T \propto \sqrt{l}$

So, if length becomes half, time period will be $\frac{T}{\sqrt{2}}$

136. Solar cell, also called photovoltaic cell, any device that directly converts the energy of light into electrical energy through the photovoltaic effect. The overwhelming majority of solar cells are fabricated from silicon with increasing efficiency and lowering cost as the materials range from amorphous (noncrystalline) to polycrystalline to crystalline (single crystal) silicon forms. Unlike batteries or fuel cells, solar cells do not utilize chemical reactions or require fuel to produce electric power, and, unlike electric generators, they do not have any moving parts. Solar cells, whether used in a central power station, a satellite, or a calculator, have the same basic structure.

137. The powers, duties and rights of Panchayati Raj have been discussed in Article 243G of the Indian Constitution. The regulation of land revenue is not the subject matter of the Panchayats. The every village panchayat may levy in its area a property tax, a profession tax, an advertisement tax and an entertainment tax. Panchayati Raj Institution (PRI) is a system of rural local self-government in India.

138. It is believed that the Mauryans maintained a huge army. The army consisted of 6,00,000 infantry, 30,000 cavalry, 9,000 elephants, and 8,000 chariots. In Mauryan administration the security of frontier forts was the responsibility of Anta-Mahamattas. The Dhamma Mahamatras were officers who were supposed to look after the interests of people from all religions and also spread the message of Dhamma.

139. Hesteryurveda is a treatise on the lifestyle of elephants. This book classifies elephants as wild and domesticated. It is a complete science of elephants considering all the facts about wild and domesticated elephants. This Samhita was composed by Palakapya. Hastyayurveda deals with the topics like the genealogical, physical, mental, and intellectual characteristics of elephants, techniques of tracing and capturing elephants from forests, nourishment for healthy growth and general upkeep, taming and training them for war and work, classification of elephants on the basis of a number of characteristics and diagnosis and treatment for their diseases. Hastyayurveda is an important text on elephantlore which originated in India. A copy of which (Hastyayurveda) is available in the Raja Serfoji Saraswathi Mahal Library of Thanjavur in South India. The work consisting of over seventy two chapters deals with the anatomy of elephants and systematically with several disease of elephants grouping them suitably into different categories. It also contains valuable instruction for the healthy of growth, upkeep and training of elephants and also classification of elephants on the basis of a number of characteristics.

140. Cuttack was acquired by the British under the Treaty of Deogaon, 1803. Treaty of Deogaon, (Dec. 17, 1803), pact concluded by Sir Arthur Wellesley (later 1st duke of Wellington) between Raghuji Bhonsle II the Maratha Raja of Berar and the British East India Company.

Treaty of Deogaon (19 December 1803) with Raghuji Bhonsle II:

- Bhonsle ceded the province of Orissa to English.
- Agreed to share revenues to the westward of the river Wardha and south of the hills (Narnaulla and Gawilgarh are situated here).
- Bhonsle retained two forts with a revenue below four lakhs.
- The province of western Berar was ceded to Nizam.
- He has to respect all the treaties concluded by the English.
- No European and American can be entertained without the consent of British Government.

141. Maharashtra has the largest network of National Highways with 17,757 km. It is true; the level of economic development is one of the reasons for the maximum share of national highways in Maharashtra. Nature of terrain and level of economic development affect the density of roads in such way that Construction of roads in plains is easy and cheaper than compare to hilly and mountainous areas, that's why Indo-Gangetic plains have a high density of roads.

142. Quinary activities are services that focus on the creation, rearrangement and interpretation of new and existing ideas; data interpretation and the use and evaluation of new technologies. The highest level of policymakers or decision-makers performs quinary activities. These are referred to as "gold collar" professionals. They create, rearrange and interpret new and existing ideas, use and evaluate new technologies e.g., senior business executives, government officials, research scientists, financial and legal consultants, etc.

143. It is an innovative scheme to develop the regional aviation market. The scheme is aimed at enhancing connectivity to remote and regional areas of the country and making air travel affordable. It is a key component of Centre's National Civil Aviation Policy led by Prime Minister Narendra Modi and launched in June 2016. Under the scheme, nearly half of the seats in Udan flights are offered at subsidised fares, and the participating carriers are provided a certain amount of viability gap funding (VGF) - an amount shared between the Centre and the concerned states. The scheme will be jointly funded by the central government and state governments.

144. The Brahmani is formed by the confluence of the Sankh and South Koel rivers, and flows through the districts of Sundargarh, Deogarh, Angul, Dhenkanal, Cuttack, Jajapur and Kendrapara. Together with the river Baitarani, it forms a large delta before emptying into the Bay of Bengal at Dhamra.

The famous falls formed by River Sharavati is Jog Falls. Sharavati is a river which originates and flows entirely within the state of Karnataka in India. It is one of the few westward flowing rivers of India and a major part of the river basin lies in the Western Ghats. The famous Jog Falls, located about 24 km from Sagara, are formed by this river. Tamirabharani is the only perennial river in Tamil Nadu.

145. SONAR technology uses ultrasonic waves, whose frequency is greater than 20,000 Hz. Many animals use this techniques for navigation purpose. These waves don't lies in audible range. The full form of SONAR is Sound Navigation and Ranging. It is a technique involving the use of propagation of sound for navigation, and it also can be used for distant object detection and interaction with other objects. SONAR has a wide range of application areas undersea such as submarine interaction and submarine route planning.

146. Speed of sound order: Solid > Liquid > Gas.

This means speed of sound will be higher in steel, than in water, than in air. Speed of sound increases with increase in temperature. The speed of sound increases with increase in temperature of the medium.

Molecules at higher temperatures have more energy, they vibrate faster. Because of faster molecular vibration the sound waves travel faster. The speed of sound is also affected by other factors such as humidity and air pressure.

147. Cochlea changes the sound vibration in electrical signal form and send to brain for further processing. The cochlea is filled with a fluid that moves in response to the vibrations from the oval window. As the fluid moves, 25,000 nerve endings are set into motion. These nerve endings transform the vibrations into electrical impulses that then travel along the eighth cranial nerve (auditory nerve) to the brain. When the pressure variations strike the ear, they find their way through the external auditory canal to the tympanic membrane, setting it into vibration. The signal is thus converted to mechanical vibrations in solid matter.

These vibrations of the tympanic membrane are transmitted to the ossicles, which in turn transmit them to the cochlea. Here, the signal undergoes a second change of nature, being converted into pressure variations within the liquid. These are then transformed again by specialised hair cells, which convert the liquid waves into nervous signals. Inside the cochlea, the tectorial membrane moves along with the pressure variations of the cochlear fluid. This membrane is in contact with the cilia on the top of the hair cells. There are two kinds of hair cells. The outer hair cells are the actual receptors. When the tectorial membrane moves, so does the hair on the outer cells. This movement is then encoded into electrical signals and goes to the brain through the cochlear nerve.

148. A filament is made up of a metal having a high melting point because a bulb lights up only by heating the filament. The heated filament is the source of light, and if the melting point of the filament's metal is low, it may melt.

Copper, aluminium, and lead are not used as filament metal since they have a relatively low melting point. Tungsten has high resistivity and high melting point. It doesn't not react with oxygen easily even at high temperature.

Hence, Tungsten metal is selected for making filaments of electric bulbs as tungsten can sustain high temperature and has a high melting point. Tungsten is easily alloyed with chromium, nickel, molybdenum, titanium, etc. to yield a number of hard facing, heat and corrosion resistant alloys. It is also used for various other purposes such as electric bulb filaments, paints, ceramics, textiles, etc.

149. Applying law of conservation on momentum,

$P_i = P_f$

$0 = 1 \times v + 10/1000 \times 300$

For two or more bodies in an isolated system acting upon each other, their total momentum remains constant unless an external force is applied.

Therefore, momentum can neither be created nor destroyed. The principle of conservation of momentum is a direct consequence of Newton's third law of motion. Consider this example of a balloon, the particles of gas move rapidly colliding with each other and the walls of the balloon, even though the particles themselves move faster and slower when they lose or gain momentum when they collide, the total momentum of the system remains the same.

150. Microphone is a type of transducer that converts sound energy into electrical signals. A microphone intercepts sound and converts it into electrical signal form. This signal then transferred for further processing.

Consider a case when we speak on mic in front of a large audience, when we speak, so we release sound signals these signals behave as input signals for the mic which is a transducer that converts these sound signals into electrical signals and the output of this mic is connected to external speakers which again converted these electrical signals into sound signals which is what we heard. There are several types of microphone available in the market which all possess different methods to convert the air pressure variations of a sound wave into electrical signals. The most common type of microphone available is a dynamic microphone which uses a coil of wire suspended in a magnetic field.

The first microphone which was invented by David Edward Hughes is a carbon microphone in the 1870s. But Edison was awarded by the first patent after a long legal dispute in mid-1877. But most of the historians give credit to Hughes instead of Edison. Thomas Elva Edison redefined the carbon microphone into his carbon button transmitter of 1886.

The first ever microphone was used in concert at the New York metropolitan opera house in 1910. Most microphones use either an electromagnetic or an electrostatic technique to convert sound waves into electrical signals. The dynamic microphone is constructed with a small magnet that oscillates inside a coil attached to the diaphragm. When a sound wave causes the diaphragm of the microphone to vibrate, the relative motion of the magnet and coil creates an electrical signal by magnetic induction.

PAPER II: MATHEMATICS

1. There are 5 odd numbers 1, 3, 5, 7, 9

Therefore, there are $^5C_1$, ways of choosing one number

$^5C_1$ ways of choosing 2nd number

$^5C_1$ ways of choosing 3rd number

and $^5C_1$ ways choosing other number

Hence, by multiplication principle the required number of ways

$= {}^5C_1 \times {}^5C_1 \times {}^5C_1 \times {}^5C_1 = 5^4$

$= (5^2)^2 = 25 \times 25 = 625.$

2. Value of $\sum_{r=0}^{n} 2^r C(n,r)$

We have,

$$(1 + x)^n = C_0 + C_1x + C_2x^2 + C_3x^3 + ... + C_nx^n$$

Putting $x = 2$, we get,

$$C_0 + C_1(2) + C_2(4) + C_3(8) + ... + C_n(2)^n = (1 + 2)^n = 3^n$$

Hence, $\sum_{r=0}^{n} 2^r C(n,r) = 3^n$.

3. The number of such arrangements

$$= \frac{10!}{2!2!}$$

$$= \frac{10 \times 9 \times 8 \times 7 \times 6 \times 5 \times 4 \times 3 \times 2 \times 1}{2 \times 2}$$

$$= 907200.$$

5.
$$\Delta = \begin{vmatrix} a_{11} & a_{12} & a_{13} \\ a_{21} & a_{22} & a_{23} \\ a_{31} & a_{32} & a_{33} \end{vmatrix}$$

$\because$ $a_{13} = yz,\ a_{23} = zx,\ a_{33} = xy$

and minors of $a_{13} = (z - y),\ a_{23} = (z - x)$ and $a_{33} = (y - x)$

$\therefore$ Value of $\Delta = (z - y)(z - x)(y - x)$.

6. $\because$
$$A = \begin{bmatrix} 1 & 0 & 0 \\ 0 & \cos\theta & \sin\theta \\ 0 & \sin\theta & -\cos\theta \end{bmatrix}$$

$\therefore$
$$|A| = \begin{vmatrix} 1 & 0 & 0 \\ 0 & \cos\theta & \sin\theta \\ 0 & \sin\theta & -\cos\theta \end{vmatrix}$$

$|A| = 0$

1. $\therefore$ A + adj A is a null matrix. (True)
2. A^{-1} + adj, A is a null matrix. (True)
3. $A - A^{-1}$ is a null matrix. (True)

Hence, 1, 2, 3 is correct.

7.
$X = [\ ]3 \times 3$

$Y = [\ ]2 \times 3$

$Z = [\ ]3 \times 2$

1. (ZY)X is a square matrix having $3 \times 3 = 9$ entries. (True).
2. Y(XZ) is a square matrix having $2 \times 2 = 4$ entries. (True)
3. X(YZ) is not defined. (True)

Hence, 1, 2, 3 is correct.

8. If Sum and product of roots are equal in quadratic equation, then number of quadratic equations, whose sum and products of roots are equal is infinitely many.

9. 1. The set of all irrational numbers between $\sqrt{2}$ and $\sqrt{5}$ is an infinite set, it is correct.

2. The set of all odd integers less than 100 is a finite set, it is not true.

Hence, only 1 is correct.

10. I. $2 + 4 + 6 + ... + 2n = n^2 + n$

$$2[1 + 2 + 3 + ... + n] = 2\left[\frac{n(n+1)}{2}\right]$$

$$= n(n + 1) = n^2 + n$$

It is true.

II. $n^2 + n + 41$, Put $n = 1, 2, 3, ...$

$1^2 + 1 + 41 = 43$ gives a prime number

$2^2 + 2 + 41 = 47$ gives a prime number

$3^2 + 3 + 41 = 53$ gives a prime number

....

II is true

Hence, I and II both are true.

11. $\because$ $x^2 + bx + c = 0$

p, q are the roots of the equation,

$\therefore$ $p + q = -b$

$p \times q = c$

$p^2 + q^2 - 11pq = 0$

$\Rightarrow$ $p^2 + q^2 - 2pq = 9pq$

$\Rightarrow$ $(p - q)^2 = 9c$

$\Rightarrow$ $p - q = 3\sqrt{c}$.

12. $12 = 2\pi r$

$\Rightarrow$ $12 = 2 \times \frac{22}{7} r$

$\Rightarrow$ $r = \frac{12 \times 7}{2 \times 22} = \frac{21}{11}$ cm

$\Rightarrow$ $d = \frac{21}{11} \times 2 = \frac{42}{11}$ cm = 3.81 cm

$2+\sqrt{3} = 2 + 1.732$

$= 3.732 \sim 3.8$ (approx)

Hence, diameter of the circle = $2+\sqrt{3}$ cm.

13. Prime factors of 8 = 2 × 2 × 2

Prime factors of 12 = 2 × 2 × 3

Hence, required number = 6.

For Qs. No. 16-18:

$$z = \frac{1+i\sin\theta}{1-i\sin\theta}$$

$$\therefore \quad \bar{z} = \frac{1-i\sin\theta}{1+i\sin\theta}$$

16. $|z|^2 = z\times\bar{z}$

$$= \frac{1+i\sin\theta}{1-i\sin\theta}\times\frac{1-i\sin\theta}{1+i\sin\theta} = 1$$

$$|z| = \sqrt{1} = 1$$

Hence, modulus of z = 1.

17. ∵ z is purely real, then

$\therefore \quad z = \bar{z}$

$\therefore$ value of $\theta = n\pi$.

18. ∵ z is purely imaginary, then

$z + \bar{z} = 0$

$$\therefore \quad \text{Value of } \theta = \frac{(2n+1)\pi}{2}$$

For Qs. No. 19-21:

$$\because \quad \frac{P}{Q} = \frac{5n+4}{9n+6}$$

For first term: 2 × 1 – 1 = 1

19. Ratio of $\frac{\text{First term of P}}{\text{First term of Q}} = \frac{5\times1+4}{9\times1+6} = \frac{9}{15} = \frac{3}{5}$

For 2nd term: 2 × 2 – 1 = 3

Ratio of $\frac{\text{2nd term of P}}{\text{2nd term of Q}} = \frac{5\times3+4}{9\times3+6} = \frac{19}{33}$

For 10th term: 2 × 10 – 1 = 19.

20. Ratio of $\frac{\text{10th term of P}}{\text{10th term of Q}} = \frac{5\times19+4}{9\times19+6} = \frac{99}{177}$

$$= \frac{33}{59}.$$

21. d = 2nd term of P – First term of P

= 19 – 3 = 16

D = 2nd term of Q – First term of Q

= 33 – 5 = 27

Clearly, D > d.

22. $(p + qx)^9$

Co-efficients of x^3 and x^6 are equal

Co-efficient of x^3 = co-efficient of x^6

$$nC_3p^{9-3}(q)^3 = {}^9C_6p^{9-6}(q)^6$$

$$\frac{9\times8\times7}{3\times2}p^6q^3 = \frac{9\times8\times7}{3\times2}p^3p^6$$

$$p^3 = q^3$$

$$\Rightarrow \quad p = q$$

Hence, value of $q = p$.

23. $(p + qx)^9$

Here, n = 9 which is odd number

$\therefore$ Middle term = 5th term and 6th term

$$p^5\,{}^9C_4q^5 = {}^9C_5q^6p^4$$

$$\frac{p}{q} = \frac{\frac{9\times8\times7\times6}{4\times3\times2}}{\frac{9\times8\times7\times6}{4\times3\times2}} = 1$$

Hence, the ratio of middle terms = $\frac{p}{q}$.

24. $(p + qx)^9$

∵ Co-efficients of x^2 and x^4 are equal

$$nC_0p^9 + nC_1\,p^8 + qx + nC_2\,p^7x^2q^2 + {}^nC_3\,p^6x^3q^3 + {}^nC_4p^5x^4q^4 + {}^nC_5p^5q^4x^4$$

$${}^nC_2p^7q^2 = nC_5p^5q^4$$

$$\frac{9\times8\times1}{2}p^7q^2 = \frac{9\times8\times7\times6}{4\times3\times2}p^5q^4$$

$$\therefore \quad \frac{p^2}{q^2} = \frac{7}{2} = 7:2.$$

$$\Rightarrow \quad p^2 : q^2 = 7 : 2.$$

For Qs. No. 28-30:

∵ Δ be the determinant of a matrix A

$$A = \begin{bmatrix} a_{11} & a_{12} & a_{13} \\ a_{21} & a_{22} & a_{23} \\ a_{31} & a_{32} & a_{33} \end{bmatrix}$$

C_{11}, C_{12}, C_{13} are co-factors of a_{11}, a_{12}, a_{13}

$$|A| = a_{11}(a_{22}a_{33} - a_{23}a_{32}) - a_{12}(a_{21}a_{33} - a_{23}a_{31}) + a_{13}(a_{21}a_{32} - a_{22}a_{31})$$

$$= a_{11}a_{22}a_{33} - a_{11}a_{23}a_{32} - a_{12}a_{21}a_{33} + a_{12}a_{23}a_{31} + a_{13}a_{21}a_{32} - a_{13}a_{22}a_{31}$$

28. $\therefore a_{11}C_{11} + a_{12}C_{12} + a_{13}C_{13} = \Delta$.

29. Value of $a_{21}C_{11} + a_{22}C_{12} + a_{23}C_{13}$

$$= -a_{21}(a_{22}a_{33} - a_{23}a_{32}) + a_{22}(a_{21}a_{33} - a_{23}a_{31}) - a_{23}(a_{21}a_{32} - a_{22}a_{31})$$

$$= -a_{21}a_{22}a_{33} + a_{21}a_{23}a_{32} + a_{22}a_{21}a_{33} - a_{22}a_{23}a_{31} - a_{23}a_{21}a_{32} + a_{23}a_{22}a_{31} = 0.$$

30. Value of $\begin{vmatrix} a_{21} & a_{31} & a_{11} \\ a_{23} & a_{33} & a_{13} \\ a_{22} & a_{32} & a_{12} \end{vmatrix}$

$$= a_{21}(a_{33}a_{12} - a_{13}a_{32}) - a_{31}(a_{23}a_{12} - a_{13}a_{22}) + a_{11}(a_{23}a_{32} - a_{33}a_{22})$$

$$= a_{21}a_{33}a_{12} - a_{21}a_{13}a_{32} - a_{31}a_{23}a_{12} + a_{31}a_{13}a_{22} + a_{11}a_{23}a_{32} - a_{11}a_{33}a_{22}$$

$$= -\Delta.$$

For Qs. No. 37-39:

$$\because \quad A = \begin{bmatrix} 0 & \sin^2\theta & \cos^2\theta \\ \cos^2\theta & 0 & \sin^2\theta \\ \sin^2\theta & \cos^2\theta & 0 \end{bmatrix}$$

A = P + Q where P is symmetric and Q is skew symmetric matrix

$A^T = P - Q$ [$Q^T = -Q$ for skew symmetric matrix]

$2P = A + A^T$

$$P = \frac{A + A^T}{2} \text{ and } Q = \frac{A - A^T}{2}$$

$$\text{Now,} \quad A = \begin{bmatrix} 0 & \sin^2\theta & \cos^2\theta \\ \cos^2\theta & 0 & \sin^2\theta \\ \sin^2\theta & \cos^2\theta & 0 \end{bmatrix}$$

$$\therefore \quad A^T = \begin{bmatrix} 0 & \cos^2\theta & \sin^2\theta \\ \sin^2\theta & 0 & \cos^2\theta \\ \cos^2\theta & \sin^2\theta & 0 \end{bmatrix}$$

37. $\therefore \quad P = \frac{A + A^T}{2}$

$$= \frac{1}{2}\begin{bmatrix} 0 & 1 & 1 \\ 1 & 0 & 1 \\ 1 & 1 & 0 \end{bmatrix} = \begin{bmatrix} 0 & \frac{1}{2} & \frac{1}{2} \\ \frac{1}{2} & 0 & \frac{1}{2} \\ \frac{1}{2} & \frac{1}{2} & 0 \end{bmatrix}.$$

38. $\therefore \quad Q = \frac{A - A^T}{2}$

$$= \frac{1}{2}\begin{bmatrix} 0 & -\cos 2\theta & \cos 2\theta \\ \cos 2\theta & 0 & -\cos 2\theta \\ -\cos 2\theta & \cos 2\theta & 0 \end{bmatrix}$$

$$= \cos 2\theta \begin{bmatrix} 0 & -\frac{1}{2} & \frac{1}{2} \\ \frac{1}{2} & 0 & -\frac{1}{2} \\ -\frac{1}{2} & \frac{1}{2} & 0 \end{bmatrix}.$$

42. cos A + cos B + cos C

$$= \frac{b^2 + c^2 - a^2}{2bc} + \frac{a^2 + c^2 - b^2}{2ac} + \frac{b^2 + a^2 - c^2}{2ab}$$

$$= \frac{100 + 256 - 100}{2 \times 10 \times 16} + \frac{100 + 256 - 100}{2 \times 10 \times 16} + \frac{100 + 100 - 256}{2 \times 10 \times 10}$$

$$= \frac{256}{320} + \frac{256}{320} - \frac{56}{200}$$

$$= \frac{1280 + 1280 - 448}{1600} = \frac{2560 - 448}{1600} = \frac{2112}{1600} = \frac{33}{25}$$

Hence, value of cos A + cos B + cos C = $\frac{33}{25}$.

46. $\operatorname{cosec}\left(-\frac{73\pi}{3}\right)$

$$\operatorname{cosec}\left(-\frac{73 \times 180°}{3}\right) = -73 \times 60° = -4380$$

$$\frac{-4380}{360} = -12\frac{60}{360}$$

$$= \operatorname{cosec}(-60°) = -\frac{2}{\sqrt{3}}.$$

47. $\cos\left(\frac{5 \times 180°}{17}\right) + \cos\left(\frac{7 \times 180°}{17}\right) + 2\cos\frac{11 \times 180}{17} \times \cos\frac{180°}{17}$

$$= \cos\frac{900°}{17} + \cos\frac{1260}{17} + 2\cos\frac{1980}{17} \times \cos\frac{180°}{17}$$

$$= \cos\frac{180°}{17} + \cos\frac{180°}{17} + 2\cos\frac{180°}{17} \times \cos\frac{180°}{17}$$

$$= 2\cos\frac{180°}{17} + 2\cos\frac{180°}{17} \times \cos\frac{180°}{17} = (-1 + 1) = 0.$$

48. $\tan\left(\frac{3\pi}{8}\right) = \tan\left(\frac{3 \times 180°}{8}\right) = \tan\frac{540}{8} = \tan 180°$

$$= \frac{1}{5}\tan 180° = \frac{1}{5}(0) = 0$$

Hence, the value of $\tan\left(\frac{3\pi}{8}\right) = 0.$

49. $\tan^{-1}.\cot(\text{cosec}^{-1} 2)$

$= \tan^{-1}.\cot\left(\sin^{-1}\frac{1}{2}\right) = \tan^{-1}.\cot(\sin^{-1} \times \sin 30°)$

$= \tan^{-1}.\cot\left(\frac{\pi}{6}\right) = \tan^{-1}.\tan\frac{\pi}{3} = \frac{\pi}{3}.$

50. $\because \quad \cos C = \frac{a^2 + b^2 - c^2}{2ab}$

$= \frac{(4)^2 + (3)^2 - (2)^2}{2 \times 4 \times 3}$

$= \frac{21}{24} = \frac{7}{8}$

$\therefore \quad \cos 3C = 4\cos^3 C - 3\cos C$

$= 4\left(\frac{7}{8}\right)^3 - 3 \times \frac{7}{8} = 4 \times \frac{343}{512} - \frac{21}{8}$

$= \frac{343}{128} - \frac{21}{8}$

$= \frac{343 - 336}{128} = \frac{7}{128}.$

51. $\cos 36° - \cos 72°$

$= \frac{\sqrt{5}+1}{4} - \frac{\sqrt{5}-1}{4} = \frac{\sqrt{5}+1-\sqrt{5}+1}{4} = \frac{2}{4} = \frac{1}{2}$

Hence, the value of $\cos 36° - \cos 72° = \frac{1}{2}.$

52. $\because \sec x = \frac{25}{24} = \frac{h}{b}$ [x lies in fourth quadrant]

$\therefore \quad P = \sqrt{(25)^2 - (24)^2}$

$= \sqrt{(625 - 576)}$

$= \sqrt{49} = 7$

$\tan x + \sin x = \left(-\frac{7}{24}\right) + \left(-\frac{7}{25}\right)$

$= \frac{-175 - 168}{600} = \frac{-343}{600}$

Hence, value of $\tan x + \sin x = \frac{-343}{600}.$

53. $\tan^2 165° + \cot^2 165°$

$= -\tan^2 15° - \cot^2 15°$

$= \left[-\left(2-\sqrt{3}\right)\right]^2 + \left[-\left(2+\sqrt{3}\right)\right]^2$

$= \left(2-\sqrt{3}\right)^2 + \left(2+\sqrt{3}\right)^2$

$= 4 + 3 - 4\sqrt{3} + 4 + 3 + 4\sqrt{3} = 7 + 7 = 14.$

54. $\sin\left(2n\pi + \frac{5\pi}{6}\right) \times \sin\left(2n\pi - \frac{5\pi}{6}\right)$

$= \sin\left(2n\pi + \frac{5 \times 180}{6}\right) \times \sin\left(2n\pi - \frac{5 \times 180}{6}\right)$

$= \sin(2n\pi + 150°) \times \sin(2n\pi - 150°)$

$= \sin 30° \times \sin(-30°)$

$= \frac{1}{2} \times \left(-\frac{1}{2}\right) = -\frac{1}{4}.$

55. $\because 1 + 2(\sin x + \cos x)(\sin x - \cos x) = 0$

$\Rightarrow \quad 1 + 2(\sin^2 x - \cos^2 x) = 0$

$\Rightarrow \quad 1 + 2[1 - \cos^2 x - \cos^2 x] = 0$

$\Rightarrow \quad 1 + 2 - 4\cos^2 x = 0$

$\Rightarrow \quad 4\cos^2 x = 3$

$\Rightarrow \quad 2\cos x = \pm\sqrt{3}$

$\Rightarrow \quad \cos x = \pm\frac{\sqrt{3}}{2}$

$\therefore \quad x = 30°$

$x = -30°$

Hence, x take two values.

61. $\because \quad x^2 = \sqrt{3}y$

$\Rightarrow \quad x^2 = 4ay$

Here, $\quad 4a = \sqrt{3}$

$\because p$ = length of side of triangle

and q = length of the latus rectum.

$\therefore 2\sqrt{3}p = q$ is correct option.

62.

1. $(AB)^2 = (2 + 2)^2 + (-4 - 4)^2 + (-2 - 6)^2$

$= 16 + 64 + 64 = 144$

$\Rightarrow \quad AB = 12$

$(DC)^2 = (4 - 8)^2 + (6 - 14)^2 + (4 - 12)^2$

$= 16 + 64 + 64 = 144$

$\Rightarrow \quad DC = 12$

$(BC)^2 = (6)^2 + (10)^2 + (6)^2$

$= 36 + 100 + 36 = 172$

$(AD)^2 = (6)^2 + (10)^2 + (6)^2$

$= 36 + 100 + 36 = 172$

$\because \quad AB = CD$ and $BC = AD$

Hence, ABCD is rectangle.

2. Mid point of AC = $\left(\frac{6+10+10}{3}\right) = \frac{26}{3}$

Mid point of BD = $\left(\frac{6+10+10}{3}\right) = \frac{26}{3}$

Mid point of AC = Mid point of BD

Hence, Both 1 and 2 are correct.

66. Given, PQRS is a parallelogram

$$\overrightarrow{PR} = \vec{a}$$

and $\overrightarrow{QS} = \vec{b}$

$\therefore$ $\overrightarrow{PQ} = ?$

In Δ PQR,

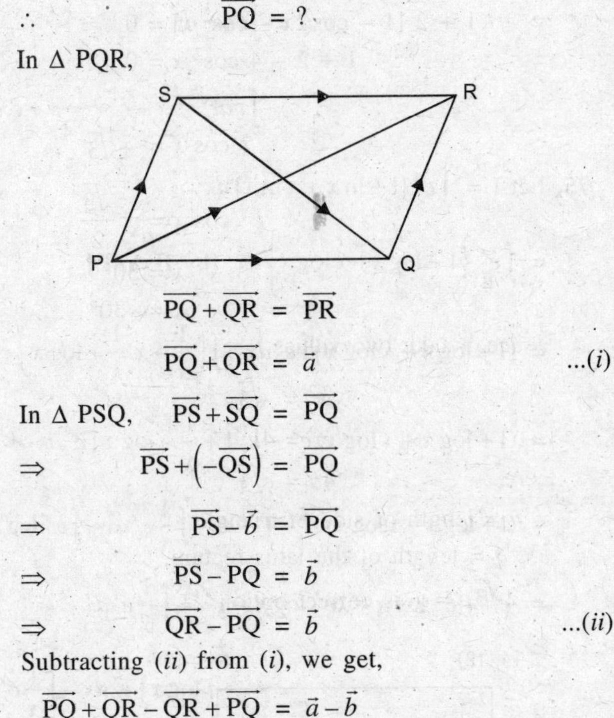

$$\overrightarrow{PQ} + \overrightarrow{QR} = \overrightarrow{PR}$$

$$\overrightarrow{PQ} + \overrightarrow{QR} = \vec{a} \quad ...(i)$$

In Δ PSQ, $\overrightarrow{PS} + \overrightarrow{SQ} = \overrightarrow{PQ}$

$\Rightarrow$ $\overrightarrow{PS} + \left(-\overrightarrow{QS}\right) = \overrightarrow{PQ}$

$\Rightarrow$ $\overrightarrow{PS} - \vec{b} = \overrightarrow{PQ}$

$\Rightarrow$ $\overrightarrow{PS} - \overrightarrow{PQ} = \vec{b}$

$\Rightarrow$ $\overrightarrow{QR} - \overrightarrow{PQ} = \vec{b} \quad ...(ii)$

Subtracting (*ii*) from (*i*), we get,

$$\overrightarrow{PQ} + \overrightarrow{QR} - \overrightarrow{QR} + \overrightarrow{PQ} = \vec{a} - \vec{b}$$

$\Rightarrow$ $2\overrightarrow{PQ} = \vec{a} - \vec{b}$

$\Rightarrow$ $\overrightarrow{PQ} = \frac{\vec{a} - \vec{b}}{2}$.

67. Let $\vec{A} = \hat{a} + 2\hat{b}$ and $\vec{B} = 5\hat{a} - 4\hat{b}$

When two vectors $\vec{A}$ and $\vec{B}$ are perpendicular to each other than the dot product is zero

i.e., $\vec{A}.\vec{B} = 0$

$\Rightarrow$ $\left(\hat{a} + 2\hat{b}\right).\left(5\hat{a} - 4\hat{b}\right) = 0$

$\Rightarrow$ $5\vec{a}.\vec{a} - 4\vec{a}.\vec{b} + 10\vec{a}.\vec{b} - 8\vec{b}.\vec{b} = 0$

$\Rightarrow$ $5 + 6\vec{a}\vec{b} - 8 = 0$

$\Rightarrow$ $-3 + 6\vec{a}\vec{b} = 0$

$\Rightarrow$ $\vec{a}\vec{b} = \frac{3}{6}$

$\Rightarrow$ $\vec{a}\vec{b} = \frac{1}{2}$

$\Rightarrow$ $|\vec{a}|.|\vec{b}|.\cos\theta = \frac{1}{2}$

$\Rightarrow$ $1 \,.\, 1 \,.\, \cos\theta = \frac{1}{2}$ [For unit vector

$\Rightarrow$ $\cos\theta = \frac{1}{2}$ $|\vec{a}| = \vec{a}.\vec{a} = 1$

$\Rightarrow$ $\cos\theta = \cos\frac{\pi}{3}$ $|\vec{b}| = \vec{b}.\vec{b} = 1]$

$\Rightarrow$ $\theta = \frac{\pi}{3}$.

68. Here, $\vec{a}$, $\vec{b}$ and $\vec{c}$ be unit vectors lying on the same plane (i.e., coplanar)

$\therefore$ $\left\{\left(3\vec{a} + 2\vec{b}\right) \times \left(5\vec{a} - 4\vec{c}\right)\right\}.\left(\vec{b} + 2\vec{c}\right)$

$= \left(15\vec{a} \times \vec{a} - 12\vec{a} \times \vec{c} + 10\vec{b} \times \vec{a} - 8\vec{b} \times \vec{c}\right).\left(\vec{b} + 2\vec{c}\right)$

$= \left(0 - 12\vec{a} \times \vec{c} + 10\vec{b} \times \vec{a} - 8\vec{b} \times \vec{c}\right).\left(\vec{b} + 2\vec{c}\right)$

$= -12\left[\vec{a}\vec{c}\vec{b}\right] - 24\left[\vec{a}\vec{c}\vec{c}\right] + 10\left[\vec{b}\vec{a}\vec{b}\right] + 20\left[\vec{b}\vec{a}\vec{c}\right] - 8\left[\vec{b}\vec{c}\vec{b}\right] - 16\left[\vec{b}\vec{c}\vec{c}\right]$

$= -12\left[\vec{a}\vec{c}\vec{b}\right] - 0 + 0 + 20\left[\vec{b}\vec{a}\vec{c}\right] - 0 - 0$

$= -12\left[\vec{a}\vec{c}\vec{b}\right] + 20\left[\vec{b}\vec{a}\vec{c}\right]$

$= 0 + 0 = 0$

[$\because$ $\vec{a}, \vec{b}, \vec{c}$ are coplanar

$\therefore$ $\left[\vec{a}, \vec{b}, \vec{c}\right] = \left[\vec{b}, \vec{a}, \vec{c}\right] = 0$.

69. Let $\vec{a} = 2x^2\hat{i} + 3x\hat{j} + \hat{k}$ and $\vec{b} = \hat{i} - 2\hat{j} + x^2\hat{k}$

The angle θ between vectors $\vec{a}$ and $\vec{b}$ is

$$\cos\theta = \frac{\vec{a}.\vec{b}}{|\vec{a}||\vec{b}|}$$

For the angle θ to be obtuse, we must have

$\cos\theta < 0$

$\Rightarrow$ $\frac{\vec{a}.\vec{b}}{|\vec{a}||\vec{b}|} < 0$

$\Rightarrow$ $\vec{a}.\vec{b} < 0$

$\Rightarrow$ $2x^2 - 6x + x^2 < 0$

$\Rightarrow$ $3x^2 - 6x < 0$

$\Rightarrow$ $3x(x - 2) < 0$

$\Rightarrow$ $0 < x < 2$.

70. We have,

$\overrightarrow{AB}$ = position vector of B – position vector of A

$= (3\hat{i}+\hat{j}+5\hat{k})-(\hat{j}+\hat{k}) = 3\hat{i}+4\hat{k}$

$\overrightarrow{BC}$ = position vector of C – position vector of B

$= (3\hat{j}+3\hat{k})-(3\hat{i}+\hat{j}+5\hat{k}) = -3\hat{i}+2\hat{j}-2\hat{k}$

and $\overrightarrow{CA}$ = position vector of A – position vector of C

$= \hat{j}+\hat{k}-(3\hat{j}+3\hat{k}) = -2\hat{j}-2\hat{k}$

Clearly, $\overrightarrow{AB}+\overrightarrow{BC}+\overrightarrow{CA}$

$= 3\hat{i}+4\hat{k}+-3\hat{i}+2\hat{j}-2\hat{k}-2\hat{j}-2\hat{k} = 0$

So, A, B and C are vertices of a triangle

Now, $\overrightarrow{BC}.\overrightarrow{CA} = (-3\hat{i}+2\hat{j}-2\hat{k}).(-2\hat{j}-2\hat{k})$

$= -4 + 4 = 0$

$\therefore \quad \overrightarrow{BC} \perp \overrightarrow{CA}$

$\Rightarrow \quad \angle BCA = \frac{\pi}{2}$

Hence, ΔABC is a right-angled triangle

Hence, $\angle C = \frac{\pi}{2}$.

72. Given, $f(x) = 4x + 1$ and $g(x) = kx + 2$

$\therefore \quad fog(x) = f(g(x)) = f(kx + 2)$

$= 4(kx + 2) + 1$

$= 4kx + 9$

and $gof(x) = g(f(x)) = g(4x + 1)$

$= k(4x + 1) + 2$

$= 4kx + k + 2$

$\because \quad fog(x) = gof(x)$

$\therefore \quad 4kx + 9 = 4kx + k + 2$

$\Rightarrow \quad 9 = k + 2$

$\Rightarrow \quad k = 9 - 2 \Rightarrow k = 7.$

73. $f(x) = \log_{10}(x^2 + 2x + 11)$

$= \frac{\log(x^2+2x+11)}{\log_{10}}$

$\Rightarrow \quad f(x) = \log(x^2 + 2x + 11)$

For Maximum and Minimum

$f(x) = 0$

$\therefore \quad \frac{2x+2}{x^2+2x+11} = 0$

$\Rightarrow \quad 2x + 2 = 0 \Rightarrow x = -1$

$\because \quad f(x) = \log_{10}(x^2 + 2x + 11)$

$\therefore \quad f(-1) = \log_{10}(1 - 2 + 11) = \log_{10}10 = 1$

Hence, the Maximum value of the function

$f(x) = 1.$

74. Let $I = \int (x^x)^2 (1+\ln x)dx$

$\Rightarrow \quad I = \int (x^x)^2 (1+\log x)dx$

Put, $x^x = t$

$\Rightarrow \quad \log x^x = \log t$

$\Rightarrow \quad x \log x = \log t$

$\Rightarrow \quad \left(x.\frac{1}{x}+\log x.1\right)dx = \frac{1}{t}dt$

$\Rightarrow \quad (1 + \log x)dx = \frac{1}{t}dt$

$\therefore \quad I = \int t^2.\frac{1}{t}dt$

$= \int t\,dt = \frac{t^2}{2}+c = \frac{x^{2x}}{2}+c.$

75. Let $I = \int e^x\{1+\ln x+x\ln x\}dx$

$= \int \underset{\text{II}}{e^x}\Big\{\underset{\text{I}}{1+\log x+x\log x}\Big\}dx$ [by ILATE]

$= (1+\log x+x\log x)\int e^x dx - \int\left(\frac{1}{x}+x.\frac{1}{x}+\log x\right)e^x dx$

$= (1+\log x+x\log x)e^x - \int\left(1+\frac{1}{x}+\log x\right)e^x dx$

$= (1+\log x+x\log x)e^x - \int e^x dx - \int \frac{1}{x}e^x dx - \int e^x \log x\,dx$

$= e^x + e^x\log x + xe^x\log x - e^x - \int\frac{1}{x}e^x dx$

$- \left[\log x\int e^x dx - \int\frac{1}{x}e^x dx\right]$

$= e^x\log x + xe^x\log x - \int\frac{1}{x}e^x dx - e^x\log x + \int\frac{1}{x}e^x dx + c$

$= xe^x\log x + c = xe^x\ln x + c$

$\Rightarrow I = xe^x\ln x + c.$

76. Let $I = \int\frac{(\cos x)^{1.5}-(\sin x)^{1.5}}{\sqrt{\sin x.\cos x}}dx$

$= \int\frac{(\cos x)^{1.5}}{\sqrt{\sin x\cos x}}dx - \int\frac{(\sin x)^{1.5}}{\sqrt{\sin x\cos x}}dx$

$\Rightarrow \quad I = \int\frac{\cos x}{\sqrt{\sin x}}dx - \int\frac{\sin x}{\sqrt{\cos x}}dx$

Put $\sin x = u \Rightarrow \cos x\,dx = du$

and $\cos x = v \Rightarrow -\sin x\,dx = dv$

$\therefore \quad I = \int\frac{du}{\sqrt{u}}+\int\frac{dv}{\sqrt{v}} = \int u^{-\frac{1}{2}}du+\int v^{-\frac{1}{2}}dv$

$= 2u^{\frac{1}{2}} + 2v^{\frac{1}{2}} + c$

$= 2\sqrt{\sin x} + 2\sqrt{\cos x} + c$.

77. Given, $y = \dfrac{x\sqrt{x^2-16}}{2} - 8\ln\left|x+\sqrt{x^2-16}\right|$

$\Rightarrow y = \dfrac{1}{2}x\sqrt{x^2-16} - 8\log\left|x+\sqrt{x^2-16}\right|$

Differentiating both sides w.r.t to x, we get,

$$\frac{dy}{dx} = \frac{1}{2}\left[x.\frac{1}{2\sqrt{x^2-16}}2x + \sqrt{x^2-16}.1\right]$$

$$-8\frac{1}{x+\sqrt{x^2-16}}\left[1+\frac{1}{2\sqrt{x^2-16}}.2x\right]$$

$$= \frac{1}{2}\left[\frac{x^2}{\sqrt{x^2-16}} + \sqrt{x^2-16}\right] - \frac{8}{x+\sqrt{x^2-16}}\left[1+\frac{x}{\sqrt{x^2-16}}\right]$$

$$= \frac{1}{2}\left[\frac{x^2+x^2-16}{\sqrt{x^2-16}}\right] - \frac{8}{x+\sqrt{x^2-16}}\left[\frac{x+\sqrt{x^2-16}}{\sqrt{x^2-16}}\right]$$

$$= \frac{1}{2}\left[\frac{2x^2-16}{\sqrt{x^2-16}}\right] - \frac{8}{\sqrt{x^2-16}}$$

$$= \frac{x^2-8}{\sqrt{x^2-16}} - \frac{8}{x^2-16} = \frac{x^2-8-8}{\sqrt{x^2-16}}$$

$$= \frac{x^2-16}{\sqrt{x^2-16}} = \frac{\sqrt{x^2-16}\sqrt{x^2-16}}{\sqrt{x^2-16}} = \sqrt{x^2-16}$$

$$\Rightarrow \frac{dy}{dx} = \sqrt{x^2-16}.$$

78. Given, $y = (x^x)x$

Taking log both sides, we get,

$\log y = \log (x^x)x$

$= x \log x^x$

$= x . x . \log x$

$\Rightarrow \log y = x^2 \log x$

Differentiating both sides, w.r.t. x, we get,

$$\frac{1}{y}\frac{dy}{dx} = x^2\frac{1}{x} + (\log x)2x$$

$$\Rightarrow \frac{1}{y}\frac{dy}{dx} = x + 2x \log x$$

$$\Rightarrow \frac{dy}{dx} = xy + 2xy \log x$$

$$\Rightarrow \frac{dy}{dx} = xy\ (1 + 2 \log x)$$

$$\Rightarrow \frac{dy}{dx} = xy\ (1 + 2 \ln x)$$

$$\Rightarrow \frac{dy}{dx} - xy\ (1 + 2 \ln x) = 0.$$

[$\because \log x = \ln x$]

79. $3(\sin x - \cos x) + 4(\cos^3 x - \sin^3 x)$

$= 3 \sin x - 3 \cos x + 4 \cos^3 x - 4 \sin^3 x$

$= 3 \sin x - 4 \sin^3 x + 4 \cos^3 x - 3 \cos x$

$= \sin 3x + \cos 3x$

$\because$ Maximum value of $a \cos x + b \sin x$ is $\sqrt{a^2+b^2}$

$\therefore$ Maximum value of $\sin 3x + \cos 3x$ is

$\sqrt{1^2+1^2} = \sqrt{2}$

Hence, required maximum value $= \sqrt{2}$.

81. Given equation,

$x - |y| = 0$ and $x - 2 = 0$

$\Rightarrow x = |y|$ and $x = 2$

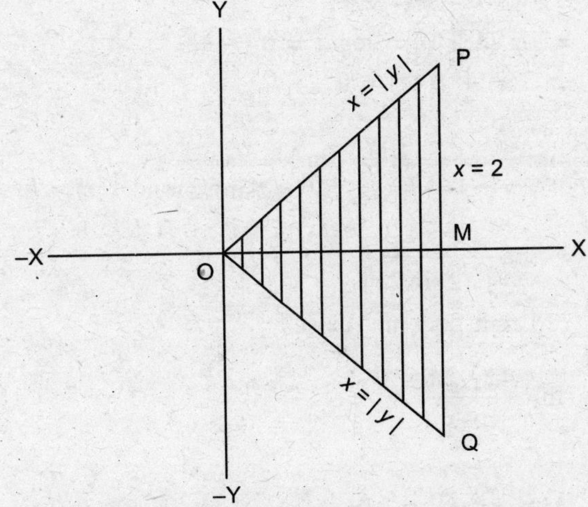

Area of the region bounded by given equation

$=$ area of ΔOPQ

$= \dfrac{1}{2}bh = \dfrac{1}{2} \times (2+2) \times 2$

[$\because$ PQ = 2 + 2 = 4, OM = 2]

= 4 sq. unit

82. Given, $f(\alpha) = \sqrt{\sec^2\alpha - 1}$

$\therefore f(\beta) = \sqrt{\sec^2\beta - 1}$

$$\therefore \frac{f(\alpha)+f(\beta)}{1-f(\alpha)f(\beta)} = \frac{\sqrt{\sec^2\alpha-1}+\sqrt{\sec^2\beta-1}}{1-\sqrt{\sec^2\alpha-1}\sqrt{\sec^2\beta-1}}$$

$$= \frac{\tan\alpha+\tan\beta}{1-\tan\alpha\tan\beta} = \tan(\alpha+\beta)$$

$$= \sqrt{\sec^2(\alpha+\beta)-1} = f(\alpha+\beta).$$

83. Given, $f(x) = \ln\left(x+\sqrt{1+x^2}\right)$

$\Rightarrow$ $f(x) = \log\left(x+\sqrt{1+x^2}\right)$

$\therefore$ $f(-x) = \log\left(-x+\sqrt{1+(-x)^2}\right)$

$= \log\left(-x+\sqrt{1+x^2}\right)$

$\Rightarrow$ $f(-x) = \log\left(-x+\sqrt{1+x^2}\right)$

Now, $f(x) + f(-x)$

$= \log\left(x+\sqrt{1+x^2}\right)+\log\left(-x+\sqrt{1+x^2}\right)$

$= \log\left(\sqrt{1+x^2}+x\right)\left(\sqrt{1+x^2}-x\right)$

$= \log\left[\left(\sqrt{1+x^2}\right)^2-x^2\right]$

$= \log\ (1 + x^2 - x^2)$

$= \log\ (1 + 0) = \log\ 1 = 0$

$\Rightarrow f(x) + f(-x) = 0.$

84. $\lim\limits_{x\to 0}\dfrac{x}{\sqrt{1-\cos 4x}} = \lim\limits_{x\to 0}\dfrac{x}{\sqrt{2\sin^2 2x}}$

$= \lim\limits_{x\to 0}\dfrac{x}{|\sqrt{2}\sin 2x|}$

$\therefore$ Limit does not exist.

85. $\lim\limits_{x\to\frac{\pi}{2}}\dfrac{4x-2\pi}{\cos x}$

$= \lim\limits_{h\to 0}\dfrac{4\left(\dfrac{\pi}{2}+h\right)-2\pi}{\cos\left(\dfrac{\pi}{2}+h\right)}$

$= \lim\limits_{h\to 0}\dfrac{2\pi+4h-2\pi}{-\sin h}$

$= \lim\limits_{h\to 0}\dfrac{4h}{-\sin h} = -4\lim\limits_{h\to 0}\dfrac{h}{\sin h}$

$= -4.\dfrac{1}{\lim\limits_{h\to 0}\dfrac{\sin h}{h}} = -4.\dfrac{1}{1} = -4.$

86. LHL of $f(x)$

$= \lim\limits_{x\to 0} f(x) = \lim\limits_{x\to 0}\dfrac{x^2+x+|x|}{x}$

$= \lim\limits_{h\to 0} f(0-h) = \lim\limits_{h\to 0}\dfrac{(-h)^2+(-h)+|-h|}{-h}$

$= \lim\limits_{h\to 0}\dfrac{h^2-h+h}{-h} = \lim\limits_{h\to 0}\dfrac{h^2}{-h}$

$= \lim\limits_{h\to 0} -h = 0$

RHL of $f(x)$

$= \lim\limits_{x\to 0^+} f(x) = \lim\limits_{h\to 0} f(0+h)$

$= \lim\limits_{h\to 0}\dfrac{h^2+h+|h|}{h} = \lim\limits_{h\to 0}\dfrac{h^2+2h}{h}$

$= \lim\limits_{h\to 0}\dfrac{h(h+2)}{h} = \lim\limits_{h\to 0}(h+2) = 0$

Clearly, $\lim\limits_{x\to 0^-} f(x) \neq \lim\limits_{x\to 0^+} f(x)$

Hence, $\lim\limits_{x\to 0} f(x)$ does not exist.

87. $\lim\limits_{h\to 0}\dfrac{\sin^2(n+h)-\sin^2 x}{h}$

$= \lim\limits_{h\to 0}\dfrac{\sin(x+h+x)\sin(x+h-x)}{h}$

$= \lim\limits_{h\to 0}\dfrac{\sin(2x+h)\sin h}{h}$

$= \lim\limits_{h\to 0}\sin(2x+h).\lim\limits_{h\to 0}\dfrac{\sin h}{h}$

$= \sin\ (2x + 0)\ .\ 1$

$= \sin\ 2x\ .\ 1$

$= \sin\ 2x.$

88. Here, $f'(x) = g(x)$ and

$f''(x) = -f(x)$

$h(x) = \{f(x)\}^2 + \{g(x)\}^2$

$\Rightarrow$ $h'(x) = 2f(x)\ f'(x) + 2g(x)\ g'(x)$

$= 2f(x)\ g(x) + 2g(x)\ f''(x)$

$= 2f(x)\ g(x) + 2g(x) - f(x)$

$= 2f(x)\ g(x) - 2f(x)\ g(x)$

$= 0$

$\Rightarrow$ $h'(x) = 0$

$\therefore$ $\int h'(x)dx = 0$

$\Rightarrow$ $h(x) = c$

$\therefore$ $h(1) = c$

and $h(2) = c$

$\therefore$ $h(1) = h(2)$

Hence, both statement 1 and 2 are correct.

90. Given, $\dfrac{d}{dx}\left(\dfrac{1+x^4+x^8}{1-x^2+x^4}\right) = ax + bx^3$

$\Rightarrow$ $\dfrac{d}{dx}\left[\dfrac{(1-x^2+x^4)(1+x^2+x^4)}{(1-x^2+x^4)}\right] = ax + bx^3$

$\Rightarrow \quad \frac{d}{dx}(1+x^2+x^4) = ax + bx^3$

$\Rightarrow \quad 2x + 4x^3 = ax + bx^3$

$\Rightarrow$ Comparing co-efficient of x and x^3

$\therefore \quad 2 = a$ and $4 = b$

Hence, $\quad 2a = b$.

91. Given, $\quad f(x) = (p \sec x)^2 + (q \operatorname{cosec} x)^2$

$\because f(x)$ attain minimum value

$\therefore \quad f(x) = 0$

$\Rightarrow 2p^2 \sec x \sec x \tan x + 2q^2 \operatorname{cosec} x - \operatorname{cosec} x \cot x = 0$

$\Rightarrow \quad 2p^2 \sec^2 x \tan x = 2q^2 \operatorname{cosec}^2 x \cot x$

$$\Rightarrow \quad \frac{q^2}{p^2} = \frac{\sec^2 x \tan x}{\operatorname{cosec}^2 x \cot x}$$

$$\Rightarrow \quad \frac{q^2}{p^2} = \tan^2 x \,.\, \tan^2 x$$

$$= (\tan^2 x)^2$$

$$\Rightarrow \quad \frac{q}{p} = \tan^2 x$$

Which is required condition.

92. $f(x) = \sum_{j=1}^{7} (x - j)^2$

$= (x-1)^2 + (x-2)^2 + (x-3)^2 + (x-4)^2 + (x-5)^2 + (x-6)^2 + (x-7)^2$

$= x^2 + 1 - 2x + x^2 + 4 - 4x + x^2 + 9 - 6x + x^2 + 16 - 8x + x^2 + 25 - 10x + x^2 + 36 - 12x + x^2 + 49 - 14x$

$= 7x^2 + 140 - 56x$

$\Rightarrow \quad f(x) = 7x^2 - 56x + 140$

For minimum value

$\therefore \quad f(x) = 0$

$\Rightarrow \quad 14x - 56 = 0$

$\Rightarrow \quad x = 4$

$\therefore$ Function attain its minimum value when $x = 4$.

94. Let $I = \int_0^1 \ln\left(\frac{1}{x} - 1\right) dx$

$$= \int_0^1 \log\left(\frac{1}{x} - 1\right) dx \quad \text{...}(i)$$

$$\left[\because \int_0^a f(x)dx = \int_0^a f(a-x)dx\right]$$

Then, $\quad I = \int_0^1 \log\left(\frac{1}{1-x} - 1\right) dx$

$$I = \int_0^1 \log\left(\frac{x}{1-x}\right) dx \quad \text{...}(ii)$$

Adding (i) and (ii), we get,

$$2I = \int_0^1 \left[\log\left(\frac{1}{x} - 1\right) + \log\left(\frac{x}{1-x}\right)\right] dx$$

$$= \int_0^1 \log\left(\frac{1-x}{x}\right).\left(\frac{x}{1-x}\right) dx$$

$$\Rightarrow \quad 2I = \int_0^1 \log 1 dx = \int_0^1 0\, dx = 0$$

$$\Rightarrow \quad I = 0.$$

95. Given, $\int_0^{\frac{\pi}{2}} (\sin^4 x + \cos^4 x)\, dx = k$

$$\therefore \quad \int_0^{20\pi} (\sin^4 x + \cos^4 x)\, dx$$

$$= \int_0^{40\pi/2} (\sin^4 x + \cos^4 x)\, dx$$

$$= 40 \int_0^{\pi/2} (\sin^4 x + \cos^4 x)\, dx$$

$= 40\, k$

By property,

$$\int_0^{2a} f(x)\, dx = 2\int_0^a f(x)\, dx$$

If $f(2a - x) = f(x)$.

99. The equation of the family of parabola having vertex at the origin and axis along positive y-axis is

$$x^2 = 4ay \quad \text{...}(i)$$

where a is a parameter

Differentiating with respect to x, we get,

$$2x = 4a\frac{dy}{dx}$$

$$\Rightarrow \quad a = \frac{2x}{4\frac{dy}{dx}}$$

$$\Rightarrow \quad a = \frac{x}{2\frac{dy}{dx}}$$

Substituting the value of a in (*i*), we get,

$$x^2 = \frac{4y \times \dfrac{x}{2\dfrac{dy}{dx}}}{}$$

$$\Rightarrow \quad 2x^2 \frac{dy}{dx} = 4xy$$

$$\Rightarrow \quad x\frac{dy}{dx} = 2y$$

$$\Rightarrow \quad x\frac{dy}{dx} - 2y = 0$$

Which is the required differential equation.

100. Given, differential equation,

$$(dy - dx) + \cos x\,(dy + dx) = 0$$

$$\Rightarrow \quad dy - dx + \cos x\, dy + \cos x\, dx = 0$$

$$\Rightarrow \quad (1 + \cos x)dy + (\cos x - 1)\, dx = 0$$

$$\Rightarrow \quad (1 + \cos x)dy = -(\cos x - 1)dx$$

$$\Rightarrow \quad \frac{dy}{dx} = \frac{-(\cos x - 1)}{1 + \cos x} = \frac{1 - \cos x}{1 + \cos x}$$

$$\Rightarrow \quad \frac{dy}{dx} = \frac{2\sin^2 \dfrac{x}{2}}{2\cos^2 \dfrac{x}{2}} = \tan^2 \frac{x}{2}$$

$$\Rightarrow \quad \frac{dy}{dx} = \tan^2 \frac{x}{2}$$

$$\Rightarrow \quad dy = \tan^2 \frac{x}{2} dx$$

$$\Rightarrow \quad \int dy = \int \tan^2 \frac{x}{2} dx$$

$$\Rightarrow \quad \int dy = \int \left(\sec^2 \frac{x}{2} - 1\right) dx$$

$$\Rightarrow \quad y = \frac{\tan \dfrac{x}{2}}{\dfrac{1}{2}} - x + c$$

$$\Rightarrow \quad y = 2\tan \frac{x}{2} - x + c$$

Which is required solution.

101. $\because$ x = The mean of squares of first n natural number

$$\Rightarrow \quad x = \frac{\dfrac{1}{6}n(n+1)(2n+1)}{n}$$

$$\Rightarrow \quad x = \frac{1}{6}(n+1)(2n+1)$$

and y = The square of mean of first n natural number

$$\Rightarrow \quad y = \left[\frac{\dfrac{1}{2}n(n+1)}{n}\right]^2 = \frac{1}{4}(n+1)^2$$

Given, $\quad \dfrac{x}{y} = \dfrac{55}{42}$

$$\Rightarrow \quad \frac{\dfrac{1}{6}(n+1)(2n+1)}{\dfrac{1}{4}(n+1)^2} = \frac{55}{42}$$

$$\Rightarrow \quad \frac{2}{3}\left(\frac{2n+1}{n+1}\right) = \frac{55}{42}$$

$$\Rightarrow \quad \frac{2n+1}{n+1} = \frac{55}{42} \times \frac{3}{2}$$

$$\Rightarrow \quad \frac{2n+1}{n+1} = \frac{55}{28}$$

$$\Rightarrow \quad 56n + 28 = 55n + 55$$

$$\Rightarrow \quad 56n - 55n = 55 - 28$$

$$\Rightarrow \quad n = 27.$$

102. $\because$ Prime numbers from 1 to 50 are 2, 3, 5, 7, 11, 13, 17, 19, 23, 29, 31, 37, 41, 43, 47

$\therefore$ Number of prime numbers from 1 to 50 = 15

$\therefore$ Number of composite numbers from 1 to 50

$$= 50 - 15$$
$$= 35$$

$\therefore$ The probability of getting a composite numbers

$$= \frac{^{35}C_1}{^{50}C_1} = \frac{35}{50} = \frac{7}{10}.$$

104. $\because$ 2 numbers x and y are chosen at random from first 10 natural numbers

$\therefore$ S = {(1, 2), ... (1, 1), (2, 3), ... (2, 10), ... (8, 1), ... (8, 10) ... (9, 1), ... (9, 10)}

$$n(\text{S}) = \frac{10(10-1)}{2} = 5 \times 9 = 45$$

E = $(x + y)$ is divisible by 4

$\because$ $\quad x + y = 4 \Rightarrow (1, 3)$

$= 8 \Rightarrow (1, 7), (2, 6), (3, 5)$

$= 12 \Rightarrow (2, 10), (3, 9), (4, 8), (5, 7)$

$= 16 \Rightarrow (6, 10), (7, 9)$

$= 20 \Rightarrow 0$

$n(\text{E}) = 10$

$$p(\text{E}) = \frac{n(\text{E})}{n(\text{S})} = \frac{10}{45} = \frac{2}{9}$$

Probability [$(x + y)$ is divisible by 4] = $\dfrac{2}{9}$.

106. 3 fair dice are tossed once

$\therefore$ n(sample space) = $6 \times 6 \times 6$

$\Rightarrow$ $n(S) = 216$

Let E = different number that are in A.P.

then, E = {(1, 2, 3), (2, 3, 4), (3, 4, 5), (4, 5, 6), (1, 3, 5), (2, 4, 6), (3, 2, 1), (4, 3, 2), (5, 4, 3), (6, 5, 4), (5, 3, 1), (6, 4, 2)}

$\Rightarrow$ $n(E) = 12$

$\therefore$ $$P(E) = \frac{n(E)}{n(S)} = \frac{12}{216} = \frac{1}{18}$$

Hence, required probability = $\frac{1}{18}$.

107. Given, $P(A) = 0.5$

$P(B) = 0.7$

and $P(A \cap B) = 0.3$

$\because$ $P(A' \cap B') = \overline{P(A \cup B)} = 1 - P(A \cup B)$

$= 1 - [P(A) + P(B) - P(A \cap B)]$

$= 1 - P(A) - P(B) + P(A \cap B)$

$P(A' \cap B) = P(B) - P(A \cap B)$

and $P(A \cap B') = P(A) - P(A \cap B)$

$\therefore$ $P(A' \cap B') + P(A' \cap B) + P(A \cap B')$

$= 1 - \cancel{P(A)} - \cancel{P(B)} + P(A \cap B) + \cancel{P(B)} - \cancel{P(A \cap B)}$

$+ \cancel{P(A)} - \cancel{P(A \cap B)}$

$= 1 - P(A \cap B)$

$= 1 - 0.3 = 0.7.$

109. Three fair dice are thrown

$\therefore$ Sample space = {(1, 1, 1), ... (6, 6, 6)}

$\Rightarrow$ $n(S) = 6 \times 6 \times 6$

$= 6^3 = 216$

Let E_1 be the total greater than 15

Then, E_1 = {(5, 5, 6), (5, 6, 5), (6, 5, 5), (4, 6, 6), (6, 4, 6), (6, 6, 4), (5, 6, 6), (6, 5, 6), (6, 6, 5), (6, 6, 6)}

$\therefore$ $n(E_1) = 10$

and E_2 be the total equal to 15

$\therefore$ E_2 = {(3, 6, 6), (6, 3, 6), (6, 6, 3), (4, 5, 6), (5, 6, 4), (6, 4, 5), (4, 6, 5), (5, 4, 6), (6, 5, 4), (5, 5, 5)}

$\therefore$ $n(E_2) = 10$

$\therefore$ The probability of getting a total greater than or equal to 15 = P = $P(E_1) + P(E_2)$

$$= \frac{n(E_1)}{n(S)} + \frac{n(E_2)}{n(S)}$$

$$= \frac{10}{216} + \frac{10}{216} = \frac{20}{216} = \frac{5}{54}.$$

110. The probability that a person hits a target = 0.5

$\Rightarrow$ $P = \frac{1}{2}$

$\therefore$ Probability of at least one hit in 4 shots

$$= \frac{1}{2} + \left(\frac{1}{2}\right)\left(\frac{1}{2}\right) + \left(\frac{1}{2}\right)\left(\frac{1}{2}\right)\left(\frac{1}{2}\right) + \left(\frac{1}{2}\right)\left(\frac{1}{2}\right)\left(\frac{1}{2}\right)\left(\frac{1}{2}\right)$$

$$= \frac{1}{2} + \frac{1}{4} + \frac{1}{8} + \frac{1}{16} = \frac{8+4+2+1}{16} = \frac{15}{16}.$$

111. Here, Total number of balls

= 2 white + 3 black + 4 red = 9

$\because$ Drawing 3 balls from the box with at least one black ball

$\therefore$ The total number of ways

$= {}^3C_1 \times {}^6C_2 + {}^3C_2 \times {}^6C_1 + {}^3C_3 \times {}^6C_0$

(By the fundamental principle of addition)

$$= 3 \times \frac{\lfloor 6}{\lfloor 2 \lfloor 4} + \frac{\lfloor 3}{\lfloor 2 \lfloor 1} \times 6 + \frac{\lfloor 3}{\lfloor 3 \lfloor 0} \times 1 = 3 \times \frac{6 \times 5}{2} + 3 \times 6 + 1 \times 1$$

$= 3 \times 3 \times 5 + 18 + 1 = 45 + 19 = 64.$

112. On an average one ship out of 5 sunk

$\therefore$ $p = \frac{1}{5}$

$\therefore$ $q = 1 - p = 1 - \frac{1}{5} = \frac{4}{5}$

and $n = 5$

Probability that exactly 3 out of 5 ships would arrive safely

$\Rightarrow$ Exactly 2 ship sunk

$\because$ $p(x) = {}^nC_x \, p^x \, q^{n-x}$

$\therefore$ $p(2) = {}^5C_2 \, p^2 \, q^3$

$$= {}^5C_2 \left(\frac{1}{5}\right)^2 \left(\frac{4}{5}\right)^3 = \frac{\lfloor 5}{\lfloor 2 \lfloor 3} \times \frac{1}{25} \times \frac{64}{125}$$

$$= \frac{5 \times 4}{2} \times \frac{1}{25} \times \frac{64}{125} = \frac{2 \times 64}{5 \times 125} = \frac{128}{625}$$

$\therefore$ Required probability = $\frac{128}{625}$.

113. A card is drawn from 52 cards

$\therefore$ $S = {}^{52}C_1$

A gambler bets that it is either a spade or an ace

$\therefore$ $$P = \frac{{}^{13}C_1 + {}^3C_1}{{}^{52}C_1} = \frac{13+3}{52} = \frac{16}{52} = \frac{4}{13}$$

$\therefore$ The odd against his winning are

$$= \left(1 - \frac{4}{13}\right) : \frac{4}{13} = \frac{9}{13} : \frac{4}{13} = 9 : 4.$$

For Qs. No. 116-117.

From given the mean marks and SD,

Co-efficient of variation = $100 \times \frac{\text{S.D.}}{\text{Mean}}$

116. Variability of marks

A. Mathematics = $100 \times \frac{15}{40} = 37.5\%$

B. Physics = $100 \times \frac{12}{28} = 42.85\%$

C. Chemistry = $100 \times \frac{14}{38} = 36.84\%$

D. Biology = $100 \times \frac{16}{36} = 44.44\%$

Here, Biology shows highest variability of marks.

117. The co-efficient of variation of marks in Mathematics

$$= 100 \times \frac{15}{40} = 37.5\%.$$

For Qs. No. 118-120.

Class	Mid Value (x_i)	f_i	C.f.	$\lvert x_i - 35 \rvert$	$f_i \lvert x_i - 35 \rvert$
0-10	5	1	1	30	30
10-20	15	2	3	20	40
20-30	25	4	7	10	40
30-40	35	6	13	0	0
40-50	45	4	17	10	40
50-60	55	3	20	20	60

$$N = \Sigma f_i = 20, \Sigma f_i \lvert x_i - 35 \rvert = 210$$

Here, N = 20

So, $\frac{N}{2} = \frac{20}{2} = 10$

and the c.f. just greater than $\frac{N}{2}$ is 13.

Thus, 30–40 is the median class

$\therefore$ Median = $l + \frac{\frac{N}{2} - F}{f} \times h$

Where, $l = 30$, $h = 10$, $f = 6$, F = 7

$\Rightarrow$ Median = $30 + \frac{10-7}{6} \times 10$

$= 30 + \frac{3}{6} \times 10$

$= 30 + 5 = 35.$

118. The Median of the distribution = 35.

119. Mean deviation about the Median

$$= \frac{1}{N}\Sigma f_i \lvert x_i - 35 \rvert = \frac{1}{20} \times 210 = \frac{21}{2} = 10.5.$$

120. M.D. about Mean:

Class	f_i	Mid point (x_i)	$d_i = \frac{x_i - 35}{10}$	$f_i d_i$	$\lvert x_i - \bar{x} \rvert$	$f_i \lvert x_i - \bar{x} \rvert$
0-10	1	5	–3	–3	$\frac{59}{2}$	$\frac{59}{2}$
10-20	2	15	–2	–4	$\frac{39}{2}$	39
20-30	4	25	–1	–4	$\frac{19}{2}$	38
30-40	6	35	0	0	$\frac{1}{2}$	3
40-50	4	45	1	4	$\frac{21}{2}$	42
50-60	3	55	2	6	$\frac{41}{2}$	$\frac{123}{2}$

$$N = \Sigma f_i = 20$$

$$\Sigma f_i d_i = -1$$

$$\Sigma f_i \lvert x_i - \bar{X} \rvert = 213$$

Complete $\bar{X}$ by step-deviation method

$\therefore$ $\bar{X} = a + h\left(\frac{1}{N}\sum_{i=1}^{n} f_i d_i\right)$

Where, $d_i = \frac{x_i - a}{h}$

a = assumed mean = 35

and h = common factor = 10

$\therefore$ $\bar{X} = a + h\left(\frac{1}{N}\sum_{i=1}^{n} f_i d_i\right)$

$= 35 + 10\left(\frac{1}{20} \times -1\right) = 35 + -\frac{1}{2} = \frac{69}{2}$

$\therefore$ Mean deviation about the mean

$$= \frac{1}{N}\Sigma f_i \lvert x_i - \bar{X} \rvert = \frac{1}{20} \times 213 = 10.65.$$

Previous Papers (Solved)

NATIONAL DEFENCE ACADEMY & NAVAL ACADEMY

NDA & NA – Entrance Exam, 2022 (I)

PAPER I : GENERAL ABILITY TEST

PART A : ENGLISH LANGUAGE

SPOTTING ERRORS

Directions (Qs. No. 1-10): *Each item in this section has a sentence with three parts labelled A, B and C. Read each sentence to find out whether there is any error in any part and indicate your response in the Answer Sheet against the corresponding letter i.e., A or B or C. If you find no error, your response should be indicated as D.*

1. A company of five thousand soldiers, (A)/ having marched tirelessly for over five days, (B)/ have just moved into their cantonment. (C)/ No error (D)

2. Every person who believes in principles (A)/ must stand up to fight (B)/ for their convictions. (C)/ No error (D)

3. The Olympic Games reflects (A)/ the highest spirit of (B)/ human endeavour and achievement. (C)/ No error (D)

4. The principal of the school (A)/ stressed the need for discipline (B)/ amongst the students. (C)/ No error (D)

5. Failure is the stepping stone to success; (A)/ however, successive failures are not (B)/ successive stepping stones to success. (C)/ No error (D)

6. India's strengths are (A)/ its diversity of culture and (B)/ the spirit of tolerance in it's people. (C)/ No error (D)

7. Once considered ninth planet of the solar system, (A)/ Pluto is today listed as the (B)/ largest dwarf planet of the solar system. (C)/ No error (D)

8. The greatest glory in life (A)/ is to be able to realize ones dreams and ambitions (B)/ without trampling on those of others. (C)/ No error (D)

9. To be able to manage one's (A)/ anger is a reflection of an individual's (B)/ psychological maturity. (C)/ No error (D)

10. A honest mistake (A)/ is no more than that; (B)/ just an honest mistake. (C)/ No error (D)

IDIOMS AND PHRASES

Directions (Qs. No. 11-20): *Given below are some idioms/ phrases followed by four alternative meanings to each. Choose the most appropriate answer from among the options A, B, C, or D.*

11. Counting your chickens
A. confident of success
B. greedily accumulating wealth
C. being careful about spending money
D. getting scared because of danger

12. The icing on the cake
A. baked food that is delicate and delicious with a topping
B. extra benefit over and above an already good deal
C. getting what you asked for
D. more than what is needed

13. A stitch in time
A. tailoring one's efforts efficiently
B. making an effort to succeed
C. inability to take timely decision
D. timely action that prevents a negative outcome

14. At sixes and sevens
A. on top of the situation
B. state of denial
C. state of total confusion
D. well-planned and prepared

15. Talking twenty to the dozen
A. talking hurriedly and rapidly
B. talking too much
C. talking without making sense
D. talking out of turn

16. Under the weather
A. walking in the rain
B. controlled by the elements
C. browbeaten by the heat
D. unwell

17. To sit on the fence
A. to act promptly
B. to be lazy
C. to be undecided
D. to sit without doing anything

18. Once in a blue moon
A. romantic moment
B. occasionally
C. rarely
D. often

19. Through thick and thin
A. in genuine friendship
B. through the best of everything
C. among people both fat and slim
D. through difficult times

20. Like chalk and cheese'
A. very different from each other
B. without any blemish
C. pure white in colour
D. very like each other

ORDERING OF WORDS IN A SENTENCE

Directions (Qs. No. 21-30): *Each of the following items in this section consists of a sentence, the parts of which have been jumbled. These parts have been labelled P, Q, R and S. Given below each sentence are four sequences namely A, B, C and D. You are required to re-arrange the jumbled parts of the sentence and mark your answer accordingly.*

21. P. but perhaps the best way is to agree
Q. there are many ways of dealing
R. with them without excessive argumentation
S. with intransigent customers

The correct sequence should be:
A. QPRS B. QSPR
C. PSQR D. RSQP

22. P. in the years following
Q. India achieved remarkable economic development
R. liberalization in the year 1991
S. the landmark reforms inaugurated via

The correct sequence should be:
A. PQRS B. PRSQ
C. SPRQ D. QPSR

23. P. was the victory secured by the women's hockey team
Q. in the arena of sport, perhaps
R. against Australia in the Tokyo Olympics
S. the greatest moment in Indian Olympic history

The correct sequence should be:
A. SPQR B. RPQS
C. QSPR D. QRPS

24. P. in terms of GDP and GNP,
Q. for gauging the success of a nation
R. which are the two major determinants
S. economic progress is determined

The correct sequence should be:
A. SQRP B. RPQS
C. SPRQ D. QRPS

25. P. with the aplomb of a stage artist,
Q. that they are not men of straw
R. they can twist and shake their wobbly heads
S. mesmerizing the gullible into believing

The correct sequence should be:
A. PRQS B. RPSQ
C. SPQR D. QRPS

26. P. of its rain-soaked verdure
Q. and on the other there are
R. on the one hand there is the immense beauty
S. the artifacts of its visible modernity

The correct sequence should be:
A. PRQS B. QRSP
C. SPQR D. RPQS

27. P. are often rooted
Q. the causes
R. of extreme poverty
S. in the inequalities of social systems

The correct sequence should be:
A. QRPS B. QRSP
C. SRQP D. SRPQ

28. P. a person by the way
Q. he behaves and
R. you must judge
S. not by the way he looks

The correct sequence should be:
A. RPQS B. QRSP
C. RSQP D. QPSR

29. P. to the greatest number of people
Q. that causes the least discomfort
R. whenever in doubt
S. always opt for the option

The correct sequence should be:
A. RQPS B. QRSP
C. RSQP D. QPSR

30. P. brought by bad times
Q. against the despondency
R. our greatest defence
S. faith and belief are

The correct sequence should be:
A. RQPS B. SRQP
C. RSQP D. QPRS

ANTONYMS

Directions (Qs. No. 31-40): *Each item in this section consists of a sentence with an underlined word followed by four options. Select the option that is* **opposite in meaning** *to the underlined word and mark your response in your Answer Sheet accordingly.*

31. He is essentially a crude person.
A. coarse B. refined
C. eager D. balanced

32. His confidence is high.
A. diffidence B. eagerness
C. steadfastness D. endurance

33. His integrity is noticed.
A. skilfulness B. ability
C. dependability D. dishonesty

34. She is a benevolent individual.
A. clever B. muddled
C. malevolent D. ambivalent

35. His sartorial manner is judged.
A. unstylish B. uncompromising
C. common D. crude

36. This piece of art is authentic.
A. genuine B. expensive
C. rare D. fake

37. The deluge affected the population.
A. cloudburst B. drought
C. deforestation D. drizzle

38. His dedication is known to all.
A. clarity B. hostility
C. apathy D. anger

39. His perspicacity was remarkable.
A. smartness B. dullness
C. dedication D. deviousness

40. He has a penchant for spicy food.
A. tendency B. affinity
C. fear D. dislike

SYNONYMS

Directions (Qs. No. 41-50): *Each item in this section consists of a sentence with an underlined word followed by four options. Select the option that is* **nearest in meaning** *to the underlined word and mark your response in your Answer Sheet accordingly.*

41. After a good meal, it is important to pay a compliment to the chef.
A. tip B. praise
C. admonish D. revile

42. His work is laudable.
A. praiseworthy B. laughable
C. bold D. loud

43. Raj is a competent carpenter.
A. capable B. exceptional
C. inadept D. clumsy

44. He is diligent in submitting assignments.
A. dilly-dallying B. procrastinating
C. intelligent D. conscientious

45. He appears to be reticent.
A. expansive B. jolly
C. silent D. withdrawn

46. He is always jovial.
A. cheerful B. callous
C. garrulous D. credulous

47. Mohan remains morose these days.
A. introspective B. generous
C. chirpy D. sullen

48. He was a reluctant learner.
A. enthusiastic B. eager
C. unwilling D. fearful

49. Amit is optimistic about the prospects of his investments.
A. pessimistic B. uncaring
C. carefree D. sanguine

50. Sachin is very cooperative by nature.
A. complaisant B. covert
C. complacent D. conniving

PART B : GENERAL KNOWLEDGE

51. What is the mass of a material, whose specific heat capacity is 400 J/ (kg °C) for a rise in temperature from 15 °C to 25 °C, when heat received is 20 kJ?
A. 0.1 kg B. 1 kg
C. 10 kg D. 5 kg

52. The specific latent heat of vaporization of a substance is the quantity of heat needed to change unit mass from:
A. liquid to vapour with a change of temperature
B. liquid to vapour without a change of temperature
C. vapour to liquid without a change of temperature
D. vapour to liquid with a change of temperature

53. Evaporation from the surface of a given liquid takes place more rapidly when:
A. the temperature is high and the surface area of the liquid is large
B. the temperature is low and the surface area of the liquid is large

C. the temperature is low and the surface area of the liquid is small
D. the temperature is high and the surface area of the liquid is small

54. Which of the following statements correctly explains/explain the existence of a positive force between two electric charges?
1. Both the charges are positive.
2. Both the charges are negative.
3. Both the charges are oppositely charged.

Select the correct answer using the code given below:
A. 1 only B. 2 only
C. 1 and 2 only D. 1, 2 and 3

55. An electric wire of resistance 50 ohm is cut into five equal wires. These wires are then connected in parallel. What is the equivalent resistance of this combination?
A. 2 ohm B. 10 ohm
C. 0.5 ohm D. 5 ohm

56. The electric field lines from an isolated positively charged conducting sphere are:
A. tangential to the conducting surface
B. at right angles to the conducting surface and towards the centre of the sphere
C. at any angle to the conducting surface
D. at right angles to the conducting surface and outwards from the centre of the sphere

57. Which one of the following is *not* a solution?
A. Alloy B. Milk
C. Air D. Sugar

58. Refining of petroleum is carried out using which one of the following techniques?
A. Evaporation B. Fractional distillation
C. Separating funnel D. Sublimation

59. Which one of the following is a chemical change?
A. Dissolving sugar in water
B. Melting of ice
C. Crystallization
D. Milk turning sour

60. Which one of the following is the correct molecular formula of ammonium carbonate if the valency of ammonium ion is (+1) and carbonate anion is (–2)?
A. $(NH_4)_2 CO_3$ B. $NH_4 (CO_3)_2$
C. $(NH_3)_2CO_3$ D. NH_4CO_3

61. Which one of the following is a covalent compound?
A. Calcium oxide B. Sodium nitride
C. Silicon carbide D. Zinc sulphide

62. The mass number of argon is 40. Which one of the following statements is correct?
A. The number of protons in argon is 22.
B. The number of neutrons in argon is 18.
C. The number of electrons in argon is 18.
D. The sum of numbers of protons and electrons in argon is 40.

63. Which one of the following is the correct order of the valencies of elements Ne, Si, N and Mg?
A. Ne < Mg < N < Si B. Si < N < Mg < Ne
C. Ne < N < Si < Mg D. Mg < Ne < N < Si

64. The frequency of an alternating current is 3 Hz. It implies that
A. there are 6 cycles/s B. there are 3 cycles/s
C. there are 2 cycles/s D. there is only 1 cycle/s

65. Which one of the following correctly represents the SI unit of resistivity?
A. Ω B. Ω/m
C. Ω cm D. Ω m

66. What is the current required to light a 60 W incandescent bulb in a domestic supply of 240 V?
A. 0.5 A B. 0.25 A
C. 1.0 A D. 5.0 A

67. The magnetic field produced by a current-carrying straight wire at a point outside the wire depends
A. inversely on the distance from it
B. directly on the distance from it
C. inversely at short distances and directly at large distances from it
D. directly on the distance (at short distances) and inversely on the distance (at long distances) from it

68. What is the dimension of gravitational constant?
A. ML^3T^{-2} B. $M^{-1}L^3T^{-2}$
C. $M^2L^{-2}T^{-2}$ D. $M^2L^{-1}T^{-2}$

69. A ball is thrown vertically upward with a speed of 40 m/s. The time taken by the ball to reach the maximum height would be approximately:
A. 2 s B. 3 s
C. 4 s D. 5 s

70. The time period of a 1 m long pendulum approximates to:
A. 6 s B. 4 s
C. 2 s D. 1 s

71. Which of the following statements about living and non-living being is/are correct?
1. While living being can demonstrate growth and repair, non-living being cannot.
2. While living being demonstrates metabolic processes, non-living being does not.

Select the correct answer using the code given below:
A. 1 only B. 2 only
C. Both 1 and 2 D. Neither 1 nor 2

72. Which one of the following plant plastids stores starch, oil and protein granules?
A. Chloroplast B. Leucoplast
C. Chromoplast D. Xanthoplast

73. Which one of the following statements about 'vacuoles' is ***not*** correct?
A. In plants, there is a large central vacuole that may occupy 90% of total cell volume.
B. In plant cells, vacuoles provide turgidity and rigidity.
C. In Amoeba, vacuoles have role in nutrition.
D. Vacuoles are absent in animal cells.

74. In aquatic plants, large air sacs give them buoyancy effects. These sacs are surrounded by which one of the following types of tissues?
A. Parenchyma B. Collenchyma
C. Sclerenchyma D. Complex tissue

75. Which one of the following belongs to 'Pisces'?
A. Dogfish B. Jellyfish
C. Silverfish D. Starfish

76. Which one of the following groups is called 'amphibians of plant kingdom'?
A. Bryophytes B. Thallophytes
C. Pteridophytes D. Gymnosperms

77. Which one of the following is caused by a bacterial pathogen?
A. AIDS B. Dengue fever
C. COVID-19 D. Typhoid fever

78. The twinkling of a star is due to the atmospheric:
A. diffraction of starlight
B. reflection of starlight
C. refraction of starlight
D. dispersion of starlight

79. A mass M is dragged by a pulley on a horizontal plane by a force anti-parallel to its displacement. The work done in pulling the mass M is:
A. zero B. positive
C. infinite D. negative

80. A 5 N force is defined when a mass of 10 kg is accelerated with:
A. 5.0 cm/s^2 B. 0.5 m/s^2
C. 0.5 cm/s^2 D. 5.0 m/s^2

81. A boy of mass 52 kg jumps with a horizontal velocity of 2 m/s onto a stationary cart of mass 3 kg. The cart is fixed with frictionless wheels. Which one of the following would be the speed of the cart?
A. 2.15 m/s B. 1.89 m/s
C. 1.51 m/s D. 2.51 m/s

82. The energy possessed by a body due to its change in position or shape is called:
A. thermal energy B. potential energy
C. kinetic energy D. electric energy

83. A sound wave has a frequency of 1 kHz and wavelength 50 cm. How long will it take to travel 1 km?
A. 5 s B. 4 s
C. 3 s D. 2 s

84. For an element with atomic number 35, which one of the following will be the correct number of electrons in its valence shell based on Bohr's model of an atom?
A. 1 B. 3
C. 5 D. 7

85. Which one of the following is ***not*** an example of a redox reaction?
A. $AlCl_3 + 3H_2O \rightarrow Al(OH)_3 + 3HCl$
B. $2NaH \rightarrow 2Na + H_2$
C. $4Fe + 3O_2 \rightarrow 2Fe_2O_3$
D. $CuSO_4 + Zn \rightarrow Cu + ZnSO_4$

86. Which one of the following allotropes of carbon is isomorphous with crystalline silicon?
A. Coke B. Diamond
C. Graphite D. Coal

87. Which one of the following is the colour of hydrogen gas?
A. Light yellow B. Orange
C. Black D. Colourless

88. Which one of the following is ***not*** a pigment?
A. Zinc oxide B. Chalk
C. White lead D. Silica

89. Which one of the following statements about fertilizers is ***not*** correct?
A. Urea is a phosphorus-containing fertilizer.
B. Application of fertilizer to the soil increases fertility of the soil.
C. Urea can be prepared by action of ammonia and carbon dioxide under high pressure and at high temperature.
D. Urea contains more nitrogen than other fertilizers.

90. Which one of the following statements is ***not*** correct?
A. Most carbon compounds are good conductors of electricity.
B. Bonding in organic compounds is covalent.
C. Graphite is used as a lubricant.
D. Diamond is an allotrope of carbon.

91. Which one of the following reactions is an example of decomposition reaction?
A. $CH_4\,(g) + 2O_2\,(g) \rightarrow CO_2\,(g) + 2H_2O\,(g)$
B. $2AgCl(s) \xrightarrow{\text{Sunlight}} 2Ag(s) + Cl_2\,(g)$
C. $CuO + H_2 \xrightarrow{\text{Heat}} Cu + H_2O$
D. $Fe(s) + CuSO_4\,(aq) \rightarrow FeSO_4\,(aq) + Cu(s)$

92. Which one of the following is the mechanism of action of oral contraceptive pills?
A. They kill the egg
B. They kill the sperm
C. They kill the zygote
D. They inhibit the release of egg

93. Which one of the following plants has unisexual flowers?
A. Papaya B. Hibiscus
C. Mustard D. Sunflower

94. A cell is unable to synthesize lipids. Which of its cell organelles might be defective?
A. Smooth endoplasmic reticulum
B. Golgi bodies
C. Lysosomes
D. Mitochondria

95. All objects experience a buoyancy when they are immersed in a fluid. Buoyancy is:
A. a downward force B. a downward pressure
C. an upward force D. an upward pressure

96. According to Fleming's right-hand rule, if the forefinger indicates the direction of magnetic field and thumb shows the direction of motion of conductor, then the stretched middle finger will predict the direction of:
A. force acting on the conductor
B. electric field
C. induced current
D. current

97. Two resistors R_1 and R_2 arranged in parallel combination in an electrical closed circuit are made of the same material and of same thickness. If the length of R_2 is twice the length of R_1, then the total resistance R satisfies:
A. $3R = 2R_1$ B. $3R = 2R_2$
C. $2R = 3R_1$ D. $2R = 3R_2$

98. What is the magnification produced by a concave lens of focal length 10 cm, when an image is formed at a distance of 5 cm from the lens?
A. 2.0 B. 1.0
C. 0.5 D. 0.33

99. A wooden box of mass 2 kg and dimensions (30 cm × 15 cm × 10 cm) is placed on a table with sides 30 cm and 10 cm touching the tabletop. Which one of the following is the approximate pressure exerted on the table?
A. 111.1 N/m^2 B. 222.2 N/m^2
C. 333.3 N/m^2 D. 666.6 N/m^2

100. Why are the tyres of aircrafts made of conducting rubber?
1. So that the charge accumulated on the aircraft in flight, by rubbing the air, can easily be transferred to ground on landing.
2. So that the charge accumulated due to the operation of various electronic equipments in the aircraft in flight can easily be transferred to ground on landing.

Select the correct answer using the code given below:
A. 1 only
B. 2 only
C. Both 1 and 2
D. Neither 1 nor 2

101. *Arthashastra*, the classical work of Indian political thought, focuses primarily on:
A. economy B. culture
C. statecraft D. monarchy

102. When did *Charaka Samhita* originate?
A. 6th Century BCE
B. 3rd to 2nd Century BCE
C. 4th Century BCE
D. 5th Century BCE

103. Early Buddhist sculptors did not show Buddha in human form. Through which of the following symbols was Buddha's presence shown by the early sculptors?
A. Empty Seat and Stupa only
B. Wheel and Tree only
C. Wheel, Tree and Stupa only
D. Empty Seat, Wheel, Tree and Stupa

104. The Parliament of India is primarily based on the model of:
A. German Parliament B. British Parliament
C. American Congress D. French Parliament

105. Who among the following had the shortest span in office as the Prime Minister of India?
A. Lal Bahadur Shastri
B. Chaudhary Charan Singh
C. Chandra Shekhar
D. H.D. Deve Gowda

106. Which one of the following does ***not*** fall under the jurisdiction of the apex court of India?
A. Original Jurisdiction
B. Appellate Jurisdiction
C. Collegiate Jurisdiction
D. Advisory Jurisdiction

107. According to the Indian Meteorological Department, which of the following is/are the feature/features of cloudburst?
1. Heavy precipitation in short period of time in a limited geographical area
2. It occurs generally during monsoon period and triggers flash flood and landslides

Select the correct answer using the code given below:
A. 1 only B. 2 only
C. Both 1 and 2 D. Neither 1 nor 2

108. In a group discussion on shape and size of the Earth, three students stated the following points:
1. Student 1 : The shape of the Earth is basically an oblate spheroid.
2. Student 2 : The polar diameter of the Earth is more than the equatorial diameter.
3. Student 3 : Bulge along the equatorial region is due to revolution of the Earth.

Who among the above students is/are correct?
A. Student 1 only
B. Student 1 and Student 2 only
C. Student 2 and Student 3 only
D. Student 1, Student 2 and Student 3

109. While watching news, you hear about a place, of which you had never heard earlier. You want to know more about the place and you want to locate it on the map. Which of the following is/are required for you to be able to locate the place on the map?
A. Only latitude of the place
B. Only longitude of the place
C. Both longitude and latitude of the place
D. Latitude, longitude and altitude of the place

110. Which one of the following statements with respect to Global Positioning System (GPS) is ***not*** correct?
A. It is based on network of satellites orbiting above the Earth.
B. It is based on the system of triangulation.
C. GPS receivers provide location in terms of latitude, longitude and altitude.
D. It provides information exclusively for military operations.

111. Which one of the following is ***not*** a Constitutional Commission of India?
A. The National Commission for Scheduled Castes
B. The National Commission for Scheduled Tribes
C. The National Commission for Backward Classes
D. The National Commission for Women

112. Which Chinese traveller in ancient India wrote the diary called 'Records of the Travels to Middle India'?
A. Wang Xuance B. Xuanzang
C. Yijing D. Li Yibiao

113. The elections to the Lower House of the Parliament of India, held in 2019, constituted the:
A. 14th Lok Sabha B. 15th Lok Sabha
C. 16th Lok Sabha D. 17th Lok Sabha

114. Panchayati Raj Institutions are primarily the institutions of:
A. Popular Government
B. Self-Government
C. Federal Government
D. Quasi-Government

115. Which of the following is/are the right/rights mentioned in the 'American Declaration of Independence'?
1. Life 2. Liberty
3. Pursuit of Happiness 4. Fraternity

Select the correct answer using the code given below:
A. 1 only B. 1 and 2 only
C. 1, 2 and 3 D. 2, 3 and 4

116. Who among the following American Presidents described democracy as "Government of the People, for the People and by the People"?
A. Abraham Lincoln B. Thomas Jefferson
C. George Washington D. John F. Kennedy

117. Inhabitants are unaware of the speed of rotation of the planet Earth because:
1. the angular velocity is constant for each place on the Earth's surface
2. the atmosphere rotates with the Earth
3. there are no nearby objects, either stationary or moving at a rate different from that of the Earth

Which of the above is/are the correct explanation(s)?
A. 1 only B. 1 and 2 only
C. 2 and 3 only D. 1, 2 and 3

118. While travelling to a hilly region, you notice a massive boulder, which was loosened by heavy rains and moved downhill. This has resulted due to which of the following processes?
1. Mass wasting 2. Erosion
3. Weathering

Select the correct answer using the code given below:
A. 1 only B. 1 and 2 only
C. 2 and 3 only D. 1, 2 and 3

119. Which of the following statements in respect of landslides are correct?
1. These occur only on gentle slopes during rain.
2. They generally occur in clay-rich soil.
3. Earthquakes trigger landslides.

Select the correct answer using the code given below.
A. 1 and 2 only B. 1 and 3 only
C. 2 and 3 only D. 1, 2 and 3

120. Consider the following features about a geographical phenomenon:
1. Torrents of snow and ice roaring down a steep mountain side.
2. It is hazardous to skiers and mountaineers.
3. It involves a mix of falling, rolling, sliding and flowing of materials.

Which of the following phenomena can be identified with the above features?
A. Slump and earthflow B. Avalanche
C. Landslide D. Rockslide

121. The real beginning of western education in India can be dated from:
A. the Charter Act of 1813
B. the Charter Act of 1793
C. the Sarda Act of 1929
D. the Macaulay's Minute on Indian Education, 1835

122. The term 'Industrial Revolution' was first used by:
A. J.A. Blanqui B. T.S. Ashton
C. Arnold Toynbee D. R.H. Tawney

123. The Khudai Khidmatgar (Servants of the God) was organized by:
A. Mahatma Gandhi
B. Khan Abdul Ghaffar Khan
C. M.A. Jinnah
D. M.M. Malaviya

124. The Mahad Satyagraha of 1927 was organized by:
A. B.R. Ambedkar B. Mahatma Gandhi
C. S.C. Bose D. Lokmanya Tilak

125. The Satyashodhak Samaj (Truth-Seeking Society) was set up by:
A. Vinoba Bhave B. Jyotiba Phule
C. B.R. Ambedkar D. C. Rajagopalachari

126. The 13th Century text *Lekhapaddhati* gives us information on which one of the following topics?
A. Art of writing B. Essay writing
C. Legal document D. Epigraphic style

127. Nkrumah was one of the five leaders, who comprised the core of the Non-Aligned Movement (NAM). He was the leader of which country in Africa?
A. Nigeria B. Kenya
C. Uganda D. Ghana

128. The idea of Planning in Independent India was drawn from:
A. the Bombay Plan
B. the demand made by peasants
C. the demand made by workers' unions
D. the Gandhian vision of India's future

129. Nisarga, Gati, Nivar, Tauktae and Yaas are names of:
A. new fighter aircrafts B. tourist places
C. weather stations D. cyclones

130. Which one of the following States/ UTs was connected with the Indian Railways network in the year 2021?
A. Mizoram B. Ladakh
C. Manipur D. Sikkim

131. The forests of Uttarakhand, Kullu Valley in Himachal Pradesh and Dzukou Valley in Nagaland and Manipur were in the news on account of which one of the following reasons?
A. Deforestation
B. Forest fire
C. Poaching of wild animals
D. Illegal mining

132. Which one of the following is correct in respect of total number of States and Union Territories in India?
A. 28 States and 8 Union Territories
B. 27 States and 9 Union Territories
C. 30 States and 6 Union Territories
D. 29 States and 7 Union Territories

133. Snow, sleet and hail are the forms of:
A. precipitation B. condensation
C. transpiration D. evaporation

134. Which one of the following is likely to be the most prevalent form of weathering in hot-tropical desert areas?
A. Mechanical B. Chemical
C. Biological D. Leaching

135. Which one of the following cities was the first to attain the status of a 'megacity'?
A. London B. Paris
C. New York D. Washington

136. In India, rigid and stable elevated lands, denuded rocks and series of scarps are the features of which of the following?
A. Northern mountains B. Peninsular plateau
C. Northern plains D. Coastal plains

137. A person had visited a region in India and found trees, such as Khair, Neem, Khejri and Palas. Which one of the following regions is she/he expected to have visited?
A. Malabar Coast B. Garo Hills
C. Sunderban Delta D. Desert Region

138. Consider the following statements:
1. Rocks do not remain in their original form for long and undergo transformation.
2. Transformation of rocks is caused by weathering, erosion and metamorphic action.

Which of the statements given above is/are correct?
A. 1 only B. 2 only
C. Both 1 and 2 D. Neither 1 nor 2

139. Weathering, mass wasting, erosion and transportation are indicators of which one of the following processes?
A. Denudation B. Endogenetic process
C. Diastrophism D. Mountain building

140. If you want to observe moraines, eskers and outwash plains, which one of the following Union Territories you may have to visit?
A. Andaman and Nicobar Islands
B. Lakshadweep
C. Puducherry
D. Ladakh

141. Legendary Kathak dancer Pandit Birju Maharaj died recently. He was the doyen of which one of the following Gharanas of Kathak?
A. Jaipur B. Raigarh
C. Lucknow D. Banaras

142. In a first, India is to export BrahMos missile to:
A. Bhutan B. Philippines
C. Maldives D. Nepal

143. Who among the following is the Head of the Committee appointed by the Supreme Court of India to enquire into the circumstances that led to the Prime Minister of India's convoy being stuck for several minutes on a flyover in Punjab recently?
A. Justice Indu Malhotra
B. Justice Ashok Bhushan
C. Justice Navin Sinha
D. Justice Rohinton Fali Nariman

144. Who among the following retired from test cricket by bagging a wicket on the last ball of his career?
A. AB de Villiers
B. Michael Hussey
C. Quinton de Kock
D. Ross Taylor

145. Who among the following is appointed as the tenth Chairman of the Indian Space Research Organization (ISRO) recently?
A. A.S. Kiran Kumar B. K. Sivan
C. K. Radhakrishnan D. S. Somanath

146. According to the Forest Survey Report, 2021, area-wise which one of the following States has the largest forest cover in India?
A. Odisha B. Madhya Pradesh
C. Arunachal Pradesh D. Chhattisgarh

147. Who among the following is the Chairperson of the Goods and Services Tax Council?
A. The Prime Minister of India
B. The Union Finance Minister
C. The Speaker of the Lok Sabha
D. The President of India

148. The International Union for Conservation of Nature (IUCN) has recently categorized the Red Sanders (Red Sandalwood) into:
A. deficient category
B. endangered category
C. near-threatened category
D. critically endangered category

149. The Government of India has decided to observe 'Veer Baal Diwas' on:
A. 6th October B. 26th November
C. 26th December D. 6th December

150. On 14th January, 2022, which one of the following ministries has organized a global Surya Namaskar Demonstration programme?
A. The Ministry of Culture
B. The Ministry of AYUSH
C. The Ministry of Health and Family Welfare
D. The Ministry of Tourism

PAPER II : MATHEMATICS

1. If $\Delta_1 = \begin{vmatrix} 1 & p & q \\ 1 & q & r \\ 1 & r & p \end{vmatrix}$ and $\Delta_2 = \begin{vmatrix} 1 & 1 & 1 \\ q & r & p \\ r & p & q \end{vmatrix}$ where $p \neq q \neq r$, then $\Delta_1 + \Delta_2$ is:
A. 0
B. always positive
C. always negative
D. positive if p, q, r are positive else negative

2. If $(a - b)(b - c)(c - a) = 2$ and $abc = 6$, then what is the value of $\begin{vmatrix} a & b & c \\ a^2 & b^2 & c^2 \\ a^3 & b^3 & c^3 \end{vmatrix}$?
A. 3
B. 12
C. 14
D. 15

3. Under which of the following conditions does the determinant $\begin{vmatrix} a & b & c \\ b & c & a \\ c & a & b \end{vmatrix}$ vanish?
1. $a + b + c = 0$
2. $a^3 + b^3 + c^3 = 3abc$
3. $a^2 + b^2 + c^2 - ab - bc - ca = 0$

Select the correct answer using the code given below:
A. 1 and 2 only B. 2 and 3 only
C. 1 and 3 only D. 1, 2 and 3

4. Consider the following in respect of the matrices:

$A = \begin{bmatrix} m & n \end{bmatrix}$, $B = \begin{bmatrix} -n & -m \end{bmatrix}$ and $C = \begin{bmatrix} m \\ -m \end{bmatrix}$

1. CA = CB
2. AC = BC
3. C(A + B) = CA + CB

Which of the above statements is/are correct?
A. 1 only B. 2 only
C. 2 and 3 D. 1 and 2

5. If $A = \begin{bmatrix} 2\sin\theta & \cos\theta & 0 \\ -2\cos\theta & \sin\theta & 0 \\ -1 & 1 & 1 \end{bmatrix}$, then, what is A(*adj* A) equal to?
A. Null matrix B. –I
C. I D. 2I
where, I is the identity matrix.

6. For what value of k is the matrix

$$\begin{bmatrix} 2\cos 2\theta & 2\cos 2\theta & 6 \\ 1-2\sin^2\theta & 2\cos^2\theta-1 & 3 \\ k & 2k & 1 \end{bmatrix}$$ singular?

A. 0 only B. 1 only
C. 2 only D. Any real value

7. Let A be a non-singular matrix and B = *adj* A. Which of the following statements is/are correct?
1. AB = BA
2. AB is a scalar matrix
3. AB can be a null matrix

Select the correct answer using the code given below:
A. 1 only B. 1 and 2 only
C. 2 only D. 1, 2 and 3

8. Consider the following statements in respect of square matrices A and B of same order:
1. If AB is a null matrix, then at least one of A and B is a null matrix.
2. If AB is an identity matrix, then BA = AB.

Which of the above statements is/are correct?
A. 1 only
B. 2 only
C. Both 1 and 2
D. Neither 1 nor 2

9. If A is the identity matrix of order 3 and B is its transpose, then what is the value of the determinant of the matrix C = A + B?
A. 1 B. 2
C. 4 D. 8

10. Let A and B be non-singular matrices of the same order such that AB = A and BA = B. Which of the following statements is/are correct?
1. $A^2 = A$
2. $AB^2 = A^2B$

Select the correct answer using the code given below:
A. 1 only B. 2 only
C. Both 1 and 2 D. Neither 1 nor 2

11. How many terms are there in the expansion of $\left(1+\frac{2}{x}\right)^9\left(1-\frac{2}{x}\right)^9$?
A. 9 B. 10
C. 19 D. 20

12. Consider the following statements in respect of the expansion of $(x + y)^{10}$:
1. Among all the coefficients of the terms, the coefficient of the 6th term has the highest value.
2. The coefficient of the 3rd term is equal to coefficient of the 9th term.

Which of the above statements is/are correct?
A. 1 only B. 2 only
C. Both 1 and 2 D. Neither 1 nor 2

13. If C(3n, 2n) = C(3n, 2n – 7), then what is the value of C(n, n – 5)?
A. 42 B. 35
C. 28 D. 21

14. What is the value of

C(51, 21) – C(51, 22) + C(51, 23) – C(51, 24) + C(51, 25) – C(51, 26) + C(51, 27) – C(51, 28) + C(51, 29) – C(51, 30)?
A. C(51, 25)
B. C(51, 27)
C. C(51, 51) – C(51, 0)
D. C(51, 25) – C(51, 27)

15. How many odd numbers between 300 and 400 are there in which none of the digits is repeated?
A. 32 B. 36
C. 40 D. 45

16. How many permutations are there of the letters of the word 'TIGER' in which the vowels should not occupy the even positions?
A. 72 B. 36
C. 18 D. 12

17. Let α and β be the roots of the equation $x^2 + px + q = 0$. If α^3 and β^3 are the roots of the equation $x^2 + mx + n = 0$, then what is the value of $m + n$?
A. $p^3 + q^3 + pq$ B. $p^3 + q^3 - pq$
C. $p^3 + q^3 + 3pq$ D. $p^3 + q^3 - 3pq$

18. Let α and β be the roots of the equation

$x^2 - ax - bx + ab - c = 0$.

What is the quadratic equation whose roots are a and b?
A. $x^2 - \alpha x - \beta x + \alpha\beta + c = 0$
B. $x^2 - \alpha x - \beta x + \alpha\beta - c = 0$
C. $x^2 + \alpha x + \beta x + \alpha\beta + c = 0$
D. $x^2 + ax + \beta x + \alpha\beta - c = 0$

19. If the roots of the equation

$x^2 - ax - bx - cx + bc + ca = 0$

are equal, then which one of the following is correct?

A. $a + b + c = 0$ B. $a - b + c = 0$
C. $a + b - c = 0$ D. $-a + b + c = 0$

20. Let α and β (α > β) be the roots of the equation $x^2 - 8x + q = 0$. If $\alpha^2 - \beta^2 = 16$, then what is the value of q?

A. –15 B. –10
C. 10 D. 15

21. What is the maximum value of n such that 5^n divides (30! + 35!), where n is a natural number?

A. 4 B. 6
C. 7 D. 8

22. What is the value of

$2(2 \times 1) + 3(3 \times 2 \times 1) + 4(4 \times 3 \times 2 \times 1) + 5(5 \times 4 \times 3 \times 2 \times 1) + ... + 9(9 \times 8 \times 7 \times 6 \times 5 \times 4 \times 3 \times 2 \times 1) + 2$?

A. 11! B. 10!
C. 10 + 10! D. 11 + 10!

23. If A = {{1, 2, 3}}, then how many elements are there in the power set of A?

A. 1 B. 2
C. 4 D. 8

24. If a, b, c are in GP where $a > 0, b > 0, c > 0$, then which of the following are correct?

1. a^2, b^2, c^2 are in GP.
2. $\frac{1}{a}, \frac{1}{b}, \frac{1}{c}$ are in GP.
3. $\sqrt{a}, \sqrt{b}, \sqrt{c}$ are in GP.

Select the correct answer using the code given below:

A. 1 and 2 only B. 2 and 3 only
C. 1 and 3 only D. 1, 2 and 3

25. If $\frac{a+b}{2}, b, \frac{b+c}{2}$ are in HP, then which one of the following is correct?

A. a, b, c are in AP
B. a, b, c are in GP
C. $a + b, b + c, c + a$ are in GP
D. $a + b, b + c, c + a$ are in AP

26. What is value of $\cot^2 15° + \tan^2 15°$?

A. 12 B. 14
C. $8\sqrt{3}$ D. 4

27. In a triangle ABC, sin A – cos B – cos C = 0. What is angle B equal to?

A. $\frac{\pi}{6}$ B. $\frac{\pi}{4}$
C. $\frac{\pi}{3}$ D. $\frac{\pi}{2}$

28. If $\alpha + \beta = \frac{\pi}{4}$ and 2 tan α = 1, then what is tan 2 β equal to?

A. $\frac{1}{3}$ B. $\frac{2}{3}$
C. $\frac{3}{4}$ D. $\frac{3}{5}$

29. If tan (45° + θ) = 1 + sin 2 θ, where $-\frac{\pi}{4} < \theta < \frac{\pi}{4}$, then what is the value of cos 2 θ?

A. 0 B. $\frac{1}{2}$
C. 1 D. 2

30. Let, sin 2 θ = cos 3 θ, where θ is acute angle. What is the value of 1 + 4 sin θ? (given that $\sin 18° = \frac{\sqrt{5}-1}{4}$)

A. $\sqrt{3}$ B. 2
C. $\sqrt{5}$ D. 3

31. If $\tan\theta = -\frac{5}{12}$, then what can be the value of sin θ?

A. $\frac{5}{13}$ but cannot be $-\frac{5}{13}$
B. $-\frac{5}{13}$ but cannot be $\frac{5}{13}$
C. $\frac{5}{13}$ or $-\frac{5}{13}$
D. None of the above

32. What is the value of $\cos^4\frac{7\pi}{8} + \cos^4\frac{5\pi}{8}$?

A. $\frac{3}{2}$ B. $\frac{3}{4}$
C. $\frac{3}{8}$ D. $\frac{3}{16}$

33. What is $\sin^2\left(\frac{\pi}{4}+\theta\right) - \sin^2\left(\frac{\pi}{4}-\theta\right)$ equal to?

A. sin 2 θ B. cos 2 θ
C. 2 sin θ D. 2 cos θ

34. A vertical tower stands on a horizontal plane and is surmounted by a vertical flagstaff of height h. At a point on the plane the angles of elevation of the bottom and top of the flagstaff are θ and 2θ respectively. What is the height of the tower?

A. h cos θ B. h sin θ
C. h cos 2 θ D. h sin 2 θ

35. The shadow of a tower becomes x metre longer, when the angle of elevation of sun changes from 60° to θ. If the height of the tower is $\sqrt{3x}$ metre, then which one of the following is correct?
A. $0 < \theta < 30°$ B. $30° < \theta < 45°$
C. $45° < \theta < 60°$ D. $60° < \theta < 90°$

36. If $\tan^{-1}\left(\frac{1}{2}\right) + \tan^{-1}\left(\frac{x}{3}\right) = \frac{\pi}{4}$, where $0 < x < 6$, then what is x equal to?
A. 1 B. 2
C. 3 D. 5

37. If $3\sin^{-1}x + \cos^{-1}x = \pi$, then what is x equal to?
A. 0 B. $\frac{1}{2}$
C. $\frac{1}{\sqrt{2}}$ D. $\frac{1}{\sqrt{3}}$

38. If $\tan\alpha + \tan\beta = 1 - \tan\alpha \,.\, \tan\beta$, where $\tan\alpha \,.\, \tan\beta \neq 1$, then which of the following is one of the values of $(\alpha + \beta)$?
A. $\frac{\pi}{6}$ B. $\frac{\pi}{4}$
C. $\frac{\pi}{3}$ D. $\frac{\pi}{2}$

39. If $(1 + \tan\theta)(1 + \tan 9\theta) = 2$, then what is the value of $\tan(10\theta)$?
A. 0 B. 1
C. 2 D. Infinite

40. What is the value of
$\sin 0° + \sin 10° + \sin 20° + \sin 30° + ... + \sin 360°$?
A. –1 B. 0
C. 1 D. 2

41. Consider all the subsets of the set A = {1, 2, 3, 4}. How many of them are supersets of the set {4}?
A. 6 B. 7
C. 8 D. 9

42. Consider the following statements in respect of two non-empty sets A and B:
1. $x \in \{A \cup B) \Rightarrow x \in A$ or $x \in B$
2. $x \in \{A \cap B) \Rightarrow x \in A$ and $x \in B$

Which of the above statements is/are correct?
A. 1 only B. 2 only
C. Both 1 and 2 D. Neither 1 nor 2

43. Consider the following statements in respect of two non-empty sets A and B:
1. $A \cup B = A \cap B$ iff $A = B$
2. $A \Delta B = \varphi$ iff $A = B$

Which of the above statements is/are correct?
A. 1 only B. 2 only
C. Both 1 and 2 D. Neither 1 nor 2

44. Consider the following statements in respect of the relation R in the set $\mathbb{N}$ of natural numbers defined by xRy if $x^2 - 5xy + 4y^2 = 0$:
1. R is reflexive 2. R is symmetric
3. R is transitive

Which of the above statements is/are correct?
A. 1 only B. 2 only
C. 1 and 2 only D. 1, 2 and 3

45. Consider the following statements in respect of any relation R on a set A:
1. If R is reflexive, then R^{-1} is also reflexive
2. If R is symmetric, then R^{-1} is also symmetric
3. If R is transitive, then R^{-1} is also transitive

Which of the above statements are correct?
A. 1 and 2 only B. 2 and 3 only
C. 1 and 3 only D. 1, 2 and 3

46. What is the principal argument of $\frac{1}{1+i}$ where $i = \sqrt{-1}$?
A. $-\frac{3\pi}{4}$ B. $-\frac{\pi}{4}$
C. $\frac{\pi}{4}$ D. $\frac{3\pi}{4}$

47. What is the modulus of $\left(\frac{\sqrt{-3}}{2} - \frac{1}{2}\right)^{200}$?
A. $\frac{1}{4}$ B. $\frac{1}{2}$
C. 1 D. 2^{200}

48. Consider the following statements:
1. $\frac{n!}{3!}$ is divisible by 6, where $n > 3$
2. $\frac{n!}{3!} + 3$ is divisible by 7, where $n > 3$

Which of the above statements is/are correct?
A. 1 only B. 2 only
C. Both 1 and 2 D. Neither 1 nor 2

49. In how many ways can a team of 5 players be selected out of 9 players so as to exclude two particular players?
A. 14 B. 21
C. 35 D. 42

50. In the expansion of $\left(x + \frac{1}{x}\right)^{2n}$, what is the $(n + 1)$th term from the end (when arranged in descending powers of x)?
A. $C(2n, n)x$ B. $C(2n, n-1)x$
C. $C(2n, n)$ D. $C(2n, n-1)$

51. If the sum of the first 9 terms of an AP is equal to sum of the first 11 terms, then what is the sum of the first 20 terms?

A. 20 B. 10
C. 2 D. 0

52. If the 5th term of an AP is $\frac{1}{10}$ and its 10th term is $\frac{1}{5}$, then what is the sum of first 50 terms?

A. 25 B. 25.5
C. 26 D. 26.5

53. What is $(1110011)_2 \div (10111)_2$ equal to?

A. $(101)_2$ B. $(1001)_2$
C. $(111)_2$ D. $(1011)_2$

54. If $x^3 + y^3 = (100010111)_2$ and $x + y = (11111)_2$, then what is $(x - y)^2 + xy$ equal to?

A. $(1101)_2$ B. $(1001)_2$
C. $(1011)_2$ D. $(1111)_2$

55. Consider the inequations

$5x - 4y + 12 < 0$, $x + y < 2$, $x < 0$ and $y > 0$.

Which one of the following points lies in the common region?

A. (0, 0) B. (–2, 4)
C. (–1, 4) D. (–1, 2)

56. Consider the following statements in respect of the function $y = [x]$, $x \in (-1, 1)$ where [.] is the greatest integer function:

1. Its derivative is 0 at $x = 0.5$
2. It is continuous at $x = 0$

Which of the above statements is/are correct?

A. 1 only B. 2 only
C. Both 1 and 2 D. Neither 1 nor 2

57. What is the degree of the differential equation

$$1+\left(\frac{dy}{dx}\right)^2=\left(\frac{d^2y}{dx^2}\right)^{\frac{4}{3}} ?$$

A. $\frac{4}{3}$ B. 2
C. 3 D. 4

58. A radioactive substance decays at a rate proportional to the amount of substance present. If half of the substance decays in 100 years, then what is the decay constant (proportionality constant)?

A. $\frac{\ln 2}{100}$ B. $\frac{\ln 5}{100}$
C. $\frac{\ln 10}{100}$ D. $\frac{2\ln 2}{100}$

59. What is the domain of the function $f(x)=\sqrt{1-(x-1)^2}$?

A. (0, 1) B. [–1, 1]
C. (0, 2) D. [0, 2]

60. The area of the region bounded by the parabola $y^2 = 4kx$, where $k > 0$ and its latus rectum is 24 square units. What is the value of k?

A. 1 B. 2
C. 3 D. 4

61. What is $\int_0^{\frac{\pi}{4}} \frac{dx}{(\sin x+\cos x)^2}$ equal to?

A. $-\frac{1}{2}$ B. $\frac{1}{2}$
C. 1 D. $\frac{3}{2}$

62. What is $\int(\sin x)^{-1/2}(\cos x)^{-3/2}\,dx$ equal to?

A. $\sqrt{\tan x}+c$ B. $2\sqrt{\tan x}+c$
C. $\sqrt{\cot x}+c$ D. $\sqrt{2\tan x}+c$

63. If $I_1=\int\frac{e^x dx}{e^x+e^{-x}}$ and $I_2=\int\frac{dx}{e^{2x}+1}$, then what is $I_1 + I_2$ equal to?

A. $\frac{x}{2}+c$ B. $x + c$
C. $\ln(e^x + e^{-x}) + c$ D. $\ln(e^x - e^{-x}) + c$

64. What is $\int_{-2}^{-1}\frac{x}{|x|}dx$ equal to?

A. –2 B. –1
C. 1 D. 2

65. How many extreme values does

$\sin 4x + 2x$, where $0 < x < \frac{\pi}{2}$ have?

A. 1 B. 2
C. 4 D. 8

66. What is the maximum value of the function $f(x)=\frac{1}{\tan x+\cot x}$, where $0<x<\frac{\pi}{2}$?

A. $\frac{1}{4}$ B. $\frac{1}{2}$
C. 1 D. 2

67. If $4f(x)-f\left(\frac{1}{x}\right)=\left(2x+\frac{1}{x}\right)\left(2x-\frac{1}{x}\right)$, then what is $f(2)$ equal to?

A. 0 B. 1
C. 2 D. 4

68. If $f(x) = 4x + 3$, then what is $f \circ f \circ f\ (-1)$ equal to?

A. -1 B. 0
C. 1 D. 2

69. If $x^y y^x = 1$, then what is $\frac{dy}{dx}$ at (1, 1) equal to?

A. -1 B. 0
C. 1 D. 4

70. If $y = (x^x)^x$, then what is the value of $\frac{dy}{dx}$ at $x = 1$?

A. $\frac{1}{2}$ B. 1
C. 2 D. 4

71. Let $y = [x + 1]$, $-4 < x < -3$ where [.] is the greatest integer function. What is the derivative of y with respect to x at $x = -3.5$?

A. -4 B. -3.5
C. -3 D. 0

72. If $\frac{dy}{dx} = (\ln 5)y$ with $y(0) = \ln 5$, then what is $y(1)$ equal to?

A. 0 B. 5
C. 2 ln5 D. 5 ln5

73. Consider the following in respect of the function $f(x) = 10^x$:

1. Its domain is $(-\infty, \infty)$
2. It is a continuous function
3. It is differentiable at $x = 0$

Which of the above statements are correct?

A. 1 and 2 only
B. 2 and 3 only
C. 1 and 3 only
D. 1, 2 and 3

74. What is $\lim_{x \to 0} x^3 (\text{cosec } x)^2$ equal to?

A. 0 B. $\frac{1}{2}$
C. 1 D. Limit does not exist

75. What is $\lim_{x \to 1} \frac{x^3 - 1}{\sqrt{x} - 1}$ equal to?

A. 0 B. 3
C. 6 D. Limit does not exist

76. In which one of the following intervals is the function $f(x) = \frac{x^3}{3} - \frac{7x^2}{2} + 6x + 5$ decreasing?

A. $(-\infty, 1)$ only B. (1, 6)
C. $(6, \infty)$ only D. $(-\infty, 1) \cup (6, \infty)$

77. If the derivative of the function $f(x) = \frac{m}{x} + 2nx + 1$ vanishes at $x = 2$, then what is the value of $m + 8n$?

A. -2
B. 0
C. 2
D. Cannot be determined due to insufficient data

78. What is the area included in the first quadrant between the curves $y = x$ and $y = x^3$?

A. $\frac{1}{8}$ square unit B. $\frac{1}{4}$ square unit
C. $\frac{1}{2}$ square unit D. 1 square unit

79. If $xy = 4225$ where x, y are natural numbers, then what is the minimum value of $x + y$?

A. 130 B. 260
C. 2113 D. 4226

80. What does the equation $x\frac{dy}{dx} - 2y = 0$ represent?

A. A family of straight lines
B. A family of circles
C. A family of parabolas
D. A family of ellipses

81. If the points with coordinates $(-5, 0)$, $(5p^2, 10p)$ and $(5q^2, 10q)$ are collinear, then what is the value of pq where $p \neq q$?

A. -2 B. -1
C. 1 D. 2

82. What is the equation of the straight line which passes through the point $(1, -2)$ and cuts off equal intercepts from the axes?

A. $x + y - 1 = 0$ B. $x - y - 1 = 0$
C. $x + y + 1 = 0$ D. $x - y - 2 = 0$

83. What is the equation of the circle which touches both the axes in the first quadrant and the line $y - 2 = 0$?

A. $x^2 + y^2 - 2x - 2y - 1 = 0$
B. $x^2 + y^2 + 2x + 2y + 1 = 0$
C. $x^2 + y^2 - 2x - 2y + 1 = 0$
D. $x^2 + y^2 - 4x - 4y + 4 = 0$

84. What is the equation of the parabola with focus $(-3, 0)$ and directrix $x - 3 = 0$?

A. $y^2 = 3x$ B. $x^2 = 12y$
C. $y^2 = 12x$ D. $y^2 = -12x$

85. What is the distance between the foci of the ellipse $x^2 + 2y^2 = 1$?

A. 1 B. $\sqrt{2}$
C. 2 D. $2\sqrt{2}$

86. Let a, b, c be the lengths of sides BC, CA, AB respectively of a triangle ABC. If p is the perimeter and q is the area of the triangle, then what is $p(p-2a)\tan\left(\frac{A}{2}\right)$ equal to?

A. q B. $2q$
C. $3q$ D. $4q$

87. A straight line passes through the point of intersection of $x + 2y + 2 = 0$ and $2x - 3y - 3 = 0$. It cuts equal intercepts in the fourth quadrant. What is the sum of the absolute values of the intercepts?

A. 2 B. 3
C. 4 D. 6

88. Under which one of the following conditions are the lines $ax + by + c = 0$ and $bx + ay + c = 0$ parallel ($a \neq 0, b \neq 0$)?

A. $a - b = 0$ only B. $a + b = 0$ only
C. $a^2 - b^2 = 0$ D. $ab + 1 = 0$

89. What is the equation of the locus of the mid-point of the line segment obtained by cutting the line $x + y = p$, (where p is a real number) by the coordinate axes?

A. $x - y = 0$ B. $x + y = 0$
C. $x - y = p$ D. $x + y = p$

90. If the point (x, y) is equidistant from the points $(2a, 0)$ and $(0, 3a)$ where $a > 0$, then which one of the following is correct?

A. $2x - 3y = 0$
B. $3x - 2y = 0$
C. $4x - 6y + 5a = 0$
D. $4x - 6y - 5a = 0$

Directions (Qs. No. 91-93): *Consider the following for the next three items that follow:*

The plane $6x + ky + 3z - 12 = 0$ where $k \neq 0$ meets the coordinate axes at A, B and C respectively. The equation of the sphere passing through the origin and A, B, C is $x^2 + y^2 + z^2 - 2x - 3y - 4z = 0$.

91. What is the value of k?

A. 3 B. 4
C. 6 D. 12

92. If p is the perpendicular distance from the centre of the sphere to the plane, then which one of the following is correct?

A. $0 < p < 0.5$ B. $0.5 < p < 1$
C. $1 < p < 1.5$ D. $p > 1.5$

93. What is the equation of the line through the origin and the centre of the sphere?

A. $x = y = z$ B. $2x = 3y = 4z$
C. $6x = 3y = 4z$ D. $6x = 4y = 3z$

Directions (Qs. No. 94 and 95): *Consider the following for the next two items that follow:*

Let the plane $\frac{2x}{k}+\frac{2y}{3}+\frac{z}{3}=2$ pass through the point $(2, 3, -6)$.

94. What are the direction ratios of a normal to the plane?

A. $< 3, 2, 1 >$ B. $< 2, 3, 6 >$
C. $< 6, 3, 2 >$ D. $< 1, 2, 3 >$

95. If p, q and r are the intercepts made by the plane on the coordinate axes respectively, then what is $(p + q + r)$ equal to?

A. 10 B. 11
C. 12 D. 13

96. If $4\hat{i}+\hat{j}-3\hat{k}$ and $p\hat{i}+q\hat{j}-2\hat{k}$ are collinear vectors, then what are the possible values of p and q respectively?

A. 4, 1 B. 1, 4
C. $\frac{8}{3},\frac{2}{3}$ D. $\frac{2}{3},\frac{8}{3}$

97. If $\vec{a}$, $\vec{b}$, $\vec{c}$ are the position vectors of the vertices A, B, C respectively of a triangle ABC and G is the centroid of the triangle, then what is $\overline{AG}$ equal to?

A. $\frac{\vec{a}+\vec{b}+\vec{c}}{3}$ B. $\frac{2\vec{a}-\vec{b}-\vec{c}}{3}$

C. $\frac{\vec{b}+\vec{c}-2\vec{a}}{3}$ D. $\frac{\vec{a}-2\vec{b}-2\vec{c}}{3}$

98. Consider the following statements:

1. Dot product over vector addition is distributive
2. Cross product over vector addition is distributive
3. Cross product of vectors is associative

Which of the above statements is/are correct?

A. 1 only B. 2 only
C. 1 and 2 only D. 1, 2 and 3

99. Let $\vec{a}$, $\vec{b}$, $\vec{c}$ be three non-zero vectors such that $\vec{a}\times\vec{b}=\vec{c}$. Consider the following statements:

1. $\vec{a}$ is unique if $\vec{b}$ and $\vec{c}$ are given.
2. $\vec{c}$ is unique if $\vec{a}$ and $\vec{b}$ are given.

Which of the above statements is/are correct?

A. 1 only B. 2 only
C. Both 1 and 2 D. Neither 1 nor 2

100. Let $\vec{a}$ and $\vec{b}$ be two unit vectors such that $|\vec{a}-\vec{b}|<2$. If 2θ is the angle between $\vec{a}$ and $\vec{b}$, then which one of the following is correct?

A. $0 < \sin\theta < 1$ only B. $-\frac{1}{2}<\sin\theta<\frac{1}{2}$ only
C. $-1 < \sin\theta < 0$ only D. $-1 < \sin\theta < 1$

101. Two digits out of 1, 2, 3, 4, 5 are chosen at random and multiplied together. What is the probability that the last digit in the product appears as 0?

A. $\frac{1}{10}$ B. $\frac{1}{5}$

C. $\frac{2}{5}$ D. $\frac{4}{5}$

102. The frequency curve (assuming unimodal) corresponding to the data obtained in an experiment is skewed to the left. What conclusion can be drawn from the curve?

A. Mean > Median > Mode
B. Mean > Mode > Median
C. Median > Mean > Mode
D. Mode > Median > Mean

103. The variance of five positive observations is 3.6. If four of the observations are 2, 2, 4, 5 then what is the remaining observation?

A. 4 B. 5
C. 7 D. 9

104. What is the arithmetic mean of 50 terms of an AP with first term 4 and common difference 4?

A. 50 B. 51
C. 100 D. 102

105. What is the coefficient of mean deviation of 21, 34, 23, 39, 26, 37, 40, 20, 33, 27 (taken from mean)?

A. 0.11 B. 0.22
C. 0.33 D. 0.44

Directions (Qs. No. 106-108): *Consider the following for the next three items that follow:*

The algebraic sum of the deviations of a set of values $x_1, x_2, x_3, \ldots, x_n$ measured from 100 is –20 and the algebraic sum of the deviations of the same set of values measured from 92 is 140.

106. What is the mean of the values?

A. 91 B. 96
C. 98 D. 99

107. What is the algebraic sum of the deviations of the same set of values measured from 99?

A. 0 B. 10
C. 20 D. 40

108. If the algebraic sum of the deviations of the same set of values measured from y is 180, then what is the value of y?

A. 80 B. 85
C. 90 D. 95

Directions (Qs. No. 109-111): *Consider the following data for the next three items that follow:*

The marks obtained by 51 students in a class are in AP with its first term 4 and common difference 3.

109. What is the mean of the marks?

A. 67 B. 71
C. 75 D. 79

110. What is the median of the marks?

A. 79.5 B. 79
C. 78.5 D. 77

111. What is the sum of the deviations measured from the median?

A. –1 B. 0
C. 1 D. 2

Directions (Qs. No. 112-114): *Consider the following data for the next three items that follow:*

There are 90 applicants for a job. Some of them are graduates. Some of them have less than three years experience.

	Number of graduates	**Number of non-graduates**
At least 3 years experience	18	9
Less than 3 years experience	36	27

Let G be the event that the first applicant interviewed is a graduate and T be the event that first applicant interviewed has at least 3 years experience.

112. What is $P(G \cap \overline{T})$ equal to?

A. $\frac{1}{5}$ B. $\frac{2}{5}$

C. $\frac{3}{5}$ D. $\frac{4}{5}$

113. What is $P(G \mid \overline{T})$ equal to?

A. $\frac{2}{7}$ B. $\frac{3}{7}$

C. $\frac{4}{7}$ D. $\frac{5}{7}$

114. What is $P(\overline{T} \mid \overline{G})$ equal to?

A. $\frac{1}{4}$ B. $\frac{1}{3}$

C. $\frac{3}{5}$ D. $\frac{3}{4}$

Directions (Qs. No. 115-117): *Consider the following data for the next three items that follow:*

The incidence of suffering from a disease among workers in an industry has a chance of $33\frac{1}{3}\%$.

115. What is the probability that exactly 3 out of 6 workers suffer from a disease?

A. $\frac{80}{729}$ B. $\frac{10}{81}$

C. $\frac{10}{243}$ D. $\frac{160}{729}$

116. What is the probability that no one out of 6 workers suffers from a disease?

A. $\frac{665}{729}$ B. $\frac{64}{729}$

C. $\frac{4}{243}$ D. $\frac{1}{729}$

117. What is the probability that at least one out of 6 workers suffer from a disease?

A. $\frac{728}{729}$ B. $\frac{665}{729}$

C. $\frac{653}{729}$ D. $\frac{596}{729}$

Directions (Qs. No. 118-120): *Consider the following for the next three items that follow:*

Class	0-20	20-40	40-60	60-80	80-100
Frequency	17	$p + q$	32	$p - 3q$	19

The total frequency is 120. The mean is 50.

118. What is the value of p?

A. 25 B. 26

C. 27 D. 28

119. What is the value of q?

A. 1 B. 2

C. 3 D. 4

120. If the frequency of each class is doubled, then what would be the mean?

A. 25 B. 50

C. 75 D. 100

ANSWERS

PAPER-I : GENERAL ABILITY TEST

1	2	3	4	5	6	7	8	9	10
C	C	A	C	D	C	A	B	B	A
11	**12**	**13**	**14**	**15**	**16**	**17**	**18**	**19**	**20**
A	B	D	C	A	D	C	C	D	A
21	**22**	**23**	**24**	**25**	**26**	**27**	**28**	**29**	**30**
B	D	C	C	B	D	A	A	C	B
31	**32**	**33**	**34**	**35**	**36**	**37**	**38**	**39**	**40**
B	A	D	C	A	D	B	C	B	D
41	**42**	**43**	**44**	**45**	**46**	**47**	**48**	**49**	**50**
B	A	A	D	D	A	D	C	D	A
51	**52**	**53**	**54**	**55**	**56**	**57**	**58**	**59**	**60**
D	B	A	C	A	D	B	B	D	A
61	**62**	**63**	**64**	**65**	**66**	**67**	**68**	**69**	**70**
C	C	A	B	D	B	A	B	C	C
71	**72**	**73**	**74**	**75**	**76**	**77**	**78**	**79**	**80**
C	B	D	A	A	A	D	C	D	B
81	**82**	**83**	**84**	**85**	**86**	**87**	**88**	**89**	**90**
B	B	D	D	A	B	D	D	A	A
91	**92**	**93**	**94**	**95**	**96**	**97**	**98**	**99**	**100**
B	D	A	A	C	C	A	C	D	D
101	**102**	**103**	**104**	**105**	**106**	**107**	**108**	**109**	**110**
C	B	D	B	B	C	C	A	C	D

111	112	113	114	115	116	117	118	119	120
D	B	D	B	C	A	B	D	C	B
121	**122**	**123**	**124**	**125**	**126**	**127**	**128**	**129**	**130**
D	C	B	A	B	C	D	A	D	C
131	**132**	**133**	**134**	**135**	**136**	**137**	**138**	**139**	**140**
B	A	A	A	C	B	D	C	A	D
141	**142**	**143**	**144**	**145**	**146**	**147**	**148**	**149**	**150**
C	B	A	D	D	B	B	B	C	B

PAPER-II : MATHEMATICS

1	2	3	4	5	6	7	8	9	10
C	B	D	C	D	D	B	B	D	B
11	**12**	**13**	**14**	**15**	**16**	**17**	**18**	**19**	**20**
B	C	D	C	D	B	D	A	C	D
21	**22**	**23**	**24**	**25**	**26**	**27**	**28**	**29**	**30**
C	B	B	D	B	B	D	C	C	C
31	**32**	**33**	**34**	**35**	**36**	**37**	**38**	**39**	**40**
C	B	A	C	B	A	C	B	B	B
41	**42**	**43**	**44**	**45**	**46**	**47**	**48**	**49**	**50**
C	D	C	A	D	B	C	D	B	C
51	**52**	**53**	**54**	**55**	**56**	**57**	**58**	**59**	**60**
D	B	A	B	D	A	D	A	D	C
61	**62**	**63**	**64**	**65**	**66**	**67**	**68**	**69**	**70**
B	B	B	B	B	B	D	A	A	B
71	**72**	**73**	**74**	**75**	**76**	**77**	**78**	**79**	**80**
D	D	D	A	C	B	D	B	A	C
81	**82**	**83**	**84**	**85**	**86**	**87**	**88**	**89**	**90**
C	C	C	D	B	D	A	C	A	C
91	**92**	**93**	**94**	**95**	**96**	**97**	**98**	**99**	**100**
B	B	D	A	B	C	C	C	B	D
101	**102**	**103**	**104**	**105**	**106**	**107**	**108**	**109**	**110**
A	D	C	D	B	D	A	C	D	B
111	**112**	**113**	**114**	**115**	**116**	**117**	**118**	**119**	**120**
B	B	C	D	D	B	B	C	A	B

EXPLANATORY ANSWERS

PAPER I : GENERAL KNOWLEDGE

51. Q = $mc\,\Delta T$ ...(*i*)

Where, m = Mass of the material,

c = Specific heat capacity of the material,

ΔT = Temperature raised

Given: $\Delta T = 25°C - 15°C = 10°C$,

$c = 400$ J/(kg °C); Q = 20 kJ

Using equation (*i*)

$\Rightarrow \quad 20000 = m \times 400 \times 10$

$$\Rightarrow \qquad m = \frac{20000}{400 \times 10}$$

$$\therefore \qquad m = 5 \text{ kg}$$

So, the correct answer is option (D).

52. Amount of heat required to change unit mass of liquid into vapour state without change in its temperature is known as specific latent heat of vaporisation.

Latent heat of vaporisation is a physical property of a substance. When a material in liquid state changes its phase from liquid to vapour, the energy absorbed in the process; is known as specific latent heat of vaporisation.

53. A substance that has a larger surface area will evaporate faster, as there are more surface molecules per unit of volume that are potentially able to escape. The higher the temperature of the substance, the greater the kinetic energy of the molecules at its surface and therefore the faster the rate of their evaporation.

55. Resistance of a wire is directly proportional to its length.

So, when we cut the wire into 5 equal parts, the resistance of each part will be 10 Ω.

On connecting these wires in parallel, the net resistance will be:

$$\frac{1}{R} = \frac{1}{10} + \frac{1}{10} + \frac{1}{10} + \frac{1}{10} + \frac{1}{10}$$

$$\Rightarrow \qquad R = 2\ \Omega.$$

56. Since for a conducting solid sphere, the charge is only present at the surface, so the electric field intensity inside the conducting solid sphere is zero. This can be proven using Gauss's law.

According to Gauss law, the total electric flux linked with a closed Gaussian surface called Gaussian surface is $\frac{1}{E_0}$ times the charge enclosed by the closed surface.

If we draw a Gaussian sphere inside the conducting sphere for $r < R$ then, there is no charge enclosed inside the Gaussian surface.

$\Rightarrow \phi = 0$

No electric flux is involved with the Gaussian sphere so there will be no electric field lines inside the Gaussian sphere but for the representation purpose, these lines will be perpendicular to the spherical surface and radially outside the surface as the conducting sphere is positively charged (Since the conducting sphere can be treated as an equipotential surface).

Hence, option (D) is correct.

57. A solution is a homogeneous mixture containing two or more substances. In a solution, the solute particles cannot be separated from the solvent. Examples: Salt solution, sugar solution, coke, vinegar, seawater, air, and metal alloys like brass, etc.

A colloid is a heterogeneous mixture. Milk is not a solution. It is a colloid because the fat will get separated from the milk and raise to the top.

58. Petroleum is a mixture of various constituents such as petroleum gas, petrol, diesel, kerosene, lubricating oil, paraffin wax, etc. whose boiling points are different. The process of separation of various constituents or fractions of petroleum is done by fractional distillation in fractionating columns. The process of heating a mixture of liquids having different boiling points and then separating them by cooling is called fractional distillation.

59. If the chemical composition is changing, then it is a chemical change, and if the chemical composition is remaining the same, then it is a physical change. Growth of a plant, rusting of iron, cooking of food, milk turning sour, digestion of food, and burning the candle are chemical changes because in these cases the chemical composition of the substance changes.

A chemical change results from a chemical reaction, while a physical change is when matter changes forms but not chemical identity. The five conditions of chemical change are colour change, formation of a precipitate, formation of a gas, odour change, temperature change.

61. Covalent bonds are mostly found in organic compounds. They are non-metallic weaker bonds. Compounds having covalent bonds occur in liquid or gaseous states if in solid, they are soft solids. They are bad conductors of heat and electricity. Compounds having covalent bonds have low melting and boiling points. Covalent compounds are insoluble in water and organic solvents. Covalent bonds are of two types—*sigma* (strong) and *pi* (weak).

Calcium Oxide: It is an ionic compound. It is a white or greyish white solid substance. It can absorb carbon dioxide from the atmosphere easily.

Sodium Nitride: It is an ionic compound. It has a gap that is usually found in semiconductors. It is formed from metal to non-metal interactions.

Silicon Carbide: Silicon carbide has a strong covalent bond between them. It is also known as the covalent network solid. It has oxidation resistance and thermal shock resistance.

Zinc Sulphide: It is an ionic compound. It is usually black in colour due to various impurities and is thus used as a pigment. It is used as a window in optics.

62. Given, Mass number of argon (Ar) = M = 40 and atomic number (Z) = 18

Number of protons in an atom = Z = 18

Number of electrons in an atom = Z = 18

Number of neutrons in an atom (N) = M – Z

⇒ N = 40 – 18 = 22.

63. Magnesium (Mg): Magnesium is an element with the atomic number 12. It is a metal and its valency is +2.

Nitrogen (N): Nitrogen is non-metal with atomic number 7. Its valency is either –3 or –5.

Silicon (Si): Silicon has atomic number 14. It shows the valency of –4 or +4.

Neon (Ne): Neon is chemically inactive due to its stable configuration. Its valency is zero.

Order of valencies: Ne < Mg < N < Si.

64. If an alternating current is said to have a frequency of 3 Hz (see diagram below), that indicates its waveform repeats 3 times in 1 second.

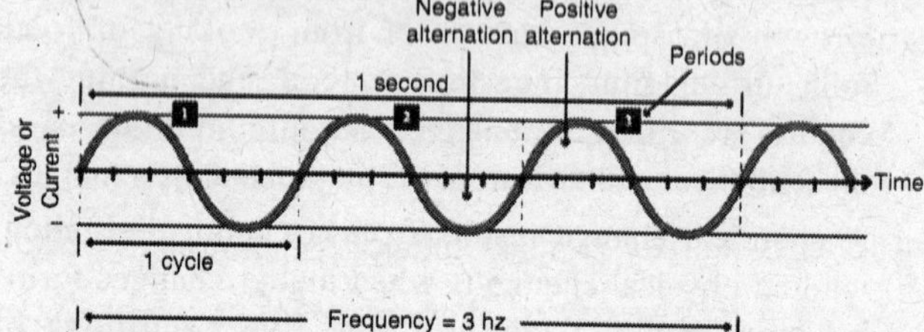

65. Electrical resistivity is an intrinsic property that quantifies how strongly a given material opposes the flow of electric current. A low resistivity indicates a material that readily allows the movement of electric charge.

Resistivity is commonly represented by the Greek letter ρ (rho).

$$\rho = \frac{R \times A}{L}$$

Hence, from the above relation we can see that the SI unit of electrical resistivity is the ohm-meter (Ω-m).

66. Given, power consumption by a bulb (P) is 60 W and source (V) is 240 V.

We know, Current (I) = $\frac{P}{V} = \frac{60}{240} = 0.25$ A.

So, the current drawn by the bulb will be 0.25 A.

68. From Newton's law of gravitation,

$$\text{Force (F)} = [\text{GmM}] \times r^{-2}$$

Gravitational Constant (G)

$$= F \times r^2 \times [\text{Mm}]^{-1} \quad ...(i)$$

Since, Force (F) = Mass × Acceleration

$$= M \times [LT^{-2}]$$

∴ The dimensional formula of force = $M^1L^1T^{-2}$ ...(*ii*)

On substituting equation (*ii*) in equation (*i*) we get,

Gravitational Constant (G)

$$= F \times r^2 \times [\text{Mm}]^{-1}$$

Or, $$G = [M^1 L^1T^{-2}] \times [L]^2 \times [M]^{-2}$$
$$= [M^{-1} L^3 T^{-2}].$$

Therefore, the gravitational constant is dimensionally represented as $M^{-1} L^3 T^{-2}$.

69. Initial velocity, u = 40 m/sec, at maximum height the ball comes at rest hence, final velocity v = 0 m/sec. Acceleration in this case is the acceleration due to gravity which is working in the opposite direction (downward) of the motion (upward).

Hence, $a = -g$
$= -10$ m/sec^2.

Now, Using the first equation of motion:

⇒ $v = u + at$

⇒ $0 = 40 + (-10)t$

⇒ $10t = 40$

⇒ $t = 4$ sec

Hence, the time taken to reach the maximum height is 4 sec.

70. Time period of a pendulum, $T = 2\pi\sqrt{\frac{L}{g}}$

Where, L is the length of the pendulum and g is the acceleration due to gravity.

Given, L = 1 m, g = 10 m/sec^2,

Also, $\pi = 3.14 \approx \sqrt{10}$

⇒ $$T = 2\pi\sqrt{\left(\frac{1}{10}\right)} = 2\sqrt{10}.\frac{1}{\sqrt{10}}$$
$$= 2 \text{ sec.}$$

Hence, the time period of the pendulum approximates to 2 sec.

72. Plastids are present only in plant cells. They are differentiated into three different types on the basis of the colour, *i.e.*, type of pigment found in them.

1. Leucoplasts
2. Chromoplast
3. Chloroplast

Leucoplast are the colourless plastids of varied shapes and sizes with stored nutrients in the form of carbohydrates, lipids, and proteins. These are as follows:

Amyloplasts: These are the carbohydrate-containing leucoplasts that store starch, e.g., tuber of potato, grain of rice, and wheat.

Elaioplasts: These are the leucoplasts that store oils and fats e.g., rose.

Aleuroplasts: These are protein storing leucoplasts, e.g., castor endosperm.

73. Vacuoles are membrane-bound cell organelles, which are present in both plants and animal cells and also in some fungal cells, protist and bacterial cells. Compared to other cells, animal cells have smaller vacuoles, as they do not require the storage of more water, organic and inorganic for the proper functioning of the cell.

76. Bryophytes are small non-vascular plants. They are called amphibians of the plant kingdom because these plants are found near freshwater. But their sperms also called antherozoids are flagellate and need water to swim and reach the eggs in order to fertilize it. Hence they need water for sexual reproduction.

77. AIDS: The word AIDS stands for Acquired Immuno Deficiency Syndrome. AIDS is caused by the Human Immunodeficiency Virus (HIV). HIV belongs to the group retrovirus. Transmission of HIV occurs through following ways—By sexual contact with the infected person. By transfusion of contaminated blood and blood products. By sharing infected needles. From infected mother to her child through placenta.

Dengue fever: It is caused by virus Flavivirus. Dengue is transmitted by the bite of a mosquito infected with one of the four dengue virus serotypes. There is no vaccine or any specific medicine to treat dengue. People who have dengue fever should rest and drink plenty of fluids. It is a febrile illness that affects infants, young children and adults with symptoms appearing 3-14 days after the infective bite.

COVID-19: The COVID-19 pandemic, also known as the coronavirus pandemic, is a global pandemic of coronavirus disease 2019 caused by a coronavirus (SARS-CoV-2) that causes severe acute respiratory syndrome. The majority of people infected with the virus will experience mild to moderate respiratory illness and will recover without the need for special treatment. Some, however, will become critically ill and require medical attention.

Typhoid fever: It is caused by pathogenic bacterium *Salmonella typhi.* It is spread by contaminated food and water. It generally enters the small intestine and then migrates to other organs through blood. Typhoid fever can be confirmed by widal test.

78. The atmospheric refraction occurs in a medium of gradually changing refractive index. The path of rays of light coming from the star goes on varying slightly. The apparent position of the star fluctuates and the star appears to twinkle.

79. Work (W) is said to be done by a force when the force acting on it causes the object to displace.
Mathematically it is given by:

$\Rightarrow \quad W = \vec{F}.\vec{d} = Fd\cos\theta \quad ...(i)$

Where, F = The magnitude of the force vector, d = The magnitude of the displacement vector.
Here the pull force F is applied in the antiparallel direction to the displacement of the mass on the plane.
Referring to the diagram,

So, the displacement and pulling force vectors will be in the antiparallel direction to each other as the angle between them will be 180°.

$\because \quad \theta = 180°$

$\Rightarrow \quad \cos 180° = -1$

So, using equation (i), the work done in pulling the mass M will be negative as the magnitude of the force and displacement vector can not be negative.

80. Force is defined as mass times acceleration.

$F = m \times a \quad ...(i)$

Where, F = Force, m = Mass of body, a = Acceleration
Given: m = 1 kg, F = 5 N
Using equation (i),

$\Rightarrow \quad 5 = 10 \times a$

$\Rightarrow \quad a = 0.5 \text{ m/s}^2.$

84. The atomic number (Z) of an atom is the total number of protons or electrons present in that atom. Niels Bohr proposed an early model of the atom as a Nucleus at the center containing protons and neutrons being orbited by electrons in different shells. Bohr named these shells K (nearest to the Nucleus), L, M, N, and so on as shown in the figure below.

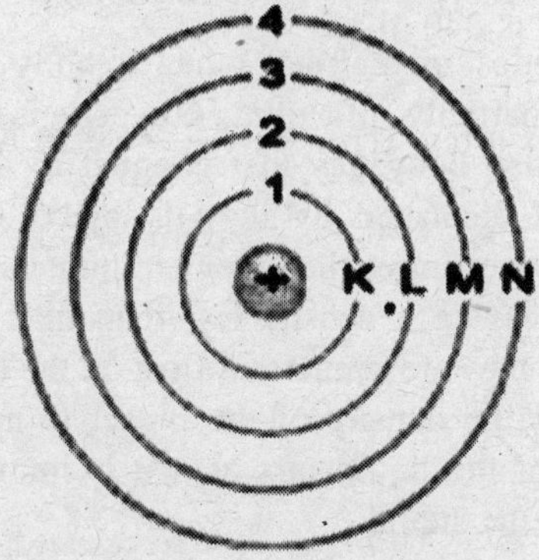

These shells contain only a fixed number of electrons like K contains only 2 electrons, L only 8 electrons,

M contains 18 electrons and so on. These states are stable states for any orbit and hence if the last shell (valance shell) of an atom contains these numbers of electrons they are said to be stable atoms.

Given, Z = 35

K = 2, L = 8, M = 18, N = 7 (Valance Shell)

Hence, the valance shell of this atom contains 7 electrons.

86. In crystallography crystals are described as **isomorphous** if they are closely similar in shape. Diamond and crystalline silicon are isomorphous because they both have three dimensional tetrahedral structure.

87. Hydrogen is the most abundant gas in the universe. The chemical element hydrogen has the symbol H and the atomic number 1. It is the very first element in the periodic table. The hydrogen nucleus contains one proton but no neutron. It is insoluble in water and lighter than the air. In nature, hydrogen gas is colourless, odourless, non-toxic, and tasteless. It is a combustible gas, but it does not support combustion.

88. Silica, or silicon dioxide, occurs as crystalline Quartz in its purest form. Although silica is not commonly used as a pigment, it can be found in grounds, primers, and wood fillers. Silica is a mineral that is used in the production of glass, water glass, abrasives, ceramics, and enamelware.

92. Contraceptive pills or tablets are oral pills for birth control. They are used to avoid pregnancy. Birth control pills contain man-made forms of two crucial female hormones estrogen and progestin. Ovulation is the natural process of realising the eggs from the ovaries.

The combination of these two hormones prevents the process of ovulation. There are different types of contraceptive pills for males and females. Contraceptive pills inhibit the release of the eggs and thus stop the process of fertilization.

95. Archimedes' principle: When a body is immersed fully or partially in a fluid, it experiences an upward force called buoyancy that is equal to the weight of the fluid displaced by it. All objects experience a force of buoyancy when they are immersed in a fluid. Objects having a density less than that of the liquid in which they are immersed, float on the surface of the liquid. If the density of the object is more than the density of the liquid in which it is immersed then it sinks in the liquid.

97. Combination is parallel, material is same (ρ = constant), thickness is same (A = Constant), and $l_2 = 2l_1$.

$$\Rightarrow \quad R_1 = \frac{\rho l_1}{A} \text{ and } R_2 = \frac{\rho l_2}{A}$$

$$\Rightarrow \quad \frac{R_1}{R_2} = \frac{\rho l_1}{A}\cdot\frac{A}{\rho l_2} = \frac{l_1}{l_2} = \frac{l_1}{2l_1} = \frac{1}{2}$$

$$\Rightarrow \quad R_2 = 2R_1$$

Since the combination is parallel, so total resistance R is:

$$\Rightarrow \quad \frac{1}{R} = \frac{1}{R_1} + \frac{1}{2R_1} = \frac{3}{2R_1}$$

Hence, $3R = 2R_1$ is the correct relation.

99. Thrust on the top of the table is due to the weight of the wooden block.

Now, Weight of the block,

$$\Rightarrow \quad F = mg \quad ...(i)$$

$$\Rightarrow \quad \text{Pressure (P)} = F / A \quad ...(ii)$$

Where A = Cross-section of the block touching the surface, m = Mass of the wooden block.

m = 2 kg

A = 30 cm × 10 cm.

= 0.30 m × 0.10 m

= 0.03 m^2,

Dimensions of block = 30 cm × 15 cm × 10 cm

Using equation (*i*),

$$\Rightarrow \quad F = mg = 2 \times 10 = 20 \text{ N}$$

Using equation (*ii*),

$$\Rightarrow \quad P = 20/0.03 = 666.67 \text{ N/m}^2.$$

100. Airplanes use tires made of conductive rubber to neutralize electricity. Electricity is created naturally through friction — and airplane tires are exposed to a lot of friction during takeoffs and landings. The friction between an airplane's tires and the runway can lead to a build up of electricity. When taking off, an airplane's tires may accumulate electricity that can damage the airplane's electronic components.

Airplanes contain hundreds if not thousands of electrical components, many of which are highly sensitive to electrical discharge. If a stray of electrical charge reaches one of these components, the component may fail. The use of conductive rubber tires prevents this from happening.

Even though conductive rubber allows electricity to flow through it, it prevents the build up of electricity. With conductive rubber tires, electricity will travel to the ground rather than accumulating in the tires. The friction-created electricity won't build up in the airplane's tires. When made of conductive rubber, the tires will expel it to the ground.

103. In the Buddhist art of the pre-Christian era, the Buddha was presented through symbols like an empty throne, the bodhi tree, a pair of footprints and a wheel. In the first century B.C., India's artists, who had worked in the perishable media of brick, wood, thatch, and bamboo, adopted stone on a very wide scale. Stone railings and gateways, covered with relief sculptures, were added to stupas. Favourite themes were events from the historic life of the Buddha, as well as from his previous lives, which were believed to be number 550.

106. Jurisdiction is the authority given to a legal body like a court to administer justice within a defined field of responsibility. The Supreme Court of India has three types of jurisdictions – original, appellate and advisory as provided in Articles 131, 133 – 136 and 143 respectively of the Indian Constitution.

110. The Global Positioning System (GPS), originally Navistar GPS, is a satellite-based radio navigation system owned by the United States government and operated by the United States Space Force. It is one of the global navigation satellite systems (GNSS) that provides geo-location and time information to a GPS receiver anywhere on or near the Earth where there is an unobstructed line of sight to four or more GPS satellites. Obstacles such as mountains and buildings can block the relatively weak GPS signals.

The GPS does not require the user to transmit any data, and it operates independently of any telephonic or Internet reception, though these technologies can enhance the usefulness of the GPS positioning information.

The GPS provides critical positioning capabilities to military, civil, and commercial users around the world. The United States government created the system, maintains and controls it, and makes it freely accessible to anyone with a GPS receiver.

114. Panchayati Raj Institution (PRI) is a system of rural local self-government in India. The Panchayati Raj now functions as a system of governance in which gram panchayats are the basic units of local administration. The system has three levels: Gram Panchayat (village level). Mandal Parishad or Block Samiti or Panchayat Samiti (block level), and Zila Parishad (district level).

115. The United States Declaration of Independence, formally 'The unanimous Declaration of the thirteen United States of America', is the pronouncement adopted by the Second Continental Congress meeting in Philadelphia, Pennsylvania, on July 4, 1776. Enacted during the American Revolution, the Declaration explains why the Thirteen Colonies at war with the Kingdom of Great Britain regarded themselves as thirteen independent sovereign states, no longer under British rule. With the Declaration, these new states took a collective first step in forming the United States of America.

The Declaration of Independence states three basic ideas:

- God made all men equal and gave them the rights of life, liberty, and the pursuit of happiness.
- The main business of government is to protect these rights.
- If a government tries to withhold these rights, the people are free to revolt and to set up a new government.

122. Industrial Revolution, in modern history, is the process of change from an agrarian and handicraft economy to one dominated by industry and machine manufacturing. These technological changes introduced novel ways of working and living and fundamentally transformed society. This process began in Britain in the 18th century and from there spread to other parts of the world. Although used earlier by French writers, the term Industrial Revolution was first popularized by the English economic historian Arnold Toynbee (1852–83) to describe Britain's economic development from 1760 to 1840. Since Toynbee's time the term has been more broadly applied as a process of economic transformation than as a period of time in a particular setting.

125. Satyashodhak Samaj (Truth-seekers' Society) was a social reform society founded by Jyotiba Phule in Pune, Maharashtra, on 24 September 1873. It espoused a mission of education and increased social rights and political access for underprivileged groups, focused especially on women, Shudras, and Dalits, in Maharashtra. Jyotirao's wife Savitribai was the head of women's section of the society. The Samaj disbanded during the 1930s as leaders left to join the Indian National Congress party.

128. The concept of planned economic development was taken from the Soviet economic model, which established state control over industries and economic structure. The idea of planning was also endorsed by a group of industrialist who framed Bombay Plan and believed that the state must play a major role in industrial and other economic investments.

133. The most common types of precipitation are rain, hail, and snow. Rain is precipitation that falls to the surface of the Earth as water droplets. Raindrops form around microscopic cloud condensation nuclei, such as a particle of dust or a molecule of pollution. Rain that falls from clouds but freezes before it reaches the ground is called sleet or ice pellets.

135. A magacity is called such type of city whose urban population is more than 10 million. New York City and Tokyo were the first known megacities, both reaching an urban conglomeration of over 10 million by the 1950s.

137. These occur in the areas which receive rainfall less than 50 cm and desert areas. It includes semi-arid areas of south west Punjab, Haryana, Rajasthan, Gujarat, Madhya Pradesh and Uttar Pradesh. These consist of a variety of grasses and shrubs. In these forests, plants remain leafless for most part of the year and give an expression of scrub vegetation. Important species found are babool, ber and wild date palm, khair, neem, khejri, palasm etc.

138. The three processes that change one rock to another are crystallization, metamorphism, and erosion and sedimentation, Any rock can transform into any other rock by passing through one or more of these processes. This creates the rock cycle which is a process in which rocks are continuously transformed between the three rock types igneous, sedimentary and metamorphic.

140. Moraines, eskers and outwash plains can be observed in the union territory of Ladakh. Outwash plains and eskers form due to the flow of meltwater in front of (outwash plains) or beneath (eskers) that glacier ice. They are composed of glacial sediments that have been reworked by flowing water. The moraine lies about 3 km north of Leh at 3650 m altitude. The irrigated and relatively fertile outwash fan stands in sharp contrast to the adjacent aluvial fans and mountains ides that are devoid of most vegetation.

142. India got its first ever export order for BrahMos missiles on when the Philippines' Defence Ministry signed USD 374 million contract with the BrahMos Aerospace Pvt Ltd (BAPL) to supply undisclosed number of missiles. The BAPL, an India-Russian joint venture, produces the supersonic cruise missile BrahMos that can be launched from submarines, ships, aircraft, or from land platforms. The USD 374 million contract is to supply shore-based anti-ship BrahMos missiles to the Phillippines' Navy.

143. The Supreme Court appointed an inquiry committee under its former judge Justice Indu Malhotra to probe the security breach during Prime Minister Narendra Modi's visit to Punjab on January 5, 2022.

A bench headed by Chief Justice of India said that the committee will also include the Registrar General of the Punjab and Haryana Court, the Director General of the National Investigation Agency or an officer nominated by him not below the rank of Inspector General, and ADGP (Security) of Punjab Police.

Setting up the panel, the bench also including Justices Surya Kant and Hima Kohli said the matter "cannot be left to one-sided enquiries" and that it must be looked into by a judicially trained mind to submit a comprehensive report for the consideration of the court.

147. The current Finance Minister Nirmala Sitaraman is the current chairman of the GST Council. The Governing body of the GST is the GST Council. The GST Council has 31 members representing the States and Union Territories.

148. The International Union for Conservation of Nature's (IUCN) recently categorised the Red Sanders (or Red Sandalwood) again into the 'endangered' category in its Red List. It was classified as 'near threatened' in 2018. Red Sanders usually grow in the rocky, degraded and fallow lands with Red Soil and hot and dry climate.

149. Prime Minister Narendra Modi declared that December 26 shall henceforth be marked as Veer Baal Diwas to pay homage to the courage of the Sahibzades, four sons of Guru Gobind Singh, the last Sikh Guru.

150. The Ministry of AYUSH organized a global Surya Namaskar Demonstration programme on 14 January 2022 for 75 lakh people globally (on the day of Makar Sakranti to commemorate the journey of the sun to the Northern Hemisphere). This occasion commemorates thanksgiving to 'Mother Nature' for bestowing health, wealth and happiness. On this day, the 'Surya Namaskar' is offered as a salutation to the Sun to exhibit one's gratitude for each of its rays as it nurtures all living beings. The Sun, as the primary source of energy, is critical not only for the continuation of the food-chain but it also energizes the mind and body of human beings. Scientifically, the Surya Namaskar has been known to develop immunity and improve vitality, which is significant to our health during pandemic conditions. Exposure to the Sun further provides the human body with Vitamin D, which has been widely recommended in all medical branches around the world.

PAPER II : MATHEMATICS

2. Let, $\Delta = \begin{vmatrix} a & b & c \\ a^2 & b^2 & c^2 \\ a^3 & b^3 & c^3 \end{vmatrix}$

Taking a, b and c common from c_1, c_2 and c_3 respectively

Then, $\Delta = abc\begin{vmatrix} 1 & 1 & 1 \\ a & b & c \\ a^2 & b^2 & c^2 \end{vmatrix}$

Applying $c_2 \to c_2 - c_1$ and $c_3 \to c_3 - c_1$

$\Rightarrow \quad \Delta = abc\begin{vmatrix} 1 & 0 & 0 \\ a & b-a & c-a \\ a^2 & b^2-a^2 & c^2-a^2 \end{vmatrix}$

taking $(b - a)$ and $(c - a)$ common from c_2 and c_3 respectively

$\Rightarrow \quad \Delta = abc(b-a)(c-a)\begin{vmatrix} 1 & 0 & 0 \\ a & 1 & 1 \\ a^2 & b+a & c+a \end{vmatrix}$

$\Rightarrow \quad \Delta = abc(b-a)(c-a)\times 1\times\begin{vmatrix} 1 & 1 \\ b+a & c+a \end{vmatrix}$

$\Rightarrow \quad \Delta = abc\ (b - a)\ (c - a)\ (c + a - b - a)$

$\Rightarrow \quad \Delta = abc\ (a - b)\ (b - c)\ (c - a) \quad ...(i)$

Given, $(a - b)\ (b - c)\ (c - a) = 2$ and $abc = 6$

From (i),

$\therefore \quad \Delta = 6 \times 2 = 12$

Hence, the value of $\Delta = 12$.

3. Let, $\Delta = \begin{vmatrix} a & b & c \\ b & c & a \\ c & a & b \end{vmatrix}$

Applying $c_1 \to c_1 + c_2 + c_3$

Then, $\Delta = \begin{vmatrix} a+b+c & b & c \\ b+c+a & c & a \\ c+a+b & a & b \end{vmatrix}$

$\Rightarrow \quad \Delta = (a+b+c)\begin{vmatrix} 1 & b & c \\ 1 & c & a \\ 1 & a & b \end{vmatrix}$

Applying $R_2 \to R_2 - R_1$ and $R_3 \to R_3 - R_1$

$\Rightarrow \quad \Delta = (a+b+c)\begin{vmatrix} 1 & b & c \\ 0 & c-b & a-c \\ 0 & a-b & b-c \end{vmatrix}$

$\Rightarrow \quad \Delta = (a+b+c)\times 1\times\begin{vmatrix} c-b & a-c \\ a-b & b-c \end{vmatrix}$

[Expanding along c_1]

$\Rightarrow \quad \Delta = (a + b + c)\ [-(b - c)^2 - (a - c)\ (a - b)]$

$= -(a + b + c)\ [a^2 + b^2 + c^2 - ab - bc - ca]$

given, condition, Δ = vanish $\Rightarrow \Delta = 0$

$\therefore -(a + b + c)\ (a^2 + b^2 + c^2 - ab - bc - ca) = 0$

$\Rightarrow a + b + c = 0$ and $a^2 + b^2 + c^2 - ab - bc - ca = 0$

$\because a^3 + b^3 + c^3 - 3abc$

$= (a + b + c)\ (a^2 + b^2 + c^2 - ab - bc - ca)$

$\therefore a^3 + b^3 + c^3 = 3abc\ [a + b + c = 0]$

Hence, code 1, 2 and 3 are correct.

4. Here, Matrices:

$A = [m \quad n]$, $B = [-n \quad -m]$ and $C = \begin{bmatrix} m \\ -m \end{bmatrix}$

1. CA = CB

$\Rightarrow \quad \begin{bmatrix} m \\ -m \end{bmatrix}[m \quad n] = \begin{bmatrix} m \\ -m \end{bmatrix}[-n \quad -m]$

$\Rightarrow \quad \begin{bmatrix} m^2+mn \\ -m^2+mn \end{bmatrix} = \begin{bmatrix} -mn-m^2 \\ mn+m^2 \end{bmatrix}$

$\Rightarrow \quad -\begin{bmatrix} -m^2-mn \\ m^2+mn \end{bmatrix} = \begin{bmatrix} -m^2-mn \\ m^2+mn \end{bmatrix} \Rightarrow CA \neq CB$

2. AC = BC

$\Rightarrow \quad [m \quad n]\begin{bmatrix} m \\ -m \end{bmatrix} = [-n \quad -m]\begin{bmatrix} m \\ -m^2 \end{bmatrix}$

$\Rightarrow \quad [m^2 - mn] = [-mn + m^2]$

$\Rightarrow \quad [m^2 - mn] = [m^2 - mn] \Rightarrow AC = BC$

3. C(A + B) = CA + CB

$\Rightarrow \quad \begin{bmatrix} m \\ -m^2 \end{bmatrix}[m-n \quad n-m] = \begin{bmatrix} m^2+mn \\ -m^2-mn \end{bmatrix} + \begin{bmatrix} -mn-m^2 \\ mn+m^2 \end{bmatrix}$

$\Rightarrow \quad \begin{bmatrix} m^2-mn+mn-m^2 \\ -m^2+mn-mn+m^2 \end{bmatrix} = \begin{bmatrix} m^2+mn-mn-m^2 \\ -m^2-mn+mn+m^2 \end{bmatrix}$

$\Rightarrow \quad \begin{bmatrix} 0 \\ 0 \end{bmatrix} = \begin{bmatrix} 0 \\ 0 \end{bmatrix}$

$\Rightarrow \quad C(A + B) = CA + CB$

Hence, Statements (2) and (3) are correct.

5. Given, $A = \begin{bmatrix} 2\sin\theta & \cos\theta & 0 \\ -2\cos\theta & \sin\theta & 0 \\ -1 & 1 & 1 \end{bmatrix}$

Let C_{ij} be the cofactor of a_{ij} in $A = [a_{ij}]$

Then, $C_{11} = (-1)^{1+1}(\sin\theta - 0) = \sin\theta$

$C_{12} = 2\cos\theta,\ C_{13} = \sin\theta - \cos\theta$

$C_{21} = -\cos\theta,\ C_{22} = 2\sin\theta$

$C_{23} = -2\sin\theta - \cos\theta$

$C_{31} = 0,\ C_{32} = 0,\ C_{33} = 2$

$$\therefore \quad \text{Adj } A = \begin{bmatrix} \sin\theta & 2\cos\theta & \sin\theta - 2\cos\theta \\ -\cos\theta & 2\sin\theta & -2\sin\theta - \cos\theta \\ 0 & 0 & 2 \end{bmatrix}^T$$

$$= \begin{bmatrix} \sin\theta & -\cos\theta & 0 \\ 2\cos\theta & 2\sin\theta & 0 \\ \sin\theta - 2\cos\theta & -2\sin\theta - \cos\theta & 2 \end{bmatrix}$$

$$\therefore \quad A(\text{adj } A) = \begin{bmatrix} 2\sin\theta & \cos\theta & 0 \\ -2\cos\theta & \sin\theta & 0 \\ -1 & 1 & 1 \end{bmatrix}\begin{bmatrix} \sin\theta & -\cos\theta & 0 \\ 2\cos\theta & 2\sin\theta & 0 \\ \sin\theta - 2\cos\theta & -2\sin\theta - \cos\theta & 2 \end{bmatrix}$$

$$= \begin{bmatrix} 2\sin^2\theta + 2\cos^2\theta + 0 & -2\sin\theta\cos\theta + 2\sin\theta\cos\theta & 0+0+2 \\ -2\sin\theta\cos\theta + 2\sin\theta\cos\theta + 0 & 2\cos^2\theta + 2\sin^2\theta + 0 & 0+0+0 \\ -\sin\theta + 2\cos\theta + \sin\theta - 2\cos\theta & \cos\theta + 2\sin\theta - 2\sin\theta - \cos\theta & 0+0+2 \end{bmatrix}$$

$$= \begin{bmatrix} 2 & 0 & 0 \\ 0 & 2 & 0 \\ 0 & 0 & 2 \end{bmatrix} = 2\begin{bmatrix} 1 & 0 & 0 \\ 0 & 1 & 0 \\ 0 & 0 & 1 \end{bmatrix} = 2I$$

Hence, $A(\text{adj } A) = 2I$.

11. $\left(1+\frac{2}{x}\right)^9\left(1-\frac{2}{x}\right)^9 = \left[1^2 - \left(\frac{2}{x}\right)^2\right]^9$

$$= \left(1-\frac{4}{x}\right)^9$$

$\because$ The expansion of $(x + a)^n$ has $(n + 1)$ terms

$\therefore$ The expansion of $\left(1-\frac{4}{x}\right)^9$ has $(9 + 1) = 10$ terms.

12. We know that the $(r + 1)^{th}$ term in the expansion of $(x + a)$ is

$$T_{r+1} = {}^nC_r\, x^{n-r}\, a^r$$

$\therefore$ In the expansion of $(x + y)^{10}$

6th term $= T_6 = T_{5+1} = {}^{10}C_5\, x^{10-5}y^5$

$= {}^{10}C_5\, x^5\, y^5$

$\because \quad {}^{10}C_4 = 210$ and ${}^{10}C_6 = 210$

$\therefore$ Co-efficient of 6th term $= {}^{10}C_5 = 252$

(1) The coefficient of the 6th term has the highest value

Now, $T_3 = T_{2+1} = {}^{10}C_2\, x^8\, y^2$

$T_9 = T_{8+1} = {}^{10}C_8\, x^2\, y^8$

$\therefore$ The co-efficient of 3rd term = the co-efficient of the 9th term

$$\Rightarrow \quad {}^{10}C_2 = {}^{10}C_8 \Rightarrow \frac{\lfloor 10}{\lfloor 2 \lfloor 8} = \frac{\lfloor 10}{\lfloor 8 \lfloor 2}$$

(2) The co-efficient of the 3rd term = the co-efficient of the 9th term.

13. Given, $C(3n, 2n) = C(3n, 2n - 7)$

$\Rightarrow \quad {}^{3n}C_{2n} = {}^{3n}C_{2n-7}$

$\Rightarrow \quad 3n = 2n + 2n - 7$

[If ${}^nC_x = {}^nC_y$, then $x + y = n$]

$\Rightarrow \quad 3n = 4n - 7$

$\Rightarrow \quad -n = -7$

$\Rightarrow \quad n = 7$

$\therefore \quad C(n, n-5) = {}^nC_{n-5}$

$$= \frac{\lfloor n}{\lfloor n-5 \lfloor n-n+5}$$

$$= \frac{\lfloor n}{\lfloor n-5 \lfloor 5} = \frac{\lfloor 7}{\lfloor 7-5 \lfloor 5}$$

$$= \frac{\lfloor 7}{\lfloor 2 \lfloor 5} = \frac{7.6 \lfloor 5}{2 \lfloor 5}$$

$$= \frac{42}{2} = 21.$$

15. Here, $a = 301,\ d = 2,\ t_n = 399$

$\because \quad t_n = a + (n-1)d$

$\Rightarrow \quad 399 = 301 + 2(n - 1)$

$\Rightarrow \quad 2(n - 1) = 399 - 301 = 98$

$\Rightarrow \quad n - 1 = 49 \Rightarrow n = 1 + 49 \Rightarrow n = 50$

Now, odd numbers which of the digit is repeated 311, 333, 355, 377, 399.

Hence, the required number of digits = 50 – 5 = 45.

17. Given, α and β be the roots of the equation

$x^2 + px + q = 0$

$\Rightarrow \quad \alpha + \beta = -p,\ \alpha\beta = q$

and α^3 and β^3 be the roots of the equation

$x^2 + mx + n = 0$

$\Rightarrow \quad \alpha^3 + \beta^3 = -m,\ \alpha^3\beta^3 = n$

$\therefore \quad m + n = -(\alpha^3 + \beta^3) + \alpha^3\beta^3$
$= -[(\alpha + \beta)(\alpha^2 + \beta^2 - \alpha\beta)] + \alpha^3\beta^3$
$= -(\alpha + \beta)[(\alpha + \beta)^2 - 2\alpha\beta - \alpha\beta] + \alpha^3\beta^3$
$= -(\alpha + \beta)[(\alpha + \beta)^2 - 3\alpha\beta] + \alpha^3\beta^3$
$= -(-p)[(-p)^2 - 3(q)] + (\alpha\beta)^3$
$= p[p^2 - 3q] + q^3$
$= p^3 - 3pq + q^3$
$= p^3 + q^3 - 3pq.$

18. $\because$ α and β be the roots of the equation
$x^2 - ax - bx + ab - c = 0$
$\Rightarrow \quad x^2 - (a + b)x + ab - c = 0$
$\therefore \quad \alpha + \beta = -\left[\frac{-(a+b)}{1}\right]$
$\Rightarrow \quad \alpha + \beta = a + b$
and $\quad \alpha\beta = \frac{ab-c}{1} = ab - c$

Now, the quadratic equation whose roots are a and b
$\Rightarrow \quad x^2 - (a + b)x + ab = 0$
$\Rightarrow \quad x^2 - (\alpha + \beta)x + \alpha\beta + c = 0 \quad [ab = \alpha\beta + c]$
$\Rightarrow \quad x^2 - \alpha x - \beta x + \alpha\beta + c = 0.$

19. Let α and β be the roots of the equation
$x^2 - ax - bx - cx + bc + ca = 0$
$\Rightarrow \quad x^2 - (a + b + c)x + c(a + b) = 0$
Then, $\quad \alpha + \beta = a + b + c$
and $\quad \alpha\beta = c(a + b)$
According to the question,
$\alpha = \beta$
$\Rightarrow \quad \alpha^2 = \beta^2$
$\Rightarrow \quad \alpha^2 - \beta^2 = 0$
$\Rightarrow \quad (\alpha + \beta)^2 - 4\alpha\beta = 0$
$\Rightarrow \quad (a + b + c)^2 - 4c(a + b)$
$\Rightarrow (a + b)^2 + c^2 + 2(a + b)c - 4c(a + b) = 0$
$\Rightarrow \quad (a + b)^2 + c^2 - 2c(a + b) = 0$
$\Rightarrow \quad (a + b - c)^2 = 0$
$\Rightarrow \quad a + b - c = 0.$

20. α and β be the roots of the equation
$x^2 - 8x + 9 = 0$
$\Rightarrow \quad \alpha + \beta = 8$ and $\alpha\beta = 9$
Given, $\quad \alpha^2 - \beta^2 = 16$
$\Rightarrow \quad (\alpha - \beta)(\alpha + \beta) = 16$
$\Rightarrow \quad (\alpha - \beta) . 8 = 16$
$\Rightarrow \quad \alpha - \beta = 2$
$\Rightarrow \quad (\alpha - \beta)^2 = 4$
$\Rightarrow \quad \alpha^2 + \beta^2 - 2\alpha\beta = 4$
$\Rightarrow \quad (\alpha + \beta)^2 - 2\alpha\beta - 2\alpha\beta = 4$
$\Rightarrow \quad (\alpha + \beta)^2 - 4\alpha\beta = 4$
$\Rightarrow \quad (8)^2 - 49 = 4$
$\Rightarrow \quad 64 - 49 = 4$
$\Rightarrow \quad 64 - 4 = 49$
$\Rightarrow \quad 60 = 49$
$\Rightarrow \quad 9 = 15.$

22. $2(2 \times 1) + 3(3 \times 2 \times 1) + 4(4 \times 3 \times 2 \times 1) + 5(5 \times 4 \times 3 \times 2 \times 1) + ... + 9(9 \times 8 \times 7 \times 6 \times 5 \times 4 \times 3 \times 2 \times 1) + 2$
$= 2\lfloor 2 + 3\lfloor 3 + 4\lfloor 4 + 5\lfloor 5 + ... + 9\lfloor 9 + 2$
$= (3-1)\lfloor 2 + (4-1)\lfloor 3 + (5-1)\lfloor 4 + (6-1)\lfloor 5 + (7-1)\lfloor 6 + (8-1)\lfloor 7 + (9-1)\lfloor 8 + (10-1)\lfloor 9 + 2$
$= 3\lfloor 2 - \lfloor 2 + 4\lfloor 3 - \lfloor 3 + 5\lfloor 4 - \lfloor 4 + 6\lfloor 5 - \lfloor 5 + 7\lfloor 6 - \lfloor 6 + 8\lfloor 7 - \lfloor 7 + 9\lfloor 8 - \lfloor 8 + 10\lfloor 9 - \lfloor 9 + 2$
$= \lfloor 3 - \lfloor 2 + \lfloor 4 - \lfloor 3 + \lfloor 5 - \lfloor 4 + \lfloor 6 - \lfloor 5 + \lfloor 7 - \lfloor 6 + \lfloor 8 - \lfloor 7 + \lfloor 9 - \lfloor 8 + \lfloor 10 - \lfloor 9 + \lfloor 2$
$= \lfloor 10.$

24. Given, a, b, c are in G.P.
$\Rightarrow \quad \frac{b}{a} = \frac{c}{b} \Rightarrow b^2 = ac$

1. a^2, b^2, c^2 are in G.P.
$\Rightarrow \quad \frac{b^2}{a^2} = \frac{c^2}{b^2} \Rightarrow \frac{b}{a} = \frac{c}{b} \Rightarrow b^2 = ac$

2. $\frac{1}{a}, \frac{1}{b}, \frac{1}{c}$ are in G.P.
$\Rightarrow \quad \frac{1}{b} \times \frac{a}{1} = \frac{1}{c} \times \frac{b}{1} \Rightarrow \frac{a}{b} = \frac{b}{c} \Rightarrow b^2 = ac$

3. $\sqrt{a}, \sqrt{b}, \sqrt{c}$ are in G.P.
$\Rightarrow \quad \frac{\sqrt{b}}{\sqrt{a}} = \frac{\sqrt{c}}{\sqrt{b}} \Rightarrow \frac{b}{a} = \frac{c}{b} \Rightarrow b^2 = ac$

Hence, 1, 2 and 3 are correct.

25. Given, $\frac{a+b}{2}, b, \frac{b+c}{2}$ are in H.P.
$\Rightarrow \frac{2}{a+b}, \frac{1}{b}, \frac{2}{b+c}$ are in A.P.
$\Rightarrow \quad \frac{2}{b} = \frac{2}{a+b} + \frac{2}{b+c}$
$\Rightarrow \quad \frac{2}{b} = \frac{2(a+b+b+c)}{(a+b)(b+c)}$
$\Rightarrow \quad \frac{1}{b} = \frac{(a+2b+c)}{(a+b)(b+c)}$

$\Rightarrow \quad b(a + 2b + c) = (a + b)(b + c)$

$\Rightarrow \quad \cancel{ab} + 2b^2 + \cancel{bc} = \cancel{ab} + ac + b^2 + \cancel{bc}$

$\Rightarrow \quad 2b^2 = ac + b^2$

$\Rightarrow \quad 2b^2 - b^2 = ac \Rightarrow b^2 = ac$

$\Rightarrow$ *a, b, c* are in G.P.

26. $\cot^2 15° + \tan^2 15°$

$= \cot^2 (90 - 75°) + \tan^2 (90 - 75°)$

$= \tan^2 75° + \cot^2 75°$

$= \tan^2 (45° + 30°) + \cot^2 (45° + 30°)$

$$= \left[\frac{\tan 45° + \tan 30°}{1 - \tan 45° \tan 30°}\right]^2 + \left[\frac{1 - \tan 45° \tan 30°}{\tan 45° + \tan 30°}\right]^2$$

$$= \left[\frac{1 + \frac{1}{\sqrt{3}}}{1 - \frac{1}{\sqrt{3}}}\right]^2 + \left[\frac{1 - \frac{1}{\sqrt{3}}}{1 + \frac{1}{\sqrt{3}}}\right]^2 = \left[\frac{\sqrt{3}+1}{\sqrt{3}-1}\right]^2 + \left[\frac{\sqrt{3}-1}{\sqrt{3}+1}\right]^2$$

$$= \frac{3+1+2\sqrt{3}}{3+1-2\sqrt{3}} + \frac{3+1-2\sqrt{3}}{3+1+2\sqrt{3}} = \frac{4+2\sqrt{3}}{4-2\sqrt{3}} + \frac{4-2\sqrt{3}}{4+2\sqrt{3}}$$

$$= \frac{2+\sqrt{3}}{2-\sqrt{3}} + \frac{2-\sqrt{3}}{2+\sqrt{3}} = \frac{\left(2+\sqrt{3}\right)^2 + \left(2-\sqrt{3}\right)^2}{\left(2-\sqrt{3}\right)\left(2+\sqrt{3}\right)}$$

$$= \frac{4+3+4\sqrt{3}+4+3-4\sqrt{3}}{4-3} = \frac{7+7}{1} = 14.$$

27. In a triangle ABC,

$\sin A - \cos B - \cos C = 0$

$\Rightarrow \quad \sin A = \cos B + \cos C$

$\Rightarrow \quad 2\sin\frac{A}{2}\cos\frac{A}{2} = 2\cos\frac{B+C}{2}\cos\frac{B-C}{2}$

$\Rightarrow \quad \cancel{2\sin\frac{A}{2}}\cos\frac{A}{2} = \cancel{2\sin\frac{A}{2}}\cos\frac{B-C}{2}$

$\Rightarrow \quad \cos\frac{A}{2} = \cos\frac{B-C}{2}$

$$\left[\cos\frac{B+C}{2} = \cos\left(\frac{\pi}{2} - \frac{A}{2}\right) = \sin\frac{A}{2}\right]$$

$\Rightarrow \quad \frac{A}{2} = \frac{B-C}{2}$

$\Rightarrow \quad A = B - C$

$\Rightarrow \quad B = A + C$

$\because \quad A + B + C = \pi$

$\therefore \quad A + C + B = \pi$

$\Rightarrow \quad B + B = \pi$

$\Rightarrow \quad 2B = \pi$

$\Rightarrow \quad B = \frac{\pi}{2}.$

28. Given, $\alpha + \beta = \frac{\pi}{4}$ and $2 \tan \alpha = 1$

$\therefore \quad \tan 2\beta = \tan 2\left(\frac{\pi}{4} - \alpha\right)$

$= \tan\left(\frac{\pi}{2} - 2\alpha\right)$

$$= \cot 2\alpha = \frac{1}{\tan 2\alpha} = \frac{1}{\frac{2\tan\alpha}{1-\tan^2\alpha}}$$

$$= \frac{1-\tan^2\alpha}{2\tan\alpha}$$

$$= \frac{1-\left(\frac{1}{2}\right)^2}{2\times\frac{1}{2}} = \frac{1-\frac{1}{4}}{1} = \frac{3}{4}.$$

29. Given, $\tan(45° + \theta) = 1 + \sin 2\theta$

$\Rightarrow \quad \frac{\tan 45° + \tan\theta}{1 - \tan 45° \tan\theta} = 1 + \sin 2\theta$

$\Rightarrow \quad \frac{1+\tan\theta}{1-\tan\theta} - 1 = \sin 2\theta$

$\Rightarrow \quad \frac{1+\tan\theta - 1 + \tan\theta}{1-\tan\theta} = \frac{2\tan\theta}{1+\tan^2\theta}$

$\Rightarrow \quad \frac{2\tan\theta}{1-\tan\theta} = \frac{2\tan\theta}{1+\tan^2\theta}$

$\Rightarrow \quad 1 - \tan\theta = 1 + \tan^2\theta$

$\Rightarrow \quad \tan^2\theta + \tan\theta = 0$

$\Rightarrow \quad \tan\theta(\tan\theta + 1) = 0$

$\Rightarrow \quad \tan\theta = 0, \tan\theta = -1 = \tan\left(-\frac{\pi}{4}\right)$

$\Rightarrow \quad \theta = 0$ or $-\frac{\pi}{4}$ $\left[\because \frac{-\pi}{4} < \theta < \frac{\pi}{4}\right]$

$\therefore \quad \theta = 0$

Hence, $\cos 2\theta = \cos 0° = 1.$

30. $\because \quad \sin 2\theta = \cos 3\theta$

$\therefore \quad 2\sin\theta\cos\theta = 4\cos^3\theta - 3\cos\theta$

$\Rightarrow \quad 2\sin\theta\cos\theta = \cos\theta(4\cos^2\theta - 3)$

$\Rightarrow \quad 2\sin\theta = 4\cos^2\theta - 3$

$\Rightarrow \quad 2\sin\theta = 4(1-\sin^2\theta) - 3$

$\Rightarrow \quad 4 - 4\sin^2\theta - 3 - 2\sin\theta = 0$

$\Rightarrow \quad -4\sin^2\theta - 2\sin\theta + 1 = 0$

$\Rightarrow \quad 4\sin^2\theta + 2\sin\theta - 1 = 0$

$\therefore \quad \sin\theta = \dfrac{-2\pm\sqrt{4+16}}{2\times 4} = \dfrac{-2\pm\sqrt{20}}{8}$

$\Rightarrow \quad \sin\theta = \dfrac{-2\pm 2\sqrt{5}}{8} = \dfrac{-1\pm\sqrt{5}}{4}$

$\Rightarrow \quad \sin\theta = \dfrac{-1\pm\sqrt{5}}{4} \left[\text{Given, } \sin 18° = \dfrac{\sqrt{5}-1}{4}\right]$

Hence, $1 + 4\sin\theta = 1 + 4\times\dfrac{\sqrt{5}-1}{4}$

$= 1 + \sqrt{5} - 1 = \sqrt{5}.$

31. Given, $\tan\theta = -\dfrac{5}{12}$

$\therefore \quad \sec\theta = \sqrt{1+\tan^2\theta}$

$= \sqrt{1+\left(\dfrac{-5}{12}\right)^2} = \sqrt{1+\dfrac{25}{144}}$

$= \sqrt{\dfrac{169}{144}} = \dfrac{13}{12}$

$\Rightarrow \quad \cos\theta = \dfrac{12}{13}$

$\therefore \quad \sin\theta = \sqrt{1-\cos^2\theta}$

$= \sqrt{1-\left(\dfrac{12}{13}\right)^2} = \sqrt{1-\dfrac{144}{169}} = \sqrt{\dfrac{25}{169}}$

$\Rightarrow \quad \sin\theta = \pm\dfrac{5}{13}$

Hence, the value of $\sin\theta = \dfrac{5}{13}$ or $\dfrac{-5}{13}$.

33. $\sin^2\left(\dfrac{\pi}{4}+\theta\right) - \sin^2\left(\dfrac{\pi}{4}-\theta\right)$

$[\because \sin^2 A - \sin^2 B = \sin(A+B)\sin(A-B)]$

$= \sin\left(\dfrac{\pi}{4}+\theta+\dfrac{\pi}{4}-\theta\right)\sin\left(\dfrac{\pi}{4}+\theta-\dfrac{\pi}{4}+\theta\right)$

$= \sin\left(\dfrac{\pi}{4}+\dfrac{\pi}{4}\right)\sin(\theta+\theta)$

$= \sin\dfrac{\pi}{2}\sin 2\theta = 1 \,.\, \sin 2\theta = \sin 2\theta.$

34. Let AB be a vertical tower and PA be a vertical flagstaff of height h

and $\angle ACB = \theta$, $\angle PCB = 2\theta$

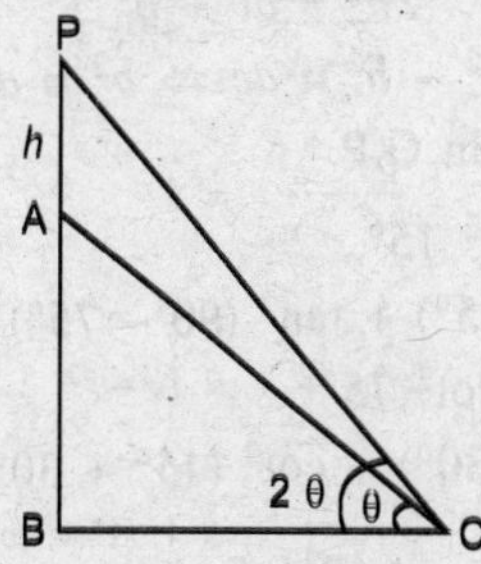

In ΔABC, $\tan\theta = \dfrac{AB}{BC} \Rightarrow BC = \dfrac{AB}{\tan\theta}$ ...(*i*)

In ΔPBC, $\tan 2\theta = \dfrac{PB}{BC} \Rightarrow BC = \dfrac{PB}{\tan 2\theta}$ ...(*ii*)

From (*i*) and (*ii*),

$\dfrac{AB}{\tan\theta} = \dfrac{PB}{\tan 2\theta} \Rightarrow \dfrac{AB}{\tan\theta} = \dfrac{PA+AB}{\tan 2\theta}$

$\Rightarrow \quad AB\tan 2\theta = PA\tan\theta + AB\tan\theta$

$\Rightarrow \quad AB(\tan 2\theta - \tan\theta) = PA\tan\theta$

$\Rightarrow \quad AB\left(\dfrac{2\tan\theta}{1-\tan^2\theta} - \tan\theta\right) = h\tan\theta$

$\Rightarrow \quad AB\left(\dfrac{2\tan\theta - \tan\theta + \tan^3\theta}{1-\tan^2\theta}\right) = h\tan\theta$

$\Rightarrow \quad \dfrac{AB(\tan\theta+\tan^3\theta)}{1-\tan^2\theta} = h\tan\theta$

$\Rightarrow \quad \dfrac{AB(1+\tan^2\theta)}{1-\tan^2\theta} = h$

$\Rightarrow AB = h\left(\dfrac{1-\tan^2\theta}{1+\tan^2\theta}\right) = h\cos 2\theta$

Hence, the height of the tower = AB = $h\cos 2\theta$.

36. Given, $\tan^{-1}\left(\dfrac{1}{2}\right) + \tan^{-1}\left(\dfrac{x}{3}\right) = \dfrac{\pi}{4}$

$\Rightarrow \quad \tan^{-1}\dfrac{\dfrac{1}{2}+\dfrac{x}{3}}{1-\left(\dfrac{1}{2}\right)\left(\dfrac{x}{3}\right)} = \dfrac{\pi}{4}$

$\Rightarrow \quad \tan^{-1}\dfrac{\dfrac{3+2x}{6}}{\dfrac{6-x}{6}} = \dfrac{\pi}{4}$

$$\Rightarrow \quad \tan^{-1}\frac{3+2x}{6-x} = \frac{\pi}{4}$$

$$\Rightarrow \quad \frac{3+2x}{6-x} = \tan\frac{\pi}{4}$$

$$\Rightarrow \quad \frac{3+2x}{6-x} = 1$$

$$\Rightarrow \quad 3 + 2x = 6 - x$$

$$\Rightarrow \quad 2x + x = 6 - 3$$

$$\Rightarrow \quad 3x = 3$$

$$\Rightarrow \quad x = 1 \ (0 < x < 6).$$

37. Given, $3\sin^{-1} x + \cos^{-1} x = \pi$

$\Rightarrow 2\sin^{-1} x + (\sin^{-1} x + \cos^{-1} x) = \pi$

$$\Rightarrow \quad 2\sin^{-1} x + \frac{\pi}{2} = \pi$$

$$\Rightarrow \quad 2\sin^{-1} x = \pi - \frac{\pi}{2}$$

$$\Rightarrow \quad 2\sin^{-1} x = \frac{\pi}{2}$$

$$\Rightarrow \quad \sin^{-1} x = \frac{\pi}{4}$$

$$\Rightarrow \quad x = \sin\frac{\pi}{4}$$

$$\Rightarrow \quad x = \frac{1}{\sqrt{2}}.$$

38. Given, $\tan\alpha + \tan\beta = 1 - \tan\alpha \,.\, \tan\beta$

$$\Rightarrow \quad \frac{\tan\alpha + \tan\beta}{1 - \tan\alpha\tan\beta} = 1$$

$$\Rightarrow \quad \tan(\alpha + \beta) = \tan\frac{\pi}{4}$$

$$\Rightarrow \quad \alpha + \beta = \frac{\pi}{4}.$$

39. Given, $(1 + \tan\theta)(1 + \tan 9\theta) = 2$

$\Rightarrow 1 + \tan\theta + \tan 9\theta + \tan\theta \tan 9\theta = 2$

$\Rightarrow \tan\theta + \tan 9\theta = 2 - 1 - \tan\theta \tan 9\theta$

$\Rightarrow \tan\theta + \tan 9\theta = 1 - \tan\theta \tan 9\theta$

$$\therefore \quad \tan 10\theta = \tan(\theta + 9\theta)$$

$$= \frac{\tan\theta + \tan 9\theta}{1 - \tan\theta\tan 9\theta}$$

$$= \frac{1 - \tan\theta\tan 9\theta}{1 - \tan\theta\tan 9\theta} = 1.$$

46. Let $\quad z = \dfrac{1}{1+i}$

then, $\quad z = \dfrac{1}{1+i} = \dfrac{1}{1+i} \times \dfrac{1-i}{1-i} = \dfrac{1-i}{1-i^2} = \dfrac{1-i}{1+1}$

$$= \frac{1-i}{2} = \frac{1}{2} - \frac{1}{2}i$$

$$\therefore \quad |z| = \sqrt{\left(\frac{1}{2}\right)^2 + \left(-\frac{1}{2}\right)^2}$$

$$= \sqrt{\frac{1}{4} + \frac{1}{4}} = \sqrt{\frac{2}{4}} = \frac{1}{\sqrt{2}}$$

Let α be the acute angle given by

$$\tan\alpha = \left|\frac{\text{Im}(z)}{\text{Re}(z)}\right|$$

then, $\quad \tan\alpha = \left|\dfrac{-1/2}{1/2}\right| = 1 \Rightarrow \alpha = \dfrac{\pi}{4}$

We observe that $\text{Re}(z) = \dfrac{1}{2} > 0$

and $\text{Im}(z) = -\dfrac{1}{2} < 0$

So, the point representing z lies in the fourth quadrant

$$\therefore \quad \arg(z) = -\alpha = -\frac{\pi}{4}$$

Hence, $\quad |z| = \dfrac{1}{\sqrt{2}}$ and $\arg(z) = -\dfrac{\pi}{4}$.

49. Here, out of 9 players so as to exclude 2 particular players

$\therefore$ The number of players $= 9 - 2 = 7$

$\therefore$ Out of 7 players, 5 players can be selected in $^7C_5$ ways

$\therefore$ Required number of ways $^7C_5$

$$= \frac{\lfloor 7}{\lfloor 5 \lfloor 7-5}$$

$$= \frac{\lfloor 7}{\lfloor 5 \lfloor 2} = \frac{7 \times 6 \times \lfloor 5}{2\lfloor 5} = \frac{42}{2} = 21.$$

50. In the expansion of $\left(x + \dfrac{1}{x}\right)^{2n}$

the number of terms $= 2n + 1$

So, the $(n + 1)$th term from the end

$= [2n + 1 - (n + 1) + 1]$th term

$= (2n + 1 - n - 1 + 1)$th term

$= (n + 1)$th term from the beginning

$\therefore$ Required term $= T_{n+1}$

$$= {}^{2n}C_n (x)^{2n-n} \,.\, \left(\frac{1}{x}\right)^n$$

$$= {}^{2n}C_n \,.\, x^n \,.\, x^{-n}$$

$$= {}^{2n}C_n \,.\, x^{n-n}$$

$$= {}^{2n}C_n \,.\, x^0 = {}^{2n}C_n \,.\, 1$$

$$= {}^{2n}C_n = C(2n, n).$$

52. Let a be the 1st term and d be the common difference of an A.P.

Then, 5th term $= \frac{1}{10}$

$\Rightarrow \quad t_5 = a + 4d = \frac{1}{10}$ ...(i)

and 10th term $= \frac{1}{5}$

$\Rightarrow \quad t_{10} = a + 9d = \frac{1}{5}$ ...(ii)

from (ii) - (i)

$(a + 9d) - (a + 4d) = \frac{1}{5} - \frac{1}{10}$

$\Rightarrow \quad 5d = \frac{2-1}{10}$

$\Rightarrow \quad 5d = \frac{1}{10} \Rightarrow d = \frac{1}{50}$

From (i), $\quad a = \frac{1}{10} - 4d = \frac{1}{10} - 4 \times \frac{1}{50}$

$= \frac{1}{10} - \frac{2}{25} = \frac{5-4}{50} = \frac{1}{50}$

$\Rightarrow \quad a = \frac{1}{50}$

$\therefore$ The sum of first 50 terms

$= \frac{50}{2}[2a + (50-1)d]$

$= 25\left[2 \times \frac{1}{50} + 49 \times \frac{1}{50}\right]$

$= 25 \times \frac{1}{50}[2 + 49]$

$= \frac{1}{2} \times 51 = 25.5$

Hence, $\quad S_{50} = 25.5.$

57. Given, differential equation,

$$1 + \left(\frac{dy}{dx}\right)^2 = \left(\frac{d^2y}{dx^2}\right)^{4/3}$$

$$\Rightarrow \quad \left[1 + \left(\frac{dy}{dx}\right)^2\right]^3 = \left(\frac{d^2y}{dx^2}\right)^4$$

The order of highest order differential co-efficient is 2

So, its order is 2.

Clearly, the power of the highest order differential co-efficient is 4.

So, its degree is 4.

61. Let, $\quad I = \int_0^{\frac{\pi}{4}} \frac{dx}{(\sin x + \cos x)^2}$

$$= \int_0^{\frac{\pi}{4}} \frac{dx}{\sin^2 x + \cos^2 x + 2\sin x \cos x}$$

$$= \int_0^{\frac{\pi}{4}} \frac{dx}{1 + \sin 2x} = \int \frac{dx}{1 + \frac{2\tan x}{1 + \tan^2 x}}$$

$$= \int_0^{\frac{\pi}{4}} \frac{dx}{\frac{1 + \tan^2 x + 2\tan x}{1 + \tan^2 x}} = \int_0^{\frac{\pi}{4}} \frac{(1 + \tan^2 x)dx}{1 + \tan^2 x + 2\tan x}$$

$$= \int_0^{\frac{\pi}{4}} \frac{\sec^2 x\, dx}{(1 + \tan x)^2}$$

Put $1 + \tan x = t \Rightarrow \sec^2 x\, dx = dt$

$$= \int_0^{\frac{\pi}{4}} \frac{dt}{t^2}$$

$$= \int_0^{\frac{\pi}{4}} t^{-2} dt = \left[\frac{-1}{t}\right]_0^{\pi/4} = \left[\frac{-1}{1 + \tan x}\right]_0^{\pi/4}$$

then, $\int_0^{\frac{\pi}{4}} \frac{dx}{(\sin x + \cos x)^2} = \left[\frac{-1}{1 + \tan x}\right]_0^{\pi/4}$

$$= \frac{-1}{1+1} + \frac{1}{1+0} = \frac{-1}{2} + 1 = \frac{1}{2}.$$

62. Let, $\quad I = \int (\sin x)^{-1/2} (\cos x)^{-3/2} dx$

$$= \int \frac{1}{(\sin x)^{1/2} (\cos x)^{3/2}} dx$$

$$= \int \frac{1}{(\sin x)^{1/2} (\cos x)^2 (\cos x)^{-1/2}} dx$$

$$= \int \frac{\sec^2 x\, dx}{(\sin x)^{1/2} (\cos x)^{-1/2}}$$

$$= \int \frac{\sec^2 x\, dx}{(\tan x)^{1/2}}$$

Put $\tan x = t \Rightarrow \sec^2 x\, dx = dt$

$$= \int \frac{dt}{(t)^{1/2}} = \int t^{-1/2} dt$$

$$= \frac{t^{-1/2}+1}{-1/2+1}+c = \frac{t^{1/2}}{1/2}+c$$

$$= 2t^{1/2}+c = 2\sqrt{\tan x}+c\,.$$

67. Given, $4f(x) - f\left(\frac{1}{x}\right) = \left(2x+\frac{1}{x}\right)\left(2x-\frac{1}{x}\right)$

$\Rightarrow \quad 4f(x) - f\left(\frac{1}{x}\right) = (2x)^2 - \frac{1}{x^2}$

$\Rightarrow \quad 4f(x) - f\left(\frac{1}{x}\right) = 4x^2 - \frac{1}{x^2}$

$\Rightarrow \quad 4f(x) = 4x^2$ and $f\left(\frac{1}{x}\right) = \frac{1}{x^2}$

$\Rightarrow \quad 4f(2) = 4(2)^2$

$\Rightarrow \quad 4f(2) = 4 \times 4$

$\Rightarrow \quad f(2) = \frac{4 \times 4}{4}$

$\Rightarrow \quad f(2) = 4.$

69. Given, $x^y\, y^x = 1$

Taking log both sides, we get,

$\log x^y + \log y^x = \log 1$

$\Rightarrow \quad y \log x + x \log y = 0$

Differentiating w.r.t. to x, we get,

$$y.\frac{1}{x}+\log x.\frac{dy}{dx}+x.\frac{1}{y}\frac{dy}{dx}+\log y.1 = 0$$

$\Rightarrow \quad \frac{dy}{dx}\left(\log x+\frac{x}{y}\right) = -\log y-\frac{y}{x}$

$\Rightarrow \quad \frac{dy}{dx} = \frac{-\left(\log y+\frac{y}{x}\right)}{\left(\log x+\frac{x}{y}\right)}$

$\Rightarrow \quad \left(\frac{dy}{dx}\right)_{(1,1)} = \frac{-\left(\log 1+\frac{1}{1}\right)}{\left(\log 1+\frac{1}{1}\right)} = \frac{-(0+1)}{(0+1)} = \frac{-1}{1} = -1$

Hence, $\frac{dy}{dx}$ at $(1, 1) = -1$.

70. Given, $y = (x^x)^x$

taking log

$\Rightarrow \quad \log y = \log (x^x)^x$

$\Rightarrow \quad \log y = x \log x^x$

$\Rightarrow \quad \log y = x\,.\,x \log x$

$\Rightarrow \quad \log y = x^2 \log x$

Differentiating both sides w.r.t. x, we get,

$$\frac{1}{y}\frac{dy}{dx} = x^2.\frac{1}{x}+(\log x).2x$$

$\Rightarrow \quad \frac{dy}{dx} = \frac{x+2x\log x}{1/y}$

$= y(x + 2\,x \log x)$

$= (x^x)^x\,(x + 2x \log x)$

$\Rightarrow \quad \frac{dy}{dx}$ at $1 = (1^1)^1\,(1 + 2 \times 1 \log 1)$

$= 1(1 + 2 \times 0)$

$= 1(1 + 0) = 1(1) = 1.$

74. $\lim\limits_{x\to 0} x^3(\operatorname{cosec} x)^2$

$= \lim\limits_{x\to 0} x^3(\operatorname{cosec}^2 x)$

$= (0)^3\,(\operatorname{cosec}^2 0)$

$= 0.$

75. $\lim\limits_{x\to 1}\frac{x^3-1}{\sqrt{x}-1}$

$= \lim\limits_{x\to 1}\frac{(x-1)(x^2+x+1)}{\sqrt{x}-1}$

$= \lim\limits_{x\to 1}\frac{\left(\sqrt{x}-1\right)\left(\sqrt{x}+1\right)\left(x^2+x+1\right)}{\left(\sqrt{x}-1\right)}$

$= \lim\limits_{x\to 1}\left(\sqrt{x}+1\right)\left(x^2+x+1\right)$

$= (1 + 1)(1^2 + 1 + 1)$

$= (2)\,(3) = 6.$

77. Given, $f(x) = \frac{m}{x}+2nx+1$

$\Rightarrow \quad f'(x) = \frac{-m}{x^2}+2n$

$\Rightarrow \quad f'(2) = \frac{-m}{(2)^2}+2n$

$\Rightarrow \quad 0 = \frac{-m}{4}+2n$

$\Rightarrow \quad 2n = \frac{m}{4}$

$\Rightarrow \quad m = 8n$

$\therefore \quad m + 8n = 8n + 8n = 16n$

Hence, the value of $m + 8n$ cannot be determined due to insufficient data.

78. The equation of the given curves are

$$y = x \quad ...(i)$$

and $$y = x^3 \quad ...(ii)$$

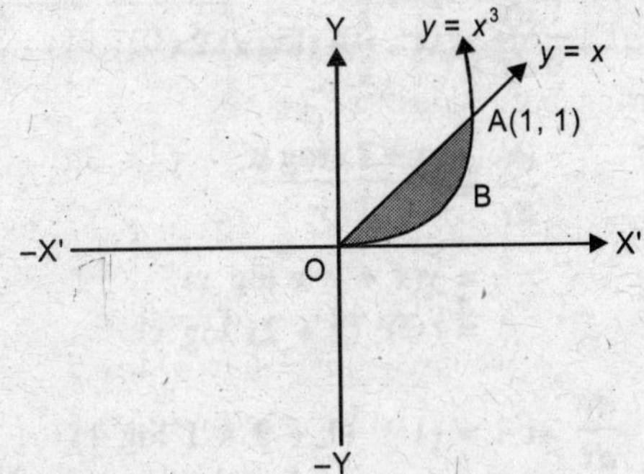

Solving (*i*) and (*ii*) the two curves intersect at O(0, 0) and A(1, 1)

∴ Required area = Area OBAO

$$= \int_0^1 |y_2 - y_1| dx$$

$$= \int_0^1 (y_2 - y_1) dx$$

$$= \int_0^1 (x - x^3) dx$$

$$= \left[\frac{x^2}{2} - \frac{x^4}{4}\right]_0^1$$

$$= \frac{1}{2} - \frac{1}{4}$$

$$= \frac{1}{4} \text{ sq. unit}$$

Hence, required area in first quadrant

$$= \frac{1}{4} \text{ square unit.}$$

81. Given, A(–5, 0), B($5p^2$, $10p$) and C($5q^2$, $10q$) are collinear

∴ Area of ΔABC = 0

$$\frac{1}{2}\begin{vmatrix} -5 & 0 & 1 \\ 5p^2 & 10p & 1 \\ 5q^2 & 10q & 1 \end{vmatrix} = 0$$

$$\Rightarrow -5(10p - 10q) + 0 + 1(50\,p^2q - 50pq^2) = 0$$

$$\Rightarrow -50p + 50q + 50p^2q - 50pq^2 = 0$$

$$\Rightarrow -p + q + p^2q - pq^2 = 0$$

$$\Rightarrow p^2q - pq^2 = p - q$$

$$\Rightarrow pq(p - q) = (p - q)$$

$$\Rightarrow pq = 1.$$

82. Given, the straight line passing through the point (1, –2) and cuts off equal intercepts from the axes

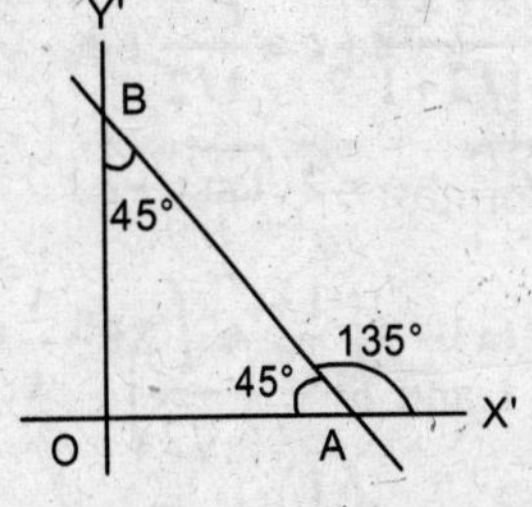

∴ $$m = \text{slope of the line}$$
$$= \tan 135°$$
$$= \tan (90° + 45°)$$
$$= -\cot 45° = -1$$

and $$x_1 = 1, y_1 = -2$$

So, the equation of the line is

$$y - y_1 = m(x - x_1)$$

$$\Rightarrow y - (-2) = -1(x - 1)$$

$$\Rightarrow y + 2 = -x + 1$$

$$\Rightarrow y + 2 + x - 1 = 0$$

$$\Rightarrow x + y + 1 = 0$$

Which is the equation of straight line.

84. Let P(x, y) be any point on the parabola whose focus in S(–3, 0) and the directrix $x - 3 = 0$.

Draw PM perpendicular from P on the directrix, then by definition

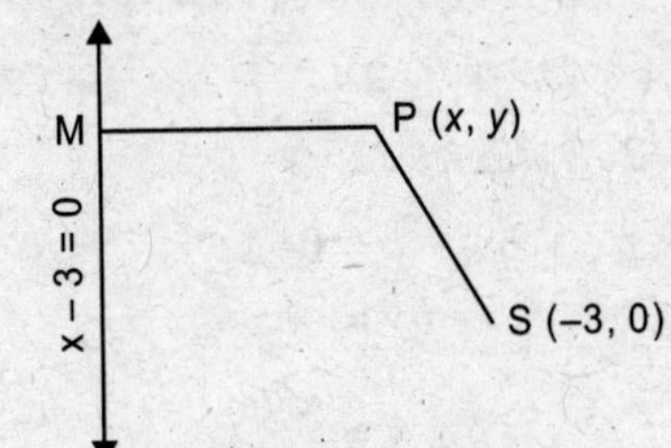

$$SP = PM$$

$$\Rightarrow SP^2 = PM^2$$

$$\Rightarrow (x + 3)^2 + (y - 0)^2 = \left|\frac{x - 3}{\sqrt{1^2 + 0^2}}\right|^2$$

$$\Rightarrow (x + 3)^2 + y^2 = (x - 3)^2$$

$$\Rightarrow x^2 + 9 + 6x + y^2 = x^2 + 9 - 6x$$

$$\Rightarrow y^2 + 6x + 6x = 0$$

$$\Rightarrow y^2 + 12x = 0$$

$$\Rightarrow y^2 = -12x.$$

85. Given, equation of the ellipse is

$$x^2 + 2y^2 = 1$$

$$\Rightarrow \frac{x^2}{1} + \frac{y^2}{\frac{1}{2}} = 1$$

$\Rightarrow \quad \dfrac{x^2}{1^2}+\dfrac{y^2}{\left(\dfrac{1}{\sqrt{2}}\right)^2} = 1$

This is the form of $\dfrac{x^2}{a^2}+\dfrac{y^2}{b^2}=1$

where, $a^2 = 1$ and $b^2 = \left(\dfrac{1}{\sqrt{2}}\right)^2$

$\Rightarrow a = 1$ and $b = \dfrac{1}{\sqrt{2}}$ clearly $a > b$

Let e be the eccentricity of the ellipse

Then, $\quad e = \sqrt{1-\dfrac{b^2}{a^2}} = \sqrt{1-\dfrac{\left(\dfrac{1}{\sqrt{2}}\right)^2}{1^2}}$

$= \sqrt{1-\dfrac{1}{2}} = \sqrt{\dfrac{1}{2}} = \dfrac{1}{\sqrt{2}}$

$\therefore$ The co-ordinates of the foci are $(ae, 0)$ and $(-ae, 0)$

i.e., $\left(\dfrac{1}{\sqrt{2}}, 0\right)$ and $\left(\dfrac{-1}{\sqrt{2}}, 0\right)$

$\therefore$ Required distance

$= \sqrt{\left[\dfrac{1}{\sqrt{2}}-\left(\dfrac{-1}{\sqrt{2}}\right)\right]^2+0^2} = \sqrt{\left(\dfrac{1}{\sqrt{2}}+\dfrac{1}{\sqrt{2}}\right)^2}$

$= \dfrac{1}{\sqrt{2}}+\dfrac{1}{\sqrt{2}} = \dfrac{1+1}{\sqrt{2}} = \dfrac{2}{\sqrt{2}} = \sqrt{2}.$

88. Given, $\quad ax + by + c = 0 \quad ...(i)$

$\Rightarrow \quad by = -ax - c$

$\Rightarrow \quad y = \dfrac{-a}{b}x-\dfrac{c}{b}$

$\therefore \quad m_1 = \text{slope} = \dfrac{-a}{b}$

and $\quad bx + ay + c = 0 \quad ...(ii)$

$\Rightarrow \quad ay = -bx - c$

$\Rightarrow \quad y = \dfrac{-b}{a}x-\dfrac{c}{a}$

$\therefore \quad m_2 = \dfrac{-b}{a}$

$\because$ Line (i) and (ii) are parallel

$\therefore$ Their slopes are equal

$\therefore \quad m_1 = m_2$

$\Rightarrow \quad \dfrac{-a}{b} = \dfrac{-b}{a}$

$\Rightarrow \quad a^2 = b^2$

$\Rightarrow \quad a^2 - b^2 = 0.$

90. Let the point $P(x, y)$ is equidistant from the points $A(2a, 0)$ and $B(0, 3a)$

Then, $\quad PA = PB$

$\Rightarrow \quad \sqrt{(x-2a)^2+(y-0)^2} = \sqrt{(x-0)^2+(y-3a)^2}$

Squaring both sides, we get,

$\Rightarrow \quad (x - 2a)^2 + y^2 = x^2 + (y - 3a)^2$

$\Rightarrow \quad x^2+4a^2-4ax+y^2 = x^2+y^2+9a^2-6ay$

$\Rightarrow \quad 4a^2 - 4ax = 9a^2 - 6ay$

$\Rightarrow \quad 9a^2 - 4a^2 = 6ay - 4ax$

$\Rightarrow \quad 5a^2 = a(6y - 4x)$

$\Rightarrow \quad 5a = 6y - 4x$

$\Rightarrow \quad 5a + 4x - 6y = 0$

$\Rightarrow \quad 4x - 6y + 5a = 0.$

96. Given, $4\hat{i}+\hat{j}-3\hat{k}$ and $p\hat{i}+q\hat{j}-2\hat{k}$ are collinear

$\therefore p\hat{i}+q\hat{j}-2\hat{k} = \mu\left(4\hat{i}+\hat{j}-3\hat{k}\right)$

$\Rightarrow \quad p = 4\mu,\ q = \mu,\ -2 = -3\mu \Rightarrow \mu = \dfrac{2}{3}$

$\therefore \quad p = 4\times\dfrac{2}{3}$

$= \dfrac{8}{3}$

and $\quad q = \mu$

$= \dfrac{2}{3}$

Hence, the possible values of p and q are $\dfrac{8}{3}$ and $\dfrac{2}{3}$.

103. Given, $N = 5$, and $\sigma^2 = 3.6$

Let a be the fifth observation

We know that,

$\bar{x} = \dfrac{\text{Sum of observation}}{\text{Number of observation}}$

$\Rightarrow \quad \bar{x} = \dfrac{2+2+4+5+a}{5}$

$\Rightarrow \quad 5\bar{x} = 13 + a$

$\Rightarrow \quad a = 5\bar{x} - 13 \quad ...(i)$

$\because \quad \sigma^2 = \dfrac{\sum_{i=1}^{5}(x_i-\bar{x})^2}{N} = 3.6$

$\Rightarrow \left(2-\bar{X}\right)^2+\left(2-\bar{X}\right)^2+\left(4-\bar{X}\right)^2+\left(5-\bar{X}\right)^2+\left(a-\bar{X}\right)^2$

$= 5 \times 3.6$

$\Rightarrow\ 4+\bar{X}^2-4\bar{x}+4+\bar{X}^2-4\bar{X}+16+\bar{X}^2-8\bar{X}+$

$+\bar{X}^2-10\bar{X}+a^2+\bar{X}^2-2a\bar{X} = 18$

$\Rightarrow\ 49+5\bar{X}^2-26\bar{X}+a^2-2a\bar{X} = 18$ ...(*ii*)

Putting the value of a in (*ii*)

$\Rightarrow\ 49+5\bar{X}^2-26\bar{X}+(5\bar{X}-13)^2-2(5\bar{X}-13)\bar{X} = 18$

$\Rightarrow\ 49+5\bar{X}^2-26\bar{X}+25\bar{X}^2-130\bar{X}+169-10\bar{X}^2+26\bar{X} = 18$

$\Rightarrow\ 218+20\bar{X}^2-130\bar{X} = 18$

$\Rightarrow\ 20\bar{X}^2-130\bar{X}+200 = 0$

$\Rightarrow\ 2\bar{X}^2-13\bar{X}+20 = 0$

$\Rightarrow\ 2\bar{X}^2-8\bar{X}-5\bar{X}+20 = 0$

$\Rightarrow\ 2\bar{X}(\bar{X}-4)-5(\bar{X}-4) = 0$

$\Rightarrow\ (\bar{X}-4)(2\bar{X}-5) = 0$

$\Rightarrow\ \bar{x} = 4,\ \bar{X} = \frac{5}{2}$

Putting the value of $\bar{x}$ in (*i*)

$\therefore\ a = 5 \times 4 - 13 = 7$

and $a = 5\times\frac{5}{2}-13$

$= 12.5 - 13 = -0.5$

As the observations are positive

$a = -0.5$ is not possible

Hence, the required remaining observation = a = 7.

104. Given, 1st term = a = 4

Common difference = d = 4

Number of terms = n = 50

$\because$ Sum of n terms in A.P. = $S_n = \frac{n}{2}[2a+(n-1)d]$

$S_{50} = \frac{50}{2}[2\times4+(50-1)\times4]$

$= 25\ [8 + 49 \times 4]$

$= 25\ [8 + 196]$

$= 25 \times 204$

$\Rightarrow\ S_{50} = 25 \times 204$

Hence, required arithmetic mean

$= \frac{\text{Sum of all the observations}}{\text{Total number of observations}}$

$= \frac{S_{50}}{50}$

$= \frac{25\times204}{50} = 102.$

106. $\Sigma(x_i - 100) = -20$

$\Rightarrow\ \Sigma x_i - 100n = -20$

$\Rightarrow\ y - 100n = -20$ ...(*i*)

Again, $\Sigma(x_i - 92) = 140$

$\Rightarrow\ \Sigma x_i - 92n = 140$

$\Rightarrow\ y - 92n = 140$ ...(*ii*)

Solving (*i*) and (*ii*), we get,

$8n = 160$

$n = 20$

Putting the value of n in (*i*), we get,

$y - 100 \times 20 = -20$

$y = 2000 - 20$

$= 1980$

$\text{Mean} = \frac{\Sigma x_i}{n} = \frac{y}{n}$

$= \frac{1980}{20} = 99$

Hence, the mean of the values = 99.

107. We know that the sum of observations

$x_1 + x_2 + x_3 + ... + x_n = 1980$ ...(*i*)

Total number of observations

$n = 20$ ...(*ii*)

Sum of the observations $x_1, x_2, x_3, ..., x_n$ from 99

$(x_1 - 99) + (x_2 - 99) + ... + (x_n - 99)$

$\Rightarrow x_1 + x_2 + x_3 + ... + x_n - 99n$ ...(*iii*)

Putting the values of equations (*i*) and (*ii*) in (*iii*) we get,

$1980 - 99 \times 20 = 1980 - 1980 = 0$

Hence, the sum of the deviations of the same set of values measured from 99 = 0.

108. $\because\ x_1 + x_2 + x_3 + ... + x_n = 1980$ ...(*i*)

and total number of observations

$n = 20$ ...(*ii*)

Sum of deviations $x_1, x_2, x_3, ..., x_n$ from y is 180

$\Rightarrow (x_1 - y) + (x_2 - y) + ... + (x_n - y) = 180$

$\Rightarrow x_1 + x_2 + ... + x_n - n_y = 180$ ...(*iii*)

Putting the values of equations (*i*) and (*ii*) in (*iii*), we get,

$1980 - 20 \times y = 180$

$\Rightarrow\ 1980 - 180 = 20y$

$\Rightarrow\ 20y = 1800$

$\Rightarrow\ y = 90$

Hence, the value of y = 90.

109. Given, $a = 4$, $d = 3$, $n = 51$

Sum of n terms in AP = $S_n = \frac{n}{2}[2a+(n-1)d]$

$$\Rightarrow \quad S_{51} = \frac{51}{2}[2 \times 4 + (51-1) \times 3]$$

$$= \frac{51}{2}[8 + 50 \times 3]$$

$$= \frac{51}{2}[8 + 150]$$

$$= \frac{51}{2}[158]$$

$$= 51 \times 79$$

Hence, the mean of the marks

$$= \frac{\text{Sum of all the observations}}{\text{Total number of observations}}$$

$$= \frac{51 \times 79}{51} = 79.$$

110. The median of the marks

= the mean of the marks = 79.

111. The nth term of an AP

$$\Rightarrow \quad T_n = a + (n-1)d$$

$$\Rightarrow \quad T_n = 4 + (51-1) \times 3$$

$$\Rightarrow \quad T_n = 154$$

So, AP must be 4, 7, 10, ..., 151, 154

Now, sum of n terms in AP

$$\Rightarrow \quad S_n = \frac{n}{2}[2a + (n-1)d]$$

$$= \frac{51}{2}[2 \times 4 + (51-1) \times 3]$$

$$\Rightarrow \quad S_n = 4029$$

Mean = 79

Hence, sum of the deviations of the marks measured from median = $\Sigma(X - \mu)$

X = each value of the data set

μ = the mean of the data set

$= (4 - 79) + (7 - 79) + (10 - 79) + \ldots + (151 - 79) + (154 - 79)$

$= (-75) + (-72) + (-69) + \ldots + 72 + 75 = 0$

Hence, the sum of the medians measured from the median is 0.

118.

Class	f_1	Mid-value (x_i)	$f_i x_i$
0-20	17	10	170
20-40	$p + q$	30	$30(p + q)$
40-60	32	50	1600
60-80	$p - 3q$	70	$70(p - 39)$
80-100	19	90	1710
	$N = \Sigma f_i$		$\Sigma f_i x_i = 3480 + 30(p + q) + 70(p - 39)$

N = 120

Total frequency = 120

$$\Sigma f_i = 68 + 2p - 2q = 120$$

$$\Rightarrow \quad 2p - 2q = 52$$

$$\Rightarrow \quad p - q = 26 \quad \ldots(i)$$

$$\text{Mean} = \bar{X} = \frac{\Sigma f_i x_i}{N}$$

$$= \frac{3480 + 30p + 30q + 70p - 210q}{120}$$

$$50 = \frac{3480 + 100p - 180q}{120}$$

$$\Rightarrow \quad 100p - 180q = 6000 - 3480 = 2520$$

$$\Rightarrow \quad 5p - 9q = 126 \quad \ldots(ii)$$

From (i) and (ii)

$$\Rightarrow 5p - 9(p - 26) = 126$$

$$\Rightarrow 5p - 9p + 234 = 126$$

$$\Rightarrow \quad -4p = 126 - 234 = -108$$

$$\Rightarrow \quad p = 27.$$

119. Putting the value of p in (i)

$$27 - 9 = 26$$

$$\Rightarrow \quad 9 = 27 - 26$$

$$\Rightarrow \quad 9 = 1$$

120. If the frequency of each class is double then, mean would be same

Hence, mean = 50.

Previous Papers (Solved)

NATIONAL DEFENCE ACADEMY & NAVAL ACADEMY

NDA & NA – Entrance Exam, 2021 (II)

PAPER I : GENERAL ABILITY TEST

PART A : ENGLISH LANGUAGE

SPOTTING ERRORS

Directions (Qs. No. 1-10): *Each item in this section has a sentence with three parts labelled A, B and C. Read each sentence to find out whether there is any error in any part and indicate your response in the Answer Sheet against the corresponding letter i.e., A or B or C. If you find no error, your response should be indicated as D.*

1. Nursery classes (A)/ for the children (B)/ starts on April every year. (C)/ No Error (D)

2. The pollution level is very (A)/ high in our city, and/ (B) becomes a health hazard. (C)/ No Error (D)

3. India is a country of linguistic (A)/ and cultural diversity with (B)/ multiple ethnic and social groups. (C) No Error (D)

4. Why does the lapse rate (A)/ effect the tendency (B)/ of air to rise? (C)/ No Error (D)

5. The thorax is the upper part (A)/ of your body from the neck down (B)/ to the bottom of the ribs and diaphragm. (C)/ No Error (D)

6. The practical uses of astrology (A)/ have seldom been seriously (B)/ studied outside India. (C)/ No Error (D)

7. She collected (A)/ some armful medicines and (B)/ poured them down a drain. (C)/ No Error (D)

8. In many countries, the United Nations (A)/ or other internationally organised (B)/ peacekeeping forces are trying to keep the peace. (C)/ No Error (D)

9. Early cities rely on food and water (A)/ from the surrounding countryside, (B)/ but today cities often depend on distant sources. (C)/ No Error (D)

10. Climate change, whether it is (A)/ natural or human-induced, (B)/ is stressful for the people. (C)/ No Error (D)

IDIOMS AND PHRASES

Directions (Qs. No. 11-20): *Given below are some idioms/ phrases followed by four alternative meanings to each. Choose the most appropriate answer from among the options A, B, C, or D.*

11. Once-over
A. To do something quickly
B. To do something elaborately
C. To do something perforce
D. To do something for others

12. A bag of bones
A. An extremely fat person
B. An extremely thin person
C. A wealthy person
D. A healthy person

13. Muddy the waters
A. To spread dirt around
B. To make a situation easy
C. To make one's life happy
D. To make the situation complicated

14. To level with
A. To be honest
B. To be on a plain
C. To cheat someone
D. To take revenge

15. Show your hand
A. To tell people about the past
B. To tell people about the future
C. To tell people about them
D. To tell people about your plans

16. To pull up
A. To lift heavy weights
B. To check oneself
C. To shorten the distance
D. Too short of destination

17. Be out of action
A. To get punishment
B. To get reward
C. To become dysfunctional
D. To become superactive

18. Learning from the school of hard knocks
A. Learning things from experience
B. Learning things from others
C. Learning things from environment
D. Learning things through difficult experiences

19. Raise some hackles
A. To annoy
B. To make someone happy
C. To do a great task
D. To sit idle

20. A man of letters
A. An excellent artist
B. A scholar in literature
C. An outstanding sportsman
D. A known novelist

ORDERING OF WORDS IN A SENTENCE

Directions (Qs. No. 21-30): *Each of the following items in this section consists of a sentence, the parts of which have been jumbled. These parts have been labelled P, Q, R and S. Given below each sentence are four sequences namely A, B, C and D. You are required to re-arrange the jumbled parts of the sentence and mark your answer accordingly.*

21. P. symbolic of peace, and prosperity
Q. the Gupta Empire in India is
R. represented through numismatic archaeological
S. and literary evidences of multiple kinds

The correct sequence should be:
A. QPRS B. QSRP
C. PSQR D. RSQP

22. P. the transportation system so that it
Q. and not just the affluent section of society
R. provides mobility to everyone
S. there are many ways to restructure

The correct sequence should be:
A. PQRS B. RQPS
C. SPRQ D. QRPS

23. P. and accurately displays spatial
Q. relationships between landforms and water bodies
R. the globe shows Earth's spherical shape
S. and comparative distance between locations

The correct sequence should be:
A. PQRS B. RPQS
C. SPQR D. QRPS

24. P. the function of the capillaries
Q. and other material to all the cells in
R. is to take nutrients, oxygen
S. the body and to take away their waste material

The correct sequence should be:
A. PRQS B. RPQS
C. SPQR D. QRPS

25. P. like mine
Q. even to someone with
R. a tin ear
S. her singing sounded pretty melodious

The correct sequence should be:
A. PRQS B. RPQS
C. SPQR D. QRPS

26. P. the sorry state of affairs in the modern factories
Q. the Government of India
R. under the British was pro-capitalist
S. though it took some half-hearted steps to mitigate

The correct sequence should be:
A. PRQS B. QRSP
C. SPQR D. QPSR

27. P. of extreme poverty among its people
Q. economic policies was the prevalence
R. a major characteristic of British rule in India
S. and the net result of British

The correct sequence should be:
A. PRQS B. QRSP
C. RSQP D. QPSR

28. P. you can't judge
Q. very intelligent, but
R. a book by its cover
S. he doesn't look

The correct sequence should be:
A. SQPR B. QRSP
C. RSQP D. QPSR

29. P. membership and partisanship as well as
Q. can be found in the decline in party
R. evidence of a crisis in party politics
S. in the rise of anti party groups and movements

The correct sequence should be:
A. RQPS B. QRSP
C. RSQP D. QPSR

30. P. government, market and voluntary organisations
Q. mixture of contributions from
R. the provision of public goods
S. and services can be regarded as a complex

The correct sequence should be:
A. RQPS B. QRSP
C. RSQP D. QPSR

SYNONYMS

Directions (Qs. No. 31-40): *Each item in this section consists of a sentence with an underlined word followed by four options. Select the option that is* **nearest in meaning** *to the underlined word and mark your response in your Answer Sheet accordingly.*

31. He is essentially a lowbrow person.
A. coarse B. proud
C. passionate D. pathetic

32. His nostalgia is deep.
A. excitement B. longing
C. happiness D. ability

33. His truancy is detrimental.
A. loyalty B. integrity
C. honesty D. absenteeism

34. He is a maleficent person.
A. generous B. cunning
C. criminal D. friendly

35. His solemnity is celebrated.
A. greed B. desire
C. trust D. dignity

36. His bounty is limitless.
A. benevolence B. gallantry
C. nepotism D. chivalry

37. The Holocaust was experienced by millions.
A. celebration B. destruction
C. construction D. beautiful

38. His aversion is known to all.
A. hospitality B. hostility
C. humility D. humbleness

39. To be able to decipher something is wonderful.
A. decode B. encode
C. simulate D. animate

40. It is the opportune time to think about investment in the real estate sector.
A. honorary B. appropriate
C. difficult D. unsuitable

ANTONYMS

Directions (Qs. No. 41-50): *Each item in this section consists of a sentence with an underlined word followed by four options. Select the option that is* **opposite in meaning** *to the underlined word and mark your response in your Answer Sheet accordingly.*

41. His opinion is lopsided.
A. partial B. crooked
C. unequal D. balanced

42. His work is praiseworthy.
A. admirable B. condemnable
C. commendable D. creditable

43. His deeds had retrograde results.
A. progressive B. negative
C. retreating D. reverse

44. He always offers palatable solutions.
A. acceptable B. agreeable
C. unacceptable D. pleasant

45. His views on the subject are microscopic.
A. broad-based B. minute
C. precise D. fine

46. He is always obdurate in his behaviour towards other people.
A. flexible B. callous
C. insensible D. obnoxious

47. Mohan always had profound respect for Sohan.
A. deep B. extreme
C. sincere D. superficial

48. We were living in turbulent times.
A. destructive B. unstable
C. calm D. stormy

49. Amit is a dogmatic person.
A. assertive B. amenable
C. bold D. rigid

50. Sachin is very fickle in his behaviour.
A. stable B. capricious
C. mercurial D. vacillating

PART B : GENERAL KNOWLEDGE

51. Which one from among the following planets is largest in size?
A. Earth B. Venus
C. Mars D. Mercury

52. Match List-I with List-II and select the correct answer using the code given below the lists:

List-I (Place)	List-II (Feature)
(*a*) Mumbai	(*i*) Queen of the Arabian Sea
(*b*) Visakhapatnam	(*ii*) Biggest port of India
(*c*) Chennai	(*iii*) Land-locked harbour
(*d*) Kochi	(*iv*) Oldest port on the Eastern Coast

Codes:

	(*a*)	(*b*)	(*c*)	(*d*)
A.	(*ii*)	(*iv*)	(*iii*)	(*i*)
B.	(*ii*)	(*iii*)	(*iv*)	(*i*)
C.	(*i*)	(*iii*)	(*iv*)	(*ii*)
D.	(*i*)	(*iv*)	(*iii*)	(*ii*)

53. Which one of the following is a crater lake in India?
A. Lonar Lake B. Sambhar Lake
C. Chilika Lake D. Vembanad Lake

54. Fine-grained bed of ephemeral lake in a desert is also known as:
A. Playa B. Oasis
C. Drumlin D. Natural levee

55. Which one of the following factors does ***not*** affect the distribution of groundwater?
A. Amount of precipitation
B. Rate of evaporation
C. Ability of the ground surface to allow water to infiltrate into the groundwater system
D. Distance from the sea

56. The Constitution (35th Amendment) Act of 1974 is related to which one of the following States?
A. Mizoram B. Sikkim
C. Nagaland D. Arunachal Pradesh

57. Which one of the following best describes the electoral system of India?
A. First-Past-the-Post System
B. Proportional Representation
C. Mixed System
D. General Ticket

58. Which one of the following is a non-justiciable right?
A. Right to adequate livelihood
B. Right against exploitation
C. Right of accused
D. Right to life and personal liberty

59. Which one of the following is ***not*** a writ ?
A. Mandamus B. Habeas Corpus
C. Certiorari D. Severability

60. Which one of the following is ***not*** a part of Fundamental Rights?
A. Right to education
B. Right to establish educational institutions by minorities
C. Right to be conferred with titles
D. Right against untouchability

61. Which one of the following is ***not*** a function of the Constitution of India?
A. To ensure participation of good people in politics
B. To guarantee a set of rights to citizens
C. To define the power of the different organs of government
D. To create conditions for a just society

62. Which one of the following statements about biodiversity is ***not*** correct?
A. The term 'biodiversity' was coined by Walter G. Rosen in 1986.
B. The term 'biodiversity hotspots' was coined by Norman Myers in 1988.
C. The regions having richest biodiversity are called 'biodiversity hotspots'.
D. More than 100 hotspots of biodiversity are identified in the world.

63. The Earth's atmosphere is mainly heated by which one of the following?
A. Short wave solar radiation
B. Reflected solar radiation
C. Long wave terrestrial radiation
D. Scattered solar radiation

64. Which one of the following is the correct sequence of layers as we move from the Earth's surface upwards?
A. Troposphere, Stratosphere, Thermosphere, Mesosphere
B. Troposphere, Stratosphere, Mesosphere, Thermosphere
C. Thermosphere, Mesosphere, Stratosphere, Troposphere
D. Stratosphere, Mesosphere, Troposphere, Thermosphere

65. Which one of the following is ***not*** a soil forming factor?
A. Parent material B. Topography
C. Climate D. Human habitation

66. Which of the following best describes the Lithosphere?
A. Upper and lower mantle
B. Crust and core
C. Crust and upper mantle
D. Lower mantle and core

67. Which one of the following countries has the maximum time difference from Greenwich Mean Time (GMT)?
A. India B. Nepal
C. Sri Lanka D. Bhutan

68. Which of the following is ***not*** a feature of the Constitution of India?
A. It provides a set of basic rules.
B. It specifies the power of the Government.
C. It is the supreme law of the land.
D. It specifies the supremacy of the judiciary.

69. Which one of the following statements about the Attorney General of India is ***not*** correct?
A. He has the right of audience only in the Supreme Court of India.
B. He shall receive such remuneration as the President may determine.
C. He shall be qualified to be appointed as a Judge of the Supreme Court.
D. He shall give advice to the Government of India on all legal matters.

70. Who among the following described the Directive Principles of State Policy as the novel feature of the Constitution of India?

A. Jawaharlal Nehru B. Rajendra Prasad
C. S.N. Mukherjee D. B.R. Ambedkar

71. Which of the following statements about the Indian Councils Act of 1861 is/are correct?

1. It enlarged the Governor General's Council for the purpose of making laws.
2. The Governor General was not authorised to' increase the number of members.

Select the correct answer using the code given below:

A. 1 only B. 2 only
C. Both 1 and 2 D. Neither 1 nor 2

72. Which one of the following statements about *Tattvabodhini Patrika* is correct?

A. It promoted a systematic study of India's past in the Bengali language.
B. It promoted a systematic study of India's past through Sanskrit sources.
C. It promoted a systematic study of India's past through Persian sources.
D. It promoted a systematic study of India's past through Western sources.

73. In which one of the following years did the British demarcate a large area of land as *Damin-i-koh* for settling the Santhals?

A. 1810 B. 1793
C. 1885 D. 1832

74. The Tropic of Cancer does ***not*** pass through which one of the following States?

A. Manipur B. West Bengal
C. Gujarat D. Jharkhand

75. Which of the following pairs of crop and product is/are correctly matched?

1. Food crop : Ragi
2. Cash crop : Jute
3. Plantation crop : Coconut

Select the correct answer using the code given below:

A. 1 only B. 2 and 3 only
C. 1, 2 and 3 D. 3 only

76. Which one of the following coalfields is ***not*** located in Jharkhand?

A. Jharia B. Ramgarh
C. Deogarh D. Umaria

77. Which one of the following is the longest parallel of latitude?

A. Tropic of Cancer
B. Tropic of Capricorn
C. Arctic Circle
D. Equator

78. The periodic rise and fall of ocean water in response to gravitational forces is called:

A. Current B. Waves
C. Tides D. Tsunami

79. Which of the following statements about the first Indian Factory Act passed in 1881 is/are correct?

1. The Act dealt primarily with the problem of child labour.
2. The Act laid down that children between 7 years and 12 years of age would not work for more than 9 hours a day.

Select the correct answer using the code given below:

A. 1 only B. 2 only
C. Both 1 and 2 D. Neither 1 nor 2

80. Which of the following statements about Mahatma Gandhi's anti-untouchability campaign is/are correct?

1. The All India Harijan Sevak Sangh was founded for this purpose.
2. The campaign was to root out untouchability, since it did not enjoy the sanction of the Hindu shastras.

Select the correct answer using the code given below:

A. 1 only B. 2 only
C. Both 1 and 2 D. Neither 1 nor 2

81. The founders of the *Paramhansa Mandali* founded in Maharashtra believed in which one of the following?

A. Social distancing along caste lines
B. Glorification of caste system
C. Forbidding widow remarriage
D. One God and in breaking caste rules

82. Which one of the following statements about the *ishtahars* issued during the Revolt of 1857 is correct?

A. They glorified the Muslim rule in India.
B. They glorified the co-existence of different communities under the Mughal Empire.
C. They glorified the message of Islam.
D. They glorified the role of Queen Victoria.

83. During the Industrial Revolution, who among the following designed the 'flying shuttle loom'?

A. Samuel Crompton
B. Edmund Cartwright
C. John Kay
D. Richard Arkwright

84. Match List-I with List-II and select the correct answer using the code given below the lists:

List-I (Dam)	**List-II (State)**
(*a*) Hirakud	(*i*) Gujarat
(*b*) Panchet	(*ii*) Bihar
(*c*) Kosi	(*iii*) Odisha
(*d*) Ukai	(*iv*) Jharkhand

Codes:

	(a)	(b)	(c)	(d)
A.	(iii)	(iv)	(ii)	(i)
B.	(iii)	(ii)	(iv)	(i)
C.	(i)	(ii)	(iv)	(iii)
D.	(i)	(iv)	(ii)	(iii)

85. Which one of the following features is the result of erosion and deposition work of a river?
A. Pothole B. Oxbow lake
C. Levee D. Rapid

86. Which one of the following is ***not*** a feature of agriculture in India?
A. Subsistence agriculture
B. Pressure of population on agriculture
C. Dependence upon Monsoon
D. Predominance of cash crops

87. Which one of the following is ***not*** a specified Sub-Mission of the National Livestock Mission?
A. Livestock development
B. Pig development in north-western region
C. Fodder and feed development
D. Skill development, technology transfer and extension

88. Who among the following wrote the famous text *'A Discourse on Political Economy'*?
A. Montesquieu B. Voltaire
C. Rousseau D. Adam Smith

89. Which of the following statements about the resolution adopted in the Karachi session of the Indian National Congress with regard to fundamental rights and economic policy is/are correct?
1. It was opposed by Ambalal Sarabhai.
2. Its 20 points included demands for civil liberties and adult suffrage.

Select the correct answer using the code given below:
A. 1 only B. 2 only
C. Both 1 and 2 D. Neither 1 nor 2

90. Which of the following statements about the Law Commission headed by Lord Macaulay is/are correct?
1. It attempted to codify the laws.
2. It was opposed to uniform system of Courts.

Select the correct answer using the code given below:
A. 1 only
B. 2 only
C. Both 1 and 2
D. Neither 1 nor 2

91. Dingko Singh, an Asian Games gold medallist, who died recently, was associated with which one of the following games?
A. Swimming B. Boxing
C. Archery D. Gymnastics

92. Who among the following is the lone Indian Cricketer included in the ICC Hall of Fame special inductions to mark the inaugural ICC World Test Championship Final?
A. Dilip Vengsarkar B. Ravi Shastri
C. Mohinder Amarnath D. Vinoo Mankad

93. Which one of the following nations is not a permanent member of G7?
A. India B. Canada
C. France D. Italy

94. Operation Olivia, an initiative to protect Olive Ridley turtles, is undertaken by:
A. Indian Navy
B. Indian Coast Guard
C. Ministry of Environment, Forest and Climate Change
D. Ministry of Earth Sciences

95. Who among the following is the winner of the French Open 2021 Men's Singles Final?
A. Novak Djokovic B. Rafael Nadal
C. Stefanos Tsitsipas D. Daniil Medvedev

96. Economist Rebeca Grynspan, who recently became the first woman to be appointed as the head of the United Nations Conference on Trade and Development (UNCTAD), hails from:
A. Germany B. Poland
C. Costa Rica D. Mexico

97. 'Belt and Road Initiative' is a foreign policy initiative of:
A. China
B. United States of America
C. Canada
D. Japan

98. Which one of the following is the theme of the International Day of Yoga 2021?
A. Yoga at home and yoga with family
B. Yoga for climate action
C. Yoga for well-being
D. Yoga for peace

99. Kenneth Kaunda, who died recently at the age of 97, was the former president of:
A. Brazil B. Mexico
C. Zambia D. South Sudan

100. The maiden Indian Navy - European Union Naval Force (IN-EUNAVFOR) Exercise (2021) was conducted in:
A. Gulf of Mannar B. Gulf of Aden
C. Gulf of Khambhat D. Gulf of Aqaba

101. The pH value of Milk of Magnesia is approximately:
A. Zero B. 7
C. 10 D. 14

102. Which one of the following compounds is used in 'black and white' photography?
A. AgF B. AgBr
C. AgCl D. Ag_2SO_4

103. What is the number of water molecules present in a Ferrous Sulphate crystal?
A. 1 B. 3
C. 5 D. 7

104. What is the colour of the precipitate obtained by passing CO_2 gas through lime water?
A. Green B. Blue
C. White D. Brown

105. Which one of the following pairs of elements is liquid at room temperature and at normal pressure?
A. Gallium and Bromine B. Mercury and Bromine
C. Gallium and Mercury D. Gallium and Caesium

106. Which one of the following methods can be used to separate anthracene from a mixture of salt and anthracene?
A. Distillation B. Sublimation
C. Evaporation D. Chromatography

107. Shoots of plant show upward movement and it can be designated to be:
A. Negatively phototropic
B. Positively chemotropic
C. Positively hydrotropic
D. Negatively geotropic

108. Which one of the following statements about the process of photosynthesis is correct?
A. Chemical energy is converted into light energy.
B. Carbon dioxide is oxidised to form carbohydrate.
C. Water molecule splits into hydrogen and oxygen.
D. Light energy is directly used to split water.

109. How are evergreen plants with woody stems having naked seed classified?
A. Angiosperms B. Monocotyledons
C. Pteridophytes D. Gymnosperms

110. Which one of the following tissues is known as basic packing tissue and found in xylem and phloem?
A. Collenchyma B. Parenchyma
C. Sclerenchyma D. Vessels

111. Girth of stem of a plant increases due to division of cells in:
A. apical meristem only.
B. lateral meristem only.
C. apical and intercalary meristem.
D. both apical and lateral meristem.

112. Different varieties of the same gene are called:
A. Genotypes B. Sib pairs
C. Alleles D. Isomers

113. Which one of the following viruses used to be responsible for highly infectious disease Smallpox?
A. Adenovirus B. Variola virus
C. Aichi virus D. Coxsackie virus

114. Buoyancy is a/an:
A. upward pressure B. downward pressure
C. downward force D. upward force

115. Weight and mass of an object are defined with Newton's laws of motion. Which among the following is true?
A. Weight is a constant of proportionality.
B. Mass is a constant of proportionality.
C. Mass is not a constant of proportionality.
D. Weight is a universal constant.

116. Fundamental laws of physics require:
A. conservation of energy and non-conservation of charge.
B. conservation of charge and non-conservation of linear momentum.
C. conservation of charge and non-conservation of energy.
D. conservation of energy, momentum and charge.

117. Work is said to be one Joule when a force of:
A. 4 N moves an object by 25 cm.
B. 2 N moves an object by 1 m.
C. 1 N moves an object by 1 cm.
D. 1 N moves an object by 50 cm.

118. A uniform motion of a car along a circular path experiences:
A. a change in speed due to a change in its direction of motion.
B. a change in velocity due to a change in its direction of motion.
C. a change in momentum due to no change in its direction of motion.
D. a constant momentum due to a change in its direction of motion.

119. Three equal resistors are connected in parallel configuration in a closed electrical circuit. Then the total resistance in the circuit becomes
A. one-third of the individual resistance.
B. two-third of the individual resistance.
C. equal to the individual resistance.
D. three times of the individual resistance.

120. Rutherford's alpha-particle (α) scattering experiment was responsible for the discovery of which one of the following?
A. Electron B. Proton
C. Atomic Nucleus D. Neutron

121. What is the maximum number of electrons in the M-Shell?
A. 6 B. 8
C. 18 D. 32

122. Chlorine occurs in nature in two isotopic forms of masses 35 u and 37 u in the ratio of 3 : 1 respectively. What is the average atomic mass of the Chlorine atom?
A. 36.1 u B. 35.5 u
C. 36.5 u D. 35.1 u

123. Which one of the following elements' isotopes is used in the treatment of cancer?
A. Iodine B. Sodium
C. Cobalt D. Uranium

124. To protect steel and iron from rusting, a thin layer of which one of the following metals is applied?
A. Magnesium B. Zinc
C. Aluminium D. Lead

125. Cinnabar is an ore of which one of the following?
A. Copper B. Zinc
C. Mercury D. Manganese

126. Imagine a current-carrying straight conductor with magnetic field of lines in anti-clockwise direction. Then the direction of current is determined by
A. the Right-Hand Thumb rule and it would be in the downward direction.
B. the Left-Hand Thumb rule and it would be in the downward direction.
C. the Right-Hand Thumb rule and it would be in the upward direction.
D. the Left-Hand Thumb rule and it would be in the upward direction.

127. The device used to produce electric current is known as:
A. motor B. generator
C. ammeter D. galvanometer

128. Myopia is a defect in human vision where an image of a:
A. nearby object is focused beyond the retina.
B. nearby object is focused before the retina.
C. distant object is focused before the retina.
D. distant object is focused beyond the retina.

129. Tyndall effect is a phenomenon of:
A. scattering of light by the colloidal particles.
B. refraction of light by the colloidal particles.
C. dispersion of light by dust particles.
D. refraction of light by dust particles.

130. Twinkling of stars is primarily due to the atmospheric:
A. refraction B. reflection
C. polarization D. dispersion

131. Cornea in human eye:
A. is a light sensitive screen.
B. is a muscular diaphragm.
C. contains blood vessels.
D. is composed of proteins and cells.

132. Power of a lens of focal length 25 cm is:
A. +2.5 Dioptre B. +3 Dioptre
C. +4 Dioptre D. +5 Dioptre

133. What is the total number of chambers in the stomach of domestic animals like cattle, buffalo, goat and sheep?
A. Four B. Two
C. One D. Three

134. Intestinal bacteria are main source of which one of the following vitamins?
A. Vitamin E B. Vitamin C
C. Vitamin B_{12} D. Vitamin A

135. Which one of the following hormones is responsible for the development of female sexual characters?
A. Prolactin B. Estrogen
C. Oxytocin D. Progesterone

136. Spherical mirror formula relating an object distance 'u', image distance 'v' and focal length of mirror 'f' may be applied to a plane mirror when:
A. focal length goes to infinity.
B. focal length goes to zero.
C. image distance goes to zero.
D. image distance goes to infinity.

137. Nuclear energy is generated by:
A. nuclear fission and its expression was proposed by Einstein.
B. nuclear fission and its expression was proposed by Rutherford.
C. nuclear fusion and its expression was proposed by Bohr.
D. nuclear fusion and its expression was proposed by Heisenberg.

138. Reverberation is a phenomenon associated with a:
A. multiple refraction of sound.
B. multiple reflection of sound.
C. single refraction of sound.
D. single reflection of sound.

139. Which among the following is true for propagation of sound waves?
A. Sound can travel in vacuum and it is a transverse wave in air.
B. Sound cannot travel in vacuum and it is a longitudinal wave in air.
C. Sound can travel in vacuum and it is a longitudinal wave in air.
D. Sound cannot travel in vacuum and it is a transverse wave in air.

140. A tennis ball is thrown in the vertically upward direction and the ball attains a maximum height of 20 m. The ball was thrown approximately with an upward velocity of:
A. 8 m/s B. 12 m/s
C. 16 m/s D. 20 m/s

141. An object of mass 2000 g possesses 100 J kinetic energy. The object must be moving with a speed of:
A. 10.0 m/s B. 11.1 m/s
C. 11.2 m/s D. 12.1 m/s

142. Which one of the following ions is *not* iso-electronic with F^-?

A. O^{2-} B. Na^+
C. Ne D. N^-

143. What is the total number of covalent bonds in methanol?

A. 3 B. 4
C. 5 D. 6

144. Which one of the following is the chemical formula of Plaster of Paris?

A. $CaSO_4 . \frac{1}{2}H_2O$ B. $CaSO_4 . 2\ H_2O$
C. $CaSO_4 . 5\ H_2O$ D. $CaSO_4 . 4\ H_2O$

145. The unit of the ratio between thrust and impulse is same as that of:

A. frequency B. speed
C. wavelength D. acceleration

146. Which one of the following figures correctly shows the path of a ray of light through a glass prism?

A. 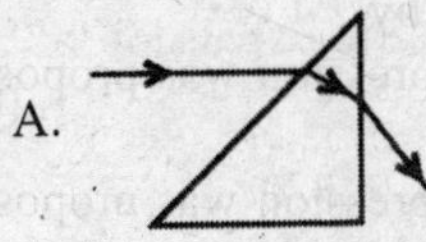
B. 
C. 
D. 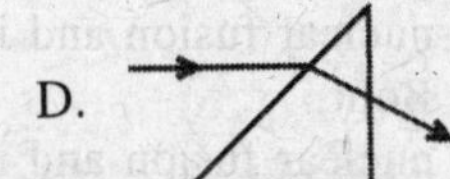

147. When a light beam falls on a triangular glass prism, a band of colours is obtained. Which one of the following statements is correct in this regard?

A. Red light bends the most, as the refractive index of glass for red light is greatest.
B. Red light bends the most, as the refractive index of glass for red light is lowest.
C. Violet light bends the most, as the refractive index of glass for violet light is greatest.
D. Violet light bends the most, as the refractive index of glass for violet light is lowest.

148. The image of an object formed by a plane mirror is:

A. erect, real and larger.
B. erect, virtual and same size.
C. inverted, virtual and same size.
D. inverted, real and smaller.

149. Which one of the following is *not* a conservative force?

A. Frictional force
B. Electric force
C. Gravitational force
D. Spring force

150. A negative work is done when an applied force F and the corresponding displacement S are:

A. perpendicular to each other.
B. parallel to each other.
C. anti-parallel to each other.
D. equal in magnitude.

PAPER II : MATHEMATICS

1. If $x^2 + x + 1 = 0$, then what is the value of $x^{199} + x^{200} + x^{201}$?

A. –1 B. 0
C. 1 D. 3

2. If x, y, z are in GP, then which of the following is/are correct?

1. $\ln(3x)$, $\ln(3y)$, $\ln(3z)$ are in AP
2. $xyz + \ln(x)$, $xyz + \ln(y)$, $xyz + \ln(z)$ are in HP.

Select the correct answer using the code given below.

A. 1 only B. 2 only
C. Both 1 and 2 D. Neither 1 nor 2

3. If $\log_{10}2$, $\log_{10}(2^x - 1)$, $\log_{10}(2^x + 3)$ are in AP, then what is x equal to?

A. 0 B. 1
C. $\log_2 5$ D. $\log_5 2$

4. Let S = {2, 3, 4, 5, 6, 7, 9}. How many different 3-digit numbers (with all digits different) from S can be made which are less than 500?

A. 30 B. 49
C. 90 D. 147

5. If p = (1111 ... up to n digits), then what is the value of $9p^2 + p$?

A. $10^n\ p$ B. $2p\ .\ 10^n$
C. $10^n\ p - 1$ D. $10^n\ p + 1$

6. The quadratic equation $3x^2 - (k^2 + 5k)\ x + 3k^2 - 5k = 0$ has real roots of equal magnitude and opposite sign. Which one of the following is correct?

A. $0 < k < \frac{5}{3}$ B. $0 < k < \frac{3}{5}$ only
C. $\frac{3}{5} < k < \frac{5}{3}$ D. No such value of k exist

7. If $a_n = n(n!)$, then what is $a_1 + a_2 + a_3 + ... + a_{10}$ equal to?

A. 10! – 1 B. 11! + 1
C. 10! + 1 D. 11! – 1

8. If p and q are the non-zero roots of the equation $x^2 + px + q = 0$, then how many possible values can q have?

A. Nil B. One
C. Two D. Three

9. If $\Delta = \begin{vmatrix} a & b & c \\ d & e & f \\ g & h & i \end{vmatrix}$ then what is $\begin{vmatrix} 3d+5g & 4a+7g & 6g \\ 3e+5h & 4b+7h & 6h \\ 3f+5i & 4c+7i & 6i \end{vmatrix}$ equal to?

A. Δ B. 7Δ
C. 72Δ D. -72Δ

10. If $\frac{1}{b+c}, \frac{1}{c+a}, \frac{1}{a+b}$ are in HP, then which of the following is/are correct?

1. a, b, c are in AP
2. $(b + c)^2, (c + a)^2, (a + b)^2$ are in GP

Select the correct answer using the code given below.

A. 1 only B. 2 only
C. Both 1 and 2 D. Neither 1 nor 2

11. If $A = \begin{bmatrix} 1 & a \\ 0 & 1 \end{bmatrix}$ where $a \in \mathbb{N}$,

then what is $A^{100} - A^{50} - 2A^{25}$ equal to?

A. –2I B. –I
C. 2I D. I

where I is the identity matrix.

12. If $\begin{vmatrix} a & -b & a-b-c \\ -a & b & -a+b-c \\ -a & -b & -a-b+c \end{vmatrix} - kabc = 0 \quad (a \neq 0, b \neq 0, c \neq 0)$

then what is the value of k?

A. –4 B. –2
C. 2 D. 4

13. What is $\sum_{n=1}^{8n+7} i^n$ equal to, where $i = \sqrt{-1}$?

A. –1 B. 1
C. i D. $-i$

14. If $z = x + iy$, where $i = \sqrt{-1}$, then what does the equation $z\bar{z} + |z|^2 + 4(z + \bar{z}) - 48 = 0$ represent?

A. Straight line B. Parabola
C. Circle D. Pair of straight lines

15. Which one of the following is a square root of $2a + 2\sqrt{a^2 + b^2}$, where $a, b \in \mathbb{R}$?

A. $\sqrt{a+ib} + \sqrt{a-ib}$ B. $\sqrt{a+ib} - \sqrt{a-ib}$
C. $2a + ib$ D. $2a - ib$

where $i = \sqrt{-1}$.

16. If $\sin \theta$ and $\cos \theta$ are the roots of the equation $ax^2 + bx + c = 0$, then which one of the following is correct?

A. $a^2 + b^2 - 2ac = 0$ B. $-a^2 + b^2 + 2ac = 0$
C. $a^2 - b^2 + 2ac = 0$ D. $a^2 + b^2 + 2ac = 0$

17. If C(n, 4), C(n, 5) and C(n, 6) are in AP, then what is the value of n?

A. 7 B. 8
C. 9 D. 10

18. How many 4-letter words (with or without meaning) containing two vowels can be constructed using only the letters (without repetition) of the word 'LUCKNOW'?

A. 240 B. 200
C. 150 D. 120

19. Suppose 20 distinct points are placed randomly on a circle. Which of the following statements is/are correct?

1. The number of straight lines that can be drawn by joining any two of these points is 380.
2. The number of triangles that can be drawn by joining any three of these points is 1140.

Select the correct answer using the code given below:

A. 1 only B. 2 only
C. Both 1 and 2 D. Neither 1 nor 2

20. How many terms are there in the expansion of

$$\left(\frac{a^2}{b^2} + \frac{b^2}{a^2} + 2\right)^{21}$$ where $a \neq 0$, $b \neq 0$?

A. 21 B. 22
C. 42 D. 43

21. For what values of k is the system of equations

$$2k^2x + 3y - 1 = 0,\ 7x - 2y + 3 = 0,$$
$$6kx + y + 1 = 0$$

consistent?

A. $\frac{3 \pm \sqrt{11}}{10}$ B. $\frac{21 \pm \sqrt{161}}{10}$

C. $\frac{3 \pm \sqrt{7}}{10}$ D. $\frac{4 \pm \sqrt{11}}{10}$

22. The inverse of a matrix A is given by

$$\begin{bmatrix} -2 & 1 \\ \frac{3}{2} & -\frac{1}{2} \end{bmatrix}$$

What is A equal to?

A. $\begin{bmatrix} 1 & 2 \\ 3 & 4 \end{bmatrix}$ B. $\begin{bmatrix} 1 & -2 \\ -3 & 4 \end{bmatrix}$

C. $\begin{bmatrix} 1 & 2 \\ 3 & -4 \end{bmatrix}$ D. $\begin{bmatrix} -1 & 2 \\ 3 & 4 \end{bmatrix}$

23. What is the period of the function $f(x) = \ln(2 + \sin^2 x)$?

A. $\frac{\pi}{2}$ B. π
C. 2π D. 3π

24. If $\sin(A + B) = 1$ and $2\sin(A - B) = 1$, where $0 < A, B < \frac{\pi}{2}$, then what is $\tan A : \tan B$ equal to?

A. 1 : 2 B. 2 : 1
C. 1 : 3 D. 3 : 1

25. Consider a regular polygon with 10 sides. What is the number of triangles that can be formed by joining the vertices which have no common side with any of the sides of the polygon?

A. 25 B. 50
C. 75 D. 100

26. Consider all the real roots of the equation $x^4 - 10x^2 + 9 = 0$. What is the sum of the absolute values of the roots?

A. 4 B. 6
C. 8 D. 10

27. Consider the expansion of $(1 + x)^n$. Let p, q, r and s be the coefficients of first, second, nth and $(n + 1)$th terms respectively. What is $(ps + qr)$ equal to?

A. $1 + 2n$ B. $1 + 2n^2$
C. $1 + n^2$ D. $1 + 4n$

28. Let $\sin^{-1} x + \sin^{-1} y + \sin^{-1} z = \frac{3\pi}{2}$ for $0 \le x, y, z \le 1$.

What is the value of $x^{1000} + y^{1001} + z^{1002}$?

A. 0 B. 1
C. 3 D. 6

29. Let $\sin x + \sin y = \cos x + \cos y$ for all $x, y \in \mathbb{R}$. What is $\tan\left(\frac{x}{2} + \frac{y}{2}\right)$ equal to?

A. 1 B. 2
C. $\sqrt{2}$ D. $2\sqrt{2}$

30. Let $A = \begin{bmatrix} 0 & 2 \\ -2 & 0 \end{bmatrix}$ and $(mI + nA)^2 = A$ where m, n are positive real numbers and I is the identity matrix. What is $(m + n)$ equal to?

A. 0 B. $\frac{1}{2}$
C. 1 D. $\frac{3}{2}$

31. What is the value of the following:

$$\cot\left[\sin^{-1}\frac{3}{5} + \cot^{-1}\frac{3}{2}\right]$$

A. $\frac{6}{17}$ B. $\frac{7}{16}$
C. $\frac{16}{7}$ D. $\frac{17}{6}$

32. Let $4\sin^2 x = 3$, where $0 \le x \le \pi$. What is $\tan 3x$ equal to?

A. –2 B. –1
C. 0 D. 1

33. Let p, q and 3 be respectively the first, third and fifth terms of an AP. Let d be the common difference. If the product (pq) is minimum, then what is the value of d?

A. 1 B. $\frac{3}{8}$
C. $\frac{9}{8}$ D. $\frac{9}{4}$

34. Consider the following statements in respect of the roots of the equation $x^3 - 8 = 0$:

1. The roots are non-collinear.
2. The roots lie on a circle of unit radius.

Which of the above statements is/are correct?

A. 1 only
B. 2 only
C. Both 1 and 2
D. Neither 1 nor 2

35. Let the equation $\sec x \cdot \operatorname{cosec} x = p$ have a solution, where p is a positive real number. What should be the smallest value of p?

A. $\frac{1}{2}$ B. 1
C. 2 D. Minimum does not exist

36. For what value of θ, where $0 < \theta < \frac{\pi}{2}$, does $\sin\theta + \sin\theta\cos\theta$ attain maximum value?

A. $\frac{\pi}{2}$ B. $\frac{\pi}{3}$
C. $\frac{\pi}{4}$ D. $\frac{\pi}{6}$

37. Consider the following statements in respect of sets:

1. The union over intersection of sets is distributive.
2. The complement of union of two sets is equal to intersection of their complements.
3. If the difference of two sets is equal to empty set, then the two sets must be equal.

Which of the above statements are correct?

A. 1 and 2 only B. 2 and 3 only
C. 1 and 3 only D. 1, 2 and 3

38. Consider three sets X, Y and Z having 6, 5 and 4 elements respectively. All these 15 elements are distinct. Let $S = (X - Y) \cup Z$. How many proper subsets does S have?

A. 255 B. 256
C. 1023 D. 1024

39. Consider the following statements in respect of relations and functions:

1. All relations are functions but all functions are not relations.
2. A relation from A to B is a subset of Cartesian product A × B.
3. A relation in A is a subset of Cartesian product A × A.

Which of the above statements are correct?

A. 1 and 2 only B. 2 and 3 only
C. 1 and 3 only D. 1, 2 and 3

40. If $\log_{10} 2\log_2 10 + \log_{10} (10^x) = 2$, then what is the value of x?

A. 0 B. 1
C. $\log_2 10$ D. $\log_5 2$

41. Let ABC be a triangle. If cos2A + cos2B + cos2C = –1 then which one of the following is correct?

A. sin A sin B sin C = 0
B. sin A sin B cos C = 0
C. cos A sin B sin C = 0
D. cos A cos B cos C = 0

42. What is the value of the following determinant?

$$\begin{vmatrix} \cos C & \tan A & 0 \\ \sin B & 0 & -\tan A \\ 0 & \sin B & \cos C \end{vmatrix}$$

A. – 1 B. 0
C. 2 tan A sin B sin C D. – 2 tan A sin B sin C

43. Suppose set A consists of first 250 natural numbers that are multiples of 3 and set B consists of first 200 even natural numbers. How many elements does A ∪ B have?

A. 324 B. 364
C. 384 D. 400

44. Let S_k denote the sum of first k terms of an AP. What is $\frac{S_{30}}{S_{20} - S_{10}}$ equal to?

A. 1 B. 2
C. 3 D. 4

45. If the roots of the equation $4x^2 - (5k + 1)x + 5k = 0$ differ by unity, then which one of the following is a possible value of k?

A. – 3 B. – 1
C. $-\frac{1}{5}$ D. $-\frac{3}{5}$

46. Consider the digits 3, 5, 7, 9. What is the number of 5-digit numbers formed by these digits in which each of these four digits appears?

A. 240 B. 180
C. 120 D. 60

47. How many distinct matrices exist with all four entries taken from {1, 2}?

A. 16 B. 24
C. 32 D. 48

48. If $i = \sqrt{-1}$, then how many values does i^{-2n} have for different $n \in \mathbb{Z}$?

A. One B. Two
C. Four D. Infinite

49. If $x = \frac{a}{b-c}, y = \frac{b}{c-a}, z = \frac{c}{a-b}$ then what is the value of the following?

$$\begin{vmatrix} 1 & -x & x \\ 1 & 1 & -y \\ 1 & z & 1 \end{vmatrix}$$

A. 0 B. 1
C. abc D. $ab + bc + ca$

50. Consider the following in respect of the matrix

$$A = \begin{vmatrix} 1 & 1 & 1 \\ 1 & 1 & 1 \\ 1 & 1 & 1 \end{vmatrix}$$

1. Inverse of A does not exist
2. $A^3 = A$
3. $3A = A^2$

Which of the above are correct?

A. 1 and 2 only B. 2 and 3 only
C. 1 and 3 only D. 1, 2 and 3

Directions (Qs. No. 51 and 52): *Consider the following for the next two (02) items that follow.*

A circle is passing through the points (5, –8), (–2, 9) and (2, 1)

51. What are the coordinates of the centre of the circle?

A. (–2, –50) B. (–50, –20)
C. (–24, –58) D. (–58, –24)

52. If r is the radius of the circle, then which one of the following is correct?

A. $r < 10$ B. $10 < r < 30$
C. $30 < r < 60$ D. $r > 60$

Directions (Qs. No. 53 and 54): *Consider the following for the next two (02) items that follow.*

The two vertices of an equilateral triangle are (0, 0) and (2, 2).

53. Consider the following statements:

1. The third vertex has at least one irrational coordinate.
2. The area is irrational.

Which of the above statements is/are correct?

A. 1 only B. 2 only
C. Both 1 and 2 D. Neither 1 nor 2

54. The difference of coordinates of the third vertex is:

A. 0 B. $\sqrt{3}$

C. $2\sqrt{2}$ D. $2\sqrt{3}$

Directions (Qs. No. 55 and 56): *Consider the following for the next two (02) items that follow.*

The coordinates of three consecutive vertices of a parallelogram ABCD are A(1, 3), B(–1, 2) and C(3, 5).

55. What is the equation of the diagonal BD?

A. $2x - 3y + 2 = 0$ B. $3x - 2y + 5 = 0$
C. $2x - 3y + 8 = 0$ D. $3x - 2y - 5 = 0$

56. What is the area of the parallelogram?

A. 1 square unit B. $\frac{3}{2}$ square unit

C. 2 square unit D. $\frac{5}{2}$ square unit

Directions (Qs. No. 57 and 58): *Consider the following for the next two (02) items that follow.*

The equations of the sides AB, BC and CA of a triangle ABC are $x - 2 = 0$, $y + 1 = 0$ and $x + 2y - 4 = 0$ respectively.

57. What is the equation of the altitude through B on AC?

A. $x - 3y + 1 = 0$ B. $x - 3y + 4 = 0$
C. $2x - y + 4 = 0$ D. $2x - y - 5 = 0$

58. What are the coordinates of circumcentre of the triangle?

A. (4, 0) B. (2, 1)
C. (0, 4) D. (2, –1)

Directions (Qs. No. 59 and 60): *Consider the following for the next two (02) items that follow.*

The two ends of the latus rectum of a parabola are (–2, 4) and (–2, –4).

59. What is the maximum number of parabolas that can be drawn through these two points as end points of latus rectum?

A. Only one B. Two
C. Four D. Infinite

60. Consider the following statements in respect of such parabolas:

1. One of the parabolas passes through the origin (0, 0).
2. The focus of one of the parabolas lies at (–2, 0).

Which of the above statements is/are correct?

A. 1 only B. 2 only
C. Both 1 and 2 D. Neither 1 nor 2

61. The locus of a point P(x, y, z) which moves in such a way that $z = 7$ is a

A. line parallel to x-axis
B. line parallel to y-axis
C. line parallel to z-axis
D. plane parallel to xy-plane

62. Consider the following statements:

1. A line in space can have infinitely many direction ratios.
2. It is possible for certain line that the sum of the squares of direction cosines can be equal to sum of its direction cosines.

Which of the above statements is/are correct?

A. 1 only B. 2 only
C. Both 1 and 2 D. Neither 1 nor 2

63. The xy-plane divides the line segment joining the points (–1, 3, 4) and (2, –5, 6)

A. internally in the ratio 2 : 3
B. internally in the ratio 3 : 2
C. externally in the ratio 2 : 3
D. externally in the ratio 2 : 1

64. The number of spheres of radius r touching the coordinate axes is:

A. 4 B. 6
C. 8 D. infinite

65. ABCDEFGH is a cuboid with base ABCD. Let A(0, 0, 0), B(12, 0, 0), C(12, 6, 0) and G(12, 6, 4) be the vertices. If α is the angle between AB and AG; β is the angle between AC and AG, then what is the value of $\cos 2\alpha + \cos 2\beta$?

A. $\frac{40}{49}$ B. $\frac{64}{49}$

C. $\frac{120}{49}$ D. $\frac{160}{49}$

66. Let $\vec{a}, \vec{b}$ and $\vec{c}$ be unit vectors such that $\vec{a} \times \vec{b}$ is perpendicular to $\vec{c}$. If θ is the angle between $\vec{a}$ and $\vec{b}$, then which of the following is/are correct?

1. $\vec{a} \times \vec{b} = \sin\theta \vec{c}$ 2. $\vec{a}.(\vec{b} \times \vec{c}) = 0$

Select the correct answer using the code given below.

A. 1 only B. 2 only
C. Both 1 and 2 D. Neither 1 nor 2

67. If $\vec{a} + 3\vec{b} = 3\hat{i} - \hat{j}$ and $2\vec{a} + \vec{b} = \hat{i} - 2\hat{j}$, then what is the angle between $\vec{a}$ and $\vec{b}$?

A. 0 B. $\frac{\pi}{6}$

C. $\frac{\pi}{3}$ D. $\frac{\pi}{2}$

68. If $(\vec{a} + \vec{b})$ is perpendicular to $\vec{a}$ and magnitude of $\vec{b}$ is twice that of $\vec{a}$, then what is the value of $(4\vec{a} + \vec{b}).\vec{b}$ equal to?

A. 0 B. 1
C. $8|\vec{a}|^2$ D. $8|\vec{b}|^2$

69. Let $\vec{a}, \vec{b}$ and $\vec{c}$ be three vectors such that $\vec{a}, \vec{b}$ and $\vec{c}$ are coplanar. Which of the following is/are correct?

1. $(\vec{a} \times \vec{b}) \times \vec{c}$ is coplanar with $\vec{a}$ and $\vec{b}$
2. $(\vec{a} \times \vec{b}) \times \vec{c}$ is perpendicular to $\vec{a} \times \vec{b}$

Select the correct answer using the code given below.

A. 1 only B. 2 only
C. Both 1 and 2 D. Neither 1 nor 2

70. If the position vectors of A and B are $\left(\sqrt{2}-1\right)\hat{i} - \hat{j}$ and $i + \left(\sqrt{2}+1\right)\hat{j}$ respectively, then what is the magnitude of $\overline{AB}$?

A. $2\sqrt{2}$ B. $3\sqrt{2}$
C. $2\sqrt{3}$ D. $3\sqrt{3}$

71. If $y = (1 + x)(1 + x^2)(1 + x^4)(1 + x^8)(1 + x^{16})$ then what is $\frac{dy}{dx}$ at $x = 0$ equal to?

A. 0 B. 1
C. 2 D. 4

72. If $y = \cos x \,.\, \cos 4x \,.\, \cos 8x$, then what is $\frac{1}{y}\frac{dy}{dx}$ at $x = \frac{\pi}{4}$ equal to?

A. – 1 B. 0
C. 1 D. 3

73. Let $f(x)$ be a polynomial function such that $f \circ f(x) = x^4$. What is $f'(1)$ equal to?

A. 0 B. 1
C. 2 D. 4

74. What is $\lim_{n \to \infty} \frac{a^n + b^n}{a^n - b^n}$ where $a > b > 1$, equal to?

A. –1 B. 0
C. 1 D. Limit does not exist

75. Let $f(x)\begin{cases} 1+\frac{x}{2k}, & 0 < x < 2 \\ kx, & 2 \le x < 4 \end{cases}$

If $\lim_{x \to 2} f(x)$ exists, then what is the value of k?

A. – 2 B. – 1
C. 0 D. 1

76. Consider the following statements in respect of $f(x) = |x| - 1$:

1. $f(x)$ is continuous at $x = 1$
2. $f(x)$ is differentiable at $x = 0$.

Which of the above statements is/are correct?

A. 1 only B. 2 only
C. Both 1 and 2 D. Neither 1 nor 2

77. If $f(x) = \frac{[x]}{|x|}, x \neq 0$, where $[\cdot]$ denotes the greatest integer function, then what is the right-hand limit of $f(x)$ at $x = 1$?

A. –1
B. 0
C. 1
D. Right-hand limit of $f(x)$ at $x = 1$ does not exist

78. Consider the following statements in respect of the function $f(x) = \sin\left(\frac{1}{x^2}\right), x \neq 0$:

1. It is continuous at $x = 0$, if $f(0) = 0$.
2. It is continuous at $x = \frac{2}{\sqrt{\pi}}$.

Which of the above statements is/are correct?

A. 1 only B. 2 only
C. Both 1 and 2 D. Neither 1 nor 2

79. What is the range of the function $f(x) = 1 - \sin x$ defined on entire real line?

A. (0, 2) B. [0, 2]
C. (–1, 1) D. [–1, 1]

80. What is the slope of the tangent of $y = \cos^{-1}(\cos x)$ at $x = -\frac{\pi}{4}$?

A. –1 B. 0
C. 1 D. 2

81. What is the integral of $f(x) = 1 + x^2 + x^4$ with respect to x^2?

A. $x + \frac{x^3}{3} + \frac{x^5}{5} + C$ B. $\frac{x^3}{3} + \frac{x^5}{5} + C$
C. $x^2 + \frac{x^4}{4} + \frac{x^6}{6} + C$ D. $x^2 + \frac{x^4}{2} + \frac{x^6}{3} + C$

82. Consider the following statements in respect of the function $f(x) = x^2 + 1$ in the interval (1, 2):

1. The maximum value of the function is 5.
2. The minimum value of the function is 2.

Which of the above statements is/are correct?

A. 1 only B. 2 only
C. Both 1 and 2 D. Neither 1 nor 2

83. If $f(x)$ satisfies $f(1) = f(4)$, then what is $\int_1^4 f'(x)dx$ equal to?

A. –1 B. 0
C. 1 D. 2

84. What is $\int_0^{\frac{\pi}{2}} e^{\ln(\cos x)} dx$ equal to?

A. –1 B. 0
C. 1 D. 2

85. If $\int \sqrt{1-\sin 2x}\, dx = A \sin x + B \cos x + C$, where $0 < x < \frac{\pi}{4}$, then which one of the following is correct?

A. A + B = 0 B. A + B – 2 = 0
C. A + B + 2 = 0 D. A + B – 1 = 0

86. What is the order of the differential equation of all ellipses whose axes are along the coordinate axes?

A. 1 B. 2
C. 3 D. 4

87. What is the degree of the differential equation of all circles touching both the coordinate axes in the first quadrant?

A. 1 B. 2
C. 3 D. 4

88. What is the differential equation of $y = A - \frac{B}{x}$?

A. $xy_2 + y_1 = 0$ B. $xy_2 + 2y_1 = 0$
C. $xy_2 - 2y_1 = 0$ D. $2xy_2 + y_1 = 0$

89. What is $\int_0^{\pi} \ln\left(\tan\frac{x}{2}\right) dx$ equal to?

A. 0 B. $\frac{1}{2}$
C. 1 D. 2

90. Where does the tangent to the curve $y = e^x$ at the point (0, 1) meet x-axis?

A. (1, 0) B. (–1, 0)
C. (2, 0) D. $\left(-\frac{1}{2}, 0\right)$

91. Consider the following statements in respect of the function $f(x) = x + \frac{1}{x}$:

1. The local maximum value of $f(x)$ is less than its local minimum value.
2. The local maximum value of $f(x)$ occurs at $x = 1$.

Which of the above statements is/are correct?

A. 1 only B. 2 only
C. Both 1 and 2 D. Neither 1 nor 2

92. What is the maximum area of a rectangle that can be inscribed in a circle of radius 2 units?

A. 4 square units B. 6 square units
C. 8 square units D. 16 square units

93. What is $\int \frac{dx}{x(x^2+1)}$ equal to?

A. $\frac{1}{2}\ln\left(\frac{x^2}{x^2+1}\right)+C$ B. $\ln\left(\frac{x^2}{x^2+1}\right)+C$
C. $\frac{3}{2}\ln\left(\frac{x^2}{x^2+1}\right)+C$ D. $\frac{1}{2}\ln\left(\frac{x^2+1}{x^2}\right)+C$

94. What is the derivative of e^{e^x} with respect to e^x?

A. e^{e^x} B. e^x
C. $e^{e^x} e^x$ D. ee^x

95. What is the condition that $f(x) = x^3 + x^2 + kx$ has no local extremum?

A. $4k < 1$ B. $3k > 1$
C. $3k < 1$ D. $3k \leq 1$

96. If $f(x) = 2^x$, then what is $\int_2^{10} \frac{f'(x)}{f(x)} dx$ equal to?

A. 4 ln 2 B. ln 4
C. ln 5 D. 8 ln 2

97. If $\int_{-2}^{0} f(x)dx = k$, then $\int_{-2}^{0} |f(x)|\, dx$ is:

A. less than k
B. greater than k
C. less than or equal to k
D. greater than or equal to k

98. If the function $f(x) = x^2 - kx$ is monotonically increasing in the interval $(1, \infty)$, then which one of the following is correct?

A. $k < 2$ B. $2 < k < 3$
C. $3 < k < 4$ D. $k > 4$

99. What is the area bounded by $y = [x]$, where $[\cdot]$ is the greatest integer function, the x-axis and the lines $x = -1.5$ and $x = -1.8$?

A. 0.3 square unit
B. 0.4 square unit
C. 0.6 square unit
D. 0.8 square unit

100. The tangent to the curve $x^2 = y$ at (1, 1) makes an angle θ with the positive direction of x-axis. Which one of the following is correct?

A. $\theta < \frac{\pi}{6}$ B. $\frac{\pi}{6} < \theta < \frac{\pi}{4}$
C. $\frac{\pi}{4} < \theta < \frac{\pi}{3}$ D. $\frac{\pi}{3} < \theta < \frac{\pi}{2}$

101. Consider the following relations for two events E and F:

1. $P(E \cap F) \geq P(E) + P(F) - 1$
2. $P(E \cup F) = P(E) + P(F) + (E \cap F)$
3. $P(E \cup F) \leq P(E) + P(F)$

Which of the above relations is/are correct?

A. 1 only B. 2 only
C. 1 and 3 only D. 1, 2 and 3

102. If $P(A \mid B) < P(A)$, then which one of the following is correct?

A. $P(B \mid A) < P(B)$ B. $P(B \mid A) > P(B)$
C. $P(B \mid A) = P(B)$ D. $P(B \mid A) > P(A)$

103. When the measure of central tendency is available in the form of mean, which one of the following is the most reliable and accurate measure of variability?

A. Range B. Mean deviation
C. Standard deviation D. Quartile deviation

104. A problem is given to three students A, B and C, whose probabilities of solving the problem independently are $\frac{1}{2}, \frac{3}{4}$ and p respectively. If the probability that the problem can be solved is $\frac{29}{32}$, then what is the value of p?

A. $\frac{2}{5}$ B. $\frac{2}{3}$
C. $\frac{1}{3}$ D. $\frac{1}{4}$

105. In a cricket match, a batsman hits a six 8 times out of 60 balls he plays. What is the probability that on a ball played he does not hit a six?

A. $\frac{2}{3}$ B. $\frac{1}{15}$
C. $\frac{2}{15}$ D. $\frac{13}{15}$

Directions (Qs. No. 106 and 107): *Consider the following for the next two (02) items that follow.*

Two regression lines are given as $3x - 4y + 8 = 0$ and $4x - 3y - 1 = 0$.

106. Consider the following statements:

1. The regression line of y on x is $y = \frac{3}{4}x + 2$.
2. The regression line of x on y is $x = \frac{3}{4}y + \frac{1}{4}$.

Which of the above statements is/are correct?

A. 1 only B. 2 only
C. Both 1 and 2 D. Neither 1 nor 2

107. Consider the following statements:

1. The coefficient of correlations r is $\frac{3}{4}$.
2. The means of x and y are 3 and 4 respectively.

Which of the above statements is/are correct?

A. 1 only B. 2 only
C. Both 1 and 2 D. Neither 1 nor 2

Directions (Qs. No. 108 and 109): *Consider the following for the next two (02) items that follow.*

The marks obtained by 60 students in a certain subject out of 75 are given below:

Marks	Number of students
15-20	4
20-25	5
25-30	11
30-35	6
35-40	5
40-45	8
45-50	9
50-55	6
55-60	4
60-65	2

108. What is the median?

A. 35 B. 38
C. 39 D. 40

109. What is the mode?

A. 27.27 B. 27.73
C. 27.93 D. 28.27

110. What is the mean of natural numbers contained in the interval [15, 64]?

A. 36.8 B. 38.3
C. 39.5 D. 40.3

111. For the set of numbers $x, x, x + 2, x + 3, x + 10$ where x is a natural number, which of the following is/are correct?

1. Mean > Mode
2. Median > Mean

Select the correct answer using the code given below.

A. 1 only B. 2 only
C. Both 1 and 2 D. Neither 1 nor 2

112. The mean of 10 observations is 5.5. If each observation is multiplied by 4 and subtracted from 44, then what is the new mean?

A. 20 B. 22
C. 34 D. 44

113. If g is the geometric mean of 2, 4, 8, 16, 32, 64, 128, 256, 512, 1024, then which one of the following is correct?

A. $8 < g < 16$ B. $16 < g < 32$
C. $32 < g < 64$ D. $g < 64$

114. If the harmonic mean of 60 and x is 48, then what is the value of x?

A. 32 B. 36
C. 40 D. 44

115. What is the mean deviation of first 10 even natural numbers?

A. 5 B. 5.5
C. 10 D. 10.5

116. If $\sum_{i=1}^{10} x_i = 110$ and $\sum_{i=1}^{10} x_i^2 = 1540$, then what is the variance?

A. 22 B. 33
C. 44 D. 55

117. 3-digit numbers are formed using the digits 1, 3, 7 without repetition of digits. A number is randomly selected. What is the probability that the number is divisible by 3?

A. 0 B. $\frac{1}{3}$
C. $\frac{1}{4}$ D. $\frac{1}{8}$

118. What is the probability that the roots of the equation $x^2 + x + n = 0$ are real, where $n \in \mathbb{N}$ and $n < 4$?

A. 0
B. $\frac{1}{4}$
C. $\frac{1}{3}$
D. $\frac{1}{2}$

119. If A and B are two events such that P(not A) = $\frac{7}{10}$, P(not B) = $\frac{3}{10}$ and P(A | B) = $\frac{3}{14}$, then what is P(B | A) equal to?

A. $\frac{11}{14}$ B. $\frac{9}{14}$
C. $\frac{1}{4}$ D. $\frac{1}{2}$

120. Seven white balls and three black balls are randomly placed in a row. What is the probability that no two black balls are placed adjacently?

A. $\frac{7}{15}$ B. $\frac{8}{15}$
C. $\frac{11}{15}$ D. $\frac{13}{15}$

ANSWERS

PAPER-I : GENERAL ABILITY TEST

1	2	3	4	5	6	7	8	9	10
C	C	D	B	B	C	B	C	A	C
11	**12**	**13**	**14**	**15**	**16**	**17**	**18**	**19**	**20**
A	B	D	A	D	B	C	D	A	B
21	**22**	**23**	**24**	**25**	**26**	**27**	**28**	**29**	**30**
A	C	B	A	D	B	C	A	A	C
31	**32**	**33**	**34**	**35**	**36**	**37**	**38**	**39**	**40**
D	B	D	B	D	A	B	B	A	B
41	**42**	**43**	**44**	**45**	**46**	**47**	**48**	**49**	**50**
D	B	A	C	A	A	D	C	B	A
51	**52**	**53**	**54**	**55**	**56**	**57**	**58**	**59**	**60**
A	B	A	A	D	B	A	A	D	C
61	**62**	**63**	**64**	**65**	**66**	**67**	**68**	**69**	**70**
A	D	C	B	D	C	D	D	A	D

71	72	73	74	75	76	77	78	79	80
A	A	D	A	C	D	D	C	C	C
81	82	83	84	85	86	87	88	89	90
D	B	C	A	B	D	B	C	B	A
91	92	93	94	95	96	97	98	99	100
B	D	A	B	A	C	A	C	C	B
101	102	103	104	105	106	107	108	109	110
C	B	D	C	B	B	D	C	D	B
111	112	113	114	115	116	117	118	119	120
B	C	B	D	B	D	A	B	A	C
121	122	123	124	125	126	127	128	129	130
C	B	C	B	C	C	C	C	A	A
131	132	133	134	135	136	137	138	139	140
D	C	A	C	B	A	A	B	B	D
141	142	143	144	145	146	147	148	149	150
A	D	C	A	A	A	C	B	A	C

PAPER-II : MATHEMATICS

1	2	3	4	5	6	7	8	9	10
B	A	C	C	A	D	D	B	D	A
11	12	13	14	15	16	17	18	19	20
B	A	A	C	A	C	A	A	B	D
21	22	23	24	25	26	27	28	29	30
B	A	B	D	B	C	C	C	A	D
31	32	33	34	35	36	37	38	39	40
A	C	C	A	C	B	A	C	B	B
41	42	43	44	45	46	47	48	49	50
D	B	C	C	C	A	C	B	A	C
51	52	53	54	55	56	57	58	59	60
D	D	C	D	C	C	D	A	B	C
61	62	63	64	65	66	67	68	69	70
D	C	C	C	B	A	D	A	C	C
71	72	73	74	75	76	77	78	79	80
B	A	C	C	D	A	C	B	B	A
81	82	83	84	85	86	87	88	89	90
D	D	B	C	B	B	B	B	A	B
91	92	93	94	95	96	97	98	99	100
A	C	A	A	B	D	D	A	C	D
101	102	103	104	105	106	107	108	109	110
C	A	C	D	D	C	A	C	B	C
111	112	113	114	115	116	117	118	119	120
A	B	C	C	A	B	A	A	D	A

EXPLANATORY ANSWERS

PAPER I : GENERAL KNOWLEDGE

51. The Size of all planets in order are:

- Mercury
- Mars
- Venus
- Earth
- Neptune
- Uranus
- Saturn
- Jupiter

53. Lonar Lake is the world's third-largest crater formed by a meteorite hit in less than a million years ago. It is also the largest impact crater in India. The lake, which was formed due to the meteorite strike nearly 56,000 years ago, has attracted scientists and tourists from across the world.

This crater of 1.8 km diameter was created when an impact meteor or asteroid collided with Earth in an extremely high-velocity of around 90,000 kmph. The crater is situated inside the small Lonar Sanctuary around 500 km away from Mumbai in Buldhana District of Maharashtra. The lake is spread across 113-hectare of land.

The lake's water is considered to be unique as it is both saline and alkaline. Due to this, the lake supports no marine life barring some species of algae.

54. Playa, also called pan, flat, or dry lake, flat-bottom depression found in interior desert basins and adjacent to coasts within arid and semi-arid regions, periodically covered by water that slowly filtrates into the ground water system or evaporates into the atmosphere, causing the deposition of salt, sand, and mud along the bottom and around the edges of the depression.

Playas are among the flattest known landforms. Their slopes are generally less than 0.2 metre per kilometre. When filled with only a few centimetres of water, many kilometres of surface may be inundated. It is the process of inundation that develops and maintains the near-perfect flatness so characteristic of these arid-region landforms.

56. The Constitution (35th Amendment) Act of 1974 terminated the protectorate status of Sikkim and conferred the status of an associate state of the Indian Union.

The Tenth Schedule was added laying down the terms and conditions of association of Sikkim with the Indian Union.

Thirty Sixth Amendment Act, 1975 made Sikkim a full-fledged State of the Indian Union and omitted the Tenth Schedule.

57. First-Past-the-Post System best describes the electoral system of India. In a first-past-the-post electoral system (FPTP or single-member plurality voting or SMP), voters cast their vote for a candidate of their choice, and the candidate who receives the most votes wins (even if the top candidate gets less than 50%, which can happen when there are more than two popular candidates).

FPTP is a plurality voting method, and is primarily used in systems that use single-member electoral divisions. FPTP is used as the primary form of allocating seats for legislative elections in about a third of the world's countries, mostly in the English-speaking world. The phrase is a metaphor from British horse racing, where there is a post at the finish line (though there is no specific percentage "finish line" required to win in this voting system, only being furthest ahead in the race).

59. A writ petition can be termed as a formal written order issued by a judicial authority who possesses the authority to do so. The meaning of the word 'Writs' means command in writing in the name of the Court. It is a legal document issued by the court that orders a person or entity to perform a specific act or to cease performing a specific action or deed. In India, writs are issued by the Supreme Court under Article 32 of the Constitution of India and by the High Court under Article 226 of the Constitution of India.

Articles 32 and 226 specifically provide for five kinds of writs. These writs are issued in different circumstances and have different implications. They are:

- Habeas Corpus
- Mandamus
- Prohibition
- Certiorari
- Quo-Warranto

64. Earth's atmosphere can be divided into five main layers. Excluding the exosphere, Earth has four primary layers, which are the troposphere, stratosphere, mesosphere, and thermosphere.

From highest to lowest, the five main layers are:

Exosphere: 700 to 10,000 km

Thermosphere: 80 to 700 km

Mesosphere: 50 to 80 km

Stratosphere: 12 to 50 km

Troposphere: 0 to 12 km

65. Soil Forming Factors:

- **Parent material:** Few soils weather directly from the underlying rocks. These "residual" soils have the same general chemistry as the original rocks. More commonly, soils form in materials that have moved in from elsewhere. Materials may have moved many miles or only a few feet. Windblown "loess" is common in the Midwest. It buries "glacial till" in many areas. Glacial till is material ground up and moved by a glacier. The material in which soils form is called "parent material". In the lower part of the soils, these materials may be relatively unchanged from when they were deposited by moving water, ice, or wind.

  Sediments along rivers have different textures, depending on whether the stream moves quickly or slowly. Fast-moving water leaves gravel, rocks, and sand. Slow-moving water and lakes leave fine textured material (clay and silt) when sediments in the water settle out.

- **Climate:** Soils vary, depending on the climate. Temperature and moisture amounts cause different patterns of weathering and leaching. Wind redistributes sand and other particles especially in arid regions. The amount, intensity, timing, and kind of precipitation influence soil formation. Seasonal and daily changes in temperature affect moisture effectiveness, biological activity, rates of chemical reactions, and kinds of vegetation.

- **Topography:** Slope and aspect affect the moisture and temperature of soil. Steep slopes facing the sun are warmer, just like the south-facing side of a house. Steep soils may be eroded and lose their topsoil as they form. Thus, they may be thinner than the more nearly level soils that receive deposits from areas upslope. Deeper, darker coloured soils may be expected on the bottom land.

66. The lithosphere is the solid, outer part of the Earth. The lithosphere includes the brittle upper portion of the mantle and the crust, the outermost layers of Earth's structure. It is bounded by the atmosphere above and the asthenosphere (another part of the upper mantle) below.

Although the rocks of the lithosphere are still considered elastic, they are not viscous. The asthenosphere is viscous, and the lithosphere-asthenosphere boundary (LAB) is the point where geologists and rheologists-scientists who study the flow of matter-mark the difference in ductility between the two layers of the upper mantle. Ductility measures a solid material's ability to deform or stretch under stress. The lithosphere is far less ductile than the asthenosphere.

There are two types of lithosphere: oceanic lithosphere and continental lithosphere. Oceanic lithosphere is associated with oceanic crust, and is slightly denser than continental lithosphere.

68. Salient Features of the Indian constitution are as follows:

- Lengthiest constitution in the world
- Sovereignty resides in the people
- Parliamentary form of Government
- Unique blend of rigidity and flexibility
- Fundamental Rights
- Directive principles of the state policy
- Quasi-federal in nature
- Adult suffrage
- Independence of Judiciary
- Judicial Review
- Fundamental duties
- Sovereign
- Democracy
- Republic
- Secular
- Single citizenship
- Uniformity in Basic Administration
- It is the supreme law of the land
- Lawyer's paradise
- Judicial Review and parliament sovereignty
- It provides a set of basic rules
- It specifies the power of the Government.

69. The Attorney General for India is the central government's chief legal advisor, and its primary lawyer in the Supreme Court of India. He is a part of the Union Executive.

He is appointed by the President of India under Article 76(1) of the Constitution and holds office during the pleasure of the President. He must be a person qualified to be appointed as a Judge of the Supreme Court. He should be an Indian Citizen. He must have either completed 5 years in High Court of any Indian state as a judge or 10 years in High Court as an advocate. He may be an eminent jurist too, in the view of the President. He shall receive such remuneration as the President may determine.

The Attorney General is necessary for giving advice to the Government of India in legal matters referred to him. He also performs other legal duties assigned to him by the President.

The Attorney General has the right of audience in all Courts in India as well as the right to participate in the proceedings of the Parliament, though not to vote.

The Attorney General appears on behalf of Government of India in all cases (including suits, appeals and other proceedings) in the Supreme Court in which Government of India is concerned.

He also represents the Government of India in any reference made by the President to the Supreme Court under Article 143 of the Constitution.

70. The Directive Principles of State Policy are enumerated in Part IV of the Constitution from Articles 36 to 51. The framers of the Constitution borrowed this idea from the Irish Constitution of 1937, which had copied it from the Spanish Constitution.

Dr. B.R. Ambedkar described these principles as 'novel features' of the Indian Constitution. The directive Principles along with the Fundamental Rights contain the philosophy of the Constitution and are the soul of the Constitution. Granville Austin has described the Directive Principles and the Fundamental Rights as the 'Conscience of the Constitution'.

71. Provisions of the Indian Councils Act 1861:

- For the executive functions of the Council, a fifth member was added. Now there were five members for home, military, law, revenue and finance. (A sixth member for public works was added in 1874.)
- Lord Canning, who was the Governor-General and Viceroy at the time, introduced the portfolio system. In this system, each member was assigned a portfolio of a particular department.
- For legislative purposes, the Governor-General's Council was enlarged. Now, there were to be between 6 and 12 additional members (nominated by the Governor-General).
- There were appointed for a period of 2 years. Out of these, at least half of the additional members were to be non-official (British or Indian).
- Their functions were confined to legislative measures.
- Lord Canning nominated three Indians to the Council in 1862 namely, the Raja of Benares, the Maharaja of Patiala and Sir Dinkar Rao.
- Any bill related to public revenue or debt, military, religion or foreign affairs could not be passed without the Governor-General's assent.
- The Viceroy had the power to overrule the council if necessary.
- The Governor-General also had the power to promulgate ordinances without the council's concurrence during emergencies.
- The Secretary of State for India in Britain could also dissolve any act passed by the Governor-General's Council.

73. The Santals are the most numerous tribe in eastern India. According to their traditions, they were a wandering tribe until they settled down in Chhotanagpur and the adjacent districts. That was around the middle of the 18th century.

Towards the end of the century, as the pressure of population was keenly felt and the jungles were being cleared, they moved up towards the virgin forests in and around the Rajmahal Hills. The Permanent Settlement of 1793 forced the landlords to improve productivity of the land. The Santals were increasingly used for land reclamation and improvement. In 1832, the government set apart a large area in Damin-i-Koh for the settlement of the Santals.

74. The Tropic of Cancer passes through eight states in India:

1. Gujarat (Jasdan)
2. Rajasthan (Kalinjarh)
3. Madhya Pradesh (Shajapur)
4. Chhattisgarh (Sonhat)
5. Jharkhand (Lohardaga)
6. West Bengal (Krishnanagar)
7. Tripura (Udaipur)
8. Mizoram (Champhai)

Tropic of Cancer crosses Mahi River twice, first in Madhya Pradesh from where it flows towards Rajasthan and enters Gujarat where it cuts for the second time.

76. Umaria Coalfield is located in *Umaria* district in the Indian state of Madhya Pradesh in the valley of the Umrer River, a tributary of the Son River. Umaria Coalfield is a part of Central India Coalfields. The latter is spread over the districts of Surguja, Koriya (both in Chhattisgarh), Shahdol and Umaria (both in Madhya Pradesh). There are fourteen coalfields in this group, namely Korar, Umaria, Johilla (Nowrozabad), Sohagpur, Sonhat, Jhilimili, Chirimiri, Sendurgarh, Koreagarh, Damhamunda, Panchbahini, Hasdeo-Arand, Lakhanpur and Bishrampur.

Umaria Coalfield, which was owned by Rewa Coalfields Limited, was nationalized in 1973.

77. All parallel circles from the equator to the poles are known as parallels of latitudes. The equator depicts the zero degrees latitude. Therefore, equator is the longest circle of latitude. All parallels north of the equator are called north latitudes and all parallels south of the equator are called south latitudes. The equator is the circle that is equidistant from the North Pole and South Pole. It divides the Earth into the Northern Hemisphere and the Southern Hemisphere.

78. The rise and fall of sea water due to gravitational forces of the sun and the moon are called tides. In fact, tides are the most uniformly varying phenomenon in the ocean.

83. Flying shuttle, Machine that represented an important step toward automatic weaving. It was invented by John Kay in 1733. In previous looms, the shuttle was thrown, or passed, through the threads by hand, and wide fabrics required two weavers seated side by side passing the shuttle between them. Kay mounted his shuttle on wheels in a track and used paddles to shoot the shuttle from side to side when the weaver jerked a cord. Using the flying shuttle, one weaver could weave fabrics of any width more quickly than two could before.

Weaving, production of fabric by interlacing two sets of yarns so that they cross each other, normally at right angles, usually accomplished with a hand- or power-operated loom.

88. Rousseau wrote the famous text "A Discourse on Political Economy".

Jean-Jacques Rousseau (1712-1778) was a Genevan philosopher, writer, and composer of the 18th century. His political philosophy influenced the Enlightenment in France and across Europe, as well as aspects of the French Revolution and the overall development of modern political and educational thought.

Rousseau's novel Emile, or On Education is a treatise on the education of the whole person for citizenship. His sentimental novel Julie, or the New Heloise was of importance to the development of pre-romanticism and romanticism in fiction. His Discourse on Inequality and The Social Contract are cornerstones in modern political and social thought.

During the period of the French Revolution, Rousseau was the most popular philosophers among members of the Jacobin Club.

90. Law Commissions in India have a pre-independence origin. The first Law Commission was formed in 1834 as a result of the Charter Act, 1833 under the chairmanship of TB Macaulay.

The first commission's recommendations resulted in the codification of the Indian Penal Code and the Criminal Procedure Code.

93. The Group of 7 (G7) is an informal group of seven countries - the United States, Canada, France, Germany, Italy, Japan and the United Kingdom, the heads of which hold an annual summit with European Union and other invitees. Unlike other bodies such as NATO, the G7 has no legal existence, permanent secretariat or official members. It also has no binding impact on policy and all decisions and commitments made at G7 meetings need to be ratified independently by governing bodies of member states.

The G7 draws its roots from a meeting between the current G7 members, excluding Canada, that took place in 1975. At the time, the global economy was in a state of recession due to the OPEC oil embargo.

The President of the European Commission was asked to join the meetings in 1977 and following the collapse of the Soviet Union in 1991 and a subsequent thaw in relations between the East and West, Russia was also invited to join the group in 1998. Thereafter the group was named the G8 until 2014, when Russia was expelled for its annexation of Crimea from Ukraine.

97. The Belt and Road Initiative, known in Chinese and formerly in English as One Belt One Road or OBOR for short, is a global infrastructure development strategy adopted by the Chinese government in 2013 to invest in nearly 70 countries and international organizations. The initiative was incorporated into the Constitution of China in 2017. The Chinese government calls the initiative "a bid to enhance regional connectivity and embrace a brighter future". The project has a target completion date of 2049, which will coincide with the centennial anniversary of the People's Republic of China (PRC)'s founding.

101. Milk of Magnesia is the magnesium compound which acts as an antacid. The term milk of magnesia was first used by English pharmacist Charles Henry Phillips in 1872.

Milk of Magnesia is basic in nature. The pH value of the Milk of Magnesia is 10.5.

The scale used to express the acidic or alkaline nature of a substance based on the concentration of hydrogen ions in its solution is called a pH scale. pH scale was discovered by Soren Sorensen. The pH value of the acids are less than 7 (0 to 7). The pH value of the Bases are greater than 7 (7 to 14)..The pH value of the neutral substance is equal to 7. The pH value of the pure water is 7. The pH value of the blood is close to 7.4.

102. Silver Bromide used in black and white photography.

$$\underset{\text{Silver bromide}}{2AgBr(s)} + \text{light} \rightarrow \underset{\text{Silver}}{2Ag(s)} + \underset{\text{Bromine}}{Br_2(g)}$$

As the above reaction are sensitive to light, they are used in black and white photography.

105. Bromine and mercury are the two elements that remain liquid at room temperature and standard pressure.

Mercury has an atomic number 80 and its symbol is Hg while bromine has an atomic number 35 and its symbol is Br. Bromine is a reddish-brown liquid while mercury is a shiny silvery metal. Mercury is commonly known as Quick Silver.

108. Photosynthesis is a process by which phototrophs convert light energy into chemical energy, which is later used to fuel cellular activities. The chemical energy is stored in the form of sugars, which are created from water and carbon dioxide.

Photosynthesis reaction involves two reactants, carbon dioxide and water. These two reactants yield two products, namely, oxygen and glucose. Hence, the photosynthesis reaction is considered to be an endothermic reaction.

Following is the photosynthesis formula:

$$6CO_2 + 6H_2O \rightarrow C_6H_{12}O_6 + 6O_2$$

110. Parenchyma cells occurs in xylem and phloem of 'vascular bundles'. These are living polygonal cells with a big central vacuole and intercellular spaces amidst them.

Parenchymatous cells are responsible to create ground pith and tissue. It comprising of chloroplasts and that's why it is termed as chlorenchyma and it helps in photosynthesis.

Parenchyma which comprises of the big air voids is called aerenchyma. 'Buoyancy' is the main purpose of aerenchyma. Some of these cells perform as storage chambers for starch in fruits and vegetables.

112. Genes are sections of DNA that determine certain traits or characteristics. Genes encode for proteins that influence things like the immune system, skin pigmentation, hormone production, and eye colour.

Genes are inherited from an offspring's parents, and they are responsible for features being passed down from one generation to the next. An organism's genotype consists of its entire set of genes. Every human has a unique genotype, which explains the vast variety in human appearance and biology.

When genes mutate, they can take on multiple forms, with each form differing slightly in the sequence of their base DNA.

These gene variants still code for the same trait (*i.e.*, hair color), but they differ in how the trait is expressed (i.e. brown vs blonde hair). Different versions of the same gene are called alleles.

113. Smallpox is an acute contagious disease caused by the Variola virus, a member of the Orthopoxvirus family. It was one of the most devastating diseases known to humanity and caused millions of deaths before it was eradicated. It is believed to have existed for at least 3000 years.

The smallpox vaccine, created by Edward Jenner in 1796, was the first successful vaccine to be developed. He observed that milkmaids who previously had caught cowpox did not catch smallpox and showed that a similar inoculation could be used to prevent smallpox in other people.

The World Health Organization launched an intensified plan to eradicate smallpox in 1967. Widespread immunization and surveillance were conducted around the world for several years. The last known natural case was in Somalia in 1977. In 1980 WHO declared smallpox eradicated—the only infectious disease to achieve this distinction.

114. The buoyant force is always present in a fluid, whether an object floats, sinks or remains suspended. The buoyant force is a result of pressure exerted by the fluid. Buoyant Force is the upward force that acts in the direction opposite to that of weight.

So, it will always act in the upward direction.

118. Uniform circular motion: The circular motion in which the speed of the particle does not change or remains constant is called uniform circular motion.

When a car is moving in a circle, the direction of motion or speed changes at every point.

At point A, the direction of the velocity is in the upward direction. At point B, the direction of the velocity is in the leftward direction. At point C, the direction of the velocity is in the downward direction.

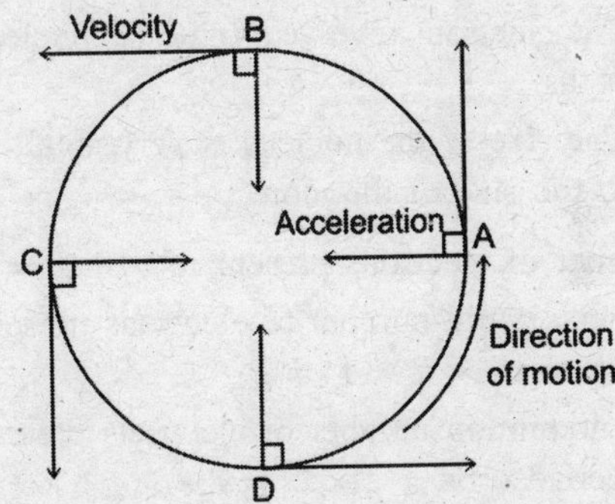

So the direction of velocity is changing at every point. The velocity of the car comes to the initial direction after one complete circle.

Given that a car is moving in a uniform circular motion. So when a car is moving in a uniform circular motion, it means it is moving with a constant speed, and its direction changes. The direction of motion is changing continuously, so velocity is not constant.

120. Rutherford's alpha-particle scattering experiment was responsible for the discovery of the atomic nucleus.

Rutherford's alpha-particle scattering experiment: Ernest Rutherford was interested in knowing how the electrons are arranged within an atom. Rutherford designed an experiment for this. In this experiment, fast-moving alpha (α)-particles were made to fall on a thin gold foil: He selected a gold foil because he wanted as thin a layer as possible.

This gold foil was about 1000 atoms thick. α-particles are doubly charged helium ions. Since they have a mass of 4 u, the fast-moving α-particles have a considerable amount of energy.

It was expected that α-particles would be deflected by the sub-atomic particles in the gold atoms. Since the α-particles were much heavier than the protons, he did not expect to see large deflections.

But, the α-particle scattering experiment gave totally unexpected results. The following observations were made:

- Most of the fast-moving α-particles passed straight through the gold foil.
- Some of the α-particles were deflected by the foil by small angles.
- Surprisingly one out of every 12000 particles appeared to rebound.

On the basis of his experiment, Rutherford put forward the nuclear model of an atom, which had the following features:

- There is a positively charged centre in an atom called the nucleus. Nearly all the mass of an atoms resides in the nucleus.
- The electrons revolve around the nucleus in circular paths.
- The size of the nucleus is very small as compared to the size of the atom.

121. Number of electrons present in n shell = $2n^2$

The maximum number of electrons present in K shell or first orbit = $2 \times 1^1 = 2$

The maximum number of electrons present in L shell or second orbit = $2 \times 2^2 = 8$

The maximum number of electrons present in M shell or third orbit = $2 \times 3^2 = 18$

123. Isotope and their uses:

- Radioactive Isotopes are used for medicinal purposes.
- They are used for the detection of tumors, blood clots, etc.
- Cobalt-60 Isotope of Cobalt is used in cancer treatments.
- Iodine-131 Isotope of iodine helps in the treatment of goiter.
- Arsenic-74, an isotope of arsenic, is used for determining the presence of a tumor.
- Sodium-24 is used for the detection of blood clots.

125. Cinnabar is the most common and is the chief ore of mercury with the formula HgS.

Metals	Ores
Mercury (Hg)	Cinnabar
Lead (Pb)	Galena
Tin (Sn)	Cassiterite
Antimony (Sb)	Stibnite
Zinc (Zn)	Calamine
Arsenic (As)	Arsenopyrite

128. Myopia means near-sightedness, the image doesn't form at retina but at a place before retina. Myopia occurs when the length of the eyeball gets increased, relative to the focusing power of the cornea and lens of the eye. Concave lens is used to correct this defect.

129. The Tyndall effect is the phenomenon in which the particles in a colloid scatter the beams of light that are directed at them. This effect is exhibited by all colloidal solutions and some very fine suspensions. Therefore, it can be used to verify if a given solution is a colloid. The intensity of scattered light depends on the density of the colloidal particles as well as the frequency of the incident light.

When a beam of light passes through a colloid, the colloidal particles present in the solution do not allow the beam to completely pass through. The light collides with the colloidal particles and is scattered (it deviates from its normal trajectory, which is a straight line). This scattering makes the path of the light beam visible.

Generally, blue light is scattered to a greater extent when compared to red light. This is because the wavelength of blue light is smaller than that of red light. This is the reason why the smoke released by motorcycles sometimes appears blue.

The Tyndall effect was first discovered by (and is named after) the Irish physicist John Tyndall. The diameters of the particles that cause the Tyndall effect can range from 40 to 900 nanometers (1 nanometer = 10^{-9} meter). In comparison, the wavelength of the visible light spectrum ranges from 400 to 750 nanometers.

130. The twinkling of a star is due to atmospheric refraction of starlight. The starlight, on entering the earth's atmosphere, undergoes refraction continuously before it reaches the earth. The atmospheric refraction occurs in a medium of gradually changing refractive index. Since the atmosphere bends starlight towards the normal, the apparent position of the star is slightly different from its actual position. The star appears slightly higher (above) than its actual position when viewed near the horizon since the stars are very distant, they approximate point-sized sources of light. As the path of rays of light coming from the star goes on varying slightly, the apparent position of the star fluctuates and the amount of starlight entering eye flickers—the star sometimes appear brighter and sometimes fainter, which is twinkling effect.

131. The cornea is the transparent part of the eye that covers the front portion of the eye. It covers the pupil (the opening at the center of the eye), iris (the colored part of the eye), and anterior chamber (the fluid-filled inside of the eye). The cornea's main function is to refract, or bend, light. The cornea is responsible for focusing most of the light that enters the eye.

The cornea is composed of proteins and cells. It does not contain blood vessels, unlike most of the tissues in the human body. Blood vessels may cloud the cornea, which may prevent it from refracting light properly and may adversely affect vision.

Since there are no nutrient-supplying blood vessels in the cornea, tears and the aqueous humor (a watery fluid) in the anterior chamber provide the cornea with nutrients.

The cornea is comprised of five layers: the epithelium, Bowman's layer, the stroma, Descemet's membrane, and the endothelium.

The first layer, the epithelium, is a layer of cells covering the cornea. It absorbs nutrients and oxygen from tears and conveys it to the rest of the cornea. It contains free nerve endings. It also prevents foreign matter from entering the eye.

The cornea tends to repair itself quickly from minor abrasions. However, deeper abrasions may cause scars to form on the cornea, which causes the cornea to lose its transparency, leading to visual impairment.

132. Power of a lens is expressed as the inverse of focal length, where a focal length of 1 meter is equal to one diopter. So a 25 cm. focal length (0.25 meters) has a power of 4 diopters.

133. Generally, the four-chambered rumen is found in Cattle, Sheep, Deer, Goat. Except for Camel which has three-chambered rumen.

- **Rumen:** In this feed is subjected to microbial fermentation. In ruminants, this enlarged part is the biggest compartment in their four-chambered stomach. The temperature of the rumen is 38-40 degrees C. This is ideal for the growth of micro-organisms and they flourish as they are grown in an incubator.
- **Reticulum:** It is a smaller sac partially separated from the rumen. This organ has a thick well-resembling honeycomb. The contents of rumen and reticulum mix freely. The reticulum is connected to the omasum, the third compartment of the stomach through an opening on the right side of the reticulum.
- **Omasum:** This organ has many layers of muscular leaves giving it the resemblance to a book. After fermentation, the ingest passes through the reticule-omasal orifice into the omasum. With the help of muscular leaves having horny papillae, the ingesta is squeezed out. Water and fatty acid so squeeze out are absorbed.
- **Abomasum:** It is the true stomach in the ruminant. From this organ onwards the digestion taking place in ruminants is similar to that of non-ruminants.

135. Estrogen and progesterone are the sex hormones in females. Estrogen is responsible for the development of secondary sexual characters in females and progesterone is required to maintain pregnancy and delivery.

Estrogen is the reproductive hormone in females that assists in endometrial regrowth, ovulation, and calcium absorption; it is also responsible for the secondary sexual characteristics of females. These include breast development, flaring of the hips, and a shorter period necessary for bone maturation.

137. Nuclear energy is generated by nuclear fission and its expression was proposed by Einstein.

Nuclear fission is a reaction where the nucleus of an atom splits into two or more smaller nuclei, while releasing energy.

For instance, when hit by a neutron, the nucleus of an atom of uranium-235 splits into a barium nucleus and a krypton nucleus and two or three neutrons. These extra neutrons will hit other surrounding uranium-235 atoms, which will also split and generate additional neutrons in a multiplying effect, thus generating a chain reaction in a fraction of a second.

Each time the reaction occurs, there is a release of energy in the form of heat and radiation. The heat can be converted into electricity in a nuclear power plant, similarly to how heat from fossil fuels such as coal, gas and oil is used to generate electricity.

The connection between energy and matter is represented by Albert Einstein's famous equation introduced as $E = m \cdot c^2$.

138. Reverberation is the phenomenon of persistence of sound after it is stopped by surfaces such as furniture, people, walls, etc. within a closed space, causing multiple reflections. These reflections build up with each reflection and persist for a finite time and then decay gradually as they are slowly absorbed by the objects in the space enclosed.

143. Methanol is CH_3OH

So, carbon is attached to 3 H and 1 OH with 4 covalent bonds. O and H in OH are bonded with 1 covalent bond.

So, there are total 5 covalent bonds.

144. Plaster of Paris (POP) is a quick-setting gypsum plaster consisting of a fine white powder (calcium sulfate hemihydrate), which hardens when moistened and allowed to dry.

It is also known as the Plaster of Paris because for the preparation of POP, the abundant gypsum was first found near the capital city of France *i.e.*, Paris.

The chemical formula of the Plaster of Paris is $CaSO_4 \cdot \frac{1}{2} H_2O$

Application of Plaster of Paris as follows:

- It is used as a building material as a protective coating on walls and ceillings.
- It is used as moulding and vesting agent for decorative elements.
- It is also used for aesthetic touch to the construction elements.
- It is also used as plaster in orthopaedics and as a filling material by dentists etc.

145. **Thrust:** The force acting perpendicular to the surface of the object is called thrust. When any object is put into the water then the object will replace the water the same as it's volume and the cause of which there is a force acting upwards, to balance this weight is called the thrust force. Thrust is a kind of pull force, which is applied by the medium on the object. It is a type of force so the SI unit of thrust is Newton (N). The dimensional formula of Thrust is $[MLT^{-2}]$. The effect of thrust is more on the smaller surface area than the thrust acting on a larger surface area.

Thrust Force (F_T) = Pressure (P) × Area (A)

Impulse: When a large force acts for a very small time, it causes a change in momentum. This is called impulse.

Impulse (J) = Force × time duration

= Change in momentum.

Dimension = MLT^{-1}.

The dimension of impulse is the same as momentum. The dimensional formula of Thrust is $[MLT^{-2}]$ and the Dimension of impulse is $[MLT^{-1}]$.

The unit of the ratio between thrust and impulse is:

$$\frac{\text{Thrust}}{\text{Impulse}} = \frac{MLT^{-2}}{MLT^{-1}} = T^{-1}$$

T^{-1} is the unit of frequency.

148. The image formed by a plane mirror is always virtual (meaning that the light rays do not actually come from the image), upright, and of the same shape and size as the object it is reflecting. A virtual image is a copy of an object formed at the location from which the light rays appear to come.

Image formed by plane mirrors are:

- Virtual
- Behind the mirror
- Erect (means not inverted)
- Same size as the object
- At same distance from the mirror as the object is from the mirror.

149. A conservative force is a force with the property that the total work done in moving a particle between two points is independent of the taken path. Equivalently, if a particle travels in a closed-loop, the total work done by a conservative force is zero.

Examples: Magnetic force, Electrostatic force, Gravitational force etc.

Force of friction is not a conservative force since the work done by it depends on the path taken.

150. **Work done by a force:** Work is said to be done by a force on a body when there is a displacement of the body due to that force. The magnitude of work done is given as:

$$W = F.S. \cos \theta$$

where, W = Magnitude of work done by the force (F) in joule, F = magnitude of force, in newton, S cos θ = component of the Displacement in the direction of the force, in meter.

Positive and negative work: When the force and the displacement are in the same direction, work done is positive.

When the force and displacement are in opposite direction, work done is negative.

Zero work done: Work done is zero if force and displacement are perpendicular to each other or if the displacement of the body is zero.

We know that the work done by a force on a body is given as:

$$\Rightarrow W = FS \times \cos \theta \quad ...(i)$$

By equation (*i*) we can say that the work done will be negative when the value of cosθ is negative and it only possible when force (F) and the corresponding displacement S are anti-parallel to each other *i.e.*, θ = 180°

$$\Rightarrow W = FS \times \cos 180° = -FS \; [\because \cos 180° = -1]$$

PAPER II : MATHEMATICS

1. Given, $x^2 + x + 1 = 0$

$$\therefore \quad x^{199} + x^{200} + x^{201} = x^{199}(1 + x + x^2) = x^{199}(0) = 0.$$

2. Given, x, y, z are in GP

$$\therefore \quad y^2 = xz$$

1. In $(3x)$, In $(3y)$, In $(3z)$ are in AP

$\Rightarrow \log(3x), \log(3y), \log(3z)$ are in AP

$\Rightarrow \log(3y) - \log(3x) = \log(3z) - \log(3y)$

$$\Rightarrow \quad \log\frac{3y}{3x} = \log\frac{3z}{3y}$$

$$\Rightarrow \quad \frac{3y}{3x} = \frac{3z}{3y}$$

$$\Rightarrow \quad \frac{y}{x} = \frac{z}{y} \Rightarrow y^2 = xz$$

2. $xyz + \text{In}(x), xyz + \text{In}(y), xyz + \text{In}(z)$ are in HP

$$\therefore \quad xyz + \text{In}(y) = \frac{2[xyz + \text{In}(x)][xyz + \text{In}(z)]}{xyz + \text{In}(x) + xyz + \text{In}(z)}$$

Hence, (1) is correct.

9. Given, $A = \begin{vmatrix} a & b & c \\ d & e & f \\ g & h & i \end{vmatrix}$

$$\therefore \begin{vmatrix} 3d+5g & 4a+7g & 6g \\ 3e+5h & 4b+7h & 6h \\ 3f+5i & 4c+7i & 6i \end{vmatrix}$$

$$= \begin{vmatrix} 3d & 4a+7g & 6g \\ 3e & 4b+7h & 6h \\ 3f & 4c+7i & 6i \end{vmatrix} + \begin{vmatrix} 5g & 4a+7g & 6g \\ 5h & 4b+7h & 6h \\ 5i & 4c+7i & 6i \end{vmatrix}$$

$$= \begin{vmatrix} 3d & 4a & 6g \\ 3e & 4b & 6h \\ 3f & 4c & 6i \end{vmatrix} + \begin{vmatrix} 3d & 7g & 6g \\ 3e & 7h & 6h \\ 3f & 7i & 6i \end{vmatrix} + \begin{vmatrix} 5g & 4a & 6g \\ 5h & 4b & 6h \\ 5i & 4c & 6i \end{vmatrix} + \begin{vmatrix} 5g & 7g & 6g \\ 5h & 7h & 6h \\ 5i & 7i & 6i \end{vmatrix}$$

$$= 3\times4\times6\begin{vmatrix} d & a & g \\ e & b & h \\ f & c & i \end{vmatrix} + 7\times6\begin{vmatrix} 3d & g & g \\ 3e & h & h \\ 3f & i & i \end{vmatrix} + 5\times6\begin{vmatrix} g & 4a & g \\ h & 4b & h \\ i & 4c & i \end{vmatrix} + 5\times7\times6\begin{vmatrix} g & g & g \\ h & h & h \\ i & i & i \end{vmatrix}$$

[If any two rows (columns) of a determinant are interchanged, then the value of the determinant changed by minus sign only.]

$$= 72(-1)\begin{vmatrix} a & d & g \\ b & e & h \\ c & f & i \end{vmatrix} + 42\times0 + 30\times0 + 210\times0$$

[The value of determinant remains unchange if its rows and columns are interchanged]

$$= -72\begin{vmatrix} a & b & c \\ d & e & f \\ g & h & i \end{vmatrix} + 0 = -72\begin{vmatrix} a & b & c \\ d & e & f \\ g & h & i \end{vmatrix}$$

$$= -72\Delta.$$

10. Given, $\frac{1}{b+c}, \frac{1}{c+a}, \frac{1}{a+b}$ are in HP

$\therefore b + c, c + a, a + b$ are in AP

$$\Rightarrow \quad c + a - (b + c) = a + b - (c + a)$$

$$\Rightarrow \quad c + a - b - c = a + b - c - a$$

$$\Rightarrow \quad a - b = b - c$$

$$\Rightarrow \quad a + c = 2b$$

$$\Rightarrow \quad b = \frac{a+c}{2}$$

1. a, b, c are in AP

$$\Rightarrow \quad b = \frac{a+c}{2}$$

2. $(b + c)^2, (c + a)^2, (a + b)^2$ are in GP

$$\Rightarrow \quad \frac{(c+a)^2}{(b+c)^2} = \frac{(a+b)^2}{(c+a)^2}$$

$$\Rightarrow \quad \frac{c+a}{b+c} = \frac{a+b}{c+a}$$

$$\Rightarrow \quad (c + a)^2 = (a + b)(b + c)$$

$$\Rightarrow \quad c^2 + a^2 + 2ca = ab + ca + b^2 + bc$$

$$\Rightarrow c^2 + a^2 + 2ca - ca = b^2 + ab + bc$$

$$\Rightarrow \quad c^2 + a^2 + ca = b^2 + ab + bc$$

$$\Rightarrow \quad c^2 + a^2 + ca = b(a + b + c)$$

$$\Rightarrow \quad b = \frac{c^2 + a^2 + ca}{a+b+c}$$

Hence, only (1) is correct.

12. Given, $\begin{vmatrix} a & -b & a-b-c \\ -a & b & -a+b-c \\ -a & -b & -a-b+c \end{vmatrix} - kabc = 0 \quad \text{...(i)}$

Let $\Delta = \begin{vmatrix} a & -b & a-b-c \\ -a & b & -a+b-c \\ -a & -b & -a-b+c \end{vmatrix}$

Applying, $R_1 \to R_1 + R_2$

$R_2 \to R_2 + R_3$

Then, $\Delta = \begin{vmatrix} 0 & 0 & -2c \\ -2a & 0 & -2a \\ -a & -b & -a-b+c \end{vmatrix}$

Expanding R_1

$\therefore \quad \Delta = 0 + 0 - 2c(2ab - 0)$

$\Rightarrow \quad \Delta = -4abc$

Putting the value of Δ in (*i*), we get,

$-4abc - kabc = 0$

$\Rightarrow \quad 4abc + kabc = 0$

$\Rightarrow \quad 4 + k = 0$

$\Rightarrow \quad k = -4.$

14. Given, $z = x + iy$, where $i = \sqrt{-1}$

$\Rightarrow \quad \overline{z} = x - iy$

and $|z| = \sqrt{x^2 + y^2}$

$\Rightarrow \quad |z|^2 = \left(\sqrt{x^2 + y^2}\right)^2$

$\Rightarrow \quad |z|^2 = x^2 + y^2$

$\therefore \quad z\overline{z} + |z|^2 + 4(z + \overline{z}) - 48 = 0$

$\Rightarrow (x + iy)(x - iy) + x^2 + y^2 + 4(x + iy + x - iy) - 48 = 0$

$\Rightarrow \quad x^2 + y^2 + x^2 + y^2 + 4(2x) - 48 = 0$

$\Rightarrow \quad 2x^2 + 2y^2 + 8x - 48 = 0$

Which represents equation of circle.

17. Given, C(*n*, 4), C(*n*, 5) and C(*n*, 6) are in AP

$\Rightarrow \frac{\lfloor n}{\lfloor 4 \lfloor n-4}, \frac{\lfloor n}{\lfloor 5 \lfloor n-5}$ and $\frac{\lfloor n}{\lfloor 6 \lfloor n-6}$ are in AP

$\Rightarrow \frac{\lfloor 1}{\lfloor 4 \lfloor n-4}, \frac{\lfloor 1}{\lfloor 5 \lfloor n-5}$ and $\frac{\lfloor 1}{\lfloor 6 \lfloor n-6}$ are in AP

$\Rightarrow \frac{1}{\lfloor 4 (n-4)(n-5) \lfloor n-6}, \frac{1}{5 \lfloor 4 (n-5) \lfloor n-6}$ and $\frac{1}{6.5 \lfloor 4 \lfloor n-6}$ are in AP

$\Rightarrow \frac{1}{(n-4)(n-5)}, \frac{1}{5(n-5)}$ and $\frac{1}{30}$ are in AP

$\Rightarrow \quad \frac{1}{5(n-5)} - \frac{1}{(n-4)(n-5)} = \frac{1}{30} - \frac{1}{5(n-5)}$

$\Rightarrow \quad \frac{n-4-5}{5(n-4)(n-5)} = \frac{n-5-6}{30(n-5)}$

$\Rightarrow \quad 30(n-9) = 5(n-4)(n-11)$

$\Rightarrow \quad 6(n-9) = n^2 - 15n + 44$

$\Rightarrow \quad n^2 - 15n + 44 - 6n + 54 = 0$

$\Rightarrow \quad n^2 - 21n + 98 = 0$

$\Rightarrow \quad n^2 - 7n - 14n + 98 = 0$

$\Rightarrow \quad n(n-7) - 14(n-7) = 0$

$\Rightarrow \quad (n-7)(n-14) = 0$

$\Rightarrow \quad n = 7 \text{ or } 14.$

20. $\left(\frac{a^2}{b^2} + \frac{b^2}{a^2} + 2\right)^{21} = \left(\frac{a^4 + b^4 + 2a^2b^2}{a^2b^2}\right)^{21}$

$= \left[\frac{(a^2 + b^2)^2}{a^2b^2}\right]^{21}$

$= \left[\left(\frac{a^2 + b^2}{ab}\right)^2\right]^{21} = \left(\frac{a}{b} + \frac{b}{a}\right)^{42}$

Hence, the number of term in the given expansion $= (n + 1) = 42 + 1 = 43$

i.e., one more than the index.

22. Given, $A^{-1} = \begin{bmatrix} -2 & 1 \\ \frac{3}{2} & \frac{-1}{2} \end{bmatrix}$

Let $B = A^{-1} = \begin{bmatrix} -2 & 1 \\ +\frac{3}{2} & -\frac{1}{2} \end{bmatrix}$

Then, $|B| = \begin{vmatrix} -2 & 1 \\ -\frac{3}{2} & -\frac{1}{2} \end{vmatrix}$

$= -2 \times \frac{-1}{2} - 1 \times \frac{3}{2}$

$= 1 - \frac{3}{2} = -\frac{1}{2}$

$\Rightarrow \quad |B| = -\frac{1}{2} \neq 0$

So, B is a non-singular matrix and therefore it is invertible

Let C_{ij} be cofactor of b_{ij} in B. Then, the cofactors of elements of B are

$C_{11} = -\frac{1}{2}, C_{12} = -\frac{3}{2}$

$C_{21} = -1$ and $C_{22} = -2$

$\therefore \quad adj B = \begin{bmatrix} -\frac{1}{2} & -\frac{3}{2} \\ -1 & -2 \end{bmatrix}^T = \begin{bmatrix} -\frac{1}{2} & -1 \\ -\frac{3}{2} & -2 \end{bmatrix}$

Hence, $B^{-1} = \frac{1}{|B|} adj\, B = \frac{1}{-\frac{1}{2}}\begin{bmatrix} -\frac{1}{2} & -1 \\ -\frac{3}{2} & -2 \end{bmatrix}$

$\Rightarrow$ $B^{-1} = -2\begin{bmatrix} -\frac{1}{2} & -1 \\ -\frac{3}{2} & -2 \end{bmatrix} = \begin{bmatrix} 1 & 2 \\ 3 & 4 \end{bmatrix}$

$(A^{-1})^{-1} = \begin{bmatrix} 1 & 2 \\ 3 & 4 \end{bmatrix} \Rightarrow A = \begin{bmatrix} 1 & 2 \\ 3 & 4 \end{bmatrix}$

Hence, $A = (A^{-1})^{-1} = \begin{bmatrix} 1 & 2 \\ 3 & 4 \end{bmatrix}$.

24. Given, $\sin(A + B) = 1$

$\Rightarrow$ $\sin A \cos B + \cos A \sin B = 1$ ...(*i*)

and $2\sin(A - B) = 1$

$\Rightarrow$ $\sin(A - B) = \frac{1}{2}$

$\Rightarrow$ $\sin A \cos B - \cos A \sin B = \frac{1}{2}$ ...(*ii*)

From adding (*i*) and (*ii*)

$2\sin A \cos B = 1 + \frac{1}{2}$

$\Rightarrow$ $\sin A \cos B = \frac{3}{4}$ ...(*iii*)

Subtracting (*ii*) from (*i*), we get,

$2\cos A \sin B = 1 - \frac{1}{2}$

$\Rightarrow$ $2\cos A \sin B = \frac{1}{2}$

$\Rightarrow$ $\cos A \sin B = \frac{1}{4}$ ...(*iv*)

On dividing (*iii*) by (*iv*)

$\frac{\sin A \cos B}{\cos A \sin B} = \frac{3}{4} \times \frac{4}{1}$

$\Rightarrow$ $\tan A \cot B = \frac{3}{1}$

$\Rightarrow$ $\frac{\tan A}{\tan B} = \frac{3}{1}$

$\Rightarrow$ $\tan A : \tan B = 3 : 1$.

27. Given, expression $= (1 + x)^n$

$\therefore$ General term $= T_{r+1} = {}^nC_r\, x^r$

$\therefore$ First term $= T_{0+1} = {}^nC_0\, x^0$,

Second term $= T_{1+1} = {}^nC_1\, x^1$,

nth term $= T_{(n-1)+1} = {}^nC_{n-1}\, x^{n-1}$

$(n + 1)$th term $= T_n = {}^nC_n\, x^n$

According to question,

Coefficient of first term $= p$

${}^nC_0 = p$

Coefficient of second term $= q$

${}^nC_1 = q$

Coefficient of nth term $= r$

${}^nC_{n-1} = r$

and Coefficient of $(n + 1)$th term $= s$

$\therefore$ ${}^nC_n = s$

$\therefore$ $ps + qr = {}^nC_0 \cdot {}^nC_n + {}^nC_1 \cdot {}^nC_{n-1}$

$= 1 \cdot 1 + n \cdot n$

$= 1 + n^2$.

28. $\sin^{-1} x + \sin^{-1} y + \sin^{-1} z$

$= \frac{3\pi}{2}$ for $0 \le x, y, z \le 1$

$\Rightarrow$ $\frac{\pi}{2} + \frac{\pi}{2} + \frac{\pi}{2} = 3\frac{\pi}{2}$

Let, $\sin^{-1} x = \frac{\pi}{2} \Rightarrow x = \sin\frac{\pi}{2} \Rightarrow x = 1$

$\sin^{-1} y = \frac{\pi}{2} \Rightarrow y = \sin\frac{\pi}{2} \Rightarrow y = 1$

and $\sin^{-1} z = \frac{\pi}{2} \Rightarrow z = \sin\frac{\pi}{2} \Rightarrow z = 1$

$\therefore x^{1000} + y^{1001} + z^{1002} = 1^{1000} + 1^{1001} + 1^{1002}$

$= 1 + 1 + 1 = 3$.

29. $\because$ $\sin x + \sin y = \cos x + \cos y$ for all $x, y \in \mathbb{R}$

$\Rightarrow$ $2\sin\frac{x+y}{2}\cos\frac{x-y}{2} = 2\cos\frac{x+y}{2}\cos\frac{x-y}{2}$

$\Rightarrow$ $\sin\frac{x+y}{2} = \cos\frac{x+y}{2}$

$\Rightarrow$ $\frac{\sin\frac{x+y}{2}}{\cos\frac{x+y}{2}} = 1$

$\Rightarrow$ $\tan\frac{x+y}{2} = 1$

$\Rightarrow$ $\tan\left(\frac{x}{2} + \frac{y}{2}\right) = 1$.

31. Let $\sin^{-1}\frac{3}{5} = x$, then $\sin x = \frac{3}{5}$

$\therefore$ $\cos x = \sqrt{1 - \sin^2 x}$

$\Rightarrow$ $\cos x = \sqrt{1 - \frac{9}{25}} = \sqrt{\frac{16}{25}} = \frac{4}{5}$

$\therefore$ $\tan x = \frac{\sin x}{\cos x} = \frac{3/5}{4/5} = \frac{3}{4}$

$$\Rightarrow \quad x = \tan^{-1}\frac{3}{4}$$

$$\therefore \quad \sin^{-1}\frac{3}{5}+\cos^{-1}\frac{3}{2} = \tan^{-1}\frac{3}{4}+\cot^{-1}\frac{3}{2}$$

$$= \tan^{-1}\frac{3}{4}+\tan^{-1}\frac{2}{3}$$

$$= \tan^{-1}\frac{\frac{3}{4}+\frac{2}{3}}{1-\frac{3}{4}\times\frac{2}{3}} = \tan^{-1}\frac{\frac{17}{12}}{1-\frac{1}{2}}$$

$$= \tan^{-1}\frac{17}{12}\times\frac{2}{1} = \tan^{-1}\frac{17}{6}$$

$$\therefore \cot\left[\sin^{-1}\frac{3}{5}+\cot^{-1}\frac{3}{2}\right]$$

$$= \cot\left[\tan^{-1}\frac{17}{6}\right] = \cot\left[\cot^{-1}\frac{6}{17}\right] = \frac{6}{17}.$$

32. $\because \quad 4\sin^2 x = 3$

$$\therefore \quad \sin^2 x = \frac{3}{4}$$

$$\Rightarrow \quad \cos^2 x = 1-\sin^2 x = 1-\frac{3}{4} = \frac{1}{4}$$

$$\therefore \quad \tan^2 x = \frac{\sin^2 x}{\cos^2 x} = \frac{3/4}{1/4} = 3$$

$$\Rightarrow \quad \tan^2 x = 3 \Rightarrow \tan x = 3^{1/2}$$

$$\Rightarrow \quad \tan^3 x = 3^{3/2}$$

$$\therefore \quad \tan^3 x = \frac{3\tan x - \tan^3 x}{1-3\tan^2 x} = \frac{3\times 3^{1/2}-3^{3/2}}{1-3\times 3}$$

$$= \frac{3^{3/2}-3^{3/2}}{1-9} = \frac{0}{-8} = 0$$

Hence, $\tan^3 x = 0$.

40. Given, $\log_{10} 2 \log_2 10 + \log_{10}(10^x) = 2$

$$\Rightarrow \quad \log_{10}10 + x\log_{10}10 = 2$$

$$\Rightarrow \quad 1 + x\,.\,1 = 2$$

$$\Rightarrow \quad 1 + x = 2 \Rightarrow x = 2-1 \Rightarrow x = 1.$$

41. $\because \quad \cos 2A + \cos 2B + \cos 2C = -1$

$$\Rightarrow \quad \cos 2A + \cos 2B + \cos 2C + 1 = 0$$

$$\Rightarrow \quad 2\cos(A+B)\cos(A-B) + 2\cos^2 C = 0$$

$$\Rightarrow \quad 2\cos(\pi - C)\cos(A-B) + 2\cos^2 C = 0$$

$$\Rightarrow \quad -2\cos C\cos(A-B) + 2\cos^2 C = 0$$

$$\Rightarrow \quad -2\cos C[\cos(A-B) - \cos C] = 0$$

$$\Rightarrow -2\cos C[\cos(A-B) + \cos(A+B)] = 0$$

$$\Rightarrow \quad -2\cos C[2\cos A\cos B] = 0$$

$$\Rightarrow \quad -4\cos A\cos B\cos C = 0$$

$$\Rightarrow \quad \cos A\cos B\cos C = 0.$$

44. Here, S_k denote the sum of first k terms of an AP

$$\therefore \quad \frac{S_{30}}{S_{20}-S_{10}}$$

$$= \frac{\frac{30}{2}[2a+(30-1)d]}{\frac{20}{2}[2a+(20-1)d]-\frac{10}{2}[2a+(10-1)d]}$$

$$= \frac{15(2a+29d)}{10[2a+19d]-5[2a+9d]}$$

$$= \frac{15[2a+29d]}{20a+190d-10a-45d}$$

$$= \frac{15[2a+29d]}{10a+145d} = \frac{15[2a+29d]}{5[2a+29d]} = 3.$$

45. Given, equation, $4x^2-(5k+1)x+5k=0$

Here, $a=4$, $b=-(5k+1)$, $c=5k$

$$\therefore \quad D = b^2-4ac$$

$$= (5k+1)^2 - 4\times 4\times 5k$$

$$= 25k^2+10k+1-80k$$

$$= 25k^2-70k+1$$

$$x = \frac{-b\pm\sqrt{D}}{2a}$$

$$= \frac{(5k+1)\pm\sqrt{25k^2-70k+1}}{2\times 4}$$

$$= \frac{(5k+1)\pm\sqrt{25k^2-70k+1}}{8}$$

Given, the roots of the equation differ by unity.

$$\frac{5k+1+\sqrt{25k^2-70k+1}}{8}+\frac{5k+1-\sqrt{25k^2-70k+1}}{8} = 1$$

$$\Rightarrow \quad \frac{5k+1+\sqrt{25k^2-70k+1}-(5k+1)+\sqrt{25k^2-70k+1}}{8} = 1$$

$$\Rightarrow \quad 2\sqrt{25k^2-70k+1} = 8$$

$$\Rightarrow \quad \sqrt{25k^2-70k+1} = 4$$

$$\Rightarrow \quad 25k^2-70k+1 = 16$$

$$\Rightarrow \quad 25k^2-70k-15 = 0$$

$$\Rightarrow \quad 5k^2-14k-3 = 0$$

$$\Rightarrow \quad 5k^2-15k+k-3 = 0$$

$$\Rightarrow \quad 5k(k-3)+1(k-3) = 0$$

$$\Rightarrow \quad (k-3)(5k+1) = 0$$

$$\Rightarrow \quad k = 3, -\frac{1}{5}$$

Hence, value of k is $-\frac{1}{5}$, 3.

48. Given, $i = \sqrt{-1} = (-1)^{1/2}$

$\therefore \quad i^{-2n} = \dfrac{1}{i^{2n}} = \dfrac{1}{(-1)^{\frac{1}{2}.2n}}$

$\because n = 1 \therefore \quad \dfrac{1}{(-1)^{\frac{1}{2}.2}} = \dfrac{1}{(-1)^1} = \dfrac{1}{-1} = -1$

$n = 2 \therefore \quad \dfrac{1}{(-1)^{\frac{1}{2}.4}} = \dfrac{1}{(-1)^2} = \dfrac{1}{1} = 1$

$n = 3 \therefore \quad \dfrac{1}{(-1)^{\frac{1}{2}.6}} = \dfrac{1}{(-1)^3} = \dfrac{1}{-1} = -1$

$n = 4 \therefore \quad \dfrac{1}{(-1)^{\frac{1}{2}.8}} = \dfrac{1}{(-1)^4} = \dfrac{1}{1} = 1$

.....

.....

Hence, the number of values are –1 and 1.

50. Given, Matrix $A = \begin{bmatrix} 1 & 1 & 1 \\ 1 & 1 & 1 \\ 1 & 1 & 1 \end{bmatrix}$

$\therefore \quad |A| = \begin{vmatrix} 1 & 1 & 1 \\ 1 & 1 & 1 \\ 1 & 1 & 1 \end{vmatrix} = 0$

Thus A is a singular matrix and therefore it is not invertible

1. Inverse of A does not exist → correct

2. $A^3 = A$

$\because \quad A^2 = \begin{bmatrix} 1 & 1 & 1 \\ 1 & 1 & 1 \\ 1 & 1 & 1 \end{bmatrix}\begin{bmatrix} 1 & 1 & 1 \\ 1 & 1 & 1 \\ 1 & 1 & 1 \end{bmatrix}$

$= \begin{bmatrix} 1+1+1 & 1+1+1 & 1+1+1 \\ 1+1+1 & 1+1+1 & 1+1+1 \\ 1+1+1 & 1+1+1 & 1+1+1 \end{bmatrix}$

$= \begin{bmatrix} 3 & 3 & 3 \\ 3 & 3 & 3 \\ 3 & 3 & 3 \end{bmatrix} = 3\begin{bmatrix} 1 & 1 & 1 \\ 1 & 1 & 1 \\ 1 & 1 & 1 \end{bmatrix}$

$A^3 = A^2 - A$

$= 3\begin{bmatrix} 1 & 1 & 1 \\ 1 & 1 & 1 \\ 1 & 1 & 1 \end{bmatrix}\begin{bmatrix} 1 & 1 & 1 \\ 1 & 1 & 1 \\ 1 & 1 & 1 \end{bmatrix} = 3\begin{bmatrix} 3 & 3 & 3 \\ 3 & 3 & 3 \\ 3 & 3 & 3 \end{bmatrix}$

$= 3 \times 3\begin{bmatrix} 1 & 1 & 1 \\ 1 & 1 & 1 \\ 1 & 1 & 1 \end{bmatrix} = 9\begin{bmatrix} 1 & 1 & 1 \\ 1 & 1 & 1 \\ 1 & 1 & 1 \end{bmatrix}$

Hence, $A^3 = A \rightarrow$ not correct

3. $3A = A^2$

$\because \quad 3A = 3\begin{bmatrix} 1 & 1 & 1 \\ 1 & 1 & 1 \\ 1 & 1 & 1 \end{bmatrix}$

and $\quad A^2 = \begin{bmatrix} 1 & 1 & 1 \\ 1 & 1 & 1 \\ 1 & 1 & 1 \end{bmatrix}\begin{bmatrix} 1 & 1 & 1 \\ 1 & 1 & 1 \\ 1 & 1 & 1 \end{bmatrix}$

$= \begin{bmatrix} 3 & 3 & 3 \\ 3 & 3 & 3 \\ 3 & 3 & 3 \end{bmatrix} = 3\begin{bmatrix} 1 & 1 & 1 \\ 1 & 1 & 1 \\ 1 & 1 & 1 \end{bmatrix}$

Hence, $3A = A^2 \rightarrow$ correct.

51. Let the required circle be

$x^2 + y^2 + 2gx + 2fy + c = 0 \quad ...(i)$

It passes through the points (5, –8), (2, –9) and (2, 1)

Therefore,

$89 + 10g - 16f + c = 0 \quad ...(ii)$

$85 + 4g - 18f + c = 0 \quad ...(iii)$

$5 + 4g + 2f + c = 0 \quad ...(iv)$

Subtracting (*iii*) from (*ii*), we get

$4 + 14g - 34f = 0$

$\Rightarrow \quad 7g - 17f = -2 \quad ...(v)$

Subtracting (*iv*) from (*iii*), we get

$80 - 8g + 16f = 0$

$\Rightarrow \quad 8g - 16f = 80$

$\Rightarrow \quad g - 2f = 10$

$\Rightarrow \quad g = 2f + 10 \quad ...(vi)$

From (*v*) and (*vi*),

$7(2f + 10) - 17f = -2$

$\Rightarrow \quad 14f + 70 - 17f = -2$

$\Rightarrow \quad 70 - 3f = -2$

$\Rightarrow \quad 3f = 72 \Rightarrow f = 24$

From (*vi*), $\quad g = 2 \times 24 + 10 = 48 + 10 = 58$

Hence, the coordinates of the centre are $(-g, -f)$ *i.e.*, (–58, –24).

52. Putting g = 58 and f = 24 in (iv), we get,

$5 + 4(58) + 2(24) + c = 0$

$\Rightarrow \quad 5 + 232 + 48 + c = 0$

$\Rightarrow \quad 285 + c = 0$

$\Rightarrow \quad c = -285$

$\therefore \quad \text{Radius} = \sqrt{g^2 + f^2 - c}$

$= \sqrt{(58)^2 + (24)^2 + 285}$

$$= \sqrt{3364+576+285}$$

$$= \sqrt{4225} = 65$$

Hence, $r = 65 > 60$

$\Rightarrow$ $r = 60.$

55. Given, the coordinates of three vertices of a parallelogram ABCD are A(1, 3), B(–1, 2) and C(3, 5)

Let D is (x, y)

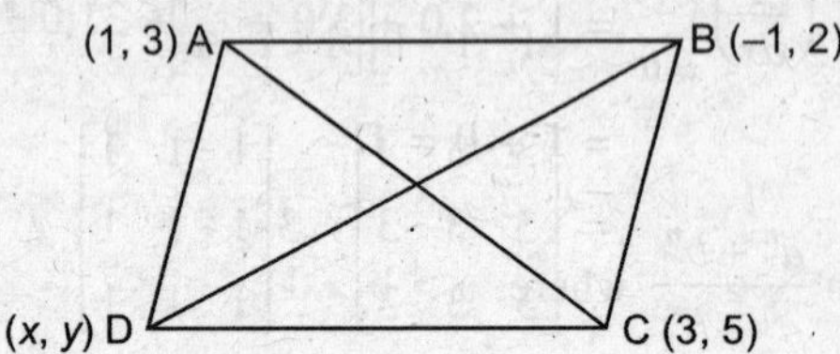

$\because$ Area of ΔABD

$$= \frac{1}{2}\left|\{x_1(y_2-y_3)+x_2(y_3-y_1)+x_3(y_1-y_3)\}\right|$$

Here, Area of ΔABD = Area of ΔBCD

$$\Rightarrow \frac{1}{2}\left|\{1(2-y)+-1(y-3)+x(3-2)\}\right|$$

$$= \frac{1}{2}\left|\{-1(5-y)+3(y-2)+x(2-5)\}\right|$$

$$\Rightarrow 2-y-y+3+x = -5+y+3y-6-3x$$

$$\Rightarrow 5-2y+x = -11+4y-3x$$

$$\Rightarrow 16 = 6y-4x$$

$$\Rightarrow 3y-2x = 8$$

$$\Rightarrow 2x-3y = -8$$

$$\Rightarrow 2x-3y+8 = 0$$

Which is the equation of the diagonal BD.

56. Area of $\Delta ABC = \frac{1}{2}\left|\{1(2-5)+-1(5-3)+3(3-2)\}\right|$

$$= \frac{1}{2}|-3-2+3| = \frac{1}{2}|-2| = \frac{1}{2}\times 2$$

$= 1$ sq. units

Hence, the area of the parallelogram

$= 2 \times$ area of ΔABC

$= 2 \times 1 = 2$ sq. units.

57. Given, the equation of the sides AB, BC and CA of a triangle ABC are

$x - 2 = 0$ ...(*i*)

$y + 1 = 0$ ...(*ii*)

and $x + 2y - 4 = 0$ ...(*iii*)

Solving the equation, from (*i*) and (*ii*),

$$x = 2,\ y = -1.$$

$\therefore$ Vertex B as B(2, –1)

from (*ii*) and (*iii*), $y = -1$

$$\therefore \quad x = 4-2y = 4-2\times -1 = 4+2 = 6$$

$\therefore$ Vertex C as C(6, –1)

from (*i*) and (*iii*), $x = 2$

$$\therefore \quad y = \frac{4-x}{2} = \frac{4-2}{2} = \frac{2}{2} = 1$$

$\therefore$ Vertex A as A(2, 1)

$\because$ Slope of side AC

$$x+2y-4 = 0$$

$$\Rightarrow 2y = x+4$$

$$\Rightarrow y = \frac{1}{2}x+2 \Rightarrow y = mx+c$$

$$\therefore \quad m = \frac{1}{2}$$

$$\therefore \text{ Slope of altitude BM} = \frac{1}{m} = \frac{1}{1/2} = 2$$

$\therefore$ Equation of altitude BM is

$$y - y_1 = 2(x - x_1)$$

$$\Rightarrow y+1 = 2(x-2)$$

$$\Rightarrow y+1 = 2x-4$$

$$\Rightarrow 2x-4-y-1 = 0$$

$$\Rightarrow 2x-y-5 = 0$$

Which is equation of the altitude through B on AC.

58. Circumcentre: Let (x, y) be the co-ordinates of the circumcentre 0 (say)

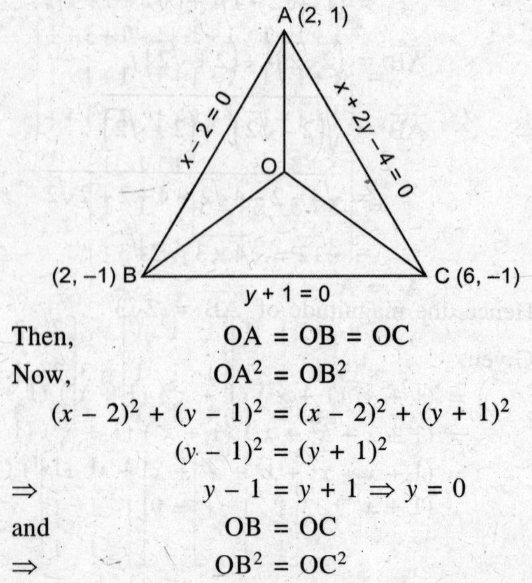

Then, OA = OB = OC

Now, $OA^2 = OB^2$

$$(x-2)^2+(y-1)^2 = (x-2)^2+(y+1)^2$$

$$(y-1)^2 = (y+1)^2$$

$$\Rightarrow y-1 = y+1 \Rightarrow y = 0$$

and OB = OC

$\Rightarrow$ $OB^2 = OC^2$

$\Rightarrow (x-2)^2 + (x+1)^2 = (x-6)^2 + (x+1)^2$

$\Rightarrow (x-2)^2 = (x-6)^2$

$\Rightarrow x^2 + 4 - 4x = x^2 + 36 - 12x$

$\Rightarrow 4 - 4x - 36 + 12x = 0$

$\Rightarrow 8x - 32 = 0$

$\Rightarrow x = 4$

Hence, the co-ordinates of circumcentre are (4, 0).

67. Given, $\vec{a}+3\vec{b} = 3\hat{i}-\hat{j}$

$\Rightarrow 2\vec{a}+6\vec{b} = 6\hat{i}-2\hat{j}$ ...(i)

and $2\vec{a}+\vec{b} = \hat{i}-2\hat{j}$ ...(ii)

From (i)–(ii), $5\vec{b} = 5\hat{i}+0$

$\Rightarrow \vec{b} = \hat{i}$

From (ii), $2\vec{a}+\hat{i} = \hat{i}-2\hat{j}$

$\Rightarrow 2\vec{a} = -2\hat{j}$

$\Rightarrow \vec{a} = -\hat{j}$

Let θ be the angle between $\vec{a}$ and $\vec{b}$

Then, $\cos\theta = \dfrac{\vec{a}.\vec{b}}{|\vec{a}||\vec{b}|} = \dfrac{0}{(1)(1)} = \dfrac{0}{1} = 0$

$\Rightarrow \cos\theta = 0$

$\Rightarrow \cos\theta = \cos\dfrac{\pi}{2}$

$\Rightarrow \theta = \dfrac{\pi}{2}$.

70. ∵ $\overrightarrow{AB}$ = the position vector of B – the position vector of A

$= \hat{i}+(\sqrt{2}+1)\hat{j}-[(\sqrt{2}-1)\hat{i}-\hat{j}]$

$= \hat{i}+(\sqrt{2}+1)\hat{j}-(\sqrt{2}-1)\hat{i}+\hat{j}$

$= (1-\sqrt{2}+1)\hat{i}+(\sqrt{2}+1+1)\hat{j}$

$\overrightarrow{AB} = (2\sqrt{2})\hat{i}+(2+\sqrt{2})\hat{j}$

$\Rightarrow \overrightarrow{AB} = \sqrt{(2-\sqrt{2})^2+(2+\sqrt{2})^2}$

$= \sqrt{4+2-4\sqrt{2}+4+2+2\sqrt{2}}$

$= \sqrt{12} = \sqrt{4\times 3} = 2\sqrt{3}$

Hence, the magnitude of $\overrightarrow{AB} = 2\sqrt{3}$.

71. Given,

$y = (1+x)(1+x^2)(1+x^4)(1+x^8)(1+x^{16})$

$= (1+x+x^2+x^3)(1+x^4)(1+x^8)(1+x^{16})$

$= (1+x+x^2+x^3+x^4+x^5+x^6+x^7)(1+x^8)(1+x^{16})$

$= (1+x+x^2+x^3+x^4+x^5+x^6+x^7+x^8+x^9+x^{10}+x^{11}+x^{12}+x^{13}+x^{14}+x^{15})(1+x^{16})$

$\Rightarrow y = 1+x+x^2+x^3+x^4+x^5+x^6+x^7+x^8+x^9+x^{10}+x^{11}+x^{12}+x^{13}+x^{14}+x^{15}+x^{16}+x^{17}+x^{18}+x^{19}+x^{20}+x^{21}+x^{22}+x^{23}+x^{24}+x^{25}+x^{26}+x^{27}+x^{28}+x^{29}+x^{30}+x^{31}$

$\Rightarrow \dfrac{dy}{dx} = 0+1+2x+3x+4x^3+5x^4+\ldots+31x^{30}$

$\Rightarrow \left(\dfrac{dy}{dx}\right)_{x=0} = 1+2.0+3.0+\ldots+31.0$

$= 1+0 = 1.$

74. $\lim\limits_{n\to\infty}\dfrac{a^n+b^n}{a^n-b^n}$ where, a > b > 1

$= \lim\limits_{n\to\infty}\dfrac{a^n-b^n+2b^n}{a^n-b^n} = \lim\limits_{n\to\infty}\left(1+\dfrac{2b^n}{a^n-b^n}\right)$

$= 1+2\lim\limits_{n\to\infty}\dfrac{\frac{b^n}{b^n}}{\frac{a^n-b^n}{b^n}} = 1+2\lim\limits_{n\to\infty}\dfrac{1}{\left(\frac{a}{b}\right)^n-1}$

$= 1+2.\dfrac{1}{\infty} = 1+2.0+1+0 = 1.$

88. $y = A-\dfrac{B}{x}$

Differentiating both sides with respect to x, we get

$\dfrac{dy}{dx} = 0-B.\dfrac{-1}{x^2}$

$\Rightarrow y_1 = \dfrac{B}{x^2}$

Multiplying both sides by x

$xy_1 = \dfrac{B}{x}$

Differentiating both sides with respect to x, we get,

$xy_2+y_1.1 = B.\dfrac{-1}{x^2}$

$\Rightarrow xy_2+y_1 = \dfrac{-B}{x^2}$

$\Rightarrow xy_2+y_1 = -y_1$ $\left[\because y_1 = \dfrac{B}{x^2}\right]$

$\Rightarrow xy_2+y_1+y_1 = 0$

$\Rightarrow xy_2+2y_1 = 0$

Which is required differential equation.

89. Let $I = \int_0^{\pi} \ln\left(\tan\frac{x}{2}\right) dx$

$$= \int_0^{\pi} \log\left(\tan\frac{x}{2}\right) dx \quad ...(i)$$

Then, $I = \int_0^{\pi} \log\tan\left(\frac{\pi - x}{2}\right) dx$

$$\left[\text{using } \int_0^a f(x)dx = \int_0^a f(a-x)dx\right]$$

$$= \int_0^{\pi} \log\tan\left(\frac{\pi}{2} - \frac{x}{2}\right) dx$$

$$= \int_0^{\pi} \log\left(\cot\frac{x}{2}\right) dx \quad ...(ii)$$

Adding (*i*) and (*ii*), we get,

$$2I = \int_0^{\pi} \left(\log\tan\frac{x}{2} + \log\cot\frac{x}{2}\right) dx$$

$$\Rightarrow \quad 2I = \int_0^{\pi} \log\left(\tan\frac{x}{2} \times \cot\frac{x}{2}\right) dx$$

$$\Rightarrow \quad 2I = \int_0^{\pi} \log 1\, dx = \int_0^{\pi} 0\, dx = 0$$

$$\Rightarrow \quad 2I = 0 \Rightarrow I = 0.$$

92. Let ABCD be a rectangle inscribed in a given circle with centre at O and radius 2.

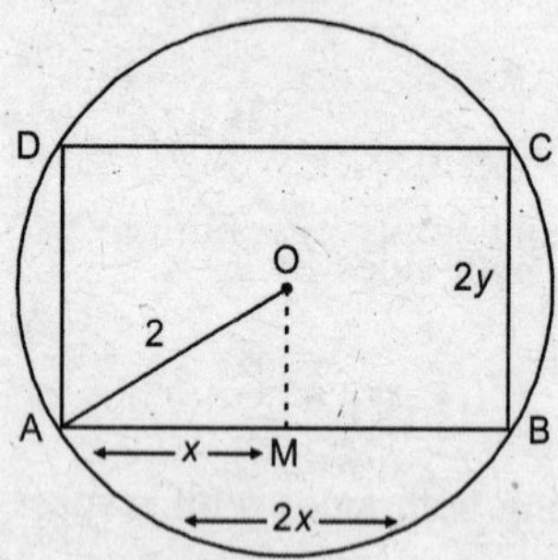

Let AB = $2x$ and BC = $2y$

Applying Pythagoras theorem in right triangle OAM.

$$OA^2 = AM^2 + OM^2$$

$$\Rightarrow \quad 2^2 = x^2 + y^2$$

$$\Rightarrow \quad y = \sqrt{4 - x^2} \quad ...(i)$$

Let A be the area of the rectangle ABCD. Then,

$$A = 4xy = 4 \times \sqrt{4 - x^2}$$

$$\Rightarrow \quad \frac{dA}{dx} = 4\left[\sqrt{4 - x^2} - \frac{x^2}{\sqrt{4 - x^2}}\right] = 4\left[\frac{4 - 2x^2}{\sqrt{4 - x^2}}\right]$$

The critical point of A are given by $\frac{dA}{dx} = 0$

$$\therefore \quad \frac{dA}{dx} = 0 \Rightarrow 4\left[\frac{4 - 2x^2}{\sqrt{4 - x^2}}\right] = 0$$

$$\Rightarrow \quad 4 - 2x^2 = 0 \Rightarrow 2 - x^2 = 0 \Rightarrow x = \sqrt{2}$$

Now, $\frac{dA}{dx} = 4\left[\frac{4 - 2x^2}{\sqrt{4 - x^2}}\right] = 8\left[\frac{2 - x^2}{\sqrt{4 - x^2}}\right]$

$$= 8(2 - x^2)(4 - x^2)^{-\frac{1}{2}}$$

$$\Rightarrow \quad \frac{d^2A}{dx^2} = 8\left\{(4 - x^2)^{\frac{-1}{2}}.(-2x) + (2 - y^2).\left(\frac{-1}{2}\right)(4 - x^2)^{\frac{-3}{2}}.(-2x)\right\}$$

$$\Rightarrow \quad \frac{d^2A}{dx^2} = 8\left\{\frac{-2x}{\sqrt{4 - x^2}} + \frac{(2 - x^2)x}{(4 - x^2)^{3/2}}\right\}$$

$$\Rightarrow \left(\frac{d^2A}{dx^2}\right)_{x=\sqrt{2}} = 8\left\{\frac{-2\sqrt{2}}{\sqrt{4 - 2}} + \frac{(2 - 2)\sqrt{2}}{(4 - 2)^{3/2}}\right\}$$

$$= 8\left\{\frac{-2\sqrt{2}}{\sqrt{2}} + 0\right\} = -16$$

$$\Rightarrow \quad -16 < 0$$

$\Rightarrow$ Thus A is maximum.

Putting $x = \sqrt{2}$ in (*i*), we get $y = \sqrt{2}$

Hence, Maximum area of a rectangle

$$= 2x \times 2y = 4xy$$

$$= 4.\sqrt{2}.\sqrt{2} = 8 \text{ sq. units.}$$

93. Let $I = \int \frac{dx}{x(x^2 + 1)} = \int \frac{x\,dx}{x^2(x^2 + 1)}$

Put, $x^2 + 1 = t$

$$\Rightarrow \quad 2xdx = dt \Rightarrow xdx = \frac{1}{2}dt$$

Then, $I = \int \frac{\frac{1}{2}dt}{(t - 1)(t)} = \frac{1}{2}\int \frac{dt}{t(t - 1)}$

$$= \frac{1}{2}\int\left(\frac{1}{t - 1} - \frac{1}{t}\right) dt = \frac{1}{2}\left[\int \frac{dt}{t - 1} - \int \frac{1}{t}dt\right]$$

$$= \frac{1}{2}\left[\log(t - 1) - \log t\right] + c = \frac{1}{2}\log\frac{t - 1}{t} + c$$

$$= \frac{1}{2}\log\frac{x^2 + 1 - 1}{x^2 + 1} + c$$

$$= \frac{1}{2}\log\frac{x^2}{x^2 + 1} + c.$$

94. Let, $u = e^{e^x}$, put $t = e^x \Rightarrow \frac{dt}{dx} = e^x$

$\Rightarrow \quad u = e^t$

$\Rightarrow \quad \frac{du}{dx} = e^t \frac{dt}{dx}$

$= e^t \cdot e^x$

$= e^{e^x} . e^x = e^x . e^{e^x}$

and $\quad v = e^x$

$\Rightarrow \quad \frac{dv}{dx} = e^x$

Hence, the derivative of u with respect to v

$$\Rightarrow \quad \frac{\frac{du}{dx}}{\frac{dv}{dx}} = \frac{e^x . e^{e^x}}{e^x} = e^{e^x}.$$

104. Given, A, B, C be the respective events of solving the problems

Then, $\quad P(A) = \frac{1}{2}, P(B) = \frac{3}{4}$ and $P(C) = P$

Clearly, A, B, C are independent events

$\therefore$ Required probability $= P(A \cup B \cup C)$

$= 1 - P(\bar{A}) P(\bar{B}) P(\bar{C})$

$\therefore \quad \frac{29}{32} = 1 - \left(1 - \frac{1}{2}\right)\left(1 - \frac{3}{4}\right)(1 - P)$

$\Rightarrow \quad \frac{29}{32} = 1 - \frac{1}{2} \times \frac{1}{4}(1 - P)$

$\Rightarrow \quad \frac{29}{32} = 1 - \frac{1}{8}(1 - P)$

$\Rightarrow \quad \frac{1}{8}(1 - P) = 1 - \frac{29}{32}$

$\Rightarrow \quad \frac{1}{8}(1 - P) = \frac{3}{32}$

$\Rightarrow \quad 1 - P = \frac{3}{32} \times 8$

$\Rightarrow \quad 1 - P = \frac{3}{4}$

$\Rightarrow \quad P = 1 - \frac{3}{4}$

$\Rightarrow \quad P = \frac{1}{4}.$

105. Here, $\quad n(S) = 60$

Let E = event of he does not hit a six

Then, $\quad n(E) = 60 - 8$

$\Rightarrow \quad n(E) = 52$

$\therefore \quad P(E) = \frac{n(E)}{n(S)} = \frac{52}{60}$

$\Rightarrow \quad P(E) = \frac{13}{15}.$

108.

Marks	Number of students (f_i)	C.f.
15-20	4	4
20-25	5	9
25-30	11	20
30-35	6	26
35-40	5	31
40-45	8	39
45-50	9	48
50-55	6	54
55-60	4	58
60-65	2	60
	$\Sigma f_i = 60$	

Here, N = 60 and $\frac{N}{2} = 30$

The class whose cumulative frequency is either equal to $\frac{N}{2}$ or is just greater than $\frac{N}{2}$ is called Median class

i.e., Just greater than $\frac{N}{2} = 31$

and Median class = 35-40

For a continuous distribution

$$\text{Median} = M_d = l + \frac{\frac{N}{2} - C}{f} \times h$$

$$= 35 + \frac{30 - 26}{5} \times 5$$

$$= 35 + 4 = 39$$

Where, l = lower limit of median class

f = frequency of the median class

N = Total frequency = Σf_i

C = c.f. of the class just before the median class

h = length of the median class.

109. Here, maximum frequency = 11 is called modal class

i.e, Modal class $\Rightarrow$ 25-30

Mode for continuous distribution,

$$M_o = l + \frac{f_0 - f_1}{2f_0 - f_1 - f_2} \times h$$

$$= 25 + \frac{11-5}{2\times 11 - 5 - 6} \times 5$$

$$= 25 + \frac{6}{22-11} \times 5 = 25 + \frac{6}{11} \times 5$$

$$= 25 + \frac{30}{11} = 25 + 2.727272$$

$$= 27.727272 = 27.73$$

where, l = lower limit of the modal class

f_0 = frequency of modal class

f_1 = frequency of the pre-modal class

f_2 = frequency of the post-modal class

h = length of the class-interval.

110. Here, first term = a = 15, d = 1, t_n = 64

$\because$ $t_n = a + (n - 1)d$

$\therefore$ $64 + 15 + (n - 1) . 1$

$\Rightarrow$ $n - 1 = 64 - 15$

$\Rightarrow$ $n - 1 = 49$

$\Rightarrow$ $n = 49 + 1$

$\Rightarrow$ $n = 50$

$\because$ $S_n = \frac{n}{2}[2a + (n-1)d]$

$\therefore$ $S_{50} = \frac{50}{2}[2 \times 15 + (50-1).1]$

$= 25[30 + 49]$

$= 25 \times 79$

Hence, $\text{Mean} = \frac{\text{Sum of natural number in the inteval [15, 64]}}{\text{Number of terms}}$

$= \frac{25 \times 79}{50} = \frac{79}{2} = 39.5.$

112. $\because$ The sum of 10 observation = 10 × 5.5 = 55

Given, each observation is multiplied by 4 and subtracted from 44

= 44 × 10 − 55 × 4

= 440 − 220 = 220

Hence, the new mean = $\frac{220}{10} = 22.$

114. $\because$ Harmonic Mean = 48

$$\frac{2ab}{a+b} = 48$$

$\Rightarrow$ $\frac{2 \times 60 \times x}{60 + x} = 48$

$\Rightarrow$ $\frac{2 \times 5 \times x}{60 + x} = 4$

$\Rightarrow$ $5x = 2(60 + x)$

$\Rightarrow$ $5x = 120 + 2x$

$\Rightarrow$ $5x - 2x = 120$

$\Rightarrow$ $3x = 120$

$\Rightarrow$ $x = 40.$

115. $\because$ Mean deviation of first n even natural number

$$= \frac{2n}{4} = \frac{2 \times 10}{4} = \frac{20}{4} = 5.$$

116. Given, $\sum_{i=1}^{10} x_i = 110$ and $\sum_{i=1}^{10} x_i^2 = 1540$

$\because$ $\text{Var}(x) = \frac{1}{n}\sum_{i=1}^{n} x_i^2 - \left\{\frac{1}{n}\sum_{i=1}^{n} x_i\right\}^2$

$= \frac{1}{10}(1540) - \left\{\frac{1}{10}(110)\right\}^2$

$= 154 - (11)^2$

$= 154 - 121 = 33.$

119. Given, $P(\text{not } A) = \frac{7}{10}$

$\Rightarrow$ $P(A) = 1 - \frac{7}{10} = \frac{3}{10}$

$P(\text{not } B) = \frac{3}{10}$

$\Rightarrow$ $P(B) = 1 - \frac{3}{10} = \frac{7}{10}$

and $P\left(\frac{A}{B}\right) = \frac{13}{14}$

$\because$ $P\left(\frac{A}{B}\right) = \frac{P(A \cap B)}{P(B)}$

$\therefore$ $\frac{13}{14} = \frac{P(A \cap B)}{7/10}$

$\Rightarrow$ $P(A \cap B) = \frac{3}{14} \times \frac{7}{10} = \frac{3}{20}$

and $P\left(\frac{B}{A}\right) = \frac{P(A \cap B)}{P(A)}$

$\Rightarrow$ $P\left(\frac{B}{A}\right) = \frac{3/20}{3/10} = \frac{3}{20} \times \frac{10}{3} = \frac{1}{2}$

$\Rightarrow$ $P\left(\frac{B}{A}\right) = \frac{1}{2}.$

Previous Papers (Solved)

NATIONAL DEFENCE ACADEMY & NAVAL ACADEMY

NDA & NA – Entrance Exam, 2021 (I)

PAPER I : GENERAL ABILITY TEST

PART A : ENGLISH LANGUAGE

SYNONYMS

Directions (Qs. No. 1-10): *Each item in this section consists of a sentence with an underlined word followed by four words. Select the option that is* ***nearest in meaning*** *to the underlined word and mark your response in your Answer Sheet accordingly.*

1. Her smile was contagious.
A. arrogant B. disrespectful
C. sarcastic D. catching

2. Her dynamic nature impressed everyone.
A. cenduring B. attentive
C. evolutionary D. jealous

3. She was lamenting her destiny.
A. celebrating B. bemoaning
C. blaming D. making

4. Under his leadership the company grew in an organic manner.
A. natural B. speedy
C. unusual D. disciplined

5. His charm lies in his oratory.
A. deceit B. eloquence
C. looks D. nobility

6. She is a patron of art and culture.
A. entrepreneur B. admirer
C. critique D. backer

7. Arrogance is a hallmark of his nature.
A. concern B. unpretentiousness
C. conceit D. simplicity

8. She undertook a reconnaissance of the entire issue.
A. revaluation B. ratification
C. investigation D. regularisation

9. My daughter is my replica.
A. pride B. clone
C. love D. original

10. The sardonic nature of her stories made her stand out among the contemporary writers.
A. compassionate B. insightful
C. mocking D. comic

ANTONYMS

Directions (Qs. No. 11-20): *Each item in this section consists of a sentence with an underlined word followed by four words. Select the option that is opposite in meaning to the underlined word and mark your response in your Answer Sheet accordingly.*

11. He found her extremely attractive and charming.
A. unnatural B. modern
C. repulsive D. disapproving

12. The sky is boundless.
A. high B. vast
C. expansive D. finite

13. The sky is clear today.
A. bright B. opaque
C. cloudless D. blue

14. I have a fascination for deep waters.
A. dark B. light
C. dangerous D. shallow

15. My boss has been too generous.
A. stingy B. rough
C. evil D. hostile

16. Spring is a time of plenty.
A. ugliness B. scarcity
C. roughness D. dryness

17. He is an industrious workman.
A. active B. productive
C. lazy D. disloyal

18. Plants grow in abundance here.
A. shrivel B. stretch
C. spread D. enlarge

19. She rarely comes here.
A. seldom B. never
C. always D. frequently

20. She is a rather crooked woman.
A. polite
B. generous
C. straightforward
D. happy

IDIOMS AND PHRASES

Directions (Qs. No. 21-30): *Given below are some idioms/phrases followed by four alternative meanings to each. Choose the response A, B, C or D, whichever is the most appropriate expression and mark your response in your Answer Sheet accordingly.*

21. Overstep the mark
A. To tell people how successful you are
B. To step into someone else's areas of expertise
C. To upset someone by doing/saying more than you should
D. To do something in an excited way

22. Palsy-walsy friends
A. Good friends
B. Friends who help each other in difficult situations
C. Friends by choice, and not by chance
D. Unfriendly

23. Open a Pandora's box
A. To do something that causes a lot of new problems that you did not expect
B. To do something out of compulsion
C. To do something beyond expectation
D. To do something out of the box, that causes awards and ceremonies for you

24. Pull your socks up
A. To get well-dressed for the occasion
B. Improve your work or behaviour
C. To speak in an honest way without hesitation
D. To be in control of an organization, often secretly

25. To get under somebody's skin
A. To deceive someone
B. To admire someone
C. To annoy someone
D. To support someone

26. Turn topsy-turvy
A. To completely change something
B. To completely evaluate something
C. To enjoy yourself greatly
D. To exhaust yourself completely

27. A clarion call
A. A trumpet call
B. An intimidating voice
C. A strong request
D. An urgent order

28. Fire in the belly
A. Fear and hatred
B. Powerful ambition
C. Love and dedication
D. Lethargy and indifference

29. A hunky-dory situation
A. There are serious issues among people
B. There are no problems and people are happy
C. There is war and bloodshed all over
D. There is no work, only enjoyment

30. Give somebody a leg up
A. To pull someone down
B. To deceive and betray someone
C. To help someone for their livelihood
D. To help someone to be successful

SPOTTING ERRORS

Directions (Qs. No. 31-40): *Each item in this section has a sentence with three underlined parts labelled A, B and C. Read each sentence to find out whether there is any error in any underlined part and indicate your response in the Answer Sheet against the corresponding letter i.e., A or B or C. If you find no error, your response should be indicated as D.*

31. You don't have (A)/a monopoly on suffering; (B)/ other people don't have problems too. (C)/ No error (D)

32. If you say that someone (A)/ you admire has feet of clay, (B)/ you mean that they have hidden faults. (C)/ No error (D)

33. He refused to change (A)/ his decision; (B)/ he refused it point out. (C)/ No error (D)

34. The importance of trade in Mughal times reinforced (A)/ the cultural definition of wealth as something (B)/ comprising of movable property. (C)/ No error (D)

35. In the nineteenth century, (A)/ most traditional scholars (B)/ tried to stay clear from the imperial Government. (C)/ No error (D)

36. He began his discussion by pointing over (A)/ that men and women (B)/ had different biological functions. (C)/ No error (D)

37. Though he is poor, (A)/ but he is (B)/ honest. (C)/ No error (D)

38. My mother (A)/ has been doing (B)/ everything for the family. (C)/ No error (D)

39. When learning to dive (A)/ it is important (B)/ to relax in between and take breaks. (C)/ No error (D)

40. I have the opportunity (A)/ to study (B)/ in America next year. (C)/ No error (D)

FILL IN THE BLANKS

Directions (Qs. No. 41-50): *Each of the following sentences in this section has a blank space and four words or group of words given after the sentence. Select the word or group of words you consider most appropriate for the blank space and indicate your response on the Answer Sheet accordingly.*

41. There was a time when West Germany was a distinct ________.
A. policy B. polity
C. abstract D. hierarchy

42. I was ______ with the film; I had expected it to be better.
A. disappointed B. disappointing
C. annoying D. prejudiced

43. It was a ________ experience. Everybody was shocked.
A. terrified B. horrified
C. terrifying D. denouncing

44. Elephants ______ when they perceive danger.
A. trumpet B. frolic
C. whine D. sing

45. The first film on Tagore was such a success that now they are going to make a ________.
A. serial B. sequence
C. sequel D. sequential

46. The United Nations had _______ 2020 as the International Year of Plant Health.
A. ruled B. ordered
C. foretold D. declared

47. My brother is _______ punctual, but he is late today.
A. normatively B. primarily
C. normally D. basically

48. My son is very _______ ; he trusts everyone.
A. fallible B. gullible
C. sensible D. credible

49. Mahatma Gandhi was a lover of humanity and a ________ believer in the goodness of human nature.
A. staunch B. powerful
C. cheerful D. hopeful

50. I wish I ______ her before we met.
A. know B. have known
C. knew D. known

PART B : GENERAL KNOWLEDGE

51. Consider the following statements about Light year:
1. Light year is a unit for measurement of very large distances.
2. Light year is a unit for measurement of very large time intervals.
3. Light year is a unit for measurement of intensity of light.

Which of the statements given above is/are correct?
A. 1, 2 and 3 B. 2 and 3 only
C. 1 and 2 only D. 1 only

52. Which one of the following regarding density of water at atmospheric pressure is correct?
A. Density of water at 4°C is 1000 kg/m^3.
B. Density of water at 0°C is 1000 kg/m^3.
C. Density of water at 0°C is 100 kg/m^3.
D. Density of water at 4°C is 10 kg/m^3.

53. Which of the following pairs of physical phenomenon and the discoverer is/are correctly matched?
1. James Chadwick : Photoelectric effect
2. Albert Einstein : Neutron
3. Marie Curie : Radium

Select the correct answer using the code given below:
A. 1, 2 and 3 B. 1 and 2 only
C. 2 and 3 only D. 3 only

54. LED (a semi-conductor device) is an abbreviation that stands for
A. Licence for Energy Detector
B. Light Energy Device
C. Light Emitting Diode
D. Lost Energy Detector

55. The statement "friction force is a contact force while magnetic force is a non-contact force" is
A. always true
B. true only at 0°C
C. a false statement
D. either true or false depending upon the temperature of the surroundings.

56. Which one of the following is the chemical formula of Hypobromous acid?
A. $HBrO_4$ B. HOBr
C. HBr D. $HBrO_3$

57. The composition of gases in exosphere is
A. Helium and Hydrogen
B. Neon and Oxygen
C. Neon and Hydrogen
D. Helium and Neon

58. Which one of the following is ***not*** used as a raw material in the manufacture of glass?
A. Soda B. Alumina
C. Borax D. Gypsum

59. In electrolytic refining of copper, the electrolyte is a solution of

A. acidified copper chloride
B. acidified copper sulphate
C. potassium chloride
D. sodium sulphate

60. Solder is an alloy of
A. Cu and Sn B. Fe and Zn
C. Pb and Sn D. Ag and Zn

61. Which one of the following statements about dihydrogen (H_2) is ***not*** correct?
A. H_2 is lighter than air and insoluble in water.
B. H_2 is inert at room temperature due to high H – H bond dissociation enthalpy.
C. H_2 reacts with alkali metals at high temperature to yield metal hydrides.
D. A mixture of NO_2 and H_2 is known as Syngas.

62. Which of the following sets of elements has the same valency?
A. Na, Mg, Ca B. Na, Mg, Al
C. Mg, Ca, K D. Mg, Ca, Ba

63. Which one of the following is the lowest possible temperature?
A. 0° Celsius B. –073° Celsius
C. –173° Celsius D. –273° Celsius

64. Numerically two thermometers, one in Fahrenheit scale and another in Celsius scale shall read same at
A. – 40° B. 0°
C. –273° D. 100°

65. The image we see in plane mirror is
A. real and thus can be photographed.
B. virtual and nearer than the object.
C. virtual and is laterally inverted.
D. real but cannot be photographed.

66. Which one of the following colours may be obtained by combining green and red colours?
A. Blue B. Magenta
C. Pink D. Yellow

67. Which of the following are the primary colours of light?
A. Yellow, Red and Green
B. Blue, Red and Green
C. Violet, Red and Yellow
D. Indigo, Violet and Green

68. According to the New Cartesian Sign Convention, which one of the following is correct in respect of the formula $\frac{1}{f}=\frac{1}{v}+\frac{1}{u}$, where symbols have their usual meanings?
A. It applies only to spherical mirrors.
B. It applies only to spherical lenses.
C. It applies to spherical mirrors as well as spherical lenses.
D. It is an invalid formula.

69. Movement of materials to different parts of cytoplasm and nucleus is generally carried out by
A. Ribosomes
B. Mitochondria
C. Lysosomes
D. Endoplasmic reticulum

70. In mitochondria, ATP synthesizing chemical reactions take place in the
A. Outer membrane
B. Matrix
C. Inner membrane
D. DNA of mitochondria

71. Squamous epithelial cells are found in the inner lining of
A. Oesophagus
B. Small intestine
C. Ducts of salivary gland
D. Kidney

72. Transformation of meristematic cells into specific permanent tissues occurs by the process of
A. Cell differentiation
B. Cell division
C. Cell multiplication
D. Cell regeneration

73. The gaseous product of a process in plants is a requirement for another vital process that releases energy. Given below are four combinations of the process and product. Identify the correct answer.
A. Respiration and Nitric oxide
B. Transpiration and Water vapour
C. Photosynthesis and Oxygen
D. Germination and Carbon dioxide

74. In a dicot pot herb, vaseline/vegetable oil was applied on the upper surface of one leaf (Experimental leaf 1) and on the lower surface of another leaf (Experimental leaf 2). Vaseline/Vegetable oil was not applied on the control leaf. The plant was deliberately not watered for several days. Which leaf will dry up last?
A. Experimental leaf 1
B. Experimental leaf 2
C. Control leaf
D. All the leaves will dry up simultaneously

75. Which one of the following statements is ***not*** correct for light rays?
A. Light travels at different speeds in different media.
B. Light travels at almost 300 million metres per second in air.
C. Light speeds down as it leaves a water surface and enters the air.
D. Light speeds up as it leaves a glass surface and enters the air.

76. A glass prism splits white light into different colours. This phenomenon is called dispersion of light by prism. Which one of the following statements is correct?
A. Red light will deviate the most and it is because of the reflection of light.
B. Violet light will deviate the most and it is because of the refraction of light.
C. Red light will deviate the most and it is because of the refraction of light.
D. Violet light will deviate the most and it is because of the reflection of light.

77. A current of 1.0 A is drawn by a filament of an electric bulb for 10 minutes. The amount of electric charge that flows through the circuit is
A. 0.1 C B. 10 C
C. 600 C D. 800 C

78. Which one of the following formulas does ***not*** represent electrical power?
A. I^2 R B. I R^2
C. V I D. V^2/R

79. The sound created in a big hall persists because of the repeated reflections. The phenomenon is called
A. Reverberation B. Dispersion
C. Refraction D. Diffraction

80. When light is scattered by a molecule and the frequency of the scattered light is changed, this phenomenon is called
A. Rayleigh scattering
B. Raman effect
C. Photoelectric effect
D. Rutherford scattering

81. Which one of the following statements about the cleansing action of soap is ***not*** true?
A. The oil and dirt gets collected in the centre of the micelle.
B. Soap micelles scatter light.
C. Soaps are ammonium salts of long chain carboxylic acids.
D. Soap forms insoluble precipitates with the calcium and magnesium ions in hard water.

82. Hydrogenation of vegetable oils using nickel catalyst is an example of
A. Substitution reaction
B. Elimination reaction
C. Addition reaction
D. Free-radical polymerization

83. Which one of the following materials is ***not*** an allotrope of carbon?
A. Diamond B. Graphene
C. Fly ash D. Fullerene

84. Which one of the following reactions does ***not*** result in the evolution of hydrogen gas?
A. Reaction of zinc metal with dilute sulphuric acid solution
B. Mixing water to Plaster of Paris
C. Heating zinc metal with sodium hydroxide solution
D. Reaction of potassium metal with water

85. Which one of the following acids is predominantly found in tomatoes?
A. Acetic acid B. Tartaric acid
C. Oxalic acid D. Lactic acid

86. Which one of the following conclusions could ***not*** be derived from Rutherford's α-particle scattering experiment?
A. Most of the space in the atom is empty.
B. The radius of the atom is about 10^5 times the radius of the nucleus.
C. Electrons move in a circular path of fixed energy called orbits.
D. Nearly all the mass of the atom resides in the nucleus.

87. Reaction of quick lime (CaO) with water to produce slaked lime ($Ca(OH)_2$) is an example of
A. Displacement reaction
B. Endothermic reaction
C. Decomposition reaction
D. Exothermic reaction

88. Which one of the following is ***not*** a bio-mass energy source?
A. Wood B. Nuclear reactor
C. Gobar gas D. Coal

89. Twinkling of stars is due to
A. particular frequencies of the starlight.
B. reflection of starlight from the oceanic surface.
C. atmospheric refraction of starlight.
D. magnetic field of Earth.

90. Which one of the following ***cannot*** be the unit of frequency of a sound wave?
A. dB B. s^{-1}
C. Hz D. min^{-1}

91. 'Beats' is a phenomenon that occurs when frequencies of two harmonic waves are
A. equal.
B. far apart.
C. multiples of each other.
D. nearly same.

92. Light waves are incident on an air-glass boundary. Some of the light waves are reflected and some are refracted in the glass. Which one of the following properties is the same for the incident wave and the refracted wave?
A. Speed B. Direction
C. Brightness D. Frequency

93. Which one of the following statements is true for a simple harmonic oscillator?
A. Force acting is directly proportional to the displacement from the mean position and is in same direction.
B. Force acting is directly proportional to the displacement from the mean position and is in opposite direction.
C. Acceleration of the oscillator is constant.
D. The velocity of the oscillator is not periodic.

94. During seed germination, the part of the embryo which grows into root is
A. Radicle B. Plumule
C. Cotyledon D. Epicotyl

95. In a typical flower, germinating pollen grains pass through several parts of the gynoecium before they reach the ovule. A list of the parts of gynoecium is given below in different combinations. Choose the combination that represents the correct sequence of pollen tube pathway/journey:
A. Style, Stigma, Ovary
B. Stigma, Style, Ovary
C. Pistil, Stigma, Ovary
D. Ovary, Pistil, Style

96. If human blood is placed in a 2% detergent solution, what will happen to the RBC?
A. The RBC will shrink.
B. The RBC will swell and become turgid.
C. The RBC will swell and burst.
D. The RBC will lyse.

97. The major source of vitamins and minerals for vegetarians is
A. black gram and wheat.
B. rice and mustard.
C. vegetables and fruits.
D. soya bean and milk.

98. If a ray of light enters from a rarer medium to a denser medium at zero angle of incidence, it would
A. reflect back B. go straight
C. turn towards right D. bend at 45°

99. Mirage is an illustration of
A. only dispersion of light.
B. only reflection of light.
C. only total internal reflection of light.
D. both refraction and total internal reflection of light.

100. Common salt (NaCl) is ***not*** used as a raw material for preparation of which one of the following compounds?
A. Bleaching powder
B. Baking soda
C. Plaster of Paris
D. Washing soda

101. Which one of the following Harappan sites was a specialised centre for making shell objects?
A. Lothal B. Balakot
C. Amri D. Kot Diji

102. Which one of the following was ***not*** a part of the *dhamma* of King Ashoka?
A. Honouring the king
B. Tolerance of religions other than one's own
C. Respecting Brahmanas
D. Promoting the welfare of his subjects

103. Which of the following statements about *Saguna* bhakti traditions is/are correct?
1. *Saguna* bhakti traditions focus on the worship of specific deities such as Vishnu or his avatars.
2. In *Saguna* bhakti traditions, Gods and Goddesses are conceptualised in anthropomorphic forms.

Select the correct answer using the code given below:
A. 1 only B. 2 only
C. Both 1 and 2 D. Neither 1 nor 2

104. At which one of the following places was a Shiva temple ***not*** constructed under the patronage of the Chola rulers?
A. Chidambaram
B. Thanjavur
C. Gangaikonda Cholapuram
D. Naneghat

105. Which of the following statements about the Deccan Riots Commission is/are correct?
1. The Commission did not hold enquiries in the districts which were not affected.
2. The Commission did record the statements of ryots, sahukars and eye-witnesses.

Select the correct answer using the code given below:
A. 1 only B. 2 only
C. Both 1 and 2 D. Neither 1 nor 2

106. Which one of the following is the correct meaning of *ziyarat*?
A. Pilgrimage to the tombs of sufi saints
B. The practice of revenue farming
C. The death anniversary of a sufi shaikh
D. A form of Islamic divorce

107. Keppel Island is completely bleached mainly due to the expansion of
A. Starfish B. Blue whale
C. Octopus D. Sea horse

108. Which one of the following rivers is ***not*** a tributary of river Brahmaputra?
A. River Manas
B. River Kameng
C. River Mahananda
D. River Subansiri

109. Which one of the following is ***not*** a minor plate?
A. Cocos Plate B. Nazca Plate
C. Caroline Plate D. Antarctic Plate

110. Advantage(s) of tectonic activity in Iceland include(s):
1. Source of natural geothermal energy
2. Creation of new land
3. Attraction of tourists

Select the correct answer using the code given below:
A. 1 only B. 2 and 3 only
C. 1 and 3 only D. 1, 2 and 3

111. The process whereby certain minerals absorb water, expand and change is called as
A. Hydration B. Oxidation
C. Hydrolysis D. Carbonation

112. Which one of the following is the longest Latitude?
A. 90 degree Latitude
B. 23.5 degree Latitude
C. 0.0 degree Latitude
D. 66.5 degree Latitude

113. If it is 12.00 Noon in India, on which meridian will it be 7.00 am of the same day?
A. 7.5 degree E. Longitude
B. 7.5 degree W. Longitude
C. 75 degree E. Longitude
D. 75 degree W. Longitude

114. Who among the following was considered to be the preceptor of Mirabai?
A. Dadu B. Raidas
C. Ramanand D. Surdas

115. Consider the following statements about the *Mahanavami Dibba*:
1. It was the name of a giant box of sweets distributed at the Mahanavami festival.
2. It was the name of a massive platform with a base covered with relief carvings.

Which of the statements given above is/are correct?
A. 1 only B. 2 only
C. Both 1 and 2 D. Neither 1 nor 2

116. Which one of the following statements about the *Ain-i-Akbari* is ***not*** correct?
A. It was written by Abu'l Fazl.
B. It is a part of a larger work called *Akbar Nama*.
C. It describes the Mughal Empire as having a diverse population and a composite culture.
D. It was later revised by Sadullah Khan on the orders of Shah Jahan.

117. Swami Dayanand Saraswati
1. was opposed to the worship of idols of Gods and Goddesses.
2. regarded the Vedas as infallible.
3. had met and had discussions with Ishwar Chandra Vidyasagar.

Which of the statements given above are correct?
A. 1, 2 and 3 B. 2 and 3 only
C. 1 and 3 only D. 1 and 2 only

118. Consider the following statements:
1. Muhammadan Anglo-Oriental College was founded at Aligarh by Sayyid Ahmad Khan.
2. Sayyid Ahmad Khan was a great believer in religious toleration, and Hindus, Parsis and Christians had contributed to the funds of his college.

Which of the statements given above is/are correct?
A. 1 only B. 2 only
C. Both 1 and 2 D. Neither 1 nor 2

119. Basket-of-eggs topography is related to
A. Drumlins B. Eskers
C. Cirques D. Moraines

120. Which one of the following planets has the highest density?
A. Mercury B. Venus
C. Jupiter D. Earth

121. Point of Origin of Earthquake Wave is known as
A. Epicentre B. Focus
C. Photosphere D. Seismic Zone

122. The maximum depth of Lithosphere is found in the
A. Pacific Ocean
B. Siberian Plain
C. Patagonian Desert
D. Himalayan Mountains

123. A large body of magmatic material that cools in the deeper depth of the Earth's crust and develops in the form of large domes is known as
A. Batholiths B. Lacoliths
C. Lopoliths D. Phacoliths

124. Which one of the following Oil Refineries is ***not*** located in Assam?
A. Tatipaka B. Numaligarh
C. Bongaigaon D. Digboi

125. Where and when did Mahatma Gandhi make his first public appearance in India on coming back from South Africa after two decades?
A. Champaran in 1917
B. Lucknow in 1916
C. Banaras Hindu University in 1916
D. Ahmedabad in 1918

126. When and where was the demand for "Purna Swaraj" or complete independence made by the Indian National Congress?

A. Bombay, 1885 B. Lahore, 1929
C. Kheda, 1917 D. Bombay, 1942

127. Which one of the following provides for the complete equality of men and women in India?
A. Articles 14 and 15 of the Constitution of India
B. Fifth Schedule of the Constitution of India
C. The Indian Independence Act
D. Article 20 of the Constitution of India

128. Which of the following statements about the non-permanent members of the Security Council of the United Nations is/are correct ?
1. Their total number is now 10, but was originally only 6.
2. They are elected for a term of two years only.

Select the correct answer using the code given below:
A. 1 only B. 2 only
C. Both 1 and 2 D. Neither 1 nor 2

129. At which of the following was the American Declaration of Independence adopted on 4 July, 1776?
A. Washington Conference
B. San Francisco Conference
C. Second Continental Congress
D. First Continental Congress

130. Who among the following was the head of the Government that was overthrown by the Bolsheviks in the 1917 Revolution?
A. Alexander Kerensky
B. Prince Lvov
C. Grand Duke Sergei
D. Tsar Nicholas II

131. Which one of the following is ***not*** a form of condensation?
A. Dew B. Fog
C. Frost D. Sleet

132. Which one of the following clouds is a rain-bearing cloud?
A. Cumulus cloud B. Stratus cloud
C. Nimbus cloud D. Cirrus cloud

133. In which one of the following countries is intensive subsistence agriculture ***not*** predominantly practised?
A. India B. Japan
C. Canada D. Indonesia

134. The Headquarters of South-Eastern Railway is located at
A. Bilaspur B. Secunderabad
C. Kolkata D. Bhubaneswar

135. Bharatmala Pariyojana is related to
A. interlinking of Northern and Southern Indian rivers in a garland shape.
B. networks of National Highways in India.
C. interlinking of all cities of India through Railways.
D. interlinking of all industrial regions of India through pipelines.

136. The natural vegetation which covers the maximum geographical areas of India is
A. Tropical deciduous forests
B. Tropical thorn forests
C. Montane forests
D. Tropical evergreen forests

137. River Beas, flowing from Himachal and Punjab, joins the river
A. Indus B. Satluj
C. Chenab D. Ravi

138. With regard to the Constitution of India, which one of the following statements is ***not*** correct?
A. The words — Socialist and Secular, were not originally part of the Constitution.
B. The Preamble states the objects of the Constitution of India.
C. The Preamble is enforceable in a Court of Law.
D. A Republic refers to the people as the source of all authority under the Constitution.

139. Which one of the following is ***not*** a power of the Speaker of the Lok Sabha?
A. Speaker shall preside over the House of the People.
B. Speaker will cast vote in the first instance in the House.
C. Speaker will have power to maintain order within the House of the People.
D. Speaker can adjourn the House or suspend the meeting till there is a quorum.

140. Which one of the following is included in Article 51A (Part IV A) of the Constitution of India?
A. Fundamental Duties
B. Suspension of Fundamental Rights
C. Special Powers of Governors
D. Writs

141. As per the data up to November, 2020, released by the Union Finance Ministry, which one of the following countries ranks 1 in terms of ODI (Outward Direct Investment) for the year 2020-21?
A. USA
B. Singapore
C. Mauritius
D. United Kingdom

142. 'Exercise Desert Knight – 21' is a bilateral air exercise between the Indian Air Force and the Air Force of which one of the following countries?
A. USA B. France
C. Britain D. Israel

143. Tableau of which one of the following States/Union Territory was adjudged best in the Republic Day Parade, 2021?

A. Ladakh B. Uttar Pradesh
C. Tripura D. Uttarakhand

144. In the recently concluded elections in December 2020, Faustin-Archange Touadera has won a second term in office as President of one of the following countries. Identify the country.
A. Central African Republic
B. Republic of South Africa
C. Republic of Ghana
D. Republic of Mozambique

145. Which one of the following statements is ***not*** correct in respect of the 'Legion of Merit' award?
A. This award is conferred by the President of the United States of America.
B. This award was conferred to the Prime Minister of India in December, 2020.
C. This was also awarded to the Prime Minister of Australia, Scott Morrison.
D. It is the highest civilian award of the United States of America.

146. Which one of the following statements is most appropriate about 'Exercise Kavach'?
A. It is a military exercise of the Indian Army only.
B. It is a joint military exercise involving the Indian Army and the Indian Navy only.
C. It is a joint military exercise involving the Indian Army, the Indian Navy and the Indian Air Force only.
D. It is a joint military exercise involving the Indian Army, the Indian Navy, the Indian Air Force and also the Indian Coast Guard.

147. Recently a state of emergency has been declared in which one of the following countries?
A. Maldives B. Bhutan
C. Nepal D. Myanmar

148. Which one of the following teams is the winner of the Syed Mushtaq Ali Trophy, 2021?
A. Uttar Pradesh
B. Punjab
C. Tamil Nadu
D. Baroda

149. Which country has replaced Maldives to host the 2023 Indian Ocean Island Games?
A. Madagascar
B. Sri Lanka
C. India
D. Mauritius

150. Identify the correct reason, out of the following, about Claire Polosak for being in the news:
A. She has been honoured with the Pulitzer Prize.
B. She recently won a Grand Slam championship.
C. She became the first female match official to conduct a men's cricket test match.
D. She has been conferred with the Gandhi Peace Prize.

PAPER II : MATHEMATICS

1. The smallest positive integer n for which

$$\left(\frac{1-i}{1+i}\right)^{n^2} = 1$$

where $i = \sqrt{-1}$, is
A. 2 B. 4
C. 6 D. 8

2. The value of x, satisfying the equation

$\log_{\cos x} \sin x = 1$, where $0 < x < \frac{\pi}{2}$, is

A. $\frac{\pi}{12}$ B. $\frac{\pi}{3}$

C. $\frac{\pi}{4}$ D. $\frac{\pi}{6}$

3. If Δ is the value of the determinant

$$\begin{vmatrix} a_1 & b_1 & c_1 \\ a_2 & b_2 & c_2 \\ a_3 & b_3 & c_3 \end{vmatrix}$$

then what is the value of the following determinant?

$$\begin{vmatrix} pa_1 & b_1 & qc_1 \\ pa_2 & b_2 & qc_2 \\ pa_3 & b_3 & qc_3 \end{vmatrix}$$

($p \neq 0$ or 1, $q \neq 0$ or 1)
A. $p\Delta$ B. $q\Delta$
C. $(p + q)\Delta$ D. $pq\Delta$

4. If $C_0, C_1, C_2, ..., C_n$ are the coefficients in the expansion of $(1 + x)^n$, then what is the value of $C_1 + C_2 + C_3 + ... + C_n$?
A. 2^n B. $2^n - 1$
C. 2^{n-1} D. $2^n - 2$

5. If $a + b + c = 4$ and $ab + bc + ca = 0$, then what is the value of the following determinant?

$$\begin{vmatrix} a & b & c \\ b & c & a \\ c & a & b \end{vmatrix}$$

A. 32 B. –64
C. –128 D. 64

6. The number of integer values of k, for which the equation $2 \sin x = 2k + 1$ has a solution, is
A. zero B. one
C. two D. four

7. If $a_1, a_2, a_3, \ldots, a_9$ are in GP, then what is the value of the following determinant?

$$\begin{vmatrix} \ln a_1 & \ln a_2 & \ln a_3 \\ \ln a_4 & \ln a_5 & \ln a_6 \\ \ln a_7 & \ln a_8 & \ln a_9 \end{vmatrix}$$

A. 0 B. 1
C. 2 D. 4

8. If the roots of the quadratic equation $x^2 + 2x + k = 0$ are real, then
A. $k < 0$ B. $k \leq 0$
C. $k < 1$ D. $k \leq 1$

9. If $n = 1001$, then what is the value of the following?

$$\frac{1}{\log_2 n} + \frac{1}{\log_3 n} + \frac{1}{\log_4 n} + \ldots + \frac{1}{\log_{100} n}$$

A. 0 B. 1
C. 2 D. 3

10. If $Z = 1 + i$, where $i = \sqrt{-1}$, then what is the modulus of $Z + \frac{2}{Z}$?
A. 1 B. 2
C. 3 D. 4

11. If A and B are two matrices such that AB is of order $n \times n$, then which one of the following is correct?
A. A and B should be square matrices of same order.
B. Either A or B should be a square matrix.
C. Both A and B should be of same order.
D. Orders of A and B need not be the same.

12. How many matrices of different orders are possible with elements comprising all prime numbers less than 30?
A. 2 B. 3
C. 4 D. 6

13. Let

$$A = \begin{vmatrix} p & q \\ r & s \end{vmatrix}$$

where p, q, r and s are any four different prime numbers less than 20. What is the maximum value of the determinant?
A. 215 B. 311
C. 317 D. 323

14. If A and B are square matrices of order 2 such that det(AB) = det(BA), then which one of the following is correct?
A. A must be a unit matrix.
B. B must be a unit matrix.
C. Both A and B must be unit matrices.
D. A and B need not be unit matrices.

15. What is
$\cot 2x \cot 4x - \cot 4x \cot 6x - \cot 6x \cot 2x$
equal to?
A. –1 B. 0
C. 1 D. 2

16. If $\tan x = -\frac{3}{4}$ and x is in the second quadrant, then what is the value of $\sin x \cdot \cos x$?
A. $\frac{6}{25}$ B. $\frac{12}{25}$
C. $-\frac{6}{25}$ D. $-\frac{12}{25}$

17. What is the value of the following?

$$\text{cosec}\left(\frac{7\pi}{6}\right)\sec\left(\frac{5\pi}{3}\right)$$

B. $\frac{4}{3}$ C. 4
C. –4 D. $-\frac{4}{\sqrt{3}}$

18. If the determinant

$$\begin{vmatrix} x & 1 & 3 \\ 0 & 0 & 1 \\ 1 & x & 4 \end{vmatrix} = 0$$

then what is x equal to?
A. –2 or 2 B. –3 or 3
C. –1 or 1 D. 3 or 4

19. What is the value of the following?
tan 31° tan 33° tan35° ... tan 57° tan 59°
A. –1 B. 0
C. 1 D. 2

20. If

$$f(x) = \begin{vmatrix} 1 & x & x+1 \\ 2x & x(x-1) & x(x+1) \\ 3x(x-1) & 2(x-1)(x-2) & x(x+1)(x-1) \end{vmatrix}$$

then what is $f(-1) + f(0) + f(1)$ equal to?
A. 0 B. 1
C. 100 D. –100

21. The equation $\sin^{-1}x - \cos^{-1}x = \frac{\pi}{6}$ has
A. no solution

B. unique solution
C. two solutions
D. infinite number of solutions

22. What is the value of the following?

(sin 24° + cos 66°) (sin 24° – cos 66°)

A. –1 B. 0
C. 1 D. 2

23. A chord subtends an angle 120° at the centre of a unit circle. What is the length of the chord?

A. $\sqrt{2}-1$ units B. $\sqrt{3}-1$ units
C. $\sqrt{2}$ units D. $\sqrt{3}$ units

24. What is

(1 + cot θ – cosec θ) (1 + tan θ + sec θ)

equal to?

A. 1 B. 2
C. 3 D. 4

25. What is

$$\frac{1+\tan^2\theta}{1+\cot^2\theta}-\left(\frac{1-\tan\theta}{1-\cot\theta}\right)^2$$

equal to?

A. 0 B. 1
C. 2 tan θ D. 2 cot θ

26. What is the interior angle of a regular octagon of side length 2 cm ?

A. $\frac{\pi}{2}$ B. $\frac{3\pi}{4}$
C. $\frac{3\pi}{5}$ D. $\frac{3\pi}{8}$

27. If 7 sin θ + 24 cos θ = 25, then what is the value of (sin θ + cos θ)?

A. 1 B. $\frac{26}{25}$
C. $\frac{6}{5}$ D. $\frac{31}{25}$

28. A ladder 6 m long reaches a point 6 m below the top of a vertical flagstaff. From the foot of the ladder, the elevation of the top of the flagstaff is 75°. What is the height of the flagstaff?

A. 12 m B. 9 m
C. $(6+\sqrt{3})$ m D. $(6+3\sqrt{3})$ m

29. The shadow of a tower is found to be x metre longer, when the angle of elevation of the sun changes from 60° to 45°. If the height of the tower is $5(3+\sqrt{3})$m, then what is x equal to?

A. 8 m B. 10 m
C. 12 m D. 15 m

30. If 3 cos θ = 4 sin θ, then what is the value of tan (45° + θ) ?

A. 10 B. 7
C. $\frac{7}{2}$ D. $\frac{7}{4}$

31. $\tan^{-1}x + \cot^{-1}x = \frac{\pi}{2}$ holds, when

A. $x \in$ R
B. $x \in$ R – (–1, 1) only
C. $x \in$ R – {0} only
D. $x \in$ R – [–1, 1] only

32. If tan A = $\frac{1}{7}$, then what is cos 2A equal to?

A. $\frac{24}{25}$ B. $\frac{18}{25}$
C. $\frac{12}{25}$ D. $\frac{6}{25}$

33. The sides of a triangle are m, n and $\sqrt{m^2+n^2+mn}$. What is the sum of the acute angles of the triangle?

A. 45° B. 60°
C. 75° D. 90°

34. What is the area of the triangle ABC with sides a = 10 cm, c = 4 cm and angle B = 30°?

A. 16 cm² B. 12 cm²
C. 10 cm² D. 8 cm²

35. Consider the following statements:

1. A = {1, 3, 5} and B = {2, 4, 7} are equivalent sets.
2. A = {1, 5, 9} and B = {1, 5, 5, 9, 9} are equal sets.

Which of the above statements is/are correct?

A. 1 only B. 2 only
C. Both 1 and 2 D. Neither 1 nor 2

36. Consider the following statements:

1. The null set is a subset of every set.
2. Every set is a subset of itself.
3. If a set has 10 elements, then its power set will have 1024 elements.

Which of the above statements are correct?

A. 1 and 2 only B. 2 and 3 only
C. 1 and 3 only D. 1, 2 and 3

37. Let R be a relation defined as xRy if and only if $2x + 3y = 20$, where $x, y \in$ N. How many elements of the form (x, y) are there in R?

A. 2 B. 3
C. 4 D. 6

38. Consider the following statements:

1. A function $f : \mathbb{Z} \to \mathbb{Z}$, defined by $f(x) = x + 1$, is one-one as well as onto.

2. A function $f : \mathbb{N} \to \mathbb{N}$, defined by $f(x) = x + 1$, is one-one but not onto.

Which of the above statements is/are correct?

A. 1 only
B. 2 only
C. Both 1 and 2
D. Neither 1 nor 2

39. Consider the following in respect of a complex number Z :

1. $\overline{(Z^{-1})} = (\overline{Z})^{-1}$
2. $ZZ^{-1} = |Z|^2$

Which of the above is/are correct?

A. 1 only B. 2 only
C. Both 1 and 2 D. Neither 1 nor 2

40. Consider the following statements in respect of an arbitrary complex number Z :

1. The difference of Z and its conjugate is an imaginary number.
2. The sum of Z and its conjugate is a real number.

Which of the above statements is/are correct?

A. 1 only B. 2 only
C. Both 1 and 2 D. Neither 1 nor 2

41. What is the modulus of the complex number where $i^{2n+1}(-i)^{2n-1}$, where $n \in \mathbb{N}$ and $i = \sqrt{-1}$?

A. –1 B. 1
C. $\sqrt{2}$ D. 2

42. If α and β are the roots of the equation $4x^2 + 2x - 1 = 0$, then which one of the following is correct?

A. $\beta = -2\alpha^2 - 2\alpha$ B. $\beta = 4\alpha^2 - 3\alpha$
C. $\beta = \alpha^2 - 3\alpha$ D. $\beta = -2\alpha^2 + 2\alpha$

43. If one root of $5x^2 + 26x + k = 0$ is reciprocal of the other, then what is the value of k?

A. 2 B. 3
C. 5 D. 8

44. In how many ways can a team of 5 players be selected from 8 players so as not to include a particular player?

A. 42 B. 35
C. 21 D. 20

45. What is the coefficient of the middle term in the expansion of $(1 + 4x + 4x^2)^5$?

A. 8064 B. 4032
C. 2016 D. 1008

46. What is $C(n, 1) + C(n, 2) + ... + C(n, r)$ equal to?

A. $2 + 2^2 + 2^3 + ... + 2^n$
B. $1 + 2 + 2^2 + 2^3 + ... + 2^n$
C. $1 + 2 + 2^2 + 2^3 + ... + 2^{n-1}$
D. $2 + 2^2 + 2^3 + ... + 2^{n-1}$

47. What is the sum of the coefficients of first and last terms in the expansion of $(1 + x)^{2n}$, where n is a natural number?

A. 1 B. 2
C. n D. $2n$

48. If the first term of an AP is 2 and the sum of the first five terms is equal to one-fourth of the sum of the next five terms, then what is the sum of the first ten terms?

A. –500 B. –250
C. 500 D. 250

49. Consider the following statements:

1. If each term of a GP is multiplied by same non-zero number, then the resulting sequence is also a GP.
2. If each term of a GP is divided by same non-zero number, then the resulting sequence is also a GP.

Which of the above statements is/are correct?

A. 1 only B. 2 only
C. Both 1 and 2 D. Neither 1 nor 2

50. How many 5-digit prime numbers can be formed using the digits 1, 2, 3, 4, 5 if the repetition of digits is not allowed?

A. 5 B. 4
C. 3 D. 0

51. If $f(x + 1) = x^2 - 3x + 2$, then what is $f(x)$ equal to?

A. $x^2 - 5x + 4$ B. $x^2 - 5x + 6$
C. $x^2 + 3x + 3$ D. $x^2 - 3x + 1$

52. If x^2, x, –8 are in AP, then which one of the following is correct?

A. $x \in \{-2\}$ B. $x \in \{4\}$
C. $x \in \{-2, 4\}$ D. $x \in \{-4, 2\}$

53. The third term of a GP is 3. What is the product of its first five terms?

A. 81
B. 243
C. 729
D. cannot be determined due to insufficient data

54. The element in the ith row and the jth column of a determinant of third order is equal to $2(i + j)$. What is the value of the determinant?

A. 0 B. 2
C. 4 D. 6

55. With the numbers 2, 4, 6, 8, all the possible determinants with these four different elements are constructed. What is the sum of the values of all such determinants?

A. 128 B. 64
C. 32 D. 0

56. What is the radius of the circle $4x^2 + 4y^2 - 20x + 12y - 15 = 0$?

A. 14 units B. 10.5 units
C. 7 units D. 3.5 units

57. A parallelogram has three consecutive vertices (–3, 4), (0, –4) and (5, 2). The fourth vertex is
A. (2, 10) B. (2, 9)
C. (3, 9) D. (4, 10)

58. If the lines $y + px = 1$ and $y - qx = 2$ are perpendicular, then which one of the following is correct?
A. $pq + 1 = 0$ B. $p + q + 1 = 0$
C. $pq - 1 = 0$ D. $p - q + 1 = 0$

59. If A, B and C are in AP, then the straight line $Ax + 2By + C = 0$ will always pass through a fixed point. The fixed point is
A. (0, 0) B. (–1, 1)
C. (1, –2) D. (1, –1)

60. If the image of the point (–4, 2) by a line mirror is (4, –2), then what is the equation of the line mirror?
A. $y = x$ B. $y = 2x$
C. $4y = x$ D. $y = 4x$

61. Consider the following statements in respect of the points $(p, p - 3)$, $(q + 3, q)$ and (6, 3):
1. The points lie on a straight line.
2. The points always lie in the first quadrant only for any value of p and q.

Which of the above statements is/are correct?
A. 1 only B. 2 only
C. Both 1 and 2 D. Neither 1 nor 2

62. What is the acute angle between the lines $x - 2 = 0$ and $\sqrt{3}x - y - 2 = 0$?
A. 0° B. 30°
C. 45° D. 60°

63. The point of intersection of diagonals of a square ABCD is at the origin and one of its vertices is at A (4, 2). What is the equation of the diagonal BD?
A. $2x + y = 0$ B. $2x - y = 0$
C. $x + 2y = 0$ D. $x - 2y = 0$

64. If any point on a hyperbola is (3 tan θ, 2 sec θ), then what is the eccentricity of the hyperbola?
A. $\frac{3}{2}$ B. $\frac{5}{2}$
C. $\frac{\sqrt{11}}{2}$ D. $\frac{\sqrt{13}}{2}$

65. Consider the following with regard to eccentricity (e) of a conic section:
1. $e = 0$ for circle
2. $e = 1$ for parabola
3. $e < 1$ for ellipse

Which of the above are correct?
A. 1 and 2 only B. 2 and 3 only
D. 1 and 3 only D. 1, 2 and 3

66. What is the angle between the two lines having direction ratios ⟨6, 3, 6⟩ and ⟨3, 3, 0⟩?
A. $\frac{\pi}{6}$ B. $\frac{\pi}{4}$
C. $\frac{\pi}{3}$ D. $\frac{\pi}{2}$

67. If l, m, n are the direction cosines of the line $x - 1 = 2(y + 3) = 1 - z$, then what is $l^4 + m^4 + n^4$ equal to?
A. 1 B. $\frac{11}{27}$
C. $\frac{13}{27}$ D. 4

68. What is the projection of the line segment joining A(1, 7, –5) and B(–3, 4, –2) on y-axis?
A. 5 B. 4
C. 3 D. 2

69. What is the number of possible values of k for which the line joining the points $(k, 1, 3)$ and $(1, -2, k + 1)$ also passes through the point (15, 2, –4)?
A. Zero B. One
C. Two D. Infinite

70. The foot of the perpendicular drawn from the origin to the plane $x + y + z = 3$ is
A. (0, 1, 2) B. (0, 0, 3)
C. (1, 1, 1) D. (–1, 1, 3)

71. A vector $\vec{r} = a\hat{i} + b\hat{j}$ is equally inclined to both x and y axes. If the magnitude of the vector is 2 units, then what are the values of a and b respectively?
A. $\frac{1}{2}, \frac{-1}{2}$ B. $\frac{1}{\sqrt{2}}, \frac{1}{\sqrt{2}}$
C. $\sqrt{2}, \sqrt{2}$ D. 2, 2

72. Consider the following statements in respect of a vector $\vec{c} = \vec{a} + \vec{b}$, where $|\vec{a}| = |\vec{b}| \neq 0$:
1. $\vec{c}$ is perpendicular to $(\vec{a} - \vec{b})$.
2. $\vec{c}$ is perpendicular to $(\vec{a} \times \vec{b})$.

Which of the above statements is/are correct?
A. 1 only B. 2 only
C. Both 1 and 2 D. Neither 1 nor 2

73. If $\vec{a}$ and $\vec{b}$ are two vectors such that $|\vec{a} + \vec{b}| = |\vec{a} - \vec{b}| = 4$, then which one of the following is correct?
A. $\vec{a}$ and $\vec{b}$ must be unit vectors.
B. $\vec{a}$ must be parallel to $\vec{b}$.
C. $\vec{a}$ must be perpendicular to $\vec{b}$.
D. $\vec{a}$ must be equal to $\vec{b}$.

74. If $\vec{a}$, $\vec{b}$ and $\vec{c}$ are coplanar, then what is $(2\vec{a}\times 3\vec{b})\cdot 4\vec{c}+(5\vec{b}\times 3\vec{c})\cdot 6\vec{a}$ equal to?

A. 114 B. 66
C. 0 D. −66

75. Consider the following statements:
1. The cross product of two unit vectors is always a unit vector.
2. The dot product of two unit vectors is always unity.
3. The magnitude of sum of two unit vectors is always greater than the magnitude of their difference.

Which of the above statements are ***not*** correct?

A. 1 and 2 only B. 2 and 3 only
C. 1 and 3 only D. 1, 2 and 3

76. If

$$\lim_{x\to a}\frac{a^x-x^a}{x^a-a^a}=-1$$

then what is the value of a?

A. −1 B. 0
C. 1 D. 2

77. A particle starts from origin with a velocity (in m/s) given by the equation $\frac{dx}{dt}=x+1$. The time (in second) taken by the particle to traverse a distance of 24 m is

A. ln 24 B. ln 5
C. 2 ln 5 D. 2 ln 4

78. What is

$$\int_0^a \frac{f(a-x)}{f(x)+f(a-x)}dx$$

equal to?

A. a B. $2a$
C. 0 D. $\frac{a}{2}$

79. What is

$$\lim_{x\to -1}\frac{x^3+x^2}{x^2+3x+2}$$

equal to?

A. 0 B. 1
C. 2 D. 3

80. If

$$\int_0^a [f(x)+f(-x)]dx=\int_{-a}^a g(x)dx$$

then what is $g(x)$ equal to?

A. $f(x)$ B. $f(-x)+f(x)$
C. $-f(x)$ D. None of the above

81. What is the area bounded by $y=\sqrt{16-x^2}$, $y\ge 0$ and the x-axis?

A. 16π square units
B. 8π square units
C. 4π square units
D. 2π square units

82. The curve $y=-x^3+3x^2+2x-27$ has the maximum slope at

A. $x=-1$ B. $x=0$
C. $x=1$ D. $x=2$

83. A 24 cm long wire is bent to form a triangle with one of the angles as 60°. What is the altitude of the triangle having the greatest possible area?

A. $4\sqrt{3}$ cm B. $2\sqrt{3}$ cm
C. 6 cm D. 3 cm

84. If $f(x)=e^{|x|}$, then which one of the following is correct?

A. $f'(0)=1$ B. $f'(0)=-1$
C. $f'(0)=0$ D. $f'(0)$ does not exist

85. What is

$$\int\frac{dx}{\sec x+\tan x}$$

equal to?

A. ln (sec x) + ln |sec x + tan x| + c
B. ln (sec x) − ln |sec x + tan x| + c
C. sec x tan x − ln |sec x − tan x| + c
D. ln |sec x + tan x| − ln |sec x| + c

86. What is

$$\int\frac{dx}{\sec^2(\tan^{-1}x)}$$

equal to?

A. $\sin^{-1}x+c$ B. $\tan^{-1}x+c$
C. $\sec^{-1}x+c$ D. $\cos^{-1}x+c$

87. If $x+y=20$ and $P=xy$, then what is the maximum value of P?

A. 100 B. 96
C. 84 D. 50

88. What is the derivative of

$$\sin(\ln x)+\cos(\ln x)$$

with respect to x at $x=e$?

A. $\frac{\cos 1-\sin 1}{e}$ B. $\frac{\sin 1-\cos 1}{e}$
C. $\frac{\cos 1+\sin 1}{e}$ D. 0

89. If $x=e^t\cos t$ and $y=e^t\sin t$, then what is $\frac{dx}{dy}$ at $t=0$ equal to?

A. 0 B. 1
C. $2e$ D. −1

90. What is the maximum value of sin 2x · cos 2x?

A. $\frac{1}{2}$ B. 1
C. 2 D. 4

91. What is the derivative of e^x with respect to x^e?

A. $\frac{xe^x}{ex^e}$ B. $\frac{e^x}{x^e}$

C. $\frac{xe^x}{x^e}$ D. $\frac{e^x}{ex^e}$

92. If a differentiable function $f(x)$ satisfies

$$\lim_{x\to -1}\frac{f(x)+1}{x^2-1}=-\frac{3}{2}$$

then what is $\lim_{x\to -1} f(x)$ equal to?

A. $-\frac{3}{2}$ B. -1

C. 0 D. 1

93. If the function

$$f(x)=\begin{cases} a+bx, & x<1 \\ 5, & x=1 \\ b-ax, & x>1 \end{cases}$$

is continuous, then what is the value of $(a + b)$?

A. 5 B. 10

C. 15 D. 20

94. Consider the following statements in respect of the function $f(x) = \sin x$:

1. $f(x)$ increases in the interval $(0, \pi)$.
2. $f(x)$ decreases in the interval $\left(\frac{5\pi}{2}, 3\pi\right)$.

Which of the above statements is/are correct?

A. 1 only
B. 2 only
C. Both 1 and 2
D. Neither 1 nor 2

95. What is the domain of the function $f(x) = 3^x$?

A. $(-\infty, \infty)$ B. $(0, \infty)$

C. $[0, \infty)$ D. $(-\infty, \infty) - \{0\}$

96. If the general solution of a differential equation is $y^2 + 2cy - cx + c^2 = 0$, where c is an arbitrary constant, then what is the order of the differential equation?

A. 1 B. 2

C. 3 D. 4

97. What is the degree of the following differential equation?

$$x=\sqrt{1+\frac{d^2y}{dx^2}}$$

A. 1
B. 2
C. 3
D. Degree is not defined

98. Which one of the following differential equations has the general solution $y = ae^x + be^{-x}$?

A. $\frac{d^2y}{dx^2}+y=0$ B. $\frac{d^2y}{dx^2}-y=0$

C. $\frac{d^2y}{dx^2}+y=1$ D. $\frac{dy}{dx}-y=0$

99. What is the solution of the following differential equation?

$$\ln\left(\frac{dy}{dx}\right)+y=x$$

A. $e^x + e^y = c$ B. $e^{x+y}e^y = c$

C. $e^x - e^y = c$ D. $e^{x-y} = c$

100. What is $\int e^{(2\ln x+\ln x^2)}dx$ equal to?

A. $\frac{x^4}{4}+c$ B. $\frac{x^3}{3}+c$

C. $\frac{2x^5}{5}+c$ D. $\frac{x^5}{5}+c$

101. Consider the following measures of central tendency for a set of N numbers:

1. Arithmetic mean
2. Geometric mean

Which of the above uses/use all the data?

A. 1 only B. 2 only

C. Both 1 and 2 D. Neither 1 nor 2

102. The numbers of Science, Arts and Commerce graduates working in a company are 30, 70 and 50 respectively. If these figures are represented by a pie chart, then what is the angle corresponding to Science graduates?

A. 36° B. 72°

C. 120° D. 168°

103. For a histogram based on a frequency distribution with unequal class intervals, the frequency of a class should be proportional to

A. the height of the rectangle
B. the area of the rectangle
C. the width of the rectangle
D. the perimeter of the rectangle

104. The coefficient of correlation is independent of

A. change of scale only
B. change of origin only
C. both change of scale and change of origin
D. neither change of scale nor change of origin

105. The following table gives the frequency distribution of number of peas per pea pod of 198 pods:

Number of peas	1	2	3	4	5	6	7
Frequency	4	33	76	50	26	8	1

What is the median of this distribution?

A. 3 B. 4
C. 5 D. 6

106. If M is the mean of n observations $x_1 - k$, $x_2 - k$, $x_3 - k$, .., $x_n - k$, where k is any real number, then what is the mean of $x_1, x_2, x_3, ..., x_n$?

A. M B. M + k
C. M − k D. kM

107. What is the sum of deviations of the variate values 73, 85, 92, 105, 120 from their mean?

A. −2 B. −1
C. 0 D. 5

108. Let x be the HM and y be the GM of two positive numbers m and n. If $5x = 4y$, then which one of the following is correct?

A. $5m = 4n$ B. $2m = n$
C. $4m = 5n$ D. $m = 4n$

109. If the mean of a frequency distribution is 100 and the coefficient of variation is 45%, then what is the value of the variance?

A. 2025 B. 450
C. 45 D. 4.5

110. Let two events A and B be such that P(A) = L and P(B) = M. Which one of the following is correct?

A. $P(A|B) < \frac{L+M-1}{M}$ B. $P(A|B) > \frac{L+M-1}{M}$

C. $P(A|B) \geq \frac{L+M-1}{M}$ D. $P(A|B) = \frac{L+M-1}{M}$

111. For which of the following sets of numbers do the mean, median and mode have the same value?

A. 12, 12, 12, 12, 24
B. 6, 18, 18, 18, 30
C. 6, 6, 12, 30, 36
D. 6, 6, 6, 12, 30

112. The mean of 12 observations is 75. If two observations are discarded, then the mean of the remaining observations is 65. What is the mean of the discarded observations?

A. 250
B. 125
C. 120
D. Cannot be determined due to insufficient data

113. If k is one of the roots of the equation $x(x + 1) + 1 = 0$, then what is its other root?

A. 1 B. $-k$
C. k^2 D. $-k^2$

114. The geometric mean of a set of observations is computed as 10. The geometric mean obtained when each observation x_i is replaced by $3x_i^4$ is

A. 810 B. 900
C. 30000 D. 81000

115. If $P(A \cup B) = \frac{5}{6}$, $P(A \cap B) = \frac{1}{3}$ and $P(\overline{A}) = \frac{1}{2}$, then which of the following is/are correct?

1. A and B are independent events.
2. A and B are mutually exclusive events.

Select the correct answer using the code given below.

A. 1 only B. 2 only
C. Both 1 and 2 D. Neither 1 nor 2

116. The average of a set of 15 observations is recorded, but later it is found that for one observation, the digit in the tens place was wrongly recorded as 8 instead of 3. After correcting the observation, the average is

A. reduced by $\frac{1}{3}$ B. increased by $\frac{10}{3}$

C. reduced by $\frac{10}{3}$ D. reduced by 50

117. A coin is tossed twice. If E and F denote occurrence of head on first toss and second toss respectively, then what is $P(E \cup F)$ equal to?

A. $\frac{1}{4}$ B. $\frac{1}{2}$

C. $\frac{3}{4}$ D. $\frac{1}{3}$

118. In a binomial distribution, the mean is $\frac{2}{3}$ and variance is $\frac{5}{9}$. What is the probability that random variable X = 2?

A. $\frac{5}{36}$ B. $\frac{25}{36}$

C. $\frac{25}{54}$ D. $\frac{25}{216}$

119. If the mode of the scores 10, 12, 13, 15, 15, 13, 12, 10, x is 15, then what is the value of x?

A. 10 B. 12
C. 13 D. 15

120. If A and B are two events such that $P(A) = \frac{3}{4}$ and $P(B) = \frac{5}{8}$, then consider the following statements:

1. The minimum value of $P(A \cup B)$ is $\frac{3}{4}$.
2. The maximum value of $P(A \cap B)$ is $\frac{5}{8}$.

Which of the above statements is/are correct?

A. 1 only B. 2 only
C. Both 1 and 2 D. Neither 1 nor 2

ANSWERS

PAPER-I - GENERAL ABILITY TEST

1	**2**	**3**	**4**	**5**	**6**	**7**	**8**	**9**	**10**
D	C	B	A	B	D	C	C	B	C
11	**12**	**13**	**14**	**15**	**16**	**17**	**18**	**19**	**20**
C	D	B	D	A	B	C	A	D	C
21	**22**	**23**	**24**	**25**	**26**	**27**	**28**	**29**	**30**
C	A	A	B	C	A	C	B	B	D
31	**32**	**33**	**34**	**35**	**36**	**37**	**38**	**39**	**40**
C	C	C	C	C	A	B	D	C	D
41	**42**	**43**	**44**	**45**	**46**	**47**	**48**	**49**	**50**
B	A	C	A	C	D	C	B	A	C
51	**52**	**53**	**54**	**55**	**56**	**57**	**58**	**59**	**60**
D	A	D	C	A	B	A	D	B	C
61	**62**	**63**	**64**	**65**	**66**	**67**	**68**	**69**	**70**
D	D	D	A	C	D	B	A	A	C
71	**72**	**73**	**74**	**75**	**76**	**77**	**78**	**79**	**80**
A	A	C	D	C	B	C	B	A	B
81	**82**	**83**	**84**	**85**	**86**	**87**	**88**	**89**	**90**
C	C	C	B	C	C	D	B	C	A
91	**92**	**93**	**94**	**95**	**96**	**97**	**98**	**99**	**100**
D	D	B	A	B	A	C	B	D	C
101	**102**	**103**	**104**	**105**	**106**	**107**	**108**	**109**	**110**
B	A	C	D	C	A	A	C	D	C
111	**112**	**113**	**114**	**115**	**116**	**117**	**118**	**119**	**120**
A	C	D	B	B	D	D	C	A	D
121	**122**	**123**	**124**	**125**	**126**	**127**	**128**	**129**	**130**
B	A	A	A	C	B	A	C	C	A
131	**132**	**133**	**134**	**135**	**136**	**137**	**138**	**139**	**140**
D	C	C	C	B	A	B	C	B	A
141	**142**	**143**	**144**	**145**	**146**	**147**	**148**	**149**	**150**
B	B	B	A	D	D	D	C	A	C

PAPER-II - MATHEMATICS

1	**2**	**3**	**4**	**5**	**6**	**7**	**8**	**9**	**10**
A	C	D	B	B	C	A	D	B	B
11	**12**	**13**	**14**	**15**	**16**	**17**	**18**	**19**	**20**
D	C	C	C	C	D	C	C	C	A
21	**22**	**23**	**24**	**25**	**26**	**27**	**28**	**29**	**30**
B	B	D	B	A	B	D	*	B	B
31	**32**	**33**	**34**	**35**	**36**	**37**	**38**	**39**	**40**
A	A	B	C	C	D	B	C	A	C

41	42	43	44	45	46	47	48	49	50
A	A	C	C	A	A	B	B	C	D
51	**52**	**53**	**54**	**55**	**56**	**57**	**58**	**59**	**60**
B	C	B	A	D	D	A	C	D	B
61	**62**	**63**	**64**	**65**	**66**	**67**	**68**	**69**	**70**
A	*	A	D	D	B	B	C	C	C
71	**72**	**73**	**74**	**75**	**76**	**77**	**78**	**79**	**80**
C	C	C	C	A	C	C	D	B	A
81	**82**	**83**	**84**	**85**	**86**	**87**	**88**	**89**	**90**
B	C	A	D	D	B	A	A	B	A
91	**92**	**93**	**94**	**95**	**96**	**97**	**98**	**99**	**100**
A	A	A	B	A	A	A	B	C	D
101	**102**	**103**	**104**	**105**	**106**	**107**	**108**	**109**	**110**
A	B	B	C	A	B	C	D	A	C
111	**112**	**113**	**114**	**115**	**116**	**117**	**118**	**119**	**120**
B	B	C	C	A	C	C	D	D	C

EXPLANATORY ANSWERS

PAPER I- GENERAL ABILITY TEST

51. • Light-year is a unit of distance. It's defined by how far a beam of light travels in one year - a distance of six trillion miles. It is often used to measure distance of stars.

- Light-year, in astronomy is the distance travelled by light moving in a vacuum in the course of one year, at its accepted velocity of 299,792,458 metres per second (186,282 miles per second).
- A light-year equals about 9.46073×10^{12} km (5.87863×10^{12} miles), or 63,241 astronomical units.

52. The mass per unit volume is called density *i.e.*,

Density = mass/volume

Density of water is maximum at 4°C at atmospheric pressure *i.e.* 1000 kg/m^3.

53. Marie Curie discovered polonium and radium in 1989. In 1903 curie together with Henri Becquerel won the Nobel Prize for Physics for discovering radioactivity. In 1911 she won the Second Nobel Prize for Chemistry for isolating pure radium.

In May 1932 James Chadwick announced that the core also contained a new uncharged particle, which he called the neutron.

Albert Einstein is best known for his equation $E = mc^2$, which states that energy and mass (matter) are the same thing, just in different forms. He is also known for his discovery of the photoelectric effect, for which he won the Nobel Prize for Physics in 1921.

54. LED stands for Light Emitting Diode. It is a optical semiconductor devices that convert electrical energy into light energy or photons. It acts just like a normal p-n junction diode. LEDs are made of gallium, phosphorus and arsenic materials instead of silicon or germanium materials. Since silicon or germanium diodes do not produce energy in the form of light like to p-n junction diodes. LEDs works only in forward bias condition. An LED has three layers: a *p*-type semiconductor and an *n*-type semiconductor separated by a depletion layer.

55. • Friction is a contact force when two surfaces interact. The static friction case in similar for when the two surfaces are stationary relative to each other in static friction the frictional force is whatever value it needs to be to prevent sliding up to some maximum value.

- Magnetic forces are non-contact forces, they pull or push on objects without touching them. Magnets are only attracted to a few 'magnetic' metals and not all matter. They are attracted to and repel other magnets.

56. Hypobromous acid is weak and unstable acid with chemical formula of HOBr, where bromine atom is in the +1 oxidation state. It is also called bromanol or hydroxide bromine. When bromine reacts with water, hypobromous acid is formed

$$Br_2 + H_2O \rightleftharpoons HOBr + HBr$$

Hypobromous acid is used as a deodorant, oxidizer and bleach.

57. The exosphere layer is mainly composed of extremely low densities of hydrogen, helium and several heavier molecules including nitrogen, oxygen and carbon dioxide closer to the exobase. The atoms and molecules are so far apart that they can travel hundreds kilometers without colliding with another.

The exosphere contains most of satellites orbiting earth. Thus, the exosphere no longer behaves like a gas, and the particles constantly escape into space. At this distance, radiation pressure from sunlight exerts more force on hydrogen atoms than does the pull of Earth's gravity.

58.
- Glass is made from natural and abundant raw materials (sand, soda ash and limestone) that are melted at very high temperature to form a new material glass.
- Alumina is often used in the production of glass products, lending improved strength; it has even been studied for its potential in treating an unbreakable glass.
- Glass manufactures add to borax to the silica base to significantly lower melting temperature and viscosity, inhibit crystallization of the glass, control thermal expansion and inhibit devitrification.

59. Electrolytic renfining is the process of refining impure metals by using electricity. In this process impure metal is made as the anode and a strip of pure metal is made the cathode. A solution of a soluble salt of the same metal is taken as the electrolyte.

In electrolytic refining of copper, the electrolyte is a solution of acidified copper sulphate. The anode is impure copper, whereas the cathode is a strip of pure copper on passing electric current, pure copper is deposited on the cathode. Anode $Cu(s) \rightarrow Cu^{2+} + 2e^-$

Cathode: Cu^{2+} (aq) $+ 2e^- \rightarrow Cu(s)$

60. Solder is a metal alloy usually made of tin (Sn) and lead (Pb) which is melted using a hot iron.

Alloys commonly used for electrical soldering are 60/40 Sn-Pb, which melts at 188°C (370°F), and 63/37 Sn-Pb used principally in electrical/electronic work. This mixture is a eutectic alloy of these metals, which has the lowest melting point (183°C or 361°F) of all the tin-lead alloys.

The solder composition, being free of lead and other known toxic metals, has a composition range of 0.5-4.0% antimony, 0.5-4.0% zinc, 0.1-3.0% silver, 0.1-2.0% copper and 86.8-98% tin, is especially adaptable for pulmbing applications where solder joints are exposed to potable water.

61. Dihydrogen is the most abundant element is the universe. The mixture of CO and H_2 is called water gas. As this mixture of CO and H_2 is used for the synthesis of methanol and a number of hydrocarbons, it is also synthesis gas of Syngas.

62.

Element	Atomic no.	Valency
Sodium (Na)	11	1
Potassium (K)	19	1
Magnesium (Mg)	12	2
Calcium (Ca)	20	2
Barium (Ba)	56	2
Aluminium (Al)	13	3

63. Highest the number in the negative scale, lower the temperature.

At zero kelvin (–273 degrees Celsius) the particles stop moving and all disorder disappears. Thus, nothing can be colder than absolute zero on the Kelvin scale.

64. Since, the Celsius and Fahrenheit scales are two different units of temperature basd on different scales.

From the formula, $\frac{C}{5} = \frac{F-32}{9}$

Let us assume, the Celsius and Fahrenheit scale coincide at $x°$

$$\therefore \quad \frac{x}{5} = \frac{x-32}{9}$$

$$\Rightarrow \quad 9x = 5x - 160$$

$$\Rightarrow \quad 4x = -160$$

$$\therefore \quad x = -40°$$

65. The image formed by a plane mirror is always virtual upright, and of the same shape and size as the object it is reflecting.

An image forned by a plane mirror has the following characteristics:

- Virtual and erect.
- Behind the mirror.
- The size of the image is equal to the size of the object.
- Laterally inverted image.

66. The three primary colours in additive mixing are red, green, and blue. If all three primary colours of light are mixed in equal proportions, the result is neutral (gray or while). If the red and green lights mix, the result is yellow.

Red, green and blue are primary colours and all other colours can be created from them. If mixing red and green, produce yellow colour.

67. The three primary colours of light: red, green and blue. They are defined as primary because they can be combined to form a various range of colours. In painting, red, green and blue are regarded as primary colours.

68. The **formula** is a relation between the object distance *u*, image distance *v* and the focal length from the pole of the mirror. The **formula** is valid for the images is spherical mirror. Mirror formula, $\frac{1}{v}+\frac{1}{u}=\frac{1}{f}$. In lenses, there comes minus in place of addition.

Lens formula, $\frac{1}{v}-\frac{1}{u}=\frac{1}{f}$.

69. The nucleus is separated from the cytoplasm by a membrane called the nuclear membrane. This membrane is also porous and allows the movement of materials between the cytoplasm and the inside of the nucleus. The movement of materials to different parts of the cytoplasm and nucleus is generally carried out by **ribosomes**.

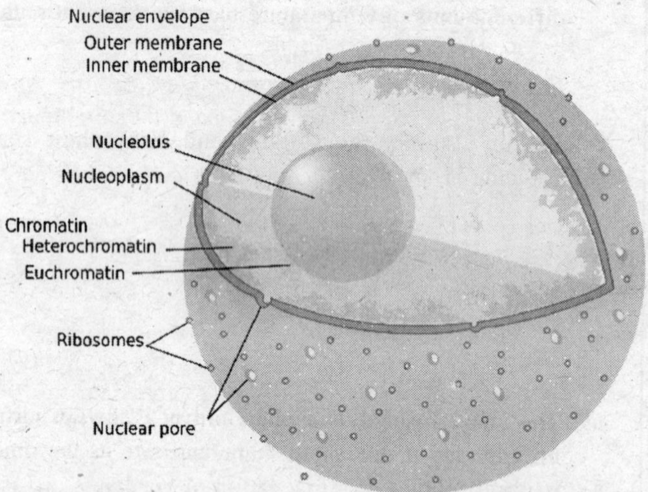

70. Mitochondria are made up of two membranes: the outer and inner mitochondrial membranes. The inner mitochondrial membrane is folded several times to form cristae and contains F_0–F_1 particles, which are the electro transport system's particles. The inner membrane is likewise densely packed with proteins involved in ATP generation, and here is frequently where ATP is produced.

Adenosine triphosphate (ATP) is the energy currency for cellular processes. ATP provides energy for both energy-consuming endergonic reactions and energy-releasing exergonic reactions, which require a small input of energy.

71. An epithelial cell has a free surface which faces either a body fluid or outside environment and thus providing covering or a lining for some parts of the body.

Squamous epithelial cells are flat and are usually found lining surface that require a smooth flow of fluid, such as your blood vessels.

Squamous epithelium has cells that are wider than their height (flat and scale-like). Squamous epithelial cell is found as the lining of the mouth, oesophagus and including blood vessels and in the alveoli of the lungs.

72. The permanent tissues always differentiate from the meristematic cells, during the process of growth. These meristematic cells lose the ability to divide and take up a specific role. This process of taking up a permanent shape, size and a function is called cellular differentiation. The permanent tissues are formed by the differentiated cells, which become specialised to perform specific functions like protection, support, storage and conduction.

73. Pants produces oxygen through the process of photosynthesis and prepare their food for survival. The oxygen is used in the respiration process which takes place in mitochondria of the cell.

74. Stomata help the plants to take up carbon dioxide (CO_2) which they use in photosynthesis or the process of food-making. Plants need stomata to release the oxygen (O_2) formed during photosynthesis too.

Therefoe, when the stomata are blocked, transpiration would not occur, and the leaves will remain fresh for a longer period.

On experimental leaf 2. Vaseline was applied underneath the leaf, thus stomata get completely blocked thereby preventing transpiration. Thus it'll dry up last.

On Experimental leaf 1, the vaseline was applied on the upper surface, so the stomata would not be affected much and transpire a little slower than usual. Thus, it'll dry up a little slower.

Control leaf had no vaseline, so it'll function as usual in transpiration with water content already available. Thus, it'll dry up first.

75. As, speed of light in a medium (v)

$$= \frac{\text{Speed of light in vaccum (c)}}{\text{Refractive index } (\mu)}$$

As the speed of light in a vacuum is constant therefore we can say that speed of light in a medium is inversely proportional to the refractive index of the medium.

Thus, the speed of light travels at different speeds in different media.

The speed of light in the air is 3×10^8 m/s.

When the light is travelling from water to air and as we know that the refractive index of water (1.33) and that of air (1.008), it means the water is a denser medium and air is a rarer medium.

Whenever light goes from water to air, the frequency of light and phase of light does not change.

However, the velocity of light and wavelength of light change (increases) because the light is travelling from denser medium (μ_{water} = 1.33) to rarer medium (μ_{air} = 1.008). Thus, option (C) is incorrect.

76. Since, bending of light is inversely proportional to the wavelength of the light.

i.e., Bending $\propto \frac{1}{\text{Wavelength}}$

- Different colours bend differently on passing through a prism and the bending colour depends on wavelength.
- Higher wavelengths bend less, whereas shorter wavelength bend more.
- Violet light has the least wavelength and hence it bends the most and red has the highest wavelength, so it bends the least.

77. Given, current, I = 1.0 A

Time, $t = 10$ minutes $= 10 \times 60$ second $= 600$ seconds

$\therefore$ Electric charge (Q)

$$Q = I \times t = 1 \times 600 = 600 \text{ C}$$

$[\because V = IR]$

78. As

$$P = VI$$
$$= IRI = I^2R$$
$$= \frac{V^2}{R^2} \times R \qquad \left(I = \frac{V}{R}\right)$$
$$= \frac{V^2}{R}$$

Hence, (B) is incorrect answer.

79. A sound created in a big hall will persist by repeated reflections from the walls until it is reduced to a value where it is no longer audible. The repeated reflections that result in this persistence of sound is called reverberation.

80. The process of scattering of light particles by molecules of medium. The scattering occurs due to a change in the wavelength of light as it enters the medium. If light is scattered by molecule and the frequency of the scattered light is changed, this phenomenon is called Raman effect. Rayleigh scattering is a form of elastic scattering in which incident light and scattered light has same frequency.

81. Soap are sodium or potassium salts of long chain fatty acids.

Soap is a kind of molecule in which both the ends (Hydrophilic end and Hydrophobic end) have different properties.

Hard water contains calcium and magnesium ions, which react with the surfactant anion to give these metallic or lime soaps. In this reaction, the sodium cation in soap is replaced by calcium to form calcium stearate.

The first one is the hydrophilic end which dissolves water and is attracted to it whereas the second one is the hydrophobic end that is dissolved in hydrocarbons and is water repulsive in nature. If on the surface of the water, soap is present then the hydrophobic tail which is not soluble in water will align along the water surface.

The soap solution appears cloudy as it forms a colloidal solution which scatters light.

82. The hydrogenation process of vegetable oils was originally introduced to convert some of the unsaturated fatty acids in vegetable oils, as well as marine or animal fats to make them more stable to oxidation.

In this process, the unsaturated double bonds in the fatty acids of the oil molecules react with hydrogen atoms in the presence of a catalyst. Nickel (Ni) catalyst is used in commercial hydrogenation of edible oils. Other catalysts, such as platinum (Pt), palladium (Pd), copper (Cu), etc., have also been applied in hydrogenation applications. These are not used in commercial hydrogenation of edible oils. Addition reaction is used for hydrogenation of vegetable oils in the presence of nickel catalyst.

83. If an element exists in more than one crystalline form, is called allotropes.

The two most common allotropes of carbon are diamond and graphite.

Graphene is a two dimensional one atom thick allotrope of carbon. Electrons in graphene behave as massless relativistic particles.

Hence, Fly ash is not an allotrope of carbon.

84. The reaction between zinc and sulphuric acid produces zinc sulphate and hydrogen gas. In the reaction, bubbles of hydrogen gas should be seen, and the zinc metal will dissolve to form aqueous zinc sulfate

$$Zn + H_2SO_4 \rightarrow ZnSO_4 + H_2$$

When zinc metal is heated with sodium hydroxide solution then Sodium zincate and hydrogen gas are formed. All the metals do not react with bases to form salt and hydrogen gas.

$$Zn(s) + 2NaOH(aq) \rightarrow Na_2ZnO_2(aq) + H_2(g)\uparrow$$

Potassium metal reacts with water to form a colourless solution of potassium hydroxide (KOH) and hydrogen gas (H_2).

$$2K + 2H_2O \rightarrow 2KOH + H_2$$

Heating of gypsum at a particular temperature of 373 K is responsible for production of Plaster of Paris. Mixing of Plaster of Paris and water can be represented as

$$CaSO_4 \cdot 1/2H_2O + H_2O \rightarrow CaSO_4 \cdot 2H_2O$$

85. Tomato contains more than 10 types of acids such as citric acid, malic acid, ascorbic acids and oxalic acid, but two accounts for a large percentage of the total: citric acid and malic acid. It also contains another essential acid, ascorbic acid, which is better known by its common name: vitamin C. All three acid have a role in protecting our health and sustaining energy.

Citric and malic acids are the main organic acids in tomato. Other organic acids may be added as well. Commercial malic acid usually contains small amounts of fumaric acid. Due to the high UV absorption coefficient of fumaric acid, an additional peak is usually visible in standards containing malic acid.

87. The reaction in which energy is released in the form of light or heat is called exothermic reaction.

When quicklime is added to water, it forms slaked lime along with the evolution of heat. There will be a rise in the temperature of the bucket. Calcium oxide reacts with water to form calcium hydroxide, also called slaked lime.

$$CaO + H_2O \rightarrow Ca(OH)_2$$

88. Nuclear reactor is not a source of biomass energy.

Biomass is a renewable source of energy. Its initial energy comes from the sun, and plants or algae biomass can regrow in a relatively short amount of time. Trees, crops, and municipal solid waste are consistently available and can be managed sustainably.

89. The twinkling of a star is due to atmospheric refraction of starlight. The starlight, on entering the earth's atmosphere, undergoes refraction continuously before it reaches the earth.

As light from a star rates through atmosphere, it bounces and bumps through the different layers, bending the light before you see it. Since the hot and cold layers of air keep moving, the bending of the light changes too, which causes the star's appearance to wobble or twinkle.

90. All are unit of frequency except sound wave. Decibel (dB) is the unit of loudness of sound.

91. When two sound waves of nearly same frequencies, travelling in a medium, superimpose on each other, the intensity of the resultant sound at a particular position rises and falls regularly with time. This phenomenon of regular variation in the intensity of sound with time at a particular position is called beats. The number of beats produced per second is called a beat frequency.

Clearly from the above, the phenomenon of wave of sound intensity when two waves of nearly the same frequencies and amplitudes travelling in the medium, are superimposed on each other is called beats.

93. In Simple Harmonic Motion (SHM) the acceleration of the system and therefore the force is directly proportional to the displacement and acts in the opposite direction of the displacement.

94. The radicle is the first part of a seedling (a growing plant embryo) to emerge from the seed during the process of germination. It is the embryonic root of the plant, and grows downward in the soil (the shoot emerges from the plumule). The radicle is the embryonic root inside the seed.

96. A solution that has higher concentration to a region of lower cencentration is called hypertonic solution.

Salt in RBC = 0.9% and salt in detergent = 2%, it is hypertonic solution.

RBC is placed in a hypertonic solution and having more water, while detergent having less concentration of water. Hence, due to Osmosis, water from RBC would diffuse to detergent solution and RBC will shrink.

98. As angle of incidence is zero so ray of light along the normal will be undeviated.

When light travels from a denser medium to a rarer medium, it bends away from the normal. This behaviour follows from Snell's Law. As you have seen earlier, the larger angle must be in the medium having the lower index of refraction.

99. A mirage is a naturally occurring optical phenomenon in which light rays bend via refraction to produce a displaced image of distant objects or the sky.

When the reflected light ray reaches our eyes, it appears as coming from the sky or tree. This inverted image creates an optical illusion of the presence of water or the presence of islands etc. Thus, the mirage is an example of refraction of light and total internal reflection.

101. Balakot is one of four known ancient coastal sites in Pakistan. These sites remained unexcavated until the opportunity arose in 1973 to launch a project at Balakot. Fishbones and shells dominate the faunal remains. People engaged in the manufacturing of jewelry, especially bangles and perhaps inlays for wooden furniture, from shells. Thus, it was a specialised centre for making shell objects.

Lothal was discovered by S.R. Rao in 1955. It is located in Gujarat near the Bhogavo river. It is considered a port city of Indus valley civilization, as a dock is present adjacent to the river.

Amri is an archaeological site dating back to 3600 BC with the remains of a pre-Harappan fortified town. The site is located south of Mohenjo-Daro near Sindh, Pakistan.

Kot Diji is located on the left bank of the Indus River in the Sindh province of Pakistan. It was a pre-Harappan site and continued its presence during the Harappan period. Storage jars, toy carts, terracotta figurines of animals and mother goddess, pottery with different designs, etc. were found.

102. Ashoka was the great Mauryan ruler and grandson of the dynasty's founder Chandragupta Maurya.

He became a Buddhist in the 9th year of his reign *i.e.*, a year after the conquest of Kalinga. Dhamma is Prakrit form of the Sanskrit word 'Dharma'. Ashoka's dhamma was neither a new religion nor a new political philosophy, it was a way of life.

Ashoka denounced all useless ceremonies and sacrifices held under the influence of superstition. One of the striking features of Ashoka's edicts is that he regards himself as a father figure for the people. Thus, honoring the king was not dhamma.

103. The Saguna bhakti insists on worshiping as a personal god. The worshipers believe in the reincarnation, of their living god and they worship them in the form of human being like Lord Krishna and Rama.

Saguna bhakti is worship of God with form and nirguna is worship of God without form. He or she is none other than God himself because God is a name attributed to the Supreme Self when it chooses to assume name and form.

104. During the reign of the Satavahana (c. 200 BCE -190 CE), the Naneghat pass was one of the trade routes. It connected the Konkan coast communities with Deccan high plateau through Junnar. It was made by Satavahana Queen NAGANIKA.

The temple was constructed during the 10th Century when Chidambaram used to be the capital of the Chola dynasty. The Cholas considered Lord Shiva as Nataraj as their family deity. The Nataraj temple has undergone damage, renovation and expansion throughout the 2nd millennium.

105. The Deccan Riots Commission

When the revolt spread in the Deccan, the Government of Bombay was initially unwilling to see it as anything serious. But the Government of India, worried by the memory of 1857, pressurised the Government of Bombay to set up a commission of enquiry to investigate into the causes of the riots. The commission produced a report that was presented to the British Parliament in 1878.

This report, referred to as the Deccan Riots Report, provides historians with a range of sources for the study of the riot. The commission held enquiries in the districts where the riots spread, recorded statements of *ryots, sahukars* and eyewitnesses, compiled statistical data on revenue rates, prices and interest rates in different regions, and collated the reports sent by district collectors.

106. Ziyarat is an Arabic term which literally means "visit", and is used to refer to a form of pilgrimage to sites associated with Muhammad's, family members and descendants (including Sufi Imam), his companions and other venerated figures in Islam such as the prophets, Sufi Saints and Islamic scholars.

113. Current time in India = 12 : 00 Noon

Required time at Meridian = 7 : 00

$\therefore$ Difference = 5 hrs behind

$\therefore$ It is west direction

Since, earth takes 24 hrs for one complete rotation.

Then, 24 hrs = 360°

$$\therefore \quad 1 \text{ hr} = \frac{360}{24} = 15^\circ$$

$\because$ Earth rotates 15° in 1 hr

$\therefore$ Earth rotates in 5 hrs = 5 × 15 = 75°

Thus, 75° W Longitude.

115. Mahanavami Dibba is a beautiful stone platform located within the Royal Enclosure of Hampi. Thus, statement 1 is incorrect.

Mahanavami Dibba is also called as Dasara Dibba.

It was built during the Vijayanagara period by King Krishnadevaraya to commemorate his victory over Udaygiri.

It was the place where the King of Vijayanagar used to celebrate the festival of Dasara (Dussehra).

The Dasara Dibba is in a ruined state now with damaged carvings on the side of the platform. Hence statement 2 is correct.

124. The oil refinery has been set up at Tatipaka in the East Godavari district of Andhra Pradesh. This is ONGC's first venture of producing petro-products through distillation of crude oil. This oil refinery is designed to produce naphtha, kerosene, diesel and reduced crude oil. Hence, it is not located in Assam.

125. Mahatma Gandhi's first public address in India was on the occasion of the opening ceremony of the Banaras Hindu University in February 1916, which was distinguished by the presence of many magnets and princes and of the Viceroy himself.

126. The Indian National Congress, on 19th December 1929, passed the historic 'Purna Swaraj' – (total independence) resolution – at its Lahore session. A public declaration was made on 26 January, 1930 – a day which the Congress Party urged Indians to celebrate as 'Independence Day'. The declaration was passed due to the breakdown of negotiations between leaders of the freedom movement and the British over the question of dominion status for India.

127. **Article 14:** The State shall not deny to any person equality before the law or the equal protection of the laws within the territory of India, on grounds of religion, race, caste, sex or place of birth.

Article 15: The State shall not discriminate against any citizen on grounds only of religion, race, caste, sex, place of birth or any of them.

128. Along with the five permanent members, the Security Council of the United Nations has temporary members that hold their seats on a rotating basis by geographic region. Non-permanent members may be involved in global security briefings. In its first two decades, the Security Council had six non-permanent members, the first of which were Australia, Brazil, Egypt, Mexico, the Netherlands, and Poland. In 1965, the number of non-permanent members was expanded to ten. Estonia (2021); India (2022); Ireland (2022); Kenya (2022); Mexico (2022); Niger (2021); Norway (2022); Saint Vincent and the Grenadines (2021) Tunisia (2021); Viet Nam (2021).

129. The 4th of July—also known as Independence Day or July 4th—has been a federal holiday in the United States since 1941, but the tradition of Independence Day celebrations goes back to the 18th century and the American Revolution. On July 2nd, 1776, the Continental Congress voted in favour of independence, and two days later delegates from the 13 colonies adopted the Declaration of Independence, a historic document drafted by Thomas Jefferson.

131. Condensation depends upon the relative humidity of the air and the amount of cooling. Precipitation consisting of small ice pellets formed by the freezing of raindrops or of melted snowflakes is called sleet. Sleet is liquid water that freezes before it hits the ground. Therefore, it is not the form of condensation.

132. Cloud is a mass of minute water droplets or tiny crystals of ice formed by the condensation of the water vapour in free air at considerable elevations. As the clouds are formed at some height over the surface of the earth, they take various shapes. According to their height, expanse, density and transparency or opaqueness clouds are grouped under four types:

1. **Cirrus:** Cirrus clouds are formed at high altitudes (8,000 – 12,000 m). They are thin and detatched clouds having a feathery appearance. They are always white in colour.
2. **Cumulus:** Cumulus clouds look like cotton wool. They are generally formed at a height of 4,000 – 7,000 m. They exist in patches and can be seen scattered here and there. They have a flat base.
3. **Stratus:** As their name implies, these are layered clouds covering large portions of the sky. These clouds are generally formed either due to loss of heat or the mixing of air masses with different temperatures.
4. **Nimbus:** Nimbus clouds are black or dark gray. They form at middle levels or very near to the surface of the earth. These are extremely dense and opaque to the rays of the sun. Sometimes, the clouds are so low that they seem to touch the ground. Nimbus clouds are shapeless masses of thick vapour.

134. The South Eastern Railway (SER) is one of the 18 railway zones in India and Part of Eastern Railways. It is headquartered at Garden Reach, Kolkata, West Bengal, India.

135. Bharatmala Pariyojana is an umbrella program for the highways sector that focuses on optimizing efficiency of freight and passenger movement across the country by bridging critical infrastructure gaps through effective interventions. It is related to networks of National Highways in India.

136. Tropical Deciduous Forests are the most widespread forests of India and are popularly known as Monsoon Forests. Tropical deciduous forests are found in the regions, which receive rainfall between 70 and 200 cm.

137. The river Beas rises at an elevation of 14,308 feet (4,361 metres) at Rohtang Pass in the western (Punjab) Himalayas in central Himachal Pradesh.

Finally the river Beas joins the river Sutlej at the south-western boundary of Kapurthala (Punjab) after a total course of 470 kilometers.

143. The Ram Temple tableau of Uttar Pradesh that was on display during the Republic Day 2021 has bagged the first prize among all tableaux. The theme of Uttar Pradesh's tableau was 'Ayodhya: Cultural Heritage of Uttar Pradesh'. The cultural heritage of ancient holy town Ayodhya, a replica of a Ram temple, a glimpse of 'Deepotsav' and various stories from Ramayana epic were depicted in the tableau.

146. Exercise Kavach is a Joint Military exercise involving assets of the Indian Army, Indian Navy, Indian Air Force, and Indian Coast Guard. The exercise was conducted under the aegis of the Andaman and Nicobar Command. Andaman and Nicobar command is the only Joint Forces Command of the country. It aims to fine-tune joint war-fighting capabilities of the tri-services and SOPs towards enhancing operational synergy. Exercise Kavach will also help in executing multi-domain, high-intensity offensive and defensive maneuvers in the Andaman Sea and Bay of Bengal.

149. Madagascar replaced the Maldives as host of the 2023 Indian Ocean Island Games.

The event was awarded to the Maldives last year, but members of the IOIG Federation voted to move the Games to Madagascar.

This decision was taken due to concerns over the COVID-19 pandemic.

The first edition took place in 1979 and it takes place every 4 years.

It pools together island nations and territories of Mauritius, Seychelles, Comoros, Madagascar, Mayotte, Reunion, and the Maldives.

PAPER II- MATHEMATICS

1. Given, $\left(\frac{1-i}{1+i}\right)^{n^2} = 1$

Multiplying above equation by $(1 - i)$ in N^r & D^r, we get

$$\therefore \quad \left(\frac{(1-i)(1-i)}{(1+i)(1-i)}\right)^{n^2} = 1$$

$$\Rightarrow \left(\frac{(1)^2+(1)^2-2i}{1-(i)^2}\right)^{n^2} = 1$$

$$\Rightarrow \left(\frac{-2i}{2}\right)^{n^2} = 1 \Rightarrow (-i)^{n^2} = 1$$

If $n = 2$ then $(-i)^{2^2} = (-i)^4 = 1$

Thus, $n = 2$.

2. Given, $\text{Log}_{\cos x} \sin x = 1$

$$\Rightarrow \frac{\log \sin x}{\log \cos x} = 1$$

If $x = \frac{\pi}{4}$ then $\frac{\log \sin \frac{\pi}{4}}{\log \cos \frac{\pi}{4}} = \frac{\log\left(\frac{1}{\sqrt{2}}\right)}{\log\left(\frac{1}{\sqrt{2}}\right)} = 1$

Hence, value of $x = \frac{\pi}{4}$

3. Given, $A = \begin{vmatrix} a_1 & b_1 & c_1 \\ a_2 & b_2 & c_2 \\ a_3 & b_3 & c_3 \end{vmatrix}$

$$\text{So,} \begin{vmatrix} pa_1 & b_1 & qc_1 \\ pa_2 & b_2 & qc_2 \\ pa_3 & b_3 & qc_3 \end{vmatrix} = p \cdot q \cdot \begin{vmatrix} a_1 & b_1 & c_1 \\ a_2 & b_2 & c_2 \\ a_3 & b_3 & c_3 \end{vmatrix}$$

$$= p \cdot q \cdot \Delta = pq\Delta$$

4. We know, $(1 + x)^n = C_0 + C_1x + C_2x^2 + C_3x^3 + \ldots + C_nx^n$

If, $x = 1$,

Then, $(1 + 1)^n = C_0 + C_1 + C_2 + C_3 + \ldots + C_n$

$\Rightarrow 2^n = 1 + C_1 + C_2 + C_3 + \ldots + C_n$

$\{\because {}^nC_0 = {}^nC_n = 1\}$

Hence, $C_1 + C_2 + C_3 + \ldots + C_n = 2^n - 1$

5. Given, $(a + b + c) = 4$ and $ab + bc + ca = 0$

We have,

$$\begin{vmatrix} a & b & c \\ b & c & a \\ c & a & b \end{vmatrix} = a(bc - a^2) - b(b^2 - ac) + c(ab - c^2)$$

$= a(bc - a^2) + b(ac - b^2) + c(ab - c^2)$

$= abc - a^3 + abc - b^3 + abc - c^3$

$= 3\,abc - a^3 - b^3 - c^3$

$= -(a^3 + b^3 + c^3 - 3abc) = -(a + b + c)^3$

Since, $a + b + c = 4$

then, $-(a+b+c)^3$
$= -(4)^3 = -64.$

6. We know $-\sqrt{a^2+b^2} \le a\sin x + b\cos x \le \sqrt{a^2+b^2}$

$\Rightarrow \sqrt{2^2+0^2} \le 2\sin x + 0\cos x \le \sqrt{2^2+0^2}$

$\Rightarrow \quad -2 \le 2\sin x \le 2$

$\Rightarrow \quad -2 \le 2k+1 \le 2$

$\Rightarrow \quad -3 \le 2k \le 1$

$\Rightarrow \quad -1.5 \le k \le 0.5$

$\therefore \quad k \le 0, -1$

Therefore the number of values of k is two.

7. Since, a_1, a_2, a_3 .... a_q are in GP.

$$\therefore \frac{a_4}{a_1} = \frac{a_5}{a_2} = \frac{a_6}{a_3} ...... = r^3$$

where r = common ration

We have, $\begin{vmatrix} \ln a_1 & \ln a_2 & \ln a_3 \\ \ln a_4 & \ln a_5 & \ln a_6 \\ \ln a_7 & \ln a_8 & \ln a_9 \end{vmatrix}$

$$= \begin{vmatrix} \ln a_4 - \ln a_1 & \ln a_5 - \ln a_2 & \ln a_6 - \ln a_3 \\ \ln a_7 - \ln a_4 & \ln a_8 - \ln a_5 & \ln a_9 - \ln a_6 \\ \ln a_7 & \ln a_8 & \ln a_9 \end{vmatrix}$$

$(R_1 \to R_2 - R_1 \text{ and } R_2 \to R_3 - R_2)$

$$= \begin{vmatrix} \ln \frac{a_4}{a_1} & \ln \frac{a_5}{a_2} & \ln \frac{a_6}{a_3} \\ \ln \frac{a_7}{a_4} & \ln \frac{a_8}{a_5} & \ln \frac{a_9}{a_6} \\ \ln a_7 & \ln a_8 & \ln a_9 \end{vmatrix}$$

After solving, we get,

$$\begin{vmatrix} \ln r^3 & \ln r^3 & \ln r^3 \\ \ln r^3 & \ln r^3 & \ln r^3 \\ \ln a_7 & \ln a_8 & \ln a_9 \end{vmatrix} = 0$$

Hence, the value of given determinant is 0.

8. Root are real, if $D \ge 0$

$b^2 - 4ac \ge 0$

Given, $x^2 + 2x + k = 0$

On comparing in general form

$a = 1, b = 2, c = k$

$\therefore \quad 2^2 - 4 \times 1 \times k \ge 0$

$\Rightarrow \quad 4 - 4k \ge 0$

$\Rightarrow \quad (1-k) \ge 0 \Rightarrow k \le 1.$

9. Given,

$$\frac{1}{\log_2 n} + \frac{1}{\log_3 n} + \frac{1}{\log_4 n} + \frac{1}{\log_5 n} .... + \frac{1}{\log_{100} n}$$

Since, $\frac{1}{\log_a b} = \log_b a$

$= \log_n 2 + \log_n 3 + \log_n 4 + ... + \log_n 100$

$= \log_n (2\cdot3\cdot4\cdot5 ... 100) = \log_n 100!$

Since, $n = 100!$

Thus, $\log_{100!} 100! = 1.$

10. Given, $Z = 1 + i$

We have, $\left|Z + \frac{2}{Z}\right| = \left|(1+i) + \frac{2}{(1+i)}\right|$

$$= \left|(1+i) + \frac{2(1-i)}{(1+i)(1-i)}\right|$$

$$= \left|(1+i) + \frac{2(1-i)}{2}\right| = |1+i+1-i| = 2$$

Hence, $\left|Z + \frac{2}{Z}\right| = 2$

11. Let A is matrix of order $n \times a$

and B is matrix of order $b \times n$

Now,

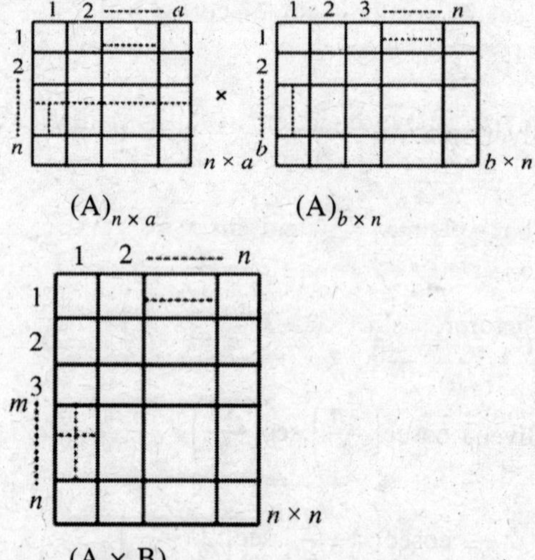

Thus, orders A and B need not to be the same.

13. Given, $A = \begin{vmatrix} p & q \\ r & s \end{vmatrix}$, where (p, q, r, s) four prime numbers < 20

$\therefore (p, q, r, s) = (2, 3, 5, 7, 11, 13, 17 \text{ and } 19)$

Now, $A = p\cdot s - q\cdot r$

For maximum value of A *i.e.*, A_{max}, the product $(p\cdot s)$ should be max and product $(q\cdot r)$ should be min.

$\therefore$ The max value i.e., $A_{max} = p\cdot s - q\cdot r$

$= 19 \times 17 - 2 \times 3$

$= 323 - 6 = 317.$

14. We have $A = \begin{vmatrix} 2 & 0 \\ 0 & 2 \end{vmatrix}_{2\times2}$

and $B = \begin{vmatrix} 1 & 0 \\ 0 & 4 \end{vmatrix}_{2\times2}$

After solving, we get

$|A| = 4$ and $|B| = 4$

Now, $\det(A\cdot B) = \begin{vmatrix} 2 & 0 \\ 0 & 2 \end{vmatrix} \cdot \begin{vmatrix} 1 & 0 \\ 0 & 4 \end{vmatrix} = \begin{vmatrix} 2 & 0 \\ 0 & 8 \end{vmatrix} = 16$

and $\det(B\cdot A) = \begin{vmatrix} 1 & 0 \\ 0 & 4 \end{vmatrix} \cdot \begin{vmatrix} 2 & 0 \\ 0 & 2 \end{vmatrix} = \begin{vmatrix} 2 & 0 \\ 0 & 8 \end{vmatrix} = 16$

Since $\det(A\cdot B) = \det(B\cdot A)$.

Therefore, A and B need not be unit matrices.

15. Given, $\cot 2x \cot 4x - \cot 4x \cot 6x - \cot 6x \cot 2x$

$= \cot 2x \cot 4x - \cot 6x[\cot 4x + \cot 2x]$

$= \cot 2x \cot 4x - \cot(2x + 4x)[\cot 4x + \cot 2x]$

$= \cot 2x \cot 4x - \dfrac{\cot 2x \cot 4x - 1}{(\cot 2x + \cot 4x)} \times [\cot 4x + \cot 2x]$

$= \cot 2x \cot 4x - (\cot 2x \cot 4x - 1)$

$= \cot 2x \cot 4x - \cot 2x \cot 4x + 1$

$= 1.$

16. Given, $\tan x = -\dfrac{3}{4}$ $\quad (\because 90° < x < 180°)$

Then, $\sin x = \dfrac{3}{5}$ and $\cos x = -\dfrac{4}{5}$

Therefore, $\sin x \cdot \cos x = \dfrac{3}{5}\left(-\dfrac{4}{5}\right) = -\dfrac{12}{25}$.

17. Given, $\operatorname{cosec}\left(\dfrac{7\pi}{6}\right).\sec\left(\dfrac{5\pi}{3}\right)$

$= \operatorname{cosec}\left(\pi + \dfrac{\pi}{6}\right).\sec\left(2\pi - \dfrac{\pi}{3}\right)$

$= -\operatorname{cosec}\dfrac{\pi}{6}\sec\dfrac{\pi}{3}$

$= \operatorname{cosec} 30° \sec 60°$

$= (-2)(2) = -4.$

18. Given, $\begin{vmatrix} x & 1 & 3 \\ 0 & 0 & 1 \\ 1 & x & 4 \end{vmatrix} = 0$

$\therefore\ x(0 - x) + 1(1 - 0) + (0 - 0) = 0$

$\Rightarrow\ -x^2 + 1 = 0$

$\therefore\ x = \pm 1$

Hence, values of x are -1 and 1.

19. Given,

$\tan 31° \tan 33° \tan 35° \ldots \tan 55° \tan 57° \tan 59°$

$= \tan(90° - 59°) \tan 59° \tan(90° - 58°) \tan 58° \ldots\ldots \tan 45°$

$= \cot 59° \tan 59° \cot 58° \tan 58° \ldots \tan 45° = 1 \times 1 \times 1 = 1$

20. Given,

$$f(x) = \begin{vmatrix} 1 & x & x+1 \\ 2x & x(x-1) & x(x+1) \\ 3x(x-1) & 2(x-1)(x-2) & x(x+1)(x-1) \end{vmatrix}$$

If $x = -1$,

then, $C_3 \rightarrow \begin{bmatrix} -1+1 \\ -1(-1+1) \\ -1(-1+1)(-1-1) \end{bmatrix} = \begin{bmatrix} 0 \\ 0 \\ 0 \end{bmatrix}$

If $f = 0$, then $f(0) = (0)$

If $x = 1$, then,

$R_3 \rightarrow [3(1 - 1)2(1 - 1)(1 - 2)(1 + 1)(1 - 1)$

$= [0\ 0\ 0]$

$\therefore\ f(-1) + f(0) + f(1) = 0.$

21. Given, $\sin^{-1}x - \cos^{-1}x = \dfrac{\pi}{6}$ ...(*i*)

Since, $\sin^{-1} x + \cos^{-1} x = \dfrac{\pi}{2}$ ...(*ii*)

On adding, Equation (*i*) & (*ii*), we get

$\sin^{-1} x - \cos^{-1} x = \dfrac{\pi}{6}$

$2 \sin^{-1} x = \dfrac{2\pi}{6}$

$\therefore\ \sin^{-1} x = \dfrac{\pi}{3}$

Thus, it is unique solution.

22. Given, $(\sin 24° + \cos 66°)(\sin 24° - \cos 66°)$

$= \sin^2 24° - \cos^2 66°$

$= \sin^2 24° - \cos^2(90° - 24°)$

$= \sin^2 24° - \sin^2 24° = 0.$

24. Given, $(1 + \cot\theta - \operatorname{cosec}\theta)(1 + \tan\theta + \sec\theta)$

$= \left(\dfrac{1+\cos\theta}{\sin\theta} - \dfrac{1}{\sin\theta}\right)\left(\dfrac{1+\sin\theta}{\cos\theta} + \dfrac{1}{\cos\theta}\right)$

$= \left(\dfrac{\sin\theta + \cos\theta - 1}{\sin\theta}\right)\left(\dfrac{\sin\theta + \cos\theta + 1}{\cos\theta}\right)$

$= \dfrac{(\sin\theta + \cos\theta)^2 - 1^2}{\sin\theta \cdot \cos\theta}$

$= \dfrac{\sin^2\theta + \cos^2\theta + 2\sin\theta\cdot\cos\theta - 1}{\sin\theta\cdot\cos\theta}$

$\left[\because\ \sin^2\theta + \cos^2\theta = 1\right]$

$$= \frac{1+2\sin\theta\cdot\cos\theta-1}{\sin\theta\cdot\cos\theta}$$

$$= \frac{2\sin\theta\cdot\cos\theta}{\sin\theta\cdot\cos\theta} = 2$$

25. Given, $\frac{1+\tan^2\theta}{1+\cot^2\theta} - \left(\frac{1-\tan\theta}{1-\cot\theta}\right)^2$

$$= \frac{1+\tan^2\theta}{1+\frac{1}{\tan^2\theta}} - \left(\frac{1-\tan\theta}{1-\frac{1}{\tan\theta}}\right)^2$$

$$= \frac{1+\tan^2\theta}{\frac{\tan^2\theta-1}{\tan^2\theta}} - \left(\frac{1-\tan\theta}{\frac{\tan\theta-1}{\tan\theta}}\right)^2$$

$$= \frac{\tan^2\theta(1+\tan^2\theta)}{(\tan^2\theta+1)} - (\tan\theta)^2 \times \left(\frac{1-\tan\theta}{1-\tan\theta}\right)^2$$

$= \tan^2\theta - \tan^2\theta = 0$

26. Number of sides for regular octagon $n = 8$

Interior angle of n-sides polygon

$$= \frac{(n-2)\times\pi}{n} = \frac{(8-2)\times\pi}{8} = \frac{6\pi}{8} = \frac{3\pi}{4}$$

27. Given, $7\sin\theta + 24\cos\theta = 25$

$$\Rightarrow \frac{7}{25}\cdot\sin\theta + \frac{24}{25}\cdot\cos\theta = 1$$

Now, $(7)^2 + (24)^2 = (25)^2$

$\therefore$ Let $\frac{7}{25} = \cos x$ and $\frac{24}{25} = \sin x$

Since, $\sin\theta\cdot\cos x + \cos\theta\cdot\sin x = 1$

$$\Rightarrow \sin(\theta+x) = \sin\frac{\pi}{2}$$

$$\Rightarrow 0 + x = \frac{\pi}{2} \Rightarrow \theta = \left(\frac{\pi}{2} - x\right)$$

Hence, $\sin\theta + \cos\theta$

$$= \sin\left(\frac{\pi}{2} - x\right) + \cos\left(\frac{\pi}{2} - x\right)$$

$$= \cos x + \sin x = \frac{7}{25} + \frac{24}{25} = \frac{31}{25}.$$

29. Given height of tower $= 5(3+\sqrt{3})$m

When elevation of Sun is 60° = the length is BC shadow

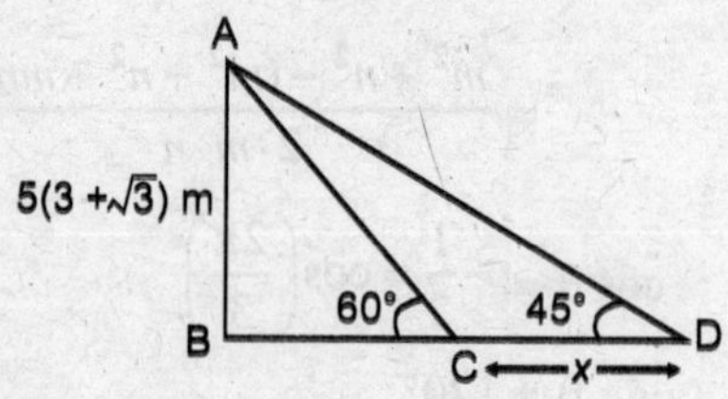

In ΔABC,

$$BC = AB\cdot\cot(60°)$$

$$= 5(3+\sqrt{3}).\frac{1}{\sqrt{3}} = 5(\sqrt{3}+1)\text{m}$$

The lenght of shadow. When elevation of Sun is 45° = BD

In ΔABD,

$$BD = AB\cdot\cot 45°$$

$$= 5(3+\sqrt{3}).1 = 5(3+\sqrt{3})\text{m}$$

$$\because \quad x = BD - BC$$

$$= 5(3+\sqrt{3}) - 5(\sqrt{3}+1)$$

$$= 15 - 5 = 10 \text{ m}$$

30. Given, $3\cos\theta = 4\sin\theta$

$$\Rightarrow \frac{\sin\theta}{\cos\theta} = \frac{3}{4} \Rightarrow \tan\theta = \frac{3}{4}$$

$$\therefore \tan(45° + \theta) = \frac{\tan 45° + \tan\theta}{1 - \tan 45°\cdot\tan\theta}$$

$$= \frac{1+\frac{3}{4}}{1-\frac{3}{4}} = \frac{7}{1} = 7.$$

32. Gvien, $\tan A = \frac{1}{7}$,

$$\therefore \cos 2A = \frac{1-\tan^2 A}{1+\tan^2 A} = \frac{1-\left(\frac{1}{7}\right)^2}{1+\left(\frac{1}{7}\right)^2}$$

$$= \frac{1-\frac{1}{49}}{1+\frac{1}{49}} = \frac{48}{50} = \frac{24}{25}$$

33.

A, θ, m, n, B, C, $\sqrt{m^2+n^2+mn}$

Using cosine rule in ΔABC,

$$\cos\theta = \frac{(AB)^2 + (AC)^2 - (BC)^2}{2\cdot(AB)\cdot(AC)}$$

$$= \frac{m^2+n^2-(m^2+n^2+mn)}{2\cdot m\cdot n}$$

$\therefore \quad \cos\theta = -\frac{1}{2} = \cos\left(\frac{2\pi}{3}\right)$

$\therefore \quad \theta = 120°$

Hence, sum of other two acute angles

$= 180° - 120° = 60°.$

34. Since, area of $\Delta ABC = \frac{1}{2}\times a\times c\times \sin(\angle B)$

$= \frac{1}{2}\times 10\times 4\times \sin(30°)$

$= \frac{1}{2}\times 10\times 4\times \frac{1}{2} = 10\text{ cm}^2$

37. Given, $2x + 3y = 20 \Rightarrow y = \frac{20-2x}{3}$

As $(x, y) \in N$

If $x = 1$, then $y = \frac{20-2}{3} = 6$, (x, y)

$= (1, 6) \in N$

If $x = 4$, then $y = \frac{20-8}{3} = 4$, (x, y)

$= (4, 4) \in N$

If $x = 7$, then $y = \frac{20-14}{3} = 2$, (x, y)

$= (7, 2) \in N$

Therefore, number of elements form (x, y) in R = 3.

39. Given, complex numbers are:

$Z = x + iy,\ \bar{Z} = x - iy$

and $Z^{-1} = \frac{1}{Z} = \frac{1}{x+iy}$

For 1,

$\overline{(Z^{-1})} = \overline{\left(\frac{1}{x+iy}\right)} = \overline{\left(\frac{x-iy}{x^2+y^2}\right)} = \left(\frac{x+iy}{x^2+y^2}\right)$

and $(\bar{Z})^{-1} = (x-iy)^{-1} = \frac{1}{x-iy} = \frac{x+iy}{x^2+y^2}$

$\therefore \ \overline{(Z^{-1})} = (\bar{Z})^{-1}.$

For 2, $Z\cdot Z^{-1} = (x+iy)\left(\frac{1}{x-iy}\right)$

$= \frac{(x-iy)(x+iy)}{(x-iy)(x+iy)} = \frac{(x+iy)}{x^2+y^2} = |Z|^2$

$\therefore \quad ZZ^{-1} = |Z^2|$

Thus, both (1) and (2) are correct.

41. Given,

$(i)^{2n+1}(-i)^{2n-1}$

Put $n = 1$, $(n \in N)$

$(i)^3(-i)^1 = i^2\cdot i = (-1)i(-i)$

$= (-1)(-i^2) = -1(1) = -1.$

45. Given, $(1 + 4x + 4x^2)^5 = [(1 + 2x)^2]^5$

$= (1 + 2x)^{10}$

For middle term $r = \frac{10}{2} = 5$

$\therefore$ Middle term $= {}^{10}C_5(1)^5(2x)^5 = \frac{10!}{5!5!}\cdot 2^5\cdot x^5$

$= \frac{10!}{5!5!}32x^5 = 8064\,x^5$

$\therefore$ The co-efficient of middle term is 8064.

48. Given, $a_0 = 2$

$S_5 = \frac{1}{4}(S_{10} - S_5)$

$\Rightarrow \quad 4S_5 + S_5 = S_{10}$

$\Rightarrow \quad 5S_5 = S_{10}$

$\Rightarrow \quad 5\times\frac{5}{2}[a_0 + a_0 + 4d] = \frac{10}{2}[a_0 + a_0 + 4d]$

$\Rightarrow \quad 5 \times [2a_0 + 4d] = 2 \times [2a_0 \times 9d]$

$\Rightarrow \quad 10a_0 + 20d = 4a_0 + 18d$

$\Rightarrow \quad a_0 = -\frac{d}{3}$

$\therefore \quad d = -3a_0 = -3 \times 2 = 6$

$\therefore \quad S_{10} = \frac{10}{2}[a_0 + a_0 + 9d]$

$= 5[2a_0 + 9d] = 5[4 - 54]$

$(a_0 = 2,\ d = -6)$

$\therefore \quad S_{10} = 5 \times (-50) = -250.$

51. Given, $f(x - 1) = x^2 - 3x + 2$

$= (x^2 + 2x + 1) - 5x - 5 + 6$

$= (x + 1)^2 - 5(x + 1) + 6$

Hence, $f(x) = x^2 - 5x + 6.$

52. Given, x^2, x, -8 are in A.P.

$\therefore\ 2x = x^2 - 8$

$\Rightarrow x^2 - 2x + 1 - 9 = 0$

$\Rightarrow x^2 - 2x + 1 = 9$

$\Rightarrow (x - 1)^2 = 9$

$\therefore\ (x - 1) = \pm 3$

$\Rightarrow x - 1 = -3,\ x = -2$ and $x - 1 = 3$

$\Rightarrow x = 4$

Thus, $x \in |-2, 4|$.

53. Let G.P. is $\frac{3}{r^2}, \frac{3}{r}, 3, 3r$ and $3r^2$

$\therefore$ Product of first five terms

$= \frac{3}{r^2}\cdot\frac{3}{r}\cdot 3\cdot 3r\cdot 3r^2 = (3)^5 = 243.$

54. Given, $2(i + j)$, then determinant

$$= \begin{vmatrix} 4 & 6 & 8 \\ 6 & 8 & 10 \\ 8 & 10 & 12 \end{vmatrix} = 2\begin{vmatrix} 2 & 3 & 4 \\ 3 & 4 & 5 \\ 4 & 5 & 6 \end{vmatrix}$$

$$= 2[2(24 - 25) + 3(20 - 18) + 4(15 - 16)] = 0.$$

56. Given equation of

$$4x^2 + 4y^2 - 20x + 12y - 15 = 0$$

$$\Rightarrow x^2 + y^2 - 5x + 3y - \frac{15}{4} = 0$$

$$\because \text{ Radius} = \sqrt{(-g)^2 + (-f)^2 - C}$$

Where, $g = -\frac{5}{2}$, $f = \frac{3}{2}$ and $C = -\frac{15}{4}$

$$\because \text{ Radius} = \sqrt{\left(\frac{5}{2}\right)^2 + \left(-\frac{3}{2}\right)^2 - \left(-\frac{15}{4}\right)}$$

$$= \sqrt{\frac{25+9+15}{4}} = \frac{7}{2} = 3.5 \text{ units.}$$

57. Let ABCD is a parallelogram and O is the point of intersection of two diagonals.

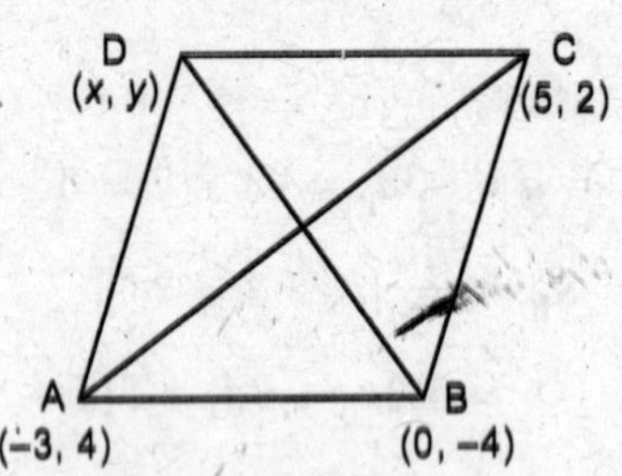

$$\text{Point 'O'} = \left(\frac{-3+5}{2}, \frac{4+2}{2}\right) = (1, 3)$$

Since, point 'O' bisects the diagonal BD

$$1 = \frac{x+0}{2} \Rightarrow x = 2$$

and $\quad 3 = \frac{y-4}{2} \Rightarrow y - 4 = 6 \therefore y = 10$

Hence, the fourth vertices $D(x, y) = (2, 10)$.

62. Given equation of line $x - 2 = 0$

$$\text{Slope, } m_1 = \tan\theta_1 = \frac{1}{0} = \infty$$

$$\therefore \tan\theta_1 = \tan 90° \Rightarrow \theta_1 = 90°$$

and other equation of line,

$$\sqrt{3}x - y - 2 = 0$$

$$\therefore \text{ Slope, } m_2 = \tan\theta_2 = \frac{\sqrt{3}}{1}$$

$$\Rightarrow \tan\theta_2 = \tan 60° \Rightarrow \theta_2 = 60°$$

Thus, the angle between lines = 90° – 60° = 30°.

63.

D, C, O (0, 0), A (4, 2), B

$$\therefore \text{ Slope of diagonal BD} = \frac{-(4-0)}{(2-0)} = -2$$

Since, equation of line passes through origin and its slope $m = -2$

We have, $\quad y = mx$

$$\Rightarrow \quad y = -2x$$

$$\Rightarrow \quad 2x + y = 0.$$

64. The equation of hyperbola is $\frac{x^2}{a^2} - \frac{y^2}{b^2} = 1$

and eccentricity, $e = \sqrt{1 + \frac{a^2}{b^2}}$

Since, point $(3 \tan\theta, 2 \sec\theta)$ lies on the hyperbola,

then, $\frac{3^2 \tan^2\theta}{a^2} - \frac{2^2 \sec^2\theta}{b^2} = 1$

$$\Rightarrow \frac{9\tan^2\theta}{a^2} - \frac{4\sec^2\theta}{b^2} = 1$$

This is true for $a^2 = 9$ and $b^2 = 4$

Hence, eccenticity, $(e) = \sqrt{1 + \frac{9}{4}} = \sqrt{\frac{4+9}{4}} = \frac{\sqrt{13}}{2}$

66. Given, $(a_1, b_1, c_1) = (6, 3, 6)$

and $(a_2, b_2, c_2) = (3, 3, 0)$

We know that, angle between two lines,

$$\cos\theta = \frac{a_1a_2 + b_1b_2 - c_1c_2}{\sqrt{a_1^2 + b_1^2 + c_1^2} \cdot \sqrt{a_2^2 + b_2^2 + c_2^2}}$$

$$\therefore \quad \cos\theta = \frac{6\times3 + 3\times3 + 0}{\sqrt{6^2 + 3^2 + 6^2} \cdot \sqrt{3^2 + 3^2 + 0}}$$

$$= \frac{27}{\sqrt{81}\sqrt{18}}$$

$$= \frac{27}{9 \cdot 3\sqrt{2}} = \frac{1}{\sqrt{2}}$$

$$\therefore \quad \theta = \cos^{-1}\left(\frac{1}{\sqrt{2}}\right) = \frac{\pi}{4}$$

67. Let $x - 1 = (y - 3) = 1 - z = k$

$$\therefore \quad l = k, m = \frac{k}{2} \text{ and } n = k$$

Using equation $l^2 + m^2 + n^2 = 1$

$$k^2+\left(\frac{k}{2}\right)^2+k^2=1\Rightarrow 2k^2+\frac{k^2}{4}=1$$

$$\Rightarrow \frac{9k^2}{4}\Rightarrow k=\frac{2}{3}$$

Hence, $l=\frac{2}{3}$, $m=\frac{1}{3}$ and $n=\frac{2}{3}$

Then, $l^4+m^4+n^4$

$$=\left(\frac{2}{3}\right)^4+\left(\frac{1}{3}\right)^4+\left(\frac{2}{3}\right)^4$$

$$=\frac{16}{81}+\frac{1}{81}+\frac{16}{81}=\frac{33}{81}=\frac{11}{27}.$$

71. Given, $\vec{r}=a\hat{i}+b\hat{j}$

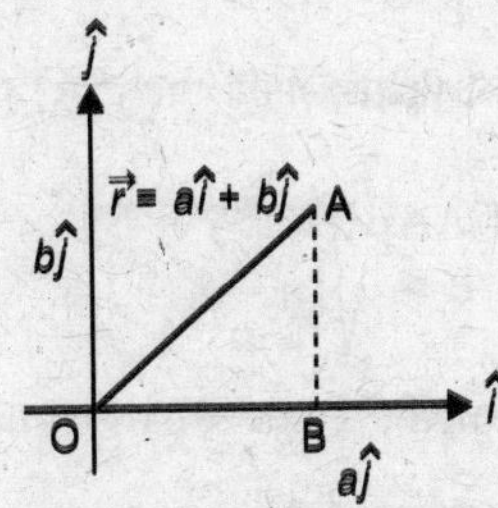

$$|\vec{r}|=\sqrt{a^2+b^2}=2$$

$\Rightarrow a^2+b^2=4$ ...(*i*)

Since, $\vec{r}$ is equally inclined to both axes, we get

$\therefore a=b$

Again from equation (*i*), we get

$$a^2+a^2=4$$

$$\Rightarrow \quad a=\sqrt{2} \text{ and } b=\sqrt{2}$$

Thus, the values of a and b are $\sqrt{2}$ and $\sqrt{2}$.

73. Given, $|\vec{a}+\vec{b}|=|\vec{a}-\vec{b}|=4$

On squaring both sides, we get

$$|\vec{a}+\vec{b}|^2=|\vec{a}-\vec{b}|^2$$

$$\Rightarrow |\vec{a}|^2|\vec{b}|^2+2\vec{a}\cdot\vec{b}=|\vec{a}|^2+|\vec{b}|^2-2\vec{a}\cdot\vec{b}$$

$\therefore \vec{a}\cdot\vec{b}=0.$

75. Let $\vec{a}$ and $\vec{b}$ are two unit vectors, then their cross product

$$\vec{a}\times\vec{b}=|\vec{a}|\cdot|\vec{b}|\cdot\sin\theta\cdot\hat{n}$$

Thus, statement 1 is true.

2. Dot product of a and b, $\vec{a}\cdot\vec{b}=|\vec{a}|\cdot|\vec{b}|\cdot\cos\theta$

Thus statement 2 is true.

3. We have $|\vec{a}+\vec{b}|>|\vec{a}-\vec{b}|$

Squaring on both sides, we get

$$|\vec{a}+\vec{b}|^2>|\vec{a}-\vec{b}|^2=|\vec{a}|^2+|\vec{b}|^2+2\vec{a}\cdot\vec{b}>|\vec{a}|^2+|\vec{b}|^2$$
$$-2\vec{a}\cdot\vec{b}$$

$\Rightarrow \vec{a}\cdot\vec{b}>0$

$\therefore |\vec{a}|\cdot|\vec{b}|\cdot\cos\theta>0$

$\therefore$ Statement 3 is false

Thus, statements 1 and 2 are correct.

76. Given, $\lim\limits_{x\to a}\frac{a^x-x^a}{x^a-a^a}$

$\left(\frac{0}{0}\text{ form, by L'Hospital rule}\right)$

$$\Rightarrow \lim_{x\to a}\frac{a^x-x^a}{x^a-a^a}=\lim_{x\to a}\frac{a^x\cdot\ln a-a\cdot x^{a-1}}{a\cdot x^{a-1}-0}$$

$$=\frac{a^a\cdot\ln a-a^a}{a^a}=\ln a-1$$

$\therefore \ln a-1=-1\Rightarrow \ln a=0$

Hence, $a=(e)^0=1$.

77. Given, $\frac{dx}{dt}=x+1$

or $\frac{dx}{x+1}=dt$

Now, integrating on both sides, we get

$$\int\frac{dx}{x+1}=\int dt$$

$$\ln(x+1)=t+c$$

At $t=0$, $x=0$ (origin point)

Hence, $\ln(0+1)=0+c\Rightarrow c=0$

Thus, $\ln(x+1)=t$

If $x=24$ m

then, $t=\ln(24+1)$

$=\ln(25)=\ln(5)^2=2\ln(5)$

78. Given, $\text{I}=\int_0^a\frac{f(a-x)}{f(x)+f(a-x)}dx$

$$=\int_0^a\frac{f(a+0-a+x)}{f(a+0-x)+f(a+0-a+x)}dx$$

$$=\int_0^a\frac{f(x)}{f(a-x)+f(x)}dx$$

$$2\text{I}=\int_0^a\frac{f(a-x)+f(x)}{f(a-x)+f(x)}dx=[x]_0^a=a$$

Hence, $\text{I}=\frac{a}{2}$

79. Given, $\lim_{x\to -1} \frac{x^3+x^2}{x^2+3x+2}$

From, L'Hospital rule,

$$\lim_{x\to -1} \frac{3x^2+2x}{2x+3} = \frac{3(-1)^2+2(-1)}{2(-1)+3} = \frac{3-2}{-2+3} = 1.$$

80. Given, $\int_0^a [f(x)+f(-x)]dx = \int_{-a}^a g(x)dx$

$$= \int_{-a}^0 g(x)\cdot dx + \int_0^a g(x)\cdot dx$$

$$= \int_0^a g(-x)\cdot dx + \int_0^a g(x)\cdot dx$$

$$= \int_0^a [g(x)+g(-x)]\cdot dx$$

Hence, $f(x) = g(x)$.

81. Given, $y = \sqrt{16-x^2}$, $y \geq 0$,

$\therefore \quad 16 - x^2 \geq 0$

$\Rightarrow \quad x^2 = 16$

$\Rightarrow \quad x = \pm 4$

$\therefore \quad x \in [-4, 4]$

Now, using from $I = \int \sqrt{a^2-x^2}\cdot dx$

$$= \frac{x\sqrt{a^2-x^2}}{2} + \frac{a^2}{2}\sin^{-1}\left(\frac{x}{a}\right)^2 + C$$

Since $a^2 = 16$.

Thus, area bounded by the curve,

$$I = \int_{-4}^{4} \sqrt{(4)^2-x^2}\cdot dx$$

$$= \left[\frac{x\sqrt{16-x^2}}{2}\right]_{-4}^{4} + \frac{16}{2}\left[\sin^{-1}\left(\frac{x}{4}\right)\right]_{-4}^{4}$$

$$= 0 + 8\cdot\left[\sin^{-1}\left(\frac{4}{4}\right) - \sin^{-1}\left(-\frac{4}{4}\right)\right]$$

$$= 8\left[\sin^{-1}(1) + \sin^{-1}(1)\right]$$

$$= 8 \times 2\sin^{-1}(1)$$

$$= 16\cdot\sin^{-1}(1) = 16\cdot\frac{\pi}{2} = 8\pi \text{ sq. units}$$

82. Given $y = -x^3 + 3x^2 + 2x - 27$

$\therefore$ Slope $= \frac{dy}{dx} = -3x^2 + 6x + 2$

Differentiate again, $\frac{d^2y}{dx^2} = -6x + 6$

Hence, the maximum slope, $\frac{d^2y}{dx^2} = 0$

$\Rightarrow \quad 6(-x+1) = 0$

$\Rightarrow \quad 6x = 6$

$\therefore \quad x = 1$

Thus, the maximum slope at $x = 1$.

83.

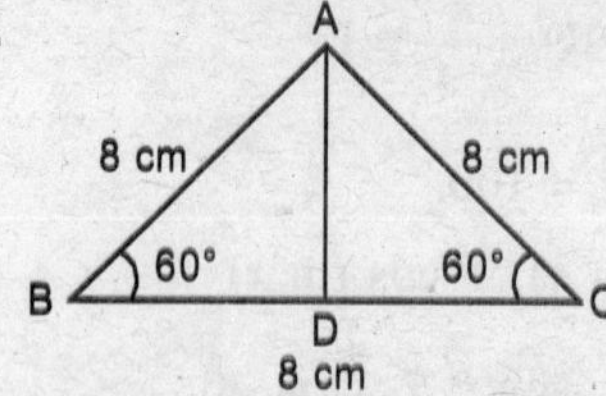

It is equilateral triangle.

Sides of equilateral triangle

$$AB = BC = CA = \frac{24}{3} = 8 \text{ cm}$$

Now, area of $\Delta ABC = \frac{\sqrt{3}}{4}(\text{side})^2$

$$= \frac{\sqrt{3}}{4}(8)^2 = 16\sqrt{3} \text{ cm}^2$$

Let AD is the altitude of the ΔABC.

Since, area of $\Delta ABC = \frac{1}{2} \times BC \times AD$

$\therefore \quad 16\sqrt{3} = \frac{1}{2} \times 8 \times AD$

$\Rightarrow \quad 4AD = 16\sqrt{3}$

$\therefore \quad AD = 4\sqrt{3}$ cm.

85. Let $\quad f(x) = \int \frac{dx}{\sec x + \tan x}$

$$= \int \frac{(\sec x - \tan x)}{(\sec x + \tan x)(\sec x - \tan x)}\cdot dx$$

$$= \int \frac{(\sec x - \tan x)}{\sec^2 x - \tan^2 x}\cdot dx$$

$$= \int (\sec x - \tan x)\, dx$$

$$\therefore \int f(x)\, dx = \int \sec x \cdot dx - \int \tan x\, dx$$

$$= \ln|\sec x + \tan x| - \ln|\sec x| + c.$$

86. Given, $\int \frac{dx}{\sec^2(\tan^{-1} x)}$

Let $\tan^{-1} x = t \Rightarrow \tan t = x$

$\because \sec^2 t = 1 + \tan^2 t = 1 + x^2$

$$\therefore \int \frac{dx}{\sec^2(\tan^{-1} x)} = \int \frac{dx}{1+x^2} = \tan^{-1} x + C$$

87. Given, $x + y = 20$ and $P = xy$

A.M. of x and $y = \frac{x+y}{2} = \frac{20}{2} = 10$

G.M. of x and $y = \sqrt{xy} = \sqrt{P}$

Since, AM ≥ G.M.

$\therefore\ 10 \geq \sqrt{P}$

Thus, $P_{max} = (10)^2 = 100.$

88. Given, $y = \sin(\ln x)) + \cos(\ln x)$

$$\therefore \frac{dy}{dx} = \frac{d}{dx}(\sin(\ln x)) + \frac{d}{dx}(\cos(\ln x))$$

$$= \cos(\ln x)\cdot\frac{1}{x} + \left[-\sin(\ln x)\cdot\frac{1}{x}\right]$$

$$= \frac{\cos(\ln x) - \sin(\ln x)}{x}$$

$$\left.\frac{dy}{dx}\right|_{x=e} = \frac{\cos(\ln e) - \sin(\ln e)}{e} = \frac{(\cos 1) - \sin(1)}{e}$$

Hence, derivative of $\sin(\ln n) + \cos(\ln x)$

$$= \frac{\cos 1 - \sin 1}{e}$$

89. Given, $x = e^t \cdot \cos t \Rightarrow \frac{dx}{dt} = e^t \cdot \cos t - e^t \cdot \sin t$

and $y = e^t \cdot \sin t \Rightarrow \frac{dy}{dt} = e^t \cdot \sin t + e^t \cdot \cos t$

$$\therefore \frac{dx}{dy} = \frac{\frac{dx}{dt}}{\frac{dy}{dt}} = \frac{e^t(\cos t - \sin t)}{e^t(\sin t + \cos t)} = \frac{\cos t - \sin t}{\sin t + \cos t}$$

$$\therefore \left.\frac{dx}{dy}\right|_{t=0} = \frac{\cos 0 - \sin 0}{\sin 0 + \cos 0} = \frac{1-0}{0+1} = 1$$

90. Given, $y = \sin 2x \cdot \cos 2x$

$$\therefore \frac{dy}{dx} = \frac{d}{dx}(\sin 2x)\cdot\cos 2x + \frac{d}{dx}(\cos 2x)\cdot\sin 2x$$

$$= \cos^2 2x - \sin^2 2x = \cos 4x$$

$[\because \cos^2 A - \sin^2 A = \cos 2A]$

Therefore, for maximum value

$$\frac{dy}{dx} = 0 \Rightarrow \cos 4x = 0$$

$$\Rightarrow \quad \cos 4x = \cos\frac{\pi}{2} \quad \left[\because \cos\frac{\pi}{2} = 0\right]$$

$$\Rightarrow \quad 4x = \frac{\pi}{2}$$

$$\therefore \quad x = \frac{\pi}{8}$$

Again, $\frac{d^2y}{dx^2} = -4\cdot\sin 4x$

At $x = \frac{\pi}{8}, \frac{d^2y}{dx^2} = -4\cdot\sin\frac{\pi}{2} = -4$

For y_{max} at $x = \frac{\pi}{8}$

$$\therefore \quad y_{max} = \sin 2\left(\frac{\pi}{8}\right)\cdot\cos 2\left(\frac{\pi}{8}\right)$$

$$= \sin\frac{\pi}{4}\cdot\cos\frac{\pi}{4} = \frac{1}{\sqrt{2}}\cdot\frac{1}{\sqrt{2}} = \frac{1}{2}.$$

91. Let $f(x) = e^x$ then,

$$f(x) = \frac{d}{dx}e^x = e^x$$

Now, $g(x) = x^e$

$$g'(x) = \frac{d}{dx}e^x = x^{e-1}$$

$$\therefore \text{Required derivative} = \frac{f'(x)}{g'(x)} = \frac{e^x}{ex^{e-1}} = \frac{xe^x}{ex^e}$$

92. Given, $\lim_{x\to -1}\frac{f(x)+1}{x^2-1} = \frac{-3}{2}$

$$\therefore \quad \frac{f'(x)}{2x} = \frac{-3}{2}$$

$$\Rightarrow \quad f'(x) = 3x$$

Now, integrating on both sides, we get

$$f(x) = \frac{-3}{2}x^2 + c \quad \text{where } c = \text{Constant}$$

$$\therefore \lim_{x\to -1} f(x) = \lim_{x\to -1}\left[\frac{-3}{2}x^2 + c\right] = \frac{-3}{2}$$

93. Given, $f(x) = \begin{cases} a+bx, & x<1 \\ 5, & x=1 \\ b-ax, & x>1 \end{cases}$, is continuous

$$\lim_{x\to 1^-} f(x) = \lim_{x\to 1^+} f(x) = f(1)$$

$$\lim_{x\to 1^-}(a+bx) = \lim_{x\to 1^+}(b-ax) = 5$$

$a + b = 5$ ...(*i*)

and $b - a = 5$ ...(*ii*)

From equations (*i*) and (*ii*), we get $b = 5$ and $a = 0$

$\therefore \quad a + b = 0 + 5 = 5$

95. Given $f(x) = 3^x$

The domain of the expression is all the real numbers except, where the expression is undefined.

In this case, there is no real number that makes the expression undefined.

Interval notation [−∞, ∞]

Hence, the domain of the function

$f(x) = 3^x$ is [−∞, ∞].

96. Given, $y^2 + 2cy - cx + c^2 = 0$

$\Rightarrow (y^2 + 2cy + c^2) - cx = 0$

$\Rightarrow (y + c)^2 = cx$

$\Rightarrow 2(y + c)y' = c$

$\Rightarrow c = \dfrac{2yy'}{1-2y'}$

Putting this in the given equation, we get

$$\left(y+\frac{2yy'}{1-2y'}\right)^2 = \frac{2yy'}{1-2y'}x$$

$\Rightarrow y^2 = 2xyy'\ (1 - 2y')$

$\Rightarrow y^2 - 2xyy' + 4xy(y') = 0$

97. Given, $x = \sqrt{1+\dfrac{dy^2}{dx^2}} \Rightarrow x^2 = 1+\dfrac{d^2y}{dx^2}$

Therefore, degree of the D.E. is 1

98. Given, $y = ae^x + be^{-x}$

Differentiate wrt to x, we get

$$\frac{dy}{dx} = ae^x - be^{-x}$$

Again differentiate, $\dfrac{d^2y}{dx^2} = ae^x + be^{-x}$

$\Rightarrow \quad \dfrac{d^2y}{dx^2} = y$

Hence, $\dfrac{d^2y}{dx^2} - y = 0$

99. Given, $\ln\left(\dfrac{dy}{dx}\right) + y = x$

$\therefore \quad \ln\left(\dfrac{dy}{dx}\right) = x - y$

$\therefore \quad e^{x-y} = \dfrac{dy}{dx}$

$\Rightarrow \quad \dfrac{e^x}{e^y} = \dfrac{dy}{dx}$

$\Rightarrow e^x \cdot dx = e^y \cdot dy$

Integrating on both sides, we get

$$\int e^x \cdot dx = \int e^y \cdot dy$$

$\Rightarrow \quad e^x = e^y + c$

$\Rightarrow \quad e^x - e^y = c$

100. Let, $I = \int e^{(2\ln x + \ln x^2)} dx$

$$= \int e^{(\ln x + \ln x^2)} \cdot dx = \int e^{(2\ln x^2)} \cdot dx$$

$$= \int e^{(\ln x^4)} \cdot dx = \int x^4 \cdot dx = \frac{x^5}{5} + c$$

101. 1. Arithmetic mean = $\dfrac{\text{Sum of observations}}{\text{Number of observations}}$

2. Geometric mean = $\sqrt{\text{Product of } n \text{ observations}}$

There are three most commonly used to measure central tendency are:

(*i*) Arithmetic mean

(*ii*) Median

(*iii*) Mode

102. Numbers science graduate = 30

Numbers of Arts graduate = 70 and numbers of commerce graduate = 50

Total graduates = 30 + 70 + 50 = 150.

$\therefore$ Science graduate = $\left(\dfrac{30}{150}\right) \times 360° = 72°$

104. The coefficient of correlation is independent on change of scale and origin of the variables x and y. Change of origin means some value has been added or subtracted in the observation.

105.

Number of peas	Frequency	Cummulative frequency
1	4	4
2	33	37
3	76	113
4	50	163
5	26	189
6	8	197
7	1	198

Since, N = 198 (even), the median will be mean values at $\dfrac{198}{2} = 99$th

Position and 99 + 1 = 100th position

From the table, both 99th and 100th values are 3. Thus, median is 3.

107. Mean = $\dfrac{73+85+92+105+120}{5} = \dfrac{475}{5} = 95$

Hence, sum of the deviations from the mean

= (95 − 73) + (95 − 85) + (95 − 92) + (95 − 105) + (95 − 180)

= 22 + 10 + 3 − 10 − 25 = 35 − 35 = 0.

108. According to question, HM of $x = \frac{2m \cdot n}{m+n}$

and GM of $y = \sqrt{m \cdot n}$

Since, $5x = 4y$

$\therefore \quad 5 \cdot \frac{(2m \cdot n)}{m+n} = 4 \cdot \sqrt{m \cdot n}$

$\because \quad \left[\text{A.M. of } m \text{ and } n = \frac{m+n}{2}\right]$

$\Rightarrow \frac{5m \cdot n}{2\sqrt{m \cdot n}} = m+n$

$\Rightarrow \frac{5}{2}\sqrt{m \cdot n} = (m+n)$

$\Rightarrow \frac{5}{2} = \sqrt{\frac{m}{n}} + \sqrt{\frac{n}{m}}$

Let $\sqrt{\frac{m}{n}} = \text{P}$

then, $\frac{5}{2} = \text{P} + \frac{1}{\text{P}}$

$\Rightarrow 2(\text{P}^2 + 1) = 5\text{P}.$

$\Rightarrow 2\text{P}^2 - 5\text{P} + 2 = 0$

$\Rightarrow (\text{P} - 2)(2\text{P} - 1) = 0$

$\therefore$ P = 2 or $\frac{1}{2}$

$\therefore \quad \sqrt{\frac{m}{n}} = 2 \quad \Rightarrow \quad m = 4n$

109. As co-efficient of variation (C.V.) = $\frac{\text{S.D.}}{\text{Mean}}$

$\therefore \quad \frac{45}{100} = \frac{\text{S.D.}}{100} \Rightarrow \text{S.D.} = 45$

Hence, value of variance = $(\text{S.D.})^2$

$= (45)^2 = 2025.$

110. As, $\text{P(A|B)} = \frac{\text{P(A} \cap \text{B)}}{\text{P(B)}}$

Since, $\text{P(A} \cup \text{B)} = \text{P(A)} + \text{P(B)} - \text{P(A} \cup \text{B)}$

For max. value of probability is 1,

i.e., $\text{P(A} \cup \text{B)} \le 1$

$\therefore \text{P(A)} + \text{P(B)} - (\text{P(A} \cup \text{B)} \le 1$

$\Rightarrow \text{L} + \text{M} - \text{P(A} \cup \text{B)} \le 1$

$\therefore \text{P(A} \cap \text{B)} \ge \text{L} + \text{M} - 1$

Since, $\text{P(A|B)} = \frac{\text{P(P} \cap \text{B)}}{\text{P(B)}}$

Thus, $\text{P(AB)} \ge \frac{\text{L}+\text{M}-1}{\text{M}}$

112. We have, Mean of discarded observations

$= \frac{\text{Sum of 12 observations} - \text{Sum of 10 observations}}{2}$

$= \frac{12 \times 72 - 10 \times 65}{2}$

$= \frac{900 - 650}{2}$

$= \frac{250}{2} = 125$

113. Given, equation $x(x + 1) + 1 = 0$

$\Rightarrow \quad x^2 + x + 1 = 0$

$\therefore a = 1, b = 1$ and $c = 1$

As k is the root of equation,

$\therefore \quad k^2 + k + 1 = 0$

$k^2 = -k - 1 \quad$ ...(*i*)

The some of roots $= \frac{-1}{1} = -1$

$\alpha + k = -1$

$\alpha = -1 - k$ or $\alpha = -k - 1$

From equation (*i*), we get

$\alpha = k^2$

Thus, other root is k^2.

115. Given, $\text{P(P} \cup \text{B)} = \frac{5}{6}$

$\text{P(A} \cap \text{B)} = \frac{1}{3}$

and $\text{P}(\overline{\text{A}}) = \frac{1}{2}$

As, $\text{P(A)} = 1 - \text{P}(\overline{\text{A}}) = 1 - \frac{1}{2} = \frac{1}{2}$

and $\text{P(B)} = \text{P(A} \cup \text{B)} - \text{P(A)} + \text{P(A} \cap \text{B)}$

$= \frac{5}{6} - \frac{1}{2} + \frac{1}{3} = \frac{5-3+1}{6} = \frac{2}{3}$

Again, $\text{P(A} \cap \text{B)} = \text{P(A)} \cdot \text{P(B)}$

$= \frac{1}{2} \times \frac{2}{3} = \frac{1}{3}$

Thus, A and B are independent events.

117. We have, $\text{P(E)} = \frac{1}{2}$ and $\text{P(F)} = \frac{1}{2}$

As, $\text{P(E} \cup \text{F)} = \text{P(E)} + \text{P(F)} - \text{P(E} \cap \text{F)}$

Since, E & F are two independent events

Then, $\text{P(E} \cap \text{F)} = \text{P(E)}.\text{P(F)}$

Thus, $\text{P(E} \cup \text{F)} = \frac{1}{2} + \frac{1}{2} - \frac{1}{2}.\frac{1}{2} = 1 - \frac{1}{4} = \frac{3}{4}$

118. Given, mean (NP) = $\frac{2}{3}$

and variance (NPQ) = $\frac{5}{9}$

But, $\frac{\text{Variance (NPQ)}}{\text{meant (NP)}} = Q = \frac{\frac{5}{9}}{\frac{2}{3}} = \frac{5}{6}$

As, $P = 1 - Q = 1 - \frac{5}{6} = \frac{1}{6}$

Here, number of trial, $n \times \frac{1}{6} = \frac{2}{3}$

Since, random variable X = 2

∴ Required probability = $^4C_2(P)^{4-2}Q^2$

$$= {}^4C_2 \times \left(\frac{1}{6}\right)^2 \times \left(\frac{5}{6}\right)^2 = 6 \times \frac{1}{36} \times \frac{25}{36} = \frac{25}{216}.$$

119. Given scores 10, 12, 13, 15, 15, 13, 12, 10, x and Mode = 15

Frequency of scores 12 = 2

Frequency of scores 15 = 2

But for mode to be 15

Hence, x should be 15.

120. Given, $P(A) = \frac{3}{4}$ and $P(B) = \frac{5}{8}$

As, $P(A \cup B) = P(A) + P(B) - P(A \cap B)$

The minimum value of $P(A \cup B) = \frac{3}{4}$

and the max. value of $P(A \cap B) = \frac{3}{4}$

Thus, both statements (1) and (2) are correct.

Previous Papers (Solved)

NATIONAL DEFENCE ACADEMY & NAVAL ACADEMY

NDA & NA – Entrance Exam, 2020 (I) & (II)*

PAPER I : GENERAL ABILITY TEST

PART A : ENGLISH LANGUAGE

ANTONYMS

Directions (Qs. No. 1-10): *Each item in this section consists of a sentence with an underlined word followed by four words. Select the option that is* ***opposite in meaning*** *to the underlined word and mark your response in your Answer sheet accordingly.*

1. He nodded absently throughout the meeting.
A. capably B. alertly
C. agitatedly D. dreamily

2. I fully believe that the cornerstone of good policy is an electorate that is educated on the national issues.
A. cerebral B. enlightened
C. ignorant D. erudite

3. For important medical decisions, even finding a doctor you trust is not enough.
A. significant B. trivial
C. basic D. probable

4. Planets move in their orbits.
A. push B. rotate
C. stall D. flow

5. Temperature is a measure of internal energy of an object and is frequently expressed by physicists in units of Kelvin.
A. found B. told
C. distributed D. concealed

6. People argue about why Venus is so much warmer than the Earth.
A. friendlier B. colder
C. wilder D. heavier

7. Scientists are concerned whether the oceans and land biosphere will take up as much carbon in the future as they presently do.
A. worried B. indifferent
C. curious D. puzzled

8. The biggest debate among scientists today is about *cloud feedback*.
A. contend B. moot
C. wrangle D. agreement

9. The Earth's climate sensitivity is conventionally defined as the equilibrium temperature increase caused by a doubling of carbon dioxide.
A. imperviousness B. willingness
C. responsiveness D. closeness

10. The oceans carry a huge amount of heat from the tropics to the high altitudes.
A. significant B. major
C. tiny D. dormant

ORDERING OF WORDS IN A SENTENCE

Directions (Qs. No. 11-20): *Each of the following items in this section consists of a sentence(s), the parts of which have been jumbled. These parts have been labelled as P, Q, R and S. Given below each sentence are four sequences namely A, B, C and D. You are required to rearrange the jumbled parts of the sentence and mark your response accordingly.*

11. P. several years ago,
Q. course on climate change at Texas A&M University
R. Professor Andrew Dessler created an introductory
S. for freshmen and sophomores
A. P R Q S B. Q R P S
C. S Q R P D. P Q R S

12. P. I realize that solving the climate change problem
Q. than solving
R. will be much harder
S. the ozone depletion problem
A. P R Q S B. Q R P S
C. S Q R P D. P Q R S

13. P. although the temperature of this layer of the
Q. when directly comparing the satellite
R. measurements of temperature
S. atmosphere should generally track the surface temperature, we must be careful
A. P R Q S B. P S Q R
C. S Q R P D. P Q R S

*A common examination for both NDA & NA Exam (I) and (II), 2020 held on 06/09/2020.

14. P. the element heats up,
Q. eventually reaching high temperatures
R. glowing like a dark orange that radiates
S. the visible range,
A. P Q S R B. Q P S R
C. S Q R P D. P R S Q

15. P. two people argue about why Venus is so much warmer
Q. to the Sun, so it absorbs more solar energy. The second argues
R. that it's because Venus has a thick, greenhouse-gas rich atmosphere
S. than the Earth. The first argues that it's because Venus is closer
A. P S Q R B. Q R P S
C. S Q R P D. P Q R S

16. P. are now used by more than a thousand firms
Q. and are growing in popularity
R. in the United States and Europe
S. gain sharing-plans
A. P R Q S B. Q R P S
C. P R S Q D. S P R Q

17. P. adversity without succumbing
Q. to the clouds of doubt and jealousy
R. between friends which is subjected to both prosperity and
S. the essay 'Of Friendship' by Francis Bacon celebrated the intimacy
A. P R Q S B. Q R P S
C. S R P Q D. P Q R S

18. P. friends without which the world is
Q. make friends and a person wills to want true
R. it is miserable solitude that compels a person to
S. nothing other than a place of wilderness
A. P R Q S B. Q R P S
C. R Q P S D. P Q R S

19. P. takes the longest
Q. that never started
R. the job
S. to finish
A. P R Q S B. R Q P S
C. S Q R P D. P Q R S

20. P. to what you can create
Q. control, shift your energy
R. instead of worrying about
S. what you cannot
A. P R S Q B. Q R S P
C. S Q R P D. R S Q P

SYNONYMS

Directions (Qs. No. 21-30): *Each item in this section consists of a sentence with an underlined word/words followed by four words. Select the option that is **nearest in meaning** to the underlined word and mark your response on your Answer sheet accordingly.*

21. She got the divorce within no time.
A. detachment B. breaking down
C. annulment D. punishment

22. He was known for his gentle disposition.
A. harmful B. amiable
C. cunning D. adjusting

23. The harder we kick, the better the ball bounces back.
A. recoils B. deflates
C. inflates D. ascends

24. I plan and execute.
A. desire B. debate
C. accomplish D. discard

25. He listened to me with equanimity.
A. carelessly B. excitedly
C. patiently D. half-heartedly

26. The whole thing was a futile exercise.
A. costly B. pointless
C. indecisive D. successful

27. He was too cunning for her.
A. capable B. fit
C. intelligent D. dodgy

28. This decision is crucial for me.
A. momentous B. natural
C. primitive D. inept

29. The media went into a frenzy about the case.
A. silent B. creative
C. berserk D. wrong

30. He has been yearning to go home.
A. declining B. demanding
C. begging D. hankering

PREPOSITIONS

Directions (Qs. No. 31-40): *Each item in this section has a sentence with a missing preposition. Select the correct preposition from the given options and mark your response on your Answer Sheet accordingly.*

31. Simulations of the 20th century by climate models that exclude the observed increase .... greenhouse gases fail to simulate the increase in temperature over the second half of the 20th century.
A. of B. in
C. by D. to

32. In extremely poor societies, children can be put to work .... a young age and are therefore a source of income.
A. in B. on
C. by D. at

33. People who are averse .... hard work, generally do not succeed in life.
A. to B. about
C. at D. on

34. I have known her .... a long time.
A. since B. for
C. at D. before

35. I accepted the offer .... certain conditions.
A. on B. in
C. by D. within

36. She is a woman .... humble origin.
A. off B. of
C. from D. within

37. There is no cure .... the common cold.
A. for B. of
C. to D. on

38. I ran .... John yesterday, and it was a pleasant surprise.
A. by B. off
C. beside D. into

39. My grandmother enjoyed boating .... the lovely lake.
A. in B. on
C. beside D. within

40. He visits the needy to relieve them .... their sufferings and poverty.
A. from B. off
C. of D. on

SPOTTING ERRORS

Directions (Qs. No. 41-50): *Each item in this section has a sentence with three underlined parts labelled as (A), (B) and (C). Read each sentence to find out whether there is any error in any underlined part and indicate your response on the Answer sheet against the corresponding letter i.e., (A) or (B) or (C). If you find no error, your response should be indicated as (D).*

41. This building (A)/ comprises of six houses, (B)/ three parking lots and one basement (C)/ No error. (D)

42. I look forward (A)/ to meet (B)/ you. (C)/ No error. (D)

43. I cannot (A)/ cope up (B)/ with this pressure (C)/ No error. (D)

44. I came (A)/to this place (B)/ by walk. (C)/ No error. (D)

45. What is (A)/ the time (B)/ in your watch? (C)/ No error. (D)

46. The price of my dress (A)/ is higher than that of (B)/ yours. (C)/ No error. (D)

47. My friend's (A)/ daughter-in-laws (B)/ have come. (C)/ No error. (D)

48. I prefer (A)/ seafood (B)/ than Mediterranean food. (C)/ No error. (D)

49. We were (A)/ discussing about (B)/ the issue. (C)/ No error. (D)

50. Dispose off (A)/ the garbage (B)/ from the shelves. (C)/ No error. (D)

PART B : GENERAL KNOWLEDGE

51. New Zealand is considered part of which one of the following island groups?
A. Micronesia
B. Melanesia
C. Polynesia
D. Hawaii Island chain

52. Which of the following statements with regard to *Pradhan Mantri Krishi Sinchayee Yojana* (PMKSY) is/are correct?
1. PMKSY was launched during 2015-16.
2. The basic aim of PMKSY is to enhance physical access of water on farm.
3. One of the main objectives of PMKSY is to achieve convergence of investments in irrigation at the field level.

Select the correct answer using the code given below:
A. 1 only B. 1 and 2 only
C. 2 and 3 only D. 1, 2 and 3

53. According to Article 79 of the Constitution of India, which of the following is/are described as a part of Parliament of India?
1. The House of the People
2. The Council of States
3. The President of India

Select the correct answer using the code given below:
A. 1 only B. 1 and 2 only
C. 2 and 3 only D. 1, 2 and 3

54. The Five Year Plan was first launched in:
A. China B. USSR
C. India D. Bhutan

55. The call for *Garibi Hatao* was incorporated in:
A. Fourth Five Year Plan
B. Fifth Five Year Plan
C. Sixth Five Year Plan
D. Seventh Five Year Plan

56. Match List-I with List-II and select the correct answer using the code given below the Lists:

List-I (Major Objective)	**List-II (Five Year Plan)**
(*a*) Faster and more inclusive growth	1. First
(*b*) Faster, more inclusive and sustainable growth	2. Fifth
(*c*) Correction of disequilibrium caused by Second World War	3. Eleventh
(*d*) Attaining self-reliance	4. Twelfth

Code:

	(*a*)	(*b*)	(*c*)	(*d*)
A.	3	1	4	2
B.	3	4	1	2
C.	2	4	1	3
D.	2	1	4	3

57. Which one of the following Directive Principles was inserted by the Constitution (42nd Amendment) Act, 1976?
A. The State shall minimise inequalities in income
B. Equal justice and free legal aid
C. Promotion of co-operative societies
D. Provision for early childhood care

58. A common High Court for two or more states can be established by:
A. a law passed by the Parliament
B. an order of the Supreme Court of India
C. an order of the President of India
D. an amendment to the Constitution of India

59. In the year 1928, a committee of Congress leaders drafted a Constitution for India. The Committee was headed by:
A. Mahatma Gandhi B. T.B. Sapru
C. Motilal Nehru D. Jawaharlal Nehru

60. Which one of the following statements about Jaipal Singh is NOT correct?
A. He was a member of the Constituent Assembly
B. He founded the Adivasi Maha Sabha
C. He was the captain of the first Indian national hockey team
D. He campaigned for a separate state of Chhattisgarh

61. What is 'Tikki Mausi' in the context of Malnutrition?
A. A specially packaged food item
B. A mascot
C. Name of a scheme
D. Name given to the healthcare providers

62. Which one of the following was the theme of the World Tourism Day, 2019?
A. Sustainable tourism
B. Tourism and the digital transformation
C. Tourism : responding to the challenge of climate change
D. Tourism and jobs : a better future for all

63. Which one of the following countries has hosted the Army Exercise TSENTR, 2019?
A. Russia B. China
C. Kazakhstan D. Kyrgyzstan

64. Which one of the following countries is called the 'country of winds'?
A. India B. China
C. Denmark D. Germany

65. Which one of the following is the oldest scientific department of Government of India?
A. Department of Biotechnology
B. Survey of India
C. India Meteorological Department
D. DRDO

66. 'Naseem-Al-Bahr' is a bilateral naval exercise between India and:
A. United Arab Emirates B. Iran
C. Saudi Arabia D. Oman

67. Koneru Humpy excels in which one of the following sports?
A. Boxing B. Table Tennis
C. Chess D. Billiards

68. Which one of the following was the official mascot of Khelo India Youth Games, 2020?
A. Vijaya B. Yaya
C. Rongmon D. Ammu

69. In January 2020, a passenger aircraft crashed in Iran soon after taking off from Tehran's Imam Khomeini airport killing about 170 people onboard. The airplane belongs to:
A. Qatar Airways
B. Ukraine International Airlines
C. Singapore Airlines
D. Cathay Pacific

70. MILAN, a multilateral naval exercise, 2020 was hosted by which one of the following cities?
A. Port Blair B. Kochi
C. Visakhapatnam D. Panaji

71. Chalk and marble are different forms of:
A. Calcium hydrogen carbonate
B. Calcium carbonate
C. Calcium acetate
D. Sodium carbonate

72. The number of maximum electrons in N Shell is:
A. 2 B. 8
C. 18 D. 32

73. Vinegar is also known as:
A. ethanoic acid B. nitric acid
C. sulphuric acid D. tartaric acid

74. A liquid is kept in a glass beaker. Which one of the following statements is correct regarding the pressure exerted by the liquid column at the base of the beaker?
A. The pressure depends on the area of the base of the beaker
B. The pressure depends on the height of liquid column
C. The pressure does not depend on the density of the liquid
D. The pressure neither depends on the area of the base of the beaker nor on the height of liquid column

75. Which of the following statements is NOT correct regarding the travel of sound waves?
A. Sound waves can travel through water
B. Sound waves can travel through air
C. Sound waves can travel through steel
D. Sound waves can travel through vacuum

76. Deendayal Port is located at:
A. Kerala B. Gujarat
C. Maharashtra D. Goa

77. Which one of the following cities is associated with Biosafety Protocol to the Convention on Biological Diversity (2000)?
A. Geneva B. Nairobi
C. Cartagena D. Rio de Janeiro

78. Krishna Raja Sagara Dam/Reservoir is developed on:
A. river Krishna B. river Tungabhadra
C. river Godavari D. river Kavery

79. Which one of the following Indian states does NOT share international border with two or more countries?
A. Arunachal Pradesh B. Assam
C. Mizoram D. Tripura

80. According to Census of India, 2011, which one among the following is the least populated state in India?
A. Maharashtra B. Madhya Pradesh
C. Odisha D. Punjab

81. The speakers of major Indian languages belong to how many language families?
A. Two B. Three
C. Four D. Six

82. Where did Gandhiji initially forge the techniques of *Satyagraha*?
A. England B. South Africa
C. North Africa D. India

83. Who was the Viceroy of India at the time of Gandhiji's Dandi march?
A. Lord Irwin B. Lord Linlithgow
C. Lord Reading D. Lord Willingdon

84. Which one among the following American newsmagazines was highly sceptical of Gandhiji's Dandi march initially but within a week completely changed its opinion and saluted him as a Saint and Statesman?
A. Saturday Evening Post
B. Readers Digest
C. Time
D. Life

85. In which of the following years were passenger trains introduced in England?
A. 1823 B. 1825
C. 1848 D. 1861

86. The correct relation between the radius of curvature R and focal length f of a spherical mirror is:
A. $R = f$ B. $R = 2f$
C. $R = 3f$ D. $R = 4f$

87. A lemon kept in water in a glass tumbler appears to be larger than its actual size. It is because of:
A. reflection of light B. scattering of light
C. refraction of light D. polarization of light

88. Light enters the eye through a thin membrane called:
A. retina B. cornea
C. pupil D. iris

89. Name the scientist who first used a glass prism to obtain the spectrum of sunlight.
A. C.V. Raman B. Lord Rayleigh
C. Isaac Newton D. S. Chandrasekhar

90. The cost of energy to operate an industrial refrigerator that consumes 5 kW power working 10 hours per day for 30 days will be:
(Given that the charge per kW.h of energy = ₹ 4)
A. ₹ 600 B. ₹ 6,000
C. ₹ 1,200 D. ₹ 1,500

91. Which one of the following statements regarding magnetic field is NOT correct?
A. Magnetic field is a quantity that has direction and magnitude
B. Magnetic field lines are closed curves
C. Magnetic field lines are open curves
D. No two magnetic field lines are found to cross each other

92. Which one of the following statements is **NOT** correct?
A. Buckminsterfullerene is an allotrope of carbon
B. Diamond is a good conductor of electricity
C. Graphite is a good conductor of electricity
D. In graphite, each carbon atom is linked to three other carbon atoms

93. How many covalent bonds are present in a Chloropropane molecule having molecular formula, C_3H_7Cl?
A. 6 B. 8
C. 9 D. 10

94. Which one of the following is the most fundamental characteristic of an element?
A. Melting point B. Atomic number
C. Colour D. Atomic weight

95. Neutrons were discovered by:
A. James Chadwick B. Ernest Rutherford
C. J.J. Thomson D. John Dalton

96. Atomic mass of an element is equal to the sum of number of:
A. electrons and protons only
B. protons and neutrons only
C. electrons and neutrons only
D. electrons, protons and neutrons

97. Which one of the following element's isotope is used in the treatment of cancer?
A. Uranium B. Cobalt
C. Sodium D. Iodine

98. Which one of the following cell organelles may play a role in expelling excess water and wastes in case of unicellular organisms?
A. Lysosome B. Vacuole
C. Golgi body D. Endoplasmic reticulum

99. Which one of the following terms describes the practice of growing two or more crops simultaneously on the same piece of land?
A. Crop rotation B. Mixed cropping
C. Intercropping D. Mixed farming

100. Which one of the following statements is correct about effects of antibiotics on viruses?
A. Viruses are "non-living" entities but it can interact with antibiotics
B. Taking antibiotics cures viral infections
C. Viruses do not possess metabolic pathways on which antibiotics can function, whereas bacteria have such pathways
D. Viruses are resistant to antibiotics

101. The Panama Canal opened in 1914, links:
A. Red Sea and Mediterranean Sea
B. Atlantic Ocean and Pacific Ocean
C. Indian Ocean and Pacific Ocean
D. Adriatic Sea and Black Sea

102. The United Nations Charter was signed by 51 original members of the United Nations in 1945 at the:
A. Hague Conference
B. London Conference
C. San Francisco Conference
D. Berlin Conference

103. Land Revenue Records maintained in India have categorized land-use into:
A. 6 categories B. 9 categories
C. 15 categories D. 21 categories

104. Dry land farming in India is largely confined to areas with rainfall less than:
A. 100 cm B. 85 cm
C. 80 cm D. 75 cm

105. For an area to be excluded from the drought-prone category, what percentage of its gross cropped area should be under irrigation?
A. 10 per cent or more
B. 20 per cent or more
C. 25 per cent or more
D. 30 per cent or more

106. Which one of the following is NOT a current of Pacific Ocean?
A. Oyashio current B. Alaska current
C. Agulhas current D. California current

107. The duration of monsoon in India extends for an average period of:
A. 80-140 days B. 100-120 days
C. 90-130 days D. 100-140 days

108. Which one of the following is the natural vegetation of South east China?
A. Subtropical broadleaf evergreen forest
B. Tropical broadleaf evergreen forest
C. Tropical deciduous forest
D. Temperate evergreen forest

109. Which one of the following is a cold local wind?
A. Santa Ana B. Chinook
C. Mistral D. Loo

110. What was the consequence of Permanent Settlement on rural society in Bengal?
A. The zamindars invested capital and enterprise to improve agriculture along lines of British yeoman farmers
B. A group of rich peasants known as jotedars succeeded in consolidating their position in the villages
C. The ryots prospered as a result of fixed revenue levy imposed on them
D. The system of Collectorate introduced by the Company for exercising supervisory control on zamindars failed to take off

111. What was *Damin-i Koh* in Rajmahal area?
A. A large area of land demarcated and declared to be the land of the Santhals
B. The land of the Paharias cultivated exclusively for paddy
C. The British territory marked for their military camp
D. The land earmarked for locating settled agriculturists

112. Which one of the following statements about the Revolt of 1857 is correct?
A. It was a Revolt carefully organised and planned by the Rajas, Nawabs and Taluqdars
B. Rumours and prophecies did not play any role in its outbreak and spread
C. The rebel proclamations in 1857 repeatedly appealed to all sections of the population irrespective of their caste and creed.
D. The British succeeded in quickly and easily controlling the rebels

113. Which one among the following was NOT a *Panch Sheel* principle?
A. Peaceful Co-existence
B. Mutual respect for territorial integrity
C. Nuclear deterrence
D. Non-interference in internal affairs

114. Who among the following had organised, in 1904, a secret society of revolutionaries named *Abhinav Bharat*?
A. Khudiram Bose
B. Shyamji Krishna Verma
C. Har Dayal
D. Vinayak Damodar Savarkar

115. The principle that the framing of the new Constitution for independent India should be primarily (though not solely) the responsibility of Indians themselves, was for the first time conceded in the:
A. Government of India Act, 1935
B. August Offer of Viceroy Linlithgow
C. Cripps Proposals
D. Cabinet Mission

116. Which one of the following is a major environmental issue in eastern Canada?
A. Acid precipitation
B. Groundwater depletion
C. Land degradation
D. Desertification

117. Which one of the following mountains lies in between Caspian Sea and Black Sea?
A. Caucasus　　B. Carpathians
C. Apennine　　D. Elburz

118. Bagalihar, Dulhasti and Salal hydro power projects have been developed on which of the following rivers?
A. Chenab and Jhelum　　B. Chenab and Indus
C. Ravi　　D. Chenab only

119. Which of the following statements with regard to Biosphere Reserve is/are correct?
1. The idea of Biosphere Reserve was initiated by UNESCO in 1973-74.
2. There are 18 designated Biosphere Reserves in India.
3. All Biosphere Reserves in India have been included in world network of Biosphere Reserves of UNESCO.

Select the correct answer using the code given below:
A. 1 only　　B. 2 only
C. 1 and 2 only　　D. 1, 2 and 3

120. Which one of the following countries does NOT have direct access to the sea/ocean?
A. Syria　　B. Jordan
C. Azerbaijan　　D. Armenia

121. In an incandescent electric bulb, the filament of the bulb is made up of which metal?
A. Aluminium　　B. Copper
C. Tungsten　　D. Silver

122. Two equal resistors R are connected in parallel, and a battery of 12 V is connected across this combination. A dc current of 100 mA flows through the circuit as shown below:

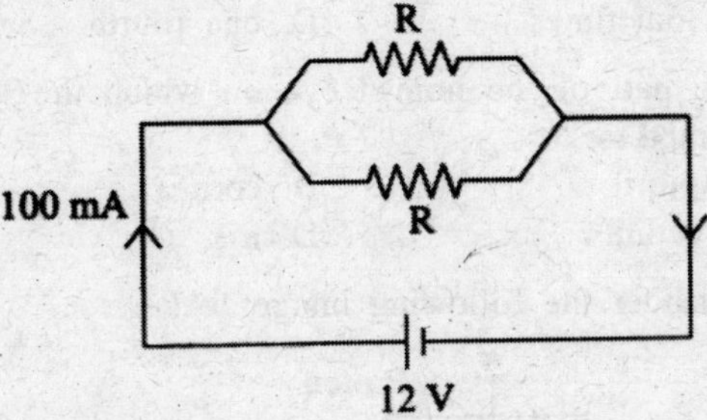

The value of R is:
A. 120 Ω　　B. 240 Ω
C. 60 Ω　　D. 100 Ω

123. Which one of the following is NOT the unit of energy?
A. Joule　　B. Watt-hr
C. Newton-metre　　D. kg-metre/sec^2

124. Which one of the following statements is NOT correct?
A. Biomass is a renewable source of energy
B. Gobar gas is produced when cowdung, crop residues, vegetable waste and sewage are allowed to decompose in the absence of oxygen
C. Biogas generation reduces soil and water pollution
D. Heating capacity of biogas is very low

125. In prokaryotic organisms, nuclear region is not surrounded by a membrane. This undefined nuclear region is known as:
A. Nucleic acid　　B. Nucleoid
C. Nucleolus　　D. Nucleosome

126. Which one of the following plant tissues has dead cells?
A. Epidermis　　B. Parenchyma
C. Collenchyma　　D. Sclerenchyma

127. Cartilage is NOT found in:
A. larynx　　B. nose
C. ear　　D. urinary bladder

128. Two planets orbit the Sun in circular orbits, with their radius of orbit as $R_1 = R$ and $R_2 = 4R$. Ratio of their periods (T_1/T_2) around the Sun will be:

A. $\frac{1}{16}$ B. $\frac{1}{8}$

C. $\frac{1}{4}$ D. $\frac{1}{2}$

129. A metallic wire having resistance of 20 Ω is cut into two equal parts in length. These parts are then connected in parallel. The resistance of this parallel combination is equal to:

A. 20 Ω B. 10 Ω

C. 5 Ω D. 15 Ω

130. Light of uniform intensity impinges perpendicularly on a totally reflecting surface. If the area of the surface is halved, the radiation force on it will become:

A. double B. half

C. four times D. one fourth

131. The part of the human eye on which the image is formed is:

A. pupil B. cornea

C. retina D. iris

132. Consider the following image:

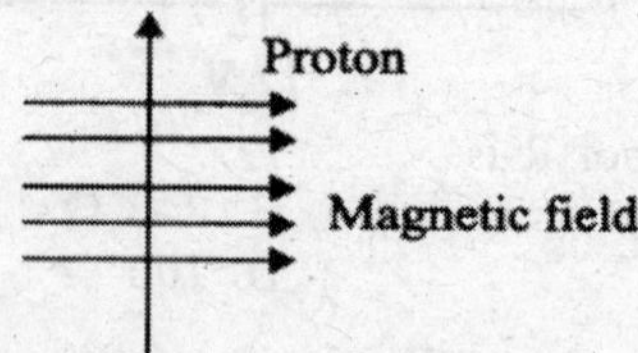

A proton enters a magnetic field at right angles to it, as shown above. The direction of force acting on the proton will be:

A. to the right B. to the left

C. out of the page D. into the page

133. Which one of the following statements about sound is NOT correct?

A. Sound travels at a speed slower than the speed of light

B. Sound waves are transverse waves

C. Sound waves are longitudinal waves

D. Sound travels faster in moist air than in dry air

134. When the short circuit condition occurs, the current in the circuit:

A. becomes zero

B. remains constant

C. increases substantially

D. keeps on changing randomly

135. Which one of the following is NOT a component of human male reproductive system?

A. Cervix B. Urethra

C. Seminal vesicle D. Vas deferens

136. Which one of the following is NOT a reason of decrease in biodiversity?

A. Large scale deforestation

B. Exploitation of forest produce

C. Maintaining sacred groves

D. Encroachment in forest areas

137. Which one of the following is NOT a cause of depletion in groundwater?

A. Afforestation

B. Loss of forests

C. Excessive pumping of groundwater

D. Construction of large scale concrete buildings

138. Which one of the following types of radiations has the smallest wavelength?

A. Microwaves B. Infra-red

C. Visible light D. X-rays

139. The instrument used for detecting the presence of electric current in a circuit is:

A. Refractometer B. Galvanometer

C. Viscometer D. Diffractometer

140. Which one of the following is the largest composition in biogas?

A. Carbon dioxide B. Methane

C. Hydrogen D. Hydrogen sulphide

141. The Sun appears reddish during sunrise and sunset. The phenomenon in optics which is responsible for this appearance of the Sun is:

A. Reflection B. Total internal reflection

C. Scattering D. Interference

142. A lens has a power of +2.0 Dioptre. Which one of the following statements about the lens is true?

A. The lens is concave and has a focal length of 0.5 metre

B. The lens is convex and has a focal length of 2.0 metre

C. The lens is convex and has a focal length of 0.5 metre

D. The lens is concave and has a focal length of 2.0 metre

143. At nearly 70°C, sodium bicarbonate shows the property of gradually decomposing, which makes it usable in bakery products. The product of decomposition responsible for this use of sodium bicarbonate is:

A. Carbon dioxide B. Hydrogen

C. Water vapour D. Oxygen

144. Number of molecules of water of crystallization in copper sulphate, sodium carbonate and Gypsum are:

A. 5, 10 and 2 respectively

B. 10, 2 and 5 respectively

C. 5, 2 and 10 respectively

D. 2, 5 and 10 respectively

145. Which one of the following is the correct sequence of change in colours when a turmeric stain on white clothes is scrubbed by soap and then washed with water?
A. Yellow – Pink – Blue
B. Yellow – Reddish Brown – Yellow
C. Yellow – Reddish Brown – Blue
D. Yellow – Blue – Pink

146. Which one of the following statements regarding Bleaching powder and D.D.T. is correct?
A. Both are inorganic compounds
B. Both are organic compounds
C. Both contain chlorine
D. Both contain calcium

147. Which one of the following is the best example of desiccant?
A. Silica gel
B. Polystyrene
C. Sodium chloride
D. Sodium carbonate

148. Which one of the following was the first mineral acid discovered?
A. Sulphuric acid B. Hydrochloric acid
C. Nitric acid D. Phosphoric acid

149. The refractive index of fused quartz is 1.46 and that of sapphire is 1.77. If v_q is the speed of light in quartz and v_s is the speed of light in sapphire, then which one of the following relations is correct?
A. $v_q > v_s$ B. $v_s > v_q$
C. $v_s = v_q$ D. $v_s = \frac{v_q}{2}$

150. In case of a concave mirror, if an object is kept between principal focus F and pole P of the mirror, then which one of the following statements about the image is NOT correct?
A. The image will be virtual
B. The image will be enlarged or magnified
C. The image will be formed at infinity
D. The image will be erect

PAPER II : MATHEMATICS

1. If matrix A = $\begin{bmatrix} 1-i & i \\ -i & 1-i \end{bmatrix}$ where $i = \sqrt{-1}$, then which one of the following is correct?
A. A is hermitian
B. A is skew-hermitian
C. $(\bar{A})^T + A$ is hermitian
D. $(\bar{A})^T + A$ is skew-hermitian

2. The term independent of x in the binomial expansion of $\left(\frac{2}{x^2} - \sqrt{x}\right)^{10}$ is equal to
A. 180 B. 120
C. 90 D. 72

3. If $(1 + 2x - x^2)^6 = a_0 + a_1x + a_2x^2 + ... + a_{12}x^{12}$, then what is $a_0 - a_1 + a_2 - a_3 + a_4 - ... + a_{12}$ equal to?
A. 32 B. 64
C. 2048 D. 4096

4. If C(20, n + 2) = C(20, n – 2), then what is n equal to?
A. 18 B. 25
C. 10 D. 12

5. For how many values of k, is the matrix $\begin{bmatrix} 0 & k & 4 \\ -k & 0 & -5 \\ -k & k & -1 \end{bmatrix}$ singular?
A. Only one B. Only two
C. Only four D. Infinite

6. The number $(1101101 + 1011011)_2$ can be written in decimal system as:
A. $(198)_{10}$ B. $(199)_{10}$
C. $(200)_{10}$ D. $(201)_{10}$

7. What is the value of
$\frac{1}{10}\log_5 1024 - \log_5 10 + \frac{1}{5}\log_5 3125$?
A. 0 B. 1
C. 2 D. 3

8. If $x = \log_c(ab)$, $y = \log_a(bc)$, $z = \log_b(ca)$, then which of the following is correct?
A. $xyz = 1$
B. $x + y + z = 1$
C. $(1 + x)^{-1} + (1 + y)^{-1} + (1 + z)^{-1} = 1$
D. $(1 + x)^{-2} + (1 + y)^{-2} + (1 + z)^{-2} = 1$

9. Let A = $\begin{bmatrix} x+y & y \\ 2x & x-y \end{bmatrix}$, B = $\begin{bmatrix} 2 \\ -1 \end{bmatrix}$ and C = $\begin{bmatrix} 3 \\ 2 \end{bmatrix}$. **If AB** = C, then what is the value of the determinant of the matrix A?
A. –10 B. –14
C. –24 D. –34

10. If $1.5 \le x \le 4.5$, then which one of the following is correct?
A. $(2x - 3)(2x - 9) > 0$
B. $(2x - 3)(2x - 9) < 0$
C. $(2x - 3)(2x - 9) \ge 0$
D. $(2x - 3)(2x - 9) \le 0$

11. Let S = {1, 2, 3, ...}. A relation R on S × S is defined by xRy if $\log_a x > \log_a y$ when $a = \frac{1}{2}$.
Then the relation is:
A. reflexive only
B. symmetric only
C. transitive only
D. both symmetric and transitive

12. What is the value of the determinant $\begin{vmatrix} i & i^2 & i^3 \\ i^4 & i^6 & i^8 \\ i^9 & i^{12} & i^{15} \end{vmatrix}$ where $i = \sqrt{-1}$?
A. 0 B. −2
C. $4i$ D. $-4i$

13. Let $A = \begin{bmatrix} a & h & g \\ h & b & f \\ g & f & c \end{bmatrix}$ and $B = \begin{bmatrix} x \\ y \\ z \end{bmatrix}$, then what is AB equal to?

A. $\begin{bmatrix} ax+hy+gz \\ y \\ z \end{bmatrix}$

B. $\begin{bmatrix} ax+hy+gz \\ hx+by+fz \\ z \end{bmatrix}$

C. $\begin{bmatrix} ax+hy+gz \\ hx+by+fz \\ gx+fy+cz \end{bmatrix}$

D. $[ax + hy + gz \quad hx + by + fz \quad gx + fy + cz]$

14. What is the number of ways in which the letters of the word 'ABLE' can be arranged so that the vowels occupy even places?
A. 2 B. 4
C. 6 D. 8

15. What is the maximum number of points of intersection of 5 non-overlapping circles?
A. 10 B. 15
C. 20 D. 25

Directions (Qs. No. 16-18): *Consider the following Venn diagram, where X, Y and Z are three sets. Let the number of elements in Z be denoted by n(Z) which is equal to 90.*

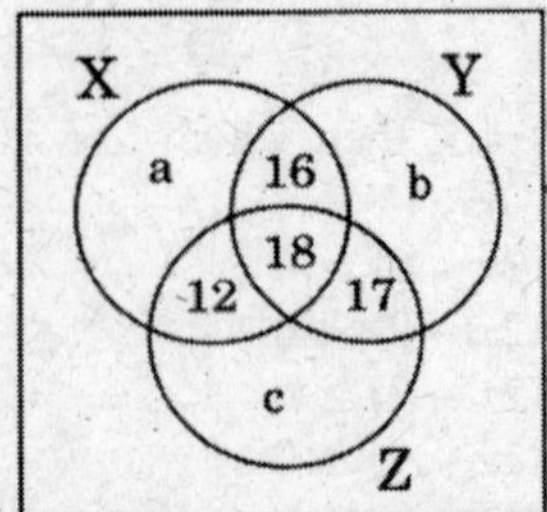

16. If the number of elements in Y and Z are in the ratio 4 : 5, then what is the value of b?
A. 18 B. 19
C. 21 D. 23

17. What is the value of
$n(X) + n(Y) + n(Z) - n(X \cap Y) - n(Y \cap Z) - n(X \cap Z) + n(X \cap Y \cap Z)$?
A. $a + b + 43$ B. $a + b + 63$
C. $a + b + 96$ D. $a + b + 106$

18. If the number of elements belonging to neither X, nor Y, nor Z is equal to p, then what is the number of elements in the complement of X?
A. $p + b + 60$ B. $p + b + 40$
C. $p + a + 60$ D. $p + a + 40$

Directions (Qs. No. 19 and 20): *Read the following information and answer the questions that follow:*

Let $\frac{\tan 3A}{\tan A} = K$, where $\tan A \neq 0$ and $K \neq \frac{1}{3}$.

19. What is $\tan^2 A$ equal to?
A. $\frac{K+3}{3K-1}$ B. $\frac{K-3}{3K-1}$
C. $\frac{3K-3}{K-3}$ D. $\frac{K+3}{3K+1}$

20. For real values of tan A, K ***cannot*** lie between:
A. $\frac{1}{3}$ and 3 B. $\frac{1}{2}$ and 2
C. $\frac{1}{5}$ and 5 D. $\frac{1}{7}$ and 7

Directions (Qs. No. 21 and 22): *Read the following information and answer the questions that follow:*

ABCD is a trapezium such that AB and CD are parallel and BC is perpendicular to them. Let ∠ADB = θ, ∠ABD = α, BC = p and CD = q.

21. Consider the following:
1. AD sin θ = AB sin α
2. BD sin θ = AB sin (θ + α)

Which of the above is/are correct?
A. 1 only B. 2 only
C. Both 1 and 2 D. Neither 1 nor 2

22. What is AB equal to?
A. $\frac{(p^2+q^2)\sin\theta}{p\cos\theta+q\sin\theta}$ B. $\frac{(p^2-q^2)\cos\theta}{p\cos\theta+q\sin\theta}$
C. $\frac{(p^2+q^2)\sin\theta}{q\cos\theta+p\sin\theta}$ D. $\frac{(p^2-q^2)\cos\theta}{q\cos\theta+p\sin\theta}$

23. If $\tan\theta = \frac{\cos 17° - \sin 17°}{\cos 17° + \sin 17°}$, then what is the value of θ?
A. 0° B. 28°
C. 38° D. 52°

24. A and B are positive acute angles such that cos 2B = 3 sin² A and 3 sin 2A = 2 sin 2B. What is the value of (A + 2B)?

A. $\frac{\pi}{6}$ B. $\frac{\pi}{4}$

C. $\frac{\pi}{3}$ D. $\frac{\pi}{2}$

25. What is
$\sin 3x + \cos 3x + 4\sin^3 x - 3\sin x + 3\cos x - 4\cos^3 x$
equal to?

A. 0 B. 1

C. 2 sin 2x D. 4 cos 4x

26. The value of ordinate of the graph of $y = 2 + \cos x$ lies in the interval:

A. [0, 1] B. [0, 3]

C. [–1, 1] D. [1, 3]

27. What is the value of

8 cos 10° . cos 20° . cos 40°?

A. tan 10° B. cot 10°

C. cosec 10° D. sec 10°

28. What is the value of cos 48° – cos 12°?

A. $\frac{\sqrt{5}-1}{4}$ B. $\frac{1-\sqrt{5}}{4}$

C. $\frac{\sqrt{5}+1}{2}$ D. $\frac{1-\sqrt{5}}{8}$

29. Consider the following statements:

1. If ABC is a right-angled triangle, right-angled at A and if sin B = $\frac{1}{3}$, then cosec C = 3.
2. If b cos B = c cos C and if the triangle ABC is not right-angled, then ABC must be isosceles.

Which of the above statements is/are correct?

A. 1 only B. 2 only

C. Both 1 and 2 D. Neither 1 nor 2

30. Consider the following statements:

1. If in a triangle ABC, A = 2B and $b = c$, then it must be an obtuse-angled triangle.
2. There exists no triangle ABC with A = 40°, B = 65° and $\frac{a}{c}$ = sin 40° cosec 15°.

Which of the above statements is/are correct?

A. 1 only B. 2 only

C. Both 1 and 2 D. Neither 1 nor 2

Directions (Qs. No. 31-33): *Read the following information and answer the questions that follow:*

Let $a\sin^2 x + b\cos^2 x = c$; $b\sin^2 y + a\cos^2 y = d$ and $p\tan x = q\tan y$.

31. What is $\tan^2 x$ equal to?

A. $\frac{c-b}{a-c}$ B. $\frac{a-c}{c-b}$

C. $\frac{c-a}{c-b}$ D. $\frac{c-b}{c-a}$

32. What is $\frac{d-a}{b-d}$ equal to?

A. $\sin^2 y$ B. $\cos^2 y$

C. $\tan^2 y$ D. $\cot^2 y$

33. What is $\frac{p^2}{q^2}$ equal to?

A. $\frac{(b-c)(b-d)}{(a-d)(a-c)}$ B. $\frac{(a-d)(c-a)}{(b-c)(d-b)}$

C. $\frac{(d-a)(c-a)}{(b-c)(d-b)}$ D. $\frac{(b-c)(b-d)}{(c-a)(a-d)}$

Directions (Qs. No. 34-36): *Read the following information and answer the questions that follow:*

Let $t_n = \sin^n\theta + \cos^n\theta$.

34. What is $\frac{t_3 - t_5}{t_5 - t_7}$ equal to?

A. $\frac{t_1}{t_3}$ B. $\frac{t_3}{t_5}$

C. $\frac{t_5}{t_7}$ D. $\frac{t_1}{t_7}$

35. What is $t_1^2 - t_2$ equal to?

A. cos 2θ B. sin 2θ

C. 2 cos θ D. 2 sin θ

36. What is the value of t_{10} where θ = 45°?

A. 1 B. $\frac{1}{4}$

C. $\frac{1}{16}$ D. $\frac{1}{32}$

Directions (Qs. No. 37-39): *Read the following information and answer the questions that follow:*

Let α = β = 15°.

37. What is the value of sin α + cos β?

A. $\frac{1}{\sqrt{2}}$ B. $\frac{1}{2\sqrt{2}}$

C. $\frac{\sqrt{3}}{2\sqrt{2}}$ D. $\frac{\sqrt{3}}{\sqrt{2}}$

38. What is the value of sin 7α – cos 7β?

A. $\frac{1}{\sqrt{2}}$ B. $\frac{1}{2\sqrt{2}}$

C. $\frac{\sqrt{3}}{2\sqrt{2}}$ D. $\frac{\sqrt{3}}{\sqrt{2}}$

39. What is $\sin(\alpha + 1°) + \cos(\beta + 1°)$ equal to?

A. $\sqrt{3}\cos 1° + \sin 1°$ B. $\sqrt{3}\cos 1° - \frac{1}{2}\sin 1°$

C. $\frac{1}{\sqrt{2}}\left(\sqrt{3}\cos 1° - \sin 1°\right)$ D. $\frac{1}{2}\left(\sqrt{3}\cos 1° + \sin 1°\right)$

40. If $\sin x + \sin y = \cos y - \cos x$, where $0 < y < x < \frac{\pi}{2}$, then what is $\tan\left(\frac{x-y}{2}\right)$ equal to?

A. 0 B. $\frac{1}{2}$

C. 1 D. 2

41. If A is a matrix of order 3 × 5 and B is a matrix of order 5 × 3, then the order of AB and BA will respectively be:

A. 3 × 3 and 3 × 3 B. 3 × 5 and 5 × 3

C. 3 × 3 and 5 × 5 D. 5 × 3 and 3 × 5

42. If p^2, q^2 and r^2 (where $p, q, r > 0$) are in GP, then which of the following is/are correct?

1. p, q and r are in GP.
2. $\ln p$, $\ln q$ and $\ln r$ are in AP.

Select the correct answer using the code given below:

A. 1 only B. 2 only

C. Both 1 and 2 D. Neither 1 nor 2

43. If $\cot \alpha$ and $\cot \beta$ are the roots of the equation $x^2 - 3x + 2 = 0$, then what is $\cot(\alpha + \beta)$ equal to?

A. $\frac{1}{2}$ B. $\frac{1}{3}$

C. 2 D. 3

44. The roots α and β of a quadratic equation, satisfy the relations $\alpha + \beta = \alpha^2 + \beta^2$ and $\alpha\beta = \alpha^2\beta^2$. What is the number of such quadratic equations?

A. 0 B. 2

C. 3 D. 4

45. What is the argument of the complex number $\frac{1-i\sqrt{3}}{1+i\sqrt{3}}$, where $i = \sqrt{-1}$?

A. 240° B. 210°

C. 120° D. 60°

46. What is the modulus of the complex number $\frac{\cos\theta + i\sin\theta}{\cos\theta - i\sin\theta}$, where $i = \sqrt{-1}$?

A. $\frac{1}{2}$ B. 1

C. $\frac{3}{2}$ D. 2

47. Consider the proper subsets of {1, 2, 3, 4}. How many of these proper subsets are superset of the set {3}?

A. 5 B. 6

C. 7 D. 8

48. Let p, q and r be three distinct positive real numbers. If $D = \begin{vmatrix} p & q & r \\ q & r & p \\ r & p & q \end{vmatrix}$, then which one of the following is correct?

A. $D < 0$ B. $D \le 0$

C. $D > 0$ D. $D \ge 0$

49. What is the sum of the last five coefficients in the expansion of $(1 + x)^9$ when it is expanded in ascending powers of x?

A. 256 B. 512

C. 1024 D. 2048

50. Consider the following in respect of a non-singular matrix of order 3:

1. A (adj A) = (adj A) A
2. |adj A| = |A|

Which of the above statements is/are correct?

A. 1 only B. 2 only

C. Both 1 and 2 D. Neither 1 nor 2

51. The center of the circle $(x - 2a)(x - 2b) + (y - 2c)(y - 2d) = 0$ is:

A. $(2a, 2c)$ B. $(2b, 2d)$

C. $(a + b, c + d)$ D. $(a - b, c - d)$

52. The point $(1, -1)$ is one of the vertices of a square. If $3x + 2y = 5$ is the equation of one diagonal of the square, then what is the equation of the other diagonal?

A. $3x - 2y = 5$ B. $2x - 3y = 1$

C. $2x - 3y = 5$ D. $2x + 3y = -1$

53. Let P(x, y) be any point on the ellipse $25x^2 + 16y^2 = 400$. If Q(0, 3) and R(0, –3) are two points, then what is (PQ + PR) equal to?

A. 12 B. 10

C. 8 D. 6

54. If the circumcentre of the triangle formed by the lines $x + 2 = 0$, $y + 2 = 0$ and $kx + y + 2 = 0$ is $(-1, 1)$, then what is the value of k?

A. –1 B. –2

C. 1 D. 2

55. In the parabola, $y^2 = x$, what is the length of the chord passing through the vertex and inclined to the x-axis at an angle θ?

A. $\sin\theta$, $\sec^2\theta$ B. $\cos\theta$, $\csc^2\theta$

C. $\cot\theta$, $\sec^2\theta$ D. $2\tan\theta$, $\csc^2\theta$

56. Under which condition, are the points (a, b), (c, d) and $(a - c, b - d)$ collinear?

A. $ab = cd$ B. $ac = bd$

C. $ad = bc$ D. $abc = d$

57. Let ABC be a triangle. If D(2, 5) and E(5, 9) are the mid-points of the sides AB and AC respectively, then what is the length of the side BC?

A. 8 B. 10
C. 12 D. 14

58. If the foot of the perpendicular drawn from the point (0, k) to the line $3x - 4y - 5 = 0$ is (3, 1), then what is the value of k?

A. 3 B. 4
C. 5 D. 6

59. What is the obtuse angle between the lines whose slopes are $2-\sqrt{3}$ and $2+\sqrt{3}$?

A. 105° B. 120°
C. 135° D. 150°

60. If $3x - 4y - 5 = 0$ and $3x - 4y + 15 = 0$ are the equations of a pair of opposite sides of a square, then what is the area of the square?

A. 4 square units B. 9 square units
C. 16 square units D. 25 square units

61. What is the length of the diameter of the sphere whose centre is at (1, –2, 3) and which touches the plane $6x - 3y + 2z - 4 = 0$?

A. 1 unit B. 2 units
C. 3 units D. 4 units

62. What is the perpendicular distance from the point (2, 3, 4) to the line $\frac{x-0}{1}=\frac{y-0}{0}=\frac{z-0}{0}$?

A. 6 units B. 5 units
C. 3 units D. 2 units

63. If a line has direction ratios $< a + b, b + c, c + a >$, then what is the sum of the squares of its direction cosines?

A. $(a + b + c)^2$ B. $2(a + b + c)$
C. 3 D. 1

64. Into how many compartments do the coordinate planes divide the space?

A. 2 B. 4
C. 8 D. 16

65. What is the equation of the plane which cuts an intercept 5 units on the z-axis and is parallel to xy-plane?

A. $x + y = 5$ B. $z = 5$
C. $z = 0$ D. $x + y + z = 5$

66. If $\hat{a}$ is a unit vector in the xy-plane making an angle 30° with the positive x-axis, then what is $\hat{a}$ equal to?

A. $\frac{\sqrt{3}\hat{i}+\hat{j}}{2}$ B. $\frac{\sqrt{3}\hat{i}-\hat{j}}{2}$

C. $\frac{\hat{i}+\sqrt{3}\hat{j}}{2}$ D. $\frac{\hat{i}-\sqrt{3}\hat{j}}{2}$

67. Let A be a point in space such that $|\overline{OA}| = 12$, where O is the origin. If $\overline{OA}$ is inclined at angles 45° and 60° with x-axis and y-axis respectively, then what is $\overline{OA}$ equal to?

A. $6\hat{i}+6\hat{j}\pm\sqrt{2}\,\hat{k}$ B. $6\hat{i}+6\sqrt{2}\hat{j}\pm 6\hat{k}$

C. $6\sqrt{2}\,\hat{i}+6\hat{j}\pm 6\hat{k}$ D. $3\sqrt{2}\,\hat{i}+3\hat{j}\pm 6\hat{k}$

68. Two adjacent sides of a parallelogram are $2\hat{i}-4\hat{j}+5\hat{k}$ and $\hat{i}-2\hat{j}-3\hat{k}$. What is the magnitude of dot product of vectors which represent its diagonals?

A. 21 B. 25
C. 31 D. 36

69. If $|\vec{a}\times\vec{b}|^2+|\vec{a}\cdot\vec{b}|^2=144$ and $|\vec{a}|=4$, then what is $|\vec{b}|$ equal to?

A. 3 B. 4
C. 6 D. 8

70. If the vectors $\vec{a}=2\hat{i}-3\hat{j}+\hat{k}$, $\vec{b}=\hat{i}+2\hat{j}-3\hat{k}$ and $\vec{c}=\hat{j}+p\hat{k}$ are coplanar, then what is the value of p?

A. 1 B. –1
C. 5 D. –5

71. What is $\lim_{x\to 1}\frac{x+x^2+x^3-3}{x-1}$ equal to?

A. 1 B. 2
C. 3 D. 6

72. The radius of a circle is increasing at the rate of 0.7 cm/sec. What is the rate of increase of its circumference?

A. 4.4 cm/sec B. 8.4 cm/sec
C. 8.8 cm/sec D. 15.4 cm/sec

73. If $\lim_{x\to 1}\frac{x^4-1}{x-1}=\lim_{x\to k}\frac{x^3-k^3}{x^2-k^2}$, where $k \neq 0$, then what is the value of k?

A. $\frac{2}{3}$ B. $\frac{4}{3}$

C. $\frac{8}{3}$ D. 4

74. The order and degree of the differential equation

$$k\frac{dy}{dx}=\int\left[1+\left(\frac{dy}{dx}\right)^2\right]^{\frac{2}{3}}dx$$ are respectively

A. 1 and 1 B. 2 and 3
C. 2 and 4 D. 1 and 4

75. What is $\lim_{x\to 0}\frac{\sin x\log(1-x)}{x^2}$ equal to?

A. –1 B. zero

C. $-e$ D. $-\frac{1}{e}$

76. If $f(x) = 3x^2 - 5x + p$ and $f(0)$ and $f(1)$ are opposite in sign, then which of the following is correct?
A. $-2 < p < 0$ B. $-2 < p < 2$
C. $0 < p < 2$ D. $3 < p < 5$

77. If $e^{\theta\varphi} = c + 4\theta\varphi$, where c is an arbitrary constant and φ is a function of θ, then what is $\varphi\, d\theta$ equal to?
A. $\theta\, d\varphi$ B. $-\theta\, d\varphi$
C. $4\theta\, d\varphi$ D. $-4\theta\, d\varphi$

78. If $p(x) = (4e)^{2x}$, then what is $\int p(x)dx$ equal to?
A. $\frac{p(x)}{1+2\ln 2}+c$ B. $\frac{p(x)}{2(1+2\ln 2)}+c$
C. $\frac{2p(x)}{1+\ln 4}+c$ D. $\frac{p(x)}{1+\ln 2}+c$

79. What is the value of $\int_0^{\pi/4}(\tan^3 x+\tan x)dx$?
A. $\frac{1}{4}$ B. $\frac{1}{2}$
C. 1 D. 2

80. Let $y = 3x^2 + 2$. If x changes from 10 to 10.1, then what is the total change in y?
A. 4.71 B. 5.23
C. 6.03 D. 8.01

81. If $f(x)=\frac{\sin x}{x}$, where $x \in \mathbb{R}$, is to be continuous at $x = 0$, then the value of the function at $x = 0$.
A. should be 0 B. should be 1
C. should be 2 D. cannot be determined

82. The solution of the differential equation $dy = (1 + y^2)\, dx$ is:
A. $y = \tan x + c$ B. $y = \tan (x + c)$
C. $\tan^{-1} (y + c) = x$ D. $\tan^{-1} (y + c) = 2x$

83. What is $\int(e^{\log x}+\sin x)\cos x\, dx$ equal to?
A. $\sin x+x\cos x+\frac{\sin^2 x}{2}+c$
B. $\sin x-x\cos x+\frac{\sin^2 x}{2}+c$
C. $x\sin x+\cos x+\frac{\sin^2 x}{2}+c$
D. $x\sin x-x\cos x+\frac{\sin^2 x}{2}+c$

84. What is the domain of the function $f(x) = \cos^{-1}(x - 2)$?
A. $[-1, 1]$ B. $[1, 3]$
C. $[0, 5]$ D. $[-2, 1]$

85. What is the area of the region enclosed between the curve $y^2 = 2x$ and the straight line $y = x$?
A. $\frac{1}{2}$ B. 1
C. $\frac{2}{3}$ D. 2

86. If $f(x) = 2x - x^2$, then what is the value of $f(x + 2) + f(x - 2)$ when $x = 0$?
A. -8 B. -4
C. 8 D. 4

87. If $x^m y^n = a^{m+n}$, then what is $\frac{dy}{dx}$ equal to?
A. $\frac{my}{nx}$ B. $-\frac{my}{nx}$
C. $\frac{mx}{ny}$ D. $-\frac{ny}{mx}$

88. What is $\int\frac{dx}{x(x^n+1)}$ equal to?
A. $\frac{1}{n}\ln\left(\frac{x^n}{x^n+1}\right)+c$ B. $\ln\left(\frac{x^n+1}{x^n}\right)+c$
C. $\ln\left(\frac{x^n}{x^n+1}\right)+c$ D. $\frac{1}{n}\ln\left(\frac{x^n+1}{x^n}\right)+c$

89. What is the minimum value of $|x - 1|$, where $x \in R$?
A. 0 B. 1
C. 2 D. -1

90. What is the value of k such that integration of $\frac{3x^2+8-4k}{x}$ with respect to x, may be a rational function?
A. 0 B. 1
C. 2 D. -2

91. Consider the following statements for $f(x) = e^{-|x|}$:
1. The function is continuous at $x = 0$.
2. The function is differentiable at $x = 0$.
Which of the above statements is/are correct?
A. 1 only B. 2 only
C. Both 1 and 2 D. Neither 1 nor 2

92. What is the maximum value of $\sin x \cdot \cos x$?
A. 2 B. 1
C. $\frac{1}{2}$ D. $2\sqrt{2}$

93. What is $\lim_{x\to 0}\frac{3^x+3^{-x}-2}{x}$ equal to?
A. 0 B. 1
C. 1 D. Limit does not exist

94. What is the derivative of $\tan^{-1}x$ with respect to $\cot^{-1}x$?
A. -1 B. 1
C. $\frac{1}{x^2+1}$ D. $\frac{x}{x^2+1}$

95. The function $u(x, y) = c$ which satisfies the differential equation

$x(dx - dy) + y(dy - dx) = 0$, is:

A. $x^2 + y^2 = xy + c$ B. $x^2 + y^2 = 2xy + c$
C. $x^2 - y^2 = xy + c$ D. $x^2 - y^2 = 2xy + c$

96. What is the minimum value of $3\cos\left(A+\frac{\pi}{3}\right)$ where $A \in R$?

A. –3 B. –1
C. 0 D. 3

97. Consider the following statements:

1. The function $f(x) = \ln x$ increases in the interval $(0, \infty)$.
2. The function $f(x) = \tan x$ increases in the interval $\left(-\frac{\pi}{2}, \frac{\pi}{2}\right)$.

Which of the above statements is/are correct?

A. 1 only B. 2 only
C. Both 1 and 2 D. Neither 1 nor 2

98. Which one of the following is correct in respect of the graph of $y = \frac{1}{x-1}$?

A. The domain is $\{x \in \mathbb{R} \mid x \neq 1\}$ and the range is the set of reals.
B. The domain is $\{x \in \mathbb{R} \mid x \neq 1\}$, the range is $\{y \in \mathbb{R} \mid y \neq 0\}$ and the graph intersects y-axis at (0, –1).
C. The domain is the set of reals and the range is the singleton set {0}.
D. The domain is $\{x \in \mathbb{R} \mid x \neq 1\}$ and the range is the set of points on the y-axis.

99. What is the solution of the differential equation $\ln\left(\frac{dy}{dx}\right) = x$?

A. $y = e^x + c$ B. $y = e^{-x} + c$
C. $y = \ln x + c$ D. $y = 2 \ln x + c$

100. Let l be the length and b be the breadth of a rectangle such that $l + b = k$. What is the maximum area of the rectangle?

A. $2k^2$ B. k^2
C. $\frac{k^2}{2}$ D. $\frac{k^2}{4}$

101. The numbers 4 and 9 have frequencies x and $(x - 1)$ respectively. If their arithmetic mean is 6, then what is the value of x?

A. 2 B. 3
C. 4 D. 5

102. If three dice are rolled under the condition that no two dice show the same face, then what is the probability that one of the faces is having the number 6?

A. $\frac{5}{6}$ B. $\frac{5}{9}$
C. $\frac{1}{2}$ D. $\frac{5}{12}$

103. If $P(A \cup B) = \frac{5}{6}$, $P(A \cap B) = \frac{1}{3}$ and $P(\text{not } A) = \frac{1}{2}$, then which one of the following is ***not*** correct?

A. $P(B) = \frac{2}{3}$
B. $P(A \cap B) = P(A)P(B)$
C. $P(A \cup B) > P(A) + P(B)$
D. $P(\text{not } A \text{ and not } B) = P(\text{not } A)\, P(\text{not } B)$

104. The sum of deviations of n number of observations measured from 2.5 is 50. The sum of deviations of the same set of observations measured from 3.5 is –50. What is the value of n?

A. 50 B. 60
C. 80 D. 100

105. A data set of n observations has mean 2M, while another data set of $2n$ observations has mean M. What is the mean of the combined data sets?

A. M B. $\frac{3M}{2}$
C. $\frac{2M}{3}$ D. $\frac{4M}{3}$

Directions (Q.No. 106-108): *Read the following information and answer the questions that follow.*

Marks	Number of students	
	Physics	Mathematics
10-20	8	10
20-30	11	21
30-40	30	38
40-50	26	15
50-60	15	10
60-70	10	6

106. The difference between number of students under Physics and Mathematics is largest for the interval:

A. 20-30 B. 30-40
C. 40-50 D. 50-60

107. Consider the following statements:

1. Modal value of the marks in Physics lies in the interval 30-40.
2. Median of the marks in Physics is less than that of marks in Mathematics.

Which of the above statements is/are correct?

A. 1 only B. 2 only
C. Both 1 and 2 D. Neither 1 nor 2

108. What is the mean of marks in Physics?

A. 38.4 B. 39.4
C. 40.9 D. 41.6

109. What is the standard deviation of the observations $-\sqrt{6}, -\sqrt{5}, -\sqrt{4}, -1, 1, \sqrt{4}, \sqrt{5}, \sqrt{6}$?

A. $\sqrt{2}$ B. 2
C. $2\sqrt{2}$ D. 4

110. If $\Sigma x_i = 20$, $\Sigma x_i^2 = 200$ and $n = 10$ for an observed variable x, then what is the coefficient of variation?

A. 80 B. 100
C. 150 D. 200

111. What is the probability that February of a leap year selected at random, will have five Sundays?

A. $\frac{1}{5}$ B. $\frac{1}{7}$
C. $\frac{2}{7}$ D. 1

112. The arithmetic mean of 100 observations is 40. Later, it was found that an observation '53' was wrongly read as '83'. What is the correct arithmetic mean?

A. 39.8 B. 39.7
C. 39.6 D. 39.5

113. A husband and wife appear in an interview for two vacancies for the same post. The probability of the husband's selection is $\frac{1}{7}$ and that of the wife's selection is $\frac{1}{5}$. If the events are independent, then the probability of which one of the following is $\frac{11}{35}$?

A. At least one of them will be selected
B. Only one of them will be selected
C. None of them will be selected
D. Both of them will be selected

114. A dealer has a stock of 15 gold coins out of which 6 are counterfeits. A person randomly picks 4 of the 15 gold coins. What is the probability that all the coins picked will be counterfeits?

A. $\frac{1}{91}$ B. $\frac{4}{91}$
C. $\frac{6}{91}$ D. $\frac{15}{91}$

115. A committee of 3 is to be formed from a group of 2 boys and 2 girls. What is the probability that the committee consists of 2 boys and 1 girl?

A. $\frac{2}{3}$ B. $\frac{1}{4}$
C. $\frac{3}{4}$ D. $\frac{1}{2}$

116. In a lottery of 10 tickets numbered 1 to 10, two tickets are drawn simultaneously. What is the probability that both the tickets drawn have prime numbers?

A. $\frac{1}{15}$ B. $\frac{1}{2}$
C. $\frac{2}{15}$ D. $\frac{1}{5}$

117. Let X and Y represent prices (in ₹) of a commodity in Kolkata and Mumbai respectively. It is given that $\bar{X} = 65$, $\bar{Y} = 67$, $\sigma_X = 2.5$, $\sigma_Y = 3.5$ and $r(X, Y) = 0.8$. What is the equation of regression of Y on X?

A. Y = 0.175X – 5 B. Y = 1.12X – 5.8
C. Y = 1.12X – 5 D. Y = 0.17X + 5.8

118. Consider a random variable X which follows Binomial distribution with parameters $n = 10$ and $p = \frac{1}{5}$. Then Y = 10 – X follows Binomial distribution with parameters n and p respectively given by:

A. $5, \frac{1}{5}$ B. $5, \frac{2}{5}$
C. $10, \frac{3}{5}$ D. $10, \frac{4}{5}$

119. If A and B are two events such that P(A) = 0.6, P(B) = 0.5 and P(A ∩ B) = 0.4, then consider the following statements:

1. $P(\bar{A} \cup B) = 0.9$.
2. $P(\bar{B} \mid \bar{A}) = 0.6$.

Which of the above statements is/are correct?

A. 1 only B. 2 only
C. Both 1 and 2 D. Neither 1 nor 2

120. Three cooks X, Y and Z bake a special kind of cake, and with respective probabilities 0.02, 0.03 and 0.05, it fails to rise. In the restaurant where they work, X bakes 50%, Y bakes 30% and Z bakes 20% of cakes. What is the proportion of failures caused by X?

A. $\frac{9}{29}$ B. $\frac{10}{29}$
C. $\frac{19}{29}$ D. $\frac{28}{29}$

ANSWERS

PAPER-I - GENERAL ABILITY TEST

1	2	3	4	5	6	7	8	9	10
B	C	B	C	D	B	B	D	A	C
11	12	13	14	15	16	17	18	19	20
A	A	B	D	A	D	C	C	B	D
21	22	23	24	25	26	27	28	29	30
C	B	A	C	C	B	D	A	C	D
31	32	33	34	35	36	37	38	39	40
B	D	A	B	A	B	A	D	B	C
41	42	43	44	45	46	47	48	49	50
B	B	B	C	C	D	B	C	B	A
51	52	53	54	55	56	57	58	59	60
C	D	D	B	B	B	B	A	C	D
61	62	63	64	65	66	67	68	69	70
B	D	A	C	B	D	C	A	B	*
71	72	73	74	75	76	77	78	79	80
B	D	A	B	D	B	C	D	D	D
81	82	83	84	85	86	87	88	89	90
C	B	A	C	B	B	C	B	C	B
91	92	93	94	95	96	97	98	99	100
C	B	D	B	A	B	B	B	B	C
101	102	103	104	105	106	107	108	109	110
B	C	B	D	D	C	B	A	C	B
111	112	113	114	115	116	117	118	119	120
A	C	C	D	B	A	A	D	C	D
121	122	123	124	125	126	127	128	129	130
C	B	D	D	B	D	D	B	C	B
131	132	133	134	135	136	137	138	139	140
C	D	B	C	A	C	A	D	B	B
141	142	143	144	145	146	147	148	149	150
C	C	A	A	B	C	A	C	A	C

PAPER-II - MATHEMATICS

1	2	3	4	5	6	7	8	9	10
C	A	B	C	D	C	A	C	B	D
11	12	13	14	15	16	17	18	19	20
C	D	C	B	C	C	D	A	B	A
21	22	23	24	25	26	27	28	29	30
C	A	B	D	A	D	B	B	B	D
31	32	33	34	35	36	37	38	39	40
A	C	B	A	B	C	D	D	*	C
41	42	43	44	45	46	47	48	49	50
C	C	B	C	A	B	C	A	A	A

51	52	53	54	55	56	57	58	59	60
C	C	B	C	B	C	B	C	B	C
61	**62**	**63**	**64**	**65**	**66**	**67**	**68**	**69**	**70**
D	B	D	C	B	A	C	C	A	B
71	**72**	**73**	**74**	**75**	**76**	**77**	**78**	**79**	**80**
D	A	C	B	A	C	B	B	B	C
81	**82**	**83**	**84**	**85**	**86**	**87**	**88**	**89**	**90**
B	B	C	B	C	A	B	A	A	C
91	**92**	**93**	**94**	**95**	**96**	**97**	**98**	**99**	**100**
A	C	A	A	B	A	C	B	A	D
101	**102**	**103**	**104**	**105**	**106**	**107**	**108**	**109**	**110**
B	C	C	D	D	C	A	C	B	D
111	**112**	**113**	**114**	**115**	**116**	**117**	**118**	**119**	**120**
B	B	A	A	D	C	B	D	D	B

EXPLANATORY ANSWERS

PAPER II- MATHEMATICS

2. Let $(r + 1)$th term be independent of x in the given expression

Now, $$T_{r+1} = {}^{10}C_r\left(\frac{2}{x^2}\right)^{10-r}\left(-\sqrt{x}\right)^r$$

$$= {}^{10}C_r(2)^{10-r}.\ x^{-20+2r}.\ (-1)^r x^{1/2r}$$

$$= {}^{10}C_r 2^{10-r}.(-1)^r x^{-20+\frac{5}{2}r} \quad ...(i)$$

This term will be independent of x, if

$$-20+\frac{5}{2}r = 0$$

$$\Rightarrow \quad \frac{5}{2}r = 20$$

$$\Rightarrow \quad r = \frac{40}{5} = 8$$

So, $(8 + 1)$th term *i.e.*, 9th term is independent of x, putting $r = 8$ in (i) we get,

$$T_9 = {}^{10}C_8.2^{10-8}.(-1)^8$$

$$= {}^{10}C_8.2^2.(+1)$$

$$= 4.\frac{\lfloor 10}{\lfloor 8\ \lfloor 10-8}$$

$$= 4.\frac{10\times 9}{2}$$

$$= 180.$$

4. Given that

$$C(20, n + 2) = C(20, n - 2)$$

$$\Rightarrow \quad {}^{20}C_{n+2} = {}^{20}C_{n-2}$$

$$\left[\because n_{c_x} = n_{c_y}\ \therefore n = x + y\right]$$

$$\Rightarrow \quad 20 = n + 2 + n - 2$$

$$\Rightarrow \quad 20 = 2n$$

$$\Rightarrow \quad n = 10.$$

5. Given, $\begin{bmatrix} 0 & k & 4 \\ -k & 0 & -5 \\ -k & k & -1 \end{bmatrix}$ is a singular matrix

$$\therefore \quad \begin{vmatrix} 0 & k & 4 \\ -k & 0 & -5 \\ -k & k & -1 \end{vmatrix} = 0$$

$\Rightarrow 0 - k(k - 5k) + 4(-k - 0) = 0$

$\Rightarrow -k(-4k) - 4k = 0$

$\Rightarrow 4k^2 - 4k = 0$

$\Rightarrow 4k(k - 1) = 0$

$\Rightarrow 4k = 0$ or, $k - 1 = 0$

$\Rightarrow k = \frac{0}{4} = 0$, or, $k = 1$

7. $\frac{1}{10}\log_5 1024 - \log_5 10 + \frac{1}{5}\log_5 3125$

$= \frac{1}{10}\log_5 2^{10} - \log_5 10 + \frac{1}{5}\log_5 5^5$

$= \frac{1}{10}.10\log_5 2 - \log_5 10 + \frac{1}{5}.5\log_5 5$

$= \log_5 2 - \log_5 2 - \log_5 5 + \log_5 5$

$= 0.$

9. Given, AB = C

$\therefore \quad \begin{bmatrix} x+y & y \\ 2x & x-y \end{bmatrix}\begin{bmatrix} 2 \\ -1 \end{bmatrix} = \begin{bmatrix} 3 \\ 2 \end{bmatrix}$

$\Rightarrow \quad \begin{bmatrix} 2x+2y-y \\ 4x-x+y \end{bmatrix} = \begin{bmatrix} 3 \\ 2 \end{bmatrix}$

$\Rightarrow \quad \begin{bmatrix} 2x+y \\ 3x+y \end{bmatrix} = \begin{bmatrix} 3 \\ 2 \end{bmatrix}$

$\therefore \quad 2x + y = 3 \quad ...(i)$

$3x + y = 2 \quad ...(ii)$

From (*i*) and (*ii*), we get

$3 - 2x = 2 - 3x$

$\Rightarrow \quad 3 - 2 = 2x - 3x$

$\Rightarrow \quad 1 = - x$

$\Rightarrow \quad x = - 1$

From (*i*),

$y = 3 - 2x$

$= 3 - 2 (- 1)$

$= 3 + 2$

$= 5$

$\therefore \quad A = \begin{bmatrix} x+y & y \\ 2x & x-y \end{bmatrix}$

$= \begin{bmatrix} -1+5 & 5 \\ 2\times-1 & -1-5 \end{bmatrix}$

$= \begin{bmatrix} 4 & 5 \\ -2 & -6 \end{bmatrix}$

$\therefore \quad |A| = \begin{vmatrix} 4 & 5 \\ -2 & -6 \end{vmatrix}$

$= - 24 - (-10)$

$= - 24 + 10$

$= - 14$

Hence, the value of the determinant of the matrix A = – 14.

12. Let $\Delta = \begin{vmatrix} i & i^2 & i^3 \\ i^4 & i^6 & i^8 \\ i^9 & i^{12} & i^{15} \end{vmatrix}$ where $i = \sqrt{-1}$

$= \begin{vmatrix} i & -1 & -i \\ 1 & -1 & 1 \\ i & 1 & -i \end{vmatrix}$

$= i(i - 1) - (-1) (- i - i) - i(1 + i)$

$= i^2 - i + 1(-2i) - i - i^2$

$= - 1 - i - 2i - i + 1$

$= - i - 2i - i$

$= - 4i.$

13. $AB = \begin{bmatrix} a & h & g \\ h & b & f \\ g & f & c \end{bmatrix}\begin{bmatrix} x \\ y \\ z \end{bmatrix} = \begin{bmatrix} ax+hy+gz \\ hx+by+fz \\ gx+fy+cz \end{bmatrix}$

14. Here, the number of letters in the word 'ABLE' = 4

We have to find the total number of arrangements of these 4 letters so that vowels occupy even places.

There are two vowels A and E and two even places 2nd and 4th.

The remaining two letters (B, L)

Hence, by the fundamental principle of counting the total number of arrangements = $\underline{|2} \times \underline{|2}$

$= 2 \times 2 = 4.$

16. The given that

$\dfrac{n(Y)}{n(Z)} = \dfrac{4}{5}$

$\Rightarrow \quad \dfrac{16+18+17+b}{90} = \dfrac{4}{5}$

$\Rightarrow \quad \dfrac{51+b}{90} = \dfrac{4}{5}$

$\Rightarrow \quad 51 + b = \dfrac{90 \times 4}{5} = 18 \times 4 = 72$

$\Rightarrow b = 72 - 51 = 21.$

17. $n(X) + n(Y) + n(Z) - n(X \cap Y) - n(Y \cap Z) - n(X \cap Z) + n(X \cap Y \cap Z)$

$= a + 12 + 18 + 16 + b + 16 + 18 + 17 + 90 - (16 + 18) - (17 + 18) - (12 + 18) + 18$

$= a + 46 + b + 51 + 90 - 34 - 35 - 30 + 18$

$= a + b + 97 + 108 - 99$

$= a + b + 205 - 99$

$= a + b + 106$

19. Here, $\dfrac{\tan 3A}{\tan A} = K$

$\Rightarrow \quad \dfrac{\dfrac{3\tan A - \tan^3 A}{1 - 3\tan^2 A}}{\tan A} = K$

$\Rightarrow \quad \dfrac{\tan A(3 - \tan^2 A)}{\tan A(1 - 3\tan^2 A)} = K$

$\Rightarrow \quad \dfrac{3 - \tan^2 A}{1 - 3\tan^2 A} = K$

$\Rightarrow \quad 3 - \tan^2 A = K - K\, 3\tan^2 A$

$\Rightarrow \quad 3 - K = \tan^2 A - K\, 3\tan^2 A$

$\Rightarrow \quad 3 - K = \tan^2 A(1 - 3K)$

$\Rightarrow \quad \tan^2 A = \dfrac{3-K}{1-3K} = \dfrac{K-3}{3K-1}$

$\Rightarrow \quad \tan^2 A = \dfrac{K-3}{3K-1}.$

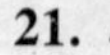

21. 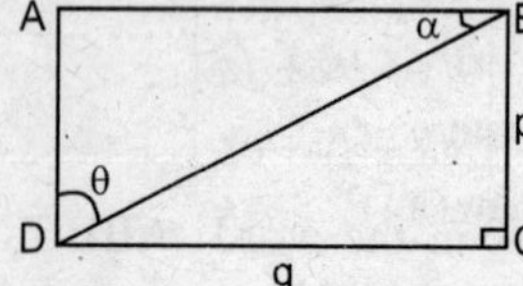

Given,

ABCD is a trapezium

Such that AB || CD

BC ⊥ CD,

Let AD is perpendicular to them.

In ΔBAD,

$$\sin\theta = \frac{BA}{BD}$$

$$\Rightarrow \quad BD = \frac{BA}{\sin\theta} \quad ...(i)$$

and
$$\sin\alpha = \frac{AD}{BD}$$

$$\Rightarrow \quad BD = \frac{AD}{\sin\alpha} \quad ...(ii)$$

From (*i*) and (*ii*), we get

$$\frac{BA}{\sin\theta} = \frac{AD}{\sin\alpha}$$

$$\Rightarrow \quad AD \sin\theta = BA \sin\alpha$$

$$\Rightarrow \quad AD \sin\theta = AB \sin\alpha \quad ...(1)$$

From (*i*),

$$BD \sin\theta = BA$$

$$\Rightarrow \quad BD\sin\theta = AB \qquad [\because \text{In } \Delta ABD$$

$$= AB\sin 90° \qquad 90° + \theta + \alpha = 180°$$

$$= AB\sin(\theta+\alpha) \qquad \theta + \alpha = 90°]$$

$$\Rightarrow BD \sin\theta = AB \sin(\theta + \alpha) \quad ...(2)$$

Thus, (1) and (2) are cosider.

22. 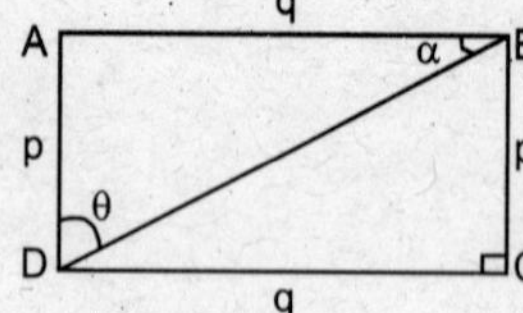

From (*i*),

$$AB = BD \sin\theta$$

Checking the options

(A) $\dfrac{(p^2+q^2)\sin\theta}{p\cos\theta + q\sin\theta}$

$$= \frac{(BD)^2 \sin\theta}{\dfrac{p.p}{BD} + \dfrac{q.q}{BD}}$$

$$= \frac{(BD)^2\sin\theta}{\dfrac{p^2+q^2}{BD}}$$

$$= \frac{(BD)^2\sin\theta}{p^2+q^2}.BD$$

$$= \frac{(BD)^2\sin\theta.BD}{(BD)^2}$$

$$= BD\sin\theta$$

Hence, AB = BD sin θ

Therefore, $AB = \dfrac{(p^2+q^2)\sin\theta}{p\cos\theta+q\sin\theta}$.

23. Given that,

$$\tan\theta = \frac{\cos 17° - \sin 17°}{\cos 17° + \sin 17°}$$

Dividing N^r and D^r by cos 17°

$$\therefore \quad \tan\theta = \frac{\dfrac{\cos 17° - \sin 17°}{\cos 17°}}{\dfrac{\cos 17° + \sin 17°}{\cos 17°}}$$

$$= \frac{1 - \tan 17°}{1 + \tan 17°}$$

$$= \frac{\tan 45° - \tan 17°}{1 + \tan 45° \tan 17°}$$

$$= \tan(45° - 17°)$$

$$= \tan 28°$$

$$\Rightarrow \tan\theta = \tan 28° \qquad \left[\tan(A-B) = \frac{\tan A - \tan B}{1 + \tan A \tan B}\right]$$

$$\Rightarrow \theta = 28°.$$

24. Given that,

$$\cos 2B = 3\sin^2 A \quad ...(i)$$

and
$$3\sin 2A = 2\sin 2B$$

$$\Rightarrow \quad 2\sin 2B = 3\sin 2A \quad ...(ii)$$

Dividing (*ii*) by (*i*), we get

$$\frac{2\sin 2B}{\cos 2B} = \frac{3\sin 2A}{3\sin^2 A}$$

$$\Rightarrow \quad 2\tan 2B = \frac{2\sin A\cos A}{\sin^2 A}$$

$$\Rightarrow \quad \tan 2B = \frac{\sin A\cos A}{\sin^2 A}$$

$$\Rightarrow \quad \tan 2B = \frac{\cos A}{\sin A}$$

$$\Rightarrow \quad \tan 2B = \cot A$$

$$\Rightarrow \quad \tan 2B = \tan(90° - A)$$

$\Rightarrow \quad 2B = 90° - A$

$\Rightarrow \quad 2B + A = 90°$

$\Rightarrow \quad A + 2B = \frac{\pi}{2}.$

25. $\sin 3x + \cos 3x + 4 \sin^3 x - 3 \sin x + 3 \cos x - 4 \cos^3 x$

$= \sin 3x + \cos 3x - (3 \sin x - 4 \sin^3 x) - (4 \cos^3 x - 3 \cos x)$

$= \sin 3x + \cos 3x - \sin 3x - \cos 3x$

$= 0.$

31. $a \sin^2 x + b \cos^2 x = c$

$\Rightarrow a \sin^2 x + b (1 - \sin^2 x) = c$

$\Rightarrow a \sin^2 x + b - b \sin^2 x = c$

$\Rightarrow (a - b) \sin^2 x = c - b$

$\Rightarrow \sin^2 x = \frac{c-b}{a-b}$ ...(*i*)

Again, $a \sin^2 x + b \cos^2 x = c$

$\Rightarrow a(1 - \cos^2 x) + b \cos^2 x = c$

$\Rightarrow a - a \cos^2 x + b \cos^2 x = c$

$\Rightarrow a - c = a \cos^2 x - b \cos^2 x$

$\Rightarrow a - c = (a - b) \cos^2 x$

$\Rightarrow \cos^2 x = \frac{a-c}{a-b}$ ...(*ii*)

From (*i*) divided by (*ii*) we get,

$$\frac{\sin^2 x}{\cos^2 x} = \frac{\frac{c-b}{a-b}}{\frac{a-c}{a-b}} = \frac{c-b}{a-c}$$

$\Rightarrow \tan^2 x = \frac{c-b}{a-c}.$

32. $b \sin^2 y + a \cos^2 y = d$

$\Rightarrow b \sin^2 y + a (1 - \sin^2 y) = d$

$\Rightarrow b \sin^2 y + a - a \sin^2 y = d$

$\Rightarrow (b - a) \sin^2 y = d - a$

$\Rightarrow \sin^2 y = \frac{d-a}{b-a}$ ...(*i*)

Again, $b \sin^2 y + a \cos^2 y = d$

$\Rightarrow b (1 - \cos^2 y) + a \cos^2 y = d$

$\Rightarrow b - b \cos^2 y + a \cos^2 y = d$

$\Rightarrow b - d = b \cos^2 y - a \cos^2 y$

$\Rightarrow b - d = (b - a) \cos^2 y$

$\Rightarrow \cos^2 y = \frac{b-d}{b-a}$ ...(*ii*)

From (*i*) divided by (*ii*) we get,

$$\frac{\sin^2 y}{\cos^2 y} = \frac{\frac{d-a}{b-a}}{\frac{b-d}{b-a}} = \frac{d-a}{b-d}$$

$\Rightarrow \tan^2 y = \frac{d-a}{b-d}$

$\Rightarrow \frac{d-a}{b-d} = \tan^2 y.$

33. $p \tan x = q \tan y$

$\Rightarrow \frac{p}{q} = \frac{\tan y}{\tan x}$

$\Rightarrow \frac{p^2}{q^2} = \frac{\tan^2 y}{\tan^2 x}$ [by Q(32) and Q(31)]

$$= \frac{\frac{d-a}{b-d}}{\frac{c-b}{a-c}}$$

$$= \frac{d-a}{b-d} \times \frac{a-c}{c-b}$$

$$= \frac{-(a-d) \times -(c-a)}{-(b-c) \times -(d-b)}$$

$$= \frac{(a-d)(c-a)}{(b-c)(d-b)}$$

$\Rightarrow \frac{p^2}{q^2} = \frac{(a-d)(c-a)}{(b-c)(d-b)}.$

34. $\because t_n = \sin^n \theta + \cos^n \theta$

$\therefore t_3 = \sin^3 \theta + \cos^3 \theta$

$t_5 = \sin^5 \theta + \cos^5 \theta$

$t_7 = \sin^7 \theta + \cos^7 \theta$

$$\therefore \frac{t_3 - t_5}{t_5 - t_7} = \frac{\sin^3 \theta + \cos^3 \theta - (\sin^5 \theta + \cos^5 \theta)}{\sin^5 \theta + \cos^5 \theta - (\sin^7 \theta + \cos^7 \theta)}$$

$$= \frac{\sin^3 \theta - \sin^5 \theta + \cos^3 \theta - \cos^5 \theta}{\sin^5 \theta - \sin^7 \theta + \cos^5 \theta - \cos^7 \theta}$$

$$= \frac{\sin^3 \theta(1 - \sin^2 \theta) + \cos^3 \theta(1 - \cos^2 \theta)}{\sin^5 \theta(1 - \sin^2 \theta) + \cos^5 \theta(1 - \cos^2 \theta)}$$

$$= \frac{\sin^3 \theta \cos^2 \theta + \cos^3 \theta \sin^2 \theta}{\sin^5 \theta \cos^2 \theta + \cos^5 \theta \sin^2 \theta}$$

$$= \frac{\sin^2 \theta \cos^2 \theta(\sin \theta + \cos \theta)}{\sin^2 \theta \cos^2 \theta(\sin^3 \theta + \cos^3 \theta)}$$

$$= \frac{\sin \theta + \cos \theta}{\sin^3 \theta + \cos^3 \theta}$$

$$= \frac{t_1}{t_3}.$$

35. $\because t_n = \sin^n \theta + \cos^n \theta$

$\therefore t_1 = \sin \theta + \cos \theta$

$\therefore t_2 = \sin^2 \theta + \cos^2 \theta$

$\therefore t_1^2 - t_2 = (\sin \theta + \cos \theta)^2 - (\sin^2 \theta + \cos^2 \theta)$

$= \sin^2 \theta + \cos^2 \theta + 2\sin \theta \cos \theta - \sin^2 \theta - \cos^2 \theta$

$= 2 \sin \theta \cos \theta$

$= \sin 2\theta.$

36. $t_n = \sin^n \theta + \cos^n \theta$

$t_{10} = \sin^{10} \theta + \cos^{10} \theta$

when $\theta = 45°$

$$t_{10} = \sin^{10} 45° + \cos^{10} 45°$$
$$= \left(\frac{1}{\sqrt{2}}\right)^{10} + \left(\frac{1}{\sqrt{2}}\right)^{10}$$
$$= 2\left(\frac{1}{\sqrt{2}}\right)^{10}$$
$$= 2\left[\left(\frac{1}{\sqrt{2}}\right)^2\right]^5$$
$$= 2\left(\frac{1}{2}\right)^5$$
$$= 2\left(\frac{1}{32}\right)$$
$$= \frac{1}{16}.$$

37. Let $\alpha = \beta = 15°$

$\sin \alpha + \cos \beta$

$= \sin 15° + \cos 15°$

$= \sin (45° - 30°) + \cos (45° - 30°)$

$= \sin 45° \cos 30° - \cos 45° \sin 30° + \cos 45° \cos 30° + \sin 45° \sin 30°$

$$= \frac{1}{\sqrt{2}}.\frac{\sqrt{3}}{2} - \frac{1}{\sqrt{2}}.\frac{1}{2} + \frac{1}{\sqrt{2}}.\frac{\sqrt{3}}{2} + \frac{1}{\sqrt{2}}.\frac{1}{2}$$
$$= \frac{\sqrt{3}}{2\sqrt{2}} + \frac{\sqrt{3}}{2\sqrt{2}}$$
$$= 2\left(\frac{\sqrt{3}}{2\sqrt{2}}\right)$$
$$= \frac{\sqrt{3}}{\sqrt{2}}.$$

38. Let $\alpha = \beta = 15°$

Then, the value of $\sin 7\alpha - \cos 7\beta$

$= \sin 105° - \cos 105°$

$= \sin (60° + 45°) - \cos (60° + 45°)$

$= \sin 60° \cos 45° + \cos 60° \sin 45° - [\cos 60° \cos 45° - \sin 60° \sin 45°]$

$$= \frac{\sqrt{3}}{2} \times \frac{1}{\sqrt{2}} + \frac{1}{2} \times \frac{1}{\sqrt{2}} - \left(\frac{1}{2} \times \frac{1}{\sqrt{2}} - \frac{\sqrt{3}}{2} \times \frac{1}{\sqrt{2}}\right)$$
$$= \frac{\sqrt{3}}{2\sqrt{2}} + \frac{1}{2\sqrt{2}} - \frac{1}{2\sqrt{2}} + \frac{\sqrt{3}}{2\sqrt{2}}$$
$$= \frac{\sqrt{3}}{2\sqrt{2}} + \frac{\sqrt{3}}{2\sqrt{2}}$$
$$= \frac{2\sqrt{3}}{2\sqrt{2}}$$
$$= \frac{\sqrt{3}}{\sqrt{2}}.$$

40. Given, $\sin x + \sin y = \cos y - \cos x$

$$\Rightarrow 2\sin\left(\frac{x+y}{2}\right)\cos\left(\frac{x-y}{2}\right) = 2\sin\left(\frac{y+x}{2}\right)\sin\left(\frac{x-y}{2}\right)$$
$$\Rightarrow \sin\left(\frac{x+y}{2}\right)\cos\left(\frac{x-y}{2}\right) = \sin\left(\frac{x+y}{2}\right)\sin\left(\frac{x-y}{2}\right)$$
$$\Rightarrow \cos\left(\frac{x-y}{2}\right) = \sin\left(\frac{x-y}{2}\right)$$
$$\Rightarrow \frac{\sin\left(\frac{x-y}{2}\right)}{\cos\left(\frac{x-y}{2}\right)} = 1$$
$$\Rightarrow \tan\left(\frac{x-y}{2}\right) = 1.$$

41. Given, $A = [a_{ij}]_{3\times5}$, $B = [b_{ij}]_{5\times3}$

$AB = [c_{ij}]_{3\times3}$

and $BA = [d_{ij}]_{5\times5}$.

42. Given, p^2, q^2 and r^2 are in G.P.

$$\therefore \quad \frac{q^2}{p^2} = \frac{r^2}{q^2}$$
$$\Rightarrow \quad q^4 = p^2r^2$$
$$\Rightarrow \quad q^2 = pr \quad ...(i)$$

I. p, q and r in G.P.

$$\therefore \frac{q}{p} = \frac{r}{q}$$
$$\Rightarrow q^2 = pr$$

II. Now, $\ln p$, $\ln q$ and $\ln r$ are in A.P.

$$\therefore \quad \frac{\ln p + \ln r}{2} = \frac{\ln pr}{2} = \frac{\ln q^2}{2} \quad \text{[from (i)]}$$
$$= \frac{2\ln q}{2} = \ln q$$

Hence, $\ln p$, $\ln q$ and $\ln r$ are in A.P.

43. Given, $\cot \alpha$ and $\cot \beta$ are the roots of the equation $x^2 - 3x + 2 = 0$

$$\therefore \quad x = \frac{-b \pm \sqrt{b^2 - 4ac}}{2a}$$
$$= \frac{-(-3) \pm \sqrt{3^2 - 4 \times 1 \times 2}}{2}$$
$$= \frac{3 \pm 1}{2}$$
$$= 2, 1$$

$\therefore$ Roots are $\cot \alpha = 2$ and $\cot \beta = 1$

$$\therefore \cot(\alpha + \beta) = \frac{\cot\alpha \cot\beta - 1}{\cot\beta + \cot\alpha} = \frac{2\times 1 - 1}{1+2}$$

$$= \frac{2-1}{3} = \frac{1}{3}.$$

45. Let $$Z = \frac{1-i\sqrt{3}}{1+i\sqrt{3}} = \frac{1-i\sqrt{3}}{1+i\sqrt{3}} \times \frac{1-i\sqrt{3}}{1-i\sqrt{3}}$$

$$= \frac{\left(1-i\sqrt{3}\right)^2}{1^2-\left(i\sqrt{3}\right)^2} = \frac{1^2+\left(i\sqrt{3}\right)^2 - 2\times 1\times i\sqrt{3}}{1-(-3)}$$

$$= \frac{1-3-i2\sqrt{3}}{1+3} = \frac{-2-i2\sqrt{3}}{4}$$

$$= \frac{-1-i\sqrt{3}}{2} = \frac{-1}{2} - \frac{i\sqrt{3}}{2}$$

$\therefore$ $\text{Re}(z) = \frac{-1}{2}$ and $\text{Im}(z) = \frac{-\sqrt{3}}{2}$

Let α be the angle

Then, $$\tan\alpha = \left|\frac{\text{Im}(z)}{\text{Re}(z)}\right|$$

$$\Rightarrow \tan\alpha = \left|\frac{-\frac{\sqrt{3}}{2}}{-\frac{1}{2}}\right|$$

$$= \left|\sqrt{3}\right|$$

$$= \sqrt{3}$$

$$= \tan 60°$$

$\Rightarrow \alpha = 60° = \frac{\pi}{3}$

Here, $\text{Re}(z) < 0$ and $\text{Im}(z) < 0$, so, point representing z lies in the third quadrant.

$$\therefore \arg(z) = \pi + \alpha$$
$$= 180° + 60°$$
$$= 240°.$$

46. Let $$Z = \frac{\cos\theta + i\sin\theta}{\cos\theta - i\sin\theta}$$

$$= \frac{\cos\theta + i\sin\theta}{\cos\theta - i\sin\theta} \times \frac{\cos\theta + i\sin\theta}{\cos\theta + i\sin\theta}$$

$$= \frac{(\cos\theta + i\sin\theta)^2}{\cos^2\theta - (i\sin\theta)^2}$$

$$= \frac{\cos^2\theta + i^2\sin^2\theta + 2\cos\theta\, i\sin\theta}{\cos^2\theta + \sin^2\theta}$$

$$= \frac{\cos^2\theta - \sin^2\theta + i2\cos\theta\sin\theta}{1}$$

$$\Rightarrow Z = (\cos^2\theta - \sin^2\theta) + i\,2\cos\theta\sin\theta$$

$$\therefore |Z| = \sqrt{\{\text{Re}(z)\}^2 + \{\text{Im}(z)\}^2}$$

$$= \sqrt{(\cos^2\theta - \sin^2\theta)^2 + 4\cos^2\theta\sin^2\theta}$$

$$= \sqrt{(\cos^2\theta + \sin^2\theta)^2}$$

$$= \cos^2\theta + \sin^2\theta$$

$$= 1$$

Hence, the modules of $Z = |Z| = 1$.

48. Given, $$D = \begin{vmatrix} p & q & r \\ q & r & p \\ r & p & q \end{vmatrix}$$

$c_1 \to c_1 + c_2 + c_3$

$$\therefore D = \begin{vmatrix} p+q+r & q & r \\ p+q+r & r & p \\ p+q+r & p & q \end{vmatrix}$$

$$= (p+q+r)\begin{vmatrix} 1 & q & r \\ 1 & r & p \\ 1 & p & q \end{vmatrix}$$

$R_1 \to R_1 - R_2$, $R_2 \to R_2 - R_3$

$$= (p+q+r)\begin{vmatrix} 0 & q-r & r-p \\ 0 & r-p & p-q \\ 1 & p & q \end{vmatrix}$$

$$= (p + q + r)\,[0 - 0 + \{(q - r)(p - q) - (r - p)^2\}]$$

$$= (p + q + r)\,(pq - q^2 - pr + qr - r^2 - p^2 + 2pr)$$

$$= (p + q + r)\,(-p^2 - q^2 - r^2 + pq + pr + qr)$$

$$= -(p + q + r)\,(p^2 + q^2 + r^2 - pq - qr - qr)$$

$$\Rightarrow D = -(p^3 + q^3 + r^3 - 3\,pqr)$$

Hence, $D < 0$.

49. Expression $= (1 + x)^9$

$$= {}^9C_0 1^9 x^0 + {}^9C_1 x^1 + {}^9C_2 x^2 + {}^9C_3 x^3 + {}^9C_4 x^4 + {}^9C_5 x^5 + {}^9C_6 x^6 + {}^9C_7 x^7 + {}^9C_8 x^8 + {}^9C_9 x^9$$

Now, the sum of the last five co-efficients

$$= {}^9C_5 + {}^9C_6 + {}^9C_7 + {}^9C_8 + {}^9C_9$$

$$= {}^{9+1}C_6 + {}^{9+1}C_8 + 1$$

$$= {}^{10}C_6 + {}^{10}C_8 + 1 \qquad [{}^nC_{r-1} + {}^nC_r = {}^{n+1}C_r]$$

$$= \frac{\lfloor 10}{\lfloor 6\,\lfloor 4} + \frac{\lfloor 10}{\lfloor 8\,\lfloor 2} + 1$$

$$= \frac{10\times 9\times 8\times 7}{4\times 3\times 2\times 1} + \frac{10\times 9}{2} + 1$$

$$= 10 \times 3 \times 7 + 5 \times 9 + 1$$

$$= 210 + 45 + 1$$

$$= 256.$$

50. I. $\because$ A(adj A) = |A| 1

and (adj A) A = |A| 1

$\therefore$ A(adj A) = (adj A)A

II. |adj A| $\neq$ |A|.

51. Given,

$(x - 2a)(x - 2b) + (y - 2c)(y - 2d) = 0$

$\Rightarrow x^2 - 2bx - 2ax + 4ab + y^2 - 2dy - 2cy + 4cd = 0$

$\Rightarrow x^2 + y^2 - (2a + 2b)x - (2c + 2d)y + 4ab + 4cd = 0$

$\Rightarrow x^2 + y^2 + 2\{-(a + b)\} + 2\{-(c + d)y + 4(b + cd) = 0$

The general equation of a circle is

$x^2 + y^2 + 2gx + 2fy + c = 0$ whose centre of the circle $= (-g, -f)$

Hence, the centre of the given circle is $\{(a + b), (c + d)\}$.

52. Given, the equation of one diagonal of the square is

$$3x + 2y = 5$$

$$\Rightarrow \quad y = -\frac{3}{2}x + \frac{5}{2}$$

Here, $m_1 = \frac{-3}{2}$

$\because$ $m_1 m_2 = -1$

$\therefore$ $m_2 = \frac{-1}{m_1} = \frac{2}{3}$

As one diagonal of a square is perpendicular to other diagonal.

So, the equation of the other diagonal is

$$2x - 3y = 5.$$

56. The points (a, b), (c, d) and $(a - c, b - d)$ are collinear

$$\therefore \begin{vmatrix} a & b & 1 \\ c & d & 1 \\ a-c & b-d & 1 \end{vmatrix} = 0$$

$\Rightarrow a(d - b + d) - c(b - b + d) + (a - c)(b - d) = 0$

$\Rightarrow a(2d - b) - c(d) + ab - ad - bc + cd = 0$

$\Rightarrow 2ad - ab - cd + ab - ad - bc + cd = 0$

$\Rightarrow ad - bc = 0$

$\Rightarrow ad = bc.$

58.

P(0, k)
(3, 1)
A M B
3x – 4y – 5 = 0

Given, the foot of the perpendicular drawn from the point P(0, k) to the line AB

$3x - 4y - 5 = 0$ is M(3, 1)

Slope of PM $= \frac{k-1}{0-3}$ and slope of AB $= \frac{3}{4}$

$$\left[\because 4y = 3x - 5 \Rightarrow y = \frac{3}{4}x - \frac{5}{4}\right]$$

$\because$ $m_1 m_2 = -1$

$\Rightarrow \left(\frac{k-1}{-3}\right)\left(\frac{3}{4}\right) = -1$

$\Rightarrow \left(\frac{k-1}{3}\right)\left(\frac{3}{4}\right) = 1$

$\Rightarrow \frac{k-1}{4} = 1$

$\Rightarrow k - 1 = 4$

$\Rightarrow k = 4 + 1 = 5$

Hence, $k = 5$.

59. Let slope of lines are $m_1 = 2 - \sqrt{3}$ and $m_2 = 2 + \sqrt{3}$

Then, $\tan\theta = \pm\frac{m_1 - m_2}{1 + m_1 m_2}$

$\Rightarrow \tan\theta = \pm\frac{2 - \sqrt{3} - (2 + \sqrt{3})}{1 + (2 - \sqrt{3})(2 + \sqrt{3})}$

$= \pm\frac{2 - \sqrt{3} - 2 - \sqrt{3}}{1 + 4 - 3}$

$= \pm\frac{-2\sqrt{3}}{2}$

$= \pm(-\sqrt{3})$

$= \pm\sqrt{3}$

$\Rightarrow \tan\theta = -\sqrt{3}$

$= -\tan 60°$

$= \tan(180 - 60)$ $[\tan(180 - \theta) = -\tan\theta]$

$= \tan 120°$

$\Rightarrow \tan\theta = \tan 120°$

$\therefore \theta = 120°$

Hence, the obtuse angle between the lines is 120°.

62. Let L be the foot of the perpendicular drawn from the point (2, 3, 4) to the given line.

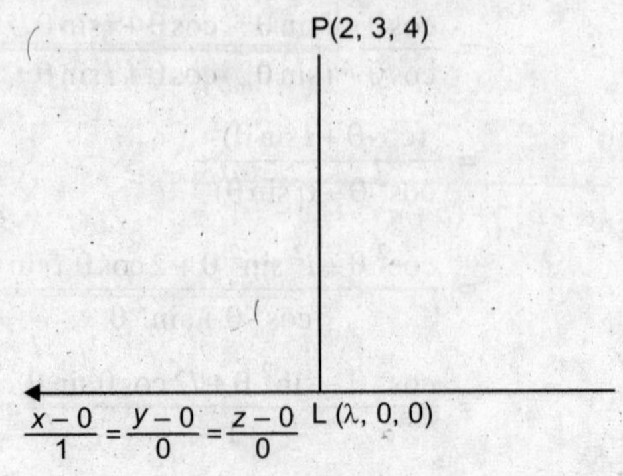

The co-ordinates of a general point

$$\frac{x-0}{1}=\frac{y-0}{0}=\frac{z-0}{0}=\lambda(\text{say})$$

or $x = \lambda$, $y = 0$, $z = 0$

Let the co-ordinates of L be $(\lambda, 0, 0)$

Therefore, direction ratio of PL are proportional to $\lambda - 2, 0 - 3, 0 - 4$ *i.e.*, $\lambda - 2, -3, -4$

Direction ratios of the given line are proportional to 1, 0, 0

But, PL is perpendicular to the given line

$\therefore\ 1(\lambda - 2) + 0(-3) + 0(-4) = 0$

$\Rightarrow \lambda - 2 = 0$

$\Rightarrow \lambda = +2$

Putting $\lambda = 2$ in $(\lambda, 0, 0)$, the co-ordinates of L are $(2, 0, 0)$

$$\therefore \quad PL = \sqrt{(2-2)^2+(0-3)^2+(0-4)^2} = \sqrt{0+9+16} = \sqrt{25} = 5$$

Hence, perpendicular distance = 5.

63. Given, direction ratio of a line is $< a + b, b + c, c + a >$

$\therefore$ Direction cosine are,

$$\frac{a+b}{\sqrt{(a+b)^2+(b+c)^2+(c+a)^2}},\ \frac{b+c}{\sqrt{(a+b)^2+(b+c)^2+(c+a)^2}},\ \frac{c+a}{\sqrt{(a+b)^2+(b+c)^2+(c+a)^2}}$$

Now, the sum of the squares of its direction cosines

$$= \left[\frac{a+b}{\sqrt{(a+b)^2+(b+c)^2+(c+a)^2}}\right]^2 + \left[\frac{b+c}{\sqrt{(a+b)^2+(b+c)^2+(c+a)^2}}\right]^2 + \left[\frac{c+a}{\sqrt{(a+b)^2+(b+c)^2+(c+a)^2}}\right]^2$$

$$= \frac{(a+b)^2}{(a+b)^2+(b+c)^2+(c+a)^2} + \frac{(b+c)^2}{(a+b)^2+(b+c)^2+(c+a)^2} + \frac{(c+a)^2}{(a+b)^2+(b+c)^2+(c+a)^2}$$

$$= \frac{(a+b)^2+(b+c)^2+(c+a)^2}{(a+b)^2+(b+c)^2+(c+a)^2} = 1$$

68.

Let ABCD be a parallelogram such that $\overline{AB} = \vec{a}$ and $\overline{BC} = \vec{b} = \hat{i} - 2\hat{j} - 3\hat{k}$

$= 2\hat{i} - 4\hat{j} + 5\hat{k}$

Then, $\overline{AB} + \overline{BC} = \overline{AC}$

$$\Rightarrow \quad \overline{AC} = \vec{a}+\vec{b} = 2\hat{i}-4\hat{j}+5\hat{k}+\hat{i}-2\hat{j}-3\hat{k}$$

$$\Rightarrow \quad \overline{AC} = 3\hat{i}-6\hat{j}+2\hat{k}$$

and $\overline{AB}+\overline{BD} = \overline{AB}$

$$\Rightarrow \quad \overline{BD} = \overline{AD}-\overline{AB} = \vec{b}-\vec{a} = \hat{i}-2\hat{j}-3\hat{k}-(2\hat{i}-4\hat{j}+5\hat{k}) = \hat{i}-2\hat{j}-3\hat{k}-2\hat{i}+4\hat{j}-5\hat{k}$$

$$\Rightarrow \quad \overline{BD} = -\hat{i}+2\hat{j}-8\hat{k}$$

$$\therefore \quad \left(\overline{AC}\cdot\overline{BD}\right) = (3\hat{i}-6\hat{j}+2\hat{k})(-\hat{i}+2\hat{j}-8\hat{k}) = (3)(-1)+(-6)(2)+(2)(-8) = -3-12-16 = -31$$

$$\therefore \left|\left(\overline{AC}\cdot\overline{BD}\right)\right| = |-31| = 31.$$

69. Given that

$$|\vec{a}\times\vec{b}|^2 + |\vec{a}\cdot\vec{b}|^2 = 144 \quad ...(i)$$

and $|\vec{a}| = 4 \quad \therefore |\vec{b}| = ?$

We know that

$$|\vec{a}\times\vec{b}|^2 + |\vec{a}\cdot\vec{b}|^2 = |\vec{a}|^2|\vec{b}|^2 \quad ...(ii)$$

From (*i*) and (*ii*) we get,

$$|\vec{a}|^2|\vec{b}|^2 = 144 \quad [|\vec{a}| = 4]$$

$$\Rightarrow \quad 4^2|\vec{b}|^2 = 144$$

$$\Rightarrow \quad |\vec{b}|^2 = \frac{144}{16} = 9$$

$$\Rightarrow \quad |\vec{b}|^2 = 3^2$$

$$\Rightarrow \quad |\vec{b}| = 3.$$

70. Given that

$\vec{a} = 2\hat{i} - 3\hat{j} + \hat{k}$, $\vec{b} = \hat{i} + 2\hat{j} - 3\hat{k}$ and $\vec{c} = \hat{j} + p\hat{k}$

We know that vectors $\vec{a}, \vec{b}, \vec{c}$ are coplanar if their scalar triple product is zero

i.e., $\left[\vec{a}\ \vec{b}\ \vec{c}\right] = 0$

Here, $\left[\vec{a}\ \vec{b}\ \vec{c}\right] = \begin{bmatrix} 2 & -3 & 1 \\ 1 & 2 & -3 \\ 0 & 1 & p \end{bmatrix} = 0$

$\Rightarrow 2(2p + 3) - 1(-3p - 1) + 0 = 0$

$\Rightarrow 4p + 6 + 3p + 1 = 0$

$\Rightarrow 7p + 7 = 0$

$\Rightarrow 7p = -7$

$\Rightarrow p = \dfrac{-7}{7} = -1$

Hence, the value of p is -1.

71. $\lim\limits_{x\to 1} \dfrac{x + x^2 + x^3 - 3}{x - 1}$

$= \lim\limits_{x\to 1} \dfrac{x^3 + x^2 + x - 3}{x - 1}$

$= \lim\limits_{x\to 1} \dfrac{(x-1)(x^2 + 2x + 3)}{(x-1)}$

$= \lim\limits_{x\to 1} x^2 + 2x + 3$

$= 1^2 + 2(1) + 3$

$= 1 + 2 + 3$

$= 6.$

72. Let r be the radius and c be the circumference of the circle at any time t.

Then, $c = 2\pi r$ and given, $\dfrac{dr}{dt} = 0.7$ cm/sec

Now, $c = 2\pi r$

$\Rightarrow \dfrac{dc}{dt} = 2\pi \dfrac{dr}{dt}$

$= 2 \times \dfrac{22}{7} \times 0.7$

$= 44 \times 0.1$

$= 4.4$ cm/sec.

73. Given, $\lim\limits_{x\to 1} \dfrac{x^4 - 1}{x - 1} = \lim\limits_{x\to k} \dfrac{x^3 - k^3}{x^2 - k^2}$

$\Rightarrow \lim\limits_{x\to 1} \dfrac{(x^2-1)(x^2+1)}{x-1} = \lim\limits_{x\to k} \dfrac{(x-k)(x^2+kx+k^2)}{(x-k)(x+k)}$

$\Rightarrow \lim\limits_{x\to 1} \dfrac{(x-1)(x+1)(x^2+1)}{(x-1)} = \lim\limits_{x\to k} \dfrac{(x^2+kx+k^2)}{(x+k)}$

$\Rightarrow \lim\limits_{x\to 1} (x+1)(x^2+1) = \lim\limits_{x\to k} \dfrac{x^2+kx+k^2}{x+k}$

$\Rightarrow (1+1)(1^2+1) = \dfrac{k^2 + k.k + k^2}{k+k}$

$\Rightarrow (2)(2) = \dfrac{k^2 + k^2 + k^2}{2k}$

$\Rightarrow 4 = \dfrac{3k^2}{2k}$

$\Rightarrow 8k = 3k^2$

$\Rightarrow k = \dfrac{8}{3}.$

75. $\lim\limits_{x\to 0} \dfrac{\sin x \log(1-x)}{x^2}$

$\left[\begin{aligned} &\because \log(1+x) = x - \frac{x^2}{2} + \frac{x^3}{3} - \frac{x^4}{4} + \ldots \\ &\therefore \log(1-x) = -x - \frac{x^2}{2} - \frac{x^3}{3} - \frac{x^4}{4} + \ldots \end{aligned}\right]$

$= \lim\limits_{x\to 0} \dfrac{\sin x\left[-x - \dfrac{x^2}{2} - \dfrac{x^3}{3} - \dfrac{x^4}{4} \ldots\right]}{x^2}$

$= \lim\limits_{x\to 0} \dfrac{\sin x}{x} \cdot \lim\limits_{x\to 0} \dfrac{x\left[-1 - \dfrac{x}{2} - \dfrac{x^2}{3} - \dfrac{x^3}{4} \ldots\right]}{x}$

$= 1 \cdot \lim\limits_{x\to 0} \left[-1 - \dfrac{x}{2} - \dfrac{x^2}{3} - \dfrac{x^3}{4} \ldots\right]$

$= -1 - 0 - 0 - 0 - \ldots$

$= -1 - 0$

$= -1.$

79. Let $I = \displaystyle\int_0^{\frac{\pi}{4}} (\tan^3 x + \tan x)dx = \int_0^{\frac{\pi}{4}} \tan x(\tan^2 x + 1)dx$

$\Rightarrow I = \displaystyle\int_0^{\frac{\pi}{4}} \tan x \sec^2 x\, dx$

Put $\tan x = t$

$\sec^2 x\, dx = dt$

$\because x = 0 \therefore t = 0$

$\because x = \dfrac{\pi}{4} \therefore t = 1$

$\Rightarrow I = \displaystyle\int_0^1 t\, dt = \left[\frac{t^2}{2}\right]_0^1$

$= \left[\dfrac{1^2}{2} - 0\right] = \dfrac{1}{2}.$

80. Let $y = 3x^2 + 2$

Then, $y_{10} = 3(10)^2 + 2 = 3(100) + 2 = 300 + 2 = 302$

and $y_{10.1} = 3(10.1)^2 + 2 = 3(102.01) + 2 = 306.03 + 2 = 308.03$

Hence, the total change in $y = y_{10.1} - y_{10}$

$= 308.03 - 302$

$= 6.03.$

82. Given, differential equation

$$dy = (1 + y^2)dx$$

$$\Rightarrow \quad \frac{dy}{1+y^2} = dx$$

$$\Rightarrow \quad \int \frac{dy}{1+y^2} = \int dx$$

$$\Rightarrow \quad \tan^{-1} y = x + c$$

Where c is a constant

$$\Rightarrow \quad y = \tan(x + c).$$

83. Let $I = \int (e^{\log x} + \sin x)\cos x \, dx$

$= \int (x + \sin x)\cos x \, dx \qquad [e^{\log x} = x]$

$= \int x\cos x \, dx + \int \sin x \cos x \, dx$

$= x\int \cos x \, dx - \int 1.\sin x \, dx + \frac{1}{2}\int 2\sin x \cos x \, dx$

$= x\sin x - (-\cos x) + \frac{1}{2}\int \sin 2x \, dx$

$= x\sin x + \cos x + \frac{1}{2} - \frac{\cos 2x}{2} + c$

$= x\sin x + \cos x - \frac{1}{4}(1 - 2\sin^2 x) + c$

$= x\sin x + \cos x - \frac{1}{4} + \frac{1}{2}\sin^2 x + c$

$= x\sin x + \cos x + \frac{1}{2}\sin^2 x + \left(c - \frac{1}{4}\right)$

$= x\sin x + \cos x + \frac{1}{2}\sin^2 x + c.$

85.

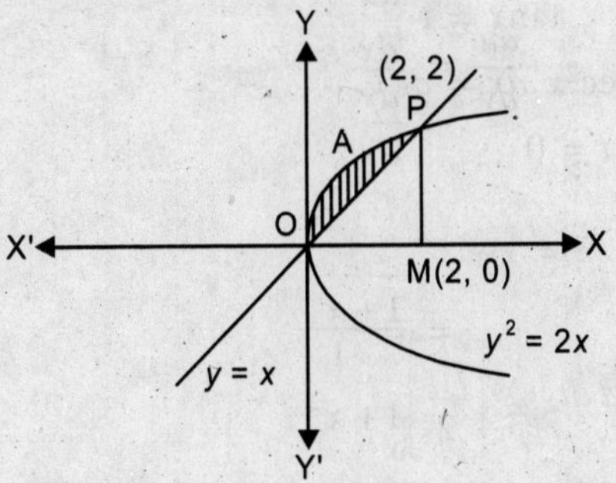

The equation of the given curve are

$$y^2 = 2x \qquad \text{...}(i)$$

and $$y = x \qquad \text{...}(ii)$$

The equation $y^2 = 2x$ represents a parabola in standard form and the equation $y = x$ represents a line passing through the origin.

From (i) and (ii) we get,

$$x^2 = 2x$$

$$\Rightarrow \quad x = 2$$

$$\therefore \quad y = 2 \text{ (from } (ii))$$

We find that

$x = 0 \Rightarrow y = 0$

and $x = 2 \Rightarrow y = 2$

So, the points of intersection of the given curves are (0, 0) and (2, 2)

The area of the region enclosed between curves (i) and (ii)

= area of OAPM – area of OPM

$= \int_0^2 \sqrt{2x}\, dx - \int_0^2 x \, dx$

$= \left[\frac{\sqrt{2}x^{\frac{1}{2}+1}}{\frac{1}{2}+1}\right]_0^2 - \left[\frac{x^2}{2}\right]_0^2$

$= \sqrt{2}\frac{2}{3}\left[x^{\frac{3}{2}}\right]_0^2 - \left[\frac{x^2}{2}\right]_0^2$

$= \frac{2\sqrt{2}}{3}(2)^{\frac{3}{2}} - \frac{(2)^2}{2}$

$= \frac{2\sqrt{2}}{3}\cdot 2\sqrt{2} - 2$

$= \frac{8}{3} - 2$

$= \frac{8-6}{3}$

$= \frac{2}{3}$ square units.

86. Given that

$$f(x) = 2x - x^2$$

$\therefore \quad f(x + 2) = 2(x + 2) - (x + 2)^2$

$= 2x + 4 - (x^2 + 4x + 4)$

$= 2x + 4 - x^2 - 4x - 4$

$= -x^2 - 2x$

and $\quad f(x - 2) = 2(x - 2) - (x - 2)^2$

$= 2x - 4 - (x^2 - 4x + 4)$

$= 2x - 4 - x^2 + 4x - 4$

$= -x^2 + 6x - 8$

$\therefore\quad f(x + 2) + f(x - 2) = -x^2 - 2x + (-x^2) + 6x - 8$

$= -2x^2 + 4x - 8$

Now, $f(x + 2) + f(x - 2)$ when $x = 0$

$= -2(0) + 4(0) - 8$

$= 0 + 0 - 8$

$= -8.$

87. Given that,

$$x^m y^n = a^{m+n}$$

Taking log on both sides, we get,

$$m\log x + n\log y = (m + n) \log a$$

Differentiating both sides with respect to x we get,

$$m \times \frac{1}{x} + n \times \frac{1}{y}\frac{dy}{dx} = (m + n).0$$

$$\Rightarrow \quad \frac{m}{x} + \frac{n}{y}\frac{dy}{dx} = 0$$

$$\Rightarrow \quad \frac{n}{y}\frac{dy}{dx} = \frac{-m}{x}$$

$$\Rightarrow \quad \frac{dy}{dx} = \frac{-m}{x} \times \frac{y}{n}$$

$$\Rightarrow \quad \frac{dy}{dx} = \frac{-my}{nx}.$$

88. We have

$$I = \int \frac{dx}{x(x^n + 1)}$$

$$= \int \frac{dx}{x(x^n + 1)} \times \frac{x^{n-1}}{x^{n-1}}$$

$$= \int \frac{x^{n-1}}{x^n(x^n + 1)} dx$$

Let $x^n + 1 = t$ then, $nx^{n-1}\, dx = dt$

$$\Rightarrow \quad dx = \frac{dt}{nx^{n-1}}$$

$$\therefore \quad I = \int \frac{1dt}{nx^n t} \qquad \left[\because x^n + 1 = t \;\; \therefore x^n = t - 1\right]$$

$$= \frac{1}{n}\int \frac{1dt}{(t-1)t}$$

$$= \frac{1}{n}\int \frac{1dt}{t^2 - t}$$

$$= \frac{1}{n}\int \frac{1dt}{t^2 - t + \frac{1}{4} - \frac{1}{4}}$$

$$= \frac{1}{n}\int \frac{dt}{\left(t - \frac{1}{2}\right)^2 - \left(\frac{1}{2}\right)^2}$$

$$= \frac{1}{n} \times \frac{1}{2\left(\frac{1}{2}\right)} \log\left|\frac{t - \frac{1}{2} - \frac{1}{2}}{t - \frac{1}{2} + \frac{1}{2}}\right| + c$$

$$= \frac{1}{n}\log\left|\frac{t-1}{t}\right| + c$$

$$= \frac{1}{n}\log\left|\frac{x^n + 1 - 1}{x^n + 1}\right| + c$$

$$= \frac{1}{n}\log\left|\frac{x^n}{x^n + 1}\right| + c.$$

89. Let $f(x) = |x - 1|$, where $x \in$ R

Since the minimum value of modulus function is z

So, the minimum value of $f(x)$ is 0.

93. $$\lim_{x\to 0} \frac{3^x + 3^{-x} - 2}{x} = \lim_{x\to 0} \frac{3^x + \frac{1}{3^x} - 2}{x}$$

$$= \lim_{x\to 0} \frac{3^{2x} + 1 - 2x\,3^x}{x \cdot 3^x}$$

$$= \lim_{x\to 0} \left(\frac{3^x - 1}{x}\right)^2 \cdot \frac{x}{3^x}$$

$$= \log 3 \lim_{x\to 0} \frac{x}{3^x}$$

$$= \log 3\left(\frac{0}{3^0}\right)$$

$$= \log 3(0)$$

$$= 0.$$

94. Let $u = \tan^{-1}x$ and $v = \cot^{-1}x$

Then, $\frac{du}{dx} = \frac{1}{1+x^2}$ and $\frac{dv}{dx} = \frac{-1}{1+x^2}$

$$\frac{du}{dv} = \frac{\frac{du}{dx}}{\frac{dv}{dx}}$$

$$= \frac{\frac{1}{1+x^2}}{\frac{-1}{1+x^2}}$$

$$= \frac{1}{1+x^2} \times \frac{1+x^2}{-1}$$

$$= -1$$

Hence, the derivative of $\tan^{-1}x$ with respect to $\cot^{-1}x$ is $\frac{du}{dv} = -1$.

99. $\ln\left(\frac{dy}{dx}\right) = x$

$\Rightarrow \quad \log\left(\frac{dy}{dx}\right) = x$

$\Rightarrow \quad e^x = \frac{dy}{dx}$

$\Rightarrow \quad dy = e^x\,dx$

Taking integration on both sides, we get,

$$\int dy = \int e^x\,dx$$

$\Rightarrow \quad y = e^x + c.$

100. Given, $l + b = k$

$\because$ Area of rectangle $= l \times b$

$A = lb$

$\Rightarrow \quad A = l(k - l)$

Differentiating both sides w.r.t. l we get,

$$\frac{dA}{dl} = (k - l) + l(0 - 1)$$
$$= k - l - l$$
$$= k - 2l$$

For maximum $\frac{dA}{dl} = 0$

$\Rightarrow \quad k - 2l = 0$

$\Rightarrow \quad l = \frac{k}{2}$

Now, $\frac{d^2A}{dl^2} = -2 < 0$

$\therefore$ A is maximum at $l = \frac{k}{2}$

Hence, value of Maximum area

$$A = \frac{k}{2}\left(k - \frac{k}{2}\right)$$
$$= \frac{k}{2}\left(\frac{k}{2}\right)$$
$$= \frac{k^2}{4}.$$

101. The given that, arithmetic mean = 6

$\therefore \quad \frac{4 \times x + 9 \times (x-1)}{x + x - 1} = 6$

$\Rightarrow \quad 4x + 9x - 9 = 6(2x - 1)$

$\Rightarrow \quad 13x - 9 = 12x - 6$

$\Rightarrow \quad 13x - 12x = 9 - 6$

$\Rightarrow \quad x = 3.$

102. Let S be the sample space

Then, $n(S) = 6 \times 6 \times 6 = 216$

Let E = Event of getting no two face have same number *i.e.*, $n(E) = 6 \times 5 \times 4 = 120$

and Let F = Event of getting one of the face have 6 number.

i.e., $n(F) = (1 \times 5 \times 4) \times 3 = 60$

$\therefore \quad n(E \cap F) = 60$

$\therefore \quad p\left(\frac{F}{E}\right) = \frac{p(F \cap E)}{p(E)}$

$$= \frac{\frac{n(F \cap E)}{n(S)}}{\frac{n(E)}{n(S)}}$$

$$= \frac{\frac{60}{216}}{\frac{120}{216}}$$

$$= \frac{60}{120}$$

$$= \frac{1}{2}.$$

103. Given, $P(A \cup B) = \frac{5}{6}$, $P(A \cap B) = \frac{1}{3}$ and P(not A) $= \frac{1}{2}$

$\Rightarrow \quad P(\bar{A}) = \frac{1}{2}$

$\Rightarrow \quad P(A) = 1 - P(\bar{A})$

$$= 1 - \frac{1}{2}$$
$$= \frac{1}{2}$$

$\because P(A \cup B) = P(A) + P(B) - P(A \cap B)$

$\Rightarrow \quad \frac{5}{6} = \frac{1}{2} + P(B) - \frac{1}{3}$

$\Rightarrow \quad \frac{5}{6} = \frac{3-2}{6} + P(B)$

$\Rightarrow \quad \frac{5}{6} = \frac{1}{6} + P(B)$

$\Rightarrow \quad P(B) = \frac{5}{6} - \frac{1}{6}$

$$= \frac{4}{6}$$
$$= \frac{2}{3}$$

(C) is not correct

$$P(A \cup B) > P(A) + P(B)$$

$$\frac{5}{6} > \frac{1}{2} + \frac{2}{3}$$

$$\Rightarrow \quad \frac{5}{6} > \frac{3+4}{6}$$

$$\Rightarrow \quad \frac{5}{6} > \frac{7}{6}$$

It is not correct.

104. Given that, $\Sigma(xi - 2.5) = 50$

and $\quad \Sigma(xi - 3.5) = -50$

$\Rightarrow \quad \Sigma xi - (2.5)n = 50 \quad$ ...(*i*)

$\Rightarrow \quad \Sigma xi - (3.5)n = -50 \quad$ ...(*ii*)

Subtracting equation (*ii*) from equation (*i*), we get,

$$-(2.5)n + (3.5)n = 50 + 50$$

$$\Rightarrow \quad 1n = 100$$

$$\Rightarrow \quad n = 100.$$

105. Given, $\bar{x}_1 = 2M$, $\bar{x}_2 = M$

and $n_1 = n$ and $n_2 = 2n$

$\therefore$ The mean of the combined data set

$$= \frac{n_1\bar{x}_1 + n_2\bar{x}_2}{n_1 + n_2}$$

$$= \frac{n \times 2M + 2n \times M}{n + 2n}$$

$$= \frac{4nM}{3n}$$

$$= \frac{4}{3}M.$$

109. Given, observation,

$-\sqrt{6}, -\sqrt{5}, -\sqrt{4}, -1, 1, \sqrt{4}, \sqrt{5}, \sqrt{6}$

$$\text{Mean} = \frac{-\sqrt{6} - \sqrt{5} - \sqrt{4} - 1 + 1 + \sqrt{4} + \sqrt{5} + \sqrt{6}}{8}$$

$$= \frac{0}{8}$$

$$= 0$$

Now, standard deviation, $\sigma = \sqrt{\dfrac{\Sigma(xi - \bar{x})^2}{n}}$

$$\Rightarrow \sigma = \sqrt{\frac{\left(-\sqrt{6}-0\right)^2 + \left(-\sqrt{5}-0\right)^2 + \left(-\sqrt{4}-0\right)^2 + (-1-0)^2 + (1-0)^2 + \left(\sqrt{4}-0\right)^2 + \left(\sqrt{5}-0\right)^2 + \left(\sqrt{6}-0\right)^2}{8}}$$

$$= \sqrt{\frac{6+5+4+1+1+4+5+6}{8}}$$

$$= \sqrt{\frac{32}{8}} = \sqrt{4} = 2.$$

110. Given that, $\Sigma xi = 20$, $\Sigma x_i^2 = 200$ and $n = 10$

We know that,

$$\text{Co-efficient of variation} = \frac{\sigma}{\bar{x}} \times 100$$

Now, $\quad \text{Mean } (\bar{x}) = \dfrac{\Sigma xi}{n}$

$$= \frac{20}{10}$$

$$= 2$$

and standard deviation,

$$\sigma = \frac{1}{n}\sqrt{n\Sigma x_i^2 - (\Sigma xi)^2}$$

$$= \frac{1}{10}\sqrt{10 \times 200 - (20)^2}$$

$$= \frac{1}{10}\sqrt{2000 - (20)^2}$$

$$= \frac{1}{10}\sqrt{2000 - 400}$$

$$= \frac{1}{10}\sqrt{1600}$$

$$= \frac{1}{10} \times 40$$

$$= 4$$

Hence, co-efficient of variation $= \dfrac{4}{2} \times 100 = 200.$

111. $\because$ February of a leap year = 29 days

29 days = 4 weeks + 1 day

Here, 4 Sunday and 1 extra day,

Extra days, it may be Sunday or Monday or Tuesday or Wednesday or Thursday or Friday or Saturday.

Hence, P(getting 5 Sundays in the February) $= \dfrac{1}{7}$.

112. Total sum of 100 observation = 40 × 100 = 4000 an observation '53' was wrongly read as '83'

$\therefore$ Total sum of correct 100 observation

$$= 4000 - 83 + 53$$

$$= 4000 - 30$$

$$= 3970$$

Hence, correct arithmetic mean

$$= \frac{3970}{100}$$

$$= 39.70.$$

113. Let husband = H and wife = W

Then, $P(H) = \frac{1}{7}$

$\Rightarrow \quad P(\bar{H}) = 1 - \frac{1}{7}$

$= \frac{6}{7}$

and $P(W) = \frac{1}{5}$

$\Rightarrow \quad P(\bar{W}) = 1 - \frac{1}{5}$

$= \frac{4}{5}$

Now, probability of none of them is selected

$= P(\bar{H} \cap \bar{W})$

$= P(\bar{H})P(\bar{W})$

$= \frac{6}{7} \times \frac{4}{5}$

$= \frac{24}{35}$

∴ Probability that at least one of them is selected = 1 – P(None of them is selected)

$= 1 - \frac{24}{35} = \frac{35-24}{35} = \frac{11}{35}$

Hence, at least one of them will be selected.

114. Given that,

Number of gold coins = 15 and the number of counterfeits coins = 6

Then, probability of getting 4 coins are counterfeits

$= \frac{^6C_4}{^{15}C_4}$

$= \frac{\frac{\lfloor 6}{\lfloor 4 \lfloor 6-4}}{\frac{\lfloor 15}{\lfloor 4 \lfloor 15-4}}$

$= \frac{\lfloor 6}{\lfloor 4 \lfloor 2} \times \frac{\lfloor 4 \lfloor 11}{\lfloor 15}$

$= \frac{\lfloor 6}{\lfloor 2} \times \frac{\lfloor 11}{\lfloor 15}$

$= \frac{6 \times 5 \times 4 \times 3 \times \lfloor 2}{\lfloor 2} \times \frac{\lfloor 11}{15 \times 14 \times 13 \times 12 \times \lfloor 11}$

$= \frac{6 \times 5 \times 4 \times 3 \times 1}{15 \times 14 \times 13 \times 12 \times 1}$

$= \frac{6 \times 5}{15 \times 14 \times 13}$

$= \frac{2}{14 \times 13}$

$= \frac{1}{7 \times 13}$

$= \frac{1}{91}.$

115. Here, the number of persons = 2 boys + 2 girls = 4

∴ Probability of getting a committee of 3 persons

$= \frac{^2C_2 \times ^2C_1}{^4C_3}$

$= \frac{1 \times 2}{\frac{\lfloor 4}{\lfloor 3 \lfloor 4-3}}$

$= \frac{2}{\frac{\lfloor 4}{\lfloor 3}}$

$= \frac{2}{4}$

$= \frac{1}{2}.$

116. Here, total number of lottery tickets = 10 and the prime number from 1 to 10 are {2, 3, 5, 7}

Hence, probability of drawing 2 prime number tickets

$= \frac{^4C_2}{^{10}C_2}$

$= \frac{\frac{\lfloor 4}{\lfloor 2 \lfloor 4-2}}{\frac{\lfloor 10}{\lfloor 2 \lfloor 10-2}}$

$= \frac{\frac{\lfloor 4}{\lfloor 2}}{\frac{\lfloor 10}{\lfloor 8}}$

$= \frac{\lfloor 4}{\lfloor 2} \times \frac{\lfloor 8}{\lfloor 10}$

$= \frac{4 \times 3}{10 \times 9}$

$= \frac{2 \times 1}{5 \times 3}$

$= \frac{2}{15}.$

117. Given that, $\bar{x} = 65$, $\bar{y} = 67$

$\sigma_x = 2.5$, $\sigma_y = 3.5$ and $r(x, y) = 0.8$

The equation of regression of y on x is

$$y - \bar{y} = \frac{r\sigma_y}{\sigma_x}(x - \bar{x})$$

$$\Rightarrow \quad y - 67 = 0.8 \times \frac{3.5}{2.5}(x - 65)$$

$$\Rightarrow \quad y - 67 = 0.8 \times \frac{7}{5}(x - 65)$$

$$\Rightarrow \quad y - 67 = \frac{5.6}{5}(x - 65)$$

$$\Rightarrow \quad y - 67 = 1.12\ (x - 65)$$

$$\Rightarrow \quad y - 67 = 1.12x - 1.12 \times 65$$

$$\Rightarrow \quad y = 1.12x - 72.8 + 67$$

$$\Rightarrow \quad y = 1.12x - 5.8.$$

118. Given that, $n = 10$, $P = \frac{1}{5}$, $y = 10 - x$

$$\therefore \quad B(X, n, P) = B\left(X, 10, \frac{1}{5}\right)$$

$$\Rightarrow \quad B(X, n, P) = {}^nC_x P^x(1 - P)^{n-x}$$

$$= {}^{10}C_x\left(\frac{1}{5}\right)^x\left(1 - \frac{1}{5}\right)^{10-x}$$

$$= {}^{10}C_{10-x}\left(\frac{4}{5}\right)^{10-x}\left(\frac{1}{5}\right)^x \quad [\because {}^nC_r = {}^nC_{n-r}]$$

$$= {}^{10}C_y\left(\frac{4}{5}\right)^y\left(\frac{1}{5}\right)^{10-y} \quad [\because y = 10 - x]$$

$$= B(Y, n, P)$$

Where, $n = 10$ and $P = \frac{4}{5}$.

119. Given that,

$P(A) = 0.6$, $P(B) = 0.5$ and $P(A \cap B) = 0.4$

1. $P(\bar{A} \cup B) = 0.9$

$$\because \quad P(\bar{A} \cup B) = 1 - P(A) + P(A \cap B)$$
$$= 1 - 0.6 + 0.4$$
$$= 1 - 0.2$$
$$= 0.8$$

Which is incorrect.

2. $P\left(\frac{\bar{B}}{\bar{A}}\right) = 0.6$

$$\because \quad P\left(\frac{\bar{B}}{\bar{A}}\right) = \frac{P(\bar{B} \cap \bar{A})}{P(\bar{A})}$$

$$= \frac{P(\overline{A \cup B})}{P(\bar{A})}$$

$$= \frac{1 - P(A \cup B)}{1 - P(A)}$$

$$= \frac{1 - [P(A) + P(B) - P(A \cap B)]}{1 - P(A)}$$

$$= \frac{1 - [0.6 + 0.5 - 0.4]}{1 - 0.6}$$

$$= \frac{1 - [1.1 - 0.4]}{0.4}$$

$$= \frac{1 - 0.7}{0.4}$$

$$= \frac{0.3}{0.4}$$

$$= \frac{3}{4}$$

$$= 0.75$$

Which is incorrect.

Hence, neither 1 or 2.

120. Let A bakes X-type of cake, B bakes Y-type of cake and C bakes Z-type of cake.

Then $P(A) = 50\% = \frac{50}{100} = \frac{1}{2}$

$P(B) = 30\% = \frac{30}{100} = \frac{3}{10}$

and $P(C) = 20\% = \frac{20}{100} = \frac{1}{5}$

$P\left(\frac{X}{A}\right) = 0.02$, $P\left(\frac{X}{B}\right) = 0.03$ and $P\left(\frac{X}{C}\right) = 0.05$

According to Baye's theorem,

$$P\left(\frac{A}{X}\right) = \frac{P(A)P\left(\frac{X}{A}\right)}{P(A)P\left(\frac{X}{A}\right) + P(B)P\left(\frac{X}{B}\right) + P(C)P\left(\frac{X}{C}\right)}$$

$$= \frac{\frac{1}{2} \times 0.02}{\frac{1}{2} \times 0.02 + \frac{3}{10} \times 0.03 + \frac{1}{5} \times 0.05}$$

$$= \frac{1.00}{1.00 + 0.90 + 1.00}$$

$$= \frac{1}{2.9}$$

$$= \frac{10}{29}.$$

Previous Papers (Solved)

NATIONAL DEFENCE ACADEMY & NAVAL ACADEMY

NDA & NA – Entrance Exam, 2019 (II)*

PAPER I : GENERAL ABILITY TEST

PART A : ENGLISH LANGUAGE

SYNONYMS

Directions (Qs. No. 1-10): *Each item in this section consists of a sentence with an underlined word followed by four options. Select the option that is **nearest in meaning** to the underlined word and mark your response in your Answer Sheet accordingly.*

1. He is always **anxious**.
A. worried B. dispassionate
C. sluggish D. torpid

2. The poems of Kabir are **ecstatic** in nature.
A. efficacious B. eerie
C. rapturous D. reverential

3. Ravi loves **seclusion**. Therefore, he lives in the mountains.
A. nature B. scripture
C. seafaring D. solitariness

4. Hitler was a **despot**.
A. conservative B. dictator
C. passionate D. monstrous

5. The imagery used in the poem is **vivid**.
A. lively B. inert
C. ebullient D. caustic

6. A human being is always **vulnerable** to other human beings.
A. resilient B. elastic
C. defenceless D. crude

7. His language is political and **vitriolic**.
A. imaginative B. sprightly
C. vivacious D. abusive

8. The Managing Director of the company declared that he is **broke** and there is a need to seek support from the government.
A. bankrupt B. rich
C. making profit D. having liabilities

9. He loves doing **nasty** things.
A. nice B. fastidious
C. foul D. finicky

10. He could not **muster** courage to speak the truth before his friend.
A. injure B. spoil
C. gather D. maim

ANTONYMS

Directions (Qs. No. 11-20): *Each item in this section consists of a sentence with an underlined word followed by four options. Select the option that is **opposite in meaning** to the underlined word and mark your response in your Answer Sheet accordingly.*

11. His conversations are always **absurd**.
A. farcical B. foolish
C. preposterous D. rational

12. The politician was a **dissident**.
A. agitator B. rebel
C. conformist D. revolutionary

13. He wrote an **incisive** article on corruption in politics.
A. vague B. penetrating
C. trenchant D. precise

14. Rakesh is an eccentric **prodigal**.
A. extravagant B. profligate
C. wasteful D. thrifty

15. Friendship is always **reciprocal**.
A. mutual B. one-sided
C. shared D. corresponding

16. The debate was highly **stimulating**.
A. arousing B. invigorating
C. boring D. stirring

17. malaria is **widespread** disease.
A. endemic B. pervasive
C. common D. rare

18. The bill received a **vehement** resistance from the opposition party in the Parliament.

* Exam Held on 17/11/2019

A. animated B. apathetic
C. fervent D. vigorous

19. He has been **obstinate** since his childhood.
A. stubborn B. dogged
C. amenable D. rigid

20. Mahatma Gandhi was one of the most **prominent** leaders of his times.
A. renowned B. distinguishable
C. eminent D. unknown

SPOTTING ERRORS

Directions (Qs. No. 21-30): *Each item in this section has a sentence with three parts labelled A, B and C. Read each sentence to find out whether there is any error in any part and indicate your response in the Answer Sheet against the corresponding letter i.e., A or B or C. If you find no error, your response should be indicated as D.*

21. He had arrived at Cairo (A)/ a few months before (B)/ protests shook the Arab world. (C)/ No Error (D)

22. Most of us who are older competitive runners (A)/ are not able to race anywhere at the same speed (B)/ as we do when we were 30. (C)/ No Error (D)

23. Work hard (A)/ least you do not (B)/ fail. (C)/ No Error (D)

24. The Eastern Ghats are home of 2600 plant species (A)/ and this habitat fragmentation (B)/ can pose a serious threat to endemic plants. (C)/ No Error (D)

25. Turbidity current is a fast-moving current (A)/ that sweeps down submarine canyons, (B)/ carrying sand and mud into the deep sea. (C)/ No Error (D)

26. Every one (A)/ of the boys (B)/ love to ride. (C)/ No Error (D)

27. Neither praise nor blame (A)/ seem (B)/ to affect him. (C)/ No Error (D)

28. Many a man (A)/ has succumbed (B)/ to this temptation. (C)/ No Error (D)

29. A time slot of fifteen minutes (A)/ are allowed (B)/ to each speaker. (C)/ No Error (D)

30. He asked (A)/ whether either of the brothers (B)/ were at home. (C)/ No Error (D)

IDIOMS AND PHRASES

Directions (Qs. No. 31-35): *Given below are some idioms/ phrases followed by four alternative meanings to each. Choose the response A, B, C or D which is the most appropriate expression.*

31. Be over the hill
A. To be on a mountain top
B. To travel in the jungle
C. To be too old to do things
D. To do something in the most complete way

32. Bite your tongue
A. To stop yourself from saying something because it would be better not to
B. To bite off your tongue while eating
C. To feel sorry
D. To ask someone something that you want

33. Turn a blind eye
A. To run away
B. To begin to behave in a more positive manner
C. To change a situation
D. To choose to ignore behaviour that you know is wrong

34. Yellow journalism
A. Paid storytelling
B. Government reports published on yellow coloured papers
C. Writings in newspapers that try to influence people's opinion by using strong language and false information
D. Journalism which agrees completely with the policies of the governments and capitalists

35. To be in seventh heaven
A. To fly in the air
B. To be extremely happy
C. To be completely alone
D. To visit a place which is in the list of the seven wonders of the world

ORDERING OF WORDS IN A SENTENCE

Directions (Qs. No. 36-40): *Each of the following items in this section consists of a sentence, the parts of which have been jumbled. These parts have been labelled P, Q, R and S. Given below each sentence are four sequences namely A, B, C and D. You are required to re-arrange the jumbled parts of the sentence and mark your answer accordingly.*

36. P. closely monitor the situation
Q. by the disturbing allegations
R. we are deeply concerned
S. and will continue to
A. RQSP B. SPQR
C. SPRQ D. PRSQ

37. P. relieve nausea, pain and strees
Q. aromatherapy may also help
R. using lavender oil on their skin
S. but patients are cautioned against
A. RQPS B. SQPR
C. QPSR D. RPSQ

38. P. without any mandate of law
Q. the plea filed through the advocate
R. online is illegal and

S. submitted that the sale of drugs and prescription medicines

A. RQSP B. QSRP
C. QRSP D. PRSQ

39. P. humans and machines have co-existed
Q. dating back to the invention of
R. the potter's wheel in ancient Mesopotamia
S. at the physical level for millennia

A. RSPQ B. QSPR
C. QRPS D. PSQR

40. P. a sell-off as US Treasury yields
Q. surged to multi-year highs
R. on robust economic data
S. global markets also witnessed

A. RSQP B. PQSR
C. QRPS D. SPQR

COMPREHENSION

Directions (Qs. No. 41-45): *In this section, you have a short passage. After the passage, you will find some items based on the passage. First, read the passage and then answer the items based on it. You are required to select your answers based on the contents of the passage and opinion of the author only.*

Studies serve for delight, for ornament, and for ability. Their chief use for delight, is in privateness and retiring; for ornament, is in discourse; and for ability, is in the judgement, and disposition of business. For expert men can execute, and perhaps judge of particulars, one by one; but the general counsels, and the plots and marshalling of affairs, come best from those that are learned. To spend too much time in studies is sloth; to use them too much for ornament, is affectation; to make judgement wholly by their rules, is the humor of a scholar. They perfect nature, and are perfected by experience: for natural abilities are like natural plants, that need pruning, by study; and studies themselves do give forth directions too much at large, except they be bounded in by experience. Crafty men condemn studies, simple men admire them, and wise men use them; for they teach not their own use; but that is a wisdom without them, and above them, won by observation. Read not to contradict and confute; nor to believe and take for granted; nor to find talk and discourse; but to weigh and consider.

41. According to the author, why should one study?
A. To gather information about the world
B. To pass the time in a creative way
C. For pleasure, enhanced capability and holistic growth
D. To become only worldly wise

42. Why does the author not recommend too much of studies?
A. Because it reflects idleness
B. Because it requires too much money
C. Because it is dangerous for the health of the mind
D. Because it makes men crafty

43. According to the author, how can the studies be perfected?

A. By reflection B. By application
C. By conversation D. By experience

44. Which kind of human beings denounce studies?

A. Innocent B. Cunning
C. Stupid D. Wise

45. According to the author, one should read to
A. only argue
B. only believe
C. evaluate and understand
D. preach and believe

FILL IN THE BLANKS

Directions (Qs. No. 46-50): *Each of the following sentences in this section has a blank space and four words or group of words given after the sentence. Select the word or group of words you consider most appropriate for the blank space and indicate your response on the Answer Sheet accordingly.*

46. The Election Commission on Saturday _____ that the Assembly elections in five States will be held from November 12 to December 7.

A. pronounced B. announced
C. promulgated D. issued

47. The victims were fruit vendors and they were going in an auto when they ______ an accident on the way.

A. met with B. ran into
C. experienced D. heard

48. Scores of villagers are ______ a sit-in protest against the construction of a new underpass.

A. performing B. sitting
C. staging D. standing

49. It is common for patients to stop ______ medicine as soon as they start feeling better.

A. eating B. gulping
C. swallowing D. taking

50. A four-year-old girl got a new lease of life after doctors at a hospital ______ a cancerous tumour from one of her kidneys.

A. rejuvenated B. removed
C. displaced D. replaced

PART B : GENERAL KNOWLEDGE

51. A thin disc and a thin ring, both have mass M and radius R. Both rotate about axes through their center of mass and are perpendicular to their surfaces at the same angular velocity. Which of the following is true?

A. The ring has higher kinetic energy
B. The disc has higher kinetic energy
C. The ring and the disc have the same kinetic energy
D. Kinetic energies of both the bodies are zero since they are not in linear motion

52. Let there be an object having some chemicals in it. It starts moving with a uniform velocity v and a chemical reaction starts happening. In this case, which of the following statement/s is/are correct?

1. Chemical reactions happening in the system cannot change the velocity v of the centre of mass of the object.
2. Chemical reactions happening in the system cannot change kinetic energy of the particles inside with respect to the centre of mass of object.

Select the correct answer using the code given below:

A. 1 only B. 2 only
C. Both 1 and 2 D. Neither 1 nor 2

53. In which of the following phenomena do heat waves travel along a straight line with the speed of light?
A. Thermal conduction
B. Thermal convection
C. Thermal radiation
D. Both thermal conduction and radiation

54. Which one of the following statements regarding Ohm's law is ***not*** correct?
A. Ohm's law is an assumption that current through a conductor is always directly proportional to the potential difference applied to it.
B. A conducting device obeys Ohm's law when the resistance of a device is independent of magnitude and polarity of applied potential difference.
C. A conducting material obeys Ohm's law when the resistance of material is independent of the magnitude and direction of applied electric field.
D. All homogeneous materials obey Ohm's law irrespective of whether the field is within range of strong.

55. When a ball bounces off the ground, which of the following changes suddenly?

(Assume no loss of energy to the floor)

A. Its speed B. Its momentum
C. Its kinetic energy D. Its potential energy

56. Which one of the following compounds does ***not*** exhibit a different oxidation number of the same element?
A. Pb_3O_4 B. Fe_3O_4
C. Fe_2O_3 D. Mn_3O_4

57. Which one of the following statements about glass is ***not*** correct?
A. Glass is often said to be a supercooled liquid.
B. Glass has no definite melting point.
C. Soda glass is harder than pyrex glass.
D. Boron is present in pyrex glass.

58. Which one of the following statements is correct?
A. Both boiling and evaporation are surface phenomena.
B. Boiling is a surface phenomenon, but evaporation is a bulk phenomenon.
C. Both boiling and evaporation are bulk phenomena.
D. Boiling is a bulk phenomenon, but evaporation is a surface phenomenon.

59. Which one of the following statements about diamond and graphite is ***not*** correct?
A. Diamond has a tetrahedral structure, whereas graphite has a hexagonal planar structure.
B. Both physical and chemical properties of diamond and graphite are different.
C. Graphite is soft but diamond is hard.
D. Graphite is a good conductor of electricity while diamond is not.

60. The raw materials used for the manufacture of Portland cement are:
A. Lime, silica and sulphur dioxide
B. Lime, silica and carbon dioxide
C. Lime, silica and alumina
D. Lime, silica and boric acid

61. Which one of the following statements about water is ***not*** true?
A. Hydrogen bonds are present in liquid water.
B. Water has a high boiling point.
C. Water has a high heat of fusion.
D. Water is a non-polar molecule.

62. A sample of 'soft soap' contains:
A. Caesium B. Potassium
C. Calcium D. Magnesium

63. If an object moves at a non-zero constant acceleration for a certain interval of time, then the distance it covers in that time:
A. depends on its initial velocity.
B. is independent of its initial velocity.
C. increases linearly with time.
D. depends on its initial displacement.

64. A solid disc and a solid sphere have the same mass and same radius. Which one has the higher moment of inertia about its centre of mass?
A. The disc
B. The sphere
C. Both have the same moment of inertia
D. The information provided is not sufficient to answer the question

65. Two substances of densities ρ_1 and ρ_2 are mixed in equal volume and their relative density is 4. When they are mixed in equal masses, relative density is 3. The

values of ρ_1 and ρ_2 respectively are:
A. 6, 2 B. 3, 5
C. 12, 4 D. 9, 3

66. A car starts from Bengaluru, goes 50 km in a straight line towards south, immediately turns around and returns to Bengaluru. The time taken for this round trip is 2 hours. The magnitude of the average velocity of the car for this round trip:
A. is 0.
B. is 50 km/hr.
C. is 25 km/hr.
D. cannot be calculated without knowing acceleration.

67. "The sum of emf's and potential differences around a closed loop equals zero" is a consequence of:
A. Ohm's law.
B. Conservation of charge.
C. Conservation of momentum.
D. Conservation of energy.

68. A student measures certain lengths using a meter scale having least count equal to 1 mm. Which one of the following measurements is more precise?
A. 0.50 mm B. 29.07 cm
C. 0.925 m D. 910 mm

69. If the work done on the system or by the system is zero, which one of the following statements for a gas kept at a certain temperature is correct?
A. Change in internal energy of the system is equal to flow of heat in or out of the system.
B. Change in internal energy of the system is less than heat transferred.
C. Change in internal energy of the system is more than the heat flow.
D. Cannot be determined.

70. Consider the following part of an electric circuit:

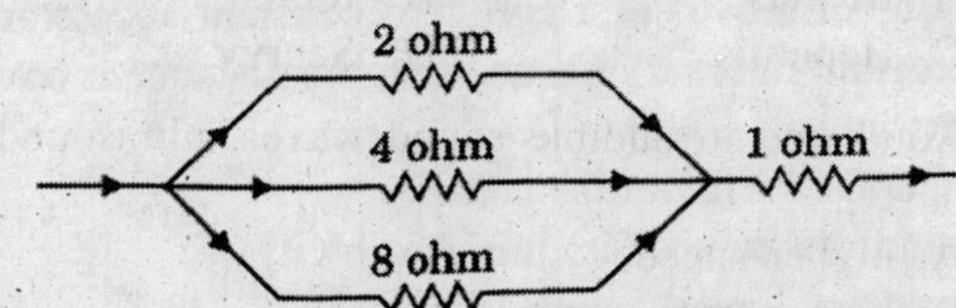

The total electrical resistance in the given part of the electric circuit is:
A. $\frac{15}{8}$ ohm B. $\frac{15}{7}$ ohm
C. 15 ohm D. $\frac{17}{3}$ ohm

71. Which one of the following statements regarding lenses is ***not*** correct?
A. A convex lens produces both real and virtual images.
B. A concave lens produces both real and virtual images.
C. A convex lens can produce images equal, greater and smaller than the size of the object.
D. A concave lens always produces images smaller than the size of the object.

72. 10 g of ice at –10°C is mixed with 10 g of water at 0°C. The amount of heat required to raise the temperature of mixture to 10°C is:
A. 400 cal B. 550 cal
C. 1050 cal D. 1200 cal

73. Which one of the following does ***not*** represent the salt, Calcium carbonate?
A. Lime water B. Limestone
C. Chalk D. Marble

74. Soaps clean surfaces on the principle based on:
A. Viscosity B. Floatation
C. Elasticity D. Surface tension

75. Which one of the following substances is ***not*** a mixture?
A. Tin B. Sea water
C. Soil D. Air

76. Which one of the following is termed as 'Dry ice'?
A. Ice present in ice-cream
B. Solid water at Antarctica
C. Solid state of carbon dioxide
D. Solid water of ionosphere

77. Net movement of water from a dilute to a concentrated solution through a selectively permeable membrane is called:
A. Diffusion B. Dispersion
C. Osmosis D. Absorption

78. Blood is a type of:
A. Epithelial tissue B. Muscular tissue
C. Nervous tissue D. Connective tissue

79. Mitochondria are able to produce their own:
A. Nucleus B. Proteins
C. Chloroplasts D. Digestive enzymes

80. Which one of the following statements is correct?
A. Xylem consists of tracheids, vessels, xylem parenchyma and xylem fibres.
B. Flexibility in plants is due to sclerenchyma.
C. Parenchyma have no intercellular spaces.
D. Xylem consists of sieve plate, sieve tube and companion cells.

81. Who among the following popularized the use of embryological characters in taxonomy?
A. Carl Linnaeus
B. Panchanan Maheshwari
C. Birbal Sahni
D. Bentham and Hooker

82. Water is heated with a coil of resistance R connected to domestic supply. The rise of temperature of water will depend on:
1. Supply voltage

2. Current passing through the coil
3. Time for which voltage is supplied

Select the correct answer from among the following:

A. 1, 2 and 3 B. 1 and 2 only
C. 1 only D. 2 and 3 only

83. A pendulum clock is lifted to a height where the gravitational acceleration has a certain value g. Another pendulum clock of same length but of double the mass of the bob is lifted to another height where the gravitational acceleration is g/2. The time period of the second pendulum would be:

A. $\sqrt{2}$ T B. $\frac{1}{\sqrt{2}}$ T
C. $2\sqrt{2}$ T D. T

84. The loudness of sound depends upon the:
A. velocity of sound waves in the medium.
B. amplitude of the sound waves.
C. frequency of the sound waves.
D. frequency and velocity of the sound waves.

85. Two bodies of mass M each are placed R distance apart. In another system, two bodies of mass 2M each are placed $\frac{R}{2}$ distance apart. If F be the gravitational force between the bodies in the first system, then the gravitational force between the bodies in the second system will be

A. 16 F B. 1 F
C. 4 F D. None of the above

86. Light rays move in straight lines. But through an optical fibre, they can move in any type of zigzag path because:
A. the holes through the fibre are extremely fine.
B. light rays are absorbed at the entry end and relieved at the exit end of the fibre.
C. scattering of light occurs inside the fibre.
D. successive total internal reflections occur as a ray moves through the fibre.

87. Which one of the following statements regarding cathode rays in *not* correct?
A. Cathode ray particles are electrons.
B. Cathode ray particles start from anode and move towards cathode.
C. In the absence of electrical and magnetic fields, cathode rays travel in straight lines.
D. Television picture tubes are cathode ray tubes.

88. A very large volume of hydrogen can be acco-mmodated by making:
A. non-metallic hydrides.
B. hydrogen peroxide.
C. non-stoichiometric hydrides.
D. alkali metal hydrides.

89. Which one of the following is *not* a monatomic element?
A. Copper B. Helium
C. Iodine D. Barium

90. Which one of the following represents the correct order of electron releasing tendency of metals?
A. Zn > Cu > Ag B. Ag > Cu > Zn
C. Cu > Zn > Ag D. Cu > Ag > Zn

91. Which one of the following is the major constituent of biogas?
A. Carbon dioxide B. Nitrous oxide
C. Methane D. Oxygen

92. Thyroid gland produces a hormone called "Thyroxine" which:
A. controls blood glucose levels.
B. controls ovulation.
C. controls metabolic rate.
D. maintains pregnancy.

93. Which one of the following is a bacterium that causes disease in the human body?
A. *Varicella zoster*
B. *Trypanosoma gambiense*
C. *Salmonella typhi*
D. *Plasmodium falciparum*

94. Which one of the following statements regarding viruses is *not* true?
A. Viruses need living cells to reproduce.
B. All viruses are parasites.
C. Viruses can synthesize their food through photosynthesis.
D. Viruses are similar to chemical substances outside the host.

95. Which one of the following diseases may be caused by the deficiency of vitamin C?
A. Rickets B. Rabies
C. Hepatitis D. Scurvy

96. Compared to audible sound waves, ultrasound waves have:
A. higher speed.
B. higher frequency.
C. longer wavelength.
D. both higher speed and frequency.

97. A rigid body of mass 2 kg is dropped from a stationary ballon kept at a height of 50 m from the ground. The speed of the body when it just touches the ground and the total energy when it is dropped from the balloon are respectively:

(acceleration due to gravity = 9.8 m/s^2)

A. 980 ms^{-1} and 980 J
B. $\sqrt{980}$ ms^{-1} and $\sqrt{980}$ J
C. 980 ms^{-1} and $\sqrt{980}$ J
D. $\sqrt{980}$ ms^{-1} and 980 J

98. The temperature of a place on one sunny day is 113 in Fahrenheit scale. The Kelvin scale reading of this temperature will be:

A. 318 K B. 45 K
C. 62.8 K D. 335.8 K

99. Radiations coming from the Sun are mostly in the form of:

A. light only.
B. light and long wavelength infrared.
C. light and short wavelength infrared.
D. both short and long wavelength infrared.

100. Which of the following are the characteristics of electromagnetic waves?

1. They are elastic waves.
2. They can also move in vacuum.
3. They have electric and magnetic compon-ents which are mutually perpendicular.
4. They move with a speed equal to 3 lakh meters per second.

Select the correct answer using the code given below:

A. 1, 2, 3 and 4 B. 1, 2 and 4 only
C. 2 and 3 only D. 3 and 4 only

101. Which one of the following is a non-metallic mineral?

A. Iron B. Mica
C. Copper D. Bauxite

102. Which one of the following is a Rabi crop in the Northern States of India?

A. Rice B. Bajra
C. Barley D. Ragi

103. The rivers of North-West Europe are good examples of:

A. parallel pattern of drainage.
B. radial pattern of drainage.
C. barbed pattern of drainage.
D. trellis pattern of drainage.

104. Which one of the following ocean currents is a cold current?

A. South Atlantic Drift
B. Mozambique Current
C. East Australian Current
D. Caribbean Current

105. Paradeep Port is located on the delta of river:

A. Rihand B. Ganga
C. Mahanadi D. Baitarani

106. Which one of the following hypothesis/theory explains the origin of the universe?

A. Nebular hypothesis B. Binary theory
C. Big Bang theory D. Planetesimal hypothesis

107. Which among the following struggles, based on Gandhi's philosophy of Satyagraha, involved the industrial working class?

A. Champaran B. Kheda
C. Ahmedabad D. Bardoli

108. Consider the following statements related to the Virashaiva tradition in Karnataka:

1. The Virashaiva movement was led by a Brahmana named Basavanna, a minister in the court of the Kalachuri ruler in the twelfth century.
2. The Virashaivas encouraged practices, approved by the Dharmashastras, like post-puberty marriages and remarriage of widows.

Which of the statement/s given above is/are correct?

A. 1 only B. 2 only
C. Both 1 and 2 D. Neither 1 nor 2

109. Consider the following statements related to Wellesley's administration:

1. In the six years of Wellesley's adminis-tration, the army accounted for 42.5 per cent of the Company's total expenditure.
2. Wellesley's administrative measures were restricted to the affairs of the Company and had nothing to do with the commerical and military affairs of the Indian ruling families.

Which of the statement/s given above is/are correct?

A. 1 only B. 2 only
C. Both 1 and 2 D. Neither 1 nor 2

110. Consider the following statements concerning the Russian Revolution:

1. The Bolsheviks believed that in a repressive society like Tsarist Russia, the party should be disciplined and should control the number of its members.
2. The Mensheviks believed that the party should be opened to all (as in Germany).

Which of the statement/s given above is/are correct?

A. 1 only B. 2 only
C. Both 1 and 2 D. Neither 1 nor 2

111. Which of the following was/were among the decisions taken by the First Continental Congress held in Philadelphia in September 1774?

1. It rejected a plan for a colonial union under the British authority.
2. It drew up a statement of grievances.
3. It agreed upon a scheme to stop trade between the Colonies and England.

Select the correct answer using the code given below:

A. 1 and 3 only B. 2 only
C. 1 and 2 only D. 1, 2 and 3

112. Which one of the following land territories of Indonesia is ***not*** touched by the Equator?

A. Sumatra B. Sulawesi
C. Java D. Kalimantan

113. Which one of the following sedimentary rocks is organically formed?
A. Shale B. Chert
C. Halite D. Chalk

114. According to the Koppen climatic classification, the letter code Cfa denotes:
A. Tropical wet climate.
B. Humid subtropical climate.
C. Tundra climate.
D. Tropical wet and dry climate.

115. In which one of the following folds is the axial plane found to be virtually horizontal?
A. Isoclinal B. Anticlinal
C. Recumbent D. Monoclinal

116. How many Ramsar conservation sites have been enlisted from India so far?
A. 12 B. 16
C. 27 D. 62

117. The Munda language group belongs to which family?
A. Austric B. Dravidian
C. Sino-Tibetan D. Indo-European

118. Which one of the following statements about the Suez Canal is ***not*** correct?
A. The Suez Canal was constructed in 1869.
B. It links the Mediterranean Sea and the Red Sea.
C. It has a six lock system and ships cross the different levels through these locks.
D. It has given Europe a new gateway to the Indian Ocean.

119. Which among the following statements is ***not*** correct about the Reign of Terror?
A. The Jacobins dashed out the Girondists with the help of sans-culottes.
B. The Jacobins were in league with the French clergy.
C. The arrest for anti-revolutionary activities was by law restricted to the political class.
D. The Reign of Terror came to an end with the execution of Robespierre by guillotine in July 1794.

120. Who among the following was the first Indian to qualify for the Indian Civil Service?
A. Satyendranath Tagore
B. Surendranath Banerjee
C. R.C. Dutt
D. Subhas Chandra Bose

121. Which among the following was/were among the factors for England to experience the Industrial Revolution first?
1. The scientific inventions had paved the way for Industrial Revolution.
2. It had favourable social and political structures in place.
3. Navigable rivers had made inland transport easier.
4. It had seen the ascendancy of capitalist practices.

Select the correct answer using the code given below:
A. 1 and 3 only B. 1, 3 and 4 only
C. 4 only D. 1, 2, 3 and 4

122. Article 46 of the Constitution of India refers to the promotion of educational and economic interests of:
A. religious minorities.
B. Scheduled Castes, Scheduled Tribes and other weaker sections.
C. displaced persons from large irrigation projects.
D. the economically deprived.

123. Who was the Education Minister in the first Cabinet of independent India?
A. Sarvepalli Radhakrishnan
B. Sardar Vallabhbhai Patel
C. Maulana Abul Kalam Azad
D. Acharya Narendra Dev

124. Who among the following died in exile?
A. Rani Laxmibai B. Bahadur Shah Zafar
C. Tantia Tope D. Nana Saheb

125. The normal lapse rate of temperature of Earth's atmosphere drops to 0°C at the:
A. upper part of ionosphere.
B. upper boundary of the tropopause.
C. lower part of mesosphere.
D. upper boundary of stratopause.

126. The headquarters of National Research Laboratory for Conservation of Cultural Property (NRLC) is located at:
A. New Delhi B. Lucknow
C. Kolkata D. Bhopal

127. Loktak lake is situated in the State of:
A. Sikkim B. Manipur
C. Odisha D. Mizoram

128. Stalactite, stalagmite and pillars are the depositional landforms of:
A. running water B. wind
C. glacier D. underground water

129. A deep valley characterized by steep step-like slope is known as:
A. U-shaped valley B. Blind valley
C. Gorge D. Canyon

130. Which one of the following is a major plate?
A. Pacific Plate B. Cocos Plate
C. Arabian Plate D. Philippine Plate

131. Lithosphere consists of:
A. upper and lower mantle.
B. crust and core.
C. crust and uppermost solid mantle.
D. mantle and core.

132. The principal component(s) of Nehru-Mahalanobis strategy of economic development was/were:

1. Restructuring economic dependency on metropolitan capitalism into independent economic development.
2. Transition from semi-feudal agriculture to capitalist farming.

Select the correct answer using the code given below:

A. 1 only B. 2 only
C. Both 1 and 2 D. Neither 1 nor 2

133. The provisions of the Fifth Schedule of the Constitution of India shall ***not*** apply to the administration and control of the Scheduled Areas and Scheduled Tribes in:

1. Chhattisgarh, Jharkhand and Odisha
2. Assam and Tripura
3. Meghalaya and Mizoram

Select the correct answer using the code given below:

A. 1 only B. 1 and 2 only
C. 2 and 3 only D. 1, 2 and 3

134. Consider the following statements related to Dayanand's idea of social reform:

1. Dayanand's reform envisaged a social order, where different castes performed functions suitable to their status determined by merit.
2. Dayanand's 'robust Vedic counterpart' challenged the masculine West that had enslaved the Aryavarta.

Which of the statement/s given above is/are correct?

A. 1 only B. 2 only
C. Both 1 and 2 D. Neither 1 nor 2

135. Consider the following statements concerning the American War of Independence:

1. The Americans raised the slogan, 'No taxation without representation'.
2. The American merchants resorted to the boycott of the British products.

Select the correct answer using the code given below:

A. 1 only B. 2 only
C. Both 1 and 2 D. Neither 1 nor 2

136. The first UDAY (Utkrisht Double Decker Air-Conditioned Yatri) Express train runs between:

A. Delhi and Kalka
B. Bengaluru and Coimbatore
C. Chennai and Visakhapatnam
D. Chennai and Bengaluru

137. Who among the following were selected for the Rajiv Gandhi Khel Ratna Award 2019?

A. Vijay Kumar and Yogeshwar Dutt
B. Sakshi Malik and Jitu Rai
C. Virat Kohli and Mirabai Chanu
D. Bajrang Punia and Deepa Malik

138. Betel leaf of which one of the following States has been accorded a GI tag recently?

A. Andhra Pradesh B. Madhya Pradesh
C. Kerala D. Mizoram

139. SAMARTH is a flagship skill development scheme of which one of the following Ministries?

A. Ministry of Textiles
B. Ministry of Agriculture and Farmers Welfare
C. Ministry of Skill Development and Entrepr-eneurship
D. Ministry of Human Resource Development

140. CORAS is a separate Commando Unit of:

A. National Security Guard
B. Central Industrial Security Force
C. Railway Protection Force
D. Central Reserve Police Force

141. Which one of the following statements is ***not*** true about Ijarah system?

A. It was a system of revenue farming.
B. It encouraged the role of middlemen.
C. Under this system, land revenue was fixed for the peasant.
D. The ijaradar paid a fixed amount to the State treasury.

142. During the Swadeshi movement, a National College was started in Calcutta under the princi-palship of:

A. Rabindranath Tagore
B. Aurobindo Ghosh
C. Rajani Kant Sen
D. Syed Abu Mohammad

143. The ruins of Vijayanagara (Hampi) were brought to public light in the year 1800 by the following British surveyor and engineer:

A. James Prinsep B. Colin Mackenzie
C. James Rennell D. Charles Metcalfe

144. Which country among the following was ***not*** a part of the Third Coalition against Napoleon?

A. Russia B. Prussia
C. Sweden D. France

145. Which one of the following pairs of travellers and their nationality is ***not correctly matched?***

A. Ibn Battuta – Moroccan
B. Duarte Barbosa – Portuguese
C. Jean Baptiste Tavernier – Dutch
D. Niccolao Manucci – Venetian

146. World Humanitarian Day is celebrated on:

A. 26th June B. 17th July
C. 19th August D. 27th September

147. Which one of the following is the name given to the lander of Chandrayaan-2?

A. Vigyan B. Anusandhan
C. Pragyan D. Vikram

148. Along with Pranab Mukherjee, how many more persons were conferred the Bharat Ratna Award in the year 2019?

A. One B. Two
C. Three D. Four

149. Aishwarya Pissay excels in which one of the following sports?
A. Badminton B. Boxing
C. Motorsports D. Chess

150. Which one of the following films was adjudged as the Best Feature Film in the 66th National Film Awards?
A. Bulbul Can Sing B. Hellaro
C. Badhaai Ho D. Uri

PAPER II : MATHEMATICS

1. If both p and q belong to the set $\{1, 2, 3, 4\}$, then how many equations of the form $px^2 + qx + 1 = 0$ will have real roots?
A. 12 B. 10
C. 7 D. 6

2. What is the value of
$1 - 2 + 3 - 4 + 5 - \ldots + 101$?
A. 51 B. 55
C. 110 D. 111

3. If A, B and C are subsets of a given set, then which one of the following relations is ***not*** correct?
A. $A \cup (A \cap B) = A \cup B$
B. $A \cap (A \cup B) = A$
C. $(A \cap B) \cup C = (A \cup C) \cap (B \cup C)$
D. $(A \cup B) \cap C = (A \cap C) \cup (B \cap C)$

4. If the sum of first n terms of a series is $(n + 12)$, then what is its third term?
A. 1 B. 2
C. 3 D. 4

5. What is the value of k for which the sum of the squares of the roots of $2x^2 - 2(k - 2)x - (k + 1) = 0$ is minimum?
A. -1 B. 1
C. $\frac{3}{2}$ D. 2

6. If the roots of the equation
$a(b - c)x^2 + b(c - a)x + c(a - b) = 0$
are equal, then which one of the following is correct?
A. a, b and c are in AP
B. a, b and c are in GP
C. a, b and c are in HP
D. a, b and c do not follow any regular pattern

7. If $|x^2 - 3x + 2| > x^2 - 3x + 2$, then which one of the following is correct?
A. $x \leq 1$ or $x \geq 2$
B. $1 \leq x \leq 2$
C. $1 < x < 2$
D. x is any real value except 3 and 4

8. A geometric progression (GP) consists of 200 terms. If the sum of odd terms of the GP is m, and the sum of even terms of the GP is n, then what is its common ratio?
A. m/n B. n/m
C. $m + (n/m)$ D. $n + (m/n)$

9. If a set A contains 3 elements and another set B contains 6 elements, then what is the minimum number of elements that $(A \cup B)$ can have?
A. 3 B. 6
C. 8 D. 9

10. What is the number of diagonals of an octagon?
A. 48 B. 40
C. 28 D. 20

11. What is the value of the determinant
$$\begin{vmatrix} 1! & 2! & 3! \\ 2! & 3! & 4! \\ 3! & 4! & 5! \end{vmatrix}?$$
A. 0 B. 12
C. 24 D. 36

12. What are the values of x that satisfy the equation
$$\begin{vmatrix} x & 0 & 2 \\ 2x & 2 & 1 \\ 1 & 1 & 1 \end{vmatrix} + \begin{vmatrix} 3x & 0 & 2 \\ x^2 & 2 & 1 \\ 0 & 1 & 1 \end{vmatrix} = 0?$$
A. $-2 \pm \sqrt{3}$ B. $-1 \pm \sqrt{3}$
C. $-1 \pm \sqrt{6}$ D. $-2 \pm \sqrt{6}$

13. If $x + a + b + c = 0$, then what is the value of
$$\begin{vmatrix} x+a & b & c \\ a & x+b & c \\ a & b & x+c \end{vmatrix}?$$
A. 0
B. $(a + b + c)^2$
C. $a^2 + b^2 + c^2$
D. $a + b + c - 2$

14. If $A = \begin{bmatrix} 1 & -1 \\ -1 & 1 \end{bmatrix}$, then the expression $A^3 - 2A^2$ is:
A. a null matrix B. an identity matrix
C. equal to A D. equal to $-A$

15. Let m and $n (m < n)$ be the roots of the equation $x^2 - 16x + 39 = 0$. If four terms p, q, r and s are inserted between m and n to form an AP, then what is the value of $p + q + r + s$?
A. 29 B. 30
C. 32 D. 35

16. Under which one of the following conditions will the quadratic equation $x^2 + mx + 2 = 0$ always have real roots?

A. $2\sqrt{3} \le m^2 < 8$ B. $\sqrt{3} \le m^2 < 4$
C. $m^2 \ge 8$ D. $m^2 \le \sqrt{3}$

17. What is the value of

$$\left[\frac{i+\sqrt{3}}{2}\right]^{2019} + \left[\frac{i-\sqrt{3}}{2}\right]^{2019} ?$$

A. 1 B. –1
C. $2i$ D. $-2i$

18. If α and β are the roots of $x^2 + x + 1 = 0$, then what is $\sum_{j=0}^{3}\left(\alpha^j + \beta^j\right)$ equal to?

A. 8 B. 6
C. 4 D. 2

19. In a school, 50% students play cricket and 40% play football. If 10% of students play both the games, then what per cent of students play neither cricket nor football?

A. 10% B. 15%
C. 20% D. 25%

20. If $A = \{x : 0 \le x \le 2\}$ and $B = \{y; y \text{ is a prime number}\}$, then what is $A \cap B$ equal to?

A. ∅ B. {1}
C. {2} D. {1, 2}

21. If $x = 1 + i$, then what is the value of $x^6 + x^4 + x^2 + 1$?

A. $6i - 3$ B. $-6i + 3$
C. $-6i - 3$ D. $6i + 3$

22. What is the value of

$$2+\cfrac{1}{2+\cfrac{1}{2+\cfrac{1}{2+\ldots\infty}}} ?$$

A. $\sqrt{2}-1$ B. $\sqrt{2}+1$
C. 3 D. 4

23. If $P(n, r) = 2520$ and $C(n, r) = 21$, then what is the value of $C(n + 1, r + 1)$?

A. 7 B. 14
C. 28 D. 56

24. How many terms are there in the expansion of $(1 + 2x + x^2)^5 + (1 + 4y + 4y^2)^5$?

A. 12 B. 20
C. 21 D. 22

25. If the middle term in the expansion of $\left(x^2 + \frac{1}{x}\right)^{2n}$ is $184756x^{10}$, then what is the value of n?

A. 10 B. 8
C. 5 D. 4

26. If $A = \begin{pmatrix} 1 & 2 \\ 2 & 3 \\ 3 & 4 \end{pmatrix}$ and $B = \begin{pmatrix} 1 & 2 \\ 2 & 1 \end{pmatrix}$, then which one of the following is correct?

A. Both AB and BA exist
B. Neither AB nor BA exists
C. AB exists but BA does not exist
D. AB does not exist but BA exists

27. If $n!$ has 17 zeros, then what is the value of n?

A. 95
B. 85
C. 80
D. No such value of n exists

28. Let $A \cup B = \{x | (x - a)(x - b) > 0, \text{ where } a < b\}$. What are A and B equal to?

A. $A = \{x | x > a\}$ and $B = \{x | x > b\}$
B. $A = \{x | x < a\}$ and $B = \{x | x > b\}$
C. $A = \{x | x < a\}$ and $B = \{x | x < b\}$
D. $A = \{x | x > a\}$ and $B = \{x | x < b\}$

29. If the constant term in the expansion of $\left(\sqrt{x} - \frac{k}{x^2}\right)^{10}$ is 405, then what can be the values of k?

A. ±2 B. ±3
C. ±5 D. ±9

30. What is $C(47, 4) + C(51, 53) + C(50, 3) + C(49, 3) + C(48, 3) + C(47, 3)$ equal to?

A. C(47, 4) B. C(52, 5)
C. C(52, 4) D. C(47, 5)

31. Let a, b, c be in AP and $k \ne 0$ be a real number. Which of the following are correct?

1. ka, kb, kc are in AP.
2. $k - a, k - b, k - c$ are in AP
3. $\frac{a}{k}, \frac{b}{k}, \frac{c}{k}$ are in AP

Select the correct answer using the code given below:

A. 1 and 2 only
B. 2 and 3 only
C. 1 and 3 only
D. 1, 2 and 3

32. How many two-digit numbers are divisible by 4?

A. 21 B. 22
C. 24 D. 25

33. Let S_n be the sum of the first n terms of an AP. If $S_{2n} = 3n + 14n^2$, then what is the common difference?

A. 5 B. 6
C. 7 D. 9

34. If 3rd, 8th and 13th terms of a GP are p, q and r respectively, then which one of the following is correct?

A. $q^2 = pr$ B. $r^2 = pq$
C. $pqr = 1$ D. $2q = p + r$

35. What is the solution of $x \le 4$, $y \ge 0$ and $x \le -4$, $y \le 0$?

A. $x \ge -4$, $y \le 0$ B. $x \le 4$, $y \ge 0$
C. $x \le -4$, $y = 0$ D. $x \ge -4$, $y = 0$

36. If $x^{\log_7 x} > 7$ where $x > 0$, then which one of the following is correct?

A. $x \in (0, \infty)$ B. $x \in \left(\frac{1}{7}, 7\right)$
C. $x \in \left(0, \frac{1}{7}\right) \cup (7, \infty)$ D. $x \in \left(\frac{1}{7}, 0\right)$

37. How many real roots does the equation $x^2 + 3|x| + 2 = 0$ have?

A. Zero B. One
C. Two D. Four

38. Consider the following statements in respect of the quadratic equation

$$4(x - p)(x - q) - r^2 = 0,$$

where p, q and r are real numbers:

1. The roots are real
2. The roots are equal if $p = q$ and $r = 0$

Which of the above statements is/are correct?

A. 1 only B. 2 only
C. Both 1 and 2 D. Neither 1 nor 2

39. Let S = {2, 4, 6, 8, ..., 20}. What is the maximum number of subsets does S have?

A. 10 B. 20
C. 512 D. 1024

40. A binary number is represented by $(cdccddcccddd)_2$, where $c > d$. What is its decimal equivalent?

A. 1848 B. 2048
C. 2842 D. 2872

41. If cosec $\theta = \frac{29}{21}$ where $0 < \theta < 90°$, then what is the value of $4 \sec\theta + 4 \tan\theta$?

A. 5 B. 10
C. 15 D. 20

42. Consider the following statements:

1. $\cos\theta + \sec\theta$ can never be equal to 1.5.
2. $\tan\theta + \cot\theta$ can never be less than 2.

Which of the above statements is/are correct?

A. 1 only B. 2 only
C. Both 1 and 2 D. Neither 1 nor 2

43. A ladder 9 m long reaches a point 9 m below the top of a vertical flagstaff. From the foot of the ladder, the elevation of the flagstaff is 60°. What is the height of the flagstaff?

A. 9 m B. 10.5 m
C. 13.5 m D. 15 m

44. What is the length of the chord of a unit circle which subtends an angle θ at the centre?

A. $\sin\left(\frac{\theta}{2}\right)$ B. $\cos\left(\frac{\theta}{2}\right)$
C. $2\sin\left(\frac{\theta}{2}\right)$ D. $2\cos\left(\frac{\theta}{2}\right)$

45. What is $\tan\left\{2\tan^{-1}\left(\frac{1}{3}\right)\right\}$ equal to?

A. $\frac{2}{3}$ B. $\frac{3}{4}$
C. $\frac{3}{8}$ D. $\frac{1}{9}$

46. What is the scalar projection of $\vec{a} = \hat{i} - 2\hat{j} + \hat{k}$ on $\vec{b} = 4\hat{i} - 4\hat{j} + 7\hat{k}$?

A. $\frac{\sqrt{6}}{9}$ B. $\frac{19}{9}$
C. $\frac{9}{19}$ D. $\frac{\sqrt{6}}{19}$

47. If the magnitude of the sum of two non-zero vectors is equal to magnitude of their difference, then which one of the following is correct?

A. The vectors are parallel
B. The vectors are perpendicular
C. The vectors are anti-parallel
D. The vectors must be unit vectors

48. Consider the following equations for two vectors $\vec{a}$ and $\vec{b}$.

1. $(\vec{a} + \vec{b}) \cdot (\vec{a} - \vec{b}) = |\vec{a}|^2 - |\vec{b}|^2$
2. $(|\vec{a} + \vec{b}|)(|\vec{a} - \vec{b}|) = |\vec{a}|^2 - |\vec{b}|^2$
3. $|\vec{a} \cdot \vec{b}| + |\vec{a} \times \vec{b}| = |\vec{a}|^2 |\vec{b}|^2$

Which of the above statements are correct?

A. 1, 2 and 3 B. 1 and 2 only
C. 1 and 3 only D. 2 and 3 only

49. Consider the following statements:

1. The magnitude of $\vec{a} \times \vec{b}$ is same as the area of a triangle with sides $\vec{a}$ and $\vec{b}$
2. If $\vec{a} \times \vec{b} = \vec{0}$ where $\vec{a} \ne 0, \vec{b} \ne \vec{0}$, then $\vec{a} = \lambda\vec{b}$

Which of the above statements is/are correct?

A. 1 only
B. 2 only
C. Both 1 and 2
D. Neither 1 nor 2

50. If $\vec{a}$ and $\vec{b}$ are unit vectors and θ is the angle between them, then what is $\sin^2\left(\frac{\theta}{2}\right)$ equal to?

A. $\frac{|\vec{a}+\vec{b}|^2}{4}$
B. $\frac{|\vec{a}-\vec{b}|^2}{4}$
C. $\frac{|\vec{a}+\vec{b}|^2}{2}$
D. $\frac{|\vec{a}-\vec{b}|^2}{2}$

51. The equation $ax + by + c = 0$ represents a straight line:

A. for all real numbers a, b and c
B. only when $a \neq 0$
C. only when $b \neq 0$
D. only when at least one of a and b is non-zero

52. What is the angle between the lines $x \cos \alpha + y \sin \alpha = a$ and $x \sin \beta - y \cos \beta = a$?

A. $\beta - \alpha$
B. $\pi + \beta - \alpha$
C. $\frac{(\pi+2\beta+2\alpha)}{2}$
D. $\frac{(\pi-2\beta+2\alpha)}{2}$

53. What is the distance betwen the points P($m \cos 2\alpha$, $m \sin 2\alpha$) and Q($m \cos 2\beta$, $m \sin 2\beta$)?

A. $|2m \sin (\alpha - \beta)|$
B. $|2m \cos (\alpha - \beta)|$
C. $|m \sin (2\alpha - 2\beta)|$
D. $|m \sin (2\alpha - 2\beta)|$

54. An equilateral triangle has one vertex at (–1, –1) and another vertex at $(-\sqrt{3}, \sqrt{3})$. The third vertex may lie on

A. $(-\sqrt{2}, \sqrt{2})$
B. $(\sqrt{2}, -\sqrt{2})$
C. (1, 1)
D. (1, –1)

55. If the angle between the lines joining the end points of minor axis of the ellipse $\frac{x^2}{a^2}+\frac{y^2}{b^2}=1$ with one of its foci is $\frac{\pi}{2}$, then what is the eccentricity of the ellipse?

A. $\frac{1}{2}$
B. $\frac{1}{\sqrt{2}}$
C. $\frac{\sqrt{3}}{2}$
D. $\frac{1}{2\sqrt{2}}$

56. A point on a line has coordinates $(p + 1, p - 3, \sqrt{2}p)$ where p is any real number. What are the direction cosines of the line?

A. $\frac{1}{2}, \frac{1}{2}, \frac{1}{\sqrt{2}}$
B. $\frac{1}{\sqrt{2}}, \frac{1}{2}, \frac{1}{2}$
C. $\frac{1}{\sqrt{2}}, \frac{1}{2}, -\frac{1}{2}$
D. Cannot be determined due to insufficient data

57. A point on the line $\frac{x-1}{1}=\frac{y-3}{2}=\frac{z+2}{7}$ has coordinates:

A. (3, 5, 4)
B. (2, 5, 5)
C. (–1, –1, 5)
D. (2, –1, 0)

58. If the line $\frac{x-4}{1}=\frac{y-2}{1}=\frac{z-k}{2}$ lies on the plane $2x - 4y + z = 7$, then what is the value of k?

A. 2
B. 3
C. 5
D. 7

59. A straight line passes through the point (1, 1, 1) makes an angle 60° with the positive direction of z-axis, and the cosine of the angles made by it with the positive directions of the y-axis and the x-axis are in the ratio $\sqrt{3}:1$. What is the acute angle between the two possible positions of the line?

A. 90°
B. 60°
C. 45°
D. 30°

60. If the points (x, y, –3), (2, 0, –1) and (4, 2, 3) lie on a straight line, then what are the values of x and y respectively?

A. 1, –1
B. –1, 1
C. 0, 2
D. 3, 4

61. What is the minimum value of

$$\frac{a^2}{\cos^2 x}+\frac{b^2}{\sin^2 x}$$ where $a > 0$ and $b > 0$?

A. $(a + b)^2$
B. $(a - b)^2$
C. $a^2 + b^2$
D. $|a^2 + b^2|$

62. If the angles of a triangle ABC are in AP and $b : c = \sqrt{3}:\sqrt{2}$, then what is the measure of angle A?

A. 30°
B. 45°
C. 60°
D. 75°

63. If tan A – tan B = x and cot B – cot A = y, then what is the value of cot (A – B)?

A. $\frac{1}{x}+\frac{1}{y}$
B. $\frac{1}{y}-\frac{1}{x}$
C. $\frac{xy}{x+y}$
D. $1+\frac{1}{xy}$

64. What is $\sin (\alpha + \beta) - 2 \sin \alpha \cos \beta + \sin (\alpha - \beta)$ equal to?

A. 0
B. $2 \sin \alpha$
C. $2 \sin \beta$
D. $\sin \alpha + \sin \beta$

65. If 2 tan A = 3 tan B = 1, then what is tan(A – B) equal to?
A. $\frac{1}{5}$ B. $\frac{1}{6}$
C. $\frac{1}{7}$ D. $\frac{1}{9}$

66. What is cos 80° + cos 40° – cos 20° equal to?
A. 2 B. 1
C. 0 D. –19

67. If angle C of a triangle ABC is a right angle, then what is tan A + tan B equal to?
A. $\frac{a^2-b^2}{ab}$ B. $\frac{a^2}{bc}$
C. $\frac{b^2}{ca}$ D. $\frac{c^2}{ab}$

68. What is $\cot\left(\frac{A}{2}\right)-\tan\left(\frac{A}{2}\right)$ equal to?
A. tan A B. cot A
C. 2 tan A D. 2 cot A

69. What is cot A + cosec A equal to?
A. $\tan\left(\frac{A}{2}\right)$ B. $\cot\left(\frac{A}{2}\right)$
C. $2\tan\left(\frac{A}{2}\right)$ D. $2\cot\left(\frac{A}{2}\right)$

70. What is tan 25° tan 15° + tan 15° tan 50° + tan 25° tan 50° equal to?
A. 0 B. 1
C. 2 D. 4

71. What is the area of the region bounded by $|x| < 5$, $y = 0$ and $y = 8$?
A. 40 square units B. 80 square units
C. 120 square units D. 160 square units

72. Consider the following statements in respect of the function $f(x) = \sin\left(\frac{1}{x}\right)$ for $x \neq 0$ and $f(0) = 0$:
1. $\lim_{x\to 0} f(x)$ exists
2. $f(x)$ is continuous at $x = 0$

Which of the above statements is/are correct?
A. 1 only B. 2 only
C. Both 1 and 2 D. Neither 1 nor 2

73. What is the value of $\lim_{x\to 0}\frac{\sin x^\circ}{\tan 3x^\circ}$?
A. $\frac{1}{4}$ B. $\frac{1}{3}$
C. $\frac{1}{2}$ D. 1

74. What is the degree of the differential equation
$$\frac{d^3y}{dx^3}+\left(\frac{dy}{dx}\right)^2-x^2\left(\frac{d^4y}{dx^4}\right)=0?$$
A. 1 B. 2
C. 3 D. 4

75. Which one of the following is the second degree polynomial function $f(x)$ where $f(0) = 5$, $f(-1) = 10$ and $f(1) = 6$?
A. $5x^2 - 2x + 5$ B. $3x^2 - 2x - 5$
C. $3x^2 - 2x + 5$ D. $3x^2 - 10x + 5$

Directions (Q. Nos. 76 to 78): *Read the following information and answer the three items that follow:*

A curve $y = me^{mx}$ where $m > 0$ intersects y-axis at a point P.

76. What is the slope of the curve at the point of intersection P?
A. m B. m^2
C. $2m$ D. $2m^2$

77. How much angle does the tangent at P make with y-axis?
A. $\tan^{-1} m^2$ B. $\cot^{-1}(1 + m^2)$
C. $\sin^{-1}\left(\frac{1}{\sqrt{1+m^4}}\right)$ D. $\sec^{-1}\sqrt{1+m^4}$

78. What is the equation of tangent to the curve at P?
A. $y = mx + m$ B. $y = -mx + 2m$
C. $y = m^2x + 2m$ D. $y = m^2x + m$

Directions (Q. Nos. 79 and 80): *Read the following information and answer the two items that follow:*

Let $f(x) = x^2$, $g(x) = \tan x$ and $h(x) = \ln x$.

79. For $x = \frac{\sqrt{\pi}}{2}$, what is the value of $[ho(gof)](x)$?
A. 0 B. 1
C. $\frac{\pi}{4}$ D. $\frac{\pi}{2}$

80. What if $[fo(fof)](2)$ equal to?
A. 2 B. 8
C. 16 D. 256

81. What is $\int\frac{dx}{2x^2-2x+1}$ equal to?
A. $\frac{\tan^{-1}(2x-1)}{2}+c$
B. $2\tan^{-1}(2x-1)+c$
C. $\frac{\tan^{-1}(2x+1)}{2}+c$
D. $\tan^{-1}(2x-1)+c$

82. What is $\int \frac{dx}{x(1+\ln x)^n}$ equal to $(n \neq 1)$?

A. $\frac{1}{(n-1)(1+\ln x)^{n-1}}+c$

B. $\frac{1-n}{(1+\ln x)^{1-n}}+c$

C. $\frac{n+1}{(1+\ln x)^{n+1}}+c$

D. $-\frac{1}{(n-1)(1+\ln x)^{n-1}}+c$

83. Which one of the following is the differential equation that represents the family of curves $y=\frac{1}{2x^2-c}$ where c is an arbitrary constant?

A. $\frac{dy}{dx}=4xy^2$ B. $\frac{dy}{dx}=\frac{1}{y}$

C. $\frac{dy}{dx}=x^2y$ D. $\frac{dy}{dx}=-4xy^2$

Directions (Q. Nos. 84 and 85): *Read the following information and answer the two items that follow:*

Consider the equation $x^y = e^{x-y}$

84. What is $\frac{dy}{dx}$ at $x = 1$ equal to?

A. 0 B. 1

C. 2 D. 4

85. What is $\frac{d^2y}{dx^2}$ at $x = 1$ equal to?

A. 0 B. 1

C. 2 D. 4

Directions (Q. Nos. 86 to 88): *Read the following information and answer the three items that follow:*

Consider the function $f(x) = g(x) + h(x)$ where $g(x) = \sin\left(\frac{x}{4}\right)$ and $h(x)=\cos\left(\frac{4x}{5}\right)$

86. What is the period of the function $g(x)$?

A. π B. 2π

C. 4π D. 8π

87. What is the period of the function $h(x)$?

A. π B. $\frac{4\pi}{5}$

C. $\frac{5\pi}{2}$ D. $\frac{3\pi}{2}$

88. What is the period of the function $f(x)$?

A. 10π B. 20π

C. 40π D. 80π

Directions (Q. Nos. 89 and 90): *Read the following information and answer the two items that follow:*

Consider the function

$$f(x) = 3x^4 - 20x^3 - 12x^2 + 288x + 1$$

89. In which one of the following intervals is the function increasing?

A. (–2, 3) B. (3, 4)

C. (–3, –2) D. (–4, –3)

90. In which one of the following intervals is the function decreasing?

A. (–2, 3) B. (3, 4)

C. (4, 6) D. (6, 9)

Directions (Q. Nos. 91 to 93): *Read the following information and answer the three items that follow:*

Let $f(x) = x^2 + 2x - 5$ and $g(x) = 5x + 30$

91. What are the roots of the equation $g[f(x)] = 0$?

A. 1, –1 B. –1, –1

C. 1, 1 D. 0, 1

92. Consider the following statements:

1. $f[g(x)]$ is a polynomial of degree 3.
2. $g[g(x)]$ is a polynomial of degree 2.

Which of the above statements is/are correct?

A. 1 only B. 2 only

C. Both 1 and 2 D. Neither 1 nor 2

93. If $h(x) = 5f(x) - xg(x)$, then what is the derivative of $h(x)$?

A. –40 B. –20

C. –10 D. 0

Directions (Q. Nos. 94 and 95): *Read the following information and answer the two items that follow:*

Consider the integrals

$$I_1 = \int_0^{\pi} \frac{x\,dx}{1+\sin x} \text{ and } I_2 = \int_0^{\pi} \frac{(\pi-x)dx}{1-\sin(\pi+x)}$$

94. What is the value of I_1?

A. 0 B. $\frac{\pi}{2}$

C. π D. 2π

95. What is the value of $I_1 + I_2$?

A. 2π B. π

C. $\frac{\pi}{2}$ D. 0

96. The differential equation which represents the family of curves given by $\tan y = c(1 - e^x)$ is:

A. $e^x \tan y\, dx + (1 - e^x)\, dy = 0$

B. $e^x \tan y\, dx + (1 - e^x) \sec^2 y\, dy = 0$

C. $e^x (1 - e^x)\, dx + \tan y\, dy = 0$

D. $e^x \tan y\, dy + (1 - e^x)\, dx = 0$

97. What is the derivative of $2^{(\sin x)^2}$ with respect to $\sin x$?

A. $\sin x\, 2^{(\sin x)^2} \ln 4$ B. $2 \sin x\, 2^{(\sin x)^2} \ln 4$

C. $\ln (\sin x)\, 2^{(\sin x)^2}$ D. $2 \sin x \cos x\, 2^{(\sin x)^2}$

98. For what value of k is the function

$$f(x) = \begin{cases} 2x + \frac{1}{4}, & x < 0 \\ k, & x = 0 \\ \left(x + \frac{1}{2}\right)^2, & x > 0 \end{cases}$$ continuous?

A. $\frac{1}{4}$ B. $\frac{1}{2}$

C. 1 D. 2

99. What is the area of the region enclosed between the curve $y^2 = 2x$ and the straight line $y = x$?

A. $\frac{2}{3}$ square units B. $\frac{4}{3}$ square units

C. $\frac{1}{3}$ square units D. 1 square units

100. If $f(x) = \frac{x^3}{3} - \frac{5x^2}{2} + 6x + 7$ increases in the interval T and decreases in the interval S, then which one of the following is correct?

A. T = $(-\infty, 2) \cup (3, \infty)$ and S = $(2, 3)$

B. T = ϕ and S = $(-\infty, \infty)$

C. T = $(-\infty, \infty)$ and S = ϕ

D. T = $(2, 3)$ and S = $(-\infty, 2) \cup (3, \infty)$

101. A coin is biased so that heads comes up thrice as likely as tails. For three independent tosses of a coin, what is the probability of getting at most two tails?

A. 0.16 B. 0.48

C. 0.58 D. 0.98

102. A bag contains 20 books out of which 5 are defective. If 3 of the books are selected at random and removed from the bag in succession without replacement, then what is the probability that all three books are defective?

A. 0.009 B. 0.016

C. 0.026 D. 0.047

103. The median of the observations 22, 24, 33, 37, $x + 1$, $x + 3$, 46, 47, 57, 58 in ascending order is 42. What are the values of 5th and 6th observations respectively?

A. 42, 45 B. 41, 43

C. 43, 46 D. 40, 40

104. Arithmetic mean of 10 observations is 60 and sum of squares of deviations from 50 is 5000. What is the standard deviation of the observations?

A. 20 B. 21

C. 22.36 D. 24.70

105. If p and q are the roots of the equation $x^2 - 30x + 221 = 0$, what is the value of $p^3 + q^3$?

A. 7010 B. 7110

C. 7210 D. 7240

106. For the variables x and y, the two regression lines are $6x + y = 30$ and $3x + 2y = 25$. What are the values of $\bar{x}$, $\bar{y}$ and r respectively?

A. $\frac{20}{3}, \frac{35}{9}, -0.5$ B. $\frac{20}{3}, \frac{35}{9}, 0.5$

C. $\frac{35}{9}, \frac{20}{3}, -0.5$ D. $\frac{35}{9}, \frac{20}{3}, 0.5$

107. The class marks in a frequency table are given to be 5, 10, 15, 20, 25, 30, 35, 40, 45, 50. The class limits of the first five classes are:

A. 3 – 7, 7 – 13, 13 – 17, 17 – 23, 23 – 27

B. 2.5 – 7.5, 7.5 – 12.5, 12.5 – 17.5, 17.5 – 22.5, 22.5 – 27.5

C. 1.5 – 8.5, 8.5 – 11.5, 11.5 – 18.5, 18.5 – 21.5, 21.5 – 28.5

D. 2 – 8, 8 – 12, 12 – 18, 18 – 22, 22 – 28

108. The mean of 5 observations is 4.4 and variance is 8.24. If three of the five observations are 1, 2 and 6, then what are the other two observations?

A. 9, 16 B. 9, 4

C. 81, 16 D. 81, 4

109. If a coin is tossed till the first head appears, then what will be the sample space?

A. {H}

B. {TH}

C. {T, HT, HHT, HHHT, ...}

D. {H, TH, TTH, TTTH, ...}

110. Consider the following discrete frequency distribution:

x	1	2	3	4	5	6	7	8
f	3	15	45	57	50	36	25	9

What is the value of median of the distribution?

A. 4 B. 5

C. 6 D. 7

111. Two dice are thrown simultaneously. What is the probability that the sum of the numbers appearing on them is a prime number?

A. $\frac{5}{12}$ B. $\frac{1}{2}$

C. $\frac{7}{12}$ D. $\frac{2}{3}$

112. If 5 of a Company's 10 delivery trucks do not meet emission standards and 3 of them are chosen for inspection, then what is the probability that none of the trucks chosen will meet emission standards?

A. $\frac{1}{8}$ B. $\frac{3}{8}$

C. $\frac{1}{12}$ D. $\frac{1}{4}$

113. There are 3 coins in a box. One is a two-headed coin; another is a fair coin; and third is biased coin that comes up heads 75% of time. When one of the three coins is selected at random and flipped, it shows heads. What is the probability that it was the two-headed coin?

A. $\frac{2}{9}$ B. $\frac{1}{3}$

C. $\frac{4}{9}$ D. $\frac{5}{9}$

114. Consider the following statements:

1. If A and B are mutually exclusive events, then it is possible that $P(A) = P(B) = 0.6$.
2. If A and B are any two events such that $P(A|B) = 1$, then $P(\bar{B} \mid \bar{A}) = 1$.

Which of the above statements is/are correct?

A. 1 only B. 2 only

C. Both 1 and 2 D. Neither 1 nor 2

115. If a fair die is rolled 4 times, then what is the probability that there are exactly 2 sixes?

A. $\frac{5}{216}$ B. $\frac{25}{216}$

C. $\frac{125}{216}$ D. $\frac{175}{216}$

116. Mean of 100 observations is 50 and standard deviation is 10. If 5 is added to each observation, then what will be the new mean and new standard deviation respectively?

A. 50, 10 B. 50, 15

C. 55, 10 D. 55, 15

117. If the range of a set of observations on a variable X is known to be 25 and if $Y = 40 + 3X$, then what is the range of the set of corresponding observations on Y?

A. 25 B. 40

C. 75 D. 115

118. If V is the variance and M is the mean of first 15 natural numbers, then what is $V + M^2$ equal to?

A. $\frac{124}{3}$ B. $\frac{148}{3}$

C. $\frac{248}{3}$ D. $\frac{124}{9}$

119. A car travels first 60 km at a speed of $3v$ km/hr and travels next 60 km at $2v$ km/hr. What is the average speed of the car?

A. $2.5v$ km/hr

B. $2.4v$ km/hr

C. $2.2v$ km/hr

D. $2.1v$ km/hr

120. The mean weight of 150 students in a certain class is 60 kg. The mean weight of boys is 70 kg and that of girls is 55 kg. What are the number of bous and girls respectively in the class?

A. 75 and 75

B. 50 and 100

C. 70 and 80

D. 100 and 50

ANSWERS

PAPER-I : GENERAL ABILITY TEST

1	2	3	4	5	6	7	8	9	10
A	C	D	B	A	C	D	A	C	C
11	**12**	**13**	**14**	**15**	**16**	**17**	**18**	**19**	**20**
D	C	A	D	B	C	A	B	C	D
21	**22**	**23**	**24**	**25**	**26**	**27**	**28**	**29**	**30**
A	C	B	A	C	C	B	D	B	C
31	**32**	**33**	**34**	**35**	**36**	**37**	**38**	**39**	**40**
C	A	D	C	B	A	C	B	D	D
41	**42**	**43**	**44**	**45**	**46**	**47**	**48**	**49**	**50**
C	A	D	B	C	B	A	C	D	B
51	**52**	**53**	**54**	**55**	**56**	**57**	**58**	**59**	**60**
D	B	C	D	B	B	C	D	B	C

61	62	63	64	65	66	67	68	69	70
D	B	A	A	A	A	D	C	A	B
71	**72**	**73**	**74**	**75**	**76**	**77**	**78**	**79**	**80**
B	C	A	D	A	C	C	D	B	A
81	**82**	**83**	**84**	**85**	**86**	**87**	**88**	**89**	**90**
B	A	A	B	A	D	B	C	C	A
91	**92**	**93**	**94**	**95**	**96**	**97**	**98**	**99**	**100**
C	C	C	C	D	B	D	A	C	C
101	**102**	**103**	**104**	**105**	**106**	**107**	**108**	**109**	**110**
B	C	C	A	C	C	C	C	B	C
111	**112**	**113**	**114**	**115**	**116**	**117**	**118**	**119**	**120**
C	C	D	B	C	C	A	C	D	A
121	**122**	**123**	**124**	**125**	**126**	**127**	**128**	**129**	**130**
B	B	C	B	D	B	B	D	A	A
131	**132**	**133**	**134**	**135**	**136**	**137**	**138**	**139**	**140**
C	C	C	B	C	B	D	C	A	C
141	**142**	**143**	**144**	**145**	**146**	**147**	**148**	**149**	**150**
C	B	B	C	C	C	D	C	C	B

PAPER-II : MATHEMATICS

1	2	3	4	5	6	7	8	9	10
C	A	A	A	C	C	C	B	B	D
11	**12**	**13**	**14**	**15**	**16**	**17**	**18**	**19**	**20**
C	D	A	A	C	C	C	D	C	C
21	**22**	**23**	**24**	**25**	**26**	**27**	**28**	**29**	**30**
C	B	C	C	A	C	D	B	B	C
31	**32**	**33**	**34**	**35**	**36**	**37**	**38**	**39**	**40**
D	B	C	A	C	C	A	C	D	D
41	**42**	**43**	**44**	**45**	**46**	**47**	**48**	**49**	**50**
B	A	C	C	B	B	B	C	B	B
51	**52**	**53**	**54**	**55**	**56**	**57**	**58**	**59**	**60**
D	D	A	C	B	A	B	D	B	A
61	**62**	**63**	**64**	**65**	**66**	**67**	**68**	**69**	**70**
A	D	A	A	C	C	D	D	B	B
71	**72**	**73**	**74**	**75**	**76**	**77**	**78**	**79**	**80**
B	D	B	A	C	B	A	D	A	D
81	**82**	**83**	**84**	**85**	**86**	**87**	**88**	**89**	**90**
D	D	D	A	B	D	C	C	A	B
91	**92**	**93**	**94**	**95**	**96**	**97**	**98**	**99**	**100**
B	D	B	C	A	B	A	A	A	A
101	**102**	**103**	**104**	**105**	**106**	**107**	**108**	**109**	**110**
D	A	B	A	B	C	B	B	D	B
111	**112**	**113**	**114**	**115**	**116**	**117**	**118**	**119**	**120**
A	C	C	C	B	C	C	C	B	B

EXPLANATORY ANSWERS

PAPER I : GENERAL KNOWLEDGE

51. When a diver jumps from the spring board, he curls his body by rolling his arms and legs in. By doing so, he decreases his moment of inertia and hence angular speed increases to conserve the angular momentum.

53. The energy emitted by a body, in the form of radiation on account of its temperature, is called thermal radiation. These radiations are heat radiations and travel along straight lines with the speed of light.

55. Momentum is a commonly used term in sports. A team that has the momentum is on *the move* and is going to take some effort to stop. A team that has a lot of momentum is really *on the move* and is going to be *hard to stop*. Momentum is a physics term; it refers to the quantity of motion that an object has. A sports team that is *on the move* has the momentum. If an object is in motion (*on the move*) then it has momentum.

Momentum can be defined as "mass in motion." All objects have mass; so if an object is moving, then it has momentum - it has its mass in motion. The amount of momentum that an object has is dependent upon two variables: how much *stuff* is moving and how fast the *stuff* is moving. Momentum depends upon the variables mass and velocity. In terms of an equation, the momentum of an object is equal to the mass of the object times the velocity of the object.

Momentum (p) = mass (m) × velocity (v)

where m is the mass and v is the velocity. The equation illustrates that momentum is directly proportional to an object's mass and directly proportional to the object's velocity.

56. Iron(II,III) oxide is the chemical compound with formula Fe_3O_4. It occurs in nature as the mineral magnetite. It is one of a number of iron oxides, the others being iron(II) oxide (FeO), which is rare, and iron(III) oxide (Fe_2O_3) also known as hematite. It contains both Fe^{2+} and Fe^{3+} ions and is sometimes formulated as $FeO \cdot Fe_2O_3$. This iron oxide is encountered in the laboratory as a black powder. It exhibits permanent magnetism and is ferrimagnetic, but is sometimes incorrectly described as ferromag-netic. Its most extensive use is as a black pigment. For this purpose, it is synthesized rather than being extracted from the naturally occurring mineral as the particle size and shape can be varied by the method of production.

57. Soda Lime Glass: Hard glass contains potassium instead of sodium, has a higher melting point, and greater resistance to reagents and as such it is more suitable for chemical apparatus. Flint glass is potash-lead glass having a high refractive index and, therefore, suitable for optical purposes.

Pyrex Glass: Pyrex glass or borosilicate was created with the addition of boron to the mixture. Pyrex is more resistant to heat as the thermal expansion coefficient of Pyrex is about one-third of soda-lime silica glass. It also has high durability against chemicals. Pyrex is also lighter in weight. Pyrex-Wafers are an ideal solution for anodic bonding processes, as the thermal coefficient of expansion alomst perfectly matches that of silicon. Apart from this, pyrex also has good acid resistance and a high optical transmission over a wide wavelength range. It can be ground, polished, and coated according to customer-specific requirements.

58. Boiling: It is a bulk phenomenon. Particles from bulk (whole) of the liquid change into vapour state.

Boiling point: The constant temperature at which a liquid changes into gas/vapour is known as its boiling point. Boiling point of water is 100°C or (273 + 100) = 373 K.

Condensation point of gas also depends upon the surrounding pressure. More will be the pressure more closer will be molecules and thus greater will be the intermolecular forces of attraction. Thus more will be the surrounding pressure more easily gas gets condensed in to liquid.

Difference between Boiling and Evaporation:

(*i*) Boiling takes place only at a particular temperature for a liquid. Whereas evaporation occurs at all temperatures.

(*ii*) Boiling is Bulk phenomena *i.e.*, the bubble formation occurs even below the surface. Whereas evaporation is surface phenomena, *i.e.*, bubble formation occurs only on the surface of liquid.

59. The various such forms of the element are called allotropes of that element. Allotropes always exhibit different physical properties but possess same chemical properties.

The allotropes of carbon are of two types — the crystalline and amorphous carbon. Diamond and graphite are crystalline carbon. Charcoal coke, lamp black soot, etc are amorphous or non-crystalline carbon.

Allotropes of an element consists of only one kind of atoms with their different arrangement having different physical properties but same chemical properties.

Pure carbon occurs in the natural form of two allotropes, namely diamond and graphite. Diamond and graphite are chemically identical, both consisting of carbon atoms only. Diamond and graphite differ only in the arrangement of carbon atoms in their crystals. This leads to the difference in their appearance and many other physical properties.

60. Chemical Composition of Portland Cements: The raw material that is used in the manu-facturing of Portland cement mainly consists of lime, silica, alumina and iron oxide.

In the cement, the oxide content is about 90%. The oxide composition of ordinary Portland cement is given below:

Common Name	Oxide	Appropriate Composition Limits (in %)
Lime	CaO	60-66
Silica	SiO_2	19-25
Alumina	Al_2O_3	3-8
Iron oxide	Fe_2O_3	1-5
Magnesia	MgO	0-5
Alkalies		
Soda	Na_2O	0.5-1
Potassa	K_2O	0.5-1
Sulphur Trioxide	SO_3	1-3

61. Water is a polar molecule and also acts as a polar solvent. When a chemical species is said to be "polar," this means that the positive and negative electrical charges are unevenly distributed. The positive charge comes from the atomic nucleus, while the electrons supply the negative charge. It's the movement of electrons that determines polarity. Here's how it works for water.

Water (H_2O) is polar because of the bent shape of the molecule. The shape means most of the negative charge from the oxygen on side of the molecule and the positive charge of the hydrogen atoms is on the other side of the molecule. This is an example of polar covalent chemical bonding. When solutes are added to water, they may be affected by the charge distribution.

62. Soaps are sodium or potassium salts of some long chain carboxylic acids. Sodium salts of fatty acids are known as hard soaps and potassium salts of fatty acids are known as soft soaps. Hard soaps are prepared from cheap oils, fats and sodium hydroxide. They contain free alkali and are used for washing purposes. Soft soaps are prepared from good oils and potassium hydroxide. They do not contain free alkali, produce more lather and are used as toilet soaps, shaving creams and shampoos. Soap is prepared by heating vegetable oil or animal fat containing Glyceryl stearate with concentrated sodium hydroxide solution. Hydrolysis of fat takes place and a mixture of sodium salts of fatty acids and glycerol is formed. The salts of fatty acids thus formed are used as soap. The alkaline hydrolysis of oils and fats forming soaps is commonly known as saponification.

63. Initial velocity is the rate that the position of an object changes relative to time. Forces acting on an object cause it to accelerate. This acceleration changes the velocity. The initial velocity, *vi* is the velocity of the object before acceleration causes a change.

65. When the substances are mixed in equal volumes, then

$$4 = \frac{V\rho_1 + V\rho_2}{2V}$$

$$\Rightarrow \quad \rho_1 + \rho_2 = 2 \times 4 \quad ...(1)$$

When the two substances are mixed in equal masses, then

$$\frac{m}{\rho_1} + \frac{m}{\rho_2} = \frac{2m}{3}$$

$$\therefore \quad \frac{1}{\rho_1} + \frac{1}{\rho_2} = \frac{2}{3} \quad ...(2)$$

$$\text{or} \quad \frac{\rho_1 + \rho_2}{\rho_1\rho_2} = \frac{2}{3}$$

$$\text{or} \quad \frac{8}{\rho_1\rho_2} = \frac{2}{3}$$

$$\text{or} \quad \rho_1\rho_2 = 12 \quad ...(3)$$

$$\text{Now,} \quad \rho_1 - \rho_2 = [(\rho_1 + \rho_2)^2 - 4\rho_1\rho_2]^{1/2}$$

$$= [64 - 48]^{1/2} = 4 \quad ...(4)$$

Solving equation (3) and (4), we get

$$\rho_1 = 6$$

and

$$\rho_2 = 2$$

66. $\text{Velocity} = \dfrac{\text{displacement}}{\text{Time}}$

Given

time = 2 hours

Displacement = 50 km

$$\text{Average velocity} = \frac{\text{Total displacement}}{\text{Total Time}}$$

Average Velocity = 50 – 50 = 0

67. As we know all about Kirchhoff's law. It is the fundamental law to circuit theory. This law quantifies that how charge flows through a circuit and how voltage varies around a loop.

According to Kirchhoff's first law (current law or conservation of charge), charge flowing into a junction must be equal to current flowing out of it.

Kirchhoff's 2nd law (voltage law or conservation of energy), the sum of all voltage around any closed loop of a circuit must be equals zero.

The sum of emfs and potential differences around a closed loop equals zero is a consequence of conservation of charge and also that conservation of energy.

71. Image Formed by a Lens

	Object	*Image*	*Real or virtual*	*Magnified or diminished*	*Erect or inverted*
Convex lens	at infinity	at F	real	diminished	inverted
	beyond 2F	between F and 2F	real	diminished	inverted
	at 2F	at 2F	real	diminished	inverted
	between F & 2F	beyond 2F	real	magnified	inverted
	at F	at infinity	—	—	—
	between F & O	on the same side	virtual	magnified	erect
Concave lens	all positions	within F on the same side	virtual	diminished	erect

73. Calcium carbonate is a chemical compound with the formula $CaCO_3$. It is a common substance found in rocks as the minerals calcite and aragonite (most notably as limestone, which is a type of sedimentary rock consisting mainly of calcite) and is the main component of pearls and the shells of marine organisms, snails, and eggs. Calcium carbonate is the active ingredient in agricultural lime and is created when calcium ions in hard water react with carbonate ions to create limescale. It is medicinally used as a calcium supplement or as an antacid, but excessive consumption can be hazardous and cause poor digestion.

74. Detergents and soaps are used for cleaning because pure water can't remove oily, organic soiling. Soap cleans by acting as an emulsifier. Basically, soap allows oil and water to mix so that oily grime can be removed during rinsing. Detergents were developed in response to the shortage of the animal and vegetable fats used to make soap during World Wat I and World War II. Detergents are primarily surfactants, which could be produced easily from petrochemicals. Surfactants lower the surface tension of water, essentially making it 'wetter' so that it is less likely to stick to itself and more likely to interact with oil and grease. Modern detergents contain more than surfactants Cleaning products may also contain engines to degarde protein-based stains, bleaches to de-colour stains and add power to cleaning agents, and blue dyes to counter yellowing. Like soaps, detergents have hydrophobic or water-hating molecular chains and hydrophilic or water-loving components.

75. Tin is a chemical element with the symbol Sn and atomic number 50. Tin is a silvery metal that characteristically has a faint yellow hue. Tin, like indium, is soft enough to be cut without much force. When a bar of tin is bent, the so-called tin cry can be heard as a result of sliding tin crystals reforming; this trait is shared by indium, cadmium, and frozen mercury. Pure tin after solidifying keeps a mirror-like appearance similar to most metals. However, in most tin alloys, the metal solidifies with a dull gray colour. Tin is a post-transition metal in group 14 of the periodic table of elements. It is obtained chiefly from the mineral cassiterite, which contains stannic oxide, SnO_2.

76. Dry Ice is frozen carbon dioxide, a normal part of our earth's atmosphere. It is the gas that we exhale during breathing and the gas that plants use in photosynthesis. It is also the same gas commonly added to water to make soda water. This gas is often captured during industrial processes and recycled to make Dry Ice.

Dry Ice is particularly useful for freezing, and keeping things frozen because of its very cold temperature: –109.3°F or –78.5°C. Dry Ice is widely used because it is simple to freeze and easy to handle using insulated gloves. Dry Ice changes directly from a solid to a gas -sublimation in normal atmospheric conditions without going through a wet liquid stage. Therefore it gets the name "dry ice."

77. Osmosis is a special case of diffusion, which involves the mo·ement of water molecules through a differentially permeable membrane from a region with a lot of water molecules to a region with fewer water molecules. A differentially permeable membrane is a membrane that allows some substances to pass through but not others. You may also find the membrane being called a semi-permeable or selectively permeable membrane. The cell membrane that surrounds biological cells is differentially permeable.

A differentially permeable membrane contains minute pores. Water molecules are able to pass through these pores. However, the particles of many other substances, which may be dissolved in the water, are unable to pass through. When two solutions, e.g. sucrose solutions, which have different concentrations, are separated by a differentially permeable membrane, the water molecules will diffuse through the pores in the membrane from the more dilute solution to the more concentrated solution. The sucrose molecules, however, do not move because they are unable to pass through the pores in the membrane. The volume of the more dilute solution decreases and the volume of the more concentrated solution increases.

78. Connective tissue provides structural frame-work and support to various structures of animal body. Blood, bone and cartilage are specialised connective tissue.

Blood is a fluid connective tissue. It helps in transportation of various substances between organs.

Bone and cartilage is skeletal connective tissue that support the body, protect various organs and help in locomotion.

80. Xylem is a complex tissue. The cells are thick-walled and many of them are dead cells. Xylem is mainly concerned with the conduction of water and minerals. It also provides mechanical support to the plant. As a conducting strand, xylem forms a continuous channel through the roots, stem, leaves and other aerial parts.

Xylem consists of four types of cells—**xylem vessels, tracheids, xylem fibres** and **xylem parenchyma**.

84. The loudness of a sound depends upon the amplitude. Loudness of a sound depends on the amplitude of the vibration producing that sound. Greater is the amplitude of vibration, louder is the sound produced by it.

85. Force of gravition between two bodies $F = G\, M_1M_2/R_2$, based on this the force of gravitation in the second case will be, $F_2 = 16 \times G\, M_1M_2/R_2 = 16F$

86. Fiber optics: With fiber optics, light entering one side of a glass or plastic fiber of optical quality is transmitted to the other end by the process of total internal reflection. Light rays that strike the core at the acceptance angle are reflected back and forth inside the core and travel to the other end of the fiber in a zigzag path of sucessive reflections.

In use, a single, large-diameter fiber is impractical because it lacks flexibility. To increase flexibility, a large number of small-diameter fibers are clustered together in a *bundle*. In order to prevent light leaking from one fiber to another, each is coated with a transparent sheath that has a lower *refractive* index than the fiber. The sheathing process protects the surfaces of the fiber and allows the bundle to be embedded into other materials without loss of light from the sides.

87. Cathode rays (electron beam or e-beam) are streams of electrons observed in discharge tubes. If an evacuated glass tube is equipped with two electrodes and a voltage is applied, glass behind the positive electrode is observed to glow, due to electrons emitted from the cathode (the electrode connected to the negative terminal of the voltage supply). They were first observed in 1869 by German physicist Julius Plücker and Johann Wilhelm Hittorf, and were named in 1876 by Eugen Goldstein *Kathodenstrahlen*, or cathode rays. In 1897, British physicist J.J. Thomson showed that cathode rays were composed of a previously unknown negatively charged particle, which was later named the *electron*. Cathode ray tubes (CRTs) use a focused beam of electrons deflected by electric or magnetic fields to render an image on a screen.

89. Some elements— for example, helium and neon–consist of single atoms that are not connected to each other—that is, they are **monatomic elements**. In contrast, oxygen, in its most common form, contains two atoms in each molecule, connected to each other by a chemical bond. We write the formula for an oxygen molecule as O_2, with the subscript showing the number of atoms in the molecule. Six other elements also occur as diatomic molecules (that is, they contain two atoms of the same element per molecule): hydrogen (H_2), nitrogen (N_2), fluorine (F_2), chlorine (Cl_2), bromine (Br_2), and iodine (I_2). It is important to understand that under normal conditions, free atoms of O, H, N, F, Cl, Br, and I do not exist. Rather, these seven elements occur only as diatomic elements.

90. This competition for release of electrons incidently remainds us of the competition for release of protons among acids. The similarity suggests that we might develop a table in which metals and their ions are listed on the basis of their tendency to release electrons just as we do in the case of acids to indicate the strength of the acids. As a matter of fact we have already made certain comparisons. By comparison we have come to know that zinc releases electrons to copper and copper releases electrons to silver and, therefore, the electron releasing tendency of the metals is in the order : $Zn > Cu > Ag$. We would love to make our list more vast and design a metal activity series or electro-chemical series.

91. Biogas is primarily methane (CH_4) and carbon dioxide (CO_2) and may have small amounts of hydrogen sulphide (H_2S), moisture and siloxanes. The gases methane, hydrogen, and carbon monoxide (CO) can be combusted or oxidized with oxygen. This energy release allows biogas to be used as a fuel; it can be used for any heating purpose, such as cooking. It can also be used in a gas engine to convert the energy in the gas into electricity and heat.

92. The Thyroid Gland: Thyroid is two-lobed gland, located at the front of the larynx and trachea in the neck. Two thyroid hormones–thyroxine (T_4) and trilodothyroxine (T_3), increase the rate of cellular metabolism. Dietary iodine is required to make thyroxine and trilodothyroxine. Different cells within the thyroid produce a third hormone—calcitonin, which lowers blood calcium levels under certain conditions. The main effect of thyroxine is control the BMR (Base Metabolic Rate). Thyroxine (T_4) contains four atoms of iodine; it is secreted in greater amounts but is less potent than triiodothyroxine (T_3), which has only three atoms of iodine. Iodine is actively transported into the thyroid gland, and it may reach a concentration as much as twenty five times greater than that of the blood. The thyroid hormones bind to many different cell types, where they speed metabolism by increasing supplies of enzymes needed for cellular respiration. Under thyroid stimulation, gas exchange in the lungs is faster, the small intenstine absorbs nutrients more rapidly and the fat levels in cells and in blood plasma diminish.

93. *Salmonella typhi* is a bacteria that causes Typhoid infection in humans. The infection is transmitted by contaminated food and drinking water.

95. Scurvy is a disease caused by a severe deficiency of vitamin C, hence it is also called the chronic vitamin C deficiency disorder. It is an ancient disease that developed during the 15th to 18th centuries or during the early times of Greek and Egyptians. It is a very rare disease and most commonly seen in undeveloped countries with the lack of proper nutrients. Vitamin C is a water-soluble vitamin which plays a vital role in repairing, production, regeneration, and maintenance of tissues, bones, blood vessels, and skin. It is a powerful antioxidant, which helps in protecting against heart-related disorders, a variety of cancers and neutralizes the effects of nitrites. Vitamin C also absorbs iron and prevents scurvy, and decreases LDL or bad cholesterol and triglycerides.

96. Sound is the mechanical vibrations of particles of the material medium. The human ear is sensitised to hear the sound waves between 20 Hz to 20 kHz, which is known as the *audible range*. Sound waves with frequencies above 20 kHz (above the audible range) are known as *ultrasonic waves*. The energy of ultrasonic waves is large on account of high frequency; so they can propagate through larger distance. The propagation also depends on the elastic properties and the density of the medium. Due to their smaller wavelength as compared to audible sound, a large number of ultrasonic applications are possible in almost all branches of technology, engineering and medicine. There are three types of ultrasonic waves depending on the mode of vibration of the particles of the medium with the propagation direction of the wave. They are (*i*) longitudinal or compressional type of waves, (*ii*) transverse or shear waves and (*iii*) surface or Rayleigh waves.

98. Equation used for the Fahrenheit to Celsius to Kelvin conversion; $K = (y\ °F - 32) \times 5/9 + 273.15 = 318K$.

101. There are over three thousand different minerals. On the basis of composition, minerals are classified mainly as metallic and non-metallic minerals.

- **Metallic** minerals contain metal in raw form. Metals are hard substances that conduct heat and electricity and have a characteristic lustreor shine. Iron ore, bauxite, manganese ore are some examples. Metallic minerals may be ferrous or non-ferrous. **Ferrous** minerals like iron ore, manganese and chromites contain iron. A **non-ferrous** mineral does not contain iron but may contain some other metal such as gold, silver, copper or lead.
- **Non-metallic** minerals do not contain metals. Limestone, mica and gypsum are examples of such minerals. The mineral fuels like coal and petroleum are also non-metallic minerals.

102. Rabi crops are sown in winter from October to December and harvested in summer from April to June. Some of the important rabi crops are wheat, barley, peas, gram and mustard. Though, these crops are grown in large parts of India, states from the north and northwestern parts such as Punjab, Haryana, Himachal Pradesh, Jammu and Kashmir, Uttarakhand and Uttar Pradesh are important for the production of wheat and other rabi crops. Availability of precipitation during winter months due to the western temperate cyclones helps in the success of these crops. However, the success of the green revolution in Punjab, Haryana, western Uttar Pradesh and parts of Rajasthan has also been an important factor in the growth of the above mentioned rabi crops.

105. Paradeep Port is located at confluence of river Mahanadi in Bay of Bengal in Odisha. It was the first major port on East Coast commissioned in independent India.

106. The most popular argument regarding the origin of the universe is the Big Bang Theory. It is also called 'Expanding Universe Hypothesis'. The Big Bang Theory considers the following stages in the development of the universe: In the beginning, all matter forming the universe existed in one place in the form of a "tiny ball" (singular atom) with an unimaginably small volume, infinite temperature and infinite density. At the Big Bang the "tiny ball" exploded violently. This lad to a huge expansion. It is now generally accepted that the event of Big Bang took place 13.7 billion years before the present. The expansion continues even to the present day. As it grew, some energy was converted into matter. There was particularly rapid expansion within fractions of a second after the bang. Thereafter, the expansion has slowed down. Within first three minutes from the Big Bang event, the first atom began to form.

107. Gandhi returned to India in January 1915. The Sabarmati Ashram in Ahmedabad, Gujarat, became an example of community living, as Gandhi fought for the indigo cultivators of Champaran and the workers of Ahmedabad mills. The direction of the Indian freedom movement changed a great deal with Gandhi emerging as a mass leader. The Gandhian era truly began in Indian politics in April 1919, when he called for a general strike against the draconian Rowlatt Act (British colonial legislation in India extending "emergency measures" to control public unrest).

108. The twelfth century witnessed the emergence of a new movement in Karnataka, led by a Brahmana named Basavanna (1106-68) who was a minister in the court of a Kalachuri ruler. His followers were known as Virashaivas (heroes of Shiva) or Lingayats (wearers of the linga). Lingayats continue to be an important community in the region to date. They worship Shiva in his manifestation as a linga, and men usually wear a small linga in a silver case on a loop strung over the left shoulder.

The Lingayats challenged the idea of caste and the "pollution" attributed to certain groups by Brahmanas. They also questioned the theory of rebirth. These won their followers amongst those who were marginalised within the Brahmanical social order. The Lingayats also encouraged certain practices disapproved in the Dharmashastras, such as post-puberty marriage and the remarriage of widows. Our understanding of the Virashaiva tradition is derived from vachanas (literally, sayings) composed in Kannada by women and men who joined the movement.

110. The Russian Social Democratic Labour Party was founded in 1898 by the socialists who respected Marx's ideas. It set up a newspaper, mobilized workers and organized strikes. Socialists formed the Socialist Revolutionary Party in 1900. This party struggled for peasants' right and demanded that land belonging to nobles be transferred to peasants. Vladimir Lenin (who led the Bolshevik group) thought that in a repressive society like Tsarist Russia, the party should be disciplined and should control the number and quality of its members.

Mensheviks were the minority group of the workers of Russia. They believed in parliamentary methods and participation in elections. They thought that the party should be open to all. They favoured parties as were existing in France and Germany, which took part in elections to the legislatures. Whereas the Bolsheviks argued that the working class should lead the revolution in alliance with the peasantry, the Mensheviks envisaged its being led by the bourgeoisie and favoured alliances with the liberals.

113. The word 'sedimentary' is derived from the Latin word sedimentum, which means settling. Rocks (igneous, sedimentary and metamorphic) of the earth's surface are exposed to denudational agents, and are broken up into various sizes of fragments. Such fragments are transported by different exogenous agencies and deposited. These deposits through compaction turn into rocks. This process is called lithification. In many sedimentary rocks, the layers of deposits retain their characteristics even after lithification. Hence, we see a number of layers of varying thickness in sedimentary rocks like sandstone, shale etc.

Depending upon the mode of formation, sedimentary rocks are classified into three major groups: (*i*) mechanically formed — sandstone, conglomerate, limestone, shale, loess etc. are examples; (*ii*) organically formed — geyserite, chalk, limestone, coal etc. are some examples; (*iii*) chemically formed — chert, limestone, halite, potash etc. are some examples.

114. **Climatic Types According to Koeppen**

Group	*Type*	*Letter Code*	*Characteristics*
A-Tropical Humid Climate	Tropical wet	Af	No dry season
	Tropical monsoon	Am	Monsoonal, short dry season
	Tropical wet and dry	Aw	Winter dry season
B-Dry Climate	Subtropical stepper	BSh	Low-latitude semi arid or dry
	Subtropical desert	BWh	Low-latitude arid or dry
	Mid-latitude stepper	BSk	Mid-latitude semi arid or dry
	Mid-latitude desert	BWk	Mid-latitude arid or dry
C-Warm temperate (Mid-latitude) Climates	Humid subtropical	Cfa	No dry season, warm summer
	Mediterranean	Cs	Dry hot summer
	Marine west coast	Cfb	No dry season, warm and cool summer
D-Cold Snow-forest Climates	Humid continental	Df	No dry season, severe winter
	Subarctic	Dw	Winter dry and very severe
E-Cold Climates	Tundra	ET	No true summer
	Polar ice cap	EF	Perennial ice
H-Highland	Highland	H	Highland with snow cover

115. Position of axial plane:

- **Symmetrical folds:** A symmetrical fold may be an anticline or syncline.
- **Asymmetrical folds:** These folds, anticlines or synclines in which the limbs are unequal in length and dip unequally on either side are termed asymmetrical.
- **Overturned folds:** These are actually folds with inclined axial plane in which both the limbs are dipping essentially in the same general direction.
- **Isoclinal folds:** These are groups of folds in which the limbs are dipping essentially in the same direction and at equal angles. Consequ-ently their axial planes are essentially parallel.
- **Recumbent folds:** These can be treated as extreme types of overturned folds in which the axial plane acquires a horizontal attitude. In such folds one limb comes to lie vertically above the other.
- **Conjugate folds:** In certain cases a pair of folds that are apparently related to each other may have mutually inclined axial planes. The individual folds themselves may be anticlinal or synclinal or their modifications.
- **Box fold**: It may be described as a special type of folds with exceptionally flattened dip and steeply inclined limbs almost forming three sides of a rectangle.

116. India currently has 27 sites designated as Wetlands of International Importance (Ramsar Sites), with a surface area of 11121.31 sq.km including Wular lake in Jammu and Kashmir. Ramsar sites are wetlands of international importance.

117. The Munda language are a group of Austroasiatic languages spoken in central and eastern India by several million people. The Munda peoples are generally believed to represent the so-called "tribal" autochthons of their current areas of inhabitation. Originally, Munda-speaking peoples probably extended over a somewhat larger area before being marginalized into the relatively remote hill country and forested areas in the states of Odisha, Madhya Pradesh, and isolated pockets in adjacent areas of Chhattisgarh, West Bengal, Uttar Pradesh, Andhra Pradesh, and Maharashtra by the encroachment of Indo-Aryan-speakers and, at an earlier period, Dravidian-speakers. The one exception to this is in the newly constituted and nearly tribal-dominant state Jharkhand (capital Ranchi).

120. Satyendranath Tagore was selected for the Indian Civil Service in June, 1863. He completed his probationary training and returned to India in November 1864. He was posted as Judge, Satara after this examination.

122. Promotion of Educational and economic interests of Scheduled Castes, Scheduled Tribes and other weaker sections (Article 46): The state shall promote with special care the educational and economic interests of the weaker sections of the people, and, in particular, of the scheduled Castes and the Scheduled Tribes, and shall protect them from social injustice and all forms of exploitation.

123. Maulana Abdul Kalam Azad was a great scholar and a freedom fighter. He was an influential leader of Congress, who opposed partition of India and advocated Hindu-Muslim unity. He was a member of Constituent Assembly and became an education minister in the first cabinet of independent India.

126. National Reasearch Laboratory for Conservation of Cultural Property (NRLC) was stablished in 1976, as a subordinate office of the Department of Culture, and is recognized by the Department of Science and Technology as a scientific institution of the Government of India. The NRLC aims to develop conservation of cultural property in the country. It provides conservation services and technical advice in matters concerning conservation to museums, archives, archaeology departments and other similar institutions, imparts training in different aspects of conservation, carries out research in methods and materials of conservation, disseminates knowledge in conservation and provides library services to conservators of the country. The headquarters of NRLC is situated at Lucknow. A regional centre of the NRLC, the Regional Conservation Laboratory is functioning at Mysore for conservation.

127. Loktak Lake: Situated in the state of Manipur, it is the largest fresh water lake in Northeast India. It is also called the only Floating Island Lake in the world due to the floating *phumdis* (floating islands) on it. It was designated a wetland of international importance under the Ramsar Convention in 1990. It serves as a source of water for hydro-power generation, irrigation and drinking water for Imphal and its surrounding towns. The lake is also a source of livelihood for the rural fishermen who live in the surrounding areas and on floating islands which are actually heterogeneous mass of vegetation, soil and organic matter.

128. The underground water dissolves a large quantity of minerals but the same is deposited elsewhere later on. Fllowing features are formed due to depositional work of underground water:

1. **Stalactite:** The water, containing limestone in solution, seeps through the roof of the caverns in the form of a continuous chain of drops. A portion of the drops hangs on the roof and on the evaporation of water, a small deposit of limestone is left behind contributing to the formation of a *stalactite*. A stalactite grows downwards from the roof. Its thickness is maximum near the roof and it thins out downwards.

2. **Stalagmite:** The remaining portion of the drop falls to the floor of the cavern. This also evaporates, leaving behind a small deposit of limestone aiding the formation of *stalagmite*, thicker and flatter, rising upwards from the floor. Its thickness is maximum at the floor of the cavern and it thins out upwards.
3. **Cavern Pillars or Columns:** Sometimes a stalactitie from above and stalagmite from below develop towards each other and combine together to form a pillar. This is known as *cavern pillar* or *column.*

131. A lithosphere is the rigid, outermost shell on Earth. It is composed of the crust and the portion of the upper mantle that behaves elastically on time scales of thousands of years or greater. The outermost shell of a rocky planet, the crust, is defined on the basis of its chemistry and mineralogy. This includes the crust and the uppermost mantle, which constitute the hard and rigid outer layer of the Earth. The uppermost part of the lithosphere that chemically reacts to the atmosphere, hydrosphere and biosphere through the soil forming process is called the pedosphere.

133. Article 244 (1) of the constitution, provides for the application of Fifth Schedule provisions to the administration and control of the Scheduled Areas and Scheduled Tribes in any State other than the State of Assam, Meghalaya, Tripura and Mizoram.

The fifth Schedule gives significant powers and responsibilities to the Governor of the States under it, in order to protect the tribal identity and provide significant say to the tribals in administration, by extending powers to the governor.

136. The first Uday was a specially-designed air-conditioned chair car coaches which started service between Coimbatore and Bangalore in June, 2018. It was inaugurated by the then Minister of State (MoS) for railways, Rejen Gohain.

138. Geographical Indications Registry under Department for Promotion of Industry and Internal Trade (DPIIT) has accorded Geographical Indication (GI) tag to Tirur betel leaf from Kerala, Tawlhlohpuan fabric and Mizo Puanchei shawl/textile from Mizoram. GI product is recognised as originating from specific geographical origin possessing qualities or reputation related to its origin. This tag is exclusive and similar item originating from different location is not allowed to use it.

139. Samarth (Scheme For Capacity Building In Textile Sector) is a flagship skill development scheme approved in continuation to the Integrated Skill Development Scheme for 12th FYP, Cabinet Committee of Economic Affairs. The industry is facing shortage of skilled workers and provides many opportunities for unemployed youth in the country who are trained in the sector. To address the issue, Central government of India has launched Scheme for Capacity Building in Textile Sector (SCBTS) and named it SAMARTH Scheme.

The objectives of the scheme are to provide demand-driven, placement oriented skilling programme to incentivize the efforts of the industry in creating jobs in the organized textile and related sectors to promote skilling and skill up-gradation in the traditional sectors through respective sectoral divisions/organizations of Ministry of Textile; and to provide livelihood to all sections of the society across the country.

143. The Discovery of Hampi: The ruins at Hampi were brought to light in 1800 by an engineer and antiquarian named Colonel Colin Mackenzie. An employee of the English East India Company, he prepared the first survey map of the site. Much of the initial information he received was based on the memories of priests of the Virupaksha temple and the shrine of Pampadevi. Subsequently, from 1856, photographers began to record the monuments which enabled scholars to study them. As early as 1836 epigraphists began collecting several dozen inscriptions found at this and other temples at Hampi. In an effort to reconstruct the history of the city and the empire, historians collated information from these sources with accounts of foreign travellers and other literature written in Telugu, Kannada, Tamil and Sanskrit.

145. Among the best known of the Portuguese writers is Duarte Barbosa, who wrote a detailed account of trade and society in south India. Later, after 1600, we find growing numbers of Dutch, English and French travellers coming to India. One of the most famous was the French jeweller Jean-Baptiste Tavernier, who travelled to India at least six times. He was particularly fascinated with the trading conditions in India, and compared India to Iran and the Ottoman empire. Some of these travellers, like the Italian doctor Manucci, never returned to Europe, and settled down in India.

146. The world humanitarian day is observed annually on August 19, as on the same day in 2003, a terrorist attack at the UN headquarters in Baghdad led to the killing of UN's top repress-entative to Iraq, Sergio Vieira de Mello and 21 of his colleagues.

148. The 2019 Bharat Ratna award has been bestowed upon former President Pranab Mukherjee, Nanaji Deshmukh and singer Bhupen Hazarika. Nanaji Deshmukh and singer Bhupen Hazarika were awarded Bharat Ratna posthumously.

149. Aishwarya Pissay (born 14 August, 1995) is an Indian circuit and off-road motorcycle racer. She has become the first-ever Indian athlete to win a world title in motorsport on motorcycles. The TVS talent participated at the FIM Bajas World Cup and secured the 1st place in the women's category and 2nd in the junior's category. She is the first Indian woman to win 6 National titles in Circuit Racing and Rally Championship combined.

150. Hellaro (Gujarati) has won the Best Feature Film award at the 66th National Film awards for year 2018. While, Ayushmann Khurrana and Vicky Kaushal share the Best Actor Award for Andhadhun and Uri: The Surgical Strikes, respectively. Keerthi Suresh bagged Best Actress award for Mahanati. 'Uri' director Aditya Dhar won in the Best Director category.

PAPER II : MATHEMATICS

1. For $px^2 + qx + 1 = 0$ to have real roots we must have

$q^2 - 4p \geq 0$

$\Rightarrow \quad q^2 \geq 4p$

If $p = 1$ then $q^2 \geq 4 \Rightarrow q = 2, 3, 4$

If $p = 2$ then $q^2 \geq 8 \Rightarrow q = 3, 4$

If $p = 3$ then $q^2 \geq 12 \Rightarrow q = 4$

If $p = 4$ then $q^2 \geq 16 \Rightarrow q = 4$

Thus the number of equations of the form $px^2 + qx + 1 = 0$ which have real root is 7.

2. $1 - 2 + 3 - 4 + 5 - ... + 101$

$= (1 + 3 + 5 + ... + 101) - (2 + 4 + ... + 100)$

$= \frac{51}{2}[2\cdot 1+(51-1)\cdot 2]-\frac{50}{2}[2\cdot 2+(50-1)2]$

$= 51[1 + 50] - 50[2 + 49]$

$= 51 \times 51 - 50 \times 51$

$= 51(51 - 50)$

$\left\{S_n = \frac{n}{2}[2a+(n-1)d]\right\}$

$= 51 \times 1 = 51$

4. Given, $S_n = n + 12$

$\because \quad T_n = S_n - S_{n-1}$

$\therefore \quad T_3 = S_3 - S_{3-1}$

$\Rightarrow \quad T_3 = S_3 - S_2$

$\Rightarrow \quad T_3 = (3 + 12) - (2 + 12)$

$\Rightarrow \quad T_3 = 15 - 14$

$\Rightarrow \quad T_3 = 1$

Hence, third term = 1

5. $2x^2 - 2(k - 2)x - (k + 1) = 0$

Let α and β are roots

then $\alpha + \beta = k - 2, \alpha\beta = -\frac{(k+1)}{2}$

$\therefore \quad \alpha^2 + \beta^2 = (\alpha + \beta)^2 - 2\alpha\beta$

$= (k-2)^2 - 2\left[-\frac{(k+1)}{2}\right]$

$= (k - 2)^2 + (k + 1)$

$= k^2 + 4 - 4k + k + 1$

$= k^2 - 3k + 5$

Min^m, when $k = \frac{3}{2}$ $\left[\begin{array}{l} ax^2+bx+c \\ \text{Min}^m, a>0 \\ x=-\frac{b}{2a} \end{array}\right]$

6. $a(b - c)x^2 + b(c - a)x + c(a - b) = 0$

Given roots of the equation are equal

$x = 1 \therefore \alpha = \beta = 1$

$\alpha + \beta = 2 = -\frac{b(c-a)}{a(b-c)}$

and $\quad \alpha\beta = 1 \cdot 1 = 1 = \frac{c(a-b)}{a(b-c)}$

$\Rightarrow \quad ac - bc = ab - ac$

$\Rightarrow \quad 2ac = b(a + c)$

$\Rightarrow \quad b = \frac{2ac}{a+c}$

$\Rightarrow a, b, c$ are in H.P.

$\left[\begin{array}{l} ax^2+bx+c=0 \\ \text{if } a+b+c=0, \text{ then } x=1 \\ \text{one } root \text{ and } x=\frac{c}{a} \end{array}\right]$

7. Given that,

$|x^2 - 3x + 2| > x^2 - 3x + 2$

$\therefore x^2 - 3x + 2 > x^2 - 3x + 2$

or, $x^2 - 3x + 2 < -(x^2 - 3x + 2)$

$\Rightarrow x^2 - 3x + 2 + (x^2 - 3x + 2) < 0$

$\Rightarrow 2(x^2 - 3x + 2) < 0$

$\Rightarrow x^2 - 3x + 2 < 0$

$\Rightarrow (x - 1)(x - 2) < 0$

$\Rightarrow 1 < x < 2$

8. Let a be the first term and r be the c.r. of G.P. given the sum of odd terms of the G.P. = m

$\therefore a + ar^2 + ar^4 + ar^6 + ... + ar^{198} = m$

$\Rightarrow a[1 + r^2 + r^4 + r^6 + ... + r^{198}] = m$

$$\Rightarrow a\left[1\frac{\{(r^2)^{100}-1\}}{r^2-1}\right] = m$$

$$\Rightarrow a\left[\frac{r^{200}-1}{r^2-1}\right] = m \quad ...(i)$$

and the sum of even terms = n

$[ar + ar^3 + ar^5 + ... + ar^{199}] = n$

$\Rightarrow ar[1 + r^2 + r^4 + ... + r^{198}] = n$

$$\Rightarrow ar\left[\frac{1\{(r^2)^{100}-1\}}{r^2-1}\right] = n$$

$$\Rightarrow ar\left[\frac{r^{200}-1}{r^2-1}\right] = n \quad ...(ii)$$

From, dividing (i) by (ii), we get

$$\frac{a\left[\frac{r^{200}-1}{r^2-1}\right]}{ar\left[\frac{r^{200}-1}{r^2-1}\right]} = \frac{m}{n} \Rightarrow \frac{1}{r} = \frac{m}{n} \Rightarrow r = \frac{n}{m}$$

Hence, common ratio = $\frac{n}{m}$

9. Given that, A = $\{a, b, c\}$

and B = $\{a, b, c, d, e, f\}$

$\therefore$ (A $\cup$ B) = $\{a, b, c\} \cup \{a, b, c, d, e, f\}$

= $\{a, b, c, d, e, f\}$

$\therefore n(A \cup B) = 6$

10. The number of side of an octagon = 8

Here, $n = 8$

$\because$ Number of diagonals = ${}^nC_2 - n$

$\therefore$ Diagonals in octagon = ${}^8C_2 - 8$

$$= \frac{\lfloor 8}{\lfloor 2 \lfloor 8-2} - 8 = \frac{\lfloor 8}{\lfloor 2 \lfloor 6} - 8$$

$$= \frac{8\times 7\lfloor 6}{2\lfloor 6} - 8$$

$= 4 \times 7 - 8 = 28 - 8 = 20$

11. Let $\Delta = \begin{vmatrix} \lfloor 1 & \lfloor 2 & \lfloor 3 \\ \lfloor 2 & \lfloor 3 & \lfloor 4 \\ \lfloor 3 & \lfloor 4 & \lfloor 5 \end{vmatrix}$

$$= \begin{vmatrix} \lfloor 1 & 2\lfloor 1 & 3\cdot 2\lfloor 1 \\ \lfloor 2 & 3\lfloor 2 & 4\cdot 3\lfloor 2 \\ \lfloor 3 & 4\lfloor 3 & 5\cdot 4\lfloor 3 \end{vmatrix} \text{ taking common } \lfloor 1\cdot\lfloor 2\cdot\lfloor 3$$

$$= \lfloor 1\times\lfloor 2\times\lfloor 3\begin{vmatrix} 1 & 2 & 6 \\ 1 & 3 & 12 \\ 1 & 4 & 20 \end{vmatrix}$$

Applying $R_1 \to R_1 - R_2$, $R_2 \to R_2 - R_3$

$$= 1\times 2\times 6\begin{vmatrix} 0 & -1 & -6 \\ 0 & -1 & -8 \\ 1 & 4 & 20 \end{vmatrix}$$

$= 12[0 - 0 + 1(8 - 6)]$

$= 12 \times 2 = 24$

12. $\begin{vmatrix} x & 0 & 2 \\ 2x & 2 & 1 \\ 1 & 1 & 1 \end{vmatrix} + \begin{vmatrix} 3x & 0 & 2 \\ x^2 & 2 & 1 \\ 0 & 1 & 1 \end{vmatrix} = 0$

$\Rightarrow x(2 - 1) - 0 + 2(2x - 2) + 3x(2 - 1)$

$+ 0 + 2(x^2 - 0) = 0$

$\Rightarrow x + 4x - 4 + 3x + 2x^2 = 0$

$\Rightarrow 2x^2 + 8x - 4 = 0$

$\Rightarrow x^2 + 4x - 2 = 0$

$$\Rightarrow x = \frac{-4\pm\sqrt{16+8}}{2\times 1} = \frac{-4\pm\sqrt{24}}{2}$$

$$= \frac{-4\pm 2\sqrt{6}}{2} = -2\pm\sqrt{6}$$

Hence, $x = -2\pm\sqrt{6}$

13. Given, $x + a + b + c = 0$

Let $\Delta = \begin{vmatrix} x+a & b & c \\ a & x+b & c \\ a & b & x+c \end{vmatrix}$

Applying $C_1 \to C_1 + C_2 + C_3$

$$= \begin{vmatrix} x+a+b+c & b & c \\ x+a+b+c & x+b & c \\ x+a+b+c & b & x+c \end{vmatrix}$$

Taking common $(x + a + b + c)$ from C_1

$$= (x+a+b+c)\begin{vmatrix} 1 & b & c \\ 1 & x+b & c \\ 1 & b & x+c \end{vmatrix}$$

$$= 0\cdot\begin{vmatrix} 1 & b & c \\ 1 & x+b & c \\ 1 & b & x+c \end{vmatrix} = 0$$

14. Given, $A = \begin{bmatrix} 1 & -1 \\ -1 & 1 \end{bmatrix}$

$$\therefore \quad A^2 = \begin{bmatrix} 1 & -1 \\ -1 & 1 \end{bmatrix}\begin{bmatrix} 1 & -1 \\ -1 & 1 \end{bmatrix}$$

$$= \begin{bmatrix} 1+1 & -1-1 \\ -1-1 & 1+1 \end{bmatrix}$$

And, $A^3 = A^2 \cdot A = 2\begin{bmatrix} 1 & -1 \\ -1 & 1 \end{bmatrix}\begin{bmatrix} 1 & -1 \\ -1 & 1 \end{bmatrix}$

$= 2\begin{bmatrix} 1+1 & -1-1 \\ -1-1 & 1+1 \end{bmatrix}$

$= 2\begin{bmatrix} 2 & -2 \\ -2 & 2 \end{bmatrix} = 4\begin{bmatrix} 1 & -1 \\ -1 & 1 \end{bmatrix}$

$\therefore A^3 - 2A^2 = 4\begin{bmatrix} 1 & -1 \\ -1 & 1 \end{bmatrix} - 2\cdot 2\begin{bmatrix} 1 & -1 \\ -1 & 1 \end{bmatrix}$

$= 4\left\{\begin{bmatrix} 1 & -1 \\ -1 & 1 \end{bmatrix} - \begin{bmatrix} 1 & -1 \\ -1 & 1 \end{bmatrix}\right\}$

$= 4\begin{bmatrix} 0 & 0 \\ 0 & 0 \end{bmatrix} = \begin{bmatrix} 0 & 0 \\ 0 & 0 \end{bmatrix}$ = a null matrix

15. $x^2 - 16x + 39 = 0$

$\Rightarrow x - 3x - 13x + 39 = 0$

$\Rightarrow x(x - 3) - 13(x - 3) = 0$

$\Rightarrow (x - 3)(x - 13) = 0$

either, $x - 3 = 0$ or, $x - 13 = 0$

$\therefore \quad x = 3$ or $x = 13$

Here, $m = 3$ and $n = 13$, $(m < n)$

Given, four terms p, q, r and s are inserted between m and n to form in A.P.

$\therefore$ 3, 5, 7, 9, 11, 13 are in A.P.

$\therefore \quad p = 5, q = 7, r = 9, s = 11$

$\therefore P + Q + R + S = 5 + 7 + 9 + 11 = 32$

16. $x^2 + mx + 2 = 0$

The quadratic equation always have real roots.

$\therefore \quad b^2 - 4ac \geq 0$

$\Rightarrow \quad m^2 - 4 \times 1 \times 2 \geq 0$

$\Rightarrow \quad m^2 - 8 \geq 0$

$\Rightarrow \quad m^2 \geq 8$

17. $\left[\frac{i+\sqrt{3}}{2}\right]^{2019} + \left[\frac{i-\sqrt{3}}{2}\right]^{2019}$

$= \left[\left(\frac{i+\sqrt{3}}{2}\right)^3\right]^{673} + \left[\left(\frac{i-\sqrt{3}}{2}\right)^3\right]^{673}$

$= \left[\frac{i^3 + 3\cdot i^2 \cdot \sqrt{3} + 3\cdot i \cdot (\sqrt{3})^2 + 3\sqrt{3}}{8}\right]^{673}$

$+ \left[\frac{i^3 - 3\cdot i^2 \cdot \sqrt{3} + 3\cdot i \cdot \sqrt{3}^2 - 3\sqrt{3}}{8}\right]^{673}$

$= \left[\frac{-i - 3\sqrt{3} + 9i + 3\sqrt{3}}{8}\right]^{673} + \left[\frac{-i + 3\sqrt{3} + 9i - 3\sqrt{3}}{8}\right]^{673}$

$= \left[\frac{8i}{8}\right]^{673} + \left[\frac{8i}{8}\right]^{673}$ $\quad [i^2 = -1, i^3 = -i = i^4 = 1]$

$= [i]^{673} + [i]^{673} = 2[i]^{673}$

$= 2[i^4]^{168} \times i = 2[1]^{168} \times i$

$= 2 \times i = 2i$

18. Given equation

$x^2 + x + 1 = 0$

$\therefore x = \frac{-1 \pm \sqrt{1^2 - 4}}{2\cdot 1} = \frac{-1 \pm \sqrt{-3}}{2} = \frac{-1 \pm \sqrt{3}i}{2}$

Given that α and β are roots of equation.

$\therefore \quad \alpha = \frac{-1-\sqrt{3}i}{2}$ and $\beta = \frac{-1+\sqrt{3}i}{2}$

Now, $\sum_{j=0}^{3}(\alpha^j + \beta^j) = \alpha^\circ + \beta^\circ + \alpha^1 + \beta^1$

$+ \alpha^2 + \beta^2 + \alpha^3 + \beta^3$

$= 1 + 1 + \frac{-1-\sqrt{3}i}{2} + \frac{-1+\sqrt{3}i}{2}$

$+ \left(\frac{-1-\sqrt{3}i}{2}\right)^2 + \left(\frac{-1+\sqrt{3}i}{2}\right)^2$

$+ \left(\frac{-1-\sqrt{3}i}{2}\right)^3 + \left(\frac{-1+\sqrt{3}i}{2}\right)^3$

$= 2 + \frac{-1-\sqrt{3}i-1+\sqrt{3}i}{2} + \left(\frac{1+\sqrt{3}i}{2}\right)^2 + \left(\frac{1-\sqrt{3}i}{2}\right)^2$

$+ -\left(\frac{1+\sqrt{3}i}{2}\right)^3 - \left(\frac{1-\sqrt{3}i}{2}\right)^3$

$= 2 - 1 + \left(\frac{1+\sqrt{3}i}{2}\right)^2\left(1 - \frac{1+\sqrt{3}i}{2}\right)$

$+ \left(\frac{1-\sqrt{3}i}{2}\right)^2\left(1 - \frac{1-\sqrt{3}i}{2}\right)$

$= 1 + \frac{(1-3+2\sqrt{3}i)}{4}\left(\frac{1-\sqrt{3}i}{2}\right) + \frac{(1-3-2\sqrt{3}i)}{4}\frac{(1+\sqrt{3}i)}{2}$

$= 1 + \frac{(-1+\sqrt{3}i)}{2}\frac{(1-\sqrt{3}i)}{2} + \frac{-(1+\sqrt{3}i)}{2}\frac{(1+\sqrt{3}i)}{2}$

$= 1 - \frac{1}{4}(1-3-2\sqrt{3}i) - \frac{1}{4}(1-3+2\sqrt{3}i)$

$= 1 - \frac{1}{4}(-2-2\sqrt{3}i-2+2\sqrt{3}i)$

$= 1 - \frac{1}{4}(-2-2) = 1 - \frac{1}{4}(-4)$

$= 1 + 1 = 2$

19. Let A = cricket player and B = football player

Then, $n(A) = 50\%$, $n(B) = 40\%$,

$n(A \cup B) = 10\%$

$\therefore\ n(A \cup B) = n(A) + n(B) - n(A \cap B)$
$= 50 + 40 - 10$
$= 90 - 10 = 80\%$

$\therefore$ per cent of students play either cricket or football = 80%

$\therefore$ per cent of students play neither cricket nor football
$= 100 - n(A \cup B)$
$= 100 - 80\% = 20\%$

20. Given, A = {0, 1, 2} and B = {2, 3; 5, ...}
Then, $(A \cap B) = \{0, 1, 2\} \cap \{2, 3, 5, ...\} = \{2\}$

21. Given, $x = (1 + i)$
then, $x^2 = (1 + i)^2 = 1 + i^2 + 2i = 1 - 1 + 2i = 2i,$
$x^4 = (1 + i)^4 = (2i)^2 = 4i^2 = 4 \times -1 = -4$
and $x^6 = x^4 \times x^2 = -4(2i) = -8i$
$\therefore\ x^6 + x^4 + x^2 + 1 = -8i + (-4) + 2i + 1$
$= -6i - 3$

22. Let $2+\cfrac{1}{2+\cfrac{1}{2+\cfrac{1}{2+...\alpha}}} = x$

Then, $x = 2+\frac{1}{x}$

$\Rightarrow\ x = \frac{2x+1}{x}$

$\Rightarrow x^2 - 2x - 1 = 0$

$\Rightarrow\ x = \frac{-(-2)\pm\sqrt{4+4}}{2}$

$= \frac{2\pm2\sqrt{2}}{2} = 1\pm\sqrt{2}$

$\Rightarrow\ x = 1+\sqrt{2}$ or $x = 1-\sqrt{2}$

Hence, $x = \sqrt{2}+1$ $\left[x = 1-\sqrt{2}\text{ is ignoring}\right]$

23. Given, P(n, r) = 2520

$\Rightarrow\ \frac{\lfloor n}{\lfloor n-r} = 2520$ ...(*i*)

and C(n, r) = 21

$\Rightarrow\ \frac{\lfloor n}{\lfloor r \lfloor n-r} = 21$ ...(*ii*)

From dividing (*i*) by (*ii*) we get

$\frac{\lfloor n}{\lfloor n-r} \times \frac{\lfloor r \lfloor n-r}{\lfloor n} = \frac{2520}{21}$

$\Rightarrow\ \lfloor r = \frac{360}{3} = 120$

$\Rightarrow\ \lfloor 5 = 5 \cdot 4 \cdot 3 \cdot 2 \cdot 1 = 120$

$\Rightarrow\ r = 5$

From (*i*) $\frac{\lfloor n}{\lfloor n-5} = 2520$

$\Rightarrow\ \frac{n(n-1)(n-2)(n-3)(n-4)\lfloor n-5}{\lfloor n-5} = 2520$

$\Rightarrow n(n - 1)(n - 2)(n - 3)(n - 4) = 2520$

$\Rightarrow 7 \times 6 \times 5 \times 4 \times 3 \times 2 = 2520$

$\therefore\ n = 7$

Now, $C(n + 1, r + 1) = C(7 + 1, 5 + 1)$

$= C(8, 6) = \frac{\lfloor 8}{\lfloor 6 \lfloor 8-6}$

$= \frac{\lfloor 8}{\lfloor 6 \lfloor 2} = \frac{8\times7}{2} = 4 \times 7 = 28$

24. $(1 + 2x + x^2)^5 + (1+ 4y + 4y^2)^5$
$= [(1 + x)^2]^5 + [(1 + 2y)^2]^5$
$= (1 + x)^{10} + (1+ 2y)^{10}$
$= ({}^{10}C_0\,(1)^{10-0} \cdot x^0 + {}^{10}C_1 \cdot 1 \cdot x^1 + ... + {}^{10}C_{10} \cdot 1 \cdot x^{10})$
$+ ({}^{10}C_0 \cdot 1 \cdot y^0 + {}^{10}C_1 \cdot 1 \cdot y^1 + ... + {}^{10}C_{10} \cdot 1 \cdot y^{10})$
$= 1 + {}^{10}C_1 \cdot x + ... + 1 \cdot x^{10} + 1 + {}^{10}C_1 \cdot y + ... + y^{10}$
$= (2 + {}^{10}C_1\, x + ... + x^{10}) + ({}^{10}C_1\, y + ... + y^{10})$

Here, the number of terms = 11 + 10 = 21

25. The given expression $= \left(x^2 + \frac{1}{x}\right)^{2n}$

Here, n = 2n, which is an even number.

So, $\left(\frac{2n}{2}+1\right)$th *i.e.*, (n + 1)th term is the middle term

Now, $T_{n+1} = {}^{2n}C_n (x^2)^{2n-n} \cdot \left(\frac{1}{x}\right)^n$

$= {}^{2n}C_n (x^2)^n \times x^{-n} = {}^{2n}C_n \cdot x^{2n} \cdot x^{-n}$
$= {}^{2n}C_n \cdot x^{2n-n}$
$= {}^{2n}C_n \cdot x^n$

Given, Middle term = $184756\, x^{10}$

${}^{2n}C_n\, x^n = 184756\, x^{10}$

$\Rightarrow\ \frac{\lfloor 2n}{\lfloor n \lfloor 2n-n} x^n = 184756\, x^{10}$

$\Rightarrow\ \frac{\lfloor 2n}{\lfloor n \lfloor n} x^n = 184756\, x^{10}$

$\Rightarrow\ \frac{\lfloor 20}{\lfloor 10 \lfloor 10} x^{10} = 184756\, x^{10}$

Hence, $n = 10$

26. Given that,

$$A = \begin{pmatrix} 1 & 2 \\ 2 & 3 \\ 3 & 4 \end{pmatrix} \text{ and } B = \begin{pmatrix} 1 & 2 \\ 2 & 1 \end{pmatrix}$$

i.e., $A = [a_{ij}]_{3\times2}$ and $B = [b_{ij}]_{2\times2}$

$\Rightarrow \quad AB = [a_{ij}\ b_{ij}]_{3\times 2}$

$\therefore$ AB exists

$B \times A = [b_{ij}]_{2\times 2} \times [a_{ij}]_{3\times 2}$

$\therefore$ BA does not exists

29. Let $(r + 1)$th term in the expansion of $\left(\sqrt{x}-\frac{k}{x^2}\right)^{10}$ be independent of x

Now, $T_{r+1} = {}^{10}C_r(\sqrt{x})^{10-r}\cdot\left(\frac{-k}{x^2}\right)^r$

$= {}^{10}C_r x^{5-\frac{r}{2}}\cdot k^r\cdot x^{-2r}$

$= {}^{10}C_r x^{5-\frac{r}{2}-2r}\cdot k^r$

$\Rightarrow \quad T_{r+1} = {}^{10}C_r x^{5-\frac{5r}{2}}\cdot k^r \quad \ldots(i)$

This will be independent of x,

if $5-\frac{5r}{2} = 0$

$\Rightarrow \frac{10-5r}{2} = 0$

$\Rightarrow 10 - 5r = 0$

$\Rightarrow 5r = 10$

$\Rightarrow r = \frac{10}{5} = 2$

Putting $r = 2$ in (i), we get

$T_3 = {}^{10}C_2\, k^2$

It is given that the term independent of x is equal to 405

$\therefore \quad {}^{10}C_2\, k^2 = 405 \Rightarrow \frac{\lfloor 10}{\lfloor 2 \lfloor 8}k^2 = 405$

$\Rightarrow \frac{10.9}{2}k^2 = 405$

$\Rightarrow k^2 = \frac{405}{45} = 9$

$\Rightarrow k^2 = 9$

$\Rightarrow k = \sqrt{9}$

$\Rightarrow k = \pm 3$

30. C(47, 4) + C(51, 3) + C(50, 3) + C(49, 3) + C(48, 3) + C(47, 3)

$= {}^{47}C_4 + {}^{51}C_3 + {}^{50}C_3 + {}^{49}C_3 + {}^{48}C_3 + {}^{47}C_3$

$= {}^{47}C_3 + {}^{47}C_4 + {}^{48}C_3 + {}^{49}C_3 + {}^{50}C_3 + {}^{51}C_3$

$= ({}^{47}C_3 + {}^{47}C_4) + {}^{48}C_3 + {}^{49}C_3 + {}^{50}C_3 + {}^{51}C_3$

$[{}^nC_{r-1} + {}^nC_r = {}^{n+1}C_r]$

$= {}^{47+1}C_4 + {}^{48}C_3 + {}^{49}C_3 + {}^{50}C_3 + {}^{51}C_3$

$= ({}^{48}C_4 + {}^{48}C_3) + {}^{49}C_3 + {}^{50}C_3 + {}^{51}C_3$

$= {}^{48+1}C_4 + {}^{49}C_3 + {}^{50}C_3 + {}^{51}C_3$

$= ({}^{49}C_4 + {}^{49}C_3) + {}^{50}C_3 + {}^{51}C_3$

$= {}^{49+1}C_4 + {}^{50}C_3 + {}^{51}C_3$

$= ({}^{50}C_4 + {}^{50}C_3) + {}^{51}C_3$

$= {}^{50+1}C_4 + {}^{51}C_3$

$= {}^{51}C_4 + {}^{51}C_3 \quad [{}^nC_{r-1} + {}^nC_r = {}^{n+1}C_r]$

$= {}^{51+1}C_4 = {}^{52}C_4 = C(52, 4)$

31. As a, b, c, are in A.P.

So, $b - a = c - b$

(1) ka, kb, kc are in A.P.

$\Rightarrow kb - ka = kc - kb$

$\Rightarrow k(b - a) = k(c - b)$

$\Rightarrow b - a = c - b$

(2) $k - a, k - b, k - c$ are in A.P.

$\Rightarrow k - b - (k - a) = k - c - (k - b)$

$\Rightarrow k - b - k + a = k - c - k + b$

$\Rightarrow a - b = b - c \Rightarrow -(b - a) = -(c - b)$

$\Rightarrow b - a = c - b$

(3) $\frac{a}{k}, \frac{b}{k}, \frac{c}{k}$ are in A.P.

$\Rightarrow \frac{b}{k}-\frac{a}{k} = \frac{c}{k}-\frac{b}{k}$

$\Rightarrow \frac{1}{k}(b-a) = \frac{1}{k}(c-b)$

$\Rightarrow b - a = c - b$

Hence, (1), (2) and (3) are in A.P.

32. As, A number is divisible by 4 if the number formed by its last two digits is divisible by 4.

So, two-digits number are divisible by 4

= 12, 16, 20, 24, 28, 32, 36, 40, 44, 48, 52, 56, 60, 64, 68, 72, 76, 80, 84, 88, 92, 96

Hence, the number of two digit numbers = 22

33. Given that, $S_{2n} = 3n + 14n^2$

When, $n = \frac{n}{2}$ then $S_n = \frac{3n}{2}+\frac{14n^2}{4}$

$\Rightarrow S_n = \frac{3n}{2}+\frac{7n^2}{2}$

$\Rightarrow S_n = \frac{1}{2}n(3+7n)$

$\therefore S_{n-1} = \frac{1}{2}(n-1)[3+7(n-1)]$

$\Rightarrow S_{n-1} = \frac{1}{2}(n-1)[3+7n-7]$

$= \frac{1}{2}(n-1)(7n-4)$

$\because T_n = S_n - S_{n-1}$

$$= \frac{1}{2}n(3+7n) - \frac{1}{2}(n-1)(7n-4)$$

$$\Rightarrow T_n = \frac{1}{2}[3n + 7n^2 - 7n^2 + 4n + 7n - 4]$$

$$\Rightarrow \quad T_n = \frac{1}{2}(14n-4) = 7n - 2$$

$$\Rightarrow \quad T_1 = 7 \times 1 - 2 = 5$$

$$\Rightarrow \quad T_2 = 7 \times 2 - 2 = 12$$

$\therefore$ the common difference

$$= T_2 - T_1 = 12 - 5 = 7$$

i.e., $\quad d = 7$

34. Let a be the first term and k be the common ratio of a G.P.

Then, 3rd term $= t_3 = ak^{3-1} = p$

$\Rightarrow \quad ak^2 = p \quad$ ...(*i*)

8th term $= t_8 = ak^{8-1} = q$

$\Rightarrow \quad ak^7 = q \quad$ ...(*ii*)

and, 13th term $= t_{13} = ak^{13-1} = r$

$\Rightarrow \quad ak^{12} = r \quad$ ...(*iii*)

From (*ii*), divided by (*i*), we get

$$\frac{ak^7}{ak^2} = \frac{q}{p} \Rightarrow k^5 = \frac{q}{p} \quad \text{...(iv)}$$

From (*iii*), divided by (*ii*), we get

$$\frac{ak^{12}}{ak^7} = \frac{r}{q} \Rightarrow k^5 = \frac{r}{q} \quad \text{...(v)}$$

From (*i*) and (*ii*), we get

$$\frac{q}{p} = \frac{r}{q} \Rightarrow q^2 = pr$$

39. S = {2, 4, 6, 8, ..., 20}

Here, $\quad n(S) = 10$

$\therefore$ The maximum number of subset

$$= 2^{10} = 2^5 \times 2^5$$

$$= 32 \times 32 = 1024$$

40. Binary numbers are represented by 0's and 1's

Given, $c > d$

$\therefore (cdccddcccddd)_2 = (101100111000)_2$

$(101100111000)_2 = (1 \times 2^{11}) + (0 \times 2^{10}) + (1 \times 2^9) + (1 \times 2^8) + (0 \times 2^7) + (0 \times 2^6) + (1 \times 2^5) + (1 \times 2^4) + (1 \times 2^3) + (0 \times 2^2) + (0 \times 2^1) + (0 \times 2^0)$

$$= 2^{11} + 2^9 + 2^8 + 2^5 + 2^4 + 2^3$$

$$= 2^3 + 2^4 + 2^5 + 2^5 (2^3 + 2^4 + 2^6)$$

$$= 8 + 16 + 32 + 32(8 + 16 + 64)$$

$$= 56 + 32(88)$$

$$= 56 + 2816 = (2872)$$

$$\therefore (101100111000)_2 = (2872)_{10}$$

41. Given, cosec $\theta = \dfrac{29}{21}$

$$\therefore \quad \sin\theta = \frac{21}{29}$$

$$\therefore \quad \cos\theta = \sqrt{1-\sin^2\theta} = \sqrt{1-\left(\frac{21}{29}\right)^2}$$

$$= \sqrt{\left(1-\frac{21}{29}\right)\left(1+\frac{21}{29}\right)}$$

$$= \sqrt{\frac{8}{29} \times \frac{50}{29}} = \sqrt{\frac{8 \times 2 \times 25}{29 \times 29}}$$

$$= \frac{4 \times 5}{29} = \frac{20}{29}$$

$$\therefore \quad \tan\theta = \frac{\sin\theta}{\cos\theta} = \frac{\frac{21}{29}}{\frac{20}{29}} = \frac{21}{20}$$

$$\therefore 4\sec\theta + 4\tan\theta = \frac{4}{\cos\theta} + \frac{4\sin\theta}{\cos\theta}$$

$$= \frac{4}{\frac{20}{29}} + 4 \times \frac{21}{20}$$

$$= 4 \times \frac{29}{20} + 4 \times \frac{21}{20}$$

$$= 4\left(\frac{29}{20} + \frac{21}{20}\right) = 4\left(\frac{29+21}{20}\right)$$

$$= 4 \times \frac{50}{20} = 4 \times \frac{5}{2} = 10$$

43. Let A ladder = AD = 9 m

and $\quad$ CD = 9 m

$\therefore \quad$ CD = AD = 9 am

BC = height of the flagstaff

$\because$ ΔACD is isosceles triangle

$\angle$CAB = 60°

$\therefore \quad \angle$ACB = $\angle$CAD = 30°

$\therefore \quad \angle$BAD = 30°

In ΔABD,

$$\sin 30° = \frac{BD}{AD}$$

$$\Rightarrow \quad \frac{1}{2} = \frac{BD}{9}$$

$$\Rightarrow \quad BD = \frac{9}{2}\text{ m} = 4.5\text{ m}$$

Therefore, BC = BD + DC

= 4.5 + 9 m = 13.5 m

45. $\tan\left\{2\tan^{-1}\left(\frac{1}{3}\right)\right\} \quad \left[2\tan^{-1}x = \tan^{-1}\frac{2x}{1-x^2}\right]$

Here, $2\tan^{-1}\frac{1}{3} = \tan^{-1}\left[\frac{2\cdot\frac{1}{3}}{1-\left(\frac{1}{3}\right)^2}\right]$

$= \tan^{-1}\left(\frac{\frac{2}{3}}{1-\frac{1}{9}}\right) = \tan^{-1}\left(\frac{\frac{2}{3}}{\frac{9-1}{9}}\right)$

$= \tan^{-1}\left(\frac{2}{3}\times\frac{9}{8}\right) = \tan^{-1}\left(\frac{3}{4}\right)$

$\therefore \tan\left\{2\tan^{-1}\left(\frac{1}{3}\right)\right\} = \tan\left\{\tan^{-1}\left(\frac{3}{4}\right)\right\}$

[$\tan(\tan^{-1}\theta) = \theta$]

$= \frac{3}{4}$

46. We know that, projection of $\vec{a}$ on $\vec{b} = \frac{\vec{a}\cdot\vec{b}}{|\vec{b}|}$

Here, $\vec{a} = \vec{i}-2\vec{j}+\vec{k}$ and $\vec{b} = 4\vec{i}-4\vec{j}+7\vec{k}$

$\therefore \quad \vec{a}\cdot\vec{b} = (\vec{i}-2\vec{j}+\vec{k})\cdot(4\vec{i}-4\vec{j}+7\vec{k})$

$= 1(4) + (-2)(-4) + 1(7)$

$= 4 + 8 + 7 = 19$

and $\quad |\vec{b}| = \sqrt{4^2+(-4)^2+7^2}$

$= \sqrt{16+16+49} = \sqrt{81} = 9$

Hence, projection of $\vec{a}$ on $\vec{b} = \frac{\vec{a}\cdot\vec{b}}{|\vec{b}|} = \frac{19}{9}$

52. Given, equation of lines are

$x\cos\alpha + y\sin\alpha = a$

and $\quad x\sin\beta - y\cos\beta = a$

$\Rightarrow \quad y\sin\alpha = -x\cos\alpha + a$

and $y\cos\beta = x\sin\beta - a$

$\Rightarrow \quad y = -\frac{x\cos\alpha}{\sin\alpha}+\frac{a}{\sin\alpha}$

and $\quad y = -\frac{x\sin\beta}{\cos\beta}-\frac{a}{\cos\beta}$

Let m_1 and m_2 be the slope of two given lines

Then, $\quad m_1 = -\frac{\cos\alpha}{\sin\alpha}$ and $m_2 = \frac{\sin\beta}{\cos\beta}$

Let θ be the angle between the lines

Then, $\tan\theta = \left|\frac{m_1-m_2}{1+m_1m_2}\right|$

$= \left|\frac{\frac{-\cos\alpha}{\sin\alpha}-\frac{\sin\beta}{\cos\beta}}{1+\frac{-\cos\alpha}{\sin\alpha}\cdot\frac{\sin\beta}{\cos\beta}}\right|$

$= \left|\frac{-(\cos\alpha\cos\beta+\sin\alpha\sin\beta)}{\sin\alpha\cos\beta-\cos\alpha\sin\beta}\right|$

$= \left|\frac{-\cos(\alpha-\beta)}{\sin(\alpha-\beta)}\right| = |-\cot(\alpha-\beta)|$

$= \pm[-\cot(\alpha-\beta)]$

$\therefore \quad \tan\theta = \pm\cot(\alpha-\beta) \quad \left[\tan\left(\frac{\pi}{2}+\theta\right) = -\cot\theta\right]$

$\tan\theta = -\cot(\alpha-\beta)$

$= \tan\left[\frac{\pi}{2}+(\alpha-\beta)\right]$

$\therefore \quad \tan\theta = \tan\left[\frac{\pi}{2}+(\alpha-\beta)\right]$

$\therefore \quad \theta = \frac{\pi}{2}+(\alpha-\beta) = \frac{\pi+2\alpha-2\beta}{2}$

$= \frac{\pi-2\beta+2\alpha}{2}$

53. Given, P($m\cos 2\alpha$, $m\sin 2\alpha$) and Q($m\cos 2\beta$, $m\sin 2\beta$)

Distance PQ $= \sqrt{\text{(Difference of abscisse)}^2 + \text{(diff. of ordinates)}^2}$

$= \sqrt{(m\cos 2\beta - m\cos 2\alpha)^2 + (m\sin 2\beta - m\sin 2\alpha)^2}$

$= \sqrt{m^2(\cos^2 2\beta+\cos^2 2\alpha-2\cos 2\beta\cos 2\alpha) + m^2(\sin^2 2\beta+\sin^2 2\alpha-2\sin 2\beta\sin 2\alpha)}$

$= \sqrt{m^2(\cos^2 2\beta+\sin^2 2\beta)+(\cos^2 2\alpha+\sin^2 2\alpha) - 2(\cos 2\beta\cos 2\alpha+\sin 2\beta\sin 2\alpha)}$

$= \sqrt{m^2[1+1-2\cos(2\alpha-2\beta)]}$

$= \sqrt{m^2[2-2\cos(2\alpha-2\beta)]}$

$= \sqrt{2m^2[1-\cos(2\alpha-2\beta)]}$

$= \sqrt{2m^2\cdot 2\sin^2\left(\frac{2\alpha-2\beta}{2}\right)}$

$= \sqrt{4m^2\sin^2(\alpha-\beta)} \quad [1-\cos 2\theta = 2\sin^2\theta]$

$= \pm[2m\sin(\alpha-\beta)]$

$= |2m\sin(\alpha-\beta)|$

57. $\frac{x-1}{1} = \frac{y-3}{2} = \frac{z+2}{7} \quad \ldots(i)$

$\Rightarrow \quad \frac{x-x_1}{a} = \frac{y-y_1}{b} = \frac{z-z_1}{c}$

A point on the line (*i*)
its co-ordinates
$(1 + 1, 2 + 3, 7 - 2)$
$= (2, 5, 5)$

58. Given line, $\frac{x-4}{1} = \frac{y-2}{1} = \frac{z-k}{2}$ lies on the plane $2x - 4y + z = 7$

$\therefore$ $(4, 2, k)$ Satisfy the plane

$\therefore 2 \times 4 - 4 \times 2 + k = 7$

$\Rightarrow 8 - 8 + k = 7$

$\Rightarrow \quad k = 7$

60. Given that, $A = (x, y, -3)$, $B(2, 0, -1)$ and $C(4, 2, 3)$ lie on a straight line

Let B divide AC in the ratio $\lambda : 1$

Then, co-ordinate of B are

$$\left[\frac{\lambda\cdot 4+1\cdot x}{\lambda+1}, \frac{\lambda\cdot 2+1\cdot y}{\lambda+1}, \frac{\lambda\cdot 3+1\cdot -3}{\lambda+1}\right]$$

$$= \left[\frac{4\lambda+x}{\lambda+1}, \frac{2\lambda+y}{\lambda+1}, \frac{3\lambda-3}{\lambda+1}\right]$$

But, co-ordinate of B are given as $(2, 0, -1)$

$$\therefore \quad \frac{4\lambda+x}{\lambda+1} = 2, \ \frac{2\lambda+y}{\lambda+1} = 0, \ \frac{3\lambda-3}{\lambda+1} = -1$$

$\Rightarrow 4\lambda + x = 2\lambda + 2,$

$2\lambda + y = 0, \qquad 3\lambda - 3 = -\lambda - 1$

$\Rightarrow 2\lambda + x = 2, \qquad 4\lambda = 3 - 1 = 2$

$\Rightarrow x = 2 - 2\lambda, \qquad \lambda = \frac{2}{4} = \frac{1}{2}$

$$= 2 - 2\cdot\frac{1}{2} = 2 - 1 = 1$$

and $2\lambda + y = 0$

$$\therefore y = -2\lambda = -2\cdot\frac{1}{2} = -1$$

Hence, value of x and y are 1 and -1

61. $\frac{a^2}{\cos^2 x} + \frac{b^2}{\sin^2 x}$

$\Rightarrow a^2 \sec^2 x + b^2 \operatorname{cosec}^2 x$

$\Rightarrow a^2 (1 + \tan^2 x) + b^2 (1 + \cot^2 x)$

$\Rightarrow a^2 + b^2 + a^2 \tan^2 x + b^2 \cot^2 x$

$\Rightarrow a^2 + b^2 + 2ab \because a^2 \tan^2 x + b^2 \cot^2 x \geq 2ab$

$= (a + b)^2$

$\text{Min}^m \left(\frac{a^2}{\cos^2 x} + \frac{b^2}{\sin^2 x}\right)$ value $= (a + b)^2$

62. $\because$ A, B, C are in A.P.,

and $\quad b : c = \sqrt{3} : \sqrt{2}$

$\Rightarrow \quad 2B = A + C,$

$A + B + C = 180° \qquad \ldots(i)$

$\Rightarrow \quad B = 60°$

$$\frac{\sin B}{b} = \frac{\sin C}{c} \Rightarrow \frac{\sin 60°}{\sqrt{3}} = \frac{\sin C}{\sqrt{2}}$$

$$\Rightarrow \quad \frac{\frac{\sqrt{3}}{2}}{\sqrt{3}} = \frac{\sin C}{\sqrt{2}}$$

$$\Rightarrow \quad \frac{1}{2} = \frac{\sin C}{\sqrt{2}} \Rightarrow \sin C = \frac{1}{\sqrt{2}}$$

$$\Rightarrow \quad \sin 45° = \frac{1}{\sqrt{2}}$$

$\Rightarrow \quad C = 45°$

From (*i*)

$A + B + C = 180°$

$\Rightarrow A + 60° + 45° = 180°$

$\Rightarrow \quad A = 180° - 105° = 75°$

63. Given, $\tan A - \tan B = x$

and, $\cot B - \cot A = y$

$$\Rightarrow \quad \frac{1}{\tan B} - \frac{1}{\tan A} = y \Rightarrow \frac{\tan A - \tan B}{\tan A \tan B} = y$$

$$\Rightarrow \quad \frac{x}{\tan A \tan B} = y \Rightarrow \tan A \cdot \tan B = \frac{x}{y}$$

$$\therefore \cot(A - B) = \frac{1}{\tan(A-B)} = \frac{1}{\frac{\tan A - \tan B}{1 + \tan A \tan B}}$$

$$= \frac{1 + \tan A \cdot \tan B}{\tan A - \tan B} = \frac{1 + \frac{x}{y}}{x}$$

$$= \frac{y+x}{xy} = \frac{y}{xy} + \frac{x}{xy} = \frac{1}{x} + \frac{1}{y}$$

Hence, the value of $\cot(A - B)$ is $\frac{1}{x} + \frac{1}{y}$

64. $\sin(\alpha + \beta) - 2 \sin \alpha \cos \beta + \sin(\alpha - \beta)$

$= \sin \alpha \cos \beta + \cos \alpha \sin \beta$
$\quad - 2 \sin \alpha \cos \beta + \sin \alpha \cos \beta$
$\quad - \cos \alpha \sin \beta$

$= 2 \sin \alpha \cos \beta - 2 \sin \alpha \cos \beta$
$\quad + \cos \alpha \sin \beta - \cos \alpha \sin \beta$

$= 0 + 0 = 0$

65. Given that,

$2 \tan A = 3 \tan B = 1$

$$\therefore \quad \tan A = \frac{1}{2} \text{ and } \tan B = \frac{1}{3}$$

$$\therefore \tan(A - B) = \frac{\tan A - \tan B}{1 + \tan A \tan B}$$

$$= \frac{\frac{1}{2} - \frac{1}{3}}{1 + \frac{1}{2} \times \frac{1}{3}}$$

$$= \frac{\frac{3-2}{6}}{1 + \frac{1}{6}} = \frac{\frac{1}{6}}{\frac{6+1}{6}} = \frac{1}{7}$$

66. $\cos 80° + \cos 40° - \cos 20°$

$$= 2\cos\frac{80° + 40°}{2}\cos\frac{80 - 40}{2} - \cos 20°$$

$$\left[\cos A + \cos B = 2\cos\frac{A+B}{2}\cos\frac{A-B}{2}\right]$$

$$= 2 \cos 60° \cos 20° - \cos 20° \qquad \left[\cos 60° = \frac{1}{2}\right]$$

$$= 2 \cdot \frac{1}{2}\cos 20° - \cos 20°$$

$$= \cos 20° - \cos 20° = 0$$

67. Given that ΔABC is a right angle triangle, at C

Then, $a^2 + b^2 = c^2$ (by Pythagoras theorem)

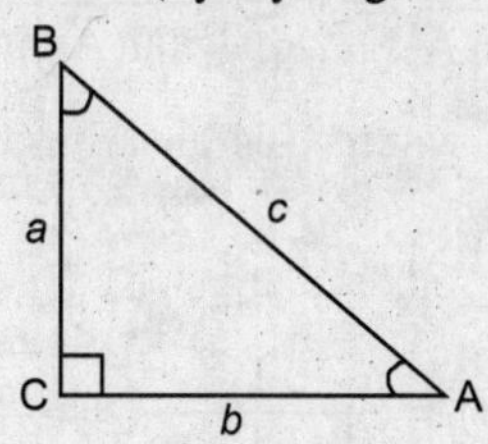

$$\therefore \tan A + \tan B = \frac{BC}{AC} + \frac{AC}{BC}$$

$$= \frac{a}{b} + \frac{b}{a} = \frac{a^2 + b^2}{ab} = \frac{c^2}{ab}$$

68. $$\cot\left(\frac{A}{2}\right) - \tan\left(\frac{A}{2}\right) = \frac{\cos\left(\frac{A}{2}\right)}{\sin\left(\frac{A}{2}\right)} - \frac{\sin\left(\frac{A}{2}\right)}{\cos\left(\frac{A}{2}\right)}$$

$$= \frac{\cos^2\left(\frac{A}{2}\right) - \sin^2\left(\frac{A}{2}\right)}{\sin\left(\frac{A}{2}\right)\cos\left(\frac{A}{2}\right)} \qquad [\cos^2\theta - \sin^2\theta = \cos 2\theta]$$

$$= \frac{\cos A}{\sin\left(\frac{A}{2}\right)\cos\left(\frac{A}{2}\right)} \qquad [\sin 2\theta = 2\sin\theta\cos\theta]$$

$$= \frac{2\cos A}{2\sin\left(\frac{A}{2}\right)\cos\left(\frac{A}{2}\right)} = \frac{2\cos A}{\sin A} = 2\cot A$$

69. $$\cot A + \operatorname{cosec} A = \frac{\cos A}{\sin A} + \frac{1}{\sin A}$$

$$= \frac{\cos A + 1}{\sin A} = \frac{2\cos^2\left(\frac{A}{2}\right)}{2\sin\left(\frac{A}{2}\right)\cos\left(\frac{A}{2}\right)}$$

$$= \frac{\cos\left(\frac{A}{2}\right)}{\sin\left(\frac{A}{2}\right)} = \cot\left(\frac{A}{2}\right)$$

70. $\because 15° + 25° + 50° = 90°$

$\therefore 15° + 25° = 90° - 50°$

$\therefore \tan(15° + 25°) = \tan(90° - 50°)$

$$\Rightarrow \frac{\tan 15° + \tan 25°}{1 - \tan 15° \tan 25°} = \cot 50°$$

$$\Rightarrow \frac{\tan 15° + \tan 25°}{1 - \tan 15° \tan 25°} = \frac{1}{\tan 50°}$$

$\Rightarrow (\tan 15° + \tan 25°) \tan 50° = 1 - \tan 15° \tan 25°$

$\Rightarrow \tan 15° \tan 50° + \tan 25° \tan 50° = 1 - \tan 15° \tan 25°$

$\Rightarrow \tan 15° \tan 50° + \tan 25° \tan 50° + \tan 15° \tan 25° = 1$

$\Rightarrow \tan 25° \tan 15° + \tan 15° \tan 50° + \tan 25° \tan 50° = 1$

71. $|x| < 5 \Rightarrow -5 < x < 5,\ y = 0,\ y = 8$

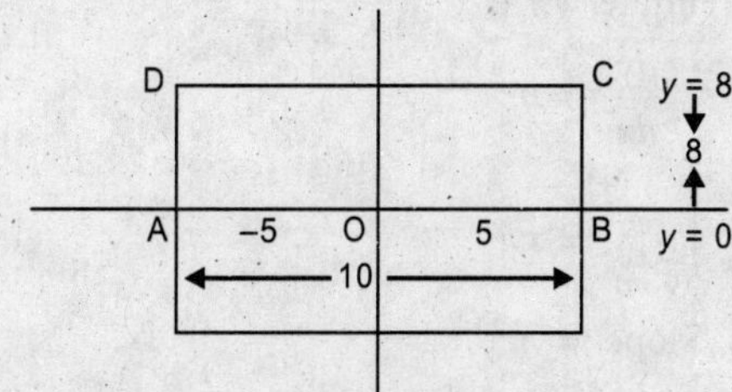

Here, BC = y = AD = 8, AB = CD = 10

Area of ABCD = 10 × 8

= 80 square units

73. $$\lim_{x\to 0}\frac{\sin x}{\tan 3x°} = \lim_{x\to 0}\frac{\frac{\sin x°}{x°}}{\frac{\tan 3x°}{3x°}\cdot 3}$$

$$= \frac{1}{3}\frac{\lim\limits_{x\to 0}\frac{\sin x°}{x°}}{\lim\limits_{x\to 0}\frac{\sin 3x°}{3x°}} = \frac{1}{3}\cdot\frac{1}{1} = \frac{1}{3}$$

74. Given differential equation

$$\frac{d^3y}{dx^3} + \left(\frac{dy}{dx}\right)^2 - x^2\left(\frac{d^4y}{dx^4}\right) = 0$$

Here, the power of highest order derivative

$\left(\frac{d^4y}{dx^4}\right)$ is 1

So, it is a differential equation of degree 1.

75. Check options

$$f(x) = 3x^2 - 2x + 5$$
$$f(0) = 0 - 0 + 5 = 5$$
$$f(-1) = 3(-1)^2 - 2(-1) + 5 = 3 + 2 + 5 = 10$$
$$f(1) = 3(1)^2 - 2(1) + 5 = 3 - 2 + 5 = 1 + 5 = 6$$

∴ The second degree polynomial is

$$f(x) = 3x^2 - 2x + 5$$

76. $y = me^{mx}$, $m > 0$

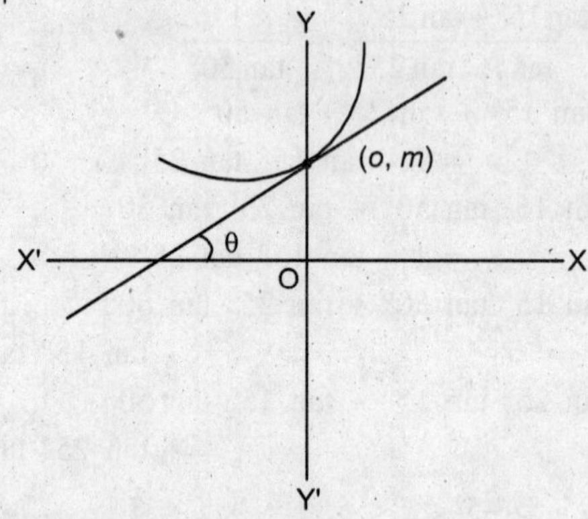

Differentiate w.r.t. x, we get

$$\therefore \quad \frac{dy}{dx} = m^2 e^{mx}$$

$$\left(\frac{dy}{dx}\right)_{(0,\, m)} = m^2$$

$$\therefore \quad \text{Slope} = m^2$$

77. $\tan\theta = m^2$

$$\Rightarrow \quad \theta = \tan^{-1}(m^2)$$

78. $Y - Y_1 = \frac{dy}{dx}(x - x_1) \quad [(x_1, y_1) = (0, m)]$

$$\Rightarrow \quad y - m = m^2(x - 0)$$
$$\Rightarrow \quad y = m^2x + m$$

which is eq. of tangent.

79. $f(x) = x^2$, $g(x) = \tan x$ and $h(x) = \text{In } x$

$[ho\ (gof)]\ (x)$ at $x = \frac{\sqrt{\pi}}{2}$

$\Rightarrow \text{In}\ [\tan(x^2)] \Rightarrow \text{In}\left(\tan\frac{\pi}{4}\right) = 0$

80. $[fo\ (fof)]\ x = [(x^2)^2]^2 = x^8$

$\Rightarrow [fo\ (fof)]^2 = (2)^8 = 256$.

81. Let $\quad I = \int \frac{dx}{2x^2 - 2x + 1} \quad \left[\int \frac{dx}{x^2 + a^2} = \frac{1}{a}\tan^{-1}\frac{x}{a}\right]$

$$= \frac{1}{2}\int \frac{dx}{x^2 - x + \frac{1}{2}}$$

$$= \frac{1}{2}\int \frac{dx}{x^2 - 2\cdot x\cdot\frac{1}{2} + \frac{1}{4} + \frac{1}{2} - \frac{1}{4}}$$

$$= \frac{1}{2}\int \frac{dx}{\left(x - \frac{1}{2}\right)^2 + \frac{1}{4}}$$

$$= \frac{1}{2}\int \frac{dx}{\left(x - \frac{1}{2}\right)^2 + \left(\frac{1}{2}\right)^2}$$

$$= \frac{1}{2}\cdot\frac{1}{\frac{1}{2}}\tan^{-1}\frac{\left(x - \frac{1}{2}\right)}{\frac{1}{2}} + c$$

$$= \frac{1}{2}\cdot 2\tan^{-1}\left(\frac{2x - 1}{2}\right)\cdot\frac{2}{1} + c$$

$$= \tan^{-1}(2x - 1) + c$$

83. Given that,

$y = \frac{1}{2x^2 - c}$, where c is an arbitrary const

$$\Rightarrow \quad 2x^2 - c = \frac{1}{y} \Rightarrow c = 2x^2 - \frac{1}{y}$$

$$\because \quad y = \frac{1}{2x^2 - c}$$

$$\Rightarrow \quad y(2x^2 - c) = 1$$

Differentiating both sides w.r.t. to x, we get

$$y\frac{d(2x^2 - c)}{dx} + (2x^2 - c)\frac{dy}{dx} = 0$$

$$\Rightarrow \quad y(4x - 0) + (2x^2 - c)\frac{dy}{dx} = 0$$

$$\Rightarrow \quad \frac{dy}{dx} = \frac{-4xy}{2x^2 - c}$$

$$= \frac{-4xy}{2x^2 - \left(2x^2 - \frac{1}{y}\right)}$$

$$= \frac{-4xy}{2x^2 - 2x^2 + \frac{1}{y}}$$

$$= \frac{-4xy}{\frac{1}{y}} = -4xy\cdot y = -4xy^2$$

84. Equation is $x^y = e^{x-y}$

taking log both sides, we get

$$\log x^y = \log e^{x-y}$$

$\Rightarrow \quad y \log x = (x-y)\log e \qquad [\log e = 1]$

$\Rightarrow \quad y \log x = (x-y) \qquad ...(i)$

Differentiating both sides w.r.t. x, we get

$$\therefore \quad y\cdot\frac{1}{x}+\log x\frac{dy}{dx} = 1-\frac{dy}{dx} \qquad \left[\text{from } (i)\ y=\frac{x}{1+\log x}\right.$$

$$\Rightarrow \log x\frac{dy}{dx}+\frac{dy}{dx} = 1-\frac{y}{x}$$

$$\Rightarrow \frac{dy}{dx}(\log x+1) = 1-\frac{y}{x}$$

$$= 1-\frac{x}{1+\log x}\cdot\frac{1}{x}=1-\frac{1}{1+\log x}$$

$$\Rightarrow \quad \frac{dy}{dx} = \frac{1+\log x-1}{(1+\log x)}\cdot\frac{1}{(1+\log x)}$$

$$= \frac{\log x}{(1+\log x)^2} \qquad ...(ii)$$

$$\therefore \left(\frac{dy}{dx}\right)_{x=1} = \frac{\log 1}{(1+\log 1)^2}$$

$$= \frac{0}{(1+0)^2}=\frac{0}{1}=0$$

85. $\dfrac{dy}{dx} = \dfrac{\log x}{(1+\log x)^2}$ [from (ii)]

$$\Rightarrow \frac{d^2y}{dx^2} = \frac{(1\log x)^2\cdot\frac{1}{x}-\log x\cdot 2(1+\log x)\cdot\left(0+\frac{1}{x}\right)}{(1+\log x)^2}$$

$$= \frac{(1+\log x)^2\cdot\frac{1}{x}-\frac{2}{x}\log x(1+\log x)}{(1+\log x)^2}$$

$$\therefore \left(\frac{d^2y}{dx^2}\right)_{x=1} = \frac{(1+\log 1)^2\cdot\frac{1}{1}-\frac{2}{1}\log 1(1+\log 1)}{(1+\log 1)^2}$$

$$= \frac{1-2\cdot 0}{(1+0)^2}=\frac{1-0}{1}=1$$

89. $f(x) = 3x^4 - 20x^3 - 12x^2 + 288x + 1$

$\Rightarrow f'(x) = 12x^3 - 60x^2 - 24x + 288$

$= 12(x^3 - 5x^2 - 2x + 24)$

$= 12[x^3 + 2x^2 - 7x^2 - 14x + 12x + 24]$

$= 12[x^2(x + 2) - 7x(x + 2) + 12(x + 2)]$

$= 12(x + 2)(x^2 - 7x + 12)$

$= 12(x + 2)(x - 3)(x - 4)$

For $f(x)$ to be increasing, we must have

$$f'(x) > 0$$

$\Rightarrow 12(x + 2)(x - 3)(x - 4) > 0$

$\Rightarrow x < -2$ or $x > 3$

$\Rightarrow x \in (-2, 3)$

So, $f(x)$ is increasing on $(-2, 3)$

90. $f(x) = 3x^4 - 20x^3 - 12x^2 + 288x + 1$

$\Rightarrow f'(x) = 12x^3 - 60x^2 - 24x + 288$

$= 12(x^3 - 5x^2 - 2x + 24)$

$= 12(x + 2)(x - 3)(x - 4)$

For $f(x)$ to be decreasing, we must have

$$f'(x) < 0$$

$\Rightarrow 12(x + 2)(x - 3)(x - 4) < 0$

$\Rightarrow (x - 3)(x - 4) < 0$

$\Rightarrow 3 < x < 4$

$\Rightarrow x \in (3, 4)$

So, $f(x)$ is increasing on $(3, 4)$

91. $f(x) = x^2 + 2x - 5$ and $g(x) = 5x + 30$

$\therefore \quad g[f(x)] = 0$

$\Rightarrow 5(x^2 + 2x - 5) + 30 = 0$

$\Rightarrow 5x^2 + 10x - 25 + 30 = 0$

$\Rightarrow 5x^2 + 10x + 5 = 0$

$\Rightarrow 5x^2 + 5x + 5x + 5 = 0$

$\Rightarrow 5x(x + 1) + 5(x + 1) = 0$

$\Rightarrow (5x + 5)(x + 1) = 0$

$\Rightarrow 5(x + 1)(x + 1) = 0$

either $(x + 1) = 0$ or $x + 1 = 0$

$\therefore \quad x = -1$ or $x = -1$

Hence, the roots of the equation $g[f(x)] = 0$ is -1 and -1.

92. 1. $f[g(x)] = (5x + 30)^2 + 2(5x + 30) - 5$

$= 25x^2 + 900 + 300x + 10x + 60 - 5$

$= 25x^2 + 310x + 955$

Here, $f[g(x)]$ is a polynomial of degree 2

2. $g[g(x)] = 5(5x + 30) + 30 = 25x + 150 + 30$

$= 25x + 180$

Here $g[g(x)]$ is polynomial of degree 1.

93. Here, $5f(x) = 5(x^2 + 2x - 5) = 5x^2 + 10x - 25$

and $\quad xg(x) = x[5x + 30] = 5x^2 + 30x$

$\therefore \quad h(x) = 5f(x) - xg(x)$

$= 5x^2 + 10x - 25 - (5x^2 + 30x)$

$= 5x^2 + 10x - 25 - 5x^2 - 30x$

$= -20x - 20$

$\Rightarrow \quad h(x) = -20x - 20$

Differentiating both sides w.r.t. to x, we get

$$h'(x) = -20 - 0 = -20$$

94. $\mathrm{I}_1 = \displaystyle\int_0^{\pi}\frac{x\,dx}{1+\sin x} \qquad ...(i)$

$$\Rightarrow \mathrm{I}_1 = \int_0^{\pi}\frac{\pi-x}{1+\sin(\pi-x)}dx \left[\because \int_0^a f(x)dx = \int_0^a f(a-x)dx\right]$$

$$\Rightarrow \quad I_1 = \int_0^{\pi} \frac{\pi - x}{1+\sin x} dx \quad ...(ii)$$

Adding (*i*) and (*ii*), we get

$$\Rightarrow \quad 2I_1 = \int_0^{\pi} \frac{x+\pi-x}{1+\sin x} dx$$

$$\Rightarrow \quad 2I_1 = \pi \int_0^{\pi} \frac{1}{1+\sin x} dx$$

$$\left[\int_0^{2a} f(x)dx = \int_0^{a} \{f(x)+f(2a-x)\} dx\right]$$

$$\Rightarrow 2I_1 = \pi \int_0^{\frac{\pi}{2}} \left[\frac{1}{1+\sin x} + \frac{1}{1+\sin(\pi-x)}\right] dx$$

$$\Rightarrow \quad 2I_1 = \pi \int_0^{\frac{\pi}{2}} \left[\frac{1}{1+\sin x} + \frac{1}{1+\sin x}\right] dx$$

$$\Rightarrow \quad 2I_1 = 2\pi \int_0^{\frac{\pi}{2}} \frac{1}{1+\sin x} dx$$

$$\Rightarrow \quad 2I_1 = 2\pi \int_0^{\frac{\pi}{2}} \frac{1-\sin x}{1-\sin^2 x} dx$$

$$\Rightarrow \quad 2I_1 = 2\pi \int_0^{\frac{\pi}{2}} (\sec^2 x - \tan x \sec x) dx$$

$$\Rightarrow \quad 2I_1 = 2\pi [\tan x - \sec x]_0^{\pi/2}$$

$$= 2\pi \left[\frac{\sin x - 1}{\cos x}\right]_0^{\pi/2}$$

$$= 2\pi \left[\frac{\sin^2 x - 1}{\cos x(\sin x + 1)}\right]_0^{\pi/2}$$

$$\Rightarrow \quad 2I_1 = 2\pi \left[\frac{-\cos^2 x}{\cos x(1+\sin x)}\right]_0^{\pi/2}$$

$$= 2\pi \left[\frac{-\cos x}{1+\sin x}\right]_0^{\pi/2}$$

$$= 2\pi(0 + 1) = 2\pi$$

$$\Rightarrow \quad 2I_1 = 2\pi \therefore I_1 = \pi \Rightarrow \int_0^{\pi} \frac{x\,dx}{1+\sin x} = \pi$$

95. $I_2 = \int_0^{\pi} \frac{(\pi - x)dx}{1-\sin(\pi+x)}$

$$= \int_0^{\pi} \frac{\pi\,dx}{1-\sin x} - \int_0^{\pi} \frac{x\,dx}{1-\sin x}$$

$$I_2 = 2\pi - I_1 \quad \text{[from Q(94)]}$$

$$\Rightarrow \quad I_1 + I_2 = 2\pi$$

Hence, value of $I_1 + I_2 = 2\pi$

96. Given that, family of curve

$$\tan y = c(1 - e^x) \quad ...(i)$$

differentiating w.r.t. x, we get

$$\sec^2 \frac{dy}{dx} = c(0 - e^x)$$

$$\Rightarrow \sec^2 y\, dy = -ce^x\, dx \quad \left[\text{from } (i)\ c = \frac{\tan y}{1-e^x}\right]$$

$$\Rightarrow \sec^2 y\, dy = -\frac{\tan y e^x}{1-e^x} dx$$

$$\Rightarrow (1 - e^x) \sec^2 y\, dy = -\tan y\, e^x\, dx$$

$$\Rightarrow (1 - e^x) \sec^2 y\, dy + \tan y\, e^x\, dx = 0$$

$$\Rightarrow e^x \tan y\, dx + (1 - e^x) \sec^2 y\, dy = 0$$

97. Let $u = 2^{(\sin x)^2}$ and $v = \sin x$

then, $$\frac{du}{dx} = 2^{(\sin x)^2} \cdot \log e^2 \cdot 2 \sin x \cos x$$

and $$\frac{dv}{dx} = \cos x$$

$$\frac{du}{dv} = \frac{\frac{du}{dx}}{\frac{dv}{dx}} = \frac{2^{(\sin x)^2} \cdot \log e^2 \cdot 2 \sin x \cos x}{\cos x}$$

$$= \sin x \cdot 2^{(\sin x)^2} \cdot 2 \log e^2$$

98. (L.H.L. of $x = 0$)

$$= \lim_{x\to 0^-} f(x) = \lim_{x\to 0^-} \left(2x + \frac{1}{4}\right)$$

$$= 2\times 0 + \frac{1}{4} = \frac{1}{4}$$

(R.H.L. of $x = 0$)

$$= \lim_{x\to 0^+} f(x) = \lim_{x\to 0^+} \left(x + \frac{1}{2}\right)^2$$

$$= \left(0 + \frac{1}{2}\right)^2 = \left(\frac{1}{2}\right)^2 = \frac{1}{4}$$

and $f(0) = k$

Since $f(x)$ is continuous at $x = 0$

$$\therefore \lim_{x\to 0^-} f(x) = \lim_{x\to 0^+} f(x) = f(0)$$

$$\Rightarrow \quad \frac{1}{4} = \frac{1}{4} = k$$

Hence value of k is $\frac{1}{4}$

99. Given that

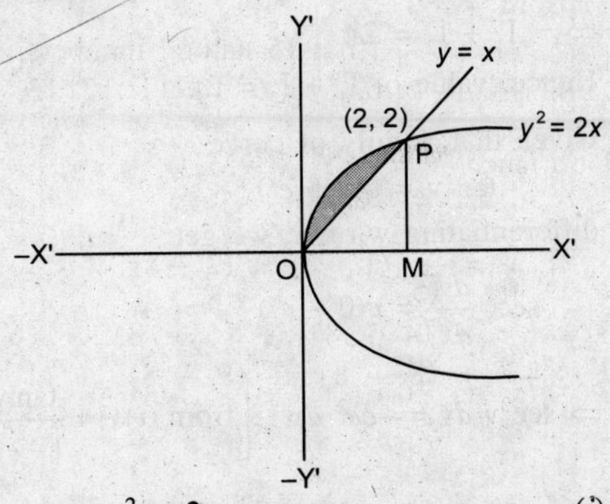

$$y^2 = 2x \quad ...(i)$$

and $$y = x \quad ...(ii)$$

The eq. (*i*) in a eq. of parabola in standard form and eq. $y = x$ a st. line passing through origin having slope I.

The point of intersection of (*i*) and (*ii*), we get

$$x^2 = 2x$$

$\Rightarrow \quad x^2 - 2x = 0$

$\Rightarrow \quad x(x - 2) = 0$

either $\quad x = 0$ or $x - 2 = 0$

or, $\quad x = 2$

$\therefore \quad y = x \quad \therefore y = 2$

Now, required area = area of shaded region

$$A = \int_0^2 (y_2 - y_1)dx = \int_0^2 (\sqrt{2x} - x)dx$$

$$= \int_0^2 \left(\sqrt{2}x^{\frac{1}{2}} - x\right)dx$$

$$= \left(\sqrt{2}\frac{x^{\frac{3}{2}}}{\frac{3}{2}} - \frac{x^2}{2}\right)_0^2$$

$$= \frac{2\sqrt{2}}{3}(2)^{\frac{3}{2}} - \frac{4}{2}$$

$$= \frac{8}{3} - 2 = \frac{8-6}{3} = \frac{2}{3} \text{ square units}$$

105. $x^2 - 30x + 221 = 0$

$\Rightarrow x^2 - 13x - 17x + 221 = 0$

$\Rightarrow x(x - 13) - 17(x - 13) = 0$

$\Rightarrow (x - 13)(x - 17) = 0$

$\Rightarrow$ either $x - 13 = 0$ or $x - 17 = 0$

$\Rightarrow \quad x = 13$ or $x = 17$

Given that *p* and *q* are the roots of the eq.

Then, $p = 13$ and $q = 17$

$\therefore \quad p^3 + q^3 = (13)^3 + (17)^3$

$= 2197 + 4913 = 7110$

108. Let *x* and *y* be the remaining two observations.

Then $\overline{X}$ = mean = 4.4

$\Rightarrow \quad \frac{1+2+6+x+y}{5} = 4.4$

$\Rightarrow 9 + x + y = 22$

$\Rightarrow \quad x + y = 22 - 9 = 13 \quad ...(i)$

and variance = 8.24

$\Rightarrow \quad \frac{1}{5}(1^2 + 2^2 + 6^2 + x^2 + y^2) - \text{Mean}^2 = 8.24$

$\Rightarrow \quad \frac{1}{5}(1 + 4 + 36 + x^2 + y^2) - (4.4)^2 = 8.24$

$\Rightarrow \quad \frac{1}{5}(41 + x^2 + y^2) - 19.36 = 8.24$

$\Rightarrow \quad \frac{1}{5}(41 + x^2 + y^2) = 8.24 + 19.36 = 27.60$

$\Rightarrow 41 + x^2 + y^2 = 27.60 \times 5 = 138$

$\Rightarrow \quad x^2 + y^2 = 138 - 41 = 97$

Now, $(x + y)^2 + (x - y)^2 = 2(x^2 + y^2)$

$\Rightarrow 169 + (x - y)^2 = 2(97)$

$\Rightarrow (x - y)^2 = 194 - 169 = 25$

$\Rightarrow x - y = \pm 5 \quad ...(ii)$

from (*i*) and (*ii*), we get, if $x - y = 5$

Then, $2x = 18 \Rightarrow x = 9$

and $\quad 2y = 8 \Rightarrow y = 4$

If $x - y = -5 \;\therefore\; 2x = 8 \Rightarrow x = 4$

and $\quad 2y = 18 \Rightarrow y = 9$

Hence, the remaining two observations are 9 and 4

or 4 and 9

110.

x	*f*	*c.f*
1	3	3
2	15	18
3	45	63
4	57	120
5	50	170
6	36	206
7	25	231
8	9	240

$$N = \Sigma f = 240$$

$$\therefore \quad \frac{N}{2} = \frac{240}{2} = 120$$

The cumulative frequency just greater than $\frac{N}{2}$

i.e., 120 is 170

The correspondiong value of the variable(*x*) is 5

So, Median = 5

111. When two dice are thrown

Then, Sample space

S = {(1, 1), (1, 2), ..., (1, 6), (2, 1, (2, 2), ..., (2, 6), (3, 1), (3, 2), ..., (3, 6), (4, 1), (4, 2), ..., (4, 6), (5, 1), (5, 2), ..., (5, 6), (6, 1), (6, 2), ..., (6, 6)}

$\therefore \quad n(S) = 36$

Let A be the event getting the sum as a prime number *i.e.*, 2, 3, 5, 7, 11 as the sum

Then, A = {(1, 1), (1, 2), (2, 1), (1, 4), (4, 1), (2, 3), (3, 2), (1, 6), (6, 1), (2, 5), (5, 2), (3, 4), (4, 3), (6, 5), (5, 6)}

Favourable number of elementary events = 15

i.e., $\quad n(A) = 15$

So, the required probability $= \frac{15}{36} = \frac{5}{12}$

115. Given, A fair die is rolled 4 times

$\therefore \quad n = 4$

Probability of one 6 $= \frac{1}{6} = p$

$\therefore$ Prob. of not 6 $= 1 - \frac{1}{6} = \frac{5}{6} = q$

$\therefore$ Prob. (exactly 2 sixes) $= {}^4C_2 \times p^2 \times q^2$

$$= \frac{\lfloor 4}{\lfloor 2 \lfloor 2} \cdot \left(\frac{1}{6}\right)^2 \cdot \left(\frac{5}{6}\right)^2$$

$$= \frac{4 \cdot 3 \cdot 2 \cdot 1}{2 \cdot 2} \times \frac{1}{6^2} \times \frac{5^2}{6^2}$$

$$= \frac{6 \times 25}{6^2 \times 6^3} = \frac{25}{6 \times 6^2} = \frac{25}{216}$$

116. Given, $n = 100$

$\bar{x} = 50, \sigma = 10$

$\because$ 5 is added to each observation

$\therefore$ new mean = 55

& standard deviation remains same

$\therefore \quad$ S.D. = 10

118. As, sum of first n natural number

$$= \frac{n(n+1)}{2}$$

So, sum of first 15 natural number

$$= \frac{15(15+1)}{2} = \frac{15 \times 16}{2} = 15 \times 8$$

$\therefore$ M = Mean of first 15 natural number

$$= \frac{15 \times 8}{15} = 8$$

$\therefore \quad M = 8$

[first 15 natural numbers, 1, 2, 3, 4, 5, 6, 7, 8, 9, 10, 11, 12, 13, 14, 15]

Now, variance, $V = \frac{1}{n}\sum (xi - M)^2$

$\therefore \quad V = \frac{1}{15}[(1-8)^2 + (2-8)^2 + (3-8)^2 + (4-8)^2 + (5-8)^2 + (6-8)^2 + (7-8)^2 + (8-8)^2 + (9-8)^2 + (10-8)^2 + (11-8)^2 + (12-8)^2 + (13-8)^2 + (14-8)^2 + (15-8)^2 +]$

$\Rightarrow \quad V = \frac{1}{15}[49 + 36 + 25 + 16 + 9 + 4 + 1 + 0 + 1 + 4 + 9 + 16 + 25 + 36 + 49]$

$$= \frac{1}{15}[280] = \frac{56}{3}$$

$\therefore \quad V + M^2 = \frac{56}{3} + 8^2 = \frac{56}{3} + 64$

$$= \frac{56 + 192}{3} = \frac{248}{3}$$

119. Average speed $= \frac{2xy}{x+y}$

$$= \frac{2 \times 3v \times 2v}{3v + 2v} \text{ km/hr}$$

$$= \frac{12v^2}{5v} \text{ km/hr}$$

$$= 2.4v \text{ km/hr}$$

120. Let the number of boys = x

Then the number of girls = $150 - x$

$\therefore 150 \times 60 = x \times 70 + (150 - x) \times 55$

$\Rightarrow \quad 9000 = 70x + 8250 - 55x$

$\Rightarrow \quad 9000 = 15x + 8250$

$\Rightarrow \quad 15x = 9000 - 8250$

$\Rightarrow \quad 15x = 750$

$\Rightarrow \quad x = \frac{750}{15} = 50$

= the number of boys = x = 50

and the number of girls

$= 150 - x$

$= 150 - 50$

$= 100$

Previous Papers (Solved)

NATIONAL DEFENCE ACADEMY & NAVAL ACADEMY

NDA & NA – Entrance Exam, 2019 (I)

PAPER I : GENERAL ABILITY TEST

PART A : ENGLISH LANGUAGE

SPOTTING ERRORS

Directions (Qs. No. 1-10): *Each item in this section has a sentence with three underlined parts labelled (A), (B) and (C). Read each sentence to find out whether there is any error in any underlined part and indicate your response in the Answer sheet against the corresponding letter i.e., (A) or (B) or (C). If you find no error, your response should be indicated as (D).*

1. Opening his letters, (A)/ reading them carefully and sending for his clerk, (B)/ he dictated answer, with them. (C)/ No error. (D)

2. He was my school friend, (A)/ but becoming a great man, (B)/ he has grown proud enough to forget his old friends. (C)/ No error. (D)

3. Rabindranath Tagore, (A)/ a Nobel laureate and the author of the national anthem, (B)/ found Shantiniketan. (C)/ No error. (D)

4. The art of printing was introduced into England (A)/ during the reign of Edward IV (B)/ by William Caxton, a native of Kent. (C)/ No error. (D)

5. From thirty years (A)/ he devoted himself to public affairs (B)/ without taking a holiday. (C)/ No error. (D)

6. If Ramesh will be promoted (A)/ he will get (B)/ a higher salary. (C)/ No error. (D)

7. My brother goes (A)/ to the office (B)/ five day week. (C)/ No error. (D)

8. If you lend Mohan a pen (A)/ he will lend it to someone else (B)/ and never you will get it back. (C)/ No error. (D)

9. One of most widely spread (A)/ bad habits (B)/ is the use of tobacco. (C)/ No error. (D)

10. A great part (A)/ of Arabia (B)/ is desert. (C)/ No error. (D)

SYNONYMS

Directions (Qs. No. 11-20): *Each item in this section consists of a sentence with an underlined word followed by four words or group of words. Select the option that is* ***nearest in meaning*** *to the underlined word/words and mark your response in your Answer sheet accordingly.*

11. Some people complain when they encounter a small misfortune in the course of their thoroughly happy life.

A. run into
B. run away
C. run down
D. run with

12. This world is full of miseries.

A. indifferent love
B. perfect happiness
C. great suffering
D. moderate sympathies

13. A glance at a beautiful object gives us delight.

A. wisdom
B. happiness
C. purity
D. peace

14. It is terrible for people to die of starvation.

A. starch
B. staple
C. plenty
D. hunger

15. The university has constituted a grievance redressal committee to look into the matter.

A. depression
B. complaint
C. abrasion
D. gratefulness

16. Rakesh delivered a slanderous speech.

A. abusive
B. praiseworthy
C. moderate
D. inspiring

17. Suddenly, the sky was darkened by a gigantic bird.

A. winged
B. small
C. tiny
D. enormous

18. To abolish poverty would be to destroy the soil upon which mankind produces the virtues conducive to higher civilization.

A. detest
B. eradicate
C. nurture
D. assimilate

19. The Arabs who are not in the cities live in the desert throughout the year, shifting from one oasis to another.

A. sandbank
B. mound
C. dune
D. spring

20. The various facets of life can be found reflected in a large city.

A. several
B. similar
C. valuable
D. singular

ANTONYMS

Directions (Qs. No. 21-30): *Each item in this section consists of a sentence with an underlined word followed by four words. Select the option that is* ***Opposite in meaning*** *to the underlined word/words and mark your response in your Answer sheet accordingly.*

21. Ramesh is a very dubious character.
A. shady B. suspicious
C. trustworthy D. doubtful

22. Do not indulge in unmindful activities, please.
A. vigilant B. careless
C. stupid D. fatuous

23. He is suffering from a curable disease.
A. remediable B. treatable
C. terminal D. operable

24. He was born on a very auspicious day.
A. propitious B. fortunate
C. ominous D. opportune

25. He has deeper hostility towards Mohan.
A. animosity B. belligerence
C. malice D. friendship

26. His life is rather monotonous.
A. exciting B. dreary
C. tedious D. uneventful

27. Macbeth is a morally repulsive character.
A. abominable B. attractive
C. obnoxious D. ugly

28. The serene beauty of Kashmir had a soothing effect on his mind.
A. placid B. pleasing
C. tranquil D. turbulent

29. Life is transient in nature.
A. brief B. momentary
C. eternal D. short-lived

30. Sohan is a vain person.
A. modest B. arrogant
C. conceited D. proud

IDIOMS AND PHRASES

Directions (Qs. No. 31-35): *Given below are some idioms/ phrases followed by four alternative meanings to each. Choose the response (A), (B), (C) or (D) which is the most appropriate expression.*

31. A dark horse
A. a black coloured horse
B. a person who wins a race or competition although no one expected him to
C. a person who keeps secrets
D. an ignorant person

32. A show-stopper
A. someone who stops the show
B. someone who organizes the show
C. a performance that is extremely good
D. a fashionable person

33. A jack of all trades
A. someone who has many skills
B. a confident and not very serious young man
C. someone who has hit the jackpot
D. a great businessman

34. Fight tooth and nail
A. to quarrel with someone
B. to attack someone with a lot of force
C. to try hard to prevent something from happening
D. to try very hard to achieve something

35. Fair and square
A. in an honest way
B. in a critical way
C. neither very good nor very bad
D. in a foolish way

ORDERING OF SENTENCES

Directions (Qs. No. 36 and 37): *In this section each item consists of six sentences of a passage. The first and sixth sentences are given in the beginning as S1 and S6. The middle four sentences in each have been jumbled up and labelled P, Q, R and S. You are required to find the proper sequence of the four sentences and mark your response accordingly on the Answer sheet.*

36. S1 : We do not know what to do with our knowledge.
S6 : In the course of time they may rule over us altogether.
P : For example, we are unable to manage our machines.
Q : We already find it difficult to do without machines.
R : Machines should be fed properly and waited upon attentively; otherwise they refuse to work or cause destruction.
S : Science has given us superhuman powers, which we do not use properly.

The proper sequence should be:
A. S P R Q B. P S Q R
C. Q R P S D. S R P Q

37. S1 : The British rule in India has brought about moral, material, cultural and spiritual ruination of this great county.
S6 : We are not to kill anybody but it is our *dharma* to see that the curse of this Government is blotted out.
P : I regard this rule as a curse.
Q : Sedition has become my religion.

R : Ours is a non-violent battle.
S : I am out to destroy this system of Government.

The proper sequence should be:

A. S P R Q B. P S Q R
C. Q R P S D. S R P Q

ORDERING OF WORDS IN A SENTENCE

Directions (Qs. No. 37-40): *Each of the following items in this section consists of a sentence, the parts of which have been jumbled. These parts have been labelled P, Q, R and S. Given below each sentence are four sequences namely (A), (B), (C) and (D). You are required to rearrange the jumbled parts of the sentence and mark your response accordingly.*

38. P. The urban local body elections
Q. unidentified gunmen
R. and injured another during
S. shot dead two workers

A. Q S R P B. P Q S R
C. S P R Q D. R P S Q

39. P. both intense political and
Q. this state has a history of
R. of syncretic accomplishments
S. religious contestation and

A. S Q P R B. P Q S R
C. S Q R P D. Q P S R

40. P. the father also
Q. in his quest for justice
R. by the system
S. feels let down

A. S Q P R B. P S R Q
C. S Q R P D. P Q R S

COMPREHENSION

Directions (Qs. No. 41-45): *In this section you have a passage. After the passage, you will find some items based on the passage. First, read the passage and answer the items based on it. You are required to select your answers based on the contents of the passage and opinion of the author only.*

Passage

I do not wish to suggest that because we were one nation we had no differences, but it is submitted that our leading men travelled throughout India either on foot or in bullock-carts. They learned one another's languages and there was no aloofness amongst them. What do you think could have been the intention of those farseeing ancestors of ours who established Setubandha (Rameshwar) in the South, Jagannath in the East and Hardwar in the North as places of pilgrimage? You will admit they were no fools. They knew that worship of God could have been performed just as well at home. They taught us that those whose hearts were aglow with righteousness had the Ganges in their own homes. But they saw that India was one undivided land so made by nature. They, therefore, argued that it must be one nation. Arguing thus, they established holy places in various parts of India, and fired the people with an idea of nationality in a manner unknown in other parts of the world. And we Indians are one as no two Englishmen are. Only you and I and others who consider ourselves civilized and superior persons imagine that we are many nations. It was after the advent of railways that we began to believe in distinctions, and you are at liberty now to say that it is through the railways that we are beginning to abolish those distinctions. An opium-eater may argue the advantage of opium-eating from the fact that he began to understand the evil of the opium habit after having eaten it. I would ask you to consider well what I had said on the railways.

41. According to the author, India:
A. has never been one nation
B. has been an aggregate of several nations
C. has always been one nation along with differences
D. became a nation after the British came

42. Why did the great sages of India establish pilgrimages in the different corners of the country?
A. Because they wanted to push people to travel to different places
B. Because they could observe the underlying unity of the country as mage by nature
C. Because they themselves had travelled to these places
D. Because they wanted people to be religious everywhere

43. In the passage, the author's attitude towards the railways is:

A. critical B. sympathetic
C. indifferent D. apathetic

44. What does the author mean when he says that "whose hearts were aglow with righteousness had the Ganges in their own homes"?
A. One need not visit the Ganges to take holy bath
B. The Ganges has been polluted, so one should bath at home
C. One should take a holy dip in the Ganges to purify one's heart
D. The purity of heart is superior to observance of any ritual

45. The paragraph is written in a:

A. dialogic style B. prescriptive style
C. descriptive style D. analytical style

FILL IN THE BLANK

Directions (Qs. No. 46-50): *Each of the following sentences in this section has a blank space and four words or group of words given after the sentence. Select the word or group* *of words you consider most appropriate for the blank space and indicate your response on the Answer sheet accordingly.*

46. ______ forests prevent erosion.
A. Lean B. Dense
C. Sparse D. Tidy

47. Three people were arrested and an illegal arms unit was ______ by the police in a raid.
A. revealed B. searched
C. discovered D. busted

48. A woman got into the car and ______ .
A. drove off B. broke down
C. rode in D. drove in

49. The lecture was not very interesting. In fact I ______ in the middle of it.
A. showed off B. put off
C. dozed off D. plugged off

50. The cops ______ murder by kin.
A. suspect B. afford
C. manage D. administer

PART B : GENERAL KNOWLEDGE

51. Which one of the following cell organelles does NOT possess nucleic acid?
A. Nucleolus B. Chloroplast
C. Ribosome D. Plasma Membrane

52. Which one of the following cell organelles does NOT possess its own genetic material encoding proteins?
A. Ribosome B. Nucleus
C. Mitochondria D. Chloroplast

53. Which one of the following is NOT a component of conducting tissue in plants?
A. Fibres B. Tracheids
C. Pericycle D. Sieve tubes

54. Which one of the following organisms has vascular tissues?
A. Cladophora B. Penicillium
C. Marsilea D. Anabaena

55. Which one of the following organisms represents the primary consumer category in an ecosystem?
A. Caterpillar B. Crabapple tree
C. Frog D. Sparrowhawk

56. Spring tides refer to:
A. greatest difference in the sea level at high and low tides
B. lowest difference in the sea level at high and low tides
C. no difference in the sea level at high and low tides
D. counteraction of gravitational pull of the Sun to that of Moon

57. Which one of the following energy is stored in the links between the atoms?
A. Nuclear energy B. Chemical energy
C. Potential energy D. Thermal energy

58. The light energy escaping from the Sun can be spread by:
A. a shower of rain drops
B. a plane mirror
C. a convex lens
D. a combination of a convex lens and a concave lens

59. The correct sequence of energy transfer that occurs when an apple falls to the ground is:
A. Gravitational potential energy → heat energy to air → kinetic energy → heat energy to ground and apple → sound energy
B. Gravitational potential energy → sound energy → kinetic energy → heat energy to air → heat energy to ground and apple
C. Gravitational potential energy → kinetic energy → heat energy to air → heat energy to ground and apple → sound energy
D. Gravitational potential energy → kinetic energy → sound energy → heat energy to air → heat energy to ground and apple

60. Which one of the following minerals is used as a fuel in nuclear power stations?
A. Bauxite B. Quartz
C. Feldspar D. Pitchblende

61. Which one of the following is NOT a synthetic detergent?
A. $CH_3(CH_2)_{10}CH_2OSO_3^-Na^+$
B. $[CH_3(CH_2)_{15} - N - (CH_3)_3]^+Br^-$
C. $CH_3(CH_2)_{16}COO^-Na^+$
D. $CH_3(CH_2)_{16}COO(CH_2CH_2O)_nCH_2CH_2OH$

62. Which one of the following is an example of a clean fuel?
A. Coke B. Propane
C. Petrol D. Wax

63. Which one of the following metals does NOT react with cold water?
A. Calcium (Ca) B. Potassium (K)
C. Magnesium (Mg) D. Sodium (Na)

64. In which of the following pairs are the ions isoelectronic?
A. Mg^{2+}, Ar B. Na^+, O^{2-}
C. Al^{3+}, Cl^- D. K^+, Ne

65. Which one of the following is used as a binder in paints?
A. Titanium dioxide B. Novolac
C. Phthalocyanine D. Silicones

66. Which one of the following is NOT true in reference to Air mass?
A. Air mass forms either in tropical or in polar region
B. Air mass develops on continents as well as over ocean
C. Air mass develops in a cyclonic condition
D. Air mass changes the weather conditions

67. National Water Academy, a centre of excellence in training and capacity building in water resource, is located at:
A. New Delhi B. Kolkata
C. Pune D. Chennai

68. "Campos" and "Llanos", Tropical Savanna grasslands are generally found in:
A. Australia B. Central Africa
C. South America D. East Asia

69. "Viticulture" is a common feature of which one of the following Australian cities?
A. Adelaide B. Darwin
C. Hobart D. Brisbane

70. "Shamal" warm and dry wind is a "Local" wind found in:
A. East Asia B. West Coast of Africa
C. Sahara of Africa D. Mesopotamia

71. "Inversion of Rainfall" is associated with:
A. Orographic rainfall
B. Convectional rainfall
C. Cyclonic rainfall (Tropical)
D. Cyclonic rainfall (Temperate)

72. Who was the author of the book 'History of British India'?
A. Charles Grant B. John Stuart Mill
C. James Mill D. William Jones

73. The Azamgarh Proclamation of August 25, 1857 stressed on which one of the following issues?
A. Hindu-Muslim divide
B. Support to the English Government
C. The return of the Badshahi
D. The imposition of heavy Jumas (revenue demand)

74. Which Viceroy had made the observation, "It's a beautiful world if it wasn't for Gandhi ..."?
A. Lord Irwin B. Lord Wavell
C. Lord Mountbatten D. Lord Willingdon

75. Which Indian businessman favoured 'healthy capitalism' in helping Gandhiji to work towards a 'common object'?
A. Ghanshyam Das Birla B. Ambalal Sarabhai
C. Sir Biren Mookerjee D. T.T.K. Krishnamachari

76. The art piece "In Memoriam" was a creation of which one of the following European painters?
A. Thomas Jones Barker B. Joseph Noel Paton
C. Thomas Daniell D. Charles D'Oyly

77. Which one of the following can charge an insulator?
A. Current electricity B. Static electricity
C. Magnetic field D. Gravitational field

78. At 20°C, the speed of sound in water is approximately:
A. 330 m/s B. 800 m/s
C. 1500 m/s D. 5000 m/s

79. Which one of the following could be the melting point of iron?
A. 25°C B. 37°C
C. 500°C D. 1500°C

80. Let us consider a copper wire having radius r and length l. Let its resistance be R. If the radius of another copper wire is $2r$ and the length is $l/2$ then the resistance of this wire will be:
A. R B. 2R
C. R/4 D. R/8

81. Basic scientific principle behind a nuclear reactor is:
A. Nuclear fusion
B. Controlled nuclear fusion
C. Uncontrolled nuclear fission
D. Controlled nuclear fission

82. Which one of the following statements is NOT correct for the given reaction?

$$Fe(s) + CuSO_4(aq) \rightarrow FeSO_4(aq) + Cu(s)$$

A. Iron is the reducing agent
B. The solution turns green in colour after the reaction
C. Copper is a more reactive metal than iron
D. The reaction is an example of a redox reaction

83. Which one of the following is an organic acid?
A. Hydrochloric acid B. Nitric acid
C. Acetic acid D. Sulphuric acid

84. Dinitrogen (N_2) and dioxygen (O_2) are the main constituents of air but they do not react with each other to form oxides of nitrogen because:
A. the reaction requires initiation by a catalyst
B. oxides of nitrogen are unstable
C. the reaction is endothermic and requires very high temperature
D. the stoichiometry of N_2 and O_2 in air is not ideal for the reaction to take place

85. Who among the following has explained the phenomenon of photoelectric effect?
A. Max Planck B. Albert Einstein
C. Neils Bohr D. Ernest Rutherford

86. The equivalent weight of oxalic acid in $C_2H_2O_4.2H_2O$ is:
A. 45 B. 63
C. 90 D. 126

87. Which one of the following is NOT a west flowing river?
A. Periyar B. Bharatpuzha
C. Pamba D. Tamraparni

88. Which one of the following rivers was earlier known as "Vitasta"?
A. Tista B. Jhelum
C. Tungabhadra D. Bharatpuzha

89. River Sarda drains in the Northern Plains of Uttar Pradesh. Before entering in the Plains, Sarda is known as:
A. Saraswati B. Bhagirathi
C. Kali D. Pindar

90. "Mission Indradhanush" is related to:
A. Bullet train project
B. Agriculture development
C. Women empowerment
D. Full immunization

91. Which of the following is/are environmental effects of Rotation of the Earth?
1. Daily or diurnal rhythm in daylight and air temperature.
2. Flow path of both air and water are turned consistently in a side-ward direction.
3. The movement of the tides.

Select the correct answer using the code given below:
A. 1 and 2 only B. 1 and 3 only
C. 1, 2 and 3 D. 3 only

92. Who among the following historians have described the Quit India movement as a 'spontaneous revolution'?
A. Gordon Johnson B. David Arnold
C. F.G. Hutchins D. Peter Robb

Directions (Qs. No. 93-95): *The following 3 (three) items consist of two statements, Statement-I and Statement-II. Examine these two statements carefully and select the correct answer using the code given below:*

Code:
A. Both the statements are individually true and Statement II is the correct explanation of Statement I
B. Both the statements are individually true and Statement II is NOT the correct explanation of Statement I
C. Statement I is true but Statement II is false
D. Statement I is false but Statement II is true

93. Statement I : Abul Fazl shaped, represented and articulated the ideas associated with the reign of Akbar.
Statement II : The qualities of Abul Fazl impressed Akbar who found the former suitable as an adviser and spokesperson for his policies.

94. Statement I : The Kisan manifesto adopted by the All India Kisan Sabha in August 1936 contained radical demands.
Statement II : The All India Kisan Sabha was a part of the Congress and maintained close relationship with the Provincial Congress Committees.

95. Statement I : The British ruled India through a modern bureaucracy headed by the Indian Civil Service, whose members were recruited through merit based on open competition.
Statement II : The Indian Civil Service was based on the whole hearted participation of Indians.

96. Two metallic wires A and B are made using copper. The radius of wire A is r while its length is l. A dc voltage V is applied across the wire A, causing power dissipation P. The radius of wire B is $2r$ and its length is $2l$ and the same dc voltage V is applied across it causing power dissipation P_1. Which one of the following is the correct relationship between P and P_1?
A. $P = 2P_1$ B. $P = P_1/2$
C. $P = 4P_1$ D. $P = P_1$

97. Consider the following statements about a solenoid:
1. The magnetic field strength in a solenoid depends upon the number of turns per unit length in the solenoid.
2. The magnetic field strength in a solenoid depends upon the current flowing in the wire of the solenoid.
3. The magnetic field strength in a solenoid depends upon the diameter of the solenoid.

Which of the statements given above are correct?
A. 1, 2 and 3 B. 1 and 3 only
C. 2 and 3 only D. 1 and 2 only

98. Light year is a unit of measurement of:
A. very large distances
B. time interval in years
C. amount of light received on earth in a year
D. mass of atoms

99. The focal length of the objective lens of a telescope is 50 cm. If the magnification of the telescope is 25, then the focal length of the eye-piece is:
A. 12.5 cm B. 5 cm
C. 2 cm D. 10 cm

100. Which one of the following forces is non-central and non-conservative?
A. Frictional force B. Electric force
C. Gravitational force D. Mechanical force

101. On exposure to moist air, copper gains a green coat on its surface due to formation of which one of the following compounds?
A. Copper carbonate B. Copper oxide
C. Copper sulphate D. Copper nitrate

102. Which one of the following will NOT produce carbon dioxide on reacting with an aqueous solution of hydrochloric acid?
A. Limestone B. Quick Lime
C. Chalk D. Marble

103. Which one of the following substances is NOT a mixture?

A. Ice　　B. Ice-cream
C. Air　　D. Honey

104. Which one of the following is an example of Salt-Crystal growth?

A. Chemical weathering
B. Physical weathering
C. Biological weathering
D. Bio-chemical weathering

105. Which one of the following is the correct sequence of proved coal reserves in the Indian States in decreasing order?

A. Jharkhand, Chhattisgarh, Odisha, West Bengal
B. Jharkhand, Odisha, Chhattisgarh, West Bengal
C. Odisha, West Bengal, Jharkhand, Chhattisgarh
D. Odisha, Chhattisgarh, West Bengal, Jharkhand

106. Consider the following statements relating to Richter scale:

1. It was devised in 1935 by Charles F. Richter.
2. It describes the quantity of energy released by a single earthquake.
3. Richter Scale has no upper limit.

Which of the statements given above is/are correct?

A. 1 only　　B. 1 and 2 only
C. 2 and 3 only　　D. 1, 2 and 3

107. Which one of the following ocean currents is NOT a cold ocean current?

A. Canary current　　B. California current
C. Kuroshio current　　D. Oyashio current

108. What is the time gap in occurrence of two successive tides at a given place on the ocean surface?

A. 12 hours　　B. 12 hours 26 minutes
C. 24 hours　　D. 24 hours 52 minutes

109. Tooth enamel is made up of which one of the following calcium compounds?

A. Calcium carbonate
B. Calcium sulphate
C. Calcium hydroxide
D. Calcium phosphate

110. Suppose there are two planets, 1 and 2, having the same density but their radii are R_1 and R_2 respectively, where $R_1 > R_2$. The accelerations due to gravity on the surface of these planets are related as:

A. $g_1 > g_2$　　B. $g_1 < g_2$
C. $g_1 = g_2$　　D. Can't say anything

111. The Sun is seen little before it rises and for a short while after it sets. This is because of:

A. total internal reflection
B. atmospheric refraction
C. apparent shift in the direction of Sun
D. dispersion

112.

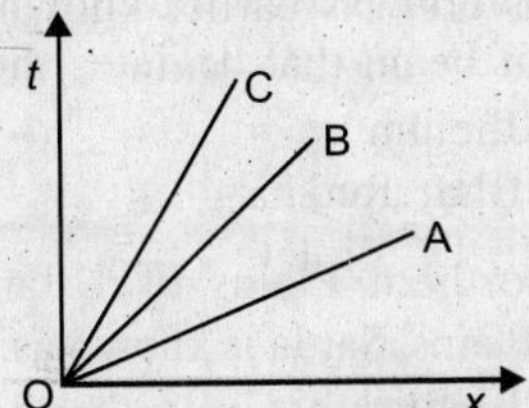

The figure shown above gives the time (t) versus position (x) graphs of three objects A, B and C. Which one of the following is the correct relation between their speeds V_A, V_B and V_C, respectively at any instant ($t > 0$)?

A. $V_A < V_B < V_C$　　B. $V_A > V_B > V_C$
C. $V_A = V_B = V_C \neq 0$　　D. $V_A = V_B = V_C = 0$

113. 1 dyne (a unit of force in CGS system) equals to:

A. 10^3 g cm/s²　　B. 10^{-3} g cm/s²
C. 10^5 kg m/s²　　D. 10^{-5} kg m/s²

114.

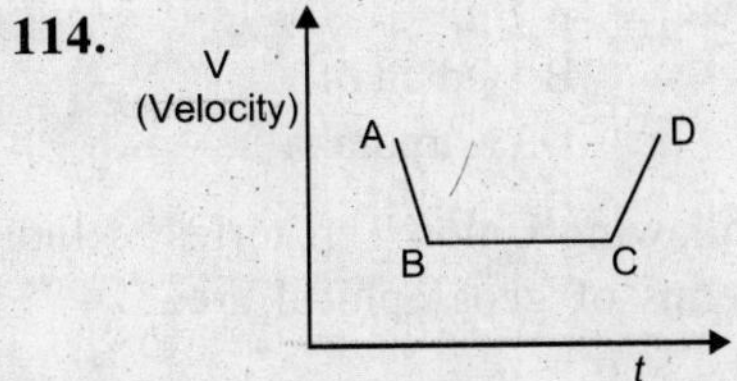

In the given velocity (V) versus time (t) graph, accelerated and decelerated motions are respectively represented by line segments:

A. CD and BC　　B. BC and AB
C. CD and AB　　D. AB and CD

115. Which one of the following statements regarding a thermos flask is NOT correct?

A. The walls of flask are separated by vacuum and made of glass which is a poor conductor of heat
B. The glass walls themselves have shiny surfaces
C. The surface of inner wall radiates good amount of heat and the surface of outer wall absorbs some of the heat that is radiated from the inner wall
D. The cork supports are poor conductors of heat

116. 'Black hole' is a:

A. huge black star which has zero acceleration due to gravity on its surface
B. star which has moderate acceleration due to gravity on its surface
C. star which has collapsed into itself and has large acceleration due to gravity on its surface
D. star which has collapsed into itself and has zero acceleration due to gravity on its surface

117. The formula for conversion between Fahrenheit and Celsius is

°F = X + (1.8 × °C)

Wha. is factor X?

A. [illegible]　　B. 22
C. 98　　D. 42

118. When a beam of white light passes through a glass prism, the colour of light beam that deviates the least is:

A. Blue B. Red
C. Green D. Violet

119. LIGO stands for:

A. Laser Interferometer Gravitational wave Observatory
B. Light Interferometer Gravitational wave Observatory
C. Light Induced Gravity Observatory
D. Laser Induced Gaseous Optics

120. A fuse wire must be:

A. conducting and of low melting point
B. conducting and of high melting point
C. insulator and of high melting point
D. insulator and of low melting point

121. Kamarajar Port was commissioned in 2001 to handle thermal coal requirements. It is situated along the coast of which Indian State?

A. Andhra Pradesh B. Odisha
C. Tamil Nadu D. Karnataka

122. Which one of the following Union Territories of India is the smallest in terms of geographical area?

A. Daman and Diu
B. Chandigarh
C. Dadra and Nagar Haveli
D. Lakshadweep

123. Which one of the following can be said to be essentially related to 'Polar Front Theory'?

A. Anticyclone
B. Tropical Cyclone
C. Temperate Cyclone
D. Inter Tropical Convergence

124. Brahmaputra and Indus rivers are antecedent rivers. Which one of the following may be the true definition of an antecedent drainage?

A. Which follows the initial slope of the Himalaya
B. Which existed before the Himalayan range came into existence
C. Which followed the dip or rock beds of the Himalaya
D. Which followed the strikes of rock beds of the Himalaya

125. The Karachi resolution of Congress in 1931 advocated which one of the following issues?

A. State shall not own or control key industries and services
B. State shall handover the key industries and services to the Indian business groups
C. State should allow the Indian business group to invest fifty per cent of the capital
D. State shall own or control key industries and services

126. The treaty of Schönbrunn (1809) was signed after which one of the following battles?

A. Battle of Austerlitz B. Battle of Tilsit
C. Battle of Wagram D. Battle of Lisbon

127. Which of the following statements about The New Model Unions is/are correct?

1. The New Model Unions were formed in the 1850s
2. The New Model Unions were formed in the 1880s
3. The New Model Unions comprised a Labour Party idea
4. The New Model Unions excluded women in the 1920s

Select the correct answer using the code given below:

A. 1 B. 2
C. 3 and 4 D. 3 only

128. The Truman Doctrine of 1947 was announced to achieve which one of the following?

A. Containment of the USSR
B. Increasing agricultural production in the USA
C. Offering friendship to Europe
D. Strengthening the UNO

129. Which of the following statements is/are correct?

1. In 1948, Burma was admitted to the United Nations and immediately supported the USA in the Cold War.
2. In 1948, Burma joined the United Nations but refused to denounce China as the aggressor in the Korean War.

Select the correct answer using the code given below:

A. 1 only B. 2 only
C. Both 1 and 2 D. Neither 1 nor 2

130. Who among the following presented 'The April Theses' to the Russian people in 1917?

A. Stalin B. Trotsky
C. Bukharin D. Lenin

131. An Election Commissioner can be removed from office on the recommendation of:

A. The Chief Justice of India
B. The Chief Election Commissioner
C. The President of India
D. The Parliament

132. Which one of the following statements regarding the Rajya Sabha is NOT correct?

A. Its members are elected by the elected members of the Legislative Assembly of a State
B. The election follows the system of proportional representation by means of a single transferable vote
C. 1/3rd of its members retire after every two years
D. It is a permanent body, but can be dissolved earlier by the President

133. Fundamental right guaranteed under which one of the following Articles of the Constitution of India is available only to the citizens of India?

A. Article 19 B. Article 20
C. Article 21 D. Article 22

134. The treaty of Yandabo was signed in:
A. 1826 B. 1825
C. 1824 D. 1823

135. In the Manusmriti which form of marriage results from the "Voluntary union of a maiden and her lover"?
A. Eighth form B. Fifth form
C. Seventh form D. Sixth form

136. Consider the following description of the Samadhi of a former Prime Minister of India:
Central Samadhi platform comprises nine-square black polished granite solid stone blocks, capped with a 'Diya' in the centre. The number nine holds significance and represents the navarasas, navaratras and navagrahas. Then placement of the nine-square Samadhi is in a circular lotus shaped pattern. The nine-square platform is accessed in four cardinal directions by pathways made in white composite tiles so that the floor does not get heated.
Identify the Samadhi:
A. Shakti Sthal B. Shantivan
C. Sadaiv Atal D. Veer Bhumi

137. IMBEX is a joint exercise conducted regularly between Armies of India and:
A. Malaysia B. Maldives
C. Mauritius D. Myanmar

138. Who among the following was awarded The Hindu Prize in Fiction category for the year 2018?
A. Neelum Saran Gour B. N Kalyan Raman
C. Manoranjan Byapari D. Arunav Sinha

139. Who among the following was appointed as head of the seven member committee to look into revenue shortfall being faced by the states after the GST roll-out in India and suggest steps for augmenting collections?
A. Himanta Biswa Sharma
B. Thomas Isaac
C. Sushil Modi
D. Capt Abhimanyu

140. The 15th Pravasi Bharatiya Divas, 2019 was held in:
A. New Delhi B. Gandhi Nagar
C. Prayagraj D. Varanasi

141. Which one of the following cities was named by UNESCO as World Capital of Architecture for 2020?
A. Tokyo B. Johannesburg
C. Rio de Janerio D. New Delhi

142. Who among the following was named ICC's emerging player of the year 2018?
A. Rishabh Pant B. Josh Hazlewood
C. Hasan Ali D. Mustafizur Rahman

143. India's first private sector Howitzer gun-making unit is located at:
A. Jamshedpur B. Kolkata
C. Hazira D. Gwalior

144. Which of the following pairs of old names and new names of islands in India is/are correctly matched?
1. Ross Island : Shaheed Dweep
2. Neil Island : Netaji Subhas Chandra Bose Dweep
3. Havelock Island : Swaraj Dweep
Select the correct answer using the code given below:
A. 1, 2 and 3 B. 2 and 3 only
C. 1 and 2 only D. 3 only

145. Who among the following was posthumously conferred with the Ashoka Chakra, India's highest peacetime gallantry award, in 2019?
A. Jyoti Prakash Nirala B. Nazir Ahmad Wani
C. Hangpan Dada D. Mohan Nath Goswami

146. As per code of the nomenclature, which one of the following is the correct way of writing a biological name?
A. *Amoeba Proteus* B. *Amoeba proteus*
C. *amoeba proteus* D. *Amoeba Proteus*

147. Which one of the following statements regarding Electrocardiogram is correct?
A. Electrocardiogram is graphical representation of electrical activity of cornea
B. Electrocardiogram is graphical representation of activity of kidney
C. Electrocardiogram is graphical representation of activity of brain
D. Electrocardiogram is graphical representation of electrical activity of heart

148. Which one of the following statements regarding Penicillin is correct?
A. Penicillin resistant bacteria can store this antibiotic in vacuole
B. Penicillin resistant bacteria can degrade this antibiotic by an enzyme called β-lactamase
C. Penicillin resistant bacteria can degrade this antibiotic by an enzyme called lactic acid dehydrogenase
D. Penicillin is not absorbed by bacteria; so most bacteria are resistant

149. Which one of the following organelles of mammalian cell is rich in hydrolytic enzymes?
A. Mitochondria B. Ribosomes
C. Lysosome D. Nucleus

150. Which one of the following statements regarding Cholera is correct?
A. Cholera is a disease that causes loss of memory
B. Cholera is a disease of muscles due to consumption of alcohol
C. Cholera is a disease due to consumption of contaminated food or water
D. Cholera is a genetic disease

PAPER II : MATHEMATICS

1. What is the value of

$$\frac{\sin 34° \cos 236° - \sin 56° \sin 124°}{\cos 28° \cos 88° + \cos 178° \sin 208°}?$$

A. –2 B. –1
C. 2 D. 1

2. tan 54° can be expressed as:

A. $\frac{\sin 9° + \cos 9°}{\sin 9° - \cos 9°}$ B. $\frac{\sin 9° - \cos 9°}{\sin 9° + \cos 9°}$

C. $\frac{\cos 9° + \sin 9°}{\cos 9° - \sin 9°}$ D. $\frac{\sin 36°}{\cos 36°}$

Directions (Qs. No. 3-5): *Consider the following for the next 03 (three) items:*

If $p = X \cos\theta - Y \sin\theta$, $q = X \sin\theta + Y \cos\theta$ and $p^2 + 4pq + q^2 = AX^2 + BY^2$, $0 \le \theta \le \frac{\pi}{2}$.

3. What is the value of θ?

A. $\frac{\pi}{2}$ B. $\frac{\pi}{3}$

C. $\frac{\pi}{4}$ D. $\frac{\pi}{6}$

4. What is the value of A?

A. 4 B. 3
C. 2 D. 1

5. What is the value of B?

A. –1 B. 0
C. 1 D. 2

Directions (Qs. No. 6-7): *Consider the following for the next 02 (two) items:*

It is given that $\cos(\theta - \alpha) = a$, $\cos(\theta - \beta) = b$.

6. What is $\cos(\alpha - \beta)$ equal to?

A. $ab + \sqrt{1-a^2}\sqrt{1-b^2}$ B. $ab - \sqrt{1-a^2}\sqrt{1-b^2}$

C. $a\sqrt{1-b^2} - b\sqrt{1-a^2}$ D. $a\sqrt{1-b^2} + b\sqrt{1-a^2}$

7. What is $\sin^2(\alpha - \beta) + 2ab\cos(\alpha - \beta)$ equal to?

A. $a^2 + b^2$ B. $a^2 - b^2$
C. $b^2 - a^2$ D. $-(a^2 + b^2)$

8. If $\sin\alpha + \cos\alpha = p$, then what is $\cos^2(2\alpha)$ equal to?

A. p^2 B. $p^2 - 1$
C. $p^2(2 - p^2)$ D. $p^2 + 1$

9. What is the value of $\sin^{-1}\frac{4}{5} + \sec^{-1}\frac{5}{4} - \frac{\pi}{2}$?

A. $\frac{\pi}{4}$ B. $\frac{\pi}{2}$

C. π D. 0

10. If $\sin^{-1}\frac{2p}{1+p^2} - \cos^{-1}\frac{1-q^2}{1+q^2} = \tan^{-1}\frac{2x}{1-x^2}$, then what is x equal to?

A. $\frac{p+q}{1+pq}$ B. $\frac{p-q}{1+pq}$

C. $\frac{pq}{1+pq}$ D. $\frac{p+q}{1-pq}$

11. If $\tan\theta = \frac{1}{2}$ and $\tan\varphi = \frac{1}{3}$, then what is the value of $(\theta + \varphi)$?

A. 0 B. $\frac{\pi}{6}$

C. $\frac{\pi}{4}$ D. $\frac{\pi}{2}$

12. If $\cos A = \frac{3}{4}$, then what is the value of $\sin\left(\frac{A}{2}\right)\sin\left(\frac{3A}{2}\right)$?

A. $\frac{5}{8}$ B. $\frac{5}{16}$

C. $\frac{5}{24}$ D. $\frac{7}{32}$

13. What is the value of tan 75° + cot 75°?

A. 2 B. 4
C. $2\sqrt{3}$ D. $4\sqrt{3}$

14. What is the value of cos 46° cos 47° cos 48° cos 49° cos 50° ... cos 135°?

A. –1 B. 0
C. 1 D. Greater than 1

15. If $\sin 2\theta = \cos 3\theta$, where $0 < \theta < \frac{\pi}{2}$, then what is $\sin\theta$ equal to?

A. $\frac{\sqrt{5}+1}{4}$ B. $\frac{\sqrt{5}-1}{4}$

C. $\frac{\sqrt{5}+1}{16}$ D. $\frac{\sqrt{5}-1}{16}$

16. What is the nth term of the sequence 25, –125, 625, –3125, ... ?

A. $(-5)^{2n-1}$ B. $(-1)^{2n} 5^{n+1}$
C. $(-1)^{2n-1} 5^{n+1}$ D. $(-1)^{n-1} 5^{n+1}$

17. Suppose X = {1, 2, 3, 4} and R is a relation on X. If R = {(1, 1), (2, 2), (3, 3), (1, 2), (2, 1), (2, 3), (3, 2)}, then which one of the following is correct?
A. R is reflexive and symmetric, but not transitive
B. R is symmetric and transitive, but not reflexive
C. R is reflexive and transitive, but not symmetric
D. R is neither reflexive nor transitive, but symmetric

18. A relation R is defined on the set N of natural numbers as $xRy \Rightarrow x^2 - 4xy + 3y^2 = 0$. Then which one of the following is correct?
A. R is reflexive and symmetric, but not transitive
B. R is reflexive and transitive, but not symmetric
C. R is reflexive, symmetric and transitive
D. R is reflexive, but neither symmetric nor transitive

19. If $A = \{x \in Z : x^3 - 1 = 0\}$ and $B = \{x \in Z : x^2 + x + 1 = 0\}$, where Z is set of complex numbers, then what is $A \cap B$ equal to?
A. Null set
B. $\left\{\frac{-1+\sqrt{3}i}{2}, \frac{-1-\sqrt{3}i}{2}\right\}$
C. $\left\{\frac{-1+\sqrt{3}i}{4}, \frac{-1-\sqrt{3}i}{4}\right\}$
D. $\left\{\frac{1+\sqrt{3}i}{2}, \frac{1-\sqrt{3}i}{2}\right\}$

20. Consider the following statements for the two non-empty sets A and B:
1. $(A \cap B) \cup (A \cap \bar{B}) \cup (\bar{A} \cap B) = A \cap B$
2. $(A \cup (\bar{A} \cap \bar{B})) = A \cup B$

Which of the above statements is/are correct?
A. 1 only
B. 2 only
C. Both 1 and 2
D. Neither 1 nor 2

21. Let X be a non-empty set and let A, B, C be subsets of X. Consider the following statements:
1. $A \subset C \Rightarrow (A \cap B) \subset (C \cap B), (A \cup B) \subset (C \cup B)$
2. $(A \cap B) \subset (C \cap B)$ for all sets $B \Rightarrow A \subset C$
3. $(A \cup B) \subset (C \cup B)$ for all sets $B \Rightarrow A \subset C$

Which of the above statements are correct?
A. 1 and 2 only
B. 2 and 3 only
C. 1 and 3 only
D. 1, 2 and 3

22. If $B = \begin{bmatrix} 3 & 2 & 0 \\ 2 & 4 & 0 \\ 1 & 1 & 0 \end{bmatrix}$, then what is adjoint of B equal to?
A. $\begin{bmatrix} 0 & 0 & 0 \\ 0 & 0 & 0 \\ -2 & -1 & 8 \end{bmatrix}$
B. $\begin{bmatrix} 0 & 0 & -2 \\ 0 & 0 & -1 \\ 0 & 0 & 8 \end{bmatrix}$
C. $\begin{bmatrix} 0 & 0 & 2 \\ 0 & 0 & 1 \\ 0 & 0 & 0 \end{bmatrix}$
D. It does not exist

23. What are the roots of the equation $|x^2 - x - 6| = x + 2$?
A. –2, 1, 4
B. 0, 2, 4
C. 0, 1, 4
D. –2, 2, 4

24. If $A = \begin{bmatrix} 0 & 1 \\ 1 & 0 \end{bmatrix}$, then the matrix A is a/an:
A. Singular matrix
B. Involutory matrix
C. Nilpotent matrix
D. Idempotent matrix

25. If $\begin{vmatrix} x & -3i & 1 \\ y & 1 & i \\ 0 & 2i & -i \end{vmatrix} = 6 + 11i$, then what are the values of x and y respectively?
A. –3, 4
B. 3, 4
C. 3, –4
D. –3, –4

26. The common roots of the equations $z^3 + 2z^2 + 2z + 1 = 0$ and $z^{2017} + z^{2018} + 1 = 0$ are:
A. $-1, \omega$
B. $1, \omega^2$
C. $-1, \omega^2$
D. ω, ω^2

27. If $C(20, n + 2) = C(20, n - 2)$, then what is n equal to?
A. 8
B. 10
C. 12
D. 16

28. There are 10 points in a plane. No three of these points are in a straight line. What is the total number of straight lines which can be formed by joining the points?
A. 90
B. 45
C. 40
D. 30

29. The equation $px^2 + qx + r = 0$ (where p, q, r, all are positive) has distinct real roots a and b. Which one of the following is correct?
A. $a > 0, b > 0$
B. $a < 0, b < 0$
C. $a > 0, b < 0$
D. $a < 0, b > 0$

30. If $A = \{\lambda, \{\lambda, \mu\}\}$, then the power set of A is:
A. $\{\phi, \{\phi\}, \{\lambda\}, \{\lambda, \mu\}\}$
B. $\{\phi, \{\lambda\}, \{\{\lambda, \mu\}\}, \{\lambda, \{\lambda, \mu\}\}\}$
C. $\{\phi, \{\lambda\}, \{\lambda, \mu\}, \{\lambda, \{\lambda, \mu\}\}\}$
D. $\{\{\lambda\}, \{\lambda, \mu\}, \{\lambda, \{\lambda, \mu\}\}\}$

31. If the roots of the equation $x^2 + px + q = 0$ are tan 19° and tan 26°, then which one of the following is correct?
A. $q - p = 1$
B. $p - q = 1$
C. $p + q = 2$
D. $p + q = 3$

32. What is the fourth term of an AP of n terms whose sum is $n(n + 1)$?
A. 6
B. 8
C. 12
D. 20

33. What is $(1 + \tan\alpha \tan\beta)^2 + (\tan\alpha - \tan\beta)^2 - \sec^2\alpha \sec^2\beta$ equal to?
A. 0
B. 1
C. 2
D. 4

34. If $p = \text{cosec}\ \theta - \cot \theta$ and $q = (\text{cosec}\ \theta + \cot \theta)^{-1}$, then which one of the following is correct?
A. $pq = 1$
B. $p = q$
C. $p + q = 1$
D. $p + q = 0$

35. If the angles of a triangle ABC are in the ratio 1 : 2 : 3, then the corresponding sides are in the ratio:
A. 1 : 2 : 3
B. 3 : 2 : 1
C. $1 : \sqrt{3} : 2$
D. $1 : \sqrt{3} : \sqrt{2}$

36. Consider the following statements:
1. For an equation of a line, $x \cos \theta + y \sin \theta = p$, in normal form, the length of the perpendicular from the point (α, β) to the line is $|\alpha \cos \theta + \beta \sin \theta + p|$.
2. The length of the perpendicular from the point (α, β) to the line $\frac{x}{a} + \frac{y}{b} = 1$ is $\left|\frac{a\alpha + b\beta - ab}{\sqrt{a^2 + b^2}}\right|$.

Which of the above statements is/are correct?
A. 1 only
B. 2 only
C. Both 1 and 2
D. Neither 1 nor 2

37. A circle is drawn on the chord of a circle $x^2 + y^2 = a^2$ as diameter. The chord lies on the line $x + y = a$: What is the equation of the circle?
A. $x^2 + y^2 - ax - ay + a^2 = 0$
B. $x^2 + y^2 - ax - ay = 0$
C. $x^2 + y^2 + ax + ay = 0$
D. $x^2 + y^2 + ax + ay - 2a^2 = 0$

38. The sum of the focal distance of a point on an ellipse is constant and equal to the:
A. length of minor axis
B. length of major axis
C. length if latus rectum
D. sum of the lengths of semi-major and semi-minor axes

39. The equation $2x^2 - 3y^2 - 6 = 0$ represents:
A. a circle
B. a parabola
C. an ellipse
D. a hyperbola

40. The two parabolas $y^2 = 4ax$ and $x^2 = 4ay$ intersect:
A. at two points on the line $y = x$
B. only at the origin
C. at three points one of which lies on $y + x = 0$
D. only at $(4a, 4a)$

41. The points (1, 3) and (5, 1) are two opposite vertices of a rectangle. The other two vertices lie on the line $y = 2x + c$. What is the value of c ?
A. 2
B. –2
C. 4
D. –4

42. If the lines $3y + 4x = 1$, $y = x + 5$ and $5y + bx = 3$ are concurrent, then what is the value of b?
A. 1
B. 3
C. 6
D. $\frac{1}{2}$

43. What is the equation of the straight line which is perpendicular to $y = x$ and passes through (3, 2)?
A. $x - y = 5$
B. $x + y = 5$
C. $x + y = 1$
D. $x - y = 1$

44. The straight lines $x + y - 4 = 0$, $3x + y - 4 = 0$ and $x + 3y - 4 = 0$, form a triangle, which is:
A. isosceles
B. right-angled
C. equilateral
D. scalene

45. The circle $x^2 + y^2 + 4x - 7y + 12 = 0$, cuts an intercept on y-axis equal to:
A. 1
B. 3
C. 4
D. 7

Directions (Qs. No. 46-47): *Consider the following for the next 02 (two) items that follows.*

In a school, all the students play at least one of three indoor games—chess, carrom and table tennis. 60 play chess, 50 play table tennis, 48 play carrom, 12 play chess and carrom, 15 play carrom and table tennis, 20 play table tennis and chess.

46. What can be the minimum number of students in the school?
A. 123
B. 111
C. 95
D. 63

47. What can be the maximum number of students in the school?
A. 111
B. 123
C. 125
D. 135

48. If A is an identity matrix of order 3, then its inverse (A^{-1}):
A. is equal to null matrix
B. is equal to A
C. is equal to 3A
D. does not exist

49. A is a square matrix of order 3 such that its determinant is 4. What is the determinant of its transpose?
A. 64
B. 36
C. 32
D. 4

50. From 6 programmers and 4 typists, an office wants to recruit 5 people. What is the number of ways this can be done so as to recruit at least one typist?
A. 209
B. 210
C. 246
D. 242

51. What is the number of terms in the expansion of $[(2x - 3y)^2 (2x + 3y)^2]^2$?
A. 4
B. 5
C. 8
D. 16

52. In the expansion of $(1 + ax)^n$, the first three terms are respectively 1, $12x$ and $64x^2$. What is n equal to?
A. 6
B. 9
C. 10
D. 12

53. The numbers 1, 5 and 25 can be three terms (not necessarily consecutive) of:
A. only one AP
B. more than one but finite numbers of APs
C. infinite number of APs
D. finite number of GPs

54. The sum of $(p + q)^{th}$ and $(p - q)^{th}$ terms of an AP is equal to:
A. $(2p)^{th}$ term B. $(2q)^{th}$ term
C. Twice the pth term D. Twice the qth term

55. If A is a square matrix of order $n > 1$, then which one of the following is correct?
A. det (–A) = det A
B. det (–A) = $(-1)^n$ det A
C. det (–A) = – det A
D. det (–A) = n det A

56. What is the least value of $25 \operatorname{cosec}^2 x + 36 \sec^2 x$?
A. 1 B. 11
C. 120 D. 121

Directions (Qs. No. 57-58): *Consider the following for the next 02 (two) items that follows.*

Let A and B be (3 × 3) matrices with det A = 4 and det B = 3.

57. What is det (2AB) equal to?
A. 96 B. 72
C. 48 D. 36

58. What is det $(3AB^{-1})$ equal to?
A. 12 B. 18
C. 36 D. 48

Directions (Qs. No. 59-60): *Consider the following for the next 02 (two) items that follows.*

A complex number is given by $z = \dfrac{1+2i}{1-(1-i)^2}$

59. What is the modulus of z?
A. 4 B. 2
C. 1 D. $\frac{1}{2}$

60. What is the principal argument of z?
A. 0 B. $\frac{\pi}{4}$
C. $\frac{\pi}{2}$ D. π

61. What is the general solution of the differential equation

$$\frac{dy}{dx} + \frac{x}{y} = 0?$$

A. $x^2 + y^2 = c$ B. $x^2 - y^2 = c$
C. $x^2 + y^2 = cxy$ D. $x + y = c$

62. The value of k which makes

$$f(x) = \begin{cases} \sin x & x \neq 0 \\ k & x = 0 \end{cases}$$ continuous at $x = 0$, is:

A. 2 B. 1
C. –1 D. 0

63. What is the minimum value of $a^2x + b^2y$ where $xy = c^2$?
A. abc B. $2abc$
C. $3abc$ D. $4abc$

64. What is $\int e^{x\ln(a)}dx$ equal to?
A. $\dfrac{a^x}{\ln(a)} + c$ B. $\dfrac{e^x}{\ln(a)} + c$
C. $\dfrac{e^x}{\ln(ae)} + c$ D. $\dfrac{ae^x}{\ln(a)} + c$

65. What is the area of one of the loops between the curve $y = c \sin x$ and x-axis?
A. c B. $2c$
C. $3c$ D. $4c$

66. If $\sin\theta + \cos\theta = \sqrt{2}\cos\theta$, then what is $(\cos \theta - \sin \theta)$ equal to?
A. $-\sqrt{2}\cos\theta$ B. $-\sqrt{2}\sin\theta$
C. $\sqrt{2}\sin\theta$ D. $2 \sin \theta$

67. In a circle of diameter 44 cm, the length of a chord is 22 cm. What is the length of minor arc of the chord?
A. $\dfrac{484}{21}$ cm B. $\dfrac{242}{21}$ cm
C. $\dfrac{121}{21}$ cm D. $\dfrac{44}{7}$ cm

68. If $\sin\theta = -\frac{1}{2}$ and $\tan\theta = \frac{1}{\sqrt{3}}$, then in which quadrant does θ lie?
A. First B. Second
C. Third D. Fourth

69. How many three-digit even numbers can be formed using the digits 1, 2, 3, 4 and 5 when repetition of digits is *not* allowed?
A. 36 B. 30
C. 24 D. 12

70. The angle of elevation of a tower of height h from a point A due South of it is x and from a point B due East of A is y. If AB = z, then which one of the following is correct?
A. $h^2 (\cot^2 y - \cot^2 x) = z^2$
B. $z^2 (\cot^2 y - \cot^2 x) = h^2$
C. $h^2 (\tan^2 y - \tan^2 x) = z^2$
D. $z^2 (\tan^2 y - \tan^2 x) = h^2$

71. From a deck of cards, cards are taken out with replacement. What is the probability that the fourteenth card taken out is an ace?

A. $\frac{1}{51}$ B. $\frac{4}{51}$

C. $\frac{1}{52}$ D. $\frac{1}{13}$

72. If A and B are two events such that P(A) = 0.5, P(B) = 0.6 and $P(A \cap B) = 0.4$, then what is $P(\overline{A \cup B})$ equal to?

A. 0.9 B. 0.7

C. 0.5 D. 0.3

73. A problem is given to three students A, B and C whose probabilities of solving the problem are $\frac{1}{2}, \frac{3}{4}$ and $\frac{1}{4}$ respectively. What is the probability that the problem will be solved if they all solve the problem independently?

A. $\frac{29}{32}$ B. $\frac{27}{32}$

C. $\frac{25}{32}$ D. $\frac{23}{32}$

74. A pair of fair dice is rolled. What is the probability that the second dice lands on a higher value than does the first?

A. $\frac{1}{4}$ B. $\frac{1}{6}$

C. $\frac{5}{12}$ D. $\frac{5}{18}$

75. A fair coin is tossed and an unbiased dice is rolled together. What is the probability of getting a 2 or 4 or 6 along with head?

A. $\frac{1}{2}$ B. $\frac{1}{3}$

C. $\frac{1}{4}$ D. $\frac{1}{6}$

76. The centroid of the triangle with vertices A(2, –3, 3), B(5, –3, –4) and C(2, –3, –2) is the point:

A. (–3, 3, –1) B. (3, –3, –1)

C. (3, 1, –3) D. (–3, –1, –3)

77. What is the radius of the sphere $x^2 + y^2 + z^2 - 6x + 8y - 10z + 1 = 0$?

A. 5 B. 2

C. 7 D. 3

78. The equation of the plane passing through the intersection of the planes $2x + y + 2z = 9$, $4x - 5y - 4z = 1$ and the point (3, 2, 1) is:

A. $10x - 2y + 2z = 28$ B. $10x + 2y + 2z = 28$

C. $10x + 2y - 2z = 28$ D. $10x - 2y - 2z = 24$

79. The distance between the parallel planes $4x - 2y + 4z + 9 = 0$ and $8x - 4y + 8z + 21 = 0$ is:

A. $\frac{1}{4}$ B. $\frac{1}{2}$

C. $\frac{3}{2}$ D. $\frac{7}{4}$

80. What are the direction cosines of z-axis?

A. < 1, 1, 1 > B. < 1, 0, 0 >

C. < 0, 1, 0 > D. < 0, 0, 1 >

81. If $\vec{a} = \hat{i} - 2\hat{j} + 5\hat{k}$ and $\vec{b} = 2\hat{i} + \hat{j} - 3\hat{k}$ then what is $(\vec{b} - \vec{a}).(3\vec{a} + \vec{b})$ equal to?

A. 106 B. –106

C. 53 D. –53

82. If the position vectors of points A and B are $3\hat{i} - 2\hat{j} + \hat{k}$ and $2\hat{i} + 4\hat{j} - 3\hat{k}$ respectively, then what is the length of $\overrightarrow{AB}$?

A. $\sqrt{14}$ B. $\sqrt{29}$

C. $\sqrt{43}$ D. $\sqrt{53}$

83. If in a right-angled triangle ABC, hypotenuse AC = p, then what is $\overrightarrow{AB} . \overrightarrow{AC} + \overrightarrow{BC} . \overrightarrow{BA} + \overrightarrow{CA} . \overrightarrow{CB}$ equal to?

A. p^2 B. $2p^2$

C. $\frac{p^2}{2}$ D. p

84. The sine of the angle between vectors $\vec{a} = 2\hat{i} - 6\hat{j} - 3\hat{k}$ and $\vec{b} = 4\hat{i} + 3\hat{j} - \hat{k}$ is:

A. $\frac{1}{\sqrt{26}}$ B. $\frac{5}{\sqrt{26}}$

C. $\frac{5}{26}$ D. $\frac{1}{26}$

85. What is the value of λ for which the vectors $3\hat{i} + 4\hat{j} - \hat{k}$ and $-2\hat{i} + \lambda\hat{j} + 10\hat{k}$ are perpendicular?

A. 1 B. 2

C. 3 D. 4

86. What is the derivative of $\sec^2(\tan^{-1} x)$ with respect to x?

A. $2x$ B. $x^2 + 1$

C. $x + 1$ D. x^2

87. If $f(x) = \log_{10}(1 + x)$, then what is $4f(4) = 5f(1) - \log_{10} 2$ equal to?

A. 0 B. 1

C. 2 D. 4

88. A function f defined by $f(x) = \ln\left(\sqrt{x^2+1} - x\right)$ is:

A. an even function
B. an odd function
C. Both even and odd function
D. Neither even nor odd function

89. The domain of the function f defined by $f(x) = \log_x 10$ is:

A. $x > 10$ B. $x > 0$ excluding $x = 10$
C. $x \geq 10$ D. $x > 0$ excluding $x = 1$

90. $\lim_{x\to 0} \frac{1-\cos^3 4x}{x^2}$ is equal to:

A. 0 B. 12
C. 24 D. 36

91. If A, B, C are three events, then what is the probability that at least two of these events occur together?

A. $P(A \cap B) + P(B \cap C) + P(C \cap A)$
B. $P(A \cap B) + P(B \cap C) + P(C \cap A) - P(A \cap B \cap C)$
C. $P(A \cap B) + P(B \cap C) + P(C \cap A) - 2P(A \cap B \cap C)$
D. $P(A \cap B) + P(B \cap C) + P(C \cap A) - 3P(A \cap B \cap C)$

92. If two variables X and Y are independent, then what is the correlation coefficient between them?

A. 1 B. −1
C. 0 D. None of the above

93. Two independent events A and B are such that $P(A \cup B) = \frac{2}{3}$ and $P(A \cap B) = \frac{1}{6}$. If $P(B) < P(A)$, then what is $P(B)$ equal to?

A. $\frac{1}{4}$ B. $\frac{1}{3}$
C. $\frac{1}{2}$ D. $\frac{1}{6}$

94. The mean of 100 observations is 50 and the standard deviation is 10. If 5 is subtracted from each observation and then it is divided by 4, then what will be the new mean and the new standard deviation respectively?

A. 45, 5 B. 11.25, 1.25
C. 11.25, 2.5 D. 12.5, 2.5

95. If two fair dice are rolled then what is the conditional probability that the first dice lands on 6 given that the sum of numbers on the dice is 8?

A. $\frac{1}{3}$ B. $\frac{1}{4}$
C. $\frac{1}{5}$ D. $\frac{1}{6}$

96. Two symmetric dice flipped with each dice having two sides painted red, two painted black, one painted yellow and the other painted white. What is the probability that both land on the same colour?

A. $\frac{3}{18}$ B. $\frac{2}{9}$
C. $\frac{5}{18}$ D. $\frac{1}{3}$

97. There are n socks in a drawer, of which 3 socks are red. If 2 of the socks are chosen randomly and the probability that both selected socks are red is $\frac{1}{2}$, then what is the value of n?

A. 3 B. 4
C. 5 D. 6

98. Two cards are chosen at random from a deck of 52 playing cards. What is the probability that both of them have the same value?

A. $\frac{1}{17}$ B. $\frac{3}{17}$
C. $\frac{5}{17}$ D. $\frac{7}{17}$

99. In eight throws of a die, 5 or 6 is considered a success. The mean and standard deviation of total number of successes is respectively given by:

A. $\frac{8}{3}, \frac{16}{9}$ B. $\frac{8}{3}, \frac{4}{3}$
C. $\frac{4}{3}, \frac{4}{3}$ D. $\frac{4}{3}, \frac{16}{9}$

100. A and B are two events such that $\bar{A}$ and $\bar{B}$ are mutually exclusive. If $P(A) = 0.5$ and $P(B) = 0.6$, then what is the value of $P(A \mid B)$?

A. $\frac{1}{5}$ B. $\frac{1}{6}$
C. $\frac{2}{5}$ D. $\frac{1}{3}$

101. Consider the following statements:

1. The algebraic sum of deviations of a set of values from their arithmetic mean is always zero.
2. Arithmetic mean > Median > Mode for a symmetric distribution.

Which of the above statements is/are correct?

A. 1 only B. 2 only
C. Both 1 and 2 D. Neither 1 nor 2

102. Let the correlation coefficient between X and Y be 0.6. Random variables Z and W are defined as $Z = X + 5$ and $W = \frac{Y}{3}$. What is the correlation coefficient between Z and W?

A. 0.1 B. 0.2
C. 0.36 D. 0.6

103. If all the natural numbers between 1 and 20 are multiplied by 3, then what is the variance of the resulting series?

A. 99.75 B. 199.75
C. 299.25 D. 399.25

104. What is the probability that an interior point in a circle is closer to the center than to the circumference?

A. $\frac{1}{4}$ B. $\frac{1}{2}$
C. $\frac{3}{4}$ D. It cannot be determined

105. If A and B are two events, then what is the probability of occurrence of either event A or event B?

A. P(A) + P(B) B. $P(A \cup B)$
C. $P(A \cap B)$ D. P(A) P(B)

106. For $r > 0, f(r)$ is the ratio of perimeter to area of a circle of radius r. Then $f(1) + f(2)$ is equal to:

A. 1 B. 2
C. 3 D. 4

107. If $f(x) = 3^{1+x}$, then $f(x)\,f(y)\,f(z)$ is equal to:

A. $f(x + y + z)$ B. $f(x + y + z + 1)$
C. $f(x + y + z + 2)$ D. $f(x + y + z + 3)$

108. The number of real roots for the equation $x^2 + 9|x| + 20 = 0$ is:

A. Zero B. One
C. Two D. Three

109. If $f(x) = \sin(\cos x)$, then $f'(x)$ is equal to:

A. cos (cos x) B. sin (–sin x)
C. (sin x) cos (cos x) D. (–sin x) cos (cos x)

110. The domain of the function $f(x)=\sqrt{(2-x)(x-3)}$ is:

A. $(0, \infty)$ B. $[0, \infty)$
C. [2, 3] D. (2, 3)

111. The solution of the differential equation $\frac{dy}{dx}=\cos(y-x)+1$ is:

A. $e^x\,[\sec(y-x)-\tan(y-x)]=c$
B. $e^x\,[\sec(y-x)+\tan(y-x)]=c$
C. $e^x \sec(y-x)\tan(y-x)=c$
D. $e^x = c\sec(y-x)\tan(y-x)$

112. $\int_0^{\frac{\pi}{2}} |\sin x-\cos x|\,dx$ is equal to:

A. 0 B. $2(\sqrt{2}-1)$
C. $2\sqrt{2}$ D. $2(\sqrt{2}+1)$

113. If $y = a\cos 2x + b\sin 2x$, then:

A. $\frac{d^2y}{dx^2}+y=0$ B. $\frac{d^2y}{dx^2}+2y=0$
C. $\frac{d^2y}{dx^2}-4y=0$ D. $\frac{d^2y}{dx^2}+4y=0$

114. A given quantity of metal is to be cast into a half cylinder (*i.e.*, with a rectangular base and semicircular ends). If the total surface area is to be minimum, then the ratio of the height of the half cylinder to the diameter of the semicircular ends is:

A. $\pi : (\pi + 2)$ B. $(\pi + 2) : \pi$
C. 1 : 1 D. None of the above

115. $\int_0^{\frac{\pi}{2}} e^{\sin x}\cos x\,dx$ is equal to:

A. $e + 1$ B. $e - 1$
C. $e + 2$ D. e

116. If $f(x)=\frac{x-2}{x+2}$, $x \neq -2$, then what is $f^{-1}(x)$ equal to?

A. $\frac{4(x+2)}{x-2}$ B. $\frac{x+2}{4(x-2)}$
C. $\frac{x+2}{x-2}$ D. $\frac{2(1+x)}{1-x}$

117. What is $\int \ln(x^2)\,dx$ equal to?

A. $2x\ln(x) - 2x + c$ B. $\frac{2}{x}+c$
C. $2x\ln(x) + c$ D. $\frac{2\ln(x)}{x}-2x+c$

118. The minimum distance from the point (4, 2) to $y^2 = 8x$ is equal to:

A. $\sqrt{2}$ B. $2\sqrt{2}$
C. 2 D. $3\sqrt{2}$

119. The differential equation of the system of circles touching the y-axis at the origin is:

A. $x^2+y^2-2xy\frac{dy}{dx}=0$ B. $x^2+y^2+2xy\frac{dy}{dx}=0$
C. $x^2-y^2+2xy\frac{dy}{dx}=0$ D. $x^2-y^2-2xy\frac{dy}{dx}=0$

120. Consider the following in respect of the differential equation:

$$\frac{d^2y}{dx^2}+2\left(\frac{dy}{dx}\right)^2+9y=x$$

1. The degree of the differential equation is 1.
2. The order of the differential equation is 2.

Which of the above statements is/are correct?

A. 1 only B. 2 only
C. Both 1 and 2 D. Neither 1 nor 2

ANSWERS

PAPER-I - GENERAL ABILITY TEST

1	2	3	4	5	6	7	8	9	10
C	A	C	A	A	A	C	C	A	A
11	**12**	**13**	**14**	**15**	**16**	**17**	**18**	**19**	**20**
A	C	B	D	B	A	D	B	D	A
21	**22**	**23**	**24**	**25**	**26**	**27**	**28**	**29**	**30**
C	A	C	C	D	A	B	D	C	A
31	**32**	**33**	**34**	**35**	**36**	**37**	**38**	**39**	**40**
B	C	A	B	A	B	B	A	D	B
41	**42**	**43**	**44**	**45**	**46**	**47**	**48**	**49**	**50**
B	B	A	D	D	B	C	A	C	A
51	**52**	**53**	**54**	**55**	**56**	**57**	**58**	**59**	**60**
D	A	C	C	A	A	B	A	C	D
61	**62**	**63**	**64**	**65**	**66**	**67**	**68**	**69**	**70**
D	B	C	B	D	A	C	C	A	D
71	**72**	**73**	**74**	**75**	**76**	**77**	**78**	**79**	**80**
A	C	C	D	A	B	B	C	D	D
81	**82**	**83**	**84**	**85**	**86**	**87**	**88**	**89**	**90**
D	C	C	C	B	B	D	B	C	D
91	**92**	**93**	**94**	**95**	**96**	**97**	**98**	**99**	**100**
C	C	A	A	C	B	D	A	B	A
101	**102**	**103**	**104**	**105**	**106**	**107**	**108**	**109**	**110**
A	B	A	B	B	B	C	B	D	A
111	**112**	**113**	**114**	**115**	**116**	**117**	**118**	**119**	**120**
B	B	D	C	C	C	A	B	A	A
121	**122**	**123**	**124**	**125**	**126**	**127**	**128**	**129**	**130**
C	D	C	B	D	C	A	A	C	D
131	**132**	**133**	**134**	**135**	**136**	**137**	**138**	**139**	**140**
B	D	A	A	B	C	D	A	C	D
141	**142**	**143**	**144**	**145**	**146**	**147**	**148**	**149**	**150**
C	A	C	D	B	B	D	B	C	C

PAPER-II - MATHEMATICS

1	2	3	4	5	6	7	8	9	10
A	C	C	B	A	A	A	C	D	B
11	**12**	**13**	**14**	**15**	**16**	**17**	**18**	**19**	**20**
C	B	B	B	B	D	D	C	B	D
21	**22**	**23**	**24**	**25**	**26**	**27**	**28**	**29**	**30**
D	A	D	B	A	D	B	B	B	C
31	**32**	**33**	**34**	**35**	**36**	**37**	**38**	**39**	**40**
A	B	A	B	C	D	B	B	D	A
41	**42**	**43**	**44**	**45**	**46**	**47**	**48**	**49**	**50**
D	C	B	A	A	B	B	B	D	C

51	52	53	54	55	56	57	58	59	60
B	B	C	C	B	D	A	C	C	A
61	62	63	64	65	66	67	68	69	70
A	D	B	A	B	C	A	C	C	A
71	72	73	74	75	76	77	78	79	80
D	D	A	C	C	B	C	A	A	D
81	82	83	84	85	86	87	88	89	90
B	D	A	B	D	A	D	D	D	C
91	92	93	94	95	96	97	98	99	100
C	C	B	C	C	C	B	A	B	A
101	102	103	104	105	106	107	108	109	110
A	D	C	A	B	C	C	A	D	C
111	112	113	114	115	116	117	118	119	120
D	B	D	A	B	D	A	B	C	C

EXPLANATORY ANSWERS

PAPER I - GENERAL KNOWLEDGE

51. The **plasma membrane** is a phospholipid bilayer with embedded proteins that encloses every living cell. This membrane blocks uncontrolled movements of water-soluble materials into or out of the cell. The various proteins embedded in the phospholipid bilayer penetrate into and through the bilayer three-dimensionally. It is the proteins of the membrane that are responsible for the specific functions of the plasma membrane. These functions include controlling the flow of nutrients and ions into and out of the cells, mediating the response of a cell to external stimuli (a process called signal transduction), and interacting with bordering cells. All membranous eukaryotic cell organelles have the common feature of a phospholipid bilayer, although the proteins differ in each case.

52. Ribosomes are the molecular machines responsible for protein synthesis. A ribosome is made out of RNA and proteins, and each ribosome consists of two separate RNA-protein complexes, known as the small and large subunits. The large subunit sits on top of the small subunit, with an RNA template sandwiched between the two. (A ribosome looks a little like a hamburger with a puffy bun on top, an RNA "patty" threading through it.)

55. Within an ecological food chain, Consumers are categorized into primary consumers, secondary consumers, tertiary consumers. Primary consumers are herbivores, feeding on plants. Caterpillars, insects, grasshoppers, termites and hummingbirds are all examples of primary consumers because they only eat producers (plants). There are certain primary consumers that are called specialists because they only eat one type of producers an example of this would be the koala because it feeds only on eucalyptus leaves. Primary consumers who feed on many kinds of plants are called generalists. Secondary consumers, on the other hand, are carnivores, and prey on other animals. Omnivores, who feed on both plants and animals, can also be considered a secondary consumer. Tertiary consumers, sometimes also known as apex predators, are usually at the top of food chains, capable of feeding on secondary consumers and primary consumers. Tertiary consumers can be either fully carnivorous or omnivorous. Humans are a great example of a tertiary consumer. Secondary and Tertiary producers both must hunt for their food so they are referred to as predators.

56. **Tidal range** is the height difference between high tide and low tide. Tides are the rise and fall of sea levels caused by gravitational forces exerted by the Moon and Sun and the rotation of Earth. Tidal range is not constant but changes depending on the locations of the Moon and Sun.

57. **Chemical Energy** is the energy stored in the bonds between atoms and molecules. Food, fuel, and the energy stored in the chemicals inside a battery are examples.

Nuclear Energy is the energy stored in the nucleus of an atom - the energy that holds the nucleus together. The energy in the nucleus of a uranium atom or in the nuclei of atoms in our Sun are examples.

Mechanical Potential Energy is energy stored in objects due to shape or position. Compressed springs, stretched rubber bands, an apple hanging from a tree, and a parked car at the top of a hill are examples.

Thermal Energy or heat is the vibration or movement of atoms and molecules in substances. Heat from a campfire is an example.

58. Light Energy: Light is the energy that we detect with our eyes. The light energy escaping from the Sun can be spread out by a prism or a shower of raindrops into light of different wavelengths. This forms the colours of the rainbow because our eyes see different wavelengths of light as different colours.

60. Pitchblende used as a fuel in nuclear power station. Pitchblende, also known by the name uraninite, is a mineral comprised mainly of oxides of the element uranium, UO_2, and UO_3. It is the primary ore of uranium. The mineral is black in colour, like 'pitch'. The term 'blende' came from the German miners who believed it contained many different metals all blended together. Pitchblende contains many other radioactive elements that can be traced back to the decay of uranium, such as radium, lead, helium, and several actinide elements. In fact, the first discovery of helium on Earth was in pitchblende. Spontaneous fission of uranium-238 leads to the presence of minute quantities of the extremely rare elements technetium (200 pg/kg) and promethium (4 fg/kg). Pitchblende was the source of discovery for several elements. In 1789, Martin Heinrich Klaproth discovered and identified uranium as a new element from pitchblende. In 1898, Marie and Pierre Curie discovered the element radium while working with pitchblende. In 1895, William Ramsay was the first to isolate helium from pitchblende.

61. Neutral or non-ionic detergents. These are esters of high molecular mass alcohols with fatty acids. These can also be obtained by treatment of long chain alcohols by with excess of ethylene oxide in presence of a base. For example, polyethylene glycol stearate,

$CH_3(CH_2)_{16}COO(CH_2CH_2O)_nCH_2CH_2OH$

Polyethylene glycol stearate.

62. Also known as liquefied petroleum gas (LPG) or propane auto gas, propane is a cleaner-burning alternative fuel that's been used for decades to power light-, medium- and heavy-duty propane vehicles.

Propane is a three-carbon alkane gas (C_3H_8). It is stored under pressure inside a tank as a colourless, odorless liquid. As pressure is released, the liquid propane vapourizes and turns into gas that is used in combustion. An odorant, ethyl mercaptan, is added for leak detection.

63. Magnesium does not react with cold water. It reacts with hot water to form magnesium hydroxide and hydrogen. It also starts floating due to the bubbles of hydrogen gas sticking to its surface. Metals like aluminium, iron and zinc do not react either with cold or hot water. But they react with steam to form the metal oxide and hydrogen.

65. Resin or Binder, is the main constituent material that holds all the ingredients together, it forms the film and it is the only component that must be present; all other components are optional although rarely are no further compounds present as it is a combination of the components that produce the desired properties of the final paint film.

The function of binder is to give protection to the substrate and to the components within the film. It ensures that resin, fillers, pigments etc are homogeneously dispersed and strongly influences the key properties such as gloss, durability, flexibility and toughness.

The binder can be made up of one or more basic resin or polymer systems, either synthetic or natural resin systems. Typical types of binders include polyesters, polyurethanes, acrylics, polyesters, silicates, epoxies, oils, melamine resins, depending upon the substrate and cured performance required.

67. National Water Academy (NWA) was set up in Central Water Commission by the Ministry of Water Resources, RD and GR, Govt. of India in the year 1988, to impart training to the in-service engineers of various Central/ State organizations involved in the Development & Management of Water Resources. It was established under USAID assistance and strengthened with the subsequent assistance received from the World Bank.

The NWA is envisaged to function as a 'Center of Excellence' in training water resources personnel. It is addressing the wider training needs of water resources engineers of States and Central Agencies in the fields of planning, design, evaluation, construction, operation and monitoring of water resources projects. In its national role, the NWA is concentrating on conducting training courses for all water sector personnel, in the specialized and emerging areas, for which the existing State or other institutes are not adequately equipped to meet the needs. Apart from this, in regard to the Central Water Commission, other offices of the Ministry of Water Resources, and for States not having adequate training facilities, it is conducting induction and refresher courses in all relevant areas of the water sector.

68. Los Llanos is a vast tropical grassland plain situated to the east of the Andes in Colombia and Venezuela, in north-western South America. It is an eco region of the flooded grasslands and savannas biome.

The Llanos' main river is the Orinoco, which forms part of the border between Colombia and Venezuela and is the major river system of Venezuela.

The principal region of grassland in South America is in the southeast portion of the continent; it can be divided into the Pampas of Argentina and the campos of the adjacent areas of Uruguay and Brazil.

69. The wines from Adelaide Hills are shaped by the coolness of the region's altitude, its changing seasons and the skill and passion of its winemakers. There were vines planted in the Adelaide Hills as early as the 1870s but due to the challenges of cool-climate viticulture in those early days, most vines were removed by the 1930s. The rebirth of the Adelaide Hills region started in 1970s and gained pace with the rise in popularity of cool climate wines in the 1980s and 1990s.

The cooler climate defines the Adelaide Hills and provides them with a distinctive point of difference to other South Australian regions that has allowed it to spearhead the evolution of Australian wine in recent years. Its wine making evolution continues to this day, and it is now a hotbed of creativity; home to bold, boundary-pushing grape growers and winemakers.

70. Shamal warm and dry wind is a local wind found in Mesopotamia. A shamal is a north-westerly wind blowing over Iraq and the Persian Gulf states (including Saudi Arabia and Kuwait), often strong during the day, but decreasing at night. This weather effect occurs anywhere from once to several times a year, mostly in summer but sometimes in winter. The resulting wind typically creates large sandstorms that impact Iraq, most sand having been picked up from Jordan and Syria.

71. Orographic Rainfall: The orographic rainfall occurs due to the ascent of air forced by the mountain barrier. The mountain barrier should be across the wind direction. So that the moist air is forced in obstruction to move upward and get cooled. In Rajasthan, the Aravalli is not an obstructing barrier to the highly moist air coming from Arabian Sea and that is why they don't play very important role in rainfalls. Thus they produce a Rain shadow area. A rain shadow is a dry area on the lee side of a mountainous area. The mountains block the passage of rain-producing weather systems, casting a "shadow" of dryness behind them. In south India, the Mangalore is located on the western windward slope and gets 2000 mm of rainfall. But Bangalore is in rain shadow area and that is why receives less than 500 mm of rainfall.

Please note that the amount of rainfall increases with increasing height of the barrier such as mountain, but this is up to a certain limit. After that there is a marked decrease due to lesser moisture content of the air and this phenomenon is called "Inversion of Rainfall".

72. James Mill was a Scottish historian, economist, political theorist, and philosopher. He is counted among the founders of the Ricardian school of economics. His son, John Stuart Mill, was also a noted philosopher of liberalism, utilitarianism and the civilizing mission of the British Empire.

Mill preferred to take a more theoretical approach to social subjects than the empirical one common at the time. His best known literary work is his *History of British India,* in which he describes the acquisition of the Indian Empire by England and later the United Kingdom.

74. Lord Willingdon, Viceroy of India, writing about Gandhi in 1933:

"It's a beautiful world if it wasn't for Gandhi who is really a perfect nuisance...At the bottom of every move he makes which he always says is inspired by God, one discovers the political manoeuvre....I see the American Press is saying what a wonderful man he is in that if he threatens to starve there is a terrible hullaballoo over here. It's true, but the fact is that we live in the midst of very unpractical, mystical and superstitious folk who look upon Gandhi as something holy, whereas I look upon him as the biggest humbug alive."

76. In 1857, British rule in India was challenged when Indian sepoy troops of the British Indian Army began a year-long insurrection against the British. To the British, the most shocking aspect of the events in India was the massacre of white women and children by Indian men. There was extensive coverage in the press and illustrated journals, which stimulated calls for revenge. Paton's famous painting In Memoriam was dedicated by the artist to the Christian heroism of "British Ladies in India during the Mutiny of 1857." In 1858, the first version of the painting, which depicted Indian sepoy troops bursting through the door, was exhibited at the Royal Academy of Art in London. The painting aroused immediate debate, as it was thought to suggest that British women were about to be raped by Indian soldiers. The review in The Illustrated London News on May, 15, 1858 stated: "The subject is too revolting... The picture is one which ought not to have been hung." Although British women and children were known to have died during the insurrection, there was no evidence of rape. The artist painted out the Indian soldiers in the original painting, and substituted Scottish highlanders. It was this version that was engraved and sold, leaving intact the myth of the British woman as sexually inviolable by colonial men.

78. Speed of Sound in Water - in SI units

Temperature 't' (°C)	Speed of Sound 'c' (m/s)
0	1403
5	1427
10	1447
20	1481
30	1507
40	1526
50	1541
60	1552
70	1555
80	1555
90	1550
100	1543

79. Iron is a metal, an element of group VIII of the periodic table. It is a lustrous, ductile, malleable, silver-gray in colour. It is the tenth most abundant element in the universe. It is found in a major amount at the core of the Earth in a molten form.

Properties of iron:

- It rusts in damp air, but not in the dry air.
- It dissolves readily in dilute acids.
- At room temperature, this metal is in the form of ferrite or α-form.
- At 910°C, it changes to γ-iron, which is much softer in nature.
- It melts at 1536°C and boils at 2861°C.
- Being a metal is magnetic in nature.

83. Acetic acid is a colourless liquid organic compound with the chemical formula CH_3COOH. When undiluted, it is sometimes called glacial acetic acid. Vinegar is no less than 4% acetic acid by volume, making acetic acid the main component of vinegar apart from water. Acetic acid has a distinctive sour taste and pungent smell. In addition to household vinegar, it is mainly produced as a precursor to polyvinyl acetate and cellulose acetate. It is classified as a weak acid since it only partially dissociates in solution, but concentrated acetic acid is corrosive and can attack the skin.

85. The photoelectric effect is a phenomenon in physics. The effect is based on the idea that electromagnetic radiation is made of a series of particles called photons. When a photon hits an electron on a metal surface, the electron can be emitted. The emitted electrons are called photoelectrons. The effect is also called the Hertz Effect, because it was discovered by Heinrich Rudolf Hertz, but this name is not used often.

The photoelectric effect has helped physicists understand the quantum nature of light and electrons. The concept of wave-particle duality was developed because of the photoelectric effect. Albert Einstein proposed the Laws of Photoelectric Effect and Won the Nobel Prize for Physics, 1921.

88.

Rig-Vedic Name	**Modern Name**
Sindhu	Indus
Vitasta	Jhelum
Askini	Chenab
Purushni	Ravi
Vipas	Beas
Sutudri, Shutudri	Satluj or Sutlej
Gumal/Gomal	Gomati
Krumu	Kurram
Drishdvati	Ghagghar
Suwastu	Swat

89. The **Kali River** originates in the Doon Valley and passes through Saharanpur, Muzaffarnagar and Bagpat districts, before merging with Hindon River (at Barnava, Bagpat), which goes on to merge with the Yamuna River (near Delhi), which itself goes to merge with the Ganga River, which finally merges with the Bay of Bengal. The total length of the river from its origin up to its confluence with the Hindon river is 150 km. The river is named Kali, because of the Hindu Goddess Kali.

90. Mission Indradhanush: To strengthen and re-energize the programme and achieve full immunization coverage for all children and pregnant women at a rapid pace, the Government of India launched "Mission Indradhanush" in December 2014.

Mission Indradhanush's Goal: The ultimate goal is to ensure full immunization with all available vaccines for children up to two years of age and pregnant women. The Government has identified 201 high focus districts across 29 states that have the highest number of partially immunized and unimmunized children.

91. The earth rotates on its axis taking approximately 24 hours to complete one rotation. This has important environmental consequences.

1. Rotation creates a diurnal cycle of light and darkness, temperature, and humidity changes.
2. Rotation requires the creation of standardized time zones. There are 24, one for each hour of the earth's rotation.
3. Rotation causes the tides—the twice daily rise and fall of sea level. Tides are complicated because they are the result of both the gravity of the moon and the gravity of the sun. Sometimes the sun and the moon are lined up with the earth, but most of

the time they are not. Tides are highest when the earth, sun and moon are in a straight line.

4. The Coriolis Force: Rotation causes a deflection of ocean and air currents. The earth rotates much faster than the winds or currents move. This causes a large deflection in the direction that winds move and ultimately results in rotation around low pressure cells and high pressure cells. It also causes large rotating pools of water in the oceans called gyres. The Coriolis force only operates on large features.

98. The **light-year** is a unit of length used to express astronomical distances and measures about 9.46 trillion kilometres (9.46×10^{12} km). As defined by the International Astronomical Union (IAU), a light-year is the distance that light travels in vacuum in one Julian year (365.25 days). Because it includes the word "year", the term light-year is sometimes misinterpreted as a unit of time.

The light-year is most often used when expressing distances to stars and other distances on a galactic scale, especially in non specialist and popular science publications. The unit most commonly used in professional astrometry is the parsec (symbol: pc, about 3.26 light-years; the distance at which one astronomical unit subtends an angle of one second of arc).

100. Conservative force, in physics, any force, such as the gravitational force between the Earth and another mass, whose work is determined only by the final displacement of the object acted upon. The total work done by a conservative force is independent of the path resulting in a given displacement and is equal to zero when the path is a closed loop. Stored energy, or potential energy, can be defined only for conservative forces. Non-conservative forces, such as friction, that depend on other factors, such as velocity, are dissipative, and no potential energy can be defined for them.

Non-conservative force examples:

- Frictional forces
- Viscous forces
- Induction forces
- Air resistance force
- Tension in a string
- Normal force
- Propulsion force of the rocket
- Propulsion force of the boat

101. Copper metal when exposed to air turns green in colour due to corrosion. When copper vessel is exposed to air in rainy season, the metal reacts with gases and moisture and atmospheric gases to form a mixture of copper carbonate and copper hydroxide. This gives a green colour to the surface of copper metal.

The reaction is as follows:

$2Cu + HO + CO + O \rightarrow Cu(OH) + CuCO_3$.

103. In chemistry, a mixture forms when two or more substances are combined such that each substance retains its own chemical identity. Chemical bonds between the components are neither broken nor formed. Note that even though the chemical properties of the components haven't changed, a mixture may exhibit new physical properties, like boiling point and melting point. For example, mixing together water and alcohol produces a mixture that has a higher boiling point and lower melting point than alcohol (lower boiling point and higher boiling point than water) but Ice substance is not a mixture.

104. Physical weathering, also called mechanical weathering or disaggregation, is the class of processes that causes the disintegration of rocks without chemical change. The primary process in physical weathering is abrasion (the process by which clasts and other particles are reduced in size). However, chemical and physical weathering often go hand in hand. Physical weathering can occur due to temperature, pressure, frost etc. For example, cracks exploited by physical weathering will increase the surface area exposed to chemical action, thus amplifying the rate of disintegration.

105. Coal reserves in the Indian states in decreasing order

S. No.	State
1.	Jharkhand
2.	Odisha
3.	Chhattisgarh
4.	West Bengal
5.	Madhya Pradesh

106. Richter scale: The Richter magnitude scale was developed in 1935 by Charles F. Richter of the California Institute of Technology as a mathematical device to compare the size of earthquakes. The magnitude of an earthquake is determined from the logarithm of the amplitude of waves recorded by seismographs. Adjustments are included for the variation in the distance between the various seismographs and the epicenter of the earthquakes. On the Richter Scale, magnitude is expressed in whole numbers and decimal fractions. For example, a magnitude 5.3 might be computed for a moderate earthquake, and a strong earthquake might be rated as magnitude 6.3. Because of the logarithmic basis of the scale, each whole number increase in magnitude represents a tenfold increase in measured amplitude; as an estimate of energy, each whole number step in the magnitude scale corresponds to the release of about 31 times more energy than the amount associated with the preceding whole number value.

107. The Kuroshio is a warm northeasterly ocean current off the coast of Japan. This current is also called the gulf stream of the Pacific or Japan Current. Kuroshio means "the black stream" in Japanese, named after the deep ultramarine colour of the high salinity water, which is found flowing north of the current's axis. The system includes the following branches: Kuroshio, up to 35 degrees N; Kuroshio extension, extending eastward into two branches up to 160 degrees E longitude; North Pacific current, a further eastward continuation, which throws branches to the south as far as 150 degrees W; Tsushima current, branches of the main current that run into the Japan Sea, along the west coast of Japan; and Kuroshio counter-current, the large swirl or eddy on the east and south east of the Kuroshio.

108. Tides

- Tide are the **periodical rise and fall of the sea levels,** once or twice a day, caused by the combined effects of the gravitational forces exerted by the sun, the moon and the rotation of the earth.
- They are a vertical movement of waters and are different from movements of ocean water caused by meteorological effects like the winds and atmospheric pressure changes.
- The moon's gravitational pull to a great extent is the major cause of the occurrence of tides (the moon's gravitational attraction is more effective on the earth than that of the sun).
- Sun's gravitational pull and the centrifugal force due to the rotation of earth are the other forces which act along with the moon's gravitational pull.
- The highest tides in the world occur in the Bay of Fundi in Canada.
- When the tide is channeled between islands or into bays and estuaries, they are termed as Tidal Currents.
- The regular interval between two high or two low tides is 12 hours 26 minutes.

109. Tooth enamel is the hardest, most highly mineralized substance in the body. It forms the outer, most visible layer of each tooth. Enamel is composed of hydroxyapatite, a mineral compound of calcium and phosphate. The colour can vary from light yellow to grayish-blue to white. Because it is semi-translucent, enamel is only partially responsible for the colour of your teeth.

Enamel plays a very important role in protecting teeth from decay, so it is essential to do everything possible to prevent your enamel from eroding. Tooth enamel forms a strong barrier that shields the inner layers of teeth from the effects of acids and plaque. It also protects these sensitive inner layers from foods and beverages that are very hot or very cold.

111. Atmospheric refraction is the deviation of light or other electromagnetic wave from a straight line as it passes through the atmosphere due to the variation in air density as a function of height. This refraction is due to the velocity of light through air, decreasing with increased density. Atmospheric refraction near the ground produces mirages. Such refraction can also raise or lower, or stretch or shorten, the images of distant objects without involving mirages. Turbulent air can make distant objects appear to twinkle or shimmer. The term also applies to the refraction of sound. Atmospheric refraction is considered in measuring the position of both celestial and terrestrial objects.

Atmospheric refraction becomes more severe when temperature gradients are strong, and refraction is not uniform when the atmosphere is heterogeneous, as when turbulence occurs in the air. This causes suboptimal seeing conditions, such as the twinkling of stars and various deformations of the Sun's apparent shape soon before sunset or after sunrise.

113. The dyne is defined as "the force required to accelerate a mass of one gram at a rate of one centimetre per second". An equivalent definition of the dyne is "that force which, acting for one second, will produce a change of velocity of one centimetre per second in a mass of one gram".

One dyne is equal to 10 micronewtons, 10^{-5} N or to 10 nsn (nanosthenes) in the old metre-tonne-second system of units.

$1 \text{ dyn} = 1 \text{ g.cm/s}^2 = 10^{-5} \text{ kg.m/s}^2 = 10^{-5} \text{ N}$

$1 \text{ N} = 1 \text{ kg.m/s}^2 = 10^5 \text{ g.cm/s}^2 = 10^5 \text{ dyn}$

118. The dispersion of white light occurs because the colours of white light travel at different speeds through the glass prism. Since the different colours travel at different speeds, they are refracted by different angles on passing through the glass prism. The red colour has the maximum speed in glass prism, so the red colour is deviated the least.

119. The **Laser Interferometer Gravitational-Wave Observatory (LIGO)** is a large-scale physics experiment and observatory to detect cosmic gravitational waves and to develop gravitational wave observations as an astronomical tool. Two large observatories were built in the United States with the aim of detecting gravitational waves by laser interferometry. These can detect a change in the 4 km mirror spacing of less than a ten-thousandth the charge diameter of a proton. The initial LIGO observatories were funded by the National Science Foundation (NSF) and were conceived, built and are operated by Caltech and MIT.

120. The primary use of an electric fuse is to protect electrical equipment from excessive current and to prevent short circuits or mismatched loads. Electrical fuses play the role of miniature circuit breakers. Apart from protecting equipment, they are also used as safety measures to prevent any safety hazards to humans.

The fuse wire in an electrical fuse is selected in such a way that it does not face any damage when the normally stipulated amount of current flows through the circuit. Under normal conditions, the fuse wire is a part of the circuitry, contributing to a complete loop for charges to flow through it. However, when an excessive amount of current flows through the fuse wire, the heating effect of current causes the fuse wire to melt. This is because the fuse wire is chosen such that it has a low melting point. This causes the loop to break thereby stopping the flow of charges in the circuit.

121. Ennore Port (officially renamed Kamarajar Port Limited) was originally conceived as a satellite port to the Chennai Port, primarily to handle thermal coal to meet the requirement of Tamil Nadu Electricity Board (TNEB) and was endowed with large chunks of land (about 2,000 acres). The scope was expanded taking into account subsequent developments such as the plan of Government of Tamil Nadu to set up a 1,880 mW LNG power project in association with a private consortium, a large petrochemical park and a naphtha cracker plant. Ennore Port was commissioned by the then Prime Minister of India Sh. Atal Bihari Vajpayee on 1 February 2001. The port was set up under the Companies Act, keeping it outside the scope of the Tariff Authority for Major Ports, the tariff regulator for 11 of the 12 ports owned by the Indian government.

122. **Area of India : 3,287,240 sq. km.***

Largest State	Rajasthan	342,239 sq. km
Smallest State	Goa	3,702 sq. km
Largest Union Territory	Andaman & Nicobar Islands	8,249 sq. km
Smallest Union Territory	Lakshadweep	32 sq. km
Largest District	Kachchh (Gujarat)	45,652 sq. km
Smallest District	Mahe (Pondicherry)	9 sq. km

* The area figure exclude 78,114 sq.km under the illegal occupation of Pakistan, 5,180 sq. km illegally handed over by Pakistan to China and 37,555 sq.km under the illegal occupation of China in Ladakh district.

125. The Karachi session was presided by Sardar Patel. The congress adopted a resolution on Fundamental Rights and Economic Policy which represented the Party's Social, Economic and Political programme. It was later known as Karachi Resolution. Nehru had originally drafted it, but some Congress leaders thought it was too radical and it was redrafted. We have been told that MN Roy also played a role in drafting this resolution, but Nehru himself later said that MN Roy had nothing to do with it. In any case, the redrafted resolution made the Karachi Session memorable, because for the first time, the Karachi Session memorable, because for the first time, the resolution tried to define what would be the meaning of Swaraj for common people.

Some important aspects of these resolutions were:

- Basic civil rights of freedom of speech, Freedom of Press, Freedom of assembly, Freedom of association.
- Equality before law.
- Elections on the basis of Universal Adult Franchise.
- Free and compulsory primary education.
- Substantial reduction in rent and taxes.
- Better conditions for workers including a living wage, limited hours of work.
- Protection of women and peasants.
- Government ownership or control of key industries, mines, and transport.
- Protection of Minorities.

126. The Treaty of Schönbrunn, sometimes known as the Peace of Schönbrunn or Treaty of Vienna, was signed between France and Austria at Schönbrunn Palace near Vienna on 14 October 1809. The treaty ended the Fifth Coalition during the Napoleonic Wars, after Austria had been defeated at the decisive Battle of Wagram on 5-6 July.

127. **New Model Trade Unions** (NMTU) were a variety of Trade Unions prominent in the 1850s and 1860s in the UK. The term was coined by Sidney and Beatrice Webb in their *History of Trade Unionism* (1894), although later historians have questioned how far New Model Trade Unions represented a 'new wave' of unionism, as portrayed by the Webbs.

128. The Truman Doctrine was an American foreign policy whose stated purpose was to counter Soviet geopolitical expansion during the Cold War. It was announced to Congress by President Harry S. Truman on March 12, 1947, and further developed on July 12, 1948, when he pledged to contain threats in Greece and Turkey. Direct American military force was usually not involved, but Congress appropriated financial aid to support the economies and militaries of Greece and

Turkey. More generally, the Truman Doctrine implied American support for other nations allegedly threatened by Soviet communism. The Truman Doctrine became the foundation of American foreign policy, and led, in 1949, to the formation of NATO, a military alliance that is still in effect.

130. April Theses, Russian Aprelskiye Tezisy, in Russian history, program developed by Lenin during the Russian Revolution of 1917, calling for Soviet control of state power; the theses, published in April 1917, contributed to the July Days uprising and also to the Bolshevik coup d'etat in October 1917.

131. The Chief Election Commissioner cannot be removed from his post easily on account of any political reasons. This is necessary so as to preserve the independence of election commission. Chief Election Commissioner of India can be removed from his office by the Parliament with a two-thirds majority in both the Lok Sabha and the Rajya Sabha on the grounds of proved misbehaviour or incapacity. Other Election Commissioners can be removed by the President of India on the recommendation of the Chief Election Commissioner. A Chief Election Commissioner has never been impeached in India.

132. Rajya Sabha is a permanent House and is not subject to dissolution. However, one-third Members of Rajya Sabha retire after every second year. A member who is elected for a full term serves for a period of six years. The election held to fill a vacancy arising otherwise than by retirement of a member on the expiration of his term of office is called 'Bye-election'. A member elected in a bye-election remains member for the remainder of the term of the member who had resigned or died or disqualified to be member of the House under the Tenth Schedule.

134. The Treaty of Yandabo was the peace treaty that ended the First Anglo-Burmese War. The treaty was signed on 24 February 1826, nearly two years after the war formally broke out on 5 March 1824, by General Sir Archibald Campbell on the British side, and the Governor of Legaing Maha Min Hla Kyaw Htin from the Burmese side. With the British army at Yandabo village, only 80 km from the capital Ava, the Burmese were forced to accept the British terms without discussion.

135. According to Hinduism there are eight different types of Hindu marriages. The first four were considered proper. Rakshasa and Gandharva marriage was regarded acceptable to Kshatriyas as was Asura marriage for Vaishyas and Shudras. The eights types are:

1. **Brahma marriage:** The Brahma marriage is the marriage of one's daughter, after decking her with costly garments and with presents of jewels, to a man of good conduct learned in the Vedas, and invited by oneself.
2. **Daiva marriage:** The Daiva rite is the marriage of one's daughter, decked with ornaments to a priest who duly officiates at a religious ceremony, during the course of its performance.
3. **Arsha marriage:** Arsha marriage is when the father gives away his daughter, after receiving from the bridegroom a cow and a bull or two pairs of either as bride price.
4. **Prajapatya marriage:** Prajapatya is when a girl's father gives her in marriage to the bridegroom, treating him with respect, and addresses them: 'May both of you perform together your duties'.
5. **Gandharva marriage:** The voluntary union of a maiden and her lover which springs from sexual desire is called Gandharva marriage.
6. **Asura marriage:** Asura marriage is when the bridegroom receives a maiden, after having given of his own free will as much wealth as he can afford, to the bride and her kinsmen.
7. **Rakshasa marriage:** Rakshasa marriage is the marriage of a maiden involving her forcible abduction from her home after her kinsmen have been slain or wounded.
8. **Paishacha marriage:** When a man by stealth seduces a girl who is sleeping, intoxicated, or mentally challenged, it is called Paishacha marriage. This is condemned in the Manusmriti as a base and sinful act.

136. "Sadaiv Atal", the Samadhi of Bharat Ratna and former PM Atal Behari Vajpayee which dedicated to the nation on 25th Dec, 2018—reflects Atalji's personality as a poet, humanist, statesman and a great leader. The central Samadhi platform comprises of nine square black polished granite solid stone blocks, capped with a 'diya' in the center. The number nine holds significance and represents the *navarasas, navaratras* and *navagrahas.* The placement of the nine square Samadhi is in a circular lotus shaped pattern. The nine-square platform is accessed in four cardinal directions by pathways made in white composite tiles so that the floor does not get heated. The Samadhi is enclosed by nine bas-relief walls which have inscriptions of the prose/poetry of Atalji which can be read by the visitor while taking a pradakshina on the outer circular path.

Atalji's thoughts and vision are a source of great inspiration to the people of the Country. In order to enable the people to pay their respects to the great soul, an initiative to develop his Samadhi was taken up by the Society—"Atal Smriti Nyas Society" (registered under the Societies Registration Act XXI of 1860) formed by eminent persons. The founding members of the Society include Smt. Sumitra Mahajan, Shri Lalji Tandon, Shri O.P Kohli, Shri Vajubhai Rudabhai Vala, Shri Vijay Kumar Malhotra, Shri Ram Lal Ji and Shri Ram Bahadur Rai.

139. Bihar Deputy Chief Minister Sushil Modi will head the 7-member committee to look into revenue shortfall being faced by the states after the GST roll-out and suggest steps for augmenting collections.

140. The 15th Pravasi Bharatiya Divas will be held in holy city if Varanasi (Uttar Pradesh) from January 21 to January 23, 2019. Its theme will be "Role of Indian Diaspora in building a New India". The mega event will be organised by Ministry of External Affairs (MEA) in association with Uttar Pradesh government. It will be inaugurated by Prime Minister Narendra Modi and his Mauritian counterpart Pravind Jugnauth.

141. The Brazilian city of Rio de Janeiro has been named as the World Capital of Architecture for 2020 by the UNESCO (United Nations Educational, Scientific, and Cultural Organization). Rio will be the first city to receive the title under a program launched together by UNESCO and the International Union of Architects (UIA) in 2018. The city will host the 27th edition of the World Congress of the International Union of Architects (UIA) in July 2020, an event that occurs every three years. According to UNESCO, the World Capital of Architecture is intended to become an international forum for debates about pressing global challenges from the perspectives of culture, cultural heritage, urban planning and architecture.

142. Rishabh Pant is a professional Indian cricketer who plays for India, Delhi, and the Delhi Capitals in the Indian Premier League. In December 2015, he was named in India's squad for the 2016 Under-19 Cricket World Cup. On 1 February 2016, during the tournament, he hit an 18-ball fifty, the fastest at this level. He made his Twenty20 International (T20I) debut for India in January 2017, his Test debut in August 2018, and his One Day International (ODI) debut in October 2018. In January 2019, Pant was named the ICC Emerging Player of the Year at the 2018 ICC Awards.

143. On 19th January, Prime Minister Narendra Modi inaugurated the India' first Armoured Systems Complex (ASC) built by a private company-Larsen & Toubro (L&T) - at Hazira in Surat, Gujarat. This is the India's first private facility where the K9 Vajra self-propelled Howitzer guns will be manufactured.

144. Ross Island, officially known as Netaji Subhash Chandra Bose Island, is an island of the Andaman Islands. It belongs to the South Andaman administrative district, Andaman and Nicobar Islands. The island is situated 3 km east from central Port Blair. The historic ruins are a tourist attraction.

Neil Island, officially Shaheed Island, is an island of the Andaman Islands, located in Ritchie's Archipelago. It belongs to the South Andaman administrative district, part of the Indian union territory of Andaman and Nicobar Islands. The island lies 36 km northeast from Port Blair.

Havelock Island, officially Swaraj Island, is the one of the largest islands that comprise a chain of islands to the east of Great Andaman in the Andaman Islands. It belongs to the South Andaman administrative district, part of the Indian union territory of Andaman and Nicobar Islands. The island is 41 km northeast of the capital city, Port Blair.

147. Electrocardiography is the process of producing an electrocardiogram (ECG), a recording—a graph of voltage versus time—of the electrical activity of the heart using electrodes placed on the skin. These electrodes detect the small electrical changes that are a consequence of cardiac muscle depolarization followed by repolariza-tion during each cardiac cycle (heartbeat). Changes in the normal ECG pattern occur in numerous cardiac abnormalities, including cardiac rhythm disturbances (such as atrial fibrillation and ventricular tachycardia), inadequate coronary artery blood flow, and electrolyte disturbances (such as hypokalemia and hyperkalemia).

148. Beta-lactamases are a family of enzymes involved in bacterial resistance to beta-lactam antibiotics. They act by breaking the beta-lactam ring that allows penicillin-like antibiotics to work. Strategies for combating this form of resistance have included the development of new beta-lactam antibiotics that are more resistant to cleavage and the development of the class of enzyme inhibitors called beta-lactamase inhibitors. Although β-lactamase inhibitors have little antibiotic activity of their own, they prevent bacterial degradation of beta-lactam antibiotics and thus extend the range of bacteria the drugs are effective against.

150. Transmission is usually through the fecal-oral route of contaminated food or water caused by poor sanitation. Most cholera cases in developed countries are a result of transmission by food, while in the developing world it is more often water. Food transmission can occur when people harvest seafood such as oysters in waters infected with sewage, as *Vibrio cholerae* accumulates in planktonic crustaceans and the oysters eat the zooplankton.

PAPER II- MATHEMATICS

1. We have,

$$= \frac{\sin 34°\cos 236° - \sin 56°\sin 124°}{\cos 28°\cos 88° + \cos 178°.\sin 208°}$$

$$= \frac{\sin 34°\cos(180°+56°) - \sin(90°-34°)\sin(180°-56°)}{\cos 28°\cos(90°-2°) - \cos(180°-28°)\sin(180°+28°)}$$

$$= \frac{\sin 34°(-\cos 56°) - \cos 34°\sin 56°}{\cos 28°\sin 2° + (-\cos 2°)(-\sin 28°)}$$

$$= \frac{-(\sin 34°\cos 56° + \cos 34°\sin 56°)}{\cos 28°\sin 2° + \cos 2°\sin 28°}$$

$$= \frac{-\sin(34°+56°)}{\sin(28°+2°)} = \frac{-\sin 90°}{\sin 30°} = \frac{-1}{\left(\frac{1}{2}\right)} = -2.$$

2. We have,

$$\tan 54° = \tan (45° + 9°)$$

$$= \frac{\tan 45° + \tan 9°}{1 - \tan 45°.\tan 9°}$$

$$= \frac{1+\tan 9°}{1-\tan 9°}$$

$$= \frac{1+\frac{\sin 9°}{\cos 9°}}{1-\frac{\sin 9°}{\cos 9°}} = \frac{\cos 9° + \sin 9°}{\cos 9° - \sin 9°}.$$

For Qs. 3-5.

We have, $p = X\cos\theta - Y\sin\theta$

$q = X\sin\theta + Y\cos\theta$

$p^2 = X^2\cos^2\theta + Y^2\sin^2\theta - 2XY\sin\theta\cos\theta$

$q^2 = X^2\sin^2\theta + Y^2\cos^2\theta + 2XY\sin\theta\cos\theta$

$p^2 + q^2 = X^2(\sin^2\theta + \cos^2\theta) + Y^2(\sin^2\theta + \cos^2\theta)$

$p^2 + q^2 = X^2 + Y^2$

$pq = (X\cos\theta)(Y\sin\theta) + (X\cos\theta)(Y\cos\theta) - (Y\sin\theta)(X\sin\theta) - (Y\sin\theta)(Y\cos\theta)$

$pq = X^2\sin\theta\cos\theta + XY\cos^2\theta - XY\sin^2\theta - Y^2\sin\theta\cos\theta$

$4pq = 2X^2\sin 2\theta - 2Y^2\sin 2\theta + 4XY\cos 2\theta$

$p^2 + q^2 + 4pq = X^2(1 + 2\sin 2\theta) + Y^2(1 - 2\sin 2\theta) + 4XY\cos 2\theta$

Compare with $AX^2 + BY^2$

We get, $A = 1 + 2\sin 2\theta$

$B = 1 - 2\sin 2\theta$

$4XY\cos 2\theta = 0$

3. $\because$ $4XY\cos 2\theta = 0$

$\because$ $XY \neq 0$

$\therefore$ $\cos 2\theta = 0$

$\cos 2\theta = \cos\frac{\pi}{2}$

$2\theta = \frac{\pi}{2}$

$\theta = \frac{\pi}{4} \Rightarrow 0 \le \theta \le \frac{\pi}{2}.$

4. $\because$ $A = 1 + 2\sin 2\theta$

$\theta = \frac{\pi}{4}$

$A = 1 + 2\sin 2\times\frac{\pi}{4}$

$= 1 + 2\sin\frac{\pi}{2}$

$= 1 + 2 = 3.$

5. $\because$ $B = 1 - 2\sin 2\theta$

$\because$ $\theta = \frac{\pi}{4}$

$\therefore$ $B = 1 - 2\sin\frac{\pi}{2}$

$= 1 - 2 = -1.$

For Qs. 6-7.

$\cos(\theta - \alpha) = a$

$\theta - \alpha = \cos^{-1} a$ ...(*i*)

$\cos(\theta - \beta) = b$

$\theta - \beta = \cos^{-1} b$ ...(*ii*)

6. Equation (*ii*) – equation (*i*)

$-\beta + \alpha = \cos^{-1} b - \cos^{-1} a$

$\alpha - \beta = \cos^{-1}\left(ab + \sqrt{1-a^2}\sqrt{1-b^2}\right)$

$\cos(\alpha - \beta) = ab + \sqrt{1-a^2}.\sqrt{1-b^2}$

7. $\sin^2(\alpha - \beta) = 1 - \cos^2(\alpha - \beta)$

$= 1 - \left[ab + \sqrt{1-a^2}.\sqrt{1-b^2}\right]^2$

$= 1 - a^2b^2 - (1-a^2)(1-b^2) - 2ab\sqrt{1-a^2}.\sqrt{1-b^2}$

$2ab\cos(\alpha - \beta) = 2ab\left(ab + \sqrt{1-a^2}.\sqrt{1-b^2}\right)$

$= 2a^2b^2 + 2ab\sqrt{1-a^2}.\sqrt{1-b^2}$

$\sin^2(\alpha - \beta) + 2ab\cos(\alpha - \beta)$

$$= 1 + a^2b^2 - (1 - a^2)(1 - b^2)$$
$$= 1 + a^2b^2 - [1 - b^2 - a^2 + a^2b^2]$$
$$= 1 + a^2b^2 - 1 + b^2 + a^2 - a^2b^2$$
$$= a^2 + b^2.$$

8. We have,

$$\sin\alpha + \cos\alpha = p$$

Taking square of both sides

$$\sin^2\alpha + \cos^2\alpha + 2\sin\alpha\cos\alpha = p^2$$
$$1 + \sin 2\alpha = p^2$$
$$\sin 2\alpha = p^2 - 1$$

$\because$ $\cos^2 2\alpha = 1 - \sin^2 2\alpha$

$$= 1 - (p^2 - 1)^2$$
$$= 1 - (p^4 + 1 - 2p^2)$$
$$= -p^4 + 2p^2$$
$$= p^2(2 - p^2).$$

9. $\sin^{-1}\frac{4}{5} + \sec^{-1}\frac{5}{4} - \frac{\pi}{2}$

$$= \sin^{-1}\frac{4}{5} + \cos^{-1}\frac{4}{5} - \frac{\pi}{2}$$

$$= \frac{\pi}{2} - \frac{\pi}{2} = 0. \qquad \left[\because \sin^{-1}\theta + \cos^{-1}\theta = \frac{\pi}{2}\right]$$

10. We have,

$$\sin^{-1}\frac{2p}{1+p^2} - \cos^{-1}\frac{1-q^2}{1+q^2} = \tan^{-1}\frac{2x}{1-x^2}$$
$$2\tan^{-1}p - 2\tan^{-1}q = 2\tan^{-1}x$$
$$\tan^{-1}p - \tan^{-1}q = \tan^{-1}x$$
$$\tan^{-1}\frac{p-q}{1+pq} = \tan^{-1}x$$

$\therefore$ $\frac{p-q}{1+pq} = x.$

11. We have, $\tan\theta = \frac{1}{2}$

$$\tan\phi = \frac{1}{3}$$
$$\tan(\theta + \phi) = \frac{\tan\theta + \tan\phi}{1 - \tan\theta.\tan\phi}$$
$$= \frac{\frac{1}{2} + \frac{1}{3}}{1 - \frac{1}{2}\times\frac{1}{3}} = \frac{\frac{5}{6}}{\frac{5}{6}}$$
$$\tan(\theta + \phi) = 1$$
$$\theta + \phi = \tan^{-1}(1) = \frac{\pi}{4}.$$

12. We have, $\cos A = \frac{3}{4}$

$$\frac{2}{2}\sin\left(\frac{A}{2}\right).\sin\left(\frac{3A}{2}\right)$$
$$= \frac{1}{2}\left[\cos\left(\frac{A}{2} - \frac{3A}{2}\right) - \cos\left(\frac{A}{2} + \frac{3A}{2}\right)\right]$$
$$= \frac{1}{2}[\cos(-A) - \cos 2A]$$

$[\because 2\sin A\sin B = \cos(A - B) - \cos(A + B)]$

$$= \frac{1}{2}\left[\cos A - 2\cos^2 A + 1\right]$$

Put $\cos A = \frac{3}{4}$,

$$= \frac{1}{2}\left[\frac{3}{4} - 2\times\left(\frac{3}{4}\right)^2 + 1\right]$$
$$= \frac{1}{2}\left[\frac{3}{4} - \frac{9}{8} + 1\right]$$
$$= \frac{1}{2}\left[\frac{6 - 9 + 8}{8}\right]$$
$$= \frac{1}{2}\left[\frac{5}{8}\right] = \frac{5}{16}.$$

13. We have, $\tan 75° + \cot 75°$

$$= \tan(30° + 45°) + \cot(30° + 45°)$$
$$= \frac{\tan 30° + \tan 45°}{1 - \tan 30°\tan 45°} + \frac{\cot 30°\cot 45° - 1}{\cot 30° + \cot 45°}$$
$$= \frac{\frac{1}{\sqrt{3}} + 1}{1 - \frac{1}{\sqrt{3}}\times 1} + \frac{\sqrt{3}\times 1 - 1}{\sqrt{3} + 1}$$
$$= \frac{1 + \sqrt{3}}{\sqrt{3} - 1} + \frac{\sqrt{3} - 1}{1 + \sqrt{3}}$$
$$= \frac{\left(1 + \sqrt{3}\right)^2 + \left(\sqrt{3} - 1\right)^2}{\left(\sqrt{3}\right)^2 - (1)^2} = \frac{2\left(\left(\sqrt{3}\right)^2 + (1)^2\right)}{3 - 1}$$
$$= \frac{2(3+1)}{2} = 4.$$

14. $\because \cos 46°\cos 47°\cos 48°\cos 49° \ldots \cos 90° \ldots \cos 185°$

$\because \cos 90° = 0$

$\therefore$ The value of the given expression will be zero.

15. We have,

$$\sin 2\theta = \cos 3\theta$$
$$\sin 2\theta = \cos(\theta + 2\theta)$$
$$\sin 2\theta = \cos\theta . \cos 2\theta - \sin\theta . \sin 2\theta$$
$$2\sin\theta\cos\theta = \cos\theta(1 - 2\sin^2\theta) - 2\sin^2\theta\cos\theta$$
$$2\sin\theta = 1 - 2\sin^2\theta - 2\sin^2\theta$$
$$4\sin^2\theta + 2\sin\theta - 1 = 0$$
$$\sin\theta = \frac{-2 \pm \sqrt{(2)^2 - 4(4)(-1)}}{2 \times 4}$$
$$\sin\theta = \frac{-2 \pm \sqrt{4+16}}{8}$$
$$\sin\theta = \frac{-1 \pm \sqrt{5}}{4}$$
$$\sin\theta = \frac{\sqrt{5}-1}{4}$$
$$\because \quad 0 < \theta < \frac{\pi}{2}.$$

16. We have, 25, –125, 625, –3125, ...

$$\because \quad \frac{T_2}{T_1} = \frac{T_3}{T_2} = r = -5$$
$$a = 25$$

$\because$ The given series in an GP

$$n\text{th term of GP} = ar^{n-1}$$
$$= 25(-5)^{n-1}$$
$$= (5)^2(-5)^{n-1}$$
$$= (-1)^{n-1} 5^{2+n-1}$$
$$= (-1)^{n-1} 5^{n+1}.$$

17. We have,

X = {1, 2, 3, 4}

R = {(1, 1), (2, 2), (3, 3), (1, 2), (2, 1), (2, 3), (3, 2)}

(*i*) Reflexive : A relation R is Reflexive

$(a, a) \in R \ \forall \ a \in X$

$\because (4, 4) \notin R$

$\therefore$ Relation is not Reflexive.

(*ii*) Symmetric: A Relation is Symmetric

If $(a, b) \in R \Rightarrow (b, a) \in R \ \forall \ a, b \in X$

$\because (1, 2) \in R \Rightarrow (2, 1) \in R$

$\therefore$ The relation is symmetric.

(*iii*) Transitive: A relation is transitive iff

$(a, b) \in R$ and $(b, c) \in R$

$(a, c) \in R \ \forall \ a, b, c \in X$

$\because (1, 2) \in R$ and $(2, 3) \in R$

$\therefore$ Relation is not Transitive.

18. A = {(1, 1), (2, 2), (3, 3), (1, 2), (1, 3), (2, 3) ....}

$$xRy = x^2 - 4xy + 3y^2 = 0$$

(*i*) Reflexive : A relation is reflexive

$(a, a) \in R \ \forall \ a \in A$

$(1, 1) \Rightarrow (1)^2 - 4 \times 1 \times 1 + 3(1)^2 = 1 - 4 + 3 = 0$

$(2, 2) \Rightarrow (2)^2 - 4 \times 2 \times 2 + 3(2)^2 = 4 - 16 + 12 = 0$

$\therefore$ Given Relation is Reflexive.

(*ii*) Symmetric : A Relation is Symmetric if

$(a, b) \in R \Rightarrow (b, a) \in R$

$$x^2 - 4xy + 3y^2 = y^2 - 4(y)(x) + 3x^2$$
$$2y^2 = 2x^2$$
$$y^2 = x^2$$
$$y = x$$

[$\because$ R defined on the set N]

$\therefore$ (1, 1), (2, 2), (3, 3), (4, 4) satisfy the condition

$\therefore$ Given relation is symmetric.

(*iii*) Transitive : A relation is Transitive iff

$(a, b) \in R$ and $(b, c) \in R \Rightarrow (a, c) \in R \ \forall \ a, b, c \in A$

$a \quad b$

$(1, 1) \Rightarrow (1)^2 - 4(1)(1) + 3(1^2) = 1 - 4 + 3 = 0$

$b \quad c$

$(1, 1) \Rightarrow (1)^2 - 4(1)(1) + 3(1^2) = 1 - 4 + 3 = 0$

$a \quad c$

$(1, 1) \Rightarrow (1)^2 - 4(1)(1) + 3(1^2) = 1 - 4 + 3 = 0$

$\therefore$ Given relation is transitive.

19. We have,

$$A = \{x \in Z : x^3 - 1 = 0\}$$
$$\because \quad x^3 - 1 = 0$$
$$(x - 1)(x^2 + 1 + x) = 0$$
$$x = 1, \frac{-1 \pm \sqrt{1-4}}{2}$$
$$x = 1, \frac{-1+\sqrt{3}i}{2}, \frac{-1-\sqrt{3}i}{2}$$
$$\therefore \quad A = \left\{1, \frac{-1+\sqrt{3}i}{2}, \frac{-1-\sqrt{3}i}{2}\right\}$$
$$B = \{x \in Z; x^2 + x + 1 = 0\}$$
$$\because \quad x^2 + x + 1 = 0$$
$$x = \frac{-1 \pm \sqrt{3}i}{2}$$
$$B = \left\{\frac{-1+\sqrt{3}i}{2}, \frac{-1-\sqrt{3}i}{2}\right\}$$
$$A \cap B = \left\{\frac{-1+\sqrt{3}i}{2}, \frac{-1-\sqrt{3}i}{2}\right\}.$$

20. Using Ven diagram:

Statement-1:

$A \cap B =$

$A \cap \overline{B} =$

$\overline{A} \cap B =$

$\therefore (A \cap B) \cup (A \cap \overline{B}) \cup (\overline{A} \cap B) =$

$= A \cup B$

Statement-2: $\overline{A} =$

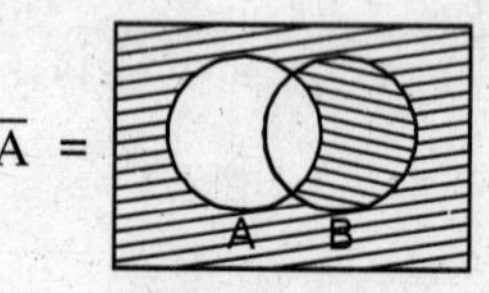

$\overline{B} =$

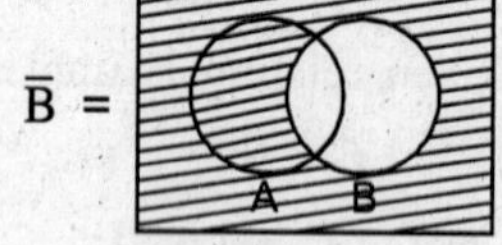

$\overline{A} \cap \overline{B} =$

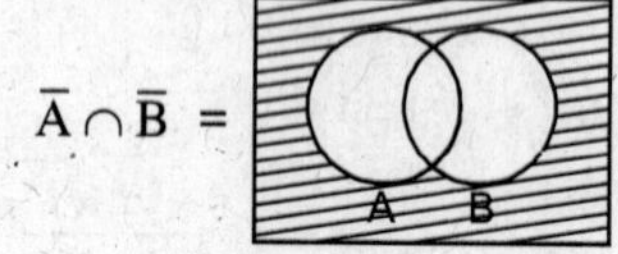

$A \cup (\overline{A} \cap \overline{B}) =$

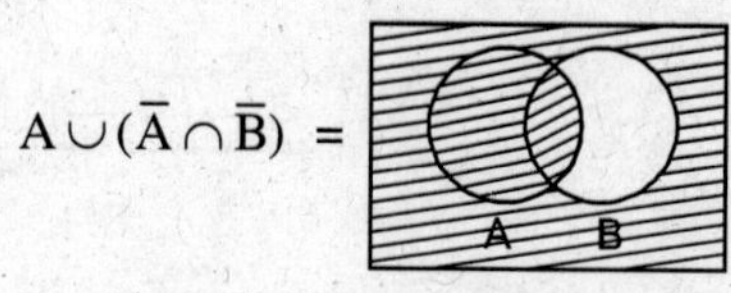

$A \cup B =$

$\therefore A \cup (\overline{A} \cap \overline{B}) \neq A \cup B$

$\therefore$ Only Statement-1 is true.

22. We have, $B = \begin{bmatrix} 3 & 2 & 0 \\ 2 & 4 & 0 \\ 1 & 1 & 0 \end{bmatrix}$

Co-factors of the given matrix

$M_{11} = \begin{vmatrix} 4 & 0 \\ 1 & 0 \end{vmatrix} = 0, \quad M_{12} = \begin{vmatrix} 2 & 0 \\ 1 & 0 \end{vmatrix} = 0$

$M_{13} = \begin{vmatrix} 2 & 4 \\ 1 & 1 \end{vmatrix} = 2 - 4 = -2$

$M_{21} = \begin{vmatrix} 2 & 0 \\ 1 & 0 \end{vmatrix} = 0, \quad M_{22} = \begin{vmatrix} 3 & 0 \\ 1 & 0 \end{vmatrix} = 0$

$M_{23} = \begin{vmatrix} 3 & 2 \\ 1 & 1 \end{vmatrix} = 3 - 2 = 1$

$M_{31} = \begin{vmatrix} 2 & 0 \\ 4 & 0 \end{vmatrix} = 0, \quad M_{32} = \begin{vmatrix} 3 & 0 \\ 2 & 0 \end{vmatrix} = 0,$

$M_{33} = \begin{vmatrix} 3 & 2 \\ 2 & 4 \end{vmatrix} = 12 - 4 = 8$

$$\text{adj}(B) = \begin{bmatrix} 0 & 0 & -2 \\ 0 & 0 & -1 \\ 0 & 0 & 8 \end{bmatrix}^T \quad \left[\because \begin{bmatrix} + & - & + \\ - & + & - \\ + & - & + \end{bmatrix}\right]$$

$$= \begin{bmatrix} 0 & 0 & 0 \\ 0 & 0 & 0 \\ -2 & -1 & 8 \end{bmatrix}.$$

23. $|x^2 - x - 6| = x + 2$

$x^2 - x - 6 = \pm (x + 2)$

I. $x^2 - x - 6 = x + 2$

$x^2 - 2x - 8 = 0$

$x^2 - 4x + 2x - 8 = 0$

$x(x - 4) + 2(x - 4) = 0$

$(x + 2)(x - 4) = 0$

$x = -2, 4$

II. $x^2 - x - 6 = -(x + 2)$

$x^2 - 4 = 0$

$x^2 = 4$

$x = \pm 2$

$\therefore \quad x = -2, 2, 4.$

24. A matrix is singular if $|A| = 0$

A matrix is involuntry if $A^2 = I$

A matrix is nilpotent if $A^m = 0$, $m \in I^+$

A matrix is idempotent if $A^2 = A$

We have, $A = \begin{bmatrix} 0 & 1 \\ 1 & 0 \end{bmatrix}$

$|A| = 0 - 1 = -1$

(not a singular matrix)

$A^2 = A.A$

$$= \begin{bmatrix} 0 & 1 \\ 1 & 0 \end{bmatrix}\begin{bmatrix} 0 & 1 \\ 1 & 0 \end{bmatrix} = \begin{bmatrix} 0 & 1 \\ 1 & 0 \end{bmatrix} = 2$$

$\therefore$ Given matrix is an involuntry matrix.

25. $\begin{bmatrix} x & -3i & 1 \\ y & 1 & i \\ 0 & 2i & -i \end{bmatrix} = 6 + 11i$

$= x(-i - 2i^2) - (-3i)(-yi - 0) + 1(2yi - 0)$
$= -xi + 2x - 3yi^2 + 2yi$
$= -xi + 2x + 3y + 2yi$
$= (2x + 3y) + (-x + 2y)i$

Compare with $6 + 11i$, we get,

$$2x + 3y = 6 \quad ...(i)$$
$$-x + 2y = 11 \quad ...(ii)$$

After solving equations (*i*) and (*ii*), we get,

$$x = -3, y = 4.$$

26. We have,
$z^3 + 2z^2 + 2z + 1 = 0$
and $z^{2017} + z^{2018} + 1 = 0$
Check from the option,

A. $-1, \omega$

$$(-1)^3 + 2(-1)^2 + 2(-1) + 1 = -1 + 2 - 2 + 1 = 0$$
$$\omega^3 + 2\omega^2 + 2\omega + 1 = 0$$
$$(-1)^{2017} + (-1)^{2018} + 1 = -1 + 1 + 1 = 1 \neq 0$$

$\therefore$ -1 is not the root of $z^{2017} + z^{2018} + 1 = 0$
$\therefore$ Option A is wrong.

B. $1, \omega^2$

$$(1)^3 + 2(1)^2 + 2(1) + 1 = 1 + 2 + 2 + 1 = 6 \neq 0$$

$\therefore$ 1 is not the root of $z^3 + 2z^2 + 2z + 1 = 0$
$\therefore$ Option B is wrong.

C. $-1, \omega^2$

$\because$ -1 is not the root of $z^{2017} + z^{2018} + 1 = 0$
$\therefore$ Option C is wrong.

D. ω, ω^2

$$(\omega)^3 + 2(\omega^2) + 2\omega + 1 = \omega^3 + 2\omega^2 + 2\omega + 1 = 0$$
$$(\omega^2)^3 + 2(\omega^2)^2 + 2\omega^2 + 1 = \omega^6 + 2\omega^4 + 2\omega^2 + 1$$
$$= 1 + 2\omega + 2\omega^2 + 1$$
$$= 2 + 2\omega + 2\omega^2$$
$$= 2(1 + \omega + \omega^2) = 0$$
$$(\omega)^{2017} + (\omega)^{2018} + 1 = (\omega^3)^{672}\omega + (\omega^3)^{672}.\omega^2 + 1$$
$$= (1)^{672}.\omega + (1)^{672}.\omega^2 + 1$$
$$= \omega + \omega^2 + 1 = 0$$
$$(\omega^2)^{2017} + (\omega^2)^{2018} + 1 = \omega^{4034} + \omega^{4036} + 1$$
$$= (\omega^3)^{1344}.\omega^2 + (\omega^3)^{1345}.\omega + 1$$
$$= (1)^{1344}.\omega^2 + (1)^{1345}.\omega + 1$$
$$= \omega^2 + \omega + 1 = 0$$

This satisfy the condition, so, ω and ω^2 are the common roots.

Hence, option (D) is the correct option.

27. ${}^{20}C_{n+2} = {}^{20}C_{n-2}$

We know the property,

$$ {}^nC_x = {}^nC_y $$
$$ x + y = n $$
$$\therefore (n + 2) + (n - 2) = 20$$
$$2n = 20$$
$$n = 10.$$

28. A line can be formed by joining the two points

$\therefore$ Required Number of lines $= {}^{10}C_2$

$$= \frac{10!}{2!(10-2)!} = \frac{10!}{2! \times 8!}$$
$$= \frac{10 \times 9 \times 8!}{2 \times 8!} = \frac{90}{2} = 45.$$

30. $A = \{\lambda, \{\lambda, \mu\}\}$

The Power set of $A = \{\phi, \{\lambda\}, \{\lambda, \mu\}, \{\lambda, \{\lambda, \mu\}\}\}$

Hence, option C is the correct answer.

31. Sum of roots, $\tan 19° + \tan 26° = -p$

Product of roots, $\tan 19° . \tan 26° = q$

$$\tan (19° + 26°) = \frac{\tan 19° + \tan 26°}{1 - \tan 19° \tan 26°}$$
$$\tan 45° = \frac{-p}{1-q}$$
$$1 = \frac{-p}{1-q}$$
$$1 - q = -p$$
$$q - p = 1.$$

32. $S_n = n(n + 1)$

$S_1 = 1(1 + 1) = 2 \Rightarrow$ First term
$S_2 = 2(2 + 1) = 6 \Rightarrow$ Second term $= 6 - 2 = 4$
$\therefore$ $a = 2, d = 4 - 2 = 2$
nth term of an AP $= a + (n - 1)d$
Fourth term of an AP $= 2 + (4 - 1) \times 2$
$= 2 + 3 \times 2$
$= 2 + 6 = 8.$

33. $(1 + \tan \alpha \tan \beta)^2 + (\tan \alpha - \tan \beta)^2 - \sec^2\alpha \sec^2\beta$

$= 1 + \tan^2 \alpha \tan^2 \beta + 2 \tan \alpha \tan \beta + \tan^2 \alpha + \tan^2 \beta - 2\tan \alpha \tan \beta - \sec^2 \alpha \sec^2 \beta$
$= 1 + \tan^2 \alpha + \tan^2 \beta + \tan^2 \alpha + \tan^2\beta - \sec^2 \alpha \sec^2 \beta$
$= 1 + \tan^2 \alpha (1 + \tan^2 \beta) + \tan^2 \beta - \sec^2 \alpha \sec^2 \beta$
$= (1 + \tan^2 \beta) + \tan^2 \alpha \sec^2 \beta - \sec^2 \alpha \sec^2 \beta$
$= \sec^2 \beta + (\sec^2 \alpha - 1) \sec^2 \beta - \sec^2 \alpha \sec^2 \beta$
$= \sec^2 \beta + \sec^2 \alpha \sec^2 \beta - \sec^2 \beta - \sec^2 \alpha \sec^2 \beta$
$= 0.$

34. $p = \text{cosec } \theta - \cot \theta$

$q = (\text{cosec } \theta + \cot \theta)^{-1}$

$$= \frac{1}{\text{cosec}\,\theta + \cot\theta} \times \frac{\text{cosec}\,\theta - \cot\theta}{\text{cosec}\,\theta - \cot\theta}$$

$$= \frac{\text{cosec}\,\theta - \cot\theta}{\text{cosec}^2\,\theta - \cot^2\theta}$$

$$q = \frac{\text{cosec}\,\theta - \cot\theta}{1} \quad [\because \text{cosec}^2\,\theta - \cot^2\theta = 1]$$

$q = p.$

35. Let the angles of triangle are x, $2x$ and $3x$

$x + 2x + 3x = 180°$

$6x = 180°$

$x = 30°$

$\therefore$ Angles of Triangles are 30°, 60° and 90°

Corresponding Side Ratio

$= \sin A° : \sin B° : \sin C°$

$= \sin 30° : \sin 60° : \sin 90°$

$$= \frac{1}{2} : \frac{\sqrt{3}}{2} : 1$$

$= 1 : \sqrt{3} : 2.$

36. We know that,

Perpendicular distance from a point, $(x_1\ y_1)$ to a line $ax + by + c = 0$

$$= \left|\frac{ax_1 + by_1 + c}{\sqrt{a^2 + b^2}}\right|$$

Statement-1: $\left|\dfrac{\alpha\cos\theta + \beta\sin\theta - p}{\sqrt{\cos^2\theta + \sin^2\theta}}\right|$

$= |\alpha \cos \theta + \beta \sin \theta - p|$

Statement-2: $xb + ay - ab = 0$

$$= \left|\frac{\alpha b + \beta a - ab}{\sqrt{a^2 + b^2}}\right|$$

$$= \left|\frac{b\alpha + a\beta - ab}{\sqrt{a^2 + b^2}}\right|$$

Hence, neither 1 nor 2 statement is correct.

37. Give that,

$x^2 + y^2 = a^2$ is circle

Centre = (0, 0)

Radius = a

$x + y = a$

$$\frac{x}{a} + \frac{y}{a} = 1$$

(0, a) B

O

1

O

A (a, 0)

(0, 0)

Centre of new circle $\left(\dfrac{a}{2}, \dfrac{a}{2}\right)$

$$AB = \sqrt{(0-a)^2 + (a-0)^2}$$

$$= \sqrt{2}\,a$$

$$\text{Radius} = \frac{AB}{2}$$

$$= \frac{\sqrt{2}a}{2} = \frac{a}{\sqrt{2}}$$

Equation of circle is

$$\left(x - \frac{a}{2}\right)^2 + \left(y - \frac{a}{2}\right)^2 = \left(\frac{a}{\sqrt{2}}\right)^2$$

$$x^2 + \frac{a^2}{4} - 2.x.\frac{a}{2} + y^2 + \frac{a^2}{4} - 2.y.\frac{a}{2} = \frac{a^2}{2}$$

$$x^2 + \frac{a^2}{2} - xa + y^2 - ya = \frac{a^2}{2}$$

$x^2 + y^2 - ax - ay = 0.$

39. $2x^2 - 3y^2 - 6 = 0$

Compare with $ax^2 + 2hxy + by^2 + 2gx + 2fy + c = 0$

$a = 2,\ h = 0,\ b = -3,\ g = 0,\ f = 0,\ c = -6$

$$\Delta = \begin{vmatrix} a & h & g \\ h & b & f \\ g & f & c \end{vmatrix} = \begin{vmatrix} 2 & 0 & 0 \\ 0 & -3 & 0 \\ 0 & 0 & -6 \end{vmatrix}$$

$\Delta = 2(-3)(-6) = 36$

$\Delta \neq 0$

$h^2 = 0$

$ab = (2)(-3) = -6$

$\because$ $h^2 > ab$

$\because$ $\Delta \neq 0,$

and $h^2 > ab$

$\therefore$ The given equation represent hyperbola.

40.

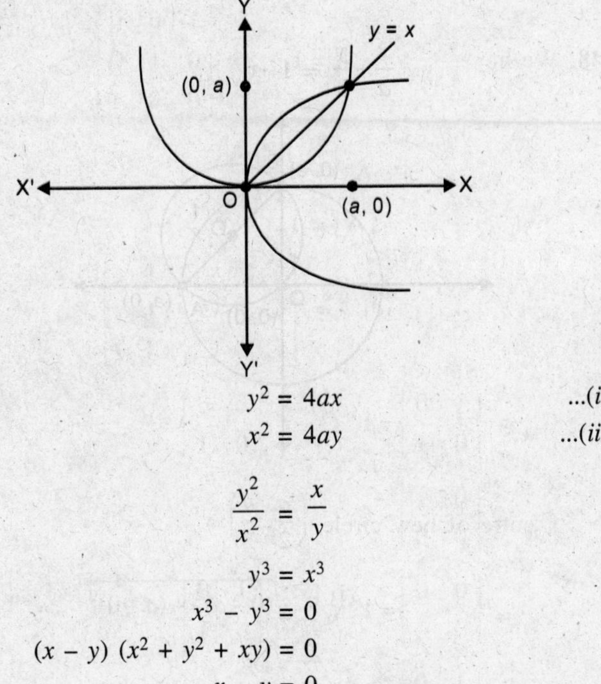

$$y^2 = 4ax \qquad ...(i)$$

$$x^2 = 4ay \qquad ...(ii)$$

$$\frac{y^2}{x^2} = \frac{x}{y}$$

$$y^3 = x^3$$

$$x^3 - y^3 = 0$$

$$(x - y)(x^2 + y^2 + xy) = 0$$

$$x - y = 0$$

$$x = y$$

∴ Parabola cut at two points on the lines $y = x$.

41. The mid-point of diagonal BD lie on the line

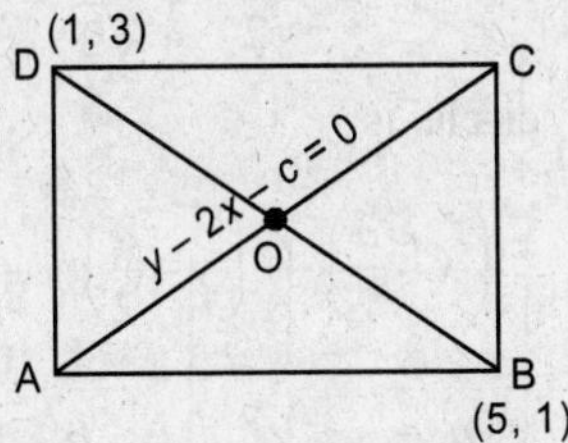

$$y - 2x - c = 0 \qquad ...(i)$$

Mid-point co-ordinate of diagonal BD

$$\left(\frac{1+5}{2}, \frac{3+1}{2}\right) = (3, 2)$$

Point (3, 2) will satisfy the equation (*i*)

$$2 - 2 \times 3 - c = 0$$

$$2 - 6 - c = 0$$

$$-4 - c = 0$$

$$c = -4.$$

42. Three lines are concurrent if

$$\begin{vmatrix} 4 & 3 & -1 \\ -1 & 1 & -5 \\ b & 5 & -3 \end{vmatrix} = 0$$

$$4(-3 + 25) - 3(3 + 5b) - 1(-5 - b) = 0$$

$$88 - 9 - 15b + 5 + b = 0$$

$$84 - 14b = 0$$

$$14b = 84$$

$$b = 6.$$

43. ∵ Slope of the equation $y = x$ is 1 (m_1)

The slope of perpendicular line = −1

[∵ $m_1 \times m_2 = -1$]

∵ Equation of line

$$(y - 2) = (-1)(x - 3)$$

$$y - 2 = -x + 3$$

$$x + y = 5.$$

44. Co-ordinate of B

$$x + y = 4 \qquad ...(i)$$

$$x + 3y = 4 \qquad ...(ii)$$

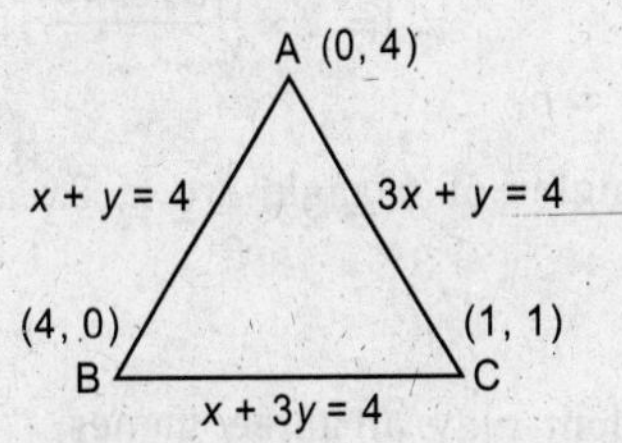

After solving (*i*) & (*ii*) we get,

$$y = 0, x = 4$$

∴ Co-ordinate of B = (4, 0)

Co-ordinate of A,

$$x + y = 4 \qquad ...(iii)$$

$$3x + y = 4 \qquad ...(iv)$$

After solving (*ii*) & (*iv*), we get,

$$x = 0, y = 4$$

∴ Co-ordinate of A = (0, 4)

Co-ordinate of C,

$$3x + y = 4 \qquad ...(v)$$

$$x + 3y = 4 \qquad ...(vi)$$

After solving (*v*) & (*vi*), we get,

$$x = 1, y = 1$$

∴ Co-ordinate of C (1, 1)

$$AB = \sqrt{(0-4)^2 + (4-0)^2} = \sqrt{32} = 4\sqrt{2}$$

$$BC = \sqrt{(1-0)^2 + (1-4)^2} = \sqrt{1+9} = \sqrt{10}$$

$$AC = \sqrt{(1-4)^2 + (1-0)^2} = \sqrt{9+1} = \sqrt{10}$$

∵ BC = AC

∴ given Δ is an iso-sceles.

45. $x^2 + y^2 + 4x - 7y + 12 = 0$

Compare with the equation,

$x^2 + y^2 + 2gx + 2fy + c = 0$

∵ $2g = 4$, ∴ $g = 2$,

∵ $2f = -7$,

∴ $f = -\frac{7}{2}$

$c = 12$

Intercept length on y-axis

$$= 2\sqrt{f^2 - c}$$

$$= 2\sqrt{\left(-\frac{7}{2}\right)^2 - 12}$$

$$= 2\sqrt{\frac{49}{4} - 12}$$

$$= 2 \times \sqrt{\frac{49-48}{4}}$$

$$= 2 \times \frac{1}{2} = 1.$$

For Qs. 46-47.

Let x student play all three games

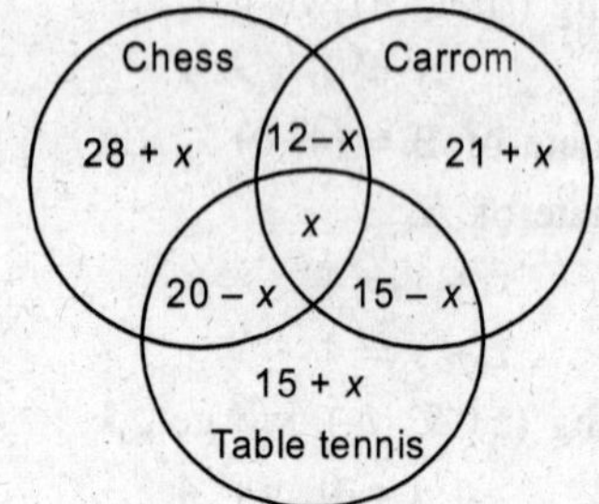

Number of students who play chess only

$$= 60 - (12 - x + x + 20 - x)$$
$$= 60 - 32 + x$$
$$= 28 + x$$

Number of students who play carrom only

$$= 48 - (12 - x + x + 15 - x)$$
$$= 48 - 27 + x$$
$$= 21 + x$$

Number of students who play table tennis only

$$= 50 - (20 - x + x + 15 - x)$$
$$= 50 - (35 - x)$$
$$= 15 + x$$

Total number of students in the school

$$= 28 + x + 12 - x + x + 20 - x + 21 + x + 15 - x + 15 + x$$
$$= 111 + x$$

46. For minimum number of students $n(A \cap B \cap C)$ *i.e.*,

$$x = 0$$

$\therefore$ Total minimum students = 111.

47. For maximum number of students

$n(A \cap B \cap C) = x$

Total maximum students

$$= 111 + 12 = 123.$$

48. We have, $A = I_{3 \times 3} = \begin{bmatrix} 1 & 0 & 0 \\ 0 & 1 & 0 \\ 0 & 0 & 1 \end{bmatrix}$

$$A^{-1} = \frac{\text{Adj } A}{|A|}$$

$|A| = 1,$

$$\text{Adj } A = \begin{bmatrix} C_{11} & C_{12} & C_{13} \\ C_{21} & C_{22} & C_{23} \\ C_{31} & C_{32} & C_{33} \end{bmatrix}$$

$$C_{11} = \begin{vmatrix} 1 & 0 \\ 0 & 1 \end{vmatrix} = 1,\ C_{12} = \begin{vmatrix} 0 & 0 \\ 0 & 1 \end{vmatrix} = 0$$

$$C_{13} = \begin{vmatrix} 0 & 1 \\ 0 & 0 \end{vmatrix} = 0$$

$$C_{21} = \begin{vmatrix} 0 & 0 \\ 0 & 1 \end{vmatrix} = 1,\ C_{22} = \begin{vmatrix} 1 & 0 \\ 0 & 1 \end{vmatrix} = 1,$$

$$C_{23} = \begin{vmatrix} 1 & 0 \\ 0 & 0 \end{vmatrix} = 0$$

$$C_{31} = \begin{vmatrix} 0 & 0 \\ 0 & 1 \end{vmatrix} = 0,\ C_{32} = \begin{vmatrix} 1 & 0 \\ 0 & 0 \end{vmatrix} = 0,$$

$$C_{33} = \begin{vmatrix} 1 & 0 \\ 0 & 1 \end{vmatrix} = 1$$

Sign will be $\begin{bmatrix} + & - & + \\ - & + & - \\ + & - & + \end{bmatrix} = \begin{bmatrix} 1 & 0 & 0 \\ 0 & 1 & 0 \\ 0 & 0 & 1 \end{bmatrix}$

$$\text{Adj } A = \begin{bmatrix} 1 & 0 & 0 \\ 0 & 1 & 0 \\ 0 & 0 & 1 \end{bmatrix}^{+} = \begin{bmatrix} 1 & 0 & 0 \\ 0 & 1 & 0 \\ 0 & 0 & 1 \end{bmatrix} = A$$

$$A^{-1} = \frac{A}{1} = A.$$

49. $\because$ We know that,

$$\det(A) = \det(A^T)$$

$$\therefore \quad \det(A^T) = 4.$$

50. (1T, 4P), (2T, 3P), (3T, 2P), (4T, 1P)

$$= {}^4C_1 \times {}^6C_4 + {}^4C_2 \times {}^6C_3 + {}^4C_3 \times {}^6C_2 + {}^4C_4 \times {}^6C_1$$

$$= 4 \times \frac{6!}{2!\,4!} + \frac{4!}{2!\,2!} \times \frac{6!}{3!\,3!} + \frac{4!}{3!\,1!} \times \frac{6!}{2!\,4!} + 1 \times 6$$

$$= 4 \times \frac{6 \times 5}{2 \times 1} + 6 \times \frac{6 \times 5 \times 4}{3 \times 2} + 4 \times \frac{6 \times 5}{2} + 6$$

$$= 2 \times 6 \times 5 + 6 \times 5 \times 4 + 2 \times 6 \times 5 + 6$$

$$= 60 + 120 + 60 + 6 = 246.$$

51. We have, $[(2x-3y)^2 (2x+3y)^2]^2$
$= [(2x-3y)(2x+3y)]^{2\times 2}$
$= (4x^2 - 9y^2)^4$
We know that the total number of term in $(x-a)^n$ is $n+1$
$\therefore$ Total term in the given expression is equal to
$= 4 + 1 = 5.$

52. We have, $(1+ax)^n$

$$\text{First term} = {}^nC_0(1)^n = {}^nC_0 = 1$$
$$\text{Second term} = {}^nC_1(1)^{n-1}(ax) = {}^nC_1(ax)$$
$${}^nC_1(ax) = 12x \quad ...(i)$$
$$\text{Third term} = {}^nC_2(1)^{n-2}(ax)^2$$
$${}^nC_2 a^2x^2 = 64x^2 \quad ...(ii)$$

put value of $ax = \dfrac{12x}{{}^nC_1}$ from equation (i)

$${}^nC_2 \times \left(\frac{12x}{{}^nC_1}\right)^2 = 64x^2$$
$${}^nC_2 \times \frac{144x^2}{\left({}^nC_1\right)^2} = 64x^2$$
$$\frac{{}^nC_2}{\left({}^nC_1\right)^2} = \frac{64}{144}$$
$$\frac{\dfrac{n!}{2!(n-2)!}}{\dfrac{n!\times n!}{(n-1)!(n-1)!}} = \frac{64}{144}$$
$$\frac{n!\times(n-1)!\times(n-1)!}{2\times n!\times n!\times(n-2)!} = \frac{64}{144}$$
$$\frac{(n-1)!\times(n-1)(n-2)!}{2\times n(n-1)!(n-2)!} = \frac{64}{144}$$
$$\frac{n-1}{2n} = \frac{64}{144}$$
$$144n - 144 = 128n$$
$$144n - 128n = 144$$
$$16n = 144$$
$$n = 9.$$

54. Let first term of an AP is 'a' and Common difference is d
$S_{(p+q)th} + S_{(p-q)th}$
$= (a + (p+q-1)d) + (a + (p-q-1)d)$
$= (a + pd + qd - d) + (a + pd - qd - d)$
$= 2a + 2pd - 2d$
$= 2[a + (p-1)d]$
$= 2 \times p$th term.

56. $25\ \text{cosec}^2 x + 36 \sec^2 x$
$= 25(1 + \cot^2 x) + 36(1 + \tan^2 x)$
$= 25 + 25\cot^2 x + 36 + 36\tan^2 x$
$= 61 + 25\cot^2 x + 36\tan^2 x$
$= 61 + 25 \times \dfrac{1}{\tan^2 x} + 36\tan^2 x$

We know that $a\tan^2 x + \dfrac{b}{\tan^2 x}$

minimum value $= 2\sqrt{ab}$
$= 61 + 2\sqrt{25\times 36}$
$= 61 + 2\times 5\times 6$
$= 61 + 60 = 121.$

57. We know the following property of determinant
If A & B are $n \times n$ order square matrix
Then, (i) $\det(AB) = \det(A) \times \det(B)$
(ii) $\det(KA) = K^n \det(A)$
(iii) $\det(A^{-1}) = \dfrac{1}{\det(A)}$

$\det(2AB) = 2^3 \times \det A \times \det B$
$= 8 \times 4 \times 3 = 96$

Hence, option (A) is the correct.

58. $\det(3AB^{-1}) = 3^3 \det A \times \dfrac{1}{\det B}$

$= 27 \times 4 \times \dfrac{1}{3} = 36$

Hence, option (C) is the correct.

For Qs. No. 59-60.

We have, $z = \dfrac{1+2i}{1-(1-i)^2}$

$$z = \frac{1+2i}{1-(1+i^2-2i)} = \frac{1+2i}{1+2i}$$
$$z = 1$$
$$z = 1 + 0i.$$

59. $|z| = \sqrt{x^2+y^2}$

$= \sqrt{(1)^2+(0)^2} = \sqrt{1} = 1.$

60. $\text{Arg}(z) = \tan^{-1}\left(\dfrac{y}{x}\right)$

$= \tan^{-1}\left(\dfrac{0}{1}\right) = \tan^{-1}(0) = 0°.$

61. We have, $\dfrac{dy}{dx}+\dfrac{x}{y} = 0$

$$\frac{dy}{dx} = -\frac{x}{y}$$

$$ydy = -x\,dx$$

Taking integration both side

$$\int y\,dy = -\int x\,dx$$

$$\frac{y^2}{2} = -\frac{x^2}{2}+c_1$$

$$y^2 + x^2 = 2c_1$$

$$y^2 + x^2 = c$$

Where c is a constant.

62. A function is continuous

iff LHL = RHL = Value of the function

$$\lim_{h\to 0^-} f(x) = \lim_{h\to 0^+} f(x) = f(0)$$

$$\lim_{h\to 0} f(0-h) = \lim_{h\to 0} f(0+h) = f(0)$$

$$\lim_{h\to 0} \sin h = k$$

$$k = 0.$$

63. Let $F(x) = a^2x + b^2y$ ...(*i*)

Given that, $xy = c^2$

$$y = \frac{c^2}{x}$$

Put in equation (*i*), we get,

$$F(x) = a^2x+\frac{b^2c^2}{x} \quad ...(ii)$$

$$F'(x) = a^2-\frac{b^2c^2}{x^2}$$

For maxima and minima

$$F'(x) = 0$$

$$a^2-\frac{b^2c^2}{x^2} = 0$$

$$x^2 = \frac{b^2c^2}{a^2}$$

$$x = \frac{bc}{a}$$

Put in equation (*ii*), we get,

$$= a^2\times\left(\frac{bc}{a}\right)+\frac{b^2c^2}{\frac{bc}{a}}$$

$$= a\times b\times c + a\times b\times c$$

64. We have, $\int e^{x\ln(a)} = \int e^{\ln(a)^x}\,dx$

$$= \int a^x\,dx = \frac{a^x}{\ln(a)}+c.$$

65.

Required Area $= \displaystyle\int_0^{\pi} c.\sin x.dx = c\int_0^{\pi}\sin x.dx$

$$= c\left[-\cos x\right]_0^{\pi}$$

$$= c\left[-\cos\pi+\cos 0\right]$$

$$= c[-(-1)+1]$$

$$= c(1+1)$$

$$= 2c$$

Hence, Required Area of one loop will be $2c$.

66. We have,

$$\sin\theta+\cos\theta = \sqrt{2}\cos\theta \quad ...(i)$$

$$\cos\theta-\sin\theta = x \quad ...(ii)$$

Equation (*i*) + equation (*ii*),

$$(\sin\theta+\cos\theta)^2+(\cos\theta-\sin\theta)^2 = 2\cos^2\theta+x^2$$

$$2\sin^2\theta+2\cos^2\theta = 2\cos^2\theta+x^2$$

$$2-2\cos^2\theta = x^2$$

$$2(1-\cos^2\theta) = x^2$$

$$x^2 = 2\sin^2\theta$$

$$x = \sqrt{2}\sin\theta.$$

67. ∵ Radius $(r) = \dfrac{44}{2} = 22$ cm

∵ OA = OB = r

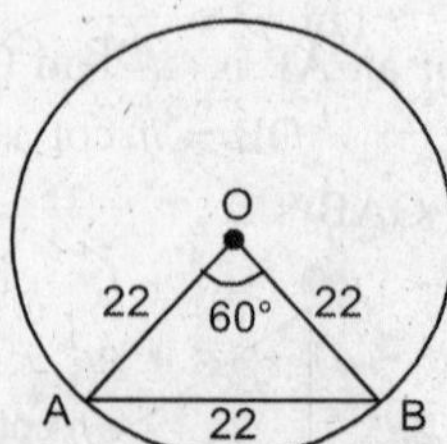

∴ ΔOAB is an equilateral triangle

∴ ∠AOB = 60°

$\therefore$ length of minor arc $= \dfrac{2\pi r\theta}{360°}$

$$= \frac{2 \times \frac{22}{7} \times 22 \times 60}{360} = \frac{484}{21} \text{ cm.}$$

69. $\therefore$ A number is even number if its unit place digit is even

2!	3!	2, 4

Total ways when repetition is not allowed

$= 2! \times 3! \times 2!$

$= 2 \times 6 \times 2 = 24.$

70. There are two right angle triangle in the given figure

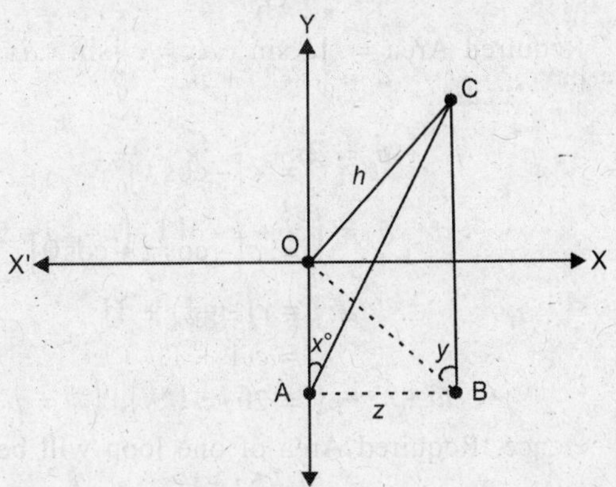

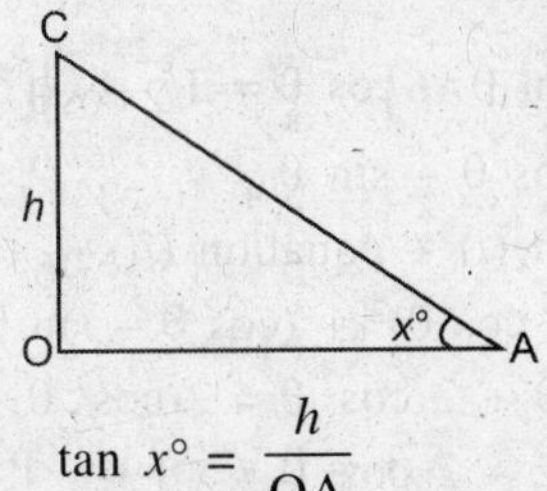

$$\tan x° = \frac{h}{OA}$$

$$OA = h \cot x$$

C

h

O

y°

B

$$\tan y° = \frac{h}{OB}$$

$$OB = h \cot y$$

In triangle OAB

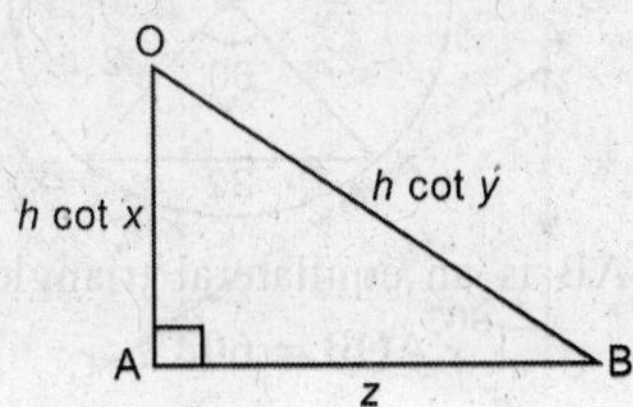

By Pythagorus Theorem

$$h^2 \cot^2 y = h^2 \cot^2 x + z^2$$

$$\therefore \quad z^2 = h^2 (\cot^2 y - \cot^2 x).$$

72. Given that, $P(A) = 0.5$, $P(B) = 0.6$

$P(A \cap B) = 0.4$

$\because \quad P(A \cup B) = P(A) + P(B) - P(A \cap B)$

$P(A \cup B) = 0.5 + 0.6 - 0.4$

$= 1.1 - 0.4 = 0.7$

$P(\overline{A \cup B}) = 1 - P(A \cup B)$

$= 1 - 0.7 = 0.3.$

73. P(Problem will be solved)

= 1 – P(Problem will not be solved)

$= 1 - P(\bar{A})\,P(\bar{B})\,P(\bar{C})$

$= 1 - (P - P(A))(1 - P(B))(1 - P(C))$

$= 1 - \left(1 - \frac{1}{2}\right)\left(1 - \frac{3}{4}\right)\left(1 - \frac{1}{4}\right)$

$= 1 - \frac{1}{2} \times \frac{1}{4} \times \frac{3}{4}$

$= 1 - \frac{3}{32} = \frac{32 - 3}{32} = \frac{29}{32}.$

74. Total case $= 6 \times 6 = 36$

Total favourable case

= {(1, 2), (1, 3), (1, 4), (1, 5), (1, 6), (2, 3), (2, 4), (2, 5), (2, 6), (3, 4), (3, 5), (3, 6), (4, 5), (4, 6), (5, 6)}

Required probability $= \frac{15}{36} = \frac{5}{12}.$

75. (2, H) or (4, H) or (6, H)

$= \frac{1}{6} \times \frac{1}{2} + \frac{1}{6} \times \frac{1}{2} + \frac{1}{6} \times \frac{1}{2}$

$= \frac{1}{12} + \frac{1}{12} + \frac{1}{12}$

$= \frac{3}{12} = \frac{1}{4}.$

76. Centroid of the Triangle ABC,

$= \left(\frac{x_1 + x_2 + x_3}{3}, \frac{y_1 + y_2 + y_3}{3}, \frac{z_1 + z_2 + z_3}{3}\right)$

$= \left(\frac{2+5+2}{3}, \frac{-3-3-3}{3}, \frac{3-4-2}{3}\right)$

$= \left(\frac{9}{3}, \frac{-9}{3}, \frac{-3}{3}\right)$

$= (3, -3, -1).$

77. $x^2 + y^2 + z^2 - 6x + 8y - 10z + 1 = 0$

Compare with $x^2 + y^2 + z^2 + 2gx + 2fy + 2hz + c = 0$

$\Rightarrow g = -3, f = 4, h = -5$

Centre of sphere = $(-g, -f, -h)$

Centre of sphere = $(3, -4, 5)$

$$\text{Radius of sphere} = \sqrt{g^2 + f^2 + h^2 - c}$$

$$= \sqrt{(3)^2 + (-4)^2 + (5)^2 - 1}$$

$$= \sqrt{9 + 16 + 25 - 1}$$

$$= \sqrt{50 - 1} = \sqrt{49} = 7.$$

78. Combined equation of two plane

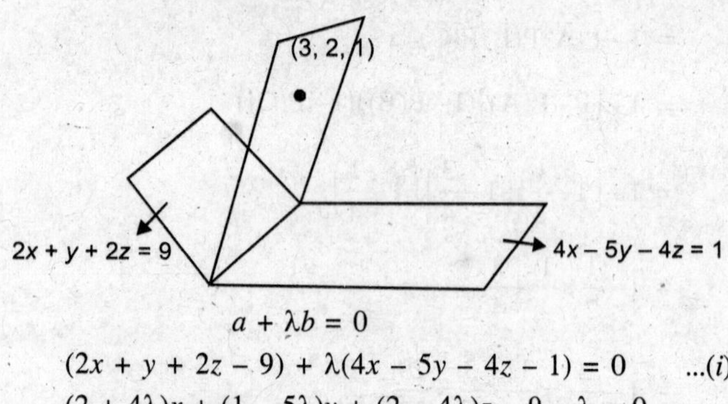

$$a + \lambda b = 0$$

$(2x + y + 2z - 9) + \lambda(4x - 5y - 4z - 1) = 0$ ...(*i*)

$(2 + 4\lambda)x + (1 - 5\lambda)y + (2 - 4\lambda)z - 9 - \lambda = 0$

$\because$ This is passes through (3, 2, 1) which is satisfy this

$(2 + 4\lambda) \times 3 + (1 - 5\lambda) \times 2 + (2 - 4\lambda) \times 1 - 9 - \lambda = 0$

$6 + 12\lambda + 2 - 10\lambda + 2 - 4\lambda - 9 - \lambda = 0$

$1 - 3\lambda = 0$

$$\lambda = \frac{1}{3}$$

Put $\lambda = \frac{1}{3}$ in equation (*i*)

$$(2x + y + 2z - 9) + \frac{1}{3}(4x - 5y - 4z - 1) = 0$$

$$(6x + 3y + 6z - 27) + (4x - 5y - 4z - 1) = 0$$

$$10x - 2y + 2z - 28 = 0$$

$$10x - 2y + 2z = 28.$$

79. We have two planes equation

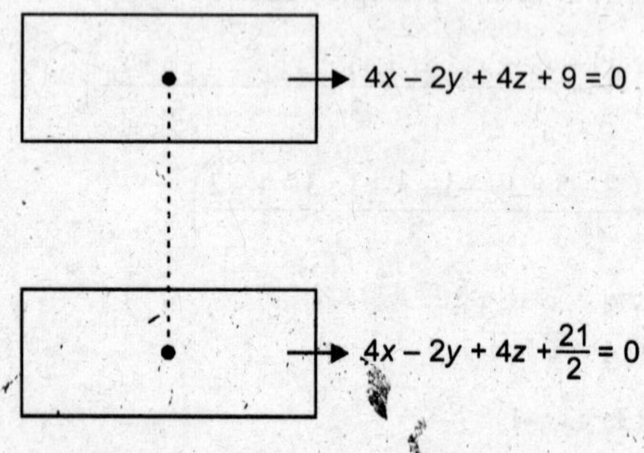

$4x - 2y + 4z + 9 = 0$ and

$$4x - 2y + 4z + \frac{21}{2} = 0$$

Required distance between two planes

$$= \left| \frac{\frac{21}{2} - 9}{\sqrt{(4)^2 + (-2)^2 + (4)^2}} \right|$$

$$= \left| \frac{\frac{3}{2}}{\sqrt{16 + 4 + 16}} \right| = \left| \frac{3}{2 \times \sqrt{36}} \right|$$

$$= \frac{3}{2 \times 6} = \frac{1}{4}.$$

81. We have,

$$\vec{a} = \hat{i} - 2\hat{j} + 5\hat{k}$$

$$\vec{b} = 2\hat{i} + \hat{j} - 3\hat{k}$$

$$\vec{b} - \vec{a} = (2\hat{i} + \hat{j} - 3\hat{k}) - (\hat{i} - 2\hat{j} + 5\hat{k})$$

$$= \hat{i} + 3\hat{j} - 8\hat{k}$$

$$3\vec{a} + \vec{b} = (3\hat{i} - 6\hat{j} + 15\hat{k}) + (2\hat{i} + \hat{j} - 3\hat{k})$$

$$= 5\hat{i} - 5\hat{j} + 12\hat{k}$$

$$(\vec{b} - \vec{a}).(3\vec{a} + \vec{b}) = (\hat{i} + 3\hat{j} - 8\hat{k})(5\hat{i} - 5\hat{j} + 12\hat{k})$$

$$= 5 + 3(-5) + (-8)(12)$$

$$= 5 - 15 - 96$$

$$= -106.$$

82.

$$\overrightarrow{AB} = \text{P.V. of B} - \text{P.V. of A}$$

$$= (2\hat{i} + 4\hat{j} - 3\hat{k}) - (3\hat{i} - 2\hat{j} + \hat{k})$$

$$= (2\hat{i} + 4\hat{j} - 3\hat{k} - 3\hat{i} + 2\hat{j} - \hat{k})$$

$$= (-\hat{i} + 6\hat{j} - 4\hat{k})$$

$$\text{Length of } \overrightarrow{AB} = |\overrightarrow{AB}| = \sqrt{(-1)^2 + (6)^2 + (-4)^2}$$

$$= \sqrt{1 + 36 + 16} = \sqrt{53}.$$

83. We have,

$$AC = |\overrightarrow{AC}| = P$$

$$\overrightarrow{AB}+\overrightarrow{BC} = \overrightarrow{AC}$$

$$\overrightarrow{AB}.\overrightarrow{AC}+\overrightarrow{BC}.\overrightarrow{AC} = \overrightarrow{AC}.\overrightarrow{AC}$$

$$\overrightarrow{AB}.\overrightarrow{AC}+\overrightarrow{CB}.\overrightarrow{CA} = |\overrightarrow{AC}|^2$$

$$\overrightarrow{AB}.\overrightarrow{AC}+\overrightarrow{CB}.\overrightarrow{CA} = p^2 \quad ...(i)$$

$$\overrightarrow{BC}.\overrightarrow{BA} = |\overrightarrow{BC}|.|\overrightarrow{BA}|.\cos 90° = 0$$

$$\therefore \overrightarrow{AB}.\overrightarrow{AC}+\overrightarrow{BC}.\overrightarrow{BA}+\overrightarrow{CB}.\overrightarrow{CA}$$

$$= \left(\overrightarrow{AB}.\overrightarrow{AC}+\overrightarrow{CB}.\overrightarrow{CA}\right)+\left(\overrightarrow{BC}.\overrightarrow{BA}\right)$$

$$= p^2 + 0$$

$$= p^2.$$

84. We have, $\vec{a} = 2\hat{i}-6\hat{j}-3\hat{k}$

$$\vec{b} = 4\hat{i}+3\hat{j}-\hat{k}$$

$$\vec{a}.\vec{b} = |\vec{a}|.|\vec{b}|\cos\theta$$

$$\left(2\hat{i}-6\hat{j}-3\hat{k}\right).\left(4\hat{i}+3\hat{j}-\hat{k}\right)$$

$$= \sqrt{(2)^2+(-6)^2+(-3)^2}\times\sqrt{(4)^2+(3)^2+(-1)^2}\cos\theta$$

$$8 - 18 + 3 = \sqrt{4+36+9}\times\sqrt{16+9+1}\cos\theta$$

$$\cos\theta = \frac{-7}{\sqrt{49}\times\sqrt{26}}$$

$$\cos\theta = \frac{-1}{\sqrt{26}}$$

$$\sin\theta = \sqrt{1-\cos^2\theta}$$

$$= \sqrt{1-\left(-\frac{1}{\sqrt{26}}\right)^2}$$

$$= \sqrt{1-\frac{1}{26}} = \sqrt{\frac{25}{26}}$$

$$\sin\theta = \frac{5}{\sqrt{26}}.$$

85. Two vectors are perpendicular if

$$\vec{a}.\vec{b} = 0$$

$$\left(3\hat{i}+4\hat{j}-\hat{k}\right).\left(-2\hat{i}+\lambda\hat{j}+10\hat{k}\right) = 0$$

$$(3)(-2) + 4\lambda + (-1)(10) = 0$$

$$-6 + 4\lambda - 10 = 0$$

$$4\lambda = 16$$

$$\lambda = 4.$$

86. $y = \sec^2(\tan^{-1} x)$

$$y = (\sec(\tan^{-1} x))^2$$

Let $\tan^{-1} x = A$

$\sqrt{1+x^2}$, x, A°, 1

$$\therefore \tan A = x = \frac{\text{Perpendicular}}{\text{Base}}$$

$$\because (\sec A) = \frac{\text{hypotenuse}}{\text{base}} = \frac{\sqrt{1+x^2}}{1}$$

$$y = (\sec A)^2$$

$$y = (1+x)^2$$

$$\frac{dy}{dx} = 2x.$$

87. We have, $f(x) = \log_{10}(1+x)$

$$f(4) = \log_{10} 5$$

$$f(1) = \log_{10} 2$$

$$4f(4) + 5f(1) - \log_{10} 2$$

$$= 4\times\log_{10} 5 + 5\log_{10} 2 - \log_{10} 2$$

$$= 4\log_{10} 5 + 4\log_{10} 2$$

$$= 4(\log_{10} 5 + \log_{10} 2)$$

$$= 4(\log_{10}(5\times 2))$$

$$= 4\times\log_{10} 10$$

$$= 4\times 1 = 4.$$

88. $f(x) = \ln\left(\sqrt{x^2+1}-x\right)$

$$f(-x) = \ln\left(\sqrt{(-x)^2+1}-(-x)\right)$$

$$= \ln\left(\sqrt{x^2+1}+x\right)$$

Even function if $f(x) = f(-x)$

Odd function if $f(x) = -f(x)$

$\therefore f(x)$ is neither even nor odd.

89. $f(x) = \log_x 10$

A Logarithm function is defined

$\log_a x$, $x > 0$, $a > 0$, $a \neq 1$

$\therefore x > 0$ excluding $x = 1$.

90. $\lim\limits_{x\to 0}\frac{1-\cos^3 4x}{x^2}$ $\quad \frac{0}{0}$ Form

Apply 'L'Hospital Rule,

$$= \lim_{x\to 0}\frac{-3\cos^2 4x(-\sin 4x)4}{2x}$$

$$= \lim_{x\to 0} \frac{12\cos^2 4x \sin 4x}{2x} \qquad \frac{0}{0} \text{ Form,}$$

Again Apply L'Hospital Rule,

$$= \lim_{x\to 0} \frac{12\left[(2\cos 4x.(-\sin 4x)4)\sin 4x + \cos^2 4x \cos 4x.4\right]}{2}$$

$$= \frac{12(0+1\times 1\times 4)}{2}$$

$$= \frac{48}{2} = 24.$$

91. At least two events occur

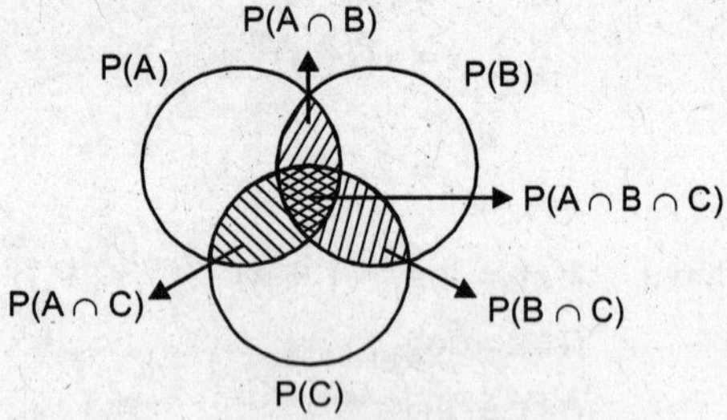

(2 event occur) or (3 event occur)

$P(A \cap B) + P(B \cap C) + P(C \cap A)$

[Three times count $P(A \cap B \cap C)$]

$\therefore P(A \cap B) + P(B \cap C) + P(C \cap B) - 2P(A \cap B \cap C)$.

93. Two events A and B are independent

If $\quad P(A \cap B) = P(A)\,P(B)$

$$P(A)\,P(B) = \frac{1}{6} \qquad ...(i)$$

$$P(A \cup B) = P(A) + P(B) - P(A \cap B)$$

$$\frac{2}{3} = P(A) + P(B) - \frac{1}{6}$$

$$\left[\because \text{Given } P(A \cap B) = \frac{1}{6}\right]$$

$$P(A) + P(B) = \frac{5}{6} \qquad ...(ii)$$

$$P(A) - P(B) = \sqrt{(P(A)+P(B))^2 - 4P(A)P(B)}$$

$$= \sqrt{\left(\frac{5}{6}\right)^2 - 4\times\frac{1}{6}}$$

$$= \sqrt{\frac{25}{36} - \frac{4}{6}}$$

$$P(A) - P(B) = \sqrt{\frac{25-24}{36}} = \sqrt{\frac{1}{36}}$$

$$P(A) - P(B) = \frac{1}{6} \qquad ...(iii)$$

Equation (*ii*) – equation (*iii*)

$$2 \times P(B) = \frac{5}{6} - \frac{1}{6}$$

$$2 \times P(B) = \frac{4}{6}$$

$$P(B) = \frac{2}{6} = \frac{1}{3}$$

$$P(A) = \frac{1}{2}. \qquad [\text{Given } P(B) < P(A)]$$

94. Given that, Mean of 100 observations = 50

Mean of 100 observations after subtracted 5 from each observation = 50 – 5 = 45

Mean of 100 observations after divided by 4 from each observation $= \frac{45}{4} = 11.25$

The standard deviation will not change after adding and subtracting in the given observation but standard deviation will change after multiply and divide.

$\therefore$ New Standard Deviation $= \frac{10}{4} = 2.5.$

95. There the following case:

(2, 4), (3, 5), (4, 4), (5, 3), (6, 2)

These event already occured favourable case

= (6, 2) = 1

Required probability $= \frac{1}{5}$.

96. 2 Side → Red

2 Side → Black

1 Side → Yellow

1 Side → White

$\because$ Total face in dice = 6

$\therefore$ Required Probability

$$= \frac{2}{6}\times\frac{2}{6} + \frac{2}{6}\times\frac{2}{6} + \frac{1}{6}\times\frac{1}{6} + \frac{1}{6}\times\frac{1}{6}$$

$$= \frac{4}{36} + \frac{4}{36} + \frac{1}{36} + \frac{1}{36}$$

$$= \frac{10}{36}$$

$$= \frac{5}{18}.$$

97. Required Probability

$$= \frac{^3C_2}{^nC_2} = \frac{\frac{3!}{2!1!}}{\frac{n!}{2!(n-2)!}} = \frac{6(n-2)!}{n!}$$

$$= \frac{6(n-2)!}{n(n-1)(n-2)!}$$

$$= \frac{6}{n(n-1)}$$

According to question,

$$\frac{6}{n(n-1)} = \frac{1}{2}$$

$$n(n-1) = 12$$

$$n^2 - n - 12 = 0$$

$$n^2 - 4n + 3n - 12 = 0$$

$$n(n-4) + 3(n-4) = 0$$

$$(n+3)(n-4) = 0$$

$$n \neq -3,$$

$\therefore$ $n = 4.$

98. (A, A, A, A), (K, K, K, K), (Q, Q, Q, Q), (J, J, J, J), (10, 10, 10, 10), ... 13 set of card, each have 4 same card

$$\text{Required probability} = \frac{^{13}C_1 \times {^4C_2}}{^{52}C_2}$$

$$= \frac{13 \times \frac{\lfloor 4}{\lfloor 2 \times \lfloor 2}}{\frac{\lfloor 52}{\lfloor 50 \lfloor 2}}$$

$$= \frac{13 \times \lfloor 4 \times \lfloor 50 \times \lfloor 2}{\lfloor 2 \times \lfloor 2 \times \lfloor 52}$$

$$= \frac{13 \times \lfloor 50 \times 24}{2 \times 52 \times 51 \times \lfloor 50} = \frac{1}{17}.$$

99. We have, $n = 8$

$$p = \frac{2}{6} = \frac{1}{3}$$

$$q = 1 - p = 1 - \frac{1}{3} = \frac{2}{3}$$

$\because$ $\text{Mean} = np = 8 \times \frac{1}{3} = \frac{8}{3}$

$$\text{Standard Deviation} = \sqrt{npq}$$

$$= \sqrt{8 \times \frac{1}{3} \times \frac{2}{3}} = \sqrt{\frac{16}{9}} = \frac{4}{3}.$$

100. Given that $\bar{A}$ and $\bar{B}$ are mutually exclusive

$$P(\bar{A} \cap \bar{B}) = 0$$

$$P(\overline{A \cup B}) = 0$$

$$1 - P(A \cup B) = 0$$

$$P(A \cup B) = 1$$

and $P(A) = 0.5,\ P(B) = 0.6$

$\because$ $P(A \cup B) = P(A) + P(B) - P(A \cap B)$

$$1 = 0.5 + 0.6 - P(A \cap B)$$

$$P(A \cap B) = 1.1 - 1$$

$$P(A \cap B) = 0.1$$

$\because$ $P(A/B) = \frac{P(A \cap B)}{P(A)}$

$$= \frac{0.1}{0.5} = \frac{1}{5}.$$

101. 1. The algebraic sum of deviations of a set of values from their arithmetic mean is always zero.

2. In Symmetric distribution,

Mean = Median = Mode

Hence, only 1 statement is true.

104. Let A circle of radius r

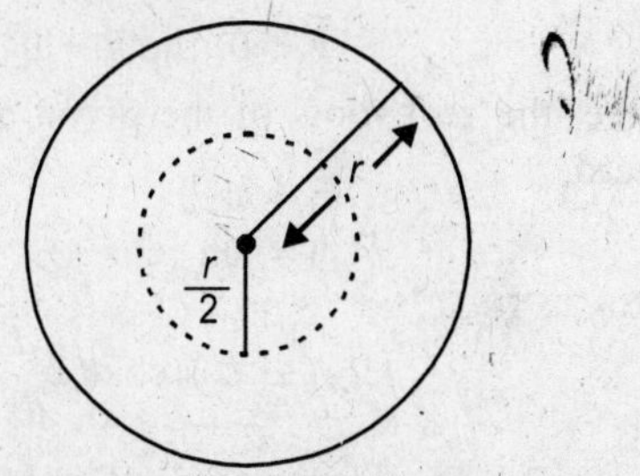

A interior point in a circle will be closer to centre if it is inside a circle which has radius half of the given circle

$$\text{Required Probability} = \frac{\pi\left(\frac{r}{2}\right)^2}{\pi r^2} = \frac{1}{4}.$$

106. Perimeter of a circle = $2\pi r$

Area of a circle = πr^2

$$f(r) = \frac{2\pi r}{\pi r^2},\ r > 0$$

$$f(r) = \frac{2}{r},\ r > 0$$

$$f(1) + f(2) = \frac{2}{1} + \frac{2}{2}$$

$$= 2 + 1 = 3.$$

107. We have,

$$f(x) = 3^{1+x}$$
$$f(y) = 3^{1+y}$$
$$f(z) = 3^{1+z}$$
$$f(x) f(y) f(z) = 3^{1+x} . 3^{1+y} . 3^{1+z}$$
$$= 3^{1+x+1+y+1+z}$$
$$= 3^{3+x+y+z}$$
$$= 3^{1+(2+x+y+z)}$$
$$= f(x+y+z+2)$$
$$\therefore \quad f(x) . f(y) . f(z) = f(x+y+z+2).$$

108. $x^2 + 9|x| + 20 = 0$

Case-I: If $x \geq 0$

$$x^2 + 9x + 20 = 0$$
$$x^2 + 5x + 4x + 20 = 0$$
$$x(x+5) + 4(x+5) = 0$$
$$(x+4)(x+5) = 0$$
$$x = -4, -5$$

$\because$ $x \geq 0$, $\therefore$ roots = 0.

Case-II: $x < 0$

$$x^2 - 9x + 20 = 0$$
$$x^2 - 5x - 4x + 20 = 0$$
$$x(x-5) - 4(x-5) = 0$$
$$(x-4)(x-5) = 0$$
$$x = 4, 5$$

$\because$ $x < 0$, roots = 0.

Hence, the real roots of the given quadratic equation is zero.

109.

$$f(x) = \sin(\cos x)$$
$$f'(x) = \cos(\cos x)\frac{d}{dx}\cos x$$
$$f'(x) = \cos(\cos x)(-\sin x)$$
$$f'(x) = (-\sin x)\cos(\cos x).$$

110. We have, $f(x) = \sqrt{(2-x)(x-3)}$

$$(2-x)(x-3) \geq 0$$
$$(x-2)(x-3) \leq 0$$
$$2 \leq x \leq 3$$

$\therefore$ Domain will be [2, 3].

111. We have, $\frac{dy}{dx} = \cos(y-x) + 1$

$$\Rightarrow \quad \frac{dy}{dx} - 1 = \cos(y-x)$$

Let $y - x = t$

$$\frac{dy}{dx} - 1 = \frac{dt}{dx}$$

$$\therefore \quad \frac{dt}{dx} = \cot t$$

$$\frac{dt}{\cos t} = dx$$

$$\sec t\, dt = dx$$

Taking Integration of both side, we get

$$\int \sec t . dt = \int dx$$

$$\log(\sec t + \tan t) = x + c_1$$

Where c_1 is a constant

$$\sec t + \tan t = e^{x + c1}$$
$$\sec t + \tan t = e^x . e^{c_1}$$
$$\frac{1}{e^c}(\sec t + \tan t) = e^x$$

Where $\frac{1}{e^c}$ is a constant

$$c(\sec(y-x) + \tan(y-x)) = e^x.$$

112. We have,

$$\int_0^{\pi/2} |\sin x - \cos x|\, dx$$

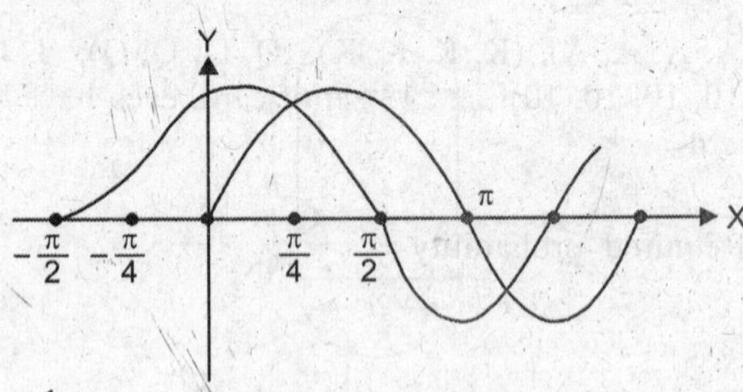

$$= \int_0^{\pi/4} |\sin x - \cos x|\, dx + \int_{\pi/4}^{\pi/2} |\sin x - \cos x|\, dx$$

$$= \int_0^{\pi/4} (\cos x - \sin x)\, dx + \int_{\pi/4}^{\pi/2} (\sin x - \cos x)\, dx$$

$$= [\sin x + \cos x]_0^{\pi/4} + [-\cos x - \sin x]_{\pi/4}^{\pi/2}$$

$$= \left[\left(\sin\frac{\pi}{4} + \cos\frac{\pi}{4}\right) - (\sin 0° + \cos 0°)\right]$$

$$+ \left[\left(-\cos\frac{\pi}{2} - \sin\frac{\pi}{2}\right) - \left(-\cos\frac{\pi}{4} - \sin\frac{\pi}{4}\right)\right]$$

$$= \left[\left(\frac{1}{\sqrt{2}} + \frac{1}{\sqrt{2}}\right) - (0+1)\right] + \left[(-0-1) - \left(-\frac{1}{\sqrt{2}} - \frac{1}{\sqrt{2}}\right)\right]$$

$$= \left[\frac{2}{\sqrt{2}} - 1\right] + \left[-1 - \left(-\frac{2}{\sqrt{2}}\right)\right]$$

$$= \left[\sqrt{2}-1\right]+\left[-1+\sqrt{2}\right]$$

$$= 2\sqrt{2}-2 = 2\left(\sqrt{2}-1\right).$$

113. We have, $y = a \cos 2x + b \sin 2x$

$$\frac{dy}{dx} = -2a \sin 2x + 2b \cos 2x$$

$$\frac{d^2y}{dx^2} = -4a \cos 2x - 4b \sin 2x$$

$$\frac{d^2y}{dx^2} = -4(a \cos 2x + b \sin 2x)$$

$$\frac{d^2y}{dx^2} = -4y$$

$$\frac{d^2y}{dx^2}+4y = 0$$

114. Let the radius and height of cylinder is r and h

$\because$ Volume is constant

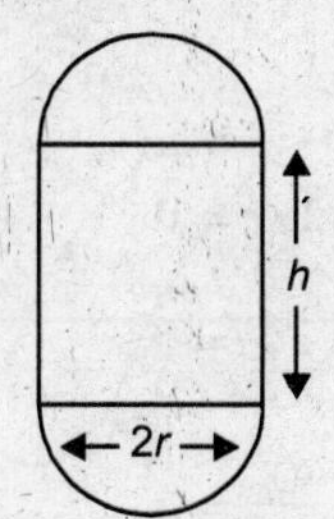

$$V = \frac{\pi r^2 h}{2}$$

$$h = \frac{2V}{\pi r^2} \quad ...(i)$$

Total Surface Area

$$T = \pi rh + \pi r^2 + 2r \times h$$

Put $h = \frac{2V}{\pi r^2}$, we get,

$$T = \pi r \times \frac{2V}{\pi r^2} + \pi r^2 + 2r \times \frac{2V}{\pi r^2}$$

$$T = \frac{2V}{r} + \pi r^2 + \frac{4V}{\pi r}$$

For maxima, minima

$$\frac{dT}{dr} = 2V\left[-\frac{1}{r^2}\right]+2\pi r+\frac{4V}{\pi}\left[-\frac{1}{r^2}\right]$$

$$\frac{dT}{dr} = 0$$

$$-\frac{2V}{r^2}+2\pi r-\frac{4V}{\pi r^2} = 0$$

$$-2V\pi + 2\pi^2 r^3 - 4V = 0$$

$$-V\pi + \pi^2 r^3 - 2V = 0$$

$$r^3 = \frac{V(\pi+2)}{\pi^2} \quad \text{Put } V = \frac{\pi r^2 h}{2}$$

$$r^3 = \frac{\pi r^2 h}{2}\frac{(\pi+2)}{\pi^2}$$

$$\frac{r}{h} = \frac{\pi+2}{2\pi}$$

$$\frac{2r}{h} = \frac{\pi+2}{\pi}$$

$$\frac{d}{h} = \frac{\pi+2}{\pi}$$

$$\therefore \quad \frac{h}{d} = \frac{\pi}{\pi+2}.$$

115. $\int_0^{\pi/2} e^{\sin x} \cos x \, dx$

Let, $\sin x = t$

$\cos x \, dx = dt$

if $x = 0$, $t = \sin 0 = 0$

if $x = \frac{\pi}{2}$, $t = \sin\frac{\pi}{2} = 1$

$$\therefore \quad \int_0^1 e^t . dt = \left[e^t\right]_0^1 = e^1 - e^0 = e-1.$$

116. $f(x) = \frac{x-2}{x+2}$

Let, $y = \frac{x-2}{x+2}$

$$yx + 2y = x - 2$$

$$2y + 2 = x - yx$$

$$x(1 - y) = 2y + 2$$

$$x = \frac{2y+2}{1-y}$$

$$x = \frac{2(y+1)}{1-y}$$

$$f^{-1}(x) = \frac{2(x+1)}{1-x}.$$

117. $\int \ln(x^2).1.dx$
I II

$= \ln(x^2)\int dx - \int\left\{\frac{d}{dx}\ln(x^2)\int 1.dx\right\}dx$

$= \ln(x^2)x - \int\left\{\frac{2x}{x^2}\times x\right\}dx$

$= x.\ln(x^2) - \int 2\,dx$

$= x.\ln(x^2) - 2x + c$

$= 2x.\ln(x) - 2x + c$

Hence, option (A) is the correct.

118. Let the point on parabola $y^2 = 8x$ is $A(x, y)$

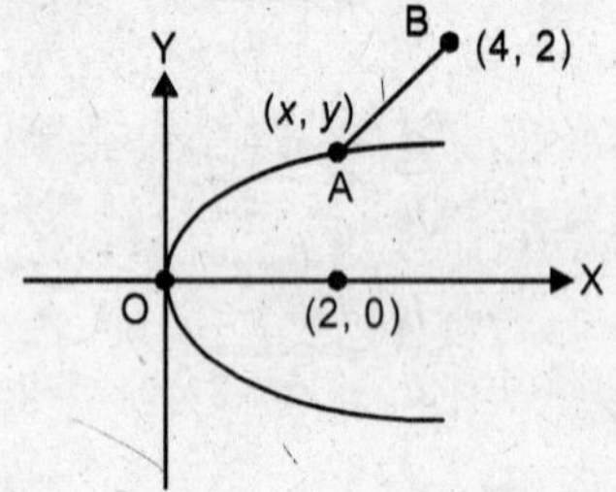

Distance between $A(x, y)$ and $B(4, 2)$

$$D = \sqrt{(2-y)^2 + (4-x)^2}$$

$$D^2 = 4 + y^2 + 4y + 16 + x^2 - 8x$$

Put $y = \sqrt{8x}$ and let $D^2 = P$

$$P = 4 + 8x - 4\sqrt{8x} + 16 + x^2 - 8x$$

$$P = x^2 - 8\sqrt{2}\left(\sqrt{x}\right) + 20 \quad ...(i)$$

For maxima minima

$$\frac{dP}{dx} = 2x - 8\times\sqrt{2}\times\frac{1}{2\sqrt{x}}$$

$$\frac{dP}{dx} = 2x - \frac{4\sqrt{2}}{\sqrt{x}}$$

$$\frac{dP}{dx} = 0,$$

$$2x - \frac{4\sqrt{2}}{\sqrt{x}} = 0$$

$$x = \frac{2\sqrt{2}}{\sqrt{x}}$$

$$x^{3/2} = 2^{3/2}$$

$$x = 2$$

Put in equation (i), we get,

$$P = (2)^2 - 8\sqrt{2}\left(\sqrt{2}\right) + 20$$

$$P = 4 - 16 + 20$$

$$P = 8$$

$\because \quad D^2 = 8$

$\Rightarrow \quad D = 2\sqrt{2}.$

119. $(x - a)^2 + y^2 = a^2$

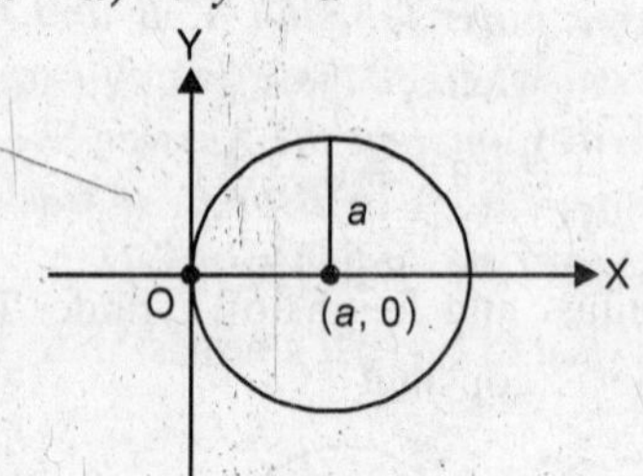

$$x^2 + a^2 - 2ax + y^2 = a^2$$

$$x^2 + y^2 - 2ax = 0 \quad ...(i)$$

$$2x + 2y\frac{dy}{dx} - 2a = 0$$

$$x + y\frac{dy}{dx} = a$$

Put the value of arbitrary constant 'a' in equation (i)

$$x^2 + y^2 - 2x\left(x + y\frac{dy}{dx}\right) = 0$$

$$x^2 + y^2 - 2x^2 - 2xy\frac{dy}{dx} = 0$$

$$-x^2 + y^2 - 2xy\frac{dy}{dx} = 0$$

$$x^2 - y^2 + 2xy\frac{dy}{dx} = 0.$$

Previous Papers (Solved)

NATIONAL DEFENCE ACADEMY

ENTRANCE EXAMINATION–2018 (II)*

PAPER I : GENERAL ABILITY TEST

PART A - ENGLISH LANGUAGE

SPOTTING ERRORS

Directions (Qs. No. 1-5): *Each item in this section has a sentence with three parts labelled A, B and C. Read each sentence to find out whether there is any error in any part and indicate your response in the Answer Sheet against the corresponding letter i.e., A or B or C. If you find no error, your response should be indicated as D.*

1. He appears (A)/ to be (B)/ a honest man. (C)/ No Error (D)
2. One of the members (A)/ expressed doubt if (B)/ the Minister was an atheist. (C)/ No Error (D)
3. This view has been taken (A)/ by one of the ablest persons (B)/ who has written on this subject. (C)/ No Error (D)
4. Slow and steady (A)/ owns the race, (B)/ as the wise would say. (C)/ No Error (D)
5. We often hear people say (A)/ that most human beings have not evolved (B)/ or grow up enough to stick to truth or non-violence. (C)/ No Error (D)

SYNONYMS

Directions (Qs. No. 6-10): *Each item in this section consists of a sentence with an underlined word/words followed by four words. Select the option that is* ***nearest in meaning*** *to the underlined word/words and mark your response in your Answer Sheet accordingly.*

6. The Industrial Revolution saw a **massive** rise in the population of Europe.
   A. enormous B. erroneous
   C. hazardous D. perilous
7. I had some deepest **convictions** reflected in my work.
   A. ideas and opinions B. firm beliefs
   C. prejudices D. biases
8. This boy is very **timid**.
   A. courageous B. shy
   C. clever D. dull
9. My friend is as **stubborn** as a mule.
   A. observant B. obnoxious
   C. obstinate D. corpulent
10. His behaviour was deliberately **provocative**.
    A. exciting desire B. infuriating
    C. pitiable D. creating frustration

ANTONYMS

Directions (Qs. No. 11-15): *Each item in this section consists of a sentence with an underlined word/words followed by four words. Select the option that is* ***opposite in meaning*** *to the underlined word/words and mark your response in your Answer Sheet accordingly.*

11. Too many cooks **spoil** the broth.
    A. tarnish B. wreck
    C. embellish D. upset
12. He is **biased** against the students from cities.
    A. open B. prejudiced
    C. liked D. impartial
13. It is easy to be an **orthodox**.
    A. idolatrous B. intelligent
    C. malignant D. heterodox
14. **Permit** me to present you with a book.
    A. allow B. enclose
    C. prohibit D. persuade
15. None but the **brave** deserves the fair.
    A. ugly person B. coward
    C. jealous person D. weak person

COMPREHENSION

Directions (Qs. No. 16-25): *In this section, you have two short passages. After each passage, you will find some items based on the passage. First, read a passage and answer the items based on it. You are required to select your answers based on the contents of the passage and opinion of the author only.*

* Exam Held on 09/09/2018

Passage-I

"Now, ladies and gentlemen," said the conjuror, "having shown you that the cloth is absolutely empty, I will proceed to take from it a bowl of goldfish. Presto!"

All around the hall people were saying, "Oh, how wonderful! How does he do it?"

But the Quick Man on the front seat said in a big whisper to the people near him, "He-had-it-up-his-sleeve."

Then the people nodded brightly at the Quick Man and said, "Oh, of course"; and everybody whispered round the hall, "He-had-it-up-his-sleeve."

"My next trick," said the conjuror, "is the famous Hindostanee rings. You will notice that the rings are apparently separate; at a blow they all join (clang, clang, clang) – Presto!"

There was a general buzz of stupefaction till the Quick Man was heard to whisper, "He-must-have-had-another-lot-up-his-sleeve."

Again everybody nodded and whispered, "The-rings-were-up-his-sleeve."

The brow of the conjuror was clouded with a gathering frown.

"I will now," he continued, "show you a most amusing trick by which I am enabled to take any number of eggs from a hat. Will some gentleman kindly lend me his hat? Ah, thank you – Presto!"

He extracted seventeen eggs, and for thirty-five seconds the audience began to think that he was wonderful. Then the Quick Man whispered along the front bench, "He-has-a-hen-up-his-sleeve," and all the people whispered it on. "He-has-a-lot-of-hens-up-his-sleeve."

The egg trick was ruined.

It went on like that all through. It transpired from the whispers of the Quick Man that the conjuror must have concealed up his sleeve, in addition to the rings, hens, and fish, several packs of cards, a loaf of bread, a doll's cradle, a live guinea pig, a fifty-cent piece, and a rocking chair.

16. "The brow of the conjuror was clouded with a gathering frown." The sentence means that the conjuror
- A. was very pleased
- B. was very sad
- C. was rather angry
- D. was very afraid

17. "The egg trick was ruined." This means that
- A. eggs were all broken
- B. people were unconvinced
- C. conjuror was disappointed
- D. the trick could not be performed

18. According to the Quick Man, the conjuror
- A. had everything bought for production
- B. produced things with the magic he knew
- C. had things in the large sleeves of his coat
- D. created an illusion of things with his magic

19. The author believes that the Quick Man was really
- A. foolish
- B. clever
- C. wrong
- D. right

20. The conjuror extracted seventeen eggs from the hat of
- A. the Quick Man
- B. his own
- C. one gentleman from the audience
- D. None of the above

Passage-II

Magda: Good morning, Mrs. Smiles. It's wet, isn't it?

Mrs. Smiles: Yes, it is, isn't it? How are you today? All right. You haven't been studying too hard, have you? You look a bit pale.

Magda: I don't, do I? Well, I haven't been out much lately. I don't like this weather a bit. Why, we haven't had a dry day for weeks, have we?

Mrs. Smiles: No, I don't think we have. Let's see, you'll be going back home next month, won't you?

Magda: Oh no, I'm not going back yet. My sister's coming over first.

Mrs. Smiles: Oh, is she? You're looking forward to that, I expect. How long is it since you saw her?

Magda: Nearly a year now. Yes, I am looking forward to it very much.

Mrs. Smiles: She's coming over here to study?

Magda: Yes, that's right. I shan't go back home until she's settled down. I don't think I ought to, ought I?

Mrs. Smiles: Well, no, she's younger than you are, is she?

Magda: Yes, she's only eighteen.

21. Magda had not been out much lately because
- A. she had not been keeping well
- B. she was busy with her studies
- C. the weather had been unpleasant
- D. her sister had come over to stay

22. Magda was not going back home yet because
- A. it had been raining heavily
- B. her sister was coming over
- C. her studies were not completed
- D. she was not feeling well

23. Mrs. Smiles says, "You're looking forward to that." This means, Magda was ________ her sister's arrival.
- A. expecting with pleasure
- B. preparing hard for
- C. thinking greatly about
- D. watching with joy

24. Magda's sister was coming to
    A. visit her sister
    B. help Mrs. Smiles
    C. settle down in England
    D. pursue her studies

25. Mrs. Smiles and Magda are
    A. classmates
    B. school friends
    C. neighbours
    D. sisters-in-law

FILL IN THE BLANKS

Directions (Qs. No. 26-35): *Each of the following sentences in this section has a blank space and four words or groups of words given after the sentence. Select whichever word or group of words you consider most appropriate for the blank space and indicate your response on the Answer Sheet accordingly.*

26. We fail to understand your reasons for __________ the college without completing the degree.
    A. attending
    B. joining
    C. leaving
    D. refusing

27. She ________ her energy and started shouting only when she heard the noise of bulldozers and cranes.
    A. checked
    B. conserved
    C. maintained
    D. controlled

28. The British ________ all over Africa and Asia collapsed in the first half of the twentieth century.
    A. hegemony
    B. domicile
    C. residence
    D. inheritance

29. The football match has to be ________ because of the weather.
    A. called off
    B. continued
    C. put off
    D. turned off

30. If I were rich, _______ a lot.
    A. I'll travel
    B. I can travel
    C. I would travel
    D. I travelled

31. They apologized ________ me for what happened.
    A. to
    B. at
    C. for
    D. with

32. If you are tired of swimming, just _________ for a while.
    A. struggle
    B. stroke
    C. float
    D. streak

33. He had _______ spoken for two minutes when there was a commotion in the crowd.
    A. even
    B. hardly
    C. often
    D. little

34. I would not commit myself ______ that course of action.
    A. of
    B. to
    C. by
    D. with

35. The soldiers waiting to go into battle for the first time were full of _________.
    A. apprehension
    B. consideration
    C. anticipation
    D. frivolity

IDIOMS AND PHRASES

Directions (Qs. No. 36-40): *Given below are some idioms/ phrases followed by four alternative meanings to each. Choose the response A, B, C or D which is the most appropriate expression.*

36. A red-letter day
    A. a trivial day
    B. a very important or significant day
    C. a day of bloodshed and violence
    D. a mourning day

37. The gift of the gab
    A. ability to speak easily and confidently
    B. ability to spoil something
    C. ability to sell things
    D. gift from a sacred institution

38. Walk a tightrope
    A. to be forced to leave your job
    B. to be ready to fall
    C. to act very carefully
    D. to invite danger

39. To be in a fix
    A. to receive strong criticism
    B. to support oneself
    C. to fix problems
    D. to be in a difficult situation

40. To fish in troubled waters
    A. to borrow money
    B. to steal belongings of
    C. to get benefit in bad situation
    D. to extend a helping hand

ORDERING OF SENTENCES

Directions (Qs. No. 41-45): *Each of the following items in this section consists of a sentence the parts of which have been jumbled. These parts have been labelled P, Q, R and S. Given below each sentence are four sequences namely A, B, C and D. You are required to rearrange the jumbled parts of the sentence and mark your answer accordingly.*

41. Domestic fires in Indian villages
    P: as the heat is dispersed
    Q: an unhealthy smoke accumulates in unventilated houses
    R: are wasteful
    S: lit in Chulhas

The correct sequence should be:
A. PQSR B. PQRS
C. SPQR D. SRPQ

42. Bold rocks near at hand
P: makes a fine forest for the imagination
Q: than distant Alps
R: are more inspiring
S: and the thick fern upon a heath
The correct sequence should be:
A. QRSP B. RSQP
C. RQSP D. SRQP

43. Newton discovered that
P: due to the gravitational pull
Q: of the earth
R: the apple falls
S: on the ground
The correct sequence should be:
A. QPRS B. RSPQ
C. QSPR D. SQRP

44. The knocking
P: were still in the house
Q: for some time
R: although the echoes of it
S: ceased
The correct sequence should be:
A. SRPQ B. SQRP
C. PQSR D. RSPQ

45. The history of mankind is
P: and steady progress
Q: continuous change
R: the history of
S: from barbarism to refinement
The correct sequence should be:
A. PQRS B. RQPS
C. QSPR D. SQRP

CLOZE COMPREHENSION

Directions (Qs. No. 46-50): *In the following passage, there are some blank spaces with four words or groups of words given. Select whichever word or group of words you consider most appropriate for the blank space and indicate your response on the Answer accordingly.*

The honeybee is a very unusual kind of insect. __(46)__ other insects which live alone, the honeybee lives as a/an __(47)__ of a community. These bees live together in what is known as a bee __(48)__. The head of the bees is called the queen bee. She is __(49)__ than the rest of the bees. Her main task is to __(50)__ eggs.

46. A. Unlike B. Similar to
C. With D. Like

47. A. group B. individual
C. member D. troop

48. A. house B. home
C. army D. colony

49. A. heaviest B. heavier
C. largest D. larger

50. A. lay B. hatch
C. make D. bear

PART B - GENERAL KNOWLEDGE

Directions (Qs. No. 51-56): *The following items consist of two statements. Statement I and Statement II. Examine these two statements carefully and select the correct answer using the code given below.*

Code:
A. Both the statements are individually true and Statement II is the correct explanation of Statement I.
B. Both the statements are individually true, but Statement II is not the correct explanation of Statement I.
C. Statement I is true, but Statement II is false.
D. Statement I is false, but Statement II is true.

51. Statement I: The pitch of the sound wave depends upon its frequency.

Statement II: The loudness of the sound wave depends upon its amplitude.

52. Statement I: Sound wave cannot propagate in vacuum.

Statement II: Sound waves are elastic waves and require a medium to propagate.

53. Statement I: The Government of India Act, 1935 introduced Dyarchy at the Centre.

Statement II: The provincial autonomy was granted to the Provinces.

54. Statement I: Mughal Painting reached its climax during the reign of Jahangir.

Statement II: Aurangzeb's Court was adorned by some of the best known artists of the Mughal School of Painting.

55. Statement I: Phytoplankton produce most of the organic carbon in the ocean.

Statement II: Algae are produced in the cold water biome.

56. Statement I: Geostrophic wind blows above a height of 600 metres, parallel to the isobars.

Statement II: Geostrophic wind is the horizontal wind velocity, in which the Coriolis force balances the horizontal pressure force.

57. Which one of the following groups of cellular organelles contains DNA?
A. Mitochondria, nucleus, chloroplast
B. Mitochondria, Golgi bodies, nucleus
C. Mitochondria, plasma membrane, nucleus
D. Chloroplast, nucleus, ribosomes

58. One of the additional functions of Smooth Endoplasmic Reticulum (SER) is
A. protein synthesis
B. lipid synthesis
C. storage of biomolecules
D. detoxification of toxic substances

59. Damage to the apical meristem of a growing young plant will affect the
A. length of the plant
B. colour of the flower
C. colour of the leaves
D. taste of the fruits

60. Which of the following kingdoms has/have only unicellular organisms?
A. Monera only
B. Protista only
C. Monera and Protista both
D. Protista and Fungi both

61. Which one of the following is a waterborne disease?
A. Jaundice B. Tuberculosis
C. Rabies D. Arthritis

62. The atomic number of an element is 8. How many electrons will it gain to form a compound with sodium?
A. One B. Two
C. Three D. Four

63. A sample of oxygen contains two isotopes of oxygen with masses 16 u and 18 u respectively. The proportion of these isotopes in the sample is 3 : 1. What will be the average atomic mass of oxygen in this sample?
A. 17.5 u B. 17 u
C. 16 u D. 16.5 u

64. Which one of the following is a heterogeneous mixture?
A. Hydrochloric acid B. Vinegar
C. Milk D. Soda water

65. What is the formula mass of anhydrous sodium carbonate? (Given that the atomic masses of sodium, carbon and oxygen are 23 u, 12 u and 16 u respectively)
A. 286 u B. 106 u
C. 83 u D. 53 u

66. Which one of the following is called 'syngas'?
A. $C(s) + H_2O(g)$ B. $CO(g) + H_2O(g)$
C. $CO(g) + H_2(g)$ D. $NO_2(g) + H_2(g)$

67. The frequency of ultrasound waves is
A. less than 20 Hz
B. between 20 Hz and 2 kHz
C. between 2 kHz and 20 kHz
D. greater than 20 kHz

68. The magnetic field strength of a current-carrying wire at a particular distance from the axis of the wire
A. depends upon the current in the wire
B. depends upon the radius of the wire
C. depends upon the temperature of the surroundings
D. None of the above

69. A stainless steel chamber contains Ar gas at a temperature T and pressure P. The total number of Ar atoms in the chamber is n. Now Ar gas in the chamber is replaced by CO_2 gas and the total number of CO_2 molecules in the chamber is $n/2$ at the same temperature T. The pressure in the chamber now is P′. Which one of the following relations holds true? (Both the gases behave as ideal gases)
A. $P' = P$ B. $P' = 2P$
C. $P' = \frac{P}{2}$ D. $P' = \frac{P}{4}$

70. Which one of the following is the correct relation between Å and nm?
A. $1 \text{ nm} = 10^{-1}$ Å B. 1 nm = 10 Å
C. 1 nm = 1 Å D. $1 \text{ nm} = 10^{-2}$ Å

71. The full form of LED is
A. Light Emitting Diode
B. Light Emitting Device
C. Light Enhancing Device
D. Light Enhancing Diode

72. If a free electron moves through a potential difference of 1 kV, then the energy gained by the electron is given by
A. 1.6×10^{-19} J B. 1.6×10^{-16} J
C. 1×10^{-19} J D. 1×10^{-16} J

73. Consider the following places of India:
1. Itanagar
2. Imphal
3. Agartala
4. Aizawl

Which one of the following is the correct chronological order of the above places in terms of sunrise time?
A. 3 – 2 – 1 – 4
B. 2 – 1 – 4 – 3
C. 1 – 4 – 3 – 2
D. 4 – 3 – 2 – 1

74. Which one of the following is known as uplands of delta region?
A. Bef B. Bils
C. Peh D. Chars

75. Consider the following Wildlife Sanctuaries of India:
1. Shikari Devi
2. Bhadra
3. Simlipal
4. Pachmarhi

Which one of the following is the correct order of the above Wildlife Sanctuaries in terms of their location from south to north?
A. 1 – 2 – 3 – 4
B. 2 – 4 – 3 – 1
C. 2 – 3 – 4 – 1
D. 3 – 1 – 2 – 4

76. Which one of the following statements about temperature is correct?
A. Temperature decreases with height in the stratosphere.
B. Temperature is constant at different heights in the stratosphere.
C. Temperature increases with height in the troposphere at an average rate of 6.5°C per kilometre.
D. Temperature decreases with height in the troposphere at an average rate of 6.4°C per kilometre.

77. Which one of the following is known as a zone of sharp salinity change in the vertical section of ocean?
A. Thermocline B. Halocline
C. Photic zone D. Pycnocline

78. Permanent hardness of water **cannot** be removed by which one of the following methods?
A. Treatment with washing soda
B. Calgon's method
C. Boiling
D. Ion exchange method

79. Which one of the following reactions will give NO (nitric oxide) gas as one of the products?
A. $3Cu + 8HNO_3$ (dilute) →
B. $Cu + 4HNO_3$ (conc.) →
C. $4Zn + 10HNO_3$ (dilute) →
D. $Zn + 4HNO_3$ (conc.) →

80. Which one of the following is a tribasic acid?
A. Hydrochloric acid
B. Nitric acid
C. Sulphuric acid
D. Phosphoric acid

81. Which one of the following statements is **not** correct?
A. All carbons in diamond are linked by carbon-carbon single bond.
B. Graphite is layered structure in which layers are held together by weak van der Waals forces.
C. Graphite layers are formed by hexagonal rings of carbon atoms.
D. Graphite layers are held together by carbon-carbon single bond.

82. Which one of the following is called dry ice?
A. Solid carbon dioxide
B. Liquid carbon dioxide
C. Liquid nitrogen
D. Liquid ammonia

83. The acidic semidigested food coming out of the stomach is neutralized by
A. pancreatic juice
B. duodenal secretion
C. large intestine secretion
D. bile juice

84. The oxygenated blood from the lungs is received by the
A. left auricle B. left ventricle
C. right auricle D. right ventricle

85. The oxygen evolved during photosynthesis comes from splitting of
A. water B. carbon dioxide
C. oxygen D. light

86. Which one of the following depicts the correct circuit of a reflex arc?
A. Effector—sensory neuron—spinal cord—motor neuron—receptor
B. Receptor—sensory neuron—spinal cord—motor neuron—effector
C. Receptor—sensory neuron—brain—motor neuron—effector
D. Sensory neuron—receptor—brain—effector—motor neuron

87. If one set of chromosomes for a given plant is represented as N; in case of double fertilization, the zygote and the endosperm nucleus of a diploid plant would have how many sets of chromosomes respectively?
A. N and 2 N B. 2 N and 2 N
C. N and 3 N D. 2 N and 3 N

88. Consider the following circuit:

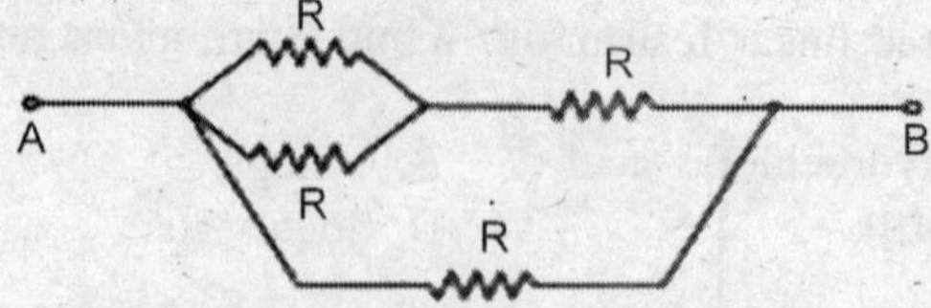

Which one of the following is the value of the resistance between points A and B in the circuit given above?
A. $\frac{2}{5}R$ B. $\frac{3}{5}R$
C. $\frac{3}{2}R$ D. 4R

89. The absolute zero temperature is 0 Kelvin. In °C unit, which one of the following is the absolute zero temperature?

A. 0°C B. −100°C
C. −273.15°C D. −173.15°C

90. Consider the following statements about visible light, UV light and X-rays:

1. The wavelength of visible light is more than that of X-rays.
2. The energy of X-ray photons is higher than that of UV light photons.
3. The energy of UV light photons is less than that of visible light photons.

Which of the statements given above is/are correct?

A. 1, 2 and 3 B. 1 and 2 only
C. 2 and 3 only D. 1 only

91. The time period of oscillation of a simple pendulum having length L and mass of the bob m is given as T. If the length of the pendulum is increased to 4 L and the mass of the bob is increased to 2 m, then which one of the following is the new time period of oscillation?

A. T B. 2T
C. 4T D. $\frac{T}{2}$

92. The connecting cable of electrical appliances like electric iron, water heater or room heater contains three insulated copper wires of three different colours—red, green and black. Which one of the following is the correct colour code?

A. Red—live wire, Green—neutral wire, Black—ground wire
B. Red—live wire, Green—ground wire, Black—live wire
C. Red—live wire, Green—ground wire, Black—neutral wire
D. Red—ground wire, Green—live wire, Black—neutral wire

93. The graphs between current (I) and voltage (V) for three linear resistors 1, 2 and 3 are given below:

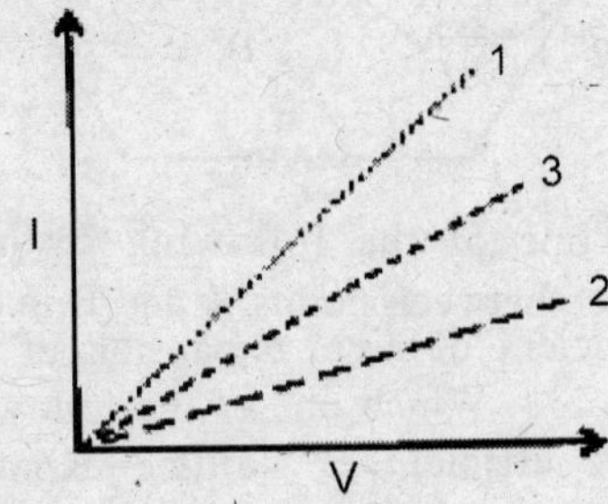

If R_1, R_2 and R_3 are the resistances of these resistors, then which one of the following is correct?

A. $R_1 > R_2 > R_3$
B. $R_1 < R_3 < R_2$
C. $R_3 < R_1 < R_2$
D. $R_3 > R_2 > R_1$

94. Consider the following statements about a microscope and a telescope:

1. Both the eyepiece and the objective of a microscope are convex lenses.
2. The focal length of the objective of a telescope is larger than the focal length of its eyepiece.
3. The magnification of a telescope increases with the increase in focal length of its objective.
4. The magnification of a microscope increases with the increase in focal length of its objective.

Which of the statements given above are correct?

A. 1 and 3 only B. 1 and 4
C. 2, 3 and 4 D. 1, 2 and 3

95. A planet has a mass M_1 and radius R_1. The value of acceleration due to gravity on its surface is g_1. There is another planet 2, whose mass and radius both are two times that of the first planet. Which one of the following is the acceleration due to gravity on the surface of planet 2?

A. g_1 B. $2g_1$
C. $\frac{g_1}{2}$ D. $\frac{g_1}{4}$

96. Match List-I with List-II and select the correct answer using the code given below the Lists:

List-I (River Basin)	**List-II (Town)**
(*a*) Bhagirathi	1. Lansdowne
(*b*) Alaknanda	2. Narendra Nagar
(*c*) Nayar	3. Uttarkashi
(*d*) Ganga	4. Pauri

Code:

	(*a*)	(*b*)	(*c*)	(*d*)
A.	3	1	4	2
B.	3	4	1	2
C.	2	4	1	3
D.	2	1	4	3

97. Match List-I with List-II and select the correct answer using the code given below the Lists:

List-I (Local Wind)	**List-II (Place)**
(*a*) Yamo	1. Sudan
(*b*) Black Roller	2. France
(*c*) Bise	3. Japan
(*d*) Haboob	4. North America

Code:

	(*a*)	(*b*)	(*c*)	(*d*)
A.	1	4	2	3
B.	1	2	4	3
C.	3	4	2	1
D.	3	2	4	1

98. 'Majuli', the river island, is located in which one of the following rivers?

A. Jamuna B. Padma
C. Ganga D. Brahmaputra

99. Which one of the following Indian States has recorded negative growth of population as per Census 2011?

A. Manipur B. Mizoram
C. Tripura D. Nagaland

100. Which one of the following types of cloud is characterized by continuous precipitation?

A. Cirrocumulus B. Cumulus
C. Nimbostratus D. Cumulonimbus

101. Match List-I with List-II and select the correct answer using the code given below the Lists:

List-I (Major Port)	**List-II (Location)**
(*a*) Kolkata	1. Landlocked area
(*b*) Mormugao	2. In the delta region
(*c*) Visakhapatnam	3. On the riverside
(*d*) Paradip	4. On the entrance of the estuary

Code:

	(*a*)	(*b*)	(*c*)	(*d*)
A.	3	1	4	2
B.	3	4	1	2
C.	2	4	1	3
D.	2	1	4	3

102. Which one of the following is **not** an agent of metamorphism?

A. Heat B. Compression
C. Decomposition D. Solution

103. The solution of which one of the following will have pH less than 7?

A. NaOH B. KCl
C. $FeCl_3$ D. NaCl

104. Which one of the following is an oxidation-reduction reaction?

A. $NaOH + HCl \rightarrow NaCl + H_2O$
B. $CaO + H_2O \rightarrow Ca(OH)_2$
C. $2Mg + O_2 \rightarrow 2MgO$
D. $Na_2SO_4 + BaCl_2 \rightarrow BaSO_4 + 2NaCl$

105. Which one of the following is **not** used as fertilizer?

A. Ammonium nitrate
B. Ammonium sulphide
C. Ammonium phosphate
D. Ammonium sulphate

106. Which one of the following is the chemical formula of gypsum?

A. $CaSO_4.2H_2O$ B. Ca_2SiO_4
C. $2CaSO_4.H_2O$ D. $CaSO_4$

107. Which one of the following statements about the law of conservation of mass is correct?

A. A given compound always contains exactly same proportion of elements.
B. When gases combine in a reaction, they do so in a simple ratio by volume, provided all gases are at room temperature.
C. Matter can neither be created nor destroyed.
D. Equal volumes of all gases at same temperature and pressure contain equal number of molecules.

108. The wavelength of X-rays is of the order of

A. 1 Å B. 1 μm
C. 1 mm D. 1 cm

109. Consider the following velocity and itme graph:

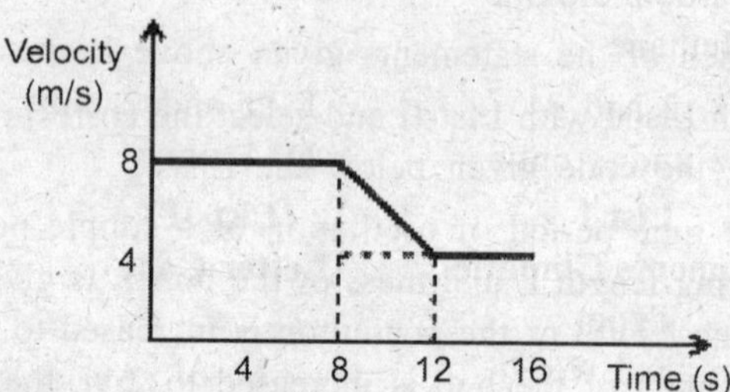

Which one of the following is the value of average acceleration from 8s to 12s?

A. 8 m/s^2 B. 12 m/s^2
C. 2 m/s^2 D. –1 m/s^2

110. If the focal length of a convex lens is 50 cm, which one of the following is its power?

A. +2 dioptre B. +0.02 dioptre
C. –0.5 dioptre D. +0.5 dioptre

111. A ball is released from rest and rolls down an inclined plane, as shown in the following figure, requiring 4s to cover a distance of 100 cm along the plane:

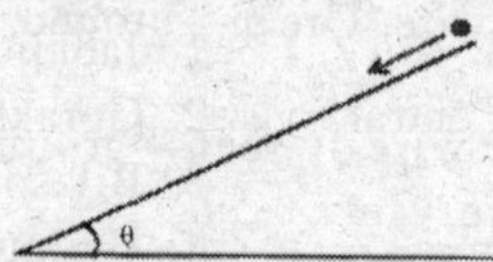

Which one of the following is the correct value of angle θ that the plane makes with the horizontal? (g = 1000 cm/s^2)

A. $\theta = \sin^{-1}\left(\frac{1}{9.8}\right)$ B. $\theta = \sin^{-1}\left(\frac{1}{20}\right)$

C. $\theta = \sin^{-1}\left(\frac{1}{80}\right)$ D. $\theta = \sin^{-1}\left(\frac{1}{100}\right)$

112. The coefficient of areal expansion of a material is 1.6×10^{-5} K^{-1}. Which one of the following gives the value of coefficient of volume expansion of this material?

A. 0.8×10^{-5} K^{-1} B. 2.4×10^{-5} K^{-1}
C. 3.2×10^{-5} K^{-1} D. 4.8×10^{-5} K^{-1}

113. The refractive indices of two media are denoted by n_1 and n_2, and the velocities of light in these two media are respectively v_1 and v_2. If n_2/n_1 is 1.5, which one of the following statements is correct?

A. v_1 is 1.5 times v_2
B. v_2 is 1.5 times v_1
C. v_1 is equal to v_2
D. v_1 is 3 times v_2

114. Which one of the following greenhouse gases is in largest concentration in the atmosphere?

A. Chlorofluorocarbon
B. Nitrous oxide
C. Carbon dioxide
D. Methane

115. Match List-I with List-II and select the correct answer using the code given below the Lists:

List-I (Koppen's Climatic Type)	List-II (Letter Code)
(*a*) Tropical wet	1. Af
(*b*) Mid-latitude desert	2. Cs
(*c*) Mediterranean	3. Df
(*d*) Humid continental	4. BWk

Code:

	(*a*)	(*b*)	(*c*)	(*d*)
A.	1	4	2	3
B.	1	2	4	3
C.	3	2	4	1
D.	3	4	2	1

116. Match List-I with List-II and select the correct answer using the code given below the Lists:

List-I (Railway Zone)	List-II (Headquarters)
(*a*) West Central	1. Jabalpur
(*b*) South East Central	2. Gorakhpur
(*c*) East Central	3. Bilaspur
(*d*) North Eastern	4. Hajipur

Code:

	(*a*)	(*b*)	(*c*)	(*d*)
A.	2	3	4	1
B.	1	4	3	2
C.	2	4	3	1
D.	1	3	4	2

117. Which one of the following is the correct descending order of Indian States in terms of sex ratio as per Census 2011?

A. Mizoram — Manipur — Tripura — Meghalaya
B. Tripura — Manipur — Meghalaya — Mizoram
C. Meghalaya — Manipur — Mizoram — Tripura
D. Manipur — Meghalaya — Tripura — Mizoram

118. Steppe (temperate continental) climate is **not** experienced in which one of the following places?

A. Pretoria
B. Saskatchewan
C. Perth
D. Buenos Aires

119. Which one of the following is **not** a process of chemical weathering?

A. Solution
B. Carbonation
C. Oxidation
D. Exfoliation

120. Which one of the following statements is correct for a plane mirror?

A. Its focal length is zero
B. The size of the image of an object placed in front of the mirror is slightly less than that of the object
C. The image is virtual, erect and laterally inverted
D. Its focal length is 200 cm

121. An object is placed in front of a convex mirror. Which one of the following statements is correct?

A. It will never form an inverted image
B. The image moves towards the focus when the object moves towards the mirror
C. Depending on the position of the object with respect to the mirror, the image can be inverted and real
D. The size of the image becomes larger than that of the object when the object is placed at a distance equal to half the focal length

122. A circular coil of radius R having N number of turns carries a steady current I. The magnetic induction at the centre of the coil is 0.1 tesla. If the number of turns is doubled and the radius is halved, which one of the following will be the correct value for the magnetic induction at the centre of the coil?

A. 0.05 tesla
B. 0.2 tesla
C. 0.4 tesla
D. 0.8 tesla

123. Which one among the following is **not** a Fundamental Right under the Constitution of India?

A. Right to equality
B. Right to freedom
C. Right to citizenship
D. Right against exploitation

124. Which one of the following crops was introduced by the Portuguese in India?

A. Opium
B. Coffee
C. Betel leaf
D. Chili

125. Consider the following statements about merchant guilds of South India:

1. Ayyavole merchant guild was originally established in Aihole.
2. Manigraman merchant guild was subordinated to the Anjuvannam merchant guild in the 13th century.

Which of the statements given above is/are correct?

A. 1 only
B. 2 only
C. Both 1 and 2
D. Neither 1 nor 2

126. Which one of the following pairs is correctly matched?

	Bhakti Saint		**Philosophy**
A.	Shankara	:	Avadhuta
B.	Ramananda	:	Kevaladvaita
C.	Ramanuja	:	Vishishtadvaita
D.	Chaitanya	:	Advaita

127. When did the Stamp Act Congress consisting of delegates from 9 of the 13 colonies of America meet in New York City?

A. 1763 B. 1764
C. 1765 D. 1766

128. Who among the following travellers was from Italy and visited Vijayanagar Kingdom in the fifteenth century?

A. Nikitin B. Fa-Hien
C. Bernier D. Nicolo Conti

129. Where did the French East India Company first establish its factory in India?

A. Calicut B. Surat
C. Pondicherry D. Masulipatnam

130. The Central Vigilance Commission was established on the recommendation of which one of the following Committees?

A. Santhanam Committee
B. Dinesh Goswami Committee
C. Tarkunde Committee
D. Narasimham Committee

131. Match List-I with List-II and select the correct answer using the code given below the Lists:

List-I (Author)	**List-II (Book)**
(*a*) Bal Gangadhar Tilak	1. *The Arctic Home in the Vedas*
(*b*) Dadabhai Naoroji	2. *Hind Swaraj*
(*c*) Mahatma Gandhi	3. *The Discovery of India*
(*d*) Jawaharlal Nehru	4. *Poverty and Un-British Rule in India*

Code:

	(*a*)	(*b*)	(*c*)	(*d*)
A.	3	4	2	1
B.	3	2	4	1
C.	1	4	2	3
D.	1	2	4	3

132. Which one of the following is the Official Mascot of the FIFA World Cup, 2018?

A. Fuleco B. Zakumi
C. Pille D. Zabivaka

133. The Headquarters of the proposed National Sports University (as per the National Sports University **Ordinance, 2018**) will be set up in

A. Chhattisgarh B. Manipur
C. Kerala D. West Bengal

134. Sentosa island, which was in news recently, is located in

A. Singapore B. China
C. Australia D. Sri Lanka

135. India, in June 2018, asserted that any mega connectivity project must respect sovereignty and territorial integrity of the countries. The project referred to above is

A. North-South Corridor Project
B. Belt and Road Initiative
C. Chabahar Port
D. Panama Canal Expansion

136. Who among the following is **not** a member of G7?

A. France B. Germany
C. Russia D. Japan

137. Who among the following leaders started the Indian Home Rule League?

A. Gopal Krishna Gokhale
B. Mahatma Gandhi
C. Bal Gangadhar Tilak
D. J.B. Kripalani

138. Every Judge of the Supreme Court of India is appointed by

A. the Supreme Court Collegium
B. the Cabinet
C. the President of India
D. the Lok Sabha

139. The Nehru-Mahalanobis Strategy of Development was implemented for the first time by which one of the following Five-year Plans?

A. First Five-Year Plan
B. Second Five-Year Plan
C. Third Five-Year Plan
D. Seventh Five-Year Plan

140. Which one of the following is **not** a part of the Directive Principles of State Policy as enshrined in the Constitution of India?

A. Equal justice and free legal aid
B. Protection of monuments and places and objects of national importance
C. Protection of personal law
D. Separation of Judiciary from Executive

141. The word 'socialist' was inserted into the Preamble to the Constitution of India through which one of the following Amendment Acts?

A. 41st Amendment Act
B. 42nd Amendment Act
C. 43rd Amendment Act
D. 44th Amendment Act

142. The place of English East India Company settlement in Madras was known as
A. Fort William
B. Fort St. George
C. Elphinstone Circle
D. Marble Palace

143. Which one of the following Indian States (other than Himalayan or NE States) ranked first in the Composite Water Management Index as per the report issued by the NITI Aayog in June 2018?
A. Madhya Pradesh B. Karnataka
C. Gujarat D. Maharashtra

144. Who among the following is the ex officio Chairman of the North Eastern Council?
A. The President of India
B. The Prime Minister of India
C. The Union Home Minister
D. The Union Minister of State (Independent Charge), Ministry of Development of North Eastern Region

145. Which one of the following is the theme of the World Blood Donor Day, 2018?
A. Blood connects us all
B. Be there for someone else. Give blood. Share life
C. Give blood. Give now. Give often
D. Thank you for saving my life

146. 'Seva Bhoj Yojana', a scheme of the Government of India that seeks to reimburse Central share of CGST and IGST on Food/Prasad/Langar/Bhandara offered by religious institutions, is introduced recently by which one of the following Ministries?
A. The Ministry of Culture
B. The Ministry of Home Affairs
C. The Ministry of Consumer Affairs, Food and Public Distribution
D. The Ministry of Social Justice and Empowerment

147. Dr. Bindeshwar Pathak, who was awarded Nikkei Asia Prize, 2018 for Culture and Community, is the founder of
A. Bachpan Bachao Andolan
B. PRS Legislative Research
C. Sulabh Sanitation and Social Reform Movement
D. Smile Foundation

148. Article 352 of the Constitution of India contains provisions related to
A. financial emergency
B. failure of constitutional machinery in States
C. suspension of the enforcement of rights conferred in Part III of the Constitution
D. general emergency

149. The Theosophical Society was led by
A. A.O. Hume B. Arthur Griffith
C. Annie Besant D. Lord Dufferin

150. Which one of the following statements about Bipin Chandra Pal is correct?
A. He was a member of the moderate group of Congress.
B. He was a member of the extremist group of Congress.
C. He was the Minister of Defence in the first Government of independent India.
D. He was the Chief Minister of West Bengal.

PAPER II : MATHEMATICS

1. What is the value of $\log_7 \log_7 \sqrt{7\sqrt{7\sqrt{7}}}$ equal to?
A. $3 \log_2 7$ B. $1 - 3 \log_2 7$
C. $1 - 3 \log_7 2$ D. $\frac{7}{8}$

2. If an infinite GP has the first term x and the sum 5, then which of the following is correct?
A. $x < -10$ B. $-10 < x < 0$
C. $0 < x < 10$ D. $x > 10$

3. Consider the following expressions:
1. $x + x^2 - \frac{1}{x}$
2. $\sqrt{ax^2 + bx + x - c + \frac{d}{x} - \frac{e}{x^2}}$
3. $3x^2 - 5x + ab$
4. $\frac{2}{x^2 - ax + b^3}$
5. $\frac{1}{x} - \frac{2}{x+5}$

Which of the above are rational expressions?
A. 1, 4 and 5 only B. 1, 3, 4 and 5 only
C. 2, 4 and 5 only D. 1 and 2 only

4. A square matrix A is called orthogonal if
A. $A = A^2$ B. $A' = A^{-1}$
C. $A = A^{-1}$ D. $A = A'$
Where A′ is the transpose of A.

5. If A, B and C are subsets of a Universal set, then which one of the following is **not** correct?
A. $A \cup (B \cap C) = (A \cup B) \cap (A \cup C)$
B. $A' \cup (A \cup B) = (B' \cap A)' \cup A$

C. $A' \cup (B \cup C) = (C' \cap B)' \cap A'$
D. $(A \cap B) \cup C = (A \cup C) \cap (B \cup C)$
Where A' is the complement of A.

6. Let x be the number of integers lying between 2999 and 8001 which have at least two digits equal. Then x is equal to
A. 2480 B. 2481
C. 2482 D. 2483

7. The sum of the series $3-1+\frac{1}{3}-\frac{1}{9}+....$ is equal to
A. $\frac{20}{9}$ B. $\frac{9}{20}$
C. $\frac{9}{4}$ D. $\frac{4}{9}$

Directions (Q. Nos. 8 and 9): *Consider the information given below and answer that follow:*

A survey was conducted among 300 students. It was found that 125 students like to play cricket, 145 students like to play football and 90 students like to play tennis. 32 students like to play exactly two games out of the three games.

8. How many students like to play all the three games?
A. 14 B. 21
C. 28 D. 35

9. How many students like to play exactly only one game?
A. 196 B. 228
C. 254 D. 268

10. If α and $\beta(\neq 0)$ are the roots of the quadratic equation $x^2 + \alpha x - \beta = 0$, then the quadratic expression $-x^2 + \alpha x + \beta$ where $x \in \mathbf{R}$ has
A. Least value $-\frac{1}{4}$
B. Least value $-\frac{9}{4}$
C. Greatest value $\frac{1}{4}$
D. Greatest value $\frac{9}{4}$

11. What is the coefficient of the middle term in the binomial expansion of $(2 + 3x)^4$?
A. 6 B. 12
C. 108 D. 216

12. For a square matrix A, which of the following properties hold?
1. $(A^{-1})^{-1} = A$
2. $\det(A^{-1}) = \frac{1}{\det A}$
3. $(\lambda A)^{-1} = \lambda A^{-1}$ where λ is a scalar

Select the correct answer using the code given below:
A. 1 and 2 only B. 2 and 3 only
C. 1 and 3 only D. 1, 2 and 3

13. Which one of the following factors does the expansions of the determinant $\begin{vmatrix} x & y & 3 \\ x^2 & 5y^3 & 9 \\ x^3 & 10y^5 & 27 \end{vmatrix}$ contain?
A. $x - 3$ B. $x - y$
C. $y - 3$ D. $x - 3y$

14. What is the adjoint of the matrix $\begin{pmatrix} \cos(-\theta) & -\sin(-\theta) \\ -\sin(-\theta) & \cos(-\theta) \end{pmatrix}$?
A. $\begin{pmatrix} \cos\theta & -\sin\theta \\ -\sin\theta & \cos\theta \end{pmatrix}$
B. $\begin{pmatrix} \cos\theta & \sin\theta \\ \sin\theta & \cos\theta \end{pmatrix}$
C. $\begin{pmatrix} \cos\theta & \sin\theta \\ -\sin\theta & \cos\theta \end{pmatrix}$
D. $\begin{pmatrix} \cos\theta & -\sin\theta \\ \sin\theta & \cos\theta \end{pmatrix}$

15. What is the value of
$$\left(\frac{-1+i\sqrt{3}}{2}\right)^{3n} + \left(\frac{-1-i\sqrt{3}}{2}\right)^{3n}$$
where $i = \sqrt{-1}$?
A. 3 B. 2
C. 1 D. 0

16. There are 17 cricket players, out of which 5 players can bowl. In how many ways can a team of 11 players be selected so as to include 3 bowlers?
A. C(17, 11)
B. C(12, 8)
C. C(17, 5) × C(5, 3)
D. C(5, 3) × C(12, 8)

17. What is the value of $\log_9 27 + \log_8 32$?
A. $\frac{7}{2}$ B. $\frac{19}{6}$
C. 4 D. 7

18. If A and B are two invertible square matrices of same order, then what is $(AB)^{-1}$ equal to?

A. $B^{-1}A^{-1}$ B. $A^{-1}B^{-1}$
C. $B^{-1}A$ D. $A^{-1}B$

19. If $a + b + c = 0$, then one of the solutions of

$$\begin{vmatrix} a-x & c & b \\ c & b-x & a \\ b & a & c-x \end{vmatrix} = 0 \text{ is}$$

A. $x = a$

B. $x = \sqrt{\frac{3(a^2+b^2+c^2)}{2}}$

C. $x = \sqrt{\frac{2(a^2+b^2+c^2)}{3}}$

D. $x = 0$

20. What should be the value of x so that the matrix $\begin{pmatrix} 2 & 4 \\ -8 & x \end{pmatrix}$ does not have an inverse?

A. 16 B. –16
C. 8 D. –8

21. The system of equations
$2x + y - 3z = 5$,
$3x - 2y + 2z = 5$ and
$5x - 3y - z = 16$
A. is inconsistent
B. is consistent, with a unique solution
C. is consistent, with infinitely many solutions
D. has its solution lying along x-axis in three-dimensional space

22. Which one of the following is correct in respect of the cube roots of unity?
A. They are collinear
B. They lie on a circle of radius $\sqrt{3}$
C. They form an equilateral triangle
D. None of the above

23. If u, v and w (all positive) are the pth, qth and rth terms of a GP, then the determinant of the matrix

$$\begin{pmatrix} \ln u & p & 1 \\ \ln v & q & 1 \\ \ln w & r & 1 \end{pmatrix} \text{ is}$$

A. 0
B. 1
C. $(p - q)(q - r)(r - p)$
D. $\ln u \times \ln v \times \ln w$

24. Let the coefficient of the middle term of the binomial expansion of $(1 + x)^{2n}$ be α and those of two middle terms of the binomial expansion of $(1 + x)^{2n-1}$ be β and γ. Which one of the following relations is correct?

A. $\alpha > \beta + \gamma$ B. $\alpha < \beta + \gamma$
C. $\alpha = \beta + \gamma$ D. $\alpha = \beta\gamma$

25. Let $A = [x \in \mathbf{R} : -1 \le x \le 1]$, $B = [y \in \mathbf{R} : -1 \le y \le 1]$ and S be the subset of $A \times B$, defined by $S = [(x, y) \in A \times B : x^2 + y^2 = 1]$.

Which one of the following is correct?
A. S is a one-one function from A into B
B. S is a many-one function from A into B
C. S is a bijective mapping from A into B
D. S is not a function

26. Let T_r be the rth term of an AP for $r = 1, 2, 3, \ldots$. If for some distinct positive integers m and n we have $T_m = 1/n$ and $T_n = 1/m$, then what is T_{mn} equal to?
A. $(mn)^{-1}$ B. $m^{-1} + n^{-1}$
C. 1 D. 0

27. Suppose $f(x)$ is such a quadratic expression that it is positive for all real x.

If $g(x) = f(x) + f'(x) + f''(x)$, then for any real x.
A. $g(x) < 0$ B. $g(x) > 0$
C. $g(x) = 0$ D. $g(x) \ge 0$

28. Consider the following in respect of matrices A, B and C of same order:
1. $(A + B + C)' = A' + B' + C'$
2. $(AB)' = A'B'$
3. $(ABC)' = C'B'A'$

where A' is the transpose of the matrix A.

Which of the above are correct?
A. 1 and 2 only B. 2 and 3 only
C. 1 and 3 only D. 1, 2 and 3

29. The sum of the binary numbers $(11011)_2$, $(10110110)_2$ and $(10011x0y)_2$ is the binary number $(101101101)_2$. What are the values of x and y?
A. $x = 1, y = 1$ B. $x = 1, y = 0$
C. $x = 0, y = 1$ D. $x = 0, y = 0$

30. Let matrix B be the adjoint of a square matrix A, l be the identity matrix of same order as A. If $k (\neq 0)$ is the determinant of the matrix A, then what is AB equal to?
A. l B. kl
C. k^2l D. $\left(\frac{1}{k}\right)l$

31. If $(0.2)^x = 2$ and $\log_{10} 2 = 0.3010$, then what is the value of x to the nearest tenth?
A. –10.0 B. –0.5
C. –0.4 D. –0.2

32. The total number of 5-digit numbers that can be composed of distinct digits from 0 to 9 is
A. 45360 B. 30240
C. 27216 D. 15120

33. What is the determinant of the matrix $\begin{pmatrix} x & y & y+z \\ z & x & z+x \\ y & z & x+y \end{pmatrix}$?

A. $(x-y)(y-z)(z-x)$
B. $(x-y)(y-z)$
C. $(y-z)(z-x)$
D. $(z-x)^2(x+y+z)$

34. If A, B and C are the angles of a triangle and

$$\begin{vmatrix} 1 & 1 & 1 \\ 1+\sin A & 1+\sin B & 1+\sin C \\ \sin A+\sin^2 A & \sin B+\sin^2 B & \sin C+\sin^2 C \end{vmatrix} = 0,$$

then which one of the following is correct?

A. The triangle ABC is isosceles
B. The triangle ABC is equilateral
C. The triangle ABC is scalene
D. No conclusion can be drawn with regard to the nature of the triangle

35. Consider the following in respect of matrices A and B of same order:

1. $A^2 - B^2 = (A + B)(A - B)$
2. $(A - I)(I + A) = O \Leftrightarrow A^2 = I$

where I is the identity matrix and O is the null matrix.

Which of the above is/are correct?

A. 1 only
B. 2 only
C. Both 1 and 2
D. Neither 1 nor 2

36. What is $\dfrac{2\tan\theta}{1+\tan^2\theta}$ equal to?

A. $\cos 2\theta$
B. $\tan 2\theta$
C. $\sin 2\theta$
D. $\operatorname{cosec} 2\theta$

37. If $\sec(\theta - \alpha)$, $\sec\theta$ and $\sec(\theta + \alpha)$ are in AP, where $\cos\alpha \neq 1$, then what is the value of $\sin^2\theta + \cos\alpha$?

A. 0
B. 1
C. –1
D. $\dfrac{1}{2}$

38. If $A + B + C = 180°$, then what is $\sin 2A - \sin 2B - \sin 2C$ equal to?

A. $-4 \sin A \sin B \sin C$
B. $-4 \cos A \sin B \cos C$
C. $-4 \cos A \cos B \sin C$
D. $-4 \sin A \cos B \cos C$

39. A balloon is directly above one end of a bridge. The angle of depression of the other end of the bridge from the balloon is 48°. If the height of the balloon above the bridge is 122 m, then what is the length of the bridge?

A. 122 sin 48° m
B. 122 tan 42° m
C. 122 cos 48° m
D. 122 tan 48° m

40. A is an angle in the fourth quadrant. If satisfies the trigonometric equation $3(3 - \tan^2 A - \cot A)^2 = 1$. Which one of the following is a value of A?

A. 300°
B. 315°
C. 330°
D. 345°

41. The top of a hill observed from the top and bottom of a building of height h is at angles of elevation $\dfrac{\pi}{6}$ and $\dfrac{\pi}{3}$ respectively. What is the height of the hill?

A. $2h$
B. $\dfrac{3h}{2}$
C. h
D. $\dfrac{h}{2}$

42. What is/are the solution(s) of the trigonometric equation $\operatorname{cosec} x + \cot x = \sqrt{3}$, where $0 < x < 2\pi$?

A. $\dfrac{5\pi}{3}$ only
B. $\dfrac{\pi}{3}$ only
C. π only
D. $\pi, \dfrac{\pi}{3}, \dfrac{5\pi}{3}$

43. If $\theta = \dfrac{\pi}{8}$, then what is the value of $(2\cos\theta + 1)^{10}$ $(2\cos 2\theta - 1)^{10}(2\cos\theta - 1)^{10}(2\cos 4\theta - 1)^{10}$?

A. 0
B. 1
C. 2
D. 4

44. If $\cos\alpha$ and $\cos\beta$ $(0 < \alpha < \beta < \pi)$ are the roots of the quadratic equation $4x^2 - 3 = 0$, then what is the value of $\sec\alpha \times \sec\beta$?

A. $-\dfrac{4}{3}$
B. $\dfrac{4}{3}$
C. $\dfrac{3}{4}$
D. $-\dfrac{3}{4}$

45. Consider the following values of x:

1. 8
2. –4
3. $\dfrac{1}{6}$
4. $-\dfrac{1}{4}$

Which of the above values of x is/are the solution(s) of the equation

$\tan^{-1}(2x) + \tan^{-1}(3x) = \dfrac{\pi}{4}$?

A. 3 only
B. 2 and 3 only
C. 1 and 4 only
D. 4 only

46. If the second term of a GP is 2 and the sum of its infinite terms is 8, then the GP is

A. $8, 2, \dfrac{1}{2}, \dfrac{1}{8}, ...$
B. $10, 2, \dfrac{2}{5}, \dfrac{2}{25}, ...$
C. $4, 2, 1, \dfrac{1}{2}, \dfrac{1}{2^2}, ...$
D. $6, 3, \dfrac{3}{2}, \dfrac{3}{4}, ...$

47. If a, b, c are in AP or GP or HP, then $\frac{a-b}{b-c}$ is equal to

A. $\frac{b}{a}$ or 1 or $\frac{b}{c}$

B. $\frac{c}{a}$ or $\frac{c}{b}$ or 1

C. 1 or $\frac{a}{b}$ or $\frac{a}{c}$

D. 1 or $\frac{a}{b}$ or $\frac{c}{a}$

48. What is the sum of all three-digit numbers that can be formed using all the digits 3, 4 and 5, when repetition of digits is **not** allowed?

A. 2664 B. 3882
C. 4044 D. 4444

49. The ratio of roots of the equations $ax^2 + bx + c = 0$ and $px^2 + qx + r = 0$ are equal. If D_1 and D_2 are respective discriminants, then what is $\frac{D_1}{D_2}$ equal to?

A. $\frac{a^2}{p^2}$ B. $\frac{b^2}{q^2}$

C. $\frac{c^2}{r^2}$ D. None of the above

50. If $A = \sin^2\theta + \cos^4\theta$, then for all real θ, which one of the following is correct?

A. $1 \le A \le 2$ B. $\frac{3}{4} \le A \le 1$

C. $\frac{13}{16} \le A \le 1$ D. $\frac{3}{4} \le A \le \frac{13}{16}$

51. The equation of a circle whose end points of a diameter are (x_1, y_1) and (x_2, y_2) is

A. $(x - x_1)(x - x_2) + (y - y_1)(y - y_2) = x^2 + y^2$
B. $(x - x_1)^2 + (y - y_1)^2 = x_2y_2$
C. $x^2 + y^2 + 2x_1x_2 + 2y_1y_2 = 0$
D. $(x - x_1)(x - x_2) + (y - y_1)(y - y_2) = 0$

52. The second degree equation $x^2 + 4y^2 - 2x - 4y + 2 = 0$ represents

A. A point
B. An ellipse of semi-major axis 1
C. An ellipse with eccentricity $\frac{\sqrt{3}}{2}$
D. None of the above

53. The angle between the two lines $lx + my + n = 0$ and $l'x + m'y + n' = 0$ is given by $\tan^{-1}\theta$. What is θ equal to?

A. $\left|\frac{lm' - l'm}{ll' - mm'}\right|$ B. $\left|\frac{lm' + l'm}{ll' + mm'}\right|$

C. $\left|\frac{lm' - l'm}{ll' + mm'}\right|$ D. $\left|\frac{lm' + l'm}{ll' - mm'}\right|$

54. Consider the following statements:

1. The distance between the lines $y = mx + c_1$ and $y = mx + c_2$ is $\frac{|c_1 - c_2|}{\sqrt{1+m^2}}$.
2. The distance between the lines $ax + by + c_1 = 0$ and $ax + by + c_2 = 0$ is $\frac{|c_1 - c_2|}{\sqrt{a^2 + b^2}}$.
3. The distance between the lines $x = c_1$ and $x = c_2$ is $|c_1 - c_2|$.

Which of the above statements are correct?

A. 1 and 2 only B. 2 and 3 only
C. 1 and 3 only D. 1, 2 and 3

55. What is the equation of straight line passing through the point of intersection of the lines $\frac{x}{2} + \frac{y}{3} = 1$ and $\frac{x}{3} + \frac{y}{2} = 1$, and parallel to the line $4x + 5y - 6 = 0$?

A. $20x + 25y - 54 = 0$
B. $25x + 20y - 54 = 0$
C. $4x + 5y - 54 = 0$
D. $4x + 5y - 45 = 0$

56. What is the distance of the point (2, 3, 4) from the plane $3x - 6y + 2z + 11 = 0$?

A. 1 unit B. 2 units
C. 3 units D. 4 units

57. Coordinates of the points O, P, Q and R are respectively (0, 0, 0), (4, 6, $2m$), (2, 0, $2n$) and (2, 4, 6). Let L, M, N and K be points on the sides OR, OP, PQ and QR respectively such that LMNK is a parallelogram whose two adjacent sides LK and LM are each of length $\sqrt{2}$. What are the values of m and n respectively?

A. 6, 2 B. 1, 3
C. 3, 1 D. None of the above

58. The line $\frac{x-1}{2} = \frac{y-2}{3} = \frac{z-3}{4}$ is given by

A. $x + y + z = 6$, $x + 2y - 3z = -4$
B. $x + 2y - 2z = -1$, $4x + 4y - 5z - 3 = 0$
C. $3x + 2y - 3z = 0$, $3x - 6y + 3z = -2$
D. $3x + 2y - 3z = -2$, $3x - 6y + 3z = 0$

59. Consider the following statements:

1. The angle between the planes $2x - y + z = 1$ and $x + y + 2z = 3$ is $\frac{\pi}{3}$.

2. The distance between the planes $6x - 3y + 6z + 2 = 0$ and $2x - y + 2z + 4 = 0$ is $\frac{10}{9}$.

Which of the above statements is/are correct?

A. 1 only B. 2 only
C. Both 1 and 2 D. Neither 1 nor 2

60. Consider the following statements:

Statement I: If the line segment joining the points P(m, n) and Q(r, s) subtends an angle α at the origin, then $\cos\alpha = \frac{ms - nr}{\sqrt{(m^2+n^2)(r^2+s^2)}}$.

Statements II: In any triangle ABC, it is true that $a^2 = b^2 + c^2 - 2bc \cos A$.

Which one of the following is correct in respect of the above two statements?

A. Both Statement I and Statement II are true and Statement II is the correct explanation of Statement I
B. Both Statement I and Statement II are true, but Statement II is not the correct explanation of Statement I
C. Statement I is true, but Statement II is false
D. Statement I is false, but Statement II is true

61. What is the area of the triangle with vertices $\left(x_1, \frac{1}{x_1}\right), \left(x_2, \frac{1}{x_2}\right), \left(x_3, \frac{1}{x_3}\right)$?

A. $|(x_1 - x_2)(x_2 - x_3)(x_3 - x_1)|$
B. 0
C. $\left|\frac{(x_1 - x_2)(x_2 - x_3)(x_3 - x_1)}{x_1x_2x_3}\right|$
D. $\left|\frac{(x_1 - x_2)(x_2 - x_3)(x_3 - x_1)}{2x_1x_2x_3}\right|$

62. If y-axis touches the circle $x^2 + y^2 + gx + fy + \frac{c}{4} = 0$, then the normal at this point intersects the circle at the point

A. $\left(-\frac{g}{2}, -\frac{f}{2}\right)$ B. $\left(-g, -\frac{f}{2}\right)$
C. $\left(-\frac{g}{2}, f\right)$ D. $(-g, -f)$

63. Let $|\vec{a}| \neq 0, |\vec{b}| \neq 0$.
$(\vec{a}+\vec{b})\cdot(\vec{a}+\vec{b}) = |\vec{a}|^2 + |\vec{b}|^2$
holds if and only if

A. $\vec{a}$ and $\vec{b}$ are perpendicular
B. $\vec{a}$ and $\vec{b}$ are parallel
C. $\vec{a}$ and $\vec{b}$ are inclined at an angle of 45°
D. $\vec{a}$ and $\vec{b}$ are anti-parallel

64. If $\vec{r} = x\hat{i} + y\hat{j} + z\hat{k}$, then what is $\vec{r}\cdot(\hat{i}+\hat{j}+\hat{k})$ equal to?

A. x B. $x + y$
C. $-(x + y + z)$ D. $(x + y + z)$

65. A unit vector perpendicular to each of the vectors $2\hat{i} - \hat{j} + \hat{k}$ and $3\hat{i} - 4\hat{j} - \hat{k}$ is

A. $\frac{1}{\sqrt{3}}\hat{i} + \frac{1}{\sqrt{3}}\hat{j} - \frac{1}{\sqrt{3}}\hat{k}$
B. $\frac{1}{\sqrt{2}}\hat{i} + \frac{1}{2}\hat{j} + \frac{1}{2}\hat{k}$
C. $\frac{1}{\sqrt{3}}\hat{i} - \frac{1}{\sqrt{3}}\hat{j} - \frac{1}{\sqrt{3}}\hat{k}$
D. $\frac{1}{\sqrt{3}}\hat{i} + \frac{1}{\sqrt{3}}\hat{j} + \frac{1}{\sqrt{3}}\hat{k}$

66. If $|\vec{a}| = 3$, $|\vec{b}| = 4$ and $|\vec{a} - \vec{b}| = 5$, then what is the value of $|\vec{a} + \vec{b}|$?

A. 8 B. 6
C. $5\sqrt{2}$ D. 5

67. Let $\vec{a}, \vec{b}$ and $\vec{c}$ be three mutually perpendicular vectors each of unit magnitude. If $\vec{A} = \vec{a} + \vec{b} + \vec{c}$, $\vec{B} = \vec{a} - \vec{b} + \vec{c}$ and $\vec{C} = \vec{a} - \vec{b} - \vec{c}$, then which one of the following is correct?

A. $|\vec{A}| > |\vec{B}| > |\vec{C}|$
B. $|\vec{A}| = |\vec{B}| \neq |\vec{C}|$
C. $|\vec{A}| = |\vec{B}| = |\vec{C}|$
D. $|\vec{A}| \neq |\vec{B}| \neq |\vec{C}|$

68. What is $(\vec{a} - \vec{b}) \times (\vec{a} + \vec{b})$ equal to?

A. $\vec{0}$ B. $\vec{a} \times \vec{b}$
C. $2(\vec{a} \times \vec{b})$ D. $|\vec{a}|^2 - |\vec{b}|^2$

69. A spacecraft located at $\hat{i} + 2\hat{j} + 3\hat{k}$ is subjected to a force $\lambda\hat{k}$ by firing a rocket. The spacecraft is subjected to a moment of magnitude

A. λ B. $\sqrt{3}\lambda$
C. $\sqrt{5}\lambda$ D. None of the above

70. In a triangle ABC, if taken in order, consider the following statements:

1. $\overrightarrow{AB}+\overrightarrow{BC}+\overrightarrow{CA}=\vec{0}$
2. $\overrightarrow{AB}+\overrightarrow{BC}-\overrightarrow{CA}=\vec{0}$
3. $\overrightarrow{AB}-\overrightarrow{BC}+\overrightarrow{CA}=\vec{0}$
4. $\overrightarrow{BA}-\overrightarrow{BC}+\overrightarrow{CA}=\vec{0}$

How many of the above statements are correct?

A. One B. Two
C. Three D. Four

71. Let the slope of the curve $y = \cos^{-1}(\sin x)$ be $\tan\theta$. Then the value of θ in the interval (0, π) is

A. $\frac{\pi}{6}$ B. $\frac{3\pi}{4}$
C. $\frac{\pi}{4}$ D. $\frac{\pi}{2}$

72. If $f(x) = \frac{\sqrt{x-1}}{x-4}$ defines a function on **R**, then what is its domain?

A. $(-\infty, 4) \cup (4, \infty)$ B. $[4, \infty)$
C. $(1, 4) \cup (4, \infty)$ D. $[1, 4) \cup (4, \infty)$

73. Consider the function

$$f(x) = \begin{cases} \frac{\sin 2x}{5x} & \text{if } x \neq 0 \\ \frac{2}{15} & \text{if } x = 0 \end{cases}$$

Which one of the following is correct in respect of the function?

A. It is not continuous at $x = 0$
B. It is continuous at every x
C. It is not continuous at $x = \pi$
D. It is continuous at $x = 0$

74. For the function $f(x) = |x - 3|$, which one of the following is **not** correct?

A. The function is not continuous at $x = -3$
B. The function is continuous at $x = 3$
C. The function is differentiable at $x = 0$
D. The function is differentiable at $x = -3$

75. If the function $f(x) = \frac{2x - \sin^{-1} x}{2x + \tan^{-1} x}$ is continuous at each point in its domain, then what is the value of $f(0)$?

A. $-\frac{1}{3}$ B. $\frac{1}{3}$
C. $\frac{2}{3}$ D. 2

76. If $f(x) = \sqrt{25 - x^2}$, then what is $\lim_{x\to 1} \frac{f(x) - f(1)}{x - 1}$ equal to?

A. $-\frac{1}{\sqrt{24}}$ B. $\frac{1}{\sqrt{24}}$
C. $-\frac{1}{4\sqrt{3}}$ D. $\frac{1}{4\sqrt{3}}$

77. If $y = \tan^{-1}\left(\frac{5 - 2\tan\sqrt{x}}{2 + 5\tan\sqrt{x}}\right)$, then what is $\frac{dy}{dx}$ equal to?

A. $-\frac{1}{2\sqrt{x}}$ B. 1
C. −1 D. $\frac{1}{2\sqrt{x}}$

78. Which one of the following is correct in respect of the function

$f(x) = x \sin x + \cos x + \frac{1}{2}\cos^2 x$?

A. It is increasing in the interval $\left(0, \frac{\pi}{2}\right)$
B. It remains constant in the interval $\left(0, \frac{\pi}{2}\right)$
C. It is decreasing in the interval $\left(0, \frac{\pi}{2}\right)$
D. It is decreasing in the interval $\left(\frac{\pi}{4}, \frac{\pi}{2}\right)$

79. What is $\lim_{\theta\to 0} \frac{\sqrt{1 - \cos\theta}}{\theta}$ equal to?

A. $\sqrt{2}$ B. $2\sqrt{2}$
C. $\frac{1}{\sqrt{2}}$ D. $-\frac{1}{2\sqrt{2}}$

80. A function $f : A \to \mathbf{R}$ is defined by the equation $f(x) = x^2 - 4x + 5$ where A = (1, 4). What is the range of the function?

A. (2, 5) B. (1, 5)
C. [1, 5) D. [1, 5]

81. What is $\int_a^b [x]dx + \int_a^b [-x]\,dx$ equal to, where [.] is the greatest integer function?

A. $b - a$ B. $a - b$
C. 0 D. $2(b - a)$

82. What is $\int_2^8 |x - 5|\,dx$ equal to?

A. 2 B. 3
C. 4 D. 9

83. What is $\int \sin^3 x \cos x \, dx$ equal to?

A. $\cos^4 x + c$ B. $\sin^4 x + c$

C. $\frac{(1-\sin^2 x)^2}{4}+c$ D. $\frac{(1-\cos^2 x)^2}{4}+c$

where c is the constant of integration.

84. What is $\int e^{\ln(\tan x)} dx$ equal to?

A. $\ln|\tan x| + c$ B. $\ln|\sec x| + c$

C. $\tan x + c$ D. $e^{\tan x} + c$

where c is the constant of integration.

85. What is $\int_{-1}^{1}\left\{\frac{d}{dx}\left(\tan^{-1}\frac{1}{x}\right)\right\}dx$ equal to?

A. 0 B. $-\frac{\pi}{4}$

C. $-\frac{\pi}{2}$ D. $\frac{\pi}{2}$

86. In which one of the following intervals is the function $f(x) = x^2 - 5x + 6$ decreasing?

A. $(-\infty, 2]$ B. $[3, \infty)$

C. $(-\infty, \infty)$ D. $(2, 3)$

87. The differential equation of the family of curves $y = p\cos(ax) + q\sin(ax)$, where p, q are arbitrary constants, is

A. $\frac{d^2y}{dx^2} - a^2y = 0$ B. $\frac{d^2y}{dx^2} - ay = 0$

C. $\frac{d^2y}{dx^2} + ay = 0$ D. $\frac{d^2y}{dx^2} + a^2y = 0$

88. The equation of the curve passing through the point $(-1, -2)$ which satisfies $\frac{dy}{dx} = -x^2 - \frac{1}{x^3}$, is

A. $17x^2y - 6x^2 + 3x^5 - 2 = 0$

B. $6x^2y + 17x^2 + 2x^5 - 3 = 0$

C. $6xy - 2x^2 + 17x^5 + 3 = 0$

D. $17x^2y + 6xy - 3x^5 + 5 = 0$

89. What is the order of the differential equation whose solution is

$y = a\cos x + b\sin x + ce^{-x} + d$, where a, b, c and d are arbitrary constants?

A. 1 B. 2

C. 3 D. 4

90. What is the solution of the differential equation $\ln\left(\frac{dy}{dx}\right) = ax + by$?

A. $a\,e^{ax} + b\,e^{by} = c$

B. $\frac{1}{a}e^{ax} + \frac{1}{b}e^{by} = c$

C. $a\,e^{ax} + b\,e^{-by} = c$

D. $\frac{1}{a}e^{ax} + \frac{1}{b}e^{-by} = c$

where c is an arbitrary constant.

91. If $u = e^{ax}\sin bx$ and $v = e^{ax}\cos bx$, then what is $u\frac{du}{dx} + v\frac{dv}{dx}$ equal to?

A. $a\,e^{2ax}$ B. $(a^2 + b^2)\,e^{ax}$

C. $ab\,e^{2ax}$ D. $(a + b)e^{ax}$

92. If $y = \sin(\ln x)$, then which one of the following is correct?

A. $\frac{d^2y}{dx^2} + y = 0$

B. $\frac{d^2y}{dx^2} = 0$

C. $x^2\frac{d^2y}{dx^2} + x\frac{dy}{dx} + y = 0$

D. $x^2\frac{d^2y}{dx^2} - x\frac{dy}{dx} + y = 0$

93. A flower-bed in the form of a sector has been fenced by a wire of 40 m length. If the flower-bed has the greatest possible area, then what is the radius of the sector?

A. 25 m B. 20 m

C. 10 m D. 5 m

94. What is the minimum value of $[x(x-1)+1]^{\frac{1}{3}}$, where $0 \le x \le 1$?

A. $\left(\frac{3}{4}\right)^{\frac{1}{3}}$ B. 1

C. $\frac{1}{2}$ D. $\left(\frac{3}{8}\right)^{-\frac{1}{3}}$

95. If $y = |\sin x|^{|x|}$, then what is the value of $\frac{dy}{dx}$ at $x = -\frac{\pi}{6}$?

A. $\frac{2^{-\frac{\pi}{6}}(6\ln 2 - \sqrt{3}\pi)}{6}$

B. $\frac{2^{\frac{\pi}{6}}(6\ln 2 + \sqrt{3}\pi)}{6}$

C. $\frac{2^{-\frac{\pi}{6}}(6\ln 2 + \sqrt{3}\pi)}{6}$

D. $\frac{2^{\frac{\pi}{6}}(6\ln 2 - \sqrt{3}\pi)}{6}$

96. What is $\frac{d\sqrt{1-\sin 2x}}{dx}$ equal to, where $\frac{\pi}{4} < x < \frac{\pi}{2}$?

A. $\cos x + \sin x$
B. $-(\cos x + \sin x)$
C. $\pm(\cos x + \sin x)$
D. None of the above

97. What is $\int \frac{dx}{a^2 \sin^2 x + b^2 \cos^2 x}$ equal to?

A. $c + \frac{1}{ab}\tan^{-1}\left(\frac{a \tan x}{b}\right)$

B. $c - \frac{1}{ab}\tan^{-1}\left(\frac{b \tan x}{a}\right)$

C. $c + \frac{1}{ab}\tan^{-1}\left(\frac{b \tan x}{a}\right)$

D. None of the above

where c is the constant of integration.

98. Let $f(x + y) = f(x) f(y)$ and $f(x) = 1 + xg(x)\phi(x)$, where $\lim_{x\to 0} g(x) = a$ and $\lim_{x\to 0} \phi(x) = b$. Then what is $f'(x)$ equal to?

A. $1 + abf(x)$
B. $1 + ab$
C. ab
D. $abf(x)$

99. What is the solution of the differential equation $\frac{dx}{dy} = \frac{x+y+1}{x+y-1}$?

A. $y - x + 4 \ln (x + y) = c$
B. $y + x + 2 \ln (x + y) = c$
C. $y - x + \ln (x + y) = c$
D. $y + x + 2 \ln (x + y) = c$

where c is an arbitrary constant.

100. What is $\lim_{x\to\frac{\pi}{6}} \frac{2\sin^2 x + \sin x - 1}{2\sin^2 x - 3\sin x + 1}$ equal to?

A. $-\frac{1}{2}$
B. $-\frac{1}{3}$
C. -2
D. -3

101. If two dice are thrown and at least one of the dice shows 5, then the probability that the sum is 10 or more is

A. $\frac{1}{6}$
B. $\frac{4}{11}$
C. $\frac{3}{11}$
D. $\frac{2}{11}$

102. The correlation coefficient computed from a set of 30 observations is 0.8. Then the percentage of variation not explained by linear regression is

A. 80%
B. 20%
C. 64%
D. 36%

103. The average age of a combined group of men and women is 25 years. If the average age of the group of men is 26 years and that of the group of women is 21 years, then the percentage of men and women in the group is respectively

A. 20, 80
B. 40, 60
C. 60, 40
D. 80, 20

104. If $\sin \beta$ is the harmonic mean of $\sin \alpha$ and $\cos \alpha$, and $\sin \theta$ is the arithmetic mean of $\sin \alpha$ and $\cos \alpha$, then which of the following is/are correct?

1. $\sqrt{2} \sin\left(\alpha + \frac{\pi}{4}\right) \sin\beta = \sin 2\alpha$
2. $\sqrt{2} \sin\theta = \cos\left(\alpha - \frac{\pi}{4}\right)$

Select the correct answer using the code given below:

A. 1 only
B. 2 only
C. Both 1 and 2
D. Neither 1 nor 2

105. Let A, B and C be three mutually exclusive and exhaustive events associated with a random experiment. If $P(B) = 1.5\,P(A)$ and $P(C) = 0.5\,P(B)$, then $P(A)$ is equal to

A. $\frac{3}{4}$
B. $\frac{4}{13}$
C. $\frac{2}{3}$
D. $\frac{1}{2}$

106. In a bolt factory, machines X, Y, Z manufacture bolts that are respectively 25%, 35% and 40% of the factory's total output. The machines X, Y, Z respectively produce 2%, 4% and 5% defective bolts. A bolt is drawn at random from the product and is found to be defective. What is the probability that it was manufactured by machine X?

A. $\frac{5}{39}$
B. $\frac{14}{39}$
C. $\frac{20}{39}$
D. $\frac{34}{39}$

107. 8 coins are tossed simultaneously. The probability of getting at least 6 heads is

A. $\frac{7}{64}$
B. $\frac{57}{64}$
C. $\frac{37}{256}$
D. $\frac{229}{256}$

108. Three groups of children contain 3 girls and 1 boy; 2 girls and 2 boys; 1 girl and 3 boys. One child is selected at random from each group. The probability that the three selected consist of 1 girl and 2 boys is

A. $\frac{13}{32}$ B. $\frac{9}{32}$

C. $\frac{3}{32}$ D. $\frac{1}{32}$

109. Consider the following statements:

1. If 10 is added to each entry on a list, then the average increases by 10.
2. If 10 is added to each entry on a list, then the standard deviation increases by 10.
3. If each entry on a list is doubled, then the average doubles.

Which of the above statements are correct?

A. 1, 2 and 3 B. 1 and 2 only

C. 1 and 3 only D. 2 and 3 only

110. The variance of 25 observations is 4. If 2 is added to each observation, then the new variance of the resulting observations is

A. 2 B. 4

C. 6 D. 8

111. If $x_i > 0$, $y_i > 0$ $(i = 1, 2, 3, ... n)$ are the values of two variables X and Y with geometric means P and Q respectively, then the geometric mean of $\frac{X}{Y}$ is

A. $\frac{P}{Q}$ B. antilog $\left(\frac{P}{Q}\right)$

C. $n(\log P - \log Q)$ D. $n(\log P + \log Q)$

112. If the probability of simultaneous occurrence of two events A and B is p and the probability that exactly one of A, B occurs is q, then which of the following is/are correct?

1. $P(\bar{A}) + P(\bar{B}) = 2 - 2p - q$
2. $P(\bar{A} \cap \bar{B}) = 1 - p - q$

Select the correct answer using the code given below:

A. 1 only B. 2 only

C. Both 1 and 2 D. Neither 1 nor 2

113. If the regression coefficient of Y on X is –6, and the correlation coefficient between X and Y is $-\frac{1}{2}$, then the regression coefficient of X on Y would be

A. $\frac{1}{24}$ B. $-\frac{1}{24}$

C. $-\frac{1}{6}$ D. $\frac{1}{6}$

114. The set of bivariate observations (x_1, y_1), (x_2, y_2), ... (x_n, y_n) are such that all the values are distinct and all the observations fall on a straight line with non-zero slope. Then the possible values of the correlation coefficient between x and y are

A. 0 and 1 only B. 0 and –1 only

C. 0, 1 and –1 D. –1 and 1 only

115. Two integers x and y are chosen with replacement from the set [0, 1, 2, ..., 10]. The probability that $|x - y| > 5$ is

A. $\frac{6}{11}$ B. $\frac{35}{121}$

C. $\frac{30}{121}$ D. $\frac{25}{121}$

116. An analysis of monthly wages paid to the workers in two firms A and B belonging to the same industry gives the following result:

	Firm A	Firm B
Number of workers	500	600
Average monthly wage	₹ 1860	₹ 1750
Variance of distribution of wages	81	100

The average of monthly wages and variance of distribution of wages of all the workers in the firms A and B taken together are

A. ₹ 1860, 100

B. ₹ 1750, 100

C. ₹ 1800, 81

D. None of the above

117. Three dice having digits 1, 2, 3, 4, 5 and 6 on their faces are marked I, II and III and rolled. Let x, y and z represent the number on die-I, die-II and die-III respectively. What is the number of possible outcomes such that $x > y > z$?

A. 14 B. 16

C. 18 D. 20

118. Which one of the following can be obtained from an ogive?

A. Mean B. Median

C. Geometric mean D. Mode

119. In any discrete series (when all values are not same) if x represents mean deviation about mean and y represents standard deviation, then which one of the following is correct?

A. $y \geq x$ B. $y \leq x$

C. $x = y$ D. $x < y$

120. In which one of the following cases would you except to get a negative correlation?

A. The ages of husbands and wives

B. Shoe size and intelligence

C. Insurance companies' profits and the number of claims they have to pay

D. Amount of rainfall and yield of crop

ANSWERS

PAPER I : GENERAL ABILITY TEST

1	2	3	4	5	6	7	8	9	10
C	B	C	B	C	A	B	B	C	A
11	12	13	14	15	16	17	18	19	20
C	D	D	C	B	C	B	C	A	C
21	22	23	24	25	26	27	28	29	30
C	B	A	D	C	C	B	A	A	C
31	32	33	34	35	36	37	38	39	40
A	C	B	B	A	B	A	C	D	C
41	42	43	44	45	46	47	48	49	50
D	C	B	A	B	A	C	D	D	A
51	52	53	54	55	56	57	58	59	60
B	A	A	A	B	C	A	D	A	C
61	62	63	64	65	66	67	68	69	70
A	B	D	C	C	C	D	A	C	B
71	72	73	74	75	76	77	78	79	80
A	B	A	B	B	D	B	C	A	D
81	82	83	84	85	86	87	88	89	90
D	A	A	A	A	B	D	B	C	B
91	92	93	94	95	96	97	98	99	100
B	C	B	D	C	B	C	D	D	D
101	102	103	104	105	106	107	108	109	110
B	C	C	C	B	A	C	A	D	A
111	112	113	114	115	116	117	118	119	120
C	B	A	C	A	D	C	C	D	C
121	122	123	124	125	126	127	128	129	130
A	C	C	D	C	C	C	D	B	A
131	132	133	134	135	136	137	138	139	140
C	D	B	A	B	C	C	C	B	C
141	142	143	144	145	146	147	148	149	150
B	B	C	C	A	A	C	C	C	B

PAPER II : MATHEMATICS

1	2	3	4	5	6	7	8	9	10
C	C	A	B	C	B	C	A	C	D
11	12	13	14	15	16	17	18	19	20
D	A	A	A	B	D	B	A	D	B
21	22	23	24	25	26	27	28	29	30
B	C	A	C	D	C	B	C	B	B
31	32	33	34	35	36	37	38	39	40
C	C	D	B	B	C	A	D	B	A
41	42	43	44	45	46	47	48	49	50
B	B	B	A	A	C	C	A	B	B
51	52	53	54	55	56	57	58	59	60
D	A	C	B	A	A	C	B	C	D

61	62	63	64	65	66	67	68	69	70
D	B	A	D	A	D	C	C	C	A
71	**72**	**73**	**74**	**75**	**76**	**77**	**78**	**79**	**80**
B	D	A	A	B	A	A	A	C	C
81	**82**	**83**	**84**	**85**	**86**	**87**	**88**	**89**	**90**
B	D	D	B	C	A	D	B	D	D
91	**92**	**93**	**94**	**95**	**96**	**97**	**98**	**99**	**100**
A	C	C	A	A	A	A	D	C	D
101	**102**	**103**	**104**	**105**	**106**	**107**	**108**	**109**	**110**
C	B	D	C	B	A	C	A	C	B
111	**112**	**113**	**114**	**115**	**116**	**117**	**118**	**119**	**120**
A	C	B	D	C	D	D	B	D	C

EXPLANATORY ANSWERS

PAPER II : MATHEMATICS

1. $$\sqrt{7\sqrt{7\sqrt{7}}} = 7^{\frac{2^3-1}{2^3}} = 7^{\frac{7}{8}}$$

$$\therefore \quad \log_7 \log_7 \sqrt{7\sqrt{7\sqrt{7}}} = \log_7 \log_7 (7)^{\frac{7}{8}}$$

$$= \log_7 \left[\frac{7}{8}\log_7 7\right]$$

$$= \log_7 \frac{7}{8} = \log_7 7 - \log_7 8$$

$$= 1 - \log_7 (2)^3 = 1 - 3\log_7 2.$$

2. We know that,

Sum of infinite GP $= \dfrac{a}{1-r}$ where $|r| < |$

$$5 = \frac{x}{1-r}$$

$$\frac{x}{5} = 1 - r$$

$$r = 1 - \frac{x}{5}$$

$$\because \quad |r| < 1$$

$$-1 < r < 1$$

$$-1 < 1 - \frac{x}{5} < 1$$

$$-2 < -\frac{x}{5} < 0$$

$$-10 < -x < 0$$

$$0 < x < 10.$$

5. Checking through option

(*a*) $A \cup (B \cap C)$ $\quad (A \cup B) \cap (A \cup C)$

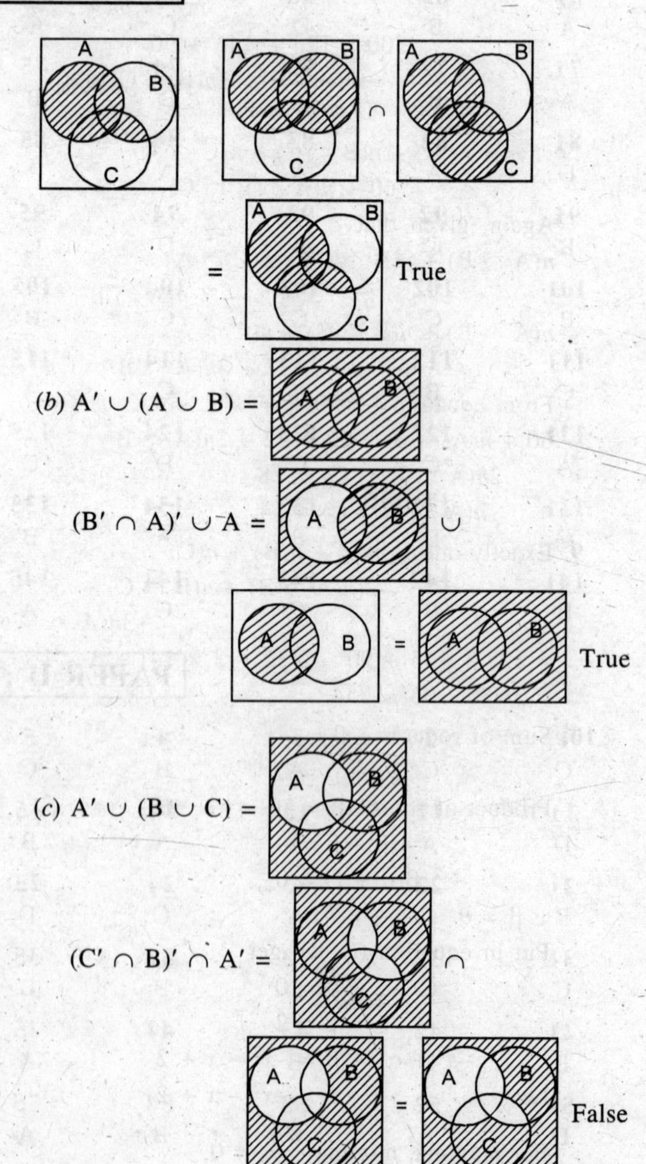

6. The no. with all distinct digits

$= 5 \times 9 \times 8 \times 7 = 2520$

$\therefore \quad x = 5001 - 2520$

$= 2481.$

7. $3 - 1 + \frac{1}{3} - \frac{1}{9} +$ .... is an infinite G.P. series.

Sum of infinite GP $= \frac{a}{1-r}$ where $| r | < |$

$a = 3, \ r = -\frac{1}{3}$

$\text{Sum} = \frac{3}{1-\left(-\frac{1}{3}\right)} = \frac{9}{4}.$

8. We know

$n(A \cup B \cup C) = n(A) + n(B) + n(C) - n(A \cap B) - n(B \cap C) - n(C \cap A) + n(A \cap B \cap C)$

$300 = 125 + 145 + 90 - (n(A \cap B) + n(B \cap C) + n(C \cap A)) + n(A \cap B \cap C)$

$\therefore n(A \cap B) + n(B \cap C) + n(C \cap A) = 60 + n(A \cap B \cap C)$ ...(*i*)

Again, given that

$n(A \cap B) + n(B \cap C) + n(C \cap A) - 3\, n(A \cap B \cap C) = 32$

$n(A \cap B) + n(B \cap C) + n(C \cap A) = 32 + 3n(A \cap B \cap C)$ ...(*ii*)

From equation (*i*) and (*ii*)

$60 + n(A \cap B \cap C) = 32 + 3n(A \cap B \cap C)$

$2n(A \cap B \cap C) = 28$

$n(A \cap B \cap C) = 14.$

9. Exactly one $= n(A) + n(B) + n(C) - 2[n(A \cap B) + n(B \cap C) + n(C \cap A)] + 3n(A \cap B \cap C)$

$= 125 + 145 + 90 - 2[32 + 3 \times 14] + 3 \times 14$

$= 360 - 106 = 254.$

10. Sum of roots $\alpha + \beta = -\alpha$

$2\alpha + \beta = 0$ ...(*i*)

Product of roots $\alpha\beta = -\beta$

$\alpha\beta + \beta = 0$

$\beta(\alpha + 1) = 0$

$\because \beta \neq 0, \quad \therefore \alpha = -1$

Put in equation (*i*), we get

$-2 + \beta = 0$

$\beta = 2$

$\therefore \quad -x^2 + \alpha x + \beta = -x^2 - x + 2$

Let $\quad \Delta = -x^2 - x + 2$ ...(*ii*)

For maxima, minima $\frac{d\Delta}{dx} = 0,$

$-2x - 1 = 0$

$x = -\frac{1}{2}$

$\because \quad \frac{d^2\Delta}{dx^2} = -2 \ (-\text{Ve})$

So, we get maxima at $x = -\frac{1}{2}$

Put equation (*ii*) we get,

$= -\left(-\frac{1}{2}\right)^2 - \left(-\frac{1}{2}\right) + 2 = -\frac{1}{4} + \frac{1}{2} + 2 = \frac{9}{4}.$

11. Coefficient of the middle term

$= {}^4C_2(2)^2 \times (3)^2$

$= 6 \times 4 \times 9 = 216.$

13. We have,

$\begin{vmatrix} x & y & 3 \\ x^2 & 5y^3 & 9 \\ x^3 & 10y^5 & 27 \end{vmatrix}$ Apply $C_1 \to C_1 - C_3$ we get

$\begin{vmatrix} x-3 & y & 3 \\ x^2-9 & 5y^3 & 9 \\ x^3-27 & 10y^5 & 27 \end{vmatrix} = (x-3)$

$\begin{vmatrix} 1 & y & 3 \\ x+3 & 5y^3 & 9 \\ x^2+9+3x & 10y^5 & 27 \end{vmatrix}$

$\therefore x - 3$ is a factor of the given determinant.

14. We have, $A = \begin{bmatrix} \cos(-\theta) & -\sin(-\theta) \\ -\sin(-\theta) & \cos(-\theta) \end{bmatrix}$

$A = \begin{bmatrix} \cos\theta & +\sin\theta \\ +\sin\theta & \cos\theta \end{bmatrix}$

$\text{Adj } A = \begin{bmatrix} \cos\theta & -\sin\theta \\ -\sin\theta & \cos\theta \end{bmatrix}$

15. $\because \quad w = \frac{-1+i\sqrt{3}}{2}$ and $w^2 = \frac{-1-i\sqrt{3}}{2}$

Then, $\quad = (w)^{3n} + (w^2)^{3n}$

$= (w^3)^n + (w^3)^{2n}$ $\quad [\because w^3 = 1]$

$= (1)^n + (1)^{2n}$

$= 1 + 1 = 2.$

16. In 17 cricket player, Bowler = 5, other = 12

So, we can choose 3 bowler out of 5 bowler and rest player (11 – 3 = 8) from other 12 players.

$\therefore$ Required No. of ways $= {}^{12}C_3 \times {}^5C_3$

$= C(5, 3) \times C(12, 3).$

17. We have $\log_9 27 + \log_8 32$

$= \log_{3^2}(3)^2 + \log_{2^3}(2^5)$

$$\left[\log(a^n)^b = \frac{1}{n}\log_a b \log(a)^b = b\log a\right]$$

$= \frac{3}{2}\log_3 3 + \frac{5}{3}\log_2 2$

$= \frac{3}{2} + \frac{5}{3} = \frac{9+10}{6} = \frac{19}{6}.$

19. $\begin{vmatrix} a-x & c & b \\ c & b-x & a \\ b & a & c-x \end{vmatrix} = 0$

Apply $C_1 \to C_1 + C_2 + C_3$ we get

$(a+b+c-x)\begin{vmatrix} 1 & c & b \\ 1 & b-x & a \\ 1 & a & c-x \end{vmatrix} = 0$

$\because \begin{vmatrix} 1 & c & b \\ 1 & b-x & a \\ 1 & a & c-x \end{vmatrix} \neq 0$

$\therefore \quad (a+b+c-x) = 0$

Given that $a + b + c = 0$

$\therefore \quad x = 0.$

20. Matrix does not have an inverse if $|A| = 0$

$\therefore \begin{vmatrix} 2 & 4 \\ -8 & x \end{vmatrix} = 0$

$2x + 32 = 0$

$x = -16.$

21. Since $\begin{vmatrix} 2 & 1 & -3 \\ 3 & -2 & 2 \\ 5 & -3 & -1 \end{vmatrix} = 26 \neq 0$

$\therefore$ System is consistent with unique solution.

22. Cube roots of unity 1, $w\left(-\frac{1}{2}, \frac{\sqrt{3}}{2}\right)$, $w^2\left(-\frac{1}{2}, -\frac{\sqrt{3}}{2}\right)$

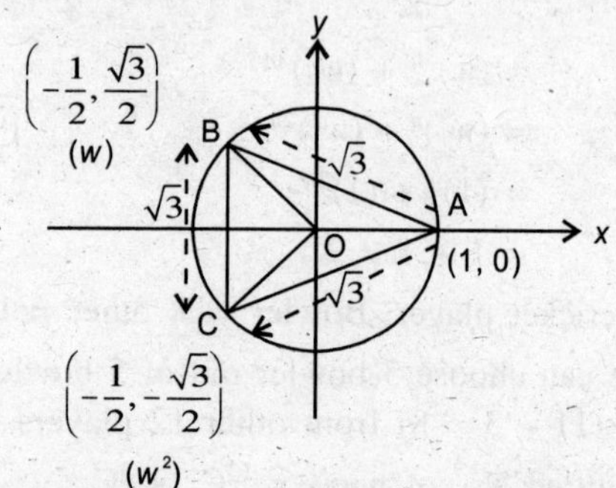

$\therefore$ Cube roots of unity form an equilateral triangle.

23. $\because$ We know that of u, v, w are in GP, then $\log u$, $\log v$, $\log w$ are in A.P.

$\therefore \begin{vmatrix} \log u & p & 1 \\ \log v & q & 1 \\ \log w & r & 1 \end{vmatrix} = 0$

24. $(1+x)^{2n} \Rightarrow$ Coefficient of the middle term $\alpha = {}^{2n}C_n$

$(1+x)^{2n-1} \Rightarrow$ Two middle terms coefficient

$\beta = {}^{2n-1}C_n$

$\gamma = {}^{2n-1}C_{n-1}$

$\beta + \gamma = {}^{2n-1}C_n + {}^{2n-1}C_{n-1}$

$= {}^{2n}C_n = \alpha$

$\beta + \gamma = \alpha \quad [\because {}^nC_r + {}^nC_{r-1} = {}^{n+1}C_r]$

25. $S = [(x, y) \in A \times B : x^2 + y^2 = 1]$

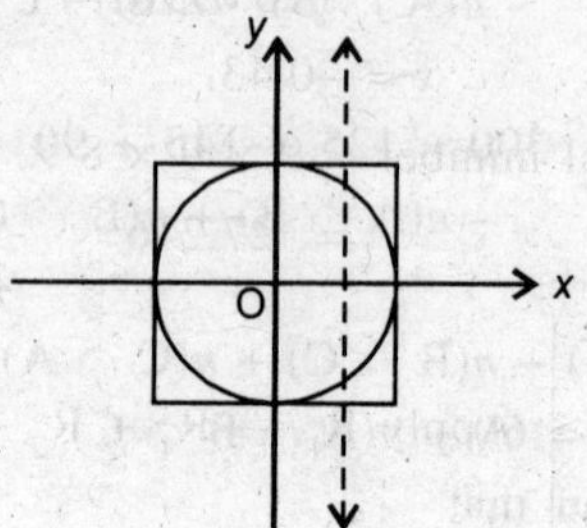

$\therefore$ S is not a function by vertical line test.

26. We have, $T_m = \frac{1}{n}$ and $T_n = \frac{1}{m}$

Let first term = a and common difference 'd'

Then, $a + (m-1)d = \frac{1}{n}$ ...(1)

$a + (n-1)d = \frac{1}{m}$ ...(2)

After solving equation (1) and (2) we get

$a = d = \frac{1}{mn}$

$T_{mn} = \frac{1}{mn} + (mn-1) \times \frac{1}{mn}$

$T_{mn} = 1.$

27. Let $f(x) = ax^2 + bx + c,\ a > 0,\ b^2 < 4ac$

$[\because f(x) > 0]$

Now, $g(x) = (ax^2 + bx + c) + (2ax + b) + (2a)$

$g(x) = ax^2 + (b + 2a)x + 2a + b + c$

Now, $(b + 2a)^2 - 4a(2a + b + c)$

$= b^2 + 4ab + 4a^2 - 8a^2 - 4ab - 4ac$

$= b^2 - 4ac - 4a^2 < 0$

$\Rightarrow g(x) > 0.$

29.
$$\begin{array}{r} 101101101 \\ -10110110 \\ \hline 10110111 \\ -11011 \\ \hline 10011100 \end{array}$$
$\therefore\ x = 1, y = 0.$

31. We have, $(0.2)^x = 2$

Taking log both sides, we get

$$x \log_{10}(0.2) = \log_{10}2$$
$$x \log_{10}\left(\frac{2}{10}\right) = \log_{10}2$$
$$x[\log_{10}2 - \log_{10}10] = \log_{10}2$$
$$x[0.3010 - 1] = 0.3010$$
$$x(-0.6990) = 0.3010$$
$$x = \frac{0.3010}{(-0.6990)}$$
$$x = -0.43.$$

32. Required total number $= 9 \times 9 \times 8 \times 7 \times 6$
$= 27{,}216$

33. $\begin{vmatrix} x & y & y+z \\ z & x & z+x \\ y & z & x+y \end{vmatrix}$ Apply $R_1 \to R_1 + R_2 + R_3$ we get

$$= \begin{vmatrix} x+y+z & x+y+z & 2(x+y+z) \\ z & x & z+x \\ y & z & x+y \end{vmatrix}$$
$$= (x+y+z)\begin{vmatrix} 1 & 1 & 2 \\ z & x & z+x \\ y & z & x+y \end{vmatrix}$$
$$= (x+y+z)(z-x)^2.$$

34. We have,

$$\begin{vmatrix} 1 & -1 & 1 \\ 1+\sin A & 1+\sin B & 1+\sin C \\ \sin A+\sin^2 A & \sin B+\sin^2 B & \sin C+\sin^2 C \end{vmatrix} = 0$$

Apply, $R_1 \to R_1 - R_2$, $R_3 \to R_3 - R_2$ we get

$$\begin{vmatrix} -\sin A & -\sin B & -\sin C \\ 1+\sin A & 1+\sin B & 1+\sin C \\ \sin^2 A-1 & \sin^2 B-1 & \sin^2 C-1 \end{vmatrix} = 0$$

Apply, $R_2 \to R_2 + R_1$ we get

$$\Rightarrow \begin{vmatrix} -\sin A & -\sin B & -\sin C \\ 1 & 1 & 1 \\ -\cos^2 A & -\cos^2 B & -\cos^2 C \end{vmatrix} = 0$$

Apply, $R_3 \to R_3 + R_2$ we get

$$\begin{vmatrix} \sin A & \sin B & \sin C \\ 1 & 1 & 1 \\ \sin^2 A & \sin^2 B & \sin^2 C \end{vmatrix} = 0$$

$\Rightarrow \sin A = \sin B = \sin C \Rightarrow \Delta$ is equilateral.

35. Matrix product is commutative (*i.e.*, AB = BA). If both are diagonal matries of same order.

$\Rightarrow\quad A^2 - B^2 = (A + B)(A - B)$ is not true

Next, $(A - I)(A + I) = 0$

$\Rightarrow\ A^2 + AI - IA - I^2 = 0 \qquad [\because AI = IA]$

$\Rightarrow\ A^2 = I^2$ is correct.

37. $\because$ Sec $(\theta - \alpha)$, sec θ and sec $(\theta + \alpha)$ are in A.P. then,

$$2\sec\theta = \sec(\theta-\alpha) + \sec(\theta+\alpha)$$
$$\frac{2}{\cos\theta} = \frac{1}{\cos(\theta-\alpha)} + \frac{1}{\cos(\theta+\alpha)}$$
$$\frac{2}{\cos\theta} = \frac{\cos(\theta+\alpha)+\cos(\theta-\alpha)}{\cos(\theta+\alpha)\cdot\cos(\theta-\alpha)}$$
$$\Rightarrow \frac{2}{\cos\theta} = \frac{2\cos\theta\cdot\cos\alpha}{\cos^2\theta-\sin^2\theta}$$
$$\Rightarrow \cos^2\theta.\cos\alpha = \cos^2\theta - \sin^2\alpha$$
$$\Rightarrow \sin^2\alpha = \cos^2\theta(1-\cos\alpha)$$
$$\Rightarrow \cos^2\theta = \frac{\sin^2\alpha}{1-\cos\alpha}$$
$$\Rightarrow \cos^2\theta = 1+\cos\alpha$$
$$\Rightarrow 1-\sin^2\theta = 1+\cos\alpha$$
$$\Rightarrow \sin^2\theta + \cos\alpha = 0.$$

38. $\sin 2A - \sin 2B - \sin 2C$

$= 2\cos(A+B).\sin(A-B) + \sin(2A+2B)$

$= 2\cos(A+B).\sin(A-B) + 2\sin(A+B).\cos(A+B)$

$= 2\cos(A+B)[\sin(A-B) + \sin(A+B)]$

$= -2\cos C[2\sin A.\cos B]$

$= -4\sin A\cos B.\cos C.$

39. Let the length of Bridge = 'l'

In Δ ABC,

$$\tan 48° = \frac{122}{l}$$
$$l = \frac{122}{\tan 48}$$
$$l = \frac{122}{\tan(90-42)} = \frac{122}{\cot 42}$$
$$= 122\tan 42°\text{ m.}$$

40. Checking through options

(A) $\qquad 300° = -60°$

So, $3(3 - \tan^2 A - \cot A)^2$

$= 3(3 - \tan^2(-60°) - \cot(-60°))^2$

$= 3\left(3-3+\frac{1}{\sqrt{3}}\right)^2$

$= 3 \times \frac{1}{3} = 1.$

41. In Δ EDC,

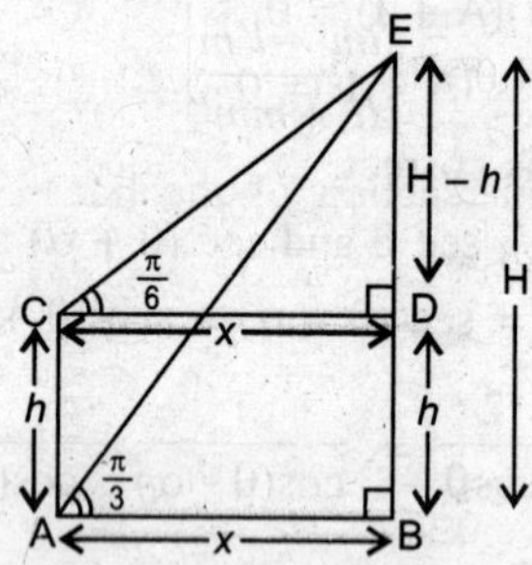

$$\tan\frac{\pi}{6} = \frac{H-h}{x}$$

$$x = \frac{H-h}{\tan\frac{\pi}{6}} \quad ...(1)$$

In Δ ABE,

$$\tan\frac{\pi}{3} = \frac{H}{x}$$

$$x = \frac{H}{\tan\frac{\pi}{3}} \quad ...(2)$$

From equation (1) and (2)

$$\frac{H-h}{\tan\frac{\pi}{6}} = \frac{H}{\tan\frac{\pi}{3}}$$

$$\sqrt{3}(H-h) = \frac{H}{\sqrt{3}}$$

$$3(H - h) = H$$

$$3H - 3h = H$$

$$2H = 3h$$

$$H = \frac{3}{2}h.$$

42. We have,

$\operatorname{cosec} x + \cot x = \sqrt{3}$

$\operatorname{cosec} x - \cot x = \frac{1}{\sqrt{3}}$ $[\because \operatorname{cosec}^2 x - \cot^2 x = 1]$

$\Rightarrow \quad 2 \operatorname{cosec} x = \sqrt{3}+\frac{1}{\sqrt{3}} = \frac{4}{\sqrt{3}}$

$\Rightarrow \quad \operatorname{cosec} x = \frac{2}{\sqrt{3}}$

$\Rightarrow \quad \sin x = \frac{\sqrt{3}}{2}$

Possible values of $x = \frac{\pi}{3}, \frac{2\pi}{3}$

$\therefore$ Solution $= \frac{\pi}{3}$

43. $[(2\cos\theta + 1)(2\cos\theta - 1)]^{10} [2\cos 2\theta - 1]^{10}$

$[2\cos 4\theta - 1)]^{10}$ $\theta = \frac{\pi}{8}$

$= (4\cos^2\theta - 1)^{10}(2\cos 2\theta - 1)^{10}(2\cos 4\theta - 1)^{10}$

$= \left(4\cos^2\frac{\pi}{8}-1\right)^{10}\left(2\cos\frac{\pi}{4}-1\right)^{10}\left(2\cos\frac{\pi}{2}-1\right)^{10}$

$= \left(4\times\frac{2+\sqrt{2}}{4}-1\right)^{10}\left(2\times\frac{1}{\sqrt{2}}-1\right)^{10}(0-1)^{10}$

$= \left[(\sqrt{2}+1)(\sqrt{2}-1)\right]^{10}$

$= \left[(\sqrt{2})^2-(1)^2\right]^{10} = (2 - 1)^{10} = 1^{10} = 1.$

44. Product of roots $\cos\alpha.\cos\beta = -\frac{3}{4}$

$$\frac{1}{\cos\alpha\cdot\cos\beta} = -\frac{4}{3}$$

$$\sec\alpha\cdot\sec\beta = -\frac{4}{3}.$$

45. We have,

$$\tan^{-1}(2x) + \tan^{-1}(3x) = \frac{\pi}{4}$$

$$\tan^{-1}\left(\frac{2x+3x}{1-(2x)(3x)}\right) = \frac{\pi}{4}$$

$$\frac{5x}{1-6x^2} = \tan\frac{\pi}{4} = 1$$

$$5x = 1 - 6x^2$$

$$6x^2 + 5x - 1 = 0$$

$$(6x - 1)(x + 1) = 0$$

$$x = \frac{1}{6},\ x = -1 \text{ (Rejected)}$$

46. Given that $ar = 2$, (second term of a GP)

Sum of infinite term $\Rightarrow \frac{a}{1-r} = 8$

$\Rightarrow \quad \frac{ar}{r-r^2} = 8$

$\Rightarrow \quad \dfrac{2}{r-r^2} = 8$

$\Rightarrow \quad \dfrac{1}{r-r^2} = 4$

$\Rightarrow \quad 4r^2 - 4r + 1 = 0$

$\Rightarrow \quad r = \dfrac{1}{2}$

$\therefore$ GP is 4, 2, 1, $\dfrac{1}{2}, \dfrac{1}{2^2}$.

47. a, b, c, ε AP $\Rightarrow a - b = b - c$

$\Rightarrow \quad \dfrac{a-b}{b-c} = 1$

a, b, c, ε GP $\Rightarrow \dfrac{a}{b} = \dfrac{b}{c} = \dfrac{a-b}{b-c}$

a, b, c, ε HP $\Rightarrow b = \dfrac{2ac}{a+c}$

$ab + bc = 2ac$

$\Rightarrow \quad ab - ac = ac - bc$

$\Rightarrow \quad a(b - c) = (a - b)c$

$\Rightarrow \quad \dfrac{a-b}{b-c} = \dfrac{a}{c}$

$\therefore \quad \dfrac{a-b}{b-c} = 1$ or $\dfrac{a}{b}$ or $\dfrac{a}{c}$.

48. Required sum of three digit numbers
$= 543 + 534 + 453 + 435 + 354 + 345$
$= 2664$.

49. $\dfrac{D_1}{D_2}$ = (ratio of coefficient of $x)^2$

$= \left(\dfrac{b}{q}\right)^2 = \dfrac{b^2}{q^2}$.

50. We have,

$A = \sin^2\theta + \cos^4\theta$

$= \sin^2\theta + (1 - \sin^2\theta)^2$

Let $\sin^2\theta = x$

$A = x^2 - x + 1, 0 \le x \le 1$

$= \left(x - \dfrac{1}{2}\right)^2 + \dfrac{3}{4}$

$A(0) = A(1) = 1$

So, $\dfrac{3}{4} \le A \le 1$.

52. We have,

$x^2 + 4y^2 - 2x - 4y + 2 = 0$

$(x^2 - 2x + 1) + (4y^2 - 4y + 1) = 0$

$\Rightarrow (x - 1)^2 + (2y - 1)^2 = 0$

$\Rightarrow x = 1, y = \dfrac{1}{2}$

It is a point.

53. $m_1 = -\dfrac{l}{m}$, and $m_2 = -\dfrac{l'}{m'}$

$\tan^{-1}\theta = \tan^{-1}\left|\dfrac{m_2 - m_1}{1 + m_1 m_2}\right|$

$\tan^{-1}\theta = \tan^{-1}\left|\dfrac{-\dfrac{l'}{m'} + \dfrac{l}{m}}{1 + \dfrac{ll'}{mm'}}\right|$

$\theta = \left|\dfrac{lm' - l'm}{ll' + mm'}\right|$

55. Point of intersection of the lines

$\dfrac{x}{2} + \dfrac{y}{3} = 1$ and $\dfrac{x}{3} + \dfrac{y}{2} = 1$ is $\left(\dfrac{6}{5}, \dfrac{6}{5}\right)$

Let equation of line be $4x + 5y + k = 0$

Putting $\left(\dfrac{6}{5}, \dfrac{6}{5}\right)$; $k = -\dfrac{54}{5}$

$\therefore$ Equation of line is $20x + 25y - 54 = 0$.

56. Distance $= \left|\dfrac{3 \times 2 - 6 \times 3 + 2 \times 4 + 11}{\sqrt{(3)^2 + (-6)^2 + (2)^2}}\right|$

$= \left|\dfrac{6 - 18 + 8 + 11}{\sqrt{49}}\right| = 1$.

58. Direction cosines of the line are 2, 3, 4 going through the option

$2(1) + 3(2) + 4(-2) = 0$

$2(4) + 3(4) - 4(5) = 0$.

59. Angle between planes

$\cos^{-1}\left(\dfrac{2 - 1 + 2}{6}\right) = \cos^{-1}\left(\dfrac{1}{2}\right) = \dfrac{\pi}{3}$

Distance between planes

$= \dfrac{\left|\dfrac{2}{3} - 4\right|}{\sqrt{9}} = \dfrac{10}{3 \times 3} = \dfrac{10}{9}$.

61. Area

$= \dfrac{1}{2}\left|x_1\left(\dfrac{1}{x_2} - \dfrac{1}{x_3}\right) + x_2\left(\dfrac{1}{x_3} - \dfrac{1}{x_1}\right) + x_3\left(\dfrac{1}{x_1} - \dfrac{1}{x_2}\right)\right|$

$= \dfrac{1}{2}\left|\dfrac{x_1(x_3 - x_2)}{x_2 x_3} + \dfrac{x_2(x_1 - x_3)}{x_1 x_3} + \dfrac{x_3(x_2 - x_1)}{x_1 x_2}\right|$

$= \dfrac{1}{2}\left|\dfrac{-x_1^2(x_2 - x_3) - x_2^2(x_3 - x_1) - x_3^2(x_1 - x_2)}{x_1 x_2 x_3}\right|$

$= \left|\dfrac{(x_1 - x_2)(x_2 - x_3)(x_3 - x_1)}{2(x_1 x_2 x_3)}\right|$

62.

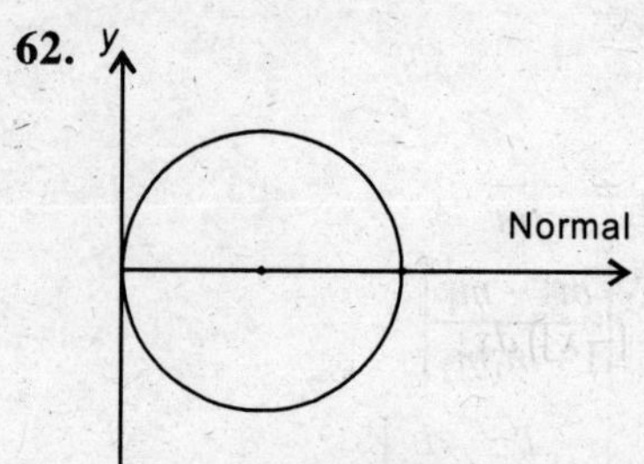

63. $(\vec{a}+\vec{b})\cdot(\vec{a}+\vec{b}) = a^2+2\vec{a}\cdot\vec{b}+b^2$

$$a^2+2\vec{a}\cdot\vec{b}+b^2 = a^2+b^2$$

$$2\vec{a}\cdot\vec{b} = 0$$

$$\vec{a}\cdot\vec{b} = 0$$

$\therefore$ $\vec{a} \perp \vec{b}$.

64. $\vec{r}\cdot(\hat{i}+\hat{j}+\hat{k})$

$= (x\hat{i}+y\hat{j}+z\hat{k})\cdot(\hat{i}+\hat{j}+\hat{k})$

$= x + y + z.$

65. $$\begin{vmatrix} \hat{i} & \hat{j} & \hat{k} \\ 2 & -1 & 1 \\ 3 & -4 & -1 \end{vmatrix} = \hat{i}(1+4)-\hat{j}(-2-3)+\hat{k}(-8+3)$$

$$= 5\hat{i}+5\hat{j}-5\hat{k}$$

Unit vector $= \dfrac{5}{5\sqrt{3}}\hat{i}+\dfrac{5}{5\sqrt{3}}\hat{j}-\dfrac{5}{5\sqrt{3}}\hat{k}$

$$= \frac{1}{\sqrt{3}}\hat{i}+\frac{1}{\sqrt{3}}\hat{j}-\frac{1}{\sqrt{3}}\hat{k}.$$

66. We know that

$$|\vec{a}+\vec{b}|^2+|\vec{a}-\vec{b}|^2 = 2\{|\vec{a}|^2+|\vec{b}|^2\}$$

$$= 2\{(3)^2+(4)^2\}$$

$$= 2 \times 25$$

$$= 50$$

$$|\vec{a}+\vec{b}|^2+(5)^2 = 50$$

$$|\vec{a}+\vec{b}|^2 = 50 - 25$$

$$|\vec{a}+\vec{b}|^2 = 25$$

$$\vec{a}+\vec{b} = 5.$$

67. Let $\vec{a}=\hat{i},\ \vec{b}=\hat{j},\ \vec{c}=\hat{k}$

Then, $\vec{A} = \hat{i}+\hat{j}+\hat{k},$

$$|\vec{A}| = \sqrt{1+1+1} = \sqrt{3}$$

$$\vec{B} = \hat{i}-\hat{j}+\hat{k},$$

$$|\vec{B}| = \sqrt{1+1+1} = \sqrt{3}$$

$$\vec{C} = \hat{i}-\hat{j}-\hat{k},$$

$$|\vec{C}| = \sqrt{1+1+1} = \sqrt{3}$$

$$|\vec{A}| = |\vec{B}| = |\vec{C}|.$$

68. We have, $(\vec{a}-\vec{b})\times(\vec{a}+\vec{b})$

$= \vec{a}\times\vec{a}+\vec{a}\times\vec{b}-\vec{b}\times\vec{a}-\vec{b}\times\vec{b}$

$= 0+\vec{a}\times\vec{b}+\vec{a}\times\vec{b}-0$

$= 2(\vec{a}\times\vec{b}).$

69. Moment $\vec{\tau} = \vec{r}\times \text{F}$

$$= (\hat{i}+2\hat{j}+3\hat{k})\times\lambda\hat{k}$$

$$= 2\lambda\hat{i}-\lambda\hat{j}$$

$$|\vec{\tau}| = \sqrt{4\lambda^2+\lambda^2}$$

$$= \sqrt{5\lambda^2} = \sqrt{5}\lambda.$$

71. We have,

$$y = \cos^{-1}(\sin x)$$

$$= \cos^{-1}\cos\left(\frac{\pi}{2}-x\right)$$

$$= \frac{\pi}{2}-x$$

Compare with $y = mx + c$,

$$m = \tan\theta = -1$$

$$\theta = \frac{3\pi}{4}\quad [\theta\varepsilon(0,\pi)]$$

72. $f(x)$ is defined if $x \geq 1$ and $x \neq 4$

$\therefore$ Domain $= [1, 4) \cup (4, \infty]$.

73. $\because \displaystyle\lim_{h\to0^-}\frac{f(0-h)}{h} = \lim_{h\to0^+}\frac{f(0+h)}{h} \neq f(0)$

$\therefore \displaystyle\lim_{x\to0}\frac{\sin 2x}{5x} = \frac{2}{5} \neq \frac{2}{15}$

$\Rightarrow$ $f(x)$ is not continuous at $x = 0$.

75. $$f(0) = \lim_{x\to0}\frac{2x-\sin^{-1}x}{2x+\tan^{-1}x}$$

$$= \lim_{x\to0}\frac{2-\dfrac{\sin^{-1}x}{x}}{2+\dfrac{\tan^{-1}x}{x}}$$

$$= \frac{2-1}{2+1} = \frac{1}{3}.$$

76. We have, $f(x) = \sqrt{25-x^2}$

$$f'(x) = \frac{-2x}{2\sqrt{25-x^2}}$$

$$= \frac{-x}{\sqrt{25-x^2}}$$

$$f'(1) = \frac{-1}{\sqrt{24}}$$

$\lim_{x\to1} \frac{f(x)-f(1)}{x-1}$ Apply L'Hospital Rule

$$\lim_{x\to1} f'(x) = f'(1) = -\frac{1}{\sqrt{24}}.$$

77. $y = \tan^{-1}\left(\frac{5-2\tan\sqrt{x}}{2+5\tan\sqrt{x}}\right)$

$$y = \tan^{-1}\left(\frac{\frac{5}{2}-\tan\sqrt{x}}{1+\frac{5}{2}\tan\sqrt{x}}\right)$$

$$y = \tan^{-1}\frac{5}{2} - \tan^{-1}\tan\sqrt{x}$$

$$y = \tan^{-1}\frac{5}{2} - \sqrt{x}$$

$$\therefore \quad \frac{dy}{dx} = -\frac{1}{2\sqrt{x}}.$$

78. We have,

$$f(x) = x\sin x + \cos x + \frac{1}{2}\cos^2 x$$

$$f'(x) = x\cos x + \sin x - \sin x - \sin x.\cos x$$

$$= \cos x\,(x - \sin x)$$

$\cos x(x - \sin x) > 0$ in $\left(0, \frac{\pi}{2}\right)$.

79. $\lim_{\theta\to0} \frac{\sqrt{1-\cos\theta}}{\theta} = \lim_{\theta\to0} \frac{\sqrt{2}\sin\left(\frac{\theta}{2}\right)}{\theta}$

$$= \frac{\sqrt{2}}{2} = \frac{1}{\sqrt{2}}.$$

80. $f(x) = x^2 - 4x + 5 = (x-2)^2 + 1$

$f(1) = 2$, $f(4) = 5$

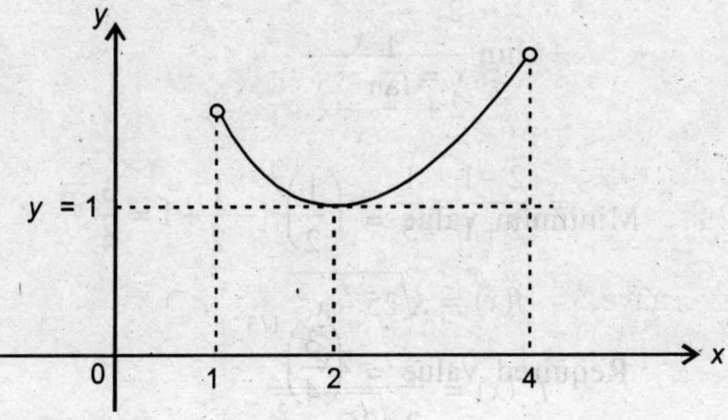

Range $f(x) = [1, 5)$.

81. $\int_a^b [x]dx + \int_a^b [-x]dx$

$$= \int_a^b ([x]+[-x])\,dx$$

$$= \int_a^b (-1)\,dx = a - b.$$

82. $\int_2^8 |x-5|\,dx = 2 \times \frac{1}{2} \times 3 \times 3 = 9.$

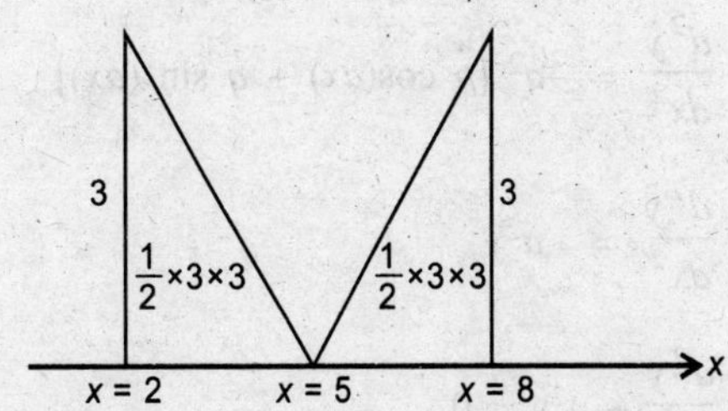

83. Let $t = \sin x$

$dt = \cos x.\,dx$

Then, $\int \sin^3 x \cdot \cos x \cdot dx = \int t^3 dt$

$$= \frac{t^4}{4} + c$$

$$= \frac{\sin^4 x}{4} + c$$

$$= \frac{(1-\cos^2 x)^2}{4} + c.$$

84. $\int e^{\ln(\tan x)}dx = \int \tan x \cdot dx$

$$= \ln|\sec x| + c$$

85. $\int_{-1}^{1}\left(\frac{d}{dx}\tan^{-1}\frac{1}{x}\right)dx = \int_{-1}^{1}\left(\frac{d}{dx}\cot^{-1}x\right)dx$

$$= \int_{-1}^{1} \frac{-1}{(1+x^2)}dx$$

$$= -2\int_0^1 \frac{1}{1+x^2}dx$$

$$= -2\left[\tan^{-1}x\right]_0^1$$

$$= -2 \times \frac{\pi}{4} = -\frac{\pi}{2}.$$

86. $f(x) = x^2 - 5x + 6$

$\Rightarrow \quad f'(x) = 2x - 5$

$\Rightarrow \quad f'(x) < 0$

$\Rightarrow \quad 2x - 5 < 0$

$\Rightarrow \quad x < \frac{5}{2} \quad (-\infty, 2].$

87. $y = p \cos ax + q \sin ax$

$\Rightarrow \quad \frac{dy}{dx} = -pa \sin ax + qa \cos ax$

$\Rightarrow \quad \frac{d^2y}{dx^2} = -pa^2 \cos ax - qa^2 \sin ax$

$\Rightarrow \quad \frac{d^2y}{dx^2} = -a^2 [p \cos(ax) + q \sin (ax)]$

$\Rightarrow \quad \frac{d^2y}{dx^2} = -a^2y$

$\Rightarrow \quad \frac{d^2y}{dx^2} + a^2y = 0.$

88. We have, $\frac{dy}{dx} = -x^2 - \frac{1}{x^3}$

$\Rightarrow \quad \int dy = \int\left(-x^2 - \frac{1}{x^3}\right) dx$

$\Rightarrow \quad y = -\frac{x^3}{3} + \frac{1}{2x^2} + c$

Putting (–1, –2) we get

$-2 = \frac{1}{3} + \frac{1}{2} + c$

$c = -\frac{17}{6}$

$\therefore \quad y = -\frac{x^3}{3} + \frac{1}{2x^2} - \frac{17}{6}$

$\Rightarrow \quad 6x^2y = -2x^5 + 3 - 17x^2$

$\Rightarrow \quad 6x^2y + 17x^2 + 2x^5 - 3 = 0.$

89. Order = 4 ($\because$ No of arbitrary constants = 4)

90. $\frac{dy}{dx} = e^{ax + by}$

$= e^{ax}. e^{by}$

$\Rightarrow \quad e^{ax} . dx - e^{-by} dy = 0$

Integrating both sides

$\frac{1}{a}e^{ax} + \frac{1}{b}e^{-by} = c.$

91. $u\frac{du}{dx} + v\frac{dv}{dx}$

$= e^{ax} \sin bx[ae^{ax}. \sin bx + be^{ax}.\cos bx] + e^{ax} . \cos bx \, [ae^{ax}.\cos bx - be^{ax}.\sin bx]$

$= e^{2ax}[a \sin^2 bx + b \sin bx.\cos bx + a \cos^2 bx - b \sin bx.\cos bx]$

$= ae^{2ax}.$

92. $y = \sin(\log x)$

$\frac{dy}{dx} = \frac{\cos(\log x)}{x}$

$\Rightarrow \quad x\left(\frac{dy}{dx}\right) = \cos (\log x)$

Again differentiating

$\Rightarrow \quad x\frac{d^2y}{dx^2} + \frac{dy}{dx} = -\frac{\sin(\log x)}{x}$

$\Rightarrow \quad x\frac{d^2y}{dx^2} + \frac{dy}{dx} = -\frac{y}{x}$

$\Rightarrow \quad x^2\frac{d^2y}{dx^2} + x\frac{dy}{dx} + y = 0.$

93.

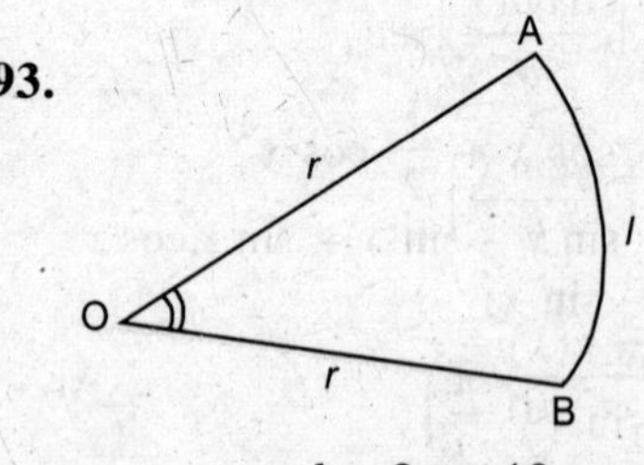

$l + 2r = 40$

Area is maximum,

When, $\quad l + 2r = 20$

$\Rightarrow \quad r = 10.$

94. $[x(x - 1) + 1]^{1/3}$ is minimum when $x^2 - x + 1$ is minimum, $0 \le x \le 1$

for minimum $\frac{dy}{dx} = 0, \; 2x - 1 = 0$

$x = \frac{1}{2}$

$\therefore \quad$ Minimum value $= \left(\frac{1}{2}\right)^2 - \frac{1}{2} + 1 = \frac{3}{4}$

Required value $= \left(\frac{3}{4}\right)^{1/3}.$

95. $y = |\sin x|^{|x|}$

$y = (-\sin x)^{-x}$

$\log y = (-x)\log(-\sin x)$

$$\frac{1}{y}\cdot\frac{dy}{dx} = \frac{-x}{-\sin x}(-\cos x) + \log(-\sin x)(-1)$$

$$\frac{dy}{dx} = (-\sin x)^{-x}\left[\frac{x}{\sin x}(-\cos x) - \log(-\sin x)\right]$$

$$\left(\frac{dy}{dx}\right)_{x=-\frac{\pi}{6}} = \left(\frac{1}{2}\right)^{\frac{\pi}{6}}\left[-\frac{\pi}{6}\sqrt{3} - \log\frac{1}{2}\right]$$

$$= 2^{-\frac{\pi}{6}}\left(\frac{6\log 2 - \sqrt{3}\pi}{6}\right).$$

96. For $\frac{\pi}{4} < x < \frac{\pi}{2}$, $\sqrt{1-\sin 2x} = \sin x - \cos x$

$$\frac{d}{dx}(\sin x - \cos x) = \cos x + \sin x.$$

97. $$I = \frac{1}{a^2}\int \frac{\sec^2 x}{\tan^2 x + \left(\frac{b}{a}\right)^2}$$

$$= \frac{1}{a^2}\times\frac{a}{b}\tan^{-1}\left(\frac{a\tan x}{b}\right) + c$$

$$= c + \frac{1}{ab}\tan^{-1}\left(\frac{a\tan x}{b}\right).$$

98. $$f'(x) = \lim_{h\to 0}\frac{f(x+h) - f(x)}{h}$$

$$= \lim_{h\to 0}\frac{f(x)f(h) - f(x)}{h}$$

$$= \lim_{h\to 0}\frac{f(x)[f(h) - 1]}{h}$$

$$= \lim_{h\to 0}\frac{f(x)[h\,g(h)\,\phi(h)]}{h}$$

$= abf(x)$.

99. Let $t = x + y$

$$\frac{dt}{dy} = \frac{dx}{dy} + 1$$

So, $$\frac{dt}{dy} - 1 = \frac{t+1}{t-1}$$

$$\frac{dt}{dy} = \frac{t+1+t-1}{t-1}$$

$$= \frac{2t}{t-1}$$

$$\Rightarrow \int\frac{t-1}{t}dt = 2\int dy$$

$$\Rightarrow t - \log t = 2y + c_1$$

$$\Rightarrow x + y - \log(x+y) - 2y = c_1$$

$$\Rightarrow x - y - \log(x+y) = c_1$$

$$\Rightarrow y - x + \log(x+y) = -c_1 = c.$$

100. $$\lim_{x\to\frac{\pi}{6}}\frac{(\sin x + 1)(2\sin x - 1)}{(\sin x - 1)(2\sin x - 1)} = \frac{\frac{1}{2}+1}{\frac{1}{2}-1} = -3.$$

101. $n(s) = 36$

A = {(1, 5), (2, 5), (3, 5), (4, 5), (5, 5), (6, 5), (5, 1), (5, 2), (5, 3), (5, 4), (5, 6)}

B = {(5, 5), (6, 4), (4, 6), (6, 5), (5, 6), (6, 6)}

A ∩ B = {(5, 5), (6, 5), (5, 6)}

$$P\left(\frac{B}{A}\right) = \frac{3}{11}.$$

103. Let no. of men = x and

No. of women = y

Then, $26x + 21y = 25(x + y)$

$26x + 21y = 25x + 25y$

$x = 4y$

$$\frac{x}{y} = \frac{4}{1}$$

$$\text{Men percentage} = \frac{4}{(4+1)}\times 100 = 80\%$$

$$\text{Women percentage} = \frac{1}{(4+1)}\times 100$$

$= 20\%$.

104. Given that $\sin\beta = \frac{2\sin\alpha\cdot\cos\alpha}{\sin\alpha + \cos\alpha}$

and, $2\sin\theta = \sin\alpha + \cos\alpha$

Statement 1: $\sqrt{2}\sin\left(\alpha + \frac{\pi}{4}\right)\cdot\sin\beta$

$$= (\sin\alpha + \cos\alpha)\frac{2\sin\alpha\cdot\cos\alpha}{(\sin\alpha + \cos\alpha)}$$

$= 2\sin\alpha\,.\,\cos\alpha$

$= \sin 2\alpha$.

Statement 2:

$$\cos\left(\alpha - \frac{\pi}{4}\right) = \frac{1}{\sqrt{2}}(\sin\alpha + \cos\alpha)$$

$$= \frac{2\sin\theta}{\sqrt{2}}$$

$$= \sqrt{2}\sin\theta.$$

105. $P(A) + P(B) + P(C) = 1$

$$P(A) + \frac{3}{2}P(A) + \frac{1}{2} \times \frac{3}{2} P(A) = 1$$

$$\frac{13}{4} P(A) = 1$$

$$\Rightarrow \quad P(A) = \frac{4}{13}.$$

106. Required probability $= \dfrac{25 \times 2}{25 \times 2 + 35 \times 4 + 40 \times 5}$

$$= \frac{5}{39}.$$

107. Required probability

$$= \left({}^8C_6 + {}^8C_7 + {}^8C_8\right)\left(\frac{1}{2}\right)^8$$

$$= (28 + 8 + 1) \times \frac{1}{256} = \frac{37}{256}.$$

108. Required probability

$$= \left(\frac{3}{4} \times \frac{2}{4} \times \frac{3}{4}\right) + \left(\frac{1}{4} \times \frac{2}{4} \times \frac{3}{4}\right) + \left(\frac{1}{4} \times \frac{2}{4} \times \frac{1}{4}\right)$$

$$= \frac{26}{64} = \frac{13}{32}.$$

110. Variance will not change by adding or substracting a fixed value to all the elements.

111. $(x_1 \cdot x_2 .... x_n)^{\frac{1}{n}} = P$

$$(y_1 \cdot y_2 .... y_n)^{\frac{1}{n}} = Q$$

$$\left(\frac{x_1 \cdot x_2 .... x_n}{y_1 \cdot y_2 .... y_n}\right)^{\frac{1}{n}} = \frac{(x_1 \cdot x_2 .... x_n)^{\frac{1}{n}}}{(y_1 \cdot y_2 .... y_n)^{\frac{1}{n}}} = \frac{P}{Q}.$$

112. $P(A) + P(B) - 2P(A \cap B) = q$

$$P(A \cap B) = p$$

$$P(A) + P(B) = 2p + q$$

$$1 - P(\bar{A}) + 1 - P(\bar{B}) = 2p + q$$

$$P(\bar{A}) + P(\bar{B}) = 2 - 2p - q$$

$$P(\bar{A} \cap \bar{B}) = 1 - P(A \cup B)$$

$$= 1 - (q + p)$$

$$= 1 - p - q.$$

113. $byx = -6$

$$r = -\frac{1}{2}$$

$$\left(-\frac{1}{2}\right)^2 = -6 \times bxy$$

$$bxy = -\frac{1}{24}.$$

116. Combined Average

$$= \frac{500 \times 1860 + 600 + 1750}{1100}$$

$$= 1800$$

Combined variance

$$= \frac{500(81 + 3600) + 600(100 + 2500)}{1100}$$

$$= \frac{(5 \times 3681) + (6 \times 2600)}{1100} \simeq 3092.$$

117. No. of possible outcomes

$$= 10 + 6 + 3 + 1 = 20.$$

119. x = M.D and y = S.D

$$\Rightarrow \quad M.D = \frac{4}{5} S.D.$$

$$x < y.$$

Previous Papers (Solved)

NATIONAL DEFENCE ACADEMY

ENTRANCE EXAMINATION–2018 (I)

PAPER I : GENERAL ABILITY TEST

PART A - ENGLISH LANGUAGE

SYNONYMS

Directions (Qs. No. 1-10): *Each item in this section consists of a sentence with an underlined word/words followed by four words. Select the option that is* ***nearest in meaning*** *to the underlined word/words and mark your response in your Answer Sheet accordingly.*

1. I do not want you to lead a life of sycophancy as you did during the foreign rule.
A. admiration B. love
C. appreciation D. flattery

2. In India, it has become easy to attack cultural artefacts these days.
A. beckon B. assault
C. belch D. appreciate

3. A local court granted bail to the criminal on Thursday.
A. confessed B. donated
C. allowed D. yielded

4. The judge told that he would analyze the evidence and then deliver the verdict.
A. liberate B. surrender
C. transfer D. pronounce

5. The growth and development of the peasant movement was indissolubly linked with the national struggle for freedom.
A. firmly B. vaguely
C. individually D. steadily

6. Weather conditions have been improving over the past few days.
A. mending B. amending
C. becoming better D. advancing

7. The confusion on the interlocutor's face was gratifying.
A. government officer
B. party worker
C. dialogist
D. revolutionary

8. He spends his money lavishly.
A. hesitatingly B. generously
C. foolishly D. carefully

9. The government's new policies will come into force from the next fiscal year.
A. calendar B. academic
C. financial D. leap

10. Abundant food was available for the soldiers in the mess.
A. little B. plentiful
C. delicious D. wholesome

ANTONYMS

Directions (Qs. No. 11-20): *Each item in this section consists of a sentence with an underlined word/words followed by four words. Select the option that is* ***opposite in meaning*** *to the underlined word/words and mark your response in your Answer Sheet accordingly.*

11. The country's economy must be geared to wartime requirements.
A. subordinated to B. related to
C. adjusted to D. unlinked to

12. Why does fire attract insects?
A. discharge B. destroy
C. repel D. remove

13. The party was excellent, and I would like to thank all the people concerned.
A. cared B. attentive
C. dependable D. uninvolved

14. He is very serious by temperament.
A. grave B. trivial
C. sober D. stupid

15. There are a few miscellaneous items to discuss in this meeting.
A. pure B. mixed
C. homogenous D. discordant

16. Due to the postal strike, the outgoing mail got delayed.
A. urgent B. incoming
C. ordinary D. speedy

17. He had a fine ear for music.
A. small B. close
C. coarse D. smooth

18. There is no likeness between him and his brother.
A. unlikeliness B. unlikelihood
C. dissimilarity D. disaffinity

19. Cultural diversity in the working place is good for business.
A. uniformity B. conformity
C. identity D. similarity

20. The company was liquidated within five years.
A. bankrupt B. closed down
C. flourishing D. privatised

SPOTTING ERRORS

Directions (Qs. No. 21-25): *Each item in this section has a sentence with three parts labelled (A), (B) and (C). Read each sentence to find out whether there is any error in any part and indicate your response in the Answer Sheet against the corresponding letter i.e., (A) or (B) or (C). If you find no error, your response should be indicated as (D).*

21. The politician lost face in his constituency (A)/ when he broke the pre-election promises (B)/ he made to his people. (C)/ No error. (D)

22. At the request of the Defence Attorney, (A)/the jury were called (B)/and their individual verdicts were recorded. (C)/ No error. (D)

23. Frank Lloyd Wright has been acclaimed (A)/by colleagues (B)/as the greater of all modern architects. (C)/ No error. (D)

24. In my younger days (A)/ I could run four miles (B)/at a stretch. (C)/ No error. (D)

25. The owner (A)/as well as his servants (B)/is honest. (C)/ No error. (D)

IDIOMS AND PHRASES

Directions (Qs. No. 26-30): *Given below are some idioms/ phrases followed by four alternative meanings to each. Choose the response (A), (B), (C) or (D) which is the most appropriate expression.*

26. Cry over spilt milk
A. Complaining about a loss in the past
B. Too much inquisitive about something
C. When something is done badly to save money
D. Dealing with a problem only in an emergency situation

27. Cut the mustard
A. Prepare spices out of mustard seeds
B. To come up to expectations
C. Making absurd expectations
D. Very enthusiastic

28. Devil's advocate
A. A dangerous person
B. To present a counter argument
C. Very argumentative person
D. Creating an unpleasant situation

29. Don't count your chickens before the eggs have hatched
A. If you are not good at something, better to avoid that
B. Don't make plans for something that might not happen
C. Not to come up to expectations
D. Don't put all your resources in one possibility

30. Give the benefit of doubt
A. To be partial to someone
B. To be judgmental
C. Regard someone as innocent until proven otherwise
D. Say something exactly right

ORDERING OF SENTENCES

Directions (Qs. No. 31-35): *In this section each item consists of six sentences of a passage. The first and sixth sentences are given in the beginning as SI and S6. The middle four sentences in each have been jumbled up and labelled P, Q, R and S. You are required to find the proper sequence of the four sentences and mark your response accordingly on the Answer Sheet.*

31. S1 : The Subsidiary Alliance system was extremely advantageous to the British.
S6 : They controlled the defence and the foreign relations of the protected ally.
P : They could now maintain a large army at the cost of Indian states
Q : if any war occurred in the territories
R : either of the British ally or of the Britishers
S : This enabled them to fight wars far away from their own territories
The proper sequence should be:
A. P Q R S B. P S Q R
C. Q R P S D. S R P Q

32. S1 : In reality, by signing a Subsidiary Alliance, an Indian state virtually signed away its independence.
S6 : In fact, the Indian ruler lost all vestiges of sovereignty in external matters.
P : of maintaining diplomatic relations
Q : It lost the right of self defence
R : with its neighbours
S : and of settling its disputes

The proper sequence should be:
A. P Q R S B. R S P Q
C. Q P S R D. Q S R P

33. S1 : A mighty popular Revolt broke out in Northern and Central India in 1857.
S6 : Millions of peasants, artisans and soldiers fought heroically and wrote a glorious chapter.
P : Sepoys, or the Indian soldiers of the Company's army
Q : but soon engulfed wide regions and involved the masses
R : and nearly swept away the British rule
S : It began with a mutiny of the
The proper sequence should be:
A. R S P Q B. P Q R S
C. S R P Q D. Q R P S

34. S1 : The Indian Civil Service gradually developed into one of the most efficient and powerful civil services in the world.
S6 : though these qualities obviously served British, and not Indian interests.
P : and often participated in the making of policy
Q : independence, integrity and hard work
R : They developed certain traditions of
S : Its members exercised vast power
The proper sequence should be:
A. P Q R S B. Q R S P
C. R S Q P D. S P R Q

35. S1 : The ruin of Indian handicrafts was reflected in the ruin of the towns and cities which were famous for their manufactures.
S6 : Centres were developed and laid waste.
P : Dacca, Surat, Murshidabad and many other rising industrial
Q : ravages of war and plunder, failed to
R : survive British conquest
S : Cities which had withstood the
The proper sequence should be:
A. P Q R S B. S Q R P
C. S R P Q D. Q R S P

COMPREHENSION

Directions (Qs. No. 36-45): *In this section you have few short passages. After each passage, you will find some items based on the passage. First, read a passage and answer the items based on it. You are required to select your answers based on the contents of the passage and opinion of the author only.*

Passage

The rule of the road means that in order that the liberties of all may be preserved, the liberties of everybody must be curtailed. When the policeman, say, at a road-crossing steps into the middle of the road and puts out his hand, he is the symbol not of tyranny but of liberty. You have submitted to a curtailment of private liberty in order that you may enjoy a social order which makes your liberty a reality. We have both liberties to preserve — our individual liberty and our social liberty. That is, we must have a judicious mixture of both. I shall not permit any authority to say that my child must go to this school or that, shall specialize in science or arts. These things are personal. But if I say that my child shall have no education at all, then society will firmly tell me that my child must have education whether I like it or not.

36. According to the author, the "rule of the road" implies:
A. the rule regulating the traffic on the road
B. the principle on which a road is constructed to ensure safe traffic
C. unrestricted freedom for all to lead a happy life
D. restricted individual freedom to ensure freedom for all

37. The author thinks that when a policeman signals you to stop on a road-crossing, he is:
A. behaving in a whimsical manner
B. interfering with your freedom to use the road
C. protecting the liberty of all to use the road
D. mischievously creating hurdles in your way from some personal motive

38. The author is of the view that we should:
A. have absolute individual liberty without any restrictions imposed by the society
B. have everything controlled by the society without any kind of individual liberty
C. try to strike a sensible balance between our individual liberty and our social liberty
D. have more of social liberty than individual liberty

39. The author holds that:
A. educating or not educating his child is a matter of personal liberty
B. educating or not educating his child is also a matter of social liberty
C. choosing the school for his child is a matter of social liberty
D. choosing the subject of study for his child is a matter of social liberty

40. The most suitable title of the passage would be:
A. The Policeman at a Road Crossing
B. The Laws of the Road
C. Importance of Liberty
D. Education of Children

Passage

My most interesting visitor comes at night, when the lights are still burning — a tiny bat who prefers to fly in through the open door, and will use the window only if there is no alternative. His object in entering the house is to snap up the moths that cluster around the lamps. All the bats I have seen fly fairly high, keeping near the ceiling; but this particular bat flies in low, like a dive bomber, zooming in and out of chair legs and under tables. Once, he passed straight between my legs. Has his radar gone wrong, I wondered, or is he just plain crazy?

41. Consider the following statements:
1. The tiny bat flew in low like a dive-bomber.
2. The tiny bat like all bats keeps near the ceiling.
3. It has lost direction because its radar has gone wrong.
4. It wants to entertain the author with its skill in flying.

Which of the above statements may be assumed to be true from the information given in the passage?

A. 1 only B. 1 and 3
C. 2 and 4 D. 3 and 4

42. The bat entered the room:
A. because there was no alternative
B. to eat the moths round the lamps
C. as it had gone mad
D. as it preferred to fly in through the open door

43. After comparing the habits of the tiny bat with those of other bats, the author was:
A. sure that this bat had lost its direction
B. not sure of its preferences
C. surprised to find that it was an expert flier
D. unable to give the correct explanation for its behaviour

44. The author calls the tiny bat an "interesting visitor". This means
A. the bat visits him at night
B. the bat is interested in the moths
C. this bat has peculiar qualities
D. this bat surprises him by zooming in and out like a dive-bomber

45. What, according to you, can be the most suitable title for the passage?
A. Someone visits me
B. Night of Mysteries
C. My Nocturnal Visitor
D. A Funny Visitor

FILL IN THE BLANK

Directions (Qs. No. 46-50): *Each of the following sentences in this section has a blank space and four words or group of words given after the sentence. Select the word or group of words you consider most appropriate for the blank space and indicate your response on the Answer Sheet accordingly.*

46. The tired traveller ________ on in the hope of finding some resting place.
A. strolled B. scurried
C. paraded D. plodded

47. The car was damaged beyond repair in the ________ accident.
A. outrageous B. ghastly
C. nasty D. heinous

48. They gave a ________ dinner to celebrate the occasion, which impressed every guest.
A. austere B. public
C. sumptuous D. summary

49. Once the ________ manuscript is received by the publishers, it is typed in double space.
A. total B. full
C. complete D. filled

50. I am used to ____________ in queues.
A. stand
B. standing
C. stand up
D. standing still

PART B - GENERAL KNOWLEDGE

51. Which one of the following statements is correct?
A. Any energy transfer that does not involve temperature difference in some way is not heat
B. Any energy transfer always requires a temperature difference
C. On heating the length and volume of the object remain exactly the same
D. Whenever there is a temperature difference, heat is the only way of energy transfer

52. If T is the time period of an oscillating pendulum, which one of the following statements is NOT correct?
A. The motion repeats after time T only once
B. T is the least time after which motion repeats itself
C. The motion repeats itself after nT, where n is a positive integer
D. T remains the same only for small angular displacements

53. If an object moves with constant velocity, then which one of the following statements is NOT correct?
A. Its motion is along a straight line
B. Its speed changes with time
C. Its acceleration is zero
D. Its displacement increases linearly with time

54. An object is moving with uniform acceleration a. Its initial velocity is u and after time t its velocity is v. The equation of its motion is $v = u + at$. The velocity

(along y-axis) time (along x-axis) graph shall be a straight line
A. passing through origin
B. with x-intercept u
C. with y-intercept u
D. with slope u

55. What is the net force experienced by a bar magnet placed in a uniform magnetic field?
A. Zero
B. Depends upon length of the magnet
C. Never zero
D. Depends upon temperature

56. Which one of the following has maximum inertia?
A. An atom B. A molecule
C. A one-rupee coin D. A cricket ball

57. Which one of the following is the value of 1 kWh of energy converted into joules?
A. 1.8×10^6 J B. 3.6×10^6 J
C. 6.0×10^6 J D. 7.2×10^6 J

58. Which one of the following statements about gravitational force is NOT correct?
A. It is experienced by all bodies in the universe
B. It is a dominant force between celestial bodies
C. It is a negligible force for atoms
D. It is same for all pairs of bodies in our universe

59. Whether an object will float or sink in a liquid, depends on
A. mass of the object only
B. mass of the object and density of liquid only
C. difference in the densities of the object and liquid
D. mass and shape of the object only

60. Which one of the following devices is non-ohmic?
A. Conducting copper coil
B. Electric heating coil
C. Semi conductor diode
D. Rheostat

61. Which one of the following is the natural phenomenon based on which a simple periscope works?
A. Reflection of light
B. Refraction of light
C. Dispersion of light
D. Total internal reflection of light

62. Which one of the following frequency ranges is sensitive to human ears?
A. 0 – 200 Hz
B. 20 – 20,000 Hz
C. 200 – 20,000 Hz only
D. 2,000 – 20,000 Hz only

63. The accidental touch of Nettle leaves creates a burning sensation, which is due to inject of:
A. Hydrochloric acid B. Methanoic acid
C. Citric acid D. Sulphuric acid

64. Which of the following properties is true for a tooth paste?
A. It is acidic
B. It is neutral
C. It is basic
D. It is made up of Calcium phosphate, the material of tooth enamel

65. Which one of the following gives the highest amount of hydrogen ions (H^+)?
A. Sodium hydroxide solution
B. Milk of magnesia
C. Lemon juice
D. Gastric juice

66. Brine is an aqueous solution of:
A. NaCl B. NaOH
C. $NaHCO_3$ D. Na_2CO_3

67. Which one of the following is the chemical formula of Washing Soda?
A. $NaHCO_3$ B. $Na_2CO_3.10H_2O$
C. $Na_2CO_3.5H_2O$ D. NaOH

68. Which one of the following is NOT true for bleaching powder?
A. It is used as a reducing agent in chemical industries
B. It is used for bleaching wood pulp in paper factories
C. It is used for disinfecting drinking water
D. It is used for bleaching linen in textile industry

69. AIDS is caused by a virus whose genetic material is:
A. single stranded circular DNA
B. double stranded DNA
C. single stranded RNA
D. double stranded RNA

70. Which one of the following is an organelle that is NOT found in prokaryotic cells?
A. Cell wall B. Mitochondria
C. Plasma membrane D. Ribosome

71. Which one of the following parts of body does NOT take part in the process of breathing?
A. Bronchi B. Bowman's capsule
C. Diaphragm D. Trachea

72. Which one of the following statements about classification of plants is correct?
A. Thallophytes have well differentiated body design
B. *Funaria* is a fungus
C. All Pteridophytes are Phanerogams
D. Vascular system is not found among Bryophytes

73. Which one of the following is the correct sequence of levels of hierarchy of classification of organisms from higher to lower?
A. Phylum – Class – Order – Family – Genus
B. Phylum – Class – Family – Order – Genus
C. Family – Order – Class – Species – Genus
D. Class – Family – Order – Species – Genus

74. Which one of the following statements about meristematic tissues in plants is correct?
A. These are dead tissues and form wood
B. They provide flexibility to plant due to their thickened walls
C. These are present in the bark of a tree only
D. Growth occurs in plants due to division of cells of these tissues

75. Which one of the following Union Territories has the highest female literacy rate?
A. Chandigarh
B. Lakshadweep
C. Andaman and Nicobar Islands
D. Puducherry

76. Consider the following statements about Roaring Forties:
1. They are strong Westerly winds found in the oceans of Southern Hemisphere.
2. The strong east to west air currents are caused by the combination of air being displaced from the Equator towards the South Pole and the earth's rotation and abundance of landmasses to serve as wind breaks.

Which of the statements given above is/are correct?
A. 1 only B. 2 only
C. Both 1 and 2 D. Neither 1 nor 2

77. Consider the following statements:
1. The doldrums is a low pressure area around Equator where the prevailing winds are calm.
2. Chinook is a hot and dry wind that blows in winter and therefore raises the temperature in a short time.

Which of the statements given above is/are correct?
A. 1 only B. 2 only
C. Both 1 and 2 D. Neither 1 nor 2

78. Which one of the following is the driest desert of the world?
A. Atacama B. Gobi
C. Sahara D. Kalahari

79. Which of the following statements about latent heat for a given substance is/are correct?
1. It is fixed at a given temperature.
2. It depends upon the temperature and volume.
3. It is independent of temperature and volume.
4. It depends on the temperature but independent of volume.

Select the correct answer using the code given below:
A. 2 B. 1 and 3
C. 4 only D. 1 and 4

80. Which one of the following statements about the mass of a body is correct?
A. It changes from one place to another
B. It is same everywhere
C. It depends on its shape
D. It does not depend on its temperature

81. A ball balanced on a vertical rod is an example of:
A. stable equilibrium B. unstable equilibrium
C. neutral equilibrium D. perfect equilibrium

82. Which of the following statements about a fluid at rest in a cup is/are correct?
1. Pressure is same at all the points in the fluid.
2. Pressure is exerted on the walls.
3. Pressure exists everywhere in the fluid.

Select the correct answer using the code given below.
A. 1 and 2 only B. 2 and 3 only
C. 1 only D. 1, 2 and 3

83. Which one of the following devices is used to measure atmospheric pressure?
A. Ammeter B. Barometer
C. Potentiometer D. Lactometer

84. Which one of the following is the number of water molecules that share with two formula unit $CaSO_4$ in Plaster of Paris?
A. One B. Two
C. Five D. Ten

85. How is carbon black obtained?
A. By heating wood at high temperature in absence of air
B. By heating coal at high temperature in absence of air
C. By burning hydrocarbons in a limited supply of air
D. By heating coal at high temperature in presence of air

86. Which one of the following properties is NOT true for graphite?
A. Hybridisation of each carbon atom is sp^3
B. Hybridisation of each carbon atom is sp^2
C. Electrons are delocalized over the whole sheet of atoms
D. Each layer is composed of hexagonal rings

87. Which one of the following is the purest form of Carbon?
A. Charcoal B. Coke
C. Fullerene D. Carbon black

88. The Poisonous nature of Carbon monoxide (CO) is due to its
A. Insolubility in water
B. Ability to form a complex with haemoglobin
C. Ability to reduce some metal oxides
D. Property of having one sigma bond

89. Which one of the following elements is needed in the human body to transfer electrical signals by nerve cells?

A. Lithium B. Sodium
C. Rubidium D. Caesium

90. Who among the following first discovered cell?
A. Robert Brown B. Robert Hooke
C. Leeuwenhoek D. Rudolf Virchow

91. Which one of the following group of organisms forms a food chain?
A. Grass, human and fish
B. Grass, goat and human
C. Tree, tree cutter and tiger
D. Goat, cow and human

92. Which one of the following types of tissues will have contractile proteins?
A. Nervous tissue B. Muscle tissue
C. Bone tissue D. Blood tissue

93. If by an unknown accident the acid secreting cells of the stomach wall of an individual are damaged, digestion of which one of the following biomolecule will be affected to a greater extent?
A. Protein only
B. Lipid
C. Carbohydrate only
D. Protein and Carbohydrate

94. In which one of the following places, Headquarters of a Railway Zone is located?
A. Kanpur B. Lucknow
C. Hajipur D. New Jalpaiguri

95. Which of the following statements about Indian Academy of Highway Engineers is/are correct?
1. It is a registered society.
2. It is a collaborative body of both Central Government and State Governments.

Select the correct answer using the code given below:
A. 1 only B. 2 only
C. Both 1 and 2 D. Neither 1 nor 2

96. Which one of the following is NOT a tributary of Indus River?
A. Beas B. Ravi
C. Chenab D. Tawi

97. Which one among the following is the largest tiger reserve of India in terms of area of the core/critical tiger habitat?
A. Manas
B. Pakke
C. Nagarjunasagar Srisailam
D. Periyar

98. Which one of the following is NOT a coastal depositional feature?
A. Tombolo B. Sand bar
C. Stack D. Spit

99. Which of the following is/are coastal erosional feature(s)?
1. Notch 2. Sea Arch
3. Cliff 4. Hook

Select the correct answer using the code given below:
A. 1, 2 and 3 B. 2, 3 and 4
C. 2 and 3 only D. 1 only

100. Chemical weathering of rocks is much greater in a place with:
A. cold and dry climate
B. hot and humid climate
C. hot and dry climate
D. cold and humid climate

101. Which of the following statements about specific heat of a body is/are correct?
1. It depends upon mass and shape of the body
2. It is independent of mass and shape of the body
3. It depends only upon the temperature of the body

Select the correct answer using the code given below:
A. 1 only B. 2 and 3
C. 1 and 3 D. 2 only

102. Which one of the following is an example of the force of gravity of the earth acting on a vibrating pendulum bob?
A. Applied force B. Frictional force
C. Restoring force D. Virtual force

103. Which one of the following statements about the refractive index of a material medium with respect to air is correct?
A. It can be either positive or negative
B. It can have zero value
C. It is unity for all materials
D. It is always greater than one

104. Which one of the following statements about magnetic field lines is NOT correct?
A. They can emanate from a point
B. They do not cross each other
C. Field lines between two poles cannot be precisely straight lines at the ends
D. There are no field lines within a bar magnet

105. Two convex lenses with power 2 dioptre are kept in contact with each other. The focal length of the combined lens system is:
A. 0.10 m B. 2 m
C. 4 m D. 0.25 m

106. Which one of the following alkali metals has lowest melting point?
A. Sodium B. Potassium
C. Rubidium D. Caesium

107. Which one of the following metals is alloyed with sodium to transfer heat in a nuclear reactor?

A. Potassium B. Calcium
C. Magnesium D. Strontium

108. Which one of the following metals is used in the filaments of photoelectric cells that convert light energy into electric energy?
A. Tungsten B. Copper
C. Rubidium D. Aluminium

109. Which of the following statements about Ring of Fire is/are correct?
1. It is a zone of convergence plate boundaries
2. It is an active seismic and volcanic zone
3. It is associated with deep trench

Select the correct answer using the code given below:
A. 1 and 2 only B. 2 and 3 only
C. 1 only D. 1, 2 and 3

110. Which one of the following Himalayan vegetation species is found between the altitudes of 1800 to 2600 metres?
A. Saal B. Chir
C. Spruce D. Deodar

111. Which one of the following rivers is NOT a tributary of river Cauvery?
A. Hemavati B. Arkavati
C. Indravati D. Amravati

112. Which of the following conditions is/are essential for tea cultivation?
1. Tropical and sub-tropical climate
2. Heavy rainfall ranging from 150 cm to 250 cm
3. Soil should contain good amount of lime

Select the correct answer using the code given below:
A. 1, 2 and 3 B. 1 and 2 only
C. 2 and 3 only D. 1 only

113. Bharatmala Project is related to:
A. Improving road connectivity
B. Interlinking ports and railways
C. Interlinking of rivers
D. Interlinking major cities with gas pipelines

114. Which one of the following is a local wind that blows out from Siberia?
A. Bora B. Purga
C. Mistral D. Blizzard

115. Which one of the following centres is NOT known for iron and steel industry?
A. Bhadravati B. Salem
C. Vishakhapatnam D. Renukoot

116. Which of the following are essential prerequisites for establishment of a thermal power station?
1. Availability of fossil fuels
2. Proximity to a river, lake or sea
3. Good transport network
4. Proximity to an urban centre

Select the correct answer using the code given below:
A. 1, 2 and 3 B. 2 and 4
C. 2 and 3 only D. 1 and 3 only

117. Which of the following statements about 'Aadi Mahotsav' held recently in New Delhi is/are correct?
1. The theme of the festival was 'A Celebration of the Spirit of Tribal Culture, Cuisine and Commerce'.
2. The festival was organized by the Ministry of Tourism, Government of India.

Select the correct answer using the code given below:
A. 1 only B. 2 only
C. Both 1 and 2 D. Neither 1 nor 2

118. Light year is a unit for measurement of:
A. age of universe
B. very small time intervals
C. very high temperature
D. very large distance

119. Which of the following statements about electromagnetic waves, sound waves and water waves is/are correct?
1. They exhibit reflection
2. They carry energy
3. They exert pressure
4. They can travel in vacuum

Select the correct answer using the code given below:
A. 1, 2 and 3 B. 2 and 4
C. 1 and 3 only D. 1 only

120. Thermal capacity of a body depends on the
A. mass of the body only
B. mass and shape of the body only
C. density of the body
D. mass, shape and temperature of the body

121. Who among the following first used the term 'Industrial Revolution' in English to describe the changes that occurred in British industrial development between 1760 and 1820?
A. Karl Marx B. Georges Michelet
C. Arnold Toynbee D. Friedrich Engels

122. Which one of the following statements about the Olympe de Gouges (1748-1793) is correct?
A. She declared that although citizens should have equal rights, they are not entitled to the same honours by the State
B. She was a supporter of the Jacobin government
C. She was jailed for treason by the National Assembly
D. She declared that the nation is the union of woman and man.

123. Who among the following built a model steam engine in 1698 called "Miner's Friend" to drain mines?
A. Thomas Savery B. Thomas Newcomen
C. James Watt D. Richard Arkwright

124. Which one of the following statements about Renaissance" Humanist culture is NOT true?
A. It slackened the control of religion over human life
B. It believed that human nature was many-sided
C. It was concerned with good manners
D. It criticized material wealth, power and glory

125. Who gifted the *Badshah Nama* to King George in 1799?
A. Abul Fazl B. Abdul Hamid Lahori
C. Nawab of Awadh D. William Jones

126. What is the name of the award given to meritorious men in the Mughal Court in the form of a robe of honour that was once worn by the Emperor?
A. Sarapa B. Patka
C. Padma murassa D. Khilat

127. Who among the following social reformer started a society for the encouragement of widow remarriage in 1866 in Maharashtra?
A. Bal Gangadhar Tilak B. Jyotirao Phule
C. Vishnushastri Pandit D. Pandita Ramabai

128. Name the first major voluntary association representing primarily Indian landlord interests that was set up in Calcutta in 1851?
A. British Indian Association
B. Landholder's Society
C. Madras Native Association
D. Bombay Association

129. Who among the following introduced the Permanent Settlement of Bengal in 1793?
A. Lord Cornwallis B. Lord Ripon
C. Robert Clive D. John Adam

130. Name the rebel who fought against the British in the battle of Chinhat in the course of the 1857 Revolt?
A. Ahmadullah Shah B. Shah Mal
C. Mangal Pandey D. Kunwar Singh

131. Who among the following are the two civil servants who assisted the Constituent Assembly in framing the Constitution of India?
A. B.N. Rau and K.M. Munshi
B. S.N. Mukherjee and Alladi Krishnaswamy Aiyar
C. B.N. Rau and S.N. Mukherjee
D. K.M. Munshi and Alladi Krishnaswamy Aiyar

132. Which member of the Constituent Assembly proposed the resolution that the National Flag of India be a "horizontal tricolour of saffron, white and dark green in equal proportion", with a wheel in navy blue at the centre?
A. Jawaharlal Nehru B. B.R. Ambedkar
C. Rajendra Prasad D. Sardar Vallabhbhai Patel

133. Which of the following is/are NOT historical biography/biographies?
1. Dipavamsa
2. Harshacharita
3. Vikramankadevacharita
4. Prithvirajavijaya

Select the correct answer from the code given below:
A. 1 only B. 2 and 3 only
C. 2, 3 and 4 only D. 1, 2, 3 and 4

134. Which of the following pairs are correctly matched?

Traveller	*Country from*
1. Marco Polo	Italy
2. Ibn Battuta	Morocco
3. Nikitin	Russia
4. Seydi Ali Reis	Turkey

Select the correct answer using the code given below:
A. 1, 2 and 3 only B. 2 and 3 only
C. 1, 2, 3 and 4 D. 1 and 4 only

135. Which of the following clans are included in the Agnikula Rajputs?
1. Pratiharas 2. Chaulukyas
3. Paramaras 4. Chahamanas

Select the correct answer from the code given below:
A. 1 and 3 only B. 1, 3 and 4 only
C. 1, 2, 3 and 4 D. 2, and 4 only

136. Who among the following was the author of Humayun Nama?
A. Roshanara Begum
B. Ruquaiya Sultan Begum
C. Gulbadan Begum
D. Gauhara Begum

137. Which one of the following about the Parliament of India is NOT correct?
A. The Parliament consists of the President, the Lok Sabha and the Rajya Sabha
B. There are no nominated members in the Lok Sabha
C. The Rajya Sabha cannot be dissolved
D. Some members of the Rajya Sabha are nominated by the President

138. Which one of the following statements with regard to the Comptroller and Auditor General (CAG) of India is NOT correct?
A. He is appointed by the President of India
B. He can be removed from office in the same way as the judge of the Supreme Court of India
C. The CAG is eligible for further office under the Government of India after he has ceased to hold his office
D. The salary of the CAG is charged upon the Consolidated Fund of India

139. The Superintendence, direction and control of elections in India is vested in
A. The Supreme Court of India

B. The Parliament of India
C. The Election Commission of India
D. The Chief Election Commissioner

140. Which of the following provision(s) of the Constitution of India became effective from 26th November, 1949?
1. Elections
2. Citizenship
3. Emergency provisions
4. Appointment of the Judges

Select the correct answer using the code given below:
A. 1 only B. 1 and 2 only
C. 1, 2 and 3 D. 2 and 4

141. Which of the following statements regarding construction of Rohtang tunnel is NOT correct?
A. It is located at an altitude of 5,000 feet
B. It will provide all-year connectivity to Lahaul and Spiti Valley
C. The tunnel is being built by the Border Roads Organization
D. It will reduce the length of the Leh-Manali highway by approximately 50 km

142. Who among the following recently became the first woman pilot in Indian Navy?
A. Astha Segal B. Roopa A.
C. Sakthi Maya S. D. Shubhangi Swaroop

143. Who among the following Indians did NOT hold the title of Miss World?
A. Reita Faria B. Sushmita Sen
C. Diana Hayden D. Yukta Mookhey

144. Which one of the following countries has failed to qualify for the first time in 60 years for the FIFA World Cup to be held in Russia in the year 2018?
A. Mexico B. Iran
C. Saudi Arabia D. Italy

145. The Defence Technology and Trade Initiative (DTTI) is a forum for dialogue on defence partnership between India and:
A. Russia B. United State of America
C. Israel D. France

146. As per the policy applicable in 2017, how much Foreign Direct Investment (FDI) is permitted in the defence sector in India?
A. 49 per cent through the automatic route
B. 26 per cent through the government route
C. 26 per cent through the automatic route and beyond that up to 49 per cent through the government route
D. 75 per cent through the automatic route

147. Which one of the following countries did NOT participate in the 21st edition of Exercise Malabar?
A. United States of America
B. Japan
C. India
D. Australia

148. Justice Dalveer Bhandari of India was recently re-elected to the International Court of Justice after Christopher Greenwood pulled out before 12th round of voting. Christopher Greenwood was a nominee of
A. Canada B. Russia
C. Britain D. USA

149. In order to review the Income Tax Act, 1961 and to draft a new Direct Tax Law in consonance with economic needs of the country, the Government of India in November, 2017 has constituted a Task Force. Who among the following is made the convenor of it?
A. Shri Arvind Subramanian
B. Shri Arbind Modi
C. Shri Amitabh Kant
D. Dr. Bibek Debroy

150. The 5th Global Conference on Cyber Space (GCCS) was held in New Delhi in November, 2017. Which of the following statements about GCCS is/are correct?
1. The 4th version of GCCS was held in London.
2. The main theme of GCCS 2017 is 'Cyber4All: A Secure and Inclusive Cyberspace for Sustainable Development'.
3. 'Bindu' is the logo of GCCS 2017.

Select the correct answer using the code given below:
A. 1 only B. 2 only
C. 2 and 3 only D. 1, 2 and 3

PAPER II : MATHEMATICS

1. If $n \in N$, then $121^n - 25^n + 1900^n - (-4)^n$ is divisible by which one of the following?
A. 1904 B. 2000
C. 2002 D. 2006

2. If $n = (2017)!$, then what is

$$\frac{1}{\log_2 n} + \frac{1}{\log_3 n} + \frac{1}{\log_4 n} + ... + \frac{1}{\log_{2017} n}$$ equal to?

A. 0 B. 1
C. $\frac{n}{2}$ D. n

3. In the expansion of $(1 + x)^{43}$, if the coefficients of $(2r + 1)^{th}$ and $(r + 2)^{th}$ terms are equal, then what is the value of r $(r \neq 1)$?
A. 5 B. 14
C. 21 D. 22

4. What is the principal argument of $(-1 - i)$, where $i = \sqrt{-1}$?

A. $\frac{\pi}{4}$ B. $-\frac{\pi}{4}$

C. $-\frac{3\pi}{4}$ D. $\frac{3\pi}{4}$

5. Let α and β be real numbers and z be a complex number. If $z^2 + \alpha z + \beta = 0$ has two distinct non-real roots with $\text{Re}(z) = 1$, then it is necessary that:

A. $\beta \in (-1, 0)$ B. $|\beta| = 1$

C. $\beta \in (1, \infty)$ D. $\beta \in (0, 1)$

6. Let A and B be subsets of X and $C = (A \cap B') \cup (A' \cap B)$, where A' and B' are complements of A and B respectively in X. What is C equal to?

A. $(A \cup B') - (A \cap B')$ B. $(A' \cup B) - (A' \cap B)$

C. $(A \cup B) - (A \cap B)$ D. $(A' \cup B') - (A' \cap B')$

7. How many numbers between 100 and 1000 can be formed with the digits 5, 6, 7, 8, 9, if the repetition of digits is not allowed?

A. 3^5 B. 5^3

C. 120 D. 60

8. The number of non-zero integral solutions of the equation $|1 - 2i|^x = 5^x$ is:

A. Zero (No solution) B. One

C. Two D. Three

9. If the ratio of AM to GM of two positive numbers a and b is 5 : 3, then $a : b$ is equal to:

A. 3 : 5 B. 2 : 9

C. 9 : 1 D. 5 : 3

10. If the coefficients of a^m and a^n in the expansion of $(1 + a)^{m+n}$ are α and β, then which one of the following is correct?

A. $\alpha = 2\beta$ B. $\alpha = \beta$

C. $2\alpha = \beta$ D. $\alpha = (m + n)\beta$

11. If $x + \log_{15}(1 + 3^x) = x \log_{15}5 + \log_{15}12$, where x is an integer, then what is x equal to?

A. –3 B. 2

C. 1 D. 3

12. How many four-digit numbers divisible by 10 can be formed using 1, 5, 0, 6, 7 without repetition of digits?

A. 24 B. 36

C. 44 D. 64

Directions (Qs. No. 13 and 14): *Consider the information given below and answer the two items (02) that follow:*

In a class, 54 students are good in Hindi only, 63 students are good in Mathematics only and 41 students are good in English only. There are18 students who are good in both Hindi and Mathematics. 10 students are good in all three subjects.

13. What is the number of students who are good in either Hindi or Mathematics but not in English?

A. 99 B. 107

C. 125 D. 130

14. What is the number of students who are good in Hindi and Mathematics but not in English?

A. 18 B. 12

C. 10 D. 8

15. If α and β are different complex numbers with $|\alpha| = 1$, then what is $\left|\frac{\alpha - \beta}{1 - \overline{\alpha}\beta}\right|$ equal to?

A. $|\beta|$ B. 2

C. 1 D. 0

16. The equation $|1 - x| + x^2 = 5$ has:

A. a rational root and an irrational root

B. two rational roots

C. two irrational roots

D. no real roots

17. The binary number expression of the decimal number 31 is:

A. 1111 B. 10111

C. 11011 D. 11111

18. What is $i^{1000} + i^{1001} + i^{1002} + i^{1003}$ equal to (where $i = \sqrt{-1}$)?

A. 0 B. i

C. $-i$ D. 1

19. What is

$$\frac{1}{\log_2 N} + \frac{1}{\log_3 N} + \frac{1}{\log_4 N} + \ldots + \frac{1}{\log_{100} N}$$

equal to $(N \neq 1)$?

A. $\frac{1}{\log_{100!} N}$ B. $\frac{1}{\log_{99!} N}$

C. $\frac{99}{\log_{100!} N}$ D. $\frac{99}{\log_{99!} N}$

20. The modulus-amplitude form of $\sqrt{3} + i$, where $i = \sqrt{-1}$ is:

A. $2\left(\cos\frac{\pi}{3} + i\sin\frac{\pi}{3}\right)$ B. $2\left(\cos\frac{\pi}{6} + i\sin\frac{\pi}{6}\right)$

C. $4\left(\cos\frac{\pi}{3} + i\sin\frac{\pi}{3}\right)$ D. $4\left(\cos\frac{\pi}{6} + i\sin\frac{\pi}{6}\right)$

21. What is the number of non-zero terms in the expansion of $\left(1 + 2\sqrt{3}x\right)^{11} + \left(1 - 2\sqrt{3}x\right)^{11}$ (after simplification)?

A. 4 B. 5

C. 6 D. 11

22. What is the greatest integer among the following by which the number $5^5 + 7^5$ is divisible?

A. 6 B. 8
C. 11 D. 12

23. If $x = 1 - y + y^2 - y^3 + ...$ up to infinite terms, where $|y| < 1$, then which one of the following is correct?

A. $x = \frac{1}{1+y}$ B. $x = \frac{1}{1-y}$

C. $x = \frac{y}{1+y}$ D. $x = \frac{y}{1-y}$

24. What is the inverse of the matrix

$$A = \begin{pmatrix} \cos\theta & \sin\theta & 0 \\ -\sin\theta & \cos\theta & 0 \\ 0 & 0 & 1 \end{pmatrix}?$$

A. $\begin{pmatrix} \cos\theta & -\sin\theta & 0 \\ \sin\theta & \cos\theta & 0 \\ 0 & 0 & 1 \end{pmatrix}$ B. $\begin{pmatrix} \cos\theta & 0 & -\sin\theta \\ 0 & 1 & 0 \\ \sin\theta & 0 & \cos\theta \end{pmatrix}$

C. $\begin{pmatrix} 1 & 0 & 0 \\ 0 & \cos\theta & -\sin\theta \\ 0 & \sin\theta & \cos\theta \end{pmatrix}$ D. $\begin{pmatrix} \cos\theta & \sin\theta & 0 \\ -\sin\theta & \cos\theta & 0 \\ 0 & 0 & 1 \end{pmatrix}$

25. If A is a 2 × 3 matrix and AB is a 2 × 5 matrix, then B must be a:

A. 3 × 5 matrix B. 5 × 3 matrix
C. 3 × 2 matrix D. 5 × 2 matrix

26. If $A = \begin{pmatrix} 1 & 2 \\ 2 & 3 \end{pmatrix}$ and $A^2 - kA - I_2 = O$, where I_2 is the 2 × 2 identity matrix, then what is the value of k?

A. 4 B. –4
C. 8 D. –8

27. What is the number of triangles that can be formed by choosing the vertices from a set of 12 points in a plane, seven of which lie on the same straight line?

A. 185 B. 175
C. 115 D. 105

28. What is $C(n, r) + 2C(n, r - 1) + C(n, r - 2)$ equal to?

A. $C(n + 1, r)$ B. $C(n - 1, r + 1)$
C. $C(n, r + 1)$ D. $C(n + 2, r)$

29. Let $[x]$ denote the greatest integer function. What is the number of solutions of the equation $x^2 - 4x + [x] = 0$ in the interval $[0, 2]$?

A. Zero (No solution) B. One
C. Two D. Three

30. A survey of 850 students in a University yields that 680 students like music and 215 like dance. What is the least number of students who like both music and dance?

A. 40 B. 45
C. 50 D. 55

31. What is the sum of all two-digit numbers which when divided by 3 leave 2 as the remainder?

A. 1565 B. 1585
C. 1635 D. 1655

32. If $0 < a < 1$, the value of $\log_{10}a$ is negative. This is justified by:

A. Negative power of 10 is less than 1
B. Negative power of 10 is between 0 and 1
C. Negative power of 10 is positive
D. Negative power of 10 is negative

33. The third term of a GP is 3. What is the product of the first five terms?

A. 216
B. 226
C. 243
D. Cannot be determined due to insufficient data

34. If x, 3/2, z are in AP; x, 3, z are in GP; then which one of the following will be in HP?

A. x, 6, z B. x, 4, z
C. x, 2, z D. x, 1, z

35. What is the value of the sum $\sum_{n=2}^{11}\left(i^n + i^{n+1}\right)$, where $i = \sqrt{-1}$?

A. i B. $2i$
C. $-2i$ D. $1 + i$

36. If $\sin x = \frac{1}{\sqrt{5}}$, $\sin y = \frac{1}{\sqrt{10}}$, where $0 < x < \frac{\pi}{2}$, $0 < y < \frac{\pi}{2}$, then what is $(x + y)$ equal to?

A. π B. $\frac{\pi}{2}$

C. $\frac{\pi}{4}$ D. 0

37. What is $\frac{\sin 5x - \sin 3x}{\cos 5x + \cos 3x}$ equal to?

A. $\sin x$ B. $\cos x$
C. $\tan x$ D. $\cot x$

38. What is $\sin 105° + \cos 105°$ equal to?

A. $\sin 50°$ B. $\cos 50°$
C. $\frac{1}{\sqrt{2}}$ D. 0

39. In a triangle ABC if $a = 2$, $b = 3$ and $\sin A = \frac{2}{3}$, then what is angle B equal to?

A. $\frac{\pi}{4}$ B. $\frac{\pi}{2}$

C. $\frac{\pi}{3}$ D. $\frac{\pi}{6}$

40. What is the principal value of $\sin^{-1}\left(\sin\frac{2\pi}{3}\right)$?

A. $\frac{\pi}{4}$ B. $\frac{\pi}{2}$

C. $\frac{\pi}{3}$ D. $\frac{2\pi}{3}$

41. If x, $x - y$ and $x + y$ are the angles of a triangle (not an equilateral triangle) such that $\tan(x - y)$, $\tan x$ and $\tan(x + y)$ are in GP, then what is x equal to?

A. $\frac{\pi}{4}$ B. $\frac{\pi}{3}$

C. $\frac{\pi}{6}$ D. $\frac{\pi}{2}$

42. ABC is a triangle inscribed in a circle with centre O. Let $\alpha = \angle BAC$, where $45° < \alpha < 90°$. Let $\beta = \angle BOC$. Which one of the following is correct?

A. $\cos\beta = \frac{1-\tan^2\alpha}{1+\tan^2\alpha}$

B. $\cos\beta = \frac{1+\tan^2\alpha}{1-\tan^2\alpha}$

C. $\cos\beta = \frac{2\tan\alpha}{1+\tan^2\alpha}$

D. $\sin\_\beta = 2\sin^2\alpha$

43. If a flag-staff of 6 m height placed on the top of a tower throws a shadow of $2\sqrt{3}$ m along the ground, then what is the angle that the sun makes with the ground?

A. 60° B. 45°

C. 30° D. 15°

44. What is $\tan^{-1}\left(\frac{1}{4}\right)+\tan^{-1}\left(\frac{3}{5}\right)$ equal to?

A. 0 B. $\frac{\pi}{4}$

C. $\frac{\pi}{3}$ D. $\frac{\pi}{2}$

45. A spherical balloon of radius r subtends an angle α at the eye of an observer, while the angle of elevation of its centre is β. What is the height of the centre of the balloon (neglecting the height of the observer)?

A. $\frac{r\sin\beta}{\sin\left(\frac{\alpha}{2}\right)}$ B. $\frac{r\sin\beta}{\sin\left(\frac{\alpha}{4}\right)}$

C. $\frac{r\sin\left(\frac{\beta}{2}\right)}{\sin\alpha}$ D. $\frac{r\sin\alpha}{\sin\left(\frac{\beta}{2}\right)}$

46. If $\frac{\sin(x+y)}{\sin(x-y)} = \frac{a+b}{a-b}$, then what is $\frac{\tan x}{\tan y}$ equal to?

A. $\frac{a}{b}$ B. $\frac{b}{a}$

C. $\frac{a+b}{a-b}$ D. $\frac{a-b}{a+b}$

47. If $\sin\alpha + \sin\beta = 0 = \cos\alpha + \cos\beta$, where $0 < \beta < \alpha < 2\pi$, then which one of the following is correct?

A. $\alpha = \pi - \beta$ B. $\alpha = \pi + \beta$

C. $\alpha = 2\pi - \beta$ D. $2\alpha = \pi + 2\beta$

48. Suppose cos A is given. If only one value of $\cos\left(\frac{A}{2}\right)$ is possible, then A must be:

A. An odd multiple of 90°

B. A multiple of 90°

C. An odd multiple of 180°

D. A multiple of 180°

49. If $\cos\alpha + \cos\beta + \cos\gamma = 0$, where $0 < \alpha \le \frac{\pi}{2}$, $0 < \beta \le \frac{\pi}{2}$, $0 < \gamma \le \frac{\pi}{2}$, then what is the value of $\sin\alpha + \sin\beta + \sin\gamma$?

A. 0 B. 3

C. $\frac{5\sqrt{2}}{2}$ D. $\frac{3\sqrt{2}}{2}$

50. The maximum value of

$\sin\left(x+\frac{\pi}{5}\right)+\cos\left(x+\frac{\pi}{5}\right)$, where $x \in \left(0, \frac{\pi}{2}\right)$, is attained at:

A. $\frac{\pi}{20}$ B. $\frac{\pi}{15}$

C. $\frac{\pi}{10}$ D. $\frac{\pi}{2}$

51. What is the distance between the points which divide the line segment joining (4, 3) and (5, 7) internally and externally in the ratio 2 : 3?

A. $\frac{12\sqrt{17}}{5}$ B. $\frac{13\sqrt{17}}{5}$

C. $\frac{\sqrt{17}}{5}$ D. $\frac{6\sqrt{17}}{5}$

52. What is the angle between the straight lines $(m^2 - mn)y = (mn + n^2)x + n^3$ and $(mn + m^2)y = (mn - n^2)x + m^3$, where $m > n$?

A. $\tan^{-1}\left(\frac{2mn}{m^2+n^2}\right)$ B. $\tan^{-1}\left(\frac{4m^2n^2}{m^4-n^4}\right)$

C. $\tan^{-1}\left(\frac{4m^2n^2}{m^4+n^4}\right)$ D. 45°

53. What is the equation of the straight line cutting off an intercept 2 from the negative direction of y-axis and inclined at 30° with the positive direction of x-axis?

A. $x-2\sqrt{3}y-3\sqrt{2}=0$ B. $x+2\sqrt{3}y-3\sqrt{2}=0$

C. $x+\sqrt{3}y-2\sqrt{3}=0$ D. $x-\sqrt{3}y-2\sqrt{3}=0$

54. What is the equation of the line passing through the point of intersection of the lines $x + 2y - 3 = 0$ and $2x - y + 5 = 0$ and parallel to the line $y - x + 10 = 0$?

A. $7x - 7y + 18 = 0$ B. $5x - 7y + 18 = 0$

C. $5x - 5y + 18 = 0$ D. $x - y + 5 = 0$

55. Consider the following statements:

1. The length p of the perpendicular from the origin to the line $ax + by = c$ satisfies the relation $p^2 = \frac{c^2}{a^2+b^2}$.
2. The length p of the perpendicular from the origin to the line $\frac{x}{a}+\frac{y}{b}=1$ satisfies the relation $\frac{1}{p^2}=\frac{1}{a^2}+\frac{1}{b^2}$.
3. The length p of the perpendicular from the origin to the line $y = mx + c$ satisfies the relation $\frac{1}{p^2}=\frac{1+m^2+c^2}{c^2}$.

Which of the above is/are correct?

A. 1, 2 and 3 B. 1 only

C. 1 and 2 only D. 2 only

56. What is the equation of the ellipse whose vertices are (± 5, 0) and foci are at (± 4, 0)?

A. $\frac{x^2}{25}+\frac{y^2}{9}=1$ B. $\frac{x^2}{16}+\frac{y^2}{9}=1$

C. $\frac{x^2}{25}+\frac{y^2}{16}=1$ D. $\frac{x^2}{9}+\frac{y^2}{25}=1$

57. What is the equation of the straight line passing through the point (2, 3) and making an intercept on the positive y-axis equal to twice its intercept on the positive x-axis?

A. $2x + y = 5$ B. $2x + y = 7$

C. $x + 2y = 7$ D. $2x - y = 1$

58. Let the coordinates of the points A, B, C be (1, 8, 4), (0, –11, 4) and (2, –3, 1) respectively. What are the coordinates of the point D which is the foot of the perpendicular from A on BC?

A. (3, 4, –2) B. (4, –2, 5)

C. (4, 5, –2) D. (2, 4, 5)

59. What is the equation of the plane passing through the points (–2, 6, –6), (–3, 10, –9) and (–5, 0, –6)?

A. $2x - y - 2z = 2$ B. $2x + y + 3z = 3$

C. $x + y + z = 6$ D. $x - y - z = 3$

60. A sphere of constant radius r through the origin intersects the coordinate axes in A, B and C. What is the locus of the centroid of the triangle ABC?

A. $x^2 + y^2 + z^2 = r^2$

B. $x^2 + y^2 + z^2 = 4r^2$

C. $9(x^2 + y^2 + z^2) = 4r^2$

D. $3(x^2 + y^2 + z^2) = 2r^2$

61. The coordinates of the vertices P, Q and R of a triangle PQR are (1, –1, 1), (3, –2, 2) and (0, 2, 6) respectively. If ∠ RQP = θ, then what is ∠ PRQ equal to?

A. 30° + θ B. 45° – θ

C. 60° – θ D. 90° – θ

62. The perpendiculars that fall from any point of the straight line $2x + 11y = 5$ upon the two straight lines $24x + 7y = 20$ and $4x - 3y = 2$ are:

A. 12 and 4 respectively

B. 11 and 5 respectively

C. Equal to each other

D. Not equal to each other

63. The equation of the line, when the portion of it intercepted between the axes is divided by the point (2, 3) in the ratio of 3 : 2, is

A. Either $x + y = 4$ or $9x + y = 12$

B. Either $x + y = 5$ or $4x + 9y = 30$

C. Either $x + y = 4$ or $x + 9y = 12$

D. Either $x + y = 5$ or $9x + 4y = 30$

64. What is the distance between the straight lines $3x + 4y = 9$ and $6x + 8y = 15$?

A. 3/2 B. 3/10

C. 6 D. 5

65. What is the equation to the sphere whose centre is at (–2, 3, 4) and radius is 6 units?

A. $x^2 + y^2 + z^2 + 4x - 6y - 8z = 7$

B. $x^2 + y^2 + z^2 + 6x - 4y - 8z = 7$

C. $x^2 + y^2 + z^2 + 4x - 6y - 8z = 4$

D. $x^2 + y^2 + z^2 + 4x + 6y + 8z = 4$

66. If $\vec{a}$ and $\vec{b}$ are vectors such that $|\vec{a}|=2, |\vec{b}|=7$ and $\vec{a}\times\vec{b}=3\hat{i}+2\hat{j}+6\hat{k}$, then what is the acute angle between $\vec{a}$ and $\vec{b}$?

A. 30° B. 45°

C. 60° D. 90°

67. Let $\vec{p}$ and $\vec{q}$ be the position vectors of the points P and Q respectively with respect to origin O. The points

R and S divide PQ internally and externally respectively in the ratio 2 : 3. If $\overline{OR}$ and $\overline{OS}$ are perpendicular, then which one of the following is correct?

A. $9p^2 = 4q^2$ B. $4p^2 = 9q^2$

C. $9p = 4q$ D. $4p = 9q$

68. What is the moment about the point $\hat{i}+2\hat{j}-\hat{k}$ of a force represented by $3\hat{i}+\hat{k}$ acting through the point $2\hat{i}-\hat{j}+3\hat{k}$?

A. $-3\hat{i}+11\hat{j}+9\hat{k}$ B. $3\hat{i}+2\hat{j}+9\hat{k}$

C. $3\hat{i}+4\hat{j}+9\hat{k}$ D. $\hat{i}+\hat{j}+\hat{k}$

69. If $\vec{a}+2\vec{b}+3\vec{c}=\vec{0}$ and

$$\vec{a}\times\vec{b}+\vec{b}\times\vec{c}+\vec{c}\times\vec{a}=\lambda(\vec{b}\times\vec{c}),$$

then what is the value of λ?

A. 2 B. 3

C. 4 D. 6

70. If the vectors $\vec{k}$ and $\vec{A}$ are parallel to each other, then what is $k\vec{k}\times\vec{A}$ equal to?

A. $k^2\vec{A}$ B. $\vec{0}$

C. $-k^2\vec{A}$ D. $\vec{A}$

71. Which one of the following is correct in respect of the function $f:\mathbb{R}\rightarrow\mathbb{R}^+$ defined as $f(x)=|x+1|$?

A. $f(x^2)=[f(x)]^2$

B. $f(|x|)=|f(x)|$

C. $f(x+y)=f(x)+f(y)$

D. None of the above

72. Suppose $f:\mathbb{R}\rightarrow\mathbb{R}$ is defined by $f(x)=\dfrac{x^2}{1+x^2}$. What is the range of the function?

A. [0, 1) B. [0, 1]

C. (0, 1] D. (0, 1)

73. If $f(x)=|x|+|x-1|$, then which one of the following is correct?

A. $f(x)$ is continuous at $x=0$ and $x=1$

B. $f(x)$ is continuous at $x=0$ but not at $x=1$

C. $f(x)$ is continuous at $x=1$ but not at $x=0$

D. $f(x)$ is neither continuous at $x=0$ nor at $x=1$

74. Consider the function $f(x)=\begin{cases}x^2\ln(x) & x\neq 0\\ 0 & x=0\end{cases}$. What is $f'(0)$ equal to?

A. 0 B. 1

C. -1 D. It does not exist

75. What is the area of the region bounded by the parabolas $y^2=6(x-1)$ and $y^2=3x$?

A. $\dfrac{\sqrt{6}}{3}$ B. $\dfrac{2\sqrt{6}}{3}$

C. $\dfrac{4\sqrt{6}}{3}$ D. $\dfrac{5\sqrt{6}}{3}$

Directions (Qs. No. 76-78): *Consider the following information for the next three (03) items that follow:*

Three sides of a trapezium are each equal to 6 cm. Let $\alpha\in\left(0,\dfrac{\pi}{2}\right)$ be the angle between a pair of adjacent sides.

76. If the area of the trapezium is the maximum possible, then what is α equal to?

A. $\dfrac{\pi}{6}$ B. $\dfrac{\pi}{4}$

C. $\dfrac{\pi}{3}$ D. $\dfrac{2\pi}{5}$

77. If the area of the trapezium is maximum, what is the length of the fourth side?

A. 8 cm B. 9 cm

C. 10 cm D. 12 cm

78. What is the maximum area of the trapezium?

A. $36\sqrt{3}$ cm^2 B. $30\sqrt{3}$ cm^2

C. $27\sqrt{3}$ cm^2 D. $24\sqrt{3}$ cm^2

79. What is $\int_0^{\pi} e^x\sin x\,dx$ equal to?

A. $\dfrac{e^\pi+1}{2}$ B. $\dfrac{e^\pi-1}{2}$

C. $e^\pi+1$ D. $\dfrac{e^\pi+1}{4}$

80. If $f(x)=\dfrac{x^2-9}{x^2-2x-3}, x\neq 3$ is continuous at $x=3$, then which one of the following is correct?

A. $f(3)=0$ B. $f(3)=1.5$

C. $f(3)=3$ D. $f(3)=-1.5$

81. What is $\int_1^{e} x\ln x\,dx$ equal to?

A. $\dfrac{e+1}{4}$ B. $\dfrac{e^2+1}{4}$

C. $\dfrac{e-1}{4}$ D. $\dfrac{e^2-1}{4}$

82. What is $\int_0^{\sqrt{2}}[x^2]dx$ equal to (where [.] is the greatest integer function)?

A. $\sqrt{2}-1$ B. $1-\sqrt{2}$

C. $2(\sqrt{2}-1)$ D. $\sqrt{3}-1$

83. What is the maximum value of 16 sin θ – 12 sin² θ?

A. $\frac{3}{4}$ B. $\frac{4}{3}$

C. $\frac{16}{3}$ D. 4

84. If $f : \mathbb{R} \to S$ defined by

$f(x) = 4 \sin x - 3 \cos x + 1$ is onto, then what is S equal to?

A. [–5, 5] B. (–5, 5)

C. (–4, 6) D. [–4, 6]

85. For f to be a function, what is the domain of f, if

$f(x) = \frac{1}{\sqrt{|x|-x}}$?

A. (–∞, 0) B. (0, ∞)

C. (–∞, ∞) D. (–∞, 0]

86. What is the solution of the differential equation $x\,dy - y\,dx = 0$?

A. $xy = c$ B. $y = cx$

C. $x + y = c$ D. $x - y = c$

87. What is the derivative of the function

$f(x) = e^{\tan x} + \ln(\sec x) - e^{\ln x}$ at $x = \frac{\pi}{4}$?

A. $\frac{e}{2}$ B. e

C. $2e$ D. $4e$

88. Which one of the following differential equations has a periodic solution?

A. $\frac{d^2x}{dt^2} + \mu x = 0$ B. $\frac{d^2x}{dt^2} - \mu x = 0$

C. $x\frac{dx}{dt} + \mu t = 0$ D. $\frac{dx}{dt} + \mu xt = 0$

Where $\mu > 0$

89. What is the period of the function $f(x) = \sin x$?

A. $\frac{\pi}{4}$ B. $\frac{\pi}{2}$

C. π D. 2π

90. What is $\int \frac{dx}{2^x - 1}$ equal to?

A. $\ln(2^x - 1) + c$ B. $\frac{\ln(1-2^{-x})}{\ln 2} + c$

C. $\frac{\ln(2^{-x}-1)}{2\ln 2} + c$ D. $\frac{\ln(1+2^{-x})}{\ln 2} + c$

91. The order and degree of the differential equation $y^2 = 4a(x - a)$, where 'a' is an arbitrary constant, are respectively:

A. 1, 2 B. 2, 1

C. 2, 2 D. 1, 1

92. What is the value of $\int_{-\pi/4}^{\pi/4} (\sin x - \tan x)dx$?

A. $-\frac{1}{\sqrt{2}} + \ln\left(\frac{1}{\sqrt{2}}\right)$ B. $\frac{1}{\sqrt{2}}$

C. 0 D. $\sqrt{2}$

93. If $\int_a^b x^3 dx = 0$ and $\int_a^b x^2 dx = \frac{2}{3}$, then what are the values of a and b respectively?

A. –1, 1 B. 1, 1

C. 0, 0 D. 2, –2

94. What is $\int_0^1 x(1-x)^9 dx$ equal to?

A. $\frac{1}{110}$ B. $\frac{1}{132}$

C. $\frac{1}{148}$ D. $\frac{1}{240}$

95. What is $\lim_{x\to 0} \frac{\tan x}{\sin 2x}$ equal to?

A. $\frac{1}{2}$ B. 1

C. 2 D. Limit does not exist

96. What is $\lim_{h\to 0} \frac{\sqrt{2x+3h} - \sqrt{2x}}{2h}$ equal to?

A. $\frac{1}{2\sqrt{2x}}$ B. $\frac{3}{\sqrt{2x}}$

C. $\frac{3}{2\sqrt{2x}}$ D. $\frac{3}{4\sqrt{2x}}$

97. If $f(x)$ is an even function, where $f(x) \neq 0$, then which one of the following is correct?

A. $f'(x)$ is an even function

B. $f'(x)$ is an odd function

C. $f'(x)$ may be an even or odd function depending on the type of function

D. $f'(x)$ is a constant function

98. If $y = e^{x^2} \sin 2x$, then what is $\frac{dy}{dx}$ at $x = \pi$ equal to?

A. $(1+\pi)e^{\pi^2}$ B. $2\pi e^{\pi^2}$

C. $2e^{\pi^2}$ D. e^{π^2}

99. What is the solution of:
$(1 + 2x)\, dy - (1 - 2y)\, dx = 0$?
A. $x - y - 2xy = c$ B. $y - x - 2xy = c$
C. $y + x - 2xy = c$ D. $x + y + 2xy = c$

100. What are the order and degree, respectively, of the differential equation

$$\left(\frac{d^3y}{dx^3}\right)^2 = y^4 + \left(\frac{dy}{dx}\right)^5 ?$$

A. 4, 5 B. 2, 3
C. 3, 2 D. 5, 4

101. In a Binomial distribution, the mean is three times its variance. What is the probability of exactly 3 successes out of 5 trials?

A. $\frac{80}{243}$ B. $\frac{40}{243}$
C. $\frac{20}{243}$ D. $\frac{10}{243}$

102. Consider the following statements:
1. $P(\bar{A} \cup B) = P(\bar{A}) + P(B) - P(\bar{A} \cap B)$
2. $P(A \cap \bar{B}) = P(B) - P(A \cap B)$
3. $P(A \cap B) = P(B)\, P(A \mid B)$

Which of the above statements are correct?
A. 1 and 2 only B. 1 and 3 only
C. 2 and 3 only D. 1, 2 and 3

103. If the correlation coefficient between x and y is 0.6, covariance is 27 and variance of y is 25, then what is the variance of x?

A. $\frac{9}{5}$ B. $\frac{81}{25}$
C. 9 D. 81

104. The probabilities that a student will solve question A and question B are 0.4 and 0.5 respectively. What is the probability that he solves at least one of the two questions?
A. 0.6 B. 0.7
C. 0.8 D. 0.9

105. Let $\bar{x}$ be the mean of $x_1, x_2, x_3, \ldots, x_n$. If $x_i = a + cy_i$ for some constants a and c, then what will be the mean of $y_1, y_2, y_3, \ldots, y_n$?

A. $a + c\bar{x}$ B. $a - \frac{1}{c}\bar{x}$
C. $\frac{1}{c}\bar{x} - a$ D. $\frac{\bar{x} - a}{c}$

106. Consider the following statements:
1. If the correlation coefficient $r_{xy} = 0$, then the two lines of regression are parallel to each other.
2. If the correlation coefficient $r_{xy} = +1$, then the two lines of regression are perpendicular to each other.

Which of the above statements is/are correct?
A. 1 only B. 2 only
C. Both 1 and 2 D. Neither 1 nor 2

107. If $4x - 5y + 33 = 0$ and $20x - 9y = 107$ are two lines of regression, then what are the values of $\bar{x}$ and $\bar{y}$ respectively?
A. 12 and 18 B. 18 and 12
C. 13 and 17 D. 17 and 13

108. Consider the following statements:
1. Mean is independent of change in scale and change in origin.
2. Variance is independent of change in scale but not in origin.

Which of the above statements is/are correct?
A. 1 only B. 2 only
C. Both 1 and 2 D. Neither 1 nor 2

109. Consider the following statements:
1. The sum of deviations from mean is always zero.
2. The sum of absolute deviations is minimum when taken around median.

Which of the above statements is/are correct?
A. 1 only B. 2 only
C. Both 1 and 2 D. Neither 1 nor 2

110. What is the median of the numbers

4.6, 0, 9.3, –4.8, 7.6, 2.3, 12.7, 3.5, 8.2, 6.1, 3.9, 5.2?
A. 3.8 B. 4.9
C. 5.7 D. 6.0

111. In a test in Mathematics, 20% of the students obtained "first class". If the data are represented by a Pie-Chart, what is the central angle corresponding to "first class"?
A. 20° B. 36°
C. 72° D. 144°

112. The mean and standard deviation of a set of values are 5 and 2 respectively. If 5 is added to each value, then what is the coefficient of variation for the new set of values?
A. 10 B. 20
C. 40 D. 70

113. A train covers the first 5 km of its journey at a speed of 30 km/hr and the next 15 km at a speed of 45 km/hr. What is the average speed of the train?
A. 35 km/hr B. 37.5 km/hr
C. 39.5 km/hr D. 40 km/hr

114. Two fair dice are rolled. What is the probability of getting a sum of 7?

A. $\frac{1}{36}$ B. $\frac{1}{6}$
C. $\frac{7}{12}$ D. $\frac{5}{12}$

115. If A and B are two events such that $2P(A) = 3P(B)$, where $0 < P(A) < P(B) < 1$, then which one of the following is correct?

A. $P(A \mid B) < P(B \mid A) < P(A \cap B)$
B. $P(A \cap B) < P(B \mid A) < P(A \mid B)$
C. $P(B \mid A) < P(A \mid B) < P(A \cap B)$
D. $P(A \cap B) < P(A \mid B) < P(B \mid A)$

116. A box has ten chits numbered 0, 1, 2, 3, ..., 9. First, one chit is drawn at random and kept aside. From the remaining, a second chit is drawn at random. What is the probability that the second chit drawn is "9"?

A. $\frac{1}{10}$ B. $\frac{1}{9}$
C. $\frac{1}{90}$ D. None of the above

117. One bag contains 3 white and 2 black balls, another bag contains 5 white and 3 black balls, If a bag is chosen at random and a ball is drawn from it, what is the chance that it is white?

A. $\frac{3}{8}$ B. $\frac{49}{80}$
C. $\frac{8}{13}$ D. $\frac{1}{2}$

118. Consider the following in respect of two events A and B:

1. $P(A \text{ occurs but not } B) = P(A) - P(B)$ if $B \subset A$
2. $P(A \text{ alone or } B \text{ alone occurs}) = P(A) + P(B) - P(A \cap B)$
3. $P(A \cup B) = P(A) + P(B)$ if A and B are mutually exclusive

Which of the above is/are correct?

A. 1 only B. 1 and 3 only
C. 2 and 3 only D. 1 and 2 only

119. A committee of three has to be chosen from a group of 4 men and 5 women. If the selection is made at random, what is the probability that exactly two members are men?

A. $\frac{5}{14}$ B. $\frac{1}{21}$
C. $\frac{3}{14}$ D. $\frac{8}{21}$

120. The standard deviation σ of the first N natural numbers can be obtained using which one of the following formulae?

A. $\sigma = \frac{N^2 - 1}{12}$ B. $\sigma = \sqrt{\frac{N^2 - 1}{12}}$
C. $\sigma = \sqrt{\frac{N - 1}{12}}$ D. $\sigma = \sqrt{\frac{N^2 - 1}{6N}}$

ANSWERS

PAPER-I - GENERAL ABILITY TEST

1	2	3	4	5	6	7	8	9	10
D	B	C	D	A	C	C	B	C	B
11	**12**	**13**	**14**	**15**	**16**	**17**	**18**	**19**	**20**
D	C	D	B	C	B	C	C	A	C
21	**22**	**23**	**24**	**25**	**26**	**27**	**28**	**29**	**30**
C	D	C	B	D	A	B	C	B	C
31	**32**	**33**	**34**	**35**	**36**	**37**	**38**	**39**	**40**
B	C	A	D	B	D	C	C	B	C
41	**42**	**43**	**44**	**45**	**46**	**47**	**48**	**49**	**50**
A	B	D	C	C	D	B	C	C	B
51	**52**	**53**	**54**	**55**	**56**	**57**	**58**	**59**	**60**
A	A	B	C	A	D	B	D	C	C
61	**62**	**63**	**64**	**65**	**66**	**67**	**68**	**69**	**70**
A	B	B	D	D	A	B	A	C	B
71	**72**	**73**	**74**	**75**	**76**	**77**	**78**	**79**	**80**
B	D	A	D	B	A	C	A	D	B
81	**82**	**83**	**84**	**85**	**86**	**87**	**88**	**89**	**90**
B	B	B	A	C	A	D	B	B	B

91	92	93	94	95	96	97	98	99	100
B	B	B	C	C	D	C	C	A	B
101	102	103	104	105	106	107	108	109	110
B	C	D	D	D	D	A	C	D	B
111	112	113	114	115	116	117	118	119	120
C	B	A	B	D	A	A	D	A	D
121	122	123	124	125	126	127	128	129	130
C	C	A	D	C	A	C	A	A	A
131	132	133	134	135	136	137	138	139	140
C	A	A	C	C	C	B	C	C	B
141	142	143	144	145	146	147	148	149	150
A	D	B	D	B	A	D	C	B	B

PAPER-II - MATHEMATICS

1	2	3	4	5	6	7	8	9	10
B	B	B	C	C	C	D	A	C	B
11	12	13	14	15	16	17	18	19	20
C	A	C	D	C	A	D	A	A	B
21	22	23	24	25	26	27	28	29	30
C	D	A	A	A	A	A	D	B	B
31	32	33	34	35	36	37	38	39	40
C	B	C	A	C	C	C	C	B	C
41	42	43	44	45	46	47	48	49	50
B	A	A	B	A	A	B	C	B	A
51	52	53	54	55	56	57	58	59	60
A	B	D	C	C	A	B	C	A	C
61	62	63	64	65	66	67	68	69	70
D	C	D	B	A	A	A	A	D	B
71	72	73	74	75	76	77	78	79	80
D	A	A	A	C	C	D	C	A	B
81	82	83	84	85	86	87	88	89	90
B	A	C	D	A	B	C	A	D	B
91	92	93	94	95	96	97	98	99	100
A	C	A	A	A	D	B	C	A	C
101	102	103	104	105	106	107	108	109	110
A	B	D	B	D	D	C	B	C	B
111	112	113	114	115	116	117	118	119	120
C	B	D	B	A	A	B	B	A	B

EXPLANATORY ANSWERS

PAPER I- GENERAL ABILITY TEST

57. One kilowatt-hour is equal to 3600000 joules: 1 kWh = 3600000 J = $3.6.10^6$ J = 3.6 MJ

58. Gravitational force is known to exist between all bodies in this universe. Due to existence of gravitational force between the earth and the moon, moon should experience a pull towards the earth and vice versa. It is experienced by all bodies in the universe. It is a dominant force between celestial bodies.

59. Whether an object sinks or floats depends on the density of the object and the fluid in which it is immersed. An object that is denser than a fluid will sink in the fluid while an object that is less dense will float. A floating object is said to be buoyant. Archimedes was first to understand that buoyancy is a force and stated so in an important principle that bears his name. Archimedes' Principle states that any object immersed in or floating in a fluid is buoyed up by a force equal to the weight of displaced fluid.

If the density of an object is less than that of the liquid in which it is kept, then the object will float, *i.e.*, when the buoyant force is more than gravitational force, But if the density of the object is more than that of the liquid in which it is kept, then the object will float, *i.e.*, buoyant force is less than gravitational force.

60. The device that does not follow ohm's law is known as a **non-ohmic device** (*i.e.*, the resistance is different for different currents passing through it).

Examples of non ohmic devices are: thermistors, crystal rectifiers, vacuum tube etc.

The resistance offered by a semi-conductor diode is an example of non-ohmic device.

61. Light reflected from an object enables us to see the object when it is in the line of sight. Periscopes have long been used in order to see the objects that are not in direct line of sight. Periscopes are optical devices that use the laws of reflection.

Simple periscopes use two mirrors inclined at an angle of 45 degrees while complex ones use prisms instead of mirrors providing magnification as well. The mirrors are placed at 45 degrees facing each other. When light falls on one mirror, it is reflected back and falls on the other mirror and gets reflected to the observer's eyes. It helps view over, around or through an object.

62. The human ear can respond to minute pressure variations in the air if they are in the audible frequency range, roughly **20 Hz - 20 kHz.**

Usually "sound" is used to mean sound which can be perceived by the human ear, *i.e.*, "sound" refers to audible sound unless otherwise classified. A reasonably standard definition of audible sound is that it is a pressure wave with frequency between 20 Hz and 20,000 Hz and with an intensity above the standard threshold of hearing. Since the ear is surrounded by air, or perhaps under water, the sound waves are constrained to be longitudinal waves. Normal ranges of sound pressure and sound intensity may also be specified.

Frequency:	20 Hz – 20,000 Hz	(corresponds with pitch)
Intensity:	10^{-12} – 10 watts/m^2	(0 to 130 decibels)
Pressure:	2×10^{-5} – 60 Newtons/m^2	2×10^{-10} – .0006 atmospheres

63. The Accidental touch of nettle leaves creates a burning sensation because it **injects** formic acid, acetylcholine and histamine when its cell sap are under pressure.

A nettle-leaf-hair sting are acidic, as methanoic acid is injected into the body, which causes severe pain and an itching sensation. Applying a baking soda solution (a base) on the skin soothes the pain by neutralising the acid. Thus, the effect of these stings is neutralised.

64. Water—toothpaste contain between 20-42 per cent water to help keep it from drying out. Abrasives—most brands contain at least 50 per cent abrasives. This is one ingredient that helps your teeth get clean. Baking soda, calcium carbonate, calcium phosphates, alumina, and silica are examples of abrasives.

Abrasives constitute at least 50% of a typical toothpaste. These insoluble particles help remove plaque from the teeth. The removal of plaque and calculus helps minimize cavities and periodontal disease. Representative abrasives include particles of aluminum hydroxide ($Al(OH)_3$), calcium carbonate ($CaCO_3$), various calcium hydrogen phosphates, various silicas and zeolites, and hydroxyapatite ($Ca_5(PO_4)_3OH$).

65. Gastric juice is a digestive fluid formed in the stomach and is composed of hydrochloric acid (HCl), potassium chloride (KCl) and sodium chloride (NaCl).

The acid plays a key role in digestion of proteins, by activating digestive enzymes, and making ingested proteins unravel so that digestive enzymes break down the long chains of amino acids. Gastric acid is produced by cells in the lining of the stomach, which are coupled in feedback systems to increase acid production when needed.

Gastric Juice gives the highest amount of hydrogen ions. Even the process of titrating gastric contents back to a hydrogen ion concentration corresponding to the ingested food may seem of less meaning on close scrutiny than at first sight.

66. Brine is a solution of sodium chloride (NaCl) and water (H_2O). The process of electrolysis involves using an electric current to bring about a chemical change and make new chemicals. The **electrolysis** of brine is a large-scale process used to manufacture chlorine from salt. Two other useful chemicals are obtained during the process, sodium hydroxide (NaOH) and hydrogen (H_2).

It is important that the chlorine and sodium hydroxide produced in the process are separated they react when they come into contact with each other.

67. The chemical name of washing soda is **sodium carbonate decahydrate,** and its chemical formula is $Na_2CO_3.10H_2O$. So washing soda is hydrated salt of sodium carbonate containing 10 molecules of water of crystallization.

68. Bleaching powder is chemically, calcium oxychloride ($CaOCl_2$). Bleaching powder is manufactured using Backmann's plant in which slack lime and Chlorine are made to react to create Bleaching Powder. Bleaching powder is a yellowish white powder with a strong smell of chlorine. When exposed to air, bleaching powder gives a smell of chlorine. This is because bleaching powder reacts with carbon dioxide from the atmosphere to produce calcium carbonate and chlorine.

69. HIV is one of the group of a typical viruses called retroviruses that maintain their genetic information in the form of ribonucleic acid (RNA). Through the use of an enzyme known as reverse transcriptase, HIV and other retroviruses are capable of producing deoxyribonucleic acid (DNA) from RNA, whereas most cells carry out the opposite process, transcribing the genetic material of DNA into RNA. The activity of the enzyme enables the genetic information of HIV to become integrated permanently into the genome (chromosomes) of a host cell.

70. **Eukaryotic** cells contain **membrane**-bound organelles, such as the nucleus, while prokaryotic cells do not. Differences in cellular structure of prokaryotes and eukaryotes include the presence of **mitochondria** and **chloroplasts**, the cell wall, and the structure of chromosomal DNA.

Mitochondria are large organelles containing DNA and surrounded by a double membrane. The inner membrane is highly convoluted, with deep folds called cristae.

The membranes divide the mitochondrion into two compartments, the central matrix, and the intermembrane space. DNA, in the form of a circular or linear molecule, is found in the matrix.

The mitochondrial DNA encodes many of the components for mitochondrial function, while nuclear DNA encodes the remaining components. Components of the protein synthesizing machinery specific for mitochondria—ribosomes, tRNAs and specific proteins and enzymes—are also found in the matrix.

72. As all living organisms in this ecosystem are divided into a few major kingdoms. Plants are also further classified into different sub-kingdoms and are mainly based on their certain characteristic features and plant taxonomy.

The Classification of Plants are mainly based on two features:

- Botanical type
- Values or geographical or ecological communities.

The main purpose of classifying plants is to ensure that the right plants are correctly named or identified regardless of where one is on earth.

Plant Classification

- The evergreens are plants that retain leaves at all times (all year round).
- Woody plants can also be grouped as deciduous or evergreen.
- Deciduous plants are seasonal plants which shed its leaves at the end of the growing season, either during the winter season in the temperate climate or during the dry season in the tropical climate.

Bryophytes do not have true vascular tissues and are therefore called 'non-vascular plants'. They, however, have the embryo stage present in their life cycle. Bryophytes do not have flowers or seeds and reproduce through spores.

The bryophytes are of botanical interest because their ancestors apparently were among the first land plants. The existing species today have some green algal features and some vascular plant attributes making them intermediates—more complex than green algae, but not quite vascular plants. Once thought to be monophyletic, the bryophytes are now recognized as having three independent lineages.

73. In biological classification, the **order** is:

a taxonomic rank used in the classification of organisms and recognized by the nomenclature codes. Other well-known ranks are life, domain, kingdom, phylum, class, family, genus, and species, with order fitting in between class and family. An immediately higher rank, **superorder,** may be added directly above order, while **suborder** would be a lower rank.

74. Meristematic tissues, or simply **meristems,** are tissues in which the cells remain forever young and divide actively throughout the life of the plant. When a meristematic cell divides in two, the new cell that remains in the meristem is called an **initial,** the other the **derivative.**

A **meristem** is the tissue in most plants containing undifferentiated cells **(meristematic cells),** found in zones of the plant where growth can take place.

Meristematic cells give rise to various organs of the plant and keep the plant growing. There are three types of meristematic tissues: *apical* (at the tips), *intercalary* (in the middle) and *lateral* (at the sides).

There are two types of apical meristem tissue: **shoot apical meristem** (SAM), which gives rise to organs like the leaves and flowers, and **root apical meristem** (RAM), which provides the meristematic cells for future root growth.

Growth occurs in plants due to division of cells of these tissues.

75. Among the Union Territories, Lakshadweep has the highest literacy rate of 91.85%. Male literacy rate is 95.56% whereas female literacy rate is 87.95%. Lakshadweep has registered a decadal growth of 5.19 percentage point.

76. The **Roaring Forties** are strong westerly winds found in the Southern Hemisphere, generally between the latitudes of 40 and 50 degrees. The strong west-to-east air currents are caused by the combination of air being displaced from the Equator towards the South Pole, the Earth's rotation, and the scarcity of landmasses to serve as windbreaks.

77. The **doldrums** is a colloquial expression derived from historical maritime usage, which refers to those parts of the Atlantic Ocean and the Pacific Ocean affected by a low-pressure area around the equator where the prevailing winds are calm.

The doldrums are also noted for calm periods when the winds disappear altogether, trapping sailing ships for periods of days or weeks.

In the cold winter months of regions east of the Rocky Mountains, a strong, dry, warm wind sometimes blows from the mountains across the land. These winds, known as Chinook winds, can bring quick temperature changes.

78. The **Atacama Desert** (Spanish: *Desierto de Atacama*) is a plateau in South America, covering a 1000-km (600-mi) strip of land on the Pacific coast, west of the Andes mountains. It is the driest desert in the world, as well as the only true desert to receive less precipitation than the polar deserts.

79. **Latent heat** is thermal energy released or absorbed, by a body or a thermodynamic system, during a constant-temperature process—usually the first-order phase transition.

- **Latent heat** is the heat energy per mass unit required for a phase change to occur. If we think about substances at a molecular level, gaseous molecules have more vibration than liquid molecules. So when you add heat to a liquid, you are actually causing the molecules to vibrate.

The latent heat is the energy required to change the molecular movement. Each substance has a unique latent heat value.

Latent heat is fixed at a given temperature. It depends on the temperature but independent of volume.

80. **Mass** is both a property of a physical body and a measure of its resistance to acceleration (a change in its state of motion) when a net force is applied. It also determines the strength of its mutual gravitational attraction to other bodies. The basic SI unit of **mass** is the kilogram (kg). **The mass of a body is the quantity of matter it contains.** It is same everywhere.

81. When the center of gravity of a body lies above the point of suspension or support, the body is said to be in unstable equilibrium.

A ball balanced on a vertical rod is an example of Unstable equilibrium.

If thin rod standing vertically is slightly disturbed from its position it will not come back to its original position. This type of equilibrium is called unstable equilibrium, other example of unstable equilibrium are vertically standing cylinder and funnel etc.

83. A **barometer** is a scientific instrument used in meteorology to measure atmospheric pressure. Pressure tendency can forecast short-term changes in the weather. Numerous measurements of air pressure are used within surface weather analysis to help find surface troughs, high pressure systems and frontal boundaries.

Barometers and pressure altimeters (the most basic and common type of altimeter) are essentially the same instrument, but used for different purposes. An altimeter is intended to be transported from place to place matching the atmospheric pressure to the corresponding altitude, while a barometer is kept stationary and measures subtle pressure changes caused by weather.

85. **Carbon black** (subtypes are acetylene black, channel black, furnace black, lamp black and thermal black) is a material produced by the incomplete combustion of heavy petroleum products such as FCC tar, coal tar, ethylene cracking tar, with the addition of a small amount of vegetable oil. Carbon black is a form of paracrystalline carbon that has a high surface-area-to-volume ratio, albeit lower than that of activated carbon.

It is dissimilar to soot in its much higher surface-area-to-volume ratio and significantly lower (negligible and non-bioavailable) PAH (polycyclic aromatic hydrocarbon) content. However, carbon black is widely used as a model compound for diesel soot for diesel oxidation experiments.

Carbon black is mainly used as a reinforcing filler in tires and other rubber products. In plastics, paints, and inks, carbon black is used as a colour pigment.

86. **Graphite** archaically referred to as **plumbago,** is a crystalline allotrope of carbon, a semimetal, a native element mineral, and a form of coal. Graphite is the most stable form of carbon under standard conditions. Therefore, it is used in thermochemistry as the standard state for defining the heat of formation of carbon compounds.

In the graphite crystal, the s orbital mixes with two p orbitals only, and each of the new three sp^2 orbitals points to one of the three vertices of a triangle which lies in the x-y plane (for instance). Three electrons occupy these orbitals and one electron stays in the p_z orbital which is directed perpendicular to the x-y plane.

88. Every poison has a particular trait that causes it to be poisonous. In the case of carbon monoxide, the trait has to do with **hemoglobin** in the blood.

Hemoglobin is made up of complex proteins that bind to iron atoms. The structure of the protein and its iron atom causes oxygen to bind to the iron atom very loosely. When blood passes through the lungs, the iron atoms in the hemoglobin bind to oxygen atoms. When the blood flows into areas of the body that are lacking in oxygen, the iron atoms release their oxygen. The difference in oxygen pressure in the lungs and in the parts of the body needed oxygen is very slight. The hemoglobin is very finely tuned to absorb and release oxygen at just the right times.

89. The sodium-potassium pump is an important mechanism that is needed for nerve function. It works by pumping three sodium ions -- charged molecules -- out of the nerve cell, allowing two potassium ions to enter the cell, giving the nerve a charge because it has more positive ions outside than inside. The sodium-potassium pump triggers an electrical impulse that bounces from one nerve cell to the next transmitting messages between your brain and spinal cord and the rest of your body.

Calcium is known as the bone-building mineral, but this nutrient also plays a key role in transmitting nerve impulses that contract the muscles in your body and heart.

90. The cell was first discovered and named by **Robert Hooke** in 1665. He remarked that it looked strangely similar to cellula or small rooms which monks inhabited, thus deriving the name. However what **Hooke** actually saw was the dead cell walls of plant cells (cork) as it appeared under the microscope.

92. Muscle cells (myocytes) are elongated cells ranging from several millimetres to about 10 centimetres in length and from 10 to 100 micrometres in width. These cells are joined together in tissues that may be either striated or smooth, depending on the presence or absence, respectively, of organized, regularly repeated arrangements of myofibrillar contractile proteins called myofilaments.

94.

S.No.	Railway Zone	Zone Headquarters	Railway Divisions
1.	Northern Railway	Delhi	Delhi, Ambala, Firozpur, Lucknow NR, Moradabad
2.	Northeast Frontier Railway	Guwahati	Alipurduar, Katihar, Rangiya, Lumding, Tinsukia
3.	Eastern Railway	Kolkata	Howrah, Sealdah, Asansol, Malda
4.	South Eastern Railway	Kolkata	Adra, Chakradharpur, Kharagpur, Ranchi
5.	South Central Railway	Secunderabad	Secunderabad, Hyderabad, Vijaya-wada, Guntakal Guntur, Nanded
6.	Southern Railway	Chennai	Chennai, Tiruchirappalli, Madurai, Palakkad, Salem, Thiruvananthapuram
7.	Central Railway	Mumbai	Mumbai, Bhusawal, Pune, Solapur, Nagpur
8.	Western Railway	Mumbai	Mumbai WR, Ratlam, Ahmedabad, Rajkot, Bhavnagar, Vadodara
9.	South Western Railway	Hubballi	Hubballi, Bengaluru, Mysuru
10.	North Western Railway	Jaipur	Jaipur, Ajmer, Bikaner, Jodhpur
11.	West Central Railway	Jabalpur	Jabalpur, Bhopal, Kota
12.	North Central Railway	Allahabad	Allahabad, Agra, Jhansi
13.	South East Central Railway	Bilaspur	Bilaspur, Raipur, Nagpur SEC
14.	East Coast Railway	Bhubaneswar	Khurda Road, Sambalpur, Waltair
15.	East Central Railway	Hajipur	Danapur, Dhanbad, Mughalsarai, Samastipur, Sonpur
16.	Konkan Railway		Navi Mumbai
17.	Kolkata Metro Railway	Kolkata	Kolkata

95. Indian Academy of Highway Engineers (formerly NITHE): The Academy is the Premium National Training Institute for sharing of knowledge and pooling of experience on the entire range of subjects dealing with the construction and maintenance of roads; bridges; tunnels and road transportation including technology, equipment, research, planning, finance, taxation, organization and all connected policy issues.

In more specific terms, the objectives of the Academy are: To impart training to professionals of Highway Sector at entry level and during service at different levels of Central & State Govts., Public and Private sectors. To help highway sector engineers build up character and develop an all-round personality as a part of Human Resource Development. To assist various organizations in developing their training institutes and training of their faculty. To promote co-operation and foster exchange of knowledge, ideas and experience in all the sphere of highway engineering among engineers in India and Abroad.

96. Tawi is a river that flows through the city of Jammu, Kashmir.

Tawi river is a major left bank tributary of Chenab River. The river originates from the lapse of Kali Kundi glacier and adjoining area south-west of Bhadarwah in Doda District. Tawi river catchment is delinated by latitude 320 35' -330 5' N and longitude 740 35' - 750 45' E.

97. Nagarjunsagar-Srisailam Tiger Reserve is the largest tiger reserve in India. The reserve spreads over five districts, Kurnool District, Prakasam District, Guntur District, Nalgonda District and Mahbubnagar district. The total area of the tiger reserve is 3,568 km^2 (1,378 sq mi). The core area of this reserve is 1,200 km^2 (460 sq mi).

98. Coastal landforms of deposition occur where the accumulation of sand and shingle is greater than it is removed. This is particularly the case where constructive waves are prevalent or where there is an abundant amount of beach material supplied. Beach, Bars, Barriers, Offshore bar, Longshore bar, Spits, Hook, Tombolo etc. are main coastal depositional feature.

A stack or **sea stack** is a geological landform consisting of a steep and often vertical column or columns of rock in the sea near a coast, formed by wave erosion. Stacks are formed over time by wind and water, processes of coastal geomorphology. They are formed when part of a headland is eroded by hydraulic action, which is the force of the sea or water crashing against the rock.

100. The process of chemical weathering generally occurs in the soil where water and minerals are in constant contact. Agents of weathering are oxygen, air pollution, water, carbonic acid, and strong acids. They combine with the minerals in rocks to form clays, iron oxides, and salts, which are the endpoints of chemical weathering.

The rates of chemical weathering depend on many factors. First, the more water in the system, the faster the weathering. Second, the higher the temperature, the faster the weathering. So, the fastest rates of chemical weathering tend to occur in the hot, humid tropics. Third, the more mineral surface area exposed in the rock by joints, the faster the weathering. The increased number of cracks in the rock will allow the agents of water and oxygen to interact more intensely with the minerals.

Finally, the type of minerals in the rock will also dictate rates. For example, rocks with less quartz and more calcium feldspars (mafic igneous rocks) will weather faster than rocks with more quartz and sodium feldspars (felsic igneous rocks).

101. The amount of heat radiated by the body depends on its surface temperature and area.

The heat content of a body is a measure of the total kinetic energy of the molecules of the body. It depends only upon the temperature of the body. It is independent of mass and shape of the body.

102. A simple pendulum consists of a relatively massive object hung by a string from a fixed support. It typically hangs vertically in its equilibrium position. The massive object is affectionately referred to as the *pendulum bob.* When the bob is displaced from equilibrium and then released, it begins its back and forth vibration about its fixed equilibrium position. The motion is regular and repeating, an example of periodic motion.

The restoring force causes the vibrating object to slow down as it moves away from the equilibrium position and to speed up as it approaches the equilibrium position. It is this restoring force that is responsible for the vibration.

103. Refractive index of a medium with respect to air is the ratio of the velocity of light in air to the velocity of the light in the medium.

It is also the ratio of the refractive index of the medium with respect to vacuum to the refractive index of air with respect to vacuum.

107. Sodium-potassium alloy, colloquially called NaK is an alloy of two alkali metals sodium (Na, atomic number 11) and potassium (K, atomic number 19) and which is usually liquid at room temperature. Various commercial grades are available. NaK is highly reactive with water (like its constituent elements) and may catch fire when exposed to air, so must be handled with special precautions.

A liquid metal cooled nuclear reactor, liquid metal fast reactor or LMFR is an advanced type of nuclear reactor where the primary coolant is a liquid metal. Liquid metal cooled reactors were first adapted for nuclear submarine use but have also been extensively studied for power generation applications.

109. The Ring of Fire is a string of volcanoes and sites of seismic activity, or earthquakes, around the edges of the Pacific Ocean. Roughly 90% of all earthquakes occur along the Ring of Fire, and the ring is dotted with 75% of all active volcanoes on Earth. It is associated with deep trench.

111. Kaveri or Cauvery flows in Karnataka and Tamil Nadu. The river covers a distance of about 765 km and flows through the state of Karnataka and Tamil Nadu. On its journey to the Bay of Bengal, the river is joined by its tributaries, which include Shimsa, Hemavathi, Honnuhole, Arkavathi, Kapila, Lakshmana Theertha, Kabini, Lokapavani, Bhavani, Noyil and Amaravathy.

Indravati River—this river is a stream of the river Godavari. Its starting point is found to be the Ghats of Dandakaranya range.

112. Tea is the dried leaf of a tropical shrub, which was native to the hill slopes of Monsoon Asia. Tea is an evergreen plant. It grows both in tropical and subtropical regions. The tea plant grows well in hot and humid climate. Actually, there is an intimate relationship between climate, yield per hectare and the quality of tea.

- **Temperature:** 21°C to 29°C is ideal for the production of tea. High temperature is required in summer. The lowest temperature for the growth of tea is 16°C.
- **Rainfall:** 150-250 cm of rainfall is required for tea cultivation.
- **Soil:** Tea shrubs require fertile mountain soil mixed with lime and iron. The soil should be rich in humus.
- **Land:** Tea cultivation needs well drained land. Stagnation of water is not good for tea plants. Heavy rainfall but no stagnancy of water, such mountain slopes are good for tea cultivation.

113. Bharatmala Pariyojana is a centrally-sponsored and funded road and highways project of the Government of India. The total investment for 83,677 km (51,994 mi) committed new highways is estimated at 5.35 lakh crore, making it the single largest outlay for a government road construction scheme.

Bharatmala will look to improve connectivity particularly on economic corridors, border areas and far flung areas with an aim of quicker movement of cargo and boosting exports.

114. The **buran** in Russian is a wind which blows across Iran, eastern Asia, specifically Xinjiang, Siberia, and Kazakhstan. Over the tundra, it is also known as purga. It is a wind of cold air, sometimes very strong, characteristic of the steppes of the Sarmatic plain, to the west of the Urals.

115. The iron and steel industry is one of the most important industries in India. The manufacture of steel is regarded as one of the key industries. It is a prerequisite for modern industrial development. Large amounts of iron and steel is required for constructing bridges, rail tracts, railway rolling stock, ships, vehicles, various machines, power plants, airports, etc.

Jamshedpur, Bhilai, Rourkela, Durgapur, Bhadravati, Salem, Vishakhapatnam are centers important centers for iron and steel industry.

Renukoot is a center for aluminium industry. It is well known for the Hindalco aluminium plant.

116. Thermal power station is the most conventional source of electric power. Thermal power plant is also referred as **coal thermal power plant** and steam turbine **power plant.**

118. A **light-year** is a unit of length, equal to just under 10 trillion kilometers (10×10^{15} meters, 10 petameters or about 6 trillion miles). As defined by the International Astronomical Union (IAU), a light-year is the distance that light travels in a vacuum in one Julian year.

The light-year is often used to measure distances to stars and other distances on a galactic scale, especially in non-specialist and popular science publications.

123. Thomas Savery, English engineer and inventor who built the first steam engine.

A military engineer by profession, Savery was drawn in the 1690s to the difficult problem of pumping water out of coal mines. Using principles adduced by the French physicist Denis Papin and others, Savery patented (1698) a machine consisting of a closed vessel filled with water into which steam under pressure was introduced, forcing the water to a higher level; when the water was expelled, a sprinkler condensed the steam, producing a vacuum capable of drawing up more water through a valve below.

124. Renaissance humanism is the study of classical antiquity, at first in Italy and then spreading across Western Europe in the 14th, 15th, and 16th centuries. The term *Renaissance humanism* is contemporary to that period—Renaissance(rebirth) and "humanist".

It slackened the control of religion over human life. It believed that human nature was many sided. It was concerned with good manners.

Renaissance humanism was a response to the utilitarian approach and what came to be depicted as the "narrow pedantry" associated with medieval scholasticism. Humanists sought to create a citizenry able to speak and write with eloquence and clarity and thus capable of engaging in the civic life of their communities and persuading others to virtuous and prudent actions. This was to be accomplished through the study of the *studia humanitatis,* today known as the humanities: grammar, rhetoric, history, poetry, and moral philosophy.

125. In 1799, The Nawab (provincial governor) of Oudh in northern India sent the *Padshahnama,* to King George III of England. Today, the imperial illustrated manuscript of the *Padshahnama* of Lahori is preserved in the Royal Library at Windsor Castle. The manuscripts of the *Padshahnamas* of Qazvini and Waris are preserved in the British Library.

128. The **British Indian Association** was established on 31 October, 1851. Its formation was a major event of 19th-century India. Its establishment meant Indians had come together and could no longer be ignored. It developed enormous hopes amongst the Indians about their future.

129. The Permanent Settlement (also Permanent Settlement of Bengal) was introduced by Lord Cornwallis in 1793. It was an agreement between the British East India Company and the Landlords of Bengal to settle the Land Revenue to be raised. Lord Cornwallis came to India as the Governor General.

The Permanent Settlement was one of the most famous measures of Lord Cornwallis. It was agreed that the landlords would have perpetual and hereditary rights over the land, so long as they pay the fixed revenue to the British Government.

130. **Ahmadullah Shah** famous as Maulavi of Faizabad, was leading figures of the Indian Rebellion of 1857. Maulavi Ahmadullah Shah was known as the Lighthouse of Rebellion in Awadh region.

The Battle of Chinhat was fought on the morning of June 30, 1857, between British forces and Indian rebels, at near Chinhat, Awadh. The British were led by The Chief Commissioner of Awadh, Sir Henry Lawrence. The insurgent force, which consisted of mutineers from the East India Company's army and retainers of local landowners, was led by Barkat Ahmad, a mutineer officer of the Company's army.

132. The flag was proposed by Nehru at the Constituent Assembly on 22 July, 1947 as a horizontal tricolour of deep saffron, white and dark green in equal proportions, with the Ashoka wheel in blue in the centre of the white band. Nehru also presented two flags, one in Khadi-silk and the other in Khadi-cotton, to the assembly. The resolution was approved unanimously. It served as the national flag of the Dominion of India between 15 August, 1947 and 26 January, 1950, and has served as the flag of the Republic of India since then.

133. The ***Dipavamsa*** is the oldest historical record of Sri Lanka. The chronicle is believed to be compiled from Atthakatha and other sources around the 3-4th century. Together with the *Mahavamsa,* it is the source of many accounts of ancient history of Sri Lanka and India. Its importance resides not only as a source of history and legend, but also as an important early work in Buddhist and Pali literature.

Harshacharita, Vikramankadevacharita, and Prithvirajvijya are historical biographies.

135. In Indian culture, the **Agnivanshi** are people who claim descent from Agni, the Vedic god of fire. The Agnivanshi lineage is one of the three lineages into which the Rajput clans are divided, the others being the Suryavanshi (descended from Surya, the sun god) and the Chandravanshi (descended from Chandra, the moon god). According to medieval legends, there are four Agnivanshi clans: Chauhans (Chahamanas), Parihars (Pratiharas), Parmars (Paramaras) and Solankis (Chaulukyas).

136. **Gulbadan Begum** was a Mughal princess and the youngest daughter of Emperor Babur, the founder of the Mughal Empire and the first Mughal emperor. She is best known as the author of *Humayun-Nama,* the account of the life of her half-brother, Emperor Humayun, which she wrote on the request of her nephew, Emperor Akbar.

137. The **Parliament of India** is the supreme legislative body of the Republic of India. The Parliament is composed of the President of India and the houses. It is a bicameral legislature with two houses: the Rajya Sabha (Council of States) and the Lok Sabha (House of the People).

The **Lok Sabha** (House of the People) is the lower house of India's bicameral Parliament, with the upper house being the Rajya Sabha. The maximum strength of the House allotted by the Constitution of India is 552. Currently the house has 545 seats which is made up by election of up to 543 elected members and at a maximum, 2 nominated members of the Anglo-Indian Community by the President of India.

The **Rajya Sabha** or **Council of States** is the upper house of the Parliament of India. Membership of Rajya Sabha is limited by the Constitution to a maximum of 250 members, and current laws have provision for 245 members. Most of the members of the House are indirectly elected by state and territorial legislatures using single transferable votes, while the President can appoint 12 members for their contributions to art, literature, science, and social services. Members sit for staggered six-year terms, with one-third of the members retiring every two years.

138. The CAG is mentioned in the Constitution of India under Article 148 - 151.

The **Comptroller and Auditor General (CAG) of India** is an authority, established by Article 148 of the Constitution of India, which audits all receipts and expenditure of the Government of India and the state governments, including those of bodies and authorities substantially financed by the government. The Comptroller and Auditor-General of India is appointed by the President of India following a recommendation by the Prime Minister. He can be removed from office in the same way as the judge of the Supreme Court of India. The salary of the CAG is charged upon the Consolidated fund of India.

139. The Superintendence, direction and control of elections in India is vested in The Election Commission of India. The **Election Commission of India** is an autonomous constitutional authority responsible for administering election processes in India. The body administers elections to the Lok Sabha, Rajya Sabha, State Legislative Assemblies in India, and the offices of the President and Vice President in the country.

140. The constitution came into force on 26 January 1950, some provisions relating to Citizenship, Elections, provisional parliament, temporary & transitional provisions were given immediate effect on 26 November, 1949.

141. **Rohtang Tunnel** is a road tunnel being built under the Rohtang Pass in the eastern Pir Panjal range of the Himalayas on the Leh-Manali Highway. The tunnel is at 3,100 metres (10,171 ft) elevation whereas the Rohtang Pass is at 3,978 metres (13,051 ft) elevation 51 km (32 mi) away from Manali. It will provide all year connectivity to Lahaul and Spiti Valley.

The tunnel is being built by the Border Roads Organization. It will reduce the length of the Leh Manali highway by approximately 50 km.

146. **Defence sector -** 100% FDI is permitted in the defence sector against 49% as permitted earlier. Investment up to 49% is permitted under the automatic route. Any investment beyond that would fall under the government route 'wherever it is likely to result in access to modern technology or for other reasons to be recorded' as against 'wherever it is likely to result in access to modern and state-of-art technology in the country'.

147. The 2017 Malabar exercise was the 21st edition of the exercise and conducted from 10 to 17 July 2017. This edition involved navies from India, USA and Japan. The exercise included a harbor phase at Chennai from 10 to 13 July 2017 and a sea phase from 14 to 17 July 2017 in the Bay of Bengal. This edition focused on Aircraft Carrier operations, Air defense, Anti-submarine warfare (ASW), Surface warfare, Visit Board Search and Seizure (VBSS), Search and Rescue (SAR), joint and tactical procedures. There was also joint training between the naval special forces of the Indian and US Navies at INS Karna, Visakhapatnam. A total of 16 ships, 2 submarines and 95 aircraft participated in this exercise. It was the first exercise between the three countries which involved three aircraft carriers.

149. During the Rajaswa Gyan Sangam held on 1st and 2nd September, 2017, the Prime Minister Shri Narendra Modi had observed that the Income-tax Act, 1961 (the Act) was drafted more than 50 years ago and it needs to be re-drafted. Accordingly, in order to review the Act and to draft a new Direct Tax Law in consonance with economic needs of the country, the Government has constituted a Task Force with the following Members:

(*i*) Shri Arbind Modi, Member (Legislation), CBDT - Convener

(*ii*) Shri Girish Ahuja, practicing Chartered Accountant and non-official Director, State Bank of India;

(*iii*) Shri Rajiv Memani, Chairman & Regional Managing Partner of E&Y;

(*iv*) Shri Mukesh Patel, Practicing Tax Advocate, Ahmedabad;

(*v*) Ms. Mansi Kedia, Consultant, ICRIER, New Delhi;

(*vi*) Shri G.C. Srivastava, Retd. IRS (1971 Batch) and Advocate.

PAPER II- MATHEMATICS

1. $n \in N$

$= 121^n - 25^n + 1900^n - (-4)^n$

$n = 1, 2, 3, 4, ...$

Put, $n = 1$, we get

$= (121)^1 - (25)^1 + (1900)^1 - (-4)^1$

$= 121 - 25 + 1900 + 4 = 2000$

So, The given exp. divisible by 2000.

2. Given, $n = (2017)!$

$$= \frac{1}{\log_2 n} + \frac{1}{\log_3 n} + \frac{1}{\log_4 n} + ... + \frac{1}{\log_{2017} n}$$

$$\left[\because \frac{1}{\log_a b} = \log_b a\right]$$

$= \log_n 2 + \log_n 3 + \log_n 4 + \log_n 5 + ... + \log_n 2017$

$[\because \log_n 1 = 0]$

$= \log_n 1 + \log_n 2 + \log_n 3 + ... + \log_n 2017$

$[\log_n a \times \log_n b = \log_n ab]$

$= \log_n (1 \times 2 \times 3 \times .... \times 2017)$

$= \log_n (2017!)$

$= \log_n (n) = 1.$

3. We know in $(1 + x)^n$

$r + 1^{\text{th}}$ term, $T_{r+1} = {}^nC_r . x^r$

So, According to question,

$$T_{2r+1} = {}^nC_{2r}$$

$$T_{r+2} = {}^nC_{r+1}$$

$$T_{r+1} = T_{r+2}$$

$$^{43}C_{2r} = {}^{43}C_{r+1} \qquad [\because {}^nC_x = {}^nC_y \quad x + y = n]$$

$$2r + r + 1 = 43$$

$$3r = 42$$

$$r = 14.$$

4. $z = -1 - i$ compare with

$$z = x + iy$$

$$x = -1, y = -1$$

$$\text{argument } (z) = \theta = \tan^{-1}\left(\frac{y}{x}\right)$$

$$\text{argument } z = \tan^{-1}\left(\frac{-1}{-1}\right) = \tan^{-1}(1)$$

$$\arg(z) = \frac{\pi}{4}$$

Which lies in the interval $(-\pi, \pi]$

if $x < 0$ and $y < 0$ then principal value of argument

$$\arg(z) = -(\pi - \theta)$$

$$\arg(z) = -\left(\pi - \frac{\pi}{4}\right)$$

$$\arg(z) = -\frac{3\pi}{4}.$$

5. Given, $z^2 + \alpha z + \beta = 0$

$$z = \frac{-\alpha \pm \sqrt{\alpha^2 - 4\beta}}{2}$$

$$z = \frac{-\alpha \pm i\sqrt{4\beta - \alpha^2}}{2}$$

compare with $x + iy$

$\text{Re}(z) = x$

Given $\text{Re}(z) = 1$

So, $-\frac{\alpha}{2} = 1, \quad \alpha = -2$

$\because \quad \alpha^2 - 4\beta = 4 - 4\beta$

$4 - 4\beta < 0$

$-\beta < 0$

$\beta > 0$ iff $\beta \in (1, \infty)$.

6. We can solve this through Venn diagram

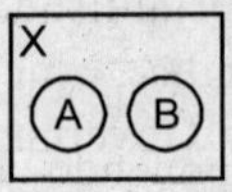

We know

$A \cap B' =$ 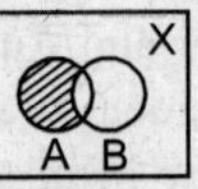

$A' \cap B =$ 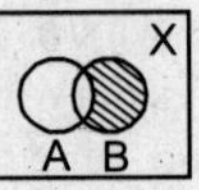

$(A \cap B') \cup (A' \cap B) =$ 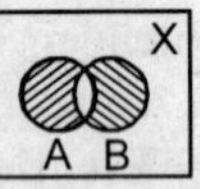

$= (A \cup B) - (A \cap B).$

7. All Numbers between 100 and 1000 are 3-digit

By digit {5, 6, 7, 8, 9} we can formed 5 digit number

Number of ways to arrange these five digit taking three at once

$$^5P_3 = \frac{5!}{(5-3)!}$$

$$= \frac{5 \times 4 \times 3 \times 2!}{2!}$$

$$= 5 \times 4 \times 3 = 60.$$

8. Given that, $|1 - 2i|^x = 5^x$

$$\left(\sqrt{(1)^2 + (-2)^2}\right)^x = 5^x$$

$$(5)^{x/2} = 5^x$$

$$\frac{x}{2} = x$$

$$x = 0.$$

9. $\text{AM} = \frac{a+b}{2}$

$\text{GM} = \sqrt{ab}$

Given, $\frac{\text{AM}}{\text{GM}} = \frac{5}{3}$

$$\frac{a+b}{2 \times \sqrt{ab}} = \frac{5}{3}$$

Apply Componendo and Dividendo

$$\frac{a+b+2\sqrt{ab}}{a+b-2\sqrt{ab}} = \frac{5+3}{5-3}$$

$$\frac{\left(\sqrt{a}+\sqrt{b}\right)^2}{\left(\sqrt{a}-\sqrt{b}\right)^2} = \frac{8}{2} = 4$$

$$\frac{\sqrt{a}+\sqrt{b}}{\sqrt{a}-\sqrt{b}} = \frac{2}{1}$$

Again apply Componendo and Dividendo

$$\frac{\sqrt{a}}{\sqrt{b}} = \frac{2+1}{2-1}$$

$$\frac{\sqrt{a}}{\sqrt{b}} = \frac{3}{1}$$

$$\frac{a}{b} = \frac{9}{1}.$$

10. $(1 + x)^n$

r^{th} Coefficient $T_{r+1} = {}^nC_r x^r$

$(1 + a)^{m+n}$,

Given, coefficient of a^m is α and a^n is β

$${}^{m+n}C_m = \alpha \quad ...(i)$$

$${}^{m+n}C_n = \beta \quad ...(ii)$$

On dividing, we get

$$\frac{\frac{(m+n)!}{n!m!}}{\frac{(m+n)!}{n!m!}} = \frac{\alpha}{\beta}$$

$$\alpha = \beta$$

Or

We know, ${}^{m+n}C_m = {}^{m+n}C_n$

So, $\alpha = \beta$.

11. If $x + \log_{15}(1 + 3^x)$

$= x.\log_{15}5 + \log_{15}12$

$x = \log_{15}5^x + \log_{15}12 - \log_{15}(1 + 3^x)$

$$x = \log_{15}\frac{5^x \times 12}{1+3^x}$$

$$15^x = \frac{5^x \times 12}{1+3^x}$$

$$15^x(1 + 3^x) = 12.5^x$$

$$15^x + 15^x.3^x = 12.5^x$$

$$(5 \times 3)^x + (5 \times 3)^x.3^x = 12.5^x$$

$$5^x.3^x + 5^x.3^x.3^x = 12.5^x$$

$$5^x(3^x + 3^{2x}) = 12.5^x$$

$$3^{2x} + 3^x - 12 = 0$$

Let $3^x = t$

$$t^2 + t - 12 = 0$$

$$t^2 + 4t - 3t - 12 = 0$$

$$t(t + 4) - 3(t + 4) = 0$$

$$(t - 3)(t + 4) = 0$$

$$t = 3,\ t \neq 4$$

$$3^x = 3^1$$

$$x = 1.$$

12. We know a number is divisible by 10 when its unit digit is zero

We have to fixed unit digit

Since, in question says digit without repeatation, *i.e.*,

$\Rightarrow$1, 5, 6, 7 (Arrange these digit), 0 (fixed)

So, rest 4 digit can be arrange in 4! manner

So, Total number which is divisible by 10

$$4! = 4 \times 3 \times 2 \times 1 = 24.$$

13. Number of Students who are good either in Hindi or in Mathematics

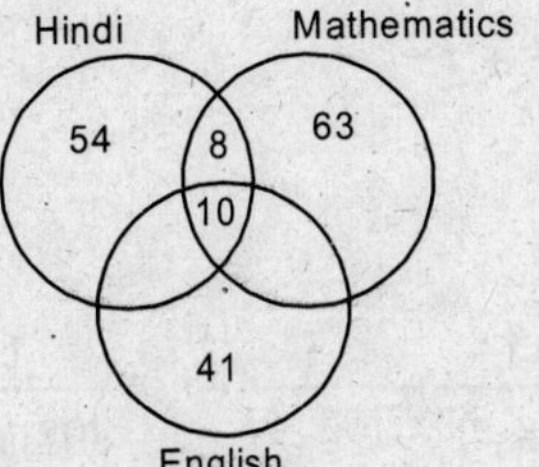

$= 54 + 8 + 63 = 125.$

14. Number of students who are good in Hindi and Mathematics but not in English = '8'.

16. $|1 - x| + x^2 = 5$

If, $x \leq 1$, then $|1 - x| = 1 - x$

$$1 - x + x^2 = 5$$

$$x^2 - x - 4 = 0$$

$$x = \frac{1 \pm \sqrt{1-4\times1(-4)}}{2}$$

$$= \frac{1 \pm \sqrt{1+16}}{2}$$

$$x = \frac{1 \pm \sqrt{17}}{2}$$

$$x = \frac{1-\sqrt{17}}{2} \text{ (irrational)}$$

$$x \neq \frac{1+\sqrt{17}}{2} \quad [\because x \leq 1]$$

If, $x > 1$, $|1 - x| = -(1 - x) = x - 1$

$$x - 1 + x^2 = 5$$

$$= x^2 + x - 6$$

$$= x^2 + 3x - 2x = 6$$

$$= (x + 3)(x - 2)$$

$$x = 2,\ x \neq -3,\ \because x > 1$$

We get two values of $x = \frac{1-\sqrt{17}}{2}, 2$

So, we get a rational root and an irrational roots.

17.

2	31	
2	15	1
2	7	1
2	3	1
	1	1

$(31)_{10} = (11111)_2$.

18. $i^{1000} + i^{1001} + i^{1002} + i^{1003}$

We know $i^4 = 1$, $i^2 = -1$

$= i^{4 \times 250} + i^{4 \times 250 + 1} + i^{4 \times 250 + 2} + i^{4 \times 250 + 3}$

$= 1 + i + i^2 + i^3$ $\quad [\because i^3 = -i]$

$= 1 + i - 1 - i$ $\quad [i^2 = -1]$

$= 0.$

19. $\frac{1}{\log_2 N} + \frac{1}{\log_3 N} + \frac{1}{\log_4 N} + \ldots + \frac{1}{\log_{100} N} = ?$

$= \log_N 2 + \log_N 3 + \log_N 4 + \ldots \log_N 100$

$= \log_N (2 \times 3 \times 4 \times \ldots 100)$

$= \log_N (1 \times 2 \times 3 \times 4 \times \ldots 100)$

$= \log_N 100!$

$= \frac{1}{\log_{100!} N}$. $\quad \left[\because \log_a b = \frac{1}{\log_b a}\right]$

20. $\left(\sqrt{3} + i\right)$ Compare with $x + iy$

$x = \sqrt{3}, \; y = 1$

then, $r = \sqrt{x^2 + y^2}$

$= \sqrt{\left(\sqrt{3}\right)^2 + (1)^2} = \sqrt{4} = 2$

$\theta = \tan^{-1}\left(\frac{y}{x}\right)$

$= \tan^{-1}\left(\frac{1}{\sqrt{3}}\right) = \frac{\pi}{6}$

We know Modulas amplitude form

$= r(\cos\theta + i \sin\theta)$

$= 2\left(\cos\frac{\pi}{6} + i \sin\frac{\pi}{6}\right)$.

21. We know the number of non-zero term of the expression, $(a + bx)^n + (a - bx)^n$

if $n \to$ odd $= \frac{n+1}{2}$

if $n \to$ even $= \frac{n+2}{2}$

In the question $n = 11$ (odd)

Number of non-zero terms

$= \frac{11+1}{2} = \frac{12}{2} = 6.$

22. We know $(a^n + b^n)$ is divisible by $(a + b)$ if n is odd number

Given $(5^5 + 7^5)$

So, it is divisible by $5^5 + 7^5 = 12$.

23. $x = 1 - y + y^2 - y^3 + \ldots \infty \; |y| < 1$

$r = \frac{T_2}{T_1} = -y, \; a = 1$

[$\because$ We know the sum of infinite series of GP $a + ar + ar^2 + \ldots \infty$]

$S_\infty = \frac{a}{1-r} \; |r| < 1$

$S_\infty = \frac{a}{1-r} = \frac{1}{1-(-y)}$

$S_\infty = \frac{1}{1+y}$.

24. $A = \begin{pmatrix} \cos\theta & \sin\theta & 0 \\ -\sin\theta & \cos\theta & 0 \\ 0 & 0 & 1 \end{pmatrix}$

$|A| = \cos\theta(\cos\theta) - (\sin\theta)(\sin\theta)$

$|A| = \cos^2\theta + \sin^2\theta = 1$

$\text{Adj } A = \begin{bmatrix} A_{11} & A_{21} & A_{31} \\ A_{12} & A_{22} & A_{32} \\ A_{13} & A_{23} & A_{33} \end{bmatrix}$

$\text{Adj } A = \begin{bmatrix} \cos\theta & -\sin\theta & 0 \\ \sin\theta & \cos\theta & 0 \\ 0 & 0 & 1 \end{bmatrix}$

$A^{-1} = \frac{\text{Adj} A}{|A|} = \begin{bmatrix} \cos\theta & -\sin\theta & 0 \\ \sin\theta & \cos\theta & 0 \\ 0 & 0 & 1 \end{bmatrix}$.

25. We know $\quad A_{ij} + B_{jk} = [AB]_{ik}$

Given, $\quad A_{2 \times 3} \times B_{3 \times 5} = [A.B]_{2 \times 5}$

(A) 3×5 matrix.

26. $A^2 - kA - I_2 = 0$

$$\begin{bmatrix}1&2\\2&3\end{bmatrix}\begin{bmatrix}1&2\\2&3\end{bmatrix}-k\begin{bmatrix}1&2\\2&3\end{bmatrix}-\begin{bmatrix}1&0\\0&1\end{bmatrix}=\begin{bmatrix}0&0\\0&0\end{bmatrix}$$

$$\begin{bmatrix}5&8\\8&13\end{bmatrix}-\begin{bmatrix}k&2k\\2k&3k\end{bmatrix}-\begin{bmatrix}1&0\\0&1\end{bmatrix}=\begin{bmatrix}0&0\\0&0\end{bmatrix}$$

$$\begin{bmatrix}4-k&8-2k\\8-2k&12-3k\end{bmatrix}=\begin{bmatrix}0&0\\0&0\end{bmatrix}$$

$$4 - k = 0$$
$$k = 4.$$

27. We know, given n distinct points in a plane in which m is collinear ($m \geq 3$) then,
the number of triangle formed $= {}^nC_3 - {}^mC_3$
$n = 12$ $m = 7$

$$^{12}C_3 - {}^7C_3$$
$$= {}^{12}C_9 - {}^7C_4 \quad [\because {}^nC_r = {}^nC_{n-r}]$$
$$= \frac{\lfloor 12}{\lfloor 9 \times \lfloor 3} - \frac{\lfloor 7}{\lfloor 4 \times \lfloor 3}$$
$$= \frac{12\times 11\times 10}{3\times 2\times 1} - \frac{7\times 6\times 5}{3\times 2}$$
$$= 2 \times 110 - 7 \times 5$$
$$= 220 - 35 = 185$$

28. $C(n, r) + 2C(n, r - 1) + C(n, r - 2)$
$= {}^nC_r + 2 \times {}^nC_{r-1} + {}^nC_{r-2}$
$= {}^nC_r + {}^nC_{r-1} + {}^nC_{r-1} + {}^nC_{r-2}$
$= {}^{n+1}C_r + {}^{n+1}C_{r-1}$
$[\because {}^nC_r + {}^nC_{r-1} = {}^{n+1}C_r]$
$= {}^{n+2}C_r$
$= C(n + 2, r)$.

29. $x^2 - 4x + [x] = 0$ $[0, 2]$

Case-I, $0 \leq x < 1$, $[x] = 0$

$$x^2 - 4x + 0 = 0$$
$$x(x - 4) = 0$$
$$x = 0, 4$$

Case-II, $1 \leq x < 2$, $[x] = 1$

$$x^2 - 4x + 1 = 0$$
$$x^2 = \frac{16 \pm \sqrt{16-4}}{2\times 1}$$
$$= \frac{16 \pm \sqrt{12}}{2}$$
$$x = 8 \pm \sqrt{3}$$

Case-III, $2 \leq x < 3$, $[x] = 2$

$$x^2 - 4x + 2 = 0$$
$$x = \frac{16 \pm \sqrt{16-8}}{2}$$
$$= \frac{16 \pm \sqrt{8}}{2} = 8 \pm \sqrt{2}$$
$$x = 8 \pm \sqrt{2}$$

So, There are one solution $0 \leq x < 1$.

30. $n(M \cup D) = 850$
$n(M) = 680$
$n(D) = 215$
$n(M \cap D) = ?$
$n(M \cup D) = n(M) + n(D) - n(M \cap D)$
$850 = 680 + 215 - n(M \cap D)$

Number of student who like both $n(M \cap D)$
$= 680 + 215 - 850$
$= 895 - 850 = 45.$

31. Two digit number which is divided by 3 leaves remain 2
= 11, 14, 17, 20, 23, ..., 98
Total number of term

$$= \frac{\text{Last number} - \text{First number}}{\text{Common difference}}$$
$$= \frac{98 - 11}{3}$$
$$n = \frac{87}{3} = 29 \quad (n = \text{odd})$$

Total term $= n + 1 = 29 + 1 = 30$

$$\text{Sum} = \frac{n}{2}[\text{first no. + last no.}]$$
$$= \frac{30}{2}[11 + 98]$$
$$= 15 \times [109] = 1635.$$

33. Given, Third term of G.P. = 3

$$ar^2 = 3$$
$$a \times ar \times ar^2 \times ar^3 \times ar^4 = a^5 r^{10}$$
$$= (ar^2)^5$$
$$= 3^5 = 243.$$

34. Given that, x, $\frac{3}{2}$, z are in AP

$$x + z = 3 \qquad ...(i)$$

[We know if a, b, c are in AP, then $2b = a + c$]
x, 3, z are in GP [if a, b, c are in GP, then $b^2 = ac$]

$$xz = 9$$
$$\frac{x + z}{xz} = \frac{3}{9}$$

$$\frac{1}{z}+\frac{1}{x} = \frac{1}{3}$$

$$\frac{1}{z}+\frac{1}{x} = \frac{2}{6} \quad \left[\frac{2}{b}=\frac{1}{a}+\frac{1}{c} \text{ are in H.P.}\right]$$

i.e., x, 6, z are in H.P.

35. $\sum_{n=2}^{11}(i^n + i^{n+1})$

$= (i^2 + i^3) + (i^3 + i^4) + (i^4 + i^5) + \ldots (i^{11} + i^{12})$
$= i^2 + 2i^3 + 2i^4 + 2i^5 + \ldots + 2i^{11} + i^{12}$
$= i^2 + i^{12} + 2(i^3 + i^4 + i^5 + \ldots + i^{11})$
$= -1 + 1 + 2i^3(1 + i + i^2 + i^3 + i^4 + i^5 + i^6 + i^7 + i^8)$
$= 0 - 2i(1 + i - 1 - i + 1 + i - 1 - i + 1)$
$= -2i.$ $\quad (\because c^2 = -1 \text{ and } i^4 = 1)$

36. Given, $\sin x = \frac{1}{\sqrt{5}}$,

$\sin y = \frac{1}{\sqrt{10}}$

condition, $0 < x < \frac{\pi}{2}, 0 < y < \frac{\pi}{2}$

$\cos x = \sqrt{1-\sin^2 x}$

$\cos x = \sqrt{1-\frac{1}{5}} = \frac{2}{\sqrt{5}}$

$\cos y = \sqrt{1-\sin^2 y}$

$= \sqrt{1-\frac{1}{10}} = \frac{3}{\sqrt{10}}$

$\sin (x + y) = \sin x.\cos y + \cos x \sin y$

$= \frac{1}{\sqrt{5}}\times\frac{3}{\sqrt{10}}+\frac{2}{\sqrt{5}}\times\frac{1}{\sqrt{10}}$

$\sin (x + y) = \frac{3}{\sqrt{50}}+\frac{2}{\sqrt{50}}$

$\sin (x + y) = \frac{5}{\sqrt{50}} \Rightarrow \sqrt{\frac{25}{50}}$

$\sin (x + y) = \frac{1}{\sqrt{2}}$

$x + y = \sin^{-1}\left(\frac{1}{\sqrt{2}}\right)$

$x + y = \frac{\pi}{4}.$

37. $\frac{\sin 5x - \sin 3x}{\cos 5x + \cos 3x}$

$= \frac{2\cos\left(\frac{5x+3x}{2}\right).\sin\left(\frac{5x-3x}{2}\right)}{2\cos\left(\frac{5x+3x}{2}\right).\cos\left(\frac{5x-3x}{2}\right)}$

$= \frac{\sin x}{\cos x}$

$= \tan x.$

38. $\sin (105°) + \cos (105°)$
$= \sin (60° + 45°) + \cos (60° + 45°)$
$= \sin 60°. \cos 45° + \cos 60° . \sin 45°$
$+ \cos 60° . \cos 45° - \sin 60° . \sin 45°$

$= \frac{\sqrt{3}}{2}\times\frac{1}{\sqrt{2}}+\frac{1}{2}\times\frac{1}{\sqrt{2}}+\frac{\sqrt{1}}{2}\times\frac{1}{\sqrt{2}}-\frac{\sqrt{3}}{2}\times\frac{1}{\sqrt{2}}$

$= \frac{1}{2\sqrt{2}}+\frac{1}{2\sqrt{2}}$

$= \frac{1+1}{2\sqrt{2}} = \frac{2}{2\sqrt{2}} = \frac{1}{\sqrt{2}}.$

39. $a = 2, b = 3, \sin A = \frac{2}{3}, B = ?$

We know sine rule

$\frac{a}{\sin A} = \frac{b}{\sin B}$

$\frac{2}{\left(\frac{2}{3}\right)} = \frac{3}{\sin B}$

$\sin B = 1$

$B = 90° = \frac{\pi}{2}.$

42. We know:

Angle made by a chord (*i.e.*, BC) at centre is two times angle made by the same chord at the circle circumference

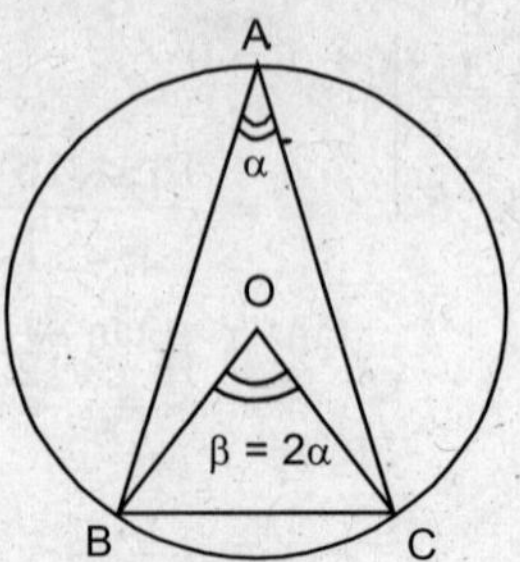

i.e., $\angle BOC = 2 \times \angle BAC$

$\beta = 2\alpha$ [Taking cos of both side]

$\cos\beta = \cos 2\alpha$

$$\cos\beta = \frac{1-\tan^2\alpha}{1+\tan^2\alpha}.$$

$$\left[\because \cos 2\alpha = \frac{1-\tan^2\alpha}{1+\tan^2\alpha}\right]$$

43. Let the angle makes with the ground α height of tower 'h' and BD = x

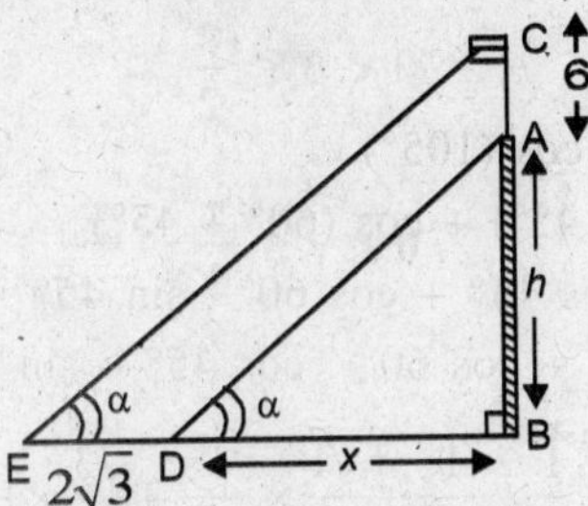

In ΔABD, $\tan\alpha = \dfrac{h}{x}$ ...(*i*)

In ΔCBE, $\tan\alpha = \dfrac{h+6}{x+2\sqrt{3}}$ ...(*ii*)

From equation (*i*) and (*ii*)

$$\frac{h}{x} = \frac{h+6}{x+2\sqrt{3}}$$

$$hx+2\sqrt{3}h = hx+6x$$

$$\frac{h}{x} = \frac{6}{2\sqrt{3}}$$

$$\frac{h}{x} = \frac{3}{\sqrt{3}} = \sqrt{3}$$

From equation (*i*),

$$\tan\alpha = \sqrt{3}.$$

$$\alpha = 60°.$$

44. $\tan^{-1}\left(\frac{1}{4}\right)+\tan^{-1}\left(\frac{3}{5}\right)$

$$\therefore \tan^{-1}\left(\frac{\frac{1}{4}+\frac{3}{5}}{1-\frac{1}{4}\times\frac{3}{5}}\right)$$

$$\because \tan^{-1}x + \tan^{-1}y = \tan^{-1}\left(\frac{x+y}{1-xy}\right)$$

$$= \tan^{-1}\left(\frac{\frac{17}{20}}{\frac{17}{20}}\right)$$

$$= \tan^{-1}(1)$$

$$= \frac{\pi}{4}.$$

45. Let O be the centre of balloon of radius r

So, $\angle ACO = \angle BCO = \dfrac{\alpha}{2}$

In right angle ΔOBC

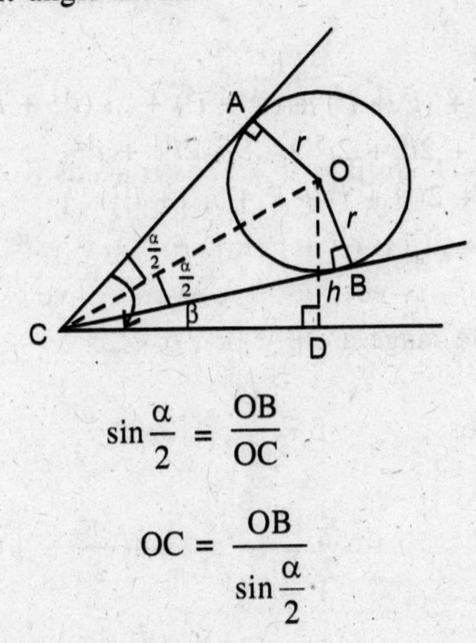

$$\sin\frac{\alpha}{2} = \frac{OB}{OC}$$

$$OC = \frac{OB}{\sin\frac{\alpha}{2}}$$

$$OC = \frac{r}{\sin\frac{\alpha}{2}}$$

In right angle ΔODC

$$\sin\beta = \frac{OD}{OC}$$

$$\sin\beta = \frac{h}{OC}$$

$$h = OC\sin\beta$$

$$h = \frac{r}{\sin\frac{\alpha}{2}}\times\sin\beta$$

$$h = \frac{r\sin\beta}{\sin\frac{\alpha}{2}}.$$

46. $\dfrac{\sin(x+y)}{\sin(x-y)} = \dfrac{a+b}{a-b}$

Apply Componendo Dividendo

$$\Rightarrow \frac{\sin(x+y)+\sin(x-y)}{\sin(x+y)-\sin(x-y)} = \frac{(a+b)+(a-b)}{(a+b)-(a-b)}$$

$$\Rightarrow \frac{2\sin\left(\frac{x+y+x-y}{2}\right).\cos\left(\frac{x+y-x+y}{2}\right)}{2\cos\left(\frac{x+y+x-y}{2}\right).\sin\left(\frac{x+y-x+y}{2}\right)} = \frac{1}{2}$$

$$\Rightarrow \quad \frac{\sin x.\cos y}{\cos x.\sin y} = \frac{a}{b}$$

$$\Rightarrow \quad \frac{\left(\frac{\sin x}{\cos x}\right)}{\left(\frac{\sin y}{\cos y}\right)} = \frac{a}{b}$$

$$\Rightarrow \quad \frac{\tan x}{\tan y} = \frac{a}{b}.$$

47. $\sin \alpha + \sin \beta = 0 = \cos \alpha + \cos \beta$

$\Downarrow$ 0 +ve, $\Downarrow$ 0 −ve, $\Downarrow$ 0 +ve, $\Downarrow$ 0 −ve

$\because$ Angle range are $0 < \beta < \alpha < 2\pi$

Suppose: $\beta = \frac{\pi}{2}, \quad \alpha = \frac{3\pi}{2}$

$$\sin\frac{\pi}{2} = 1, \quad \sin\frac{3\pi}{2} = -1$$

$$\cos\frac{\pi}{2} = 0, \quad \cos\frac{3\pi}{2} = -1$$

which is satisfy the equation,

$$\frac{3\pi}{2} = \pi + \frac{\pi}{2}$$

$$\alpha = \pi + \beta.$$

48. $\cos A = 2\cos^2\frac{A}{2} - 1$

$$\cos\frac{A}{2} = \sqrt{\frac{1}{2}(\cos A + 1)}$$

For one value is possible $\cos\frac{A}{2} \geq 0$

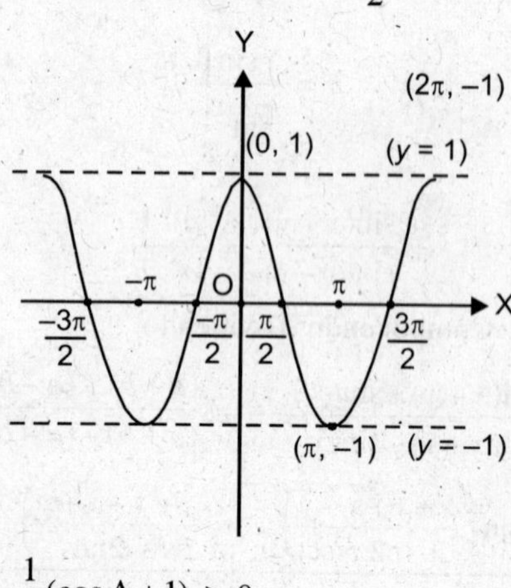

$$\frac{1}{2}(\cos A + 1) \geq 0$$

$$\cos A + 1 \geq 0$$

$$\cos A \geq -1$$

$A = \pi, 3\pi, 5\pi, 7\pi$

A must be odd multiple of 'π'.

49. $\cos \alpha + \cos \beta + \cos \gamma = 0$

$\Downarrow$ 0, $\Downarrow$ 0, $\Downarrow$ 0

where, $0 < \alpha \leq \frac{\pi}{2}$

$$0 < \beta \leq \frac{\pi}{2}$$

$$0 < \gamma \leq \frac{\pi}{2}$$

$$\alpha = \beta = \gamma = \frac{\pi}{2} \qquad \left[\because \cos\frac{\pi}{2} = 0\right]$$

$\therefore \sin \alpha + \sin \beta + \sin \gamma$

$$= \sin\frac{\pi}{2} + \sin\frac{\pi}{2} + \sin\frac{\pi}{2}$$

$$= 1 + 1 + 1$$

$$= 3.$$

50. We know $\sin x + \cos x$

$$-\sqrt{1^2 + 1^2} \leq \sin x + \cos x \leq \sqrt{1^2 + 1^2}$$

$$-\sqrt{2} \leq \sin x + \cos x \leq \sqrt{2}$$

So, the maximum value of

$$\sin x + \cos x = \sqrt{2}$$

$$x = \frac{\pi}{4}$$

So, for maximum value of

$$\sin\left(x + \frac{\pi}{5}\right) + \cos\left(x + \frac{\pi}{5}\right)$$

$\Downarrow \frac{\pi}{4}$, $\Downarrow \frac{\pi}{4}$

$$x + \frac{\pi}{5} = \frac{\pi}{4}$$

$$x = \frac{\pi}{4} - \frac{\pi}{5}$$

$$x = \frac{\pi}{20}.$$

51. A (4, 3) —— $m = 2$ —— P (x, y) —— $n = 3$ —— B (5, 7) - - - - Q (x_2, y_2)

Case–I,

When divide internally

$$P(x_1, y_1) = \left(\frac{10+12}{2+3}, \frac{14+9}{2+3}\right)$$

$$= \left(\frac{22}{5}, \frac{23}{5}\right)$$

when divide externally,

$$Q(x_2, y_2) = \left(\frac{10-12}{2-3}, \frac{14-9}{2-3}\right) = (2, -5)$$

Distance between two points (x_1, y_1) and (x_2, y_2) is

$$d = \sqrt{(y_2 - y_1)^2 + (x_2 - x_1)^2}$$

$$d = \sqrt{\left(-5 - \frac{23}{5}\right)^2 + \left(2 - \frac{22}{5}\right)^2}$$

$$d = \sqrt{\left(-\frac{48}{5}\right)^2 + \left(-\frac{12}{5}\right)^2}$$

$$d = \sqrt{\frac{2304}{25} + \frac{144}{25}}$$

$$d = \sqrt{\frac{2448}{25}}$$

$$d = \sqrt{\frac{144 \times 17}{25}}$$

$$d = \frac{12\sqrt{17}}{5}$$

52. $(m^2 - mn)y = (mn + n^2)x + n^3$

$$m_1 = \frac{mn + n^2}{m^2 - mn} = \frac{n}{m}\left(\frac{m+n}{m-n}\right)$$

$(mn + m^2)y = (mn - n^2)x + m^3$

$$m_2 = \frac{mn - n^2}{mn + m^2} = \frac{n}{m}\left[\frac{m-n}{m+n}\right]$$

$$m_1 - m_2 = \frac{n}{m}\left[\frac{m+n}{m-n} - \frac{m-n}{m+n}\right]$$

$$= \frac{n}{m}\left[\frac{(m+n)^2 - (m-n)^2}{m^2 - n^2}\right]$$

$$= \frac{n}{m}\left[\frac{4mn}{m^2 - n^2}\right].$$

$$m_1 - m_2 = \frac{4n^2}{m^2 - n^2}$$

$$m_1 \times m_2 = \frac{n}{m} \times \left(\frac{m+n}{m-n}\right) \times \frac{n}{m}\left(\frac{m-n}{m+n}\right)$$

$$m_1 \times m_2 = \frac{n^2}{m^2}$$

We know,

$$\tan\theta = \left|\frac{m_1 - m_2}{1 + m_1 m_2}\right| = \left|\frac{\frac{4n^2}{m^2 - n^2}}{1 + \frac{n^2}{m^2}}\right|$$

$$\tan\theta = \frac{\frac{4n^2}{m^2 - n^2}}{\frac{m^2 + n^2}{m^2}}$$

$$\tan\theta = \frac{4m^2n^2}{(m^2 - n^2)(m^2 + n^2)} = \frac{4m^2n^2}{m^4 - n^4}$$

$$\theta = \tan^{-1}\left(\frac{4m^2n^2}{m^4 - n^4}\right).$$

53. $C = -2$, $m = \tan 30° = \frac{1}{\sqrt{3}}$

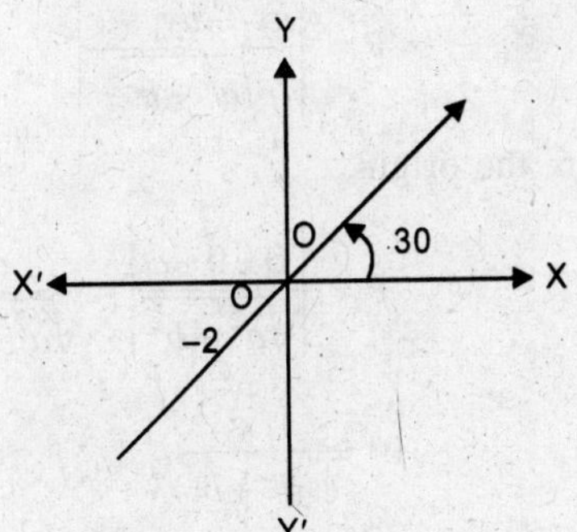

So, the equation, $y = mx + c$

$$y = \frac{1}{\sqrt{3}}x - 2$$

$$\sqrt{3}y = x - 2\sqrt{3}$$

$$x - \sqrt{3}y - 2\sqrt{3} = 0.$$

54. Point of Intersection of two lines

$x + 2y - 3 = 0$ ...(*i*)

$2x - y + 5 = 0$ ...(*ii*)

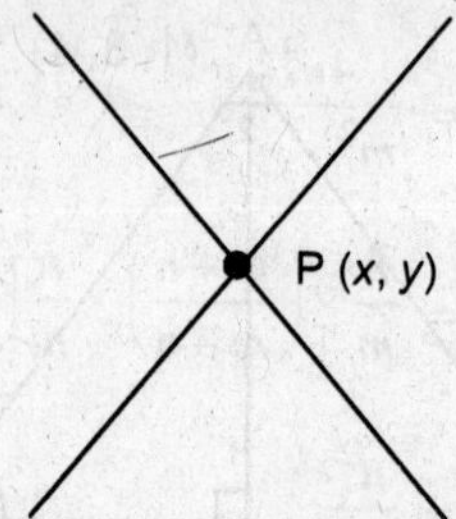

After solving these two equations we get,

$$\left(-\frac{7}{5}, \frac{22}{10}\right)$$

Two lines || (parallel) when their gradients are same

$$m_1 = m_2 = 1$$

[line || (parallel) to $y - x + 10 = 0$]

The equation of line,

$$(y - y_1) = m(x - x_1)$$

$$y - \frac{22}{10} = 1\left(x + \frac{7}{5}\right)$$

$$\frac{10y - 22}{10} = \frac{5x + 7}{5}$$

$$10y - 22 = 10x + 14$$

$$10x - 10y + 36 = 0$$

$$5x - 5y + 18 = 0.$$

55. We know the perpendicular distance from point $(x_1\ y_1)$ to a line $ax + by + c = 0$

is $$P = \left|\frac{ax_1 + by_1 + c}{\sqrt{a^2 + b^2}}\right|$$

(A) From the origin,

$$P = \left|\frac{0 + 0 + c}{\sqrt{a^2 + b^2}}\right| = \frac{c}{\sqrt{a^2 + b^2}}$$

i.e., $$P^2 = \frac{c}{a^2 + b^2}$$

(B) $$\frac{x}{a} + \frac{y}{b} = 1$$

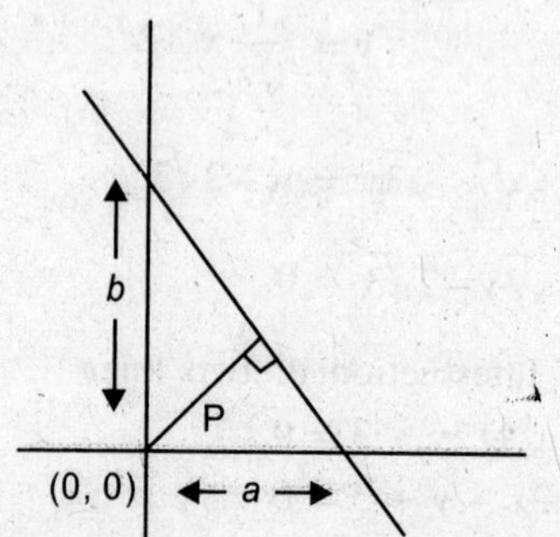

$$bx + ay = ab$$

$$P = \left|\frac{0 + 0 - ab}{\sqrt{a^2 + b^2}}\right|$$

$$P = \left|\frac{-ab}{\sqrt{a^2 + b^2}}\right|$$

$$= \frac{ab}{\sqrt{a^2 + b^2}}$$

$$P^2 = \frac{a^2b^2}{a^2 + b^2}$$

$$\frac{1}{P^2} = \frac{a^2 + b^2}{a^2 + b^2}$$

$$\frac{1}{P^2} = \frac{1}{a^2} + \frac{1}{b^2}.$$

(C) $$y - mx - c = 0$$

$$P = \left|\frac{0 - 0 - c}{\sqrt{1 + m^2}}\right|$$

$$P^2 = \frac{c^2}{1 + m^2}$$

Hence, 1 and 2 statements are correct.

56. Ellipse vertices $(\pm 5, 0)$

foci $(\pm 4, 0)$

(*i*) vertices $A(5, 0)$ $A_1(-5, 0)$

Foci $S(ae, 0) = (4, 0)$

$S_1(-ae, 0) = (-4, 0)$

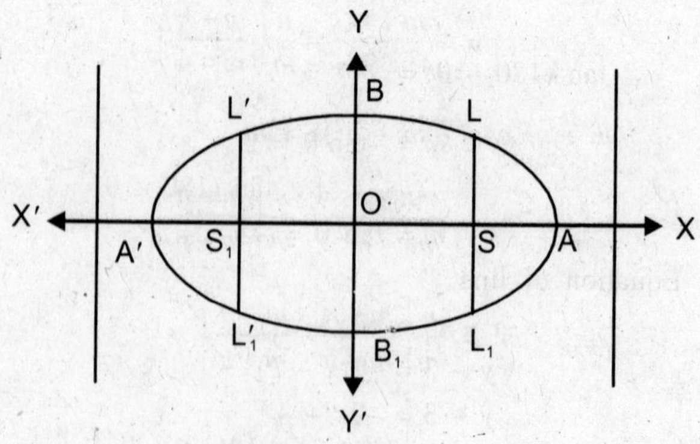

So, $$ae = 4$$

$$e = \frac{4}{5} \text{ eccentricity}$$

$$e = \sqrt{1-\frac{b^2}{a^2}}$$

$$\frac{4}{5} = \sqrt{1-\frac{b^2}{25}}$$

$$\frac{16}{25} = \frac{25-b^2}{25}$$

$$b^2 = 25 - 16$$

$$b = \sqrt{9} = \pm 3$$

$$b = 3$$

$0 < b < a$

So, equation of ellipse

$$\frac{x^2}{a^2}+\frac{y^2}{b^2} = 1$$

$$\frac{x^2}{25}+\frac{y^2}{9} = 1.$$

57. Point (2, 3)

Gradient of line

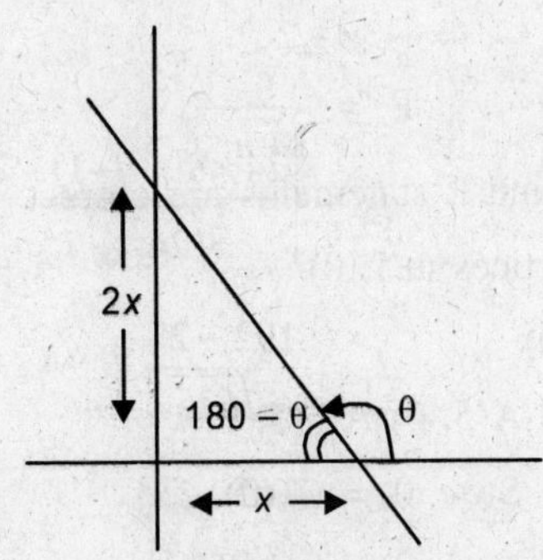

$$m = \tan\theta$$

$$\tan(180 - \theta) = \frac{2x}{x}$$

$$m = -\tan\theta = 2$$

$$[\because \tan(180 - \theta) = -\tan\theta]$$

$$m = \tan\theta = -2$$

Equation of line

$$y - y_1 = m(x - x_1)$$

$$y - 3 = -2(x - 2)$$

$$y - 3 = -2x + 4$$

$$2x + y = 7.$$

58. $\overline{BC} = 2\hat{i}+8\hat{j}-3\hat{k}$

$\overline{DA} = (1-x)\hat{i}+(8-y)\hat{j}+(4-z)\hat{k}$

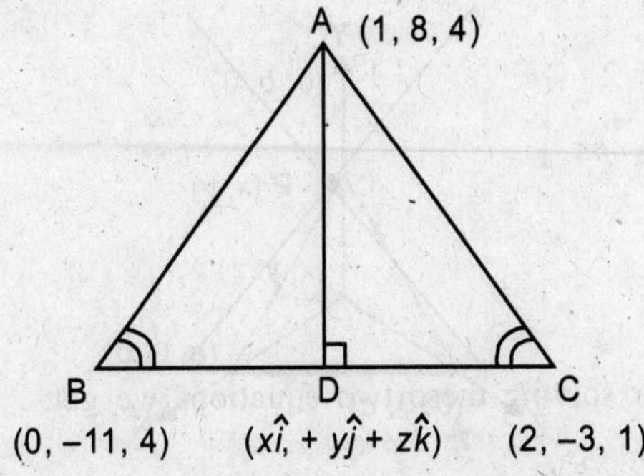

Given,

$$\overline{BC}\cdot\overline{DA} = 0$$

$$2(1 - x) + 8(8 - y) - 3(4 - z) = 0$$

$$2 - 2x + 64 - 8y - 12 + 3z = 0$$

$$-2x - 8y + 3z + 54 = 0$$

Option (C) (4, 5, –2) put in equation

$(-8 - 40 - 6) + 54 = 0$

So, the foot from A on BC = (4, 5, –2).

59. We know the equation of plane passing through three points $(x_1\ y_1\ z_1)\ (x_2\ y_2\ z_2)\ (x_3\ y_3\ z_3)$

is $$\begin{vmatrix} x-x_1 & y-y_1 & z-z_1 \\ x_2-x_1 & y_2-y_1 & z_2-z_1 \\ x_3-x_1 & y_3-y_1 & z_3-z_1 \end{vmatrix} = 0$$

Point given $\begin{pmatrix} -2, & 6 & -6 \\ x_1 & y_1 & z_1 \end{pmatrix}$ $\begin{pmatrix} -3, & 10 & -9 \\ x_2 & y_2 & z_2 \end{pmatrix}$ and $\begin{pmatrix} -5, & 0 & -6 \\ x_3 & y_3 & z_3 \end{pmatrix}$

$$\begin{vmatrix} x+2 & y-6 & z+6 \\ -1 & 4 & -3 \\ -3 & -6 & 0 \end{vmatrix} = 0$$

$$(x + 2)[0 - 18] - (y - 6)[0 - 9]$$

$$+ (z + 6)[6 + 12) = 0$$

$$-18(x + 2) + 9(y - 6) + 18(z + 6) = 0$$

$$-18x - 36 + 9y - 54 + 18z + 108 = 0$$

$$-18x + 9y + 18z + 18 = 0$$

$$2x - y - 2z - 2 = 0$$

$$2x - y - 2z = 2.$$

60. Let the coordinate of centroid (x, y, z)

We know the equation of sphere

$x^2 + y^2 + z^2 + 2ux + 2vy + 2wz + c = 0$

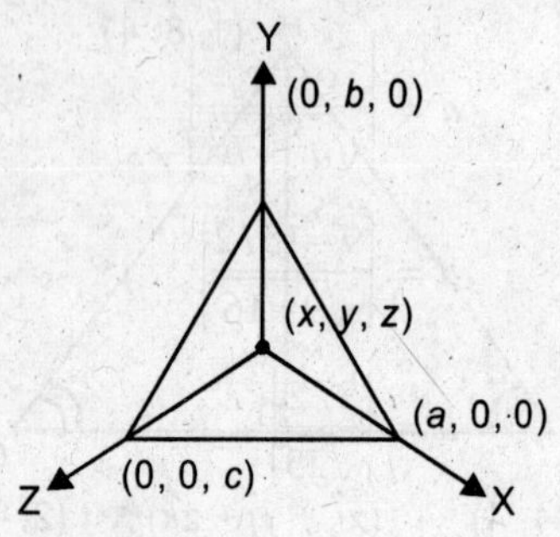

x-axis $(a, 0, 0)$

$$a^2 + 2ua = 0$$

$$u = -\frac{a}{2}$$

Similarly, $v = -\frac{b}{2}$,

$$w = -\frac{c}{2}$$

Radius of sphere 'r' $= \sqrt{u^2 + v^2 + w^2}$

$$r^2 = \frac{a^2}{4} + \frac{b^2}{4} + \frac{c^2}{4}$$

$$a^2 + b^2 + c^2 = 4r^2 \quad ...(i)$$

Coordinate of centroid,

$$x = \frac{a}{3} \qquad a = 3x$$

$$y = \frac{b}{3} \qquad b = 3y$$

$$z = \frac{c}{3} \qquad c = 3z$$

Put in equation (i)

$$(3x)^2 + (3y)^2 + (3z)^2 = 4r^2$$

$$9x^2 + 9y^2 + 9z^2 = 4r^2$$

$$9(x^2 + y^2 + z^2) = 4r^2.$$

61. $\overrightarrow{PQ} = 2i - j + k$

$$\overrightarrow{PR} = -i + 3j + 5k$$

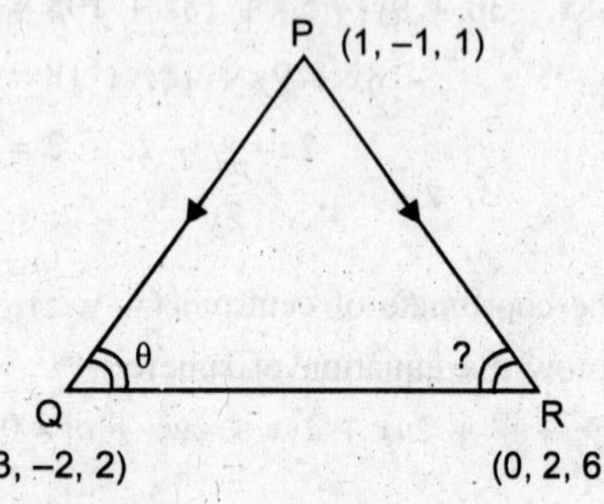

$$\cos \angle QPR = \frac{\overrightarrow{PQ}.\overrightarrow{PR}}{|\overrightarrow{PQ}|.|\overrightarrow{PR}|}$$

$$\cos \angle QPR = 0$$

$$\angle QPR = \cos^{-1}(0)$$

$$\angle QPR = 90^\circ$$

We know the sum of three angle of a triangle = 180°

$$\theta + \angle QPR + \angle PRQ = 180^\circ$$

$$\theta + 90 + \angle PRQ = 180$$

So, $\angle PRQ = 90 - \theta.$

62. Let us, assume a point $(8, -1)$ is on line $2x + 11y = 5$ which is satisfies if

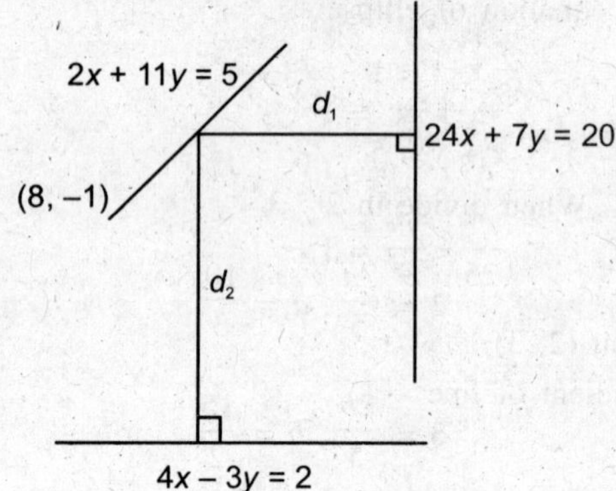

then, $d_1 = \left|\frac{24 \times 8 + 7(-1) - 20}{\sqrt{24^2 + 7^2}}\right|$

$$d_1 = \frac{192 - 27}{\sqrt{625}}$$

$$= \frac{165}{25} = \frac{33}{5}$$

$$d_2 = \left|\frac{4(8) - 3(-1) - 2}{\sqrt{4^2 + (3)^2}}\right|$$

$$= \left|\frac{32 + 3 - 2}{5}\right|$$

$$d_2 = \frac{33}{5}$$

So, $d_1 = d_2.$

63. Case-I: When divide 3 : 2

$$2 = \frac{2a}{5}, \ a = 5$$

$$3 = \frac{3b}{5}, \ b = 5$$

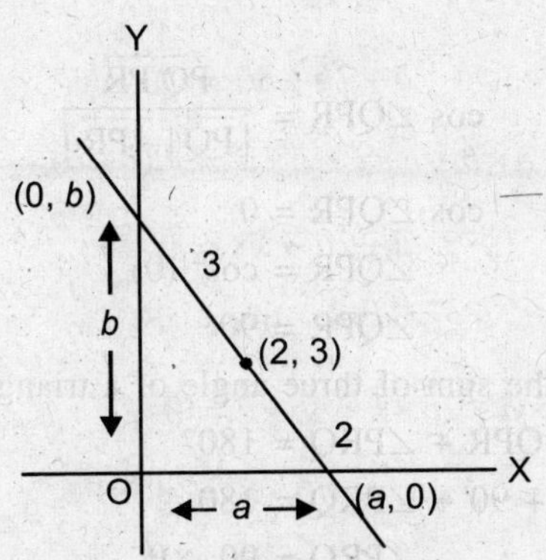

We know the line intercepted

Form $\frac{x}{a}+\frac{y}{b}=1$

$$\frac{x}{5}+\frac{y}{5}=1$$

$$x+y=5$$

Case-II. When divide in 2 : 3

$$2=\frac{3a}{5},\ a=\frac{10}{3}$$

$$3=\frac{2b}{5},\ b=\frac{15}{2}$$

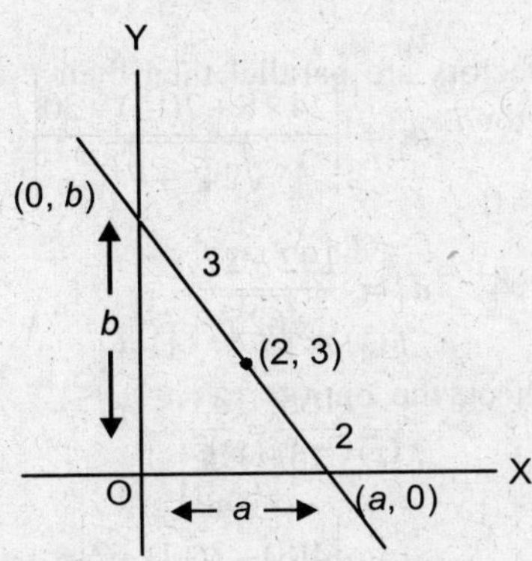

$$\frac{x}{a}+\frac{y}{b}=1$$

$$\frac{3x}{10}+\frac{2y}{15}=1$$

$$9x+4y=30$$

So, either $x+y=5$

or $9x+4y=30.$

64. $3x+4y=9$

$$6x+8y=15$$

$$\Rightarrow \quad 3x+4y=\frac{15}{2}$$

$\because m_1=m_2$, So, both lines are parallel

We know distance between two parallel line

$$d=\left|\frac{c_1-c_2}{\sqrt{a^2+b^2}}\right|$$

$$d=\left|\frac{9-15/2}{\sqrt{9+16}}\right|$$

$$d=\left|\frac{3/2}{\sqrt{25}}\right|$$

$$d=\frac{3}{10}.$$

65. Given that Sphere centre (–2, 3, 4) and radius 'r' = 6 unit

$\because$ We know the equation of sphere with Centre (a, b, c) with radius r is

$$(x-a)^2+(y-b)^2+(z-c)^2=r^2$$

$$(x+2)^2+(y-3)^2+(z-4)^2=(6)^2$$

$$x^2+4+4x+y^2+9-6y+z^2+16-8z=36$$

$$x^2+y^2+z^2+4x-6y-8z+29-36=0$$

$$x^2+y^2+z^2+4x-6y-8z=7.$$

66. $|\vec{a}|=2,\ |\vec{b}|=7$

$$\vec{a}\times\vec{b}=3\hat{i}+2\hat{j}+6\hat{k}$$

$$|\vec{a}\times\vec{b}|=\sqrt{3^2+2^2+6^2}$$

$$=\sqrt{49}=7$$

Angle $\quad \sin\theta=\frac{|\vec{a}\times\vec{b}|}{|\vec{a}|.|\vec{b}|}$

$$\sin\theta=\frac{7}{2\times 7}$$

$$\sin\theta=\frac{1}{2}$$

$$\sin\theta=\sin\frac{\pi}{6}\quad [0<\theta<90]$$

$$\theta=30°.$$

67. I. When divide Internally

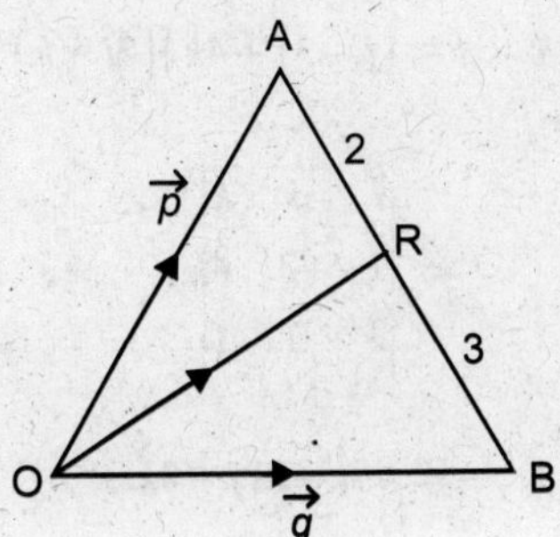

$$\overrightarrow{OR} = \frac{2q+3p}{2+3}$$

$$\overrightarrow{OR} = \frac{2q+3p}{5}$$

II. When divide externally

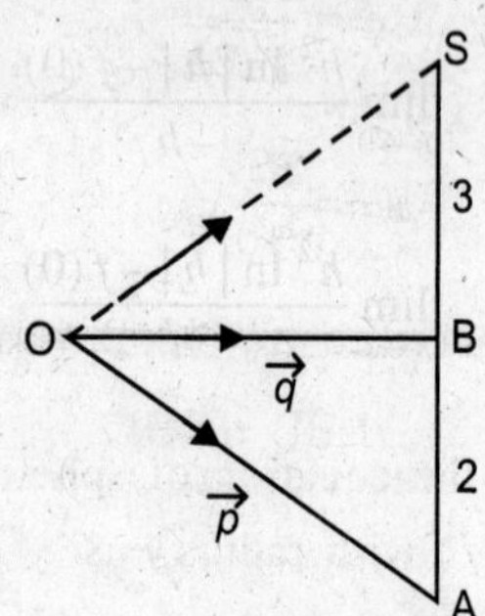

$$\overrightarrow{OS} = \frac{2q-3p}{2-3}$$

$$\overrightarrow{OS} = 3p - 2q$$

Given, the $\overrightarrow{OR}$ and $\overrightarrow{OS}$ are perpendicular

$$\overrightarrow{OR} \cdot \overrightarrow{OS} = 0$$

$$\left(\frac{2q+3p}{5}\right)(3p-2q) = 0$$

$$(2q + 3p)(3p - 2q) = 0$$

$$6pq - 4q^2 + 9p^2 - 6pq = 0$$

$$9p^2 = 4q^2.$$

68. F = $3i + k$

Point 0 about which moment is to be taken is $i + 2j - k$

$\therefore \quad r = \overrightarrow{OP}$ = Pv of P – Pv of O

$$= \left(2\hat{i} - \hat{j} + 3\hat{k}\right) - \left(\hat{i} + 2\hat{j} - \hat{k}\right)$$

$$r = \hat{i} - 3\hat{j} + 4\hat{k}$$

Hence, the moment is

$$r \times f = \left(\hat{i} - 3\hat{j} + 4\hat{k}\right)\left(3\hat{i} + \hat{k}\right)$$

$$= \begin{vmatrix} \hat{i} & \hat{j} & \hat{k} \\ 1 & -3 & 4 \\ 3 & 0 & 1 \end{vmatrix}$$

$$= -3\hat{i} + 11\hat{j} + 9\hat{k}.$$

69. We have, $\quad \vec{a} + 2\vec{b} + 3\vec{c} = \vec{0}$ and

$$\vec{a}\times\vec{b} + \vec{b}\times\vec{c} + \vec{c}\times\vec{a} = \lambda(\vec{b}\times\vec{c})$$

$$\vec{a} + 2\vec{b} + 3\vec{c} = \vec{0}$$

$$\vec{b}\times(\vec{a} + 2\vec{b} + 3\vec{c}) = \vec{b}\times\vec{0}$$

$$\vec{b}\times\vec{a} + 2\vec{b}\times\vec{b} + 3\vec{b}\times\vec{c} = 0$$

$$\vec{b}\times\vec{a} = -3\vec{b}\times\vec{c}$$

$$\vec{a}\times\vec{b} = 3\vec{b}\times\vec{c} \quad ...(i)$$

$$\vec{a} + 2\vec{b} + 3\vec{c} = \vec{0}$$

$$\vec{c}\times\left(\vec{a} + 2\vec{b} + 3\vec{c}\right) = \vec{c}\times\vec{0}$$

$$\vec{c}\times\vec{a} + 2\vec{c}\times\vec{b} + 0 = 0$$

$$\vec{c}\times\vec{a} = -2\vec{c}\times\vec{b}$$

$$\vec{c}\times\vec{a} = 2\vec{b}\times\vec{c} \quad ...(ii)$$

$$\vec{a}\times\vec{b} + \vec{b}\times\vec{c} + \vec{c}\times\vec{a} = \lambda(\vec{b}\times\vec{c})$$

$$3\vec{b}\times\vec{c} + \vec{b}\times\vec{c} + 2\vec{b}\times\vec{c} = \lambda(\vec{b}\times\vec{c})$$

$$6(\vec{b}\times\vec{c}) = \lambda(\vec{b}\times\vec{c})$$

$$\lambda = 6.$$

70. If two vectors are parallel then their cross product is zero vector *i.e.*,

$$k\vec{k}\times\vec{A} = \vec{0}.$$

71. $f : \mathbb{R} \to \mathbb{R}^+$

$$f(x) = |x + 1|$$

Now, Check the option

(A) $\quad f(x)^2 = [f(x)]^2$

$$|x^2 + 1| \neq (|x + 1|)^2$$

(B) $\quad f(|x|) = |f(x)|$

$$||x| + 1| = ||x + 1||$$

$$||x| + 1| \neq ||x + 1||$$

(C) $\quad f(x + y) = f(x) + f(y)$

$$|x + y + 1| \neq |x + 1| + |y + 1|$$

So, None of the above is the correct answer.

72. $f : \mathbb{R} \to \mathbb{R}$

$$f(x) = \frac{x^2}{1+x^2}$$

Let $\quad y = \dfrac{x^2}{1+x^2}$

$$y + yx^2 = x^2$$

$$x^2 = \frac{y}{1-y}$$

$$x = \sqrt{\frac{y}{1-y}}$$

This function is valid $\frac{y}{1-y} \geq 0$

But $1 - y \neq 0$, $y \neq 1$

So, The range of $f(x) = [0, 1)$

$$0 \leq f(x) < 1.$$

73. $f(x) = |x| + |x - 1|$

Check continuity at $x = 0$, $x = 1$

Ist, $x = 0$ $\quad f(0) = 1$

$$f(0 + h) = |h| + |h - 1|$$

$$f(0 - h) = |h| + |-h - 1|$$

L.H.L $\lim_{h \to 0} \frac{f(0-h) - f(0)}{-h}$

$$= \lim_{h \to 0} \frac{|h| + |-h-1| - 1}{-h} = 1$$

R.H.L $\lim_{h \to 0} \frac{f(0+h) - f(0)}{h}$

$$= \lim_{h \to 0} \frac{|h| + |h-1| - 1}{h} = 1$$

$$\text{L.H.L.} = \text{R.H.L} = f(0)$$

So, function $f(x)$ is continuous at $x = 0$

Now, $\quad x = 1$

$$f(1) = 1$$

$$f(1 + h) = |1 + h| + |h|$$

$$f(1 - h) = |1 - h| + |h|$$

L.H.L. $\lim_{h \to 0} \frac{f(1-h) - f(1)}{-h}$

$$= \lim_{h \to 0} \frac{|1-h| + |h| - 1}{-h} = 1$$

R.H.L. $\lim_{h \to 0} \frac{f(1+h) - f(1)}{h}$

$$= \lim_{h \to 0} \frac{|1+h| + |h| - 1}{h} = 1$$

$$\text{L.H.L.} = \text{R.H.L.} = f(1)$$

So, function $f(x)$ is continuous at $x = 1$.

74. $f(x) = \begin{cases} x^2 \ln|x| & x \neq 0 \\ 0 & x = 0 \end{cases}$

$\because \quad f(0) = 0$

$$f(0 + h) = h^2 \ln|h|$$

$$f(0 - h) = h^2 \ln|h|$$

L.H.L. $\lim_{h \to 0} \frac{h^2 \ln|h| - f(0)}{-h} = 0$

R.H.L. $\lim_{h \to 0} \frac{h^2 \ln|h| - f(0)}{h} = 0$

$\because \quad \text{LHL} = \text{RHL}$

$$= f(a)$$

So, $\quad f'(0) = 0.$

75. $\quad y^2 = 6(x - 1)$

$$y^2 = 3x$$

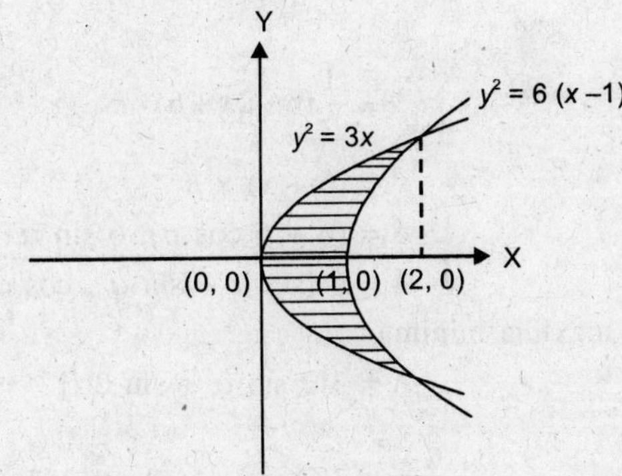

After solving, $\quad 3x = 6(x - 1)$

$$x = 2$$

Area of Bounded Region

$$= \int_0^2 \sqrt{3}\sqrt{x}\,dx - \int_1^2 \sqrt{6}\sqrt{x-1}\,dx$$

$$= \sqrt{3}\left[\frac{x^{3/2}}{\frac{3}{2}}\right]_0^2 - \sqrt{6}\left[\frac{(x-1)^{3/2}}{\frac{3}{2}}\right]_1^2$$

$$= \sqrt{3}\left[\frac{2}{3}.(2)^{3/2}\right] - \sqrt{6}\left[\frac{2}{3}\right]$$

$$= \frac{4\sqrt{6} - 2\sqrt{6}}{3} = \frac{2\sqrt{6}}{3}$$

So required area

$$= 2 \times \frac{2\sqrt{6}}{3} = \frac{4\sqrt{6}}{3}.$$

For Qs. No. 76-78.

Let ABCD is a trapezium with height 'h'

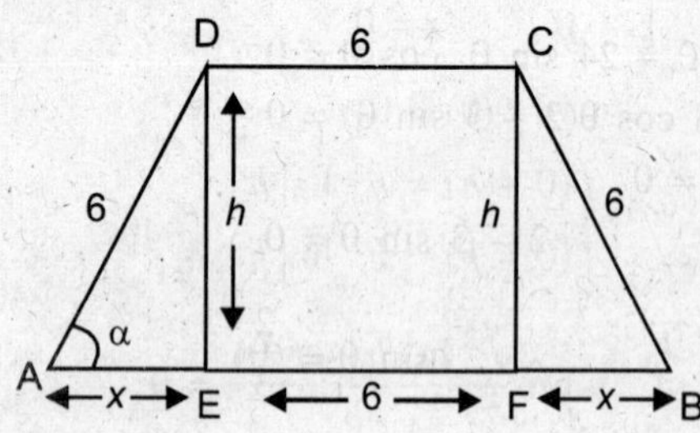

$$\sin\alpha = \frac{h}{6}$$

$$h = 6\sin\alpha$$

$$\cos\alpha = \frac{x}{6}$$

$$x = 6\cos\alpha$$

Area of Trapezium = $\frac{1}{2}$ (sum of || side) × height

$$= \frac{1}{2}(6+2x+6)\times h$$

$$= (6 + x) \times h$$

$$\Delta = (6 + 6\cos\alpha).\ 6\sin\alpha$$

$$\Delta = 6[\sin\alpha + \sin\alpha\ .\ \cos\alpha]$$

For maxima minima

$$\Delta = 3[2\sin\alpha + \sin 2\alpha]$$

$$\frac{d\Delta}{d\alpha} = 3[2\cos\alpha + 2\cos 2\alpha]$$

$$= 6[\cos\alpha + 2\cos^2\alpha - 1]$$

$$\frac{d\Delta}{dx} = 0$$

$$6[2\cos^2\alpha + \cos\alpha - 1] = 0$$

$$\cos\alpha = \frac{1}{2}$$

$$\cos\alpha = -1$$

We don't take this value $\alpha \in \left(0, \frac{\pi}{2}\right)$

$$\alpha = \frac{\pi}{3}.$$

76. If Area is maximum $\alpha = \frac{\pi}{3}$.

77. Length of fourth side

$$= 2x + 6$$

$$= 2 \times 6\cos\alpha + 6$$

$$= 12.\cos\frac{\pi}{3}+6$$

$$= 12\times\frac{1}{2}+6$$

$$= 12 \text{ cm.}$$

78. Maximum Area of trapezium

$$\Delta = (6 + 6\cos\alpha).6\sin\alpha$$

$\alpha = \frac{\pi}{3}$ $\qquad \Delta = 6\sin\frac{\pi}{3}\left(6+6\cos\frac{\pi}{3}\right)$

$$= 6\times\frac{\sqrt{3}}{2}\left(6+6\times\frac{1}{2}\right)$$

$$= 3\sqrt{3}(9)$$

$$\Delta = 27\sqrt{3} \text{ cm}^2.$$

79. Let, $I = \int_0^\pi e^x.\sin x.dx$

$$I = \left[e^x(-\cos x)\right]_0^\pi - \int_0^\pi e^x(-\cos x).dx$$

$$I = \left[-e^\pi\cos\pi + e^0.\cos 0\right] + \int_0^\pi e^x.\cos x.dx$$

$$I = \left[e^\pi + 1\right] + \left[e^x.\sin x\right]_0^\pi - \int_0^\pi e^x.\sin x.dx$$

$$2I = \left(e^\pi + 1\right) + \left[e^\pi.\sin\pi - e^0.\sin 0\right]$$

$$2I = e^\pi + 1 + 0 - 0$$

$$I = \frac{e^\pi + 1}{2}.$$

80. If $f(x) = \frac{x^2-9}{x^2-2x-3}, x \neq 3$

A function is continuous at $x = a$ iff

$$\lim_{x\to a} f(x) = 0$$

$$\lim_{x\to 3}\frac{x^2-9}{x^2-2x-3} = \lim_{x\to 3}\frac{2x}{2x-2}$$

$$= \frac{6}{4} = \frac{3}{2} = 1.5$$

So function is continuous if $f(3) = 1.5$.

81. $\int_1^e x.\ln x.dx$

$$= \left[\ln x.\frac{x^2}{2}\right]_1^e - \int_1^e \left[\frac{d}{dx}.\ln x.\int x.dx\right]dx$$

$$= \left[\ln e\left(\frac{e^2}{2}\right) - \ln 1 \times \frac{1}{2}\right] - \int_1^e \frac{1}{x} \times \frac{x^2}{2}.dx$$

$$= \left[1.\frac{e^2}{2} - 0\right] - \frac{1}{2}\left[\frac{x^2}{2}\right]_1^e$$

$$= \frac{e^2}{2} - \frac{1}{2}\left[\frac{e^2}{2} - \frac{1}{2}\right]$$

$$= \frac{e^2}{2} - \frac{e^2}{4} + \frac{1}{4}$$

$$= \frac{e^2}{4} + \frac{1}{4}$$

$$= \frac{e^2+1}{4}.$$

82. $\int_0^{\sqrt{2}} [x^2].dx$

We know that,

$0 < x < 1 \Rightarrow 0 < x^2 < 1$, $[x] = 0$

$1 < x < \sqrt{2} \Rightarrow 1 < x^2 < 2$, $[x] = 1$

$$\int_0^{\sqrt{2}} [x^2]dx = \int_0^1 [x]dx + \int_1^{\sqrt{2}} [x]dx$$

$$= \int_0^1 0.dx + \int_1^{\sqrt{2}} 1.dx$$

$$= 0 + [x]_1^{\sqrt{2}}$$

$\Rightarrow \sqrt{2} - 1$.

83. Let, $y = 16 \sin\theta - 12 \sin^2\theta$

Differentiate w.r.t. θ

$$\frac{dy}{d\theta} = 16 \cos\theta - 12 \times (2 \sin\theta).\cos\theta$$

$$\frac{dy}{d\theta} = 16 \cos\theta - 24 \sin\theta.\cos\theta$$

For Maxima minima $\frac{dy}{d\theta} = 0$

$16 \cos\theta - 24 \sin\theta. \cos\theta = 0$

$8 \cos\theta(2 - 3 \sin\theta) = 0$

If $\cos\theta \neq 0$

$2 - 3 \sin\theta = 0$

$\sin\theta = \frac{2}{3}$

Put in equation $= 16 \times \frac{2}{3} - 12 \times \left(\frac{4}{9}\right)$

$$= \frac{96-48}{9}$$

$$= \frac{48}{9} = \frac{16}{3}.$$

84. We know that maximum and minimum value of $a \sin\theta + b \sin\theta + c$

Minimum value $= -\left(\sqrt{a^2+b^2}\right) + c$

Maximum value $= \sqrt{a^2+b^2} + c$

So, given function is

$$f(x) = 4 \sin x - 3 \cos x + 1$$

Maximum value $= \sqrt{(4)^2 + (-3)^2} + 1 = 6$

Minimum value $= -\left(\sqrt{(4)^2+(-3)^2}\right) - 1 = -4$

So, $S \varepsilon [-4, 6]$.

85. $f(x) = \frac{1}{\sqrt{|x| - x}}$

$\because$ For domain $|x| - x$ must be positive and it is possible iff $x \varepsilon (-\infty, 0)$ *i.e.*, zero and negative value of x.

86. We have, $xdy - ydx = 0$

We can write this as,

$$xdy = ydx$$

$$\frac{1}{y}.dy = \frac{dx}{x}$$

$$\frac{dy}{y} = \frac{dx}{x}$$

Take integration of both sides

$$\int \frac{dy}{y} = \int \frac{dx}{x}$$

$\log y = \log x + c$ where c is constant

$\log y - \log x = c$

$$\log \frac{y}{x} = c$$

$$\frac{y}{x} = e^c$$

$e^c \rightarrow$ is constant

$$y = xc.$$

87. $f(x) = e^{\tan x} + \ln(\sec x) - e^{\ln x}$

Differentiate w.r.t. x

$$= e^{\tan x}.\sec^2 x + \frac{1}{\sec x}\sec x.\tan x - e^{\ln x}.\frac{1}{x}$$

$$= e^{\tan x}.\sec^2 x + \tan x - \frac{e^{\ln x}}{x}$$

Putting $x = \frac{\pi}{4}$

$$= e.2 + 1 - \frac{e^{\ln\frac{\pi}{4}}}{\frac{\pi}{4}} \qquad [e^{\ln x} = x]$$

$$= 2e + 1 - \frac{4}{\pi} \times \frac{\pi}{4}$$

$= 2e + 1 - 1$

$= 2e.$

89. Graph of $y = \sin x$

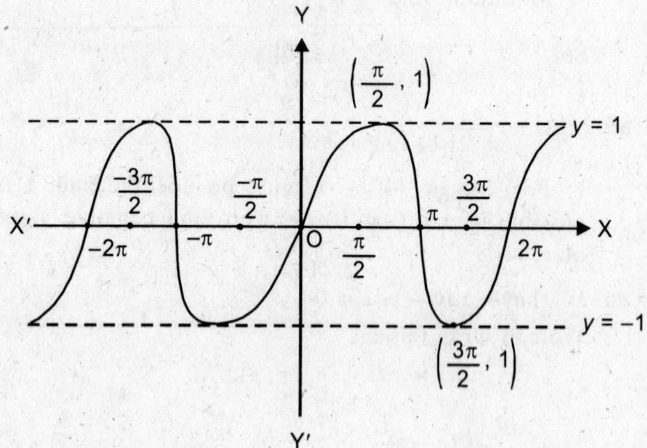

Period $= 2\pi$.

90. $\int \frac{dx}{2^x - 1}$

Multiply and divide by 2^{-x}, we get,

$$\int \frac{2^{-x}}{1 - 2^{-x}}.dx$$

Let, $\quad 1 - 2^{-x} = t$

$$2^{-x} \log 2 = \frac{dt}{dx}$$

$$2^{-x}.dx = \frac{dt}{\log 2}$$

$$= \frac{1}{\log 2}\int \frac{1}{t}.dt$$

$$= \frac{1}{\log 2}[\log t] + c$$

$$= \frac{1}{\log 2}\log\left(1 - 2^{-x}\right) + c.$$

91. $y^2 = 4a(x - a)$, where a is constant

$$y^2 = 4ax - 4a^2 \qquad ...(i)$$

Differentiate $w.r.t.$ x

$$2.y\frac{dy}{dx} = 4a$$

$$a = \frac{y}{2}\frac{dy}{dx}$$

Value of 'a' put in equation (i)

$$y^2 = 4 \times \left(\frac{y}{2}.\frac{dy}{dx}\right)x - 4\left[\frac{y}{2}.\frac{dy}{dx}\right]^2$$

$$y^2 = 2xy.\frac{dy}{dx} - y^2\left[\frac{dy}{dx}\right]^2$$

$$y^2\left[\left(\frac{dy}{dx}\right)^2 + 1\right] - y\left(\frac{dy}{dx}\right) = 0$$

Order = 1

Degree = 2.

92. $\int_{\frac{-\pi}{4}}^{\frac{\pi}{4}} (\sin x - \tan x)dx$

$$= \int_{\frac{-\pi}{4}}^{\frac{\pi}{4}} \sin x\,dx - \int_{\frac{-\pi}{4}}^{\frac{\pi}{4}} \tan x\,dx$$

$$= [-\cos x]_{\frac{-\pi}{4}}^{\frac{\pi}{4}} - [-\log\cos x]_{\frac{-\pi}{4}}^{\frac{\pi}{4}}$$

$$= \left[-\cos\frac{\pi}{4} + \cos\left(-\frac{\pi}{4}\right)\right] - \left[-\log\cos\frac{\pi}{4} + \log\cos\left(-\frac{\pi}{4}\right)\right]$$

$$= \left(-\cos\frac{\pi}{4}+\cos\frac{\pi}{4}\right)-\left(-\log\cos\frac{\pi}{4}+\log\cos\frac{\pi}{4}\right)$$

$= 0.$

93. We have, $\int_a^b x^3.dx = 0$

$$\left[\frac{x^4}{4}\right]_a^b = 0$$

$$\frac{b^4}{4}-\frac{a^4}{4} = 0$$

$$b^4 - a^4 = 0 \quad ...(i)$$

$$(b - a)(b + a)(b^2 + a^2) = 0$$

$$b = a,\ b = -a,\ \ b^2 \neq a^2$$

and $\int_a^b x^2 dx = \frac{2}{3}$

$$\left[\frac{x^3}{3}\right]_a^b = \frac{2}{3}$$

$$\left[\frac{b^3}{3}-\frac{a^3}{3}\right] = \frac{2}{3}$$

$$b^3 - a^3 = 2 \quad ...(ii)$$

Put value $b = -a$ in the equation,

$$(-a)^3 - a^3 = 2$$

$$-2a^3 = 2$$

$$a^3 = -1$$

$$a = -1$$

$$b = 1$$

Hence, the value of a and b are -1, 1 respectively.

95. $\lim_{x\to 0}\frac{\tan x}{\sin 2x}$ $\quad \frac{0}{0}$ form apply L Hospital rule

$$= \lim_{x\to 0}\frac{\frac{d}{dx}\tan x}{\frac{d}{dx}\sin 2x}$$

$$= \lim_{x\to 0}\frac{\sec^2 x}{2.\cos 2x}$$

$$= \frac{\sec^2 0°}{2\times\cos 0°} = \frac{1}{2}.$$

96. $\lim_{h\to 0}\frac{\sqrt{2x+3h}-\sqrt{2x}}{2h}$

$$= \lim_{h\to 0}\frac{\sqrt{2x+3h}-\sqrt{2x}}{2h}\times\frac{\sqrt{2x+3h}+\sqrt{2x}}{\sqrt{2x+3h}+\sqrt{2x}}$$

$$= \lim_{h\to 0}\frac{\left(\sqrt{2x+3h}\right)^2-\left(\sqrt{2x}\right)^2}{2h\left(\sqrt{2x+3h}+\sqrt{2x}\right)}$$

$$= \lim_{h\to 0}\frac{2x+3h-2x}{2h\left(\sqrt{2x+3h}+\sqrt{2x}\right)}$$

$$= \lim_{h\to 0}\frac{3h}{2h\left(\sqrt{2x+3h}+\sqrt{2x}\right)}$$

$$= \lim_{h\to 0}\frac{3}{2\left(\sqrt{2x+3h}+\sqrt{2x}\right)}$$

$$= \frac{3}{2\left(\sqrt{2x+0}+\sqrt{2x}\right)}$$

$$= \frac{3}{2\times 2\sqrt{2x}}$$

$$= \frac{3}{4\sqrt{2x}}.$$

97. $f(x)$ – even function

Let, $\quad f(x) = \cos x,\ f(x) = x^2$

$\quad f'(x) = -\sin x,\ f'(x) = 2x$

$\therefore$ If $f(x)$ is an even function then $f'(x)$ is an odd function.

98. $\quad y = e^{x^2}.\sin 2x$

$$\frac{dy}{dx} = e^{x^2}.\left[\frac{d}{dx}.\sin 2x\right]+\sin 2x\left[\frac{d}{dx}.e^{x^2}\right]$$

$$\frac{dy}{dx} = e^{x^2}\left[\cos 2x.(2)\right]+\sin 2x\left[e^{x^2}.2x\right]$$

$$= 2\times e^{x^2}.\cos 2x+2x\sin 2x.e^{x^2}$$

$$\left(\frac{dy}{dx}\right)_{x=\pi} = 2\times e^{\pi^2}.\cos 2\pi+2\pi\sin 2\pi e^{\pi^2}$$

$$= 2\times e^{\pi^2}. \quad \left[\begin{array}{l}\because \sin 2\pi = 0\\ \cos 2\pi = 1\end{array}\right]$$

99. $(1 + 2x)dy - (1 - 2y)dx = 0$

$$(1 + 2x)dy = (1 - 2y)dx$$

$$\frac{1}{1-2y}dy = \frac{1}{1+2x}dx$$

Taking integration of both sides

$$\int \frac{1}{1-2y}dy = \int \frac{1}{1+2x}dx$$

$$\log(1 - 2y)(-2) = \log(1 + 2x).2 + c$$

$$-2 \log(1 - 2y) - 2\log (1 + 2x) = 0$$

$$-2[\log(1 - 2y) + \log(1 + 2x)] = c$$

$$-2[\log (1 - 2y)(1 + 2x)] = c$$

$$(1 - 2y) (1 + 2x) = e^{-c/2}$$

$$1 + 2x - 2y - 4xy = e^{-c/2}$$

$$2(x - y - 2xy) = e^{-c/2} - 1$$

$$(x - y - 2xy) = \frac{e^{-c/2} - 1}{2} = \text{constant}$$

$$x - y - 2xy = c.$$

100. $$\left(\frac{d^3y}{dx^3}\right)^2 = y^4 + \left(\frac{dy}{dx}\right)^5$$

Order = 3

Degree = 2.

101. Gives, Mean = np

Variance = npq

Given, mean = 3 × variance

$$np = 3 \times npq$$

$$q = \frac{1}{3}$$

$$p = \frac{2}{3}$$

$n = 5, r = 3$

$\because \quad p(X = r) = {}^nC_r\, p^r q^{n-r}$

$\therefore \quad p(X = 3) = {}^5C_3.\left(\frac{2}{3}\right)^3.\left(\frac{1}{3}\right)^2$

$$= \frac{5\times4}{2\times1}\left(\frac{8}{27}\right)\times\frac{1}{9} = \frac{80}{243}.$$

103. Given, correlation coefficient 'r' = 0.6

$$\text{cov}(x, y) = 27$$

$$\text{Var}_y = 25$$

$$\text{Var}_x = ?$$

We know,

$$\text{Coefficient of correlation '}r\text{'} = \frac{\text{cov}(x,y)}{\sqrt{\text{Var}_x \text{Var}_y}}$$

$$0.6 = \frac{27}{\sqrt{25\times \text{Var}_x}}$$

$$0.6\times5\times\sqrt{\text{Var}_x} = 27$$

$$\sqrt{\text{Var}_x} = 9$$

$$\text{Var}_x = 81.$$

Hence, option (D) is correct.

104. Given,

$$P(A) = 0.4 = \frac{4}{10}$$

$$P(B) = 0.5 = \frac{5}{10}$$

The probability to solve at least one of the two question

$$= 1 - P\left(\frac{\bar{A}}{\bar{B}}\right)$$

$$= 1 - \frac{6}{10}\times\frac{5}{10}$$

$$= 1 - \frac{6}{20}$$

$$= 1 - 0.3$$

$$= 0.7$$

105. $$\bar{x} = \frac{x_1 + x_2 + x_3 + ...x_n}{n}$$

$$x_i = a + c\,y_i$$

$$i = 1, 2, 3, ... n$$

$$x_1 = a + c\,y_1$$

$$x_2 = a + c\,y_2$$

$$x_3 = a + c\,y_3$$

... ...

$$x_n = (a) + c\,y_n$$

$$x_1 + x_2 + x_3 + ... + x_n = na + c(y_1 + y_2 + y_3 + ... y_n)$$

Divided by n

$$\frac{(x_1 + x_2 + x_3 + ...x_n)}{n} = a + c\frac{(y_1 + y_2 + y_3 + ...y_n)}{n}$$

$$\bar{x} = a + c\bar{y}$$

$$\bar{y} = \frac{\bar{x} - a}{c}.$$

106. We know $r = \sqrt{b_{xy} b_{yx}}$, and Angle between two regression lines

$$\tan \theta = \frac{(1-r)^2}{|r|} \frac{\sigma_x \sigma_y}{\sigma_x^2 \times \sigma_y^2}$$

(*a*) if $r = 0$, $\theta = \frac{\pi}{2}$,

The two regression lines are perpendicular to each other. Actually, they are parallel to the axes, regression line of y on x is parallel to the x-axis and of x on y is parallel to y-axis.

(*b*) If $r = 1$ or -1, $\theta = 0$

So the regression line coincide.

107. We get the mean value $\bar{x}$ and $\bar{y}$ after solving the two lines of regression

$$4x - 5y + 33 = 0$$

$$20x - 9y = 107$$

After solving this, we get

$$\bar{x} = 13$$

and $\bar{y} = 17.$

110. Arrange in ascending order

–4.8, 0, 2.3, 3.5, 3.9, 4.6, 5.2, 6.1, 7.6, 8.2, 9.3, 12.1

$n = 12$ (even)

$$\text{Median} = \frac{1}{2}\left[\frac{n}{2}\text{th term} + \left(\frac{n}{2}+1\right)\text{th term}\right]$$

$$= \frac{1}{2}[\text{6th term} + \text{7th term}]$$

$$= \frac{1}{2}[4.6 + 5.2]$$

$$= \frac{1}{2}[9.8] = 4.9.$$

111. $\text{Central Angle} = \dfrac{\text{Frequency} \times 360^\circ}{\text{Total frequency}}$

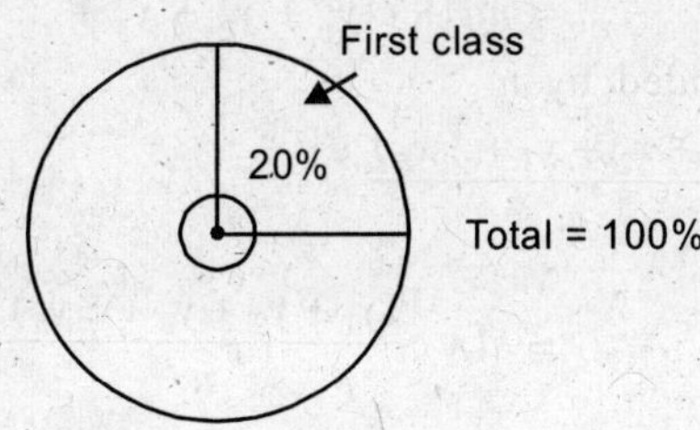

$$= \frac{20}{100} \times 360^\circ$$

Central Angle = 72°.

112. Given, $\bar{x} = 5$

Standard deviation, $\sigma = 2$

If 5 is added to each value

New mean $\bar{x} = 5 + 5 = 10$

$\sigma = 2$ (No change)

We know Coefficient of variation

$$= \frac{\sigma}{x} \times 100$$

$$= \frac{2}{10} \times 100 = 20.$$

113. Average Speed

$$= \frac{\text{Total distance}}{\text{Total time taken to cover distance}}$$

$$\text{Average speed} = \frac{5+15}{\frac{5}{30}+\frac{15}{45}}$$

$$= \frac{20}{\frac{1}{6}+\frac{1}{3}} = \frac{20 \times 6}{3}$$

= 40 km/h.

114. Favourable case

= {(1, 6) (2, 5) (3, 4) (5, 2) (6, 1) (4, 3)}

= 6

Total outcomes = 6 × 6 = 36

$$\text{Probability} = \frac{6}{36} = \frac{1}{6}.$$

117.

3W+ 2B	5W+ 3B

Probability to select a bag from two bag

$$= \frac{1}{2}$$

Probability to select a white ball from bag first

$$= \frac{3}{5}$$

Probability to select a white ball from bag second

$$= \frac{5}{8}$$

$$= \frac{3}{5} \times \frac{1}{2} + \frac{5}{8} \times \frac{1}{2}$$

$$= \frac{3}{10} + \frac{5}{16}$$

$$= \frac{24+25}{80} = \frac{49}{80}.$$

118. P(A occurs but not B) = P(A) – P(B)

when $B \subset A$

If two events are mutually exclusive then

$$P(A \cap B) = 0$$

Hence, $P(A \cup B) = P(A) + P(B)$.

119.

4 Men + 5 Women

The Probability that exactly two members are men

$$= \frac{{}^4C_2 \times {}^5C_1}{{}^9C_3}$$

$$= \frac{\frac{\lfloor 4}{\lfloor 2 \lfloor 2} \times \frac{\lfloor 5}{\lfloor 4}}{\frac{\lfloor 9}{\lfloor 3 \lfloor 6}}$$

After solving $= \frac{5}{14}$.

120. We know that,

$$\sigma = \sqrt{\frac{\Sigma x^2}{N} - \left(\frac{\Sigma x}{N}\right)^2}$$

$$\sigma = \sqrt{\frac{N(N+1)(2N+1)}{6N} - \left(\frac{N(N+1)}{2N}\right)^2}$$

$$\sigma = \sqrt{\frac{N(N+1)(2N+1)}{6N} - \frac{N^2(N+1)^2}{4N^2}}$$

$$\sigma = \sqrt{\frac{(N+1)(2N+1)}{6} - \frac{(N+1)^2}{4}}$$

$$\sigma = \sqrt{\frac{2(2N^2+3N+1) - 3(N^2+1+2N)}{12}}$$

$$\sigma = \sqrt{\frac{4N^2+6N+2-3N^2-3-6N}{12}}$$

$$\sigma = \sqrt{\frac{N^2-1}{12}}.$$

Previous Papers (Solved)

NATIONAL DEFENCE ACADEMY & NAVAL ACADEMY

NDA & NA – Entrance Exam, 2017 (II)

PAPER I : GENERAL ABILITY TEST

PART A : ENGLISH LANGUAGE

SYNONYMS

Directions (Qs. 1-10): *Each item in this section consists of a sentence with an* **bold** *word/words followed by four options. Select the option that is* **nearest in meaning** *to the* **bold** *word/words and mark your response in your Answer Sheet accordingly.*

1. The discussion was **wound up** after a long and fruitful exchange of views.
A. postponed B. cut short
C. interrupted D. concluded

2. He was fully **alive to** the need for making adjustments.
A. concerned about B. worried about
C. aware of D. indifferent about

3. The police officer tried to **intimidate** the witness but in vain.
A. inform B. reward
C. frighten D. persuade

4. We must adopt **drastic** measures to control population growth.
A. simple B. dramatic
C. realistic D. severe

5. He is extremely **meticulous** in his approach.
A. simple B. careful
C. fair D. reasonable

6. The experts' **minute** examination brought to light some important clues.
A. quick B. detailed
C. superficial D. prolonged

7. The decision of the Union Government to **repeal** the Urban Land Ceiling Act has been welcomed by all.
A. suppress B. amend
C. cancel D. withhold

8. This is his **maiden** appearance on the screen.
A. first B. last
C. girlish D. shy

9. At the end of the marathon everybody was **exhausted**.
A. weakened B. honoured
C. satisfied D. tired

10. He gave me a **counterfeit** coin.
A. rare B. fake
C. unmatured D. inferior

ANTONYMS

Directions (Qs. 11 to 20): *Each item in this section consists of a sentence with an* **bold** *word/words followed by four options. Select the option that is* **opposite in meaning** *to the* **bold** *word/words and mark your response in your Answer Sheet accordingly.*

11. My mother has been working hard for the last two weeks and she feels **run down**.
A. morbid B. energetic
C. exhausted D. emotional

12. The President condemned the act of **violence** during the celebration of the festival.
A. reason B. instigation
C. restraint D. sobriety

13. The students made a **generous** contribution to the flood relief fund.
A. niggard B. selfish
C. spendthrift D. indecent

14. He was just **idle** by temperament.
A. employed B. occupied
C. industrious D. happy

15. Most of the decisions taken by the officer were **unjust**.
A. serious B. lenient
C. correct D. imbecile

16. He is a loving father and takes great **delight** in his children.
A. revolt B. dissatisfaction
C. enjoyment D. disgust

17. He was quite **concerned** about his son's career.
A. unrelated B. indifferent
C. dispassionate D. carefree

18. They are **confident** of success.
A. imprudent B. impatient
C. diffident D. reluctant

19. We **carried on** the search for the missing person.
A. delayed B. reconsidered
C. broke up D. called off

20. This T.V. has many **indigenous** components.
A. Indian B. foreign
C. unnatural D. genuine

SELECTING WORDS

Directions (Qs. 21-30): *In the following passage, at certain points you are given a choice of four words marked A, B, C and D, one of which fits the meaning of the passage. Choose the best word out of the four. Mark the letter, viz., A, B, C or D, relating to this word on your Answer Sheet. Examples K and L have been solved for you.*

The .... (K) .... was in the school in Shimla. .... (L) .... was homesick.

K. A. boy B. horse
C. dog D. cow

L. A. She B. It
C. He D. Her

Explanation: *Out of the list given in item K, only, 'boy' is the correct answer because usually, a boy, and not a horse, a dog or a cow, attends school. So 'A' is to be marked on the Answer Sheet for item K. A boy is usually referred to as 'he', so for item L, 'C' is the correct answer. Notice that to solve the first item K you have to read the rest of the sentence and then see what fits best.*

Passage

After this incident I went to Nainital, and returned after nearly a month. I had ... **(21)** ... taken ... **(22)** ... my clothes when I saw Gangu standing ... **(23)** ... a new baby. He was ... **(24)** ... with joy. Even Nanda ... **(25)** ... not have ... **(26)** ... such joy ... **(27)** ... getting Krishna. His face had the same ... **(28)** ... that ... **(29)** ... on the face of a ... **(30)** ... man after a full meal.

21. A. hardly B. barely
C. merely D. rarely

22. A. out B. away
C. off D. on

23. A. by B. near
C. with D. at

24. A. jumping B. bursting
C. dancing D. singing

25. A. could B. would
C. should D. ought

26. A. experimented B. shown
C. felt D. heard

27. A. at B. in
C. on D. into

28. A. light B. glow
C. sense D. hope

29. A. comes B. appears
C. rises D. shows

30. A. starved B. starving
C. hungry D. satisfied

ORDERING OF WORDS IN A SENTENCE

Directions (Qs. 31-35): *Each of the following items in this section consists of a sentence, the parts of which have been jumbled. These parts have been labelled P, Q, R and S. Given below each sentence are four sequences namely A, B, C and D. You are required to re-arrange the jumbled parts of the sentence and mark your response accordingly.*

31. The spirit of man
P : has slowly and painfully surmounted
Q : and his growing intelligence
R : all the obstacles that have come in his way
S : has faced all kinds of dangers.
The correct sequence should be:
A. Q P S R B. S Q P R
C. R P Q S D. P R Q S

32. After our school boys had won a well-contested hockey match
P : so that they might communicate the news of their victory to the headmaster
Q : who is a keen sportsman
R : they came to school in high spirits
S : and takes a very lively interest in school games.
The correct sequence should be:
A. Q P S R B. S Q P R
C. R P Q S D. P R Q S

33. Even a leisurely game like cricket
P : demanding grace rather than strength
Q : and over the rough tactics of the Australian team that visited England in 1921
R : as we saw in the controversy over body-line bowling
S : can cause much ill-will.
The correct sequence should be:
A. P S R Q B. R S P Q
C. S R Q P D. Q P R S

34. Scientists point out
P : of sunspot activity
Q : that it is an aftermath that
R : has now reached its peak
S : of the eleven-year cycle.
The correct sequence should be:
A. R S P Q B. P Q S R
C. Q R P S D. Q S P R

35. As the ship streams from San Diego
P : as walls of gray water from a distant storm in the North Pacific

Q : making the greener among us miserable with sea sickness
R : rock and toss the ship
S : those of us aboard have a personal demonstration of powerful ocean movement.

The correct sequence should be:

A. P Q R S
B. S R P Q
C. S P R Q
D. Q S R P

SPOTTING ERRORS

Directions (Qs. 36-40): *Each item in this section has a sentence with three underlined parts labelled A, B and C. Read each sentence to find out whether there is any error in any underlined part and indicate your response in the Answer Sheet against the corresponding letter i.e., A or B or C. If you find no error, your response should be indicated as D.*

36. (A)/ An electrical circuit (B)/ is the complete path (C)/ traversed by electric current. (D)/ No error.

37. (A)/ He waved us a by-by (B)/ as he boarded the train (C)/ which disappeared into the tunnel. (D)/ No error.

38. (A)/ There was great deal that had to be scrapped, that must be scrapped; (B)/ but surely India could not have been what she undoubtedly was, (C)/ and could not have continued a cultured existence for thousands of years. (D)/ No error.

39. (A)/ With regard to interior decoration, it is the attention given to the less overt aspects of using space (B)/ that give it life, an identity, a quality (C)/ that makes it exciting and unusual. (D)/ No error.

40. (A)/ A small parcel (B)/ of novels is (C)/ better than none. (D)/ No error.

FILL IN THE BLANKS

Directions (Qs. 41-50): *Each of the following sentences in this section has a blank space and four words or group of words given after the sentence. Select the word or group of words you consider most appropriate for the blank space and indicate your response on the Answer Sheet accordingly.*

41. He looks as if he .... weary.

A. is
B. was
C. would be
D. were

42. My house is insured .... theft and fire.

A. for
B. against
C. in
D. towards

43. The result of the prolonged discussion was ....

A. disappointment
B. disappointing
C. disappointed
D. to disappoint

44. You are lucky .... in the 20th century.

A. by being born
B. to have been born
C. for being born
D. to have born

45. Sita is true to ....

A. word
B. her words
C. the words
D. words

46. Years .... since I saw her last.

A. have passed
B. had passed
C. had been passing
D. have been passing

47. When he heard the terrible noise he asked me what was .... on.

A. happening
B. being
C. getting
D. going

48. Could you lend me some money? I am very .... of cash at the moment.

A. down
B. low
C. short
D. scarce

49. I saw her when she was standing .... the side of the old statue.

A. by
B. at
C. in
D. beyond

50. True friends never .... their loved ones in adversity.

A. abuse
B. criticize
C. befool
D. desert

PART B : GENERAL KNOWLEDGE

51. Which one of the following was set as a target of average growth of GDP of India over the plan period 2012-2017 by the Approach Paper to the Twelfth Five Year Plan?

A. 7 per cent
B. 8 per cent
C. 9 per cent
D. 10 per cent

52. Which one of the following is ***not*** a subject that has been devolved to the Panchayati Raj Institutions by the 11th Schedule of the Constitution of India?

A. Non-conventional energy resources
B. Roads
C. Higher education
D. Libraries

53. Who among the following used the term Industrial Revolution for the first time in English to describe the changes that occurred in the British industrial development between 1760 and 1820?

A. Friedrich Engels
B. Eric Hobsbawm
C. Arnold Toynbee
D. Georges Michelet

54. Who among the following is the author of the book *"The Indian Struggle, 1920–1934"*?

A. Maulana Abul Kalam
B. Jayprakash Narayan
C. Subhash Chandra Bose
D. Manabendra Nath Roy

55. Which one of the following about the Swadeshi Campaign in 1896 is *not* correct?
A. Its centre was Maharashtra
B. Its main participants were students
C. It opposed the levy of tariff on imports
D. It publicly burnt foreign clothes

56. Which one of the following associations was founded in London by Dadabhai Naoroji in 1866?
A. The Bengal British India Society
B. The East India Association
C. The British Indian Association
D. The Madras Native Association

57. Mariana Trench is located in the ocean floor of:
A. Southern Atlantic Ocean
B. Western Pacific Ocean
C. Eastern Pacific Ocean
D. Northern Atlantic Ocean

58. Taklamakan Desert is situated in:
A. Western Asia
B. Southern fringe of Sahara in Africa
C. South America
D. Central Asia

59. Rudraprayag is situated at the confluence of rivers Alaknanda and.
A. Bhagirathi B. Mandakini
C. Nandakini D. Dhauliganga

60. Arrange the following Indian cities according to their locations from west to east:
1. Bilaspur 2. Jodhpur
3. Bhopal 4. Ranchi

Select the correct answer using the code given below:
A. 3-2-1-4 B. 2-3-1-4
C. 4-1-2-3 D. 2-1-3-4

61. The Kashmir region receives additional amount of precipitation during the winter brought by:
A. South-west Monsoon B. Western Disturbances
C. Retreating Monsoon D. Temperate Cyclone

62. Which part of India has the Kalakot tertiary coal field?
A. Brahmaputra river basin of Assam
B. Damodar river basin of Jharkhand and West Bengal
C. Himalayan mountain region
D. Cardamom hills in Kerala

63. Tendons through which muscles are connected to bones are tightly compacted bundles of which one of the following long fibrous protein?
A. Fibrin B. Collagen
C. Elastin D. Cellulose

64. Which one of the following is the scientific name of the causal organism of elephantiasis?
A. *Ascaris lumbricoides* B. *Culex pipiens*
C. *Wuchereria bancrofti* D. *Fasciola hepatica*

65. Melanin is the natural pigment that gives colour to human skin, hair and the iris. It provides protection against:
A. Ultraviolet radiation
B. Infrared radiation
C. X-ray radiation
D. Short wave radio radiation

66. Intake of which one of the following food components should be minimized by patients having Gouty Arthritis due to elevated serum uric acid level?
A. Food fibres B. Nucleic acids
C. Lipids D. Carbohydrates

67. Which one of the following statements about microbes is *not* correct?
A. They are used in sewage treatment plants.
B. They are used in industrial fermenters for the production of beverages.
C. No antibiotic has been obtained from any microbe.
D. They are used to get many bioactive molecules for the treatment of diseases.

68. Golden rice is a genetically-modified crop plant where the incorporated gene is meant for biosynthesis of:
A. Omega-3 fatty acids B. Vitamin A
C. Vitamin B D. Vitamin C

69. An object moves in a circular path with a constant speed. Which one of the following statements is correct?
A. The centripetal acceleration of the object is smaller for a gentle curve (*i.e.*, curve of larger radius) than that for a sharp curve (*i.e.*, curve of smaller radius).
B. The centripetal acceleration is greater for a gentle curve than that for a sharp curve.
C. The centripetal acceleration is the same for both, the gentle and sharp curves.
D. The centripetal acceleration causes the object to slow down.

70. The force acting on a particle of mass m moving along the x-axis is given by $F(x) = Ax^2 - Bx$. Which one of the following is the potential energy of the particle?
A. $2Ax - B$ B. $-\frac{x^2}{6}(2Ax - 3B)$
C. $Ax^3 - Bx^2$ D. Zero

71. The symbol of SI unit of inductance is H. It stands for:
A. Holm B. Halogen
C. Henry D. Hertz

72. In a vacuum, a five-rupee coin, a feather of a sparrow bird and a mango are dropped simultaneously from the same height. The time taken by them to reach the bottom is t_1, t_2 and t_3 respectively. In this situation, we will observe that:
A. $t_1 > t_2 > t_3$ B. $t_1 > t_3 > t_2$
C. $t_3 > t_1 > t_2$ D. $t_1 = t_2 = t_3$

73. Electron emission from a metallic surface by application of light is known as:
A. Thermionic emission B. Photoelectric emission
C. High field emission D. Autoelectronic emission

74. How long does light take to reach the Earth from the Sun?
A. About 4 minutes B. About 8 minutes
C. About 24 minutes D. About 24 hours

75. Radioactivity is measured by:
A. GM Counter B. Polarimeter
C. Calorimeter D. Colorimeter

76. The mirrors used as rear-view mirrors in vehicles are:
A. concave B. convex
C. cylindrical D. plane

77. Which one of the following waves is used for detecting forgery in currency notes?
A. Ultraviolet waves B. Infrared waves
C. Radio waves D. Microwaves

78. The majority charge carriers in a *p*-type semiconductor are:
A. free electrons B. conduction electrons
C. ions D. holes

79. The ionization energy of hydrogen atom in the ground state is:
A. 13.6 MeV B. 13.6 eV
C. 13.6 Joule D. Zero

80. When pure water boils vigorously, the bubbles that rise to the surface are composed primarily of:
A. air B. hydrogen
C. hydrogen and oxygen D. water vapour

81. Which compound, when dissolved in water, conducts electricity and forms a basic solution?
A. HCl B. CH_3COOH
C. CH_3OH D. NaOH

82. The principal use of hydrofluoric acid is:
A. in etching glass
B. as a bleaching agent
C. as an extremely strong oxidizing agent
D. in the preparation of strong organic fluorine compounds

83. The species that has the same number of electrons as ${}^{35}_{17}Cl$ is:
A. ${}^{32}_{16}S$ B. ${}^{34}_{16}S^+$
C. ${}^{40}_{18}Ar^+$ D. ${}^{35}_{16}S^{2-}$

84. The compound $C_6H_{12}O_4$ contains:
A. 22 atoms per mole
B. twice the mass per cent of H as compared to the mass per cent of C
C. six times the mass per cent of C as compared to the mass per cent of H
D. thrice the mass per cent of H as compared to the mass per cent of O

85. The proposition 'equal volumes of different gases contain equal numbers of molecules at the same temperature and pressure' is known as
A. Avogadro's hypothesis
B. Gay-Lussac's hypothesis
C. Planck's hypothesis
D. Kirchhoff's theory

86. Which one of the following statements about the Ilbert Bill is correct?
A. It proposed that the Indian magistrates would try Europeans in criminal cases.
B. It allowed Indians to file criminal cases against Europeans.
C. It authorized Indian ICS officers to try Europeans in courts.
D. It was an agitation led by Ilbert in support of the nationalists.

87. Who among the following can attend the meetings of both Houses of Parliament while ***not*** being a member of either House?
A. The Solicitor General of India
B. The Vice-President of India
C. The Comptroller and Auditor General of India
D. The Attorney General of India

88. Who among the following was believed to be a leader of the Sanyasis and Fakirs conspiring against the British in 1857?
A. Mangal Pandey B. Bahadur Shah II
C. Queen Zeenat Mahal D. Nana Sahib

89. Who among the following was the founder of the Avadh Kingdom in the 18th century?
A. Murshid Quli Khan B. Saadat Khan
C. Alivardi Khan D. Sarfaraz Khan

90. Who among the following was the founder of the Young Bengal Movement?
A. Henry Vivian Derozio
B. David Hare
C. Dwarkanath Tagore
D. Prasanna Kumar Tagore

91. Which one of the following statements about the Quit India Movement is ***not*** correct?
A. It broke out in August 1942.
B. Ahmedabad Textile Mills went on strike for more than three months.
C. Muslim League and Hindu Mahasabha actively participated in the movement.
D. Communist Party did not support the movement.

92. Who among the following is the winner of the Singapore Open Superseries Badminton Men's Singles title 2017?
A. Kidambi Srikanth B. Lin Dan
C. B. Sai Praneeth D. Kento Momota

93. Koradi Thermal Power Station is located in:
A. Nagpur B. Raipur
C. Mumbai D. Secunderabad

94. Which one of the following is the theme of the International Day for Monuments and Sites (World Heritage Day) 2017?
A. The Heritage of Sport
B. Cultural Heritage and Sustainable Tourism
C. Past and Present Heritage
D. Heritage and Science

95. In April 2017, USA dropped MOAB (Massive Ordnance Air Blast popularly known as the Mother of All Bombs) in the suspected hideouts of militants in which one of the following countries?
A. Iran B. Syria
C. Afghanistan D. Somalia

96. Who among the following is the Chairman of the Interdisciplinary Committee constituted recently by the Government of India to examine framework for virtual currencies?
A. Secretary, Department of Financial Services
B. Special Secretary, Department of Revenue
C. Special Secretary, Department of Economic Affairs
D. Deputy Governor, Reserve Bank of India

97. SAMPADA scheme is being implemented by the Ministry of:
A. Finance
B. Housing and Urban Affairs
C. Food Processing Industries
D. Earth Sciences

98. The shortest day length that occurs in the Northern hemisphere is on:
A. 21st March B. 23rd September
C. 22nd November D. 22nd December

99. The Indian Railways have gone in for qualitative improvements since independence. Which of the following have taken place in recent years?
1. Gauge conversion
2. Track electrification
3. Automatic signals
Select the correct answer using the codes given below:
A. 1 and 2 only B. 2 and 3 only
C. 1 and 3 only D. 1, 2 and 3

100. In India, maximum amount of rainfall is received from:
A. Western Disturbances B. North-east Monsoon
C. South-west Monsoon D. Retreating Monsoon

101. Which set of the following biosphere reserves in India is included in the World Network of Biosphere Reserves?
A. Gulf of Mannar, Nokrek, Panchmarhi and Simlipal
B. Gulf of Mannar, Kanchanjunga, Nokrek and Seshachalam
C. Nilgiri, Nokrek, Panchmarhi and Panna
D. Nilgiri, Nokrek, Panchmarhi and Seshachalam

102. Which of the following statements about magnetite ore of iron is/are correct?
1. It is known as black ore.
2. It contains 60% to 70% of pure iron.
3. It possesses magnetic properties.
Select the correct answer using the code given below:
A. 1 only B. 2 and 3 only
C. 1 and 3 only D. 1, 2 and 3

103. Which one of the following vitamins has a role in blood clotting?
A. Vitamin A B. Vitamin D
C. Vitamin E D. Vitamin K

104. The term 'Probiotic' is applied to:
A. Organic food
B. Antacid
C. Antibiotic
D. Live microbial food supplement

105. Which one of the following microbes causes acidification and curding of milk?
A. Lactic Acid *Bacillus*
B. *Clostridium botulinum*
C. *Vibrio cholerae*
D. *Saccharomyces cerevisiae*

106. Who among the following shared the Nobel Prize in 1962 along with Francis Crick and James Watson for their discoveries concerning the molecular structure of nucleic acids?
A. Erwin Chargaff
B. Maurice Hugh Frederick Wilkins
C. Rosalind Franklin
D. Phoebus Levene

107. Water boils at a lower temperature at high altitudes, because:
A. the air pressure is less
B. outside temperature is less
C. latent heat is less
D. None of the above

108. Concave mirror is used in headlights of vehicles, because it:
A. focuses light from the bulb onto nearby vehicles
B. sends parallel rays
C. fits well into the shape of the headlight
D. is cheaper than other mirrors

109. If some object is weighed when submerged in water, what will happen to its weight compared to its weight in air?
A. Increase
B. Decrease
C. Remain exactly the same
D. Increase or decrease cannot be predicted

110. Light year is a measure of:
A. time
B. distance
C. total amount of light falling on the Earth in a year
D. average intensity of light falling on the Earth in a year

111. Which one of the following statements about a satellite orbiting around the Earth is correct?
A. Satellite is kept in orbit by remote control from ground station.
B. Satellite is kept in orbit by retro-rocket and solar energy keeps it moving around the Earth.
C. Satellite requires energy from solar panels and solid fuels for orbiting.
D. Satellite does not require any energy for orbiting.

112. Which one of the following statements about energy is correct?
A. Energy can be created as well as destroyed.
B. Energy can be created but not destroyed.
C. Energy can neither be created nor destroyed.
D. Energy cannot be created but can be destroyed.

113. Step-up transformers are used for:
A. increasing electrical power
B. decreasing electrical power
C. decreasing voltage
D. increasing voltage

114. Which one among the following waves carries the maximum energy per photon?
A. X-rays
B. Radio waves
C. Light waves
D. Microwave

115. How much CO_2 is produced on heating of 1 kg of carbon?
A. $\frac{11}{3}$ kg B. $\frac{3}{11}$ kg
C. $\frac{4}{3}$ kg D. $\frac{3}{4}$ kg

116. Zinc is used to protect iron from corrosion because zinc is:
A. more electropositive than iron
B. cheaper than iron
C. a bluish white metal
D. a good conductor of heat and electricity

117. Which one of the following gases is placed second in respect of abundance in the Earth's atmosphere?
A. Oxygen B. Hydrogen
C. Nitrogen D. Carbon dioxide

118. Which one of the following is a chemical change?
A. Cutting of hair
B. Graying of hair naturally
C. Swelling of resin in water
D. Cutting of fruit

119. Which one among the following chemicals is used as washing soda?
A. Calcium carbonate B. Calcium bicarbonate
C. Sodium carbonate D. Sodium bicarbonate

120. Why is potassium permanganate used for purifying drinking water?
A. It kills germs
B. It dissolves the impurities
C. It is a reducing agent
D. It is an oxidizing agent

121. Consider the following movements:
1. Moplah Rebellion
2. Bardoli Satyagraha
3. Champaran Satyagraha
4. Salt Satyagraha

Which one of the following is the correct chronological order of the above in ascending order?
A. 1-3-4-2 B. 3-1-2-4
C. 2-3-1-4 D. 4-2-1-3

122. Which one of the following travelogues has given an insight on the reign of Muhammad Bin Tughlaq?
A. Ibn Battuta's *Rihla*
B. Francois Bernier's *Travels in the Mogul Empire*
C. Niccolao Manucci's *Storia do Mogor*
D. Tavernier's *Travels in India*

123. Which one of the following was ***not*** a Chishti Sufi saint?
A. Khwaja Moinuddin
B. Baba Fariduddin Ganj-i-Shakar
C. Nizamuddin Auliya
D. Shaikh Bahauddin Zakariya

124. In April 2017, India celebrated 100 years of Mahatma Gandhi's:
A. Satyagraha in Kheda
B. Dandi March
C. Satyagraha in Champaran
D. Return from South Africa

125. A rainbow is produced due to which one of the following phenomena?
A. Dispersion of light
B. Interference of light
C. Diffraction of light
D. Scattering of light by atmospheric dust

126. Bats detect obstacles in their path by receiving the reflected:
A. Infrasonic waves B. Ultrasonic waves
C. Radio waves D. Microwaves

127. The statement that 'heat cannot flow by itself from a body at a lower temperature to a body at a higher temperature', is known as:
A. Zeroth law of thermodynamics
B. First law of thermodynamics
C. Second law of thermodynamics
D. Third law of thermodynamics

128. Which one of the following waves does ***not*** belong to the category of the other three?
A. X-rays B. Micro waves
C. Radio waves D. Sound waves

129. Which one of the following statements is ***not*** correct?
A. Human eye is a refracting system containing a diverging lens.
B. The retina of the human eye contains millions of light sensitive cells, called *rods* and *cones,* which convert the light into electrical messages.
C. Every image that is focused on the retina is upside down.
D. We need both eyes to judge the relative positions of objects accurately.

130. Which one of the following statements is ***not*** correct?
A. Ultrasonic waves cannot get reflected, refracted or absorbed.
B. Ultrasonic waves are used to detect the presence of defects like cracks, porosity, etc. in the internal structure of common structure materials.
C. Ultrasonic waves can be used for making holes in very hard materials like diamond.
D. Ultrasonic waves cannot travel through vacuum.

131. According to the Travel and Tourism Competitiveness Index (TTCI) 2017 released by the World Economic Forum, among the 136 economies across the world, India ranked
A. 50th B. 40th
C. 30th D. 20th

132. Which one of the following is the theme of the World Health Day, 2017 celebrated by the World Health Organization?
A. Diabetes
B. Food Safety
C. Depression: Let's Talk
D. Ageing and Health

133. Which one of the following Ministries has launched a new programme on Interdisciplinary Cyber Physical Systems (ICPS) to foster and promote R&D?
A. Ministry of Earth Sciences
B. Ministry of Science and Technology
C. Ministry of Information and Broadcasting
D. Ministry of New and Renewable Energy

134. Consider the following statements about the Nagara style of temple architecture:
1. This style of temples are commonly found in the areas between Himalayas and Vindhyas.
2. The most striking feature of this style is its pyramidal shikhara.

Which of the statements given above is/are correct?
A. 1 only B. 2 only
C. Both 1 and 2 D. Neither 1 nor 2

135. Ashoka's connection with Buddhism is evident from which one of the following edicts?
A. Major Rock Edict 13 B. Rock Edict 6
C. Minor Rock Edict 1 D. Pillar Edict 4

136. The Cabinet Mission Plan for India envisaged a
A. Federation
B. Confederation
C. Unitary form of Government
D. Union of States

137. The creation of the institution of Lokpal was first recommended by:
A. Law Commission
B. Santhanam Committee
C. Shah Commission
D. Administrative Reforms Commission

138. Which one of the following is a cause of acid rains?
A. Ozone B. Ammonia
C. Sulphur dioxide D. Carbon monoxide

139. The desirable range of pH for drinking water is
A. 6.5 to 8.5 B. 5.0 to 6.5
C. 6.5 to 7.0 D. 7.0 to 8.5

140. Consider the following reaction:

$CH_4 + 2O_2 \rightarrow CO_2 + 2H_2O$

Which of the following about the reaction given above is/are correct?
1. Carbon is oxidized. 2. Hydrogen is oxidized.
3. Hydrogen is reduced. 4. Carbon is reduced.

Select the correct answer using the code given below:
A. 1 only B. 1 and 2 only
C. 2 and 3 only D. 2 and 4 only

141. Sunrise in eastern Arunachal Pradesh would be about how many hours before the sunrise in western Gujarat?
A. One hour B. Two hours
C. Three hours D. Four hours

142. Consider the following States of India in terms of percentage of forest area in relation to the total area of the State:
1. Karnataka 2. Odisha
3. Kerala 4. Andhra Pradesh

Which one of the following is the correct descending order?

A. 1-2-4-3 B. 3-1-2-4
C. 3-2-1-4 D. 2-3-1-4

143. Which one of the following States in India has the longest coastline?

A. Odisha B. Tamil Nadu
C. Karnataka D. West Bengal

144. Which one of the following States in India has the largest area under forest cover?

A. Maharashtra B. Chhattisgarh
C. Madhya Pradesh D. Andhra Pradesh

145. Which one of the following is *not* an igneous rock?

A. Gabbro B. Granite
C. Dolomite D. Basalt

146. The Coriolis effect is the result of:

A. Pressure gradient
B. Earth's axis of inclination
C. Earth's rotation
D. Earth's revolution

147. Where is Mekong Delta located?

A. Thailand B. Cambodia
C. Myanmar D. Vietnam

148. Which one of the following pairs of rivers and tributaries is ***not*** correctly matched?

A. Godavari : Indravati
B. Ganga : Penganga
C. Krishna : Bhima
D. Luni : Sukri

149. Consider the following characteristics of a tropical cyclone:

1. A warm sea temperature of > 26°C
2. High relative humidity of atmosphere at a height of > 700 m
3. Atmospheric instability

The above mentioned characteristics are associated with which one of the following cycles of its development?

A. Formulation and initial stage
B. Modification stage
C. Full maturity
D. Decay

150. In the Mesopotamian records, which one of the following terms was used for the Indus Valley (Harappans)?

A. Dilmun B. Meluha
C. Magan D. Failaka

PAPER II : MATHEMATICS

1. If $x + \log_{10}(1 + 2^x) = x \log_{10} 5 + \log_{10} 6$ then x is equal to:

A. 2, –3 B. 2 only
C. 1 D. 3

2. The remainder and the quotient of the binary division $(101110)_2 \div (110)_2$ are respectively:

A. $(111)_2$ and $(100)_2$ B. $(100)_2$ and $(111)_2$
C. $(101)_2$ and $(101)_2$ D. $(100)_2$ and $(100)_2$

3. The matrix A has x rows and $x + 5$ columns. The matrix B has y rows and $11 - y$ columns. Both AB and BA exist. What are the values of x and y respectively?

A. 8 and 3 B. 3 and 4
C. 3 and 8 D. 8 and 8

4. If $S_n = nP + \frac{n(n-1)Q}{2}$, where S_n denotes the sum of the first n terms of an AP, then the common difference is:

A. P + Q B. 2P + 3Q
C. 2Q D. Q

5. The roots of the equation: $(q - r)x^2 + (r - p)x + (p - q) = 0$ are

A. $\frac{(r-p)}{(q-r)}, \frac{1}{2}$ B. $\frac{(p-q)}{(q-r)}, 1$

C. $\frac{(q-r)}{(p-q)}, 1$ D. $\frac{(r-p)}{(p-q)}, \frac{1}{2}$

6. If E is the universal set and A = B ∪ C, then the set E – (E – (E – (E – (E – A)))) is same as the set:

A. B′ ∪ C′ B. B ∪ C
C. B′ ∩ C′ D. B ∩ C

7. If A = {x : x is a multiple of 2}, B = {x : x is a multiple of 5} and C = {x : x is a multiple of 10}, then A ∩ (B ∩ C) is equal to:

A. A
B. B
C. C
D. {x : x is a multiple of 100}

8. If α and β are the roots of the equation $1 + x + x^2 = 0$, then the matrix product

$$\begin{bmatrix} 1 & \beta \\ \alpha & \alpha \end{bmatrix}\begin{bmatrix} \alpha & \beta \\ 1 & \beta \end{bmatrix}$$

is equal to:

A. $\begin{bmatrix} 1 & 1 \\ 1 & 2 \end{bmatrix}$ B. $\begin{bmatrix} -1 & -1 \\ -1 & 2 \end{bmatrix}$

C. $\begin{bmatrix} 1 & -1 \\ -1 & 2 \end{bmatrix}$ D. $\begin{bmatrix} -1 & -1 \\ -1 & -2 \end{bmatrix}$

9. If $|a|$ denotes the absolute value of an integer, then which of the following are correct?

1. $|ab| = |a||b|$
2. $|a + b| \le |a| + |b|$
3. $|a - b| \ge ||a| - |b||$

Select the correct answer using the code given below:

A. 1 and 2 only B. 2 and 3 only
C. 1 and 3 only D. 1, 2, and 3

10. How many different permutations can be made out of the letters of the word 'PERMUTATION'?

A. 19958400 B. 19954800
C. 19952400 D. 39916800

11. If $A = \begin{bmatrix} 4i-6 & 10i \\ 14i & 6+4i \end{bmatrix}$ and $k = \frac{1}{2i}$, where $i = \sqrt{-1}$, then kA is equal to:

A. $\begin{bmatrix} 2+3i & 5 \\ 7 & 2-3i \end{bmatrix}$ B. $\begin{bmatrix} 2-3i & 5 \\ 7 & 2+3i \end{bmatrix}$

C. $\begin{bmatrix} 2-3i & 7 \\ 5 & 2+3i \end{bmatrix}$ D. $\begin{bmatrix} 2+3i & 5 \\ 7 & 2+3i \end{bmatrix}$

12. The sum of all real roots of the equation $|x - 3|^2 + |x - 3| - 2 = 0$ is:

A. 2 B. 3
C. 4 D. 6

13. It is given that the roots of the equation $x^2 - 4x - \log_3 P = 0$ are real. For this, the minimum value of P is:

A. $\frac{1}{27}$ B. $\frac{1}{64}$

C. $\frac{1}{81}$ D. 1

14. If A is a square matrix, then the value of adj A^T – (adj $A)^T$ is equal to

A. A
B. $2|A|I$, where I is the identity matrix
C. null matrix whose order is same as that of A
D. unit matrix whose order is same as that of A

15. The value of the product

$6^{\frac{1}{2}} \times 6^{\frac{1}{4}} \times 6^{\frac{1}{8}} \times 6^{\frac{1}{16}} \times \ldots$ up to infinite terms is:

A. 6 B. 36
C. 216 D. 512

16. The value of the determinant

$$\begin{vmatrix} \cos^2\frac{\theta}{2} & \sin^2\frac{\theta}{2} \\ \sin^2\frac{\theta}{2} & \cos^2\frac{\theta}{2} \end{vmatrix}$$

for all values of θ, is

A. 1 B. $\cos\theta$
C. $\sin\theta$ D. $\cos 2\theta$

17. The number of terms in the expansion of $(x + a)^{100} + (x - a)^{100}$ after simplification is:

A. 202 B. 101
C. 51 D. 50

18. In the expansion of $(1 + x)^{50}$, the sum of the coefficients of odd powers of x is:

A. 2^{26} B. 2^{49}
C. 2^{50} D. 2^{51}

19. If a, b, c are non-zero real numbers, then the inverse of the matrix $A = \begin{bmatrix} a & 0 & 0 \\ 0 & b & 0 \\ 0 & 0 & c \end{bmatrix}$ is equal to:

A. $\begin{bmatrix} a^{-1} & 0 & 0 \\ 0 & b^{-1} & 0 \\ 0 & 0 & c^{-1} \end{bmatrix}$ B. $\frac{1}{abc}\begin{bmatrix} a^{-1} & 0 & 0 \\ 0 & b^{-1} & 0 \\ 0 & 0 & c^{-1} \end{bmatrix}$

C. $\frac{1}{abc}\begin{bmatrix} 1 & 0 & 0 \\ 0 & 1 & 0 \\ 0 & 0 & 1 \end{bmatrix}$ D. $\frac{1}{abc}\begin{bmatrix} a & 0 & 0 \\ 0 & b & 0 \\ 0 & 0 & c \end{bmatrix}$

20. A person is to count 4500 notes. Let a_n denote the number of notes he counts in the nth minute. If $a_1 = a_2 = a_3 = .. = a_{10} = 150$, and $a_{10}, a_{11}, a_{12}, \ldots$ are in AP with the common difference –2, then the time taken by him to count all the notes is:

A. 24 minutes B. 34 minutes
C. 125 minutes D. 135 minutes

21. The smallest positive integer n for which $\left(\frac{1+i}{1-i}\right)^n = 1$, is:

A. 1 B. 4
C. 8 D. 16

22. If we define a relation R on the set N × N as (a, b) R $(c, d) \Leftrightarrow a + d = b + c$ for all $(a, b), (c, d) \in N \times N$, then the relation is:

A. symmetric only
B. symmetric and transitive only
C. equivalence relation
D. reflexive only

23. If $y = x + x^2 + x^3 + ...$ up to infinite terms, where $x < 1$, then which one of the following is correct?

A. $x = \frac{y}{1+y}$ B. $x = \frac{y}{1-y}$

C. $x = \frac{1+y}{y}$ D. $x = \frac{1-y}{y}$

24. If α and β are the roots of the equation $3x^2 + 2x + 1 = 0$, then the equation whose roots are $\alpha + \beta^{-1}$ and $\beta + \alpha^{-1}$ is:

A. $3x^2 + 8x + 16 = 0$

B. $3x^2 - 8x - 16 = 0$

C. $3x^2 + 8x - 16 = 0$

D. $x^2 + 8x + 16 = 0$

25. The value of $\frac{1}{\log_3 e} + \frac{1}{\log_3 e^2} + \frac{1}{\log_3 e^4} + ...$ up to infinite terms is:

A. $\log_e 9$ B. 0

C. 1 D. $\log_e 3$

26. A tea party is arranged for 16 people along two sides of a long table with eight chairs on each side. Four particular men wish to sit on one particular side and two particular men on the other side. The number of ways they can be seated is:

A. $24 \times 8! \times 8!$ B. $(8!)^3$

C. $210 \times 8! \times 8!$ D. $16!$

27. The system of equations $kx + y + z = 1$, $x + ky + z = k$ and $x + y + kz = k^2$ has no solution if k equals:

A. 0 B. 1

C. –1 D. –2

28. If $1.3 + 2.3^2 + 3.3^3 + ... + n.3^n = \frac{(2n-1)3^a + b}{4}$ then a and b are respectively:

A. n, 2 B. n, 3

C. $n + 1$, 2 D. $n + 1$, 3

29. In ΔPQR, $\angle R = \frac{\pi}{2}$. If $\tan\left(\frac{P}{2}\right)$ and $\tan\left(\frac{Q}{2}\right)$ are the roots of the equation $ax^2 + bx + c = 0$, then which one of the following is correct?

A. $a = b + c$ B. $b = c + a$

C. $c = a + b$ D. $b = c$

30. If $\left|z - \frac{4}{z}\right| = 2$, then the maximum value of $|z|$ is equal to:

A. $1+\sqrt{3}$ B. $1+\sqrt{5}$

C. $1-\sqrt{5}$ D. $\sqrt{5}-1$

31. The angle of elevation of a stationary cloud from a point 25 m above a lake is 15° and the angle of depression of its image in the lake is 45°. The height of the cloud above the lake level is:

A. 25 m B. $25\sqrt{3}$ m

C. 50 m D. $50\sqrt{3}$ m

32. The value of tan 9° – tan 27° – tan 63° + tan 81° is equal to:

A. –1 B. 0

C. 1 D. 4

33. The value of $\sqrt{3}\,\text{cosec}\,20° - \sec 20°$ is equal to:

A. 4 B. 2

C. 1 D. –4

34. Angle α is divided into two parts A and B such that $A - B = x$ and $\tan A : \tan B = p : q$. The value of $\sin x$ is equal to:

A. $\frac{(p+q)\sin\alpha}{p-q}$ B. $\frac{p\sin\alpha}{p+q}$

C. $\frac{p\sin\alpha}{p-q}$ D. $\frac{(p-q)\sin\alpha}{p+q}$

35. The value of $\sin^{-1}\left(\frac{3}{5}\right) + \tan^{-1}\left(\frac{1}{7}\right)$ is equal to:

A. 0 B. $\frac{\pi}{4}$

C. $\frac{\pi}{3}$ D. $\frac{\pi}{2}$

36. The angles of elevation of the top of a tower from the top and foot of a pole are respectively 30° and 45°. If h_T is the height of the tower and h_P is the height of the pole, then which of the following are correct?

1. $\frac{2h_P h_T}{3+\sqrt{3}} = h_P^2$ 2. $\frac{h_T - h_P}{\sqrt{3}+1} = \frac{h_P}{2}$

3. $\frac{2(h_P + h_T)}{h_P} = 4 + \sqrt{3}$

Select the correct answer using the code given below:

A. 1 and 3 only B. 2 and 3 only

C. 1 and 2 only D. 1, 2 and 3

37. In a triangle ABC, $a - 2b + c = 0$. The value of $\cot\left(\frac{A}{2}\right)\cot\left(\frac{C}{2}\right)$ is:

A. $\frac{9}{2}$ B. 3

C. $\frac{3}{2}$ D. 1

38. $\sqrt{1+\sin A} = -\left(\sin\frac{A}{2}+\cos\frac{A}{2}\right)$ is true if:

A. $\frac{3\pi}{2} < A < \frac{5\pi}{2}$ only B. $\frac{\pi}{2} < A < \frac{3\pi}{2}$ only

C. $\frac{3\pi}{2} < A < \frac{7\pi}{2}$ D. $0 < A < \frac{3\pi}{2}$

39. In triangle ABC, if $\frac{\sin^2 A+\sin^2 B+\sin^2 C}{\cos^2 A+\cos^2 B+\cos^2 C} = 2$ then the triangle is:

A. right-angled B. equilateral
C. isosceles D. obtuse-angled

40. The principal value of $\sin^{-1} x$ lies in the interval:

A. $\left(-\frac{\pi}{2}, -\frac{\pi}{2}\right)$ B. $\left[-\frac{\pi}{2}, \frac{\pi}{2}\right]$

C. $\left[0, \frac{\pi}{2}\right]$ D. $[0, \pi]$

41. The points (a, b), $(0, 0)$, $(-a, -b)$ and (ab, b^2) are:

A. the vertices of a parallelogram
B. the vertices of a rectangle
C. the vertices of a square
D. collinear

42. The length of the normal from origin to the plane $x + 2y - 2z = 9$ is equal to:

A. 2 units B. 3 units
C. 4 units D. 5 units

43. If α, β and γ are the angles which the vector $\overline{OP}$ (O being the origin) makes with positive direction of the coordinate axes, then which of the following are correct?

1. $\cos^2\alpha + \cos^2\beta = \sin^2\gamma$
2. $\sin^2\alpha + \sin^2\beta = \cos^2\gamma$
3. $\sin^2\alpha + \sin^2\beta + \sin^2\gamma = 2$

Select the correct answer using the code given below:

A. 1 and 2 only
B. 2 and 3 only
C. 1 and 3 only
D. 1, 2 and 3

44. The angle between the lines $x + y - 3 = 0$ and $x - y + 3 = 0$ is α and the acute angle between the lines $x-\sqrt{3}y+2\sqrt{3}=0$ and $\sqrt{3}x-y+1=0$ is β. Which one of the following is correct?

A. $\alpha = \beta$
B. $\alpha > \beta$
C. $\alpha < \beta$
D. $\alpha = 2\beta$

45. Let $\vec{\alpha} = \hat{i}+2\hat{j}-\hat{k}$, $\vec{\beta} = 2\hat{i}-\hat{j}+3\hat{k}$ and $\vec{\gamma} = 2\hat{i}+\hat{j}+6\hat{k}$ be three vectors. If $\vec{\alpha}$ and $\vec{\beta}$ are both perpendicular to the vector $\vec{\delta}$ and $\vec{\delta}\cdot\vec{\gamma} = 10$, then what is the magnitude of $\vec{\delta}$?

A. $\sqrt{3}$ units B. $2\sqrt{3}$ units

C. $\frac{\sqrt{3}}{2}$ units D. $\frac{1}{\sqrt{3}}$ units

46. If $\hat{a}$ and $\hat{b}$ are two unit vectors, then the vector $(\hat{a}+\hat{b})\times(\hat{a}\times\hat{b})$ is parallel to:

A. $(\hat{a}-\hat{b})$ B. $(\hat{a}+\hat{b})$

C. $(2\hat{a}-\hat{b})$ D. $(2\hat{a}+\hat{b})$

47. A force $\vec{F} = \hat{i}+3\hat{j}+2\hat{k}$ acts on a particle to displace it from the point $A(\hat{i}+2\hat{j}-3\hat{k})$ to the point $B(3\hat{i}-\hat{j}+5\hat{k})$. The work done by the force will be:

A. 5 units B. 7 units
C. 9 units D. 10 units

48. For any vector $\vec{a}$

$|\vec{a}\times\hat{i}|^2 + |\vec{a}\times\hat{j}|^2 + |\hat{a}\times\hat{k}|^2$ is equal to:

A. $|\vec{a}|^2$ B. $2|\vec{a}|^2$

C. $3|\vec{a}|^2$ D. $4|\vec{a}|^2$

49. A man running round a racecourse notes that the sum of the distances of two flag-posts from him is always 10 m and the distance between the flag-posts is 8 m. The area of the path he encloses is:

A. 18π square metres B. 15π square metres
C. 12π square metres D. 8π square metres

50. The distance of the point (1, 3) from the line $2x + 3y = 6$, measured parallel to the line $4x + y = 4$, is:

A. $\frac{5}{\sqrt{13}}$ units B. $\frac{3}{\sqrt{17}}$ units

C. $\sqrt{17}$ units D. $\frac{\sqrt{17}}{2}$ units

51. If the vectors $a\hat{i}+\hat{j}+\hat{k}$, $\hat{i}+b\hat{j}+\hat{k}$ and $\hat{i}+\hat{j}+c\hat{k}$ $(a, b, c \neq 1)$ are coplanar, then the value of $\frac{1}{1-a}+\frac{1}{1-b}+\frac{1}{1-c}$ is equal to:

A. 0 B. 1
C. $a + b + c$ D. abc

52. The point of intersection of the line joining the points (–3, 4, –8) and (5, –6, 4) with the XY-plane is:

A. $\left(\frac{7}{3}, -\frac{8}{3}, 0\right)$ B. $\left(-\frac{7}{3}, -\frac{8}{3}, 0\right)$

C. $\left(-\frac{7}{3}, \frac{8}{3}, 0\right)$ D. $\left(\frac{7}{3}, \frac{8}{3}, 0\right)$

53. If the angle between the lines whose direction ratios are ⟨2, –1, 2⟩ and ⟨x, 3, 5⟩ is $\frac{\pi}{4}$, then the smaller value of x is:

A. 52 B. 4
C. 2 D. 1

54. The position of the point (1, 2) relative to the ellipse $2x^2 + 7y^2 = 20$ is:

A. outside the ellipse
B. inside the ellipse but not at the focus
C. on the ellipse
D. at the focus

55. The equation of a straight line which cuts off an intercept of 5 units on negative direction of y-axis and makes an angle 120° with positive direction of x-axis is:

A. $y+\sqrt{3}x+5=0$ B. $y-\sqrt{3}x+5=0$

C. $y+\sqrt{3}x-5=0$ D. $y-\sqrt{3}x-5=0$

56. The equation of the line passing through the point (2, 3) and the point of intersection of lines $2x - 3y + 7 = 0$ and $7x + 4y + 2 = 0$ is:

A. $21x + 46y - 180 = 0$
B. $21x - 46y + 96 = 0$
C. $46x + 21y - 155 = 0$
D. $46x - 21y - 29 = 0$

57. The equation of the ellipse whose centre is at origin, major axis is along x-axis with eccentricity $\frac{3}{4}$ and latus rectum 4 units is:

A. $\frac{x^2}{1024}+\frac{7y^2}{64}=1$ B. $\frac{49x^2}{1024}+\frac{7y^2}{64}=1$

C. $\frac{7x^2}{1024}+\frac{49y^2}{64}=1$ D. $\frac{x^2}{1024}+\frac{y^2}{64}=1$

58. The equation of the circle which passes through the points (1, 0), (0, –6) and (3, 4) is:

A. $4x^2 + 4y^2 + 142x + 47y + 140 = 0$
B. $4x^2 + 4y^2 - 142x - 47y + 138 = 0$
C. $4x^2 + 4y^2 - 142x + 47y + 138 = 0$
D. $4x^2 + 4y^2 + 150x - 49y + 138 = 0$

59. A variable plane passes through a fixed point (a, b, c) and cuts the axes in A, B and C respectively. The locus of the centre of the sphere OABC, O being the origin, is

A. $\frac{x}{a}+\frac{y}{b}+\frac{z}{c}=1$ B. $\frac{a}{x}+\frac{b}{y}+\frac{c}{z}=1$

C. $\frac{a}{x}+\frac{b}{y}+\frac{c}{z}=2$ D. $\frac{x}{a}+\frac{y}{b}+\frac{z}{c}=2$

60. The equation of the plane passing through the line of intersection of the planes $x + y + z = 1$, $2x + 3y + 4z = 7$, and perpendicular to the plane $x - 5y + 3z = 5$ is given by:

A. $x + 2y + 3z - 6 = 0$
B. $x + 2y + 3z + 6 = 0$
C. $3x + 4y + 5z - 8 = 0$
D. $3x + 4y + 5z + 8 = 0$

61. The inverse of the function $y = 5^{\ln x}$ is:

A. $x = y^{\frac{1}{\ln 5}}, y > 0$ B. $x = y^{\ln 5}, y > 0$

C. $x = y^{\frac{1}{\ln 5}}, y < 0$ D. $x = 5 \ln y, y > 0$

62. A function is defined as follows:

$$f(x) = \begin{cases} -\frac{x}{\sqrt{x^2}}, & x \neq 0 \\ 0, & x = 0 \end{cases}$$

Which one of the following is correct in respect of the above function?

A. $f(x)$ is continuous at $x = 0$ but not differentiable at $x = 0$
B. $f(x)$ is continuous as well as differentiable at $x = 0$
C. $f(x)$ is discontinuous at $x = 0$
D. None of the above

63. If $y = (\cos x)^{(\cos x)^{(\cos x)^{\cdots}}}$, then $\frac{dy}{dx}$ is equal to:

A. $-\frac{y^2 \tan x}{1 - y \ln(\cos x)}$ B. $\frac{y^2 \tan x}{1 + y \ln(\cos x)}$

C. $\frac{y^2 \tan x}{1 - y \ln(\sin x)}$ D. $\frac{y^2 \tan x}{1 + y \ln(\sin x)}$

64. Consider the following:

1. $x + x^2$ is continuous at $x = 0$
2. $x + \cos\frac{1}{x}$ is discontinuous at $x = 0$
3. $x^2 + \cos\frac{1}{x}$ is continuous at $x = 0$

Which of the above are correct?

A. 1 and 2 only B. 2 and 3 only
C. 1 and 3 only D. 1, 2 and 3

65. Consider the following statements:

1. $\frac{dy}{dx}$ at a point on the curve gives slope of the tangent at that point.
2. If $a(t)$ denotes acceleration of a particle, then $\int a(t)dt + c$ gives velocity of the particle.
3. If $s(t)$ gives displacement of a particle at time t, then $\frac{ds}{dt}$ gives its acceleration at that instant.

Which of the above statements is/are correct?

A. 1 and 2 only B. 2 only
C. 1 only D. 1, 2 and 3

66. If $y = \sec^{-1}\left(\frac{x+1}{x-1}\right) + \sin^{-1}\left(\frac{x-1}{x+1}\right)$, then $\frac{dy}{dx}$ is equal to:

A. 0 B. 1
C. $\frac{x-1}{x+1}$ D. $\frac{x+1}{x-1}$

67. What is $\int \tan^{-1}(\sec x + \tan x)dx$ equal to?

A. $\frac{\pi x}{4} + \frac{x^2}{4} + c$ B. $\frac{\pi x}{2} + \frac{x^2}{4} + c$
C. $\frac{\pi x}{4} + \frac{\pi x^2}{4} + c$ D. $\frac{\pi x}{4} - \frac{x^2}{4} + c$

68. A function is defined in $(0, \infty)$ by:

$$f(x) = \begin{cases} 1 - x^2 & \text{for } 0 < x \le 1 \\ \ln x & \text{for } 1 < x \le 2 \\ \ln 2 - 1 + 0.5x & \text{for } 2 < x < \infty \end{cases}$$

Which one of the following is correct in respect of the derivative of the function, *i.e.*, $f'(x)$?

A. $f'(x) = 2x$ for $0 < x \le 1$
B. $f'(x) = -2x$ for $0 < x \le 1$
C. $f'(x) = -2x$ for $0 < x < 1$
D. $f'(x) = 0$ for $0 < x < \infty$

69. Which one of the following is correct in respect of the function

$$f(x) = x(x - 1)(x + 1)?$$

A. The local maximum value is larger than local minimum value
B. The local maximum value is smaller than local minimum value
C. The function has no local maximum
D. The function has no local minimum

70. Consider the following statements:

1. Derivative of $f(x)$ may not exist at some point.
2. Derivative of $f(x)$ may exist finitely at some point
3. Derivative of $f(x)$ may be infinite (geometrically) at some point.

Which of the above statements are correct?

A. 1 and 2 only B. 2 and 3 only
C. 1 and 3 only D. 1, 2 and 3

71. The maximum value of $\frac{\ln x}{x}$ is:

A. e B. $\frac{1}{e}$
C. $\frac{2}{e}$ D. 1

72. The function $f(x) = |x| - x^3$ is:

A. odd B. even
C. both even and odd D. neither even nor odd

73. If $l_1 = \frac{d}{dx}(e^{\sin x})$

$$l_2 = \lim_{h \to 0} \frac{e^{\sin(x+h)} - e^{\sin x}}{h}$$

$$l_3 = \int e^{\sin x} \cos x\, dx$$

then which one of the following is correct?

A. $l_1 \neq l_2$ B. $\frac{d}{dx}(l_3) = l_2$
C. $\int l_3 dx = l_2$ D. $l_2 = l_3$

74. The general solution of

$$\frac{dy}{dx} = \frac{ax + h}{by + k}$$

represents a circle only when

A. $a = b = 0$ B. $a = -b \neq 0$
C. $a = b \neq 0,\ h = k$ D. $a = b \neq 0$

75. If $\lim_{x \to \frac{\pi}{2}} \frac{\sin x}{x} = l$ and $\lim_{x \to \infty} \frac{\cos x}{x} = m$, then which one of the following is correct?

A. $l = 1,\ m = 1$ B. $l = \frac{2}{\pi},\ m = \infty$
C. $l = \frac{2}{\pi},\ m = 0$ D. $l = 1,\ m = \infty$

76. What is $\int_0^{2\pi} \sqrt{1 + \sin\frac{x}{2}}\, dx$ equal to?

A. 8 B. 4
C. 2 D. 0

77. The area bounded by the curve $|x| + |y| = 1$ is:

A. 1 square unit B. $2\sqrt{2}$ square units
C. 2 square units D. $2\sqrt{3}$ square units

78. If x is any real number, then $\frac{x^2}{1+x^4}$ belongs to which one of the following intervals?

A. (0, 1) B. $\left(0, \frac{1}{2}\right]$
C. $\left(0, \frac{1}{2}\right)$ D. [0, 1]

79. The left-hand derivative of
$f(x) = [x] \sin(\pi x)$ at $x = k$
where k is an integer and $[x]$ is the greatest integer function, is

A. $(-1)^k (k-1)\pi$ B. $(-1)^{k-1} (k-1)\pi$
C. $(-1)^k k\pi$ D. $(-1)^{k-1} k\pi$

80. If $f(x) = \frac{x}{2} - 1$, then on the interval $[0, \pi]$ which one of the following is correct?

A. $\tan [f(x)]$, where [.] is the greatest integer function, and $\frac{1}{f(x)}$ are both continuous
B. $\tan [f(x)]$, where [.] is the greatest integer function, and $f^{-1}(x)$ are both continuous
C. $\tan [f(x)]$, where [.] is the greatest integer function; and $\frac{1}{f(x)}$ are both discontinuous
D. $\tan [f(x)]$, where [.] is the greatest integer function, is discontinuous but $\frac{1}{f(x)}$ is continuous

81. The order and degree of the differential equation

$$\left[1+\left(\frac{dy}{dx}\right)^2\right]^3 = \rho^2 \left[\frac{d^2y}{dx^2}\right]^2$$ are respectively:

A. 3 and 2 B. 2 and 2
C. 2 and 3 D. 1 and 3

82. If $y = \cos^{-1}\left(\frac{2x}{1+x^2}\right)$, then $\frac{dy}{dx}$ is equal to:

A. $-\frac{2}{1+x^2}$ for all $|x| < 1$
B. $-\frac{2}{1+x^2}$ for all $|x| > 1$
C. $\frac{2}{1+x^2}$ for all $|x| < 1$
D. None of the above

83. The set of all points, where the function $f(x) = \sqrt{1-e^{-x^2}}$ is differentiable, is:

A. $(0, \infty)$ B. $(-\infty, \infty)$
C. $(-\infty, 0) \cup (0, \infty)$ D. $(-1, \infty)$

84. Match List-I with List-II and select the correct answer using the code given below the lists:

List-I ***(Function)***	***List-II*** ***(Maximum value)***
(*a*) $\sin x + \cos x$	1. $\sqrt{10}$
(*b*) $3 \sin x + 4 \cos x$	2. $\sqrt{2}$
(*c*) $2 \sin x + \cos x$	3. 5
(*d*) $\sin x + 3 \cos x$	4. $\sqrt{5}$

Code:

	(*a*)	(*b*)	(*c*)	(*d*)
A.	2	3	1	4
B.	2	3	4	1
C.	3	2	1	4
D.	3	2	4	1

85. If $f(x) = x\left(\sqrt{x} - \sqrt{x+1}\right)$, then $f(x)$ is:

A. continuous but not differentiable at $x = 0$
B. differentiable at $x = 0$
C. not continuous at $x = 0$
D. None of the above

86. Which one of the following graphs represents the function $f(x) = \frac{x}{x}$, $x \neq 0$?

A.
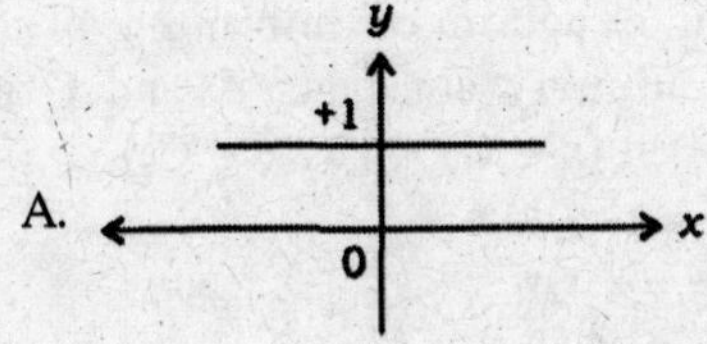

B.
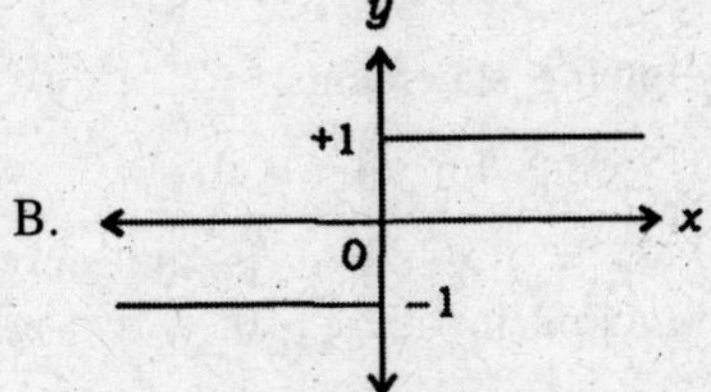

C.
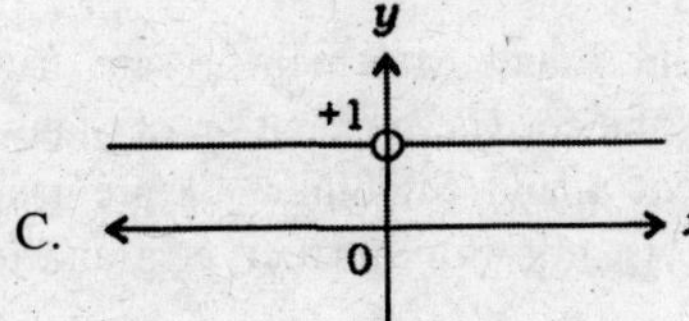

D. None of the above

87. Let $f(n) = \left[\frac{1}{4} + \frac{n}{1000}\right]$, where $[x]$ denotes the integral part of x. Then the value of $\sum_{n=1}^{1000} f(n)$ is:

A. 251 B. 250
C. 1 D. 0

88. $\int (\ln x)^{-1} dx - \int (\ln x)^{-2} dx$ is equal to:

A. $x(\ln x)^{-1} + c$ B. $x(\ln x)^{-2} + c$
C. $x(\ln x) + c$ D. $x(\ln x)^2 + c$

89. A cylindrical jar without a lid has to be constructed using a given surface area of a metal sheet. If the capacity of the jar is to be maximum, then the diameter of the jar must be k times the height of the jar. The value of k is

A. 1 B. 2
C. 3 D. 4

90. The value of $\int_0^{\frac{\pi}{4}} \sqrt{\tan x}\, dx + \int_0^{\frac{\pi}{4}} \sqrt{\cot x}\, dx$ is equal to:

A. $\frac{\pi}{4}$ B. $\frac{\pi}{2}$
C. $\frac{\pi}{2\sqrt{2}}$ D. $\frac{\pi}{\sqrt{2}}$

91. Let g be the greatest integer function. Then the function $f(x) = (g(x))^2 - g(x^2)$ is discontinuous at:

A. all integers
B. all integers except 0 and 1
C. all integers except 0
D. all integers except 1

92. The differential equation of minimum order by eliminating the arbitrary constants A and C in the equation $y = A\,[\sin(x + C) + \cos(x + C)]$ is:

A. $y'' + (\sin x + \cos x)y' = 1$
B. $y'' = (\sin x + \cos x)y'$
C. $y'' = (y')^2 + \sin x \cos x$
D. $y'' + y = 0$

93. Consider the following statements:

Statement I : $x > \sin x$ for all $x > 0$

Statement II : $f(x) = x - \sin x$ is an increasing function for all $x > 0$.

Which one of the following is correct in respect of the above statements?

A. Both Statement I and Statement II are true and Statement II is the correct explanation of Statement I
B. Both Statement I and Statement II are true and Statement II is not the correct explanation of Statement I
C. Statement I is true but Statement II is false
D. Statement I is false but Statement II is true

94. The solution of the differential equation $\frac{dy}{dx} = \frac{y\phi'(x) - y^2}{\phi(x)}$ is:

A. $y = \frac{x}{\phi(x) + c}$ B. $y = \frac{\phi(x)}{x} + c$
C. $y = \frac{\phi(x) + c}{x}$ D. $y = \frac{\phi(x)}{x + c}$

95. If $f(x) = \frac{4x + x^4}{1 + 4x^3}$ and $g(x) = \ln\left(\frac{1+x}{1-x}\right)$, then what is the value of $f \circ g\left(\frac{e-1}{e+1}\right)$ equal to?

A. 2 B. 1
C. 0 D. $\frac{1}{2}$

96. The value of the determinant $\begin{vmatrix} 1-\alpha & \alpha-\alpha^2 & \alpha^2 \\ 1-\beta & \beta-\beta^2 & \beta^2 \\ 1-\gamma & \gamma-\gamma^2 & \gamma^2 \end{vmatrix}$ is equal to:

A. $(\alpha - \beta)(\beta - \gamma)(\alpha - \gamma)$
B. $(\alpha - \beta)(\beta - \gamma)(\gamma - \alpha)$
C. $(\alpha - \beta)(\beta - \gamma)(\gamma - \alpha)(\alpha + \beta + \gamma)$
D. 0

97. The adjoint of the matrix $A = \begin{vmatrix} 1 & 0 & 2 \\ 2 & 1 & 0 \\ 0 & 3 & 1 \end{vmatrix}$ is:

A. $\begin{bmatrix} -1 & 6 & 2 \\ -2 & 1 & -4 \\ 6 & 3 & 1 \end{bmatrix}$ B. $\begin{bmatrix} 1 & 6 & -2 \\ -2 & 1 & 4 \\ 6 & -3 & 1 \end{bmatrix}$

C. $\begin{bmatrix} 6 & 1 & 2 \\ 4 & -1 & 2 \\ 6 & 3 & -1 \end{bmatrix}$ D. $\begin{bmatrix} -6 & 2 & 1 \\ 4 & -2 & 1 \\ 3 & 1 & -6 \end{bmatrix}$

98. If $A = \begin{pmatrix} -2 & 2 \\ 2 & -2 \end{pmatrix}$, then which one of the following is correct?

A. $A^2 = -2A$ B. $A^2 = -4A$
C. $A^2 = -3A$ D. $A^2 = 4A$

99. Geometrically $\text{Re}(z^2 - i) = 2$, where $i = \sqrt{-1}$ and Re is the real part, represents

A. circle B. ellipse
C. rectangular hyperbola D. parabola

100. If $p + q + r = a + b + c = 0$, then the determinant
$\begin{vmatrix} pa & qb & rc \\ qc & ra & pb \\ rb & pc & qa \end{vmatrix}$ equals:

A. 0 B. 1
C. $pa + qb + rc$ D. $pa + qb + rc + a + b + c$

101. A committee of two persons is selected from two men and two women. The probability that the committee will have exactly one woman is:

A. $\frac{1}{6}$ B. $\frac{2}{3}$
C. $\frac{1}{3}$ D. $\frac{1}{2}$

102. Let a die be loaded in such a way that even faces are twice likely to occur as the odd faces. What is the probability that a prime number will show up when the die is tossed?

A. $\frac{1}{3}$ B. $\frac{2}{3}$
C. $\frac{4}{9}$ D. $\frac{5}{9}$

103. Let the sample space consist of non-negative integers up to 50, X denote the numbers which are multiples of 3 and Y denote the odd numbers. Which of the following is/are correct?

1. $P(X) = \frac{8}{25}$
2. $P(Y) = \frac{1}{2}$

Select the correct answer using the code given below.
A. 1 only B. 2 only
C. Both 1 and 2 D. Neither 1 nor 2

104. For two events A and B, let $P(A) = \frac{1}{2}$, $P(A \cup B) = \frac{2}{3}$ and $P(A \cap B) = \frac{1}{6}$. What is $P(\bar{A} \cap B)$ equal to?

A. $\frac{1}{6}$ B. $\frac{1}{4}$
C. $\frac{1}{3}$ D. $\frac{1}{2}$

105. Consider the following statements:
1. Coefficient of variation depends on the unit of measurement of the variable.
2. Range is a measure of dispersion.
3. Mean deviation is least when measured about median.

Which of the above statements are correct?
A. 1 and 2 only B. 2 and 3 only
C. 1 and 3 only D. 1, 2 and 3

106. Given that the arithmetic mean and standard deviation of a sample of 15 observations are 24 and 0 respectively. Then which one of the following is the arithmetic mean of the smallest five observations in the data?
A. 0 B. 8
C. 16 D. 24

107. Which one of the following can be considered as appropriate pair of values of regression coefficient of y on x and regression coefficient of x on y?
A. (1, 1) B. (–1, 1)
C. $\left(-\frac{1}{2}, 2\right)$ D. $\left(\frac{1}{3}, \frac{10}{3}\right)$

108. Let A and B be two events with $P(A) = \frac{1}{3}$, $P(B) = \frac{1}{6}$ and $P(A \cap B) = \frac{1}{12}$. What is $P(B \mid \bar{A})$ equal to?

A. $\frac{1}{5}$ B. $\frac{1}{7}$
C. $\frac{1}{8}$ D. $\frac{1}{10}$

109. In a binomial distribution, the mean is $\frac{2}{3}$ and the variance is $\frac{5}{9}$. What is the probability that X = 2?

A. $\frac{5}{36}$ B. $\frac{25}{36}$
C. $\frac{25}{216}$ D. $\frac{25}{54}$

110. The probability that a ship safely reaches a port is $\frac{1}{3}$. The probability that out of 5 ships, at least 4 ships would arrive safely is

A. $\frac{1}{243}$ B. $\frac{10}{243}$
C. $\frac{11}{243}$ D. $\frac{13}{243}$

111. What is the probability that at least two persons out of a group of three persons were born in the same month (disregard year)?

A. $\frac{33}{144}$ B. $\frac{17}{72}$
C. $\frac{1}{144}$ D. $\frac{2}{9}$

112. It is given that $\overline{X} = 10$, $\overline{Y} = 90$, $\sigma_X = 3$, $\sigma_Y = 12$ and $r_{XY} = 0.8$. The regression equation of X on Y is:

A. Y = 3.2X + 58 B. X = 3.2Y + 58
C. X = –8 + 0.2Y D. Y = –8 + 0.2X

113. If $P(B) = \frac{3}{4}$, $P(A \cap B \cap \overline{C}) = \frac{1}{3}$ and $P(\overline{A} \cap B \cap \overline{C}) = \frac{1}{3}$, then what is $P(B \cap C)$ equal to?

A. $\frac{1}{12}$ B. $\frac{3}{4}$
C. $\frac{1}{15}$ D. $\frac{1}{9}$

114. The following table gives the monthly expenditure of two families:

	Expenditure (in ₹)	
Items	*Family A*	*Family B*
Food	3,500	2,700
Clothing	500	800
Rent	1,500	1,000
Education	2,000	1,800
Miscellaneous	2,500	1,800

In constructing a pie diagram to the above data, the radii of the circles are to be chosen by which one of the following ratios?

A. 1 : 1 B. 10 : 9
C. 100 : 91 D. 5 : 4

115. If a variable takes values 0, 1, 2, 3, ..., *n* with frequencies

1, C(*n*, 1), C(*n*, 2), C(*n*, 3), ..., C(*n*, *n*)

respectively, then the arithmetic mean is:

A. $2n$ B. $n + 1$
C. n D. $\frac{n}{2}$

116. In a multiple-choice test, an examinee either knows the correct answer with probability *p*, or guesses with probability 1 – *p*. The probability of answering a question correctly is $\frac{1}{m}$, if he or she merely guesses. If the examinee answers a question correctly, the probability that he or she really knows the answer is:

A. $\frac{mp}{1+mp}$ B. $\frac{mp}{1+(m-1)p}$
C. $\frac{(m-1)p}{1+(m-1)p}$ D. $\frac{(m-1)p}{1+mp}$

117. If x_1 and x_2 are positive quantities, then the condition for the difference between the arithmetic mean and the geometric mean to be greater than 1 is:

A. $x_1 + x_2 > 2\sqrt{x_1 x_2}$ B. $\sqrt{x_1} + \sqrt{x_2} > \sqrt{2}$
C. $\left|\sqrt{x_1} - \sqrt{x_2}\right| > \sqrt{2}$ D. $x_1 + x_2 < 2\left(\sqrt{x_1 x_2} + 1\right)$

118. Consider the following statements:

1. Variance is unaffected by change of origin and change of scale.
2. Coefficient of variance is independent of the unit of observations.

Which of the statements given above is/are correct?

A. 1 only B. 2 only
C. Both 1 and 2 D. Neither 1 nor 2

119. Five sticks of length 1, 3, 5, 7 and 9 feet are given. Three of these sticks are selected at random. What is the probability that the selected sticks can form a triangle?

A. 0.5 B. 0.4
C. 0.3 D. 0

120. The coefficient of correlation when coefficients of regression are 0.2 and 1.8 is:

A. 0.36 B. 0.2
C. 0.6 D. 0.9

ANSWERS

PAPER-I : GENERAL ABILITY TEST

1	2	3	4	5	6	7	8	9	10
D	C	C	D	B	B	C	A	D	B
11	**12**	**13**	**14**	**15**	**16**	**17**	**18**	**19**	**20**
B	D	A	B	C	D	B	C	D	B
21	**22**	**23**	**24**	**25**	**26**	**27**	**28**	**29**	**30**
A	C	C	B	B	C	C	B	B	B
31	**32**	**33**	**34**	**35**	**36**	**37**	**38**	**39**	**40**
B	C	A	C	C	B	A	A	A	D

41	42	43	44	45	46	47	48	49	50
D	A	B	D	D	A	D	C	A	D
51	**52**	**53**	**54**	**55**	**56**	**57**	**58**	**59**	**60**
C	C	C	C	C	B	B	D	B	B
61	**62**	**63**	**64**	**65**	**66**	**67**	**68**	**69**	**70**
B	C	B	C	A	B	C	B	A	B
71	**72**	**73**	**74**	**75**	**76**	**77**	**78**	**79**	**80**
C	D	B	B	A	B	A	D	B	C
81	**82**	**83**	**84**	**85**	**86**	**87**	**88**	**89**	**90**
D	A	C	C	A	A	D	A	B	A
91	**92**	**93**	**94**	**95**	**96**	**97**	**98**	**99**	**100**
C	C	A	B	C	C	C	D	A	C
101	**102**	**103**	**104**	**105**	**106**	**107**	**108**	**109**	**110**
A	C	D	D	A	B	A	B	B	B
111	**112**	**113**	**114**	**115**	**116**	**117**	**118**	**119**	**120**
D	C	D	A	A	A	A	B	C	D
121	**122**	**123**	**124**	**125**	**126**	**127**	**128**	**129**	**130**
B	A	D	C	A	B	C	D	A	D
131	**132**	**133**	**134**	**135**	**136**	**137**	**138**	**139**	**140**
B	C	B	C	A	D	D	C	C	A
141	**142**	**143**	**144**	**145**	**146**	**147**	**148**	**149**	**150**
B	C	B	B	C	C	D	B	A	B

PAPER-II – MATHEMATICS

1	2	3	4	5	6	7	8	9	10
C	B	A	D	B	C	C	B	D	A
11	**12**	**13**	**14**	**15**	**16**	**17**	**18**	**19**	**20**
A	D	C	C	A	B	C	B	B	B
21	**22**	**23**	**24**	**25**	**26**	**27**	**28**	**29**	**30**
B	C	A	A	A	C	D	D	C	B
31	**32**	**33**	**34**	**35**	**36**	**37**	**38**	**39**	**40**
B	D	A	D	B	C	B	A	A	B
41	**42**	**43**	**44**	**45**	**46**	**47**	**48**	**49**	**50**
D	B	C	B	B	A	C	B	B	D
51	**52**	**53**	**54**	**55**	**56**	**57**	**58**	**59**	**60**
B	A	B	A	A	B	B	C	C	A
61	**62**	**63**	**64**	**65**	**66**	**67**	**68**	**69**	**70**
A	C	A	D	A	A	D	B	A	D
71	**72**	**73**	**74**	**75**	**76**	**77**	**78**	**79**	**80**
B	D	B	B	C	A	C	B	A	C
81	**82**	**83**	**84**	**85**	**86**	**87**	**88**	**89**	**90**
B	A	C	B	B	D	A	A	B	D
91	**92**	**93**	**94**	**95**	**96**	**97**	**98**	**99**	**100**
D	D	B	B	B	B	B	B	C	A
101	**102**	**103**	**104**	**105**	**106**	**107**	**108**	**109**	**110**
B	C	D	A	A	D	A	C	C	C
111	**112**	**113**	**114**	**115**	**116**	**117**	**118**	**119**	**120**
B	C	A	B	D	B	C	B	C	C

EXPLANATORY ANSWERS

PAPER-I : GENERAL ABILITY TEST

51. The Draft Approach to the 12th Five Year Plan (2012-2017) has been approved by the National Development Council last month. The theme of the Approach Paper is "faster, sustainable and more inclusive growth". The Approach Paper in broader sense laid down the major targets of the Twelfth Plan, the key challenges in meeting them and the broad approach to be followed to achieve the stated objectives. It proposes a growth target of 8 per cent. However in view of the uncertainties in the global economy, and challenges in the domestic economy, achieving the growth rate of 9 per cent may not be feasible unless difficult decisions are taken. And this uncertainty was also discussed in the process.

Though the government is yet to finalise growth targets for the 12th Plan period, the Planning Commission was contemplating to raise the economic growth target to 9 per cent during the five year period, up from 8.2 per cent likely in the current Plan.

53. **Industrial Revolution,** in modern history, the process of change from an agrarian and handicraft economy to one dominated by industry and machine manufacturing. This process began in Britain in the 18th century and from there spread to other parts of the world. Although used earlier by French writers, the term *Industrial Revolution* was first popularized by the English economic historian Arnold Toynbee (1852–83) to describe Britain's economic development from 1760 to 1840. Since Toynbee's time the term has been more broadly applied.

54. ***The Indian Struggle, 1920–1942*** is a two-part book by the Indian nationalist leader Netaji Subhash Chandra Bose that covers the 1920–1942 history of the Indian independence movement to end British imperial rule over India. Banned in India by the British colonial government, *The Indian Struggle* was published in the country only in 1948 after India became independent.

The first part of *The Indian Struggle* covering the years 1920–1934 was published in London in 1935 by Lawrence and Wishart. The second part dealing with 1935–1942 was written by Bose during the Second World War.

55. In Maharashtra a effective Swadeshi Campaign in 1896, its main participants were students and it publicity burnt foreign clothes.

56. The East India Association was founded by Dadabhai Naoroji in 1866, in collaboration with Indians and retired British officials in London. It superseded the London Indian Society and was a platform for discussing matters and ideas about India, and to provide representation for Indians to the Government. Naoroji delivered the first lecture to the Association on 2 May 1867. The Association's first President was Lord Lyveden.

57. The **Mariana Trench** or **Marianas Trench** is the deepest part of the world's oceans. It is located in the western Pacific Ocean, an average of 200 kilometres to the east of the Mariana Islands, in the Western Pacific East of Philippines. It is a crescent-shaped scar in the Earth's crust, and measures about 2,550 km (1,580 mi) long and 69 km wide on average.

58. Taklamakan Desert is situated in central Asia. Taklamakan is a desert in southwest Xinjiang Uyghur Autonomous Region, northwest China. It is bounded by the Kunlun Mountains to the south, the Pamir Mountains and Tian Shan to the west and north, and the Gobi Desert to the east.

59. Rudraprayag is one of the Panch Prayag (five confluences) of Alaknanda River, the point of confluence of rivers Alaknanda and Mandakini. Kedarnath, a Hindu holy town is located 86 km from Rudraprayag. The man eating Leopard of Rudraprayag hunted and written about by Jim Corbett dwelled here.

61. A **Western Disturbance** is an extratropical storm originating in the Mediterranean region that brings sudden winter rain to the northwestern parts of the Indian subcontinent. It is a non-monsoonal precipitation pattern driven by the westerlies. The moisture in these storms usually originates over the Mediterranean Sea and the Atlantic Ocean. Extratropical storms are a global phenomena with moisture usually carried in the upper atmosphere, unlike their tropical counterparts where the moisture is carried in the lower atmosphere. In the case of the subcontinent, moisture is sometimes shed as rain when the storm system encounters the Himalayas.

62. Tertiary coal fields share only 1% of coal production of India. Such fields occur in Assam, Arunachal Pradesh, Meghalaya and Nagaland and also in small quantities in Jammu & Kashmir. It is extracted from Darangiri, Cherrapunji, Mewlong and Langrin (Meghalaya); Makum, Jaipur and Nazira in upper Assam, Namchik – Namphuk (Arunachal Pradesh) and Kalakot (Jammu and Kashmir).

Tertiary coal is the lignite coal. Lignite also occurs in the coastal areas of Tamil Nadu, Pondicherry, Gujarat and Jammu and Kashmir. The coal is of inferior quality with around 30 to 50% carbon. India's largest ignite deposits are at Neyveli in Tamil Nadu.

63. **Collagen** is the main structural protein in the extracellular space in the various connective tissues in animal bodies. As the main component of connective tissue, it is the most abundant protein in mammals, making up from 25% to 35% of the whole-body protein content. Collagen consists of amino acids wound together to form triple-helices to form of elongated fibrils. It is mostly found in fibrous tissues such as tendons, ligaments and skin.

64. **Lymphatic filariasis**, also known as **elephantiasis**, is a human disease caused by parasitic worms known as filarial worms.

Wuchereria bancrofti is a human parasitic roundworm that is the major cause of lymphatic filariasis. It is one of the three parasitic worms, together with *Brugia malayi* and *B. timori*, that infect the lymphatic system to cause lymphatic filariasis.

65. **Melanin** is a broad term for a group of natural pigments found in most organisms. Melanin is produced by the oxidation of the amino acid tyrosine, followed by polymerization. The melanin pigments are produced in a specialized group of cells known as melanocytes.

In the human skin, melanogenesis is initiated by exposure to UV radiation, causing the skin to turn tan. Melanin is an effective absorbent of light; the pigment is able to dissipate over 99.9% of absorbed UV radiation.

66. Gout is a rheumatic condition resulting from the deposition of monosodium urate crystals (tophi) in the joints or soft tissues. It is usually associated with elevated serum uric acid levels (greater than 7 mg/dL). The diagnosis is based on uric acid crystals found in the joints, tissues, or body fluids, as well as on gouty attacks or flares characterized by intense pain, swelling, redness, and heat.

Intake of Nucleic acid food components should be minimized by patients having Gouty Arthritis due to elevated serum uric acid level.

68. **Golden rice** is a variety of rice (*Oryza sativa*) produced through genetic engineering to biosynthesize beta-carotene, a precursor of vitamin A, in the edible parts of rice. It is intended to produce a fortified food to be grown and consumed in areas with a shortage of dietary vitamin A.

73. The process by which free electrons are emitted from the metal surface by the application of light is called photoelectric emission.

It is also defined as, the process by which free electrons are released from the metal when it absorbs light energy. Photoelectric emission is also called as photoemission or photoelectron emission or photoelectric effect.

In this method, light or photons is used to remove the free electrons from the solid metal. Hence, the free electrons emitted from the solid metal are called photoelectrons and current produced due to this process is called photoelectric current.

74. The sun's light takes about 8 minutes and 20 seconds to reach the Earth after it has been emitted from the sun's surface. The time it takes for light to reach planets in our Solar System (not the Milky Way, which is our galaxy) varies from about 3 minutes for Mercury, to about 5.3 hours for Pluto. There is nothing out in space to prevent the sun's light from going infinitely far, in principle. In practice, the sun is only 4.5 billion years old, so its light can only extend 4.5 billion light years away from us right now. But there's nothing to stop that light from expanding outwards forever, as time goes on. The sun's radius is about 100 times that of the Earth, meaning that about 1.12 million Earths could fit inside it, as could about 930 Jupiter's.

76. A convex mirror has an outward curve, meaning that the reflecting surface is focussed towards the source of light falling onto it. Such mirrors create a virtual image of the object and this image is lightly diminished as compared to the object's actual size. This is why in some of the cars, the passenger side-mirror is generally inscribed with a warning, which states that "Objects in the mirror are closer than they appear". The convex mirror produces an upright image of any object and offers a wide viewing area as compared to the plane mirror. The usage of this type of mirror can be perceived on the car rear-view mirror, side-view mirror and even the motorcycles. These mirrors in the vehicles help in cutting down the blind spots as long as the object is in their focus.

77. Ultraviolet waves or UV rays are used for detecting fake and forged currency. The paper currency has a strip that is embedded in the note. This strip cannot be forged like that in the original currency.

So, to check for detecting forgery in currency notes, UV rays are used.

An authentic paper currency will fluoresce when it is illuminated by long wave ultraviolet light. The embedded stripe will fluoresce in accordance with the colour chart.

78. **Majority** and minority **carriers**. The more abundant **charge carriers** are called **majority carriers**, which are primarily responsible for current transport in a piece of **semiconductor**. In ***n*-type semiconductors** they are electrons, while in ***p*-type semiconductors** they are holes. The less abundant charge carriers are called **minority carriers**; in n-type semiconductors they are holes, while in p-type semiconductors they are electrons.

82. **Hydrofluoric acid** is a solution of hydrogen fluoride (HF) in water. It is a precursor to almost all fluorine compounds, including pharmaceuticals such as fluoxetine (Prozac), diverse materials such as PTFE (Teflon), and elemental fluorine itself. It is a colourless solution that is highly corrosive, capable of dissolving many materials, especially oxides.

Hydrofluoric acid has a variety of uses in industry and research. It is used as a starting material or intermediate in industrial chemistry, mining, refining, glass finishing, silicon chip manufacturing, and in cleaning.

85. **Avogadro's law** (sometimes referred to as **Avogadro's hypothesis** or **Avogadro's principle**) is an experimental gas law relating volume of a gas to the amount of substance of gas present. A modern statement of Avogadro's law is:

Avogadro's law states that, "equal volumes of all gases, at the same temperature and pressure, have the same number of molecules".

86. The 'Ilbert Bill' was a bill introduced in 1883 under the reign of the Viceroy Lord Ripon (who earned the epithet Ripon-The good) which was written by Sir C.P Ilbert (The law member of the Viceroy's Council). According to the said Act, Indian judges could try a European accused.

Ilbert Bill, in the history of India, a controversial measure proposed in 1883 that sought to allow senior Indian magistrates to preside over cases involving British subjects in India. The bill, severely weakened by compromise, was enacted by the Indian Legislative Council on Jan. 25, 1884. The bitter controversy surrounding the measure deepened antagonism between British and Indians and was a prelude to the formation of the Indian National Congress the following year.

87. The Attorney General (AG) is appointed by the president. He must be a person who is qualified to be appointed a judge of the Supreme Court. In other words, he must be a citizen of India and he must have been a judge of some high court for five years or an advocate of some high court for ten years or an eminent jurist, in the opinion of the president.

In the performance of his official duties, the Attorney General has the right of audience in all courts in the territory of India. Further, he has the right to speak and to take part in the proceedings of both the Houses of Parliament or their joint sitting and any committee of the Parliament of which he may be named a member, but without a right to vote. He enjoys all the privileges and immunities that are available to a member of Parliament.

89. **Awadh** is a region in the modern Indian state of Uttar Pradesh. Its inhabitants are referred to as Awadhis.

It was established as one of the twelve original subahs under 16th-century Mughal emperor Akbar and became a hereditary tributary polity around 1722 AD, with Faizabad as its initial capital and Saadat Ali Khan as its first Subadar Nawab and progenitor of a dynasty of Nawabs of Awadh.

90. Young Bengal Movement was launched by Henry Louis Vivian Derozio (1809-1831), who had come to Calcutta in 1826 and was appointed in the Hindu College as a teacher of English literature and History. Besides this he edited *Hesperus* and *Calcutta Literary Gazette*. He was connected with *India Gazette* as well.

Derozio was one of those rare teachers whose attachment to knowledge, love of truth, and hatred of evil made a profound impression upon those who came in contact with him. Like Socrates, he pursued what was right and was accused of misguiding the youth.

91. The **Quit India Movement** or the **India August Movement**, was a movement launched at the Bombay session of the All-India Congress Committee by Mahatma Gandhi on 8 August 1942, during World War II, demanding an end to British Rule of India.

The British had the support of the Viceroy's Council (which had a majority of Indians), of the All India Muslim League, the princely states, the Indian Imperial Police, the British Indian Army and the Indian Civil Service. Many Indian businessmen profiting from heavy wartime spending did not support Quit India Movement.

93. **Koradi Thermal Power Station** (KTPS) is located at Koradi near Nagpur, Maharashtra. The power plant is one of the four major power plants in Vidarbha – a power surplus region of India. The power station began operations in 1974 and is one of the nine active power stations operated by Maharashtra State Power Generation Company Limited (Mahagenco), a subsidiary of Government of Maharashtra owned Maharashtra State Electricity Board.

94. The 2017 World Heritage Day was observed across the world on 18 April 2017. The theme for the year is Cultural Heritage & Sustainable Tourism. The theme for the 2017 World Heritage Day was chosen in relation to the United Nations International Year of Sustainable Tourism for Development and in the context of the 2030 Agenda for Sustainable Development and the

Sustainable Development Goals. The day is aims at raising awareness of the importance of protecting and preserving various sites around the world that have achieved world heritage status.

97. Government of India (GOI) has approved a new Central Sector Scheme SAMPADA (Scheme for Agro Marine Processing and Development of Agro-Processing Clusters), with an allocation of ₹ 6000 crores for the period 2016-20 coterminous with the 14th Finance Commission cycle. The SAMPADA will be implemented by Ministry of Food Processing Industries (MOFPI).

100. The south-west monsoon occur from June through September. The northern and central Indian subcontinent heat up considerably during the hot summers. This causes a low pressure area over the northern and central Indian subcontinent. To fill this void, the moisture-laden winds from the Indian Ocean (South-west) rush into the subcontinent.

On reaching the southernmost point of the Indian Peninsula, the moisture-laden winds divide into two parts: the Arabian Sea Branch and the Bay of Bengal Branch.

101. Ten of the eighteen biosphere reserves are a part of the World Network of Biosphere Reserves, based on the UNESCO Man and the Biosphere (MAB) Programme list.

Name	*States*	*Year*
Nilgiri Biosphere Reserve	Tamil Nadu, Kerala, Karnataka	2000
Gulf of Mannar Biosphere Reserve	Tamil Nadu	2001
Sundarbans Biosphere Reserve	West Bengal	2001
Nanda Devi Biosphere Reserve	Uttarakhand	2004
Nokrek Biosphere Reserve	Meghalaya	2009
Pachmarhi Biosphere Reserve	Madhya Pradesh	2009
Simlipal Biosphere Reserve	Odisha	2009
Great Nicobar Biosphere Reserve	Great Nicobar	2013
Achanakmar-Amarkantak Biosphere Reserve	Chhattisgarh, Madhya Pradesh	2012
Agasthyamalai Biosphere Reserve	Kerala and Tamil Nadu	2016

In 2009, India designated Cold Desert of Himachal Pradesh as a biosphere reserve. On September 20, 2010, the Ministry of Environment and Forests designated Seshachalam Hills as the 17th biosphere reserve. Panna (Madhya Pradesh) was scheduled to become the 18th on August 25, 2011.

102. The iron minerals that are at present used as ores are **hematite, magnetite, limonite,** and **siderite**; also, occasionally **ankerite, goethite,** and **turgite**. Hematite is the most important iron ore.

The iron content of the pure minerals is as follows:

Mineral	*Formula*	*% of Iron*
Hematite	Fe_2O_3	70.0
Magnetite	Fe_3O_4	72.4
Limonite	$2Fe_2O_3.3H_2O$	59.8
Siderite	$FeCO_3$	48.2

Magnetite is a mineral and one of the main iron ores. With the chemical formula Fe_3O_4, it is one of the oxides of iron. Magnetite is ferrimagnetic; it is attracted to a magnet and can be magnetized to become a permanent magnet itself. It is the most magnetic of all the naturally-occurring minerals on Earth.

Small grains of magnetite occur in almost all igneous and metamorphic rocks. Magnetite is black or brownish-black with a metallic luster, has a Mohs hardness of 5–6 and leaves a black streak.

103. **Vitamin K** is a group of structurally similar, fat-soluble vitamins the human body requires for complete synthesis of certain proteins that are prerequisites for blood coagulation (K via German for *Koagulation*) and which the body also needs for controlling binding of calcium in bones and other tissues.

104. Probiotics are microorganisms that provide health benefits when consumed. Probiotics are live bacteria and yeasts that are beneficial in preventing several health conditions. They are usually consumed as supplements and are also referred to as good bacteria. Probiotics restore the balance of bacteria in the gut when it has become disrupted through long-term antibiotic use or gastrointestinal disease.

107. **High-altitude** cooking is the opposite of pressure cooking in that the **boiling point of water** is **lower** at **higher altitudes** due to the decreased atmospheric pressure. This may require an increase in cooking times or **temperature** and alterations of recipe ingredients.

108. Concave mirrors are commonly used in not only vehicles headlights but also in torches and search-lights to get powerful parallel beams of light to focus the light at the longer distances by placing the source of light at the focus of the Concave mirrors.

112. In physics, the **law of conservation of energy** states that the total energy of an isolated system in a given frame of reference remains constant — it is said to be *conserved* over time. In other words, this law means that energy can neither be created nor destroyed; rather, it can only be transformed from one form to another.

113. Transformers "step up" or **"step down"** voltage according to the ratios of primary to secondary wire turns. A **transformer** designed to increase voltage from primary to secondary is called a **step-up transformer**. A **transformer** designed to reduce voltage from primary to secondary is called a **step-down transformer.**

A **transformer** that **increases voltage** from primary to secondary (more secondary winding turns than primary winding turns) is called a **step-up transformer**. ... As a **step-down** unit, this **transformer** converts **high-voltage**, low-current power into **low-voltage, high-**current power.

A transformer designed to increase voltage from primary to secondary is called a *step-up* transformer. A transformer designed to reduce voltage from primary to secondary is called a *step-down* transformer.

The transformation ratio of a transformer will be equal to the square root of its primary to secondary inductance (L) ratio.

114. Electromagnetic radiation can be described in terms of a stream of mass-less particles, called photons, each travelling in a wave-like pattern at the speed of light. Each photon contains a certain amount of energy. The different types of radiation are defined by the amount of energy found in the photons. Radio waves have photons with low energies, microwave photons have a little more energy than radio waves, infrared photons have still more, then visible, ultraviolet, X-rays, and, the most energetic of all, gamma-rays.

116. Galvanising is a method of rust prevention. The iron or steel object is coated in a thin layer of zinc. This stops oxygen and water reaching the metal underneath - but the zinc also **acts** as a **sacrificial** metal. Zinc is more **reactive** than iron, so it oxidises in preference to the iron object.

117. According to NASA, the gases in Earth's atmosphere include:

- Nitrogen — 78 per cent
- Oxygen — 21 per cent
- Argon — 0.93 per cent
- Carbon dioxide — 0.04 per cent
- Trace amounts of neon, helium, methane, krypton and hydrogen, as well as water vapour.

118. Graying of hair naturally is a chemical change. Hair colour is produced by cells known as melanocytes, which migrate into the hair bulb as the hair follicles develop in utero. The melanocytes produce pigment that is incorporated into the growing hair fibres to produce hair in a bewildering array of natural shades.

Hair colour depends on the presence and ratios of two groups of melanins: eumelanins (brown and black pigments) and pheomelanins (red and yellow pigments). While variations in the ratio of these pigments can produce an large number of colours and tones, siblings often have strikingly similar hair colour.

119. Sodium carbonate is a chemical name for soda ash and washing soda.

Sodium carbonate is a household chemical with a variety of different uses. Its chemical formula, Na_2CO_3, is similar to that of baking soda, $NaHCO_3$. But baking soda is a nontoxic chemical commonly used in food preparation, while sodium carbonate is toxic and should not be consumed. Instead, it's a common cleaning product sometimes used in laundry detergent and pool cleaners.

The principal applications of sodium carbonate are in the manufacture of glass and the production of chemicals. It is also used in processing wood pulp to make paper, in making soaps and detergents, in refining aluminium, in water softening, and in many other applications. It can help remove alcohol and grease stains from clothing, as well as calcifications in everything from coffee pots and espresso makers to boilers and hot water heaters.

120. Potassium permanganate is an inorganic chemical compound and medication. As a medication it is used for cleaning wounds and dermatitis.

It has the chemical formula $KMnO_4$. It is a strong oxidizing agent. It dissolves in water to give intensely pink or purple solutions, the evaporation of which leaves prismatic purplish-black glistening crystals.

Potassium permanganate is an oxidant, but a poor disinfectant. It's often used in well water to control odour and taste, remove manganese, iron and colour from the water, and to control biological growth that is considered a "nuisance," such as the Asiatic clam, according to the Environmental Protection Agency. The substance is most often used as a pre-treatment before water is filtered, and is better at removing sulphide odours from water than chlorine.

121.

Movement	–	**Year**
Champaran Satyagraha	–	1917
Moplah Rebellion	–	1921
Bardoli Satyagraha	–	1928
Salt Satyagraha	–	1930

122. Ibn Battuta was a Berber Muslim scholar and traveller, who was born in Tangier, Morocco. He is considered one of the greatest travellers of all time, and is well known for the account of his travels and excursions. The full title of the book of his journeys is *Tuhfat al-anzar fi gharaaib al-amsar wa ajaaib al-asfar* (A gift to those who contemplate the wonders of cities and the marvels of travelling), but it is commonly referred to as *Ibn Battuta's Rihla*.

The ***Rihla*** travel practice originated in Middle Ages Morocco and served to connect Muslims of Morocco to the collective consciousness of the *ummah* across the Islamic world, thereby generating a larger sense of community.

123. The **Chishti** Order is primarily followed in Afghanistan and Indian subcontinent. It was the first of the four main Sufi orders (Chishti, Qadiriyya, Suhrawardiyya and Naqshbandi) to be established in this region. Moinuddin Chishti introduced the Chishti Order in Lahore (Punjab) and Ajmer (Rajasthan), sometime in the middle of the 12th century CE. Baba Farid, Nizamuddin Auliya, Bakhtiyar Kaki, also was a important Chisti sufi.

The founder of **suhrawardi silsila** was shekh sihabuddin umar suhrawardi. **Bahauddin Zakariya**, and also known as **Baha-ul-Haq** and **Hazrat Bahauddin Zakariya Multani**, was a Sufi of Suhrawardiyyaorder (tariqa).

125. A **rainbow** is a meteorological phenomenon that is caused by reflection, refraction and dispersion of light in water droplets resulting in a spectrum of light appearing in the sky. It takes the form of a multicoloured circular arc. Rainbows caused by sunlight always appear in the section of sky directly opposite the sun.

126. **Ultrasound** is sound waves with frequencies higher than the upper audible limit of human hearing. Ultrasound is no different from 'normal' (audible) sound in its physical properties, except in that humans cannot hear it. This limit varies from person to person and is approximately 20 kilohertz (20,000 hertz) in healthy, young adults. Ultrasound devices operate with frequencies from 20 kHz up to several gigahertz.

Ultrasound is used in many different fields. Ultrasonic devices are used to detect objects and measure distances. Ultrasound imaging or sonography is often used in medicine. In the nondestructive testing of products and structures, ultrasound is used to detect invisible flaws. Industrially, ultrasound is used for cleaning, mixing, and to accelerate chemical processes. Animals such as bats and porpoises use ultrasound for locating prey and obstacles.

127. Thermodynamics is the study of heat and energy. At its heart are laws that describe how energy moves around within a system, whether an atom, a hurricane or a black hole. The first law describes how energy cannot be created or destroyed, merely transformed from one kind to another. The second law, however, is probably better known and even more profound because it describes the limits of what the universe can do.

This law is about inefficiency, degeneration and decay. It tells us all we do is inherently wasteful and that there are irreversible processes in the universe.

The second law can be expressed in several ways, the simplest being that heat will naturally flow from a hotter to a colder body.

131. India was ranked 40th among the 136 economies across the world in 2017 Travel and Tourism Competitiveness Index (TTCI) released by the World Economic Forum (WEF).

In this edition of index, India has jumped 12 places from earlier 52nd position in 2015. But it lagged behind its other Asian peers like Japan (4th) and China (13th).

Top 10 Countries in 2017 TTCI: Spain (1st), France (2nd), Germany (3rd), Japan (4th), the United Kingdom (5th), the United States (6th), Australia (7th), Italy (8th), Canada (9th) and Switzerland (10th).

132. World Health Day, celebrated on 7 April every year to mark the anniversary of the founding of the World Health Organization, provides us with a unique opportunity to mobilize action around a specific health topic of concern to people all over the world. The theme of our 2017 World Health Day campaign is depression.

Depression affects people of all ages, from all walks of life, in all countries. It causes mental anguish and impacts on people's ability to carry out even the simplest everyday tasks, with sometimes devastating consequences for relationships with family and friends and the ability to earn a living. At worst, depression can lead to suicide, now the second leading cause of death among 15-29-year olds.

134. Nagara temples are found in the northern part of India. Nagara temples have two distinct features:

- In plan, the temple is a square with a number of graduated projections in the middle of each side giving a cruciform shape with a number of re-entrant angles on each side.
- In elevation, a Shikhara, *i.e.*, tower gradually inclines inwards in a convex curve, using a concentric rotating-squares and circles principle.

Temples built between the 7th and the 14th centuries CE in the nagara style had mandapas (pavilions). The projections in the plan are also carried upwards to the top of the Shikhara and, thus, there is strong emphasis on vertical lines in elevation.

The Nagara style is widely distributed over a greater part of India, exhibiting distinct varieties and ramifications in lines of evolution and elaboration according to each locality. An example of Nagara architecture is the Kandariya Mahadeva Temple at khajuraho.

135. The list of major rock edicts:

Rock Edict I: Prohibits animal slaughter. Bans festive gatherings and killings of animals. Only two peacocks and one deer were killed in Asoka's kitchen. He wished to discontinue this practice of killing two peacocks and one deer as well.

Major Rock Edict II: Provides for care for man and animals, describes about Chola, Pandyas, Satyapura and Keralputra Kingdoms of South India.

Major Rock Edict III: Issued after 12 years of Asoka's coronation. It says that the Yuktas (subordinate officers and Pradesikas (district Heads) along with Rajukas (Rural officers) shall go to the all areas of kingdom every five years and spread the Dhamma Policy of Asoka.

Major Rock Edict IV: Dhammaghosa is ideal to the mankind and not the Bherighosa. Impact of Dhamma on society.

Major Rock Edict V: Concerns about the policy towards slaves. He mentions in this rock edict "Every Human is my child". Appointment of Dhammamahamatras is mentioned in this edict.

Major Rock Edict VI: Describes King's desire to get informed about the conditions of the people constantly. Talks about welfare measures.

Major Rock Edict VII: Requests tolerance for all religions - "To foster one's own sect, depreciating the others out of affection for one's own, to exalt its merit, is to do the worst harm to one's own sect."

The Kandahar Greek Edict of Asoka is a portion of a Major Rock Edict in Greek recovered in Kandahar, Afghanistan, in 1963.

Major Rock Edict VIII: Describes Asoka's first Dhamma Yatra to Bodhgaya & Bodhi Tree.

Major Rock Edict IX: Condemns popular ceremonies. Stress in ceremonies of Dhamma.

Major Rock Edict X: Condemns the desire for fame and glory. Stresses on popularity of Dhamma.

Major Rock Edict XI: Elaborates Dhamma Major.

Rock Edict XII: Directed and determined request for tolerance among different religious sects. Also written in Greek in the Kandahar Greek Edict of Asoka (last portion).

Major Rock Edict XIII: It is the largest inscription from the edict. King considered the victory by "Dhamma" to be the foremost victory; mention the Dhamma victory on the Greek being named Antiochus; it also mentions the Dhamma victory over the following foreign brings- Ptolemy II Philadelphus- King of Egypt (285-247 BC) Alexander – King of Epirus (273-255 BC) Antigonous Gonatus- King of Macedonia (276-239 BC) Magas - King of Cyrene. It also mentions the Dhamma victory in south over the Cholas and Pandyas as far as Ceylon. Also written in Greek in the Kandahar Greek Edict of Asoka (first portion).

Major Rock Edict XIV: Describes engraving of inscriptions in different parts of country.

136. The United Kingdom **Cabinet Mission** of 1946 to India aimed to discuss the transfer of power from the British government to the Indian leadership, with the aim of preserving India's unity and granting it independence.

- The cabinet mission plan of 1946 proposed that there *shall be a Union of India which was to be empowered to deal with the defense, foreign affairs and communications.*
- The cabinet mission **recommended an undivided India** and turned down the Muslim league's demand for a separate Pakistan. The Cabinet **mission restricted the Communal representation.**
- It provided that all the members of the Interim cabinet would be Indians and there would be minimum interference by the Viceroy.
- It also provided for formation of the constituent assembly on democratic principle of population.
- It recognized Indian Right to cede from the Commonwealth.

138. Acid rain is a rain or any other form of precipitation that is unusually acidic, meaning that it has elevated levels of hydrogen ions (low pH). It can have harmful effects on plants, aquatic animals and infrastructure. Acid rain is caused by emissions of sulphur dioxide and nitrogen oxide, which react with the water molecules in the atmosphere to produce acids.

142.

State	–	**% of forested area**
Kerala	–	49.50
Odisha	–	32.34
Krnataka	–	18.99
Andhra Pradesh	–	15.27

143. The total length of coastline along each of the coastal State/UT in the country is as follows:

State/UT	Length of coastline (in km)
(*i*) Gujarat	1214.7
(*ii*) Maharashtra	652.6
(*iii*) Goa, Daman and Diu	160.5
(*iv*) Karnataka	280.0
(*v*) Kerala	569.7
(*vi*) Tamil Nadu	906.9
(*vii*) Pudducherry	30.6
(*viii*) Andhra Pradesh	973.7
(*ix*) Odisha	476.4
(*x*) West Bengal	157.5
(*xi*) Lakshadweep Islands	132.0
(*xii*) Andaman & Nicobar Islands	1962.0
Total Coastline	**7516.6**

145. Igneous rock or **magmatic rock**, is one of the three main rock types, the others being sedimentary and metamorphic. Igneous rock is formed through the cooling and solidification of magma or lava. The magma can be derived from partial melts of existing rocks in either a planet's mantle or crust. Typically, the melting is caused by one or more of three processes: an increase in temperature, a decrease in pressure, or a change in composition. Solidification into rock occurs either below the surface as intrusive rocks or on the surface as extrusive rocks. Igneous rock may form with crystallization to form granular, crystalline rocks, or without crystallization to form natural glasses. Granite, Gabbro, Basalt, Obsidian etc. is a example of Igneous rock.

Dolomite is a example of Sedimentary rock.

146. The **Coriolis force** is an inertial force that acts on objects that are in motion relative to a rotating reference frame. In a reference frame with clockwise rotation, the force acts to the left of the motion of the object. In one with anticlockwise rotation, the force acts to the right. Deflection of an object due to the Coriolis force is called the **Coriolis effect**.

148. The **Godavari** is India's second longest river after the Ganga. It has its source in Triambakeshwar, Maharashtra. In terms of length, catchment area and discharge, the Godavari river is the largest in peninsular India, and had been dubbed as the **Dakshina Ganga** – the South Ganges river. Pravada, Purna, Pranhita, Manpra, Wardha, Penganga, Indravati are its main tributaries.

Ganga is a trans-boundary river of Asia which flows through the nations of India and Bangladesh. The 2,525 km (1,569 mi) river rises in the eastern Himalayas in the Indian state of Uttarakhand, and flows south and east through the Gangetic Plain of North India into Bangladesh, where it empties into the Bay of Bengal. It is the third largest river in the world by discharge.

Its main tributaries are Yamuna, Gomati, Ghaghra, Ramganga, Gandak, Koshi and Mahanadi.

PAPER-II : MATHEMATICS

1. $x + \log_{10}(1 + 2^x) = x \log_{10} 5 + \log_{10} 6$

$\Rightarrow \quad x(1 - \log_{10}5) = \log_{10} 6 - \log_{10}(1 + 2^x)$

$\Rightarrow x(\log_{10}10 - \log_{10}5) = \log_{10}\left(\dfrac{6}{1+2^x}\right)$

$\Rightarrow \quad x \log_{10}2 = \log_{10}\left(\dfrac{6}{1+2^x}\right) \Rightarrow x = 1.$

2. $(101110)_2 = (46)_{10}$ and $(110)_2 = (6)_{10}$

Quotient $= (7)_{10} = (111)_2$

Remainder $= (4)_{10} = (100)_2$.

3. For AB and BA to be exist

$x + 5 = y$ and $11 - y = x$

Solving these, $x = 8$ and $y = 3$.

4. $S_n = nP + \dfrac{n(n-1)Q}{2}$

$\therefore$ Common difference $(d) = 2 \times \dfrac{Q}{2} = Q.$

5. Sum of coefficients

$= q - r + r - p + p - q = 0$

$\Rightarrow$ 1 is a root

Another root $= \dfrac{p-q}{q-r}$.

6. $E - (E - (E - (E - (E - A))))$

$= E - (E - (E - (E - A')))$

$= E - (E - (E - A))$

$= E - (E - A')$

$= E - A = A'$

$= (B \cup C)'$

$= B' \cap C'.$

7. Here, $C \subset A$ and $C \subset B$

$C = A \cap B$

$= A \cap (B \cap C)$

$= A \cap C = C.$

8. α, β are roots of $x^2 + x + 1 = 0$

$\Rightarrow \quad \alpha = \omega, \beta = \omega^2$

$$\begin{bmatrix} 1 & \beta \\ \alpha & \alpha \end{bmatrix}\begin{bmatrix} \alpha & \beta \\ 1 & \beta \end{bmatrix} = \begin{bmatrix} \alpha+\beta & \beta+\beta^2 \\ \alpha^2+\alpha & \alpha\beta+\alpha\beta \end{bmatrix}$$

$$= \begin{bmatrix} \omega+\omega^2 & \omega^2+\omega \\ \omega^2+\omega & 2\omega^2 \end{bmatrix} = \begin{bmatrix} -1 & -1 \\ -1 & 2 \end{bmatrix}.$$

9. All are true.

10. 'T' is repeated twice.

So Number of permutaions $= \dfrac{(11)!}{2!} = 19958400.$

11. $k = \dfrac{1}{2i} = \dfrac{-i}{2}$

$$kA = \begin{bmatrix} (4i-6)\left(\frac{-i}{2}\right) & 10i\left(\frac{-i}{2}\right) \\ 14i\left(\frac{-i}{2}\right) & (6+4i)\left(\frac{-i}{2}\right) \end{bmatrix}$$

$$= \begin{bmatrix} 2+3i & 5 \\ 7 & 2-3i \end{bmatrix}.$$

12. $|x-3|^2 + |x-3| - 2 = 0$

Let $\quad |x-3| = y$

$\Rightarrow \quad y^2 + y - 2 = 0$

$\Rightarrow \quad y = \dfrac{-1 \pm \sqrt{1+8}}{2} = \dfrac{-1 \pm 3}{2}$

$\Rightarrow \quad y = 1$ or -2

(–2 Rejected as y is +ve)

$\Rightarrow \quad y = 1$

$\Rightarrow \quad |x-3| = 1$

$\Rightarrow \quad x - 3 = 1$ or $x - 3 = -1$

$\Rightarrow \quad x = 4$ or 2

$\therefore \quad$ Sum of roots = 6.

13. $\quad x^2 - 4x - \log_3^P = 0$

$$D = 16 + 4\log_3^P \geq 0$$

$\Rightarrow \quad \log_3^P \geq \dfrac{-16}{4} \geq -4$

$\Rightarrow \quad P \geq 3^{-4} \geq \dfrac{1}{81}$

$\therefore \quad$ Minimum value $= \dfrac{1}{81}$.

14. $\quad \text{Adj } A^T = (\text{adj } A)^T$

$\Rightarrow \quad \text{Adj } A^T - (\text{adj } A)^T = 0.$

15. $6^{\frac{1}{2}} \times 6^{\frac{1}{4}} \times 6^{\frac{1}{8}} \times 6^{\frac{1}{16}} .....\infty$

$$6^{\frac{1}{2}+\frac{1}{4}+\frac{1}{8}+\frac{1}{16}+....\infty} = 6^{\frac{1/2}{1-1/2}} = 6^1 = 6.$$

16. $\begin{vmatrix} \cos^2 \frac{\theta}{2} & \sin^2 \frac{\theta}{2} \\ \sin^2 \frac{\theta}{2} & \cos^2 \frac{\theta}{2} \end{vmatrix} = \left(\cos^4 \frac{\theta}{2} - \sin^4 \frac{\theta}{2}\right)$

$$= \left(\cos^2 \frac{\theta}{2} + \sin^2 \frac{\theta}{2}\right)\left(\cos^2 \frac{\theta}{2} - \sin^2 \frac{\theta}{2}\right) = \cos \theta.$$

17. $(x + a)^{100} + (x - a)^{100}$

Numbers of terms = 101 – 50 = 51.

18. In $(1 + x)^{50}$

$$C_1 + C_3 + C_5 + ... = \frac{1}{2} \times 2^{50} = 2^{49}$$

$\because \quad C_0 + C_1 + C_2 + ... C_n = 2^n.$

19. $A = \begin{bmatrix} 1 & 0 & 0 \\ 0 & b & 0 \\ 0 & 0 & c \end{bmatrix} a = \text{diag } [a, b, c]$

$$A^{-1} = \text{diag}^{-1} [a, b, c] = \frac{1}{|A|} \text{ diag } [a^{-1}, b^{-1}, c^{-1}]$$

$$= \frac{1}{abc}\begin{bmatrix} a^{-1} & 0 & 0 \\ 0 & b^{-1} & 0 \\ 0 & 0 & c^{-1} \end{bmatrix}.$$

20. Let us assume that total minutes $= x$

For first nine minutes $= 150 \times 9$

Let the remaining minutes $= y = x - 9$

Now $(150 \times 9) + \dfrac{y}{2}[2 \times 150 + (y - 1)(-2)] = 4500$

$$\frac{y}{2}(302 - 2y) = 3150$$

$\Rightarrow \quad y^2 - 151y + 3150 = 0$

$\Rightarrow \quad (y - 126)(y - 25) = 0$

$\Rightarrow \quad y = 25$ or 126 (Rejected)

So, $\quad x = y + 9 = 25 + 9 = 34$ minutes.

21. $\left(\dfrac{1+i}{1-i}\right)^n = i^n = 1 \Rightarrow n = 4.$

22. $(a, b) R (c, d) \Leftrightarrow a + b = b + c$

$a + a = a + a$

$\Rightarrow \quad (a, a) R (a, a) \Rightarrow$ R is reflexive

Next, Let $(a, b) R (c, d) \Rightarrow a + b = b + c$

$\Rightarrow \quad c + b = d + a \Rightarrow (c, d) R (a, b)$

$\Rightarrow$ R is symmetric.

Next, Let $(a, b) R (c, d)$ and $(c, d) R (e, f)$

$\Rightarrow \quad a + b = b + c$ and $c + f = d + e$

$\Rightarrow \quad a + d + c + f = b + c + d + e$

$\Rightarrow \quad a + f = b + e \Rightarrow (a, b) R (e, f)$

$\Rightarrow$ R is transitive $\Rightarrow$ R is an equivalence relation.

23. $y = \frac{x}{1-x} \Rightarrow x = \frac{y}{1+y}$.

24. $3x^2 + 2x + 1 = 0$

$\Rightarrow \quad \alpha + \beta = -\frac{2}{3},\ \alpha\beta = \frac{1}{3}$

$S = \alpha + \beta + \frac{1}{\alpha} + \frac{1}{\beta} = -\frac{2}{3} - 2 = \frac{-8}{3}$

$P = (\alpha + \beta^{-1})(\beta + \alpha^{-1})$

$= \alpha\beta + 2 + \frac{1}{\alpha\beta} = \frac{16}{3}$

Required equation is $x^2 - Sx + P = 0$

$x^2 + \frac{8}{3}x + \frac{16}{3} = 0$

$\Rightarrow \quad 3x^2 + 8x + 16 = 0.$

25. $\log_e 3 + \frac{1}{2}\log_e 3 + \frac{1}{4}\log_e 3 + \ldots$

$= (\log_e 3)\left[1 + \frac{1}{2} + \frac{1}{4} + \ldots\infty\right] = (\log_e 3)\frac{1}{1-1/2}$

$= 2\log_e 3 = \log_e 9.$

26. $\frac{8!}{4!}\frac{8}{6!}10! = 8! \times 8! \times \frac{10 \times 9 \times 8 \times 7}{4!} = 210 \times (8!)^2.$

27. $\begin{vmatrix} k & 1 & 1 \\ 1 & k & 1 \\ 1 & 1 & k \end{vmatrix} = 0$

$\Rightarrow \quad k(k^2 - 1) - (k - 1) + (1 - k) = 0$

$\Rightarrow \quad k(k + 1) - 1 - 1 = 0$

$\Rightarrow \quad k^2 + k - 2 = 0 \Rightarrow k = 1, -2$

For $k = 1$, first two equations will become same.

$\Rightarrow \quad k = -2.$

28. $S_n = \frac{ab}{1-r} + \frac{dbr(1-r^{n-1})}{(1-r)^2}$

$1.3 + 2.3^2 + \ldots.n.3^n$

$= \frac{\{(2n-1)3^{n+1} + 3\}}{4}$

$\frac{(2n-1)3^a + b}{4} = \frac{(2n-1)3^{n+1} + 3}{4}$

$a = n + 1,\ b = 3.$

29. $\frac{P}{2} + \frac{Q}{2} = 45°$

$\tan\left(\frac{P}{2} + \frac{Q}{2}\right) = \frac{\tan\frac{P}{2} + \tan\frac{Q}{2}}{1 - \tan\frac{P}{2}\tan\frac{Q}{2}} = 1$

$\frac{-b}{a} = 1 - \frac{c}{a} = \frac{a-c}{a} \Rightarrow a + b = c.$

30. $\left|z - \frac{4}{z}\right| \geq |z| - \left|\frac{4}{z}\right|$

$\Rightarrow \quad 2 \geq |z| - \frac{4}{|z|}$

$\Rightarrow \quad |z|^2 - 2|z| - 4 \leq 0$

$\Rightarrow \quad |z| = \frac{2 + 2\sqrt{5}}{2}$

$= 1 + \sqrt{5}$

(neglecting –ve value)

31. $\tan 15° = 2 - \sqrt{3} = \frac{x}{x + 50}$

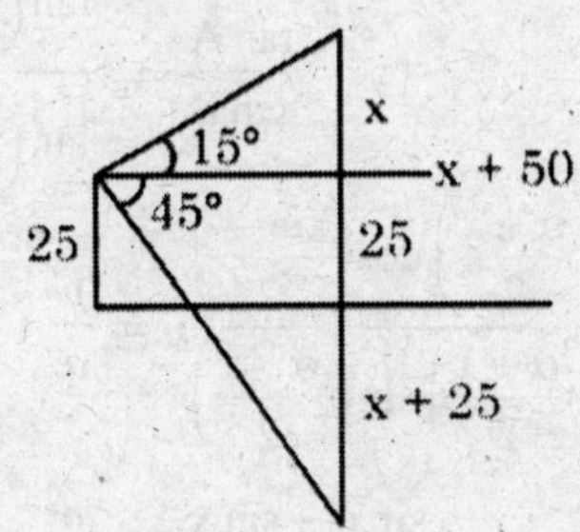

$\Rightarrow \quad (2 - \sqrt{3} - 1)x = -50(2 - \sqrt{3})$

$\Rightarrow \quad x = \frac{-50(2 - \sqrt{3})}{(1 - \sqrt{3})}$

$\Rightarrow \quad x + 25 = \frac{-50(2 - \sqrt{3}) + 25(1 - \sqrt{3})}{1 - \sqrt{3}}$

$= \frac{-100 + 50\sqrt{3} + 25 - 25\sqrt{3}}{1 - \sqrt{3}}$

$= \frac{-75 + 25\sqrt{3}}{1 - \sqrt{3}} = \frac{25(3 - \sqrt{3})}{(\sqrt{3} - 1)}$

$= 25\sqrt{3}.$

32. $\tan 9° - \tan 27° - \tan 63° + \tan 81°$

$= (\tan 9° + \cot 9°) - (\tan 27° + \cot 27°)$

$= \frac{\cos(9° - 9°)}{\sin 9° \cos 9°} - \frac{\cos(27° - 27°)}{\sin 27°.\cos 27°}$

$= \frac{2}{\sin 18°} - \frac{2}{\sin 54°}$

$= \frac{2(\sin 54° - \sin 18°)}{\sin 18°.\sin 54°}$

$= \frac{2.2\cos 36°.\sin 18°}{\sin 18°.\sin 54°} = 4.$

33. $\sqrt{3}\,\text{cosec}\,20° - \sec 20°$

$$= \frac{\sqrt{3}}{\sin 20°} - \frac{1}{\cos 20°} = 2\left(\frac{\sqrt{3}\cos 20° - \sin 20°}{2\sin 20°.\cos 20°}\right)$$

$$= 2\times 2\left(\frac{\sin 60°.\cos 20° - \cos 60°.\sin 20°}{\sin 40°}\right)$$

$$= 2\times 2\frac{\sin(60° - 20°)}{\sin 40°} = 4.$$

34. $\alpha = A + B$ and $x = A - B$

$$\Rightarrow A = \frac{x+\alpha}{2},\ B = \frac{\alpha - x}{2}$$

$$\frac{\tan A}{\tan B} = \frac{\tan\left(\frac{x+\alpha}{2}\right)}{\tan\left(\frac{\alpha - x}{2}\right)} = \frac{p}{q}$$

$$\Rightarrow \frac{2\sin\left(\frac{\alpha+x}{2}\right)\cos\left(\frac{\alpha-x}{2}\right)}{2\cos\left(\frac{\alpha+x}{2}\right)\sin\left(\frac{\alpha-x}{2}\right)} = \frac{p}{q}$$

$$\Rightarrow \frac{\sin\alpha + \sin x}{\sin\alpha - \sin x} = \frac{p}{q}$$

$$\Rightarrow \frac{\sin\alpha + \sin x + \sin\alpha - \sin x}{\sin\alpha + \sin x - \sin\alpha + \sin x} = \frac{p+q}{p-q}$$

$$\Rightarrow \frac{2\sin\alpha}{2\sin x} = \frac{p+q}{p-q}$$

$$\Rightarrow \sin x = \frac{(p-q)\sin\alpha}{p+q}.$$

35. $\sin^{-1}\frac{3}{5} + \tan^{-1}\frac{1}{7} = \tan^{-1}\frac{3}{4} + \tan^{-1}\frac{1}{7}$

$$= \tan^{-1}\frac{\frac{3}{4}+\frac{1}{7}}{1-\frac{3}{4}.\frac{1}{7}} = \tan^{-1}\frac{21+4}{28-3}$$

$$= \tan^{-1}\frac{25}{25} = \tan^{-1}1 = \frac{\pi}{4}.$$

36. Let the distance between pole & tower is 'b'.

Now, $\frac{h_T}{b} = \tan 45° = 1 \Rightarrow h_T = b$

$$\frac{h_T - h_P}{b} = \tan 45° = \frac{1}{\sqrt{3}}$$

$$\Rightarrow \frac{h_T - h_P}{h_T} = \frac{1}{\sqrt{3}}$$

$$\Rightarrow \frac{h_T - h_P}{h_T - (h_T - h_P)} = \frac{1}{\sqrt{3}-1}$$

$$\Rightarrow \frac{h_T - h_P}{h_P} = \frac{\sqrt{3}+1}{2}$$

$\Rightarrow$ Statement '2' is correct.

$$\frac{h_T - h_P + 2h_P}{h_P} = \frac{\sqrt{3}+1+4}{2}$$

$$\Rightarrow \frac{h_T + h_P}{h_P} = \frac{5+\sqrt{3}}{2}$$

$\Rightarrow$ Statement '3' is incorrect.

$\therefore$ Option 'C' is right choice.

37. $a + c = 2b$

$$= \cot\frac{A}{2}.\cot\frac{C}{2}$$

$$= \sqrt{\frac{s(s-a)}{(s-b)(s-c)} \times \frac{s(s-c)}{(s-a)(s-b)}}$$

$$= \frac{s}{s-b} = \frac{2s}{2s-2b} = \frac{a+b+c}{a+b+c-2b} = \frac{3b}{b} = 3.$$

38. $\sqrt{1+\sin A} = \left|\sin\frac{A}{2} + \cos\frac{A}{2}\right|$

$$= \begin{cases} \sin\frac{A}{2} + \cos\frac{A}{2}, & 2n\pi - \frac{\pi}{4} \le 2n\pi + \frac{3\pi}{4} \\ -\left(\sin\frac{A}{2} + \cos\frac{A}{2}\right), & \text{otherwise} \end{cases}$$

So, $\sqrt{1+\sin A} = -\left(\sin\frac{A}{2} + \cos\frac{A}{2}\right)$

When $\frac{3\pi}{4} < \frac{A}{2} < \frac{5\pi}{4}$

$$\Rightarrow \frac{3\pi}{2} < A < \frac{5\pi}{2}$$

39. $\sin^2 A + \sin^2 B + \sin^2 C$

$= 2\cos^2 A + 2\cos^2 B + 2\cos^2 C$

$\Rightarrow \cos^2 A + \cos^2 B + \cos^2 C = 1$

$\Rightarrow \frac{3}{2} + \frac{1}{2}(\cos 2A + \cos 2B + \cos 2C) = 1$

$\Rightarrow \cos 2A + \cos 2B + \cos 2C = -1$

$\Rightarrow 2\cos(A + B)\cos(A - B) = -(1 + \cos 2C)$

$\Rightarrow -2\cos C\cos(A - B) = -2\cos^2 C$

$\Rightarrow \cos(A - B) = \cos C$

$\Rightarrow A - B = C$

Again, $A + B + C = \pi$

$\Rightarrow A + B + A - B = \pi$

$\Rightarrow A = \frac{\pi}{2}$

$\Rightarrow \Delta$ is right angled.

40. Range of $\sin^{-1} x$ is $\left[-\frac{\pi}{2}, \frac{\pi}{2}\right]$

$\Rightarrow \sin^{-1} x \in \left[-\frac{\pi}{2}, \frac{\pi}{2}\right]$.

41. All given points lie on the line of equation $ay = bx$

$\Rightarrow$ All points are collinear.

42. $x + 2y - 2z = 9$

$$\Rightarrow \quad \text{Length of normal} = \frac{9}{\sqrt{1^2 + 2^2 + (-2)^2}} = 3.$$

43. $\cos^2 \alpha + \cos^2 \beta + \cos^2 \gamma = 1$

$$\Rightarrow \quad \cos^2 \alpha + \cos^2 \beta = 1 - \cos^2 \gamma = \sin^2 \gamma$$

$\Rightarrow$ Statement 1 is correct

$$\cos^2 \alpha + \cos^2 \beta + \cos^2 \gamma = 1$$

$$\Rightarrow 1 - \sin^2 \alpha + 1 - \sin^2 \beta + 1 - \sin^2 \gamma = 1$$

$$\Rightarrow \quad \sin^2 \alpha + \sin^2 \beta + \sin^2 \gamma = 2$$

$\Rightarrow$ Statement 3 is correct.

44. $\angle$ between $x + y - 3 = 0$ and $x - y + 3 = 0$ is $90°$

$\Rightarrow \alpha = 90°$

As, β is acute, therefore $\alpha > \beta$.

45. Let $\quad \vec{\delta} = a\hat{i} + b\hat{j} + c\hat{k}$

$$\vec{\alpha}.\vec{\delta} = 0 \Rightarrow a + 2b - c = 0 \quad ...(i)$$

$$\Rightarrow \quad \vec{\beta}.\vec{\delta} = 0$$

$$\Rightarrow \quad 2a - b + 3c = 0 \quad ...(ii)$$

From (i) and (ii) $\quad \dfrac{a}{5} = \dfrac{b}{-5} = \dfrac{c}{-5}$

$$\Rightarrow \quad \frac{a}{1} = \frac{b}{-1} = \frac{c}{-1} = \lambda \text{ (say)}$$

$$\Rightarrow \quad a = \lambda,\ b = -\lambda,\ c = -\lambda$$

Again, $\quad \vec{\delta}.\vec{\lambda} = 10$

$$\Rightarrow \quad 2a + b + 6c = 2\lambda - \lambda - 6\lambda = -5\lambda = 10$$

$$\Rightarrow \quad \lambda = -2$$

$$\therefore \quad \vec{\delta} = -2\hat{i} + 2\hat{j} + 2\hat{k}$$

$$\Rightarrow \quad |\vec{\delta}| = \sqrt{12} = 2\sqrt{3}.$$

46.
$$(\hat{a}+\hat{b})\times(\hat{a}\times\hat{b}) = \hat{a}\times(\hat{a}\times\hat{b}) + \hat{b}\times(\hat{a}\times\hat{b})$$
$$= (\hat{a}.\hat{b})\hat{a} - (\hat{a}.\hat{a})\hat{b} + (\hat{b}.\hat{b})\hat{a} - (\hat{b}.\hat{a})\hat{b}$$
$$= k\hat{a} - \hat{b} + \hat{a} - k\hat{b} = (k+1)(\hat{a} - \hat{b}).$$

47. $\quad \overline{AB} = 2\hat{c} - 3\hat{j} + 8\hat{k}$

Work done $= \vec{F}.\overline{AB} = 1 \times 2 + 3(-3) + 2(8)$

$= 2 - 9 + 16 = 9$ units.

48. Let, $\quad \vec{a} = x\hat{i} + y\hat{j} + 3\hat{k}$

$$|\vec{a}\times\hat{i}|^2 = z^2 + y^2$$

$$|\vec{a}\times\hat{j}|^2 = x^2 + z^2$$

$$|\vec{a}\times\hat{k}|^2 = x^2 + y^2$$

$$\therefore \ 2(x^2 + y^2 + z^2) = 2|\vec{a}|^2.$$

49.

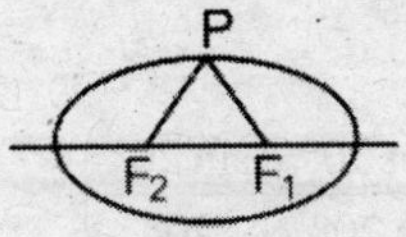

$$PF_1 + PF_2 = 10$$

$$\Rightarrow \quad 2a = 10 \Rightarrow a = 5$$

$$F_1F_2 = 8$$

$$\Rightarrow \quad 2c = 8 \Rightarrow c = 4$$

$$a^2 = b^2 + c^2 \Rightarrow b^2 = 3^2 \Rightarrow b = 3$$

$$\text{Area} = \pi ab = \pi \times 3 \times 5 = 15\pi.$$

50.

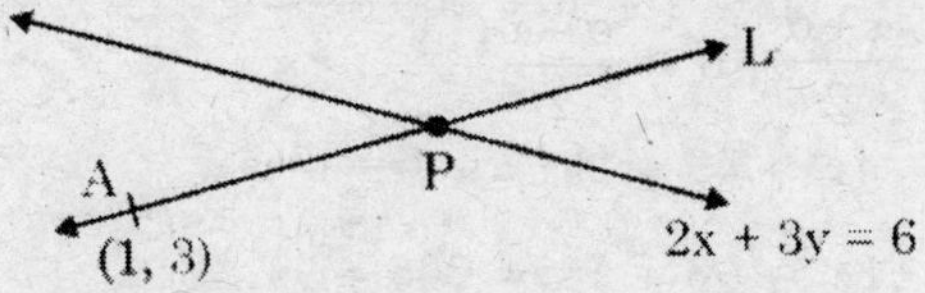

Equation of line L is

$$y - 3 = -4(x - 1)$$

$$\Rightarrow \quad y - 3 = -4x + 4$$

$$\Rightarrow \quad 4x + y = 7$$

Solving equations, $\quad x = \dfrac{3}{2},\ y = 1$

$$\therefore \quad AP = \sqrt{\left(\frac{3}{2}-1\right)^2 (1-3)^2} = \sqrt{\frac{1}{4}+4} = \frac{\sqrt{17}}{2}.$$

51.
$$\begin{vmatrix} a & 1 & 1 \\ 1 & b & 1 \\ 1 & 1 & c \end{vmatrix} = 0$$

$\Rightarrow C_2 \to C_2 - C_1,\ C_3 \to C_3 - C_1$

$$\begin{vmatrix} a & 1-a & 1-a \\ 1 & b-1 & 0 \\ 1 & 0 & c-1 \end{vmatrix} = 0$$

$$\Rightarrow a(b-1)(c-1) - (1-a)(c-1) - (1-a)(b-1) = 0$$

Dividing by $(1 - a)(1 - b)(1 - c)$, we get

$$\frac{a}{1-a} + \frac{1}{1-b} + \frac{1}{1-c} = 0$$

$$\Rightarrow \quad \frac{1}{1-b} + \frac{1}{1-c} = -\frac{a}{1-a}$$

Adding $\dfrac{1}{1-a}$ on both sides

$$\frac{1}{1-a} + \frac{1}{1-b} + \frac{1}{1-c} = 1.$$

52. (–3, 4, –8) (5, –6, 4)

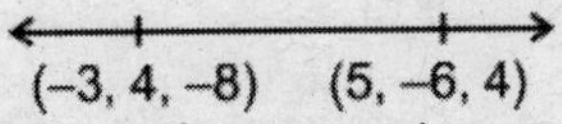

Equation of line is

$$\frac{x+3}{8} = \frac{y-4}{-10} = \frac{z+8}{12} = \lambda \text{ (say)}$$

$\Rightarrow \quad x = 8\lambda - 3$

$y = -10\lambda + 4$

$z = 12\lambda - 8$

Since line intersects XY plane, so, $z = 0$

$\Rightarrow \quad \lambda = \frac{2}{3} \quad \therefore x = \frac{7}{3}, y = \frac{-8}{3}$

$\Rightarrow$ Point $\left(\frac{7}{3}, \frac{-8}{3}, 0\right)$.

53. $2x - 3 + 10 = 3\sqrt{\frac{34+x^2}{2}}$

$4x^2 + 49 + 28x = \frac{9(34+x^2)}{2}$

$8x^2 + 98 + 56x = 306 + 9x^2$

$x^2 - 56x + 208 = 0$

$x = \frac{+56 \pm \sqrt{3136-832}}{2}$

$= 28 \pm 24 = 4, 52.$

54. $2(1)^2 + 7(2)^2 - 20 = 2 + 28 - 20 > 0$

$\therefore$ Point lies outside the ellipse.

55.

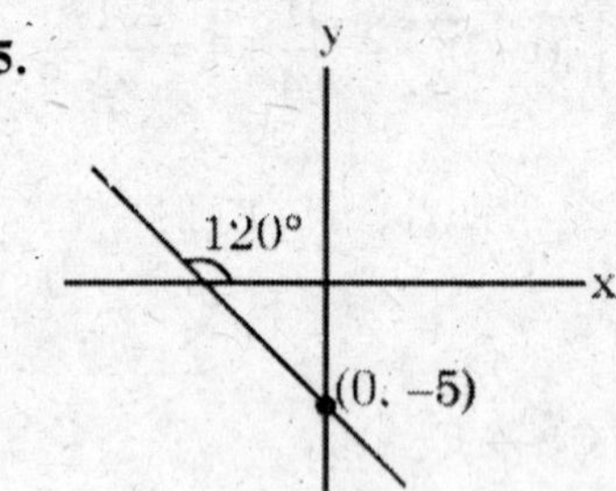

$m = \tan 120° = -\sqrt{3}$

$y + 5 = -\sqrt{3}x$

$\Rightarrow \quad y + \sqrt{3}x + 5 = 0.$

56. Required Line

$(2x - 3y + 7) + \lambda(7x + 4y + 2) = 0 \quad ...(i)$

Putting (2, 3)

$\Rightarrow \quad (4 - 9 + 7) + \lambda(14 + 12 + 2) = 0$

$\Rightarrow \quad \lambda = -\frac{1}{14}$

$(28x - 7x) + (-42y - 4y)(98 - 2) = 0$

$21x - 46y + 96 = 0.$

57. $b^2 = 2a, c^2 = \frac{9}{16}a^2$

We know, $\quad a^2 = b^2 + c^2$

So, $\quad a^2 = 2a + \frac{9}{16}a^2$

$\Rightarrow \quad a = \frac{32}{7}, b^2 = \frac{64}{7}$

Equation of ellipse, $\quad \frac{x^2}{a^2} + \frac{y^2}{b^2} = 1$

Putting values of a and b, $\quad \frac{49x^2}{1024} + \frac{7y^2}{64} = 1.$

58.

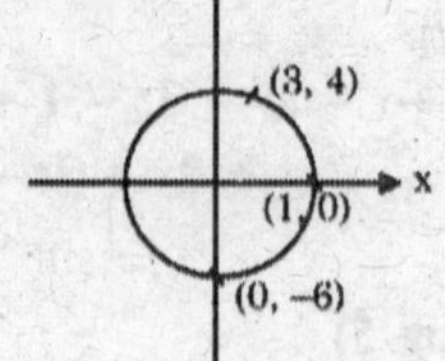

Let equation of circle is

$x^2 - x + y^2 + 6y + \lambda(-y - 6 + 6x) = 0$

Putting (3, 4), we get

$9 - 3 + 16 + 24 + \lambda(-4 - 6 + 18) = 0$

$\Rightarrow \quad 46 + 8\lambda = 0$

$\Rightarrow \quad \lambda = \frac{-23}{4}$

$\therefore \quad x^2 - x + y^2 + 6y - \frac{23}{4}(-y - 6 + 6x) = 0$

$\Rightarrow 4x^2 + 4y^2 - 4x + 24y + 23y + 138 - 138x = 0$

$\Rightarrow \quad 4x^2 + 4y^2 - 142x + 47y + 138 = 0.$

59.

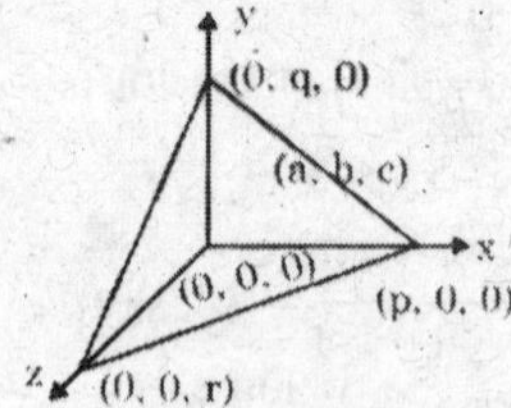

Equation of plane is

$\frac{x}{p} + \frac{y}{q} + \frac{z}{r} = 1$

It passes through (a, b, c)

$\Rightarrow \quad \frac{a}{p} + \frac{b}{q} + \frac{c}{r} = 1$

Equation of sphere is given by

$x^2 + y^2 + z^2 - pz - qy - rz = 0$

With its centre at (x_c, y_c, z_c) such that

$x_c = \frac{p}{2}, y_c = \frac{q}{2}, z_c = \frac{r}{2}$

$\Rightarrow \quad p = 2x_c, q = 2y_c, r = 2z_c$

$\therefore$ Locus of centre $\Rightarrow \frac{a}{x} + \frac{b}{y} + \frac{c}{z} = 2.$

60. Let $P_1 : \quad x + y + z - 1 = 0$

$P_2 : 2x + 3y + 4z - 7 = 0$

Equation of plane passing through the line of intersection of P_1 and P_2 is given by

$x + y + z - 1 + \lambda(2x + 3y + 4z - 7) = 0$

$\Rightarrow x(1 + 2\lambda) + y(1 + 3\lambda) + z(1 + 4\lambda) - 1 - 7\lambda = 0$

This is perpendicular to $x - 5y - 3z - 5 = 0$

$$\Rightarrow \quad 1(1 + 2\lambda) - 5(1 + 3\lambda) + 3(1 + 4\lambda) = 0$$

$$\Rightarrow \quad 1 + 2\lambda - 5 - 15\lambda + 3 + 12\lambda = 0$$

$$\Rightarrow \quad -\lambda - 1 = 0$$

$$\Rightarrow \quad \lambda = -1$$

$\therefore$ Equation of plane is $-x - 2y - 3z - 1 + 7 = 0$

$$\Rightarrow \quad x + 2y + 3z - 6 = 0.$$

61. $$y = 5^{\log x}$$

$$\Rightarrow \quad \log y = (\log x)(\log 5)$$

$$\Rightarrow \quad \log x = \frac{\log y}{\log 5} = \log y^{\frac{1}{\log 5}} \Rightarrow x = y^{\frac{1}{\log 5}}$$

$y > 0$.

62. $$f(x) = \begin{cases} -\dfrac{x}{|x|}, & x \neq 0 \\ 0, & x = 0 \end{cases} = \begin{cases} -1, & x > 0 \\ 1, & x < 0 \\ 0 & x = 0 \end{cases}$$

$f(x)$ is discontinuous at $x = 0$.

63. $$y = (\cos x)^y$$

$$\Rightarrow \quad \log y = y \log \cos x$$

Differentiating both sides,

$$\frac{1}{y}\frac{dy}{dx} = y.(-\tan x) + \log\cos x.\frac{dy}{dx}$$

$$\Rightarrow \quad \left(\frac{1}{y} - \log\cos x\right)\frac{dy}{dx} = -y \tan x$$

$$\Rightarrow \quad \frac{dy}{dx} = \frac{-y^2 \tan x}{1 - y\log\cos x}.$$

66. $$\cos^{-1}\frac{x-1}{x+1} + \sin^{-1}\frac{x-1}{x+1} = \frac{\pi}{2}$$

$$\Rightarrow \quad \frac{dy}{dx} = 0.$$

67. $$\int \tan^{-1}(\sec x + \tan x)dx = \int \tan^{-1}\left\{\tan\left(\frac{\pi}{4} - \frac{x}{2}\right)\right\}dx$$

$$= \int\left(\frac{\pi}{4} - \frac{x}{2}\right)dx = \frac{\pi x}{4} - \frac{x^2}{4} + c.$$

68. $$f(x) = \begin{cases} 1 - x^2, & 0 < x \le 1 \\ \log x, & 1 < x \le 2 \\ \log 2 - 1 + 0.5x & 2 < x < \infty \end{cases}$$

$$f'(x) = -2x,\ 0 < x \le 1.$$

69. $$f(x) = x(x^2 - 1)$$

$$f'(x) = x(2x) + (x^2 - 1) = 3x^2 - 1$$

$$f''(x) = 6x$$

At $\quad f'(x) = 0 \Rightarrow x = \pm\dfrac{1}{\sqrt{3}}$

$$f(x)_{\max} = f\left(\frac{-1}{\sqrt{3}}\right) = \frac{-1}{\sqrt{3}}\left(\frac{1}{3} - 1\right) = \frac{2}{3\sqrt{3}}$$

$$f(x)_{\min} = f\left(\frac{1}{\sqrt{3}}\right) = \frac{1}{\sqrt{3}}\left(\frac{1}{3} - 1\right) = \frac{-2}{3\sqrt{3}}.$$

70. All statements are correct.

71. $$f(x) = \frac{\ln x}{x}$$

$$f'(x) = \frac{\left(\frac{1}{x}\right)x - \ln x}{x^2} = \frac{1 - \ln x}{x^2}$$

$$f''(x) = \frac{-\frac{1}{x}.x^2 - 2x(1 - \ln x)}{x^4}$$

$$= \frac{-x - 2x(1 - \ln x)}{x^4} = \frac{-[1 + 2 - 2\ln x]}{x^3}$$

$$= \frac{-(3 - 2\ln x)}{x^3}$$

At, $\quad f'(x) = 0 \Rightarrow \ln x = 1 \Rightarrow x = e$

$$f''(e) = \frac{-(3-2)}{e^3} = -\frac{1}{e^3} < 0$$

$$f(x)_{\max} = f(e) = \frac{\ln e}{e} = \frac{1}{e}.$$

72. $$f(x) = \begin{cases} x - x^3, & x \ge 0 \\ -x - x^3, & x < 0 \end{cases}$$

$$f(-x) = \begin{cases} x + x^3, & x \ge 0 = f(x) \\ x + x^3, & x < 0 = -f(x) \end{cases}$$

Neither even nor odd.

73. $$\ell_1 = \frac{d}{dx}e^{\sin x}$$

$$\ell_2 = \lim_{h \to 0}\frac{e^{\sin(x+h)} - e^{\sin x}}{h} = \frac{d}{dx}e^{\sin x} = \ell_1$$

$$\ell_3 = \int e^{\sin x}\cos x dx = \int e^t dt = e^t + c = e^{\sin x} + c$$

$$\frac{d}{dx}(\ell_3) = \frac{d}{dx}e^{\sin x} = \ell_2.$$

74. $$\frac{dy}{dx} = \frac{ax + h}{by + k}$$

$$\int(by + k)dy = \int(ax + h)dx$$

$$\frac{by^2}{2} + ky = \frac{ax^2}{2} + hx + c$$

$$\frac{ax^2}{2} - \frac{by^2}{2} + hx - ky + c = 0$$

$$a = -b \neq 0.$$

75. $\lim_{x\to\pi/2} \frac{\sin x}{x} = L \Rightarrow L = \frac{2}{\pi}$

$m = 0.$

76. $\int_0^{2\pi} \sqrt{1+\sin\frac{x}{2}}\,dx = \int_0^{2\pi} \left|\sin\frac{x}{4}+\cos\frac{x}{4}\right| dx$

$= 4\left[\sin\frac{x}{4}-\cos\frac{x}{4}\right]_0^{2\pi} = 8.$

77.

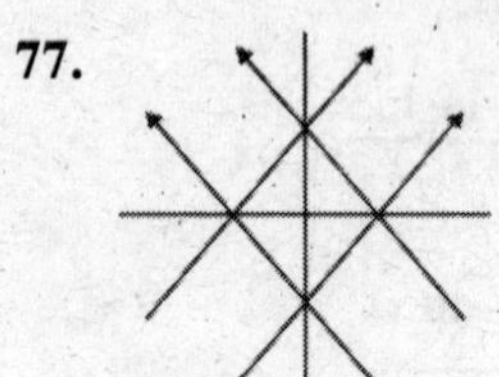

Area $= 4\times\frac{1}{2}\times 1 = 2$ sq. unit.

78. $y = \frac{x^2}{1+x^4} \Rightarrow y \geq 0$

Also, $y = \frac{x^2}{1+x^4} = \frac{1}{x^2+\frac{1}{x^2}}$

$\Rightarrow \quad y \leq \frac{1}{2} \Rightarrow y \in \left[0, \frac{1}{2}\right].$

79. L.H.D.

$= \lim_{h\to 0} \frac{[k-h]\sin\pi(k-h)-[k]\sin k\pi}{-h}$

$= \lim_{h\to 0} \frac{(k-1)\sin(k\pi-\pi h)}{-h} = \lim_{h\to 0} \pm\frac{(k-1)\sin(\pi h)}{-h}$

$= \mp(k-1)\pi = (-1)^k (k-1)\pi.$

80. $f(x) = \frac{x}{2}-1,\ [0, \pi]$

$\tan[f(x)] = \tan\left[\frac{x}{2}-1\right]$

$\frac{1}{f(x)} = \frac{1}{\frac{x}{2}-1}$ is discontinuous at $x = 2$

Also, $\tan[f(x)]$ is discontinuous for $x = 2$ in $[0, \pi]$.

81. $\left[1+\left(\frac{dy}{dx}\right)^2\right]^3 = p^2\left[\frac{d^2y}{dx^2}\right]^2$

Order = 2, Degree 2.

82. $y = \cos^{-1}\left(\frac{2x}{1+x^2}\right) = \frac{\pi}{2}-\sin^{-1},\left(\frac{2x}{1+x^2}\right)$

$= \frac{\pi}{2}-2\tan^{-1}x, |x|<1.$

83. $f'(x) = \frac{-2x\left(-e^{-x^2}\right)}{2\sqrt{1-e^{-x^2}}} = \frac{xe^{-x^2}}{\sqrt{1-e^{-x^2}}}$

Which is defined $\forall\ x \in R$, except $x = 0$

$\Rightarrow f(x)$ is differentiable on $(-\infty, 0) \cup (0, \infty)$.

84. $f(x) = \sin x + \cos x \Rightarrow$ maximum value $= \sqrt{2}$

(A) $\to$ (2)

$f(x) = 3\sin x + 4\cos x$

$\Rightarrow$ maximum value $= \sqrt{3^2+4^2} = 5$

(B) $\to$ (3)

$f(x) = 2\sin x + \cos x$

$\Rightarrow$ maximum value $= \sqrt{4+1} = \sqrt{5}$

(C) $\to$ (4)

$f(x) = \sin x + 3\cos x$

maximum value $= \sqrt{1+9} = \sqrt{10}$

(D) $\to$ (1).

85. L.H. Lt = R.H. Lt = $f(0) = 0$

$\Rightarrow f(x)$ is continuous at $x = 0$

L.H.D. = R.H.D. = –1

$\Rightarrow f(x)$ is differentiable at $x = 0$.

86. $f(x) = \frac{x}{x}, \neq 0 \Rightarrow y = 1, x \neq 0$

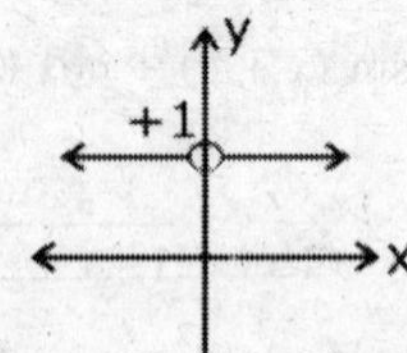

87. $f(n) = \left[\frac{1}{4}+\frac{n}{1000}\right]$

$\therefore \sum_{n=1}^{1000} +(n)$

$= \left[\frac{1}{4}+\frac{1}{1000}\right]+\left[\frac{1}{4}+\frac{2}{1000}\right]+\left[\frac{1}{4}+\frac{1}{1000}\right]+.....+\left[\frac{1}{4}+\frac{1000}{1000}\right]$

$= 0+0+0+....\left[\frac{1}{4}+\frac{750}{1000}\right]+\left[\frac{1}{4}+\frac{750}{1000}\right]+....+\left[\frac{1}{4}+\frac{1000}{1000}\right]$

$= 1 + 1 + 1 + ... + 1$ (251 times)

$= 251.$

88. $\int\left[\frac{1}{\log x}-\frac{1}{(\log x)^2}\right]dx$

Putting $\log x = t$

$\Rightarrow \quad x = e^t \Rightarrow dx = e^t\,dt$

$\int e^t\left[\frac{1}{t}-\frac{1}{t^2}\right]dt = \frac{e^t}{t}+c = \frac{x}{\log x}+c.$

89. The height and the radius of the base of an open cylinder of given surface area and maximum volume are equal. *i.e.,* radius = height.

$\Rightarrow$ Diameter = 2 × height $\Rightarrow k = 2$.

90. $$\int_0^{\pi/4}\sqrt{\tan x}+\int_0^{\pi/4}\sqrt{\cot x}\,dx = \int_0^{\pi/4}\left(\sqrt{\tan x}+\sqrt{\cot x}\right)dx$$

$$= \int_0^{\pi/4}\frac{\sin x+\cos x}{\sqrt{\sin x\cos x}}dx = \sqrt{2}\int_0^{\pi/4}\frac{(\sin x+\cos x)}{\sqrt{1-(\sin x-\cos x)^2}}dx$$

Putting $\sin x - \cos x = t$

$\Rightarrow$ $dt = (\sin x + \cos x)dx$

when $x = 0$, $t = -1$ and $x = \dfrac{\pi}{4}$, $t = 0$

$$= \sqrt{2}\int_{-1}^{0}\frac{1}{\sqrt{1-t^2}}dt = \sqrt{2}\int_{-1}^{0}\left[\sin^{-1}t\right]_{-1}^{0}$$

$$= \sqrt{2}\left[0-(-\pi/2)\right] = \frac{\pi}{\sqrt{2}}.$$

91. $g(x) = [x], f(x) = [x]^2 - [x]$

$f(x)$ is discontinuous at every integers except $x = 1$.

92. $$y = A[\sin(x+c)+\cos(x+c)]$$

$$\frac{dy}{dx} = A[\cos(x+c)-\sin(x+c)]$$

$$\frac{d^2y}{dx^2} = -A[\sin(x+c)+\cos(x+c)] = -y$$

$$\Rightarrow \frac{d^2y}{dx^2}+y = 0.$$

94. $$\frac{dy}{dx}-\frac{y\phi'(x)}{\phi(x)} = \frac{-y^2}{\phi(x)}$$

$$\Rightarrow \frac{1}{y^2}.\left(\frac{dy}{dx}\right)-\frac{1}{y}.\frac{\phi'(x)}{\phi(x)} = -\frac{1}{\phi(x)}$$

Put, $$t = -\frac{1}{y}$$

We get, $$\frac{dt}{dx} = \frac{1}{y^2}\left(\frac{dy}{dx}\right)$$

$$\Rightarrow \frac{dt}{dx}+\frac{\phi'(x)}{\phi(x)}t = -\frac{1}{\phi(x)}$$

$$\text{I.F.} = e^{\int\frac{\phi'(x)}{\phi(x)}dx} = e^{\log\phi(x)} = \phi(x)$$

Solution of differential equation is

$$t\,.\,\phi(x) = \int-\frac{1}{\phi(x)}\times\phi(x)dx$$

$$\Rightarrow -\frac{1}{y}\phi(x) = -x \Rightarrow \frac{\phi(x)}{y} = x \Rightarrow y = \frac{\phi(x)}{x}+c.$$

95. $$f(x) = \frac{4x+x^4}{1+4x^3},\ g(x) = \ln\left(\frac{1+x}{1-x}\right)$$

$$g\left(\frac{e-1}{e+1}\right) = \ln\left[\frac{e+1+e-1}{e+1-e+1}\right] = \ln\left(\frac{2e}{2}\right) = 1$$

$$f\circ g\left(\frac{e-1}{e+1}\right) = f(1) = \frac{4+1}{1+4} = 1.$$

96. $$\begin{vmatrix}1-\alpha & \alpha-\alpha^2 & \alpha^2\\ 1-\beta & \beta-\beta^2 & \beta^2\\ 1-\gamma & \gamma-\gamma^2 & \gamma^2\end{vmatrix}$$

$$C_1 \to C_1 + C_2 + C_3 = \begin{vmatrix}1 & \alpha-\alpha^2 & \alpha^2\\ 1 & \beta-\beta^2 & \beta^2\\ 1 & \gamma-\gamma^2 & \gamma^2\end{vmatrix}$$

$$C_2 \to C_2 + C_3 = \begin{vmatrix}1 & \alpha & \alpha^2\\ 1 & \beta & \beta^2\\ 1 & \gamma & \gamma^2\end{vmatrix}$$

$= (\alpha - \beta)(\beta - \gamma)(\gamma - \alpha)$.

97. $$A = \begin{bmatrix}1 & 0 & 2\\ 2 & 1 & 0\\ 0 & 3 & 1\end{bmatrix}$$

$C_{11} = 1$ $\quad C_{12} = -2$ $\quad C_{13} = 6$

$C_{21} = 6$ $\quad C_{22} = 1$ $\quad C_{23} = -3$

$C_{31} = -2$ $\quad C_{32} = 4$ $\quad C_{33} = 1$

$$\therefore \text{Adj A} = \begin{bmatrix}1 & 6 & -2\\ -2 & 1 & 4\\ 6 & -3 & 1\end{bmatrix}.$$

98. $$A^2 = \begin{bmatrix}-2 & 2\\ 2 & -2\end{bmatrix}\begin{bmatrix}-2 & 2\\ 2 & -2\end{bmatrix} = \begin{bmatrix}8 & -8\\ -8 & 8\end{bmatrix}$$

$$= -4\begin{bmatrix}-2 & 2\\ 2 & -2\end{bmatrix} = -4A$$

99. Let, $$z = x + iy$$

$$z^2 - i = x^2 - y^2 + 2xyi - i$$

$$= x^2 - y^2 + (2xy - 1)i$$

$$\text{Re}(z^2 - i) = 2 \Rightarrow x^2 - y^2 = 2$$

This equation represents rectangular hyperbola.

100. $p + q + r = a + b + c = 0$

$$= \begin{vmatrix}pa & qb & rc\\ qc & ra & pb\\ rb & pc & qa\end{vmatrix}$$

$= pqr(a^3 + b^3 + c^3) - abc(p^3 + q^3 + r^3)$

$= pqr(3abc) - abc(3pqr)$

$= 0$ ($\because a^3 + b^3 + c^3 = 3abc$ $p^3 + q^3 + r^3 = 3pqr$).

101. $n(s) = {}^4C_2 = \frac{4\times 3}{2} = 6$

$n(E) = {}^2C_1 \times {}^2C_1 = 2 \times 2 = 4$

$P(E) = \frac{4}{6} = \frac{2}{3}$.

102. Possible primes are 2, 3, 5

$\frac{2}{3}\times\frac{1}{3}+\frac{1}{3}\times\frac{2}{3}=\frac{4}{9}$.

103. $n(X) = 16$, $n(Y) = 25$ and $S = 51$

$\Rightarrow \quad P(X) = \frac{16}{51}, P(Y) = \frac{25}{51}$.

104. $P(A \cup B) = P(A) + P(B) - P(A \cup B)$

$P(B) = \frac{2}{3}-\frac{1}{2}+\frac{1}{6}=\frac{1}{3}$

$\therefore \quad P(\bar{A}\cap B) = \frac{1}{3}-\frac{1}{6}=\frac{1}{6}$.

105. Statement 1 and statement 2 are correct.
Mean derivation is least when measured about mean, therefore statement 3 is wrong.

106. As standard deviation is '0', therefore all observations will be equal to 24.

$\Rightarrow$ Average of any five observations = 24.

107. Regression coefficient of y on x
= regression coefficient of x on y
$\Rightarrow$ (x, y) lies on $(y = x)$ line.

108. $P(A) = \frac{1}{3}$, $P(B) = \frac{1}{6}$, $P(A \cap B) = \frac{1}{12}$

$$P(B\,|\,\bar{A}) = \frac{P(B\cap\bar{A})}{P(\bar{A})}$$

$$P(B\cap\bar{A}) = P(B)-P(A\cap B)=\frac{1}{12}$$

$$P(\bar{A}) = \frac{2}{3} \therefore P\left(\frac{B}{\bar{A}}\right) = \frac{1/12}{2/3}=\frac{1}{8}.$$

109. $np = \frac{2}{3}$, $npq = \frac{5}{9}$

$\Rightarrow \quad q = \frac{5}{9}\times\frac{3}{2}=\frac{5}{6} \Rightarrow p = \frac{1}{6}, n = 4$

$$p(x=2) = {}^4C_2\left(\frac{1}{6}\right)^2\times\left(\frac{5}{6}\right)^2 = 6\times\frac{1}{36}\times\frac{25}{36}=\frac{25}{216}.$$

110. $p(\text{all reach safely}) = \left(\frac{1}{3}\right)^5$

$p(\text{4 reach safely}) = 5\times\left(\frac{1}{3}\right)^4\left(\frac{2}{3}\right)$

$p(\text{at least 4 reach safely}) = \frac{11}{243}$.

111. $p(\text{none born in same month}) = \frac{12\times11\times10}{12\times12\times12}$

$p(\text{at least two born in same month})$

$= 1-\frac{12\times11\times10}{12\times12\times12}=\frac{144-110}{144}=\frac{17}{72}$.

112. $\bar{x} = 10$, $\bar{y} = 90$, $\sigma x = 3$, $\sigma y = 12$, $r_{xy} = 0.8$

Regression equation x on y is

$\Rightarrow \quad x-10 = r\frac{\sigma x}{\sigma y}(y-90)$

$\Rightarrow \quad x - 10 = 0.8\times\frac{3}{12}(y-90)$

$\Rightarrow \quad x - 10 = 0.2\,(y - 90) \Rightarrow x = -8 + 0.2y$.

113. $P(B\cap\bar{C}) = P(A\cap B\cap\bar{C})+P(\bar{A}\cap B\cap\bar{C})$

$= \frac{1}{3}+\frac{1}{3}=\frac{2}{3}$

$P(B) = P(B\cap C)+P(B\cap\bar{C})$

$\Rightarrow \quad P(B \cap C) = P(B)-P(B\cap\bar{C}) = \frac{3}{4}-\frac{2}{3}=\frac{1}{12}$.

114. Total expenditure of A = 10,000
Total expenditure of B = 8,100
So, area of A : area of B = 10,000 : 8100 = 100 : 81
$\Rightarrow$ radii of A : radii of B = $\sqrt{100}:\sqrt{81}=10:9$.

115. The arithmetic mean will always be between minimum and maximum value so out of the given option, '$n/2$' is possible value.

116. P(to know correct answer) = p
P(to guess correct answer) = $(1 - p) \times (1/m)$

P(to answer correctly) = $p+\frac{1-p}{m}$

So, required probability = $\frac{p}{p+\frac{1-p}{m}}=\frac{mp}{1+p(m-1)}$.

117. $\frac{x_1+x_2}{2}-\sqrt{x_1x_2}>1 \Rightarrow \frac{x_1+x_2}{2} > \sqrt{x_1x_2}+1$

$\Rightarrow \quad x_1 + x_2 > 2\sqrt{x_1x_2}+2$

$\Rightarrow \quad x_1+x_2-2\sqrt{x_1x_2} > 2$

$\Rightarrow \quad \left(\sqrt{x_1}-\sqrt{x_2}\right)^2 > 2$

$\Rightarrow \quad \left|\sqrt{x_1}-\sqrt{x_2}\right| > \sqrt{2}$.

119. $n(S) = {}^5C_3 = 10 \qquad n(E) = {}^4C_3 - 1 = 3$
$P(E) = 3/10 = 0.3$

120. Coefficient of correlation = $\sqrt{0.2\times1.8}=0.6$.

Previous Papers (Solved)

NATIONAL DEFENCE ACADEMY & NAVAL ACADEMY

NDA & NA – Entrance Exam, 2017 (I)

PAPER I : GENERAL ABILITY TEST

PART A : ENGLISH LANGUAGE

SELECTING WORDS

Directions (Qs. 1-10) : *Each of the following items in this section has a sentence with a blank space and four words or groups of words given after the sentence. Select whichever word or group of words you consider most appropriate for the blank space and indicate your response on the Answer Sheet accordingly.*

1. I .... you to be at the party this evening.
A. look forward to B. hope
C. expect D. think

2. When I met John yesterday, it was the first time I .... him since Christmas.
A. saw B. have seen
C. had seen D. have been seeing

3. He .... to listen to my arguments and walked away.
A. denied B. disliked
C. prevented D. refused

4. The flow of blood was so .... that the patient died.
A. intense B. adequate
C. profuse D. extensive

5. You have never .... me about your experiences in America.
A. said B. told
C. explained D. spoken

6. I always felt hungry .... I heard the dinner bell.
A. as much as B. as well as
C. as soon as D.. as close as

7. Although they took every precaution, they could not .... the accident.
A. defer B. allow
C. avoid D. block

8. The ambitious nobleman .... to marry the King's daughter.
A. transpired B. perspired
C. aspired D. expired

9. The dictator of that country was a monster of wickedness, insatiable in his .... for blood and plunder.
A. idea B. vision
C. lust D. intention

10. Please don't give me any more, I have had ....
A. few B. too little
C. little D. enough

ANTONYMS

Directions (Qs. 11 to 15): *In this section, each item consists of a sentence with a word **bold** and is followed by four words. Select the word that is **most opposite** in meaning to the **bold** word and indicate your response in the Answer Sheet accordingly.*

11. My first lecture in the classroom was a **fiasco**.
A. success B. joy
C. fun D. disaster

12. It was indeed **arduous** to cross streets in New York.
A. pleasant B. effortless
C. interesting D. risky

13. Unlike his brother, he is **affable**.
A. reserved B. gullible
C. irritable D. lovable

14. The birth of his child decidedly proved to be an **auspicious** event in his life.
A. precious B. ominous
C. useless D. unforgettable

15. The witness **corroborated** word for word the statement of the victim.
A. accepted B. confirmed
C. denied D. repeated

SYNONYMS

Directions (Qs. 16-20): *In this section, each item consists of a sentence with a word **bold** and is followed by four words or groups of words. Select the word or group of words that is **most similar** in meaning to the **bold** word and indicate your response in the Answer Sheet accordingly.*

16. It is unwise to **sever** diplomatic relations with a neighbouring country over small matters.

A. engage B. estrange
C. cut off D. twist

17. Bad tendencies are to be **countered** by good ones until all that is evil disappears.
A. opposed B. balanced
C. reduced D. bypassed

18. The police fired **indiscriminately** at the crowd, killing many innocent women and children.
A. continuously B. without distinguishing
C. foolishly D. rapidly

19. Businessmen who lack **acumen** cannot be expected to be very successful.
A. fairness B. sharpness
C. boldness D. righteousness

20. His **candid** opinions have won him many friends.
A. kind B. courteous
C. generous D. frank

SENTENCE IMPROVEMENT

Directions (Qs. 21-30): *In this section, look at the **bold** part of each sentence. Below each sentence are given three possible substitutions for the **bold** part. If one of them (A), (B) or (C) is better than the **bold** part, indicate your response on the Answer Sheet against the corresponding letter (A), (B) or (C). If none of the substitutions improves the sentence, indicate (D) as your response on the Answer Sheet. Thus a 'No improvement' response will be signified by the letter (D).*

21. I disliked him not so much for his meanness **but for** his dishonesty.
A. as for B. but because
C. but due to D. No improvement

22. He preferred death **rather than** imprisonment.
A. for B. to
C. than D. No improvement

23. They kept the idea **secretly**.
A. secretive B. secret
C. secretively D. No improvement

24. He ought not to **tell** me your secret, but he did.
A. telling B. have told
C. having told D. No improvement

25. If I don't know the meaning of a word, I **look it after** in the dictionary.
A. look it out B. look it for
C. look it up D. No improvement

26. Mr. and Mrs. Rao stay **in their home** every evening.
A. at home B. inside home
C. within their home D. No improvement

27. When we saw him last, he **ran** to catch a bus.
A. has run B. had run
C. was running D. No improvement

28. She **cut a sad figure** in her first performance on the stage.
A. made a sorry figure B. cut a sorry face
C. cut a sorry figure D. No improvement

29. Last evening I went to the optician and bought **spectacles**.
A. a spectacle B. two spectacles
C. a pair of spectacles D. No improvement

30. I would like **to avail** a fifteen days' holiday this summer.
A. to avail of B. to avail myself of
C. to avail myself D. No improvement

SPOTTING ERRORS

Directions (Qs. 31-35): *Each item in this section has a sentence with three underlined parts labelled (A), (B) and (C). Read each sentence to find out whether there is any error in any underlined part and indicate your response in the Answer Sheet against the corresponding letter, i.e., (A) or (B) or (C). If you find no error, your response should be indicated as (D).*

31. (A)/ I can fly (B)/ if I will be (C)/ a bird (D)/ No error.

32. (A)/ As soon as (B)/ the train arrived (C)/ the passengers entered the compartments (D)/ No error.

33. (A)/ Never (B)/ I have (C)/ seen such a town (D)/ No error.

34. (A)/ He goes to his office (B)/ by bicycle (C)/ every day (D)/ No error.

35. (A)/ Far from being appreciated (B)/ his conduct was discussed (C)/ and sharply commented (D)/ No error.

COMPREHENSION

Directions (Qs. 36-41): *In this section, you have two short passages. Read the passages and answer the items that follow. You are required to select your answers based on the contents of the passage and opinion of the author only.*

Passage - 1

We had just passed Tenali, where I roused myself in order to hear the name of the station. As I was falling asleep again, a violent jolt shot me into the arms of somebody in the seat opposite. The engine with one wheel broken was lying across the track and beside it was the luggage van, likewise, derailed. Groaning, wheezing, gasping, sputtering in its death agony, the engine was like a fallen horse which, snorting, trembling in every limb, its flanks heaving, its chest labouring, seems incapable of making the smallest effort to struggle on to its legs again.

36. The author had roused himself as he wanted to
A. get off
B. meet someone

C. know the name of the station
D. keep himself awake

37. The engine stopped because
A. the driver had stopped it
B. one of the wheels was broken
C. there was a halting place
D. there was no fuel

38. The engine is compared to a fallen horse because
A. it was groaning like a horse
B. it was lying across the track
C. it could make no effort to stand upright
D. it had a broken wheel

Passage - 2

I was beginning to tire a little now. I had been cutting steps continuously for two hours, and Tenzing, too, was moving very slowly. As I chipped steps around still another corner, I wondered rather dully just how long we could keep it up. Our original zest had now quite gone and it was turning more into a grim struggle. I then realised that the ridge ahead, instead of still monotonously rising, now dropped sharply away, and far below I could see the North Col and Rongbuk glacier. I looked upwards to see a narrow ridge running up to a snowy summit. A few more whacks of the ice-axe in the firm snow and we stood on top.

39. Which of the following is the most appropriate description of the area in which the narrator had been moving?
A. A steep rocky slope
B. A peak with a flight of steps
C. A high peak covered with snow
D. A long ridge

40. 'I had been cutting steps continuously for two hours' suggests that
A. the climber was unskilled in the art of making steps
B. he had to cut the steps out of snow before climbing up which was necessarily a slow process
C. the slowness was caused by the fact that as soon as he cut the steps they were again covered with snow
D. he had to work suspended from a ledge

41. 'It was turning more into a grim struggle' would mean
A. that after the long exertion he was feeling so weak that any further climbing meant a hard struggle with the forces of nature
B. that Tenzing was making the task more difficult
C. that strong cold wind was pushing him down from above and that he had to struggle with the forces of nature
D. that he was in a mood to give up ultimately

ORDERING OF WORDS IN A SENTENCE

Directions (Qs. 42-50): *Each of the following items in this section consists of a sentence the parts of which have been jumbled. These parts have been labelled P, Q, R and S. Given below each sentence are four sequences namely (A), (B), (C) and (D). You are required to re-arrange the jumbled parts of the sentence and mark your response accordingly.*

42. (P)/ Farm workers (Q)/ spend (R)/ outdoors (S)/ most of their time
The proper sequence should be
A. P Q R S B. P R Q S
C. P Q S R D. R P Q S

43. (P)/ He (Q)/ shuffled the papers (R)/ in a drawer (S)/ together
The proper sequence should be
A. P Q S R B. P Q R S
C. P S Q R D. R S P Q

44. (P)/ Do you think (Q)/ will (R)/ this soap (S)/ shrink woollen clothes?
The proper sequence should be
A. P Q R S B. P R Q S
C. Q R P S D. Q P R S

45. (P)/ We advised (Q)/ the hijackers to surrender (R)/ to the police (S)/ themselves
The proper sequence should be
A. P Q R S B. P R Q S
C. P Q S R D. R P Q S

46. (P)/ Sports cars (Q)/ appeal (R)/ to some motorists only (S)/ with noisy exhausts
The proper sequence should be
A. R Q S P B. P S Q R
C. R S P Q D. P Q S R

47. (P)/ He (Q)/ almost (R)/ planned the entire strategy of operation (S)/ single-handed
The proper sequence should be
A. R S P Q. B. P R Q S
C. S Q R P D. Q P S R

48. (P)/ She has (Q)/ more (R)/ intelligence (S)/ than we suspected her to possess
The proper sequence should be
A. P Q S R B. P R Q S
C. P S Q R D. P Q R S

49. (P)/ They (Q)/ should implant (R)/ in the minds of young children (S)/ sound principles
The proper sequence should be
A. P Q R S B. P Q S R
C. R P Q S D. P R Q S

50. (P)/ When I was a student (Q)/ I learnt swimming at the age of 15 (R)/ of class X (S)/ in a government school
The proper sequence should be
A. P Q R S
B. P R Q S
C. Q P R S
D. Q S P R

PART B : GENERAL KNOWLEDGE

51. Which one of the following devices changes low voltage alternating current to high voltage alternating current and vice-versa?

A. Generator B. Motor
C. Transformer D. Vibrator

52. An optical illusion which occurs mainly in deserts during hot summer is based on the principle of

A. Reflection B. Interference
C. Dispersion D. Total internal reflection

53. At which place Earth's magnetic field becomes horizontal?

A. Magnetic meridian B. Magnetic equator
C. Geographical pole D. Tropic of Cancer

54. The speed of a car travelling on a straight road is listed below at successive intervals of 1 s:

Time (s)	0	1	2	3	4
Speed (m/s)	0	2	4	6	8

Which of the following is/are correct?

The car travels

1. with a uniform acceleration of 2 m/s^2
2. 16 m in 4 s
3. with an average speed of 4 m/s.

Select the correct answer using the code given below :

A. 1, 2 and 3 B. 2 and 3 only
C. 1 and 2 only D. 1 only

55. The speed of a body that has Mach number more than 1 is

A. supersonic B. subsonic
C. 300 m/s D. about 10 m/s

56. Molecules of which of the following has cage like structure?

1. Diamond
2. Graphite
3. Fullerenes

Select the correct answer using the code given below :

A. 1, 2 and 3 B. 2 and 3 only
C. 2 only D. 3 only

57. Temporary hardness in water is due to which one of the following of Calcium and Magnesium?

A. Hydrogen carbonates
B. Carbonates
C. Chlorides
D. Sulphates

58. Stung by hairs of nettle leaves causes burning pain. This is due to the injection of

A. Acetic acid B. Methanoic acid
C. Sulphuric acid D. Hydrochloric acid

59. Which one of the following elements is least reactive with water?

A. Lithium B. Sodium
C. Potassium D. Cesium

60. Rutherford's alpha-particle scattering experiment was responsible for the discovery of

A. Electron B. Proton
C. Nucleus D. Helium

61. Glass is a

A. liquid
B. colloid
C. non-crystalline amorphous solid
D. crystalline solid

62. Cell wall of any fungus is different from plants in having

A. cellulose B. chitin
C. cholesterol D. glycogen

63. Sleeping sickness is a parasitic disease of humans and other animals. It is caused by

A. Histomonas B. Trypanosoma
C. Angomonae D. Naegleria

64. Which one of the following agencies enforces the laws on food security in India?

A. FDA B. WHO
C. FSSAI D. FAO

65. Dengue virus causes high fever, rashes and reduces the number of a particular type of blood cells. Those blood cells are

A. Monocytes B. Platelets
C. Eosinophils D. Neutrophils

66. Kidney secretes an enzyme, which changes plasma protein angiotensinogen into angiotensin. The enzyme is

A. Renin B. Nitrogenase
C. Hydrolase D. Mono-oxygenase

67. Red blood cells (RBCs) have

A. no nucleus, no mitochondria and no endoplasmic reticulum
B. nucleus, mitochondria and endoplasmic reticulum
C. nucleus, mitochondria but no endoplasmic reticulum
D. no mitochondria but endoplasmic reticulum is present

68. According to the Census 2011, the density of population in which one among the following States is the lowest?

A. Sikkim B. Nagaland
C. Manipur D. Mizoram

69. Headquarters of the World Meteorological Organization is located in

A. Washington B. Geneva
C. Moscow D. London

70. Match List-I with List-II and select the correct answer using the codes given below the Lists:

List-I (Industry)	List-II (Place)
(*a*) Petrochemical	1. Coimbatore
(*b*) Aircraft	2. Pinjore
(*c*) Machine tools	3. Bengaluru
(*d*) Cotton textiles	4. Bongaigaon

Codes:

	(*a*)	(*b*)	(*c*)	(*d*)
A.	4	3	2	1
B.	4	2	3	1
C.	1	2	3	4
D.	1	3	2	4

71. Consider the following statements pertaining to Coffee plantation in India :

1. Need warm and moist climate with a spell of dry weather during the ripening period
2. Rolling fields having good drainage
3. Strong sunshine over hilly slopes exceeding temperature 35°C
4. Karnataka is the leading producer in India

Which of the statements given above are correct?

A. 1 and 4 only B. 1, 2 and 3
C. 3 and 4 D. 1, 2 and 4

72. Dr. Urjit Patel, who has been appointed, recently as Governor of Reserve Bank of India, was holding which position immediately prior to this appointment?

A. Chief Economist, IMF
B. Deputy Governor, Reserve Bank of India
C. Chief Economic Advisor to the Government of India
D. Professor of Economics at Harvard University

73. Who among the following personalities is NOT a Governor of any Indian State?

A. Najma Heptulla B. Ram Nath Kovind
C. Acharya Dev Vrat D. Arvind Subramaniam

74. Which of the following cricket teams was defeated by India to lift the Women's Twenty 20 Asia Cup 2016?

A. Bangladesh B. Sri Lanka
C. Pakistan D. Afghanistan

75. Which one of the following was the venue of 2nd BRICS Youth Summit of the Ministers, Officials and Youth Delegations?

A. New Delhi B. Mumbai
C. Shillong D. Guwahati

76. Which one among the following States of India has recently proposed to frame the first Internal Security Act to deal with the challenges of terrorism, insurgency, communalism and caste violence?

A. Maharashtra B. Gujarat
C. Uttar Pradesh D. Chhattisgarh

77. The World Humanitarian Day is being observed every year on which date?

A. 24 October B. 19 August
C. 10 December D. 8 March

78. Surge pricing takes place when a service provider

A. raises the price of its product or service as demand outstrips supply
B. follows preset prices immune to demand and supply dynamics
C. fixes a minimum price for its services
D. fixes an average price on the basis of transactions carried over a day

79. By fulfilling which of the following conditions can a political party claim the status of a national party?

1. It secures at least six per cent (6%) of the valid votes polled in any four or more states, at a general election to the House of the People or, to the State Legislative Assembly
2. It wins at least four seats in the House of the People from any State or States or wins at least two per cent (2%) seats in the House of the People (*i.e.*, 11 seats in the existing House having 543 members), and these members are elected from at least three different States
3. The party in question has got recognition as a state party in at least two states
4. It must have its headquarters in New Delhi

Select the correct answer using the code given below :

A. 1, 2 and 3 B. 2 and 4
C. 1 and 2 only D. 1, 3 and 4

80. In its emphasis on enhancing human capabilities, which one among the following does NOT figure in the Twelfth Five-Year Plan?

A. Life and longevity
B. Education
C. Delivery of Public Service
D. Skill development

81. Which one of the following is NOT a target of the 12th Five-Year Plan?

A. Real GDP Growth Rate of 8 per cent
B. Agriculture Growth Rate of 5 per cent
C. Manufacturing Growth Rate of 10 per cent
D. Increase in green cover by 1 million hectare every year during the Plan period

82. Which one of the following statements is NOT correct?

A. In the conduction mode of transference of heat, the molecules of solid pass heat from one molecule to another without moving from their positions
B. The amount of heat required to raise the temperature of a substance is called its specific heat capacity
C. The process of heat transfer in liquids and gases is through convection mode
D. The process of heat transfer from a body at higher temperature to a body at lower temperature without heating the space between them is known as radiation

83. The amount of heat required to change a liquid to gaseous state without any change in temperature is known as
A. specific heat capacity
B. mechanical equivalent of heat
C. latent heat of vaporization
D. quenching

84. The following figure shows displacement versus time curve for a particle executing simple harmonic motion :

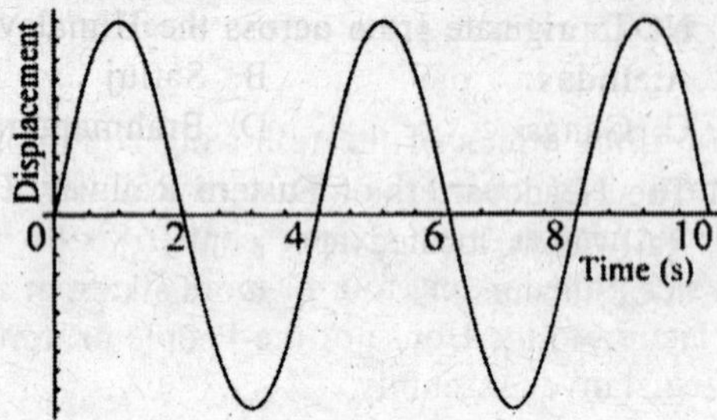

Which one of the following statements is correct?
A. Phase of the oscillating particle is same at $t = 1s$ and $t = 3s$
B. Phase of the oscillating particle is same at $t = 2s$ and $t = 8s$
C. Phase of the oscillating particle is same at $t = 3s$ and $t = 7s$
D. Phase of the oscillating particle is same at $t = 4s$ and $t = 10s$

85. Match List-I with List-II and select the correct answer using the codes given below the Lists:

List-I (Disease)	**List-II (Remedy)**
(*a*) Hypermetropia	1. Concave lens
(*b*) Presbyopia	2. Bifocal lens
(*c*) Myopia	3. Surgery
(*d*) Cataract	4. Convex lens

Codes:

	(*a*)	(*b*)	(*c*)	(*d*)
A.	4	2	1	3
B.	4	1	2	3
C.	3	1	2	4
D.	3	2	1	4

86. A circular coil of single turn has a resistance of 20 Ω. Which one of the following is the correct value for the resistance between the ends of any diameter of the coil?
A. 5 Ω B. 10 Ω
C. 20 Ω D. 40 Ω

87. In a solenoid, the current flowing through the wire is I and number of turns per unit length is n. This gives a magnetic field B inside the solenoid. If numbers of turn per unit length is increased to $2n$, what will be the value of magnetic field in the solenoid?
A. B B. $2B$
C. $B/2$ D. $B/4$

88. Which one of the following statements is correct about the magnification of an optical microscope?
A. Magnification increases with the increase in focal length of eyepiece
B. Magnification increases with the increase in focal length of objective
C. Magnification does not depend upon the focal length of eyepiece
D. Magnification decreases with the increase in focal length of eyepiece

89. A homogeneous mixture contains two liquids. How are they separated?
A. By filtration B. By evaporation
C. By distillation D. By condensation

90. Which one of the following elements forms highest number of compounds?
A. Oxygen B. Hydrogen
C. Chlorine D. Carbon

91. Which one of the following elements corrodes rapidly?
A. Aluminium B. Iron
C. Zinc D. Silver

92. 20 g of common salt is dissolved in 180 g of water. What is the mass percentage of the salt in the solution?
A. 5% B. 9%
C. 10% D. 15%

93. The valency of an element depends upon the
A. total number of protons in an atom
B. mass number of an atom
C. total number of neutrons in an atom
D. total number of electrons in the outer most shell of an atom

94. Match List-I with List-II and select the correct answer using the codes given below the Lists :

List-I (Noble gas)	**List-II (Use)**
(*a*) Argon	1. In lights for advertising display
(*b*) Neon	2. Airport landing lights and in light houses
(*c*) Krypton	3. Light in photographer's flash gun
(*d*) Xenon	4. In tungsten filament to last longer

Codes:

	(*a*)	(*b*)	(*c*)	(*d*)
A.	3	1	2	4
B.	3	2	1	4
C.	4	2	1	3
D.	4	1	2	3

95. Colour vision in human eyes is the function of photoreceptor cells named
A. Rods B. Cones
C. Blind spot D. Fovea

96. Which one of the following statements is NOT correct?
A. All proteins are enzymes
B. Mostly enzymes are proteins
C. All fats are energy rich compounds
D. Glucose is a common carbohydrate

97. Sugarcane is one of the important cash crops in India. It is grown to obtain
A. Starch B. Glucose
C. Fructose D. Sucrose

98. The colourful part of the Sunflower or Marigold plant is
A. Flower B. Inflorescence
C. Fruit D. Seed

99. Match List-I with List-II and select the correct answer using the codes given below the Lists:

List-I (Mineral)	List-II (Leading State)
(*a*) Manganese	1. Uttarakhand
(*b*) Gypsum	2. Karnataka
(*c*) Limestone	3. Rajasthan
(*d*) Magnesite	4. Odisha

Codes:

	(*a*)	(*b*)	(*c*)	(*d*)
A.	1	3	2	4
B.	1	2	3	4
C.	4	2	3	1
D.	4	3	2	1

100. Which one among the following is the correct order of tiger reserves situated from North to South in India?
A. Corbett - Simlipal - Sariska - Periyar
B. Periyar - Sariska - Simlipal - Corbett
C. Corbett - Sariska - Simlipal - Periyar
D. Periyar - Simlipal - Sariska - Corbett

101. Which of the following are correct with regard to Indian Monsoonal Rainfall?
1. Largely governed by the topographical features
2. Regional and seasonal variation in the distribution of rainfall
3. Heavy downpour resulting in considerable runoff
4. Beginning and end of rain is regular and on time

Select the correct answer using the codes given below:
A. 1 and 2 only B. 1, 2 and 3
C. 3 and 4 only D. 2, 3 and 4

102. Match List-I with List-II and select the correct answer using the codes given below the Lists :

List-I (Type of Climate)	List-II (State)
(*a*) Monsoon with Short Dry Season (Amw)	1. Uttar Pradesh and Bihar
(*b*) Cold Humid Winter with Short Summer (Dfc)	2. Tamil Nadu Coast
(*c*) Monsoon with Dry Winter (Cwg)	3. Arunachal Pradesh
D. Monsoon with Dry Summer (As)	4. Kerala and Karnataka Coast

Codes:

	(*a*)	(*b*)	(*c*)	(*d*)
A.	4	3	1	2
B.	4	1	3	2
C.	2	1	3	4
D.	2	3	1	4

103. Which one of the following Himalayan rivers does NOT originate from across the Himalayas?
A. Indus B. Satluj
C. Ganga D. Brahmaputra

104. The Headquarters of Eastern Railway Zone of Indian Railway is located at
A. Bhubaneswar B. Kolkata
C. Hajipur D. Guwahati

105. Which one among the following countries is the largest trading partner of India in external trade for the year 2015-2016?
A. United States of America
B. United Kingdom
C. United Arab Emirates
D. China

106. The radii of curvature of the faces of a double convex lens are 10 cm and 20 cm. The refractive index of the glass is 1.5. What is the power of this lens (in units of dioptre)?
A. + 7.5 D B. − 7.5 D
C. + 2.5 D D. + 5.0 D

107. The time period of a simple pendulum made using a thin copper wire of length L is T. Suppose the temperature of the room in which this simple pendulum is placed increases by 30°C, what will be the effect on the time period of the pendulum?
A. T will increase slightly
B. T will remain the same
C. T will decrease slightly
D. T will become more than 2 times

108. Which one of the following physical quantity has the same unit as that of pressure?
A. Angular momentum B. Stress
C. Strain D. Work

109. Which one of the following statements is correct with regard to the material of electrical insulators?
A. They contain no electrons
B. Electrons do not flow easily through them
C. They are crystals
D. They have more number of electrons than the protons on their surface

110. Which one of the following physical quantities does NOT affect the resistance of a cylindrical resistor?
A. The current through it
B. Its length

C. The resistivity of the material used in the resistor
D. The area of cross-section of the cylinder

111. Which one of the following statements regarding King Krishnadevaraya is NOT correct?
A. He was a great scholar of Telugu and Sanskrit
B. Foreign travellers Paes and Nuniz visited his court
C. Barbosa praised him for the great justice and equity prevailing in his empire
D. He wrote his magnum opus Amuktamalyada in Sanskrit

112. Match List-I with List-II and select the correct answer using the codes given below the Lists:

List-I (Amendment to the Constitution of India)	**List-II (Subject)**
(*a*) 52nd Amendment Act, 1985	1. Reduction of voting age from 21 to 18
(*b*) 73rd Amendment Act, 1992	2. Right to Education
(*c*) 61st Amendment Act, 1988	3. Panchayati Raj
(*d*) 86th Amendment Act, 2006	4. Disqualification on grounds of defection

Codes:

	(*a*)	(*b*)	(*c*)	(*d*)
A.	4	1	3	2
B.	4	3	1	2
C.	2	3	1	4
D.	2	1	3	4

113. Which one of the following was NOT a cause of the Revolt of 1857?
A. The rumour that the British had mixed the bone dust of cows and pigs into the flour being sold in the market
B. The prophecy that British rule would come to an end on the centenary of the Battle of Plassey on 23rd June, 1857
C. Popular discontent with British rule
D. The prophecy that the end of British rule would lead to the end of the Kali Yuga and the return of Ram Rajya

114. Which one of the following was NOT a feature of the Subsidiary Alliance of Lord Wellesley?
A. The British were responsible for protecting the ally from any external threats
B. All internal threats were to be handled by the ally alone, with no help from the British
C. The ally was to provide resources for maintaining a British armed contingent stationed in its territory
D. The ally could not enter into any agreement with other rulers without the permission of the British

115. Match List-I with List-II and select the correct answer using the codes given below the Lists:

List-I (Place)	**List-II (Mineral)**
A. Lakwa	1. Copper
B. Malanjkhand	2. Petroleum
C. Kalakot	3. Zinc
D. Zawar	4. Coal

Codes:

	(*a*)	(*b*)	(*c*)	(*d*)
A.	3	4	1	2
B.	3	1	4	2
C.	2	1	4	3
D.	2	4	1	3

116. Which of the following are the major coral reef areas of India?
1. Gulf of Kachchh
2. Gulf of Mannar
3. Lakshadweep
4. Andaman and Nicobar Islands

Select the correct answer using the codes given below:
A. 1 and 3 only B. 2 and 4 only
C. 1, 2 and 3 only D. 1, 2, 3 and 4

117. Which of the following regions is/are NOT known for cotton-textile industry?
1. Mumbai - Pune region
2. Madurai - Coimbatore region
3. Dhanbad - Jamshedpur region
4. Indore - Ujjain region

Select the correct answer using the codes given below:
A. 1 and 3 B. 2 and 3
C. 1, 2 and 4 D. 3 only

118. Which one of the following States does NOT have the Headquarters of any Railway Zone?
A. Jharkhand B. Chhattisgarh
C. Odisha D. Bihar

119. Suppose a rod is given a negative charge by rubbing it with wool. Which one of the following statements is correct in this case?
A. The positive charges are transferred from rod to wool
B. The positive charges are transferred from wool to rod
C. The negative charges are transferred from rod to wool
D. The negative charges are transferred from wool to rod

120. Which one of the following is the correct relation between frequency f and angular frequency ω?
A. $f = \pi\omega$ B. $\omega = 2\pi f$
C. $f = 2\omega/\pi$ D. $f = 2\pi\omega$

121. A Kelvin thermometer and a Fahrenheit thermometer both give the same reading for a certain sample. What would be the corresponding reading in a Celsius thermometer?

A. 574 B. 301
C. 273 D. 232

122. If the potential difference applied to an X-ray tube is doubled while keeping the separation between the filament and the target as same, what will happen to the cutoff wavelength?
A. Will remain same
B. Will be doubled
C. Will be halved
D. Will be four times of the original wavelength

123. Which one of the following statements is true for the relation $F = \frac{Gm_1m_2}{r^2}$?
(All symbols have their usual meanings)
A. The quantity G depends on the local value of g, acceleration due to gravity
B. The quantity G is greatest at the surface of the Earth
C. The quantity G is used only when earth is one of the two masses
D. The quantity G is a universal constant

124. Why is it difficult to measure the coefficient of expansion of a liquid than solid?
A. Liquids tend to evaporate at all temperatures
B. Liquids conduct more heat
C. Liquids expand too much when heated
D. Their containers also expand when heated

125. Radon is
A. an inert gas B. an artificial fibre
C. an explosive D. a metal

126. The chemical name of baking soda is
A. Na_2CO_3 B. $NaHCO_3$
C. $CaCO_3$ D. NaOH

127. Which one of the following elements is used in pencil-lead?
A. Zinc B. Lead
C. Carbon (Graphite) D. Tin

128. Who among the following is one of the authors of the book "Philosophy of the Bomb?"
A. Bhagat Singh B. Jawaharlal Nehru
C. Surya Sen D. Yashpal

129. Which of the following statements about the Chittagong group is NOT correct?
A. Its membership included a large number of youth including Ganesh Ghosh, Lokenath Baul and Anant Singh
B. Its leader Surya Sen had been a lawyer in Dhaka before joining the group
C. Surya Sen and his group were closely associated with Congress work in Chittagong
D. This group had prepared an action plan to occupy the armouries in Chittagong

130. Which one of the following was a significant feature of the Quit India Movement?
A. Women did not play an important role in the movement
B. Nasik in Maharashtra was an important regional base during the movement
C. It was marked by anti-zamindar violence
D. It was marked by the emergence of parallel governments in different parts of India

131. Which one of the following characteristics does NOT describe the Khilafat movement?
A. Mahatma Gandhi sought to link it to the Non-Cooperation movement
B. It was not supported by the Congress
C. It demanded that the Turkish Sultan must retain control over Muslim sacred places in the erstwhile Ottoman empire
D. It was led by Muhammad Ali and Shaukat Ali

132. Which one of the following was NOT a feature of railways in colonial India?
A. The main purpose of the setting up of railways in India was to serve the interest of the empire
B. British capital investments were invited with 15% guaranteed interest to be paid if necessary from Indian revenues
C. The construction work disturbed ecology
D. The construction of the railways was planned, in such a way that it connected the internal markets with the ports, but provided no interconnection between internal market cities

133. Which colonial administrator made the following declaration about the partition of Bengal in 1904? "Bengal united is a power. Bengal divided will pull in different ways. That is perfectly true and one of the merits of the scheme"
A. Lord Curzon B. H. H. Risley
C. Lord Minto D. Sir Lancelot Hare

134. Who launched the Bardoli Satyagraha on 4th February, 1928?
A. Mahatma Gandhi B. Vallabhbhai Patel
C. Rajendra Prasad D. Kalyanji Mehta

135. Which one of the following Princely States did NOT support the Congress during the course of the Civil Disobedience Movement?
A. Bhavnagar B. Mysore
C. Junagadh D. Kathiawar

136. Which one of the following is a feature of thought and philosophy of the Kandukuri Viresalingam?
A. He believed that science and morality were unconnected to truth
B. He believed in universal education
C. He believed that language had no role in inculcating morality in students

D. He did not attempt to build a national consciousness on a cultural base

137. Name the calligrapher in Akbar's court who was honoured with the title "Zarrin Kalam" or Golden Pen.

A. Abul Fazl

B. Tansen

C. Muhammad Husayn

D. Muhammad Kasim

138. Which one of the following sections of the Golden Quadrilateral Highway in India is the longest in terms of route distance?

A. Delhi - Kolkata B. Kolkata - Chennai

C. Chennai - Mumbai D. Mumbai - Delhi

139. Match List-I with List-II and select the currect answer using the codes given below the Lists :

List-I (Classification of resources)	List-II (Example)
(*a*) Basic inexhaustible resource	1. Hydel power
(*b*) Conventional non-renewable resource	2. Coal
(*c*) Non-conventional renewable resource	3. Solar energy
(*d*) Non-conventional non-renewable resource	4. Natural gas

Codes:

	(*a*)	(*b*)	(*c*)	(*d*)
A.	3	2	1	4
B.	3	1	2	4
C.	4	1	2	3
D.	4	2	1	3

140. Match List-I with List-II and select the correct answer using the codes given below the Lists:

List-I (Mineral deposit)	List-II (State)
(*a*) Gypsum	1. Odisha
(*b*) Graphite	2. Gujarat
(*c*) Fluorspar	3. Arunachal Pradesh
(*c*) Nickel	4. Rajasthan

Codes:

	(*a*)	(*b*)	(*c*)	(*d*)
A.	1	3	2	4
B.	1	2	3	4
C.	4	3	2	1
D.	4	2	3	1

141. Which one of the following pairs of Tribe and State is NOT correctly matched?

A. Tharu : Madhya Pradesh

B. Adi : Arunachal Pradesh

C. Irula : Kerala

D. Shaharia : Rajasthan

142. If the absolute refractive indices of glass and water are 3/2 and 4/3 respectively, what will be the ratio of velocity of light in glass and water?

A. 3 : 4 B. 4 : 3

C. 8 : 7 D. 8 : 9

143. A positive charge $+q$ is placed at the centre of a hollow metallic sphere of inner radius a and outer radius b. The electric field at a distance r from the centre is denoted by E. In this regard, which one of the following statements is correct?

A. $E = 0$ for $a < r < b$

B. $E = 0$ for $r < a$

C. $E = q/4\pi\varepsilon_0 r$ for $a < r < b$

D. $E = q/4\pi\varepsilon_0 a$ for $r < a$

144. Consider the following Indian States :

1. Bihar – 8.60
2. Rajasthan – 5.66
3. Jammu and Kashmir – 1.04
4. Haryana – 2.09

Which one of the following is the correct ascending order of the above States on the basis of percentage of State's population to total population of India (based on census 2011)?

A. 3 - 4 - 1 - 2 B. 4 - 2 - 1 - 3

C. 3 - 4 - 2 - 1 D. 2 - 3 - 4 - 1

145. Who among the following was the author of *Badshah Nama*?

A. Abdul Hamid Lahori

B. Abul Fazl

C. Shah Jahan

D. Sadullah Khan

146. Which one of the following statements about Fatehpur Sikri is NOT correct?

A. It was located on the direct road to Ajmer

B. Akbar commissioned the building of a marble tomb for Sheikh Salim Chisti next to the Friday mosque at Fatehpur Sikri

C. The arched gateway or Bulund Darwaza was meant to remind visitors of the Mughal victory in Gujarat

D. In 1585, the capital of the Mughal emperor shifted from Fatehpur Sikri to Delhi

147. Which one of the following cities hosted the 3rd World Trauma Congress recently?

A. New Delhi B. Dacca

C. Singapore D. Bangkok

148. Which one of the following is NOT one of the objectives of Act East Policy?

A. To promote economic cooperation, cultural ties and develop strategic relationship with countries in the Asia-Pacific region

B. To promote peace and amity with the neighbouring countries of Asia

C. To place emphasis on India-ASEAN cooperation in India's domestic agenda

D. To provide enhanced connectivity to the North East of India

149. Arrange the following countries in ascending order on the basis of the total medals earned by them in Rio Olympic 2016:

1. United States
2. China
3. Great Britain
4. Russia

Select the correct answer using the codes given below :

A. 1, 2, 3, 4 B. 1, 3, 2, 4
C. 4, 3, 2, 1 D. 4, 3, 1, 2

150. Which one of the following is NOT an objective of the National Civil Aviation Policy 2016?

A. Establish an integrated eco-system which will lead to significant growth of civil aviation sector
B. To promote tourism, increase employment and lead to a balanced regional growth
C. Ensure safety, security and sustainability of all sectors through the use of technology
D. Enhance regional connectivity through fiscal support and infrastructure development

PAPER II : MATHEMATICS

1. Let S be the set of all persons living in Delhi. We say that x, y in S are related if they were born in Delhi on the same day. Which one of the following is correct?

A. The relation is an equivalent relation
B. The relation is not reflexive but it is symmetric and transitive
C. The relation is not symmetric but it is reflexive and transitive
D. The relation is not transitive but it is reflexive and symmetric

2. Let A = {1, 2, 3, 4, 5, 6, 7, 8, 9, 10}. Then the number of subsets of A containing two or three elements is

A. 45 B. 120
C. 165 D. 330

3. The value of $i^{2n} + i^{2n+1} + i^{2n+2} + i^{2n+3}$, where $i = \sqrt{-1}$, is

A. 0 B. 1
C. i D. $-i$

4. If the difference between the roots of the equation $x^2 + kx + 1 = 0$ is strictly less than $\sqrt{5}$, where $|k| \geq 2$, then k can be any element of the interval

A. $(-3, -2] \cup [2, 3)$ B. $(-3, 3)$
C. $[-3, -2] \cup [2, 3]$ D. None of the above

5. If the roots of the equation $x^2 + px + q = 0$ are in the same ratio as those of the equation $x^2 + lx + m = 0$, then which one of the following is correct?

A. $p^2m = l^2q$ B. $m^2p = l^2q$
C. $m^2p = q^2l$ D. $m^2p^2 = l^2q$

6. The value of $\left(\frac{-1+i\sqrt{3}}{2}\right)^n + \left(\frac{-1-i\sqrt{3}}{2}\right)^n$ where n is not a multiple of 3 and $i = \sqrt{-1}$, is

A. 1 B. -1
C. i D. $-i$

7. Three-digit numbers are formed from the digits 1, 2 and 3 in such a way that the digits are not repeated. What is the sum of such three-digit numbers?

A. 1233 B. 1322
C. 1323 D. 1332

8. What is the sum of the series 0.3 + 0.33 + 0.333 + ... n terms?

A. $\frac{1}{3}\left[n - \frac{1}{9}\left(1 - \frac{1}{10^n}\right)\right]$ B. $\frac{1}{3}\left[n - \frac{2}{9}\left(1 - \frac{1}{10^n}\right)\right]$

C. $\frac{1}{3}\left[n - \frac{1}{3}\left(1 - \frac{1}{10^n}\right)\right]$ D. $\frac{1}{3}\left[n - \frac{1}{9}\left(1 + \frac{1}{10^n}\right)\right]$

9. If 1, ω, ω^2 are the cube roots of unity, then $(1 + \omega)(1 + \omega^2)(1 + \omega^3)(1 + \omega + \omega^2)$ is equal to

A. -2 B. -1
C. 0 D. 2

10. If the sum of m terms of an AP is n and the sum of n terms is m, then the sum of $(m + n)$ terms is

A. mn B. $m + n$
C. $2(m + n)$ D. $-(m + n)$

11. The modulus and principal argument of the complex number $\frac{1+2i}{1-(1-i)^2}$ are respectively

A. 1, 0 B. 1, 1
C. 2, 0 D. 2, 1

12. If the graph of a quadratic polynomial lies entirely above x-axis, then which one of the following is correct?

A. Both the roots are real
B. One root is real and the other is complex
C. Both the roots are complex
D. Cannot say

13. If $|z + 4| \leq 3$, then the maximum value of $|z + 1|$ is

A. 0 B. 4
C. 6 D. 10

14. The number of roots of the equation $z^2 = 2\bar{z}$ is

A. 2 B. 3
C. 4 D. zero

15. If $\cot \alpha$ and $\cot \beta$ are the roots of the equation $x^2 + bx + c = 0$ with $b \neq 0$, then the value of $\cot(\alpha + \beta)$ is

A. $\frac{c-1}{b}$ B. $\frac{1-c}{b}$

C. $\frac{b}{c-1}$ D. $\frac{b}{1-c}$

16. The sum of the roots of the equation $x^2 + bx + c = 0$ (where b and c are non-zero) is equal to the sum of the reciprocals of their squares. Then $\frac{1}{c}, b, \frac{c}{b}$ are in

A. AP B. GP

C. HP D. None of the above

17. The sum of the roots of the equation $ax^2 + x + c = 0$ (where a and c are non-zero) is equal to the sum of the reciprocals of their squares. Then a, ca^2, c^2 are in

A. AP B. GP

C. HP D. None of the above

18. The value of [C(7, 0) + C(7, 1)] + [C(7, 1) + C(7, 2)] + ... + [C(7, 6) + C(7, 7)] is

A. 254 B. 255

C. 256 D. 257

19. The number of different words (eight-letter words) ending and beginning with a consonant which can be made out of the letters of the word 'EQUATION' is

A. 5200 B. 4320

C. 3000 D. 2160

20. The fifth term of an AP of n terms, whose sum is $n^2 - 2n$, is

A. 5 B. 7

C. 8 D. 15

21. The sum of all the two-digit odd numbers is

A. 2475 B. 2530

C. 4905 D. 5049

22. The sum of the first n terms of the series

$$\frac{1}{2}+\frac{3}{4}+\frac{7}{8}+\frac{15}{16}+...$$

is equal to

A. $2^n - n - 1$ B. $1 - 2^{-n}$

C. $2^{-n} + n - 1$ D. $2^n - 1$

23. Consider the following in respect of sets A and B:

1. $(A - B) \cup B = A$
2. $(A - B) \cup A = A$
3. $(A - B) \cap B = \phi$
4. $A \subseteq B \Rightarrow A \cup B = B$

Which of the above are correct?

A. 1, 2 and 3 B. 2, 3 and 4

C. 1, 3 and 4 D. 1, 2 and 4

24. In the binary equation

$(1p101)_2 + (10q1)_2 = (100r\,00)_2$

where p, q and r are binary digits, what are the possible values of p, q and r respectively?

A. 0, 1, 0 B. 1, 1, 0

C. 0, 0, 1 D. 1, 0, 1

25. If S = $\{x : x^2 + 1 = 0, x \text{ is real}\}$, then S is

A. {–1} B. {0}

C. {1} D. an empty set

26. The expansion of $(x - y)^n$, $n \geq 5$ is done in the descending powers of x. If the sum of the fifth and sixth terms is zero, then $\frac{x}{y}$ is equal to

A. $\frac{n-5}{6}$ B. $\frac{n-4}{5}$

C. $\frac{5}{n-4}$ D. $\frac{6}{n-5}$

27. If $A = \begin{bmatrix} \alpha & 2 \\ 2 & \alpha \end{bmatrix}$ and det $(A^3) = 125$, then α is equal to

A. ± 1 B. ± 2

C. ± 3 D. ± 5

28. If B is a non-singular matrix and A is a square matrix, then the value of det $(B^{-1}AB)$ is equal to

A. det (B) B. det (A)

C. det (B^{-1}) D. det (A^{-1})

29. If $a \neq b \neq c$, then one value of x which satisfies the equation $\begin{vmatrix} 0 & x-a & x-b \\ x+a & 0 & x-c \\ x+b & x+c & 0 \end{vmatrix} = 0$ is given by

A. a B. b

C. c D. 0

30. If $A = \begin{bmatrix} \cos\alpha & \sin\alpha \\ -\sin\alpha & \cos\alpha \end{bmatrix}$ then what is AA^T equal to (where A^T is the transpose of A)?

A. Null matrix

B. Identity matrix

C. A

D. – A

31. The equations

$$x + 2y + 3z = 1$$
$$2x + y + 3z = 2$$
$$5x + 5y + 9z = 4$$

A. have the unique solution

B. have infinitely many solutions

C. are inconsistent

D. None of the above

32. $A = \begin{bmatrix} x+y & y \\ x & x-y \end{bmatrix}, B = \begin{bmatrix} 3 \\ -2 \end{bmatrix}$ and $C = \begin{bmatrix} 4 \\ -2 \end{bmatrix}$. If AB = C, then what is A^2 equal to?

A. $\begin{bmatrix} 4 & 8 \\ -4 & -16 \end{bmatrix}$ B. $\begin{bmatrix} 4 & -4 \\ 8 & -16 \end{bmatrix}$

C. $\begin{bmatrix} -4 & -8 \\ 4 & 12 \end{bmatrix}$ D. $\begin{bmatrix} -4 & -8 \\ 8 & 12 \end{bmatrix}$

33. What is the value of the determinant

$$\begin{vmatrix} 1 & 1 & 1 \\ 1 & 1+xyz & 1 \\ 1 & 1 & 1+xyz \end{vmatrix}?$$

A. $1 + x + y + z$ B. $2xyz$
C. $x^2y^2z^2$ D. $2x^2y^2z^2$

34. If $\begin{vmatrix} x & y & 0 \\ 0 & x & y \\ y & 0 & x \end{vmatrix} = 0$, then which one of the following is correct?

A. $\frac{x}{y}$ is one of the cube roots of unity
B. x is one of the cube roots of unity
C. y is one of the cube roots of unity
D. $\frac{x}{y}$ is one of the cube roots of -1

35. Consider the set A of all matrices of order 3 × 3 with entries 0 or 1 only. Let B be the subset of A consisting of all matrices whose determinant is 1. Let C be the subset of A consisting of all matrices whose determinant is –1. Then which one of the following is correct?
A. C is empty
B. B has as many elements as C
C. $A = B \cup C$
D. B has thrice as many elements as C

36. If $A = \begin{bmatrix} \cos\theta & \sin\theta \\ -\sin\theta & \cos\theta \end{bmatrix}$, then what is A^3 equal to?

A. $\begin{bmatrix} \cos 3\theta & \sin 3\theta \\ -\sin 3\theta & \cos 3\theta \end{bmatrix}$ B. $\begin{bmatrix} \cos^3\theta & \sin^3\theta \\ -\sin^3\theta & \cos^3\theta \end{bmatrix}$

C. $\begin{bmatrix} \cos 3\theta & -\sin 3\theta \\ \sin 3\theta & \cos 3\theta \end{bmatrix}$ D. $\begin{bmatrix} \cos^3\theta & -\sin^3\theta \\ \sin^3\theta & \cos^3\theta \end{bmatrix}$

37. What is the order of

$$[x\ y\ z]\begin{bmatrix} a & h & g \\ h & b & f \\ g & f & c \end{bmatrix}\begin{bmatrix} x \\ y \\ z \end{bmatrix}?$$

A. 3 × 1 B. 1 × 1
C. 1 × 3 D. 3 × 3

38. If $A = \begin{bmatrix} 0 & 1 \\ 1 & 0 \end{bmatrix}$, then the value of A^4 is

A. $\begin{bmatrix} 1 & 0 \\ 0 & 1 \end{bmatrix}$ B. $\begin{bmatrix} 1 & 1 \\ 0 & 0 \end{bmatrix}$

C. $\begin{bmatrix} 0 & 0 \\ 1 & 1 \end{bmatrix}$ D. $\begin{bmatrix} 0 & 1 \\ 1 & 0 \end{bmatrix}$

39. If $\sin A = \frac{3}{5}$, where $450° < A < 540°$, then $\cos\frac{A}{2}$ is equal to

A. $\frac{1}{\sqrt{10}}$ B. $-\sqrt{\frac{3}{10}}$
C. $\frac{\sqrt{3}}{\sqrt{10}}$ D. None of the above

40. What is $\frac{1}{\sin 10°} - \frac{\sqrt{3}}{\cos 10°}$ equal to?
A. 0 B. 1
C. 2 D. 4

41. From the top of a lighthouse, 100 m high, the angle of depression of a boat is $\tan^{-1}\left(\frac{5}{12}\right)$. What is the distance between the boat and the lighthouse?
A. 120 m B. 180 m
C. 240 m D. 360 m

42. The maximum value of

$$\sin\left(x+\frac{\pi}{6}\right)+\cos\left(x+\frac{\pi}{6}\right)$$

in the interval $\left(0, \frac{\pi}{2}\right)$ is attained at

A. $\frac{\pi}{12}$ B. $\frac{\pi}{6}$
C. $\frac{\pi}{3}$ D. $\frac{\pi}{2}$

43. If $K = \sin\left(\frac{\pi}{18}\right)\sin\left(\frac{5\pi}{18}\right)\sin\left(\frac{7\pi}{18}\right)$, then what is the value of K?

A. $\frac{1}{2}$ B. $\frac{1}{4}$
C. $\frac{1}{8}$ D. $\frac{1}{16}$

44. The expression $\frac{\sin\alpha+\sin\beta}{\cos\alpha+\cos\beta}$ is equal to

A. $\tan\left(\frac{\alpha+\beta}{2}\right)$ B. $\cot\left(\frac{\alpha+\beta}{2}\right)$
C. $\sin\left(\frac{\alpha+\beta}{2}\right)$ D. $\cos\left(\frac{\alpha+\beta}{2}\right)$

45. If $\sin\theta = 3\sin(\theta + 2\alpha)$, then the value of $\tan(\theta + \alpha) + 2\tan\alpha$ is equal to
A. – 1 B. 0
C. 1 D. 2

46. What is the value of tan 18°?

A. $\frac{\sqrt{5}-1}{\sqrt{10+2\sqrt{5}}}$ B. $\frac{\sqrt{5}-1}{\sqrt{10+\sqrt{5}}}$

C. $\frac{\sqrt{10+2\sqrt{5}}}{\sqrt{5}-1}$ D. $\frac{\sqrt{10+\sqrt{5}}}{\sqrt{5}-1}$

47. Let x, y, z be positive real numbers such that x, y, z are in GP and $\tan^{-1} x$, $\tan^{-1} y$ and $\tan^{-1} z$ are in AP. Then which one of the following is correct?

A. $x = y = z$ B. $xz = 1$

C. $x \neq y$ and $y = z$ D. $x = y$ and $y \neq z$

48. If $\tan(\alpha + \beta) = 2$ and $\tan(\alpha - \beta) = 1$, then $\tan(2\alpha)$ is equal to

A. -3 B. -2

C. $-\frac{1}{3}$ D. 1

49. Consider the following for triangle ABC:

1. $\sin\left(\frac{B+C}{2}\right) = \cos\left(\frac{A}{2}\right)$
2. $\tan\left(\frac{B+C}{2}\right) = \cot\left(\frac{A}{2}\right)$
3. $\sin(B + C) = \cos A$
4. $\tan(B + C) = -\cot A$

Which of the above are correct?

A. 1 and 3 B. 1 and 2

C. 1 and 4 D. 2 and 3

50. If $\sec\theta - \operatorname{cosec}\theta = \frac{4}{3}$, then what is $(\sin\theta - \cos\theta)$ equal to?

A. -2 only B. $\frac{1}{2}$ only

C. Both -2 and $\frac{1}{2}$ D. Neither $\frac{1}{2}$ nor -2

51. If a vertex of a triangle is (1, 1) and the midpoints of two sides of the triangle through this vertex are (–1, 2) and (3, 2), then the centroid of the triangle is

A. $\left(-\frac{1}{3}, \frac{7}{3}\right)$ B. $\left(-1, \frac{7}{3}\right)$

C. $\left(\frac{1}{3}, \frac{7}{3}\right)$ D. $\left(1, \frac{7}{3}\right)$

52. The incentre of the triangle with vertices $A(1, \sqrt{3})$, $B(0, 0)$ and $C(2, 0)$ is

A. $\left(1, \frac{\sqrt{3}}{2}\right)$ B. $\left(\frac{2}{3}, \frac{1}{\sqrt{3}}\right)$

C. $\left(\frac{2}{3}, \frac{\sqrt{3}}{2}\right)$ D. $\left(1, \frac{1}{\sqrt{3}}\right)$

53. If the three consecutive vertices of a parallelogram are (–2, –1), (1, 0) and (4, 3), then what are the coordinates of the fourth vertex?

A. (1, 2) B. (1, 0)

C. (0, 0) D. (1, –1)

54. The two circles $x^2 + y^2 = r^2$ and $x^2 + y^2 - 10x + 16 = 0$ intersect at two distinct points. Then which one of the following is correct?

A. $2 < r < 8$ B. $r = 2$ or $r = 8$

C. $r < 2$ D. $r > 2$

55. What is the equation of the circle which passes through the points (3, –2) and (–2, 0) and having its centre on the line $2x - y - 3 = 0$?

A. $x^2 + y^2 + 3x + 2 = 0$

B. $x^2 + y^2 + 3x + 12y + 2 = 0$

C. $x^2 + y^2 + 2x = 0$

D. $x^2 + y^2 = 5$

56. What is the ratio in which the point $C\left(-\frac{2}{7}, -\frac{20}{7}\right)$ divides the line joining the points A(–2, –2) and B(2, – 4)?

A. 1 : 3 B. 3 : 4

C. 1 : 2 D. 2 : 3

57. What is the equation of the ellipse having foci (±2, 0) and the eccentricity $\frac{1}{4}$?

A. $\frac{x^2}{64} + \frac{y^2}{60} = 1$ B. $\frac{x^2}{60} + \frac{y^2}{64} = 1$

C. $\frac{x^2}{20} + \frac{y^2}{24} = 1$ D. $\frac{x^2}{24} + \frac{y^2}{20} = 1$

58. What is the equation of the straight line parallel to $2x + 3y + 1 = 0$ and passes through the point (–1, 2)?

A. $2x + 3y - 4 = 0$ B. $2x + 3y - 5 = 0$

C. $x + y - 1 = 0$ D. $3x - 2y + 7 = 0$

59. What is the acute angle between the pair of straight lines $\sqrt{2}x + \sqrt{3}y = 1$ and $\sqrt{3}x + \sqrt{2}y = 2$?

A. $\tan^{-1}\left(\frac{1}{2\sqrt{6}}\right)$ B. $\tan^{-1}\left(\frac{1}{\sqrt{2}}\right)$

C. $\tan^{-1}(3)$ D. $\tan^{-1}\left(\frac{1}{\sqrt{3}}\right)$

60. If the centroid of a triangle formed by $(7, x)$, $(y, -6)$ and (9, 10) is (6, 3), then the values of x and y are respectively

A. 5, 2 B. 2, 5

C. 1, 0 D. 0, 0

61. A straight line with direction cosines $\langle 0, 1, 0 \rangle$ is

A. parallel to x-axis

B. parallel to y-axis

C. parallel to z-axis

D. equally inclined to all the axes

62. (0, 0, 0), $(a, 0, 0)$ $(0, b, 0)$ and $(0, 0, c)$ are four distinct points. What are the coordinates of the point which is equidistant from the four points?

A. $\left(\frac{a+b+c}{3}, \frac{a+b+c}{3}, \frac{a+b+c}{3}\right)$

B. (a, b, c)

C. $\left(\frac{a}{2}, \frac{b}{2}, \frac{c}{2}\right)$

D. $\left(\frac{a}{3}, \frac{b}{3}, \frac{c}{3}\right)$

63. The points P(3, 2, 4), Q(4, 5, 2), R(5, 8, 0) and S(2, –1, 6) are

A. vertices of a rhombus which is not a square
B. non-coplanar
C. collinear
D. coplanar but not collinear

64. The line passing through the points (1, 2, –1) and (3, –1, 2) meets the *yz*-plane at which one of the following points?

A. $\left(0, -\frac{7}{2}, \frac{5}{2}\right)$ B. $\left(0, \frac{7}{2}, \frac{1}{2}\right)$

C. $\left(0, -\frac{7}{2}, -\frac{5}{2}\right)$ D. $\left(0, \frac{7}{2}, -\frac{5}{2}\right)$

65. Under which one of the following conditions are the lines $x = ay + b$; $z = cy + d$ and $x = ey + f$; $z = gy + h$ perpendicular?

A. $ae + cg - 1 = 0$ B. $ae + bf - 1 = 0$
C. $ae + cg + 1 = 0$ D. $ag + ce + 1 = 0$

66. If $\vec{a} = \hat{i} - \hat{j} + \hat{k}$, $\vec{b} = 2\hat{i} + 3\hat{j} + 2\hat{k}$ and $\vec{c} = \hat{i} + m\hat{j} + n\hat{k}$ are three coplanar vectors and $|\vec{c}| = \sqrt{6}$, then which one of the following is correct?

A. $m = 2$ and $n = \pm 1$ B. $m = \pm 2$ and $n = -1$
C. $m = 2$ and $n = -1$ D. $m = \pm 2$ and $n = 1$

67. Let ABCD be a parallelogram whose diagonals intersect at P and let O be the origin. What is $\overrightarrow{OA} + \overrightarrow{OB} + \overrightarrow{OC} + \overrightarrow{OD}$ equal to?

A. $2\overrightarrow{OP}$ B. $4\overrightarrow{OP}$
C. $6\overrightarrow{OP}$ D. $8\overrightarrow{OP}$

68. ABCD is a quadrilateral whose diagonals are AC and BD. Which one of the following is correct?

A. $\overrightarrow{BA} + \overrightarrow{CD} = \overrightarrow{AC} + \overrightarrow{DB}$
B. $\overrightarrow{BA} + \overrightarrow{CD} = \overrightarrow{BD} + \overrightarrow{CA}$
C. $\overrightarrow{BA} + \overrightarrow{CD} = \overrightarrow{AC} + \overrightarrow{BD}$
D. $\overrightarrow{BA} + \overrightarrow{CD} = \overrightarrow{BC} + \overrightarrow{AD}$

69. If $\vec{a} \times \vec{b} = \vec{c}$ and $\vec{b} \times \vec{c} = \vec{a}$, then which one of the following is correct?

A. $\vec{a}, \vec{b}, \vec{c}$ are orthogonal in pairs and $|\vec{a}| = |\vec{c}|$ and $|\vec{b}| = 1$
B. $\vec{a}, \vec{b}, \vec{c}$ are non-orthogonal to each other
C. $\vec{a}, \vec{b}, \vec{c}$ are orthogonal in pairs but $|\vec{a}| \neq |\vec{c}|$
D. $\vec{a}, \vec{b}, \vec{c}$ are orthogonal in pairs but $|\vec{b}| \neq 1$

70. If $\vec{a} = 2\hat{i} + 3\hat{j} + 4\hat{k}$ and $\vec{b} = 3\hat{i} + 2\hat{j} - \lambda\hat{k}$ are perpendicular, then what is the value of λ?

A. 2 B. 3
C. 4 D. 5

71. What is $\lim_{x \to 0} \frac{e^x - (1+x)}{x^2}$ equal to?

A. 0 B. $\frac{1}{2}$
C. 1 D. 2

72. What is $\int_0^{\frac{\pi}{2}} \frac{d\theta}{1+\cos\theta}$ equal to?

A. $\frac{1}{2}$ B. 1
C. $\sqrt{3}$ D. None of the above

73. What is $\int \frac{dx}{x(x^7+1)}$ equal to?

A. $\frac{1}{2}\ln\left|\frac{x^7-1}{x^7+1}\right| + c$ B. $\frac{1}{7}\ln\left|\frac{x^7+1}{x^7}\right| + c$

C. $\ln\left|\frac{x^7-1}{7x}\right| + c$ D. $\frac{1}{7}\ln\left|\frac{x^7}{x^7+1}\right| + c$

74. The function $f: X \to Y$ defined by $f(x) = \cos x$, where $x \in X$, is one-one and onto if X and Y are respectively equal to:

A. $[0, \pi]$ and $[-1, 1]$ B. $\left[-\frac{\pi}{2}, \frac{\pi}{2}\right]$ and $[-1, 1]$
C. $[0, \pi]$ and $(-1, 1)$ D. $[0, \pi]$ and $[0, 1]$

75. If $f(x) = \frac{x}{x-1}$, then what is $\frac{f(a)}{f(a+1)}$ equal to?

A. $f\left(-\frac{a}{a+1}\right)$ B. $f(a^2)$

C. $f\left(\frac{1}{a}\right)$ D. $f(-a)$

76. What is $\int \frac{(x^{e-1} + e^{x-1})dx}{x^e + e^x}$ equal to?

A. $\frac{x^2}{2} + c$ B. $\ln(x + e) + c$

C. $\ln(x^e + e^x) + c$ D. $\frac{1}{e}\ln(x^e + e^x) + c$

77. Let $f : [-6, 6] \rightarrow \mathbb{R}$ be defined by $f(x) = x^2 - 3$. Consider the following:

1. $(f \circ f \circ f)(-1) = (f \circ f \circ f)(1)$
2. $(f \circ f \circ f)(-1) - 4(f \circ f \circ f)(1) = (f \circ f)(0)$

Which of the above is/are correct?

A. 1 only B. 2 only
C. Both 1 and 2 D. Neither 1 nor 2

78. Let $f(x) = px + q$ and $g(x) = mx + n$. Then $f(g(x)) = g(f(x))$ is equivalent to

A. $f(p) = g(m)$ B. $f(q) = g(n)$
C. $f(n) = g(q)$ D. $f(m) = g(p)$

79. If $F(x) = \sqrt{9 - x^2}$, then what is

$$\lim_{x \to 1} \frac{F(x) - F(1)}{x - 1}$$

equal to?

A. $-\frac{1}{4\sqrt{2}}$ B. $\frac{1}{8}$
C. $-\frac{1}{2\sqrt{2}}$ D. $\frac{1}{2\sqrt{2}}$

80. What is $\frac{d^2x}{dy^2}$ equal to?

A. $-\left(\frac{d^2y}{dx^2}\right)^{-1}\left(\frac{dy}{dx}\right)^{-3}$ B. $\left(\frac{d^2y}{dx^2}\right)^{-1}\left(\frac{dy}{dx}\right)^{-2}$
C. $-\left(\frac{d^2y}{dx^2}\right)\left(\frac{dy}{dx}\right)^{-3}$ D. $\left(\frac{d^2y}{dx^2}\right)^{-1}$

81. Let $f(x) : \begin{cases} x, & x \text{ is rational} \\ 0, & x \text{ is irrational} \end{cases}$

and $g(x) : \begin{cases} 0, & x \text{ is rational} \\ x, & x \text{ is irrational} \end{cases}$

If $f : \mathbb{R} \rightarrow \mathbb{R}$ and $g: \mathbb{R} \rightarrow \mathbb{R}$, then $(f - g)$ is

A. one-one and into B. neither one-one nor onto
C. many-one and onto D. one-one and onto

82. What is the length of the longest interval in which the function $f(x) = 3\sin x - 4\sin^3 x$ is increasing?

A. $\frac{\pi}{3}$ B. $\frac{\pi}{2}$
C. $\frac{3\pi}{2}$ D. π

83. If $x\,dy = y(dx + y dy)$; $y(1) = 1$ and $y(x) > 0$, then what is $y(-3)$ equal to?

A. 3 B. 2
C. 1 D. 0

84. What is the maximum value of the function $f(x) = 4\sin^2 x + 1$?

A. 5 B. 3
C. 2 D. 1

85. Let $f(x)$ be an indefinite integral of $\sin^2 x$.
Consider the following statements:

Statement 1:
The function $f(x)$ satisfies $f(x + \pi) = f(x)$ for all real x.

Statement 2:
$\sin^2(x + \pi) = \sin^2 x$ for all real x.

Which one of the following is correct in respect of the above statements?

A. Both the statements are true and Statement 2 is the correct explanation of Statement 1
B. Both the statements are true but Statement 2 is not the correct explanation of Statement 1
C. Statement 1 is true but Statement 2 is false
D. Statement 1 is false but Statement 2 is true

86. What are the degree and order respectively of the differential equation

$$y = x\left(\frac{dy}{dx}\right)^2 + \left(\frac{dx}{dy}\right)^2 ?$$

A. 1, 2 B. 2, 1
C. 1, 4 D. 4, 1

87. What is the differential equation corresponding to $y^2 - 2ay + x^2 = a^2$ by eliminating a?

A. $(x^2 - 2y^2)p^2 - 4pxy - x^2 = 0$
B. $(x^2 - 2y^2)p^2 + 4pxy - x^2 = 0$
C. $(x^2 + 2y^2)p^2 - 4pxy - x^2 = 0$
D. $(x^2 + 2y^2)p^2 - 4pxy + x^2 = 0$

where $p = \frac{dy}{dx}$.

88. What is the general solution to the differential equation
$$ydx - (x + 2y^2)dy = 0?$$

A. $x = y^2 + cy$ B. $x = 2cy^2$
C. $x = 2y^2 + cy$ D. None of the above

89. Let $f(x + y) = f(x)f(y)$ for all x and y. Then what is $f'(5)$ equal to [where $f'(x)$ is the derivative of $f(x)$]?

A. $f(5)f'(0)$ B. $f(5) - f'(0)$
C. $f(5)f(0)$ D. $f(5) + f'(0)$

90. If $f(x)$ and $g(x)$ are continuous functions satisfying $f(x) = f(a - x)$ and $g(x) + g(a - x) = 2$, then what is $\int_0^a f(x)g(x)dx$ equal to?

A. $\int_0^a g(x)dx$ B. $\int_0^a f(x)dx$
C. $2\int_0^a f(x)dx$ D. 0

91. What is the solution of the differential equation

$$\ln\left(\frac{dy}{dx}\right) - a = 0?$$

A. $y = xe^a + c$ B. $x = ye^a + c$
C. $y = \ln x + c$ D. $x = \ln y + c$

92. Let $f(x)$ be defined as follows:

$$f(x) = \begin{cases} 2x+1, & -3 < x < -2 \\ x-1, & -2 \le x < 0 \\ x+2, & 0 \le x < 1 \end{cases}$$

Which one of the following statements is correct in respect of the above function?

A. It is discontinuous at $x = -2$ but continuous at every other point.
B. It is continuous only in the interval $(-3, -2)$.
C. It is discontinuous at $x = 0$ but continuous at every other point.
D. It is discontinuous at every point.

93. Consider the following statements:

1. If $\lim_{x \to a} f(x)$ and $\lim_{x \to a} g(x)$ both exist, then $\lim_{x \to a} \{f(x)g(x)\}$ exists.
2. If $\lim_{x \to a} \{f(x)g(x)\}$ exists, then both $\lim_{x \to a} f(x)$ and $\lim_{x \to a} g(x)$ must exist.

Which of the above statements is/are correct?

A. 1 only B. 2 only
C. Both 1 and 2 D. Neither 1 nor 2

94. Which one of the following functions is neither even nor odd?

A. $x^2 - 1$ B. $x + \frac{3}{x}$
C. $|x|$ D. $x^2(x - 3)$

95. What is the derivative of $\log_{10}(5x^2 + 3)$ with respect to x?

A. $\frac{x \log_{10} e}{5x^2 + 3}$ B. $\frac{2x \log_{10} e}{5x^2 + 3}$
C. $\frac{10x \log_{10} e}{5x^2 + 3}$ D. $\frac{10x \log_e 10}{5x^2 + 3}$

96. Let $f(a) = \frac{a-1}{a+1}$.

Consider the following:

1. $f(2a) = f(a) + 1$
2. $f\left(\frac{1}{a}\right) = -f(a)$

Which of the above is/are correct?

A. 1 only B. 2 only
C. Both 1 and 2 D. Neither 1 nor 2

97. What is the maximum area of a triangle that can be inscribed in a circle of radius a?

A. $\frac{3a^2}{4}$ B. $\frac{a^2}{2}$
C. $\frac{3\sqrt{3}a^2}{4}$ D. $\frac{\sqrt{3}a^2}{4}$

98. Let $f(x) = x + \frac{1}{x}$, where $x \in (0, 1)$. Then which one of the following is correct?

A. $f(x)$ fluctuates in the interval
B. $f(x)$ increases in the interval
C. $f(x)$ decreases in the interval
D. None of the above

99. Suppose the function $f(x) = x^n$, $n \neq 0$ is differentiable for all x. Then n can be any element of the interval

A. $(1, \infty)$ B. $(0, \infty)$
C. $\left(\frac{1}{2}, \infty\right)$ D. None of the above

100. What is $\int_{e^{-1}}^{e^2} \left|\frac{\ln x}{x}\right| dx$ equal to?

A. $\frac{3}{2}$ B. $\frac{5}{2}$
C. 3 D. 4

101. The variance of 20 observations is 5. If each observation is multiplied by 3, then what is the new variance of the resulting observations?

A. 5 B. 10
C. 15 D. 45

102. The mean of a group of 100 observations was found to be 20. Later it was found that four observations were incorrect, which were recorded as 21, 21, 18 and 20. What is the mean if the incorrect observations are omitted?

A. 18 B. 20
C. 21 D. 22

103. A committee of two persons is constituted from two men and two women. What is the probability that the committee will have only women?

A. $\frac{1}{6}$ B. $\frac{1}{3}$
C. $\frac{1}{2}$ D. $\frac{2}{3}$

104. A question is given to three students A, B and C whose chances of solving it are $\frac{1}{2}, \frac{1}{3}$ and $\frac{1}{4}$ respectively. What is the probability that the question will be solved?

A. $\frac{1}{24}$ B. $\frac{1}{4}$
C. $\frac{3}{4}$ D. $\frac{23}{24}$

105. The mean weight of 150 students in a certain class is 60 kg. The mean weight of boys in the class is 70 kg and that of girls is 55 kg. What is the number of boys in the class?

A. 50 B. 55
C. 60 D. 100

106. For two dependent events A and B, it is given that P(A) = 0.2 and P(B) = 0.5. If $A \subseteq B$, then the values of conditional probabilities P(A|B) and P(B|A) are respectively

A. $\frac{2}{5}, \frac{3}{5}$

B. $\frac{2}{5}, 1$

C. $1, \frac{2}{5}$

D. Information is insufficient

107. A point is chosen at random inside a circle. What is the probability that the point is closer to the centre of the circle than to its boundary?

A. $\frac{1}{5}$ B. $\frac{1}{4}$

C. $\frac{1}{3}$ D. $\frac{1}{2}$

108. If two regression lines between height (x) and weight (y) are $4y - 15x + 410 = 0$ and $30x - 2y - 825 = 0$, then what will be the correlation coefficient between height and weight?

A. $\frac{1}{3}$ B. $\frac{1}{2}$

C. $\frac{2}{3}$ D. $\frac{3}{4}$

109. In an examination, 40% of candidates got second class. When the data are represented by a pie chart, what is the angle corresponding to second class?

A. 40° B. 90°
C. 144° D. 320°

110. Consider the following statements:

Statement 1:

Range is not a good measure of dispersion.

Statement 2:

Range is highly affected by the existence of extreme values.

Which one of the following is correct in respect of the above statements?

A. Both Statement 1 and Statement 2 are correct and Statement 2 is the correct explanation of Statement 1

B. Both Statement 1 and Statement 2 are correct but Statement 2 is not the correct explanation of Statement 1

C. Statement 1 is correct but Statement 2 is not correct

D. Statement 2 is correct but Statement 1 is not correct

111. A card is drawn from a well-shuffled ordinary deck of 52 cards. What is the probability that it is an ace?

A. $\frac{1}{13}$ B. $\frac{2}{13}$

C. $\frac{3}{13}$ D. $\frac{1}{52}$

112. If the data are moderately non-symmetrical, then which one of the following empirical relationships is correct?

A. 2 × Standard deviation = 5 × Mean deviation
B. 5 × Standard deviation = 2 × Mean deviation
C. 4 × Standard deviation = 5 × Mean deviation
D. 5 × Standard deviation = 4 × Mean deviation

113. Data can be represented in which of the following forms?

1. Textual form
2. Tabular form
3. Graphical form

Select the correct answer using the codes given below.

A. 1 and 2 only B. 2 and 3 only
C. 1 and 3 only D. 1, 2 and 3

114. For given statistical data, the graphs for less than ogive and more than ogive are drawn. If the point at which the two curves intersect is P, then abscissa of point P gives the value of which one of the following measures of central tendency?

A. Median B. Mean
C. Mode D. Geometric mean

115. Consider the following statements:

1. Two events are mutually exclusive if the occurrence of one event prevents the occurrence of the other.
2. The probability of the union of two mutually exclusive events is the sum of their individual probabilities.

Which of the above statements is/are correct?

A. 1 only B. 2 only
C. Both 1 and 2 D. Neither 1 nor 2

116. If the regression coefficient of x on y and y on x are $-\frac{1}{2}$ and $-\frac{1}{8}$ respectively, then what is the correlation coefficient between x and y?

A. $-\frac{1}{4}$ B. $-\frac{1}{16}$

C. $\frac{1}{16}$ D. $\frac{1}{4}$

117. A sample of 5 observations has mean 32 and median 33. Later it is found that an observation was recorded incorrectly as 40 instead of 35. If we correct the data, then which one of the following is correct?

A. The mean and the median remain the same

B. The median remains the same but the mean will decrease

C. Both the mean and the median will decrease

D. The mean remains the same but the median will decrease

118. If two fair dice are thrown, then what is the probability that the sum is neither 8 nor 9?

A. $\frac{1}{6}$ B. $\frac{1}{4}$

C. $\frac{3}{4}$ D. $\frac{5}{6}$

119. Let A and B be two mutually exclusive events with $P(A) = \frac{1}{3}$ and $P(B) = \frac{1}{4}$. What is the value of $P(\bar{A} \cap \bar{B})$?

A. $\frac{1}{6}$ B. $\frac{1}{4}$

C. $\frac{1}{3}$ D. $\frac{5}{12}$

120. The mean and the standard deviation of a binomial distributions are 12 and 2 respectively. What is the number of trials?

A. 2 B. 12

C. 18 D. 24

ANSWERS

PAPER-I : GENERAL ABILITY TEST

1	**2**	**3**	**4**	**5**	**6**	**7**	**8**	**9**	**10**
C	A	D	C	B	C	C	C	C	D
11	**12**	**13**	**14**	**15**	**16**	**17**	**18**	**19**	**20**
A	B	A	B	C	C	B	B	B	D
21	**22**	**23**	**24**	**25**	**26**	**27**	**28**	**29**	**30**
A	B	B	B	B	A	C	C	C	C
31	**32**	**33**	**34**	**35**	**36**	**37**	**38**	**39**	**40**
B	C	B	B	B	C	B	C	C	B
41	**42**	**43**	**44**	**45**	**46**	**47**	**48**	**49**	**50**
A	C	A	B	C	B	B	D	B	C
51	**52**	**53**	**54**	**55**	**56**	**57**	**58**	**59**	**60**
C	D	B	A	A	D	C	B	A	C
61	**62**	**63**	**64**	**65**	**66**	**67**	**68**	**69**	**70**
C	B	B	C	B	A	A	*	B	A
71	**72**	**73**	**74**	**75**	**76**	**77**	**78**	**79**	**80**
D	B	D	C	D	A	B	A	C	C
81	**82**	**83**	**84**	**85**	**86**	**87**	**88**	**89**	**90**
B	B	C	C	A	A	B	D	C	D
91	**92**	**93**	**94**	**95**	**96**	**97**	**98**	**99**	**100**
B	C	D	A	B	A	D	B	D	C
101	**102**	**103**	**104**	**105**	**106**	**107**	**108**	**109**	**110**
B	A	C	B	D	A	A	B	B	A
111	**112**	**113**	**114**	**115**	**116**	**117**	**118**	**119**	**120**
D	B	A	B	C	B	D	A	D	B
121	**122**	**123**	**124**	**125**	**126**	**127**	**128**	**129**	**130**
B	C	D	D	A	B	C	*	C	D
131	**132**	**133**	**134**	**135**	**136**	**137**	**138**	**139**	**140**
B	B	B	B	B	B	C	B	A	C
141	**142**	**143**	**144**	**145**	**146**	**147**	**148**	**149**	**150**
A	D	AC	A	A	A	A	D	C	A

PAPER-II : MATHEMATICS

1	**2**	**3**	**4**	**5**	**6**	**7**	**8**	**9**	**10**
A	C	A	A	A	B	D	A	C	D
11	**12**	**13**	**14**	**15**	**16**	**17**	**18**	**19**	**20**
A	C	C	A	B	C	A	A	B	B

21	22	23	24	25	26	27	28	29	30
A	C	B	A	D	B	C	B	D	B
31	32	33	34	35	36	37	38	39	40
A	D	C	D	C	A	B	A	D	D
41	42	43	44	45	46	47	48	49	50
C	A	C	A	B	A	A	A	B	C
51	52	53	54	55	56	57	58	59	60
D	D	A	A	A	B	A	A	A	B
61	62	63	64	65	66	67	68	69	70
B	C	C	D	C	D	B	B	A	B
71	72	73	74	75	76	77	78	79	80
B	B	D	B	B	D	C	C	C	C
81	82	83	84	85	86	87	88	89	90
D	B	A	A	A	D	B	C	A	B
91	92	93	94	95	96	97	98	99	100
A	C	D	B	C	B	D	C	A	A
101	102	103	104	105	106	107	108	109	110
D	B	A	C	A	B	B	B	C	A
111	112	113	114	115	116	117	118	119	120
A	C	B	A	C	A	B	C	D	C

EXPLANATORY ANSWERS

PAPER-I : GENERAL ABILITY TEST

51. Transformer: A transformer is an electrical device which converts large alternating current (a.c.) into small alternating current (a.c.) at high voltage (a.c.) and vice-versa. The transformers which convert low voltage into higher ones are called the step up transformers, while those which convert high voltage into lower ones are called step down transformers.

52. When any light ray enters from optically denser medium to optically rarer medium then due to refraction, light ray bends away from the normal. But as well as the values of angles of incidence are increased, the light bending away from the normal becomes more and more away. Thus value of angle of refraction is in increasing order. But for a definite angle of incidence the angle of refraction becomes 90° and here the angle of incidence is called critical angle.

Thus; index of refraction (μ) = $\frac{1}{\sin C}$

Thereby, $\sin C = \frac{1}{\mu}$, where C = critical angle

53. The positions of the magnetic poles can be defined in at least two ways: locally or globally. One way to define a pole is as a point where the magnetic field is vertical. This can be determined by measuring the inclination, as described above. The inclination of the Earth's field is 90° (downwards) at the North Magnetic Pole and –90° (upwards) at the South Magnetic Pole. The two poles wander independently of each other and are not directly opposite each other on the globe. The *magnetic equator* is the line where the inclination is zero (the magnetic field is horizontal).

The global definition of the Earth's field is based on a mathematical model. If a line is drawn through the centre of the Earth, parallel to the moment of the best-fitting magnetic dipole, the two positions where it intersects the Earth's surface are called the North and South geomagnetic poles. If the Earth's magnetic field were perfectly dipolar, the geomagnetic poles and magnetic dip poles would coincide and compasses would point towards them. However, the Earth's field has a significant non-dipolar contribution, so the poles do not coincide and compasses do not generally point at either.

55. Supersonic travel is a rate of travel of an object that exceeds the speed of sound (Mach 1). For objects travelling in dry air of a temperature of 20°C at sea level, this speed is approximately 343 m/s, 1,125 ft/s, 768 mph, 667 knots, or 1,235 km/h. Speeds greater than five times the speed of sound (Mach 5) are often referred to as hypersonic. Flights during which only some parts of the air surrounding an object, such as the ends of rotor blades, reach supersonic speeds are called transonic. This occurs typically somewhere between Mach 0.8 and Mach 1.23.

56. Buckminsterfullerene (or bucky-ball) is a spherical fullerene molecule with the formula C_{60}. It has a cage-like fused-ring structure (truncated icosahedron) which resembles a soccer ball (football), made of twenty hexagons and twelve pentagons, with a carbon atom at each vertex of each polygon and a bond along each polygon edge.

57. There are two types of water hardness: temporary and permanent hardness. Temporary hardness is due to the presence of calcium hydrogencarbonate $Ca(HCO_3)_{2(aq)}$ and magnesium hydrogencarbonate $Mg(HCO_3)_{2(aq)}$.

Both calcium hydrogencarbonate and magnesium hydrogencarbonate decompose when heated. The original insoluble carbonate is reformed. This happens when water is boiled.

60. Rutherford's Atomic Model: Rutherford in 1911 conducted an experiment to detect the inner composition or configuration of an atom and it is called Rutherford's α-particles scattering experiment. He rejected the conclusions and facts detected by Dalton regarding the atomic theory and propounded a comprehensive theory which is called Rutherford atomic model.

This model has following conclusions:

(*i*) In an atom there is a central massive part and it is called nucleus which is surrounded by the electrons and in this nucleus proton and neutron are packed together.

(*ii*) The atom is spherical and most of its part is empty.

(*iii*) The size of the nucleus is very small with comparison to the entire atom.

(*iv*) Rutherford predicted empirically that the electrons rotate in the various orbits around the nucleus while the electron and proton of the nucleus has a coulomb force of attraction which is equal to the centripetal force to remain the electron orbiting in the circular orbits.

61. Glass: Firstly the glass was manufactured in Egypt. Basically glass is the homogeneous mixture of the silicates of various alkalined metals of non-crystallined and transparent or less transparent substances. Ordinary glass is manufactured by the composition of various substances like silica, bleaching powder, oxides of alkaline metals, calcium oxide (lime), etc. These constituents of the glass are transformed into fine micro powder and after fusing these are melted into the furnaces at moderate temperature and ordinary glass is prepared by a suitable cooling mechanism of the molten or liquid glass. Thus ordinary glass is a non-crystallined substance of ultra cooled liquid glass.

62. Chitin $(C_8H_{13}O_5N)n$ is a long-chain polymer of an N-acetylglucosamine, a derivative of glucose, and is found in many places throughout the natural world. It is a characteristic component of the cell walls of fungi, the exoskeletons of arthropods such as crustaceans (*e.g.*, crabs, lobsters and shrimps) and insects, the radulae of molluscs, and the beaks and internal shells of cephalopods, including squid and octopuses and on the scales and other soft tissues of fish and amphibians. The structure of chitin is comparable to the polysaccharide cellulose, forming crystalline nanofibrils or whiskers. In terms of function, it may be compared to the protein keratin. Chitin has proved versatile for several medicinal, industrial and biotechnological purposes.

63. Trypanosoma is a genus of kinetoplastids, a monophyletic group of unicellular parasitic flagellate protozoa. The name is derived from the Greek *trypano* (borer) and *soma* (body) because of their corkscrew-like motion. Most trypanosomes are heteroxenous and most are transmitted via a vector. Some, such as *Trypanosoma equiperdum*, are spread by direct contact. The majority of species are transmitted by blood-feeding invertebrates, but there are different mechanisms among the varying species. In an invertebrate host they are generally found in the intestine, but normally occupy the bloodstream or an intracellular environment in the mammalian host. Trypanosomes infect a variety of hosts and cause various diseases, including the fatal human diseases sleeping sickness, caused by *Trypanosoma brucei*, and Chagas disease, caused by *Trypanosoma cruzi*.

64. Food Safety and Standards Authority of India (FSSAI) is an autonomous body established under the Ministry of Health & Family Welfare, Government of India. The FSSAI has been established under the Food Safety and Standards Act, 2006 which is a consolidating statute related to food safety and regulation in India. FSSAI is responsible for protecting and promoting public health through the regulation and supervision of food safety.

65. Dengue fever is a mosquito-borne tropical disease caused by the dengue virus. Symptoms typically begin three to fourteen days after infection. This may include a high fever, headache, vomiting, muscle and joint pains, and a characteristic skin rash. Recovery generally takes two to seven days. In a small proportion of cases, the disease develops into the life-threatening dengue hemorrhagic fever, resulting in bleeding, low levels of blood platelets and blood plasma leakage, or into dengue shock syndrome, where dangerously low blood pressure occurs.

66. Renin, also known as an angiotensinogenase, is a protein and enzyme secreted by the kidneys that participates in the body's renin-angiotensin aldosterone system (RAAS)—also known as the renin-angiotensin-aldosterone axis—that mediates extracellular volume (i.e., that of the blood plasma, lymph and interstitial fluid), and arterial vasoconstriction. Thus, it regulates the body's mean arterial blood pressure.

67. Red Blood Cells (RBCs) or Erythrocytes are biconcave cells which don't have a nucleus. They are responsible for transporting oxygen from the lungs to tissues with the help of respiratory pigment haemoglobin, which is the main constituent of RBCs. In the embryonic stage RBC is produced in liver, spleen and lymph nodes (all the three). Up to 20 years of age, they are produced in bone marrow of long bones such as femur. After 20 years they are produced in the bone marrows of membranous bones. RBCs complete a circulation in the body in 20 seconds. Their life span is 100-120 days. Their main constituent haemoglobin is made of four polypeptide chains and four heme (iron) groups. The spleen is the main organ where old red blood cells are destroyed. During the destruction of red blood cells, the heme groups turn into bilirubin and this substance is then captured by the liver and later excreted to the bowels as a part of bile.

69. The World Meteorological Organization (WMO) is an intergovernmental organization with a membership of 191 Member States and Territories. It originated from the International Meteorological Organization (IMO), which was founded in 1873. Established by the ratification of the WMO Convention on 23 March 1950, WMO became the specialised agency of the United Nations for meteorology (weather and climate), operational hydrology and related geophysical sciences a year later. Its current Secretary-General is Petteri Taalas and the President of the World Meteorological Congress, its supreme body, is David Grimes. The Organization is headquartered in Geneva, Switzerland.

70. **The Bongaigaon Refinery & Petrochemicals Ltd.** (BRPL) is a petroleum refinery company in India. It was incorporated on February 20, 1974 by the government of India.

HAL was established as Hindustan Aircraft in Bangalore on 23 Dec 1940. Hindustan Aircraft Company was duly incorporated under the Mysore Companies Act as a private Ltd Company. Walchand-Tulsidas-Khatau Ltd was the Managing agency.

HMT Limited, formerly Hindustan Machine Tools Limited, is a state-owned manufacturing company under the Ministry of Heavy Industries and Public Enterprises in India. Six manufacturing units situated at Bangalore (Mother unit), Kochi, Hyderabad (2 units), Pinjore and Ajmer to back up sales and services. HMT Machine Tool marketing is spread across India serving Defence, Government, Private Manufacturing Industries and Educational Institutions.

Coimbatore is a city in southern India, a major commercial and business hub in the state of Tamil Nadu. It is the highest revenue yielding district in the state even ahead of Chennai, thus making it one of the fastest-growing metro cities in India.

Economy of Coimbatore is heavily influenced by Information Technology, Engineering & Textiles. Coimbatore is called the Manchester of South India due to its extensive textile industry, fed by the surrounding cotton fields.

72. Urjit Ravindra Patel is an Indian economist, who has currently been serving as Governor of the Reserve Bank of India (RBI) since September 2016. Previously, as an RBI deputy governor, he looked after monetary policy, economic policy research, statistics and information management, deposit insurance, communication and Right to Information. Appointed by the Narendra Modi government, Patel succeeded Raghuram Rajan as RBI governor on 4 September 2016.

73. **Dr. Najma Akbarali Heptulla** is an Indian politician and the current governor of Manipur. She is a former vice-president of the Bharatiya Janata Party (BJP), and a five time member of the Rajya Sabha, the Upper House of the Indian parliament, between 1986 and 2012, and Deputy Chairman of the Rajya Sabha for sixteen years.

Ram Nath Kovind is a current Governor of Bihar. Kovind is a politician from the Bharatiya Janata Party-BJP.

Acharya Dev Vrat is the Governor of Himachal Pradesh, serving since August 2015. He is an Arya Samaj *pracharak* and served previously as the principal of a Gurukul in Kurukshetra, Haryana. Being the Governor of Himachal Pradesh, he is also the ex-officio Chancellor of state universities of Himachal Pradesh.

Arvind Subramanian is an Indian economist and the current Chief Economic Adviser to the Government of India, having taken charge of the position on 16 October 2014 succeeding Raghuram Rajan.

74. The Indian Women's cricket team has won the 2016 Women's Twenty 20 Asia Cup cricket tournament by defeating arch-rival Pakistan by 17 runs in the final at Bangkok, Thailand. With this win, India won their 6th Asia Cup crown.

75. The 2nd edition of BRICS Youth Summit 2016 was organized at Guwahati, Assam from 1st to 3rd July, 2016. The 2016 theme is "Youth as bridge for Intra-BRICS Exchanges". The summit adopted the 'Guwahati BRICS Youth Summit 2016 Call to Action' and urged the youth of the five member nations to come together for working towards this goal. The 1st BRICS Youth Summit was held in Kazan, Russia in 2015.

76. Maharashtra has become the first Indian state to draft its own internal security act "2016 Maharashtra Protection of Internal Security Act (MPISA)". The draft act has defined internal security as a situation posing threat to state within its borders, either caused or provoked, prompted, or proxy by a hostile foreign power, perpetrated even by such groups that use a failed, failing or weak hostile foreign power, causing insurgency, terrorism or any other subversive act targeting innocent citizens, causing animosity between groups, violence, destroy, or attempt to destroy public and private establishments.

77. The United Nations' (UN) World Humanitarian Day is held on August 19 each year. The day honours all humanitarians who have worked in the promotion of the humanitarian cause, and those who have lost their lives in the cause of duty. It aims to increase public awareness about humanitarian assistance activities worldwide and the importance of international cooperation.

79. Election Commission of India (ECI) is the only authority that grants National Party or State Party status to any political party in the country. A political party is able to get status of National Party when it:

- Secures at least 6% of the valid votes polled in any four or more states, in the Lok Sabha election or to the State Legislative Assembly and (ii) In addition, it wins at least 4 seats in the Lok Sabha from any State or States.
- Wins at least 2% seats in the Lok Sabha (*i.e.*, 11 seats in the existing Lok Sabha having 543 members) and these members are elected from at least three different States.
- It is recognised as a State party in at least four States.

81. 12th Five Year Plan lists various growth indicators as follows:

- It aims at average GDP growth rate of 8%
- It seeks to achieve 4% growth in agricultural sector
- It aims at reducing head-count poverty by 10%
- It aims at eliminating gender and social gap in education
- Increasing infrastructure investment to 9% of GDP
- Achieving universal road connectivity and access to power for all villages
- Increase public spending from 1% (11th plan) to 2.5% of GDP by the end of 12th
- For the purpose of providing electricity to households it aims at addition of 88,000 MW electricity generation capacity and 55,000 MW of renewable energy capacity.
- Eliminate gender and social gap in school enrolment
- Improving child sex ratio (0-6) to 950
- Increasing Gross Irrigated area from 90 million hectares to 103 million hectares
- Increase rural tele-density to 70%, currently it is 40.81%

82. Heat is required to raise the temperature of a given amount of substance, and the quantity of heat depends on the temperature change. The heat capacity (C) of a sample of substance is the quantity of heat needed to raise the temperature of the sample of substance one degree celsius (or one kelvin). Changing the temperature of the sample from an initial temperature t_i to a final temperature t_f requires heat equal to

$$q = C\Delta t$$

83. When we boil water to evaporate it, what we observe. We observe that when we boil water to evaporate it at 100°C, all the given heat is absorbed by the liquid. This absorbed heat is called latent heat of vaporization and taken by vapour molecules. Similarly, when we melt ice, it is converted into water because ice molecules absorb this heat. This is called latent heat of fusion.

85. Myopia or Short Sightedness: The person suffering from myopia cannot be able to see the far flung object but easily see the near most object. The myopia affected person uses concave lens of suitable focal length so that now image starts to form at retina.

Hypermetropia or Long Sightedness: The person suffering from hypermetropia cannot be able to see the nearest object but see the object located at the remote places. The hypermetropia affected person uses convex lens of suitable focal length so that now image starts to form at retina.

Presbyopia: In old age, the accommodation power of eye is diminished or ended, dut to which a person is neither capable to see the near object nor the far flung object. The presbyopia affected person uses bifocal lens of suitable focal lengh.

Cataract: A cataract is a clouding of the lens in the eyes which leads to a decrease in vision. Cataracts often develop slowly and can affect one or both eyes. Surgery is needed only if the cataracts are causing problems and generally results in an improved quality of life.

89. Process of Distillation: By the process of distillation mainly the mixture of the liquids are separated and specially those components mixtures are separated which have a substantial gap among the boiling points of the liquid mixture. In this process the component liquids are vapourised and transported to another place where these are cooled and transformed into the liquid state. Thus liquid mixtures are separated and purified and in the complete process two processes vapourisation and condensation are involved.

90. Carbon in nature occurs abundantly in both free and compounds forms. In free state it occurs as diamond, graphite and coke, while in compound forms it appears as metallic carbonate, bicarbonate, CO_2, hydrocarbon, protein, carbohydrate and other complex compounds. The number of compounds of carbon are more than 5 lakhs while the number of compounds of other elements are nearly 50 thousand. Carbon is a unique element of its group which has a special characteristic to form C–C bond and it is called catanation property of carbon. There are various allotrops of carbon like diamond, graphite, coal, etc., whose chemical properties are same but physical properties are different. Carbon exists in both crystalline and non-crystalline forms.

93. The valency of an element is the number of hydrogen atoms that can combine with or replace (either directly or indirectly) one atom of the element. In other words, the valency of an element is the number of electrons an atom of the element uses to combine with atoms of other elements — it is the combining power of an atom of the element. In an atom, the valence electrons are the electrons that can be used in combining with other atoms — these are the electrons in the orbitals of the outermost shell (also called valence shell).

94. Helium (He), Neon (Ne), Argon (Ar), Krypton (Kr), Xenon (Xe) and Radon (Rn) have been placed in zero group of the modern long form of periodic table. These are called inert gases because they are chemically inactive.

Neon (Ne): This gas is frequently used in fluorescent bulbs and in glazing advertisement. This is also utilized in Neon lamp through which symbolic indication is provided to the aircraft's pilot at the aerodrome or airport. Infact this light of the lamp extremely shines in the fog. Thus neon is today used frequently in discharge lamps and fluorescent bulbs which are utilised vigorously in the advertisement.

Argon (Ar): This is the most abundantly occurring gas in the atmosphere. It is used in filling ordinary electric bulbs because in the presence of this gas filaments of the bulb have longer life and remain intact even after the regular and longer use. This gas is also used in high temperature metallurgical operations and the processes involve behind it or in creating vacuum (being evacuated) in the arch welding of the alloys.

Xenon (Xe): Xenon is a non-metal chemical element. It has the chemical symbol Xe and atomic number 54. It is one of the few elements that are a gas at standard temperature and pressure. Xenon is used in flash lamps and arc lamps and as a general anaesthetic.

Krypton (Kr): It is a member of group 18 (noble gases) elements. A colourless, odourless, tasteless noble gas, krypton occurs in trace amounts in the atmosphere and is often used with other rare gases in fluorescent lamps.

95. Colour vision is the ability of an organism or machine to distinguish objects based on the wavelengths (or frequencies) of the light they reflect, emit, or transmit. Colours can be measured and quantified in various ways; indeed, a person's perception of colours is a subjective process whereby the brain responds to the stimuli that are produced when incoming light reacts with the several types of cone cells in the eye. In essence, different people see the same illuminated object or light source in different ways.

96. Proteins are large biomolecules, or macromolecules, consisting of one or more long chains of amino acid residues. Proteins perform a vast array of functions within organisms, including catalysing metabolic reactions, DNA replication, responding to stimuli, and transporting molecules from one location to another. Proteins differ from one another primarily in their sequence of amino acids, which is dictated by the nucleotide sequence of their genes, and which usually results in protein folding into a specific three-dimensional structure that determines its activity.

100. The correct order of tiger reserves situated from North to South in India.

Jim Corbett National Park is the oldest national park in India and was established in 1936 as Hailey National Park to protect the endangered Bengal tiger. It is located in Nainital district of Uttarakhand and was named after Jim Corbett who played a key role in its establishment. The park was the first to come under the Project Tiger initiative.

Sariska Tiger Reserve is a national park and tiger reserve located in the Alwar district of the state of Rajasthan, India. The topography of the protected area comprises scrub-thorn arid forests, rocky landscapes, dry deciduous forests, rocks, grasses and hilly cliffs. This area was a hunting preserve of the Alwar state and it was declared a wildlife reserve in 1955.

Simlipal National Park is a national park and a tiger reserve in the Mayurbhanj district in the Indian state of Odisha. It is a part of the Similipal-Kuldiha-Hadgarh Elephant Reserve popularly known as Mayurbhanj Elephant Reserve, which includes three protected areas: Similipal Tiger Reserve, Hadgarh Wildlife Sanctuary and Kuldiha Wildlife Sanctuary. Simlipal National Park derives its name from the abundance of *semul* (red silk cotton trees) that bloom here.

Periyar National Park and Wildlife Sanctuary (PNP) is a protected area near Thekkady in the districts of Idukki, Kottayam and Pathanamthitta in Kerala, India. It is notable as both an elephant reserve and a tiger reserve.

102. Climatic Regions of India According to Koeppen's Scheme

Type of Climate	*Areas*
Amw Monsoon with short dry season	West coast of India south of Goa
As - Monsoon with dry summer	Coromandel coast of Tamil Nadu
Aw - Tropical savannah	Most of the Peninsular plateaus, south of the Tropic of Cancer
Bwhw - Semi-arid steppe climate	North-western Gujarat, some parts of western Rajasthan and Punjab
Bwhw - Hot desert	Extreme western Rajasthan
Cwg - Monsoon with dry winter	Ganga plain, eastern Rajasthan, northern Madhya Pradesh, most of North-east India
Dfc - Cold humid winter with short summer	Arunachal Pradesh
E - Polar type	Jammu and Kashmir, Himachal Pradesh and Uttarakhand

104. Railway Zones in India

Sl. No.	*Name*	*Code*	*Year of Establishment*	*Headquarters*
1	Central Railway	CR	1951	Mumbai
2	East Central Railway	ECR	2001	Hajipur
3	East Coast Railway	ECoR	2001	Bhubaneswar
4	Eastern Railway	ER	1952	Kolkata
5	North Central Railway	NCR	2003	Allahabad
6	North Eastern Railway	NER	1952	Gorakhpur
7	North Western Railway	NWR	2002	Jaipur
8	Northeast Frontier Railway	NFR	1958	Guwahati
9	Northern Railway	NR	1952	Delhi
10	South Central Railway	SCR	1966	Secunderabad
11	South East Central Railway	SECR	2003	Bilaspur
12	South Eastern Railway	SER	1955	Kolkata
13	South Weastern Railway	SWR	2003	Hubli
14	Southern Railway	SR	1951	Chennai
15	West Central Railway	WCR	2003	Jabalpur
16	Western Railway	WR	1951	Mumbai
17	Kolkata Metro Railway	KMR	2009	Kolkata

108. The dimension of stress is that of pressure, and therefore its coordinates are commonly measured in the same units as pressure: *viz.,* pascals (Pa, *i.e.,* newtons per square metre) in the International System, or pounds per square inch (psi) in the Imperial system. Because mechanical stresses easily exceed a million Pascals, MPa, which stands for mega pascal, is a common unit of stress.

109. An electrical insulator is a material whose internal electric charges do not flow freely; very little electric current will flow through it under the influence of an electric field. This contrasts with other materials, semiconductors and conductors, which conduct electric current more easily. The property that distinguishes an insulator is its resistivity; insulators have higher resistivity than semiconductors or conductors.

111. Krishnadevaraya was the emperor of the Vijayanagara Empire from 1509 to 1530. He was the third ruler of the Tuluva Dynasty. Presiding over the empire at its zenith, he is regarded as an icon by many Indians. Portuguese travellers Domingo Paes and Fernao Nuniz also visited the Vijayanagara Empire during his reign. Krishna Deva Raya benefited from the able prime minister Timmarusu, who was regarded by the emperor as a father figure and was responsible for his coronation. The rule of Krishnadevaraya was an age of prolific literature in many languages, although it is also known as a golden age of Telugu literature. Many Telugu, Sanskrit, Kannada and Tamil poets enjoyed the patronage of the emperor. *Amuktamalyada* is an epic poem in Telugu composed by Krishnadevaraya of the Vijayanagar Dynasty. *Amuktamalyada* translates to one who wears and gives away garlands. Considered as a masterpiece, Amuktamalyada describes the story of wedding of the Hindu Lord Vishnu and Andal the Tamil Alvar poet and daughter of Periyalvar, at Srirangam.

112. 52nd Amendment Act, 1985: Anti Defection Law - Provide disqualification of members from parliament and assembly in case of defection from one party to other. However, parts of the 10th Schedule to the Constitution of India was struck down by the Supreme Court in the case of Kihoto Hollohan v. Zachillhu 1992 SCR (1) 686, for being in contravention with Article 368 of the Constitution.

61st Amendment Act, 1988: The Act provides for reducing voting age from 21 to 18 years by amending Article 326 of the Constitution to provide to the unrepresented youth of the country an opportunity to give vent to their feeling and help them become a part of political process.

73rd Amendment Act, 1993: Statutory provisions for Panchyati Raj as third level of administration in villages.

86th Amendment Act, 2006: Provides Right to Education until the age of fourteen and Early childhood care until the age of six.

113. The Indian Rebellion of 1857 had diverse political, economic, military, religious and social causes.

The sepoys, a generic term used for native Indian soldiers of the Bengal Army derived from the Persian word *sepahi* meaning "infantry soldier", had their own list of grievances against the British East India Company administration, caused mainly by the ethnic gulf between the European officers and their Indian troops. The spark that led to a mutiny in several sepoy companies was the issue of new gunpowder cartridges for the Enfield rifle in February, 1857. A rumour was spread that the cartridges were made from cow and pig fat. Loading the Enfield required tearing open the greased cartridge with one's teeth. This would have insulted both Hindu and Muslim religious practices; cows were considered holy by Hindus while pigs were considered unclean by Muslims.

114. The doctrine of subsidiary alliance was framed by Lord Wellesley, British Governor-General in India from 1798 to 1805. Early in his governorship Wellesley adopted a policy of non-intervention in the princely states, but he later adopted the policy of forming subsidiary alliances. This policy was to play a major role in British expansion in India. According to the terms of a subsidiary alliance, princely rulers were not allowed to have an independent armed force. They were to be protected by the East India Company, but had to pay for the 'subsidiary forces' that the company was supposed to maintain for the purpose of this protection. If the Indian rulers failed to make the payment, then part of their territory was taken away as penalty.

116. Coral reefs in India are one of the most ancient and dynamic ecosystems of India. The coral reefs not only provide a sanctuary to a myriad of marine life but also play a key role in protecting the coastline from erosion. India has about 7517 km of coastline including islands but mainland coast is 6100 km.

Andaman and Nicobar Islands: Situated in the Bay of Bengal, exclusively fringing reefs of about 500 islands, most of these islands have a healthy biodiversity.

Gulf of Kutch: Exclusively consists of fringing reefs. The reefs are relatively less developed due to large range of temperature and high salinity. The harbours have less biodiversity. The entire Gulf of Kutch is also known as a marine national park.

Gulf of Mannar: Fringing reefs with a chain of 21 islands from Rameswaram in the north to Thoothukudi (Tuticorin) in the south. This part of the gulf forms part of the Gulf of Mannar biosphere reserve.

Lakshadweep: Exclusively coral atolls with 36 islands, of which 10 are inhabited.

Others: Tarkarli in Malwan, Maharashtra is a smaller reef. There are some coral reefs around small inlets in the western part of the Gulf of Khambat. Angria Bank is a coral reef off Vijaydurg in Maharashtra. There is a coral reef in Netrani Island in Karnataka.

120. In physics, angular frequency ω is a scalar measure of rotation rate. It refers to the angular displacement per unit time (*e.g.*, in rotation) or the rate of change of the phase of a sinusoidal waveform (*e.g.*, in oscillations and waves), or as the rate of change of the argument of the since function. Angular frequency (or angular speed) is the magnitude of the vector quantity angular velocity. The term 'angular frequency vector' $\bar{\omega}$ is sometimes used as a synonym for the vector quantity angular velocity. One revolution is equal to 2π radians, hence

$$\omega = \frac{2\pi}{T} = 2\pi f,$$

where,

ω is the angular frequency or angular speed (measured in radians per second),

T is the period (measured in seconds),

f is the ordinary frequency (measured in hertz) sometimes symbolised with ν).

121. Let's suppose, the X is such a reading

$$\frac{X-273}{100} = \frac{X-32}{180}$$

$$\Rightarrow \quad 9(X-273) = 5(X-32)$$

$$\Rightarrow \quad X = \frac{9\times 273 - 5\times 32}{4}$$

$$\Rightarrow \quad X = 574K \text{ or } 574°F$$

$$= (574 - 273)°C$$

$$= 301°C$$

123. In 1687, English mathematician Sir Isaac Newton published *Principia*, which hypothesizes the Inverse-Square low of universal gravitation. In his one words "I deduced that the force which keeps the planets in their orbs must reciprocally as the squares of their distances from the centres about which they revolve and thereby compared the force requisite to keep the Moon in her orb with the force of gravity at the surface of the Earth; and found them answer pretty nearly." The equation is the following:

$$F = G\frac{m_1m_2}{r^2}$$

where, F is the Force, m_1 and m_2 are the masses of the objects interacting, r is the distance between the centres of the masses and G is the gravitational constant.

125. Radon is a chemical element with symbol Rn and atomic number 86. It is a radioactive, colourless, odourless, tasteless noble gas (inert gas). It occurs naturally as an intermediate step in the normal radioactive decay chains through which thorium and uranium slowly decay into lead; radon, itself, is a decay product of radium. Its most stable isotope, ^{222}Rn, has a half-life of 3.8 days. Since thorium and uranium are two of the most common radioactive elements on Earth, and since their isotopes have very long half-lives, on the order of billions of years, radon will be present long into the future in spite of its short half-life as it is continually being regenerated.

126. Sodium bicarbonate is a chemical compound with the formula $NaHCO_3$. It is a salt composed of sodium ions and bicarbonate ions. Sodium bicarbonate is a white solid that is crystalline but often appears as a fine powder. It has a slightly salty, alkaline taste resembling that of washing soda (sodium carbonate). The natural mineral form is nahcolite. It is a component of the mineral natron and is found dissolved in many mineral springs.

127. Most pencil cores are made of graphite mixed with a clay binder which leaves grey or black marks that can be easily erased. Graphite pencils are used for both writing and drawing and result in durable markings: though writing is easily removable with an eraser, it is otherwise resistant to moisture, most chemicals, ultraviolet radiation, and natural aging.

129. The Chittagong armoury raid, also known as the Chittagong uprising, was an attempt on 18 April 1930 to raid the armoury of police and auxiliary forces from the Chittagong armoury in the Bengal Presidency of British India (now in Bangladesh) by armed Indian independence fighters led by Surya Sen. The raiders were members of revolutionary groups who favoured armed uprisings as a means to achieve India's independence from British colonial rule. They were inspired by the 1916 Easter Rising in Ireland and led by Surya Sen. The group included Ganesh Ghosh, Lokenath Bal, Ambika Chakrobarty, Harigopal Bal (Tegra), Ananta Singh, Anand Prasad Gupta, Pritilata Waddedar, Kalpana Dutta, Binod Bihari Chowdhury, Subodh Roy, Debi Prasad Gupta and many others.

130. On Aug. 8, 1942, the Congress in its meeting at Gowaleya Tank, Bombay passed a resolution known as 'Quit India' resolution, whereby Gandhiji asked the British to quit India and gave a call for 'Do or die' (Either free India or die in the attempt) to his countrymen. On Aug. 9, 1942 all the prominent leaders like Gandhi, Nehru, Patel, etc., were arrested but the rest leaders (J.P., Lohiya, Aruna Ali, Usha Mehta, etc.) continued the revolutionary struggle. Violence spread throughout the country, several government offices were destroyed and damaged, the telegraph wires were cut and communication paralyzed. The parallel government was established in some places, viz., 1. Balia (UP), 2. Tamulak (Bengal), 3. Satara (Maharashtra), 4. Talcher (Odisha), etc. The movement was, however, crushed by the government.

133. The decision to effect the Partition of Bengal was announced in July 1905, by the Viceroy of India, Lord Curzon. The partition took place on 16 October, 1905 and separated the largely Muslim eastern areas from the largely Hindu western areas. The Hindus of West Bengal who dominated Bengal's business and rural life complained that the division would make them a minority in a province that would incorporate the province of Bihar and Odisha. Hindus were outraged at what they recognised as a "divide and rule" policy, where the colonisers turned the native population against itself in order to rule, even though Curzon stressed it would produce administrative efficiency. H.H. Risley, the Home Secretary of the Government of India was the most outspoken in this regard. He said, "Bengal united is power. Bengal divided will pull several different ways".

134. The Bardoli Satyagraha of 1928, in the state of Gujarat, India during the period of the British Raj, was a major episode of civil disobedience and revolt in the Indian Independence Movement. The movement was eventually led by Vallabhbhai Patel, and its success gave rise to Patel becoming one of the main leaders of the independence movement.

135. The Salt March, also known as the Dandi March and the Dandi Satyagraha, was an act of nonviolent civil disobedience in colonial India initiated by Mohandas Karamchand Gandhi to produce salt from the seawater in the coastal village of Dandi, as was the practice of the local populace until British officials introduced taxation on salt production, deemed their sea-salt reclamation activities illegal, and then repeatedly used force to stop it. The 24-day march began from 12 March 1930 and continued till 6 April 1930 as a direct action campaign of tax resistance and nonviolent protest against the British salt monopoly, and it gained worldwide attention which gave impetus to the Indian independence movement and started the nationwide Civil Disobedience Movement.

The debate over federation and the future constitutional status of the princely states along with the Civil Disobedience movement stimulated political activity among popular politicians from the princely states. The South Indian States' People's Conference met in Travancore in January 1929, and the All-India States' People's Conference held its second session in Bombay on May 25-26, 1929. During the 1930s there was also a proliferation of regional states' people's groups in Punjab and in Rajasthan and more extensive political mobilization in existing organizations in Kathiawar, Travancore, Cochin, and Mysore. Many such groups sought closer ties with and more active support from Congress.

136. Kandukuri Veeresalingam (16 April 1848 – 27 May 1919) was a social reformer who first brought about a renaissance in Telugu people and Telugu literature. He was influenced by the ideals of Brahmo Samaj particularly those of Keshub Chunder Sen. He got involved in the cause of social reforms. In 1876 he started a journal and wrote the first prose for women. He encouraged education for women, and started a school in Dowlaishwaram in 1874. He started a social organisation called Hitakarini (Benefactor).

137. Honoured with the title Zarrinqalam (gold pen), Muhammad Husain Kashmiri was one of the acclaimed calligraphers of the court of Akbar Shah in the late 16th and early 17th century. He was a master of Nasta'liq and a pupil of 'Abd al-'Aziz. Abul fazl 'Alami in A'in-i Akbari considers his handwriting to be equal to that of Mir 'Ali.

138. Golden Quadrilateral is a network of highways connecting India's four top metropolitan cities, *viz.*, Delhi, Mumbai, Chennai and Kolkata, thereby, forming a quadrilateral. The largest highway project in India, the Golden Quadrilateral project was launched in 2001 as part of National Highways Development Project (NHDP).

No.	*Segment*	*Length Completed*	*Total Length*
1.	Delhi-Kolkata	1,453 km (903 mi)	1,453 km (903 mi)
2.	Chennai-Mumbai	1,290 km (800 mi)	1,290 km (800 mi)
3.	Kolkata-Chennai	1,684 km (1,046 mi)	1,684 km (1,046 mi)
4.	Mumbai-Delhi	1,419 km (882 mi)	1,419 km (882 mi)
	Total	5,846 km (3,633 mi)	5,846 km (3,633 mi)

139. The definition of **inexhaustible resources** is a natural resource that is not an endless supply. Examples of these resources are geothermal energy, air and solar radiation. In general, most of the natural resources can be depleted. Inexhaustible resources are a resource that is present with unlimited amounts in the nature; they cannot be depleted or exhausted by human activity. Inexhaustible resource is known as a renewable resource. This includes water, sand clay, water as well as solar energy.

A non-renewable resource is a resource that does not renew itself at a sufficient rate for sustainable economic extraction in meaningful human time-frames. An example is carbon-based, organically-derived fuel. The original organic material, with the aid of heat and pressure, becomes a fuel such as oil or gas. Earth minerals and metal ores, fossil fuels (coal, petroleum, natural gas) and groundwater in certain aquifers are all considered non-renewable resources, though individual elements are almost always conserved.

Renewable energy is energy that is collected from renewable resources, which are naturally replenished on a human timescale, such as sunlight, wind, rain, tides, waves, and geothermal heat. Renewable energy often provides energy in four important areas: electricity generation, air and water heating/cooling, transportation, and rural (off-grid) energy services.

Non-renewable Resource: A non-renewable resource is a resource of economic value that cannot be readily replaced by natural means on a level equal to its consumption. Most fossil fuels, such as oil, natural gas and coal are considered non-renewable resources in the sense that their use is not sustainable because their formation takes billions of years.

141. The Tharu tribe are spread in the terai and bhawar regions of Uttar Pradesh (including Uttarakhand). The origin of the term 'Tharu' is debatable. According to one school, the term is associated with the *Atharvaveda*. Initially called 'Athru' the tribes later began to be called Tharu. The term 'Tharu' means 'stuck up'. The Tharu have stuck up in the region to make a livelihood, braving frequent malaria epidemics.

142. $\frac{Cg}{Cw} = \frac{C/Cw}{C/Cg} = \frac{\mu w}{\mu g} = \frac{4}{3} \times \frac{2}{3} = \frac{8}{9}$

$\therefore$ 8 : 9

144.

State	*Population*	*% share in total population of the country*
Jammu & Kashmir	12,541,302	1.04
Haryana	25,351,462	2.09
Rajasthan	68,548,437	5.66
Bihar	104,099,452	8.60

145. Abdul Hamid Lahori was a traveller and historian during the period of Shah Jahan who later became a court historian of Shah Jahan. He wrote the book *Padshahnama* also referred as *Badshahnama*, about the reign of Shah Jahan. He has described Shah Jahan's life and activities during the first twenty years of his reign in this book in great detail.

146. Fatehpur Sikri is a city in the Agra District of Uttar Pradesh, India. The city was founded in 1569 by the Mughal Emperor Akbar, and served as the capital of the Mughal Empire from 1571 to 1585, when it was abandoned. After his military victories were over Chittor and Ranthambore, Akbar decided to shift his capital from Agra to a new location 23 miles (37 km) west south-west, to honour the Sufi saint Salim Chishti. Here, he commenced the construction of a planned walled city, which took the next fifteen years in planning and construction, with a series of royal palaces, harem, courts, a mosque, private quarters and other utility buildings. He named the city Fatehabad, with Fateh, a word of Arabic origin in Persian, meaning "victorious." It was later called Fatehpur Sikri. It is at Fatehpur Sikri that the legends of Akbar and his famed courtiers, the nine jewels or Navaratnas, were born. Fatehpur Sikri is one of the best preserved examples of Mughal architecture in India.

147. India is hosting the 3rd edition of World Trauma Congress (WTC), which is recently inaugurated by Union Health Minister J.P Nadda at Vigyan Bhavan in New Delhi on August 18, 2016. The main purpose of the WTC is to exchange ideas, experiences and lessons learned about the role of internationally accepted systems and protocols in the field of trauma care, mass causality incidents and disasters.

148. The objective of "Act East Policy" is to promote economic cooperation, cultural ties and develop strategic relationship with countries in the Asia-Pacific region through continuous engagement at bilateral, regional and multilateral levels thereby providing enhanced connectivity to the State of North Eastern Region including Arunachal Pradesh with other countries in our neighbourhood. The North East of India has been a priority in our Act East Policy (AEP). AEP provides an interface between North East India including the state of Arunachal Pradesh and the ASEAN region. Various plans at bilateral and regional levels include steady efforts to develop and strengthen connectivity of Northeast with the ASEAN region through trade, culture, people-to-people contacts and physical infrastructure (road, airport, telecommunication, power, etc.). Some of the major projects include Kaladan Multi-modal Transit Transport Project, the India-Myanmar-Thailand Trilateral Highway Project, Rhi-Tiddim Road Project, Border Haats, etc.

149. The 2016 summer olympics, officially known as the games of the XXXI Olympiad was a major international multi-sport event held in Rio-de-Janeiro, Brazil, from 5 August to 21 August 2016.

Final Total Medal

Rank	Country	Total
1	United States	121
2	China	67
3	Great Britain	70
4	Russia	56

150. Objective of the National Civil Aviation Policy 2016:

- Establish an integrated eco-system which will lead to significant growth of civil aviation sector, which in turn would promote tourism, increase employment and lead to a balanced regional growth.
- Ensure safety, security and sustainability of aviation sector through the use of technology and effective monitoring.
- Enhance regional connectivity through fiscal support and infrastructure development.
- Enhance ease of doing business through deregulation, simplified procedures and e-governance.
- Promote the entire aviation sector chain in a harmonised manner covering cargo, MRO, general aviation, aerospace manufacturing and skill development.

PAPER-II : MATHEMATICS

1. Let S be the set of all persons living in Delhi

R = {(x, y): x and y were born in Delhi on same day}

∴ R is an equivalent relation.

2. Required no. of Students

$$= {}^{10}C_2 + {}^{10}C_3$$

$$= \frac{10\times9\times8!}{2!\times8!}+\frac{10\times9\times8\times7!}{3!\times7!}$$

$$= 45+\frac{10\times9\times8}{3\times2}$$

$$= 45 + 120 = 165$$

3. $\because i^{2n} + i^{2n+1} + i^{2n+2} + i^{2n+3}$
$= i^{2n} + i^{2n} \times i + i^{2n} \times i^2 + i^{2n} \times i^3$
$= i^{2n}[1 + i + i^2 + i^3]$
$= i^{2n}[1 + i - 1 - i]$
$= i^{2n}(0) = 0$

4. $(\alpha - \beta)^2 < 5$
$\Rightarrow k^2 - 4 < 5 \Rightarrow k^2 < 9$
$\Rightarrow -3 < k < 3$ ...(*i*)
Next, $|k| \geq 2 \Rightarrow k \leq -2$ or $k \geq 2$ ...(*ii*)
From (*i*) and (*ii*)
$k \in (-3, -2] \cup [2, 3)$

5. Let α, β are the roots of the equation $x^2 + px + q = 0$ and a, b are the roots of the equation $x^2 + lx + m = 0$
Then, $\alpha + \beta = -p, \alpha \times \beta = q$
$a + b = -l, a \times b = m$

Now, $\dfrac{\alpha}{\beta} = \dfrac{a}{b}$ (given)

$$\Rightarrow \frac{\alpha+\beta}{\alpha-\beta} = \frac{a+b}{a-b}$$

$$\Rightarrow \frac{(\alpha+\beta)^2}{(\alpha-\beta)^2} = \frac{(a+b)^2}{(a-b)^2}$$

$$\Rightarrow \frac{p^2}{p^2-2q} = \frac{l^2}{l^2-2m} \Rightarrow p^2m = l^2q$$

6. $\left(\dfrac{-1+\sqrt{3}i}{2}\right)^n + \left(\dfrac{-1-\sqrt{3}i}{2}\right)^n$

$= (w)^n + (w^2)^n$

Put $n = 1, 2, 4$ (not multiple of 3)
$(w)^1 + (w^2)^1 = w + w^2 = -1$ $[\because 1 + w + w^2 = 0]$
$(w)^2 + (w^2)^2 = w^2 + w^4 = w^2 + w^3.w = w^2 + w$
$= -1$ $[w^3 = 1]$

Hence, the value of $\left(\dfrac{-1+i\sqrt{3}}{2}\right)^n + \left(\dfrac{-1-i\sqrt{3}}{2}\right)^n$

$= -1$

7. Required sum $= 12\,(10^0 + 10^1 + 10^2)$
$= 12 \times (1 + 10 + 100)$
$= 12 \times 111 = 1332$

8. $0.3 + 0.33 + 0.333 + ...$

$$= \frac{3}{10} + \frac{33}{100} + \frac{333}{1000} + ...$$

$$= \frac{3}{9}\left[\frac{9}{10} + \frac{99}{100} + \frac{999}{1000} + ...\right]$$

$$= \frac{1}{3}\left[\left(1-\frac{1}{10}\right) + \left(1-\frac{1}{100}\right) + \left(1-\frac{1}{1000}\right) + ...\right]$$

$$= \frac{1}{3}\left[n - \frac{\frac{1}{10}\left(1-\frac{1}{10^n}\right)}{\frac{9}{10}}\right] = \frac{1}{3}\left[n - \frac{1}{9}\left(1-\frac{1}{10^n}\right)\right]$$

9. $(1 + w)(1 + w^2)(1 + w^3)(1 + w + w^2)$
$= (1 + w)(1 + w^2)(1 + w^3)(0)$ $[\because 1 + w + w^2 = 0]$
$= 0$ [Zero multiplied by any number is zero]

10. In an AP
If $S_m = n$ and $S_n = m$
Then, $S_{m+n} = -(m + n)$

11. $\dfrac{1+2i}{1-(1+i^2-2i)} = \dfrac{1+2i}{1+2i} = 1$

$r \cos \theta = 1$
$r \sin \theta = 0$
$r^2(\cos^2\theta + \sin^2\theta) = 1$
$r = 1$
$\cos\theta = 1 = \cos 0°$
$\theta = 0°$
(1, 0)

12. If graph of quadratic lies entirely above x-axis then, $D > 0$. Hence, both roots are complex.

13. We have, $|z + 4| \leq 3$
Now, $|z + 1| = |z + 4 - 3| \leq |z + 4| + |-3|$
$\Rightarrow |z + 1| \leq 3 + 3 = 6$ $[\because |z + 4| \leq 3]$
Hence, maximum value of $|z + 1| = 6$

14. $Z^2 = 2\bar{Z}$
Let $Z = x + iy$
Now, $Z^2 = x^2 - y^2 + 2ixy$
According to the question,
$x^2 - y^2 + 2ixy = 2x - 2iy \Rightarrow x = -1$ and $y = \pm 3$
Hence, $Z = -1 + \sqrt{3}i$ and $Z = -1 - \sqrt{3}i$ are two roots.

15. $x^2 + bx + c = 0$
$\because \cot\alpha$ and $\cot\beta$ are the roots of the equation
$\therefore \cot\alpha + \cot\beta = -b$
$\cot\alpha \times \cot\beta = c$

$$\cot(\alpha + \beta) = \frac{\cot\alpha \times \cot\beta - 1}{\cot\beta + \cot\alpha}$$

$$= \frac{c-1}{-b} = \frac{-(1-c)}{-b}$$

$$= \frac{1-c}{b}$$

16. $x^2 + bx + c = 0$
Let α, β are the roots of the given equation.
$\alpha + \beta = -b$ and $\alpha \times \beta = c$

$$\alpha + \beta = \frac{1}{\alpha^2} + \frac{1}{\beta^2}$$

$\Rightarrow \quad -b = \dfrac{\beta^2+\alpha^2}{(\alpha\beta)^2} = \dfrac{(\alpha+\beta)^2-2\alpha\beta}{(\alpha\beta)^2}$

$\Rightarrow \quad -b = \dfrac{b^2-2c}{c^2}$

$\Rightarrow \quad -bc^2 = -(2c - b^2)$

$2c = b^2 + bc^2$

Now, $\dfrac{1}{c}, b, \dfrac{c}{b}$ are in H.P.

$\therefore c, \dfrac{1}{b}, \dfrac{b}{c}$ are in A.P.

$\dfrac{1}{b} - c = \dfrac{b}{c} - \dfrac{1}{b}$

$\Rightarrow \quad \dfrac{1}{b} + \dfrac{1}{b} = \dfrac{b}{c} + c$

$\Rightarrow \quad \dfrac{2}{b} = \dfrac{b+c^2}{c}$

$\Rightarrow \quad 2c = b^2 + bc^2$

Hence, $\dfrac{1}{c}, b, \dfrac{c}{b}$ are in H.P.

17. Let α, β are the roots of the equation $ax^2 + x + c = 0$

$\alpha + \beta = -\dfrac{1}{a}$

$\alpha \times \beta = \dfrac{c}{a}$

$\dfrac{1}{\alpha^2} + \dfrac{1}{\beta^2} = \dfrac{\beta^2+\alpha^2}{(\alpha\beta)^2} = \dfrac{(\alpha+\beta)^2-2\alpha\beta}{(\alpha\beta)^2}$

$= \dfrac{\frac{1}{a^2} - 2\frac{c}{a}}{\frac{c^2}{a^2}} = \dfrac{\frac{1-2ac}{a^2}}{\frac{c^2}{a^2}}$

$= \dfrac{1-2ac}{c^2}$

$-\dfrac{1}{a} = \dfrac{1-2ac}{c^2}$

$\Rightarrow \quad -c^2 = a - 2a^2c$

$\Rightarrow \quad c^2 = 2a^2c - a \Rightarrow 2a^2c = c^2 + a$

a, ca^2, c^2 are in A.P.

$ca^2 - a = c^2 - ca^2$

$2ca^2 = c^2 + a$

$\Rightarrow \quad 2a^2c = c^2 + a$

Hence, a, ca^2, c^2 are in A.P.

18. $({}^7C_0 + {}^7C_1) + ({}^7C_1 + {}^7C_2) + ({}^7C_2 + {}^7C_3) + ({}^7C_3 + {}^7C_4) + ({}^7C_4 + {}^7C_5) + ({}^7C_5 + {}^7C_6) + ({}^7C_6 + {}^7C_7)$

$= (1 + 7) + (7 + 21) + (21 + 35) + (35 + 35) + (35 + 21) + (21 + 7) + (7 + 1)$

$= 8 + 28 + 56 + 70 + 56 + 28 + 8$

$= 36 + 112 + 70 + 36$

$= 72 + 112 + 70$

$= 142 + 112 = 254$

19. ${}^3P_2 \times 6! = 6 \times 720 = 4320$

20. $S_n = n^2 - 2n$

$S_0 = 0 - 0 = 0$

$S_1 = 1 - 2 = -1$

$S_2 = 4 - 4 = 0$

$S_3 = 9 - 6 = 3$

$S_4 = 16 - 8 = 8$

$S_5 = 25 - 10 = 15$

$a_1 = S_1 - S_0 = (-1) = -1$

$a_2 = S_2 - S_1 = 0 - (-1) = 0 + 1 = 1$

$a_3 = S_3 - S_2 = 3 - 0 = 3$

$a_4 = S_4 - S_3 = 8 - 3 = 5$

$a_5 = S_5 - S_4 = 15 - 8 = 7$

$\therefore -1, 1, 3, 5, 7$ are in A.P. whose 5th term = 7.

21. $11 + 13 + 15 + 17 + ... + 99$

$a = 11, d = 2$

$99 = a + (n-1)d$

$= 11 + (n-1)2$

$= 11 + 2n - 2$

$= 9 + 2n$

$\Rightarrow \quad 2n = 90 \Rightarrow n = 45$

$S_{45} = \dfrac{45}{2}[2\times11+(45-1)\times2]$

$= \dfrac{45}{2}[22+88] = \dfrac{45}{2}\times110$

$= 45 \times 55 = 2475$

22. $\dfrac{1}{2}+\dfrac{3}{4}+\dfrac{7}{8}+\dfrac{15}{16}+....$

$S_1 = \dfrac{1}{2}$

$S_2 = \dfrac{1}{2}+\dfrac{3}{4} = \dfrac{2+3}{4} = \dfrac{5}{4}$

$S_3 = \dfrac{1}{2}+\dfrac{3}{4}+\dfrac{7}{8} = \dfrac{4+6+7}{8} = \dfrac{17}{8}$

$S_4 = \dfrac{17}{8}+\dfrac{15}{16} = \dfrac{34+15}{16} = \dfrac{49}{16}$

$S_n = 2^{-n} + n - 1$

$= \dfrac{1}{2^n} + n - 1$

$S_1 = \dfrac{1}{2^1} + 1 - 1 = \dfrac{1}{2}$

$S_2 = \dfrac{1}{2^2} + 2 - 1 = \dfrac{1}{4} + 1 = \dfrac{5}{4}$

$$S_3 = \frac{1}{2^3}+3-1=\frac{1}{8}+2=\frac{17}{8}$$

$$S_4 = \frac{1}{2^4}+4-1=\frac{1}{16}+3=\frac{49}{16}$$

Hence, $\frac{1}{2}+\frac{3}{4}+\frac{7}{8}+\frac{15}{16}+.... = 2^{-n}+n-1$

26. $(x-y)^6 = {}^nC_0\, x^6 - {}^nC_1 x^5 y + {}^nC_2 x^4 y^2 - {}^nC_3 x^3 y^3 + {}^nC_4 x^2 y^4 - {}^nC_5 xy^5 + {}^nC_6 y^6$

$${}^nC_4 x^2y^4 - {}^nC_5 xy^5 = 0$$

$${}^nC_4 x^2y^4 = {}^nC_5 xy^5$$

$$\frac{x^2y^4}{xy^5} = \frac{{}^nC_5}{{}^nC_4} = \frac{{}^6C_5}{{}^6C_4}$$

$$\Rightarrow \quad \frac{x}{y} = \frac{\frac{6\times 5!}{5!\times 1}}{\frac{6\times 5\times 4!}{4!\times 2!}} = \frac{\frac{6}{1}}{\frac{15}{1}}$$

$$\Rightarrow \quad \frac{x}{y} = \frac{6}{15} = \frac{2}{5}$$

$$\therefore \quad \frac{x}{y} = \frac{n-4}{5} = \frac{6-4}{5} = \frac{2}{5}$$

Hence, $\frac{x}{y} = \frac{n-4}{5}$

29. $\begin{vmatrix} 0 & x-a & x-b \\ x+a & 0 & x-c \\ x+b & x+c & 0 \end{vmatrix} = 0$

$0[0-(x-c)(x+c)] - (x-a)[0-(x-c)(x-b)] + (x-b)(x+a)(x+c) = 0$

$0 + (x-a)(x-b)(x-c) + (x+a)(x-b)(x+c) = 0$

$(x-a)(x-b)(x-c) = -(x+a)(x-b)(x+c)$

$x^2 - cx - ax + ac = -(x^2 + cx + ax - ac)$

$x^2 - cx - ax + ac + x^2 + cx + ax - ac = 0$

$2x^2 = 0$

$x^2 = 0 \Rightarrow x = 0$

Hence, the value of $x = 0$

31. $x + 2y + 3z = 1$

$2x + y + 3z = 2$

$5x + 5y + 9z = 4$

$$D = \begin{vmatrix} 1 & 2 & 3 \\ 2 & 1 & 3 \\ 5 & 5 & 9 \end{vmatrix}$$

$= 1(9-15) - 2(18-15) + 3(10-5)$

$= -6 - 6 + 15 = 3$

$$D_1 = \begin{vmatrix} 1 & 2 & 3 \\ 2 & 1 & 3 \\ 4 & 5 & 9 \end{vmatrix}$$

$= 1(9-15) - 2(18-12) + 3(10-4)$

$= 6 - 12 + 18 = 12$

$$D_2 = \begin{vmatrix} 1 & 1 & 3 \\ 2 & 2 & 3 \\ 5 & 4 & 9 \end{vmatrix}$$

$= 1(18-12) - 1(18-15) + 3(8-10)$

$= 6 - 3 - 6 = -3$

$$D_3 = \begin{vmatrix} 1 & 2 & 1 \\ 2 & 1 & 2 \\ 5 & 5 & 4 \end{vmatrix}$$

$= 1(4-10) - 2(8-10) + 1(10-5)$

$= -6 + 4 + 5 = 3$

$\because$ D $\neq 0$ then, the system is consistent and has a unique solution given by

$$x = \frac{D_1}{D},\ y = \frac{D_2}{D} \text{ and } Z = \frac{D_3}{D}$$

$$x = \frac{12}{3} = 4$$

$$y = -\frac{3}{3} = -1$$

$$z = \frac{3}{3} = 1$$

Hence, the solutions have the unique solution.

33. $\begin{vmatrix} 1 & 1 & 1 \\ 1 & 1+xyz & 1 \\ 1 & 1 & 1+xyz \end{vmatrix}$

$= 1\left[(1+xyz)^2 - (1)^2\right] - 1\left[1(1+xyz) - 1^2\right] + 1\left[1^2 - 1(1+xyz)\right]$

$= [1 + x^2y^2z^2 + 2xyz - 1] - [1 + xyz - 1] + [1 - 1 - xyz]$

$= x^2y^2z^2 + 2xyz - xyz - xyz$

$= x^2y^2z^2 + 2xyz - 2xyz$

$= x^2y^2z^2.$

34. $\begin{vmatrix} x & y & 0 \\ 0 & x & y \\ y & 0 & x \end{vmatrix} = 0$

$\Rightarrow x(x^2 - 0) - y(0 - y^2) + 0(0 - xy) = 0$

$\Rightarrow \quad x^3 + y^3 = 0$

$\Rightarrow \quad x^3 = -y^3$

$\Rightarrow \quad \frac{x^3}{y^3} = -1$

$\Rightarrow \quad \left(\frac{x}{y}\right)^3 = -1$

$\Rightarrow \quad \frac{x}{y} = -1$

Hence, $\frac{x}{y}$ is one of the cube roots of -1.

35. By symmetry B has as many elements as C.

36. $A = \begin{bmatrix} \cos\theta & \sin\theta \\ -\sin\theta & \cos\theta \end{bmatrix}$

$\Rightarrow A^2 = \begin{bmatrix} \cos\theta & \sin\theta \\ -\sin\theta & \cos\theta \end{bmatrix}\begin{bmatrix} \cos\theta & \sin\theta \\ -\sin\theta & \cos\theta \end{bmatrix}$

$= \begin{bmatrix} \cos^2\theta - \sin^2\theta & \cos\theta.\sin\theta + \sin\theta.\cos\theta \\ -\sin\theta.\cos\theta - \sin\theta.\cos\theta & -\sin^2\theta + \cos^2\theta \end{bmatrix}$

$= \begin{bmatrix} \cos 2\theta & \sin 2\theta \\ -\sin 2\theta & \cos 2\theta \end{bmatrix}$

Similarly,

$A^3 = \begin{bmatrix} \cos 3\theta & \sin 3\theta \\ -\sin 3\theta & \cos 3\theta \end{bmatrix}$

37. $(1 \times 3)(3 \times 3)(3 \times 1) = (1 \times 1)$

38. $A = \begin{bmatrix} 0 & 1 \\ 1 & 0 \end{bmatrix}$

$\Rightarrow A^2 = \begin{bmatrix} 0 & 1 \\ 1 & 0 \end{bmatrix}\begin{bmatrix} 0 & 1 \\ 1 & 0 \end{bmatrix} = \begin{bmatrix} 1 & 0 \\ 0 & 1 \end{bmatrix}$

$\Rightarrow A^4 = I = \begin{bmatrix} 1 & 0 \\ 0 & 1 \end{bmatrix}$

39. $\sin A = \frac{3}{5}$

$\Rightarrow \cos A = -\frac{4}{5}$ ($\because$ A lies in 2nd quadrant)

$\therefore \cos^2\frac{A}{2} = \frac{1+\cos A}{2} = \frac{1}{10}$

$\Rightarrow \cos\frac{A}{2} = \frac{1}{\sqrt{10}}$ ($\frac{A}{2}$ lies in 1st Quadrant)

40. $\frac{1}{\sin 10^\circ} - \frac{\sqrt{3}}{\cos 10^\circ}$

$= \frac{\cos 10^\circ - \sqrt{3}\sin 10^\circ}{\sin 10^\circ.\cos 10^\circ}$

$= \frac{2\left[\frac{1}{2}.\cos 10^\circ - \frac{\sqrt{3}}{2}.\sin 10^\circ\right]}{\frac{2[2\sin 10^\circ.\cos 10^\circ]}{2}}$

$= \frac{2[\cos 60^\circ.\cos 10^\circ - \sin 60^\circ.\sin 10^\circ]}{\frac{\sin 20^\circ}{2}}$

$= 2 \times 2\frac{[\cos(60^\circ + 10^\circ)]}{\sin 20^\circ}$

$= 4 \times \frac{\cos 70^\circ}{\sin 20^\circ}$

$= 4 \times \frac{\cos(90^\circ - 20^\circ)}{\sin 20^\circ}$

$= 4 \times \frac{\sin 20^\circ}{\sin 20^\circ} = 4 \times 1 = 4$

41. Let $\tan^{-1}\left(\frac{5}{12}\right) = \theta$

$\Rightarrow \tan\theta = \frac{5}{12}$

$\tan\theta = \frac{100}{x}$

$\Rightarrow \frac{5}{12} = \frac{100}{x}$

$\Rightarrow 5x = 1200$

$\Rightarrow x = \frac{1200}{5} = 240$

Hence, the distance between the boat and the light house is 240 m.

42. $y = \sin\left(x + \frac{\pi}{6}\right) + \cos\left(x + \frac{\pi}{6}\right)$

$= \sqrt{2}\cos\left(x + \frac{\pi}{6} - \frac{\pi}{4}\right)$

$= \sqrt{2}\cos\left(x - \frac{\pi}{12}\right)$

$\Rightarrow y$ is maximum for $x - \frac{\pi}{12} = 0$

$\Rightarrow x = \frac{\pi}{12}$

43. $\sin\left(\frac{\pi}{18}\right).\sin\frac{5\pi}{18} \times \sin\frac{7\pi}{18} = k$

$\Rightarrow \sin 10^\circ.\sin 50^\circ.\sin 70^\circ = k$

$\Rightarrow \frac{2\sin 10^\circ.\sin 50^\circ.\sin 70^\circ}{2} = k$

$\Rightarrow [\cos(50 - 10^\circ) - \cos(50 + 10)] \times \sin 70^\circ = 2k$

$\Rightarrow [\cos 40^\circ - \cos 60^\circ] \times \sin 70^\circ = 2k$

$\Rightarrow \cos 40^\circ.\sin 70^\circ - \frac{1}{2} \times \sin 70^\circ = 2k$

$\Rightarrow \frac{2 \times \cos 40^\circ.\sin 70^\circ - 2 \times \frac{1}{2}\sin 70^\circ}{2} = 2k$

$$\Rightarrow \quad \frac{\sin(70°+40°)+\sin(70-40°)-\sin 70°}{2} = 2k$$

$$\Rightarrow \quad \sin 110° + \sin 30° - \sin 70° = 4k$$

$$\Rightarrow \quad \sin(180° - 70°) + \sin 30° - \sin 70° = 4k$$

$$\Rightarrow \quad \sin 70° + \frac{1}{2} - \sin 70° = 4k$$

$$\Rightarrow \quad \frac{1}{2} = 4k$$

$$\Rightarrow \quad k = \frac{1}{8}$$

44. $$\frac{\sin\alpha+\sin\beta}{\cos\alpha+\cos\beta} = \frac{2\sin\frac{(\alpha+\beta)}{2}.\cos\frac{(\alpha-\beta)}{2}}{2\cos\frac{(\alpha+\beta)}{2}.\cos\frac{(\alpha-\beta)}{2}}$$

$$= \frac{\sin\frac{(\alpha+\beta)}{2}}{\cos\frac{(\alpha+\beta)}{2}} = \tan\frac{(\alpha+\beta)}{2}$$

45. $$\frac{\sin(\theta+2\alpha)}{\sin\theta} = \frac{1}{3}$$

$$\Rightarrow \quad \frac{\sin(\theta+2\alpha)+\sin\theta}{\sin(\theta+2\alpha)-\sin\theta} = \frac{1+3}{1-3} = \frac{4}{-2}$$

$$\Rightarrow \quad \frac{2\sin\frac{\theta+2\alpha+\theta}{2}.\cos\frac{(\theta+2\alpha-\theta)}{2}}{2\cos\frac{(\theta+2\alpha+\theta)}{2}.\sin\frac{(\theta+2\alpha-\theta)}{2}} = -\frac{2}{1}$$

$$\Rightarrow \quad \frac{\sin(\theta+\alpha)\times\cos\alpha}{\cos(\theta+\alpha)\times\sin\alpha} = -\frac{2}{1}$$

$$\frac{\tan(\theta+\alpha)}{\tan\alpha} = -2$$

$$\Rightarrow \quad \tan(\theta+\alpha) = -2\tan\alpha$$

$$\Rightarrow \quad \tan(\theta+\alpha) + 2\tan\alpha = 0$$

46. $$\sin 18° = \frac{\sqrt{5}-1}{4}$$

$$\cos 18° = \sqrt{\frac{10+2\sqrt{5}}{4}}$$

$$\tan 18° = \frac{\sqrt{5}-1}{\sqrt{10+2\sqrt{5}}}$$

47. It is given that x,y,z are in G.P.

$\therefore \quad y^2 = xz$ ....(*i*)

Also, $\tan^{-1}x$, $\tan^{-1}y$, $\tan^{-1}z$ are in A.P.

$\therefore \quad 2\tan^{-1}y = \tan^{-1}x + \tan^{-1}z$

$$\Rightarrow \quad \tan^{-1}\left(\frac{2y}{1-y^2}\right) = \tan^{-1}\frac{(x+z)}{1-xz}$$

$$\Rightarrow \quad \frac{2y}{1-y^2} = \frac{x+z}{1-xz}$$

$$\Rightarrow \quad \frac{2y}{1-xz} = \frac{x+z}{1-xz}$$ [using (*i*)]

$$\Rightarrow \quad 2y = x + z$$ ...(*ii*)

$$\Rightarrow \quad y = \frac{x+z}{2}$$

$\therefore$ x, y, z are in A.P.

From (*i*) and (*ii*), we get, $x = y = z$

48. $$\tan 2\alpha = \tan(\alpha+\beta+\alpha-\beta)$$

$$= \frac{\tan(\alpha+\beta)+\tan(\alpha-\beta)}{1-\tan(\alpha+\beta)\tan(\alpha-\beta)}$$

$$= \frac{2+1}{1-2\times 1} = \frac{3}{-1} = -3$$

49. $$A + B + C = 180°$$

$$\frac{B+C}{2} = \frac{180°}{2} - \frac{A}{2}$$

I. $\sin\left(\frac{B+C}{2}\right) = \sin\left(90° - \frac{A}{2}\right) = \cos\frac{A}{2}$

II. $\tan\left(\frac{B+C}{2}\right) = \tan\left(90° - \frac{A}{2}\right) = \cot\frac{A}{2}$

III. $\sin(B + C) = \sin(180° - A) = \sin A$

IV. $\tan(B + C) = \tan(180° - A) = -\tan A$

Hence, I and II are correct

50. $$\because \quad \sec\theta - \csc\theta = \frac{4}{3}$$

$$\Rightarrow \quad \frac{1}{\cos\theta} - \frac{1}{\sin\theta} = \frac{4}{3}$$

$$\Rightarrow \quad \frac{\sin\theta-\cos\theta}{\cos\theta\times\sin\theta} = \frac{4}{3}$$

$$\Rightarrow \quad \sin\theta - \cos\theta = \frac{4}{3}\cos\theta.\sin\theta$$

Now, $(\sec\theta - \csc\theta)^2 = \frac{16}{9}$

$$\Rightarrow \sec^2\theta + \csc^2\theta - 2\sec\theta.\csc\theta = \frac{16}{9}$$

$$\Rightarrow \quad \frac{1}{\cos^2\theta} + \frac{1}{\sin^2\theta} - \frac{2}{\sin\theta.\cos\theta} = \frac{16}{9}$$

$$\Rightarrow \quad \frac{\sin^2\theta+\cos^2\theta-2\sin\theta.\cos\theta}{\cos^2\theta.\sin^2\theta} = \frac{16}{9}$$

$$\Rightarrow \quad \frac{1-2\sin\theta.\cos\theta}{\cos^2\theta.\sin^2\theta} = \frac{16}{9}$$

$$\Rightarrow 16\cos^2\theta.\sin^2\theta + 18\sin\theta.\cos\theta - 9 = 0$$

$$\Rightarrow 16\cos^2\theta.\sin^2\theta + 24\cos\theta.\sin\theta - 6\cos\theta.\sin\theta - 9 = 0$$

$$\Rightarrow 8\cos\theta.\sin\theta(2\cos\theta.\sin\theta + 3) - 3(2\cos\theta.\sin\theta + 3) = 0$$

$\Rightarrow (2\cos\theta.\sin\theta + 3)\ (8\cos\theta.\sin\theta - 3) = 0$

$\Rightarrow \cos\theta.\sin\theta = -\dfrac{3}{2}$ or $\cos\theta.\sin\theta = \dfrac{3}{8}$

$\therefore\ \sin\theta - \cos\theta = \dfrac{4}{3}\times\dfrac{-3}{2} = -2$

and $\sin\theta - \cos\theta = \dfrac{4}{3}\times\dfrac{3}{8} = \dfrac{1}{2}$

51.

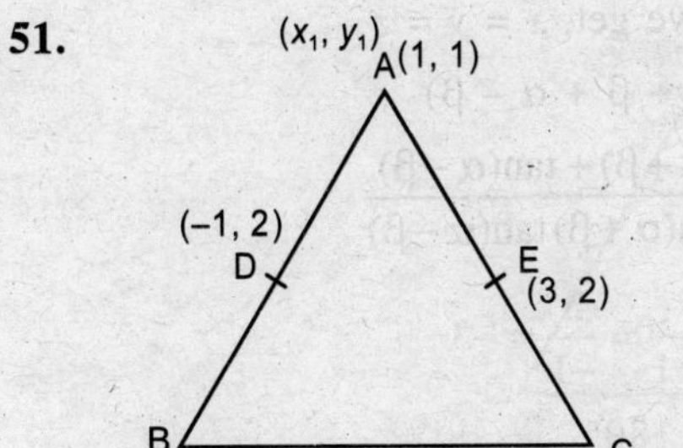

$\dfrac{1+x_2}{2} = -1$	$\dfrac{1+y_2}{2} = 2$
$1 + x_2 = 2$	$1 + y_2 = 4$
$x_2 = -3$	$y_2 = 3$
$\dfrac{1+x_3}{2} = 3$	$\dfrac{1+y_3}{2} = 2$
$1 + x_3 = 6$	$1 + y_3 = 4$
$\Rightarrow\ x_3 = 5$	$y_3 = 3$

Hence, centroid of the triangle

$$\left(\frac{x_1+x_2+x_3}{3}, \frac{y_1+y_2+y_3}{3}\right)$$

$$= \left(\frac{1-3+5}{3}, \frac{1+3+3}{3}\right)$$

$$= \left(1, \frac{7}{3}\right)$$

52.

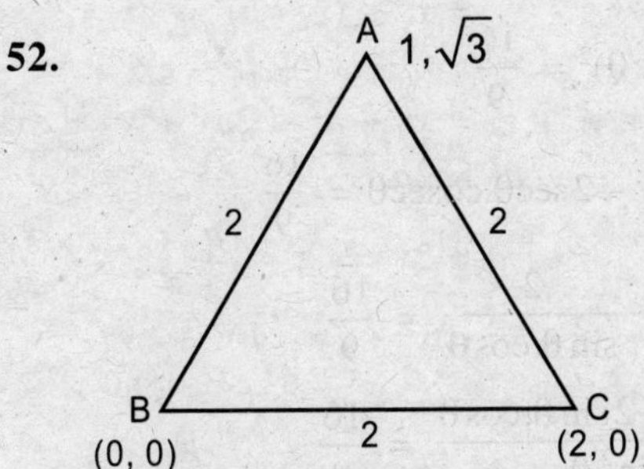

$\therefore$ Co-ordinates of the incentre are

$$\left(\frac{ax_1+bx_2+cx_3}{a+b+c}, \frac{ay_1+by_2+cy_3}{a+b+c}\right)$$

$$= \left(\frac{2\times1+2(0)+2\times2}{2+2+2}, \frac{2\times\sqrt{3}+2\times0+2\times0}{a+b+c}\right)$$

$$= \left(\frac{2+4}{6}, \frac{2\sqrt{3}+0+0}{6}\right)$$

$$= \left(1, \frac{1}{\sqrt{3}}\right)$$

53.

D (x, y), C (4, 3), A (−2, −1), B (1, 0)

$\because$ ABCD is a parallelogram

$\therefore$ mid point of AC = mid point of BD

$$\left(\frac{4-2}{2}, \frac{3-1}{2}\right) = \left(\frac{x+1}{2}, \frac{y+0}{2}\right)$$

$$\Rightarrow\quad (1, 1) = \left(\frac{x+1}{2}, \frac{y}{2}\right)$$

$$\frac{x+1}{2} = 1 \Rightarrow x = 1$$

$$\frac{y}{2} = 1 \Rightarrow y = 2$$

Hence, Co-ordinate of D = (1, 2)

54. Centres of the given circles are $C_1(5, 0)$ and $C_2(0, 0)$, and their radii are $r_1 = 3$ and $r_2 = r$. For the circles to intersect at two distinct points.

$$|r_1 - r_2| < C_1C_2 < r_1 + r_2$$

$$\Rightarrow\quad r - 3 < 5 < r + 3$$

$$\Rightarrow\quad r < 8 \text{ and } r > 2$$

$$\Rightarrow\quad 2 < r < 8$$

Hence, option (A) is correct.

55. Let centre be (h, k), then

$$\sqrt{(h-3)^2+(k+2)^2} = \sqrt{(h+2)^2+(k-0)^2}$$

and $\quad 2h - k - 3 = 0 = k = 2h - 3$

$h^2 + 9 - 6h + k^2 + 4 + 4k = h^2 + 4 + 4h + k^2$

$4k - 6h + 13 = 4h + 4$

$4k - 10h = -9$

$4(2h - 3) - 10h = -9$

$8h - 12 - 10h = -9$

$\Rightarrow\quad -2h = 3 \Rightarrow h = \dfrac{3}{2}$

$$k = 2h - 3 = 2\times\frac{3}{2} - 3 = 0$$

$$\left(\frac{3}{2}, 0\right)$$

$x^2 + y^2 + 2hx + 2ky + c = 0$

$$x^2+y^2+2\times\frac{3}{2}x+2(0)y$$

Required equation is $x^2 + y^2 + 3x + 2 = 0$

56. (–2, –2) λ (x,y) 1 (2, – 4)
A ———— C ———— B

$$x = \frac{2\lambda-2}{\lambda+1}$$

$$-\frac{2}{7} = \frac{2(\lambda-1)}{\lambda+1}$$

$$7\lambda - 7 = -\lambda - 1$$

$\Rightarrow$ $8\lambda = 6$

$\Rightarrow$ $\lambda = \frac{6}{8} = \frac{3}{4}$

Hence, required ratio is 3 : 4.

57. Let the ellipse be $\frac{x^2}{a^2}+\frac{y^2}{b^2} = 1$

It is given that $e = \frac{1}{4}$ and $ae = 2$

$\therefore$ $a = \frac{2}{\frac{1}{4}} = 8$

Now, $b^2 = a^2(1 - e^2)$

$\Rightarrow$ $b^2 = 8^2\left(1-\frac{1}{16}\right)$

$\Rightarrow$ $b^2 = 64\times\frac{15}{16} = 60$

Hence, the required ellipse is

$$\frac{x^2}{64}+\frac{y^2}{60} = 1$$

58. Equation of line parallel to
$2x + 3y + 1 = 0$ is
$2x + 3y + \lambda = 0$

But it passes through (–1, 2)

$\therefore$ $2(-1) + 3(2) + \lambda = 0$

$\Rightarrow$ $-2 + 6 + \lambda = 0$

$\Rightarrow$ $\lambda + 4 = 0$

$\Rightarrow$ $\lambda = -4$

$\therefore$ Required equation is $2x + 3y - 4 = 0$

59. The given equations of lines are

$$\sqrt{2}x+\sqrt{3}y = 1$$

$$\sqrt{3}x+\sqrt{2}y = 2$$

$a_1 = \sqrt{2}$, $b_1 = \sqrt{3}$, $c_1 = 1$

$a_2 = \sqrt{3}$, $b_2 = \sqrt{2}$, $c_2 = 2$

$$\theta = \tan^{-1}\left|\frac{a_2b_1-a_1b_2}{a_1a_2+b_1b_2}\right|$$

$$= \tan^{-1}\left|\frac{\sqrt{3}\times\sqrt{3}-\sqrt{2}\times\sqrt{2}}{\sqrt{2}\times\sqrt{3}+\sqrt{3}\times\sqrt{2}}\right|$$

$$= \tan^{-1}\left|\frac{3-2}{\sqrt{6}+\sqrt{6}}\right| = \tan^{-1}\frac{1}{2\sqrt{6}}$$

Hence, required angle $= \tan^{-1}\frac{1}{2\sqrt{6}}$

60.

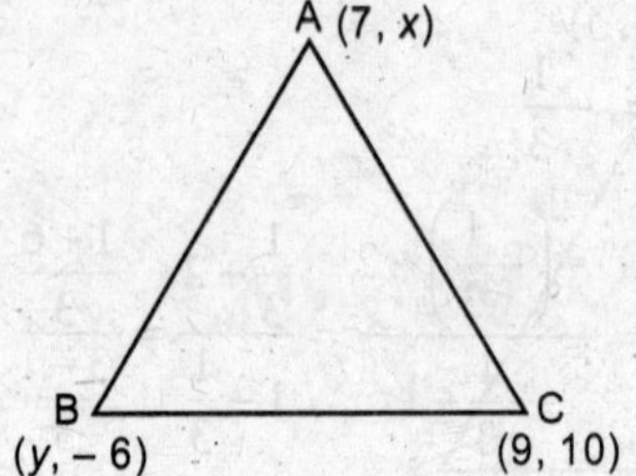

Centroid of the triangle

$$= \left(\frac{x_1+x_2+x_3}{3},\frac{y_1+y_2+y_3}{3}\right)$$

$$= \left(\frac{7+y+9}{3} = 6, \frac{x-6+10}{3} = 3\right)$$

$= y = 2, x = 5$

Hence, the centroid of the triangle
= 2, 5

61. Direction cosines of a straight line parallel to y axis are 0,1,0

Parallel to x axis are 1,0,0

Parallel to z axis are 0,01

Here, direction consines are 0,1,0

$\therefore$ It is parallel to y-axis.

62. Let the point A(x,y,z) is equidistant from the points B(0,0,0), C(a,0,0), D(0,b,0), E(0,0,C)

$\because$ AB = AC = AD = AE

$$x^2 + y^2 + z^2 = (x - a)^2 + y^2 + z^2$$
$$= x^2 + (y - b)^2 + z^2$$
$$= x^2 + y^2 + (z - c)^2$$

$$x^2 + y^2 + z^2 = x^2 + a^2 - 2ax + y^2 + z^2$$

$\Rightarrow$ $a^2 = 2ax$

$\Rightarrow$ $a = 2x \Rightarrow x = \frac{a}{2}$

Similarly, $x^2 + y^2 + z^2 = x^2 + (y - b)^2 + z^2$

$\Rightarrow$ $x^2 + y^2 + z^2 = x^2 + y^2 + b^2 - 2by + z^2$

$\Rightarrow$ $b^2 = 2by \Rightarrow y = \frac{b}{2}$

$$x^2 + y^2 + z^2 = x^2 + y^2 + c^2 + z^2 - 2cz$$

$\Rightarrow$ $c^2 = 2cz$

$\Rightarrow$ $c = 2z \Rightarrow z = \frac{c}{2}$

$\therefore$ Point is $\left(\frac{a}{2},\frac{b}{2},\frac{c}{2}\right)$

64. Suppose yz-plane divides the line joining the given points in the ratio $\lambda : 1$.

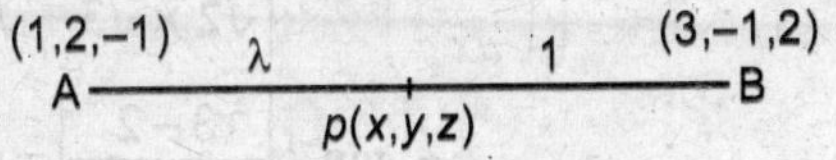

$$x = \frac{3\lambda+1}{\lambda+1},\ y = \frac{-\lambda+2}{\lambda+1},\ z = \frac{2\lambda-1}{\lambda+1}$$

$$\because \quad \frac{3\lambda+1}{\lambda+1} = 0 \Rightarrow 3\lambda = -1$$

$$\lambda = -\frac{1}{3}$$

$$y = \frac{-\left(-\frac{1}{3}\right)+2}{-\frac{1}{3}+1} = \frac{\frac{1}{3}+2}{1-\frac{1}{3}} = \frac{\frac{1+6}{3}}{\frac{3-1}{3}}$$

$$= \frac{7}{2}$$

$$z = \frac{2\left(-\frac{1}{3}\right)-1}{-\frac{1}{3}+1} = \frac{-\frac{2}{3}-1}{1-\frac{1}{3}} = \frac{-\frac{5}{3}}{\frac{2}{3}}$$

$$= -\frac{5}{2}$$

Hence, required points $\left(0, \frac{7}{2}, -\frac{5}{2}\right)$

65.
$$\frac{x-b}{a} = \frac{y-0}{1} = \frac{z-d}{c} \quad ...(i)$$

$$\frac{x-f}{e} = \frac{y-0}{1} = \frac{z-\hbar}{g} \quad ...(ii)$$

(i) and (ii) are perpendicular

$\Rightarrow ae + 1 + cg = 0$

66.
$$\begin{vmatrix} a & b & c \\ 1 & -1 & 1 \\ 2 & 3 & 2 \\ 1 & m & n \end{vmatrix} = 0$$

$1(3n - 2m) + 1(2n - 2) + 1(2m - 3) = 0$

$3n - 2m + 2n - 2 + 2m - 3 = 0$

$5n - 5 = 0$

$\Rightarrow \quad 5n = 5 \Rightarrow n = 1$

$\sqrt{c} = \sqrt{1+m^2+n^2}$

$6 = 1 + m^2 + 1$

$\Rightarrow \quad m^2 = 4$

$\Rightarrow \quad m = \pm 2$

$\therefore \quad m = \pm 2$ and $n = 1$

67. Since, the diagonals of a paralleio gram bisect each other. Therefore P is the middle point of AC and BD both.

$$\therefore \quad \overline{OA}+\overline{OC} = 2.\overline{OP}$$

$$\text{and} \quad \overline{OB}+\overline{OD} = 2.\overline{OP}$$

$$\overline{OA}+\overline{OB}+\overline{OC}+\overline{OD} = 4.\overline{OP}$$

68.

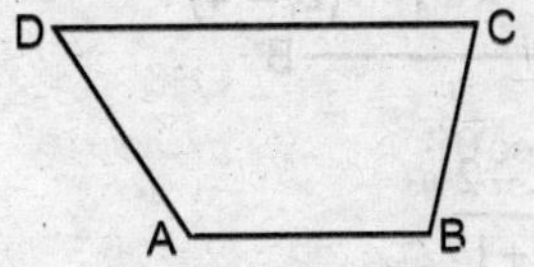

$$\overline{BA}+\overline{AD} = \overline{BD} \quad ...(i)$$

$$\overline{CD}+\overline{DA}+\overline{CA} \quad ...(ii)$$

adding (*i*) and (*ii*)

$$\overline{BA}+\overline{CA} = \overline{BD}+\overline{CA}$$

69.
$$\vec{c} = \vec{a}\times\vec{b} \Rightarrow \vec{c}\perp\vec{a} \text{ and } \vec{c}\perp\vec{b}$$

$$\vec{a} = \vec{b}\times\vec{c} \Rightarrow \vec{a}\perp\vec{b} \text{ and } \vec{a}\perp\vec{c}$$

$$\Rightarrow \quad \vec{a}\perp\vec{b}\perp\vec{c}$$

Now, $\quad \vec{a}\times\vec{b} = \vec{c}$

$$\Rightarrow \quad \left(\vec{b}\times\vec{c}\right)\times\vec{b} = \vec{c} \quad \left[\because \vec{a} = \vec{b}\times\vec{c}\right]$$

$$\Rightarrow \left(\vec{b}.\vec{b}\right)\vec{c} - \left(\vec{b}.\vec{c}\right)\vec{b} = \vec{c}$$

$$\Rightarrow \quad \left|\vec{b}\right|^2\vec{c} = \vec{c} \quad \left[\because \vec{b}\perp\vec{c} \because \vec{b}.\vec{c} = 0\right]$$

$$\Rightarrow \quad \left|\vec{b}\right| = 1$$

Also $\quad \vec{c} = \vec{a}\times\vec{b} \Rightarrow \left|\vec{c}\right| = \left|\vec{a}\times\vec{b}\right|$

$$\Rightarrow \quad \left|\vec{c}\right| = \left|\vec{a}\right|\left|\vec{b}\right|\sin\frac{\pi}{2}$$

$$\Rightarrow \quad \left|\vec{c}\right| = \left|\vec{a}\right| \quad \left[\because \left|\vec{b}\right| = 1\right]$$

Hence option (A) is correct.

70. $\because \vec{a}\perp\vec{b}$

$\therefore \quad \vec{a}\cdot\vec{b} = 0$

$\therefore \quad \left(2\vec{i}+3\vec{j}+4\vec{k}\right)\cdot\left(3\vec{i}+2\vec{j}-\lambda\vec{k}\right)$

$\Rightarrow \quad 6 + 6 - 4\lambda = 0$

$$\Rightarrow \quad 4\lambda = 12 \Rightarrow \lambda = \frac{12}{4} = 3$$

71. We have,

$$\lim_{x\to 0}\frac{e^x-1-x}{x^2} = \lim_{x\to 0}\frac{e^x-1}{2x}$$

$$= \frac{1}{2} \quad \text{[using L-Hospital's rule]}$$

72. $\displaystyle\int_0^{\frac{\pi}{2}}\frac{d\theta}{1+\cos\theta}$

$$\text{Let} \quad I = \int_0^{\frac{\pi}{2}}\frac{1}{1+\cos\theta}\times\frac{1-\cos\theta}{1-\cos\theta}d\theta$$

$$= \int_0^{\frac{\pi}{2}}\frac{1-\cos\theta}{\sin^2\theta}d\theta$$

$$= \int_0^{\frac{\pi}{2}} \left[\frac{1}{\sin^2\theta} - \frac{\cos\theta}{\sin^2\theta}\right] d\theta$$

$$= \int_0^{\frac{\pi}{2}} \left[\text{cosec}^2\theta - \text{cosec}\theta \times \cot\theta\right] d\theta$$

$$= \left[-\cot\theta + \text{cosec}\,\theta\right]_0^{\frac{\pi}{2}}$$

$$= \left[-\cot\frac{\pi}{2} + \text{cosec}\frac{\pi}{2}\right] - \left(\cot 0° - \text{cosec}0°\right)$$

$= 1$

73. $\dfrac{1}{x(x^7+1)}dx$

Putting $x^7 + 1 = t$

$7x^6 dx = dt$

$$\int \frac{1}{x(x^7+1)}dx = \frac{1}{7}\int \frac{1}{t(t-1)}dt$$

$$= \frac{1}{7}\log\frac{(t-1)}{t} + c$$

$$= \frac{1}{7}\log\left(\frac{x^7+1-1}{x^7+1}\right) + c$$

$$= \frac{1}{7}\log\left(\frac{x^7}{x^7+1}\right) + c$$

75. $$\frac{f(a)}{f(a+1)} = \frac{\frac{a}{a-1}}{\frac{a+1}{a}} = \frac{a}{a-1} \times \frac{a}{a+1}$$

$$= \frac{a^2}{a^2-1} = f(a^2)$$

76. $$\int \frac{x^{e-1}+e^{x-1}}{x^e+e^x}dx = \frac{1}{e}\int \frac{ex^{e-1}+e^x}{x^e+e^x}dx$$

$$= \frac{1}{e}\log(x^e+e^x) + c$$

79. $\because$ $f(x) = \sqrt{9-x^2}$

$\Rightarrow$ $f'(x) = \dfrac{-x}{\sqrt{9-x^2}}$

Now, $\lim\limits_{x\to 1} \dfrac{f(x)-f(1)}{x-1} = f'(1)$

$\Rightarrow$ $\lim\limits_{x\to 1} \dfrac{f(x)-f(1)}{x-1} = \dfrac{-1}{\sqrt{9-1}}$

$$= \frac{-1}{\sqrt{8}} = \frac{-1}{2\sqrt{2}}$$

80. $$\frac{d^2x}{dy^2} = \frac{d}{dy}\left(\frac{1}{\left(\frac{dy}{dx}\right)}\right)$$

$$= \frac{\frac{d}{dy}\left(\frac{dy}{dx}\right)}{\left(\frac{dy}{dx}\right)^2} = \frac{\frac{d}{dx}\left(\frac{dy}{dx}\right)\times\frac{dx}{dy}}{\left(\frac{dy}{dx}\right)^2} = \left(\frac{d^2y}{dx^2}\right)\left(\frac{dy}{dx}\right)^{-3}$$

81. $(f-g)(x) = \begin{cases} x, & x \in Q \\ -x, & x \in R-Q \end{cases}$

Clearly $f - g$ is one-one and on to.

82. $f(x) = \sin 3x$

$\sin 3x$ is increasing in

$$\left[-\frac{\pi}{6}, \frac{\pi}{6}\right]$$

Interval length $= \dfrac{\pi}{3}$

83. $x\,dy = ydx + y^2dy$

$\Rightarrow$ $\displaystyle\int \frac{ydx - xdy}{y^2} = -\int dy$

$\Rightarrow$ $-y = \dfrac{x}{y} + C$

$y(1) = 1 \Rightarrow C = -2$

$\Rightarrow$ $-y = \dfrac{x}{y} - 2$

$\therefore$ $y(-3) = 3$ $(\because y(x) > 0)$

85. $$f(x) = \int \sin^2 x dx = \int\left(\frac{1-\cos 2x}{2}\right)dx$$

$$= \frac{1}{2}\left[x - \frac{1}{2}\sin 2x\right] + C$$

$f(x+\pi) \neq f(x)$ $(\because f(x)$ is not periodic)

Statement 1 false

Next, $\sin^2(\pi + x) = \sin^2 x$

Statement 2 true

86. $$y = x\left(\frac{dy}{dx}\right)^2 + \left(\frac{dy}{dx}\right)^{-2}$$

$\Rightarrow$ $y\left(\dfrac{dy}{dx}\right)^2 = x\left(\dfrac{dy}{dx}\right)^4 + 1$

Order = 1, degree = 4

87. $y^2 - 2ay + x^2 = a^2$

$\Rightarrow 2y\dfrac{dy}{dx} - 2a\dfrac{dy}{dx} + 2x = 0$

$\Rightarrow$ $\dfrac{y\frac{dy}{dx} + x}{\frac{dy}{dx}} = a$

$\Rightarrow \quad \dfrac{py+x}{p} = a$

$\Rightarrow y^2 \dfrac{-2y(py+x)}{p} + x^2 = \left(\dfrac{py+x}{p}\right)^2$

$\Rightarrow p^2y^2 - 2p^2y^2 - 2xyp + p^2x^2 = p^2y^2 + x^2 + 2xyp$

$\Rightarrow -2p^2y^2 + p^2x^2 - 4xyp - x^2 = 0$

$\Rightarrow \quad p^2(x^2 - 2y^2) - 4xyp - x^2 = 0$

88. $ydx - xdy - 2y^2dy = 0$

$\dfrac{ydx - xdy}{y^2} = 2dy$

$d\left(\dfrac{x}{y}\right) = 2y$

$\dfrac{x}{y} = 2y + c$

$x = 2y^2 + cy$

Hence, option (c) is correct.

89. $f(x + y) = f(x).f(y) \ \forall \ x, y \in R$

$\Rightarrow \quad f(0 + 0) = f(0).f(0) \Rightarrow \{f(0)\}^2 - f(0) = 0$

$\Rightarrow \quad f(0) = 1$

Next, $\quad f'(x) = \lim\limits_{h\to 0} \dfrac{f(x+h)-f(x)}{h}$

$= \lim\limits_{h\to 0} \dfrac{f(x)\cdot f(h)-f(x)}{h}$

$= f(x)\cdot \lim\limits_{h\to 0} \dfrac{f(h)-1}{h}$

$= f(x) \lim\limits_{h\to 0} \dfrac{f(h)-f(0)}{h} = f(x).f'(0)$

$\therefore \quad f'(5) = f(5).f'(0)$

90. $I = \displaystyle\int_0^a f(x)g(x)dx = \int_0^a f(a-x)\cdot g(a-x)dx$

$= \displaystyle\int_0^a f(x)\{2-g(x)\}dx = \int_0^a 2f(x)dx - \int_0^a f(x)\cdot g(x)dx$

$\Rightarrow 2I = 2\displaystyle\int_0^a f(x)dx \Rightarrow I = \int_0^a f(x)dx$

91. $\log\left(\dfrac{dy}{dx}\right) = a \Rightarrow \dfrac{dy}{dx} = e^a \Rightarrow \displaystyle\int dy = \int e^a dx$

$\Rightarrow \quad y = xe^a + c$

92. $f(x) = \begin{cases} 2x+1, & -3 < x < -2 \\ x-1, & -2 \le x < 0 \\ x+2, & 0 \le x < 1 \end{cases}$

Here $f(0^-) = -1$ and $f(0^+) = 2$ clearly $f(x)$ is discontinuous at $x = 0$ and continuous at all other points

95. $\dfrac{d}{dx}\log_{10}^{(5x^2+3)} = \dfrac{1}{5x^2+3} \times \log_{10}^{e} \times 10x = \dfrac{10x\log_{10}^{e}}{5x^2+3}$

96. $f(a) = \dfrac{a-1}{a+1}$

$f(2a) = \dfrac{2a-1}{2a+1}$

$f(a) + 1 = \dfrac{a-1}{a+1} + 1 = \dfrac{2a}{a+1}$

So, $\quad f(2a) \ne f(a) + 1$

Next, $\quad f\left(\dfrac{1}{a}\right) = \dfrac{\frac{1}{a}-1}{\frac{1}{a}+1} = \dfrac{1-a}{a+1} = -\left(\dfrac{a-1}{a+1}\right) = -f(a)$

97.

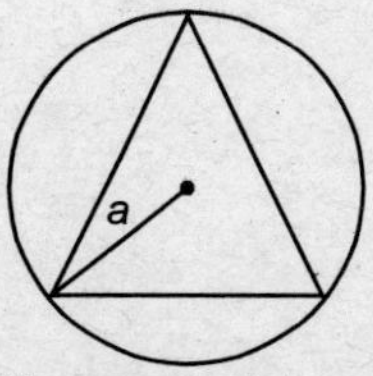

For area of Δ to be maximum, triangle should be an equilateral triangle

ℓ = length of side of equilateral triangle = $\sqrt{3}a$

$\therefore \quad \text{Area} = \dfrac{\sqrt{3}}{4}\left(\sqrt{3}a\right)^2 = \dfrac{3\sqrt{3}}{4}a^2$

98. $f(x) = x + \dfrac{1}{x} \Rightarrow f'(x) = \dfrac{x^2-1}{x^2}$

$\Rightarrow \quad f'(x) = \dfrac{(x-1)(x+1)}{x^2}$

for $\quad x \in (0, 1), f'(x) < 0$

$\Rightarrow \quad f(x)$ decreases

99. $f(x) = x^n, n \ne 0$

$\Rightarrow \quad f'(x) = nx^{n-1}$

$f(x)$ to be differentiable, $n - 1 \ge 0 \Rightarrow n \ge 1$

$\Rightarrow \quad n \in [1, \infty)$

100. $\displaystyle\int_{e^{-1}}^{e^2} \left|\dfrac{\log x}{x}\right| dx = \int_{e^{-1}}^{e^0} -\dfrac{\log x}{x}dx + \int_{e^0}^{e^2} \dfrac{\log x}{x}dx$

$= -\dfrac{1}{2}\left[(\log x)^2\right]_{e^{-1}}^{e^0} + \dfrac{1}{2}\left[(\log x)^2\right]_{e^0}^{e^2}$

$= \dfrac{1}{2} + 2 = \dfrac{5}{2}$

102. Total of 100 observation

$= 100 \times 20 = 2000$

Total of four incorrect

$= 21 + 21 + 18 + 20 = 80$

$2000 - 80 = 1920$

New mean $= \dfrac{1920}{96} = 20$

103. Required probability $= \frac{{}^2C_0 \times {}^2C_2}{{}^4C_2} = \frac{1}{6}$

104. Required probability

$= 1-\left(1-\frac{1}{2}\right)\left(1-\frac{1}{3}\right)\left(1-\frac{1}{4}\right)$

$= 1-\left(\frac{1}{2}\right)\left(\frac{2}{3}\right)\left(\frac{3}{4}\right)$

$= 1-\frac{1}{4}=\frac{3}{4}$

105. Let no. of boys = x and no. of girls = y

Total weight of 150 students = 150 × 60
= 9000

Total weight of x boys = $70x$

Total weight of y girls = $55y$

According to the question,

$[x + y = 150] \times 70$

$70x + 55y = 9000$

$70x + 70y = 10500$

$70x + 55y = 9000$

$15y = 1500 \Rightarrow y = 100$

$\therefore$ No. of boys = 150 – 100 = 50

106. $A \subseteq B \Rightarrow A \cap B = A$

$P(A/B) = \frac{P(A \cap B)}{P(B)} = \frac{P(A)}{P(B)} = \frac{0.2}{0.5} = \frac{2}{5}$

$P(B/A) = \frac{P(A \cap B)}{P(A)} = \frac{P(A)}{P(A)} = 1$

107. Required probability $= \frac{\pi\left(\frac{r}{2}\right)^2}{\pi r^2} = \frac{1}{4}$

109. Required angle $= \frac{40}{100} \times 360°$

$= 4 \times 36 = 144°$

111. Required probability

$= \frac{4}{52} = \frac{1}{13}$

114. The abscissa of the point of intersection of less than and more than ogive is median.

116. Result $= \sqrt{\left(-\frac{1}{2}\right) \times \left(\frac{-1}{8}\right)} = \frac{1}{4}$

117. $x_1 + x_2 + x_3 + x_4 + x_5$
$= 32 \times 5 = 160$

median $= \left(\frac{5+1}{2}\right)$ th term

= 3rd term

= 33

$\Rightarrow \quad x_3 = 33$

$40 - 35 = 5$

$\therefore$ New total no = 160 – 5 = 155

$\therefore$ New mean $= \frac{155}{5} = 31$

$\therefore$ Mean will decrease but median remains the same.

Hence, option (B) is correct.

118. Required probability

$= 1-\frac{9}{36} = 1-\frac{1}{4} = \frac{3}{4}$

119. $P(\bar{A} \cap \bar{B}) = 1 - P(A \cup B)$

$= 1-\left(\frac{1}{3}+\frac{1}{4}\right) = \frac{5}{12}$

120. $np = 12$ and $npq = 4$

$\Rightarrow \quad q = \frac{4}{12} = \frac{1}{3} \Rightarrow p = \frac{2}{3}$

So, $n \times \frac{2}{3} = 12 \Rightarrow n = 18$

Previous Papers (Solved)

NATIONAL DEFENCE ACADEMY & NAVAL ACADEMY

NDA & NA – Entrance Exam, 2016 (II)

PAPER I : GENERAL ABILITY TEST

PART A : ENGLISH LANGUAGE

Sentence Improvement

Directions (Qs. No. 1 to 13) : *Look at the underlined part of each sentence. Below each sentence are given three possible substitutions for the underlined part. If one of them (A), (B) or (C) is better than the underlined part, indicate your response on the Answer Sheet against the corresponding letter (A), (B) or (C). If none of the substitutions improves the sentence, indicate (D) as your response on the Answer Sheet. Thus a "No improvement" response will be signified by the letter (D).*

1. My old teacher gave many poor students money in spite of he was poor.
A. even though B. as if
C. however D. No Improvement

2. You should to read the newspapers regularly if you want to be well-informed.
A. ought B. have to
C. should be D. No Improvement

3. If he had listening to me he would not have got lost.
A. listened me B. listened to me
C. listen me D. No Improvement

4. He asked for a bank loan also he didn't have sufficient resources.
A. because B. even if
C. requiring D. No Improvement

5. I went to the shop to buy some stationeries.
A. stationery B. stationary
C. stationaries D. No Improvement

6. I have been waiting here for the last two hours.
A. from B. since
C. by D. No Improvement

7. The table needs to be painted.
A. paint B. painting
C. having paint D. No Improvement

8. It began to rain heavily just when I prepare to go out.
A. prepared B. was preparing
C. have prepared D. No Improvement

9. The couple seemed to love one another very much.
A. every other B. each
C. each other D. No Improvement

10. It is high time that we did something.
A. had done B. would do
C. have done D. No Improvement

11. If I were a millionaire, I would have helped the poor.
A. am capable of helping
B. could have helped
C. would help
D. No Improvement

12. The training programme was extended for a month.
A. from B. until
C. since D. No Improvement

13. The painting which they were looking at was done by my sister.
A. what B. that
C. whom D. No Improvement

Ordering of Words in a Sentence

Directions (Qs. No. 14 to 20) : *Each of the following items in this section consists of a sentence the parts of which have been jumbled. These parts have been labelled P, Q, R and S. Given below each sentence are four sequences namely (A), (B), (C) and (D). You are required to rearrange the jumbled parts of the sentence and mark your response accordingly.*

14. The statement
P. therefore you must listen carefully
Q. what the speaker has said
R. in order to understand
S. will be made just once
The proper sequence should be:
A. S P R Q B. S R Q P
C. R S P Q D. S P Q R

15. The small boy who
P. broke his leg Q. fell down
R. and S. climbed the wall

The proper sequence should be:

A. P S R Q B. S Q R P
C. Q S R P D. S P R Q

16. According to an engineer
P. might hit the market next year
Q. a newly developed air-cooler system
R. that employed in conventional room coolers
S. which is based on a principle radically different from
The proper sequence should be:
A. S Q R P B. R S Q P
C. Q S R P D. P Q R S

17. The clerk
P. on the desk
Q. left the money
R. in the safe
S. which he should have locked up
The proper sequence should be:
A. S R Q P B. Q R S P
C. P Q R S D. Q P S R

18. Hardly had my brother descended from the plane
P. when the people
Q. waved and cheered
R. who had come to receive him
S. from the lounge
The proper sequence should be:
A. P Q R S B. R S P Q
C. R P Q S D. P R S Q

19. The essay
P. like that of the human face
Q. because its variety is infinite
R. is a literary form
S. which is not easy to define
The proper sequence should be:
A. P Q R S B. P Q S R
C. R S Q P D. R S P Q

20. The exhibition committee
P. attractive and useful
Q. to make exhibition
R. making efforts
S. has been
The proper sequence should be:
A. Q S R P B. S R Q P
C. Q P S R D. S P Q R

Synonyms

Directions (Qs. no. 21 to 25): *Each item in this section consists of a sentence with an underlined word or words followed by four words or group of words. Select the word or group of words that is most similar in meaning to the underlined word.*

21. Hospitality is a virtue for which the natives of the East in general are highly admired.
A. Duty of a doctor
B. Generosity shown to guests
C. Cleanliness in hospitals
D. Kindness

22. House rent in cities like Mumbai or Delhi has risen to astronomical figures beyond the reach of even high-salaried people.
A. exorbitant B. commercial
C. planetary D. illogical

23. Appropriate technology holds the key to a nation's development.
A. Modern B. Suitable
C. Effective D. Growing

24. He was enamoured of his own golden voice.
A. very fond of B. concerned with
C. obsessed with D. imbued with

25. Some journalists are guilty of indulging in yellow journalism.
A. misrepresentation
B. vulgarization
C. sensational reporting
D. loud gestures

Antonyms

Directions (Qs. no. 26 to 30): *Each item in this section consists of a sentence with an underlined word or words followed by four words or group of words. Select the word or group of words that is most nearly* ***opposite*** *in meaning to the underlined word.*

26. The culprit was sentenced by the court.
A. acquitted B. punished
C. relieved D. pardoned

27. Thrifty as he is, he can well afford to live within his means.
A. careless B. instinctive
C. sentimental D. extravagant

28. Do not give him a responsible job, he is immature.
A. thoughtful B. cautious
C. calculating D. seasoned

29. I was prepared to show my hand provided he agreed to do the same.
A. to yield
B. to shake hands
C. to conceal my plan
D. to lose my ground

30. Akbar the great was a sagacious ruler.
A. haughty B. cunning
C. rude D. unwise

Spotting Errors

Directions (Qs. No. 31 to 40): *Each question in this section has a sentence with three parts labelled (A), (B) and (C). Read each sentence to find out whether there is any error in any part and indicate your response in the Answer Sheet against the corresponding letter i.e., (A) or (B) or (C). If you find no error, your response should be indicated as (D).*

31. My friend was (A)/ habitual to drive a car (B)/ at very high speed. (C)/ No error (D).

32. Being a day of national mourning (A)/ the offices were closed (B)/ and the national flag flew half mast. (C)/ No error (D).

33. If you are wanting to watch (A)/ the birds nesting (B)/ you must not let them see you. (C)/ No error (D).

34. He does not listen to (A)/ what I say, (B)/ although I am advising him for a long time. (C)/ No error (D).

35. It is most essential for us (A)/ to reach the station before noon (B)/ lest we should miss the train. (C)/ No error (D).

36. I asked him (A)/ what had brought (B)/ him there. (C)/ No error (D).

37. The guards (A)/ dare not (B)/ to harm him. (C)/ No error (D).

38. The Principal looks very worried (A)/ because students are on strike for the last fifteen days as a protest against (B)/ his disciplinary action against some miscreants. (C)/ No error (D).

39. The king was embarrassed (A)/ to find evidences (B)/ against his own queen. (C)/ No error (D).

40. As I prefer coffee than tea (A)/ my friends always take the trouble (B)/ to get me a cup of coffee whenever I visit them. (C)/ No error (D).

Selecting Words

Directions (Qs. No. 41 to 50): *Each of the following sentences has a blank space and four words given after the sentence. Select whichever word you consider most appropriate for the blank space and indicate your response on the Answer Sheet.*

41. She has been lying in bed for the last fortnight. I hope she will _______
A. come out B. pull out
C. pull through D. go out

42. The path of progress is beset _______ difficulties.
A. with B. by
C. through D. along

43. I feel _______ for those who are cruel to their children.
A. sympathy B. contempt
C. admiration D. craving

44. Both the parties were keen to have an _______ settlement of the dispute.
A. enviable B. inimical
C. worthy D. amicable

45. I have come to know that the two brothers have _______ .
A. fallen through B. fallen out
C. fallen for D. fallen short

46. Everybody finds his own work _______ whereas he feels that others have delightful jobs.
A. tedious B. fabulous
C. unprofitable D. indecent

47. The accident took place because of the criminal _______ of the driver.
A. performance B. disregard
C. negligence D. slackness

48. The belief in the _______ of vaccination is gaining ground.
A. immunity B. prevalence
C. efficacy D. workability

49. Our new leader is a _______ young man and will take us forward.
A. haughty B. intoxicated
C. fanciful D. dynamic

50. They found a world of _______ between what he said and what he did.
A. chaos B. bitterness
C. difference D. hope

PART B : GENERAL KNOWLEDGE

51. Which one of the following statements is correct?
A. Covalent bonds are directional
B. Ionic bonds are directional
C. Both covalent and ionic bonds are directional
D. Both covalent and ionic bonds are non-directional

52. When one strikes a safety match, the first step is:
A. burning of sulphur
B. decomposition of potassium chlorate into potassium chloride and oxygen
C. conversion of a small amount of red phosphorus into white phosphorus
D. burning of glue and starch

53. The LPG cooking gas contains propane and butane as the constituents. A sulphur containing compound is added to the LPG, because:

A. it lowers the cost of production
B. it enhances the efficiency of LPG
C. it facilitates easy detection of leakage of the gas
D. it assists in liquefying hydrocarbons

54. The genetic material of bacteria is found in:
A. nucleus B. cytoplasm
C. cell membrane D. ribosome

55. A horse and a donkey can breed to produce mule which is an infertile animal. The infertility is because horse and donkey belong to different:
A. class B. order
C. species D. genus

56. A plant having yellow leaves with dead spots has the deficiency of:
A. Potassium B. Magnesium
C. Nitrate D. Phosphate

57. Fluoride toothpaste is sometimes recommended beçause fluoride:
A. prevents plaque formation
B. hardens the enamel of the tooth
C. kills pathogenic bacteria
D. prevents tooth ache

58. Along a streamline flow of fluid:
A. the velocity of all fluid particles at a given instant is constant
B. the speed of a fluid particle remains constant
C. the velocity of all fluid particles crossing a given position is constant
D. the velocity of a fluid particle remains constant

59. How is the kinetic energy of a moving object affected if the net work done on it is positive?
A. Decreases B. Increases
C. Remains constant D. Becomes zero

60. A particle is executing simple harmonic motion. Which one of the following statements about the acceleration of the oscillating particle is true?
A. It is always in the opposite direction to velocity
B. It is proportional to the frequency of oscillation
C. It is minimum when the speed is maximum
D. It decreases as the potential energy increases

61. Which one of the following four particles, whose displacement x and acceleration a_x are related as follows, is executing simple harmonic motion?
A. $a_x = +3x$ B. $a_x = +3x^2$
C. $a_x = -3x^2$ D. $a_x = -3x$

62. If we plot a graph between volume V and inverse of pressure P (*i.e.*, $\frac{1}{P}$) for an ideal gas at constant temperature T, the curve so obtained is:
A. straight line B. circle
C. parabola D. hyperbola

63. Which one of the following statements is correct?
A. The speed of sound waves in a medium depends upon the elastic property of the medium but not on inertia property
B. The speed of sound waves in a medium depends upon the inertia property of the medium but not on elastic property
C. The speed of sound waves in a medium depends neither on its elastic property nor on its inertia property
D. The speed of sound waves in a medium depends both on elastic and inertia properties of the medium

64. Which one of the following statements is ***not*** correct?
A. Pitch of a sound is its characteristic by which we can generally differentiate between a male voice and a female voice
B. The loudness of sound is related to its frequency
C. A musical sound has certain well defined frequencies which are generally harmonics of a fundamental frequency
D. The timbre of a particular musical sound is related to the waveform of the sound wave

65. A particle executes linear simple harmonic motion with amplitude of 2 cm. When the particle is at 1 cm from the mean position, the magnitudes of the velocity and the acceleration are equal. Then its time period (in seconds) is
A. $\frac{2\pi}{\sqrt{3}}$ B. $\frac{\sqrt{3}}{2\pi}$
C. $\frac{\sqrt{3}}{\pi}$ D. $\frac{1}{2\pi\sqrt{3}}$

66. Which of the following items is used in the household wirings to prevent accidental fire in case of short circuit?
A. Insulated wire
B. Plastic switches
C. Non-metallic coatings on conducting wires
D. Electric fuse

67. Which of the following are the features of the ideology of utilitarianism?
1. Utilitarians believed that all value derives from land
2. The most celebrated spokesmen of utilitarianism were Jeremy Bentham and John Stuart Mill
3. Utilitarians were advocates of the idea that India could be ruled through indigenous laws and customs

4. Utilitarians were advocates of the idea of the 'greatest good for the greatest number of people'

Select the correct answer using the code given below:

A. 1 and 4 only B. 2 and 4 only
C. 1, 2 and 4 D. 2 and 3

68. Who among the following invented the powerloom that revolutionized the cotton textile industry?

A. Edmund Cartwright
B. Samuel Crompton
C. Richard Arkwright
D. James Hargreaves

69. Subsidiary Alliance was a system devised by

A. Lord Wellesley B. Lord Dalhousie
C. Lord Canning D. Lord Ripon

70. Consider the following statements:

1. Periplus is a Greek word meaning sailing around.
2. Erythraean was the Greek name for the Mediterranean Sea.

Which of the statements given above is/are correct?

A. 1 only B. 2 only
C. Both 1 and 2 D. Neither 1 nor 2

71. Who among the following was defeated by Saina Nehwal to win the women's title of the Australian Open Super Series Badminton Tournament, 2016?

A. Sun Yu B. Carolina Marin
C. Wang Yihan D. Sung Ji Hyun

72. Consider the following statements:

He was an Indian journalist, editor and author. He was associated with the Statesman, the Guardian, the Times of India etc. He received the Ramnath Goenka Lifetime Achievement Award in 2013. He died in June 2016.

The person referred to above is:

A. B.K. Karanjia
B. K.M. Mathew
C. Inder Malhotra
D. Nanasaheb Parulekar

73. Achyut Lahkar, who died recently, was a:

A. sports administrator
B. wildlife photographer
C. mobile theatre personality
D. bureaucrat

74. Recently Microsoft announced its 26.2 billion dollar acquisition of which one of the following professional networking sites?

A. PartnerUP B. PerfectBusiness
C. StartupNation D. LinkedIn

75. Which of the following statements concerning Mediterranean climatic region are correct?

1. It is found in the latitude range 30° to 45° northern and southern hemisphere.
2. Mediterranean climate experiences extreme temperature conditions.
3. In Mediterranean climate, rainfall occurs mainly during summer season.
4. In Mediterranean climate, rainfall is mainly due to Westerlies.

Select the correct answer using the code given below:

A. 1, 2 and 4 B. 1 and 4 only
C. 1, 2 and 3 D. 3 and 4

76. Arrange the following states in decreasing order of their total area under forest cover:

1. Jharkhand
2. Chhattisgarh
3. Arunachal Pradesh
4. Madhya Pradesh

Select the correct answer using the code given below:

A. 4 – 3 – 2 – 1 B. 4 – 2 – 3 – 1
C. 3 – 4 – 1 – 2 D. 2 – 1 – 3 – 4

77. Which of the following statements concerning Scheduled Castes (SC) population in India are correct?

1. The highest percentage of SC population out of the total population of the state is found in Punjab.
2. Bihar is the second largest state in respect of total SC population in India.
3. Uttar Pradesh has the highest number of SC population in India.
4. Among the Indian states, the lowest percentage of SC population out of the total population of the state is found in Goa.

Select the correct answer using the code given below:

A. 1, 2 and 3 B. 1 and 3 only
C. 2 and 4 only D. 1, 2 and 4

78. Match List–I with List–II and select the correct answer using the code given below the Lists:

List–I ***(Element)***	***List–II*** ***(Highest Valency)***
(*a*) Sulphur	1. Five
(*b*) Phosphorus	2. Six
(*c*) Lead	3. Two
(*d*) Silver	4. Four

Code:

	(*a*)	(*b*)	(*c*)	(*d*)
A.	2	4	1	3
B.	2	1	4	3
C.	3	1	4	2
D.	3	4	1	2

79. Which one of the following species is ***not*** capable of showing disproportionation reaction?

A. ClO^- B. ClO_2^-
C. ClO_3^- D. ClO_4^-

80. Combination of one volume of nitrogen with three volumes of hydrogen produces
A. one volume of ammonia
B. two volumes of ammonia
C. three volumes of ammonia
D. one and a half volumes of ammonia

81. Consider the following statements about cactus:
1. The leaves are reduced to spines.
2. The stem does the photosynthesis.

Which of the statements given above is/are correct?
A. 1 only B. 2 only
C. Both 1 and 2 D. Neither 1 nor 2

82. In which one of the following, methanogens, *i.e.*, methane producing bacteria are ***not*** present?
A. Rumen of cattle
B. Aerobic environment
C. Anaerobic sludge
D. Excreta of cattle

83. Malarial parasite is a:
A. bacteria B. protozoa
C. virus D. fungus

84. With reference to biodiversity, which of the following statements is/are correct?
1. Species richness and high degree of endemism are important criteria for identifying biodiversity hot spots.
2. Species diversity is highest in the tropics and decreases down the poles.
3. Biodiversity conservation may be *in situ* as well as *ex situ*.

Select the correct answer using the code given below:
A. 1 only B. 2 and 3 only
C. 1, 2 and 3 D. 1 and 3 only

85. It is difficult to kill viruses because they:
A. consist of tough protein coat
B. are very small in size
C. lack cellular structure
D. spend a lot of time inside the host's cells

86. When a ray of light enters a glass slab, then:
A. only the frequency changes
B. frequency and velocity change
C. frequency does not change
D. frequency and wavelength change

87. A ball is thrown vertically upward from the ground with a speed of 25.2 m/s. The ball will reach the highest point of its journey in:
A. 5.14 s B. 3.57 s
C. 2.57 s D. 1.29 s

88. One kilowatt hour is equal to:
A. 36×10^3 joule B. 36×10^5 joule
C. 10^3 joule D. 10^5 joule

89. When sound waves are propagated through a medium, the physical quantity/quantities transmitted is/are:
A. matter only
B. energy only
C. energy and matter only
D. energy, momentum and matter

90. Pressure is a scalar quantity because:
A. it is the ratio of force to area and both force and area are vectors.
B. it is the ratio of magnitude of force to area
C. it is the ratio of component of force (normal to area) to area
D. None of the above

91. A person is unable to read a newspaper without his glasses. He is most probably suffering from:
A. myopia B. presbyopia
C. astigmatism D. hypermetropia

92. The free fall acceleration *g*, increases as one proceeds, at sea level, from the equator toward either pole. The reason is:
A. Earth is a sphere with same density everywhere
B. Earth is a sphere with different density at the polar regions than in the equatorial regions
C. Earth is approximately an ellipsoid having its equatorial radius greater than its polar radius by 21 km
D. Earth is approximately an ellipsoid having its equatorial radius smaller than its polar radius by 21 km

93. Which one of the following statements is correct?
A. The measurement of mass taken by a spring weighing balance is correct at the place where the spring balance is calibrated for
B. The measurement of mass taken by a spring weighing balance is correct at all places
C. The measurement of mass taken by a spring weighing balance is correct at the places where the acceleration due to gravity is same with the place where the spring balance is calibrated for
D. A spring balance cannot be used to measure mass at any place

94. Which one of the following is ***not*** a contact force?
A. Push force B. Gravitational force
C. Frictional force D. Strain force

95. When a force of 1 newton acts on a mass of 1 kg which is able to move freely, the object moves in the direction of force with a/an:
A. speed of 1 km/s
B. acceleration of 1 m/s^2
C. speed of 1 m/s
D. acceleration of 1 km/s^2

96. Which one of the following statements is ***not*** correct?
A. The SI unit of charge is ampere-second
B. Debye is the unit of dipole moment
C. Resistivity of a wire of length l and area of cross-section a depends upon both l and a
D. The kinetic energy of an electron of mass m kg and charge e coulomb, when accelerated through a potential difference of V volt, is eV joule

97. Two balls, A and B, are thrown simultaneously, A vertically upward with a speed of 20 m/s from the ground and B vertically downward from a height of 40 m with the same speed and along the same line of motion. At what points do the two balls collide by taking acceleration due to gravity as 9.8 m/s^2?
A. The balls will collide after 3s at a height of 30.2 m from the ground
B. The balls will collide after 2s at a height of 20.1 m from the ground
C. The balls will collide after 1s at a height of 15.1 m from the ground
D. The balls will collide after 5s at a height of 20 m from the ground

98. The setting time of cement is lowered by adding:
A. oxides of aluminium
B. gypsum
C. oxides of magnesium
D. silica

99. Emulsion is known as a:
A. colloidal solution of substances having different physical states
B. true solution
C. distillation mixture for making alcohols
D. colloidal solution of two liquids

100. If one mixes up ashes with animal fat, the substance received in the crude form is called:
A. Pheromone B. Soap
C. Cement D. Concrete

101. Which of the following statements with regard to coverage rate of Aadhar cards during 2015 is/are correct?
1. The coverage rate of Aadhar cards in western India is quite high and it is above 90 per cent in Gujarat.
2. The coverage rate of Aadhar cards is the highest in southern India and it is almost 100 per cent in the staes of Telangana and Andhra Pradesh.
3. The penetration of Aadhar cards has been very low in north-eastern part of India and it is the lowest in Assam and Meghalaya.

Select the correct answer using the code given below:
A. 2 only B. 1 and 3 only
C. 2 and 3 only D. 1, 2 and 3

102. Which one of the following is the correct descending order of countries in terms of per capita availability of arable land?
A. India – China – Brazil
B. China – Brazil – India
C. Brazil – China – India
D. Brazil – India – China

103. Match List–I with List–II and select the correct answer using the code given below the Lists:

List–I (Geomorphic Agent)	***List–II (Feature)***
(*a*) Ground water	1. Plunge pool
(*b*) Running water	2. Horns
(*c*) Glacier	3. Playas
(*d*) Wind	4. Lapies

Code:

	(*a*)	(*b*)	(*c*)	(*d*)
A.	4	1	2	3
B.	3	2	1	4
C.	3	1	2	4
D.	4	2	1	3

104. Which of the following statements concerning temperature is/are correct?
1. In winter season isotherms in Northern Hemisphere are more or less circular on continents.
2. Isotherms are parallel to latitude in Southern Hemisphere in oceans.
3. Minimum temperature during winter is recorded in Northern Canada.

Select the correct answer using the code given below:
A. 1 and 2 only B. 1 and 3 only
C. 1, 2 and 3 D. 2 only

105. Which of the following statement(s) concerning natural regions of the world is/are correct?
1. Equatorial climatic regions have less urbanization.
2. Mediterranean climatic regions have high level of urbanization.
3. Equatorial climatic regions have high concentration of human population.
4. Mediterranean climatic regions practice plantation farming.

Select the correct answer using the code given below:
A. 1 and 2 only B. 1, 2 and 3
C. 2 and 4 D. 1 only

106. Which one of the following gases gives acidic solution on dissolving in water?
A. Hydrogen B. Carbon dioxide
C. Nitrogen D. Oxygen

107. How many moles of hydrogen atom are present in one mole of Aluminium hydroxide?
A. One mole B. Two moles
C. Three moles D. Four moles

108. The United Nations proclaimed 21 June as:
A. International Mother Language Day
B. International Widows' Day
C. International Day of Yoga
D. International Day against Drug Abuse and Illicit Trafficking

109. Who are Bhawana Kanth, Avani Chaturvedi and Mohana Singh?

A. Sprinters B. Rock climbers
C. Fighter pilots D. Mountaineers

110. Consider the following statements about the Constitution of India:

1. A Member of Parliament enjoys freedom of speech in the Parliament as a Parliamentary Privilege protected by the Constitution of India.
2. The Constitution has vested the power to amend the Constitution in the Parliament.

Which of the statements given above is/are correct?

A. 1 only B. 2 only
C. Both 1 and 2 D. Neither 1 nor 2

111. Which one of the following statements about the Union Executive in India is correct?

A. According to the Constitution of India, the total number of members of the Council of Ministers cannot exceed 20% of the total number of Members of the House of the People
B. The rank of the different Ministers is determined by the President
C. The Ministers are appointed by the President on the advice of the Prime Minister
D. Only a member of either House of Parliament can be appointed as a Minister

112. Which one of the following statements about Money Bill is correct?

A. A Bill shall be deemed to be a Money Bill only if it provides for imposition of fines or penalties
B. A Money Bill shall be introduced in the Rajya Sabha
C. The Rajya Sabha can reject the Money Bill
D. The Speaker of the Lok Sabha finally decides if it is a Money Bill, should any dispute about it arise

113. Which one of the following powers of the Prime Minister of India is codified in the Constitution of India itself?

A. The power of advising the President as regards the appointment of other Ministers
B. The power to allocate business amongst the Ministers
C. The power to summon the meeting of the Cabinet
D. The power to transfer a Minister from one Department to another

114. The cylindrical stone seals were used in which civilization?

A. Harappan B. Egyptian
C. Roman D. Mesopotamian

115. Which of the following statements with regards to the Civil Disobedience movement is/are correct?

1. The movement received massive response from business groups and peasantry.
2. The movement coincided with large scale labour upsurge in Maharashtra.
3. The movement was marked by the mass participation of lawyers and students.

Select the correct answer using the code given below:

A. 1 only B. 1 and 2 only
C. 2 and 3 only D. 1, 2 and 3

Directions (Qs. No. 116 to 121): *The following 6 (Six) items consist of two statements, Statement–I and Statement–II. Examine these two statements carefully and select the correct answer using the code given below:*

Code:

A. Both the statements are individually true and Statement II is the correct explanation of Statement I
B. Both the statements are individually true but Statement II is ***not*** the correct explanation of Statement I
C. Statement I is true, but Statement II is false
D. Statement I is false, but Statement II is true

116. Statement I : Variability of annual rainfall is very high in western part of Rajasthan.

Statement II : Average annual rainfall is extremely low in western Rajasthan.

117. Statement I : Ozone is a tri-atomic molecule of oxygen.

Statement II : Ozone is concentrated mainly in stratosphere.

118. Statement I : The laterite soils develop in areas with high temperature and high rainfall.

Statement II : Laterite soils are the result of intense leaching process.

119. Statement I : Too much salt content in diet could be one of the reasons for kidney failure.

Statement II : High salt may cause high blood pressure.

120. Statement I : The city of Rome revived in a spectacular way in the 15th century.

Statement II : From the 15th century onwards, artists were known individually by name, not as member of a group or a guild, in Roman society.

121. Statement I : Chartism was the political reform campaign for democratic rights which swept over Britain between 1838 and 1848.

Statement II : The trade union movement declined by the 1830s as it failed to fulfil the aspirations of the working class.

122. 'Sahel' region of Sahara desert is associated with:
A. core area of Sahara desert
B. southern moving edge of Sahara desert
C. northern fringe of Sahara desert bordering Mediterranean sea
D. another name of Sahara desert

123. Which one of the following pairs of a river and its tributary is ***not*** correctly matched?
A. Godavari – Wainganga
B. Cauvery – Bhavani
C. Narmada – Amaravati
D. Krishna – Bhima

124. In which one of the following countries, the Mediterranean type of Biome is found?
A. Chile B. Kenya
C. Argentina D. Bolivia

125. Arrange the following states in order of their decreasing population size as per the census 2011:
1. West Bengal 2. Bihar
3. Maharashtra 4. Andhra Pradesh

Select the correct answer using the code given below:
A. 2 – 3 – 1 – 4 B. 3 – 2 – 1 – 4
C. 1 – 4 – 3 – 2 D. 3 – 1 – 4 – 2

126. Match List–I with List–II and select the correct answer using the code given below the Lists:

List–I (River)	***List–II (Mouth of the river)***
(*a*) Danube	1. North sea
(*b*) Rhine	2. Black sea
(*c*) Rhone	3. Bay of Biscay
(*d*) Loire	4. Mediterranean sea

Code:

	(*a*)	(*b*)	(*c*)	(*d*)
A.	2	1	4	3
B.	3	4	1	2
C.	2	4	1	3
D.	3	1	4	2

127. Match List–I with List–II and select the correct answer using the code given below the Lists:

List–I (Process)	***List–II (Type of change)***
(*a*) Heating Camphor	1. Chemical
(*b*) Cooling of water vapour up to room temperature	2. Evaporation
(*c*) Cooking an egg	3. Condensation
(*d*) Formation of water vapour at room temperature	4. Sublimation

Code:

	(*a*)	(*b*)	(*c*)	(*d*)
A.	4	3	1	2
B.	4	1	3	2
C.	2	1	3	4
D.	2	3	1	4

128. Identify the element having zero valency:
A. Sulphur B. Phosphorous
C. Lead D. Radon

129. There are six electrons, six protons and six neutrons in an atom of an element. What is the atomic number of the element?
A. 6 B. 12
C. 18 D. 24

130. Which one of the following has different number of molecules? (All are kept at normal temperature and pressure)
A. 3 gram of Hydrogen
B. 48 gram of Oxygen
C. 42 gram of Nitrogen
D. 2 gram of Carbon

131. Which one of the following statements is ***not*** correct?
A. The longest wavelength of light visible to human eye is about 700 nm
B. The shortest wavelength of light visible to human eye is about 400 nm
C. The wavelength of gamma rays is longer than that of X-rays
D. The ability of a telescope to form separable images of close objects is called its resolving power

132. If the image of an object, formed by a concave mirror is virtual, erect and magnified, then the object is placed:
A. at the principal focus
B. at the centre of curvature
C. beyond the centre of curvature
D. between the pole of the mirror and the principal focus

133. When three resistors, each having resistance r, are connected in parallel, their resultant resistance is x. If these three resistances are connected in series, the total resistance will be:
A. $3x$ B. $3rx$
C. $9x$ D. $3/x$

134. Which of the following was/were the feature(s) of Lenin's New Economic Policy (NEP) for the Soviet Union?
1. Private retail trading was strictly forbidden.
2. Private enterprise was strictly forbidden.
3. Peasants were not allowed to sell their surplus.
4. To secure liquid capital, concessions were allowed to foreign capitalists, but the State retained the option of purchasing the products of such concerns.

Select the correct answer using the code given below:
A. 1 only B. 2 and 3
C. 1, 2 and 4 D. 4 only

135. Which of the following was/were the reasons for the defeat of British during the American War of Independence?
1. The remoteness of the American Continent and the lack of good roads.
2. The British authorities failed to rally the loyalist Americans.
3. The Americans benefited from the extraordinary military leadership of George Washington.
4. The Americans had access to superior arms and ammunition.

Select the correct answer using the code given below:
A. 1, 2 and 4 B. 3 only
C. 2 and 3 only D. 1, 2 and 3

136. The industrial revolution in England had a profound impact on the lives of people. Which of the following statements are correct about that?
1. Women were the main workers in the silk, lace-making and knitting industries.
2. Factory managers were well aware of the health risks of industrial work on children.
3. Children were often employed in textile factories.
4. The novel 'Hard Times' by Charles Dickens was a severe critique of the horrors of industrialization.

Select the correct answer using the code given below:
A. 1 and 3 only B. 1 and 2
C. 1, 3 and 4 D. 3 and 4 only

137. Consider the following statements:
1. British colonialism continued to grow steadily in the 18th and 19th centuries.
2. Raw cotton for the textile industry in Britain during the industrial revolution needed to be imported.

Which of the statements given above is/are correct?
A. 1 only B. 2 only
C. Both 1 and 2 D. Neither 1 nor 2

138. Who among the following was the author of *Neel Darpan,* published in 1860?
A. Reverend James Long
B. Michael Madhusudan Dutta
C. Raja Ram Mohan Roy
D. Dinabandhu Mitra

139. Which one of the following organizations was started by Jyotirao Phule in 1873?
A. Prarthana Samaj B. Bahujan Samaj
C. Justice Party D. Satyashodhak Samaj

140. Although used earlier by French and German writers, the term 'Industrial Revolution' in English was first popularized by:
A. Adam Smith B. Arnold Toynbee
C. James Mill D. Bertrand Russell

141. In the 19th century, the majority of the workers in Japan's modern industries were mainly:
A. Japanese men and children
B. Japanese women and Chinese men
C. Women
D. Japanese and Chinese men

142. Which of the following statements regarding recent developments in international affairs is/are correct?
1. NATO's defence ministers agree to boost support for Ukraine with a comprehensive package of assistance which will help it strengthen defence and to modernize its armed forces.
2. Israel announces plans for construction of dwelling units for Jewish settlers in a Palestinian neighbourhood of East Jerusalem.

Select the correct answer using the code given below:
A. 1 only B. 2 only
C. Both 1 and 2 D. Neither 1 nor 2

143. As per the RBI guidelines, which one of the following is the minimum tenure of Masala Bonds that an Indian company can issue offshore?
A. Five years B. Four years
C. Three years D. Two years

144. Which of the following statements about Krishi Kalyan Cess (KKC) is/are correct?
1. KKC is calculated in the same way as Service Tax is calculated.
2. The current rate of KKC is 0.50%.
3. KKC is similar to the KKS (Krishi Kalyan Surcharge).

Select the correct answer using the code given below:
A. 1, 2 and 3 B. 1 and 2 only
C. 2 and 3 only D. 1 only

145. Which country won the Thomas Cup Badminton Championship, 2016?
A. Indonesia B. Denmark
C. China D. Malaysia

146. Match List–I with List–II and select the correct answer using the code given below the Lists:

***List–I* (*Ultra mega power project at different stages of development*)**	***List–II* (*State*)**
(*a*) Sasan	1. Gujarat
(*b*) Mundra	2. Madhya Pradesh
(*c*) Tilaiya	3. Andhra Pradesh
(*d*) Krishnapattam	4. Jharkhand

Code:

	(*a*)	(*b*)	(*c*)	(*d*)
A.	2	4	1	3
B.	3	4	1	2
C.	2	1	4	3
D.	3	1	4	2

147. The world's largest biomass cookstove system for cooking in community kitchen has been installed at
A. Tirupati B. Amritsar
C. Shirdi D. Udupi

148. Which one of the following sectors is the largest contributor to carbon dioxide emissions from fuel consumption in India?
A. Electricity and heat production
B. Transport

C. Manufacturing industries and construc-tions
D. Others

149. As per census 2011, which one of the following states has the highest number of inhabitated villages?
A. Uttar Pradesh B. Odisha
C. Rajasthan D. Maharashtra

150. The property of electric current which is applicable in the fuse wire is
A. chemical effect of current
B. magnetic effect of current
C. heating effect of current
D. optical property of current

PAPER II : MATHEMATICS

Directions (Qs. No. 1 and 2): *Consider the following for the next two (02) items that follow:*

Let α and β be the roots of the equation: $x^2 - (1 - 2a^2)x + (1 - 2a^2) = 0$.

1. Under what condition does the above equation have real roots?
A. $a^2 < \frac{1}{2}$ B. $a^2 > \frac{1}{2}$
C. $a^2 \le \frac{1}{2}$ D. $a^2 \ge \frac{1}{2}$

2. Under what condition is $\frac{1}{\alpha^2} + \frac{1}{\beta^2} < 1$?
A. $a^2 < \frac{1}{2}$ B. $a^2 > \frac{1}{2}$
C. $a^2 > 1$ D. $a^2 \in \left(\frac{1}{3}, \frac{1}{2}\right)$ only

3. What is $\sqrt{\frac{1+\omega^2}{1+\omega}}$ equal to, where ω is the cube root of unity?
A. 1 B. ω
C. ω^2 D. None of the above

4. In an examination, 70% students passed in Physics, 80% students passed in Chemistry, 75% students passed in Mathematics and 85% students passed in Biology, and x% students failed in all the four subjects. What is the minimum value of x?
A. 10 B. 12
C. 15 D. None of the above

Directions (Qs. No. 5 and 6): *Consider the following for the next two (02) items that follow:*

For the system of linear equations $2x + 3y + 5z = 9$, $7x + 3y - 2z = 8$ and $2x + 3y + \lambda z = \mu$

5. Under what condition does the above system of equations have infinitely many solutions?
A. $\lambda = 5$ and $\mu \ne 9$ B. $\lambda = 5$ and $\mu = 9$
C. $\lambda = 9$ and $\mu = 5$ D. $\lambda = 9$ and $\mu \ne 5$

6. Under what condition does the above system of equations have unique solutions?
A. $\lambda = 5$ and $\mu = 9$
B. $\lambda \ne 5$ and $\mu = 7$ only
C. $\lambda \ne 5$ and μ has any real value
D. λ has any real value and $\mu \ne 9$

7. What is the number of odd integers between 1000 and 9999 with no digit repeated?
A. 2100 B. 2120
C. 2240 D. None of the above

8. What is the greatest value of the positive integer n satisfying the condition:
$$1+\frac{1}{2}+\frac{1}{4}+\frac{1}{8}+....+\frac{1}{2^{n-1}} < 2-\frac{1}{1000}?$$
A. 8 B. 9
C. 10 D. 11

Directions (Qs. No. 9 and 10): *Consider the following for the next two (02) items that follow:*

$2x^2 + 3x - \alpha = 0$ has roots -2 and β while the equation $x^2 - 3mx + 2m^2 = 0$ has both roots positive, where $\alpha > 0$ and $\beta > 0$.

9. What is the value of α?
A. 1/2 B. 1
C. 2 D. 4

10. If β, 2, $2m$ are in GP, then what is the value of $\beta\sqrt{m}$?
A. 1 B. 2
C. 4 D. 6

11. sin A + 2 sin 2A + sin 3A is equal to which of the following?
1. $4 \sin 2A \cos^2\left(\frac{A}{2}\right)$
2. $2 \sin 2A\left(\sin\frac{A}{2}+\cos\frac{A}{2}\right)^2$
3. $8 \sin A \cos A \cos^2\left(\frac{A}{2}\right)$

Select the correct answer using the code given below:
A. 1 and 2 only B. 2 and 3 only
C. 1 and 3 ony D. 1, 2 and 3

12. If $x = \sin 70° . \sin 50°$ and $y = \cos 60° . \cos 80°$, then what is xy equal to?
A. 1/16 B. 1/8
C. 1/4 D. 1/2

13. If $\sin\theta_1 + \sin\theta_2 + \sin\theta_3 + \sin\theta_4 = 4$, then what is the value of:
$\cos\theta_1 + \cos\theta_2 + \cos\theta_3 + \cos\theta_4$?
A. 0 B. 1
C. 2 D. 4

14. What is the value of:

$\left(1+\cos\frac{\pi}{8}\right)\left(1+\cos\frac{3\pi}{8}\right)\left(1+\cos\frac{5\pi}{8}\right)\left(1+\cos\frac{7\pi}{8}\right)$?

A. $\frac{1}{2}$ B. $\frac{1}{2}+\frac{1}{2\sqrt{2}}$

C. $\frac{1}{2}-\frac{1}{2\sqrt{2}}$ D. $\frac{1}{8}$

15. If $x \cos \theta + y \sin \theta = z$, then what is the value of $(x \sin \theta - y \cos \theta)^2$?

A. $x^2 + y^2 - z^2$ B. $x^2 - y^2 - z^2$

C. $x^2 - y^2 + z^2$ D. $x^2 + y^2 + z^2$

16. Let S be a set of all distinct numbers of the form $\frac{p}{q}$, where $p, q \in \{1, 2, 3, 4, 5, 6\}$. What is the cardinality of the set S?

A. 21 B. 23

C. 32 D. 36

17. If $c > 0$ and $4a + c < 2b$, then $ax^2 - bx + c = 0$ has a root in which one of the following intervals?

A. (0, 2) B. (2, 3)

C. (3, 4) D. (–2, 0)

18. If $A = \{x \in \mathbb{R} : x^2 + 6x - 7 < 0\}$ and $B = \{x \in \mathbb{R} : x^2 + 9x + 14 > 0\}$, then which of the following is/are correct?

1. $A \cap B = \{x \in \mathbb{R} : -2 < x < 1\}$
2. $A \setminus B = \{x \in \mathbb{R} : -7 < x < -2\}$

Select the correct answer using the code given below:

A. 1 only B. 2 only

C. Both 1 and 2 D. Neither 1 nor 2

19. If A is a square matrix of order 3 and det A = 5, then what is det $[(2A)^{-1}]$ equal to?

A. $\frac{1}{10}$ B. $\frac{2}{5}$

C. $\frac{8}{5}$ D. $\frac{1}{40}$

20. What is $\omega^{100} + \omega^{200} + \omega^{300}$ equal to, where ω is the cube root of unity?

A. 1 B. 3ω

C. $3\omega^2$ D. 0

21. If $\text{Re}\left(\frac{z-1}{z+1}\right) = 0$, where $z = x + iy$ is a complex number, then which one of the following is correct?

A. $z = 1 + i$ B. $|z| = 2$

C. $z = 1 - i$ D. $|z| = 1$

22. What is $[x \quad y \quad z]\begin{bmatrix} a & h & g \\ h & b & f \\ g & f & c \end{bmatrix}$ equal to?

A. $[ax+hy+gz \quad h+b+f \quad g+f+c]$

B. $\begin{bmatrix} a & h & g \\ hx & by & fz \\ g & f & c \end{bmatrix}$

C. $\begin{bmatrix} ax+hy+gz \\ hx+by+fz \\ gx+fy+cz \end{bmatrix}$

D. $[ax+hy+gz \quad hx+by+fz \quad gx+fy+cz]$

23. Out of 15 points in a plane, n points are in the same straight line. 445 triangles can be formed by joining these points. What is the value of n?

A. 3 B. 4

C. 5 D. 6

24. If $z = \left(\frac{\sqrt{3}}{2}+\frac{i}{2}\right)^{107} + \left(\frac{\sqrt{3}}{2}-\frac{i}{2}\right)^{107}$, then what is the imaginary part of z equal to?

A. 0 B. $\frac{1}{2}$

C. $\frac{\sqrt{3}}{2}$ D. 1

25. If both the roots of the equation $x^2 - 2kx + k^2 - 4 = 0$ lie between –3 and 5, then which one of the following is correct?

A. $-2 < k < 2$ B. $-5 < k < 3$

C. $-3 < k < 5$ D. $-1 < k < 3$

26. What is the number of distinct solutions of the equation $z^2 + |z| = 0$ (where z is a complex number)?

A. One B. Two

C. Three D. Five

27. How many geometric progressions is/are possible containing 27, 8 and 12 as three of its/their terms?

A. One B. Two

C. Four D. Infinitely many

28. Let R be a relation from A = {1, 2, 3, 4} to B = {1, 3, 5} such that $R = \{(a, b) : a < b, \text{ where } a \in A \text{ and } b \in B\}$. What is RoR^{-1} equal to?

A. {(1, 3), (1, 5), (2, 3), (2, 5), (3, 5), (4, 5)}

B. {(3, 1), (5, 1), (3, 2), (5, 2), (5, 3), (5, 4)}

C. {(3, 3), (3, 5), (5, 3), (5, 5)}

D. {(3, 3), (3, 4), (4, 5)}

29. A five-digit number divisible by 3 is to be formed using the digits 0, 1, 2, 3 and 4 without repetition of digits. What is the number of ways this can be done?

A. 96

B. 48

C. 32

D. No number can be formed

30. What is ${}^{47}C_4 + {}^{51}C_3 + \sum_{j=2}^{5} {}^{52-j}C_3$ equal to?

A. ${}^{52}C_4$ B. ${}^{51}C_5$

C. ${}^{53}C_4$ D. ${}^{52}C_5$

31. What is the value of $\cos(2\cos^{-1} 0.8)$?
A. 0.81 B. 0.56
C. 0.48 D. 0.28

32. The top of a hill when observed from the top and bottom of a building of height h is at angles of elevation p and q respectively. What is the height of the hill?

A. $\frac{h\cot q}{\cot q - \cot p}$ B. $\frac{h\cot p}{\cot p - \cot q}$

C. $\frac{2h\tan p}{\tan p - \tan q}$ D. $\frac{2h\tan q}{\tan q - \tan p}$

33. If $\sin 18° = \frac{\sqrt{5}-1}{4}$, then what is the value of sin 81°?

A. $\frac{\sqrt{3+\sqrt{5}}+\sqrt{5-\sqrt{5}}}{4}$ B. $\frac{\sqrt{3+\sqrt{5}}+\sqrt{5+\sqrt{5}}}{4}$

C. $\frac{\sqrt{3-\sqrt{5}}+\sqrt{5-\sqrt{5}}}{4}$ D. $\frac{\sqrt{3+\sqrt{5}}-\sqrt{5-\sqrt{5}}}{4}$

34. A moving boat is observed from the top of a cliff of 150 m height. The angle of depression of the boat changes from 60° to 45° in 2 minutes. What is the speed of the boat in metres per hour?

A. $\frac{4500}{\sqrt{3}}$ B. $\frac{4500(\sqrt{3}-1)}{\sqrt{3}}$

C. $4500\sqrt{3}$ D. $\frac{4500(\sqrt{3}+1)}{\sqrt{3}}$

35. What is $\frac{1-\tan 2°\cot 62°}{\tan 152° - \cot 88°}$ equal to?

A. $\sqrt{3}$ B. $-\sqrt{3}$
C. $\sqrt{2}-1$ D. $1-\sqrt{2}$

36. An equilateral triangle has one vertex at (0, 0) and another at $(3, \sqrt{3})$. What are the coordinates of the third vertex?

A. $(0, 2\sqrt{3})$ only
B. $(3, -\sqrt{3})$ only
C. $(0, 2\sqrt{3})$ or $(3, -\sqrt{3})$
D. Neither $(0, 2\sqrt{3})$ nor $(3, -\sqrt{3})$

37. What is the equation of the right bisector of the line segment joining (1, 1) and (2, 3)?
A. $2x + 4y - 11 = 0$ B. $2x - 4y - 5 = 0$
C. $2x - 4y - 11 = 0$ D. $x - y + 1 = 0$

38. What is the radius of the circle passing through the point (2, 4) and having centre at the intersection of the lines $x - y = 4$ and $2x + 3y + 7 = 0$?
A. 3 units B. 5 units
C. $3\sqrt{3}$ units D. $5\sqrt{2}$ units

39. What is the equation of the hyperbola having latus rectum and eccentricity 8 and $\frac{3}{\sqrt{5}}$ respectively?

A. $\frac{x^2}{25} - \frac{y^2}{20} = 1$ B. $\frac{x^2}{40} - \frac{y^2}{20} = 1$

C. $\frac{x^2}{40} - \frac{y^2}{30} = 1$ D. $\frac{x^2}{30} - \frac{y^2}{25} = 1$

40. If the point (a, a) lies between the lines $|x + y| = 2$, then which one of the following is correct?

A. $|a| < 2$ B. $|a| < \sqrt{2}$

C. $|a| < 1$ D. $|a| < \frac{1}{\sqrt{2}}$

41. What is the equation of the straight line which passes through the point of intersection of the straight lines $x + 2y = 5$ and $3x + 7y = 17$ and is perpendicular to the straight line $3x + 4y = 10$?
A. $4x + 3y + 2 = 0$ B. $4x - y + 2 = 0$
C. $4x - 3y - 2 = 0$ D. $4x - 3y + 2 = 0$

42. If (a, b) is at unit distance from the line $8x + 6y + 1 = 0$, then which of the following conditions are correct?
1. $3a - 4b - 4 = 0$ 2. $8a + 6b + 11 = 0$
3. $8a + 6b - 9 = 0$
Select the correct answer using the code given below:
A. 1 and 2 only B. 2 and 3 only
C. 1 and 3 only D. 1, 2 and 3

43. If the ellipse $9x^2 + 16y^2 = 144$ intercepts the line $3x + 4y = 12$, then what is the length of the chord so formed?
A. 5 units B. 6 units
C. 8 units D. 10 units

44. A straight line cuts off an intercept of 2 units on the positive direction of x-axis and passes through the point (–3, 5). What is the foot of the perpendicular drawn from the point (3, 3) on this line?
A. (1, 3) B. (2, 0)
C. (0, 2) D. (1, 1)

45. What is the eccentricity of rectangular hyperbola?
A. $\sqrt{2}$ B. $\sqrt{3}$
C. $\sqrt{5}$ D. $\sqrt{6}$

Directions (Qs. No. 46 to 48): *Consider the following for the next three (03) items that follow:*

Let a, x, y, z, b be in AP, where $x + y + z = 15$. Let a, p, q, r, b be in HP, where $p^{-1} + q^{-1} + r^{-1} = 5/3$.

46. What is the value of ab?
A. 10 B. 9
C. 8 D. 6

47. What is the value of xyz?
A. 120 B. 105
C. 90 D. Cannot be determined

48. What is the value of pqr?

A. $\frac{35}{243}$ B. $\frac{81}{35}$

C. $\frac{243}{35}$ D. Cannot be determined

Directions (Qs. No. 49 and 50): *Consider the following for the next two (02) items that follow:*

The sixth term of an AP is 2 and its common difference is greater than 1.

49. What is the common difference of the AP so that the product of the first, fourth and fifth terms is greatest?

A. $\frac{8}{5}$ B. $\frac{9}{5}$

C. 2 D. $\frac{11}{5}$

50. What is the first term of the AP so that the product of the first, fourth and fifth terms is greatest?

A. −4 B. −6

C. −8 D. −10

Directions (Qs. No. 51 and 52): *Consider the following for the next two (02) items that follow:*

Let $ax^3 + bx^2 + cx + d = \begin{vmatrix} x+1 & 2x & 3x \\ 2x+3 & x+1 & x \\ 2-x & 3x+4 & 5x-1 \end{vmatrix}$, then

51. What is the value of c?

A. −1 B. 34

C. 35 D. 50

52. What is the value of $a + b + c + d$?

A. 62 B. 63

C. 65 D. 68

Directions (Qs. No. 53 and 54): *Consider the following for the next two (02) items that follow:*

The interior angles of a polygon of n sides are in AP. The smallest angle is 120° and the common difference is 5°.

53. How many possible values can n have?

A. One B. Two

C. Three D. Infinitely many

54. What is the largest interior angle of the polygon?

A. 160° only B. 195° only

C. Either 160° or 195° D. Neither 160° nor 195°

55. If $m = \begin{bmatrix} 1 & 0 \\ 0 & 1 \end{bmatrix}$ and $n = \begin{bmatrix} 0 & 1 \\ -1 & 0 \end{bmatrix}$, then what is the value of the determinant of $m \cos\theta - n \sin\theta$?

A. −1 B. 0

C. 1 D. 2

56. If $f(x) = \begin{bmatrix} \cos x & -\sin x & 0 \\ \sin x & \cos x & 0 \\ 0 & 0 & 1 \end{bmatrix}$, then which of the following are correct?

1. $f(\theta) \times f(\phi) = f(\theta + \phi)$.
2. The value of the determinant of the matrix $f(\theta) \times f(\phi)$ is 1.
3. The determinant of $f(x)$ is an even function.

Select the correct answer using the code given below:

A. 1 and 2 only B. 2 and 3 only

C. 1 and 3 only D. 1, 2 and 3

57. Which of the following are correct in respect of the system of equations $x + y + z = 8$, $x - y + 2z = 6$ and $3x - y + 5z = k$?

1. They have no solution, if $k = 15$.
2. They have infinitely many solutions, if $k = 20$.
3. They have unique solution, if $k = 25$.

Select the correct answer using the code given below:

A. 1 and 2 only B. 2 and 3 only

C. 1 and 3 only D. 1, 2 and 3

58. If $A = \begin{bmatrix} 1 & -1 \\ 2 & 3 \end{bmatrix}$ and $B = \begin{bmatrix} 2 & 3 \\ -1 & -2 \end{bmatrix}$, then which of the following is/are correct?

1. $AB(A^{-1}B^{-1})$ is a unit matrix.
2. $(AB)^{-1} = A^{-1}B^{-1}$.

Select the correct answer using the code given below:

A. 1 only B. 2 only

C. Both 1 and 2 D. Neither 1 nor 2

59. If $x^{\ln\left(\frac{y}{z}\right)} \cdot y^{\ln(xz)^2} \cdot z^{\ln\left(\frac{x}{y}\right)} = y^{4\ln y}$ for any $x > 1, y > 1$ and $z > 1$, then which one of the following is correct?

A. ln y is the GM of ln x, ln x, ln x and ln z

B. ln y is the AM of ln x, ln x, ln x and ln z

C. ln y is the HM of ln x, ln x, ln x and ln z

D. ln y is the AM of ln x, ln x, ln z and ln z

60. If the number 235 in decimal system is converted into binary system, then what is the resulting number?

A. $(11110011)_2$ B. $(11101011)_2$

C. $(11110101)_2$ D. $(11011011)_2$

61. Let $f(x)$ be a function such that $f'\left(\frac{1}{x}\right) + x^3 f'(x) = 0$. What is $\int_{-1}^{1} f(x)\,dx$ equal to?

A. $2f(1)$ B. 0

C. $2f(-1)$ D. $4f(1)$

62. What is $\int \frac{x^4 - 1}{x^2\sqrt{x^4 + x^2 + 1}}\,dx$ equal to?

A. $\sqrt{\frac{x^4 + x^2 + 1}{x}} + c$ B. $\sqrt{x^4 + 2 - \frac{1}{x^2}} + c$

C. $\sqrt{x^2 + \frac{1}{x^2} + 1} + c$ D. $\sqrt{\frac{x^4 - x^2 + 1}{x}} + c$

63. What are the degree and order respectively of the differential equation satisfying $e^{y\sqrt{1-x^2} + x\sqrt{1-y^2}} = ce^x$, (where $c > 0, |x| < 1, |y| < 1$)?

A. 1, 1 B. 1, 2
C. 2, 1 D. 2, 2

64. What is the curve which passes through the point (1, 1) and whose slope is $\frac{2y}{x}$?

A. Circle B. Parabola
C. Ellipse D. Hyperbola

65. If $x\,dy = y\,dx + y^2\,dy$, $y > 0$ and $y(1) = 1$, then what is $y(-3)$ equal to?

A. 3 only B. –1 only
C. Both –1 and 3 D. Neither –1 nor 3

66. What is the order of the differential equation $\frac{dx}{dy} + \int y\,dx = x^3$?

A. 1 B. 2
C. 3 D. Cannot be determined

67. Which one of the following differential equations represents the family of straight lines which are at unit distance from the origin?

A. $\left(y - x\frac{dy}{dx}\right)^2 = 1 - \left(\frac{dy}{dx}\right)^2$

B. $\left(y + x\frac{dy}{dx}\right)^2 = 1 + \left(\frac{dy}{dx}\right)^2$

C. $\left(y - x\frac{dy}{dx}\right)^2 = 1 + \left(\frac{dy}{dx}\right)^2$

D. $\left(y + x\frac{dy}{dx}\right)^2 = 1 - \left(\frac{dy}{dx}\right)^2$

68. What is $\int e^{\sin x}\frac{x\cos^3 x - \sin x}{\cos^2 x}dx$ equal to?

A. $(x + \sec x)e^{\sin x} + c$ B. $(x - \sec x)e^{\sin x} + c$
C. $(x + \tan x)e^{\sin x} + c$ D. $(x - \tan x)e^{\sin x} + c$

69. If $\int_0^{\pi/2}\frac{dx}{3\cos x + 5} = k\cot^{-1} 2$, then what is the value of k?

A. $\frac{1}{4}$ B. $\frac{1}{2}$
C. 1 D. 2

70. What is $\int_1^3 |1 - x^4|\,dx$ equal to?

A. $-\frac{232}{5}$ B. $-\frac{116}{5}$
C. $\frac{116}{5}$ D. $\frac{232}{5}$

71. A special dice with numbers 1, –1, 2, –2, 0 and 3 is thrown thrice. What is the probability that the sum of the numbers occurring on the upper face is zero?

A. $\frac{1}{72}$ B. $\frac{1}{8}$
C. $\frac{7}{72}$ D. $\frac{25}{216}$

72. There is 25% chance that it rains on any particular day. What is the probability that there is at least one rainy day within a period of 7 days?

A. $1 - \left(\frac{1}{4}\right)^7$ B. $\left(\frac{1}{4}\right)^7$
C. $\left(\frac{3}{4}\right)^7$ D. $1 - \left(\frac{3}{4}\right)^7$

73. A salesman has a 70% chance to sell a product to any customer. The behaviour of successive customers is independent. If two customers A and B enter, what is the probability that the salesman will sell the product to customer A or B?

A. 0.98 B. 0.91
C. 0.70 D. 0.49

74. A student appears for tests I, II and III. The student is considered successful if he passes in tests I, II or I, III or all the three. The probabilities of the student passing in tests I, II and III are m, n and 1/2 respectively. If the probability of the student to be successful is 1/2, then which one of the following is correct?

A. $m(1 + n) = 1$ B. $n(1 + m) = 1$
C. $m = 1$ D. $mn = 1$

75. Three candidates solve a question. Odds in favour of the correct answer are 5 : 2, 4 : 3 and 3 : 4 respectively for the three candidates. What is the probability that at least two of them solve the question correctly?

A. $\frac{209}{343}$ B. $\frac{134}{343}$
C. $\frac{149}{343}$ D. $\frac{60}{343}$

Directions (Qs. No. 76 and 77): *Consider the following for the next two (02) items that follow:*

Let Q be the image of the point P (–2, 1, –5) in the plane $3x - 2y + 2z + 1 = 0$.

76. Consider the following:
1. The coordinates of Q are (4, –3, –1).
2. PQ is of length more than 8 units.
3. The point (1, –1, –3) is the mid-point of the line segment PQ and lies on the given plane.

Which of the above statements are correct?

A. 1 and 2 only B. 2 and 3 only
C. 1 and 3 only D. 1, 2 and 3

77. Consider the following:
1. The direction ratios of the line segment PQ are < 3, –2, 2 >.
2. The sum of the squares of direction cosines of the line segment PQ is unity.

Which of the above statements is/are correct?

A. 1 only B. 2 only
C. Both 1 and 2 D. Neither 1 nor 2

Directions (Qs. No. 78 and 79): *Consider the following for the next two (02) items that follow:*

A line L passes through the point P(5, –6, 7) and is parallel to the planes $x + y + z = 1$ and $2x - y - 2z = 3$.

78. What are the direction ratios of the line of intersection of the given planes?

A. < 1, 4, 3 > B. < –1, –4, 3 >
C. < 1, –4, 3 > D. < 1, –4, –3 >

79. What is the equation of the line L?

A. $\frac{x-5}{-1}=\frac{y+6}{4}=\frac{z-7}{-3}$ B. $\frac{x+5}{-1}=\frac{y-6}{4}=\frac{z+7}{-3}$
C. $\frac{x-5}{-1}=\frac{y+6}{-4}=\frac{z-7}{3}$ D. $\frac{x-5}{-1}=\frac{y+6}{-4}=\frac{z-7}{-3}$

Directions (Qs. No. 80 and 81): *Consider the following for the next two (02) items that follow:*

Let $\vec{a}=\hat{i}+\hat{j}$, $\vec{b}=3\hat{i}+4\hat{k}$ and $\vec{b}=\vec{c}+\vec{d}$, where $\vec{c}$ is parallel to $\vec{a}$ and $\vec{d}$ is perpendicular to $\vec{a}$.

80. What is $\vec{c}$ equal to?

A. $\frac{3(\hat{i}+\hat{j})}{2}$ B. $\frac{2(\hat{i}+\hat{j})}{3}$
C. $\frac{(\hat{i}+\hat{j})}{2}$ D. $\frac{(\hat{i}+\hat{j})}{3}$

81. If $\vec{d}=x\hat{i}+y\hat{j}+z\hat{k}$, then which of the following equations is/are correct?

1. $y - x = 4$
2. $2z - 3 = 0$

Select the correct answer using the code given below:

A. 1 only B. 2 only
C. Both 1 and 2 D. Neither 1 nor 2

Directions (Qs. No. 82 and 83): *Consider the following for the next two (02) items that follow:*

Let $\vec{a}$, $\vec{b}$ and $\vec{c}$ be three vectors such that $\vec{a}+\vec{b}+\vec{c}=\vec{0}$, and $|\vec{a}|=10, |\vec{b}|=6$ and $|\vec{c}|=14$.

82. What is $\vec{a}.\vec{b}+\vec{b}.\vec{c}+\vec{c}.\vec{a}$ equal to?

A. –332 B. –166
C. 0 D. 166

83. What is the angle between $\vec{a}$ and $\vec{b}$?

A. 30° B. 45°
C. 60° D. 75°

84. In a right-angled triangle ABC, if the hypotenuse AB = p, then what is

$\overline{AB}.\overline{AC}+\overline{BC}.\overline{BA}+\overline{CA}.\overline{CB}$ equal to?

A. p B. p^2
C. $2p^2$ D. $\frac{p^2}{2}$

85. A force $\vec{F}=3\hat{i}+2\hat{j}-4\hat{k}$ is applied at the point (1, –1, 2). What is the moment of the force about the point (2, –1, 3)?

A. $\hat{i}+4\hat{j}+4\hat{k}$ B. $2\hat{i}+\hat{j}+2\hat{k}$
C. $2\hat{i}-7\hat{j}-2\hat{k}$ D. $2\hat{i}+4\hat{j}-\hat{k}$

86. What is the domain of the function $f(x)=\frac{1}{\sqrt{|x|-x}}$?

A. $(-\infty, 0)$ B. $(0, \infty)$
C. $0 < x < 1$ D. $x > 1$

87. Consider the following in respect of the function

$$f(x)=\begin{cases}2+x, & x\geq 0\\ 2-x, & x<0\end{cases}$$

1. $\lim_{x\to 1} f(x)$ does not exist.
2. $f(x)$ is differentiable at $x = 0$.
3. $f(x)$ is continuous at $x = 0$.

Which of the above statements is/are correct?

A. 1 only B. 3 only
C. 2 and 3 only D. 1 and 3 only

88. Let f : A → ℝ, where A = ℝ\(0) is such that $f(x)=\frac{x+|x|}{x}$. On which one of the following sets is $f(x)$ continuous?

A. A
B. B = $\{x \in \mathbb{R} : x \geq 0\}$
C. C = $\{x \in \mathbb{R} : x \leq 0\}$
D. D = ℝ

89. Which one of the following statements is correct in respect of the function

$f(x) = x^3 \sin x$?

A. It has local maximum at $x = 0$
B. It has local minimum at $x = 0$
C. It has neither maximum nor minimum at $x = 0$
D. It has maximum value 1

90. What is the area bounded by the curves $|y| = 1 - x^2$?

A. $\frac{4}{3}$ square units B. $\frac{8}{3}$ square units
C. 4 square units D. $\frac{16}{3}$ square units

91. Consider the following statements:

1. The mean and median are equal in symmetric distribution.
2. The range is the difference between the maximum value and the minimum value in the data.
3. The sum of the areas of the rectangles in the histogram is equal to the total area bounded by the frequency polygon and the horizontal axis.

Which of the above statements are correct?

A. 1 and 2 only B. 2 and 3 only
C. 1 and 3 only D. 1, 2 and 3

92. The scores of 15 students in an examination were recorded as 10, 5, 8, 16, 18, 20, 8, 10, 16, 20, 18, 11, 16, 14 and 12. After calculating the mean, median and mode, an error is found. One of the values is

wrongly written as 16 instead of 18. Which of the following measures of central tendency will change?
A. Mean and median B. Median and mode
C. Mode only D. Mean and mode

93. For 10 observations on price (x) and supply (y), the following data was obtained:
$\Sigma x = 130$, $\Sigma y = 220$, $\Sigma x^2 = 2288$, $\Sigma y^2 = 5506$ and $\Sigma xy = 3467$.
What is the line of regression of y on x?
A. $y = 0.91x + 8.74$ B. $y = 1.02x + 8.74$
C. $y = 1.02x - 7.02$ D. $y = 0.91x - 7.02$

94. In a study of two groups, the following results were obtained:

	Group A	***Group B***
Sample size	20	25
Sample mean	22	23
Sample standard deviation	10	12

Which of the following statements is correct?
A. Group A is less variable than Group B because Group A's standard deviation is smaller.
B. Group A is less variable than Group B because Group A's sample size is smaller.
C. Group A is less variable than Group B because Group A's sample mean is smaller.
D. Group A is less variable than Group B because Group A's coefficient of variation is smaller.

95. Consider the following statements in respect of class intervals of grouped frequency distribution:
1. Class intervals need not be mutually exclusive.
2. Class intervals should be exhaustive.
3. Class intervals need not be of equal width.
Which of the above statements are correct?
A. 1 and 2 only B. 2 and 3 only
C. 1 and 3 only D. 1, 2 and 3

96. A medicine is known to be 75% effective to cure a patient. If the medicine is given to 5 patients, what is the probability that at least one patient is cured by this medicine?
A. $\frac{1}{1024}$ B. $\frac{243}{1024}$
C. $\frac{1023}{1024}$ D. $\frac{781}{1024}$

97. For two events, A and B, it is given that $P(A) = \frac{3}{5}$, $P(B) = \frac{3}{10}$ and $P(A \mid B) = \frac{2}{3}$. If $\overline{A}$ and $\overline{B}$ are the complementary events of A and B, then what is $P(\overline{A} \mid \overline{B})$ equal to?
A. $\frac{3}{7}$ B. $\frac{3}{4}$
C. $\frac{1}{3}$ D. $\frac{4}{7}$

98. A machine has three parts, A, B and C, whose chances of being defective are 0.02, 0.10 and 0.05 respectively. The machine stops working if any one of the parts becomes defective. What is the probability that the machine will ***not*** stop working?
A. 0.06 B. 0.16
C. 0.84 D. 0.94

99. Three independent events, A_1, A_2 and A_3 occur with probabilities $P(A_i) = \frac{1}{1+i}$, $i = 1, 2, 3$. What is the probability that at least one of the three events occurs?
A. $\frac{1}{4}$ B. $\frac{2}{3}$
C. $\frac{3}{4}$ D. $\frac{1}{24}$

100. Two variates, x and y, are uncorrelated and have standard deviations σ_x and σ_y respectively. What is the correlation coefficient between $x + y$ and $x - y$?
A. $\frac{\sigma_x \sigma_y}{\sigma_x^2 + \sigma_y^2}$ B. $\frac{\sigma_x + \sigma_y}{2\sigma_x \sigma_y}$
C. $\frac{\sigma_x^2 - \sigma_y^2}{\sigma_x^2 + \sigma_y^2}$ D. $\frac{\sigma_y - \sigma_x}{\sigma_x \sigma_y}$

101. A random sample of 20 people is classified in the following table according to their ages:

Age	***Frequency***
15–25	2
25–35	4
35–45	6
45–55	5
55–65	3

What is the mean age of this group of people?
A. 41.0 B. 41.5
C. 42.0 D. 42.5

102. If the covariance between x and y is 30, variance of x is 25 and variance of y is 144, then what is the correlation coefficient?
A. 0.4 B. 0.5
C. 0.6 D. 0.7

103. A coin is tossed three times. Consider the following events:
A : No head appears
B : Exactly one head appears
C : At least two heads appear
Which one of the following is correct?
A. $(A \cup B) \cap (A \cup C) = B \cup C$
B. $(A \cap B') \cup (A \cap C') = B' \cup C'$

C. A ∩ (B′ ∪ C′) = A ∪ B ∪ C

D. A ∩ (B′ ∪ C′) = B′ ∩ C′

104. In a series of 3 one-day cricket matches between teams A and B of a college, the probability of team A winning or drawing are 1/3 and 1/6 respectively. If a win, loss or draw gives 2, 0 and 1 point respectively, then what is the probability that team A will score 5 points in the series?

A. $\frac{17}{18}$ B. $\frac{11}{12}$

C. $\frac{1}{12}$ D. $\frac{1}{18}$

105. Let the random variable X follow B(6, p). If 16 P(X = 4) = P(X = 2), then what is the value of p?

A. $\frac{1}{3}$ B. $\frac{1}{4}$

C. $\frac{1}{5}$ D. $\frac{1}{6}$

Directions (Qs. No. 106 and 107): *Consider the following function for the next two (02) items that follow:*

$$f(x)=\begin{cases}3x^2+12x-1, & -1\le x\le 2\\ 37-x, & 2<x\le 3\end{cases}$$

106. Which of the following statements is/are correct?

1. $f(x)$ is increasing in the interval [–1, 2].
2. $f(x)$ is decreasing in the interval [2, 3]

Select the correct answer using the code given below:

A. 1 only B. 2 only

C. Both 1 and 2 D. Neither 1 nor 2

107. Which of the following statements are correct?

1. $f(x)$ is continuous at $x = 2$.
2. $f(x)$ attains greatest value at $x = 2$.
3. $f(x)$ is differentiable at $x = 2$.

Select the correct answer using the code given below:

A. 1 and 2 only B. 2 and 3 only

C. 1 and 3 only D. 1, 2 and 3

Directions (Qs. No. 108 to 110): *Consider the following for the next three (03) items that follow:*

Let $f(x) = \{|x| - |x - 1|\}^2$

108. What is $f'(x)$ equal to when $x > 1$?

A. 0 B. $2x - 1$

C. $4x - 2$ D. $8x - 4$

109. What is $f'(x)$ equal to when $0 < x < 1$?

A. 0 B. $2x - 1$

C. $4x - 2$ D. $8x - 4$

110. Which of the following equations is/are correct?

1. $f(-2) = f(5)$
2. $f''(-2) + f''(0.5) + f''(3) = 4$

Select the correct answer using the code given below:

A. 1 only B. 2 only

C. Both 1 and 2 D. Neither 1 nor 2

Directions (Qs. No. 111 to 113): *Consider the following for the next three (03) items that follow:*

Let $f(x) = [x]$, where [.] is the greatest integer function and $g(x) = \sin x$ be two real valued functions over ℝ.

111. Which of the following statements is correct?

A. Both $f(x)$ and $g(x)$ are continuous at $x = 0$.

B. $f(x)$ is continuous at $x = 0$, but $g(x)$ is not continuous at $x = 0$

C. $g(x)$ is continuous at $x = 0$, but $f(x)$ is not continuous at $x = 0$

D. Both $f(x)$ and $g(x)$ are discontinuous at $x = 0$.

112. Which one of the following statements is correct?

A. $\lim_{x\to 0}(fog)(x)$ exists.

B. $\lim_{x\to 0}(gof)(x)$ exists.

C. $\lim_{x\to 0^-}(fog)(x) = \lim_{x\to 0^-}(gof)(x)$

D. $\lim_{x\to 0^+}(fog)(x) = \lim_{x\to 0^+}(gof)(x)$

113. Which of the following statements are correct?

1. (fof) $(x) = f(x)$.
2. (gog) $(x) = g(x)$ only when $x = 0$.
3. (go(fog)) (x) can take only three values.

Select the correct answer using the code given below:

A. 1 and 2 only B. 2 and 3 only

C. 1 and 3 only D. 1, 2 and 3

Directions (Qs. No. 114 and 115): *Consider the following for the next two (02) items that follow:*

Let $f(x)=\begin{cases}\dfrac{e^x-1}{x}, & x>0\\ 0, & x=0\end{cases}$

be a real valued function.

114. Which one of the following statements is correct?

A. $f(x)$ is a strictly decreasing function in $(0, x)$.

B. $f(x)$ is a strictly increasing function in $(0, x)$.

C. $f(x)$ is neither increasing nor decreasing in $(0, x)$.

D. $f(x)$ is not decreasing in $(0, x)$.

115. Which of the following statements is/are correct?

1. $f(x)$ is right continuous at $x = 0$.
2. $f(x)$ is discontinuous at $x = 1$.

Select the correct answer using the code given below:

A. 1 only B. 2 only

C. Both 1 and 2 D. Neither 1 nor 2

Directions (Qs. No. 116 and 117): *Consider the following for the next two (02) items that follow:*

Consider the parabola $y = x^2 + 7x + 2$ and the straight line $y = 3x - 3$.

116. What are the coordinates of the point on the parabola which is closest to the straight line?

A. (0, 2) B. (–2, –8)

C. (–7, 2) D. (1, 10)

117. What is the shortest distance from the above point on the parabola to the line?

A. $\frac{\sqrt{10}}{2}$ B. $\frac{\sqrt{10}}{5}$

C. $\frac{1}{\sqrt{10}}$ D. $\frac{\sqrt{5}}{4}$

Directions (Qs. No. 118 to 120): *Consider the following for the next three (03) items that follow:*

Let $f(x) = \begin{cases} -2, & -3 \le x \le 0 \\ x-2, & 0 < x \le 3 \end{cases}$ and

$g(x) = f(|x|) + |f(x)|$

118. Which of the following statements is/are correct?

1. $g(x)$ is differentiable at $x = 0$.
2. $g(x)$ is differentiable at $x = 2$.

Select the correct answer using the code given below:

A. 1 only B. 2 only

C. Both 1 and 2 D. Neither 1 nor 2

119. What is the value of the differential coefficient of $g(x)$ at $x = -2$?

A. -1 B. 0

C. 1 D. 2

120. Which of the following statements are correct?

1. $g(x)$ is continuous at $x = 0$.
2. $g(x)$ is continuous at $x = 2$.
3. $g(x)$ is continuous at $x = -1$.

Select the correct answer using the code given below:

A. 1 and 2 only B. 2 and 3 only

C. 1 and 3 only D. 1, 2 and 3

ANSWERS

PAPER-I : GENERAL ABILITY TEST

1	**2**	**3**	**4**	**5**	**6**	**7**	**8**	**9**	**10**
A	B	B	A	A	D	D	A	C	D
11	**12**	**13**	**14**	**15**	**16**	**17**	**18**	**19**	**20**
C	D	D	D	B	C	D	A	C	B
21	**22**	**23**	**24**	**25**	**26**	**27**	**28**	**29**	**30**
B	A	B	C	C	A	D	D	C	D
31	**32**	**33**	**34**	**35**	**36**	**37**	**38**	**39**	**40**
B	A	A	C	A	D	C	B	B	A
41	**42**	**43**	**44**	**45**	**46**	**47**	**48**	**49**	**50**
C	A	B	D	B	A	C	C	D	C
51	**52**	**53**	**54**	**55**	**56**	**57**	**58**	**59**	**60**
A	C	C	A	C	B	B	C	B	C
61	**62**	**63**	**64**	**65**	**66**	**67**	**68**	**69**	**70**
D	A	D	B	A	D	B	A	A	A
71	**72**	**73**	**74**	**75**	**76**	**77**	**78**	**79**	**80**
A	C	C	D	A	A	B	B	D	B
81	**82**	**83**	**84**	**85**	**86**	**87**	**88**	**89**	**90**
C	B	B	C	C	C	C	B	B	C
91	**92**	**93**	**94**	**95**	**96**	**97**	**98**	**99**	**100**
D	C	C	B	B	C	C	B	D	B
101	**102**	**103**	**104**	**105**	**106**	**107**	**108**	**109**	**110**
D	*	A	C	B	B	C	C	C	C
111	**112**	**113**	**114**	**115**	**116**	**117**	**118**	**119**	**120**
C	D	A	D	B	B	B	A	B	B
121	**122**	**123**	**124**	**125**	**126**	**127**	**128**	**129**	**130**
C	B	C	A	B	A	A	D	A	D
131	**132**	**133**	**134**	**135**	**136**	**137**	**138**	**139**	**140**
C	D	C	C	D	D	C	D	D	B
141	**142**	**143**	**144**	**145**	**146**	**147**	**148**	**149**	**150**
C	C	C	B	B	C	C	A	A	C

PAPER-II : MATHEMATICS

1	2	3	4	5	6	7	8	9	10
D	B	B	B	B	D	C	D	C	A
11	**12**	**13**	**14**	**15**	**16**	**17**	**18**	**19**	**20**
C	A	A	D	A	B	C	C	D	D
21	**22**	**23**	**24**	**25**	**26**	**27**	**28**	**29**	**30**
D	D	C	A	D	C	D	C	D	A
31	**32**	**33**	**34**	**35**	**36**	**37**	**38**	**39**	**40**
D	B	A	B	B	C	A	D	A	B
41	**42**	**43**	**44**	**45**	**46**	**47**	**48**	**49**	**50**
D	B	A	D	A	B	B	C	A	B
51	**52**	**53**	**54**	**55**	**56**	**57**	**58**	**59**	**60**
C	B	B	C	C	D	D	D	A	B
61	**62**	**63**	**64**	**65**	**66**	**67**	**68**	**69**	**70**
B	C	A	B	C	B	C	B	B	D
71	**72**	**73**	**74**	**75**	**76**	**77**	**78**	**79**	**80**
D	D	B	A	A	C	C	C	A	A
81	**82**	**83**	**84**	**85**	**86**	**87**	**88**	**89**	**90**
D	B	C	B	C	A	D	A	C	B
91	**92**	**93**	**94**	**95**	**96**	**97**	**98**	**99**	**100**
D	D	B	C	B	C	A	C	C	B
101	**102**	**103**	**104**	**105**	**106**	**107**	**108**	**109**	**110**
B	B	D	D	C	C	C	A	D	C
111	**112**	**113**	**114**	**115**	**116**	**117**	**118**	**119**	**120**
A	D	A	B	A	B	C	B	B	D

EXPLANATORY ANSWERS

PAPER-I : GENERAL ABILITY TEST

51. **Covalent bond,** in chemistry, the interatomic linkage that results from the sharing of an electron pair between two atoms. The binding arises from the electrostatic attraction of their nuclei for the same electrons. A covalent bond forms when the bonded atoms have a lower total energy than that of widely separated atoms.

In a simplified view of an *ionic bond,* the bonding electron is not shared at all, but transferred. In this type of bond, the outer *atomic orbital* of one atom has a vacancy which allows the addition of one or more electrons. These newly added electrons potentially occupy a lower energy-state (effectively closer to more nuclear charge) than they experience in a different atom. Thus, one nucleus offers a more tightly bound position to an electron than does another nucleus, with the result that one atom may transfer an electron to the other. This transfer causes one atom to assume a net positive charge, and the other to assume a net negative charge. The bond then result from electrostatic attraction between atoms and the atoms become positive or negatively charged *ions.*

52. A match is a small stick of wood or strip of cardboard with a solidified mixture of flammable chemicals deposited on one end. When that end is struck on a rough surface, the friction generates enough heat to ignite the chemicals and produce a small flame. Some matches, called strike-anywhere matches, may be ignited by striking them on any rough surface. Other matches, called safety matches, will ignite only when they are struck on a special rough surface containing certain chemicals.

When you strike a match the red phosphorus is converted to white phosphorus for a fraction of a second, just enough to cause a spark of heat by reacting with oxygen in the surrounding air.

53. LPG is prepared by refining petroleum or "wet" natural gas, and is almost entirely derived from fossil fuel sources, being manufactured during the refining of petroleum (crude oil), or extracted from petroleum or natural gas streams as they emerge from the ground. It was first produced in 1910 by **Dr. Walter Snelling,** and the first commercial products appeared in 1912. It currently provides about 3% of all energy consumed, and burns relatively cleanly with no soot and very few sulphur emissions. As it is a gas, it does not pose ground or water pollution hazards, but it can cause air pollution. LPG has a typical specific calorific value of 46.1 MJ/kg compared with 42.5 MJ/kg for fuel oil and 43.5 MJ/kg for premium grade petrol (gasoline).

54. **Bacterial genetics** is the subfield of genetics devoted to the study of bacteria. Bacterial genetics are subtly different from eukaryotic genetics, however bacteria still serve as a good model for animal genetic studies. One of the major distinctions between bacterial and eukaryotic genetics stems from the bacteria's lack of membrane-bound organelles (this is true of all prokaryotes. While it is a fact that there are prokaryotic organelles, they are never bound by a lipid membrane, but by a shell of proteins), necessitating protein synthesis occur in the cytoplasm.

55. Horses are the species Equus caballus, while donkeys are classified as Equus asinus. Since both species are of the Equus genus, they have the same basic body shape and share many physical traits, including long muzzles and pointed ears.

Horses are known for their smooth coats, flowing manes and graceful stature, while donkeys often have wiry or bristly hair and a spiky mane. On average, donkeys grow to about 550 pounds, but the extensive breeding of horses produces sizes ranging from 660 to 4,400 pounds, according to Animal Diversity Web. Donkeys and horses have a different number of chromosomes, making them genetically incompatible. They can mate to produce mules or hinnies, but their offspring are incapable of reproducing.

In sexual organisms, two organisms belong to the same species if they are able to breed and have fertile offspring. Although horses and donkeys can have mules, they are infertile, so they are two separate species and the mule is a hybrid.

56. Magnesium is a component of the chlorophyll molecule and serves as a cofactor in most enzymes. Magnesium deficiency will exhibit a yellowing (which may turn brown) and interveinal chlorosis beginning in the older leaves. The older leaves will be the first to develop interveinal chlorosis. Starting at leaf margin or tip and progressing inward between the veins.

57. **Fluoride therapy** is the delivery of fluoride to the teeth, topically or systemically, to protect them from dental caries (cavities). Strictly speaking, fluoride therapy repairs rather than prevents damage to the teeth, causing the mineral fluorapatite to be incorporated into damaged tooth enamel. Fluorapatite is not a natural component of human teeth, although it is found in the teeth of sharks. The main mineral found in natural tooth enamel is hydroxyapatite rather than the fluorapatite created in the presence of fluoride. Even without fluoride, teeth experience alternating increases and decreases in mineral content, depending upon how acidic or basic the mouth is, and depending upon the concentration of other substances in the mouth, such as phosphate and calcium. Fluoride enhances and modifies the restoration of the mineral content of the teeth, and counteracts the breakdown of the teeth from lactic acid producing bacteria.

58. When the flow is steady, streamlines are often used to represent the trajectories of the fluid particles. A streamline is a line drawn in the fluid such that a tangent to the streamline at any point is parallel to the fluid velocity at the point. The velocity vectors at three points along streamline. The fluid veclocity can vary (in both magnitude and direction). From point to point along a streamline, but at any given point, the velocity is constant in time, as required by the condition of steady flow. In Fact, steady flow is often called streamling flow.

63. The speed of sound depends on the medium that the waves pass through, and is a fundamental property of the material. The first significant effort towards the measure of the speed of sound was made by Newton. He believed that the speed of sound in a particular substance was equal to the square root of the pressure acting on it (STP) divided by its density. The speed of sound waves in a medium depends both on elastic and inertia properties of the medium.

64. There are six experimentally separable ways in which sound waves are analysed. They are: pitch, duration, loudness, timbre, sonic texture and spatial location.

Pitch is perceived as how "low" or "high" a sound is and represents the cyclic, repetitive nature of the vibrations that make up sound. Pitch of a sound is its characteristic by which we can generally differentiate between a male voice and a female voice.

Duration is perceived as how "long" or "short" a sound is and relates to onset and offset signals created by nerve responses to sounds. The duration of a sound usually lasts from the time the sound is first noticed until the sound is identified as having changed or ceased.

Loudness is perceived as how "loud" or "soft" a sound is and relates to the totalled number of auditory nerve stimulations over short cyclic time periods, most likely over the duration of theta wave cycles. The loudness of sound is related to its amplitude.

Timbre is perceived as the quality of different sounds (*e.g.*, the thud of a fallen rock, the whir of a drill, the tone of a musical instrument or the quality of a voice) and represents the pre-conscious allocation of a sonic identity to a sound. The timber of a particular musical sound is related to the waveform of the sound wave.

Sonic texture relates to the number of sound sources and the interaction between them. The word 'texture', in this context, relates to the cognitive separation of auditory objects.

Spatial location represents the cognitive placement of a sound in an environmental context; including the placement of a sound on both the horizontal and vertical plane, the distance from the sound source and the characteristics of the sonic environment.

66. There exists two main types of short circuits; a dead short circuit and a limited short circuit.

A dead short occurs when a live wire comes in contact with a common or ground wire (or the positive and negative wires are connected in a DC circuit) and the circuit is subsequently energized. In properly fused circuits this will cause the fuse to blow and the circuit to de-energize. This type of situation does not create sufficient heat to ignite combustibles. However, it is possible that the circuit is not fused properly. If this occurs, the current can continue to pass through the wires causing them to significantly overheat. This type of situation can ignite surrounding combustibles causing a fire.

The other type of short circuit is a limited short circuit. In this case, wires come in contact such that the volume of material through which the current flows is smaller than the fusible link. This will create a spark or flash and result in melting of the copper of the wiring.

67. **Utilitarianism** is a theory about what we ought to do. It states that the best action is the one that maximizes utility. "Utility" is defined in various ways, usually in terms of the well-being of sentient entities, such as human beings and other animals. **Jeremy Bentham,** the founder of utilitarianism, gave this definition of "utility": it is the sum of all pleasure that results from an action, minus the suffering of anyone involved in the action. The philosopher **John Stuart Mill** developed this concept further. He included not only the quantity of the pleasure, but also the *quality* of pleasure. He focused on rules, instead of individual actions.

Utilitarian were advocates of the idea of the 'greatest good for the greatest number of people'. In *An Inquiry into the Original of Our Ideas of Beauty and Virtue,* Hutcheson says when choosing the most moral action, virtue is in proportion to the number of people a particular action brings happiness to. In the same way, moral evil, or vice, is proportionate to the number of people made to suffer. The best action is the one that procures the greatest happiness of the greatest numbers—and the worst is the one that causes the most misery.

68. A **power loom** is a mechanized loom powered by a line shaft, and was one of the key developments in the industrialization of weaving during the early Industrial Revolution. The first power loom was designed in 1784 by **Edmund Cartwright** and first built in 1785.

69. **Subsidiary Alliance** is a system of ruling a dominated nation. Lord Wellesley introduced it in India in the 19th century. At that time, there were local rulers in India. The system worked as follows: The (ruling) British would enter into a contract with a local ruler. This ruler had to accept many conditions; among them was that he would only deal with the British, and no other European forces, that he would allow British forces in the territory he ruled, and that he would not declare war without asking the British first.

70. A **periplus** is a manuscript document that lists the ports and coastal landmarks, in order and with approximate intervening distances, that the captain of a vessel could expect to find along a shore. It served the same purpose as the later Roman itinerarium of road stops; however, the Greek navigators added various notes, which if they were professional geographers (as many were) became part of their own additions to Greek geography.

The ***Periplus of the Erythraean Sea*** is a Greco-Roman periplus, written in Greek, describing navigation and trading opportunities from Roman Egyptian ports like Berenice along the coast of the Red Sea and others along Northeast Africa and the Sindh and South western India.

71. Indian shuttler Saina Nehwal has won the 2016 Australian Open Super Series Badminton tournament title in women's singles category. In the final match played at Sydney, Saina defeated Chinese Sun Yu by 11-21, 21-14, 21-19 score. It was Saina's first title of year 2016 season and overall second Australian Open title of her career. She won her first Australian Open title in 2014.

74. LinkedIn is an online directory of individual professionals and organizations. Individuals and companies use LinkedIn for professional networking. LinkedIn has millions of members in more than 200 countries, including executives from all Fortune 500 companies.

Individuals use LinkedIn for professional networking, connecting and job searching. Companies use LinkedIn for recruiting and for providing company information to prospective employees.

On June 13, 2016, Microsoft announced it will acquire LinkedIn for $26.2 billion, a deal expected to be completed by the end of 2016.

75. Mediterranean climate, major climate type of the Köppen classification characterized by hot, dry summers and cool, wet winters and located between about 30° and 45° latitude north and south of the Equator and on the western sides of the continents.

Mediterranean climate experiences extreme temperature condition. The majority of the regions with mediterranean climates have relatively mild winters and very warm summers. However winter and summer temperatures can vary greatly between different regions with a mediterranean climate.

76.

State	Total forest area	% of forest area
Madhya Pradesh	77,522	25.15
Arunachal Pradesh	67,321	80.39
Chhattisgarh	55,621	41.14
Jharkhand	23,473	29.45

77. As per Census-2011, the State of Punjab, has the highest percentage of Scheduled Caste population amongst all the States of the Country. The Scheduled Caste population in Punjab is 29% followed by Himachal Pradesh (25%), West Bengal (23%).

Mizoram has the lowest percentage of SC population among all the states of the country. The SC population in Mizoram in 0.1% followed by Meghalya (0.6%), Goa (1.7%).

Uttar Pradesh has the highest number of SC population in India followed by Maharastra.

81. A **cactus** is a member of the plant family **Cactaceae**, a family comprising about 127 genera with some 1750 known species of the order Caryophyllales.

The stems of most cacti are some shade of green, often bluish or brownish green. Such stems contain chlorophyll and are able to carry out photosynthesis;

The great majority of cacti have no visible leaves; photosynthesis takes place in the stems.

The absence of visible leaves is one of the most striking features of most cacti. Spines, which are modified leaves, are present on even those cacti with true leaves, showing the evolution of spines preceded the loss of leaves.

83. **Malaria** is a mosquito-borne infectious disease affecting humans and other animals caused by parasitic protozoans belonging to the *Plasmodium* type. Malaria causes symptoms that typically include fever, fatigue, vomiting, and headaches. In severe cases it can cause yellow skin, seizures, coma, or death.

85. A **virus** is a biological agent that reproduces inside the cells of living hosts. When infected by a virus, a host cell is forced to produce many thousands of identical copies of the original virus at an extraordinary rate. Unlike most living things, viruses do not have cells that divide; new viruses are assembled in the infected host cell.

90. **Pressure** is a physical quantity that is a force spread over a certain area. In other words, pressure is force per unit area. If you take the amount of force being applied on a body, divide it with the area of contact, you will arrive at the pressure being applied on the body. Pressure = force/area

Pressure is a scalar quantity. It relates the vector surface element (a vector normal to the surface) with the normal force acting on it.

91. Hypermetropia occurs when light is focused behind the retina. In reality, light cannot actually be focused behind the retina. So, the lens changes its thickness (becomes fatter or more rounded) which aims to bring the light into focus on the retina–a process called accommodation.

93. A **spring scale** or **spring balance** is a type of weighing scale. It consists of spring fixed at one end with a hook to attach an object at the other.

A spring balance can be calibrated for the accurate measurement of mass in the location in which they are used, but many spring balances are marked right on their face "Not Legal for Trade" or words of similar import due to the approximate nature of the theory used to mark the scale.

94. In physics, a **contact force,** is a force that acts at the point of contact between two objects, in contrast to body forces. Contact forces are described by Newton's laws of motion, as with all other forces in dynamics.

Push force, Frictional force, Strain force, Applied force, Air resistance force, and Normal force is a type of contact force.

98. Gypsum is an indispensable component of ordinary Portland cement. The main function of gypsum is to regulate the setting time of cement. Gypsum has a great influence on water consumption of standard consistence and strength simultaneously.

99. An **emulsion** is a mixture of two or more liquids that are normally immiscible. Emulsions are part of a more general class of two-phase systems of matter called colloids.

A colloidal solution, sometimes known as a colloidal suspension, is a solution in which a material is evenly suspended in a liquid. In other words, a colloid is a microscopically small substance that is equally dispersed throughout another material.

100. When *fatty acids* (present in animal fat or oil) are mixed with an *alkali* (present in wood ash), the alkali causes the fatty acid to split into fatty acids and glycerin. Through the process, the fatty acids that remain are chemically joined with potassium present in the alkali giving us "*potassium salts*" (potassium hydroxide) which form the basis of soap.

108. **International Day of Yoga** or commonly and unofficially referred to as **Yoga Day**, is celebrated annually on 21 June since its inception in 2015. An international day for yoga was declared unanimously by the United Nations General Assembly (UNGA) on 11 December 2014. Yoga is a physical, mental, and/ or spiritual practice attributed mostly to India. The Indian Prime Minister Narendra Modi in his UN address suggested the date of 21 June, as it is the longest day of the year in the Northern Hemisphere and shares special significance in many parts of the world.

111. The total number of ministers, including the prime minister, in the council of ministers shall not exceed 15% of the total strength of the Lok Sabha. The provision was added by the 91st Amendment Act of 2003.

Prime minister recommends persons who can be appointed as ministers by the president. The president can appointed only those persons as ministers. The Prime minister is appointed by the president, while the other ministers are appointed by the president on the advice of the prime minister. This means that the president can appoint only those persons as ministers who are recommended by the prime minister.

112. A Money Bill is one that contains provisions for taxes, appropriation of funds etc. Money Bills can be introduced only in the Lok Sabha, and the Rajya Sabha cannot make amendments to such bills passed by the Lok Sabha. The Rajya Sabha can suggest amendments, but it is the Lok Sabha's choice to accept or reject them.

Procedure for a Money Bill:

1. Money Bills can be introduced only in Lok Sabha (the directly elected 'people's house' of the Indian Parliament).
2. Money bills passed by the Lok Sabha are sent to the Rajya Sabha (the upper house of parliament, elected by the state and territorial legislatures or appointed by the president). The Rajya Sabha may not amend money bills but can recommend amendments. To make sure that Rajya Sabha doesn't amend the bill by adding some non-money matters (known as Financial Bill), the Lok Sabha Speaker certifies the bill as a money bill before sending it to the upper house, and the decision of the Speaker is binding on both the Houses. A money bill must be returned to the Lok Sabha within 14 days or the bill is deemed to have passed both houses in the form it was originally passed by the Lok Sabha.
3. When a Money Bill is returned to the Lok Sabha with the recommended amendments of the Rajya Sabha it is open to Lok Sabha to accept or reject any or all of the recommendations.
4. A money bill is deemed to have passed both houses with any recommended amendments the Lok Sabha chooses to accept, (and without any that it chooses to decline).
5. The definition of "Money Bill" is given in the Article 110 of the Constitution of India. A financial bill is not a Money Bill unless it fulfills the requirements of the Article 110.
6. The Speaker of the Lok Sabha certifies if a Finance bill is a Money Bill or not.

113. The Prime Minister shall be appointed by the President and the other Ministers shall be appointed by the President on the advice of the Prime Minister. **Article 75(1)**

114. Among the most interesting and revealing artifacts discovered from ancient **Mesopotamia** are the objects known as cylinder seals. Cylinder seals were impression stamps, often quite intricate in design, used throughout Mesopotamia.

A **cylinder seal** is a small round cylinder, typically about one inch in length, engraved with written characters or figurative scenes or both, used in ancient times to roll an impression onto a two-dimensional surface, generally wet clay. Cylinder seals were invented around 3500 BC in the Near East, at the contemporary sites of Susa in south-western Iran and Uruk in southern Mesopotamia.

115. **Civil disobedience** is the active, professed refusal to obey certain laws, demands, and commands of a government, or of an occupying international power. Civil disobedience is a symbolic or ritualistic violation of the law, rather than a rejection of the system as a whole.

The Civil Disobedience Movement led by Mahatma Gandhi, in the year 1930 was an important milestone in the history of Indian Nationalism. There are three distinct phases that mark the development of Indian Nationalism.

The movement received massive response from business groups and peasantry. The movement coincided with large scale labour upsurge in Maharashtra.

116. The annual rainfall in the state varies significantly. The Average rainfall varies throughout the state. The western part that consists of the desert receives an annual rainfall of 100 mm (about 4 inches). The general trend of Isohytes is from north-west to south-east. There is a very rapid and marked decrease in rainfall west of the Aravalli range making western Rajasthan the most arid part. The yearly total rainfall is highly variable at different places all over the state and it is most erratic in the western half with frequent spells of drought, punctuated occasionally by heavy downpour in some years, associated with the passing low pressure systems over the region.

117. The **ozone layer** or **ozone shield** is a region of Earth's stratosphere that absorbs most of the Sun's ultraviolet (UV) radiation. It contains high concentrations ozone (O_3) in relation to other parts of the atmosphere, although still small in relation to other gases in the stratosphere.

The ozone molecules formed by the reaction above absorb radiation having an appropriate wavelength between UV-C and UV-B. The tri-atomic ozone molecule becomes diatomic molecular oxygen plus a free oxygen atom.

118. Laterite has been derived from the Latin word 'Later' which means brick. The Laterite soils develop in areas with high temperature and high rainfall. These are the result of intense leaching due to tropical rains. With rain, lime and silica are leached away, and soils rich in iron oxide and aluminium compound are left behind. Humus content of the soil is removed fast by bacteria that thrives well in high temperature. These soils are poor in organic matter, nitrogen, phosphate and calcium, while iron oxide and Potash are in excess. Hence, Laterites are not suitable for cultivation; however, application of manures and fertilizers are required for making the soils fertile for cultivation.

119. Salt works on your kidneys to make your body hold on to more water.

This extra stored water raises your blood pressure and puts strain on your kidneys, arteries, heart and brain.

Your body removes unwanted fluid by filtering your blood through your kidneys. Here any extra fluid is sucked out and put into your bladder to be removed as urine.

The amount of salt you eat has a direct effect on your blood pressure. Salt makes your body hold on to water. If you eat too much salt, the extra water stored in your body raises your blood pressure. So, the more salt you eat, the higher your blood pressure.

122. The Sahel Desert is a semi-arid region that separates tropical forest from the Sahara Desert. The Sahel Desert is a strip of land stretching from the Red Sea to the Atlantic Ocean. It covers over 1 million square miles and several countries, including Sudan, Senegal and Mauritania. The topography of the Sahel Desert is mostly flat, with some mountainous regions.

123. The Amaravati River is a tributary of Kaveri River in southern India. The Amaravati River begins in the Anjanda valley of Kerala State in India. The 282-kilometre long Amaravati River begins at the Kerala/ Tamil Nadu border at the bottom of Manjampatti Valley between the Annamalai Hills and the Palni Hills.

124. The Mediterranean forests, woodlands, and scrub biome mostly occurs in, but not limited to, the Mediterranean climate zones, in the mid-latitudes;

A Mediterranean forest, the Upper Galilee

- the Mediterranean Basin
- the Chilean Matorral
- the California chaparral and woodlands eco region of California and the Baja California Peninsula
- the Western Cape of South Africa
- The sclerophyll forests in Australia, which are predominantly found in the southwest, southern and southeast Australia.

125. As per census data 2011, the total population of India is: 1,210,193,422.

Uttar Pradesh top the state wise population table with 19,95,81,477 (16.49%) people.

Maharashtra has second highest population with 11,23,72,972 (9.29%) people.

Bihar the third highest populated state in India with 10,38,04,637 (8.58%) population.

West Bengal stand at fourth with 9,13,47,736 (7.55%) population.

Andhra Pradesh is at number five with 8,46,65, 533 (7%) population.

126. The longest river within today's European Union – and second-longest on the continent – the **Danube River** originates in Germany's Black Forest, and flows in a southeasterly direction through central and eastern Europe to the Black Sea. The Danube flows through ten modern-day European nations: Romania, Hungary, Serbia, Austria, Germany, Bulgaria, Slovakia, Croatia, Ukraine and Moldova.

The **Rhine river** is one of the longest rivers in Europe. Flowing through six countries, the Rhine River has served as a link between southern and northern Europe. Originating from mountain brooks in the Swiss Alps, the Rhine travels north into Switzerland's Lake Constance (Europe's third largest), over the surging Rhine Falls. The Rhine then serves as a border between Germany and France, narrows through deep gorges and meanders through steep-sided valleys known for vineyards and castles. At the Netherlands border the Rhine splits up into tributaries that cross an extensive delta and empty into the North Sea.

The **Rhone** is one of the major rivers of Europe, rising in Switzerland, passing through Lake Geneva and running through south-eastern France. At Arles, near its mouth on the Mediterranean Sea.

The **Loire** is the longest river in France. It rises in the highlands of the southeastern quarter of the Massif Central in the Cévennes range. It flows through the Pays de la Loire to Nantes, emptying into the Bay of Biscay.

127. Chemical Change, a chemical reaction takes place and new substances are formed. Such reaction either takes energy or releases energy. Cooking of egg would denature the protein molecules; which uncoil and create cross links to become solid white.

Evaporation is the process of a substance in a liquid state changing to a gaseous state due to an increase in temperature and/or pressure. Evaporation is a fundamental part of the water cycle and is constantly occurring throughout nature.

Condensation is the process of a substance in a gaseous state transforming into a liquid state. This change is caused by a change in pressure and temperature of the substance.

Sublimation is the transition of a substance directly from the solid to the gas phase without passing through the intermediate liquid phase. Heating camphor is a example of sublimation.

129. The **atomic number** of a chemical element is the number of protons found in the nucleus of an atom of that element, and therefore identical to the charge number of the nucleus.

134. Lenin introduced the NEP in order to revive the economy. The new program signified a return to a limited capitalist system. Forced requisition of grain was replaced by a specific tax in kind; peasants could retain excess produce and sell it for a profit. Smaller businesses were permitted to operate as private enterprises. Large industries remained under state control. They operated on the open market, but the state controlled the fixing of prices and the appointment of boards of directors. Private trade and wages were restored, and compulsory labour service was abolished.

135. American War of Independence and the **Revolutionary War** in the United States, was the armed conflict between Great Britain and thirteen of its North American colonies, which had declared themselves the independent United States of America.

Five Main Reasons The British Lost The Revolutionary War

1. The Failure to Capture or Disband Washington's Army
2. Parliament Opinion On The War Was Split
3. The Franco-American Alliance
4. Lack of Loyalist Support
5. Inability to Efficiently Supply the British Army

136. The Industrial Revolution was the transition to new manufacturing processes in the period from about 1760 to sometime between 1820 and 1840. The Industrial Revolution began in Great Britain and most of the important technological innovations were British.

The Industrial Revolution brought about a greater volume and variety of factory-produced goods and raised the standard of living for many people, particularly for the middle and upper classes. Children were part of the labour force and often worked long hours and were used for such highly hazardous tasks as cleaning the machinery. In the early 1860s, an estimated one-fifth of the workers in Britain's textile industry were younger than 15.

Charles Dickens is known for writing about life during the Industrial Revolution. *Hard Times,* published in 1854, falls into this category. It focuses on the fictional town of Coketown, England and the people who live there and their struggles. Charles Dickens was a severe critique of the horrors of industrialization.

138. ***Nil Darpan*** is a Bengali play written by Dinabandhu Mitra in 1858-1859. The play was published from Dhaka in 1860, under a pseudonym of the author. The play was essential to Nilbidraha, better known as the Indigo revolt of February-March 1859 in Bengal, when farmers refused to sow indigo in their fields to protest against exploitative farming under the British Raj. It was also essential to the development of theater in Bengal and influenced Girish Chandra Ghosh, who, in 1872, would establish The National Theatre in Calcutta where the first ever play commercially staged was *Nildarpan.*

139. Satyashodhak Samaj is a society established by Jyotirao Phule in Maharastra, India, on 24 September 1873. Its purpose is to liberate the Shudra and Untouchable castes from exploitation and oppression. Through his writings and activities Mahatma Phule always condemned caste hierarchy and the privileged status of priests in it. He condemned the inequality in the religious books, orthodox nature of religion, exploitation of masses by the means of it, blind and misleading rituals, and hypocrisy in the prevalent religion. Phule established Satyashodhak Samaj with the ideals of human well-being, happiness, unity, equality, and easy religious principles and rituals.

143. The Reserve Bank of India (RBI) reduced the minimum maturity period of offshore rupee-denominated bonds or masala bonds to three years from five years earlier.

144. Krishi Kalyan Cess is a Cess which shall be levied and collected in accordance with the provision of Chapter VI of the Finance Act, 2015 called Krishi Kalyan Cess, as Service Tax on all Taxable Services at the rate of 0.50% of the value of Taxable Services. Krishi Kalyan Cess would be calculated in the same way as Service tax is calculated. Therefore, KKC would be levied on the same taxable value as service tax. KKC is not to be calculated on Service Tax but on the taxable value of the service provided.

148. "Carbon" is shorthand for greenhouse gas emissions, including CO_2, methane, nitrous oxide and F-gases. These gases are released by many different types of activity – not just the burning of fossil fuels, but also farming, deforestation and some industrial processes. Global emissions can be allocated to human activities in various ways. One of the most granular analyses is this one from the World Resources Institute (WRI), which breaks down total global emissions from 2005 into the following headline sectors:

Energy

- Electricity & heat (24.9%)
- Industry (14.7%)
- Transportation (14.3%)
- Other fuel combustion (8.6%)
- Fugitive emissions (4%)

Agriculture (13.8%)
Land use change (12.2%)
Industrial processes (4.3%)
Waste (3.2%)

PAPER-II : MATHEMATICS

1. $\because$ α, β are the roots of the equation

$$x^2 - (1 - 2a^2)x + (1 - 2a^2) = 0$$

$\because$ Roots are real

$$\therefore \quad D \geq 0$$

$$\Rightarrow \quad b^2 - 4ac \geq 0$$

$$\left[-(1-2a^2)\right]^2 - 4(1)(1-2a^2) \geq 0$$

$$\Rightarrow \quad 1 - 4a^2 + 4a^4\ 4 + 8a^2 \geq 0$$

$$\Rightarrow \quad 4a^4 + 4a^2 - 3 \geq 0$$

Put $a^2 = x$

$$4x^2 + 4x - 3 \geq 0$$

$$\Rightarrow \quad 4x^2 + 6x - 2x - 3 \geq 0$$

$$\Rightarrow \quad 2x(2x + 3) - 1(2x + 3) \geq 0$$

$$\Rightarrow \quad (2x - 1)(2x + 3) \geq 0$$

$$x \geq \frac{1}{2}$$

$$\Rightarrow \quad a^2 \geq \frac{1}{2}.$$

2. $\because$ α, β are the roots of the equation $x^2 - (1 - 2a^2)x + (1 - 2a^2) = 0$

$$\therefore \quad \alpha + \beta = -\frac{b}{a} = 1 - 2a^2$$

$$\alpha \times \beta = \frac{c}{a} = 1 - 2a^2$$

$$\because \quad \frac{1}{\alpha^2} + \frac{1}{\beta^2} = \frac{\beta^2 + \alpha^2}{\alpha^2\beta^2} = \frac{(\alpha+\beta)^2 - 2\alpha\beta}{(\alpha\beta)^2}$$

$$= \frac{(1-2a^2)^2 - 2(1-2a^2)}{(1-2a^2)^2}$$

$$\Rightarrow \quad \frac{1 + 4a^4 - 4a^2 - 2 + 4a^2}{1 + 4a^4 - 4a^2} < 1$$

$$\Rightarrow \quad 4a^4 - 1 < 1 + 4a^4 - 4a^2$$

$$\Rightarrow \quad 4a^2 > 1 + 1$$

$$\Rightarrow \quad a^2 > \frac{2}{4}$$

$$\Rightarrow \quad a^2 > \frac{1}{2}.$$

3. Let $\omega = \sqrt{\dfrac{1+\omega^2}{1+\omega}}$

Squaring both sides,

$$\omega^2 = \frac{1+\omega^2}{1+\omega}$$

$$\Rightarrow \quad \omega^2(1 + \omega) = 1 + \omega^2$$

$$\Rightarrow \quad \omega^2 + \omega^3 = 1 + \omega^2$$

$$\Rightarrow \quad \omega^2 + 1 = \omega^2 + 1 \quad [\because \omega^3 = 1]$$

Hence, $\sqrt{\dfrac{1+\omega^2}{1+\omega}} = \omega.$

7. All the digits that will be formed are 4 digit numbers. There are all together five odd numbers which can occupy the last digit to form an odd number. As soon as we place an odd number in the last place we are left with 9 numbers. But 0 can not occupy the first place as it reduce into 3 digit number. So, first place is occupied by 8 numbers. Second place with 8 numbers as 0 can be included. Third place with remaining 7 numbers as repetition is not allowed.

Thus, required number of odd numbers
$= 8 \times 8 \times 7 \times 5 = 2240.$

11. sin A + 2 sin 2A + sin 3A

$$= \left(2\sin\frac{3A+A}{2}.\cos\frac{3A-A}{2}\right) + 2\sin 2A$$

$$= 2\sin 2A \,.\, \cos A + 2\sin 2A$$

$$= 2\sin 2A\,(\cos A + 1)$$

$$= 2\sin 2A \times 2\cos^2\frac{A}{2}$$

$$= 4\sin 2A \,.\, \cos^2\frac{A}{2}$$

$$= 4[2\sin A.\cos A].\cos^2\frac{A}{2}$$

$$= 8\sin A \,.\, \cos A \,.\, \cos^2\left(\frac{A}{2}\right).$$

12. $\because \quad x = \sin 70° \,.\, \sin 50°$

$$= \cos 20° \,.\, \cos 40°$$

$$y = \cos 60° \,.\, \cos 80°$$

$$= \frac{1}{2} \times \cos 80°$$

$$xy = \frac{\cos 20°.\cos 40°.\cos 80°}{2}$$

$$= \frac{2\sin 20°.\cos 20°.\cos 40°.\cos 80°}{2 \times 2\sin 20°}$$

$$= \frac{2 \times \sin 40°.\cos 40°.\cos 80°}{2 \times 4\sin 20°}$$

$$= \frac{2 \times \sin 80°.\cos 80°}{2 \times 8\sin 20°}$$

$$= \frac{\sin 160°}{16\sin 20°} = \frac{\sin 20°}{16 \times \sin 20°} = \frac{1}{16}.$$

14. $\because$

$$\cos\frac{3\pi}{8} = \cos\left(\frac{\pi}{2} - \frac{\pi}{8}\right) = \sin\frac{\pi}{8}$$

$$\cos\frac{5\pi}{8} = \cos\left(\frac{\pi}{2} + \frac{\pi}{8}\right) = -\sin\frac{\pi}{8}$$

$$\cos\frac{7\pi}{8} = \cos\left(\pi - \frac{\pi}{8}\right) = -\cos\frac{\pi}{8}$$

$\therefore \left(1+\cos\frac{\pi}{8}\right)\left(1+\sin\frac{\pi}{8}\right)\left(1-\sin\frac{\pi}{8}\right)\left(1-\cos\frac{\pi}{8}\right)$

$$= \left(1-\cos^2\frac{\pi}{8}\right)\left(1-\sin^2\frac{\pi}{8}\right)$$

$$= \sin^2\frac{\pi}{8}.\cos^2\frac{\pi}{8}$$

$$= \frac{1}{4}\left[2\sin\frac{\pi}{8}.\cos\frac{\pi}{8}\right]^2$$

$$= \frac{1}{4}\left[\sin\frac{\pi}{4}\right]^2 = \frac{1}{4}\left[\frac{1}{\sqrt{2}}\right]^2 = \frac{1}{8}.$$

15. $\because x \cos\theta + y \sin\theta = z$

squaring both sides

$x^2 \cos^2\theta + y^2 \sin^2\theta + 2xy \sin\theta . \cos\theta = z^2$ ...(*i*)

Now $(x \sin\theta - y \cos\theta)^2 = m^2$ (suppose)

$x^2 \sin^2\theta + y^2 \cos^2\theta - 2xy \sin\theta . \cos\theta = m^2$ ...(*ii*)

Adding (*i*) and (*ii*)

$x^2 (\cos^2\theta + \sin^2\theta) + y^2 (\sin^2\theta + \cos^2\theta)$

$= z^2 + m^2$

$x^2 + y^2 = z^2 + m^2$

$\because \quad m^2 = x^2 + y^2 - z^2$

Hence, $(x \sin\theta - y \cos\theta)^2 = x^2 + y^2 - z^2$.

18. A. $x^2 + 6x - 7 = 0$

$\Rightarrow x^2 + 7x - x - 7 = 0$

$\Rightarrow x(x + 7) - 1(x + 7) = 0$

$\Rightarrow (x - 1)(x + 7) = 0$

$\Rightarrow x = 1, x = -7$

B. $x^2 + 9x + 14 = 0$

$x^2 + 7x + 2x + 14 = 0$

$x(x + 7) + 2(x + 7) = 0$

$(x + 7)(x + 2) = 0$

$x = -7, x = -2$

(*i*) $A \cap B = \{x \in \mathbb{R} : -2 < x < 1\}$

(*ii*) $A \setminus B = \{x \in \mathbb{R} : -7 < x < -2\}$

Hence, both (*i*) and (*ii*) are correct.

20. $\omega^{100} + \omega^{200} + \omega^{300}$

$= (\omega^3)^{33} \times \omega + (\omega^3)^{66} \times \omega^2 + (\omega^3)^{100}$

$= (1)^{33} \times \omega + (1)^{66} \times \omega^2 + (1)^{100}$

$= \omega + \omega^2 + 1$

$= 0 \quad [\because 1 + \omega + \omega^2 = 0]$

21. $\because \quad z = x + iy$

$$\frac{z-1}{z+1} = \frac{(x^2+y^2-1)+2iy}{(x+1)^2+y^2}$$

$$\because \quad \text{Re}\left(\frac{z-1}{z+1}\right) = 0$$

$$\Rightarrow \frac{x^2+y^2-1}{(x+1)^2+y^2} = 0$$

$\Rightarrow x^2 + y^2 = 1$

$\Rightarrow |z|^2 = 1$

$\Rightarrow |z| = 1.$

23. $\because$ 15 points are in a plane, n points are in the same straight line. 445 triangles can be formed by joining three points.

$\because \quad 445 = {}^{15}C_3 - {}^{n}C_3$

$\Rightarrow \quad {}^{n}C_3 = {}^{15}C_3 - 445$

$$= \frac{15!}{3! \times 12!} - 445$$

$$= \frac{15\times14\times13\times12!}{3\times2\times1\times12!} - 445$$

$\Rightarrow {}^{n}C_3 = 455 - 445 = 10$

$\Rightarrow {}^{n}C_3 = {}^{5}C_3$

$\Rightarrow n = 5$

Hence, the value of $n = 5$.

29. If a number is divisible by 3, the sum of the digits in it must be multiple of 3. The sum of given five numerals is $0 + 1 + 2 + 3 + 4 = 10$.

So, to make a five digit number divisible by 3, if 0 is left, no number can be formed, sum $0 + 1 + 2 + 3 + 4 = 10$ which is not divisible by 3.

Hence, no number can be formed.

30. $${}^{47}C_4 + {}^{51}C_3 + \sum_{i=2}^{5} {}^{52-i}C_3$$

The given expression on putting

$r = 2, 3, 4, 5$ is

${}^{47}C_4 + {}^{51}C_3 + {}^{50}C_3 + {}^{49}C_3 + {}^{48}C_3 + {}^{47}C_3 = $ A (say)

Combining first and last

${}^{47}C_3 + {}^{47}C_4 = {}^{48}C_4$

$\therefore \quad A = {}^{48}C_4 + {}^{51}C_3 + {}^{50}C_3 + {}^{49}C_3 + {}^{48}C_3$

Again combining first and last

$A = {}^{49}C_4 + {}^{51}C_3 + {}^{50}C_3 + {}^{49}C_3$

$= {}^{50}C_4 + {}^{51}C_3 + {}^{50}C_3$

$= {}^{51}C_4 + {}^{51}C_3 = {}^{52}C_4.$

31. Since, $2\cos^{-1} x = \cos^{-1}(2x^2 - 1)$

$\therefore \quad 2\cos^{-1} 0.8 = \cos^{-1}(2 \times 0.64 - 1)$

$= \cos^{-1}(0.28)$

$\Rightarrow \cos(2\cos^{-1} 0.8) = \cos(\cos^{-1} 0.28)$

$= 0.28.$

32.

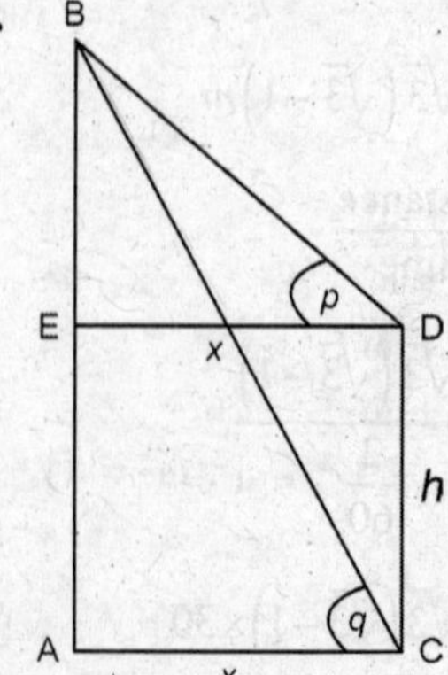

$$\cot p = \frac{x}{BE}$$

$$x = BE \cot p \quad ...(i)$$

$$\cot q = \frac{x}{AB}$$

$$\Rightarrow \quad x = AB \cot q \quad ...(ii)$$

From (*i*) and (*ii*)

$$\Rightarrow \quad AB \cot q = BE \cot p$$

$$\Rightarrow \quad AB \cot q = (AB - AE) \cot p$$

$$\Rightarrow \quad AB \cot q = AB \cot p - h \cot p$$

$$h \cot p = AB \cot p - AB \cot q$$

$$= AB (\cot p - \cot q)$$

$$\therefore \quad AB = \frac{h \cot p}{\cot p - \cot q}$$

Hence, height of the hill

$$= \frac{h \cot p}{\cot p - \cot q}.$$

34.

$$\tan 60° = \frac{150}{x}$$

$$\Rightarrow \quad \sqrt{3} = \frac{150}{x}$$

$$\Rightarrow \quad x = \frac{150}{\sqrt{3}} \times \frac{\sqrt{3}}{\sqrt{3}} = 50\sqrt{3}$$

$$\tan 45° = \frac{150}{x+y}$$

$$\Rightarrow \quad 1 = \frac{150}{x+y}$$

$$\Rightarrow \quad x + y = 150$$

$$\Rightarrow \quad y = \left(150 - 50\sqrt{3}\right)m$$

$$= 50\sqrt{3}\left(\sqrt{3}-1\right)m$$

$$\text{Speed of the boat} = \frac{\text{Distance}}{\text{time}}$$

$$= \frac{50\sqrt{3}\left(\sqrt{3}-1\right)}{\frac{2}{60}}$$

$$= 50\sqrt{3}\left(\sqrt{3}-1\right) \times 30$$

$$= 1500\sqrt{3}\left(\sqrt{3}-1\right) \text{m/hr}$$

$$= \frac{1500\sqrt{3}\left(\sqrt{3}-1\right) \times \sqrt{3}}{\sqrt{3}}$$

$$= \frac{4500\left(\sqrt{3}-1\right)}{\sqrt{3}} \text{m/hr.}$$

35. $\dfrac{1 - \tan 2°.\cot 62°}{\tan 152° - \cot 88°}$

$$= \frac{1 - \tan 2°.\tan 28°}{-\tan 28° - \tan 2°}$$

$$= \frac{1 - \tan 2°.\tan 28°}{-(\tan 28° + \tan 2°)} = \frac{1}{-\tan 30°}$$

$$= \frac{1}{-\frac{1}{\sqrt{3}}} = -\sqrt{3}.$$

36.

Let OAP be an equilateral triangle, *i.e.*,

$$OA = OP = AP$$

or

$$OA^2 = OP^2 = AP^2$$

$$(0-3)^2 + \left(0-\sqrt{3}\right)^2 = (0 - x)^2 + (0 - y)^2$$

$$= (3-x)^2 + \left(\sqrt{3}-y\right)^2$$

or

$$12 = x^2 + y^2$$

$$= x^2 + y^2 - 6x - 2\sqrt{3}y + 12 \quad ...(i)$$

$$x^2 + y^2 = 12 \quad ...(ii)$$

From (*i*) we have,

$$x^2 + y^2 - 6x - 2\sqrt{3}y + 12 = x^2 + y^2$$

$$\Rightarrow \quad 6x + 2\sqrt{3}y = 12$$

$$\Rightarrow \quad 3x + y\sqrt{3} = 6$$

$$\Rightarrow \quad y\sqrt{3} = 6 - 3x$$

$$\Rightarrow \quad y = \sqrt{3}(2-x) \quad ...(iii)$$

From (*ii*) and (*iii*), we get,

$$x^2 + 3(2 - x)^2 = 12$$

$$\Rightarrow \quad 4x^2 - 12x = 0$$

$$\Rightarrow \quad 4x(x - 3) = 0$$

$$\Rightarrow \quad x = 0, 3$$

From (*iii*) we get $y = 2\sqrt{3}$ when $x = 0$ and $y = -\sqrt{3}$ when $x = 3$

The point P is $\left(0, 2\sqrt{3}\right)$ or $\left(3, -\sqrt{3}\right)$.

37. (1, 1) A ———— P (x, y) ———— B (2, 3)

$\because$ $AP = PB$

$AP^2 = PB^2$

$\Rightarrow (x-1)^2 + (y-1)^2 = (2-x)^2 + (3-y)^2$

$\Rightarrow x^2 + 1 - 2x + y^2 + 1 - 2y$

$= 4 + x^2 - 4x + 9 + y^2 - 6y$

$\Rightarrow \quad 2x + 4y - 11 = 0$

Hence, the required equation is

$2x + 4y - 11 = 0.$

38. $x - y = 4$ ...(i)] × 2

$2x + 3y = -7$ ...(ii)

$2x - 2y = 8$

$2x + 3y = -7$

$- \quad - \quad +$

$-5y = 15$

$\therefore \quad y = -3$

Putting the value of y in (i)

then we get $x = 1$

The point of intersection of two diameters is centre which is the point C (1, –3), P (2, 4)

$\therefore$ Radius of the circle

$= \sqrt{(1-2)^2 + (-3-4)^2}$

$= \sqrt{1+49} = \sqrt{50} = 5\sqrt{2}$ units.

39. Let the equation of the hyperbola is

$$\frac{x^2}{a^2} - \frac{y^2}{b^2} = 1 \quad ...(i)$$

Then, length of the latus rectum = 8

$\Rightarrow \quad \frac{2b^2}{a} = 8$

$\Rightarrow \quad b^2 = 4a$

$\Rightarrow \quad a^2(e^2 - 1) = 4a$

$\Rightarrow \quad a(e^2 - 1) = 4$

$\Rightarrow \quad a\left(\frac{9}{5} - 1\right) = 4 \qquad \left[\because e = \frac{3}{\sqrt{5}}\right]$

$\Rightarrow \quad a\left(\frac{4}{5}\right) = 4$

$\Rightarrow \quad a = 5$

Putting the value of $a = 5$ in

$b^2 = 4a$

$\Rightarrow \quad b^2 = 4 \times 5 = 20$

Hence, the equation of the required hyperbola is

$\frac{x^2}{25} - \frac{y^2}{20} = 1.$

41. $x + 2y - 5 = 0$

$3x + 7y - 17 = 0$

Any line through the intersection of given lines is

$P + \lambda Q = 0$

$\Rightarrow \quad x + 2y - 5 + \lambda(3x + 7y - 17) = 0$

$\Rightarrow \quad x + 2y - 5 + 3\lambda x + 7\lambda y - 17\lambda = 0$

$\Rightarrow \quad x(1 + 3\lambda) + y(2 + 7\lambda) - 5 - 17\lambda = 0 \quad ...(i)$

Its slope $= -\left(\frac{1+3\lambda}{2+7\lambda}\right)$

Since, its perpendicular to the

$3x + 4y - 10 = 0$

whose slope $= -\frac{3}{4}$

Hence, using the condition

$m_1 m_2 = -1$

for the perpendicular lines

we get,

$\frac{3}{4} \times \frac{(1+3\lambda)}{2+7\lambda} = -1$

$\Rightarrow \quad 3 + 9\lambda = -8 - 28\lambda$

$\Rightarrow \quad 37\lambda = -11$

$\therefore \quad \lambda = \frac{-11}{37}$

Putting the value of λ in (i)

$x\left\{1 + 3\left(\frac{-11}{37}\right)\right\} + y\left\{2 + 7\left(\frac{-11}{37}\right)\right\} - 5 - 17\left(\frac{-11}{37}\right) = 0$

$\Rightarrow \quad x\left(1 - \frac{33}{37}\right) + y\left(2 - \frac{77}{37}\right) - 5 + \frac{187}{37} = 0$

$\Rightarrow \quad \frac{4x}{37} - \frac{3y}{37} + \frac{2}{37} = 0$

$\Rightarrow \quad 4x - 3y + 2 = 0$

Hence, the required line is $4x - 3y + 2 = 0$.

For Qs. No. 46 and 47.

$\because$ a, x, y, z, b are in A.P.

$\therefore \quad x = a + d \quad ...(i)$

$y = a + 2d \quad ...(ii)$

$z = a + 3d \quad ...(iii)$

Now, $\quad x + y + z = 3a + 6d$

$15 = 3a + 6d \quad ...(iv)$

$\therefore$ Put $a = 1$, $d = 2$

Hence, 1, 3, 5, 7, 9 are in A.P.

46. Value of $ab = 1 \times 9 = 9$.

47. Value of $xyz = 3 \times 5 \times 7 = 105$.

For Qs. No. 49, 50.

$\because$ 6th term of an A.P. = 2

$\Rightarrow \quad a + 5d = 2$

$\Rightarrow \quad 5d = 2 - a$

$d = \frac{2-a}{5}$

Put $d = \frac{8}{5}$

$$\frac{8}{5} = \frac{2-a}{5}$$

$\Rightarrow$ $8 = 2 - a$

$\Rightarrow$ $a = 2 - 8 = -6$

$\therefore -6, \frac{-22}{5}, \frac{-14}{5}, \frac{-6}{5}, \frac{2}{5}, 2$ are in A.P.

Hence, first term = –6

Common difference $= \frac{8}{5}$

Product of first term, 4th term and 6th term

$$= -6\times\frac{-6}{5}\times 2 = \frac{72}{5}$$

49. Common difference of A.P. = $\frac{8}{5}$.

50. First term of A.P. = –6.

For Qs. No. 51 and 52.

$(x + 1)[(x + 1)(5x - 1) - x(3x + 4)]$
$- 2x [(2x + 3)(5x - 1) - x(2 - x)]$
$+ 3x[(2x + 3)(3x + 4) - (x + 1)(2 - x)]$
$= (x + 1)[(5x^2 - x + 5x - 1) - 3x^2 - 4x]$
$-2x[10x^2 - 2x + 15x - 3 - 2x + x^2]$
$+ 3x[6x^2 + 8x + 9x + 12 - (2x - x^2 + 2 - x)]$
$= (x + 1)(2x^2 + 4x - 4x - 1) - 2x(11x^2$
$+ 11x -3) + 3x [7x^2 + 16x + 10]$
$= (x + 1)(2x^2 - 1) - 2x (11x^2 + 11x - 3)$
$+ 3x (7x^2 + 16x + 10)$
$= 2x^3 - x + 2x^2 - 1 - 22x^3 - 22x^2 + 6x$
$+ 21x^3 + 48x^2 + 30x$
$= x^3 + 28x^2 + 35x - 1$
$\therefore ax^3 + bx^2 + cx + d$
$= x^3 + 28x^2 + 35x - 1$

Clearly, the value of

$a = 1, b = 28, c = 35, d = -1$

51. Value of $c = 35$.

52. Value of $a + b + c + d$

$= 1 + 28 + 35 - 1 = 63.$

For Qs. No. 53, 54

Since the number of sides of the polygon be n.

Sum of the interior angles of the polygon

$= (n - 2) \times 180°$

Given that first term of A.P.

i.e., $a = 120°$ and common difference $d = 5°$.

$\Rightarrow \frac{n}{2}\{2a+(n-1)d\} = (n - 2) \times 180°$

$\Rightarrow \frac{n}{2}\{2\times120°+(n-1)\times5\} = (n - 2) \times 180°$

$\Rightarrow n(48 + n - 1) = (n - 2) \times 72$

$\Rightarrow n^2 - 25n + 144 = 0$

$\Rightarrow n^2 - 16n - 9n + 144 = 0$

$\Rightarrow n(n - 16) -9 (n - 16) = 0$

$\Rightarrow (n - 16) (n - 9) = 0$

either $n = 16$ or $n = 9$

53. Value of $n = 16$ or 9.

54. For $n = 16$,
the largest angle = 120° + 15 × 5° = 195°
For $n = 9$,
the largest angle = 120° + 8 × 5 = 160°.

55. By closely inspecting

$m = \begin{bmatrix}1 & 0\\0 & 1\end{bmatrix}$ and $n = \begin{bmatrix}0 & 1\\-1 & 0\end{bmatrix}$.

with respect to cos θ and sin θ, we conclude that
$m \cos\theta - n \sin\theta$

$$= \begin{bmatrix}1 & 0\\0 & 1\end{bmatrix}\cos\theta - \begin{bmatrix}0 & 1\\-1 & 0\end{bmatrix}\sin\theta$$

$$|m \cos\theta - n \sin\theta| = \begin{bmatrix}\cos\theta & \sin\theta\\-\sin\theta & \cos\theta\end{bmatrix}$$

$$= \cos^2\theta + \sin^2\theta = 1.$$

60. Remainder

$235 \div 2 = 117 + 1$
$117 \div 2 = 58 + 1$
$58 \div 2 = 29 + 0$
$29 \div 2 = 14 + 1$
$14 \div 2 = 7 + 0$
$7 \div 2 = 3 + 1$
$3 \div 2 = 1 + 1$
$1 \div 2 = 0 + 1$

$\therefore (235)_{10} = (11101011)_2$.

74. Let A, B, C be the events that the student is successful in tests I, II and III respectively. Then the probability that the student is successful is

$= m[(A\cap B\cap \bar{C})\cup(A\cap \bar{B}\cap C)\cup(A\cap B\cap C)]$

$= m(A\cap B\cap \bar{C}) + m(A\cap \bar{B}\cap C) + m(A\cap B\cap C)$

$= m(A)m(B)m(\bar{C}) + m(A)m(\bar{B})m(C) + m(A)m(B)m(C)$

[∵ A, B, C are independent]

$$= mn\left(1-\frac{1}{2}\right) + m(1-n)\left(\frac{1}{2}\right) + mn\left(\frac{1}{2}\right)$$

$$= \frac{mn + m - mn + mn}{2} = \frac{m(1+n)}{2}$$

But the probability that the student is successful = $\frac{1}{2}$

$\therefore \frac{m(1+n)}{2} = \frac{1}{2}$

$\Rightarrow m(1 + n) = 1.$

82. We have,

$$\vec{a}+\vec{b}+\vec{c} = 0$$

$\Rightarrow \quad (\vec{a}+\vec{b}+\vec{c}).(\vec{a}+\vec{b}+\vec{c}) = 0$

$\Rightarrow |\vec{a}|^2 + |\vec{b}|^2 + |\vec{c}|^2 + 2|\vec{a}.\vec{b}+\vec{b}.\vec{c}.+\vec{c}.\vec{a}.| = 0$

$\Rightarrow \quad 100+36+196+2|\vec{a}.\vec{b}+\vec{b}.\vec{c}.+\vec{c}.\vec{a}.| = 0$

$\Rightarrow \quad 2(\vec{a}.\vec{b}+\vec{b}.\vec{c}.+\vec{c}.\vec{a}.) = -332$

$\Rightarrow \quad \vec{a}.\vec{b}+\vec{b}.\vec{c}.+\vec{c}.\vec{a}. = \frac{-332}{2} = -166$

83. We have,

$\vec{a}+\vec{b}+\vec{c} = 0$

$\Rightarrow \quad \vec{c} = -(\vec{a}+\vec{b})$

$\Rightarrow \quad |\vec{c}|^2 = \vec{c}.\vec{c} = (\vec{a}+\vec{b}).(\vec{a}+\vec{b})$

$\Rightarrow \quad |\vec{c}|^2 = |\vec{a}|^2 + |\vec{b}|^2 + 2\vec{a}.\vec{b}$

$\Rightarrow \quad |\vec{c}|^2 = |\vec{a}|^2 + |\vec{b}|^2 + 2|\vec{a}|\,|\vec{b}|\cos\theta$

$\Rightarrow \quad 196 = 100 + 36 + 2 \times 10 \times 6 \cos\theta$

$\Rightarrow 196 - 136 = 120 \cos\theta$

$\Rightarrow \quad 60 = 120 \cos\theta$

$\therefore \quad \cos\theta = \frac{1}{2} = \cos 60°$

$\Rightarrow \quad \theta = 60°.$

84.

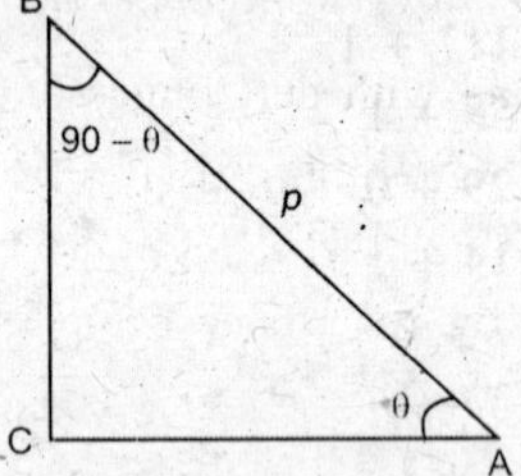

We have,

$\overrightarrow{AB}.\overrightarrow{AC}+\overrightarrow{BC}.\overrightarrow{BA}+\overrightarrow{CA}.\overrightarrow{CB}$

$= (AB)\,(AC)\cos\theta + (BC)(BA)\sin\theta + 0$

$= AB\,(AC\cos\theta + BC\sin\theta)$

$= AB\left[\frac{(AC)^2}{AB}+\frac{(BC)^2}{AB}\right]$

$= AC^2 + BC^2 = AB^2 = p^2.$

85. $F = 3\vec{i}+2\vec{j}-4\vec{k}$

$P = 1, -1, 2$

$O = (2, -1, 3)$

$r = OP = (\text{P.V. of P}) - (\text{PV of O})$

$= (i - j + 2k) - (2i - j + 3k)$

$= -i + 0j - k$

$\therefore \quad M = r \times F$

$= (-i - k) \times (3i + 2j - 4k)$

$\begin{vmatrix} i & j & k \\ -1 & 0 & -1 \\ 3 & 2 & -4 \end{vmatrix}$

$= 2\vec{i} - 7\vec{j} - 2\vec{k}.$

86. $|x| = \begin{cases} x, x \geq 0 \\ -x, x < 0 \end{cases}$

$\Rightarrow \quad |x| - x = \begin{cases} 0, x \geq 0 \\ -2x, x < 0 \end{cases}$

Hence, the domain of $f(x)\frac{1}{\sqrt{|x|-x}}$ is the set of all negative real numbers *i.e.*, $(-\infty, 0)$.

92. 5, 8, 8, 10, 10, 11, 12, 14, 16, 16, 16, 18, 18, 20, 20

$\text{Mean} = \frac{5+8+8+20+23+30+32+36+40}{15}$

$= \frac{202}{15} = 13.47$

$\text{Median} = \left(\frac{15+1}{2}\right)\text{th term}$

$= 8\text{th term} = 14$

Mode = 16

Now, 18 – 16 = 2

(Now, 18 at the place of 16)

$\text{Mean} = \frac{204}{15} = 13.6$

Mode = 18 Median = 14

Thus, we see that no change in median.

But change in mean and mode.

101.

C.I.	Frequency f_i	Midpoint x_i	$f_i x_i$
15-25	2	20	40
25-35	4	30	120
35-45	6	40	240
45-55	5	50	250
55-65	3	60	180
Total	20		830

$\text{Mean} = \frac{830}{20} = \frac{83}{2} = 41.5$

Hence, the mean age of this group of people = 41.5.

103. The sample space of the experiment is

S = {HHH, HHT, HTH, THH, HTT, THT, TTH, TTT}

and A = {TTT}, B = {HTT, THT, TTH}

C = {HHT, HTH, THH, HHH}

Now, A ∪ B ∪ C = {TTT, HTT, THT, TTH, HHT, HTH, THH, HHH} = S

Therefore, A, B and C are exhaustive events also, A ∩ B = φ, A ∩ C = φ and B ∩ C = φ

Therefore, the events are pairwise disjoint

Hence, A ∩ (B′ ∪ C′) = B′ ∩ C′ is correct option.

108. $\because \quad f(x) = \{|x| - |x-1|\}^2$

$f(x) = (x - x + 1)^2 = (1)^2$

$\therefore \quad f'(x) = 0$

109. Again, $f(x) = (-x - x + 1)^2$

$= (-2x + 1)^2$

$= 4x^2 - 4x + 1.$

$f'(x) = 8x - 4.$

Previous Papers (Solved)

NATIONAL DEFENCE ACADEMY & NAVAL ACADEMY

NDA & NA – Entrance Exam, 2016 (I)

PAPER I : GENERAL ABILITY TEST

PART A : ENGLISH LANGUAGE

Selecting Words

Directions (Qs. no. 1 to 9) : *In this section, each of the following sentences has a blank space and four words given after the sentence. Select whichever word you consider most appropriate for the blank space and indicate your response in the Answer Sheet accordingly.*

1. When the bus was at full speed, its brakes failed and an accident was ....

A. inevitable B. undeniable
C. fatal D. miserable

2. To explain his design to his visitors, the architect .... a simple plan on the blackboard.

A. built B. finalised
C. sketched D. arranged

3. Though Bonsai, a well-known art form, originated in China, it was .... by the Japanese.

A. cultivated B. finished
C. perfected D. enlarged

4. He is greatly admired for his .... behaviour.

A. decrepit B. decadent
C. decorative D. decorous

5. Would you mind .... to the Principal how the trouble started?

A. remarking B. saying
C. explaining D. talking

6. Vaccination will make people immune .... certain diseases for a given period.

A. against B. to
C. with D. for

7. The two boys looked so alike that it was impossible to .... between them.

A. discriminate B. discern
C. distinguish D. identify

8. The campers .... their tents at the base of the mountain.

A. installed B. dug
C. pitched D. established

9. The enemy had captured him and his life was at stake, still he refused to .... the state secrets.

A. divulge B. divert
C. indulge D. invert

Antonyms

Directions (Qs. no. 10 to 20) : *Each item in this section consists of an underlined word in given sentences. Each sentence is followed by four words. Select the word which is most nearly* ***opposite*** *in meaning to the underlined word.*

10. He handled the machine with deft fingers.

A. delicate B. sturdy
C. quick D. clumsy

11. I was deeply affected by his urbane behaviour.

A. rural B. rude
C. irrational D. indifferent

12. His timidity proved costly.

A. arrogance B. boldness
C. skilfulness D. cunning

13. Arrangements were made to handle the mammoth gathering tactfully.

A. significant B. small
C. unruly D. noisy

14. He was engrossed in his work when I walked in.

A. occupied B. inattentive
C. engaged D. absent

15. These are the main points of the preceding paragraph.

A. following B. previous
C. first D. last

16. He made a shrewd guess.

A. clever B. wild
C. incorrect D. discriminating

17. He is suffering from a severe cough.

A. violent B. mild
C. bad D. continuous

18. Cumulatively, the effect of these drugs is quite bad.
A. Individually B. Obviously
C. Clearly D. Collectively

19. He was conspicuous because of his colourful shirt.
A. charming B. ugly
C. small D. unnoticeable

20. He hates these continual arguments with his friend.
A. repeated B. irrational
C. occasional D. regular

Spotting Errors

Directions (Qs. no. 21 to 30): *Each question in this section has a sentence with three underlined parts labelled (A), (B) and (C). Read each sentence to find out whether there is any error in any underlined part and indicate your response in the Answer Sheet against the corresponding letter i.e., (A) or (B) or (C). If you find no error, your response should be indicated as (D).*

21. She said that (A)/ she was understanding (B)/ his point of view (C)/ very well. (D)/ No error.

22. All the houses (A)/ having been washed away (B)/ by the floods, (C)/ the villagers sought shelter in the panchayat office. (D)/ No error.

23. It is necessary for us (A)/ to familiarize with and (B)/ get used to the ways of the people (C)/ among whom we live. (D)/ No error.

24. (A)/ The mother asked the child (B)/ why did she cry out (C)/ in her sleep. (D)/ No error.

25. (A)/ I asked him that (B)/ why he was angry (C)/ but he did not answer. (D)/ No error.

26. (A)/ Had I not taken ill, I would (B)/ have sent you my research paper (C)/ much earlier. (D)/ No error.

27. The barn owl helps the farmer (A)/ by destroying rats which could, (B)/ if left unchecked do a lot of (C)/ damage to the crops. (D)/ No error.

28. He (A)/ had gone home three weeks ago and (B)/ was expected back yesterday, but he (C)/ has not come yet. (D)/ No error.

29. We (A)/ must sympathize (B)/ for others (C)/ in their troubles. (D)/ No error.

30. (A)/ The scientists in America (B)/ are trying for long (C)/ to discover the genes responsible for ageing. (D)/ No error.

Sentence Improvement

Directions (Qs. no. 31 to 40) : *In this section, look at the underlined part of each sentence. Below each sentence are given three possible substitutions for the underlined part. If one of them (A), (B) or (C), is better than the underlined part, indicate your response on the Answer Sheet against the corresponding letter (A), (B) or (C). If none of the substitutions improves the sentence, indicate (D) as your response on the Answer Sheet. Thus, a 'No improvement' response will be signified by the letter (D).*

31. When he heard the rhetorical speech of the leader, he was carried along by his enthusiasm.
A. carried aloft
B. carried down
C. carried away
D. No improvement

32. After the heavy rains last week, the water in the lake raised another two feet.
A. rose another two feet
B. arisen another two feet
C. would raise another two feet
D. No improvement

33. One can live and work in a town without being aware of the daily march of the sun across the sky without never seeing the moon and stars.
A. seldom B. hardly
C. ever D. No improvement

34. Applications of those who are graduates will be considered.
A. whom are graduates
B. whose are graduates
C. whom are only graduates
D. No improvement

35. It is raining heavily all through this week.
A. has rained B. rains
C. rained D. No improvement

36. The sparrow took no notice about the bread.
A. notice of B. notice from
C. notice to D. No improvement

37. As he spoke about his achievements, his high claims amused us.
A. big B. tall
C. long D. No improvement

38. We ought to stand for what is right.
A. stand at B. stand on
C. stand up D. No improvement

39. He enjoys to tell stories to children.
A. how to tell stories
B. telling stories
C. to narrate stories
D. No improvement

40. In a few minutes' time, when the clock strikes six, I would be waiting here for an hour.
A. shall be waiting on
B. shall have been waiting
C. shall wait
D. No improvement

Synonyms

Directions (Qs. no. 41 to 50) : *Each item in this section consists of an underlined word in given sentences. Each sentence is followed by four words. Select the word which is most* ***similar*** *in meaning to the underlined word and mark your response in the Answer Sheet accordingly.*

41. Suddenly there was a bright flash, followed by a deafening explosion.
A. dangerous B. terrifying
C. mild D. very loud

42. He showed exemplary courage during the crisis.
A. usual B. durable
C. commendable D. some

43. When the new teacher entered the classroom, he found the pupils restive.
A. at rest B. idle
C. quiet D. impatient

44. There is no dearth of talent in this country.
A. scarcity B. availability
C. plenty D. absence

45. The servants retired to their quarters.
A. entered B. went away
C. ran away D. mobilised

46. The navy gave tactical support to the marines.
A. sensitive B. strategic
C. immediate D. expert

47. A genius tends to deviate from the routine way of thinking.
A. dispute B. disagree
C. distinguish D. differ

48. He was greatly debilitated by an attack of influenza.
A. depressed B. weakened
C. worried D. defeated

49. His efforts at helping the poor are laudable.
A. welcome B. sincere
C. good D. praiseworthy

50. His conduct brought him reproach from all quarters.
A. rebuke B. sympathy
C. indifference D. remorse

PART B : GENERAL KNOWLEDGE

Directions : *The following* ***five (5)*** *items consist of two statements, Statement I and Statement II. Examine these two statements carefully and select the answers to these items using the code given below :*

Code:

A. Both the statements are individually true and Statement II is the correct explanation of Statement I.
B. Both the statements are individually true but Statement II is not the correct explanation of Statement I.
C. Statement I is true but Statement II is false.
D. Statement I is false but Statement II is true.

51. Statement I: Petroleum is a mixture of many different hydrocarbons of different densities.

Statement II: The grade of petroleum depends mainly on the relative proportion of the different hydrocarbons.

52. Statement I: There is high salinity in Red sea.

Statement II: Rate of evaporation is high in Red sea.

53. Statement I: Volcanic eruption is accompanied by earthquakes.

Statement II: Volcanoes erupt water vapours and dust particles in the atmosphere.

54. Statement I: Plantation farming has mostly been practised in humid tropics.

Statement II: The soil of humid tropics is highly fertile.

55. Statement I: India has wide variation in population density.

Statement II: Factors like agricultural productivity and history of settlements have greatly influenced the population density pattern in India.

56. A container is first filled with water and then entire water is replaced by mercury. Mercury has a density of 13.6×10^3 kg/m^3. If X is the weight of the water and Y is the weight of the mercury, then
A. X = Y B. X = 13.6 Y
C. Y = 13.6 X D. None of the above

57. Density of water is
A. maximum at 0°C B. minimum at 0°C
C. maximum at 4°C D. minimum at –4°C

58. The phosphorus used in the manufacture of safety matches is
A. Red phosphorus B. Black phosphorus
C. White phosphorus D. Scarlet phosphorus

59. Which one of the following is not a chemical change?
A. Ripening of fruits B. Curdling of milk
C. Freezing of water D. Digestion of food

60. One of the main causes of air pollution in cities is emissions from vehicles like cars and trucks. Cars emit various pollutants which are bad for human health when inhaled, like

1. Nitrogen oxides (NO_x)
2. Carbon monoxide (CO)
3. Carbon dioxide (CO_2)
4. Benzene

Which of the above pollutants are not tolerated by human beings even at very low levels?
A. 1 and 4 only
B. 1 and 2 only
C. 1, 2 and 3 only
D. 1, 2 and 4 only

61. Arrange the following centres of AIIMS from East to West:
1. Rishikesh 2. New Delhi
3. Patna 4. Bhubaneswar

Select the correct answer using the code given below:
A. 4-3-1-2 B. 4-1-3-2
C. 3-4-2-1 D. 3-2-1-4

62. Suppose the force of gravitation between two bodies of equal masses is F. If each mass is doubled keeping the distance of separation between them unchanged, the force would become
A. F B. 2 F
C. 4 F D. $\frac{1}{4}$F

63. A body has a free fall from a height of 20 m. After falling through a distance of 5 m, the body would
A. lose one-fourth of its total energy
B. lose one-fourth of its potential energy
C. gain one-fourth of its potential energy
D. gain three-fourth of its total energy

64. Soap is sodium or potassium salt of
A. Stearic acid B. Oleic acid
C. Palmitic acid D. All of the above

65. Mass of a particular amount of substance
1. is the amount of matter present in it.
2 does not vary from place to place.
3. changes with change in gravitational force.

Select the correct answer using the code given below:
A. 1, 2 and 3 B. 1 and 2 only
C. 2 and 3 only D. 1 only

66. Which of the following substances are harmful for health if present in food items?
1. Pesticide residues
2. Lead
3. Metanil yellow
4. Mercury

Select the correct answer using the code given below:
A. 1 and 2 only B. 1, 2 and 4 only
C. 3 and 4 only D. 1, 2, 3 and 4

67. In India, glacial terraces known as 'Karewas' are found in
A. Sapt Kosi Valley
B. Jhelum Valley
C. Alakananda Valley
D. Teesta Valley

68. Structurally, the Meghalaya region is a part of
A. Shiwalik Range B. Deccan Plateau
C. Greater Himalaya D. Aravalli Range

69. Two bodies A and B are moving with equal velocities. The mass of B is double that of A. In this context, which one of the following statements is correct?
A. Momentum of B will be double that of A
B. Momentum of A will be double that of B
C. Momentum of B will be four times that of A
D. Momenta of both A and B will be equal

70. During solar eclipse
A. the earth comes in between the sun and the moon
B. the moon comes in between the sun and the earth
C. the moon comes exactly halfway between the earth and the sun
D. the sun comes in between the earth and the moon

71. The S.I. unit of acceleration is
A. ms^{-1} B. ms^{-2}
C. cms^{-2} D. kms^{-2}

72. An atom of carbon has 6 protons. Its mass number is 12. How many neutrons are present in an atom of carbon?
A. 12 B. 6
C. 10 D. 14

73. Which one of the following is a reduction reaction?
A. $2\,Mg\,(s) + O_2\,(g) \rightarrow 2\,MgO\,(s)$
B. $S\,(s) + O_2\,(g) \rightarrow SO_2\,(g)$
C. $2\,HgO(s) \xrightarrow{heat} 2Hg(l) + O_2(g)$
D. $Mg\,(s) + S\,(s) \rightarrow MgS\,(s)$

74. Which of the commonly used household item(s) release Bisphenol A (BPA) which is an endocrine disruptor and bad for human health?
1. Steel utensils
2. Plastic coffee mugs
3. Aluminium utensils
4. Plastic water storage bottles

Select the correct answer using the code given below:
A. 1 only B. 1 and 2 only
C. 2 and 4 only D. 1, 2 and 3 only

75. The Nagarjuna Sagar Project is located on which one of the following rivers?
A. Godavari B. Krishna
C. Kavery D. Mahanadi

76. Consider the following statements:
1. Rajmahal highlands consists of lava flow deposits.
2 Bundelkhand gneiss belong to the oldest Achaean rocks of India.

Which of the statements given above is/are correct?
A. 1 only B. 2 only
C. Both 1 and 2 D. Neither 1 nor 2

77. An object is placed at the centre of curvature of a concave mirror of focal length 16 cm. If the object is shifted by 8 cm towards the focus, the nature of the image would be
A. real and magnified
B. virtual and magnified
C. real and reduced
D. virtual and reduced

78. A pencil is placed upright at a distance of 10 cm from a convex lens of focal length 15 cm. The nature of the image of the pencil will be
A. real, inverted and magnified
B. real, erect and magnified
C. virtual, erect and reduced
D. virtual, erect and magnified

79. Which one of the following is a conventional energy source?
A. Tidal energy B. Geothermal energy
C. Solar energy D. Biomass energy

80. Which one of the following oxides of nitrogen is known as 'anhydride' of nitric acid?
A. N_2O B. N_2O_3
C. NO_2 D. N_2O_5

81. Which one of the following is the chemical name for baking soda?
A. Sodium bicarbonate (Sodium hydrogen carbonate)
B. Sodium carbonate
C. Potassium bicarbonate (Potassium hydrogen carbonate)
D. Potassium carbonate

82. Which of the following statements about DNA is/are correct?
1. DNA is the hereditary material of all living organisms.
2. All segments of DNA code for synthesis of proteins.
3. Nuclear DNA is double helical with two nucleotide chains which run anti-parallel.
4. DNA is also found in mitochondria.
Select the correct answer using the code given below:
A. 1, 2 and 3 only B. 3 and 4 only
C. 1, 3 and 4 only D. 4 only

83. Which organisation prepares the topographical maps of India?
A. Geological Survey of India
B. Archaeological Survey of India
C. Survey of India
D. National Atlas and Thematic Mapping Organisation

84. Which one of the following is not an international boundary line?
A. Dresden Line B. Durand Line
C. Maginot Line D. 38th Parallel

85. A lady is standing in front of a plane mirror at a distance of 1 m from it. She walks 60 cm towards the mirror. The distance of her image now from herself (ignoring the thickness of the mirror) is
A. 40 cm B. 60 cm
C. 80 cm D. 120 cm

86. The brightness of a star depends on its
A. size and temperature only
B. size and distance from the earth
C. size, temperature and mass
D. size, temperature and distance from the earth

87. When a solid is heated, it turns directly into a gas. This process is called
A. Condensation B. Evaporation
C. Sublimation D. Diffusion

88. Which one of the following is water gas?
A. Mixture of carbon monoxide and hydrogen
B. Mixture of carbon monoxide and nitrogen
C. Mixture of carbon dioxide and water vapour
D. Mixture of carbon monoxide and water vapour

89. Which of the following statements are correct?
In honey bees
1. Males are haploid.
2. Workers are sterile and diploid.
3. Queen develops from diploid larvae that fed on royal jelly.
4. Honey is collected/made by males.
Select the correct answer using the code given below:
A. 1, 2, 3 and 4 B. 2 and 3 only
C. 1, 2 and 3 only D. 1 and 4 only

90. The Amarkantak Hills is the source of which of the following rivers?
1. Narmada 2. Mahanadi
3. Tapti 4. Son
Select the correct answer using the code given below:
A. 1 and 2 only B. 2 only
C. 1, 3 and 4 only D. 1, 2 and 4 only

91. Which of the following statements in the context of northern hemisphere is/are correct?
1. Vernal equinox occurs on March 21.
2. Summer solstice occurs on December 22.
3. Autumnal equinox occurs on September 23.
4. Winter solstice occurs on June 21.
Select the correct answer using the code given below:
A. 1 only B. 1 and 3 only
C. 2 and 4 only D. 1, 2 and 3 only

92. A glass vessel is filled with water to the rim and a lid is fixed to it tightly. Then it is left inside a freezer for hours. What is expected to happen?
A. The water freezes to ice and the level of ice comes down
B. The water in the glass vessel simply freezes to ice

C. The glass vessel breaks due to expansion as water freezes to ice
D. The water does not freeze at all

93. A simple circuit contains a 12 V battery and a bulb having 24 ohm resistance. When you turn on the switch, the ammeter connected in the circuit would read
A. 0.5 A B. 2 A
C. 4 A D. 5 A

94. Three resistors with magnitudes 2, 4 and 8 ohm are connected in parallel. The equivalent resistance of the system would be
A. less than 2 ohm
B. more than 2 ohm but less than 4 ohm
C. 4 ohm
D. 14 ohm

95. Suppose you have four test tubes labelled as 'A', 'B', 'C' and 'D'. 'A' contains plain water, 'B' contains solution of an alkali, 'C' contains solution of an acid, and 'D' contains solution of sodium chloride. Which one of these solutions will turn phenolphthalein solution pink?
A. Solution 'A' B. Solution 'B'
C. Solution 'C' D. Solution 'D'

96. Which one of the following oxides dissolves in water?
A. CuO B. Al_2O_3
C. Fe_2O_3 D. Na_2O

97. To prevent heart problems, blood of a normal healthy person should have
1. low cholestrol level
2. high HDL level
3. high VLDL level
4. high LDL level

Select the correct answer using the code given below:
A. 1 and 2 only B. 1, 2 and 4 only
C. 3 and 4 only D. 1, 2 and 3 only

98. Spruce and Cedar are tree varieties of
A. Equatorial forest
B. Temperate coniferous forest
C. Monsoon forest
D. Temperate deciduous forest

99. 'Sal' tree is a
A. Tropical evergreen tree
B. Tropical semi-evergreen tree
C. Dry deciduous tree
D. Moist deciduous tree

100. Matter around us can exist in three different states, namely, solid, liquid and gas. The correct order of their compressibility is
A. Liquid < Gas < Solid
B. Solid < Liquid < Gas
C. Gas < Liquid < Solid
D. Solid < Gas < Liquid

101. The temperature at which a solid melts to become a liquid at the atmospheric pressure is called its melting point. The melting point of a solid is an indication of
A. strength of the intermolecular forces of attraction
B. strength of the intermolecular forces of repulsion
C. molecular mass
D. molecular size

102. Consider the following circuit:

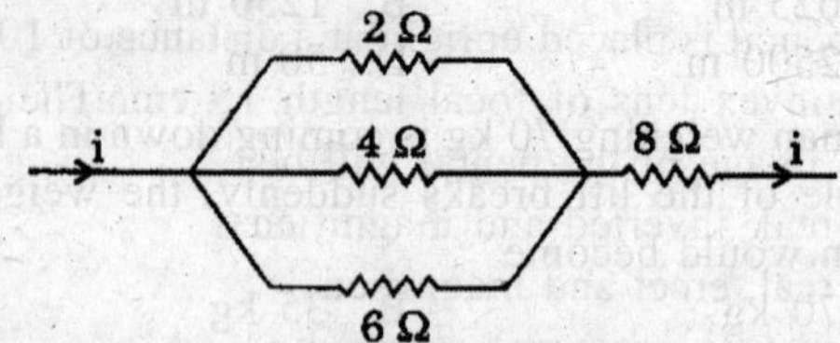

The equivalent resistance of the circuit will be
A. 12 Ω B. $8\frac{11}{12}$ Ω
C. $9\frac{1}{11}$ Ω D. $\frac{24}{25}$ Ω

103. Which one of the following elements will not react with dilute HCl to produce H_2?
A. Hg B. Al
C. Mg D. Fe

104. Which of the following pairs of vector and disease is/are correctly matched?

Vector		Disease
1. Anopheles	:	Malaria
2. *Aedes aegypti*	:	Chikungunya
3. Tsetse fly	:	Filariasis
4. Bed bugs	:	Sleeping sickness

Select the correct answer using the code given below:
A. 1, 2 and 3 only B. 1 and 2 only
C. 1 and 4 only D. 2 only

105. Consider the following statements:
1. All Echinoderms are not marine.
2. Sponges are exclusively marine.
3. Insects are found in all kinds of habitats.
4. Many primates are arboreal.

Which of the statements given above is/are correct?
A. 1, 3 and 4 only B. 3 and 4 only
C. 2 and 4 only D. 3 only

106. Areas which are engines for economic growth supported by quality infrastructure and complemented by an attractive fiscal package are known as
A. Export Processing Zones
B. Duty Free Tariff Zones
C. Special Economic Zones
D. Technology Parks

107. Deserts, fertile plains and moderately forested mountains are the characteristic features of which one of the following regions of India?

A. South-Western border along Arabian Sea
B. Coromandel Coast
C. North-Eastern Frontier
D. North-Western India

108. A racing car accelerates on a straight road from rest to a speed of 50 m/s in 25 s. Assuming uniform acceleration of the car throughout, the distance covered in this time will be

A. 625 m　　B. 1250 m
C. 2500 m　　D. 50 m

109. A man weighing 70 kg is coming down in a lift. If the cable of the lift breaks suddenly, the weight of the man would become

A. 70 kg　　B. 35 kg
C. 140 kg　　D. Zero

110. A given conductor carrying a current of 1 A produces an amount of heat equal to 2000 J. If the current through the conductor is doubled, the amount of heat produced will be

A. 2000 J　　B. 4000 J
C. 8000 J　　D. 1000 J

111. Which one of the following carbon compounds will not give a sooty flame?

A. Benzene　　B. Hexane
C. Naphthalene　　D. Anthracene

112. Match List I with List II and select the correct answer using the code given below the Lists:

List-I (Molecule)	List-II (Product of digestion)
(*a*) Proteins	1. Nitrogenous bases and pentose sugars
(*b*) Carbohydrates	2. Fatty acids and glycerol
(*c*) Nucleic acids	3. Monosaccharides
(*d*) Lipids	4. Amino acids

Codes:

	(*a*)	(*b*)	(*c*)	(*d*)
A.	2	3	1	4
B.	2	1	3	4
C.	4	1	3	2
D.	4	3	1	2

113. In Thar region, the shifting sand dunes are locally known as

A. Dhrian　　B. Daurs
C. Dhoros　　D. Dhaya

114. The impulse on a particle due to a force acting on it during a given time interval is equal to the change in its

A. force　　B. momentum
C. work done　　D. energy

115. Which one of the following statements with regard to expansion of materials due to heating is not correct?

A. As ice melts, it expands uniformly up to 4°C
B. Mercury thermometer works using the principle of expansion due to heating
C. Small gap is kept between two rails to allow for expansion due to heating
D. The length of metallic wire increases when its temperature is increased

116. Which of the following pairs is/are correctly matched?

National Park		Famous for
1. Ranthambhore	:	Tiger
2. Periyar	:	Elephant
3. Manas	:	Lion
4. Gir	:	Rhinoceros

Select the correct answer using the code given below:

A. 1, 2 and 3 only　　B. 1 and 2 only
C. 1 and 4 only　　D. 2 only

117. Which one of the following is not a form of stored energy?

A. Nuclear energy　　B. Potential energy
C. Electrical energy　　D. Chemical energy

118. The motion of a car along a straight path is shown by the following figure:

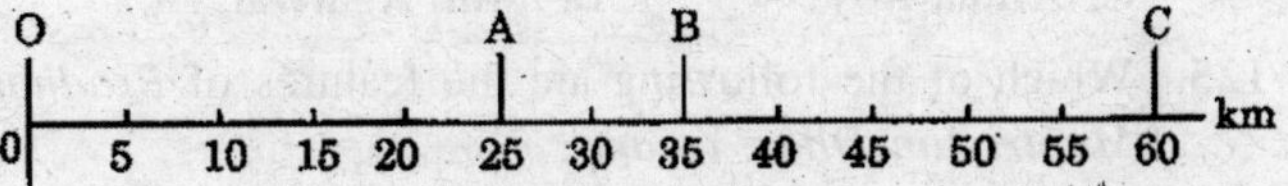

The car starts from 0 and reaches at A, B and C at different instants of time. During its motion from O to C and back to B, the distance covered and the magnitude of the displacement are, respectively

A. 25 km and 60 km
B. 95 km and 35 km
C. 60 km and 25 km
D. 85 km and 35 km

119. Jelep La pass is located in

A. Punjab Himalaya
B. Sikkim Himalaya
C. Kumaon Himalaya
D. Kashmir Himalaya

120. What is the number of mole(s) of H_2(g) required to saturate one mole benzene?

A. 1　　B. 2
C. 3　　D. 4

121. Which one of the following pairs of the Schedule in the Constitution of India and its Content is not correctly matched?

Schedule		Content
A. Eighth Schedule	:	Languages
B. Second Schedule	:	The forms of oaths and affirmations
C. Fourth Schedule	:	Allocation of seats in the Council of States
D. Tenth Schedule	:	Provisions as to disqualification on the ground of defection

122. Consider the following statements:
1. The Constitution of India empowers the Parliament to form new States and to alter the areas, boundaries or names of existing States by passing a resolution in simple majority.
2. Jammu and Kashmir has been given special status under Article 370 of the Constitution of India.

Which of the statements given above is/are correct?
A. 1 only B. 2 only
C. Both 1 and 2 D. Neither 1 nor 2

123. The Speaker of the Lok Sabha may resign his office by writing, addressed to the
A. President of India
B. Prime Minister of India
C. Vice President of India
D. Deputy Speaker of the Lok Sabha

124. Who among the following is the founder of the *'Bachpan Bachao Andolan'*?
A. Shantha Sinha B. Kailash Satyarthi
C. Aruna Roy D. Anil Agarwal

125. Which of the following are the features of *Pradhan Mantri Jan Dhan Yojana*?
1. Ensuring financial inclusion of the poor
2. Enhancing financial literacy
3. Provision for accidental insurance to account holders
4. Allowing bank accounts with zero balance

Select the correct answer using the code given below:
A. 1 and 4 only B. 1, 2 and 3 only
C. 2 and 4 only D. 1, 2, 3 and 4

126. The Election Commission recognizes a political party as a national party if
1. it secures at least six percent of the total valid votes polled in four or more States in a general election to the Lok Sabha or to the State Legislative Assemblies.
2. it wins at least four seats in a general election to the Lok Sabha from any State or States.

Select the correct answer using the code given below:
A. 1 only B. 2 only
C. Both 1 and 2 D. Neither 1 nor 2

127. Which one of the following is not a feature of the Nehru-Mahalanobis model of development strategy?
A. Development of capital goods industries
B. Major involvement of the State in the economy
C. Industrial deregulation and disinvestment in the public sector
D. Enhancing the scope and importance of the public sector

128. Which of the following best explains the stated broad vision and aspirations of the Twelfth Five Year Plan (2012-2017)?
A. Faster, Sustainable and More Inclusive Growth
B. Modernisation of Industries and Strengthening Infrastructure.
C. Enhancing Agricultural and Rural Incomes
D. Checking Inflation and Strengthening non-economic variables like Nutritional Requirements, Health and Family Planning

129. *Nabhah Sprsam Diptam* is the motto of
A. Central Industrial Security Force
B. Indian Air Force
C. ISRO
D. Indian Navy

130. Consider the following statements :
1. The Amendment procedure has been provided in Article 368 of the Constitution of India.
2. The consent of the States is mandatory for all Amendments to the Constitution of India.

Which of the statements given above is/are correct?
A. 1 only B. 2 only
C. Both 1 and 2 D. Neither 1 nor 2

131. Which of the following statements relating to the Comptroller and Auditor General (CAG) of India is/are correct?
1. The CAG can attend the sittings of the Committee on Public Accounts.
2. The CAG can attend the sittings of Lok Sabha and Rajya Sabha.
3. The jurisdiction of CAG is co-extensive with powers of the Union Government.

Select the correct answer using the code given below:
A. 1 only B. 2 and 3 only
C. 1 and 2 only D. 1, 2 and 3

132. Which of the following statements relating to election as the President of India is/are correct?
1. A person above the age of thirty-five years is eligible for election as the President of India.
2. The President of India is eligible for re-election for more than one term.
3. A person is not eligible for election as the President of India if the person holds an office of profit.

Select the correct answer using the code given below:
A. 1 and 2 only B. 2 only
C. 1, 2 and 3 D. 3 only

133. Which one of the following nations adopted its first democratic Constitution in September 2015?
A. Bhutan B. Myanmar
C. Nepal D. Singapore

134. Who among the following was defeated by Novak Djokovic in the final of the US Open Tennis Tournament Men's Singles event (2015)?
A. Tommy Robredo B. Fabio Fognini
C. Roger Federer D. Pablo Cuevas

135. The citizens of India do not have which one of the following Fundamental Rights?

A. Right to reside and settle in any part of India
B. Right to acquire, hold and dispose of property
C. Right to practice any profession
D. Right to form co-operative societies

136. Which one among the following Acts for the first time allowed Indians, at least theoretically, entry to higher posts in British Indian administration?

A. Charter Act, 1813
B. Charter Act, 1833
C. Charles Wood's Education Despatch, 1854
D. Indian Councils Act, 1861

137. Consider the following statements about Rashtrakuta kings:

1. They were ardent patrons of Shaivism and did not support other forms of religion.
2. They promoted only Sanskrit scholars and gave them large grants.

Which of the statements given above is/are correct?

A. 1 only B. 2 only
C. Both 1 and 2 D. Neither 1 nor 2

138. After a ban on unscientific coal mining and transportation of coal in this region by the National Green Tribunal, many of those engaged in the activity have been switching to turmeric farming for their livelihood. The region referred above is

A. Jaintia Hills, Meghalaya
B. Koriya, Chhattisgarh
C. Angul, Odisha
D. Bardhaman, West Bengal

139. Which of the following statements about the first Act of the Revolt of 1857 is/are true?

1. It occurred in Meerut when two sepoys stole a superior officer's rifle.
2. It began when the Rani of Jhansi declared war on the British.
3. It began when Mangal Pandey fired at a European officer in Meerut.
4. It began when Mangal Pandey fired at a European officer in Barrackpore.

Select the correct answer using the code given below:

A. 2 only B. 1, 2 and 3 only
C. 4 only D. 1 and 4 only

140. Which of the following statements about Gandhiji's *Hind Swaraj* written in 1909 is/are true?

1. *Hind Swaraj* offers a civilizational concept of the Indian nation.
2. *Hind Swaraj* states that Parliamentary democracy was necessary for the amelioration of the sufferings of Indians.
3. *Hind Swaraj* argues that Industrial capitalism was responsible for the immorality of society.

Select the correct answer .using the code given below:

A. 3 only B. 1, 2 and 3
C. 1 and 3 only D. 1 only

141. Division of labour often involves

1. specialized economic activity.
2. highly distinct productive roles.
3. involving everyone in many of the same activities.
4. individuals engage in only a single activity and are dependent on others to meet their various needs.

Select the correct answer using the code given below:

A. 1, 3 and 4 only B. 1, 2 and 4 only
C. 3 only D. 2 and 4 only

142. Who among the following is/was associated with 'Maharashtra Andhashraddha Nirmoolan Samiti'?

A. Chandi Prasad Bhatt
B. Narendra Dabholkar
C. G.D. Agrawal
D. Kailash Satyarthi

143. Consider the following statements:

1. Warren Hastings set up the Calcutta Madrassa for the study and teaching of Muslim law related subjects.
2. Jonathan Duncan started a Sanskrit College at Varanasi for the study of Hindu law and philosophy.

Which of the statements given above is/are correct?

A. 1 only B. 2 only
C. Both 1 and 2 D. Neither 1 nor 2

144. Consider the following statements about Sufism in India:

1. Pilgrimage called *ziyarat* to tombs of Sufi saints is an important feature.
2. The most influential group of Sufis in India were the Chishtis.

Which of the statements given above is/are correct?

A. 1 only B. 2 only
C. Both 1 and 2 D. Neither 1 nor 2

145. Which of the following thinkers and movements influenced the development of Gandhiji's political ideas?

1. Henry David Thoreau
2. John Ruskin
3. John Milton
4. Jainism

Select the correct answer using the code given below:

A. 1 only B. 1, 2 and 3 only
C. 1, 2 and 4 only D. 2 and 4 only

146. Consider the following statements:

1. The *Arthashastra* is the first Indian text to define a State.
2. The main concerns of the *Arthashastra* are theoretical issues like the origins of the state.

Which of the statements given above is/are correct?

A. 1 only B. 2 only
C. Both 1 and 2 D. Neither 1 nor 2

147. Which of the following is/are not FDI policy change(s) after 2010?
1. Permission of 100 per cent FDI in automotive sector.
2. Permitting foreign airlines to make FDI up to 49 per cent.
3. Permission of up to 51 per cent FDI under the government approval route in multi-brand retailing, subject to specified conditions.
4. Amendment of policy on FDI in single-brand product retail trading for aligning with global practices.

Select the correct answer using the code given below:
A. 1 only B. 2 and 4 only
C. 1 and 2 only D. 1, 2 and 3 only

148. Which of the following is/are the component/components of the Integrated Power Development Scheme launched by the Government of India recently?
1. Strengthening of sub-transmission and distribution networks in the urban areas.
2. Metering of distribution transformers/feeders/consumers in the rural areas.

Select the correct answer using the code given below:
A. 1 only B. 2 only
C. Both 1 and 2 D. **Neither** 1 nor 2

149. Which of the following statements about Brahmo Samaj is/are correct?
1. The Brahmo Marriage Act of 1872 allowed inter-caste and widow re-marriage only if the contracting parties declared themselves to be non-Hindus.
2. Keshub Chandra Sen arranged the marriage of his minor daughter with the Maharaja of Burdwan.
3. Keshub Chandra Sen's followers broke away to form the Naba Brahmo Samaj.
4. The Brahmo Samaj grew from a small elite group to a mass movement in the 19th century.

Select the correct answer using the code given below:
A. 1 only B. 1 and 2 only
C. 2 and 3 only D. 1, 2, 3 and 4

150. Which of the following statements about the aims of the United Nations is/are true?
1. To foster a mutual appreciation of each others' culture and literature among nations
2. To achieve international co-operation in solving problems of an economic, social, cultural, or humanitarian character
3. To foster relations between scholars and academics in different countries
4. To organize international conferences

Select the correct answer using the code given below:
A. 1 only B. 1, 2 and 4 only
C. 2 only D. 1, 2 and 3 only

PAPER II : MATHEMATICS

1. Suppose ω is a cube root of unity with $\omega \neq 1$. Suppose P and Q are the points on the complex plane defined by ω and ω^2. If O is the origin, then what is the angle between OP and OQ?
A. 60° B. 90°
C. 120° D. 150°

2. Suppose there is a relation * between the positive numbers x and y given by $x * y$ if and only if $x \leq y^2$. Then which one of the following is correct?
A. * is reflexive but not transitive and symmetric
B. * is transitive but not reflexive and symmetric
C. * is symmetric and reflexive but not transitive
D. * is symmetric but not reflexive and transitive

3. If $x^2 - px + 4 > 0$ for all real values of x, then which one of the following is correct?
A. $|p| < 4$ B. $|p| \leq 4$
C. $|p| > 4$ D. $|p| \geq 4$

4. If $z = x + iy = \left(\frac{1}{\sqrt{2}} - \frac{i}{\sqrt{2}}\right)^{-25}$, where $i = \sqrt{-1}$, then what is the fundamental amplitude of $\frac{z-\sqrt{2}}{z-i\sqrt{2}}$?
A. π B. $\frac{\pi}{2}$
C. $\frac{\pi}{3}$ D. $\frac{\pi}{4}$

5. If $f(x_1) - f(x_2) = f\left(\frac{x_1 - x_2}{1 - x_1x_2}\right)$ for $x_1, x_2 \in (-1, 1)$, then what is $f(x)$ equal to?
A. $\ln\left(\frac{1-x}{1+x}\right)$ B. $\ln\left(\frac{2+x}{1-x}\right)$
C. $\tan^{-1}\left(\frac{1-x}{1+x}\right)$ D. $\tan^{-1}\left(\frac{1+x}{1-x}\right)$

6. What is the range of the function
$$y = \frac{x^2}{1+x^2}$$
where, $x \in \mathbb{R}$?
A. [0, 1) B. [0, 1]
C. (0, 1) D. (0, 1]

7. A straight line intersects x and y axes at P and Q respectively. If (3, 5) is the middle point of PQ, then what is the area of the triangle OPQ?
   A. 12 square units B. 15 square units
   C. 20 square units D. 30 square units

8. If a circle of radius b units with centre at $(0, b)$ touches the line $y = x - \sqrt{2}$, then what is the value of b?
   A. $2+\sqrt{2}$ B. $2-\sqrt{2}$
   C. $2\sqrt{2}$ D. $\sqrt{2}$

For the next three (3) items that follow:

Consider the function

$$f(\theta) = 4(\sin^2 \theta + \cos^4 \theta)$$

9. What is the maximum value of the function $f(\theta)$?
   A. 1 B. 2
   C. 3 D. 4

10. What is the minimum value of the function $f(\theta)$?
   A. 0 B. 1
   C. 2 D. 3

11. Consider the following statements:
   1. $f(\theta) = 2$ has no solution.
   2. $f(\theta) = \frac{7}{2}$ has a solution.

   Which of the above statements is/are correct?
   A. 1 only B. 2 only
   C. Both 1 and 2 D. Neither 1 nor 2

For the next two (2) items that follow:

Consider the curves

$$f(x) = x|x| - 1 \text{ and } g(x) = \begin{cases} \frac{3x}{2}, & x > 0 \\ 2x, & x \le 0 \end{cases}$$

12. Where do the curves intersect?
   A. At (2, 3) only
   B. At (–1, –2) only
   C. At (2, 3) and (–1, –2)
   D. Neither at (2, 3) nor at (–1, –2)

13. What is the area bounded by the curves?
   A. $\frac{17}{6}$ square units B. $\frac{8}{3}$ square units
   C. 2 square units D. $\frac{1}{3}$ square unit

For the next two (2) items that follow:

Consider the function

$$f(x) = \frac{27(x^{2/3} - x)}{4}$$

14. How many solutions does the function $f(x) = 1$ have?
   A. One B. Two
   C. Three D. Four

15. How many solutions does the function $f(x) = -1$ have?
   A. One B. Two
   C. Three D. Four

For the next two (2) items that follow:

Consider the functions

$$f(x) = xg(x) \text{ and } g(x) = \left[\frac{1}{x}\right]$$

where, [.] is the greatest integer function.

16. What is $\int_{\frac{1}{3}}^{\frac{1}{2}} g(x)dx$ equal to?
   A. $\frac{1}{6}$ B. $\frac{1}{3}$
   C. $\frac{5}{18}$ D. $\frac{5}{36}$

17. What is $\int_{\frac{1}{3}}^{1} f(x)dx$ equal to?
   A. $\frac{37}{72}$ B. $\frac{2}{3}$
   C. $\frac{17}{72}$ D. $\frac{37}{144}$

For the next five (5) items that follow:

Consider the function

$$f(x) = |x - 1| + x^2$$

where, $x \in \mathbb{R}$.

18. Which one of the following statements is correct?
   A. $f(x)$ is continuous but not differentiable at $x = 0$
   B. $f(x)$ is continuous but not differentiable at $x = 1$
   C. $f(x)$ is differentiable at $x = 1$
   D. $f(x)$ is not differentiable at $x = 0$ and $x = 1$

19. Which one of the following statements is correct?
   A. $f(x)$ is increasing in $\left(-\infty, \frac{1}{2}\right)$ and decreasing in $\left(\frac{1}{2}, \infty\right)$
   B. $f(x)$ is decreasing in $\left(-\infty, \frac{1}{2}\right)$ and increasing in $\left(\frac{1}{2}, \infty\right)$
   C. $f(x)$ is increasing in $(-\infty, 1)$ and decreasing in $(1, \infty)$
   D. $f(x)$ is decreasing in $(-\infty, 1)$ and increasing in $(1, \infty)$

20. Which one of the following statements is correct?
   A. $f(x)$ has local minima at more than one point in $(-\infty, \infty)$

B. $f(x)$ has local maxima at more than one point in $(-\infty, \infty)$

C. $f(x)$ has local minimum at one point only in $(-\infty, \infty)$

D. $f(x)$ has neither maxima nor minima in $(-\infty, \infty)$

21. What is the area of the region bounded by x-axis, the curve $y = f(x)$ and the two ordinates $x = \frac{1}{2}$ and $x = 1$?

A. $\frac{5}{12}$ square unit B. $\frac{5}{6}$ square unit

C. $\frac{7}{6}$ square units D. 2 square units

22. What is the area of the region bounded by x-axis, the curve $y = f(x)$ and the two ordinates $x = 1$ and $x = \frac{3}{2}$?

A. $\frac{5}{12}$ square unit B. $\frac{7}{12}$ square unit

C. $\frac{2}{3}$ square unit D. $\frac{11}{12}$ square unit

For the next two (2) items that follow:

Given that

$$a_n = \int_0^{\pi} \frac{\sin^2\{(n+1)x\}}{\sin 2x} dx$$

23. Consider the following statements:

1. The sequence $\{a_{2n}\}$ is in AP with common difference zero.
2. The sequence $\{a_{2n+1}\}$ is in AP with common difference zero.

Which of the above statements is/are correct?

A. 1 only B. 2 only

C. Both 1 and 2 D. Neither 1 nor 2

24. What is $a_{n-1} - a_{n-4}$ equal to?

A. –1 B. 0

C. 1 D. 2

For the next two (2) items that follow:

Consider the equation $x + |y| = 2y$.

25. Which of the following statements are not correct?

1. y as a function of x is not defined for all real x.
2. y as a function of x is not continuous at $x = 0$.
3. y as a function of x is differentiable for all x.

Select the correct answer using the code given below.

A. 1 and 2 only B. 2 and 3 only

C. 1 and 3 only D. 1, 2 and 3

26. What is the derivative of y as a function of x with respect to x for $x < 0$?

A. 2 B. 1

C. $\frac{1}{2}$ D. $\frac{1}{3}$

For the next two (2) items that follow:

Consider the lines

$y = 3x$, $y = 6x$ and $y = 9$

27. What is the area of the triangle formed by these lines?

A. $\frac{27}{4}$ square units B. $\frac{27}{2}$ square units

C. $\frac{19}{4}$ square units D. $\frac{19}{2}$ square units

28. The centroid of the triangle is at which one of the following points?

A. (3, 6) B. $\left(\frac{3}{2}, 6\right)$

C. (3, 3) D. $\left(\frac{3}{2}, 9\right)$

For the next two (2) items that follow:

Consider the function

$f(x) = (x-1)^2 (x+1)(x-2)^3$

29. What is the number of points of local minima of the function $f(x)$?

A. None B. One

C. Two D. Three

30. What is the number of points of local maxima of the function $f(x)$?

A. None B. One

C. Two D. Three

31. Let $f(x)$ and $g(x)$ be twice differentiable functions on [0, 2] satisfying $f''(x) = g''(x)$, $f'(1) = 4$, $g'(1) = 6$, $f(2) = 3$ and $g(2) = 9$. Then what is $f(x) - g(x)$ at $x = 4$ equal to?

A. –10 B. –6

C. –4 D. 2

For the next two (2) items that follow:

Consider the curves

$y = |x-1|$ and $|x| = 2$

32. What is/are the point(s) of intersection of the curves?

A. (–2, 3) only

B. (2, 1) only

C. (–2, 3) and (2, 1)

D. Neither (–2, 3) nor (2, 1)

33. What is the area of the region bounded by the curves and x-axis?

A. 3 square units B. 4 square units

C. 5 square units D. 6 square units

For the next two (2) items that follow:

Consider the function

$$f(x) = \begin{vmatrix} x^3 & \sin x & \cos x \\ 6 & -1 & 0 \\ p & p^2 & p^3 \end{vmatrix}$$

where, p is a constant.

34. What is the value of $f'(0)$?

A. p^3 B. $3p^3$

C. $6p^3$ D. $-6p^3$

35. What is the value of p for which $f''(0) = 0$?

A. $-\frac{1}{6}$ or 0 B. -1 or 0

C. $-\frac{1}{6}$ or 1 D. -1 or 1

For the next two (2) items that follow:

Consider a triangle ABC in which

$$\cos A + \cos B + \cos C = \sqrt{3} \sin \frac{\pi}{3}$$

36. What is the value of $\sin \frac{A}{2} \sin \frac{B}{2} \sin \frac{C}{2}$?

A. $\frac{1}{2}$ B. $\frac{1}{4}$

C. $\frac{1}{8}$ D. $\frac{1}{16}$

37. What is the value of

$$\cos\left(\frac{A+B}{2}\right)\cos\left(\frac{B+C}{2}\right)\cos\left(\frac{C+A}{2}\right)?$$

A. $\frac{1}{4}$ B. $\frac{1}{2}$

C. $\frac{1}{16}$ D. None of the above

For the next two (2) items that follow:

Given that $\tan \alpha$ and $\tan \beta$ are the roots of the equation $x^2 + bx + c = 0$ with $b \neq 0$.

38. What is $\tan(\alpha + \beta)$ equal to?

A. $b(c - 1)$ B. $c(b - 1)$

C. $c(b - 1)^{-1}$ D. $b(c - 1)^{-1}$

39. What is $\sin(\alpha + \beta) \sec \alpha \sec \beta$ equal to?

A. b B. $-b$

C. c D. $-c$

For the next two (2) items that follow:

Consider the two circles

$(x - 1)^2 + (y - 3)^2 = r^2$ and

$x^2 + y^2 - 8x + 2y + 8 = 0$

40. What is the distance between the centres of the two circles?

A. 5 units B. 6 units

C. 8 units D. 10 units

41. If the circles intersect at two distinct points, then which one of the following is correct?

A. $r = 1$ B. $1 < r < 2$

C. $r = 2$ D. $2 < r < 8$

For the next two (2) items that follow:

Consider the two lines

$x + y + 1 = 0$ and $3x + 2y + 1 = 0$

42. What is the equation of the line passing through the point of intersection of the given lines and parallel to x-axis?

A. $y + 1 = 0$ B. $y - 1 = 0$

C. $y - 2 = 0$ D. $y + 2 = 0$

43. What is the equation of the line passing through the point of intersection of the given lines and parallel to y-axis?

A. $x + 1 = 0$ B. $x - 1 = 0$

C. $x - 2 = 0$ D. $x + 2 = 0$

For the next two (2) items that follow:

Consider the equation

$k \sin x + \cos 2x = 2k - 7$

44. If the equation possesses solution, then what is the minimum value of k?

A. 1 B. 2

C. 4 D. 6

45. If the equation possesses solution, then what is the maximum value of k?

A. 1 B. 2

C. 4 D. 6

For the next two (2) items that follow:

Consider the function

$$f(x) = \frac{a^{[x]+x} - 1}{[x] + x}$$

where [.] denotes the greatest integer function.

46. What is $\lim_{x \to 0} f(x)$ equal to?

A. 1 B. $\ln a$

C. $1 - a^{-1}$ D. Limit does not exist

47. What is $\lim_{x \to 0-} f(x)$ equal to?

A. 0 B. $\ln a$

C. $1 - a^{-1}$ D. Limit does not exist

For the next two (2) items that follow :

Let z_1, z_2 and z_3 be non-zero complex numbers satisfying $z^2 = iz$, where, $i = \sqrt{-1}$.

48. What is $z_1 + z_2 + z_3$ equal to?

A. i B. $-i$

C. 0 D. 1

49. Consider the following statements:

1. $z_1 z_2 z_3$ is purely imaginary.

2. $z_1 z_2 + z_2 z_3 + z_3 z_1$ is purely real.

Which of the above statements is/are correct?

A. 1 only B. 2 only

C. Both 1 and 2 D. Neither 1 nor 2

For the next two (2) items that follow:

Given that $\log_x y$, $\log_z x$, $\log_y z$ are in GP, $xyz = 64$ and x^3, y^3, z^3 are in AP.

50. Which one of the following is correct?

x, y and z are

A. in AP only
B. in GP only
C. in both AP and GP
D. neither in AP nor in GP

51. Which one of the following is correct?

xy, yz and zx are

A. in AP only
B. in GP only
C. in both AP and GP
D. neither in AP nor in GP

For the next two (2) items that follow:

Let, z be a complex number satisfying

$$\left|\frac{z-4}{z-8}\right| = 1 \text{ and } \left|\frac{z}{z-2}\right| = \frac{3}{2}$$

52. What is $|z|$ equal to?

A. 6 B. 12
C. 18 D. 36

53. What is $\left|\frac{z-6}{z+6}\right|$ equal to?

A. 3 B. 2
C. 1 D. 0

For the next two (2) items that follow :

A function $f(x)$ is defined as follows:

$$f(x) = \begin{cases} x+\pi & \text{for } x \in [-\pi, 0) \\ \pi\cos x & \text{for } x \in \left[0, \frac{\pi}{2}\right] \\ \left(x-\frac{\pi}{2}\right)^2 & \text{for } x \in \left(\frac{\pi}{2}, \pi\right] \end{cases}$$

54. Consider the following statements:

1. The function $f(x)$ is continuous at $x = 0$.
2. The function $f(x)$ is continuous at $x = \frac{\pi}{2}$.

Which of the above statements is/are correct?

A. 1 only B. 2 only
C. Both 1 and 2 D. Neither 1 nor 2

55. Consider the following statements:

1. The function $f(x)$ is differentiable at $x = 0$.
2. The function $f(x)$ is differentiable at $x = \frac{\pi}{2}$.

Which of the above statements is/are correct?

A. 1 only B. 2 only
C. Both 1 and 2 D. Neither 1 nor 2

For the next two (2) items that follow:

Let α and β ($\alpha < \beta$) be the roots of the equation $x^2 + bx + c = 0$, where, $b > 0$ and $c < 0$.

56. Consider the following:

1. $\beta < -\alpha$
2. $\beta < |\alpha|$

Which of the above is/are correct?

A. 1 only B. 2 only
C. Both 1 and 2 D. Neither 1 nor 2

57. Consider the following:

1. $\alpha + \beta + \alpha\beta > 0$
2. $\alpha^2\beta + \beta^2\alpha > 0$

Which of the above is/are correct?

A. 1 only B. 2 only
C. Both 1 and 2 D. Neither 1 nor 2

For the next three (3) items that follow:

Consider a parallelogram whose vertices are A(1, 2), B(4, y), C(x, 6) and D(3, 5) taken in order.

58. What is the value of $AC^2 - BD^2$?

A. 25 B. 30
C. 36 D. 40

59. What is the point of intersection of the diagonals?

A. $\left(\frac{7}{2}, 4\right)$ B. (3, 4)
C. $\left(\frac{7}{2}, 5\right)$ D. (3, 5)

60. What is the area of the parallelogram?

A. $\frac{7}{2}$ square units B. 4 square units
C. $\frac{11}{2}$ square units D. 7 square units

For the next four (4) items that follow:

Let, $f: \mathbb{R} \to \mathbb{R}$ be a function such that

$f(x) = x^3 + x^2 f'(1) + xf''(2) + f'''(3)$ for $x \in \mathbb{R}$

61. What is $f(1)$ equal to?

A. –2 B. –1
C. 0 D. 4

62. What is $f'(1)$ equal to?

A. –6 B. –5
C. 1 D. 0

63. What is $f'''(10)$ equal to?

A. 1 B. 5
C. 6 D. 8

64. Consider the following :

1. $f(2) = f(1) - f(0)$
2. $f''(2) - 2f'(1) = 12$

Which of the above is/are correct?

A. 1 only B. 2 only
C. Both 1 and 2 D. Neither 1 nor 2

For the next three (3) items that follow:

A plane P passes through the line of intersection of the planes $2x - y + 3z = 2$, $x + y - z = 1$ and the point (1, 0, 1).

65. What are the direction ratios of the line of intersection of the given planes?

A. $\langle 2, -5, -3\rangle$ B. $\langle 1, -5, -3\rangle$
C. $\langle 2, 5, 3\rangle$ D. $\langle 1, 3, 5\rangle$

66. What is the equation of the plane P?

A. $2x + 5y - 2 = 0$
B. $5x + 2y - 5 = 0$
C. $x + z - 2 = 0$
D. $2x - y - 2z = 0$

67. If the plane P touches the sphere $x^2 + y^2 + z^2 = r^2$, then what is r equal to?

A. $\frac{2}{\sqrt{29}}$ B. $\frac{4}{\sqrt{29}}$
C. $\frac{5}{\sqrt{29}}$ D. 1

For the next two (2) items that follow:

Consider the function

$f(x) = |x^2 - 5x + 6|$

68. What is $f'(4)$ equal to?

A. –4 B. –3
C. 3 D. 2

69. What is $f''(2.5)$ equal to?

A. –3 B. –2
C. 0 D. 2

For the next two (2) items that follow:

Let, $f(x)$ be the greatest integer function and $g(x)$ be the modulus function.

70. What is $(g \circ f)\left(-\frac{5}{3}\right) - (f \circ g)\left(-\frac{5}{3}\right)$ equal to?

A. –1 B. 0
C. 1 D. 2

71. What is $(f \circ f)\left(-\frac{9}{5}\right) + (g \circ g)(-2)$ equal to?

A. –1 B. 0
C. 1 D. 2

For the next two (2) items that follow:

Consider a circle passing through the origin and the points (a, b) and $(-b, -a)$.

72. On which line does the centre of the circle lie?

A. $x + y = 0$ B. $x - y = 0$
C. $x + y = a + b$ D. $x - y = a^2 - b^2$

73. What is the sum of the squares of the intercepts cut off by the circle on the axes?

A. $\left(\frac{a^2+b^2}{a^2-b^2}\right)^2$ B. $2\left(\frac{a^2+b^2}{a-b}\right)^2$
C. $4\left(\frac{a^2+b^2}{a-b}\right)^2$ D. None of the above

For the next two (2) items that follow :

Let, $\hat{a}, \hat{b}$ be two unit vectors and θ be the angle between them.

74. What is $\cos\left(\frac{\theta}{2}\right)$ equal to?

A. $\frac{|\hat{a}-\hat{b}|}{2}$ B. $\frac{|\hat{a}+\hat{b}|}{2}$
C. $\frac{|\hat{a}-\hat{b}|}{4}$ D. $\frac{|\hat{a}+\hat{b}|}{4}$

75. What is $\sin\left(\frac{\theta}{2}\right)$ equal to?

A. $\frac{|\hat{a}-\hat{b}|}{2}$ B. $\frac{|\hat{a}+\hat{b}|}{2}$
C. $\frac{|\hat{a}-\hat{b}|}{4}$ D. $\frac{|\hat{a}+\hat{b}|}{4}$

76. Consider the following statements:

1. There exists $\theta \in \left(-\frac{\pi}{2}, \frac{\pi}{2}\right)$ for which $\tan^{-1}(\tan\theta) \neq \theta$.
2. $\sin^{-1}\left(\frac{1}{3}\right) - \sin^{-1}\left(\frac{1}{5}\right) = \sin^{-1}\left(\frac{2\sqrt{2}(\sqrt{3}-1)}{15}\right)$

Which of the above statements is/are correct?

A. 1 only B. 2 only
C. Both 1 and 2 D. Neither 1 nor 2

77. Consider the following statements:

1. $\tan^{-1} x + \tan^{-1}\left(\frac{1}{x}\right) = \pi$
2. There exist $x, y \in [-1, 1]$, where, $x \neq y$ such that $\sin^{-1} x + \cos^{-1} y = \frac{\pi}{2}$.

Which of the above statements is/are correct?

A. 1 only B. 2 only

C. Both 1 and 2 D. Neither 1 nor 2

78. What are the order and degree respectively of the differential equation whose solution is $y = cx + c^2 - 3c^{3/2} + 2$, where c is a parameter?

A. 1, 2 B. 2, 2

C. 1, 3 D. 1, 4

79. What is

$$\int_{-2}^{2} x dx - \int_{-2}^{2} [x] dx$$

equal to, where [.] is greatest integer function?

A. 0 B. 1

C. 2 D. 4

80. If

$$\int_{-2}^{5} f(x)dx = 4 \text{ and } \int_{0}^{5} \{1 + f(x)\}dx = 7$$

then what is $\int_{-2}^{0} f(x)dx$ equal to?

A. –3 B. 2

C. 3 D. 5

81. If $\lim_{x \to 0} \phi(x) = a^2$, where $a \neq 0$, then what is $\lim_{x \to 0} \phi\left(\frac{x}{a}\right)$ equal to?

A. a^2 2. a^{-2}

C. $-a^2$ D. $-a$

82. What is $\lim_{x \to 0} e^{-\frac{1}{x^2}}$ equal to?

A. 0

B. 1

C. –1

D. Limit does not exist

83. If A is a square matrix, then what is $\text{adj}(A^{-1}) - (\text{adj } A)^{-1}$ equal to?

A. 2 | A | B. Null matrix

C. Unit matrix D. None of the above

84. What is the binary equivalent of the decimal number 0.3125?

A. 0.0111 B. 0.1010

C. 0.0101 D. 0.1101

85. Let R be a relation on the set N of natural numbers defined by 'nR$m \Leftrightarrow n$ is a factor of m'. Then which one of the following is correct?

A. R is reflexive, symmetric but not transitive

B. R is transitive, symmetric but not reflexive

C. R is reflexive, transitive but not symmetric

D. R is an equivalence relation

86. What is $\int_{0}^{4\pi} |\cos x| dx$ equal to?

A. 0 B. 2

C. 4 D. 8

87. What is the number of natural numbers less than or equal to 1000 which are neither divisible by 10 nor 15 nor 25?

A. 860 B. 854

C. 840 D. 824

88. $(a, 2b)$ is the mid-point of the line segment joining the points (10, –6) and (k, 4). If $a - 2b = 7$, then what is the value of k?

A. 2 B. 3

C. 4 D. 5

87. Consider the following statements:

1. If ABC is an equilateral triangle, then 3 tan (A + B) tan C = 1.
2. If ABC is a triangle in which A = 78°, B = 66°, then

$$\tan\left(\frac{A}{2} + C\right) < \tan A$$

3. If ABC is any triangle, then

$$\tan\left(\frac{A+B}{2}\right)\sin\left(\frac{C}{2}\right) < \cos\left(\frac{C}{2}\right)$$

Which of the above statements is/are correct?

A. 1 only B. 2 only

C. 1 and 2 D. 2 and 3

90. If A = (cos 12° – cos 36°) (sin 96° + sin 24°) and B = (sin 60° – sin 12°) (cos 48° – cos 72°), then what is $\frac{A}{B}$ equal to?

A. – 1 B. 0

C. 1 D. 2

91. What is the mean deviation from the mean of the numbers 10, 9, 21, 16, 24?

A. 5.2 B. 5.0

C. 4.5 D. 4.0

92. Three dice are thrown simultaneously. What is the probability that the sum on the three faces is at least 5?

A. $\frac{17}{18}$ B. $\frac{53}{54}$

C. $\frac{103}{108}$ D. $\frac{215}{216}$

93. Two independent events A and B have $P(A) = \frac{1}{3}$ and $P(B) = \frac{3}{4}$. What is the probability that exactly one of the two events A or B occurs?

A. $\frac{1}{4}$ B. $\frac{5}{6}$

C. $\frac{5}{12}$ D. $\frac{7}{12}$

94. A coin is tossed three times. What is the probability of getting head and tail alternately?

A. $\frac{1}{8}$ B. $\frac{1}{4}$

C. $\frac{1}{2}$ D. $\frac{3}{4}$

95. If the total number of observations is 20, $\Sigma x_i = 1000$ and $\Sigma x_i^2 = 84000$, then what is the variance of the distribution?

A. 1500 B. 1600
C. 1700 D. 1800

96. A card is drawn from a well-shuffled deck of 52 cards. What is the probability that it is queen of spade?

A. $\frac{1}{52}$ B. $\frac{1}{13}$

C. $\frac{1}{4}$ D. $\frac{1}{8}$

97. If two dice are thrown, then what is the probability that the sum on the two faces is greater than or equal to 4?

A. $\frac{13}{18}$ B. $\frac{5}{6}$

C. $\frac{11}{12}$ D. $\frac{35}{36}$

98. A certain type of missile hits the target with probability $p = 0.3$. What is the least number of missiles should be fired so that there is at least an 80% probability that the target is hit?

A. 5 B. 6
C. 7 D. None of the above

99. For two mutually exclusive events A and B, P(A) = 0.2 and $P(\bar{A} \cap B) = 0.3$. What is $P(A \mid (A \cup B))$ equal to:

A. $\frac{1}{2}$ B. $\frac{2}{5}$

C. $\frac{2}{7}$ D. $\frac{2}{3}$

100. What is the probability of 5 Sundays in the month of December?

A. $\frac{1}{7}$ B. $\frac{2}{7}$

C. $\frac{3}{7}$ D. None of the above

101. If m is the geometric mean of

$$\left(\frac{y}{z}\right)^{\log(yz)}, \left(\frac{z}{x}\right)^{\log(zx)} \text{ and } \left(\frac{x}{y}\right)^{\log(xy)}$$

then what is the value of m?

A. 1 B. 3
C. 6 D. 9

102. A point is chosen at random inside a rectangle measuring 6 inches by 5 inches. What is the probability that the randomly selected point is at least one inch from the edge of the rectangle?

A. $\frac{2}{3}$ B. $\frac{1}{3}$

C. $\frac{1}{4}$ D. $\frac{2}{5}$

103. The mean of the series $x_1, x_2, \ldots, x_n$ is $\bar{X}$. If x_2 is replaced by λ, then what is the new mean?

A. $\bar{X} - x_2 + \lambda$ B. $\frac{\bar{X} - x_2 - \lambda}{n}$

C. $\frac{\bar{X} - x_2 + \lambda}{n}$ D. $\frac{n\bar{X} - x_2 + \lambda}{n}$

104. For the data

3, 5, 1, 6, 5, 9, 5, 2, 8, 6

the mean, median and mode are x, y and z respectively. Which one of the following is correct?

A. $x = y \neq z$
B. $x \neq y = z$
C. $x \neq y \neq z$
D. $x = y = z$

105. Consider the following statements in respect of a histogram :

1. The total area of the rectangles in a histogram is equal to the total area bounded by the corresponding frequency polygon and the x-axis.
2. When class intervals are unequal in a frequency distribution, the area of the rectangle is proportional to the frequency.

Which of the above statements is/are correct?

A. 1 only B. 2 only
C. Both 1 and 2 D. Neither 1 nor 2

106. A fair coin is tossed 100 times. What is the probability of getting tails an odd number of times?

A. $\frac{1}{2}$ B. $\frac{3}{8}$

C. $\frac{1}{4}$ D. $\frac{1}{8}$

107. What is the number of ways in which 3 holiday travel tickets are to be given to 10 employees of an organization, if each employee is eligible for any one or more of the tickets?

A. 60 B. 120
C. 500 D. 1000

108. If one root of the equation $(l - m)x^2 + lx + 1 = 0$ is double the other and l is real, then what is the greatest value of m?

A. $-\frac{9}{8}$ B. $\frac{9}{8}$

C. $-\frac{8}{9}$ D. $\frac{8}{9}$

109. What is the number of four-digit decimal numbers (< 1) in which no digit is repeated?

A. 3024 B. 4536

C. 5040 D. None of the above

110. What is a vector of unit length orthogonal to both the vectors $\hat{i}+\hat{j}+\hat{k}$ and $2\hat{i}+3\hat{j}-\hat{k}$?

A. $\frac{-4\hat{i}+3\hat{j}-\hat{k}}{\sqrt{26}}$ B. $\frac{-4\hat{i}+3\hat{j}+\hat{k}}{\sqrt{26}}$

C. $\frac{-3\hat{i}+2\hat{j}-\hat{k}}{\sqrt{14}}$ D. $\frac{-3\hat{i}+2\hat{j}+\hat{k}}{\sqrt{14}}$

111. If $\vec{a}, \vec{b}$ and $\vec{c}$ are the position vectors of the vertices of an equilateral triangle whose orthocentre is at the origin, then which one of the following is correct?

A. $\vec{a}+\vec{b}+\vec{c}=\vec{0}$

B. $\vec{a}+\vec{b}+\vec{c}=$ unit vector

C. $\vec{a}+\vec{b}=\vec{c}$

D. $\vec{a}=\vec{b}+\vec{c}$

112. What is the area of the parallelogram having diagonals $3\hat{i}+\hat{j}-2\hat{k}$ and $\hat{i}-3\hat{j}+4\hat{k}$?

A. $5\sqrt{5}$ square units

B. $4\sqrt{5}$ square units

C. $5\sqrt{3}$ square units

D. $15\sqrt{2}$ square units

113. Consider the following in respect of the matrix

$$A=\begin{pmatrix}-1 & 1\\ 1 & -1\end{pmatrix}:$$

1. $A^2 = -A$
2. $A^3 = 4A$

Which of the above is/are correct?

A. 1 only

B. 2 only

C. Both 1 and 2

D. Neither 1 nor 2

114. Which of the following determinants have value 'zero'?

1. $\begin{vmatrix}41 & 1 & 5\\ 79 & 7 & 9\\ 29 & 5 & 3\end{vmatrix}$

2. $\begin{vmatrix}1 & a & b+c\\ 1 & b & c+a\\ 1 & c & a+b\end{vmatrix}$

3. $\begin{vmatrix}0 & c & b\\ -c & 0 & a\\ -b & -a & 0\end{vmatrix}$

Select the correct answer using the code given below.

A. 1 and 2 only

B. 2 and 3 only

C. 1 and 3 only

D. 1, 2 and 3

115. What is the acute angle between the lines represented by the equations

$$y-\sqrt{3}x-5=0 \text{ and } \sqrt{3}y-x+6=0?$$

A. 30° B. 45°

C. 60° D. 75°

116. The system of linear equations $kx + y + z = 1$, $x + ky + z = 1$ and $x + y + kz = 1$ has a unique solution under which one of the following conditions?

A. $k \neq 1$ and $k \neq -2$

B. $k \neq 1$ and $k \neq 2$

C. $k \neq -1$ and $k \neq -2$

D. $k \neq -1$ and $k \neq 2$

117. What is the number of different messages that can be represented by three 0's and two 1's?

A. 10 B. 9

C. 8 D. 7

118. If $\log_a(ab) = x$, then what is $\log_b(ab)$ equal to?

A. $\frac{1}{x}$ B. $\frac{x}{x+1}$

C. $\frac{x}{1-x}$ D. $\frac{x}{x-1}$

119. If $y = \log_{10} x + \log_x 10 + \log_x x + \log_{10} 10$ then what is $\left(\frac{dy}{dx}\right)_{x=10}$ equal to?

A. 10 B. 2

C. 1 D. 0

120. Suppose ω_1 and ω_2 are two distinct cube roots of unity different from 1. Then what is $(\omega_1 - \omega_2)^2$ equal to?

A. 3 B. 1

C. −1 D. −3

ANSWERS

PAPER-I : GENERAL ABILITY TEST

1	2	3	4	5	6	7	8	9	10
A	C	C	D	C	B	C	C	A	D
11	**12**	**13**	**14**	**15**	**16**	**17**	**18**	**19**	**20**
A	B	B	B	A	B	B	A	D	C
21	**22**	**23**	**24**	**25**	**26**	**27**	**28**	**29**	**30**
D	B	C	D	B	A	A	B	B	B
31	**32**	**33**	**34**	**35**	**36**	**37**	**38**	**39**	**40**
C	A	C	D	A	A	B	D	B	B
41	**42**	**43**	**44**	**45**	**46**	**47**	**48**	**49**	**50**
D	C	D	A	B	B	D	B	D	A
51	**52**	**53**	**54**	**55**	**56**	**57**	**58**	**59**	**60**
A	A	B	A	A	C	C	A	C	D
61	**62**	**63**	**64**	**65**	**66**	**67**	**68**	**69**	**70**
A	C	B	D	B	D	B	C	A	B
71	**72**	**73**	**74**	**75**	**76**	**77**	**78**	**79**	**80**
B	B	C	C	B	C	A	D	B	D
81	**82**	**83**	**84**	**85**	**86**	**87**	**88**	**89**	**90**
A	C	C	A	C	D	C	A	C	C
91	**92**	**93**	**94**	**95**	**96**	**97**	**98**	**99**	**100**
B	C	A	A	B	D	A	B	D	B
101	**102**	**103**	**104**	**105**	**106**	**107**	**108**	**109**	**110**
A	C	A	B	C	C	D	A	D	C
111	**112**	**113**	**114**	**115**	**116**	**117**	**118**	**119**	**120**
B	D	A	B	A	B	A	D	B	C
121	**122**	**123**	**124**	**125**	**126**	**127**	**128**	**129**	**130**
B	C	D	B	D	C	C	A	B	A
131	**132**	**133**	**134**	**135**	**136**	**137**	**138**	**139**	**140**
A	C	C	C	B	D	D	A	C	A
141	**142**	**143**	**144**	**145**	**146**	**147**	**148**	**149**	**150**
B	B	C	C	C	A	D	A	A	C

PAPER-II : MATHEMATICS

1	2	3	4	5	6	7	8	9	10
C	B	C	C	A	A	D	B	D	D
11	**12**	**13**	**14**	**15**	**16**	**17**	**18**	**19**	**20**
B	B	B	C	A	A	D	B	B	C
21	**22**	**23**	**24**	**25**	**26**	**27**	**28**	**29**	**30**
B	D	B	A	B	D	A	B	C	C
31	**32**	**33**	**34**	**35**	**36**	**37**	**38**	**39**	**40**
A	C	B	D	A	C	D	D	B	A
41	**42**	**43**	**44**	**45**	**46**	**47**	**48**	**49**	**50**
B	D	B	B	D	B	C	A	D	C
51	**52**	**53**	**54**	**55**	**56**	**57**	**58**	**59**	**60**
C	A	D	C	D	C	B	C	A	D
61	**62**	**63**	**64**	**65**	**66**	**67**	**68**	**69**	**70**
D	B	C	C	A	B	C	C	B	C

71	72	73	74	75	76	77	78	79	80
B	A	B	B	A	B	D	D	C	B
81	82	83	84	85	86	87	88	89	90
A	A	B	C	C	D	B	A	B	C
91	92	93	94	95	96	97	98	99	100
A	B	D	B	C	A	C	A	B	B
101	102	103	104	105	106	107	108	109	110
A	D	D	B	C	A	D	B	C	B
111	112	113	114	115	116	117	118	119	120
A	C	B	D	A	A	A	D	D	D

EXPLANATORY ANSWERS

PAPER-I : GENERAL ABILITY TEST

51. Petroleum consists of hydrocarbons of various molecular weights and other organic compounds. The name petroleum covers both naturally occurring unprocessed crude oil and petroleum products that are made up of refined crude oil. The grade of petroleum is determined on the basis of the proportion of the different hydrocarbons. So both the statements I & II are correct and Statement-II is the correct explanation of Statement-I.

52. Due to high evaporation, the Red Sea is one of the saltiest bodies of water in the world. Salinity ranges from between ~36 ‰ in the southern part because of the effect of the Gulf of Aden water and reaches 41 ‰ in the northern part, mainly due to the Gulf of Suez water and the high evaporation. The average salinity is 40 ‰. (Average salinity for the world's seawater is ~35 ‰ on the Practical Salinity Scale, or PPS; that translates to 3.5% actual dissolved salts). The salinity of the Red Sea is greater than the world average, approximately 4 percent. This is due to several factors like high rate of evaporation and very little precipitation; lack of significant rivers or streams draining into the sea and limited connection with the Indian Ocean, which has lower water salinity.

In the light of both the statements and the elaboration as given above, both the statements I and II are correct and Statement-II is the correct explanation of Statement-I.

53. Most earthquakes are caused directly beneath a volcano by the movement of magma. The magma exerts pressure on the rocks until it cracks the rock. Then the magma squirts into the crack and starts rebuilding the pressure on the rocks. Every time the rock cracks, it makes a small earthquake. These earthquakes are usually too weak to be felt but can be detected and recorded by sensitive instruments. As given in Statement-I and corroborated by the above explanation, the Statement-I is proved to be true.

The statement, "Volcanoes erupt water vapours and dust particles in the atmosphere" has no relevance with the natural fact and therefore, the Statement-II is false.

54. Plantation farming has mostly been practised in humid tropics, as a wide range of vegetation types grows in the humid tropical bioclimate (Plate 1), with numerous tree species of varying heights, canopy structure, and biomass. The most predominant vegetation of the humid tropics consists of TRF in the lowlands, moist deciduous forest in regions with a pronounced dry season, and mountain forest in the high lands. The TRF, the climax vegetation of the humid tropics is diverse and complex, and occupies about 10% of the worlds land area. Thus, it comes to knowledge that the Statement-I is true.

"The soil of humid tropics is highly fertile" as mentioned in Statement-II, is false, because tropical soils in general, are unproductive in terms of crop yields. The reason behind their being infertile are its being Oxisols (most weathered, typical tropical soils, high in iron and aluminium oxides); Ultisols (high leached); Alfisols (least weathered, younger soils, aluminium and iron soils temperate soils). Thus, it is proved that Statement-II is false.

55. Population density is a measurement of the number of people in an area. It is an average number. Like world population, India also has a wide variation in population density. Somewhere the population is dense while somewhere it is not. Density of population depends upon birth & death rate, fertility of land, job and business opportunities, law and order condition and so on. Considering all these advantages people migrate to other places, thereby making their earlier place of stay less populated and the place of their emigration densely populated. For example, around 70% of India's population lives in villages but when the density is measured in comparison to urban area, cities and towns are many-many times more densely population than rural areas. So the assertion in Statement-I is true.

The assertion in Statement-II is neither true nor does it have any relevance to the Statement-I and its explanation.

58. The phosphorus used in the manufacture of safety matches is Red phosphorus. Anton Schrötter von Kristelli discovered in 1850 that heating white phosphorus at 250 °C in an inert atmosphere produced a red allotropic form, which did not fume in contact with air. It was suggested that this would make a suitable substitute in match manufacture although it was slightly more expensive.

59. Chemical change is any change that results in the formation of new chemical substances, and the taking shape of any substance/object into new form due to chemical change is not revertible. So freezing of water is not a chemical change; it's a physical change because water becomes ice due to freezing and then again reverts to its old liquid form after being melt, which is an example of physical change.

60. Both the gases—Nitrogen dioxide and Carbon monoxide are immensely harmful to human beings and even other creatures. High levels of Nitrogen dioxide exposure can cause people coughs and breathing difficulty. People who are exposed to this gas for a long time are prone to have respiratory infections. Nitrogen dioxide reacts in the atmosphere to form acid rain, which can harm plants and animals.

Carbon monoxide makes it hard for body parts to get the oxygen they need to function well. Exposure to Carbon monoxide makes people feel dizzy and tired and causes headaches. In high concentrations, it is fatal. More often, elderly people with heart disease are hospitalised when they are exposed to higher amounts of Carbon monoxide.

61. Given below are the centres of AIIMS, illustrated in brief and arranged in directional order from East to West:

- All India Institute of Medical Sciences Bhubaneswar (AIIMS Bhubaneswar) is a medical college and medical research public university located in Bhubaneswar, Odisha. The Institute operates autonomously under the aegis of the Ministry of Health and Family Welfare (India). Previously, AIIMS Bhubaneswar was known as the Netaji Subhas Chandra Bose All India Institute of Medical Sciences, later it became AIIMS Bhubaneswar. AIIMS Bhubaneswar was inaugurated on 26 February 2014.
- AIIMS Patna (officially Jayaprakash Narayan All India Institute of Medical Sciences) is a medical college and medical research public university based in Patna, Bihar. It is under construction for almost a decade foundation of which was laid on 3 January 2004. The AIIMS, near Walmi institute at Phulwari Sharif, Patna started operating since 25 September 2012 after a series of observations by Patna High Court.
- AIIMS Rishikesh is a medical college, hospital and medical research public university, based in Rishikesh, Uttarakhand. Like other AIIMS, it also operates autonomously under the Ministry of Health and Family Welfare. It was inaugurated on 10 February 2014.
- AIIMS Delhi is a medical college and medical research public university based in New Delhi, India. The Institute was established in 1956 and operates autonomously under the Ministry of Health and Family Welfare. AIIMS was established in New Delhi after former Indian Prime Minister Jawaharlal Nehru's initial proposal to set up the institute in Calcutta (Kolkata) was turned down by the then chief minister of West Bengal, B.C. Roy. AIIMS Delhi was ranked at third place in the first list of the Times Higher Education India Reputation Rankings, published alongside the Times Higher Education World Reputation Rankings in 2013. AIIMS has been consistently ranked the top medical college in India to pursue any Medical degree by India Today in annual surveys starting in 1997 and was ranked No. 1 in 2013. It was the vision of Rajkumari Amrit Kaur, the first Health Minister of India, to establish an institute of such nature in India.

64. Soap is sodium or potassium salt of Stearic acid, which is a saturated fatty acid with an 18-carbon chain and has the IUPAC name octadecanoic acid. It is a waxy solid and its chemical formula is $C_{17}H_{35}CO_2H$. Stearic acid is mainly used in the production of detergents, soaps, and cosmetics such as shampoos and shaving cream products. Soaps are not made directly from stearic acid, but indirectly by saponification of triglycerides consisting of stearic acid esters. Esters of stearic acid with ethylene glycol, glycol stearate, and glycol distearate are used to produce a pearly effect in shampoos, soaps, and other cosmetic products.

65. Statements I and II are correct whose combined explanations are given below:

Mass of a particular amount of substance is the amount of matter present therein. In other words, it is the amount of "stuff" there is. It is easy to confuse the terms "mass" with "weight" but they are fundamentally different properties. The mass of an object does not vary from place to place. Mass can be measured by using a triple beam balance and the units to be used are grams (g) and sometimes kilograms (kg).

66. Following are the substances given with their respective codes and explanations that are harmful for health if present in food items:

(*i*) Pesticide residue refers to the pesticides that may remain on or in food after they are applied to food crops. The levels of these residues in foods are often stipulated by regulatory bodies in many countries. Exposure of the general population to these residues most commonly occurs through consumption of treated food sources, or being in close contact to areas treated with pesticides such as farms or lawns around houses.

(*ii*) Lead is present in small amounts throughout the environment due to its natural occurrence and its release into the environment by human activities, thereby making its presence in plants, including the plants grown for food. Lead poisoning is a type of metal poisoning and a medical condition in humans and other vertebrates caused by increased levels of the heavy metal lead in the body. Lead interferes with a variety of body processes and is toxic to many organs and tissues including the heart, bones, intestines, kidneys, and reproductive and nervous systems.

(*iii*) Metanil yellow is a monoazo acid dye, $C_{18}H_{14}N_3O_3SNa$, used as a cytoplasmic and connective tissue stain, which is the principal non-permitted food colour used extensively in India in foods like jalebi and laddoo etc. Metanil yellow is highly dangerous as it causes degenerative changes in the lining of the stomach, kidneys and liver. It also adversely affects the ovaries and testes, proving to be dangerous to reproductive organs. It is commonly used to add colour to food items in India. Consumption of this colour has reported symptoms of giddiness, weakness and food poisoning.

(*iv*) The toxicity of mercury depends on the form of mercury to which people are exposed. Toxic effects, especially in the case of methyl mercury, may be taking place at lower concentrations than previously thought, but this is proving difficult to establish because the suspected toxic effects are subtle and their mechanisms complex. Methyl mercury is of particular concern because it can accumulate in the food chain to reach high concentrations. It is a poison for the nervous system. Exposure during pregnancy is of most concern, because it may harm the development of the unborn baby's brain. Some studies suggest that small increases in exposure may affect the heart and circulatory system, and may cause even cancer also. The inhalation of elemental mercury vapours can cause neurological and behavioural disorders, such as tremors, emotional instability, insomnia, memory loss, neuromuscular changes and headaches. They can also harm the kidneys and thyroid. High exposures may also lead to deaths.

67. The Kashmir valley is an oval-shaped basin, trending in the NNW-SSE direction. It is bounded by lofty and glacier-chiselled mountain chains of the Himalayas. It is an inter-mountain valley fill, comprising unconsolidated gravel sand and mud succession appearing as plateaus above the present plain of Jhelum and its tributaries. These plateau-like terraces are called 'Karewas' or 'Vudra' in the local language. Despite consistent erosion since a couple of million years, about half of the valley is still occupied by the Karewa sediments, which are dominantly lacustrine in origin. Due to the rise of Pirpanjal, the drainage was impounded and a lake of about 5000 sq. km area was developed and thus formed the basin. Karewa sediments are witness to and treasure of many human civilisations and habitations.

68. Greater Himalaya is the highest range of Himalayas. This range is separated from Lesser Himalayas by Main Central Thrust and lies north of it. The world's highest peak Mount Everest and some other tallest peaks are in this range. Besides a few other states, the state of Meghalaya is also a part of Greater Himalaya. Meghalaya is mostly mountainous, with stretches of valley and highland plateaus, and it is geologically rich with rich deposits of valuable minerals like coal, limestone, uranium and sillimanite.

70. During solar eclipse, the moon comes in between the sun and the earth. However, there are 5 stages in the natural process of eclipse if it happens to be a total solar eclipse. These 5 stages are elucidated below:

(*i*) **Partial eclipse begins (first contact):** The moon's shadow starts becoming visible over the sun's disc. The sun looks as if a bite has been taken from it.

(*ii*) **Total eclipse begins (Second contact):** Almost the whole disc of the sun is covered by the moon. Observers in the path of the moon's umbra may be able to see Baily's beads and the diamond ring effect.

(*iii*) **Maximum eclipse or totality:** The moon completely covers the disc of the sun. Only the sun's corona remains visible. This is the most dramatic stage of a Total Solar Eclipse. At this time, the sky goes dark, temperatures fall drastically and birds and animals often keep quiet.

(*iv*) **Total eclipse ends (third contact):** The moon's shadow starts moving away and the sun reappears.

(*v*) **Partial eclipse ends (fourth contact):** The moon stops overlapping the sun's disc. The eclipse ends at this stage.

71. Acceleration, in physics, is the rate of change of velocity of an object. An object's acceleration is the net result of any and all forces acting on the object, as described by Newton's Second Law. The SI unit for acceleration is metre per second squared (ms^{-2}). Accelerations are vector quantities (they have magnitude and direction) and add according to the parallelogram law. As a vector, the calculated net force is equal to the product of the object's mass (a scalar quantity) and its acceleration.

74. The answers in Codes 2 and 4 are correct, which are given below with their combined explanation:

In most of the kitchens, an entire drawer are found to be full of reusable plastic containers that are used to store and reheat leftovers. After all, these things are handy, lightweight, and easy to store besides being cheap. What many people don't think about is that many of their plastic dishes and storage containers are leaching chemicals into their food, especially if they are using #3 or #7 plastics, or any hard plastic that's "shatterproof." These plastics contain Bisphenol A (BPA), a chemical that, once ingested, mimics estrogen in our bodies and are proved very harmful for human health. So the use of plastic coffee/tea mugs and plastic water storage bottles must be avoided to prevent such diseases as affect health.

75. Nagarjuna Sagar Dam was built across the Krishna river at Nagarjuna Sagar where the river is forming boundary between Nalgonda district of Telangana state and Guntur district of Andhra Pradesh state in India. The dam created a water reservoir whose gross storage capacity is 11,472,000,000 cubic metres (4.051×10^{11} cu ft). The dam is 490 feet (150 m) tall from its deepest foundation and 0.99 miles (1.6 km) long with 26 flood gates, which are 42 feet (13 m) wide and 45 feet (14 m) tall. Nagarjuna Sagar was the earliest in the series of large infrastructure projects termed as "modern temples" initiated for achieving the Green Revolution in India. It is also one of the earliest multi-purpose irrigation and hydro-electric projects in India.

76. Both the statements are correct, which are given below with their elaborations:

(*i*) Rajmahal Highlands consist of lava flow deposits and are described as the concrete base for the study of geology in Indian context. The study area has earliest Archaean to recent Quaternary rocks and sediments. One of the most important events in the study area is the volcanic eruption, which makes Rajmahal Traps. Such a huge volume of basaltic magma on the continental crust has profound effect on crustal evolution.

(*ii*) Bundelkhand Uplands (24°-26°30' N and 78° 10' - 81° 30' E) is bounded by the Yamuna river in the north, the Vindhyan Plateau in the south, the Chambal in the north-west and Panna-Ajaigarh ranges in the south-east. The region mainly consists of crystalline igneous and metamorphic rocks (the Bundelkhand gneiss). Here the lower Vindhyans are found in the form of Bhander, Rewa and Kaimur series while shales are best developed in the centre.

79. Biomass power is carbon neutral electricity generated from renewable organic waste that would otherwise be dumped in landfills, openly burned, or left as fodder for forest fires. When burned, the energy in biomass is released as heat. If you have a fireplace, you already are participating in the use of biomass as the wood you burn in it is a biomass fuel. Therefore, biomass is a conventional energy source.

80. Also known as nitrogen pentoxide, N_2O_5 is one of the binary nitrogen oxides, a family of compounds that only contain nitrogen and oxygen. It is an unstable and potentially dangerous oxidiser that once was used as a reagent when dissolved inchloroform for nitrations but has largely been superseded by NO_2BF_4 (nitronium tetrafluoroborate).

N_2O_5 is a rare example of a compound that adopts two structures depending on the conditions: most commonly, it is a salt; but under some conditions, it is a polar molecule:

$$[NO_2^+][NO_3^-] \rightleftharpoons N_2O_5$$

81. Sodium bicarbonate (IUPAC name: sodium hydrogen carbonate) is a chemical compound with the formula $NaHCO_3$. It is a salt composed of sodium ions and bicarbonate ions. Sodium bicarbonate is a white solid that is crystalline but often appears as a fine powder. It has a slightly salty, alkaline taste resembling that of washing soda (sodium carbonate). The natural mineral form is nahcolite. It is a component of the mineral natron and is found dissolved in many mineral springs. It is among the food additives encoded by European Union, identified as E 500. Since it has long been known and is widely used, the salt has many related names such as baking soda, bread soda, cooking soda, and bicarbonate of soda.

82. Following statements with their respective Codes 1, 3 and 4 are correct and their explanations are also given below:

Statement 1: DNA or deoxyribonucleic acid is the hereditary material in humans and almost all other organisms. Nearly every cell in a person's body has the same DNA. Most DNA is located in the cell nucleus (where it is called nuclear DNA), but an iota of DNA can also be found in the mitochondria (where it is called mitochondrial DNA or mtDNA).

Statement 3: Most DNA molecules consist of two biopolymer strands coiled around each other to form a double helix. The two DNA strands are known as polynucleotides since they are composed of simpler units called nucleotides. Each nucleotide is composed of a nitrogen-containing nucleobase-either cytosine

(C), guanine (G), adenine (A), or thymine (T)-as well as a sugar called deoxyribose and a phosphate group. The nucleotides are joined to one another in a chain by covalent bonds between the sugar of one nucleotide and the phosphate of the next, resulting in an alternating sugar-phosphate backbone.

Statement 4: Although most DNA is packaged in chromosomes within the nucleus, mitochondria also have a small amount of their own DNA. This genetic material is known as mitochondrial DNA or mtDNA. Mitochondria (illustration) are structures within cells that convert the energy from food into a form that cells can use. Each cell contains hundreds to thousands of mitochondria, which are located in the fluid that surrounds the nucleus (the cytoplasm).

83. Set up in 1767, the *Survey of India* is responsible for all topographic control, surveys and mapping of India. Topographic maps use contour lines to show the shape of Earth's surface. The spacing of contour lines indicates how steep a slope is. The *Survey of India* is India's central engineering agency in charge of mapping and surveying, and also one of the oldest Engineering Departments of the Government of India.

84. Dresden Line is not an international boundary line. The city of Dresden is about 100 miles south of Berlin. The autobahn goes directly from Berlin Schonefeld airport to the outskirts of Dresden meaning that the keen photographer can be at the lineside within two house of landing. Three working narrow gauge lines are to be found in the Dresden area. These are the liners from Frietal - Kipsdorf, Radebeul Ostr - Radeburg and Cranzahl - Oberwiesenrtal. All three are 750mm gauge lines, branching off from the main DB system.

86. It is true that brightness of a star depends on its size, temperature and distance from the earth. When we have a glance of sky at night, we find some stars much brighter than others. It is because of its composition and how far it is from earth. Astronomers define star brightness in terms of apparent magnitude (how bright the star appears from our planet) and absolute magnitude (how bright the star appears at a standard distance of 32.6 light years, or 10 parsecs). Astronomers also measure luminosity — the amount of energy (light) that a star emits from its surface. Measuring star brightness is an idea of yore, but today astronomers use more precise tools to obtain the calculation.

87. Sublimation is the transition of a substance directly from the solid to the gas phase without passing through the intermediate liquid phase. Sublimation is anendothermic phase transition that occurs at temperatures and pressures below a substance's triple point in its phase diagram. The reverse process of sublimation is desublimation or deposition, in which a substance passes directly from a gas to a solid phase. Sublimation has also been used as a generic term to describe phase changes between solid and gas that avoid the liquid state without specifying the direction of the transition.

88. Water gas is a mixture of carbon monoxide and hydrogen (not water). It is produced when steam is passed over red-hot coke (carbon).

$$C + H_2O = CO + H_2$$

Water gas is so named because water (steam) is a source for its production. Both CO and H_2 are inflammable gases, and so water gas is used as a fuel.

89. Statements 1, 2 and 3 are correct, which are explained below:

1. Haplodiploidy is a sex-determination system. In this system, sex is determined by the number of sets of chromosomes an individual receives. An offspring formed from the union of a sperm and an egg develops as a female, and an unfertilised egg develops as a male. This means that the males have half the number of chromosomes that a female has, and are haploid.
2. A worker bee is any female (eusocial) bee that lacks the full reproductive capacity (*i.e.* being sterile) of the colony's queen bee; under most circumstances, this is correlated to an increase in certain non-reproductive activities relative to a queen, as well. Worker bees are diploid and occur in many bee species other than honeybees, but this is by far the most familiar colloquial use of the term.
3. In the life cycle of honeybees, a worker and a queen are identical when in the egg and young larva stages. The difference between the two comes about through the feeding of the larva. Food is provisioned in to the cells of developing larvae by adult worker bees that secrete brood jelly from their mandibular glands after ingesting pollen, nectar, and bee bred. Queens are raised entirely on royal jelly, while workers are fed various combinations of larval jelly, pollen, and nectar.

90. The Amarkantak Hills is the source of the following rivers (as given with their respective codes), which are elaborated below:

1. The Narmada originates in Amarkantak Hills, the highest peak of the Vindhya Range, it flows westward through Madhya Pradesh and Gujarat before finally ending its journey in the Gulf of Khambat. The 1300 km long Narmada is the fifth longest river in India, and the oldest.
2. Apart from the Narmada, the Tapti (Tapi) is the only river that flows westward and falls into the Arabian Sea, in the Gulf of Khambat, to be precise.

With 724 km of its length, Tapti is agriculturally very important as it drains an area of over 65,145sq km spread over Madhya Pradesh, Maharashtra and Gujarat. This river originates in Amarkantak Hills at a height of 762 metres in Betul district of Madhya Pradesh (to the south of the Satpura Range). The Tapti journeys almost parallel to the Narmada, though it is much shorter in length than the Narmada and has a smaller catchment area.

3. The Son, also called the Maikalsut because its source is in the Maikal Hills, originates from a mountain called Amarkantak Hills in the Maikal Range.

91. Both Statements 1 and 2 are correct and their combined explanations are given below:

An equinox is an astronomical event in which the plane of Earth's equator passes through the centre of the Sun, which occurs twice a year, on around 21 March and 23 September. On an equinox, day and night are of approximately equal duration all over the planet. They are not exactly equal, however, due to the angular size of the sun and atmospheric refraction. To avoid this ambiguity, the word equilux is sometimes used to mean a day in which the durations of light and darkness are equal.

97. The answers in Codes 1 and 2 are correct, which are given below with their explanations:

1. High blood cholesterol is one of the major risk factors for heart disease. A risk factor is a condition that increases chance of getting a disease. In fact, the higher the blood cholesterol level, the greater the risk for developing heart disease or having a heart attack.

2. HDL (good) cholesterol protects against heart disease, so for HDL, higher numbers are better. A level less than 40 mg/dL is low and is considered a major risk factor because it increases risk for developing heart disease. HDL levels of 60 mg/dL or more help to lower the risk for heart disease.

98. Temperate coniferous forest is a terrestrial biome found in temperate regions of the world with warm summers and cool winters and adequate rainfall to sustain a forest. In most temperate coniferous forests, evergreen conifers predominate, while some are a mix of conifers and broadleaf evergreen trees and/or broadleaf deciduous trees. Temperate evergreen forests are common in the coastal areas of regions that have mild winters and heavy rainfall, or inland in drier climates or mountain areas. Coniferous forests are found in the United States, Canada, Europe, and Asia.

Besides a number of other species of tree, Spruce and Cedar trees inhabit these forests. Spruces are large trees, from about 20-60 metres (about 60-200 feet) tall when mature, and can be distinguished by their whorled branches and conical form. Cedar tree is a common name for cedar wood, used for several different trees.

100. Matter can exist in three different states, which we see in the form of solid, liquid and gas. The correct order of their compressibility is Solid < Liquid < Gas. The reason behind it is as, Solids have the highest inter-molecular face of attraction between its molecules; Liquids have medium or average inter-molecular force of attraction as compared to gases and solids: and Gases have very less inter-molecular force of attraction between its molecules.

104. The options given in Codes 1 and 2 are correctly matched and their explanations are given below:

1. Malaria is transmitted among humans by female mosquitoes of the genus Anopheles. Female mosquitoes take blood meals to carry out egg production, and such blood meals are the link between the human and the mosquito hosts in the parasite life cycle.

2. Chikungunya virus is transmitted to people through mosquito bites. Mosquitoes become infected when they feed on a person already infected with the virus. Infected mosquitoes can then spread the virus to other people through bites. Chikungunya virus is most often spread to people by Aedes aegypti and Aedes albopictus mosquitoes. These are the same mosquitoes that transmit dengue virus. They bite mostly during the daytime.

105. The statements 3 & 4 given with their explanation below, are correct:

3. Ubiquity of insects is a common phenomenon as insects are the most diverse group of animals on this planet. They are found in all kinds of habitats. Scientists estimate that there are 4 to 6 million species in existence and discover approximately 10,000 new ones every year. As invertebrates, insects have an exoskeleton instead of an internal structure. They undergo either complete or incomplete metamorphosis, undergoing radical changes in appearance between egg and adult.

4. Arboreal animals mean those which mostly live and feed on trees. Besides monkeys, lorises and all from ape family, there are also some other animals that are adapted to life in the trees. Arboreal animals spend most of their time scampering around in trees rather than on the ground, in the air, or water - sometimes they enjoy playing on trees and sometimes eating fruits of those trees.

106. Export Processing Zones (EPZ) is a type of Free Trade Zone (FTZ), set up generally in developing countries by their governments to promote industrial and commercial exports. Besides providing the benefits of FTZ, these zones offer other incentives such as exemptions from certain and business regulations. Also called Development Economic Zone or Special Economic Zone, the value of EPZ is so much as this is regarded as engine for economic growth supported by quality infrastructure and complemented by an attractive fiscal package.

107. The northern frontiers of India are defined largely by the Himalayan mountain range, where the country borders China, Bhutan, and Nepal. Its western border with Pakistan lies in the Punjab Plain and the Thar Desert. In the far northeast, the China Hills and Kachin Hills, deeply forested mountainous regions, separate India from Burma. On the east, its border with Bangladesh is largely defined by the Khasi Hills and Mizo Hills, and the watershed region of the Indo-Gangetic Plain. As a whole, the characteristic features of North-Eastern Frontiers lie in deserts, fertile plains and moderately forested mountains.

111. Hexane is an alkane of six carbon atoms, with the chemical formula C_6H_{14}. The term may refer to any of the five structural isomers with that formula, or to a mixture of them. In IUPAC nomenclature, however, hexane is the unbranched isomer (n-hexane); the other four isomers are named as methylated derivatives of pentane and butane. Hexanes are significant constituents of gasoline. They are all colourless liquids at room temperature, odourless when pure, with boiling points between 50 and 70 °C. They are widely used as cheap, relatively safe, largely unreactive, and easily evaporated non-polar solvents.

112. A. Proteins are large, complex molecules that are critical for the normal functioning of the human body. They are essential for the structure, function, and regulation of the body's tissues and organs. Proteins are made up of hundreds of smaller units called amino acids, which are attached to one another in the form of a long chain through peptide bonds. You can think of a protein as a string of beads and each bead is an amino acid.

B. Monosaccharides are the simplest carbohydrates and are often called single sugars. They are the building blocks from which all bigger carbohydrates are made. Monosaccharides have the general molecular formula $(CH_2O)_n$ where n can be 3, 5 or 6. They can be classified according to the number of carbon atoms in a molecule.

C. A set of five nitrogenous bases is used in the construction of nucleotides, which in turn build up the nucleic acids like DNA and RNA. These bases are vitally important because the sequencing of them in DNA and RNA is the way information is stored.

D. One major class of lipids is called glycerolipids, which are composed of glycerol and fatty acids. Glycerol has three carbon atoms, each of which has a hydroxyl (-OH) group bound to it. Fatty acids are fairly long linear hydrocarbon chains with a carboxylic acid group at one end. Fatty acids are named based on the number of carbon atoms and carbon-carbon double bounds in the chain.

113. The sand hills in the desert of Thar region are clothed to a certain extent with shrubs and coarse grass, and, around the villages, these afford pasture to the flocks and herds. But in this part, there are large extents of shifting sands, locally termed 'dhrian'. They vary in size from two to three miles across to ten or twelve. On them, there is no trace of vegetation, and their surface is ever changing.

116. The options given in Codes 1 and 2 are correctly matched and their descriptions are given below:

1. Protected and known for tiger reserve, Ranthambhore Park is one of the biggest and most renowned national parks in Northern India. The park is located in the Sawai Madhopur district of south-eastern Rajasthan.
2. Periyar National Park and Wildlife Sanctuary (PNP) is a protected area in the districts of Idukki, Kottayam and Pathanamthitta in Kerala, India. It is notable as an elephant reserve and also a tiger reserve.

117. Nuclear Energy is energy stored in the nucleus of an atom—the energy that holds the nucleus together; it does not mean that it can be stored somewhere else like in battery etc. The energy can be released when the nuclei are combined or split apart. Nuclear power plants split the nuclei of uranium atoms in a process called fission. The sun combines the nuclei of hydrogen atoms in a process called fusion. Scientists are working on creating fusion energy on earth, so that someday there might be fusion power plants.

119. At the height of 13,999 ft, Jelep La is a high altitude mountain pass linking Lhasa to India. It nestles between India and Tibet in the eastern part of the Sikkim in India. The word, 'Jelep La' is of Tibetan origin and it means "the lovely level pass". It is truly the most level among all the passes between Sikkim and Tibet.

121. The pairs in Code (b) is matched incorrectly, as Second Schedule does not deal in Forms of oaths and affirmation; rather it is dealt by Third Schedule. In fact, Second Schedule deals in Salary of President, Governors, Chief Judges, Judges of High Court and Supreme Court, Comptroller and Auditor General.

122. Both the statements are correct and they are elucidated below:

Article 3 of the Constitution of India empowers the Parliament to form a new state by separation of a part of territory of an established state or to unite two or more states or parts of states or by uniting any territory to a part of any state by passing a resolution in simple majority. This article provides that area of any state can reduce or increase and alter the boundaries or change the name of a state. Even though the state boundaries are subject to change, their area cannot be acquired by a foreign state.

Article 370 of the Indian Constitution is an article that grants special autonomous status to the state of Jammu and Kashmir. The article is drafted in Part XXI of the Constitution, which relates to Temporary, Transitional and Special Provisions. The state's constituent assembly was empowered to recommend the articles of the Indian Constitution to be applied to the state or to abrogate the Article 370 altogether. After the state constituent assembly has dissolved itself without recommending abrogation, the Article 370 is deemed to have become a permanent feature of the Indian Constitution.

123. The Speaker may, at any time, resign from office by writing under his/her hand to the Deputy Speaker, who plays the same role in the House in absence/place of the Speaker. The Speaker can be removed from office only on a resolution of the House passed by a majority of all the then members of the House. Such a resolution has to satisfy some conditions like: it should be specific with respect to the charges and it should not contain arguments, inferences, ironical expressions, imputations or defamatory statements, etc.

124. Kailash Satyarthi (born 'Kailash Sharma' on 11 January 1954) is an Indian advocate of children's rights and education and an activist against child labour. He founded the Bachpan Bachao Andolan (Save the Childhood Movement) in 1980 and has acted to protect the rights of more than 83,000 children from 144 countries. It is largely because of Satyarthi's work and activism that the International Labour Organisation adopted Convention No. 182 on the worst forms of child labour, which is now a principal guideline for governments around the world. His work is recognised through various national and international honours and awards, including the Nobel Peace Prize of 2014, which he shared with Malala Yousafzai of Pakistan.

125.
1. Ensuring financial Inclusion of the poor can be called as a movement, initiated by various committees of Reserve Bank of India, to achieve the goal of bringing the low-income and disadvantaged sections of economy into the ambit of banking and financial services. As part of the National Mission on Financial Inclusion, the Pradhan Mantri Jan-Dhan Yojana (PMJDY) is an integrated approach of Government of India to bring universal access to banking facilities to every household, improve financial literacy, access to credit, insurance & pension facilities to every individual.
2. So far as enhancing financial literacy is concerned, government and banks in an effective co-ordinated manner will have to launch a massive campaign to create full awareness among poor households for their better understanding of the Jan Dhan Yojana (JDY) and improve the level of education/financial literacy that can help them avail the benefits under the scheme along with the responsibilities attached to it.
3. The JDY also provides facility of accidental insurance cover up to rupee one lac without any charge for the account holder. It will focus on provision of micro-insurance and enrolment in pension services.
4. Under JDY, anyone who is Indian citizen above the age of 10 years and does not have a bank account, can open the account with zero balance. Account can be opened in any bank branch or Business Correspondent (Bank Mitr) outlet, specially designed for the purpose of opening the account under this scheme.

126. The correct answer lies in Code 1 only. A registered political party in India is recognised as a National Party only if it secures at least six per cent of the total valid votes polled in four or more states in a general election to the Lok Sabha or to the State Legislative Assemblies, Or in other words if that party fulfils any one of the following three conditions:

1. The party wins 2% of seats in the Lok Sabha (as of 2014, 11 seats) from at least 3 different States.
2. At a General Election to Lok Sabha or Legislative Assembly, the party polls 6% of votes in four States and in addition, it wins 4 Lok Sabha seats.
3. A party gets recognition as State Party in four or more States.

128. Faster, Sustainable and More Inclusive Growth best explains the broad vision and aspirations of the Twelfth Five-Year Plan (2012 - 2017). The plan aims towards the betterment of the infrastructural projects of the nation avoiding all types of bottlenecks. The document presented by the Planning Commission is aimed to attract private investments of up to US$1 trillion in the infrastructural growth in the 12th five-year plan, which will also ensure a reduction in subsidy burden of the government to 1.5 per cent from 2 per cent of the GDP (gross domestic product).

129. Nabhah Sprsam Diptam (Touching the sky with glory), which is the motto of Indian Air Force, has been taken from 11th chapter of the Gita, the discourse given by lord Krishna to Arjuna on the battlefield of Kurukshetra during the Great War of Mahabharata. The lord is showing his supreme divine form to Arjuna and the great form of the lord is reaching/touching the sky with glory, evoking fear and loss of self-control in the mind of Arjuna. Similarly, the Indian Air Force, as India's sentinels in the sky, aims to overcome the adversaries by applying aerospace power in defence of the nation.

130. Amending the Constitution of India is the process of making changes to the nation's fundamental law or supreme law. The amendment procedure has been laid down in Part XX (Article 368) of the Constitution of India. This procedure ensures the sanctity of the Constitution of India and keeps a check on arbitrary power of the Parliament of India.

132. Article 58 of the Constitution of India sets the eligibility conditions, which a presidential candidate needs to qualify to become the President of India. All the three statements consecutively given in their respective Codes 1, 2 and 3 are correct, as they are truly relevant concerning the election as the President of India.

133. Nepal is being governed as per the Constitution of Nepal, which came into effect on Sept. 20, 2015, replacing the Interim Constitution of 2007. The Constitution was drafted by the Second Constituent Assembly following the failure of the First Constituent Assembly to produce a constitution in its mandated period. The Constitution was endorsed by 90% of the total lawmakers. Out of 598 CA members, 507 voted in favour of the Constitution while 25 voted against and 66 members of the Constituent Assembly mainly representing political parties based in Terai boycotted the final debates on the Constitution as a protest against states delimitation and inclusion of minorities and Madhesi population in the national and public life.

134. In a strident night session on Arthur Ashe Stadium, after the start of play was delayed by more than three hours because of rain, Roger Federer looked to have a real chance in the third set. However, Djokovic broke the Federer serve six times and saved 19 of 23 break points as he battled his way to a 27th win in 28 Grand Slam matches in 2015.

135. Every citizen of India is given the right to freedom in Article 19 that guarantees six freedoms. However, there are a few exceptions, as per which the citizens of India do not have fundamental rights (such as) to acquire, hold and dispose of property. It includes freedom to practise any profession or to carry on any occupation, trade or business on which the State may impose reasonable restrictions in the interest of the general public. Thus, there is no right to carry on a business, which is dangerous or immoral. Also, professional or technical qualifications may be prescribed for practising any profession or carrying on any trade.

136. The Charter Act of 1833 marked the beginning of a system of government for all India. Later, it adopted a representative character, which distinguished it fundamentally from the earlier rule of despotism. It marked the beginning of the Indianisation in services. It also tried to separate and decentralise executive and legislative functions.

137. In the given two statements about Rashtrakuta kings, neither the statement given in Code 1 is correct, nor that of 2. Rashtrakuta kings were not only the patron of Shaivism, but also that of Vaishnavism and Shaktaism. Almost their all inscriptions began with an invocation to Vishnu or Shiva. The Sanjan inscriptions tell of King Amoghavarsha-I sacrificing a finger from his left hand at the Lakshmi Temple at Kolhapur to avert a calamity in his kingdom. All these evidences corroborate the fact that their deference did not confine to Shaivism only but they revered other deities also.

As far as the use of language was concerned, Kannada became more prominent as a literary language during the Rashtrakuta rule with its script and literature showing remarkable growth, dignity and productivity. This period effectively marked the end of the classical Prakrit and Sanskrit era.

138. The National Green Tribunal ban on coal mining and transportation of coal in Meghalaya's Jaintia Hills region has resulted in many of those engaged in the activity switching to turmeric farming for their livelihood. For the past one year, these coal-miners, who earlier practised unscientific mining and transportation of coal, have taken to cultivation of famed curcumin-rich Lakadong turmeric varieties at their villages in East Jaintia Hills District.

139. Statement in Code 4 is correct, as the first act of the Revolt of 1857 began after an East India Company sepoy Mangal Pandey fired at Mr. Baugh, a British officer in Barrackpore near Calcutta. The resentment against the cruelties of the British imperialism was already growing among the Indians when it was rumoured that the cartridges supplied to the soldiers had cow's and pig's fat as the device to use it was by opening its seal by mouth, which was a direct attack on the religious sentiments of both the Hindu and Muslim soldiers. When the sepoys refused to accept such cartridge, they were berated and punished that ensued the rebellion, starting with fire at the British officer by Mangal Pandey.

141. The following statements, which are given in Codes 1, 3, and 4, are correct and given with their explanations:

1. Division of labour often involves specialised economic activity, as the workers are placed to work in a particular field/activity so that they can have specialisation in their respective nature of work.
3. It involves a number of workers in the same activities so that an adequate number of them get specialised to work in a particular domain.
4. In such case, it is but natural for individuals to depend on others to meet their various needs, as they engage in only one single activity and become specialists of that particular activity rather than being all-rounder.

143. Both the statements as given below with their respective codes and elaborations are correct:

1. It's surprising to know that it was the British who introduced the modern Madrasa to India and was revived by the last Marxist government of West Bengal, which is actually predominantly Hindu. Now it is a reinvigorated institution called Aliah University for the benefit of Muslims' Education. The WB Act XXVII of 2007, passed by the state government, made this possible. Aliah Madrasah, also called Calcutta Madrasah, was established by Warren Hasting, the first Governor General of India in 1780 for the study and teaching of Muslim law related subjects. Hastings himself called it Mohammedan College of Calcutta.
2. Established in 1791 in Banaras, Government Sanskrit College was a landmark college in India from where several notable teachers emerged. In 1958, it merged with Sampurnanand Sanskrit University. In 1791, during the period of British rule in India, Jonathan Duncan, the representative of the East India Company proposed the establishment of a Sanskrit college for development and preservation of the Sanskrit Vangmaya and to show that the English people were in favour of the development of the Indian culture. This was sanctioned by Governor General Lord Cornwallis. Kashi Naresh Mahip Narayan Singh donated a huge tract of land in the southern part of Banaras for construction of the college. Thus, Sanskrit College at Varanasi came into existence.

145. Henry David Thoreau (July 12, 1817 - May 6, 1862) was an American author, poet, philosopher, abolitionist, naturalist, tax resister, development critic, surveyor, and historian. A leading transcendentalist, Thoreau is best known for his book *Walden*, a reflection upon simple living in natural surroundings, and his essay *Resistance to Civil Government* (also known as *Civil Disobedience*), an argument for disobedience to an unjust state. Thoreau's philosophy of civil disobedience later influenced the political thoughts and actions of such notable figures as Leo Tolstoy, Mahatma Gandhi, and Martin Luther King, Jr. who all had almost similar thoughts.

146. Both the statements as given below with their respective codes and elaborations are correct:

1. Written in Sanskrit, the *Arthashastra* by Kautilya is an ancient Indian treatise on statecraft, economic policy and military strategy. Likely to be the work of several authors over centuries, Kautilya, also identified as Vishnugupta and Chanakya, is traditionally credited as the author of the text. The latter was a scholar at Takshashila, the teacher and guardian of Emperor Chandragupta Maurya. However, scholars have questioned this identification.
2. The main concerns of Kautilya's *Arthashastra* are theoretical issues like the origins of the state. It depicts a bureaucratic welfare state, in fact some kind of socialised monarchy, in which the central government administers the details of the economy for the common good.

148. The government's flagship scheme, Integrated Power Development Scheme (IPDS) seeks to ensure 24×7 power for all, is aimed at strengthening the power sub-transmission and distribution network in urban areas across country, as unravelled by Union Minister of State for Power Piyush Goyal. The projects worth ₹ 3,268 crore, covering 247 towns, have been sanctioned so far under IPDS, of which projects worth ₹ 1,067 crore for 23 circles covering 91 towns have been sanctioned for Uttar Pradesh. The minister said that it included ₹ 432 crore for Kashi area and ₹ 140 crore for remaining Varanasi town.

149. Both the statements as given below with their respective codes and elaborations are correct:

1. It was the period of Keshab Chandra when he separated from Raja Ram Mohun Roy's association. Under Keshab's leadership, the Brahmo Samaj of India succeeded in getting the Government pass the Act III of 1872, which abolished early marriage of girls and polygamy, and sanctioned widow re-marriage and inter-caste marriage for those who did not profess any recognised faith such as Hinduism and Islam.
2. When Keshab Chandra gave his fourteen-year old daughter Suniti Devi in marriage to the Maharaja of Cooch Behar in 1878, it served as the last straw on the camel's back that ensued with the second schism. Those who differed set up Sadharan Brahmo Samaj in 1878. After the first schism, Devendranath's Brahmo Samaj gradually receded into the background so did Keshab Chandra's Brahma Samaj which was now called 'the new dispensation or a synthesis of all religions' or Nababidhan.

PAPER-II : MATHEMATICS

1. From cube root of unity

$$\omega = \left(\frac{-1+\sqrt{3}i}{2}\right) \text{ and } \omega^2 = \left(\frac{-1-\sqrt{3}i}{2}\right)$$

Projection of ω

$$\theta = \tan^{-1}\left(\frac{\frac{\sqrt{3}}{2}}{-\frac{1}{2}}\right) = \tan^{-1}\left(-\sqrt{3}\right)$$

$$\theta = \pi - \tan^{-1}\left(\sqrt{3}\right) = \pi - \frac{\pi}{3} = \frac{2\pi}{3}$$

Projection of ω^2

$$\alpha = \tan^{-1}\left(\frac{-\frac{\sqrt{3}}{2}}{-\frac{1}{2}}\right) = \pi + \tan^{-1}\left(\sqrt{3}\right)$$

$$= \pi + \frac{\pi}{3} = \frac{4\pi}{3}$$

So, angle between ω and ω^2

$$= \frac{4\pi}{3} - \frac{2\pi}{3} = \frac{2\pi}{3} \text{ or } = 120°.$$

3. $x^2 - Px + 4 > 0$ is true when

Discriminant $D > 0$

$$(-P)^2 - 4 \times 4 > 0$$
$$P^2 - 16 > 0$$
$$P^2 > 16$$
$$\Rightarrow \quad P > 4 \text{ and } P < -4$$
$$P = (-\infty, -4) \cup (4, \infty)$$
$$\therefore \quad |P| > 4.$$

4. $Z = x + iy = \left(\frac{1}{\sqrt{2}} - \frac{i}{\sqrt{2}}\right)^{-25}$

$$= \left(\cos\frac{\pi}{4} - i\sin\frac{\pi}{4}\right)^{-25}$$

$$= \cos\left(-\frac{25\pi}{4}\right) - i\sin\left(-\frac{25\pi}{4}\right)$$

$$= \cos\left(-\frac{\pi}{4}\right) - i\sin\left(-\frac{\pi}{4}\right)$$

$$= \frac{1}{\sqrt{2}} - i\left(-\frac{1}{\sqrt{2}}\right) = \frac{1}{\sqrt{2}} + i\left(\frac{1}{\sqrt{2}}\right)$$

$$\frac{z-\sqrt{2}}{z-i\sqrt{2}} = \frac{\frac{1}{\sqrt{2}} + i\frac{1}{\sqrt{2}} - \sqrt{2}}{\frac{1}{\sqrt{2}} + i\frac{1}{\sqrt{2}} - i\sqrt{2}}$$

$$= \frac{-\frac{1}{\sqrt{2}} + i\frac{1}{\sqrt{2}}}{\frac{1}{\sqrt{2}} - i\frac{1}{\sqrt{2}}} = \frac{e^{i\frac{3\pi}{4}}}{e^{i\left(\frac{\pi}{4}\right)}}$$

$$= e^{i\left(\frac{3\pi}{4} - \left(\frac{-\pi}{4}\right)\right)}$$

$$= e^{i\pi}$$

$\therefore$ Fundamental amplitude $= \pi$.

5. Let, $\quad f(x) = \text{In}\left(\frac{1-x}{1+x}\right)$

$$f(x_1) - f(x_2) = \text{In}\left(\frac{1-x_1}{1+x_1}\right) - \text{In}\left(\frac{1-x_2}{1+x_2}\right)$$

$$= \text{In}\left(\frac{(1-x_1)}{(1+x_1)} \times \frac{(1+x_2)}{(1-x_2)}\right)$$

$$= \text{In}\left(\frac{1-x_1+x_2-x_1x_2}{1+x_1-x_2-x_1x_2}\right) \quad ...(i)$$

$$\text{Now, } f\left(\frac{x_1-x_2}{1-x_1x_2}\right) = \text{In}\left(\frac{1-\frac{(x_1-x_2)}{1-x_1x_2}}{1+\frac{(x_1-x_2)}{1-x_1x_2}}\right)$$

$$= \text{In}\left\{\frac{1-x_1x_2-x_1+x_2}{1-x_1x_2+x_1-x_2}\right\} \quad ...(ii)$$

From (i) and (ii), we have

$$f(x_1) - f(x_2) = f\left(\frac{x_1-x_2}{1-x_1x_2}\right)$$

$$\therefore \quad f(x) = \text{In}\left(\frac{1+x}{1+x}\right).$$

6. Let, $f(x) = y$, then $y \geq 0$

and $f(x) = y$

$$\Rightarrow \quad \frac{x^2}{x^2+1} = y$$

$$\Rightarrow \quad \frac{x^2+1}{x^2} = \frac{1}{y} \text{ for } y > 0$$

$$\Rightarrow \quad \frac{1}{x^2} = \frac{1-y}{y} \Rightarrow x = \frac{\sqrt{y}}{1-y}$$

Now, $x \in R$, if $\frac{\sqrt{y}}{1-y}$ is real

$$\Rightarrow \quad \frac{y}{1-y} \geq 0$$

$$\Rightarrow \quad 0 \leq y < 1$$

$\therefore$ Range of $f(x) = [0, 1)$.

7.

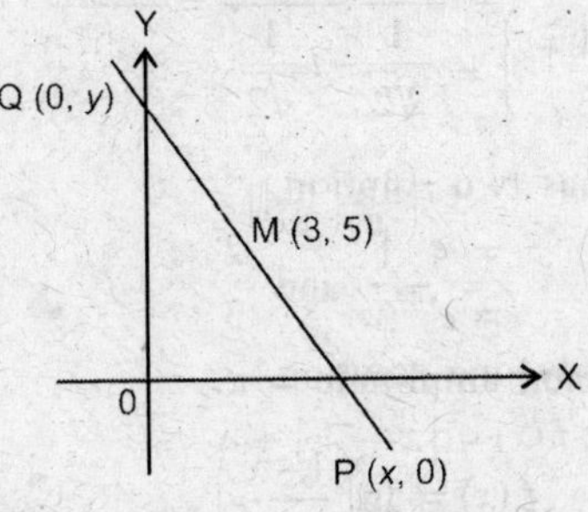

Let, Point P = $(x, 0)$

Q = $(0, y)$

$$\text{Mid point M } (3, 5) = \left(\frac{x+0}{2}, \frac{0+y}{2}\right)$$

$$\frac{x}{2} = 3 \Rightarrow x = 6$$

$$\frac{y}{2} = 5 \Rightarrow y = 10$$

$$\text{Area of triangle OPQ} = \frac{1}{2}|\text{OP.OQ}| = \frac{1}{2}|6 \times 10|$$

$$= 30 \text{ square units.}$$

8.

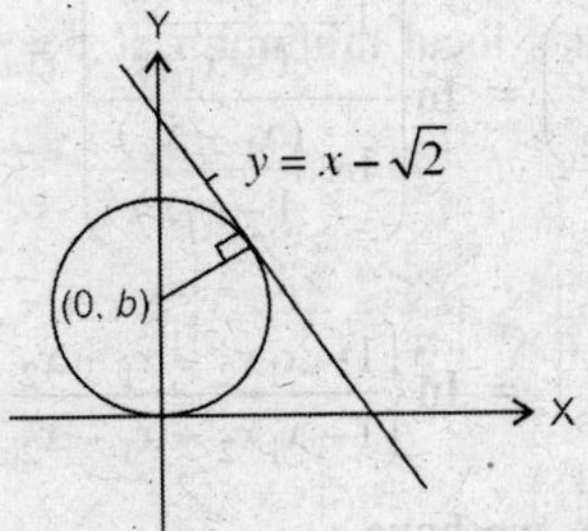

Length of perpendicular = radius

$$b = \left|\frac{x - y - \sqrt{2}}{\sqrt{1+(-1)^2}}\right|$$

$$b = \left|\frac{0 - b - \sqrt{2}}{\sqrt{2}}\right|$$

$$\left(\sqrt{2}+1\right)b = \left|-\sqrt{2}\right|$$

$$b = \left|\frac{-\sqrt{2}}{\left(\sqrt{2}+1\right)}\right| = \left|\sqrt{2}-2\right|$$

$$\therefore \quad b = 2 - \sqrt{2}.$$

For Qs. Nos. 9-11

$$\text{A} = 4(\sin^2\theta + \cos^4\theta)$$

$$\text{A} = 4\frac{(1-\cos 2\theta)}{2} + \frac{(1+\cos 2\theta)^2}{2}$$

$$= 4\left[\frac{1}{2} - \frac{\cos 2\theta}{2} + \frac{1}{4} + \frac{1}{2}\cos 2\theta + \frac{1}{4}\cos^2 2\theta\right]$$

$$= 4\left[\frac{3}{4} + \frac{1}{4}\frac{(1+\cos 4\theta)}{2}\right]$$

$$= 3 + \frac{1}{2} + \frac{1}{2}\cos 4\theta \qquad (\text{Put } \theta = 0°)$$

$$= 3 + \frac{1}{2} + \frac{1}{2} = \frac{6+1+1}{2} = \frac{8}{2} = 4.$$

9. The maximum value of $f(\theta) = 4$.

10. The minimum value of $f(\theta)$

$$= 3 + \frac{1}{2} + \frac{1}{2}(-1) \qquad [\because \cos 180° = -1]$$

$$= 3 + \frac{1}{2} - \frac{1}{2} = 3.$$

11. $f(\theta) = 2$ No any solution.

$f(\theta) = \frac{7}{2}$ is the only solution

$$3 + \frac{1}{2} + (0) = \frac{7}{2} \qquad [\because \cos 90° = 0]$$

$\therefore$ Option B is correct.

For Qs. Nos. 12-13. $f(x) = x\,|x| - 1$

$$\therefore \quad f(x) = \begin{cases} x^2 - 1, & x \geq 0 \\ -x^2 - 1, & x < 0 \end{cases}$$

and

$$g(x) = \begin{cases} \frac{3x}{2}, & x > 0 \\ 2x, & x \leq 0 \end{cases}.$$

12. For $x \geq 0$,

Point of intersection

$$x^2 - 1 = \frac{3x}{2}$$

$$\Rightarrow \quad 2x^2 - 3x - 2 = 0$$

$$2x^2 - 4x + x - 2 = 0$$

$$x = 2 \text{ and } -\frac{1}{2}$$

For, $x \geq 0 \Rightarrow x = 2$

and $y = \dfrac{3 \times 2}{2} = 3$

For, $x < 0$, Point of intersection

$$-x^2 - 1 = 2x$$

$$\Rightarrow \quad x^2 + 2x + 1 = 0$$

$$x = -1$$

For, $x = -1$, $y = 2(-1) = -2$

Point of intersection = $(-1, -2)$.

13.

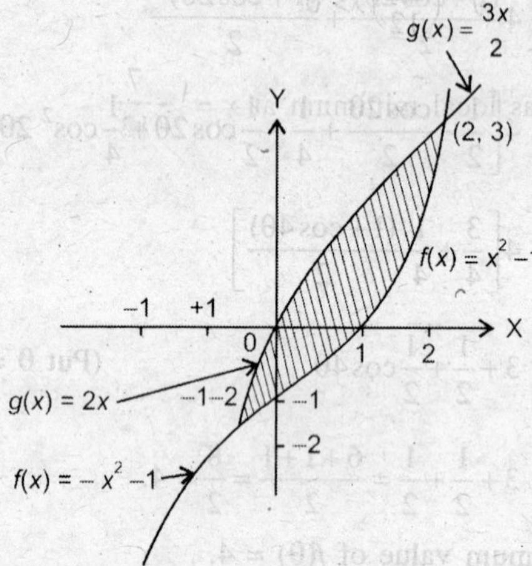

Area bounded by the curve

$$A = A_1 + A_2$$

Here, $A_1 = \left| \int_{-1}^{0} | f(x) - g(x) | dx \right|$

$$= \left| \int_{-1}^{0} (-x^2 - 1 - 2x) dx \right| = \left[\frac{-x^3}{3} - x - x^2 \right]_{-1}^{0}$$

$$= \left| -\frac{1}{3} - 1 + 1 \right| = \left| -\frac{1}{3} \right| = \frac{1}{3}$$

$$A_2 = \left| \int_{0}^{2} (g(x) - f(x)).dx \right| = \left| \int_{0}^{2} \left(\frac{3x}{2} - x^2 + 1 \right).dx \right|$$

$$= \left| \left(\frac{3x^2}{4} - \frac{x^3}{3} + x \right) \right|_{0}^{2} = \frac{3(2)^2}{4} - \frac{(2)^3}{3} + 2 = \frac{7}{3}$$

Area $A = A_1 + A_2$

$$= \frac{1}{3} + \frac{7}{3} = \frac{8}{3} \text{ square units}$$

14. $f(x) = \dfrac{27\left(x^{\frac{2}{3}} - x\right)}{4}$

when, $f(x) = 1$

then, $1 = \dfrac{27\left(x^{\frac{2}{3}} - x\right)}{4}$

$$4 = 27\left(x^{\frac{2}{3}} - x\right)$$

$$4 = 27\,(z^2 - z^3)$$

$$(z^2 - z^3) = \frac{4}{27}$$

For, $z = \dfrac{2}{3}$

$$\Rightarrow \left(\frac{2}{3}\right)^2 - \left(\frac{2}{3}\right)^3 = \frac{4 \times 3 - 8}{27} = \frac{4}{27}$$

Thus, $f(x) = 1$ have one solution,

For, $z = -\dfrac{1}{3}$

$$(z^2 - z^3) = \frac{4}{27}$$

$$\Rightarrow \left(\left(-\frac{1}{3}\right)^2 - \left(-\frac{1}{3}\right)^3 \right) = \frac{4}{27}$$

Thus, $f(x) = 1$, has two solution,

$$x = -\frac{1}{3} \text{ and } \frac{2}{3}.$$

15. $f(x) = -1$, has only one solution.

For Qs. Nos. 18-22. $f(x) = | x - 1 | + x^2$

$$\therefore \quad f(x) = \begin{cases} x^2 + x - 1, & \text{for } x \geq 1 \\ x^2 - x + 1, & \text{for } x < 1 \end{cases}$$

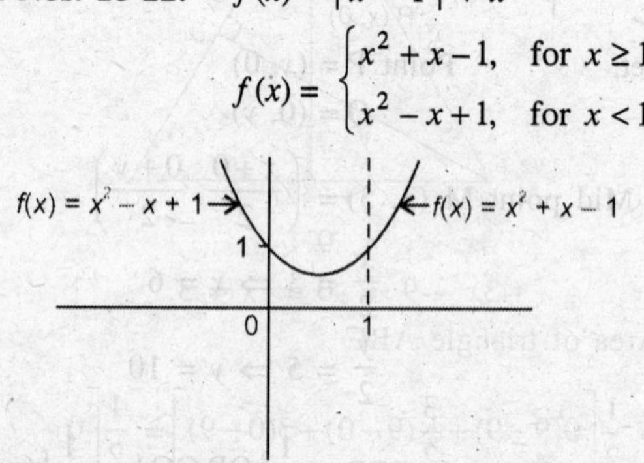

18. From graph we see that $f(x)$ is continuous at $x = 1$, but not differentiable at $x = 1$.

20. $f(x) = | x - 1 | + x^2$ has local minimum at $x = \dfrac{1}{2}$.

21. Required Area

$$A = \left| \int_{\frac{1}{2}}^{1} (x^2 - x + 1).dx \right| = \left| \frac{x^3}{3} - \frac{x^2}{2} + x \right|_{\frac{1}{2}}^{1}$$

$$= \left| \left(\frac{1 - \frac{1}{8}}{3} \right) - \left(\frac{1 - \frac{1}{4}}{2} \right) + \left(1 - \frac{1}{2} \right) \right| = \frac{5}{12} \text{ square units.}$$

22. Required area,

$$A = \left| \int_{1}^{\frac{3}{2}} (x^2 + x - 1).dx \right| = \left| \frac{x^3}{3} + \frac{x^2}{2} - x \right|_{1}^{\frac{3}{2}}$$

$$= \left|\frac{\left(\frac{27}{8}-1\right)}{3}+\frac{\left(\frac{9}{4}-1\right)}{2}-\left(\frac{3}{2}-1\right)\right|$$

$$= \left|\frac{19}{24}+\frac{5}{8}-\frac{1}{2}\right| = \frac{11}{12} \text{ Square units.}$$

23. $a_0 = \int_0^{\pi}\frac{\sin^2 x}{\sin 2x}dx = \frac{1}{2}\int_0^{\pi}\tan x.dx = \frac{1}{2}[\log(\sec x)]_0^{\pi} = 0$

$$a_1 = \int_0^{\pi}\frac{\sin^2 2x}{\sin 2x}.dx = \int_0^{\pi}\sin 2x.dx = -\left[\frac{\cos 2x}{2}\right]_0^{\pi} = 0$$

$$a_3 = \int_0^{\pi}\frac{\sin^2 4x}{\sin 2x}.dx = \int_0^{\pi}2(\sin 4x.\cos 2x).dx$$

$$= \int_0^{\pi}(\sin 6x+\sin 2x).dx = -\left[\frac{\cos 6x}{6}+\frac{\cos 2x}{2}\right]_0^{\pi} = 0$$

Thus, $\{a_n\}$ is in A.P. with C.d. = 0.

For Qs. Nos. 27-28

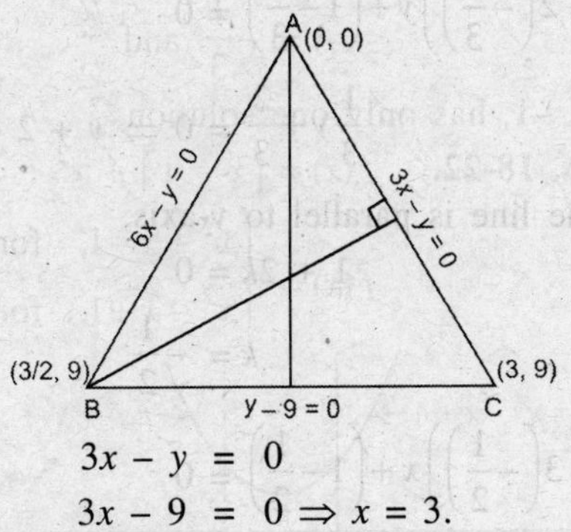

$$3x - y = 0$$
$$3x - 9 = 0 \Rightarrow x = 3.$$

27. Area of triangle ABC

$$= \frac{1}{2}\left[0(9-9)+\frac{3}{2}(9-0)+3(0-9)\right] = \frac{1}{2}\left[0+\frac{27}{2}-27\right]$$

$$= \frac{1}{2}\left[\frac{27-54}{2}\right] = \frac{27}{4} \text{ square units.}$$

28. The co-ordinate of the centroid are

$$\left(\frac{x_1+x_2+x_3}{3}, \frac{y_1+y_2+y_3}{3}\right)$$

$$= \left(\frac{0+3+\frac{3}{2}}{3}, \frac{0+9+9}{3}\right) = \left(\frac{9}{6}, \frac{18}{3}\right) = \left(\frac{3}{2}, 6\right)$$

For Qs. Nos. 29-30.

$$f(x) = (x-1)^2(x+1)(x-2)^3$$
$$f'(x) = 2(x-1)(x+1)(x-2)^3 + (x-1)^2(x-2)^3 + 3(x-1)^2(x+1)(x-2)^2$$
$$= (x-1)(x-2)^2\{2(x+1)(x-2) + (x-1)(x-2) + 3(x-1)(x+1)\}$$
$$= (x-1)(x-2)^2\{6x^2 - 5x - 5\}$$

When, $f'(x) = 0$

$$\Rightarrow \quad x = 1, 2, -\frac{7}{12}, \frac{17}{12}$$

$$f''(x) = 2(x-2)(x-1)(6x^2-5x-5) + (x-2)^2(6x^2-5x-5) + (x-1)(x-2)^2(12x-5)$$

at $x = 1$, $f''(1) < 0$

$\therefore f(x)$ has local maximum at $x = 1$

$x = \frac{-7}{12}$, $f''\left(\frac{-7}{12}\right) > 0$,

$\therefore f(x)$ has local minimum at $x = -\frac{7}{12}$

$x = \frac{17}{12}$, $f''\left(\frac{17}{12}\right) > 0$,

$\therefore f(x)$ has local maximum at $\frac{17}{12}$

29. $f(x)$ has local minimum at $x = -\frac{7}{12}$ and $x = 2$.

30. Number of points of local maxima $x = 1$ and $\frac{17}{12}$.

31. Let $f(x) = x^2 + ax + b$

and $g(x) = x^2 + px + q$

$f(2) = 4 + 2a + b = 3$

$\Rightarrow \quad 2a + b = -1$ ...(*i*)

$g(2) = 4 + 2p + q = 9$

$\Rightarrow \quad 2p + q = 5$ ...(*ii*)

Again $f'(x) = 2x + a$

$\Rightarrow \quad f'(1) = 2 + a = 4 \Rightarrow a = 2$

$g'(x) = 2x + p$

$\Rightarrow \quad g'(1) = 2 + p = 6 \Rightarrow p = 4$

From (*i*) and (*ii*), $b = -5$ and $q = -3$

Thus, $f(x) = x^2 + 2x - 5$

and $g(x) = x^2 + 4x - 3$

$\{f(x) - g(x)\} = -2x - 2$

at $x = 4$, $-2 \times (4) - 2 = -10$.

For Qs. Nos. 32-33.

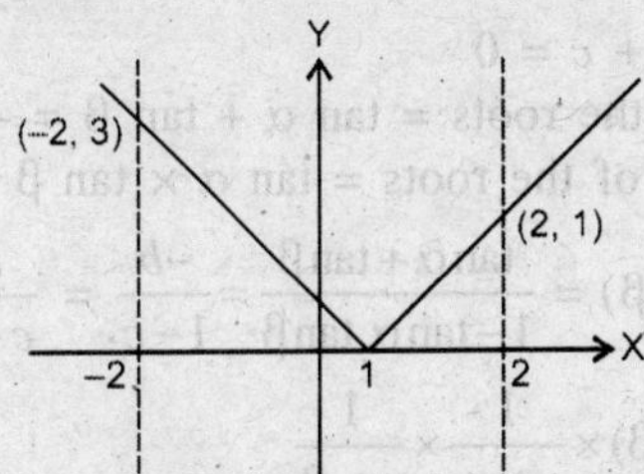

32. From graph we see that, there are two point of intersection (–2, 3) and (2, 1).

33. Area of the region bounded by the curve.

$$= \frac{1}{2}\times 3\times 2+\frac{1}{2}\times 2\times 1 = 3 + 1 = 4 \text{ sq. unit.}$$

For Qs. Nos. 34-35.

$$f(x) = \begin{vmatrix} x^3 & \sin x & \cos x \\ 6 & -1 & 0 \\ P & P^2 & P^3 \end{vmatrix}$$

34. $$f'(x) = \begin{vmatrix} 3x^2 & \cos x & -\sin x \\ 6 & -1 & 0 \\ P & P^2 & P^3 \end{vmatrix}$$

$$f'(0) = \begin{vmatrix} 0 & 1 & 0 \\ 6 & -1 & 0 \\ P & P^2 & P^3 \end{vmatrix} = -6\,P^3.$$

35. $$f''(x) = \begin{vmatrix} 6x & -\sin x & -\cos x \\ 6 & -1 & 0 \\ P & P^2 & P^3 \end{vmatrix}$$

$$f''(0) = \begin{vmatrix} 0 & 0 & -1 \\ 6 & -1 & 0 \\ P & P^2 & P^3 \end{vmatrix} = 0$$

$$-1(6P^2 + P) = 0$$

$$P = 0 \text{ or } -\frac{1}{6}.$$

For Qs. Nos. 36-37

$$\cos A + \cos B + \cos C = \sqrt{3}\sin\frac{\pi}{3}$$

$$\Rightarrow \cos A + \cos B + \cos C = \sqrt{3}\times\frac{\sqrt{3}}{2} = \frac{3}{2}$$

$$\frac{b^2+c^2-a^2}{2bc} + \frac{a^2+c^2-b^2}{2ac} + \frac{a^2+b^2-c^2}{2ab} = \frac{3}{2}$$

$= a = b = c$

$\therefore$ It is an equilateral triangle

$\therefore$ Each angle = 60°.

36. $\sin 30° \times \sin 30° \times \sin 30° = \frac{1}{2}\times\frac{1}{2}\times\frac{1}{2} = \frac{1}{8}.$

37. $\cos 60° \times \cos 60° \times \cos 60° = \frac{1}{2}\times\frac{1}{2}\times\frac{1}{2} = \frac{1}{8}.$

38. $x^2 + bx + c = 0$

Sum of the roots = $\tan\alpha + \tan\beta = -b$

Product of the roots = $\tan\alpha \times \tan\beta = c$

$$\tan(\alpha+\beta) = \frac{\tan\alpha+\tan\beta}{1-\tan\alpha.\tan\beta} = \frac{-b}{1-c} = \frac{b}{c-1} = b(c-1)^{-1}.$$

39. $$\sin(\alpha+\beta)\times\frac{1}{\cos\alpha}\times\frac{1}{\cos\beta}$$

$$= (\sin\alpha\times\cos\beta+\cos\alpha\times\sin\beta)\times\frac{1}{\cos\alpha\times\cos\beta}$$

$$= \frac{\sin\alpha\times\cos\beta}{\cos\alpha\times\cos\beta} + \frac{\cos\alpha\times\sin\beta}{\cos\alpha\times\cos\beta} = (\tan\alpha + \tan\beta) = -b.$$

For Qs. Nos. 40-41.

Circle 1 : $(x-1)^2 + (y-3)^2 = r^2$

$\Rightarrow$ $C_1 = (1, 3),\ r_1 = r$

Circle 2 : $(x-4)^2 + (y+1)^2 = 3^2$

$\Rightarrow$ $C_2 = (4, -1),\ r_2 = 3$

40. Distance between two centres

$$= \sqrt{(4-1)^2+(-1-3)^2} = \sqrt{9+16} = 5 \text{ units.}$$

41. If two circles touches internally, then, distance between two centres = 1.

So, $1 < r < 5 - 3$

or, $1 < r < 2.$

For Qs. Nos. 42-43. Equation of lines passing through point of intersection of two lines is σ

$$(x + y + 1) + k(3x + 2y + 1) = 0$$

$$(1 + 3k)x + (1 + 2k)y + (1 + k) = 0$$

42. As the line is parallel to x-axis, so

$$1 + 3k = 0 \Rightarrow k = -\frac{1}{3}$$

$$\left(1+2\left(-\frac{1}{3}\right)\right)y+\left(1-\frac{1}{3}\right) = 0$$

$$\frac{1}{3}y+\frac{2}{3} = 0 \Rightarrow y + 2 = 0$$

43. As the line is parallel to y-axis,

so, $1 + 2k = 0$

$\Rightarrow$ $k = -\frac{1}{2}$

$$\left(1+3\left(-\frac{1}{2}\right)\right)x+\left(1-\frac{1}{2}\right) = 0$$

$$-\frac{1}{2}x+\frac{1}{2} = 0 \Rightarrow x - 1 = 0.$$

For Qs. Nos. 44-45.

$$k \sin x + \cos 2x = 2k - 7$$

$$k.\sin x + 1 - 2\sin^2 x = 2k - 7$$

$$2\sin^2 x - k\sin x + 2k - 8 = 0$$

$$\sin x = \frac{k\pm\sqrt{(-k)^2-4.2.2(k-4)}}{4}$$

$$= \frac{k\pm(k-8)}{4} = \frac{k}{2}-2$$

44. For minimum value of k,

$$\sin x = -1 = \frac{k}{2}-2$$

$$k = 2.$$

45. For maximum value of k,

$$\sin x = 1 = \frac{k}{2}-2$$

$$k = 6.$$

For Qs. Nos. 46-47.

We know that as $x \to 0^+, [x] = 0$

and as $x \to 0^-, [x] = -1$

46. $\lim_{x\to 0^+} f(x) = \lim_{x\to 0^+} \frac{a^{[x]+x}-1}{[x]+x} = \lim_{x\to 0^+} \frac{a^x-1}{x}$

By L'Hospital rule,

$= \lim_{x\to 0^+} \frac{a^x . \ln a}{1} = \ln a.$

47. $\lim_{x\to 0^-} f(x) = \lim_{x\to 0^-} \frac{a^{[x]+x}-1}{[x]+x}$

$= \lim_{x\to 0^-} \frac{a^{x-1}-1}{x-1} = \frac{a^{-1}-1}{-1}$

$= 1 - a^{-1}.$

For Qs. Nos. 50-51.

$\log_x y, \log_z x, \log_y z$ are in G.P.

$$\frac{\log_z x}{\log_x y} = \frac{\log_y z}{\log_z x}$$

$$\Rightarrow \quad \frac{\log 2x}{\log(y+z)} = \frac{\log 2z}{\log(y+x)}$$

$\log 2x(y + x) = \log 2z\,(y + z)$

$2x(y + x) = 2z\,(y + z)$

$(x - z)(x + y + z) = 0 \Rightarrow x = z$

From, x^3, y^3 and z^3 are in A.P.

$2y^3 = x^3 + z^3$

$2y^3 = 2x^3 \Rightarrow x = y$

again, $xyz = 64 \Rightarrow x = y = z = 4.$

For Qs. Nos. 52-53.

Let $z = x + iy$

$$\left|\frac{z-4}{z-8}\right| = 1$$

$\Rightarrow \quad |z - 4|^2 = |z - 8|^2$

$(x - 4)^2 + y^2 = (x - 8)^2 + y^2$

$(x - 8)^2 - (x - 4)^2 = 0$

$(x - 8 + x - 4)(x - 8 - x + 4) = 0$

$(-4)(2x - 12) = 0 \Rightarrow x = 6$

Again, $\left|\frac{z}{z-2}\right| = \frac{3}{2}$

$$\left|\frac{x+iy}{(x-2)+iy}\right| = \frac{3}{2}$$

$\Rightarrow \quad 2|x + iy| = 3\{|(x - 2) + iy|\}$

$4(x^2 + y^2) = 9\{(x - 2)^2 + y^2\}$

for, $x = 6$, $y = 0$.

52. $z = x + iy = 6 + i(0)$

$|z| = 6.$

53. $\left|\frac{z-6}{z+6}\right| = \left|\frac{6-6}{6+6}\right| = 0.$

54. Check for continuity at $x = 0$

$\underset{x\to 0^-}{\text{Lt}} f(x) = \underset{x\to 0^+}{\text{Lt}} f(x) = f(0)$

$\underset{x\to 0^-}{\text{Lt}} (x+\pi) = \underset{x\to 0^+}{\text{Lt}} \pi\cos x = \pi.\cos(0)$

$\pi = \pi = \pi$

Hence, $f(x)$ is continuous at $x = 0$

Check for continuity at $x = \frac{\pi}{2}$

$\underset{x\to \frac{\pi}{2}^-}{\text{Lt}} f(x) = \underset{x\to \frac{\pi}{2}^+}{\text{Lt}} f(x) = f\left(\frac{\pi}{2}\right)$

$\underset{x\to \frac{\pi}{2}^-}{\text{Lt}} \pi\cos x = \underset{x\to \frac{\pi}{2}^+}{\text{Lt}} \left(x-\frac{\pi}{2}\right)^2 = \pi.\cos\left(\frac{\pi}{2}\right)$

$\pi.\cos\left(\frac{\pi}{2}\right) = \left(\frac{\pi}{2}-\frac{\pi}{2}\right)^2 = 0$

$0 = 0 = 0$

Thus, $f(x)$ is continuous of $x = \frac{\pi}{2}$.

For Qs. Nos. 56-57.

$\alpha + \beta = -b, \alpha.\beta = c$

As, $b > 0$ and $c < 0$

So, $\alpha + \beta < 0$ and $\alpha.\beta < 0$

and, from question, $\alpha < \beta$.

$\therefore$ α is –ve number and β is +ve number.

56. $\alpha + \beta < 0 \Rightarrow \beta < -\alpha$

or $\beta < |\alpha|$

57. $\alpha + \beta < 0$ and $\alpha\beta < 0 \Rightarrow \alpha + \beta + \alpha\beta < 0$

and $\alpha^2\beta + \beta^2\alpha = \alpha\beta(\alpha + \beta) > 0.$

58.

Mid point of AC $= \left(\frac{x+1}{2}, \frac{2+6}{2}\right) = \left(\frac{x+1}{2}, 4\right)$

Mid point of BD $= \left(\frac{3+4}{2}, \frac{y+5}{2}\right)$

Now $\frac{x+1}{2} = \frac{7}{2} \Rightarrow x = 6$

$\frac{y+5}{2} = 4 \Rightarrow 5 = 3$

$(AC)^2 - (BD)^2 = [(6-1)^2 + (6-2)^2] - [(3-4)^2 + (y-3)^2]$

$= (25 + 16) - (1 + 4) = 41 - 5 = 36$

$\therefore$ Value of $AC^2 - BD^2 = 36.$

59. Point of intersection of the diagonals

$P(x, y) = P\left(\frac{7}{2}, 4\right).$

60.

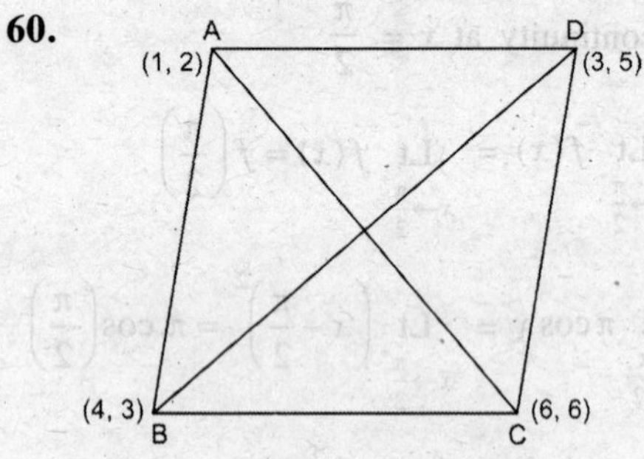

Area of parallelogram ABCD

$= \text{ar } \Delta ABC + \text{ar } \Delta ACD = 2 \text{ ar } \Delta ABC$

$= 2 \times \frac{1}{2}[x_1(y_2 - y_3) + x_2(y_3 - y_1) + x_3(y_1 - y_2)]$

$= [1(3-6) + 4(6-2) + 6(2-3)] = (-3 + 16 - 6)$

$= 7$ square units.

For Qs. No. 61-64.

$f(x) = x^3 + x^2 f'(1) + x f''(2) + f'''(3)$

$f'(x) = 3x^2 + 2x.f'(1) + f''(2)$ ...(*i*)

$f''(x) = 6x + 2f'(1)$ ...(*ii*)

$f'''(x) = 6$ ...(*iii*)

from (*ii*), $f''(2) = 6 \times 2 + 2f'(1) = 12 + 2f'(1)$

from (*i*), $f'(1) = 3 + 2f'(1) + 12 + 2f'(1)$

$\therefore$ $f'(1) = -\frac{15}{3} = -5$ ...(*iv*)

and $f''(2) = 6 \times 2 + 2(-5) = 2$ ...(*v*)

61. $f(1) = (1)^3 + (1)^2(-5) + 1(2) + 6$

$= 1 - 5 + 2 + 6 = 4.$

62. $f'(1) = -5.$

63. $f'''(10) = f'''(3) = 6.$

64. 1. $f(2) = (2)^3 + (2)^2.(-5) + 2(2) + 6$

$= 8 - 20 + 4 + 6 = -2$

$f(1) = 4, f(0) = 6$

$f(1) - f(0) = 4 - 6 = -2$

$\therefore$ $f(2) = f(1) - f(0).$

2. $f''(2) - 2f'(1) = 2 - 2(-5) = 12$

Hence, both 1 and 2 are true.

68. $f(x) = |x^2 - 5x + 6|$

$= \begin{cases} x^2 - 5x + 6, & \text{if } x \geq 3 \text{ or } x \leq 2 \\ -(x^2 - 5x + 6), & \text{if } 2 < x < 3 \end{cases}$

$f'(x) = \begin{cases} (2x - 5), & \text{if } x \geq 3 \text{ or } x \leq 2 \\ -(2x - 5), & \text{if } 2 < x < 3 \end{cases}$

$\therefore$ $f'(4) = \{2 \times 4 - 5\} = 8 - 5 = 3.$

69. $f''(x) = -2$

$\therefore$ $f''(2.5) = -2.$

For Qs. Nos. 70-71.

$f(x) = [x]$ and $g(x) = |x|$

70. $(gof)\left(\frac{-5}{3}\right) = g\left(f\left(\frac{-5}{3}\right)\right) = \left|\left[\frac{-5}{3}\right]\right| = |-2| = 2$

$(fog)\left(\frac{-5}{3}\right) = f\left(g\left(\frac{-5}{3}\right)\right) = \left[\left|\frac{-5}{3}\right|\right] = \left[\frac{5}{3}\right] = 1$

so, $(gof)\left(\frac{-5}{3}\right) - (fog)\left(\frac{-5}{3}\right) = 2 - 1 = 1.$

71. $(fof)\left(\frac{-9}{5}\right) + (gog)(-2) = f\left(f\left(-\frac{9}{5}\right)\right) + g(g(-2))$

$= f(-2) + g(2) = -2 + 2 = 0.$

For Qs. Nos. 72-73.

Equation of circle passing through origin:

$x^2 + y^2 + 2gx + 2fy = 0$

as, it is passes through (a, b) and $(-b, -a)$, then

$a^2 + b^2 + 2g.a + 2f.b = 0$ ...(*i*)

and $b^2 + a^2 - 2gb - 2fa = 0$ ...(*ii*)

from (*i*) and (*ii*), we have,

$(g + f)(a + b) = 0$

$g = -f$

and on solving for g and f, we get

$g = \frac{a^2 + b^2}{2(b-a)}$

$f = \frac{a^2 + b^2}{2(a-b)}.$

72. Centre of the circle $= (-g, -f)$

as, $g + f = 0$

$\therefore$ Centre lies on the line $x + y = 0.$

73. Intercept cut on the axis

x-axis intercept $= \frac{a^2 + b^2}{(a-b)}$

y-axis intercept $= \left(\frac{a^2 + b^2}{b-a}\right)$

Sum of squares of intercept $= 2\left(\frac{a^2 + b^2}{a-b}\right)^2.$

74. $|\vec{a}|^2 = 1,\ |\vec{b}|^2 = 1$

$\vec{a}.\vec{b} = \cos\theta$

$$\cos^2\frac{\theta}{2} = \frac{1+\cos\theta}{2} = \frac{2+2\cos\theta}{4}$$

$$= \frac{|\vec{a}|^2+|\vec{b}|^2+2(\vec{a}.\vec{b})}{4} = \left|\frac{\vec{a}+\vec{b}}{2}\right|^2$$

$$\therefore \cos\frac{\theta}{2} = \frac{|\vec{a}+\vec{b}|}{2}.$$

75. $\sin^2\frac{\theta}{2} = \frac{1-\cos\theta}{2} = \frac{2-2\cos\theta}{4}$

$$= \frac{|\vec{a}|^2+|\vec{b}|^2-2(\vec{a}.\vec{b})}{4} = \left|\frac{\vec{a}-\vec{b}}{2}\right|^2 \quad \therefore \sin\frac{\theta}{2} = \frac{|\vec{a}-\vec{b}|}{2}.$$

76. 1. $\tan^{-1}(\tan\theta) = \theta$ for $\theta \in \left(-\frac{\pi}{2}, \frac{\pi}{2}\right)$.

2. $\sin^{-1}\left(\frac{1}{3}\right) - \sin^{-1}\left(\frac{1}{5}\right)$

$$= \sin^{-1}\left(\frac{1}{3}.\sqrt{1-\left(\frac{1}{5}\right)^2} - \sqrt{1-\left(\frac{1}{3}\right)^2}.\frac{1}{5}\right)$$

$$= \sin^{-1}\left(\frac{1}{3}\times\frac{2\sqrt{6}}{5} - \frac{2\sqrt{2}}{3}\times\frac{1}{5}\right)$$

$$= \sin^{-1}\left(\frac{2\sqrt{2}(\sqrt{3}-1)}{15}\right).$$

77. 1. $\tan^{-1}\left(\frac{1}{x}\right) = \cot^{-1}(x) = \tan^{-1}(x) + \tan^{-1}\left(\frac{1}{x}\right)$

$$= \tan^{-1}(x) + \cot^{-1}(x) = \frac{\pi}{2}.$$

2. $\sin^{-1}(x) + \cos^{-1}(y) = \frac{\pi}{2}$ in $x, y \in [-1, 1]$

when $x = y$.

79. $\int_{-2}^{2} x.dx - \int_{-2}^{2} [x].dx$

$$= \left[\frac{x^2}{2}\right]_{-2}^{2} - \int_{-2}^{-1}[x].dx - \int_{-1}^{0}[x].dx - \int_{0}^{1}[x].dx - \int_{1}^{2}[x].dx$$

$$= 0 - \left[\int_{-2}^{-1} -2.dx + \int_{-1}^{0} -1.dx + \int_{0}^{1} 0.dx + \int_{1}^{2} dx\right]$$

$$= 0 - [-2(-1+2) - 1(0+1) + 0 + 1(2-1)] = 2.$$

80. $\int_{-2}^{5} f(x).dx = \int_{-2}^{0} f(x).dx + \int_{0}^{5} f(x).dx$

and $\int_{0}^{5}[1+f(x)].dx = [x]_0^5 + \int_{0}^{5} f(x).dx = 7$

$$= 5 + \int_{0}^{5} f(x).dx = 7 = \int_{0}^{5} f(x).dx = 2$$

$$\therefore \int_{-2}^{0} f(x) = \int_{-2}^{5} f(x).dx - \int_{0}^{5} f(x).dx$$

$$= 4 - 2 = 2.$$

84.

.3125 × 2	= .6250	0
.6250 × 2	= 1.2500	1
.2500 × 2	= .5000	0
.5000 × 2	= 1.1000	1
.1000 × 2	= .2000	0

$\therefore (0.3125)_{10} = (0.0101)_2.$

86. Graph of $y = |\cos x|$

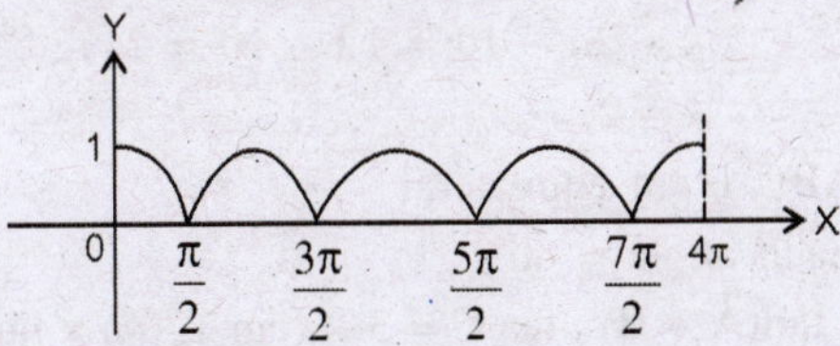

$$\int_{0}^{4\pi} |\cos x|.dx$$

$$= \int_{0}^{\pi/2} \cos x.dx + \left|\int_{\pi/2}^{3\pi/2} \cos x.dx\right| + \left|\int_{3\pi/2}^{5\pi/2} \cos x.dx\right| + \left|\int_{5\pi/2}^{7\pi/2} \cos x.dx\right| + \int_{7\pi/2}^{4\pi} \cos x.dx$$

$$= [\sin x]_0^{\pi/2} + \left|[\sin x]_{\pi/2}^{3\pi/2}\right| + \left|[\sin x]_{3\pi/2}^{5\pi/2}\right| + \left|[\sin x]_{5\pi/2}^{7\pi/2}\right| + \left|[\sin x]_{7\pi/2}^{4\pi}\right|$$

$= 1 + 2 + 2 + 2 + 1 = 8.$

87. Number of Numbers between 1 to 1000:

divisible by 10 $= \frac{1000}{10} = 100$

divisible by 15 $= \frac{1000}{15} \cong 66$

divisible by 25 $= \frac{1000}{25} = 40$

divisible by 10 & 15 $= \frac{1000}{30} \cong 33$

divisible by 10 & 25 $= \frac{1000}{50} = 20$

divisible by 15 & 25 $= \frac{1000}{75} = 13$

divisible by 10, 15 & 25 $= \frac{1000}{150} = 6$

Number of Numbers divisible by either 10, 15 or 25

$= 100 + 66 + 40 - 33 - 20 - 13 + 6 = 146$

$\therefore$ Number of numbers not divisible by 10, 15 or 25

$= 1000 - 146 = 854.$

88. (10 – 6) (*a*, 2*b*) (*k*, 4)
A C B

$$\frac{k+10}{2} = a$$

$$\frac{4-6}{2} = 2b$$

$$\frac{-2}{2} = 2b \quad \Rightarrow -1 = 2b$$

$$b = \frac{-1}{2}$$

$\because \quad a - 2b = 7$

$$a = 7 + 2b = 7+2\left(\frac{-1}{2}\right) = 7 - 1 = 6$$

$k + 10 = 2a$

$k = 2a - 10 = 12 - 10 = 2$

$\therefore \quad k = 2.$

89. I. $\because$ ABC is an equilateral

$\therefore$ Each angle = 60°

$\therefore$ 3 tan(A + B) . tan C = 3 × (tan 120°) × tan 60°

$= 3\times\left(-\sqrt{3}\right)\times\sqrt{3} = 3 \times (-3) = -9$

which is not possible.

II. $\because$ ABC is a triangle in which

$\angle A = 78°; \angle B = 66°$

$\therefore \angle C = 180° - 144° = 36°$

$$\because \tan\left(\frac{A}{2}+C\right) < \tan A$$

$\Rightarrow \tan (39° + 36°) < \tan 78°$

$\Rightarrow$ tan 75° < tan 78° which is possible.

III. $$\because \frac{A+B+C}{2} = \frac{180°}{2} = 90°$$

$$\Rightarrow \quad \frac{A+B}{2} = 90° - \frac{C}{2}$$

$$\tan\left(\frac{A+B}{2}\right) = \tan\left(90° - \frac{C}{2}\right) = \cot\frac{C}{2}$$

$$\therefore \cot\frac{C}{2}\times\sin\frac{C}{2} < \cos\frac{C}{2}$$

$$\Rightarrow \frac{\cos\frac{C}{2}}{\sin\frac{C}{2}}\times\sin\frac{C}{2} < \cos\frac{C}{2}$$

$$\Rightarrow \cos\frac{C}{2} < \cos\frac{C}{2}$$ not possible.

90. $\because$ A = (cos 12° – cos 36°) (sin 96° + sin 24°)

$$= \left[2\sin\frac{36+12}{2}.\sin\frac{36-12}{2}\right]\left[2\sin\frac{96+24}{2}\times\cos\frac{96-24}{2}\right]$$

= (2 sin 24° . sin 12°) (2 sin 60° . cos 36°)

B = (sin 60° – sin 12°) (cos 48° – cos 72°)

= (2 cos 36° × sin 24°) (2 sin 60° . sin 12°)

$$\therefore \frac{A}{B} = \frac{2\sin 24°.\sin 12°\times 2\sin 60°.\cos 36°}{2\cos 36°\times\sin 24°\times 2\sin 68°.\sin 12°}$$

$$\therefore \frac{A}{B} = 1.$$

91. $$\text{Mean} = \frac{10+9+21+16+24}{5} = \frac{80}{5} = 16$$

$$\text{M.D.} = \frac{\Sigma|x-\bar{x}|}{5} = \frac{6+7+5+0+8}{5} = \frac{26}{5} = 5.2$$

$\therefore$ Mean deviation = 5.2.

92. Probability of getting sum equal to 3 *i.e.*,

(1, 1, 1), $P(A) = \dfrac{1}{6\times6\times6}$

Probability of getting sum equal to 4 *i.e.*, (1, 1, 2), (1, 2, 1), (2, 1, 1)

$$P(B) = \frac{3}{6\times6\times6}$$

Probability of getting the sum either 3 or 4

$$= \frac{1+3}{6\times6\times6} = \frac{4}{6\times6\times6} = \frac{1}{54}$$

Probability of getting the sum atleast 5

$$= 1 - \frac{1}{54} = \frac{53}{54}.$$

93. $P(A) = \dfrac{1}{3}$, $P(A') = 1 - \dfrac{1}{3} = \dfrac{2}{3}$

$P(B) = \dfrac{3}{4}$, $P(B') = 1 - \dfrac{3}{4} = \dfrac{1}{4}$

Probability that exactly one of them occurs

= P(A).P(B′) + P(A′). P(B)

$$= \frac{1}{3}\times\frac{1}{4}+\frac{2}{3}\times\frac{3}{4} = \frac{7}{12}.$$

94. Let, A be the event of getting a head and B that of getting a tail.

Then $P(A) = \dfrac{1}{2}$, $P(B) = \dfrac{1}{2}$

Head and tail can occur alternately in the following mutually exclusive ways.

(*i*) HTH (*ii*) THT

Hence, required probability

$= P[(A \cap B \cap A) \cup (B \cap A \cap B)]$

$= P(A \cap B \cap A) + P(B \cap A \cap B)$

= P(A) P(B) P(A) + P(B) P(A) P(B)

$$= \left(\frac{1}{2}\right)^3 + \left(\frac{1}{2}\right)^3 = \frac{1}{4}.$$

96. In a deck of 52 cards, queen of spades = 1

so, required probability $= \dfrac{1}{52}.$

97. Probability of getting sum equal to 2 *i.e.,* (1, 1)

$$= \frac{1}{6\times6}$$

Probability of getting sum equal to 3 *i.e.,* (1, 2) or (2, 1) $= \frac{2}{6\times6}$

Probability of getting sum atleast 4 $= 1-\frac{1+2}{6\times6} = \frac{11}{12}$.

99. Two event A and B are mutually exclusive

if $P(A\cap B) = 0$

$P(A\cup B) = P(A) + P(B)$

Here, $P(A'\cap B) = P(B) = 0.3$

Now, $P(A/A\cup B) = \frac{P(A\cap(A\cup B))}{P(A\cup B)}$

$$= \frac{P(A)}{P(A)+P(B)} = \frac{0.2}{0.2+0.3} = \frac{2}{5}.$$

100. Number of days in December = 31 days.

Number of odd days = 3

Required probability for 5 Sundays $= \frac{2}{7}$.

102.

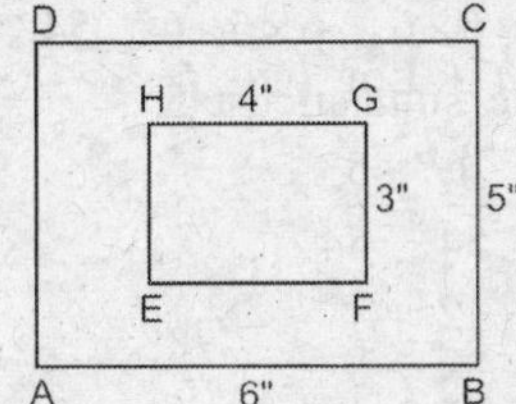

Area of the rectangle ABCD

$= 6 \times 5 = 30$ square inches

Area of the rectangle EFGH

$= 4 \times 3 = 12$ square inches

Required probability $= \frac{12}{30} = \frac{2}{5}$.

103. Sum of the Series $= n.\overline{X}$

when X_2 is replaced by λ, then

New sum of the series, $n.\overline{X} - X_2 + \lambda$

New mean $= \frac{n.\overline{X} - X_2 + \lambda}{n}$.

104. 1, 2, 3, 5, 5, 5, 6, 6, 8, 9

Mean $(x) = \frac{1+2+3+5+5+5+6+8+9}{10} = \frac{44}{10} = 4.4.$

Median $(y) = \frac{5+5}{2} = 5$

Mode $(z) = 5$ which appear maximum times $= z$

Clearly, $y = z$ But x is different.

Hence, $x \neq y = z$ is correct option.

106. Let, X denote the number of tails.

Then, X is a binomial variate with parameters $n = 100$ and $p = \frac{1}{2}$.

$\therefore p(X = r) = 100C_r\left(\frac{1}{2}\right)^{100}$

$r = 0, 1, 2, ..., 100$

Required probability $= p(X = 1) + p(X = 3) + ... + p(X = 99)$

$$= \left(\frac{1}{2}\right)^{100}\left[{}^{100}C_1 + {}^{100}C_3 + ... + {}^{100}C_{99}\right] = \frac{1}{2^{100}}[2^{99}] = \frac{1}{2}$$

107. Each of the three tickets given to the employ in 10 ways

So, required number of ways $= 10 \times 10 \times 10 = 1000$.

108. Let one root is α, then other root is 2α

Now, sum of roots $3\alpha = \frac{-l}{(l-m)}$ ...(*i*)

Product of roots $\alpha.2\alpha = \frac{1}{(l-m)}$ ...(*ii*)

from (*i*) and (*ii*), we have

$$\frac{2\alpha}{3} = -\frac{1}{l} \Rightarrow \alpha = -\frac{3}{2l}$$

$$(l-m)\left(\frac{-3}{2l}\right)^2 + l\left(-\frac{3}{2l}\right) + 1 = 0$$

$$\frac{9(l-m)}{4l^2} - \frac{3}{2} + 1 = 0$$

$$9(l-m) - 2l^2 = 0$$

$$2l^2 - 9l + 9m = 0$$

For real values of l, $D \geq 0$

$$(-9)^2 - 4.2.9m \geq 0$$

$$m \leq \frac{9}{8}$$

Greatest value of $m = \frac{9}{8}$.

109. Number of 4 digit decimal numbers in which no digits get repeated $= 10 \times 9 \times 8 \times 7 = 5040$.

110. Let third vector is $x\hat{i} + y\hat{j} + z\hat{k}$

As the vectors are orthogonal

then $x + y + z = 0$ and $2x + 3y - z = 0$

$$\text{Required vector} = \begin{vmatrix} \hat{i} & \hat{j} & \hat{k} \\ 1 & 1 & 1 \\ 2 & 3 & -1 \end{vmatrix}$$

$$= (-1-3)\hat{i} + (2+1)\hat{j} + (3-2)\hat{k}$$

$$= -4\hat{i} + 3\hat{j} + \hat{k}$$

$$\text{Unit vector} = \frac{-4\hat{i} + 3\hat{j} + \hat{k}}{\sqrt{(-4)^2 + (3)^2 + (1)^2}}$$

$$= \frac{-4\hat{i} + 3\hat{j} + \hat{k}}{\sqrt{26}}.$$

111. The position vector of the centroid of the triangle is $\frac{\vec{a}+\vec{b}+\vec{c}}{3}$.

Since the triangle is an equilateral, therefore the orthocentre coincides with the centroid and hence

$$\frac{\vec{a}+\vec{b}+\vec{c}}{3}=0 \Rightarrow \vec{a}+\vec{b}+\vec{c}=0$$

112. Area of parallelogram $= \frac{1}{2}|\vec{d}_1 \times \vec{d}_2|$

$= \frac{1}{2}\times 10\sqrt{3} = 5\sqrt{3}$ square units.

113. $A^2 = \begin{bmatrix} -1 & 1 \\ 1 & -1 \end{bmatrix}\begin{bmatrix} -1 & 1 \\ 1 & -1 \end{bmatrix} = \begin{bmatrix} 2 & -2 \\ -2 & 2 \end{bmatrix}$

$$A^3 = \begin{bmatrix} 2 & -2 \\ 2 & -2 \end{bmatrix}\begin{bmatrix} -1 & 1 \\ 1 & -1 \end{bmatrix} = \begin{bmatrix} -2-2 & 2+2 \\ 2+2 & -2-2 \end{bmatrix}$$

$$= \begin{bmatrix} -4 & 4 \\ 4 & -4 \end{bmatrix} = 4\begin{bmatrix} -1 & 1 \\ 1 & -1 \end{bmatrix}$$

$A^3 = 4A$.

114. I. $\begin{vmatrix} 41 & 1 & 5 \\ 79 & 7 & 9 \\ 29 & 5 & 3 \end{vmatrix}$

$= 41(21 - 45) - 1(237 - 261) + 5(395 - 203)$

$= 41(-24) + 24 + 5 \times 192$

$= -984 + 24 + 960 = -24 + 24 = 0$

II. $\begin{vmatrix} 1 & a & b+c \\ 1 & b & c+a \\ 1 & c & a+b \end{vmatrix}$

$= 1(b(a + b) - c(c + a)) - a(a + b - c - a) + (b + c)(c - b)$

$= ab + b^2 - c^2 - ac - a^2 - ab + ac + a^2 + bc - b^2 + c^2 - bc = 0$

III. $\begin{vmatrix} 0 & c & b \\ -c & 0 & a \\ -b & -a & 0 \end{vmatrix}$

$= 0(0 + a^2) - c(0 + ab) + b(ac + 0)$

$= 0 - abc + abc = 0$

Hence, (D) I, II, III is correct option.

115. $m_1 = \sqrt{3}$, $m_2 = \frac{1}{\sqrt{3}}$

Angle between two lines

$$\tan\theta = \left|\frac{m_1 - m_2}{1 + m_1.m_2}\right|$$

$$= \left|\frac{\sqrt{3}-\frac{1}{\sqrt{3}}}{1+\sqrt{3}.\frac{1}{\sqrt{3}}}\right| = \left|\frac{2}{2\sqrt{3}}\right| = \frac{1}{\sqrt{3}}$$

$\therefore\ \theta = \frac{\pi}{6}$ or 30°.

116. For unique solution $D \neq 0$

$$\begin{vmatrix} k & 1 & 1 \\ 1 & k & 1 \\ 1 & 1 & k \end{vmatrix} \neq 0$$

$$\begin{vmatrix} k & 0 & 1 \\ 1-k & k-1 & 0 \\ 1 & 1-k & k \end{vmatrix} \neq 0$$

{Applying $C_2 : C_2 - C_3$ and $R_2 \rightarrow R_2 - R_1$}

$k(k - 1)k + (1 - k)^2 - (k - 1) \neq 0$

$(k - 1)\{k^2 + (k - 1) - 1\} \neq 0$

$\Rightarrow\ (k - 1)^2 (k + 2) \neq 0$

$\therefore\ k \neq 1$ and $k \neq -2$.

118. $x = \text{Log}_a (ab)$

$\Rightarrow\ x = \text{Log}_a a + \text{Log}_a b$

$x = 1 + \log_a b$

$\text{Log}_a b = x - 1$

$\text{Log}_b a = \frac{1}{x-1}$

$\text{Log}_b a + 1 = \frac{1}{x-1} + 1$

$\text{Log}_b a + \text{Log}_b b = \frac{x}{x-1}$

$\text{Log}_b\, ab = \frac{x}{x-1}$.

119. $y = \text{Log}\, x + \frac{1}{\text{Log}\, x} + 1 + 1$

$$\frac{dy}{dx} = \frac{1}{x} + \left(-\frac{1}{x(\log x)^2}\right)$$

$$\left(\frac{dy}{dx}\right)_{x=10} = \frac{1}{10} - \frac{1}{10.(\text{Log}_{10})^2}$$

$$= \frac{1}{10} - \frac{1}{10} = 0.$$

120. As, w_1, w_2 are cube root of unity.

so, $1 + w_1 + w_2 = 0$

and $w_1.w_2 = 1$

$(w_1 - w_2)^2 = (w_1 + w_2)^2 - 4w_1.w_2$

$= (-1)^2 - 4 = 1 - 4 = -3.$

Previous Papers (Solved)

NATIONAL DEFENCE ACADEMY & NAVAL ACADEMY

NDA & NA – Entrance Exam, 2015 (II)

PAPER I : GENERAL ABILITY TEST

PART A : ENGLISH LANGUAGE

Directions: *In this section, look at the* **bold** *part of each sentence. Below each sentence are given three possible substitutions for the* **bold** *part. If one of them A, B or C is better than the* **bold** *part, indicate your response on the Answer Sheet against the corresponding letter A, B or C. If none of the substitutions improves the sentence, indicate D as your response on the Answer Sheet. Thus, a "No improvement" response will be signified by the letter D.*

1. **Had she been hungry,** she would have devoured the whole lot of it.
A. Unless she had been hungry
B. However she had been hungry
C. As if she had been hungry
D. No improvement

2. **Until you don't finish** the work, you won't be given leave.
A. Until you must finish B. Until finishing
C. Until you finish D. No improvement

3. The names of the defaulters have been **cut off** the register.
A. cut out B. struck out
C. struck off D. No improvement

4. This is a matter **I'd rather not talk about**.
A. of which I'd rather not talk about
B. I rather not talk about
C. that I'd rather not talk about
D. No improvement

5. Only when you left **I did sleep**.
A. I slept B. did I sleep
C. had I slept D. No improvement

6. I will be happy if you **will buy** me apples.
A. buy B. bought
C. will be buying D. No improvement

7. After I **saved** some money, I shall go abroad.
A. shall save B. should have saved
C. have saved D. No improvement

8. Can you **arrange the car** to be ready this evening?
A. arrange with the car B. arrange for the car
C. arrange that the car D. No improvement

9. Hardly **had he reached** home when the telephone rang.
A. he had reached B. did he reach
C. he reached D. No improvement

10. He is likely to win the elections **by the sweeping majority**.
A. with the sweeping majority
B. in sweeping majority
C. by a sweeping majority
D. No improvement

Directions: *Each of the following items in this section consists of a sentence the parts of which have been jumbled. These parts have been labelled P, Q, R and S. Given below each sentence are four sequences namely A, B, C and D. You are required to re-arrange the jumbled parts of the sentence and select the correct sequence.*

11. His uncle (P) for success in life, / (Q) always advised his son, / (R) who was a self-made man / (S) to depend on his own efforts.
The proper sequence should be:
A. SQPR B. RQSP
C. PRSQ D. QPSR

12. The doctor (P) did not like the behaviour of the patients/ (Q) who was very competent in his profession / (R) when they talked at length / (S) about their problems.
The proper sequence should be:
A. RPSQ B. SRPQ
C. QPRS D. PRQS

13. (P) from leadership in culture / (Q) in military situations and in face-to-face small groups / (R) leadership has wide range of expressions / (S) to leadership in politics.
The proper sequence should be:
A. RSQP B. PQRS
C. RPSQ D. SQRP

14. He sat (P) glancing occasionally / (Q) peering through the window / (R) at the figure of the old woman / (S) until he was chilled with the cold
The proper sequence should be:
A. PSRQ B. QRPS
C. SPRQ D. PRSQ

15. After the earthquake tremors, the TV showed a haggard man (P) shaking his fist at the sky / (Q) clambering over the ruins / (R) and collapsing with a howl of revolt / (S) of his house and factory.

The proper sequence should be:

A. SRQP B. QSPR
C. PQRS D. RPSQ

16. Everyone (P) acknowledges / (Q) when he considers the case calmly / (R) who knows you / (S) that you have been wronged.

The proper sequence should be:

A. RSQP B. RPQS
C. PQRS D. QRPS

Directions: *Each item in this section consists of a sentence with the **bold** word followed by four words. Select the word that is **nearest in meaning** to the **bold** word and mark your response in your Answer Sheet accordingly.*

17. Many of his acquaintances avoid him because he is so **garrulous**.

A. unreasonable B. talkative
C. quarrelsome D. proud

18. He bore the pain with great **fortitude**.

A. resignation B. defiance
C. indifference D. forbearance

19. He gave his **tacit** approval to the proposition.

A. full B. loud
C. clean D. implied

20. In spite of hard work, the farmers could only get a **meagre** yield.

A. satisfactory B. scanty
C. plenty D. normal

21. He was **exhilarated** at the outcome of the election results.

A. satisfied B. surprised
C. disappointed D. overjoyed

Directions: *Each item in this section consists of a sentence with the **bold** word followed by four words. Select the word that is **opposite in meaning** to the **bold** word and mark your response in your Answer Sheet accordingly.*

22. He **concealed** his thoughts very cleverly.

A. emphasized B. expressed
C. affirmed D. revealed

23. The proposal was **denounced** by one and all.

A. renounced B. recommended
C. announced D. commended

24. She was **skeptical** about the safety of the new drug.

A. doubtful B. certain
C. hopeful D. sanguine

25. The answers to the question were **coherent**.

A. relaxed B. loose
C. consistent D. disconnected

26. It was no **altruistic** motive that prompted him to help her.

A. selfish B. inhuman
C. brutal D. wicked

Directions: *Each of the following sentences in this section has a blank space and four words or group of words given after the sentence. Select whichever word or group of words you consider most appropriate for the blank space and indicate your response on the Answer Sheet accordingly.*

27. Man has won his dominant position on this planet by his .... of technology.

A. command B. emphasis
C. belief D. stress

28. The day was extremely hot and, in no time, my back was drenched with ....

A. prickly heat B. perspiration
C. sores D. fatigue

29. The Government is encouraging village upliftment .... in the country.

A. programmes B. designs
C. talks D. propaganda

30. Satish was endowed .... a natural talent for music.

A. in B. by
C. for D. with

31. Mr. Ghosh is very happy .... his son's excellent result.

A. for seeing B. to see
C. by seeing D. see

32. Sunlight filtering .... the stained glass window created a mosaic of colours on the floor.

A. in B. through
C. at D. into

33. Are you feeling doubtful .... your decision?

A. about B. upon
C. at D. for

34. I want to study Geology now for I .... Zoology for the last three years.

A. am studying B. have been studying
C. had studied D. had been studying

35. Increase in storage facilities has made it possible to store goods at places .... to people all over the country.

A. safe B. easy
C. proper D. convenient

36. To say that we were surprised at the cleverness of the child is an understatement; we were really ....

A. annoyed B. astounded
C. flattered D. confused

37. In spite of the old woman's repeated entreaties, he remained ....

A. ashamed B. docile
C. indifferent D. lethargic

38. There was .... competition for electoral seats.

A. diligent B. rapid
C. cut-throat D. sparse

39. The cricket team .... mainly of State players.

A. composed B. consist
C. made with D. comprises

40. His love for money is the only .... that drives him to work so hard.

A. programme B. plan
C. reason D. greed

41. According to .... sources, the Chief Minister did not consult his Cabinet Members on this issue.

A. intelligent B. simple
C. reliable D. fundamental

Directions: *Each item in this section has a sentence with three underlined parts labelled A, B and C. Read each sentence to find out whether there is any error in any underlined part and indicate your answer in the Answer Sheet against the corresponding letter i.e., A or B or C. If you find no error, your response should be indicated as D.*

42. I am told, (A)/ John is ill, (B)/ since Monday. (C)/ No error. (D)

43. I shall leave school, (A)/ as soon as, (B)/ I shall find a job. (C)/ No error (D)

44. He is a rich man, (A)/ he is owning, (B)/ a number of buildings in Bombay. (C)/ No error (D)

45. We were able to make it, (A)/ in spite of, (B)/ a bad weather. (C)/ No error (D)

46. Neither of the two letters of credit, (A)/ were useful, (B)/ when he needed it. (C)/ No error (D)

47. Little he realized, (A)/ that he wouldn't live, (B)/ to see his grandson married. (C)/ No error (D)

48. A difficult syllabus, (A)/ is supposed to hurt, (B)/ juvenile mind. (C)/ No error (D)

49. The voice of sanity and patriotism, (A)/ are important to dispel, (B)/ the prevailing confusion. (C)/ No error (D)

50. You were going to explain, (A)/ your late arrival, (B)/ isn't it? (C)/ No error (D)

PART B : GENERAL KNOWLEDGE

51. A brass ball is tied to a thin wire and swung so as to move uniformly in a horizontal circle. Which of the following statements in this regard is/are true?

1. The ball moves with constant velocity
2. The ball moves with constant speed
3. The ball moves with constant acceleration
4. The magnitude of the acceleration of the ball is constant

Select the correct answer using the code given below:

A. 1 only B. 1 and 3
C. 1, 2 and 4 D. 2 and 4 only

52. Two long wires each carrying a d.c. current in the same direction are placed close to each other. Which one of the following statements is correct?

A. The wires will attract each other
B. The wires will repel each other
C. There will be no force between the wires
D. There will be a force between the wires only at the moment when the current is switched ON or OFF

53. The first Indian Satellite, Aryabhatt, was launched in the year:

A. 1972 B. 1975
C. 1976 D. 1979

54. Which one of the following sea routes is the shortest from point to point?

A. Kolkata to Yangoon B. Kolkata to Chennai
C. Chennai to Port Blair D. Mumbai to Colombo

55. Which one of the following is *not* a Green House Gas?

A. Water vapours B. Methane
C. Ozone D. Carbon Monoxide

56. Muscle fatigue is due to the accumulation of:

A. Cholesterol B. Lactic acid
C. Lipoic acid D. Triglycerides

57. The absolute zero, i.e., temperature below which is ***not*** achievable, is about:

A. 0ºC B. –273 K
C. –273ºC D. –300ºC

58. Lightning conductors are used to protect building from lightning strikes. Which of the following statements is/are true about lightning conductors?

1. Lightning conductors create an electric field at its top so that lightning strikes it preferentially
2. Lightning conductors reduce the effect of the strike by uniformly distributing the charge (current) over the surface of the building
3. Lightning conductors take all charge (current) to deep down in the earth
4. Lightning conductors must be installed at a place taller than the building

Select the correct answer using the code given below:

A. 1 and 2 B. 3 and 4 only
C. 1, 3 and 4 D. 4 only

59. Match List-I with List-II and select the correct answer using the code given below the Lists:

List-I (Manufacturing site)	List-II (Industry)
(a) Ludhiana	1. Auto parts
(b) Kanpur	2. Woollen garments
(c) Varanasi	3. Leather
(d) Vijayawada	4. Handloom

Codes:

	(a)	(b)	(c)	(d)
A.	1	4	3	2
B.	2	3	4	1
C.	2	4	3	1
D.	1	3	4	2

60. Which one of the following is ***not*** a sea port?
A. Paradeep B. Haldia
C. Diamond Harbour D. Dhamra

61. Consider the following reaction:

$$CH_4(g) + H_2O(g) \xrightarrow{1270\text{ K}} CO(g) + 3H_2(g)$$

In the reaction given above, the mixture of CO and H_2 is:
A. natural gas B. water gas
C. producer gas D. industrial gas

62. Living things are grouped into sub-groups like plant kingdom/animal kingdom. Which one of the following is ***not*** correct for animal kingdom?
A. Cannot make their own food
B. Body contains cellulose
C. Do not have chlorophyll
D. Migrate from one place to another

63. The silvering in thermos flasks is done to avoid heat transfer by:
A. Convection
B. Conduction
C. Radiation
D. Both convection and conduction

64. The Manas National Park is situated in the State of:
A. Madhya Pradesh B. Jharkhand
C. Assam D. West Bengal

65. Addition of gypsum to cement:
A. reduces setting time of cement
B. produces very light colour cement
C. increases setting time of cement
D. shining surface is formed

66. In case of a compound microscope which of the following statements is/are correct?
1. The focal length of the eye piece is larger than the focal length of the objective
2. The focal length of the eye piece is smaller than the focal length of the objective
3. The image produced in a normal optical microscope is real
4. The image produced in a normal optical microscope is virtual

Select the correct answer using the code given below:
A. 1 only B. 1 and 4
C. 2 and 3 D. 2 and 4

67. Which one of the following statements is ***not*** correct?
A. The radius of curvature of a concave mirror is twice its focal length
B. Power of a convex lens is negative and that of a concave lens is positive
C. The radius of curvature of a plane mirror is infinity
D. When a ray of light passes from an optically denser medium to an optically rarer medium, the angle of refraction is greater than the corresponding angle of incidence

68. Identify the place that is ***not*** an oil field:
A. Naharkatiya B. Kalol
C. Ledo D. Ankleshwar

69. Ammonia (NH_3) obtained from different sources always has same proportion of Nitrogen and Hydrogen. It proves the validity of law of:
A. Reciprocal proportion B. Constant proportion
C. Multiple proportions D. None of the above

70. Which one of the following statements is ***not*** correct?
A. If the velocity and acceleration have opposite sign, the object is slowing down.
B. If the velocity is zero at an instant, the acceleration should also be zero at that instant.
C. If the velocity is zero for a time interval; the acceleration is zero at any instant within the time interval.
D. If the position and velocity have opposite sign, the object is moving towards the origin.

71. The IST meridian 82½°E passes through a number of States in India. Which one of the following sets of States is correct in this respect?
A. Uttarakhand, Uttar Pradesh, Chhatisgarh and Andhra Pradesh
B. Uttar Pradesh, Jharkhand, Chhatisgarh and Odisha
C. Uttarakhand, Uttar Pradesh, Madhya Pradesh and Chhatisgarh
D. Uttar Pradesh, Odisha, Andhra Pradesh and Chhatisgarh

72. Boric acid is an acid because its molecule:
A. accepts OH^- from water releasing proton
B. combines with proton from water molecule
C. contains replaceable H^+ ion
D. gives up a proton

73. Who among the following discovered the antibiotic producing fungus from Penicillium genus?
A. Louis Pasteur B. Sir Alexander Fleming
C. Stanley Prusiner D. Robert Hooke

74. Three equal resistances when combined in series are equivalent to 90 ohm. Their equivalent resistance when combined in parallel will be:
A. 10 ohm B. 30 ohm
C. 270 ohm D. 810 ohm

75. The following figure represents the velocity-time graph of a moving car on a road:

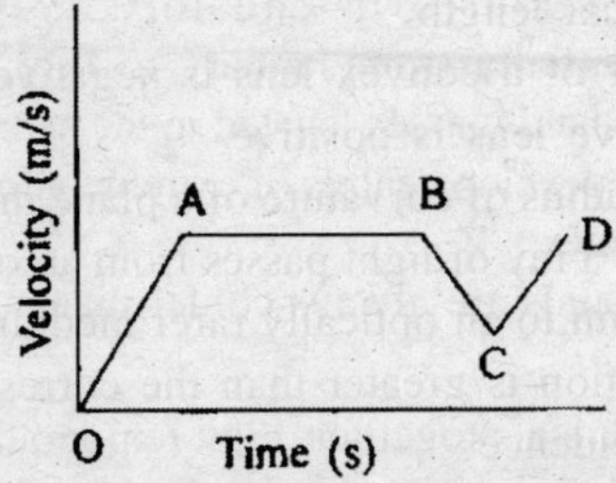

Which segment of the graph represents the retardation?

A. AB B. BC
C. CD D. None

76. Which one among the following places is ***not*** an iron-ore mining area?

A. Badampahar B. Zawar
C. Bailadila D. Anantpur

77. Match List-I with List-II and select the correct answer using the code given below the Lists:

List-I (Forest Conservation Type)	List-II (Place)
(*a*) National Park	1. Dudhwa
(*b*) Sanctuary	2. Bhitarkanika
(*c*) Biosphere Reserve	3. Chilka
(*d*) Tiger Reserve	4. Nokrek

Codes:

	(*a*)	(*b*)	(*c*)	(*d*)
A.	2	3	4	1
B.	1	4	3	2
C.	2	4	3	1
D.	1	3	4	2

78. The main constituent of Vinegar is:

A. Acetic acid B. Ascorbic acid
C. Citric acid D. Tartaric acid

79. White Phosphorus glows in the dark due to:

A. amorphous character
B. slow oxidation
C. high ignition temperature
D. good conducting property of electricity

80. Which one of the following is ***not*** an example of eukaryotic organism?

A. Yeast B. Bacteria
C. Plant D. Human being

81. Which one of the following statements is ***not*** correct?

A. The Kelvin scale of temperature is called the Absolute scale
B. Visible light radiation has wavelength range of 400-700 nm
C. The capacity to do work is called power
D. The wavelength of Gamma rays is less than that of X-rays

82. A man is sitting in a train which is moving with a velocity of 60 km/hour. His speed with respect to the train is:

A. 10/3 m/s B. 60 m/s
C. infinite D. zero

83. Match List-I with List-II and select the correct answer using the code given below the Lists:

List-I (Place)	List-II (Normal vegetation type)
(*a*) Western Ghats	1. Tropical Moist Deciduous
(*b*) Himachal Pradesh	2. Tropical Evergreen
(*c*) Haryana and Punjab	3. Himalayan Moist Forest
(*d*) Chhotanagpur Plateau	4. Tropical Thorny Forest

Codes:

	(*a*)	(*b*)	(*c*)	(*d*)
A.	2	3	4	1
B.	1	4	3	2
C.	2	4	3	1
D.	1	3	4	2

84. The term 'Regur' is used to mean:

A. Laterite soil B. Deltaic soil
C. Red soil D. Black cotton soil

85. Graphite is a much better conductor of heat and electricity than diamond. This is due to the fact that each carbon atom in graphite:

A. undergoes sp^2 hybridization and forms three sigma bonds with three neighbouring carbon atoms
B. undergoes sp^3 hybridization
C. is tetrahedrally bonded
D. is free from van der Waals force

86. Which one of the following vitamins is synthesized in our own skin?

A. Vitamin A B. Vitamin B
C. Vitamin C D. Vitamin D

87. Which one of the following is the SI unit of the thermal conductivity of a material?

A. $Wm^{-1}K^{-1}$ B. Wm/K
C. Wm^{-1}/K^{-1} D. $Js^{-1}m^{-1}K$

88. Which one of the following statements is ***not*** correct?

A. Conduction can occur easily in solids, less easily in liquids but hardly at all in gases
B. Heat energy is carried by moving particles in a convection current
C. Heat energy is carried by electromagnetic waves in radiation
D. The temperature at which a solid changes into a liquid is called the boiling point

89. Which one of the following combinations of stalactites and stalagmites occurrences is correct?

A. Stalactites hang as icicles of different diameters and stalagmites hang from the floor of the caves
B. Stalactites hang as icicles of different diameters and stalagmites rise up from the floor of the caves
C. Stalactites rise up from the floor of the caves and stalagmites hang as icicles of different diameters

D. Stalactites hang as icicles of different diameters and stalagmites also hang as icicles of different diameters

90. Which one of the following is the correct sequence about various levels of organization of Biosphere?
A. Eco system–Biosphere–Community–Population
B. Population–Organism–Eco system–Biosphere
C. Organism–Community–Population–Biosphere
D. Organism–Population–Eco system–Biosphere

91. Which of the following are the properties of an electron?
1. Electron is a constituent of cathode ray
2. Electron is a negatively charged particle
3. The mass of the electron is equal to the mass of the proton
4. Electron is deflected by the electric field but not by magnetic field

Select the correct answer using the code given below:
A. 1 and 2 only B. 1, 2 and 3
C. 3 and 4 D. 1 and 4

92. Carbon and energy requirements of autotrophic organisms are fulfilled by:
A. Photosynthesis B. Gluconeogenesis
C. Glycogenesis D. External sources

93. The resistance of a wire of length l and area of cross-section a is x ohm. If the wire is stretched to double its length, its resistance would become:
A. 2 x ohm B. 0.5 x ohm
C. 4 x ohm D. 6 x ohm

94. Which one of the following describes the Lithosphere?
A. Upper and lower mantle
B. Crust and upper mantle
C. Crust and core
D. Mantle and core

95. Which of the following statements regarding heavy water are correct?
1. It is extensively used as a moderator in nuclear reactors
2. It cannot be used in exchange reaction to study reaction mechanism
3. Viscosity of heavy water is relatively smaller than that of ordinary water
4. The dielectric constant of heavy water is smaller than that of ordinary water

Select the correct answer using the code given below:
A. 1 and 2 B. 2 and 3
C. 3 and 4 D. 1 and 4

96. Conservation of momentum in a collision between particles can be understood on the basis of:
A. Newton's first law of motion
B. Newton's second law of motion only
C. Both Newton's second law of motion and Newton's third law of motion
D. Conservation of energy

97. Which one of the following statements is ***not*** correct?
A. Temperatures decrease from the equator to poles
B. Temperatures in equatorial regions change substantially from January to July
C. Large land masses located in the subarctic and arctic zones develop centres of extremely low temperatures in winter
D. Highlands are always colder than surrounding low lands

98. To weld metals together, high temperature is required. Such a high temperature is obtained by burning:
A. Acetylene in oxygen B. LPG in oxygen
C. Methane in oxygen D. Acetylene in nitrogen

99. Two forces, one of 3 newton and another of 4 newton are applied on a standard 1 kg body, placed on a horizontal and frictionless surface, simultaneously along the x-axis and the y-axis, respectively, as shown below:

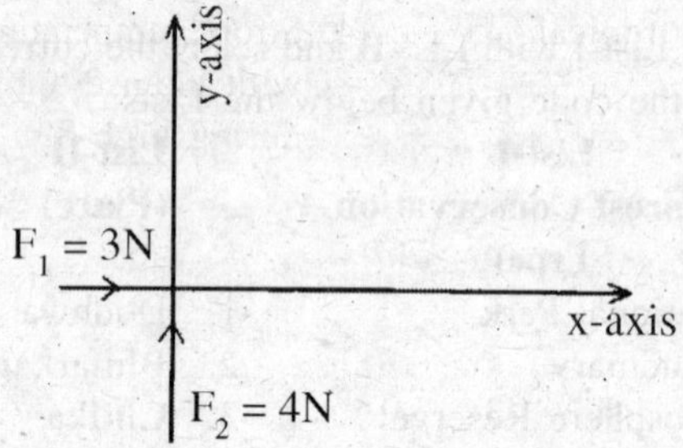

The magnitude of the resultant acceleration is:
A. 7 m/s^2 B. 1 m/s^2
C. 5 m/s^2 D. $\sqrt{7}$ m/s^2

100. Magnetic meridian is an imaginary:
A. line along north-south B. point
C. vertical plane D. horizontal plane

101. An up fold in rock is:
A. graben B. horse
C. anticline D. syncline

102. Which one of the following gases is found in highest quantity in Exosphere?
A. Hydrogen B. Helium
C. Nitrogen D. Oxygen

103. In blood, platelets are required for:
A. transporting oxygen
B. transporting carbon dioxide
C. initiating blood clotting
D. initiating degradation of urea

104. In SI unit of force 'Newton' (N) is given by (where m stands for metre and s stands for second):
A. 1 N = 1 kg/ms^2 B. 1 N = 1 kgm/s^2
C. 1 N = 1 $kg\ s^2/m$ D. 1 N = 1 $kg\ ms^2$

105. The acceleration due to gravity 'g' for objects on or near the surface of earth is related to the universal gravitational constant 'G' as ('M' is the mass of the earth and 'R' is its radius):

A. $G = g\frac{M}{R^2}$ B. $g = G\frac{M}{R^2}$

C. $M = \frac{gG}{R^2}$ D. $R = \frac{gG}{M^2}$

106. Match List-I with List-II and select the correct answer using the code given below the Lists:

List-I (Low-Latitude Climate)	List-II (Characteristic)
(*a*) Wet Equatorial	1. Uniform temperatures, mean near 27°C
(*b*) Monsoon and trade wind coastal	2. Marked temperature cycle with very high temperature before the rainy season
(*c*) Wet-dry tropical	3. Temperatures show an annual cycle with high temperature in the high-Sun season
(*d*) Dry tropical	4. Strong temperature cycle, with intense temperature during high-Sun season

Codes:

	(*a*)	(*b*)	(*c*)	(*d*)
A.	2	3	4	1
B.	1	2	3	4
C.	2	4	3	1
D.	1	3	2	4

107. Match List-I with List-II and select the correct answer using the code given below the Lists:

List-I (Element)	List-II (Use)
(*a*) Li	1. Time keeper in atomic clocks
(*b*) Na	2. Batteries
(*c*) K	3. Transfer of nerve impulses
(*d*) Cs	4. Control of the water content in the blood

Codes:

	(*a*)	(*b*)	(*c*)	(*d*)
A.	2	3	4	1
B.	1	2	3	4
C.	2	4	3	1
D.	1	3	2	4

108. Which one of the following is ***not*** a site of action in human body for the malarial parasite plasmodium?

A. Liver B. Kidney

C. Red blood cell D. Brain

109. The loudness of sound is related to:

A. its frequency B. its amplitude

C. its speed D. its pitch

110. X-rays are electromagnetic radiation whose wavelengths are of the order of:

A. 1 metre B. 10^{-1} metre

C. 10^{-5} metre D. 10^{-10} metre

111. Which one of the following pairs of properties of typical air masses is correct?

Air Mass	:	Source Region
A. Maritime Equatorial	:	Warm oceans in the equatorial zone
B. Maritime Polar	:	Warm oceans in the tropical zone
C. Continental Tropical	:	Less warm oceans in the tropical zone
D. Continental Polar	:	Moist oceans in the polar zone

112. The symbol of the element 'Tungsten' is:

A. Ta B. W

C. Tl D. Tc

113. In Egypt, ancient mummies can be found to have their arteries intact due to well preserved:

A. mineralized blood B. fibroblasts fibre

C. elastic fibre D. brown fat

114. Which one of the following statements is correct?

A. The image formed by a concave mirror for an object lying at infinity is at the principal focus, highly diminished, real and inverted

B. A ray of light parallel to the principal axis after reflection from a concave mirror appears to diverge from the principal focus of the mirror

C. The focal length of a spherical mirror is double of its radius of curvature

D. A ray of light travelling from a rarer medium to a denser medium bends away from the normal

115. Which one of the following statements is correct?

A. Rutherford's alpha-particle scattering experiment led to the discovery of electron

B. J J Thomson suggested that the nucleus of an atom contains protons

C. The atomic number of an element is the same as the number of protons in the nucleus of its atom

D. The mass number of an atom is equal to the number of electrons in its shells

116. Which one of the following statements is ***not*** correct?

A. Application of lime makes the soil acidic

B. High acidity in soil is typical of humid climate

C. Increasing soil acidity results in declining soil fertility

D. Arid climate is characterized by alkaline soil

117. The alkali metals have relatively low melting point. Which one of the following alkali metals is expected to have the highest melting point?

A. Li B. Na

C. K D. Rb

118. Which one of the following is useful in paper manufacturing industry?

A. Fibrous plants

B. Orchids

C. Non-flowering plants

D. Plants growing in high altitude

119. Which one of the following statements is ***not*** correct?
A. In steady flow of a liquid, the velocity of liquid particles reaching at a particular point is the same at all points
B. Steady flow is also called streamlined flow
C. In steady flow, each particle may not follow the same path as taken by a previous particle passing through that point
D. Two streamlines cannot intersect each other

120. According to the Geo-scientists, the shape of the earth is:
1. round
2. spherical
3. close to that of a sphere
4. an oblate ellipsoid

Select the correct answer using the code given below:
A. 2, 3 and 4 B. 1, 2 and 3
C. 1 and 2 only D. 3 and 4 only

121. The word 'Secular' was inserted into the Constitution of India by:
A. 44th Amendment Act B. 52nd Amendment Act
C. 42nd Amendment Act D. 34th Amendment Act

122. Which one of the following is ***not*** correct in the context of balance of payments of India during 2013-14?
A. India's exports were less than its imports
B. Trade balance was negative
C. Net invisibles were positive
D. Capital account balance was negative

123. Which one of the following continents accounts for the maximum share in exports from India?
A. Asia B. Europe
C. Africa D. North America

124. The two provisions of the Constitution of India that most clearly express the power of judicial review are:
A. Article 21 and Article 446
B. Article 32 and Article 226
C. Article 44 and Article 152
D. Article 17 and Article 143

125. Which one of the following statements about Subsidiary Alliance devised by Lord Wellesley in the year 1798 is ***not*** correct?
A. The territories entering into a subsidiary alliance with the British were responsible for their own internal and external protection
B. In the territory of the ally, a British armed contingent would be stationed
C. The ally would have to provide the resources for maintaining the British contingent in the territory
D. The permission of the British was needed for the ally to enter into agreements with other rulers

126. Who among the following was associated with the Mughal Court as a physician to Prince Dara Shukoh?
A. Hakim Afzal Khan B. Ibn Battuta
C. Francois Bernier D. Duarte Barbosa

127. During the Eleventh Five Year Plan (FYP), agriculture sector in India witnessed a growth rate of 3.3 per cent per annum which is higher than 2.4 per cent per annum in the previous FYP. This is largely due to better performance of:
A. Crops and Livestock B. Oilseeds and Fibres
C. Fishing and Oilseeds D. Fibres and Fishing

128. An emergency under Article 352 of the Constitution of India can be declared only during:
A. War, external aggression or internal disturbance.
B. War, external aggression or armed rebellion.
C. Failure of Constitutional Machinery in the State.
D. Financial instability in the country.

129. Which of the following statements about the Livestock sector in India is/are correct?
1. Livestock contributed about 25 per cent of gross value added in agriculture
2. It provides self-employment to a large segment of population
3. Rapid growth of livestock sector can be egalitarian and inclusive

Select the correct answer using the code given below:
A. 3 only B. 1 and 2 only
C. 2 and 3 only D. 1, 2 and 3

130. Which one of the following statements about Khilafat Movement is ***not*** correct?
A. The Khilafat Movement demanded that the Khalifa must retain control over Muslim holy places
B. The radical trend in the Khilafat Movement was represented by younger leaders like Muhammad Ali, Shaukat Ali, and Maulana Azad
C. Indian Muslim leaders used Khilafat as a symbol that could unite the Indian Muslim community
D. The Delhi conference of the Central Khilafat Committee in 1920 decided to launch a massive Non-Cooperation Movement

131. Which one of the following is ***not*** correct in the current Indian scenario?
A. Life expectancy is on the increase and is about 67 years as of now
B. Infant mortality rate is on the decline and has reached 47 per thousand
C. Maternal Mortality Rate (MMR) is on the rise due to lack of medical facilities
D. Percentage of women giving birth in health institutions is one the rise

132. The Fourth Schedule to the Constitution of India deals with:
A. provisions related to the administration of tribal areas.
B. allocation of seats in the Council of States.
C. the Union List, the State List and the Concurrent List.
D. recognized languages of the Union of India.

133. The British Officer who was a representative of the Governor General and who lived in a State which was not under direct British rule was called:

A. Collector B. Viceroy
C. Resident D. Agent

134. Which of the following features of the Permanent Settlement of 1793 is / are correct?

1. The Permanent Settlement vested land ownership rights in the peasants
2. The Permanent Settlement vested land ownership rights in the Zamindars
3. The Zamindars had to pay a fixed amount of rent by a particular date
4. The Zamindars benefited hugely from the Permanent Settlement while the peasants suffered

Select the correct answer using the code given below:

A. 1 only B. 2 and 3 only
C. 4 only D. 1, 2 and 3

135. The Vijayanagara Empire received its death blow at the battle of:

A. Talikota in 1565 B. Panipat in 1661
C. Talikota in 1665 D. Raichur in 1510

136. The 'Basic Structure Doctrine' was enunciated by the Supreme Court during the:

A. Golak Nath case
B. Maneka Gandhi case
C. Kesavananda Bharati case
D. S.R. Bommai case

137. Consider the following statements about the travellers who visited India:

1. Abdur Razzaq Samarqandi from Herat visited Delhi and Daulatabad.
2. Ibn Battuta provides detailed accounts of both Delhi and Daulatabad.
3. According to Francois Bernier there was no private property in land in Mughal India.

Which of the statements given above is/are correct?

A. 1 only B. 1, 2 and 3
C. 1 and 3 only D. 2 and 3 only

138. Which of the following statements about hill stations of colonial India is/are correct?

1. The architecture of hill stations sought to recreate the European style
2. Hill stations were developed as sanitariums where soldiers were treated for illness
3. Shimla became the official residence of the Commander in Chief of the Indian Army
4. In 1864, Shimla had to be evacuated because of a Typhoid epidemic

Select the correct answer using the code given below:

A. 1 only B. 1, 2 and 3
C. 3 and 4 D. 2 and 3 only

139. Match List-I with List-II and select the correct answer using the code given below the Lists:

List-I (Dynasty)	**List-II (Architecture)**
(*a*) Chalukyas	1. Sun Temple, Konark
(*b*) Hoysalas	2. Pattadakal Temples
(*c*) Pandyas	3. Kesava Temple, Somnathpur
(*d*) Eastern Gangas	4. Eastern *gopura* of Chidambaram Temple

Codes:

	(*a*)	(*b*)	(*c*)	(*d*)
A.	1	3	2	4
B.	1	2	3	4
C.	2	4	3	1
D.	2	3	4	1

140. The Senia tradition is:

A. musical tradition that emerged from the colonial army (Sena)
B. dance drama written by Keshab Chandra Sen
C. textile tradition of eastern UP
D. musical tradition that invoked the name of Tansen, the celebrated musician of Akbar's Court

141. Who among the following founded the Rajahmundri Social Reform Association in 1878 in support of widow remarriage?

A. Vishanshastri Pandit
B. Ishwar Chandra Vidyasagar
C. Pandita Ramabai
D. Veeresalingam Pantulu

142. The SAARC Secretariat is located at:

A. New Delhi B. Colombo
C. Kathmandu D. Karachi

143. The 19th Century Faraizi Movement in eastern Bengal developed under the leadership of:

A. Titu Rai B. Haji Shariatullah
C. Shah Sayyid Ahmad D. Dudu Miyan

144. The Indian States Committee was formed in 1928 under:

A. The Raja of Junagadh B. Ian Copland
C. Sir Harcourt Butler D. Motilal Nehru

145. The Panchayati Raj system under Part-IX of the Constitution of India does ***not*** apply to the States of:

A. Assam, Mizoram and Nagaland
B. Nagaland, Meghalaya and Tripura
C. Nagaland, Meghalaya and Mizoram
D. Sikkim, Tripura and Meghalaya

146. The First Five Year Plan (1951-1956) was drafted by:

A. P.C. Mahalanobis B. K.N. Raj
C. J.C. Kumarappa D. Jawaharlal Nehru

147. Who among the following is the author of the book, "Pakistan Paradox: Instability and Resilience"?

A. Christophe Jaffrelot B. G. Parthasarthy
C. Imran Khan D. Mamnoon Hussain

148. Which one of the following was the theme of the "International Day of United Nations Peacekeepers" for the year 2015?
A. Peacekeeping is a Global Partnership
B. UN 70 and UN Peacekeeping: Past, Present, and Future
C. Women in Peacekeeping
D. A Force for the Future

149. Indian athlete Vikas Gowda is associated with:
A. Wrestling B. Sprint
C. Discus throw D. Archery

150. The 19th Federation Cup National Senior Athletic Championships (2015) was held in:
A. Karnataka B. Haryana
C. Uttar Pradesh D. Kerala

PAPER II : MATHEMATICS

1. Let X be the set of all persons living in Delhi. The persons *a* and *b* in X are said to be related if the difference in their ages is at most 5 years. The relation is:
A. an equivalence relation
B. reflexive and transitive but not symmetric
C. symmetric and transitive but not reflexive
D. reflexive and symmetric but not transitive

2. The matrix $A = \begin{bmatrix} 1 & 3 & 2 \\ 1 & x-1 & 1 \\ 2 & 7 & x-3 \end{bmatrix}$ will have inverse for every real number x ***except*** for

A. $x = \frac{11 \pm \sqrt{5}}{2}$ B. $x = \frac{9 \pm \sqrt{5}}{2}$

C. $x = \frac{11 \pm \sqrt{3}}{2}$ D. $x = \frac{9 \pm \sqrt{3}}{2}$

3. If the value of the determinant $\begin{vmatrix} a & 1 & 1 \\ 1 & b & 1 \\ 1 & 1 & c \end{vmatrix}$ is positive, where $a \neq b \neq c$, then the value of abc
A. cannot be less than 1
B. is greater than –8
C. is less than –8
D. must be greater than 8

4. Consider the following statements in respect of the determinant

$$\begin{vmatrix} \cos^2 \frac{\alpha}{2} & \sin^2 \frac{\alpha}{2} \\ \sin^2 \frac{\beta}{2} & \cos^2 \frac{\beta}{2} \end{vmatrix}$$

where α, β are complementary angles

1. The value of the determinant is $\frac{1}{\sqrt{2}} \cos\left(\frac{\alpha - \beta}{2}\right)$.
2. The maximum value of the determinant is $\frac{1}{\sqrt{2}}$.

Which of the above statements is/are correct?
A. 1 only B. 2 only
C. Both 1 and 2 D. Neither 1 nor 2

5. What is $(1000000001)_2 - (0.0101)_2$ equal to?
A. $(512.6775)_{10}$ B. $(512.6875)_{10}$
C. $(512.6975)_{10}$ D. $(512.0909)_{10}$

6. If $A = \begin{bmatrix} 1 & 0 & -2 \\ 2 & -3 & 4 \end{bmatrix}$, then the matrix X for which 2X + 3A = 0 holds true is

A. $\begin{bmatrix} -\frac{3}{2} & 0 & -3 \\ -3 & -\frac{9}{2} & -6 \end{bmatrix}$ B. $\begin{bmatrix} \frac{3}{2} & 0 & -3 \\ 3 & -\frac{9}{2} & -6 \end{bmatrix}$

C. $\begin{bmatrix} \frac{3}{2} & 0 & 3 \\ 3 & \frac{9}{2} & 6 \end{bmatrix}$ D. $\begin{bmatrix} -\frac{3}{2} & 0 & 3 \\ -3 & \frac{9}{2} & -6 \end{bmatrix}$

7. If z_1 and z_2 are complex numbers with $|z_1| = |z_2|$, then which of the following is/are correct?
1. $z_1 = z_2$
2. Real part of z_1 = Real part of z_2
3. Imaginary part of z_1 = Imaginary part of z_2

Select the correct answer using the code given below:
A. 1 only B. 2 only
C. 3 only D. None

8. If $A = \begin{bmatrix} 1 & 1 & -1 \\ 2 & -3 & 4 \\ 3 & -2 & 3 \end{bmatrix}$ and $B = \begin{bmatrix} -1 & -2 & -1 \\ 6 & 12 & 6 \\ 5 & 10 & 5 \end{bmatrix}$, then which of the following is/are correct?
1. A and B commute.
2. AB is a null matrix.

Select the correct answer using the code given below:
A. 1 only B. 2 only
C. Both 1 and 2 D. Neither 1 nor 2

9. The number of real roots of the equation $x^2 - 3|x| + 2 = 0$ is:
A. 4 B. 3
C. 2 D. 1

10. If the sum of the roots of the equation $ax^2 + bx + c = 0$ is equal to the sum of their squares, then
A. $a^2 + b^2 = c^2$ B. $a^2 + b^2 = a + b$
C. $ab + b^2 = 2ac$ D. $ab - b^2 = 2ac$

11. If A = $\{x \in R : x^2 + 6x - 7 < 0\}$ and B = $\{x \in R : x^2 + 9x + 14 > 0\}$, then which of the following is/are correct?
1. $(A \cap B) = (-2, 1)$
2. (A/B) = (–7, –2)
Select the correct answer using the code given below:
A. 1 only B. 2 only
C. Both 1 and 2 D. Neither 1 nor 2

12. A, B, C and D are four sets such that $A \cap B = C \cap D = \phi$. Consider the following:
1. $A \cup C$ and $B \cup D$ are always disjoint.
2. $A \cap C$ and $B \cap D$ are always disjoint.
Which of the above statements is/are correct?
A. 1 only B. 2 only
C. Both 1 and 2 D. Neither 1 nor 2

13. If A is an invertible matrix of order n and k is any positive real number, then the value of $[\det(kA)]^{-1}$ det A is
A. k^{-n} B. k^{-1}
C. k^n D. nk

14. The value of the infinite product
$6^{\frac{1}{2}} \times 6^{\frac{1}{2}} \times 6^{\frac{3}{8}} \times 6^{\frac{1}{4}} \times$ ..... is
A. 6 B. 36
C. 216 D. ∞

15. If the roots of the equation $x^2 - nx + m = 0$ differ by 1, then
A. $n^2 - 4m - 1 = 0$ B. $n^2 + 4m - 1 = 0$
C. $m^2 + 4n + 1 = 0$ D. $m^2 - 4n - 1 = 0$

16. If different words are formed with all the letters of the word 'AGAIN' and are arranged alphabetically among themselves as in a dictionary, the word at the 50th place will be:
A. NAAGI B. NAAIG
C. IAAGN D. LAANG

17. The number of ways in which a cricket team of 11 players be chosen out of a batch of 15 players so that the captain of the team is always included, is:
A. 165 B. 364
C. 1001 D. 1365

18. In the expansion of $\left(\sqrt{x} + \frac{1}{3x^2}\right)^{10}$ the value of constant term (independent of x) is :
A. 5 B. 8
C. 45 D. 90

19. The value of $\sin^2 5° + \sin^2 10° + \sin^2 15° + \sin^2 20° + ... + \sin^2 90°$ is:
A. 7 B. 8
C. 9 D. $\frac{19}{2}$

20. On simplifying $\frac{\sin^3 A + \sin 3A}{\sin A} + \frac{\cos^3 A - \cos 3A}{\cos A}$, we get:
A. sin3A B. cos3A
C. sinA + cosA D. 3

21. The value of $\tan\left(2\tan^{-1}\frac{1}{5} - \frac{\pi}{4}\right)$ is:
A. $-\frac{7}{17}$ B. $\frac{5}{16}$
C. $\frac{5}{4}$ D. $\frac{7}{17}$

22. Two poles are 10 m and 20 m high. The line joining their tops makes an angle of 15° with the horizontal. The distance between the poles is approximately equal to:
A. 36.3 m B. 37.3 m
C. 38.3 m D. 39.3 m

23. If $g(x) = \frac{1}{f(x)}$ and $f(x) = x, x \neq 0$, then which one of the following is correct?
A. $f(f(f(g(g(f(x)))))) = g(g(f(g(f(x)))))$
B. $f(f(g(g(g(f(x)))))) = g(g(f(g(f(x)))))$
C. $f(g(f(g(g(f(g(x))))))) = g(g(f(g(f(x)))))$
D. $f(f(f(g(g(f(x)))))) = f(f(f(g(f(x)))))$

24. Consider the following:
1. $\sin^{-1}\frac{4}{5} + \sin^{-1}\frac{3}{5} = \frac{\pi}{2}$
2. $\tan^{-1}\sqrt{3} + \tan^{-1}1 = -\tan^{-1}(2+\sqrt{3})$
Which of the above is/are correct?
A. 1 only B. 2 only
C. Both 1 and 2 D. Neither 1 nor 2

25. If A is an orthogonal matrix of order 3 and $B = \begin{bmatrix} 1 & 2 & 3 \\ -3 & 0 & 2 \\ 2 & 5 & 0 \end{bmatrix}$, then which of the following is/are correct?
1. $|AB| = \pm 47$
2. AB = BA
Select the correct answer using the code given below:
A. 1 only B. 2 only
C. Both 1 and 2 D. Neither 1 nor 2

26. If a, b, c are the sides of a triangle ABC, then $a^{\frac{1}{p}} + b^{\frac{1}{p}} - c^{\frac{1}{p}}$ where $p > 1$, is:

A. always negative
B. always positive
C. always zero
D. positive if $1 < p < 2$ and negative if $p > 2$

27. If a, b, c are real numbers, then the value of the determinant $\begin{vmatrix} 1-a & a-b-c & b+c \\ 1-b & b-c-a & c+a \\ 1-c & c-a-b & a+b \end{vmatrix}$ is:

A. 0 B. $(a - b)(b - c)(c - a)$
C. $(a + b + c)^2$ D. $(a + b + c)^3$

28. If the point $z_1 = 1 + i$ where $i = \sqrt{-1}$ is the reflection of a point $z_2 = x + iy$ in the line $i\bar{z} - iz = 5$, then the point z_2 is:

A. $1 + 4i$ B. $4 + i$
C. $1 - i$ D. $-1 - i$

29. If $\sin x + \sin y = a$ and $\cos x + \cos y = b$, then $\tan^2\left(\frac{x+y}{2}\right) + \tan^2\left(\frac{x-y}{2}\right)$ is equal to:

A. $\dfrac{a^4 + b^4 + 4b^2}{a^2b^2 + b^4}$ B. $\dfrac{a^4 - b^4 + 4b^2}{a^2b^2 + b^4}$

C. $\dfrac{a^4 - b^4 + 4a^2}{a^2b^2 + a^4}$ D. None of these

30. A vertical tower standing on a levelled field is mounted with a vertical flag staff of length 3 m. From a point on the field, the angles of elevation of the bottom and tip of the flag staff are 30° and 45° respectively. Which one of the following gives the best approximation to the height of the tower?

A. 3.90 m B. 4.00 m
C. 4.10 m D. 4.25 m

For the next three (03) items that follow: Consider the expansion of $(1 + x)^{2n + 1}$

31. If the coefficients of x^r and x^{r+1} are equal in the expansion, then r is equal to:

A. n B. $\dfrac{2n-1}{2}$

C. $\dfrac{2n+1}{2}$ D. $n + 1$

32. The average of the coefficients of the two middle terms in the expansion is:

A. ${}^{2n+1}C_{n+2}$ B. ${}^{2n+1}C_n$
C. ${}^{2n+1}C_{n-1}$ D. ${}^{2n}C_{n+1}$

33. The sum of the coefficients of all the terms in the expansion is:

A. 2^{2n-1} B. 4^{n-1}
C. 2×4^n D. None of these

34. The nth term of an A.P. is $\dfrac{3+n}{4}$, then the sum of first 105 terms is:

A. 270 B. 735
C. 1409 D. 1470

35. A polygon has 44 diagonals. The number of its sides is:

A. 11 B. 10
C. 8 D. 7

36. If p, q, r are in one geometric progression and a, b, c are in another geometric progression, then ap, bq, cr are in:

A. Arithmetic progression B. Geometric progression
C. Harmonic progression D. None of the above

For the next two (02) items that follow: Consider a triangle ABC satisfying

$$2a\sin^2\left(\frac{C}{2}\right) + 2c\sin^2\left(\frac{A}{2}\right) = 2a + 2c - 3b$$

37. The sides of the triangle are in:

A. G.P.
B. A.P.
C. H.P.
D. Neither in G.P. nor in A.P. nor in H.P.

38. sin A, sin B, sin C are in:

A. G.P.
B. A.P.
C. H.P.
D. Neither in G.P. nor in A.P. nor in H.P.

39. If $p = \tan\left(-\frac{11\pi}{6}\right), q = \tan\left(\frac{21\pi}{4}\right)$ and $r = \cot\left(\frac{283\pi}{6}\right)$, then which of the following is/are correct?

1. The value of $p \times r$ is 2.
2. p, q and r are in G.P.

Select the correct answer using the code given below:

A. 1 only B. 2 only
C. Both 1 and 2 D. Neither 1 nor 2

40. The number of ways in which 3 holiday tickets can be given to 20 employees of an organization if each employee is eligible for any one or more of the tickets, is:

A. 1140 B. 3420
C. 6840 D. 8000

41. What is the sum of n terms of the series $\sqrt{2} + \sqrt{8} + \sqrt{18} + \sqrt{32} + ...?$

A. $\dfrac{n(n-1)}{\sqrt{2}}$ B. $\sqrt{2}n(n+1)$

C. $\dfrac{n(n+1)}{\sqrt{2}}$ D. $\dfrac{n(n-1)}{2}$

42. The coefficient of x^{99} in the expansion of $(x-1)(x-2)(x-3)\ldots(x-100)$ is:
A. 5050
B. 5000
C. –5050
D. –5000

43. $z\bar{z}+(3-i)z+(3+i)\bar{z}+1=0$ represents a circle with:
A. centre (–3, –1) and radius 3
B. centre (–3, 1) and radius 3
C. centre (–3, –1) and radius 4
D. centre (–3, 1) and radius 4

44. The number of 3-digit even numbers that can be formed from the digits 0, 1, 2, 3, 4 and 5, repetition of digits being not allowed, is:
A. 60
B. 56
C. 52
D. 48

45. If $\log_8 m + \log_8 \frac{1}{6} = \frac{2}{3}$, them m is equal to:
A. 24
B. 18
C. 12
D. 4

46. The area of the figure formed by the lines $ax + by + c = 0$, $ax - by + c = 0$, $ax + by - c = 0$ and $ax - by - c = 0$ is:
A. $\frac{c^2}{ab}$
B. $\frac{2c^2}{ab}$
C. $\frac{c^2}{2ab}$
D. $\frac{c^2}{4ab}$

47. If a line is perpendicular to the line $5x - y = 0$ and forms a triangle of area 5 square units with co-ordinate axes, then its equation is:
A. $x+5y\pm5\sqrt{2}=0$
B. $x-5y\pm5\sqrt{2}=0$
C. $5x+y\pm5\sqrt{2}=0$
D. $5x-y\pm5\sqrt{2}=0$

48. Consider any point P on the ellipse $\frac{x^2}{25}+\frac{y^2}{9}=1$ in the first quadrant. Let r and s represent its distances from (4, 0) and (–4, 0) respectively, then $(r + s)$ is equal to:
A. 10 unit
B. 9 unit
C. 8 unit
D. 6 unit

49. A straight line $x = y + 2$ touches the circle $4(x^2 + y^2) = r^2$. The value of r is:
A. $\sqrt{2}$
B. $2\sqrt{2}$
C. 2
D. 1

50. The three lines $4x + 4y = 1$, $8x - 3y = 2$, $y = 0$ are:
A. the sides of an isosceles triangle
B. concurrent
C. mutually perpendicular
D. the sides of an equilateral triangle

51. The line $3x + 4y - 24 = 0$ intersects the x-axis at A and y-axis at B. Then the circumcentre of the triangle OAB where O is the origin is:
A. (2, 3)
B. (3, 3)
C. (4, 3)
D. None of these

52. The eccentricity of the hyperbola $16x^2 - 9y^2 = 1$ is:
A. $\frac{3}{5}$
B. $\frac{5}{3}$
C. $\frac{4}{5}$
D. $\frac{5}{4}$

53. The product of the perpendiculars from the two points (± 4, 0) to the line $3x \cos\phi + 5y \sin\phi = 15$ is:
A. 25
B. 16
C. 9
D. 8

54. If the centre of the circle passing through the origin is (3, 4), then the intercepts cut off by the circle on x-axis and y-axis respectively are:
A. 3 unit and 4 unit
B. 6 unit and 4 unit
C. 3 unit and 8 unit
D. 6 unit and 8 unit

55. The lines $2x = 3y = -z$ and $6x = -y = -4z$
A. are perpendicular
B. are parallel
C. intersect at an angle 45º
D. intersect at an angle 60º

56. Two straight lines passing through the point A(3, 2) cut the line $2y = x + 3$ and x-axis perpendicularly at P and Q respectively. The equation of the line PQ is:
A. $7x + y - 21 = 0$
B. $x + 7y + 21 = 0$
C. $2x + y - 8 = 0$
D. $x + 2y + 8 = 0$

57. The radius of the sphere
$3x^2 + 3y^2 + 3z^2 - 8x + 4y + 8z - 15 = 0$ is:
A. 2
B. 3
C. 4
D. 5

58. The direction ratios of the line perpendicular to the lines with direction ratios < 1, –2, –2 > and < 0, 2, 1 > are:
A. < 2, –1, 2 >
B. < –2, 1, 2 >
C. < 2, 1, –2 >
D. < –2, –1, –2 >

59. What are the co-ordinates of the foot of the perpendicular drawn from the point (3, 5, 4) on the plane $z = 0$?
A. (0, 5, 4)
B. (3, 5, 0)
C. (3, 0, 4)
D. (0, 0, 4)

60. The lengths of the intercepts on the co-ordinate axes made by the plane $5x + 2y + z - 13 = 0$ are:
A. 5, 2, 1 unit
B. $\frac{13}{5},\frac{13}{2},13$ unit
C. $\frac{5}{13},\frac{2}{13},\frac{1}{13}$ unit
D. 1, 2, 5 unit

61. The area of the square, one of whose diagonals is $3\hat{i}+4\hat{j}$ is:
A. 12 square unit
B. 12.5 square unit
C. 25 square unit
D. 156.25 square unit

62. ABCD is a parallelogram and P is the point of intersection of the diagonals. If O is the origin, then $\overrightarrow{OA}+\overrightarrow{OB}+\overrightarrow{OC}+\overrightarrow{OD}$ is equal to:

A. $4\overrightarrow{OP}$ B. $2\overrightarrow{OP}$
C. $\overrightarrow{OP}$ D. Null vector

63. If $\vec{b}$ and $\vec{c}$ are the position vectors of the points B and C respectively, then the position vector of the point D such that $\overrightarrow{BD}=4\overrightarrow{BC}$ is:

A. $4(\vec{c}-\vec{b})$ B. $-4(\vec{c}-\vec{b})$
C. $4\vec{c}-3\vec{b}$ D. $4\vec{c}+3\vec{b}$

64. If the position vector $\vec{a}$ of the point (5, n) is such that $|\vec{a}|=13$, then the value/values of n can be:

A. ± 8 B. ± 12
C. 8 only D. 12 only

65. If $|\vec{a}|=2$ and $|\vec{b}|=3$, then $|\vec{a}\times\vec{b}|^2+|\vec{a}.\vec{b}|^2$ is equal to:

A. 72 B. 64
C. 48 D. 36

66. Consider the following inequalities in respect of vectors $\vec{a}$ and $\vec{b}$:

1. $|\vec{a}+\vec{b}|\le|\vec{a}|+|\vec{b}|$
2. $|\vec{a}-\vec{b}|\ge|\vec{a}|-|\vec{b}|$

Which of the above is/are correct?

A. 1 only B. 2 only
C. Both 1 and 2 D. Neither 1 nor 2

67. If the magnitude of difference of two unit vectors is $\sqrt{3}$, then the magnitude of sum of the two vectors is:

A. $\frac{1}{2}$ unit B. 1 unit
C. 2 unit D. 3 unit

68. If the vectors $\alpha\hat{i}+\alpha\hat{j}+\gamma\hat{k}, \hat{i}+\hat{k}$ and $\gamma\hat{i}+\gamma\hat{j}+\beta\hat{k}$ lie on a plane, where α, β and γ are distinct non-negative numbers, then γ is:

A. Arithmetic mean of α and β
B. Geometric mean of α and β
C. Harmonic mean of α and β
D. None of the above

69. The vectors $\vec{a},\vec{b},\vec{c}$ and $\vec{d}$ are such that $\vec{a}\times\vec{b}=\vec{c}\times\vec{d}$ and $\vec{a}\times\vec{c}=\vec{b}\times\vec{d}$. Which of the following is/are correct?

1. $(\vec{a}-\vec{d})\times(\vec{b}-\vec{c})=\vec{0}$
2. $(\vec{a}\times\vec{b})\times(\vec{c}\times\vec{d})=\vec{0}$

Select the correct answer using the code given below:

A. 1 only B. 2 only
C. Both 1 and 2 D. Neither 1 nor 2

70. The value of $\int_a^b \frac{x^7+\sin x}{\cos x}dx$ where $a+b=0$ is:

A. $2b - a\sin(b-a)$ B. $a + 3b\cos(b-a)$
C. $\sin a - (b-a)\cos b$ D. 0

71. If $f(x)=\sqrt{25-x^2}$, then what is $\lim_{x\to 1}\frac{f(x)-f(1)}{x-1}$ equal to?

A. $\frac{1}{5}$ B. $\frac{1}{24}$
C. $\sqrt{24}$ D. $-\frac{1}{\sqrt{24}}$

72. Consider the function

$$f(x)=\begin{cases} ax-2 & \text{for } -2<x<-1 \\ -1 & \text{for } -1\le x\le 1 \\ a+2(x-1)^2 & \text{for } 1<x<2 \end{cases}$$

What is the value of a for which $f(x)$ is continuous at $x=-1$ and $x=1$?

A. -1 B. 1
C. 0 D. 2

73. The function $f(x)=\frac{1-\sin x+\cos x}{1+\sin x+\cos x}$ is not defined at $x=\pi$. The value of $f(\pi)$ so that $f(x)$ is continuous at $x=\pi$ is:

A. $-\frac{1}{2}$ B. $\frac{1}{2}$
C. -1 D. 1

74. Consider the following functions:

1. $f(x)=\begin{cases}\frac{1}{x} & \text{if } x\ne 0\\ 0 & \text{if } x=0\end{cases}$
2. $f(x)=\begin{cases}2x+5 & \text{if } x>0\\ x^2+2x+5 & \text{if } x\le 0\end{cases}$

Which of the above functions is/are derivable at $x=0$?

A. 1 only B. 2 only
C. Both 1 and 2 D. Neither 1 nor 2

75. The domain of the function $f(x)=\frac{1}{\sqrt{|x|-x}}$ is:

A. $[0,\infty)$ B. $(-\infty,0)$
C. $[1,\infty)$ D. $(-\infty,0]$

76. Consider the following statements:

1. The function $f(x)=x^2+2\cos x$ is increasing in the interval $(0,\pi)$

2. The function $f(x) = \ln\left(\sqrt{1+x^2} - x\right)$ is decreasing in the interval $(-\infty, \infty)$

Which of the above statements is/are correct?

A. 1 only B. 2 only
C. Both 1 and 2 D. Neither 1 nor 2

77. The derivative of $\ln(x + \sin x)$ with respect to $(x + \cos x)$ is:

A. $\dfrac{1+\cos x}{(x+\sin x)(1-\sin x)}$ B. $\dfrac{1-\cos x}{(x+\sin x)(1+\sin x)}$

C. $\dfrac{1-\cos x}{(x-\sin x)(1+\cos x)}$ D. $\dfrac{1+\cos x}{(x-\sin x)(1-\cos x)}$

78. If $y = \cot^{-1}\left[\dfrac{\sqrt{1+\sin x}+\sqrt{1-\sin x}}{\sqrt{1+\sin x}-\sqrt{1-\sin x}}\right]$, where $0 < x < \dfrac{\pi}{2}$,

then $\dfrac{dy}{dx}$ is equal to:

A. $\dfrac{1}{2}$ B. 2
C. $\sin x + \cos x$ D. $\sin x - \cos x$

79. The function $f(x) = \dfrac{x^2}{e^x}$ is monotonically increasing if:

A. $x < 0$ only
B. $x > 2$ only
C. $0 < x < 2$
D. $x \in (-\infty, 0) \cup (2, \infty)$

80. If $x^a y^b = (x - y)^{a+b}$, then the value of $\dfrac{dy}{dx} - \dfrac{y}{x}$ is equal to:

A. $\dfrac{a}{b}$ B. $\dfrac{b}{a}$
C. 1 D. 0

81. If $f : \mathrm{R} \to \mathrm{R}$, $g : \mathrm{R} \to \mathrm{R}$ be two functions given by $f(x) = 2x - 3$ and $g(x) = x^3 + 5$, then $(fog)^{-1}(x)$ is equal to:

A. $\left(\dfrac{x+7}{2}\right)^{\frac{1}{3}}$ B. $\left(\dfrac{x-7}{2}\right)^{\frac{1}{3}}$

C. $\left(x-\dfrac{7}{2}\right)^{\frac{1}{3}}$ D. $\left(x+\dfrac{7}{2}\right)^{\frac{1}{3}}$

82. If $0 < a < b$, then $\displaystyle\int_a^b \frac{|x|}{x}\,dx$ is equal to:

A. $|b|-|a|$ B. $|a|-|b|$
C. $\dfrac{|b|}{|a|}$ D. 0

83. $\displaystyle\int_0^{2\pi} \sin^5\left(\frac{x}{4}\right) dx$ is equal to:

A. $\dfrac{8}{15}$ B. $\dfrac{16}{15}$
C. $\dfrac{32}{15}$ D. 0

84. If $f(x) = \dfrac{\sin\left(e^{x-2}-1\right)}{\ln(x-1)}$, then $\lim\limits_{x\to 2} f(x)$ is equal to:

A. -2 B. -1
C. 0 D. 1

85. Consider the following statements:

1. $f(x) = \ln x$ is an increasing function on $(0, \infty)$.
2. $f(x) = e^x - x(\ln x)$ is an increasing function on $(1, \infty)$.

Which of the above statements is/are correct?

A. 1 only B. 2 only
C. Both 1 and 2 D. Neither 1 nor 2

86. If $s = \sqrt{t^2+1}$, then $\dfrac{d^2s}{dt^2}$ is equal to:

A. $\dfrac{1}{s}$ B. $\dfrac{1}{s^2}$
C. $\dfrac{1}{s^3}$ D. $\dfrac{1}{s^4}$

87. Consider the following statements:

Statement 1: The function $f : \mathrm{R} \to \mathrm{R}$ such that $f(x) = x^3$ for all $x \in \mathrm{R}$ is one-one.

Statement 2: $f(a) = f(b) \Rightarrow a = b$ for all $a, b \in \mathrm{R}$ if the function f is one-one.

Which one of the following is correct in respect of the above statements?

A. Both the statements are true and Statement 2 is the correct explanation of Statement 1.
B. Both the statements are true and Statement 2 is ***not*** the correct explanation of Statement 1.
C. Statement 1 is true but Statement 2 is false.
D. Statement 1 is false but Statement 2 is true.

88. $\displaystyle\int \frac{dx}{1+e^{-x}}$ is equal to:

A. $1 + e^x + c$ B. $\ln(1 + e^{-x}) + c$
C. $\ln(1 + e^x) + c$ D. $2\ln(1 + e^{-x}) + c$

where c is the constant of integration.

89. $\displaystyle\int_{-1}^{1} x|x|\,dx$ is equal to:

A. 0 B. $\dfrac{2}{3}$
C. 2 D. -2

90. The area bounded by the coordinate axes and the curve $\sqrt{x}+\sqrt{y}=1$, is:

A. 1 square unit
B. $\frac{1}{2}$ square unit
C. $\frac{1}{3}$ square unit
D. $\frac{1}{6}$ square unit

For the next two (02) items that follow: Consider the function

$f(x)=\left(\frac{1}{x}\right)^{2x^2}$, where $x > 0$

91. At what value of x does the function attain maximum value?

A. e
B. $\sqrt{e}$
C. $\frac{1}{\sqrt{e}}$
D. $\frac{1}{e}$

92. The maximum value of the function is:

A. e
B. $e^{\frac{2}{e}}$
C. $e^{\frac{1}{e}}$
D. $\frac{1}{e}$

For the next two (02) items that follow: Consider

$f'(x)=\frac{x^2}{2}-kx+1$ such that $f(0) = 0$ and $f(3) = 15$

93. The value of k is:

A. $\frac{5}{3}$
B. $\frac{3}{5}$
C. $-\frac{5}{3}$
D. $-\frac{3}{5}$

94. $f''\left(-\frac{2}{3}\right)$ is equal to:

A. −1
B. $\frac{1}{3}$
C. $\frac{1}{2}$
D. 1

For the next two (02) items that follow: Consider the function $f(x) = -2x^3 - 9x^2 - 12x + 1$

95. The function $f(x)$ is an increasing function in the interval

A. (−2, −1)
B. (−∞, −2)
C. (−1, 2)
D. (−1, ∞)

96. The function $f(x)$ is a decreasing function in the interval:

A. (−2, −1)
B. (−∞, −2) only
C. (−1, ∞) only
D. (−∞, −2) ∪ (−1, ∞)

For the next two (02) items that follow: Consider the integrals

$A=\int_0^{\pi}\frac{\sin x\,dx}{\sin x+\cos x}$ and $B=\int_0^{\pi}\frac{\sin x\,dx}{\sin x-\cos x}$

97. Which one of the following is correct?

A. A = 2B
B. B = 2A
C. A = B
D. A = 3B

98. What is the value of B?

A. $\frac{\pi}{4}$
B. $\frac{\pi}{2}$
C. $\frac{3\pi}{4}$
D. π

For the next two (02) items that follow: Consider the function

$$f(x)=\begin{cases}-2\sin x & \text{if } x\le -\frac{\pi}{2}\\ A\sin x+B & \text{if } -\frac{\pi}{2}<x<\frac{\pi}{2}\\ \cos x & \text{if } x\ge\frac{\pi}{2}\end{cases}$$

which is continuous everywhere.

99. The value of A is:

A. 1
B. 0
C. −1
D. −2

100. The value of B is:

A. 1
B. 0
C. −1
D. −2

101. The degree of the differential equation $\frac{dy}{dx}-x=\left(y-x\frac{dy}{dx}\right)^{-4}$ is:

A. 2
B. 3
C. 4
D. 5

102. The solution of $\frac{dy}{dx}=\sqrt{1-x^2-y^2+x^2y^2}$ is:

A. $\sin^{-1} y = \sin^{-1} x + c$

B. $2\sin^{-1} y=\sqrt{1-x^2}+\sin^{-1}x+c$

C. $2\sin^{-1} y=x\sqrt{1-x^2}+\sin^{-1}x+c$

D. $2\sin^{-1} y=x\sqrt{1-x^2}+\cos^{-1}x+c$

where c is an arbitrary constant.

103. The differential equation of the family of circles passing through the origin and having centres on the x-axis is:

A. $2xy\frac{dy}{dx}=x^2-y^2$
B. $2xy\frac{dy}{dx}=y^2-x^2$
C. $2xy\frac{dy}{dx}=x^2+y^2$
D. $2xy\frac{dy}{dx}+x^2+y^2=0$

104. The order and degree of the differential equation of parabolas having vertex at the origin and focus at $(a, 0)$ where $a > 0$, are respectively:

A. 1, 1
B. 2, 1
C. 1, 2
D. 2, 2

105. $f(xy) = f(x) + f(y)$ is true for all:
A. Polynomial functions f
B. Trigonometric functions f
C. Exponential functions f
D. Logarithmic functions f

106. Three digits are chosen at random from 1, 2, 3, 4, 5, 6, 7, 8 and 9 without repeating any digit. What is the probability that the product is odd?

A. $\frac{2}{3}$ B. $\frac{7}{48}$
C. $\frac{5}{42}$ D. $\frac{5}{108}$

107. Two events A and B are such that P(not B) = 0.8, $P(A \cup B) = 0.5$ and $P(A|B) = 0.4$. Then P(A) is equal to:
A. 0.28 B. 0.32
C. 0.38 D. None of these

108. If mean and variance of a Binomial variate X are 2 and 1 respectively, then the probability that X takes a value greater than 1 is:

A. $\frac{2}{3}$ B. $\frac{4}{5}$
C. $\frac{7}{8}$ D. $\frac{11}{16}$

109. Seven unbiased coins are tossed 128 times. In how many throws would you find at least three heads?
A. 99 B. 102
C. 103 D. 104

110. A coin is tossed five times. What is the probability that heads are observed more than three times?

A. $\frac{3}{16}$ B. $\frac{5}{16}$
C. $\frac{1}{2}$ D. $\frac{3}{32}$

111. The geometric mean of the observations $x_1, x_2, x_3, \ldots. x_n$ is G_1. The geometric mean of the observations $y_1, y_2, y_3, \ldots. y_n$ is G_2. The geometric mean of observations $\frac{x_1}{y_1}, \frac{x_2}{y_2}, \frac{x_3}{y_3}, \ldots. \frac{x_n}{y_n}$ is:

A. G_1G_2 B. $\ln(G_1G_2)$
C. $\frac{G_1}{G_2}$ D. $\ln\left(\frac{G_1}{G_2}\right)$

112. The arithmetic mean of 1, 8, 27, 64, ... up to n terms is given by:

A. $\frac{n(n+1)}{2}$ B. $\frac{n(n+1)^2}{2}$
C. $\frac{n(n+1)^2}{4}$ D. $\frac{n^2(n+1)^2}{4}$

113. An unbiased coin is tossed until the first head appears or until four tosses are completed, whichever happens earlier. Which of the following statements is/are correct?
1. The probability that no head is observed is $\frac{1}{16}$.
2. The probability that the experiment ends with three tosses is $\frac{1}{8}$.

Select the correct answer using the code given below:
A. 1 only B. 2 only
C. Both 1 and 2 D. Neither 1 nor 2

114. If $x \in [0, 5]$, then what is the probability that $x^2 - 3x + 2 \geq 0$?

A. $\frac{4}{5}$ B. $\frac{1}{5}$
C. $\frac{2}{5}$ D. $\frac{3}{5}$

115. A bag contains 4 white and 2 black balls and another bag contains 3 white and 5 black balls. If one ball is drawn from each bag, then the probability that one ball is white and one ball is black is:

A. $\frac{5}{24}$ B. $\frac{13}{24}$
C. $\frac{1}{4}$ D. $\frac{2}{3}$

116. A problem in statistics is given to three students A, B and C whose chances of solving it independently are $\frac{1}{2}, \frac{1}{3}$ and $\frac{1}{4}$ respectively. The probability that the problem will be solved is:

A. $\frac{1}{12}$ B. $\frac{11}{12}$
C. $\frac{1}{2}$ D. $\frac{3}{4}$

117. An insurance company insured 2000 scooter drivers, 4000 car drivers and 6000 truck drivers. The probabilities of an accident involving a scooter driver, car driver and a truck driver are 0.01, 0.03 and 0.15 respectively. One of the insured persons meets with an accident. The probability that the person is a scooter driver is:

A. $\frac{1}{52}$ B. $\frac{3}{52}$
C. $\frac{15}{52}$ D. $\frac{19}{52}$

118. A coin is tossed 5 times. The probability that tail appears an odd number of times, is:

A. $\frac{1}{2}$ B. $\frac{1}{3}$
C. $\frac{2}{5}$ D. $\frac{1}{5}$

119. The regression coefficients of a bivariate distribution are –0.64 and –0.36. Then the correlation coefficient of the distribution is:

A. 0.48
B. –0.48
C. 0.50
D. –0.50

120. What is the probability that the sum of any two different single digit natural numbers is a prime number?

A. $\frac{5}{27}$ B. $\frac{7}{18}$
C. $\frac{1}{3}$ D. None of these

ANSWERS

PAPER-I : GENERAL ABILITY TEST

1	2	3	4	5	6	7	8	9	10
D	C	C	D	B	A	C	B	D	C
11	12	13	14	15	16	17	18	19	20
B	C	C	B	B	B	B	B	D	B
21	22	23	24	25	26	27	28	29	30
D	D	D	B	D	A	A	B	A	D
31	32	33	34	35	36	37	38	39	40
B	B	C	B	D.	B	C	C	D	C
41	42	43	44	45	46	47	48	49	50
C	B	C	B	B	B	A	B	B	C
51	52	53	54	55	56	57	58	59	60
D	A	B	C	C	B	C	B	B	C
61	62	63	64	65	66	67	68	69	70
B	B	C	C	A	B	B	C	B	B
71	72	73	74	75	76	77	78	79	80
D	A	B	A	B	B	C	A	B	B
81	82	83	84	85	86	87	88	89	90
C	D	A	D	A	D	A	D	B	D
91	92	93	94	95	96	97	98	99	100
A	A	C	B	D	C	D	A	C	A
101	102	103	104	105	106	107	108	109	110
C	A	C	B	B	A	C	D	B	D
111	112	113	114	115	116	117	118	119	120
A	B	D	A	C	A	A	A	C	A
121	122	123	124	125	126	127	128	129	130
C	D	A	B	A	C	A	B	D	D
131	132	133	134	135	136	137	138	139	140
C	B	C	B	A	C	D	B	D	D
141	142	143	144	145	146	147	148	149	150
D	C	B	D	C	D	A	B	C	A

PAPER-II : MATHEMATICS

1	2	3	4	5	6	7	8	9	10
D	A	B	C	B	D	D	B	A	C
11	12	13	14	15	16	17	18	19	20
C	D	C	B	A	B	C	A	D	D
21	22	23	24	25	26	27	28	29	30
A	B	B	C	C	B	A	A	B	C
31	32	33	34	35	36	37	38	39	40
A	B	C	D	A	B.	B	B	B	D
41	42	43	44	45	46	47	48	49	50
C	C	A	C	A	B	A	A	B	B

51	52	53	54	55	56	57	58	59	60
C	B	C	D	A	A	B	A	B	B
61	62	63	64	65	66	67	68	69	70
B	A	C	B	D	C	B	B	C	D
71	72	73	74	75	76	77	78	79	80
D	A	C	B	B	A	A	A	C	D
81	82	83	84	85	86	87	88	89	90
B	A	C	D	C	C	A	C	A	D
91	92	93	94	95	96	97	98	99	100
C	C	C	D	A	D	C	B	C	A
101	102	103	104	105	106	107	108	109	110
C	C	B	A	D	C	D	D	A	A
111	112	113	114	115	116	117	118	119	120
C	C	C	A	B	D	A	A	A	B

EXPLANATORY ANSWERS

PAPER-I : GENERAL ABILITY TEST

53. Named after an Indian astronomer, India's first satellite Aryabhatt was launched by the Soviet Union on 19 April 1975 from Kapustin Yar using a Kosmos-3M launch vehicle. It was built by the Indian Space Research Organisation (ISRO) to gain experience in building and operating a satellite in space. The launch was the result of an agreement between India and the Soviet Union directed by U.R. Rao and signed in 1972 that allowed the USSR to use Indian ports for tracking ships and launching vessels in return for launching Indian satellites.

54. Almost the geographical distance of 832 miles and a 60-hour's journey by ship from Chennai to Port Blair, it is also almost one of the shortest sea routes from India's seaports to reach Port Blair, which is a part of India.

55. Ozone is not a Greenhouse gas. It is a pale blue gas with a distinctively pungent smell. It is an allotrope of oxygen that is much less stable than the diatomic allotrope O_2, breaking down in the lower atmosphere to normal dioxygen.

56. Lactic acid is formed and accumulated in the muscle under the condition of high energy demand, rapid fluctuations of the energy requirement and insufficient supply of O_2. Muscle fatigue is considered to be due to an insufficient rate of ADP rephosphorylation resulting in a block in the activation process or in the excitation/contraction coupling.

57. Absolute zero is the point at which the fundamental particles of nature have vibrational motion, retaining only quantum mechanical, zero-point energy-induced particle motion. By international agreement, absolute zero is defined as precisely; 0 K on the Kelvin scale, which is a thermodynamic (absolute) temperature scale; and –273.15 degrees Celsius on the Celsius scale.

58. A lightning conductor (UK) or lightning rod (US, Aus.) or finial is a metal rod mounted on top of an elevated structure, such as a building, a ship, or even a tree, electrically bonded using a wire or electrical conductor to interface with ground or 'earth' through an electrode, engineered to protect the structure in the event of lightning strike. If the structure is hit by lightning, it will preferentially strike the rod and be conducted to ground through the wire, instead of passing through the structure, where it could start a fire or cause electrocution.

59. A. Ludhiana is an industrial city in the Punjab state of India. Besides having many manufacturing and other industries, Ludhiana is specifically famous all over India for production and wholesale of its woollen sweaters and cotton T-shirts. Most of the top Indian woollen apparel brands are based in Ludhiana.

B. Also known with the nicknames of "Leather City of the World" and "Manchester of the East", Kanpur, the largest city of Uttar Pradesh is famous for leather industry. Kanpur leather traders export leather goods in large volumes throughout the world. Kanpur leather traders are involved in manufacturing, exporting, and supplying of all types of finished leather products.

C. Varanasi or Banaras situated on the Ganges in Uttar Pradesh is famous for handloom, especially for Banarasi sarees, which are worn by Indian women on special occasions and celebrations. There are about one lac handloom weavers at Varanasi among whom, 40,000 are active in their business.

From Varanasi, handloom clothes are supplied to almost all over India and some parts of the world.

D. Situated on the banks of the Krishna River, in the Indian state of Andhra Pradesh, Vijayawada is famous for auto parts. It is a hub of manufacturing and supplying auto parts all over India.

60. Paradeep, Haldia and Dhamra are seaports whereas Diamond Harbour in the southern suburbs of Indian city, Kolkata, is not a seaport. Diamond Harbour, presently a picnic spot, used to be considered a safe resting spot for oceangoing ships and offered a spectacular view of Hooghly River.

62. It is correct that animals cannot make their own food; they do not have chlorophyll like plants and they migrate from one place to other in search of food. However, cellulose is not related to animal kingdom as it is a polysaccharide, $(C_6H_{10}O_5)_n$, that is composed of glucose monomers and is the main constituent of the cell walls of plants.

63. The silvering in thermos flasks is done to avoid heat transfer by radiation. The flask's glass remains silvered like a mirror to reduce infrared radiation. The combination of a vacuum and the silvering greatly reduces heat transfer by radiation.

64. Manas National Park or Manas Wildlife Sanctuary is a national park, UNESCO Natural World Heritage site, a Project Tiger Reserve, an Elephant Reserve and a Biosphere Reserve in Assam state of India. The Park is known for its rare and endangered endemic wildlife such as the Assam roofed turtle, hispid hare, golden langur and pygmy hog. Manas is famous for its population of the wild water buffaloes.

65. With the addition of quantity of gypsum to cement, initial and final setting time has different degrees of extension. When gypsum content exceeds a certain range, compressive and flexural strength decreases gradually.

67. A lens' optical power, also called dioptre, is the reciprocal of focal length expressed in metres. Dioptres define magnifying power. Convex lenses, or converging lenses, would have positive values, as they magnify objects. On the other hand, a diverging lens would have a negative dioptre, since it does the opposite: makes objects appear smaller than they are.

68. Ledo in Assam is a small town, which is known for coalmines whereas Naharkatiya in Assam; Kalol and Ankleshwar in Gujarat are known for oil field.

69. In chemical science, the law of definite (constant) proportions, often named Proust's Law, states that a chemical compound always holds exactly the same ratio of chemical elements by mass. The equivalent statement is the law of invariant composition, which in turn states that all samples of a given chemical compound have the same elementary constitution.

70. For the most part, velocity is not zero if an object is accelerating. If something is accelerating, it has to have a variable velocity. However, if the velocity is constant, the acceleration is zero (because the velocity is not changing over time); although at an instant in time, it is possible to have zero velocity whilst accelerating. For example, if you drop an object, at the instant you release it. It has zero velocity but it is accelerating. Also, if you throw an object upwards, it will by subject to an acceleration throughout its flight time, however at the very top of its trajectory, it will have zero velocity for an instant in time.

71. Indian Standard Time (IST) is the time observed throughout India and Sri Lanka, with a time offset of UTC + 05:30. IST is calculated on the basis of 82.5ºE longitude, in Shankargarh Fort, Mirzapur (25.15ºN 82.58ºE) in Allahabad district of Uttar Pradesh which is nearly on the corresponding longitude reference line. Geographically, it passes through Uttar Pradesh, Odisha, Andhra Pradesh and Chhatisgarh.

72. Due to the electron-withdrawing oxygens, other structurally analogous acids such as sulphuric acid also have an electrophilic centre atom, but these acids do not behave the way that boric acid does. These acids simply donate protons but the molecule of boric acid accepts OH from water releasing proton.

73. Sir Alexander Fleming (6 August 1881 – 11 March 1955), a Scottish biologist, pharmacologist and botanist, showed the contaminated culture to his former assistant Merlin Price, who reminded him, "That's how you discovered lysozyme." Fleming grew the mould in a pure culture and found that it produced a substance that killed numerous disease-causing bacteria. He identified the mould as being from the *Penicillium* genus. After calling it *mould juice* for a few months, he named the substance it released *penicillin* on 7 March 1929. The laboratory in which Fleming discovered and tested penicillin is preserved as the Alexander Fleming Laboratory Museum in St. Mary's Hospital, Paddington.

76. Zawar in Udaipur district of Rajasthan, India, is a township created by mining company Hindustan Zinc Limited, for extraction of zinc and lead. It is one of the oldest zinc mines of the world.

77. A. Bhitarkanika National Park is a national park in the Kendrapara district of Odisha, India. The park is home to the endangered saltwater crocodile, white crocodile, Indian python, king cobra, black ibis, darters and many other species of flora and fauna.

B. Besides being an important bird sanctuary with a vast area, Nokrek Biosphere Reserve is also a national park in West Garo Hills district of Meghalaya, India. Nokrek has a remnant population of the red panda and an important habitat of the Asian elephants. The park had eight species of cats, ranging from tiger to marbled cat but the current status of the former is uncertain.

C. Stretching over an area of 1,100 sq. kms at South-west of Puri, the Chilka Lake or Biosphere in Orissa is Asia's largest inland salt-water lagoon. Over a million birds congregate in this water body for feeding and roosting.

D. Covering an area of 1,284.3 km^2, the Dudhwa Tiger Reserve is a protected area in Uttar Pradesh, India, that stretches mainly across the Lakhimpur Kheri and Bahraich district, comprising the Dudhwa National Park, Kishanpur Wildlife Sanctuary and Katarniaghat Wildlife Sanctuary.

78. Vinegar is a liquid that consists mainly of acetic acid (CH_3COOH) and water. The acetic acid is produced by the fermentation of ethanol by acetic acid bacteria. Besides other usages, vinegar is now mainly used as cooking ingredient.

79. Often abbreviated as WP, white phosphorus is the most important form of elemental phosphorus from applications and the chemical literature perspectives. It consists of tetrahedral P 4 molecules, in which each atom is bound to the other three atoms by a single bond. Due to slow oxidation, white WP glows in the dark.

80. Almost every organism that can be seen without a microscope and some microscopic organisms are examples of eukaryotes. Eukaryotes have several cellular characteristics that distinguish them from prokaryotes like bacteria. For example, all eukaryotes have complex organelles, including a cytoskeleton, a membrane-bound nucleus and other membrane-bound organelles like mitochondria, the Golgi apparatus and chloroplasts. They also have relatively large cells, generally much larger than bacterial cells. Except bacteria, all protists, fungi, plants and animals are examples of eukaryotes.

81. In Physics, the capacity to do work is not power, as power is the rate of doing work. It is equivalent to an amount of energy consumed per unit time, whereas energy is the capacity to do work.

83. A. The Western Ghats or Sahyadri are a mountain range that runs almost parallel to the western coast of the Indian peninsula, located entirely in India. At lower elevations are the South Western Ghats in Kerala that is among the last tracts of virgin tropical evergreen forest in India.

B. Forest in Himachal Pradesh cover an area of about 21,325 sq.km i.e. about 38.3 of the total area of the state. Though the Himalayan Moist Forest ranges from the extreme north to east hilly region of India, Himachal abounds in moist forests.

C. The eco-region represents the thorn scrub forests in north-western region of the Indian subcontinent. Many ecologists consider this thorn scrub to represent a degraded state of tropical dry forests. The eco-region stretches across the border between India and Pakistan and covers parts of Gujarat, Rajasthan, Haryana, and Punjab states of India and the lower parts of Jammu & Kashmir.

D. A plateau in eastern India, the Chhotanagpur Plateau spreading approximately 65,000 sq. kms, covers much of Jharkhand state as well as adjacent parts of Odisha, West Bengal, Bihar and Chhattisgarh. It abounds in tropical moist deciduous forests.

84. The word, 'regur' originates from the Latin 'regurgitare' which means 'to overflow'. It is commonly known as 'black cotton soil' as it is perfect for growing cotton.

86. Vitamin D is recognised as a prohormone. Its unique aspect as a nutrient is that it can be synthesised by the human body through the action of sunlight. Those who live in northern latitudes have less chance to make vitamin D since, in wintertime, even at midday, the sunlight is so weak that it does not produce significant vitamin D synthesis in our skins.

88. When a solid is heated, the particles are given more energy and start to vibrate faster. At a certain temperature, the particles vibrate so much that their ordered structure breaks down. At this point, the solid melts into liquid. Thus, the temperature at which this changes from solid to liquid is called the melting point, not boiling point.

91. Electron is a constituent of cathode ray because cathode rays are emitted by the negative electrode, or cathode, in a vacuum tube. The electron is a subatomic particle, symbol e^- or β^-, with a negative elementary electric charge.

92. Life on earth is solar-powered. The chloroplasts of plants capture light energy that has travelled 160 million kilometres from the sun and convert it to chemical energy stores in sugar and other organic molecules. The process is called photosynthesis. Either directly or indirectly, almost all of the living world is nourished by Photosynthesis. An organism acquires the organic, compounds it uses for energy and carbon skeletons one of the two major modes: autotrophic or heterotrophic nutrition. Thus, carbon and energy requirements of autotrophic organisms are fulfilled by Photosynthesis.

94. Lithosphere on earth, comprises the crust and the portion of the upper mantle that behaves elastically on time scales of thousands of years or greater. The crust and the uppermost mantle constitute the hard and rigid outer layer of the earth. The lithosphere is subdivided into tectonic plates. The uppermost part of the lithosphere that chemically reacts to the atmosphere, hydrosphere and biosphere through the soil forming process is called the pedosphere.

95. A pressurised heavy-water reactor (PHWR) is a nuclear power reactor, commonly using un-enriched natural uranium as its fuel that uses heavy water (deuterium oxide D_2O) as its coolant and moderator. The heavy water coolant is kept under pressure, allowing it to be heated to higher temperatures without boiling, much as in a pressurised water reactor. While heavy water is significantly more expensive than ordinary light water, it creates greatly enhanced neutron economy, allowing the reactor to operate without fuel-enrichment facilities (offsetting the additional expenses of the heavy water) and enhancing the ability of the reactor to make use of alternate fuel cycles.

98. Acetylene gas is composed of two parts of carbon and two parts of hydrogen. When burned in the atmosphere of oxygen, it produces one of the highest flame temperatures obtainable. It is a versatile industrial fuel gas used in cutting, heating, welding, brazing, soldering, flame hardening, metallising, and stress-relieving applications. It is produced when calcium carbide is submerged into water or from petrochemical processes.

100. A meridian or line of longitude is a great circle line on the Earth's surface, passing through the North Pole and the South Pole. The position of any point on the Earth is located by its meridian longitude and its latitude. Each meridian is perpendicular to all circles of latitude. Each meridian is also the same length equal to the circumference of the Earth, as each meridian is a great circle dividing the Earth into two equal hemispheres.

102. The exosphere is the outermost layer of Earth's atmosphere, i.e. the upper limit of the atmosphere. It extends from the exobase, which is located at the top of the thermosphere at an altitude of about 700 km above sea level, to about 10,000 km. The gase found in highest quantity in the exosphere is hydrogen.

103. Platelets are the cells that circulate within our blood and bind together when they recognise damaged blood vessels. Platelets are required for initiating blood clotting; e.g., when we get a cut, the platelets bind to the site of the damaged vessel, thereby causing a blood clot. There is an evolutionary reason as to why they are there. It helps stop bleeding from the cut or affected part of the body.

106. A. Wet equatorial climate is major climate type of the Köppen classification characterised by consistently high temperatures (around 30°C), with plentiful precipitation (150-1,000 cm), heavy cloud-cover and high humidity, with very little annual temperature variation. Wet equatorial regions lie within about 12° latitude of the Equator. The climate type is denoted by the abbreviation Af in the Köppen-Geiger.

B. Monsoon and trade wind littoral or coastal climate is major climate type of the Köppen classification characterised by small annual temperature ranges, high temperatures, and plentiful precipitation (often more than wet equatorial, or Af, climates in annual total). Trade win littoral climates exhibit a short dry season, usually in the low-sun (winter season, and the highest temperatures generally occur at the end of this clear spell).

C. Wet-dry tropical is found near the equator, usually on the outer edges of Tropical wet climate areas. This type of climate corresponds to the Köppen climate classification categories "Aw" and "As". Tropical savannah climates have monthly means temperatures above 18ºC in every month of the year and typically a pronounced dry season, with the driest month having precipitation less than 60 mm and also less than (100 – [total annual precipitation {mm}/25]).

D. Dry tropical climates are found in low-latitude deserts approximately between 18° to 28° in both hemispheres. These latitude belts are centred on the tropics of Cancer and Capricorn, which lie just north and south of the equator. They coincide with the edge of the equatorial subtropical high pressure belt and trade winds. Winds are light, which allows for the evaporation of moisture in the intense heat. They generally flow downward so the area is seldom penetrated by air masses that produce rain. This makes for a very dry heat. The dry arid desert is a true desert climate, and covers 12% of the Earth's land surface.

107. A. **Li** is a symbol for lithium, which has atomic number 3. The term 'lithium battery' refers to a family of different chemistries, comprising many types of cathodes and electrolytes. The battery requires from 0.15 to 0.3 kg of lithium per kWh.

B. The $\mathbf{Na^+/K^+}$ pump is found in the membranes of many types of cells. Particularly, it plays a key role in nerve cell membranes. Notice that 3 positive ions (Na^+) are pumped out of the cell (towards ECF) for every 2 positive ions (K^+) pumped into the cell (towards ICF). This means that there are more positive charges, leaving the cell than entering it. As a result, positive charge builds up outside the cell compared to inside the cell. The difference in charge between the outside and inside of the cell allows nerve cells to generate electrical impulses, which lead to nerve impulses.

C. Though **K** element is used in control of the water content in the blood, it stands for dialyzer clearance, the rate at which blood passes through the dialyzer, expressed in millilitres per minute. K also refers to a group of structurally similar, fat-soluble vitamins the human body needs for complete synthesis of certain proteins that are required for blood coagulation. Potassium (K) in blood is a potassium test that checks how much potassium is in the blood.

D. **Cs** in modern atomic clocks stands for caesium (cesium). Modern atomic clocks only use caesium atoms as oscillators. Besides Caesium, the other material used in atomic clocks is Rubidium. The International System of Units (SI) defines one second as the time it takes a Caesium-133 atom at the ground state to oscillate exactly 9,192,631,770 times.

109. The amplitude and the frequency are two main properties of a regular vibration that affect the way it sounds. Amplitude is the size of the vibration and this determines how loud the sound is

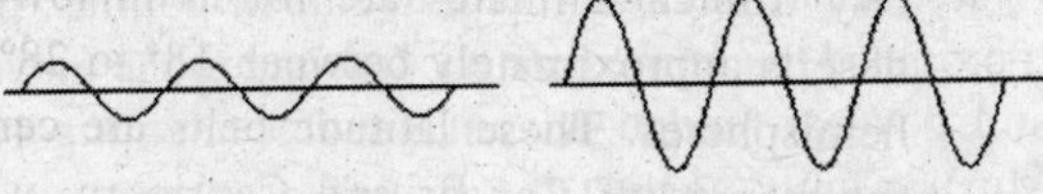

Amplitude is important when balancing and controlling the loudness of sounds, such as with the volume control on CD player. It is also the origin of the word 'amplifier', a device which increases the amplitude of a waveform.

110. X-radiation (composed of X-rays) is a form of electromagnetic radiation. Most X-rays have a wavelength ranging from 0.01 to 10 nanometres, corresponding to frequencies in the range 30 petahertz to 30 exahertz (3×30^{16} Hz to 3×10^{19} Hz) and energies in the range 100 eV to 100 keV. X-ray wavelengths are shorter than those of UV rays and typically longer than those of gamma rays.

111. Equatorial regions are located in a band around the Equator and cover about 6% of the Earth's surface. They are in lowland areas and have a hot and wet climate throughout the year. Therefore, oceans remain warm in this region.

112. Also known as wolfram, Tungsten is a chemical element with symbol W and atomic number 74. The word 'tungsten' comes from the Swedish language *tung sten*, which means *heavy stone*. In Swedish language, its name is *volfram*.

113. Brown fat or Brown Adipose Tissue (BAT) is one of the two types of fat or adipose tissue (the other being white adipose tissue, or white fat) found in mammals. In ancient Egypt, the mummies could be found to have their arteries intact due to being kept well-preserved and then BAT was used besides other materials to preserve the mummies.

115. The atomic number is the number of protons in an atom of an element. For example, krypton's atomic number is 36. This tells that an atom of krypton has 36 protons in its nucleus. Here, the noteworthy thing is that an atom of krypton contains 36 protons. If an atom does not have 36 protons, it can't be an atom of krypton.

116. Application of lime does not make the soil acidic as liming, which is the application of calcium- and magnesium-rich materials to soil in various forms, including marl, chalk, limestone, or hydrated lime that help neutralise soil acidity and increase activity of soil bacteria.

117. Having atomic number 3, Li is a symbol for lithium. Its melting and boiling point as compared to other members of the Alkali group metals is conspicuously high.

118. Fibre crops are obtained from fibrous plants. Fibre crops are traditionally used to make paper, cloth or rope etc. Fibre crops are generally harvested after a single growing season, as distinct from trees, which are typically grown for many years before being harvested for such materials as wood pulp fibre or lacebark.

119. In stream line flow each particle follow the same path and we have unique line of flow passing through a given point.

120. Though it appears to be round, the planet Earth is not, in fact, perfectly round. According to the Geo-scientists, it is spherical, close to that of a sphere and an oblate ellipsoid.

121. In India, secularism means equal treatment to all religions by the state. The 42nd Amendment of the Constitution of India, officially known as The Constitution (Forty-second Amendment) Act, 1976, was enacted during the Emergency (25 June 1975 – 21 March 1977) by the Indian National Congress government headed by Indira Gandhi, and that was the period when the words 'Secular' and 'Social' were inserted into the Constitution of India.

122. India's balance-of-payments (BoP) position improved dramatically in 2013-14, particularly in the last three quarters. This owed in large part to the measures taken by the government and the Reserve Bank of India (RBI) and in some part to the overall macroeconomic slowdown that fed into the external sector. From the last quarter of 2014, India's economy had become the world's fastest growing major economy, replacing the People's Republic of China. Thus, it would be wrong to say that during 2013-2014, India's capital account balance was negative.

123. Asia is a key destination of India's exports. Among Asian countries, India's main export partners include United Arab Emirates (12.1 per cent of the total exports), Singapore (4.5 per cent), China (4.5 per cent), Hong Kong (4 per cent), *et al.*

124. Article 32 of the Constitution of India gives citizens the right to directly approach the Supreme Court to seek remedies against the violation of their fundamental rights. Besides the Supreme Court, the high courts located in various states are also designated as constitutional courts and Article 226 permits citizens to file similar writs before the high courts.

125. The doctrine of subsidiary alliance was introduced by Lord Wellesley, British Governor-General in India from 1798 to 1805. Early in his governorship, Wellesley adopted a policy of non-intervention in the princely states, but he later adopted the policy of forming subsidiary alliances. This policy was to play a major role in British expansion in India. According to the term of this alliance, Indian rulers were not allowed to have their independent armed force. They were to be protected by the company, but had to pay for the 'subsidiary forces' that the company was supposed to maintain for the purpose of this protection. If the Indian rulers failed to make the payment, then part of their territory was taken away as penalty.

126. François Bernier (25 September 1620 – 22 September 1688), a French physician and traveller, was personal physician to Prince Dara Shikoh (28 October 1615 – 30 August 1659), the elder son of Shah Jahan. After Dara Shikoh's fall, he was attached to the court of the Emperor Aurangzeb (14 October 1618 – 20 February 1707), for around 12 years during his stay in India.

127. An important aspect of 'inclusive growth' in the Eleventh Five-year Plan (2007-2012) was its target of 4 per cent per annum growth in GDP from agriculture and allied sectors. Hence, the farmers in general in India followed mixed crop and livestock farming system due to strong linkage between these two that resulted fructuously.

128. National emergency can be declared under Article 352 by the President of India on the basis of external aggression or armed rebellion in India. Such an emergency was declared in India in 1962 (Indo-China war), 1971 (Indo-Pakistan war), and 1975 (declared by Indira Gandhi). It can be declared only on the basis of a written request by the Council of Ministers headed by the Prime Minister. Such a proclamation must be laid before both houses of Parliament, and the state of emergency expires after one month unless approved within that time by both houses sitting and voting separately. However, if the Lok Sabha (the lower house) is not in session when the state of emergency is declared, and the Rajya Sabha approves of the state of emergency, the deadline for the Lok Sabha is extended until thirty days after that house convenes. According to Article 352(6), approval by each house requires a special majority: those in favour of the motion must be two thirds of those present and voting, and amount to a majority of the entire membership of that house. A Parliamentary resolution extends the state of emergency for up to six months, and it can be extended indefinitely by further resolutions in six-monthly increments.

129. India's livestock sector is one of the largest in the world. It has 56.7% of world's buffaloes, 12.5% cattle, 20.4% small ruminants, 2.4% camel, 1.4% equine, 1.5% pigs and 3.1% poultry. In 2010-11, livestock generated outputs worth was Rs 2075 billion (at 2004-05 prices) which comprised 4% of the GDP and 26% of the agricultural GDP. The total output worth was higher than the value of food grains.

130. During 1919-22, the British opposed two mass movements – the Khilafat and Non-Cooperation. Despite emerging from separate issues, the two movements adopted a common programme of action, that of non-violence and non-cooperation. The Khilafat issue did not have any link to Indian politics, though it provided the immediate background to the movement and gave an added advantage of cementing Hindu-Muslim unity against the British.

131. India accounts for the maximum number of maternal deaths in the world as 17 per cent or nearly 50,000 of the 2.89 lakh women died as a result of complications due to pregnancy or childbearing in 2013. According to Dr. Lale Say of WHO, the major challenge faced by India is lack of accurate information about births and deaths, particularly when women give birth at home. Thus, lack of medical facilities has not been the factor behind the rise in maternal mortality rate in India.

132. There are 12 schedules to the Constitution of India, each dealing with different provisions. The Fourth Schedule contains the allocation of seats to each State and Union territory in the Rajya Sabha.

133. British Residents were posted in various Princely states – in major states or groups of states during British India. They were often appointed to a single state, as with the Resident in Lucknow, the capital of Awadh; to the Maharaja Gaekwar of Baroda; to the Maharaja Sindhya of Gwalior; to the Nizam al-Mulk of Hyderabad and so on. These were the states that did not come directly under British rule.

134. Also known as the Permanent Settlement of Bengal, the Permanent Settlement was an agreement between the East India Company and Bengali zamindars (landlords) to fix revenues to be raised from land, with far-reaching consequences for both agricultural methods and productivity in the entire Empire and the political realities of the Indian countryside. It was concluded in 1793, by the Company administration headed by Charles, Earl Cornwallis. It formed one part of a larger body of legislation enacted known as the Cornwallis Code.

135. Talikota is situated in northern Karnataka, about 80 km to the southeast from the city of Bijapur. The Battle of Talikota (26 January 1565) was a watershed battle fought between the Vijayanagara Empire and the Deccan Sultanates. It resulted in a defeat of Vijayanagara, and ended in great weakening of one of the greatest Indian Empires originating from the South before the Marathas.

136. Kesavananda Bharati Sripadagalvaru *v.* State of Kerala (case citation: (1973) 4 SCC 225) is a landmark decision of the Supreme Court of India that outlined the Basic Structure doctrine of the Constitution. Through this doctrine, Justice Hans Raj Khanna asserted that the constitution possesses a basic structure of constitutional principles and values. The Basic Structure doctrine forms the basis of power of the Indian judiciary to review, and strike down, amendments to the Constitution of India enacted by the Indian parliament, which conflict with or seek to alter this basic structure of the Constitution.

137. Muhammad Ibn Battuta (February 25, 1304 – 1368 or 1369), was an explorer of Berber descent, who is widely known as one of the greatest travellers of all time. He is known for his extensive travels, accounts of which were published in the Rihla (lit. "Journey"). Over a period of thirty years, he visited most of the known Islamic world as well as many non-Muslim lands. His journeys included trips to North Africa, the Horn of Africa, West Africa and Eastern Europe, and to the Middle East, South Asia, Central Asia, Southeast Asia and China.

François Bernier (25 September 1620 – 22 September 1688) was a French physician and traveller. He was personal physician to Shah Jahan's elder son, Prince Dara Shikoh (28 October 1615 – 30 August 1659). Later, he was attached to the court of the Emperor Aurangzeb (14 October 1618 – 20 February 1707), for around 12 years during his stay in India. His 1684 publication *Nouvelle division de la terre par les différentes espèces ou races qui l'habitent* is considered the first published post-Classical classification of humans into distinct races. He also wrote *Travels in the Mughal Empire*, which is mainly about the reigns of Dara Shikoh and Aurangzeb. It is premised on his own extensive journeys and observations, and on information from eminent Mughal courtiers who had witnessed the events at first hand.

139. A. Noted for its temples and inscriptions, Pattadakal is a great centre of Chalukya art and architecture. Pattadakal is a World Heritage site, a village and an important tourist centre in the Karnataka state is 22 km from Badami and about 10 km from Aihole, both of which are well-known for Chalukya monuments.

B. Somnathpur is a town in Karnataka state of India. It is famous for the Chennakesava or Kesava Temple built by Soma, a *Dandanayaka* (commander) in 1268 CE under Hoysala Empire King Narasimha III. At that time, the Hoysalas were the major power in South India. The Kesava Temple is one of the finest and accomplished examples of Hoysala architecture.

C. The Gopuram's (Gopura *singular*) origins can be traced back to early structures of the Tamil kings Pallavas; and by the twelfth century, under the Pandya rulers hailing from an ancient Tamil dynasty. Thus, the Pandyas' association with Eastern *Gopura* of Chidambaram Temple is historical.

D. Konark Sun Temple is a 13th-century Sun Temple at Konark in Odisha state of India. It is believed that the temple was built around 1250 CE by king Narasimhadeva I of Eastern Ganga Dynasty. The temple is in the shape of a gigantic chariot elaborately carved stone wheels, pillar and walls.

140. The word 'Senia' is related to Tansen (born 1493 or 1506 as Ramtanu Misra – died 1586 or 1589 as Tansen), the father of Indian Classical Music. The followers of Tansen's school of music are widely known as the followers of "Senia gharana" i.e. "Senia style/school of music".

141. Kandukuri Veeresalingam Pantulu (16 April 1848 – 27 May 1919), was a social reformer of Andhra Pradesh state of India. In 1878, he founded Rajahmundry Social Reform Association that laid emphasis on anti-nautch movement to discontinue the hiring of nautch girls. However, the association started focusing on widow remarriage at the later stage. Under this association, Kandukuri organised the first widow remarriage on 11 December 1881 of Gogulapati Sreeramulu and Gowramma. Despite facing severe criticism from the society, he succeeded in convincing people to accept widow remarriage.

142. Based in Kathmandu, Nepal, the SAARC Secretariat coordinates and monitors implementation of activities, prepares for and services meetings, and serves as a channel of communication between the Association and its Member States as well as other regional organisations.

143. Initiated in 1818 in eastern Bengal (now Bangladesh) by Haji Shariatullah Faraizi, the Faraizi Movement was an urge to Muslims to shun all the un-Islamic practices and act upon their obligations as true Muslims. The movement was widely received in the districts of Dhaka, Faridpur, Barisal, Mymensingh and Comilla.

144. Formed in 1928 under Motilal Nehru, The Indian States Committee was a committee of the All Parties Conference chaired by Motilal Nehru with his son Jawaharlal Nehru acting as secretary. This committee had prepared the Nehru Report in August 1928 which was a memorandum outlining a proposed new dominion status constitution for India. There were nine other members in this committee.

145. In India, the Panchayati Raj generally refers to the system introduced by constitutional amendment in 1992, although it is based upon the traditional panchayat system of South Asia. Panchayats (Extension to Scheduled Areas) Act, 1996 or PESA is a law enacted by the Government of India to cover the "Scheduled areas", which are not covered in the 73rd amendment or Panchayati Raj Act of the Indian Constitution. It is an Act to provide for the extension of the provisions of Part IX of the Constitution relating to the Panchayats and the Scheduled Areas. However, this system under Part IX of the Constitution does not apply to the states of Nagaland, Meghalaya and Mizoram.

146. India's First Five-year Plan (1951 – 1956) was drafted and presented to the Parliament of India by India's first Prime Minister, Pt. Jawaharlal Nehru for urgent attention. Launched in 1951, the First Five-year Plan mainly focused on development of the primary sector.

147. The book, *Pakistan Paradox: Instability and Resilience* is authored by a French scholar Dr. Christophe Jaffrelot, who is Research Director at CNRS and a teacher of South Asian politics and history at Sciences Po (Paris). Jaffrelot in this book has written on a fresh political history of Pakistan that explains the resilience of the state and its people and how both persevere against the odds.

148. The International Day of United Nations Peacekeepers on May 29, 2015 was observed as a day to pay tribute to all those who served (many of who have lost their lives in the cause of peace) and would continue to serve in UN peacekeeping operations. They were honoured with blue helmets as a symbol of recognition, thereby reaffirming their commitment to make them more effective in the years to come. Thus, the theme for the Day this year was "UN at 70 and UN Peacekeeping: Past, Present, and Future".

149. Discus throw is a game in which athletes throw a metal disc weighing 2 kg for men, 1 kg for women, that is 22 cm in diameter for men, and 18 cm for women, as far as possible while remaining inside a 2.5m-diameter circle. Born in Mysore (Karnataka) on 5 July 1983, Vikas Gowda is an Indian discus thrower and shot putter. He grew up in Frederick, Maryland in the USA.

150. Organised jointly by the Karnataka Amateur Athletic Association, Dakshina Kannada Athletic Association and the district administration, the 19th National Senior Athletic Championship for the Federation Cup was held at the Mangala Stadium of Mangaluru from April 30 to May 4. More than thousand athletes participated in the five-day event.

PAPER-II : MATHEMATICS

1. Let, X = (*a*, *b*, ...)

Reflexive relation:

(a, a) $\in$ X, for all a such that difference of their age's ≤ 5.

$$|a-a| = 0 \le 5$$

then, relation is reflexive.

Symmetric relation:

(a, b) $\in$ X, a, b, such that

$$|a-b| \le 5$$

for, $|a-b| \le 5$, $|(b-a)| \le 5$ also true

so, relation is symmetric as well.

Transitive relation:

(a, b) and (b, c) $\in$ X then,

$$(a-b) \le 5 \text{ and } |b-c| \le 5$$

but $|a-c| \le 10$, thus, relation is not transitive.

3. $$\begin{vmatrix} a & 1 & 1 \\ 1 & b & 1 \\ 1 & 1 & c \end{vmatrix} = \begin{vmatrix} a & 0 & 1 \\ 1 & b-1 & 1 \\ 1 & 1-c & c \end{vmatrix} \quad \{\text{Applying } C_2 \to C_2 - C_3\}$$

$$\begin{vmatrix} a & 0 & 1 \\ 1-a & b-1 & 0 \\ 1 & 1-c & c \end{vmatrix} \quad \{\text{Applying } R_2 \to R_2 - R_1\}$$

$$a(c(b-1)) + (1-a)(1-c) - (b-1)$$

$$abc - ac + 1 - a - c + ac - b + 1$$

$$abc - a - b - c + 2$$

From question, Determinant > 0

$\therefore$ $abc - (a+b+c) + 2 > 0$

$abc > (a+b+c) - 2$

$\therefore$ abc is greater than -8.

4. $$\begin{vmatrix} \cos^2\frac{\alpha}{2} & \sin^2\frac{\alpha}{2} \\ \sin^2\frac{\beta}{2} & \cos^2\frac{\beta}{2} \end{vmatrix} = \cos^2\frac{\alpha}{2}.\cos^2\frac{\beta}{2} - \sin^2\frac{\alpha}{2}.\sin^2\frac{\beta}{2}$$

$$= \cos\left(\frac{\alpha+\beta}{2}\right).\cos\left(\frac{\alpha-\beta}{2}\right)$$

As α and β are complementary angles

$\therefore \cos\left(\frac{\alpha+\beta}{2}\right) = \cos(45°) = \frac{1}{\sqrt{2}}$

Hence, $\cos\left(\frac{\alpha+\beta}{2}\right).\cos\left(\frac{\alpha-\beta}{2}\right) = \frac{1}{\sqrt{2}}.\cos\left(\frac{\alpha-\beta}{2}\right)$

and also, max. of $\cos\left(\frac{\alpha-\beta}{2}\right) = 1.$

max. of $\left\{\frac{1}{\sqrt{2}}\cos\left(\frac{\alpha-\beta}{2}\right)\right\} = \frac{1}{\sqrt{2}}$

5. $(1000000001)_2 = 2^9 + 1$

$= (513)_{10}$

$(0.0101)_2 = \frac{1}{2^2} + \frac{1}{2^4}$

$= 0.25 + 0.0625$

$= (0.3125)_{10}$

$\therefore (513)_{10} - (0.3125)_{10} = (512.6875)_{10}$.

6. $\because$ $2X + 3A = 0$

$\Rightarrow$ $2X = -3A$

$X = -\frac{3A}{2}$

$$A = \begin{bmatrix} 1 & 0 & -2 \\ 2 & -3 & 4 \end{bmatrix}$$

$$-3A = \begin{bmatrix} -3 & 0 & +6 \\ -6 & +9 & -12 \end{bmatrix}$$

$$-\frac{3A}{2} = \begin{bmatrix} -\frac{3}{2} & 0 & 3 \\ -3 & \frac{9}{2} & -6 \end{bmatrix}$$

$$\Rightarrow \quad X = \begin{bmatrix} -\frac{3}{2} & 0 & 3 \\ -3 & \frac{9}{2} & -6 \end{bmatrix}$$

9. $x^2 - 3x + 2 = 0$

$\Rightarrow$ $x^2 - 2x - x + 2 = 0$

$\Rightarrow$ $(x - 2)(x - 1) = 0$

$x = 2, 1$

Again,

$x^2 + 3x + 2 = 0$

$\Rightarrow$ $x^2 + 2x + x + 2 = 0$

$\Rightarrow$ $(x + 2)(x + 1) = 0$

$x = -2, -1$

Hence, Number of real roots = 4.

10. Let α, β are the roots of the given equation

$ax^2 + bx + c = 0$

$\alpha + \beta = -\frac{b}{a}$

$\alpha \times \beta = \frac{c}{a}$

$\alpha^2 + \beta^2 = (\alpha + \beta)^2 - 2\alpha\beta$

$= \frac{b^2}{a^2} - \frac{2c}{a} = \frac{b^2 - 2ac}{a^2}$

According to the question,

$\alpha^2 + \beta^2 = \alpha + \beta$

$\Rightarrow$ $\frac{b^2 - 2ac}{a^2} = -\frac{b}{a}$

$\Rightarrow$ $b^2 - 2ac = -ab$

$\Rightarrow$ $ab + b^2 = 2ac$

11. A : $x^2 + 6x - 7 < 0$

$(x + 7)(x - 1) < 0$

A: $x \in (-7, 1)$

B: $x^2 + 9x + 14 > 0$

$(x + 2)(x + 7) > 0$

B: $x \in (-\infty, -7) \cup (-2, \infty)$

$\therefore$ $(A \cap B) = (-2, 1)$

and $(A \mid B) = (A–B) = (-7, -2)$

14. $P = 6^{\frac{1}{2}} \times 6^{\frac{2}{4}} \times 6^{\frac{3}{8}} \times 6^{\frac{4}{16}} \times 6^{\frac{5}{32}} ....$

$= 6^{\frac{1}{2}+\frac{2}{2^2}+\frac{3}{2^3}+\frac{4}{2^4}+\frac{5}{2^5}+....\infty}$

Let, $S = \frac{1}{2} + \frac{2}{2^2} + \frac{3}{2^3} + \frac{4}{2^4} + \frac{5}{2^5} + ...$

$\frac{1}{2}S = \frac{1}{2^2} + \frac{2}{2^3} + \frac{3}{2^4} + \frac{4}{2^5} + ...$

$\left(1 - \frac{1}{2}\right)S = \frac{1}{2} + \left(\frac{2-1}{2^2}\right) + \left(\frac{3-2}{2^3}\right) + \left(\frac{4-3}{2^4}\right) + ...$

$\frac{S}{2} = \frac{1}{2} + \frac{1}{2^2} + \frac{1}{2^3} + \frac{1}{2^4} + ...$

$= \frac{\frac{1}{2}}{1 - \frac{1}{2}} = 1$

$\therefore$ $S = 2$

$P = 6^2 = 36.$

15. Let α, β are the roots of the equation

$x^2 - nx + m = 0$

$\therefore$ $\alpha + \beta = n$

$\alpha \times \beta = m$

$\because$ $\alpha - \beta = 1$

$\therefore$ $\alpha = 1 + \beta$

$\because \quad (\alpha - \beta)^2 = (\alpha + \beta)^2 - 4\alpha\beta$

$1 = n^2 - 4m$

$\Rightarrow n^2 - 4m - 1 = 0.$

16. Starting with the letter A, and arranging the other four letters, there are 4! words. These are the first 24 words. Then, starting with G, and arranging A, A, I and N in different ways, these are

$$\frac{4!}{2!1!1!} = \frac{24}{2} = 12 \text{ words.}$$

Next, the 37 word starts with I. There are 12 words starting with I. This accounts up to the 48 words. The 49th word is NAAGI. The 50th word is NAAIG.

17. Total players = 15

Selection = 11

Captain is always included

$\therefore \quad n = 14, r = 10$

$$\therefore \quad {}^{14}C_{10} = \frac{14!}{10! \times 4!} = \frac{14 \times 13 \times 12 \times 11}{4 \times 3 \times 2 \times 1}$$

$= 91 \times 11 = 1001$

Hence, required no. of ways = 1001.

18. $\left(\sqrt{x} + \frac{1}{3x^2}\right)^{10}$

$$= {}^nC_0 \left(x^{\frac{1}{2}}\right)^{10} + {}^nC_1 \left(x^{\frac{1}{2}}\right)^9 \cdot \left(\frac{1}{3x^2}\right) + {}^nC_2 \left(x^{\frac{1}{2}}\right)^8 \cdot \left(\frac{1}{3x^2}\right)^2$$

$$= {}^{10}C_2 \times \frac{1}{9} = \frac{10 \times 9}{2 \times 9} = 5$$

Hence, the required value of constant term = 5.

19. $\sin^2 5° + \sin^2 10° + \sin^2 15° + \sin^2 20° + ... + \sin^2 90°$

$= \sin^2 5° + \sin^2(90° - 5°) + \sin^2 10° + \sin^2(90° - 10°) + \sin^2 15° + \sin^2(90° - 15°) + \sin^2 20° + \sin^2(90° - 20°) + ... + \sin^2 45° + ... + \sin^2 90°$

$= \sin^2 5° + \cos^2 5° + \sin^2 10° + \cos^2 10° + \sin^2 15° + \cos^2 15° + \sin^2 20° + \cos^2 20° + \sin^2 25° + \cos^2 25° + \sin^2 30° + \cos^2 30° + ... + \sin^2 45° + ... + \sin^2 90°$

$$= 9 + \frac{1}{2} = 9\frac{1}{2} = \frac{19}{2} \quad \left[\begin{array}{l} \because \sin 90° = 1 \\ \sin 45° = \frac{1}{\sqrt{2}} \\ \sin^2\theta + \cos^2\theta = 1 \end{array}\right].$$

20. $\dfrac{\sin^3 A + \sin 3A}{\sin A} + \dfrac{\cos^3 A - \cos 3A}{\cos A}$

$$= \frac{\sin^3 A + 3\sin A - 4\sin^3 A}{\sin A} + \frac{\cos^3 A - \left(4\cos^3 A - 3\cos A\right)}{\cos A}$$

$$= \frac{3\sin A - 3\sin^3 A}{\sin A} + \frac{3\cos A - 3\cos^3 A}{\cos A}$$

$$= \frac{3\sin A\left(1 - \sin^2 A\right)}{\sin A} + \frac{3\cos A\left(1 - \cos^2 A\right)}{\cos A}$$

$= 3\cos^2 A + 3\sin^2 A$

$= 3(\cos^2 A + \sin^2 A)$

$= 3 \times 1 = 3.$

21. $\tan\left[2\tan^{-1}\frac{1}{5} - \frac{\pi}{4}\right]$

$$\because \quad 2\tan^{-1}\left(\frac{1}{5}\right) = \tan^{-1}\frac{2\left(\frac{1}{5}\right)}{1 - \left(\frac{1}{5}\right)^2}$$

$$= \tan^{-1}\frac{5}{12}$$

and $\quad \frac{\pi}{4} = \tan^{-1}(1)$

$$\therefore \tan\left[2\tan^{-1}\left(\frac{1}{5}\right) - \frac{\pi}{4}\right]$$

$$= \tan.\tan^{-1}\frac{\left(\frac{5}{12}\right) - 1}{1 + \left(\frac{5}{12}\right).1}$$

$$= \tan.\tan^{-1}\left(\frac{-7}{17}\right) = \frac{-7}{17}$$

22.

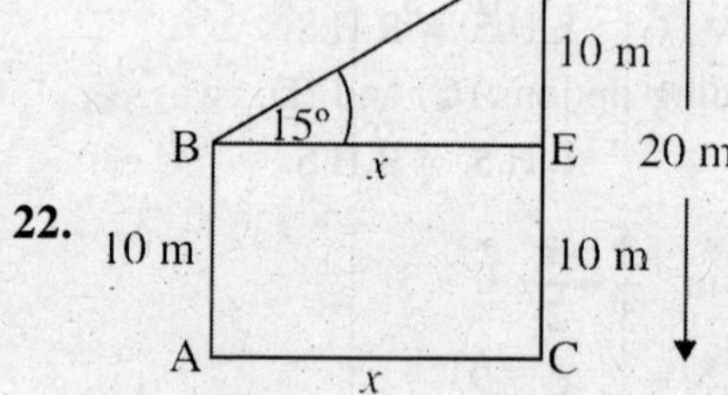

In Δ BDE,

$$\tan 15° = \frac{10}{x} \Rightarrow \frac{\sqrt{3} - 1}{\sqrt{3} + 1} = \frac{10}{x}$$

$$\Rightarrow \frac{\sqrt{3} - 1}{\sqrt{3} + 1} \times \frac{\sqrt{3} - 1}{\sqrt{3} - 1} = \frac{10}{x} \Rightarrow \frac{\left(\sqrt{3} - 1\right)^2}{2} = \frac{10}{x}$$

$$\Rightarrow \frac{4 - 2\sqrt{3}}{2} = \frac{10}{x} \Rightarrow 2 - \sqrt{3} = \frac{10}{x}$$

$$\Rightarrow x = \frac{10}{2 - \sqrt{3}} \times \frac{2 + \sqrt{3}}{2 + \sqrt{3}}$$

$$= \frac{10\left(2 + \sqrt{3}\right)}{4 - 3} = \frac{10(2 + 1.73)}{1}$$

$= 10 \times 3.73$
$= 37.3$

Hence, the distance between poles = 37.3 m.

23. (A) $g(f(x)) = \dfrac{1}{f(x)} = \dfrac{1}{x}$

$$g(g(f(x))) = \frac{1}{\frac{1}{x}} = x$$

L.H.S. $f(f(f(g(g(f(x)))))) = x$

R.H.S. $f(g(f(x))) = \dfrac{1}{x}$

$$g(f(g(f(x)))) = \frac{1}{\frac{1}{x}} = x$$

$$g(g(f(g(f(x))))) = \frac{1}{x}$$

$\therefore$ L.H.S. $\neq$ R.H.S.

(B) L.H.S.

$$g(g(f(x))) = x$$

$$g(g(g(f(x)))) = \frac{1}{x}$$

$$f(f(g(g(g(f(x)))))) = \frac{1}{x}$$

R.H.S.

$$g(f(g(f(x)))) = x$$

$$g(g(f(g(f(x))))) = \frac{1}{x}$$

$\therefore$ L.H.S. = R.H.S.

When expanding options (C) and (D), we get

L.H.S. $\neq$ R.H.S.

24. (i) $\sin^{-1}\dfrac{4}{5} + \sin^{-1}\dfrac{3}{5} = \dfrac{\pi}{2}$

Let, $\sin^{-1}\dfrac{3}{5} = x$

$\Rightarrow$ $\sin x = \dfrac{3}{5}$

$$\cos x = \sqrt{1-\sin^2 x} = \sqrt{1-\frac{9}{25}} = \frac{4}{5}$$

$\therefore$ $x = \cos^{-1}\dfrac{4}{5}$

$\therefore$ $\sin^{-1}\dfrac{3}{5} = \cos^{-1}\dfrac{4}{5}$

Now, $\sin^{-1}\dfrac{4}{5} + \sin^{-1}\dfrac{3}{5} = \sin^{-1}\dfrac{4}{5} + \cos^{-1}\dfrac{4}{5} = \dfrac{\pi}{2}$

$\therefore$ $\sin^{-1}\dfrac{4}{5} + \sin^{-1}\dfrac{3}{5} = \dfrac{\pi}{2}$ (True)

(ii) $\tan^{-1}\sqrt{3} + \tan^{-1}1 = -\tan^{-1}\left(2+\sqrt{3}\right)$

Now, $\tan^{-1}\sqrt{3} + \tan^{-1}1 = \tan^{-1}\dfrac{\sqrt{3}+1}{1-\sqrt{3}\times 1}$

$$= \tan^{-1}\left(\frac{\sqrt{3}+1}{1-\sqrt{3}} \times \frac{1+\sqrt{3}}{1+\sqrt{3}}\right)$$

$$= \tan^{-1}\frac{\left(\sqrt{3}+1\right)^2}{1-3} = \tan^{-1}\frac{\left(3+1+2\sqrt{3}\right)}{-2}$$

$$= -\tan^{-1}\left(2+\sqrt{3}\right) \text{ (True)}$$

Hence (i) and (ii) both are True.

27. $\begin{vmatrix} 1-a & a-b-c & b+c \\ 1-b & b-c-a & c+a \\ 1-c & c-a-b & a+b \end{vmatrix}$

$$= \begin{vmatrix} 1-a & a-b-c & b+c \\ a-b & 2(b-a) & a-b \\ c-a & 2(a-c) & c-a \end{vmatrix} \begin{Bmatrix} \text{Applying } R_2 \to R_2 - R_1 \\ R_3 \to R_1 - R_3 \end{Bmatrix}$$

$$= \begin{vmatrix} 1-a-b-c & a-b-c & b+c \\ 0 & 2(b-a) & a-b \\ 0 & 2(a-c) & c-a \end{vmatrix} \{\text{Applying } C_1 \to C_1 - C_3\}$$

$$= 2(1-a-b-c)\{(b-a)(c-a)-(a-b)(a-c)\} = 0.$$

28. Mid-point of the line joining points z_1 and z_2 lies on the given line,

$$\text{Mid-point} = \left(\frac{1+x}{2}, i\left(\frac{1+y}{2}\right)\right)$$

Then,

$$i\left(\frac{1+x}{2} - i\left(\frac{1+y}{2}\right)\right) - i\left(\frac{1+x}{2} + i\left(\frac{1+y}{2}\right)\right) = 5$$

or, $1 + y = 5$

$y = 4$

and $x = 1$

$\therefore$ $z_2 = 1 + 4i.$

29. $\because$ $\dfrac{a^2}{b^2} = \dfrac{(\sin x + \sin y)^2}{(\cos x + \cos y)^2} = \dfrac{\left\{2\sin\dfrac{(x+y)}{2}.\cos\dfrac{(x-y)}{2}\right\}^2}{\left\{2\cos\dfrac{(x+y)}{2}.\cos\dfrac{(x-y)}{2}\right\}^2}$

$$= \frac{\left\{\sin\dfrac{(x+y)}{2}\right\}^2}{\left\{\cos\dfrac{(x+y)}{2}\right\}^2} = \tan^2\frac{(x+y)}{2}$$

and $\dfrac{4-(a^2+b^2)}{a^2+b^2} = \dfrac{4-(2+2\sin x.\sin y+2\cos x.\cos y)}{2+2\sin x.\sin y+2\cos x.\cos y}$

$$= \frac{2-2\cos(x-y)}{2+2\cos(x-y)} = \frac{4\sin^2\left(\frac{x-y}{2}\right)}{4\cos^2\frac{(x-y)}{2}}$$

$$= \tan^2\left(\frac{x-y}{2}\right)$$

Now, $\tan^2\left(\frac{x+y}{2}\right)+\tan^2\left(\frac{x-y}{2}\right)$

$$= \frac{a^2}{b^2}+\frac{4-(a^2+b^2)}{a^2+b^2}$$

$$= \frac{a^2(a^2+b^2)+b^2\left[4-a^2-b^2\right]}{b^2(a^2+b^2)}$$

$$= \frac{a^4+a^2b^2+4b^2-a^2b^2-b^4}{a^2b^2+b^4}$$

$$= \frac{a^4-b^4+4b^2}{a^2b^2+b^4}$$

30.

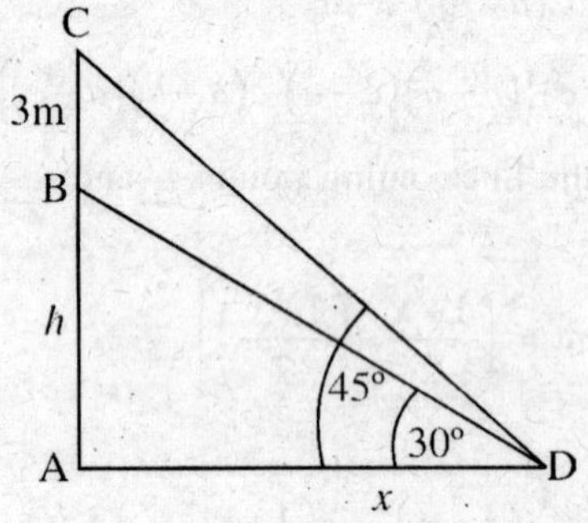

$\tan 30° = \dfrac{h}{x} \Rightarrow \dfrac{1}{\sqrt{3}} = \dfrac{h}{x}$

$\Rightarrow \quad x = \sqrt{3}\,h$ ...(i)

$\tan 45° = \dfrac{h+3}{x}$

$\Rightarrow \quad 1 = \dfrac{h+3}{x} \Rightarrow x = h+3$ ...(ii)

From (i) and (ii)

$\sqrt{3}h = h+3$

$\Rightarrow \quad \sqrt{3}h - h = 3 \Rightarrow h(\sqrt{3}-1) = 3$

$\therefore \quad h = \dfrac{3}{\sqrt{3}-1}\times\dfrac{\sqrt{3}+1}{\sqrt{3}+1} = \dfrac{3(\sqrt{3}+1)}{2}$,

$$= \frac{3(1.732+1)}{2} = \frac{3\times 2.732}{2}$$

$$= \frac{8.196}{2} = 4.093 \text{ m}$$

$$\cong 4.10 \text{ m}$$

Hence, height of the tower gives the best approximation is 4.10 m.

31. Co-efficient of $x^r = {}^{2n+1}C_r$

Co-efficient of $x^{r+1} = {}^{2n+1}C_{r+1}$

From question,

$${}^{2n+1}C_r = {}^{2n+1}C_{r+1}$$

$$\frac{(2n+1)!}{r!(2n+1-r)!} = \frac{(2n+1)!}{(r+1)!(2n+1-r-1)!}$$

$$r+1 = 2n+1-r$$

$\therefore \quad r = n.$

33. Sum of the Co-efficient

$$= (2)^{2n+1} = 2.4^n.$$

34. nth term $= \dfrac{3+n}{4}$

$\Rightarrow \quad a_n = \dfrac{3+n}{4}$

$\Rightarrow \quad a_1 = \dfrac{3+1}{4} = 1$

$\therefore \quad a = 1$ and $l = \dfrac{3+n}{4}$

$$S_n = \frac{n}{2}(a+l)$$

$$S_{105} = \frac{105}{2}\left(1+\frac{3+105}{4}\right)$$

$$= \frac{105}{2}\times 28 = 105\times 14 = 1470$$

Hence, Sum of first 105 terms = 1470.

35. Number of diagonals in a n-sided polygon

$$= \frac{n(n-3)}{2}$$

$\Rightarrow \quad 44 = \dfrac{n^2-3n}{2} \Rightarrow n^2 - 3n = 88$

$\Rightarrow \quad n^2 - 3n - 88 = 0$

$\Rightarrow \quad n^2 - 11n + 8n - 88 = 0$

$\Rightarrow n(n-11) + 8(n-11) = 0$

$(n-11)(n+8) = 0$

$\therefore \quad n = 11$

Hence, number of its sides = 11.

36. $\because$ p, q, r are in G.P.

and a, b, c are in G.P.

$\therefore$ ap, bq, cr are in G.P.

We have,

if each term of a G.P. is multiplied or divided by some fixed, non-zero number, the resulting sequence is also a G.P.

37. $2a\sin^2\frac{C}{2}+2C\sin^2\frac{A}{2} = 2a + 2c - 3b$

$\Rightarrow a(1 - \cos C) + C(1 - \cos A) = 2a + 2c - 3b$

$\Rightarrow a - a\cos C + C - C\cos A = 2a + 2c - 3b$

$\Rightarrow a + c - (a\cos C + C\cos A) = 2a + 2c - 3b$

$\Rightarrow a + c - b = 2a + 2c - 3b$

$\Rightarrow a + c = 2b$

$\Rightarrow \frac{a+c}{2} = b$

$\therefore$ a, b, c are in A.P.

38. $\because$ a, b, c are in A.P.

$\therefore$ sinA, sinB, sinC are in A.P.

39. $p=\tan\left(-\frac{11\pi}{6}\right) = \tan\left(-\frac{11}{6}\times180^\circ\right)$

$= -\tan(330^\circ)$

$= -\tan(360 - 30^\circ)$

$= \tan 30^\circ = \frac{1}{\sqrt{3}}$

$q=\tan\left(\frac{21}{4}\pi\right) = \tan\left(\frac{21\times180^\circ}{4}\right)=\tan(945^\circ)$

$= \tan(2 \times 360^\circ + 225^\circ)$

$= \tan(180 + 45^\circ)$

$= \tan 45^\circ = 1.$

$r=\cot\left(\frac{283\pi}{6}\right) = \cot\left(\frac{283}{6}\times180\right)$

$= \cot(283 \times 30) = \cot(8490^\circ)$

$= \cot(360 \times 23 + 210^\circ)$

$= \cot(210^\circ)$

$= \cot(180^\circ + 30^\circ)$

$= \cot 30^\circ = \sqrt{3}$

I. The value of $p \times r = \frac{1}{\sqrt{3}}\times\sqrt{3} = 1$.

II. $\because$ p, q, r are in G.P.

$\therefore \quad q^2 = p \times r$

$\Rightarrow \quad (1)^2 = \frac{1}{\sqrt{3}}\times\sqrt{3}=1$

Hence, only II is correct answer.

40. Each employee are eligible for any number of tickets, then, required number of ways

$= 20 \times 20 \times 20$

$= 8000.$

41. $\sqrt{2}+\sqrt{8}+\sqrt{18}+\sqrt{32}+....$ n terms.

$= \sqrt{2}(1+2+....+n)$

$= \sqrt{2}\times\frac{n(n+1)}{2}=\frac{n(n+1)}{\sqrt{2}}.$

42. Co-efficient of x^{99} in $(x - 1)(x - 2) .... (x - 100)$

$= -(1 + 2 + 3 + ... + 100)$

$= -\frac{(100\times101)}{2}=-5050.$

43. Let, $\quad z = (x + iy)$

Then,

$(x + iy)(x - iy) + (3 - i)(x + iy) + (3 + i)(x - iy) + 1 = 0$

$x^2 + y^2 + 3x + y + 3iy - xi + 3x + y + ix - 3iy + 1 = 0$

$x^2 + 6x + y^2 + 2y + 1 = 0$

$(x + 3)^2 + (y + 1)^2 - 9 = 0$

$(x + 3)^2 + (y + 1)^2 = (3)^2$

Centre : (–3, –1), radius = 3.

44.

1,2,3, 4,5	0,1,2, 3,4,5	0,2,4

Case-I : When unit place is filled by '0' then, next two place would be filled by

$^5P_2 = 20$ ways

Case-II: When unit place is filled by 2, then hundred place will be filled by 4 ways and tenth place will be filled by 4 ways.

number of ways = 4 × 4 = 16

Case-III: When unit place is filled by 4, then hundred place will be filled by 4 ways and tenth place will be filled by 4 ways

number of ways = 4 × 4 = 16.

total number = 16 + 16 + 20 = 52.

45. $\log_8\left(m\times\frac{1}{6}\right)=\frac{2}{3} \Rightarrow \frac{m}{6}=(8)^{\frac{2}{3}}$

$\Rightarrow \frac{m}{6}=(2^3)^{\frac{2}{3}}=2^2 = 4 \Rightarrow m = 6 \times 4 = 24.$

46.

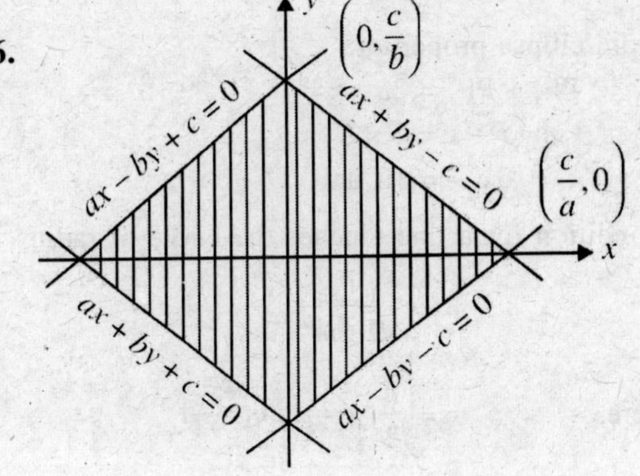

Required Area is the shaded portion

$$A = \left|4\times\frac{1}{2}\times\frac{c}{a}\times\frac{c}{b}\right|$$

$$= \frac{2c^2}{ab}.$$

47. Equation of any line ⊥ to $5x - y = 0$ is $y = -\frac{1}{5}x + C$.

where C = constant.

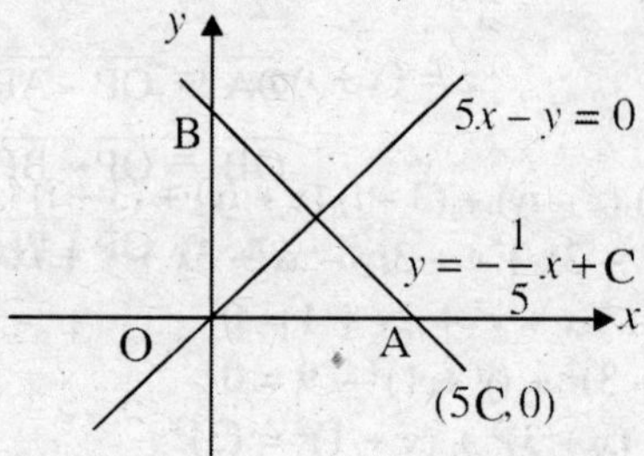

Let, the point of intersection of line with co-ordinate axis are A and B.

Then, A = (5C, 0) and B = (0, C).

Area of $\Delta OAB = \frac{1}{2}\times OA\times OB$

$$5 = -\frac{1}{2}\times 5C\times C$$

$\therefore$ $C = \pm\sqrt{2}$

Hence, required equation of line

$$y = -\frac{x}{5}\pm\sqrt{2}$$

$$x + 5y \pm 5\sqrt{2} = 0$$

48.

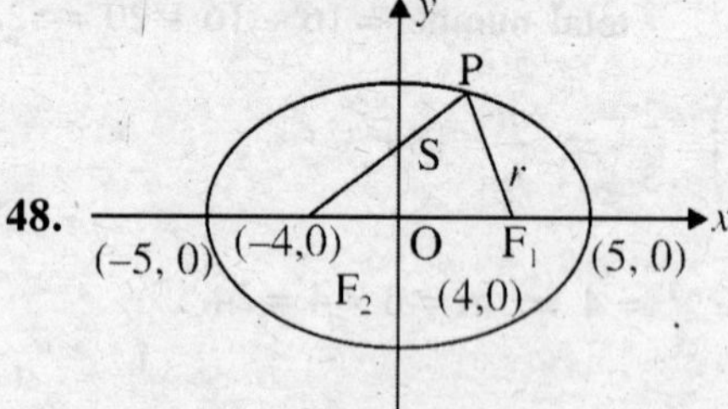

From ellipse properties.

$$PF_1 + PF_2 = 2a$$
$$r + s = 2\times 5$$
$$= 10 \text{ unit.}$$

49. Condition for a line touches the circle of radius

$$r = \frac{c}{\sqrt{1+m^2}}$$

Here, $r = \frac{r}{2}$, $c = 2$, $m = -1$

$$\therefore \quad \frac{r}{2} = \frac{2}{\sqrt{1+(-1)^2}}$$

$$r = \frac{4}{\sqrt{2}} \Rightarrow r = 2\sqrt{2}.$$

50.

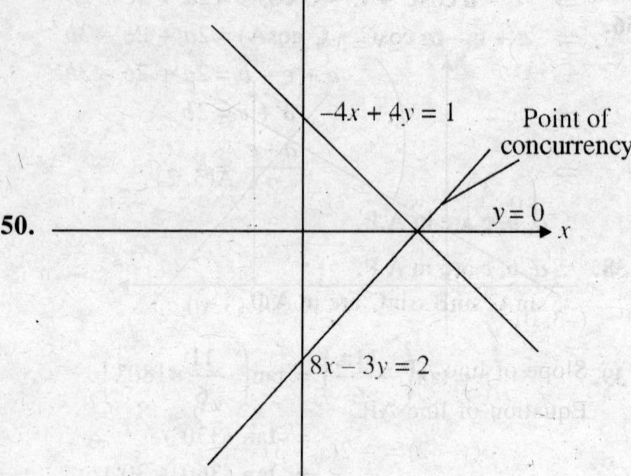

51.

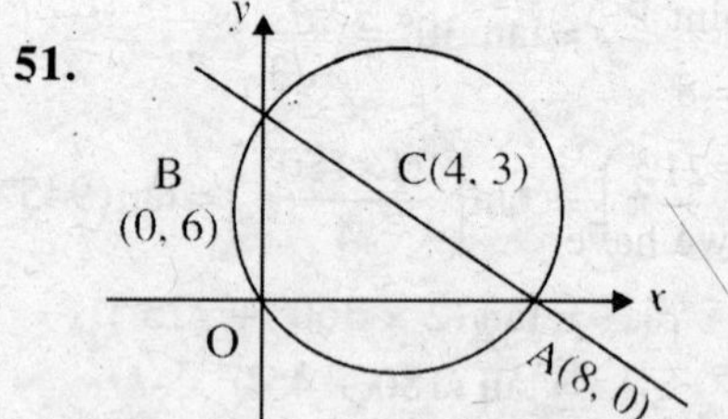

ΔOAB is a right triangle with right angle ∠AOB. Then, side AB act as a diameter to the circumcircle

its centre $= \left(\frac{8+0}{2}, \frac{0+6}{2}\right)$

$= (4, 3).$

52. Eccentricity of the hyperbola with major axis is y-axis.

$$e = \sqrt{\frac{a^2+b^2}{a^2}}$$

$$= \sqrt{\frac{16+9}{9}} = \frac{5}{3}.$$

54. Radius of the circle passing through origin and centre at (3, 4) is

$$\sqrt{(3-0)^2+(4-0)^2}$$

$$= \sqrt{9+16} = \sqrt{25} = 5 \text{ units.}$$

Equation of the circle

$$(x-3)^2 + (y-4)^2 = (5)^2$$

Intercept cut on x-axis *i.e.*, $y = 0$.

$$(x-3)^2 + (4)^2 = (5)^2$$

$$(x-3)^2 = 5^2 - 4^2$$
$$(x-3)^2 = 9$$
$$(x-3) = \pm 3$$
$$x = 0 \text{ or } 6.$$

Intercept on x-axis = 6 unit.

Similarly, on solving for y, intercept on y-axis = 8 unit.

56.

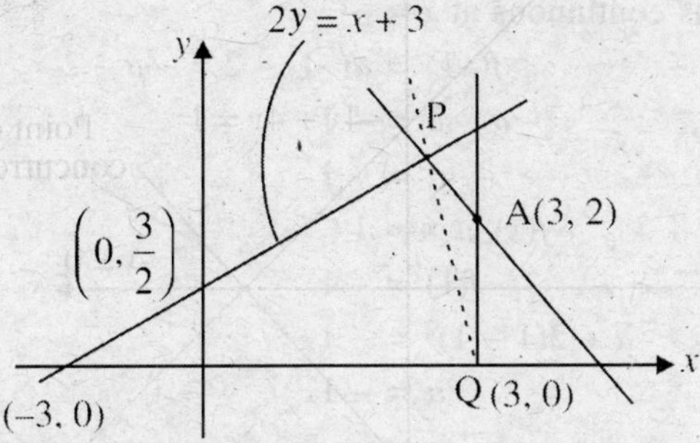

Slope of line AP = – 2

Equation of line AP.

$$(y-2) = -2(x-3)$$
$$2x + y = 8 \quad ...(i)$$

Co-ordinate of Point P :

$$2x + y = 8 \quad ...(i)$$

And $\quad x - 2y = -3 \quad ...(ii)$

From (*i*) and (*ii*), we have

$$x = \frac{13}{5},\ y = \frac{14}{5}$$

Equation of line AQ : $x = 3$

Co-ordinate of point Q = (3, 0)

$$\text{Slope of line PQ} = \frac{\frac{14}{5}-0}{\frac{13}{5}-3} = -7$$

Equation of line PQ :

$$(y-0) = -7(x-3)$$
$$7x + y - 21 = 0.$$

57. $3x^2 + 3y^2 + 3z^2 - 8x + 4y + 8z - 15 = 0.$

$$3\left(x^2 - \frac{8x}{3} + \left(\frac{4}{3}\right)^2\right) + 3\left(y^2 + \frac{4}{3}y + \left(\frac{2}{3}\right)^2\right) + 3\left(z^2 + \frac{8z}{3} + \left(\frac{4}{3}\right)^2\right)$$
$$-\frac{16}{3} - \frac{4}{3} - \frac{16}{3} - 15 = 0$$
$$\left(x - \frac{4}{3}\right)^2 + \left(4 + \frac{2}{3}\right)^2 + \left(z + \frac{4}{3}\right)^2 - 9 = 0$$

$$\text{Radius} = \sqrt{9} = 3 \text{ units.}$$

62.

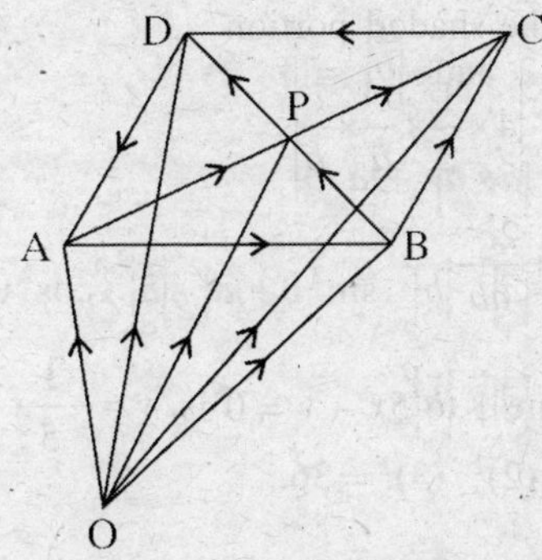

$$\overrightarrow{OA} = \overrightarrow{OP} - \overrightarrow{AP}$$
$$\overrightarrow{OB} = \overrightarrow{OP} - \overrightarrow{BP}$$
$$\overrightarrow{OC} = \overrightarrow{OP} + \overrightarrow{PC}$$
$$\overrightarrow{OD} = \overrightarrow{OP} + \overrightarrow{PD}$$

From figure, $\quad |\overrightarrow{AP}| = |\overrightarrow{PC}|$

$$|\overrightarrow{BP}| = |\overrightarrow{PD}|$$

$$\therefore \quad \overrightarrow{OA} + \overrightarrow{OB} + \overrightarrow{OC} + \overrightarrow{OD} = 4\overrightarrow{OP}.$$

63.

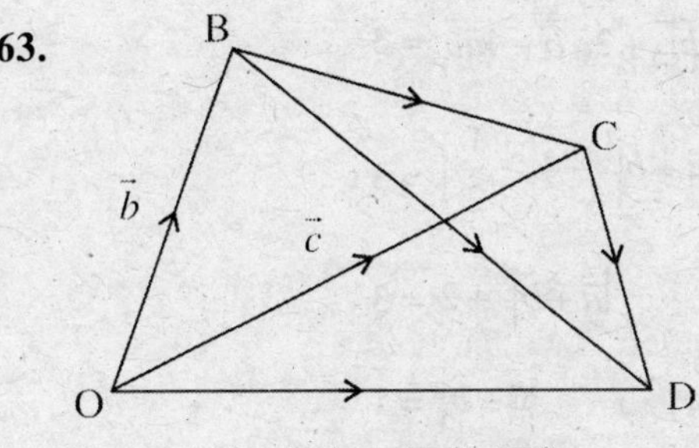

$$\overrightarrow{BC} = \overrightarrow{OC} - \overrightarrow{OB}$$
$$= \vec{c} - \vec{b}$$

and $\quad \overrightarrow{BD} = 4\overrightarrow{BC}$ (given).

again, $\quad \overrightarrow{BD} = \overrightarrow{BC} + \overrightarrow{CD}$

$$\overrightarrow{CD} = \overrightarrow{BD} - \overrightarrow{BC}$$
$$= 3\overrightarrow{BC}$$
$$= 3(\vec{c} - \vec{b})$$
$$\overrightarrow{OD} = \overrightarrow{OC} + \overrightarrow{CD}$$
$$= \vec{c} + 3(\vec{c} - \vec{b})$$
$$= 4\vec{c} - 3\vec{b}$$

64.

$$\vec{a} = 5\hat{i} + n\hat{j}$$
$$|\vec{a}| = \sqrt{5^2 + n^2}$$
$$13 = \sqrt{25 + n^2}$$
$$25 + n^2 = 169$$
$$n^2 = 144 \Rightarrow n = \pm 12$$

65. $|\vec{a}| = 2$ and $|\vec{b}| = 3$

$$= |\vec{a}\times\vec{b}|^2 + |\vec{a}.\vec{b}|^2$$

$$= |\vec{a}|^2.|\vec{b}|^2.\sin^2\theta + |\vec{a}|^2.|\vec{b}|^2.\cos^2\theta$$

$$= |\vec{a}|^2.|\vec{b}|^2$$

$$= (2)^2.(3)^2 = 36.$$

67. Let, $\vec{a}$ and $\vec{b}$ are two unit vectors.

$$|\vec{a}| = |\vec{b}| = 1$$

Then, $|\vec{a}-\vec{b}| = \sqrt{3}$

$$|\vec{a}|^2 + |\vec{b}|^2 - 2\vec{a}.\vec{b} = 3$$

$$1+1-2\vec{a}.\vec{b} = 3$$

$$\vec{a}.\vec{b} = -\frac{1}{2}$$

$$|\vec{a}|^2 + |\vec{b}|^2 + 2\vec{a}\vec{b} - 4\vec{a}\vec{b} = 3$$

$$|\vec{a}+\vec{b}|^2 - 4\left(-\frac{1}{2}\right) = 3$$

$$|\vec{a}+\vec{b}|^2 + 2 = 3$$

$$|\vec{a}+\vec{b}| = 1$$

68. As three vectors lies on a plane, then

$$\begin{vmatrix}\alpha & \alpha & \gamma\\ 1 & 0 & 1\\ \gamma & \gamma & \beta\end{vmatrix} = 0$$

$$\alpha(-\gamma) + \alpha(\gamma - \beta) + \gamma = 0$$

$$-\alpha\gamma + \alpha\gamma - \alpha\beta + \gamma^2 = 0$$

$$\gamma^2 = \alpha\beta$$

$\therefore$ $\gamma = \sqrt{\alpha\beta}$

$\therefore$ γ is the G.M. of α and β.

70. $I = \int_a^b \frac{x^7 + \sin x}{\cos x}.dx = \int_a^b \frac{(a+b-x)^7 + \sin(a+b-x)}{\cos(a+b-x)}.dx$

$$= \int_a^b \frac{-x^7 - \sin x}{\cos x}.dx$$

$$= -\int_a^b \frac{x^7 \times \sin x}{\cos x}.dx$$

Then, $I = 0$.

71. $\lim_{x\to 1}\frac{f(x)-f(1)}{x-1} = f'(1)$ [by def. of derivative]

Now, $f(x) = \sqrt{25-x^2} \Rightarrow f'(x) = -\frac{x}{\sqrt{25-x^2}}$

$\Rightarrow$ $f'(1) = -\frac{1}{\sqrt{24}}$.

72. $f(x)$ is continuous at $x = -1$.

$$f(-1) = a(-1) - 2 = -a - 2$$

then, $-a - 2 = -1$

$$a = -1$$

and $f(x)$ at $x = 1$

$$f(1) = -1$$

$$a + 2(1-1)^2 = -1$$

$$a = -1.$$

73. $f(\pi) = \lim_{x\to\pi} f(x)$

$$= \lim_{x\to\pi}\frac{1-\sin x+\cos x}{1+\sin x+\cos x}$$

By L′ Hospital rule

$$\lim_{x\to\pi} = -\frac{\cos x - \sin x}{\cos x - \sin x}$$

$$= -\frac{\cos(\pi) - \sin(\pi)}{\cos(\pi) - \sin(\pi)} = -\frac{(-1)}{-1}$$

$$= -1.$$

75. We have,

$$x = \begin{cases} x, x \geq 0\\ -x, x < 0\end{cases} \Rightarrow |x| - x = \begin{cases} 0, \geq 0\\ -2x, x < 0\end{cases}$$

Hence, the domain of $f(x) = \frac{1}{\sqrt{|x| - x}}$ is the set of all negative real numbers.
i.e., $(-\infty, 0)$.

77. Let, $y = \ln(x + \sin x)$

$$z = (x + \cos x)$$

$$\frac{dy}{dx} = \frac{d}{dx}\ln(x+\sin x)$$

$$= \frac{(1+\cos x)}{(x+\sin x)}$$

$$\frac{dz}{dx} = \frac{d}{dx}(x+\cos x) = (1 - \sin x)$$

$$\frac{dy}{dz} = \frac{(1+\cos x)}{(x+\sin x)(1-\sin x)}.$$

78. $y = \cot^{-1}\left[\frac{\sqrt{1+\sin x}+\sqrt{1-\sin x}}{\sqrt{1+\sin x}-\sqrt{1-\sin x}}\right]$

$= \cot^{-1}\frac{\left[\sqrt{1+\sin x}+\sqrt{1-\sin x}\right]}{\left\{-\sqrt{(1-\sin x)}-\sqrt{1+\sin x}\right\}}$

$= \cot^{-1}\frac{\left(\cos\frac{x}{2}+\sin\frac{x}{2}\right)+\left(\cos\frac{x}{2}-\frac{\sin x}{2}\right)}{-\left\{\left(\cos\frac{x}{2}-\sin\frac{x}{2}\right)-\left(\cos\frac{x}{2}+\sin\frac{x}{2}\right)\right\}}$

Note that,

$\sin\frac{x}{2} < \cos\frac{x}{2}$ for $0 < x < \frac{\pi}{2}$

$= \cot^{-1}\left(\cot\frac{x}{2}\right)$

$= \cot^{-1}.\cot\left(\pi+\frac{x}{2}\right)$

$\Rightarrow \quad y = \pi+\frac{x}{2}$

$\therefore \quad \frac{dy}{dx} = \frac{1}{2}.$

79. We have, $y = x^2 . e^{-x} \Rightarrow \frac{dy}{dx} = 2x\, e^{-x} - x^2e^{-x}$

for y to be increasing, $\frac{dy}{dx} > 0$

$\Rightarrow \quad e^{-x}(-x^2 + 2x) > 0 \Rightarrow x \in (0, 2)$

$\therefore \quad 0 < x < 2$

Hence, $f(x)$ is increasing if $0 < x < 2$.

80. $x^ay^b = (x-y)^{a+b}$

Taking log both sides

$a \log x + b \log y = (a + b) \log (x - y)$

$a.\frac{1}{x}+b.\frac{1}{y}\frac{dy}{dx} = (a+b).\frac{1}{x-y}\left(1-\frac{dy}{dx}\right)$

$\frac{a}{x}-\frac{a+b}{x-y} = -\left(\frac{a+b}{x-y}+\frac{b}{y}\right)\frac{dy}{dx}$

$\frac{ax-ay-ax-bx}{x(x-y)} = -\left(\frac{ay+by+bx-by}{y(x-y)}\right)\frac{dy}{dx}$

$-\frac{(bx+ay)}{x(x-y)} = -\frac{(bx+ay)}{y(x-y)}\frac{dy}{dx}$

$\Rightarrow \quad \frac{1}{x} = \frac{1}{y}\frac{dy}{dx}$

$\Rightarrow \quad \frac{dy}{dx} = \frac{y}{x}$

$\therefore \quad \frac{dy}{dx}-\frac{y}{x} = \frac{y}{x}-\frac{y}{x} = 0.$

81. $\because f : R \to R$ and $g : R \to R$ given by $f(x) = 2x - 3$ and $g(x) = x^3 + 5$ respectively, are bijections, therefore f^{-1} and g^{-1} exist.

We have, $\quad f(x) = 2x - 3$

$\therefore \quad f(x) = y$

$\Rightarrow \quad 2x - 3 = y$

$\Rightarrow \quad x = \frac{y+3}{2}$

$\Rightarrow \quad f^{-1}(y) = \frac{y+3}{2}$

Thus, f^{-1} is given by $f^{-1}(x) = \frac{x+3}{2}\ \forall x \in R$

Similarly, $\quad g^{-1}(x) = (x-5)^{\frac{1}{3}}\ \forall x \in R$

Now, $\quad (fog)^{-1}(x) = (g^{-1} of^{-1})(x) = g^{-1}(f^{-1}(x))$

$= g^{-1}\left(\frac{x+3}{2}\right) = \left(\frac{x+3}{2}-5\right)^{\frac{1}{3}}$

$= \left(\frac{x-7}{2}\right)^{\frac{1}{3}}.$

82. $\int_a^b \frac{|x|}{x}dx = |b|-|a|.$

83. $I = \int_0^{2\pi}\sin^5\left(\frac{x}{4}\right).dx = \int_0^{2\pi}\sin^4\left(\frac{x}{4}\right).\sin\left(\frac{x}{4}\right).dx$

Let, $\quad \sin^2\left(\frac{x}{4}\right) = z$

Then, $\quad dz = 2\sin\left(\frac{x}{4}\right).\cos\left(\frac{x}{4}\right).\frac{1}{4}dx$

$\sin\left(\frac{x}{4}\right)dx = \frac{2dz}{\cos\left(\frac{x}{4}\right)}$

$= \frac{2dz}{\sqrt{1-z}}$

Change of Limit

When, $\quad x = 2\pi,\ z = \sin^5\left(\frac{2\pi}{4}\right) = 1$

$$x = 0,\ z = \sin^5(0) = 0$$

$$\therefore \quad I = \int_0^{2\pi} \sin^5\left(\frac{x}{4}\right).dx = \int_0^1 \frac{2z^2}{\sqrt{1-z}}.dz$$

Again, Let $\quad 1 - 2 = k^2,\ dz = -2k.dk.$

Change of Limit

When, $\quad z = 1,\ 1 - z = k$

$$1 - 1 = k \Rightarrow k = 0$$

$$z = 0,\ 1 - z = k$$

$$1 - 0 = k \Rightarrow k = 1.$$

$$\therefore \quad \int_0^1 \frac{2z^2}{\sqrt{1-z}}.dz = 2\int_1^0 \frac{\left(1-k^2\right)^2}{k}(-2k.dk)$$

$$= -4\int_1^0 \left(1 + k^4 - 2k^2\right).dk$$

$$= -4\left[k + \frac{k^5}{5} - \frac{2}{3}k^3\right]_1^0$$

$$= -4\left[-1 - \frac{1}{5} + \frac{2}{3}\right]$$

$$= \frac{32}{15}.$$

84. $$\lim_{x\to2} f(x) = \lim_{x\to2}\frac{\sin\left(e^{x-2}-1\right)}{\ln(x-1)}$$

By L′ Hospital rule

$$\lim_{x\to2}\frac{\cos\left(e^{x-2}-1\right).e^{(x-2)}}{\frac{1}{(x-1)}}$$

$$= 1.$$

86. $$s = \sqrt{t^2+1}$$

$$\frac{ds}{dt} = \frac{2t}{2\sqrt{t^2+1}} = \frac{t}{\sqrt{t^2+1}}$$

$$\frac{d^2s}{dt^2} = \frac{\sqrt{\left(t^2+1\right)} - \frac{t.t}{\sqrt{t^2+1}}}{\left(t^2+1\right)}$$

$$= \frac{\left(t^2+1\right)-t^2}{\left(t^2+1\right)^{3/2}} = \frac{1}{\left(t^2+1\right)^{3/2}}$$

$$= \frac{1}{s^3}.$$

88. $$I = \int\frac{dx}{1+e^{-x}}$$

$$= \int\frac{e^x.dx}{1+e^x}$$

Let, $\quad 1 + e^x = z,\quad dz = e^x\,.\,dx$

$$I = \int\frac{e^x.dx}{1+e^x} = \int\frac{dz}{z} = \ln(z) + C$$

$$= \ln\left(1 + e^x\right) + C.$$

89. $$\int_{-1}^{1} x|x|dx$$

$$= -\int_{-1}^{0} x^2dx + \int_0^1 x^2dx$$

$$= -\left[\frac{x^3}{3}\right]_{-1}^{0} + \left[\frac{x^3}{3}\right]_0^1$$

$$= -\left[\frac{1}{3}\right] + \left[\frac{1}{3}\right] = 0.$$

91. At maximum value, $f'(x) = 0$.

$$f(x) = y = \left(\frac{1}{x}\right)^{2x^2}$$

$$\ln y = 2x^2\ln\left(\frac{1}{x}\right)$$

$$\frac{1}{y}.\frac{dy}{dx} = 4x.\ln\left(\frac{1}{x}\right) + \frac{2x^2}{\left(\frac{1}{x}\right)} - \left(\frac{1}{x^2}\right)$$

$$= 4x.\ln\left(\frac{1}{x}\right) - 2x$$

$$= -2x\left[1 + \ln(x)^2\right]$$

$$\frac{dy}{dx} = -y.2x\left[1 + \ln(x)^2\right]$$

$$= \left(\frac{1}{x}\right)^{2x^2}.2x\ \left[1 + \ln(x)^2\right.$$

When, $\quad \frac{dy}{dx} = 0$

$$x = 0 \text{ or } \ln(x) = -\frac{1}{2}$$

$$\Rightarrow \quad x = e^{-\frac{1}{2}}$$

$$= \frac{1}{\sqrt{e}}.$$

92. $$\int\left(\frac{1}{\sqrt{e}}\right) = \left(\frac{1}{\frac{1}{\sqrt{e}}}\right)^{2\left(\frac{1}{\sqrt{e}}\right)^2}$$

$$= \left(\sqrt{e}\right)^{\frac{2}{e}} = (e)^{\frac{1}{2}\times\frac{2}{e}}$$

$$= (e)^{\frac{1}{e}}$$

93. $$f(x) = \int\left(\frac{x^2}{2} - kx + 1\right)dx$$

$$= \left[\frac{x^3}{6} - \frac{k.x^2}{2} + x\right] + C$$

Where, C = constant.

$$f(0) = 0 \Rightarrow C = 0$$

$$f(3) = 15$$

$$\frac{(3)^3}{6} - \frac{k.(3)^2}{2} + 3 = 15$$

$$\frac{9}{2} - \frac{k.9}{2} = 12$$

$$9k = 9 - 24$$

$$= -15$$

$$k = -\frac{5}{3}.$$

94. $$f'(x) = \frac{x^2}{2} + \frac{5x}{3} + 1$$

$$f''(x) = x + \frac{5}{3}$$

$$f''\left(-\frac{2}{3}\right) = -\frac{2}{3} + \frac{5}{3} = 1.$$

For Q 95 and 96

Let, $f(x) = -2x^3 - 9x^2 - 12x + 1$

$\Rightarrow$ $y = -2x^3 - 9x^2 - 12x + 1$

$\Rightarrow$ $\frac{dy}{dx} = -6x^2 - 18x - 12$

$\because$ $f(x)$ is increasing

$\therefore$ $\frac{dy}{dx} > 0$

$\Rightarrow$ $-6x^2 - 18x - 12 > 0$

$\Rightarrow$ $x^2 + 3x + 2 > 0$

$x^2 + 2x + x + 2 > 0$

$\Rightarrow$ $x(x + 2) + 1(x + 2) > 0$

$\Rightarrow$ $(x + 1)(x + 2) > 0$

$x = -1, -2$

95. The function $f(x)$ is increasing function in the interval $(-2, -1)$.

96. $f(x)$ is decreasing

$\because$ $\frac{dy}{dx} < 0$

$\therefore$ $x = (-1, \infty)$ and $x = -2, -\infty$

$\therefore$ $f(x)$ is decreasing function in the interval $(-\infty, -2) \cup (-1, \infty)$.

99. $$f\left(-\frac{\pi}{2}\right) = -2.\sin\left(-\frac{\pi}{2}\right) = 2$$

$$= A.\sin\left(-\frac{\pi}{2}\right) + B = -A + B$$

$\therefore$ $-A + B = 2$ ...(*i*)

$$f\left(\frac{\pi}{2}\right) = \cos\left(\frac{\pi}{2}\right) = 0$$

$$= A\sin\left(\frac{\pi}{2}\right) + B = A + B$$

$\therefore$ $A + B = 0$ ...(*ii*)

From (*i*) and (*ii*), we have

A = – 1 and B = 1.

102. $\because$ $$\frac{dy}{dx} = \sqrt{1 - x^2 - y^2 + x^2y^2}$$

$$= \sqrt{(1 - x^2) - y^2(1 - x^2)}$$

$$= \sqrt{(1 - x^2)(1 - y^2)}$$

$\Rightarrow$ $$\frac{dy}{dx} = \sqrt{(1 - x^2)(1 - y^2)}$$

$\Rightarrow$ $$\int\frac{dy}{\sqrt{1 - y^2}} = \int\sqrt{1 - x^2}\,dx$$

$\Rightarrow$ $$\sin^{-1}y = \frac{1}{2}x\sqrt{1 - x^2} + \frac{1}{2}\sin^{-1}x + c$$

$\Rightarrow$ $$2\sin^{-1}y = x\sqrt{1 - x^2} + \sin^{-1}x + c.$$

103. Equation of circle passing through origin (0, 0) and having centre on X – axis at point (9, 0) is

$(x - a)^2 + y^2 = a^2$ ...(*i*)

$y^2 = a^2 - (x - a)^2$

$$y^2 = -x^2 + 2xa$$

$$\frac{x^2+y^2}{2x} = a.$$

Now, differentiating equation (*i*), w.r.t. x, we get

$$2(x-a)+2y.\frac{dy}{dx} = 0$$

$$2x-2\left(\frac{x^2+y^2}{2x}\right)+2y.\frac{dy}{dx} = 0$$

$$2x^2-x^2-y^2+2yx\frac{dy}{dx} = 0$$

$$2xy.\frac{dy}{dx} = y^2 - x^2.$$

104. Parabola having vertex at origin and focus at $(a, 0)$

$$y^2 = 4ax \Rightarrow 4x = \frac{y^2}{x}$$

Differentiating w.r.t. x, $2y.\frac{dy}{dx} = 4a$

$$2y.\frac{dy}{dx} = \frac{y^2}{x}$$

$$\Rightarrow \quad \frac{dy}{dx} = \frac{y}{2x}$$

order of d.E = 1

degree of d.E = 1.

106. Product of three numbers are odd, if all three numbers are odd. Number of ways of selecting 3 odd numbers out of 5 = ${}^5C_3$

Number of ways of selecting 3 numbers out of 9 = ${}^9C_3$

$$\text{Required probability} = \frac{{}^5C_3}{{}^9C_3}$$

$$= \frac{5}{42}.$$

107. $P(\text{not B}) = 0.8$

$\therefore \quad P(B) = 1 - 0.8 = 0.2$

$$P\left(\frac{A}{B}\right) = 0.4$$

$$\because \quad P\left(\frac{A}{B}\right) = \frac{P(A\cap B)}{P(B)}$$

$$\Rightarrow \quad .2 = \frac{P(A\cap B)}{.2}$$

$$P(A\cap B) = .2\times.2 = \frac{4}{100} = .04$$

Now, $P(A\cup B) = P(A) + n(B) - P(A\cap B)$

$\Rightarrow \quad .5 = P(A) + .2 - .04$

$\Rightarrow \quad P(A) = .3 + .04 = .34$

$\therefore \quad P(A) = 0.34.$

110. Number of times head appears more than three times = 6.

Total outcomes = $(2)^5$

$$\therefore \text{ Required probability} = \frac{6}{(2)^5} = \frac{3}{16}.$$

112. 1, 8, 27, 64, ... n terms.

Sum of $1^3 + 2^3 + 3^3 + 4^3 + ... + n^3$

$$= \frac{n^2(n+1)^2}{4}$$

$$\therefore \quad \text{A.M.} = \frac{n^2(n+1)^2}{4\times n} = \frac{n(n+1)^2}{4}.$$

115. Number of ways of selecting one white ball from bag 1 = ${}^4C_1 = 4$.

Number of ways of selecting one black ball from bag 2 = ${}^5C_1 = 5$.

Number of ways of selecting one black ball from bag 1 = ${}^2C_1 = 2$.

Number of ways of selecting one white ball from bag 2 = ${}^3C_1 = 3$.

$$\text{Required probability} = \frac{4\times5+2\times3}{{}^6C_1\times{}^8C_1}$$

$$= \frac{26}{6\times8} = \frac{13}{24}.$$

116. Probability for unsolve the question

by $\quad A = 1-\frac{1}{2} = \frac{1}{2}$

by $\quad B = 1-\frac{1}{3} = \frac{2}{3}$

by $\quad C = 1-\frac{1}{4} = \frac{3}{4}$

Probability for unsolve the problem

$$= \frac{1}{2}\times\frac{2}{3}\times\frac{3}{4} = \frac{1}{4}.$$

Probability for question to be solved

$$= 1-\frac{1}{4} = \frac{3}{4}.$$

118. Let, $\quad x$ = probability for head = $\frac{1}{2}$

y = probability for tail = $\frac{1}{2}$

$$(x + y)^5 = {}^5C_1\ y.x^4 + {}^5C_3\ y^3.x^2 + {}^5C_5\ y^5$$

$$= (5+10+1)\times\frac{1}{2^5}$$

$$= \frac{16}{32} = \frac{1}{2}.$$

119. Correlation Co-efficient

$$\sigma = \sqrt{b_{xy}.b_{yx}}$$

$$= \sqrt{(-0.64)\times(-0.36)}$$

$$= 0.48.$$

120. Single digit natural numbers :

(1, 2, 3, 4, 5, 6, 7, 8, 9)

Pair of numbers whose sum is prime number are:

(1, 2), (1, 4), (1, 6), (2, 3), (2, 5), (2, 9), (3, 4), (3, 8), (4, 7), (4, 9), (5, 6), (5, 8), (6, 7), (8, 9).

$$\therefore \quad n(E) = 14$$

$$n(S) = {}^9C_2 = 36.$$

$$\therefore \text{ Required probability } = \frac{n(E)}{n(S)} = \frac{14}{36}$$

$$= \frac{7}{18}.$$

Previous Papers (Solved)

NATIONAL DEFENCE ACADEMY & NAVAL ACADEMY

NDA & NA – Entrance Exam, 2015 (I)

PAPER I : GENERAL ABILITY TEST

PART A : ENGLISH LANGUAGE

Spotting Errors

Directions (Qs. no. 1 to 15): *In this Section, a number of sentences are given. The sentences are divided in three separate parts and each one is labelled (A), (B), (C). Read each sentence to find out whether there is an error in any part. No sentence has more than one error. When you find an error in any one of the parts (A), (B) or (C), indicate your response on the Answer Sheet at the appropriate space. You may feel that there is no error in a sentence. In that case letter '(D)' will signify a 'No error' response.*

1. Unless you stop to make noise at once, (A)/ I will have no option but to (B)/ bring the matter to the attention of the police. (C)/ No error (D).

2. He couldn't but help (A)/ shed tears at the plight of the villagers (B)/ rendered homeless by a devastating cyclone. (C)/ No error (D).

3. Since it was his first election campaign, the candidate was confused; (A)/ none could clearly understand (B)/ either the principles he stood for or the benefits he promised. (C)/ No error (D).

4. It is an established fact that the transcendental American poets and philosophers, (A)/ who lived in the latter half of the nineteenth century, (B)/ were more influenced by Indian philosophy, in particular by Upanishadic Philosophy. (C)/ No error (D).

5. No sooner did I open the door (A)/ when the rain, heavy and stormy, rushed in (B)/ making us shiver from head to foot. (C)/ No error (D).

6. After opening the door (A)/ we entered into the room (B)/ next to the kitchen. (C)/ No error (D).

7. When the dentist came in (A)/ my tooth was stopped aching (B)/ out of fear that I might lose my tooth. (C)/ No error (D).

8. Emphasis on equality of life ensures (A)/ for the health and happiness (B)/ of every individual. (C)/ No error (D).

9. The students were (A)/ awaiting for (B)/ the arrival of the chief guest. (C)/ No error (D).

10. You will come (A)/ to my party tomorrow, (B)/ isn't it? (C)/ No error (D).

11. Having read a number of stories (A)/ about space travel (B)/ his dream now is about to visit the moon. (C)/ No error (D).

12. The meeting adjourned abruptly (A)/ by the Chairman after (B)/ about three hours of deliberation. (C)/ No error (D).

13. Not one of the hundreds (A)/ of striking workers (B)/ were allowed to go near the factory. (C)/ No error (D).

14. If I had known (A)/ this earlier (B)/ I will have helped him. (C)/ No error (D).

15. Mr. Smith was accused for murder (A)/ but the court found him not guilty (B)/ and acquitted him. (C)/ No error (D).

Sentence Improvement

Directions (Qs. no. 16 to 30) : *Look at the underlined part of each sentence. Below each sentence are given three possible substitutions for the underlined part. If one of them (A), (B) or (C), is better than the underlined part, indicate your response on the Answer Sheet against the corresponding letter (A), (B) or (C). If none of the substitutions improve the sentence, indicate (D) as your response on the Answer Sheet. Thus a 'No improvement' response will be signified by the letter (D).*

16. Although India is still <u>by far</u> a poor country, it can become rich if its natural and human resources are fully utilised.

A. few and far between
B. by and large
C. by and by
D. No improvement

17. The more they earn, more they spend.
A. More they earn, more they spend
B. More they earn, the more they spend
C. The more they earn, the more they spend
D. No improvement

18. But in all these cases conversion from one scale to another is easy because scales have well-formulated.
A. can be well-formulated
B. are well-formulated
C. well-formulated
D. No improvement

19. Five years ago on this date, I am sitting in a small Japanese car, driving across Poland towards Berlin.
A. was sitting
B. sat
C. have been sitting
D. No improvement

20. The old man felled some trees in the garden with hardly no effort at all.
A. hard effort
B. hardly any effort
C. a hardly any effort
D. No improvement

21. She says she's already paid me back, but I can't remember, so I'll have to take her word.
A. to take her word true
B. to take her at her word
C. to take her word for it
D. No improvement

22. The workers are hell bent at getting what is due to them.
A. hell bent on getting
B. hell bent for getting
C. hell bent to getting
D. No improvement

23. You are warned against committing the same mistake again.
A. to commit B. for committing
C. against to commit D. No improvement

24. While we would like that all Indian children to go to school, we need to ponder why they do not.
A. that all the Indian children
B. if all the children of India
C. all Indian children
D. No improvement

25. Due to these reasons we are all in favour of universal compulsory education.
A. Out of these reasons
B. For these reasons
C. By these reasons
D. No improvement

26. When it was feared that the serfs might go too far and gain their freedom from serfdom, the Protestant leaders joined the princes at crushing them.
A. into crushing B. in crushing
C. without crushing D. No improvement

27. In India, today many of our intellectuals still talk in terms of the French revolution and the Rights of Man, not appreciating that much has happened since then.
A. much has been happening
B. much had happened
C. much might happen
D. No improvement

28. Taxpayers are to be conscious of their privileges.
A. have to B. need
C. ought to D. No improvement

29. I would have waited for you at the station if I knew that you would come.
A. had known B. was knowing
C. have known D. No improvement

30. No one could explain how a calm and balanced person like him could penetrate such a mindless act on his friends.
A. perpetuate B. perpetrate
C. precipitate D. No improvement

Ordering of Sentences

Directions (Qs. no. 31 to 36) : *In items in this section, each passage consists of six sentences. The first and the sixth sentences are given in the beginning as S1 and S6. The middle four sentences in each have been removed and jumbled up. These are labelled P, Q, R and S. You are required to find out the proper order for the four sentences and mark accordingly on the Answer Sheet.*

31. S1 : At the roadside the driver will be asked to blow through a small glass tube into a plastic bag.
S6 : The driver will be asked to go to the police station.
P : And if the colour change does not reach the line the driver cannot be punished under the new law.
Q : Inside the tube are chemically treated crystals which change colour if the driver has alcohol on his breath.
R : But if the colour change does reach the line then the test has proved positive.
S : If the colour change goes beyond a certain line marked on the tube this indicates that the driver is probably over the specified limit.

The proper sequence should be
A. P S Q R B. S Q R P
C. R P S Q D. Q S P R

32. S1 : Hope springs eternally in the heart of man.
S6 : This is the central idea of the poem.
P : But hope is everlasting.
Q : Love, friendship and youth perish.
R : It is nursed by the glorious elements of nature.
S : Man derives hope from nature in his gallant struggle after some noble ideal.

The proper sequence should be
A. Q P R S B. S R Q P
C. R S Q P D. Q P S R

33. S1 : Mr. Sherlock Holmes and Doctor Watson were spending a weekend in a University town.
S6 : It was clear that something very unusual happened.
P : One evening they received a visit from an acquaintance, Mr. Hilton Soames.
Q : On that occasion he was in a state of great agitation.
R : They were staying in furnished rooms, close to the library.
S : Mr. Soames was a tall, thin man of a nervous and excitable nature.

The proper sequence should be
A. P R S Q B. R P S Q
C. P Q R S D. R P Q S

34. S1 : The machines that drive modern civilisation derive their power from coal and oil.
S6 : Nuclear energy may also be effectively used in this respect.
P : But they are not inexhaustible.
Q : These sources may not be exhausted very soon.
R : A time may come when some other sources have to be tapped and utilised.
S : Power may, of course, be obtained in future from forests, water, wind and withered vegetables.

The proper sequence should be
A. P Q R S B. Q P R S
C. S R Q P D. S P Q R

35. S1 : The body can never stop.
S6 : It comes from food.
P : To support this endless activity, the body needs all the fuel for action.
Q : Sometimes it is more active than at other times, but it is always moving.
R : Even in the deepest sleep we must breathe.
S : The fuel must come from somewhere.

The proper sequence should be
A. P Q R S B. P R Q S
C. Q R P S D. S R Q P

36. S1 : American idealism is essentially a belief in the idea of progress.
S6 : This sense they have inherited from the English.
P : Therefore, he believes that, because of human effort, the future will be better than the past.
Q : But if Americans are usually optimistic, they are not wholly unrealistic.
R : The American tends to view history as a record of human achievement.
S : They have some common sense practicality.

The proper sequence should be
A. P Q R S B. P Q S R
C. R P Q S D. P R Q S

Selecting Words

Directions (Qs. no. 37 to 42) : *In the following passage at certain points you are given a choice of three words marked (A), (B) and (C), one of which fits the meaning of the passage. Choose the best word out of the three. Mark the letter, viz., (A), (B) or (C), relating to this word on your Answer Sheet. Examples K and L have been solved for you.*

K. The ...(K)... was in the school in Shimla.
A. boy B. horse C. dog

L. ...(L)... was home sick.
A. She B. It C. He

Explanation : *Out of the list given in item K, only 'boy' is the correct answer because usually, a boy, and not a horse or a dog, attends school. So '(a)' is to be marked on the Answer Sheet for item K. A boy is usually referred to as 'he', so for item L, '(c)' is the correct answer. Notice that to solve the first item K you have to read the rest of the sentence and then see what fits best.*

PASSAGE

After having slept for an hour, Bond decided to go out into the city and try to find his contact. After changing his suit, he carefully locked his room and stepped out of the hotel. No one was around. But he had walked only for a few minutes when it suddenly ...(37)... to him that he was being ...(38)... by someone. There was really no ...(39)... for it except a very slight ...(40)... of footsteps. He was now walking ...(41)... the main street, which was crowded ...(42)... people. He became exremely aware of the danger of people threatening him.

37. A. felt B. occurred C. happened
38. A. followed B. shot C. looked
39. A. reason B. cause C. evidence
40. A. weight B. sound C. hurting
41. A. from B. down C. over
42. A. with B. by C. in

Synonyms

Directions (Qs. no. 43 to 46) : *Each item in this section consists of a sentence with an underlined word followed by four words or group of words. Select the word or group of words that is most* ***similar*** *in meaning to the underlined word.*

43. He was fired for negligence on duty.
A. relieved of his job
B. scolded
C. rebuked
D. attacked

44. Democracy is not the standardising of everyone so as to obliterate all peculiarity.
A. demolish B. extinguish
C. erase D. change

45. Divine grace is truly ineffable.
A. that which cannot be rubbed out
B. incapable of being understood
C. that which is too great to be expressed in words
D. too powerful to be defeated

46. The convocation address was very edifying.
A. tedious B. in need of editing
C. instructive D. exciting

Antonyms

Directions (Qs. no. 47 to 50) : *Each item in this section consists of a sentence with an underlined word, followed by four words. Select the word that is most nearly* ***opposite*** *in meaning to the underlined word.*

47. John is always shabbily dressed.
A. decently B. beautifully
C. extravagantly D. scantily

48. The new manager of the Bank is urbane in his manners.
A. civilised B. slow
C. rude D. foolish

49. It is necessary to develop thrifty habits to be able to lead a comfortable life.
A. expensive B. extravagant
C. economical D. good

50. Many people suffer because of pride.
A. lowliness B. submission
C. humility D. obedience

PART B : GENERAL KNOWLEDGE

Directions : *The following* ***eight (8)*** *items consist of two statements, Statement I and Statement II. You are to examine these two statements carefully and select the answers to these items using the code given below :*

Code:
A. Both the statements are individually true and Statement II is the correct explanation of Statement I.
B. Both the statements are individually true but Statement II is ***not*** the correct explanation of Statement I
C. Statement I is true but Statement II is false
D. Statement I is false but Statement II is true

51. Statement I: Growth of plants is smooth with a complete fertilizer.
Statement II: A complete fertilizer always contains N, P, K.

52. Statement I: The granules of modern gunpowder (also called black powder) are typically coated with Graphite.
Statement II: Graphite prevents the build-up of electrostatic charge.

53. Statement I: Colour of nitrogen dioxide changes to colourless at low temperature.
Statement II: At low temperature Nitrogen tetroxide (N_2O_4) is formed which is colourless.

54. Statement I: Diamond is very bright.
Statement II: Diamond has very low refractive index.

55. Statement I: Oxygen gas is easily produced at a faster rate by heating a mixture of potassium chlorate and manganese dioxide than heating potassium chlorate alone.
Statement II: Manganese dioxide acts as a negative catalyst.

56. Statement I: A body weighs less on a hill top than on earth's surface even though its mass remains unchanged.
Statement II: The acceleration due to gravity of the earth decreases with height.

57. Statement I: While putting clothes for drying up, we spread them out.
Statement II: The rate of evaporation increases with an increase in surface area.

58. Statement I: Due to diffused or irregular reflection of light, a closed room gets light even if no direct sunlight falls inside the room.
Statement II: Irregular reflection, where the reflected rays are not parallel, does not follow the laws of reflection.

59. Ultrasonic waves of frequency 3×10^5 Hz are passed through a medium where speed of sound is 10 times that in air (Speed of sound in air is 300 m/s). The wavelength of this wave in that medium will be of the order of
A. 1 cm B. 10 cm
C. 100 cm D. 0.1 cm

60. If radius of the earth were to shrink by 1%, its mass remaining the same, g would decrease by nearly

A. 1% B. 2%
C. 3% D. 4%

61. The displacement-time graph of a particle acted upon by a constant force is

A. a straight line
B. a circle
C. a parabola
D. any curve depending upon initial conditions

62. Which one of the following is ***not*** a result of surface tension?

A. Nearly spherical drop of rain
B. Capillary rise
C. Removal of dirt by soap or detergent
D. Flow of a liquid

63. Match List-I with List-II and select the correct answer using the codes given below the Lists:

List-I (Compound)	**List-II (Nature)**
(*a*) Sodium hydroxide	1. Strong acid
(*b*) Calcium oxide	2. Alkali
(*c*) Acetic acid	3. Weak acid
(*d*) Hydrochloric acid	4. Base

Codes:

	(*a*)	(*b*)	(*c*)	(*d*)
A.	2	3	4	1
B.	2	4	3	1
C.	1	4	3	2
D.	1	3	4	2

64. Which one of the following statements is ***not*** correct?

A. Kerala is the largest producer of natural rubber in India
B. Neyveli is an important thermal power generating area of Tamil Nadu
C. Ratnagiri Bauxite mining area is located in Karnataka
D. Assam is the largest tea producing state in India

65. Match List-I with List-II and select the correct answer using the codes given below the Lists:

List-I (Paper industry centre)	**List-II (State)**
(*a*) Kamptee	1. Karnataka
(*b*) Rajahmundry	2. Maharashtra
(*c*) Shahdol	3. Andhra Pradesh
(*d*) Belagola	4. Madhya Pradesh

Codes:

	(*a*)	(*b*)	(*c*)	(*d*)
A.	1	4	3	2
B.	2	3	4	1
C.	1	3	4	2
D.	2	4	3	1

66. The newly formed state of Telengana is surrounded by

A. 5 States B. 4 States
C. 6 States D. 3 States

67. Energy is required for maintenance of life. It is obtained by a process called

A. Metabolism
B. Phagocytosis
C. Photorespiration
D. Decomposition

68. All life forms contain "molecules of life". These are

A. Carbohydrates B. Proteins
C. Nucleic acids D. All of the above

69. If a charged particle (+ q) is projected with certain velocity parallel to the magnetic field, then it will

A. trace helical path
B. trace circular path
C. continue its motion without any change
D. come to rest instantly

70. Optical fibres, though bent in any manner, allows light to pass through. What is the inference that one can draw from it?

A. The concept that light travels in straight path is wrong
B. Light can flow through the optical fibres
C. Light can travel through the fibres because of their ductility
D. Light can travel through the fibres due to multiple total internal reflections

71. Which one among the following happens when a swing rises to a certain height from its rest position?

A. Its potential energy decreases while kinetic energy increases
B. Its kinetic energy decreases while potential energy increases
C. Both potential and kinetic energy decrease
D. Both potential and kinetic energy increase

72. Which one among the following is used in making gunpowder?

A. Magnesium sulphate B. Potassium nitrate
C. Sodium stearate D. Calcium sulphate

73. The cleaning action of soap and detergent in water is due to the formation of

A. Micelle B. Salt
C. Base D. Acid

74. The chemical used as a fixer/developer in photography is

A. Sodium sulphate B. Sodium sulphide
C. Sodium thiosulphate D. Sodium sulphite

75. Rain shadow effect is associated with

A. Cyclonic rainfall B. Orographic rainfall
C. Convectional rainfall D. Frontal rainfall

76. Match List-I with List-II and select the correct answer using the codes given below the Lists:

List-I (Place)	List-II (Industry)
(*a*) Jabalpur	1. Petro-chemical industry
(*b*) Bengaluru	2. IT industry
(*c*) Mathura	3. Paper industry
(*d*) Ballarpur	4. Automobile industry

Codes:

	(*a*)	(*b*)	(*c*)	(*d*)
A.	4	1	2	3
B.	3	2	1	4
C.	4	2	1	3
D.	3	1	2	4

77. Which one of the following irrigation canals is the most important in terms of area coverage in Haryana?
A. Bhakra canal
B. The Western Yamuna canal
C. Jawaharlal Nehru canal
D. Gurgaon canal

78. Which one of the following is the smallest unit showing the properties of life such as capacity for metabolism, response to the environment, growth and reproduction?
A. Gene B. Chromosome
C. Nucleus D. Cell

79. In plants, which one of the following gases is released during Photosynthesis?
A. Carbon dioxide B. Oxygen
C. Hydrogen D. Methane

80. Match List-I with List-II and select the correct answer using the codes given below the Lists:

List-I (Physical quantity)	List-II (Unit)
(*a*) Distance	1. Mole
(*b*) Amount of material	2. Coulomb
(*c*) Amount of electrical charge	3. Light year
(*d*) Energy	4. Watt hour

Codes:

	(*a*)	(*b*)	(*c*)	(*d*)
A.	3	1	2	4
B.	3	2	1	4
C.	4	2	1	3
D.	4	1	2	3

81. A ray of light when refracted suffers change in velocity. In this context, which one among the following statements is correct?
A. Velocity increases as the ray passes from a rarer to a denser medium
B. Velocity decreases as the ray passes from a denser to a rarer medium
C. Velocity decreases as the ray passes from a rarer to a denser medium
D. Change of velocity does not depend on the nature of medium

82. An object is placed 10 cm in front of a convex lens of focal length 15 cm. The image produced will be
A. Real and magnified
B. Virtual and magnified
C. Virtual and reduced in size
D. Real and reduced in size

83. Why is Graphite used in electrolytic cells?
A. Graphite is soft and can be easily moulded into electrodes
B. Graphite is made of layers of carbon atoms which can slide
C. Graphite is inert to most of the chemicals and remains intact in electrolytic cells
D. Graphite is a good conductor of electricity

84. Washing Soda is the common name for
A. Calcium Carbonate
B. Magnesium Carbonate
C. Sodium Carbonate
D. Potassium Carbonate

85. Which one of the following Indian states has the highest proportion of area under forest cover?
A. Madhya Pradesh B. Sikkim
C. Meghalaya D. Mizoram

86. Match List-I with List-II and select the correct answer using the codes given below the Lists:

List-I (National Park/ Wildlife Sanctuary)	List-II (State)
(*a*) Chandra Prabha	1. Uttarakhand
(*b*) Silent Valley	2. Chhattisgarh
(*c*) Valley of flowers	3. Uttar Pradesh
(*d*) Indravati	4. Kerala

Codes:

	(*a*)	(*b*)	(*c*)	(*d*)
A.	2	1	4	3
B.	3	4	1	2
C.	2	4	1	3
D.	3	1	4	2

87. To a perpendicular to the plane of ecliptic, Earth's axis of rotation makes an angle of 23.5 degrees. Had this angle been zero degree, which one among the following would result?
A. There would have been no season
B. The length of day and night would have been the same throughout the year
C. The length of the day and night would have been the same all over the earth
D. All of the above

88. Gametophytes of sexually reproducing flowering plants are
A. Haploid B. Diploid
C. Tetraploid D. Polyploid

89. The seeds of flowering plants are made up of
A. Ovary and ovary wall
B. Embryo, food reserves and coat
C. Cotyledons
D. Zygotes

90. A person stands on his two feet over a surface and experiences a pressure P. Now the person stands on only one foot. He would experience a pressure of magnitude.
A. 4 P B. P
C. ½ P D. 2 P

91. A solid is melted and allowed to cool and solidify again. The temperature is measured at equal intervals of time. The graph below shows the change of temperature with time.

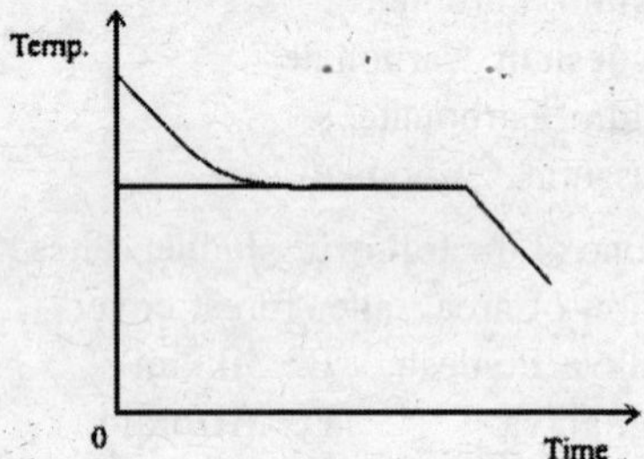

The part of the curve that is practically horizontal is due to
A. latent heat given away by the liquid
B. specific heat given away by the liquid
C. thermal capacity changes with time keeping temperature constant
D. change in density during transformation

92. A deep sea diver may hurt his ear drum during diving because of
A. lack of oxygen
B. high atmospheric pressure
C. high water pressure
D. All of the above

93. When you walk on a woollen carpet and bring your finger near the metallic handle of a door an electric shock is produced. This is because
A. charge is transferred from your body to the handle
B. a chemical reaction occurs when you touch the handle
C. the temperature of the human body is higher than that of the handle
D. the human body and the handle arrive at thermal equilibrium by the process

94. Which one among the following does ***not*** wet the walls of the glass vessel in which it is kept?
A. Water B. Alcohol
C. Mercury D. Phenol

95. Permanent hardness of water is due to the presence of
A. sulphates of sodium and potassium
B. sulphates of magnesium and calcium
C. carbonates of sodium and magnesium
D. bicarbonates of magnesium and calcium

96. In the reaction $ZnO + C \rightarrow Zn + CO$, 'C' acts as
A. an acid B. a base
C. an oxidising agent D. a reducing agent

97. Which of the following are the characteristics of organic farming?
1. Use of chemical fertilizers to improve soil fertility.
2. Frequent decomposing and fallowing.
3. Use of herbs to control pests.
4. Higher productivity per hectare.

Select the correct answer using the code given below:
A. 1 and 4 only B. 1, 3 and 4
C. 2 and 3 only D. 2, 3 and 4

98. 'Yakuts' are the nomadic herders of
A. Gobi B. Sahara
C. Tundra D. Kalahari

99. A farmer in a semi-arid area claims that his farming practice is very environment friendly. Which of the following practices on his farm can justify his claim?
1. Planting a tree belt.
2. Practising crop rotation.
3. Carrying out a large scale irrigation system.
4. Using organic fertilizers.

Select the correct answer using the code given below:
A. 3 and 4 only B. 1, 2 and 4
C. 1, 3 and 4 B. 1 and 2 only

100. The luxuriant growth of natural vegetation in tropical rainforest is due to
1. fertile soil.
2. hot and wet climate throughout the year.
3. intense sunlight for photosynthesis.
4. seasonal change to facilitate nutrient absorption.

Select the correct answer using the code given below:
A. 1 and 4 only B. 2 and 3 only
C. 1, 2 and 3 only B. 1, 2, 3 and 4

101. Which endocrine gland requires iodine to synthesize a particular hormone whose deficiency may cause goitre disease?
A. Hypothalamus B. Pancreas
C. Thymus D. Thyroid gland

102. Which one of the following is ***not*** a part of nerves?
A. Axons B. Connective tissues
C. Schwann cells D. Smooth muscles

103. The product of conductivity and resistivity of a conductor
A. depends on pressure applied
B. depends on current flowing through conductor
C. is the same for all conductors
D. varies from conductor to conductor

104. We use CFL to save electrical energy and to provide sufficient light. The full form of CFL is

A. Condensed filament light
B. Compact filament lamp
C. Condensed fluorescent lamp
D. Compact fluorescent lamp

105. When the sun is 30° above the horizon, shadow of one tree is 17.3 m long. What is the height of this tree?

A. 20 m B. 17.30 m
C. 10 m D. 1.73 m

106. When heat rays are reflected from Earth, gases like Carbon dioxide, Nitrous oxide do not allow them to escape back to the space causing our planet to heat up. These gases are known as

A. Noble gas B. Green-house gas
C. Hot gas D. Blue gas

107. A spring can be used to determine the mass *m* of an object in two ways : (i) by measuring the extension in the spring due to the object; and (ii) by measuring the oscillation period for the given mass. Which of these methods can be used in a space-station orbiting Earth?

A. Both
B. Only the extension method
C. Only the oscillation method
D. Neither

108. Match List-I with List-II and select the correct answer using the codes given below the Lists:

List-I (Region)	**List-II (Vegetation)**
(*a*) Selvas	1. Conifers
(*b*) Savannas	2. Mosses and Lichens
(*c*) Taiga	3. Epiphytes
(*d*) Tundra	4. Grasses and trees

Codes:

	(*a*)	(*b*)	(*c*)	(*d*)
A.	4	1	2	3
B.	3	2	1	4
C.	3	4	1	2
D.	4	2	1	3

109. Which of the following statements with regard to the western coastal plain of India are correct?

1. It is a narrow belt.
2. It is an example of submerged coastal plain.
3. It provides natural conditions for development of ports.
4. It has well developed deltas.

Select the correct answer using the code given below :

A. 1, 2 and 3 only B. 1 and 2 only
C. 1, 2, 3 and 4 D. 3 and 4 only

110. Which one of the following weather conditions indicates a sudden fall in barometer reading?

A. Stormy weather B. Calm weather
C. Cold and dry weather D. Hot and sunny weather

111. Match List-I with List-II and select the correct answer using the codes given below the Lists:

List-I (Island)	**List-II (Location)**
(*a*) Continental island	1. Mauritius
(*b*) Coral island	2. Madagascar
(*c*) Volcanic island	3. Andaman and Nicobar islands
(*d*) Mountain island	4. Maldives

Codes:

	(*a*)	(*b*)	(*c*)	(*d*)
A.	2	4	1	3
B.	2	1	4	3
C.	3	1	4	2
D.	3	4	1	2

112. Consider the following diagram :

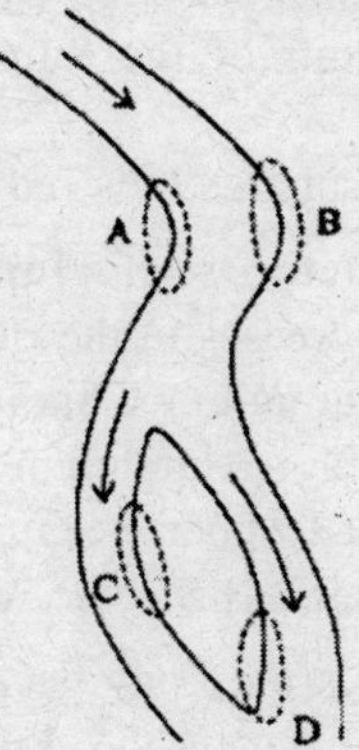

In which one among the following lettered areas of the diagram would erosion most likely change the shapes of the riverbed?

A. A B. B
C. C D. D

113. Match List-I with List-II and select the correct answer using the codes given below the Lists:

List-I (Cloud)	**List-II (Characteristic)**
(*a*) Cirrus	1. Rain giving
(*b*) Stratus	2. Feathery appearance
(*c*) Nimbus	3. Vertically growing
(*d*) Cumulus	4. Horizontally spreading

Codes:

	(*a*)	(*b*)	(*c*)	(*d*)
A.	3	1	4	2
B.	3	4	1	2
C.	2	4	1	3
D.	2	1	4	3

114. The concept of demographic transition provides a model for

A. analyzing government responses to changing pattern of population growth

B. explaining major patterns of global population movement throughout the history
C. analyzing spatial variations in the distribution, growth and movement of population over time
D. examining the relationship between economic development and natural population change

115. Precursor of which one of the following vitamins comes from β-carotene?
A. Vitamin A B. Vitamin C
C. Vitamin D D. Vitamin K

116. 'Lub-dup' sound is produced due to action of
A. Large intestine B. Lungs
C. Heart D. Oesophagus

117. The Sun is observed to be reddish when it is near the horizon, i.e., in the morning and the evening. This is because
A. red light is least scattered by atmosphere
B. red light is most scattered by atmosphere
C. it is the colour of the Sun in the morning and evening
D. Earth's atmosphere emits red light

118. Thermal conductivity of aluminium, copper and stainless steel increases in the order
A. Copper < Aluminium < Stainless Steel
B. Stainless Steel < Aluminium < Copper
C. Aluminium < Copper < Stainless Steel
D. Copper < Stainless Steel < Aluminium

119. Perspiration cools the body because
A. presence of water on the skin is cooling
B. evaporation requires latent heat
C. water has a high specific heat
D. water is a poor conductor of heat

120. The radius of the Moon is about one-fourth that of the Earth and acceleration due to gravity on the Moon is about one-sixth that on the Earth. From this, we can conclude that the ratio of the mass of Earth to the mass of the Moon is about
A. 10 B. 100
C. 1,000 D. 10,000

121. Which of the following country/countries successfully inserted a spacecraft into Mars' orbit by maiden attempt?
A. USA B. USA and Russia
C. India D. China

122. The European Space Agency (ESA) successfully landed a spacecraft on a speeding comet that lies 310 million miles away from Earth. As a result, the scientists may find out
A. the age of the Sun
B. the age of the Universe
C. new fundamental atomic particles
D. the role of the comets in bringing organic matter and water to Earth

123. Who among the following Nobel laureates has recently announced to put his Nobel Medal under auction?
A. Kailash Satyarthi
B. JD Watson
C. Mikhail Sergeyevich Gorbachev
D. Jody Williams

124. Which one among the following statements with regard to a climate deal adopted between USA and China in November 2014 is ***not*** correct?
A. China committed to cap its output of carbon pollution by the year 2030 or earlier
B. China committed to increase its use of zero emission energy to 20% by the year 2030
C. USA agreed to reduce its emissions by 26%–28% below its year 2005 levels in the year 2025
D. Both the countries agreed to completely phase out coal technologies by the year 2020

125. Which one among the following books is centered around 'environment'?
A. The Late, Great Planet Earth
B. Silent Spring
C. Here I Stand
D. And Then One Day

126. Who among the following cricket players has ***not*** died while playing a match?
A. Wasim Raja B. Phillip Hughes
C. Raman Lamba D. Vijay Hazare

127. Which one among the following films was conferred the 'Golden Peacock' award in the 45th International Film Festival of India (2014)?
A. Ek Hazarachi Note B. A Short Story
C. Leviathan D. Ajeyo

128. Which one among the following films was awarded the best motion picture (Drama) in the 72nd Golden Globe Awards?
A. The Theory of Everything
B. Boyhood
C. Still Alice
D. Birdman

129. East Zone won the prestigious Deodhar Trophy cricket tournament 2014-15 by defeating
A. South Zone B. Central Zone
C. West Zone D. North Zone

130. Which one of the following books won the Man Booker Prize 2014?
A. History of the Rain
B. The Lives of Others
C. The Narrow Road to the Deep North
D. How to be Both

131. The Second Five Year Plan that called for the establishment of Socialist pattern of society was commonly referred to as the
A. Harrod-Domar Plan B. Mahalanobis Plan
C. Nehru Plan D. Peoples Plan

132. Harappan crafts display an amazing degree of standardization. According to Kenoyer, what was the possible reason for such an achievement?

A. Availability of raw materials at local level
B. Centralized markets for crafts
C. Specialized training centres for craftsmen
D. State control

133. Consider the following statements about Ashokan rock edicts :

1. Major Rock Edict XIII records Ashoka's remorse at the sufferings caused by his Kalinga campaign.
2. Major Rock Edict X records Ashoka's visit to Lumbini.
3. Major Rock Edict XII refers to *Dhamma Mahamattas* as a new categroy of officers instituted by Ashoka.
4. Major Rock Edict XII speaks about showing tolerance towards all sects.

Which of the statements given above are correct?

A. 1 and 4 only B. 2 and 3 only
C. 3 and 4 only D. 1, 3 and 4

134. Which one of the following is the common element among Rajagriha, Vaishali and Pataliputra?

A. Pali canon of the *Sthaviravadins* was compiled there
B. Ashokan Major Rock Edicts were found there
C. Places where Buddhist Councils were held
D. Places associated with the compilation of Buddhist canons of the Mahasanghikas

135. Which one among the following sects was associated with Gosala Maskariputra?

A. Vajrayana B. Ajivikas
C. Sthaviravadins D. Mahasanghikas

136. Consider the following statements about the early modern technology in India:

1. The Portuguese brought European movable metal types to Goa in 1550.
2. The first Indian script of which types were prepared was Tamil.
3. The English Company's first experiment with printing press was at Calcutta.
4. The English Company imported printing press to India in 1674-75 at the request of Bhimji Parak.

Which of the statements given above are correct?

A. 1 and 2 only B. 2 and 3
C. 3 and 4 D. 1, 2 and 4

137. Which of the following statement(s) is/are true for Olympe de Gouges?

1. She was one of the most important politically active woman in revolutionary France.
2. She was one of the members of the Committee that drafted the Declaration of Rights of Man and Citizen
3. She wrote the Declaration of the Rights of Woman and Citizen.

Select the correct answer using the code given below:

A. 1 only B. 3 only
C. 1 and 2 D. 1 and 3

138. Arrange the following inventions in the field of cotton industry in chronological order (starting with the earliest):

1. James Hargreaves's Spinning Jenny
2. John Kay's Flying Shuttle
3. Samuel Crompton's Mule
4. Richard Arkwright's Water Frame

Select the correct answer using the code given below:

A. 1, 3, 4, 2 B. 2, 1, 4, 3
C. 4, 1, 3, 2 D. 2, 4, 1, 3

139. While opposing the Public Safety Bill, 1928 who among the following said that it was 'a direct attack on Indian nationalism, on the Indian National Congress' and as 'the Slavery of India, Bill No. 1'?

A. Motilal Nehru B. Lala Lajpat Rai
C. T Prakasam D. Diwan Chaman Lal

140. Soon after the formation of Indian National Congress, the British became suspicious of nationalists. Who among the following called Congress representing only the elite—'a microscopic minority'?

A. Lord Napier B. Lord Dufferin
C. Lord Ripon D. Lord Lytton

141. What is the common element among Ram Prasad Bismil, Roshan Singh and Rajendra Lahiri?

A. They threw a bomb in the Central Legislative Assembly on 8 April, 1929
B. They were the founder members of Swaraj Party
C. They were the founders of Hindustan Republican Association
D. They were associated with Kakori Conspiracy case

142. Which of the following is/are ***not*** fundamental right(s) under the Constitution of India?

1. Right to education.
2. Right to work.
3. Right to form associations.
4. Right to practise any profession.

Select the correct answer using the code given below:

A. 1 and 2 B. 2 and 4
C. 2 only D. 1 and 3

143. Mahatma Gandhi's Hind Swaraj is essentially

A. a critique of Western modernity
B. an outline of his philosophy of Satyagraha
C. an invocation to Indians to free themselves from the British
D. a blueprint of Gram Swaraj

144. The Seventh Schedule of the Constitution of India contains

A. provisions regarding the administration of tribal areas
B. the Union List, the State List and the Concurrent List

C. a list of recognized languages
D. provisions about the disqualification of Members of Legislatures on grounds of defection

145. Pochampally in Nalgonda district of Telengana became famous in April, 1951 because
A. the Bhoodan movement was launched there by Vinoba Bhave
B. the landless peasants rose up in arms against the landlords
C. it witnessed violent anti-Hindi agitation
D. Silk weavers' cooperative was formed for the first time in India

146. Who among the following was ***not*** associated with the Sarvodaya movement?
A. Jaya Prakash Narayan B. Acharya Vinoba Bhave
C. Dhirendra Mazumdar D. GV Apparao

147. Article 368 of the Constitution of India deals with
A. the powers of the Parliament of India to amend the Constitution
B. financial emergency
C. reservation of seats for Scheduled Castes and Scheduled Tribes in the Lok Sabha
D. Official Language of the Union of India

148. Which among the following is ***not*** a basic feature of the Constitution of India?
A. Fundamental rights
B. Independence of judiciary
C. Federalism
D. The unquestioned right of the Parliament to amend any part of the Constitution

149. Which one among the following is ***not*** a fundamental duty?
A. To abide by the Constitution of India and respect the national flag and national anthem
B. To safeguard public property
C. To protect the Sovereignty, Unity and Integrity of India
D. To render compulsory military service

150. Which of the following are the basic features of the Constitution (73rd Amendment) Act?
1. Provides for a three-tier structure of panchayats in the village, intermediary and district levels.
2. Reservation of seats for Scheduled Castes and Scheduled Tribes and women in all the tiers of panchayats.
3. Election to panchayats under the supervision of the State Election Commissions.
4. Introduction of the 11th Schedule to the Constitution

Select the correct answer using the code given below :
A. 1, 2 and 3 only B. 3 and 4 only
C. 1, 2, 3 and 4 D. 2 and 4 only

PAPER II : MATHEMATICS

1. Let X be the set of all persons living in a city. Persons x, y in X are said to be related as $x < y$ if y is at least 5 years older than x. Which one of the following is correct?
A. The relation is an equivalence relation on X.
B. The relation is transitive but neither reflexive nor symmetric
C. The relation is reflexive but neither transitive nor symmetric
D. The relation is symmetric but neither transitive nor reflexive

2. Which one of the following matrices is an elementary matrix?

A. $\begin{bmatrix} 1 & 0 & 0 \\ 0 & 0 & 0 \\ 0 & 0 & 1 \end{bmatrix}$ B. $\begin{bmatrix} 1 & 5 & 0 \\ 0 & 1 & 0 \\ 0 & 0 & 1 \end{bmatrix}$

C. $\begin{bmatrix} 0 & 2 & 0 \\ 1 & 0 & 0 \\ 0 & 0 & 1 \end{bmatrix}$ D. $\begin{bmatrix} 1 & 0 & 0 \\ 0 & 1 & 0 \\ 0 & 5 & 2 \end{bmatrix}$

3. Consider the following statements in respect of the given equation :
$(x^2 + 2)^2 + 8x^2 = 6x(x^2 + 2)$
1. All the roots of the equation are complex.
2. The sum of all the roots of the equation is 6.

Which of the above statements is/are correct?
A. 1 only B. 2 only
C. Both 1 and 2 D. Neither 1 nor 2

4. In solving a problem that reduces to a quadratic equation, one student makes a mistake in the constant term and obtains 8 and 2 for roots. Another student makes a mistake only in the coefficient of first-degree term and finds –9 and –1 for roots. The correct equation is
A. $x^2 - 10x + 9 = 0$ B. $x^2 + 10x + 9 = 0$
C. $x^2 - 10x + 16 = 0$ D. $x^2 - 8x - 9 = 0$

5. If $A = \begin{bmatrix} 2 & 7 \\ 1 & 5 \end{bmatrix}$ then what is $A + 3A^{-1}$ equal to?
A. 3I B. 5I
C. 7I D. None of the above

where I is the identity matrix of order 2.

6. In a class of 60 students, 45 students like music, 50 students like dancing, 5 students like neither. Then the number of students in the class who like both music and dancing is

A. 35 B. 40
C. 50 D. 55

7. If $\log_{10} 2$, $\log_{10}(2^x - 1)$ and $\log_{10}(2^x + 3)$ are three consecutive terms of an AP, then the value of x is

A. 1 B. $\log_5 2$
C. $\log_2 5$ D. $\log_{10} 5$

8. The matrix $\begin{bmatrix} 0 & -4+i \\ 4+i & 0 \end{bmatrix}$ is

A. symmetric B. skew-symmetric
C. Hermitian D. skew-Hermitian

9. Let Z be the set of integers and aRb, where a, $b \in$ Z if and only if $(a - b)$ is divisible by 5.

Consider the following statements :

1. The relation R partitions Z into five equivalent classes.
2. Any two equivalent classes are either equal or disjoint.

Which of the above statements is/are correct?

A. 1 only B. 2 only
C. Both 1 and 2 D. Neither 1 nor 2

10. If $z = \frac{-2(1+2i)}{3+i}$ where $i = \sqrt{-1}$, then the argument $\theta(-\pi < \theta \le \pi)$ of z is

A. $\frac{3\pi}{4}$ B. $\frac{\pi}{4}$
C. $\frac{5\pi}{6}$ D. $-\frac{3\pi}{4}$

11. If m and n are the roots of the equation $(x + p)(x + q) - k = 0$, then the roots of the equation $(x - m)(x - n) + k = 0$ are

A. p and q B. $1/p$ and $1/q$
C. $-p$ and $-q$ D. $p + q$ and $p - q$

12. What is the sum of the series 0.5 + 0.55 + 0.555 + ... to n terms?

A. $\frac{5}{9}\left[n - \frac{2}{9}\left(1 - \frac{1}{10^n}\right)\right]$

B. $\frac{1}{9}\left[5 - \frac{2}{9}\left(1 - \frac{1}{10^n}\right)\right]$

C. $\frac{1}{9}\left[n - \frac{5}{9}\left(1 - \frac{1}{10^n}\right)\right]$

D. $\frac{5}{9}\left[n - \frac{1}{9}\left(1 - \frac{1}{10^n}\right)\right]$

13. If 1, ω, ω^2 are the cube roots of unity, then the value of $(1 + \omega)(1 + \omega^2)(1 + \omega^4)(1 + \omega^8)$ is

A. –1 B. 0
C. 1 D. 2

14. Let A = {1, 2, 3, 4, 5, 6, 7, 8, 9, 10}. Then the number of subsets of A containing exactly two elements is

A. 20 B. 40
C. 45 D. 90

15. What is the square root of i, where $i = \sqrt{-1}$?

A. $\frac{1+i}{2}$ B. $\frac{1-i}{2}$
C. $\frac{1+i}{\sqrt{2}}$ D. None of the above

16. The decimal number $(127{\cdot}25)_{10}$, when converted to binary number, takes the form

A. $(1111111{\cdot}11)_2$ B. $(1111110{\cdot}01)_2$
C. $(1110111{\cdot}11)_2$ D. $(1111111{\cdot}01)_2$

17. Consider the following in respect of two non-singular matrices A and B of same order :

1. det (A + B) = det A + det B
2. $(A + B)^{-1} = A^{-1} + B^{-1}$

Which of the above statements is/are correct?

A. 1 only B. 2 only
C. Both 1 and 2 D. Neither 1 nor 2

18. If

$$X = \begin{bmatrix} 3 & -4 \\ 1 & -1 \end{bmatrix}, B = \begin{bmatrix} 5 & 2 \\ -2 & 1 \end{bmatrix} \text{ and } A = \begin{bmatrix} p & q \\ r & s \end{bmatrix}$$

satisfy the equation AX = B, then the matrix A is equal to

A. $\begin{bmatrix} -7 & 26 \\ 1 & -5 \end{bmatrix}$ B. $\begin{bmatrix} 7 & 26 \\ 4 & 17 \end{bmatrix}$

C. $\begin{bmatrix} -7 & -4 \\ 26 & 13 \end{bmatrix}$ D. $\begin{bmatrix} -7 & 26 \\ -6 & 23 \end{bmatrix}$

19. What is $\sum_{r=0}^{1} {}^{n+r}C_n$ equal to?

A. ${}^{n+2}C_1$ B. ${}^{n+2}C_n$
C. ${}^{n+3}C_n$ D. ${}^{n+2}C_{n+1}$

20. How many words can be formed using all the letters of the word 'NATION' so that all the three vowels should never come together?

A. 354 B. 348
C. 288 D. None of the above

21. $(x^3 - 1)$ can be factorised as

A. $(x - 1)(x - \omega)(x + \omega^2)$
B. $(x - 1)(x - \omega)(x - \omega^2)$
C. $(x - 1)(x + \omega)(x + \omega^2)$
D. $(x - 1)(x + \omega)(x - \omega^2)$

where ω is one of the cube roots of unity.

22. What is $\left[\dfrac{\sin\frac{\pi}{6}+i\left(1-\cos\frac{\pi}{6}\right)}{\sin\frac{\pi}{6}-i\left(1-\cos\frac{\pi}{6}\right)}\right]^3$

where $i=\sqrt{-1}$, equal to?

A. 1 B. –1

C. i D. $-i$

23. Let

$$A=\begin{bmatrix} x+y & y \\ 2x & x-y \end{bmatrix},\ B=\begin{bmatrix} 2 \\ -1 \end{bmatrix} \text{ and } C=\begin{bmatrix} 3 \\ 2 \end{bmatrix}$$

If AB = C, then what is A^2 equal to?

A. $\begin{bmatrix} 6 & -10 \\ 4 & 26 \end{bmatrix}$ B. $\begin{bmatrix} -10 & 5 \\ 4 & 24 \end{bmatrix}$

C. $\begin{bmatrix} -5 & -6 \\ -4 & -20 \end{bmatrix}$ D. $\begin{bmatrix} -5 & -7 \\ -5 & 20 \end{bmatrix}$

24. The value of $\begin{vmatrix} 1 & 1 & 1 \\ 1 & 1+x & 1 \\ 1 & 1 & 1+y \end{vmatrix}$ is

A. $x+y$ B. $x-y$

C. xy D. $1+x+y$

25. If A = {x : x is a multiple of 3} and B = {x : x is a multiple of 4} and C = {x : x is a multiple of 12}, then which one of the following is a null set?

A. $(A \setminus B) \cup C$ B. $(A \setminus B) \setminus C$

C. $(A \cap B) \cap C$ D. $(A \cap B) \setminus C$

26. If $(11101011)_2$ is converted to decimal system, then the resulting number is

A. 235 B. 175

C. 160 D. 126

27. What is the real part of $(\sin x + i \cos x)^3$

where $i=\sqrt{-1}$?

A. $-\cos 3x$ B. $-\sin 3x$

C. $\sin 3x$ D. $\cos 3x$

28. If $E(\theta)=\begin{bmatrix} \cos\theta & \sin\theta \\ -\sin\theta & \cos\theta \end{bmatrix}$ then $E(\alpha)\,E(\beta)$ is equal to

A. $E(\alpha\beta)$ B. $E(\alpha-\beta)$

C. $E(\alpha+\beta)$ D. $-E(\alpha+\beta)$

29. Let A = {x, y, z} and B = {p, q, r, s}. What is the number of distinct relations from B to A?

A. 4096 B. 4094

C. 128 D. 126

30. If $2p + 3q = 18$ and $4p^2 + 4pq - 3q^2 - 36 = 0$ then what is $(2p + q)$ equal to?

A. 6 B. 7

C. 10 D. 20

31. Let θ be a positive angle. If the number of degrees in θ is divided by the number of radians in θ, then an irrational number $180/\pi$ results. If the number of degrees in θ is multiplied by the number of radians in θ, then an irrational number $125\pi/9$ results. The angle θ must be equal to

A. 30° B. 45°

C. 50° D. 60°

32. In a triangle ABC, $a = (1+\sqrt{3})$ cm, $b = 2$ cm and angle C = 60°. Then the other two anlges are

A. 45° and 75° B. 30° and 90°

C. 105° and 15° D. 100° and 20°

For the next two (2) items that follow :

Let α be the root of the equation $25\cos^2\theta + 5\cos\theta - 12 = 0$,

where $\frac{\pi}{2} < \alpha < \pi$.

33. What is $\tan\alpha$ equal to?

A. –3/4 B. 3/4

C. –4/3 D. –4/5

34. What is $\sin 2\alpha$ equal to?

A. 24/25 B. –24/25

C. –5/12 D. –21/25

35. The angle of elevation of the top of a tower from a point 20 m away from its base is 45°. What is the height of the tower?

A. 10 m B. 20 m

C. 30 m D. 40 m

36. The equation

$\tan^{-1}(1+x) + \tan^{-1}(1-x) = \frac{\pi}{2}$ is satisfied by

A. $x = 1$ B. $x = -1$

C. $x = 0$ D. $x = 1/2$

37. The angles of elevation of the top of a tower standing on a horizontal plane from two points on a line passing through the foot of the tower at distances 49 m and 36 m are 43° and 47° respectively. What is the height of the tower?

A. 40 m B. 42 m

C. 45 m D. 47 m

38. $(1 - \sin A + \cos A)^2$ is equal to

A. $2(1-\cos A)(1+\sin A)$

B. $2(1-\sin A)(1+\cos A)$

C. $2(1-\cos A)(1-\sin A)$

D. None of the above

39. What is $\dfrac{\cos\theta}{1-\tan\theta}+\dfrac{\sin\theta}{1-\cot\theta}$ equal to?

A. $\sin\theta - \cos\theta$ B. $\sin\theta + \cos\theta$

C. $2\sin\theta$ D. $2\cos\theta$

For the next three (3) items that follow :
Consider $x = 4\tan^{-1}\left(\frac{1}{5}\right)$, $y = \tan^{-1}\left(\frac{1}{70}\right)$ and $z = \tan^{-1}\left(\frac{1}{99}\right)$.

40. What is x equal to?
A. $\tan^{-1}\left(\frac{60}{119}\right)$ B. $\tan^{-1}\left(\frac{120}{119}\right)$
C. $\tan^{-1}\left(\frac{90}{169}\right)$ D. $\tan^{-1}\left(\frac{170}{169}\right)$

41. What is $x - y$ equal to?
A. $\tan^{-1}\left(\frac{828}{845}\right)$ B. $\tan^{-1}\left(\frac{8287}{8450}\right)$
C. $\tan^{-1}\left(\frac{8281}{8450}\right)$ D. $\tan^{-1}\left(\frac{8287}{8471}\right)$

42. What is $x - y + z$ equal to?
A. $\frac{\pi}{2}$ B. $\frac{\pi}{3}$
C. $\frac{\pi}{6}$ D. $\frac{\pi}{4}$

For the next three (3) items that follow :
Consider the triangle ABC with vertices A(–2, 3), B(2, 1) and C(1, 2).

43. What is the circumcentre of the triangle ABC?
A. (–2, –2) B. (2, 2)
C. (–2, 2) D. (2, –2)

44. What is the centroid of the triangle ABC?
A. $\left(\frac{1}{3}, 1\right)$ B. $\left(\frac{1}{3}, 2\right)$
C. $\left(1, \frac{2}{3}\right)$ D. $\left(\frac{1}{2}, 3\right)$

45. What is the foot of the altitude from the vertex A of the triangle ABC?
A. (1, 4) B. (–1, 3)
C. (–2, 4) D. (–1, 4)

46. The point on the parabola $y^2 = 4ax$ nearest to the focus has its abscissa
A. $x = 0$ B. $x = a$
C. $x = a/2$ D. $x = 2a$

47. A line passes through (2, 2) and is perpendicular to the line $3x + y = 3$. Its y-intercept is
A. 3/4 B. 4/3
C. 1/3 D. 3

48. The hyperbola $\frac{x^2}{a^2} - \frac{y^2}{b^2} = 1$ passes through the point $(3\sqrt{5}, 1)$ and the length of its latus rectum is $\frac{4}{3}$ units. The length of the conjugate axis is
A. 2 units B. 3 units
C. 4 units D. 5 units

49. The perpendicular distance between the straight lines $6x + 8y + 15 = 0$ and $3x + 4y + 9 = 0$ is
A. 3/2 units B. 3/10 unit
C. 3/4 unit D. 2/7 unit

50. The area of a triangle, whose vertices are (3, 4), (5, 2) and the point of intersection of the lines $x = a$ and $y = 5$, is 3 square units. What is the value of a?
A. 2 B. 3
C. 4 D. 5

51. The length of perpendicular from the origin to a line is 5 units and the line makes an angle 120° with the positive direction of x-axis. The equation of the line is
A. $x + \sqrt{3}y = 5$ B. $\sqrt{3}x + y = 10$
C. $\sqrt{3}x - y = 10$ D. None of the above

52. The equation of the line joining the origin to the point of intersection of the lines $\frac{x}{a} + \frac{y}{b} = 1$ and $\frac{x}{b} + \frac{y}{a} = 1$ is
A. $x - y = 0$ B. $x + y = 0$
C. $x = 0$ D. $y = 0$

For the next two (2) items that follow : The projections of a directed line segment on the coordinate axes are 12, 4, 3 respectively.

53. What is the length of the line segment?
A. 19 units B. 17 units
C. 15 units D. 13 units

54. What are the direction cosines of the line segment?
A. $\langle 12/13, 4/13, 3/13 \rangle$
B. $\langle 12/13, -4/13, 3/13 \rangle$
C. $\langle 12/13, -4/13, -3/13 \rangle$
D. $\langle -12/13, -4/13, 3/13 \rangle$

For the next two (2) items that follow : From the point P(3, –1, 11), a perpendicular is drawn on the line L given by the equation $\frac{x}{2} = \frac{y-2}{3} = \frac{z-3}{4}$. Let Q be the foot of the perpendicular.

55. What are the direction ratios of the line segment PQ?
A. $\langle 1, 6, 4 \rangle$ B. $\langle -1, 6, -4 \rangle$
C. $\langle -1, -6, 4 \rangle$ D. $\langle 2, -6, 4 \rangle$

56. What is the length of the line segment PQ?

A. $\sqrt{47}$ units B. 7 units

C. $\sqrt{53}$ units D. 8 units

For the next two (2) items that follow : A triangular plane ABC with centroid (1, 2, 3) cuts the coordinate axes at A, B, C respectively.

57. What are the intercepts made by the plane ABC on the axes?

A. 3, 6, 9 B. 1, 2, 3

C. 1, 4, 9 D. 2, 4, 6

58. What is the equation of the plane ABC?

A. $x + 2y + 3z = 1$ B. $3x + 2y + z = 3$

C. $2x + 3y + 6z = 18$ D. $6x + 3y + 2z = 18$

For the next two (2) items that follow : A point P (1, 2, 3) is one vertex of a cuboid formed by the coordinate planes and the planes passing through P and parallel to the coordinate planes.

59. What is the length of one of the diagonals of the cuboid?

A. $\sqrt{10}$ units B. $\sqrt{14}$ units

C. 4 units D. 5 units

60. What is the equation of the plane passing through P(1, 2, 3) and parallel to xy-plane?

A. $x + y = 3$ B. $x - y = -1$

C. $z = 3$ D. $x + 2y + 3z = 14$

61. If $G(x) = \sqrt{25-x^2}$, then what is

$$\lim_{x\to 1}\frac{G(x)-G(1)}{x-1} \text{ equal to?}$$

A. $-\frac{1}{2\sqrt{6}}$ B. $\frac{1}{5}$

C. $-\frac{1}{\sqrt{6}}$ D. $\frac{1}{\sqrt{6}}$

62. Consider the following statements :

1. $y=\frac{e^x+e^{-x}}{2}$ is an increasing function on $[0, \infty]$.

2. $y=\frac{e^x-e^{-x}}{2}$ is an increasing function on $(-\infty, \infty)$.

Which of the above statements is/are correct?

A. 1 only B. 2 only

C. Both 1 and 2 D. Neither 1 nor 2

63. For each non-zero real number x, let $f(x) = \frac{x}{|x|}$. The range of f is

A. a null set

B. a set consisting of only one element

C. a set consisting of two elements

D. a set consisting of infinitely many elements

64. Consider the following statements :

1. $f(x) = [x]$, where $[\cdot]$ is the greatest integer function, is discontinuous at $x = n$, where $n \in Z$.

2. $f(x) = \cot x$ is discontinuous at $x = n\pi$, where $n \in Z$.

Which of the above statements is/are correct?

A. 1 only B. 2 only

C. Both 1 and 2 D. Neither 1 nor 2

65. What is the derivative of $\tan^{-1}\left(\frac{\sqrt{1+x^2}-1}{x}\right)$ with respect to $\tan^{-1} x$?

A. 0 B. 1/2

C. 1 D. x

66. If $f(x) = \log_e\left(\frac{1+x}{1-x}\right)$, $g(x) = \frac{3x+x^3}{1+3x^2}$ and $g \circ f(t) = g(f(t))$, then what is $g \circ f\left(\frac{e-1}{e+1}\right)$ equal to?

A. 2 B. 1

C. 0 D. 1/2

For the next two (2) items that follow :

Given a function $f(x)=\begin{cases}-1 & \text{if } x\le 0\\ ax+b & \text{if } 0<x<1\\ 1 & \text{if } x\ge 1\end{cases}$ where a, b are constants. The function is continuous everywhere.

67. What is the value of a?

A. -1 B. 0

C. 1 D. 2

68. What is the value of b?

A. -1 B. 1

C. 0 D. 2

69. Consider the following functions :

1. $f(x) = x^3$, $x \in \mathbb{R}$

2. $f(x) = \sin x$, $0 < x < 2\pi$

3. $f(x) = e^x$, $x \in \mathbb{R}$

Which of the above functions have inverse defined on their ranges?

A. 1 and 2 only B. 2 and 3 only

C. 1 and 3 only D. 1, 2 and 3

For the next two (2) items that follow :

The integral $\int\frac{dx}{a\cos x+b\sin x}$ is of the form $\frac{1}{r}\ln\left[\tan\left(\frac{x+\alpha}{2}\right)\right]$.

70. What is r equal to?

A. $a^2 + b^2$ B. $\sqrt{a^2+b^2}$

C. $a + b$ D. $\sqrt{a^2-b^2}$

71. What is α equal to?

A. $\tan^{-1}\left(\frac{a}{b}\right)$ B. $\tan^{-1}\left(\frac{b}{a}\right)$

C. $\tan^{-1}\left(\frac{a+b}{a-b}\right)$ D. $\tan^{-1}\left(\frac{a-b}{a+b}\right)$

For the next two (2) items that follow :

Consider the function $f(x) = \frac{x^2-1}{x^2+1}$, where $x \in \mathbb{R}$.

72. At what value of x does $f(x)$ attain minimum value?

A. –1 B. 0

C. 1 D. 2

73. What is the minimum value of $f(x)$?

A. 0 B. 1/2

C. –1 D. 2

For the next two (2) items that follow : Consider the function

$$f(x) = \begin{cases} \frac{\alpha \cos x}{\pi - 2x} & \text{if } x \neq \frac{\pi}{2} \\ 3 & \text{if } x = \frac{\pi}{2} \end{cases}$$

which is continuous at $x = \frac{\pi}{2}$, where α is a constant.

74. What is the value of α?

A. 6 B. 3

C. 2 D. 1

75. What is $\lim_{x \to 0} f(x)$ equal to?

A. 0 B. 3

C. $\frac{3}{\pi}$ D. $\frac{6}{\pi}$

For the next two (2) items that follow : Consider the line $x = \sqrt{3}y$ and the circle $x^2 + y^2 = 4$.

76. What is the area of the region in the first quadrant enclosed by the x-axis, the line $x = \sqrt{3}$ and the circle?

A. $\frac{\pi}{3} - \frac{\sqrt{3}}{2}$ B. $\frac{\pi}{2} - \frac{\sqrt{3}}{2}$

C. $\frac{\pi}{3} - \frac{1}{2}$ D. None of the above

77. What is the area of the region in the first quadrant enclosed by the x-axis, the line $x = \sqrt{3}y$ and the circle?

A. $\frac{\pi}{3}$ B. $\frac{\pi}{6}$

C. $\frac{\pi}{3} - \frac{\sqrt{3}}{2}$ D. None of the above

For the next two (2) items that follow : Consider the curves $y = \sin x$ and $y = \cos x$.

78. What is the area of the region bounded by the above two curves and the lines $x = 0$ and $x = \frac{\pi}{4}$?

A. $\sqrt{2} - 1$ B. $\sqrt{2} + 1$

C. $\sqrt{2}$ D. 2

79. What is the area of the region bounded by the above two curves and the lines $x = \frac{\pi}{4}$ and $x = \frac{\pi}{2}$?

A. $\sqrt{2} - 1$ B. $\sqrt{2} + 1$

C. $2\sqrt{2}$ D. 2

For the next two (2) items that follow: Consider the function $f(x) = 0.75x^4 - x^3 - 9x^2 + 7$.

80. What is the maximum value of the function?

A. 1 B. 3

C. 7 D. 9

81. Consider the following statements :

1. The function attains local minima at $x = -2$ and $x = 3$.
2. The function increases in the interval (–2, 0).

Which of the above statements is/are correct?

A. 1 only B. 2 only

C. Both 1 and 2 D. Neither 1 nor 2

For the next three (3) items that follow : Consider the parametric equation

$$x = \frac{a(1-t^2)}{1+t^2}, \quad y = \frac{2at}{1+t^2}$$

82. What does the equation represent?

A. It represents a circle of diameter a

B. It represents a circle of radius a

C. It represents a parabola

D. None of the above

83. What is $\frac{dy}{dx}$ equal to?

A. $\frac{y}{x}$ B. $-\frac{y}{x}$

C. $\frac{x}{y}$ D. $-\frac{x}{y}$

84. What is $\frac{d^2y}{dx^2}$ equal to?

A. $\frac{a^2}{y^2}$ B. $\frac{a^2}{x^2}$

C. $-\frac{a^2}{x^2}$ D. $-\frac{a^2}{y^3}$

85. Consider the following statements :

1. The general solution of $\frac{dy}{dx} = f(x) + x$ is of the form $y = g(x) + c$, where c is an arbitrary constant.

2. The degree of $\left(\frac{dy}{dx}\right)^2 = f(x)$ is 2.

Which of the above statements is/are correct?

A. 1 only B. 2 only
C. Both 1 and 2 D. Neither 1 nor 2

86. What is $\int \frac{dx}{\sqrt{x^2 + a^2}}$ equal to?

A. $\ln\left|\frac{x + \sqrt{x^2 + a^2}}{a}\right| + c$

B. $\ln\left|\frac{x - \sqrt{x^2 + a^2}}{a}\right| + c$

C. $\ln\left|\frac{x^2 + \sqrt{x^2 + a^2}}{a}\right| + c$

D. None of the above

where c is the constant of integration.

For the next four (4) items that follow : Consider the integral $I_m = \int_0^{\pi} \frac{\sin 2mx}{\sin x} dx$, where m is a positive integer.

87. What is I_1 equal to?

A. 0 B. 1/2
C. 1 D. 2

88. What is $I_2 + I_3$ equal to?

A. 4 B. 2
C. 1 D. 0

89. What is I_m equal to?

A. 0 B. 1
C. m D. $2m$

90. Consider the following :

1. $I_m - I_{m-1}$ is equal to 0.
2. $I_{2m} > I_m$

Which of the above is/are correct?

A. 1 only B. 2 only
C. Both 1 and 2 D. Neither 1 nor 2

For the next two (2) items that follow :

Given that $\frac{d}{dx}\left(\frac{1 + x^2 + x^4}{1 + x + x^2}\right) = Ax + B$

91. What is the value of A?

A. –1 B. 1
C. 2 D. 4

92. What is the value of B?

A. –1 B. 1
C. 2 D. 4

For the next two (2) items that follow : Given that

$$\lim_{x \to \infty}\left(\frac{2 + x^2}{1 + x} - Ax - B\right) = 3$$

93. What is the value of A?

A. –1 B. 1
C. 2 D. 3

94. What is the value of B?

A. –1 B. 3
C. –4 D. –3

95. What is the solution of the differential equation $\frac{ydx - xdy}{y^2} = 0$?

A. $xy = c$ B. $y = cx$
C. $x + y = c$ D. $x - y = c$

where c is an arbitrary constant.

96. What is the solution of the differential equation $\sin\left(\frac{dy}{dx}\right) - a = 0$?

A. $y = x \sin^{-1} a + c$
B. $x = y \sin^{-1} a + c$
C. $y = x + x \sin^{-1} a + c$
D. $y = \sin^{-1} a + c$

where c is an arbitrary constant.

97. What is the solution of the differential equation $\frac{dx}{dy} + \frac{x}{y} - y^2 = 0$?

A. $xy = x^4 + c$ B. $xy = y^4 + c$
C. $4xy = y^4 + c$ D. $3xy = y^3 + c$

where c is an arbitrary constant.

98. What is $\int \frac{xe^x dx}{(x+1)^2}$ equal to?

A. $(x + 1)^2 e^x + c$ B. $(x + 1) e^x + c$
C. $\frac{e^x}{x+1} + c$ D. $\frac{e^x}{(x+1)^2} + c$

where c is the constant of integration.

99. The adjacent sides AB and AC of a triangle ABC are represented by the vectors $-2\hat{i} + 3\hat{j} + 2\hat{k}$ and $-4\hat{i} + 5\hat{j} + 2\hat{k}$ respectively. The area of the triangle ABC is

A. 6 square units B. 5 square units
C. 4 square units D. 3 square units

100. A force $\vec{F} = 3\hat{i} + 4\hat{j} - 3\hat{k}$ is applied at the point P, whose position vector is $\vec{r} = 2\hat{i} - 2\hat{j} - 3\hat{k}$. What is the magnitude of the moment of the force about the origin?

A. 23 units B. 19 units
C. 18 units D. 21 units

101. Given that the vectors $\vec{\alpha}$ and $\vec{\beta}$ are non-collinear. The values of x and y for which $\vec{u} - \vec{v} = \vec{w}$ holds true if $\vec{u} = 2x\vec{\alpha} + y\vec{\beta}$, $\vec{v} = 2y\vec{\alpha} + 3x\vec{\beta}$ and $\vec{w} = 2\vec{\alpha} - 5\vec{\beta}$, are

A. $x = 2, y = 1$ B. $x = 1, y = 2$
C. $x = -2, y = 1$ D. $x = -2, y = -1$

102. If $|\vec{a}| = 7$, $|\vec{b}| = 11$ and $|\vec{a} + \vec{b}| = 10\sqrt{3}$, then $|\vec{a} - \vec{b}|$ is equal to

A. 40 B. 10
C. $4\sqrt{10}$ D. $2\sqrt{10}$

103. Let α, β, γ be distinct real numbers. The points with position vectors $\alpha\hat{i} + \beta\hat{j} + \gamma\hat{k}$, $\beta\hat{i} + \gamma\hat{j} + \alpha\hat{k}$ and $\gamma\hat{i} + \alpha\hat{j} + \beta\hat{k}$

A. are collinear
B. form an equilateral triangle
C. form a scalene triangle
D. form a right-angled triangle

104. If $\vec{a} + \vec{b} + \vec{c} = \vec{0}$, then which of the following is/are correct?

1. $\vec{a}, \vec{b}, \vec{c}$ are coplanar.
2. $\vec{a} \times \vec{b} = \vec{b} \times \vec{c} = \vec{c} \times \vec{a}$

Select the correct answer using the code given below :

A. 1 only B. 2 only
C. Both 1 and 2 D. Neither 1 nor 2

105. If $|\vec{a} + \vec{b}| = |\vec{a} - \vec{b}|$, then which one of the following is correct?

A. $\vec{a} = \lambda\vec{b}$ for some scalar λ
B. $\vec{a}$ is parallel to $\vec{b}$
C. $\vec{a}$ is perpendicular to $\vec{b}$
D. $\vec{a} = \vec{b} = \vec{0}$

106. The mean and the variance of 10 observations are given to be 4 and 2 respectively. If every observation is multiplied by 2, the mean and the variance of the new series will be respectively

A. 8 and 20 B. 8 and 4
C. 8 and 8 D. 80 and 40

107. Which one of the following measures of central tendency is used in construction of index numbers?

A. Harmonic mean B. Geometric mean
C. Median D. Mode

108. The correlation coefficient between two variables X and Y is found to be 0.6. All the observations on X and Y are transformed using the transformations U = 2 – 3X and V = 4Y + 1. The correlation coefficient between the transformed variables U and V will be

A. – 0.5 B. + 0.5
C. – 0.6 D. + 0.6

109. Which of the following statements is/are correct in respect of regression coefficients?

1. It measures the degree of linear relationship between two variables.
2. It gives the value by which one variable changes for a unit change in the other variable.

Select the correct answer using the code given below :

A. 1 only B. 2 only
C. Both 1 and 2 D. Neither 1 nor 2

110. A set of annual numerical data, comparable over the years, is given for the last 12 years.

Consider the following statements :

1. The data is best represented by a broken line graph, each corner (turning point) representing the data of one year.
2. Such a graph depicts the chronological change and also enables one to make a short-term forecast.

Which of the above statements is/are correct?

A. 1 only B. 2 only
C. Both 1 and 2 D. Neither 1 nor 2

111. Two men hit at a target with probabilities 1/2 and 1/3 respectively. What is the probability that exactly one of them hits the target?

A. 1/2 B. 1/3
C. 1/6 D. 2/3

112. Two similar boxes B_i (i = 1, 2) contain (i + 1) red and (5 – i – 1) black balls. One box is chosen at random and two balls are drawn randomly. What is the probability that both the balls are of different colours?

A. 1/2 B. 3/10
C. 2/5 D. 3/5

113. In an examination, the probability of a candidate solving a question is 1/2. Out of given 5 questions in the examination, what is the probability that the candidate was able to solve at least 2 questions?

A. 1/64 B. 3/16
C. 1/2 D. 13/16

114. If $A \subseteq B$, then which one of the following is ***not*** correct?

A. $P(A \cap \bar{B}) = 0$

B. $P(A|B) = \dfrac{P(A)}{P(B)}$

C. $P(B|A) = \dfrac{P(B)}{P(A)}$

D. $P(A|(A \cup B)) = \dfrac{P(A)}{P(B)}$

115. The mean and the variance in a binomial distribution are found to be 2 and 1 respectively. The probability P (X = 0) is

A. 1/2 B. 1/4
C. 1/8 D. 1/16

116. The mean of five numbers is 30. If one number is excluded, their mean becomes 28. The excluded number is

A. 28 B. 30
C. 35 D. 38

117. If A and B are two events such that $P(A \cup B) = \frac{3}{4}$, $P(A \cap B) = \frac{1}{4}$ and $P(\bar{A}) = \frac{2}{3}$, then what is P(B) equal to?

A. 1/3 B. 2/3
C. 1/8 D. 2/9

118. The 'less than' ogive curve and the 'more than' ogive curve intersect at

A. median B. mode
C. arithmetic mean D. None of the above

119. In throwing of two dice, the number of exhaustive events that '5' will never appear on any one of the dice is

A. 5 B. 18
C. 25 D. 36

120. Two cards are drawn successively without replacement from a well-shuffled pack of 52 cards. The probability of drawing two aces is

A. 1/26 B. 1/221
C. 4/223 D. 1/13

ANSWERS

PAPER-I : GENERAL ABILITY TEST

1	2	3	4	5	6	7	8	9	10
A	A	D	C	B	B	B	B	B	C
11	12	13	14	15	16	17	18	19	20
C	A	C	C	A	D	C	B	A	B
21	22	23	24	25	26	27	28	29	30
A	A	D	C	B	B	D	C	A	B
31	32	33	34	35	36	37	38	39	40
D	A	B	B	C	C	B	A	C	B
41	42	43	44	45	46	47	48	49	50
B	A	A	C	C	C	A	C	B	C
51	52	53	54	55	56	57	58	59	60
D	A	A	C	C	A	A	C	*	B
61	62	63	64	65	66	67	68	69	70
C	D	B	C	B	B	A	D	C	D
71	72	73	74	75	76	77	78	79	80
B	B	A	C	B	C	B	D	B	A
81	82	83	84	85	86	87	88	89	90
C	B	D	C	A	B	A	A	B	D
91	92	93	94	95	96	97	98	99	100
A	B	A	C	B	D	C	C	B	B
101	102	103	104	105	106	107	108	109	110
D	D	C	D	C	B	C	C	A	A
111	112	113	114	115	116	117	118	119	120
B	*	C	A	A	C	A	B	B	B
121	122	123	124	125	126	127	128	129	130
C	*	B	D	B	D	C	B	C	C
131	132.	133	134	135	136	137	138	139	140
B	D	A	C	B	D	D	B	B	B
141	142	143	144	145	146	147	148	149	150
D	C	A	B	A	D	A	D	D	C

PAPER-II : MATHEMATICS

1	2	3	4	5	6	7	8	9	10
B	B	C	A	D	B	C	D	C	D
11	**12**	**13**	**14**	**15**	**16**	**17**	**18**	**19**	**20**
C	D	C	C	A	D	D	A	D	C
21	**22**	**23**	**24**	**25**	**26**	**27**	**28**	**29**	**30**
B	C	A	C	*	A	B	C	A	C
31	**32**	**33**	**34**	**35**	**36**	**37**	**38**	**39**	**40**
C	A	A	B	B	C	B	B	B	B
41	**42**	**43**	**44**	**45**	**46**	**47**	**48**	**49**	**50**
C	D	B	B	D	A	B	C	B	D
51	**52**	**53**	**54**	**55**	**56**	**57**	**58**	**59**	**60**
B	A	D	A	B	C	A	D	B	C
61	**62**	**63**	**64**	**65**	**66**	**67**	**68**	**69**	**70**
A	C	C	C	B	B	D	A	C	B
71	**72**	**73**	**74**	**75**	**76**	**77**	**78**	**79**	**80**
A	B	C	A	D	A	A	A	A	C
81	**82**	**83**	**84**	**85**	**86**	**87**	**88**	**89**	**90**
C	B	D	D	C	A	A	D	A	A
91	**92**	**93**	**94**	**95**	**96**	**97**	**98**	**99**	**100**
C	A	B	C	B	A	D	C	D	A
101	**102**	**103**	**104**	**105**	**106**	**107**	**108**	**109**	**110**
A	D	B	C	C	C	B	*	*	*
111	**112**	**113**	**114**	**115**	**116**	**117**	**118**	**119**	**120**
A	D	D	C	D	D	B	A	C	B

EXPLANATORY ANSWERS

PAPER-I : GENERAL ABILITY TEST

52. Gunpowder, also known as black powder, is a chemical explosive the earliest known. It is a mixture of sulphur, charcoal and potassium nitrate (saltpeter). The sulphur and charcoal act as fuels and the saltpeter is an oxidizer. To reduce the likelihood of accidental ignition by static electricity, the granules of modern black powder are typically coated with graphite, which prevents the build-up of electrostatic charge.

54. Diamond is renowned as a material with superlative physical qualities, most of which originate from the strong covalent bonding between its atoms. In particular, diamond has the highest hardness and thermal conductivity of any bulk material. Diamonds also possess and extremely high refractive index and fairly high dispersion.

59. Frequency (η) = 3×10^5 Hz

Velocity $v = \eta.\lambda$

$$3000 = (3 \times 10^5).\lambda$$

$$\therefore \lambda = \frac{3000}{3 \times 10^5} = 0.01 \text{ m} = 1 \text{ cm}$$

60. Acceleration due to gravity,

$$g = \frac{GM}{R^2}$$

when R is reduced by 1%.

$$R' = R - \frac{R}{100} = 0.99\,R$$

$$g' = \frac{GM}{(0.99R)^2}$$

Per cent decrease in g

$$= \left(\frac{g' - g}{g}\right) \times 100$$

$$= \left(\frac{\frac{GM}{(0.99R)^2} - \frac{GM}{R^2}}{\frac{GM}{R^2}}\right) \times 100$$

$$= \left\{\left(\frac{1}{0.99}\right)^2 - 1\right\} \times 100 = 2\%$$

61. Displacement – time equation for a moving particle

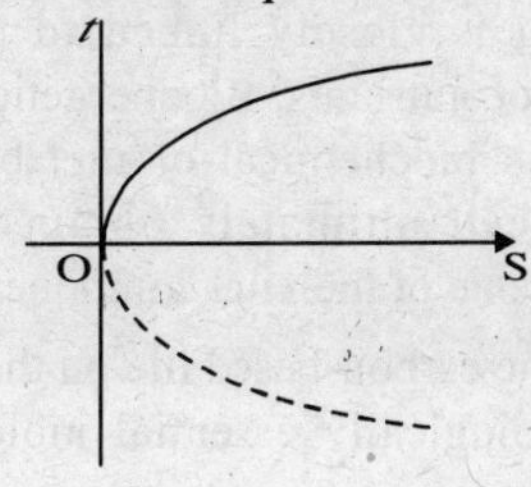

$$S = ut + \frac{1}{2}at^2$$

where, S = displacement

u = initial velocity

a = acceleration

t = time of motion

As, force is constant so, a is constant applied

$\therefore S \propto t^2 \quad \Rightarrow S = kt^2$

where k = constant

This is a parabolic graph.

62. The cohesive forces between liquid molecules are responsible for the phenomenon known as surface tension. The molecules at the surface donot have other like molecules on all sides of them and consequently they cohere more strongly to those directly associated with them on the surface. This forms a surface 'film' which makes it more difficult to move an object through the surface than to move it when it is completely submerged. Examples of surface tension are walking on water by small insects, floating of needle in water, soaps and detergents, clinical test for jaundice, inflating the Alveoli, washing with cold water.

64. Ratnagiri is a port city on the Arabian sea coast in Ratnagiri District in the southwestern part of Maharashtra, India. The Sahyadri mountains border Ratnagiri to the east. Heavy rainfall results in highly eroded landscape in the coastal region, but fertile alluvial valleys in the region produce abundant rice, coconuts, cashewnuts and fruits.

66. Telangana is bordered by the states of Maharashtra, Chattisgarh to the north, Karnataka to the west and Andhra Pradesh to the south, east and north east. Telangana has an area of 114,840 square kms and a population of 3,52,86,757 crore (2011 census). Telangana has three National Parks : Kasu Brahmananda Reddy National Park in Hyderabad district, Mahavir Harina Vanasthali National Park and Mrugvani National Park in Ranga Reddy district.

67. Metabolism is a term that is used to describe all chemical reactions involved in maintaining the living state of the cells and the organism. Metabolism can be conveniently divided into two categories:

- Catabolism : the breakdown of molecules to obtain energy.
- Anabolism : the synthesis of all compounds needed by the cells.

Metabolism is closely linked to nutrition and the availability of nutrients, Bioenergetics is a term which describes the biochemical or metabolic pathways by which the cell ultimately obtains energy. Energy formation is one of the vital components of metabolism.

68. Crucial to the carbon-based life on the Earth are several types of biologically essential molecules. The basic types of molecules are carbohydrates, lipids, proteins and nucleic acids. The chemistry of these carbon-based molecules is included in the field of organic chemistry with specific life-related processes forming the field of chemistry.

72. Potassium nitrate, also known as saltpeter or niter, is a chemical compound consisting of potassium, nitrogen and oxygen. While it has many applications, including use as a fertilizer, its most important usage historically has been a component of gunpowder. Over time, its use as an explosive has been made nearly obsolete by dynamite and TNT.

73. Micelles are lipid molecules that arrange themselves in a spherical form in aqueous solutions. Micelles usually form in soap molecules. Soap often form as micelles because they contain only one hydrocarbon chain instead of two. Therefore they make up the soap property. Micelles act as emulsifiers that allows a compound that is usually insoluble in water to dissolve.

74. Sodium thiosulphate ($Na_2S_2O_3$), also spelled sodium thiosulphate, is an inorganic compound. The solid is an efflorescent (loses water readily) crystalline substance that dissolves well in water. It is also called sodium hyposulphite or "hypo". The applications of sodium thiosulphate are :

- Iodometry
- Photographic processing
- Gold extraction
- Aluminium cation reaction
- Organic chemistry
- Neutralizing bleach and chlorinated water

75. A rain shadow effect is caused by mountains that block the rain producing clouds from continuing beyond the peak of the mountain. As air passes over the peak, it decreases in elevation and increases in temperature. As the air temperature increases, the water vapour in the atm osphere evaporates causing little or no rain to form on the back side of the m ountain.

77. The Western Yamuna Canal takes off from the right bank of the Yamuna at Tajewala. It was built by Feroze Shah Tughlaq. The total length of the canal along with its distributaries is 3200 km and it irrigates about 4 lakh hectares in Ambala, Kurushetra, Karnal, Panipat, Rohtak, Sirsa, Faridabad and Jind districts. It's important branches are, the Delhi, the Hansa and Sirsa branch.

Gurgaon Canal takes off from the Yamuna at Okhla in Delhi. It was started in 1970 and it irrigates 1.2 lakh hectares in Gurgaon and Faridabad districts.

78. Cell is the smallest unit showing the properties of life such as capacity for metabolism, response to the environment, growth and reproduction. The cell was discovered by Robert Hooke in 1665. Cells are the smallest unit of life that can replicate independently, and are often called the "building blocks of life".

83. An electrolytic cell is an electrochemical cell that undergoes a redox reaction when electrical energy is applied. It is most often used to decompose chemical compounds, in a process called electrolysis. Graphite is used in electrolytic cells because it is a good conductor of electricity.

84. Sodium carbonate (also known as washing soda, soda ash and soda crystals), $Na_2 CO_3$ is the sodium salt of carbonic acid (soluble in water). It is used as a water softener in laundering. It competes with the magnesium and calcium ions in hard water and prevents them from bonding with the detergent used.

86. Chandra Prabha Wild Life Sanctuary has been endowed with beautiful picnic spots, dense forest, and scenic waterfalls like Raj Dari and Dev Dari and a dam nearly called Chandra Prabha Dam. The Sanctuary was established in 1957 and is situated at Chandoli, near Varanasi in Uttar Pradesh.

The Silent Valley National Park with an area of 90 sq km is located in the northeastern corner of Palakkad district. It rises abruptly to the Nilgiri Plateau in the north and overlooks the plains of Mannarkkad in the South. The core of the Nilgiri Biosphere Reserve is the Silent Valley National Park.

Valley of flowers is a National Park located 300 kms, North of Rishikesh, near Badrinath. It was declared as a National Park in 1982.

Indrawati National Park is located in the Dantewada district of Chattisgarh State. In 1981, it attained the status of a National Park and a Tiger Reserve in 1983.

88. The gameophyte is the multicellular structure (plant) that is haploid, containing a single set of chromosomes in each cell. The gametophyte produces male on female gametes (or both), by a process of cell division called mitosis.

94. Mercury is a heavy, silver-white metal. It is a poor conductor of heat. Mercury has a freezing point of –38.83°C and a boiling point of 356.73°C, both exceptionally low for a metal, and it is the only elemental metal known to melt at a generally cold temperature. Mercury does not wet the walls of the glass vessel in which it is kept.

96. In the reaction $ZnO + C \rightarrow Zn + CO$

Oxidation number of 'C' atom changes from 'O' to + 4 i.e. there is increase in oxidation number.

Hence 'C' atom oxidise and so it act as reducing agent.

97. Organic Farming system in India is not new and is being followed from ancient time. It is a method of farming system which primarily aimed at cultivating the land and raising crops in such a way, as to keep the soil alive and in good health by use of organic wastes (crop, animal and farm wastes, aquatic wastes) and other biological materials along with beneficial microbes (biofertilizers) to release nutrients to crops for increased sustainable production in an ecofriendly pollution free environment.

98. The Yakuts are the indigenous people of the Republic of Sakha in the northeast of Siberia. They are the nomadic herders of the Tundra region in Siberia. Today there are about 400,000 Yakuts living in the vast region that covers an area of about 31,03,200 sq. km.

99. A Farmer in a semi-arid area claims that his farming practise is very environment friendly. The following practices on his farm can justify his claim :

- Planting a Tree Belt
- Practising crop rotation
- Using organic fertilizers

Practise of carrying out a large scale irrigation system is not environment friendly because irrigation in semi-arid area results in salinization (deposite of salt) of soil.

100. The luxuriant growth of natural vegetation in tropical rainforest is due to hot and wet climate throughout the year and intense sunlight for photosynthesis.

101. The thyroid is a butterfly-shaped gland that sits low on the front of the neck. The thyroid secretes several hormones, collectively called thyroid hormones. The main hormone is thyroxine, also called T4. Thyroid hormones act throughout the body, influencing metabolism, growth and development and body temperature.

104. A compact fluorescent lamp is designed to replace an incandescent lamp. The lamps use a tube which is curved or folded to fit into the space of an incandescent bulb, and a compact electronic ballast in the base of the lamp. A CFL lamp has a higher purchase price than an ordinary lamp but can save over five times it purchase price in electricity costs over the lamp's lifetime. Like all fluorescent lamps, CFLs contain toxic mercury which complicates their disposal.

105. Height of the tree AB = h m

Angle of elevation of sum $\angle$ ACB = 30°

From Δ ABC,

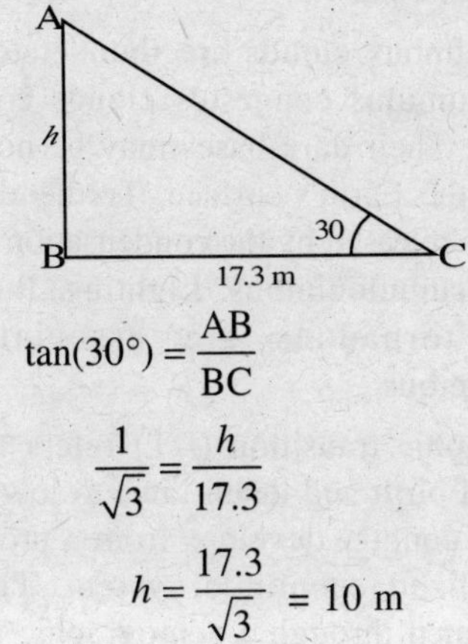

$$\tan(30°) = \frac{AB}{BC}$$

$$\frac{1}{\sqrt{3}} = \frac{h}{17.3}$$

or, $$h = \frac{17.3}{\sqrt{3}} = 10 \text{ m}$$

106. When heat rays are reflected from Earth, gases like carbon dioxide, Nitrous oxide donot allow them to escape back to the space causing our planet to heat up. These gases are known as greenhouse gases.

109. The Western Coastal Plain is a narrow strip of land that is sandwiched between the western Ghats and the Arabian Sea. The strip begins in Gujarat in the north and extends across the states of Maharashtra, Goa, Karnataka and Kerala. The features of western coastal plains of India are :

(a) The whole plains is intersected by mountain ridges.
(b) Deltas are not formed in the western coastal plain.
(c) It provides natural conditions for making ports.
(d) It is relatively rocky with sand and sand dunes. It is mainly formed by coarse grained soil and thus is infertile. It slopes abruptly down to the sea.

113. Cirrus clouds are thin, wispy clouds that usually form above 18,00 feet. These clouds are blown by strong westerly winds aloft into streamers known as "mares tails". Cirrus clouds generally move from west to east across the sky and usually point to fair weather. Cirrus clouds form when water vapour undergoes deposition and forms ice crystals. Cirrus clouds are thin because they form in the higher levels of the atmosphere where little water vapour is present.

Stratus clouds are uniform gray clouds that usually cover the entire sky. They can form when very weak, upward vertical air currents lift a thin layer of air high enough to initiate condensation. Stratus clouds also form when a layer of air is cooled from below to its dew point temperature and water vapour condenses into liquid droplets. Stratus clouds look like a layer of fog that never reaches the ground.

Nimbus or Nimbostratus clouds are dark low-level clouds accompanied by light to moderately falling precipitation. These clouds are primarily composed of water droplets since their bases generally lie below 6500 feet (2000 metres). However, when temperatures are cold enough, these clouds may also contain ice particles and snow.

Cumulonimbus clouds are thunderstorm clouds that form if cumulus congestus clouds continue to grow vertically. Their dark bases may be no more than 300 m above the Earth's surface. Tremendous amounts of energy are released by the condensation of water vapour within a cumulonimbus. Lighting, thunder and even violent tornadoes are associated with the cumulonimbus.

114. Demographic transition (DT) refers to the transition from high birth and death rates to low birth and death rates as a country develops from a pre-industrial to an industrialized economic system. This is typically demonstrated through a demographic transition model (DTM). The theory is based on an interpretation of demographic history developed in 1929 by the American demographer Warren Thomson. Thompson observed changes, or transitions, in bith and death rates in industrialized societies over the previous 200 years.

It has to be remembered that the Demographic Transition Model (DTM) is only a model and cannot necessarily predict the future. It does however give an indication of what the future birth and death rates may be for an underdeveloped country, together with the total population size.

115. Beta-carotene is a pigment found in plants that gives them their colour. The name beta-carotene is derived from the Latin name for carrot. It gives yellow and orange fruits and vegetables their rich colours.

In the body, beta-carotene is changed into vitamin A (retinol). We need vitamin A for good vision and eye health, for a strong immune system and for healthy skin and mucous membranes. Beta-carotene is an antioxidant. It protects the body from damaging molecules called free radicals.

117. Sunlight is composed of seven colours-Violet, Indigo, Blue, Green, Yellow, Orange and Red. In the mornings and evenings, when the Sun is near the horizon, the rays have to travel about fifty time's longer path in the atmosphere to reach us than it does in the noon. The dust, smoke and water vapour present in the atmosphere scatter away these colours differently. Violet, Indigo and Blue are scattered most and red and orange are scattered least. That is why most of these two colours reach our eyes. As a result, the rising and setting sun appears red.

118. In physics, thermal conductivity (often denoted K, A or K) is the property of a material to conduct heat. It is evaluated primarily in terms of Fourier's Law for heat conduction. Heat transfer occurs at a lower rate across materials of low thermal conductivity. Correspondingly, materials of high thermal conductivity are widely used in heat sink applications and materials of low thermal conductivity are used as thermal insulation.

121. The Mars Orbiter Mission (MOM) also called Mangalyaan is a space probe orbiting Mars since 24 September 2014. It is India's first interplanetary mission and ISRO has become the fourth space agency to reach Mars, after the Soviet space program, NASA and the European Space Agency.

The Scientific objectives of the Mars Orbiter Mission are :

- Exploration of Mars surface features by studying the morphology, topography and mineralogy.
- Study the constituents of Martian atmosphere including methane and CO_2 using remote sensing techniques.

- Study the dynamics of the upper atmosphere of Mars, effects of solar wind and radiation and the escape of volatilities to outer space.

122. The European Space Agency's Philae lander on the Rosetta spacecraft successfully touched a speeding comet that lies 310 million miles away from Earth. The Rosetta mission is charged with helping scientists learn more about comets, mysterious, icy wanders that are left over from the dawn of the solar system billions of years ago. Some research also suggests that comets could be responsible for bringing water to Earth early in the planet's history.

124. The U.S. China Joint Announcement on climate change was made in Beijing on 12 November 2014. The Highlights of the Agreement are :

- The United States intends to achieve an economy-wide target of reducing its emissions by 26%-28% below its 2005 level in 2025 and to make best efforts to reduce its emissions by 28%.
- China intends to achieve the peaking of CO_2 emissions around 2030 and to make best efforts to peak early and intends to increase the share of non-fossil fuels in primary energy consumption to around 20% by 2030.

126. Vijay Hazare (11 March 1915 – 18 December 2014) was an Indian cricket player from the state of Maharashtra. He captained the Indian cricket team in 14 matches between 1951 and 1953. He did not die while playing a match. Wasim Raja, Philip Hughes and Raman Lamba had died while playing a match.

127. The Russia Film 'Leviathan' bagged Golden Peacock award for Best Film at the 45th International Film Festival of India (IFFI) 2014. IFFI founded in 1952, is one of the most significant film festivals in Asia. It is held in Goa, since 2004. The first edition of IFFI was held in Mumbai from 24 January to 1 February 1952, the Festival was sebsequently taken to Madras, Delhi and Calcutta.

128. 'Boyhood' was awarded the best motion picture (Drama) in the 72nd Golden Globe Awards. Boyhood is a 2014 American Independent coming-of-age drama film, written and directed by Richard Linklater.

129. The Narrow Road to the Depth North' book won the Man Booker Prize 2014. The Narrow Road to the Deep North is a love story unfolding over half a century between a doctor and his uncle's wife. The book was written by Richard Flanagan.

131. At the time of the Formulation of the Second Five Year Plan, Professor P.C. Mahalanobis prepared a growth model with which he showed that to achieve a rapid long-term rate of growth it would be essential to devote a major part of the investment outlay to building of basic heavy industries.

Mahalanobis was of the opinion that without adequate investment in basic heavy industries, it would not be possible to achieve rapid self-reliant economic growth. Therefore highest priority must be given to development of industries.

134. The First Buddhist Council was held soon after the Mahaparinirvana of the Buddha around 483 BC under the patronage of king Ajatshatru with the monk Mahakasyappa presiding at Rajgriha, in the Sattapani cave. The idea was to preserve Buddha's teachings (Sutta) and rules for disciples (Vinaya).

The second Buddhist Council was held in 383 BC at Vaishali under the patronage of king Kalasoka and under the presidency of Sabakami. The idea of the council was to settle a dispute on Vinaya Pitaka, the code of discipline.

The Third Buddhist council was held in 250 BC at Pataliputra under the patronage of king Ashoka and under the presidency of Moggaliputta Tissa.

The Fourth Buddhist Council was held at Kundalvana, Kashmir in 72 AD under the patronage of Kushan king Kanishka and the President of this council was Vasumitra. This council distinctively divided Buddhism into two sects—Hinayana and Mahayana.

137. Olympe de Gouges (7 May 1748-3 November 1793), born Marie Gouze was a French playwright and political activist whose feminist and abolitionist writings reached a large audience. The following statements are true for Olympe De Gouges :

- She was one of the most important politically active woman in revolutionary France.
- She wrote the Declaration of the Rights of women and the Female citizen.

139. Lala Lajpat Rai while opposing the Public Safety Bill, 1928 said that it was 'a direct attack on Indian nationalism, on the Indian National Congress' and as 'the slavery of India, Bill No. 1'. On October 30, 1928 to boycott the arrival of the members of the Simon Commission in Lahore, a peaceful procession, headed by Lala Lajpat Rai was launched. The police targeted Lala Lajpat Rai and hit him on the head, due to the injuries, Lala Lajpat Rai died.

141. The idea that objects of the political dacoties must be to secure money belonging to the Government was that of Ram Prasad Bismil. The idea was accepted and it followed a plan that a running train at Kakori on the Lucknow-Saharanpur section should be looted. The Railway was carrying the Government chest and it was plundered successfully by ten Hindustan Republican Association (HRA) revolutionaries. But the whole plot was unearthed. Thirty people were arrested in connection with the case. Ram Prasad Bismil, Roshan Singh and Rajendra Lahiri were associated with Kakori conspiracy case.

142. The following are Fundamental Rights under the Constitution of India:

(a) Right to education - Art 21-A

(b) Right to form associations-Act 19

(c) Right to practise any profession-Art 19

143. Hind Swaraj is a book written by M.K. Gandhi is 1909. In it he expresses his views on Swaraj, modern civilization etc. M.K. Gandhi wrote this book in his native language, Gujarati, while travelling from London to South Africa. Gandhi's Hindi Swaraj takes the form of a dialogue between two characters, 'The Reader and The Editor'. In the text he is deeply critical of western civilization, claiming, "India is being ground down, not under the English heel, but under that of modern civilization."

148. The Supreme Court recognized Basic Structure concept for the first time in the historic Kesavananda Bharti case in 1973. The Supreme Court held that Article 368 even before the 24th Amendment contained the power as well as the procedure for amendment. The Supreme Court declared that Article 368 did not enable Parliament to alter the basic structure of the constitution and Parliament could not use its amending powers under Article 368 to damage, destroy or abrogate the basic features of the constitution.

Some of the basic features of the constitution are :

- Supremacy of the Constitution
- Republican and democratic form of government
- Fundamental Rights
- Independence of Judiciary
- Secular character of the Constitution
- Federal character of the Constitution
- Separation of powers between the legislative, judiciary and the executive.

150. The Salient features of the 73rd Constitutional Amendment Act are :

(*i*) Provides for a three-tier structure of Panchayats in the village, intermediary and district levels.

(*ii*) Reservation of seats for Scheduled Castes and Scheduled Tribes and women in all tiers of Panchayats.

(*iii*) Election to Panchayats under the supervision of the State Election Commissions.

(*iv*) Introduction of the 11th Schedule to the Constitution.

PAPER-II : MATHEMATICS

4. Let the correct equation is $x^2 + bx + c = 0$

when wrong term is constant term,

then, sum of roots of the equation

$$-b = (8 + 2) = 10$$

when, wrong term is x – co-efficient term,

then, product of roots of the equation

$$c = (-9)(-1) = 9$$

Hence, the required equation is

$$x^2 - 10x + 9 = 0$$

5. $A = \begin{bmatrix} 2 & 7 \\ 1 & 5 \end{bmatrix}$, $|A| = 2 \times 5 - 7 \times 1$

$$= 10 - 7 = 3$$

$$A^{-1} = \frac{Adj\,(A)}{|A|} = \frac{\begin{bmatrix} 5 & -1 \\ -7 & 2 \end{bmatrix}}{3} = \frac{1}{3}\begin{bmatrix} 5 & -1 \\ -7 & 2 \end{bmatrix}$$

Now, $3A^{-1} = \begin{bmatrix} 5 & -1 \\ -7 & 2 \end{bmatrix}$

$$A + 3A^{-1} = \begin{bmatrix} 2 & 7 \\ 1 & 5 \end{bmatrix} + \begin{bmatrix} 5 & -1 \\ -7 & 2 \end{bmatrix}$$

$$= \begin{bmatrix} 7 & 6 \\ -6 & 7 \end{bmatrix}$$

6. A – student likes music

B – student likes dance

$n(A) = 45, n(B) = 50$

$n(A \cup B) = 60 - 5 = 55$

from, $n(A \cup B) = n(A) + n(B) - n(A \cap B)$

$$55 = 45 + 50 - n(A \cap B)$$

$n(A \cap B) = 95 - 55 = 40$

7. From question, given terms are in A.P.

$2 \log_{10}(2^x - 1) = \log_{10} 2 + \log_{10}(2^x + 3)$

$\log_{10}(2^x - 1)^2 = \log_{10} 2\,(2^x + 3)$

or, $\log_{10}(2^x - 1)^2 - \log_{10} 2(2^x + 3) = 0$

$$\log_{10}\left(\frac{(2^x - 1)^2}{2(2^x + 3)}\right) = 0$$

$$\frac{(2^x - 1)^2}{2(2^x + 3)} = 10^0 = 1$$

$\therefore\ (2^x - 1)^2 = 2(2^x + 3)$

Let $2^x = z$

$(z - 1)^2 = 2(z + 3)$

$z^2 - 2z + 1 = 2z + 6$

$z^2 - 4z - 5 = 0$

$(z - 5)(z + 1) = 0 \Rightarrow z = -1$ and 5

But $2^x \neq -1 \ \forall\ x \in R$

$\therefore\ 2^x = 5 \ \Rightarrow x = \log_2 5$

10. $z = \dfrac{-2(1+2i)}{3+i}$

$= \dfrac{-2(1+2i)}{(3+i)} \times \dfrac{(3-i)}{(3-i)}$

$= \dfrac{-2(5+5i)}{9+1}$

$= \dfrac{-10\,(1+i)}{10} = -(1+i)$

Argument $(z) = \tan(\theta) = \left(\dfrac{-1}{-1}\right)$

$\theta = -\pi + \dfrac{\pi}{4} = -\dfrac{3\pi}{4}$

11. $(x + p)(x + q) - k = 0$

$x^2 + (p + q)x + pq - k = 0$

sum of roots, $(m + n) = -(p + q)$ ...(i)

Product of roots $m{\cdot}n = pk - k$

$\therefore\ mn + k = pq$ ...(ii)

Again, from equation,

$(x - m)(x - n) + k = 0$

$\Rightarrow x^2 - (m + n)x + mn + k = 0$

Let two roots of this equation are a and b,

then $a + b = m + n = -(p + q)$ ...(iii)

$ab = m{\cdot}n + k = p{\cdot}q$ ...(iv)

from (iii) and (iv),

$(a - b) = \sqrt{(a+b)^2 - 4ab}$

$= \sqrt{\{-(p+q)\}^2 - 4p{\cdot}q}$

$a - b = (q - p)$ ...(v)

From, (iii) and (v), we get

$a = -p$ and $b = -q$

Hence, two roots of the later equation are $-p$ and $-q$.

13. $(1 + \omega)(1 + \omega^2)(1 + \omega^4)(1 + \omega^8)$

As ω is a cube root of unity

$\therefore\ \omega^4 = \omega$ and $\omega^8 = \omega^2$

$(1 + \omega)(1 + \omega^2)(1 + \omega)(1 + \omega^2)$

$(1 + \omega)^2 (1 + \omega^2)^2$

$(-\omega^2)^2 (-\omega)^2$

$\omega^4{\cdot}\omega^2 = \omega^6 = 1$

14. No. of elements = 10

No. of ways of containing only two elements

$= {}^{10}C_2$

$= \dfrac{10!}{2!(10-2)!} = \dfrac{10 \times 9}{2} = 45$

16.

2	127	1
2	63	1
2	31	1
2	15	1
2	7	1
2	3	1
	1	

$\therefore\ (127)_{10} = (1111111)_2$

$0.25 \times 2 = 0.50$ 0 $\therefore\ (0.25)_{10} = (0.01)_2$

$0.50 \times 2 = 1.00$ 1

Hence, $(127.25)_{10} = (1111111.01)_2$

18. A X = B

$\begin{bmatrix} p & q \\ r & s \end{bmatrix}\begin{bmatrix} 3 & -4 \\ 1 & -1 \end{bmatrix} = \begin{bmatrix} 5 & 2 \\ -2 & 1 \end{bmatrix}$

$\begin{bmatrix} 3p+q & -4p-q \\ 3r+s & -4r-s \end{bmatrix} = \begin{bmatrix} 5 & 2 \\ -2 & 1 \end{bmatrix}$

$3p + q = 5,\quad 4p + q = -2,$

$3r + s = -2,\quad 4r + s = -1$

From above equation.

$p = -7,\ q = 26,\ r = 1,\ s = -5$

Hence, $A = \begin{bmatrix} -7 & 26 \\ 1 & -5 \end{bmatrix}$

19. ${}^nC_n + {}^{n+1}C_n$

$= \dfrac{n!}{0!n!} + \dfrac{(n+1)!}{n!1!}$

$= 1 + n + 1 = n + 2$

Now, ${}^{n+2}C_{n+1} = \dfrac{(n+2)!}{(n+1)!1!} = (n+2)$

Hence, $\sum_{r=0}^{1} {}^{n+r}C_n = {}^{n+2}C_{n+1}$

20. When all the vowels come together, treating as a single letter, Number of letters = 4

So, number of words formed, when all the vowels come together $= \dfrac{4!3!}{2!}$

Total number of words formed when all letters are randomly arrange $= \dfrac{6!}{2!}$

Hence, required number of words $= \dfrac{(6! - 4!3!)}{2!}$

$= \left(\dfrac{720-144}{2}\right) = 288$

21. $(x^3 - 1) = (x - 1)(x^2 + x + 1)$

$= (x-1)\left(x - \left(\dfrac{1-\sqrt{3}i}{2}\right)\right)\left(x - \left(\dfrac{1+\sqrt{3}i}{2}\right)\right)$

$= (x - 1)(x - \omega)(x - \omega^2)$

here, ω and ω^2 are cube roots of unity

$$\omega = \frac{-1-\sqrt{3}i}{2} \text{ and } \omega^2 = \frac{-1+\sqrt{3}i}{2}$$

22. $$\left[\frac{\sin\frac{\pi}{6}+i\left(1-\cos\frac{\pi}{6}\right)}{\sin\frac{\pi}{6}-i\left(1-\cos\frac{\pi}{6}\right)}\right]^3$$

$$\left[\frac{\sin\frac{\pi}{6}+i\left(2\sin^2\frac{\pi}{12}\right)}{\sin\frac{\pi}{6}-i\left(2\sin^2\frac{\pi}{12}\right)}\right]^3$$

$$= \left[\frac{2\sin\frac{\pi}{12}}{2\sin\frac{\pi}{12}}\right]^3\left[\frac{\cos\frac{\pi}{12}+i\cdot\sin\frac{\pi}{12}}{\cos\frac{\pi}{12}-i\cdot\sin\frac{\pi}{12}}\right]^3$$

$$= \frac{\cos\frac{\pi}{4}+i\cdot\sin\frac{\pi}{4}}{\cos\frac{\pi}{4}-i\cdot\sin\frac{\pi}{4}}$$

$$\frac{\left(\cos\frac{\pi}{4}+i\sin\frac{\pi}{4}\right)\left(\cos\frac{\pi}{4}+i\sin\frac{\pi}{4}\right)}{\left(\cos\frac{\pi}{4}-i\sin\frac{\pi}{4}\right)\left(\cos\frac{\pi}{4}+i\sin\frac{\pi}{4}\right)}$$

$$\frac{\left(\cos\frac{\pi}{2}+i\sin\frac{\pi}{2}\right)}{\left(\cos^2\frac{\pi}{4}+\sin^2\frac{\pi}{4}\right)} = i$$

23. $$\begin{bmatrix} x+y & y \\ 2x & x-y \end{bmatrix}\begin{bmatrix} 2 \\ -1 \end{bmatrix} = \begin{bmatrix} 3 \\ 2 \end{bmatrix}$$

$$\begin{bmatrix} 2(x+y)-y \\ 2(2x)-1(x-y) \end{bmatrix} = \begin{bmatrix} 3 \\ 2 \end{bmatrix}$$

$$\begin{bmatrix} 2x+y \\ 3x+y \end{bmatrix} = \begin{bmatrix} 3 \\ 2 \end{bmatrix}$$

$2x + y = 3$ and $3x + y = 2$

From above equation, $x = -1$, $y = 5$

$$A = \begin{bmatrix} x+y & y \\ 2x & x-y \end{bmatrix} = \begin{bmatrix} -1+5 & 5 \\ 2(-1) & -1-5 \end{bmatrix} = \begin{bmatrix} 4 & 5 \\ -2 & -6 \end{bmatrix}$$

$$A^2 = \begin{bmatrix} 4 & 5 \\ -2 & -6 \end{bmatrix}\begin{bmatrix} 4 & 5 \\ -2 & -6 \end{bmatrix} = \begin{bmatrix} 16-10 & 20-30 \\ -8+12 & -10+36 \end{bmatrix}$$

$$= \begin{bmatrix} 6 & -10 \\ 4 & 26 \end{bmatrix}$$

24. $$\begin{vmatrix} 1 & 1 & 1 \\ 1 & 1+x & 1 \\ 1 & 1 & 1+y \end{vmatrix} = \begin{vmatrix} 1 & 0 & 0 \\ 1 & x & 0 \\ 1 & 0 & y \end{vmatrix}$$

Applying $C_2 \to C_2 - C_1$

$C_3 \to C_3 - C_1$

$= xy$

26. (11101011) /2

$= 2^7 + 2^6 + 2^5 + 0 + 2^3 + 0 + 2^1 + 2^0$

$= 128 + 64 + 32 + 8 + 2 + 1$

$= 235$

28. $$E(\alpha)\cdot E(\beta) = \begin{bmatrix} \cos\alpha & \sin\alpha \\ -\sin\alpha & \cos\alpha \end{bmatrix}\begin{bmatrix} \cos\beta & \sin\beta \\ -\sin\beta & \cos\beta \end{bmatrix}$$

$$= \begin{bmatrix} \cos\alpha\cdot\cos\beta-\sin\alpha\cdot\sin\beta & \cos\alpha\cdot\sin\beta+\sin\alpha\cdot\cos\beta \\ -\sin\alpha\cdot\cos\beta-\cos\alpha\cdot\sin\beta & -\sin\alpha\cdot\sin\beta+\cos\alpha\cdot\cos\beta \end{bmatrix}$$

$$= \begin{bmatrix} \cos(\alpha+\beta) & \sin(\alpha+\beta) \\ -\sin(\alpha+\beta) & \cos(\alpha+\beta) \end{bmatrix} = E(\alpha+\beta)$$

30. $2p + 3q = 18$

$4p^2 + 4pq - 3q^2 - 36 = 0$

Let $2p + q = z$, then, $2p + 3q = 18$

$2p + q + 2q = 18$

$z + 2q = 18$ ...(*i*)

$4p^2 + 4pq + q^2 - 4q^2 - 36 = 0$

$(2p + q)^2 - 4q^2 - 36 = 0$

$z^2 - 4q^2 = 36$

$(z + 2q)(z - 2q) = 36$

$18(z - 2q) = 36$

$\Rightarrow z - 2q = 2$ ...(*ii*)

From (*i*) and (*ii*), we get $z = 10$

$2p + q = 10$

31. θ degree $= \frac{\pi}{180}\cdot\theta$ radian

from question,

$$\theta\cdot\left(\frac{\pi}{180}\cdot\theta\right) = \frac{125\pi}{9}$$

$$\theta^2 = \frac{125}{9}\times 180 = 2500° \Rightarrow \theta = 50°$$

32. From Cosine rule

$$\cos C = \frac{a^2+b^2-c^2}{2ab}$$

$C^2 = a^2 + b^2 - 2ab\cos C$

$= (1+\sqrt{3})^2 + (2)^2 - 2\cdot(1+\sqrt{3})\cdot 2\cdot\cos 60°$

$= 4+2\sqrt{3}+4-2-2\sqrt{3}$

$= 6$

$C = \sqrt{6}$ cm

From, sine rule,

$$\frac{b}{\sin B}=\frac{c}{\sin C}$$

$$\therefore \sin B=\frac{b}{c}\cdot\sin C$$

$$=\frac{2}{\sqrt{6}}\sin 60^\circ$$

$$=\frac{2}{\sqrt{2}\cdot\sqrt{3}}\cdot\frac{\sqrt{3}}{2}=\frac{1}{\sqrt{2}}$$

$\therefore$ B = 45°

and A = 180° – 45° – 60°

= 75°

For Qs. 33 and 34 :

$25\cos^2\alpha + 5\cos\alpha - 12 = 0$

$$\cos\alpha=\frac{-5\pm\sqrt{5^2-4\cdot 25\cdot(-12)}}{2.25}$$

$$=\frac{-5\pm\sqrt{25+1200}}{50}$$

$$=\frac{-5\pm\sqrt{1225}}{50}$$

$$=\frac{-5\pm 35}{50}=\frac{3}{5}\text{ or }\frac{-4}{5}$$

For $\alpha\in\left(\frac{\pi}{2},\pi\right)$, $\cos\alpha=\frac{-4}{5}$

33. $\therefore \tan\alpha=-\frac{3}{4}$

34. $\sin 2\alpha = 2\sin\alpha\cdot\cos\alpha$

$$=2\cdot\left(\frac{3}{5}\right)\left(-\frac{4}{5}\right)=-\frac{24}{25}$$

35.

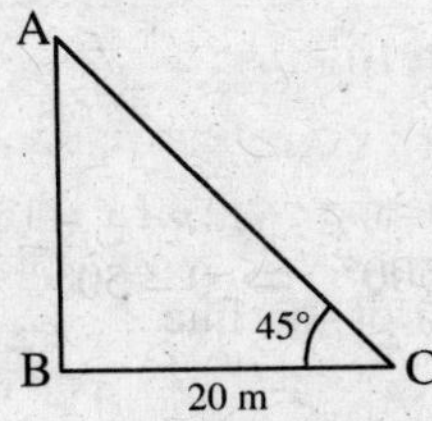

From Δ ABC, height of the tower AB

= BC · tan 45°

= 20 × 1 = 20 m

36. $\tan^{-1}(1+x)+\tan^{-1}(1-x)=\frac{\pi}{2}$

$$\tan^{-1}\left(\frac{1+x+1-x}{1-(1+x)(1-x)}\right)=\frac{\pi}{2}$$

$$\tan^{-1}\left(\frac{2}{1-1+x^2}\right)=\frac{\pi}{2}$$

$$\frac{1}{x^2}=\tan\left(\frac{\pi}{2}\right)=\infty \qquad \therefore x=0$$

38. $(1 - \sin A + \cos A)^2$

$(1 - \sin A)^2 + \cos^2 A + 2\cos A\cdot(1 - \sin A)$

$(1 - \sin A)^2 + \cos^2 A + 2\cos A - 2\sin A\cdot\cos A$

$1 + \sin^2 A - 2\sin A + \cos^2 A + 2\cos A - \sin 2A$

$2 - 2\sin A + 2\cos A - \sin 2A$

$2(1 - \sin A) + 2\cos A(1 - \sin A)$

$= 2(1 - \sin A)(1 + \cos A)$

39. $\frac{\cos\theta}{1-\tan\theta}+\frac{\sin\theta}{1-\cot\theta}$

$$\frac{\cos\theta\cdot\cos\theta}{\cos\theta-\sin\theta}+\frac{\sin\theta\cdot\sin\theta}{\sin\theta-\cos\theta}$$

$$\frac{\cos^2\theta-\sin^2\theta}{\cos\theta-\sin\theta}=\sin\theta+\cos\theta$$

For Qs. 40 to 42 :

$$x=4\tan^{-1}\left(\frac{1}{5}\right),\ y=\tan^{-1}\left(\frac{1}{70}\right),\ z=\tan^{-1}\left(\frac{1}{99}\right)$$

40. $\frac{x}{4}=\tan^{-1}\left(\frac{1}{5}\right) \Rightarrow \tan\left(\frac{x}{4}\right)=\frac{1}{5}$

$$\tan\left(\frac{x}{2}\right)=\frac{2\tan\left(\frac{x}{4}\right)}{1-\tan^2\left(\frac{x}{4}\right)}=\frac{\frac{2}{5}}{1-\left(\frac{1}{5}\right)^2}=\frac{\frac{2}{5}}{1-\frac{1}{25}}$$

$$=\frac{10}{24}=\frac{5}{12}$$

$$\text{Now, }\tan(x)=\frac{2\tan\left(\frac{x}{2}\right)}{1-\tan^2\left(\frac{x}{2}\right)}=\frac{2\times\frac{5}{12}}{1-\left(\frac{5}{12}\right)^2}=\frac{120}{119}$$

$$\therefore x=\tan^{-1}\left(\frac{120}{119}\right)$$

41. $\tan(x-y)=\frac{\tan x-\tan y}{1+\tan x\cdot\tan y}=\frac{\frac{120}{119}-\frac{1}{70}}{1+\frac{120}{119}\cdot\frac{1}{70}}$

$$=\frac{8400-119}{8330+120}=\frac{8281}{8450}$$

$$\therefore (x-y)=\tan^{-1}\left(\frac{8281}{8450}\right)$$

42. $\tan(x-y+z) = \dfrac{\tan(x-y)+\tan z}{1-\tan(x-y)\cdot\tan z}$

$$= \frac{\dfrac{8281}{8450}+\dfrac{1}{99}}{1-\dfrac{8281}{8450}\cdot\dfrac{1}{99}}$$

$$= \frac{819819+8450}{836550-8281} = \frac{828269}{828269} = 1$$

$\therefore (x-y+z) = \tan^{-1}(1) = \dfrac{\pi}{4}$

44. Centroid of the triangle ABC

$$= \left(\frac{x_1+x_2+x_3}{3}, \frac{y_1+y_2+y_3}{3}\right)$$

$$= \left(\frac{-2+2+1}{3}, \frac{3+1+2}{3}\right)$$

$$= \left(\frac{1}{3}, 2\right)$$

45.

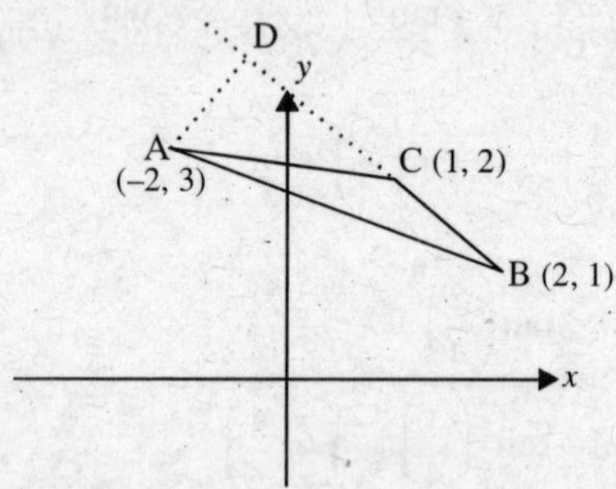

Let AD is the perpendicular drawn from point A on side BC.

D is the foot of the ⊥.

Slop of line AD = $-\dfrac{1}{\text{slope of line BC}}$

$$= -\frac{1}{\dfrac{(2-1)}{(1-2)}} = -\frac{1}{(-1)} = 1$$

Equation of Line AD : $(y-3) = (x+2)$

$x - y + 5 = 0$ ...(*i*)

Again, equation of BC : $(y-1) = -1(x-2)$

$x + y - 3 = 0$ ...(*ii*)

from (*i*) and (*ii*), we get

$x = -1, y = 4$

Hence, foot of the altitude = (–1, 4).

46. Nearest point to the focus of a parabola, that lies on the parabola is its vertex points.

For the given equation, vertex point is (0, 0).

47. Slope of the perpendicular line = $\dfrac{1}{3}$

equation of the perpendicular line through point (2, 2) is $(y-2) = \dfrac{1}{3}(x-2)$

$\Rightarrow x - 3y + 4 = 0$

It is *y*-intercept = $\dfrac{4}{3}$

49. The perpendicular distance between two given lines are

$$\frac{3(0)+4(0)+9}{\sqrt{(3)^2+(4)^2}} - \frac{6(0)+8(0)+15}{\sqrt{6^2+8^2}}$$

$$\frac{9}{5} - \frac{15}{10} = \frac{18-15}{10} = \frac{3}{10} \text{ units}$$

50. Area of the triangle A = 3 (given)

$$3 = \frac{1}{2}\begin{vmatrix} a & 5 & 1 \\ 3 & 4 & 1 \\ 5 & 2 & 1 \end{vmatrix}$$

$6 = a(4-2) + 5(5-3) + 1(6-20)$

$6 = 2a + 10 - 14$

$\therefore a = 5$

51. Equation of any line with slope $m = \tan 120°$

$y = \tan 120° . x + C$

$y = -\sqrt{3}\cdot x + C$

$\sqrt{3}x + y + C' = 0$ ...(*i*)

Length of perpendicular from origin

$$5 = \left|\frac{\sqrt{3}(0)+(0)+C'}{\sqrt{(\sqrt{3})^2+(1)^2}}\right|$$

$$5 = \left|\frac{C^1}{2}\right| \Rightarrow |C^1| = 10$$

$\therefore$ Equation of that line : $\sqrt{3}x + y = 10$

52. Point of intersection of the line

$\dfrac{x}{a} + \dfrac{y}{b} = 1$ and $\dfrac{x}{b} + \dfrac{y}{a} = 1$

$\dfrac{x}{a^2} + \dfrac{y}{ab} = \dfrac{1}{a}$ and $\dfrac{x}{b^2} + \dfrac{y}{ab} = \dfrac{1}{b}$

$\dfrac{x}{a^2} - \dfrac{x}{b^2} = \dfrac{1}{a} - \dfrac{1}{b} \Rightarrow x\left(\dfrac{1}{a} + \dfrac{1}{b}\right) = 1$

$x = \dfrac{ab}{a+b} = y$

Point of intersection = $\left(\dfrac{ab}{a+b}, \dfrac{ab}{a+b}\right)$

Equation of line through (0, 0)

and $\left(\dfrac{ab}{a+b}, \dfrac{ab}{a+b}\right)$ is $y = x$

$\Rightarrow x - y = 0$

53. Length of the line segment

$$d = \sqrt{l^2 + m^2 + n^2}$$

$$= \sqrt{12^2 + 4^2 + 3^2}$$

$$= \sqrt{169} = 13 \text{ units}$$

54. direction cosines = $\left(\dfrac{l}{d}, \dfrac{m}{d}, \dfrac{n}{d}\right)$

$$= \left(\frac{12}{13}, \frac{4}{13}, \frac{3}{13}\right)$$

57. Let co-ordinate of the points A, B, C are $(x, 0, 0)$, $(0, y, 0)$ and $(0, 0, z)$ respectively.

Centroids (1, 2, 3) = $\left(\dfrac{x+0+0}{3}, \dfrac{0+y+0}{3}, \dfrac{0+0+z}{3}\right)$

$\therefore\ x = 3,\ y = 6$ and $z = 9$

58. Equation of the plane with intercept (a, b, c) :

$$\frac{x}{a} + \frac{y}{b} + \frac{z}{c} = 1$$

here, $(a, b, c) = (3, 6, 9)$

$\therefore$ Equation of the plane $\dfrac{x}{3} + \dfrac{y}{6} + \dfrac{z}{9} = 1$

or, $6x + 3y + 2z = 18$

59. Length of the cuboid

$$= \sqrt{(1-0)^2 + (2-0)^2 + (3-0)^2}$$

$$= \sqrt{14} \text{ units}$$

60. Equation of plane passing through (1, 2, 3) and parallel to xy-plane :

$$= x + y = 3$$

61. $\displaystyle\lim_{x\to 1} \frac{G(x) - G(1)}{x-1} = \lim_{x\to 1} \frac{\sqrt{25 - x^2} - \sqrt{24}}{x-1}$

This is in $\dfrac{0}{0}$ form,

Applying L'Hospital rule, we have

$$\lim_{x\to 1} \frac{\left(\dfrac{-2x}{2\sqrt{25-x^2}}\right)}{1}$$

$$\lim_{x\to 1} -\frac{x}{\sqrt{25-x^2}} = -\frac{1}{\sqrt{24}} = -\frac{1}{2\sqrt{6}}$$

63. for $x > 0$

$f(x) = \dfrac{x}{x} = 1$, $\quad R\{f(x)\} = 1$

for $x < 0$

$f(x) = \dfrac{x}{-x} = -1$, $\quad R\{f(x)\} = -1$

Hence, range of f = [–1 and 1].

65. Let $y = \tan^{-1}\left(\dfrac{\sqrt{1+x^2} - 1}{x}\right)$

$$\tan y = \frac{\sqrt{1+x^2} - 1}{x}$$

and $\tan^{-1} x = z \quad \Rightarrow x = \tan z$

$$= \quad \tan y = \frac{\sqrt{1 + \tan^2 z} - 1}{\tan z}$$

$$= \quad \frac{\sec z - 1}{\tan z} = \tan\left(\frac{z}{2}\right)$$

$$y = n\pi + \left(\frac{z}{2}\right)$$

Differentiating y w.r.t. z,

$$\frac{dy}{dz} = \frac{1}{2}$$

66. -

$$g\text{o}f\left(\frac{e-1}{e+1}\right) = g\left(\log_e\left(\frac{1 + \frac{e-1}{e+1}}{1 - \frac{e-1}{e+1}}\right)\right)$$

$$= g(\log_e(e))$$

$$= g(1) = \frac{3+1}{1+3} = 1$$

67.

$$f(x) = \begin{cases} -1 & \text{if} \quad x \le 0 \\ ax + b & \text{if} \quad 0 < x < 1 \\ 1 & \text{if} \quad x \ge 1 \end{cases}$$

$\displaystyle\lim_{x\to 0^-} f(x) = \lim_{x\to 0^+} f(x)$

$\therefore\ a(0) + b = -1$

$b = -1$

and $\displaystyle\lim_{x\to 1^-} f(x) = \lim_{x\to 1^+} f(x)$

$\therefore\ a(1) + b = 1$

$a + b = 1$

$a - b = 1 \quad \Rightarrow a = 2$

69. 1. $f(x) = x^3$, $f(-x) = (-x)^3 = -x^3 = -f(x)$

$\therefore\ f(x) = x^3$ is a odd and one to one function

2. $f(x) = \sin(x)$, $f(-x) = \sin(-x) = \sin x = -f(x)$

$\therefore\ f(x) = \sin x$ is one-to-one odd function, in the given domain $0 < x < 2\pi$.

3. $f(x) = e^x, f(-x) = e^{-x} = \frac{1}{e^x} \neq -f(x)$

$f(x)$ is not a odd function.

Hence, function given in (1) and (2) are only have inverse.

For Qs. 72 and 73 :

$$f(x) = \frac{x^2 - 1}{x^2 + 1}$$

$$f'(x) = \frac{(x^2+1)\frac{d}{dx}(x^2-1) - (x^2-1)\frac{d}{dx}(x^2+1)}{(x^2+1)^2}$$

$$= \frac{(x^2+1)(2x) - (x^2-1)(2x)}{(x^2+1)^2} = \frac{4x}{(x^2+1)^2}$$

72. For minimum value, $f'(x) = 0$

$$\frac{4x}{(x^2+1)^2} = 0 \Rightarrow x = 0$$

73. $f(0) = \frac{0-1}{0+1} = -1$

74. $f(x) = \frac{\alpha \cos x}{\pi - 2x}$

$$\lim_{x \to \frac{\pi}{2}} f(x) = \lim_{x \to \frac{\pi}{2}} \frac{\alpha . \cos x}{\pi - 2x}$$

By L'Hospital rule

$$\lim_{x \to \frac{\pi}{2}} \frac{\alpha \cos x}{\pi - 2x} = \lim_{x \to \frac{\pi}{2}} \frac{-\alpha \cdot \sin x}{-2} = 3$$

$$\frac{\alpha \cdot \sin\left(\frac{\pi}{2}\right)}{2} = 3$$

$$\frac{\alpha}{2} = 3 \quad \Rightarrow \alpha = 6$$

75. $\lim_{x \to 0} f(x) = \lim_{x \to 0} \frac{6 \cos x}{\pi - 2x} = \frac{6}{\pi}$

77. Line $x = \sqrt{3}\, y$, has slope $m = \frac{1}{\sqrt{3}} = \tan\theta$

$\therefore\ \theta = 30°$

Area of the sector of a circle with angle $\theta = 30°$

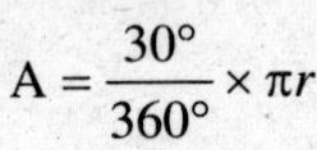

$$A = \frac{30°}{360°} \times \pi r^2$$

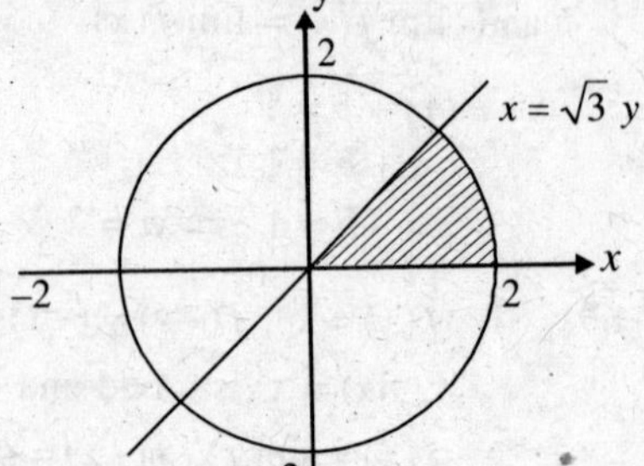

here $r = 2$

$$\therefore \quad A = \frac{30°}{360°} \times \pi(2)^2 = \frac{\pi}{3}$$

76. Required area is the shadded Portion
= Area of sector ($\theta = 30°$) of circle
– Area of triangle AOB.

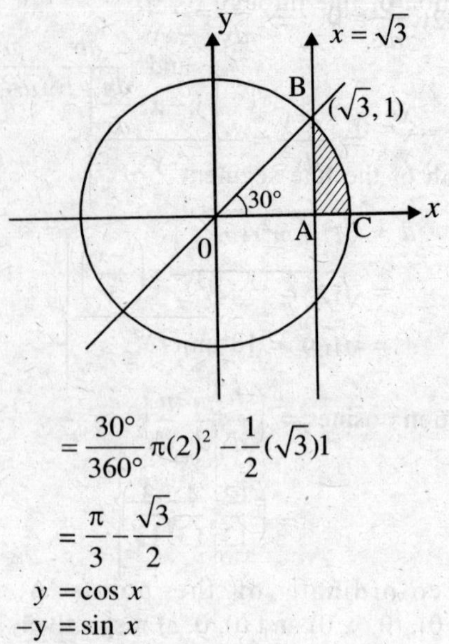

$$= \frac{30°}{360°}\pi(2)^2 - \frac{1}{2}(\sqrt{3})1$$

$$= \frac{\pi}{3} - \frac{\sqrt{3}}{2}$$

$y = \cos x$

$-y = \sin x$

For Qs. 80 and 81 :

$f(x) = 0.75\, x^4 - x^3 - 9x^2 + 7$

For extremum value, $f'(x) = 0$

$f'(x) = 0.75 \times 4x^3 - 3x^2 - 18x = 0$

$3x(x^2 - x - 6) = 0$

$3x(x - 3)\,(x + 2) = 0$

$x = 0, -2$ and 3

$f''(x) = 9x^2 - 6x - 18$

80. $f''(x) = 9x^2 - 6x - 18$

$f''(0) = -18 < 0$

So, $f(x)$ is maximum for $x = 0$

$f(0) = 0 - 0 - 0 + 7 = 7$

81. At $x = -2$ and 3,

$f''(-2) = 9(-2)^2 - 6(-2) - 18 = 30 > 0$

$f''(3) = 9(3)^2 - 6(3) - 18 = 45 > 0$

$\therefore f(x)$ has local minimum at $x = -2$ and 3 and function is increasing from $x = -2$ to 0.

For Qs. 82 to 84 :

$$x = \frac{a(1-t^2)}{1+t^2}, \quad y = \frac{2at}{1+t^2}$$

Let $t = \tan\theta$

$$x = \frac{a(1-\tan^2\theta)}{1+\tan^2\theta}, \quad y = \frac{(a)2\tan\theta}{1+\tan^2\theta}$$

$x = a\cdot\cos 2\theta, \quad y = a\cdot\sin^2\theta$

82. Squaring and adding,

$x^2 + y^2 = a^2(\cos^2 2\theta + \sin^2 2\theta)$

$x^2 + y^2 = a^2$

This is equation of a circle with radius a.

83. $x^2 + y^2 = a^2$

Differentiating both sides w.r.t. x, we get

$$2x + 2y.\frac{dy}{dx} = 0 \Rightarrow \frac{dy}{dx} = -\frac{x}{y}$$

84. $\frac{dy}{dx} = -\frac{x}{y} \Rightarrow \frac{d^2y}{dx^2} = -\left\{\frac{y - x\cdot\frac{dy}{dx}}{y^2}\right\}$

$$= -\left\{\frac{y - x\left(\frac{-x}{y}\right)}{y^2}\right\}$$

$$= -\left\{\frac{y + \frac{x^2}{y}}{y^2}\right\}$$

$$= -\left\{\frac{y^2 + x^2}{y^3}\right\} = -\frac{a^2}{y^3}$$

87. $I_m = \int_0^{\pi} \frac{\sin 2mx}{\sin x}\cdot dx$

for $m = 1$

$$I_1 = \int_0^{\pi} \frac{\sin 2x}{\sin x}\cdot dx = 2\int_0^{\pi} \cos x \cdot dx$$

$$= 2[\sin x]_0^{\pi} = 0$$

88. $I_2 = \int_0^{\pi} \frac{\sin 4x}{\sin x}\cdot dx = \int_0^{\pi} \frac{2\sin 2x\cdot\cos 2x}{\sin x}\cdot dx$

$$= 4\int_0^{\pi} \cos x\cdot\cos 2x\cdot dx$$

$$= 2\int_0^{\pi} (\cos 3x + \cos x)\cdot dx$$

$$= 2\left[\frac{\sin 3x}{3} + \sin x\right]_0^{\pi} = 0$$

$$I_3 = \int_0^{\pi} \frac{\sin 6x}{\sin x}\cdot dx$$

$$= 2\int_0^{\pi} \frac{(\sin 3x)\cdot\cos(3x)}{\sin x}\cdot dx$$

$$= 2\int_0^{\pi} (3 - 4\sin^2 x)\cdot\cos 3x\cdot dx$$

$$= 2\int_0^{\pi} 3\cos 3x - 4\int_0^{\pi} 2\sin^2 x\cdot\cos 3x\cdot dx$$

$$= 6\left[\frac{\sin 3x}{3}\right]_0^{\pi} - 4\int_0^{\pi} (1 - \cos 2x)\cdot\cos 3x\cdot dx$$

$$= 0 - 4\int_0^{\pi} \cos 3x\cdot dx + 2\int_0^{\pi} 2\cos 2x\cdot\cos 3x\cdot dx$$

$$= 0 + 2\int_0^{\pi} (\cos 5x + \cos x)\cdot dx$$

$$= 0 + 2\left[\frac{\sin 5x}{5} + \sin x\right]_0^{\pi} = 0$$

For Qs. 91 and 92 :

$(1 + x + x^2)^2 = 1 + x^2 + x^4 + 2x + 2x^3 + 2x^2$

$\therefore\ (1 + x^2 + x^4) = (1 + x + x^2)^2 - 2x(1 + x + x^2)$

$= (1 + x + x^2)(1 - x + x^2)$

Now, $\frac{d}{dx}\left(\frac{1 + x^2 + x^4}{1 + x + x^2}\right) = \frac{d}{dx}\left[\frac{(1 + x + x^2)(1 - x + x^2)}{(1 + x + x^2)}\right]$

$$= \frac{d}{dx}(1 - x + x^2) = 2x - 1$$

$\therefore\ A = 2$ and $B = -1$

For Qs. 93 and 94 :

$$\lim_{x\to\infty}\left(\frac{2 + x^2}{1 + x} - A\cdot x - B\right)$$

$$\lim_{x\to\infty}\left(\frac{2 + x^2 - A\cdot x(1 + x) - B(1 + x)}{1 + x}\right)$$

$$\lim_{x\to\infty}\left(\frac{x^2 - Ax^2 - Ax - Bx + 2 - B}{1 + x}\right)$$

By L' Hospital rule,

$$\lim_{x\to\infty}\left(\frac{2x - 2Ax - A - B}{1}\right)$$

For Limit to be defined,

$2x - 2Ax = 0 \quad \Rightarrow A = 1$

Also, From question, limit value is 3.

$-A - B = 3$

$-1 - B = 3 \quad \Rightarrow B = -4$

95. $\frac{y\,dx - x\,dy}{y^2} = 0$

$y\,dx - x\,dy = 0$

$$\frac{dy}{y} = \frac{dx}{x}$$

Integrating both sides, we have

$$\int\frac{dy}{y} = \int\frac{dx}{x}$$

$\text{In } y = \text{In } x + \text{In } c$

$\text{In } y = \text{In } Cx \quad \Rightarrow y = Cx$

96. $\sin\left(\frac{dy}{dx}\right) - a = 0$

$$\frac{dy}{dx} = \sin^{-1}(a)$$

$$dy = \sin^{-1}(a) \cdot dx$$

$$y = x \cdot \sin^{-1}(a) + C$$

97. $\frac{dx}{dy} + \frac{x}{y} - y^2 = 0$

$$\text{I.F.} = e^{\int \frac{1}{y} dy} = e^{\ln y} = y$$

General solution,

$$x \cdot (\text{I.F.}) = \int Q \cdot (\text{I.F.}) dy$$

$$x \cdot y = \int y^2 \cdot y \cdot dy$$

$$xy = \frac{y^4}{4} + C$$

$$\Rightarrow 4xy = y^4 + C.$$

98. $\text{I} = \int \frac{x \cdot e^x}{(x+1)^2} \cdot dx$

$$\int \frac{(x+1)e^x - e^x}{(x+1)^2} \cdot dx$$

$$\text{I} = \int \frac{e^x}{(x+1)} \cdot dx - \int \frac{e^x}{(x+1)^2} \cdot dx \quad ...(i)$$

$$u = \frac{1}{(x+1)} \text{ and } v = e^x$$

$$\frac{dy}{dx} = -\frac{1}{(x+1)^2}$$

$$\int u.v.dx = u \cdot \int v.dx - \int \left(\frac{dy}{dx} . \int v.dx\right) \cdot dx$$

$$= \frac{1}{(x+1)} \int e^x \cdot dx - \int -\left(\frac{1}{(x+1)^2} \int e^x \cdot dx\right) \cdot dx$$

$$= \frac{1}{(x+1)} \cdot e^x + \int \frac{e^x}{(x+1)^2} \cdot dx + C$$

from (*i*)

$$\text{I} = \frac{e^x}{x+1} + C$$

99. Area of the triangle ABC

$$= \frac{1}{2} \left|\overrightarrow{AB} \times \overrightarrow{AC}\right|$$

$$= \frac{1}{2} \begin{vmatrix} \hat{i} & \hat{j} & \hat{k} \\ -2 & 3 & 2 \\ -4 & 5 & 2 \end{vmatrix}$$

$$= \frac{1}{2} \left|-4\hat{i} - 4\hat{j} + 2\hat{k}\right|$$

$$= \frac{1}{2} \left|\sqrt{(-4)^2 + (-4)^2 + 2^2}\right|$$

$$= \frac{1}{2} \times 6 = 3 \text{ square units}$$

100. Momentum $= \left|\vec{F} \times \vec{r}\right|$

$$= \left|\left(3\hat{i} + 4\hat{j} - 3\hat{k}\right) \times \left(2\hat{i} - 2\hat{j} - 3\hat{k}\right)\right|$$

$$= \left|-18\hat{i} + 3\hat{j} - 14\hat{k}\right|$$

$$= \sqrt{529}$$

$$= 23 \text{ units}$$

101. $\vec{\alpha}$ and $\vec{\beta}$ are non-collinear,

$$2x\vec{\alpha} + y\vec{\beta} - 2y\vec{\alpha} - 3x\vec{\beta} = 2\vec{\alpha} - 5\vec{\beta}$$

$$(2x - 2y)\vec{\alpha} + (y - 3x)\vec{\beta} = 2\vec{\alpha} - 5\vec{\beta}$$

$\therefore$ $2x - 2y = 2 \Rightarrow x - y = 1$ ...(*i*)

and $y - 3x = -5 \Rightarrow 3x - y = 5$ ...(*ii*)

from (*i*) and (*ii*), we have,

$$x = 2 \text{ and } y = 1$$

102. $\left|\vec{a} + \vec{b}\right|^2 = \left|\vec{a}\right|^2 + \left|\vec{b}\right|^2 + 2\vec{a} \cdot \vec{b}$

$$(10\sqrt{3})^2 = (7)^2 + (11)^2 + 2\vec{a} \cdot \vec{b}$$

$$300 = 49 + 121 + 2\vec{a} \cdot \vec{b}$$

$$\therefore \quad \vec{a} \cdot \vec{b} = 65$$

Now, $\left|\vec{a} - \vec{b}\right|^2 = \left|\vec{a}\right|^2 + \left|\vec{b}\right|^2 - 2\vec{a} \cdot \vec{b}$

$$= (7)^2 + (11)^2 - 130$$

$$= 49 + 121 - 130 = 40$$

$$\left|\vec{a} - \vec{b}\right| = \sqrt{40} = 2\sqrt{10}$$

103. Points are collinear, if $\Delta = 0$

$$\begin{vmatrix} \alpha & \beta & \gamma \\ \beta & \gamma & \alpha \\ \gamma & \alpha & \beta \end{vmatrix} = 0$$

$$\alpha(\beta\gamma - \alpha^2) + \beta(\alpha.\gamma - \beta^2) + \gamma(\alpha\beta - \gamma^2) = 0$$

$$3\ \alpha\beta\gamma - \alpha^3 - \beta^3 - \gamma^3 = 0$$

which is not satisfy for given value.

So, Points are not collinear.

Points form an equilateral triangle, if three parts are equidistance apart and form equal angles with others. Length of each lines are equal, which is

$$= \sqrt{(\alpha - \beta)^2 + (\beta - \gamma)^2 + (\gamma - \alpha)^2}$$

Also, angle between any two lines are

$$\theta = \cos^{-1}\left\{\frac{\alpha\beta + \beta\gamma + \alpha\gamma}{\alpha^2 + \beta^2 + \gamma^2}\right\}$$

Hence, Points form equilateral triangle.

105. $|\vec{a}+\vec{b}| = |\vec{a}-\vec{b}|$

Squaring both sides, we get

$$|\vec{a}+\vec{b}|^2 = |\vec{a}-\vec{b}|^2$$

$$|\vec{a}|^2 + |\vec{b}|^2 + 2\vec{a}\cdot\vec{b} = |\vec{a}|^2 + |\vec{b}|^2 - 2\vec{a}\cdot\vec{b}$$

$$4\vec{a}\cdot\vec{b} = 0$$

$$\therefore \quad \vec{a} \perp \vec{b}$$

111. Probability for A hit the target $= \frac{1}{2}$

Probability for A not hit the target $= \frac{1}{2}$

Probability for B hit the target $= \frac{1}{3}$

Probability for B not hit the target $= \frac{2}{3}$

Probability that exactly one person (either A or B) hit the target

$$= \frac{1}{2}\times\frac{2}{3}+\frac{1}{2}\times\frac{1}{3} = \frac{3}{2\times 3} = \frac{1}{2}$$

112. Probability of choosing one box $= \frac{1}{2}$

Total number of balls $= 5 - i - 1 + i + 1 = 5$

number of red balls $= i + 1 = 2$ or 3

for $i = 1, 2$

and, number of black balls $= 5 - i - 1$

$= 3$ or 2

for $= i = 1, 2$

Now, Probability of choosing two different balls, from any of two boxes

$$= \frac{1}{2}\left[\frac{{}^2C_1 \times {}^3C_1}{{}^5C_2} + \frac{{}^3C_1 \times {}^2C_1}{{}^5C_2}\right]$$

$$= \frac{1}{2}\times\left[\frac{3}{5}+\frac{3}{5}\right] = \frac{1}{2}\times\frac{6}{5} = \frac{3}{5}$$

113. Probability for solving a question $x = \frac{1}{2}$

Probability not solving a question

$$y = 1 - \frac{1}{2} = \frac{1}{2}$$

From binomial distribution :

$$(x+y)^n = {}^nC_0 x^n + {}^nC_1 x^{n-1} y + {}^nC_2 x^{n-2} y^2 + {}^nC_3 x^{n-3} y^3 + {}^nC_r x^{n-r} y^r$$

Here $n = 5$ and $r = 2$

Required probability

$${}^5C_2\left(\frac{1}{2}\right)^{5-2}\cdot\left(\frac{1}{2}\right)^3 + {}^5C_3\left(\frac{1}{2}\right)^{5-3}\cdot\left(\frac{1}{2}\right)^2 + {}^5C_4\left(\frac{1}{2}\right)^{5-4}\cdot\left(\frac{1}{2}\right) + {}^5C_5\left(\frac{1}{2}\right)^5$$

$$= \left({}^5C_2 + {}^5C_3 + {}^5C_4 + {}^5C_5\right)\left(\frac{1}{2}\right)^5$$

$$= (10+10+5+1)\frac{1}{32}$$

$$= \frac{26}{32} = \frac{13}{16}$$

114. $A \subseteq B \quad \Rightarrow n(A) \subseteq n(B)$

$\therefore A \cap B = A$ and $A \cup B = B$

(a) $P(A \cap \bar{B}) = 0$, AS $A \subseteq B$

$\therefore A \cap \bar{B} = 0$ {Correct}

(b) $P(A \mid B) = \frac{P(A \cap B)}{P(B)} = \frac{P(A)}{P(B)}$ {Correct}

(c) $P(B \mid A) = \frac{P(B \cap A)}{P(A)} = \frac{P(A)}{P(A)} = 1$ {Incorrect}

(d) $P(A|(A \cup B)$

$$= \frac{P(A \cap (A \cup B))}{P(A \cup B)} = \frac{P(A)}{P(B)} \text{ \{Correct\}}$$

116. Sum of five numbers = 30 × 5 = 150

Sum of four numbers = 28 × 4 = 112

Hence, fifth number = 150 − 112 = 38

117. $P(\bar{A}) = \frac{2}{3}$, $P(A) = 1 - P(\bar{A})$

$$= 1 - \frac{2}{3} = \frac{1}{3}$$

Now, $P(A \cup B) = P(A) + P(B) - P(A \cap B)$

$P(B) = P(A \cup B) - P(A) + P(A \cap B)$

$$= \frac{3}{4} - \frac{1}{3} + \frac{1}{4} = \frac{2}{3}$$

119. Total number of outcome in throwing two dice $= (6)^2 = 36$

Event that 5 appears on atleast one die face

= (1, 5), (2, 5), (3, 5), (4, 5), (5, 5), (6, 5), (5, 1), (5, 2), (5, 3), (5, 4), (5, 6)

Number of such events = 11

Hence, required number of such exhaustive event = 36 − 11 = 25

120. Number of aces in pack of 52 cards = 4

Number of ways of selecting any two ace cards from 4 aces $= {}^4C_2 = 6$

Number of ways of selecting any two cards from 52 cards pack.

$$= {}^{52}C_2 = 1326$$

Hence, required probability

$$= \frac{{}^4C_2}{{}^{52}C_2} = \frac{6}{1326} = \frac{1}{221}$$

Previous Papers (Solved)

NATIONAL DEFENCE ACADEMY & NAVAL ACADEMY

NDA & NA – Entrance Exam, 2014 (II)

PAPER I : GENERAL ABILITY TEST

PART A : ENGLISH LANGUAGE

Synonyms

Directions (Qs. No. 1 to 10) : *In this section, you find a number of sentences, parts of which are underlined. For each underlined part, four words are listed below. Choose the word nearest in meaning to the underlined part and indicate your response in the Answer Sheet.*

1. We should always try to maintain and promote communal <u>amity.</u>
A. bondage B. contention
C. friendship D. understanding

2. Many species of animals have become <u>extinct</u> during the last hundred years.
A. aggressive B. non-existent
C. scattered D. feeble

3. True religion does not require one to <u>proselytise</u> through guile or force.
A. translate B. hypnotise
C. attack D. convert

4. That the plan is both inhuman and <u>preposterous</u> needs no further proof.
A. heartless B. impractical
C. absurd D. abnormal

5. The attitude of the Western countries towards the third-world countries is rather <u>callous</u> to say the least.
A. passive B. unkind
C. cursed D. unfeeling

6. Whatever the <u>verdict</u> of history may be, Chaplin will occupy a unique place in its pages.
A. judgment B. voice
C. outcome D. prediction

7. He <u>corroborated</u> the statement of his brother.
A. confirmed B. disproved
C. condemned D. seconded

8. Whatever opinion he gives is <u>sane.</u>
A. rational B. obscure
C. wild D. arrogant

9. The story is too fantastic to be <u>credible.</u>
A. believable B. false
C. readable D. praiseworthy

10. Catching snakes can be <u>hazardous</u> for people untrained in the art.
A. tricky B. harmful
C. difficult D. dangerous

Selecting Words

Directions (Qs. No. 11 to 20) : *In this section, each of the following sentences has a blank space and four words are given after the sentence. Select whichever word you consider the most appropriate for the blank space and indicate your response on the Answer Sheet.*

11. You haven't had your lunch yet, ...you?
A. are B. aren't
C. have D. haven't

12. Life is to death as pleasure is to............ .
A. poverty B. suffering
C. anguish D. pain

13. The French .... reputed to have a very good sense of humour.
A. is B. was
C. are D. will be

14. 'Please' and 'Thank you' are the little courtesies by which we keep the .... of life oiled and running smoothly.
A. path B. machine
C. garden D. river

15. Many of the advances of civilization have been conceived by young people just on the .... of adulthood.
A. boundary B. threshold
C. peak D. horizon

16. The more your action and thought are allied and ...., the happier you grow.

A. divergent B. unraveled
C. integrated D. invincible

17. He .... in wearing the old-fashioned coat in spite of his wife's disapproval.
A. insists B. persists
C. desists D. resists

18. It is not what you say that ...., but what you do.
A. matches B. implies
C. matters D. moves

19. Physically we are now all neighbours, but psychologically we are .... to each other.
A. primitives B. complementary
C. strangers D. cowards

20. The old 'Nature' versus .... debate regarding crime continues even today.
A. 'Man' B. 'Universe'
C. 'Culture' D. 'Nurture'

Sentence Improvement

Directions (Qs. No. 21 to 30) : *In this section, look at the underlined part of each sentence. Below each sentence are given three possible substitutions for the underlined part. If one of them, i.e., A, B or C is better than the underlined part, indicate your response on the Answer Sheet against the corresponding letter A, B or C. If none of the substitutions improves the sentence, indicate D as your response on the Answer Sheet. Thus a 'No improvement' response will be signified by the letter D.*

21. As the parties failed to reach any agreement, the meeting broke through.
A. broke out B. broke away
C. broke up D. No improvement

22. If I have reached there by this time tomorrow, I will write to you immediately.
A. reached B. reach
C. am reaching D. No improvement

23. My friend met me, unexpectedly, when I looked for a taxi, desperately.
A. had looked B. was looking
C. had been looking D. No improvement

24. Her learning makes up towards her want of beauty.
A. for B. to
C. against D. No improvement

25. If he got his enemy in his hand, he would have crushed him to death.
A. has got B. was getting
C. had got D. No improvement

26. Please ask your son to turn off the radio so that it is not quite so loud.
A. in B. back
C. down D. No improvement

27. He said that when I have worked for him for six months I would get a pay rise.
A. had worked B. have had worked
C. did work D. No improvement

28. I am looking forward to joining your organization.
A. join B. join in
C. having joined D. No improvement

29. I am not sure why she is wanting to see him.
A. she wants B. is she wanting
C. she want D. No improvement

30. Everybody who finished writing can go home.
A. had finished B. have finished
C. has finished D. No improvement

Spotting Errors

Directions (Qs. No. 31 to 40) : *In this section, each question has a sentence with three underlined parts labelled A, B and C. Read each sentence to find out whether there is any error in any underlined part and indicate your response in the Answer Sheet against the corresponding letter, i.e., A or B or C. If you find 'No error', your response should be indicated as D.*

31. It was nearly thirty years ago, (A)/ since this magazine (B)/ was first published. (C)/ No error (D).

32. Ten years ago he was having an income (A)/ of over ten thousand rupees a month; (B)/ he must indeed be a wealthy man by now. (C)/ No error (D).

33. In spite of the fact (A)/ that the meeting was about to end, (B)/ he insisted to ask several questions. (C)/ No error (D).

34. Hardly had he entered into the room (A)/ and taken his seat, (B)/ when the girls began to giggle. (C)/ No error (D).

35. I was disappointed (A)/ when I came for seeing you last evening (B)/ but could not find you at home. (C)/ No error (D).

36. The number of jobs (A)/ that would be satisfactory in all respects (B)/ are small. (C)/ No error (D).

37. I have found the man (A)/ whom I know (B)/ is the thief. (C)/ No error (D).

38. There is no reason (A)/ why he should not come (B)/ since he is in town and is free. (C)/ No error (D).

39. It is high time (A)/ we cried a halt to the existing corrupt practices (B)/ followed in the educational sphere. (C)/ No error (D).

40. The situation is perilous (A)/ but if we are prepared promptly to act, (B)/ there is still one chance of escape. (C)/ No error (D).

Antonyms

Directions (Qs. No. 41 to 50) : *In this section, each item consists of a sentence with an underlined word. It is followed by four words, one of which is closest to the* **opposite** *in meaning of the underlined word. Choose the word and indicate your response in the Answer Sheet.*

41. His short but pointed speech was applauded by all sections of the audience.
A. disapproved B. misunderstood
C. praised D. welcomed

42. In ancient India, scholars had no interest in political power or material growth.
A. internal B. spiritual
C. psychic D. celestial

43. A friendly dog met us at the farm gate.
A. helpful B. understanding
C. quiet D. hostile

44. He is extremely intelligent but proud.
A. dull B. weak
C. ignorant D. arrogant

45. The young leader was reluctant to shoulder the responsibilities of the ministerial office.
A. wanting B. willing
C. anxious D. eager

46. He abandoned his family.
A. supported B. encouraged
C. pleased D. saved

47. History abounds in instances of courage.
A. shines B. lacks
C. suffices D. fails

48. Adversity teaches man to be humble and self-reliant.
A. Sincerity B. Animosity
C. Curiosity D. Prosperity

49. Like poverty, affluence can sometimes create its own problems.
A. indigence B. opulence
C. sorrow D. exuberance

50. The habit of squandering money should not be encouraged.
A. discarding B. hoarding
C. donating D. stealing

PART B : GENERAL KNOWLEDGE

51. Light waves are
A. electro-mechanical waves
B. electro-magnetic waves
C. electro-optical waves
D. magneto-optical waves

52. A sample of carbon dioxide that undergoes a transformation from solid to liquid and then to gas would undergo
A. a change in mass
B. a change in density
C. a change in composition
D. no change in physical properties

53. Which one of the following pairs of power projects is ***not*** correctly matched?
A. Papanasam—Hydropower
B. Neyveli—Hydropower
C. Ukai—Thermal power
D. Rana Pratap Sagar—Hydropower

54. A particle is moving in a circular path of radius r at a constant speed v. Which one of the following graphs correctly represents its acceleration a?

A. B.

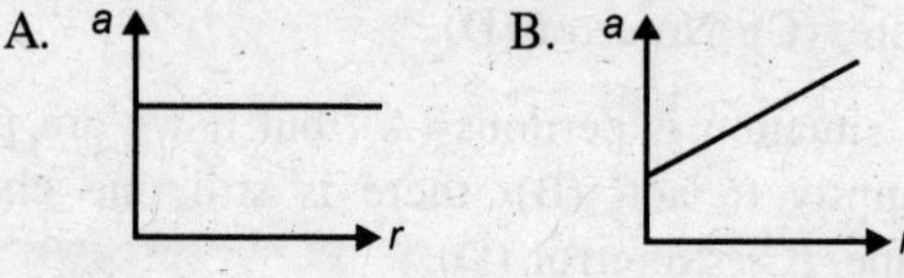

C. 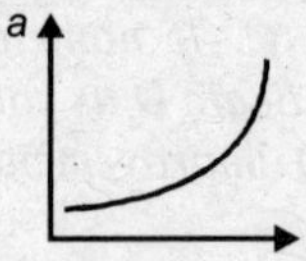 D.

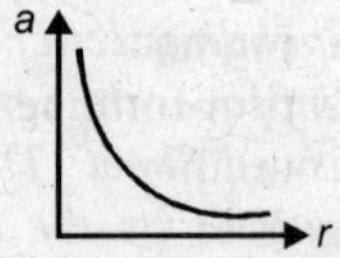

55. Which of the following element combinations will form ionic compounds?
1. Ca (Z = 20) and Ti (Z = 22)
2. Si (Z = 14) and Br (Z = 35)
3. Mg (Z = 12) and Cl (Z = 17)

Select the correct answer using the code given below.
A. 2 only B. 3 only
C. 2 and 3 only D. 1, 2 and 3

56. In the term GIS, 'G' stands for
A. Global B. Geographic
C. Goodness D. Geological

57. A thermodynamic process where no heat is exchanged with the surroundings is
A. isothermal B. adiabatic
C. isobaric D. isotropic

58. A compound X_2O_3 contains 31.58% oxygen by weight. The atomic mass of X is
A. 34.66 g mol^{-1} B. 45.01 g mol^{-1}
C. 52.00 g mol^{-1} D. 104.00 g mol^{-1}

59. Which one of the following is the eorrect sequence of oil refineries in India in respect of their time of establishment (starting from the earliest)?

A. Barauni—Haldia—Guwahati—Mathura
B. Barauni—Mathura—Guwahati—Haldia
C. Guwahati—Haldia—Mathura—Barauni
D. Guwahati—Barauni—Haldia—Mathura

60. Which one of the following circuit elements is an active component?
A. Resistor B. Transistor
C. Inductor D. Capacitor

61. Which one among the following contains the most neutrons?
A. $^{59}_{26}Fe$ B. $^{61}_{29}Cu$
C. $^{61}_{30}Zn$ D. $^{61}_{30}Zn^{2+}$

62. Movements of tides are mostly determined by
A. albedo effect
B. wind velocity
C. rotation of the Earth
D. revolution of the Earth

63. Fahrenheit and Celsius are the two scales used for measuring temperature. If the numerical value of a temperature recorded in both the scales is found to be same, what is the temperature?
A. – 40° B. + 40°
C. + 72° D. – 72°

64. Turpentine oil in paints is used as a
A. pigment
B. film-forming material
C. thinner
D. drier

65. Match List-I with List-II and select the correct answer using the code given below the Lists:

List-I (Textile industry)	***List-II (Place)***
(*a*) Woolen textile	1. Sualkuchi
(*b*) Cotton textile	2. Rishra
(*c*) Silk textile	3. Ludhiana
(*d*) Jute textile	4. Davangere

Code:

	(*a*)	(*b*)	(*c*)	(*d*)
A.	3	4	1	2
B.	2	1	4	3
C.	2	4	1	3
D.	3	1	4	2

66. Which one among the following is a plant hormone?
A. Insulin B. Thyroxin
C. Gibberellin D. Estrogen

67. Quartzite is metamorphosed from
A. limestone B. plutonic rock
C. sandstone D. shale

68. Which one of the following processes explains the splitting of a beam of white light into its constituent colours?
A. Dispersion B. Reflection
C. Diffraction D. Polarization

69. The very high heat of vaporization of water is mainly a result of
A. van der Waals forces
B. covalent bonds
C. interionic attraction
D. hydrogen bonding

70. Which of the following groups of plants can be used as indicators of SO_2 pollution of air?
A. Ferns B. Mentha
C. Lichens D. Hornworts

71. The permanent wind that blows from the horse latitude to the equatorial region is known as
A. westerly B. trade wind
C. doldrum D. easterly

72. Two bodies A and B having masses m and $4m$ respectively are moving with equal linear momentum. The ratio of kinetic energies between A and B is
A. 1 : 4 B. 4 : 1
C. 1 : 1 D. 1 : 2

73. Optical glass used in the construction of spectacles is made by
A. flint glass B. Crookes glass
C. quartz glass D. hard glass

74. Which one of the following cell organelles is absent in animal cell?
A. Cell membrane B. Endoplasmic reticulum
C. Cell wall D. Mitochondria

75. Which one of the following is a warm ocean current?
A. Labrador current B. Kuroshio current
C. Peru current D. Benguela current

76. A force applied on a body is represented as

$$\vec{F} = 6\hat{i} - 8\hat{j} + 10\hat{k}$$

and accelerates it at 1 m/s². The mass of the body is
A. 10 kg B. $10\sqrt{2}$ kg
C. $2\sqrt{10}$ kg D. 8 kg

77. The burning sensation of a beesting can be stopped by rubbing the affected area with soap. This is because
A. a beesting is acidic and soap, an alkali, neutralizes it
B. a beesting is alkaline and soap, an acid, neutralizes it
C. soap cleans the affected area and removes the sting
D. soap acts as an anesthetic and dulls the sensation

78. Consider the following statements:
1. Carbohydrates are the only source of energy to humans.

2. Fats give maximum energy on oxidation as compared to other foods.

Which of the statements given above is/are correct?
A. 1 only B. 2 only
C. Both 1 and 2 D. Neither 1 nor 2

79. The place located at the confluence of Alaknanda and Bhagirathi rivers is
A. Badrinath B. Rishikesh
C. Rudraprayag D. Devprayag

80. Which one of the following is ***not*** a function of Liver?
A. Conversion of glucose into glycogen
B. Production of urea
C. Destruction of dead and wornout red blood cells
D. Absorption of food and excess water from the undigested food

81. Which one of the following is the correct sequence of economic sectors in terms of their contribution to the GDP of India in decreasing order?
A. Service—Industry—Agriculture
B. Agriculture—Industry—Service
C. Industry—Service—Agriculture
D. Agriculture—Service—Industry

82. A force $\vec{F}$, acting on an electric charge q, in presence of an electromagnetic field, moves the charge parallel to the magnetic field with velocity $\vec{v}$. Then $\vec{F}$ is equal to (where $\vec{E}$ and $\vec{B}$ are electric field and magnetic field respectively)
A. $q\vec{E}$ B. $q(\vec{v}\times\vec{B})$
C. $q(\vec{v}\times\vec{E})$ D. $q\vec{B}$

83. What is the oxidizing agent in the following equation?

$$HAsO_2\,(aq) + Sn^{2+}\,(aq) + H^+\,(aq) \rightarrow As\,(s) + Sn^{4+}\,(aq) + H_2O\,(l)$$

A. $HAsO_2$ (aq) B. Sn^{2+} (aq)
C. H^+ (aq) D. Sn^{4+} (aq)

84. Which one of the following is not a part of female reproductive system?
A. Fallopian tube B. Cervix
C. Urethra D. Vagina

85. If a news is broadcast from London at 1 : 45 p.m. on Monday, at what time and on what day it will be heard at Dhaka (90° E)?
A. 7 : 45 p.m. on Monday
B. 7 : 45 a.m. on Monday
C. 7 : 45 p.m. on Tuesday
D. 7 : 45 a.m. on Sunday

86. Which of the following are the correct parameters for the common domestic power supply in India?
A. 220 V, 110 Hz B. 220 V, 50 Hz
C. 110 V, 220 Hz D. 110 V, 50 Hz

87. Which one of the following substances is most likely to be used as soap?
A. $CH_3\,(CH_2)_{12}COOCH_3$
B. $CH_3\,(CH_2)_5O(CH_2)_5CH_3$
C. $CH_3\,(CH_2)_{12}COONa$
D. $CH_3\,(CH_2)_{12}\,CHCl_2$

88. Which one of the following animals is cold-blooded?
A. Dolphin B. Shark
C. Whale D. Porpoise

89. Match List-I with List-II and select the correct answer using the code given below the Lists:

List-I (Geographical feature)	***List-II (Type of geographic process)***
(*a*) Cirque	1. Erosional feature of wind
(*b*) Yardang	2. Depositional feature of glacier
(*c*) Barkhan	3. Depositional feature of wind
(*d*) Drumlin	4. Erosional feature of glacier

Code:

	(*a*)	(*b*)	(*c*)	(*d*)
A.	4	1	3	2
B.	4	3	1	2
C.	2	3	1	4
D.	2	1	3	4

90. A ray of light travels from a medium of refractive index n_1 to a medium of refractive index n_2. If angle of incidence is i and angle of refraction is r, then $\frac{\sin i}{\sin r}$ is equal to
A. n_1 B. n_2
C. $\frac{n_2}{n_1}$ D. $\frac{n_1}{n_2}$

91. A sample of gas is to be identified by means of its behaviour in the presence of a glowing splint. Which of the following gases will neither itself burn nor cause the splint to burn?
A. Oxygen B. Nitrogen
C. Hydrogen D. Methane

92. Leprosy is caused by
A. virus B. bacteria
C. protozoa D. retrovirus

93. A topographical map with scale 1 : 50000 indicates 1 cm to
A. 50 km B. 500 m
C. 50 m D. 5 km

94. Light waves projected on oil surface show seven colours due to the phenomenon of
A. polarization B. refraction
C. reflection D. interference

95. A monatomic species that has 18 electrons and a net charge of 2^- has
A. the same number of electrons as a neutral argon atom
B. more protons than electrons
C. 2 unpaired electrons
D. 20 protons

96. Consider the following statements about Indian Regional Navigation Satellite System (IRNSS) :
1. IRNSS is a constellation of five satellites, which were launched by PSLV.
2. It is an independent regional navigation satellite system designed to provide position information in the Indian region.

Which of the statements given above is/are correct?
A. 1 only B. 2 only
C. Both 1 and 2 D. Neither 1 nor 2

97. The National Defence Academy has foreign cadets from which of the following countries?
1. Bhutan 2. Bangladesh
3. Nepal 4. Afghanistan

Select the correct answer using the code given below.
A. 1, 2, 3 and 4 B. 1, 3 and 4 only
C. 3 and 4 only D. None of these

98. From which one among the following countries has India recently (May 2014) recalled its troops, who went for a joint combat exercise in the country?
A. Malaysia B. Thailand
C. Egypt D. Singapore

99. Who among the following was associated with the formulation of the basic ideas of the *Mahayana* Buddhism?
A. Nagarjuna B. Kashyapa Matanga
C. Menander D. Kanishka

100. Consider the following statements about Harappan Culture :
1. The Harappan Culture matured in Sind and Punjab.
2. It spread from there to Southwards and Eastwards.
3. The area, where it spread, was bigger than Egypt and Mesopotamia.

Which of the statements given above is/ are correct?
A. 1 and 2 only B. 2 and 3 only
C. 3 only D. None of these

101. Megasthenes was a
A. Greek ambassador to the court of Chandragupta Maurya
B. Greek trader during Ashoka's time
C. Greek trader in the Gupta period
D. Chinese pilgrim during Harsha's time

102. By the late 19th century, India was one of the largest producers and exporters of
A. cotton yarn and wheat
B. sugar and rice
C. sugar and alcohol
D. iron and steel

103. Which one of the following is the correct sequence of appearance of the poet-saints of the Bhakti-Sufi tradition?
A. Basavanna—Appar—Mira Bai—**Lal Ded**
B. Appar—Mira Bai—Lal Ded—Basavanna
C. Appar—Basavanna—Lal Ded—Mira Bai
D. Basavanna—Mira Bai—Lal Ded—Appar

104. Who among the following did not bring trading ships to the port of Surat in pre-British times?
A. Portuguese and English
B. Russian and German
C. English and Arab
D. French and Arab

105. The Factory Act of 1891 in India was enacted to
A. improve the condition of labour in India
B. ensure greater governmental control over industry in India
C. provide a level playing field for English manufacturers
D. enable greater political control over Indian industry

106. Which of the following statements is correct?
A. The Presiding Officer of the Rajya Sabha is elected every year
B. The Presiding Officer of the Rajya Sabha is elected for a term of 5 years
C. The Presiding Officer of the Rajya Sabha is elected for a term of 6 years
D. The Vice President of India is the Ex Officio Presiding Officer of the Rajya Sabha

107. Who among the following was not a member of the Drafting Committee of the Constitution of India?
A. B. R. Ambedkar
B. K. M. Munshi
C. Krishnaswamy Iyer
D. M. K. Gandhi

108. Who among the following was not a member of the 'Big Four' in the Congress of Vienna (1815)?
A. Great Britain B. Russia
C. Austria D. France

109. The Stamp Act Congress consisting of delegates from nine of the thirteen colonies met in 1765 at
A. Philadelphia B. New York City
C. Boston D. Providence

110. Which of the following American colonies did not attend the first Continental Congress held in Philadelphia?
A. Rhode Island B. Connecticut
C. Georgia D. Maryland

111. The Bolshevik Revolution started in Russia during the reign of

A. Czar Alexander I
B. Czar Alexander II
C. Czar Alexander III
D. Czar Nicholas II

112. Which of the following is/are not related to fundamental duties?

1. To cherish and follow the noble ideals which inspired our national struggle for freedom
2. To value and preserve the rich heritage of our composite culture
3. To promote the educational and economic interests of the weaker sections of the people, especially the Scheduled Castes and Scheduled Tribes
4. To protect all monuments of historic interest and national importance

Select the correct answer using the code given below.

A. 1 and 2 B. 2 and 3
C. 3 and 4 D. 4 only

113. Joint sittings of the two Houses of Indian Parliament are held to

A. elect the President of India
B. elect the Vice President of India
C. adopt a Constitution Amendment Bill
D. consider and pass a Bill on which the two Houses disagree

114. The President of India can issue proclamation of Emergency

A. on the advice of the Prime Minister
B. on the advice of the Council of Ministers
C. in his own discretion
D. when the decision of the Union Cabinet for the issue of such proclamation has been communicated to him in writing

115. Which of the following statements is/are correct about the working of the Permanent Settlement in Bengal?

1. The traditional Zamindars lost their lands.
2. The reason for the Zamindars' inability to pay up land revenues was that the Ryots defaulted on payment of revenue.
3. A new group of farmers–the Jotedars–became influential.
4. The Collector replaced the Zamindars as the alternative focus of authority.

Select the correct answer using the code given below.

A. 1 only B. 1 and 4 only
C. 2 and 3 only D. 1, 2, 3 and 4

Directions : *The following seven (7) items consist of two statements, Statement I and Statement II. You are to examine these two statements carefully and select the answers to these items using the code given below :*

Code:

A. Both the statements are individually true and Statement II is the correct explanation of Statement I
B. Both the statements are individually true but Statement II is not the correct explanation of Statement I
C. Statement I is true but Statement II is false
D. Statement I is false but Statement II is true

116. **Statement I :** Grand Banks are one of the major fishing grounds of the world due to the presence of a vast continental shelf.
Statement II : Planktons grow in the shallow waters.

117. **Statement I :** Amoeba is a unicellular organism and the single cell performs all functions of a living organism.
Statement II : Cell is the fundamental unit of living organism.

118. **Statement I :** The first coins to bear the names and images of rulers were issued by the Kushanas.
Statement II : The first gold coins were issued by the Kushanas.

119. **Statement I :** Jahandar Shah's reign came to an early end in January 1713.
Statement II : He was defeated at Agra by Farrukhsiyar, his nephew.

120. **Statement I :** The defects of the Regulating Act and the exigencies of British politics necessitated the passing of the Pitt's India Act.
Statement II : The Pitt's India Act gave the British Government supreme control over the Company's affairs and its administration in India.

121. **Statement I :** It is not necessary that every bar magnet has one North Pole and one South Pole.
Statement II : Magnetic poles occur in pair.

122. **Statement I :** A body moving in a circular path is acted upon by the centripetal force.
Statement II : Centripetal force acting on the body is doing work to keep it rotating in the circular path.

123. Which of the following statements is/are correct?

1. The tropical cyclones of China Sea are called typhoons.
2. The tropical cyclones of the West Indies are called tornadoes.
3. The tropical cyclones of Australia are called willy-willies.
4. Formation of an anticyclone results in stormy weather condition.

Select the correct answer using the code given below.

A. 1, 2, 3 and 4 B. 1, 2 and 4 only
C. 1 and 3 only D. 3 only

124. Which one of the following is ***not*** an ASEAN member?
A. Cambodia B. Laos
C. Myanmar D. Taiwan

125. Heat given to a body which raises its temperature by 1° C is known as
A. water equivalent
B. thermal capacity
C. specific heat
D. temperature gradient

126. Consider the following reaction :
$x As_2S_3 + y O_2 \rightarrow z As_2O_3 + w SO_2$
What is y (the coefficient for O_2) when this equation is balanced using whole number coefficients?
A. 5 B. 7
C. 9 D. 11

127. Growth and repair of damaged tissue involve
A. mitotic cell division only
B. both mitotic and meiotic cell divisions
C. meiotic cell division only
D. amitotic cell division only

128. Rotterdam of Netherlands is largely famous for
A. textiles B. dairying
C. shipbuilding D. paper industry

129. If the motion of an object is represented by a straight line parallel to the time axis in a distance-time graph, then the object undergoes
A. an accelerated motion
B. a decelerated motion
C. a uniform non-zero velocity motion
D. a zero velocity motion

130. How many grams of $MgCO_3$ contain 24.00 g of oxygen? (The molar mass of $MgCO_3$ is 84.30 g mol^{-1})
A. 42.15 g B. 84.30 g
C. 126.00 g D. 154.00 g

131. Kerosene oil rises in a wick of lantern because of
A. buoyancy of air
B. diffusion of the oil through the wick
C. capillary action in the wick
D. gravitational pull of the wick

132. If the reaction of 1.0 mol NH_3 (g) and 1.0 mol O_2 (g)
$4NH_3 (g) + 5O_2 (g) \rightarrow 4NO (g) + 6H_2O (l)$
is carried to completion, then
A. all the O_2 (g) is consumed
B. 4.0 mol NO (g) is produced
C. 1.5 mol H_2O (l) is produced
D. all the NH_3 (g) is consumed

133. Which of the following sequences is correct for rainfall?
A. Slow ascent of air → slow condensation → heavy downpour
B. Rapid ascent of air → large raindrops → heavy downpour
C. Pressure decreased → air compressed → heavy downpour
D. Descent of air → air warmed → heavy downpour

134. The working of a microwave oven involves
A. absorption of microwaves by matter
B. reception of microwaves by optical fibre
C. microwave amplification by stimulated emission of radiation
D. transmission of microwaves through a metal

135. What would be the total population at the end of the year if population at the beginning of the year is 5000 and population changed during the year is– birth 250, death 60, immigration 30 and emigration 15?
A. 5205 B. 5235
C. 5310 D. 5180

136. Two cars A and B have masses m_A and m_B respectively, with $m_A > m_B$. Both the cars are moving in the same direction with equal kinetic energy. If equal braking force is applied on both, then before coming to rest
A. A will cover a greater distance
B. B will cover a greater distance
C. both will cover the same distance
D. distance covered by them will depend on their respective velocities

137. If the length of the Equator is about 40000 km and the velocity of rotation is about 1700 km per hour, what would be the velocity of rotation at the Pole?
A. Zero B. 850 km/hr
C. 1700 km/hr D. 3400 km/hr

138. A bullet is fired vertically up from a 400 m tall tower with a speed 80 m/s. If g is taken as 10 m/s², the time taken by the bullet to reach the ground will be
A. 8 s B. 16 s
C. 20 s D. 24 s

139. A cyclotron accelerates particles of mass m and charge q. The energy of particles emerging is proportional to
A. $\frac{q^2}{m}$ B. $\frac{q}{m^2}$
C. $\frac{q^2}{m^2}$ D. q

140. The electric field inside a perfectly conducting hollow object is
A. 4π
B. infinite
C. zero
D. dependent upon the shape of the object

141. The densities of three liquids are D, 2D and 3D. What will be the density of the resulting mixture if equal volumes of the three liquids are mixed?

A. 6 D B. 1.4 D
C. 2 D D. 3 D

142. A particle is moving with uniform acceleration along a straight line ABC, where AB = BC. The average velocity of the particle from A to B is 10 m/s and from B to C is 15 m/s. The average velocity for the whole journey from A to C in m/s is

A. 12 B. 12.5
C. 13 D. 13.5

143. The dimension of 'impulse' is the same as that of

A. pressure
B. angular momentum
C. work
D. linear momentum

144. Consider the following statements :

1. China won both Thomas Cup and Uber Cup Badminton Tournaments, 2014.
2. The Uber Cup is the World Team Championship for women and the Thomas Cup is for men.

Which of the statements given above is/are correct?

A. 1 only
B. 2 only
C. Both 1 and 2
D. Neither 1 nor 2

145. Consider the following statements about Drishti system :

1. It is a sophisticated instrument to assess the runway visual range.
2. This system is developed by Airports Authority of India.

Which of the statements given above is/are correct?

A. 1 only B. 2 only
C. Both 1 and 2 D. Neither 1 nor 2

146. Which of the following about Malavath Poorna is correct?

A. First Indian swimmer to cross Suez Canal
B. Youngest woman to scale Everest
C. First Indian to win FIDE World Junior Championship
D. Winner of Young Scientist Award, 2014

147. Which one among the following countries was the top contributor to India's FDI for the year 2013-14?

A. Mauritius B. Singapore
C. USA D. Japan

148. Which of the following statements about SIMBEX 14 is/are correct?

1. It was a bilateral naval exercise between Indian navy and Sri Lankan navy.
2. It was the 21st in the series.
3. It was conducted in the Andaman Sea.

Select the correct answer using the code given below.

A. 1, 2 and 3 B. 2 and 3 only
C. 2 only D. 1 and 3 only

149. Consider the following statements :

1. *Mobile Seva,* the National Mobile Governance Initiative of Department of Electronics and Information Technology of India, has won the United Nations Public Service Award, 2014.
2. The innovative initiative is aimed at mainstreaming mobile governance in the country.

Which of the statements given above is/are correct?

A. 1 only B. 2 only
C. Both 1 and 2 D. Neither 1 nor 2

150. Consider the following statements about Prithvi-II Missile :

1. It is a nuclear-capable ballistic missile.
2. It has a maximum range of 100 km.
3. It is India's first native made ballistic missile.

Which of the statements given above is/are correct?

A. 1, 2 and 3 B. 1 only
C. 1 and 3 only D. 2 and 3 only

PAPER II : MATHEMATICS

Directions (Qs. No. 1 to 3): *For the next three questions that follow:*

Consider the function $f(x) = \begin{cases} x^2 - 5, & x \le 3 \\ \sqrt{x+13}, & x > 3 \end{cases}$

1. What is $\lim_{x \to 3} f(x)$ equal to?

A. 2 B. 4
C. 5 D. 13

2. Consider the following statements:

1. The function is discontinuous at $x = 3$.
2. The function is not differentiable at $x = 0$.

Which of the above statements is/are correct?

A. 1 only B. 2 only
C. Both 1 and 2 D. Neither 1 nor 2

3. What is the differential coefficient of $f(x)$ at $x = 12$?

A. $\frac{5}{2}$ B. 5
C. $\frac{1}{5}$ D. $\frac{1}{10}$

Directions (Qs. No. 4 to 6): *For the next three questions that follow:*

The line $2y = 3x + 12$ cuts the parabola $4y = 3x^2$.

4. Where does the line cut the parabola?
A. At (–2, 3) only
B. At (4, 12) only
C. At both (–2, 3) and (4, 12)
D. Neither at (–2, 3) nor at (4, 12)

5. What is the area enclosed by the parabola and line?
A. 27 square unit B. 36 square unit
C. 48 square unit D. 54 square unit

6. What is the area enclosed by the parabola, the line and the y-axis in the first quadrant?
A. 7 square unit B. 14 square unit
C. 20 square unit D. 21 square unit

7. Consider the function

$$f(x) = \begin{cases} \dfrac{\tan kx}{x}, & x < 0 \\ 3x + 2k^2, & x \geq 0 \end{cases}$$

What is the non-zero value of k for which the function is continuous at $x = 0$?
A. $\frac{1}{4}$ B. $\frac{1}{2}$
C. 1 D. 2

8. Consider the following statements:
1. The function $f(x) = [x]$, where [.] is the greatest integer function defined on **R**, is continuous at all points *except* at $x = 0$.
2. The function $f(x) = \sin|x|$ is continuous for all $x \in$ **R**.

Which of the above statements is/are correct?
A. 1 only B. 2 only
C. Both 1 and 2 D. Neither 1 nor 2

Directions (Qs. No. 9 and 10): *For the next two questions that follow:*

Consider the curve $x = a(\cos\theta + \theta\sin\theta)$ and $y = a(\sin\theta - \theta\cos\theta)$.

9. What is $\frac{dy}{dx}$ equal to?
A. $\tan\theta$ B. $\cot\theta$
C. $\sin 2\theta$ D. $\cos 2\theta$

10. What is $\frac{d^2y}{dx^2}$ equal to?
A. $\sec^2\theta$ B. $-\text{cosec}^2\theta$
C. $\frac{\sec^3\theta}{a\theta}$ D. None of these

11. What is the area of the parabola $y^2 = 4bx$ bounded by its latus rectum?
A. $\frac{2b^2}{3}$ square unit B. $\frac{4b^2}{3}$ square unit
C. b^2 square unit D. $\frac{8b^2}{3}$ square unit

12. If $y = x \ln x + xe^x$, then what is the value of $\frac{dy}{dx}$ at $x = 1$?
A. $1 + e$ B. $1 - e$
C. $1 + 2e$ D. None of these

13. What is $\lim_{x\to 0} \frac{\log_5(1+x)}{x}$ equal to?
A. 1 B. $\log_5 e$
C. $\log_e 5$ D. 5

14. What is $\lim_{x\to 0} \frac{5^x - 1}{x}$ equal to?
A. $\log_e 5$ B. $\log_5 e$
C. 5 D. 1

15. What is $\lim_{n\to\infty} \frac{1+2+3+...+n}{1^2+2^2+3^2+...n^2}$ equal to?
A. 5 B. 2
C. 1 D. 0

Directions (Qs. No. 16 and 17): *For the next two questions that follow:*

Let S_n denote the sum of first n terms of an AP and $3S_n = S_{2n}$.

16. What is $S_{3n} : S_n$ equal to?
A. 4 : 1 B. 6 : 1
C. 8 : 1 D. 10 : 1

17. What is $S_{3n} : S_{2n}$ equal to ?
A. 2 : 1 B. 3 : 1
C. 4 : 1 D. 5 : 1

18. What is the length of the latus rectum of the ellipse $25x^2 + 16y^2 = 400$?
A. $\frac{25}{2}$ B. $\frac{25}{4}$
C. $\frac{16}{5}$ D. $\frac{32}{5}$

Directions (Qs. No. 19 and 20): *For the next two questions that follow:*

Consider the circles $x^2 + y^2 + 2ax + c = 0$ and $x^2 + y^2 + 2by + c = 0$.

19. What is the distance between the centres of the two circles?
A. $\sqrt{a^2+b^2}$ B. $a^2 + b^2$
C. $a + b$ D. $2(a + b)$

20. The two circles touch each other if

A. $c = \sqrt{a^2 + b^2}$ B. $\frac{1}{c} = \frac{1}{a^2} + \frac{1}{b^2}$

C. $c = \frac{1}{a^2} + \frac{1}{b^2}$ D. $c = \frac{1}{a^2 + b^2}$

21. A(3, 4) and B(5, –2) are two points and P is a point such that PA = PB. If the area of triangle PAB is 10 square unit, what are the coordinates of P?
A. (1, 0) only B. (7, 2) only
C. (1, 0) or (7, 2) D. Neither (1, 0) nor (7, 2)

22. What is the product of the perpendiculars drawn from the points $\left(\pm\sqrt{a^2 - b^2}, 0\right)$ upon the line $bx \cos \alpha + ay \sin \alpha = ab$?
A. a^2 B. b^2
C. $a^2 + b^2$ D. $a + b$

23. Which one of the following is correct in respect of the equations $\frac{x-1}{2} = \frac{y-2}{3}$ and $2x + 3y = 5$?
A. They represent two lines which are parallel
B. They represent two lines which are perpendicular
C. They represent two lines which are neither parallel nor perpendicular
D. The first equation does not represent a line

Directions (Qs. No. 24 to 26): *For the next three questions that follow:*

Consider a sphere passing through the origin and the points (2, 1, –1), (1, 5, –4), (–2, 4, –6).

24. What is the radius of the sphere?

A. $\sqrt{12}$ B. $\sqrt{14}$
C. 12 D. 14

25. What is the centre of the sphere?
A. (–1, 2, –3) B. (1, –2, 3)
C. (1, 2, –3) D. (–1, –2, –3)

26. Consider the following statements:
1. The sphere passes through the point (0, 4, 0).
2. The point (1, 1, 1) is at a distance of 5 unit from the centre of the sphere.

Which of the above statements is/are correct?
A. 1 only B. 2 only
C. Both 1 and 2 D. Neither 1 nor 2

Directions (Qs. No. 27 and 28): *For the next two questions that follow:*

The line joining the points (2, 1, 3) and (4, –2, 5) cuts the plane $2x + y - z = 3$.

27. Where does the line cut the plane?
A. (0, –4, –1) B. (0, –4, 1)
C. (1, 4, 0) D. (0, 4, 1)

28. What is the ratio in which the plane divides the line?
A. 1 : 1 B. 2 : 3
C. 3 : 4 D. None of the above

Directions (Qs. No. 29 and 30): *For the next two questions that follow:*

Consider the plane passing through the points A(2, 2, 1), B(3, 4, 2) and C(7, 0, 6).

29. Which one of the following points lies on the plane?
A. (1, 0, 0) B. (1, 0, 1)
C. (0, 0, 1) D. None of these

30. What are the direction ratios of the normal to the plane?
A. < 1, 0, 1 > B. < 0, 1, 0 >
C. < 1, 0, –1 > D. None of these

31. The function $f : N \to N$, N being the set of natural numbers, defined by $f(x) = 2x + 3$ is
A. injective and surjective
B. injective but not surjective
C. not injective but surjective
D. neither injective nor surjective

32. What is $\frac{(1+i)^{4n+5}}{(1-i)^{4n+3}}$ equal to, where n is a natural number and $i = \sqrt{-1}$?
A. 2 B. $2i$
C. $-2i$ D. i

33. What is the number of ways in which one can post 5 letters in 7 letter boxes?
A. 7^5 B. 3^5
C. 5^7 D. 2520

34. What is the number of ways that a cricket team of 11 players can be made out of 15 players?
A. 364 B. 1001
C. 1365 D. 32760

35. A and B are two sets having 3 elements in common. If $n(A) = 5$, $n(B) = 4$, then what is $n(A \times B)$ equal to?
A. 0 B. 9
C. 15 D. 20

36. If $f(x) = ax + b$ and $g(x) = cx + d$ such that $f(g(x)) = g(f(x))$, then which one of the following is correct?
A. $f(c) = g(a)$ B. $f(a) = g(c)$
C. $f(c) = g(d)$ D. $f(d) = g(b)$

37. If A and B are square matrices of second order such that $|A| = -1$, $|B| = 3$, then what is $|3AB|$ equal to?
A. 3 B. –9
C. –27 D. None of these

Directions (Qs. No. 38 to 40): *For the next three questions that follow:*

Consider the function $f(x) = \frac{x-1}{x+1}$.

38. What is $\frac{f(x)+1}{f(x)-1}+x$ equal to?

A. 0 B. 1
C. $2x$ D. $4x$

39. What is $f(2x)$ equal to?

A. $\frac{f(x)+1}{f(x)+3}$ B. $\frac{f(x)+1}{3f(x)+1}$

C. $\frac{3f(x)+1}{f(x)+3}$ D. $\frac{f(x)+3}{3f(x)+1}$

40. What is $f(f(x))$ equal to?

A. x B. $-x$

C. $-\frac{1}{x}$ D. None of these

Directions (Qs. No. 41 and 45): *For the next five questions that follow:*

Consider the expansion $\left(x^2+\frac{1}{x}\right)^{15}$.

41. What is the independent term in the given expansion?

A. 2103 B. 3003
C. 4503 D. None of these

42. What is the ratio of coefficient of x^{15} to the term independent of x in the given expansion?

A. 1 B. $\frac{1}{2}$

C. $\frac{2}{3}$ D. $\frac{3}{4}$

43. Consider the following statements:
1. There are 15 terms in the given expansion.
2. The coefficient of x^{12} is equal to that of x^3.

Which of the above statements is/are correct?

A. 1 only B. 2 only
C. Both 1 and 2 D. Neither 1 nor 2

44. Consider the following statements:
1. The term containing x^2 does not exist in the given expansion.
2. The sum of the coefficients of all the terms in the given expansion is 2^{15}.

Which of the above statements is/are correct?

A. 1 only B. 2 only
C. Both 1 and 2 D. Neither 1 nor 2

45. What is the sum of the coefficients of the middle terms in the given expansion?

A. C(15, 9) B. C(16, 9)
C. C(16, 8) D. None of these

46. Suppose A and B are two events. Event B has occurred and it is known that P(B) < 1. What is $P(A|B^c)$ equal to?

A. $\frac{P(A)-P(B)}{1-P(B)}$ B. $\frac{P(A)-P(AB)}{1-P(B)}$

C. $\frac{P(A)+P(B^c)}{1-P(B)}$ D. None of these

Directions (Qs. No. 47 to 50): *For the next four questions that follow:*

Consider events A, B, C, D, E of the sample space S = (n : n is an integer such that $10 \le n \le 20$) given by:

A is the set of all even numbers.

B is the set of all prime numbers.

C = {15}.

D is the set of all integers ≤ 16.

E is the set of all double digit numbers expressible as a power of 2.

47. A, B and D are

A. Mutually exclusive events but not exhaustive events
B. Exhaustive events but not mutually exclusive events
C. Mutually exclusive and exhaustive events
D. Elementary events

48. A, B and C are

A. Mutually exclusive events but not exhaustive events
B. Exhaustive events but not mutually exclusive events
C. Mutually exclusive and exhaustive events
D. Elementary events

49. B and C are

A. Mutually exclusive events but not exhaustive events
B. Compound events
C. Mutually exclusive and exhaustive events
D. Elementary events

50. C and E are

A. Mutually exclusive events but not elementary events
B. Exhaustive events but not mutually exclusive events
C. Mutually exclusive and exhaustive events
D. Elementary and mutually exclusive events

51. Consider the following statements in respect of histogram:
1. The histogram is a suitable representation of a frequency distribution of a continuous variable.
2. The area included under the whole histogram is the total frequency.

Which of the above statements is/are correct?

A. 1 only B. 2 only
C. Both 1 and 2 D. Neither 1 nor 2

52. The regression lines will be perpendicular to each other if the coefficient of correlation r is equal to

A. 1 only B. 1 or –1
C. –1 only D. 0

53. For any two events A and B, which one of the following holds?

A. $P(A \cap B) \leq P(A) \leq P(A \cup B) \leq P(A) + P(B)$
B. $P(A \cup B) \leq P(A) \leq P(A \cap B) \leq P(A) + P(B)$
C. $P(A \cup B) \leq P(B) \leq P(A \cap B) \leq P(A) + P(B)$
D. $P(A \cap B) \leq P(B) \leq P(A) + P(B) \leq P(A \cup B)$

54. The probability that in a random arrangement of the letters of the word 'UNIVERSITY' the two I's do ***not*** come together is

A. $\frac{4}{5}$ B. $\frac{1}{5}$
C. $\frac{1}{10}$ D. $\frac{9}{10}$

55. There are 4 white and 3 black balls in a box. In another box, there are 3 white and 4 black balls. An unbiased dice is rolled. If it shows a number less than or equal to 3, then a ball is drawn from the second box, otherwise from the first box. If the ball drawn is black, then the probability that the ball was drawn from the first box is

A. $\frac{1}{2}$ B. $\frac{6}{7}$
C. $\frac{4}{7}$ D. $\frac{3}{7}$

56. If $\bar{x}$ and $\bar{y}$ are the means of two distributions such that $\bar{x} < \bar{y}$ and $\bar{z}$ is the mean of the combined distribution, then which one of the following statements is correct?

A. $\bar{x} < \bar{y} < \bar{z}$ B. $\bar{x} > \bar{y} > \bar{z}$
C. $\bar{z} = \frac{\bar{x}+\bar{y}}{2}$ D. $\bar{x} < \bar{z} < \bar{y}$

57. What is the mean deviation about the mean for the data 4, 7, 8, 9, 10, 12, 13, 17 ?

A. 2.5 B. 3
C. 3.5 D. 4

58. The variance of 20 observations is 5. If each observation is multiplied by 2, then what is the new variance of the resulting observations?

A. 5 B. 10
C. 20 D. 40

59. Two students X and Y appeared in an examination. The probability that X will qualify the examination is 0.05 and Y will qualify the examination is 0.10. The probability that both will qualify the examination is 0.02. What is the probability that only one of them will qualify the examination?

A. 0.15 B. 0.14
C. 0.12 D. 0.11

60. A fair coin is tossed four times. What is the probability that at most three tails occur?

A. $\frac{7}{8}$ B. $\frac{15}{16}$
C. $\frac{13}{16}$ D. $\frac{3}{4}$

61. What is $\sqrt{1+\sin 2\theta}$ equal to?

A. $\cos\theta - \sin\theta$ B. $\cos\theta + \sin\theta$
C. $2\cos\theta + \sin\theta$ D. $\cos\theta + 2\sin\theta$

62. A lamp post stands on a horizontal plane. From a point situated at a distance 150 m from its foot, the angle of elevation of the top is 30°. What is the height of the lamp post?

A. 50 m B. $50\sqrt{3}$ m
C. $\frac{50}{\sqrt{3}}$ m D. 100 m

63. If cot A = 2 and cot B = 3, then what is the value of A + B?

A. $\frac{\pi}{6}$ B. π
C. $\frac{\pi}{2}$ D. $\frac{\pi}{4}$

64. What is $\sin^2 66\frac{1}{2}^\circ - \sin^2 23\frac{1}{2}^\circ$ equal to?

A. sin 47° B. cos 47°
C. 2 sin 47° D. 2 cos 47°

65. What is $\sin^{-1}\frac{3}{5} + \sin^{-1}\frac{4}{5}$ equal to?

A. $\frac{\pi}{2}$ B. $\frac{\pi}{3}$
C. $\frac{\pi}{4}$ D. $\frac{\pi}{6}$

66. What is $\frac{\cos 7x - \cos 3x}{\sin 7x - 2\sin 5x + \sin 3x}$ equal to?

A. $\tan x$ B. $\cot x$
C. $\tan 2x$ D. $\cot 2x$

67. In a triangle ABC, $c = 2$, A = 45°, $a = 2\sqrt{2}$, then what is C equal to?

A. 30° B. 15°
C. 45° D. None of these

68. In a triangle ABC, sin A – cos B = cos C, then what is B euqal to?

A. π
B. $\frac{\pi}{3}$

C. $\frac{\pi}{2}$
D. $\frac{\pi}{4}$

69. If $\frac{\sin(x+y)}{\sin(x-y)} = \frac{a+b}{a-b}$, then what is $\frac{\tan x}{\tan y}$ equal to?

A. $\frac{b}{a}$
B. $\frac{a}{b}$
C. ab
D. 1

70. If sin A sin (60° – A) sin (60° + A) = k sin 3A, then what is k equal to?

A. $\frac{1}{4}$
B. $\frac{1}{2}$
C. 1
D. 4

71. The line $y = \sqrt{3}$ meets the graph $y = \tan x$, where $x \in \left(0, \frac{\pi}{2}\right)$, in k points. What is k equal to?

A. One
B. Two
C. Three
D. Infinity

72. Which one of the following is one of the solutions of the equation tan 2θ. tan θ = 1?

A. $\frac{\pi}{12}$
B. $\frac{\pi}{6}$
C. $\frac{\pi}{4}$
D. $\frac{\pi}{3}$

Directions (Qs. No. 73 to 75): *For the next three questions that follow:*

Given that $16 \sin^5 x = p \sin 5x + q \sin 3x + r \sin x$.

73. What is the value of p ?

A. 1
B. 2
C. –1
D. –2

74. What is the value of q?

A. 3
B. 5
C. 10
D. –5

75. What is the value of r?

A. 5
B. 8
C. 10
D. –10

76. If $|\vec{a}| = 2$, $|\vec{b}| = 5$ and $|\vec{a} \times \vec{b}| = 8$, then what is $\vec{a} \cdot \vec{b}$ equal to?

A. 6
B. 7
C. 8
D. 9

77. If $|\vec{a} + \vec{b}| = |\vec{a} - \vec{b}|$, then which one of the following is correct?

A. $|\vec{a}| = |\vec{b}|$
B. $\vec{a}$ is parallel to $\vec{b}$
C. $\vec{a}$ is perpendicular to $\vec{b}$
D. $\vec{a}$ is a unit vector

78. What is the area of the triangle OAB where O is the origin, $\overline{OA} = 3\hat{i} - \hat{j} + \hat{k}$ and $\overline{OB} = 2\hat{i} + \hat{j} - 3\hat{k}$?

A. $5\sqrt{6}$ square unit
B. $\frac{5\sqrt{6}}{2}$ square unit
C. $\sqrt{6}$ square unit
D. $\sqrt{30}$ square unit

79. Which one of the following is the unit vector perpendicular to both $\vec{a} = -\hat{i} + \hat{j} + \hat{k}$ and $\vec{b} = -\hat{i} - \hat{j} + \hat{k}$?

A. $\frac{\hat{i} + \hat{j}}{\sqrt{2}}$
B. $\hat{k}$
C. $\frac{\hat{j} + \hat{k}}{\sqrt{2}}$
D. $\frac{\hat{i} - \hat{j}}{\sqrt{2}}$

80. What is the interior acute angle of the parallelogram whose sides are represented by the vectors $\frac{1}{\sqrt{2}}\hat{i} + \frac{1}{\sqrt{2}}\hat{j} + \hat{k}$ and $\frac{1}{\sqrt{2}}\hat{i} - \frac{1}{\sqrt{2}}\hat{j} + \hat{k}$?

A. 60°
B. 45°
C. 30°
D. 15°

81. For what value of λ are the vectors $\lambda\hat{i} + (1+\lambda)\hat{j} + (1+2\lambda)\hat{k}$ and $(1-\lambda)\hat{i} + \lambda\hat{j} + 2\hat{k}$ perpendicular?

A. $-\frac{1}{3}$
B. $\frac{1}{3}$
C. $\frac{2}{3}$
D. 1

Directions (Qs. No. 82 to 85): *For the next four questions that follow:*

$\vec{a} + \vec{b} + \vec{c} = \vec{0}$ such that $|\vec{a}|3, |\vec{b}| = 5$ and $|\vec{c}| = 7$.

82. What is the angle between $\vec{a}$ and $\vec{b}$?

A. $\frac{\pi}{6}$
B. $\frac{\pi}{4}$
C. $\frac{\pi}{3}$
D. $\frac{\pi}{2}$

83. What is $\vec{a} \cdot \vec{b} + \vec{b} \cdot \vec{c} + \vec{c} \cdot \vec{a}$ equal to?

A. –83
B. $-\frac{83}{2}$
C. –75
D. $-\frac{75}{2}$

84. What is cosine of the angle between $\vec{b}$ and $\vec{c}$?

A. $\frac{11}{12}$ B. $\frac{13}{14}$

C. $-\frac{11}{12}$ D. $-\frac{13}{14}$

85. What is $|\vec{a}+\vec{b}|$ equal to?

A. 7 B. 8

C. 10 D. 11

86. What is $\int_0^{\frac{\pi}{2}} \frac{dx}{a^2\cos^2 x + b^2 \sin^2 x}$ equal to?

A. $2ab$ B. $2\pi ab$

C. $\frac{\pi}{2ab}$ D. $\frac{\pi}{ab}$

Directions (Qs. No. 87 and 88): *For the next two questions that follow:*

A cylinder is inscribed in a sphere of radius *r*.

87. What is the height of the cylinder of maximum volume?

A. $\frac{2r}{\sqrt{3}}$ B. $\frac{r}{\sqrt{3}}$

C. $2r$ D. $\sqrt{3}r$

88. What is the radius of the cylinder of maximum volume?

A. $\frac{2r}{\sqrt{3}}$ B. $\frac{\sqrt{2}r}{\sqrt{3}}$

C. r D. $\sqrt{3}r$

Directions (Qs. No. 89 and 90): *For the next two questions that follow:*

Consider the function $f''(x) = \sec^4 x + 4$ with $f(0) = 0$ and $f'(0) = 0$.

89. What is $f'(x)$ equal to?

A. $\tan x - \frac{\tan^3 x}{3} + 4x$

B. $\tan x + \frac{\tan^3 x}{3} + 4x$

C. $\tan x + \frac{\sec^3 x}{3} + 4x$

D. $-\tan x - \frac{\tan^3 x}{3} + 4x$

90. What is $f(x)$ equal to?

A. $\frac{2\ln\sec x}{3} + \frac{\tan^2 x}{6} + 2x^2$

B. $\frac{3\ln\sec x}{2} + \frac{\cot^2 x}{6} + 2x^2$

C. $\frac{4\ln\sec x}{3} + \frac{\sec^2 x}{6} + 2x^2$

D. $\ln\sec x + \frac{\tan^4 x}{12} + 2x^2$

Directions (Qs. No. 91 to 93): *For the next three questions that follow:*

Consider $I = \int_0^{\pi} \frac{x\,dx}{1+\sin x}$

91. What is I equal to?

A. $-\pi$ B. 0

C. π D. 2π

92. What is $\int_0^{\pi} \frac{(\pi - x)dx}{1+\sin x}$ equal to?

A. π B. $\frac{\pi}{2}$

C. 0 D. 2π

93. What is $\int_0^{\pi} \frac{dx}{1+\sin x}$ equal to?

A. 1 B. 2

C. 4 D. -2

Directions (Qs. No. 94 and 95): *For the next two questions that follow:*

Consider $\int x\tan^{-1} x\,dx = A(x^2+1)\tan^{-1} x + Bx + C$, where C is the constant of integration.

94. What is the value of A?

A. 1 B. $\frac{1}{2}$

C. $-\frac{1}{2}$ D. $\frac{1}{4}$

95. What is the value of B?

A. 1 B. $\frac{1}{2}$

C. $-\frac{1}{2}$ D. $\frac{1}{4}$

Directions (Qs. No. 96 and 97): *For the next two questions that follow:*

Consider the integral $I = \int_0^{\pi} \ln(\sin x)\,dx$

96. What is $\int_0^{\pi/2} \ln(\sin x)\,dx$ equal to?

A. 4 I B. 2 I

C. I D. $\frac{I}{2}$

97. What is $\int_0^{\pi/2} \ln(\cos x)\, dx$ equal to?

A. $\frac{I}{2}$ B. I
C. 2 I D. 4 I

Directions (Qs. No. 98 and 99): *For the next two questions that follow:*

A rectangular box is to be made from a sheet of 24 inch length and 9 inch width cutting out identical squares of side length *x* from the four corners and turning up the sides.

98. What is the value of *x* for which the volume is maximum?
A. 1 inch B. 1.5 inch
C. 2 inch D. 2.5 inch

99. What is the maximum volume of the box?
A. 200 cubic inch B. 400 cubic inch
C. 100 cubic inch D. None of these

100. What is the degree of the differential equation $\left(\frac{d^3y}{dx^3}\right)^{3/2} = \left(\frac{d^2y}{dx^2}\right)^2$?
A. 1 B. 2
C. 3 D. 4

101. What is the solution of the equation $\ln\left(\frac{dy}{dx}\right) + x = 0$?
A. $y + e^x = c$ B. $y - e^{-x} = c$
C. $y + e^{-x} = c$ D. $y - e^x = c$
where *c* is an arbitrary constant.

102. Eliminating the arbitrary constants B and C in the expression $y = \frac{2}{3C}(Cx-1)^{3/2} + B$, we get

A. $x\left[1+\left(\frac{dy}{dx}\right)^2\right] = \frac{d^2y}{dx^2}$

B. $2x\left(\frac{dy}{dx}\right)\frac{d^2y}{dx^2} = 1+\left(\frac{dy}{dx}\right)^2$

C. $\left(\frac{dy}{dx}\right)\frac{d^2y}{dx^2} = 1$

D. $\left(\frac{dy}{dx}\right)^2 + 1 = \frac{d^2y}{dx^2}$

Directions (Qs. No. 103 to 105): *For the next three questions that follow:*

Let $f(x) = ax^2 + bx + c$ such that $f(1) = f(-1)$ and *a*, *b*, *c* are in Arithmetic Progression.

103. What is the value of *b*?
A. –1
B. 0
C. 1
D. Cannot be determined due to insufficient data

104. $f'(a), f'(b), f'(c)$ are in
A. A.P.
B. G.P.
C. H.P.
D. Arithmetico-geometric progression

105. $f''(a), f''(b), f''(c)$ are
A. in A.P. only
B. in G.P. only
C. in both A.P. and G.P.
D. neither in A.P. nor in G.P.

106. Every quadratic quation $ax^2 + bx + c = 0$ where $a, b, c \in \mathbf{R}$, $a \neq 0$ has
A. exactly one real root
B. at least one real root
C. at least two real roots
D. at most two real roots

107. The relation S is defined on the set of integers Z as *x*S*y* if integer *x* divides integer *y*. Then
A. S is an equivalence relation
B. S is only reflexive and symmetric
C. S is only reflexive and transitive
D. S is only symmetric and transitive

108. If $a \neq b \neq c$ are all positive, then the value of the determinant $\begin{vmatrix} a & b & c \\ b & c & a \\ c & a & b \end{vmatrix}$ is
A. non-negative B. non-positive
C. negative D. positive

109. Let A and B be two matrices such that AB = A and BA = B. Which of the following statements are correct?
1. $A^2 = A$
2. $B^2 = B$
3. $(AB)^2 = AB$

Select the correct answer using the code given below:
A. 1 and 2 only B. 2 and 3 only
C. 1 and 3 only D. 1, 2 and 3

110. What is $(1001)_2$ equal to?
A. $(5)_{10}$ B. $(9)_{10}$
C. $(17)_{10}$ D. $(11)_{10}$

111. What is $\left(\frac{\sqrt{3}+i}{\sqrt{3}-i}\right)^6$ equal to where $i = \sqrt{-1}$?
A. 1 B. $\frac{1}{6}$
C. 6 D. 2

112. Let *z* be a complex number such that $|z| = 4$ and arg $z = \frac{5\pi}{6}$. What is *z* equal to?

A. $2\sqrt{3}+2i$ B. $2\sqrt{3}-2i$
C. $-2\sqrt{3}+2i$ D. $-\sqrt{3}+i$
where $i = \sqrt{-1}$

113. If $\begin{vmatrix} 6i & -3i & 1 \\ 4 & 3i & -1 \\ 20 & 3 & i \end{vmatrix} = x + iy$, where $i = \sqrt{-1}$, then what is x equal to?
A. 3 B. 2
C. 1 D. 0

114. If α, β are the roots of $ax^2 + bx + c = 0$ and $\alpha + h$, $\beta + h$ are the roots of $px^2 + qx + r = 0$, then what is h equal to?
A. $\frac{1}{2}\left(\frac{b}{a}-\frac{q}{p}\right)$ B. $\frac{1}{2}\left(-\frac{b}{a}+\frac{q}{p}\right)$
C. $\frac{1}{2}\left(\frac{b}{p}+\frac{q}{a}\right)$ D. $\frac{1}{2}\left(-\frac{b}{p}+\frac{q}{a}\right)$

115. If the matrix A is such that $\begin{pmatrix} 1 & 3 \\ 0 & 1 \end{pmatrix} A = \begin{pmatrix} 1 & 1 \\ 0 & -1 \end{pmatrix}$, then what is A equal to?
A. $\begin{pmatrix} 1 & 4 \\ 0 & -1 \end{pmatrix}$ B. $\begin{pmatrix} 1 & 4 \\ 0 & 1 \end{pmatrix}$
C. $\begin{pmatrix} -1 & 4 \\ 0 & -1 \end{pmatrix}$ D. $\begin{pmatrix} 1 & -4 \\ 0 & -1 \end{pmatrix}$

116. Consider the following statements:
1. Determinant is a square matrix.
2. Determinant is a number associated with a square matrix.

Which of the above statements is/are correct?
A. 1 only B. 2 only
C. Both 1 and 2 D. Neither 1 nor 2

117. If A is an invertible matrix, then what is det (A^{-1}) equal to?
A. det A B. $\frac{1}{\det A}$
C. 1 D. None of these

118. From the matrix equation AB = AC, where A, B, C are the square matrices of same order, we can conclude B = C provided
A. A is non-singular
B. A is singular
C. A is symmetric
D. A is skew symmetric

119. If $A = \begin{pmatrix} 4 & x+2 \\ 2x-2 & x+1 \end{pmatrix}$ is symmetric, then what is x equal to?
A. 2 B. 3
C. −1 D. 5

120. If $\begin{vmatrix} a & b & 0 \\ 0 & a & b \\ b & 0 & a \end{vmatrix} = 0$, then which one of the following is correct?
A. $\frac{a}{b}$ is one of the cube roots of unity
B. $\frac{a}{b}$ is one of the cube roots of −1
C. a is one of the cube roots of unity
D. b is one of the cube roots of unity

ANSWERS

PAPER-I : GENERAL ABILITY TEST

1	2	3	4	5	6	7	8	9	10
C	B	D	C	D	A	A	A	A	D
11	**12**	**13**	**14**	**15**	**16**	**17**	**18**	**19**	**20**
C	D	C	B	B	C	A	C	C	D
21	**22**	**23**	**24**	**25**	**26**	**27**	**28**	**29**	**30**
A	B	B	A	C	C	B	D	A	C
31	**32**	**33**	**34**	**35**	**36**	**37**	**38**	**39**	**40**
A	A	C	A	B	C	C	B	D	C
41	**42**	**43**	**44**	**45**	**46**	**47**	**48**	**49**	**50**
A	B	D	A	B	A	B	D	A	B
51	**52**	**53**	**54**	**55**	**56**	**57**	**58**	**59**	**60**
B	B	B	D	B	B	B	C	D	B
61	**62**	**63**	**64**	**65**	**66**	**67**	**68**	**69**	**70**
A	B	A	C	D	C	C	A	D	C

71	72	73	74	75	76	77	78	79	80
B	B	A	C	B	B	A	B	D	D
81	**82**	**83**	**84**	**85**	**86**	**87**	**88**	**89**	**90**
A	A	C	C	A	B	C	B	D	C
91	**92**	**93**	**94**	**95**	**96**	**97**	**98**	**99**	**100**
B	B	B	D	A	C	B	B	D	D
101	**102**	**103**	**104**	**105**	**106**	**107**	**108**	**109**	**110**
A	A	C	B	A	D	D	A	C	C
111	**112**	**113**	**114**	**115**	**116**	**117**	**118**	**119**	**120**
D	A	D	D	C	B	B	B	A	C
121	**122**	**123**	**124**	**125**	**126**	**127**	**128**	**129**	**130**
D	A	A	D	C	C	A	C	D	A
131	**132**	**133**	**134**	**135**	**136**	**137**	**138**	**139**	**140**
C	C	B	A	A	C	A	C	A	C
141	**142**	**143**	**144**	**145**	**146**	**147**	**148**	**149**	**150**
C	A	D	A	A	B	B	B	C	C

PAPER-II : MATHEMATICS

1	2	3	4	5	6	7	8	9	10
B	D	D	C	A	C	B	B	A	C
11	**12**	**13**	**14**	**15**	**16**	**17**	**18**	**19**	**20**
D	C	B	A	D	B	A	D	A	B
21	**22**	**23**	**24**	**25**	**26**	**27**	**28**	**29**	**30**
C	B	B	B	A	A	D	D	A	C
31	**32**	**33**	**34**	**35**	**36**	**37**	**38**	**39**	**40**
B	A	A	C	D	D	C	A	C	C
41	**42**	**43**	**44**	**45**	**46**	**47**	**48**	**49**	**50**
B	A	B	C	C	B	C	C	A	D
51	**52**	**53**	**54**	**55**	**56**	**57**	**58**	**59**	**60**
C	D	A	A	D	D	B	C	B	B
61	**62**	**63**	**64**	**65**	**66**	**67**	**68**	**69**	**70**
B	B	D	B	A	B	A	C	B	A
71	**72**	**73**	**74**	**75**	**76**	**77**	**78**	**79**	**80**
A	B	A	D	C	A	C	B	A	A
81	**82**	**83**	**84**	**85**	**86**	**87**	**88**	**89**	**90**
A	C	B	D	A	C	B	B	B	A
91	**92**	**93**	**94**	**95**	**96**	**97**	**98**	**99**	**100**
C	A	B	B	C	D	A	C	A	C
101	**102**	**103**	**104**	**105**	**106**	**107**	**108**	**109**	**110**
C	B	B	D	C	D	C	C	D	B
111	**112**	**113**	**114**	**115**	**116**	**117**	**118**	**119**	**120**
A	C	D	A	A	B	B	A	D	B

EXPLANATORY ANSWERS

PAPER-II : MATHEMATICS

16. Given relation implies

$$2a = (n + 1)d$$

$$\therefore \quad \frac{S_{3n}}{S_n} = 3\left[\frac{2a+(3n-1)d}{2a+(n-1)d}\right] = 3 \times 2 = 6$$

$$\therefore \quad S_{3n} : S_n = 6 : 1.$$

17. $$\frac{S_{3n}}{S_{2n}} = \frac{3[2a+(3n-1)d]}{2[2a+(2n-1)d]}$$

$$= \frac{3}{2}\left[\frac{nd + d + 3nd - d}{nd + d + 2nd - d}\right] = \frac{3}{2} \times \frac{4}{3} = 2$$

$\therefore$ $S_{3n} : S_{2n} = 2 : 1$.

18. $\frac{25x^2}{400} = \frac{16y^2}{400} = \frac{400}{400} \Rightarrow \frac{x^2}{16} + \frac{y^2}{25} = 1$

Here $a^2 = 16$, $b^2 = 25$

Length of latus rectum of ellipse

$$= \frac{2a^2}{b} = \frac{2 \times 16}{5} = \frac{32}{5}.$$

54. The total number of arrangements of the letters of the word 'UNIVERSITY' is $\frac{10!}{2!}$ as there are two I's.

Regarding 2I's as one letter, number of ways of arrangement in which both I's are together = 9!

So, the number of ways in which 2 I's are not together

$$= \frac{10!}{2!} - 9!$$

Hence, the required probability

$$= \frac{\frac{10!}{2!} - 9!}{\frac{10!}{2!}} = 1 - \frac{2!\,9!}{10!} = \frac{4}{5}.$$

57. $\because$ Mean $= \frac{4+7+8+9+10+12+13+17}{8} = \frac{80}{8} = 10$

$\therefore$ Mean deviation

$$= \frac{|4-10|+|7-10|+|8-10|+|9-10|+|10-10| +|12-10|+|13-10|+|17-10|}{8}$$

$$= \frac{6+3+2+1+0+2+3+7}{8} = \frac{24}{8} = 3.$$

61. $\sqrt{1+\sin 2\theta} = \sqrt{\sin^2\theta + \cos^2\theta + 2\sin\theta.\cos\theta}$

$= \sqrt{(\sin\theta + \cos\theta)^2}$

$= \sin\theta + \cos\theta$

$= \cos\theta + \sin\theta$.

62.

B

h

A

30°

C

150m

$\tan 30° = \frac{h}{150}$

$\Rightarrow \frac{1}{\sqrt{3}} = \frac{h}{150}$

$\Rightarrow h = \frac{150}{\sqrt{3}} \times \frac{\sqrt{3}}{\sqrt{3}} = 50\sqrt{3}\,m$

$\therefore$ Height of the lamp post $= 50\sqrt{3}\,m$.

63. $\cot A = 2 \therefore \tan A = \frac{1}{2}$

and $\cot B = 3 \therefore \tan B = \frac{1}{3}$

$$\tan(A+B) = \frac{\tan A + \tan B}{1 - \tan A.\tan B} = \frac{\frac{1}{2}+\frac{1}{3}}{1-\frac{1}{2}\times\frac{1}{3}}$$

$\Rightarrow \tan(A+B) = \frac{5}{6} \times \frac{6}{5} = 1$

$\Rightarrow \tan(A+B) = \tan\frac{\pi}{4}$

$\Rightarrow A + B = \frac{\pi}{4}$.

64. $\sin 90°. \sin(43°) = \sin(90° - 47°) = \cos 47°$.

65. Let $\sin^{-1}\frac{3}{5} = x$

$\Rightarrow \sin x = \frac{3}{5}$ $\qquad \therefore \cos x = \frac{4}{5}$

and $\sin^{-1}\frac{4}{5} = y$

$\Rightarrow \sin y = \frac{4}{5}$ $\qquad \therefore \cos y = \frac{3}{5}$

$\sin(x+y) = \sin x.\cos y + \cos x.\sin y$

$= \frac{3}{5}\times\frac{3}{5}+\frac{4}{5}\times\frac{4}{5} = \frac{9}{25}+\frac{16}{25} = \frac{25}{25} = 1$

$\therefore \sin(x+y) = \sin\frac{\pi}{2}$

$\Rightarrow x + y = \frac{\pi}{2}$

$\Rightarrow \sin^{-1}\frac{3}{5} + \sin^{-1}\frac{4}{5} = \frac{\pi}{2}$.

66. $\frac{\cos 7x - \cos 3x}{\sin 7x + \sin 3x - 2\sin 5x}$

$= \frac{-2\sin 5x.\sin 2x}{2\sin 5x.\cos 2x - 2\sin 5x}$

$= \frac{-2\sin 5x.\sin 2x}{-2\sin 5x(1-\cos 2x)} = \frac{\sin 2x}{2\sin^2 x}$

$= \frac{2\sin x.\cos x}{2\sin x.\sin x} = \cot x$.

67. $\frac{a}{\sin A} = \frac{b}{\sin B} = \frac{c}{\sin C}$

$\frac{2\sqrt{2}}{\sin 45°} = \frac{2}{\sin C}$

$$\Rightarrow \frac{\frac{2\sqrt{2}}{1}}{\sqrt{2}} = \frac{2}{\sin C}$$

$$\Rightarrow 4 \sin C = 2$$

$$\Rightarrow \sin C = \frac{2}{4} = \frac{1}{2} = \sin 30°$$

$$\Rightarrow C = 30°$$

68. $\because \sin A - \cos B = \cos C$ (given)

$$\Rightarrow \cos B + \cos C = \sin A$$

$$\Rightarrow 2\cos\frac{B+C}{2}\cdot\cos\frac{B-C}{2} = \sin A$$

$$\Rightarrow 2\sin\frac{A}{2}\cdot\cos\frac{(B-C)}{2} = 2\sin\frac{A}{2}\cdot\cos\frac{A}{2}$$

$$\Rightarrow \cos\frac{(B-C)}{2} = \cos\frac{A}{2}$$

$$\Rightarrow \frac{B-C}{2} = \frac{A}{2}$$

$$\Rightarrow B - C = A$$

$$\Rightarrow B = A + C$$

$$\because A + B + C = 180°$$

$$\Rightarrow B + B = 180°$$

$$\Rightarrow 2B = 180°$$

$$\Rightarrow B = 90° = \frac{\pi}{2}$$

69. $\dfrac{\sin(x+y)+\sin(x-y)}{\sin(x+y)-\sin(x-y)} = \dfrac{a+b+a-b}{a+b-a+b}$

$$\frac{2\sin\left(\frac{x+y+x-y}{2}\right)\cdot\cos\left(\frac{x+y-x+y}{2}\right)}{2\cos\left(\frac{x+y+x-y}{2}\right)\cdot\sin\left(\frac{x+y-x+y}{2}\right)} = \frac{2a}{2b}$$

$$\Rightarrow \frac{\sin x\cdot\cos y}{\cos x\cdot\sin y} = \frac{a}{b}$$

$$\Rightarrow \tan x \times \cot y = \frac{a}{b}$$

$$\Rightarrow \tan x \times \frac{1}{\tan y} = \frac{a}{b} \Rightarrow \frac{\tan x}{\tan y} = \frac{a}{b}$$

70. $\sin A\,.\,(\sin^2 60° - \sin^2 A) = k \sin 3A$

$$\sin A\left(\left(\frac{\sqrt{3}}{2}\right)^2 - \sin^2 A\right) = k \sin 3A$$

$$\sin A\left(\frac{3}{4} - \sin^2 A\right) = k \sin 3A$$

$$\frac{3\sin A - 4\sin^3 A}{4} = k \sin 3A$$

$$\frac{\sin 3A}{4} = \frac{k \sin 3A}{1}$$

$$4k = 1$$

$$k = \frac{1}{4}$$

72. $\tan 2\theta\,.\,\tan\theta = 1$

$$\Rightarrow \frac{2\tan\theta}{1-\tan^2\theta} \times \tan\theta = 1$$

$$2\tan^2\theta = 1 - \tan^2\theta$$

$$3\tan^2\theta = 1$$

$$\Rightarrow \tan^2\theta = \frac{1}{3}$$

$$\Rightarrow \tan\theta = \frac{1}{\sqrt{3}} = \tan 30°$$

$$\Rightarrow \theta = 30° = \frac{\pi}{6}$$

93. $\displaystyle\int_0^\pi \frac{dx}{1+\sin x} = \int_0^\pi \frac{1-\sin x}{\cos^2 x}dx = \int_0^\pi (\sec^2 x - \sec x.\tan x)dx$

$$= [\tan x - \sec x]_0^\pi - [\tan\pi - \sec\pi + 1] = [0 + 1 + 1] = 2.$$

For Q. No. 94 and 95

$$\int x\cdot\tan^{-1} x\, dx = A(x^2+1)\tan^{-1}x + Bx + C$$

Let $I = \int x\cdot\tan^{-1} x\, dx$

$$= \tan^{-1} x\cdot\left(\frac{x^2}{2}\right) - \int\frac{1}{1+x^2}\cdot\frac{x^2}{2}dx$$

$$= \frac{x^2}{2}\cdot\tan^{-1} x - \frac{1}{2}\int\frac{x^2}{1+x^2}dx$$

$$= \frac{x^2}{2}\cdot\tan^{-1} x - \frac{1}{2}\int\frac{(1+x^2)-1}{1+x^2}dx$$

$$= \frac{x^2}{2}\cdot\tan^{-1} x - \frac{1}{2}\left[\int 1\,dx - \int\frac{1}{1+x^2}dx\right]$$

$$= \frac{x^2}{2}\cdot\tan^{-1} x - \frac{1}{2}\left[x - \tan^{-1} x\right] + C$$

$$= \frac{x^2}{2}\cdot\tan^{-1} x - \frac{1}{2}x + \frac{1}{2}\tan^{-1} x + C$$

$$= \left(\frac{x^2+1}{2}\right)\tan^{-1} x - \frac{x}{2} + C$$

94. Value of $A = \frac{1}{2}$

95. Value of $B = -\frac{1}{2}$

NATIONAL DEFENCE ACADEMY & NAVAL ACADEMY

NDA & NA – Entrance Exam, 2014 (I)

PAPER I : GENERAL ABILITY TEST

PART A : ENGLISH LANGUAGE

Directions (Qs. 1 to 11): *Read each sentence to find out whether there is any grammatical error in it. The error, if any, will be in one part of the sentence. The letter of that part is the answer. If there is no error, the answer is 'D'. (Ignore the errors of punctuation, if any).*

1. (A) The pile of books/(B) are/(C) missing./(D) No error

2. (A) Either he/(B) or I/(C) are wrong./(D) No error

3. (A) Please/(B) tell to him/(C) to do his work./(D) No error

4. (A) Though he is good/(B) he is/(C) mischievous./(D) No error

5. (A) The thief/(B) hit me/(C) suddenly and hardly./(D) No error

6. (A) The number of books/(B) in our library/(C) is less./(D) No error

7. (A) The general said,/(B) "Soldiers, do not fire/(C) till I will give the order."/(D) No error

8. (A) Neither of the candidates/(B) are/(C) good./(D) No error

9. (A) This machine/(B) is more efficient/(C) than any other equipments in the workshop./(D) No error

10. (A) The tin deposits in that area/(B) would probably be exhausted/(C) in to near future./(D) No error

11. (A) The operation of this machine/(B) is different/(C) to that of the other./(D) No error

Directions (Qs. 12 to 23): *Look at the* ***bold*** *part of each sentence. Below each sentence three possible substitutions are given for the* ***bold*** *part. If one of them, i.e., A, B or C is better than the* ***bold*** *part, indicate your response on the Answer Sheet against the corresponding letter. If none of the substitutions improves the sentence, indicate D as your response on the Answer Sheet.*

12. I don't remember exactly **when did I go** to Simla last year.
A. when I did go B. when I was going
C. when I went D. No improvement

13. **Even** he worked hard, he failed in the examination.
A. Since B. Although
C. For D. No improvement

14. He was asked **to arbitrate with** two merchants in a dispute.
A. to arbitrate between B. to arbitrate at
C. to arbitrate D. No improvement

15. He is definitely the cleverer **among** the two.
A. in B. of
C. than D. No improvement

16. He **is resembling** his father.
A. has resembled B. was resembling
C. resembles D. No improvement

17. Would you mind **closing** the window?
A. to close B. in closing
C. for closing D. No improvement

18. I **can be** grateful if you could write to me about it.
A. would be B. should be
C. must be D. No improvement

19. A majority of the passengers **could have been saved** if the driver had applied the brakes in time.
A. had been saved B. may have been saved
C. could have saved D. No improvement

20. He **is living** in this house for the past ten years.
A. was living B. had been living
C. has been living D. No improvement

21. He **is knowing** the secret.
A. knows B. has been knowing
C. was knowing D. No improvement

22. The meeting has been **put off** to Friday next.
A. put on B. put out
C. put for D. No improvement

23. If you **will come with me** I shall be happy.
A. come with me B. had come with me
C. came with me D. No improvement

Directions (Qs. 24 to 27): *Each of the items in this section contains a blank followed by words listed as A, B, C and D. Choose the most appropriate word to fill in the blank and indicate your response in the Answer Sheet accordingly.*

24. When the police arrived, the thief .... away.
A. strolled B. moved
C. galloped D. ran

25. His .... as an officer was not quite satisfactory.
A. acting B. doing
C. deed D. record

26. The two children stood at the .... of the table.
A. conclusion B. terminal
C. end D. termination

27. The old man was .... weak to open the door.
A. very B. far
C. much D. too

Directions (Qs. 28 to 31): *Each question in this section consists of a word printed in capital letters followed by words listed as A, B, C and D. Choose from these the word that has most nearly the meaning* ***opposite*** *to the word in capital letters and indicate your response in the Answer Sheet accordingly.*

28. FRAIL
A. strong B. big
C. old D. weak

29. INDIGENOUS
A. genuine B. foreign
C. indigent D. indignant

30. POVERTY
A. prosperity B. adversary
C. adversity D. diversity

31. WHOLESOME
A. complete B. unhealthy
C. incomprehensible D. few

Directions (Qs. 32 to 38): *Read the following short passages. After each passage, you will find several questions based on what is stated or implied in the passages. Answer the questions that follow each passage.*

PASSAGE-I

In a free country, the man who reaches the position of leader is usually one of outstanding character and ability. Moreover, it is usually possible to foresee that he will reach such a position, since early in life one can see his qualities of character. But this is not always true in the case of a dictator; often he reaches his position of power through chance, very often through the unhappy state of his country. It is possible that Hitler would never have become the leader of Germany if that country had not been driven to despair.

32. In a free country, one who becomes a leader
A. must be of outstanding character and ability
B. must show qualities of character from an early age
C. is generally of a remarkable character and ability
D. must see that his country is free from despair

33. Hitler became a leader because
A. he exhibited leadership qualities
B. Germany was a free country
C. Germany was in despair
D. Germans wanted a dictator

34. The passage seems to suggest that
A. despair sometimes leads to dictatorship
B. Hitler was no leader
C. a leader is chosen only by a free country
D. a leader foresees his future position

PASSAGE-II

The dog is a very intelligent animal and it can be trained for many duties. Some dogs work with the police and the army as sentries and trackers, and there are medals that are awarded to dogs for bravery in action. Other dogs act as seeing-eyes for the blind, and some breeds are specially trained for rescue work among mountains and snow. Jobs like herding sheep and cattle and guarding homes are also done by them. Whenever man lives and works in the Arctic Circle, in the desert, in the jungle, in the moors or mountains, the dog is his faithful companion and help. A common mongrel may possess these qualities just as much as the aristocratic bloodhound.

35. The passage tells us that dogs
A. can be trained to do different kinds of work
B. are capable of difficult work
C. are of different types
D. alone are a great help to man

36. Medals are awarded to some dogs for
A. their brave deeds
B. working with the police
C. serving as sentries
D. being able to perform difficult work

37. The passage implies that
A. only dogs are faithful but not man
B. man would have felt helpless without dogs
C. the dog has certain qualities that make it man's trustworthy companion
D. dogs can do almost anything

38. The phrase 'aristocratic bloodhound' in the passage means
A. the dog kept by wealthy people
B. a pedigree dog
C. a dog fond of blood
D. any big dog

Directions (Qs. 39 to 50): *In the following passage, at certain points you are given a choice of three words marked A, B and C, one of which fits the meaning of the passage. Choose the best word out of the three. Mark the letter, viz. A, B, or C, relating to this word on your Answer Sheet. Examples* ***K*** *and* ***L*** *have been solved for you.*

K. The A. boy was in the school in Simla
B. horse
C. dog

L. A. She was homesick.
B. It
C. He

Explanation: Out of the list given in item **K**, only, 'boy' is the correct answer because usually, a boy, and not a horse or a dog, attends school. So 'A' is to be marked on the Answer Sheet for item **K**. A boy is usually referred to as 'he', so for item **L**, 'C' is the correct answer. Notice that to solve the first item **K**, you have to read the rest of the sentence and then see what fits the best.

PASSAGE

Drobny defied the critics. He had played through the Wimbledon fortnight and reached the final. Could he win just one more match and take the crown, or would he fail again at the last test and justify those who said that he lacked that little extra something that makes the champion? His opponent was the Australian Ken Rosewall, ...(39)... brilliant youngster and already a master ...(40)... worldwide experience behind him. Jaroslav Drobny, ...(41)... son of a Czech carpenter who ...(42)... started the boy off at the ...(43)... of five with a wooden 'bat' in lieu ...(44)... a racquet, went on ...(45)... the famous Centre Court at Wimbledon ...(46)... day with the full knowledge that this ...(47)... be the game of his ...(48)... . He had kept on trying, and ...(49)... could keep on trying, but ...(50)... would become fewer and fewer. He knew that he had to gain an advantage from the start, and he had this young rival set off against him.

39. A. that
B. a
C. the

40. A. with
B. of
C. for

41. A. a
B. that
C. the

42. A. had
B. was
C. has

43. A. age
B.. stage
C. career

44. A. for
B. of
C. to

45. A. to
B. for
C. with

46. A. in
B. on
C. that

47. A. can
B. must
C. would

48. A. life
B. age
C. day

49. A. he
B. one
C. you

50. A. games
B. matches
C. opportunities

PART B : GENERAL KNOWLEDGE

51. Which of the following statements about the Progressive Writers' Association, which created a generation of creative people, is/are correct?
1. It thought critically about the poverty and hunger of the Indian people.
2. It brought out the positive developments of colonialism.
3. Its creative pursuits began with a critical evaluation of Gandhian politics.
4. It planned India's development model.

Select the correct answer using the code given below.
A. 1 only B. 2 and 3
C. 1 and 4 D. 1 and 3

52. E.V. Ramaswami Naicker was associated with
1. reforming Brahminism
2. the Self-Respect Movement
3. the Low Caste Movement
4. the Communist Movement

Select the correct answer using the code given below.
A. 1, 2, 3 and 4 B. 1 and 3 only
C. 1 and 4 only D. 2 and 3 only

53. Consider the following statements about 'Param Vir Chakra':
1. It is the highest peacetime gallantry award.
2. It is the replacement of British Victoria Cross.
3. It can be awarded to civilians.

Which of the statements given above is/are correct?
A. 1 only B. 2 only
C. 2 and 3 only D. 1, 2 and 3

54. Gandhiji's 'Harijan Campaign' sought to
1. attack caste system as a whole
2. open wells, roads, temples, etc., to Harijans
3. encourage social work among Harijans

Select the correct answer using the code given below.
A. 1 and 2 B. 2 and 3
C. 1 and 3 D. 3 only

55. The Salt Satyagraha called by Mahatma Gandhi saw the
1. violation of salt laws along coastal India
2. participation of women
3. upward swing when it came to the working class joining in

Select the correct answer using the code given below.
A. 1 and 3 only B. 2 only
C. 1 and 2 only D. 1, 2 and 3

56. What was the code name for the Indian Air Force operations during the Kargil Conflict of 1999?
A. Operation Vijay
B. Operation Meghdoot
C. Operation Indradhanush
D. Operation Safed Sagar

57. During the Civil Disobedience Movement, tribals in Chota Nagpur
1. gave up opium consumption

2. wore Khadi
3. gave up drinking liquor and eating meat

Select the correct answer using the code given below.

A. 1 and 3 only B. 1 only
C. 1, 2 and 3 D. 2 and 3 only

58. Which of the following was/were the new feature/features visible in the Quit India Movement (1942)?

1. Large-scale movements in some of the industrial areas
2. Large-scale mass involvement in some of the Princely States
3. Increase in the activities of the Kisan Sabha

Select the correct answer using the code given below.

A. 1, 2 and 3 B. 1 only
C. 1 and 3 only D. 3 only

59. The Financial Sector Legislative Reforms Commission report submitted recently, among others, contained which of the following proposals?

1. All regulators will have an empowered board, the role of each of the members has been defined.
2. The Commission envisages an important process of judicial review of the regulations.
3. The draft code does not mention about executive powers.

Select the correct answer using the code given below.

A. 1 and 2 only B. 2 only
C. 1 and 3 only D. 1, 2 and 3

60. The Swadeshi Movement evoked serious responses in

A. Madras and Hyderabad
B. Bengal and Maharashtra
C. Bihar and Orissa
D. the Princely States

61. Who among the following was associated with the Gudem-Rampa Rebellion?

A. Birsa Munda B. Kushal Konwar
C. Alluri Sitarama Raju D. Mangal Pandey

62. The Bali Ministerial Declaration and the ministerial decisions that were adopted on 7th December, 2013 contained several issues. Which of the following are related to the Least-Developed Countries?

1. Preferential Rules of Origin for Least-Developed Countries
2. Operationalization of the Waiver Concerning Preferential Treatment to Services
3. Duty-Free and Quota-Free (DFQF) Market Access for Least-Developed Countries

Select the correct answer using the code given below.

A. 1, 2 and 3 B. 1 and 2 only
C. 1 and 3 only D. 2 and 3 only

63. The 'Doctrine of Lapse' was a policy that aimed to

A. control the rebellions in the Princely States
B. extend the military strength of the British
C. regulate the landlords
D. extend the territorial boundaries of the English East India Company

64. The Permanent Settlement of 1793 introduced

A. peasant rights
B. bourgeois property rights in land to Zamindars
C. shipping rights for the English East India Company
D. rights for women to have property rights

65. Which of the following is/are true relating to the Lokpal Bill, 2013, which was assented to by the President on 1st January, 2014?

1. It provides for creation of antigraft ombudsman to investigate corruption charges against public functionaries including the Prime Minister, Ministers and Members of the Parliament.
2. The Bill makes it incumbent upon States to make within a year their own law for setting up Lokayuktas on the lines of the Lokpal Bill.
3. States are free not to set up Lokayuktas, if they do not so desire.

Select the correct answer using the code given below.

A. 1 and 2 only B. 2 and 3 only
C. 1 only D. 1, 2 and 3

66. Who among the following was associated with the Hindustan Socialist Republican Association?

A. Subhash Chandra Bose
B. Mahatma Gandhi
C. Bhagat Singh
D. Laxmi Sehgal

67. The Indian National Army was organized to fight against

A. Germany and Japan B. the British in India
C. Japan D. Russia

68. Which of the following is/are true relating to Nelson Mandela?

1. He was the first President of South Africa.
2. Mandela spent 18 years in prison on Robben Island.
3. Mandela became the President in 1990 after his release from the prison.

Select the correct answer using the code given below.

A. 1 and 3 only B. 2 and 3 only
C. 2 only D. 1, 2 and 3

69. The Non-Cooperation Movement was withdrawn after the

A. First World War
B. Chauri-Chaura Incident
C. Bardoli Satyagraha
D. Gandhi-Irwin Pact

70. Which of the following books was written by B.R. Ambedkar?

A. *The Discovery of India*
B. *My Life*
C. *Buddha or Karl Marx*
D. *Hind Swaraj*

71. Which of the following is/are correct relating to the North-Eastern Region Community Resource Management Project for upland areas?

1. It is a livelihood and rural development project aimed to transform the lives of the poor and marginalized tribal families in North-East India.
2. This Project is initiated exclusively by the North-Eastern Council.

Select the correct answer using the code given below.

A. 1 only B. 2 only
C. Both 1 and 2 D. Neither 1 nor 2

72. Which of the following statements are true for the Fundamental Right to Life and Personal Liberty as guaranteed under Article 21 of the Constitution of India?

1. The Right is available to citizens as well as aliens.
2. It covers protection against arbitrary executive and legislative action.
3. It includes the right to live with human dignity.
4. It can be taken away according to the procedure established by law.

Select the correct answer using the code given below.

A. 1, 2 and 3 only B. 2, 3 and 4 only
C. 1, 2, 3 and 4 D. 1 and 4 only

73. Consider the following statements:

1. 'SAMARTH 2014', a national festival for showcasing the abilities of persons with disabilities, was organized recently in New Delhi by the Ministry of Culture.
2. India is a party to the United Nations Convention on the Rights of Persons with Disabilities.

Which of the statements given above is/are correct?

A. 1 only B. 2 only
C. Both 1 and 2 D. Neither 1 nor 2

74. Consider the following statements about 'Sahayog Kaijin':

1. It is a joint exercise of the Coast Guards of India and Japan.
2. Its 13th edition was held recently off Chennai Port.

Which of the statements given above is/are correct?

A. 1 only B. 2 only
C. Both 1 and 2 D. Neither 1 nor 2

75. Consider the following statements about grand slam tennis tournaments:

1. There are four grand slam annual tennis tournaments.
2. The first grand slam of a year is the US Open.
3. The Australian and the US tournaments are played on grass court.

Which of the statements given above is/are correct?

A. 1, 2 and 3 B. 1 and 2 only
C. 1 only D. 2 and 3 only

Directions: *The following six (6) items consist of two statements, Statement I and Statement II. You are to examine these two statements carefully and select the answers to these items using the code given below:*

Code:

A. Both the statements are individually true and Statement II is the correct explanation of Statement I
B. Both the statements are individually true but Statement II is ***not*** the correct explanation of Statement I
C. Statement I is true but Statement II is false
D. Statement I is false but Statement II is true

76. Statement I : Minerals are formed by slow cooling of the magma.

Statement II : Very small crystals are formed when lava cools quickly on the surface.

77. Statment I : The Kullu Valley in Himachal Pradesh receives copious snowfall during winter.

Statement II : The Kullu Valley receives moisture-bearing wind of the Western Disturbances during winter.

78. Statement I : The hills with dense vegetation cover do not experience heavy soil erosion.

Statement II : The vegetation cover helps infiltration of rainwater and binding of soils.

79. Statement I : The decrease of air temperature with increasing altitudes in the atmosphere is called the vertical temperature gradient.

Statement II : In Troposphere, air temperature decrease with increasing altitude due to radiation from the Earth.

80. Statement I : Chemical weathering processes are found more active in hot and humid environment.

Statement II : High temperature and rainfall help in the process of decomposition of rocks.

81. Statement I : The acceleration due to gravity decreases with increase in height from the surface of the Earth.

Statement II : The acceleration due to gravity is inversely proportional to the square of the distance from the centre of the Earth.

82. The number of valence electrons in the O^{2-} ion is

A. 4 B. 6
C. 8 D. 10

83. Within an animal cell, the most abundant inorganic constituent of protoplasm is

A. sodium and potassium salt
B. water
C. iron
D. phosphate

84. Two conducting wires A and B are made of same material. If the length of B is twice that of A and the radius of

circular cross-section of A is twice that of B, then their resistances R_A and R_B are in the ratio
A. 2 : 1 B. 1 : 2
C. 1 : 8 D. 1 : 4

85. Consider the following statements:
A real image
1. can be formed on a screen
2. is always magnified and inverted
Which of the statements given above is/are correct?
A. 1 only B. 2 only
C. Both 1 and 2 D. Neither 1 nor 2

86. Which one of the following is the correct electronic configuration of chlorine?
A. 2, 7, 8 B. 2, 8, 7
C. 2, 8, 8 D. 7, 8, 2

87. In honey, which one among the following sugars predominates?
A. Sucrose B. Fructose
C. Galactose D. Maltose

88. During short-circuiting, the current flowing in the electrical circuit
A. reduces substantially
B. does not change
C. increases instantaneously
D. varies continuously

89. The number of aluminium ions present in 54 g of aluminium (atomic weight 27) is
A. 2 B. 18
C. 1.1×10^{24} D. 1.2×10^{24}

90. What is 'breakbone fever' most commonly known as?
A. Typhoid B. Rhinitis
C. Yellow fever D. Dengue

91. Van de Graaff generator is used for
A. accelerating charged particles
B. generating large currents
C. generating electric field
D. generating high-frequency voltage

92. The most stable form of carbon is
A. diamond B. graphite
C. fullerene D. coal

93. Which one among the following is *not* a sexually transmitted disease?
A. Syphilis B. Gonorrhea
C. Scurvy D. Hepatitis B

94. The summer and winter seasons in a year are caused by
A. aphelion (farthest) and perihelion (nearest) positions of the Earth from the Sun during the annual revolution
B. rotation of the Earth on its axis
C. variation in solar insolation
D. revolution of the Earth on its inclined axis

95. The latest discovered state of matter is
A. solid
B. Bose-Einstein condensate
C. plasma
D. liquid

96. Which of the following pairs represents isoelectronic ions?
A. Na^+, K^+ B. K^+, Mg^{2+}
C. Mg^{2+}, Ca^{2+} D. Ca^{2+}, S^{2-}

97. After diagnosis of disease in a person, the doctor advises the patient iron and folic acid tablets. The person is suffering from
A. osteoporosis
B. anaemia
C. goitre
D. protein-energy malnutrition

98. Which one among the following is the coral group of islands of India?
A. Andaman B. Nicobar
C. Minicoy D. Lakshadweep

99. Bernoulli's principle is based on which one among the following laws?
A. Conservation of mass
B. Conservation of momentum
C. Conservation of angular momentum
D. Conservation of energy

100.

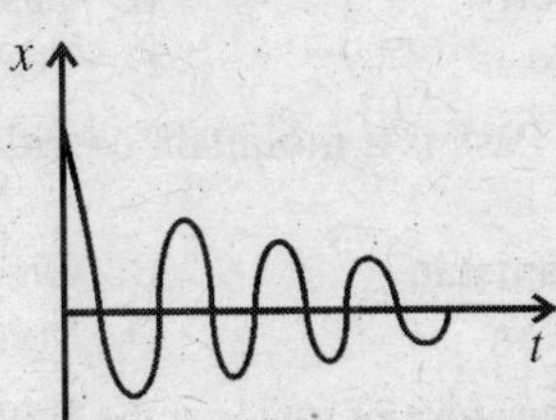

The displacement (x)-time (t) graph given above approximately represents the motion of a
A. simple pendulum placed in vacuum
B. simple pendulum immersed in water
C. simple pendulum placed in outer space
D. point mass moving in air

101. Dihydrogen can be prepared on a commercial scale by the action of steam on hydrocarbons, when a mixture of CO and H_2 gas is formed. It is known as
A. water gas B. producer gas
C. industrial gas D. fuel gas

102. Dropsy is a disease caused due to adulteration in
A. Ghee B. Arhar Dal
C. Mustard oil D. Turmeric powder

103. Consider the following surface winds:
1. Doldrums 2. Trade winds
3. Westerlies 4. Polar winds
Which one among the following is the idealized global pattern of these winds from the Equator to the Pole?
A. 1-2-3-4 B. 1-3-2-4
C. 2-1-4-3 D. 3-1-2-4

104.

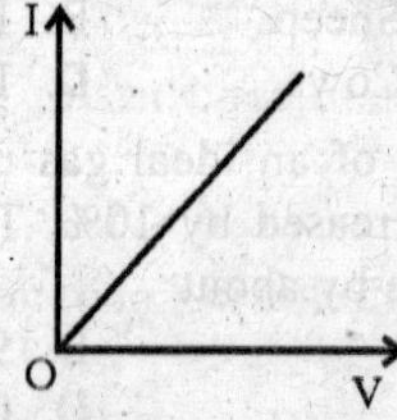

The current (I)-voltage (V) plot of a certain electronic device is given above. The device is

A. a semiconductor
B. a conductor which obeys Ohm's law
C. a superconductor
D. an insulator

105. Which of the following statements about hydrogen is/are correct?

1. Hydrogen has three isotopes of which protium is the most common.
2. Hydrogen ion (H^+) exists freely in solution.
3. Dihydrogen, H_2, acts as a reducing agent.

Select the correct answer using the code given below.

A. 1, 2 and 3 B. 1 only
C. 1 and 3 only D. 3 only

106. Leaves of which of the following plants are ***not*** used for the rearing of silkworms?

A. Mulberry B. Castor
C. Oak D. Teak

107. Taungup Pass is a mountain corridor connecting India with

A. Afghanistan B. China
C. Pakistan D. Myanmar

108. The temperature of water at the bottom of a lake whose upper surface has frozen to ice would be around

A. – 10°C B. 0°C
C. 4°C D. – 4°C

109. Which of the following statements is correct?

A. Fullerenes have only six-membered carbon rings
B. Fullerenes are cage-like molecules
C. Diamond is thermodynamically the most stable allotrope of carbon
D. Graphite is slippery and hard, and is therefore used as a dry lubricant in machines

110. Which one among the following groups is the most abundant in terms of number of species identified?

A. Fungi B. Green plants
C. Bacteria D. Insects

111. Consider the following statements:

1. Crystallization is a form of mechanical weathering.
2. Hydration causes granular disintegration.
3. Frost action is synonymous with freeze-thaw action.

Which of the statements given above are correct?

A. 1 and 2 only B. 2 and 3 only
C. 1 and 3 only D. 1, 2 and 3

112. Lapland is a cultural region largely within the Arctic Circle in the north of the Scandinavian Peninsula. Who inhabited the Lapland?

A. Sami people B. Padaung people
C. Hamar people D. Himba people

113. If speed of light in air is 3×10^8 m/s, the speed of light in glass (with refractive index 1.5) would be

A. 2×10^8 m/s B. 4.5×10^8 m/s
C. 3×10^8 m/s D. 1.5×10^8 m/s

114. While looking at an image formed by a convex lens (one half of the lens is covered with a black paper), which one of the following will happen to the image?

A. Half of the image will be visible
B. Intensity of the image will be diminished
C. Image will be inverted now
D. One can see an image of smaller size

115. Which of the following acids is a mineral acid?

A. Citric acid B. Hydrochloric acid
C. Ascorbic acid D. Tartaric acid

116. Considering the locations of mountains in India, which one among the following is in right sequence from south to north?

A. Doddabetta, Kailash, Dhaulagiri, Vindhyachal
B. Doddabetta, Vindhyachal, Dhaulagiri, Kailash
C. Dhaulagiri, Kailash, Doddabetta, Vindhyachal
D. Dhaulagiri, Vindhyachal, Doddabetta, Kailash

117. A balloon filled up with gas would only go up in air if it is filled up with

A. a gas whose density is lower than air
B. a gas whose density is higher than air
C. cold air
D. water vapour

118. Planet A has double the radius than that of Planet B. If the mass of Planet A is 4 times heavier than the mass of Planet B, which of the following statements regarding weight of an object is correct?

A. Heavier on Planet A than on Planet B
B. Heavier on Planet B than on Planet A
C. Same on both the Planets
D. Cannot be measured on Planet B

119. Which of the following is correct regarding the reaction of fluorine with water?

$2F_2(g) + 2H_2O(l) \rightarrow 4H^+(aq) + 4F^-(aq) + O_2(g)$

A. Fluorine is oxidized to F^-
B. Water is oxidized to O_2
C. Water is reduced to H^+
D. Oxidation state of fluorine does not change

120. The site of cellular respiration in animal cell is

A. ribosome B. mitochondria
C. endoplasmic reticulum D. lysosome

121. Which one among the following lakes is situated on the west coast of India?
A. Chilika B. Ashtamudi
C. Pulicat D. Kolleru

122. Sound waves are similar to the waves
A. of laser light passing through air
B. generated in a stretched wire by hitting or plucking the wire
C. generated in a pipe filled with air by moving the piston attached to the pipe up and down
D. generated by the mobile phone towers

123. A sound wave has frequency of 2 kHz and wavelength of 35 cm. If an observer is 1.4 km away from the source, after what time interval could the observer hear the sound?
A. 2 s B. 20 s
C. 0.5 s D. 4 s

124. Which of the following is/are amphoteric?
A. $Al(OH)_3(s)$ and $Fe(OH)_3(s)$
B. $Al(OH)_3(s)$ and $HCO^-_3(aq)$
C. $Ba(OH)_2(s)$ and $NaOH(aq)$
D. $Al(OH)_3(s)$ only

125. Which of the following statements about vitamins are correct?
1. Vitamin C is essential to make connective tissue in body.
2. Vitamin D is needed for synthesis of eye pigment.
3. Vitamin B_{12} helps in maturation of RBC.
4. Vitamin C is required to make use of calcium absorbed from the intestine.

Select the correct answer using the code given below.
A. 1 and 2 B. 1 and 3
C. 2 and 4 D. 1 and 4

126. What is the correct sequence from the smallest to the largest grain of the following types of clastic rocks?
A. Shale, sandstone, conglomerate, siltstone
B. Shale, siltstone, sandstone, conglomerate
C. Conglomerate, sandstone, shale, siltstone
D. Sandstone, siltstone, conglomerate, shale

127. Which one among the following waves bats use to detect the obstacles in their flying path?
A. Infrared waves B. Electromagnetic waves
C. Ultrasonic waves D. Radio waves

128. A fuse is used in an electric circuit to
A. break the circuit when excessive current flows through the circuit
B. break the circuit when power gets off
C. indicate if the current is flowing uninterrupted
D. complete the circuit for flow of current

129. The most of the mass of the atom can be found in
A. electrons B. charges
C. nucleus D. electron cloud

130. The Faroe is a group of islands lying in the Atlantic Ocean between Scotland and Iceland. This island group is also known as
A. Island of Sheep B. Island of Goats
C. Island of Cows D. Island of Buffaloes

131. The pressure of an ideal gas undergoing isothermal change is increased by 10%. The volume of the gas must decrease by about
A. 0.1% B. 9%
C. 10% D. 0.9%

132. Tuareg is a pastoral nomad living in the desert of
A. Kalahari B. Sahara
C. Arabia D. Patagonia

133. A passenger in a moving train tosses a coin upward which falls behind him. It implies that the motion of the train is
A. accelerated B. uniform
C. retarded D. along the circular tracks

134. The mass number of an atom is determined by
A. adding the number of neutrons and number of electrons
B. adding the number of protons and number of electrons
C. the number of protons only
D. adding the number of neutrons and number of protons

135. Match List-I with List-II and select the correct answer using the code given below the Lists:

List-I (Region)	List-II (Characteristic vegetation)
(*a*) Selvas	1. Tropophytes
(*b*) Savanna	2. Mosses and lichens
(*c*) Tundra	3. Epiphytes
(*d*) Monsoon land	4. Grasses and trees

Code:

	(*a*)	(*b*)	(*c*)	(*d*)
A.	3	2	4	1
B.	1	4	2	3
C.	1	2	4	3
D.	3	4	2	1

136. In optical instruments, the lenses are used to form image by the phenomenon of
A. reflection B. refraction
C. scattering D. diffusion

137. Note the following balanced chemical equation:

$$2CO + O_2 \rightleftharpoons 2CO_2$$

Which one of the following statements is significant in relation to the above chemical equation?
A. One can add to a vessel only 2 mol of CO for each mol of O_2 added
B. No matter how much of these two reagents are added to a vessel, 1 mol of O_2 is consumed
C. When they react, CO reacts with O_2 in a 2 : 1 mol ratio
D. When 2 mol of CO and 1 mol of O_2 are placed in a vessel, they will react to give 1 mol of CO_2

138. Which of the following is/are the most likely cause/ causes of sheet-flood found in western part of Rajasthan?

1. Scanty rainfall
2. Sudden high intensity rain
3. Loose sandy soil with scanty vegetation

Select the correct answer using the code given below.

A. 1 only B. 1 and 2 only
C. 2 and 3 only D. 1, 2 and 3

139. Mulching, an agronomic measure of soil conservation, is very effective because it

1. protects soil from gully erosion
2. protects soil from sheetwash and wind erosion
3. helps soil to retain moisture and nutrients

Select the correct answer using the code given below.

A. 1 only B. 1 and 2 only
C. 2 and 3 only D. 1, 2 and 3

140. How many cubic centimetres (cm^3) are in a cubic metre (m^3)?

A. 10^3 B. 10^6
C. 10^9 D. 10^{12}

141. A semiconducting device is connected in a series circuit with a battery and a resistance. Current is found to pass through the circuit. If the polarity of the battery is reversed, the current drops to zero. The device may be

A. *p*-type semiconductor
B. *n*-type semiconductor
C. an intrinsic semiconductor
D. *p-n* junction

142. A fertilizer contains 20% nitrogen by mass. To provide a fruit tree with an equivalent of 1 kg of nitrogen, the quantity of fertilizer required is

A. 20 kg B. 0.20 kg
C. 0.05 kg D. 5 kg

143. Why is hydrolysis an effective form of chemical decomposition of bedrock in humid tropics?

1. Humid tropics experience high temperature and humidity.
2. There is high diurnal range in temperature.

Select the correct answer using the code given below.

A. 1 only B. 2 only
C. Both 1 and 2 D. Neither 1 nor 2

144. If the distance S covered by a moving car in rectilinear motion with a speed v in time t is given by $S = vt$, then the car undergoes

A. a uniform acceleration
B. a non-uniform acceleration
C. a uniform velocity
D. a non-uniform velocity

145. The phenomenon of electromagnetic induction implies a production of induced

A. resistance in a coil when the magnetic field changes with time
B. current in a coil when an electric field changes with time
C. current in a coil when a magnetic field changes with time
D. voltage in a coil when an electric field changes with time

146. Which one among the following is ***not*** a characteristic of a federal system?

A. There are two distinct levels of government
B. The responsibilities and powers of each level of government are clearly defined in a written Constitution
C. There is no separation of powers between the legislative and executive branches of government
D. A Supreme Court is entrusted with the responsibility of interpreting these provisions and arbitrating in matters of dispute

147. The Constitution of India guarantees the Fundamental Right to Freedom of Religion to all its citizens. Which among the following is ***not*** true for this Right?

A. It gives freedom of conscience and freedom to profess, practice and propagate any religion
B. It gives freedom to establish and maintain institution for religious and charitable purposes
C. The Right is subject to public order, morality and health
D. The State cannot make any law which abrogates this Right for citizens

148. The Scheduled Castes and Scheduled Tribes (Prevention and Atrocities) Act, 1989 may be seen as giving effect to which of the following Fundamental Rights?

1. Equality before the Law
2. Right against Discrimination
3. Abolition of Untouchability
4. Right to Freedom of Religion

Select the correct answer using the code given below.

A. 1, 2 and 3 only B. 2 and 3 only
C. 2, 3 and 4 only D. 1, 2, 3 and 4

149. Under which of the following Acts is the National Population Register being created?

A. The Citizenship Act of India, 1955 as amended in 2004
B. The Census Act, 1948
C. The UID Act, 2010
D. None of the above

150. Which one among the following is ***not*** true about Bal Gangadhar Tilak?

A. He started the New English School in Poona
B. He founded the Shri Shivaji Fund Committee for celebration of Shiv Jayanti
C. He preached the cult of self-reliance
D. He transformed the household worshipping of Ganesha into a public event

PAPER II : MATHEMATICS

1. Let X be the set of all citizens of India. Elements x, y in X are said to be related if the difference of their age is 5 years. Which one of the following is correct?
A. The relation is an equivalence relation on X.
B. The relation is symmetric but neither reflexive nor transitive.
C. The relation is reflexive but neither symmetric nor transitive.
D. None of the above

2. Consider the following relations from A to B where A = $\{u, v, w, x, y, z\}$ and B = $\{p, q, r, s\}$.
1. $\{(u, p), (v, p), (w, p), (x, q), (y, q), (z, q)\}$
2. $\{(u, p), (v, q), (w, r), (z, s)\}$
3. $\{(u, s), (v, r), (w, q), (u, p), (v, q), (z, q)\}$
4. $\{(u, q), (v, p), (w, s), (x, r), (y, q), (z, s)\}$

Which of the above relations are ***not*** functions?
A. 1 and 2 B. 1 and 4
C. 2 and 3 D. 3 and 4

3. If α and β are the roots of the equation $ax^2 + bx + c = 0$, where $a \neq 0$, then $(a\alpha + b)(a\beta + b)$ is equal to:
A. ab B. bc
C. ca D. abc

4. Let S denote set of all integers. Define a relation R on S as 'aRb if $ab > 0$ where $a, b \in$ S'. Then R is:
A. Reflexive but neither symmetric nor transitive relation
B. Reflexive, symmetric but not transitive relation
C. An equivalence relation
D. Symmetric but neither reflexive nor transitive relation

5. The roots of the equation $2a^2x^2 - 2abx + b^2 = 0$ when $a < 0$ and $b > 0$ are:
A. Sometimes complex B. Always irrational
C. Always complex D. Always real

6. What is the sum of the two numbers $(11110)_2$ and $(1010)_2$?
A. $(101000)_2$ B. $(110000)_2$
C. $(100100)_2$ D. $(101100)_2$

7. Let N denote the set of all non-negative integers and Z denote the set of all integers. The function $f : Z \to N$ given by $f(x) = |x|$ is:
A. One-one but not onto
B. Onto but not one-one
C. Both one-one and onto
D. Neither one-one nor onto

8. If P and Q are two complex numbers, then the modulus of the quotient of P and Q is:
A. Greater than the quotient of their moduli
B. Less than the quotient of their moduli
C. Less than or equal to the quotient of their moduli
D. Equal to the quotient of their moduli

9. Let $z = x + iy$ where x, y are real variables and $i = \sqrt{-1}$. If $|2z - 1| = |z - 2|$, then the point z describes:
A. A circle B. An ellipse
C. A hyperbola D. A parabola

10. The sum of an infinite GP is x and the common ratio r is such that $|r| < 1$. If the first term of the GP is 2, then which one of the following is correct?
A. $-1 < x < 1$ B. $-\infty < x < 1$
C. $1 < x < \infty$ D. None of the above

11. A box contains 3 white and 2 black balls. Two balls are drawn at random one after the other. If the balls are not replaced, what is the probability that both the balls are black?
A. 2/5 B. 1/5
C. 1/10 D. None of the above

12. For two variables x and y, the two regression coefficients are $b_{yx} = -3/2$ and $b_{xy} = -1/6$. The correlation coefficient between x and y is:
A. $-1/4$ B. $1/4$
C. $-1/2$ D. $1/2$

13. The variance of numbers $x_1, x_2, x_3, \ldots x_n$ is V. Consider the following statements:
1. If every x_i is increased by 2, the variance of the new set of numbers is V.
2. If the numbers x_i is squared, the variance of the new set is V^2.

Which of the following statements is/are correct?
A. 1 only B. 2 only
C. Both 1 and 2 D. Neither 1 nor 2

14. What is the mean of the squares of the first 20 natural numbers?
A. 151.5 B. 143.5
C. 65 D. 72

15. p, q, r, s, t are five numbers such that the average of p, q and r is 5 and that of s and t is 10. What is the average of all the five numbers?
A. 7.75 B. 7.5
C. 7 D. 5

16. The cumulative frequency of the largest observed value must always be:
A. Less than the total number of observations
B. Greater than the total number of observation
C. Equal to total number of observations
D. Equal to mid point of the last class interval

17. It has been found that if A and B play a game 12 times, A wins 6 times, B wins 4 times and they draw twice. A and B take part in a series of 3 games. The probability that they win alternately, is:
A. 5/12 B. 5/36
C. 19/27 D. 5/27

18. Out of 7 consonants and 4 vowels, words are to be formed by involving 3 consonants and 2 vowels. The number of such words formed is:
A. 25200 B. 22500
C. 10080 D. 5040

19. Let X denote the number of scores which exceed 4 in 18 tosses of a symmetrical die. Consider the following statements:
1. The arithmetic mean of X is 6.
2. The standard deviation of X is 2.
Which of the above statements is/are correct?
A. 1 only B. 2 only
C. Both 1 and 2 D. Neither 1 nor 2

20. How many different words can be formed by taking four letters out of the letters of the word 'AGAIN' if each word has to start with A?
A. 6 B. 12
C. 24 D. None of the above

21. The sum of the series formed by the sequence 3, $\sqrt{3}$, 1, ... upto infinity is:
A. $\frac{3\sqrt{3}\left(\sqrt{3}+1\right)}{2}$ B. $\frac{3\sqrt{3}\left(\sqrt{3}-1\right)}{2}$
C. $\frac{3\left(\sqrt{3}+1\right)}{2}$ D. $\frac{3\left(\sqrt{3}-1\right)}{2}$

22. If $|z+\bar{z}|=|z-\bar{z}|$, then the locus of z is:
A. A pair of straight lines
B. A line
C. A set of four straight lines
D. A circle

23. The number 251 in decimal system is expressed in binary system by:
A. 11110111 B. 11111011
C. 11111101 D. 11111110

24. What is the argument of the complex number $\frac{(1+i)(2+i)}{3-i}$ where $i=\sqrt{-1}$?
A. 0 B. $\frac{\pi}{4}$
C. $-\frac{\pi}{4}$ D. $\frac{\pi}{2}$

25. Consider the following statements in respect of the matrix $A = \begin{bmatrix} 0 & 1 & 2 \\ -1 & 0 & -3 \\ -2 & 3 & 0 \end{bmatrix}$
1. The matrix A is skew-symmetric.
2. The matrix A is symmetric.
3. The matrix A is invertible.
Which of the above statements is/are correct?
A. 1 only B. 3 only
C. 1 and 3 D. 2 and 3

26. Consider two matrices $A = \begin{bmatrix} 1 & 2 \\ 2 & 1 \\ 1 & 1 \end{bmatrix}$ and $B = \begin{bmatrix} 1 & 2 & -4 \\ 2 & 1 & -4 \end{bmatrix}$.
Which one of the following is correct?
A. B is the right inverse of A
B. B is the left inverse of A
C. B is the both sided inverse of A
D. None of the above

27. One of the roots of $\begin{vmatrix} x+a & b & c \\ a & x+b & c \\ a & b & x+c \end{vmatrix} = 0$ is:
A. abc B. $a+b+c$
C. $-(a+b+c)$ D. $-abc$

28. If A is any matrix, then the product AA is defined only when A is a matrix of order $m \times n$ where
A. $m > n$ B. $m < n$
C. $m = n$ D. $m \leq n$

29. The determinant of an odd order skew symmetric matrix is always:
A. Zero B. One
C. Negative D. Depends on the matrix

30. If any two adjacent rows or columns of a determinant are interchanged in position, the value of the determinant:
A. Becomes zero B. Remains the same
C. Changes its sign D. Is doubled

Directions (Qs. 31 to 33): *In a survey of 25 students, it was found that 15 had taken Mathematics, 12 had taken Physics and 11 had taken Chemistry, 5 had taken Mathematics and Chemistry, 9 had taken Mathematics and Physics, 4 had taken Physics and Chemistry and 3 had taken all the three subjects.*

31. The number of students who had taken only Physics is:
A. 2 B. 3
C. 5 D. 6

32. The number of students who had taken only two subjects is:
A. 7 B. 8
C. 9 D. 10

33. Consider the following statements:
1. The number of students who had taken only one subject is equal to the number of students who had taken only two subjects.
2. The number of students who had taken at least two subjects is four times the number of students who had taken all the three subjects.
Which of the above statements is/are correct?
A. 1 only B. 2 only
C. Both 1 and 2 D. Neither 1 nor 2

Directions (Qs. 34 to 36): *In the expansion of* $\left(x^3 - \frac{1}{x^2}\right)^n$, *where n is a positive integer, the sum of the coefficients of* x^5 *and* x^{10} *is 0.*

34. What is n equal to?
A. 5 B. 10
C. 15 D. None of the above

35. What is the value of the independent term?
A. 5005 B. 7200
C. –5005 D. –7200

36. What is the sum of the coefficients of the two middle terms?
A. 0 B. 1
C. –1 D. None of the above

Directions (Qs. 37 to 39): *Given that C(n, r) : C(n, r + 1) = 1 : 2 and C(n, r + 1) : C(n, r + 2) = 2 : 3.*

37. What is n equal to?
A. 11 B. 12
C. 13 D. 14

38. What is r equal to?
A. 2 B. 3
C. 4 D. 5

39. What is P(n, r) : C(n, r) equal to?
A. 6 B. 24
C. 120 D. 720

40. The complete solution of $3\tan^2 x = 1$ is given by:
A. $x = n\pi \pm \frac{\pi}{3}$ B. $x = n\pi + \frac{\pi}{3}$ only
C. $x = n\pi \pm \frac{\pi}{6}$ D. $x = n\pi + \frac{\pi}{6}$ only
where $n \in Z$

41. What is the value of cos 36°?
A. $\frac{\sqrt{5}-1}{4}$ B. $\frac{\sqrt{5}+1}{4}$
C. $\frac{\sqrt{10+2\sqrt{5}}}{4}$ D. $\frac{\sqrt{10-2\sqrt{5}}}{4}$

42. Consider the following statements:
1. Value of sin θ oscillates between –1 and 1.
2. Value of cos θ oscillates between 0 and 1.

Which of the above statements is/are correct?
A. 1 only B. 2 only
C. Both 1 and 2 D. Neither 1 nor 2

43. If x and y are positive and $xy > 1$, then what is $\tan^{-1} x + \tan^{-1} y$ equal to?
A. $\tan^{-1}\left(\frac{x+y}{1-xy}\right)$ B. $\pi + \tan^{-1}\left(\frac{x+y}{1-xy}\right)$
C. $\pi - \tan^{-1}\left(\frac{x+y}{1-xy}\right)$ D. $\tan^{-1}\left(\frac{x-y}{1+xy}\right)$

44. Consider the following statements:
1. $n\left(\sin^2 67\frac{1^\circ}{2} - \sin^2 22\frac{1^\circ}{2}\right) > 1$ for all positive integers $n \geq 2$.
2. If x is any positive real number, then $nx > 1$ for all positive integers $n \geq 2$.

Which of the above statements is/are correct?
A. 1 only B. 2 only
C. Both 1 and 2 D. Neither 1 nor 2

45. Consider the following statements:
1. If 3θ is an acute angle such that sin 3θ = cos 2θ, then the measurement of θ in radian equals to $\frac{\pi}{10}$.
2. One radian is the angle subtended at the centre of a circle by an arc of the same circle whose length is equal to the diameter of that circle.

Which of the above statements is/are correct?
A. 1 only B. 2 only
C. Both 1 and 2 D. Neither 1 nor 2

46. From an aeroplane above a straight road the angles of depression of two positions at a distance 20 m apart on the road are observed to be 30° and 45°. The height of the aeroplane above the ground is:
A. $10\sqrt{3}$ m B. $10(\sqrt{3}-1)$ m
C. $10(\sqrt{3}+1)$ m D. 20 m

47. Consider the following statements:
1. There exists no triangle ABC for which sin A + sin B = sin C.
2. If the angles of a triangle are in the ratio 1 : 2 : 3, then its sides will be in the ratio $1 : \sqrt{3} : 2$.

Which of the above statements is/are correct?
A. 1 only B. 2 only
C. Both 1 and 2 D. Neither 1 nor 2

48. Consider the following statements:
1. sin | x | + cos | x | is always positive.
2. $\sin(x^2) + \cos(x^2)$ is always positive.

Which of the above statements is/are correct?
A. 1 only B. 2 only
C. Both 1 and 2 D. Neither 1 nor 2

49. What is $\frac{1+\sin A}{1-\sin A} - \frac{1-\sin A}{1+\sin A}$ equal to?
A. sec A – tan A B. 2 sec A . tan A
C. 4 sec A . tan A D. 4 cosec A . cot A

50. What is $\frac{\cot 224^\circ - \cot 134^\circ}{\cot 226^\circ + \cot 316^\circ}$ equal to?
A. –cosec 88° B. –cosec 2°
C. –cosec 44° D. –cosec 46°

51. Consider the following statements:

1. $\tan^{-1} 1 + \tan^{-1} (0.5) = \pi/2$
2. $\sin^{-1} (1/3) + \cos^{-1} (1/3) = \pi/2$

Which of the above statements is/are correct?

A. 1 only B. 2 only
C. Both 1 and 2 D. Neither 1 nor 2

52. If A + B + C = π, then what is cos (A + B) + cos C equal to?

A. 0 B. 2 cos C
C. cos C – sin C D. 2 sin C

53. What is cos 20° + cos 100° + cos 140° equal to?

A. 2 B. 1
C. 1/2 D. 0

54. What is $\sin^{-1} \sin \frac{3\pi}{5}$ equal to?

A. $\frac{3\pi}{5}$ B. $\frac{2\pi}{5}$
C. $\frac{\pi}{5}$ D. None of the above

55. What is $\sin^2(3\pi) + \cos^2(4\pi) + \tan^2(5\pi)$ equal to?

A. 0 B. 1
C. 2 D. 3

56. Consider the following statements:

1. (0, 5)
2. (2, –1)
3. (3, –4)

Which of the above lie on the line $3x + y = 5$ and at a distance $\sqrt{10}$ from (1, 2)?

A. 1 only B. 2 only
C. 1 and 2 only D. 1, 2 and 3

57. What is the equation of the line through (1, 2) so that the segment of the line intercepted between the axes is bisected at this point?

A. $2x - y = 4$ B. $2x - y + 4 = 0$
C. $2x + y = 4$ D. $2x + y + 4 = 0$

58. What is the equation of straight line passing through the point (4, 3) and making equal intercepts on the coordinate axes?

A. $x + y = 7$ B. $3x + 4y = 7$
C. $x - y = 1$ D. None of the above

59. What is the equation of the line midway between the lines $3x - 4y + 12 = 0$ and $3x - 4y = 6$?

A. $3x - 4y - 9 = 0$ B. $3x - 4y + 9 = 0$
C. $3x - 4y - 3 = 0$ D. $3x - 4y + 3 = 0$

60. What is the sum of the major and minor axes of the ellipse whose eccentricity is 4/5 and length of latus rectum is 14.4 unit?

A. 32 unit B. 48 unit
C. 64 unit D. None of the above

Directions (Qs. 61 to 63): *A straight line passes through (1, –2, 3) and perpendicular to the plane 2x + 3y – z = 7.*

61. What are the direction ratios of normal to plane?

A. < 2, 3, –1 > B. < 2, 3, 1 >
C. < –1, 2, 3 > D. None of the above

62. Where does the line meet the plane?

A. (2, 3, –1) B. (1, 2, 3)
C. (2, 1, 3) D. (3, 1, 2)

63. What is the image of the point (1, –2, 3) in the plane?

A. (2, –1, 5) B. (–1, 2, –3)
C. (5, 4, 1) D. None of the above

Directions (Qs. 64 and 65): *Consider the spheres $x^2 + y^2 + z^2 - 4y + 3 = 0$ and $x^2 + y^2 + z^2 + 2x + 4z - 4 = 0$.*

64. What is the distance between the centres of the two spheres?

A. 5 unit B. 4 unit
C. 3 unit D. 2 unit

65. Consider the following statements:

1. The two spheres intersect each other.
2. The radius of first sphere is less than that of second sphere.

Which of the above statements is/are correct?

A. 1 only B. 2 only
C. Both 1 and 2 D. Neither 1 nor 2

Directions (Qs. 66 to 68): *The vertices of a triangle ABC are A(2, 3, 1), B(–2, 2, 0) and C(0, 1, –1).*

66. What is the cosine of angle ABC?

A. $\frac{1}{\sqrt{3}}$ B. $\frac{1}{\sqrt{2}}$
C. $\frac{2}{\sqrt{6}}$ D. None of the above

67. What is the area of the triangle?

A. $6\sqrt{2}$ square unit B. $3\sqrt{2}$ square unit
C. $10\sqrt{3}$ squre unit D. None of the above

68. What is the magnitude of the line joining mid points of the sides AC and BC?

A. $\frac{1}{\sqrt{2}}$ unit B. 1 unit
C. $\frac{3}{\sqrt{2}}$ unit D. 2 unit

Directions (Qs. 69 and 70): *Consider the vectors $\vec{a} = \hat{i} - 2\hat{j} + \hat{k}$ and $\vec{b} = 4\hat{i} - 4\hat{j} + 7\hat{k}$.*

69. What is the scalar projection of $\vec{a}$ on $\vec{b}$?

A. 1 B. 19/9
C. 17/9 D. 23/9

70. What is the vector perpendicular to both the vectors?

A. $-10\hat{i}-3\hat{j}+4\hat{k}$ B. $-10\hat{i}+3\hat{j}+4\hat{k}$
C. $10\hat{i}-3\hat{j}+4\hat{k}$ D. None of the above

Directions (Qs. 71 and 72): *Let a vector $\vec{r}$ make angles 60°, 30° with x and y-axis respectively.*

71. What angle does $\vec{r}$ make with z-axis?

A. 30° B. 60°
C. 90° D. 120°

72. What are the direction cosines of $\vec{r}$?

A. $\left\langle \frac{1}{2}, \frac{\sqrt{3}}{2}, 0 \right\rangle$ B. $\left\langle \frac{1}{2}, -\frac{\sqrt{3}}{2}, 0 \right\rangle$

C. $\left\langle \frac{1}{\sqrt{2}}, -\frac{1}{\sqrt{2}}, 0 \right\rangle$ D. $\left\langle -\frac{1}{2}, \frac{\sqrt{3}}{2}, 0 \right\rangle$

Directions (Qs. 73 and 74): *Let* $|\vec{a}|=7$, $|\vec{b}|=11$, $|\vec{a}+\vec{b}|=10\sqrt{3}$

73. What is $|\vec{a}-\vec{b}|$ equal to?

A. $2\sqrt{2}$ B. $2\sqrt{10}$
C. 5 D. 10

74. What is the angle between $(\vec{a}+\vec{b})$ and $(\vec{a}-\vec{b})$?

A. $\frac{\pi}{2}$ B. $\frac{\pi}{3}$

C. $\frac{\pi}{6}$ D. None of the above

75. A line passes through the points (6, –7, –1) and (2, –3, 1). What are the direction ratios of the line?

A. < 4, – 4, 2 > B. < 4, 4 , 2 >
C. < – 4, 4, 2 > D. < 2, 1, 1 >

76. What is $\lim_{x \to 0} \frac{(1+x)^n - 1}{x}$ equal to?

A. 0 B. 1
C. n D. n – 1

77. What is $\lim_{x \to 0} \frac{x}{\sqrt{1-\cos x}}$ equal to?

A. $\sqrt{2}$ B. $-\sqrt{2}$

C. $\frac{1}{\sqrt{2}}$ D. Limit does not exist

78. What is the derivative of $\sqrt{\frac{1+\cos x}{1-\cos x}}$?

A. $\frac{1}{2}\sec^2\frac{x}{2}$ B. $-\frac{1}{2}\text{cosec}^2\frac{x}{2}$

C. $-\text{cosec}^2\frac{x}{2}$ D. None of the above

79. What is $\int_0^1 \frac{e^{\tan^{-1}x}dx}{1+x^2}$ equal to?

A. $e^{\frac{\pi}{4}}-1$ B. $e^{\frac{\pi}{4}}+1$
C. $e-1$ D. e

80. What is the slope of the tangent to the curve $y = \sin^{-1}(\sin^2 x)$ at $x = 0$?

A. 0 B. 1
C. 2 D. None of the above

81. The solution of $\frac{dy}{dx} = |x|$ is:

A. $y=\frac{x|x|}{2}+c$ B. $y=\frac{|x|}{2}+c$

C. $y=\frac{x^2}{2}+c$ D. $y=\frac{x^3}{2}+c$

where c is an arbitrary constant

82. What is the solution of $\frac{dy}{dx}+2y=1$ satisfying $y(0) = 0$?

A. $y=\frac{1-e^{-2x}}{2}$ B. $y=\frac{1+e^{-2x}}{2}$

C. $y=1+e^x$ D. $y=\frac{1+e^x}{2}$

Directions (Qs. 83 and 84): *Consider the curve* $y = e^{2x}$.

83. What is the slope of the tangent to the curve at (0, 1)?

A. 0 B. 1
C. 2 D. 4

84. Where does the tangent to the curve at (0, 1) meet the x-axis?

A. (1, 0) B. (2, 0)
C. (–1/2, 0) D. (1/2, 0)

Directions (Qs. 85 and 86): *Consider an ellipse* $\frac{x^2}{a^2}+\frac{y^2}{b^2}=1$.

85. What is the area of the greatest rectangle that can be inscribed in the ellipse?

A. ab B. 2 ab
C. $ab/2$ D. $\sqrt{ab}$

86. What is the area included between the ellipse and the greatest rectangle inscribed in the ellipse?

A. $ab(\pi - 1)$ B. $2ab(\pi - 1)$
C. $ab(\pi - 2)$ D. None of the above

Directions (Qs. 87 and 88): *Consider the integrals*

$$I_1 = \int_{\frac{\pi}{6}}^{\frac{\pi}{3}} \frac{dx}{1+\sqrt{\tan x}} \text{ and } I_2 = \int_{\frac{\pi}{6}}^{\frac{\pi}{3}} \frac{\sqrt{\sin x}\,dx}{\sqrt{\sin x}+\sqrt{\cos x}}.$$

87. What is $I_1 - I_2$ equal to?

A. 0 B. $2I_1$
C. π D. None of the above

88. What is I_1 equal to?

A. $\pi/24$ B. $\pi/18$
C. $\pi/12$ D. $\pi/6$

Directions (Qs. 89 and 90): *Consider the function* $f(x)=\dfrac{1-\sin x}{(\pi-2x)^2}$, where $x\neq\dfrac{\pi}{2}$ and $f\left(\dfrac{\pi}{2}\right)=\lambda$.

89. What is $\lim_{x\to\frac{\pi}{2}} f(x)$ equal to?

A. 1 B. 1/2
C. 1/4 D. 1/8

90. What is the value of λ if the function is continuous at $x=\dfrac{\pi}{2}$?

A. 1/8 B. 1/4
C. 1/2 D. 1

91. If $f(9) = 9$ and $f'(9) = 4$, then what is $\lim_{x\to 9}\dfrac{\sqrt{f(x)}-3}{\sqrt{x}-3}$ equal to?

A. 36 B. 9
C. 4 D. None of the above

92. What is $\int_{-\frac{\pi}{2}}^{\frac{\pi}{2}} x\sin x\,dx$ equal to?

A. 0 B. 2
C. –2 D. π

93. What is the general solution of the differential equation $x\,dy - y\,dx = y^2$?

A. $x = cy$
B. $y^2 = cx$
C. $x + xy - cy = 0$
D. None of the above

where c is an arbitrary constant

94. Consider the following statements:

1. The function $f(x)=\sqrt[3]{x}$ is continuous at all x except at $x = 0$.
2. The function $f(x) = [x]$ is continuous at $x = 2.99$ where [.] is the bracket function.

Which of the above statements is/are correct?

A. 1 only B. 2 only
C. Both 1 and 2 D. Neither 1 nor 2

95. Consider the following statements:

1. The function $f(x) = |x|$ is not differentiable at $x = 1$.
2. The function $f(x) = e^x$ is differentiable at $x = 0$.

Which of the above statements is/are correct?

A. 1 only B. 2 only
C. Both 1 and 2 D. Neither 1 nor 2

96. If $z = f\circ f(x)$ where $f(x) = x^2$, then what is $\dfrac{dz}{dx}$ equal to?

A. x^3 B. $2x^3$
C. $4x^3$ D. $4x^2$

Directions (Qs. 97 and 98): *Consider the function* $f(x)=\dfrac{x^2-x+1}{x^2+x+1}$.

97. What is the maximum value of the function?

A. 1/2 B. 1/3
C. 2 D. 3

98. What is the minimum value of the function?

A. 1/2 B. 1/3
C. 2 D. 3

Directions (Qs. 99 to 101): *Let f(x) be a function defined in* $1\le x<\infty$ *by*

$$f(x)=\begin{cases}2-x & \text{for } 1\le x\le 2\\ 3x-x^2 & \text{for } x>2\end{cases}.$$

99. Consider the following statements:

1. The function is continuous at every point in the interval $[1, \infty]$.
2. The function is differentiable at $x = 1.5$.

Which of the above statements is/are correct?

A. 1 only B. 2 only
C. Both 1 and 2 D. Neither 1 nor 2

100. What is the differentiable coefficient of $f(x)$ at $x = 3$?

A. 1 B. 2
C. –1 D. –3

101. Consider the following statements:

1. $f'(2 + 0)$ does not exist.
2. $f'(2 - 0)$ does not exist.

Which of the above statements is/are correct?

A. 1 only B. 2 only
C. Both 1 and 2 D. Neither 1 nor 2

102. What is $\int_0^{\frac{\pi}{2}} \ln(\tan x)\,dx$ equal to?

A. ln 2 B. – ln 2
C. 0 D. None of the above

Directions (Qs. 103 to 105): *The general solution of the differential equation* $(x^2 + x + 1)dy + (y^2 + y + 1)dx = 0$ *is* $(x + y + 1) = A(1 + Bx + Cy + Dxy)$ *where B, C and D are constants and A is parameter.*

103. What is B equal to?

A. –1 B. 1
C. 2 D. None of the above

104. What is C equal to?

A. 1 B. –1
C. 2 D. None of the above

105. What is D equal to?
A. –1 B. 1
C. 2 D. None of the above

106. Consider the following statements:
1. The function $f(x) = \sin x$ decreases on the interval $(0, \pi/2)$.
2. The function $f(x) = \cos x$ increases on the interval $(0, \pi/2)$.

Which of the above statements is/are correct?
A. 1 only B. 2 only
C. Both 1 and 2 D. Neither 1 nor 2

107. What is the number of arbitrary constants in the particular solution of differential equation of third order?
A. 0 B. 1
C. 2 D. 3

108. What is the equation of a curve passing through (0, 1) and whose differential equation is given by $dy = y \tan x\, dx$?
A. $y = \cos x$ B. $y = \sin x$
C. $y = \sec x$ D. $y = \text{cosec } x$

109. Consider the following statements in respect of the differential equation $\frac{d^2y}{dx^2} + \cos\left(\frac{dy}{dx}\right) = 0$:
1. The degree of the differential equation is not defined.
2. The order of the differential equation is 2.

Which of the above statements is/are correct?
A. 1 only B. 2 only
C. Both 1 and 2 D. Neither 1 nor 2

110. What is the equation of parabola whose vertex is at (0, 0) and focus is at (0, –2)?
A. $y^2 + 8x = 0$ B. $y^2 - 8x = 0$
C. $x^2 + 8y = 0$ D. $x^2 - 8y = 0$

Directions (Qs. 111 to 114): *Number X is randomly selected from the set of odd numbers and Y is randomly selected from the set of even numbers of the set {1, 2, 3, 4, 5, 6, 7}. Let Z = (X + Y).*

111. What is P(Z = 5) equal to?
A. 1/2 B. 1/3
C. 1/4 D. 1/6

112. What is P(Z = 10) equal to?
A. 0 B. 1/2
C. 1/3 D. 1/5

113. What is P(Z > 11) equal to?
A. 0 B. 1/4
C. 1/6 D. 1/12

114. What is P(Z is the product of two prime numbers) equal to?
A. 0 B. 1/2
C. 1/4 D. None of the above

Directions (Qs. 115 to 117): *The number of telephone calls received in 245 successive one minute intervals at an exchange is given below in the following frequency distribution.*

Number of calls	0	1	2	3	4	5	6	7
Frequency	14	21	25	43	51	40	39	12

115. What is the mean of the distribution?
A. 3.76 B. 3.84
C. 3.96 D. 4.05

116. What is the median of the distribution?
A. 3.5 B. 4
C. 4.5 D. 5

117. What is the mode of the distribution?
A. 3 B. 4
C. 5 D. 6

Directions (Qs. 118 to 120): *The mean and standard deviation of 100 items are 50, 5 and that of 150 items are 40, 6 respectively.*

118. What is the combined mean of all 250 items?
A. 43 B. 44
C. 45 D. 46

119. What is the combined standard deviation of all 250 items?
A. 7.1 B. 7.3
C. 7.5 D. 7.7

120. What is the variance of all the 250 items?
A. 50.6 B. 53.3
C. 55.6 D. 59.3

ANSWERS

PAPER-I : GENERAL ABILITY TEST

1	2	3	4	5	6	7	8	9	10
B	C	B	B	C	C	C	B	C	C
11	**12**	**13**	**14**	**15**	**16**	**17**	**18**	**19**	**20**
C	D	B	A	B	C	D	A	D	C
21	**22**	**23**	**24**	**25**	**26**	**27**	**28**	**29**	**30**
A	D	A	D	D	C	D	A	B	A

31	**32**	**33**	**34**	**35**	**36**	**37**	**38**	**39**	**40**
B	A	C	B	A	A	C	B	B	B
41	**42**	**43**	**44**	**45**	**46**	**47**	**48**	**49**	**50**
C	A	A	B	A	C	C	A	A	B
51	**52**	**53**	**54**	**55**	**56**	**57**	**58**	**59**	**60**
C	D	B	B	C	D	B	D	D	B
61	**62**	**63**	**64**	**65**	**66**	**67**	**68**	**69**	**70**
C	C	D	B	A	C	B	C	B	C
71	**72**	**73**	**74**	**75**	**76**	**77**	**78**	**79**	**80**
A	C	B	A	B	B	A	A	A	A
81	**82**	**83**	**84**	**85**	**86**	**87**	**88**	**89**	**90**
A	C	B	C	A	B	B	C	D	D
91	**92**	**93**	**94**	**95**	**96**	**97**	**98**	**99**	**100**
A	B	C	D	C	D	B	D	D	B
101	**102**	**103**	**104**	**105**	**106**	**107**	**108**	**109**	**110**
A	C	A	B	C	D	D	C	C	C
111	**112**	**113**	**114**	**115**	**116**	**117**	**118**	**119**	**120**
A	A	A	B	B	B	A	C	B	B
121	**122**	**123**	**124**	**125**	**126**	**127**	**128**	**129**	**130**
B	C	A	B	B	D	C	A	C	A
131	**132**	**133**	**134**	**135**	**136**	**137**	**138**	**139**	**140**
C	B	A	D	D	B	C	C	C	B
141	**142**	**143**	**144**	**145**	**146**	**147**	**148**	**149**	**150**
D	D	B	C	C	C	D	B	A	B

PAPER-II : MATHEMATICS

1	**2**	**3**	**4**	**5**	**6**	**7**	**8**	**9**	**10**
B	C	C	C	C	A	B	C	A	A
11	**12**	**13**	**14**	**15**	**16**	**17**	**18**	**19**	**20**
C	D	A	B	C	C	B	A	A	C
21	**22**	**23**	**24**	**25**	**26**	**27**	**28**	**29**	**30**
A	A	B	D	A	D	C	C	A	C
31	**32**	**33**	**34**	**35**	**36**	**37**	**38**	**39**	**40**
A	C	B	C	C	A	D	C	B	C
41	**42**	**43**	**44**	**45**	**46**	**47**	**48**	**49**	**50**
B	A	B	C	A	C	C	D	C	B
51	**52**	**53**	**54**	**55**	**56**	**57**	**58**	**59**	**60**
B	A	D	B	B	C	C	C	D	C
61	**62**	**63**	**64**	**65**	**66**	**67**	**68**	**69**	**70**
A	D	C	C	C	A	B	C	B	A
71	**72**	**73**	**74**	**75**	**76**	**77**	**78**	**79**	**80**
C	A	B	D	C	C	A	B	A	A
81	**82**	**83**	**84**	**85**	**86**	**87**	**88**	**89**	**90**
A	A	C	C	B	C	A	C	D	A
91	**92**	**93**	**94**	**95**	**96**	**97**	**98**	**99**	**100**
C	B	D	B	B	C	D	B	B	D
101	**102**	**103**	**104**	**105**	**106**	**107**	**108**	**109**	**110**
D	C	A	B	C	D	D	C	C	C
111	**112**	**113**	**114**	**115**	**116**	**117**	**118**	**119**	**120**
D	A	D	C	A	B	B	B	C	C

EXPLANATORY ANSWERS

PAPER-I : GENERAL ABILITY TEST

82. Number of valence electrons in O with atomic number = 8

$K = 2\ (1s^2)$

$L = 6\ (2s^2\ 2p^4)$

In case of O^{2-}

$K = 2\ (1s^2)$

$L = 8\ (2s^2\ 2p^6)$

Hence, valence electrons = 8.

84. Resistance $R = \frac{\rho \cdot l}{A}$

$l_B = 2l_A$ also $r_A = 2r_B$

$\therefore A_A = 4A_B$

$\therefore \frac{R_A}{R_B} = \frac{l_A \cdot A_B}{l_B \cdot A_A}$

$= \frac{1}{2} \cdot \frac{1}{4} = 1 : 8$

86. Cl atomic number is 17.

$\therefore$ E.C. $K = 2\ (1s^2)$

$L = 8\ (2s^2\ 2p^6)$

$M = 7\ (3s^2\ 3p^5)$

$= 2, 8, 7.$

89. Number of mols of Aluminium ions in $= \frac{54}{27} = 2$ mols

Now, 1 mol = 6.1×10^{23} ions

$\therefore$ 2 mol = 1.2×10^{24} ions.

96. $Ca^{2+} \div$ Number of electrons = 20 – 2 = 18

$S^{2-} \div$ Number of electrons = 16 + 2 = 18.

99. Bernoulli's equation relates the speed of fluid at a point, the pressure at that point and height of that point above a reference level. It is just the application of work-energy theorem in the case of fluid flow.

100. From the graph, the particle has come to rest after time $t = t_1$. Hence, this is example of S.H.M. immersed in water.

104. Ohm's law state that voltage (V) $\propto$ current (I).

or, $V = R.I$

where R = Resistance of the conductor.

108. The anomalous expansion of water has a favourable effect for animals living in water. Since, the water density is maximum at 4°C, water at the bottom of the lakes remains at 4°C in winter even if that at the surface freezes. This allows marine animals to remain alive and move near the bottom.

113. Speed of light in glass $= \frac{\text{Speed of light in air}}{\text{Refractive index}}$

$= \frac{3 \times 10^8}{1.5} = 2 \times 10^8$ m/s.

118. $R_A = 2R_B$

and $M_A = 4M_B$

Weight $W_A = \frac{C_2 M_A m}{R_A^2}$

$= \frac{4 \cdot GM_B m}{4R_B^2}$

$= \frac{GM_B m}{R_B^2} = W_B$

$\therefore W_A = W_B$.

119. Increase in oxidation state is oxidation. Here, oxidation state of oxygen atom changes from –2 to 0. Hence, water is oxidised to O_2.

123. Speed of sound wave

$v = \nu \cdot \lambda$

$= 2 \times 10^3 \times 35 \times 10^{-2}$

$= 700$ m/sec

Required time interval

$t = \frac{1.4 \times 10^3}{700} = 2$ sec.

128. Fuse is a conducting wire of high resistance and low melting point so that when a large current passes through it, it melted down and protect the circuit or electric appliance from damage.

129. Mass of the atom is its mass of protons and neutrons which is found in the nucleus.

131. In isothermal process

$\Delta T = 0$

$\therefore$ PV = Constant

$P \propto \frac{1}{V}$

From $P_1V_1 = P_2V_2$

here $P_2 = \left(1 + \frac{10}{100}\right) P_1 = 1.1\ P_1$

$\therefore$ Change in volume

$\frac{V_1 - V_2}{V_1} = \frac{1}{11}$

Percentage decrease = 9.09%.

133. Due to acceleratory motion of train the passenger moved forward, while the tossed coin fell freely and landed behind him.

134. Mass number (A) = Number of protons (p) + Number of neutrons (n).

136. In optical instruments, the rays passes through the lens and form the image after refraction.

137. When they react, CO reacts with O_2 in 2 : 1 mol ratio and form 2 mols of CO_2.

140. $1\ m^3 = 1 \times (10^2)^3 \cdot cm^3$
$= 10^6\ cm^3$.

141. p-n junction is a diode, which allows to pass the current in only one direction.

142. To provide 1 kg of N_2.

The quantity of fertilizer required $= \dfrac{1 \times 100}{20} = 5$ kg.

144. As from the formula

$$S = vt \pm \frac{1}{2}at^2$$

here, $a = 0 \Rightarrow S = vt$

∴ motion is uniform velocity motion.

145. Faraday's law of electromagnetic induction says that "whenever the flux of magnetic field through the area bounded by a closed conducting loop changes, an emf is produced in the loop, which induces a current in the coil".

PAPER-II : MATHEMATICS

3. ∵ α, β are the roots of the given equation $ax^2 + bx + c = 0$

∴ Sum of roots $= \alpha + \beta = -\dfrac{b}{a}$

and product of the roots $= \alpha \times \beta = \dfrac{c}{a}$

Now, value of $(a\alpha + b)(a\beta + b)$

$= a^2\alpha\beta + ab\,\alpha + ab\,\beta + b^2$

$= a^2(\alpha\beta) + ab(\alpha + \beta) + b^2$

$= a^2\left(\dfrac{c}{a}\right) + ab\left(-\dfrac{b}{a}\right) + b^2 = ac - b^2 + b^2 = ac.$

10. First term of G.P. $= a = 2$ and common ratio $= r$

Sum of ∞ terms $= \dfrac{a}{1-r} = \dfrac{2}{1-r}$

∵ $-1 < r < 1$

∴ $-1 < x < 1$ is correct answer.

14. $1^2 + 2^2 + 3^2 + \ldots\ldots\ldots + 20^2$

$= \dfrac{n(n+1)(2n+1)}{6}$ $\left[\because 1^2 + 2^2 + \ldots + n^2 = \dfrac{n(n+1)(2n+1)}{6}\right]$

$= \dfrac{20 \times 21 \times 41}{6}$

Required mean value $= \dfrac{20 \times 21 \times 41}{6 \times 20} = \dfrac{287}{2} = 143.5.$

15. There are 5 numbers as p, q, r, s and t.

Sum of three numbers as $(p + q + r) = 5 \times 3 = 15$

Sum of s and t numbers $= 10 \times 2 = 20$

Sum of all 5 numbers $= 15 + 20 = 35$

Average of these numbers $= \dfrac{35}{5} = 7$.

16. The cumulative frequency of the largest observed value must always be equal to total number of observations.

18. Three consonants out of 7 and 2 vowels out of 4 can be chosen in ${}^7C_3 \times {}^4C_2$ ways. Since each group contains 5 letters which can be arranged among themselves in 5! ways. Hence, the required number of words

$= \left({}^7C_3 \times {}^4C_2\right) \times 5! = \dfrac{7!}{3!\,4!} \times \dfrac{4!}{2! \times 2!} \times 5!$

$= \dfrac{7 \times 6 \times 5 \times 4!}{3 \times 2 \times 4!} \times \dfrac{4 \times 3 \times 2!}{2 \times 1 \times 2!} \times 5 \times 4 \times 3 \times 2 \times 1$

$= 35 \times 6 \times 120 = 35 \times 720 = 25200.$

21. $3, \sqrt{3}, 1, \ldots \infty$ are in G.P.

Here, $a = 3$, and $r = \dfrac{1}{\sqrt{3}}$

Sum of infinity terms

$= \dfrac{a}{1-r} = \dfrac{3}{1 - \dfrac{1}{\sqrt{3}}} = \dfrac{3}{\dfrac{\sqrt{3}-1}{\sqrt{3}}}$

$= \dfrac{3\sqrt{3}}{\sqrt{3}-1} \times \dfrac{\sqrt{3}+1}{\sqrt{3}+1} = \dfrac{3\sqrt{3}\left(\sqrt{3}+1\right)}{3-1}$

$= \dfrac{3\sqrt{3}\left(\sqrt{3}+1\right)}{2}$.

22. Let $z = x + iy$.

Then, $|z + \bar{z}| = |z - \bar{z}|$

$\Rightarrow |2x| = |2iy|$

$\Rightarrow |x| = |y| \Rightarrow x = \pm y$

Hence, the locus of z is a pair of straight lines.

24. $\dfrac{(1+i)(2+i)}{3-i} = \dfrac{1(2+i)+i(2+i)}{3-i}$

$= \dfrac{2+i+2i+i^2}{3-i} = \dfrac{2+3i-1}{3-i}$

$= \dfrac{1+3i}{3-i} \times \dfrac{3+i}{3+i} = \dfrac{1(3+i)+3i(3+i)}{9-i^2}$

$= \dfrac{3+i+9i+3i^2}{9+1}$

$= \dfrac{3+10i-3}{10} = \dfrac{0+10i}{10}$

$= 0 + i = \cos\dfrac{\pi}{2} + i\sin\dfrac{\pi}{2}$

Argument, $\theta = \dfrac{\pi}{2}$.

27. $\begin{vmatrix} x+a & b & c \\ a & x+b & c \\ a & b & x+c \end{vmatrix} = 0$

$(x + a)\ [(x + b)\ (x + c) - bc] - b\ [a(x + c) - ac]$
$+ c[ab - a(x + b)]$
$= (x + a)\ [x^2 + xc + bx + bc - bc] - b\ [ax + ac - ac]$
$+ c[ab - ax - ab]$
$= (x + a)\ [x^2 + xc + bx] - abx - acx$
$= x^3 + x^2c + bx^2 + ax^2 + acx + abx - abx - acx$
$= x^3 + x^2\ c + bx^2 + ax^2$
$= x^2\ (x + a + b + c)$
Now, $x^2\ (x + a + b + c) = 0$
$\Rightarrow x + a + b + c = 0$
$\Rightarrow x = - a - b - c$
Hence, one of the root is $-(a + b + c)$.

34. $\left(x^3 - \dfrac{1}{x^2}\right)^n$

$= {}^nC_0\left(x^3\right)^n - {}^nC_1\left(x^3\right)^{n-1}\cdot\left(\dfrac{1}{x^2}\right) + {}^nC_2\left(x^3\right)^{n-2}\cdot\left(\dfrac{1}{x^2}\right)^2$

$- {}^nC_3\left(x^3\right)^{n-3}\left(\dfrac{1}{x^2}\right)^3 + {}^nC_4\left(x^3\right)^{n-4}\left(\dfrac{1}{x^2}\right)^4 - {}^nC_5\left(x^3\right)^{n-5}$

$\left(\dfrac{1}{x^2}\right)^5 + {}^nC_6\left(x^3\right)^{n-6}\left(\dfrac{1}{x^2}\right)^6 - {}^nC_7\left(x^3\right)^{n-7}\cdot\left(\dfrac{1}{x^2}\right)^7$

$+ {}^nC_8\left(x^3\right)^{n-8}\left(\dfrac{1}{x^2}\right)^8 - {}^nC_9\left(x^3\right)^{n-9}\cdot\left(\dfrac{1}{x^2}\right)^9$

$\therefore\ {}^nC_8 - {}^nC_7 = 0$ $\quad\left[\begin{array}{l}\because\ {}^nC_x = {}^nC_y \\ \therefore\quad n = x + y\end{array}\right]$

$\Rightarrow {}^nC_8 = {}^nC_7 \Rightarrow n = 8 + 7 \Rightarrow n = 15$

Hence, $n = 15$.

35. Value of the independent term

$= -{}^nC_9\left(x^3\right)^{n-9}\left(\dfrac{1}{x^2}\right)^9 = -{}^{15}C_9\left(x^3\right)^{15-9}\left(\dfrac{1}{x^2}\right)^9$

$= -{}^{15}C_9\ x^{18-18} = -{}^{15}C_9 x^0 = -{}^{15}C_9 = -\dfrac{15!}{9!\times 6!}$

$= \dfrac{-15\times 14\times 13\times 12\times 11\times 10\times 9!}{9!\times 6\times 5\times 4\times 3\times 2\times 1}$

$= -91 \times 55 = -5005.$

For the three questions (37 to 39):

$\dfrac{{}^nC_r}{{}^nC_{r+1}} = \dfrac{1}{2}$ (given)

$\Rightarrow \dfrac{\dfrac{n!}{r!\,(n-r)!}}{\dfrac{n!}{(r+1)!\,(n-r-1)!}} = \dfrac{1}{2}$

$\Rightarrow \dfrac{(r+1)!\,(n-r-1)!}{r!\,(n-r)!} = \dfrac{1}{2}$

$\Rightarrow \dfrac{(r+1)\cdot r!\,(n-r-1)!}{r!\,(n-r)\,(n-r-1)!} = \dfrac{1}{2}$

$\Rightarrow \quad n - r = 2\ (r + 1)$
$\Rightarrow \quad n - r = 2r + 2$
$\Rightarrow \quad n = 3r + 2$ ...(*i*)

Again, $\dfrac{{}^nC_{r+1}}{{}^nC_{r+2}} = \dfrac{2}{3}$

$\Rightarrow \dfrac{\dfrac{n!}{(r+1)!\,(n-r-1)!}}{\dfrac{n!}{(r+2)!\,(n-r-2)!}} = \dfrac{2}{3}$

$\Rightarrow \dfrac{(r+2)!\,(n-r-2)!}{(r+1)!\,(n-r-1)!} = \dfrac{2}{3}$

$\Rightarrow \dfrac{(r+2)\,(r+1)!\,(n-r-2)!}{(r+1)!\,(n-r-1)\,(n-r-2)!} = \dfrac{2}{3}$

$2(n - r - 1) = 3\ (r + 2)$
$\Rightarrow \quad 2n - 2r - 2 = 3r + 6$
$\Rightarrow \quad 2n = 5r + 8$ ...(*ii*)

Multiply equation (*i*) by 2

$2n = 6r + 4$ ...(*iii*)

From equations (*ii*) and (*iii*)

$6r + 4 = 5r + 8$
$\Rightarrow \quad r = 4$

Putting the value of r in equation (*ii*)

$2n = 5(4) + 8$
$\Rightarrow \quad 2n = 20 + 8$
$\Rightarrow \quad 2n = 28$
$\Rightarrow \quad n = 14.$

37. Value of $n = 14$.

38. Value of $r = 4$.

39. $^nP_r : {}^nC_r = \dfrac{^nP_r}{^nC_r}$

$$\frac{\dfrac{n!}{(n-r)!}}{\dfrac{n!}{r!\,(n-r)!}} = \frac{n!}{(n-r)!} \times \frac{r!(n-r)!}{n!}$$

$$= r! = 4! \qquad [\because r = 4]$$

$$= 4 \times 3 \times 2 \times 1 = 24.$$

40. $3 \tan^2 x = 1$

$\Rightarrow \quad \tan^2 x = \dfrac{1}{3}$

$\tan x = \pm\dfrac{1}{\sqrt{3}} = \pm\tan\dfrac{\pi}{6}$

$\Rightarrow \quad x = n\pi \pm \dfrac{\pi}{6}.$

41. $\cos 36° = \dfrac{\sqrt{5}+1}{4}.$

43. $\tan^{-1} x + \tan^{-1} y = \dfrac{\tan^{-1}(x+y)}{1-xy}$

But $xy > 1$

$\therefore \tan^{-1} x + \tan^{-1} y = \pi + \tan^{-1}\dfrac{(x+y)}{1-xy}.$

45. $\sin 3\theta = \cos 2\theta$

$\Rightarrow \cos(90° - 3\theta) = \cos 2\theta$

$\Rightarrow 90° - 3\theta = 2\theta$

$\Rightarrow 5\theta = 90°$

$\Rightarrow \theta = 18°$

$\therefore 180° = \pi$ radian

$\therefore 18° = \dfrac{\pi}{180} \times 18 = \dfrac{\pi}{10}$ radian

1 is true.
2 is not true.

46.

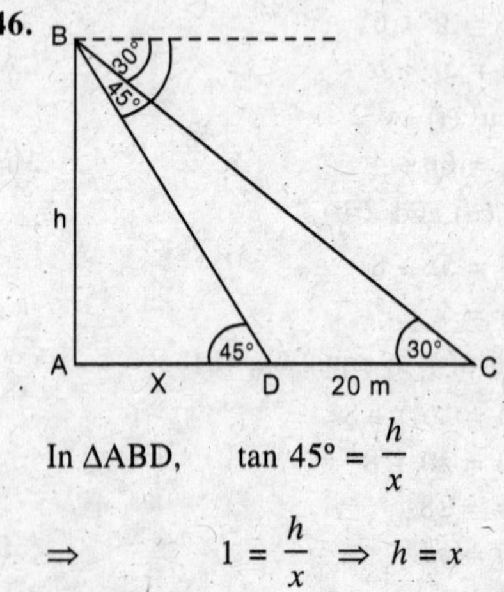

In ΔABD, $\tan 45° = \dfrac{h}{x}$

$\Rightarrow \quad 1 = \dfrac{h}{x} \Rightarrow h = x$

In Δ ABC,

$\tan 30° = \dfrac{h}{x+20}$

$\Rightarrow \dfrac{1}{\sqrt{3}} = \dfrac{h}{x+20} = \dfrac{h}{h+20} \quad (\because x = h)$

$\Rightarrow \sqrt{3}h = h + 20 = (\sqrt{3}h - h) = 20$

$\Rightarrow h\left(\sqrt{3}-1\right) = 20$

$\Rightarrow \quad h = \dfrac{20}{\sqrt{3}-1} \times \dfrac{\sqrt{3}+1}{\sqrt{3}+1} = \dfrac{20\left(\sqrt{3}+1\right)}{2}$

$\Rightarrow \quad h = 10\left(\sqrt{3}+1\right)$

Hence, height of the aeroplane above the ground $= 10\left(\sqrt{3}+1\right)$ m.

49. $\dfrac{1+\sin A}{1-\sin A} - \dfrac{1-\sin A}{1+\sin A}$

$$= \frac{(1+\sin A)^2 - (1-\sin A)^2}{(1-\sin A)\,(1+\sin A)}$$

$$= \frac{(1+2\sin A+\sin^2 A)-(1-2\sin A+\sin^2 A)}{1-\sin^2 A}$$

$$= \frac{1+2\sin A+\sin^2 A-1+2\sin A-\sin^2 A}{\cos^2 A}$$

$$= \frac{4\sin A}{\cos A \times \cos A} = 4 \sec A \cdot \tan A.$$

51. 1. $\tan^{-1} 1 + \tan^{-1} (0.5) = \dfrac{\pi}{2}$. It is not true.

2. $\sin^{-1}\left(\dfrac{1}{3}\right) + \cos^{-1}\left(\dfrac{1}{3}\right) = \dfrac{\pi}{2}$

It is true because $\sin^{-1} x + \cos^{-1} x = \dfrac{\pi}{2}$.

52. $\because \quad A + B + C = \pi$

$A + B = \pi - C$

$\cos (A + B) = \cos (\pi - C)$

$\Rightarrow \cos (A + B) = -\cos C$

Now, $\cos (A + B) + \cos C$

$= -\cos C + \cos C = 0.$

53. $\cos 20° + \cos 100° + \cos 140°$

$= 2\cos\dfrac{120°}{2}\cdot\cos\dfrac{80°}{2} + \cos 140°$

$= 2\cos 60°\cdot\cos 40° + \cos 140°$

$= 2 \times \dfrac{1}{2} \times \cos 40° + \cos 140°$

$= \cos 40° + \cos 140°$

$= \cos 40° + \cos (180° - 40°)$

$= \cos 40° - \cos 40° = 0.$

54. $\sin^{-1} \times \sin\frac{3\pi}{5} = \sin^{-1}\left[\sin\left(\pi - \frac{2\pi}{5}\right)\right]$

$= \sin^{-1} \cdot \sin\frac{2\pi}{5} = \frac{2\pi}{5}$.

55. $\sin^2 (3\pi) + \cos^2 (4\pi) + \tan^2 (5\pi)$

$= (0)^2 + (1)^2 + \frac{\sin^2(5\pi)}{\cos^2(5\pi)}$

$= 0 + 1 + 0 = 1$ $\left[\begin{array}{l}\because \sin n\pi = 0 \\ \cos n\pi = (-1)^n\end{array}\right]$

For the two questions (66 and 67):

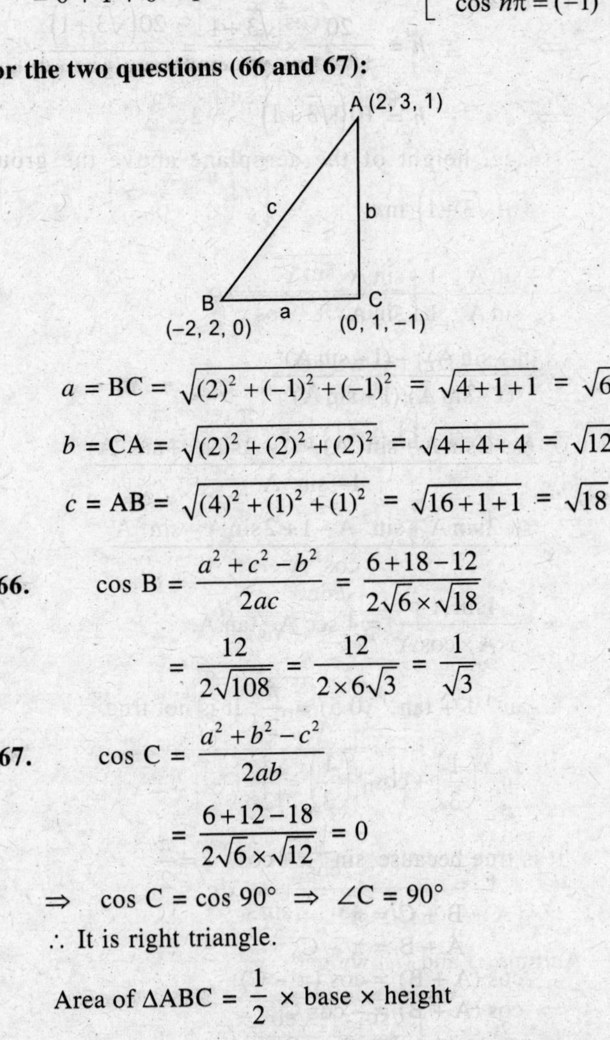

$a = BC = \sqrt{(2)^2 + (-1)^2 + (-1)^2} = \sqrt{4+1+1} = \sqrt{6}$

$b = CA = \sqrt{(2)^2 + (2)^2 + (2)^2} = \sqrt{4+4+4} = \sqrt{12}$

$c = AB = \sqrt{(4)^2 + (1)^2 + (1)^2} = \sqrt{16+1+1} = \sqrt{18}$.

66. $\cos B = \frac{a^2 + c^2 - b^2}{2ac} = \frac{6+18-12}{2\sqrt{6}\times\sqrt{18}}$

$= \frac{12}{2\sqrt{108}} = \frac{12}{2\times 6\sqrt{3}} = \frac{1}{\sqrt{3}}$

67. $\cos C = \frac{a^2 + b^2 - c^2}{2ab}$

$= \frac{6+12-18}{2\sqrt{6}\times\sqrt{12}} = 0$

$\Rightarrow$ $\cos C = \cos 90° \Rightarrow \angle C = 90°$

$\therefore$ It is right triangle.

Area of $\Delta ABC = \frac{1}{2} \times$ base $\times$ height

$= \frac{1}{2}\times\sqrt{6}\times\sqrt{12} = \frac{1}{2}\times\sqrt{72}$

$= \frac{1}{2}\times 6\sqrt{2} = 3\sqrt{2}$ square unit.

76. $\lim_{x\to 0} \frac{(1+x)^n - 1}{x}$

$\frac{(1+x)^1 - 1}{x} = \frac{1+x-1}{x} = \frac{x}{x} = 1$

$\frac{(1+x)^2 - 1}{x} = \frac{1+2x+x^2-1}{x} = \frac{x(2+x)}{x}$

$\frac{(1+x)^3 - 1}{x} = \frac{1+3x+3x^2+x^3-1}{x}$

$= \frac{3x+3x^2+x^3}{x} = \frac{x(3+3x+x^2)}{x}$

$\therefore \lim_{x\to 0} \frac{(1+x)^n - 1}{x} = \frac{1+n\cdot x+\ldots-1}{x}$

$= \frac{nx + \text{highest power of } x}{x}$

$= \frac{x(n + \text{highest power of } x)}{x}$

$= n +$ highest power of x

$= n$

77. $\lim_{x\to 0} \frac{x}{\sqrt{1-\cos x}} \times \frac{\sqrt{1+\cos x}}{\sqrt{1+\cos x}}$

$= \lim_{x\to 0} \frac{x\left(\sqrt{1+\cos x}\right)}{\sqrt{1-\cos^2 x}} = \lim_{x\to 0} \frac{x\sqrt{(1+\cos x)}}{\sin x}$

$= \lim_{x\to 0} \frac{x}{\sin x} \times \lim_{x\to 0} \sqrt{1+1} = 1\times\sqrt{2} = \sqrt{2}$.

78. $y = \sqrt{\frac{1+\cos x}{1-\cos x}} = \sqrt{\frac{2\cos^2\frac{x}{2}}{2\sin^2\frac{x}{2}}}$

$= \sqrt{\frac{\cos^2\frac{x}{2}}{\sin^2\frac{x}{2}}} = \frac{\cos\frac{x}{2}}{\sin\frac{x}{2}} = \cot\frac{x}{2}$

Differentiating both sides with respect to x.

$\frac{dy}{dx} = -\frac{1}{2}\operatorname{cosec}^2\frac{x}{2}$.

79. $\int_0^1 \frac{e^{\tan^{-1} x}}{1+x^2} dx$

Substituting $t = \tan^{-1} x$

$\Rightarrow$ $\frac{dt}{dx} = \frac{1}{1+x^2}$

$\Rightarrow$ $dt = \frac{dx}{1+x^2}$

when $x = 0, t = \tan^{-1}(0)$

$= 0$

for $x = 1, t = \tan^{-1}(1) = \frac{\pi}{4}$

$\Rightarrow$ $\int_0^1 \frac{e^{\tan^{-1} x}}{1+x^2} dx = \int_0^{\frac{\pi}{4}} e^t dt = \left(e^t\right)_0^{\frac{\pi}{4}} = e^{\frac{\pi}{4}} - 1$.

85. The equation of the ellipse is

$$\frac{x^2}{a^2}+\frac{y^2}{b^2}=1 \quad ...(i)$$

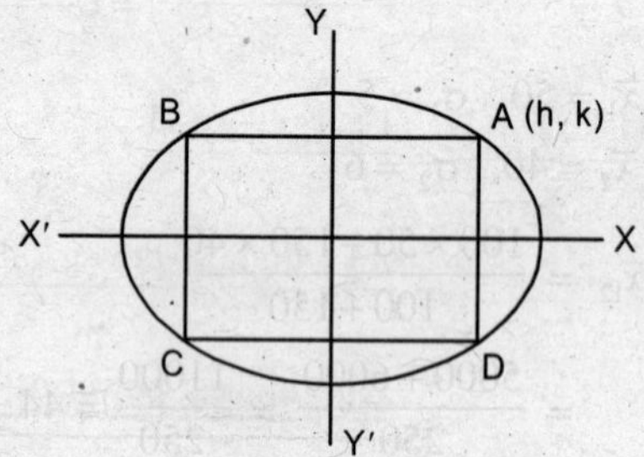

Let ABCD be the rectangle inscribed in the ellipse.

Let AB = $2h$, AD = $2k$

$\therefore$ Area of the rectangle is

$$A = 4\,hk$$

or $A^2 = 16\,h^2k^2 \quad ...(ii)$

Since, (h, k) lies on the ellipse (i)

$$\therefore \quad \frac{h^2}{a^2}+\frac{k^2}{b^2} = 1 \quad ...(iii)$$

from (ii) and (iii)

$$A^2 = 16h^2b^2\left(1-\frac{h^2}{a^2}\right)$$

$$\therefore \quad \frac{d(A^2)}{dh} = 16b^2\left(2h-\frac{4h^3}{a^2}\right)$$

$$\frac{d^2}{dh^2}(A^2) = 16b^2\left(2-\frac{12h^2}{a^2}\right)$$

For maxima and minima $\frac{d(A^2)}{dh} = 0$

$$\Rightarrow 16b^2\left(2h-\frac{4h^3}{a^2}\right) = 0$$

$$\Rightarrow \quad h = 0, \ \pm\frac{a}{\sqrt{2}}$$

At $h=\frac{a}{\sqrt{2}}$, $k=\frac{b}{\sqrt{2}}$ · $\frac{d^2}{dh^2}(A^2)<0$

So, A is maximum

$\therefore$ Maximum area A = $4\,hk$

$$= 4\times\frac{a}{\sqrt{2}}\times\frac{b}{\sqrt{2}}=2ab.$$

For the two questions (87 and 88):

Consider the integrals

$$I_1 = \int_{\pi/6}^{\pi/3}\frac{dx}{1+\sqrt{\tan x}}$$

and $$I_2 = \int_{\pi/6}^{\pi/3}\frac{\sqrt{\sin x}\,dx}{\sqrt{\sin x}+\sqrt{\cos x}}$$

Let $$I_1 = \int_{\pi/6}^{\pi/3}\frac{dx}{1+\sqrt{\tan x}}$$

$$= \int_{\pi/6}^{\pi/3}\frac{\sqrt{\cos x}}{\sqrt{\cos x}+\sqrt{\sin x}}dx \quad ...(i)$$

$$= \int_{\pi/6}^{\pi/3}\frac{\sqrt{\cos\left(\frac{\pi}{2}-x\right)}}{\sqrt{\cos\left(\frac{\pi}{2}-x\right)}+\sqrt{\sin\left(\frac{\pi}{2}-x\right)}}dx$$

$$\left[\because\left(\frac{\pi}{6}+\frac{\pi}{3}-x\right)=\left(\frac{\pi}{2}-x\right)\right]$$

$$= \int_{\pi/6}^{\pi/3}\frac{\sqrt{\sin x}}{\sqrt{\sin x}+\sqrt{\cos x}}dx \quad ...(ii)$$

Adding (i) and (ii) we get

$$2I_1 = \int_{\pi/6}^{\pi/3}1\,dx=[x]_{\frac{\pi}{6}}^{\frac{\pi}{3}}=\frac{\pi}{3}-\frac{\pi}{6}=\frac{\pi}{6}$$

$$\therefore \quad I_1 = \frac{\pi}{12}$$

$$I_2 = \int_{\pi/6}^{\pi/3}\frac{\sqrt{\sin x}}{\sqrt{\sin x}+\sqrt{\cos x}}dx \quad ...(i)$$

$$I_2 = \int_{\pi/6}^{\pi/3}\frac{\sqrt{\sin\left(\frac{\pi}{2}-x\right)}}{\sqrt{\sin\left(\frac{\pi}{2}-x\right)}+\sqrt{\cos\left(\frac{\pi}{2}-x\right)}}dx$$

$$I_2 = \int_{\pi/6}^{\pi/3}\frac{\sqrt{\cos x}}{\sqrt{\cos x}+\sqrt{\sin x}}dx \quad ...(ii)$$

Adding (i) and (ii) we get

$$2I_2 = \int_{\pi/6}^{\pi/3}\frac{\sqrt{\sin x}+\sqrt{\cos x}}{\sqrt{\sin x}+\sqrt{\cos x}}dx$$

$$\Rightarrow \quad 2I_2 = \int_{\pi/6}^{\pi/3}1\,dx=[x]_{\frac{\pi}{6}}^{\frac{\pi}{3}}=\frac{\pi}{3}-\frac{\pi}{6}=\frac{\pi}{6}$$

$$\therefore \quad I_2 = \frac{\pi}{12}.$$

87. $I_1 - I_2 = \frac{\pi}{12}-\frac{\pi}{12}=0.$

88. $I_1 = \frac{\pi}{12}.$

91. $4=\lim_{x\to 9}\dfrac{f(x)-9}{x-9}$

$$\Rightarrow 4=\lim_{x\to 9}\left[\frac{\sqrt{f(x)}-3}{\sqrt{x}-3}\right]\lim_{x\to 9}\left[\frac{\sqrt{f(x)}+3}{\sqrt{x}+3}\right]$$

$$\Rightarrow \lim_{x\to 9}\frac{\sqrt{f(x)}-3}{\sqrt{x}-3}.$$

$$\Rightarrow \lim_{x\to 9}\frac{\frac{1}{\sqrt{f(x)}}f'(x)}{\frac{1}{\sqrt{x}}}=\frac{\frac{4}{3}}{\frac{1}{3}}=4.$$

115.

x	f	fx
0	14	0
1	21	21
2	25	50
3	43	129
4	51	204
5	40	200
6	39	234
7	12	84
	245	922

Mean $=\dfrac{922}{245}=3.76$.

116.

x	f	cf
0	14	14
1	21	35
2	25	60
3	43	103
4	51	154
5	40	194
6	39	233
7	12	245

Here n = 245 which is odd number.

Hence, median $=\left(\dfrac{n+1}{2}\right)$th term $=\left(\dfrac{246}{2}\right)$th term

= 123th term

Hence, median = 4.

117. From the given table it is clear that 51 has the highest frequency 4.

Hence, mode of the given frequency distribution is 4.

118. Here,

$n_1=100,\ \bar{x}_1=50,\ \sigma_1=5$

$n_2=150,\ \bar{x}_2=40,\ \sigma_2=6$

$$\bar{x}_{12}=\frac{100\times 50+150\times 40}{100+150}$$

$$=\frac{5000+6000}{250}=\frac{11000}{250}=44$$

Hence, combined mean of all 250 items = 44.

119. Here,

$n_1=100,\ \bar{x}_1=50,\ \sigma_1=5$

$n_2=150,\ \bar{x}_2=40,\ \sigma_2=6$

Combined SD = σ_{12}

$$=\sqrt{\frac{n_1\left(\sigma_1^2+D_1^2\right)+n_2\left(\sigma_2^2+D_2^2\right)}{n_1+n_2}}$$

$$\sigma_{12}=\sqrt{\frac{100\left[5^2+(50-44)^2\right]+150\left[6^2+(40-44)^2\right]}{100+150}}$$

$$=\sqrt{\frac{100[25+36]+150(36+16)}{250}}$$

$$\begin{bmatrix}D_1=(\bar{x}_1-\bar{x}_{12})\\ D_2=(\bar{x}_2-\bar{x}_{12})\end{bmatrix}$$

$$=\sqrt{\frac{100\times 61+150\times 52}{250}}$$

$$=\sqrt{\frac{6100+7800}{250}}=\sqrt{\frac{13900}{250}}$$

$$=\sqrt{\frac{1390}{25}}=\sqrt{55.6}=7.45\cong 7.5$$

Hence, combined standard deviation of 250 items = 7.5.

120. Required variance

$$=\frac{100[25+36]+150(36+16)}{250}$$

$$=\frac{6100+7800}{250}=\frac{1390}{25}=55.6.$$

Previous Papers (Solved)

NATIONAL DEFENCE ACADEMY & NAVAL ACADEMY

NDA & NA – Entrance Exam, 2013 (II)

PAPER I : GENERAL ABILITY TEST

PART A : ENGLISH LANGUAGE

Directions (For the 10 items which follow):

(*i*) *In this section, a number of sentences are given. The sentences are divided in three separate parts and each one is labelled A, B, C. Read each sentence to find out whether there is an error in any part. No sentence has more than one error. When you find an error in any one of the parts A, B or C, indicate your responses on the Answer Sheet at the appropriate space. You may feel that there is no error in a sentence. In that case, D will signify a 'No error' response.*

(*ii*) *Error may be in grammar, word usage or idioms. There may be a word missing or there may be a word which should be removed.*

(*iii*) *You are* ***not*** *required to correct the error. You are required only to indicate your response on the answer sheet.*

1. (A) Suppose if you were left alone/(B) to live on a desert island/(C) what would you do?/(D) No error

2. (A) He wondered that what/(B) would be the next move of his opponents/(C) who had vowed to see him dislodged from power./(D) No error

3. (A) The nation should be greatful/(B) to the armed forces/(C) for protecting them./(D) No error

4. (A) I do not know/(B) what is he doing/(C) to solve the problem. /(D) No error

5. (A) For so many years/(B) it is almost his habit/(C) to go to the bed at 10 p.m. daily/(D) No error

6. (A) He took/(B) down after/(C) his father./(D) No error

7. (A) His honesty/(B) has never been/(C) called to question./(D) No error

8. (A) I see her/(B) most weekends/(C) but not very often between./(D) No error

9. (A) The chancellor/(B) was present/(C) on both occasions./(D) No error

10. (A) The deliberations by/(B) the committee/(C) are completely confidential./(D) No error

Directions (For the 10 items which follow) : *Each of the following items consists of a sentence followed by four words or group of words. Select the* ***synonym*** *of the word (occurring in the sentence in capital letters) as per the context.*

11. A wise man puts past RANCOUR behind and moves ahead.
A. Dislike B. Hatred
C. Division D. Criticism

12. Many of the villagers were ISOLATED by heavy showers of rains.
A. Destroyed B. Separated from others
C. Battered D. Devasted

13. A series of COLUMNS supporting a large porch is typical of medieval architecture.
A. Statues B. Arches
C. Pillars D. Murals

14. Trees that BLOCK the view of oncoming traffic should be cut down.
A. Alter B. Obstruct
C. Improve D. Spoil

15. The landscape changed ABRUPTLY after the snowfall.
A. Suddenly B. Sharply
C. Favourably D. Slightly

16. We saw a SCINTILLATING fireworks display.
A. Fascinating B. Unforgettable
C. Beautiful D. Sparkling

17. The PACT has been in effect for twenty years.
A. Treaty B. Monarchy
C. Lease D. Trend

18. He had a reputation of being a PRUDENT businessman.
A. Skilful B. Wealthy
C. Careful D. Dishonest

19. There was a signpost where the two paths CONVERGE.
A. Separate B. Intersect
C. Merge D. Diverge

20. The violence erupted because of the ZEALOT.
A. Enthusiastic B. Brave
C. Timid D. Fanatic

Directions (For the 10 items which follow): *Each of the following items consists of a sentence followed by four words or group of words. Select the* ***antonym*** *of the word (occurring in the sentence in capital letters) as per the context.*

21. His CANDID remarks impressed the authorities.
A. Blunt B. Guarded
C. Sincere D. Unconventional

22. The guilty appealed to the jury to CONDONE his punishment.
A. Accept B. Forgive
C. Condemn D. Criticize

23. His family SEVERED ties with him for marrying inter-caste.
A. Joined B. Included
C. Detached D. Disrupted

24. It is easy to understand his FUZZY thoughts.
A. Misty B. Vague
C. Clear D. Useful

25. He drove his car through SLIMY road to reach your office.
A. Ugly B. Clean
C. Beautiful D. Slippery

26. We are ANXIOUS to avoid any problems with regard to this.
A. Cool B. Composed
C. Careless D. Worried

27. The railway lines are EXTENDED and we are quite happy about it.
A. Protracted B. Widened
C. Curtailed D. Elongated

28. There was a fire this morning. They were lucky to ESCAPE it.
A. Arrest B. Elude
C. Evade D. Conceive

29. Domestic violence is a very INHUMAN act.
A. Indifferent B. Compasssionate
C. Terrible D. Ferocious

30. His ELOQUENT speech helped him bag the award.
A. Lucid B. Vivid
C. Short D. Inarticulate

Directions (For the 10 items which follow): *Supply suitable preposition/phrasal verb in the blank of each item.*

31. Universities in Germany and Denmark will have an input .... the project.
A. for B. into
C. about D. at

32. He gave me a leg .... when I was completely new to the business.
A. up B. down
C. off D. for

33. You should have nothing to do with those criminals; they all have violent attitudes and long records. They are men .... the same kidney.
A. with B. in
C. of D. on

34. He didn't have the guts to stand .... his friend when he was in trouble.
A. with B. for
C. by D. beside

35. He broke out of the prison .... dressing as a woman.
A. in B. as
C. by D. with

36. When electricity failed, emergency generators ....
A. cut out B. cut off
C. cut on D. cut in

37. We need two more hands to .... the heavy rush of work.
A. cope up B. cope with
C. cope to D. cope in

38. Twenty-five candidates .... each other for the first prize.
A. compete for B. compete with
C. compete to D. compete on

39. We must eliminate the .... rich and poor.
A. disparity between B. disparity for
C. disparity in D. disparity from

40. As an innovator, he .... the beaten track and explored new religions.
A. deviated from B. deviated to
C. deviated in D. deviated for

Directions (For the next 04 items that follow) : *Read the passage and answer the questions that follow:*

It has often been said that the scale of natural phenomena in India and her total dependence on the monsoon, have helped to form the character of her people. Even today, major disasters, such as flood, famine and plaque, are hard to check, and in older times, their control was almost impossible. Many other ancient civilizations, such as those of the Greeks, Romans and Chinese, had to contend with hard winters, which encouraged sturdiness and resourcefulness. India, on the other hand, was blessed by a bounteous nature, who demanded little of man in return for sustenance, but in her terrible anger could not be appeased by any human effort. Hence it has been suggested, the Indian character has tended to quietism, accepting fortune and misfortune alike without complaint.

41. The author's main argument is
A. description of natural phenomena of India
B. unpredictability of Indian monsoon
C. correlation between the climate and the character of the inhabitants of a region
D. hardahips caused by natural calamities

42. Which one of the following civilizations did ***not*** have to face hardships due to bad winter?
A. Indian B. Greek
C. Chinese D. Roman

43. The expression "India, on the other hand, was blessed by a bounteous nature ...." means
A. Indian soil is fertile
B. India is a land of flora and fauna
C. Indian people have been rewarded more generously by nature in proportion to their efforts
D. Indian soil is suited for growing a variety of crops

44. Which trait of Indian character has been formed by the monsoon?
A. Fatalism B. Sturdiness
C. Asceticism D. Epicureanism

Directions (For the next 06 items that follow) : *In the following sentences, some parts of the sentences have been jumbled up. You are required to rearrange these parts which are labelled P, Q, R, S to produce the correct sentence. Choose the proper sequence and mark in your answer sheet acoordingly.*

45. (P) she/ (Q) and neither have I/ (R) the assignment yet/ (S) hasn't finished
The correct sequence should be
A. QRSP B. QPSR
C. PQSR D. PSRQ

46. (P) himself/ (Q) a child/ (R) can usually feed/ (S) by the age of six months
The correct sequence should be
A. QPRS B. SRQP
C. PQRS D. QRPS

47. Every experience in life makes (P) on some of the cells/ (Q) or other nerve centres/ (R) of the brain/ (S) an impression
The correct sequence should be
A. SPRQ B. QRSP
C. RSPQ D. PSQR

48. You'll (P) know how to do it/ (Q) have to/ (R) because she does not/ (S) help her
The correct sequence should be
A. QSPR B. SRPQ
C. QPRS D. QSRP

49. Would you (P) like to come/ (Q) on Saturday/ (R) at the International House/ (S) to a concert
The correct sequence should be
A. PQRS B. PSQR
C. RSPQ D. PQSR

50. It is (P) to be admitted/ (Q) not necessary that/ (R) to an engineering college/ (S) you qualify an entrance examination
The correct sequence should be
A. SRQP B. QSPR
C. QRPS D. SRPQ

PART B : GENERAL KNOWLEDGE

51. Consider the following statements about the National Cyber Security Policy, approved by the Union Cabinet in May 2013:
1. The policy focuses on manpower training.
2. It aims to create a secured computing environment across the country.

Which of the statements given above is/are correct?
A. 1 only B. 2 only
C. Both 1 and 2 D. Neither 1 nor 2

52. Which of the following statements about Dr. Aparajita Datta is/are correct?
1. She is a wildlife biologist.
2. She has been working for the conservation of hornbills in the dense tropical forests of Arunachal Pradesh.
3. She was honoured with the Whitley Award, also known as Green Oscar, in the year 2013 in London.

Select the correct answer using the code given below:
A. 1, 2 and 3
B. 2 and 3 only
C. 1 and 2 only
D. 3 only

53. Who among the following won the Men's Singles title of the Madrid Open Tennis Tournament, 2013?
A. Novak Djokovic
B. Rafael Nadal
C. Roger Federer
D. Stanislas Wawrinka

54. Which one among the following films was presented the Best Feature Film award in the 60th National Film Awards?
A. *Dekh Indian Circus* B. *Vicky Donor*
C. *Paan Singh Tomar* D. *Chittagong*

55. Which one among the following is an indigenously built Weapon System Integrated helicopter handed over to the Indian Army in February 2013 by Hindustan Aeronautics Ltd.?
A. Varun B. Indra
C. Rudra D. Shiva

56. Who among the following is the Chairman of the Fourteenth Finance Commission?
A. Abhijit Sen
B. Y.V. Reddy
C. Amartya Sen
D. Montek Singh Ahluwalia

57. Which of the following statements about 'Chit Fund' in India is/are correct?

1. It is kind of savings scheme.
2. There are no Acts regulating the activities relating to Chit Funds in India.

Select the correct answer using the code given below:

A. 1 only B. 2 only
C. Both 1 and 2 D. Neither 1 nor 2

58. Who among the following is the author of the book *Pax Indica : India and the World of the 21st Century?*

A. Shashi Tharoor B. Salman Khurshid
C. S.M. Krishna D. Pranab Mukherjee

59. Which one among the following about Prof. C.N.R. Rao is ***not*** correct?

A. He worked mainly in solid-state and structural chemistry
B. He is the head of the Scientific Advisory Council to the President of India
C. He was conferred with China's top science award for the year 2013 for his contributions in boosting Sino-Indian scientific cooperation
D. He is a member of the US National Academy of Sciences

60. Identify the person from the information given below: He was a popular Urdu poet and Hindi lyricist, who worked extensively in Hindi films. He was a Padma Shri and won two Filmfare awards. The President of India recently released a commemorative postage stamp on his birth anniversary at Rashtrapati Bhavan.

A. Khayyam B. Sahir Ludhianvi
C. Ali Sardar Jafri D. Salik Lucknawi

Directions : *The following **07 (Seven)** items consist of two statements, Statement I and Statement II. You are to examine these two statements carefully and select the answers to these items using the code given below:*

Code :

A. Both the statements are individually true and Statement II is the correct explanation of Statement I.
B. Both the Statements are individually true but Statement II is ***not*** the correct explanation of Statement I.
C. Statement I is true but Statement II is false.
D. Statement I is false but Statement II is true.

61. Statement I : The process of decay and disintegration of rocks in situ is called weathering.

Statement II : Weathering takes place both mechanically and chemically.

62. Statement I : Doldrums is a calm belt between 5° N and 5° S of the equator.

Statement II : The sun rays strike almost vertically over the equator throughout the year.

63. Statement I : In the 19th century, India was the largest British colony.

Statement II : India became a big market for British manufactured goods and a field of investment for foreign capital in the 19th century.

64. Statement I : Glass is not considered as a true compound.

Statement II : Glass does not have a definite melting point.

65. Statement I : Limestone decomposes when it is heated in air.

Statement II : Increase in the content of CO_2 in the atmosphere in recent years is mainly due to the using of limestone in the manufacture of cement.

66. Statement I : Very little hydrogen is produced when sulphuric acid is added to calcium.

Statement II : The salt that is produced, calcium sulphate, is insoluble.

67. Statement I : Zinc is used for galvanization to protect iron from rusting.

Statement II : Zinc is more reactive towards oxygen than iron.

68. Which of the following are the results of El Nino?

1. Reduction in the amount of planktons which further reduces the number of fish in the sea.
2. Irregularities in the evaporation of sea water.
3. Distortion of equatorial atmospheric circulation.

Select the correct answer using the code given below:

A. 1 and 2 only B. 2 and 3 only
C. 1 and 3 only D. 1, 2 and 3

69. 'Esker' is a geomorphic feature developed by

A. mechanical weathering B. river action
C. glaciofluvial deposits D. aeolian deposits

70. It is known that the atmosphere is divided into some layers. In which one among the following layers, is the percentage composition of Helium gas maximum?

A. Troposphere B. Stratosphere
C. Exosphere D. Ionosphere

71. The rigid lithospheric slabs are known as 'Plates'. What would be the result, if the oceanic plate collides with the continental plate?

1. Oceanic plate is forced below the continental plate.
2. Continental plate is forced below the oceanic plate.
3. Continental and oceanic plates never collide.

Select the correct answer using the code given below:

A. 1 only B. 2 only
C. 1 and 2 only D. 1, 2 and 3

72. Consider the following layers of the atmosphere:

1. Troposphere 2. Stratosphere
3. Mesosphere 4. Thermosphere

Which one among the following is the correct sequence of the layers with increasing altitude from the Earth's surface?

A. 1-2-3-4 B. 2-1-3-4
C. 3-2-1-4 D. 4-2-3-1

73. Match List-I with List-II and select the correct answer using the codes given below the lists:

List-I *(Land from of peninsular India)*	List-II *(Predominant rock)*
(*a*) Marwar upland	1. Quartzites, Shales, Schists
(*b*) Bundelkhand upland	2. Sandstone, Shale, Limestone
(*c*) Meghalaya upland	3. Granite and Gneise
(*d*) Maharashtra plateau	4. Basalt

Codes :

	(*a*)	(*b*)	(*c*)	(*d*)
A.	2	3	1	4
B.	2	1	3	4
C.	4	3	1	2
D.	4	1	3	2

74. Jawahar tunnel on Jammu-Srinagar highway passes through

A. Pir Panjal range B. Karakoram range
C. Zaskar range D. Dhauladhar range

75. What would be the date and local time of a place located at 88°30' E longitude when the local time at 0° longitude is 19-00 hrs. of 28th February 2013?

A. 23-54 hrs. of 28th February
B. 00-54 hrs. of 1st March
C. 23-30 hrs. of 28th February
D. 00-44 hrs. of 1st March

76. Which of the following statements about tornadoes are correct?

Tornadoes usually spin

1. anticlockwise in the northern homisphere.
2. clockwise in the southern hemisphere.
3. clockwise in the northern hemisphere.
4. anticlockwise in the southern hemisphere.

Select the correct answer using the code given below:

A. 1 and 3 B. 1 and 2
C. 2 and 4 D. 2 and 3

77. Which one among the following terms is used to describe a plant that grows only in a mountainous environment?

A. Orophyte B. Geophyte
C. Epiphyte D. Bryophyte

78. Which of the following statements is/are correct?

1. Air close to the Earth's surface is heavier.
2. Air close to the Earth's surface contains larger quantity of water vapour and dust particles.

Select the correct answer using the code given below:

A. 1 only B. 2 only
C. Both 1 and 2 D. Neither 1 nor 2

79. Match List-I with List-II and select the correct answer using the codes given below the lists:

List-I *(Mineral)*	*List-II* *(Location in Map)*
(*a*) Mica	
(*b*) Chromite	
(*c*) Magnesite	
(*d*) Zinc	

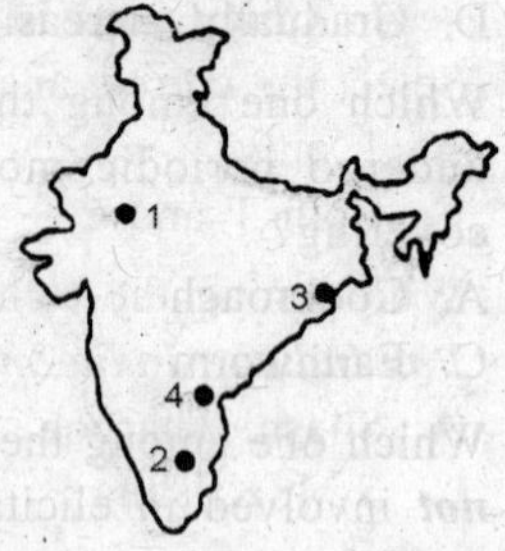

Codes :

	(*a*)	(*b*)	(*c*)	(*d*)
A.	1	2	3	4
B.	1	3	2	4
C.	4	2	3	1
D.	4	3	2	1

80. The term 'albedo' implies the

A. capacity to absorb solar radiation.
B. capacity to modify the path of solar radiation
C. proportion of the shortwave solar radiation reflected by a surface.
D. amount of solar radiation returned to air by a surface.

81. Which of the following statements are correct?

1. Assam produces nearly 80% of jute in India.
2. Jute grows well on loamy soil
3. Hot and humid conditions are ideal for growing jute.
4. Jute is commonly cultivated with wheat in rotation.

Select the correct answer using the code given below:

A. 1, 2 and 3 B. 2, 3 and 4
C. 2 and 3 only D. 1 and 4 only

82. The Indian Standard Time is ahead of Greenwich Mean Time by

A. 3 hrs and 30 minutes B. 4 hrs and 30 minutes
C. 5 hrs and 30 minutes D. 6 hrs and 30 minutes

83. Which of the following is the main characteristic of Mediterranean climate?

A. High temperature throughout the year
B. Rainfall throughout the year
C. Rain in winter season
D. Convectional rain

84. Which one, among the following atmospheric gases, filters out most of the ultraviolet radiation of the Sun?

A. Oxygen B. Nitrogen
C. Helium D. Ozone

85. Which one among the following is ***not*** a factor that affects direction of wind?

A. Pressure gradient B. Friction
C. Magnetism D. Coriolis effect

86. Presbyopia is a visual defect caused by
A. Elongation of the eye ball
B. Shortened curvature of the eye lens
C. Weakening of the ciliary muscles
D. Gradually increasing flexibility of the eye lens

87. Which one among the following animals does ***not*** undergo periodic moulting of their external body covering?
A. Cockroach B. Cobra
C. Earthworm D. Dragonfly

88. Which one among the following organs in humans is ***not*** involved in elicitation of immune response?
A. Thymus B. Brain
C. Spleen D. Lymph Nodes

89. From which part of turmeric, is the turmeric powder obtained?
A. Dried rhizome B. Dried root
C. Dried fruit D. Seed

90. Which one among the following substances is ***never*** excreted out through urine under normal circumstances in any healthy individual?
A. Urea B. Sodium
C. Amino acid D. Potassium

91. Which one among the following animals gives birth to the biggest baby?
A. Elephant B. Rhinoceros
C. Blue whale D. Hippopotamus

92. Muscles of which one among the following body parts contract slowly but can remain contracted for a longer time?
A. Face B. Arms
C. Intestine D. Legs

93. Solutions of three enzymes were prepared namely lipase, trypsin and amylase, in order to remove stains from a piece of cloth. Out of these three enzyme solutions, only lipase could completely remove the stain. This indicates that the stain was due to
A. Oil
B. Protein
C. Mixture of protein and oil
D. Starch containing plant pigment

94. Which one among the following diseases is ***not*** caused by polluted water?
A. Dysentery B. Jaundice
C. Typhoid D. Tuberculosis

95. Which one among the following animals is a mammal?
A. Great Indian Bustard B. Gharial
C. Platypus D. Hornbill

96. Which of the following statements with regard to the 'Fifth Report' is/are correct?
1. It was submitted to the British Parliament in 1813 for consideration.
2. It became the basis of intense parliamentary debates on the nature of the East India Company's rule in India.
3. It was primarily on the economic conditions of the urban and industrial centres of India.

Select the correct answer using the code given below:
A. 1 and 3 only B. 1 and 2 only
C. 2 only D. 1, 2 and 3

97. Consider the following statements about *Salt Satyagraha*:
1. It was a form of Civil Disobedience.
2. It was the first nationalist activity in which women participated in large numbers.
3. Gandhiji first experimented with *Salt Satyagraha* in South Africa.

Which of the statements given above is/are correct?
A. 1 only B. 2 only
C. 1 and 2 only D. 1, 2 and 3

98. Which of the following statements about *Ryotwari* system is/are correct?
1. The government collected the revenue directly from the individual cultivators.
2. The cultivators were not recognized in law as the owners of the land.

Select the correct answer using the code given below:
A. 1 only B. 2 only
C. Both 1 and 2 D. Neither 1 nor 2

99. Which of the following statements about Russia is/are correct?
1. Russia emerged as the first socialist state in the world.
2. Socialist state in Russia was established by Bolsheviks in 1917.

Select the correct answer using the codes given below:
A. 1 only B. 2 only
C. Both 1 and 2 D. Neither 1 nor 2

100. Consider the following statements:
1. Dadabhai Naoroji first put forward 'the theory of drain of wealth'.
2. The Indian National Congress adopted a resolution to criticize the drain of wealth in its annual session at Calcutta in 1896.

Which of the statements given above is/are correct?
A. 1 only B. 2 only
C. Both 1 and 2 D. Neither 1 nor 2

101. Which of the following statements about Quit India Movement of 1942 is/are correct?
1. The movement was massive in character.
2. One of the unique features of the movement was the participation of the communists at the local level defying the official stand of the Communist party.
3. It was a completely non-violent movement.

Select the correct answer using the code given below:

A. 1 only B. 1 and 2

C. 2 only D. 1 and 3

102. Consider the following statements:

1. Annie Besant was the first woman President of the Indian National Congress.
2. The historic Lucknow session of the Congress in 1916 was presided by Madan Mohan Malviya.
3. Mahatma Gandhi presided over the annual session of Congress only once at Belgaum in 1924.

Which of the statements given above is/are correct?

A. 1, 2 and 3 B. 2 and 3 only

C. 1 and 3 only D. 1 only

103. Match List-I with List-II and select the correct answer using the code given below the lists:

List-I *(Book/Journal)*	*List-II* *(Author/Editor)*
(*a*) Bande Mataram	1. Aurobindo Ghosh
(*b*) New India	2. Mahatma Gandhi
(*c*) India Today	3. Bipin Chandra Pal
(*d*) Young India	4. R.P. Dutt

Code:

	(*a*)	(*b*)	(*c*)	(*d*)
A.	1	4	3	2
B.	1	3	4	2
C.	2	3	4	1
D.	2	4	3	1

104. For Mahatma Gandhi, Satyagraha is

1. a political force.
2. a philosophy of life.
3. an ideology of action.

Select the correct answer using the code given below:

A. 1 and 2 only B. 2 and 3 only

C. 1 and 3 only D. 1, 2 and 3

105. What was the common element among the following three newspapers?

1. The Servant of India
2. Dnyan Prakash
3. Hitawad

A. They were newspapers brought out by the Indian National Congress

B. They were newspapers under the influence of socialism

C. They were newspapers of moderate views brought out by the Servants of India Society

D. They represented the Trade Union Movement in India

106. "... it has reduced us politically to serfdom. It has sapped the foundations of our culture ... it has degraded us spiritually." This was Mahatma Gandhi complaining of the ill-effect on Indians of which action/policy of the colonial government?

A. Salt tax B. Inadequate franchise

C. Press Act D. Rowlatt Act

107. The Indian National Congress was founded during the Viceroyalty of

A. Lord Lytton B. Lord Ripon

C. Lord Dufferin D. Lord Mayo

108. *Kandh* Revolt against the British was led by

A. Chakra Bishoyi B. Dandasena

C. Tomma Dora D. Birsa Munda

109. The implementation of factory legislation in India in the nineteenth century was a result of the pressure on the Government of India from

A. the trade unionists in India

B. the socialists in India

C. the manufacturers from Lancashire and Manchester

D. the Indian National Congress

110. Who among the following was the President of Indian National Congress when India attained independence?

A. Jawaharlal Nehru

B. Vallabhbhai Patel

C. Maulana Azad

D. Acharya Kripalani

111. Who among the following has described the uprising of 1857 as the First India War of Independence?

A. S.N. Sen

B. R.C. Majumdar

C. B.G. Tilak

D. V.D. Savarkar

112. Arrange the following events of Indian freedom movement in correct sequence beginning from the earliest:

1. Second Round Table Conference
2. Communal Award
3. Poona Pact
4. Simon Commission

Select the correct answer using the code given below:

A. 1-2-3-4 B. 4-3-2-1

C. 4-1-2-3 D. 3-2-1-4

113. Consider the following statements:

1. Morley – Minto reforms ended the official majority in state legislative assemblies.
2. Despite the Government of India Act, 1909 the non-officials were elected to local bodies indirectly.

Which of the statements given above is/are correct?

A. 1 only B. 2 only

C. Both 1 and 2 D. Neither 1 nor 2

114. No Indian "shall by reason only of his religion, place of birth, descent, colour or any of them be disabled from holding any office or employment under the company." This was a pledge first given by the

A. Charter Act of 1813

B. Charter Act of 1833

C. Queen's Proclamation of 1858

D. Indian Civil Service Act of 1861

115. A beautiful rainbow on the sky is due to the
A. dispersion of sunlight from a water droplet only
B. reflection of sunlight from a water droplet only
C. reflection and refraction of sunlight from a water droplet only
D. refraction, dispersion and reflection of sunlight from a water droplet.

116. The weight of an object may be assigned by using Newton's
A. first law of motion B. second law of motion
C. third law of motion D. laws of gravitation

117. A current of 0-5 A is drawn by a filament of an electric bulb for 20 minutes. The amount of electric charge that flows through the circuit is
A. 1 C B. 10 C
C. 600 C D. 300 C

118. Which one among the following properties of a proton may change while it moves freely in a magnetic field?
A. Speed B. Charge
C. Mass D. Velocity

119. Power required by a boy of mass 30 kg to run up a staircase of 40 steps in 10 seconds is (Height of each step is 15 cm)
(Take g = 10 m/s^2)
A. 1800 Watt B. 180 Watt
C. 18000 Watt D. 18 Watt

120.

The figure given above shows the temperature (T) – time (t) plot when we start heating a piece of naphthalene. The temperature (T*) at the plateau of the curve signifies
A. boiling point of naphthalene
B. freezing point of naphthalene
C. melting point of naphthalene
D. the temperature when naphthalene undergoes a chemical change upon heating

121. A piece of paper and a coin both having the same mass are dropped from the 10th floor of a building. The piece of paper would take more time to reach the ground because
A. gravitational pull on the paper is less than the coin
B. buoyant force on the piece of paper is more than that on the coin
C. buoyant force on the coin is more and acts in the downward direction
D. the piece of paper takes a longer path to reach the ground

122. During sunrise and sunset, sun appears reddish-orange because
A. during that time sun emits only reddish-orange light
B. all other colours are absorbed by the atmosphere
C. reddish-orange light is least scattered by the atmosphere
D. all other colours apart from reddish-orange are reflected back by the atmosphere

123. Ohm's law can also be taken as a statement for
A. conservation of energy
B. conservation of electric charge
C. conservation of angular momentum
D. non-conservation of momentum of the flowing charges

124. Motion of a particle can be described in x-direction by $x = a \sin wt$, and y-direction by $y = b \cos wt$. The particle is moving on
A. a circular path of radius 'a'
B. a circular path of radius 'b'
C. an elliptical path
D. a straight line

125.

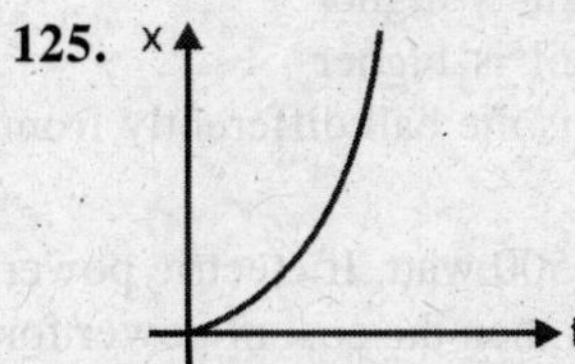

The plot given above represents displacement 'x' of a particle with time 't'. The particle is
A. moving with uniform velocity
B. moving with acceleration
C. moving with deceleration
D. executing a periodic motion

126. A bullet of mass 20 gm is fired in the horizontal direction with a velocity 150 m/s from a pistol of mass 1 kg. Recoil velocity of the pistol is
A. 3 m/s B. 3 km/s
C. 300 m/s D. 1/3 m/s

127.

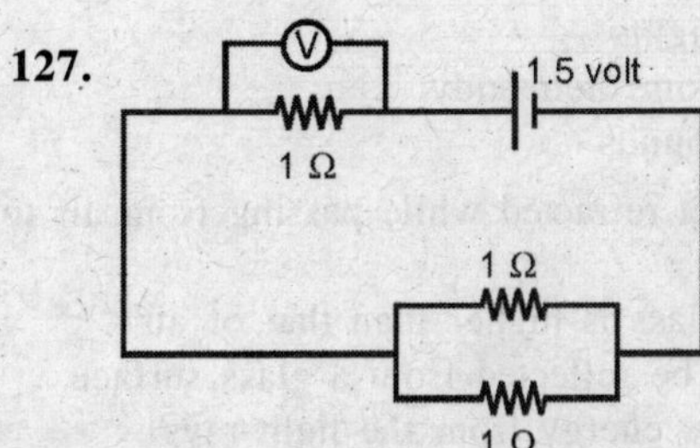

What should be the reading of the voltmeter V in the circuit given above?
(All the resistances are equal to 1Ω and the battery is of 1.5 volt)
A. 1.5 volt B. 0.66 volt
C. 1 volt D. 2 volt

128. 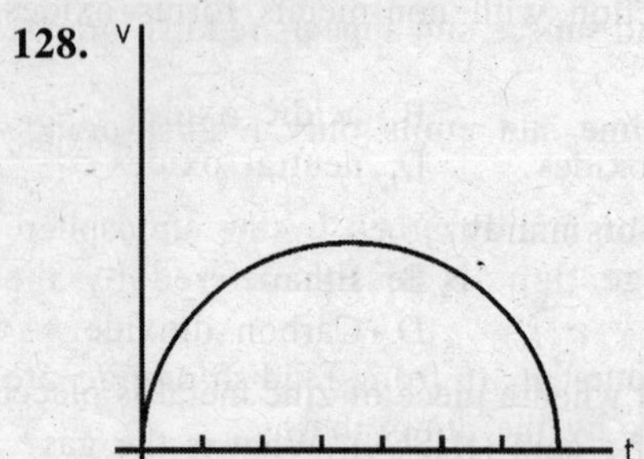

The plot given above represents the velocity of a particle (in m/s) with time (in seconds). Assuming that the plot represents a semi-circle, distance traversed by the particle at the end of 7 seconds is approximately

A. 19 m B. 7 m
C. 3.2 m D. 4.75 m

129. Suppose we have an iron nail and an iron ball of same mass. When submerged in water, the iron ball may float but the nail always sinks. This is because

A. buoyant force on the ball is larger than that of the nail due to their shapes
B. viscous force on the ball is higher
C. viscous force on the nail is higher
D. gravitational force affects the ball differently from the nail

130. An electric heater is rated 1500 watt. If electric power costs ₹ 2 per kilo-watt-hour, then the cost of power for 10 hours running of the heater is

A. ₹ 30 B. ₹ 15
C. ₹ 150 D. ₹ 25

131. The ceilings of a concert hall are generally curved

A. because they reflect the sound to the audience
B. because they can absorb noise
C. to have better aeration in the hall
D. as any sound from outside cannot pass through a curved ceiling

132. Bats can know about their prey at a distance even in the night by emitting

A. infrared lights
B. ultraviolet lights
C. chemicals from their body
D. ultrasonic sounds

133. Rays of light get refracted while passing from air to glass because

A. density of glass is higher than that of air
B. they cannot be reflected from a glass surface
C. glass absorbs energy from the light rays
D. speed of light in glass is less than the speed of light in air

134. White light while passing through a glass prism breaks up into light of different colours because

A. refractive index of glass for different colours of light is different
B. glass prism absorbs white light and emits lights of several colours in different directions
C. of total internal reflection of white light on surfaces of the prism
D. of the interference of different colours inside the prism

135. 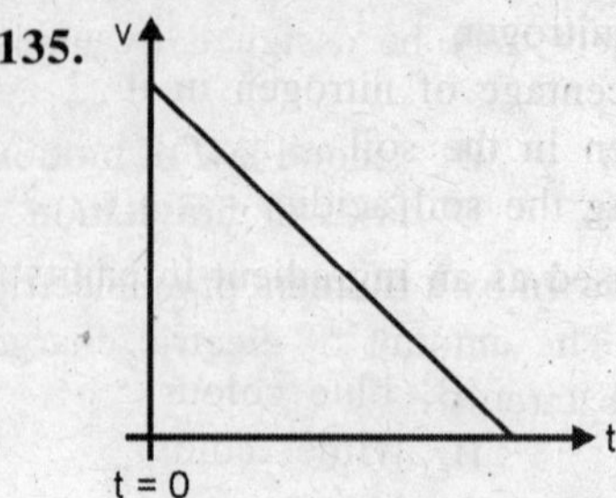

Which one among the following situations is best represented by the velocity – time plot shown above?

A. Uniform motion of a particle on a circle
B. Accelerated motion of a particle which has a non-zero initial velocity
C. Decelerated motion of a particle which has an initial non-zero velocity
D. Decelerated motion of a particle which has no initial velocity

136. When long dry hair is brushed the strands often move away from each other because while brushing

A. air is being blown through the strands
B. static electric charges are being induced on the hair
C. mechanical energy is being transferred into heat energy
D. the gravitational attraction among the strands becomes smaller

137. If the length of a simple pendulum is being increased by 4-fold, time period of oscillation will be

A. decreased by 4-fold
B. increased by 4-fold
C. decreased to half of the initial value
D. increased by a factor of 2 of its initial value

138. A pressure cooker works on the principle of

A. elevation of boiling point of water by application of pressure
B. making the foodgrains softer by application of pressure
C. making the foodgrains softer by application of pressure and temperature
D. keeping the foodgrains inside steam for a longer time

139. Pressure of a gas increase due to increase of its temperature because at higher temperature

A. gas molecules repel each other more
B. potential energy of the gas molecules is higher
C. kinetic energies of the gas molecules are higher
D. gas molecules attract each other more

140. The presence of sulphur in gunpowder
A. decreases the ignition temperature
B. increases the final temperature
C. increases explosiveness of the gunpowder
D. makes the powder smokeless

141. Calcium ammonium nitrate (CAN) is a popular nitrogen fertilizer because it is
A. slow supplier of nitrogen
B. having more percentage of nitrogen in it
C. fixing the nitrogen in the soil
D. capable of making the soil acidic

142. Chromium oxide is used as an ingredient in paints to obtain
A. green colour B. blue colour
C. red colour D. violet colour

143. A mixture of sodium chlorides and naphthalene can be separated by
A. extraction with hot water
B. extraction with cold water
C. sublimation
D. steam distillation

144. The pH of the solution obtained by dissolving pure sodium chloride in water is
A. acidic
B. basic
C. neutral
D. dependent on the amount of sodium chloride dissolved in water

145. Oxygen on reaction with non-metals forms oxides, which are
A. basic oxides B. acidic oxides
C. amphoteric oxides D. neutral oxides

146. Biogas consists of mainly
A. Methane B. Ethane
C. Butane D. Carbon dioxide

147. A gas is evolved when a piece of zinc metal is placed in dilute sulphuric acid (H_2SO_4). What is the gas?
A. Hydrogen B. Oxygen
C. Water vapour D. Sulphur dioxide

148. Turmeric (*Haldi*) rapidly becomes colourless on addition of
A. Baking soda B. Vinegar
C. Lemon juice D. Alcohol

149. Metalloids are
A. alloys of alkali metals with other metals
B. colloids of metals
C. elements having some properties of both metals and non-metals
D. metals heavier than lead

150. Two reactants in a flask produce bubbles of gas; it turns lime water into milky. The reactants in the flask are
A. Zinc and hydrochloric acid
B. Magnesium carbonate and hydrochloric acid
C. Magnesium nitrate and hydrochloric acid
D. Magnesium sulphate and hydrochloric acid

PAPER II : MATHEMATICS

1. What is the seventh term of the sequence 0, 3, 8, 15, 24, ... ?
A. 63 B. 48
C. 35 D. 33

2. What is tan 15° equal to?
A. $2-\sqrt{3}$
B. $2+\sqrt{3}$
C. $1-\sqrt{3}$
D. $1+\sqrt{3}$

3. Consider the following:
1. $\tan\left(\frac{\pi}{6}\right)$ 2. $\tan\left(\frac{3\pi}{4}\right)$
3. $\tan\left(\frac{5\pi}{4}\right)$ 4. $\tan\left(\frac{2\pi}{3}\right)$

What is the correct order?
A. 1 < 4 < 2 < 3 B. 4 < 2 < 1 < 3
C. 4 < 2 < 3 < 1 D. 1 < 4 < 3 < 2

4. If $\cos x = \frac{1}{3}$, then what is sin *x*.cot*x*.cosec*x*.tan*x* equal to?
A. $\frac{2}{3}$ B. $\frac{3}{2}$
C. 2 D. 1

5. What is $\log_{81} 243$ equal to?
A. 0.75 B. 1.25
C. 1.5 D. 3

6. If the three vertices of the parallelogram ABCD are A(1, *a*), B(3, *a*), C(2, *b*), then D is equal to
A. (3, *b*) B. (6, *b*)
C. (4, *b*) D. (5, *b*)

7. The value of *k* for which the lines $2x + 3y + a = 0$ and $5x + ky + a = 0$ represent family of parallel lines is
A. 3 B. 4.5
C. 7.5 D. 15

8. What is the equation of the line which passes through (4, –5) and is perpendicular to $3x + 4y + 5 = 0$?
A. $4x - 3y - 31 = 0$ B. $3x - 4y - 41 = 0$
C. $4x + 3y - 1 = 0$ D. $3x + 4y + 8 = 0$

9. The foci of the hyperbola $4x^2 - 9y^2 - 1 = 0$ are

A. $(\pm\sqrt{13}, 0)$ B. $\left(\pm\frac{\sqrt{13}}{6}, 0\right)$

C. $\left(0, \pm\frac{\sqrt{13}}{6}\right)$ D. None of the above

10. For what value of k are the two straight lines $3x + 4y = 1$ and $4x + 3y + 2k = 0$ equidistant from the point (1, 1)?

A. $\frac{1}{2}$ B. 2

C. –2 D. $-\frac{1}{2}$

11. A point P moves such that its distances from (1, 2) and (–2, 3) are equal. Then the locus of P is

A. straight line B. parabola
C, ellipse D. hyperbola

12. The equation of the locus of a point which is equidistant from the axes is

A. $y = 2x$ B. $x = 2y$
C. $y = \pm x$ D. $2y + x = 0$

13. What angle does the line segment joining (5, 2) and (6, –15) subtend at (0, 0)?

A. $\frac{\pi}{6}$ B. $\frac{\pi}{4}$

C. $\frac{\pi}{2}$ D. $\frac{3\pi}{4}$

14. The length of latus rectum of the ellipse $4x^2 + 9y^2 = 36$ is

A. $\frac{4}{3}$ B. $\frac{8}{3}$

C. 6 D. 12

15. What is the equation to the straight line passing through (5, –2) and (–4, 7)?

A. $5x - 2y = 4$ B. $-4x + 7y = 9$
C. $x + y = 3$ D. $x - y = -1$

16. What is $\sin^2 20^\circ + \sin^2 70^\circ$ equal to?

A. 1 B. 0

C. –1 D. $\frac{1}{2}$

17. What is the value of the determinant

$$\begin{vmatrix} 1 & bc & a(b+c) \\ 1 & ca & b(c+a) \\ 1 & ab & c(a+b) \end{vmatrix}?$$

A. 0 B. abc
C. $ab + bc + ca$ D. $abc\,(a + b + c)$

18. Consider the following:

1. $A \cup (B \cap C) = (A \cap B) \cup (A \cap C)$
2. $A \cap (B \cup C) = (A \cup B) \cap (A \cup C)$

Which of the above is/are correct?

A. 1 only B. 2 only
C. Both 1 and 2 D. Neither 1 nor 2

19. Let n be a positive integer and $(1 + x)^n = a_0 + a_1x + a_2x^2 + ... + a_nx^n$

What is $a_0 + a_1 + a_2 + ... + a_n$ equal to?

A. 1 B. 2^n
C. 2^{n-1} D. 2^{n+1}

20. If α, β are the roots of the equation $ax^2 + bx + b = 0$, then what is the value of $\sqrt{\frac{\alpha}{\beta}} + \sqrt{\frac{\beta}{\alpha}} + \sqrt{\frac{b}{a}}$?

A. –1 B. 0
C. 1 D. 2

21. A number in binary system is 110001. It is equal to which one of the following numbers in decimal system?

A. 45 B. 46
C. 48 D. 49

22. The roots of the equation $x^2 - 8x + 16 = 0$

A. are imaginary B. are distinct and real
C. are equal and real D. cannot be ascertained

23. What is $\tan^{-1}\left(\frac{1}{2}\right) + \tan^{-1}\left(\frac{1}{3}\right)$ equal to?

A. $\frac{\pi}{2}$ B. $\frac{\pi}{3}$

C. $\frac{\pi}{4}$ D. $\frac{\pi}{6}$

24. What is $(1 - \sin^2\theta)(1 + \tan^2\theta)$ equal to?

A. $\sin^2\theta$ B. $\cos^2\theta$
C. $\tan^2\theta$ D. 1

25. How many terms are there in the expansion of $(1 + 2x + x^2)^{10}$?

A. 11 B. 20
C. 21 D. 30

26. The sum of the first five terms and the sum of the first ten terms of an AP are same. Which one of the following is the correct statement?

A. The first term must be negative
B. The common difference must be negative
C. Either the first term or the common difference is negative but not both
D. Both the first term and the common difference are negative

27. If A = {1, 3, 5, 7}, then what is the cardinality of the power set P(A)?

A. 8 B. 15
C. 16 D. 17

28. What is the difference in the roots of the equation $x^2 - 10x + 9 = 0$?

A. 2 B. 3
C. 5 D. 8

29. If $8x - 9y = 20$ and $7x - 10y = 9$, then what is $2x - y$ equal to?

A. 10 B. 11
C. 12 D. 13

30. The quadratic equation $x^2 + bx + 4 = 0$ will have real roots if

A. $b \leq -4$ only B. $b \geq 4$ only
C. $-4 < b < 4$ D. $b \leq -4$, $b \geq 4$

31. What is the positive square root of $7+4\sqrt{3}$?

A. $\sqrt{3}-1$ B. $\sqrt{3}+1$
C. $\sqrt{3}-2$ D. $\sqrt{3}+2$

32. If A = {1, 2}, B = {2, 3} and C = {3, 4}, then what is the cardinality of $(A \times B) \cap (A \times C)$?

A. 8 B. 6
C. 2 D. 1

33. If α, β are the roots of the equation $x^2 + x + 2 = 0$, then what is $\frac{\alpha^{10}+\beta^{10}}{\alpha^{-10}+\beta^{-10}}$ equal to?

A. 4096 B. 2048
C. 1024 D. 512

34. If a and b are rational and b is not perfect square, then the quadratic equation with rational coefficients whose one root is $3a+\sqrt{b}$ is

A. $x^2-6ax+9a^2-b=0$ B. $3ax^2+x-\sqrt{b}=0$
C. $x^2+3ax+\sqrt{b}=0$ D. $\sqrt{b}x^2+x-3a=0$

35. If A is a finite set having n elements, then the number of relations which can be defined in A is

A. 2^n B. n^2
C. 2^{n^2} D. n^n

36. If the positive integers a, b, c, d are in AP, then the numbers abc, abd, acd, bcd are in

A. HP B. AP
C. GP D. None of the above

37. Which one of the following is an example of non-empty set?

A. Set of all even prime numbers
B. $(x : x^2 - 2 = 0$ and x is rational)
C. $\{x : x$ is a natural number, $x < 8$ and simultaneously $x > 12\}$
D. $\{x : x$ is a point common to any two parallel lines$\}$

38. What is one of the square roots of $3 + 4i$, where $i = \sqrt{-1}$?

A. $2 + i$ B. $2 - i$
C. $-2 + i$ D. $-3 - i$

39. The number 83 is written in the binary system as

A. 100110 B. 101101
C. 1010011 D. 110110

40. The relation R in the set Z of integers given by R = $\{(a, b) : a - b$ is divisible by 5$\}$ is

A. reflexive
B. reflexive but not symmetric
C. symmetric and transitive
D. an equivalence relation

41. What is $\sum_{r=0}^{n} C(n, r)$ equal to?

A. $2^n - 1$ B. n
C. $n!$ D. 2^n

42. What is 0.9 + 0.09 + 0.009 + ... equal to?

A. 1 B. 1.01
C. 1.001 D. 1.1

43. How many real roots does the quadratic equation $f(x) = x^2 + 3|x| + 2 = 0$ have?

A. One B. Two
C. Four D. No real root

44. In a group of 50 people, two tests were conducted, one for diabetes and one for blood pressure. 30 people were diagnosed with diabetes and 40 people were diagnosed with high blood pressure. What is the minimum number of people who were having diabetes and high blood pressure?

A. 0 B. 10
C. 20 D. 30

45. Consider the following statements:

1. The product of two non-zero matrices can never be identity matrix.
2. The product of two non-zero matrices can never be zero matrix.

Which of the above statements is/are correct?

A. 1 only B. 2 only
C. Both 1 and 2 D. Neither 1 nor 2

46. What is the area of the parabola $x^2 = y$ bounded by the line $y = 1$?

A. $\frac{1}{3}$ square unit B. $\frac{2}{3}$ square unit
C. $\frac{4}{3}$ square units D. 2 square units

47. What is the area bounded by $y = \tan x$, $y = 0$ and $x = \frac{\pi}{4}$?

A. ln 2 square units B. $\frac{\ln 2}{2}$ square units
C. 2(ln 2) square units D. None of the above

48. What is $\int (x\cos x + \sin x)dx$ equal to?

A. $x \sin x + c$ B. $x \cos x + c$

C. $-x \sin x + c$ D. $-x \cos x + c$

where c is an arbitrary constant.

49. What is $\int_0^2 e^{\ln x} dx$ equal to?

A. 1

B. 2

C. 4

D. None of the above

50. If the angle between the vectors $\hat{i} - m\hat{j}$ and $\hat{j} + \hat{k}$ is $\frac{\pi}{3}$, then what is the value of m?

A. 0 B. 2

C. –2 D. None of the above

51. What is the vector perpendicular to both the vectors $\hat{i} - \hat{j}$ and $\hat{i}$?

A. $\hat{i}$ B. $-\hat{j}$

C. $\hat{j}$ D. $\hat{k}$

52. The position vectors of the points A and B are respectively $3\hat{i} - 5\hat{j} + 2\hat{k}$ and $\hat{i} + \hat{j} - \hat{k}$. What is the length of AB?

A. 11 B. 9

C. 7 D. 6

53. The vectors $\hat{i} - 2x\hat{j} - 3y\hat{k}$ and $\hat{i} + 3x\hat{j} + 2y\hat{k}$ are orthogonal to each other. Then the locus of the point (x, y) is

A. hyperbola B. ellipse

C. parabola D. circle

54. What is the value of p for which the vector $p(2\hat{i} - \hat{j} + 2\hat{k})$ is of 3 units length?

A. 1 B. 2

C. 3 D. 6

55. If $\vec{a} = 2\hat{i} + 2\hat{j} + 3\hat{k}$, $\vec{b} = -\hat{i} + 2\hat{j} + \hat{k}$ and $\vec{c} = 3\hat{i} + \hat{j}$ are three vectors such that $\vec{a} + t\vec{b}$ is perpendicular to $\vec{c}$, then what is t equal to?

A. 8 B. 6

C. 4 D. 2

56. The mean of 20 observations is 15. On checking, it was found that two observation were wrongly copied as 3 and 6. If wrong observations are replaced by correct values 8 and 4, then the correct mean is

A. 15 B. 15.15

C. 15.35 D. 16

57. The arithmetic mean of the squares of the first n natural numbers is

A. $\frac{n(n+1)(2n+1)}{6}$ B. $\frac{n(n+1)(2n+1)}{2}$

C. $\frac{(n+1)(2n+1)}{6}$ D. $\frac{(n+1)(2n+1)}{3}$

58. Consider the following statements:

1. Both the regression coefficients have same sign.
2. If one of the regression coefficients is greater than unity, the other must be less than unity.

Which of the above statements is/are correct?

A. 1 only

B. 2 only

C. Both 1 and 2

D. Neither 1 nor 2

59. Which one of the following measures is determined only after the construction of cumulative frequency distribution?

A. Arithmetic mean B. Mode

C. Median D. Geometric mean

60. Coefficient of correlation is the measure of

A. central tendency

B. dispersion

C. both central tendency and dispersion

D. neither central tendency nor dispersion

61. What is $\lim_{x \to 0} \frac{1 - \cos x}{x}$ equal to?

A. 0 B. $\frac{1}{2}$

C. 1 D. 2

62. What is $\lim_{x \to 0} \frac{\cos x}{\pi - x}$ equal to?

A. 0 B. π

C. $\frac{1}{\pi}$ D. 1

63. What is $\lim_{x \to 0} \frac{\sin 2x + 4x}{2x + \sin 4x}$ equal to?

A. 0 B. $\frac{1}{2}$

C. 1 D. 2

64. The maximum value of the function $f(x) = x^3 + 2x^2 - 4x + 6$ exists at

A. $x = -2$ B. $x = 1$

C. $x = 2$ D. $x = -1$

65. The minimum value of the function $f(x) = |x - 4|$ exists at

A. $x = 0$ B. $x = 2$

C. $x = 4$ D. $x = -4$

66. What is $\int_1^2 \ln x\, dx$ equal to?

A. ln 2

B. 1

C. $\ln\left(\frac{4}{e}\right)$

D. $\ln\left(\frac{e}{4}\right)$

67. What is $\int \frac{dx}{\sqrt{4+x^2}}$ equal to?

A. $\ln\left|\sqrt{4+x^2}+x\right|+c$

B. $\ln\left|\sqrt{4+x^2}-x\right|+c$

C. $\sin^{-1}\left(\frac{x}{2}\right)+c$

D. None of the above

where c is an arbitrary constant.

68. What is the order of the differential equation

$$\left(\frac{dy}{dx}\right)^2+\frac{dy}{dx}-\sin^2 y=0?$$

A. 1

B. 2

C. 3

D. Undefined

69. $y = 2\cos x + 3\sin x$ satisfies which of the following differential equations?

1. $\frac{d^2y}{dx^2}+y=0$

2. $\left(\frac{dy}{dx}\right)^2+\frac{dy}{dx}=0$

Select the correct answer using the code given below.

A. 1 only

B. 2 only

C. Both 1 and 2

D. Neither 1 nor 2

70. The differential equation of all circles whose centres are at the origin is

A. $\frac{dy}{dx}=\frac{y}{x}$

B. $\frac{dy}{dx}=\frac{x}{y}$

C. $\frac{dy}{dx}=-\frac{x}{y}$

D. None of the above

71. What is $\int \sin^2 x dx+\int \cos^2 x\, dx$ equal to?

A. $x + c$

B. $\frac{x^2}{2}+c$

C. $x^2 + c$

D. None of the above

where c is an arbitrary constant.

72. What is $\int e^{e^x} e^x dx$ equal to?

A. $e^{e^x}+c$

B. $2e^{e^x}+c$

C. $e^{e^x}e^x+c$

D. $2e^{e^x}e^x+c$

where c is an arbitrary constant.

73. What is the area bounded by the lines $x = 0$, $y = 0$ and $x + y + 2 = 0$?

A. $\frac{1}{2}$ square unit

B. 1 square unit

C. 2 square units

D. 4 square units

74. What is the derivative of sin(sin x)?

A. cos(cos x)

B. cos(sin x)

C. cos(sin x) cos x

D. cos(cos x) cos x

75. What is the derivative of $|x-1|$ at $x = 2$?

A. –1

B. 0

C. 1

D. Derivative does not exist

76. If three events A, B, C are mutually exclusive, then which one of the following is correct?

A. $P(A \cup B \cup C) = 0$

B. $P(A \cup B \cup C) = 1$

C. $P(A \cap B \cap C) = 0$

D. $P(A \cap B \cap C) = 1$

77. What is the variance of the first 11 natural numbers?

A. 10

B. 11

C. 12

D. 13

78. If A and B are independent events such that $P(A)=\frac{1}{5}$, $P(A\cup B)=\frac{7}{10}$, then what is $P(\bar{B})$ equal to?

A. $\frac{2}{7}$

B. $\frac{3}{7}$

C. $\frac{3}{8}$

D. $\frac{7}{9}$

79. In a binomial distribution the occurrence and the non-occurrence of an event are equally likely and the mean is 6. The number of trials required is

A. 15

B. 12

C. 10

D. 6

80. A die is tossed twice. What is the probability of getting a sum of 10?

A. $\frac{1}{18}$

B. $\frac{1}{6}$

C. $\frac{1}{12}$

D. $\frac{5}{12}$

81. Three dice are thrown. What is the probability of getting a triplet?

A. $\frac{1}{6}$

B. $\frac{1}{18}$

C. $\frac{1}{36}$

D. $\frac{1}{72}$

82. Consider the following statements:
1. If A and B are exhaustive events, then their union is the sample space.
2. If A and B are exhaustive events, then their intersection must be an empty event.

Which of the above statements is/are correct?
A. 1 only B. 2 only
C. Both 1 and 2 D. Neither 1 nor 2

83. Consider the following statements:
1. The algebraic sum of the deviations of a set of n values from its arithmetic mean is zero.
2. In the case of frequency distribution, mode is the value of the variable which corresponds to maximum frequency.

Which of the statements given above is/are correct?
A. 1 only B. 2 only
C. Both 1 and 2 D. Neither 1 nor 2

84. Which one of the following may be the parameter of a binomial distribution?
A. $np = 2$, $npq = 4$ B. $n = 4$, $p = \frac{3}{2}$
C. $n = 8$, $p = 1$ D. $np = 10$, $npq = 8$

85. What is the number of outcomes when a coin is tossed and then a die is rolled only in case a head is shown on the coin?
A. 6 B. 7
C. 8 D. None of the above

86. If $P(A) = \frac{2}{3}$, $P(B) = \frac{2}{5}$, and $P(A \cup B) - P(A \cap B) = \frac{2}{5}$, then what is $P(A \cap B)$ equal to?
A. $\frac{3}{5}$ B. $\frac{5}{11}$
C. $\frac{1}{3}$ D. None of the above

87. What is the probability that there are 5 Mondays in the month of February 2016?
A. 0 B. $\frac{1}{7}$
C. $\frac{2}{7}$ D. None of these

88. Consider the following statements:
1. Pie diagrams are suitable for categorical data.
2. The arc length of a sector of a pie diagram is proportional to the value of the component represented by the sector.

Which of the statements given above is/are correct?
A. 1 only
B. 2 only
C. Both 1 and 2
D. Neither 1 nor 2

89. In a relay race, there are six teams A, B, C, D, E and F. What is the probability that A, B, C finish first, second, third respectively?
A. $\frac{1}{2}$ B. $\frac{1}{12}$
C. $\frac{1}{60}$ D. $\frac{1}{120}$

90. The variance of 20 observations is 5. If each observation is multiplied by 2, then what is the new variance of the resulting observations?
A. 5 B. 10
C. 20 D. 40

91. What is the angle between the lines $x + y = 1$ and $x - y = 1$?
A. $\frac{\pi}{6}$ B. $\frac{\pi}{4}$
C. $\frac{\pi}{3}$ D. $\frac{\pi}{2}$

92. The axis of the parabola $y^2 + 2x = 0$ is
A. $x = 0$ B. $y = 0$
C. $x = 2$ D. $y = 2$

93. The radius of the circle $x^2 + y^2 + x + c = 0$ passing through the origin is
A. $\frac{1}{4}$ B. $\frac{1}{2}$
C. 1 D. 2

94. The centroid of the triangle with vertices (2, 3), (–2, –5) and (3, 5) is at
A. (1, 1) B. (2, –1)
C. (1, –1) D. (1, 2)

95. The equation of the line, the reciprocals of whose intercepts on the axes are m and n, is given by
A. $nx + my = mn$ B. $mx + ny = 1$
C. $mx + ny = mn$ D. $mx - my = 1$

96. If θ is the acute angle between the diagonals of a cube, then which one of the following is correct?
A. $\theta = 30^\circ$ B. $\theta = 45^\circ$
C. $2\cos\theta = 1$ D. $3\cos\theta = 1$

97. What is the equation of the sphere with unit radius having centre at the origin?
A. $x^2 + y^2 + z^2 = 0$ B. $x^2 + y^2 + z^2 = 1$
C. $x^2 + y^2 + z^2 = 2$ D. $x^2 + y^2 + z^2 = 3$

98. What is the sum of the squares of direction cosines of x-axis?
A. 0 B. $\frac{1}{3}$
C. 1 D. 3

99. What is the distance of the line $2x + y + 2z = 3$ from the origin?
A. 1 unit B. 1.5 units
C. 2 units D. 2.5 units

100. If the projections of a straight line segment on the coordinate axes are 2, 3, 6, then the length of the segment is

A. 5 units B. 7 units
C. 11 units D. 49 units

101. Consider the following functions:

1. $f(x) = e^x$, where $x > 0$
2. $g(x) = |x - 3|$

Which of the above functions is/are continuous?

A. 1 only B. 2 only
C. Both 1 and 2 D. Neither 1 nor 2

102. What is the derivative of x^3 with respect to x^2?

A. $3x^2$ B. $\frac{3x}{2}$
C. x D. $\frac{3}{2}$

103. What is $\lim_{x\to 2} \frac{2-x}{x^3-8}$ equal to?

A. $\frac{1}{8}$ B. $-\frac{1}{8}$
C. $\frac{1}{12}$ D. $-\frac{1}{12}$

104. A function $f:\mathbb{R}\to\mathbb{R}$ is defined as $f(x) = x^2$ for $x \geq 0$ and $f(x) = -x$ for $x < 0$.

Consider the following statements in respect of the above function:

1. The function is continuous at $x = 0$.
2. The function is differentiable at $x = 0$.

Which of the above statements is/are correct?

A. 1 only B. 2 only
C. Both 1 and 2 D. Neither 1 nor 2

105. If $f(x) = 2x^2 + 3x - 5$, then what is $f'(0) + 3f'(-1)$ equal to?

A. –1 B. 0
C. 1 D. 2

106. Consider the following statements:

1. The matrix $\begin{pmatrix} 1 & 2 & 1 \\ a & 2a & 1 \\ b & 2b & 1 \end{pmatrix}$ is singular.

2. The matrix $\begin{pmatrix} c & 2c & 1 \\ a & 2a & 1 \\ b & 2b & 1 \end{pmatrix}$ is non-singular.

Which of the above statements is/are correct?

A. 1 only
B. 2 only
C. Both 1 and 2
D. Neither 1 nor 2

107. The cofactor of the element 4 in the determinant $\begin{vmatrix} 1 & 2 & 3 \\ 4 & 5 & 6 \\ 5 & 8 & 9 \end{vmatrix}$ is

A. 2 B. 4
C. 6 D. –6

108. If A is a square matrix of order 3 with $|A| \neq 0$, then which one of the following is correct?

A. $|\text{adj } A| = |A|$ B. $|\text{adj } A| = |A|^2$
C. $|\text{adj } A| = |A|^3$ D. $|\text{adj } A|^2 = |A|$

109. Let $A = \{a, b, c, d\}$ and $B = \{x, y, z\}$. What is the number of elements in $A \times B$?

A. 6 B. 7
C. 12 D. 64

110. If $C(28, 2r) = C(28, 2r - 4)$, then what is r equal to?

A. 7 B. 8
C. 12 D. 16

111. If A is a subset of B, then which one of the following is correct?

A. $A^c \subseteq B^c$ B. $B^c \subseteq A^c$
C. $A^c = B^c$ D. $A \subseteq A \cap B$

112. If $A = \begin{pmatrix} i & 0 \\ 0 & -i \end{pmatrix}$, $B = \begin{pmatrix} 0 & -1 \\ 1 & 0 \end{pmatrix}$, $C = \begin{pmatrix} 0 & i \\ i & 0 \end{pmatrix}$ where $i = \sqrt{-1}$, then which one of the following is correct?

A. AB = –C
B. AB = C
C. $A^2 = B^2 = C^2 = I$, where I is the identity matrix
D. BA ≠ C

113. Let f be a function from the set of natural numbers to the set of even natural numbers given by $f(x) = 2x$. Then f is

A. one to one but not onto
B. onto but not one-one
C. both one-one and onto
D. neither one-one nor onto

114. If $2A = \begin{pmatrix} 2 & 1 \\ 3 & 2 \end{pmatrix}$, then what is A^{-1} equal to?

A. $\begin{pmatrix} 2 & -1 \\ -3 & 2 \end{pmatrix}$ B. $\frac{1}{2}\begin{pmatrix} 2 & -1 \\ -3 & 2 \end{pmatrix}$
C. $\frac{1}{4}\begin{pmatrix} 2 & -1 \\ -3 & 2 \end{pmatrix}$ D. None of the above

115. If $\begin{pmatrix} 2 & 3 \\ 4 & 1 \end{pmatrix} \times \begin{pmatrix} 5 & -2 \\ -3 & 1 \end{pmatrix} = \begin{pmatrix} 1 & -1 \\ 17 & \lambda \end{pmatrix}$ then what is λ equal to?

A. 7 B. –7
C. 9 D. –9

116. What is the angle (in circular measure) between the hour hand and the minute hand of a clock when the time is half past 4?

A. $\frac{\pi}{3}$

B. $\frac{\pi}{4}$

C. $\frac{\pi}{6}$

D. None of the above

117. The angles of elevation of the top of a tower from two places situated at distances 21 m and x m from the base of the tower are 45° and 60° respectively. What is the value of x?

A. $7\sqrt{3}$ B. $7-\sqrt{3}$

C. $7+\sqrt{3}$ D. 14

118. What is $\frac{\cos 54°}{\tan 36°}+\frac{\tan 20°}{\cot 70°}$ equal to?

A. 0 B. 1

C. 2 D. 3

119. A person standing on the bank of a river observes that the angle subtended by a tree on the opposite of bank is 60°. When he retires 40 m from the bank, he finds the angle to be 30°. What is the breadth of the river?

A. 60 m B. 40 m

C. 30 m D. 20 m

120. If the angles of a triangle are 30° and 45° and the included side is $(\sqrt{3}+1)$, then what is the area of the triangle?

A. $\frac{\sqrt{3}+1}{2}$ B. $2(\sqrt{3}+1)$

C. $\frac{\sqrt{3}+1}{3}$ D. $\frac{\sqrt{3}-1}{2}$

ANSWERS

PAPER-I : GENERAL ABILITY TEST

1	2	3	4	5	6	7	8	9	10
A	A	C	B	C	B	C	C	C	A
11	**12**	**13**	**14**	**15**	**16**	**17**	**18**	**19**	**20**
B	B	C	B	A	D	A	C	B	D
21	**22**	**23**	**24**	**25**	**26**	**27**	**28**	**29**	**30**
A	C	A	C	B	B	C	A	B	D
31	**32**	**33**	**34**	**35**	**36**	**37**	**38**	**39**	**40**
A	A	C	C	C	D	B	B	A	A
41	**42**	**43**	**44**	**45**	**46**	**47**	**48**	**49**	**50**
C	A	C	A	D	D	A	D	B	B
51	**52**	**53**	**54**	**55**	**56**	**57**	**58**	**59**	**60**
B	A	B	C	C	B	C	A	B	B
61	**62**	**63**	**64**	**65**	**66**	**67**	**68**	**69**	**70**
A	B	A	D	A	B	C	D	C	D
71	**72**	**73**	**74**	**75**	**76**	**77**	**78**	**79**	**80**
A	A	A	A	B	B	A	C	D	D
81	**82**	**83**	**84**	**85**	**86**	**87**	**88**	**89**	**90**
C	C	C	D	C	C	C	B	A	C
91	**92**	**93**	**94**	**95**	**96**	**97**	**98**	**99**	**100**
C	C	A	D	C	A	C	C	C	A
101	**102**	**103**	**104**	**105**	**106**	**107**	**108**	**109**	**110**
A	C	B	B	C	B	C	A	A	D
111	**112**	**113**	**114**	**115**	**116**	**117**	**118**	**119**	**120**
D	C	C	C	D	D	C	D	B	C
121	**122**	**123**	**124**	**125**	**126**	**127**	**128**	**129**	**130**
B	C	A	C	B	A	C	A	A	A

131	132	133	134	135	136	137	138	139	140
A	B	D	A	C	B	D	A	C	C
141	**142**	**143**	**144**	**145**	**146**	**147**	**148**	**149**	**150**
A	A	C	C	B	A	A	A	C	B

PAPER-II : MATHEMATICS

1	2	3	4	5	6	7	8	9	10
B	A	B	D	B	C	C	A	B	D
11	**12**	**13**	**14**	**15**	**16**	**17**	**18**	**19**	**20**
A	C	C	B	C	A	A	D	B	B
21	**22**	**23**	**24**	**25**	**26**	**27**	**28**	**29**	**30**
D	C	C	D	C	C	C	D	A	D
31	**32**	**33**	**34**	**35**	**36**	**37**	**38**	**39**	**40**
D	C	C	A	C	A	A	A	C	D
41	**42**	**43**	**44**	**45**	**46**	**47**	**48**	**49**	**50**
D	A	D	C	D	B	B	A	B	D
51	**52**	**53**	**54**	**55**	**56**	**57**	**58**	**59**	**60**
D	C	D	A	A	B	C	C	C	B
61	**62**	**63**	**64**	**65**	**66**	**67**	**68**	**69**	**70**
A	C	C	A	C	C	A	A	A	C
71	**72**	**73**	**74**	**75**	**76**	**77**	**78**	**79**	**80**
A	A	C	C	C	C	A	C	B	C
81	**82**	**83**	**84**	**85**	**86**	**87**	**88**	**89**	**90**
C	A	C	D	B	C	B	C	D	C
91	**92**	**93**	**94**	**95**	**96**	**97**	**98**	**99**	**100**
D	B	B	A	B	D	B	C	A	B
101	**102**	**103**	**104**	**105**	**106**	**107**	**108**	**109**	**110**
C	B	D	A	B	A	C	B	C	B
111	**112**	**113**	**114**	**115**	**116**	**117**	**118**	**119**	**120**
B	A	C	B	B	B	A	C	D	A

EXPLANATORY ANSWERS

PAPER-II : MATHEMATICS

1. 0, 3, 8, 15, 24, 35, 48

$3-0=3$, $8-3=5$, $15-8=7$, $24-15=9$, $35-24=11$, $48-35=13$

Hence, seventh term is 48.

2. From formula

$$\tan(A-B)=\frac{\tan A-\tan B}{1+\tan A\cdot\tan B}$$

$$\tan(15°)=\tan(45°-30°)$$

$$=\frac{\tan 45°-\tan 30°}{1+\tan 45°+\tan 30°}$$

$$=\frac{1-\frac{1}{\sqrt{3}}}{1+1\cdot\frac{1}{\sqrt{3}}}=\frac{(\sqrt{3}-1)}{(\sqrt{3}+1)}\times\frac{(\sqrt{3}-1)}{(\sqrt{3}-1)}$$

$$=\frac{(\sqrt{3}-1)^2}{(\sqrt{3})^2-(1)^2}=\frac{3+1-2\sqrt{3}}{3-1}$$

$$=\frac{4-2\sqrt{3}}{2}=2-\sqrt{3}$$

3. From trigonometric values

1. $\tan\left(\frac{\pi}{6}\right)=\frac{1}{\sqrt{3}}$

2. $\tan\left(\frac{3\pi}{4}\right)=\tan\left(\pi-\frac{\pi}{4}\right)=\tan\left(\frac{\pi}{4}\right)=-1$

3. $\tan\left(\frac{5\pi}{4}\right)=\tan\left(\pi+\frac{\pi}{4}\right)=\tan\left(\frac{\pi}{4}\right)=1$

4. $\tan\left(\frac{2\pi}{3}\right) = \tan\left(\pi - \frac{\pi}{3}\right) = \tan\left(\frac{\pi}{3}\right) = -\sqrt{3}$

Hence, correct ascending order is 4 < 2 < 1 < 3.

4. $\cos x = \frac{1}{3}$

$\sin x . \cot x . \text{cosec } x . \tan x$

$= \sin x \cdot \frac{1}{\tan x} \cdot \frac{1}{\sin x} \cdot \tan x = 1$

5. $\text{Log}_{81} 243 = \text{Log}_{(3)^4} (3)^5$

From Log properties,

$$\text{Log}_{(b)^y} (a)^x = \frac{x}{y} \text{Log}_b a$$

Similarly, $\text{Log}_{(3)^4} (3)^5 = \frac{5}{4} \text{Log}_3 3$

$$= \frac{5}{4} = 1.25$$

6. Note: In the given question, it should be 'D (2, *b*), then c is equal to' in place of 'C (2, *b*), then D is equal to' and so we will get correct option C (4, *b*).

7. Family of lines having slopes $m_1, m_2, m_3 \ldots\ldots m_n$ respectively are in parallel if $m_1 = m_2 = m_3 = \ldots\ldots = m_n$.

Given equations are:

$$2x + 3y + a = 0 \Rightarrow y = -\frac{2}{3}x - \frac{a}{3}$$

$$\text{and } 5x + ky + a = 0 \Rightarrow y = -\frac{5}{k}x - \frac{a}{k}$$

Slopes are $m_1 = -\frac{2}{3}$ and $m_2 = -\frac{5}{k}$

two lines are parallel, if

$$-\frac{2}{3} = -\frac{5}{k}$$

or, $k = \frac{5 \times 3}{2} = 7.5$

8. Given line is $3x + 4y + 5 = 0$

or, $y = -\frac{3}{4}x - \frac{5}{4}$

Slope of line $(m) = -\frac{3}{4}$

Product of Slopes of two perpendicular lines = –1

Let slope of required line is m'.

then $m \cdot m' = -1$

$$\left(-\frac{3}{4}\right) \cdot m' = -1$$

$$m' = \frac{4}{3}$$

From formula, equation of line with slope (P) and passing through point (α, β) is

$$(y - \beta) = p \cdot (x - \alpha)$$

Here, $P = \frac{4}{3}, (\alpha, \beta) = (4, -5)$

$$(y - (-5)) = \frac{4}{3}(x - 4)$$

or, $3y + 15 = 4x - 16$

or, $4x - 3y - 31 = 0$

9. Standard equation of hyperbola

$$\frac{x^2}{a^2} - \frac{y^2}{b^2} = 1$$

with foci $S(ae, 0)$ and $S'(-ae, 0)$

Given equation is

$$4x^2 - 9y^2 = 1$$

or, $\frac{x^2}{\left(\frac{1}{4}\right)} - \frac{y^2}{\left(\frac{1}{9}\right)} = 1$

Here, $a^2 = \frac{1}{4}, \quad b^2 = \frac{1}{9}$

From hyperbola properties,

$$b^2 = a^2e^2 - a^2$$

or, $a^2e^2 = b^2 + a^2$

$$= \frac{1}{9} + \frac{1}{4} = \frac{13}{36}$$

or, $ae = \pm\frac{\sqrt{13}}{6}$

Hence, $\boxed{\text{foci} : \left(\pm\frac{\sqrt{13}}{6}, 0\right)}$

10. As two lines are equidistant from point (1, 1) so, length of perpendicular from point (1, 1) to two given lines would be equal.

From formula, length of perpendicular from given point (α, β) on line $ax + by + c = 0$ is:

$$\frac{a\alpha + b\beta + c}{\sqrt{a^2 + b^2}}$$

According to the question,

$$\frac{3(1) + 4(1) - 1}{\sqrt{(3)^2 + (4)^2}} = \frac{4(1) + 3(1) + 2k}{\sqrt{(4)^2 + (3)^2}}$$

or, $\frac{3 + 4 - 1}{5} = \frac{4 + 3 + 2k}{5}$

$$6 = 7 + 2k$$

$\Rightarrow$ $k = -\frac{1}{2}$

11. Let point P is (α, β)

According to the question,

$$\sqrt{(\alpha-1)^2+(\beta-2)^2} = \sqrt{(\alpha-(-2))^2+(\beta-3)^2}$$

Squaring both sides,

$$(\alpha - 1)^2 + (\beta - 2)^2 = (\alpha + 2)^2 + (\beta - 3)^2$$

$$\alpha^2 + \beta^2 - 2\alpha - 4\beta + 5 = \alpha^2 + \beta^2 + 4\alpha - 6\beta + 13$$

or, $6\alpha - 2\beta + 8 = 0$

$\Rightarrow$ $3\alpha - \beta + 4 = 0$

Locus of point P is a straight line whose equation is:

$$3x - y + 4 = 0$$

12. As the required line is equidistant from the axes, so its has equal inclination with two axes. Slope of such line $(m) = \pm \tan (45°) = \pm 1$.

Equation of such line will passes through origin.

Hence, locus of a point equidistant from two axes will be

$$y - 0 = \pm 1\ (x - 0)$$

$$y = \pm x$$

13. Let point A = (5, 2), B = (6, –15) and O = (0, 0).

Slope of line OA = $m_1 = \dfrac{2-0}{5-0} = \dfrac{2}{5}$

Slope of line OB = $m_2 = \dfrac{-15-0}{6-0} = \dfrac{-15}{6}$

Angle between two lines with slopes m_1 and m_2 is

$$\tan(\theta) = \frac{m_1 - m_2}{1+m_1\cdot m_2}$$

$$= \frac{\frac{2}{5}-\left(-\frac{15}{6}\right)}{1+\frac{2}{5}\cdot\left(-\frac{15}{6}\right)} = \frac{\frac{2}{5}+\frac{15}{6}}{1-1}$$

$$\tan(\theta) = \infty \Rightarrow \theta = \frac{\pi}{2}$$

14. Standard equation of ellipse is:

$$\frac{x^2}{a^2}+\frac{y^2}{b^2} = 1$$

Length of latus rectum = $\dfrac{2b^2}{a}$

Given equation is

$$4x^2 + 9y^2 = 36$$

or, $\dfrac{x^2}{9}+\dfrac{y^2}{4} = 1$

$$a^2 = 9, \quad b^2 = 4$$

Length of latus rectum = $\dfrac{2\times 4}{3} = \dfrac{8}{3}$

15. Slope of required line

$$m = \frac{7-(-2)}{-4-5} = \frac{9}{-9} = -1$$

equation of line

$$(y - (-2)) = -1(x - 5)$$

$$y + 2 = -x + 5$$

or, $x + y - 3 = 0$

16. $\sin^2 20° + \sin^2 70°$

or, $\sin^2 20° + \sin^2 (90° - 20°)$

or, $\sin^2 20° + \cos^2 (20°) = 1$.

17. $\begin{vmatrix} 1 & bc & a(b+c) \\ 1 & ca & b(c+a) \\ 1 & ab & c(a+b) \end{vmatrix}$

$= \begin{vmatrix} 1 & bc & ab+bc+ca \\ 1 & ca & bc+ab+ca \\ 1 & ab & ac+bc+ab \end{vmatrix}$ {Applying $C_3 \to C_3 + C_2$}

$= (ab + bc + ca)\begin{vmatrix} 1 & bc & 1 \\ 1 & ca & 1 \\ 1 & ab & 1 \end{vmatrix}$

$= (ab + bc + ca)\begin{vmatrix} 1 & bc & 0 \\ 1 & ca & 0 \\ 1 & ab & 0 \end{vmatrix}$

{Applying $C_3 \to C_3 - C_1$}

$= (ab + bc + ca) = 0$

18. Distributive properties of three non-empty sets are:

$$A \cup (B \cap C) = (A \cup B) \cap (A \cup C)$$

and $A \cap (B \cup C) = (A \cap B) \cup (A \cap C)$

Hence, neither (1) nor (2) are correct.

19. Plug in $x = 1$, we get

$(1 + 1)^n = a_0 + a_1 + a_2 + \ldots\ldots + a_n = (2)^n$

20. $\sqrt{\dfrac{\alpha}{\beta}}+\sqrt{\dfrac{\beta}{\alpha}}+\sqrt{\dfrac{b}{a}} = \dfrac{\alpha+\beta}{\sqrt{\alpha\cdot\beta}}+\sqrt{\dfrac{b}{a}}$

Sum of roots of given equation $ax^2 + bx + b = 0$

$$\alpha + \beta = -\frac{b}{a}$$

so, $\dfrac{-\frac{b}{a}}{\sqrt{\frac{b}{a}}}+\sqrt{\dfrac{b}{a}} = -\sqrt{\dfrac{b}{a}}+\sqrt{\dfrac{b}{a}} = 0$

21. 110001

$= 1 \times 2^5 + 1 \times 2^4 + 0 \times 2^3 + 0 \times 2^2 + 0 \times 2^1 + 1 \times 2^0$

$= 32 + 16 + 0 + 0 + 0 + 1 = 49$

22. Discriminant (D) = $b^2 - 4a.c$

$= (-8)^2 - 4.1.16$

$= 64 - 64 = 0$

for D = 0,

two roots are real & equal.

23. We know that

$$\tan^{-1} m + \tan^{-1} n = \tan^{-1}\left(\frac{m+n}{1-m\cdot n}\right)$$

Here, $m = \frac{1}{2}$, $n = \frac{1}{3}$

$$\tan^{-1}\left(\frac{1}{2}\right) + \tan^{-1}\left(\frac{1}{3}\right)$$

$$= \tan^{-1}\left(\frac{\frac{1}{2}+\frac{1}{3}}{1-\frac{1}{2}\cdot\frac{1}{3}}\right) = \tan^{-1}\left(\frac{5}{5}\right)$$

$$= \tan^{-1}(1) = \frac{\pi}{4}$$

24. $(1 - \sin^2\theta)(1 + \tan^2\theta)$

$$\cos^2\theta \,.\, \sec^2\theta = \cos^2\theta\cdot\frac{1}{\cos^2\theta} = 1$$

25. $(1+2x+x^2)^{10} = \{(1+x)^2\}^{10} = (1+x)^{20}$

We know that number of terms in the expansion of $(1 + x)^n$ are $n + 1$

so, required number of terms = 20 + 1 = 21.

26. Let first term and common difference are a and d respectively.

Sum of first five terms = Sum of first ten terms

$$\frac{5}{2}(2a+(5-1)d) = \frac{10}{2}(2a+(10-1)d)$$

or, $5(a + 2d) = 5(2a + 9d)$

or, $a + 7d = 0$

This is true, only when either a or d is negative but not both together.

27. The number of elements in the finite set A is denoted by n(A) is called cardinal number.

Number of elements in power set P(A)

$= (2)^4 = 16$

Hence, cardinality of P(A) = 16.

28. Sum of roots $\alpha + \beta = 10$

Product of roots $\alpha\cdot\beta = 9$

$$\alpha - \beta = \sqrt{(\alpha+\beta)^2 - 4\alpha\cdot\beta}$$

$$= \sqrt{(10)^2 - 4\times 9}$$

$$= \sqrt{100-36} = \sqrt{64}$$

$\alpha - \beta = 8$

Difference of roots = 8.

29. Substracting two given equations.

$$\begin{array}{r} 8x - 9y = 20 \\ 7x - 10y = 9 \\ - \quad + \quad - \\ \hline x + y = 11 \end{array}$$

or, $x = 11 - y$

Plug in $x = 11 - y$ into

$8x - 9y = 20$

$8(11 - y) - 9y = 20$

$88 - 8y - 9y = 20$

or, $17y = 68 \Rightarrow y = 4$

and, $x = 11 - 4 = 7$

$2x - y = 2(7) - 4 = 10$

30. Quadratic equation have real roots if discriminant D > 0

$b^2 - 4.1.4 \geq 0$

or, $b^2 \geq 16$

or, $b \geq 4$ and $b \leq -4$

31. Let $P^2 = 7 + 4\sqrt{3}$

$= (2)^2 + (\sqrt{3})^2 + 2.2.\sqrt{3}$

$= (2+\sqrt{3})^2$

Hence, positive square root

$P = (\sqrt{3}+2)$

32. (A × B) = {(1, 2), (1, 3), (2, 2), (2, 3)}

(A × C) = {(1, 3), (1, 4), (2, 3), (2, 4)}

(A × B) ∩ (A × C) = {(1, 3), (2, 3)}

Cardinality = 2

33. From given equation,

$\alpha + \beta = -1$ and $\alpha\cdot\beta = 2$

$$\frac{\alpha^{10}+\beta^{10}}{\alpha^{-10}+\beta^{-10}} = \frac{\alpha^{10}+\beta^{10}}{\frac{\alpha^{10}+\beta^{10}}{(\alpha\cdot\beta)^{10}}}$$

$= (\alpha\cdot\beta)^{10} = (2)^{10} = 1024$

34. We know that, in a quadratic equation with rational co-efficient, surd roots occur in conjugate pairs.

So, other root will be $3a - \sqrt{b}$.

Quadratic equation will be

x^2 – (sum of roots)x + Product of roots = 0

$$x^2 - \left(3a - \sqrt{b} + 3a - \sqrt{b}\right)x + \left(3a+\sqrt{b}\right)\left(3a-\sqrt{b}\right) = 0$$

or, $x^2 - 6ax + 9a^2 - b = 0$

35. The cartesian product (A × A) contains $n \times n = n^2$ elements.

Number of relation definded in A is equal to the number of subsets of (A × A) which is equal to 2^{n^2}.

36. a, b, c, d are in A.P.

then, $\frac{1}{a}, \frac{1}{b}, \frac{1}{c}, \frac{1}{d}$ are in H.P.

or, $\frac{abcd}{a}, \frac{abcd}{b}, \frac{abcd}{c}, \frac{abcd}{d}$ are in H.P.

or, bcd, acd, abd, abc are in H.P.

37. (A) $x = \{2\}$

(B) $x^2 - 2 = 0 \Rightarrow x = \pm\sqrt{2}$, but x is rational so, $x = \{\}$

(C) $x : \{x < 8 \cap x > 12\} \Rightarrow x = \{\}$

(D) $x : \{\}$, As no common point exist for any two parallel line.

38. Let $I^2 = 3 + 4i$

$= (2)^2 + (i)^2 + 2.2.i$

$= (2 + i)^2$

Square root I = $(2 + i)$

39. Writing 83 into sum of power of 2.

$83 = 64 + 16 + 2 + 1$

$= 2^6 + 2^4 + 2^1 + 2^0$

$= 1010011$

40. A relation 'R' is called equivalence relation, if it is reflexive, symmetric and transitive together.

R = $\{(a, a) : a - a$ is divisible by $5\}$. It is reflexive relation.

Again, R = $\{(a, b) : a - b$ is divisible by $5\}$ also $(b - a)$ is divisible by 5. So it is symmetric relation.

Again, R = $(a, c) : a - c$ is divisible by 5, then $b - c$ is also divisible by 5, so it is transitive. Hence 'R' is equivalence relation.

41. $(1 + x)^n = {}^nC_0 + {}^nC_1\, x + {}^nC_2\, x^2 + \ldots\ldots + {}^nC_n\, x^n$

for $x = 1$

$(2)^n = {}^nC_0 + {}^nC_1 + {}^nC_2 + {}^nC_3 + \ldots\ldots + {}^nC_n$

$$\sum_{r=0}^{n} C(n,r) = (2)^n.$$

42. $S = \frac{9}{10} + \frac{9}{100} + \frac{9}{1000} \ldots\ldots \infty$

This is sum of infinite terms G.P. with common ratio

$r = \frac{1}{10}$

$$S = \frac{\frac{9}{10}}{1 - \frac{1}{10}} = \frac{\frac{9}{10}}{\frac{9}{10}} = 1$$

43. Case-1, when $x > 0$, $|x| = x$

$f(x) = x^2 + 3x + 2 = 0$

$(x + 2)(x + 1) = 0 \qquad x = -1$ and -2

But $x > 0$,

Hence, no roots exist.

Case-II, when $x < 0$, $|x| = -x$

$f(x) = x^2 - 3x + 2 = 0$

$(x - 2)(x - 1) = 0 \qquad x = +1, 2$

But $x < 0$,

Hence, no real roots exist again.

44. Let diabetes and blood pressure is denoted by d and b respectively.

so, $n(d \cup b) = 50$

$n(d) = 30$ and $n(b) = 40$

From, $n(d \cup b) = n(d) + n(b) - n(d \cap b)$

$50 = 30 + 40 - n(d \cap b)$

$n(d \cap b) = 70 - 50 = 20$

46.

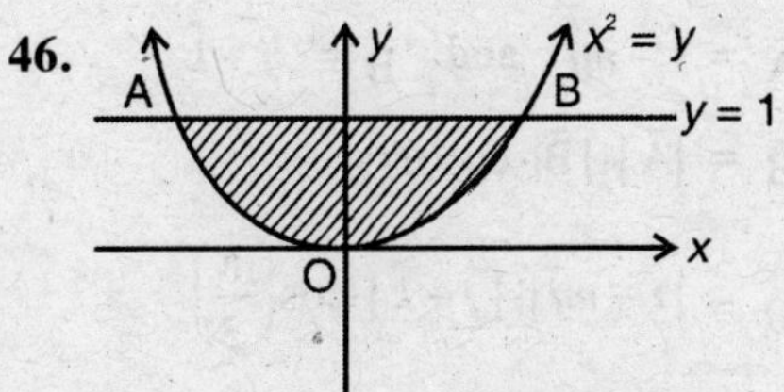

Required area is area AOB

$$= \int_0^1 \sqrt{y} \cdot dy = \left[\frac{(y)^{3/2}}{3/2}\right]_0^1$$

$= \frac{2}{3}$ square units

47.

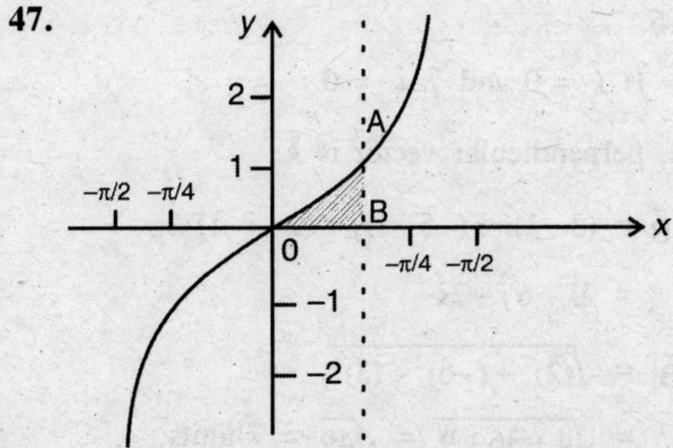

Required area is the shaded portion OAB.

$$= \int_0^{\frac{\pi}{4}} \tan(x) \cdot dx = [\ln(\sec(x))]_0^{\pi/4}$$

$= \ln \sec\left(\frac{\pi}{4}\right) - \ln \sec(0)$

$= \ln\left(\sqrt{2}\right) - \ln(1)$

$= \frac{1}{2}\ln(2) - 0 = \frac{\ln(2)}{2}$

48. $\int (x\cos x + \sin x)\cdot dx$

$= \int x\cos x\cdot dx + \int \sin x\cdot dx$

$= x\cdot \sin x + \cos x - \cos x + C$

$= x \sin x + C$

49. $I = \int_0^2 e^{\ln x}\cdot dx$

Let $e^{\ln(x)} = y$

or, $\ln(x) = \ln(y)$

$x = y \Rightarrow dx = dy$

$$I = \int_0^2 y\cdot dy = \left[\frac{y^2}{2}\right]_0^2 = 2 - 0 = 2$$

50. Let $\vec{A} = \hat{i} - m\hat{j}$ and $\vec{B} = \hat{j} + \hat{k}$

$\vec{A}\cdot\vec{B} = |\vec{A}|\cdot|\vec{B}|\cdot\cos(\theta)$

$$(\hat{i} - m\hat{j})\cdot(\hat{j}+\hat{k}) = |\hat{i} - m\hat{j}|\cdot|\hat{j}+\hat{k}|\cdot\cos\left(\frac{\pi}{3}\right)$$

$$-m = \left|\sqrt{1+m^2}\right|\cdot\left|\sqrt{1^2+1^2}\right|\cdot\frac{1}{2}$$

or, $-\sqrt{2}\,m = \sqrt{1+m^2}$

Squaring both sides, we get

$2m^2 = 1 + m^2 \Rightarrow m^2 = 1$

$m = \pm 1$

51. Two vectors are perpendicular if its dot product equals to zero.

$(\hat{i} - \hat{j})\cdot\hat{k} = 0$ and $\hat{i}\cdot\hat{k} = 0$

Hence, perpendicular vector is $\hat{k}$.

52. $\overline{AB} = (3-1)\hat{i} + (-5-1)\hat{j} + (2-(-1))\hat{k}$

$= 2\hat{i} - 6\hat{j} + 3\hat{k}$

$|\overline{AB}| = \sqrt{(2)^2 + (-6)^2 + (3)^2}$

$= \sqrt{4+36+9} = \sqrt{49} = 7$ units.

53. Two vectors are orthogonal, if its dot product or scalar product = 0.

$\left(\hat{i} - 2x\hat{j} - 3y\hat{k}\right)\cdot\left(\hat{i} + 3x\hat{j} + 2y\hat{k}\right) = 0$

$1 - 6x^2 - 6y^2 = 0$ or, $x^2 + y^2 = \dfrac{1}{6}$

This is a circle.

54. Length of given vector

$P\left|(2\hat{i} - \hat{j} + 2\hat{k})\right| = 3$

$P\cdot\sqrt{(2)^2 + (1)^2 + (2)^2} = 3$

$P\cdot 3 = 3 \Rightarrow P = 1$

55. $\vec{a} + t\vec{b} = \left(2\hat{i} + 2\hat{j} + 3\hat{k}\right) + t\left(-\hat{i} + 2\hat{j} + \hat{k}\right)$

$= (2-t)\hat{i} + (2+2t)\hat{j} + (3+t)\hat{k}$

According to the question,

$(\vec{a} + t\vec{b})\cdot\vec{c} = 0$

$(2 - t) . 3 + (2 + 2t) . 1 = 0$

$8 - t = 0 \Rightarrow t = 8$

56. Difference in values = (8 + 4) – (6 + 3) = 3

Mean difference = $\dfrac{3}{20} = 0.15$

Hence, correct mean = 15.15

57. A.M.

$$= \frac{\text{sum of square of 1st } n \text{ natural numbers}}{n}$$

$$= \frac{n(n+1)(2n+1)}{6n} = \frac{(n+1)(2n+1)}{6}$$

61. $\lim\limits_{x\to 0}\dfrac{1-\cos x}{x}\times\dfrac{(1+\cos x)}{(1+\cos x)}$

$$= \lim_{x\to 0}\frac{1-\cos^2 x}{x(1+\cos x)} = \lim_{x\to 0}\frac{\sin^2 x}{x\cdot(1+\cos x)}$$

$$= \lim_{x\to 0}\frac{x}{(1+\cos x)}\cdot\frac{\sin^2(x)}{x^2}$$

$$= \frac{0}{(1+1)}\cdot 1 = 0$$

62. $\lim\limits_{x\to 0}\dfrac{\cos x}{\pi - x} = \dfrac{\cos(0)}{\pi - 0} = \dfrac{1}{\pi}.$

63. $\lim\limits_{x\to 0}\dfrac{\sin 2x + 4x}{2x + \sin 4x}$

$$= \lim_{x\to 0}\frac{\dfrac{2\cdot\sin 2x}{2x} + \dfrac{4x}{x}}{\dfrac{2x}{x} + \dfrac{4\cdot\sin 4x}{4x}}$$

$$= \frac{2+4}{2+4} = \frac{6}{6} = 1$$

64. $f(x) = x^3 + 2x^2 - 4x + 6$

$f'(x) = 3x^2 + 4x - 4$

For extremum values of $f(x)$, $f'(x) = 0$

$3x^2 + 4x - 4 = 0$

$(3x - 2)(x + 2) = 0 \Rightarrow x = -2, \dfrac{2}{3}$

$f''(x) = 6x + 4$

for $x = -2$, $f''(-2) = 6(-2) + 4$

$= -8 < 0$

Hence, $f(x)$ is maximum at $x = -2$.

65. From graphical method:
Graph of $f(x) = |x - 4|$

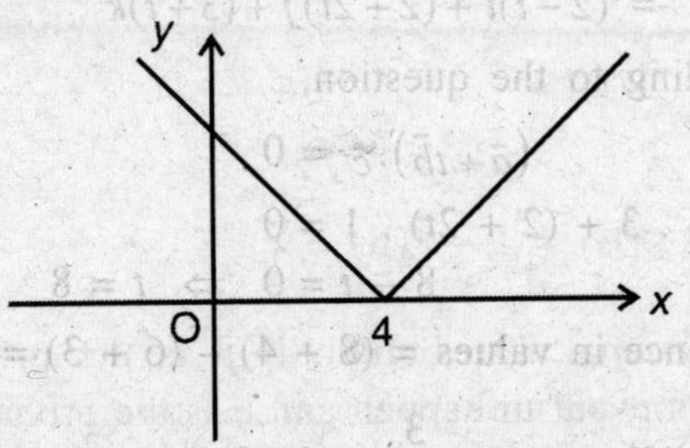

It is clear from the graph, minimum values of $f(x)$ is 0 at $x = 4$.

66. $I = \int_1^2 \ln(x) \cdot dx$

From integration by parts formula

$$u = \ln(x), \quad v = 1$$

$$\int uvdx = u\int v.dx - \int\left(\frac{du}{dx}\cdot\int v.dx\right)dx$$

$$I = \ln x \cdot \int_1^2 dx - \int_1^2\left(\frac{d}{dx}(\ln x)\cdot\int dx\right)\cdot dx$$

$$= [\ln x \cdot (x)]_1^2 - \int_1^2 \frac{1}{x}\cdot x \cdot dx$$

$$= [x \cdot \ln(x) - x]_1^2$$

$$= 2 . \ln(2) - 2 - 1 . \ln 1 + 1$$

$$= \ln (2)^2 - 1$$

$$= \ln (4) - \ln e = \ln\left(\frac{4}{e}\right).$$

67. $I = \int \frac{dx}{\sqrt{x^2+4}} = \int \frac{dx}{\sqrt{x^2+(2)^2}}$

Let $x = 2\tan\theta$

$dx = 2\sec^2\theta \, d\theta$

$$\int \frac{2\sec^2\theta \cdot d\theta}{\sqrt{2^2(1+\tan^2\theta)}} = \int \sec\theta \cdot d\theta$$

$$= \ln(\sec\theta + \tan\theta) + C = \ln\left(x+\sqrt{x^2+4}\right) + C$$

68. The order of a differential equation is the order of the highest differential co-efficient which occurs in it. Here order of differential equation is 1.

69. $\frac{dy}{dx} = -2 . \sin x + 3 \cos x$

and $\frac{d^2y}{dx^2} = -2 . \cos x - 3 \sin x$

$= -(2 \cos x + 3 \sin x)$

$= -y$

Hence, $\frac{d^2y}{dx^2} + y = 0$ satisfied

Again, $\left(\frac{dy}{dx}\right)^2 + \frac{dy}{dx} = 0$

$$\frac{dy}{dx}\left(\frac{dy}{dx}+1\right) = 0$$

either $\frac{dy}{dx} = 0$

or $\frac{dy}{dx} = -1$

i.e., $-2 \sin x + 3 \cos x = 0$

or, $-2 \sin x + 3 \cos x = -1$

or, $2 \sin x = 3 \cos x$

$$\tan x = \frac{3}{2}$$

This is satisfied for $x = \tan^{-1}\left(\frac{3}{2}\right)$

70. Standard equation of circle where centre is at the origin is

$$x^2 + y^2 = r^2$$

Differentiating both sides w.r.t. x, we get

$$2x + 2y\cdot\frac{dy}{dx} = 0$$

or, $\frac{dy}{dx} = -\frac{x}{y}$

71. $\int \sin^2 x \cdot dx + \int \cos^2 x \cdot dx$

$= \int(\sin^2 x + \cos^2 x)\cdot dx = \int dx = x + c$

72. $I = \int e^{e^x}\cdot e^x \cdot dx$

Let $e^{e^x} = y$

then, $e^x = \ln(y)$

and, $e^x.dx = \frac{1}{y}\cdot dy$

$$I = \int y \cdot \frac{1}{y}\cdot dy$$

$$= \int dy = y + c$$

$$= e^{e^x} + c$$

73.

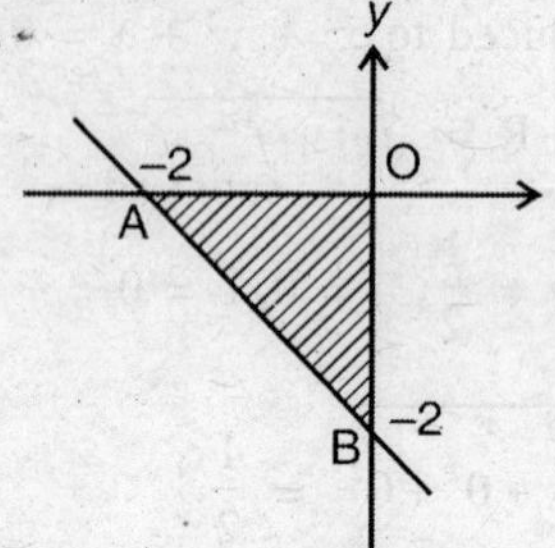

Required area is the shaded triangle OAB, its area

$$A = \frac{1}{2}|OA|\cdot|OB|$$

$$= \frac{1}{2}|2|\cdot|2| = 2 \text{ square units.}$$

74. $y = \sin(\sin x)$

$$\frac{dy}{dx} = \frac{d}{dx}(\sin(\sin x))$$

$$= \cos(\sin x) \cdot \cos x$$

75. at $x = 2$, $|x - 1| = x - 1$

$$y = x - 1 \Rightarrow \frac{dy}{dx} = 1$$

76. A set of events is said to be mutually exclusive if the occurrence of one of them precludes the occurrence of any of the remaining events.

In set theory notation, events $A_1, A_2, A_3 \ldots\ldots A_m$ are mutually exclusive if $A_i \cap A_j = \phi$ for $i \neq j$ and $1 \leq i, j \leq m$.

77. Variance : The square of standard deviation is called the variance (σ^2)

$$\therefore \quad \sigma^2 = \frac{\Sigma(x - \bar{X})^2}{n},$$

where $\bar{X}$ = mean of given data

$\bar{x}$ = mean of 1st eleven natural numbers.

$$= \frac{11 \times 12}{2 \times 11} = 6$$

$$\therefore \sigma^2 = \frac{(1-6)^2 + (2-6)^2 + (3-6)^2 + \ldots\ldots + (11-6)^2}{11}$$

$$= \frac{2[1^2 + 2^2 + 3^2 + 4^2 + 5^2]}{11}$$

$$= \frac{2 \times 5 \times 6 \times 11}{11 \times 6} = 10.$$

78. As A and B are independent events, so

$P(A \cap B) = P(A) \cdot P(B)$

Now, from

$P(A \cup B) = P(A) + P(B) - P(A \cap B)$

$$\frac{7}{10} = \frac{1}{5} + P(B) - \frac{1}{5} \cdot P(B)$$

or, $$\frac{1}{2} = \frac{4}{5}P(B)$$

$$\Rightarrow \quad P(B) = \frac{5}{8}$$

$$P(\bar{B}) = 1 - P(B) = \frac{3}{8}$$

79. In Binomial distribution, if p is the probability of certain event to happen and q is the probability of its failure in a single trial then $p + q = 1$.

Here given $p = q$

(As both events are equally likely)

so, $$p = \frac{1}{2}$$

Now, mean μ = (Number of trials) $\times$ p

$$6 = n \cdot \frac{1}{2}$$

or, $n = 12$

80. Sample event = (4, 6), (5, 5), (6, 4),

$n(E) = 3$

Sample space = 6×6, $n(s) = 36$

$$p(E) = \frac{n(E)}{n(s)} = \frac{3}{36} = \frac{1}{12}.$$

81. Sample event = (1, 1, 1), (2, 2, 2), (3, 3, 3), (4, 4, 4), (5, 5, 5), (6, 6, 6)

$n(E) = 6$

Sample space = $6 \times 6 \times 6$, $n(s) = 216$

$$p(\varepsilon) = \frac{n(E)}{n(s)} = \frac{6}{216} = \frac{1}{36}$$

82. Exhaustive events: A system of events is said to be exhaustive if on each performance of the experiment at least one of the events of the system is must to occur.

For example, on tossing a coin, the events {H} and {T} form an exhaustive events.

83. Here both statements are true.

84. In Binomial distribution,

mean (μ) > Variance $(\sigma)^2$

i.e., $np > npq$

and $0 \leq p \leq 1$

Hence, correct option is (D).

85. The set of all possible outcomes in a random experiment is called sample space.

Here, total number of possible outcomes

$= 1 + 6 = 7.$

86. P(A ∪ B) – P(A ∩ B)

$= P(A) + P(B) - 2P(A \cap B) = \frac{2}{5}$

$= \frac{2}{3} + \frac{2}{5} - 2P(A \cap B) = \frac{2}{5}$

$\therefore P(A \cap B) = \frac{1}{3}.$

87. Month of February 2016 would be of 29 days. If the month of February starts with Monday, then till 28th February, it would be 4 Mondays.

Now, probability that Monday will be on 29th February is $\frac{1}{7}$.

88. Both statements (1) and (2) are correct.

89. Probability that A comes first = $\frac{1}{6}$

Probability that B comes second = $\frac{1}{5}$

Probability that C comes third = $\frac{1}{4}$

Required probability = $\frac{1}{6} \times \frac{1}{5} \times \frac{1}{4} = \frac{1}{120}$

90. Variance $(\sigma^2) = \sum_{i=1}^{n} f(x_i - \bar{X})^2$

when each observation is multiplied by m, then,

Variance $(\sigma^2) = \sum_{i=1}^{n} m^2 f(x_i - \bar{X})^2$

Here, $m = 2$, so, new variance (σ^2)

$= 2^2 \times 5 = 20.$

91. Slope of line $x + y = 1 \Rightarrow y = -x + 1$

$m_2 = -1$

Slope of line $x - y = 1 \Rightarrow y = x - 1$

$m_2 = 1$

Angle between two lines

$$\tan(\theta) = \frac{m_1 - m_2}{1 + m_1 . m_2}$$

$$= \frac{1-(-1)}{1+(-1).1} = \frac{2}{0} = \infty$$

Hence, $\theta = 90°$.

92. $y^2 + 2x = 0 \Rightarrow y^2 = -2x$

Axis of this parabola is x-axis *i.e.*, $y = 0$

93. $x^2 + y^2 + x + c = 0$

As, this circle is passing through origin, so

$0 + 0 + 0 + c = 0 \Rightarrow c = 0$

Hence, equation reduced to $x^2 + y^2 + x = 0$

Radius of the circle R = $\sqrt{g^2 + f^2 - c}$

Here, $2g = 1 \Rightarrow g = \frac{1}{2}$, $f = 0$, $c = 0$

$$\text{Radius } R = \sqrt{\left(\frac{1}{2}\right)^2 + 0^2 + 0^2} = \frac{1}{2}.$$

94. Centroid point (x, y)

$$x = \frac{x_1 + x_2 + x_3}{3}, \quad y = \frac{y_1 + y_2 + y_3}{3}$$

$$x = \frac{2 - 2 + 3}{3} = 1,$$

$$y = \frac{3 - 5 + 5}{3} = 1$$

Centroid $(x, y) = (1, 1)$.

95. Equation of line in intercept form

$$\frac{x}{p} + \frac{y}{q} = 1,$$

where, p and q are intercept cut out by line on x-axis & y-axis respectively.

Given that $\frac{1}{p} = m$ and $\frac{1}{q} = n$

so, equation of line : $mx + ny = 1$.

96. If 'θ' be the angle between the diagonals of a cube, then

$$\cos(\theta) = \frac{1(-1)+(-1)(1)+1(1)}{\sqrt{1+1+1} \cdot \sqrt{1+1+1}}$$

$$= \frac{-1}{\sqrt{3} \cdot \sqrt{3}} = -\frac{1}{3}$$

$$\theta = \cos^{-1}\left(-\frac{1}{3}\right) = \cos^{-1}\left(\frac{1}{3}\right)$$

or, $3 \cos(\theta) = 1$.

98. Angle made by x-axis with x-axis, y-axis and z-axis are 0°, 90° & 90° respectively, therefore its direction cosines are cos(0°), cos(90°), cos(90°) *i.e.*, 1, 0, 0.

Sum of the square of direction cosines

$= (1)^2 + (0)^2 + (0)^2 = 1$

99. Distance of line drawn from origin

$$= \left| \frac{2(0) + 0 + 2(0) - 3}{\sqrt{(2)^2 + (1)^2 + (2)^2}} \right|$$

$$\frac{3}{3} = 1.$$

100. Length of line segment $= \sqrt{p^2+q^2+r^2}$

$= \sqrt{2^2+3^2+6^2} = \sqrt{49} = 7$ units.

101. The simplest way to check continuity is by graphical method.

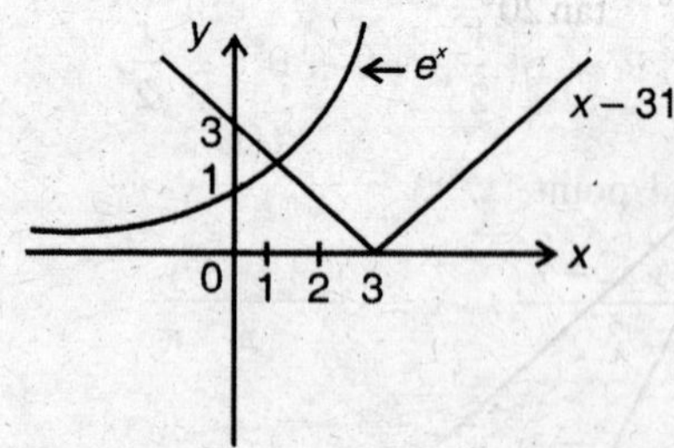

We see from the graph that both functions are continuous function.

102. Let $p = x^3,\ q = x^2$

Now, $\frac{dp}{dx} = 3x^2,\ \frac{dq}{dx} = 2x$

derivative of p w.r.t. q is $\frac{dp}{dq}$

$$= \frac{\frac{dp}{dx}}{\frac{dq}{dx}} = \frac{3x^2}{2x} = \frac{3}{2}x$$

103. $\lim_{x\to 2} \frac{2-x}{x^3-8}$

This is in the $\frac{0}{0}$ form, we use L'Hospital rule

$$\lim_{x\to 2} \frac{-1}{3x^2} = \frac{-1}{3(2)^2} = -\frac{1}{12}$$

104. Test of continuity at $x = 0$

$R\ f(x) = \lim_{x\to 0^+} x^2 = 0$

$L\ f(x) = \lim_{x\to 0^-} (-x) = 0$

also, $f(0) = (0)^2 = 0$

Hence, $f(x)$ is continuous at $x = 0$

Differentiability

$f'(x)$ for $(x > 0) = 2x \Rightarrow f'(0) = 0$

$f'(x)$ for $(x < 0) = -1 \Rightarrow f'(0) = -1$

Hence, $f(x)$ is not differentiable at $x = 0$.

105. $f'(x) = 2 \times 2x + 3 = 4x + 3$

$f'(0) + 3f'(-1) = 4(0) + 3 + 3\,[4(-1) + 3]$

$= 3 - 12 + 9 = 0$

106. A square matrix is said to be singular if its determinant is zero & non-singular if its determinant is not equal to zero.

$$\begin{vmatrix} 1 & 2 & 1 \\ a & 2a & 1 \\ b & 2b & 1 \end{vmatrix} = \begin{vmatrix} 1 & 2 & 1 \\ a-b & 2(a-b) & 0 \\ 1-b & 2(1-b) & 0 \end{vmatrix}$$

{Applying $R_2 \to R_2 - R_3$; $R_3 \to R_1 - R_3$}

$$= (a-b)(1-b)\begin{vmatrix} 1 & 2 & 1 \\ 1 & 2 & 0 \\ 1 & 2 & 0 \end{vmatrix}$$

$= (a - b)(1 - b)(2 - 2) = 0$ It is singular.

Again, $\begin{vmatrix} c & 2c & 1 \\ a & 2a & 1 \\ b & 2b & 1 \end{vmatrix} = \begin{vmatrix} c & 2c & 1 \\ a-b & 2(a-b) & 0 \\ b-c & 2(b-c) & 0 \end{vmatrix}$

{Applying $R_2 \to R_2 - R_3$; $R_3 \to R_3 - R_2$}

$$= (a-b)(b-c)\begin{vmatrix} c & 2c & 1 \\ 1 & 2 & 0 \\ 1 & 2 & 0 \end{vmatrix}$$

$= (a - b)(b - c)(2 - 2) = 0$

It is singular.

107. The co-factor of an element a_{ij} of det A is equal to $(-1)^{i+j}$ times its minor. Co-factor

$$C_{ij} = (-1)^{i+j} M_{ij}$$

$$C_{21} = (-1)^{2+1}\begin{vmatrix} 2 & 3 \\ 8 & 9 \end{vmatrix}$$

$= -1\,(18 - 24) = 6$

108. As $|A| \neq 0$, It is non-singular matrix.

Hence, $|\text{Adj } A| = |A|^2$

109. Number of elements in A × B

$n(A \times B) = n(A) \times n(B)$

$= 4 \times 3 = 12$

110. ${}^{28}C_{2r} = {}^{28}C_{2r-4}$

$\Rightarrow 2r + 2r - 4 = 28$

$\Rightarrow 4r = 32$

$r = 8$

111. As A is a subset of B, so every elements of A is an elements of B.

Hence, A is subset of $A \cap B$.

i.e., $A \subset A \cap B$. But $A \not\subset A \cap B$

$A \subseteq B$ then $B^C \subseteq A^C$

112. $A \cdot B = \begin{vmatrix} i & 0 \\ 0 & -i \end{vmatrix}\begin{vmatrix} 0 & -1 \\ 1 & 0 \end{vmatrix}$

$$= \begin{vmatrix} 0 & -i \\ -i & 0 \end{vmatrix} = -C$$

113.

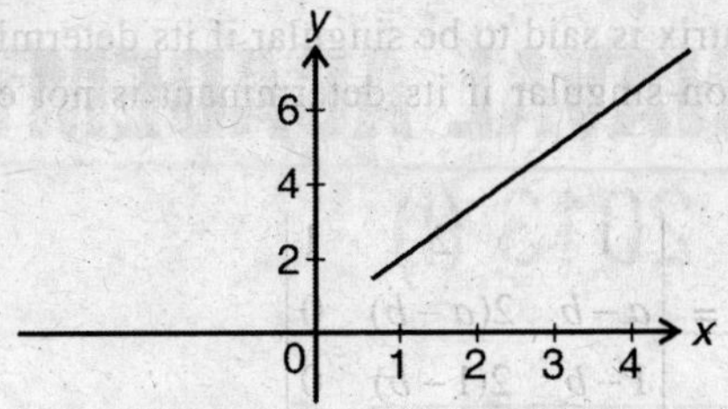

$f(x) = 2x$

Graph of $f(x) = 2x$

This is graph for one-one and onto function.

115. $\begin{vmatrix} 2 & 3 \\ 4 & 1 \end{vmatrix} \begin{vmatrix} 5 & -2 \\ 3 & 1 \end{vmatrix} = \begin{vmatrix} 1 & -1 \\ 17 & \lambda \end{vmatrix}$

$= \begin{vmatrix} 2\times5-3\times3 & -2\times2+3\times1 \\ 4\times5-1\times3 & -4\times2+1\times1 \end{vmatrix} = \begin{vmatrix} 1 & -1 \\ 17 & \lambda \end{vmatrix}$

$= \begin{vmatrix} 1 & -1 \\ 17 & -7 \end{vmatrix} = \begin{vmatrix} 1 & -1 \\ 17 & \lambda \end{vmatrix}$

$\therefore \quad \lambda = -7$

116. Angle rotated by minute hand in 30 minutes

$= \frac{30}{60} \times 360° = 180°$

Angle rotated by hour hand when it is at 4.5

$= \frac{4.5}{12} \times 360° = 135°$

Angle between two hands = 180° – 135° = 45°

117.

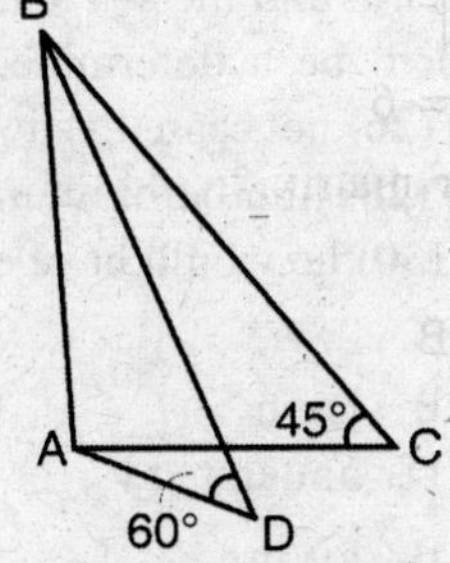

Let AB is a tower,

Given that AC = 21 m and AD = x m

From ΔABC, $\tan(45°) = \frac{AB}{AC}$

$1 = \frac{AB}{21}$

$\therefore \quad AB = 21$ m

Again, from ΔABD,

$\tan(60°) = \frac{AB}{AD} \Rightarrow \sqrt{3} = \frac{21}{x}$

$x = 7\sqrt{3}$ m.

118. $\frac{\cot 54°}{\tan 36°} + \frac{\tan 20°}{\cot 70°}$

$\frac{\tan(90° - 54°)}{\tan 36°} + \frac{\tan 20°}{\tan(90° - 70°)}$

$\frac{\tan 36°}{\tan 36°} + \frac{\tan 20°}{\tan 20°} = 1 + 1 = 2.$

119.

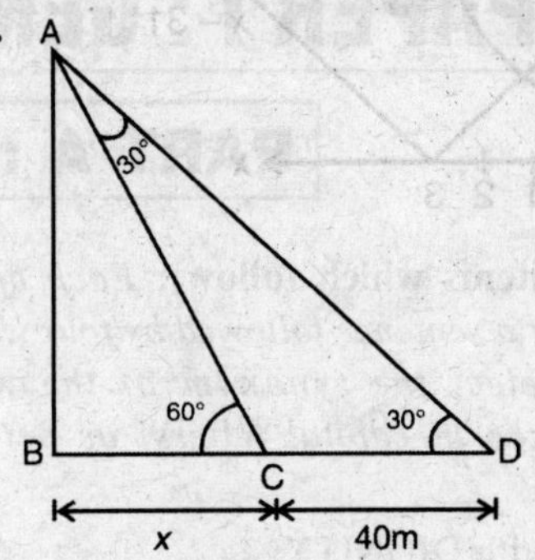

From ΔACD, ∠CAD = ∠CDA = 30°

$\therefore \quad AC = CD = 40$ m.

Now, from ΔABC,

$\cos(60°) = \frac{BC}{AC} \Rightarrow BC = AC \cdot \frac{1}{2}$

$= 40 \times \frac{1}{2} = 20$ m.

120.

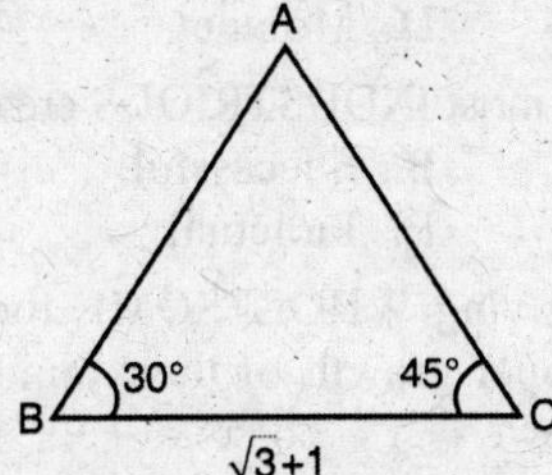

From sine formula $\frac{a}{\sin A} = \frac{b}{\sin B}$

$\Rightarrow \frac{\sqrt{3}+1}{\sin(180° - (30° + 45°))} = \frac{AC}{\sin 30°}$

or, $\frac{\sqrt{3}+1}{\sin 75°} = \frac{b}{1/2}$

or, $\frac{\sqrt{3}+1}{\left(\frac{\sqrt{3}+1}{2\sqrt{2}}\right)} = \frac{b}{1/2} \Rightarrow b = \sqrt{2}$

Area of triangle ΔABC $= \frac{1}{2} \cdot a.b.\sin(c)$

$= \frac{1}{2} \cdot (\sqrt{3}+1)(\sqrt{2}) \cdot \sin(45°)$

$= \frac{\sqrt{3}+1}{2}$ square units.

Previous Papers (Solved)

NATIONAL DEFENCE ACADEMY & NAVAL ACADEMY

NDA & NA – Entrance Exam, 2013 (I)

PAPER I : GENERAL ABILITY TEST

PART A : ENGLISH LANGUAGE

Directions (For the 10 items which follow): *Each of the following items consists of a sentence followed by four words or groups of words. Select the* **synonym** *of the word (occurring in the sentence in capital letters) as per the context.*

1. One must live life with DIGNITY.
A. Nobility B. Eminence
C. Honour D. Rank

2. Europe, America and Japan have taken to the field of science with SINGULAR vigour and activity.
A. Peculiar B. Outstanding
C. Familiar D. Single

3. Our age is preeminently an AGE of science.
A. Era B. Date
C. Generation D. Moment

4. Ant is believed to be the most INDUSTRIOUS creature.
A. Sensible B. Successful
C. Diligent D. Punctual

5. The schools insist on giving WHOLESOME food to the children for the proper growth of their mind and body.
A. Whole crops B. Nourishing
C. Fit D. Sound

6. As I look around I see the crumbling ruins of a proud civilization strewn like a vast heap of FUTILITY.
A. Irrelevance B. Absurdity
C. Pointlessness D. Downtrodden

7. Mark Antony's EULOGY of Caesar is finely recorded by Shakespeare in his play.
A. Prayer B. Honour
C. Praise D. Denunciation

8. By 1918, Gandhiji had established himself as a leader with a UNIQUE way of protesting exploitation and injustice.
A. Different B. Exceptional
C. Excellent D. Good

9. Your INTERVENTION was required.
A. Interference B. Interruption
C. Disturbance D. Connection

10. It is difficult to DISCERN the sample on the slide without adjusting the microscope.
A. Discard B. Arrange
C. Determine D. Debate

Directions for the Close Comprehension Passage (For the 20 items which follow) : *Supply suitable word in the blank of each item which is followed by four words or groups of words.*

In a few seconds we ran the boat into a little bay, where we made her fast to a piece of coral, and running up the beach, entered the ranks of the penguins armed with our sticks and spears. We were greatly surprised to **(11)** that instead of attacking us or **(12)** signs of fear at our **(13)** these strange birds do not move **(14)** their places until we took hold **(15)** them, merely **(16)** their eyes on us **(17)** wonder as we passed. There **(18)** one old penguin, however that **(19)** to walk slowly towards the sea, and Peterkin **(20)** it into his head that he **(21)** try to stop it, so he **(22)** between it and the sea and **(23)** his stick in its face. But this **(24)** to be a determined old **(25)**. It would not go back; in fact, it **(26)** not cease to advance, but **(27)** with Peterkin bravely, and **(28)** him before it until it **(29)** the sea. Had Peterkin used his **(30)** he would have easily killed it.

11. A. find B. learn
C. hear D. understand

12. A. showing B. giving
C. revealing D. conveying

13. A. arrival B. entry
C. approach D. alight

14. A. in B. at
C. from D. on

15. A. off B. of
C. from D. on

16. A. opened B. turned
C. closed D. showed

17. A. with B. out of
C. in D. on

18. A. lived B. existed
C. was D. persisted

19. A. commenced B. began
C. continued D. stalked

20. A. carried B. bore
C. took D. thought

21. A. would B. could
C. should D. won't

22. A. interposed B. ran
C. arrived D. jumped

23. A. moved B. pointed
C. waved D. watched

24. A. appeared B. happened
C. proved D. seemed

25. A. bird B. animal
C. creature D. pet

26. A. should B. would
C. could D. must

27. A. battled B. struggled
C. contested D. snugged

28. A. chased B. drove
C. moved D. lashed

29. A. touched B. arrived at
C. reached D. jumped

30. A. baton B. stick
C. spear D. club

Directions (For the 10 items which follow):

(i) In this section, a number of sentences are given. The sentences are divided in three separate parts and each one is labelled (A), (B) and (C). Read each sentence to find out whether there is an error in any divided part. No sentence has more than one error. When you find an error in any one of the divided parts (A), (B) or (C), indicate your response on the Answer Sheet at the appropriate space. You may feel that there is no error in a sentence. In that case, (D) will signify a 'No error' response .

(ii) Errors may be in grammar, word usage or idioms. There may be a word missing or there may be a word which should be removed.

(iii) You are ***not*** required to correct the error. You are required ***only*** to indicate your response on the Answer Sheet.

31. If you will work hard (A)/ you will always (B)/ succeed. (C)/ No error (D)

32. She has been teaching (A)/ the same lesson (B)/ since five days. (C)/ No error (D)

33. Many a boy were happy (A)/ dancing at the victory (B)/ of our cricket team in Australia. (C)/ No error (D)

34. Imagine living (A)/ with someone (B)/ who never stops talk. (C)/ No error (D)

35. I was shocked (A)/ when he told me (B)/ that the old woman died by cancer. (C)/ No error (D)

36. To the men who worked so hard in the project, (A)/ the news was (B)/ profound disappointing. (C)/ No error (D)

37. Even though she lost the beauty contest, (A)/ she was still more prettier (B)/ than the other girls. (C)/ No error (D)

38. The novel is interesting, (A)/ informative (B)/ and it is easy to read. (C)/ No error (D)

39. The differential attractions of the sun and the moon have a direct effect (A)/ in the rising and falling (B)/ of the tides. (C)/ No error (D)

40. Despite of the pills (A)/ which are available, (B)/ many people still have trouble sleeping. (C)/ No error (D)

Directions (For the 10 items which follow): *Each of the following items consists of a sentence followed by four words. Select the **antonym** of the word (occurring in the sentence in capital letters) as per the context.*

41. Her illness ENERVATED the whole family.
A. Enhanced B. Exhausted
C. Weakened D. Energized

42. The teacher INSERTED another picture to illustrate the point.
A. Deducted B. Added
C. Removed D. Reclined

43. The committee rejected his LUDICROUS proposal.
A. Absurd B. Reasonable
C. Farcical D. Stupid

44. Children ADORE the cricket players.
A. Discuss B. Condemn
C. Benefit D. Check

45. These people are sunk in abysmal ignorance and their illiteracy is simply COLOSSAL.
A. Intolerable B. Huge
C. Small D. Silly

46. Previously per capita income used to INCREASE by seven rupees per year.
A. Dwindle B. Diminish
C. Mitigate D. Profit

47. In the modern times, we find that most social relationships are rather ARTIFICIAL.
A. Decent B. Genuine
C. Excellent D. Adorable

48. Social LIBERTY may be instrumental in the emotional growth of a person.
A. Constraint B. Slavery
C. Compulsion D. Obligation

49. Education is most ESSENTIAL for the all-round development of a person.
A. Unimportant B. Disdainful
C. Customary D. Redundant

50. He was extremely MODEST in company.
A. Curious B. Virtuous
C. Unassuming D. Immodest

PART B : GENERAL KNOWLEDGE

51. The pH of fresh milk is 6. When it turns sour, the pH
A. becomes < 6
B. remains the same, i.e., 6
C. becomes > 6
D. becomes neutral, i.e., 7

52. The displacement of a particle is given by $x = \cos^2 \omega t$. The motion is
A. simple harmonic
B. periodic but not simple harmonic
C. non-periodic
D. None of the above

53. A motor vehicle is moving on a circle with a uniform speed. The net acceleration of the vehicle is
A. zero
B. towards the centre of the circle
C. away from the centre along the radius of the circle
D. perpendicular to the radius and along the velocity

54. An object is undergoing a non-accelerated motion. Its rate of change in momentum is
A. a non-zero constant B. zero
C. not a constant D. None of the above

55. 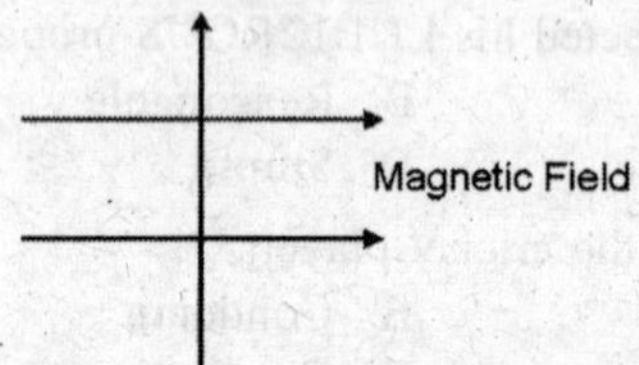

The motion of an electron in presence of a magnetic field is depicted in the figure given above. The force acting on the electron will be directed
A. into the page
B. out of the page
C. opposite to the motion of the electron
D. along the motion of the electron

56. Imagine a current-carrying wire with the direction of current downward or into the page. The direction of magnetic field lines is
A. clockwise B. anticlockwise
C. into the page D. out of the page

57. The main thinking part of the brain is
A. midbrain B. hypothalamus
C. forebrain D. hindbrain

58. Which one among the following hormones stimulates the plant cells to grow in a manner such that the plant appears to be bent towards light?
A. Cytokinin B. Auxin
C. Gibberellin D. Abscisic acid

59. Magnetic Resonance Imaging (MRI) is used in medical diagnosis to obtain images of our internal body organs. This is primarily possible because
A. our body possesses a permanent magnet
B. MRI uses an external magnet to generate a magnetic field in our body
C. MRI uses an external electric field to generate magnetic field in our body
D. ions' motion along our nerve cells generates magnetic fields

60. The motion of a particle is given by a straight line in the graph given above drawn with displacement (x) and time (t). Which one among the following statements is correct?

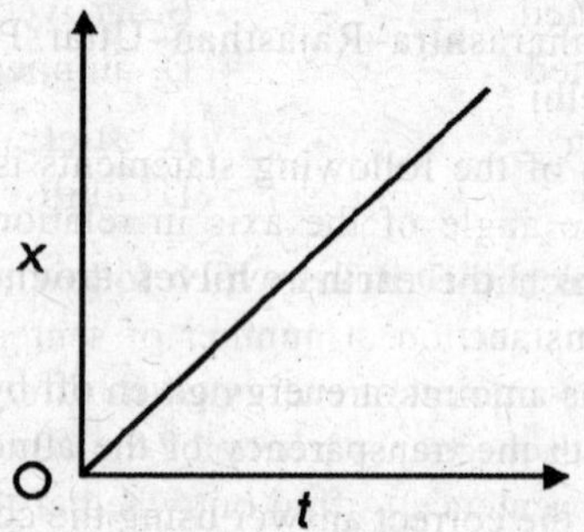

A. The velocity of the particle is uniform
B. The velocity of the particle is non-uniform
C. The speed is uniform and the particle is moving on a circular path
D. The speed is non-uniform and the particle is moving on a straight line path

61. The human eye is like a camera and hence it contains a system of lens. The eye lens forms
A. a straight or upright, real image of the object on the retina
B. an inverted, virtual image of the object on the retina
C. an inverted, real image of the object on the retina
D. a straight or upright, real image of the object on the iris

62. Match List-I with List-II and select the correct answer using the codes given below the Lists:

List-I (Rock Type)	List-II (Composition)
(*a*) Sandstone	1. Rock formed from peat or other organic deposits

(*b*) Limestone	2. Clay, breaking easily into flat flake plates
(*c*) Coal	3. Calcium carbonate formed by precipitation
(*d*) Shale	4. Cemented sand grains

Codes:

	(*a*)	(*b*)	(*c*)	(*d*)
A.	4	1	3	2
B.	2	3	1	4
C.	2	1	3	4
D.	4	3	1	2

63. The 'Golden Quadrilateral' which connects Delhi, Mumbai, Chennai and Kolkata passes through
A. Amritsar–Ahmedabad–Pune–Patna
B. Jaipur–Porbandar–Hyderabad–Varanasi
C. Vadodara–Pune–Visakhapatnam–Varanasi
D. Nagpur–Bhopal–Surat–Amritsar

64. Delhi-Mumbai Industrial Corridor connects the political and business capital of India. Arrange the States from highest to lowest in terms of the length of the corridor passing through them.
A. Maharashtra–Gujarat–Rajasthan–NCR of Delhi
B. NCR of Delhi–Uttar Pardesh–Rajasthan–Maharashtra
C. Rajasthan–Gujarat–Maharashtra–NCR of Delhi
D. Maharashtra–Rajasthan–Uttar Pradesh–NCR of Delhi

65. Which of the following statements is/are true?
1. The angle of the axis in relation to the plane in which the earth revolves around the sun is not constant.
2. The amount of energy given off by the sun changes with the transparency of the atmosphere.

Select the correct answer using the codes given below.
A. 1 only B. 2 only
C. Both 1 and 2 D. Neither 1 nor 2

66. A car is moving with a uniform speed. However its momentum is changing. Then the car
A. may be on an elliptical path
B. is moving on a straight path without acceleration
C. is moving on a straight path with acceleration
D. is moving without any acceleration

67. Ohm's law defines
A. a resistance
B. current only
C. voltage only
D. Both B and C

68. Which of the following statements about sexual reproduction in flowering plants are correct?
1. Stamen is present in the centre of a flower.
2. Stamen produces pollen grains in the a ovary.
3. The swollen bottom part of carpel is the ovary.
4. The fusion of germ cells gives rise to zygote.

Select the correct answer using the code given below.
A. 2, 3 and 4 only B. 2 and 4 only
C. 1 and 3 only D. 1, 2, 3 and 4 only

69. The complete digestion of carbohydrates, proteins and fats occurs in
A. stomach B. liver
C. small intestine D. large intestine

70. Which one among the following statements about a healthy diet is correct?
A. Regular eating of high-energy snacks between meals is healthy since it provides energy and vitamins in plenty
B. Fruits and vegetables make a good choice because their energy content is high
C. A balanced diet must contain plenty of fat and protein with little carbohydrates and fibre
D. An optimal quantity of fat, protein carbohydrate with adequate amount of water and fibre makes a healthy diet

71. The Nobel Prize in Medicine for the year 2012 has been awarded to John B. Gurdon and Shinya Yamanaka for the discovery that
A. mature specialized cells can be reprogrammed to become immature cells
B. stem cells can be programmed to develop individual body organs
C. dendritic cells have a critical role in the development of adaptive immunity
D. thymus cells have a critical role in the development of innate immunity

72. The sex of a newborn baby is determined by the chromosome inherited from
A. the mother B. the father
C. mother's mother D. father's father

73. Arrange the following events that took place in the first decade of the 20th century in chronological order:
1. Indian National Congress, Bombay Session
2. Establishment of All India Muslim League
3. Partition of Bengal
4. Indian National Congress, Surat Session

Select the correct answer using the code given below.
A. 1-2-3-4 B. 1-3-2-4
C. 4-3-2-1 D. 2-4-1-3

74. Match List-I with List-II and select the correct answer using the codes given below the Lists:

List-I (Peasant Movement)	**List-II (Region)**
(*a*) Mappila outbreak	1. Maharashtra
(*b*) Ramosi peasant force	2. Bengal
(*c*) Kuka revolt	3. Malabar
(*d*) Pabna revolt	4. Punjab

Codes:

	(a)	(b)	(c)	(d)
A.	3	1	4	2
B.	3	4	1	2
C.	2	4	1	3
D.	2	1	4	3

75. Consider the following statements about Periyar E.V. Ramaswamy:

1. He was a politician, social activist and an important figure in the Dravidian movement in South India.
2. He championed the cause of caste upliftment, nationalism and the rights of women.
3. He was contemporary of the Maharashtran anti-caste reformer, Jyotiba Phule.

Which of the statements given above is/are correct?

A. 1 only B. 3 only
C. 1 and 3 D. 1 and 2

76. Two atoms are said to be isotopes if

A. they have the same atomic number but different mass numbers
B. they have the same number of neutrons but different mass numbers
C. the sum of the number of protons and neutrons is the same, but the number of protons is different
D. they have the same number of neutrons but different modes of radioactive decay

77. The phenomenon of radioactivity was discovered by

A. Marie Curie B. Pierre Curie
C. Henri Becquerel D. J.J. Thomson

78. The principle of cleaning by soap is

A. surface tension B. floatation
C. viscosity D. elasticity

79. Sodium stearate is a salt and is used

A. in gunpowder B. in paint
C. to make soap D. to make fertilizer

80. The pure form of carbon is

A. diamond B. graphite
C. charcoal D. fullerene

81. Which one among the following countries was least affected by the tsunami that hit the Indonesian Ocean on 26th December, 2004?

A. Indonesia B. Malaysia
C. Sri Lanka D. India

82. Which one among the following statements is ***not*** true about Bahadur Shah Jafar II?

A. The rebels of 1857 proclaimed their loyalty to him
B. He was killed by Lt. Hodson, a cavalry officer in Delhi
C. He was reluctant to lead the Revolt of 1857 in the beginning
D. He was a poet

83. Which one among the following statements is true about Lord Curzon?

A. He had full sympathy for the Congress
B. He introduced the Subsidiary Alliance
C. He succeeded Lord Canning as the Viceroy of India
D. He separated the divisions of Dacca, Chittagong and Rajshahi from the province of Bengal and annexed them to Assam.

84. Which one among the following statements about Civil Disobedience Movement is correct?

A. It started with Gandhiji's march to Champaran
B. Under Gandhi-Irwin agreement the, Congress agreed to give up Civil Disobedience Movement
C. The British Government was quite soft towards the movement from the beginning
D. There were no violent incidents during the movement

85. The greatest stylistic forms of temple architecture during the early medieval period were the Nagara, the Dravida and the Vesara. Which of the following was the geographical spread of the Dravida style?

A. Between Vindhyan and Krishna rivers
B. Between Krishna and Kaveri rivers
C. Between Vindhyan and Kaveri rivers
D. Between Godavari and Krishna rivers

86. Consider the following statement:

"No Indian could have started the Indian National Congress... if the founder of the Congress had not been a great Englishman and a distinguished ex-official, such was the distrust of political agitation in those days that the authority would have at once found some way or the other to suppress the movement."

Who among the following gave the statement on the establishment of Indian National Congress?

A. W. Wedderburn B. G.K. Gokhale
C. R. Palme Dutt D. Allan Octavian Hume

87. Which one among the following is the chemical formula of gypsum which is an ingredient of cement?

A. Ca_2SiO_4 B. $CaSO_4.2H_2O$
C. CaO D. $CaSO_4.3H_2O$

88. Which of the following statements in connection with the properties of water is/are correct?

1. Water has higher specific heat in comparison with other liquid.
2. Water has no dipole moment.
3. Water has low heat of vaporization.

Select the correct answer using the code given below.

A. 1 only B. 2 and 3
C. 1 and 3 D. 3 only

89. The bond which is present between water molecules is

A. electrovalent bond B. covalent bond
C. hydrogen bond D. van der Waals bond

90. Water is a good solvent. This is due to high

A. dielectric constant of water
B. surface tension of water
C. specific heat of water
D. heat of fusion of water

91. Which of the following statements regarding the property of hard water is/are correct?

(1) Temporary hardness of water is due to the presence of soluble magnesium and calcium hydrogen carbonate.

(2) Temporary hardness of water can be removed by boiling.

(3) Calgon's method is applied to remove temporary hardness of water.

(4) Permanent hardness of water is removed by Clark's method.

Select the correct answer using the code given below:

A. 1 and 2 only B. 1, 2 and 3

C. 3 and 4 D. 2 only

92. An ant is moving on thin (negligible thickness) circular wire. How many coordinates do you require to completely describe the motion of the ant?

A. One B. Two

C. Three D. Zero

93. If *d* denotes the distance covered by a car in time *t* and $\bar{S}$ denotes the displacement by the car during the same time, then :

A. $d \leq |\bar{S}|$ B. $d = |\bar{S}|$ only

C. $d \geq |\bar{S}|$ D. $d < |\bar{S}|$

94. A current-carrying wire is known to produce magnetic lines of force around the conducting straight wire. The direction of the lines of force may be described by :

A. left-hand thumb rule for up-current and right-hand thumb rule for down-current

B. right-hand thumb rule for up-current and left-hand thumb rule for down-current

C. right-hand thumb rule for both up and down currents

D. left-hand thumb rule for both up and down currents

95. If an object undergoes a uniform circular motion, then its

A. acceleration remains uniform

B. velocity changes

C. speed changes

D. velocity remains uniform

96. A force F is applied on a body (which moves on a straight line) for a duration of 3 s. The momentum of the body changes from 10 g cm/s to 40 g cm/s. The magnitude of the force F is

A. 10 dynes B. 10 newtons

C. 120 dynes D. 12 dynes

97. Which among the following areas is conducive for well irrigation?

A. Rocky and uneven surface of Peninsular India

B. Dry tracts of Rajasthan and Gujarat

C. Brackish groundwater region of Uttar Pradesh

D. Deltaic regions of Mahanadi, Godavari and Krishna

98. Humid climate, ready market and availability of cheap and skilled labour are the conditions conducive for the production of cotton cloth. Which of the following States of India will have the highest cotton cloth production?

A. Gujarat B. Karnataka

C. Maharashtra D. Punjab

99. The requirement of water is highest in which one among the following industries?

A. Iron and steel B. Oil refining

C. Paper from wood D. Rayon

100. Which of the following statements regarding hurricanes is/are correct?

1. They develop over the ocean between 8° – 15° N.
2. They are almost absent in the South Atlantic Ocean.
3. They do not develop close to the equator.

Select the correct answer using the code given below.

A. 1 only B. 2 and 3 only

C. 1 and 3 only D. 1, 2 and 3

101. Joint Parliamentary Sessions in India are chaired by the

A. President of India

B. Vice-President of India who is the Chairman of the Rajya Sabha

C. Speaker of the Lok Sabha

D. Prime Minister of India

102. Which one among the following is ***not*** a function of the Comptroller and Auditor General of India?

A. Auditing the transactions of Centre and State Governments relating to contingency funds and public accounts

B. Compiling the accounts of Defence

C. Auditing the accounts of institutions financed by the Government

D. Compiling the accounts of States

103. Specific gravity of silver is 11 and specific gravity of iron is 8. Which one among the following is the approximate relative density of silver with respect to iron?

A. 1.4 B. 0.7

C. 3.0 D. 2.8

104. Metal used to make wires for safety fuses must have

A. very low resistivity and high melting point

B. high resistivity and low melting point

C. low resistivity and low melting point

D. high resistivity and high melting point

105. A positively charged particle projected towards west is deflected towards north by a magnetic field. The direction of the magnetic field is

A. towards south B. towards east

C. in downward direction D. in upward direction

106. Which one among the following films won the prestigious Golden Globe Award, 2013 in the best motion picture—Drama category?

A. *Life of Pi* B. *Argo*
C. *Lincoln* D. *Les Miserables*

107. Ward Cunningham is famous for developing for the first time
A. 'Wiki', the free encyclopedia on Internet
B. a computer language called 'Java'
C. a digital camera
D. a software which can take Hebrew language as input

108. *Catch me if you can* is a Hollywood movie made on the life of Frank Abagnale who was
A. a famous lawyer B. a famous swimmer
C. a famous sprinter D. an infamous imposter

109. Who among the following is a sportsperson who has won the maximum number of gold medals in Summer Olympic Games?
A. Paavo Nurmi B. Carl Lewis
C. Michael Phelps D. Mark Spitz

110. Anthony De Mello Trophy is associated with test cricket series played between
A. Australia and India
B. England and India
C. England and Australia
D. South Africa and India

111. Which one among the following European countries has the maximum number of running nuclear reactors?
A. Germany B. Switzerland
C. France D. Norway

112. Which one among the following has completed thirty years of its development on 1st January, 2013?
A. Transmission Control Protocol/Internet Protocol (TCP/IP)
B. Computer Network
C. Social Networking Sites
D. Network Control Protocol (NCP)

113. Which of the following statements is/are correct?
1. The 14th Finance Commission was constituted under the Chairmanship of Shri Vijay Kelkar.
2. The 14th Finance Commission has been specifically asked also to recommend how non-priority PSUs be relinquished.

Select the correct answer using the code given below.
A. 1 only B. 2 only
C. Both 1 and 2 D. Neither 1 nor 2

114. Which of the following statements is/are correct?
1. UN General Assembly in November 2012 adopted a resolution banning death penalty.
2. India voted against the resolution.

Select the correct answer using the code given below.
A. 1 only B. 2 only
C. Both 1 and 2 D. Neither 1 nor 2

115. Which one among the following stock exchanges was closed for two continuous days in October 2012 due to the devastating effects of hurricane Sandy?
A. New York Stock Exchange
B. Toronto Stock Exchange
C. National Stock Exchange of Australia
D. London Stock Exchange

Directions : *The following* ***eight*** *(8) items consist of two statements, Statement I and Statement II. You are to examine these two statements carefully and select the answers to these items using the codes given below :*

Code:
A. Both the statements are individually true and Statement II is the correct explanation of Statement I.
B. Both the statements are individually true but Statement II is ***not*** the correct explanation of Statement I
C. Statement I is true but Statement II is false
D. Statement I is false but Statement II is true

116. **Statement I:** Insolation is greatest when the sun is directly overhead and the sun's rays are vertical.

Statement II: When the sun is lower in the sky, the same amount of solar energy spreads over a greater area of ground surface, so insolation is lower.

117. **Statement I:** The Russian Revolution of 1917 inspired the Indian working class movement.

Statement II: The Non-Cooperation Movement (1921-22) saw the involvement of the Indian working class.

118. **Statement I:** Intellectual criteria which informed the reform movements were rationalism and religious universalism.

Statement II: Social relevance was not judged by a rationalist critique.

119. **Statement I:** Hard water does not give lather with soap.

Statement II: Calcium and magnesium salts present in hard water form precipitate with soap.

120. **Statement I:** Evapotranspiration helps in classifying the climatic types.

Statement II: Only temperature affects evapotranspiration, hence it can be used for classifying the climatic types.

121. **Statement I:** There is a large-scale fluctuation of oil flow from oil wells prior to earthquakes.

Statement II: Tectonic stress accumulates to a certain level, the pore pressure within a deep oilbearing stratum reaches its breaking strength causing oil to sprout along the oil wells.

122. **Statement I :** The potential energy that results from pushing water above mean sea level is transferred to kinetic energy that initiates the horizontal propagation of tsunami waves.

Statement II: The vertical displacement of sea-water due to abrupt and jerky movements of fault blocks on sea-bed gives birth to tsunamis.

123. **Statement I:** Indian economy has experienced slower growth rate during the years 2010-11 and 2011-12.

Statement II: Indian economy has experienced weakening industrial growth during the period.

124. Consider the following diseases :

1. Cholera   2. Tuberculosis
3. Filaria   4. Typhoid

Which of the above diseases are caused by bacteria?

A. 1 and 3 only   B. 2 and 4 only
C. 1, 3 and 4   D. 1, 2 and 4

125. Consider the following statements in relation to plant tissue 'chlorenchyma':

1. It is formed by the palisade and spongy mesophyll.
2. It is a form of parenchyma which contains chloroplasts.
3. It serves to transport organic solutes made by photosynthesis.
4. It is a thin transparent layer which has chiefly a protective function.

Which of the statements given above is/are correct?

A. 1 and 3 only   B. 1 and 2 only
C. 2 and 4   D. 1 only

126. Consider the following statements regarding osmosis in animal cells :

1. If the water potential of the solution surrounding the cell is too high, the cell shrinks.
2. If the water potential of the solution surrounding the cell is too low, the cell swells and bursts.
3. It is important to maintain a constant water potential inside the animal body.
4. In animal cells, water potential far exceeds the solute potential.

Which of the statements given above is/are correct?

A. 1 and 2   B. 3 only
C. 4 only   D. 2 and 3

127. In India, increase in population and diversion of agricultural land for non-agricultural purposes have resulted in the decrease of

A. forested land   B. cultivable wasteland
C. net sown area   D. double-cropped area

128. Radioactive decay provides an internal source of heat for the earth. This helps in the formation of which type of rocks?

A. Igneous   B. Sedimentary
C. Metamorphic   D. All of the above

129. Sun emits energy in the form of electromagnetic radiation. The following help in the generation of solar energy. Arrange them in the right sequence beginning from the starting of the cycle :

1. Hydrogen is converted to helium at very high temperatures and pressures.
2. The energy finds its way to sun's surface.
3. A vast quantity of energy is generated by nuclear fusion.

Select the correct answer using the code given below.

A. 1-2-3   B. 2-3-1
C. 3-2-1   D. 1-3-2

130. The greatest seasonal contrast of insolation on the earth is in which of the following latitudinal zones?

A. Equatorial   B. Tropical
C. Temperate   D. Polar

131. Consider the following statements :

1. The *Ain-i Akbari* is the third book in the *Akbarnama* written during the reign of the Mughal Emperor, Akbar.
2. Abul Fazl was the author of the first two books of the *Akbarnama,* while Akbar was the author of the third.
3. The best known accounts of illustrated Mughal official reports are the *Akbarnama* and the *Babarnama*.

Which of the statements given above is/are correct?

A. 1 only   B. 1 and 3 only
C. 3 only   D. 1, 2 and 3

132. Consider the following statements :

1. Gandhiji's Salt Satyagraha in 1930 was against the State monopoly of the manufacture and sale of salt.
2. The American news magazine 'Time' covered the progress of Gandhiji's walk to Dandi on the Salt Satyagraha.
3. The Viceroy of India at the time of the Salt Satyagraha was Lord Ripon.
4. Gandhiji did not complete the Dandi March due to ill-health.

Which of the statements given above is/are correct?

A. 1, 2 and 3   B. 4 only
C. 2 only   D. 1 and 2 only

133. Consider the following statements:

1. Gandhiji's launched the Rowlatt Satyagraha in 1919 because of the British measures to impose censorship on the Press.
2. Gandhiji launched the Rowlatt Satyagraha because of the British policy of permitted detention without trial.
3. The Rowlatt Act was restricted to Bombay and Madras Presidency.
4. The agitation against the Rowlatt Act reached climax with the Jallianwala Bagh Massacre in Amritsar.

Which of the statements given above is/are correct?

A. 1, 2 and 3   B. 2 and 3 only
C. 1, 2 and 4   D. 1 and 4 only

134. The acid contained in vinegar is

A. acetic acid   B. ascorbic acid
C. citric acid   D. tartaric acid

135. Which one among the following is ***not*** a chemical change?

A. Curdling of milk B. Ripening of fruit
C. Evaporation of water D. Burning of coal

136. The acid in gastric juice is

A. acetic acid B. nitric acid
C. hydrochloric acid D. sulphuric acid

137. An object is placed at the focus of a concave mirror. The image will be

A. real, inverted, same size at the focus
B. real, upright, same size at the focus
C. virtual, inverted, highly enlarged at infinity
D. real, inverted, highly enlarged at infinity

138. An optician prescribes a power = –0.5 dioptre. The corresponding lens must be a

A. convex lens of focal length 2 m
B. convex lens of focal length 50 cm
C. concave lens of focal length 2 m
D. concave lens of focal length 50 cm

139. A current I flows through a potential difference V in an electrical circuit containing a resistance R. The product of V and I, i.e., VI may be understood as

A. resistance R
B. heat generated by the circuit
C. thermal power radiated by the circuit
D. rate of change of resistance

140. When the winds blow from all sides to the central low in an anticlockwise direction, then this phenomenon is known as

A. anti-tropical cyclones of southern hemisphere
B. temperate cyclones of northern hemisphere
C. tropical cyclones of northern hemisphere
D. tropical cyclones of southern hemisphere

141. The diagram given below shows the schematic relations of temperature and precipitation of tropical climatic type over land:

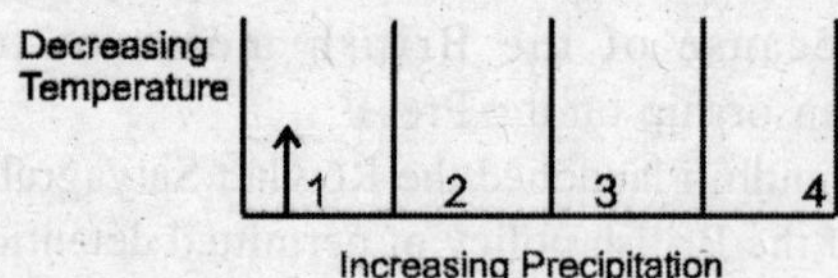

Arrange the climatic types in the correct sequence from left to right :

1. Monsoon topics 2. Wet and dry tropics
3. Arid and semiarid 4. Rainy tropics

Select the correct answer using the code given below.

A. 1-4-2-3 B. 4-3-2-1
C. 2-1-3-4 D. 3-2-1-4

142. Which of the following statements relating to tsunami is/are correct?

As the tsunamis leave the deep water of the open sea and travel towards shallow water

1. the speed is reduced considerably
2. they attain enormous height
3. they appear as a gentle rise and fall of the sea

Select the correct answer using the code given below.

A. 1 and 2 only B. 2 and 3 only
C. 1 only D. 1, 2 and 3

143. Consider the following statements about the Indo-Saracenic architecture:

1. It combined the Indian with the European style of architecture in the beginning of the 20th century.
2. The Gateway of India in Mumbai is the most famous example of this style.
3. There are many famous examples of this style in the colonial cities of Bombay (Mumbai) and Madras (Chennai).
4. It takes its imputation from ancient Greece.

Which of the statements given above is/are correct?

A. 1, 2 and 3 B. 2 and 3 only
C. 1 and 2 only D. 4 only

144. Which of the following statements is/are correct?

Under Article 200 of the Constitution of India, the Governor of a State may

1. withhold his assent to a bill passed by the State Legislature
2. reserve the bill passed by the State Legislature for reconsideration of the President
3. return the bill, other than a money bill, for reconsideration of the Legislature

Select the correct answer using the code given below.

A. 1 only B. 1 and 2 only
C. 2 and 3 only D. 1, 2 and 3

145. Point out the difference between the local government in India before and after the Constitutional Amendments in 1992 :

1. It has become mandatory to hold regular elections to the local government bodies.
2. 1/3rd positions are reserved for women.
3. Elected officials exercise supreme power in the government.

Select the correct answer using the code given below.

A. 1 only B. 1 and 2 only
C. 1, 2 and 3 D. 2 and 3 only

146. The President of India is elected by proportional representative system by a single transferrable vote. This implies that

A. elected MPs and MLAs of States have different number of votes
B. all MPs and MLAs of States have one vote each
C. all MPs and MLAs of States have equal number of votes
D. MPs of the Lok Sabha have equal number of votes

147. A particle is moving freely. Then its

A. kinetic energy is always greater than zero
B. potential energy is greater than zero and kinetic energy is less than zero

C. potential energy is less than zero and kinetic energy is greater than zero

D. potential energy is zero and kinetic energy is less than zero

148. The displacement of a particle at time t is given by

$$\vec{x} = a\hat{i} + bt\hat{j} + \frac{c}{2}t^2\hat{k}$$

where a, b and c are positive constants. Then the particle is

A. accelerated along $\hat{k}$-direction

B. decelerated along $\hat{k}$-direction

C. decelerated along $\hat{j}$-direction

D. accelerated along $\hat{j}$-direction

149. Gravitational force shares a common feature with electromagnetic force. In both cases, the force is

A. between massive and neutral objects

B. between charged objects

C. a short range

D. a long range

150. The spread in colours in a rainbow on sky is primarily due to

A. dispersion of sunlight

B. reflection of sunlight

C. refraction of sunlight

D. total internal reflection of sunlight

PAPER II : MATHEMATICS

1. The sum of the direction cosines of z-axis is

A. 0 B. 1/3

C. 1 D. 3

2. What is the area of the triangle whose vertices are (0, 0, 0), (1, 2, 3) and (–3, –2, 1)?

A. $3\sqrt{5}$ square unit B. $6\sqrt{5}$ square unit

C. 6 square unit D. 12 square unit

3. What is the distance between the planes $x - 2y + z - 1 = 0$ and $-3x + 6y - 3z + 2 = 0$?

A. 3 unit B. 1 unit

C. 0 D. None of these

4. If a line makes 30° with the positive direction of x-axis, angle β with the positive direction of y-axis and angle γ with the positive direction of z-axis, then what is $\cos^2\beta + \cos^2\gamma$ equal to?

A. 1/4 B. 1/2

C. 3/4 D. 1

5. What should be the value of k for which the equation $3x^2 + 3y^2 + (k + 1)z^2 + x - y + z = 0$ represents the sphere?

A. 3 B. 2

C. 1 D. –1

6. Consider the following statements in respect of a function $f(x)$:

1. $f(x)$ is continuous at $x = a$ iff $\lim_{x\to a} f(x)$ exists.

2. If $f(x)$ is continuous at a point, then $\frac{1}{f(x)}$ is also continuous at that point.

Which of the above, statements is/are correct?

A. 1 only B. 2 only

C. Both 1 and 2 D. Neither 1 nor 2

7. If $2x^3 - 3y^2 = 7$, what is $\frac{dy}{dx}$ equal to $(y \neq 0)$?

A. $\frac{x^2}{2y}$ B. $\frac{x}{2y}$

C. $\frac{x^2}{y}$ D. None of the above

8. The derivative of $|x|$ at $x = 0$

A. is 1 B. is –1

C. is 0 D. does not exist

9. Consider the function $f(x) = \begin{cases} x^2, & x > 2 \\ 3x - 2, & x \le 2 \end{cases}$. Which one of the following statements is correct in respect of the above function?

A. $f(x)$ is derivable but not continuous at $x = 2$.

B. $f(x)$ is continuous but not derivable at $x = 2$.

C. $f(x)$ is neither continuous nor derivable at $x = 2$.

D. $f(x)$ is continuous as well as derivable at $x = 2$.

10. Consider the following statements :

1. $\lim_{x\to 0} \sin\frac{1}{x}$ does not exist.

2. $\lim_{x\to 0} \sin\frac{1}{x}$ exists.

Which of the above statements is/are correct?

A. 1 only B. 2 only

C. Both 1 and 2 D. Neither 1 nor 2

11. What is $\lim_{x\to 0} \frac{\sin x - \tan x}{x}$ equal to?

A. 0 B. 1

C. –1 D. 1/2

12. What is $\lim_{x\to 0} \frac{1 - \sqrt{1 + x}}{x}$ equal to?

A. 1/2 B. –1/2

C. 1 D. –1

13. If $y = \sin(ax + b)$, then what is $\frac{d^2y}{dx^2}$ at $x = -\frac{b}{a}$, where a, b are constants and $a \neq 0$?

A. 0 B. –1
C. $\sin(a - b)$ D. $\sin(a + b)$

14. What is the range of the function $f(x) = \frac{|x|}{x}$, $x \neq 0$?

A. Set of all real numbers B. Set of all integers
C. {–1, 1} D. {–1, 0, 1}

15. If $y = x^x$, what is $\frac{dy}{dx}$ at $x = 1$ equal to ?

A. 0 B. 1
C. –1 D. 2

16. The angle of elevation of the top of a tower of height H from the foot of another tower in the same plane is 60° and the angle of elevation of the top of the second tower from the foot of the first tower is 30°. If h is the height of the other tower, then which one of the following is correct ?

A. $H = 2h$ B. $H = \sqrt{3}h$
C. $H = 3h$ D. None of these

17. If $\operatorname{cosec}\theta + \cot\theta = c$, then what is $\cos\theta$ equal to?

A. $\frac{c}{c^2-1}$ B. $\frac{c}{c^2+1}$
C. $\frac{c^2-1}{c^2+1}$ D. None of these

18. If $\sin\theta + 2\cos\theta = 1$, then what is $2\sin\theta - \cos\theta$ equal to?

A. 0 B. 1
C. 2 D. 4

19. If $A + B = 90°$, then what is $\sqrt{\sin A \sec B - \sin A \cos B}$ equal to?

A. sin A B. cos A
C. tan A D. 0

20. What is $\tan^4 A - \sec^4 A + \tan^2 A + \sec^2 A$ equal to?

A. 0 B. 0
C. 2 D. –1

21. Which one of the following points lies inside a circle of radius 6 and centre at (3, 5)?

A. (–2, –1) B. (0, 1)
C. (–1, –2) D. (2, –1)

22. What is the equation of a straight line which passes through (3, 4) and the sum of whose x and y intercepts is 14?

A. $4x + 3y = 24$ B. $x + y = 14$
C. $4x - 3y = 0$ D. $3x + 4y = 25$

23. The equation of the ellipse whose vertices are at (±5, 0) and foci at (±4, 0) is

A. $\frac{x^2}{25}+\frac{y^2}{9}=1$ B. $\frac{x^2}{9}+\frac{y^2}{25}=1$
C. $\frac{x^2}{16}+\frac{y^2}{25}=1$ D. $\frac{x^2}{25}+\frac{y^2}{16}=1$

24. The point whose abscissa is equal to its ordinate and which is equidistant from A(–1, 0) and B(0, 5) is

A. (1, 1) B. (2, 2)
C. (–2, –2) D. (3, 3)

25. The difference of focal distances of any point on a hyperbola is equal to

A. latus rectum B. semi-transverse axis
C. transverse axis D. semi-latus rectum

26. What is the area of the triangle whose vertices are (3, 0), (0, 4) and (3, 4)?

A. 6 square unit B. 7.5 square unit
C. 9 square unit D. 12 square unit

27. A straight line passes through the points (5, 0) and (0, 3), the length of the perpendicular from the point (4, 4) on the line is

A. $\frac{\sqrt{17}}{2}$ B. $\sqrt{\frac{17}{2}}$
C. $\frac{15}{\sqrt{34}}$ D. $\frac{17}{2}$

28. What is the inclination of the line $\sqrt{3}x - y - 1 = 0$?

A. 30° B. 60°
C. 135° D. 150°

29. What is the angle between the planes $2x - y - 2z + 1 = 0$ and $3x - 4y + 5z - 3 = 0$?

A. $\frac{\pi}{6}$ B. $\frac{\pi}{4}$
C. $\frac{\pi}{3}$ D. $\frac{\pi}{2}$

30. If the straight line $\frac{x-x_0}{\ell} = \frac{y-y_0}{m} = \frac{z-z_0}{n}$ is parallel to the plane $ax + by + cz + d = 0$ then which one of the following is correct?

A. $\ell + m + n = 0$ B. $a + b + c = 0$
C. $\frac{a}{\ell}+\frac{b}{m}+\frac{c}{n}=0$ D. $a\ell + bm + cn = 0$

31. What is $\sqrt{-i}$ where $i = \sqrt{-1}$ equal to?

A. $\pm\frac{1-i}{\sqrt{2}}$ B. $\pm\frac{1+i}{\sqrt{2}}$
C. $\pm\frac{1-i}{2}$ D. $\pm\frac{1+i}{2}$

32. What is the argument of the complex number $(-1 - i)$ where $i = \sqrt{-1}$?

A. $\frac{5\pi}{4}$ B. $-\frac{5\pi}{4}$
C. $\frac{3\pi}{4}$ D. None of these

33. If $4^x - 6.2^x + 8 = 0$, then the values of x are

A. 1, 2 B. 1, 1
C. 1, 0 D. 2, 2

34. A bag contains balls of two colours, 3 black and 3 white. What is the smallest number of balls which must be drawn from the bag, without looking, so that among these there are two of the same colour?

A. 2 B. 3
C. 4 D. 5

35. What is the sum of the coefficients in the expansion of $(1 + x)^n$?

A. 2^n B. $2^n - 1$
C. 2^{n-1} D. $n + 1$

36. If P(77, 31) = x and C(77, 31) = y, then which one of the following is correct?

A. $x = y$ (b) $2x = y$
(c) $77x = 31y$ (d) $x > y$

37. The binary representation of the decimal number 45 is

A. 110011 B. 101010
C. 1101101 D. 101101

38. If the roots of a quadratic equation $ax^2 + bx + c = 0$ are α and β, then the quadratic equation having roots α^2 and β^2 is

A. $x^2 - (b^2 - 2ac)\,x + c = 0$
B. $a^2x^2 - (b^2 - 2ac)\,x + c = 0$
C. $ax^2 - (b^2 - 2ac)\,x + c^2 = 0$
D. $a^2x^2 - (b^2 - 2ac)\,x + c^2 = 0$

39. If the roots of the equation $3ax^2 + 2bx + c = 0$ are in the ratio 2:3, then which one of the following is correct?

A. $8ac = 25b$ B. $8ac = 9b^2$
C. $8b^2 = 9ac$ D. $8b^2 = 25ac$

40. Two straight line paths are represented by the equations $2x - y = 2$ and $-4x + 2y = 6$. Then the paths will

A. cross each other at one point
B. not cross each other
C. cross each other at two points
D. cross each other at infinitely many points

41. For what value of k, the equations $3x - y = 8$ and $9x - ky = 24$ will have infinitely many solutions?

A. 6 B. 5
C. 3 D. 1

42. If the numbers $n - 3$, $4n - 2$, $5n + 1$ are in AP, what is the value of n ?

A. 1 B. 2
C. 3 D. 4

43. $(x + 1)^2 - 1 = 0$ has

A. one real root B. two real roots
C. two imaginary roots D. four real roots

44. If A and B are two non-singular square matrices such that AB =A, then which one of the following is correct

A. B is an identity matrix
B. B $= A^{-1}$
C. B $= A^2$
D. Determinant of B is zero

45. What is the value of the minor of the element 9 in the determinant $\begin{vmatrix} 10 & 19 & 2 \\ 0 & 13 & 1 \\ 9 & 24 & 2 \end{vmatrix}$?

A. –9 B. –7
C. 7 D. 0

46. The marks obtained by 13 students in a test are 10, 3, 10, 12, 9, 7, 9, 6, 7, 10, 8, 6, 7. The median of this data is

A. 7 B. 8
C. 9 D. 10

47. Consider the following statements:

1. Both variance and standard deviation are measures of variability in the population.
2. Standard deviation is the square of the variance.

Which of the above statements is/are correct?

A. 1 only B. 2 only
C. Both 1 and 2 D. Neither 1 nor 2

48. The harmonic mean H of two numbers is 4 and the arithmetic mean A and geometric mean G satisfy the equation $2A + G^2 = 27$. The two numbers are

A. 6, 3 B. 9, 5
C. 12, 7 D. 3, 1

49. Consider the following frequency distribution:

Class interval	0-10	10-20	20-30	30-40	40-50
Frequency	14	x	27	y	15

If the total of the frequencies is 100 and mode is 25, then which one of the following is correct ?

A. $x = 2y$ B. $2x = y$
C. $x = y$ D. $x = 3y$

50. In how many ways can the letters of the word 'GLOOMY' be arranged so that the two O's should not be together?

A. 240 B. 480
C. 600 D. 720

51. Consider a random experiment of throwing together a die and two coins. The associated sample space has

A. 8 points B. 12 points
C. 24 points D. 36 points

52. In throwing a six faced die, let A be the event that an even number occurs, B be the event that an odd number occurs and C be the event that a number greater than 3 occurs. Which one of the following is correct ?

A. A and C are mutually exclusive
B. A and B are mutually exclusive
C. B and C are mutually exclusive
D. A, B and C are mutually exclusive

53. What is the probability of getting a sum of 7 with two dice?
A. 1/6 B. 1/3
C. 1/12 D. 5/36

54. Four coins are tossed simultaneously. What is the probability of getting exactly 2 heads?
A. 1/2 B. 1/4
C. 1/8 D. 3/8

55. A bag contains 5 black and 3 white balls. Two balls are drawn at random one after the other without replacement. What is the probability that both are white?
A. 1/28 B. 1/14
C. 3/28 D. None of the above

56. If A and B are any two events such that $P(\bar{A}) = 0.4$, $P(\bar{B}) = 0.3$, $P(A \cup B) = 0.9$, then what is the value of $P(\bar{A} \cup \bar{B})$ equal to?
A. 0.2 B. 0.5
C. 0.6 D. 0.7

57. A fair coin is tossed repeatedly. The probability of getting a result in the fifth toss different from those obtained in the first four tosses is
A. 1/2 B. 1/32
C. 31/32 D. 1/16

58. If X follows a binomial distribution with parameters $n = 100$ and $p = 1/3$, then $P(X = r)$ is maximum when
A. $r = 16$ B. $r = 32$
C. $r = 33$ D. $r = 34$

59. Two numbers are successively drawn from the set U = {1, 2, 3, 4, 5, 6, 7, 8}, the second being drawn without replacing the first. The number of elementary events in the sample is
A. 64 B. 56
C. 32 D. 14

60. The binomial distribution has
A. only one parameter B. two parameters
C. three parameters D. four parameters

61. The roots of the equation $\begin{vmatrix} 1 & t-1 & 1 \\ t-1 & 1 & 1 \\ 1 & 1 & t-1 \end{vmatrix} = 0$ are
A. 1, 2 B. –1, 2
C. 1, –2 D. –1, –2

62. The value of the determinant $\begin{vmatrix} m & n & p \\ p & m & n \\ n & p & m \end{vmatrix}$
A. is a perfect cube B. is a perfect square
C. has linear factor D. is zero

63. The determinant of an orthogonal matrix is
A. ±1 B. 2
C. 0 D. ±2

64. If D is a determinant of order 3 and D' is the determinant obtained by replacing the elements of D by their cofactors, then which one of the following is correct ?
A. $D' = D^2$ B. $D' = D^3$
C. $D' = 3D^2$ D. $D' = 3D^3$

65. Consider the following statements:
1. A matrix is not a number
2. Two determinants of different orders may have the same value.

Which of the above statements is/are correct?
A. 1 only B. 2 only
C. Both 1 and 2 D. Neither 1 nor 2

66. What is the value of tan 105°?
A. $\frac{\sqrt{3}+1}{\sqrt{3}-1}$ B. $\frac{\sqrt{3}+1}{1-\sqrt{3}}$
C. $\frac{\sqrt{3}-1}{\sqrt{3}+1}$ D. $\frac{\sqrt{3}+2}{\sqrt{3}-1}$

67. If $\tan A = x + 1$ and $\tan B = x - 1$, then $x^2 \tan(A - B)$ has the value :
A. 1 B. x
C. 0 D. 2

68. What is the value of $(\sin^4\theta - \cos^4\theta + 1)\,\text{cosec}^2\theta$?
A. –2 B. 0
C. 1 D. 2

69. If d is the number of degrees contained in an angle, m is the number of minutes and s is the number of seconds, then the value of $(s - m)/(m - d)$ is
A. 1 B. 60
C. 1/60 D. None of these

70. The expression $\frac{\cot x + \text{cosec}\, x - 1}{\cot x - \text{cosec}\, x + 1}$ is equal to
A. $\frac{\sin x}{1-\cos x}$ B. $\frac{1-\cos x}{\sin x}$
C. $\frac{1+\cos x}{\sin x}$ D. $\frac{\sin x}{1+\cos x}$

71. What is $\frac{1-\tan^2 \frac{x}{2}}{1+\tan^2 \frac{x}{2}}$ equal to?
A. $\sin x \cdot \cos x$ B. $\tan x$
C. $\sin x$ D. $\cos x$

72. In any triangle ABC, $a = 18$, $b = 24$ and $c = 30$. Then what is sin C equal to?
A. 1/4 B. 1/3
C. 1/2 D. 1

73. If $\sin^{-1}\left(\frac{2a}{1+a^2}\right) + \sin^{-1}\left(\frac{2b}{1+b^2}\right) = 2\tan^{-1}x$, then x is equal to

A. $\frac{a-b}{1+ab}$ B. $\frac{a-b}{1-ab}$

C. $\frac{2ab}{a+b}$ D. $\frac{a+b}{1-ab}$

74. A man walks 10 m towards a lamp post and notices that the angle of elevation of the top of the post increases from 30° to 45°. The height of the lamp post is

A. 10 m B. $(5\sqrt{3}+5)$m

C. $(5\sqrt{3}-5)$m D. $(10\sqrt{3}+10)$m

75. The shadow of a tower standing on a level plane is found to be 50 m longer when the Sun's elevation is 30° than when it is 60°. The height of the tower is

A. 25 m B. $25\sqrt{3}$ m

C. 50 m D. None of these

76. What is the degree of the differential equation

$$\left(\frac{d^4y}{dx^4}\right)^{\frac{3}{5}}-5\frac{d^3y}{dx^3}+6\frac{d^2y}{dx^2}-8\frac{dy}{dx}+5=0?$$

A. 5 B. 4

C. 3 D. 2

77. The general solution of the differential equation $x\frac{dy}{dx}+y=0$ is

A. $xy = c$ B. $x = cy$

C. $x + y = c$ D. $x^2 + y^2 = c$

where c is an orbitrary constant.

78. What is the area of the triangle bounded by the sides $x = 0$, $y = 0$ and $x + y = 2$?

A. 1 square unit B. 2 square unit

C. 4 square unit D. 8 square unit

79. The general solution of the differential equation $\ell n\left(\frac{dy}{dx}\right)+x=0$ is

A. $y = e^{-x} + c$ B. $y = -e^{-x} + c$

C. $y = e^{x} + c$ D. $y = -e^{x} + c$

80. If $\vec{\beta}$ is perpendicular to both $\vec{\alpha}$ and $\vec{\gamma}$ where $\vec{\alpha}=\hat{k}$ and $\vec{\gamma}=2\hat{i}+3\hat{j}+4\hat{k}$, then what is $\vec{\beta}$ equal to?

A. $3\hat{i}+2\hat{j}$ B. $-3\hat{i}+2\hat{j}$

D. $2\hat{i}-3\hat{j}$ D. $-2\hat{i}+3\hat{j}$

81. For any vector $\vec{\alpha}$, what is $(\vec{\alpha}\cdot\hat{i})\hat{i}+(\vec{\alpha}\cdot\hat{j})\hat{j}+(\vec{\alpha}\cdot\hat{k})\hat{k}$ equal to?

A. $\vec{\alpha}$ B. $3\vec{\alpha}$

C. $-\vec{\alpha}$ D. $\vec{0}$

82. If the magnitude of $\vec{a}\times\vec{b}$ equals to $\vec{a}\cdot\vec{b}$, then which one of the following is correct?

A. $\vec{a}=\vec{b}$

B. The angle between $\vec{a}$ and $\vec{b}$ is 45°

C. $\vec{a}$ is parallel to $\vec{b}$

D. $\vec{a}$ is perpendicular to $\vec{b}$

83. If $|\vec{a}|=\sqrt{2}, |\vec{b}|=\sqrt{3}$ and $|\vec{a}+\vec{b}|=\sqrt{6}$, then what is $|\vec{a}-\vec{b}|$ equal to?

A. 1 B. 2

C. 3 D. 4

84. Which one of the following vectors is normal to the vector $\hat{i}+\hat{j}+\hat{k}$?

A. $\hat{i}+\hat{j}-\hat{k}$ B. $\hat{i}-\hat{j}+\hat{k}$

C. $\hat{i}-\hat{j}-\hat{k}$ D. None of the above

85. If θ is the angle between the vectors $4(\hat{i}-\hat{k})$ and $\hat{i}+\hat{j}+\hat{k}$, then what is (sin θ + cos θ) equal to?

A. 0 B. $\frac{1}{2}$

C. 1 D. 2

86. The average marks obtained by the students in a class are 43. If the average marks obtained by 25 boys are 40 and the average marks obtained by the girl students are 48, then what is the number of girl students in the class?

A. 15 B. 17

C. 18 D. 20

87. Marks obtained by 7 students in a subject are 30, 55, 75, 90, 50, 60, 39. The number of students securing marks less than the mean marks is

A. 7 B. 6

C. 5 D. 4

88. Variance is always independent of the change of

A. origin but not scale B. scale only

C. both origin and scale D. None of the above

89. If two lines of regression are perpendicular, then the correlation coefficient r is

A. 2 B. $\frac{1}{2}$

C. 0 D. None of the above

90. The standard deviation of the observations 5, 5, 5, 5, 5 is

A. 0 B. 5

C. 20 D. 25

91. The function $f(x) = x^2 - 4x$, $x \in [0, 4]$ attains minimum value at

A. $x = 0$ B. $x = 1$
C. $x = 2$ D. $x = 4$

92. The curve $y = xe^x$ has minimum value equal to

A. $-\frac{1}{e}$ B. $\frac{1}{e}$
C. $-e$ D. e

93. Consider the following statements :

1. The derivative where the function attains maxima or minima must be zero.
2. If a function is differentiable at a point, then it must be continuous at that point.

Which of the above statements is/are correct?

A. 1 only B. 2 only
C. Both 1 and 2 D. Neither 1 nor 2

94. What is the differential coefficient of $\log_x x$?

A. 0 B. 1
C. $\frac{1}{x}$ D. x

95. What is $\int_0^2 \frac{dx}{x^2+4}$ equal to?

A. $\frac{\pi}{2}$ B. $\frac{\pi}{4}$
C. $\frac{\pi}{8}$ D. None of the above

96. What is $\int_{-a}^{a} (x^3 + \sin x)\,dx$ equal to?

A. a B. $2a$
C. 0 D. 1

97. What is $\int_0^1 xe^x\,dx$ equal to?

A. 1 B. -1
C. 0 D. e

98. What is $\int e^{\ln x}\,dx$ equal to?

A. $xe^{\ln x} + c$ B. $-xe^{-\ln x} + c$
C. $x + c$ D. $\frac{x^2}{2} + c$

where c is constant of integration.

99. What is $\int_{-\frac{\pi}{6}}^{\frac{\pi}{6}} \frac{\sin^5 x \cos^3 x}{x^4}\,dx$ is equal to?

A. $\frac{\pi}{2}$ B. $\frac{\pi}{4}$
C. $\frac{\pi}{8}$ D. 0

100. What is $\int \frac{dx}{x \ln x}$ equal to ?

A. $\ln(\ln x) + c$ B. $\ln x + c$
C. $(\ln x)^2 + c$ D. None of the above

where c is the constant of integration.

101. What is the area of the region enclosed by $y = 2|x|$ and $y = 4$?

A. 2 square unit B. 4 square unit
C. 8 square unit D. 16 square unit

102. What is the area of the parabola $y^2 = x$ bounded by its latus rectum ?

A. $\frac{1}{12}$ square unit B. $\frac{1}{6}$ square unit
C. $\frac{1}{3}$ square unit D. None of the above

103. The derivative of $\sec^2 x$ with respect to $\tan^2 x$ is

A. 1 B. 2
C. $2 \sec x \tan x$ D. $2 \sec^2 x \tan x$

104. The differential equation of the curve $y = \sin x$ is

A. $\frac{d^2y}{dx^2} + y\frac{dy}{dx} + x = 0$ B. $\frac{d^2y}{dx^2} + y = 0$
C. $\frac{d^2y}{dx^2} - y = 0$ B. $\frac{d^2y}{dx^2} + x = 0$

105. The degree and order respectively of the differential equation $\frac{dy}{dx} = \frac{1}{x+y+1}$ are

A. 1, 1 B. 1, 2
C. 2, 1 D. 2, 2

Directions : *For the next six (06) questions that follow:*

In a state with a population of 75×10^6, 45% of them know Hindi, 22% know English, 18% know Sanskrit, 12% know Hindi and English, 8% know English and Sanskrit, 10% know Hindi and Sanskrit and 5% know all the three languages.

106. What is the number of people who do not know any of the above three languages ?

A. 3×10^6 B. 4×10^6
C. 3×10^7 D. 4×10^7

107. What is the number of people who know Hindi only?

A. 21×10^6 B. 25×10^6
C. 28×10^6 D. 3×10^7

108. What is the number of people who know Sanskrit only?
A. 5×10^6 B. 45×10^5
C. 4×10^6 D. None of the above

109. What is the number of people who know English only?
A. 5×10^6 B. 45×10^5
C. 4×10^6 D. None of the above

110. What is the number of people who know only one language?
A. 3×10^6 B. 4×10^6
C. 3×10^7 D. 4×10^7

111. What is the number of people who know only two languages?
A. 11.25×10^5 B. 11.25×10^6
C. 12×10^5 D. 12.5×10^5

112. What is the degree of the equation $\frac{1}{x-3} = \frac{1}{x+2} - \frac{1}{2}$?
A. 0 B. 1
C. 2 D. 3

113. Which one of the following is a null set?
A. {0} B. {{{}}}
C. {{}} D. $\{x \mid x^2 + 1 = 0, x \in R\}$

114. If A = {x, y}, B = {2, 3}, C = {3, 4}, then what is the number of elements in A × (B ∪ C)?
A. 2 B. 4
C. 6 D. 8

115. What is the value of $\log_y x^5 \log_x y^2 \log_z z^3$?
A. 10 B. 20
C. 30 D. 60

116. If A is a relation on a set R, then which one of the following is correct ?
A. $R \subseteq A$ B. $A \subseteq R$
C. $A \subseteq (R \times R)$ D. $R \subseteq (A \times A)$

117. Let N be the set of natural numbers and $f : N \to N$ be a function given by $f(x) = x + 1$ for $x \in N$. Which one of the following is correct?
A. f is one-one and onto
B. f is one-one but not onto
C. f is only onto
D. f is neither one-one nor onto

118. If the sum of the roots of a quadratic equation is 3 and the product is 2, then the equation is
A. $2x^2 - x + 3 = 0$ B. $x^2 - 3x + 2 = 0$
C. $x^2 + 3x + 2 = 0$ D. $x^2 + 3x - 2 = 0$

119. If α and β are the roots of the equation $x^2 + bx + c = 0$, then what is the value of $\alpha^{-1} + \beta^{-1}$?
A. $-\frac{b}{c}$ B. $\frac{b}{c}$
C. $\frac{c}{b}$ D. $-\frac{c}{b}$

120. The area of a rectangle whose length is five more than twice its width is 75 square unit. The length is
A. 5 unit B. 10 unit
C. 15 unit D. 20 unit

ANSWERS

PAPER-I : GENERAL ABILITY TEST

1	2	3	4	5	6	7	8	9	10
C	A	A	C	B	C	C	B	A	C
11	**12**	**13**	**14**	**15**	**16**	**17**	**18**	**19**	**20**
A	A	A	C	B	B	B	C	B	D
21	**22**	**23**	**24**	**25**	**26**	**27**	**28**	**29**	**30**
B	D	B	C	C	B	B	C	C	C
31	**32**	**33**	**34**	**35**	**36**	**37**	**38**	**39**	**40**
A	C	A	C	C	C	B	C	B	C
41	**42**	**43**	**44**	**45**	**46**	**47**	**48**	**49**	**50**
D	C	B	B	C	B	B	B	A	D
51	**52**	**53**	**54**	**55**	**56**	**57**	**58**	**59**	**60**
A	A	B	B	B	A	C	B	B	A
61	**62**	**63**	**64**	**65**	**66**	**67**	**68**	**69**	**70**
C	B	C	C	A	A	A	C	C	D
71	**72**	**73**	**74**	**75**	**76**	**77**	**78**	**79**	**80**
A	B	B	A	D	A	C	A	C	B
81	**82**	**83**	**84**	**85**	**86**	**87**	**88**	**89**	**90**
C	B	D	B	D	D	B	A	C	A
91	**92**	**93**	**94**	**95**	**96**	**97**	**98**	**99**	**100**
B	B	C	C	B	A	D	C	A	A

101	102	103	104	105	106	107	108	109	110
D	B	A	C	D	A	A	B	C	B
111	112	113	114	115	116	117	118	119	120
C	A	D	C	A	B	B	D	A	C
121	122	123	124	125	126	127	128	129	130
A	B	A	D	B	B	C	D	D	B
131	132	133	134	135	136	137	138	139	140
D	D	C	A	C	C	D	C	B	D
141	142	143	144	145	146	147	148	149	150
D	B	B	D	B	B	A	A	D	A

PAPER-II : MATHEMATICS

1	2	3	4	5	6	7	8	9	10
C	A	D	A	B	D	C	D	B	C
11	12	13	14	15	16	17	18	19	20
A	B	A	C	B	C	C	C	B	A
21	22	23	24	25	26	27	28	29	30
B	A	A	B	C	A	B	B	D	D
31	32	33	34	35	36	37	38	39	40
A	A	A	C	A	D	D	D	D	B
41	42	43	44	45	46	47	48	49	50
C	A	B	A	B	B	D	A	C	A
51	52	53	54	55	56	57	58	59	60
C	B	A	D	C	C	D	C	B	B
61	62	63	64	65	66	67	68	69	70
B	C	A	A	C	B	D	D	B	C
71	72	73	74	75	76	77	78	79	80
D	D	D	B	B	C	A	B	B	B
81	82	83	84	85	86	87	88	89	90
A	B	B	D	C	A	D	A	C	A
91	92	93	94	95	96	97	98	99	100
C	A	B	A	C	C	A	D	D	A
101	102	103	104	105	106	107	108	109	110
C	B	A	B	A	C	A	D	D	C
111	112	113	114	115	116	117	118	119	120
B	C	D	C	C	C	B	B	A	C

EXPLANATORY ANSWERS

PAPER-II : MATHEMATICS

1. Direction cosines are 0, 0, 1

Sum = 1

2. Area $= \frac{1}{2}\left|\overrightarrow{AB} \times \overrightarrow{AC}\right|$

$$= \frac{1}{2}\begin{vmatrix} i & j & k \\ 1 & 2 & 3 \\ -3 & -2 & 1 \end{vmatrix}$$

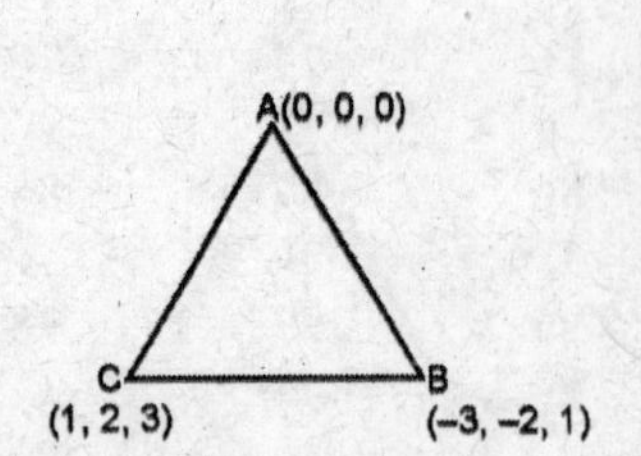

$$= \frac{1}{2}\left(8\hat{i} - 10\hat{j} + 4\hat{k}\right)$$

$$= \frac{1}{2}\sqrt{64+16+100}$$

$$= \frac{1}{2}\left(6\sqrt{5}\right)$$

$$= 3\sqrt{5}$$

3. $x - 2y + z = 1$ ...(i)

$x - 2y + z = \frac{2}{3}$ ...(ii)

$$\text{Distance} = \left|\frac{1-\frac{2}{3}}{\sqrt{1+4+1}}\right| = \frac{1}{3\sqrt{6}}$$

4. $\cos^2 30° + \cos^2 \beta + \cos^2 \gamma = 1$

$\Rightarrow \quad \cos^2 \beta + \cos^2\gamma = \frac{1}{4}$

5. $k + 1 = 3 \quad \Rightarrow \quad k = 2$

7. $6x^2 - 6y\frac{dy}{dx} = 0$

$$\frac{dy}{dx} = \frac{x^2}{y}$$

8.

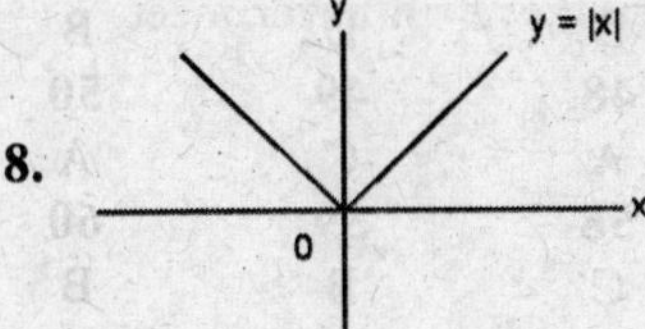

RHD = 1 at $x = 0$ LHD = –1 at $x = 0$

9. Let $f(2 + h) = 4$ as $h \to 0$

Let $f(2 - h) = 4$ as $h \to 0$

Let $f(2) = 4$

continuous at $x = 2$

$f'(2^+) = 4,\ f'(2^-) = 3$

11. $\lim\limits_{x\to 0} \frac{\cos x - \sec^2 x}{1} = 1 - 1 = 0$

12. $\lim\limits_{x\to 0} \frac{-\frac{1}{2\sqrt{1+x}}}{1} = -\frac{1}{2}$

13. $\frac{dy}{dx} = a\cos(ax + b)$

$$\frac{d^2y}{dx^2} = -a^2\sin(ax + b) = -a^2\sin(0) = 0$$

14. $x > 0;\ f(x) = \frac{x}{x} = 1$

$x < 0;\ f(x) = -\frac{x}{x} = -1$

Range = {–1, 1}

15. $y = x^x \quad \Rightarrow \quad \ln y = x\ln x$

$$\frac{1}{y}\cdot\frac{dy}{dx} = 1 + \ln x$$

$$\frac{dy}{dx} = y\ln ex$$

$$\left.\frac{dy}{dx}\right|_{x=1} = 1.\ln e = 1$$

16.

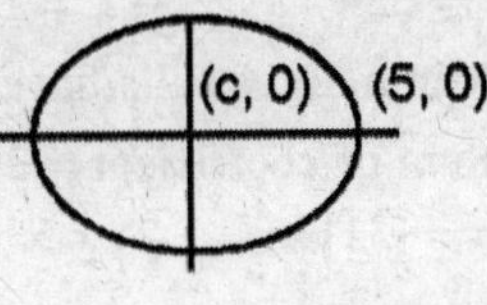

$\frac{H}{\alpha} = \sqrt{3}$ and $\frac{h}{\alpha} = \frac{1}{\sqrt{3}}$

$\Rightarrow \quad \frac{H}{h} = 3 \quad \Rightarrow H = 3h$

17. $\frac{1+\cos\theta}{\sin\theta} = c \Rightarrow \cot\frac{\theta}{2} = c \Rightarrow \cos\theta = \frac{1-\frac{1}{c^2}}{1+\frac{1}{c^2}} = \frac{c^2-1}{c^2+1}$

18. $\sin\theta + 2\cos\theta = 1$ ...(i)

$2\sin\theta - \cos\theta = \alpha$ (let) ...(ii)

Squaring and adding

$1 + 4 = 1 + \alpha^2 \Rightarrow \alpha^2 = 4 \Rightarrow \alpha = 2.$

19. $\sqrt{\sin A\ \text{cosec}A - \sin A \sin A} = \sqrt{1-\sin^2 A} = \cos A.$

20. $(\tan^2A + \sec^2A)(\tan^2A - \sec^2A) + \tan^2A + \sec^2A$

$= -(\tan^2A + \sec^2A) + \tan^2A + \sec^2A = 0.$

21. $S \equiv (x - 3)^2 + (y - 5)^2 - 36$

for inside circle S < 0 for (0, 1).

22. $\frac{x}{a} + \frac{y}{b} = 1 \Rightarrow \frac{3}{a} + \frac{4}{b} = 1$ ...(i)

$a + b = 14$ ...(ii)

From (i) and (ii)

$a = 6$ and $b = 8$

or $a = 7$ and $b = 7$

$4x + 3y = 24$

or $x + y = 7$

23. $a = 5$ and $ae = 4$

(c, 0) (5, 0)

$e = \frac{4}{5}$

$$e^2 = 1 - \frac{b^2}{a^2}$$

$$\frac{16}{25} = 1 - \frac{b^2}{25}$$

$$\Rightarrow \frac{b^2}{25} = \frac{9}{25} \qquad \Rightarrow b^2 = 9$$

$$\frac{x^2}{25} + \frac{y^2}{9} = 1$$

24. P(0, 0)

$(a + 1)^2 + a^2 = a^2 + (a - 5)^2$

$2a^2 + 2a + 1 = 2a^2 - 10a + 25$

$12a = 24 \quad ; \quad a = 2$

P(2, 2)

26. $\text{Area} = \frac{1}{2}\left|\begin{vmatrix} 3 & 0 & 1 \\ 0 & 4 & 1 \\ 3 & 4 & 1 \end{vmatrix}\right| = \frac{1}{2}|3(4-4)+1(0-12)| = 6$

27. $\frac{x}{5} + \frac{y}{3} = 1$

$3x + 5y - 15 = 0$

$$P = \left|\frac{3 \cdot 4 + 5 \cdot 4 - 15}{\sqrt{34}}\right| = \left|\frac{17}{\sqrt{34}}\right|$$

$$P = \sqrt{\frac{17}{2}}$$

28. $\tan\theta = \sqrt{3} \qquad \Rightarrow \theta = 60^\circ$

29. $\cos\theta = \frac{2(3)+(-1)(-4)+5(-2)}{\sqrt{2^2+1^2+2^2}\sqrt{3^2+4^2+5^2}} = 0$

$$\theta = \frac{\pi}{2}$$

30. If the line is parallel to the plane then $a\ell + bm + cn = 0$

31. $\sqrt{-i} = \sqrt{e^{-i\pi/2}} = \pm e^{\frac{-i\pi}{4}}\left(\frac{1-i}{\sqrt{2}}\right)$

32. $z = -1 - i \quad ;$ argument lies in III quadrant

$\therefore \quad \arg(z) = \pi + \tan^{-1}\left|\frac{-1}{-1}\right| = \frac{5\pi}{4}$

33. Put $2^x = t \quad ; \quad t^2 - 6t + 8 = 0$

$t = 2, 4 \quad ; \quad x = 1, 2$

34. Minimum 4 balls have to be drawn.

35. Sum of coefficient = 2^n

36. $x = (31!\ y) \quad \therefore \quad x > y$

37. $101101 = 2^0 + 1 \times 2^2 + 1 \times 2^3 + 1 \times 2^5 = 45$

38. Required equation is $x^2 - x(\alpha^2 + \beta^2) + (\alpha\beta)^2 = 0$

$x^2 - x[(\alpha + \beta)^2 - 2\alpha\beta] + (\alpha\beta)^2 = 0$

$$x^2 - x\left(\frac{b^2}{a^2} - \frac{2c}{a}\right) + \frac{c^2}{a^2} = 0$$

$$\Rightarrow \quad a^2x^2 - x(b^2 - 2ac) + c^2 = 0$$

39. Let roots of equation $3ax^2 + 2bx + c = 0$ are 2α, 3α

$$2\alpha + 3\alpha = -\frac{2b}{3a} \quad \Rightarrow \quad \alpha = -\frac{2b}{15a}$$

$$2\alpha \,.\, 3\alpha = \frac{c}{3a} \quad \Rightarrow \quad \alpha^2 = \frac{c}{18a}$$

$$\therefore \quad \left(\frac{-2b}{15a}\right)^2 = \frac{c}{18a} \quad \Rightarrow \quad \frac{4b^2}{225a^2} = \frac{c}{18a}$$

$$8b^2 = 25ac$$

40. Both lines are parallel so they will never meet

41. For infinite solution $\frac{3}{9} = \frac{-1}{-k} = \frac{8}{24}$

$k = 3$

42. $\because$ $(n - 3)$, $4n - 2$, $5n + 1$ are in A.P.

$2(4n - 2) = (n - 3) + 5n + 1$

$8n - 4 = 6n - 2 \quad \Rightarrow n = 1$

43. $(x + 1)^2 - 1 = 0 \quad \Rightarrow \quad x + 1 = \pm 1$

$x = 0, -2$ two real roots

44. A and B are 2 non singular matrix so A^{-1} and B^{-1} are defined

$A^{-1}AB = A^{-1}A \quad \Rightarrow \quad B = I$

45. Minor of element 9 = $\begin{vmatrix} 19 & 2 \\ 13 & 1 \end{vmatrix} = -7$

46. 3, 6, 6, 7, 7, 7, 8, 9, 9, 10, 10, 10, 12

Ans = 8

47. $\sigma = (\text{S.D.})^2$

48. 2A + AH = 27

A (2 + 4) = 27

$$A = \frac{9}{2}$$

$a + b = 9$

$a \times b = AH = 18$

$a = 3$ and $b = 6$ or $a = 6$ and $b = 3$

49. $14 + x + 27 + y = 15 = 100$

$x + y = 44$

$\therefore x = y$ is only possibility

50. .... GLMY 00

$4 \times {}^5C_2 = 240$

51. $6 \times 2 \times 2 = 24$ sample points

53. Total case $= 6 \times 6 = 36$

Favourable = (1, 6), (2, 5), (3, 4), (4, 3), (5, 2), (6, 1)

Probability $= \dfrac{6}{36} = \dfrac{1}{6}$

54. $^4C_2 \times \left(\dfrac{1}{2}\right)^2 \times \left(\dfrac{1}{2}\right)^2 = \dfrac{6}{16} = \dfrac{3}{8}$

55. $\dfrac{^3C_2}{^8C_2} = \dfrac{3}{28}$

56. $P(\overline{A} \cup \overline{B}) = P(\overline{A}) + P(\overline{B}) - P(\overline{A} \cap \overline{B})$

$= P(\overline{A}) + P(\overline{B}) - P(\overline{A \cup B})$

$= P(\overline{A}) + P(\overline{B}) - (1 - P(A \cup B)) = .4 + .3 - (1 - .9) = .6$

57. P(HHHHT or TTTTH) = P(HHHHT) + P(TTTTH)

$= \left(\dfrac{1}{2}\right)^5 \times \left(\dfrac{1}{2}\right)^2 = \dfrac{1}{16}$

58. $P(x = r) = (r + 1)^{th}$ term of $(q + p)^{th}$

$m = \dfrac{n+1}{1+\dfrac{p}{q}} = \dfrac{101}{1+2} = 33\dfrac{2}{3}$

$[m] = 33$

t_{34} will be greatest

$\therefore \quad x = 3$

59. $^5C_2 \times 2! = 56$

60. Binomial distribution has two parameters n and p, where n is number of trials and p is probability of success.

61. $1(t - 2) - (t - 1)\ (t - 1)^2 - 1] + 1\ (t - 2) = 0$

$(t - 2)\ [1 - (t - 1)\ (t) + 1] = 0$

$(t - 2)\ (t^2 - t - 2) = 0$

$(t - 2)\ (t - 2)\ (t + 1) = 0$

$t = 2,\ t = -1$

62. $(m+n+p)\begin{vmatrix} 1 & n & p \\ 1 & m & n \\ 1 & p & m \end{vmatrix}$

$(m+n+p)\begin{vmatrix} 1 & n & p \\ 0 & m-n & n-p \\ 0 & p-n & m-p \end{vmatrix}$

$= (m + n + p)\ (m^2 - mp - mn + np - np + p^2 + n^2 - np)$

$= (m + n + p)\ (m^2 + n^2 + p^2 - mn - np - pm)$

63. $AA^T = I$

$|AA^T| = 1$

$|A|^2 = 1$

$|A| = \pm 1$

64. $D' =$ cofactor D

$|D'| = |$cofactor D$|$

$|D'| = |D|^{3-1}$

$|D'| = |D|^2$

So $D' = D^2$

66. $\tan(105°) = \tan(60° + 45°) = \dfrac{\sqrt{3}+1}{1-\sqrt{3}}$

67. $x^2\left(\dfrac{\tan A - \tan B}{1 + \tan A \tan B}\right) = x^2\left(\dfrac{(x+1)-(x-1)}{1+(x^2-1)}\right)$

$= x^2\left(\dfrac{2}{x^2}\right) = 2$

68. $\sin^2\theta(\sin^2\theta + 1 + \cos^2\theta)\ \text{cosec}^2\theta = 2$

69. $m = 60d$

$s = 60m$

$\dfrac{s-m}{m-d} = \dfrac{60m - 60d}{m-d} = 60$

70. $\dfrac{\cot x + \text{cosec}\, x - (\text{cosec}^2 x - \cot^2 x)}{\cot x - \text{cosec}\, x + 1}$

$= \dfrac{(\cot x + \text{cosec}\, x)(1 + \cot x - \text{cosec}\, x)}{(\cot x - \text{cosec}\, x + 1)}$

$= \dfrac{1 + \cos x}{\sin x}$

72. $\cos C = \dfrac{(18)^2 + (24)^2 - (30)^2}{2 \times 18 \times 24} = \dfrac{9 + 16 - 5^2}{2 \times 3 \times 4}$

$\cos C = 0$

$\sin C = 1$

73. $a > 0,\ b > 0$

$2\tan^{-1}a + 2\tan^{-1}b = 2\tan^{-1}x$

$2\tan^{-1}\left(\dfrac{a+b}{1-ab}\right) = 2\tan^{-1}x$

$x = \dfrac{a+b}{1-ab}$

74.

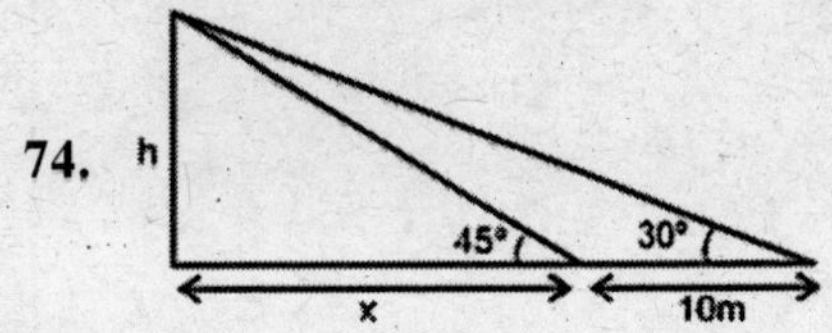

$\tan 45° = \frac{h}{x}$

$\tan 30° = \frac{h}{x+10}$

$\frac{1}{\sqrt{3}} = \frac{h}{h+10}$

$h + 10 = \sqrt{3}h$

$h = \left(\frac{10}{\sqrt{3}-1}\right)m = \frac{10(\sqrt{3}+1)}{2}$

75. $\tan 60° = \frac{h}{x}$

$\tan 30° = \frac{h}{x+50}$

$\frac{\sqrt{3}}{\frac{1}{\sqrt{3}}} = \frac{x+50}{x}$

$3x = x + 50$

$x = 25 \quad \Rightarrow h = x\sqrt{3} = 25\sqrt{3}$

76. $\left(\frac{d^4y}{dx^4}\right) = \left(\frac{5d^3y}{dx^3} + \frac{6d^2y}{dx^2}......\right)^5$

highest order = 4, degree = 3

77. $\frac{dy}{y} = -\frac{dx}{x}$

$\ln y = -\ln x + \ln c$

$\left(y = \frac{c}{x}\right)$

78.

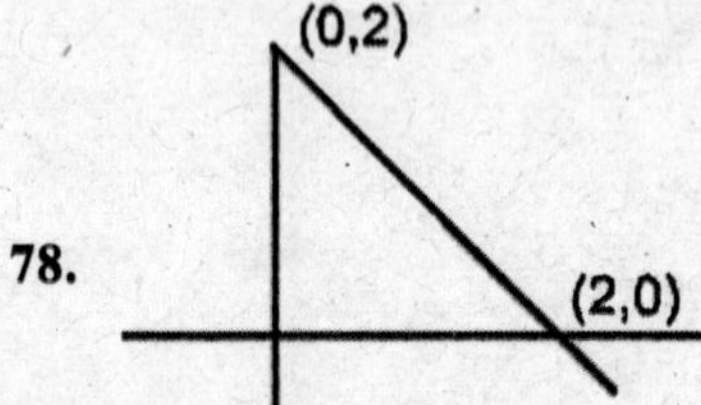

$A = \frac{1}{2} \times 2 \times 2 = 2$

79. $\frac{dy}{dx} = e^{-x}$

$y = -e^{-x} + c$

80. $\vec{B} = \pm\begin{vmatrix} \hat{i} & \hat{j} & \hat{k} \\ 0 & 0 & 1 \\ 2 & 3 & 4 \end{vmatrix}$

$\vec{B} = \pm 1(3\hat{i} - 2\hat{j}) = \pm(3\hat{i} - 2\hat{j})$

81. $\vec{\alpha} = a_1\hat{i} + a_2\hat{j} + a_3\hat{k}$

take dot with $\hat{i}$, $\hat{j}$ and $\hat{k}$ on both sides you get

$\vec{\alpha}.\hat{i} = a_1, \quad a_2 = \vec{\alpha}.\hat{j}, \quad a_3 = \vec{\alpha}.\hat{k}$

$\vec{\alpha} = (\vec{\alpha}.\hat{i})\hat{i} + (\vec{\alpha}.\hat{j})\hat{j} + (\vec{\alpha}.\hat{k})\hat{k}$

82. $|\vec{a} \times \vec{b}| = |\vec{a}.\vec{b}|$

$|\vec{a}||\vec{b}|\sin\theta = |\vec{a}||\vec{b}|\cos\theta$

$\tan\theta = 1 \quad \Rightarrow \quad \theta = \frac{\pi}{4}$

83. $|\vec{a}+\vec{b}|^2 + |\vec{a}-\vec{b}|^2 = 2\left(|\vec{a}|^2 + |\vec{b}|^2\right)$

$6 + |\vec{a}-\vec{b}|^2 = 2(2+3)$

$|\vec{a}-\vec{b}| = 2$

84. $\vec{a}.(\hat{i}+\hat{j}+\hat{k}) = 0$

Hence (D) none of these

85. $\cos\theta = 4(\hat{i}-\hat{k}).(\hat{i}+\hat{j}+\hat{k}) = 0$

$\theta = \frac{\pi}{2}$

$\cos\theta + \sin\theta = 1$

86. Number of girls student be x

$43 = \frac{25 \times 40 + x \times 48}{x+25}$

$43x + 43 \times 25 = 25 \times 40 + x \times 48$

$5x = 3 \times 25$

$x = 15$

87. $\bar{x} = \frac{30+55+75+90+50+60+39}{7}$

$= \frac{399}{7} = 57$

number of students = 4

90. $x = 5$

$$\sigma^2 = \sum_{i=1}^{5} \frac{(x_1 - \bar{x})^2}{N} = 0$$

91. $f(2) = 4 - 8$

$= -4$

$x = 2$

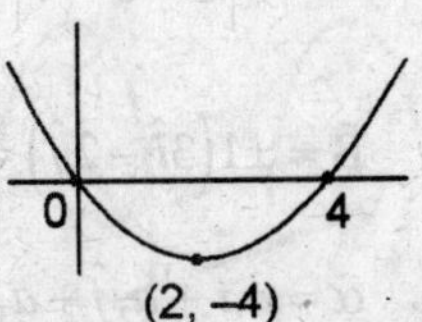

92. $y = xe^x$

$$\frac{dy}{dx} = e^x + xe^x = e^x(1 + x) = 0$$

$x = -1$

$$\frac{d^2y}{dx^2} = e^x + e^x(1 + x)$$

$$\left(\frac{d^2y}{dx^2}\right)_{(x=-1)} = \frac{1}{e} + 0 > 0$$

$$y_{\min} = (-1)e^{-1} = -\frac{1}{e}$$

93. 1. Not necessarily true

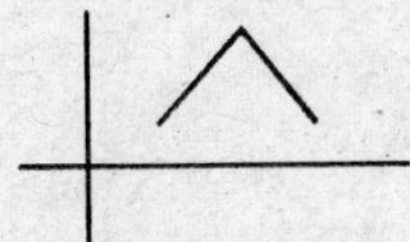

2. True

94. $y = \log_x x$

$y = 1$ for $x > 0$ and $x \neq 1$

$$\frac{dy}{dx} = 0$$

95. $$\int_0^2 \frac{dx}{x^2 + 4} = \frac{1}{2}\left[\tan^{-1}\frac{x}{2}\right]_0^2 = \frac{1}{2}\left[\frac{\pi}{4} - 0\right] = \frac{\pi}{8}$$

96. $$\int_{-a}^{a} (x^3 + \sin x)dx = 0 \qquad (\because \text{ odd function})$$

97. $$\int_0^1 \underset{I}{x}\,\underset{II}{e^x}\,dx = xe^x - \int_0^1 1.e^x dx = [xe^x - e^x]_0^1 = (e - e) - [0 - 1] = 1$$

98. $$\int e^{\ln x} dx = \frac{x^2}{2} + c$$

99. $$\int_{\frac{\pi}{6}}^{\pi/6} \frac{\sin^5 x.\cos^3 x}{x^4} dx = 0 \qquad (\because \text{ odd function})$$

100. $$\int \frac{dx}{x \ln x}$$

Put $\ln x = t$

$$\frac{1}{x} dx = dt$$

$$\int \frac{1}{t} dt = \ln t + c = \ln \ln x + c$$

101.

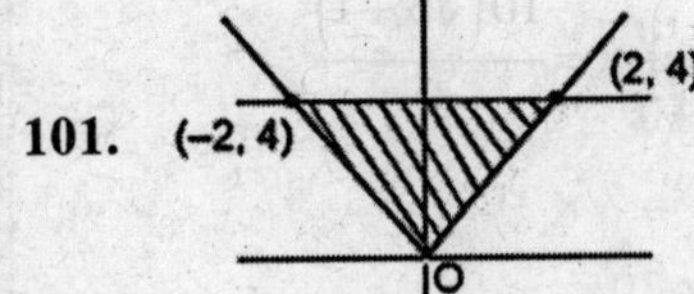

Area = 2 × 4 = 8 sq. unit

102.

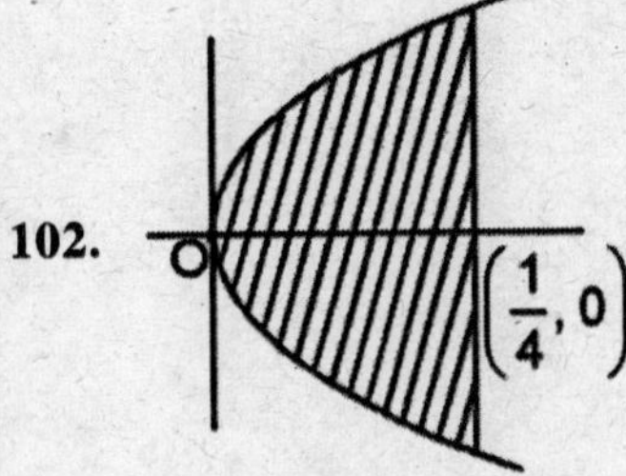

$$\text{Area} = 2\int_0^{1/4} \sqrt{x}\, dx$$

$$= 2.\frac{2}{3}\left[x^{3/2}\right]_0^{1/4}$$

$$= \frac{4}{3}\left[\frac{1}{8} - 0\right] = \frac{1}{6} \text{sq. unit}$$

103. $v = \sec^2 x$, $z = \tan^2 x$

$$\frac{dv}{dz} = \frac{dv/dx}{dz/dx} = \frac{2\sec x.\sec x \tan x}{2\tan x.\sec^2 x} = 1$$

104. $y = \sin x$

$$\frac{dy}{dx} = \cos x \qquad \frac{d^2y}{dx^2} = -\sin x$$

$$\therefore \quad y + \frac{d^2y}{dx^2} = 0$$

105. $$\frac{dy}{dx} = \frac{1}{x + y + 1}$$

106. 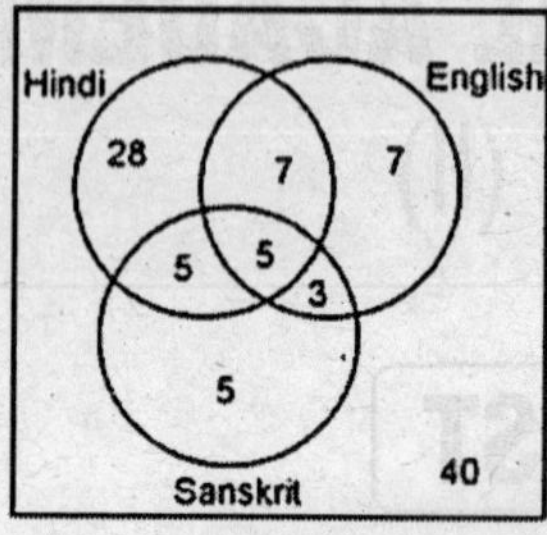

40% of total population = $0.4 \times 75 \times 10^6 = 3 \times 10^7$

107. $.28 \times 75 \times 10^6 = 21 \times 10^6$

108. $.05 \times 75 \times 10^6 = 3.75 \times 10^6$

109. $.07 \times 75 \times 10^6 = 5.25 \times 10^6$

110. $.4 \times 75 \times 10^6 = 30 \times 10^6 = 3 \times 10^7$

111. $.15 \times 75 \times 10^6 = 11.25 \times 10^6$

112. $\dfrac{1}{x-3} = \dfrac{1}{x+2} - \dfrac{1}{2}$

$2(x + 2) = (x - 3)$

$2x + 4 + x^2 - 3x = 0$

$x^2 - x + 4 = 0$

113. For any $x \in R$,

$|x| x^2 + 1$ cann't be zero.

114. $A \times (B \cup C)$

$\{x, y\} \times (2, 3, 4) = 6$

115. $\log_y x^5 . \log_x y^2 . \log_z z^2 = \dfrac{5\ln x}{\ln y} \times \dfrac{2\ln y}{\ln x} \times \dfrac{3\ln z}{\ln z} = 30$

116. Obvious

117. 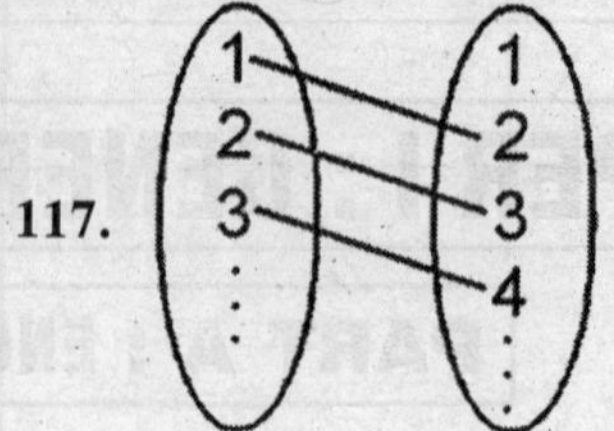

f is one-one but not onto

118. $x^2 - 3x + 2 = 0$

119. $\dfrac{1}{\alpha} + \dfrac{1}{\beta} = \dfrac{\alpha + \beta}{\alpha\beta} = \dfrac{-b}{c}$

120. Let width = x

so length = $2x + 5$

$\therefore$ $x(2x + 5) = 75$

$2x^2 + 5x - 75 = 0$

$2x^2 + 15x - 10x - 75 = 0$

$(x - 5)(2x + 15) = 0$

$x = 5, -\dfrac{15}{2}$

$\therefore$ length = $2x + 5 = 15$ unit

Previous Papers (Solved)

NATIONAL DEFENCE ACADEMY & NAVAL ACADEMY

NDA & NA – Entrance Exam, 2012 (II)

PAPER I : GENERAL ABILITY TEST

PART A : ENGLISH LANGUAGE

COMPREHENSION

Directions (Qs. 1 to 8) : *Read the following* ***two passages*** *and answer the questions that follow each passage.*

Passage-1

There was a farewell ceremony on her day at school, to which my parents and I were invited. It was a touching ceremony in a solemn kind of way. The City Corporation sent a representative and so did the two main political parties. There were many speeches and my grandmother was garlanded by a girl from every class. Then the head-girl, a particular favourite of hers, unveiled the farewell present the girls had bought for her by subscription. It was a large marble model of the Taj Mahal; it had a bulb inside and could be lit up like a table lamp. My grandmother made a speech too, but she couldn't finish it properly, for she began to cry before she got to the end of it and to stop to wipe away her tears. I turned away when she began dabbing at her eyes with a huge green handkerchief, and discovered, to my surprise, that many of the girls sitting around me were wiping their eyes too. I was very jealous, I remember. I had always taken it for granted that it was my own special right to love her; I did not know how to cope with the discovery that my right had been infringed by a whole school.

1. The farewell ceremony described in the passage is for the

A. author's mother used to teach at his/her school
B. mother of head-girl teaching at her school
C. grandmother of head-girl no longer teaching at her school
D. grandmother of the author who used to teach at his/her school

2. The farewell ceremony made everyone feel

A. sad
B. unhappy
C. happy
D. bad

3. Before the writer attended the ceremony he/she had thought

A. he/she was the only child who loved his/her grandmother
B. all the girls in the school loved his/her grandmother
C. only a few girls in the school loved his/her grandmother
D. only his/her parents loved his/her grandmother

Passage-2

It is no doubt true that we cannot go through life without sorrow. There can be no sunshine without shadow, we must not complain that roses have thorns but rather be grateful that thorns bear flowers. Our existence here is so complex that we must expect much sorrow and suffering. Yet it is certain that no man was ever discontented with the world who did his duty in it. The world is like a looking glass; if you smile, it smiles; if you frown, it frowns back. Always try, then, to look at the bright side of things. There are some persons whose very presence seems like a ray of sunshine and brightens the whole room. Life has been described as a comedy to those who think and a tragedy to those who feel.

4. The author says that we cannot go through life without sorrow because

A. it is our fate
B. we are always discontented
C. life is a tragedy
D. human life is very complex

5. According to the author, no man can be discontented with the world if he

A. is determined to be happy
B. is sincere in discharging his duties
C. has a healthy attitude to life
D. likes sunshine

6. The expression "life is a tragedy to those who feel" means that it is tragedy to those who

A. think about the world
B. believe in fate
C. do not understand the world
D. are sensitive and emotional

7. The author says, "There are some persons whose very presence seems like a ray of sunshine and brightens that whole room." The reason for this is that they

A. have the capacity to love
B. talk more of roses and less of thorns

C. are happy and spread happiness
D. look good and behave well

8. What is the author's message in this passage?
A. Look at the bright side of things
B. Our existence is so complex
C. The world is a looking glass
D. Expect much sorrow and suffering

REARRANGING PARTS OF SENTENCE

Directions (Qs. 9 to 20) : *In the following sentences, some parts of the sentences have been jumbled up. You are required to rearrange these parts which are labelled P, Q, R, S to produce the correct sentence. Choose the proper sequence and mark in your answer sheet accordingly.*

9. P : he had
Q : 'no' to him
R : such a winning smile
S : that I could not say
The correct sequence should be
A. Q P R S B. R P Q S
C. S P Q R D. P R S Q

10. P : he nodded
Q : he understood
R : as though
S : everything
The correct sequence should be
A. P R Q S B. P S Q R
C. Q R S P D. S P R Q

11. P : the child burned down
Q : the house
R : by playing
S : with matches
The correct sequence should be
A. R S P Q B. Q S P R
C. R P S Q D. Q P S R

12. P : in his innocence
Q : I believed
R : of the charge
S : and aquittal
The correct sequence should be
A. S Q R P B. Q P S R
C. P R S Q D. R P Q S

13. My little sister
P : in school
Q : instead of reading books
R : who was quite intelligent
S : played with dolls
The correct sequenc should be
A. P R S Q B. R S P Q
C. Q P S R D. P R Q S

14. P : for having stood first
Q : last year
R : at the B.A. examination
S : he was awarded gold medal
The correct sequence should be
A. P Q R S B. S P R Q
C. P R Q S D. S R Q P

15. We are proud that
P : as our chief guest
Q : our Mayor
R : is a former student of this college
S : who is presiding over today's function
The correct sequence should be
A. P Q R S B. Q P S R
C. P Q S R D. Q S P R

16. At the end of the morning exercise,
P : the soldiers
Q : to get ready to leave
R : were asked
S : for an unknown destination
The correct sequence should be
A. P Q R S B. R S P Q
C. S R Q P D. P R Q S

17. After having got up from bed
P : the Magistrate
Q : to bring coffee
R : ordered the attendant
S : immediately
The correct sequence should be
A. P Q R S B. S P Q R
C. S P R Q D. P R Q S

18. P : to resolve it
Q : than
R : it is easier
S : to talk about a problem
The correct sequence should be
A. R P Q S B. Q P R S
C. P Q S R D. R S Q P

19. P : to my client
Q : that I speak
R : immediately
S : it is important
The correct sequence should be
A. S R Q P B. S Q P R
C. S P Q R D. P S Q R

20. You had better
P : of getting a good response
Q : so that
R : we will be sure
S : work hard
The correct sequence should be
A. R S Q P B. S Q R P
C. S Q P R D. R P Q S

SPOTTING ERRORS

Directions (Qs. 21 to 30) :

(*i*) In this section, a number of sentences are given. The sentences are broken in three separate parts and each one is labelled A, B, C. Read each sentence to find out whether there is an error in any part. No sentences has more than one error. When you find an error in any one of the parts A, B, C, indicate your responses on the Answer Sheet at the appropriate space. You may feel that there is no error in a sentences. In that case, D will signify a 'No error' response.

(*ii*) Errors may be in grammar, word usage or idioms. There may be a word missing or there may be a word which should be removed.

(*iii*) You are **not** required to correct the error. You are required only to indicate your response on the answer sheet.

21. A. None of the applicants have turned up
B. for the interview
C. on time
D. No error

22. A. Her mother did not reply
B. when I asked her
C. why was she weeping
D. No error

23. A. The oxygen content of Mars is not
B. sufficient enough to support life
C. as we know it
D. No error

24. A. He told his friend that
B. each of them
C. should be able to carry out the orders oneself
D. No error

25. A. If the police would have worked
B. in time
C. the riot would not have occurred
D. No error

26. A. The flag is risen in the morning
B. and taken down at night
C. by the guards
D. No error

27. A. I have seen him
B. going to the theatre
C. with his friends yesterday evening
D. No error

28. A. He was charged of murder
B. though the evidence did everything
C. to convince the judge of his innocence
D. No error

29. A. Neither he nor his brother
B. is a good student
C. but both are good players
D. No error

30. A. He has taken charge
B. as principal of our college
C. three years ago
D. No error

Directions (Qs. 31 to 40) : *Each of the following items consists of a sentence followed by four words or group of words. Select the* ***antonym*** *of the word (occurring in the sentences in capital letters) as per the context.*

31. A small ALTERCATION between the children started off a riot.
A. quarrel B. friendly discussion
C. contest D. race

32. He agreed reluctantly to sign the form but looked ILL AT EASE.
A. embarrassed B. comfortable
C. welcome D. easy

33. My mother has been working hard for the last two weeks and she feels RUN DOWN.
A. energetic B. cold
C. emotional D. morbid

34. The three states signed a pact to have COLLECTIVE economy.
A. distributive B. disintegrative
C. individual D. divided

35. He was deeply hurt by her CURT reply.
A. abrupt B. short
C. expansive D. rude

36. He was asked to ACCELERATE the pace of work.
A. check B. control
C. slacken D. supervise

37. The child was ABDUCTED when he was going to school.
A. seized B. set free
C. kidnapped D. ransomed

38. The baby has a very DELICATE body.
A. crude B. strong
C. hard D. bony

39. The government has ENHANCED the tuition fees in schools and colleges.
A. magnified B. aggravated
C. decreased D. augmented

40. He aims at PERFECTION in whatever job he undertakes.
A. deficiency B. immaturity
C. badness D. completeness

Directions (Qs. 41 to 50) : *Each of the following items consists of a sentence followed by four words or group of words. Select the* ***synonym*** *of the word or words (occurring in the sentences in capital letters) as per the context.*

41. MOMENTOUS changes are taking place in the social and economic life of India.
A. notorious B. momentary
C. official D. enormous

42. His condition DETERIORATED day-by-day.
A. went bad B. grew worse
C. went down D. grew bad

43. She is pretty INSIPID young lady
A. clever B. lazy
C. dull D. lean

44. It is the difficulty or SCARCITY of a thing that it makes it precious.
A. poverty B. absence
C. insufficiency D. disappearance

45. We should not allow ADVERSITY to discourage us.
A. poverty B. darkness
C. time of trouble D. unfriendly criticism

46. He is very OBLIGING by nature.
A. helpful B. nice
C. thankful D. compelling

47. She thought that RUNNING INTO her old friend was a stroke of fate.
A. meeting by chance B. colliding
C. travelling with D. quarrelling with

48. He was a CHARISMATIC leader.
A. exceptionally fascinating
B. particularly popular
C. compulsively pleasant
D. strangely haunting

49. She was completely ENGROSSED in her work.
A. disturbed B. absorbed
C. fatigued D. successful

50. He is an INDEFATIGABLE worker.
A. tired B. tireless
C. brave D. skilful

PART B : GENERAL KNOWLEDGE

51. Air is
A. always a compound
B. always a mixture
C. a compound in pollution free zones
D. a mixture in industrial zones

52. Consider the following figure :

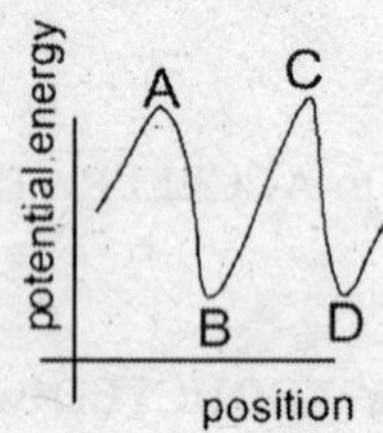

Which of the following labelled points in the figure given above indicate unstable state of an object?
A. Point A only B. Point B only
C. Points A and C D. Points B and D

53. Which one among the following is an electrochemical cell that cannot be charged?
A. Electrolytic cell B. Storage cell
C. Primary cell D. Fuel cell

54. Which one among the following is the correct order of power consumption for light of equal intensity?
A. CFL tube < Fluorescent tube < Incandescent bulb < Light emitting diode
B. Light emitting diode < CFL tube < Fluorescent tube < Incandescent bulb
C. CFL tube < Fluorescent tube < Light emitting diode < Incandescent bulb
D. Incandescent bulb < Light emitting diode < Fluorescent tube < CFL tube

55. One feels heavier in a lift when the lift
A. is going down steadily B. just begins to go up
C. is moving up steadily D. descends freely

56. A swinging pendulum has its maximum acceleration at
A. the bottom of the swing
B. the two extremities of the swing
C. every point on the swing
D. no particular portion of the pendulum

57. Which one among the following statements about thermal conductivity is correct?
A. Steel > Wood > Water B. Steel > Water > Wood
C. Water > Steel > Wood D. Water > Wood > Steel

58. The process of nuclear fusion in the sun requires
A. very high temperature and very high pressure
B. low temperature and high pressure
C. high temperature and low pressure
D. very high temperature and no pressure

59. Which one among the following is the true represeptation of (*i*) variable DC potential (*ii*) rheostat and (*iii*) AC ammeter respectively?

A. (*i*)

(*ii*)

(*iii*)

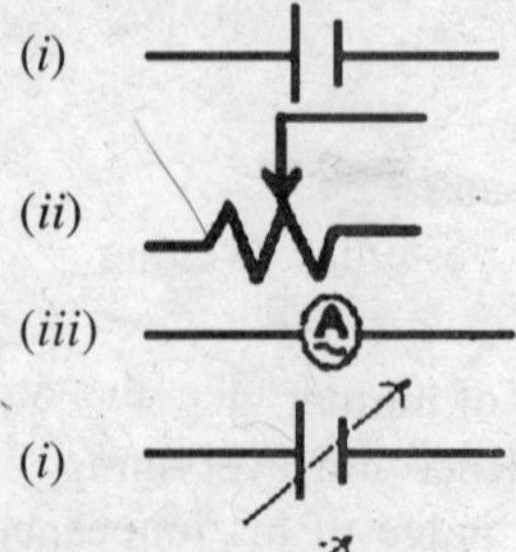

B. (*i*)

(*ii*)

(*iii*)

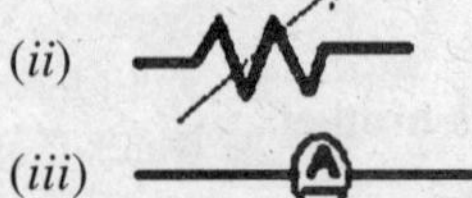

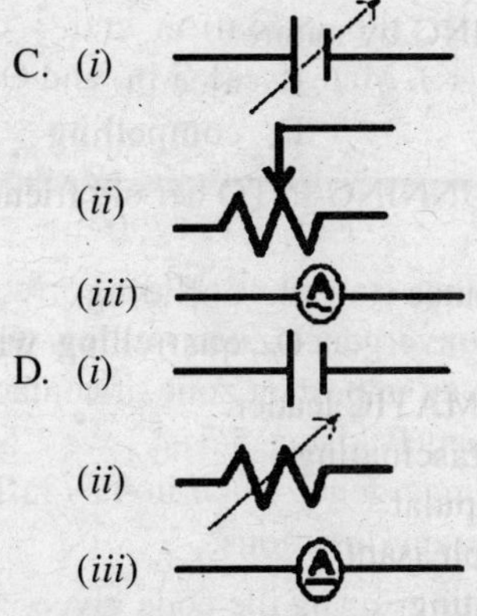

60. In India, distribution of electricity for domestic purpose is done in the form of

A. 220 V; 50 Hz B. 110 V; 60 Hz
C. 220 V; 60 Hz D. 110 V; 50 Hz

61. The earth's magnetic field is approximately

A. 1 Tesla B. 2 Gauss
C. 10^4 Tesla D. 1 Gauss

62. Yellow colour light is used as fog light because yellow colour

A. light is most scattered by fog
B. has the longest wavelength among all colours
C. has the longest wavelength among all colours except red and orange but the red colour is already used for brake light and stop light whereas orange colour is avoided, due to its similarity with red
D. has the shortest wavelength among all colours not already reserved for other purpose

63. A hot object loses heat to its surroundings in the form of heat radiation. The rate of loss of heat depends on the

A. temperature of the object
B. temperature of the surroundings
C. temperature difference between the object and its surroundings
D. average temperature of the object and its surroundings

64. The mirror used for the head light of a car is

A. spherical concave B. plane
C. cylindrical D. parabolic concave

65. An iron ball and a wooden ball of the same radius are released from a height 'H' in vacuum. The time taken to reach the ground will be

A. more for the iron ball
B. more for the wooden ball
C. equal for both
D. in the ratio of their weights

66. Match List-I with List-II and select the correct answer using the codes given below the Lists :

List-I (River)	**List-II (Sea)**
(*a*) Volga	1. Sea of Azov
(*b*) Dnieper	2. Black Sea
(*c*) Rhine	3. Caspian Sea
(*d*) Don	4. Mediterranean Sea

Codes :

	(*a*)	(*b*)	(*c*)	(*d*)
A.	1	4	2	3
B.	1	2	4	3
C.	3	2	4	1
D.	3	4	2	1

67. Which one among the following transitions is associated with the largest change in energy in hydrogen atom?

A. $n = 5$ to $n = 3$ B. $n = 2$ to $n = 1$
C. $n = 3$ to $n = 2$ D. $n = 4$ to $n = 2$

68. Match List-I with List-II and select the correct answer using the codes given below the Lists :

List-I (Compound)	**List-II (Use)**
(*a*) Cellulose nitrate	1. Soft soap
(*b*) Potassium sulphate	2. Gun powder
(*c*) Potassium salt of fatty acids	3. Fertilizer
(*d*) Calcium oxide	4. Glass

Codes :

	(*a*)	(*b*)	(*c*)	(*d*)
A.	2	3	1	4
B.	2	1	3	4
C.	4	1	3	2
D.	4	3	1	2

69. Which one among the following does not have an allotrope?

A. Oxygen B. Sulphur
C. Nitrogen D. Carbon

70. Match List-I with List-II and select the correct answer using the codes given below the Lists :

List-I (Scientist)	**List-II (Discovery)**
(*a*) Goldstein	1. Atomic theory
(*b*) Chadwick	2. Proton
(*c*) J.J. Thomson	3. Neutron
(*d*) John Dalton	4. Electron

Codes :

	(*a*)	(*b*)	(*c*)	(*d*)
A.	2	3	4	1
B.	2	4	3	1
C.	1	4	3	2
D.	1	3	4	2

71. Consider the following statements :

1. Diamond is hard and graphite is soft.
2. Diamond is soft and graphite is hard.
3. Diamond is a bad conductor but graphite is a good conductor.
4. Diamond is a good conductor but graphite is a bad conductor.

Which of the statements given above is/are correct?

A. 1 and 3 B. 1 only

C. 2 and 3 D. 1 and 4

72. The most important raw material used in the manufacture of cement are

A. Potassium nitrate, charcoal and sulphur

B. Limestone, clay and gypsum

C. Transition metal oxides, sodium hydroxide or potassium hydroxide

D. Limestone, sodium carbonate and silica

73. Which one among the following equations is correctly balanced?

A. $NaOH + Al + H_2O \rightarrow 2H_2 + NaAlO_2$

B. $2NaOH + 2Al + 2H_2O \rightarrow 3H_2 + 2NaAlO_2$

C. $2NaOH + 2Al + 3H_2O \rightarrow 4H_2 + 2NaAlO_2$

D. $2NaOH + 2Al + H_2O \rightarrow H_2 + 2NaAlO_2$

74. Three elements Na, S and O combine to form a compound Na_2SO_3. What is the valency of S in this compound?

A. 2+ B. 4+

C. 6+ D. 8+

75. Which one among the following is the equivalent weight of sulphuric acid?
(Atomic weight : H = 1, S = 32, O = 16)

A. 98 B. 60

C. 100 D. 49

76. Deionised water is produced by

A. Calgon process

B. ion-exchange resin process

C. Clark's process

D. Permutit process

77. Which one among the following is a double salt?

A. $K_4[Fe(CN)_6]$

B. $K_2SO_4.Al_2(SO_4)_3.24H_2O$

C. $CuSO_4.5H_2O$

D. NaCl

78. Which one among the following is the correct order the strength of acids?

A. $H_2SO_4 > H_3PO_3 > CH_3COOH$

B. $H_3PO_3 > H_2SO_4 > CH_3COOH$

C. $CH_3COOH > H_3PO_3 > H_2SO_4$

D. $CH_3COOH > H_2SO_4 > H_3PO_3$

79. Given below is an approximate composition of a substance :

CaO	60-70%
SiO_2	20-25%
Al_2O_3	5-10%
Fe_2O_3	2-3%

The substance is

A. Plaster of Paris B. Cement

C. Marble stone D. Quartz

80. In $KMnO_4$ molecule, the oxidation states of the elements Potassium (K), Manganese (Mn) and Oxygen (O) are respectively

A. +1, +5, –2 B. +1, +7, –2

C. 0, 0, 0 D. +1, +7, 0

81. Which of the following statements is/are correct?

1. Inter-Tropical Convergence Zone is a low pressure belt which forms an important zone of contact over Northern India and Pakistan.
2. Inter-Tropical convergence Zone invites inflow of winds from different directions.

Select the correct answer using the code given below :

A. 1 only B. 2 only

C. Both 1 and 2 D. Neither 1 nor 2

82. Consider the following characteristics of industries :

1. They can be located in a wide variety of places.
2. They are not dependent on any specific raw material.
3. They are generally not polluting industries.
4. The most important factor in their location is accessibility.

Which one of the following types of industries has the above characteristics?

A. Market oriented B. Foot loose

C. Sunset D. Sunrise

83. Consider the following statements regarding El Nino effect on Indian Monsoon :

1. The surface temperature goes up in the Southern Pacific Ocean and there is deficient rainfall in India.
2. The Walker Circulation shifts eastward from its normal position and reduces monsoon rainfall in India.

Which of the statements given above is/are correct?

A. 1 only B. 2 only

C. Both 1 and 2 D. Neither 1 nor 2

84. In which among the following terrains the bore wells and canals can be dug easily?

A. Gneiss, granites and basaltic terrain of Peninsular India

B. Rolling and dotted hilly terrain of North-East India

C. Soft alluvium of the Northern Plains

D. Confined aquifer below the normal water table

85. Wide range and variability in rainfall, torrential in character, reversal of winds and uncertain arrival are the characteristics of

A. Westerlies B. Trade winds

C. Monsoon D. Anti trade winds

86. Which of the following statements is/are correct?

1. The local time of Itanagar (Arunachal Pradesh) is about two hours ahead than Dwarka (Gujarat).
2. The local time at Chennai (Tamil Nadu) and Lucknow (Uttar Pradesh) is almost same.
3. The local time of Mumbai (Maharashtra) is one hour ahead than Kolkata (West Bengal).

Select the correct answer using the code given below :

A. 1 and 2 only B. 2 only

C. 1 and 3 only D. 1, 2 and 3

87. Mackeral sky is associated with cloud type

A. Cumulo-nimbus B. Strato-cumulus

C. Alto-cumulus D. Cirro-cumulus

88. The average surface temperature of the earth's surface is

A. 10°C B. 15°C

C. 8°C D. 5°C

89. Match List-I with List-II and select the correct answer using the codes given below the Lists :

List-I
(Atomic power station)

(*a*) Narora

(*b*) Rana Pratap Sagar

(*c*) Tarapur

(*d*) Kalpakkam

List-II
(Position in map)

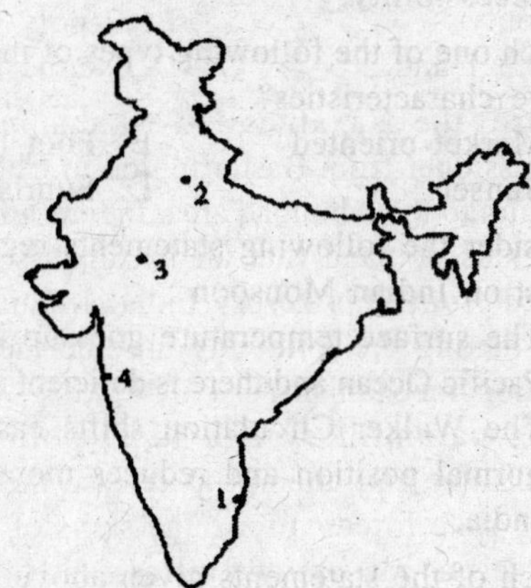

Codes :

	(*a*)	(*b*)	(*c*)	(*d*)
A.	2	4	3	1
B.	1	3	4	2
C.	2	3	4	1
D.	1	4	3	2

90. Ferral's law is related to deflection of

A. cold air-mass

B. hot air-mass

C. monsoon air-mass

D. trade wind and ocean currents

91. The grassland region of South Africa is known as

A. Selvas B. Downs

C. Veldt D. Llaons

92. In India, the Tropical Savanah (AW) type of climate prevails largely in

A. Rajasthan desert region

B. Penisular plateau region

C. Jammu & Kashmir region

D. North-Eastern region

93. The Nokrek biosphere reserve is located in

A. Arunachal Pradesh B. Assam

C. Sikkim D. Meghalaya

94. Match List-I with List-II and select the correct answer using the codes given below the Lists :

List-I (Place)	**List-II (Industry)**
(*a*) Jabalpur	1. Petro-chemical
(*b*) Bengaluru	2. Information technology
(*c*) Modinagar	3. Paper
(*d*) Ballarpur	4. Automobile

Codes :

	(*a*)	(*b*)	(*c*)	(*d*)
A.	4	1	2	3
B.	3	1	2	4
C.	3	2	1	4
D.	4	2	1	3

95. Where is Aghil Pass located?

A. Nepal Himalayas B. Sikkim Himalayas

C. Eastern Himalayas D. Trans Himalayas

96. The Jury Act of 1827 was opposed by many Indians. One of the grounds for opposing it was that it denied both to the Hindus and Mohammedans the honor of a seat on the Grand Jury. Which among the following was known for his opposition to the Jury Act?

A. Gopal Krishna Gokhale B. Lord Sinha

C. Sir Syed Ahmed Khan D. Raja Rammohan Roy

97. Plan Balkan was

A. A plan devised by Mountbatten to transfer power of separate provinces or confederation of provinces, with the Bengal and Punjab Assemblies being given the options to vote for partition of their provinces

B. The plan devised by Pethick Lawrence to give autonomy to Indian princes and provinces

C. A plan devised by the Muslim League and the Congress to provide autonomy to Indian provinces to form confederations.

D. A plan devised by Mountbatten to allow Indian princes the freedom to either be independent or to join either India or Pakistan

98. Which one among the following prominently rose in revolt against the British in 1857?

A. Punjab Army B. Madras Regiment

C. Bengal Army D. Awadh Regiment

99. The first Prime Minister of India in 1947 was appointed by

A. the Governor General

B. The President of India

C. Mahatma Gandhi

D. a committee headed by Dr. Rajendra Prasad

100. Which one among the following statements is correct? The press in democracy must

A. be free and impartial

B. be committed to the policies of the government
C. highlight the achievement of the government without criticizing its policies
D. criticize the policies of the government

101. Telescopes are placed in space to view distant galaxies primarily to
A. get closer to the observed objects
B. avoid the absorption of light or other radiations in the atmosphere of the earth
C. avoid light pollution from the earth's populated areas
D. avoid steering the telescope against the earth's motion

102. SONAR is mostly used by
A. Doctors B. Engineers
C. Astronauts D. Navigators

103. A bucket full of water is kept in a room and it cools from 75°C to 70°C in time T_1 minutes, from 70°C to 65°C in time T_2 minutes, and from 65°C to 60°C in time T_3 minutes, then
A. $T_1 = T_2 = T_3$ B. $T_1 < T_2 < T_3$
C. $T_1 > T_2 > T_3$ D. $T_1 < T_3 < T_2$

104. For a simple pendulum, the graph between T^2 and L (where T is the time period & L is the length) is
A. straight line passing through origin
B. parabolic
C. circle
D. none of the above

105. When an electrical safety fuse is rated (marked) as 16 A, it means it
A. will not work if current is less than 16 A
B. has a resistance of 16 Ω
C. will work if the temperature is more than 16°C
D. will be blown (break) if current exceeds 16 A

106. Who among the following was recently (May 2012) elected as Chair of the Asian Development Bank's Board of Governors?
A. Pranab Mukherjee
B. Montek Singh Ahluwalia
C. Duvvuri Subbarao
D. Aditya Puri

107. Consider the following statements:
1. Justice Dalveer Bhandari was recently elected as the President of International Court of Justice.
2. Justice Bhandari was a senior Judge of the Supreme Court of India.

Which of the statements given above is/are correct?
A. 1 only B. 2 only
C. Both 1 and 2 D. Neither 1 nor 2

108. Consider the following names in field of Indian cinema :
Vidya Balan
Soumitra Chatterjee
Tapan Sinha
V.K. Murthy

Which of the following statement is/are correct?
1. All of them are winners of Dadasaheb Phalke award.
2. While Tapan Sinha is a film director V.K. Murthy is known cinematography.
3. Soumitra Chatterjee was the last to get the Dadasaheb Phalke awards.

Select the correct answer using the code given below:
A. 1, 2 and 3 B. 2 and 3 only
C. 3 only D. 1 and 2 only

109. Who among the following was awarded the first Tagore Award for Cultural Harmony for the year 2012?
A. Jasraj B. Ravi Shankar
C. Nikhil Banerjee D. Bhimsen Joshi

110. Consider the following about the budget proposals for the year 2012-2013 :
1. Service tax rate raised and covers all services including those in the negative list.
2. Increase in defence allocation over the previous year.

Which of the statements given above is/are correct?
A. 1 only B. 2 only
C. Both 1 and 2 D. Neither 1 nor 2

111. Suppose, the Naxalites have kidnapped a Deputy Commissioner from Baster region in Chhattisgarh and taken him to the Abujmad area. In return for his release, the Naxals demand that all Naxal prisoners must be released from jails across India. In such a situation which among the following may be the best conflict resolution mechanism?
1. The paramilitary and local police attack the Naxalites and attempt to release the kidnapped.
2. The state forces offer huge sums of money to the Naxals as ransom and release all Naxal prisoners.
3. The state forces engaged the Naxals in a dialogue while simultaneously sending in a commando force to release the prisoners.
4. The state forces utilize local mediators to engage with the Naxals to workout a resolution process for release of the kidnapped.

Select the correct answer using the code given below :
A. 1, 3 and 4 B. 2 and 3
C. 3 and 4 only D. 4 only

112. A high level committee set up by the Ministry of Housing and Urban poverty alleviation conducted a survey of the slum populations in India's states. Which one among the following states was identified as being the one with highest slum population?
A. Andhra Pradesh B. Madhya Pradesh
C. Maharashtra D. Tamil Nadu

113. The UN has recently passed a resolution against human right violation in a South Asian country. Which of the following was the country?
A. Nepal B. India
C. Pakistan D. Sri Lanka

114. Prof. Vijay Raghavan, an Indian scientist, who has been elected Fellow of Royal Society in the year 2012, is a renowned

A. Biotechnologist B. Chemist
C. Agricultural scientist D. Missile engineer

115. Operation Cactus is the name given to Indian Military intervention in

A. Maldives B. Sri Lanka
C. Bangladesh D. Bhutan

Directions : *The following two items consist of two statements, statement I and statement II. You are to examine these two statements carefully and select the answer to these items using the code given below :*

A. Both statements are individually true and statement II is the correct explanation of statement I.
B. Both statements are individually true but statement II is not the correct explanation of statement I.
C. Statement I is true but statement II is false.
D. Statement I is false but statement II is true.

116. Statement I : Red blood cells burst when placed in water.

Statement II : Due to phenomenon of osmosis water enters into red blood cells.

117. Statement I : Indigo formed the basis of a flourishing sector of commercial agriculture by the beginning of the 19th century.

Statement II : The Indigo Commission was set up to enquire into the grievances of the indigo cultivators in 1860.

118. Which one of the following water borne disease is not caused by bacteria?

A. Cholera B. Typhoid
C. Bacillary dysentery D. Hepatitis A

119. The process of conventional earlobe piercing does not lead to bleeding. This is because the

A. Heart does not supply blood to earlobes
B. cartilages found in ear lobe has lesser blood supply unlike other body parts
C. earlobes consist of dead non-dividing tissue
D. needle used for ear piercing is sterilized

120. After entering the human body through mosquito bite, the malarial parasite (plasmodium) shows initial multi-plication in

A. Spinal cord B. Blood
C. Liver D. Spleen

121. Which one among the following parts of blood carries the function of body defence?

A. Platelets B. White Blood Cells
C. Haemoglobin D. Red Blood Cells

122. Which one among the following is not included in major clinical sign as a case definition of AIDS in children < 12 years of age?

A. Persistent cough for more than 1 month
B. Loss of weight
C. Chronic diarrhoea
D. Prolonged fever

123. Polio disease is caused by

A. Bacteria B. Fungi
C. Virus D. Worm

124. Which one among the following is the hardest part of our body?

A. Skull bones of head B. Thumb nails
C. Enamel of teeth D. Spinal vertebra

125. Which of the following group is present in animal cells?

A. Mitochondria, Cell membrane, Cell wall, Cytoplasm
B. Chloroplast, Cytoplasm, Vacuole, Nucleus
C. Nucleus, Cell membrane, Mitochondria, Cytoplasm
D. Vacuole, Cell membrane, Nucleus, Mitochondria

126. Which one among the following statement is correct? In digestive system of living organisms

A. glucose is broken down into glycerol
B. glucose is converted into glycogen
C. glucose is broken down into carbon dioxide and water
D. proteins are broken down into amino acids

127. Which one among the following rocks does not belong to the same group?

A. Shale B. Limestone
C. Slate D. Sandstone

128. Match List-I with List-II and select the correct answer using the codes given below the lists :

List-I (World Heritage site)	List-II (State)
(*a*) Brihadisvara Temple	1. Maharashtra
(*b*) Ellora Caves	2. Karnataka
(*c*) Hampi	3. Tamil Nadu
(*d*) Mahabodhi Temple	4. Bihar

Codes :

	(*a*)	(*b*)	(*c*)	(*d*)
A.	4	1	2	3
B.	4	2	1	3
C.	3	2	1	4
D.	3	1	2	4

129. Match List-I with List-II and select the correct answer using the codes given below the Lists :

List-I (Himalayan Peak)	List-II (State)
A. K2	1. Uttarakhand
(*b*) Nanda Devi	2. Jammu & Kashmir
(*c*) Tara Pahar	3. Sikkim
(*d*) Kanchenjunga	4. Himachal Pradesh

Codes :

	(*a*)	(*b*)	(*c*)	(*d*)
A.	2	4	1	3
B.	2	1	4	3
C.	3	1	4	2
D.	3	4	1	2

130. The Deccan Trap Formation was caused by
A. Shield eruption B. Composite eruption
C. Caldera eruption D. Flood basalt eruption

131. Match List-I with List-II and select the correct answer using the codes given below the Lists :

List-I (Magnet)	**List-II (Property)**
(*a*) Artificial magnet	1. Long lived
(*b*) Permanent magnet	2. Last for infinitely long period
(*c*) Temporary magnet	3. Short lived
(*d*) Earth as a magnet	4. Induced magnet

Codes :

	(*a*)	(*b*)	(*c*)	(*d*)
A.	3	1	4	2
B.	3	4	1	2
C.	2	1	4	3
D.	2	4	1	3

132. A body weighs 5 kg on equator. At the poles it is likely to weigh
A. 5 kg
B. less than 5 kg but not zero
C. 0 kg
D. more than 5 kg

133. The polarity of an unmarked horse shoe magnet can be determined by using
A. a charged glass rod
B. a magnetic compass
C. an electroscope
D. another unmarked bar magnet

134. A staircase has 5 steps each 10 cm high and 10 cm wide. What is the minimum horizontal velocity to be given to the ball so that it hits directly the lowest plane from the top of the staircase? ($g = 10\ ms^{-2}$)
A. $2\ ms^{-1}$ B. $1\ ms^{-1}$
C. $\sqrt{2}\ ms^{-1}$ D. $\frac{1}{2}\ ms^{-1}$

135. Consider the following statements :
1. If a piece of bar magnet is broken into two equally long pieces, the pieces will not lose the magnetic properties.
2. Magnetic properties of a substance lie in the atomic level.

Which of the statements given above is/are correct?
A. 1 only B. 2 only
C. Both 1 and 2 D. Neither 1 nor 2

136. Consider the following circuit :

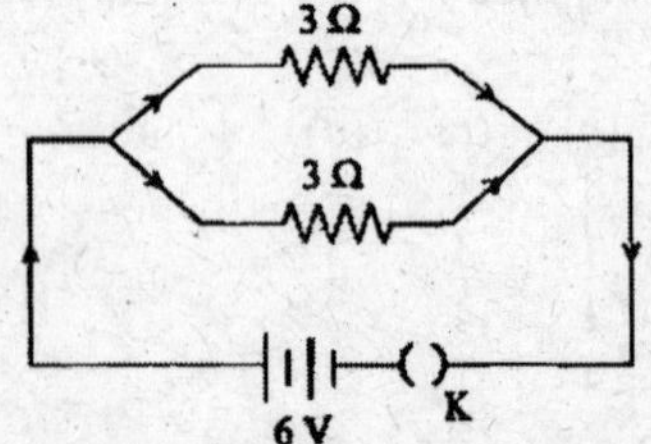

The current flowing through each of the resistors connected in the above circuit is
A. 2 A B. 1 A
C. 9 A D. 4 A

137. Consider the following statements :
The state government shall appoint a Finance Commission to review the financial position of the Panchayats and to make recommendations as to
1. The distribution between the state and Panchayats of the net proceeds of taxes, tolls and fees leviable by the states.
2. The determination of the taxes, duties, tolls and fees which may be assigned to the Panchayats.
3. The principles that will determine grant-in-aid to the Panchayats.

Which of the statements given above is/are correct?
A. 1 only B. 2 and 3 only
C. 1 and 3 only D. 1, 2 and 3

138. Which one among the following monuments was earlier known as 'All India War Memorial'?
A. Gateway of India B. India Gate
C. Charminar D. Lal Quila

139. Which of the following statements regarding the Preamble of the Constitution of India is/are correct?
1. The Preamble is an integral part of the Constitution.
2. The words 'secular' and 'socialist' have been a part of the Preamble since its inception.

Select the correct answer using the code given below :
A. 1 only B. 2 only
C. Both 1 and 2 D. Neither 1 nor 2

140. Normally the Parliament can legislate on the subjects enumerated in
A. the Union List
B. the Concurrent List
C. the State List
D. the Union as well as Concurrent List

141. Which one among the following statements relating to the Home Rule movement is not correct?
A. The movement, instead of going forward after its great advance in 1917, gradually declined in 1918
B. Annie Besant, the leader of the movement did not oppose the entry of Extremists
C. The movement became weaker and weaker because of the continuous differences of opinion among the nationalist leaders
D. The movement was again revived by Mahatma Gandhi

142. Why did Gandhiji go to Champaran?
A. To launch a Satyagraha movement
B. To launch a non-cooperation movement
C. To enquire into the grievances of the indigo cultivators
D. To fight against the zamindars

143. Which one among the following was the fundamental cause of the first Karnataka War between the British and the French?
A. Participation of the English and the French in the native politics of Karnataka
B. The ambition of Dupleix to drive out the English from the South
C. The trade rivalry between the English and the French
D. The war of Austrian succession because of which Britain and France became each other's enemy in every part of the world

144. Which one among the following cities was the best producer of silk cloth under Gupta reign?
A. Pataliputra B. Murshidabad
C. Ghazipur D. Varanasi

145. Which one among the following is not correct about the cave paintings at Ajanta?
A. Scenes have no dividing frame and blend into each other
B. Scenes are both religious and secular in nature
C. The influence of the Gandhara art is seen
D. Scenes mostly depict tales from Jatakas

146. Vice-President of India is elected by an electoral college consisting of
A. members of both Houses of Parliament
B. members of Rajya Sabha only
C. elected members of both Houses of Parliament
D. elected members of Lok Sabha only

147. Who among the following has a right to speak and otherwise take part in proceedings of either House of Parliament and to be a member of any parliamentary committee but is not entitled to vote?
A. Chairman, Finance Commission
B. The Attorney General
C. The Comptroller and Auditor General
D. The Chief Election Commissioner

148. Which one among the following countries is not touched by the Stilwell Road constructed during the World War II?
A. Myanmar B. Thailand
C. China D. India

149. Which one among the following wars ended by the Treaty of Salbai?
A. First Maratha War B. Second Maratha War
C. Third Maratha War D. Fourth Mysore War

150. Navroze is a festival celebrated in India by the
A. Hindus B. Muslims
C. Parsis D. Christians

PAPER II : MATHEMATICS

1. If the roots of a quadratic equation are $m + n$ and $m - n$, then the quadratic equation will be :
A. $x^2 + 2mx + m^2 - mn + n^2 = 0$
B. $x^2 + 2mx + (m - n)^2 = 0$
C. $x^2 - 2mx + m^2 - n^2 = 0$
D. $x^2 + 2mx + m^2 - n^2 = 0$

2. If α, β are the roots of $x^2 + px - q = 0$ and γ, δ are roots of $x^2 - px + r = 0$ then what is $(\beta + \gamma)(\beta + \delta)$ equal to?
A. $p + r$ B. $p + q$
C. $q + r$ D. $p - q$

3. Consider the following statements :
1. The sum of cubes of first 20 natural numbers is 44400.
2. The sum of squares of first 20 natural numbers is 2870.

Which of the above statements is/are correct?
A. 1 only B. 2 only
C. Both 1 and 2 D. Neither 1 nor 2

4. Consider the following statements :

1. $\left(\omega^{10} + 1\right)^7 + \omega = 0$
2. $\left(\omega^{105} + 1\right)^{10} = p^{10}$ for some prime number p

where $\omega \neq 1$ is a cubic root of unity.
Which of the above statements is/are correct?
A. 1 only
B. 2 only
C. Both 1 and 2
D. Neither 1 nor 2

5. What is the sum of first eight terms of the series $1 - \frac{1}{2} + \frac{1}{4} - \frac{1}{8} + ...$?
A. $\frac{89}{128}$ B. $\frac{57}{384}$
C. $\frac{85}{128}$ D. None of the above

6. The number of permutations that can be formed from all the letters of the word 'BASEBALL' is :
A. 540 B. 1260
C. 3780 D. 5040

7. The relation 'has the same father as' over the set of children is :
A. only reflexive
B. only symmetric
C. only transitive
D. an equivalence relation

8. If the roots of the quadratic equation $3x^2 - 5x + p = 0$ are real and unequal, then which one of the following is correct?

A. $p = \frac{25}{12}$ B. $p < \frac{25}{12}$
C. $p > \frac{25}{12}$ D. $p \leq \frac{25}{12}$

9. The decimal representation of the number $(1011)_2$ in binary system is :

A. 5 B. 7
C. 9 D. 11

10. The decimal number $(57.375)_{10}$ when converted to binary number takes the form :

A. $(111001.011)_2$ B. $(100111.110)_2$
C. $(110011.101)_2$ D. $(111011.011)_2$

11. If $(\log_3 x)(\log_x 2x)(\log_{2x} y) = \log_x x^2$, then what is y equal to?

A. 4.5 B. 9
C. 18 D. 27

12. Let P = {1, 2, 3} and a relation on set P is given by the set R = {(1, 2), (1, 3), (2, 1), (1, 1), (2, 2), (3, 3), (2, 3)}. Then R is :

A. Reflexive, transitive but not symmetric
B. Symmetric, transitive but not reflexive
C. Symmetric, reflexive but not transitive
D. None of the above

13. The value of the sum $\sum_{n=1}^{13}\left(i^n + i^{n+1}\right)$ where $i = \sqrt{-1}$ is :

A. i B. $-i$
C. 0 D. $i - 1$

Directions (Qs. 14 and 15): *For the next two (02) questions that follows:*

The sum of first 10 terms and 20 terms of an AP are 120 and 440 respectively.

14. What is its first term?

A. 2 B. 3
C. 4 D. 5

15. What is the common difference?

A. 1 B. 2
C. 3 D. 4

16. If a non-empty set A contains n elements, then its power set contains how many elements?

A. n^2 B. 2^n
C. $2n$ D. $n + 1$

17. Let A = {$x \in$ W, the set of whole numbers and $x < 3$}, B = {$x \in$ N, the set of natural numbers and $2 \leq x < 4$} and C = {3, 4}, then how many elements will $(A \cup B) \times C$ contain?

A. 6 B. 8
C. 10 D. 12

18. What is the modulus of $\frac{\sqrt{2}+i}{\sqrt{2}-i}$ where $i = \sqrt{-1}$?

A. 3 B. 1/2
C. 1 D. None of the above

19. What is the number of diagonals which can be drawn by joining the angular points of a polygon of 100 sides?

A. 4850 B. 4950
C. 5000 D. 10000

20. The angles of a triangle are in AP and the least angle is 30°. What is the greatest angle (in radian)?

A. $\frac{\pi}{2}$ B. $\frac{\pi}{3}$
C. $\frac{\pi}{4}$ D. π

21. If each element in a row of a determinant is multiplied by the same factor r, then the value of the determinant?

A. is multiplied by r^3 B. is increased $3r$
C. remains unchanged D. is multiplied by r

22. The inverse of a diagonal matrix is a :

A. symmetric matrix B. skew-symmetric matrix
C. diagonal matrix D. None of the above

23. If $A = \begin{bmatrix} 3 & 4 \\ 5 & 6 \\ 7 & 8 \end{bmatrix}$ and $B = \begin{bmatrix} 3 & 5 & 7 \\ 4 & 6 & 8 \end{bmatrix}$, then which one of the following is correct?

A. B is the inverse of A B. B is the adjoint of A
C. B is the transpose of A D. None of the above

24. If the sum of matrices $\begin{bmatrix} x \\ x \\ y \end{bmatrix}, \begin{bmatrix} y \\ y \\ z \end{bmatrix}$ and $\begin{bmatrix} z \\ 0 \\ 0 \end{bmatrix}$ is the matrix $\begin{bmatrix} 10 \\ 5 \\ 5 \end{bmatrix}$, then what is the value of y?

A. –5 B. 0
C. 5 D. 10

25. If the matrix AB is a zero matrix, then which one of the following is correct?

A. A must be equal to zero matrix or B must be equal to zero matrix
B. A must be equal to zero matrix and B must be equal to zero matrix
C. It is not necessary that either A is zero matrix or B is zero matrix
D. None of the above

26. If the matrix $\begin{bmatrix} \alpha & 2 & 2 \\ -3 & 0 & 4 \\ 1 & -1 & 1 \end{bmatrix}$ is ***not*** invertible, then :

A. $\alpha = -5$ B. $\alpha = 5$
C. $\alpha = 0$ D. $\alpha = 1$

27. The value of the determinant $\begin{vmatrix} x^2 & 1 & y^2+z^2 \\ y^2 & 1 & z^2+x^2 \\ z^2 & 1 & x^2+y^2 \end{vmatrix}$ is :

A. 0 B. $x^2 + y^2 + z^2$
C. $x^2 + y^2 + z^2 + 1$ D. None of the above

28. A square matrix $[a_{ij}]$ such that $a_{ij} = 0$ for $i \neq j$ and $a_{ij} = k$ where k is a constant for $i = j$ is called :

A. diagonal matrix, but not scalar matrix
B. scalar matrix
C. unit matrix
D. None of the above

29. What is the value of sin 15°?

A. $\frac{\sqrt{3}-1}{2\sqrt{2}}$ B. $\frac{\sqrt{3}+1}{2\sqrt{2}}$
C. $\frac{\sqrt{3}-1}{\sqrt{3}+1}$ D. $\frac{\sqrt{3}+1}{\sqrt{3}-1}$

30. If $4 \sin^2 \theta = 1$, where $0 < \theta < 2\pi$, how many values does θ take?

A. 1 B. 2
C. 4 D. None of the above

31. What is the value of sin 18° cos 36° equal to?

A. 4 B. 2
C. 1 D. $\frac{1}{4}$

32. What is $\sin\left[\sin^{-1}\left(\frac{3}{4}\right) + \sin^{-1}\left(\frac{4}{5}\right)\right]$ equal to?

A. 0 B. $\frac{1}{2}$
C. 1 D. 2

33. If $\sec \alpha = \frac{13}{5}$ where $270° < \alpha < 360°$, then what is sin α equal to?

A. $\frac{5}{13}$ B. $\frac{12}{13}$
C. $\frac{-12}{13}$ D. $\frac{-13}{12}$

34. What is tan (–585°) equal to?

A. 1 B. –1
C. $-\sqrt{2}$ D. $-\sqrt{3}$

35. Consider the following statements :

1. The value of cos 46° – sin 46° is positive.
2. The value of cos 44° – sin 44° is negative.

Which of the above statements is/are correct?

A. 1 only B. 2 only
C. Both 1 and 2 D. Neither 1 nor 2

36. The line making an angle (–120°) with x-axis is situated in the :

A. first quadrant B. second quadrant
C. third quadrant D. fourth quadrant

37. The angle subtended at the centre of a circle of radius 3 cm by an arc of length 1 cm is :

A. $\frac{30°}{\pi}$ B. $\frac{60°}{\pi}$
C. 60° D. None of the above

38. If $\sin A = \frac{2}{\sqrt{5}}$ and $\cos B = \frac{1}{\sqrt{10}}$ where A and B are acute angles, then what is A + B equal to?

A. 135° B. 90°
C. 75° D. 60°

39. The top of a hill observed from the top and bottom of a building of height h is at angles of elevation α and β respectively. The height of the hill is :

A. $\frac{h \cot \beta}{\cot \beta - \cot \alpha}$ B. $\frac{h \cot \alpha}{\cot \alpha - \cot \beta}$
C. $\frac{h \tan \alpha}{\tan \alpha - \tan \beta}$ D. None of the above

40. From the top of a lighthouse 70 m high with its base at sea level, the angle of depression of a boat is 15°. The distance of the boat from the foot of the lighthouse is :

A. $70(2-\sqrt{3})$m B. $70(2+\sqrt{3})$m
C. $70(3-\sqrt{3})$m D. $70(3+\sqrt{3})$m

41. The locus of a point equidistant from three collinear points is :

A. a straight line B. a pair of points
C. a point D. the null set

42. The equation of the locus of a point which is always equidistant from the points (1, 0) and (0, –2) is :

A. $2x + 4y + 3 = 0$ B. $4x + 2y + 3 = 0$
C. $2x + 4y - 3 = 0$ D. $4x + 2y - 3 = 0$

43. The points (5, 1), (1, –1) and (11, 4) are :

A. collinear
B. vertices of right angled triangle
C. vertices of equilateral triangle
D. vertices of an isosceles triangle

44. What is the perpendicular distance between the parallel $3x + 4y = 9$ and $9x + 12y + 28 = 0$?

A. 7/3 units B. 8/3 units
C. 10/3 units D. 11/3 units

45. Let p, q, r, s be the distances from origin of the points (2, 6), (3, 4), (4, 5) and (–2, 5) respectively. Which one of the following is a whole number?

A. p B. q
C. r D. s

46. From the point (4, 3) a perpendicular is dropped on the x-axis as well as on the y-axis. If the lengths of perpendiculars are p, q respectively, then which one of the following is correct?

A. $p = q$ B. $3p = 4q$
C. $4p = 3q$ D. $p + q = 5$

47. What is the value of λ if the straight line $(2x + 3y + 4) + \lambda(6x - y + 12) = 0$ is parallel to y-axis?

A. 3 B. –6
C. 4 D. –3

48. The line $y = 0$ divides the line joining the points (3, –5) and (–4, 7) in the ratio :

A. 3 : 4 B. 4 : 5
C. 5 : 7 D. 7 : 9

49. The sum of the focal distances of a point on the ellipse $\frac{x^2}{4}+\frac{y^2}{9}=1$ is :

A. 4 units B. 6 units
C. 8 units D. 10 units

50. The eccentricity e of an ellipse satisfies the condition :

A. $e < 0$ B. $0 < e < 1$
C. $e = 1$ D. $e > 1$

51. The equation of a straight line which makes an angle 45° with the x-axis with y-intercept 101 units is :

A. $10x + 101y = 1$ B. $101x + y = 1$
C. $x + y - 101 = 0$ D. $x - y + 101 = 0$

52. If the points (2, 4), (2, 6) and $(2 + \sqrt{3}, k)$ are the vertices of an equilateral triangle, then what is the value of k?

A. 6 B. 5
C. –3 D. 1

53. If the distance between the point (7, 1, –3) and (4, 5, λ) is 13 units, then what is one of the values of λ?

A. 20 B. 10
C. 9 D. 8

54. If a line OP of length r (where 'O' is the origin) makes an angle α with x-axis and lies in the xz-plane, then what are the coordinates of P?

A. $(r \cos \alpha, 0, r \sin \alpha)$ B. $(0, 0, r \sin \alpha)$
C. $(r \cos \alpha, 0, 0)$ D. $(0, 0, r \cos \alpha)$

55. What is the distance of the point (1, 2, 0) from yz-plane is :

A. 1 unit B. 2 units
C. 3 units D. 4 units

56. What are the direction cosines of a line which is equally inclined to the positive directions of the axes?

A. $\left\langle \frac{1}{\sqrt{3}}, \frac{1}{\sqrt{3}}, \frac{1}{\sqrt{3}} \right\rangle$ B. $\left\langle -\frac{1}{\sqrt{3}}, \frac{1}{\sqrt{3}}, \frac{1}{\sqrt{3}} \right\rangle$

C. $\left\langle -\frac{1}{\sqrt{3}}, -\frac{1}{\sqrt{3}}, \frac{1}{\sqrt{3}} \right\rangle$ D. $\left\langle \frac{1}{3}, \frac{1}{3}, \frac{1}{3} \right\rangle$

57. What is the angle between the lines $\frac{x-2}{1} = \frac{y+1}{-2} = \frac{z+2}{1}$ and $\frac{x-1}{1} = \frac{2y+3}{3} = \frac{z+5}{2}$?

A. $\frac{\pi}{2}$ B. $\frac{\pi}{3}$

C. $\frac{\pi}{6}$ D. None of the above

58. What is the equation to the plane through (1, 2, 3) parallel to $3x + 4y - 5z = 0$?

A. $3x + 4y + 5z + 4 = 0$ B. $3x + 4y - 5z + 14 = 0$
C. $3x + 4y - 5z + 4 = 0$ D. $3x + 4y - 5z - 4 = 0$

59. What are the direction ratios of the line of intersection of the planes $x = 3z + 4$ and $y = 2z - 3$?

A. $\langle 1,2,3 \rangle$ B. $\langle 2,1,3 \rangle$
C. $\langle 3,2,1 \rangle$ D. $\langle 1,3,2 \rangle$

60. What is the equation to the straight line passing through (a, b, c) and parallel to z-axis?

A. $\frac{x-a}{1} = \frac{y-b}{0} = \frac{z-c}{0}$

B. $\frac{x-a}{0} = \frac{y-b}{0} = \frac{z-c}{1}$

C. $\frac{x-a}{0} = \frac{y-b}{1} = \frac{z-c}{0}$

D. $\frac{x-a}{0} = \frac{y-b}{1} = \frac{z-c}{1}$

61. What is $\lim_{x \to 0} \frac{\sqrt{1+x}-1}{x}$ equal to?

A. 0 B. $\frac{1}{2}$
C. 1 D. $-\frac{1}{2}$

62. What is $\lim_{x \to 0} \frac{2(1-\cos x)}{x^2}$ equal to?

A. 0 B. $\frac{1}{2}$
C. $\frac{1}{4}$ D. 1

63. Consider the following:

1. $\lim_{x \to 0} \frac{1}{x}$ exists.
2. $\lim_{x \to 0} e^{\frac{1}{x}}$ does not exist.

Which of the above is/are correct?
A. 1 only B. 2 only
C. Both 1 and 2 D. Neither 1 nor 2

64. If $x^m + y^m = 1$ such that $\frac{dy}{dx} = -\frac{x}{y}$, then what should be the value of m?
A. 0 B. 1
C. 2 D. None of the above

65. Which one of the following is correct in respect of the function $f(x) = \frac{x^2}{|x|}$ for $x \neq 0$ and $f(0) = 0$?
A. $f(x)$ is discontinuous every where
B. $f(x)$ is continuous every where
C. $f(x)$ is continuous at $x = 0$ only
D. $f(x)$ is discontinuous at $x = 0$ only

66. What is $\lim_{x \to 2} \frac{x-2}{x^2-4}$ equal to?
A. 0 B. $\frac{1}{4}$
C. $\frac{1}{2}$ D. 1

67. The radius of a circle is uniformly increasing at the rate of 3 cm/s. What is the rate of increase in area, when the radius is 10 cm?
A. 6π cm²/s B. 10π cm²/s
C. 30π cm²/s D. 60π cm²/s

68. Let $f : R \to R$ be a function whose inverse is $\frac{x+5}{3}$. What is $f(x)$ equal to?
A. $f(x) = 3x + 5$ B. $f(x) = 3x - 5$
C. $f(x) = 5x - 3$ D. $f(x)$ does not exist

69. Consider the following statements :
1. If $y = \ln(\sec x + \tan x)$, then $\frac{dy}{dx} = \sec x$.
2. If $y = \ln(\text{cosec } x - \cot x)$, then $\frac{dy}{dx} = \text{cosec } x$.

Which of the above is/are correct?
A. 1 only B. 2 only
C. Both 1 and 2 D. Neither 1 nor 2

70. If $f(x) = 2^{\sin x}$, then what is the derivative of $f(x)$?
A. $2^{\sin x} \ln 2$ B. $(\sin x)\, 2^{\sin x - 1}$
C. $(\cos x) 2^{\sin x - 1}$ D. None of the above

71. The function $f(x) = x^3 - 3x^2 + 6$ is an increasing function for :
A. $0 < x < 2$ B. $x < 2$
C. $x > 2$ or $x < 0$ D. all x

72. Consider the following statements :
1. If $f(x) = x^3$ and $g(y) = y^3$ then $f = g$.
2. Identity function is not always a bijection.

Which of the above statements is/are correct?
A. 1 only B. 2 only
C. Both 1 and 2 D. Neither 1 nor 2

73. Let $A = \{x \in R \,|x \geq 0|\}$. A function $f : A \to A$ is defined by $f(x) = x^2$. Which one of the following is correct?
A. The function does not have inverse
B. f is its own inverse
C. The function has an inverse but f is not its own inverse
D. None of the above

74. If $y = \ln\left(e^{mx} + e^{-mx}\right)$, then what is $\frac{dy}{dx}$ at $x = 0$ equal to?
A. -1 B. 0
C. 1 D. 2

75. What is the minimum value of $|x|$?
A. -1 B. 0
C. 1 D. 2

76. What is $\int a^x e^x dx$ equal to?
A. $\frac{a^x e^x}{\ln a} + c$ B. $a^x e^x + c$
C. $\frac{a^x e^x}{\ln(ae)} + c$ D. None of the above
where c is the constant of integration.

77. What is $\int_{-1}^{1} x|x| dx$ equal to?
A. 2 B. 1
C. 0 D. -1

78. What is $\int_0^1 \frac{\tan^{-1} x}{1+x^2} dx$ equal to?
A. $\frac{\pi^2}{8}$ B. $\frac{\pi^2}{32}$
C. $\frac{\pi}{4}$ D. $\frac{\pi}{8}$

79. What is $\int_0^{\pi/2} \sin 2x \ln(\cot x) dx$ equal to?
A. 0 B. $\pi \ln 2$
C. $-\pi \ln 2$ D. $\frac{\pi \ln 2}{2}$

80. What is the area of the portion of the curve $y = \sin x$, lying between $x = 0$, $y = 0$ and $x = 2\pi$?
A. 1 square unit B. 2 square units
C. 4 square units D. 8 square units

81. What is $\int \frac{\ln x}{x} dx$ equal to?
A. $\frac{(\ln x)^2}{2} + c$ B. $\frac{(\ln x)}{2} + c$
C. $(\ln x)^2 + c$ D. None of the above
where c is the constant of integration.

82. What is the area of the region bounded by the lines $y = x$, $y = 0$ and $x = 4$?

A. 4 square units B. 8 square units
C. 12 square units D. 16 square units

83. What is $\int\left(\frac{1}{\cos^2 x} - \frac{1}{\sin^2 x}\right)dx$ equal to?

A. $2 \operatorname{cosec} 2x + c$ B. $-2 \cot 2x + c$
C. $2 \sec 2x + c$ D. $-2 \tan 2x + c$

where c is the constant of integration.

84. What is the degree of the differential equation $\frac{d^3y}{dx^3} + 2\left(\frac{d^2y}{dx^2}\right) - \frac{dy}{dx} + y = 0$?

A. 6 B. 3
C. 2 D. 1

85. Consider a differential equation of order m and degree n. Which one of the following pairs is ***not*** feasible?

A. (3, 2) B. (2, 3/2)
C. (2, 4) D. (2, 2)

86. The differential equation representing the family of curves $y = a \sin (\lambda x + \alpha)$ is :

A. $\frac{d^2y}{dx^2} + \lambda^2 y = 0$ B. $\frac{d^2y}{dx^2} - \lambda^2 y = 0$

C. $\frac{d^2y}{dx^2} + \lambda y = 0$ D. None of the above

87. The differential equation $y\frac{dy}{dx} + x = a$ where 'a' is any constant represents :

A. A set of straight lines B. A set of ellipses
C. A set of circles D. None of the above

88. For the differential equation $\left(\frac{dy}{dx}\right)^2 - x\left(\frac{dy}{dx}\right) + y = 0$, which one of the following is not its solution?

A. $y = x - 1$ B. $4y = x^2$
C. $y = x$ D. $y = -x - 1$

89. What is the general solution of the differential equation $x^2dy + y^2dx = 0$?

A. $x + y = c$ B. $xy = c$
C. $c(x + y) = xy$ D. None of the above

where c is the constant of integration

90. What is the general solution of the differential equation $e^x \tan y dx + (1 - e^x) \sec^2 y dy = 0$?

A. $\sin y = c(1 - e^x)$ B. $\cos y = c(1 - e^x)$
C. $\cot y = c(1 - e^x)$ D. None of the above

where c is the constant of integration.

91. EFGH is a rhombus such that the angle EFG is 60°. The magnitude of vectors $\overrightarrow{FH}$ and $\{m\overrightarrow{EG}\}$ are equal where m is a scalar. What is the value of m?

A. 3 B. 1.5
C. $\sqrt{2}$ D. $\sqrt{3}$

92. If $\vec{a} \cdot \vec{b} = 0$ and $\vec{a} \times \vec{b} = \vec{0}$ then which one of the following is correct?

A. $\vec{a}$ is parallel to $\vec{b}$
B. $\vec{a}$ is perpendicular to $\vec{b}$
C. $\vec{a} = \vec{0}$ or $\vec{b} = \vec{0}$
D. None of the above

93. The vectors $\vec{a} \times (\vec{b} \times \vec{a})$ is coplanar with :

A. $\vec{a}$ only B. $\vec{b}$ only
C. Both $\vec{a}$ and $\vec{b}$ D. Neither $\vec{a}$ nor $\vec{b}$

94. Consider the following :

1. $4\hat{i} \times 3\hat{i} = \vec{0}$
2. $\frac{4\hat{i}}{3\hat{i}} = \frac{4}{3}$

Which of the above is/are correct?

A. 1 only B. 2 only
C. Both 1 and 2 D. Neither 1 nor 2

95. What is the value of λ for which $(\lambda\hat{i} + \hat{j} - \hat{k}) \times (3\hat{i} - 2\hat{j} + 4\hat{k}) = (2\hat{i} - 11\hat{j} - 7\hat{k})$?

A. 2 B. -2
C. 1 D. 7

96. The magnitude of the scalar p for which the vector $p(-3\hat{i} - 2\hat{j} + 13\hat{k})$ is of unit length is :

A. $\frac{1}{8}$ B. $\frac{1}{64}$

C. $\sqrt{182}$ D. $\frac{1}{\sqrt{182}}$

97. The vector $2\hat{j} - \hat{k}$ lies :

A. in the plane of XY B. in the plane of YZ
C. in the plane of XZ D. along the X-axis

98. ABCD is a parallelogram. If $\overline{AB} = \vec{a}$, $\overline{BC} = \vec{b}$, then what is $\overline{BD}$ equal to?

A. $\vec{a} + \vec{b}$ B. $\vec{a} - \vec{b}$
C. $-\vec{a} - \vec{b}$ D. $-\vec{a} + \vec{b}$

99. What is the geometric mean of the sequence 1, 2, 4, 8, ..., 2^n?

A. $2^{n/2}$ B. $2^{(n+1)/2}$
C. $2^{(n+1)} - 1$ D. $2^{(n-1)}$

100. The mean of 10 observations is 5. If 2 is added to each observation and then multiplied by 3, then what will be the new mean?
A. 5 B. 7
C. 15 D. 21

101. What is the mean of first n odd natural numbers?
A. n B. $(n + 1)/2$
C. $n(n + 1)/2$ D. $n + 1$

102. The arithmetic mean of numbers a, b, c, d, e is M. What is the value of $(a - M) + (b - M) + (c - M) + (d - M) + (e - M)$?
A. M B. $a + b + c + d + e$
C. 0 D. 5M

103. The algebraic sum of the deviations of 20 observations measured from 30 is 2. What would be the mean of the observations?
A. 30 B. 32
C. 30.2 D. 30.1

104. The median of 27 observations of a variable is 18. Three more observations are made and the values of these observations are 16, 18 and 50. What is the median of these 30 observations?
A. 18
B. 19
C. 25.5
D. Can not be determined due to insufficient data

105. Frequency curve may be :
A. symmetrical B. positive skew
C. negative skew D. All of the above

106. The monthly family expenditure (in percentage) on different items are as follows :

Food	Rent	Cloth	Transport	Education	Others
38	19	18	—	9	6

If the total monthly expenditure is ₹ 9000, then what is the expenditure on transport?
A. ₹ 180 B. ₹ 1000
C. ₹ 900 D. ₹ 360

107. If the mean of few observations is 40 and standard deviation is 8, then what is the coefficient of variation?
A. 1% B. 10%
C. 20% D. 30%

108. What is the standard deviation of 7, 9, 11, 13, 15?
A. 2.4 B. 2.5
C. 2.7 D. 2.8

109. Which of one of the following is a measure of dispersion?
A. Mean B. Median
C. Mode D. Standard deviation

110. Let X and Y be two related variables. The two regression lines are given by $x - y + 1 = 0$ and $2x - y + 4 = 0$. The two regression lines pass through the point :
A. (–4, –3) B. (–6, –5)
C. (3, –2) D. (–3, –2)

111. If P(E) denotes the probability of an event E, then E is called certain event if :
A. P(E) = 0 B. P(E) = 1
C. P(E) is either 0 or 1 D. P(E) = 1/2

112. What is the probability that a leap year selected at random will contain 53 Mondays?
A. $\frac{2}{5}$ B. $\frac{2}{7}$
C. $\frac{1}{7}$ D. $\frac{5}{7}$

113. If A and B are two events such that $P(A \cup B) = \frac{3}{4}$, $P(A \cap B) = \frac{1}{4}$, $P(\overline{A}) = \frac{2}{3}$ where $\overline{A}$ is the complement of A, then what is P(B) equal to?
A. $\frac{1}{3}$ B. $\frac{2}{3}$
C. $\frac{1}{9}$ D. $\frac{2}{9}$

114. Three coins are tossed simultaneously. What is the probability that they will fall two heads and one tail?
A. $\frac{1}{3}$ B. $\frac{1}{2}$
C. $\frac{1}{4}$ D. $\frac{3}{8}$

115. Which one of the following is correct?
A. An event having no sample point is called an elementary event
B. An event having one sample point is called an elementary event
C. An event having two sample points is called an elementary event
D. An event having many sample points is called an elementary event

116. What is the most probably number of successes in 10 trials with probability of success 2/3?
A. 10 B. 7
C. 5 D. 4

Directions: *For the nex two (02) questions that follow:*
An urn contains one black ball and one gree ball. A second urn contains one white and one green ball. One ball is drawn at random from each urn.

117. What is the probability that both balls are of same colour?
A. $\frac{1}{2}$ B. $\frac{1}{3}$
C. $\frac{1}{4}$ D. $\frac{2}{3}$

118. What is the probability of getting at least one green ball?

A. $\frac{1}{2}$ B. $\frac{1}{3}$

C. $\frac{2}{3}$ D. $\frac{3}{4}$

Directions: *For the next two (02) questions that follow:*

The dice each numbered from 1 to 6 are thrown together. Let A and B be two events given by

A: even number on the first die

B: number on the second die is greater than 4

119. What is P(A ∪ B) equal to?

A. $\frac{1}{2}$ B. $\frac{1}{4}$

C. $\frac{2}{3}$ D. $\frac{1}{6}$

120. What is P(A ∩ B) equal to?

A. $\frac{1}{2}$ B. $\frac{1}{4}$

C. $\frac{2}{3}$ D. $\frac{1}{6}$

ANSWERS

PAPER-I – GENERAL ABILITY TEST

1	**2**	**3**	**4**	**5**	**6**	**7**	**8**	**9**	**10**
D	A	A	D	B	D	C	A	D	A
11	**12**	**13**	**14**	**15**	**16**	**17**	**18**	**19**	**20**
A	B	B	B	D	D	D	D	B	B
21	**22**	**23**	**24**	**25**	**26**	**27**	**28**	**29**	**30**
D	C	B	C	A	A	A	A	D	A
31	**32**	**33**	**34**	**35**	**36**	**37**	**38**	**39**	**40**
B	B	A	D	C	C	B	B	C	A
41	**42**	**43**	**44**	**45**	**46**	**47**	**48**	**49**	**50**
D	B	C	C	C	C	A	A	B	B
51	**52**	**53**	**54**	**55**	**56**	**57**	**58**	**59**	**60**
B	C	C	B	B	B	B	A	C	A
61	**62**	**63**	**64**	**65**	**66**	**67**	**68**	**69**	**70**
D	C	C	D	C	C	B	A	C	A
71	**72**	**73**	**74**	**75**	**76**	**77**	**78**	**79**	**80**
A	D	B	B	D	A	B	A	B	B
81	**82**	**83**	**84**	**85**	**86**	**87**	**88**	**89**	**90**
B	B	C	C	C	A	C	B	C	D
91	**92**	**93**	**94**	**95**	**96**	**97**	**98**	**99**	**100**
C	B	D	C	D	D	D	C	A	A
101	**102**	**103**	**104**	**105**	**106**	**107**	**108**	**109**	**110**
A	D	B	B	B	A	C	B	B	B
111	**112**	**113**	**114**	**115**	**116**	**117**	**118**	**119**	**120**
A	C	D	A	A	A	B	D	B	C
121	**122**	**123**	**124**	**125**	**126**	**127**	**128**	**129**	**130**
B	A	C	C	C	D	C	D	B	A
131	**132**	**133**	**134**	**135**	**136**	**137**	**138**	**139**	**140**
A	B	D	B	C	B	D	B	A	D
141	**142**	**143**	**144**	**145**	**146**	**147**	**148**	**149**	**150**
D	C	D	B	C	C	B	B	A	C

PAPER-II – MATHEMATICS

1	**2**	**3**	**4**	**5**	**6**	**7**	**8**	**9**	**10**
C	C	B	B	C	D	D	B	D	A
11	**12**	**13**	**14**	**15**	**16**	**17**	**18**	**19**	**20**
B	C	D	B	B	B	B	C	A	A
21	**22**	**23**	**24**	**25**	**26**	**27**	**28**	**29**	**30**
A	C	C	B	C	A	A	B	A	C

31	32	33	34	35	36	37	38	39	40
D	C	C	B	D	(*)	B	A	B	B
41	**42**	**43**	**44**	**45**	**46**	**47**	**48**	**49**	**50**
D	A	A	D	B	C	A	A	B	B
51	**52**	**53**	**54**	**55**	**56**	**57**	**58**	**59**	**60**
D	B	C	A	A	A	A	C	C	B
61	**62**	**63**	**64**	**65**	**66**	**67**	**68**	**69**	**70**
B	D	B	C	B	B	D	B	C	D
71	**72**	**73**	**74**	**75**	**76**	**77**	**78**	**79**	**80**
C	A	C	B	B	C	C	B	A	C
81	**82**	**83**	**84**	**85**	**86**	**87**	**88**	**89**	**90**
A	B	A	D	B	A	C	C	C	D
91	**92**	**93**	**94**	**95**	**96**	**97**	**98**	**99**	**100**
D	C	C	A	A	D	B	D	B	D
101	**102**	**103**	**104**	**105**	**106**	**107**	**108**	**109**	**110**
A	C	D	A	D	C	C	D	D	D
111	**112**	**113**	**114**	**115**	**116**	**117**	**118**	**119**	**120**
B	A	B	D	B	B	C	D	C	D

*Data Insufficient

EXPLANATORY ANSWERS

PAPER II- MATHEMATICS

1. $\because$ Roots are $m + n$ and $m - n$

Sum of roots $= m + n + m - n = 2m$

Product of roots $= (m + n)(m - n) = m^2 - n^2$

$x^2 -$ (Sum of roots)$x +$ Product of roots $= 0$

$x^2 - 2mx + m^2 - n^2 = 0.$

2. $\because$ α, β are the roots of $x^2 + px - q = 0$

$\therefore\ \alpha + \beta = -p$ and $\alpha \times \beta = -q$

γ, δ are roots of $x^2 - px + r = 0$

$\therefore\ \gamma + \delta = +p$ and $\gamma \times \delta = r$

$(\beta + \gamma)(\beta + \delta) = \beta^2 + \beta\delta + \beta\gamma + \delta\gamma$

$= \beta^2 + \beta(\delta + \gamma) + r = \beta^2 + p\beta + r$

$= q + r$

[$\because$ β is the root of $x^2 + px - q = 0\ \therefore\ \beta^2 + p\beta = q$]

3. $\because\quad 1^3 + 2^3 + 3^3 + \ldots\ldots + n^3 = \left(\frac{n(n+1)}{2}\right)^2$

$\therefore\ 1^3 + 2^3 + 3^3 + \ldots\ldots + 20^3 = \left(\frac{20.21}{2}\right)^2$

$= (10 \times 21)^2 = 44100$

$1^2 + 2^2 + 3^3 + \ldots\ldots + n^2 = \frac{1}{6}n(n+1)(2n+1)$

$\therefore\quad 1^2 + 2^2 + \ldots\ldots + 20^2 = \frac{1}{6}20.21.41 = 2870$

5. $1 - \frac{1}{2} + \frac{1}{4} - \frac{1}{8} + \ldots\ldots\ldots$

Sum of first 'n' terms of G.P.

$$S_n = 1 \cdot \frac{\left(1 - \left(-\frac{1}{2}\right)^8\right)}{1 - \left(-\frac{1}{2}\right)} = \frac{1 - \frac{1}{256}}{1 + \frac{1}{2}}$$

$$= \frac{\frac{255}{256}}{\frac{3}{2}} = \frac{85}{128}.$$

9. $(1011)_2 = 1 \times 2^3 + 0 \times 2^2 + 1 \times 2^1 + 1 \times 2^0$

$= 8 + 0 + 2 + 1$

$= (11)_{10} = 11.$

10. $(57.375)_{10} = (111001.011)_2$

$(57)_{10} = (111001)_2$

$(.375)_{10} = (.011)_2.$

11. $\frac{\log x}{\log 3} \cdot \frac{\log 2x}{\log x} \cdot \frac{\log y}{\log 2x} = 2$

$\therefore\ \log_3 y = 2$

$\Rightarrow\quad y = 9.$

12. $\because$ R = {(1, 2), (1, 3), (2, 1), (1, 1), (2, 2), (3, 3), (2, 3)}

Relation is reflexive

$\because$ it contains (1, 1), (2, 2), (3, 3),

symmetric

$\because$ (1, 2) (2, 1)

hence relation is symmetric, reflexive but not transitive.

13. $\sum_{n=1}^{13}\left(i^n + i^{n+1}\right) = (i + i^2) + (i^2 + i^3)\ ....\ (i^{13} + i^{14})$

$= i + 2\{i^2 + i^3 + ...+ i^{13}\} + i^{14}$

$= i + i^{14} = i - 1$

$\because (i^2 + i^3\ ....\ i^{13} = 0).$

16. Power set is set of all subsets

$\therefore$ no. of subsets will be 2^n.

17. A = {0, 1, 2}, B = {2, 3}, C = {3, 4}

$\therefore$ A ∪ B = {0, 1, 2, 3}

$\therefore$ no. of elements in (A ∪ B) × C will be 8.

18. $\frac{\sqrt{2}+i}{\sqrt{2}-i} = \frac{\sqrt{2}+i}{\sqrt{2}-i}\times\frac{\sqrt{2}+i}{\sqrt{2}+i} = \frac{\left(\sqrt{2}+i\right)^2}{2+1}$

$= \frac{2-1+2\sqrt{2}i}{3} = \frac{1+2\sqrt{2}i}{3} = \frac{1}{3}+\frac{2\sqrt{2}i}{3}$

$r\cos\theta = \frac{1}{3}$ ...(*i*)

$r\sin\theta = \frac{2\sqrt{2}}{3}$ ...(*ii*)

Squaring (*i*) and (*ii*) then adding

$r^2(\cos^2\theta + \sin^2\theta) = \frac{1}{9}+\frac{8}{9} = \frac{9}{9}$

$r^2(1) = 1 \Rightarrow r^2 = 1 \Rightarrow r = 1$

$\therefore$ Modulus of $\frac{\sqrt{2}+i}{\sqrt{2}-i} = 1.$

21. If each element of a row (column) of a determinant is multiplied by a constant *k*, then the value of the new determinant is k^3 times the value of the original determinant.

22. The inverse of a diagonal matrix is a diagonal matrix.

23. $A = \begin{bmatrix}3 & 4\\5 & 6\\7 & 8\end{bmatrix}, A^T = \begin{bmatrix}3 & 5 & 7\\4 & 6 & 8\end{bmatrix}, B = \begin{bmatrix}3 & 5 & 7\\4 & 6 & 8\end{bmatrix}$

$\therefore$ B is the transpose of A.

24.

$x + y + z = 10$

$x + y + 0 = 5$

$y + z + 0 = 5$

$5 + z = 10$

$\Rightarrow z = 5$

$y + z = 5$

$y = 5 - 5 = 0.$

25. If $A = \begin{bmatrix}2 & 0\\0 & 0\end{bmatrix}, B = \begin{bmatrix}0 & 0\\2 & 0\end{bmatrix}$ then, $AB = \begin{bmatrix}0 & 0\\0 & 0\end{bmatrix}$

Here A ≠ 0, B ≠ 0 but AB = 0.

26. $\begin{vmatrix}\alpha & 2 & 2\\-3 & 0 & 4\\1 & -1 & 1\end{vmatrix} = 0$

$\Rightarrow \alpha(0 + 4) - 2(-3 - 4) + 2(3 - 0) = 0$

$\Rightarrow 4\alpha + 14 + 6 = 0$

$\Rightarrow 4\alpha = -20$

$\alpha = -5.$

28. In a scalar matrix, $a_{ij} = \begin{cases}0 & \text{for } i \neq j\\k & \text{for } i = j\end{cases}$

Example $\begin{bmatrix}4 & 0 & 0\\0 & 4 & 0\\0 & 0 & 4\end{bmatrix}$

29. $\sin 15° = \sin(45° - 30°)$

$= \sin 45°\,.\cos 30° - \cos 45°\,.\sin 30°$

$= \frac{1}{\sqrt{2}}.\frac{\sqrt{3}}{2} - \frac{1}{\sqrt{2}}.\frac{1}{2}$

$= \frac{\sqrt{3}}{2\sqrt{2}} - \frac{1}{2\sqrt{2}} = \frac{\sqrt{3}-1}{2\sqrt{2}}.$

30. $4\sin^2\theta = 1 \Rightarrow \sin^2\theta = \frac{1}{4}$

$\Rightarrow \sin\theta = \pm\frac{1}{2}$

θ = 30°, 150°, 210°, 330°.

31. $\sin 18° \times \cos 36° = \frac{\sqrt{5}-1}{4}\times\frac{\sqrt{5}+1}{4}$

$= \frac{5-1}{16} = \frac{4}{16} = \frac{1}{4}.$

32. $\sin\left[\sin^{-1}\left(\frac{3}{5}\right)+\sin^{-1}\left(\frac{4}{5}\right)\right]$

$= \sin\left[\sin^{-1}\left(\frac{3}{5}\right)+\cos^{-1}\left(\frac{3}{5}\right)\right]$

$\left[\because \sin^{-1}x + \cos^{-1}x = \frac{\pi}{2}\right]$

$= \sin\left[\frac{\pi}{2}\right] = 1.$

33. $\because \sec\alpha = \frac{13}{5} = \frac{h}{b}$

$\therefore \sin\alpha = \frac{P}{h} = \frac{12}{13}$

But α is in 4th quadrant

$\therefore \sin\alpha = -\frac{12}{13}.$

34. $\tan(-585°) = \tan(-585° + 2 \times 360°)$

$= \tan(-585° + 720°)$

$= \tan 135° = -\tan 45° = -1.$

37. $l = 1$ cm

$r = 3$ cm

$\theta = \frac{l}{r} = \frac{1}{3}$ radian

π radian $= 180°$

$\frac{1}{3}$ radian $= \frac{180}{\pi} \times \frac{1}{3} = \frac{60°}{\pi}.$

38. $\sin A = \frac{2}{\sqrt{5}}$

$\therefore \cos A = \sqrt{1-\sin^2 A} = \sqrt{1-\frac{4}{5}} = \frac{1}{\sqrt{5}}$

$\cos B = \frac{1}{\sqrt{10}}$

$\therefore \sin B = \sqrt{1-\cos^2 B} = \frac{3}{\sqrt{10}}$

$\sin(A + B) = \sin A \times \cos B + \cos A \times \sin B$

$= \frac{2}{\sqrt{5}} \times \frac{1}{\sqrt{10}} + \frac{1}{\sqrt{5}} \times \frac{3}{\sqrt{10}}$

$= \frac{2}{5\sqrt{2}} + \frac{3}{5\sqrt{2}} = \frac{5}{5\sqrt{2}} = \frac{1}{\sqrt{2}}$

$\sin(A + B) = \sin\frac{\pi}{4}$

$A + B = 45°$ or $135°$.

39. AB is hill and CD is building

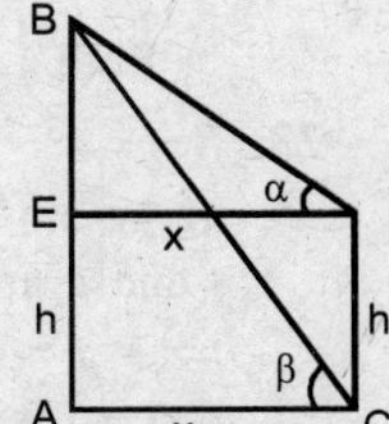

$\tan\beta = \frac{AB}{x}$

$\Rightarrow \cot\beta = \frac{x}{AB}$

$\tan\alpha = \frac{AB - h}{x}$

$\Rightarrow \cot\alpha = \frac{x}{AB - h}$

$\frac{\cot\beta}{\cot\alpha} = \frac{\frac{x}{AB}}{\frac{x}{AB-h}} = \frac{x}{AB} \times \frac{AB-h}{x} = \frac{AB-h}{AB}$

$AB\cot\alpha - h\cot\alpha = AB\cot\beta$

$AB(\cot\alpha - \cot\beta) = h\cot\alpha$

$\Rightarrow AB = \frac{h\cot\alpha}{\cot\alpha - \cot\beta}.$

40. AB is a lighthouse.

Let AC = x m.

$\tan 15° = \frac{70}{x}$

$\frac{\sqrt{3}-1}{\sqrt{3}+1} = \frac{70}{x}$

$x = \frac{70(\sqrt{3}+1)}{\sqrt{3}-1}$

$= \frac{70(\sqrt{3}+1)}{\sqrt{3}-1} \times \frac{\sqrt{3}+1}{\sqrt{3}+1} = \frac{70 \times 2(2+\sqrt{3})}{2}$

$\Rightarrow x = 70(2+\sqrt{3})$ m.

42. A (1, 0), C (x, y), B (0, –2)

$AC^2 = BC^2$

$\Rightarrow (x-1)^2 + (y-0)^2 = (x-0)^2 + (y+2)^2$

$\Rightarrow x^2 - 2x + 1 + y^2 = x^2 + y^2 + 4y + 4$

$-2x - 4y - 3 = 0 \Rightarrow 2x + 4y + 3 = 0.$

43. $AB = \sqrt{16+4} = 2\sqrt{5}$

$BC = \sqrt{100+25} = 5\sqrt{5}$

$CA = \sqrt{36+9} = 3\sqrt{5}$

BC = AB + AC

$\therefore$ points are collinear.

Area of $\Delta ABC = 0$.

44. $3x + 4y - 9 = 0$ ...(1)

$3x + 4y + \frac{28}{3} = 0$ ...(2)

distance between parallel lines $= \frac{\left|\frac{28}{3}+9\right|}{\sqrt{3^2+4^2}}$

$\Rightarrow \frac{55}{15} \Rightarrow \frac{11}{3}$ units.

45. $p = \sqrt{2^2+6^2} \Rightarrow \sqrt{40}$

$q = \sqrt{3^2+4^2} = 5$

$r = \sqrt{4^2+5^2} = \sqrt{41}$

$s = \sqrt{2^2+5^2} = \sqrt{29}.$

53. $\sqrt{(7-4)^2+(1-5)^2+(\lambda+3)^2} = 13$

$9 + 16 + \lambda^2 + 9 + 6\lambda = 169$

$\lambda^2 + 6\lambda - 135 = 0$

$\lambda = 9, -15.$

54. The coordinate of P will be $(r\cos\alpha, 0, r\sin\alpha)$

$\because$ y coordinate will be zero.

57. $\frac{x-2}{1} = \frac{y+1}{-2} = \frac{z+2}{1}$

Direction ratios are proportional to 1, –2, 1

$$\frac{x-1}{1} = \frac{y+\frac{3}{2}}{\frac{3}{2}} = \frac{z+5}{2}$$

Direction ratios are proportional to $1, \frac{3}{2}, 2$

$$\cos\theta = \frac{a_1a_2 + b_1b_2 + c_1c_2}{\sqrt{a_1^2+b_1^2+c_1^2}\sqrt{a_2^2+b_2^2+c_2^2}}$$

$$= \frac{(1)(1)+(-2)\left(\frac{3}{2}\right)+(1)(2)}{\sqrt{1^2+(-2)^2-1^2}\sqrt{1^2+\left(\frac{3}{2}\right)^2+(2)^2}}$$

$$\Rightarrow \quad \theta = \frac{\pi}{2}.$$

58. Let equation of plane parallel to

$3x + 4y - 5z = 0$ is

$3x + 4y - 5z + \lambda = 0$

$\because$ it passes through (1, 2, 3)

$\therefore$ $3(1) + 4(2) - 5(3) + \lambda = 0$

$\Rightarrow$ $3 + 8 - 15 + \lambda = 0$

$\Rightarrow$ $\lambda = 4$

$\therefore$ equation of plane is $3x + 4y - 5z + 4 = 0$.

59. $x = 3z + 4$

and $y = 2z - 3$

$\Rightarrow$ $\frac{x-4}{3} = z$

and $\frac{y+3}{2} = z$

$\Rightarrow$ $\frac{x-4}{3} = \frac{y+3}{2} = \frac{z}{1}$

$\therefore$ Direction ratios are proportional to <3, 2, 1>.

61. $$\lim_{x\to 0}\frac{\sqrt{1+x}-1}{x}\times\frac{\sqrt{1+x}+1}{\sqrt{1+x}+1}$$

$$= \lim_{x\to 0}\frac{1+x-1}{x\left(\sqrt{1+x}+1\right)} = \frac{x}{x\left(\sqrt{1+x}+1\right)} = \frac{1}{2}.$$

62. $$\lim_{x\to 0}\frac{2(1-\cos x)}{x^2} = \lim_{x\to 0}\frac{2\times 2\sin^2 x/2}{x^2}$$

$$= \lim_{x\to 0}\left(\frac{\sin x/2}{x/2}\right)^2 = 1.$$

64. $x^m + y^m = 1$

$$m\,x^{m-1} + m\,y^{m-1}\cdot\frac{dy}{dx} = 0$$

$$\frac{dy}{dx} = \left(-\frac{x}{y}\right)^{m-1}$$

$$\left(-\frac{x}{y}\right)^1 = \left(-\frac{x}{y}\right)^{m-1}$$

$\Rightarrow$ $m - 1 = 1$ $\therefore$ $m = 2$.

65. $f(x)$ is continuous every where.

66. $$\lim_{x\to 2}\frac{x-2}{(x+2)(x-2)} = \frac{1}{4}.$$

67. $\frac{dr}{dt} = 3$ cm/s

Area of circle $= \pi r^2$

$$\frac{dA}{dt} = 2\pi r\frac{dr}{dt} = 2\pi r(3)$$

$$= 6\pi r = 6\pi(10) = 60\pi \text{ cm}^2\text{/s}.$$

69. $y = \log_e(\sec x + \tan x)$

$$\therefore \quad \frac{dy}{dx} = \frac{1}{\sec x + \tan x}\cdot\frac{d}{dx}(\sec x + \tan x)$$

$$= \frac{1}{\sec x + \tan x}\times(\sec x\cdot\tan x + \sec^2 x)$$

$$= \frac{(\sec x + \tan x)\sec x}{(\sec x + \tan x)} = \sec x$$

$y = \log_e(\text{cosec } x - \cot x)$

$$\frac{dy}{dx} = \frac{1}{\text{cosec } x - \cot x}\cdot\frac{d}{dx}(\text{cosec } x - \cot x)$$

$$= \frac{1}{\text{cosec } x - \cot x}\times(-\text{cosec } x\cdot\cot x + \text{cosec}^2 x)$$

$$= \frac{\text{cosec } x(\text{cosec } x - \cot x)}{(\text{cosec } x - \cot x)} = \text{cosec } x$$

$\therefore$ Both 1 and 2 are correct.

72. $f(x) = x^3$

$g(y) = y^3$

f and g are identical functions

$\Rightarrow$ $f = g$

$f(x) = x$ is an identity function and identity function is always one-one-onto.

74. $$y = \log_e\left(e^{mx} + e^{-mx}\right)$$

$$\frac{dy}{dx} = \frac{1}{\left(e^{mx} + e^{-mx}\right)}\cdot\left(e^{mx}\cdot m + e^{-mx}(-m)\right)$$

$$= \frac{1}{\left(e^{mx} + e^{-mx}\right)}\left(e^{mx} - e^{-mx}\right)$$

$$\left(\frac{dy}{dx}\right)_{x=0} = 0.$$

75. 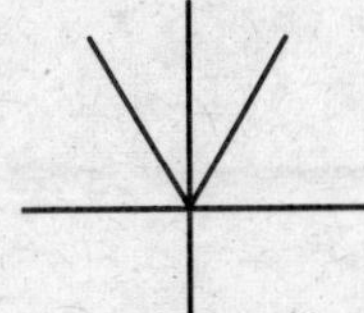

min. value of $|x|$ is 0.

76. $\int a^x e^x dx = \int \left(ae^x\right) dx = \dfrac{(ae)^x}{\log_e(ae)} + c.$

79. $I = \int_0^{\pi/2} \sin 2x \,.\, \ln(\cot x) dx$ equal to?

$\because \; f\left(\dfrac{\pi}{2} - x\right) = -f(x)$

$$\left\{\int_0^{2a} f(x)dx = 0, \text{ if } f(2a-x) = -f(x)\right\}$$

$\therefore \qquad I = 0.$

80. Area $= 2\int_0^{\pi} \sin x dx = 2\left[-\cos x\right]_0^{\pi}$

$= -2\,(-1 - 1) = 4.$

82. 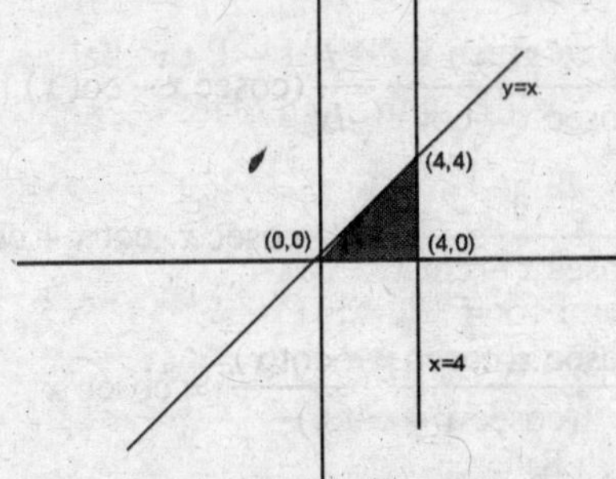

Area $= \dfrac{1}{2} \times 4 \times 4 = 8$ square unit.

84. $\dfrac{d^3y}{dx^3} + 2\left(\dfrac{d^2y}{dx^2}\right)^2 - \dfrac{dy}{dx} + y = 0$

degree = 1.

89. $x^2\, dy + y^2\, dx = 0$

$x^2\, dy = -y^2\, dx$

$\dfrac{dx}{x^2} + \dfrac{dy}{y^2} = 0$

on integrating, we get

$-\dfrac{1}{x} - \dfrac{1}{y} = C_1$

where C_1 is constant of integration

$\dfrac{x+y}{xy} = -C_1$

$x + y = -C_1(xy)$

$\Rightarrow \; \dfrac{1}{-C_1}(x+y) = xy$

$\Rightarrow \; C(x+y) = xy \qquad$ where $C = \dfrac{1}{-C_1}$

93. $\bar{a} \times \left(\bar{b} \times \bar{a}\right)$

$\Rightarrow \; (\bar{a}\cdot\bar{a})\bar{b} - (\bar{a}\cdot\bar{b})\bar{a}$

$\Rightarrow \; \lambda\bar{b} - \mu\bar{a}$ = coplanar with $\bar{a}$ & $\bar{b}$.

94. 1. $4\hat{i} \times 3\hat{i} = 0$

2. $\dfrac{4\hat{i}}{3\hat{i}} = \dfrac{4}{3}$

$\because$ division of vector not applicable

$\therefore$ only I[st] is correct.

95. $|(\lambda\hat{i} + \hat{j} - k) \times (3\hat{i} - 2\hat{j} + 4k) = 2\hat{i} - 11\hat{j} - 7\hat{k}$

$$\begin{vmatrix} \hat{i} & \hat{j} & k \\ \lambda & 1 & -1 \\ 3 & -2 & 4 \end{vmatrix} = 2\hat{i} - 11\hat{j} - 7\hat{k}$$

$\hat{i}(4-2) - \hat{j}(4\lambda + 3) + \hat{k}(-2\lambda - 3) = 2\hat{i} - 11\hat{j} - 7\hat{k}$

from above $4\lambda + 3 = 11$

$\therefore \; \lambda = 2.$

96. $\left|p(-3\hat{i} - 2\hat{j} + 13\hat{k})\right| = 1$

$\therefore \quad p\sqrt{9 + 4 + 169} = 1$

$\therefore \quad p = \dfrac{1}{\sqrt{182}}.$

97. Given vector is $2\hat{j} - \hat{k}$

hence, it lies in YZ plane only.

98. $\overrightarrow{BC} = \overrightarrow{AD}$

$\overrightarrow{AB} + \overrightarrow{BD} = \overrightarrow{AD}$

$\therefore \quad \overrightarrow{BD} = \overrightarrow{AD} - \overrightarrow{AB}$

$\Rightarrow \quad \bar{b} - \bar{a}.$

D C b A B a

99. We know that geometric mean of $a_1, a_2, a_3, \ldots\ldots\ldots a_n$ is $(a_1\, a_2\, a_3 \ldots\ldots\ldots a_n)^{1/n}$

$= 2^{\frac{n(n+1)}{2}\cdot\frac{1}{n}} = 2^{\frac{n+1}{2}}.$

101. Sum of first n odd natural numbers

$S = 1 + 3 + 5 + \ldots\ldots\ldots + (2n - 1)$

$S = \dfrac{n}{2}(1 + 2n - 1) = n^2$

mean $= \dfrac{\text{sum of observations}}{\text{number of observations}} = \dfrac{n^2}{n} = n$

102. Mean $= \dfrac{a+b+c+d+e}{5} = M$

New mean

$$= \frac{(a - M) + (b - M) + (c - M) + (d - M) + (e - M)}{5}$$

$$= \left(\frac{a + b + c + d + e}{5}\right) - M = M - M$$

New mean = 0.

103. Standard deviation = 30

algebraic sum with deviation = $\sum xi - h = 2$

$$\text{Mean} = \frac{\sum xi - h}{20} + h = \frac{2}{20} + 30$$

= 30 + 0.1 = 30.1.

106. Expenditure on transport = $\frac{10}{100} \times 9000$

= 90 × 10 = ₹ 900.

108. $\text{S.D.} = \sigma = \sqrt{\frac{1}{n}\Sigma(x - \bar{x})^2}$

$$= \sqrt{\frac{1}{n}[16 + 4 + 4 + 16]} = \sqrt{\frac{40}{5}} = \sqrt{8}$$

$$= 2\sqrt{2} = 2 \times 1.4 = 2.8.$$

109. Standard deviation is a measure of dispersion.

111. If P(E) = 1 then E is called certain event.

112. A leap year contain 366 days *i.e.,* 52 weeks and 2 days, clearly there are 52 Mondays in 52 weeks.

For the remaining two days, we may have any of the following two days.

(*i*) Monday and Tuesday
(*ii*) Tuesday and Wednesday
(*iii*) Wednesday and Thursday
(*iv*) Thursday and Friday
(*v*) Friday and Saturday
(*vi*) Saturday and Sunday
(*vii*) Sunday and Monday

Now for 53 Mondays, one of the two days must be Monday.

Hence, the required probability = $\frac{2}{7}$.

113. $P(A \cup B) = \frac{3}{4}$, $P(A \cap B) = \frac{1}{4}$

$$P(\bar{A}) = \frac{2}{3} \Rightarrow P(\bar{A}) = 1 - P(A)$$

$$\Rightarrow P(A) = 1 - P(\bar{A}) = 1 - \frac{2}{3} = \frac{1}{3}$$

$$P(A \cup B) = P(A) + P(B) - P(A \cap B)$$

$$\Rightarrow \frac{3}{4} = \frac{1}{3} + P(B) - \frac{1}{4}$$

$$\Rightarrow \frac{3}{4} + \frac{1}{4} - \frac{1}{3} = P(B)$$

$$\Rightarrow \frac{4}{4} - \frac{1}{3} = P(B)$$

$$\Rightarrow P(B) = 1 - \frac{1}{3} = \frac{2}{3}.$$

114. Sample space

= {*TTT, TTH, THT, HTT, THH, HTH, HHT, HHH*}

P (two head and one tail) = $\frac{3}{8}$.

116. $p(r) = {}^nC_r \cdot p^r \cdot q^{n-r}$

$n = 10$, $p = 2/3$, $q = 1/3$.

117. Since, ball should be of same colour

So, colour is green

Ways of selecting a green ball from I[st] urn = 1/2

Ways of selecting a green ball from IInd urn = 1/2

Now, probability that both balls should be of same colour = $\frac{1}{2 \times 2} = \frac{1}{4}$.

118. P (at least one green ball) = 1 – P (no ball is green)

= 1 – P (*i.e.,* ball is white and black)

$$= 1 - \frac{1}{2} \times \frac{1}{2} = 1 - \frac{1}{4} = \frac{3}{4}.$$

119. A : even numbers = {2, 4, 6}

B : number > 4 = {5, 6} A ∩ B = {6}

$$P(A \cap B) = \frac{1}{6}$$

$$P(A) = \frac{3}{6} = \frac{1}{2}$$

$$P(B) = \frac{2}{6} = \frac{1}{3}$$

$$P(A \cup B) = P(A) + P(B) - P(A \cap B)$$

$$= \frac{1}{2} + \frac{1}{3} - \frac{1}{6} = \frac{3 + 2 - 1}{6}$$

$$= \frac{4}{6} = \frac{2}{3}.$$

120. $P(A \cap B) = \frac{1}{6}$

A ∩ B) = {6}.

Previous Papers (Solved)

NATIONAL DEFENCE ACADEMY & NAVAL ACADEMY

NDA & NA – Entrance Exam, 2012 (I)

PAPER I : GENERAL ABILITY TEST

PART A : ENGLISH LANGUAGE

SPOTTING ERRORS

Directions (Qs. 1 to 10) :

(i) In this section, a number of sentences are given. The sentences are underlined in three separate parts and each one is labelled A, B and C. Read each sentence to find out whether there is an error in any underlined part. No sentence has more than one error. When you find an error in any one of the underlined parts A, B or C, indicate your response on the Answer Sheet at the appropriate space. You may feel that there is no error in a sentence. In that case, letter D will signify a 'No error' response.

(ii) Errors may be in grammar, word usage or idioms. There may be a word missing or there may be a word which should be removed.

*(iii) You are **not** required to correct the error. You are required **only** to indicate your response on the Answer Sheet.*

1. (A) Let us/(B) bring this discussion/(C) to close./(D) No error

2. (A) Each of them/(B) have a different version/(C) of the crime./(D) No error

3. (A) I and Gopal/(B) went to the meeting/(C) together./(D) No error

4. (A) Latin is not only hard to write/(B) but also/(C) to read./(D) No error

5. (A) In most villages/(B) the roads are rough;/(C) isn't it?/(D) No error

6. (A) Despite of continuing pain/(B) she worked at her temporary summer job/(C) most of the week./(D) No error

7. (A) As soon the film started/(B) I developed/(C) an irritating headache./(D) No error

8. (A) He applied for an employment/(B) in/(C) an office./(D) No error

9. (A) Though we drove fast, the train left,/(B) before we could reach/(C) the station./(D) No error

10. (A) One Indian virtue that has impressed me greatly/(B) and touched me deeply/(C) was the Indian people's freedom of rancour./(D) No error.

Directions (Qs. 11 to 20) : *Each of the following items consists of a sentence followed by four words or groups of words. Select the **synonym** of the word or words (occurring in the sentence in capital letters) as per the context.*

11. The convict's INGENUOUS explanation brought tears in every eye.

A. Candid B. Secret
C. Insincere D. Consistent

12. The ENORMITY of the population problem is irksome.

A. Intensity B. Vastness
C. Cruelty D. Fragility

13. EXAGGERATION of facts would always lead to confusion.

A. Simplification B. Negation
C. Emancipation D. Amplification

14. After his father's death, he became INSOLVENT.

A. Rich B. Poor
C. Bankrupt D. Nonchalant

15. He INDUCES human beings to want things they don't want.

A. Influences B. Dictates
C. Persuades D. Appreciates

16. His information is not AUTHENTIC.

A. Real B. Reliable
C. Believable D. Genuine

17. He is not CUT OUT to be a teacher.

A. Trained B. Suited
C. Selected D. Guided

18. The Chief Minister REPRIMANDED the officers for their methods of handling the public.

A. Adulated B. Scolded severely
C. Disapproved of D. Suspended

*Exam held on 15 April, 2012.

19. Sin is the sole calamity that a wise man should APPREHEND.
A. Give up B. Discourage
C. Comprehend D. Fear

20. We must be proud of our cultural HERITAGE.
A. Things we make for ourselves
B. Things we have lost
C. Things we have from the past
D. Things we do for others

Directions (Qs. 21 to 30) : *Each of the following items consists of a sentence followed by four words. Select the* ***antonym*** *of the word (occurring in the sentence in capital letters) as per the context.*

21. The COMPLAINANT was not supportive of providing all facts in the court.
A. Defendant B. Advocate
C. Indulgence D. Servant

22. Living in a SOLITARY place brings in some kind of satisfaction.
A. Limited B. Exotic
C. Healthy D. Populous

23. They spent a DISTURBED night after hearing the tragic news.
A. Restless B. Sleepless
C. Mournful D. Peaceful

24. We have CREATED a beautiful new house from out of the old ruin.
A. Destroyed B. Built
C. Constructed D. Planned

25. A large number of designer clothes are REVOLTING.
A. Inviting B. Beautiful
C. Fashionable D. Delightful

26. Though they are twins, they look very DIFFERENT.
A. Regular B. Same
C. Similar D. Uniform

27. RECESSION is a major cause of unemployment.
A. Education B. Inflation
C. Poverty D. Computerization

28. He finally CONCEDED that he was involved in smuggling.
A. Admitted B. Accepted
C. Denied D. Concealed

29. The accused emphatically DENIED the charge in the court.
A. Accepted B. Agreed
C. Asserted D. Affirmed

30. This cloth is a COARSE of touch.
A. Delicate B. Rough
C. Painful D. Harsh

REARRANGING PARTS OF A SENTENCE

Directions (Qs. 31 to 40) : In the following sentences, *parts of the sentences have been jumbled up. You are required to rearrange these parts which are labelled P, Q, R and S to produce the correct sentence. Choose the proper sequence and mark in your Answer Sheet accordingly.*

31. P : even when
Q : are well informed
R : people engaged in a conversation
S : their conversation may be dull
The correct sequence should be
A. Q – S – P – R B. P – R – Q – S
C. S – R – Q – P D. S – Q – R – P

32. P : a pressure cooker
Q : fits tightly on the top
R : consists of a very strong vessel
S : made of an aluminium alloy with a lid that
The correct sequence should be
A. P – R – S – Q B. R – S – P – Q
C. Q – S – P – R D. P – Q – S – R

33. P : is to convince your reader
Q : the aim of an argumentative essay
R : you have taken on a subject is right
S : that the position
The correct sequence should be
A. S – Q – P – R B. R – Q – S – P
C. P – Q – S – R D. Q – P – S – R

34. P : there is only one way
Q : the world can be
R : in which
S : made safe from the war
The correct sequence should be
A. R – Q – S – P B. P – R – Q – S
C. P – Q – S – R D. S – P – R – Q

35. P : the conspiracy
Q : got wind of
R : the Government
S : against the king's life
The correct sequence should be
A. P – Q – R – S B. R – Q – P – S
C. P – S – Q – R D. S – P – Q – R

36. P : to death penalty is that
Q : in preventing the crime
R : the important objection
S : it has not succeeded
The correct sequence should be
A. P – R – S – Q B. P – S – R – Q
C. R – P – S – Q D. Q – S – P – R

37. P : choice carefully
Q : when you want to use
R : make your
S : a graphic representation for your data
The correct sequence should be
A. Q – R – S – P B. S – R – Q – P
C. P – R – Q – S D. Q – S – R – P

38. P : he would like to see some changes
Q : but as a junior lecturer
R : he does not cut much ice
S : in the curriculum
The correct sequence should be
A. P – Q – R – S B. Q – P – S – R
C. Q – R – P – S D. P – S – Q – R

39. P : he simply starves
Q : even when there are good crops
R : but if the crops fail
S : he lives from hand to mouth
The correct sequence should be
A. S – Q – R – P B. P – Q – R – S
C. S – R – Q – P D. S – P – Q – R

40. P : providence had helped me
Q : to retain my true identity and
R : changed the course of my life
S : in the process
The correct sequence should be
A. P – S – Q – R B. P – Q – S – R
C. R – S – Q – P D. P – R – Q – S

COMPREHENSION

Directions (Qs. 41 to 50) : Read the following three passages and answer the items that follow each passage.

Passage-1

Even in the most primitive societies, the great majority of people satisfy a large part of their material needs by exchanging goods and services. Very few people indeed can make for themselves everything they need—all their food, their clothes, their housing, their tools. Ever since men started living in communities, they have been satisfying their needs by means of specialization and exchange; increasingly each individual has concentrated on what he can do best, and has produced more of the special goods or services in which he has concentrated, than he can consume himself. The surplus he has exchanged with other members of the community, acquiring, in exchange the things he needs that others have produced.

41. According to the passage, the great majority of people can satisfy their needs today by
A. providing things for themselves
B. exchanging goods and services
C. concentrating on what they can do best
D. individual specialization

42. Exchange of goods becomes possible only when
A. there is no specialization
B. goods are produced in surplus
C. primitive societies become modern
D. individuals make things for themselves

43. Specialization and exchange began when men started
A. big industries
B. concentrating on their work
C. producing things for individual use
D. living in communities

44. Exchange of goods and services becomes necessary because
A. man is a social being
B. reciprocity is the law of life
C. trade and commerce are means of progress
D. we cannot produce everything we need ourselves

Passage–2

What interests many people is the possibility of finding an Earth-like planet, and many science fiction stories have been woven around the possibility of there existing a planet somewhere in the universe which is an exact replica of the Earth. There are too many variable quantities for this to be a possibility worth considering. What is possible, if planetary systems are common as they seem to be, is the existence of planets where the conditions are similar to conditions on the Earth and to which our form of life could rapidly adapt. If life had gained a foothold on such a planet, it is possible that life closely paralleling our own planet could have developed.

What sort of conditions is necessary for life as we know it to develop? First of all of course a suitable planetary body essential. Given this, then two vital conditions must be satisfied. The temperature must be neither too hot nor too cold, since intense heat breaks down organic molecules and severe cold prevents activity from going on. Too much short-wave radiation also upsets living organisms. The other prerequisite is a suitable atmosphere sufficiently dense to give protection from radiation and meteorites and containing oxygen and water vapour in reasonable quantities.

45. This passage suggests that there
A. cannot be another planet like the Earth
B. are other planets like the Earth mentioned only in stories
C. may be other planets like the Earth in this universe
D. is a planet which is exactly like the Earth

46. The hypothesis about the possibility of planets parallel to the Earth gets its strength from the fact that
A. the scientists have discovered them
B. books have been written about them
C. the planetary system exists
D. many people have shown interest in it

47. The statement, "If life had gained a foothold on such a planet" means that
A. if there is life on the planet, it would be like ours
B. if we go there, we can develop it like this Earth
C. even if we try, we cannot go and live there
D. it is impossible for life to develop there

Passage–3

"The doctor's coming in a minute, Inspector", said Miss Smith.

"Yes, thank you for phoning, Miss Smith. It was very kind of you ..... the lady's name is Mrs. West, you say, ..."

"Yes, that's right."

"And what about Mr. West?"

"Doctor West, Inspector."

"Oh, I see .... Well, Doctor West, then. Do you know where he is?"

"Not exactly, Inspector. He never told Mrs. West where he was going. You see, they hated each other."

"What do you mean?"

"Well, Doctor West thought that Mrs. West was in love with another man, and everyone knows Doctor West went to see another woman."

48. The conversation appears to be taking place
A. in a street where an accident has just occurred
B. in a hotel where Mrs. West suddenly became ill
C. in Mrs. West's house where the police are enquiring into lady's murder
D. in Mrs. West's house where a theft has taken place the night before

49. The questions the Inspector asks are
A. inquisitive B. foolish
C. disturbing D. searching

50. "You see, they hated each other." "What do you mean?" The Inspector seems
A. to know Doctor West's secret
B. surprised to get the information
C. not to have understood Miss Smith
D. not impressed by Miss Smith's information

PART B : GENERAL KNOWLEDGE

Directions (Qs. 51 to 59) : The following nine (09) items consists of two statements, Statement I and Statement II. You are to examine these two statements carefully and select the answers to these items using the codes given below:

Code:
A. Both the statements are individually true and Statement II is the correct explanation of Statement I
B. Both the statements are individually true but Statement II is ***not*** the correct explanation of Statement I
C. Statement I is true but Statement II is false
D. Statement I is false but Statement II is true

51. Statement I : In the year 1946, the Council of the Muslim League accepted the Cabinet Mission Plan.
Statement II : The Muslim League proposed to join the Interim Government.

52. Statement I : The blue colour of copper sulphate crystal disappears when it is heated strongly.
Statement II : Due to heating, water of crystalization of crystal is lost.

53. Statement I : After cutting an apple or a banana, the colour of the cut surface becomes brown.
Statement II : Polyphenolic compounds present in fruits get oxidized in air and show colour.

54. Statement I : At high temperature, hyd-rogen can reduce PbO to elemental lead.
Statement II : Hydrogen has great affinity to oxygen.

55. Statement I : Conversion of blue copper sulphate to black cupric oxide on heating is a physical change.
Statement II : A change in which chemical composition does not change is called physical change.

56. Statement I : Water is a high boiling point liquid.
Statement II : Hydrogen bonding in water is responsible for high boiling point of water.

57. Statement I : Convex mirror is used as a driver mirror.
Statement II : Images formed by convex mirror are diminished in size.

58. Statement I : A thermos flask is made of double-walled glass bottles.
Statement II : Metals are good conductors while gas and air are poor conductors of heat.

59. Statement I : Bats can catch their prey in the darkness of night.
Statement II : Bats can produce and also detect ultrasound.

60. The Indian Standard Time (IST) is based on
A. 90° E meridian
B. 82½° E meridian
C. 75° E meridian
D. 0° meridian

61. Collision-coalescence process of precipitation is applicable to
A. those clouds which do not extend beyond the freezing level
B. those clouds which extend beyond the freezing level
C. all types of clouds
D. cumulonimbus clouds

62. Match List-I with List-II and select the correct answer using the codes given below the Lists:

List-I (Map showing ocean current)	*List-II (Name of ocean current*
(d)	1. Kuroshio
(c)	2. Humboldt
(b)	3. Benguela
(a)	4. Oyashio

Codes:

	(*a*)	(*b*)	(*c*)	(*d*)
A.	2	1	3	4
B.	4	3	1	2
C.	4	1	3	2
D.	2	3	1	4

63. Which one among the following nutrients is a structural component of the cell wall of plants?

A. Manganese B. Potassium
C. Phosphorus D. Calcium

64. Balanced diet should have approximately

A. 1/5 protein, 3/5 fat and 1/5 carbohydrate
B. 3/5 protein, 1/5 fat and 1/5 carbohydrate
C. 1/5 protein, 1/5 fat and 3/5 carbohydrate
D. 1/2 protein, 1/4 fat and 1/4 carbohydrate

65. Which one among the following statements is correct?

A. All arteries carry oxygenated blood
B. All veins carry oxygenated blood
C. Except the pulmonary artery, all other arteries carry oxygenated blood
D. Except the pulmonary vein, all other veins carry oxygenated blood

66. What are the cold-blooded animals?

A. Animals with blood without haemoglobin
B. Animals who are not ferocious
C. Animals whose body temperature remains constant
D. Animals whose body temperature varies according to the temperature of atmosphere

67. Sickle-cell anaemia is a disease caused due to the abnormality in

A. white blood cells
B. red blood cells
C. thrombocytes
D. blood plasma composition

68. Carbohydrates are stored in plants and animals in the form of

A. cellulose and glucose respectively
B. starch and glycogen respectively
C. starch and glucose respectively
D. cellulose and glycogen respectively

69. Which of the following statements regarding oxidation and reduction are correct?

1. In oxidation, loss of electron takes place whereas in reduction, gain of electron takes place.
2. In oxidation, gain of electron takes place whereas in reduction, loss of electron takes place.
3. Oxidizing agent decreases the oxidation number but reducing agent increases the oxidation number.
4. Oxidizing agent increases the oxidation number but reducing agent reduces the oxidation number.

Select the correct answer using the code given below:

Code:

A. 1 and 3 B. 2 and 4
C. 2 and 3 D. 1 and 4

70. Which one among the following is correct regarding ^{20}Ne, $^{23}Na^{+}$, $^{19}F^{-}$, and $^{24}Mg^{2+}$?

A. They are isomers of each other
B. They are isotopes of each other
C. They are isoelectronic with each other
D. All of the above

71. Which of the following pairs is/are correctly matched?

1. Isotopes : Atoms with same atomic number but different atomic mass
2. Isobars : Atoms with same number of neutrons but different atomic number
3. Isotones : Atoms with same mass number but different atomic number

Select the correct answer using the code given below:

Code:

A. 1, 2 and 3 B. 1 only
C. 1 and 2 only D. 2 only

72. Sometimes, indigestion is caused by the secretion of too much hydrochloric acid in the stomach. To ease the pain caused, a tablet can be taken that reacts to reduce the amount of acid present. Which one among the following would be ***inappropriate*** for a manufacturer to include as a major reactant in the tablet?

A. $CaCO_3$ B. $MgCO_3$
C. NaOH D. $Mg(OH)_2$

73. Muhammad bin Tughlaq's experiment of introducing token currency could not succeed on account of

A. rejection of token coins by foreign merchants
B. shortage of copper for minting token coins
C. large-scale minting of spurious coins
D. poor quality of token currency

74. The Parliament can legislate on the subjects in the State List if the

A. President issues an order authorizing it to do so
B. Supreme Court gives authority to the Parliament in this regard
C. Rajya Sabha passes a resolution by two-thirds of its members present and voting, declaring it expedient to legislate on a State matter in the national interest
D. Prime Minister issues a special order

75. The writ of certiorari is issued by a superior court to
A. an inferior court to stop further proceedings in a particular case
B. an inferior court to transfer the record of proceedings in a case for review
C. an officer to show his/her right to hold a particular office
D. a public authority to produce a person detained by it before the court within 24 hours

76. Schemes run under the National Rural Employment Guarantee Act are sponsored
A. by the Central Government alone
B. partly by the Central Government and partly by the State Government
C. by Centre, State and Panchayat bodies together
D. on public-private partnership basis

77. The World Bank was created immediately after the Second World War. Its activities are focused on the developing countries. Which among the following are the activities of the Bank?
1. Human development
2. Agriculture and rural development
3. Environmental protection and governance
4. Loans and grants to the member countries

Select the correct answer using the code given below:

Code:
A. 1, 2 and 3 only   B. 3 and 4 only
C. 2 and 4 only   D. 1, 2, 3 and 4

78. A refracting telescope consists of
A. one concave mirror and one convex lens
B. two convex lenses of equal focal length
C. two concave mirrors of different focal lengths
D. two convex lenses of unequal focal lengths

79. The nucleus of a singly ionized carbon atom contains
A. 6 protons and 6 neutrons
B. 5 protons and 6 nutrons
C. 6 protons, 6 neutrons and 6 electrons
D. 12 protons, 6 neutrons and 6 electrons

80. Two similarly charged bodies are kept 5 cm apart in air. If the second body is shifted away from the first by another 5 cm, their force of repulsion will be
A. doubled
B. halved
C. quadrupled
D. reduced to one-fourth

81. A glass of water does not turn into ice as it reaches 0°C. It is because
A. water does not solidify at 0°C
B. a certain amount of heat must be supplied to the glass of water so as to solidify
C. a certain amount of heat must be taken out from the glass of water so as to solidify
D. water solidifies at 0 K only

82. The main power supply in India is at 220 V, whereas that in the US is at 110 V. Which one among the following statements in this regard is correct?
A. 110 V is safer but more expensive to maintain
B. 110 V is safer and cheaper to maintain
C. 110 V leads to lower power loss
D. 110 V works better at higher latitudes

83. The equatorial rain forest is also known as
A. Savanna   B. Campos
C. Selva   D. Lanose

84. Match List-I with List-II and select the correct answer using the code given below the Lists:

List-I (Port)	***List-II (Special feature)***
(*a*) Kandla	1. Deepest land-locked protected port
(*b*) Kochi	2. Located at mouth of lagoon
(*c*) Vishakhapatnam	3. Tidal port
(*d*) Kolkata	4. Inland riverine port

Code:

	(*a*)	(*b*)	(*c*)	(*d*)
A.	3	1	2	4
B.	3	2	1	4
C.	4	1	2	3
D.	4	2	1	3

85. The Earth's surface receives maximum energy at 12 noon but the maximum temperature never occurs at 12 noon. State which of the following reasons are correct.
1. Transformation of solar energy into heat requires some time.
2. The loss of energy through long-wave radiations from the Earth's surface exceeds the energy received from the Sun at 4:00 p.m.
3. Energy received by the Earth from solar radiations continues to exceed the energy lost by outgoing long-wave radiations from the Earth's surface up to 4:00 pm.

Select the correct answer using the code given below:

Code:
A. 1 and 2 only   B. 2 and 3 only
C. 1 and 3 only   D. 1, 2 and 3

86. Certain parts of a plant can be bent easily without breaking. This flexibility in certain parts, like leaf and stem, can be attributed to the abundance of
A. parenchyma   B. collenchyma
C. sclerenchyma   D. xylem and phloem

87. Which of the following is ***not*** a micronutrient for a plant?
A. Iron   B. Magnesium
C. Molybdenum   D. Manganese

88. Which of the following statements is/are correct?
1. Ligaments are highly flexible.
2. Ligaments connect muscles and bones.
3. Ligaments contain very little matrix.

Select the correct answer using the code given below:

Code:

A. 1, 2 and 3 B. 1 and 3 only
C. 2 and 3 only D. 1 only

89. Cell membrane is selectively permeable because

A. it is made up of selected organic molecules
B. it does not allow transport of some substances from region of higher concentration to the region of lower concentration
C. the movement of organic molecules occurs only at specific concentration
D. it allows the movement of certain molecules in and out of the cell while the movement of other molecules is prevented

90. The following equation is an example of a redox reaction, in which Cl_2 is the oxidising agent and $FeBr_3$ is the reducing agent:

$$2FeBr_3(aq) + 3Cl_2(g) = 2FeCl_3(aq) + 3Br_2(l)$$

Which one among the following statements is ***incorrect*** for this redox reaction?

A. Oxidizing agents are themselves reduced
B. Reducing agents gain or appear to gain electrons
C. Reducing agents are themselves oxidized
D. Oxidizing agents oxidize other substances.

91. Which one among the following nitrogen compounds has the least percentage of nitrogen by mass?

A. $(NH_4)_3PO_4$ B. NH_3
C. NH_4OH D. NH_4NO_3

92. Which one among the following is the correct order of amount of lime (CaO), silica (SiO_2), alumina (Al_2O_3) and ferric oxide (Fe_2O_3) in Portland cement?

A. $CaO > SiO_2 > Al_2O_3 > Fe_2O_3$
B. $SiO_2 > CaO > Fe_2O_3 > Al_2O_3$
C. $Al_2O_3 > SiO_2 > CaO > Fe_2O_3$
D. $Fe_2O_3 > Al_2O_3 > SiO_2 > CaO$

93. Which one among the following transitions of electron of hydrogen atom emits radiation of the shortest wavelength?

A. $n = 2$ to $n = 1$ B. $n = 3$ to $n = 2$
C. $n = 4$ to $n = 3$ D. $n = 5$ to $n = 4$

94. Which one among the following is the most appropriate statement with respect to the atomic weight of an element?

A. The atomic weight of an element is the sum total of the number of protons and neutrons present in the atom of the element
B. Unlike mass number, the atomic weight of an element can be a fraction
C. The atomic weight of an element is a whole number
D. The atomic weight of all the atoms in an element is the same

95. During the discussion on the Demands for Grants, motions can be moved to reduce the amount of a demand. Such a motion is called a 'cut-motion'. Which of the following categories are classified as 'cut-motion'?

1. Disapproval of policy cut
2. Economy cut
3. Token cut

Select the correct answer using the code given below:

Code:

A. 1 and 2 only B. 2 and 3 only
C. 1, 2 and 3 D. 1 and 3 only

96. Which of the statements given below is/are correct?

1. The Speaker immediately vacates his/her office whenever the State Legislative Assembly is dissolved.
2. No Member of a State Legislative Assembly shall be liable to any proceeding in any court in respect of anything said or any vote given by him/her in the legislature.

Select the correct answer using the code given below:

Code:

A. 1 only B. 2 only
C. Both 1 and 2 D. Neither 1 nor 2

97. Consider the following statements about Cripps Proposals of 1942:

1. Provision was to be made for participation of Indian States in the Constitution-making body.
2. British Government undertook to accept and implement the Constitution.
3. All provinces of British India were to give an undertaking about the acceptance of the Constitution.
4. In the ongoing World War, no resources of British India would be used.

Which of the statements given above is/are correct?

Code:

A. 1 and 2 only B. 2 only
C. 1, 2 and 4 D. 1, 3 and 4

98. Which one among the following was ***not*** one of the causes of the Third Anglo-Maratha War?

A. The Maratha Chiefs, particularly the Peshwa desired to throw off the restrictions imposed on them by the treaties with the English
B. The determination of the English to give a finishing blow to the Maratha power
C. The Pindari designs to seek support from the Marathas to drive the English away from India
D. The attack of Peshwa Baji Rao on the residency at Khirki

99. William Bentinck attempted to reform Hindu society by suppressing/abolishing social evils. Which one among the following was ***not*** included in them?

A. Sati B. Infanticide
C. Thugi D. Slavery

100. *Karam* is a festival celebrated to worship *Karam Devta*, the God of power. Which one among the following tribal communities in India traditionally celebrates this festival?

A. Santhals B. Karbi
C. Meenas D. Bhils

101. The terra-cotta plough of the Harappan civilization was found at

A. Mohenjodaro B. Banawali
C. Kalibangan D. Lothal

102. Which one among the following works of Mahatma Gandhi provides a critique of modern machine-oriented civilization?

A. *The Story of My Experiments with Truth*
B. *Hind Swaraj*
C. *Constructive Programme*
D. *Anasakti Yoga* (Commentary on 'Gita')

103. An object is in uniform circular motion on a plane. Suppose that you measure its displacement from the centre along one direction, say, along the *x*-axis. Which one among the following graphs could represent this displacement (*x*)?

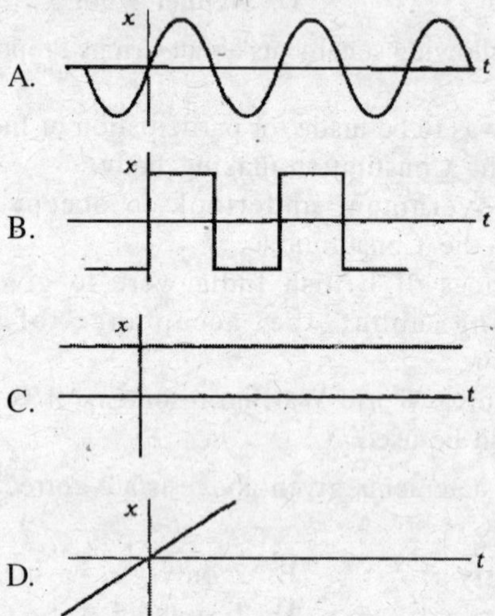

104. The penetrating power of X-rays can be increased by

A. increasing the current in the filament
B. decreasing the potential difference between the cathode and the anode
C. decreasing the current in the filament
D. increasing the potential difference between the cathode and the anode

105.

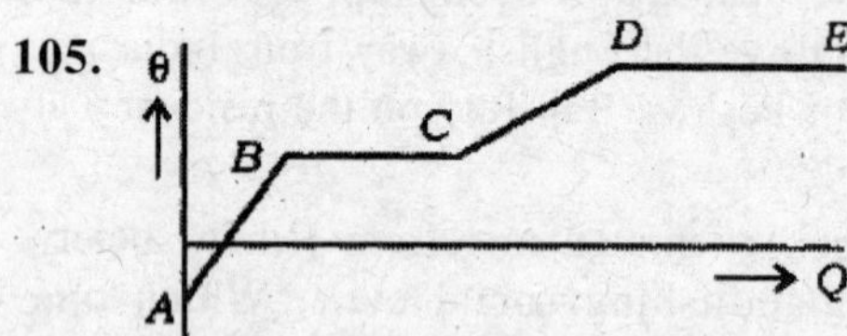

The graph given above indicates change in temperature (θ) when heat (*Q*) was given to a substance. Which among the following parts of the graph correctly depict the latent heat of the substance?

A. *AB* and *BC* B. *BC* and *DE*
C. *CD* and *DE* D. *DE* and *AB*

106. When a solid object is immersed in water, there is a loss in its weight. This loss is

A. equal to the weight of the water displaced
B. less than the weight of the water displaced
C. greater than the weight of the water displaced
D. not related to the weight of the water displaced

107. Body *A* of mass 2 kg and another body *B* of mass 4 kg and of same material are kept in the same sunshine for some interval of time. If the rise in temperature is equal for both the bodies, then which one among the following in this regard is correct?

A. Heat absorbed by *B* is double because its mass is double
B. Heat absorbed by *A* is double because its mass is half
C. Heat absorbed by both *A* and *B* is equal because the quantity of heat absorbed does not depend upon mass
D. Heat absorbed by *B* is four times than the heat absorbed by *A* because the quantity of heat absorbed is proportional to square of the mass

108. For a steel boat floating on a lake, the weight of the water displaced by the boat is

A. less than the weight of the boat
B. more than the weight of the boat
C. equal to the weight of the part of the boat which is below the water level of the lake
D. equal to the weight of the boat

109. Consider the following coal mines of India:

1. Bokaro 2. Adilabad
3. Raniganj 4. Bishrampur

Select the correct sequence of the above from east to west.

A. 1–3–4–2 B. 3–1–4–2
C. 3–1–2–4 D. 1–3–2–4

110. Which one among the following agricultural crops/groups of crops may be grown in abundant in lowlands and river deltas of fertile alluvial soil where there is high summer temperature and rainfall varies from 180 cm to 250 cm?

A. Wheat and sugarcane
B. Cotton
C. Maize and coarse crops
D. Rice, jute and tea

111. Arrange the following tropical forest groups in the correct order of sequence based on area covered in India beginning from the largest covered area:

1. Moist deciduous 2. Dry deciduous
3. Wet evergreen 4. Semi-evergreen

Select the correct answer using the code given below:

Code:

A. 1–2–3–4 B. 3–4–2–1
C. 1–3–2–4 D. 4–3–2–1

112. Which one among the following is the major reason for low agricultural productivity in dry regions of India?
A. Constraints of financial resources
B. Rural indebtedness
C. Dependence on erratic monsoon
D. Small size of landholdings

113. Which one among the following groups is referred to as types of precipitation?
A. Fog, Dew and Rain B. Air, Water and Soil
C. Fog, Water and Rain D. Dew, Soil and Rain

114. Which one among the following is the most important source of fish catch in India?
A. Deep-sea fisheries
B. Coastal fisheries
C. Inland natural fisheries
D. Inland cultural fisheries

115. In which one among the following areas of South-East Asia, there is largest concentration of peasant population?
A. Areas of intensive shifting cultivation
B. Highland areas where the climate is cooler and healthier
C. Cleared lowlands in forest areas
D. Areas where the grain farming is practised

116. The largest number of temperate cyclones originate mostly over the
A. Indian Ocean B. North Atlantic Ocean
C. North Pacific Ocean D. Arctic Ocean

117. Which one among the following statements is *not* correct?
A. More than 50% of world's animal species are found in tropical rain forest
B. One-third of land surface is arid or semi-arid
C. Floating plants (phytoplankton) in the ocean produce over half the world's oxygen
D. World's important deserts are located across the equator

118. Which one among the following statements regarding Chinook winds is *not* correct?
A. They rise from the Pacific Ocean
B. After crossing the Rockies, they descend to the east of the mountains
C. They bring rainfall in the Prairies
D. These winds are beneficial to wheat cultivation

119. Consider the following statements relating to planning in India:
1. In the year 1938, the National Planning Committee was set up in India under the chairmanship of Jawaharlal Nehru.
2. The Bombay Plan was prepared by the Indian industrialists.
3. Acharya Kripalani prepared the Gandhian Plan.

Which of the statements given above is/are correct?
A. 1 only B. 2 only
C. 1 and 2 only D. 1, 2 and 3

120. Which one among the following statements regarding the Government of India Act, 1935 is ***not*** correct?
A. Provincial Autonomy came into existence
B. Bicameral legislatures were provided in six provinces
C. The principles of communal electorates and weightages were further extended
D. The States were compelled to enter the Federation

121. Consider the following statements relating to Jain literature:
1. The sacred books of the Jainas are known as *Siddhanta* or *Agama.*
2. The language of the earliest Jain texts is eastern dialect of Pali known as *Ardha Magadhi.*

Which of the statements given above is/are correct?
A. 1 only B. 2 only
C. Both 1 and 2 D. Neither 1 nor 2

122. Which one among the following was a newspaper founded and edited by Raja Rammohan Roy?
A. *The Calcutta Gazette*
B. *Mirat-ul Akhbar*
C. *Harijan*
D. *The Bharat Mihir*

123. Which one among the following is ***not*** produced by sound waves in air?
A. Polarization B. Diffraction
C. Reflection D. Refraction

124. A body attached to a spring balance weighs 10 kg on the Earth. The body attached to the same spring balance is taken to a planet where gravity is half that of the Earth. The balance will read
A. 20 kg B. 10 kg
C. 5 kg D. 2.5 kg

125. The resistance of a wire is 10 Ω. If it is stretched ten times, the resistance will be
A. 1 W B. 10 W
C. 100 W D. 1000 W

126. If the focal length of the biconvex lens is 25 cm, then the power of the lens will be
A. +4 dioptre B. –4 dioptre
C. +0.04 dioptre D. –0.04 dioptre

127. A compound slab is composed of two paralled layers of different materials, with thickness 3cm and 2 cm. The temperatures of the outer faces of the compound slab are maintained at 100°C and 0°C. If conductivities are 0.36 and 0.16 then the temperature of the Junction is:
A. 40°C B. 60°C
C. 100°C D. 50°C

128. The torque on a rectangular coil placed in a uniform magnetic field is large when the
A. number of turns is large
B. number of turns is less
C. plane of the coil is perpendicular to the magnetic field
D. area of the coil is small

129. Two metallic wires *A* and *B* are of same material and have equal length. If the cross-sectional area of *B* is double that of *A*, then which one among the following is the electrical resistance of *B*?
A. Twice that of *A* B. 4 times that of *A*
C. $\frac{1}{4}$ that of *A* D. $\frac{1}{2}$ that of *A*

130. Two thin lenses of focal lengths 20 cm and 25cm are placed in contact. The effection power of the combination is:
A. 45 dioptres B. 9 dioptres
C. $\frac{1}{9}$ dioptres D. 6 dioptres

131. The Damuda series of Gondwana system has three stages, namely, Raniganj, Barren Rocks and Barakar. The middle stage is called Barren because
A. it consists of coal and not iron
B. it consists of iron and not coal
C. it consists of neither coal nor iron
D. it is a sedimentary layer consisting of shale and clay

132. The cyclonic storm occurring over the Caribbean Sea is known as
A. Typhoon B. Willy-Willy
C. Hurricane D. Cyclone

133. Match List-I with List-II and select the correct answer using the code given below the Lists:

***List-I* (Mountain pass)**	***List-II* (State)**
(*a*) Zoji La	1. Himachal Pradesh
(*b*) Lipulekh	2. Sikkim
(*c*) Shipki La	3. Uttarakhand
(*d*) Nathu La	4. Jammu and Kashmir

Code:

	(*a*)	(*b*)	(*c*)	(*d*)
A.	2	1	3	4
B.	2	3	1	4
C.	4	1	3	2
D.	4	3	1	2

134. Where do you find the Isle of Youth?
A. Near Cuba B. Near Bahamas
C. Near Jamaica D. Near Saint Lucia

135. For which among the following house appliances, magnet is an essential part?
A. Calling bell B. Fan
C. Washing machine D. All of the above

136. Consider the following statements:
Hypermetropia is a defect of vision in which
1. a person cannot see the distant objects clearly
2. a person cannot see the near objects clearly
3. the near point of the eye gets shifted away from the normal position
4. the far point of the eye gets shifted towards the eye

Which of the statements given above are correct?
A. 1 and 3 B. 2 and 4
C. 1 and 4 D. 2 and 3

137. To obtain the powerful parallel beams of light from a vehicle's headlight, one must use
A. front surface silvered plane mirror
B. back surface silvered plane mirror
C. concave mirror
D. convex mirror

138. Which one among the following is the major constituent of soda lime glass?
A. Sodium oxide B. Calcium oxide
C. Calcium carbonate D. Silica

139. Which among the following about Mahatma Gandhi's Non-Cooperation Movement are correct?
1. Refusal to attend Government Durbars and official functions
2. Participation in elections
3. Participation in rallies for the boycott of foreign goods
4. Surrender of titles

Select the correct answer using the code given below:

Code:
A. 1, 2 and 3 B. 1, 3 and 4
C. 2, 3 and 4 D. 1 and 4 only

140. Gandhiji's call for breaking Salt Laws was in response to the
A. Non-Cooperation Movement
B. Civil Disobedience Movement
C. Khilafat Movement
D. Quit India Movement

141. The Suez Canal, the Strait of Hormuz and the Strait of Gibraltar are important because they
A. prevent attacks on bordering nations
B. prohibit the movement of ships carrying nuclear weapons
C. unite Russian access to warm water points
D. control access to vital trade routes

142. Which one among the following is the largest exporter of small arms in the world?
A. Russia B. The United States
C. China D. France

143. Which among the following islands in the South China Sea are the source of conflict between several countries?

A. Marshall Islands
B. Solomon Islands
C. Kuril Islands
D. Spratly Islands

144. In recent past, the Indian Navy has deployed its fleet ships to patrol near the Gulf of Aden to
A. show off its naval might to neighbouring countries
B. indicate dominant intentions in the Indian Ocean region
C. carry out anti-piracy role
D. exercise operational readiness in international water

145. The only operational Naval Base exclusively controlled by the Indian Navy is located at
A. Puducherry
B. Okha
C. Karwar
D. Kakinada

146. Who among the following led India to their first overseas test victory in cricket?
A. C.K. Nayadu
B. M.A.K. Pataudi
C. Sunil Gavaskar
D. Bishen Singh Bedi

147. Who among the following was conferred the highest Bangladesh award—the *Bangladesh Swadhinata Sammanona* in the year 2011?
A. Indira Gandhi
B. Rajiv Gandhi
C. Jyoti Basu
D. Satyajit Ray

148. *Dhanush*, a missile inducted into the Indian Navy
A. is a customized and naval variant of *Prithvi* missile
B. has a range of 700 km
C. can be launched from an aircraft
D. cannot carry nuclear warheads

149. India commissioned its first indigenously built stealth warship INS Shivalik and inducted into the Indian Navy recently, thus joining the elite group of countries capable of constructing such vessels. Which among the following other countries are in the elite group?
1. Russia
2. The United States
3. Germany
4. The United Kingdom

Select the correct answer using the code given below:

Code:
A. 1, 2 and 3
B. 1, 2 and 4
C. 2 and 4 only
D. 1 and 3 only

150. Which of the following statements is/are correct?
1. The Indian Army is organized into five Regional Commands.
2. The Headquarters of Northern Command is located at Lucknow.

Select the correct answer using the code given below:

Code:
A. 1 only
B. 2 only
C. Both 1 and 2
D. Neither 1 nor 2

PAPER II : MATHEMATICS

1. What is the sum of the squares of the roots of the equation $x^2 + 2x - 143 = 0$?
A. 170
B. 180
C. 190
D. 290

2. Let U = $\{x \in N : 1 \le x \le 10\}$ be the universal set, N being the set of natural numbers. If A = {1, 2, 3, 4} and B = {2, 3, 6, 10} then what is the complement of (A – B)?
A. {6, 10}
B. {1, 4}
C. {2, 3, 5, 6, 7, 8, 9, 10}
D. {5, 6, 7, 8, 9, 10}

3. The solution of the simultaneous linear equations $2x + y = 6$ and $3y = 8 + 4x$ will also be satisfied by which one of the following linear equations?
A. $x + y = 5$
B. $2x + y = 9$
C. $2x - 3y = 10$
D. $2x + 3y = 6$

4. Let A = {x : x is a square of a natural number and x is less than 100} and B is a set of even natural numbers. What is the cardinality of $A \cap B$?
A. 4
B. 5
C. 9
D. None of the above

5. If $A = \begin{pmatrix} 1 & 2 \\ 2 & 3 \end{pmatrix}$ and $B = \begin{pmatrix} 1 & 0 \\ 1 & 0 \end{pmatrix}$ then what is determinant of AB?
A. 0
B. 1
C. 10
D. 20

6. What is $\begin{vmatrix} -a^2 & ab & ac \\ ab & -b^2 & bc \\ ac & bc & -c^2 \end{vmatrix}$ equal to?
A. $4abc$
B. $4a^2bc$
C. $4a^2b^2c^2$
D. $-4a^2b^2c^2$

7. What is the distance between the lines $3x + 4y = 9$ and $6x + 8y = 18$?
A. 0
B. 3 units
C. 9 units
D. 18 units

8. The number 292 in decimal system is expressed in binary system by
A. 100001010
B. 100010001
C. 100100100
D. 101010000

9. What is the arithmetic mean of first 16 natural numbers with weights being the number itself?
A. 17/2
B. 33/2
C. 11
D. 187/2

10. What is the mode for the data 20, 20, 20, 21, 21, 21 21, 22, 22, 22, 22, 22, 22, 22, 23, 23, 23, 23, 23, 24, 24, 25?

A. 7 B. 21
C. 22 D. 25

11. A and B are two matrices such that AB = A and BA = B then what is B^2 equal to?

A. B B. A
C. I D. –I
where I is the identity matrix

12. The geometric mean and harmonic mean of two non-negative observations are 10 and 8 respectively. Then what is the arithmetic mean of the observations equal to?

A. 4 B. 9
C. 12.5 D. 25

13. Consider the following statements:

1. A continuous variable can take all values in an interval.
2. A random variable which takes a finite number of values is necessarily discrete.
3. Construction of a frequency distribution is based on data which are discrete.

Which of the above statements are correct?

A. 1 and 2 only B. 2 and 3 only
C. 1 and 3 only D. 1, 2 and 3

14. What is the nth term of the sequence 1, 5, 9, 13, 17, ... ?

A. $2n - 1$ B. $2n + 1$
C. $4n - 3$ D. None of the above

15. What does the series

$1+3^{-\frac{1}{2}}+3+\frac{1}{3\sqrt{3}}+...$ represent?

A. AP B. GP
C. HP D. None of the above

16. If p, q, r are in AP as well as GP, then which one of the following is correct?

A. $p = q \neq r$ B. $p \neq q \neq r$
C. $p \neq q = r$ D. $p = q = r$

17. What is the perimeter of the triangle with vertices A(–4, 2), B(0, –1) and C(3, 3)?

A. $7+3\sqrt{2}$ B. $10+5\sqrt{2}$
C. $11+6\sqrt{2}$ D. $5+\sqrt{2}$

18. If the mid point between the points $(a + b, a - b)$ and $(-a, b)$ lies on the line $ax + by = k$, what is k equal to?

A. a/b B. $a + b$
C. ab D. $a - b$

19. The acute angle which the perpendicular from origin on the line $7x - 3y = 4$ makes with the x-axis is

A. zero B. positive but not $\pi/4$
C. negative D. $\pi/4$

20. Out of 500 first year students, 260 passed in the first semester and 210 passed in the second semester. If 170 did not pass in either semester, how many passed in both semesters?

A. 80 B. 40
C. 70 D. 140

21. If a matrix A has inverses B and C, then which one of the following is correct?

A. B may not be equal to C
B. B should be equal to C
C. B and C should be unit matrices
D. None of the above

22. Three dice are thrown. What is the probability that the same number will appear on each of them?

A. 1/6 B. 1/18
C. 1/24 D. 1/36

For the next ***Two (2)*** *questions that follow:*

The equation formed by multiplying each root of $ax^2 + bx + c = 0$ by 2 is $x^2 + 36x + 24 = 0$.

23. What is $b : c$ equal to?

A. 3 : 1 B. 1 : 2
C. 1 : 3 D. 3 : 2

24. Which one of the following is correct?

A. $bc = a^2$ B. $bc = 36\ a^2$
C. $bc = 72\ a^2$ D. $bc = 108\ a^2$

For the next ***Three (3)*** *questions that follow:*

Let sin (A + B) = 1 and sin (A – B) = 1/2, where A, B $\in \left[0, \frac{\pi}{2}\right]$

25. What is the value of A?

A. $\frac{\pi}{6}$ B. $\frac{\pi}{3}$
C. $\frac{\pi}{4}$ D. $\frac{\pi}{8}$

26. What is tan (A + 2B). tan (2A + B) equal to?

A. –1 B. 0
C. 1 D. 2

27. What is $\sin^2 A - \sin^2 B$ equal to?

A. 0 B. 1/2
C. 1 D. 2

28. If the latus rectum of an ellipse is equal to half of the minor axis, then what is its eccentricity?

A. $2/\sqrt{3}$ B. $1/\sqrt{3}$
C. $\sqrt{3}/2$ D. $1/\sqrt{2}$

29. What is the probability that a leap year selected at random contains 53 Mondays?

A. 1/7 B. 2/7
C. 7/366 D. 26/183

30. What is the decimal number representation of the binary number $(11101.001)_2$?

A. 30.125 B. 29.025
C. 29.125 D. 28.025

31. What is the equation of line passing through (0, 1) and making an angle with the *y*-axis equal to the inclination of the line $x - y = 4$ with *x*-axis?

A. $y = x + 1$ B. $x = y + 1$
C. $2x = y + 2$ D. None of the above

32. What is $\tan\left(\frac{\pi}{12}\right)$ equal to?

A. $2-\sqrt{3}$ B. $2+\sqrt{3}$
C. $\sqrt{2}-\sqrt{3}$ D. $\sqrt{3}-\sqrt{2}$

33. If $\theta = 18°$, then what is the value of $4 \sin^2\theta + 2 \sin \theta$?

A. –1 B. 1
C. 0 D. 2

34. Two poles are 10 m and 20 m high. The line joining their tips makes an angle of 15° with the horizontal. What is the distance between the poles?

A. $10\left(\sqrt{3}-1\right)$ m B. $5\left(4+2\sqrt{3}\right)$ m
C. $20\left(\sqrt{3}+1\right)$ m D. $10\left(\sqrt{3}+1\right)$ m

35. The angle of elevation of a tower at a level ground is 30°. The angle of elevation becomes θ when moved 10 m towards the tower. If the height of tower is $5\sqrt{3}$ m, then what is θ equal to?

A. 45° B. 60°
C. 75° D. None of the above

36. In a triangle ABC if the angles A, B, C are in AP, then which one of the following is correct?

A. $c = a + b$ B. $c^2 = a^2 + b^2 - ab$
C. $a^2 = b^2 + c^2 - bc$ D. $b^2 = a^2 + c^2 - ac$

37. If $\sin^{-1} 1 + \sin^{-1}\frac{4}{5} = \sin^{-1} x$, then what is *x* equal to?

A. 3/5 B. 4/5
C. 1 D. 0

38. If $\operatorname{cosec} \theta - \cot \theta = \frac{1}{\sqrt{3}}$ where $\theta \neq 0$, then what is the value of $\cos \theta$?

A. 0 B. $\frac{\sqrt{3}}{2}$
C. $\frac{1}{2}$ D. $\frac{1}{\sqrt{2}}$

39. From the top of a building of height *h* metre, the angle of depression of an object on the ground is θ. What is the distance (in metre) of the object from the foot of the building?

A. $h \cot \theta$ B. $h \tan \theta$
C. $h \cos \theta$ D. $h \sin \theta$

40. If $\tan^{-1} 2$, $\tan^{-1} 3$ are two angles of a triangle, then what is the third angle?

A. $\tan^{-1} 2$ B. $\tan^{-1} 4$
C. $\pi/4$ D. $\pi/3$

41. What is the maximum value of $\sin 3\theta \cos 2\theta + \cos 3\theta \sin 2\theta$?

A. 1 B. 2
C. 4 D. 10

42. What is sin A cos A tan A + cos A sin A cot A equal to?

A. sin A B. cos A
C. tan A D. 1

43. What is the value of $\sec^2 \tan^{-1}\left(\frac{5}{11}\right)$?

A. 121/96 B. 217/921
C. 146/121 D. 267/121

44. Which one of the following is positive in the third quadrant?

A. $\sin \theta$ B. $\cos \theta$
C. $\tan \theta$ D. $\sec \theta$

45. What is the value of sin (1920°)?

A. $\frac{1}{2}$ B. $\frac{1}{\sqrt{2}}$
C. $\frac{\sqrt{3}}{2}$ D. $\frac{1}{3}$

46. The angle of elevation of the tip of a flag staff from a point 10 m due South of its base in 60°. What is the height of the flag staff correct to the nearest metre?

A. 15 m B. 16 m
C. 17 m D. 18 m

47. What is $\frac{\sin\theta}{\operatorname{cosec}\theta}+\frac{\cos\theta}{\sec\theta}$ equal to?

A. 1 B. 1/2
C. 1/3 D. 2

48. If $\tan \theta + \sec \theta = 4$, then what is the value of $\sin \theta$?

A. 8/17 B. 8/15
C. 15/17 D. 23/32

49. What is the value of

$$\cos\left\{\cos^{-1}\frac{4}{5}+\cos^{-1}\frac{12}{13}\right\}?$$

A. 63/65 B. 33/65
C. 22/65 D. 11/65

50. What is the angle subtended by 1 m pole at a distance 1 km on the ground in sexagesimal measure?

A. $\frac{9}{50\pi}$ degree B. $\frac{9}{5\pi}$ degree
C. 3.4 minute D. 3.5 minute

51. If cot A . cot B = 2, then what is the value of cos (A + B) . sec(A – B)?
A. 1/3 B. 2/3
C. 1 D. –1

52. Consider the following statements:
1. Every zero matrix is a square matrix.
2. A matrix has a numerical value.
3. A unit matrix is a diagonal matrix.
Which of the above statements is/are correct?
A. 2 only B. 3 only
C. 2 and 3 D. 1 and 3

53. If the sequence $\{s_n\}$ is a geometric progression and $s_2 s_{11} = s_p s_8$, then what is the value of p?
A. 1
B. 3
C. 5
D. Can not be determined

54. In the expansion of $(1 + x)^n$, what is the sum of even binomial coefficients?
A. 2^n B. 2^{n-1}
C. 2^{n+1} D. None of the above

55. The value of the term independent of x in the expansion of $\left(x^2 - \frac{1}{x}\right)^9$ is
A. 9 B. 18
C. 48 D. 84

56. What is the number of ways that 4 boys and 3 girls can be seated so that boys and girls alternate?
A. 12 B. 72
C. 120 D. 144

57. If the difference between the roots of $ax^2 + bx + c = 0$ is 1, then which one of the following is correct?
A. $b^2 = a(a + 4c)$ B. $a^2 = b(b + 4c)$
C. $a^2 = c(a + 4c)$ D. $b^2 = a(b + 4c)$

58. If one of the roots of the equation $x^2 + ax - b = 0$ is 1, then what is $(a - b)$ equal to?
A. –1 B. 1
C. 2 D. –2

59. If α and β are the roots of the equation $x^2 - q(1 + x) - r = 0$, then what is $(1 + \alpha)(1 + \beta)$ equal to?
A. $1 - r$ B. $q - r$
C. $1 + r$ D. $q + r$

60. If 1/4, $1/x$, 1/10 are in HP, then what is the value of x?
A. 5 B. 6
C. 7 D. 8

61. If $f(xy) = f(x)f(y)$, then $f(t)$ may be of the form:
A. $t + k$ B. $ct + k$
C. $t^k + c$ D. t^k
where k, c are constants

62. If $A + iB = \frac{4+2i}{1-2i}$ where $i = \sqrt{-1}$, then what is the value of A?
A. –8 B. 0
C. 4 D. 8

63. If $z = \bar{z}$, then which one of the following is correct?
A. The real part of z is zero.
B. The imaginary part of z is zero.
C. the real part of z is equal to imaginary part of z.
D. The sum of real and imaginary parts of z is z.

64. If A and B are two non-empty sets having n elements in common, then what is the number of common elements in the sets A × B and B × A?
A. n B. n^2
C. $2n$ D. zero

65. If A and B are any two sets, then what is A ∩ (A ∪ B) equal to?
A. Complement of A B. Complement of B
C. B D. A

66. What is the cosine of angle between the planes $x + y + z + 1 = 0$ and $2x - 2y + 2z + 1 = 0$?
A. 1/2 B. 1/3
C. 2/3 D. None of the above

67. If $A = \begin{bmatrix} 1 & 2 \\ 1 & 1 \end{bmatrix}$ and $B = \begin{bmatrix} 0 & -1 \\ 1 & 2 \end{bmatrix}$, then what is $B^{-1}A^{-1}$ equal to?
A. $\begin{bmatrix} 1 & -3 \\ -1 & 2 \end{bmatrix}$ B. $\begin{bmatrix} -1 & 3 \\ 1 & -2 \end{bmatrix}$
C. $\begin{bmatrix} -1 & 3 \\ -1 & -2 \end{bmatrix}$ D. $\begin{bmatrix} -1 & -3 \\ 1 & -2 \end{bmatrix}$

68. Which one of the following functions is differentiable for all real values of x?
A. $\frac{x}{|x|}$ B. $x|x|$
C. $\frac{1}{|x|}$ D. $\frac{1}{x}$

69. Which of the following differential equations is ***not*** linear?
A. $\frac{d^2y}{dx^2} + 4y = 0$ B. $x\frac{dy}{dx} + y = x^3$
C. $(x-y)^2 \frac{dy}{dx} = 9$ D. $\cos^2 x \frac{dy}{dx} + y = \tan x$

70. What is the sum of the squares of direction cosines of the line joining the points (1, 2, –3) and (–2, 3, 1)?
A. 0 B. 1
C. 3 D. $\frac{2}{\sqrt{26}}$

71. What is the diameter of the sphere $x^2 + y^2 + z^2 - 4x + 6y - 8z - 7 = 0$
A. 4 units B. 5 units
C. 6 units D. 12 units

72. What is the slope of the tangent to the curve $x = t^2 + 3t - 8$, $y = 2t^2 - 2t - 5$ at $t = 2$?
A. 7/6 B. 6/7
C. 1 D. 5/6

73. Which one of the following statements is correct?
A. e^x is an increasing function
B. e^x is a decreasing function
C. e^x is neither increasing nor decreasing function
D. e^x is a constant function

74. If $y = \cos t$ and $x = \sin t$, then what is $\frac{dy}{dx}$ equal to?
A. xy B. x/y
C. $-y/x$ D. $-x/y$

75. What is $\int (x^2+1)^{\frac{5}{2}} x dx$ equal to?
A. $(x^2+1)^{\frac{7}{2}} + c$ B. $\frac{2}{7}(x^2+1)^{\frac{7}{2}} + c$
C. $\frac{1}{7}(x^2+1)^{\frac{7}{2}} + c$ D. None of the above
where c is a constant of integration.

76. If $f(x) = x^2 - 6x + 8$ and there exists a point c in the interval [2, 4] such that $f'(c) = 0$, then what is the value of c?
A. 2.5 B. 2.8
C. 3 D. 3.5

77. If $\begin{vmatrix} 8 & -5 & 1 \\ 5 & x & 1 \\ 6 & 3 & 1 \end{vmatrix} = 2$, then what is the value of x?
A. 4 B. 5
C. 6 D. 8

78. What is the order of the product
$$\begin{bmatrix} x & y & z \end{bmatrix} \begin{bmatrix} a & h & g \\ h & b & f \\ g & f & c \end{bmatrix} \begin{bmatrix} x \\ y \\ z \end{bmatrix}?$$
A. 3 × 1 B. 1 × 1
C. 1 × 3 D. 3 × 3

79. What is $\int_{-\frac{\pi}{2}}^{\frac{\pi}{2}} |\sin x| dx$ equal to?
A. 2 B. 1
C. p D. 0

80. The area bounded by the curve $x = f(y)$, the y-axis and the two lines $y = a$ and $y = b$ is equal to:
A. $\int_a^b y\,dx$ B. $\int_a^b y^2\,dx$
C. $\int_a^b x\,dy$ D. None of the above

81. If $y = \frac{x+1}{x-1}$, then what is $\frac{dy}{dx}$ equal to?
A. $\frac{-2}{x-1}$ B. $\frac{-2}{(x-1)^2}$
C. $\frac{2}{(x-1)^2}$ D. $\frac{2}{(x-1)}$

82. Which one of the following statement is correct?
A. The derivative of a function $f(x)$ at a point will exist if there is one tangent to the curve $y = f(x)$ at that point and the tangent if parallel to y-axis
B. The derivative of a function $f(x)$ at a point will exist if there is one tangent to the curve $y = f(x)$ at that point and the tangent must be parallel to x-axis
C. The derivative of a function $f(x)$ at a point will exist if there is one and only one tangent to the curve $y = f(x)$ at that point and the tangent is not parallel to y-axis
D. None of the above

83. Consider the following:
1. $\int \ln 10 dx = x + c$ 2. $\int 10^x dx = 10^x + c$
where c is the constant of integration.
Which of the above is/are correct?
A. 1 only B. 2 only
C. Both 1 and 2 D. Neither 1 nor 2

84. How many tangents are parallel to x-axis for the curve $y = x^2 - 4x + 3$?
A. 1
B. 2
C. 3
D. No tangent is parallel to x-axis

85. What is $\lim_{x \to 0} x^2 \sin\left(\frac{1}{x}\right)$ equal to?
A. 0 B. 1
C. 1/2 D. Limit does not exist

86. What is $\lim_{x \to -2}\left(\frac{x+2}{x^3+8}\right)$ equal to?
A. 1/4 B. −1/4
C. 1/12 D. −1/12

87. What is the solution of the differential equation $\frac{dy}{dx} + \frac{y}{x} = 0$?
A. $xy = c$ B. $x = cy$
C. $y = cx$ D. None of the above
where c is a constant.

88. What is the degree of the differential equation $y = x\frac{dy}{dx} + \left(\frac{dy}{dx}\right)^{-1}$?

A. 1
B. 2
C. –1
D. Degree does not exist

89. What is $\int_0^1 \frac{\tan^{-1} x}{1+x^2} dx$ equal to?

A. $\frac{\pi}{4}$
B. $\frac{\pi}{8}$
C. $\frac{\pi^2}{8}$
D. $\frac{\pi^2}{32}$

90. What is the rate of change of $\sqrt{x^2+16}$ with respect to x^2 at $x = 3$?

A. 1/5
B. 1/10
C. 1/20
D. None of the above

91. If $\vec{a} = (2, 1, -1)$, $\vec{b} = (1, -1, 0)$, $\vec{c} = (5, -1, 1)$, then what is the unit vector parallel to $\vec{a}+\vec{b}-\vec{c}$ in the opposite direction?

A. $\frac{\hat{i}+\hat{j}-2\hat{k}}{3}$
B. $\frac{\hat{i}-2\hat{j}+2\hat{k}}{3}$
C. $\frac{2\hat{i}-\hat{j}+2\hat{k}}{3}$
D. None of the above

92. If the magnitudes of two vectors $\vec{a}$ and $\vec{b}$ are equal then which one of the following is correct?

A. $(\vec{a}+\vec{b})$ is parallel to $(\vec{a}-\vec{b})$
B. $(\vec{a}+\vec{b})\bullet(\vec{a}-\vec{b})=1$
C. $(\vec{a}+\vec{b})$ is perpendicular to $(\vec{a}-\vec{b})$
D. None of the above

93. Consider the following in respect of the function $f(x) = |x - 3|$:

1. $f(x)$ is continuous at $x = 3$
2. $f(x)$ is differentiable at $x = 0$.

Which of the above statements is/are correct?

A. 1 only
B. 2 only
C. Both 1 and 2
D. Neither 1 nor 2

94. If four dice are thrown together, then what is the probability that the sum of the numbers appearing on them is 25?

A. 0
B. 1/2
C. 1
D. 1/1296

95. Let O be the origin and P, Q, R be the points such that $\overrightarrow{PO}+\overrightarrow{OQ}=\overrightarrow{QO}+\overrightarrow{OR}$. Then which one of the following is correct?

A. P, Q, R are the vertices of an equilateral triangle
B. P, Q, R are the vertices of an isosceles triangle
C. P, Q, R are collinear
D. None of the above

96. What is the value of $2\log_8 2 - \frac{1}{3}\log_3 9$?

A. 0
B. 1
C. 2
D. 1/3

97. What is the value of m if the vectors $2\hat{i}-\hat{j}+\hat{k}$, $\hat{i}+2\hat{j}-3\hat{k}$ and $3\hat{i}+m\hat{j}+5\hat{k}$ are coplanar?

A. –2
B. 2
C. –4
D. 4

98. If $|\vec{a}|=10$, $|\vec{b}|=2$ and $\vec{a}\bullet\vec{b}=12$, then what is the value of $|\vec{a}\times\vec{b}|$?

A. 12
B. 16
C. 20
D. 24

99. If the vectors $\hat{i}-x\hat{j}-y\hat{k}$ and $\hat{i}+x\hat{j}-y\hat{k}$ are orthogonal to each other, then what is the locus of the point (x, y)?

A. a parabola
B. an ellipse
C. a circle
D. a straight line

100. If A is a square matrix such that $A^2 = 1$ where I is the identity matrix, then what is A^{-1} equal to?

A. A + I
B. Null matrix
C. A
D. Transpose of A

101. What is the eccentricity of the conic $4x^2 + 9y^2 = 144$?

A. $\frac{\sqrt{5}}{3}$
B. $\frac{\sqrt{5}}{4}$
C. $\frac{3}{\sqrt{5}}$
D. 2/3

102. If two rows of a determinant are identical, then what is the value of the determinant?

A. 0
B. 1
C. –1
D. Can be any real value

103. If A = {0, 1} and B = {1, 0}, then what is A × B equal to?

A. {(0, 1), (1, 0)}
B. {(0, 0), (1, 1)}
C. {(0, 1), (1, 0), (1, 1)}
D. A × A

104. What is the perpendicular distance of the point (x, y) from x-axis?

A. x
B. y
C. $|x|$
D. $|y|$

105. If ABCD is a cyclic quadrilateral then what is sin A + sin B – sin C – sin D equal to?

A. 0
B. 1
C. 2
D. 2(sin A + sin B)

106. What is the value of

sin 420°. cos 390° + cos(–300°).sin(–330°)?

A. 0
B. 1
C. 2
D. –1

107. Consider the following statements:

1. 1° in radian measure is less than 0.02 radians.
2. 1 radian in degree measure is greater than 45°.

Which of the above statements is/are correct?

A. 1 only
B. 2 only
C. Both 1 and 2
D. Neither 1 nor 2

108. What is the maximum value of $\sin^2 x$?

A. –1 B. 0
C. 1 D. Infinity

109. The sum and product of matrices A and B exist. Which of the following implications are necessarily true?

1. A and B are square matrices of same order.
2. A and B are non-singular matrices.

Select the correct answer using the code given below:

A. 1 only B. 2 only
C. Both 1 and 2 D. Neither 1 nor 2

110. What is the area of the rectangle having vertices A, B, C and D with position vectors $-\hat{i}+\frac{1}{2}\hat{j}+4\hat{k}$, $\hat{i}+\frac{1}{2}\hat{j}+4\hat{k}$, $\hat{i}-\frac{1}{2}\hat{j}+4\hat{k}$ and $-\hat{i}-\frac{1}{2}\hat{j}+4\hat{k}$?

A. 1/2 square unit B. 1 square unit
C. 2 square unit D. 4 square unit

111. The set A = $\{x : x + 4 = 4\}$ can also be represented by:

A. 0 B. φ
C. {φ} D. {0}

112. If a line makes the angles α, β, γ with the axes, then what is the value of $1 + \cos 2\alpha + \cos 2\beta + \cos 2\gamma$ equal to?

A. –1 B. 0
C. 1 D. 2

113. What is the sum of the series $1-\frac{1}{2}+\frac{1}{4}-\frac{1}{8}+\ldots$ equal to?

A. 1/2 B. 3/2
C. 2 D. 2/3

114. Consider the following statements:

1. Two independent variables are always uncorrelated.
2. The coefficient of correlation between two variables X and Y is positive when X decreases then Y decreases.

Which of the above statements is/are correct?

A. 1 only B. 2 only
C. Both 1 and 2 D. Neither 1 nor 2

115. A variate X takes values 2, 9, 3, 7, 5, 4 3, 2, 10. What is the median?

A. 2 B. 4
C. 7 D. 9

116. What are the direction ratios of normal to the plane $2x - y + 2z + 1 = 0$?

A. $\langle 2, 1, 2\rangle$ B. $\left\langle 1, -\frac{1}{2}, 1\right\rangle$
C. $\langle 1, -2, 1\rangle$ D. None of the above

For the next ***Four (4)*** *questions that follow:*

In a city, three daily newspapers A, B, C are published, 42% read A; 51% read B; 68% read C; 30% read A and B; 28% read B and C; 36% read A and C; 8% do not read any of the three newspapers.

117. What is the percentage of persons who read all the three papers?

A. 20% B. 25%
C. 30% D. 40%

118. What is the percentage of persons who read only two papers?

A. 19% B. 31%
C. 44% D. None of the above

119. What is the percentage of persons who read only one paper?

A. 38% B. 48%
C. 51% D. None of the above

120. What is the percentage of persons who read only A but neither B nor C?

A. 4% B. 3%
C. 1% D. None of the above

ANSWERS

PAPER-I : GENERAL ABILITY TEST

1	2	3	4	5	6	7	8	9	10
C	B	D	C	C	A	A	A	D	C
11	**12**	**13**	**14**	**15**	**16**	**17**	**18**	**19**	**20**
A	B	D	C	C	D	B	C	B	C
21	**22**	**23**	**24**	**25**	**26**	**27**	**28**	**29**	**30**
A	D	D	A	A	C	B	C	A	A
31	**32**	**33**	**34**	**35**	**36**	**37**	**38**	**39**	**40**
B	A	D	B	B	C	D	D	A	B
41	**42**	**43**	**44**	**45**	**46**	**47**	**48**	**49**	**50**
B	B	D	D	C	C	A	A	A	C
51	**52**	**53**	**54**	**55**	**56**	**57**	**58**	**59**	**60**
A	A	A	A	D	A	A	A	A	B
61	**62**	**63**	**64**	**65**	**66**	**67**	**68**	**69**	**70**
B	D	D	C	C	D	B	B	D	C

71	72	73	74	75	76	77	78	79	80
B	C	C	C	B	B	D	D	A	D
81	82	83	84	85	86	87	88	89	90
C	A	C	B	B	C	B	B	D	B
91	92	93	94	95	96	97	98	99	100
A	A	A	B	C	B	A	D	D	A
101	102	103	104	105	106	107	108	109	110
B	B	A	D	B	A	A	C	B	D
111	112	113	114	115	116	117	118	119	120
A	C	A	B	D	A	D	C	C	D
121	122	123	124	125	126	127	128	129	130
A	B	A	C	D	A	B	C	D	B
131	132	133	134	135	136	137	138	139	140
D	C	D	A	D	D	C	B	B	B
141	142	143	144	145	146	147	148	149	150
D	A	D	C	C	B	A	C	B	D

PAPER-II : MATHEMATICS

1	2	3	4	5	6	7	8	9	10
D	C	A	A	A	C	A	C	A	C
11	12	13	14	15	16	17	18	19	20
B	C	B	C	D	D	B	C	B	D
21	22	23	24	25	26	27	28	29	30
B	D	A	D	B	C	B	C	B	C
31	32	33	34	35	36	37	38	39	40
A	A	B	B	B	D	A	B	A	C
41	42	43	44	45	46	47	48	49	50
A	D	C	C	C	C	A	C	B	A
51	52	53	54	55	56	57	58	59	60
A	B	C	B	D	D	A	A	A	C
61	62	63	64	65	66	67	68	69	70
D	B	A	B	D	B	B	B	A	B
71	72	73	74	75	76	77	78	79	80
C	B	A	D	C	C	D	B	A	C
81	82	83	84	85	86	87	88	89	90
B	C	A	A	A	C	A	B	D	B
91	92	93	94	95	96	97	98	99	100
C	C	B	A	A	A	C	B	B	C
101	102	103	104	105	106	107	108	109	110
A	A	D	D	A	B	C	C	A	B
111	112	113	114	115	116	117	118	119	120
D	B	D	A	B	B	B	A	B	C

EXPLANATORY ANSWERS

PAPER-II : MATHEMATICS

1. If roots α, β

then $\alpha + \beta = -2$

$$\alpha\beta = -143$$

$$\alpha^2 + \beta^2 = (\alpha + \beta)^2 - 2\,\alpha\beta$$

$$= (-2)^2 - 2(-143)$$

$$= 4 + 286 = 290.$$

2. $A - B = \{1, 4\}$

$(A - B)^c = \{2, 1, 5, 6, 7, 8, 9, 10\}$

3. $2x + y = 6 \Rightarrow 2x = 6 - y$

$$3y = 8 + 2\,(2x)$$

$$3y = 8 + 2\,(6 - y)$$

$$3y = 8 + 12 - 2y$$

$$5y = 20$$

$$y = 4$$

$$\Rightarrow \quad 2x = 2$$

$$x = 1.$$

4. A = {1, 4, 9, 16, 25, 36, 49, 64, 81}
B = {even natural numbers}
A ∩ B = {4, 16, 36, 64}.

5. $\begin{bmatrix} 1 & 2 \\ 2 & 3 \end{bmatrix}\begin{bmatrix} 1 & 0 \\ 1 & 0 \end{bmatrix}$

$AB = \begin{bmatrix} 3 & 0 \\ 5 & 0 \end{bmatrix}$

(AB) = 0.

6. $\begin{vmatrix} -a^2 & ab & ac \\ ab & -b^2 & bc \\ ac & bc & -c^2 \end{vmatrix}$

$= abc\begin{vmatrix} -a & b & c \\ a & -b & c \\ a & b & -c \end{vmatrix}$

$= a^2b^2c^2\begin{vmatrix} -1 & 1 & 1 \\ 1 & -1 & 1 \\ 1 & 1 & -1 \end{vmatrix}$

$= a^2b^2c^2\begin{vmatrix} -1 & 1 & 1 \\ 0 & 0 & 2 \\ 0 & 2 & 0 \end{vmatrix}$

$= a^2b^2c^2[(-1)(-4)]$
$= 4a^2b^2c^2$.

7. $3x + 4y = 9$ ...(1)
$2(3x + 4y = 9)$ ...(2)

8.

2	292	0
2	146	0
2	73	1
2	36	0
2	18	0
2	9	1
2	4	0
2	2	0
	1	

100100100.

9. $S_{16} = \frac{16}{2}[2(1)+15(1)]$
$= 8(17)$
$= 136$

$\text{A.M.} = \frac{136}{16} = \frac{17}{2}$.

10. ∴ mode = 22.

11. AB = A
BA = B
ABA = A.

12. $\sqrt{ab} = 10$
$ab = 100$
$\frac{2ab}{a+b} = 8$
$\frac{200}{a+b} = 8$
$a + b = 25$
$(a - b)^2 = (a + b)^2 - 4ab$
$= 625 - 400$
$= 225$
$a - b = 15$
$a + b = 25$
$2a = 40$
$a = 20, b = 5$

$\text{A.M.} = \frac{20+5}{2} = 12.5$.

14. $a = 1, d = 4$
$a_n = a + (n - 1)d$
$= 1 + (n - 1)4$
$= 1 + 4n - 4$
$= 4n - 3$.

15. $1+\frac{1}{\sqrt{3}}+3+\frac{1}{3\sqrt{3}}+\ldots$

$\frac{a_2}{a_1} = \frac{1}{\sqrt{3}}$

$\frac{a_3}{a_2} = \frac{3}{1/\sqrt{3}}$

$\frac{a_4}{a_3} = \frac{1/3\sqrt{3}}{3}$.

16. A.P. → $2q = p + r$ ...(1)
G.P. → $q^2 = pr \Rightarrow 0 = \sqrt{pr}$
$2\sqrt{pr} = p + r$
$p+r-2\sqrt{pr} = 0$
$\left(\sqrt{p}\right)^2+\left(\sqrt{r}\right)^2-2\sqrt{p}.\sqrt{r} = 0$
$\left(\sqrt{p}-\sqrt{r}\right)^2 = 0$
$\sqrt{p} = \sqrt{r}$
$p = r$ ...(2)
$2q = 2p$
$q = p$ ...(3)

from (2) and (3)

$p = q = r$.

17. $AB = \sqrt{(0+4)^2 + (-1-2)^2}$

$= \sqrt{16+9} = 5$

$BC = \sqrt{9+16} = 5$

$CA = \sqrt{49+(1)^2} = \sqrt{50}$

$= 5\sqrt{2}$

$= 10 + 5\sqrt{2}$

$= 5(2+\sqrt{2})$.

18. Mid point is $\left(\frac{a+b-a}{2}, \frac{a-b+b}{2}\right)$

$= \left(\frac{b}{2}, \frac{a}{2}\right)$

it lies on $ax + by = k$

$a\left(\frac{b}{2}\right) + b\left(\frac{a}{2}\right) = k$

$k = ab$.

22. Total no. of case $= 6^3 = 216$

Fav cases = {(1, 1, 1), (2, 2, 2) (3, 3, 3), (4, 4, 4), (5, 5, 5), (6, 6, 6)}.

Probability $\frac{6}{216} = \frac{1}{36}$

For the next ***Two*** *(2) questions that follow:*

The equation formed by multiplying each root of $ax^2 + bx + c = 0$ by 2 is $x^2 + 36x + 24 = 0$.

23. Let α, β be roots of equation

$ax^2 + bx + c = 0$

$\therefore \quad \alpha + \beta = -b/a$

$\alpha\beta = c/a$

So, 2α and 2β we roots of equation

$x^2 + 36x + 24 = 0$

$2\alpha + 2\beta = -36$

$\alpha + \beta = -18$

$\Rightarrow \quad \frac{-b}{a} = -18 \Rightarrow b = 18a$

$(2\alpha) + (2\beta) = 24$

$\alpha\beta = 6$

$\frac{c}{a} = 6 \Rightarrow c = 6a$

$\therefore b : c = 3 : 1$.

24. $b = 18a$

$c = 6a$

For the next ***Three*** *(3) questions that follow:*

Let sin (A + B) = 1 and sin (A – B) = $\frac{1}{2}$,

where A, B $\in \left[0, \frac{\pi}{2}\right]$.

25. sin (A + B) = 1

sin (A + B) = sin 90°

A + B = 90°

sin (A – B) = $\frac{1}{2}$ = sin 30°

A – B = 30°

2A = 120

A = 60

B = 30.

26. tan (120°).tan(150°)

tan(90° + 30°) tan (90° + 60°)

cot 30°.cot 60°

$\sqrt{3}.\frac{1}{\sqrt{3}} = 1$.

27. $\sin^2 60° - \sin^2 30°$

$\frac{3}{4} - \frac{1}{4} = \frac{1}{2}$.

28. $\frac{2b^2}{a} = b$

$2b = a$

$b^2 = a^2(1 - e^2)$

$b^2 = 4b^2(1 - e^2)$

$\frac{1}{4} = 1 - e^2$

$e^2 = 1 - \frac{1}{4} = \frac{3}{4}$

$e = \frac{\sqrt{3}}{2}$.

29. No. of days in each year = 366

No. of complete week = 52.

No. of days left = 2.

Required probability = 2/7.

30. 11101.001

$1 \times 2^4 + 1 \times 2^3 + 1 \times 2^2 + 0 \times 2^1 + 1 \times 2^0 \bullet 0 \times 2^{-} + 0 \times 2^{-2} + 1 \times 2^{-3}$

$16 + 8 + 4 + 0 + 1 \bullet 0 + 0 + \frac{1}{8}$

29.125.

32. $\tan\left(\frac{\pi}{3} - \frac{\pi}{4}\right)$

$= \frac{\tan\frac{\pi}{3} - \tan\frac{\pi}{4}}{1 + \tan\frac{\pi}{3}\tan\frac{\pi}{4}}$

$= \frac{\sqrt{3}-1}{\sqrt{3}+1} \times \frac{\sqrt{3}-1}{\sqrt{3}-1}$

$= \frac{(\sqrt{3}-1)^2}{3-1} = \frac{4-2\sqrt{3}}{2}$

$$= \frac{2(2-\sqrt{3})}{2} = 2-\sqrt{3}.$$

34.

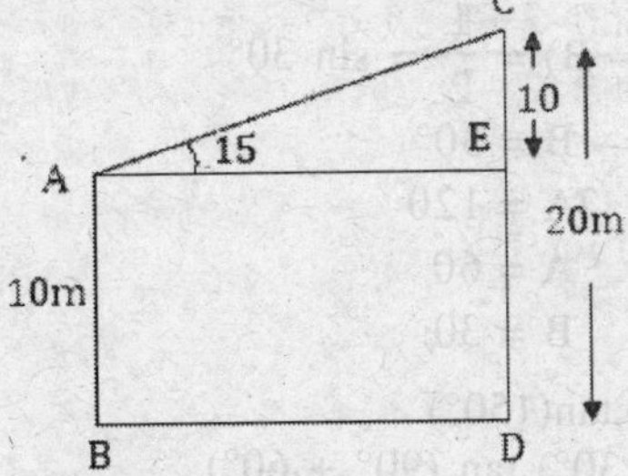

In ΔAEC,

$$\frac{CE}{AE} = \tan 15°$$

$$\frac{10}{AE} = \tan (45° - 30°)$$

$$= \frac{\tan 45° - \tan 30°}{1 + \tan 45° \tan 30°}$$

$$= \frac{1-\frac{1}{\sqrt{3}}}{1+\frac{1}{\sqrt{3}}}$$

$$\frac{10}{AE} = \frac{\sqrt{3}-1}{\sqrt{3}+1}$$

$$AE = \frac{10(\sqrt{3}+1)}{\sqrt{3}-1} \times \frac{\sqrt{3}+1}{\sqrt{3}+1}$$

$$= 10\left[\frac{3+1+2\sqrt{3}}{2}\right]$$

$$= 10\left[\frac{2(2+\sqrt{3})}{2}\right].$$

35.

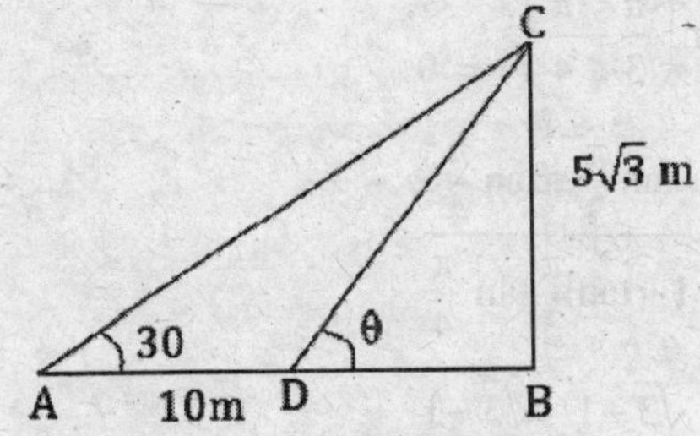

In ΔABC,

$$\frac{BC}{AB} = \tan 30°$$

$$AB = \frac{BC}{\tan 30°}$$

$$= \frac{5\sqrt{3}}{1/\sqrt{3}}$$

$$= 15$$

$$AB = 15$$

Given

$$AD = 10 \text{ m}$$

$\therefore$

$$DB = 5 \text{ m}$$

In ΔBCD,

$$\frac{BC}{BD} = \tan \theta$$

$$\frac{5\sqrt{3}}{5} = \tan \theta$$

$$\theta = 60°.$$

40.

$$\theta_1 = \tan^{-1} 2$$

$$\theta_2 = \tan^{-1} 3,\ \theta_3 = ?$$

$$\theta_1 + \theta_2 + \theta_3 = 180°$$

$$\tan^{-1} 2 + \tan^{-1} 3 + \theta_3 = 180°$$

$$\tan^{-1}\left(\frac{2+3}{1-2.3}\right) + \theta_3 = 180°$$

$$\tan^{-1}\left(\frac{5}{-5}\right) + \theta_3 = 180°$$

$$135 + \theta_3 = 180°$$

$$\theta_3 = 45.$$

41. $\sin 3\theta \cos 2\theta + \cos 3\theta \sin 2\theta$

$$= \sin (3\theta + 2\theta)$$

$$= \sin (5\theta)$$

$$-1 < \sin \theta < 1.$$

42. $\sin A \cos A . \frac{\sin A}{\cos A} + \cos A \sin A \frac{\cos A}{\sin A}$

$$\sin^2 A + \cos^2 A = 1.$$

43. $\sec^2\left(\tan^{-1}\left(\frac{5}{11}\right)\right)$

$$1+\tan^2\left(\tan^{-1}\left(\frac{5}{11}\right)\right)$$

$$1+\left[\tan\left\{\tan^{-1}\left(\frac{5}{11}\right)^2\right\}\right]$$

$$1+\frac{25}{121} \qquad \frac{121+25}{121} = \frac{146}{121}.$$

45. $\sin (1920°)$

$\sin (360 \times 5 + 120°)$

$\sin 120°$

$\sin (90° + 30°)$

$$\cos 30° = \frac{\sqrt{3}}{2}.$$

46.

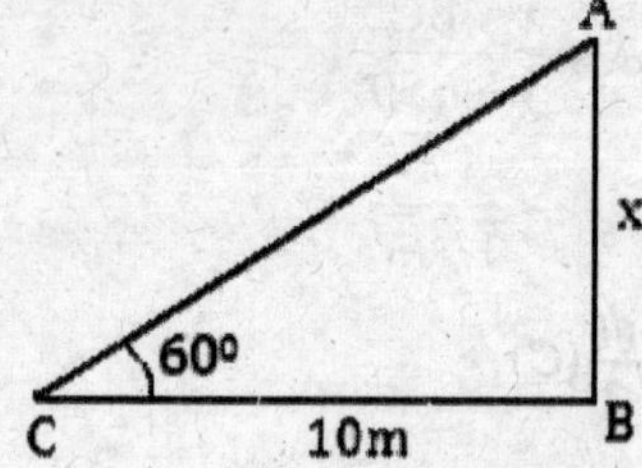

$$\tan 60° = \frac{x}{10}$$

$$\sqrt{3} = \frac{x}{10}$$

$$x = 10\sqrt{3} = 10 \times 1.732$$

$$= 17.32$$

$$\cong 17.$$

47. $\sin^2\theta + \cos^2\theta = 1.$

48. $$\frac{\sin\theta}{\cos\theta} + \frac{1}{\cos\theta} = 4$$

$$1 + \sin\theta = 4\cos\theta$$

$$(1 + \sin\theta)^2 = 16\cos^2\theta$$

$$= 16(1 - \sin^2\theta)$$

$$(1 + \sin\theta)^2 = 16(1 - \sin\theta)(1 + \sin\theta)$$

$$1 + \sin\theta = 16 - 16\sin\theta$$

$$17\sin\theta = 16 - 1$$

$$\sin\theta = \frac{15}{17}.$$

49. Put $\cos^{-1}\frac{4}{5} = A$

$$\cos A = \frac{4}{5}$$

$$\Rightarrow \quad \sin A = \frac{3}{5}$$

$$\cos^{-1}\frac{12}{13} = B$$

$$\cos B = \frac{12}{13}$$

$$\Rightarrow \quad \sin B = \frac{5}{13}.$$

Now,

$$\cos\left(\cos^{-1}\frac{4}{5} + \cos^{-1}\frac{12}{13}\right)$$

$= \cos(A + B)$

$= \cos A \cos B - \sin A \sin B$

$$= \left(\frac{4}{5}\right)\left(\frac{12}{13}\right) - \left(\frac{3}{5}\right)\left(\frac{5}{13}\right)$$

$$= \frac{48}{65} - \frac{15}{65} = \frac{33}{65}.$$

51. $$\frac{\cos(A+B)}{\cos(A-B)}$$

$$\frac{\cos A \cos B - \sin A \sin B}{\cos A \cos B + \sin A \sin B}$$

Divide N and D by sin A sin B,

$$\frac{\cot A \cot B - 1}{\cot A \cot B + 1} = \frac{2-1}{2+1} = \frac{1}{3}.$$

53. $S_2 S_{11} = S_p S_8$

$(ar)(ar^{10}) = ar^{p-1}(ar^7)$

$r^{11} = r^{7+p-1}$

$r^{11} = r^{6+p}$

$11 = 6 + p$

$p = 5$

55. $$\left(x^2 - \frac{1}{x}\right)^9$$

$$t_{r+1} = {}^9C_r (x^2)^{9-r}\left(\frac{-1}{x}\right)^r$$

$$= {}^9C_r (x)^{18-2r}(-1)^r x^{-r} \quad ...(1)$$

Put $18 - 3r = 0$

$r = 6$

Put $r = 6$, in (1),

$$t_7 = {}^9C_6(1)^6 = \frac{9!}{6!\,3!} = \frac{9.8.7.6!}{6!.3.2} = 84.$$

56. B G B G B G B

$4 \times 3 \times 3 \times 2 \times 2 \times 1 \times 1 = 144.$

57. $\alpha + \beta = -b/a$

$\alpha\beta = c/a$

$\alpha - \beta = 1$

$(\alpha + \beta)^2 - (\alpha - \beta)^2 = 4\alpha\beta$

$$\frac{b^2}{a^2} - 1 = \frac{4c}{a}$$

$$\frac{b^2 - a^2}{a^2} = \frac{4c}{a}$$

$$b^2 - a^2 = 4ac$$

$$b^2 = a^2 + 4ac$$

$$= a(a + 4c).$$

58. $(1)^2 + a(1) - b = 0$

$a - b = -1.$

59. $x^2 - qx + (-q - r) = 0$

$\alpha + \beta = q$

$\alpha\beta = -q - r$

$(1 + \alpha)(1 + \beta)$

$1 + \alpha + \beta + \alpha\beta$

$1 + q - q - r$

$1 - r.$

60. 4, x, 10 are m AP.

$2x = 4 + 10$

$$x = \frac{14}{2} = 7.$$

61. $f(xy) = (xy)^k = x^k.y^k = f(x).f(y)$.

62. $A + iB = \frac{4+2i}{1-2i} \times \frac{1+2i}{1+2i}$

$= \frac{4+2i+8i-4}{(1)^2-(2i)^2}$

$= \frac{0+10i}{5} = 2i$

A = 0.

63.
$$z = x + y$$
$$\overline{z} = x - iy$$
$$\therefore \quad (x + iy) = -(x - iy)$$
$$x + iy = -x + iy$$
$$2x = 0$$
$$\text{Re}(z) = 0.$$

65. $A \cap (A \cup B) = A$.

66. $\cos\theta = \frac{1(2)+1(-2)+1(2)}{\sqrt{1^2+1^2+1^2}.\sqrt{2^2+(-2)^2+2^2}} = \frac{2}{\sqrt{3}\,2\sqrt{3}} = \frac{1}{3}$.

67. $|A| = -1$, $|B| = 1$

$$A^{-1} = \frac{1}{|A|}\text{Adj } A = \frac{1}{-1}\begin{bmatrix} 1 & -1 \\ -2 & 1 \end{bmatrix}^T$$

$$= \begin{bmatrix} -1 & 2 \\ 1 & -1 \end{bmatrix}$$

$$B^{-1} = \frac{1}{|B|}\text{Adj} = \frac{1}{1}\begin{bmatrix} 2 & -1 \\ 1 & 0 \end{bmatrix}^T = \begin{bmatrix} 2 & 1 \\ -1 & 0 \end{bmatrix}$$

$$B^{-1}A^{-1} = \begin{bmatrix} 2 & 1 \\ -1 & 0 \end{bmatrix}\begin{bmatrix} -1 & 2 \\ 1 & -1 \end{bmatrix} = \begin{bmatrix} -1 & 3 \\ 1 & -2 \end{bmatrix}.$$

70. Always equal to 1.

71. Compare with

$x^2 + y^2 + z^2 + 2ux + 2vy + 2wz + d = 0$

$u = -2,\ v = 3,\ w = -4,\ d = -7$

radius $= \sqrt{u^2+v^2+w^2-d}$

$= \sqrt{4+9+16+7}$

$= \sqrt{36} = 6.$

72. $\frac{dx}{dt} = 2t+3,\ \frac{dy}{dt} = 4t - 2$

$\frac{dy}{dx} = \frac{dy/dt}{dx/dt} = \frac{4t-2}{2t+3}$

slope at $t = 2 = \frac{dy}{dx}/t = 2$

$= \frac{4(2)-2}{2(2)+3} = \frac{6}{7}.$

74. $\frac{dy}{dt} = -\sin t,\ \frac{dx}{dt} = \cos t$

$\frac{dy}{dx} = \frac{dy/dt}{dx/dt} = \frac{-\sin t}{\cos t} = -\frac{x}{y}.$

75. Put $x^2 + 1 = t$

$2x = dx = dt$

$x\,dx = \frac{dt}{2} \qquad \int (t)^{5/2}\frac{dt}{2}(C)$

$\frac{1}{2}\frac{t^{7/2}}{7/2} + c = \frac{1}{7}(x^2+1)^{7/2} + c.$

76.
$$f'(x) = 2x - 6$$
$$f'(c) = 0$$
$$2c - 6 = 0$$
$$2c = 6$$
$$c = 3.$$

77. $8(x - 3) + 5(5 - 6) + 1(15 - 6x) = 2$

$8x - 24 - 5 + 15 - 6x = 2$

$2x - 14 = 2$

$2x = 16 \Rightarrow x = 8.$

79. $\int_{-\frac{\pi}{2}}^{\frac{\pi}{2}} |\sin x|\,dx$

$$|\sin x| = \begin{cases} \sin x & 0 < x < \frac{\pi}{2} \\ -\sin x & -\frac{\pi}{2} < x < 0 \end{cases}$$

$= \int_{-\frac{\pi}{2}}^{0} -\sin x\,dx + \int_{0}^{\frac{\pi}{2}} \sin x\,dx$

$= -[-\cos x]_{-\pi/2}^{0} + (-\cos x)\Big|_0^{\pi/2}$

$= (\cos 0 - \cos(-\pi/2) + (-\cos \pi/2 - (-\cos 0))$

$= (1 - 0) + (-0 + 1) = 2.$

81.
$$y = \frac{x+1}{x-1}$$
$$\frac{dy}{dx} = \frac{(x-1)(1)-(x+1)1}{(x-1)^2}$$
$$= \frac{x-1-x-1}{(x-1)^2} = \frac{-2}{(x-1)^2}.$$

84.
$$y = x^2 - 4x + 3$$
$$\frac{dy}{dx} = 2x - 3$$

Tangent is ∥ to x-axis.

∴ slope = 0 ⇒ one tangent.

85. $\lim_{x\to 0}(x^2)\left[\sin\left(\frac{1}{x}\right)\right]$

since $\sin\frac{1}{x}$ is odd and x^2 approaches to zero = 0.

86. $\lim_{x\to-2} \frac{x+2}{(x)^3+(2)^3}$

$\lim_{x\to\infty} -2 \frac{x+2}{(x+2)(x^2-2x+4)}$

$= \frac{1}{(-2)^2-2(-2)+4}$ (C) $= \frac{1}{4+4+4} = \frac{1}{12}.$

87. $\frac{dy}{dx} = \frac{-y}{x}$

$\frac{dy}{y} = -\frac{dx}{x} \qquad \frac{dy}{y}+\frac{dx}{x} = 0$

integration

$\log y + \log x = \log 1 + \log C$

$\log xy = \log (1.c)$

$xy = c.$

88. $y = x\frac{dy}{dx}+\left(\frac{dy}{dx}\right)^{-1}$

Multiply by $\frac{dy}{dx} \qquad y = \frac{dy}{dx} = x\left(\frac{dy}{dx}\right)^2 + 1$

degree → 2.

89. $\int_0^1 \frac{\tan^{-1} x}{1+x^2} dx$

Put $\tan^{-1} x = t$

$\frac{1}{1+x^2} dx = dt$

$x = 0, \Rightarrow t = 0 \qquad x = 1, \Rightarrow t = \pi/4$

$\int_0^{\pi/4} t\, dt \qquad \frac{t^2}{2}\Big|_0^{\pi/4}$

$\frac{1}{2}\left[\left(\frac{\pi}{4}\right)^2 - (0)^2\right] \qquad \frac{1}{2}\left(\frac{\pi}{16}\right)^2 = \frac{\pi^2}{32}.$

96. $2.\frac{\log 2}{\log 8} - \frac{1}{3}.\frac{\log 9}{\log 3}$

$2.\frac{\log 2}{\log 2^3} - \frac{1}{3}.\frac{\log 3^2}{\log 3} \qquad 2.\frac{\log 2}{3.\log 2} - \frac{1}{3}2.\frac{\log 3}{\log 3}$

$\frac{2}{3} - \frac{2}{3} = 0.$

97. $\begin{vmatrix} 2 & -1 & 1 \\ 1 & 2 & -3 \\ 3 & m & 5 \end{vmatrix} = 0$

$2(10 + 3m) + 1(5 + 9) + 1(m - 6) = 0$

$20 + 6m + 14 + m - 6 = 0$

$7m + 28 = 0 \qquad m = -4.$

99. $1(1) + (-x)(x) + (-y)(y) = 0$

$1 - x^2 - y^2 = 0$

$x^2 + y^2 = 1.$

100. $A^2 = I$

$\Rightarrow A^2A^{-1} = IA^{-1}$

$A = A^{-1}.$

101. $\frac{x^2}{26}+\frac{y^2}{16} = 1 \qquad a^2 = 36,\ 6^2 = 16$

we have, $b^2 = a^2(1 - c^2)$

$\frac{16}{36} = 1 - e^2$

$1 - e^2 = \frac{4}{9}$ (A)

$1-\frac{4}{9} = e^2 \qquad \frac{5}{9} = e^2 \Rightarrow e = \frac{\sqrt{5}}{3}.$

103. $A \times B = \{(0, 1), (1, 1), (0, 0), (1, 0)\}$

$A \times A = \{(0, 0), (0, 1), (1, 1), (1, 0)\}$

$\therefore A \times B = A \times A.$

105. $\sin A + \sin B - \sin C - \sin D$

In cyclic quadrilateral, ABCD

$A + C = 180°, B + D = 180°$

$A = 180° - C, B = 180° - D$

$\therefore \sin(180° - C) + \sin(180° - D) - \sin C - \sin D$

$\sin C + \sin D - \sin C - \sin D = 0.$

106. $\sin(360° + 60°).\cos(360° + 30°) + \cos(360° - 60°)\{-\sin(360° - 30°)\}$

$= \sin 60°.\cos 30° + \cos 60° \sin 30°$

$= \sin(60° + 30°)$

$= \sin 90° = 1.$

110. $A\left(-1, \frac{1}{2}, 4\right) B\left(1, \frac{1}{2}, 4\right)$

$B\left(-1, \frac{1}{2}, 4\right) C\left(1, \frac{-1}{2}, 4\right)$

AB =1 BC = 1 Area (1).

112. $\cos^2 \alpha + \cos^2 \beta + \cos^2 \gamma = 1$

$\frac{1+\cos 2\alpha}{2}+\frac{1+\cos 2\beta}{2}+\frac{1+\cos 2\gamma}{2} = 1$

$3 + \cos 2\alpha + \cos 2\beta + \cos 2\gamma = 2$

$1 + \cos 2\alpha + \cos 2\beta + \cos 2\gamma = 0.$

113. $1, \frac{-1}{2}, \frac{1}{4}, \frac{-1}{8}$

$S_\infty = \frac{a}{1-r}$

$a = 1 \qquad r = -1/2$

$= \frac{1}{1-\left(\frac{-1}{2}\right)} = \frac{2}{3}.$

115. 2, 2, 3, 3, 4, 5, 7, 9, 10

median = 4.

116. $< 2, -1, 2 > \quad \Rightarrow < 1, \frac{-1}{2}, 1 >.$

Previous Papers (Solved)

NATIONAL DEFENCE ACADEMY & NAVAL ACADEMY

NDA & NA – Entrance Exam, 2011 (II)

PAPER I : GENERAL ABILITY TEST

PART A : ENGLISH LANGUAGE

SPOTTING ERRORS

Directions (For the 15 items which follow) :

(i) In this section, a number of sentences are given. The sentences are divided in three separate parts and each one is labelled A, B and C. Read each sentence to find out whether there is an error in any part. No sentence has more than one error. When you find an error in any one of the parts A, B or C, indicate your response on the separate Answer Sheet at the appropriate space. You may feel that there is no error in a sentence. In that case, letter D will signify a 'No error' response.

(ii) You are to indicate only one response for each item in your Answer Sheet. (If you indicate more than one response, your answer will be considered wrong.) Errors may be in grammar, word usage or idioms. There may be a word missing or there may be a word which should be removed.

*(iii) You are **not** required to correct the error. You are required **only** to indicate your response on the Answer Sheet.*

Examples 'P' and 'Q' have been solved for you.

P. (A) The young child/(B) singed/(C) a very sweet song./(D) No error

Q. (A) We worked/(B) very hard/(C) throughout the season./(D) No error

Explanation:

In item P, the word 'singed' is wrong. The letter under this part is (B), so (B) is the correct answer. Similarly, for item Q, (D) is the correct answer, as the sentence does not contain any error.

1. (A) It was really smart of him/(B) to have chosen the right course,/(C) *is n't it*?/(D) No error

2. (A) The doctor advised me/(B) that/(C) I am going on a salt free diet./(D) No error

3. (A) It can't be true/(B) that he has never done something wrong/(C) in his entire career./(D) No error

4. (A) He told/(B) that his brother/(C) was singer. /(D) No error

5. (A) When we reached at the station/(B) I fought my way through people and luggage/(C) and secured a place next to the window./(D) No error

6. (A) The managing director along with his staff members were present/(B) for/(C) the annual general body meeting./(D) No error

7. (A) If you will follow my instructions,/(B) you will definitely score high marks/(C) in the entrance examination./(D) No error

8. (A) In many respects,/(B) India is different/(C) than western countries./(D) No error

9. (A) The members of the family/(B) soon became/(C) aware what had taken place./(D) No error

10. (A) I have met him/(B) on Monday last/(C) and had a long discussion./(D) No error

11. (A) It is time/(B) we decide not to play cricket, /(C) for the next two years./(D) No error

12. (A) He likes/(B) the sceneries/(C) of the hills./(D) No error

13. (A) I did not know/(B) that you have left your handbag in our office/(C) when you came to see me last Friday./(D) No error

14. (A) He wanted me/(B) to bring two breads and some butter/(C) for breakfast./(D) No error

15. (A) The parents are happy to know/(B) that a number of summer programmes have been arranged/(C) for the benefit of their children./(D) No error

***Directions (For the 10 items which follow) :** Each of the following items consists of a sentence followed by four words or group of words. Select the **synonym** of the word (occurring in the sentence in capital letters) as per the context.*

16. The vehicle slowed down as they moved up the GRADIENT.

A. road with sharp bends B. bumpy, uneven path
C. slope or incline D. mountainous area

17. It is DEPLORABLE that millions of people in India are below the poverty line.
A. hateful B. regrettable
C. undesirable D. unpleasant

18. The government should PROSCRIBE that sort of literature.
A. rusticate B. excommunicate
C. ban D. outlaw

19. The volcano on the island is DORMANT.
A. cold B. inactive
C. dangerous D. old

20. A person who EQUIVOCATES should not be relied upon.
A. deceives others
B. tells lies
C. gives misleading statements
D. flatters

21. The newspaper reports were MENDACIOUS.
A. mischievous B. truthful
C. provocative D. false

22. The priest pronounced BENEDICTION.
(a) good wishes (b) blessings
(c) punishment (d) appreciation

23. Her habits are INNOCUOUS.
A. useful B. injurious
C. causing no harm D. bad

24. I INVEIGHED her for her different outlook.
A. criticized B. rebuked
C. disliked D. appreciated

25. The youth was BEFOGGED when he was interrogated loudly by the police inspector.
A. terrified B. panicky
C. surprised D. puzzled

Directions (For the 10 items which follow): *Each of the following items consists of a sentence followed by four words or group of words. Select the* ***antonym*** *of the word (occurring in the sentence in capital letters) as per the context.*

26. A few heavenly talents DARKEN the world in each generation.
A. brighten B. please
C. enlighten D. glamorize

27. An ICY reception greeted the arrivals.
A. hostile B. warm
C. pleasing D. strange

28. The young athlete is ENERGETIC enough to run ten thousand meters at a stretch.
A. inactive B. dull
C. gloomy D. lethargic

29. He has a SECURE position in the entrance examination.
A. rigid B. precarious
C. static D. secondary

30. The accused was ACQUITTED of the charge.
A. held guilty B. betrayed
C. involved D. offended

31. It is COMPULSORY that all members of the board be present at the meeting.
A. optional B. contrary
C. obligatory D. conditional

32. Events ultimately led to LUGUBRIOUS ending.
A. happy B. hopeful
C. helpful D. reassuring

33. He ACCELERATED the speed of his car.
A. retarded B. reviewed
C. recorded D. restored

34. The criminal was known to the police by VARIOUS names
A. separate B. distinct
C. identical D. similar

35. The police praised the METICULOUS arrangements made by organizers to receive the guest at the airport.
A. haphazard B. random
C. ridiculous D. shabby

REARRANGING PARTS OF A SENTENCE

Directions (For the 8 items which follow) : *In the following items, some parts of the sentence have been jumbled up. You are required to rearrange these parts which are labelled P, Q, R and S to produce the correct sentence. Choose the proper sequence and marks in your Answer Sheet accordingly.*

Example 'Z' has been solved for you.

Z. Some people believe that/(P) the effect/(Q) is very bad/ (R) on children/(S) of cinema
The correct sequence should be
A. PSRQ B. SPQR
C. SRPQ D. QSRP

Explanation:
The proper way of writing the sentence is "Some people believe that the effect of cinema on children is very bad". This is indicated by the sequence PSRQ and so (A) is the correct answer.

36. (P) they marched/ (Q) for a while under a tree/ (R) often they had rested/(S) on to their journey
The correct sequence should be
A. SRQP B. PSRQ
C. QRPS D. RQPS

37. (P) as the President entered the hall/ (Q) from his seat/ (R) to greet him/ (S) everyone got up
The correct sequence should be
A. RQPS B. QPRS
C. PSQR D. SQRP

38. (P) he took shelter/ (Q) near the lake/ (R) when there was a heavy downpour/ (S) under the large mango tree

The correct sequence should be
A. PRQS B. PSRQ
C. RSPQ D. RPSQ

39. Our educationalists/are (P) to teach children/ (Q) too often anxious/ (R) without any utility/ (S) so many languages
The correct sequence should be
A. PQRS B. QRSP
C. SRQP D. QPSR

40. (P) the rain did not prevent/ (Q) from being played/ (R) to a finish/ (S) the match
The correct sequence should be
A. PQRS B. PSQR
C. PSRQ D. SQPR

41. It has been like (P) inheriting some money/ (Q) and afterwards/ (R) marrying for love/ (S) through the wife
The correct sequence should be
A. RQPS B. PSQR
C. SPQR D. PQSR

42. His mother (P) when he was hungry/ (Q) last evening/ (R) could not feed/ (S) the baby
The correct sequence should be
A. RSPQ B. PQRS
C. SPQR D. QPRS

43. Whenever he heard the question (P) the old man/ (Q) answered/ (R) who lived in that house/ (S) that the Earth is flat
The correct sequence should be
A. PQRS B. PQSR
C. PRQS D. SPQR

COMPREHENSION

Directions (For the 07 items which follow) : In this section, you have two short passages. After each passage, you will find several questions based on the passage. First, read a passage and then answer the questions based on it. You are required to select your answers based on the contents of the passage and opinion of the auther only.

Examples 'I' and 'J' have been solved for you.

PASSAGE (EXAMPLE)

In our approach to life, be it pragmatic or otherwise, a basic fact that confronts us squarely and unmistakably is the desire for peace, security and happiness. Different forms of life at different levels of existence make up the teeming denizens of this earth of ours. And, no matter whether they belong to the higher groups such as human beings or to the lower groups such as animals, all beings primarily seek peace, comfort and security. Life is as dear to a mute creature as it is to a man. Even the lowliest insect strives for protection against dangers that threaten its life. Just as each one of us wants to live and not to die, so do all other creatures.

I. The author's main point is that
A. different forms of life are found on the earth
B. different levels of existence are possible in nature
C. peace and security are the chief goals of all living beings
D. even the weakest creature struggles to preserve its life

J. Which one of the following assumptions or steps is essential in developing the author's position?
A. All forms of life have a single overriding goal
B. The will to survive of a creature is identified with a desire for peace
C. All beings are divided into higher and lower groups
D. A parallel is drawn between happiness and life, and pain and death

Explanation:

I. The idea which represents the author's main point is "peace and security are the chief goals of all living beings", which is response (C). So (C) is the correct answer.

J. The best assumption underlying the passage is "The will to survive of a creature is identified with a desire for peace", which is response (B). So (B) is the correct answer.

Passage I

Elephants spray water over their ears to stay cool. The rhythm of an elephant's day is set largely by its watering routine. An adult needs about thirty gallons of water a day. When water is abundant there is no problem. But during droughts, elephants resort to an intriguing technique: digging wells. In a dried–up river bed they scoop out holes with their forefeet until they reach water. After waiting patiently for the sand to settle, they drink in order of seniority, calves last.

44. According to the passage, water is
A. quite important for the elephant
B. vital for the elephant's survival
C. occasionally useful for the elephant
D. often a problem for the elephant

45. According to the passage, elephants spray water over themselves
A. to have fun
B. to ward off the heat
C. to cool their heels
D. to quench their thirst

46. During droughts, elephants
A. burrow in the sand to avoid heat
B. find water in rivers
C. dig holes in the river bed to reach the water
D. find new water holes

47. When the elephants find water
A. the baby elephants drink first
B. the oldest adult drinks first

C. the largest elephant drinks first
D. the youngest adult drinks first

Passage II

One day my brother brought home a new song-bird. It was the smallest of them all, a tiny creature of a blue and a red that sparkled when brushed by the sun. But there was a problem: while the others sang, this new bird remained silent. My brother tried coaxing music out of him, in vain. He tried attacking with a stick, but the bird was unmoved. My brother first tried withholding food, but later when the incentive was offered the bird ignored it, and twice he knocked over his dish, scattering the seed.

48. One day the writer's brother brought home a bird
A. which never ate food
B. which flew so high it seemed to touch the sun
C. whose colours shone brightly in the sunlight
D. which was the largest of all the birds in his collection

49. At first his brother tried to get the bird to sing by
A. tempting with food
B. placing it in the company of the other birds while they sang
C. singing to the bird himself
D. withholding food

50. What does the word "coaxing" mean?
A. to behave rudely
B. to use violent means
C. to gently persuade
D. to beg repeatedly

PART B : GENERAL KNOWLEDGE

***Directions** : The following **six (06)** items consist of two statements, Statement I and Statement II. You are to examine these two statements carefully and select the answers to these items using the code given below:*

Code :

A. Both the statements are individually true and Statement II is the correct explanation of Statement I.
B. Both the Statements are individually true but Statement II is ***not*** the correct explanation of Statement I.
C. Statement I is true but Statement II is false.
D. Statement I is false but Statement II is true.

51. Statement I : Mahatma Gandhi launched the Rowlatt Satyagraha as an all– India mass protest.

Statement II : Rowlatt Act was passed by the British Government in 1919 to authorize the government to imprison any person without trial.

52. Statement I : A public expression of dissatisfaction with democracy indicates the success of the democratic project: it transforms people from the status of a subject into that of a citizen.

Statement II : The fact that people are complaining is itself an affirmation of the success of democracy: it shows that people have developed aware-ness and the ability to look critically at the government.

53. Statement I : The private trade of the East India Company's officials in the 18th century had flowered with the indirect patronage of the authorities of the Company.

Statement II : The extra-legal power enjoyed by the foreign merchants and the duty-free nature of their private trade virtually edged the indigenous merchants out of competition.

54. Statement I : Water (H_2O) is more polar than Hydrogen Sulphide (H_2S).

Statement II : Oxygen is more electronegative than Sulphur.

55. Statement I : Metal ions are Lewis acids.

Statement II : Metal ions are electron pair acceptors.

56. Statement I : Diamond is very hard and has high melting point.

Statement II : In diamond, each carbon is covalently bonded to four other carbon atoms to form a three-dimensional network.

57. Consider the following statements about the visit of Indian President Smt. Pratibha Patil to Mongolia in July 2011:
1. She became the first Indian President to make an official visit to the country.
2. In the area of defence, India and Mongolia agreed to expand collaboration through increased level of joint exercises and training.

Which of the statements given above is/are correct?
A. 1 only   B. 2 only
C. Both 1 and 2   D. Neither 1 nor 2

58. Who among the following, is the latest Indian to win the Pulitzer Prize for literature?
A. Jhumpa Lahiri   B. Geeta Anand
C. Gobind Behari Lal   D. Siddhartha Mukherjee

59. Indian Army's counter-insurgency school is situated in
A. Kanker   B. Srinagar
C. Tezpur   D. Vairengte

60. Match List-I with List-II and select the correct answer using the codes given below the lists:

List-I (Name of the Shipyard)	List-II (Location)
(a) Hindustan Shipyard Limited	1. Kolkata
(b) Garden Reach Shipbuilders & Engineers Limited	2. Vasco-da-Gama
(c) Goa Shipyard Limited	3. Mumbai
(d) Mazagon Dock Limited	4. Visakhapatnam

Codes:

	(a)	(b)	(c)	(d)
A.	4	2	1	3
B.	3	1	2	4
C.	4	1	2	3
D.	3	2	1	4

61. Sirocco is a name used to mean

A. a local wind B. a volcano
C. an island D. an ocean current

62. Which of the following is/are the chief characteristics of commercial grain farming of the middle latitude grasslands?

1. The size of farms are generally large.
2. Cultivation is highly mechanized.
3. It is a type of extensive farming.

Select the correct answer using the code given below:

A. 1 and 2 only B. 2 only
C. 1, 2 and 3 D. 1 and 3 only

63. Match List-I with List-II and select the correct answer using the codes given below the lists:

List-I (Desert)	List-II (Country)
(a) Kalahari	1. Angola
(b) Namib	2. Sudan
(c) Nubian	3. Botswana
(d) Atacama	4. Chile

Codes :

	(a)	(b)	(c)	(d)
A.	4	2	1	3
B.	3	2	1	4
C.	4	1	2	3
D.	3	1	2	4

64. Which one among the following statements relating to an anticyclone is correct?

A. Anticyclone is a wind system with a high pressure centre
B. In anticyclone the movement of wind is inward
C. The contribution of an anticyclone towards determining weather of an area is quite significant
D. The movement of wind is clockwise in an anticyclone of southern hemisphere

65. Tipu Sultan's major interest in building ships was to

A. fight the English at sea
B. promote trade and commerce
C. maintain diplomatic relations with Muscat (Oman)
D. establish an overseas settlement at port Basra (Iraq), which would be under his control, on lines of the European companies

66. Which among the following is/are the impact/impacts of industrial revolution in England?

1. Cottage industry was replaced by the factory system of production using machines.
2. It led to the overpopulation of villages.
3. It led to the emergence of working class movements.

Select the correct answer using the code given below:

A. 1, 2 and 3 B. 1 and 3 only
C. 1 only D. 2 and 3 only

67. The international body which was formed in Europe (in 1889) to coordinate the efforts of socialists all over Europe was called

A. Social Democratic Party
B. Commune
C. Second International
D. Labour Party

68. Which of the following statements with regard to the Federal System is/are correct?

1. In a federation, two sets of governments co-exist and there is distribution of power.
2. There is a written constitution.

Select the correct answer using the code given below:

A. 1 only B. 2 only
C. Both 1 and 2 D. Neither 1 nor 2

69. The common edible mushroom is a

A. mass of fungal spores
B. type of hypha
C. tightly packed mycelium
D. structure used for producing asexual spores

70. A biogeographic region with significant reservoir of biodiversity that is under threat from humans is called as

A. bioendangered region
B. biodiversity hotspot
C. biodiversity reservoir
D. environmentally endangered region

71. The main function of the inner bark of a woody plant is to

A. transport minerals and water from the roots to the leaves
B. act as a membrane impermeable to water and gas
C. transport food from the leaves to the other parts of the plant
D. protect the plant from herbivorous animals

72. Birds like Flamingos can stand on one leg. Which among the following statements relating to this is/are correct?

1. By standing on one leg Flamingos can conserve body heat and energy because they can reduce great deal of surface area for the loss of heat.
2. By standing on one leg, one Flamingo makes a courtship display, which is a part of ritual prior to reproduction.

Select the correct answer using the code given below:

A. 1 only B. 2 only
C. Both 1 and 2 D. Neither 1 nor 2

73. Which one among the following is the largest monkey?

A. Spider monkey B. Baboon
C. Gorilla D. Howler monkey

74. Two copper wires A and B length l and $2l$ respectively, have the same area of cross-section. The ratio of the resistivity of wire A to the resistivity of wire B is

A. 4 B. 2
C. 1 D. 1/2

75. The position – time ($x - t$) graph for motion of a body is given below:

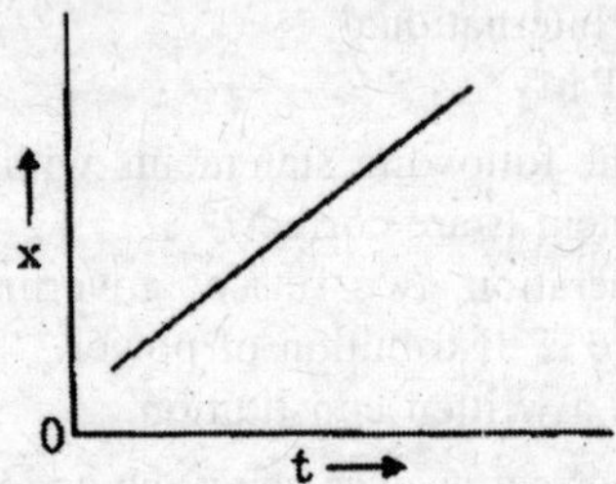

Which one among the following is depicted by the above graph?

A. Positive acceleration B. Negative acceleration
C. Zero acceleration D. None of the above

76. Which one among the following waves are called waves of heat energy?

A. Radio waves B. Infrared waves
C. Ultraviolet waves D. Microwaves

77. The phenomenon of 'trade winds' takes place due to

A. conduction of heat B. convection of heat
C. radiation D. None of the above

78. Ultrasonic waves are those sound waves having frequency

A. between 20 hertz and 1000 hertz
B. between 1000 hertz and 20000 hertz
C. more than 20 kilohertz
D. less than 20 hertz

79. Bases turn red litmus blue and acids turn blue litmus red. A student tested a liquid with a red litmus paper and it stayed red with no change. This shows that the liquid

A. must be pure water
B. must be an acid
C. is not a base
D. is neither a base nor an acid

80. The main constituent of vinegar is

A. Citric acid B. Acetic acid
C. Ascorbic acid D. Tartaric acid

81. The major component used in preparation of different types of glasses is

A. Silica B. Sodium borate
C. Calcium silicate D. Sodium silicate

82. All the elements in a group (family) have a common valency. For example, all the elements of the carbon family (carbon, silicon, germanium, tin and lead) have common valency four. However, some of these elements can also have valency two. Which of the following can have valency two?

A. Silicon, germanium and tin
B. Only germanium and tin
C. Germanium, tin and lead
D. Only tin and lead

83. Match List-I with List-II and select the correct using the code given below the lists:

List-I (Metallic oxide)	List-II (Colour imparted to glass)
(*a*) Uranium oxide	1. Red
(*b*) Cuprous oxide	2. Blue
(*c*) Cobalt oxide	3. Green
(*d*) Chromium oxide	4. Yellow

Codes :

	(*a*)	(*b*)	(*c*)	(*d*)
A.	4	1	2	3
B.	3	2	1	4
C.	4	2	1	3
D.	3	1	2	4

84. The image formed by a convex mirror of a real object is larger than the object

A. when u < 2f
B. when u > 2f
C. for all values of u
D. for no value of u

(u = object distance, f = focal length)

85. Protons and neutrons are bound in a nucleus by the

A. short range 'weak interaction'
B. short range 'strong interaction'
C. long range 'electromagnetic interaction'
D. long range 'gravitational interaction'

86. Refractive index of an optical medium changes with

1. the nature of the medium.
2. the change in the angle of incidence of the ray.
3. colour of the incident ray.

Select the correct answer using the code given below:

A. 1 and 3 only B. 2 and 3 only
C. 1 and 2 only D. 1, 2 and 3

87. A one-rupee coin is placed at the bottom of a vessel. Water is then poured into the vessel such that the depth of water becomes 20 cm. If water has refractive index 4/3, the coin would be seen at a depth of

A. 20 cm B. about 26 cm
C. 15 cm D. 25 cm

88. Momentum of a body is
1. a vector quantity.
2. a conserved quantity in an isolated system.
3. same as force in linear motion.

Select the correct answer using the code given below:
A. 1 and 3 only B. 2 and 3 only
C. 1 and 2 only D. 1, 2 only

89. Which one among the following is a correct sequence of the Indian ports from north to south?
A. Haldia – Kandla – Paradeep – Kochi
B. Kandla – Haldia – Paradeep – Kochi
C. Kandla – Haldia – Kochi – Paradeep
D. Kochi – Kandla – Haldia – Paradeep

90. Which one among the following is a correct sequence of production of coal in the Indian States in descending order?
A. Jharkhand – Madhya Pradesh – West Bengal – Meghalaya
B. West Bengal – Madhya Pradesh – Jharkhand – Meghalaya
C. Jharkhand – West Bengal – Meghalaya – Madhya Pradesh
D. Madhya Pradesh – Jharkhand – West Bengal – Meghalaya

91. Match List-I with List-II and select the correct answer using the code given below the lists:

List-I (Mineral)	List-II (State)
(*a*) Bauxite	1. Andhra Pradesh
(*b*) Mica	2. Odisha
(*c*) Copper	3. Madhya Pradesh
(*d*) Zinc	4. Rajasthan

Codes :

	(*a*)	(*b*)	(*c*)	(*d*)
A.	4	1	3	2
B.	2	1	3	4
C.	4	3	1	2
D.	2	3	1	4

92. The western coasts of India receive very high rainfall in summer mainly due to
A. Tropical location B. Nearness to sea
C. Western Ghats D. Himalayas

93. The current produced by upwelling of cold water off the coast of Chile and Peru is known as
A. El Nino B. Humboldt current
C. Agulhas current D. Canary current

94. If the ratio of the weight of a man in a stationary lift and when it is moving downwards with uniform acceleration 'a' is 3 : 2, then the value of 'a' is
A. 3g/2 B. g/3
C. g D. 2g/3

95. A body is thrown upward against the gravity 'g' with initial velocity 'u'. Which one among the following is the correct expression for its final velocity when attains the maximum height?
A. $u^2/(2g)$ B. $2g/u^2$
C. $u^2g/2$ D. None of the above

96. Which one among the following is the correct value of the gravitational force of the Earth acting on a body of mass 1kg?
A. 8.9 N B. 9.8 N
C. 89 N D. 98 N

97. A neutral (unchanged) metal ball is suspended using a non-magnetic string. A positively charged insulating rod is placed near the ball which is observed to be attracted to the rod. This is because
A. the ball becomes positively charged by induction
B. the ball becomes negatively charged by induction
C. there is a rearrangement of the electrons in the ball
D. the number of electrons in the ball is more than the number of electrons on the rod

98. It is impossible for two oscillators, each executing simple harmonic motion, to remain in phase with each other if they have different
A. time periods B. amplitudes
C. spring constants D. kinetic energy

99. Identity the correct sequence of the following events of Indian history:
1. Foundation of the Indian Muslim League
2. Surat Split
3. Partition of Bengal
4. Transfer of capital from Calcutta to Delhi

Select the correct answer using the codes given below:
A. 1-2-3-4 B. 2-3-4-1
C. 3-1-2-4 D. 4-3-2-1

100. *Neel Darpan* is a play based on the story of Indigo Rebellion of Bengal of 1860-61. Who authored it?
A. Dinabandhu Mitra
B. Bankim Chandra Chattopadhyaya
C. Sisir Kumar Ghosh and Motilal Ghosh jointly
D. Madhusudan Dutta

101. Which one among the following is ***not*** the characteristic feature of the Harappan settlement?
A. Doorways and windows generally faced the side lanes and rarely opened onto the main streets
B. Houses generally had separate bathing areas and toilets
C. The citadel was walled but the lower town was not walled
D. Drains and water chutes from the second storey were often built inside the wall

102. Which one among the following is ***not*** true with regard to Rig Veda Samhita?

A. There are about 300 non-Indo-European words in Rig Veda
B. There is a reference to *dasarajna* (battle of ten kings) in the Rig Veda
C. It is mentioned in the Rig Veda that the Bharata chief Sudas fought against a confederacy of ten tribes
D. Purus sided with Bharata in the battle of ten kings

103. The First Anglo-Burmese War was concluded by a treaty. Which one among the following is that?
A. Treaty of Bharma B. Treaty of Tamu
C. Treaty of Bhamo D. Treaty of Yandaboo

104. Rain shadow effect is associated with
A. Cyclonic rainfall
B. Orographic rainfall
C. Convectional rainfall
D. Frontal rainfall

105. Match List-I with List-II and select the correct answer using the code given below the lists:

List-I (Current)	**List-II (Feature)**
(*a*) Kuroshio current	1. Warm current in the Atlantic Ocean
(*b*) Peru current	2. Cold current in the Atlantic Ocean
(*c*) Labrador current	3. Warm current in the Pacific Ocean
(*d*) Florida current	4. Cold current in the Pacific Ocean

Codes :

	(*a*)	(*b*)	(*c*)	(*d*)
A.	3	4	2	1
B.	3	2	4	1
C.	1	4	2	3
D.	1	2	4	3

106. The intensity of insolation depends on
A. Altitude B. Nature of terrain
C. Wind D. Latitude

107. Which of the following statements is/are correct?
1. Cyclone is a low pressure system.
2. The wind movement is clockwise in the cyclone of northern hemisphere.

Select the correct answer using the code given below:
A. 1 only B. 2 only
C. Both 1 and 2 D. Neither 1 nor 2

108. Which one of the following processes of weathering belongs to both mechanical and chemical weathering?
A. Crystallization B. Exfoliation
C. Hydration D. Carbonation

109. A man was trapped in a room of a building which was up in flames. Fire-fighters had to break window panes which were filled in smoke to take him out. Once the injured person is out, he should be observed/treated for
A. Superficial burn wound
B. Electric burn wound
C. Respiratory burn
D. Internal organ injury

110. AIDS is caused by Human Immunodeficiency Virus (HIV) which is
A. Retro virus B. Lente virus
C. Arbo virus D. Immune virus

111. With regard to animal breeding, which one among the following is ***not*** correct?
A. In-breeding : Mating of more closely related animals within the same breed for 1-2 generations
B. Out-breeding : Breeding of unrelated animals of the same breed without common ancestors for 4-6 generations.
C. Cross-breeding : Superior males of one breed are mated with superior females of another breed.
D. Out-crossing : Offspring is called an 'out cross'.

112. Which one among the following statements regarding heart sound is correct?
A. Heart sounds are caused by the internal blood flow inside the heart
B. Heart sounds are caused by the external blood flow outside the heart
C. Heart sounds are caused by opening and closing of heart valves
D. Normal sounds are called 'murmurs'

113. Which one among the following cell organelles is semi-permeable?
A. Cell membrane B. Plasma membrane
C. Cell wall D. Nucleus

114. Thermometer A and B have ice points marked at 15° and 25° and steam points at 75° and 125° respectively. When thermometer A measures the temperature of a bath as 60°, the reading of B for the same bath is
A. 60° B. 75°
C. 90° D. 100°

115. Which one among the following most correctly determines the atomic number of an element?
A. Number of protons
B. Number of protons and electrons
C. Number of ions
D. Number of nucleons

116. Potential at a point due to a point charge is V. The charge is doubled and also the distance of the point from the charge is doubled. The new potential is
A. V/2 B. 4V
C. V D. 2V

117. Which one among the following is used to make periscope?

A. Concave lens B. Concave mirror
C. Plane mirror D. None of the above

118. Kilowatt-hour is the unit of
A. potential difference B. electric power
C. electric energy D. electric potential

119. A stable nucleus (light with $A < 10$) has
A. exactly the same number of neutrons and protons
B. more neutrons than protons
C. no neutrons
D. no protons

120. In oxidation
1. hydrogen is displaced from a substance.
2. an electropositive element is added to or proportion of electropositive element increases in a substance.

Select the correct answer using the code given below:
A. 1 only B. 2 only
C. Both 1 and 2 D. Neither 1 nor 2

121. When a copper rod is dipped in aqueous silver nitrate solution, the colour of the solution changes to blue. This is because
A. Cu is more easily reduced than Ag
B. Ag is more easily reduced than Cu
C. Nitrate ion acts as an oxidizing agent
D. Nitrate ion acts as a reducing agent

122. The reaction that takes place in soap making is called saponification. Basically soap is sodium or potassium salts of
A. long chain monocarboxylic acids
B. glycerol
C. long chain dicarboxylic acids
D. long chain tricarboxylic acids

123. The number of protons in a negatively charged atom (anion) is
A. more than the atomic number of the element
B. less than the atomic number of the element
C. more than the number of electrons in the atom
D. less than the number of electrons in the atom

124. The metal constituent of chlorophyll is
A. Iron B. Potassium
C. Manganese D. Magnesium

125. During explosion of gunpowder, which of the following gases are evolved in the proportion of 1 : 3?
A. Oxygen : Nitrogen
B. Nitrogen : Oxygen
C. Nitrogen : Carbon dioxide
D. Carbon dioxide : Nitrogen

126. Which of the following statements regarding Mughal paintings is/are correct?
1. The paintings of Akbar's time were mostly confined to book illustrations and portraits.
2. Mir Sayyid Ali of Herat and Khwaja Abdus Samad formed the nucleus of the Mughal School of painting which fused together the non-Islamic and Islamic elements.

Select the correct answer using the code given below:
A. 1 only B. 2 only
C. Both 1 and 2 D. Neither 1 nor 2

127. Which of the following statements regarding consolidation of British power in 18th century Bengal is/are correct?
1. The Nawab granted the Company the Nizamat powers in 1765.
2. The duties of collecting revenues and administration of justice were entrusted with the European officials of the East India Company.

Select the correct answer using the code given below:
A. 1 only B. 2 only
C. Both 1 and 2 D. Neither 1 nor 2

128. Which of the following statements about industrial revolution in Europe is ***not*** correct?
A. Britain was the first country to experience the industrial revolution
B. England was fortunate as coal and iron resources were plentifully available, as were other minerals — lead, copper and tin — that were used in industry
C. From the 1780s, the iron industry symbolized the British industrial revolution
D. In England, the movement of goods between markets was helped by a good network of rivers and an indented coastline

129. In a democracy, individual differences are encouraged because
A. individuals will place the good of the nation ahead of their own preferences
B. individuals will tend to act and think alike in the long run
C. individual differences make for diverse beneficial contributions to the common cause
D. the Constitution guarantees the right of the individual to act as he pleases

130. The Supreme Court of India has expanded the meaning of the Right to Life to include the following derivative rights. Which one among the following is ***not*** included in the Court's definition?
A. Right to food and adequate livelihood
B. Right to education
C. Right to live in a healthy environment
D. Right to health and information

131. Which of the following statements is/are correct?
1. The major constituent mineral of granite rock is quartz.
2. The major constituent mineral of sandstone rock is feldspar.
3. The major constituent mineral of limestone rock is dolomite.

Select the correct answer using the code given below:
A. 1, 2 and 3 B. 3 only
C. 1 and 2 only D. 2 and 3 only

132. Which one among the following is a primary rock?
A. Sedimentary B. Igneous
C. Metamorphic D. None of the above

133. Which one among the following is the largest temperate desert of the world?
A. Patagonian desert B. Taklamakan desert
C. Iranian desert D. Turkmen desert

134. Doldrums is a
A. Tropical wind belt
B. Tropical wind deflection belt
C. Sub-tropical wind belt
D. Tropical no-wind belt

135. The Gulf of Mannar is situated along the coast of
A. Tamil Nadu B. Kerala
C. Karnataka D. Andhra Pradesh

136. The river with highest tidal bore in India is
A. Cauvery B. Mahanadi
C. Hoogli D. Krishna

137. Which one among the following is ***not*** a mixture?
A. Graphite B. Glass
C. Brass D. Steel

138. What is the power of the lens, if the far point of a short-sighted eye is 200 cm?
A. –0.5 D B. 2 D
C. 1 D D. –1.5 D

139. Which one among the following is correct for resultant of balanced forces?
A. It is zero
B. It is non-zero
C. It varies continuously
D. None of the above

140. Three resistance coils of 1Ω, 2Ω and 3Ω are connected in series. If the combination is connected to a battery of 9 V, what is the potential drop across the resistance coil of 3Ω?
A. 2.0 volt B. 3.0 volt
C. 4.5 volt D. 6.0 volt

141. An electric lamp of 100 watt is used for 10 hours per day. The 'units' of energy consumed in one day by the lamp is
A. 1 unit B. 0.1 unit
C. 10 units D. 100 units

142. Which one among the following pairs is ***not*** correctly matched?
A. Union List : Banking
B. State List : Agriculture
C. Concurrent List : Marriage
D. Residuary List : Education

143. Which of the following statements relating to the Government of India Act of 1935 are correct?
1. It introduced provincial autonomy.
2. It proposed a federation of India.
3. It proposed for the establishment of a Federal Court.

Select the correct answer using the code given below:
A. 1, 2 and 3 B. 1 and 2 only
C. 2 and 3 only D. 1 and 3 only

144. The themes of the murals of the Ajanta Caves are
1. Decorative designs which include a variety of animals, trees and flowers.
2. Portraits of various Buddhas and Bodhisattvas.
3. Narrative scenes portraying Jataka stories.

Select the correct answer using the code given below:
A. 1, 2 and 3
B. 2 and 3 only
C. 1 and 3 only
D. 1 and 2 only

145. Consider the following statements about a report on 'Status of Tigers, Co-predators and Prey in India, 2010' released by the Ministry of Environment and Forests in July 2011:
1. India registered a 20 per cent decline in tiger population over the last survey in the year 2006.
2. The report warns that tigers are in danger due to an overall more than 12 per cent loss of habitat.

Which of the statements given above is/are correct?
A. 1 only B. 2 only
C. Both 1 and 2 D. Neither 1 nor 2

146. Government of India in July 2011 gave its nod for accepting international regulations for the prevention of air pollution emanating from ships. In this regard, which of the following statements is/are correct?
1. According to the regulations, limits have been set on Sulphur oxide and Nitrogen oxide emissions from ship exhausts.
2. India is the first country to ratify to the Convention for the Prevention of Pollution from Ships of the International Maritime Organization.

Select the correct answer using the code given below:
A. 1 only B. 2 only
C. Both 1 and 2 D. Neither 1 nor 2

147. The Supreme Court of India on July 29, 2011 directed the suspension of all mining operations and transportation in Bellary district of Karnataka till further orders. In this respect, which of the following statements is/are correct?
1. The Court was convinced that over exploration of the area had caused large scale environmental degradation.
2. The Court felt that Article 21 of the Constitution (Right to life) was violated by such exploration.

3. The Court directed the Central Government to prepare rehabilitation scheme for restoration of the forest wealth.

Select the correct answer using the code given below:

A. 1, 2 and 3 B. 2 only
C. Both 1 and 2 D. Neither 1 nor 2

148. Which one among the following statements regarding South Sudan, who officially joined the international community as an independent nation on July 9, 2011 is ***not*** correct?

A. The capital of the new nation is Juba
B. It is Africa's first post-colonial nation
C. India has stationed peacekeepers in South Sudan
D. The Nile flows through Sudan before entering South Sudan and then flowing into Egypt

149. Which one of the following statements about *Salwa Judum*, the Special Force created to counter Maoist insurgency, is ***not*** correct?

A. It was created by the Chhattisgarh Government in 2005, comprising of about 6500 Special Police Officers or Koya Commandos
B. *Salwa Judum* was initially known as Jan *Jagran Abhiyan*
C. The force was fully funded by the Chhattisgarh government
D. The Supreme Court of India in July 2011 ordered the Chhattisgarh Government to disband the Special Force and desist from using them to counter Maoist activities.

150. Why was Sucheta Kadethankar in the news recently?

A. She secured highest rank among women in Civil Services Examination 2010
B. She is the first Indian to cross the Gobi Desert
C. She is the first Indian to cross the English Channel
D. She is the first Indian to climb Mount Everest twice

PAPER II : MATHEMATICS

1. What is the value of $(1 + i)^5 + (1 - i)^5$ where $i = \sqrt{-1}$?

A. –8 B. 8
C. $8i$ D. $-8i$

2. What is the value of $\tan 9° - \tan 27° - \tan 63° + \tan 81°$?

A. 1 B. 2
C. 3 D. 4

3. If $x = y \cos\left(\frac{2\pi}{3}\right) = z \cos\left(\frac{4\pi}{3}\right)$, then what is $xy + yz + zx$ equal to?

A. –1 B. 0
C. 1 D. 2

4. If $\sin A + \sin B + \sin C = 3$ then what is $\cos A + \cos B + \cos C$ equal to?

A. –1 B. 0
C. 1 D. 3

5. At a point 15 m away from the base of a 15 m high house, the angle of elevation of the top is

A. 90° B. 60°
C. 45° D. 30°

6. The simultaneous equations $3x + 5y = 7$ and $6x + 10y = 18$ have

A. no solution
B. infinitely many solutions
C. unique solution
D. any finite number of solutions

7. What is the principal value of $\sec^{-1}\left(\frac{2}{\sqrt{3}}\right)$?

A. $\frac{\pi}{2}$ B. $\frac{\pi}{3}$
C. $\frac{\pi}{4}$ D. $\frac{\pi}{6}$

8. What is the 10th common term between the series $2 + 6 + 10 + \ldots$ and $1 + 6 + 11 + \ldots$?

A. 180 B. 186
C. 196 D. 206

9. If the 10th term of a GP is 9 and 4th term is 4, then what is its 7th term?

A. 6 B. 14
C. 27/14 D. 56/15

10. The function $y = f(x) = mx + c$ has

A. maximum point but no minimum point
B. minimum point but no maximum point
C. both maximum and minimum points
D. neither maximum point nor minimum point

11. If $\log_{10} 2$, $\log_{10} (2^x - 1)$, $\log_{10} (2^x + 3)$ are three consecutive terms of an AP, then which one of the following is correct?

A. $x = 0$ B. $x = 1$
C. $x = \log_2 5$ D. $x = \log_5 2$

12. What is the locus of points of intersection of a sphere and a plane?

A. Circle B. Ellipse
C. Parabola D. Hyperbola

13. The equation $x^2 - 4x + 29 = 0$ has one root $2 + 5i$. What is the other root? $\left(i = \sqrt{-1}\right)$

A. 2 B. 5
C. $2 + 5i$ D. $2 - 5i$

14. What are the square roots of $-2i$? $\left(i=\sqrt{-1}\right)$

A. $\pm (1 + i)$ B. $\pm (1 - i)$
C. $\pm i$ D. ± 1

15. What is the area between the curve $y = \cos 3x$, $0 \le x \le \frac{\pi}{6}$ and the co-ordinate axes?

A. 1 square unit B. $\frac{1}{2}$ square unit
C. $\frac{1}{3}$ square unit D. $\frac{1}{4}$ square unit

16. At an extreme point of a function $f(x)$, the tangent to the curve is

A. parallel to the x-axis
B. perpendicular to the x-axis
C. inclined at an angle 45° to the x-axis
D. inclined at an angle 60° to the x-axis

17. If $y=\left(1+x^{\frac{1}{4}}\right)\left(1+x^{\frac{1}{2}}\right)\left(1-x^{\frac{1}{4}}\right)$, then what is $\frac{dy}{dx}$ equal to?

A. 1 B. -1
C. x D. $\frac{1}{x^2}$

18. In binary system the decimal number 0.3 can be expressed as

A. $(0.01001 \ldots)_2$ B. $(0.10110 \ldots)_2$
C. $(0.11001 \ldots)_2$ D. $(0.10101 \ldots)_2$

19. Two letters are drawn at random from the word 'HOME'. What is the probability that both the letters are vowels?

A. 1/6 B. 5/6
C. 1/2 D. 1/3

20. If $z = 1 + i \tan \alpha$ where $\pi < \alpha < \frac{3\pi}{2}$, then what is $|z|$ equal to?

A. $\sec \alpha$ B. $-\sec \alpha$
C. $\sec^2 \alpha$ D. $-\sec^2 \alpha$

21. There are 4 candidates for the post of a lecturer in Mathematics and one is to be selected by votes of 5 men. What is the number of ways in which the votes can be given?

A. 1048 B. 1072
C. 1024 D. 625

22. What is the value of $\sum_{r=1}^{n}\frac{P(n, r)}{r!}$?

A. $2^n - 1$ B. 2^n
C. 2^{n-1} D. $2^n + 1$

23. What are the co-ordinates of the foot of the prependicular from the point (2, 3) on the line $x + y - 11 = 0$?

A. (2, 9) B. (5, 6)
C. (–5, 6) D. (6, 5)

24. What is the degree of the differential equation

$$\left(\frac{d^3y}{dx^3}\right)^{\frac{2}{3}} + 4 - 3\left(\frac{d^2y}{dx^2}\right) + 5\left(\frac{dy}{dx}\right) = 0?$$

A. 3 B. 2
C. 2/3 D. Not defined

25. What is the area enclosed by the equation $x^2 + y^2 = 2$?

A. 4π square units B. 2π square units
C. $4\pi^2$ square units D. 4 square units

26. What is $\int \frac{dx}{\sin^2 x \cos^2 x}$ equal to?

A. $\tan x + \cot x + c$
B. $\tan x - \cot x + c$
C. $(\tan x + \cot x)^2 + c$
D. $(\tan x - \cot x)^2 + c$
where c is the constant of integration.

27. The roots of the equation $\begin{vmatrix} x & \alpha & 1 \\ \beta & x & 1 \\ \beta & \gamma & 1 \end{vmatrix} = 0$ are independent of

A. α B. β
C. γ D. α, β and γ

28. Which one of the following is the mean of the data given below?

x_i	6	10	14	18	24	28	30
f_i	2	4	7	12	8	4	3

A. 17 B. 18
C. 19 D. 20

29. If $\vec{a}$ and $\vec{b}$ are two vectors such that $\vec{a} \bullet \vec{b} = 0$ and $\vec{a} \times \vec{b} = \vec{0}$, then which one of the following is correct?

A. $\vec{a}$ is parallel to $\vec{b}$
B. $\vec{a}$ is perpendicular to $\vec{b}$
C. Either $\vec{a}$ or $\vec{b}$ is a null vector
D. None of the above

30. If $y = \ln\sqrt{\tan x}$, then what is the value of $\frac{dy}{dx}$ at $x = \frac{\pi}{4}$?

A. 0 B. -1
C. 1/2 D. 1

31. The point in the interval $(0, 2\pi)$ where $f(x) = e^x \sin x$ has maximum slope is

A. $\frac{\pi}{4}$ B. $\frac{\pi}{2}$
C. π D. $\frac{3\pi}{2}$

32. If $\tan\theta = \sqrt{m}$, where m is a non-square natural number m, then $\sec 2\theta$ is
A. a negative number B. a transcendental number
C. an irrational number D. a rational number

33. In any triangle ABC, the sides are 6 cm, 10 cm and 14 cm. Then the triangle is obtuse angled with the obtuse angle equal to
A. 150º B. 135º
C. 120º D. 105º

34. In a triangle ABC, if $A = \tan^{-1} 2$ and $B = \tan^{-1} 3$, then C is equal to
A. $\frac{\pi}{3}$ B. $\frac{\pi}{4}$
C. $\frac{\pi}{6}$ D. $\frac{\pi}{2}$

35. Let α, β be the roots of the equation $(x - a)(x - b) = c$, $c \neq 0$. Then the roots of the equation $(x - \alpha)(x - \beta) + c = 0$ are
A. a, c B. b, c
C. a, b D. $a + b, a + c$

36. If the equations $x^2 - px + q = 0$ and $x^2 - ax + b = 0$ have a common root and the roots of the second equation are equal, then which one of the following is correct?
A. $aq = 2(b + p)$ B. $aq = b + p$
C. $ap = 2(b + q)$ D. $ap = b + q$

37. If $n\,!$, $3\times(n\,!)$ and $(n + 1)!$ Are in GP, then the value of n will be
A. 3 B. 4
C. 8 D. 10

38. The smallest positive integral value of n for which $\left(\frac{1-i}{1+i}\right)^n$ is purely imaginary with positive imaginary part is
A. 1 B. 3
C. 4 D. 5

39. What is the area of the triangle formed by the lines joining the vertex of the parabola $x^2 = 12y$ to the ends of the latus rectum?
A. 9 square units B. 12 square units
C. 14 square units D. 18 square units

40. What is the angle between two planes $2x - y + z = 4$ and $x + y + 2z = 6$?
A. $\frac{\pi}{2}$ B. $\frac{\pi}{3}$
C. $\frac{\pi}{4}$ D. $\frac{\pi}{6}$

41. What is the equation of the curve passing through the point $\left(0, \frac{\pi}{3}\right)$ satisfying the differential equation $\sin x \cos y\, dx + \cos x \sin y\, dy = 0$?
A. $\cos x \cos y = \frac{\sqrt{3}}{2}$ B. $\sin x \sin y = \frac{\sqrt{3}}{2}$
C. $\sin x \sin y = \frac{1}{2}$ D. $\cos x \cos y = \frac{1}{2}$

42. A husband and wife appear in an interview for two vacancies in the same post. The probability of husband's selection is 1/5 and that of wife's selection is 1/3. What is the probability that only one of them will be selected?
A. 1/5 B. 2/5
C. 3/5 D. 4/5

43. If α and β are the complex cube roots of unity, then what is the value of $(1 + \alpha)(1 + \beta)(1 + \alpha^2)(1 + \beta^2)$?
A. –1 B. 0
C. 1 D. 4

44. A tower of height 15 m stands vertically on the ground. From a point on the ground the angle of elevation of the top of the tower is found to be 30º. What is the distance of the point from the foot of the tower?
A. $15\sqrt{3}$ m B. $10\sqrt{3}$ m
C. $5\sqrt{3}$ m D. 30 m

45. If $\tan A - \tan B = x$ and $\cot B - \cot A = y$, then what is $\cot(A - B)$ equal to?
A. $\frac{1}{y} - \frac{1}{x}$ B. $\frac{1}{x} - \frac{1}{y}$
C. $\frac{1}{x} + \frac{1}{y}$ D. $-\frac{1}{x} - \frac{1}{y}$

46. There is a point inside a circle. What is the probability that this point is close to the circumference than to the centre?
A. 3/4 B. 1/2
C. 1/4 D. 1/3

47. How many diagonals will be there in an n-sided regular polygon?
A. $\frac{n(n-1)}{2}$ B. $\frac{n(n-3)}{2}$
C. $n^2 - n$ D. $\frac{n(n+1)}{2}$

48. Students of three sections of a class, having 30, 30 and 40 students appeared for a test of 100 marks. The arithmetic means of the marks of the three sections are 72.2, 69.0 and 64.1 in that order. What is the arithmetic mean of the marks of all the students of three sections?
A. 66.6 B. 67.3
C. 68.0 D. 70.6

49. What is the focal distance of any point $P(x_1, y_1)$ on the parabola $y^2 = 4ax$?
A. $x_1 + y_1$ B. x_1y_1
C. ax_1 D. $a + x_1$

50. If the vectors $-\hat{i}-2x\hat{j}-3y\hat{k}$ and $\hat{i}-3x\hat{j}-2y\hat{k}$ are orthogonal to each other, then what is the locus of the point (x, y)?

A. a straight line B. an ellipse
C. a parabola D. a circle

51. What is the value of the determinant

$$\begin{vmatrix} a-b & b+c & a \\ b-c & c+a & b \\ c-a & a+b & c \end{vmatrix}?$$

A. $a^3 + b^3 + c^3$ B. $3bc$
C. $a^3 + b^3 + c^3 - 3abc$ D. 0

52. If a, b, c, d, e, f are in AP, then $(e - c)$ is equal to which one of the following?

A. $2(c - a)$ B. $2(d - c)$
C. $2(f - d)$ D. $(d - c)$

53. Let α and β be the roots of the equation $x^2 + x + 1 = 0$. The equation whose roots are α^{19} and β^7 is

A. $x^2 - x - 1 = 0$ B. $x^2 - x + 1 = 0$
C. $x^2 + x - 1 = 0$ D. $x^2 + x + 1 = 0$

54. A vertical tower stands on a horizontal plane and is surmounted by a vertical flag staff of height h. At a point P on the plane, the angle of elevation of the bottom of the flag staff is β and that of the top is α. What is the height of the tower?

A. $\dfrac{h\tan\beta}{\tan\alpha - \tan\beta}$ B. $\dfrac{h\tan\beta}{\tan\alpha + \tan\beta}$

C. $\dfrac{h\cos\beta}{\cos\alpha - \cos\beta}$ D. $\dfrac{h}{\cos(\alpha - \beta)}$

55. If $\begin{vmatrix} p & -q & 0 \\ 0 & p & q \\ q & 0 & p \end{vmatrix} = 0$, then which one of the following is correct?

A. p is one of the cube roots of unity
B. q is one of the cube roots of unity
C. $\dfrac{p}{q}$ is one of the cube roots of unity
D. None of these

56. If (p, q) is the point on the x-axis equidistant from the points (1, 2) and (2, 3), then which one of the following is correct?

A. $p = 0, q = 4$ B. $p = 4, q = 0$
C. $p = 3/2, q = 0$ D. $p = 1, q = 0$

57. If the variance of the data 2, 4, 5, 6, 17 is v, then what is the variance of the data 4, 8, 10, 12, 34?

A. v B. $4v$
C. v^2 D. $2v$

58. If $\vec{c}$ is the unit vector perpendicular to both the vectors $\vec{a}$ and $\vec{b}$, then what is another unit vector perpendicular to both the vectors $\vec{a}$ and $\vec{b}$?

A. $\vec{c}\times\vec{a}$ B. $\vec{c}\times\vec{b}$

C. $-\dfrac{(\vec{a}\times\vec{b})}{|\vec{a}\times\vec{b}|}$ D. $\dfrac{(\vec{a}\times\vec{b})}{|\vec{a}\times\vec{b}|}$

59. If p is the length of the perpendicular drawn from the origin to the line $\dfrac{x}{a}+\dfrac{y}{b}=1$, then which one of the following is correct?

A. $\dfrac{1}{p^2}=\dfrac{1}{a^2}+\dfrac{1}{b^2}$ B. $\dfrac{1}{p^2}=\dfrac{1}{a^2}-\dfrac{1}{b^2}$

C. $\dfrac{1}{p}=\dfrac{1}{a}+\dfrac{1}{b}$ D. $\dfrac{1}{p}=\dfrac{1}{a}-\dfrac{1}{b}$

60. If the sides of a triangle are in the ratio $2:\sqrt{6}:1+\sqrt{3}$, then what is the smallest angle of the triangle?

A. 75° B. 60°
C. 45° D. 30°

61. What is the value of

$\sqrt{8+2\sqrt{8+2\sqrt{8+2\sqrt{8+\ldots\ \infty}}}}$?

A. 10 B. 8
C. 6 D. 4

62. If A = {a, b, c}, then what is the number of proper subsets of A?

A. 5 B. 6
C. 7 D. 8

63. In a random arrangement of the letters of the word 'UNIVERSITY', what is the probability that two I's do not come together?

A. 4/5 B. 1/5
C. 1/10 D. 9/10

64. If tan A = 1/2 and tan B = 1/3, then what is the value of 4A + 4B?

A. $\pi/4$ B. $\pi/2$
C. π D. 2π

65. An aeroplane flying at a height of 300 m above the ground passes vertically above another plane at an instant when the angles of elevation of two planes from the same point on the ground are 60° and 45° respectively. What is the height of the lower plane from the ground?

A. 50 m B. $\dfrac{100}{\sqrt{3}}$ m

C. $100\sqrt{3}$ m D. $150(\sqrt{3}+1)$ m

66. For what value of m are the points with position vectors $10\hat{i}+3\hat{j}$, $12\hat{i}-5\hat{j}$ and $m\hat{i}+11\hat{j}$ collinear?

A. −8
B. 4
C. 8
D. 12

67. The mean of 7 observations is 10 and that of 3 observations is 5. What is the mean of all the 10 observations?

A. 15
B. 10
C. 8.5
D. 7.5

68. What is the ratio of coefficient of x^{15} to the term independent of x in $\left(x^2+\frac{2}{x}\right)^{15}$?

A. 1/64
B. 1/32
C. 1/16
D. 1/4

69. If $a^{-1} + b^{-1} + c^{-1} = 0$ such that $\begin{vmatrix} 1+a & 1 & 1 \\ 1 & 1+b & 1 \\ 1 & 1 & 1+c \end{vmatrix} = \lambda$, then what is λ equal to?

A. $-abc$
B. abc
C. 0
D. 1

70. In a class of 125 students 70 passed in Mathematics, 55 passed in Statistics and 30 passed in both. What is the probability that a student selected at random from the class has passed in only one subject?

A. 13/25
B. 3/25
C. 17/25
D. 8/25

71. For what value of m are the vectors $2\hat{i}-3\hat{j}+4\hat{k}$, $\hat{i}+2\hat{j}-\hat{k}$ and $m\hat{i}-\hat{j}+2\hat{k}$ coplanar?

A. 0
B. 5/3
C. 1
D. 8/5

72. In a triangle ABC, $a = 8$, $b = 10$ and $c = 12$. What is angle C equal to?

A. A/2
B. 2A
C. 3A
D. 3A/2

73. If $\sin\theta = x+\frac{a}{x}$ for all $x \in R - \{0\}$, then which one of the following is correct?

A. $a \geq 4$
B. $a \geq \frac{1}{2}$
C. $a \leq \frac{1}{4}$
D. $a \leq \frac{1}{2}$

74. The equation $\tan^4 x - 2\sec^2 x + a^2 = 0$ will have at least one real solution if

A. $|a| \leq 4$
B. $|a| \leq 2$
C. $|a| \leq \sqrt{3}$
D. None of the above

75. The sides a, b, c of a triangle ABC are in arithmetic progression and 'a' is the smallest side. What is cos A equal to?

A. $\frac{3c-4b}{2c}$
B. $\frac{3c-4b}{2b}$
C. $\frac{4c-3b}{2c}$
D. $\frac{3b-4c}{2c}$

76. If $\int_1^2 \{k^2+(4-4k)x+4x^3\}\,dx \leq 12$, then which one of the following is correct?

A. $k = 3$
B. $0 \leq k < 3$
C. $k \leq 4$
D. $k = 0$

77. If p, q, r are positive integers and ω is the cube root of unity and $f(x) = x^{3p} + x^{3q+1} + x^{3r+2}$, then what is $f(\omega)$ equal to?

A. ω
B. $-\omega^2$
C. $-\omega$
D. 0

78. What is the maximum value of $3\cos x + 4\sin x + 5$?

A. 5
B. 7
C. 10
D. 12

79. If $\sin\theta = \cos^2\theta$, then what is $\cos^2\theta(1 + \cos^2\theta)$ equal to?

A. 1
B. 0
C. $\cos^2\theta$
D. $2\sin\theta$

80. What is the equation of the plane passing through the point $(1, -1, -1)$ and perpendicular to each of the planes $x - 2y - 8z = 0$ and $2x + 5y - z = 0$?

A. $7x - 3y + 2z = 14$
B. $2x + 5y - 3z = 12$
C. $x - 7y + 3z = 4$
D. $14x - 5y + 3z = 16$

81. What is the value of $\tan 15^\circ \cdot \tan 195^\circ$?

A. $7-4\sqrt{3}$
B. $7+4\sqrt{3}$
C. $7+2\sqrt{3}$
D. $7+6\sqrt{3}$

82. If the rate of change in volume of spherical soap bubble is uniform, then the rate of change in surface area varies as

A. square of radius
B. square root of radius
C. inversely proportional to radius
D. cube of the radius

83. What is $\frac{\sin x}{1+\cos x}+\frac{1+\cos x}{\sin x}$ equal to?

A. $2\tan x$
B. $2\operatorname{cosec} x$
C. $2\cos x$
D. $2\sin x$

84. Some measures of central tendency for n discrete observations are given below:

1. Arithmetic mean
2. Geometric mean
3. Harmonic mean
4. Median

A desirable property of a measure of central tendency is if every observation is multiplied by c then the measure of central tendency is also multiplied by c, where $c > 0$. Which of the above measures satisfy the property?

A. 1, 2 and 3 only
B. 1, 2 and 4 only
C. 3 and 4 only
D. 1, 2, 3 and 4

85. If $f(x) = x \ln x$, then $f(x)$ attains minimum value at which one of the following points?

A. $x = e^{-2}$ B. $x = e$
C. $x = e^{-1}$ D. $x = 2e^{-1}$

86. A variate X takes values 2, 3, 4, 2, 5, 4, 3, 2, 1. What is the mode?
A. 2 B. 3
C. 4 D. 5

87. If $z = \frac{1+2i}{2-i} - \frac{2-i}{1+2i}$, then what is the value of $z^2 + z\bar{z}$? $\left(i = \sqrt{-1}\right)$
A. 0 B. –1
C. 1 D. 8

88. What is the argument of $(1 - \sin\theta) + i\cos\theta$? $\left(i = \sqrt{-1}\right)$
A. $\frac{\pi}{2} - \frac{\theta}{2}$ B. $\frac{\pi}{2} + \frac{\theta}{2}$
C. $\frac{\pi}{4} - \frac{\theta}{2}$ D. $\frac{\pi}{4} + \frac{\theta}{2}$

89. What is the area bounded by the curve $\sqrt{x} + \sqrt{y} = \sqrt{a}(x, y \geq 0)$ and the coordinate axes?
A. $\frac{5a^2}{6}$ B. $\frac{a^2}{3}$
C. $\frac{a^2}{2}$ D. $\frac{a^2}{6}$

90. Consider the following statements in respect of the square matrices A and B of same order:
1. A and B are non-zero and AB = 0 ⇒ either |A| = 0 or |B| = 0
2. AB = 0 ⇒ A = 0 or B = 0

Which of the above statements is/are correct?
A. 1 only B. 2 only
C. Both 1 and 2 D. Neither 1 nor 2

91. For what value of k, are the lines $x + 2y - 9 = 0$ and $kx + 4y + 5 = 0$ parallel?
A. 2 B. –1
C. 1 D. 0

92. What are the points on the curve $x^2 + y^2 - 2x - 3 = 0$ where the tangents are parallel to x-axis?
A. (1, 2) and (1, –2)
B. $(0, \sqrt{3})$ and $(0, -\sqrt{3})$
C. (3, 0) and (–3, 0)
D. (2, 1) and (2, –1)

93. If sin 3A = 1, then how many distinct values can sin A assume?
A. 1 B. 2
C. 3 D. 4

94. What is the radius of the circle touching x-axis at (3, 0) and y-axis at (0, 3)?
A. 3 units B. 4 units
C. 5 units D. 6 units

95. For all $n \in$ N, $2^{4n} - 15n - 1$ is divisible by
A. 125 B. 225
C. 450 D. None of the above

96. If the roots of the equation $x^2 - 4x - \log_3 N = 0$ are real, then what is the minimum value of N?
A. 1/256 B. 1/27
C. 1/64 D. 1/81

97. The equation to sphere passing through origin and the points (–1, 0, 0), (0, –2, 0) and (0, 0, –3) is $x^2 + y^2 + z^2 + f(x, y, z) = 0$. What is $f(x, y, z)$ equal to?
A. $-x - 2y - 3z$
B. $x + 2y + 3z$
C. $x + 2y + 3z - 1$
D. $x + 2y + 3z + 1$

98. What is the area of the triangle with vertices (1, 2, 3), (2, 5, –1) and (–1, 1, 2)?
A. $\frac{\sqrt{155}}{2}$ square units
B. $\frac{\sqrt{175}}{2}$ square units
C. $\frac{\sqrt{155}}{4}$ square units
D. $\frac{\sqrt{175}}{4}$ square units

99. For what value of x does $(1\ 3\ 2)\begin{pmatrix}1 & 3 & 0\\ 3 & 0 & 2\\ 2 & 0 & 1\end{pmatrix}\begin{pmatrix}0\\ 3\\ x\end{pmatrix} = (0)$ hold?
A. –1 B. 1
C. 9/8 D. –9/8

100. If one of the roots of the equation $a(b - c)x^2 + b(c - a)x + c(a - b) = 0$ is 1, what is the second root?
A. $-\frac{b(c-a)}{a(b-c)}$ B. $\frac{b(c-a)}{a(b-c)}$
C. $\frac{c(a-b)}{a(b-c)}$ D. $-\frac{c(a-b)}{a(b-c)}$

101. What are the roots of the equation $2(y + 2)^2 - 5(y + 2) = 12$?
A. –7/2, 2 B. –3/2, 4
C. –5/3, 3 D. 3/2, 4

102. What is the value of $\log_2(\log_3 81)$?
A. 2 B. 3
C. 4 D. 9

103. If the roots of the equation $3x^2 - 5x + q = 0$ are equal, then what is the value of q?
A. 2 B. 5/12
C. 12/25 D. 25/12

104. If Φ is a null set, then which one of the following is correct?
A. Φ = 0 B. Φ = {0}
C. Φ = {Φ} D. Φ = { }

105. What is the equation of a line parallel to x-axis at a distance of 5 units below x-axis?
A. $x = 5$ B. $x = -5$
C. $y = 5$ D. $y = -5$

Note: *Study the following table and answer the next 08 (Eight) questions that follow:*

Year	*Male*			*Female*			*Total*
	Urban	*Rural*	*Total*	*Urban*	*Rural*	*Total*	
1995	280	350			310		1350
1996	370		670	180		450	
1997		130	440		190		
1998	400	280		290			
Total				1060	850		

106. What is the total population for the year 1997?
A. 810 B. 830
C. 970 D. 1030

107. What is the female urban population in the year 1995?
A. 390 B. 410
C. 430 D. 470

108. What is the urban population in the year 1997?
A. 400 B. 460
C. 490 D. 510

109. What is the total population in the year 1998?
A. 1000 B. 1020
C. 1040 D. 1050

110. What is the difference between the number of females and the number of males in the year 1995?
A. 90 B. 100
C. 110 D. 120

111. In which year is the male population minimum?
A. 1995 B. 1996
C. 1997 D. 1998

112. In which year is the female population maximum?
A. 1995 B. 1996
C. 1997 D. 1998

113. What is the percentage of rural male population (over the whole population) in the year 1998?
A. $\frac{80}{3}\%$ B. $\frac{100}{3}\%$
C. 35% D. 40%

Note : *Study the pie chart given below and answer the next 04 (four) questions that follow:*

The following pie chart gives the distribution of funds in a five year plan under the major heads of development expenditures: Agriculture (A), Industry (B), Education (C), Employment (D) and Miscellaneous (E).

The total allocation is 36,000 (in crores of rupees).

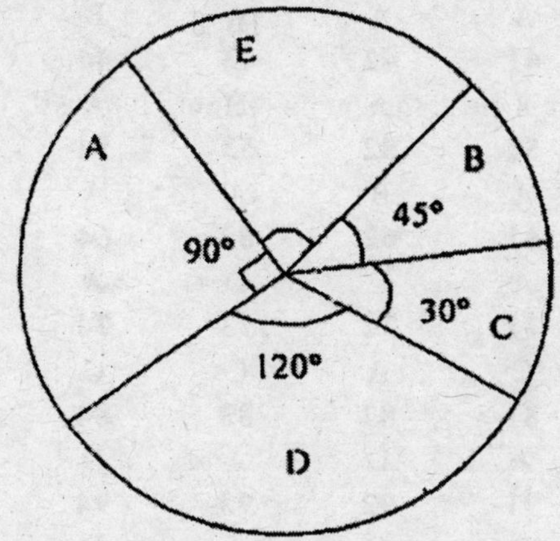

114. Which head is allocated maximum funds?
A. Agriculture B. Industry
C. Employment D. Miscellaneous

115. How much money (in crores) is allocated to Education?
A. 3000 B. 6000
C. 9000 D. 10800

116. How much money (in crores) is allocated to both Agriculture and Employment?
A. 20000 B. 21000
C. 24000 D. 27000

117. How much excess money (in crores) is allocated to Miscellaneous over Education?
A. 3600 B. 4200
C. 4500 D. 4800

118. What is the geometric mean of 10, 40 and 20?
A. 10 B. 20
C. 40 D. 70

119. What is the median of the distribution 3, 7, 6, 9, 5, 4, 2?
A. 5 B. 6
C. 7 D. 8

120. If the arithmetic and geometric means of two numbers are 10, 8 respectively, then one number exceeds the other number by
A. 8 B. 10
C. 12 D. 16

ANSWERS

PAPER-I : GENERAL ABILITY TEST

1	2	3	4	5	6	7	8	9	10
C	C	B	C	A	A	A	C	C	A
11	**12**	**13**	**14**	**15**	**16**	**17**	**18**	**19**	**20**
B	B	B	A	B	C	B	C	B	C
21	**22**	**23**	**24**	**25**	**26**	**27**	**28**	**29**	**30**
D	B	C	A	D	A	B	D	B	A
31	**32**	**33**	**34**	**35**	**36**	**37**	**38**	**39**	**40**
A	A	A	B	A	B	C	B	D	B
41	**42**	**43**	**44**	**45**	**46**	**47**	**48**	**49**	**50**
B	A	D	A	B	C	C	C	D	C
51	**52**	**53**	**54**	**55**	**56**	**57**	**58**	**59**	**60**
A	B	A	A	A	A	C	D	D	C
61	**62**	**63**	**64**	**65**	**66**	**67**	**68**	**69**	**70**
A	C	D	A	B	B	C	A	C	B
71	**72**	**73**	**74**	**75**	**76**	**77**	**78**	**79**	**80**
C	A	C	C	C	A	D	C	C	B
81	**82**	**83**	**84**	**85**	**86**	**87**	**88**	**89**	**90**
A	D	A	D	B	A	C	A	B	A
91	**92**	**93**	**94**	**95**	**96**	**97**	**98**	**99**	**100**
B	C	A	B	D	B	B	A	C	A
101	**102**	**103**	**104**	**105**	**106**	**107**	**108**	**109**	**110**
A	D	D	B	A	D	A	C	C	A
111	**112**	**113**	**114**	**115**	**116**	**117**	**118**	**119**	**120**
C	C	B	D	C	C	C	C	A	A
121	**122**	**123**	**124**	**125**	**126**	**127**	**128**	**129**	**130**
B	D	D	D	C	C	C	C	C	D
131	**132**	**133**	**134**	**135**	**136**	**137**	**138**	**139**	**140**
A	B	A	D	A	C	A	A	A	C
141	**142**	**143**	**144**	**145**	**146**	**147**	**148**	**149**	**150**
A	D	D	A	B	A	A	D	C	B

PAPER-II : MATHEMATICS

1	2	3	4	5	6	7	8	9	10
A	D	B	B	C	A	D	B	A	D
11	**12**	**13**	**14**	**15**	**16**	**17**	**18**	**19**	**20**
C	A	D	B	C	A	B	A	A	B
21	**22**	**23**	**24**	**25**	**26**	**27**	**28**	**29**	**30**
C	A	B	B	A	B	A	C	C	D
31	**32**	**33**	**34**	**35**	**36**	**37**	**38**	**39**	**40**
A	A	C	B	C	C	C	B	A	B
41	**42**	**43**	**44**	**45**	**46**	**-47**	**48**	**49**	**50**
D	B	C	A	C	A	B	C	D	D
51	**52**	**53**	**54**	**55**	**56**	**57**	**58**	**59**	**60**
C	B	D	A	C	B	B	D	A	C
61	**62**	**63**	**64**	**65**	**66**	**67**	**68**	**69**	**70**
D	C	A	C	C	C	C	B	B	A

71	72	73	74	75	76	77	78	79	80
D	D	C	C	C	A	D	C	A	D
81	**82**	**83**	**84**	**85**	**86**	**87**	**88**	**89**	**90**
A	C	B	D	C	A	A	B	D	A
91	**92**	**93**	**94**	**95**	**96**	**97**	**98**	**99**	**100**
A	A	B	A	B	D	B	A	D	C
101	**102**	**103**	**104**	**105**	**106**	**107**	**108**	**109**	**110**
A	A	D	D	D	A	B	C	D	A
111	**112**	**113**	**114**	**115**	**116**	**117**	**118**	**119**	**120**
C	A	A	C	A	B	C	B	A	C

EXPLANATORY ANSWERS

PAPER-II : MATHEMATICS

1. $(1 + i)^5 + (1 - i)^5$

$= 1 + 5c_1\ 1^4.\ i + 5c_2\ (1)^3(i)^2 + 5c_3(1)^2\ (i)^3 + 5c_4\ (1)\ (i)^4 + i^5 + 1 - 5c_1\ (1)^4\ i + 5c_2(1)^3 .\ (i)^2 - 5c_3(1)^2\ i^3 + 5c_4(1)\ (i)^4 - i^5$

$= 2 - 10 + 5 - 10 + 5 = -8.$

2. We have, $\tan 9^\circ - \tan 27^\circ - \tan 63^\circ + \tan 81^\circ$

$= (\tan 9^\circ + \tan 81^\circ) - (\tan 27^\circ + \tan 63^\circ)$

$$= \frac{1}{\cos 9^\circ . \cos 81^\circ} - \frac{1}{\cos 27^\circ . \cos 63^\circ}$$

$$= \frac{1}{\sin 9^\circ . \cos 9^\circ} - \frac{1}{\sin 27^\circ . \cos 27^\circ}$$

$$= \frac{2}{\sin 18^\circ} - \frac{2}{\sin 54^\circ}$$

$$= 2\left[\frac{\sin 54^\circ - \sin 18^\circ}{\sin 54^\circ . \sin 18^\circ}\right]$$

$$= 2\left[\frac{2\cos 36^\circ . \sin 18^\circ}{\sin 18^\circ . \cos 36^\circ}\right] = 2 \times 2 = 4.$$

5.

B
15 m
θ
A 15 m C

$$\tan\theta = \frac{AB}{AC} = \frac{15}{15} = 1$$

$\Rightarrow \quad \tan\theta = \tan 45^\circ$

$\therefore \quad \theta = 45^\circ$

$\therefore$ Angle of elevation $= 45^\circ$.

6. $\because \quad 3x + 5y = 7$

$6x + 10y = 18$

$$\frac{3}{6} = \frac{5}{10} \neq \frac{7}{18}$$

$$\frac{a_1}{a_2} = \frac{b_1}{b_2} \neq \frac{c_1}{c_2}$$

Equations have no solution.

7.
$$\sec^{-1}\left(\frac{2}{\sqrt{3}}\right) = \sec^{-1}(\sec 30^\circ)$$

$$= \sec^{-1}\left(\sec\frac{\pi}{6}\right)$$

$$= \frac{\pi}{6}.$$

9. Let first term of G.P. is a and common ratio $= r$

$\because$ 10th term of G.P. is 9

$\Rightarrow \quad ar^9 = 9 \quad ...(i)$

and $\quad ar^3 = 4 \quad ...(ii)$

Divide (i) by (ii)

$$\frac{ar^9}{ar^3} = \frac{9}{4} \Rightarrow r^6 = \frac{9}{4}$$

$$\Rightarrow \quad (r^3)^2 = \left(\frac{3}{2}\right)^2$$

$$r^3 = \frac{3}{2}$$

Putting the value of r^3 in (i)

$$ar^3 = 4$$

$$a\left(\frac{3}{2}\right) = 4 \quad \Rightarrow a = \frac{8}{3}$$

$$7^{th} \text{ term} = ar^6 = \frac{8}{3} \times \frac{9}{4} = 6.$$

13. The given equation $x^2 - 4x + 29 = 0$

Here, $a = 1,\ b = -4,\ c = 29$

$$\text{Sum of roots} = \frac{-b}{a} = 4$$

Let other root $= \beta$

According to the question,

$2 + 5i + \beta = 4$

$$\beta = 4 - 2 - 5i$$
$$\beta = 2 - 5i$$

$\therefore$ Other root $= 2 - 5i$

26. $$\int \frac{dx}{\sin^2 x \cos^2 x} = \frac{\int(\cos^2 x + \sin^2 x)dx}{\cos^2 x \sin^2 x}$$
$$= \int \text{cosec}^2 dx + \int \sec^2 x\, dx$$
$$= -\cot x + \tan x + c$$
$$= \tan x - \cot x + c.$$

28.

x_i	f_i	$x_i f_i$
6	2	12
10	4	40
14	7	98
18	12	216
24	8	192
28	4	112
30	3	90
	40	760

$$\bar{x} = \frac{\sum x_i f_i}{f_i} = \frac{760}{40} = 19$$

$\therefore$ Mean of the given data = 19.

33.

A, B, C; c = 14 cm, b = 10 cm, a = 6 cm

$$\cos C = \frac{a^2 + b^2 - c^2}{2ab} = \frac{36 + 100 - 196}{2(6)(10)}$$
$$= \frac{-60}{120} = \frac{-1}{2}$$
$$\cos C = \cos 120^\circ$$
$$C = 120^\circ.$$

34. $\tan A = 2$ and $\tan B = 3$

$$\tan(A + B) = \frac{\tan A + \tan B}{1 - \tan A \cdot \tan B} = \frac{2+3}{1-6}$$
$$= \frac{5}{-5} = -1$$

$\because$ $A + B + C = \pi$
$$A + B = \pi - C$$
$$\tan(A + B) = \tan(\pi - C) = -\tan C$$

$\therefore$ $-\tan C = -1 \Rightarrow \tan C = \tan\frac{\pi}{4}$

$$\therefore C = \frac{\pi}{4}.$$

35. The given equation $(x - a)(x - b) = c$ can be written as

$x^2 - (a + b)x + (ab - c) = 0$ ...(*i*)

$\because$ α, β are the roots of the equation

$\therefore$ $\left.\begin{array}{l}\alpha + \beta = a + b \\ \alpha\beta = ab - c\end{array}\right\}$ ...(*ii*)

If λ and δ are the roots of equation
$$(x - \alpha)(x - \beta) + c = 0$$
$$x^2 - (\alpha + \beta)x + (\alpha\beta + c) = 0$$

$\therefore$ $\lambda + \delta = \alpha + \beta = a + b$

and $\lambda.\delta = \alpha\beta + c = ab$ by ...(*ii*)

Clearly, the roots λ and δ are a and b.

37. $n!$, $3(n!)$ and $(n+1)!$ are in G.P.

$\therefore$ $[3(n!)]^2 = n! \times (n + 1)!$
$$9(n!)(n!) = n!\,(n + 1).\,n!$$
$$9 = n + 1$$
$\Rightarrow$ $n = 8.$

38. $$\left(\frac{1-i}{1+i}\right)^n = \left(\frac{1-i}{1+i} \times \frac{1-i}{1-i}\right)^n = \left[\frac{(1-i)^2}{1-i^2}\right]^n$$
$$= \left[\frac{1 - 2i + i^2}{1+1}\right]^n$$
$$= \left[\frac{1 - 2i - 1}{2}\right]^n = (-i)^n$$

if $n = 3$ then $(-i)^3 = i.$

44. Let AB is tower

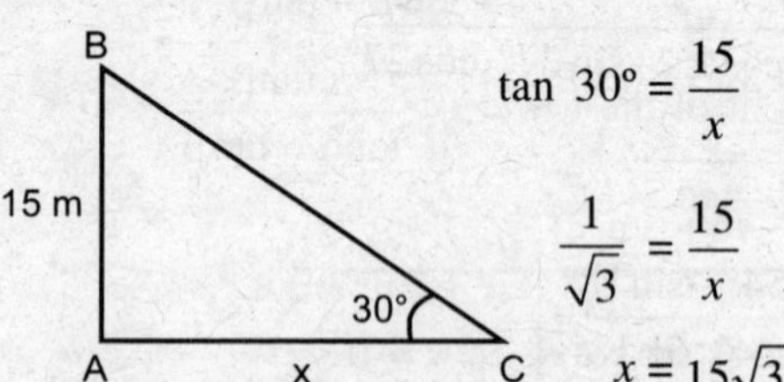

$$\tan 30^\circ = \frac{15}{x}$$
$$\frac{1}{\sqrt{3}} = \frac{15}{x}$$
$$x = 15\sqrt{3}$$

$\therefore$ Distance of the point from the foot of the tower is $15\sqrt{3}$ m.

45. $\because$ $\tan A - \tan B = x$

$\Rightarrow$ $\frac{\sin A}{\cos A} - \frac{\sin B}{\cos B} = x$

$\Rightarrow$ $\frac{\sin(A - B)}{\cos A.\cos B} = x$

$\Rightarrow$ $\sin(A - B) = x \cos A . \cos B$ ...(*i*)

$\cot B - \cot A = y$

$\frac{\cos B}{\sin B} - \frac{\cos A}{\sin A} = y$

$\Rightarrow$ $\sin(A - B) = y \sin A . \sin B$ ... (*ii*)

From (*i*) and (*ii*) $x \cos A . \cos B = y \sin A. \sin B$

$$\cot(A - B) = \frac{\cos(A - B)}{\sin(A - B)}$$
$$= \frac{\cos A.\cos B + \sin A.\sin B}{x \cos A.\cos B}$$

[$\because$ $x \cos A . \cos B = y \sin A. \sin B$]

$$= \frac{1}{x} + \frac{\sin A . \sin B}{x \cos A . \cos B}$$

$$= \frac{1}{x} + \frac{\sin A . \sin B}{y \sin A . \sin B}$$

$$= \frac{1}{x} + \frac{1}{y}$$

54. In ΔABP,

$$\tan \beta = \frac{AB}{x} \quad ...(i)$$

In ΔACP,

$$\tan \alpha = \frac{AB + h}{x} \quad ...(ii)$$

Divide (*ii*) by (*i*)

$$\frac{\tan \alpha}{\tan \beta} = \frac{\frac{AB + h}{x}}{\frac{AB}{x}}$$

$$\frac{\tan \alpha}{\tan \beta} = \frac{AB + h}{AB}$$

$$AB \tan \alpha = AB \tan \beta + h \tan \beta$$

$$AB (\tan \alpha - \tan \beta) = h \tan \beta$$

$$AB = \frac{h \tan\beta}{\tan\alpha - \tan\beta}$$

$\therefore$ Height of the tower is $\dfrac{h \tan\beta}{\tan\alpha - \tan\beta}$

56. A (1, 2) ——— M (p, q) ——— (2, 3) B

$\because$ (p,q) is on x-axis $\therefore$ $y = 0$

$\because$ $AM = MB$

$$(AM)^2 = (MB)^2$$

$\Rightarrow$ $(p - 1)^2 + (-2)^2 = (2 - p)^2 + (3)^2$

$\Rightarrow$ $p^2 - 2p + 1 + 4 = 4 + p^2 - 4p + 9$

$\Rightarrow$ $2p = 8$

$p = 4$

$\therefore$ $p = 4$, $q = 0$ is correct.

60.

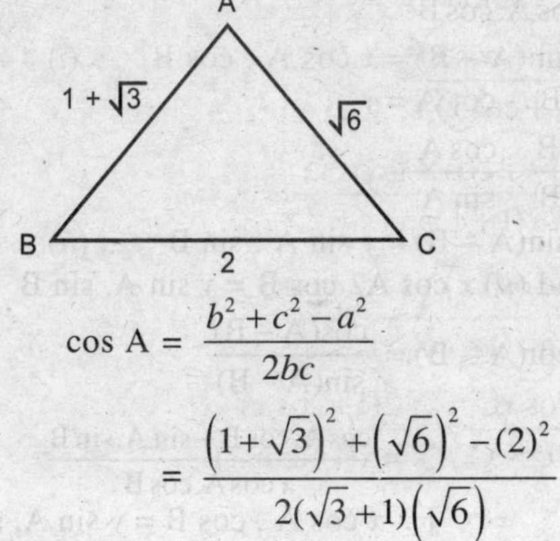

$$\cos A = \frac{b^2 + c^2 - a^2}{2bc}$$

$$= \frac{\left(1+\sqrt{3}\right)^2 + \left(\sqrt{6}\right)^2 - (2)^2}{2(\sqrt{3}+1)\left(\sqrt{6}\right)}$$

$$= \frac{1 + 3 + 2\sqrt{3} + 6 - 4}{2\left(\sqrt{3}+1\right)\left(\sqrt{6}\right)}$$

$$= \frac{2\sqrt{3} + 6}{2\left(\sqrt{3}+1\right)\left(\sqrt{6}\right)} = \frac{2\sqrt{3}\left(\sqrt{3}+1\right)}{2\left(\sqrt{3}+1\right)\left(\sqrt{6}\right)}$$

$$\cos A = \frac{1}{\sqrt{2}}$$

$$\cos A = \cos 45^\circ$$

$$A = 45^\circ.$$

61. Let $x = \sqrt{8 + 2\sqrt{8 + 2\sqrt{8 + 2\sqrt{8 + \cdots \infty}}}}$

$$x = \sqrt{8 + 2x}$$

$\Rightarrow$ $x^2 = 8 + 2x$

$\Rightarrow$ $x^2 - 2x - 8 = 0$

$\Rightarrow$ $x^2 - 4x + 2x - 8 = 0$

$x(x - 4) + 2(x - 4) = 0$

$(x - 4)(x + 2) = 0$

$x = 4, x = -2$

$\therefore$ $x = 4$ $\quad [\because x > 0]$

63. The total number of arrangements of the letters of the word 'University' is $\frac{10!}{2!}$ as there are two i's.

Regarding 2I's as one letter, number of ways of arrangement in which both I's are together = 9!

So, the number of ways in which 2I's are not together = $\frac{10!}{2!} - 9!$

Hence, the required probability

$$= \frac{\frac{10!}{2!} - 9!}{\frac{10!}{2!}}$$

$$= 1 - \frac{2!9!}{10!} = \frac{4}{5}.$$

64. $\tan A = \frac{1}{2}$, $\tan B = \frac{1}{3}$

$$\tan (A + B) = \frac{\tan A + \tan B}{1 - \tan A . \tan B}$$

$$= \frac{\frac{1}{2} + \frac{1}{3}}{1 - \frac{1}{2} \times \frac{1}{3}} = \frac{\frac{5}{6}}{\frac{5}{6}}$$

$$\tan (A + B) = 1$$

$$\tan (A + B) = \tan \frac{\pi}{4}$$

$$A + B = \frac{\pi}{4}$$

$$4(A + B) = \frac{\pi}{4} \times 4$$

$$4A + 4B = \pi.$$

65.

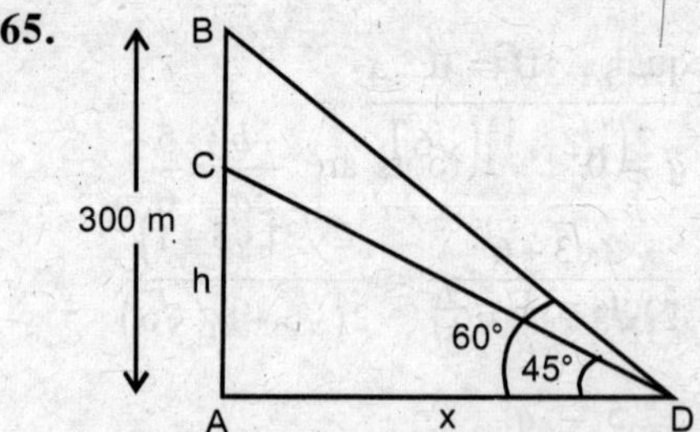

In ΔACD, $\tan 45^\circ = \dfrac{h}{x}$

$$1 = \frac{h}{x} \Rightarrow h = x$$

In Δ ABD, $\tan 60^\circ = \dfrac{300}{x}$

$$\sqrt{3} = \frac{300}{x}$$

$$\sqrt{3}x = 300$$

$$\sqrt{3}h = 300 \qquad [\because h = x]$$

$$h = \frac{300}{\sqrt{3}} \times \frac{\sqrt{3}}{\sqrt{3}}$$

$$= \frac{300\sqrt{3}}{3}$$

$$\therefore \quad h = 100\sqrt{3}$$

$\therefore$ Height of the lower plane from the ground is $100\sqrt{3}$ m.

67. Total of 7 observations = 7 × 10 = 70

Total of 3 observations = 3 × 5 = 15

Total of 10 observations = 70 + 15 = 85

$\therefore$ Mean of 10 observations = $\dfrac{85}{10} = 8.5$.

68.
$$\frac{nc_5(2^5)}{nc_{10}(2)^{10}} = \frac{\frac{15!}{5!10!}(2^5)}{\frac{15!}{10!5!}(2^{10})}$$

$$= \frac{32}{32 \times 32} = \frac{1}{32}.$$

69. We have, $\dfrac{1}{a} + \dfrac{1}{b} + \dfrac{1}{c} = 0$

$$\therefore \begin{vmatrix} 1+a & 1 & 1 \\ 1 & 1+b & 1 \\ 1 & 1 & 1+c \end{vmatrix} = abc\left(\frac{1}{a} + \frac{1}{b} + \frac{1}{c}\right) = 0$$

$\Rightarrow \lambda = 0.$

72.

A, B, C; AB = 12, AC = 10, BC = 8

$$\frac{a}{\sin A} = \frac{b}{\sin B} = \frac{c}{\sin C}$$

$$\frac{8}{\sin A} = \frac{12}{\sin C}$$

$$\Rightarrow \quad 8C = 12A$$

$$C = \frac{12A}{8} = \frac{3A}{2}.$$

75. $\because$ a, b, c are in A.P.

$$\therefore \quad b = \frac{a+c}{2} \Rightarrow a = 2b - c$$

$$\cos A = \frac{b^2 + c^2 - a^2}{2bc} = \frac{b^2 + c^2 - (2b-c)^2}{2bc}$$

$$= \frac{b^2 + c^2 - (4b^2 + c^2 - 4bc)}{2bc}$$

$$= \frac{-3b^2 + 4bc}{2bc} = \frac{b(4c-3b)}{2bc}$$

$$\therefore \quad \cos A = \frac{4c - 3b}{2c}.$$

78. Since

$$-\sqrt{3^2+4^2} \le 3\cos x + 4\sin x \le \sqrt{3^2+4^2} \ \forall x$$

$\Rightarrow -5 + 5 \le 3\cos x + 4\sin x + 5 \le 5 + 5 \ \forall x$

$\Rightarrow 0 \le 3\cos x + 4\sin x + 5 \le 10 \ \forall x$

$\therefore$ Maximum value of $3\cos x + 4\sin x + 5 = 10$.

79. $\because$ $\sin\theta = \cos^2\theta$

$$\cos^2\theta\,(1 + \cos^2\theta) = \sin\theta(1 + \sin\theta)$$

$$= \sin\theta + \sin^2\theta$$

$$= \cos^2\theta + \sin^2\theta$$

$$= 1 \qquad [\because \sin\theta = \cos^2\theta]$$

81. $\tan 15^\circ \,.\, \tan 195^\circ$

$= \tan 15^\circ \,.\, \tan(180 + 15^\circ)$

$= \tan 15^\circ \,.\, \tan 15^\circ$

$= \left(2-\sqrt{3}\right)\left(2-\sqrt{3}\right)$

$= 4 - 2\sqrt{3} - 2\sqrt{3} + 3.$

$= 7 - 4\sqrt{3}.$

83.
$$\frac{\sin x}{1+\cos x} + \frac{1+\cos x}{\sin x}$$

$$= \frac{\sin^2 x + (1+\cos x)^2}{\sin x(1+\cos x)}$$

$$= \frac{\sin^2 x + 1 + 2\cos x + \cos^2 x}{\sin x(1+\cos x)}$$

$$= \frac{(\sin^2 x + \cos^2 x) + 1 + 2\cos x}{\sin x(1+\cos x)}$$

$$= \frac{2 + 2\cos x}{\sin x(1+\cos x)} = \frac{2(1+\cos x)}{\sin x(1+\cos x)}$$

$= 2 \operatorname{cosec} x.$

87. $$z = \frac{(1+2i)^2-(2-i)^2}{(2-i)(1+2i)}$$

$$= \frac{1-4+4i-(4-1-4i)}{(2-i)(1+2i)}$$

$$= \frac{-3+4i-3+4i}{2+4i-i+2} = \frac{-6+8i}{4+3i}$$

$$= \frac{(-6+8i)}{(4+3i)} \times \frac{(4-3i)}{(4-3i)}$$

$$= \frac{-24+18i+32i+24}{16+9}$$

$$= \frac{50i}{25} = 2i$$

$$z^2 + z\bar{z} = (2i)^2 + (2i)(-2i)$$

$$= 4i^2 - 4i^2 = 0.$$

91. $\left.\begin{array}{l} x+2y=9 \\ kx+4y=-5 \end{array}\right\}$ has no solution

$$\therefore \quad \frac{a_1}{a_2} = \frac{b_1}{b_2} \neq \frac{c_1}{c_2}$$

$$\frac{1}{k} = \frac{2}{4} \quad \Rightarrow \quad 2k = 4$$

$$k = 2.$$

100. Let other root is β of the equation $a(b-c)x^2 + b(c-a)x + c(a-b) = 0$

$$\text{product of roots} = \frac{c}{a}$$

$$1 \times \beta = \frac{c(a-b)}{a(b-c)}$$

$$\therefore \quad \text{other root } (\beta) = \frac{c(a-b)}{a(b-c)}.$$

101. Let $y + 2 = x$, equation can be written as

$$2x^2 - 5x - 12 = 0$$
$$2x^2 - 8x + 3x - 12 = 0$$
$$2x(x-4) + 3(x-4) = 0$$
$$(x-4)(2x+3) = 0$$

$x = 4,$	$x = -\frac{3}{2}$
$\because\ y + 2 = 4$	$y + 2 = -\frac{3}{2}$
$y = 2$	$y = -\frac{7}{2}$

102. Let, $\log_3^{81} = x \Rightarrow 3^x = 81 = (3)^4 \Rightarrow x = 4$
and let $\log_2^4 = y \Rightarrow (2)^y = 4 = (2)^2 \Rightarrow y = 2$
$\therefore \log_2(\log_3^{81}) = 2.$

103. ∵ Roots are equal ∴ D = 0

$$3x^2 - 5x + q = 0 \quad \therefore x \text{ roots are } \frac{-b}{2a} = \frac{5}{6}$$

$$\text{Product of roots} = \frac{c}{a} = \frac{q}{3}$$

$$\frac{5}{6} \times \frac{5}{6} = \frac{q}{3}$$

$$\frac{25}{36} = \frac{q}{3} \quad \Rightarrow \quad q = \frac{25}{12}.$$

For Q. 106-113:

Year	*Male*			*Female*			*Total*
	Urban	*Rural*	*Total*	*Urban*	*Rural*	*Total*	
1995	280	350	630	410	310	720	1350
1996	370	300	670	180	270	450	1120
1997	310	130	440	180	190	370	810
1998	400	280	680	290	80	370	1050
Total	1360	1060	2420	1060	850	1910	4330

106. Total population for the year 1997

= 440 + 370 = 810.

107. Female urban population in 1995 = 410.

108. Urban population in 1997 = 310 + 180 = 490.

109. Total population in the year 1998

= 680 + 370 = 1050.

110. Difference between no. of females and the number of males in 1995 = 720 – 630 = 90.

111. In 1997 number of male population = 440 which is male's minimum population.

112. In 1995 number of female population = 720 which is female's maximum population.

113. Number of rural male population in 1998 = 280
Whole population in 1998 = 1050

$$\% = \frac{280}{1050} \times 100 = \frac{80}{3}\%$$

For (Qs. No. 114 – 117)

$$\text{Agriculture (A)} = \frac{90}{360} \times 36000$$
$$= 9000 \text{ crores}$$

$$\text{Industry (B)} = \frac{45}{360} \times 36000$$
$$= 4500 \text{ crores}$$

$$\text{Education (C)} = \frac{30}{360} \times 36000$$
$$= 3000 \text{ crores}$$

$$\text{Employment (D)} = \frac{120}{360} \times 36000$$
$$= 12000 \text{ crores}$$

$$\text{Miscellaneous (E)} = \frac{75}{360} \times 36000$$
$$= 7500 \text{ crores}$$

114. Employment is allocated *i.e.* 12000 crores maximum funds.

115. 3000 crores money is allocated to Education.

116. 12000 + 9000 = 21000 crores money is allocated to both Agriculture and Employment.

117. 7500 – 3000 = 4500 crores excess money is allocated to miscellaneous over Education.

118. Geometric mean of 10, 40 and 20 is

Here $n = 3$

$\therefore$ $\text{G.M.} = \sqrt[3]{10 \times 40 \times 20} = \sqrt[3]{8000}$

$= \left(20^3\right)^{\frac{1}{3}} = 20.$

119. 2, 3, 4, 5, 6, 7, 9

Here $n = 7$ which is odd number

$\therefore$ median = 4th term = 5.

120. Let numbers are a and b

$$\text{A.M} = \frac{a+b}{2} \Rightarrow 10 = \frac{a+b}{2}$$

$\Rightarrow$ $a + b = 20$ ...(*i*)

$$\text{G.M} = \sqrt{ab} \Rightarrow 8 = \sqrt{ab}$$

$\Rightarrow ab = 64$

$\because$ $(a - b)^2 = (a + b)^2 - 4ab$

$= (20)^2 - 4(64)$

$= 400 - 256 = 144$

$a - b = 12$ ...(*ii*)

from (*i*) and (*ii*)

$a + b = 20$

$a - b = 12$

$2a = 32 \Rightarrow a = 16, b = 4$

$\therefore$ $16 - 4 = 12$

$\therefore$ one number exceeds the other number by 12.

Previous Papers (Solved)

NATIONAL DEFENCE ACADEMY & NAVAL ACADEMY

NDA & NA – Entrance Exam, 2011 (I)

PAPER I : GENERAL ABILITY TEST

PART A : ENGLISH LANGUAGE

COMPREHENSION

Directions (Qs. 1 to 10) : *In this section, you have 03 short passages. After each passage, you will find several questions based on the passage. First, read a passage and then answer the questions based on it. You are required to select your answers based on the contents of the passage and opinion of the author only.*

Examples : 'I' and 'J' have been solved for you.

Passage (Example)

In our approach to life, be it pragmatic or otherwise, a basic fact that confronts us squarely and unmistakably is the desire for peace, security and happiness. Different forms of life at different levels of existence make up the teeming denizens of this earth of ours. And, no matter whether they belong to the higher groups such as human beings or to the lower groups such as animals, all beings primarily seek peace, comfort and security. Life is as dear to a mute creature as it is to a man. Even the lowliest insect strives for protection against dangers that threaten its life. Just as each one of us wants to live and not to die, so do all other creatures.

I. The author's main point is that

A. different forms of life are found on the earth

B. different levels of existence are possible in nature

C. peace and security are the chief goals of all living beings

D. even the weakest creature struggles to preserve its life

J. Which one of the following assumptions or steps is essential in developing the author's position?

A. All forms of life have a single overriding goal

B. The will to survive of a creature is identified with a desire for peace

C. All beings are divided into higher and lower groups

D. A parallel is drawn between happiness and life, and pain and death

Explanation :

I. The idea which represents the author's main point is "peace and security are the chief goals of all living beings", which is response (C). So (C) is the correct answer.

J. The best assumption underlying the passage is "The will to survive of a creature is identified with a desire for peace", which is response (B), so (B) is the correct answer.

Passage-I

Gandhi was not born great. He was a blundering boy, a mediocre student, a poor lawyer, an ordinary individual until he remade himself. He was a self-remade man. He had faith in himself. But above all, he had a deep, touching faith in the peasants, miners, labourers, and young unformed men and women whom he drew into his work. He fed them all an elixir of growth which often transformed nameless, uneducated people into leonine heroes. The elixir was fearlessness.

1. Consider the following assumptions:

1. Gandhi was a great man throughout his life.
2. Men are not born great, but they are made great by self effort.
3. Gandhi liked the ordinary people and neglected the rich.
4. Gandhi transformed the ordinary masses into great heroes.

Which of the above assumptions can be drawn from the above passage?

A. 2 and 4 B. 1 and 2

C. 3 and 4 D. None of these

2. Gandhi transformed the uneducated people by teaching them

A. work-mindedness B. self confidence

C. fearlessness D. heroism

3. Gandhi's attitude to the labour class was one of

A. generosity B. pity

C. compassion D. fearlessness

4. The word 'leonine' in the passage means

A. lean B. courageous

C. timid D. learning

Passage–II

The dog fence in Australia has been erected to keep out hostile invaders, in this case hordes of yellow dogs called dingoes. The empire it preserves is that of wool growers. Yet the fence casts a much broader ecological shadow. For the early explorers, a kangaroo or a wallaby sighting marked a noteworthy event. Now try ***not*** to see one. Without a native predator there is no check on the marsupial population. The kangaroos are now cursed more than the dingoes. They have become rivals of sheep, competing for water and grass. The State Governments now cull more than three million kangaroos a year to keep Australia's natural symbol from over running the pastoral lands.

5. The Fence is meant to keep the:
A. kangaroo in and the dingo out.
B. kangaroo in and the sheep out.
C. sheep in and the kangaroo out.
D. sheep in and the dingo out.

6. Australia's national symbol is:
A. Kangaroo B. Wallaby
C. Sheep D. Dingo

7. What has led to the unchecked growth of the marsupial population?
A. The building of fences
B. The absence of native predator
C. The culling of kangaroos
D. The availability of water and grass

8. The marsupial population is up in Australia because:
A. both wallaby and kangaroo count as marsupials.
B. the kangaroo consumes the water and grass of the sheep.
C. the dingo cannot get at the kangaroo.
D. the kangaroos are fenced out.

Passage–III

Not all nocturnal animals have good eyesight. Many of them concentrate on the other senses for finding their way about and for finding food. The sense of touch is very well developed in many nocturnal animals, whether they have good eyes or not. The large hairs or whiskers on the faces of cats and mice are sense organs and the animals react rapidly if these whiskers are touched. The sense of smell is also very important for nocturnal animals such as hedgehogs and field mice. The moist night air holds scent much better than dry air does.

9. Which one of the following statements is correct?
A. All nocturnal animals are blind
B. Many nocturnal animals do not have good eyesight
C. Most nocturnal animals can not see any thing in the dark
D. No nocturnal animal has good eyesight

10. The cat's whiskers are organs associated with the sense of
A. taste B. touch
C. hearing D. smell

SPOTTING ERRORS

Directions (Qs. 11 to 20) :
(i) In this section a number of sentences are given. The sentences are underlined in three separate parts and each one is labelled A, B, and C. Read each sentence to find out whether there is an error in any underlined part. No sentence has more than one error. When you find an error in any one of the underlined parts A, B or C, indicate your response on the separate Answer Sheet at the appropriate space. You may feel that there is no error in a sentence. In that case, letter D will signify a 'No error' response.
(ii) You are to indicate only one response for each item in your Answer Sheet. (If you indicate more than one response, your answer will be considered wrong.) Errors may be in grammar, word usage or idioms. There may be a word missing or there may be a word which should be removed.
*(iii) You are **not** required to correct the error. You are required **only** to indicate your response on the Answer Sheet.*

11. (A) We are meeting today afternoon/(B) to discuss the matter/(C) and reach a compromise./(D) No error.

12. (A) Either Ram or/(B) you is responsible/(C) for this action./(D) No error.

13. (A) The student flatly denied/(B) that he had copied/(C) in the examination hall./(D) No error.

14. (A) By the time you arrive tomorrow/(B) I have finished/(C) my work./(D) No error.

15. (A) The speaker stressed repeatedly on/(B) the importance of improving/(C) the condition of the slums./(D) No error.

16. (A) The captain with the members of his team/(B) are returning/(C) after a fortnight./(D) No error.

17. (A) After returning from/(B) an all-India tour/(C) I had to describe about it/(D) No error.

18. (A) The teacher asked his students/(B) if they had gone through/(C) either of the three chapters included in the prescribed text./(D) No error.

19. (A) Although they are living in the country/(B) since they were married/(C) they are now moving to the town./(D) No error.

20. (A) Do you know/(B) how old were you/(C) when you came here?/(D) No error.

Directions (Qs. 21 to 30): *Each of the following items consists of a sentence followed by four words or group of words. Select the **antonym** of the word (occurring in the sentence in capital letters) as per the context.*

21. All care is FUTILE in a cureless case.
A. waste B. expensive
C. useful D. cheap

22. REVELATION of facts became very easy when I investigated the case.
A. rejection B. elimination
C. concealment D. introduction

23. The story you have just told is INCREDIBLE
A. credible B. fantastic
C. probable D. believable

24. His assignments have taken him to many EXOTIC locations around the world.
A. wonderful B. cosmopolitan
C. irrelevant D. common

25. He has given up his VICIOUS habits.
A. godly B. virtuous
C. sublime D. friendly

26. The doctor found the patient INERT.
A. active B. lazy
C. strong D. resolute

27. The issue was raised TANGENTIALLY in the negotiations.
A. partly B. forcefully
C. candidly D. fitfully

28. ESCALATING prices are causing hardship to the poor.
A. fixed B. fluctuating
C. falling D. reasonable

29. I have MALICE towards none.
A. sympathy B. goodwill
C. friendship D. attraction

30. The boy comes of an AFFLUENT family.
A. poor B. ordinary
C. infamous D. backward

REARRANGING PARTS OF A SENTENCE

Directions (Qs. 31 to 40) : In the following items, *some parts of the sentence have been jumbled up. You are required to rearrange these parts which are labelled P, Q, R and S to produce the correct sentence. Choose the proper sequence and mark in your Answers Sheet accordingly.*

Example 'Z' has been solved for you.

Z. Some people believe that, the effect/P, is very bad/Q, on children/R, of cinema/S

The correct sequence should be
A. P – S – R – Q
B. S – P – Q – R
C. S – R – P – Q
D. Q – S – R – P

Explanation

The proper way of writing the sentence is "Some people believe that the effect of cinema on children is very bad". This is indicated by the sequence P – S – R – Q and so (A) is the correct answer.

31. In the Middle Ages
P : there was little progress
Q : either intellectual or social
R : with the result that
S : teaching became the exclusive prerogative of the church
Which one of the following is the correct sequence?
A. P – Q – R – S B. S – R – P – Q
C. P – R – S – Q D. Q – P – R – S

32. A scientist has shown that
P : when anyone holds
Q : a burning cigarette
R : near their leaves
S : plants react with fear
Which one of the following is the correct sequence?
A. P – Q – R – S B. Q – R – S – P
C. S – P – Q – R D. P – Q – S – R

33. P : because the driver lost control
Q : and hit a lamp post
R : the bus fell into a ditch
S : at a turning
Which one of the following is the correct sequence?
A. R – Q – P – S B. R – P – S – Q
C. P – Q – S – R D. S – P – R – Q

34. We want
P : every country
Q : or a foreign policy
R : to have a population policy
S : as it has an economic policy
Which one of the following is the correct sequence?
A. P – Q – R – S B. Q – R – S – P
C. P – R – S – Q D. R – Q – P – S

35. The teacher
P : and the pupils continued likewise with their repetition
Q : read the sentence again
R : the pupils knew the sentence by heart
S : until the teacher thought
Which one of the following is the correct sequence?
A. P – Q – S – R B. P – S – R – Q
C. Q – P – S – R D. Q – S – R – P

36. For dropping kilos
P : it is safe to cut your fat intake
Q : and maintaining weight loss
R : to 20% of your calories
S : even further
Which one of the following is the correct sequence?
A. P – R – Q – S B. Q – S – P – R
C. S – P – R – Q D. Q – P – R – S

37. His uncle
P : after he joined
Q : did not send
R : the college
S : money for his expenses

Which one of the following is the correct sequence?
A. Q – R – S – P B. R – S – Q – P
C. Q – S – P – R D. S – R – P – Q

38. Language is
P : to the other person
Q : communicating
R : only a means of
S : one's thoughts and emotions
Which one of the following is the correct sequence?
A. P – Q – S – R B. R – Q – S – P
C. Q – R – S – P D. S – P – Q – R

39. Whenever I see the model
P : who started it
Q : is the face of the man
R : of our factory
S : what comes to my mind
Which one of the following is the correct sequence?
A. S – R – Q – P B. R – S – Q – P
C. Q – P – R – S D. P – Q – R – S

40. P : I bought from your shop
Q : a week ago
R : to send the books
S : you have not cared
Which one of the following is the correct sequence?
A. Q – P – S – R B. Q – P – R – S
C. S – R – P – Q D. P – Q – S – R

Directions (Qs. 41 to 50) : *Each of the following items consists of a sentence followed by four words or group of words. Select the* ***synonym*** *of the word (occurring in the sentence in capital letters) as per the context.*

41. The song had a SOPORIFIC effect on the child.
A. soothing B. terrific
C. supreme D. sleep-inducing

42. His ALLEGIANCE to the Party was suspect from the very beginning.
A. servility B. obedience
C. loyalty D. passivity

43. Sympathetic criticism has a SALUTARY effect.
A. premature B. terrible
C. disastrous D. beneficial

44. His bad behaviour EVOKED punishment.
A. escaped B. called for
C. produced D. summoned

45. Please do not give any more FLIMSY pretexts for not having done the work.
A. weak B. strong
C. justified D. impulsive

46. He was the court appointed lawyer for fifty-six INDIGENT defendants.
A. Indian men B. poor
C. guilty D. untried

47. The boy said that pain had ABATED.
A. reduced B. vanished
C. increased D. stabilized

48. He became known as an IMPLACABLE foe of fundamentalism.
A. relentless B. pleasing
C. dangerous D. courageous

49. The queen was aware of the INSOLENT behaviour of the lords.
A. violent B. polite
C. insulting D. frivolous

50. Modern man is PRAGMATIC in his dealings.
A. practical B. playful
C. causal D. clever

PART B : GENERAL KNOWLEDGE

51. Which one among the following is ***not*** a reason for practising tank irrigation in the Peninsular India?
A. The undulating relief and hard rocks
B. Little percolation of rain water due to impervious rock structure
C. Most of the rivers of Peninsular India are perennial
D. There are many streams which become torrential during rainy season

52. Identify from the following states of India through which the Tropic of Cancer passes and arrange them from east to west:
1. Gujarat 2. West Bengal
3. Uttar Pradesh 4. Jharkhand
5. Madhya Pradesh 6. Bihar
7. Chhattisgarh

Select the correct answer using the code given below:
A. 2-5-7-4-1 B. 2-4-7-5-1
C. 3-2-6-7-5 D. 3-7-4-6-2

53. Hot deserts like Sahara, Arabia etc. receive very negligible amount of rainfall. This is because they:
A. do not receive moisture-bearing wind from the oceans.
B. are the most rocky and barren areas of the Earth.
C. are located on the tropical high pressure belt of the atmosphere.
D. are not on the path of the monsoons.

54. The latitude is the angular distance of a point on the Earth's surface, north of south, of the Equator as measured from the:
A. centre of the Earth.

B. Equator.
C. Tropic of Cancer of the Capricorn.
D. Poles.

55. When an Ordinary Bill is referred to a joint sitting of both the Houses of Indian Parliament, it has to be passed by a:
A. simple majority of the total number of members of both the Houses present and voting.
B. two-third majority of the total number of members of both the Houses.
C. simple majority of the total number of members of both the Houses.
D. two-third majority of the total number of members of both the Houses present and voting.

56. The Rowlatt Act was passed to:
A. bring about agrarian reforms.
B. curtail the nationalist and revolutionary activities.
C. have a favourable balance of trade.
D. put Second World War criminals on trial.

57. Which one among the following features of the Constitution of India is indicative of the fact that the real executive power is vested in the Council of Ministers headed by the Prime Minister?
A. Federalism
B. Representative Legislature
C. Universal Adult Franchise
D. Parliamentary Democracy

58. In which among the following cases the joint session of both the Houses of Parliament can be summoned?
1. To amend the Constitution
2. When a bill has been pending with one House for more than six months after it was passed by the other
3. When both the Houses disagree on the amendments to be made in a bill
4. When a bill is passed by one House and is rejected by the other

Select the correct answer using the code given below:
A. 1, 2 and 3 B. 2, 3 and 4
C. 2 and 3 only D. 1 and 4

59. The 'Bombay Plan' drafted by G.D. Birla and J.R.D. Tata emphasized:
A. that the economy should be left to the dynamic investments by the private sector in heavy industries etc.
B. the public sector investment in infrastructure and heavy industries.
C. annual planning
D. that the private sector should foot the bill for intensive and low return investments in the industrial sector.

60. Consider the following statements:
1. The Buddhists in Deccan excavated rock-cut *Chaityas* and the *Vaishnavas, Shaivas* and *Jainas* imitated these in later centuries.
2. The *Vaishnavas, Shaivas* and *Jainas* excavated temples at sites far distant from rock-cut *Chaityas.*

Which of the statements given above is/are correct?
A. 1 only B. 2 only
C. Both 1 and 2 D. Neither 1 nor 2

61. Consider the following statements:
1. The Champaran Satyagraha marked Gandhiji's second appearance in India politics as a leader of the masses.
2. The Champaran Satyagraha was launched to address the problems faced by Indigo plantation workers.

Which of the statements given above is/are correct?
A. 1 only B. 2 only
C. Both 1 and 2 D. Neither 1 nor 2

62. Consider the following statements:
1. Charles Wood's Despatch of 1854 laid exclusive emphasis on the development of higher education in India and neglected primary and secondary education
2. The Carlyle Circular issued by R.W. Carlyle sought to check the spread of revolutionary activities in educational institutions.

Which of the statements given above is/are correct?
A. 1 only B. 2 only
C. Both 1 and 2 D. Neither 1 nor 2

63. Consider the following statements about Gandhiji's thinking on enviroment:
1. His environmental thinking is rooted in his larger philosophical and moral thinking
2. He preferred sustainable environmental practices to nourish the soil and the natural world
3. He laid emphasis on the rigorous ethic of non-injury in our treatment of animals

Which of the statements given above is/are correct?
A. 1 only B. 1 and 2 only
C. 1, 2 and 3 D. 2 and 3 only

64. Which one among the following is common to the treaty of *Yandaboo* (1826), the treaty of *Salbai* (1782) and the treaty of *Gandamak* (1879)?
A. With these treaties various Indian powers formed alliances to defeat the British
B. These treaties enabled the British to control the South Asian powers
C. These treaties expedited the spread of Indian culture abroad
D. These treaties gave an essential boost to enhanced trade in South Asia

65. Which one among the following was the major demand of the *Bardoli Satyagraha* (1928) organized under the leadership of Sardar Vallabhbhai Patel?
A. Land to the Tiller
B. Increase in the rates of labour wage
C. Rollback of newly enhanced revenue rate
D. Supply of agricultural inputs to the farmers at subsidised rate

66. Which one among the following statements is ***not*** correct?
A. *Gandhara* Schood of Art owed its origin to the Indo-Greek rulers but the real patrons of the school were the Kushans, especially Kanishka
B. Rich carving, elaborate ornamentations and complex symbolism were not the main features of the *Gandhara* sculpture
C. The Graeco-roman architectural impact modified the structure of Buddhist *Stupas*
D. The artists of the *Amravati* School of Arts mainly used white marble

67. Which one among the following statements regarding the Eighth Five Year Plan in India is ***not*** correct?
A. The plan was postponed by two years because of political upheavals at the centre
B. It aimed at high growth of both agriculture and manufacturing sectors
C. Its emphasis was on growth in export and import, improvement in trade and current account deficit
D. It set before itself the two principal objectives of 'growth with stability' and 'growth with justice'

68. Which among the following statements is/are true with regard to WTO membership?
1. All WTO members automatically receive the 'most favoured nation' status
2. Over 75% of WTO members are from developing countries. WTO membership allows them access to developed markets at the lower tariff

Select the correct answer using the code given below:
A. 1 only B. 2 only
C. Both 1 and 2 D. Neither 1 nor 2

69. TRIPS (Trade Related aspects of Intellectual Property Rights) agreement is administered by:
A. United Nations Conference on Trade and Development (UNCTAD)
B. United Nations Organization (UNO)
C. Word Trade Organization (WTO)
D. World Bank (WB)

70. Consider the following statements:
1. The G20 was established in 2008 in the wake of the global financial crisis led by the USA
2. It brings together the major advanced and emerging economies to stabilize the global financial market
3. India's stand on Mutual Assessment Process (MAP) for measuring imbalances between surplus and deficit economies in the Seoul conference of G20 in the year 2010 was firmly endorsed by all the nations

Which of the statements given above is/are correct?
A. 1, 2 and 3 B. 1 and 2 only
C. 2 and 3 only D. 3 only

71. Which one among the following statements is ***not*** correct?
A. In progressive waves, the amplitude may be constant and neighbouring points are out of phase with each other
B. In air or other gases, a progressive antinode occurs at a displacement node and a progressive node occurs at a displacement antinode
C. Transverse wave can be polarized while longitudinal wave can not be polarized
D. Longitudinal wave can be polarized while transverse wave can not be polarized

72. A body initially at rest is acted upon by a constant force. The rate of change of its kinetic energy varies:
A. linearly with square root of time.
B. linearly with time.
C. linearly with square of time.
D. inversely with time.

73. A jet plane flies through air with a velocity of 2 Mach. While the velocity of sound is 332 m/s the air speed of the plane is:
A. 166 m/s B. 66.4 km/s
C. 332 m/s D. 664 m/s

74. Which one among the following statements is correct?
A. Convex mirrors are used by doctors to examine oral cavity
B. Concave mirrors are used as reflectors
C. Convex mirrors are used as reflectors
D. Convex mirrors should be used for shaving

75. Light travels in optical fibre irrespective of its shape because it is a device by which signals can be transferred from one location to another. It is based on the phenomenon of:
A. diffraction of light
B. refraction of light
C. polarization of light
D. total internal reflection of light

76. A man is at rest in the middle of a horizontal plane of perfectly smooth surface of ice. He can move himself to the shore by making use of Newton's:
A. First law of motion.
B. Second law of motion.
C. Third law of motion.
D. First, second and third laws of motion.

77. Which one among the following is the major cause of blurring and unsharp images of objects observed through very large telescope at the extreme limit of magnification?
A. Air turbulence of earth's atmosphere
B. Poor optical polish achievable on large mirrors
C. Poor tracking capacities of telescopes
D. Varying density of air in the Earth's atmosphere

78. Bats can ascertain distances, directions, nature and size of the obstacles at night. This is possible by reflection of the emitted:

A. ultrasonic waves from the bat.
B. ultrasonic waves from the distant objects.
C. supersonic waves from the bat.
D. supersonic waves from the distant objects.

79. When a moving bus suddenly applies brakes, the passengers sitting in it fall in the forward direction. This can be explained by:
A. the theory of relativity.
B. Newton's first law.
C. Newton's second law.
D. Newton's third law.

80. The material used for electric fuse is an alloy of tin and lead. This alloy should have:
A. high specific resistance and low melting point.
B. low specific resistance and high melting point.
C. low specific resistance and low melting point.
D. high specific resistance and high melting point.

81. Suppose you are standing 1 m in front of a plane mirror. What should be the minimum vertical size of the mirror so that you can see your full image in it?
A. 0.50 m B. 2 m
C. half of your height D. twie your height

82. Light travels slower in glass than in air because:
A. refractive index of air is less than that of glass.
B. refractive index of air is greater than that of glass.
C. density of glass is greater than that of air.
D. density of glass is less than that of air.

83. The lines of force of a uniform magnetic field:
A. must be convergent
B. must be divergent.
C. must be parallel to each other.
D. intersect.

84. A Jet engine works on the principle of conservation of:
A. linear momentum.
B. angular momentum.
C. energy.
D. mass.

85. The surface temperature of the Sun is nearly:
A. 2000 K B. 4000 K
C. 6000 K D. 8000 K

86. Venkataraman Ramakrishnan was jointly awarded Nobel Prize in Chemistry in the year 2009 for the:
A. theory of electron transfer.
B. studies of the structure and function of the ribosome.
C. palladium catalyzed cross couplings in organic synthesis.
D. work in the area of olefin metathesis.

87. Which one among the following statements regarding cell is ***not*** correct?
A. Shape and size of cells are related to specific function
B. Some cells have changing shapes
C. Each cell has its own capacity to perform
D. Same type of cells are present in all body tissues

88. Which one among the following Indian scientists proposed a theory for long distance transport of water in plants?
A. J.C. Bose B. Birbal Sahni
C. P. Maheshwari D. N.S. Parihar

89. To a perpendicular to the plane of ecliptic, the Earth's axis of rotation makes an angle of 23½ degrees. Had this angle been 0 degree, which one among the following would result?
A. There would have been no seasons
B. The length of day and night would have been the same throughout the year.
C. The length of day and night would have been the same all over the earth
D. All of the above

90. Jet streams are usually found in the:
A. Ozonosphere B. Mesosphere
C. Tropopause D. Ionosphere

91. There exceptionally high and low tides that occur at the time of the new moon or the full moon when the Sun, the Moon and the Earth are approximately aligned is called:
A. Spring B. Fall
C. Neap D. Diurnal

92. What is the general direction of cyclones formed in the Bay of Bengal?
A. East to west B. West to east
C. West to south D. North to south

93. The Narmada river in the Peninsular plateau flows westward with a remarkably straight channel. It is because the:
A. slope gradient in this part controls the river channel pattern.
B. river carries a huge amount of water which has created a straight channel course.
C. river forms the boundary between the Central Highlands and the Deccan Plateau.
D. river flows through the trough of a rift valley inclined westward.

94. No trees are found in Tundra biome near polar region of northern hemisphere. This is due to:
A. snowfall inhibits plant respiration.
B. frozen ice beneath the surface soil (permafrost) restricts roots growth.
C. less wind movement and inadequate sunlight.
D. low temperature which restricts development of reproductive organs.

95. Why the summer monsoon winds blow from south-western direction in the northern hemisphere?
A. The general direction of wind from the Indian Ocean is south-western
B. The presence of the doldrums around the Equator
C. The low pressure condition in north-west India
D. Due to the effect of Coriolis force

96. If the Earth's axis were perpendicular to the plane of its orbit, which one among the following would *not* have happened?
A. The North Pole will always lie in dark
B. Days and nights would be equal throughout the year
C. No change of seasons will take place
D. The sun will be perpendicular to the Equator

97. Match List-I with List-II and select the correct answer using the code given below the Lists:

List-I (Peak in the Eastern Himalaya)	*List-II (Location in the map)*
(*a*) Makalu	
(*b*) Kanchenjunga	
(*c*) Namcha Barwa	
(*d*) Mt. Everest	

Code:

	(*a*)	(*b*)	(*c*)	(*d*)
A.	2	3	4	1
B.	2	4	3	.1
C.	1	4	3	2
D.	1	3	4	2

98. Which one among the following is the best reason for the marked increase in the agricultural production in India in the past decades?
A. Increase in the area under cultivation
B. Conversion of barren land into agricultural land
C. Use of improved agricultural methods and technologies
D. Priority status given by the successive governments to atricultural sector over the industry sector

99. Which of the following statements regarding the Deccan Traps is/are correct?
1. Intense volcanic activity in the form of fissure eruption took place towards the end of Cretaceous period
2. The volcanic lava spread out in horizontal sheets
3. The regular soil found here is rich in nitrogen

Select the correct answer using the code given below:
A. 1 and 2 only B. 1, 2 and 3
C. 3 only D. 1 only

100. Consider the following statements:
1. The Himalayan vegetation varies according to both altitude and climatic conditions.
2. There are mainly two types of tropical forests that are found in the Himalayas—the tropical rainforests and the tropical deciduous forests

Which of the statements given above is/are correct?
A. 1 only B. 2 only
C. Both 1 and 2 D. Neither 1 nor 2

101. If the electrical resistance of a typical substance suddenly drops to zero, then the substance is called:
A. super conductor. B. semiconductor.
C. conductor. D. insulator.

102. A spherical air bubble is embedded in a piece of glass. For a ray of light passing through the bubble, it behaves like a:
A. converging lens.
B. diverging lens.
C. plano-converging lens.
D. plano-diverging lens.

103. 'The stars seem to be higher on the sky than they actually are'. This can be explained by:
A. atmospheric refraction.
B. dispersion of light.
C. total internal reflection.
D. diffraction of light.

104. Which one among the following is *not* a source of renewable energy?
A. Hydroelectricity B. Solar energy
C. Fuel cell D. Wind energy

105. A liquid rises to a certain length in a capillary tube. The tube is inclined to an angle of 45°. The length of the liquid column will:
A. increase.
B. decrease.
C. remain unchanged.
D. first decrease and then increase.

106. Mass of B is four times that of A. B moves with a velocity half that of A. Then B has:
A. kinetic energy equal to that of A.
B. half the kinetic energy of A.
C. twice the kinetic energy of A.
D. kinetic energy one-fourth of A.

107. In a pressure cooker cooking is faster bacause the increase in vapour pressure:
A. increase the specific heat.
B. decreases the specific heat.
C. decreases the boiling point.
D. increases the boiling point.

108. Magnets attract magnetic substances such as iron, nickel, cobalt etc. They can also repel:
A. paramagnetic substances.
B. ferromagnetic substances.
C. diamagnetic substances.
D. non-magnetic substances.

109. When a ray of light is going from one medium to another, its:
A. wavelength remains same.
B. frequency remains same.
C. frequency increases.
D. wavelength increases.

110. Which one among the following is the main ingredient in cement?

A. Gypsum B. Lime stone
C. Clay D. Ash

111. Glass is actually:
A. a crystalline solid B. an ionic solid
C. an elastic solid D. a vitrified liquid

112. Solutions in test tubes containing H_2O and aqueous NaOH can be differentiated with the help of:
A. red litmus. B. blue litmus.
C. Na_2CO_3 D. HCl (aqueous)

113. A student heated some sulphur in a spatula and collected the gas 'X'. Which one among the following is correct about 'X'?
A. X is SO_2 and it turns moist litmus to blue
B. X is SO_3 and it turns moist litmus to red
C. X is SO_2 and it turns moist litmus to red
D. X is SO_3 and it turns dry litmus to blue

114. Human stomach produces acid 'X' which helps in digestion of food. Acid 'X' is:
A. acetic acid B. methanoic acid
C. hydrochloric acid D. citric acid

115. When concentrated H_2SO_4 spilts on the surface, it should be immediately cleaned:
A. with a piece of cloth.
B. by adding cold water.
C. by adding solid Na_2CO_3.
D. by adding solid $BaCl_2$.

116. India by becoming a full-fledged member of the Financial Action Task Force:
A. will be able to access information on suspect accounts in nations such as Switzerland and UK.
B. will play an important role in law enforcement matters, investigations at an international level.
C. has also become a member of Organization for Economic Co-operation and Development.
D. all of the above.

117. Consider the following declaration and identify the person who made it using the code given below:
'The time has come when badges of honour make out shame glaring in their incongruous context of humiliation, and, I, for my part, wish to stand shorn of all special distinction, by the side of my countrymen who, for their so-called insignificance are liable to suffer degradation not fit for human beings'.
Code:
A. Mahatma Gandhi B. Jawaharlal Nehru
C. Dada Bhai Naoroji D. Rabindranath Tagore

118. Identify, using the code given below, the nationalist leader who was sentenced in the words outlined below:
'the fat that in the eyes of millions of your countrymen you are a great patriot and great leader' but *'as a man subject to the law, who has, by his own admission broken the law' you are subject to six years imprisonment*

Code :
A. C.R. Das B. Mahatma Gandhi
C. Subhash Bose D. Jawaharlal Nehru

119. Consider the following statement:
'We believe that it is the inalienable right of the Indian people as of any other people, to have freedom and to enjoy the fruits of their toil and have the necessities of life so that they may have full opportunities of growth' Identify the correct context of this statement from below:
A. Pledge of independence to be publicly taken all over India on 26 January 1930
B. Preamble of the Constitution of India adopted in 1950
C. Congress Working Committee Resolution adopted at the Special Calcutta Congress in 1920
D. Part of Speech delivered by Subhash Bose at the launch of *Azad Hind Fauj*

120. Which one among the following led to the Greece economic crisis 2010?
A. Excessive borrowing from IMF
B. Sudden depreciation of Euro
C. Unrestricted spending and cheap loans
D. Outflow of foreign capital due to political unrest

121. The Clean Development Mechanism (CDM), a mechanism to reduce green-house gas emission as per Kyoto Protocol implies that:
A. industrial countries receive carbon credits by funding carbon saving projects in another relatively affluent nation
B. industrial countries reduce their carbon emission by using environment friendly technology in production
C. developed countries invest in carbon reduction in developing countries and receive carbon credit in return
D. developed nations purchase carbon credit from other nations

122. Match List-I with List-II and select the correct answer using the code given below the Lists:

List-I (Joint exercise)	***List-II (Type)***
(*a*) Indra	1. Joint anti-terrorism exercise
(*b*) Cope India	2. Joint air force exercise
(*c*) Ind-Indo Corpat	3. Coordinated maritime patrolling
(*d*) Yudhabhyas	4. Joint army exercise

Code:

	(*a*)	(*b*)	(*c*)	(*d*)
A.	1	2	3	4
B.	1	3	2	4
C.	4	3	2	1
D.	4	2	3	1

123. Match List-I with List-II and select the correct answer using the code given below the Lists:

List-I (Ship)	List-II (Type)
(a) INS *Arihant*	1. Aircraft Carrier
(b) INS *Vikrant*	2. Landing Platform Dock
(c) INS *Shiwalik*	3. Nuclear Submarine
(d) INS *Airavat*	4. Stealth Frigate

Code:

	(a)	(b)	(c)	(d)
A.	3	4	1	2
B.	3	1	4	2
C.	2	1	4	3
D.	2	4	1	3

124. '*Milan*' is ?

1. an annual gathering of navies of Indian Ocean countries.
2. conducted at Chennai.
3. a joint anti terrorism exercise.
4. aimed at enhancing inter-operability among navies.

Select the correct answer using the code given below:

A. 1 only B. 2 and 3
C. 1 and 4 D. 3 and 4

125. Consider the following pairs:

1. *Pinaka* : 1. Multi Barrel Rocket Launcher System
2. *Nag* : 2. Anti Tank Missile System
3. *Lakshya* : 3. Unmanned Aerial Vehicle

Which of the pairs given above is/are correctly matched?

A. 1 only B. 1 and 2 only
C. 2 and 3 only D. 1, 2 and 3

126. Which one among the following is the unit raised to protect the naval assets?

A. *Sagar Rakshak Bal*
B. *Sagar Suraksha Bal*
C. *Sagar Prahari Bal*
D. *Sagar Nigrani Bal*

127. Which one among the following films won the *Nargis Dutt* award for best feature film on national integration in the 57th National Film Award in the year 2010?

A. Well Done Abba B. Lahore
C. Dilli-6 D. Paa

128. Consider the following statements with regard to the Renewable Energy Certificate (REC) Mechanism launched in November 2010 by the Government of India:

1. It enables the obligated entities to meet their renewable purchase obligation
2. It is one of the pioneering efforts in any developing country for mainstreaming the renewable energy generation through market mechanism

Which of the statements given above is/are correct?

A. 1 only B. 2 only
C. Both 1 and 2 D. Neither 1 nor 2

129. Consider the following statements with regard to the Global Hunger Index:

1. India ranks within the top ten among the developing countries in the Global Hunger Index 2010
2. According to the Global Hunger Index 2010 the proportion of undernourished in India is decreasing
3. Normally economic progress of a country measured by its gross national income and the hunger level are inversely correlated

Which of the statements given above is/are correct?

A. 1, 2 and 3 B. 2 and 3 only
C. 1 and 2 only D. 3 only

Directions: *The following Six (06) items consist of two statements, statement I and statement II. You are to examine these two statements carefully and select the answers to these items using the code given below:*

Code :

A. Both the statements are individually true and statement II is the correct explanation of statement I
B. Both the statements are individually true but statement II is ***not*** the correct explanation of statement I
C. Statement I is true but Statement II is false
D. Statement I is false but statement II is true

130. Statement I : A myopic person is advised to use concave lens

Statement II : The eye lens of a myopic person focuses the parallel rays coming from distant objects in front of the retina

131. Statement I : Oxidation in our body cell releases dangerous free radicals

Statement II : Our body itself produces anti-oxidants to neutralize harmful free radicals

132. Statement I : Decay and disintegration of rocks in situ is called weathering

Statement II : Mechanical weathering is mainly causeed by temperature variation

133. Statement I : The semi-arid tracts of India stretching from eastern Rajasthan in the north to south central Tamil Nadu are agriculturally less productive

Statement II : The semi-arid tracts are homeland to a large number of central Indian Scheduled Tribe population

134. Statement I : The Mediterranean climate is highly suitable for fruit production

Statement II : Cool and moist winters in Mediterranean regions enable ample production of fruits.

135. Statement I : In the northern hemisphere the ocean currents flowing from equator towards the north pole and from pole towards the equator are deflected to their right

Statement II : This happens due to rotation of the Earth on the axis from west to east

136. A bee-sting leaves an acid which causes pain and irritation. The injected acid is:

A. acetic acid B. sulphuric acid
C. citric acid D. methanoic acid

137. Iron nails are dipped into blue copper sulphate solution. After some time iron nails are:

A. dissolved and blue colour is discharged.
B. dissolved but blue colour is not discharged.
C. not dissolved but blue colour is not discharged.
D. not disssolved but blue colour is discharged.

138. A student by chance mixed acetone with alcohol. This mixture of acetone and alcohol can be separated by:

A. filtration.
B. separating funnel.
C. fractional crystallization.
D. fractional distillation.

139. Silver ware turns black after a period of time due to formation of:

A. nitrate coating on silver.
B. sulphide coating on silver.
C. chloride coating one silver.
D. oxide coating on silver.

140. Which of the statements given below is/are correct

Permanent hardness of water is due to the presence of soluble:

1. chloride of calcium.
2. bicarbonate of calcium.
3. sulphate of magnesium.
4. bicarbonate of magnesium.

Select the correct answer using the code given below:

A. 1 only B. 1 and 3 only
C. 2 and 4 D. 1, 2 and 3

141. Which of the following statements about diamond are correct?

1. It is used as a gem in jewellery because of its ability to reflect light
2. It is a good conductor of electricity
3. It is used for cutting glass, marble stones and other hard materials
4. It is used for drilling of rocks

Select the correct answer using the code given below:

A. 1, 3 and 4 B. 2, 3 and 4
C. 1, 2 and 3 D. 2 and 4 only

142. Which one among the following methods is ***not*** effective in removing arsenic from contaminated ground water?

A. Boiling
B. Reverse osmosis
C. Ion exchange
D. Coagulation-adsorption

143. Bronze is often used to make statues and medals whereas brass is used in making utensils, scientific apparatus and cartidges. Both brass and bronze are copper containing alloys, yet they differ in their chemical composition for additionally containing:

A. Zinc in brass and tin in bronze.
B. Chromium in brass and nickel in bronze.
C. Nickel in brass and tin in bronze.
D. Iron in brass and nickel in bronze.

144. Which of the statements about glass are correct?

1. Glass is a super-cooled liquid having infinite viscosity
2. Violet coloured glass is obtained by adding MnO_2
3. Glass is a man made silicate
4. Glass is a crystalline substance

Select the correct answer using the code given below:

A. 1, 2 and 4 B. 2, 3 and 4
C. 1, 2 and 3 D. 1 and 3 only

145. Sandalwood tree is considered a :

A. total root parasite.
B. total stem parasite.
C. stem parasite.
D. partial root parasite.

146. Which one among the following statements about stomach is ***not*** correct?

A. Stomach acts as a temporary reservoir
B. Stomach mixes food with gastric juice
C. Stomach secretes lipase and amylase in gastric juice
D. Rate of stomach emptying depends on the type of food

147. Which one of the following organs breaks fat to produce cholesterol?

A. Intestine B. Liver
C. Lungs D. Kidneys

148. Consider the following statements about comets:

1. Most comets have elongated elliptical orbits that take them close to the Sun for a part of their orbit, and then out into the further reaches of the Solar System for the remainder
2. If a comet is travelling fast enough, it may leave the Solar System

Which of the statements given above is/are correct?

A. 1 only
B. 2 only
C. Both 1 and 2
D. Neither 1 nor 2

149. An individual whose blood type is B may in an emergency donate blood to a person whose blood type is:

A. B or A B. AB or A
C. A or O D. AB or B

150. Which of the following statements is/are correct?

1. In comparison to the Jupiter, planet Earth displays eclipses more frequently
2. On Mars only partial solar eclipses are possible

Select the correct answer using the code given below:

A. 1 only B. 2 only
C. Both 1 and 2 D. Neither 1 nor 2

PAPER II : MATHEMATICS

1. What is the value of the determinant

$$\begin{vmatrix} x+1 & x+2 & x+4 \\ x+3 & x+5 & x+8 \\ x+7 & x+10 & x+14 \end{vmatrix}?$$

A. $x + 2$ B. $x^2 + 2$
C. 2 D. –2

2. Consider the following statements in respect of the function

$f(x) = x^3 - 1$, $x \in [-1, 1]$

1. $f(x)$ is increasing in $[-1, 1]$
2. $f(x)$ has no root in $(-1, 1)$

Which of the statements given above is/are correct?

A. 1 only B. 2 only
C. Both 1 and 2 D. Neither 1 nor 2

3. The largest value of
$2x^3 - 3x^2 - 12x + 5$
for $-2 \leq x \leq 2$ occurs when

A. $x = -2$ B. $x = -1$
C. $x = 2$ D. $x = 0$

4. What is $\int_0^{\pi} \frac{dx}{1+2\sin^2 x}$ equal to?

A. π B. $\frac{\pi}{3}$
C. $\frac{\pi}{\sqrt{3}}$ D. $\frac{2\pi}{\sqrt{3}}$

5. If 5 and 7 are the roots of the equation

$$\begin{vmatrix} x & 4 & 5 \\ 7 & x & 7 \\ 5 & 8 & x \end{vmatrix} = 0$$

then what is the third root?

A. –12 B. 9
C. 13 D. 14

6. In a GP of positive terms, any term is equal to one-third of the sum of next two terms. What is the common ratio of the GP?

A. $\frac{\sqrt{13}+1}{2}$ B. $\frac{\sqrt{13}-1}{2}$
C. $\frac{\sqrt{13}+1}{3}$ D. $\sqrt{13}$

7. If $(1 + \tan \theta)(1 + \tan \varphi) = 2$, then what is $(\theta + \varphi)$ equal to?

A. 30° B. 45°
C. 60° D. 90°

8. If $f(x)$ is an even function, then what is

$\int_0^{\pi} f(\cos x)dx$ equal to?

A. 0 B. $\int_0^{\frac{\pi}{2}} f(\cos x)dx$
C. $2\int_0^{\frac{\pi}{2}} f(\cos x)dx$ D. 1

9. What is the value of k for which the system of equations $kx + 2y = 5$ and $3x + y = 1$ has no solution?

A. 0 B. 3
C. 6 D. 15

10. In how many ways can 6 girls be seated in 2 empty chairs?

A. 10 B. 15
C. 24 D. 30

11. What is the value of

$$\log_{10}\left(\frac{9}{8}\right) - \log_{10}\left(\frac{27}{32}\right) + \log_{10}\left(\frac{3}{4}\right)?$$

A. 3 B. 2
C. 1 D. 0

12. Which term of the series

$$\frac{1}{4}, \frac{1}{2}, 1, \ldots$$

is –128?

A. 9th B. 10th
C. 11th D. 12th

13. What is the number of ordered pairs of non-zero positive integers (x, y) such that $x + y \leq 4$?

A. 4 B. 5
C. 6 D. 8

14. In the binary system of numbers let a = 00111 and b = 01110, then in decimal system what is b/a equal to?

A. 1 B. 2
C. 4 D. 5

15. If $\frac{1}{b-a}+\frac{1}{b-c}=\frac{1}{a}+\frac{1}{c}$ then a, b, c are in
A. AP B. GP
C. HP D. None of the above

16. What is $\int \sin^{-1}(\cos x)dx$ equal to?

A. $\frac{x\pi}{2}-\frac{x^2}{2}+k$ B. $\frac{\pi}{2}+\frac{x^2}{2}+k$

C. $-\frac{x\pi}{2}-\frac{x^2}{2}+kx$ D. $\frac{\pi}{2}-\frac{x^2}{2}+k$

where k is a constant of integration.

17. If α and β are the roots of the equation $4x^2 + 3x + 7 = 0$, then what is the value of $(\alpha^{-2} + \beta^{-2})$?
A. 47/49 B. 49/47
C. – 47/49 D. – 49/47

18. What is the equation of the line passing through (2, –3) and parallel to y-axis?
A. $y = -3$ B. $y = 2$
C. $x = 2$ D. $x = -2$

19. What is the set of points (x, y) satisfying the equations $x^2 + y^2 = 4$ and $x + y = 2$?
A. {(2, 0), (–2, 0), (0, 2)}
B. {(0, 2), (0, –2)}
C. {(0, 2), (2, 0)}
D. {(2, 0), (–2, 0), (0, 2), (0, –2)}

20. Consider the following statements:
1. The inverse of a square matrix, if exists, is unique.
2. If A and B are singular matrices of order n, then AB is also a singular matrix of order n.

Which of the statements given above is/are correct?
A. 1 only B. 2 only
C. Both 1 and 2 D. Neither 1 nor 2

21. What is the angle between the lines whose direction cosines are proportional to (2, 3, 4) and (1, –2, 1) respectively?
A. 90° B. 60°
C. 45° D. 30°

22. What is the value of k for which the following function $f(x)$ is continuous for all x?

$$f(x)=\begin{cases}\frac{x^3-3x+2}{(x-1)^2} & \text{for } x\neq 1\\ k & \text{for } x=1\end{cases}$$

A. 3 B. 2
C. 1 D. –1

23. If p, q, r are rational numbers, then the roots of the equation $x^2 - 2px + p^2 - q^2 + 2qr - r^2 = 0$ are
A. complex B. pure imaginary
C. irrational D. rational

24. If A = {1, 2, 5, 6} and B = {1, 2, 3}, then what is $(A \times B) \cap (B \times A)$ equal to?
A. {(1, 1), (2, 1), (6, 1), (3, 2)}
B. {(1, 1), (1, 2), (2, 1), (2, 2)}
C. {(1, 1), (2, 2)}
D. {(1, 1), (1, 2), (2, 5), (2, 6)}

25. What is the differential equation of all parabolas whose axes are parallel to y-axis?

A. $\frac{d^3y}{dx^3}=0$ B. $\frac{d^2x}{dy^2}=c$

C. $\frac{d^3x}{dy^3}=1$ D. $\frac{d^3x}{dx^3}=c$

where c is a constant.

For the next **five (5)** items that follow:
The students of a class are offered three language (Hindi, English and French). 15 students learn all the three languages whereas 28 students do not learn any language. The number of students learning Hindi and English but not French is twice the number of students learning Hindi and French but not English. The number of students learning English and French but not Hindi is thrice the number of students learning Hindi and French but not English. 23 students learn only Hindi and 17 students learn only English. The total number of students learning French is 46 and the total number of students learning only French is 11.

26. How many students learn precisely two languages?
A. 55 B. 40
C. 30 D. 13

27. How many students learn at least two languages?
A. 15 B. 30
C. 45 D. 55

28. What is the total strength of the class?
A. 124 B. 100
C. 96 D. 66

29. How many students learn English and French?
A. 30 B. 43
C. 45 D. 73

30. How many students learn at least one language?
A. 45 B. 51
C. 96 D. None of the above

For the next **four (4)** items that follow:
ABC is a triangle right angled at B. The hypotenuse (AC) is four times the perpendicular (BD) is four times the perpendicular (BD) drawn to its from the opposite vertex and AD < DC.

31. What is one of the acute angles of the triangle?
A. 15° B. 30°
C. 45° D. None of the above

32. What is angle ABD?
A. 15° B. 30°
C. 45° D. None of the above

33. What is $AD : DC$ equal to?
A. $(7-2\sqrt{3}):1$ B. $(7-4\sqrt{3}):1$
C. 1 : 2 D. None of these

34. What is $\tan(A - C)$ equal to?
A. 0 B. 1
C. 2 D. None of the above

35. What is the radius of the sphere
$x^2 + y^2 + z^2 - x - y - z = 0$?
A. $\sqrt{\frac{3}{4}}$ B. $\sqrt{\frac{1}{2}}$
C. $\sqrt{\frac{3}{2}}$ D. $\frac{1}{3}$

36. An experiment consists of flipping a coin and then flipping it a second time if head occurs. If a tail occurs on the first flip, then a six-faced die is tossed once. Assuming that the outcomes are equally likely, what is the probability of getting one head and one tail?
A. 1/4 B. 1/36
C. 1/6 D. 1/8

37. If, in general, the value of sin A is known, but the value of A is not known, then how many values of tan $(A/2)$ can be calculated?
A. 1 B. 2
C. 3 D. 4

38. Consider the following:
1. $\operatorname{cosec}^{-1}\left(-\frac{2}{\sqrt{3}}\right) = -\frac{\pi}{3}$
2. $\sec^{-1}\left(\frac{2}{\sqrt{3}}\right) = \frac{\pi}{6}$

Which of the above is/are correct?
A. 1 only B. 2 only
C. Both 1 and 2 D. Neither 1 nor 2

39. Consider the following statements with regard to correlation coefficient r between random variables x and y:
1. $r = +1$ or -1 means there is a linear relation between x and y.
2. $-1 \le r \le 1$ and r^2 is a measure of the linear relationship between the variables.

Which of the statements given above is/are correct?
A. 1 only B. 2 only
C. Both 1 and 2 D. Neither 1 nor 2

40. If the values of a set are measured in cm, what will be the unit of variance?
A. cm B. cm^2
C. cm^3 D. No unit

41. A box contains 6 distinct dolls. From this box, three dolls are randomly selected one by one with replacement. What is the probability of selecting 3 distinct dolls?
A. 5/54 B. 12/25
C. 1/20 D. 5/9

42. For the equation
$ax^2 + by^2 + 2hxy + 2gx + 2fy + c = 0$
where $a \neq 0$, to represent a circle, the condition will be
A. $a = b$ and $c = 0$ B. $f = g$ and $h = 0$
C. $a = b$ and $h = 0$ D. $f = g$ and $c = 0$

43. If A and B are events such that $P(A \cup B) = 0.5$, $P(\overline{B}) = 0.8$ and $P(A \mid B) = 0.4$, then what is $P(A \cap B)$ equal to?
A. 0.08 B. 0.02
C. 0.8 D. 0.2

44. Consider the following relations among the angles α, β, γ made by a vectors with the coordinate axes:
1. $\cos 2\alpha + \cos 2\beta + \cos 2\gamma = -1$
2. $\sin^2\alpha + \sin^2\beta + \sin^2\gamma = 1$

Which of the above is/are correct?
A. 1 only B. 2 only
C. Both 1 and 2 D. Neither 1 nor 2

45. Which one of the following points lies on the plane $2x + 3y - 6z = 21$?
A. (3, 2, 2) B. (3, 7, 1)
C. (1, 2, 3) D. (2, 1, –1)

46. If 3 is the root of the equation $x^2 - 8x + k = 0$, then what is the value of k?
A. –15 B. 9
C. 15 D. 24

47. Two straight lines $x - 3y - 2 = 0$ and $2x - 6y - 6 = 0$
A. never intersect
B. intersect at a single point
C. intersect at infinite number of points
D. intersect at more than one point (but finite number of points)

48. If $(a, 0)$, $(0, b)$ $(1, 1)$ are collinear, what is $(a + b - ab)$ equal to?
A. 2 B. 1
C. 0 D. –1

49. If $A = \begin{bmatrix} 3 & 1 \\ 0 & 4 \end{bmatrix}$ and $B = \begin{bmatrix} 1 & 1 \\ 0 & 2 \end{bmatrix}$

then which of the following is/are correct?
1. AB is defined
2. BA is defined
3. $AB = BA$

Select the correct answer using the code given below:
A. 1 only B. 2 only
C. 1 and 2 only D. 1, 2 and 3

50. Using the digits 1, 2, 3, 4 and 5 only once, how many numbers greater than 41000 can be formed?

A. 41 B. 48

C. 50 D. 55

51. If an angle α is divided into two parts A and B such that $A - B = x$ and $\tan A : \tan B = 2 : 1$, then what is $\sin x$ equal to?

A. $3\sin\alpha$ B. $(2\sin\alpha)/3$

C. $(\sin\alpha)/3$ D. $2\sin\alpha$

52. A man standing on the bank of a river observes that the angle of elevation of the top of a tree just on the opposite bank is 60°. The angle of elevation is 30° from a point at a distance y metres from the bank. What is the height of the tree?

A. y metres B. $2y$ metres

C. $\frac{\sqrt{3}y}{2}$ metres D. $\frac{y}{2}$ metres

53. If P, Q, R are three non-collinear points, then what is $PQ \cap PR$ equal to?

A. Null set B. $\{P\}$

C. $\{P, Q, R\}$ D. $\{Q, R\}$

54. A, B, C, D and E are coplanar points and three of them lie in a straight line. What is the maximum number of triangles that can be drawn with these points as their vertices?

A. 5 B. 9

C. 10 D. 12

55. The vector $\vec{a}$ lies in the plane of vectors $\vec{b}$ and $\vec{c}$. Which one of the following is correct?

A. $\vec{a}.(\vec{b} \times \vec{c}) = 0$ B. $\vec{a}.(\vec{b} \times \vec{c}) = 1$

C. $\vec{a}.(\vec{b} \times \vec{c}) = -1$ D. $\vec{a}.(\vec{b} \times \vec{c}) = 3$

56. What is the projection of the vector $\hat{i} - 2\hat{j} + \hat{k}$ on the vector $4\hat{i} - 4\hat{j} + 7\hat{k}$?

A. $\frac{\sqrt{5}}{2}$ B. $\frac{19}{9}$

C. $\frac{\sqrt{5}}{4}$ D. $\frac{11}{3}$

57. Which one of the following statements is correct?

A. $\sin^2 30°, \sin^2 45°, \sin^2 60°$ are in GP

B. $\cos^2 30°, \cos^2 45°, \cos^2 60°$ are in GP

C. $\cot^2 30°, \cot^2 45°, \cot^2 60°$ are in AP

D. $\tan^2 30°, \tan^2 45°, \tan^2 60°$ are in GP

58. If sum of squares of the roots of the equation $x^2 + kx - b = 0$ is $2b$, what is k equal to?

A. 1 B. b

C. $-b$ D. 0

59. If one root of the equation $ax^2 + bx + c = 0$, $a \neq 0$ is reciprocal of the other root, then which one of the following is orrect?

A. $a = c$ B. $b = c$

C. $a = -c$ D. $b = 0$

60. If ω is the imaginary cube root of unity, then what is $(2 - \omega + 2\omega^2)^{27}$ equal to?

A. $3^{27}\ \omega$ B. $-3^{27}\ \omega^2$

C. 3^{27} D. -3^{27}

61. What is the acute angle between the planes $x + y + 2z = 3$ and $-2x + y - z = 11$?

A. $\pi/5$ B. $\pi/4$

C. $\pi/6$ D. $\pi/3$

62. What is the area bounded by the curves $y = e^x$, $y = e^{-x}$ and the straight line $x = 1$?

A. $\left(e + \frac{1}{e}\right)$ square units

B. $\left(e - \frac{1}{e}\right)$ square units

C. $\left(e + \frac{1}{e} - 2\right)$ square units

D. $\left(e - \frac{1}{e} - 2\right)$ square units

63. What are the points of intersection of the curve $4x^2 - 9y^2 = 1$ with its conjugate axis?

A. (1/2, 0) and (–1/2, 0)

B. (0, 2) and (0, –2)

C. (0, 3) and (0, –3)

D. No such points exist

64. What is the locus of a point which moves equidistant from the coordinate axes?

A. $x \pm y = 0$ B. $x + 2y = 0$

C. $2x + y = 0$ D. None of the above

65. What is $\int e^x \left(\sqrt{x} + \frac{1}{2\sqrt{x}}\right) dx$ equal to?

A. $xe^x + c$ B. $e^x\left(\sqrt{x}\right) + c$

C. $2e^x\left(\sqrt{x}\right) + c$ D. $2xe^x + c$

Where c is a constant of integration.

66. Let p, q, r, s be respectively the magnitudes of the vectors $3\hat{i} - 2\hat{j}, 2\hat{i} + 2\hat{j} + \hat{k}, 4\hat{i} - \hat{j} + \hat{k}, 2\hat{i} + 2\hat{j} + 3\hat{k}$. Which one of the following is correct?

A. $r > s > q > p$ B. $s > r > p > q$

C. $r > s > p > q$ D. $s > r > q > p$

67. In a triangle ABC, if $c = 2$, $A = 120°$, $a = \sqrt{6}$, then what is C equal to?

A. 30° B. 45°
C. 60° D. 75°

68.

Class Interval	1 – 5	6 – 10	11 – 15	16 – 20
Frequency	3	7	6	5

Consider the following statements in respect of the above frequency distribution:

1. The median is contained in the modal class.
2. The distribution is bell-shaped.

Which of the above statements is/are correct?

A. 1 only B. 2 only
C. Both 1 and 2 D. Neither 1 nor 2

For the next **two (2)** items that follow:
The following table gives the continuous frequency distribution of a continuous variable X:

Class Interval	0 – 10	10 – 20	20 – 30	30 – 40	40 – 50
Frequency	5	10	20	5	10

69. What is the median of the above frequency distribution?

A. 23 B. 24
C. 25 D. 26

70. What is the mean of the above frequency distribution?

A. 25 B. 26
C. 27 D. 28

71. If the matrix $A = \begin{pmatrix} 2-x & 1 & 1 \\ 1 & 3-x & 0 \\ -1 & -3 & -x \end{pmatrix}$ is singular, then what is the solution set S?

A. $S = \{0, 2, 3\}$ B. $S = \{-1, 2, 3\}$
C. $S = \{1, 2, 3\}$ D. $S = \{2, 3\}$

72. What is the range of $f(x) = \cos 2x - \sin 2x$?

A. $[2, 4]$ B. $[-1, 1]$
C. $[-\sqrt{2}, \sqrt{2}]$ D. $(-\sqrt{2}, \sqrt{2})$

73. What is the solution of the differential equation

$$\frac{dy}{dx} + \sqrt{\frac{1-y^2}{1-x^2}} = 0?$$

A. $\sin^{-1} y + \sin^{-1} x = c$
B. $\sin^{-1} y - \sin^{-1} x = c$
C. $2\sin^{-1} y + \sin^{-1} x = c$
D. $2\sin^{-1} y - \sin^{-1} x = c$
where c is a constant.

74. If $z = 1 + \cos\frac{\pi}{5} + i\sin\frac{\pi}{5}$ then what is $|z|$ equal to?

A. $2\cos\frac{\pi}{5}$ B. $2\sin\frac{\pi}{5}$
C. $2\cos\frac{\pi}{10}$ D. $2\sin\frac{\pi}{10}$

75. If $x\hat{i} + y\hat{j} + z\hat{k}$ is a unit vector and $x : y : z = \sqrt{3} : 2 : 3$, then what is the value of z?

A. $\frac{3}{16}$ B. 3
C. $\frac{3}{4}$ D. 2

76. What is the modulus of $\frac{1}{1+3i} - \frac{1}{1-3i}$?

A. $\frac{3}{5}$ B. $\frac{9}{25}$
C. $\frac{3}{25}$ D. $\frac{5}{3}$

77. Let M be the set of men and R is a relation 'is son of' defined on M. Then R is

A. an equivalence relation
B. a symmetric relation only
C. a transitive relation only
D. None of the above

78. What is the locus of the point which is at a distance 8 units to the left of y-axis?

A. $x = 8$ B. $y = 8$
C. $x = -8$ D. $y = -8$

79. The number 10101111 in binary system is represented in decimal system by which one of the following numbers?

A. 157 B. 175
C. 571 D. 751

80. There are 4 letters and 4 directed envelopes. These 4 letters are randomly inserted into the 4 envelopes. What is the probability that the letters are inserted into the corresponding envelopes?

A. 11/12 B. 23/24
C. 1/24 D. None of these

81. The average daily income of workers of a factory including that of the owner is ₹ 110. However, if the income of the owner is excluded, the average daily income of the remaining 9 workers is ₹ 76. What is the daily income of the owner?

A. ₹ 300 B. ₹ 316
C. ₹ 322 D. ₹ 416

82. If A, B, C are non-empty sets such that $A \cap C = \Phi$, then what is $(A \times B) \cap (C \times B)$ equal to?

A. $A \times C$ B. $A \times B$
C. $B \times C$ D. Φ

83. If $A = \{4n + 2 \mid n$ is a natural number$\}$ and $B = \{3n \mid n$ is a natural number$\}$, then what is $(A \cap B)$ equal to?

A. $\{12n^2 + 6n \mid n$ is a natural number$\}$
B. $\{24n - 12 \mid n$ is a natural number$\}$

C. {60n + 30 | n is a normal number}
D. {12n – 6 | n is a natural number}

84. If the matrix $A=\begin{bmatrix}\alpha & \beta\\ \beta & \alpha\end{bmatrix}$ is such that $A^2 = 1$, then which one of the following is correct?
A. $\alpha = 0, \beta = 1$ or $\alpha = 1, \beta = 0$
B. $\alpha = 0, \beta \neq 1$ or $\alpha \neq 0, \beta = 1$
C. $\alpha = 1, \beta \neq 0$ or $\alpha \neq 1, \beta = 0$
D. $\alpha \neq 0, \beta \neq 0$

85. What is the sum of the focal distances of a point of an ellipse $\frac{x^2}{a^2}+\frac{y^2}{b^2}=1$?
A. a B. b
C. $2a$ D. $2b$

86. What is the degree of the following differential equation?

$$\left(\frac{d^3y}{dx^3}\right)^{\frac{2}{3}}+4-3\frac{d^2y}{dx^2}+5\frac{dy}{dx}=0$$

A. 1 B. 2
C. 3 D. 4

87. What is the sum of $\sqrt{3}+\frac{1}{\sqrt{3}}+\frac{1}{3\sqrt{3}}+...$?
A. $\frac{\sqrt{3}}{2}$ B. $\frac{3\sqrt{3}}{2}$
C. $\frac{2\sqrt{3}}{2}$ D. $\sqrt{3}$

88. What does the differential equation

$$y\frac{dy}{dx}+x=a$$

(where a is a constant) represent?
A. A set of circles having centre on the y-axis
B. A set of circles having centre on the x-axis
C. A set of ellipses
D. A pair of straight lines

89. If $A=\begin{bmatrix}\alpha & 0\\ 1 & 1\end{bmatrix}$ and $B=\begin{bmatrix}1 & 0\\ 2 & 1\end{bmatrix}$ such that $A^2 = B$, then what is the value of α?
A. –1 B. 1
C. 2 D. 4

90. What is the value of n, if $P(15, n - 1) : P(16, n - 2) = 3 : 4$?
A. 10 B. 12
C. 14 D. 15

91. What is the middle term in the expansion of $\left(1-\frac{x}{2}\right)^8$?
A. $\frac{35x^4}{8}$ B. $\frac{17x^5}{8}$
C. $\frac{35x^5}{8}$ D. None of these

92. What is the sum of the roots of the equations $\left(2-\sqrt{3}\right)x^2-\left(7-4\sqrt{3}\right)x+\left(2+\sqrt{3}\right)=0$?
A. $2-\sqrt{3}$ B. $2+\sqrt{3}$
C. $7-4\sqrt{3}$ D. 4

93. What is the total number of combinations of n different things taken 1, 2, 3, ..., n at a time?
A. 2^{n+1} B. 2^{2n+1}
C. 2^{n-1} D. $2^n - 1$

94. One of the roots of the equadratic equation $ax^2 + bx + c = 0$, $a \neq 0$ is positive and the other root is negative. The condition for this to happen is
A. $a > 0, b > 0, c > 0$
B. $a > 0, b < 0, c > 0$
C. $a < 0, b > 0, c < 0$
D. $a < 0, c > 0$

95. If the solution of the differential equation

$$\frac{dy}{dx}=\frac{ax+3}{2y+f}$$

represents a circle, then what is the value of a?
A. 2 B. 1
C. –2 D. –1

96. If A, B, C are in AP and $b : c = \sqrt{3}:\sqrt{2}$, then what is the value of sin C?
A. 1 B. $\frac{1}{\sqrt{3}}$
C. $\sqrt{3}$ D. $\frac{1}{\sqrt{2}}$

97. The points with position vectors

$10\hat{i}+3\hat{j},\ 12\hat{i}-5\hat{j},\ a\hat{i}+11\hat{j}$

are collinear, if the value of a is
A. –8 B. 4
C. 8 D. 12

98. What is the sine of angle between the vectors $\hat{i}+2\hat{j}+3\hat{k}$ and $-\hat{i}+2\hat{j}+3\hat{k}$?
A. $\sqrt{\frac{13}{7}}$ B. $\frac{\sqrt{13}}{17}$
C. $\frac{13}{\sqrt{7}}$ D. None of the above

99. If $\sin\left(\sin^{-1}\frac{1}{5}+\cos^{-1}x\right)=1$ then what is x equal to?

A. 0 B. 1

C. $\frac{4}{5}$ D. $\frac{1}{5}$

100. What is $\log\left(a+\sqrt{a^2+1}\right)+\log\left(\frac{1}{a+\sqrt{a^2+1}}\right)$ equal to?

A. 1 B. 0

C. 2 D. $\frac{1}{2}$

101. 5 books are to be chosen from a lot of 10 books. If m is the number of ways of choice when one specified book is always included and n is the number of ways of choice when a specified book is always excluded, then which one of the following is correct?

A. $m > n$ B. $m = n$

C. $m = n - 1$ D. $m = n - 2$

102. Which one of the following is correct in respect of the function $f(x) = |x| + x^2$?

A. $f(x)$ is not continuous at $x = 0$

B. $f(x)$ is differentiable at $x = 0$

C. $f(x)$ is continuous but not differentiable at $x = 0$

D. None of the above

103. What is the condition that one root of the equation $ax^2 + bx + c = 0$, $a \neq 0$ should be double the other?

A. $2a^2 = 9bc$ B. $2b^2 = 9ac$

C. $2c^2 = 9ab$ D. None of the above

104. Consider the following with regard to a relation R on a set of real numbers defined by xRy if and only if $3x + 4y = 5$:

1. $0\,R\,1$
2. $1\,R\,\frac{1}{2}$
3. $\frac{2}{3}\,R\,\frac{3}{4}$

Which of the above are correct?

A. 1 and 2 only B. 1 and 3 only

C. 2 and 3 only D. All of the above

105. The function $f(x)=k\sin x+\frac{1}{3}\sin 3x$ has maximum value at $x=\frac{\pi}{3}$. What is the value of k?

A. 3 B. $\frac{1}{3}$

C. 2 D. $\frac{1}{2}$

106. If $I_n = \int_0^{\frac{\pi}{4}} \tan^n x\,dx$ then what is $I_n + I_{n-2}$ equal to?

A. $1/n$ B. $1/(n-1)$

C. $n/(n-1)$ D. $1/(n-2)$

107. What is the equation of the line joining the origin with the point of intersection of the lines $4x + 3y = 12$ and $3x + 4y = 12$?

A. $x + y = 1$ B. $x - y = 1$

C. $3y = 4x$ D. $x = y$

108. If the sum of the squares of the distances of the point (x, y) from the points $(a, 0)$ and $(-a, 0)$ is $2b^2$, then which one of the following is correct?

A. $x^2 + a^2 = b^2 + y^2$ B. $x^2 + a^2 = 2b^2 - y^2$

C. $x^2 - a^2 = b^2 + y^2$ D. $x^2 + a^2 = b^2 - y^2$

109. If $f(x) = 2^x$, then what is $f''(x)$ equal to?

A. $2^x (\ln 2)^2$ B. $x(x-1)2^{x-2}$

C. $2^{x+1} (\ln 2)$ D. $2^x (\log_{10} 2)^2$

110. In an examination, there are 3 multiple-choice questions and each question has 4 choices. If a student randomly selects an answer for all the three questions, what is the probability that the student will not answer all the three questions correctly?

A. 1/64 B. 63/64

C. 1/12 D. 11/12

111. What is the geometric mean of the data 2, 4, 8, 16, 32?

A. 2 B. 4

C. 8 D. 16

112. What is the cumulative frequency curve of statistical data commonly called?

A. Cartogram B. Histogram

C. Ogive D. Pictogram

113. If A and B are two mutually exclusive events, then what is $P(AB)$ equal to?

A. 0 B. $P(A) + P(B)$

C. $P(A)\,P(B)$ D. $P(A)\,P(B\,|\,A)$

114. If $x = \sin\theta + \cos\theta$ and $y = \sin\theta.\cos\theta$, then what is the value of $x^4 - 4x^2y - 2x^2 + 4y^2 + 4y + 1$?

A. 0 B. 1

C. 2 D. None of the above

115. What is $\lim_{x\to\infty}\left(\sqrt{a^2x^2+ax+1}-\sqrt{a^2x^2+1}\right)$ equal to?

A. $\frac{1}{2}$ B. 1

C. 2 D. 0

116. What is $\int\frac{\sin\sqrt{x}}{\sqrt{x}}dx$ equal to?

A. $\frac{\cos\sqrt{x}}{2}+c$ B. $2\cos\sqrt{x}+c$

C. $\frac{-\cos\sqrt{x}}{2}+c$ D. $-2\cos\sqrt{x}+c$

where c is a constant of integration.

117. Which one of the following is the unit vector perpendicular to the vector $4\hat{i}+2\hat{j}$ and $-3\hat{i}+2\hat{j}$?

A. $\frac{\hat{i}+\hat{j}}{\sqrt{2}}$ B. $\frac{\hat{i}-\hat{j}}{\sqrt{2}}$

C. $\hat{k}$ D. $\frac{\hat{i}+\hat{j}+\hat{k}}{\sqrt{3}}$

118. Consider the following statements in respect of the vectors

$\vec{u}_1=(1,2,3)$, $\vec{u}_2=(2,3,1)$,

$\vec{u}_3=(1,3,2)$, and $\vec{u}_4=(4,6,2)$,

1. $\vec{u}_1$ is parallel to $\vec{u}_4$
2. $\vec{u}_2$ is parallel to $\vec{u}_4$
3. $\vec{u}_2$ is parallel to $\vec{u}_3$

Which of the statements given above is/are correct?

A. 1 only B. 2

C. 3 only D. 1 and 3

119. The line $mx + ny = 1$ passes through the points (1, 2) and (2, 1). What is the value of m?

A. 1 B. 3

C. $\frac{1}{2}$ D. $\frac{1}{3}$

120. What is the solution set for the equation $x^4 - 26x^2 + 25 = 0$?

A. {–5, –1, 1, 5} B. {–5, –1}

C. {1, 5} D. {– 5, 0, 1, 5}

ANSWERS

PAPER-I : GENERAL ABILITY TEST

1	2	3	4	5	6	7	8	9	10
A	C	A	B	A	A	B	A	B	B
11	**12**	**13**	**14**	**15**	**16**	**17**	**18**	**19**	**20**
A	B	D	B	A	B	C	C	B	D
21	**22**	**23**	**24**	**25**	**26**	**27**	**28**	**29**	**30**
C	C	D	D	B	A	C	C	B	A
31	**32**	**33**	**34**	**35**	**36**	**37**	**38**	**39**	**40**
A	C	B	C	C	A	C	B	B	C
41	**42**	**43**	**44**	**45**	**46**	**47**	**48**	**49**	**50**
D	C	D	B	A	B	A	A	D	A
51	**52**	**53**	**54**	**55**	**56**	**57**	**58**	**59**	**60**
C	B	D	B	A	B	B	B	B	A
61	**62**	**63**	**64**	**65**	**66**	**67**	**68**	**69**	**70**
B	B	C	B	C	B	D	D	C	C
71	**72**	**73**	**74**	**75**	**76**	**77**	**78**	**79**	**80**
D	B	D	C	D	D	C	A	B	C
81	**82**	**83**	**84**	**85**	**86**	**87**	**88**	**89**	**90**
C	A	C	A	C	B	D	A	C	C
91	**92**	**93**	**94**	**95**	**96**	**97**	**98**	**99**	**100**
A	C	C	B	C	C	B	C	A	A
101	**102**	**103**	**104**	**105**	**106**	**107**	**108**	**109**	**110**
A	B	C	C	A	A	D	C	B	A
111	**112**	**113**	**114**	**115**	**116**	**117**	**118**	**119**	**120**
D	A	C	C	C	D	D	B	A	C
121	**122**	**123**	**124**	**125**	**126**	**127**	**128**	**129**	**130**
C	A	B	C	D	B	C	C	D	A
131	**132**	**133**	**134**	**135**	**136**	**137**	**138**	**139**	**140**
B	C	B	A	A	D	A	D	D	B
141	**142**	**143**	**144**	**145**	**146**	**147**	**148**	**149**	**150**
A	A	A	C	D	C	B	C	D	C

PAPER-II – MATHEMETICS

1	2	3	4	5	6	7	8	9	10
D	A	B	B	A	B	B	C	C	B
11	12	13	14	15	16	17	18	19	20
D	B	C	B	C	A	C	C	C	C
21	22	23	24	25	26	27	28	29	30
A	A	D	B	A	C	C	C	A	C
31	32	33	34	35	36	37	38	39	40
A	A	D	D	A	A	B	D	C	B
41	42	43	44	45	46	47	48	49	50
A	C	A	A	B	C	A	C	D	B
51	52	53	54	55	56	57	58	59	60
C	C	B	B	A	B	D	D	A	D
61	62	63	64	65	66	67	68	69	70
D	C	D	D	B	C	B	C	C	B
71	72	73	74	75	76	77	78	79	80
A	C	A	C	C	A	D	C	B	C
81	82	83	84	85	86	87	88	89	90
D	D	D	A	C	B	B	B	B	C
91	92	93	94	95	96	97	98	99	100
A	A	D	D	C	D	C	B	D	B
101	102	103	104	105	106	107	108	109	110
B	C	B	C	C	B	D	D	A	B
111	112	113	114	115	116	117	118	119	120
C	C	B	A	A	D	C	B	D	A

EXPLANATORY ANSWERS

PAPER-II : MATHEMATICS

1. $$\begin{vmatrix} x+1 & x+2 & x+4 \\ x+3 & x+5 & x+5 \\ x+7 & x+10 & x+14 \end{vmatrix}$$

$c_1 \rightarrow c_2 - c_1, c_3 - c_2$

$$\begin{vmatrix} -1 & -2 & x+4 \\ -2 & -3 & x+8 \\ -3 & -4 & x+14 \end{vmatrix}$$

$$= \begin{vmatrix} 1 & 2 & x+4 \\ 2 & 3 & x+8 \\ 3 & 4 & x+14 \end{vmatrix}$$

$= R_2 - R_1, R_3 - R_2$

$$\begin{vmatrix} 1 & 2 & x+4 \\ 1 & 1 & 4 \\ 1 & 1 & 6 \end{vmatrix}$$

$= R_1 - R_2, R_2 - R_3$

$$\begin{vmatrix} 0 & 1 & x \\ 0 & 0 & -2 \\ 1 & 1 & 6 \end{vmatrix}$$

$= 1\{(-2)\} = -2.$

3. Clearly when we put $x = -1$ the value of the given polynomial is maximum.

5. $$\begin{vmatrix} x & 4 & 5 \\ 7 & x & 7 \\ 5 & 8 & x \end{vmatrix} = 0$$

$\Rightarrow x(x^2 - 56) - 7(4x - 40) + 5(28 - 5x) = 0$

$\Rightarrow x^3 - 56x - 28x + 280 + 140 - 25x = 0$

$\Rightarrow x^3 - 109x + 420 = 0$

Since 5 and 7 are the roots of the given equation so that

$x^2 - 12x + 35$ is a factor of the given equation, when we divide the given equation by $x^2 - 12x + 35$ it gives

$x + 12 = 0$

$\Rightarrow \quad x = -12.$

7. Given $(1 + \tan\theta)(1 + \tan\phi) = 2$

$\Rightarrow 1 + \tan\theta + \tan\phi + \tan\theta.\tan\phi = 2$

$\Rightarrow \tan\theta + \tan\phi = 1 - \tan\theta.\tan\phi$

$\Rightarrow \dfrac{\tan\theta + \tan\phi}{1 - \tan\theta.\tan\phi} = 1$

$\Rightarrow \tan(\theta + \phi) = \tan\dfrac{\pi}{4}$

$\Rightarrow \theta + \phi = \dfrac{\pi}{4} = 45°.$

9. The system of equation has no solution if

$$\frac{a_1}{a_2} = \frac{b_1}{b_2} \neq \frac{c_1}{c_2}$$

$\Rightarrow \dfrac{k}{3} = \dfrac{2}{1} \neq \dfrac{5}{1}$

$\Rightarrow k = 6.$

11. $\log_{10} 9 - \log_{10} 8 - \log_{10} 27 + \log_{10} 32 + \log_{10} 3 - \log_{10} 4$

$\Rightarrow 2\log_{10} 3 - 3\log_{10} 2 - 3\log_{10} 3 + 5\log_{10} 2 + \log_{10} 3 - 21\log_{10} 2$

$\Rightarrow 3\log_{10} 3 - 3\log_{10} 3 + 5\log_{10} 2 - 5\log_{10} 2$

$\Rightarrow 0.$

12. Since that given series are in G.P

Where first term $= \dfrac{1}{4}$, common ratio $= -2$

Let -128 is nth term

$\therefore \quad -128 = \dfrac{1}{4}.(-2)^{n-1}$

$-128 \times 4 = (-2)^{n-1}$

$\Rightarrow (-2)^9 = (-2)^{n-1}$

$\Rightarrow n = 9 + 1 = 10^{th}$

15. Given $\dfrac{1}{b-a} + \dfrac{1}{b-c} = \dfrac{1}{a} + \dfrac{1}{c}$

$\Rightarrow \dfrac{1}{b-a} - \dfrac{1}{c} = \dfrac{1}{a} - \dfrac{1}{b-c}$

$\Rightarrow \dfrac{c-b+a}{(b-a)c} = \dfrac{b-c-a}{a(b-c)}$

$\Rightarrow \dfrac{c-b+a}{(b-a)c} = \dfrac{-(c-b+a)}{a(b-c)}$

$\Rightarrow a(b-c) = -(b-a)c$

$\Rightarrow ab - ac = -bc + ac$

$\Rightarrow b(a+c) = 2ac$

$\Rightarrow b = \dfrac{2ac}{a+c}.$

Clearly a, b, c are in H.P.

16. $\int \sin^{-1}(\cos x)dx$

$= \int \sin^{-1}\left\{\sin\left(\dfrac{\pi}{2}\right) - x\right\}dx$

$= \int\left(\dfrac{\pi}{2} - x\right)dx \quad [\because \sin^{-1}(\sin x) = x]$

$= \dfrac{\pi}{2}x - \dfrac{x^2}{2} + c.$

22. Since the given function is continuous so that

$f(1+h) = f(1-h) = f(h)$

Now $\quad f(1+h) = \lim\limits_{h\to1} \dfrac{(1+h)^3 - 3(1+h) + 2}{(1+h-1)^2}$

$\Rightarrow \lim\limits_{h\to0} \dfrac{1 + h^3 + 3h^2 + 3h - 3 - 3h + 2}{(h)^2}$

$\therefore \quad f(x) = 3.$

24. A = {1, 2, 5, 6} and B = {1, 2, 3}

$\therefore$ A × B = {(1, 1) (1, 2) (1, 3) (2, 1) (2, 2) (2, 3) (5, 1) (5, 2) (5, 3) (6, 1) (6, 2) (6, 3)}

Again B × A = {(1, 1) (1, 2) (1, 5) (1, 6) (2, 1) (2, 2) (2, 5) (2, 6) (3, 1) (3, 2) (3, 5) (3, 6)}

$\therefore$ (A × B) ∩ (B × A) = {(1, 1) (1, 2) (2, 1) (2, 2)}

43. Since $\quad P(\overline{B}) = 0.8$

$\therefore \quad P(B) = 1 - P(\overline{B})$

$= 1 - 0.8 = 0.2$

Now $\quad P(A/B) = P(A) = 0.4$

Now $\quad P(A \cap B) = P(A).P(B)$

$= 0.4 \times 0.2 = 0.08.$

46. Since 3 is root of the equation

$\therefore \quad 3^2 - 8 \times 3 + k = 0$

$\Rightarrow \quad k = 15.$

47. $\dfrac{a_1}{a_2} = \dfrac{1}{2}, \dfrac{b_1}{b_2} = \dfrac{-3}{-6} = \dfrac{1}{2}, \dfrac{c_1}{c_2} = \dfrac{-2}{-6} = \dfrac{1}{3}$

Since $\dfrac{a_1}{a_2} = \dfrac{b_1}{b_2} \neq \dfrac{c_1}{c_2}$ (No solution)

$\therefore$ They never intersect.

48. The given points are collinear so that

$$\begin{vmatrix} a & 0 & 1 \\ 0 & b & 1 \\ 1 & 1 & 1 \end{vmatrix} = 0$$

$\Rightarrow a(b-1) + 1(-b) = 0$

$\Rightarrow ab - a - b = 0$

$\Rightarrow a + b - ab = 0.$

51. Given that $\dfrac{\tan A}{\tan B} = \dfrac{2}{1}$

$\Rightarrow \dfrac{\sin A.\cos B}{\cos A.\sin B} = \dfrac{2}{1}$

$\Rightarrow$ sinA.cosB − cosA.sinB = cosA.sinB

$\sin(A - B) = \dfrac{1}{2} \times 2\cos A.\sin B$

$= \dfrac{1}{2}\{\sin(A+B) - \sin(A-B)\}$

$\Rightarrow \sin(A-B) = \sin x = \frac{1}{2}(\sin\alpha - \sin x)$

$\Rightarrow \quad 2\sin x + \sin x = \sin\alpha$

$\Rightarrow \quad \sin x = \frac{\sin\alpha}{3}$

54. Total number of points = 5

Now a triangle has three vertices

$\therefore$ Number of triangles forms = $5c_3$

But it is given that three points are collinear. So that maximum number of triangles formed = $5c_3 - 3c_3$

$$= \frac{5\times 4}{2} - 1 = 10 - 1 = 9.$$

56. Projection of the vector $\hat{i} - 2\hat{j} + \hat{k}$ on the vector $4\hat{i} - 4\hat{j} + 7\hat{k} = \frac{(\hat{i}-2\hat{j}+\hat{k}).(4\hat{i}-4\hat{j}+7\hat{k})}{|4\hat{i}-4\hat{j}+7\hat{k}|}$

$$= \frac{4+8+7}{\sqrt{16+16+49}} = \frac{19}{\sqrt{81}} = \frac{19}{9}.$$

58. Let α, β be two roots then

$$\alpha^2 + \beta_2 = 2b \text{ (given)}$$

Now $\quad \alpha + \beta = -\frac{k}{1} = -k$

$$\alpha\beta = \frac{-b}{1} = -b$$

$\Rightarrow \quad \alpha^2 + \beta^2 = (\alpha+\beta)^2 - 2\alpha\beta$

$\Rightarrow \quad 2b = k^2 - 2(-b)$

$\Rightarrow \quad 2b = k^2 + 2b$

$\Rightarrow \quad k^2 = 0 \quad \Rightarrow k = 0.$

60. ω is the imaginary cube root of unity

Now $(2 - \omega + 2\omega^2)^{27} \quad \therefore 1 + \omega + \omega^2 = 0$

$$= \{2(1+\omega^2) - \omega\}^{27}$$

$\Rightarrow \{2(-\omega) - \omega)\}^{27}$

$$= (-3\omega)^{27} = (-3)^{27} \times \omega^{27}$$

$$= (-3)^{27} (\omega^2)^{27} = (-3)^{27}.$$

65. $\int e^x\left(\sqrt{x} + \frac{1}{2\sqrt{x}}\right)dx = \int e^x\sqrt{x}\,dx + \int\frac{e^x}{2\sqrt{x}}dx.$

$= \sqrt{x}\int e^x dx - \int\left(\frac{d}{dx}\left(\sqrt{x}\right)\int e^x dx\right)dx + \int\frac{e^x}{2\sqrt{x}}dx$

$= e^x\sqrt{x} - \int\frac{1}{2\sqrt{x}}\times e^x dx + \int\frac{e^x}{2\sqrt{x}}dx$

$= e^x\sqrt{x} + c.$

67. $c = 2$, $A = 120°$, $a = \sqrt{6}$ $C = ?$

We know that

$$\frac{a}{\sin A} = \frac{c}{\sin C}$$

$\Rightarrow \frac{\sqrt{6}}{\sin 120°} = \frac{2}{\sin C}$

$\Rightarrow \frac{\sqrt{6}}{\frac{\sqrt{3}}{2}} = \frac{2}{\sin C}$

$\Rightarrow \quad 2\sqrt{2} = \frac{2}{\sin C}$

$\Rightarrow \quad \sin C = \frac{1}{\sqrt{2}} = \sin 45°$

$\Rightarrow \quad C = 45°.$

71. Since the matrix is singular therefore,

$$\begin{vmatrix} 2-x & 1 & 1 \\ 1 & 3-x & 0 \\ -1 & -3 & -x \end{vmatrix} = 0$$

$\Rightarrow R_2 \to (R_3 + R_2)$

$$\begin{vmatrix} 2-x & 1 & 1 \\ 1 & 3-x & 0 \\ 0 & -x & -x \end{vmatrix} = 0$$

$\Rightarrow (2-x)\{-3x + x^2)\} - 1(-x + x) = 0$

$\Rightarrow (2-x)(x^2 - 3x) = 0$

$\Rightarrow x(2-x), (x-3) = 0$

$\Rightarrow x = 0, x = 2, x = 3$

73. $\frac{dy}{\sqrt{1+y^2}} + \frac{dx}{\sqrt{1-x_2}} = 0$

on integration

$\sin^{-1} y + \sin^{-1} x = C.$

74. $\quad z = 1 + \cos\frac{\pi}{5} + i\sin\frac{\pi}{5}$

$$= 2\cos^2\frac{\pi}{10} + 2\hat{i}\sin\frac{\pi}{10}.\cos\frac{\pi}{10}$$

$$z = 2\cos\frac{\pi}{10}\left\{\cos\frac{\pi}{10} + i\sin\frac{\pi}{10}\right\}$$

$\therefore \quad |z| = 2\cos\frac{\pi}{10}.$

76. Given, $\quad \frac{1}{1+3i} = \frac{1}{1-3i}$

$\therefore \quad \frac{(1-3i)-(1+3i)}{(1+3i)(1-3i)} = \frac{-6i}{1-9i^2}$

$$\frac{-6i}{10} = \frac{-3}{5}i$$

$\therefore \quad \text{Modulus} = \sqrt{(0)^2 + \left(-\frac{3}{5}\right)^2}$

$$= \frac{3}{5}.$$

80. Four letters can be placed in 4 envelops in 4! ways whereas there is only one way of placing them in their right envelops.
So that the probability that all the letters are placed in the right envelops $= \frac{1}{4!}$ ways

$$= \frac{1}{4\times3\times2} = \frac{1}{24}.$$

84. $A = \begin{bmatrix} -\alpha & \beta \\ -\beta & \alpha \end{bmatrix}$

$\therefore \quad A^2 = \begin{bmatrix} \alpha & \beta \\ \beta & \alpha \end{bmatrix} \times \begin{bmatrix} \alpha & \beta \\ \beta & \alpha \end{bmatrix}$

$\Rightarrow \quad A^2 = \begin{bmatrix} \alpha^2+\beta^2 & 2\alpha\beta \\ 2\alpha\beta & \beta^2+\alpha^2 \end{bmatrix}$

Given that $A^2 = 1$

$\Rightarrow \begin{bmatrix} \alpha^2+\beta^2 & 2\alpha\beta \\ 2\alpha\beta & \beta^2+\alpha^2 \end{bmatrix} = \begin{bmatrix} 1 & 0 \\ 0 & 1 \end{bmatrix}$

$\Rightarrow \quad \alpha^2 + \beta^2 = 1$ and $\alpha\beta = 0$

$\Rightarrow \quad \alpha = 0,\ \beta = 1$ or $\alpha = 1,\ \beta = 0$.

87. $\sqrt{3} + \frac{1}{\sqrt{3}} + \frac{1}{3\sqrt{3}} + \ldots.$

The given series is in G.P. an infinite series

Here, first term $= \sqrt{3}$

And common ratio $= \frac{1}{3}$

$\therefore$ Required sum $= \frac{\sqrt{3}}{1-\frac{1}{3}} = \frac{\sqrt{3}}{\frac{2}{3}} = \frac{3\sqrt{3}}{2}$.

89. $A = \begin{bmatrix} \alpha & 0 \\ 1 & 1 \end{bmatrix}$

$\therefore \quad A^2 = \begin{bmatrix} \alpha & 0 \\ 1 & 1 \end{bmatrix} \times \begin{bmatrix} \alpha & 0 \\ 1 & 1 \end{bmatrix}$

$\Rightarrow \quad A^2 = \begin{bmatrix} \alpha^2 & 0 \\ \alpha+1 & 1 \end{bmatrix}$

Given $\quad A^2 = I$

$\therefore \begin{bmatrix} \alpha^2 & 0 \\ \alpha+1 & 1 \end{bmatrix} = \begin{bmatrix} 1 & 0 \\ 2 & 1 \end{bmatrix}$

$\Rightarrow \quad \alpha + 1 = 2$

$\Rightarrow \quad \alpha = 1.$

90. $P(15, n-1) : P(16, n-2) = 3 : 4$

$\Rightarrow \quad \frac{15\,P_{n-1}}{16\,P_{n-2}} = \frac{3}{4}$

$\Rightarrow \quad \frac{\frac{15!}{15-x+1!}}{\frac{16!}{(16-n+2)}} = \frac{3}{4}$

$\Rightarrow \quad \frac{15!\ 18-n!}{16!\ 16-n!} = \frac{3}{4}$

$\frac{(8-n)(17-n)}{16} = \frac{3}{4}$

$n^2 - 35n + 294 = 0$

$n^2 - 21n - 14n + 294 = 0$

$n(n-21) - 14(n-21) = 0$

$\Rightarrow \quad n = 14, 21.$

91. $n = 8$ which is even.

So that their is one middle term is 5th term is middle term.

$T_{4+1} = 8C_4(1)^4\left(-\frac{x}{2}\right)^4$

$= \frac{8!}{4!\,4!}\frac{x^4}{16}$

$= \frac{8\times7\times6\times5}{4\times3\times2}\times\frac{x^4}{16}$

$= \frac{35}{8}x^4.$

92. Sum of roots $= \frac{-\left\{-\left(7=4\sqrt{3}\right)\right\}}{2-\sqrt{3}}$

$= \frac{7-4\sqrt{3}}{2-\sqrt{3}} \times \frac{2+\sqrt{3}}{2+\sqrt{3}}$

$= \frac{14+7\sqrt{3}-8\sqrt{3}-12}{1}$

$= 2-\sqrt{3}.$

96. Since $A + B + C = 180°$

Also $\quad 2B = A + C$

$\Rightarrow \quad 2B + B = 180°$

$\Rightarrow \quad B = 60°$

Now $\quad \frac{b}{\sin B} = \frac{c}{\sin C}$

$\Rightarrow \quad \frac{b}{C} = \frac{\sin B}{\sin C}$

$\Rightarrow \quad \frac{\sqrt{3}}{\sqrt{2}} = \frac{\sin 60°}{\sin C}$

$\Rightarrow \quad \sin C = \sin 60° \times \frac{\sqrt{2}}{\sqrt{3}}$

$= \frac{\sqrt{3}}{2} \times \frac{\sqrt{2}}{\sqrt{3}}$

$\Rightarrow \quad \sin C = \frac{1}{\sqrt{2}}.$

Previous Papers (Solved)

NATIONAL DEFENCE ACADEMY & NAVAL ACADEMY

NDA & NA – Entrance Exam, 2010 (II)

PAPER I : GENERAL ABILITY TEST

PART A : ENGLISH LANGUAGE

SPOTTING ERRORS

Directions (Qs. 1 to 10) :

(i) *In this section a number of sentences are given. The sentences are underlined in three separate parts and each one is labelled A, B, and C. Read each sentence to find out whether there is an error in any underlined part. No sentence has more than one error. When you find an error in any one of the underlined parts A, B or C, indicate your response on the separate Answer Sheet at the appropriate space. You may feel that there is no error in a sentence. In that case, letter D will signify a 'No error' response.*

(ii) *You are to indicate only one response for each item in your Answer Sheet. (If you indicate more than one response, your answer will be considered wrong.) Errors may be in grammar, word usage or idioms. There may be a word missing or there may be a word which should be removed.*

(iii) *You are **not** required to correct the error. You are required **only** to indicate your response on the Answer Sheet.*

1. (A) Let us congratulate him/(B) for his success/(C) in the examination./(D) No error.

2. (A) Many people prefer to travel/(B) by the road/(C) because it is less expensive./(D) No error.

3. (A) She was beside herself in joy/(B) when she came to know/(C) that she had been selected for the job./(D) No error.

4. (A) Mother tongue is as natural/(B) for the development of man's mind/(C) as mother's milk is for the development of the infant's body./(D) No error.

5. (A) The Prime Minister as well as his secretary were expected to/(B) arrive in Chennai/(C) on Saturday morning./(D) No error.

6. (A) The speaker was/(B) not only slow/(C) but also inaudible as well./(D) No error.

7. (A) The crowd surged forward/(B) to have a glimpse/(C) of their favourite leader/(D) No error.

8. (A) There is a distinctive possibility/(B) that he will leave the job/(C) once the investigation is over./(D) No error.

9. (A) Many a star/(B) are/(C) twinkling in the sky/(D) No error.

10. (A) We discussed the problem/(B) so thoroughly that/(C) I found it easy to work it out/(D) No error.

ANTONYMS

Directions (Qs. 11 to 16) : *Each of the following items consists of a sentence followed by four words. Select the* ***antonym*** *of the word (occuring in the sentence in capital letters) as per the context.*

11. What the critic said about this new book was ABSURD.

A. Interesting B. Impartial
C. Sensible D. Ridiculous

12. The issue raised in the forum can be IGNORED.

A. Removed B. Considered
C. Set aside D. Debated

13. After swallowing the frog has become LETHARGIC.

A. Aggressive B. Dull
C. Active D. Hungry

14. For the first time I saw him speaking RUDELY to her.

A. Softly B. Gently
C. Politely D. Slowly

15. Dust storms and polluted rivers have made it HAZARDOUS to breathe the air and drink the water.

A. Convenient B. Risky
C. Wrong D. Safe

16. Only hard work can ENRICH our country.

A. Impoverish B. Improve
C. Increase D. Involve

COMPREHENSION

Directions (Qs. 17 to 28) : *In this section, you have 03 short passages. After each passage, you will find several questions based on the passage. First, read a passage and then answer the questions based on it. You are required to select your answers based on the contents of the passage and opinion of the author only.*

Examples : 'I' and 'J' have been solved for you.

Passage (Example)

In our approach to life, be it pragmatic or otherwise, a basic fact that confronts us squarely and unmistakably is the desire for peace, security and happiness. Different forms of life at different levels of existence make up the teeming denizens of this earth of ours. And, no matter whether they belong to the higher groups such as human beings or to the lower groups such as animals, all beings primarily seek peace, comfort and security. Life is as dear to a mute creature as it is to a man. Even the lowliest insect strives for protection against dangers that threaten its life. Just as each one of us wants to live and not to die, so do all other creatures.

I. The author's main point is that
- A. different forms of life are found on the earth
- B. different levels of existence are possible in nature
- C. peace and security are the chief goals of all living beings
- D. even the weakest creature struggles to preserve its life

J. Which one of the following assumptions or steps is essential in developing the author's position?
- A. All forms of life have a single overriding goal
- B. The will to survive of a creature is identified with a desire for peace
- C. All beings are divided into higher and lower groups
- D. A parallel is drawn between happiness and life, and pain and death

Explanation :

I. The Idea which represents the author's main point is "peace and security are the chief goals of all living beings", which is response (C). So (C) is the correct answer.

J. The best assumption underlying the passage is "The will to survive of a creature is identified with a desire for peace", which is response (B), so (B) is the correct answer.

Passage-I

An old man with steel-rimmed spectacles and very dusty clothes sat by the side of the road. There was a pontoon bridge across the river and carts, trucks, and men, women and children were crossing it. The mule-drawn carts staggered up the steep bank from the bridge with soldiers helping to push against the spokes of the wheels. The trucks wound up and away heading out of it all. The peasants plodded along in the ankle-deep dust. But the old man sat there without moving.

17. The term "pontoon bridge" means:
- A. a temporary bridge constructed with the help of ropes
- B. a bridge made by soldiers during a war
- C. a bridge supported by floating flat-bottomed boats
- D. a bridge made with wooden planks

18. The soldiers were "helping to push against the spokes of the wheels" because:
- A. they wanted to stop the carts
- B. the spokes of the wheels were broken
- C. the mules refused to draw the carts
- D. there was a steep elevation

19. The mule-drawn carts staggered up because:
- A. there were too many mule-carts
- B. the mules were indisciplined
- C. it was a steep uphill journey
- D. the carts were blocked by the peasants

20. The reference to the old man in the beginning and the end of the passage indicates that:
- A. the writer wants to compare between the bridge and motionless old man
- B. the description that takes place between the first sentence and the last sentence is irrelevant
- C. there is an unnecessary repetition in the reference to the old man
- D. the figure of the old man is brought under a sharp focus

Passage-II

When vegetation sprouts in the desert, it is a good sign but when the ice in the Arctic and Antarctic begins to turn green, there is something terribly wrong. Reports say that an iceberg, approximately the size of New York city, has broken off from the icy continent. An Argentine team discovered huge cracks in the polar ice caps. These developments can have serious implications. If polar ice fields melt, our coastal cities might be submerged, and sea levels across the world could rise between 3.65 and 6.09 metre in different parts of the earth. This is probably due to global warming.

21. What can be considered as a "good sign" in the desert?
- A. when shrubs and trees grow there
- B. when it snows in the desert
- C. when ice caps melt and there is water
- D. when there is vegetation found in the desert

22. The melting of ice fields in the Arctic and Antarctic regions is dangerous because:
- A. the ice will turn green and poisonous
- B. it will cause huge floods which will destroy coastal regions
- C. it will create global warming and will badly affect our climate
- D. huge cracks will develop all over the world

23. Polar ice caps develop huge cracks because:
A. of the movement of the earth
B. of the breaking off of icebergs
C. of the crowding of cities like New York
D. of rising temperatures

24. What do you think the intention of the author is?
A. to describe strange phenomena in nature
B. to report findings of research teams working in the polar regions
C. to make us aware of the dangers of global warming
D. to compare developments in deserts and Arctic regions caused by global warming

Passage-III

It was a very cold evening and so few people were seen out on the streets. I did not go out myself although it was my habit not to keep indoors after sunset. So I closed all the doors and windows or my room, took the book which had been lying opened on the table, and tried to read it. The cold was getting so severe that I started shivering, so I wrapped myself up with a bigger blanket. But I could not continue reading the book because I was nearly rendered incapable of turning the pages.

25. The author's habit was to:
A. read in the evening
B. sleep in the evening
C. go out in the evening
D. play in the evening

26. If it was not so cold the author would have:
A. liked to work
B. liked to sit and look out to the streets
C. liked to read
D. liked to have a stroll

27. The author could not continue reading the book because:
A. he did not like to
B. he was feeling tired
C. he was feeling very cold
D. the lights had gone off

28. There were not many people outside because:
A. it was a rainy evening
B. it was a cold evening
C. it was a dark evening
D. there was heavy snow outside

Directions (Qs. 29 to 38) : *Each of the following items is followed by four words or group of words. Fill in the blanks with appropriate word or group of words.*

29. Your present statement does not .... what you said last week.
A. accord to B. accord in
C. accrod with D. accord for

30. I had a vague .... that the lady originally belonged to Scotland.
A. notion B. expression
C. imagination D. theory

31. The prisoner showed no .... for his crimes.
A. hatred B. obstinacy
C. remorse D. anger

32. It is inconceivable that in many schools children are subjected to physical .... in the name of discipline.
A. violation B. exercise
C. violence D. security

33. We have not yet fully realised the .... consequences of the war.
A. happy B. pleasing
C. grim D. exciting

34. Happiness consists in being .... what we have.
A. contented to B. contented with
C. contented for D. contented in

35. His rude behaviour is a .... his organization.
A. disgrace for B. disgrace on
C. disgrace upon D. disgrace to

36. No child is .... understanding. One has to wait and provide proper guidance.
A. dull to B. dull in
C. dull of D. dull for

37. I am fully .... the problems facing the industry.
A. alive with B. alive to
C. alive for D. alive on

38. The Romans were .... science.
A. bad in B. bad to
C. bad for D. bad at

REARRANGING SENTENCES INTO A PARAGRAPH

Directions (Qs. 39 to 44) : In the following items, *some parts of the sentence have been jumbled up. You are required to rearrange these parts which are labelled P, Q, R and S to produce the correct sentence. Choose the proper sequence and mark in your Answers Sheet accordingly.*

Example 'Z' has been solved for you.

Z. Some people believe that,
P : the effect
Q : is very bad
R : on children
S : of cinema

The correct sequence should be
A. P – S – R – Q B. S – P – Q – R
C. S – R – P – Q D. Q – S – R – P

Explanation

The proper way of writing the sentence is "Some people believe that the effect of cinema on children is very bad". This is indicated by the sequence P – S – R – Q and so (A) is the correct answer.

39. At the door
P : that he would have the door broken open
Q : the guard shouted
R : if the persons inside did not heed his call
S : at the top of his voice
The correct sequence should be
A. S – P – R – Q B. Q – S – P – R
C. P – R – S – Q D. P – Q – R – S

40. P : by bandits
Q : were driving through a desert area
R : a man and his daughter
S : when they were held up
The correct sequence should be
A. S – P – R – Q B. R – Q – S – P
C. S – R – P – Q D. P – Q – R – S

41. Our finest contemporary achievement
P : and toil
Q : in the provision of higher education
R : is our unprecedented expenditure of wealth
S : for all
The correct sequence should be
A. P – Q – R – S B. R – Q – P – S
C. R – P – Q – S D. P – R – Q – S

42. It seemed to him
P : like seeing one's reflection
Q : an endless quest
R : two mirrors
S : while standing between
The correct sequence should be
A. P – R – S – Q B. S – P – Q – R
C. R – S – P – Q D. Q – P – S – R

43. A series of shocks
P : is known as earthquake
Q : which can be recognised through seismic waves
R : that result from sudden earth movements or tremors
S : causing widespread destruction of life and property
The correct sequence should be
A. P – Q – R – S B. R – P – Q – S
C. R – S – P – Q D. R – Q – S – P

44. P : in this world
Q : a man has
R : it is possible that the best friend
S : may turn against him
The correct sequence should be
A. Q – P – R – S B. P – Q – R – S
C. R – Q – P – S D. Q – R – S – P

SYNONYMS

Directions (Qs. 45 to 50) : *Each of the following items consists of a sentence followed by four words. Select the* ***synonym*** *of the word (occurring in the sentence in capital letters) as per the context.*

45. His descriptions are VIVID.
A. Detailed B. Categorical
C. Clear D. Ambiguous

46. Friends have always DEPLORED my unsociable nature.
A. Deprived B. Implored
C. Denied D. Regretted

47. Despite his enormous wealth, the businessman was very FRUGAL in his habits.
A. Reckless B. Law-abiding
C. Unpredictable D. Economical

48. He was ENGROSSED in writing a story.
A. Absolved B. Absorbed
C. Interested D. Engaged

49. People fear him because of his VINDICTIVE nature.
A. Violent B. Cruel
C. Revengeful D. Irritable

50. He always has a very PRAGMATIC approach to life.
A. Practical B. Proficient
C. Potent D. Patronizing

PART B : GENERAL KNOWLEDGE

51. Sound moves with higher velocity if:
A. pressure of the medium is decreased
B. temperature of the medium is increased
C. humidity of the medium is increased
D. both B and C above

52. Which one of the following is the correct angle between the incident and reflected rays when a ray of light incident normally on a plane mirror?
A. 180° B. 90°
C. 45° D. 0°

53. Which one of the following four glass lenses is a diverging lens?

A. B.

C. D.

54. Magnetism of a bar magnet can be destroyed if it is :
1. kept in the magnetic meridian.
2. placed in a direction opposite that of the Earth's horizontal intensity.
3. heated to a temperature known as Curie temperature.

Select the correct answer using the code given below:
A. 1 and 3 only B. 2 only
C. 2 and 3 only D. 1, 2 and 3

55. Capacity of a parallel plate condenser can be doubled by:
1. doubling the areas of the plates
2. doubling the distance of separation between the plates
3. reducing the distance of separation between the plates to half the original separation
4. doubling both the areas of the plates and the distance of separation between the plates

Select the correct answer using the code given below:
A. 1 and 4 B. 1 and 3
C. 3 only D. 2 and 3

56. If two conducting spheres are separately charged and then brought in contact:
A. the total energy of the two spheres is conserved
B. the total charge on the spheres is conserved
C. both the total energy and charge are conserved
D. the final potential is always the mean of the original potential of the two spheres

57. Two pieces of metallic wire having equal length and equal volume placed in air have different resistances. The two wires must:
A. have different cross sections
B. have different temperatures
C. be of different materials
D. be of same density

58. If a heater coil is cut into two equal parts and only one part is used in the heater, the heat generated will be :
A. doubled B. four times
C. one-fourth D. halved

59. The direction of magnetic field at a point due to an infinitely long wire carrying current is:
A. parallel to the current
B. antiparallel to the current
C. along the perpendicular drawn from a point on the wire
D. perpendicular to the plane containing the conductor and the point

60. A hollow metal ball carrying an electric charge produces no electric field at points:
A. outside the sphere B. on its surface
C. inside the sphere D. only at the centre

61. A man is sitting on a rotating stool with his arms outstretched. If suddenly he folds his arm the angular velocity of the man would:
A. increase B. decrease
C. become zero D. remain constant

62. For a particle revolving in a circular path, the acceleration of the particle is:
A. along the tangent
B. along the radius
C. zero
D. along the circumference of the circle

63.

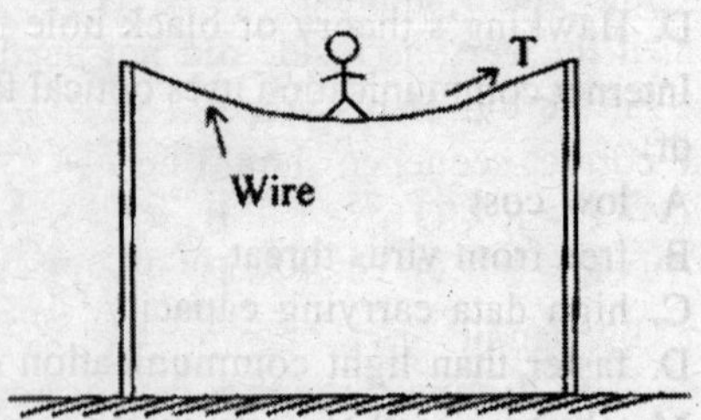

A circus performer of mass M is walking along a wire as shown in the figure given above. The tension T in the wire is : (g = acceleration due to gravity)
A. approximately Mg
B. less than Mg
C. more than Mg
D. depends on whether the performer stands on one or two feet

64.

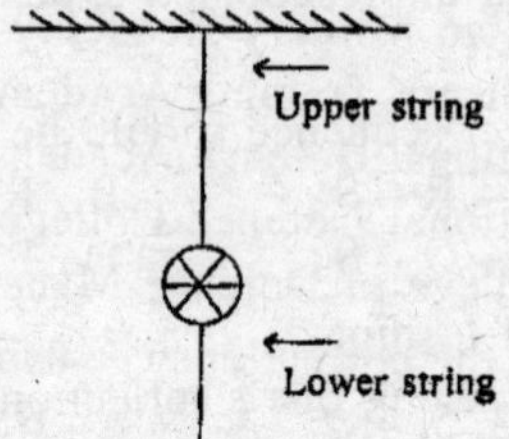

A heavy ball is suspended as shown in the figure given above. A quick jerk on the lower string will break that string but a slow pull on the lower string will break the upper string. The first result occurs because:
A. the force is too small to move the ball
B. air friction holds the ball back
C. of action and reaction
D. the ball has inertia

65. The visible light has a wavelength range from about 380 nm (violet) to 780 nm (red). If an excited object emits light with wavelength of 15 nm, to which one of the following ranges does it belong?
A. X-ray B. Gamma ray
C. Infrared D. Ultraviolet

66. Microwave oven consumes less power due to:
A. small frequency of radiation
B. short wavelength of radiation
C. large frequency as well as wavelength of radiation
D. small frequency as well as wavelength of radiation

67. The sun is constantly radiating energy and yet its surface temperature is nearly constant at 6000°C. The constancy of solar temperature is due to :
A. fission B. radioactivity
C. fusion D. black hole evaporation

68. An annular solar eclipse occurred during January 2010 with duration of annularity around 12 minutes. It is predicted that such long annular duration will not occur till the year 3043. Such prediction is possible due to:

A. Einstein's theory of relativity
B. Darwin's theory of natural selection
C. Newton's theory of gravitation
D. Hawking's theory of black hole

69. Internet communication uses optical fibre cables because of:
A. low cost
B. free from virus threat
C. high data carrying capacity
D. faster than light communication of signals

70. Metal pipes used to carry water sometimes burst in the winter. This is because:
A. water expands when it freezes
B. metal contracts more than water
C. outside of the pipe contracts more than inside
D. metal expands more than water

71. Arrange the following Military Training Institutes in India in terms of their geographical location from North to South:
1. Indian Military Academy
2. Officers' Training Academy
3. National Defence Academy
4. National Defence College
5. College of Defence Management

Select the correct answer using the code given below:
A. 1, 3, 5, 4, 2 B. 1, 4, 3, 5, 2
C. 4, 5, 3, 2, 1 D. 3, 4, 1, 2, 5

72. Which among the following statements characterized El Nino?
1. It occurs at irregular intervals
2. It carries warmer water
3. It carries less saline water
4. Its atmospheric equivalent is southern oscillation

Select the correct answer using the code given below:
A. 1 and 2 only B. 2 and 3 only
C. 3 and 4 only D. 1, 2, 3 and 4

73. Consider the following statements regarding Andaman and Nicobar Islands:
1. It enjoys equatorial climate
2. This is the only place in India where a volcano is located
3. This is the only place in India where coral bed is found

Which of the statements given above is/ are correct?
A. 1, 2 and 3 B. 1 and 2 only
C. 2 and 3 only D. 1 only

74. Which of the following has/have been declared as national waterways in India?
1. The Allahabad-Haldia stretch of river Ganga
2. The Sadiya-Dhubri stretch of river Brahmaputra
3. The Cherla-Rajamundry stretch of river Godavari

Select the correct answer using the code given below:
A. 1 and 2 only B. 2 and 3 only
C. 1 only D. 1, 2 and 3

75. Consider the following statements:
1. In a cyclone, the direction of wind flow is counter clockwise in the northern hemisphere
2. The tropical cyclone fades away when it reaches land because there is no large supply of warm moist air

Which of the statements given above is/are correct?
A. 1 only B. 2 only
C. Both 1 and 2 D. Neither 1 nor 2

76. Which among the following statements about the North Atlantic Drift is/are correct?
1. It keeps the west coast of Northern Europe ice free
2. It is responsible for the warm air mass which interacts with the cold air mass from the Polar region and causes rainfall in Western Europe
3. It meets the Labrador current near Vancouver Island and causes dense fog

Select the correct answer using the code given below:
A. 1, 2 and 3 B. 1 and 2 only
C. 2 only D. 1 and 3 only

77. Which one among the following explains the earthquakes of the eastern margins of Asia?
A. Subduction of Pacific plate under Asiatic plate
B. Subduction of African plate below European plate
C. Subduction of Indian plate under Asiatic plate
D. Subduction of American plate under the Pacific plate

78. Unlike other Meridians International Date Line is drawn zigzag in order to :
A. permit certain land areas and groups of islands to have the same calendar day
B. facilitate the sailors to adjust time in their watch
C. adjust the day in calendar while sailing from east to west and vice versa
D. make 180°E and 180°W conterminous

79. The time difference between the two cities, city A (30' N 60' E) and city B (30' N 80' E) would be:
A. 80 minutes B. 0 minute
C. 20 minutes D. 34 minutes

80. Consider the following statements:
1. The tropical year is shorter than the sidereal year
2. The solar day is longer than the sidereal day

Which of the statements given above is/are correct?
A. 1 only B. 2 only
C. Both 1 and 2 D. Neither 1 nor 2

81. Consider the following statements about rocks:
1. Shale becomes Slate through metamorphosis
2. Shale is converted to Slate when it is subjected to tremendous pressure and high temperature

Which of the statements given above is/are correct?
A. 1 only B. 2 only
C. Both 1 and 2 D. Neither 1 nor 2

82. Which of the following statements is/are correct?
1. Mumbai receives more rainfall than Pune because it is located at the windward side of Western Ghats

2. Vidarbha region experiences semiarid climate as it is located in a rain shadow region
3. In India monsoon reaches Kashmir valley at the last

Select the correct answer using the code given below:

A. 1, 2 and 3 B. 1 and 2 only
C. 2 and 3 only D. 1 only

83. Which of the following statements regarding south-west monsoon in India is/are correct?

1. Monsoon reaches the Malabar coast first
2. Rajasthan does not get rainfall from south west monsoon
3. South-west monsoon retreats when the permanent wind belts start shifting to the south

Select the correct answer using the code given below:

A. 1, 2 and 3 B. 1 and 2 only
C. 3 only D. 1 and 3 only

84. Which one of the following is the correct sequence of the four stages of water movement in a hydrological cycle?

A. Evaporation-Condensation-Precipitation- Infiltration
B. Evaporation-Precipitation-Condensation-Infiltration
C. Infiltration-Evaporation-Condensation-Precipitation
D. Condensation-Precipitation-Evaporation-Infiltration

85. Match List I with List II and select the correct answer using the code given below the Lists:

List I (Agents of erosion)	**List II** (Topographical feature)
(*a*) Running water	1. Cirque
(*b*) Glacier	2. Barchan
(*c*) Wind	3. Rift Valley
(*d*) Underground water	4. Doline
	5. Gorge

Code:

	(*a*)	(*b*)	(*c*)	(*d*)
A.	5	1	2	4
B.	5	2	1	3
C.	4	2	1	5
D.	3	4	1	2

86. Which among the following statements about Nirupam Sen is/are correct?

1. In the year 2009 he was appointed as Special Senior Adviser to the, President of the UN General Assembly on the world financial and economic crisis
2. He was formerly the Indian Ambassador to the UK

Select the correct answer using the code given below:

A. 1 only B. 2 only
C. Both 1 and 2 D. Neither 1 nor 2

87. Consider the following statement:

I can only thank a genius director like Guru Dutt for giving me an opportunity to work in his films and translate his conceptions on screen. I was able to involve (myself) in many innovative experiments he had tried. The best example is the making of 'Kagaz Ke Phool' (1959), which is the first cinemascope venture in the Indian film industry.

On receipt of a prestigious award of India the above statement was made recently by :

A. Santhosh Sivan B. Ravi K. Chandran
C. Ramachandra Babu D. V. K. Murthy

88. Consider the following statements about General V. K. Singh:

1. He is the first trained commando to take over as the Chief of the Army Staff of Indian Army
2. He belongs to the Rajputana Rifles regiment of Indian Army
3. General Singh succeeded General Deepak Kapoor

Which among the statements given above is/are correct?

A. 1, 2 and 3 B. 1 and 3 only
C. 3 only D. 1 and 2 only

89. Consider the following passage and identify the form of dance theatre referred thereto using the code given below:

This is a uniquely traditional form of dance theatre of India with a formidable classical background. The main essence of this form of dance drama is its attachment with religion, which provides the most common theme for its plays. The performance begins with a prayer offering to the lord Ganesha, which is followed by a comedy act, accompanied by the background music of the chenda and the maddale, and a tala (cymbals) played by a team of three. The narrator, who is also a part of the team is called Bhagavata, and is the producer, the director, and the head of the ceremony. His primary task involves the narration of the story through songs, introduction of the characters, and occasionally conversing with them. Another unique feature of it is the totally unrehearsed and unwritten use of dialogues, which makes it so special.

Code :

A. Cheraw B. Yakshagana
C. Devarattam D. Jatra

90. In a rare case, a record number of about 20000 employees of the Government of Kerala retired on a single day (on 31 March 2010). Which among the following statements is/are correct in this respect?

1. The mass retirement follows the Kerala government's move to allow employees retiring any day during the year to work till March 31
2. In a recent bid to reduce burden on the state exchequer, the Government of Kerala reduced the retirement age of government employees from 59 to 58 years
3. More than 50% of those retired were from the Education department

Select the correct answer using the code given below:

A. 1, 2 and 3 B. 1 and 3 only
C. 2 and 3 only D. 1 only

91. Car manufacturer Maruti has stopped selling its popular brand Maruti 800 in some major cities of India from 1st of April 2010. Which among the following statements is/are correct in this regard?
1. The engine of the car is unable to meet the stricter Bharat Stage IV norms that become mandatory in some major cities of India from that date
2. The company has decided to promote another brand of car in the small car segment in some select cities
3. The company wants to shorten its product line

Select the correct answer using the code given below:
A. 1, 2 and 3 B. 1 only
C. 2 and 3 only D. 2 only

92. In a major eco-friendly step towards renewable energy generation in India, in June 2010 seaweed sourced ethanol (ethyl alcohol), a biofuel additive in transport fuel, has been used to run a car for the first time. With regard to this which of the following statements is/are correct?
1. Experiment in this direction was carried out by the scientists of Central Salt and Marine Chemicals Research Institute (CSMCRI), Bhavnagar
2. India has become the first country in the world to produce and use green fuel to run cars

Select the correct answer using the code given below:
A. 1 only B. 2 only
C. Both 1 and 2 D. Neither 1 nor 2

93. Which of the following aspects with regard to the T-20 world cup (Men's) cricket and T-20 world cup (Women's) cricket tournaments held in the year 2010 was/were common?
1. Both the tournaments were won by England
2. The tournaments were held in West Indies
3. There was a tie match each in both the tournaments

Select the correct answer using the code given below:
A. 1 only B. 2 only
C. 1, 2 and 3 D. 2 and 3 only

94. Which amongst the following statements is/are correct about the INS Arihant ?
1. It is India's first nuclear submarine
2. It is India's first aircraft carrier
3. It has been indigenously built in India

A. 1 only B. 2 and 3 only
C. 1 and 3 only D. 2 only

95. Which among the following statements about the Zaranj-Delaram road is/are correct?
1. It was constructed by Border Road Organization in Afghanistan
2. It links India with Afghanistan via Pakistan
3. This road will open up market for Indian goods in Afghanistan via Iran

Select the correct answer using the code given below:
A. 3 only B. 1 and 3
C. 1 and 2 D. 2 only

Directions (Qs. No. 96-99): *These items are based on the following Table:*

Match List I with List II, List III and List IV and select the correct answer using the code given below:

List I (Body system)	*List II (Organ)*	*List III (Structure)*	*List IV (Function of the system)*
A. Blood Circulation	1. Bone marrow	I. Alveoli	i. Clot Formation
B. Excretory	2. Thymus	II. T-lymphocyte	ii. Perfusion of tissues
C. Alimentary	3. Intestine	III. Myocardium	iii. Support and protech of body frame
D. Skeletal	4. Lung	IV. Matrix	iv. Oxygenation
E. Blood	5. Bone	V. Nephron	v. Filtration of body waste
F. Respiratory	6. Heart	VI. Villi	vi. Absorption of nutrients
G. Neurological	7. Kidney	VII. Axon	vii. Fighting infection and foreign invasion
H. Immunological	8. Neuron	VIII. Platelets	viii. Transmission of electrical impulse

96.

	List I	List II	List III	List IV
A.	A	1	III	ii
B.	B	7	VI	v
C.	A	6	III	ii
D.	B	2	V	v

97.

	List I	List II	List III	List IV
A.	C	3	VI	vi
B.	D	1	V	iii
C.	C	2	VII	vi
D.	D	5	IV	vii

98.

	List I	List II	List III	List IV
A.	E	1	I	i
B.	F	2	I	iv
C.	E	1	IV	v
D.	F	4	I	iv

99.

	List I	List II	List III	List IV
A.	G	8	VII	vii
B.	H	2	II	iv
C.	G	8	VI	vii
D.	H	1	II	vii

100. Consider the following statements regarding the recent global outbreak of 'Swine Flu' :
1. The agent of infection is not well identified
2. The risk is higher in those who consume pork
3. It has a propensity to spread from contact with an infected person
4. Absence of an effective treatment or vaccine makes it risk for a global pandemic

Which of the statements given above is/ are correct?
A. 1, 2 and 4 B. 3 and 4
C. 2 and 3 D. 3 only

101. Which among the following are the properties of good paint?
1. The paint should be opaque and have high covering power
2. The solid particles in paint should reflect much of the destructive light to ensure long life of the paint
3. Combination of pigments, *e.g.*, white lead and TiO_2 give better result
4. Addition of plasticiser destroy the elasticity of the film and leads to cracking

Select the correct answer using the code given below:
A. 1, 2 and 4 B. 1, 2 and 3
C. 2 and 3 only D. 1 and 3 only

102. By which one among the following mechanism, soap removes dirt (soil) from cloth?
A. Soap dissolves the soil as such
B. Soap reacts with soil and converts them into soluble silicates
C. Soap takes away the oily part of the soil and thus separates the soil from the cloth
D. The soap molecules bind with the soil, lift the soil and keep it suspended which can then be rinsed away

103. Which one among the following statements is not correct about graphite?
A. It is the most stable allotrope of carbon
B. It is an electrically conducting material
C. Crystalline spherical beads of graphite have very good lubricating property under dry conditions
D. It is the highest grade of coal

104. Which one among the following is not a property of salt ?
A. Salts have ordered packing arrangements called lattices
B. Salts have low melting points but high boiling points
C. Salts are brittle
D. Salts conduct electricity when dissolved in water or even in the molten state

105. Which among the following statements with regard to pH scale is/are correct?
1. It is a logarithmic scale
2. The scale is limited to 0–14 because the ionic product of water is about 10^{-14}
3. The lower the value of pH the greater is the acidity of the solution

Select the correct answer using the code given below:
A. 1 and 2 only B. 1, 2 and 3
C. 1 and 3 only D. 2 only

106. An oxidizing agent is a substance which:
A. increases the oxidation number of an element in a given substance
B. decreases the oxidation number of an element in a given substance
C. is oxidized itself in an oxidation reduction reaction
D. loses electrons in an oxidation reduction reaction

107. Neutral water with pH about 7 becomes slightly acidic when aerated. This is because:
A. oxygen from air is dissolved in the water which makes the water acidic
B. dirt, which get contaminated with the water during aeration makes the water acidic
C. ultraviolet radiation dissociates water molecules and makes water acidic
D. carbon-dioxide from air is dissolved

108. Which one of the following statements is ***not*** correct?
A. Diesel burns with air in a diesel engine at a high temperature at which nitrogen and oxygen from air can combine whereas petrol burns at a lower temperature at which nitrogen and oxygen can not combine
B. Diesel contains some nitrogenous compounds whereas petrol does not
C. Nitrogen from air is easily dissolved in diesel but it is not soluble in petrol
D. A catalyst is used in diesel engines which contains nitrogen whereas petrol engines do not need such catalysts

109. Consider the following statements with regard to the properties of water:
1. Water is a good solvent for ionic compound but poor solvent for covalent compound
2. Water is a good solvent for covalent compound but poor solvent for ionic compound
3. Water has maximum density at the temperature 277 K

Which of the statements given above are correct?
A. 1 and 3 only B. 2 and 3 only
C. 1 and 2 only D. 1, 2 and 3

110. Calcium carbonate is naturally available as limestone and can also be synthesized from quick lime. It is seen that the composition of the elements in both the natural and synthetic calcium carbonate are same. The validity of which one among the following laws is confirmed by this observation?

A. Law of conservation of mass
B. Law of definite proportion
C. Law of multiple proportion
D. Avogadro's law

111. When aqueous solutions of two salts are mixed, the third salt formed may appear as a solid precipitates or a clear solution depending upon the solubility of its ions. It is observed that all salts of Na, K, NH_4 are soluble. All nitrates and bicarbonates are also soluble. All halides (chlorides, bromides, iodides) are soluble except those of Ag, Hg (I) and Pb. All sulphates are soluble except those of Ag, Ca, Ba and Pb. Which one among the following combinations of solutions will produce a solid precipitate?

A. Sodium sulphate and barium chloride
B. Magnesium sulphate and barium bicarbonate
C. Lithium iodide and barium chloride
D. Ammonium sulphate and potassium bromide

112. A mixture containing SiO_2, NaCl and NH_4Cl is taken for separating the constituents. The suitable steps required for this are:

A. Sublimation-dissolution-filtration-crystallization
B. Dissolution-filtration-crystallization-distillation
C. Sublimation-evaporation-dissolution-decomposition
D. Dissolution-distillation-decomposition evaporation

113. Iodized salt is a:

A. mixture of potassium iodide and common salt
B. mixture of molecular iodine and common salt
C. compound formed by combination of potassium iodide and common salt
D. compound formed by combination of molecular iodine and common salt

114. Which one among the following is a chemical process?

A. Distillation of sea (salty) water
B. Crystallization of impure salt (NaCl)
C. Production of iodine (I_2) from sea-weeds
D. Sublimation of iodine (I_2)

115. Which one among the following statements regarding the properties of mixtures and compounds is ***not*** correct?

A. A mixture shows the properties of its constituents but the properties of a compound are entirely different from its constituents
B. A mixture may be homogeneous or heterogeneous but a compound is a homogeneous substance
C. The constituents of a mixture can be separated by physical methods but those of a compound can not be separated by physical method
D. Energy is either absorbed or evolved during the preparation of a mixture but not in the preparation of a compound

116.

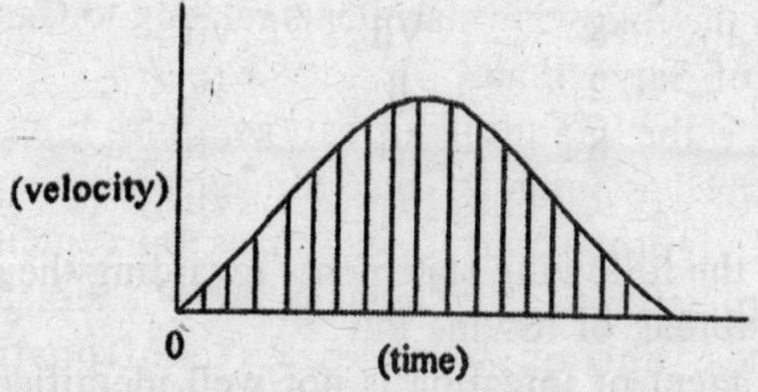

Which one of the following characteristics of the particle does the shaded area of the velocity-time graph shown above represent?

A. Momentum
B. Acceleration
C. Distance covered
D. Speed

117. A body is at rest on the surface of the earth. Which one among the following statements is correct regarding this?

A. No force is acting on the body
B. Only weight of the body acts on it
C. Net downward force is equal to the net upward force
D. None of the above statements is correct

118. A pendulum beats faster than a standard pendulum. In order to bring it to the standard beat, the length of the pendulum is to be:

A. reduced
B. increased
C. reduced and the mass of the bob increased
D. reduced and also the mass of the bob reduced

119.

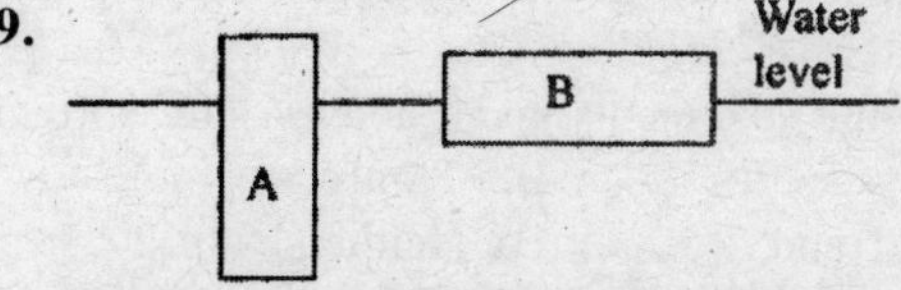

Two identical blocks of ice, A and B, float in water as shown in the figure given above. Which one among the following statements in this regard is correct?

A. Block A displaces a greater volume of water since the pressure acts on a smaller bottom area
B. Block A displaces a greater volume of water since its submerged end is lower in the water
C. Block B displaces a greater volume of water since its submerged end has a greater area in water
D. The two blocks displace equal volumes of water since they have the same specific gravity and same mass

120. When a ship floats on water:

A. it displaces no water
B. the mass of water displaced is equal to the mass of the ship
C. the mass of water displaced is lesser than the mass of the ship
D. the mass of water displaced is greater than the mass of the ship

121. Consider the following statements relating to Gandhian strategy of Satyagraha:

1. Under the Gandhian strategy, which may be described as Struggle-Truce-Struggle (S-T-S), phases of a vigorous extra-legal mass movement and confrontation with colonial authority alternate with phases, during which direct confronation is withdrawn
2. The entire political process of S-T-S was an upward spiraling one, which also assumed that the freedom struggle would pass through several stages, ending with the transfer of power by the colonial regime itself

Which of the statements given above is/are correct?

A. 1 only B. 2 only
C. Both 1 and 2 D. Neither 1 nor 2

122. Rajmohan Gandhi's book 'A Tale of Two Revolts' (2009) deals with the:

A. Taiping and Indigo revolts
B. Revolt of 1857 and the American Civil War
C. Revolt of 1857 and the Deccan Uprising
D. American Civil War and Santhal Uprising

123. Consider the following statements relating to Jawaharlal Nehru's attitude towards science and technology:

1. Nehru was convinced that science and technology were crucial to the solution of India's problems relating to underdevelopment and poverty
2. To emphasize the importance of science and scientific research, Nehru himself became the Chairman of the Council of Scientific and Industrial Research

Which of the statements given above is/are correct?

A. 1 only B. 2 only
C. Both 1 and 2 D. Neither 1 nor 2

124. "No Taxation without Representation" was the popular slogan of:

A. Indian freedom struggle
B. American war of independence
C. Russian revolution
D. French revolution

125. Which one of the following pairs is *not* correctly matched?

A. Power of Parliament	:	Creating a new State
B. Power of State Legislature	:	Altering the name of a State
C. Equality before the law	:	Both Indian and non-Indian citizens
D. Equality of opportunity	:	Indian citizen

126. Which among the following statements with regard to Raja Rammohan Roy are correct?

1. He started the Atmiya Sabha
2. He wrote the Gift of Monotheist
3. He published the Precepts of Jesus
4. He founded the Brahma Sabha

Select the correct answer using the code given below:

A. 2, 3 and 4 only
B. 1, 2 and 3 only
C. 1, 3 and 4 only
D. 1, 2, 3 and 4

127. Which one among the following was *not* a demand of the early congress (1885–1905)?

A. Indianization of the superior grades of the administrative services
B. Purna Swaraj/complete independence
C. Abolition of the Arms Act
D. Autonomy within the empire

Directions (Qs. No. 128-130): *These items are based on the passage given below:*

The myth is that the Indian National Congress was started by A.O. Hume and others under the official direction, guidance and advice of no less a person than Lord Dufferin, the Viceroy, to provide a safe, mild, peaceful and constitutional outlet or safety-valve for the rising discontent among the masses, which was inevitably leading towards a popular and violent revolution. Consequently, the revolutionary potential was nipped in the bud. Most writers accept the core of the myth, that a violent revolution was on the cards at the time and was avoided only by the foundations of the congress, ... All of them agree that the manner of its birth affected the basic character and future work of the congress in a crucial manner.

128. The colonial rulers, according to the safety valve thesis, were trying to use congress as:

A. a constitutional outlet for the mass discontent against the authorities
B. an instrument for the spread of British culture in India
C. an instrument to expand the Indian market for the products of British industries
D. an agency for social change in India

129. The author describes the safety-valve thesis as a myth because:

A. evidence are insufficient to establish the validity of the thesis.
B. the author has concluded that in the light of available materials the thesis does not hold ground.
C. the congress was a nationalist organization right from the start.
D. the violent anti-colonial movements did not come to an end with the foundation of the congress.

130. The core of the safety-valve thesis rests on the assumption that:

A. a violent anti-colonial revolution was bound to occur unless a constitutional platform like the congress was founded.

B. the congress would assist the British in administering the colony.

C. the congress leaders would constitute the colonial elite.

D. the congress as a party would assist the colonial rulers to implement political and social reforms.

131. Match List I with List II and select the correct answer using the code given below the lists:

List I *(Grassland)*	*List II* *(Country)*
(*a*) Pampas	1. Venezuela
(*b*) Veld	2. Australia
(*c*) Downs	3. South Africa
(*d*) Llanos	4. Argentina

Code:

	(*a*)	(*b*)	(*c*)	(*d*)
A.	4	3	2	1
B.	4	2	3	1
C.	1	3	2	4
D.	1	2	3	4

132. Consider the following statements:
1. In India, the largest concentration of roads is found in the northern plains
2. The ratio of surfaced road to the total road length is lower in the northern plains

Which of the statements given above is/are correct?

A. 1 only
B. 2 only
C. Both 1 and 2
D. Neither 1 nor 2

133. Which one of the following does ***not*** characterize the Himalayas?

A. Various parallel ranges of the Himalayas form a convex arc

B. There exist syntaxial bends at both the terminals of the Himalayas

C. Indus, Sutlej and Brahmaputra rivers are examples of antecedent drainage

D. The Himalayas are wider in the east than in the west

134. Which among the following statements provides the best evidence that a river is flowing through a rift valley?

A. The Chambal valley is marked by bad land topography

B. River Tapi does not have Delta but Estuary only

C. River Mahanadi flows through a gorge at Satkosia

D. River Colorado has the Grand Canyon along its valley

135. Match List I with List II and select the correct answer using the code given below the lists:

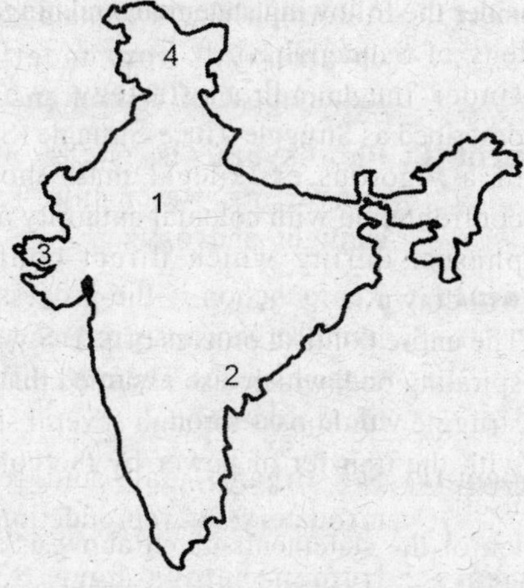

List I *(Places indicated in the map)*	*List II* *(Seismic zone)*
(*a*) 1	1. Zone V
(*b*) 2	2. Zone IV
(*c*) 3	3. Zone III
(*d*) 4	4. Zone II

Code:

	(*a*)	(*b*)	(*c*)	(*d*)
A.	2	1	3	4
B.	2	3	1	4
C.	4	3	1	2
D.	4	1	3	2

136. When dried raisins are put in plain water, they swell up. If put again in brine solution, they shrivel up. This phenomenon indicates the property of:

A. Diffusion B. Perfusion
C. Osmosis D. Fusion

137. Consider the following items
1. Proteins, Carbohydrates, and Fats
2. Vitamins
3. Minerals
4. Water

Which of the above are considered as the constituents of food?

A. 1, 2 and 4 only B. 1 and 3 only
C. 2 and 3 only D. 1, 2, 3 and 4

Directions (Qs. No. 138-141): *These items consist of two statements, statement I and statement II. You are to examine these two statements carefully and select the answers to these items using the code given below:*

Code:

A. Both the statements are individually true and statement II is the correct explanation of statement I

B. Both the statements are individually true but statement II is ***not*** the correct explanation of statement I

C. Statement I is true but statement II is false

D. Statement I is false but statement II is true

138. Statement I : Autotroph plants contain the pigment chlorophyll for meeting their requirement of carbon and energy

Statement II : Photosynthesis is the process of converting water into food using sunlight and oxygen

139. Statement I : Reproduction is the process by which living organisms produce young ones of their species. There are different forms of reproduction

Statement II : Sex organs, male and female, are mandatory for reproduction

140. Statement I : Human beings have 23 pair of chromosomes, one of which is the sex chromosome and the remaining 22 autosomes. The X-linked diseases are related to mutations on a sex chromosome

Statement II : Colour blindness results from a mutation in X chromosome

141. Statement I : Sarkaria Commission recommended that Governor of a state should be a non-political person appointed after consultation with the Chief Minister of the state

Statement II : This could be achieved through amending Article 165 of the Constitution of India

142. The Legislative Council in a state in India can be created or abolished by the:
A. Parliament on the recommendation of a Governor of the state.
B. Parliament alone.
C. Parliament after the state assembly passes the resolution to that effect.
D. Governor of the state on the recommendation of the Council of Ministers.

143. The Government Bill means a bill introduced by a:
A. Member of the Treasury bench in the Lok Sabha
B. Member of the Parliament who is not a Minister
C. Minister in the Lok Sabha
D. Minister in any House of the Parliament.

Directions. (Qs. No. 144-147): *The next four (04) items are based on the table given below: Match List I with List II, List III and List IV and select the correct answer using the code given below:*

List-I (Ruler)	*List-II (Important Battle)*	*List-III (Dynasty)*	*List-IV (Significant work)*
A. Ashoka	*1. Against several rulers of Northern and Southern India*	*I. Kushana*	*i. Writer and poet, patron of learning besides an empire builder*
B. Samudragupta	*2. Kalinga war*	*II. Maurya*	*ii. Political conquest, patron of learning*
C. Kanishka	*3. Battle of Pundravardhana*	*III. Pushpavati*	*iii. Holding the 4th Buddhist Council and patron of learning*
D. Harshavardhana	*4. Against the Chinese and the Parthians*	*IV. Gupta*	*iv. Spread of Dharma, ahimsa and welfare activities*

144.

	List-I	List-II	List-III	List-IV
A.	*A*	1	II	iv
B.	*A*	2	II	iv
C.	*B*	1	IV	iii
D.	*B*	2	IV	iii

145.

	List-I	List-II	List-III	List-IV
A.	*C*	4	I	iii
B.	*D*	3	III	i
C.	*C*	4	I	i
D.	*D*	3	III	ii

146.

	List-I	List-II	List-III	List-IV
A.	*B*	1	III	i
B.	*C*	4	IV	ii
C.	*B*	1	IV	ii
D.	*C*	4	III	i

147.

	List-I	List-II	List-III	List-IV
A.	*A*	1	II	iii
B.	*D*	3	III	ii
C.	*A*	1	II	iii
D.	*D*	3	III	i

148. Right to information of India is a:
A. Fundamental Right
B. Legal Right
C. Both Fundamental and Legal Rights
D. Neither Fundamental nor Legal Right

149. Which among the following statements are correct with regard to the Portuguese in India?
1. They had the monopoly over the Eastern trade in the 16th Century
2. They possessed Bombay in the beginning
3. They had trading settlements at Cochin, Diu and Daman
4. The Mughals denied them any trading concessions

Select the correct answer using the code given below:
A. 1, 2 and 3
B. 2, 3 and 4
C. 1, 2 and 4
D. 1 and 3 only

150. Which among the following statements with respect to the Comptroller and Auditor General of India is/are correct?
1. The procedure and grounds for his removal from the office are the same as of a Judge of Supreme Court
2. He prescribes the form in which accounts of the Union and the States are to be kept

Select the correct answer using the code given below:
Code:
A. 1 only B. 2 only
C. Both 1 and 2 D. Neither 1 nor 2

PAPER II : MATHEMATICS

1. Consider the following data:

	Factory-A	Factory-B
Mean wage of workers	₹ 540	₹ 620
Standard deviation of wages	₹ 40.50	₹ 31

What is the variability in the wages of the workers in Factory-A?
A. 100% more than the variability in the wages of the workers in Factory-*B*
B. 50% more than the variability in the wages of the workers in Factory-*B*
C. 50% less than the variability in the wages of the workers in Factory-*B*
D. 150% more than the variability in the wages of the workers in Factory-*B*

2. Let $U = \{1, 2, 3, ..., 20\}$. Let *A, B, C* be the subsets of *U*. Let *A* be the set of all numbers which are perfect squares, *B* be the set of all numbers which are multiples of 5 and *C* be the set of all numbers which are divisible by 2 and 3.
Consider the following statements:
1. *A, B, C* are mutually exclusive.
2. *A, B, C* are mutually exhaustive.
3. The number of elements in the complement set of $A \cup B$ is 12.

Which of the statements given above are correct?
A. 1 and 2 only B. 1 and 3 only
C. 2 and 3 only D. 1, 2 and 3

3. A lot of 4 white and 4 red balls is randomly divided into two halves. What is the probability that there will be 2 red and 2 white balls in each half ?
A. 18/35 B. 3/35
C. 1/2 D. None of the above

4. The distributions *X* and *Y* with total number of observations 36 and 64, and mean 4 and 3 respectively are combined. What is the mean of the resulting distribution *X* + *Y* ?
A. 3.26 B. 3.32
C. 3.36 D. 3.42

5. Consider the following data:

x	5	7	8	4	6
y	2	4	3	2	4

What is the regression equation of *y* on *x* ?
A. $y = 0.6 + 0.4\,x$ B. $y = 0.7 + 0.3\,x$
C. $y = 6 + 5\,x$ D. $y = 4 + 9\,x$

6. What is value of

$$\lim_{x \to 0} \frac{\cos(ax) - \cos(bx)}{x^2}$$

A. $a - b$ B. $a + b$
C. $\frac{b^2 - a^2}{2}$ D. $\frac{b^2 + a^2}{2}$

Directions (Q.No. 7-10): *The frequency distribution of life of 90 TV tubes whose median life is 17 months is as follows:*

Life of TV tubes (in months)	*No. of TV tubes*
0-5	3
5-10	12
10-15	x
15-20	35
20-25	y
25-30	4

7. What is the lower limit of the median class?
A. 10 B. 15
C. 20 D. 25

8. What is the missing frequency *y* ?
A. 20 B. 16
C. 15 D. 12

9. What is the cumulative frequency of the modal class?
A. 31
B. 35
C. 66
D. Cannot be determined as the given data is insufficient

10. If the area of a triangle with vertices (–3, 0), (3, 0) and (0, k) is 9 square units, then what is the value of k?
A. 3 B. 6
C. 9 D. 12

11. Consider the following statements:
If A and B are independent events, then
1. A and $\overline{B}$ are independent
2. $\overline{A}$ and B are independent
3. $\overline{A}$ and $\overline{B}$ are independent
Which of the above statements is/are correct?
A. 3 only
B. 1 and 2 only
C. 1, 2 and 3
D. None of the statements 1, 2 and 3 is correct

12. If $x = k(\theta + \sin\theta)$ and $y = k(1 + \cos\theta)$, then what is the derivative of y with respect to x at $\theta = \pi/2$?
A. –1 B. 0
C. 1 D. 2

13. What is the value of
$1 + i^2 + i^4 + i^6 + \ldots + i^{100}$
where $i = \sqrt{-1}$?
A. 0 B. 1
C. –1 D. None of the above

14. What is the value of

$$\begin{vmatrix} 1 & \omega & 2\omega^2 \\ 2 & 2\omega^2 & 4\omega^3 \\ 3 & 3\omega^3 & 6\omega^4 \end{vmatrix}$$

where ω is the cube root of unity?
A. 0 B. 1
C. 2 D. 3

15. If the cardinality of a set A is 4 and that of a set B is 3, then what is the cardinality of the set $A \,\Delta\, B$?
A. 1
B. 5
C. 7
D. Cannot be determined as the sets A and B are not given

16. From top of a lighthouse 120 m above the sea, the angle of depression of a boat is 15°. What is the distance of the boat from the lighthouse?
A. 400 m B. 421 m
C. 444 m D. 460 m

17. What is the value of

$$\frac{\sin\theta + \cos\theta - \tan\theta}{\sec\theta + \operatorname{cosec}\theta - \cot\theta}$$

when $\theta = \frac{3\pi}{4}$?
A. 0 B. 1
C. –1 D. None of the above

18. What is the value of $\sin 292\frac{1}{2}°$?
A. $\frac{1}{3}\sqrt{2+\sqrt{3}}$ B. $-\frac{1}{3}\sqrt{2-\sqrt{3}}$
C. $\frac{1}{2}\sqrt{2+\sqrt{2}}$ D. $-\frac{1}{2}\sqrt{2+\sqrt{2}}$

19. What is $\int \sec^n x \tan x \, dx$ equal to?
A. $\frac{\sec^n x}{n} + c$ B. $\frac{\sec^{n-1} x}{n-1} + c$
C. $\frac{\tan^n x}{n} + c$ D. $\frac{\tan^{n-1} x}{n-1} + c$
where c is a constant of integration.

20. What is the area bounded by the curve $y = x^2$ and the line $y = 16$?
A. 32/3 B. 64/3
C. 256/3 D. 128/3

21. What is the number of terms in the expansion of $(a + b + c)^n$, $n \in N$?
A. $n + 1$ B. $n + 2$
C. $n(n + 1)$ D. $(n+1)(n+2)/2$

22. What is the number of signals that can be sent by 6 flags of different colours taking one or more at a time?
A. 21 B. 63
C. 720 D. 1956

23. In how many ways can a committee consisting of 3 men and 2 women be formed from 7 men and 5 women?
A. 45 B. 350
C. 700 D. 4200

24. If

$\vec{a} = \hat{i} - \hat{k}$

$\vec{b} = x\hat{i} + \hat{j} + (1-x)\hat{k}$

$\vec{c} = y\hat{i} + x\hat{j} + (1+x-y)\hat{k}$

then $\vec{a}.(\vec{b} \times \vec{c})$ depends on
A. x only B. y only
C. both x and y D. neither x nor y

25. What is the probability of having 53 Sundays or 53 Mondays in a leap year ?
A. 2/7 B. 3/7
C. 4/7 D. 5/7

26. Three digital numbers are formed using the digits 0, 2, 4, 6, 8. A number is chosen at random out of these numbers. What is the probability that the number has the same digits?

A. 1/16 B. 1/25
C. 16/25 D. 1/645

27. What is the mean deviation of the data 2, 9, 9, 3, 6, 9, 4?

A. 2.23 B. 2.57
C. 3.23 D. 3.57

28. A set of n values x_1 x_2, ..., x_n has standard deviation σ. What is the standard deviation of n values $x_1 + k$, $x_2 + k$, ..., $x_n + k$?

A. σ B. $\sigma + \kappa$
C. $\sigma - \kappa$ D. $\kappa\sigma$

29. The two lines of regression are $8x - 10y = 66$ and $40x - 18y = 214$, and variance of x series is 9. What is the standard deviation of y series?

A. 3 B. 4
C. 6 D. 8

30. The standard deviation of some consecutive integers is found to be 2. Which of the following statements best describes the nature of the consecutive integers?

A. The integers are any set of eight consecutive integers
B. The integers are any set of eight consecutive positive integers
C. The integers are any set of seven consecutive intergers
D. None of the above

31. What is the interval over which the function $f(x) = 6x - x^2$, $x > 0$ is increasing?

A. (0, 3) B. (3, 6)
C. (6, 9) D. None of the above

32. What is $\int \sqrt{x} e^{\sqrt{x}} dx$ equal to ?

A. $2e^{\sqrt{x}}(x - 2\sqrt{x} + 2) + c$
B. $2e^{\sqrt{x}}(x + 2\sqrt{x} + 2) + c$
C. $2e^{\sqrt{x}}(x + 2\sqrt{x} - 2) + c$
D. $2e^{\sqrt{x}}(x - 2\sqrt{x} - 2) + c$

where c is a constant of integration.

33. What is the degree of the differential equation

$$\left(1 + \frac{dy}{dx}\right)^4 = \left(\frac{d^2y}{dx^2}\right)^2 ?$$

A. 1 B. 2
C. 4 D. 8

34. What is the general solution of

$$(1 + x^x)y dy = e^x dx ?$$

A. $y^2 = \ln[c^2(e^x + 1)]^2$
B. $y = \ln[c(e^x + 1)]$
C. $y^2 = \ln[c(e^x + 1)]$
D. None of the above

where c is a constant of integration.

35. What is the value of

$$\int_{\pi/6}^{\pi/4} \frac{dx}{\sin x \cos x} ?$$

A. $2 \ln \sqrt{3}$ B. $\ln \sqrt{3}$
C. $2 \ln 3$ D. $4 \ln 3$

36. If f and g are two increasing functions such that $f \circ g$ is defined, then which one of the following is correct ?

A. $f \circ g$ is always an increasing function
B. $f \circ g$ is always an decreasing function
C. $f \circ g$ is neither an increasing nor a decreasing function
D. None of the above

37. What is the value of

$$\int_1^2 e^x \left(\frac{1}{x} - \frac{1}{x^2}\right) dx$$

A. $e\left(\frac{e}{2} - 1\right)$ B. $e(e - 1)$
C. $e - \frac{1}{e}$ D. 0

38. Which one of the following is the differential equation to family of circles having centre at the origin?

A. $(x^2 - y^2)\frac{dy}{dx} = 2xy$
B. $(x^2 + y^2)\frac{dy}{dx} = 2xy$
C. $\frac{dy}{dx} = (x^2 + y^2)$
D. $x\,dx + y\,dy = 0$

39. What is the area under the curve $f(x) = xe^x$ above the x-axis and between the lines $x = 0$ and $x = 1$?

A. 1/2 square unit
B. 1 square unit
C. 3/2 square units
D. 2 square units

40. What does the solution of the differential equation

$$x\frac{dy}{dx} = y \text{ represent?}$$

A. Family of straight lines through the origin
B. Family of circles with their centres at the origin
C. Family of parabolas with their vertices at the origin
D. Family of straight lines having slope 1 and not passing through the origin

41. What is the coefficient of x^{17} in the expansion of

$$\left(3x - \frac{x^3}{6}\right)^9 ?$$

A. 189/8 B. 567/2
C. 21/16 D. None of the above

42. What is the derivative of $\sin^2 x$ with respect to $\cos^2 x$?
A. $\tan^2 x$ B. $\cot^2 x$
C. –1 D. 1

43. Consider the following statements:
1. $f(x) = |x - 3|$ is continuous at $x = 0$
2. $f(x) = |x - 3|$ is differentiable at $x = 0$

Which of the statements given above is/are correct?
A. 1 only B. 2 only
C. Both 1 and 2 D. Neither 1 nor 2

44. What is $(1111)_2 + (1001)_2 - (1010)_2$ equal to?
A. $(111)_2$ B. $(1100)_2$
C. $(1110)_2$ D. $(1010)_2$

45. What is $\dfrac{\sin\theta + 1}{\cos\theta}$ equal to?
A. $\dfrac{\sin\theta+\cos\theta-1}{\sin\theta+\cos\theta+1}$ B. $\dfrac{\sin\theta+\cos\theta+1}{\sin\theta+\cos\theta-1}$
C. $\dfrac{\sin\theta-\cos\theta-1}{\sin\theta+\cos\theta+1}$ D. $\dfrac{\sin\theta-\cos\theta+1}{\sin\theta+\cos\theta-1}$

46. If $f(x) = 2x + 7$ and $g(x) = x^2 + 7$, $x \in R$, then what are the values of x for which $f \circ g(x) = 25$?
A. –1, 1 B. –2, 2
C. $-\sqrt{2}, \sqrt{2}$ D. None of the above

47. What does the differential equation $y\dfrac{dy}{dx} + x = k$ (k is any constant) represent?
A. A family of circles having centre on the y-axis
B. A family of circles having centre on the x-axis
C. A family of circles touching the x-axis
D. A family of ellipses

48. What is the area of the region bounded by the curve $f(x) = 1 - \dfrac{x^2}{4}$, $x \in [-2, 2]$ and the x-axis)?
A. 8/3 square units B. 4/3 square units
C. 2/3 square unit D. 1/3 square unit

49. What is $\lim\limits_{x\to 0} \dfrac{a^x - b^x}{x}$ equal to?
A. $\ln(ab)$ B. $\dfrac{\ln a}{\ln b}$
C. $\ln\left(\dfrac{a}{b}\right)$ D. $\ln\left(\dfrac{b}{a}\right)$

50. If $\sqrt{x} + \sqrt{y} = 2$, then what is $\dfrac{dy}{dx}$ at $y = 1$ equal to?
A. 5 B. 2
C. 4 D. –1

51. For a point of inflection of $y = f(x)$, which one of the following is correct?
A. $\dfrac{dy}{dx}$ must be zero
B. $\dfrac{d^2y}{dx^2}$ must be zero
C. $\dfrac{dy}{dx}$ must be non-zero
D. $\dfrac{d^2y}{dx^2}$ must be non-zero

52. If the function

$$f(x) = \frac{x(x-2)}{x^2-4},\ x \neq \pm 2$$

is continuous at $x = 2$, then what is $f(2)$ equal to?
A. 0 B. 1/2
C. 1 D. 2

53. If $x = \cos(2t)$ and $y = \sin^2 t$, then what is $\dfrac{d^2y}{dx^2}$ equal to?
A. 0 B. $\sin(2t)$
C. $-\cos(2t)$ D. –1/2

54. What is the value of p for which the function

$$f(x) = p\sin x + \frac{\sin 3x}{3}$$

has an extremum at $x = \dfrac{\pi}{3}$?
A. 0 B. 1
C. –1 D. 2

55. What is the value of the integral

$$\int_{-1}^{1} |x|\, dx$$

A. 1 B. 0
C. 2 D. –1

56. A particular solution of a differential equation represents
A. line B. circle
C. ellipse D. curve

57. At how many points is the function $f(x) = [x]$ discontinuous?
A. 1 B. 2
C. 3 D. Infinite

58. What is

$$\int \frac{e^x(1+x)}{\cos^2(xe^x)} dx$$

equal to?
A. $xe^x + c$ B. $\cos(xe^x) + c$
C. $\tan(xe^x) + c$ D. $x\,\mathrm{cosec}(xe^x) + c$

where c is a constant of integration.

59. If at any instant t, for a sphere, r denotes the radius, S denotes the surface area and V denotes the volume, then what is $\dfrac{dV}{dt}$ equal to?

A. $\frac{1}{2}S\frac{dr}{dt}$ B. $\frac{1}{2}r\frac{dS}{dt}$

C. $r\frac{dS}{dt}$ D. $\frac{1}{2}r^2\frac{dS}{dt}$

60. If

$$f(x)=\frac{2}{3}x+\frac{3}{2},\ x\in R$$

then what is $f^{-1}(x)$ equal to?

A. $\frac{3}{2}x+\frac{2}{3}$ B. $\frac{3}{2}x-\frac{9}{4}$

C. $\frac{2}{3}x-\frac{4}{9}$ D. $\frac{2}{3}x-\frac{2}{3}$

61. The two planes $ax + by + cz + d = 0$ and $ax + by + cz + d_1 = 0$, where $d \neq d_1$, have

A. one point only in common
B. three points in common
C. infinite points in common
D. no points in common

62. A point P moves such that the difference of its distances from two given points $(c, 0)$ and $(-c, 0)$ is constant. What is the locus of the point P?

A. Circle B. Ellipse
C. Hyperbola D. Parabola

63. What is the distance of the origin from the plane $2x + 6y - 3z + 7 = 0$?

A. 1 B. 2
C. 3 D. 6

64. $PQRS$ is a parallelogram, where $\overline{PQ}=3\hat{i}+2\hat{j}-m\hat{k}$, $\overline{PS}=\hat{i}+3\hat{j}+\hat{k}$ and the area of the parallelogram is $\sqrt{90}$. What is the value of m?

A. 1 B. −1
C. 2 D. −2

65. What is the vector equally inclined to the vectors $\hat{i}+3\hat{j}$ and $3\hat{i}+\hat{j}$?

A. $\hat{i}+\hat{j}$ B. $2\hat{i}-\hat{j}$

C. $2\hat{i}+\hat{j}$ D. None of the above

66. $ABCD$ is a quadrilateral. Forces $\overline{AB}$, $\overline{CB}$, $\overline{CD}$ and $\overline{DA}$ act along its sides. What is their resultant?

A. $2\overrightarrow{CD}$ B. $2\overrightarrow{DA}$

C. $2\overrightarrow{BC}$ D. $2\overrightarrow{CB}$

67. Under which of the following conditions does a general second-degree equation

$$ax^2+2hxy+by^2+2gx+2fy+c=0(a\neq 0)$$

represent a circle?

A. $h = g,\ a = b$
B. $h = g = f,\ a = b$
C. $h = 0,\ a = b$
D. $h = 0,\ g^2 + f^2 - c = a + b$

68. What is the area of a triangle whose vertices are at $(3, -1, 2)$, $(1, -1, -3)$ and $(4, -3, 1)$?

A. $\frac{\sqrt{165}}{2}$ B. $\frac{\sqrt{135}}{2}$

C. 4 D. 2

69. What is the value of b such that the scalar product of the vector $\hat{i}+\hat{j}+\hat{k}$ with the unit vector parallel to the sum of the vectors $2\hat{i}+4\hat{j}-5\hat{k}$ and $b\hat{i}+2\hat{j}+3\hat{k}$ is unity?

A. −2 B. −1
C. 0 D. 1

70. If the latus rectum of an ellipse is equal to half its minor axis, then what is its eccentricity?

A. $\frac{1}{2}$ B. $\sqrt{3}$

C. $\frac{\sqrt{3}}{2}$ D. $\frac{1}{\sqrt{2}}$

71. If $A = \{2, 3\}$, $B = \{4, 5\}$, $C = \{5, 6\}$, then what is the number of elements in $A \times (B \cap C)$

A. 2 B. 4
C. 6 D. 8

72. What is the slope of the line perpendicular to the line $\frac{x}{4}+\frac{y}{3}=1$?

A. $\frac{3}{4}$ B. $-\frac{3}{4}$

C. $-\frac{4}{3}$ D. $\frac{4}{3}$

73. ABC is a triangle in which $BC = 10$ cm, $CA = 6$ cm and $AB = 8$ cm. Which one of the following is correct?

A. ABC is an acute-angled triangle
B. ABC is an obtuse-angled triangle
C. ABC is a right-angled triangle
D. None of the above

74. If the AM and GM between two numbers are in the ratio $m : n$, then what is the ratio between the two numbers?

A. $\frac{m+\sqrt{m^2-n^2}}{m-\sqrt{m^2-n^2}}$ B. $\frac{m+n}{m-n}$

C. $\frac{m^2-n^2}{m^2+n^2}$ D. $\frac{m^2+n^2-mn}{m^2+n^2+mn}$

75. Consider the function $f : R \to \{0, 1\}$ such that

$$f(x)=\begin{cases}1 & \text{if } x \text{ is rational}\\ 0 & \text{if } x \text{ is irrational}\end{cases}$$

Which one of the following is correct?
A. The function is one-one into
B. The function is many-one into
C. The function is one-one onto
D. The function is many-one onto

76. One of the angles of a triangle is 1/2 radian and the other is 99°. What is the third angle in radian measure?

A. $\frac{9\pi - 10}{\pi}$ B. $\frac{90\pi - 100}{7\pi}$

C. $\frac{90\pi - 10}{\pi}$ D. None of the above

77. Two poles are 10 m and 20 m high. The line joining their tops makes an angle of 15° with the horizontal. What is the approximate distance between the poles?
A. 35.3 m B. 37.3 m
C. 41 m D. 44 m

78. What is the value of

$$\sin^{-1}\frac{4}{5} + 2\tan^{-1}\frac{1}{3}?$$

A. $\frac{\pi}{3}$ B. $\frac{\pi}{2}$

C. $\frac{\pi}{4}$ D. $\frac{\pi}{6}$

79. What is $\left(\frac{\sec 18°}{\sec 144°} + \frac{\operatorname{cosec} 18°}{\operatorname{cosec} 144°}\right)$ equal to?
A. sec 18° B. cosec 18°
C. – sec 18° D. – cosec 18°

80. If α and β are positive angles such that $\alpha + \beta = \frac{\pi}{4}$, then what is (1 + tanα) (1 + tanβ) equal to
A. 0 B. 1
C. 2 D. 3

81. What is the value of (sin 50° – sin 70° + sin 10°)?

A. 1 B. $\frac{1}{\sqrt{2}}$

C. $\frac{\sqrt{3}}{2}$ D. 0

82. If

cos A + cos B = m

sin A + sin B = n

where $m, n \neq 0$, then what is sin(A + B) equal to?

A. $\frac{mn}{m^2 + n^2}$ B. $\frac{2mn}{m^2 + n^2}$

C. $\frac{m^2 + n^2}{2mn}$ D. $\frac{mn}{m + n}$

83. If $y = \sec^2\theta + \cos^2\theta$, where $0 < \theta < \frac{\pi}{2}$, then which one of the following is correct?
A. $y = 0$ B. $0 \le y \le 2$
C. $y \ge 2$ D. None of the above

84. If tan A = 3/4 and tan B = –12/5, then how many values can cot (A – B) have depending on the actual values of A and B?
A. 1 B. 2
C. 3 D. 4

85. What is the value of sin 15° sin 75°?
A. 1/4 B. 1/8
C. 1/16 D. 1

86. What is the equation to the straight line joining the origin to the point of intersection of the lines

$$\frac{x}{a} + \frac{y}{b} = 1 \text{ and } \frac{x}{b} + \frac{y}{a} = 1?$$

A. $x + y = 0$ B. $x + y + 1 = 0$
C. $x - y = 0$ D. $x + y + 2 = 0$

87. What is the equation to circle which touches both the axes and has centre on the line $x + y = 4$?
A. $x^2 + y^2 - 4x + 4y + 4 = 0$
B. $x^2 + y^2 - 4x - 4y + 4 = 0$
C. $x^2 + y^2 + 4x - 4y - 4 = 0$
D. $x^2 + y^2 + 4x + 4y - 4 = 0$

88. If the position vector of a point P with respect to origin O is $\hat{i} + 3\hat{j} - 2\hat{k}$ and that of a point Q is $3\hat{i} + \hat{j} - 2\hat{k}$, then what is the position vector of the bisector of the angle POQ?
A. $\hat{i} - \hat{j} - \hat{k}$ B. $\hat{i} + \hat{j} - \hat{k}$
C. $\hat{i} + \hat{j} + \hat{k}$ D. None of the above

89. If the straight lines $x - 2y = 0$ and $kx + y = 1$ intersect at the point $\left(1, \frac{1}{2}\right)$ then what is the value of k?
A. 1 B. 2
C. 1/2 D. –1/2

90. Let a, b and c be distinct non-negative numbers. If the vectors $a\hat{i} + a\hat{j} + c\hat{k}$, $\hat{i} + \hat{k}$, $c\hat{i} + c\hat{j} + b\hat{k}$ lie on a plane, then which one of the following is correct?
A. c is the arithmetic mean of a and b
B. c is the geometric mean of a and b
C. c is the harmonic mean of a and b
D. c is equal to zero

91. If A and B are two disjoint sets, then which one of the following is correct?
A. $A - B = A - (A \cap B)$
B. $B - A' = B \cap A$
C. $A \cap B = (A - B) \cap B$
D. All of the above

92. Consider the following statements in respect of a square matrix A and its transpose A^T.

1. $A + A^T$ is always symmetric.
2. $A - A^T$ is always anti-symmetric.

Which of the statements given above is/are correct?

A. 1 only B. 2 only
C. Both 1 and 2 D. Neither 1 nor 2

93. If α and β are the roots of the equation $x^2 - 2x + 4 = 0$, then what is the value of $\alpha^3 + \beta^3$?

A. 16 B. −16
C. 8 D. −8

94. What is the value of $(-1 + i\sqrt{3})^{48}$?

A. 1 B. 2
C. 2^{24} D. 2^{48}

95. If a matrix A is such that

$$3A^3 + 2A^2 + 5A + I = 0$$

Then what is A^{-1} equal to?

A. $-(3A^2 + 2A + 5)$ B. $3A^2 + 2A + 5I$
C. $3A^2 - 2A - 5I$ D. $-(3A^2 + 2A + 5I)$

96. What is the sum of all the coefficients in the expansion of $(1 + x)^n$?

A. 2^n B. $2^n - 1$
C. 2^{n-1} D. $2(n - 1)$

97. Let N denote the set of natural numbers and $A = \{n^2 : n \in N\}$ and $B = \{n^3 : n \in N\}$. Which one of the following is correct?

A. $A \cup B = N$
B. The complement of $(A \cup B)$ is an infinite set
C. $A \cap B$ must be a finite set
D. $A \cap B$ must be a proper subset of $\{m^6 : m \in N\}$

98. Which of the following are the two roots of the equation $(x^2 + 2)^2 + 8x^2 = 6x(x^2 + 2)$?

A. $1 \pm i$ B. $3 \pm i$
C. $1 \pm \sqrt{2}$ D. $2 \pm i\sqrt{2}$

99. What is the coefficient of x^4 in the expansion of $\left(\frac{1-x}{1+x}\right)^2$?

A. −16 B. 16
C. 8 D. −8

100. If α and β are the roots of the equation $x^2 - x + 1 = 0$, then which of the following are the roots of the equation $x^2 - x + 1 = 0$?

A. α^7 and β^{13} B. α^{13} and β^7
C. α^{20} and β^{20} D. None of the above

101. A square is drawn by joining mid-point of the sides of a square. Another square is drawn inside the second square in the same way and the process is continued indefinitely. If the side of the first square is 16 cm then what is the sum of the areas of all the squares?

A. 256 sq. cm B. 512 sq. cm
C. 1024 sq. cm D. 512/3 sq. cm

102. Let A and B be matrices of order 3 × 3. If $AB = 0$, then which of the following can be concluded?

A. $A = 0$ and $B = 0$
B. $|A| = 0$ and $|B| = 0$
C. Either $|A| = 0$ or $|B| = 0$
D. Either $A = 0$ or $B = 0$

103. The sum of an infinite geometric progression is 6. If the sum of the first two terms is 9/2, then what is the first term?

A. 1 B. 5/2
C. 3 or 3/2 D. 9 or 3

104. If A is a square matrix, then what is adj A^T – (adj $A)^T$ equal to ?

A. 2 $|A|$ B. 2 $|A|$ I
C. Null matrix D. Unit matrix

105. Which one of the following is correct?

A. sin 1° > sin 1 B. sin 1° < sin 1
C. sin 1° = sin 1 D. $\sin 1° = \frac{\pi}{180}\sin 1$

106. The relation

$R = \{(1, 1), (2, 2), (3, 3), (1, 2), (2, 3), (1, 3)\}$ on a set $A = \{1, 2, 3\}$ is

A. reflexive, transitive but not symmetric
B. reflexive, symmetric but not transitive
C. symmetric, transitive but not reflexive
D. reflexive but neither symmetric nor transitive

107. If

$$\begin{bmatrix} 1 & -3 & 2 \\ 2 & -8 & 5 \\ 4 & 2 & \lambda \end{bmatrix}$$

is not an invertible matrix, then what is the value of λ?

A. −1 B. 0
C. 1 D. 2

108. What is the number of words that can be formed from the letters of the word 'UNIVERSAL', the vowels remaining always together?

A. 720 B. 1440
C. 17280 D. 21540

109. The arithmetic mean of two numbers exceeds their geometric mean by 2 and the geometric mean exceeds their harmonic mean by 1.6. What are the two numbers?

A. 16, 4 B. 81, 9
C. 256, 16 D. 625, 25

110. What is the conjugate of $\left(\frac{1+2i}{2+i}\right)^2$?

A. $\frac{7}{25} + i\frac{24}{25}$ B. $-\frac{7}{25} - i\frac{24}{25}$
C. $-\frac{7}{25} + i\frac{24}{25}$ D. $\frac{7}{25} - i\frac{24}{25}$

111. If the equations $x^2 + kx + 64 = 0$ and $x^2 - 8x + k = 0$ have real roots, then what is the value of k?

A. 4 B. 8
C. 12 D. 16

112. What is $\left(\frac{\sqrt{3}+i}{\sqrt{3}-i}\right)^6$ equal to?

A. –1 B. 0
C. 1 D. 2

113. If

$$A = \begin{bmatrix} 0 & 1 \\ -1 & 0 \end{bmatrix}, B = \begin{bmatrix} i & 0 \\ 0 & -i \end{bmatrix}, C = \begin{bmatrix} 0 & -i \\ -i & 0 \end{bmatrix}$$

then which one of the following is ***not*** correct?

A. $A^2 = B^2$ B. $B^2 = C^2$
C. $AB = C$ D. $AB = BA$

114. If $\log_3[\log_3[\log_3 x]] = \log_3 3$, then what is the value of x?

A. 3 B. 27
C. 3^9 D. 3^{27}

115. If ω is a complex cube root of unity, then what is $\omega^{10} + \omega^{-10}$ equal to?

A. 2 B. –1
C. –2 D. 1

116. If the roots of the equation

$$(a^2 + b^2)x^2 - 2b(a+c)x + (b^2 + c^2) = 0$$

are equal, then which one of the following is correct?

A. $2b = a + c$ B. $b^2 = ac$
C. $b + c = 2a$ D. $b = ac$

117. What is the maximum number of straight lines that can be drawn with any four points in a plane such that each line contains at least two of these points?

A. 2 B. 4
C. 6 D. 12

118. If

$$x + iy = \begin{vmatrix} 6i & -3i & 1 \\ 4 & 3i & -1 \\ 20 & 3 & i \end{vmatrix}$$

then what is $x - iy$ equal to ?

A. $3 + i$ B. $1 + 3i$
C. $3i$ D. 0

119. If |A| = 8, where A is a square matrix of order 3, then what is |adj A| equal to ?

A. 16 B. 24
C. 64 D. 512

120. What is the binary number equivalent of the decimal number 32.25?

A. 100010.10 B. 100000.10
C. 100010.01 D. 100000.01

ANSWERS

PAPER-I : GENERAL ABILITY TEST

1	2	3	4	5	6	7	8	9	10
B	B	A	D	A	D	C	A	B	C
11	12	13	14	15	16	17	18	19	20
C	B	C	C	D	A	C	D	C	A
21	22	23	24	25	26	27	28	29	30
D	B	D	C	C	D	C	B	C	A
31	32	33	34	35	36	37	38	39	40
C	C	C	B	D	B	B	D	B	B
41	42	43	44	45	46	47	48	49	50
C	D	B	C	C	D	D	B	C	A
51	52	53	54	55	56	57	58	59	60
D	D	A	C	C	D	C	A	D	B
61	62	63	64	65	66	67	68	69	70
A	B	B	C	D	A	C	A	C	A
71	72	73	74	75	76	77	78	79	80
B	D	B	D	C	A	A	A	A	C
81	82	83	84	85	86	87	88	89	90
C	A	A	A	A	A	D	A	B	D
91	92	93	94	95	96	97	98	99	100
A	A	B	C	A	C	D	D	A	D
101	102	103	104	105	106	107	108	109	110
B	C	A	C	B	A	D	C	A	D

111	112	113	114	115	116	117	118	119	120
B	A	A	C	D	C	C	B	D	B
121	122	123	124	125	126	127	128	129	130
C	B	C	B	B	D	B	A	B	A
131	132	133	134	135	136	137	138	139	140
B	B	D	D	C	C	D	C	C	B
141	142	143	144	145	146	147	148	149	150
B	C	D	B	A	C	D	B	A	C

PAPER-II : MATHEMATICS

1	2	3	4	5	6	7	8	9	10
C	B	A	C	A	C	B	A	C	A
11	12	13	14	15	16	17	18	19	20
A	A	B	A	A	C	B	C	A	D
21	22	23	24	25	26	27	28	29	30
A	D	B	D	A	B	B	B	B	D
31	32	33	34	35	36	37	38	39	40
A	A	B	A	B	A	A	D	B	A
41	42	43	44	45	46	47	48	49	50
A	C	C	C	C	C	B	A	C	D
51	52	53	54	55	56	57	58	59	60
A	B	A	A	D	D	D	C	B	B
61	62	63	64	65	66	67	68	69	70
D	B	A	A	D	D	C	A	D	C
71	72	73	74	75	76	77	78	79	80
A	D	C	A	D	D	B	B	A	C
81	82	83	84	85	86	87	88	89	90
D	B	C	B	A	C	B	D	C	B
91	92	93	94	95	96	97	98	99	100
C	C	B	D	D	A	D	B	B	D
101	102	103	104	105	106	107	108	109	110
B	D	D	C	B	A	C	C	A	D
111	112	113	114	115	116	117	118	119	120
D	C	D	D	B	B	C	D	C	D

EXPLANATORY ANSWERS

PAPER-II : MATHEMATICS

2. (1) $\because$ (1) $A \cap B \cap C = 0$

$\therefore$ A, B and C are mutually exclusive

(3) $A \cup B = \{1, 4, 5, 9, 10, 15, 16, 20\}$

$(A \cup B)' = U - (A \cup B)$

$= \{2, 3, 6, 7, 8, 11, 12, 13, 14, 17, 18, 19\}$

No og element in (A ∪ B) complement is 12

Hence, Statement 1 and 3 are true.

5.

x_i	y_i	$x_i - \overline{x}$ dx_i	$y_i - \overline{y}$ dy_i	dx_i^2	dy_i^2	$dx_i \times dy_i$
5	2	–1	–1	1	1	1
7	4	1	1	1	1	1
8	3	2	0	4	0	0
4	2	–2	–1	4	1	2
6	4	0	1	0	1	0
$\overline{x} = 6$	$\overline{y} = 3$	0	0	10	4	4

$$\therefore\ y - 3 = 0.4\,(x - 6)$$

$$y = 0.4x - 2.4 + 3$$

$$y = 0.4x - .6$$

6. Using L'Hospital rule

$$\lim_{x \to 0} \frac{-a \sin ax + b \sin bx}{-2x}$$

$$\lim_{x \to 0} \frac{-a^2 \cos ax + b^2 \cos bx}{2}$$

$$= \frac{b^2 - a^2}{2}.$$

7-9. Clearly median class will 15 – 20 using formula

$$M_o = l + \frac{\frac{N}{2} - c.f.}{f} \times i$$

Also $54 + x + y = 90$

$x + y = 36 \quad ...(1)$

Again $17 = 15 + \dfrac{45 - 15 - x}{35} \times 5$

$\Rightarrow \quad 2 = \dfrac{30 - x}{y}$

$\Rightarrow \quad x = 30 - 14 = 16$

$\Rightarrow \quad y = 20$

10. $9 = \dfrac{1}{2}\begin{vmatrix} -3 & 0 & 1 \\ 3 & 0 & 1 \\ 0 & k & 1 \end{vmatrix}$

$9 = \dfrac{1}{2}\{-3(-k) - 3(-k) + 0(0)\}$

$9 = \dfrac{1}{2} \times 6k$

$\therefore k = 3$

12. $x = k(\theta + \sin\theta)$

$y = k(1 + \cos\theta)$

$\Rightarrow \dfrac{dx}{d\theta} = k(1 + \cos\theta)$

$\Rightarrow \dfrac{dy}{d\theta} = k(0 - \sin\theta)$

$\therefore \dfrac{dy}{dx} = \dfrac{-\sin\theta}{1 + \cos\theta}$

$= \dfrac{-\sin\frac{\pi}{2}}{1 + \cos\frac{\pi}{2}}$

$= \dfrac{-1}{1} = -1$

14. $\begin{vmatrix} 1 & \omega & 2\omega^2 \\ 2 & 2\omega^2 & 4 \\ 3 & 3 & 6\omega \end{vmatrix} \quad (\because \omega^3 = 1)$

$1(4\omega - 4\omega^4) - 2(6\omega^2 - 6\omega^2) + 3(4\omega - 4\omega^4)$

$1(4\omega - 4\omega) - 2(6\omega^2 - 6\omega^2) + 3(4\omega - 4\omega)$

$= 0$

16.

A, 15°, 120, 15°, B, x, C

Let required distance BC = x m.

$\therefore \tan 15° = \dfrac{120}{x}$

$x = \dfrac{120}{2 - \sqrt{3}} \times \dfrac{2 + \sqrt{3}}{2 + \sqrt{3}}$

$x = 447.6 = 444\text{m}.$

19. $\int \sec^n x \tan x \, dx$

$= \int \sec^{n-1} x . \sec x \tan x \, dx$

Put $\sec x = u$

$sec\ x.\tan x.dx = du$

$= \int u^{n-1} du = \dfrac{u^n}{n} = \dfrac{\sec^n x}{n} + c$

22. By alternation in the arrangement of flags the signals will charge the required number of signals

$= 6P_1 + 6P_2 + 6P_3 + 6P_4 + 6P_5 + 6P_6$

$= 6 + 30 + 120 + 360 + 720 + 720$

$= 1956$

23. The required ways

$= 7C_3 \times 5C_2 = 350.$

24. $\vec{a}.\vec{b} \times \vec{c}$

Now, $\vec{b} \times \vec{c} = \begin{vmatrix} \hat{i} & \hat{j} & \hat{k} \\ x & 1 & 1 - x \\ y & x & (1 + x - y) \end{vmatrix}$

$= \hat{i}(1 + x - y - x + x^2) - \hat{j}(x + x^2 - xy - y + xy) + \hat{k}(x^2 - y)$

$= \hat{i}(1 - y + x^2) - \hat{j}(x + x^2 - y) + \hat{k}(x^2 - y)$

Now $\vec{a}.(\vec{b} \times \vec{c})$

$= (\hat{i} - \hat{k})\{\hat{i}(1 - y + x^2) - \hat{j}(x + x^2 - y) + \hat{k}(x^2 - y)\}$

$= 1 - y + x^2 - (x^2 - y)$

$= 1 - y + x^2 - x^2 + y$

$= 1$

27. Mean deviation $= \dfrac{\sum |x_i - \bar{x}|}{n}$

$= \dfrac{|2-6| + |9-6| + |9-6| + |3-6| + |6-6| + |9-6| + |1-6|}{7}$

$= \dfrac{18}{7} = 2.57.$

32. $\int \sqrt{x}\, e^{\sqrt{x}} dx$

Put $\sqrt{x} = u$

$$\frac{1}{2\sqrt{x}} = du$$

$\therefore\ dx = 2\sqrt{x}\,du$

$= \int u^2 e^u du \times 2$

$= 2\left[u^2 \int e^u du - \int 2u e^u du\right]$

$= 2\left[u^2.e^u - 2\{e^u.u - e^u\}\right]$

$= 2u^2e^u - 4ue^u + 4e^u$

$= 2xe^{\sqrt{x}} - 4\sqrt{x}\,e^{\sqrt{x}} + 4e^{\sqrt{x}}$

$= 2e^{\sqrt{x}}\left(x - 2\sqrt{x} + 2\right)$

34. $y\,dy = \int \frac{e^x}{e^{x+1}} dx$

$\therefore\ \frac{y^2}{2} = \log(e^x + 1) + \log c$

$y^2 = 2\log(e^x + 1) + 2\log c$

$y^2 = \log(e^x + 1)^2 c^2$

35. $\int_{\pi/6}^{\pi/4} \frac{-dx}{\sin x.\cos x} = \int_{\pi/6}^{\pi/4} \frac{\sec^2 x}{\tan x} dx$

$= \int_{\frac{1}{\sqrt{3}}}^{1} \frac{dz}{z} = [\log z]_{\frac{1}{\sqrt{3}}}^{1}$

$= \left[\log 1 - \left(\log 1 - \log\sqrt{3}\right)\right] = \log\sqrt{3}$

37. $\int_1^2 \left(\frac{e^x}{x} - \frac{e^x}{x^2}\right) dx$

$= \int_1^2 \frac{e^x}{x} dx - \int_1^2 \frac{e^x}{x^2} dx$

$= \left[\frac{1}{x}.e^x\right]_1^2 - \int_1^2 -\frac{1}{x^2}.e^x dx - \int_1^2 \frac{e^x}{x^2} dx$

$= \frac{1}{2}e^2 - e^1 = e\left(\frac{e}{2} - 1\right)$

41. Coefficient of x^{17} in $\left(3x - \frac{x^3}{6}\right)^9$

$= 9C_4 (3x)^{9-4} \times \left(-\frac{x^3}{6}\right)^4$

$= 9C_4 \times 3^5 \times \left(-\frac{1}{6}\right)^4$

$= \frac{\underline{|9}}{\underline{|4}\underline{|5}} \times \frac{3^5}{6^4} = \frac{189}{8}$

42. Let $u = \sin^2 x$

and $v = \cos^2 x$

$\therefore\ \frac{du}{dx} = 2\sin x.\cos x$

$\frac{du}{dx} = -2\cos x.\sin x$

$\therefore\ \frac{du}{dv} = \frac{du}{dx} \times \frac{dx}{dv}$

$= \frac{2\sin x.\cos x}{-2\sin x.\cos x} = -1$

49. $\lim_{x\to 0} \frac{a^x - b^x}{x}$

$= \lim_{x\to 0} \frac{a^x \log e^a - b^x \log e^b}{1}$

(using L'Hospital's Rule)

$= \log e^a - \log e^b$

$= \log\left(\frac{a}{b}\right).$

50. $\sqrt{x} + \sqrt{y} = 2$

$\therefore\ \frac{1}{2\sqrt{x}} + \frac{1}{2\sqrt{y}}\frac{dy}{dx} = 0$

$\frac{dy}{dx} = -\frac{1}{\sqrt{x}} \times \frac{\sqrt{y}}{1}$

$\left[\begin{array}{l}\text{at } y = 1 \\ \sqrt{x} + 1 = 2 \\ \sqrt{x} = 1\end{array}\right.$

$\left(\frac{dy}{dx}\right)_{y=1} = -\frac{1}{1} \times 1$

$= -1$

53. $x = \cos^{(2t)}$ and $y = \sin^2 t$

$\therefore\ \frac{dx}{dt} = -2\sin 2t$ and $\frac{dy}{dt} = 2\sin t.\cos t$

$\therefore\ \frac{dy}{dx} = \frac{2\sin t.\cos t}{-4\sin t.\cos t} = -\frac{1}{2}$

$\therefore\ \frac{d^2y}{dx^2} = 0$

58. $\int \frac{e^x(1+x)}{\cos^2(xe^x)} dx$

Put $xe^x = z$

$\therefore\ e^x(1 + x)\,dx = dz$

$\int \frac{dz}{\cos^2 z} = \int \sec^2 z\,dz = \tan z + c$

$= \tan(xe^x) + c.$

64. Area of parallelogram = $\frac{1}{2}\left|\left(\overrightarrow{PQ}\times\overrightarrow{PS}\right)\right|$

$$\therefore \sqrt{90} = \begin{vmatrix} \hat{i} & \hat{j} & \hat{k} \\ 3 & 2 & -m \\ 1 & 3 & 1 \end{vmatrix}$$

$$= \left[\hat{i}(2+3m)-\hat{j}(3+m)+\hat{k}(9-2)\right]$$

$$\sqrt{90} = \sqrt{(2+3m)^2+(3+m)^2+49}$$

$$= \sqrt{4+12m+9m^2+9+m^2+6m+49}$$

$$\sqrt{90} = \sqrt{10m^2+18m+62}$$

$\Rightarrow 10m^2 + 18m + 62 - 90 = 0$

$\Rightarrow 10m^2 + 18m - 28 = 0$

$\Rightarrow 5m^2 + 9m - 14 = 0$

$\Rightarrow 5m^2 - 5m + 14m - 14 = 0$

$5m(m-1) + 14(m-1) = 0$

$m -\frac{14}{5}, m = 1$

70. Latus rectum = $\frac{2b^2}{a}$

minor axis = $2b$

$\therefore \quad \frac{2b^2}{a} = \frac{1}{2}\times 2b$

$b = \frac{2b^2}{a}$

$\Rightarrow \quad a = 2b$

Now from formula $b^2 = a^2(1-e^2)$

$b^2 = 4b^2(1-e^2)$

$\frac{1}{4} = 1 - e^2$

$\Rightarrow \quad e^2 = 1-\frac{1}{4}$

$e^2 = \frac{3}{4}$

$\Rightarrow \quad e = \frac{\sqrt{3}}{2}$

71. A = {2, 3}, B = {4, 5}, C = {5, 6}

B ∩ C = {5}

A × (B ∩ C) = {2, 3} × {5}

= {(2, 5) (3, 5)

∴ n {A × (B ∩ C)} = 2.

72. Given $\frac{x}{4}+\frac{y}{3}=1$

$\Rightarrow 3x + 4y = 12$

$\Rightarrow y = -\frac{3}{4}x+3$

$\therefore m_1 = -\frac{3}{4}$

Any line ⊥r to given line if

$m_1 \times m_2 = -1$

i.e., $-\frac{3}{4}\times m_2 = -1$

$m_2 = \frac{4}{3}$

74. According to question,

$$\frac{a+b}{2\sqrt{ab}} = \frac{m}{n}$$

$$\Rightarrow \frac{a+b+2\sqrt{ab}}{a+b-2\sqrt{ab}} = \frac{m+n}{m-n}$$

(By componendo and devidendo)

$$\Rightarrow \frac{\left(\sqrt{a}+\sqrt{b}\right)^2}{\left(\sqrt{a}-\sqrt{b}\right)^2} = \frac{m+n}{m-n}$$

$$\Rightarrow \frac{\sqrt{a}+\sqrt{b}}{\sqrt{a}-\sqrt{b}} = \frac{\sqrt{m+n}}{\sqrt{m-n}}$$

$$\Rightarrow \frac{2\sqrt{a}}{2\sqrt{b}} = \frac{\sqrt{m+n}+\sqrt{m-n}}{\sqrt{m+n}-\sqrt{m-n}}$$

(By componendo and devidendo)

$$\Rightarrow \frac{a}{b} = \frac{m+\sqrt{m^2-n^2}}{m-\sqrt{m^2-n^2}}$$

76. One radian = 57° (approx.)

$\frac{1}{2}$ radian = $\frac{1}{2}\times 57° = 28.5°$

∴ third angle = 180° − 99° − 28.5°

= 62.5°

180° = π radian

$\therefore \quad 1° = \frac{\pi}{180°}$ radian

$\therefore \quad 62.5° = \frac{\pi}{180°}\times 62.5$

78. $2\tan^{-1}\left(\frac{1}{3}\right) = \tan^{-1}\frac{\frac{2}{3}}{1-\frac{1}{9}} = \tan^{-1}\frac{3}{4}$.

Also $\sin^{-1}\frac{4}{5} = \tan^{-1}\frac{4}{3} = \cot^{-1}\frac{3}{4}$

$\therefore\ \tan^{-1}\frac{3}{4}+\cot^{-1}\frac{3}{4}=\frac{\pi}{2}$

79. $\frac{\cos 114°}{\cos 18°}+\frac{\sin 144°}{\sin 18°}=\frac{\sin(144+18°)}{\sin 18°.\cos 18°}$

$=\frac{\sin(180°-18°)}{\sin 18°.\cos 18°}$

$=\frac{1}{\cos 18°}$ = sec 18°.

80. $\tan(\alpha+\beta)=\frac{\tan\alpha+\tan\beta}{1-\tan\alpha.\tan\beta}$

$\tan\frac{\pi}{4}=\frac{\tan\alpha+\tan\beta}{1-\tan\alpha.\tan\beta}$

$\Rightarrow 1 = \tan\alpha + \tan\beta + \tan\alpha\ .\ \tan\beta$

$\Rightarrow 2 = (1 + \tan\alpha)(1 + \tan\beta)$

82. $mn = \sin A\ .\ \cos A + \sin A\ .\ \cos B + \cos A.\ \sin B + \cos B.\ \sin B$

$=\frac{\sin 2A}{2}+\sin(A+B)+\frac{\sin 2B}{2}$

$=\sin(A+B)+\frac{1}{2}\{2\sin(A+B).\cos(A-B)\}$

$= \sin(A + B) + \sin(A + B)\ .\ \cos(A - B)$

$mn = \sin(A + B)\ \{1 + \cos(A - B)\}$ ...(*i*)

Also $m^2 + n^2 = \cos^2 A + \cos^2 B + 2\cos A\ .\ \cos B + \sin^2 A + \sin^2 B + 2\sin A\ .\ \sin B$

$= 2 + 2\cos(A - B)$

$m^2 + n^2 = 2\{1 + \cos(A - B)\}$

$\frac{m^2+n^2}{2} = 1 + \cos(A - B)$ ...(*ii*)

From (*i*) and (*ii*)

$\sin(A+B)=\frac{2mn}{m^2+n^2}$

85. $\sin(45° - 30°)\ .\ \sin(45° + 30°)$

$= \sin^2 45° - \sin^2 30°$

$=\left(\frac{1}{\sqrt{2}}\right)^2-\left(\frac{1}{2}\right)^2=\frac{1}{2}-\frac{1}{4}=\frac{1}{4}$

89. On solving equation $x - 2y = 0$ and $kx + y = 1$

we get $y(2k + 1) = 1$

$\Rightarrow \frac{1}{2}(2k+1)=1$

$\Rightarrow 2k + 1 = 2$

$k=\frac{1}{2}$

93. $\alpha^3 + \beta^3 = (\alpha + \beta)^3 - 3\alpha\beta(\alpha + \beta)$ | since $\alpha+\beta=2$, $\alpha\beta=4$

$= (2)^3 - 3 \times 4(2)$

$= 8 - 24$

$= -16$

94. $\left\{2(-\frac{1}{2}+i\frac{\sqrt{3}}{2}\right\}^{48}$

$=2^{48}\left(\cos\frac{2\pi}{3}+i\sin\frac{\pi}{3}\right)^{48}$

$= 2^{48}(\cos 32\pi + i\sin 16\pi)$

$= 2^{48}(1 + 0) = 2^{48}$

99. Coefficient of x^4 in $(1 - 2x + x^2)(1 + x)^{-2}$

$\Rightarrow$ Coefficient of x^4 in $(1 - 2x + x^2)(1 - 2x + 3x^2 - 4x^3 + 5x^4 - ...)$

$\Rightarrow 5 + 8 + 3$

$\Rightarrow 16$

101.

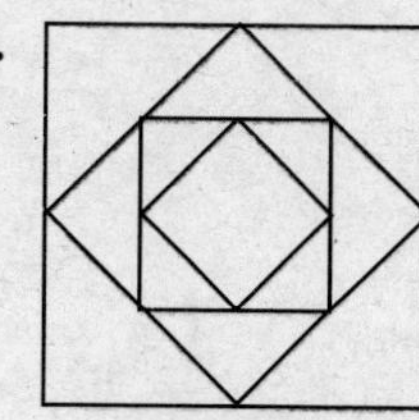

Area of given square = 256 cm^2

Now length of square drawn by joining mid points = $8\sqrt{2}$ cm

$\therefore$ Area = 128 cm^2

Next area = 64 cm^2

And so on,

Sum = 256 + 128 + 64 + 32 + ... which is in G.P

Sum $=\frac{256}{1-\frac{1}{2}}=256\times 2$

= 512 sq. cm.

103. Given $a+ar=\frac{9}{2}$

$a(1+r)=\frac{9}{2}$ ...(*i*)

Again $6 = \frac{a}{1-r}$

$\therefore \quad a = 6(1 - r)$ ...(*ii*)

from (*i*) $6(1 - r^2) = \frac{9}{2}$

$-12r^2 = -3$

$r = \pm\frac{1}{2}$

$\therefore \quad a = 6\left(1-\frac{1}{2}\right) = 3$ or $6\left(1+\frac{1}{2}\right) = 9$

$a = 9$ or 3.

108. Total number of letters = 9

Number of vowels = 4

We take vowels as 1 letter

then total number of letters = 6

Number of words form = $6P_6 = \lfloor 6$

Vowels can arrange = $4P_4 = \lfloor 4$

$\therefore$ Total number of words can be formed =

$\lfloor 6 \times \lfloor 4 = 17280$

110. $\left\{\frac{1+2i}{2+i} \times \frac{2-i}{2-i}\right\}^2$

$= \left(\frac{2-i+4i-2i^2}{4-i^2}\right)^2$

$= \left(\frac{4+3i}{5}\right)^2 = \frac{1}{25}\{16 + 24i - 9\}$

$= \frac{1}{25}(7+24i)$

$= \frac{7}{25}+\frac{24}{25}i$

Hence its cojugate = $\frac{7}{25}-\frac{24}{25}i$

115. $\therefore \omega^3 = 1$ and $1 + \omega + \omega^2 = 0$

So that

$\omega^{10} + \omega^{-10} = \omega^{10} + \frac{1}{\omega^{10}}$

$= (\omega^3)^3.\omega + \frac{1}{(\omega^3)^3.\omega}$

$= \omega + \frac{1}{\omega} = \frac{\omega^2+1}{\omega}$

$= \frac{-\omega}{\omega} = -1$

116. Since roots of the equation are equal then $b^2 - 4ac = 0$

i.e., $4b^2(a + c)^2 - 4(a^2 + b^2)(b^2 + c^2) = 0$

$\Rightarrow b^2(a^2 + 2ac + c^2) - (a^2b^2 + a^2c^2 + b^4 + b^2c^2) = 0$

$\Rightarrow a^2b^2 + 2ab^2c + b^2c^2 - a^2b^2 - a^2c^2 - b^4 - b^2c^2 = 0$

$\Rightarrow 2ab^2c - a^2c^2 - b^4 = 0$

$\Rightarrow b^4 - 2ab^2c + a^2c^2 = 0$

$\Rightarrow (b^2 - ac)^2 = 0$

$\Rightarrow b^2 = ac.$

119. Since $|A| = 8 \neq 0$

$\therefore |\text{adj A}| = |A|^{n-1}$

where n is order of the matrix

$\therefore |\text{adj A}| = |8|^{3-1} = |8|^2 = 64.$

Previous Papers (Solved)

NATIONAL DEFENCE ACADEMY & NAVAL ACADEMY

NDA & NA – Entrance Exam, 2010 (I)

PAPER I : GENERAL ABILITY TEST

PART A : ENGLISH LANGUAGE

SPOTTING ERRORS

Directions (Qs. 1 to 8) :

(i) *In this section, a number of sentences are given. The sentences are underlined in three separate parts and each one is labelled A, B, and C. Read each sentence to find out whether there is an error in any underlined part. No sentence has more than one error. When you find an error in any one of the underlined parts A, B or C, indicate your response on the separate Answer Sheet at the appropriate space. You may feel that there is no error in a sentence. In that case, letter D will signify a 'No error' response.*

(ii) *You are to indicate only one response for each item in your Answer Sheet. (If you indicate more than one response, your answer will be considered wrong.) Errors may be in grammar, word usage or idioms. There may be a word missing or there may be a word which should be removed.*

(iii) *You are not required to correct the error. You are required* ***only*** *to indicate your response on the Answer Sheet.*

1. (A) Whenever a person lost anything/(B) the poor folk around/(C) are suspected./(D) No error.
2. (A) Still impressive is that/(B) we achieve this selective attention/(C) through our latent ability to lip-read./(D) No error.
3. (A) As I entered the famous gallery/(B) my attention was at once drawn/(C) to the large sculpture in the corner./(D) No error.
4. (A) Everyday before/(B) I start work for my livelihood/(C) I do my prayer./(D) No error.
5. (A) Pooja went to her friend's house at the appointed hour; but/(B) she was told/(C) that her friend left half an hour earlier./(D) No error.
6. (A) Rekha is/(B) enough old/(C) to get married./(D) No error.
7. (A) As far as I am concerned,/(B) I shall do everything/(C) possible to help you./(D) No error.
8. (A) The person in the seat of justice/(B) should be absolutely partial/(C) and not treat his nearest and dearest with favour./(D) No error.

FILL IN THE BLANKS

Directions (Qs. 9 to 16) : *Each of the following items is followed by four words or groups of words. Fill in the blanks with the appropriate word or group of words.*

9. Although I was .... of his plans, I encouraged him, because there was no one else who was willing to help.
   A. sceptical B. remorseful
   C. fearful D. excited
10. You have no business to .... pain on a weak and poor person.
   A. inflict B. put
   C. direct D. force
11. Her uncle died in a car accident. He was quite rich. She suddenly .... all her uncle's money.
   A. succeeded B. caught
   C. gave D. inherited
12. There was a major accident. The plane crashed. The pilot .... did not see the tower.
   A. likely B. probably
   C. scarcely D. hurriedly
13. The car we were travelling in .... a mile from home.
   A. broke off B. broke down
   C. broke into D. broke up
14. What are you .... in the kitchen cupboard?
   A. looking in B. looking on
   C. looking to D. looking for
15. I did not see the point of .... waiting for them, so I went home.
   A. hanging around B. hang on
   C. hang together D. hanging up
16. He lost confidence and .... of the deal at the last minute.
   A. backed out B. backed on
   C. backed down D. backed onto

SYNONYMS

Directions (Qs. 17 to 24): *Each of the following items consists of a sentence followed by four words or groups of words. Select the* **synonym** *of the word or group of words (occurring in the sentence in capital letters) as per the context.*

17. Teaching in universities is now considered a LUCRATIVE job.
A. Risky B. Profitable
C. Honourable D. Undignified

18. The policemen kept on questioning the criminal but failed to ELICIT the truth.
A. Evoke B. Wrest
C. Obtain D. Extort

19. Very few people are IMPERVIOUS to criticism.
A. Impenetrable B. Unaffected
C. Unstoppable D. Unmindful

20. The students took COPIOUS notes during the lecture delivered by the visiting professor.
A. Extensive B. Exhaustive
C. Bounteous D. Abounding

21. After weeks of FRENETIC activity, the ground was ready for the big match.
A. Strenuous B. Hurried
C. Excited D. Hectic

22. He had the AUDACITY to interrupt the Governor of the State while the latter was addressing a gathering of academicians.
A. Courage B. Authority
C. Foolishness D. Arrogance

23. He fell into an ABYSS of despair.
A. Well B. Deep pit
C. Sea D. Hollow

24. The engineer ROUGHED OUT his ideas on a piece of paper while he talked.
A. Shaped roughly
B. Rejected
C. Drew a quick plan
D. Described inaccurately

COMPREHENSION

Directions (Qs. 25 to 34): *In this section, you have* **two** *short passages. After each passage, you will find several questions based on the passage. First, read a passage and then answer the questions based on it. You are required to select your answers based on the contents of the passage and opinion of the author only.*

PASSAGE-I

When we talk of education in our present age, we think largely in terms of schools and colleges. The man who is well-to-do spends money in sending his son to foreign lands, in the belief that some wonderful process will take place there transforming a dull fellow into a genius. Yet, the products of expensive schools and universities often fail to make good. One the other hand, the poor man who has struggled against adversity often earns the highest honour. The fact is that the true background of early education is the home. The home, the influence of the mother, the inspiring examples that are held before the child at an age while he is impressionable, are the true groundwork of character.

25. According to the passage, who helps in our character-building?
A. A foreign university
B. A well-to-do man
C. Examples that inspire
D. A man who has earned honour.

26. The proper background of early education is
A. a school.
B. a college.
C. a religious institution.
D. the home.

27. From the passage, we get an impression that the highest honour is earned by
A. a man who has received education in a foreign country.
B. a man who has struggled against adversity.
C. a man who has seen prosperity alone.
D. the son of a prosperous man.

28. A well-to-do man sends his son to foreign lands
A. because it is the fashion of the day.
B. in the belief that his dull son will be transformed into a genius.
C. so that the son may learn the customs of those countries.
D. in order to make his son familiar with the persons and places of thos countries.

29. The expression "the products of expensive schools and universities often fail to make good" means
A. they fail to make a mark in life.
B. they fail to become intelligent.
C. they fail to earn proper living.
D. they do not earn good reputation.

PASSAGE – II

The functional declines of advancing age are depressing. The heart's ability to pump blood drops about one per cent: blood flow to arms and legs decreases by thirty to forty per cent in old age. The amount of air a person can exhale after a deep breath lessens and the chest wall stiffens with age. However, recent studies have shown that most of these age-associated declines can be delayed by exercise. Exercise lowers the resting heart-rate and increases the amount of blood pumped with each beat in older people. When stress is placed on bones through exercise, calcium content rises, with the result that resistance to fracture is improved.

30. Old age is generally a depressing period, because
A. old people worry more than others.
B. old people tend to regret their past.
C. various organs of the body function less efficiently.
D. old people do very little work.

31. The strength of bones can be increased by exercise, because it
A. increases the amount of blood pumped by the heart.
B. increases calcium content in bones.
C. increases the amount of air exhaled by a person.
D. lessens the stiffness of the chest wall.

32. The word 'exhale' means
A. breathe in. B. breathe out.
C. breathe slowly. D. breath fast.

33. Which one of the following statements is correct?
A. Exercise delays natural decay of old age
B. Old-age problems increase due to exercise
C. Exercise increases the heartbeat which is dangerous
D. Exercise creates stress which is harmful to bones.

34. The chest wall becomes stiff in old age, because
A. the heart's ability to pump blood to it drops about one per cent
B. the blood flow to various organs decreases
C. the resting heart-rate becomes high
D. the person's ability to exhale sufficient air lessens

ANTONYMS

Directions (Qs. 35 to 42): *Each of the following items consists of a sentence followed by four words. Select the* ***antonym*** *of the word (occurring in the sentence in capital letters) as per the context.*

35. He is man of EXTRAVAGANT habits.
A. Sensible B. Careful
C. Economical D. Balanced

36. They employ only DILIGENT workers.
A. Unskilled B. Lazy
C. Careless D. Idle

37. His success in the preliminary examination made him COMPLACENT.
A. Discontented B. Self-satisfied
C. Curious D. Militant

38. In this competition, he has become the VICTOR
A. Beaten B. Frustrated
C. Disappointed D. Vanquished

39. His behaviour at social gatherings is LAUDABLE.
A. Condemnable B. Impolite
C. Unpleasant D. Repulsive

40. The characters in this story are not all FICTITIOUS.
A. Common B. Factual
C. Real D. Genuine

41. The RELUCTANCE of the officer was obvious.
A. Eagerness B. Hesitation
C. Enjoyment D. Unwillingness

42. He is a GENEROUS man.
A. Stingy B. Uncharitable
C. Selfish D. Ignoble

ORDERING OF WORDS IN A SENTENCE

Directions (Qs. 43 to 50): *In the following items, some parts of the sentence have been jumbled up. You are required to rearrange these parts which are labelled P, Q, R and S to produce the correct sentence. Choose the proper sequence and mark in your Answers Sheet accordingly.*

43. We are doing
P : to the people
Q : to give relief
R : all we can
S : but more funds are needed
The correct sequence should be
A. P – Q – R – S B. R – Q – P – S
C. Q – P – R – S D. S – P – Q – R

44. The man
P : when he was
Q : in the office last evening
R : could not finish
S : all his work
The correct sequence should be
A. P – Q – R – S B. Q – R – S – P
C. R – Q – P – S D. R – S – P – Q

45. The people decided
P : they were going
Q : how much
R : to spend
S : on the construction of the school building
The correct sequence should be
A. Q – P – R – S B. P – Q – R – S
C. P – R – Q – S D. S – Q – P – R

46. The man said that
P : those workers
Q : would be given a raise
R : who did not go on
S : strike last month
The correct sequence should be
A. P – Q – R – S B. P – R – S – Q
C. Q – P – R – S D. R – S – P – Q

47. I think
P : the members
Q : are basically in agreement
R : of the group
S : on the following points.
The correct sequence should be
A. R – Q – P – S B. S – Q – R – P
C. P – R – Q – S D. P – Q – S – R

48. While it was true that
P : I had

Q : to invest in industry
R : some lands and houses
S : I did not have ready cash
The correct sequence should be
A. P – Q – R – S B. P – R – S – Q
C. S – Q – P – R D. Q – P – R – S

49. P : But your help
Q : to finish this work
R : it would not have been possible
S : in time
The correct sequence should be
A. P – R – Q – S
B. S – P – Q – R
C. R – P – Q – S
D. P – Q – R – S

50. The boy
P : in the competition
Q : who was wearing spectacles
R : won many prizes
S : held in our college
The correct sequence should be
A. P – Q – R – S
B. R – P – S – Q
C. Q – R– P – S
D. Q – P – S – R

PART B : GENERAL KNOWLEDGE

51. Which one of the following pairs does *not* have the same dimension?
A. Potential energy and kinetic energy
B. Density and specific gravity
C. Focal length and height
D. Gravitational force and frictional force

52. Which one of the following graphs represents uniform motion?

A. 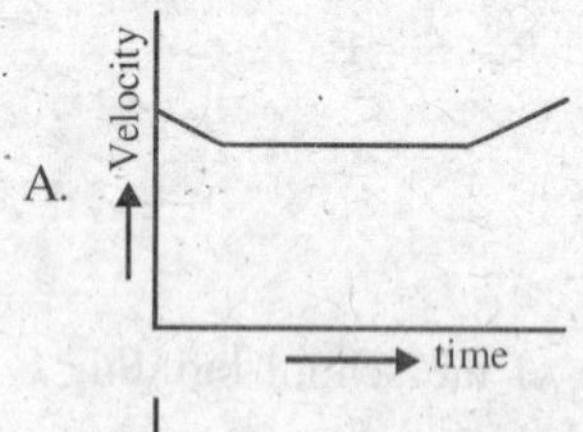

B. 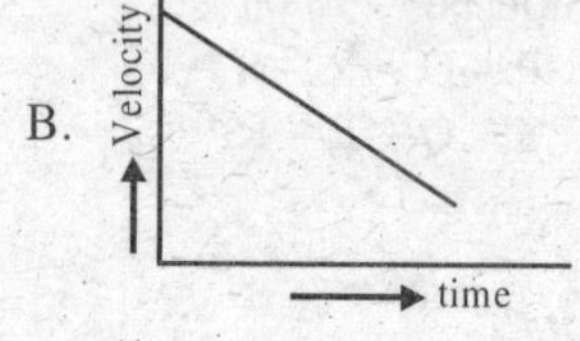

C. 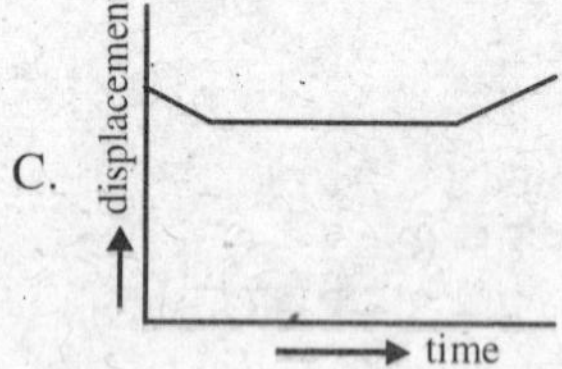

D. 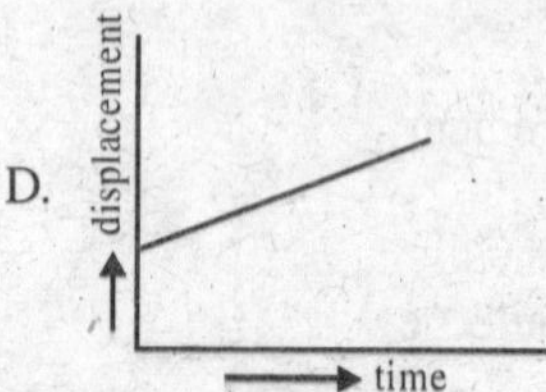

53. How many sixty watt (60 W) bulbs may be safely used in a 240-V supply with 4-ampere fuse?
A. 4 B. 8
C. 12 D. 16

54. A vessel contains oil (density ρ_1) over a liquid of density ρ_2; a homogeneous sphere of volume V floats with half of its volume immersed in the liquid and the other half in oil. The weight of the sphere is
A. $V(\rho_2 - \rho_1)/2$ B. $V(\rho_2 + \rho_1)\ g/2$
C. $V(\rho_2 - \rho_1)/2$ D. $V(\rho_2 - \rho_1)/2$

55. For a simple pendulum in simple harmonic motion, which of the following statements is/are correct?
1. The kinetic energy is maximum at the mean position.
2. The potential energy is maximum at the mean position.
3. Acceleration is maximum at the mean position.

Select the correct answer using the code given below:
Code:
A. 1 only B. 2 only
C. 1 and 3 D. 2 and 3

56. The metal atom, which is present in superphosphate, is
A. sodium (Na) B. potassium (K)
C. calcium (Ca) D. magnesium (Mg)

57. The best and the poorest conductors of heat are respectively
A. silver (Ag) and lead (Pb)
B. copper (Cu) and aluminium (Al)
C. silver (Ag) and gold (Au)
D. copper (Cu) and gold (Au)

58. Which one among the following metals is more reactive than hydrogen?
A. Mercury B. Copper
C. Silver D. Tin

59. The number of neutrons in ${}_{13}Al^{27}$ is
A. 40 B. 27
C. 14 D. 13

Directions. Qs. 60 to 63: *The following questions are based on the table given below. You are to match List-I with List-II, List-III and List-IV, and select the correct answer using the code given below:*

List-I (Element)	List-II (Property)	List-III (Property/Composition)	List-IV (Property/Composition)
(a) Diamond	1. Thermosetting Polymer	I. Rigid structure	i. Non conductor of heat
(b) Graphite	2. Monomer	II. Sheet-like structure	ii. Ester
(c) Rayon	3. Soft	III. Cellulose	iii. Conductor of heat
(d) Nylon	4. Viscose process	IV. Soft on heating	iv. Ether
(e) Carbon fibre	5. Synthetic fibre	V. Unreactive	v. Silk-like thread
(f) Polyvinyl chloride	6. High strength	VI. Corrosion	vi. Spacecraft
(g) Terylene	7. Thermoplastic	VII. Melts instead of burning	vii. Chlorine atom replaces hydrogen atom
(h) Bakelite	8. Polyester fibre	VIII. Ethylene glycol	viii. Cross-linked
	9. Hardest Natural substance	IX. Phenol and formaldehyde	ix. Terephthalic acid

60.

	List-I	List-II	List-III	List-IV
A.	(a)	9	I	i
B.	(b)	3	IV	iv
C.	(a)	9	I	ii
D.	(b)	3	II	v

61.

	List-I	List-II	List-III	List-IV
A.	(c)	4	II	i
B.	(d)	5	VII	v
C.	(c)	6	V	vi
D.	(d)	5	II	iv

62.

	List-I	List-II	List-III	List-IV
A.	(e)	6	I	vi
B.	(f)	7	IV	ix
C.	(e)	6	VI	vi
D.	(f)	3	VI	v

63.

	List-I	List-II	List-III	List-IV
A.	(g)	8	I	ix
B.	(h)	4	IV	iii
C.	(g)	8	VIII	ix
D.	(h)	1	VI	viii

64. Which one of the following is a transition metal?
A. Aluminium (Al)
B. Manganese (Mn)
C. Magnesium (Mg)
D. Calcium (Ca)

65. Which one of the following gases, present in the air near the surface of the Earth, has maximum concentration?
A. Oxygen (O_2) B. Hydrogen (H_2)
C. Nitrogen (N_2) D. Methane (CH_4)

66. Which one of the following elements will replace hydrogen from acids to form salts?
A. Sulphur (S) B. Silicon (Si)
C. Zinc (Zn) D. Phosphorus (P)

67. Which of the following represent a chemical change?
1. Magnetisation of iron
2. Condensation of liquid
3. Burning of fuel
4. Rusting of iron

Select the correct answer using the code given below:
Code:
A. 1 and 2 B. 2 and 3
C. 3 and 4 D. 1 and 4

68. Which one among the following is the correct order of reactivity of the elements?
A. Cu > Mg > Zn > Na
B. Na > Zn > Mg > Cu
C. Cu > Zn > Mg > Na
D. Na > Mg > Zn > Cu

69. Vinegar is produced from
A. ethanoic acid B. valeric acid
C. methanoic acid D. butanoic acid

70. Match List-I with List-II and select the correct answer using the code given below the Lists:

List-I	List-II
(a) Ozone gas	1. Combines with haemoglobin
(b) Nitrous oxide	2. Ultraviolet radiation
(c) Carbon dioxide	3. Component of air in small quantity
(d) Carbon monoxide	4. Visible radiation
	5. Infrared radiation

Code:

	(a)	(b)	(c)	(d)
A.	1	4	5	3
B.	2	3	5	1
C.	1	4	3	2
D.	2	5	3	1

71. Iron ore from Kudremukh is most likely to be exported through
A. Goa B. Kochi
C. Mangalore D. Ennore

72. Match List-I with List-II and select the correct answer using the code given below the Lists:

List-I (Type of vegetation)	List-II (State)
(a) Mangrove	1. Madhya Pradesh
(b) Scrub	2. Karnataka
(c) Teak	3. Rajasthan
(d) Coniferous	4. Arunachal Pradesh

Code:

	(a)	(b)	(c)	(d)
A.	4	1	3	2
B.	2	1	3	4
C.	4	3	1	2
D.	2	3	1	4

73. Arrange the following States on the basis of ascending dates of the onset of monsoon:

1. Uttar Pradesh 2. West Bengal
3. Kerala 4. Rajasthan

Select the correct answer using the code given below:

Code:

A. 2 - 3 - 1 - 4 B. 3 - 2 - 1 - 4
C. 3 - 1 - 2 - 4 D. 1 - 2 - 3 - 4

74. Which of the following are west following rivers?

1. Krishna 2. Narmada
3. Mahanadi 4. Sabarmati

Select the correct answer using the code given below:

A. 2 and 4 B. 1 and 3
C. 1 and 4 D. 2 and 3

75. Whcih of the following statements are correct?

1. In a cyclone, the area of low pressure is at the centre surrounded by the areas of high pressure.
2. In a cyclone, the areas of low pressure surround the area of high pressure.
3. In an anti-cyclone, the area of high pressure is surrounded by the areas of low pressure.
4. In an anti-cyclone, the area of low pressure is surrounded by the areas of high pressure.

Select the correct answer using the code given below:

Code

A. 1 and 2 B. 1 and 3
C. 1 and 4 D. 2 and 4

76. Which part of brain controls fine movement, maintains balance and equilibrium of the body and muscle tone in a human being?

A. Cerebrum B. Thalamus
C. Cerebellum D. Hypothalamus

77. Leishmania, the causative agent of kala-azar, multiplies asexually by

A. budding B. binary fission
C. multiple fission D. sporogony

78. Administering a vaccine provides protection by inducing synthesis of antibodies (proteins) specific to the vaccine. The cell in the body responsible for the production of antibodies is

A. granulocyte
B. lymphocyte
C. erythrocyte (red blood cell)
D. platelet

79. Biological catalysts in living organisms are known as

A. hormones B. vitamins
C. steroids D. enzymes

80. To which one of the following types of organism do mushrooms belong?

A. Algae B. Ferns
C. Fungi D. Lichens

81. Among the following elements, which one is essential for the transmission of impulses in the nerve fibre?

A. Calcium B. Iron
C. Sodium D. Zinc

82. Cure to spinal injury is likely to emerge from

A. gene therapy B. steam cell therapy
C. xenograft D. transfusion

83. Food wrapped in newspaper is likely to get contaminated with

A. lead B. aluminium
C. iron D. magnesium

84. Which one among the following produces seeds but not flowers?

A. Cashew nut B. Coffee
C. Groundnut D. Pine

85. Which among the following is *not* a true fruit?

A. Apple B. Date
C. Grape D. Plum

Directions. (Qs. 86 to 92): *The questions consist of two statements, Statement I and Statement II. You are to examine these two statements carefully and select the answers to these items using the code given below:*

Code:

A. Both the statements are individually true and Statement II is the correct explanation of Statement I.
B. Both the statements are individually true but Statement II is ***not*** the correct explanation of Statement I.
C. Statement I is true but Statement II is false.
D. Statement I is false but Statement II is true.

86. Statement I : Coalition in India is always a post-poll phenomenon.

Statement II : The United Progressive Alliance was formed after the Lok Sabha Election of 2004.

87. Statement I : The Constitution of India is a liberal Constitution.

Statement II : It provides Fundamental Rights to individuals.

88. Statement I : In order to create linguistic provinces in India the Congress Party constituted Motilal Nehru Committee in 1928.

Statement II : The Motilal Nehru Committee suggested creation of linguistic provinces in India.

89. Statement I : During the day, winds blow from sea to land.

Statement II : The land gets more heated than the surrounding sea, hence lower pressure develops over land as compared to sea.

90. Statement I : Winds are deflected to their right in the northern hemisphere and to their left in the southern hemisphere.

Statement II : The Earth's axis is inclined.

91. Statement I : Pressure gradients determine the velocity of winds.

Statement II : When isobars (lines of equal atmospheric pressure) are closely spaced, the wind velocity would be gentle.

92. Statement I : Temperatures of countries like United Kingdom, Norway, the Netherlands and Denmark are higher as compared to places located on similar latitudes during the winter.

Statement II : United Kingdom, Norway, the Netherlands and Denmark are located on the coast.

93. Consider the following statement and identify with the help of the code given below the Viceroy who made the statement and when:

In my belief, Congress is tottering to its fall and one of my great ambitions while in India is to assist it to a peaceful demise.

Code:

A. Lord Curzon, in a letter to Secretary of States in 1900.
B. Lord Curzon, while announcing the partition of Bengal.
C. Lord Dufferin, during the fare
D. Lord Minto, while addressing the Muslim delegation which met him at Shimla in 1906.

94. The Copenhagen Summit for Climate Change, 2009 saw

A. an agreement among the participants over CO_2 emission.
B. unanimity of views among the developed and BASIC bloc of countries.
C. rise of African countries as a bloc.
D. acceptance of the US as a leader to attain the objective of the Copenhagen Summit.

95. Consider the following paragraph and identify with the help of the code given below the writer referred to therein:

She is the winner of the Sahitya Akademi Award, the Jnanpith Award and is also India's first Principal Prince Claus laureate. One of the most celebrated writers of contemporary Indian literature, she is noted for her novels which include, *The Moth-Eaten Howdah of the Tusker, Pages Stained with Blood* and *The Man from Chinnamasta.*

Code:

A. Anita Desai B. Indira Goswami
C. Mahasweta Devi D. Chitra Mudgal

96. Consider the following paragraph and identify with the help of the code given below the Church referred to therein:

Considered as one of the best examples of baroque architecture in India, this World Heritage Monument is dedicated to Infant Jesus. It houses the sacred relics of St. Francis Xavier, the patron saint, who died in 1552.

Code:

A. Santa Cruz Basilica
B. St. Francis Church
C. Church of the Holy Cross
D. Basilica of Bom Jesus

97. Ms. Reena Kaushal Dhrmshaktu is the first Indian woman

A. to reach Antarctica.
B. pilot inducted in Indian Air Force.
C. to ski to the South Pole.
D. to win the gold medal in Asian Boxing Championship.

98. Which one among the following is the latest milestone of Doordarshan, the public broadcaster of India?

A. Launch of enrichment/cultural channel-DD Bharati.
B. Launch of 24 hours news channel-DD News.
C. Launch of sports channel-DD Sports.
D. Formation of Prasar Bharati (Broadcasting Corporation of India).

99. START (Strategic Arms Reduction Treaty) is a treaty between/among

A. China and Japan.
B. USA and Russia.
C. USA and European Union.
D. China, India, USA and Russia.

100. Which one of the following is ***not*** a member of BASIC bloc of countries?

A. South Africa B. China
C. India D. Australia

101. 'Pitch' is a characteristic of sound that depends upon its

A. intensity B. frequency
C. quality D. None of these

102. The ratio of the focal length of the objective to the focal length of the eyepiece is greater than one for

A. a microscope
B. a telescope
C. both microscope and telescope
D. neither microscope nor telescope

103. The effective resistance of three equal resistances, each of resistance r, connected in parallel, is

A. $3/r$ B. $r/3$
C. $3r$ D. r^3

104. A fan produces a feeling of comfort during hot weather, because

A. our body radiates more heat in air.
B. fan supplies cool air.
C. conductivity of air increases.
D. our perspiration evaporates rapidly.

105. Which one of the following statements is *correct*?
A. Only electrons reside inside the nucleus of an atom
B. Both electrons and protons reside inside the nucleus of an atom
C. Only neutrons reside inside the nucleus of an atom
D. Both protons and neutrons can reside inside the nucleus of an atom.

106. The ratio of velocity of X-rays to that of gamma rays
A. is < 1
B. is > 1
C. is 1
D. depends upon the ratio of their frequencies.

107. Which one of the following pairs of rays is electromagnetic in nature?
A. Beta rays and gamma rays
B. Cathode rays and X-rays
C. Alpha rays and X-rays
D. X-rays and gamma rays.

108. The magnetic lines of force due to a bar magnet
A. intersect inside the body of the magnet.
B. intersect at neutral points only.
C. intersect only at north and south poles.
D. cannot intersect at all.

109. The specific resistance of a conducting wire depends upon
A. length of the wire, area of cross-section of the wire and material of the wire.
B. length of the wire and area of cross-section of the wire but not on the material of the wire.
C. material of the wire only but neither on the length of the wire nor on the area of cross-section of the wire.
D. length of the wire only but neither on the area of cross-section of the wire nor on the material of the wire.

110. When X-rays are produced
A. heat is generated at the target.
B. heat is absorbed at the target.
C. the temperature of the target remains constant.
D. brilliant light is seen at the target.

111. Which one of the statements given below is ***not*** correct?
A. A vertical plane passing through the axis of a freely suspended magnet is called the magnetic meridian
B. A vertical plane passing through the axis of rotation of the Earth is called the geographical meridian.
C. The degree to which the magnetic field can penetrate a medium is known as the relative permeability of the medium.
D. The relative permeability is not a dimensionless quantity.

112. If an object is placed at the centre of curvature of a concave mirror, the position of the image is
A. at the principal focus.
B. between the principal focus and the centre of curvature.
C. at the centre of curvature.
D. beyond the centre of curvature.

113. The radius of curvature of a plane mirror
A. is zero.
B. is infinity.
C. can be anywhere between zero and infinity.
D. None of these.

114. A coin in a beaker filled with water appears raised. This phenomenon occurs because of the property of
A. reflection of light.
B. refraction of light.
C. total internal reflection of light.
D. interference of light.

115. A ray of light falls on a transparent glass plate. A part of it is reflected and a part is refracted. The reflected and refracted rays can be perpendicular to each other for
A. angle of incidence equal to 90°.
B. angle of incidence equal to zero.
C. only one angle of incidence.
D. more than one angle of incidence.

116. A man with a dark skin, in comparison with a man with a white skin, will experience
A. less heat and less cold.
B. less heat and more cold.
C. more heat and less cold.
D. more heat and more cold.

117. Which one among the following denotes the smallest temperature?
A. 1° on the Celsius scale
B. 1° on the Kelvin scale
C. 1° on the Fahrenheit scale
D. 1° on the Reaumur scale.

118. A particle oscillates in one dimension about the equilibrium position subject to a force $F_x(x)$ that has an associated potential energy $U(x)$. If k is the force constant, which one of the following relations is true?
A. $F_x(x) = -kx^2$ B. $F_x(x) = -kx$
C. $U(x) = \frac{1}{2}kx$ D. $U(x) = \frac{1}{2}k^2x$

119. When a body moves with simple harmonic motion, then the phase difference between the velocity and the acceleration is
A. 0° B. 90°
C. 180° D. 270°

120. A body is thrown vertically upwards and then falls back on the ground. Its potential energy is maximum
A. on the ground.
B. at the maximum height.
C. during the return journey.
D. both on the ground and at the maximum height.

121. Mahatma Gandhi and Rabindranath Tagore did *not* define India as a 'nation', because they were
A. appreciative of cultural divisiveness.
B. opposed to the idea of homogeneity.
C. supportive of 'oneness'.
D. critical of hegemonic culture.

122. Socialism refers to
A. state-controlled economy.
B. liquidation of the bourgeoisie.
C. removal of peasantry from administration.
D. establishment of military dictatorship.

123. According to Karl Marx, attainment of communism is possible only after
A. resolution of tension between the leader and led.
B. completion of permanent revolution.
C. emergence of exploitation-free society.
D. disappearance of difference between urban and rural areas.

124. India's 'Look East Policy'
1. was articulated during the regin of H.D. Deve Gowda as India's Prime Minister.
2. is directed towards South-East Asian countries.
3. is about controlling terrorism.
4. seeks to develop a bond among various countries on the basis of economic cooperation.

Select the correct answer using the code given below:
Code:
A. 1 and 2 B. 2 and 3
C. 2 and 4 D. 3 and 4

125. Cloudy nights are warmer than clear nights because of
A. greenhouse effect.
B. depletion of ozone layer.
C. insolation.
D. terrestrial radiation.

126. Match List-I with List-II and select the correct answer using the code given below the Lists:

List-I (Landform)	***List-II (Agent of erosion/ deposition)***
(*a*) Inselbergs	1. River
(*b*) Stalagmite	2. Glacier
(*c*) Delta	3. Underground water
(*d*) Moraines	4. Wind

Code:

	(*a*)	(*b*)	(*c*)	(*d*)
A.	4	2	1	3
B.	3	1	2	4
C.	1	2	3	4
D.	4	3	1	2

127. If it is 12 noon in a city located on 90° W longitude, what would be the time in a city located on 105° W longitude?
A. 13:00 hours B. 12:30 hours
C. 11:30 hours D. 11:00 hours

128. As we proceed from equator to poles, the daily range of temperature tends to
A. decrease B. increase
C. be constant D. fluctuate

129. Doldrums are characterised by
A. uniform low pressure
B. uniform high pressure
C. high wind velocity
D. low humidity

130. Glaciated regions are associated with
A. V-shaped valley B. U-shaped valley
C. sand dunes D. stalactites

131. Which one of the following is generally found in sedimentary rocks?
A. Basalt B. Silica
C. Shale D. Magnesium

132. The interval between two high tides is approximately
A. 4 hours B. 6 hours
C. 12 hours D. 24 hours

133. Xerophytes thrive in
A. hot and arid condition
B. cool and wet condition
C. hot and wet condition
D. cool and arid condition

134. Biodiversity is highest in
A. Tundra zone B. Prairie zone
C. Torrid zone D. Tropic zone

135. Which of the following statements is/are *correct*?
1. Lunar eclipse takes place when the Earth comes directly between the Sun and the Moon.
2. Solar eclipse happens when the Moon comes directly between the Sun and the Earth.
3. Lunar eclipse takes place when the Sun comes directly between the Earth and the Moon.
4. Solar eclipse happens when the Earth comes directly between the Sun and Moon.

Select the correct answer using the code given below:
Code:
A. 1, 2 and 3 B. 3 and 4
C. 1 and 2 only D. 2 only

136. Which of the following is/are instance(s) of violation of human rights?
1. A person was detained by the security forces while going for casting vote in Parliamentary Election.
2. A civilian was killed by the army while undertaking combing operation.

Select the correct answer using the code given below:
Code:
A. 1 only B. 2 only
C. Both 1 and 2 D. Neither 1 nor 2

137. Consider the following paragraph about one of the prominent personalities of India and identify him/her using the code given below:

One of the founder members of the Progressive Artists Group, he/she painted several important series of paintings like the Mahabharata and Ramayana, Christ and the Lamb, Peace Doves, Women with Roosters and Mother Teresa. He/She made a symbolic film through the eyes of a Painter, which fetched him/her Golden Bear in Berlin Film Festival.

Code:

A. Dhiraj Chaudhary B. Satish Gujral
C. M.F. Husain D. Amrita Shergil

138. *Operation Vajraprabar* is the joint counter-terrorism exercise between Indian Army and

A. US Army B. Chinese Army
C. Russian Army D. Nepalese Army

139. The notion of *saptanga* that was introduced in *Arthashastra* includes

A. kings, territory, administration and treasury.
B. music, dance, ragas and wrestling.
C. ministers, civil servants, subalterns and those involved in espionage.
D. aristocrats acharyas, traders and monks.

140. The immediate cause of the revival of human rights in post-Second World War period was

A. massive loss of lives in the War.
B. nuclear bombing of Hiroshima and Nagasaki by the Americans.
C. growing knowledge of brutal atrocities of Nazis over the Jews.
D. emergence of Soviet Union as a Superpower.

141. Which one of the following with regard to the Poona Pact, 1932 is ***not*** correct?

A. Adequate representation of depressed sections in government jobs
B. Reservation of seats for the depressed classes in the provincial legislature
C. Acceptance of joint electorate system
D. Reservation of seats for the depressed classes in the central legislature.

142. The Government of India Act, 1935 was based on

A. the principle of federation and parliamentary system
B. the principle of secession of the British Indian provinces
C. acceptance of independence of India
D. acceptance of the idea of a constituent assembly to draft a constitution.

143. Which of the following statements with regard to freedom struggle are correct? If

1. The British rule could prevail in India on the basis of the consent or acquiescence of many sections of Indian people.
2. The social basis of the colonial regime was among the Zamindars and upper classes.
3. The Indian National Army forced the British to withdraw from India.
4. The *Hindu Mahasabha* supported the partition of India.

Select the correct answer using the code given below:

Code:

A. 1 and 2 only
B. 2 and 3 only
C. 3 and 4 only
D. 1, 2, 3 and 4

144. Which one of the following statements with regard to 'Direct Action Day' is correct?

A. Hasan Suhrawardy presided over the 'Direct Action Day'
B. 'Direct Action' took place in Delhi
C. 'Direct Action Day' led to the Bihar riot
D. 'Direct Action' was endorsed by the Congress Party.

145. Planning in India drew on

A. the New Economic Programme of Lenin.
B. the Fabian Socialism of Sidney and Beatrice Webb.
C. the British welfare mechanism.
D. new democratic development packages.

146. The Haripura Congress (1938) remains a milestone in Indian freedom struggle, because

A. it declared war on the British Empire.
B. it anointed Jawaharlal Nehru as the future Prime Minister of India.
C. of the introduction of the idea of a planning commission.
D. of the acceptance of the Government of India Act, 1935 by the Congress.

147. The Constitution (93rd Amendment) Act deals with

A. local self-government.
B. extension of reservation in educational institutions.
C. basic structure of the Constitution of India.
D. appointment of judges in the Supreme Court of India.

148. Which of the following statements is/are ***not*** violative of the principle of federalism?

1. The President of India takes over administration of provinces under the emergency provisions.
2. The Parliament of India has exclusive power to make any law with respect to any matter not enumerated in the Concurrent List or State List.
3. The distribution of powers between the Union and Provinces is done through three different lists enumerated in the Constitution of India.

Select the correct answer using the code given below:

Code:

A. 1 and 2 B. 2 and 3
C. 3 only D. 1 and 3

149. Public Interest Litigation (PIL) may be linked with

A. judicial review.
B. judicial activism.
C. judicial intervention.
D. judicial sanctity.

150. In *Hind Swaraj*, Mahatma Gandhi was critical of railways, because they are
1. carriers of plague germs
2. instruments for frequency of famines
3. responsible for creating class division in the society
4. accident-prone

Select the correct answer using the code given below:
Code:
A. 1, 2 and 3 B. 1 and 2 only
C. 2 and 3 only D. 1 and 4

PAPER II : MATHEMATICS

1. The geometric mean of three numbers was computed as 6. It was subsequently found that, in this computation, a number 8 was wrongly read as 12. What is the correct geometric mean?
A. 4 B. $\sqrt[3]{5}$
C. $2\sqrt[3]{18}$ D. None of these

2. Let $A = \begin{bmatrix} 1 & 2 \\ 3 & 4 \end{bmatrix} = [a_{ij}]$, where $i, j, = 1, 2$. If its inverse matrix is $[b_{ij}]$, what is b_{22}?
A. –2 B. 1
C. $\frac{3}{2}$ D. $-\frac{1}{2}$

3. The angle A lies in the third quadrant and it satisfies the equation $4(\sin^2 x + \cos x) = 1$. What is the measure of the angle A?
A. 225° B. 240°
C. 210° D. None of these

4. What is the area enclosed between the curves $y^2 = 12x$ and the lines $x = 0$ and $y = 6$?
A. 2 square units B. 4 square units
C. 6 square units D. 8 square units

5. In triangle ABC, BC = $\sqrt{39}$, AC = 5 and AB = 7. What is the measure of the angle A?
A. $\frac{\pi}{4}$ B. $\frac{\pi}{3}$
C. $\frac{\pi}{2}$ D. $\frac{\pi}{6}$

6. What is the modulus of $\frac{1+2i}{1-(1-i)^2}$?
A. 1 B. $\sqrt{5}$
C. $\sqrt{3}$ D. 5

7. If the line through the points A $(k, 1, -1)$ and B$(2k, 0, 2)$ is perpendicular to the line through the points B and C$(2+2k, k, 1)$, then what is the value of k?
A. –1 B. 1
C. –3 D. 3

8. What is $\int \frac{1}{1+e^x} dx$ equal to?
A. $x - \ln x + c$ B. $x - \ln(\tan x) + c$
C. $x - \ln(1 + e^x) + c$ D. $\ln(1 + e^x) + c$
where c is constant of integration.

9. The function $f(x) = x \operatorname{cosec} x$ is
A. continuous for all values of x
B. discontinuous everywhere
C. continuous for all x except at $x = n\pi$, where n is an integer.
D. discontinuous for all x except at $x = n\pi/2$, where n is an integer.

10. What is the solution of the differential equation $a\left(x\frac{dy}{dx} + 2y\right) = xy\frac{dy}{dx}$?
A. $x^2 = kye^{\frac{y}{a}}$ B. $yx^2 = kye^{\frac{y}{a}}$
C. $y^2x^2 = kye^{\frac{y^2}{a}}$ D. None of these

11. A vector $\vec{b}$ is collinear with the vector $\vec{a} = (2, 1, -1)$ and satisfies the condition $\vec{a}.\vec{b} = 3$. What is $\vec{b}$ equal to?
A. (1, 1/2, –1/2) B. (2/3, 1/3, –1/3)
C. (1/2, 1/4, –1/4) D. (1, 1, 0)

12. What is the least positive integer n for which $\left(\frac{1+i}{1-i}\right)^n = 1$?
A. 16 B. 12
C. 8 D. 4

13. The vector $\vec{a} = x\hat{i} + y\hat{i} + z\hat{k}, \vec{b} = \hat{k}, \vec{c}$ are such that they form a right-handed system. What is $\vec{c}$ equal to?
A. $\hat{j}$ B. $y\hat{j} - x\hat{k}$
C. $y\hat{i} - x\hat{j}$ D. $x\hat{i} - y\hat{j}$

14. If $x = t^2$, $y = t^3$, then what is $\frac{d^2y}{dx^2}$ equal to?
A. 1 B. $\frac{3}{2t}$
C. $\frac{3}{4t}$ D. $\frac{3}{2}$

15. What is $\int_{-\frac{\pi}{4}}^{\frac{\pi}{4}} \tan^3 x\, dx$ equal to?
A. $\sqrt{3}$ B. $\frac{1}{3}$
C. $\frac{1}{2}$ D. 0

16. What is the number of ways of arranging the letters of the word 'BANANA' so that no two N's appear together?
A. 40 B. 60
C. 80 D. 100

17. Consider the equation $(x - p)(x - 6) + 1 = 0$ having integer coefficients. If the equation has integral roots, then what values can p have?
A. 4 or 8 B. 5 or 10
C. 6 or 12 D. 3 or 6

18. What is the equivalent binary number of the decimal number 13.625?
A. 1101.111 B. 1111.101
C. 1101.101 D. 1111.111

19. What is the value of

$$\left(\frac{i+\sqrt{3}}{-i+\sqrt{3}}\right)^{200}+\left(\frac{i-\sqrt{3}}{i+\sqrt{3}}\right)+1?$$

A. –1 B. 0
C. 1 D. 2

20. The order of a set A is 3 and that of a set B is 2. What is the number of relations from A to B?
A. 4 B. 6
C. 32 D. 64

21. What is the value of $\dfrac{\log_{\sqrt{\alpha\beta}}(H)}{\log_{\sqrt{\alpha\beta\gamma}}(H)}$?
A. $\log_{\alpha\beta}(\alpha)$ B. $\log_{\alpha\beta\gamma}(\alpha\beta)$
C. $\log_{\alpha\beta}(\alpha\beta\gamma)$ D. $\log_{\alpha\beta}(\beta)$

22. The 59th term of an AP is 449 and the 449th term is 59. Which term is equal to 0 (zero)?
A. 501th term B. 502nd term
C. 508th term D. 509th term

23. For a set A, consider the following statements:
I. $A \cup P(A) = P(A)$
II. $\{A\} \cap P(A) = (A)$
III. $P(A) - \{A\} = P(A)$
where P denotes the power set.
Which of the statements given above is/are *correct*?
A. I only B. II only
C. III only D. I, II and III

24. If the AM and HM of two numbers are 27 and 12 respectively, then what is their GM equal to?
A. 12 B. 18
C. 24 D. 27

25. If $\tan A = \dfrac{1}{2}$ and $\tan B = \dfrac{1}{3}$, then what is the value of $(A + B)$?
A. 0 B. $\dfrac{\pi}{4}$
C. $\dfrac{\pi}{2}$ D. π

26. If (4, 0) and (–4, 0) are the foci of an ellipse and the semi-minor axis is 3; then the ellipse passes through which one of the following points?
A. (2, 0) B. (0, 5)
C. (0, 0) D. (5, 0)

27. Under what condition do the planes $bx - ay = n$, $cy - bz = l$, $az - cx = m$ intersect in a line?
A. $a + b + c = 0$ B. $a = b = c$
C. $al + bm + cn = 0$ D. $l + m + n = 0$

28. What is the maximum point on the curve $x = e^x y$?
A. $(1, e)$ B. $(1, e^{-1})$
C. $(e, 1)$ D. $(e^{-1}, 1)$

29. The function $f(x) = e^x$, $x \in R$ is
A. Onto but not one-one
B. One-one onto
C. One-one but not onto
D. Neither one-one nor onto

30. If $y = \sin^{-1}\left(\dfrac{4x}{1+4x^2}\right)$, then what is $\dfrac{dy}{dx}$ equal to?
A. $\dfrac{1}{1+4x^2}$ B. $-\dfrac{1}{1+4x^2}$
C. $\dfrac{4}{1+4x^2}$ D. $\dfrac{4x}{1+4x^2}$

31. If $\begin{vmatrix} a & b & c \\ l & m & n \\ p & q & r \end{vmatrix} = 2$, then what is the value of the determinant $\begin{vmatrix} 6a & 3b & 15c \\ 2l & m & 5n \\ 2p & q & 5r \end{vmatrix}$?
A. 10 B. 20
C. 40 D. 60

32. Let X be the set of all graduates in India. Elements x and y in X are said to be related if they are graduates of the same university.
Which one of the following statements is *correct*?
A. Relation is symmetric and transitive only
B. Relation is reflexive and transitive only
C. Relation is reflexive, and symmetric only
D. Relation is reflexive, symmetric and transitive

33. If $x^2 + y^2 = 1$, then what is $\dfrac{1+x+iy}{1+x-iy}$ equal to?
A. $x - iy$ B. $x + iy$
C. $2x$ D. $-2iy$

34. Consider the following statements:
I. For any three vectors $\vec{a}, \vec{b}, \vec{c}$;

$$\vec{a}.\left[\left(\vec{b}+\vec{c}\right)\times\left(\vec{a}+\vec{b}+\vec{c}\right)\right]=0$$

II. For any three coplanar unit vectors $\vec{d}, \vec{e}, \vec{f}; \left(\vec{d} \times \vec{e}\right).\vec{f} = 1$

Which of the statements given above is/are correct?

A. I only B. II only
C. Both I and II D. Neither I nor II

Directions (35-37) : *Consider the following lists:*

Each item under List-I is associated with one or more items under List-II.

List-I (Function)	***List-II (Property)***
(*a*) sin *x*	1. Periodic function
(*b*) cos *x*	2. Non-periodic function
(*c*) tan *x*	3. Continuous at every point on $(-\infty, \infty)$
	4. Discontinuous function
	5. Differentiable at every point on $(-\infty, \infty)$
	6. Not differentiable at every point on $(-\infty, \infty)$
	7. has period π
	8. has period 2π
	9. increases on $(0, \pi/2)$
	10. decreases on $(\pi/2, \pi)$
	11. increases on $(\pi/2, \pi)$
	12. decreases on on $(\pi/2, \pi)$

35. (*a*) is associated with

A. 1, 3, 5, 8, 9, 12 B. 2, 4, 6, 8, 10, 11
C. 1, 3, 5, 7, 10, 11 D. None of the above

36. (*b*) is associated with

A. 2, 3, 5, 8, 9, 12 B. 1, 3, 5, 8, 10, 12
C. 1, 3, 5, 8, 9, 12 D. None of the above

37. (*c*) is associated with

A. 1, 4, 6, 7, 9, 11 B. 2, 4, 6, 8, 9
C. 1, 4, 6, 7, 9 D. None of the above

38. If *p* and *q* are positive integers, then which one of the following equations has $p - \sqrt{q}$ as one of its roots?

A. $x^2 - 2px - (p^2 - q) = 0$
B. $x^2 - 2px + (p^2 - q) = 0$
C. $x^2 + 2px - (p^2 - q) = 0$
D. $x^2 + 2px + (p^2 - q) = 0$

39. Given two squares of sides *x* and *y* such that $y = x + x^2$. What is the rate of change of area of the second square with respect to the area of the first square?

A. $1 + 3x + 2x^2$ B. $1 + 2x + 3x^2$
C. $1 - 2x + 3x^2$ D. $1 - 2x - 3x^2$

40. The planes $px + 2y + 2z - 3 = 0$ and $2x - y + z + 2 = 0$ intersect at an angle $\pi/4$. What is the value of p^2?

A. 24 B. 12
C. 6 D. 3

41. The growth of a quantity $N(t)$ at any instant *t* is given by $\frac{dN(t)}{dt} = \alpha N(t)$. Given that $N(t) = ce^{kj}$, *c* is a constant, what is the value of α?

A. *c* B. *k*
C. $c + k$ D. $c - k$

42. A circle is drawn with the two foci of an ellipse $\frac{x^2}{a^2} + \frac{y^2}{b^2} = 1$ at the end of the diameter. What is the equation to the circle?

A. $x^2 + y^2 = a^2 + b^2$
B. $x^2 + y^2 = a^2 - b^2$
C. $x^2 + y^2 = 2(a^2 + b^2)$
D. $x^2 + y^2 = 2(a^2 - b^2)$

43. What is the image of the point (1, 2) on the line $3x + 4y - 1 = 0$

A. $\left(-\frac{7}{5}, -\frac{6}{5}\right)$ B. $\left(\frac{7}{8}, \frac{1}{2}\right)$

C. $\left(\frac{7}{8}, -\frac{1}{2}\right)$ D. $\left(-\frac{7}{5}, -\frac{1}{2}\right)$

44. If the product of the roots of he equation $x^2 - 5x + k = 15$ is -3, then what is the value of *k*?

A. 12 B. 15
C. 16 D. 18

45. Consider the following statements:

I. Every function has a primitive.
II. A primitive of a function is unique.

Which of the statements given above is/are correct?

A. I only B. II only
C. Both I and II D. Neither I nor II

46. Let O (0, 0, 0), P (3, 4, 5), Q (*m*, *n*, *r*) and R (1, 1, 1) be the vertices of a parallelogram taken in order. What is the value of $m + n + r$?

A. 6 B. 12
C. 15 D. None of these

47. What is the solution of the differential equation $3\, e^x \tan y\, dx + (1 + e^x) \sec 2y\, dy = 0$?

A. $(1 + e^x) \tan y = c$ B. $(1 + e^x)^3 \tan y = c$
C. $(1 + e^x)^2 \tan y = c$ D. $(1 + e^x) \sec^2 y = c$

where *c* is a constant of integration.

48. What is the locus of points, the difference of whose distances from two points being constant?

A. Pair of straight lines
B. An ellipse
C. A hyperbola
D. A parabola

49. What is the differential equation for $y^2 = 4a(x-a)$?

A. $yy' - 2xyy' + y^2 = 0$
B. $yy'\ (yy' + 2x) + y^2 = 0$
C. $yy'\ (yy' - 2x) + y^2 = 0$
D. $yy' - 2xyy' + y = 0$

50. If the angle between the vector $\vec{a}$ and $\vec{b}$ is $\frac{\pi}{3}$, what is the angle between $-5\vec{a}$ and $6\vec{b}$?

A. $\frac{\pi}{6}$ B. $\frac{2\pi}{3}$

C. $\frac{2\pi}{5}$ D. $\frac{3\pi}{7}$

51. What is the degree of the differential equation $\frac{d^2y}{dx^2} - \sqrt{1+\left(\frac{dy}{dx}\right)^3} = 0$?

A. 1 B. 2
C. 3 D. 6

52. If $\int x^2 ln\,x\,dx = \frac{x^2}{m} ln\,x + \frac{x^3}{n} + c$, then what are the values of m and n respectively?

A. 1/3, –1/9 B. 3, –9
C. 3, 9 D. 3, 3

where c is a constant of integration.

53. What is the principal value of $\text{cosec}^{-1}\left(\sqrt{2}\right)$?

A. $\frac{\pi}{4}$ B. $\frac{\pi}{2}$

C. $-\frac{\pi}{4}$ D. 0

54. If $f : R \rightarrow R$, $g : R \rightarrow R$ and $g(x) = x + 3$ and $(fog)(x) = (x + 3)^2$, then what is the value of $f(-3)$?

A. –9 B. 0
C. 9 D. 3

55. What is the value of $\lim_{x\to 1}\frac{(x-1)^2}{(x-1)}$?

A. 0
B. 1
C. –1
D. The limit does not exist.

56. A balloon is pumped at the rate of 4cm^3 per second. What is the rate at which its surface area increases when its radius is 4 cm?

A. 1 cm^2/sec B. 2 cm^2/sec
C. 3 cm^2/sec D. 4 cm^2/sec

57. What is the value of $\frac{1+\tan 15°}{1-\tan 15°}$?

A. 1 B. $\frac{1}{\sqrt{2}}$

C. $\frac{1}{\sqrt{3}}$ D. $\sqrt{3}$

58. If $f(x) = kx^3 - 9x^2 + 9x + 3$ is monotonically increasing in every interval, then which one of the following is *correct*?

A. $k < 3$ B. $k \le 3$
C. $k > 3$ D. $k \ge 3$

59. If $\sin^{-1}\frac{5}{x} + \sin^{-1}\frac{12}{x} = \frac{\pi}{2}$, then what is the value of x?

A. 1 B. 7
C. 13 D. 17

60. If α, β are the roots of the quadratic equation $x^2 - x + 1 = 0$, then which one of the following is *correct*?

A. $(\alpha^4 - \beta^4)$ is real B. $2(\alpha^5 + \beta^5) = (\alpha\beta)^5$
C. $(\alpha^6 - \beta^6) = (\alpha\beta)^5$ D. $(\alpha^8 + \beta^8) = (\alpha\beta)^8$

61. If A = {a, b, c, d} then what is the number of proper subsets of A?

A. 16 B. 15
C. 14 D. 12

62. What is the number of three-digit odd numbers formed by using the digits 1, 2, 3, 4, 5, 6 if repetition of digits is allowed?

A. 60 B. 108
C. 120 D. 216

63. Let $A = \begin{pmatrix} 5 & 6 & 1 \\ 2 & -1 & 5 \end{pmatrix}$. Let there exist a matrix B such that $AB = \begin{pmatrix} 35 & 49 \\ 29 & 13 \end{pmatrix}$. What is B equal to?

A. $\begin{pmatrix} 5 & 1 & 4 \\ 2 & 6 & 3 \end{pmatrix}$ B. $\begin{pmatrix} 2 & 6 & 3 \\ 5 & 1 & 4 \end{pmatrix}$

C. $\begin{pmatrix} 5 & 2 \\ 1 & 6 \\ 4 & 3 \end{pmatrix}$ D. $\begin{pmatrix} 2 & 5 \\ 6 & 1 \\ 3 & 4 \end{pmatrix}$

64. Consider the following statements:

I. The probability that there are 53 Sundays in a leap year is twice the probability that there are 53 Sundays in a non-leap year.

II. The probability that there are 5 Mondays in the month of March is thrice the probability that there are 5 Mondays in the month of April.

Which of the statements given above is/are correct?

A. I only B. II only
C. Both I and II D. Neither I nor II

65. Consider the following statements:

I. If A′ = A, then A is a singular matrix, where A′ is the transpose of A.

II. If A is a square matrix such that $A^3 = I$, then A is non-singular.

Which of the statements given above is/are correct?

A. I only B. II only
C. Both I and II D. Neither I nor II

66. If p times the pth term of an AP is q times the qth term, then what is the $(p + q)$th term equal to?

A. $p + q$ B. pq
C. 1 D. 0

67. A team of 8 players is to be chosen from a group of 12 players. Out of the eight players one is to be elected as captain and another as vice-captain. In how many ways can this be done?

A. 27720 B. 13860
C. 6930 D. 495

68. In tossing three coins at a time, what is the probability of getting at most one head?

A. $\frac{3}{8}$ B. $\frac{7}{8}$

C. $\frac{1}{2}$ D. $\frac{1}{8}$

69. What is the sum of the coefficients of all the terms in the expansion of $(45x - 49)^4$?

A. –256 B. –100
C. 100 D. 256

70. Two balls are selected from a box containing 2 blue and 7 red balls. What is the probability that at least one ball is blue?

A. $\frac{2}{9}$ B. $\frac{7}{9}$

C. $\frac{5}{12}$ D. $\frac{7}{12}$

71. If the equation $x^2 - bx + 1 = 0$ does not possess real roots, then which one of the following is correct?

A. $-3 < b < 3$ B. $-2 < b < 2$
C. $b > 2$ D. $b < -2$

72. The probability of guessing a correct answer is $\frac{x}{12}$. If the probability of not guessing the correct answer is $\frac{2}{3}$, then what is x equal to?

A. 2 B. 3
C. 4 D. 6

73. If the system of equations $2x + 3y = 7$ and $2ax + (a + b)y = 28$ has infinitely many solutions, then which one of the following is correct?

A. $a = 2b$ B. $b = 2a$
C. $a = -2b$ D. $b = -2a$

74. If p and q are the roots of the equation $x^2 - px + q = 0$, then what are the values of p and q respectively?

A. 1, 0 B. 0, 1
C. –2, 0 D. –2, 1

75. Consider the following statements related to a variable X having a binomial distribution $b_x(n, p)$:

I. If $p = \frac{1}{2}$, then the distribution is symmetrical.

II. p remaining constant, $P(X = r)$ increases as n increases.

Which of the statements given above is/are correct?

A. I only B. II only
C. Both I and II D. Neither I nor II

76. What is the value of λ for which the vectors $\hat{i} - \hat{j} + \hat{k}$, $2\hat{i} + \hat{j} - \hat{k}$, $\lambda\hat{i} - \hat{j} + \lambda\hat{k}$, are coplanar?

A. 1 B. 2
C. 3 D. 4

77. What is the equation of the plane through z-axis and parallel to the line

$$\frac{x-1}{\cos\theta} = \frac{y+2}{\sin\theta} = \frac{z-3}{0}$$

A. $x \cot\theta + y = 0$ B. $x \tan\theta - y = 0$
C. $x + y \cot\theta = 0$ D. $x - y \tan\theta = 0$

78. If the lines $3y + 4x = 1$, $y = x + 5$ and $5y + bx = 3$ are concurrent, then what is the value of b?

A. 1 B. 3
C. 6 D. 0

79. What is the lease value of $f(x) = 2x^3 - 3x^2 - 12x + 1$ on $[-2, 2.5]$?

A. –3 B. 8
C. –19 D. –16.5

80. What is the derivative of

$$x\sqrt{a^2 - x^2} + a^2 \sin^{-1}\left(\frac{x}{a}\right)?$$

A. $\sqrt{a^2 - x^2}$ B. $2\sqrt{a^2 - x^2}$

C. $\sqrt{x^2 - a^2}$ D. $2\sqrt{x^2 - a^2}$

81. If (–5, 4) divides the line segment between the coordinate axes in the ratio 1 : 2, then what is its equation?

A. $8x + 5y + 20 = 0$ B. $5x + 8y - 7 = 0$
C. $8x - 5y + 60 = 0$ D. $5x - 8y + 57 = 0$

82. What is the value of

$$\begin{vmatrix} \cos 15° & \sin 15° \\ \cos 45° & \sin 45° \end{vmatrix} \times \begin{vmatrix} \cos 45° & \cos 15° \\ \sin 45° & \sin 15° \end{vmatrix}?$$

A. $\frac{1}{4}$ B. $\frac{\sqrt{3}}{2}$

C. $-\frac{1}{4}$ D. $-\frac{3}{4}$

83. Out of 32 persons, 30 invest in National Savings Certificates and 17 invest in shares. What is the number of persons who invest in both?

A. 13 B. 15
C. 17 D. 19

84. What are the equations of the directrices of the ellipse $25x^2 + 16y^2 = 400$?

A. $3x \pm 25 = 0$ B. $3y \pm 25 = 0$
C. $x \pm 15 = 0$ D. $y \pm 25 = 0$

85. Let A be an $n \times n$ matrix. If $\det(\lambda A) = \lambda^s \det(A)$, what is the value of s?

A. 0 B. 1
C. –1 D. n

86. Let E be the ellipse $\frac{x^2}{9} + \frac{y^2}{4} = 1$ and C be the circle $x^2 + y^2 = 9$. Let P = (1, 2) and Q = (2, 1). Which one of the following is correct?

A. Q lies inside C but outside E
B. Q lies outside both C and E
C. P lies inside both C and E
D. P lies inside C but outside E

87. What is the geometric interpretation of the identity $(\bar{a}-\bar{b})\times(\bar{a}+\bar{b})=2(\bar{a}\times\bar{b})$?

I. If the diagonals of a given parallelogram are used as sides of a second parallelogram, then the area of the second parallelogram is twice that of the given parallelogram.

II. If the semi-diagonals of a given parallelogram are used as sides of a second parallelogram, then the area of the second parallelogram is half that of the given parallelogram.

Select the correct answer using the code given below:

A. I only　　B. II only
C. Both I and II　　D. Neither I nor II

88. What is $\int_0^{\pi/2} \frac{\sin^2 x}{\sin^3 x+\cos^3 x}dx$?

A. π　　B. $\frac{\pi}{2}$
C. $\frac{\pi}{4}$　　D. 0

89. The function $f(x) = \frac{x}{x^2+1}$ from R to R is

A. One-one as well as onto
B. Onto but not one-one
C. Neither one-one nor onto
D. One-one but not onto

90. If A be a real skew-symmetric matrix of order n such that $A^2 + I = O$, I being the identity matrix of the same order as that of A, then what is the order of A?

A. 3　　B. Odd
C. Prime number　　D. Even

91. What is the value of $\sqrt{3}$ cosec 20° – sec 20°?

A. 1/4　　B. 4
C. 2　　D. 1

92. The probability distribution of random variable X with two missing probabilities p_1 and p_2 is given below:

X	P(X)
1	k
2	p_1
3	$4k$
4	p_2
5	$2k$

It is further given that $P(X \le 2) = 0.25$ and $P(X \ge 4) = 0.35$.

Consider the following statements:

I. $p_1 = p_2$　　II. $p_1 + p_2 = P(X=3)$

Which of the statements given above is/are correct?

A. I only　　B. II only
C. Both I and II　　D. Neither I nor II

93. If angles A, B, C are in AP, then what is sin A + 2 sin B + sin C equal to?

A. $4 \sin B \cos^2\left(\frac{A-C}{2}\right)$

B. $4 \sin B \cos^2\left(\frac{A-C}{4}\right)$

C. $4 \sin (2B) \cos^2\left(\frac{A-C}{2}\right)$

D. $4 \sin (2B) \cos^2\left(\frac{A-C}{4}\right)$

94. Statement I : If $-1 \le x < 0$, then $\cos(\sin^{-1} x) = -\sqrt{1-x^2}$?

Statement II : If $-1 \le x < 0$, then $\sin(\cos^{-1} x) = \sqrt{1-x^2}$

Which one of the following is *correct* in respect of the above statements?

A. Both statements I and II are independently correct and statement II is the correct explanation of statement I
B. Both statements I and II are independently correct but statement II is not the correct explanation of statement I
C. Statements I is correct but statement II is false
D. Statements I is false but statement II is correct

95. Statement I : $y = \tan^{-1}(x^{-1}) + 1$ is an increasing function of x.

Statement II : $\frac{dy}{dx}$ is positive for all values of x.

Which one of the following is *correct* in respect of the above statements?

A. Both statements I and II are independently correct and statement II is the correct explanation of statement I
B. Both statements I and II are independently correct but statement II is not the correct explanation of statement I
C. Statement I is correct but statement II is false
D. Statement I is false but statement II is correct

96. Consider the following statements in respect of circles $x^2 + y^2 - 2x - 2y = 0$ and $x^2 + y^2 = 1$:

I. The radius of the first circle is twice that of the second circle.

II. Both the circles pass through the origin.

Which of the statements given above is/are correct?

A. I only B. II only

C. Both I and II D. Neither I nor II

97. Let *a, b, c* be in AP.

Consider the following statements:

I. $\frac{1}{ab}, \frac{1}{ca}, \frac{1}{bc}$ are in AP.

II. $\frac{1}{\sqrt{b}+\sqrt{c}}, \frac{1}{\sqrt{c}+\sqrt{a}}, \frac{1}{\sqrt{a}+\sqrt{b}}$ are in AP.

Which of the statements given above is/are correct?

A. I only B. II only

C. Both I and II D. Neither I nor II

98. What is the differentiation of $\log_x x$ with respect to $ln\ x$?

A. 0 B. 1

C. $1/x$ D. x

99. What is $\tan\left(7\frac{1^\circ}{2}\right)$ equal to?

A. $\sqrt{6}+\sqrt{3}-\sqrt{2}+2$

B. $\sqrt{6}-\sqrt{3}+\sqrt{2}+2$

C. $\sqrt{6}-\sqrt{3}+\sqrt{2}-2$

D. $\sqrt{6}+\sqrt{3}+\sqrt{2}-2$

100. What is the value of $\frac{\cos 15^\circ + \cos 45^\circ}{\cos^3 15^\circ + \cos^3 45^\circ}$?

A. $\frac{1}{4}$ B. $\frac{1}{2}$

C. $\frac{1}{3}$ D. None of these

Directions (Qs. No. 101-103) : *For these questions follow:*

The vertices of a cube are (0, 0, 0), (2, 0, 0), (0, 2, 0), (0, 0, 2), (2, 2, 0), (2, 0, 2), (0, 2, 2), (2, 2, 2) respectively.

101. What is the angle between any two diagonals of the cube?

A. $\cos^{-1}(1/2)$ B. $\cos^{-1}(1/3)$

C. $\cos^{-1}(1/\sqrt{3})$ D. $\cos^{-1}(2/\sqrt{3})$

102. What is the angle between one of the edges of the cube and the diagonal of the cube intersecting the edge of the cube?

A. $\cos^{-1}(1/2)$ B. $\cos^{-1}(1/3)$

C. $\cos^{-1}(1/\sqrt{3})$ D. $\cos^{-1}(2/\sqrt{3})$

103. What is the angle between the diagonal of one of the faces of the cube and the diagonal of the cube intersecting the diagonal of the face of the cube?

A. $\cos^{-1}(1/\sqrt{3})$ B. $\cos^{-1}(2/\sqrt{3})$

C. $\cos^{-1}(\sqrt{1/3})$ D. $\cos^{-1}(\sqrt{2/3})$

104. Let $\vec{a}$ and $\vec{b}$ be two unit vectors and α be the angle between them. If $(\vec{a}+\vec{b})$ is also the unit vector, then what is the value of α?

A. $\frac{\pi}{4}$ B. $\frac{\pi}{3}$

C. $\frac{2\pi}{3}$ D. $\frac{\pi}{2}$

105. What is the value of

$$\frac{(0.101)_2^{(11)_2} + (0.011)_2^{(11)_2}}{(0.101)_2^{(10)_2} - (0.101)_2^{(01)_2}(0.011)_2^{(01)_2} + (0.011)_2^{(10)_2}}?$$

A. $(0.001)_2$ B. $(0.01)_2$

C. $(0.1)_2$ D. $(1)_2$

Directions (Qs. No. 106-108) : *Follow the table given:*

The table below gives an incomplete frequency distribution with two missing frequencies f_1 and f_2.

Value of X	*Frequency*
0	f_1
1	f_2
2	4
3	4
4	3

The total frequency is 18 and the arithmetic mean of X is 2.

106. What is the value of f_2?

A. 4 B. 3

C. 2 D. 1

107. What is the standard deviation?

A. $\frac{\sqrt{5}}{2}$ B. $\frac{\sqrt{5}}{3}$

C. $\frac{4}{3}$ D. $\frac{16}{9}$

108. What is the coefficient of variance?

A. $\frac{200}{3}$ B. $\frac{50\sqrt{5}}{9}$

C. $\frac{600}{\sqrt{5}}$ D. 150

109. What is the sum of all natural numbers between 200 and 400 which are divisible by 7?

A. 6729 B. 8712

C. 8729 D. 9276

110. The mean and variance of a binomial distribution are 8 and 4 respectively. What is P(X = 1) equal to?

A. $\frac{1}{2^{12}}$ B. $\frac{-1}{2^8}$

C. $\frac{1}{2^6}$ D. $\frac{1}{2^4}$

111. What is $\int e^{\ln x} \sin x \, dx$ equal to?

A. $e^{ln\, x}(\sin x - \cos x) + c$
B. $(\sin x - x \cos x) + c$
C. $(x \sin x + \cos x) + c$
D. $(\sin x + x \cos x) + c$
where c is a constant of integration.

112. An observed event B can occur after one of the three events A_1, A_2, A_3. If
$P(A_1) = P(A_2) = 0.4$, $P(A_3) = 0.2$ and
$P(B|A_1) = 0.25$, $P(B|A_2) = 0.4$,
$P(B|A_3) = 0.125$, what is the probability of A_1 after observing B?

A. 1/3 B. 6/19
C. 20/57 D. 2/5

113. What is $\int \frac{x^4+1}{x^2+1} dx$ equal to?

A. $\frac{x^3}{3} - x + 4 \tan^{-1} x + c$

B. $\frac{x^3}{3} + x + 4 \tan^{-1} x + c$

C. $\frac{x^3}{3} - x + 2 \tan^{-1} x + c$

D. $\frac{x^3}{3} - x - 4 \tan^{-1} x + c$

where c is a constant of integration.

114. What is the value of $\lim_{x \to \infty} \left(\frac{x+6}{x+1} \right)^{x+4}$?

A. e B. e^2
C. e^4 D. e^5

115. What is the area of the triangle with vertices (0, 2, 2), (2, 0, –1) and (3, 4, 0)?

A. 15/2 square units
B. 15 square units
C. 7/2 square units
D. 7 square units

116. If $\frac{1}{2-\sqrt{-2}}$ is one of the roots of $ax^2 + bx + c = 0$, where a, b, c are real, then what are the values of a, b, c respectively?

A. 6, –4, 1 B. 4, 6, –1
C. 3, –2, 1 D. 6, 4 1

117. If ω is a complex cube root of unity and $x = \omega^2 - \omega - 2$, then what is the value of $x^2 + 4x + 7$?

A. –2 B. – 1
C. 0 D. 1

118. If $\cos x \neq -1$, then what is $\frac{\sin x}{1+\cos x}$ equal to?

A. $-\cot\frac{x}{2}$ B. $\cot\frac{x}{2}$

C. $\tan\frac{x}{2}$ D. $-\tan\frac{x}{2}$

119. The angle of the elevation of the tip of a flag post from a point 5 m away from its base is 75. What is the approximate height of the flag post?

A. 15 m B. 17 m
C. 19 m D. 21 m

120. If A = P({1, 2}) where P denotes the power set, then which one of the following is correct?

A. $\{1, 2\} \subset A$ B. $1 \in A$
C. $\phi \notin A$ D. $\{1, 2\} \in A$

ANSWERS

PAPER-I : GENERAL ABILITY TEST

1	2	3	4	5	6	7	8	9	10
A	C	C	B	C	B	B	B	A	A
11	**12**	**13**	**14**	**15**	**16**	**17**	**18**	**19**	**20**
D	B	B	D	A	A	B	C	B	A
21	**22**	**23**	**24**	**25**	**26**	**27**	**28**	**29**	**30**
A	A	B	A	C	D	B	B	A	C
31	**32**	**33**	**34**	**35**	**36**	**37**	**38**	**39**	**40**
B	B	A	D	C	C	A	D	A	C
41	**42**	**43**	**44**	**45**	**46**	**47**	**48**	**49**	**50**
A	A	B	D	A	B	C	C	A	C
51	**52**	**53**	**54**	**55**	**56**	**57**	**58**	**59**	**60**
B	D	D	B	A	C	A	D	C	A
61	**62**	**63**	**64**	**65**	**66**	**67**	**68**	**69**	**70**
B	A	C	B	C	C	C	D	A	D

71	72	73	74	75	76	77	78	79	80
C	D	B	A	B	C	B	B	D	C
81	82	83	84	85	86	87	88	89	90
C	B	A	C	D	D	A	A	A	A
91	92	93	94	95	96	97	98	99	100
C	A	A	A	B	D	C	B	B	D
101	102	103	104	105	106	107	108	109	110
B	B	B	D	D	C	D	D	C	D
111	112	113	114	115	116	117	118	119	120
C	C	B	B	C	C	B	B	C	B
121	122	123	124	125	126	127	128	129	130
D	A	D	C	D	D	D	A	A	B
131	132	133	134	135	136	137	138	139	140
C	C	A	C	C	C	C	A	A	C
141	142	143	144	145	146	147	148	149	150
A	A	A	C	A	C	B	C	B	C

PAPER-II : MATHEMATICS

1	2	3	4	5	6	7	8	9	10
C	D	D	C	B	A	D	C	C	D
11	12	13	14	15	16	17	18	19	20
A	D	B	C	D	A	B	C	A	B
21	22	23	24	25	26	27	28	29	30
C	C	A	B	B	D	C	B	C	C
31	32	33	34	35	36	37	38	39	40
D	C	A	C	A	D	C	B	A	A
41	42	43	44	45	46	47	48	49	50
D	A	A	A	C	D	B	C	C	B
51	52	53	54	55	56	57	58	59	60
A	B	C	C	A	B	D	C	C	A
61	62	63	64	65	66	67	68	69	70
A	B	C	A	D	D	B	C	A	D
71	72	73	74	75	76	77	78	79	80
B	C	B	A	A	A	D	B	C	B
81	82	83	84	85	86	87	88	89	90
C	C	B	D	D	C	C	C	C	A
91	92	93	94	95	96	97	98	99	100
B	D	B	B	A	D	A	A	C	D
101	102	103	104	105	106	107	108	109	110
A	D	D	A	C	A	C	A	C	A
111	112	113	114	115	116	117	118	119	120
B	C	C	C	C	C	C	C	C	D

EXPLANATORY ANSWERS

PAPER-II : MATHEMATICS

2. $|A| = 4 - 6 = -2$

$$A^{-1} = [b_{ij}] = \frac{1}{-2}\begin{bmatrix} 4 & -2 \\ -3 & 1 \end{bmatrix} = \begin{bmatrix} -2 & 1 \\ \frac{3}{2} & -\frac{1}{2} \end{bmatrix}$$

$$\therefore\ b_{22} = -\frac{1}{2}$$

3. $4(\sin^2 x + \cos x) = 1$

$4(1 - \cos^2 x + \cos x) = 1$

$- \cos^2 x + \cos x = \frac{1}{4} - 1 = -\frac{3}{4}$

$\cos^2 x - \cos x - \frac{3}{4} = 0$

Multiply both sides by 4

$4\cos^2 x - 4 \cos x - 3 = 0$

Let, $a = \cos x$

$4a^2 - 4a - 3 = 0$

$4a^2 - 6a + 2a - 3 = 0$

$2a(2a - 3) + 1\,(2a - 3) = 0$

$a = -\frac{1}{2},\ a = -\frac{3}{2}$ are not valid

Now,

$\cos x = \cos(\pi - \pi/3)$

$\cos x = \cos 2\pi/3$

$x = 2\pi/3 = \frac{2 \times 180}{3} = 120°$

4.

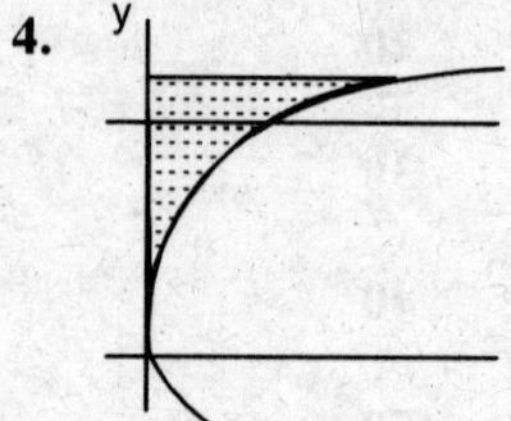

$$A = \int_0^6 \frac{y^2}{1^2} dy = \frac{1}{12}\left[\frac{y^3}{3}\right]_0^6$$

$$= \frac{1}{12 \times 3} \times (6)^3 = 6 \text{ sq. units}$$

5.

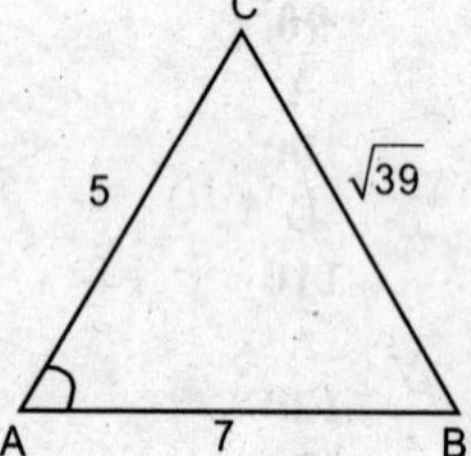

$$\cos A = \frac{(AC)^2 + AB^2 - BC^2}{2(AC)(AB)} = \frac{25 + 49 - 39}{2 \times 5 \times 7}$$

$$= \frac{74 - 39}{2 \times 5 \times 7} = \frac{35}{2 \times 35} = \frac{1}{2}$$

$$\cos A = \frac{1}{2} \therefore \text{angle } A = \frac{\pi}{3}$$

6. $\frac{1 + 2i}{1 - (1 - i)^2} = \frac{1 + 2i}{1 - (1 - i^2 - 2i)} = \frac{1 + 2i}{1 + 2i} = 1$

7. $AB = (2k - k, 0 - 1, 2 + 1)$

$= (k, -1, 3)$

$BC = (2 + 2k - 2k, k - 0, 1 - 2)$

$= (2, k, -1)$

$k \times 2 - 1 \times k - 3 = 0$

$\Rightarrow 2k - k = 3 \Rightarrow k = 3$

8. $\int \frac{1}{1 + e^x} dx$

$= \int \frac{1 + e^x - e^x}{1 + e^x} dx$

$= \int \frac{1 + e^x}{1 + e^x} dx - \int \frac{e^x}{1 + e^x} dx$

$= x - \log(1 + e^x) + c$

10. $ax \frac{dy}{dx} + 2ay = xy \frac{dy}{dx}$

or $\frac{dy}{dx} = \frac{-2ay}{ax - xy}$

$\frac{a - y}{y} dy = -2a \frac{dx}{x}$

or $\log y - y = -2a \log x + c$

or $\log y - y = \log x^{-2a} + \log k$

or $\log y - y = \log kx^{-2a}$

$\therefore \log \frac{y}{kx^{-2a}} = y$ or $e^y = \frac{y}{kx^{-2a}}$ or $ke^y = yx^{2a}$

11. $\vec{b} = \vec{a}\lambda$

$\vec{b}\lambda = 2\hat{i} + \hat{j} - \hat{k}$

$\vec{a} = 2\hat{i} + \hat{j} - \hat{k}$

$\therefore \vec{a}.\vec{b} = 4\lambda + \lambda + \lambda = 6\lambda = 3$

or $\lambda = \frac{1}{2}$ $\vec{b} = \left(\hat{i} + \frac{1}{2}\hat{j} - \frac{1}{2}\hat{k}\right)$

$= \left(1 + \frac{1}{2}, -\frac{1}{2}\right)$

12. $\left(\frac{1 + i}{1 - i}\right)^n = 1$

or $\left[\frac{(1 + i)(1 + i)}{(1 - i^2)}\right]^n = 1$

$i^n = 1 \Rightarrow n = 4$

14. $x = t^2, y = t^3$

$\therefore \frac{dx}{dt} = 2t, \frac{dy}{dt} = 3t^2$

$\therefore \frac{dy}{dx} = \frac{dy/dt}{dx/dt} = \frac{3t^2}{2t} = \frac{3}{2} \times t$

Also, $\dfrac{d^2y}{dx^2} = \dfrac{3}{2} \times 1 \times \dfrac{dt}{dx}$

$= \dfrac{3}{2} \times \dfrac{1}{2t} = \dfrac{3}{4}t$

15. $A = \int_{-\pi/4}^{\pi/4} \tan x \tan^2 x\, dx$

$= \int_{-\pi/4}^{\pi/4} \tan x(\sec^2 x - 1)\, dx$

$= \int_{-\pi/4}^{\pi/4} \tan x.\sec^2 x\, dx - \int_{-\pi/4}^{\pi/4} \tan x\, dx$

Put $\tan x = t$ or $\sec^2 x\, dx = dt$

$A = \int_{-1}^{1} t\,dt - [\log \sec x]_{-\pi/4}^{\pi/4}$

$= \left[\dfrac{t^2}{2}\right]_{-1}^{1} - [\log \sec(\pi/4) - \log \sec(-\pi/4)]$

$= 0 - \left[\log\sqrt{2} - \log\sqrt{2}\right] = 0$

16. Total alphabets = 6

Total no. of words = $\dfrac{6!}{3!2!} = \dfrac{720}{6 \times 2} = 60$

Let two 'Ns' come together.

Total no. of words = $\dfrac{5!}{3!}$

Reqd. numbers = 60 – 20 = 40.

19. $\left(\dfrac{\sqrt{3}+i}{\sqrt{3}+i} \times \dfrac{\sqrt{3}-i}{\sqrt{3}-i}\right)^{200} + \left(\dfrac{\sqrt{3}-i}{\sqrt{3}+i} \times \dfrac{\sqrt{3}-i}{\sqrt{3}-i}\right)^{200} + 1$

$= \left(\dfrac{3+i^2+2\sqrt{3}i}{3+1}\right)^{200} + \left(\dfrac{3+i^2-2\sqrt{3}i}{4}\right)^{200} + 1$

$= \left(\dfrac{1+\sqrt{3}i}{2}\right)^{200} + \left(\dfrac{1-\sqrt{3}i}{2}\right)^{200} + 1 = 1$

21. $\dfrac{\log_e H}{\log(\alpha B)^{\frac{1}{2}}} \times \dfrac{\log(\alpha\beta\gamma)^{\frac{1}{2}}}{\log H}$

$= \log \alpha\beta\gamma / \log \alpha\beta$

22. $T_{59} = a + 58d = 449$ ...(*i*)

$T_{449} = a + 448d = 59$ ...(*ii*)

from (*i*) and (*ii*)

$a + 58d = 449$

$a + 448d = 59$

$-390d = 390$

$d = -1$

$\therefore\ a = 449 + 58 = 507$

$\Rightarrow a + (n - 1)d = 0$

$(n - 1)d = -507,\ n = 508$

24. Let the two numbers be a and b.

So, $\dfrac{a+b}{2} = 27$, and $\dfrac{2ab}{a+b} = 12$

$\Rightarrow \quad a + b = 54$

and $\quad a + b = \dfrac{ab}{6}$

$\therefore \quad \dfrac{ab}{6} = 54$

$\Rightarrow \quad ab = 54 \times 6$

$\therefore \quad$ G.M. = $\sqrt{ab} = \sqrt{54\times 6} = \sqrt{9\times 6\times 6} = 18.$

26. Focus = $(\pm ae, o)$

$b = 3$, and

$2b = 6$

$ae = 4$

But $c = 4$

$\therefore\ c = \sqrt{a^2 - b^2}$

$\Rightarrow 1b = a^2 - b^2$ or $a^2 = 16 + 9$

$\therefore\ a = 5,\ b = 3$

$\therefore\ \dfrac{x^2}{25} + \dfrac{b^2}{9} = 1$

which clearly passes through (5, 0)

28. $y = xe^{-x}$

$\therefore\ \dfrac{dy}{dx} = (1 - x)e^{-x}$

$\Rightarrow \dfrac{dy}{dx} = 0 \Rightarrow 1 - x = 0$ or $x = 1$

$\Rightarrow e^x(x - 1) = 0 \Rightarrow$ & so $y = e^{-1}$

30. $y = \sin^{-1}\left[\dfrac{2(2x)}{1+(2x)^2}\right]$

Put $2x = \tan\theta$

$\therefore\ y = \sin^{-1}\left[\dfrac{2\tan\theta}{1+\tan^2\theta}\right]$

$\Rightarrow y = 2 \times \tan^{-1}\theta\ \therefore\ \dfrac{dy}{dx} = \dfrac{2\times 2}{1+4x^2}$

34.

c b a f e d

$\vec{a}[\vec{b}\times\vec{a}+\vec{b}\times\vec{b}+\vec{b}\times\vec{c}+\vec{c}\times\vec{a}+\vec{c}\times\vec{b}+\vec{c}\times\vec{c}]$

$= 0$

$\vec{a}[-\vec{c}+\vec{a}+\vec{b}-\vec{a}] = 0$

or $\vec{a}.b-\vec{a}.\vec{c} = 0$

$\therefore \vec{b} = \vec{c}$

39. $y^2 = (x + x^2)^2$

So, $A = x^2 + x^4 + 2x^3$, $B = x^3$

$\frac{dB}{dx} = 2x,\ \frac{dA}{dx} = 2x + 4x^3 + 6x^2$

$\frac{dA}{dB} = \frac{dA/dx}{dB/dx} = \frac{2x+4x^3+6x^2}{2x}$

$= 1 + 2x^2 + 3x$

40. $\cos \pi/4 = \frac{2p-2+2}{\sqrt{p^2+4+4}\times\sqrt{4+1+1}}$

$\Rightarrow \frac{1}{\sqrt{2}} = \frac{2p}{\sqrt{p^2+8}\times\sqrt{6}}$

or $\frac{1}{2} = \frac{4p^2}{6p^2+48}$

or $6p^2 + 48 = 8p^2$

or $p^2 = 24$

41. $\frac{dN(t)}{dt} = \alpha N(t)$

$\therefore \log N(t) = \alpha\, t + c$

$\Rightarrow \log N(t) = e^{\alpha t+c}$ or $ce^{kt} = e^{\alpha t+c}$

or $kt = \alpha t + c$ or $\alpha t = kt - c$, $\alpha = k - c/t$

43.

A(1, 2)

P(1) B(x, y) (2)

Let foot be B $(x_1 y_1)$

$3x + 4y = 1$ ...(*i*)

or $AB = 4/3$

Eq. of the line AB is

$\frac{y_1-2}{x_1-1} = \frac{4}{3}$ or $4x_1 - 4 = 3y_1 - 6$

or $4x_1 - 3y_1 = -2$ ...(*ii*)

Solving (*i*) and (*ii*), we get

$x_1 = \frac{-1}{5},\ y = \frac{2}{5}$.

47. $(1 + e^x) \sec^2 y dy = -3e^x \tan y dx$

$\frac{\sec^2 y}{\tan y} dy = \frac{-3e^x}{1+e^x} dx$

Using log on both side

or $\log \tan y = -3 \log(1 + e^x) + \log c$

or $\log \tan y = \log \frac{c}{(1+e^x)^3}$

or $\tan y = \frac{c}{(1+e^x)^3} \Rightarrow (1 + e^x)^3 \tan y = c$

50. $\cos\theta = \frac{\vec{a}\vec{b}}{|\vec{a}||\vec{b}|}$

$\cos\theta = \frac{.5\vec{a}.6\vec{b}}{.5\times 6} = \frac{-\vec{a}.\vec{b}}{|\vec{a}||\vec{b}|}$

$= \cos\left(\pi - \frac{\pi}{3}\right) = 2\pi/3.$

52. $\int x^2 \ln x\, dx = \frac{x^3}{m}\ln x + \frac{x^3}{n} + c$

$\Rightarrow \frac{x^2}{3}\ln x - \int \frac{1}{x}.\frac{x^3}{3} dx = \frac{x^3}{3}\ln x + \frac{x^3}{9} + c$

On comparing.

$m = 3,\ n = -9.$

56. $\frac{dV}{dt} = 4\text{cm}^3/\text{s}$

$S = 4\pi r^2,\ V = \frac{4}{3}\pi r^3$

$\frac{dS}{dt} = 8\pi r\frac{dr}{dt},\ \frac{dV}{dt} = 4\pi r^2\frac{dr}{dt}$

$4 = 4\pi(4)^2 \frac{dr}{dv}$

$\Rightarrow \frac{dV}{dt} = \frac{1}{11\pi}$

$= 8\pi \times 4 \times \frac{1}{16\pi} = 8\ \text{cm}^2/\text{s}$

58. $f(x) = kx^3 - 9x^2 + 9x + 3$

$f'(x_1 > 0) \Rightarrow 3kx^2 - 18x + 9 > 0$

or $kx^2 - 6x + 3 > 0 \Rightarrow k > 3$

59. $\sin^{-1}\pi = \pi - \sin^{-1}\frac{12}{x}$

$\sin^{-1}\pi = \cos^{-1}\frac{12}{x}$

or $\cos^{-1}\dfrac{\sqrt{x^2-25}}{-x} = \cos^{-1}\dfrac{12}{x}$

or $\dfrac{x-25}{-x} = \dfrac{12}{x}$

or $x^2 = 169 \Rightarrow x = 13$

66. $p^{th} = a + (p-1)d$

$q^{th} = a + (q-1)d$

By hypothesis

$ap + (p^2 - p)d = aq + (q^2 - q)d$

$(ap - aq) = (q^2 - q - p^2 + p)d$

or $a(p-q) = [(p-q) - (p^2 - q^2)]d$

$(p+q)\text{th} = a + (p+q-1)d$

$= [1 - (p+q)]d - [1 - (p+q)]d = 0$

68. $P = P(x=0) + P(x=1)$

$= {}^3C_0\left(\frac{1}{2}\right)^3\left(\frac{1}{2}\right)^0 + {}^3C_1\left(\frac{1}{2}\right)^2\left(\frac{1}{2}\right)^1$

$= 1\times\frac{1}{8} + 3\times\frac{1}{8} = \frac{1}{2}$

70. $P = \dfrac{{}^2C_1\times{}^7C_1}{{}^9C_2} + \dfrac{{}^2C_2\times{}^7C_0}{{}^9C_2}$

$= \dfrac{2\times 7}{36} + \dfrac{1\times 7}{36} = \dfrac{14+7}{36} = \dfrac{7}{12}$

76. $x(\hat{i} - \hat{j} + \hat{k}) + y(2\hat{i} + \hat{j} - \hat{k}) = \lambda\hat{i} - \hat{j} + \lambda\hat{k}$

$\Rightarrow (x+2y)i + (-x+y)\hat{j} + (x-y)\hat{k} = \lambda\hat{i} - \hat{j} + \lambda\hat{k}$

$x + 2y = \lambda$

$3y = 0,\ x = \lambda$

$y = 0,\ \lambda = 1$

78. Subtraction

$$\begin{array}{r} 3y + 4x = 1 \\ 3y - 3x = 15 \\ - \quad + \quad - \\ \hline 7x = -14 \end{array}$$

We get

$x = -2$

$y = -2 + 5 = 3$

$5y + bx = 3$

$5(3) + b(-2) = 3$

$\Rightarrow b = 3$

79. $f'(x) = 6x^2 - 6x - 12$

$\therefore f'(x) = 0$ gives

$\Rightarrow 6(x^2 - x - 2) = 0$

$= x(x-2) + 1(x-2) = 0$

$\Rightarrow x = -1, 2$

$f(x) = 2x^3 - 3x^2 - 12x + 1$

$f(-1) = 2(-1)^3 - 3(-1)^3 - 12(-1) + 1$

$f(2) = 16 - 12 - 24 + 1 = -19$

81.

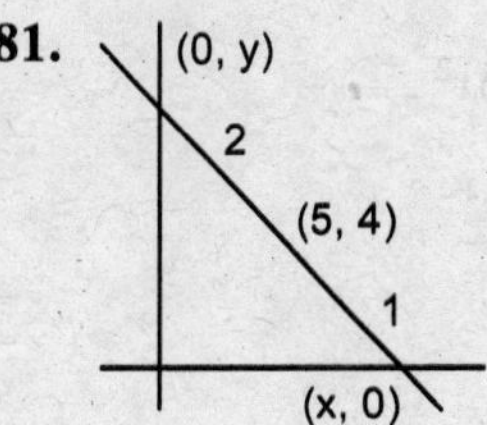

$\dfrac{2x+0}{3} = -5$ or $x = \dfrac{-15}{2}$, $\dfrac{y+0}{3} = 4 \Rightarrow y = 12$

$\therefore$ Reqd. equation is $\dfrac{2x}{-15} + \dfrac{y}{12} = 1$

or $8x - 5y + 60 = 0$

82. $\begin{vmatrix}\cos 15° & \sin 15° \\ \cos 45° & \sin 45°\end{vmatrix} \times \begin{vmatrix}\cos 45° & \cos 15° \\ \sin 45° & \sin 15°\end{vmatrix}$

$= [\cos 15° \sin 45° - \sin 15° \cos 45°] \times [\cos 45° \sin 15° - \sin 45° \cos 15°]$

$= \sin 30° \times -\sin 30°$

$= +\dfrac{1}{2} \times -\dfrac{1}{2} = -\dfrac{1}{4}$

83. $x(A)$ = Invested in National Saving Certificate = 30

$x(B)$ = Invested in shares = 17

$x(A \cup B) = 32$

$x(A \cap B)$ = No. of persons invested in both

As $x(A \cup B) = x(A) + x(B) - x(A \cap B)$

$32 = 30 + 17 - x(A \cap B)$

or $x(A \cap B) = 47 - 32 = 15$

84. $\dfrac{25x^2}{400} + \dfrac{16y^2}{400} = 1$

or $\dfrac{x^2}{16} + \dfrac{y^2}{25} = 1$

$\therefore a^2 = 16,\ b^2 = 25$

$\therefore$ Eqs. of directrices are

$y \pm 25 = 0$

88. $I = \int_0^{\pi/2} \frac{\sin^3 x}{\sin^3 x + \cos^2 x} dx$ ...(*i*)

$$I = \int_0^{\pi/2} \frac{\left\{\sin\left(\frac{\pi}{2} - x_1\right)\right\}^3}{\left\{\sin\left(\frac{\pi}{2} - x\right) +\right\}^3 + \left\{\cos\left(\frac{\pi}{2} - x\right)\right\}^3 dx} dx$$

$I = \int_0^{\pi/2} \frac{\cos^3 x}{\sin^3 x + \cos^3 x} dx$ ...(*ii*)

from equation (*i*) + (*ii*)

$$2I = \int_0^{\pi/2} \frac{\sin^3 x + \cos^3 x}{\sin^3 x + \cos^3 x} dx$$

or $2I = x = \left[\frac{\pi}{2} - 0\right] \therefore I = \frac{\pi}{4}.$

89. $f(x) = \frac{x}{x^2 + 1}$

$f(x_1) = \frac{x_1}{x_1^2 + 1}, \quad f(x_2) = \frac{x_2}{x_2^2 + 1}$

$f(x_1) = f(x_2)$

$\frac{x_1}{x_1^2 + 1} = \frac{x_2}{x_2^2 + 1}$

or $x_1 x_2^2 + x_1 = x_2 x_1^2 + x_2$

or $x_1 x_2^2 - x_2 x_1^2 = x_2 - x_1$

$x_1 x_2 = 1$

f is neither one-one nor onto.

91. $\sqrt{3} \operatorname{cosec} 20° - \sec 20°$

$= \sqrt{3} \times \frac{1}{\sin 20°} - \frac{1}{\cos 20°}$

$= \frac{\sqrt{3} \cos 20° - \sin 20°}{\sin 20° \cos 20°}$

$= \frac{\frac{\sqrt{3}}{2} \cos 20° - \frac{1}{2} \sin 20°}{\frac{1}{2} \sin 20° \cos 20°}$

$= 4 \frac{\sin(60° - 20°)}{\sin 2 \times 20°} = 4.$

92. Subtracting equation (*ii*) from equation (*i*)

$$\begin{aligned} k + P_1 &= 0.25 \quad ...(i) \\ 2k + P_2 &= 0.35 \quad ...(ii) \\ - \quad - \quad & - \\ \hline -k + P_1 - P_2 &= -0.10 \end{aligned}$$

$k + P_2 - P_1 = 0.10$ ...(*iii*)

Also

$k + P_1 + 4k + P_2 + 2k = 1$

$7k + P_1 + P_2 = 1$ ...(*iv*)

Adding the equations (*iii*) and (*iv*)

$$\begin{aligned} 7k + P_2 + P_1 &= 1 \\ k + P_2 - P_1 &= 0.10 \\ \hline 8k + 2P_2 &= 1.1 \end{aligned}$$

$4k + P_2 = 0.55$

$P_2 = 0.55 - 4k$

From (*ii*)

$2k + 0.55 - 4k = 0.35$

$k = 0.10$

Now $P_2 = 0.55 - 4 \times .10$

$P_2 = 0.15$

From (*i*), $P_1 = 0.25 - k$

$\Rightarrow P_1 = 0.15$

93. sin A + sin C + 2 sin B

$= 2\sin\left(\frac{A+C}{2}\right)\cos\left(\frac{A-C}{2}\right) + 2\sin B$

$= 2 \sin B \cos\left(\frac{A-C}{2}\right) + 2\sin B$

$= 2 \sin B \left[1 + \cos\left(\frac{A-C}{2}\right)\right]$

$= 4 \sin B \cos^2\left(\frac{A-C}{4}\right)$

100. $\frac{\cos 15° + \cos 45°}{(\cos 15°)^3 + (\cos 45°)^3}$

$= \cos (45° - 30°)$

$= \cos 45° \cos 30° + \sin 45° \sin 30°$

$= \frac{1}{\sqrt{2}} \times \frac{\sqrt{3}}{2} + \frac{1}{\sqrt{2}} \times \frac{1}{2} = \frac{\sqrt{3}+1}{2\sqrt{2}}$

$= \frac{1}{\left(\frac{\sqrt{3}+1}{2\sqrt{2}}\right)^2 + \left(\frac{1}{\sqrt{2}}\right)^2 - \frac{\sqrt{3}+1}{2\sqrt{2}} \times \frac{1}{\sqrt{2}}}$

$= \frac{1}{\frac{3+1+2\sqrt{3}+4-2\sqrt{3}-2}{8}} = \frac{8}{-2} = -4$

107. Standard deviation,

$$\sigma = \sqrt{\sum f_i x_1^2 - \left(\frac{\sum f_i x_i}{tf_i}\right)^2}$$

$$= \sqrt{104 - \left(\frac{136}{2}\right)^2} \quad \therefore \sigma = \frac{4}{3}.$$

109. $a = 203$; $L = 399$

$L = a + (n - 1)d$

$\therefore 399 = 203 + (n - 1) \times 7$

or $399 - 203 = (n - 1)7$

or $28 = n - 1 \Rightarrow n = 29$

$$\text{Sum} = \frac{29}{2}[a + L]$$

$$= \frac{29}{2}[203 + 399] = 8729$$

110. $np = 8, \quad npq = 4$

$q = \frac{1}{2}$, so $p = \frac{1}{2}$

$np = 8, n \times \frac{1}{2} = 8 \Rightarrow n = 16$

$$\therefore p(X = 1) = {}^{16}C_1\left(\frac{1}{2}\right)^{15}\left(\frac{1}{2}\right)^1$$

$$= 16 \times \left(\frac{1}{2}\right)^{16} = \frac{1}{2^{12}}.$$

112. $$P\left(\frac{A_1}{B}\right) = \frac{P(A_1) \times P\left(\frac{B}{A_1}\right)}{P(A_1) \times P\left(\frac{B}{A_1}\right) + P(A_2)P\left(\frac{B}{A_1}\right)}$$

$$= \frac{0.4 \times 0.25}{0.4 \times 0.25 + 0.4 \times 0.4 + 0.2 \times 0.125}$$

$$= \frac{\frac{4}{10} \times \frac{25}{100}}{\frac{4}{10} \times \frac{25}{100} + \frac{4}{10} \times \frac{4}{10} + \frac{2}{10} \times \frac{125}{1000}} = \frac{20}{57}$$

117. $x = w^2 - w - 2$

Consider

$x^2 + 4x + 7 = (-2w - 3)^2 + 4(-2w - 3) + 7$

$= 4w^2 + 4w + 4 = 4(w^2 + w + 1)$

$= 4 \times 0 = 0$

YOUR SPACE